The Cambridge World History of Human Disease

The Cambridge World History of Human Disease

Editor
KENNETH F. KIPLE

Executive Editor
Rachael Rockwell Graham

Associate Editors
David Frey
Brian T. Higgins
Kerry Stewart
H. Micheal Tarver
Thomas W. Wilson
Brent Zerger

Assistant Editors
Alicia Browne
Roger Hall
Paul Henggeler
Bruce O. Solheim
Dalila de Sousa

CAMBRIDGE
UNIVERSITY PRESS

PUBLISHED BY THE PRESS SYNDICATE OF THE UNIVERSITY OF CAMBRIDGE
The Pitt Building, Trumpington Street, Cambridge, United Kingdom

CAMBRIDGE UNIVERSITY PRESS
The Edinburgh Building, Cambridge CB2 2RU, UK   http://www.cup.cam.ac.uk
40 West 20th Street, New York, NY 10011-4211, USA   http://www.cup.org
10 Stamford Road, Oakleigh, Melbourne 3166, Australia

First published 1993
Reprinted 1994 (thrice), 1995, 1999

Printed in the United States of America

Typeset in Century Schoolbook

A catalogue record for this book is available from the British Library

Library of Congress Cataloguing-in-Publication Data is available

ISBN 0-521-33286-9 hardback

In Memory of

Michael Dols
Wilbur Downs
Lu Gwei-Djen
R. H. Kampmeier
Edward H. Kass
John L. Kemink
Jerry Stannard
and
Miguel M. Ornelas

Contents

Contents

Tables, Figures, and Maps

Figures

Maps

Contributors

Geoffrey C. Ainsworth
Commonwealth Mycological Institute
Kew, England

Marvin J. Allison
Medical College of Virginia
Richmond, Virginia

Roy D. Altman
University of Miami School of
  Medicine
Miami, Florida

David Arnold
School of Oriental and African
  Studies
London, England

Jon Arrizabalaga
Consejo Superior de Investigaciones
  Cientificas
Barcelona, Spain

Arthur C. Aufderheide
University of Minnesota
Duluth, Minnesota

Scott Bamber
The Australian National University
The Research School of Pacific
  Studies
Canberra, Australia

William H. Barker
University of Rochester
Rochester, New York

Thomas G. Benedek
Veterans Administration Medical
  Center
Pittsburgh, Pennsylvania

Georges C. Benjamin
Department of Human Services
Washington, D.C.

Surinder M. Bhardwaj
Kent State University
Kent, Ohio

Francis L. Black
Yale University School of Medicine
New Haven, Connecticut

Alfred Jay Bollett
Yale University
New Haven, Connecticut

Allan M. Brandt
Department of Social Medicine
University of North Carolina
Chapel Hill, North Carolina

Don R. Brothwell
University of London
London, England

Audrey K. Brown
SUNY Health Science Center
Brooklyn, New York

Peter J. Brown
Emory University
Atlanta, Georgia

Jane E. Buikstra
University of Chicago
Chicago, Illinois

Vern L. Bullough
State University College
Buffalo, New York

Ann G. Carmichael
Indiana University
Bloomington, Indiana

Kenneth J. Carpenter
University of California
Berkeley, California

K. Codell Carter
Brigham Young University
Provo, Utah

Ranes C. Chakravorty
Veterans Medical Hospital
Salem, Virginia

Peter S. Y. Chen
University of Massachusetts Medical
  School
Worcester, Massachusetts

Thomas S. N. Chen
New Jersey Medical School
Newark, New Jersey

James D. Cherry
UCLA School of Medicine
Los Angeles, California

Thomas E. Cone, Jr.
The Children's Hospital
Boston, Massachusetts

Donald B. Cooper
The Ohio State University
Columbus, Ohio

Christine E. Cronk
Southern Illinois University
Carbondale, Illinois

Alfred W. Crosby
University of Texas
Austin, Texas

Scott F. Davies
Hennepin County Medical Center
Minneapolis, Minnesota

Charles W. Denko
Case Western Reserve University
   Hospitals
Cleveland, Ohio

Christian Derouesné
Centre Hospitalier
Universitaire Henri Mondor
Créteil, France

Eric J. Devor
University of Iowa
Iowa City, Iowa

Robert Dirks
Illinois State University
Normal, Illinois

Michael W. Dols
The Wellcome Institute for the
   History of Medicine
University of Oxford
Oxford, England

Wilbur G. Downs
The Yale Medical School
New Haven, Connecticut

Jacalyn Duffin
Queen's University
Kingston, Ontario, Canada

John Duffy
University of Maryland
Baltimore, Maryland, and
Tulane University Medical School
New Orleans, Louisiana

Howard Duncan
Henry Ford Hospital
Detroit, Michigan

Fredrick L. Dunn
University of California
San Francisco, California

Herbert L. DuPont
University of Texas Health Sciences
   Center
Houston, Texas

Stephen R. Ell
University of Utah Medical Center
Salt Lake City, Utah

Peter C. English
Duke University Medical Center
Durham, North Carolina

J. Worth Estes
Boston University School of Medicine
Boston, Massachusetts

Elizabeth W. Etheridge
Longwood College
Farmville, Virginia

John Ettling
University of Houston
Houston, Texas

John Farley
Dalhousie University
Halifax, Nova Scotia, Canada

Wayne W. Farris
University of Tennessee
Knoxville, Tennessee

Daniel M. Fox
State University of New York
Stony Brook, New York

David W. Fraser
Swarthmore College
Swarthmore, Pennsylvania

Roger K. French
The Wellcome Institute for the
   History of Medicine
London, England

Nancy E. Gallagher
University of California
Santa Barbara, California

Donald E. Gilbertson
James Ford Bell Museum of Natural
   History
Minneapolis, Minnesota

Clarence E. Grim
Hypertension Research Center
C. R. Drew University of Medicine
   and Science
Los Angeles, California

Otto R. Gsell
University of Basel
Lenzerheide, Switzerland

Lu Gwei-Djen
The Needham Research Institute
Cambridge, England

Thomas L. Hall
University of California
San Francisco, California

John S. Haller, Jr.
University of Colorado
Denver, Colorado

Victoria A. Harden
NIH Historical Office and
   Dewitt Stetten, Jr., Museum of
   Natural Research
Bethesda, Maryland

Anne Hardy
The Wellcome Institute for the
   History of Medicine
London, England

Brian T. Higgins
Toledo University
Toledo, Ohio

Neal R. Holtan
St. Paul-Ramsey Medical
   Center
St. Paul, Minnesota

Donald R. Hopkins
The Carter Presidential Center
Atlanta, Georgia

Patrick D. Horne
York County Hospital
Newmarket, Ontario, Canada

Joel D. Howell
University of Michigan Medical
   Center
Ann Arbor, Michigan

Robert P. Hudson
University of Kansas
Kansas City, Kansas

Frank C. Innes
University of Windsor
Windsor, Ontario, Canada

Robert Jackson
University of Ottawa
Ottawa, Ontario, Canada

Ann Bowman Jannetta
University of Pittsburgh
Pittsburgh, Pennsylvania

William D. Johnston
Wesleyan University
Middletown, Connecticut

Robert J. T. Joy
Uniformed Services University for
   the Health Sciences
Bethesda, Maryland

R. H. Kampmeier
Vanderbilt University School of
   Medicine
Nashville, Tennessee

Mary C. Karasch
Oakland University
Rochester Hills, Michigan

Edward H. Kass
Channing Laboratory
Boston, Massachusetts

John L. Kemink
University of Michigan Medical
  Center
Ann Arbor, Michigan

Robert J. Kim-Farley
World Health Organization Ex-
  panded Program on Immunization
Commugny, Switzerland

Kenneth F. Kiple
Bowling Green State University
Bowling Green, Ohio

Joseph B. Kirsner
University of Chicago Medical
  Center
Chicago, Illinois

Ronald J. Knudson
University of Arizona School of
  Medicine
Tucson, Arizona

John Komlos
University of Pittsburgh
Pittsburgh, Pennsylvania

Norman Kretchmer
University of California
Berkeley, California

LaVerne Kuhnke
Northeastern University
Boston, Massachusetts

Stephen J. Kunitz
University of Rochester Medical
  Center
Rochester, New York

Joseph A. Kwentus
The Dartmouth Hospital
Dayton, Ohio

Donald M. Larson
University of Minnesota
Duluth, Minnesota

Charles W. LeBaron
Centers for Disease Control
Atlanta, Georgia

Robert D. Leff
University of Minnesota
Duluth, Minnesota

James C. C. Leisen
Henry Ford Hospital
Detroit, Michigan

Angela Ki Che Leung
Sun Yat-Sen Institute for Social
  Sciences and Philosophy
Nankang, Taiwan, Republic of China

Jeffrey Levin
Phipps and Levin Dentistry
Bowling Green, Ohio

Jerrold E. Levy
University of Arizona
Tuscon, Arizona

Leslie Sue Lieberman
University of Florida
Gainesville, Florida

Elizabeth Lomax
University of California
Los Angeles, California

Irvine Loudon
Green College
Oxford, England

Maryinez Lyons
University of London
London, England

W. I. McDonald
Institute for Neurology
The National Hospital
London, England

F. Landis MacKellar
Unité de Planification de la
  Population
Lome, Togo

Sally McMillen
Davidson College
Davidson, North Carolina

James McSherry
Queen's University
Kingston, Ontario, Canada

Lois N. Magner
Purdue University
West Lafayette, Indiana

Gerald Markowitz
John Jay College of Criminal Justice
City University of New York
New York, New York

Leslie B. Marshall
University of Iowa
Iowa City, Iowa

Steven C. Martin
Albert Einstein School of Medicine
Bronx, New York

Pauline M. H. Mazumdar
University of Toronto
Toronto, Canada

Melinda S. Meade
University of North Carolina
Chapel Hill, North Carolina

David F. Musto
Yale University School of Medicine
New Haven, Connecticut

Joseph Needham
The Needham Research Institute
Cambridge, England

James L. Newman
Syracuse University
Syracuse, New York

John K. Niparko
University of Michigan Medical
  Center
Ann Arbor, Michigan

Ynez Violé O'Neill
University of California
Los Angeles, California

Donald J. Ortner
National Museum of Natural History
Smithsonian Institution
Washington, D.C.

S. R. Palmer
Centre for Communicable Disease
  Surveillance
London, England

Katharine Park
Wellesley College
Wellesley, Massachusetts

Bernard M. Patten
Baylor College of Medicine
Houston, Texas

K. David Patterson
University of North Carolina
Charlotte, North Carolina

Gordon J. Piller
Leukaemia Research Fund
London, England

Jacques Poirier
Centre Hospitalier
Universitaire Henri Mondor
Créteil, France

Heather Munro Prescott
Cornell University
Ithaca, New York

Jack D. Pressman
Institute for Health, Health Care
  Policy, Aging Research
Rutgers-Princeton Program in
  Mental Health Research
New Brunswick, New Jersey

Diane Quintal
University of Ottawa
Ottawa, Ontario, Canada

Ann Ramenofsky
University of New Mexico
Albuquerque, New Mexico

Oscar D. Ratnoff
University Hospitals of Cleveland
Cleveland, Ohio

R. T. Ravenholt
World Health Surveys Incorporated
Seattle, Washington

James C. Riley
Indiana University
Bloomington, Indiana

Guenter B. Risse
University of California
San Francisco, California

David Rosner
Bernard Baruch College and
   Mt. Sinai School of Medicine
New York, New York

Richard B. Rothenberg
Centers for Disease Control
Atlanta, Georgia

Mohammed Said
Hamdard Foundation
Karachi, Pakistan

Todd L. Savitt
East Carolina University School of
   Medicine
Greenville, North Carolina

Clark T. Sawin
Veterans Administration
Boston, Massachusetts

Shigehisa Kuriyama
Emory University
Atlanta, Georgia

Victor W. Sidel
Montefiore Medical Center/Albert
   Einstein College of Medicine
Bronx, New York

Dale Smith
Uniformed Services University of
   Health Sciences
Bethesda, Maryland

Reinhard S. Speck
University of California
San Francisco, California

David E. Stannard
University of Hawaii
Honolulu, Hawaii

Jerry Stannard
University of Kansas
Lawrence, Kansas

R. Ted Steinbock
Baptist Hospital East
Louisville, Kentucky

Edward G. Stockwell
Bowling Green State University
Bowling Green, Ohio

Shōji Tatsukawa
Kitasato University
Kanagawa-Ken, Japan

David N. Taylor
Walter Reed Army Institute of
   Research
Washington, D.C.

Keith W. Taylor
Cornell University
Ithaca, New York

Steven A. Telian
University of Michigan Medical
   Center
Ann Arbor, Michigan

Gretchen Theobald
Smithsonian Institution
Washington, D.C.

Bradford Towne
Southwest Foundation for Biomedical
   Research
San Antonio, Texas

Paul U. Unschuld
Institut für Geschichte der Medizin
Ludwig-Maximilians-Universität
Munich, Germany

Oscar Urteaga-Ballón
University of San Marcos
Lima, Peru

James Whorton
University of Washington
Seattle, Washington

Lise Wilkinson
University of London
London, England

Thomas W. Wilson
Charles R. Drew University of
   Medicine and Science
Martin Luther King, Jr., General
   Hospital
Los Angeles, California

H. V. Wyatt
University of Leeds
Leeds, Yorkshire, England

Preface

Over the past few decades or so, scholars and the public alike have been made increasingly aware of the role pathogens have played in shaping the history of humankind – an awareness now underscored by Quincentenary literature and exhibitions, which depict disease as a potent ally of the Spanish explorers and conquerors of the Americas. Certainly the swath that disease cut into the ranks of the Indians, and the chain of events the thinning of those ranks set in motion, constitute a vivid example of the importance of epidemiology in the unfolding of the historical process – a process that quickly spilled over from the Western Hemisphere to influence profoundly events in Africa, Europe, and ultimately the entire globe.

Yet this example, however compelling, can be as misleading as it is instructive when it creates the impression that the forces unleashed by pathogens in the Americas were products of circumstances that render them discrete. In fact, as the pages that follow demonstrate, pathogens have wielded (and are wielding) a similar dramatic and decided power over the history of all peoples everywhere throughout the whole of humankind's stay on the planet.

To make such a demonstration in substantial detail and from many different angles is one of the major purposes of this work. Another is to provide a place to start for others who wish to elaborate a biological dimension for their own research. A final purpose is to encapsulate what this generation knows or thinks it knows about disease and history as an artifact for generations to come.

One of the most striking features of world health today that scholars of those generations (as well as our own) will doubtless struggle to explain is the widely varying differences in infant, child, and adult mortality rates from region to region (as well as within regions) and the causes that generate those rates. In those less developed areas that embrace the majority of the world's population, the diseases that winnow human ranks remain, for the most part, the very killers that brought death to distant ancestors. In the world's more developed portions, however, new maladies of old age, such as heart diseases, cancer, and Alzheimer's disease, have supplanted communicable and deficiency diseases as the greatest outlets of human life.

Such differences confront us with political, economic, social, and certainly moral questions – questions that make the study of health in the less developed world a very pressing matter indeed. For this reason we have endeavored to bring the epidemiological history of that world right up to the present. Yet because of a certain "sameness" in the history of disease of the developed countries we felt no such obligation, but rather permitted these regional treatments to "trail off" and let topical entries such as "Alzheimer's Disease," "Concepts of Cancer," "Concepts of Heart-Related Diseases," and the like continue the story into the twentieth century.

Acknowledgments

This work is the fruit of the Cambridge History and Geography of Human Disease Project that was launched in late 1985. During the six years or so it took to complete, we have accumulated a considerable amount of indebtedness. That incurred by individual authors is acknowledged in their essays. It is my pleasure, however, to acknowledge the indebtedness of the project as a whole to many splendid individuals and institutions.

Funding for the project was provided as needed by various offices on the Bowling Green State University campus from beginning to end. Louis Katzner, Dean of the Graduate School, and Gary Hess, Chair of the History Department, made certain that the project was always staffed by at least one graduate assistant, and often two, on a year-round basis. The History Department also purchased computer equipment for the project including an optical scanner, made an office available for the staff, and provided secretarial service. Indeed, I shudder to think at what stage the effort would still be without Connie Willis, Judy Gilbert, and Phyllis Wulff, who performed a myriad of tasks including the typing of hundreds of letters and retyping of dozens of essays.

In addition, Christopher Dunn, Director of Research Services, helped us struggle with fundraising problems and made "seed money" available, whereas the Faculty Research Committee provided a salary and travel funds during two of the summers spent on the project. Finally, Eloise Clark, Vice President for Academic Affairs, gave us the resources needed to meet our payrolls on two critical occasions.

Seed money from outside the university was awarded to the project in 1986 by Cambridge University Press, the Hoffman–La Roche Corporation, Pfizer Pharmaceuticals, and the Milbank Memorial Fund. These monies were absolutely crucial in the early stages of the project both to launch it and to instill in us some confidence that others besides ourselves thought the effort important. A grant from the Earhart Foundation in 1987 helped to keep the project moving, and in 1988 the generosity of the National Endowment for the Humanities (Tools Division) made available the necessary funds to see it through to completion in late 1990. I am enormously grateful to all of these very fine organizations.

The project was born of discussions with Frank Smith, our editor at Cambridge University Press, and Frank has been extraordinarily supportive of the effort from the very first. That support, however, was much more than just encouragement from the sidelines. Frank was involved with the project's conceptualization; he helped to assemble the Board of Editors, and, on more than one occasion, found authorities to write essays that I had become convinced would go unwritten. To say that without his support this project would have never been realized is merely to state the obvious.

I would also like to acknowledge the considerable effort on our behalf made by copy editors Rosalind Corman and Mary Racine who, under the direction of Sophia Prybylski, were not at all intimidated by the four thousand or so manuscript pages of the project. Rather they scrutinized each and every page, frequently calling us to task, and forcing upon us that last round of writing, checking, and double checking that is so important but so painful. On the other hand, there are those who saved us a great deal of pain, and I am most grateful to some very gifted as well as good-hearted scholars who helped us with the intricacies of accenting, spelling, even rendering languages we had absolutely no competence in. These are board members Nancy Gallagher and Paul Unschuld; Oliver Phillips of the University of Kansas; and Bowling Green colleagues Ed Chen, Larry Daly, Fujiya Kawashima, and Kriemhild Coneé Ornelas.

Three generations of graduate students at Bowling Green have labored on the project, some for considerable periods of time, checking sources, entering essays into our computer equipment, preparing indexes, and performing countless other chores, including tutoring the rest of us on increasingly complex computer hardware and software. I thank them all. If these individuals were with us for a year or more, we have listed them as the associate editors they, in fact, were. Others who were with us for only a semester appear as assistant editors, but these distinctions are in no way intended to indicate reflections on the quality of the effort they gave us.

Rachael R. Graham has been the only permanent staff member to work on the project, and, as Executive Editor, it is she who has provided the continuity that kept the project from sliding into the abyss of chaos on numerous occasions. She also imposed stylistic continuity on it by reading, with marvelously critical eyes, each of our some 200 entries countless times, researching many of them, and working with the authors to completely rewrite a few. In addition, she corresponded regularly with our authors, and even as I write these words is readying a new caption listing of tables, graphs, charts, and so forth, while at the same time helping me with the latest versions of both of the indexes. It is impossible to express adequately my gratitude for all of her considerable effort and for her unfailing, and contagious, enthusiasm that accompanied it. But I shall try anyway with a simple "Thank you, Rachael." I also thank her husband, James Q. Graham, Jr., for all of his labors on our behalf in acquiring and setting up our various pieces of computer equipment. Finally I thank him for the considerable patience he exercised during years of hearing about the project from both of us and for the very good advice he provided on many occasions, just to prove he was still listening.

I am immensely grateful as well for all of the splendid advice given, and critical reviewing done, by the board members, some of whom, like Philip Curtin and Ann Carmichael, helped to initiate the project. The board members recommended most of the authors for the project, in many cases wrote essays themselves, and read essays in their areas of expertise for scientific and historical accuracy. Because of the nature of that expertise, some, such as

Tom Benedek, Jim Cassedy, Arthur Kleinman, Steve Kunitz, Ron Numbers, Dave Patterson, and Paul Unschuld, were called upon with sufficient frequency to provoke a bit of "testiness." But the collective performance of the entire board constituted a remarkable display of the highest possible standards of scholarship, right to the end when Ann Carmichael, Nancy Gallagher, Ron Numbers, and Guenter Risse more or less cheerfully helped in reading the Name Index. In some cases revisions called for by our board members were not made, or were only partially made. Negotiations with individual authors account for some of these differences, disagreement in the reports of board members account for more, and, on occasion, editorial decisions in our office were the reason. This is all by way of saying that despite the board members' incredible amounts of selfless input, only the authors and I bear final responsibility for the essays in this volume.

This work is, of course, first and foremost the product of those who wrote it, and my admiration for, and gratitude to, our 160 or so authors is boundless. Surely, as experts in their fields with countless other things besides this project to worry about, many of them must have felt sorely put upon by our (occasional) seemingly endless demands on their time. Doubtless this was very often the case for those contributors in faraway countries, when we encountered both technical and linguistic problems of communication as drafts, revisions, advice, criticism, and corrections traveled uncertainly back and forth via telephone, faxlines, and the mail services. Yet even if we tried the patience of many, the complaints have been few, and I thank all of the authors for the tremendous effort that their work represents and the wisdom it contains.

One of the great pleasures of any new project is that it generally brings new friends, and this one brought them by the score. But a project of this magnitude is also likely to bring sadness, and so it did as seven of our authors died while the work was still in progress. The loss of Michael Dols, Wilbur Downs (a board member as well), Lu Gwei-Djen, R. H. Kampmeier, Edward H. Kass, John L. Kemink, and Jerry Stannard was a heavy one for medicine and for its history.

During the course of the project, I also lost one of the best friends any person could hope for, when Miguel M. Ornelas, Director of Affirmative Action and Handicapped Services at Bowling Green State University, passed away. And it is to his memory, and to the memory of our seven colleagues on the project, that I dedicate this book.

Introduction

Between 1860 and 1864, August Hirsch published his monumental *Handbuch der historisch-geographischen Pathologie* in two volumes. In 1881 he finished an introduction to an updated edition, which Charles Creighton translated from German into English. This opus, published by the New Sydenham Society in three volumes, appeared during the years 1883 to 1886 and was entitled *Handbook of Geographical and Historical Pathology*. The *Handbook* represented a Herculean effort to detail the distribution of diseases of historical and geographic interest in time and in place.

Our work represents a similar undertaking, but with a major difference. In the second half of the nineteenth century, the dawn of germ theory, it was still possible (as Hirsch proved) for an individual working alone to produce a compilation of this sort. Today even the contemplation of such an attempt boggles the mind. The Cambridge World History of Human Disease project was launched in 1985 as a collective effort of some 160 social and medical scientists to provide at the close of this century something of what the Hirsch volumes provided at the end of the preceding century. We hope that, like the Hirsch volumes, our own effort will aid future students of health and disease in grasping our present-day understanding of diseases in their historical, spatial, and social dimensions.

Another important purpose of the project is to make available an understandable and accessible history of disease to social scientists and humanists in their many varieties. As historians, geographers, anthropologists, and other researchers have become increasingly aware of the importance of adding a biological dimension to their work, they have found the usual medical tomes, with their unfamiliar terminology and concepts, daunting indeed. We do not, however, ignore the needs of specialists in the many fields our work encompasses. Most of the following essays have been written by specialists, and all have been refereed by one or more of our board members, who are also specialists.

Parts I Through VIII

Part I of the work presents the major historical roots and branches of medical thought from ancient times to the twentieth century, and introduces the reader to the interplay of human migration, epidemiology, and immunology. Some may be interested to learn that despite popular notions about the antiquity of Chinese medicine, it actually trailed behind medicine in the West as a systematic discipline.

Part II deals with concepts of disease in the East and in the West, as well as with concepts of complex physical and mental ailments, the emphasis being on how those concepts have changed over time. As medicine has become more a science and less an art, it has helped to tame yesterday's plagues, which capriciously brought sudden death so frequently to so many. As a result, many now have the questionable privilege of living long enough to develop cancer or heart-related illnesses, which have supplanted infectious disease and malnutrition in the developed world as the most important causes of death. Increasing life expectancy has also contributed to the growth of that branch of medicine that deals with disorders of the mind and that, as Vern Bullough points out, has tended over time to appropriate for itself the right to decide what is deviant in sexual as well as other matters.

Some chapters in Part III deal with the inheritance of disease. Certainly one can inherit genetic diseases just as one can inherit disease immunities. Some disease immunities are acquired, but even these can be viewed as a heritage of the disease environment of one's birth. Children "inherit" what might be considered special illnesses because of their age, and the heritage of human-modified environments has frequently been famine, illnesses of malnutrition, and illnesses triggered by occupation. In addition, the "heritage" of habits can often produce illness, as is made clear in the essays on substance abuse and tobaccosis (along with those on cirrhosis and emphysema in Part VIII). The remaining chapters of Part III deal with efforts outside mainstream medicine to prevent and control disease; these include public health projects and the rise of chiropractic – a system of alternative medicine.

Part IV is essentially demographic. It focuses on measuring the health of various groups by nutritional status, by morbidity, and especially by mortality. An extremely important contribution of this section derives from the methodological questions that are raised.

The following three parts provide regional histories of disease around the globe from prehistory to the present. Part V concentrates on Europe, the Middle East, Africa, and most of the Americas, whereas Part VI is devoted to Asia. We have employed two types of historical division in these sections – Western idiosyncratic divisions in Part V and the more straightforward (and convenient) divisions of "ancient," "premodern," and "modern" for Asia in Part VI. Part VII completes the regional treatment by presenting a larger picture of changing disease ecologies. In addition to encapsulating the more detailed discussions of Europe, the Americas, Africa, and Asia that appear in Parts V and VI, this section deals with two more geographic areas – the Caribbean and Australia/Oceania. Because of their diversity and relatively small populations, they were omitted from the history sections.

Collectively, the essays in Parts V through VII reveal how much more is known about the history of disease in Europe and the Americas than in the rest of the world. There are a number of reasons for this, but three stand out. One is that anthropologists and other investigators of diseases that afflicted our distant ancestors have been considerably more active in the West than elsewhere. The second is that Western medical observers have historically been more empirically oriented than their philosophically inclined counterparts elsewhere. The third reason is that Western observers have had greater opportunities to observe a greater variety of illnesses. From

the Renaissance onward, increasing urbanization created more and larger breeding grounds for disease in Europe. In addition, the expanded travel of Europeans into the larger world – travel fraught with pathogenic peril – introduced them to still more diseases. All of this seems to have stimulated a compulsiveness in the West to give names to illnesses, which was not shared by medical practitioners elsewhere.

Part VIII discusses the history and geography of the most notable diseases of humankind in alphabetical order, from AIDS through yellow fever. Most essays are divided by the subheadings *definition, distribution and incidence or prevalence, epidemiology, etiology, clinical manifestations and pathology,* and *history and geography.* However, because of the variable nature of illnesses, some essays are organized in a way that is more suitable to the topic under discussion.

In Part VIII readers will encounter some disease entities discussed under archaic names, because they occur with some frequency in historical works. In certain cases we know what disease entity or entities they were intended to describe. The term *catarrh,* for example, was used in the past (and occasionally is still used) to label a variety of conditions that produced an inflamation of the mucous membranes of the head and throat. In other instances, such as chlorosis, which was proabably often anemia, we kept the name because it specifically signifies a "disease" recognized in the past as one that struck mostly young women. However, in the case of other ephemeral diseases such as sweating sickness, typhomalarial fever, and the plague of Athens, we had no choice but to use the archaic terms because to this day we can only guess what they were.

Most of these ailments are found in Hirsch under their now archaic names. He did not, of course, discuss AIDS or other newly discovered, extremely deadly infections such as Ebola virus disease, Lassa fever, or Legionnaires' disease, or illnesses such as Alzheimer's disease that were not recognized as specific clinical entities when Hirsch wrote. Others, however, like poliomyelitis are treated in his work under a different name (in this case, epidemic cerebrospinal meningitis). Indeed, what is striking about a comparison of the illnesses discussed in our volume and those dealt with by Hirsch is how few diseases have disappeared and how few new ones have arisen to take their places in the century that divides the two efforts. Perhaps most striking of all, however, is the change in emphasis. When Hirsch wrote, the world was still ignorant of the causes of epidemic diseases. Today, it is the chronic diseases such as cancer, Alzheimer's disease, and heart-related ailments about which we are most ignorant.

Indexes, Overlap, and Illustrative Materials

By means of two detailed indexes we have attempted to make the information in this work as useful, and accessible, as possible. The larger, general index provides many cross-references and historical synonyms for diseases. The second index lists proper names and supplies the dates and a brief biographical sketch of all historical figures in medicine mentioned by more than one author. Thus, it is possible to consult an entry on, say, the perception of disease in Asia during the eighth century (Parts I and II); to turn to another entry on the impact of smallpox and other epidemic diseases in eighth-century Japan (Part VI); to read another entry that discusses smallpox as a disease entity and provides its history; to discover something about Edward Jenner in the index of names; and then, using the general index, to trace the course of smallpox over time and around the globe.

The fact that this is possible means that there is some overlap. Yet from the outset it was decided that each essay should stand on its own. Thus, some repetition was not only inevitable but even desirable. Indeed, given the variety of methods and approaches employed by the contributors, what might be thought to be duplication is often scrutiny of a question with different lenses. Still, much overlap has been avoided because of the different approaches. Medical scientists tend to emphasize subjects that social scientists do not, and among the latter, anthropologists, demographers, economists, geographers, and historians all manage to disagree (not always cheerfully) about what is important. The various disciplines have also dictated an uneven deployment of illustrative materials. Geographers use maps; demographers, charts and graphs; anthropologists, diagrams; whereas historians all too often believe that their words are descriptive enough.

Overview

Despite the diversity, some consensus can be gleaned from the essays, and the epidemiological overview presented here is an attempt to highlight some new findings and old answers as well as the many perennial questions that remain unanswered.

Hunter-gatherers and early agriculturalists of the Old World, although hardly disease free, are gener- ally held to have been free of epidemic diseases as well as of many other illnesses now regarded as "diseases of civilization." In fact, there is some agreement that the cradle of many epidemic viral ailments, such as smallpox, was ancient South Asia, which was among the first regions to develop civilizations large enough to support these ailments. From there the diseases traveled east to China and then accompanied Buddhist missionaries to Korea and Japan.

Much evidence suggests that the West was relatively free of eruptive fevers such as smallpox, measles, and rubella until the first millennium A.D., when they finally settled in. These fevers are not mentioned in Greek texts, and as Stephen Ell points out in his study of the disease ecologies of Europe, the military fortunes of the Romans and their enemies do not seem to have been influenced by the kinds of diseases that decimated later European armies – or at least this influence was not felt until very late in the Empire's decline. But at that time, the eruptive ailments had apparently taken root, as is indicated by a change in Roman strategy and by the fate of wave after wave of invaders who enjoyed initial success only to go finally into sharp decline.

It is now clear that leprosy was a serious health problem for Europeans during much of the Middle Ages. Excavations of leper cemeteries leave no doubt that those interred were suffering from that disease and not something else such as yaws, as earlier writers have argued. The reason or reasons for the disappearance of leprosy remain subject to dispute. Some researchers believe that it had to do with the rise of tuberculosis – a disease that provides some immunity to leprosy; others argue that the plague killed so many lepers that the disease itself died out.

As for the plague, a great number of the questions regarding its course in Europe remain unanswered. It is generally accepted that it originated in the Himalayan borderlands between India and China and that the plague of Justinian (542–3), which reached Europe by 547, was in fact bubonic plague. But why it disappeared from Europe for some 800 years remains a mystery. Plague certainly seems to have been active in China during this period. The circumstances of its reappearance are also obscure. Our authors note that it may have reached the West from the Middle East. But the most likely explanation is that a plague epidemic began in China in 1331, found its way to the Crimea by 1346, and then diffused over Europe. Yet how this disease could linger on for centuries, very possibly without a sylvatic focus and with little evidence of widespread rat mortality, has not been explained. Nor have the circumstances of the eventual disappearance of plague from western Europe in the late seventeenth and early eighteenth centuries been determined. Explanations ranging from a mutation of the bacillus to the rise of strong governments able to regulate trade (and, often by accident, disease) continue to be advanced.

Among scholars of diseases in the Americas, there is a noticeable tendency to accept the notion that much larger Indian populations developed in isolation from the rest of the world than has previously been believed. Indeed, even the now nearly empty Amazon basin was teeming with them. Like the Old World hunter-gatherers, these people were not disease free. Intestinal parasites, a form of tuberculosis that may have become extinct, encephalitis, and hepatitis tormented them along with some kind or kinds of treponemal infection, and in certain locales, such uniquely American ailments as Carrión's disease and Chagas' disease were present. But despite the fact that some populations were dense enough to host them, neither the Old World epidemic diseases, nor malaria or yellow fever, infected the native Americans. If the Indians lacked pathogens to kill them, they seem to have made up for it by violence, because burial sites often reveal that trauma was an important cause of death.

European diseases changed this state of affairs – abruptly in the case of Caribbean Indians, somewhat more slowly in the Inca and Aztec empires, and substantially more slowly among other groups in Brazil and North America. But it is generally conceded that, despite locale, about 90 percent of the population eventually died out before demographic recovery began. Ann Ramenofsky has pinned down at least 13 diseases that arrived in the Americas with the Europeans and Africans during the first two centuries after the discovery of the American continent: viral diseases including influenza, measles, mumps, rubella, smallpox, and yellow fever; bacterial ailments embracing pneumonia, scarlet fever, pertussis, anthrax, and bubonic plague; typhus, whose causative microorganism stands midway between a virus and bacteria; and one protozoal infection – malaria. There is general agreement that, outside of Brazil, smallpox was the most devastating disease, though there is puzzlement as to how a relatively benign disease suddenly became deadly in Europe as well as the Americas in the sixteenth century. But all authors concerned with the matter point out the devastating impact of disease after disease sweeping over a people and the social disloca-

tion caused by the death of adults who normally provided food and care for the young and the old. Malaria is blamed for having depopulated much of the interior of Brazil, which brings us to still other Old World ailments, and to Africa.

If it is generally conceded that Asia was the cradle of many of the illnesses so far discussed (i.e., diseases that probably reached humankind via domesticated animals), there is no doubt that Africa was the cradle of another group of illnesses – those of wild animals and thus diseases that in many instances antedated the human species. These African diseases include some malarial types and other protozoal infections, such as African trypanosomiasis, which first infected our primate predecessors, as well as viral infections such as yellow fever and dengue.

Malaria, of course, has plagued India and China for millennia. But Africans and those of African descent living elsewhere around the globe are almost completely refractive to vivax malaria. This suggests that they have had the longest experience with what is generally believed to be the most ancient of the malarial types to affect humans. Indeed, because black Africans are so refractory to vivax malaria, the disease has disappeared from almost all of sub-Sahara Africa. By contrast, falciparum malaria, which is the most deadly of the malarial types, is also the newest; it too seems to have an African origin (or at least to have plagued Africans the longest), because Africans have by far the greatest variety and highest frequencies of genetic defenses against it.

Nonetheless, falciparum malaria spread out across the Sahara desert to take up residence around the Mediterranean and to become a serious threat in classical times, whereas vivax malaria had diffused much earlier over much of the globe. Vivax malaria doubtless reached the New World in the blood of early Spanish conquistadors, and falciparum malaria in the blood of the first slaves to be imported, if not before. Yellow fever, by contrast, was confined to Africa until the slave trade brought it to the Americas in the mid-seventeenth century. It seems to have begun tormenting European cities only in the eighteenth century, and never became established in Asia despite a plethora of suitable vectors, as well as monkey and human hosts. One possible explanation for the latter is that Asia supports so many other group B arborviruses that there has been no room for another.

In any event, such was not the case in the Americas. Both malaria and yellow fever joined in the slaughter of Indians; in the Caribbean this African wave of disease, coming hard on the heels of the European wave, almost obliterated them. But African diseases also killed whites, while sparing blacks, who seemed immune to both. These differences in susceptibility suggested to the Europeans that neither Indians nor whites could survive hard labor in warmer regions of the hemisphere. This brought about an accelerated slave trade and, of course, an accelerated flow of African pathogens to the New World. Indeed, much of tropical and subtropical America became more an extension of the African disease environment than of the European, until late in the nineteenth century. Even smallpox arrived from African, as opposed to European, reservoirs.

Whether the Indians gave syphilis to the rest of the world is a question taken up by a number of authors in this work. The biological anthropologists report that the treponemal lesions found in the bones of pre-Columbian Indians are probably not those of syphilis (as previously thought), or at least not of syphilis as we know it today. Moreover, the ability of Indians to resist the disease, which has been taken by some as proof of its pre-Columbian presence in the Americas, can be explained to some extent by the prevalence of pinta and perhaps nonvenereal syphilis – both milder forms of treponemal disease that nonetheless would have provided some cross-immunity. Also, our authors take into account the opinion of European physicians who claimed that the syphilis they saw at the beginning of the sixteenth century was simply a more virulent form of an old disease they had always treated. In view of these circumstances it is tempting to speculate that two treponemal infections, one from the Old World and the other from the New World, somehow fused to become the disease that ravaged Europe for more than a century before becoming more benign.

Somewhere around the beginning of the eighteenth century, Europe's population began to increase and, despite fits and starts, has continued to do so. How much of this growth can be credited to improved nutrition, the abatement of disease, increasing fertility and decreasing infant and child mortality, medical intervention, the growth of nation-states and improved public health, and changes in human attitudes and behavior has long been a subject of considerable debate. Stephen Kunitz believes that all are important factors and that no single one provides a full explanation. Nonetheless, he, along with other authors considering the problem in Asia, does stress the importance of the growth of cities in which diseases could become endemic and thus transformed into childhood ailments.

Meanwhile, from the 1770s onward, the natives of Australia and Oceania were subjected with increasing ferocity to the same trial by disease that had begun almost two centuries earlier in the Americas. And according to David Stannard, the results were similar, at least in Hawaii, where he places the population decline at 90 percent and blames smallpox, as well as other epidemic illnesses and venereal disease, for both increased mortality and reduced fertility. Elsewhere the process was often more gradual and is unfortunately still ongoing in some places, such as Brazil and Colombia.

As the world's cities grew in importance, so did tuberculosis, in both Asia and the West. Our authors leave no doubt about the relationship between urbanization and tuberculosis. Yet the disease began receding while urbanization was still accelerating and long before medicine had acquired its therapeutic "magic bullet." This leaves still another unresolved medical mystery, although it would seem that the explanation lies somewhere within the parameters of improving nutrition and the development of resistance to the illness.

Crowded nineteenth-century cities with poor sanitation and impure water supplies were natural targets for another of the plagues from India – Asiatic cholera. In his essay, Reinhold Speck demonstrates the role of the British army in unwittingly unleashing the disease. He traces each of the pandemics, straightens out the problem of dating one of them, and shows how cholera did much to emphasize the importance of public health and sanitation programs.

The end of the 1800s brought an understanding of the role of vectors in a number of diseases, including malaria and yellow fever, and this along with an increase in the production of quinine permitted the Europeans finally to venture beyond the coasts into the interior of Africa. Tropical medicine became an integral part of colonizing efforts, although as both Maryinez Lyons and K. David Patterson make clear, the initial aim was not so much to help those colonized as it was to preserve the health of the colonizers. Moreover, in modifying environments to suit themselves, the latter inadvertently facilitated the spread of such illnesses as African trypanosomiasis, onchocerciasis, schistosomiasis, and leishmaniasis.

The twentieth century dawned with the principles of germ theory still being digested by the world's medical community. As our authors on Asia and Africa indicate, Western medicine has (perhaps fortunately) not always supplanted local medicine but rather has often coexisted with it. Nonetheless, the effectiveness of Western medicine in combating trauma and illnesses such as rabies, cholera, typhoid, gangrene, puerperal fever, and yaws was quickly recognized.

Yet Western medicine was completely overwhelmed as influenza became the next great plague to sweep the earth just as World War I was winding down. As Alfred Crosby emphasizes, although the case mortality rate for the disease is low, the disease killed upward of 30 million across the globe, making it perhaps the "greatest single demographic shock that the human species has ever received." Nor did the dying cease after the pandemic was over: As R. T. Ravenholt reveals in his essay on encephalitis lethargica, this illness was a peculiar sequela to the so-called Spanish flu.

After the influenza epidemic, the developed world enjoyed perhaps its first extended respite from epidemic disease since classical times. Medical science made great strides in understanding and controlling infectious illnesses. Because of the emphasis on germ theory, however, the etiologies of nutritional ailments remained elusive for a time, but eventually those of beriberi, pellagra, rickets, and scurvy were unraveled and the role of vitamins discovered. In the tropical and subtropical worlds, Rockefeller programs were launched to rid these regions of long-standing illnesses, and if hookworm disease and yellow fever were not eradicated as had been confidently expected, at least much was learned about their control.

Rickettsial diseases have always been troublesome for armies. Typhus has been credited with defeating Napoleon in Russia, and during World War I the disease killed some 2 million to 3 million soldiers and civilians. But in World War II and its aftermath, important advances were made in combating rickettsial diseases. In addition, new drugs were developed against malaria.

As the authors writing on the ailments of infants and children make evident, the young have historically suffered most from epidemic and endemic diseases. But in the past several decades this has been changed by the development of antibiotics and by accelerated worldwide programs of vaccination. In fact, as Alfred Crosby points out, in his essay on smallpox, one of these programs led by the World Health Organization appears to have ended the career of that disease, which killed so many for so long. Poliomyelitis, which briefly loomed as another of the world's great plagues, was also brought under control by similar programs, although as H. V. Wyatt reminds us, such efforts are not without some risk and the disease lingers in many parts of the world.

Unfortunately, other diseases of the young continue to be prevalent, especially in the developing world, where protein–energy malnutrition, respiratory infections, dysenteries, and helminthic and protozoal parasites, separately and working in concert, kill or retard the development of millions each year. As our specialists make clear, much headway must be made in that world against other potentially crippling ailments such as yaws, leprosy, and ophthalmia. Some malarial strains have become drug resistant, and continued dengue epidemics, carried by the same vectors that spread yellow fever, raise the very real possibility of yellow fever making a comeback in the Western Hemisphere, as it seems to be doing in parts of Africa.

In the developed world, chronic diseases such as cancer, heart-related illnesses, and Alzheimer's disease have supplanted infectious diseases as the important killers, and increasingly the role of genes in the production of these diseases has come under scrutiny. In addition, medicine has concentrated on understanding the genetic basis for such diseases as cystic fibrosis, Down syndrome, epilepsy, favism, hemophilia, Huntington's disease, leukemia, multiple sclerosis, muscular dystrophy, Parkinson's disease, sickle cell anemia, and Tay-Sachs disease. Some of these, such as sickle-cell anemia, favism, and possibly Tay-Sachs disease, are an unfortunate result of the body's evolutionary attempt to protect itself against other diseases.

As this research has gone forward, it has become clear that many other disease conditions, such as lactose intolerance and diabetes, are strongly influenced by heredity. Leslie Sue Lieberman argues that in the latter instance a "thrifty gene" left over from the feast and famine days of our hunter-gatherer ancestors may be at work. Genes also play a vital role in selecting cancer and heart disease victims or even gout patients, although in these cases genetic predisposition can often be modified by behavioral changes – and to that extent these illnesses can be viewed as human made. No wonder, then, that there has been a recent upsurge of concern about the air we breathe and the food and other substances we take into our bodies.

It may well be that environmental factors are bringing us back face to face with epidemic illnesses. For example, as more and more individuals are entering our shrinking rain forests, new and deadly viruses are being released into the rest of the world. In fact, AIDS, which almost certainly originated in nonhuman primates, has become a plague of such proportions that it may eventually be ranked along with the Black Death, smallpox, cholera, and influenza as among the most disastrous epidemic scourges of humankind. In addition, as Wilbur Downs shows, other extraordinarily lethal viruses such as Ebola, Marburg, and Lassa also lurk in these rain forests and pose a serious threat to us all.

When Hirsch wrote in the preceding century, few understood and appreciated the extent to which humans have created their own disease ecologies and their own diseases by the ways they live and the ways they manipulate their environments. As we approach the twenty-first century, we have finally begun to acquire that understanding. Whether at the same time we have acquired a sufficient appreciation of what we have done is another matter.

Kenneth F. Kiple

PART I

Medicine and Disease:
An Overview

Greece and Rome

Before the fifth century B.C., ancient Greece had physician-seers (*iatromantis*) who combined magical procedures and drug treatments, and wound healers deft at caring for battlefield trauma. Another group of practitioners were engaged in medical dietetics, a tradition that developed primarily in response to the needs of athletes. Ultimately, it encompassed not only questions regarding exercise, bathing, and relaxation, but the regulation of food and drink for all citizens. All of these traditions eventually merged around 500 B.C. into a *techne iatriche,* or healing science, that sought to define its own intellectual approach and methodology. For this purpose, the new medicine adopted a theoretical framework capable of explaining the phenomena of health and illness. The new *techne* was also heavily dependent on clinical observations from which careful inferences and generalizations were derived.

The foremost representative of classical Greek medicine was Hippocrates, a prominent practitioner and teacher who came to personify the ideal Western physician. Within a century of his death in 370 B.C., several unknown disciples wrote nearly 60 treatises, come clinical and some theoretical, on medical subjects differing widely in content and style. This collection of writings, which comprised a comprehensive and rational healing system usually known as "Hippocratic" medicine, emphasized the individual patient. Its practitioners focused exclusively on physical factors related to health and disease, including the immediate environment. Indeed, among the most famous works of the Hippocratic corpus was the treatise *Airs, Waters, and Places,* an early primer on environmental medicine. Another was *Epidemics,* a day-to-day account of certain patients, and a third was *Regimen,* a prescription of diet and life-style conducive to health.

For the ancient Greeks, health was a state of balance among four bodily humors: blood, phlegm, yellow bile, and black bile. Each had a specific bodily source, a pair of fundamental qualities, and a particular season in which it could be produced in excess. The blood, for example, was elaborated in the liver, was hot and moist, and was prone to overflow during the spring. Not only were humors the material and dynamic components of the body, but their ever-imperfect and labile mixture was responsible for a person's psychological makeup, or "temperament," as well as for deficiencies in bodily constitution that created susceptibilities to disease.

Illness thus occurred when the humoral balance was upset either by a lack of proper nourishment or by the imperfect production, circulation, and elimination of the humors. The physician's goal was to restore a healthy balance through the use of diet, rest, or exercise and a limited number of drugs, all capable of aiding the natural healing powers believed to exist in every human being.

This somewhat conservative approach of merely assisting nature and above all not harming the sick characterized the method of Hippocratic physicians. It was congruent with the rather tenuous social position of the early Greek healer, often an itinerant craftsman entirely dependent on his personal reputation because the country lacked an educational and licensing system for medical professionals. Given the elementary state of medical knowledge as reflected in the absence of properly identified disease entities, the demands made of Hippocratic healers were simple prognostications – will the patient live or die? – and ideally some amelioration of symptoms by complementing the healing forces. Unfettered by religious barriers, although coexisting with a religious healing system based on the cult of Asclepius (the god of medicine), the *techne iatriche* prospered within the flexible tenets of humoralism, a cultural system that was widely shared by healers and their patients and that allowed for the gradual inclusion of new clinical observations.

After the death of Alexander the Great in 323 B.C. and the partial dismembering of his empire, Egypt flourished under the rule of the Ptolemies. Alexandria, the chief cultural and commercial center, became famous for its library and museum, attracting manuscripts and scholars from the entire Hellenistic world. In addition to collecting medical literature, scholars such as Herophilus of Chalcedon and Erasistratus of Cos carried out systematic human dissections, identifying structures of the circulatory and nervous systems, the eye, and the female reproductive organs.

Given the limitations of contemporary medical knowledge, as the Hippocratic healing profession began to compete for upper-class patronage serious debates ensued about the value of medical theory and bedside expertise. Two "sects," the Dogmatists and Empiricists, first became involved in this dispute. The former, led by Praxagoras of Cos, emphasized the need for theoretical knowledge in medicine, especially to establish plausible explanations for the phenomena of health and disease. The Empiricists, under the guidance of Herophilus, revolted against excessive speculation and expressed skepticism about the value of medical theory, placing instead greater emphasis on bedside experience. Two centuries later, a third group of Greek physicians residing in Rome – the Methodists – espoused a simplistic view of bodily functioning and restricted their treatments to bathing, diet, massage, and a few drugs.

In Rome, healing was essentially a popular skill practiced by heads of families, slaves, and foreigners. A lack of regulations and low social status contributed to a general mistrust of physicians. An exception, however, was the respect accorded to Galen of Pergamon of the second century, a well-educated follower of Hippocratic medicine who managed to overcome the schisms of sectarianism. A prolific writer who authored hundreds of treatises, Galen also carried out anatomic dissections and physiological experiments on animals. He successfully integrated his extensive clinical experience, which he acquired mainly as a surgeon to performing gladiators, into his basic theoretical knowledge, providing medicine with a comprehensive system destined to survive for nearly 1,500 years.

Early Christian Era, East and West

After the collapse of the Roman Empire, Western medicine experienced a period of retrenchment and decline. Healing became an important act of Christian charity, a divine gift freely provided within the framework of the new church and not restricted to professional physicians. Given this religious orientation, Christians healed through the confession of sins, prayer, the laying on of hands, exorcisms, and miracles, occasionally performed by saints or church fathers.

In Byzantium, the Christian magical-religious healing flourished side by side with the earlier rational Greco-Roman medicine in spite of frequent tensions, especially because physicians often exacted exorbitant payments for their services. Several of them, including Oribasius of the fourth century, Aetius of Amida and Alexander of Tralles of the sixth century, and Paul of Aegina of the seventh century, compiled and preserved ancient medical knowledge and with their writings made Galen the central medical authority for the next 500 years.

Faced with a growing population and adverse economic conditions, the early Christian church created a number of philanthropic institutions. The provision of shelter and food for the poor and for strangers was extended to several forms of health care in houses called *xenones* (hostels) and more specifically *nosokomeia* (places for the sick). Among the first was an inn built by Bishop Basil around 375 in Caesarea, which was apparently staffed by nurses and physicians. Two decades later similar institutions opened their doors in Constantinople, and thereafter such hospitals proliferated in other major commercial cities of the Byzantine Empire.

In western Europe, monks played an important role in Christian healing as well as in the collection and preservation of medical manuscripts. Whereas Augustinian monks lived a life of isolation and prayer, the followers of Benedict created working communities that cared for their sick brethren as well as visitors and transients. Monasteries such as the cloister of Monte Cassino, founded in 529, and the cathedral schools after the year 800 became heirs to fragments of classical medical knowledge. Many Benedictine monasteries – such as St. Gall (c. 820) – continued both a *hospitale pauperum* for pilgrims and an *infirmarium* for sick monks and novices. Monasteries were constructed along important roads or in surviving Roman towns, notably in southern France and Italy. Sick care was dispensed as part of the traditional Christian good works. By contrast, medical treatment under the supervision of physicians remained sporadic.

Islam

Before the seventh century, Islamic healing consisted merely of a collection of popular health rules, or *hadiths*, known as "Muhammad's medicine" for use by devout Muslims living on the Arabic peninsula. In accordance with basic religious and philosophical ideas, this system was holistic, emphasizing both body and soul. However, as the Islamic Empire gradually expanded, a comprehensive body of Greco-Roman medical doctrine was adopted together with an extensive Persian and Hindu drug lore.

The collection, preservation, and eventual transmission of classical medical knowledge went on for several centuries. Even before the Arab conquest of 636, Nestorian Christians in Jundishapur, Persia, had played a prominent role in safeguarding Greek learning by translating many Greek works into the Syriac language. Later, under Islamic rule, these Nestorian physicians wielded great influence over the early caliphs, conducting searches for additional

Greek manuscripts in the Middle East and directing a massive translation program of scientific texts from Syriac into Arabic.

Islam's political supremacy and commercial networks made possible the collection of medicinal plants from the Mediterranean basin, Persia, and India. The eleventh-century author Abu al-Biruni composed a treatise on pharmacy in which he listed about 720 drugs. In addition, Islamic alchemy furnished a number of metallic compounds for the treatment of disease. Such expansions in materia medica and the compounding of remedies led to the establishment of a separate craft of pharmacy.

In medical theory, authors writing in Arabic merely followed and further systematized classical humoralism. Whereas al-Razi, or Rhazes, of the ninth and early tenth centuries contributed a number of original clinical works such as his treatise on smallpox and measles, the *Canon of Medicine* composed in the early eleventh century by the Persian physician Ibn Sina, or Avicenna, became the leading medical encyclopedia and was widely used until the seventeenth century. Finally, Moses Maimonides, a Jewish physician and prolific author, wrote on clinical subjects and medical ethics.

Islam significantly influenced hospital development, creating secular institutions devoted to the care of the sick. The first *bimaristan* – a Persian term meaning "house for the sick" – was established in Baghdad before the year 803 by Ibn Barmak, the famous wazir of Harun al-Rashid. It was based on Byzantine models transmitted to Jundishapur. Unlike previous and contemporary Christian institutions devoted to medical care, *bimaristan*s were private hospitals symbolizing royal prestige, wealth, and charity. Their selected inmates came from all sectors of the population and included mentally disturbed individuals. Operated by a director together with a medical staff, pharmacist, and servants, *bimaristan*s offered comprehensive medical care and educational opportunities for students serving apprenticeships. In fact, the hospitals had their own libraries, which contained copies of medical texts translated from the Greek and Syriac.

In addition to providing clinical training, medical education became more formalized. Small private schools offered a flexible curriculum of lectures and discussions, generally under the direction of famous physicians. In recognition of these cultural apprenticeships, the state issued licenses for practicing medicine to students who had successfully completed a course of theoretical and clinical studies. The traditional Islamic *hisbah* system of codes and regulations designed to enforce law and order according to the mandates of the Koran gradually extended its jurisdiction over multiple healing activities. Physicians, surgeons, bonesetters, and pharmacists were examined by the caliph's chief physician or an appointed inspector before receiving permission to practice. Unquestionably, such official efforts to establish ethical and practical standards for medical conduct and action were important steps in the professionalization of medicine.

Middle Ages

After the twelfth century, medieval medical knowledge in the Occident ceased to be based solely on a number of scattered Greek and Latin manuscripts carefully collected and preserved for centuries in monasteries and schools. A rapidly growing number of classical medical texts, including the *Canon* of Avicenna and clinical treatises of Rhazes, were translated from Arabic to Latin. Nonetheless, the theory of four humors and qualities remained the basis for explaining health and disease. It was supplemented by the notion that an essential or "radical" moisture was needed to ensure proper mental and physical functioning. Based on the natural wetness of bodily tissues, this element played an important role in explaining disease, senility, and death.

The inclusion of medicine in early university studies had momentous consequences. Teachers devised formal curricula and identified a specific body of medical knowledge to be mastered by students. For the first time, physicians could acquire an academic degree in the field of medicine, thus laying claim to greater competency and legitimacy. Among the first schools to offer medical studies was in Salerno, around 985, but the real growth in medical education occurred in the thirteenth century with the founding of three major university centers: Montpellier and Paris in France, Bologna in Italy. Because a medieval medical education stressed theory, rhetoric, and philosophical speculation, graduates acquired an unprecedented degree of prestige and status. In contrast, the practical aspects of healing lacked intellectual standing, and surgery was therefore excluded from university studies. Graduates, in turn, created select medical organizations – often under royal patronage – and worked hard to achieve a monopoly on practice.

Teaching centers became focal points for medical investigations. Human dissection, for example, began at the University of Bologna toward the end of the thirteenth century, prompted by forensic as well as medical considerations: Both lawyers and practitioners were interested in ascertaining the causes of death from foul play or epidemic disease. In 1316, a Bolognese professor, Mondino de Luzzi, wrote the first modern treatise on anatomy. This specific interest was continued at other universities, including those of Padua, Florence, and Pisa. All works on anatomy were designed to illustrate the descriptions of Galen, still the absolute authority on the subject.

In response to repeated and deadly plague epidemics – the first pandemic struck Europe between 1348 and 1350 – northern Italian city-states instituted a series of public health measures designed to protect the healthy elite from the ravages of the disease. Because poisonous miasma was blamed for the humoral imbalance that caused susceptibility to plague, authorities isolated ships whose crews and cargoes were suspected of carrying miasma. The isolation – or so-called *quarantenaria* – necessary to neutralize the offending particles lasted for 40 days. Venice and Ragusa were among the first cities to implement such measures, the former in 1348, the latter in 1377. Burial regulations, the control of water supplies, the cleansing or burning of contaminated possessions – all inaugurated a comprehensive sanitary program widely adopted by other European cities in ensuing centuries.

The emergence during the twelfth century of lay communities in which the principal focus of charitable work was care of the sick can be seen as a response to Europe's growing burden of disease. The Knights of St. John, the Teutonic Knights, and the Augustinian Brotherhood played key roles in this evolution. Hospital foundations, sponsored by the rulers of newly created kingdoms or local bishops, provided the poor, elderly, unemployed, and sick with spiritual and physical care in the form of diet and nursing. The rising prevalence of leprosy after 1200 forced the establishment of nearly 20,000 shelters to separate these stigmatized sufferers from the general population. With the onset of plague after 1348, local authorities set up quarantine stations and pesthouses aimed at isolating those suspected of harboring the disease.

Renaissance

With the revival of classical Greek learning, or humanism, during the Renaissance, Western medicine was profoundly influenced by the replacement of corrupt and incomplete texts with new Latin translations of the original Greek. However, tensions developed between the old learning and contemporary insights into the phenomena of health and disease, some of which had been previously ignored or misun-

derstood. For example, the early-sixteenth-century findings of Andreas Vesalius of Padua, based on meticulous and systematic dissections that established the foundations of modern anatomy in the West, contradicted Galen's descriptions. In fact, Vesalius demonstrated that Galen's findings were based on animal dissections – especially of the barbary ape – instead of human dissections.

Another sixteenth-century attack on classical medicine came from a Swiss practitioner, Philippus von Hohenheim, better known by his adopted name, Paracelsus. His goal was to investigate nature directly and thereby discover the hidden correspondences between the cosmos and human beings. During his many travels, Paracelsus acquired a detailed knowledge of occupational diseases. For example, he observed the ailments contracted by European miners, an unprecedented pathology without adequate classical antecedents. On the basis of his alchemical education and clinical experience, Paracelsus formulated a new theory of medicine based on the notion that the body functioned chemically under the direction of an internal "archeus," or alchemist, responsible for maintaining the proper balances and mixtures. Consequently, cures could be achieved only through the administration of chemically prepared remedies. Paracelsus strongly advocated the use of mercury in the treatment of syphilis, a potentially toxic therapy widely accepted by his contemporaries.

Equally important were the innovations in surgical technique and management of gunshot wounds by the sixteenth-century French surgeon Ambroise Paré. On the basis of new anatomic knowledge and clinical observations, Paré questioned a series of traditional assumptions concerning the treatment of injured soldiers, including venesection, cauterization, and the use of boiling oil. Paré's publications, written in the vernacular, profoundly influenced the surgical craft of his day, replacing ancient methods with procedures based on empirical knowledge.

Seventeenth Century

The classical assumptions of humoralism that had explained human functioning in health and disease for nearly two millennia in the Western world were severely challenged in the seventeenth century. During this century, the body came to be viewed as something like a machine governed by physical principles. This view was expressed by the philosopher René Descartes in a treatise published posthumously in 1662. Cartesian man had a dual nature: a physical body ruled by universal laws of matter and motion, and an immaterial soul or mind – a pure thinking entity – located in the pineal body of the brain. The body was conceived of as a vast hydraulic network of hollow pipes, moving blood and nervous fluid in the circulatory and nervous systems under the influence of the mind.

Descartes's mechanical theory spawned a mechanical school of human physiology located primarily in northern Italy, where Galileo Galilei, the great physicist, had already established a science of mechanics. Following in Galileo's footsteps, a mathematician, Giovanni A. Borelli, analyzed the phenomenon of muscular contraction and a physician, Sanctorius of Padua, studied metabolic combustion and insensible perspiration.

In England, William Harvey's experimental discovery of the blood circulation, announced in 1628, contributed to the mechanical view of living organisms while discrediting Galen's fanciful hypothesis of a humor ebb and flow. The heart was now viewed as a pump, its chambers closing tightly with the help of valves. Blood was impelled into an intricate system of vessels according to the laws of hydrodynamics and traveled in a close circle through the arterial, venous, and capillary systems.

Not only did Harvey's findings support a mechanistic view of the human organism, but his approach to the theory – which included dissections, animal experiments, and mathematical reasoning – demonstrated the potential usefulness of scientific research in resolving physiological questions. On the basis of the ideas of Pierre Gassendi, a seventeenth-century French philosopher, regarding the corpuscular nature of matter, various British investigators working in concert studied the phenomenon of respiration. By the 1670s, Robert Boyle, Robert Hooke, Richard Lower, and John Mayow had concluded that certain air particles entering the lungs and mixing with arterial blood were essential for all vital functions. At the same time, chemical fermentation studies by Jean Baptiste van Helmont and François de la Boë explained the nature of digestion. Microscopic studies, carried out by Anton van Leeuwenhoeck in Holland using a single-lens instrument with a magnification of about 300 diameters, remained unequivocal.

Although corpuscular dynamics replaced traditional humors and their qualities in the explanation of human physiology, clinical medicine failed to benefit from the new medical theories. Practitioners treating the sick could not readily apply these views to the therapeutic tasks at hand, preferring instead to prescribe their traditional cures by adhering to obsolete ideas of humoral corruption and displacement. Thomas Sydenham, a prominent English physician, urged his colleagues to ignore the conflicting theoretical views, proposing instead the careful study of individual diseases at the bedside. Sydenham's goal was the establishment of complete clinical descriptions of particular diseases, their subsequent classification, and the development of specific remedies for each identified ailment.

Eighteenth Century

In the occidental world, the Enlightenment created an optimistic outlook concerning the role and benefits of medicine. Most contemporary thinkers believed that health was a natural state to be attained and preserved. Society had to be made aware of medical possibilities through the employment of professionals who could deal expertly with all health-related problems. Governments increasingly sought to develop social policies that included the physical well-being of the public. A new medical elite took charge and began to play a more prominent role in European society.

Among the requirements of national power perceived by European authorities was a healthy and expanding population. Greater emphasis was placed on environmental health, infant and maternal welfare, military and naval hygiene, as well as mass treatment of the poorer sectors in newly erected hospitals and dispensaries. Absolutist governments established systems of "medical police." These organizations were responsible for establishing and implementing programs, such as that designed by the German physician Johann P. Frank, to monitor and enforce public and private health regulations from cradle to grave. In Britain, private philanthropy substituted for governmental action in matters of health. Although frequently utopian in its goals, the medical police movement created greater awareness of the social and economic factors conducive to disease. In turn, physicians and reformers were successful in establishing charitable institutions for care of the sick, including mothers and children. Needy ambulatory patients were seen in dispensaries and polyclinics. Although often crowded and a source of contagion, such establishments provided shelter, food, and a modest medical regimen designed to manage illness.

Efforts to control smallpox focused on a practice popular in the Orient: smallpox variolation. The virus, taken from pustules of an active case, was inoculated in healthy individuals on the assumption that this transfer would attenuate the agent and produce only a mild case of the disease in exchange for permanent immunity. In England the procedure was pioneered in 1721, but it remained controversial because of its potential for causing full-fledged, often fatal cases of smallpox and thus triggering unexpected epidemics. After the 1760s, however, simplified and safer inoculation methods found popular acceptance, and these were replaced in the 1790s by cowpox vaccination, introduced by Edward Jenner.

On the theoretical front, the eighteenth century became the age of medical systems in the Western world. It was clear that a synthesis of the isolated physical and chemical discoveries of the preceding century into a comprehensive system would be necessary to provide a rationale for and guidance to clinical activities. Spurred by success in the physical sciences, especially Newton's formulation of the laws of gravity, physicians set out to establish principles governing the phenomena of health and disease. Such efforts were as old as medicine itself. However, new models of anatomy and physiology based on Vesalius's dissections and Harvey's experiments, coupled with chemical and microscopic findings, demanded placement into an updated scaffolding.

Most eighteenth-century systematists tended to be prominent academics. As teachers and famous practitioners, they zealously promoted and defended their creations, fueling bitter controversies within the medical profession. System building conferred status and a mantle of intellectual respectability conducive to patient patronage and separation from quacks. Among those who adhered to mechanical concepts in explaining clinical events were the Dutch professor Herman Boerhaave of Leyden and the German Friedrich Hoffmann of Halle. By contrast, a colleague of Hoffmann, Georg Stahl, tried to remedy the apparent inadequacies of iatromechanism by postulating the existence of a vital principle, a soul or "anima," capable of harmoniously directing all mechanical activities in the body and thus ensuring organic unity. Two subsequent systems elaborated by the Scottish physicians William Cullen and John Brown assumed that a properly balanced and stimulated nervous system played a pivotal role in the maintenance of human health.

Efforts to classify diseases were intensified. Nosology, the systematic division of disease entities, prospered side by side with similar taxonomic efforts directed at plants and animals. Physicians such as Carl von Linné (Linnaeus), Boissier de Sauvages, and Cullen established complex classification systems designed to bring order to the myriad symptom complexes found at the bedside as well as to provide guidelines for treatment. Unfortunately, these systems remained highly subjective and dependent on the clinical experience of the nosologist who produced them. Greater accuracy and uniformity were achieved as bedside experiences were linked to structural changes observed at postmortem dissections, an approach pioneered by the Italian physician Giovanni B. Morgagni but not fully implemented until decades later in France.

Nineteenth Century

French Clinical School

Modern Western medicine emerged in France at the Paris Medical School during the first half of the nineteenth century. After the French Revolution, political developments and a new philosophical outlook radically changed the theoretical and institutional bases of medicine. Given the population explosion and urbanization, hospitals became the key locations for medical advances. Housing thousands of poor patients, the Parisian hospitals offered unique opportunities for the observation of a large number of sick individuals.

The French medical revolution was ushered in by an important change in approach. Arguing that it was not necessary to discover the ultimate causes of health and disease, early leaders of the Paris Medical School, such as Pierre J. Cabanis and Philippe Pinel, postulated that physicians could perceive the effects of disease and apprehend the relationships between the disease and the patient, accessible to observation only at the bedside. Thus, only the incontestable truths of sensory perception had validity in any attempt to understand health and disease. These phenomena were too complex and variable to be placed into the straitjacket of a specific medical theory. Stress was to be placed on practical problem solving, with sense impressions providing the only reliable data.

This skeptical empiricism gave rise to a new method: "analysis." Disease was composed of many symptoms and signs, and these confusing combinations appeared sequentially at the sickbed. The most important task was to record the regular order of such manifestations, correlate them with physical signs, and thus recognize simple patterns. Eventually, practitioners would be able to discern specific disease entities and finally classify them. Pinel urged physicians to walk the hospital wards frequently, notebook in hand, recording the hourly and daily progression of illness. The goal was better diagnosis and prognosis based on clinical events.

Emphasis on the physician's powers of observation increased the importance of physical diagnosis and expanded the techniques employed in eliciting physical signs of illness. Until this time, practitioners had relied almost entirely on their patients' accounts to reach a diagnosis. Although the clinical history remained important, French physicians began to apply new methods starting with Jean N. Corvisart's direct percussion in 1808, the employment of a stethoscope by René T. H. Laennec in 1816, and indirect percussion of the body with a plessimeter designed by Pierre A. Piorry in 1826. These procedures were, of course, also based on the premise that certain organs in the patient's diseased body suffered a number of structural changes.

Thus, another fundamental development of the Paris Medical School was pathological anatomy, the study of localized changes in bodily organs accomplished through systematic postmortem examinations of the thousands of patients who died in hospitals. Correlating clinical symptoms and signs with specific organic lesions enabled practitioners to redefine particular disease entities and understand the underlying structural defects. Such clinicopathological correspondences expanded medicine's knowledge of diseases, their effects, and natural evolution. As a corollary, French physicians became more interested in improving their diagnostic rather than their therapeutical skills.

Another tool, the "numerical method," was introduced in 1828 by Pierre C. A. Louis to compare clinical findings and identify through medical statistics general disease characteristics as well as the efficacy of traditional therapies. Although this approach initially raised a storm of protest among practitioners who felt that statistical calculations tended to obscure the significance of individual clinical variations, the method launched a new era of clinical investigation, replacing intuitive and impressionistic decision making at the bedside.

By the mid-nineteenth century, however, the French school lost its undeniable leadership in Western medical practice. Although tremendously fruitful, the clinical approach based on bedside observations and postmortem findings had its limitations. Consciously ignored were questions concerning the causes of disease and the nature of biological events surrounding the phenomena of health and disease. What had been a realistic approach in an era of speculative chemistry and physiology, imperfect microscopes, and nonexistent pharmacological knowledge around 1800 became an anachronism 50 years later. Further answers had to be sought in the laboratory, not just at the sickbed.

German Scientific Medicine

Before the eclipse of the Paris Medical School, German medicine began to emerge from its earlier, speculative period, frequently labeled "romantic." From 1800 to 1825 physicians in the politically divided German states made a serious attempt to establish a "science" of medicine using criteria from the critical philosophy of Immanuel Kant. But their efforts were doomed given the elementary state of knowledge of what we consider to be the "basic" medical sciences: anatomy, physiology, biochemistry, pathology, and pharmacology.

By the 1830s, however, the foundations had been laid for less ambitious but more fruitful investigations into the phenomena of health and disease. The 1834 Prussian–German Customs Union and extensive railroad network brought a measure of economic prosperity to the German states, enabling them to support the reform of their autonomous university system. Armed with an ideology of pure research and lack of concern for immediate practical results, German physicians went to work in academic laboratories and dissecting halls. The emphasis on and prestige accorded to the pursuit of intellectual activities was eagerly supported by the highest authorities, who perceived such scientific enterprises as enhancing national prestige.

Studies in physiology, microscopic anatomy, embryology, as well as comparative and pathological anatomy flourished. One of the key figures promoting these studies was Johannes Mueller, a physiologist searching for the ultimate truths of life behind empirical data. Although his philosophical goals remained elusive, Mueller had trained a whole generation of outstanding German scientists by the time of his death in 1858. They included Theodor Schwann, proponent of the cell theory; Emil DuBois Reymond, and Hermann von Helmholtz, famous for their discoveries in nerve electrophysiology and the physics of vision; Jakob Henle, the founder of histology; and Rudolf Virchow, the founder of cellular pathology. Indeed, these men rejected a general philosophical framework and adopted a purely reductionist viewpoint, attempting to explain all biological phenomena as merely following the laws of physics and chemistry.

Germany's university system played a central role in the development of scientific medicine in the West after 1840. Unlike the near monopoly of

French academic studies in one city, Paris, there were more than 20 institutions of higher learning scattered throughout the German states, each self-governing and intensely competitive. Since degree requirements included the submission of dissertations based on original research, the stage was set for a spectacular increase in scientific activity once the universities had established prestigious professorships and built adequate laboratory facilities. Medical research became a respectable career, made possible by the proliferation of fellowships and assistantships. Successful individuals were rewarded with academic posts and further facilities, leading to a dramatic rise in scientific professionalization and specialization.

Even in clinical disciplines German academics with proper research experience edged out outstanding practitioners. A whole generation of physicians who had trained abroad — especially in Paris — returned with a knowledge of physical diagnosis and pathological anatomy. A new bedside approach combined the French methods with German chemical and microscopic examinations based on a growing understanding of human physiology and physiopathology. Although the first key step of disease description and identification had taken place in Parisian hospitals, German physician-scientists sought to understand the mechanisms that caused pathological changes. Here the laboratory became important for biochemical analyses, microscopic observations, and animal experiments.

The quest for greater diagnostic precision was aided by the design of new tools for visualizing disease. In 1851, Helmholtz described the ophthalmoscope, an instrument capable of directly exposing eye disorders and testing visual acuity. The successful assembly of a laryngoscope by Johann N. Czermak in 1857 permitted inspection of the throat, especially the larynx and vocal cords. Visualization of the esophagus was accomplished in 1868 by Adolf Kussmaul with an esophagoscope, and the bladder came to be observed with the help of the cystoscope, invented by Max Nitze in 1877. Finally, in 1895, Wilhelm C. Roentgen, a physicist, discovered the rays that carry his name. Henceforth, X-ray photographs and fluoroscopes became common features in clinical diagnosis, especially that of chest diseases.

German advances in the basic medical sciences and clinical diagnosis were not matched at the therapeutic level. In fact, a better understanding of disease processes often led to skepticism — even nihilism — regarding possible cures. To be sure, the conceptual advances in understanding disease were impressive and promised further breakthroughs. At the same time, greater technological assistance and diagnostic complexity shifted medical care to hospitals and clinics, significantly raising costs. But the actual practice of medicine remained unaffected. Although the fledgling pharmaceutical industry began to purify a number of traditional remedies and develop a few new drugs, therapeutics lagged. Translating scientific understanding into convincing practical results had to await the development of vaccines, sera, and antisepsis based on a knowledge of bacteriology.

Germ Theory

Since the time of Hippocrates, Western practitioners had blamed factors in the atmosphere for the appearance of infectious disease. A "miasma" composed of malodorous and poisonous particles generated by the decomposition of organic matter was implicated in a broad array of fevers, including plague, malaria, and yellow fever. Speculations about the nature of these miasmatic specks waxed and waned, from Girolamo Fracastoro's *seminaria,* or "seeds of disease," in 1546, to microscopic "worms," or multiplying ferments, *zymes,* proposed by William Farr in 1842. However, physicians remained generally skeptical of theories that implicated microscopic substances in the genesis of complex disease entities. Moreover, their rudimentary microscopes only added to the confusion by revealing myriad objects.

Given the clinical behavior of the most common nineteenth-century diseases such as typhus, cholera, typhoid, and yellow fever, most physicians accepted the notion that they were not directly contagious and could occur only because of specific environmental conditions. This anticontagionist posture was strongly reinforced by political and economic groups that sought to avoid the imposition of costly quarantines. But others argued that certain contagious diseases, such as smallpox, measles, and syphilis, were indeed transmitted by living parasites.

In the 1840s, chemists, including Justus von Liebig, proposed that both contagion and miasma were actually "ferments," consisting of self-reproducing particles of a chemical nature spontaneously generated during the decomposition of organic matter. At about the same time, Henle, a German anatomist, suggested that such particles were actually alive and behaved like parasites after invading the human organism. He believed that the causes of infectious disease could be found by a careful search for these parasites, believed to be members of the plant kingdom. The proof for this causal relationship between disease and parasites was contained in Henle's three "postulates": constant presence of the parasite in the sick, its isolation from foreign admixtures, and reproduction of the particular disease in other animals through the transmission of an isolated parasite.

Thanks to the work of Louis Pasteur, a French chemist, fermentation and putrefaction were shown to be indeed mediated by living microorganisms. In 1857 Pasteur claimed that the yeast responsible for lactic fermentation was such a microorganism. In the early 1860s, Pasteur disposed of the doctrine of spontaneous generation, proving through a series of clever experiments that only by exposure to tainted air would processes of fermentation and putrefaction take place. Microbial life could not exist in any organic medium that had been sterilized and subsequently protected from outside contamination.

With the existence of microscopic germs and some of their actions firmly established, researchers such as Pasteur and the German physician Robert Koch began to study specific diseases. In 1876 Koch published his findings on anthrax, a deadly illness of animals, especially cattle and sheep. He provided the first proof that a specific microorganism could cause a particular disease in an animal. Koch's new techniques for obtaining pure cultures and staining pathogenic bacteria further advanced the fledgling field of microbiology and led to a reformulation of Henle's postulates. According to Koch, three criteria were needed to implicate a particular microorganism in the etiology of a certain disease. First, the parasite must be present in every case of the disease and under circumstances that could account for the clinical course and pathological changes of that disease. Second, this agent should not be present in any other disease as a fortuitous and nonpathogenic parasite. Finally, after being fully isolated from the sick organism and repeatedly grown in pure culture, the parasite should be able to induce the same disease if inoculated into another animal.

The last two decades of the nineteenth century witnessed an unprecedented string of bacteriological discoveries based on the Henle–Koch postulates, including the agents responsible for typhoid fever, leprosy, and malaria (1880), tuberculosis (1882), cholera (1883), diphtheria and tetanus (1884), pneumonia (1886), plague and botulism (1894), dysentery (1898), and syphilis (1905). Whereas Koch and his coworkers devoted much time to the development of technical methods for cultivating and studying bacteria, Pasteur and his collaborators turned their efforts toward determining the actual mechanisms of bacterial infection and host resistance. By 1900 not only were physicians able to diagnose the presence of specific microorganisms in the human body and hence diagnose an infectious disease, but they possessed some knowledge concerning natural and acquired immunity. In several instances, the latter could be successfully induced, a belated triumph of modern laboratory medicine.

Guenter B. Risse

Bibliography

Ackerknecht, Erwin H. 1967. *Medicine at the Paris Hospital, 1794–1848.* Baltimore.

    1982. *A short history of medicine.* Baltimore.

Ben David, E. G. J. 1960. Scientific productivity and academic organization in 19th century medicine. *Scientific Sociological Review* 25: 828–43.

Bullough, Vern. 1966. *The development of medicine as a profession.* Basel.

Cipolla, Carlo M. 1976. *Public health and the medical profession in the Renaissance.* London.

Debus, Allen G., ed. 1974. *Medicine in seventeenth century England.* Berkeley and Los Angeles.

Foster, W. D. 1970. *A history of medical bacteriology and immunology.* London.

Foucault, Michel. 1973. *The birth of the clinic,* trans. A. M. Sheridan Smith. New York.

Garrison, Fielding H. 1929. *An introduction to the history of medicine.* Philadelphia.

King, Lester S. 1958. *The medical world of the eighteenth century.* Chicago.

    1963. *The growth of medical thought.* Chicago.

Nasr, Seyyed H. 1968. *Science and civilization in Islam.* Cambridge, Mass.

Penn, M., and M. Dworkin. 1976. Robert Koch and two visions of microbiology. *Bacteriological Reviews* 40: 276–83.

Phillips, E. D. 1973. *Greek medicine.* London.

Risse, Guenter B. 1986. *Hospital life in Enlightenment Scotland.* New York.

Rothschuh, Karl E. 1973. *History of physiology,* trans. and ed. Guenter B. Risse. Huntington, N.Y.

Shryock, Richard H. 1947. *The development of modern medicine.* New York.

Singer, Charles, and E. A. Underwood. 1962. *A short history of medicine.* Oxford.

Temkin, Owsei. 1973. *Galenism: Rise and decline of a medical philosophy.* Ithaca, N.Y.

Temkin, Owsei, and C. L. Temkin, eds. 1967. *Ancient medicine.* Baltimore.

I.2
History of Chinese Medicine

Premedical Health Care

A concern with illness has been documented in China for three millennia; the earliest written evidence extant today on the theoretical and practical consequences of this concern dates from approximately the eleventh century B.C. At that time, and for centuries to come, it was assumed that the well-being of the living – be it related to success on the battlefield, to an abundant harvest, or to physical health – depended to a considerable extent on their interactions with the nonliving members of the community (i.e., with their ancestors). An adherence to specific norms was thought to guarantee social and individual health; transgressions were known to cause the wrath of the dead, who then had to be propitiated with sacrifices. The communication between the living and the nonliving that was necessary to establish the cause of an affliction and to identify an appropriate remedy was recorded on bones and turtle shells, many of which were found in the soil, especially in the province of Henan, earlier this century. Whether the belief in ancestral intervention was supplemented by a pragmatic application of drugs or other empirically valuable means of therapy was not documented in written form at this early time.

Political changes during the first millennium B.C., when the Chou dynasty fell into a period of turmoil with several centuries of civil war, may have been responsible for the rise of a new worldview. Even though a belief in the effect of ancestral curses or blessings on the health of the living has survived in Chinese culture well into the twentieth century, especially among some rural strata of the population, Chou sources indicate a change in emphasis. The physical health and illness of the individual (and, in the case of epidemics, of society) were thought of at this time predominantly as an outcome of successful protection against the possibility or manifestation of an onslaught of not only visible but also invisible enemies (i.e., demons).

In contrast to ancestors, demons, who were not related to specific living persons as deceased relatives, were not believed to desist from harming humans even if they adhered to certain moral principles. Moreover, demons could not be propitiated through sacrifice. Rather, they had to be prevented from entering and harming a human body by means of signs and symbols demonstrating an alliance with superior metaphysical powers, and they had to be removed from the body either through the casting of oral or written spells or with the help of substances designed to kill or chase away (for instance, through their odor) unwanted intruders. Several clues suggest that among the origins of acupuncture may have been attempts to pierce, with symbolic swords and lancets, afflicted, aching body regions thought to be invaded by some outside evil.

Ancestral and demonological notions of health and illness are mentioned here for two reasons. First, they have survived in Chinese culture until the present time as important aspects of the overall system of conceptualized and practical health care, particularly in the treatment of mental and children's illnesses. Second, Chinese medicine, documented since the second century B.C. and developed as a system of ideas and practices based on insights into the laws of nature rather than on metaphysics, still embodies some of the fundamental tenets of these earlier approaches to understanding health and healing, namely an emphasis on cause–effect relationships and a localistic-ontological notion of disease.

Traditional Chinese Medicine

An almost complete afterworld household, closed in 167 B.C., was unearthed from the now-well-known Ma-wang-tui site near Ch'ang-sha in Hunan between 1972 and 1974. This tomb of a noble family had been equipped with virtually everything a deceased person was thought to need in his or her subsequent existence, including 14 manuscripts on various aspects of health care. These manuscripts marked the beginning of documented Chinese medicine and revealed that it was on the verge of breaking away from metaphysical health care. Thus, we may assume that they also reflected the earliest phase in the development of medicine in China, that is, the development of a system of health care beliefs and practices focusing specifically on the illnesses of the human mind and body rather than on human social and individual existence as a whole.

The tomb dates from a period between the second century B.C. and the first century A.D., when Chinese medicine took on its basic shape. This appears to have been a quite dynamic era. As early as the first century, various schools of medical thought had been founded and had already produced diverging ideas. These were compiled under the name of the mythical Yellow Emperor and have become the classic scripture of traditional Chinese medicine, that is, the *Huang-ti nei-ching* (The inner classic of the Yellow Emperor).

An attempt at systematizing the rather heterogeneous contents of the *Huang-ti nei-ching,* and at drawing diagnostic and clinical conclusions from an assumed circulation of vapors in the human body, resulted in the second major literary work of Chinese medicine, the *Nan-ching,* probably of the first century A.D. This work is also of unknown authorship and was subsequently associated with an earlier (about the sixth century B.C.) semilegendary itinerant physician named Pien Ch'io.

Pharmaceutical knowledge was recorded with astonishing sophistication in a collection of prescriptions found among the Ma-wang-tui scripts named *Wu-shih-erh ping fang* (Prescriptions against 52 ailments) by modern researchers. At about the time of the compilation of the *Nan-ching* (and coinciding with the appearance of the materia medica of Dioscorides in A.D. 65 in the West), Chinese pharmaceutical knowledge found its own literary form when the first Chinese herbal was compiled, which became known by the title *Shen-nung pen-ts'ao ching* (The divine husbandman's classic on materia medica). Its real author is unknown, and like the other works discussed, this classic was linked to a mythical culture hero, Shen-nung, who is also credited with the development of agriculture and markets as well as with the establishment of drug lore.

Basic Perspectives
The Ma-wang-tui manuscripts, the *Huang-ti nei-ching,* the *Nan-ching,* and the *Shen-nung pen-ts'ao ching* are the main sources for our current understanding of the early developmental phase of Chinese medicine, even though the last three may have undergone considerable revisions in later centuries and cannot be considered genuine Han dynasty sources in their entirety. Still, the picture emerging from studies of these sources so far reveals the formation of several complex and multifaceted approaches to health care, all of which were associated with basic social, economic, and ideological changes preceding and following the unification of the Chinese Empire in 221 B.C.

Central to Chinese medicine is its perception of the human organism. Corresponding to the socioeconomic structure of the unified empire, the human organism was described in Han sources as a system of individual functional units that stored, distributed, and processed resources, which were brought into the organism from the outside or were developed within. The individual units were linked through a system of channels, thought to transport resources from one place to another and join the units to the outside world. The terminology used to describe the structure and workings of the organism is largely metaphoric and is based on images from the geographic, economic, and social environment of the Ch'in and Han dynasties in China.

The resources or goods to be passed through the organism were given the name *ch'i* in the *Huang-ti nei-ching.* This term denotes essential vapors thought to be the carriers of life. Similar to the development of ancient European concepts of *pneuma* and *spiritus,* the concept of *ch'i* may have originated from observations of such phenomena as suffocation and "empty vessels" (arteries = *aer tereo* = "carriers of air") in a corpse. The *Huang-ti nei-ching* described a continuous circulation of these vapors through the organism, ascribing greater importance to them than to blood. Illness occurred in an individual organism in the same way that crisis emerged in a complex state economy. This might be because one or more of the functional units failed to fulfill their duties, or were inadequately equipped with *ch'i,* or did not pass *ch'i* on. Also, the transportation system might be blocked, thereby preventing the circulation of resources. All of these problems could be caused by the person concerned – for example, through an unhealthy life-style – or by environmental conditions to which the person was unable to adapt.

The purpose of Chinese medicine, like that of all medicine, is to protect individuals from an untimely loss of health, one of their most essential possessions. According to the *Huang-ti nei-ching,* a life span of 100 years should be considered normal, and as the unknown author concluded, it is only because civilized people are unable to lead healthy lives that they must resort to medicine for help. The prevention and treatment of illness were attempted in Chinese medicine through the two basic approaches of localistic-ontological and holistic-functional reasoning.

An ontological approach views diseases either as abstract hostile entities themselves or as the result of an intrusion of some normally innocuous environmental agent into the human organism. One of the Ma-wung-tui texts suggests the existence of a tangible ontological perspective by relating the notion of small animals (such as worms or insects) entering the body to cause destruction at well-defined locations. This internal destruction was thought to become visible in the failure of bodily functions or in the destruction of external parts of the body that were associated with the internal functional units affected first. The history of leprosy in Chinese medicine, traceable from Ch'in sources written between 252 and 221 B.C., is one example of the persistence of such ontological thoughts through two millennia of Chinese medical history. It is also a good example of the early ontological notions in China that paved the way for an understanding and acceptance of Western bacteriology, morphological pathology, and, finally, chemotherapy in the nineteenth and twentieth centuries.

In addition to such tangible agents as worms and insects, the ontological perspective views the environment as filled with agents (such as heat, cold, humidity, dryness, and wind) that are essential components of nature and that may turn into "evils" that harm humans upon entering their bodies either in undue quantities or at inappropriate times. "Wind" in particular has remained a central etiologic category in Chinese medicine through the ages, and it is this very concept of wind that demonstrates the continuation and transformation of basic demonological tenets in the history of Chinese medicine. Originally conceived of as a spirit entity, the wind was believed to live in caves and cause harm to humans when it left its residence. Yet in the *Huang-ti nei-ching* there is a shift to the concept of wind as a natural phenomenon active as a result of the movement, through heaven, of a superior spirit named *T'ai-i*. Harm was caused by wind now only if it blew from what were considered inappropriate cardinal directions in the course of the year (as might be expected in an agricultural society) or if it met humans with constitutions susceptible to harm. Then, beginning with the works of Chang Chi in the second to third century A.D., the wind came to be seen solely as an environmental agent, albeit one that could strike humanity and cause a host of illnesses.

In addition to identifiable environmental influences that could change from "normal" (*cheng*) to "evil" (*hsieh*), abstract "evil" or "malicious" (*o*) entities could enter the organism and cause illness. These assaults were thought of not only as invasions of the natural environment into the human body, but also as flare-ups between various functional units within the body itself. If, for instance, *ch'i* normally filling the spleen was exhausted beyond some acceptable degree, agents from the liver might turn evil and invade the spleen to take over its territory. The language used to describe these processes, beginning with Han dynasty sources and throughout the history of Chinese medicine, reflects the experience of the long period of "Warring States" that preceded the unification of the Chinese Empire. Furthermore,

in the same way that troops move through a country from one place to another, the ontological perspective of Chinese medicine assumed that evil intruders could be transmitted from one location in the body to another. Transmission was thought to occur in accordance with clearly defined mutual relationships between the various upper and lower, inner and outer regions of the body. An early example of this thought can be found in the biography of Pien Ch'io compiled by Ssu-ma Ch'ien in 90 B.C.

Closely linked to the ontological perspective of Chinese medicine is a functional view that is recorded in medical literature beginning with Han dynasty sources. This approach to identifying and curing illness is concerned mainly with diagnosing functional disturbances in the human organism, which is considered to be a complex structure consisting of various mutually interrelated functional units. The functional view focuses on processes and on functional relationships among the subsystems constituting the organism, and it assumes that the same illness may affect several functions at the same time.

For example, a specific functional unit may be harmed by wind. There result various pathological conditions, such as aversion to wind or fever, headache, and sweating without external reason. Or the "liver" (seen here not as a tangible organ but as a set of functions) may be marked by a depletion of *ch'i*, which is accompanied by the growth of a shade in one's eyes. Treatment may be directed at the ailment in the liver, or it may be focused solely on the secondary problem in the eyes. Although the first example reminds one of Western categories such as "disease" and "symptoms," the second demonstrates that the terms *illness, disease,* and *symptom* do not entirely overlap in Chinese and Western medicine and should be used only with great care in a comparative context.

The perspectives outlined here did not preclude the realization that one individual organism might be affected at one time by two or more mutually independent illnesses, each of which had to be named and treated separately. To make matters more complicated, one identical cause could result in two simultaneous, yet separate, illnesses. Conversely, two separate causes could bring about one single illness, with each of these situations requiring, theoretically at least, different therapeutic treatments.

Diagnosis

Some of the Ma-wang-tui texts refer to various vessels thought to pervade the body without interconnection. Specific irregularities in the contents and movements of each of 11 such vessels revealed specific illnesses. The *Huang-ti nei-ching,* however, described 12 vessels, or conduits, which were interconnected. This text advocated the feeling of pulses at various locations of the body to examine movement in the individual sections of the vessel circuit and to diagnose the condition of the functional units associated with these sections. Finally, the *Nan-ching* proposed the feeling of the pulses at the wrists only and developed complicated methods for extracting detailed information on the origin, present location, and possible future courses of an illness. In addition, the *Huang-ti nei-ching* and the *Nan-ching* provided ample data on the meaning of changing colors in a person's complexion, of changes in a person's voice or mouth odor, and of changes in longing for a specific flavor. Furthermore, the *Nan-ching* recommended investigations of the condition of the skin of the lower arms and of abdominal palpitations.

These diagnostic methods were described in the literature so that an illness could be discovered and categorized from a theoretical (mainly functional) point of view. Prescription literature, by contrast, did not depend on theory. Rather, it contained listings of very simple and more or less obvious symptoms, such as headache and diarrhea. These were paired with drug prescriptions for their cures.

Theoretical Foundations and Treatment

The most impressive mode of treatment recorded in detail in the Ma-wang-tui scripts is drug therapy. More than 200 active drugs and neutral carrier substances were described, as was a highly developed pharmaceutical technology. Other therapies included massage, minor surgery, hot baths, sexual practices, dietetics, and moxa cauterization, in addition to various magical interventions. Acupuncture was not yet referred to and appeared first in the already mentioned biography of the semilegendary physician Pien Ch'io compiled by Ssu-ma Ch'ien in 90 B.C. Because no earlier documentation of needling exists in China, the origins of acupuncture, possibly the most recent mode of therapy in the history of Chinese medicine, remain unknown.

For about 1,200 years after the emergence of Chinese medicine, until the end of the Song dynasty in the thirteenth century, a dichotomy prevailed between two major currents. One was the so-called medicine of systematic correspondence; the other was pragmatic drug therapy.

The ideology of systematic correspondence appeared almost simultaneously in China and ancient Greece (possibly stimulated by a common origin, the location of which is unknown) around the sixth century B.C., when it became the theoretical underpinning of the functional approach to an understanding of health and illness.

The (most likely older) ontological understanding of illness is based on a recognition of struggle, attack, and defense as normal modes of interaction in nature. Both human behavior and the daily observation of attack and defense among other animals and plants supported this worldview.

In contrast – and this is to be regarded as one of the outstanding cultural achievements of humankind – the ideology of systematic correspondence is based on the concept of harmony as normal, and of a loss of harmony as abnormal, states of existence. Like the ontological notion, the notion of systematic correspondence drew on sufficient environmental and social evidence to be plausible; it gained legitimacy from its emphasis on the regularity of countless natural processes, a regularity that was guaranteed by the appropriate behavior and location of each perceivable phenomenon in a complex network of interrelatedness. It holds that inappropriate behavior jeopardizes this regularity, or harmony, and leads to crisis. This crisis may occur in nature, in the affairs of state, or in the life of an individual, in the last case leading to illness. Hence, this ideology is holistic in that it views both the individual physical/mental organism and the sociopolitical organism as corresponding to identical principles, and "health" is a notion transcending them.

The ideology of systematic correspondence assumes (as this designation by contemporary scholars implies) a relationship of correspondence among virtually all tangible and abstract phenomena in the universe. Phenomena of identical quality are grouped within a category, and two or more categories are linked with one another and interact with one another according to certain natural laws. Various schools emerged within the framework of systematic correspondence, advocating the existence of two (yin and yang) or five (five-phases) categories of all phenomena.

The yin–yang school was based on a perception of the unity of two antagonistic categories of all existence. Day and night are opposites, and yet they form a unity. The same applies to male and female, heaven and earth, summer and winter, above and below, dominating and submitting, and so forth. Beginning in the fourth century B.C., day, male, heaven, summer, above, and dominating were identified as qualitatively identical and were categorized as yang, their opposites as yin. The *Huang-ti nei-ching* contains more sophisticated groupings into four and six yin–yang subcategorizations, which may have developed in the meantime.

The second school, the five-phases school, recognized five categories of qualitatively identical phenomena, symbolized by five essential environmental elements: metal, wood, water, fire, and soil. These five categories represented phases in the succession, and hierarchical stages in the interaction, of certain phenomena. For example, the liver was associated with the phase of wood, and the spleen was associated with the phase of soil. Wood – for instance, as a wood spade – could move soil; hence, a specific relationship between liver and spleen could be explained as resulting from a potential of the liver to subdue the functions of the spleen.

The *Huang-ti nei-ching* and the *Nan-ching* linked these notions of systematic correspondence with physiology, etiology, and therapy. As a result, the human organism was described as a microcosm of interrelated functional units associated with the more encompassing categories of all being, and hence with the social and physical environment. Not surprisingly, the reasons for maintaining individual health, or for the emergence of illness, closely paralleled the reasons for social and environmental harmony and crisis. The only therapeutic mode within this system of ideas was acupuncture (and to a certain degree dietary means and moxa cauterization).

The *Shen-nung pen-ts'ao ching* contained virtually no references to the concepts of systematic correspondence. Pharmaceutics developed along its own lines from a description of 365 substances in Shen-nung's herbal of the first century, to 850 substances in the first government-sponsored materia medica in 659, to more than 1,700 drug descriptions in the great herbals of the northern Song published from 960 to 1126.

One reason for this dichotomy may be seen in a basic antagonism between Confucian-Legalist thinking and the Taoist worldview. Confucian-Legalist social ideology has dominated Chinese society – with varying intensity – since the early Han dynasty. One of its conceptual foundations is the belief in social order, a social order maintained by the government through law enforcement and education, both of which encourage appropriate legal and moral behavior. The medicine of systematic correspondence was built on identical tenets; health was promised to individuals if they followed a specific life-style congruent with Confucian-Legalist ethics. Needling, moxa, and dietetics were not meant to

rescue the fatally ill, but were seen as stimuli to correct aberrations from a proper path.

By contrast, drug lore promised to rescue individuals from illness regardless of whether they adhered to morality and human rites. From the Han through the T'ang dynasty, the development of pharmaceutics was closely tied to persons affiliated with Taoism. This phenomenon was obviously related not only to the Taoist quest for elixirs and drugs of immortality, but also to the value of drug lore for contradicting the Confucian-Legalist linking of social and individual well-being with an adherence to a morally legitimated life-style and to government-proclaimed laws. Taoists claimed such rites and laws to be the origins of social and individual crisis. Thus, it was only between the thirteenth and fifteenth centuries, in the aftermath of Song Neo-Confucianism, that certain Confucian-Legalist and Taoist tenets were united for a few centuries and that attempts were made to construct a pharmacology of systematic correspondence.

Literature and Specialties

Before the decline of the last of the imperial dynasties at the end of the nineteenth century, Chinese medicine developed on many levels and in many directions. Even though new insights and data were being accumulated virtually all the time, it maintained its original theoretical foundations; perhaps a peculiarity of Chinese medical history is that the concept of obsolescence remained almost entirely alien to it. Indeed, before modern Western thought made an impact, no theory or practice was ever relegated to oblivion as outdated (only in pharmaceutics do some herbals list "drugs no longer in use"). The notion of a dialectic advancement of knowledge or of "scientific revolutions" does not apply to Chinese medicine. In fact, one should speak of an expansion rather than of a progression of knowledge, because the etymology of *progress* implies that something is left behind.

More than 12,000 titles of premodern Chinese medical literature from a period of about 2,000 years are available in libraries in China and other countries today, but not even a handful of these texts have been translated into modern languages in a philologically serious way. Hence, only some very basic historical tenets of traditional Chinese medicine are known in the West, and it is imperative that access to many sources be provided so that comparisons can be made with the history of medicine in other cultures. In this connection, it is important to note that Chinese medicine developed the same specialties as did traditional European medicine. Separate sections in the often very voluminous prescription works and individual monographs were devoted to such problems as children's diseases, the diseases of women, skin problems, eye complaints, and throat ailments. The following provide a few examples: The earliest extant title concerned with the diseases of children is the *Lu-hsin ching* (Classic of the Fontanel), of unknown authorship and compiled around A.D. 907, which was presumably based on sources of the fourth century or even earlier. The oldest available text today on women's diseases and obstetrics is the *Fu-jen liang fang* (Good prescriptions for females) of 1237 by Ch'en Tzu-ming. A text, lost now, possibly dating back to T'ang times and indicating the Indian origins of Chinese ophthalmology, is the *Lung-shu p'u-sa yen lun* (Bodhisattva Nagarjuna's discourse on the eyes), and a first monograph on leprosy was published by Hsüeh Chi in 1529 under the title *Li-yang chi-yao* (Essentials of the *li*-lesions). On ailments affecting the throat, the oldest text extant is the *Yen-hou mai cheng t'ung lun* (Comprehensive discourse on vessel [movements] indicating [the condition of] the throat), of unknown authorship and dating from approximately 1278.

Although, as has been stressed, Chinese medicine emphasized an ontological perspective and was quite familiar with localistic notions of illness, only a few dissections were recorded during the imperial age, and surgery was never developed much beyond the knowledge needed for performing castrations. Cataract surgery was introduced from India as early as the T'ang dynasty, but was never really integrated into Chinese medicine or further developed, despite the great number of patients who could have benefited from such operations.

The reasons for such reluctance to explore human anatomy and develop surgery are unclear; also unclear is the reason for the failure to expand certain knowledge that reached an impressive stage at some early time but went no further. An example is the world's first treatise on forensic medicine, the *Hsi yüan lu* (The washing away of wrongs) of 1247 by Sung Tz'u. Although it preceded comparable Western knowledge by several centuries, it remained a solitary achievement, for no author is known to have built upon and improved this work. In contrast, pharmaceutical literature was continuously expanded and amended throughout Chinese history.

The Final Centuries of the Imperial Age

If the Han dynasty was marked by the initial development of Chinese medicine, the Song–Chin–Yüan period was the second most dynamic formative period in the history of Chinese medicine. The at-

tempts by K'ou Tsung-shih, who wrote about the middle of the thirteenth century, by Chang Yüan-su of the twelfth century, and most important by Wang Haogu to create a pharmacology of systematic correspondence signaled a closing of the most decisive rift that had separated the two major traditions of Chinese medicine for the preceding one and a half millennia. At the same time, however, individual schools began to appear, and these initiated an increasing specialization and fragmentation within this unified system – a process that came to an end only in the twentieth century.

The second millennium of Chinese medical history was characterized by the attempts of individual authors to reconcile their own observations and experiences with the ancient theoretical guidelines. One of the first to suggest a reductionist etiology was Liu Wan-su, a twelfth-century physician who proposed that most illnesses were caused by too much heat and who advocated cooling therapies. Chang Ts'ung-cheng, a few decades later, saw the main course of human illnesses as an intrusion of "evil influences," and he founded a school emphasizing "attack and purging" in therapy. His near contemporary, Li Kao, in contrast, thought that most illnesses were a result of a failure of spleen and stomach to perform their presumed digestive functions, and he advocated supplementation of these two units as a basic therapy. None of these schools, or any other of the many opinions published in subsequent centuries, achieved even temporary dominance. Hence, a proliferation of individual perspectives characterized the history of Chinese medicine during these final centuries rather than a succession of generally acknowledged paradigms.

This does not mean, however, that this period lacked brilliance; several authors made contributions to their respective fields that were never surpassed. The *Pen-ts'ao kang mu* (Materia medica arranged according to drug descriptions and technical aspects) of 1596 by Li Shih-chen is a most impressive encyclopedia of pharmaceutics touching on many realms of natural science. It contains more than 1,800 drug monographs and more than 11,000 prescriptions in 52 volumes. In 1601 Yang Chi-chou published his *Chen-chiu ta-ch'eng* (Complete presentation of needling and cauterization) in 10 volumes, offering a valuable survey of the literature and various schools of acupuncture and moxibustion, which is cauterization by the burning of a tuft of a combustible substance (moxa) on the skin (including a chapter on pediatric massage), of the preceding one and a half millennia.

Yet despite such monumental works, the dynamics of Chinese medical history appear to have slowed down subsequently. When in 1757 one of the most brilliant physician-intellectuals of the second millennium, Hsü Ta-ch'un, wrote his *I-hsüeh yüan liu lun* (On the origins and history of medicine), he recorded a deplorable "loss of tradition" in virtually every respect of theoretical and clinical health care.

The work of Hsü Ta-ch'un, who died in the same year, 1771, as Giovanni Battista Morgagni, the author of *De Sedibus et Causis Morborum* (On the seats and causes of diseases), illustrates the fact that traditional Chinese medicine, traditional European medicine, and even modern Western medicine have more basic theoretical foundations in common than is usually believed. Hsü Ta-ch'un, a conservative who was not influenced by Western thought and was a sharp critic of the influences of Song–Chin–Yüan thought on medicine, nonetheless wrote treatises on "intraabdominal ulcers" and, following a long tradition of military metaphors, compared the use of drugs to the use of soldiers. One may assume that he would have had few difficulties in communicating with his contemporary Morgagni or in understanding Western medicine as it later developed.

Given the internal fragmentation of traditional Chinese medicine and the fact that it contained many of the theoretical foundations of modern European and U.S. medicine, it should be no surprise that the latter was quickly accepted in China early in the twentieth century, a process stimulated by a feeling shared by many Chinese that a decent existence could be achieved only by employing Western science and technology. Only during the past four decades has there been a reassessment of the value of traditional medicine in China.

For decades, traditional Chinese medicine was held in contempt by virtually all prominent Chinese Marxist thinkers. In the 1950s and 1960s, however, it became apparent that Western medicine, with its emphasis on expertise and its many tenets that contradicted those of dialectical materialism, could not be fully integrated into a socialist society, and Chinese medicine was suddenly perceived to be a political tool. Chinese Marxist dogmatists began to point out the antagonism between Western medicine, so-called bourgeois metaphysics, and individualism, on one side, and dialectical materialism and traditional Chinese medicine, on the other. Whereas the complex formulas of traditional Chinese pharmaceutics could not be explained by modern pharmacology, the second law of dialectics as formulated by Friedrich Engels offered a satisfactory theoretical foundation.

Similarly, acupuncture anesthesia resisted modern scientific explanation, but could be understood on the basis of the dialectics of internal contradiction. Since the demise of the Cultural Revolution, such theoretical reinterpretations of traditional Chinese medicine have coexisted in China with Western medicine, with the latter dominant on virtually all levels of health care.

Efforts to preserve Chinese medicine include attempts to select those facets of that heterogeneous tradition that appear to form a coherent system, that are thought to supplement Western medicine, and that are not considered superstitious. Research on the scientific basis of traditional Chinese medicine is being pursued on many levels. Veteran doctors, however, prefer a continuation of traditional Chinese medicine in its own right. Although the dialogue between Western medicine and Chinese medicine goes on, not without tension, the Chinese population turns to both, selecting whatever it considers best for a specific problem.

Paul U. Unschuld

Bibliography

Anon. 1986. *"Nan-ching": The classic of difficult issues*, trans. P. U. Unschuld. Berkeley and Los Angeles.

Croizier, Ralph C. 1986. *Traditional medicine in modern China*. Cambridge, Mass.

Epler, D. C., Jr. 1980. Bloodletting in early Chinese medicine and its relation to the origin of acupuncture. *Bulletin of the History of Medicine* 54: 337–67.

  1988. The concept of disease in an ancient Chinese medical text, the *Discourse on Cold-Damage Disorders (Shang-han Lun)*. *Journal of the History of Medicine and Allied Sciences* 43: 8–35.

Harper, Donald. 1982. The *Wu-shih Erh Ping Fang:* Translation and prolegomena. Ph.D. thesis, University of California, Berkeley.

Hillier, S., and T. Jewell. 1983. *Health care and traditional medicine in China, 1800–1982*. London.

Huard, Pierre, and Ming Wong. 1959. *La médecine chinoise au cours des siècles*. Paris.

Hymes, R. P. 1987. Doctors in Sung and Yuan. *Chinese Science* 8: 9–76.

Lu, Gwei-djen, and Joseph Needham. 1980. *Celestial lancets: A history and rationale of acupuncture*. Cambridge.

Needham, Joseph, et al. 1970. *Clerks and craftsmen in China and the West*. Cambridge.

Spence, Jonathan. 1974. Aspects of the Western medical experience in China, 1850–1910. In *Medicine and society in China*, ed. J. Z. Bowers and E. F. Purcell, 40–54. New York.

Sun Simiao. 1985. *"Shanghan lun": Traité des [coups du froid]*, trans. into French by C. Despeux. Paris.

1987. *Prescriptions d'acuponcture valant mille onces d'or,* trans. into French by C. Despeux. Paris.

Sung Tz'u. 1981. *The washing away of wrongs,* trans. B. E. McKnight. Ann Arbor, Mich.

Unschuld, Paul U. 1978. *Approaches to ancient Chinese medicine.* Dordrecht.

1979. *Medical ethics in Imperial China.* Berkeley and Los Angeles.

1983. Die Bedeutung der Ma-wang-tui Funde für die chinesische Medizin- und Pharmaziegeschichte. In *Perspektiven der Pharmaziegeschichte,* ed. P. J. Dilg et al., 389–416. Graz.

1985. *Medicine in China: A history of ideas.* Berkeley and Los Angeles.

1986. *Medicine in China: A history of pharmaceutics.* Berkeley and Los Angeles.

1989. *Forgotten traditions of ancient Chinese medicine: Translation and annotated edition of the "I-hseh yüan liu lun" by Hsü Ta-ch'un of 1757.* Brookline, Mass.

Van Straten, N. H. 1983. *Concepts of health, disease and vitality in traditional Chinese society: A psychological interpretation.* Wiesbaden.

Wong K. Chimin and Wu Lien-Teh. 1936. *History of Chinese medicine: Being a chronicle of medical happenings in China from ancient times to the present period.* Shanghai (reprint 1973, New York).

I.3
Islamic and Indian Medicine

Islamic and Indian medicine originated in distinct cultural traditions but have been in close contact for many centuries. The terms *Islamic* and *Indian* as they refer to medicine do not describe static, idealized, or monolithic systems that can be categorized by referring to the medical texts of a distant golden age. Medical practices in Islamic and Indian cultures were, as elsewhere, eclectic and pluralistic, evolving in response to complex influences that varied according to time and place. This essay briefly traces the origins and the major components of the two traditions and compares and contrasts their institutional responses to the challenges of modern times.

Islamic medicine is based largely on the Greek medical knowledge of later antiquity and is more properly called Greco-Islamic or Galenic-Islamic medicine, reflecting the influence of Galen, whose works dominated medical learning in the eastern Hellenic world. At the time of the Muslim conquests of the seventh century A.D., the major centers of Greek medical learning in the eastern Mediterranean were flourishing.

Because of theological constraints, Greek Orthodox scholars were more interested in the Greek sciences, which included medicine and philosophy, than in literature, historiography, and other humanistic subjects. The Muslim conquerors recognized the excellence of Greek learning, and the Umayyid and Abbasid caliphs subsequently sponsored the translation of a large portion of the available scholarly works into Syriac and Arabic (Ullmann 1978).

The Hellenic culture had in large part been developed in the Near East and was an integral part of the Near Eastern culture inherited by the Muslims. The belief that the Greek sciences were transported from the Occident to the Orient, where they were preserved in Arabic translation until their eventual repatriation by the Occident, is mistaken. The infusion of Greek scholarship transformed the Arabic language and Islamic culture and must be viewed as a major historical process in which Islamic civilization energetically built on the existing Near and Middle Eastern cultures.

The major period of translation spanned the years from the ninth to the eleventh century and was a complex process that drew on several routes of cultural transmission. Even before the Muslim conquest, numerous Greek texts had been translated into Syriac, and many of these as well as a few original medical works written in Syriac were in turn translated to Arabic. The transmission of Greek scholarship into Arabic, which became the learned language, accelerated during the Abbasid era when, beginning toward the end of the eighth century, Harun al-Rashid and his successors sponsored centers of translation and learning in Baghdad. Almost all of Galen's lengthy medical texts were translated by the end of the ninth century, and Greek knowledge had also reached the Islamic world through Persian sources. The Achaemenid rulers of western Iran, who valued Greek knowledge, had founded in the third century A.D. a center of learning at Jundishapur where Greek scholars, captured in war, could work. In the fifth and sixth centuries A.D., Nestorian Christian scholars, persecuted in Greek Orthodox Byzantium, found refuge in Jundishapur, then under Sasanid rule. The Sasanid rulers sponsored numerous translations of Greek medical texts into Pahlevi. In the ninth century many of these Pahlevi texts were in turn translated into Arabic. Finally, the major Indian medical works were translated into Arabic or Persian and were accessible to Islamic physicians from a relatively early date (Ullmann 1978).

In answer to the often asked question regarding the originality of Islamic medicine, Manfred Ullmann, a specialist in Islamic medicine, has suggested that the question is inapplicable because it is inherently anachronistic. The physicians (hakims) of the Islamic Middle Ages, he observes, were not interested in discovering new knowledge, but rather in developing and commenting on the natural truths learned from the ancients (Ullmann 1978). This view, however, may overstate the case, for within the framework inherited from the Hellenic sciences, the Islamic scholars made numerous discoveries. For example, Alhazen (Ibn al-Haytham), a mathematician who worked in Cairo, used inductive, experimental, and mathematical methods inherited largely from Ptolemaic science to discount Greek and Islamic theories of light and vision and to produce a new, more accurate and intellectually sophisticated theory (Sabra 1972; Omar 1977).

A. I. Sabra (1987) has suggested that scholars study the Islamic sciences as part of Islamic civilization. The question then becomes not whether the Islamic scholars made original discoveries or how the Greek sciences were translated into Arabic and then into Latin, but rather by what process Islamic civilization appropriated, assimilated, and "naturalized" the Greek sciences.

According to the Greco-Islamic medical theories, diseases were caused by imbalances of the four humors of the body: hot, cold, moist, and dry. The matters of the four humors, blood, phlegm, and yellow and black bile, influenced the temperament of individuals. When the balance was upset, the body would become ill. Thus, an excess of blood would produce a sanguine condition, whereas an excess of phlegm would produce a phlegmatic condition, and so forth. The physician's role was to correct the imbalance, perhaps by prescribing foods or medicines with "hot" or "cold" properties or by removing excess blood. This system was essentially secular because it did not ascribe disease causation to supernatural influences. When Greek medical works referred to the Greek gods, Muslim translators simply inserted Allah when appropriate or made the gods historical figures.

Prophetic medicine can be viewed as a "science" that integrated medical knowledge derived from the hadiths, or sayings and traditions of Mohammed and his companions, and local medical customs, magical beliefs, incantations, charms with ideas and con-

cepts drawn from Greco-Islamic medicine. It was, in other words, an effort to incorporate Greek medical knowledge into an acceptable Islamic framework. The authors of prophetic medicine were generally not practicing physicians but *ulama* (specialists of Islamic theological and legal sciences), who worked out "religiously correct" compendia of medical lore. In recent years, many prophetic medical works have been printed and can be purchased in bookstores throughout the Islamic world.

Sufis, or mystics, believed that illness should be treated through prayer or other religious observances and not by medical means at all. In addition, many people believed in astrological influences on disease causation. Astrological medicine was widely practiced, and most astrological manuals had sections giving medical advice (Savage-Smith 1988). The obvious contradiction between natural causation, divine causation, and planetary control of events was never entirely resolved. The late Fazlur Rahman, the noted Muslim philosopher and scholar, while dismissing astrology, confronted the dilemma of the orthodox theological insistence on total reliance on God's will and the necessity of seeking secular medical intervention. He concluded that "the Qur'an's position appears to be that God acts through natural causation and human volition to further His purposes" and that whereas many theologians and Sufi leaders clearly advocated resignation to the will of God at all times, most, when sick, sought medical treatment (Rahman 1987). The average person presumably subscribed to a variety of medical beliefs without great concern for the obvious contradictions. In short, in emergencies, all possibilities were to be tried.

It might be said that over time the difference between Greco-Islamic medicine and daily medical practices resembled the difference between the classical Arabic and the spoken language. One was formal and was carefully studied and developed by savants for scholarly discourse. The other was informal, eclectic, and used for everyday needs.

Only a few of the major Greco-Islamic physicians will be mentioned here, in chronological order, to suggest their varied origins and interests. Mesue (Yuhanna ibn-Masawayh), court physician to four Abbasid caliphs during the late eighth and first half of the ninth centuries, was a renowned clinician and teacher who wrote influential texts on nosology and therapeutics. Joannitius (Hunayn ibn-Ishaq al-Ibadi) was a ninth-century physician who studied in Jundishapur, Basra, and Baghdad. He was proficient in Greek,

Syriac, and Arabic, and was renowned for his excellent translations of Greek medical texts, which secured his place in the history of medicine and of Islamic civilization. He also wrote monographs on ophthalmology and other subjects. His contemporary, Ali ibn Sahl Rabban al-Tabari, who worked for most of his life in Rayy, wrote a compendium of medicine based on the works of Hippocrates, Galen, Aristotle, Dioscorides, and other authors, mostly from Syriac translations. Qusta ibn-Luqa al-Balabakki, who died in 912, practiced in Baghdad and, toward the end of his life, in Armenia. He wrote on the relationship between mind and body, in addition to other medical, philosophical, and mathematical treatises. His famous contemporary, Rhazes (Abū Bakr Muhammad ibn Zakarīya al-Rāzī), was born in Rayy and practiced medicine in Baghdad and at various locations in Iran. He was a noted philosopher and alchemist who compiled the famous medical texts entitled *Kitab al-Mansuri* and *Kitab al-Hawi*. He is best known for his exceptionally precise (but not original) descriptions of diseases such as smallpox and measles. Haly Abbas (Ali ibn al-Abbas al-Majusi), who died in 994, was a physician at the Buwayhid court. He wrote the famous *Kitab al-Malaki,* one of the most concise and well-organized expositions of Greco-Islamic medicine. At about the same time, Albucasis practiced in Cordoba and wrote an encyclopedic study that contained an influential section on surgery based on Greek sources and his own findings. Avicenna (Abu-Ali al-Husayn ibn-Sina) was a polymath who during his checkered career practiced medicine at various locations in Iran. Early in the eleventh century he compiled the famous *Qanun,* a five-volume study dealing with physiology, nosology, etiology, symptomatology and therapy, simple remedies, pathology, and the preparation of compound remedies. This work is a compilation of medical knowledge of the era that was enormously influential in the Islamic world and in the West in Latin translation. He also wrote a book refuting astrology, a "science" held in ill-repute by most of the prominent physicians of the era. Averroes (Ibn Rushd) was twelfth-century Aristotelian philosopher and government official in Cordoba and Marrakesh who wrote a major medical work divided into seven parts dealing with anatomy, dietetics, pathology, nourishment, materia medica, hygiene, and therapeutics. His pupil, Maimonides (Ibn Maymun), was, like Ibn Rushd, born in Cordoba. But he left Spain following Almohad persecution and sought refuge in Cairo, where he became court physician and the official representative of Egypt's large and flourishing Jewish community. Among his medical works

is the famous *Kitab al-Fusul,* which was derived largely from Galen.

Abd al-Latif al-Baghdadi, who died in 1232, was a scientist who demonstrated that simple observation of human anatomy revealed substantial errors in Galen's anatomic descriptions. Also prominent in the thirteenth century was Ibn Nafis, who studied medicine in Damascus and became director of the Mansuri Hospital in Cairo. He wrote *al-Mujiz,* a widely used commentary on Avicenna's *Qanun.* In it he stated his famous theory of the pulmonary, or lesser, circulation of the blood, later proved correct. Finally, Ibn Abi Usaybia should be mentioned. An oculist at the Nuri Hospital in Damascus, he later worked at the Mansuri Hospital with Ibn Nafis. He compiled *Uyun al-Anba fi Tabaqat al-Atibba,* a biography of more than 400 physicians of Greco-Islamic medicine. It remains a major source on the history of Islamic medicine (Ibn Abi Usaybia 1882–4; Brockelmann 1937–49; Ullmann 1978).

These Greco-Islamic medical scholars were a diverse group, among whom were Muslims, Christians, Jews, and Zoroastrians. Persian Muslims probably outnumbered those of other origins. Although nearly all wrote their major works in Arabic, many also wrote in Syriac or Persian, as well as in Hebrew (written in either Hebraic or Arabic letters) or, later, in Turkish. Regardless of ethnic or cultural origin, all shared and contributed to the Islamic cultural tradition. Most, though by no means all, practiced medicine at some time in their careers. A few were *ulama,* or lay persons with a special interest in medicine. Women are conspicuously absent from the biobibliographies but are known to have acquired medical expertise and to have practiced medicine in medieval times (Issa 1928; Goitein 1967).

Medical education was far less structured than in modern times. Medical students studied the medical texts independently or sometimes in mosques and madrasas (schools) along with the other sciences. Often an aspiring physician studied with one or more masters and acquired practical experience through an apprenticeship. There was no formal certification system or formal curriculum. Proof of medical expertise depended on the recommendation of a physician's teachers, demonstrated familiarity with the medical texts, as well as a reputation established through practical experience. Only much later did a system of certification come into existence, in which a head doctor (*bash hakim*), appointed by the ruler, would issue an *ijaza* (permission or license) to a prospective physician testifying to his competence.

Most of the physicians discussed earlier limited the realm of their activities to the large cities, usually at court or in the homes of the wealthy. Several were directors of major hospitals in Baghdad, Damascus, Cairo, and elsewhere.

Hospitals in Islamic regions were usually funded by waqfs (religious endowments for charitable purposes). The concept of waqf funding of hospices for the sick, which may have been adapted from Byzantine custom, remained standard practice in Islamic regions until the expansion of the modern nation-state. For example, in 1662, in Tunis, the ruler Hamuda al-Muradi established a waqf funded by revenues from designated hotels, shops, public ovens, kilns, water pipes, mills, and baths and from the rent on houses. The funds were for a doctor, nurses, servants, and food for the staff and patients. In addition, the funds were to maintain the building itself, which contained 24 rooms and was intended for the sick and wounded of the army and navy and the poor who had no family to care for them. The charter of this waqf specifically stated that there was to be no distinction among Arabs, Turks, or foreigners. In Tunis and elsewhere, those who could, however, preferred to seek medical care at home from relatives and local practitioners (Gallagher 1983).

In the sixteenth and seventeenth centuries when Muslim rulers became aware of the military and commercial expansion of the European powers, they did not hesitate to recruit European physicians to their courts. Although European physicians of the era could treat most diseases no better than their Muslim counterparts, Muslim rulers, extrapolating from European advances in other fields of science and technology, suspected that the Europeans could (Gallagher 1983). The European physicians had an advantage because, although they still relied on the medical texts of Avicenna, Averroes, and Rhazes, they were more systematically educated than their Muslim counterparts. Often both Muslim and European physicians were retained at Muslim courts and were consulted according to the dictates of the ruler. European physicians at Muslim courts also sometimes served as intermediaries, interpreters, and diplomatic representatives. They were generally well compensated and held in high esteem.

A few prominent Muslim physicians also sought the new European medical knowledge. In the seventeenth century, Ibn Sallum, an important physician at the Ottoman court, relied on the works of the sixteenth- and seventeenth-century Paracelsian scholars, whose theories of chemistry (later proved wrong) had emphatically rejected the ancient Greek medical theories. Ibn Sallum translated several treatises in Paracelsian medicine from Latin to Arabic, modifying them slightly for use in Islamic regions. He is credited with being the first Muslim physician to subscribe to the new European science and was not himself trained in Greco-Islamic medicine (Savage-Smith 1987). In the eighteenth and nineteenth centuries, Muslim physicians from North Africa to Iran occasionally used European source materials to discuss the etiology and treatment of new diseases such as syphilis and cholera. Muslim scholars did not, however, understand or adopt the new experimental methods that underlay the Scientific Revolution.

The transmission of European medical knowledge was accelerated in the early nineteenth century when Muhammad Ali, the modernizing ruler of Egypt, recruited Antoine Clot-Barthelemy to organize his medical services. Clot founded a medical school in Cairo where European medicine alone was taught. European physicians were subsequently called to Istanbul, Tunis, Tehran, and other Muslim captials to organize modern medical schools and health services. By the early twentieth century, Islamic medicine, which bore little resemblance to medical practices of the medieval era, was held in official disrepute and the Greco-Islamic theories themselves had been overturned by the experimental methods and systematic observations of modern Western medicine.

The term *Indian medicine* usually refers to Hindu or Ayurvedic medicine. It is a medical tradition distinct from either Greek or Islamic medicine. Ayurvedic scholars trace its roots to verses from the ancient Vedic hymns, which contain medical doctrines, mostly of a magicoreligious character, and date from as early as the second millennium B.C. The medical doctrines based on treatment with extracts of plants (vegetable decoctions, oils, and ghees, usually prepared at home) featured in classic Ayurvedic medicine are, however, not found in the Vedic hymns. Perhaps they derived from the herbal medicines of Buddhist monks. The term *Ayurveda* may have served to legitimize the medical system by associating it with the Vedic religious tradition. The term *Veda* refers to an abstract idea of knowledge that is found in all branches of Hindu learning. *Ayur* means prolonging or preserving life or the science of longevity. Ayurveda is, in fact, a code of life. It deals with rebirth, renunciation, salvation, soul, the purpose of life, the maintenance of mental health, and of course the prevention and treatment of diseases.

The most important Ayurvedic medical texts are the *samhitas* (the four canonical texts of the Hindu scriptures) of the mythical savants Caraka and Susruta. Both are compilations of medical traditions and exist only in incomplete or copied form. Caraka's work was apparently compiled in about the first century A.D. and that of Susruta in the fourth or sixth century. Caraka described more than 200 diseases and 150 pathological conditions. He also mentioned older magical ideas along with the rational humoral approach based on drug therapy and diet. Susruta included a long chapter on surgery, which was apparently widely practiced in antiquity but was nearly unknown in later years.

The ideas of Ayurveda have permeated Hindu cultural ways of dealing with life and death and sickness and health. Whereas Greek medicine has four humors, Ayurvedic medicine has three humors, or *dosas,* wind, bile, and phlegm, which govern health and regulate bodily functions. These are the three microcosms of the three divine universal forces, wind, sun, and moon. Illness results from an imbalance of the three *dosas.* Although an essentially rational understanding of disease and treatment underlies Ayurvedic medical doctrine, Brahmin myths, gods, and demons are sometimes cited in the classic texts to explain the origins of diseases and the character of medicine. Epidemic diseases, for example, might be caused by drought, excessive rainfall, calamities sent by the gods in punishment for sins, poisonous miasmas, or the influence of planets. The body is considered to be a manifestation of divine energy and substance, and is a microcosm of the universe. Whereas Islamic medicine acknowledged its Greek and Indian origins, Ayurvedic medicine emerged from the Hindu religious and cultural tradition (Zimmer 1948; Jolly 1951; Basham 1976; Zyzk 1985).

Medical knowledge was generally transmitted from a master practitioner to his pupil. Often, medical knowledge was handed down from father to son for many generations. Medical students also studied at medical establishments attached to large temples or in schools and universities. In the ideal, Ayurvedic physicians (*vaidyas* or *vaids*) were to be Brahmin and thoroughly learned in the Sanskrit texts. In practice, they were usually from the top three castes (*varna*), Brahmin, Kshatriya, and Vaisya, but were sometimes considered to have compromised their status by the nature of their profession. Brahmins, for example, would often not accept food from a *vaidya* because he had entered the homes of persons of lower caste and had touched excrement

and other impure substances (Basham 1976). Most people, however, had no access to the formal or learned Ayurvedic medical tradition and relied on home remedies and consultation with local medical healers. With few exceptions, only the rulers, military leaders, and male members of elite castes had access to Ayurvedic medicine.

Yunani (Ionian or Greek) medicine should also be considered a part of the Indian medical tradition. Yunani medicine was probably introduced into India with the Turco-Afghan conquests of the thirteenth century and the expansion of Persian culture in the fifteenth century. Lahore, Agra, Delhi, and Lucknow became renowned centers of Islamic learning where the classic medical texts were copied, studied, and reformulated, usually in Arabic. From the thirteenth century, Indian physicians attempted to synthesize Islamic and Ayurvedic medicine and there was much borrowing between the two systems (Leslie 1976). Ayurvedic physicians learned to classify and interpret diseases in Yunani terms. They began to diagnose disease by feeling the pulse of the patient, a practice developed in Yunani but not in Ayurvedic medicine. They used mercury, which Muslim physicians had borrowed from Europe, and opium and practiced alchemy, a science not found in Ayurvedic texts. They studied the case histories found in Yunani but not in Ayurvedic texts. In turn, the Yunani physicians (hakims) borrowed extensively from the Ayurvedic pharmacopeia and adopted many Ayurvedic ideas concerning dietary principles. Both systems were widely used in India's Muslim and Hindu communities, and Muslim physicians are known to have practiced Ayurvedic medicine and Hindu physicians to have practiced Yunani medicine.

Ayurvedic medicine reached its highest point of development from the first to the sixth century A.D., considerably earlier than Islamic medicine, which reached its highest point from the ninth to the thirteenth century. Both traditions lent themselves to sophisticated reasoning, earnest speculation, and scholarly curiosity, but also to involuted argumentation, abstract distinctions, and increasingly obscurantist generalizations. In Indian as in Islamic medicine, there was no systematic experimental research. In the sixteenth and seventeenth centuries, Ayurvedic and Yunani physicians were even less exposed than were their counterparts in the Middle East and North Africa to the new ideas of the Scientific Revolution.

The British conquest of India, begun in the mid-eighteenth century, did not immediately disrupt long-standing medical traditions. In 1822 the British colonial authorities established the School of Native Doctors at Calcutta, where students could study both Ayurvedic and Western medicine. The British authorities also sponsored courses for the training of hakims and recruited them for medical relief projects. Within little more than a decade, however, the British government had decided that higher education in India would follow a Western model and the schools and courses in indigenous medicine were abandoned. In 1841 a British medical surgeon in the Bengal medical service found that only four or five Ayurvedic medical practitioners could read the Sanskrit texts (Leslie 1976; Metcalf 1985).

Even after the British suspended patronage of indigenous medical systems, a few princes continued to sponsor Ayurvedic and Yunani colleges. In 1889 the family of Hakim Ajmal Khan, the famous Muslim reformer and physician, established a Yunani school in Ballimaran and later a pharmacy that provided Yunani and Ayurvedic medicines. In 1906 Ajmal Khan established the Tibb (medical) Conference. Its purpose was to reform and develop Yunani medicine and to work with Ayurvedic physicians for their shared interests. In 1907 Ayurvedic practitioners established the All-India Ayurvedic Congress, which remains the leading Ayurvedic professional association. In 1910 Ajmal Khan expanded his earlier organization into the All-India Ayurvedic and Yunani Tibb Conference. The medical associations successfully opposed the Registration Acts that fully certified only allopathic, or Western-trained, British and Indian physicians. They also called for placing the ancient indigenous medical systems on a scientific basis (Metcalf 1985). Indigenous practitioners established links between their medical concepts and those of modern Western medicine in order to sanction them. When British authorities moved the capital to Delhi, Ajmal Khan requested and received land for an indigenous medical college. With funding from princes and merchants, the foundation stone for the Ayurvedic and Yunani Tibb College was laid in 1916 and the college was formally opened in 1921. Despite much ambivalence, both the British viceroy and Mahatma Gandhi gave their support to the college because it was an important symbol of the Indian cultural revival and of Hindu–Muslim cooperation (Metcalf 1986). The Indian National Congress, founded in 1920, called for government sponsorship of Indian medicine. In the 1920s and 1930s *vaidyas* and hakims who had formed professional associations in rural areas actively campaigned for government recognition.

Well before independence in 1947, more than 60 Ayurvedic and Yunani colleges existed throughout India and there were official Boards of Indian Medicine in Bombay, Madras, and elsewhere. After independence, Ayurvedic and Yunani physicians expected to win equal status with physicians trained in the Western medical schools, but despite strikes and other organized protests they did not do so. In 1956 the government established the Central Institute of Research in Indigenous Systems of Medicine and the Post Graduate Training Centre for Ayurveda in Gujarat State and similar institutions elsewhere. Although the number of Ayurvedic and Yunani colleges and dispensaries has multiplied since independence, government funding has been minimal. Many of the colleges teach anatomy, nosology, and other Western medical subjects in addition to the basic courses in Ayurvedic and Yunani medicine, but the result is popularly regarded as inadequate training in any medical system. Ayurvedic and Yunani practitioners, for example, often prescribe antibiotics and give injections, but without the understanding of the physician educated in Western medicine. According to Paul Brass, a political scientist specializing in modern India, the students in the indigenous medical schools are popularly perceived to have failed in secondary school or to have failed to gain admission to modern medical or professional schools (Brass 1972). For the treatment of serious ailments, Western medicine is preferred by those who can obtain and afford it. Nevertheless, the struggle for "medical equality" continues.

The process of medical professionalization in the Middle East was quite different. In Egypt in the late nineteenth century, medical works by Avicenna and others were published by Cairo's Bulaq Press. This could have been a sign of a revival or of a new institutionalization of Islamic medicine. Thus, Ullmann (1978) suggests that the manuscripts were published because they were part of a living medical tradition rather than part of medical history. It is probably truer that they were part of Egypt's nationalist revival and were valued primarily as part of its cultural heritage. Egyptian medical students studied exclusively Western medicine at the Qasr al-Ayni medical school or went abroad to study in British or French medical schools. By the post–World War I era, most governments in the Middle East required practicing physicians and pharmacists to be licensed, and medical schools specializing in Western medicine alone had been established in Istanbul, Beirut, Cairo, Tunis, Tehran, and many other major cities. In Iran, for example, the modernizing government of Reza Shah required all physicians and pharmacists to be licensed by the early 1930s. Unlicensed physicians with established practices had to take an examination that, according to Byron Good, an anthropologist specializing in Iran, covered internal medicine, pharmacology, and traditional Galenic–Islamic medicine. The license given to these (*mojaz*, or permitted) physicians was not equivalent to that given by the accredited Western medical schools but was rather comparable to the *médecin toléré* license given to indigenous practitioners in French colonies. To pass the exam, the candidates had to study European medical texts in order to familiarize themselves with the new medical theories and practices. This resulted in a modification of existing medical practices, and after the early 1930s all new physicians and pharmacists had to hold licenses from the accredited medical schools (Good 1981).

The unlicensed indigenous practitioners in Egypt, Iran, and elsewhere – health barbers, midwives, bonesetters, herbalists – continued to have clients, of course, because most people did not have access to European medicine, which was expensive and confined to the large cities. But such practitioners did not themselves organize in order to establish medical schools, pharmaceutical companies, or journals specializing in Greco-Islamic medicine.

There are several possible explanations for these very different responses to the new dominance of Western medicine. Ralph Croizier (1968), a specialist in Chinese medical systems, has suggested that Islamic medicine differed from Ayurvedic and Chinese medicine because it did not claim that it contained special knowledge unknown in the West. Indeed, unlike the Hellenic medical theories shared by both Islamic and pre-Renaissance Western medicine, the ideas of Ayurvedic medicine were nearly unknown to Western scholars until the colonial era. The unique origin of Ayurvedic medicine therefore may have distinguished it from Islamic medicine.

Another explanation may be that the Ayurvedic texts were believed to have originated in Hindu holy scripture, whereas the Greco-Islamic medical texts were clearly of non-Islamic, secular origin. Barbara Metcalf, a historian of India and Pakistan, has observed, however, that, in Muslim India, Yunani medicine was considered to be an ancillary dimension of religion and its practitioners were expected to be pious men. Yet, as she cautions, Muslim scholars were aware that Yunani medicine did not contain the truths of the religion as did the *Quran* and the hadiths, and did not consider it part of the Islamic religious sciences (Metcalf 1982).

In the Middle East, there was no competing medical system associated with a dominant indigenous religion, and Muslim, Christian, and Jewish physicians all studied the Greco-Islamic medical theories. Although Islamic medicine was not an integral part of the Islamic sciences, most people considered it to be compatible with correct Islamic values. Because not only Ayurvedic but also Yunani physicians formed professional associations, it would seem that the "unique origin" and the "religious versus secular or foreign origin" explanations can only partially explain the different responses to modern medicine and to colonial rule. An additional explanation may lie in the fact that the Middle East was closer to the European metropoles than was India, making its exposure to European political and cultural influence more intense. The main support for Ayurvedic and Yunani professional organizations has, in fact, come not from the main cities of India but from the provinces. A further explanation may be found in British colonial administrative policies. The British authorities in India initially attempted to preserve local traditions. They even combined the indigenous and European systems in their new medical schools, where courses were taught in Sanskrit and English.

The process was quite different in the Middle East and North Africa because in the nineteenth century, when the British and French established colonial rule, indigenous ruling elites such as Muhammad Ali of Egypt and his successors had for some time been trying to strengthen their own power by learning the secrets of European power. India's rulers had not had such a long exposure to European science and technology before the onset of colonial rule. Indigenous rulers in India had not, therefore, been able to emulate Muhammad Ali of Egypt or the other modernizing rulers of the Middle East, for they had been relegated to a largely ceremonial and traditional role in the British raj. The sequential establishment of colonial rule may thus have contributed to the difference in medical professionalization. Furthermore, as the nineteenth century progressed, the discovery of quinine, smallpox vaccination, new methods of public health sanitation, anesthesia, antisepsis, and other advances made the prevention and treatment of disease more effective and the modern medical profession in general more confident. The Ayurvedic and Yunani physicians, protected by British colonial policies, managed to upgrade their skills by adopting new methods of medical intervention learned from European medicine and, rather like practitioners of homeopathy and chiropractic in the West, were able to obtain a degree of official recognition.

Finally, because the ruling elites of the Middle East and North Africa had opted for European medicine long before the colonial era, indigenous practitioners in these regions, unlike their counterparts in India, had no support from their local (Muslim) rulers and none from their European colonial rulers. Because they had been represented at most by a head doctor appointed by the ruler, they had no organized means of protest. In contrast to the authoritarian, centralized political systems of the Middle East, the constitutional form of government established in India in the twentieth century lent itself to lobbying by special interest groups such as professional associations. The result is a dual system of officially recognized medical education, professional organization, and certification in India and a single system in the Middle East and North Africa. Nevertheless, in all these regions, as in the West, a wide variety of medical practitioners continue to flourish.

Apologists for the Islamic and Indian medical traditions argue that Western medicine cannot treat all diseases. They correctly observe that many diseases have a cultural component that a local healer familiar with the beliefs of the patient might treat more satisfactorily than a counterpart trained in European medicine. It is widely recognized that diseases partly caused by psychological stress can be more effectively treated by healers who understand the religious, cultural, and political beliefs of the patient. Recognizing this and, more important, the unavoidable fact that the majority of the world's population does not have access to modern medicine, the World Health Organization has been attempting to upgrade existing indigenous medical traditions rather than to replace them with modern medicine. In practice this has meant studying local remedies with the techniques of modern science in order to distinguish between effective and harmful practices and to train practitioners to modify these methods in accord with their findings. Success has been very limited, however.

Today, in India, as Charles Leslie, an anthropologist specializing in Indian medicine, has pointed out, one must distinguish between the Ayurvedic medicine of the Sanskrit classic texts; the Yunani medicine of the classic Arabic texts; the syncretic Ayurvedic and Yunani medicine of the traditional culture; contemporary professionalized Ayurvedic and Yunani medicine (both of which have borrowed from modern Western or allopathic medicine); folk medicine; popular culture; homeopathic medicine;

and learned magic-religious medicine (Leslie 1976). Yet all must be considered part of Indian medicine.

Similarly, in the Middle East, one must distinguish between the classical Islamic medical tradition; the everyday practices of the health barbers, herbalists, midwives, bonesetters, and religious healers; and, of course, Western medicine. Throughout the Islamic world, Muslim fundamentalists are especially active in the medical schools. But outside of India and, to a lesser extent, Pakistan, they have given no thought to developing Islamic medicine along Western institutional lines. They argue that medical sciences have no nationality, but that (modern or Western) medicine should be administered according to Islamic law. Thus, charitable clinics attached to fundamentalist mosques dispense Western medicine, and the fundamentalists call merely for the revival of the comprehensive worldview and the humanistic concern that, they contend, characterized the Islamic medical system. They advocate what would in the West be called the holistic approach to patient care, with modern medicine subsidized through the legal Islamic taxes and accessible to all.

Nancy E. Gallagher

Bibliography

Basham, A. L. 1976. The practice of medicine in ancient and medieval India. In *Asian medical systems,* ed. Charles Leslie, 18–43. Berkeley and Los Angeles.

Brass, Paul R. 1972. The politics of Ayurvedic education: A case study of revivalism and modernization in India. In *Education and politics in India: Studies in organization, society, and policy,* ed. Susanne H. Rudolph and Lloyd I. Rudolph, 342–71. Cambridge.

Brockelmann, C. 1937–49. *Geschichte der arabischen Litteratur.* Leiden.

Croizier, Ralph. 1968. *Traditional medicine in modern China: Science, nationalism and the tensions of cultural change.* New York.

Dols, Michael. 1984. *Medieval Islamic medicine: Ibn Ridwan's treatise "On the prevention of bodily ills in Egypt."* Berkeley and Los Angeles.

Dunn, Fred. 1976. Traditional Asian medicine and cosmopolitan medicine as adaptive systems. In *Asian medical systems,* ed. Charles Leslie, 133–58. Berkeley and Los Angeles.

Elgood, Cyril. 1951. *A medical history of Persia and the Eastern Caliphate.* Cambridge.

Filliozat, J. 1964. *The classical doctrine of Indian medicine.* Delhi.

Gallagher, N. 1983. *Medicine and power in Tunisia, 1780–1900.* Cambridge.

Goitein, Shlomo. 1967. *A Mediterranean society,* Vol. 1. Berkeley.

Good, Byron. 1981. The transformation of health care in modern Iranian history. In *Modern Iran: The dialectics of continuity and change,* ed. Michael E. Bonine and Nikki R. Keddie, 59–82. Albany, N.Y.

Gupta, B. 1976. Indigenous medicine in nineteenth- and twentieth-century Bengal. In *Asian medical systems,* ed. Charles Leslie, 368–78. Berkeley and Los Angeles.

Ibn Abi Usaybia. 1882–4. *Tabaqat al-atibba',* ed. A. Muller. Cairo.

Issa, Ahmed. 1928. *Histoire des Bimaristans (hôpitaux à l'époque islamique).* Cairo.

Jolly, Julius. 1951. *Indian medicine.* Poona.

Leslie, Charles. 1976. The ambiguities of medical revivalism in modern India. In *Asian medical systems,* ed. Charles Leslie, 356–67. Berkeley and Los Angeles.

Metcalf, Barbara Daly. 1982. *Islamic revival in British India: Deoband, 1880–1900.* Princeton, N.J.

　　1985. Nationalist Muslims in British India: The case of Hakim Ajmal Khan. *Modern Asian Studies* 19: 1–28.

　　1986. Hakim Ajmal Khan: Rais of Delhi and Muslim "leader." In *Delhi through the years: Essays in urban history, culture and society,* ed. R. E. Frykenberg, 299–315. Delhi.

Meyerhof, M. 1984. *Studies in medieval Arabic medicine.* London.

O'Flaherty, Wendy Doniger. 1980. *Karma and rebirth in classical Indian traditions.* Berkeley and Los Angeles.

Omar, Saleh Beshara. 1977. *Ibn al-Haytham's optics: A study of the origins of experimental science.* Minneapolis.

Rahman, Fazlur. 1987. *Health and medicine in the Islamic tradition.* New York.

Sabra, A. I. 1972. al-Haytham, Ibn. *Dictionary of scientific biography.* New York.

　　1987. The appropriation and subsequent naturalization of Greek science in medieval Islam, a preliminary statement. *History of Science* 25: 223–43.

Savage-Smith, E. 1987. Drug therapy of eye diseases in seventeenth-century Islamic medicine: The influence of the "New Chemistry" of the Paracelsians. *Pharmacy in History* 29: 3–28.

　　1988. Gleanings from an Arabist's workshop: Current trends in the study of medieval Islamic science and medicine. *ISIS* 79: 246–72.

Ullmann, Manfred. 1978. *Islamic medicine.* Edinburgh.

Zimmer, Henry R. 1948. *Hindu medicine.* Baltimore.

Zysk, Kenneth G. 1985. Religious healing in the Veda. *Transactions of the American Philosophical Society* 75: 7.

I.4
Disease, Human Migration, and History

There is a story told among the Kiowa Indians of North America's southern Great Plains about the arrival in their midst, in a time long past, of a stranger in a black suit and a tall hat. This missionary-appearing figure is confronted by Saynday, a mystic hero of the Kiowa.

"Who are you?" asks the stranger.

"I'm Saynday. I'm the Kiowa's Old Uncle Saynday. I'm the one who's always coming along. Who are you?"

"I'm smallpox."

"Where do you come from and what do you do and why are you here?"

"I come from far away, from across the Eastern Ocean. I am one of the white men – they are my people as the Kiowa are yours. Sometimes I travel ahead of them, and sometimes I lurk behind. But I am always their companion and you will find me in their camps and in their houses."

"What do you do?"

"I bring death. My breath causes children to wither like young plants in the spring snow. I bring destruction. No matter how beautiful a woman is, once she has looked at me she becomes as ugly as death. And to men I bring not death alone but the destruction of their children and the blighting of their wives. The strongest warriors go down before me. No people who have looked at me will ever be the same." (Crosby 1986)

Stories such as this abound among indigenous peoples throughout the world. Sometimes they are simple sayings, as among the Hawaiians: "Lawe li'ili'i ka make a ka Hawai'i, lawe nui ka make a ka haole" – "Death by Hawaiians takes a few at a time; death by white poeple takes many." Among some, such as the Maori of New Zealand, they are more cryptic: White people and their diseases are *"he taru tawhiti"* – "a weed from afar." And among still others elaborate systems of disease differentiation have emerged, as among the Southwest American Indian Pima and Papago, who distinguish *ká:cim múmkidag,* or "staying sicknesses," from *'óimmeddam,* or "wandering sicknesses." Staying sicknesses are those the Indians have always had; they are noncontagious, and whom they afflict and the appropriate response to them are well understood. Wandering sicknesses, in contrast, originated among other, distant peoples, principally white peoples; they are relatively new to the Indians, are highly contagious and indiscriminate in whom they attack, and are "wrong" because there is no way to defend against them (Bahr et al. 1974).

To some Western readers these may seem like quaint notions among simple peoples. In fact, they are clear-eyed and accurate recognitions of historical and ongoing reality. For millennia upon millennia, over most of the earth's surface, the vast majority of humankind lived in relatively isolated enclaves. Diseases, of course, existed in those enclaves, but among most peoples for most of that time, none of the diseases were so-called crowd-type ecopathogenic infections such as smallpox, yellow fever, typhoid, malaria, measles, pertussis, polio, and so on (Newman 1976). Nor for most of the history of humankind did the majority of the world's populations suffer from such afflictions as hypertension, diabetes, obesity, gallstones, renal stones, coronary heart disease, appendicitis, diverticular disease, and more, including various forms of cancer (Trowell and Burkitt 1981).

During these huge stretches of time, before humans developed the ability to move great distances into areas inhabited by other humans, population growth among these generally quite healthy people was restrained by the same phenomenon that restrained growth among other animals – limited resources. With the rise of agriculture, however, the domestication of animals, and the first appearance of urban communities in Sumeria about 5,000 years ago, the resource restraint on population growth began to loosen. But another restraint emerged – infectious disease.

Early Urban Environments

Before the domestication of various kinds of birds and mammals, hunter-gatherer societies had little everyday contact with large numbers of animals except, in some cases, dogs. As humans learned to contain, control, and breed pigs, sheep, cattle, goats, horses, and fowl, however, they were forced to share those animals' environments. Although their dietary protein intake thus increased, so too did their exposure to pox viruses, distemper, measles, influenza, and other maladies, all diseases carried by the newly domesticated creatures in their midst.

Damaging as these diseases were when first encountered, in time they became the troublesome, but relatively nonlethal childhood diseases of the evolved stockbreeding societies. The diseases, along with the animals, in effect became domesticated, but only for the specific people who had endured the lengthy immunization process. As these people moved from place to place, encountering other groups, they deposited pathogens that were disas-

trous to the newly contacted, nonimmune communities. Their travels were rarely extensive, however, at least in the early centuries of animal husbandry, agriculture, and urbanization.

A major problem at this stage of social development was founded on the concentration of humans in the new protourban centers, initially in the Middle East and later elsewhere. First, the people in such locales were dependent on those in the surrounding countryside for food supplies; any depletion of those supplies, because of drought or other natural disaster, spelled catastrophe for the urban dwellers. In addition, the concentration of a large number of people in a relatively small geographic area greatly increased the opportunity for the infectious communication of various diseases from one human host to another. On occasion, and in the short term, this resulted in epidemic outbreaks of disease. Generally, however, and in the long term, it probably meant the creation of endemic diseases that did not erupt like firestorms, but that gnawed away at the well-being of the community and in part undermined its ability to reproduce.

A larger consequence of the urbanization–disease dynamic was that urban populations were often unable to sustain themselves without external support and a steady stream of in-migration from the countryside. This was a perpetual problem from the time of the rise of urban centers until the nineteenth century; throughout this period, observes William H. McNeill (1979), "rural peasantries [were required] to produce a surplus of children as well as a surplus of food to sustain urban life and the civilized social structures cities created."

This is not to say, however, that in-migrating rural peasants were greeted as saviors of civilization. On the contrary, they were fodder to be wasted in the interests of civilization's continuance. As Lawrence Stone (1977), among others, has vividly shown, as late as the seventeenth, eighteenth, and nineteenth centuries, the centers of Western civilization were cesspools of disease, exploitation, starvation, and death. In Manchester, England, for example, for much of the nineteenth century, the mortality rate for children under 5 was around 50 percent (Forbes 1986). All during this time urban dwellers in Europe were dying of bubonic plague, smallpox, syphilis, typhus, typhoid fever, measles, bronchitis, whooping cough, tuberculosis, and other diseases (e.g., Matossian 1985), which still had not spread to what – to Europeans, at least – were the most remote portions of the globe.

Migration outward to the Caribbean, the Americas, and the Pacific from the densely packed, disease-infested urban centers of Europe and then Asia – with an involuntary assist from Africa – probably created the greatest explosion of epidemic disease and the worst human catastrophe the world has ever seen. Before turning to that holocaust, which began in the late fifteenth century, it is worth glancing at the first great disease exchange that brought both China and Rome nearly to their knees long before the peoples of the Pacific or the Americas would experience the initial forays of bacteria and viruses.

Disease and Commerce

In his well-known study *Plagues and Peoples,* and in subsequent writings as well, the historian William H. McNeill has shown that a useful way to understand the evolution of human society is to examine the complex interactions between and among microparasites and macroparasites. Microparasites, in this context, are the microscopic organisms that live off human tissue, sometimes carrying disease and death, sometimes provoking immune reactions in their host that destroy the microparasites, and sometimes developing a reciprocal relationship that allows both host and parasite to survive in a state of relative equilibrium. In the last case, the host may become a carrier of infection, capable of spreading it to others although he or she remains symptomless.

Macroparasites, in the traditional sense, are predatory animals such as lions and wolves that feed on the flesh of other animals – but McNeill suggests that, in a more metaphorical sense, humans who seize the goods of others or who compel others to provide services are also macroparasites. Like microparasites, macroparasites of this sort sometimes kill their hosts in the immediate assault, but more often they develop a long-term exploitative relationship, again a state of relative equilibrium, albeit to the much greater advantage of the parasite than the host (McNeill 1976, 1980).

Throughout the course of human evolution there have been long stretches of time when it seems that states of equilibrium have existed among the masses of people and the microparasites and macroparasites that lived off their bodies and their labor. To be sure, during these times neither the physical nor the social conditions of the majority of humankind may have been ideal, but neither were they often in a state of crisis. This was true even in the early centuries of urban society discussed earlier: Although certainly punctuated from time to time by epidemic or political upheaval – usually in tandem, the case of

Athens in the fifth century B.C. being the classic example (Shrewsbury 1950) – those early civilizations remained sufficiently separate from one another that biological and social stability was more the rule than the exception.

This began to change at about the time of the Christian Era (to use the Western chronological guidepost) as overland caravans and open-sea ships expanded trade throughout the Middle East, Asia, and Europe. The outer extremes of that new network of commerce – China and Rome – were also the least experienced in terms of previous trade interactions and cosmopolitan disease. To use the earlier-noted Pima and Papago Indian terminology, both China and Rome were well adapted to their own "staying sicknesses," but unlike the more trade-experienced peoples in much of India and the Middle East they had little experience with the "wandering sicknesses" that existed outside their realms. As a consequence, whereas most of India and the Middle East seem to have experienced no major pathogenic demographic reactions to the new expansion of commerce, China and Rome were convulsed by it.

In the late second century A.D. both Rome and China were probably overwhelmed by pestilence. In Rome the so-called Antonine plagues of A.D. 165–80 were followed less than a century later by another round of empirewide pandemic. Although it is impossible, at this distance, to determine what diseases entered Rome and caused such havoc during these times, opinion has long centered on smallpox or something similar or ancestral to it as the primary agent (Hirsch 1883; McNeill 1976). No doubt, however, other newly introduced infections (including, probably, measles) were present as well. The result was severe and prolonged population decline and, perhaps consequently, political upheaval.

A very similar epidemiological and social pattern developed in China during the same early centuries of this era (McNeill 1976). In short, the mobility of commerce, to a degree unprecedented in previous world history, introduced new and devastating waves of microparasitism to geographic locales that previously had existed in widely separated realms; the consequent population collapses probably gave rise to upheaval in the macroparasitic equilibrium (however uneasy it may already have been), with eventual deterioration and collapse of the existing political orders – the Roman and Han empires – altogether.

The European Middle Ages and After

The thousand years following the second- and third-century Roman and Chinese pandemics witnessed recurring bouts of disease upheaval, but generally these were confined to specific geographic areas. In particular, it seems that the Mediterranean world experienced major epidemiological assaults during the middle to later centuries of the first millennium A.D., due in large part to that locale's openness to migrations and seaborne contagions. To some extent in response to this, European civilization began a slow northward shift (Biraben and Le Goff 1969).

The early medieval period in northern Europe was one of a relatively large number of disease outbreaks, but few of major epidemic consequence (Bonser 1944). As McNeill (1976) notes, "A pattern of increasing frequency but declining virulence of infectious disease is exactly what a population learning to live with a new infection experiences as the accommodation between hosts and parasites moves toward a more stable, chronic state." In sum, a parasite–host equilibrium was emerging. To be sure, by modern standards mortality from endemic diseases was high – and the urban centers were still unable to maintain growth without significant in-migration from the countryside – but overall the population of Europe probably tripled during the half-millennium between 800 and 1300.

By any standards, however, the fourteenth-century population of Europe was far from robust. The famous agricultural revolution of the Middle Ages had greatly increased European nutritional levels, thus undergirding the relatively rapid population growth (White 1962), but it was a precarious foundation for population maintenance. England, for example, was hit by major famines between 1315 and 1317, although less disastrous times of starvation were common as agricultural yields declined by nearly 20 percent in the first half of the century (Braudel 1973). Then, in midcentury, plague struck.

For some centuries migrations from Europe to the Middle East had been growing, beginning with small pilgrimages and culminating in the Crusades. These population movements generated trade networks, which themselves gave impetus to the creation of new and larger urban centers in Europe – centers of extreme crowding and extraordinarily poor public health conditions. As one English legal statute of the fourteenth century described things, as a prelude to a futile effort at correction:

So much dung and filth of the garbage and entrails as well as of beasts killed, as of other corruption, be cast and put in ditches, rivers, and other waters, and also in many other places, within, about, and nigh unto divers cities, boroughs, and towns of the realm, and the suburbs of them, that the air there is greatly corrupt and infect, and

many maladies and other intolerable diseases do daily happen. (Robertson 1968)

The worst of those "many maladies and intolerable diseases" descended on Europe from China through the trade routes of the Mediterranean, moving through southern Russia and the Crimea between 1331 and 1346, finally exploding across the length and breadth of the Continent between 1346 and 1350. By the time this first wave of the bubonic plague pandemic, the Black Death, had passed, at least a third of the population of Europe had died. Then it returned in the 1360s and 1370s to kill again, though each new visitation brought progressively lower death rates as immunity to the disease began to develop.

The weight of evidence suggests that in the wake of the plague nothing remained the same. It is perhaps an exaggeration to label the Black Death the "cause" of events ranging from the Peasants' Revolt to the Reformation, as some have done, but there is no doubt that spiritual and political faith were profoundly shaken by it. Certainly this disequilibrium – when, as one nineteenth-century historian put it, "faith disappeared, or was transformed; men became at once skeptical and intolerant" (Jusserand 1891) – made an important contribution to the great social changes that occurred in Europe from the fifteenth to the seventeenth century.

During those later centuries epidemics continued to haunt the Continent, and population recovery was slow (Flinn 1981). As before, the cities could not sustain themselves without constant in-migration from the countryside. As one writer has flatly stated, during these centuries "immigration to the towns was vital if they were to be preserved from extinction" (Mols 1973). Until the eighteenth century, however, the geographic extent of most Europeans' internal urban migrations appears to have been quite small: Apart from the forced migrations caused by warfare, as one large study has shown, the majority of those people who moved at all during their lifetimes were unlikely to have migrated more than 10 miles from their original home (Clark 1979).

The crucial point, however, for present purposes at least, is that by the close of the fifteenth century, Europeans had accumulated and exposed one another to an enormous number of what had evolved into chronic infectious diseases – including measles, mumps, influenza, chicken pox, smallpox, scarlet fever, gonorrhea, and tuberculosis, to name but a few. Although occasionally breaking out in epidemic episodes, these diseases had principally become slow killers, many of them preying largely on children, nearly half of whom died before reaching their tenth birthday (Flinn 1981), or the aged.

It was neither children nor the aged, however, who manned the sailing ships that, near the turn of the fifteenth century, began the most extensive explorations and migrations the world had ever witnessed and, as already mentioned, in the process created what may well have been the worst series of human disasters in history.

Africa and the Caribbean

The massive African continent, with a commerce, migration, and disease history that was at least Europe's match, loomed large in the imagination of the earliest open-sea European explorers. With all its riches, however, as Alfred Crosby (1986) has commented, "Africa was a prize well within European reach, but it seared the hand that tried to hold it." In addition to malaria, one of the most destructive diseases humans have ever faced, so extensive was the barrage of African diseases that greeted the Europeans – in Crosby's words, "blackwater fever, yellow fever, breakbone fever, bloody flux, and a whole zoo of helminthic parasites" – that Africa quickly became known as the "white man's grave." Even as late as the nineteenth century it was routine for British troops stationed on the Gold Coast to lose half their number in a single year to the ravages of African disease, and European soldiers stationed alongside black troops in West Africa died from disease at a rate 15 to 20 times higher than their African counterparts (Curtin 1968). The Europeans, of course, returned some of these favors with diseases of their own to which the Africans had little or no resistance – in particular, syphilis and tuberculosis, which took a heavy toll among their African recipients.

Whereas some explorers plied the African trade, others ventured deep into the Atlantic. There they encountered peoples living in the most salubrious of island environments, peoples with no domesticated animals and no history of almost any of the diseases Europeans had had to live with for centuries and even millennia. In their great isolation, the natives of the Caribbean had long since come to biological terms with the relatively few microparasites in their midst. In this sense, they were probably similar to the Old World populations of thousands of years earlier. Predictably, European contact was calamitous for them. The Caribbean island natives, living in fairly dense coastal settlements, were overwhelmed by the barrage of diseases that rolled over them. Unlike even the worst epidemics the Europeans had historically had to endure, including the infamous Black Death, the biological invaders of the Caribbean came in a swarm: A variety of scourges hit them all at once. In their confined island worlds there was nowhere to hide.

The island of Hispaniola was the first to be hit. In 1492, when contacted by Columbus, its population may have been as large as 8 million; less than half a century later its people were, for all practical purposes, extinct (Cook and Borah 1971). The pattern was the same throughout the islands of the Caribbean. Diseases descended on the natives in clusters. And with no one in the community having any resistance, everyone fell sick at the same time. With no one left to haul water or feed children or provide comfort to anyone else, nutritional levels plummeted and despair swept over the populace – further reducing their resistance to infection.

As the first epidemic waves passed, longer-term illnesses like tuberculosis and gonorrhea took hold, reducing the island populations still further while undermining their reproductive potential and thus any possibility of recovery. In this condition the natives were yoked to forced labor by the Spanish invaders. With the failure of native labor to produce as desired, the Europeans turned to Africa for their work force. This spelled the end for the Caribbean's native island peoples, for the enslaved Africans brought with them the diseases that earlier had made their continent the storied "white man's grave." Whipsawed between the diseases that had been accumulating in Europe and Africa for millennia, the island natives at last ceased to be (Kiple 1984).

In the centuries that followed, down to the present, the European and African diseases did most of their damage to the populations native to the other continent – tuberculosis, smallpox, and pneumonia attacking the African immigrants, malaria and yellow fever assaulting the Europeans. Demographically, the Africans triumphed: Today the descendants of African slaves dominate the populations of the Caribbean. As Kenneth Kiple (1984) has clearly shown, however, new catastrophes now lie in wait as population pressures build in the region and the safety valve of out-migration threatens to close.

The Americas

Following their invasions of the Caribbean, the sixteenth-century European explorers headed for the American mainland. Again, they encountered peoples with no previous exposure to the diseases the Europeans bore so easily – and again the result was a holocaust.

Whereas it now appears that influenza, carried by pigs aboard Columbus's ships, may have been the initial principal killers in Hispaniola (Guerra 1985, 1988), on the American mainland the initial major cause of death was smallpox (Crosby 1972; Dobyns 1983). Death rates were much higher in coastal than in inland areas, those in the former often approaching the extermination-level rates of the Caribbean (Borah and Cook 1969). Inland areas, however, though faring somewhat better in a comparative sense, still suffered at a level that strains comprehension. The population of central Mexico, for example, appears to have dropped by one-third, from about 25 million to less than 17 million, in a single decade following European contact. Within 75 years it had fallen by 95 percent (Cook and Borah 1960; Borah and Cook 1963).

So rapidly did the viruses and bacteria spread up and down and across the North and South American continents that historians have been unable to trace their paths with any precision. It is now clear, however, that the diseases moved across the land at a much faster pace than did the men who brought them, destroying whole populations long before their very existence could be known by the European invaders (Ramenofsky 1987).

Although the overall size of the population in the Americas at the time of European contact and its subsequent rate of collapse have long been a subject of much controversy, it is becoming increasingly apparent that both numbers represent magnitudes that earlier scholars had never imagined. It is possible, in fact, that the pre-Columbian Americas contained more than 100 million persons – more than resided in Europe, including Russia – at the time of the European arrival (Dobyns 1966).

Recent regional estimates continue to support the thesis, originally propounded by Sherburne Cook and Woodrow Borah, that massive and sudden depopulation was the rule in early native European contact situations throughout the Americas: From Peru, where a population of about 9 million dropped to 600,000 during the century following contact (a 93 percent decline rate), to Nicaragua, where it fell by more than 92 percent (Cook 1981; Newson 1987); from California, where the native population declined by 95 to 98 percent before bottoming out in the nineteenth century (Thornton 1987), to Florida, where it appears to have fallen by 75 percent in only 15 years and 95 percent within the first century of European contact (Dobyns 1983); from New England, where the

Patuxet tribe was extinguished in two years and the Massachusett tribe fell by 97 percent in two decades, to Guatemala, where the highland population alone dropped by 94 percent in little more than a century (Axtell 1985; Lovell 1985). Other examples abound.

Terrible as the epidemic invasions were in all these cases, it is now becoming evident that viral and bacterial assaults, by themselves, do not sufficiently account for such large population losses. As in the Caribbean, it appears likely that in the rest of the Americas the epidemics initiated a process of collapse, which then was exacerbated by the rapid withering away of village life and social supports, along with the pervading sense of despair and helplessness that was a natural concomitant of the epidemic firestorm (Neel 1977). In addition, comparative research now suggests that the fundamental cause of the most drastic population declines may well have been an overwhelming degree of infertility directly caused by the waves of smallpox, tuberculosis, measles, and venereal infection that attacked these epidemiologically virginal populations (Stannard 1990).

The Pacific

The Pacific – from the continent of Australia to the islands of Hawaii – was the last major region of the world affected by the great era of European exploration in the sixteenth, seventeenth, and eighteenth centuries. The same lugubrious tale of explosive epidemics and drastic population decline that we have encountered in the Americas was repeated here.

The lengthy ocean voyages required to reach the Pacific screened out the danger of smallpox during the earliest years of exploration, although in time smallpox epidemics did devastate native populations throughout the entire region (for examples from Australia, Pohnpei, and Hawaii see Greer 1965; Butlin 1983; Campbell 1985; and Hanlon 1988). Influenza may have been restrained to some extent by the same distance-screening process, although influenzalike epidemics were reported in many early records and ongoing research on the spread of influenza viruses suggests ways in which the distance restraint may have been overcome (Hope-Simpson and Golubev 1987). Of greatest importance in the first decades of Western contact, however, were tuberculosis (which can explode with epidemiclike intensity in a previously uninfected population; see, e.g., Dubos 1965) and venereal diseases.

An account of the devastation visited on the Pacific is as lamentable as is the account of what happened in the Americas. In southeastern Australia about 95 percent of the aboriginal population died off in slightly more than 60 years (Butlin 1983). In New Zealand the native population fell by about 60 percent in 70 years and at least 75 percent in a century (Lewthwaite 1950; Pool 1977). In the Marquesas Islands the population dropped by 90 percent in 65 years and by 96 percent in just over a century (Dening 1980). In Hawaii the native population was halved within 25 years following Western contact and reduced by at least 95 percent in a little more than a century (Stannard 1988). There are many more examples.

As with the natives of the Caribbean and the Americas, a primary cause of the Pacific peoples' vulnerability to the introduced infections was their lack of immunity to the new diseases and the fact that they were assaulted by a barrage of them simultaneously. In addition, some genetic factors may have also played a part. Because initial populations were relatively small in each newly settled island, the evolved gene pool in each case was probably relatively small, making large-scale die-offs more likely than would be the case in populations with a more complex and heterogeneous composition. Like American Indians, who also grew from a comparatively small population of early immigrants and who were isolated from the world's gene pools and great disease experiences for a vast period of time, Polynesians, for example, show a remarkably narrow range of blood types, with an almost complete absence of type B (Morton et al., 1967; Mourant 1983).

In the Pacific, as in the Americas, the populations that were not extinguished by their contact with the West in time began to recover. Partly because of the development of acquired immunities, and partly because of amalgamation with the races that had brought the new diseases (among Hawaiians, for example, the worst health profile today remains that of so-called pure Hawaiians, whose numbers have dwindled to less than 1 percent of those at the time of Western contact), the Pacific's native people now have birthrates higher than most of the immigrant populations in their homelands.

Conclusion
It is easy, in light of the historical record, to believe that migration-caused health disasters are a thing of the past. There are, after all, few if any hermetically remote populations left on earth; and as we have seen, from Rome and China in the second century A.D. to the Pacific in the eighteenth and nineteenth centuries – as well as parts of South America in the twentieth century – virgin-soil conditions were the seedbeds of the great disease holocausts.

The problem, however, is much more complex. In addition to the fact that immigrants to many parts of the world suffer greatly increased incidences of coronary heart disease and various forms of cancer – as, for example, Japanese immigrants to the United States (Waterhouse et al. 1976; Robertson et al. 1977) – there is the ongoing tragedy of the acquired immune deficiency syndrome (AIDS), which should be sufficient to quell undue optimism. It is far from impossible, as Joshua Lederberg (1988) has noted, that the AIDS viruses will continue to mutate, perhaps even, in his words, "learning the tricks of airborne transmission," and, as he says, "it is hard to imagine a worse threat to humanity than an airborne variant of AIDS."

Of course, that may not – indeed, probably will not – happen. But it may. Even if it does not, the great ease of human mobility and migration, along with the ability of our worst diseases to sustain themselves, ensures that – with or without virgin-soil populations in the traditional sense – we have not seen the last mobility-caused infectious catastrophe.

David E. Stannard

Bibliography
Axtell, James. 1985. *The invasion within: The contest of cultures in colonial North America*. New York.
Bahr, Donald M., et al. 1974. *Piman Shamanism and staying sickness (Ká:cim Múmbidag)*. Tucson, Ariz.
Biraben, J. N., and Jacques Le Goff. 1969. La peste dans le Haut Moyen Age. *Annales: Economies, Sociétés, Civilisations* 24: 1492–1507.
Bonser, Wilfred. 1944. Epidemics during the Anglo-Saxon period. *Journal of the British Archaeological Association* 9: 48–71.
Borah, Woodrow, and Sherburne F. Cook. 1963. *The aboriginal population of central Mexico on the eve of the Spanish conquest*. Berkeley and Los Angeles.
  1969. Conquest and population: A demographic approach to Mexican history. *Proceedings of the American Philosophical Society* 113.
Braudel, Fernand. 1973. *Capitalism and material life, 1400–1800*. New York.
Butlin, N. G. 1983. *Our original aggression: Aboriginal population of southwestern Australia, 1788–1850*. Sydney.
Campbell, Judy. 1983. Smallpox in aboriginal Australia, 1829–31. *Historical Studies* 20: 536–56.
  1985. Smallpox in aboriginal Australia, the early 1830s. *Historical Studies* 21: 336–58.
Clark, P. 1979. Migration in England during the late seventeenth and early eighteenth centuries. *Past and Present* 83: 57–90.
Cook, David Noble. 1981. *Demographic collapse: Indian Peru, 1520–1620*. Cambridge.

Cook, Sherburne F., and Woodrow Borah. 1960. *The Indian population of central Mexico, 1531–1610*. Berkeley and Los Angeles.

1971. The aboriginal population of Hispaniola. In *Essays in population history: Mexico and the Caribbean*, Vol. 1, ed. S. F. Cook and W. Borah, 376–410. Berkeley and Los Angeles.

Crosby, Alfred W. 1972. *The Columbian exchange: Biological and cultural consequences of 1492*. Westport, Conn.

1986. *Ecological imperialism: The biological expansion of Europe, 900–1900*. Cambridge.

Curtin, Philip D. 1968. Epidemiology and the slave trade. *Political Science Quarterly* 83: 190–216.

Dening, Greg. 1980. *Islands and beaches – discourse on a silent land: Marquesas, 1774–1800*. Honolulu.

Dobyns, Henry F. 1966. An appraisal of techniques for estimating aboriginal American population with a new hemispheric estimate. *Current Anthropology* 7: 395–416.

1983. *Their number become thinned: Native American population dynamics in eastern North America*. Knoxville, Tenn.

Dubos, René. 1965. *Man adapting*. New Haven, Conn.

Flinn, Michael W. 1981. *The European demographic system, 1500–1820*. Baltimore.

Forbes, Thomas R. 1986. Deadly parents: Child homicide in eighteenth and nineteenth century England. *Journal of the History of Medicine and Allied Sciences* 41: 175–99.

Greer, Richard. 1965. O'ahu's ordeal: The smallpox epidemic of 1853. *Hawaii Historical Review* 1.

Guerra, Francisco. 1985. La epidemia americana de Influenza en 1493. *Revista de Indias* (Madrid) 176: 325–47.

1988. The earliest American epidemic: The influenza of 1493. *Social Science History* 12: 305–25.

Hanlon, David. 1988. *Upon a stone altar: A history of the Island of Pohnpei to 1890*. Honolulu.

Hirsch, August. 1883. *Handbook of geographical and historical pathology*, Vol. 1, trans. C. Creighton. London.

Hope-Simpson, R. E., and D. B. Golubev. 1988. A new concept of the epidemic process of influenza A virus. *Epidemiology and Infection* 99: 5–54.

Jusserand, J. J. 1891. *English wayfaring life in the Middle Ages*. London.

Kiple, Kenneth F. 1984. *The Caribbean slave: A biological history*. Cambridge.

Lederberg, Joshua. 1988. Pandemic as a natural evolutionary phenomenon. *Social Research* 55: 343–59.

Lewthwaite, Gordon. 1950. The population of Aotearoa: Its number and distribution. *New Zealand Geographer* 6: 32–52.

Lovell, W. George. 1985. *Conquest and survival in colonial Guatemala: A historical geography of the Cuchumatan Highlands, 1500–1821*. Montreal.

Matossian, Mary Kilbourne. 1985. Death in London. *Journal of Interdisciplinary History* 16: 183–97.

McNeill, William H. 1976. *Plagues and peoples*. New York.

1979. Historical patterns of migration. *Current Anthropology* 20: 95–102.

1980. *The human condition*. Princeton, N.J.

Mols, R. P. R. 1973. Population in Europe, 1500–1700. In *The Fontana economic history of Europe*, Vol. 2, ed. C. M. Cipolla. London.

Morton, Newton, et al. 1967. *Genetics of international crosses in Hawaii*. Basel.

Mourant, A. E. 1983. *Blood relations: Blood groups and anthropology*. Oxford.

Neel, J. V. 1977. Health and disease in unacculturated Amerindian populations. In *Health and disease in tribal societies*, ed. P. Hugh-Jones et al., 155–77. Amsterdam.

Neel, J. V., et al. 1970. Notes on the effect of measles and measles vaccine in a virgin-soil population of South American Indians. *American Journal of Epidemiology* 91: 418–29.

Newman, Marshall T. 1976. Aboriginal New World epidemiology and medical care, and the impact of Old World disease imports. *American Journal of Physical Anthropology* 45: 667–72.

Newson, Linda A. 1987. *Indian survival in colonial Nicaragua*. Norman, Okla.

Pool, D. Ian. 1977. *The Maori population of New Zealand, 1769–1971*. Auckland.

Ramenofsky, Ann F. 1987. *Vectors of death: The archaeology of European contact*. Albuquerque, N.M.

Robertson, D. W., Jr. 1968. *Chaucer's London*. New York.

Robertson, T. L., et al. 1977. Epidemiologic studies of coronary heart disease and stroke in Japanese men living in Japan, Hawaii, and California. *American Journal of Cardiology* 39: 239–49.

Shrewsbury, J. F. D. 1950. The plague of Athens. *Bulletin of the History of Medicine* 24: 1–25.

Stannard, David E. 1988. *Before the horror: The population of Hawai'i on the eve of Western contact*. Honolulu.

1990. Disease and infertility: A new look at the demographic collapse of native populations in the wake of Western contact. *Journal of American Studies* 24: 325–50.

Stone, Lawrence. 1977. *The family, sex and marriage in England, 1500–1800*. New York.

Thornton, Russell. 1987. *American Indian holocaust and survival: A population history since 1492*. Norman, Okla.

Trowell, H.C., and D. P. Burkitt. 1981. *Western diseases: Their emergence and prevention*. Cambridge, Mass.

Waterhouse, J., et al. 1976. *Cancer incidence in five continents*, Vol. 3. Lyon.

White, Lynn, Jr. 1962. *Medieval technology and social change*. New York.

PART II

Changing Concepts of Health and Disease

II.1
Concepts of Disease in the West

The semantic and logical quagmires that await anyone audacious enough to safari through the changing concepts of disease, illness, and health are portended by a cursory analysis of the definition formulated by the World Health Organization. "Health," we are informed, "is a state of complete physical, mental and social well-being and not merely the absence of disease or infirmity" (Caplan, Engelhardt, and McCartney 1981). Aside from the fact that this seems more realistic for a bovine than a human state of existence, problems abound in what appears to be a fairly straightforward statement. The word "complete" immediately removes the definition from the realm of human reality. What is complete mental well-being, or physical for that matter? Worse still, the phrase "complete social well-being" is so freighted with individual interpretations that it alone renders the definition useless, if not pernicious.

This essay concentrates on ideas of physical health and disease, which is not to minimize the importance of psychiatric disease, but rather to admit that concepts of mental health and illness, although sharing most of the definitional difficulties of physical health and disease, are even more difficult to handle. In large part this is because with mental illness we lack the kinds of objective tools to measure brain function that have helped, though not resolved, questions of what constitutes health and disease in the physical realm. This is not, however, to deny the interconnectedness of the psychic and the physical, which is assumed in all of what follows.

Perhaps no one sentence captures the history of changing notions about disease better than a paraphrase of Humpty Dumpty's haughty admonition: "When I use the word *disease*, it means just what I choose it to mean – neither more nor less." Disease has always been what society chooses it to mean – neither more nor less. A number of important considerations lead to this generalization. Among these are the following: (1) The definition of disease has varied with time and place in history; (2) the names assigned to diseases are ultimately abstractions, although it is useful at times to act as though they are real; (3) what we mean by diagnostic terms, as with

words in general, can be discerned more accurately by what we do with them than what we say about them.

There have been countless attempts to define illness, disease, and health (Faber 1923; Riese 1953; Lush 1961; Meador 1965; Hudson 1966; Niebyl 1971; Boorse 1975; Burns 1975; Engel 1977; Temkin 1977; Taylor 1979; King 1982; Sundström 1987). Most share certain features, but it remains a practical certainty that no mortal could come up with short definitions of these words that would satisfy all who have an interest in them.

Although they will not be treated in what follows, even traditional definitions of death are no longer sufficient. This is due, in part, to the same developments in knowledge and technology that have forced us continually to redefine our notions of health and disease. Death, according to *Webster's Third New International Dictionary*, is the "cessation of all vital functions without capability of resuscitation." But we now have a state of existence that may last many minutes in which there are no apparent vital functions, but during which the capability of resuscitation is unknown. What do we call such a state of existence? This confounding of traditional definitions by today's knowledge and technology leads to such strange article titles as "Prevention of Recurrent Sudden Death" (Rapaport 1982).

The judicious historian, after even a dampening immersion into the literature of changing concepts of disease, will conclude that the subject is unmanageable in a brief essay. Accordingly, what follows excludes non-Western concepts of disease and focuses on the tension between those who believed diseases were real entities with an existence of their own (ontologists) and the opposing camp, which held that disease should be viewed properly as illness, as a unique process in one person over time (physiologists).

The ontology–physiology tension has persisted because physicians perceive that, at a minimum, they must have a reasonably precise definition of what they mean by disease in order to distinguish themselves as professionals. Try to imagine convincing a patient to submit to exploratory abdominal surgery without using a diagnostic term; or to study pathology without the use of disease names; or to mount fund-raising campaigns without words such as *cancer* or *muscular dystrophy*. The essential contradiction that practitioners have confronted over the centuries is that understanding disease demands thinking in abstract generalizations, but the practice of medicine deals with ailing individuals.

The question of disease vis-à-vis illness is not simply an intriguing philosophical persistency, although it has been a source of much intellectual enjoyment as well as frustration. The viewpoint adopted has definite implications for what physicians do in practice. Lord H. Cohen perceived five dangers in an inordinate ontological orientation:

It promotes a "penny-in-the slot machine" approach to diagnosis by seeking for pathognomonic signs, especially the short cuts of the laboratory; . . . it suggests that diagnosis is arrived at by comparing an unknown with a catalogue of knowns; the method of recognizing an elephant by having seen one before; . . . it reduces thought to a minimum; . . . it is of little help and may be positively misleading where the disease process varies significantly from the usual; and . . . it leads to all those dangers associated with a label which Cowper implied when he wrote of those – "who to the fascination of a name, surrender judgment, hoodwinked." (Lush 1961)

In this view, the diagnostic label attached to a patient tends to dictate the treatment that follows. If the patient is jaundiced, has pain in the right upper abdomen that radiates through to the back beneath the scapula, and the X-ray demonstrates gallstones, the diagnostic label is cholelithiasis and the treatment is removal of the stones. "Surgery does the ideal thing," wrote a health columnist around 1930 in a statement of pristine ontology, "it separates the patient from his disease. It puts the patient back to bed and the disease in a bottle" (Clendening 1931). But are such patients really separated from their diseases? They retain the genetic predisposition or eating habits or whatever produced the gallstones originally. Somehow it seems insufficient to speak of separating patients and diseases with such ready surgical facility.

A complete reliance on the opposite notion of illness has hazards of a different sort. Physicians who think largely in terms of illness aptly consider the whole patient, but if they are ignorant of the natural history of the disease, they may miss the diagnosis and, for example, operate needlessly or too late.

A number of commentators have accepted as fact that disease is ultimately defined by the words and deeds of those persons constituting a given society. They agree as well that physicians usually have had an important voice in these social definitions. What is often neglected at this point is the role that the biology of diseases has played in shaping societal conceptions of the nature of disease (Risse 1979).

Granted that cultural, social, and individual considerations contribute to the expression of diseases in society, we may not overlook the importance of the biological aspects unique to diseases. A current example is the acquired immune deficiency syndrome (AIDS). The period of time between infection with the human immunodeficiency virus (HIV) and the body's development of a testable antibody response can be as long as a year. One practical consequence of this inherent characteristic of the virus is that, during this period of time, blood that tests negative for the antibody may be transfused and infect recipients. Furthermore, the period between infection with the virus and development of the clinical disease may be 8 to 10 years or longer. This trait of the HIV greatly confounds the question of who should be tested for AIDS and what a positive test means. Thus, even as we correctly emphasize the role of cultural factors in the spread of AIDS (homosexual activity and intravenous drug use), we may not forget the central importance of the biological characteristics of the virus itself.

This critical significance of the nature of the disease appears in earlier historical examples as well. One of the most intriguing mysteries in the history of disease is that the Greeks, in the words of Karl Sudhoff, were "blind to the fact of contagion" (Adams 1886; Garrison 1929). The enigma is darkened by the fact that some of the diseases they described so well are contagious – mumps and childbed fever, for example.

Nonetheless, contagionism was never completely eliminated from medical thinking after the acceptance of the Jewish Old Testament as a holy book in the Christian religion. In large part this was because of the attention accorded leprosy, which increased with the return of the Crusaders from the Middle East. The notion of disease as contagious was even more strongly reinforced by the sweeps of bubonic plague in the fourteenth century. In a passage from his work *On Plague*, the fourteenth-century Arabic physician Ibn al-Khatîb wrote, "The existence of contagion is established by experience, study, and the evidence of the senses, by trustworthy reports on transmission by garments, earrings; by the spread of it by persons from one house, by infection of a healthy sea-port by an arrival from an infected land" (Arnold 1952). Even though the writer had no inkling of the intermediate role played by the flea and common house rat in the spread of plague, the patterns of spread convinced him that the disease was contagious.

Historical Survey
As revealed by what physicians say and do, an ontological orientation dominates our late-twentieth-

century thinking, but this was not always so. Historically, the dominance of ontological and physiological thinking shifted time and again. Concepts of disease in ancient Israel, Egypt, and Mesopotamia were too diffuse and vague to fit easily into ontological or physiological compartments. In the Golden Age of Greece, however, physiological thinking is easily identified. Plato needed no formal medical experience to see the deficiencies of compartmentalizing human illness. In *Charmides* he has Socrates say the following: "If his eyes are to be cured, his head must be treated; and then again they say that to think of curing the head alone and not the rest of the body also, is the height of the folly. And arguing in this way they apply their methods to the whole body, and try to treat and heal the whole and the part together." And a bit further on, "The great error of our day in the treatment of the human body [is] that physicians separate the soul from the body" (Jowett 1892).

The Hippocratic approach was also decidedly physiological. Not only did the Hippocratics see the patient as an integrated whole, they appreciated the need to study ailing individuals in the context of their total environment, as evidenced in *Airs, Waters, Places*. Yet Hippocratic physicians could not escape the essential dichotomy between illness and disease. In part this was because they were superb clinical observers. They described a number of cases so faithfully that we can affix modern diagnostic names to them with certainty. At times they even gave specific names to these symptom complexes, such as *pneumonia* and *pleurisy*.

If the Hippocratics were so sensitive to the differences in individual episodes of illness, how did they deal with the similarities they detected in specific syndromes to which they gave names? The answer is that they considered both, but neither to the exclusion of the other (Temkin 1977). One takes account of the symptoms, because the nature of the disease is important, but so too is the unique nature of the individual. The wise physician works not with the ontological red and physiological yellow, but with the orange that results. A return to Hippocratic holism has been advocated recently under the rubric of a "biopsychosocial" model (Engel 1977).

In asking why the balance seen as ideal to the Hippocratics did not become and remain the dominant outlook, it must be remembered that Hippocratic thought did not rule the Hellenistic period. Indeed, contemporaneously with developing Hippocratism, the nearby Cnidians, although postulating an erroneous single common pathway for disease causation, constructed a system of definite disease entities. Neither approach was entirely sufficient. As has been said, "Hippocrates did the wrong thing well; the Cnidians did the right thing badly" (Jones 1952).

As Greek culture spread first to Alexandria and then to Rome, the Hippocratic tradition was but one of many Greek schools of thought. Hippocratism is cherished today because it is more congenial to modern medicine than the other competing systems of the time. In Alexandria the ontological approach was advocated by Erasistratus, who in the third century B.C. wrote books on gout, dropsy, and paralysis. In the second century A.D., Galen returned the emphasis to the Hippocratic theme, saying in effect that a disease is not only a change in a body, but also a change in a particular body. After the decline of Rome, the Hippocratic–Galenic tradition survived in the Greek-speaking East, where it was picked up and modified by the Arabs and returned to the Latin West beginning in the eleventh and twelfth centuries.

Characteristically, however, throughout Western history, neither the physiological nor the ontological notion disappeared completely, even as one or the other was dominant. In the ninth century, Rhazes was echoing the ontological when he distinguished between measles and smallpox. In the sixteenth century, Paracelsus not only broke with Galen's version of disease causation (i.e., the doctrine of the four humors) but refuted Galen's conception of the nature of disease itself. For Paracelsus there were as many specific diseases as there were "pears, apples, nuts, and medlars." In his strong opinion Paracelsus influenced the physician-chemist Jean Baptistie van Helmont, who believed disease was "due to a creative 'seed' which gets hold of a part of the material frame of the body and 'organises' it according to its own schedule of life" (Pagel 1972). For Paracelsus and van Helmont it was the disease, not the patient, that varied (Pagel 1972). The move of these two men toward ontology presaged the arrival of the "arch-ontologist" of the seventeenth century, Thomas Sydenham.

Although he never worked out a detailed system himself, Sydenham believed diseases could be classified in much the same way as Linnaeus would later group plants. In an oft-quoted passage Sydenham (1848) wrote the following:

Nature, in the production of disease, is uniform and consistent; so much so, that for the same disease in different persons the symptoms are for the most part the same; and the selfsame phenomena that you would observe in the sickness of a Socrates you would observe in the sickness of a simpleton. Just so the universal characters of a plant are extended to every individual of the species; and whoever . . . should accurately describe the colour, the taste, the smell, the figure, etc., of one single violet, would find that his description held good, there or thereabouts, for all the violets of that particular species upon the face of the earth.

To do this with any hope of accuracy, Sydenham realized that physicians must return to the Hippocratic seat at the bedside. Beginning in 1666 he used this method to execute detailed descriptions of smallpox, syphilis, dysentery, gout (his personal nemesis), and measles, which he differentiated from scarlatina.

Although he would later be acclaimed the "English Hippocrates," this honor is not related to his conception of disease. As noted, the Hippocratics described individual illnesses, which they perceived as unique events limited in time. Sydenham, conversely, strove to discover syndromes that, because of their general characteristics, could be recognized when encountered in another patient. As Henry Sigerist (1971) put it, "Hippocrates wrote the histories of sick persons, but Sydenham wrote the history of diseases."

The greatest attempt to accomplish the goal of classification that Sydenham espoused came in the eighteenth century at the hands of François Boissier de Sauvages when he published *Nosologia methodica*, in which diseases were divided into 10 classes, 40 orders, and so on, to 2,400 species (Sauvages 1768). For the most part he was unwittingly describing symptoms and syndromes, not disease entities. Yet the idea was widely emulated. It appealed to clinicians, who had only to classify their patients' conditions correctly: Proper treatment followed as a matter of course.

During the seventeenth century the iatromechanists came to the fore. This departure was led by François de la Boë, also known as Sylvius, who followed van Helmont's lead in the development of iatrochemistry and its cousin, the iatrophysics championed by Giorgio Baglivi. The details of their systems need not be explored here, neither do those of the eighteenth century, the "century of medical systems," featuring the theories of Friedrich Hoffmann, William Cullen, John Brown, and Benjamin Rush.

Though their systems were ephemeral, the ideas of these men retained one element of humoralism, which linked them to the nineteenth century. In general, they held that disease was due to an imbalance — too much or too little of something, whether stimuli, or spasm of the arteries, or nervous

fluid. In the nineteenth century, disease would be defined as a deviation from the normal. Because physiological normality had a range, disease, in a sense, was a departure from the limits of range within which health was balanced. In different terms, Brown and his eighteenth-century kin, with their ideas of too much or too little, were using deviation from the normal as the definition of disease. Their problem was that they lacked the knowledge and technology needed to confer objectivity on the various ranges of physiological normality.

The French clinical school of the first half of the nineteenth century exploited the investigative tool called the clinical–pathological correlation. This was the system used effectively by Giovanni Battista Morgagni a half-century earlier, which had led him to conclude that diseases originated locally in the organs of the body, and not in some imbalance of the vague fluidal humors. The process remains one of the most effective teaching devices in medicine — obtaining a detailed history and physical examinations, which change following the natural course of the disease, and finally submitting to the judgment of the autopsy table.

French clinicians Jean Nicolas Corvisart and René Laennec raised this exercise to such excellence that it became known as *la méthode*. In the process, many diseases that had never existed by name or had been confused with others were sorted out in such a way that they could be detected in living patients. This naturally gave great impetus to ontological thinking.

As it turned out, however, a more forceful and effective contemporary personality belonged to the antiontologist François Broussais. For Broussais, disease occurred when certain structures were excessively stimulated. Such stimulation (irritation) produced visible inflammatory lesions, which in his scheme centered in the stomach and intestines. There were then no such specific diseases as diphtheria and typhoid; these were considered merely variations of inflammations. In part due to Broussais's influence, between 1800 and 1880 ontology was pushed into the remote reaches of medical thinking. In his turn, Broussais would yield to the laboratory data produced by such physiologists as François Magendie and Claude Bernard, and even more decisively to the apparently irrefutable proof that specific microbes caused specific diseases.

As noted, an important conceptual emphasis of the nineteenth century was the idea of disease as deviation from normal. The idea existed as early as Plato's *Timaeus* and, of course, was basic to the enduring humoral pathology. The word *normal* has a number of meanings, only two of which are germane here. The first is the notion of conforming to a type, to an ideal or an object of desire, and thus is a value judgment. The second refers to something that is usual and that can be determined by enumeration (King 1982).

The problem of normality as it confounded medical practice was not a matter of accepting the definitions just given, but of fixing the ranges of normality and agreeing to the magnitude of departure from these ranges that should be labeled disease. The promise of a practical solution to this age-old problem expanded in the nineteenth century with rapidly developing methods of quantifying physiological functions.

As the century progressed, these methods came to include a host of chemical determinations and tools, such as the clinical thermometer, the X-ray, and a portable blood pressure apparatus. Their important common denominator was an unprecedented objectivity. As experience was added to these new technologies, clinicians increasingly held that old and new notions of what constitued disease must satisfy the new methods of quantification. The whole process was reinforced in the last quarter of the nineteenth century by the establishment of the concept of specific etiology with the final vindication of the germ theory of human disease. Not only were there specific diseases, but each apparently had a specific cause. No longer was the notion of disease as deviation from the normal burdened by such vague and unquantifiable etiologic agents as the four humors or nervous energy.

Now the agent responsible for the deviation from health in tuberculosis could be seen under the microscope. It could be recovered from human sputum grown in pure culture, injected into healthy guinea pigs, where it produced a characteristic tissue reaction and clinical picture, recovered from the tuberculous animal, grown again in pure culture, and on and on. More impressive proof that disease was real would be difficult to imagine. If not *diseased,* what was one to call a cavity-ridden lung from which identical pathogenic microbes could be recovered in every instance?

Social forces added to the swing back to ontology. The rise of hospital practice brought together many patients whose diseases were, for practical purposes, identical. Such devices as the ophthalmoscope and laryngoscope gave impetus to specialization, which in turn gave practitioners exposure to a large number of similar clinical pictures. Out of this conflu-

ence of developments, the ontological view returned at the turn of the twentieth century more powerfully than ever before (Faber 1923).

Still, as always, the concept of disease could not be reduced to black or white. New questions arose. What does one do with "Typhoid Mary" Mallon, whose gallbladder teemed with typhoid bacillus but caused Ms. Mallon no symptoms at all? The bacteriologist labeled this the "carrier state," which may have comforted science, but not society. Everywhere that Mary went typhoid was sure to follow. Was she diseased? Certainly in the eyes of public health authorities and society. But was she ill? Not to Mary herself.

To accommodate the increasing accuracy with which late-nineteenth-century scientists could define normality, practicing physicians had to reenlist an old friend, impairment, or as they called the updated concept, impediment. Impediment implied that, before a departure from the still-imprecise boundaries of normality could be labeled disease, a person must suffer physical or social impairment to a significant degree.

In the seventeenth century, Daniel Sennert had defined health and disease in terms of a person's ability to perform in a natural way. In the eighteenth century, Hermann Boerhaave used the presence or absence of impairment in a strikingly similar fashion. Boerhaave also specifically anticipated one of the major problems of disease as impediment: Suffering the same objective physical deficiency, persons differed in their subjective perception of impairment (King 1982). The quadriplegic confined to a wheelchair for years would feel little impairment from an attack of polio involving his lower limbs. Yet a previously healthy person would experience paraplegia as a catastrophic impediment.

Beyond this, there were differences between what scientists considered unacceptable departures from normality and how these variations were considered by patients. Enumerating blood pressure readings in thousands of persons led medical scientists to classify any determination above, say, 160 over 95 as the disease hypertension. The problem was that many patients with such elevations experienced no impediment whatever – indeed, felt perfectly well. What was the practitioner to do in this instance? He might argue that, even if these persons were not impaired at the time, there was a significant probability that they would be in the future. But, again, not always. Some persons carried their elevations without symptoms to the age of 80 and died of unrelated causes.

Confounding all this was the question of what constituted *significant* impairment. The cardiac neurotic may be almost totally impaired by a fear of the heart attack that claimed his father and grandfather at early ages. He may refuse to get out of his easy chair even though repeated thorough medical examination including sophisticated indicators of heart disease have all been negative. In practical terms, the hypertensive is diseased but not ill and the neurotic is ill but not diseased. Such a framework can satisfy the needs of the practitioner, but it likely leaves the philosopher unfulfilled.

Functional Disease

The word *function* has been in English usage for some 400 years. Earlier in medical terms it meant both the physiological activity of an organ and the psychological activity of the brain. This dual usage persisted into the 1830s, after which neurologists began classifying diseases as organic and functional, the latter reserved for conditions in which current technology could not demonstrate structural alterations (Trimble 1982).

Later in the century the concept of functional disease spread to medicine generally. Between 1867 and 1869 Adolf Kussmaul introduced a tube into the stomach to relieve gastric dilation. He realized that, in addition to relieving the patient's symptoms, the technique could be used to study the function of the stomach as well. The idea was picked up by Ottomar Rosenbach, who used the term *ventricular insufficiency* to indicate a disproportion between the muscular reserve of the stomach and the physiological demands on it. From this grew a vast range of tests designed to determine the functional capacity of a bodily structure in health and disease. The model forms the basis of much of clinical laboratory medicine today. But once again semantic confusion entered the scene as evidence that psychological activity as well as structural changes could produce profound disturbances in bodily function.

After the work of Sigmund Freud, the word *functional* returned largely to its psychological meaning, and today is used indiscriminately to mean disturbed function of the nervous system, or as a word for symptoms that do not fit prevailing diagnostic terms, as well as a euphemism for a variety of psychiatric disorders and the antithesis of what is meant by organic disease. When used without qualification, it can only lead to confusion. As was said of the sobriquet *psychogenic*, "it would be well . . . to give it decent burial, along with some of the fruitless controversies whose fire it has stoked" (Lewis 1972).

Conclusion

Many health professionals continue to define disease and health simply in terms of each other. This school of thought contends that the two are on a spectrum, their extremes – serious disease and excellent health – being at opposite ends. There is a heuristic value in this viewpoint, but it poses serious problems in the real world of medical practice. The problems are related in part to medicine's ability to fix points on the spectrum of disease more discretely than in the region of health. When patients tell health professionals that they are "not quite up to par" or are feeling "very sick," there are often objective means for translating these expressions into useful information. Beyond this, the concept of illness has reasonably finite points on the spectrum. At its extreme, hospitalized patients are classified as serious, critical, very critical, and, ultimately, deceased.

Even though the concept of relative health can be traced to the ancient Greeks, the spectrum of health (as opposed to illness) has no such clear points or distinctions (Kudlien 1973). Patients may state that they feel very good or are in excellent or perfect health, but even if there is a reason to objectify their assessments, there are no logical or technological tools for performing the task. If the examination and laboratory results are normal, a patient will generally be classified simply as healthy. Any qualification of a statement about health, such as "almost healthy," moves the patient to a point on the spectrum that coincides with slightly impaired or ill. A measure of the difficulties here is seen in one author's suggestion, then rejection, of the idea that health could be quantified by fixing a point on the scale and allowing health to be two standard deviations from the norm (Caplan et al. 1981).

One reason for this state of affairs is that, from the standpoint of time, health is on a generally unidirectional spectrum directed toward illness and death. Things are a bit more complicated than the old saw "We are all dying from the moment of conception," but the element of truth in looking at human existence in this way may help us understand why health and disease are not au fond a tension or balance. True, for many years we may be in the healthy range of the spectrum, but during this time, our unidirectional genetic program (as best we now understand it) is moving us inexorably toward disease. True, also, in a given illness episode, we may reverse the direction and return to the spectrum of subjective and objective health, but this turnabout is temporary. The key element, time, remains unidirectional. Even as we move out of a given illness to health, we are advancing toward death, much as we are both gaining and losing ground as we walk against the direction of a moving sidewalk.

In desperation someone once defined disease as something people go to doctors for. As simplistic as this seems, and as unsatisfying as it may be to medical historians and philosophers, there is more than a germ of truth in the definition. Indeed, it reminds us of the original meaning of our elusive term – dis-ease. It covers situations in which the "patient" is simply ill at ease, without regard to the finer nuances of normality and impediment. Originally the word had no connection to pathological conditions, so that one might be said to be reluctant to dis-ease oneself by attending a lecture on changing concepts of disease (Garrison 1966).

The older definition of dis-ease applies to much of what physicians do nowadays. The young graduate student is dis-eased by a pregnancy that threatens to disrupt her academic career. The ensuing elective abortion relieves her dis-ease, but it is difficult to fit a normal pregnancy into any system of illness—disease considered so far. Some might contend that the student suffers an impediment, and in career terms, that might be true. But we would seem to be headed for even murkier depths if we translated into disease the impediment occasioned by a physiological alteration so profoundly normal that the species would die out in its absence.

Many encounters between patients and physicians result from similar social and cultural pressures. The middle-aged executive who resorts to plastic surgery to eliminate his perfectly normal, and even honorable, facial wrinkles is dis-eased, as are most who undergo cosmetic surgery. And, of course, the vast majority of persons seeking psychotherapy are dis-eased, in that it is basic to human existence to experience anxiety, insecurity, loneliness, and even depression. Certainly when physicians treat persons whose complaint is not only diagnosed as normal, but almost universal, dis-ease in the older sense must be involved rather than disease as it has been analyzed in the ontological or physiological meanings.

It is properly humbling to attempt to summarize an essay that one realizes has not succeeded completely in its aim. Under these circumstances, the temptation is to suggest that the question being asked is not a proper one in the sense that it cannot be answered by logic or experiment. Indeed, one of the more cogent summaries of our conundrum was expressed in precisely these terms by Owsei Temkin:

The question: does disease exist or are there only sick persons? is an abstract one and, in that form, does not allow a meaningful answer. Disease is not simply either the one or the other. Rather it will be thought of as the circumstances require. The circumstances are represented by the patient, the physician, the public health man, the medical scientist, the pharmaceutical industry, society at large, and last but not least the disease itself. For our thinking about disease is not only influenced by internal and external factors, it is also determined by the disease situation in which we find ourselves. (Temkin 1977)

Claude Bernard (1865) held that seeking the cause of life or the essence of disease was wasting time in "pursuing a phantom. The words life, death, health, disease, have no objective reality." Here Bernard was only partly right. It is not a waste of time to struggle with these definitions. There is much to be gained if the task does nothing more than force society, and especially medical people, to think of the consequences each time they use words to describe disease and health. The process is a waste of time only if one enters into it with the exclusive goal of arriving at universal and timeless definitions.

Robert P. Hudson

Bibliography

Adams, Francis. 1886. *The genuine works of Hippocrates,* Vol. 1. New York.

Arnold, Thomas. 1952. *The legacy of Islam.* London.

Bernard, Claude. 1865. *Introduction á l'étude de la médecine expérimentale.* Paris.

Boorse, Christopher. 1975. On the distinction between disease and illness. *Philosophy and Public Affairs* 5: 49–68.

Burns, Chester R. 1975. Diseases versus healths: Some legacies in the philosophies of modern medical science. In *Evaluation and explanation in the biomedical sciences,* ed. H. T. Engelhardt, Jr., and S. F. Spicker. Boston.

Caplan, Arthur L., H. Tristram Engelhardt, Jr., and James J. McCartney. 1981. *Concepts of health and disease: Interdisciplinary perspectives.* Reading, Mass.

Clendening, Logan. 1931. *Modern methods of treatment.* St. Louis, Mo.

Engel, George L. 1977. The need for a new medical model: A challenge for biomedicine. *Science* 196: 129–36.

Faber, Knud. 1923. *Nosography in modern internal medicine.* New York.

Garrison, Fielding H. 1929. *An introduction to the history of medicine.* Philadelphia.

1966. *Contributions to the history of medicine.* New York.

Hudson, Robert P. 1966. The concept of disease. *Annals of Internal Medicine* 65: 595–601.

Jones, W. H. S. 1952. *Hippocrates,* Vol. 2. London.

Jowett, Benjamin, trans. 1892. *The dialogues of Plato,* Vol. 1. New York.

King, Lester S. 1982. *Medical thinking: A historical preface.* Princeton, N.J.

Kudlien, Fridolf. 1973. The old Greek concept of "relative" health. *Journal of the History of the Behavioral Sciences* 9: 53–9.

Lewis, Aubrey, 1972. "Psychogenic": A word and its mutations. *Psychological Medicine* 2: 209–15.

Lush, Brandon, ed. 1961. *Concepts of medicine: A collection on aspects of medicine.* New York.

Meador, Clifton K. 1965. The art and science of nondisease. *New England Journal of Medicine* 272: 92–5.

Niebyl, Peter H. 1971. Sennert, van Helmont, and medical ontology. *Bulletin of the History of Medicine* 45: 115–37.

Pagel, Walter. 1972. Van Helmont's concept of disease – to be or not to be? The influence of Paracelsus. *Bulletin of the History of Medicine* 46: 419–54.

Rapaport, Elliot. 1982. Prevention of recurrent sudden death. *New England Journal of Medicine* 306: 1359–60.

Riese, Walther. 1953. *The conception of disease, its history, its versions, and its nature.* New York.

Risse, Guenter B. 1979. Epidemics and medicine: The influence of disease on medical thought and practice. *Bulletin of the History of Medicine* 53: 505–19.

Sauvages, François Boissier de. 1768. *Nosologia methodica sistens morborum classes.* Amsterdam.

Sigerist, Henry E. 1971. *The great doctors: A biographical history of medicine.* New York.

Sundström, Per. 1987. *Icons of disease.* Kristianstads Boktryckeri.

Sydenham, Thomas. 1848. *The works of Thomas Sydenham, M.D.,* Vol. 1, ed. R. G. Latham. London.

Taylor, F. Kraupl. 1979. *The concepts of illness, disease and morbus.* London.

Temkin, Owsei. 1977. *The double face of Janus and other essays in the history of medicine.* Baltimore.

Trimble, Michael R. 1982. Functional diseases. *British Medical Journal* 285: 1768–70.

II.2 Concepts of Disease in East Asia

In the inscriptions that record the divinations of Shang dynasty China (eighteenth to eleventh centuries B.C.), we find a number of diagnostic queries like this: "Divining this tooth affliction. Should we hold a festival for Fuyi?" Fuyi refers to a Shang ancestor, and the concern about a propitiatory festival reflects the belief, frequently voiced in the oracles, that sickness arises from the anger and envy of ancestors toward their descendants (Hu 1944; Miyashita 1959). If the welfare of the dead depended on the rituals of the living, the resentments of the dead were something to which the living remained ceaselessly vulnerable.

Disease thus first appears in China embodied in dangerous others, as a menace from without. After the Shang dynasty, the focus of concern would broaden and shift from disgruntled ancestors to parasites and poisons, demons and witchcraft spells. But whomever or whatever the Chinese accused of inspiring sickness, the defining feature of the earliest conceptions of disease was their independence from a conception of the body. In other words, the peculiarities of an individual's somatic condition were no more relevant to understanding a fever or a toothache than they were for explaining why one's crops were destroyed in a storm. The fact that an affliction happened to attack the body was incidental. The vengeful spirits that brought sickness could just as easily have inflicted drought and famine.

This accounts in part for why a collection of cures such as the *Wushier bing fang* (Recipes for fifty-two ailments) of the late third century B.C. tells us so much, on the one hand, about noxious demons and the techniques for exorcizing them and teaches us so little, on the other hand, about the afflicted body itself (Harper 1982). For whether a shaman literally beat the disease out of the patient or appealed to benevolent divinities for assistance, whether demons were coaxed out with magical formulas or transferred sympathetically to other objects, the treatment of disease, like the diagnosis, concentrated on agents alien to the self. The body merely provided the stage for the drama of sickness; it was not an actor.

This was a remarkably influential vision of disease. For instance, a dictionary of the later Han dynasty (25–220), the *Shiming,* glosses *yi* (epidemic disease) as *yi* (corvée), explaining that diseases were the corvée imposed on humans by demons. From the Sui (581–618) through the Yuan (1279–1368) dynasties, professors and masters of exorcistic rituals and incantations (*zhoujin*) constituted a part of the official medical bureaucracy, alongside professors of such other medical specialties as acupuncture and massage (Kano 1987). At a more popular level, the folklore of medieval Japan abounds in accounts of beguiling fox spirits that seduce or possess young men and women and cause them to waste away, go mad, or die (Veith 1965). And even today, a Korean shaman will acknowledge in his healing chant "ghosts of the drowned, ghosts who were shot . . . maiden ghosts, bachelor ghosts" (Kendall 1985).

In the evolution of East Asian disease conceptions, therefore, the imagination of menacing outsiders represents not a transient stage of superstitions, which the rise of philosophy would supersede, but a thematic pole to which reflection on sickness would repeatedly return. At the same time, by the late Zhou (770–403 B.C.) and Warring States (403–221 B.C.) periods, suspicions of supernatural mischief were already slipping from the intellectual mainstream. In the philosophical ferment of these periods, a new conception of disease was emerging – one that would seek the origins of sickness not in the whims of some dangerous other, but in the desires of the self.

In the late Zhou and Warring States periods, disease became a reflection of somatic condition, and somatic condition, a reflection of the self. For the Confucian and Taoist philosophers of this era, the body was the dynamic product of experience, a reality continually shaped and reshaped by how one was living and had lived. *Shen,* "the body," was the same *shen* emphasized by the ideals of *xiushen,* "self-cultivation," and *deshen,* "self-possession": It was the embodied self, a lifetime of decisions and indecisions made manifest.

The failings of the body, therefore, were inseparable from failures of self-mastery. Sickness in this view had little to do with ancestral ire or demonic cruelty. It arose principally from within, from immoderation and carelessness, from gluttony and overexertion, from protracted grief and explosive anger, and sometimes from the mere imagination of dangers. One man falls ill after experiencing a terrifying dream and is cured only when a clever physician suggests that the dream was one reserved for future kings. Another suffers severe cramps after being compelled to drink a cup of wine in which he thinks he sees a snake. Only when he is made to realize that what he saw in the wine was merely the reflection of an archer's bow hanging on the wall does he recover (Li 1960). The close identification of body and self went hand in hand with a subtle awareness of the many ways in which human beings could make themselves sick.

According to the most devoted and influential students of the body, however, the real essence of disease was depletion. The experts of *yangsheng,* or "the cultivation of life," envisaged the body as the container of a precious and finite vitality. If properly conserved, this vitality could sustain one for a hundred years, free of all affliction, and free even of the ravages of age. True health found its proof in ever-youthful longevity. If most people succumbed to disabilities and senescence, and died before reaching their hundredth year, if most, in short, were sick, it was because they depleted the body by squandering this vitality.

Ghosts and malevolent spirits were not involved. Yet the body was still surrounded by enemies. Early historical and philosophical texts refer frequently to individuals struck down by wind or cold, rain or scorching heat. Wind and cold especially loomed large as noxious forces. To winds fell the blame for afflictions ranging from sneezing and headaches to paralysis and madness, and proverbial wisdom would soon have it that "the myriad ailments all arise from wind." As for cold, the study of the feverish disorders to which it gave rise would eventually become the subject of the most influential treatise of the pharmacological tradition, Zhang Ji's *Shanghan lun* (Treatise on cold afflictions), written around the end of the second century. Wind, cold, and other meteorological elements thus replaced the demons and spirits of shamanistic medicine as embodiments of the dangerous outsider. Like demons and spirits, they were objective pathogens that penetrated and roamed throughout the body; and like demons and spirits, they figured both as the cause of disease and as the disease itself.

But wind and cold differed from demons and spirits in one critical respect: Their pathogenic character was contingent on the condition of the body. They would invade only when the body was vulnerable, or more precisely, depleted. As the *Lingshu* of the Han dynasty later explained: "Unless there is depletion, wind, rain, cold and heat cannot, by themselves, injure a person. A person who suddenly encounters brisk winds or violent rains and yet does not become ill is a person without depletion" (Chen

1977). In a body brimming with vitality there was no room for noxious influences to enter.

The depletion of vitality was thus doubly noxious. It left one vulnerable to the virulence of wind, cold, and other climatic pathogens. More immediately, however, depletion was itself a form of sickness, a diminution of possibilities: It meant that even without the intrusion of alien influences the senses and limbs that should be strong and unimpaired until age 100 might already be weak or failing at age 50 or 60.

The leitmotif of *yangsheng* reflection on the body, therefore, was *bao,* "preservation" – "preserving the body" (*bao shen*), "preserving the vital essence" (*bao zhen*), "preserving life" (*bao sheng*). To maintain the body intact, to protect it against attacks from without by carefully conserving and containing vitality within – such was the heart of the "cultivation of life." But preservation was difficult. A considerable disparity separated the attentions required to preserve vitality and the ease with which it slipped away, for preservation demanded concentration whereas the outflow of vitality often accompanied the experience of pleasure. If the depletion of vitality constituted the root of disease, the roots of depletion lay in desire.

This was most apparent in sexual intercourse. Already in the sixth century B.C., we find a physician tracing the illness of the duke of Jin to his frequentation of concubines (Li 1960). Later Chinese and Japanese writings on regimen would even specify the precise number of times per month or year to which intercourse should be limited (Kaibara 1974). On few points would opinion be as unanimous: Semen was the distilled essence of life, and there could be no surer path to debility and early death than to exhaust one's supply in frequent intercourse. Although moral strictures against pleasure per se were rare, philosophers and physicians constantly warned against the physical drain of sexual indulgence. It is revealing that the response in classical China to the temptations of the flesh was not mortification, but rather the art of the bedroom (*fangzhong*) – psychophysical techniques centered around the prevention of ejaculation and the "recycling" of semen within the body (Van Gulik 1974).

The expenditure of vital essence in intercourse was, however, just one form of the intertwining of desire and depletion. Vitality could slip away from all the orifices: It flowed out of the eyes as one became absorbed in beautiful sights, and from ears as one lost oneself in rapturous harmonies. The orifices were, the *Huainan zi* explained, "the windows

of the vital spirit," and when the eyes and ears dwelled on pleasures of sight and sound, this vital spirit streamed outward, depleting the body and inviting affliction (Liu 1965). This movement of the spirit toward the desired object was the very essence of desire. Literally, as well as figuratively, desire entailed a loss of self: Physical depletion and lapses in self-possession were just different views of the unique phenomenon of sickness. Conversely, somatic integrity and emotional self-mastery coalesced in the notion of health. As the philosopher Han Fei of the early third century B.C. summarized it: "When the spirit does not flow outward, then the body is complete. When the body is complete, it is called possessed. Possessed refers to self-possessed" (Li 1960).

The secret of health thus lay in a mind devoid of desire. Such was the lesson of the "cultivation of life" in the Warring States period; and such also was the lesson of medical theory as it first crystallized in the classical treatises of the Han dynasty (206 B.C. to A.D. 220). But in the latter case the meaning of the lesson was more complex, because the meaning of disease was more complex.

Classical medicine yoked together what were in fact two conflicting images of the body and its afflictions. On the one hand, the key theoretical treatises of the Han dynasty – the *Huangdi neijing,* consisting of the *Suwen* and the *Lingshu,* and the *Nanjing* – perpetuated *yangsheng* intuitions of the vital self warding off the dangers of the world around it. Body was clearly separated from nonbody by the protective barrier of the skin, which both sealed in vitality and kept out noxious winds and cold. The two key terms of etiologic analysis, *depletion* and *repletion,* preserved in their definitions the distinction between what is healthy and proper to the body (*zheng*) and what is pathogenic and alien to it (*xie*): Depletion (*xu*) was a "deficiency in the body's vitality (*zhengqi*)," repletion (*shi*), an "excess of noxious influences (*xieqi*)."

Yet already in these definitions a new and alternative conception of disease was clearly emerging for the main distinction between depletion and repletion was not the opposition of inner and outer, but rather the complementary nature of deficiency and excess. Subtly, but surely, the earlier rhetoric of defense and attack was giving way to the new logic of balance and compensation; fears of threatening outsiders were being supplemented, and to an extent supplanted, by a conception of disease as unequal distribution.

In the schemes that articulated the emerging etiology of imbalance (the dialectic of yin and yang and the five-phase cycle [*wuxing*] of wood, fire, earth, metal, and water), the dichotomy of body and nonbody had little significance. Cosmic events and somatic events figured on the same plane: Deep grief could cause the repletion of yin and the depletion of yang, but so too could winter cold; a state of replete wood and depleted earth might involve a hyperactive liver (a wood organ), but it might also stem from easterly winds (also associated with wood). Moreover, both body and nonbody were subject to the same universal law of rhythmic change, the alternation of hot (yang) and cold (yin), the cycle of spring (wood), summer (fire), fall (metal), and winter (water). With indefinite and infinitely permeable boundaries, the body was seamlessly fused to a world ceaselessly transforming itself (Chiu 1986).

Disease in the Han dynasty became above all a seasonal phenomenon. Earlier observers had already recognized that different afflictions tended to characterize different seasons. The *Zhou li* (Rituals of the Zhou dynasty) observed, for instance, that headaches were prevalent in spring, whereas summer was characterized by the spread of scabieslike itching, autumn by malarial and other fevers, and winter by respiratory disorders (Lu and Needham 1967). Also widely noted was the fact that the same climatic pathogens of wind and cold had different effects in different seasons. Unseasonal weather, such as cold in summer, posed special dangers and often engendered epidemics.

The Han medical classics, however, went further and situated the seasonality of disease in the seasonality of the human body itself. According to the *Nanjing,* the most vigorous organ in spring should be the liver; in summer the heart should dominate; in autumn the lungs; and in winter the kidneys. In spring the pulse should begin to rise, gently, but growing like the first primaveral shoots; in summer it should be strong and overflowing; in autumn it should be slower and more constricted; and in winter it should lie deep as if in hibernation. To the discerning physician, each season exhibited its distinct physiology, and it was only with respect to this seasonal physiology that the standards separating health from sickness could be defined. The same signs, considered perfectly normal for one season, might certify disease in another.

Health, therefore, was a state of dynamic attunement in which the directions of an individual's energies paralleled the ebb and flow of the cosmos as a whole. For every season there were appropriate foods, appropriate activities, and even appropriate feelings. For example, in spring, the *Huangdi neijing* advised:

The myriad things flourish, engendered by heaven and earth together. Going to sleep at nightfall one should get up early and stride leisurely in the garden. Letting down one's hair and putting oneself at ease, one should give rise to ambitions. Engender and do not kill. Give and do not take away. Reward and do not punish. This is what is appropriate to the spirit of spring. (Chen 1977)

Failure to follow the spirit of the season, motivations and actions out of phase with cosmic transformation, resulted in deficiencies and excesses of yin and yang and the five phases, that is, in disease. The principle governing health and sickness was thus simple: Those who followed the flow (*xun*) flourished; those who opposed it, fell ill or died.

As part of the cosmos, human beings were naturally attuned to seasonal rhythms. Yet this attunement, like the intact body prized by proponents of *yangsheng,* was an ideal frequently compromised in actuality by unruly passions. The *Lushi chunqiu* explained: "What fosters life is following the flow (*xun*); but what causes life to depart from the flow (*bu xun*) is desire" (Li 1960). Desire here referred not to the depletion of vitality, but to disruptions in the smooth and balanced circulation of influences, to rigid attachments that resisted cosmic rhythms, and to impulses that deviated from the directions of seasonal change. If desire in the etiology of depletion implied a partial loss of self, desire in the etiology of imbalance entailed forgetting that the self was but one part of a much larger, ever-evolving world.

The cosmic dimensions of Han medical thought mirrored the expansive ambitions of the first great age of universal empire. In the same way that the political vision of universal empire would survive the rise and fall of subsequent dynasties, so the vision of the body as a seasonal microcosm would continue, along with *yangsheng* ideals of somatic integrity, to define medical orthodoxy for nearly two millennia. Yet the views of orthodox physicians did not by any means represent the views of all. In the chaos of the disintegrating Han empire, there emerged an alternative approach to illness that had a far greater and immediate impact on the popular imagination – an approach concerned not with the cosmic systems, but with individual morality and its consequences.

Intimations of sickness as punishment can be traced as far back as Shang fears of ancestral ire, and the moral failings of more than one emperor in the early Han dynasty (206 B.C. to A.D. 8) would be blamed later for the epidemics that devastated their people. But especially in the late Han dynasty (25–220), with the rise of religious Taoism, and the Six Dynasties (222–589) period, with the influx of Buddhism, the equation of sickness and personal transgression came to pervade popular consciousness (Kano 1987). With the diffusion of these religions, reflection on disease assumed an introspective aspect as religious healing turned increasingly toward the scrutiny of personal memory and conscience.

Zhang Lu, leader of a Taoist rebellion in the early third century, thus required the ailing first to spend time in a "chamber of silence," where they explored their consciences for the possible transgressions underlying their afflictions. Disease was the result of past sins, and recovery required the confession of these sins (Unschuld 1985). The Buddhist concept of karmic disease (*yebing*) also traced sickness (*bing*) to an individual's past actions (Sanskrit, *karma;* Chinese, *ye*). Karmic analysis diverged somewhat from Taoist intuitions in that these actions might go back many reincarnations, beyond conscious recall and beyond confession – thus explaining such puzzling phenomena as congenital diseases and the afflictions of the virtuous. But in the popular understanding, Buddhist precepts of karmic consequence and Taoist teachings of sickness and sin tended to coalesce into the same basic lessons: Good actions are rewarded, and misbehavior eventually punished; the ailments of today have their origins in the wrongdoings of yesterday.

Folk religion frequently framed these lessons in a divine bureaucracy. Unlike the often-unpredictable ancestral spirits of the Shang, the divinities of Han and Six Dynasties religion frequently resembled government officials, keeping track of a moral ledger of good and evil deeds (Eberhard 1967). For each transgression, appropriate afflictions were imposed, and days were detracted from one's allotted lifetime; meritorious acts, conversely, earned relief from sickness, and the restoration of longevity. The bureaucratic regularity of this scheme even allowed the early fourth-century Taoist Ge Hong to specify the number of days subtracted from one's life for each level of demerit.

The idea of moral accounting also formed the core of what was perhaps the most intriguing conception of disease in medieval East Asia, namely the theory of the body's three "corpses," or *shi*. Originating in China no later than the early fourth century and attaining its mature form by the Tang dynasty (618–

907), this belief posited the existence of three small creatures (*shi*) who inhabited various regions of the body and who recorded all the individual's evil yearnings and deeds. Then, once every 60 days, on the *gengshen* night of the astrological cycle, these *shi* would leave the body while the person slept, and fly up into heaven. There they would report to the heavenly emperor (*shangdi*) on the wrongdoings that they had witnessed, and the heavenly emperor would mete out punishment in the form of disease and shortened life. It was thus imperative for all who hoped to escape illness and live long lives to somehow restrain or purge these *shi*.

This was the origin of the custom whereby entire communities gathered together on *gengshen* night and stayed up until dawn to prevent the *shi* from escaping the body. The custom had many variants: Some villages would spend the night reciting Lao Zi's *Daode jing;* others would revel in drink and merriment; and in eighth-century Japan the importation of the three-*shi* theory gave Heian aristocrats an excuse for all-night music and poetry competitions. Although some philosophers, like Liu Zongyuan, denounced the idea of the *shi* as superstition, *gengshen* practices flourished and spread throughout East Asia, surviving in rural areas well into the twentieth century (Kubo 1961).

The popularity of three-*shi* etiology derived in no small part from the fact that it united many streams of East Asian reflection on disease. Though the three *shi* were originally conceived as small humanoids, they quickly became assimilated into traditions going back to the Shang about the infestation of the body by parasites and poisonous insects, and the same drugs were used against them as were habitually used to purge parasites. The notion that they would betray one only on particular nights fed, of course, into medicoastrological associations of health and cosmic rhythm. And in their role as keepers of the moral ledger, the three *shi* internalized the accounting of merits and demerits that linked sickness to sin.

Finally, the theory of the three *shi* reaffirmed the conviction that sickness was somehow tied to desire. According to some accounts, it was the presence of these *shi* that explained the pullulation of desires in the human heart; other accounts, conversely, stressed how killing off desire was the only way the *shi* could be exterminated. But all accounts of the *shi* and their dangers underlined their intimate connection to human beings as creatures of passion. Sickness and desire, which had, with different implications, been tied together by the *yangsheng* thinkers of the Warring States period and by the medical classics of the Han dynasty, were again united in medieval religion.

The physicians of the Song (960–1126) and Yuan (1279–1368) dynasties inherited a tradition of medicine that knew disease under two guises. On the one hand, there was the disease of theory, sickness as elucidated by the complementarity of somatic depletion and alien intrusion and by the system of yin and yang and the five phases. On the other hand, there was disease as it had been observed and experienced by physicians and patients over the course of a millennium. As evidenced by the sprawling seventh-century nosological compendium of Chao Yuanfang, the *Zhubing yuanhou lun* (On the origins and symptoms of all diseases), this tradition was protean and unwieldy, with seemingly limitless combinations of ever-diverse symptoms (Chao 1955). A great distance separated the perspicuity of theory from the dense tangle of experience. The key theme of Song and Yuan reflection on disease was the quest to reduce that distance.

The quest translated into two basic strategies. One strategy aimed at refining the classical etiology of depletion. Although recognizing that a complex variety of factors converged in the genesis of disease, many physicians from the Song and Yuan periods onward nonetheless sought to isolate a single crux of vulnerability. Li Gao, for instance, argued in the thirteenth century that "the hundred illnessess all arise from [disorders of] the spleen and stomach" (Beijing zhonqui xueyuan 1978). By contrast, his contemporary Wang Haogu sought the predisposing origins of sickness in depleted kidneys (conceived as the repository of semen), whereas Zhu Zhenheng of the fourteenth century focused on the tendency of human beings to experience "a superfluity of the yang element, and a deficiency of the yin" (Beijing zhonqui xueyuan). Later, in the Ming (1368–1662) and Qing (1662–1912) dynasties, still other physicians would blame the depletion of a variously defined organ known as the "gate of life" (*mingmen*) (Beijing zhongyi xueyuan 1978).

The other strategy sought to extend the classical etiology of imbalance, to articulate exhaustively the paradigms of yin and yang and the five phases so that they might provide a more adequate language for describing the rich variability of symptoms and syndromes. This produced a highly abstract perspective, which translated the concrete pathogens of wind, cold, and heat into the transparent logic of dialectical balance and seasonal rhythms; but it also produced a more unified approach to disease.

Whereas in Han medicine the marriage of the etiology of imbalance with the etiology of depletion had been at best an uneasy alliance, their strategic extensions in Song and Yuan medicine often blended smoothly together. Thus, desire, without entirely losing its long-standing associations with the depleting outflow of vitality, was recast as yang fire. Zhu Zhenheng's identification of the crux of vulnerability in excess yang and deficient yin referred, among other things, to the propensity of emotional agitation (yang) to predominate over rest and collected self-possession (yin). For him it was especially the inner feverishness (fire) generated by the tumult of passions that dispersed and dried up the moist vital essence (water) and gave rise to depletion. Similarly, Li Gao, who insisted on sound digestion as the pivot of sickness and health, analyzed the critical impact of emotional unrest in terms of the effect of fire (passions) on the earth-associated organs of the spleen and stomach. By translating in this way the analysis of depletion into the schemes of yin and yang and the five phases, these physicians framed the understanding of disease in a single comprehensive and integrated system.

The new technology of printing ensured the broad dissemination of Song and Yuan medical treatises, and these were assiduously studied not only by Chinese physicians in the Ming and Qing dynasties, but also by their counterparts in Yi dynasty Korea (1392–1910) and Tokugawa Japan (1600–1868) (Fujikawa 1980). No small part of the persisting myth of Chinese medicine as based on a timeless, monolithic theory is due to the resultant identification, throughout East Asia, of medicine with the systematizing tradition established by Song and Yuan physicians.

In reality, of course, Song and Yuan medicine itself comprised many diverging viewpoints, and subsequent periods witnessed a widening spectrum of ideas. Zhang Congzheng at the turn of the thirteenth century, for instance, rejected the prevailing focus on inner depletion and attunement and urged that intrusive attack was the primary fact of disease. His nosology, accordingly, recognized six basic kinds of disease, corresponding to the six climatic pathogens of wind, cold, fire, humidity, dryness, and heat. Later, in extensive investigations into epidemics in the Qing dynasty, Wu Youxing, born just before the middle of the seventh century, and Wu Tang, born a century later, probed even deeper into extrinsic causation. They distinguished between commonplace infiltrations of cold and other climatic agents, which occurred through the pores, and epidemic fiery afflictions (*wenbing*), which entered through the mouth and nose (Beijing zhongyi xueyan 1978).

Beyond China's borders, there were outright critics as well as devoted followers of this systemizing tradition. In the late seventeenth and eighteenth centuries, the Ancient Practice school (*kohoha*) of Japanese medicine rallied specifically around the overthrow of the Song–Yuan spirit of system. It inspired some radical conceptions of disease, such as Yoshimasu Todo's eighteenth-century theory that all disease arises from one poison and Goto Konzan's earlier notion that all disease results from stagnation in the flow of vital energy (Fujikawa 1980). Although these theories themselves did not have a lasting impact, the critical ferment they represented inspired physicians and scholars in late-eighteenth-century Japan to undertake the first serious studies of Western medicine in East Asia.

Students of medicine and health care in contemporary East Asia have stressed the persisting plurality of disease conceptions (Kleinman et at. 1975; Leslie 1976). As in the past, the advent of new approaches to disease, and in particular the introduction of ideas from the West, has led not to the abandonment of traditional assumptions, but simply to a more complex skein of beliefs and practices.

Some aspects of medical pluralism are obvious. A Korean healer who specializes in exorcizing noxious spirits may also refer patients to acupuncturists and hospitals (Kendall 1985). Acupuncture texts published in Taiwan today habitually refer to both the nosology of cosmopolitan medicine and the language of yin and yang.

There are also subtler forms of syncretism. The ostracism of tuberculosis patients and their families in early-twentieth-century Japan, for example, combined a vague understanding of modern theories of infection and heredity with traditional notions of contagious pollution and sickness as sin (Namihira 1984; Johnston 1987). But perhaps the most intriguing manifestations of the ever-present past have to do with the actual experience of illness.

Medical anthropologists have observed that patients in East Asia tend to experience all illness as illnesses of the body. That is, whereas a North American patient might complain principally of anxiety or depression, a Chinese patient will complain rather of palpitations, digestive disorders, or suffocating sensations in the chest (*men*), focusing on physical rather than emotional symptoms. Moreover, rather than seeking psychological explanations such as stress or frustration, Chinese and Japanese patients manifest a distinct preference for understanding diseases in terms of climatic and somatic etiologies – chilling wind, change of seasons, sagging stomach, acidic blood, imbalance in the autonomic nervous system, or simply weak nerves (Kleinman 1980; Ohnuki-Tierney 1984).

Such concepts as the autonomic nervous system and blood pH derive, of course, from modern science, but the general attachment to somatic symptoms and analyses surely goes back thousands of years. Desires and emotions figured centrally in traditional East Asian conceptions of disease, but they were never based in some disembodied psyche. They were invariably intertwined with somatic experience. Thus anger, for Han physicians, entailed the rise of the vital spirit, fear the sinking of the spirit, joy its relaxation, and grief its dissipation. The *yangsheng* thinkers before them saw self-possessed freedom from desire and the physical containment of vitality as one and the same reality. If, as anthropologists report, patients in East Asia manifest an unusual sensitivity to and interest in the body, this sensitivity and interest are perhaps related to a long cultural tradition that conceived of the body as the dynamic product of lived life, that is, as the embodied self.

Shigehisa Kuriyama

Bibliography

Beijing zhongyi xueyuan (Peking Academy for Chinese Medicine). 1978. *Zhongyi gejia xueshuo jiangyi*. Hong Kong.

Chao Yuanfang. 1955. *Zhubing yuanhou lun*. Beijing.

Chen Menglei. 1977. *Gujin tushu jicheng*, Vol. 42. Taipei.

Chiu, Martha Li. 1986. Mind, body, and illness in a Chinese medical tradition. Ph.D. dissertation, Harvard University.

Eberhard, Wolfram. 1967. *Guilt and sin in traditional China*. Berkeley and Los Angeles.

Fujikawa Yu. 1980. *Fujikawa Yu chosaku shu*, Vol. 1. Kyoto.

Harper, Donald. 1982. The *Wu shih erh ping fang*: Translation and prolegomena. Ph.D. dissertation, University of California, Berkeley.

Hu Houxuan. 1944. Yinren jibing kao. In *Jiaguxue Shangshi luncong*. Chengdu.

Johnston, William. 1987. Disease, medicine, and the state: A social history of tuberculosis in Japan, 1850–1950. Ph.D. dissertation, Harvard University.

Kaibara Ekiken. 1974. *Yojokun: Japanese secret of good health,* trans. Kunihiro Masao. Tokyo.

Kano Yoshimitsu. 1987. *Chugoku igaku no tanjo*. Tokyo.

Kendall, Laurel. 1985. *Shamans, housewives, and other restless spirits: Women in Korean ritual life*. Honolulu.

Kleinman, Arthur. 1980. *Patients and healers in the context of culture*. Berkeley and Los Angeles.

Kleinman, Arthur, et al. eds. 1975. *Medicine in Chinese cultures: Comparative studies of health care in Chinese and other societies*. Washington, D.C.

Kubo Noritada. 1961. *Koshin shinko no kenkyu*. Tokyo.

Leslie, Charles, ed. 1976. *Asian medical systems: A comparative study*. Berkeley and Los Angeles.

Li Fang, ed. 1960. *Taiping youlan*, Vol. 4. Shanghai.

Liu An. 1965. *Huainan zi*. In *Sibu beiyao*, Vol. 78. Taipei.

Lu Gwei-djen and Joseph Needham. 1967. Records of diseases in ancient China. In *Diseases in antiquity*, ed. D. Brothwell and A. T. Sandison, 222–37. Springfield, Ill.

Miyashita Saburo. 1959. Chugoku kodai no shippeikan to ryoho. *Toho gakuho* 30: 227–52.

Namihira Emiko. 1984. *Byoki to chiryo no bunka jinrui gaku*. Tokyo.

Ohnuki-Tierney, Emiko. 1984. *Illness and culture in contemporary Japan*. New York.

Parish, Lawrence Charles, and Sheila Gail. 1967. Ancient Korean medicine. *Transactions and Studies of the College of Physicians of Philadelphia* 38: 161–7.

Unschuld, Paul. 1985. *Medicine in China: A history of ideas*. Berkeley and Los Angeles.

Van Gulik, R. H. 1974. *Sexual life in ancient China*. Leiden.

Veith, Ilza. 1965. *Hysteria: The history of a disease*. Chicago.

Yu Yunxiu. 1972. *Gudai jibing minghou shuyi*. Taipei.

II.3
Concepts of Mental Illness in the West

We are not ourselves when nature, being oppressed, commands the mind to suffer with the body.

Shakespeare, *King Lear*

Mental disease refers, at present, to disorders of perception, cognition, emotion, and behavior. The disorder may be mild or severe, acute or chronic, and may be attributed to a defect of mind or body or of some unknown combination of the two. A diagnosis of mental illness is the judgment that an individual is impaired in his or her capacity to think, feel, or relate to others. In mild cases, the impairment may intrude on a person's ability to gain satisfaction from meeting the challenges of everyday life. In severe instances, an individual may be thought so dangerous or incompetent that sequestration within a psychiatric facility is necessary, with a resulting loss of rights normally granted to citizens.

The Problem of Mental Illness

The simple title of this section belies the extraordinary scope, complexity, and controversial state of contemporary psychiatric thought. Some have argued that if the myriad types of disorders bedeviling humankind were ranked by the net misery and incapacitation they caused, we would discover that psychiatry captures a larger share of human morbidity than does any other medical specialty. It seems ironic – if not tragic – that a clinical field of such magnitude is at the same time distinguished among its peers by a conspicuous lack of therapeutic and philosophical consensus. That the discipline lacks a set of internal standards by which to differentiate unequivocally the correct theory from the false, or the efficacious therapy from the useless, is an open secret. In a sense, if the disputing psychiatric camps are all equally able to claim truth, then none is entitled to it. Consequently, there exists not one psychiatry, but many psychiatries, a simple fact that alone has had enormous ramifications for the field's comparatively low medical status and conceptual disarray. Everywhere recognized and yet nowhere fully understood, insanity continues to challenge us as a problem that demands attention and yet defies control.

Situated so uneasily within the medical domain, the subject of mental illness poses a challenge of singular difficulty for the geographer and historian of human disease. One typically locates disease in place and time by first asking an array of standard questions: What are its immediate and predisposing causes? How does it normally progress? Upon whom is it most likely to befall? For example, in this volume any of a number of essays on infectious diseases (cholera, smallpox, plague) may begin with a tightly drawn narrative of how the disease unfolds in an untreated victim, knowable to the patient or casual observer by conspicuous signs and symptoms and to the medical investigator by the additional involvement of organ or systemic changes. We learn about the life course of the offending infectious agent and about the mechanisms by which it wreaks physiological havoc.

Once a clinical portrait and a chain of causation have been well established, it is possible to position a disease on the social as well as geographic landscape; its prevalence by age, sex, social class, and nation may be determined with some justification. At the same time, the work of the medical historian comes into focus. Paradoxically, as the present becomes clearer, so does the past. Using our clinicobiological model as a guide, we can search the historical record for answers to additional questions: When did the disease first appear and how did it migrate? Over the centuries, how wide has been its trail of morbidity? We can also reconstruct the story of when and how medicine, in fits and starts, first isolated the entity as a specific disease and then unraveled its pathogenic mechanisms. Indeed, endeavors such as this volume are indicative of the high confidence we have that our current nosology (fashioned by such triumphs as bacteriology and molecular biology) does, in fact, mirror the contours of biological reality. We are certain that typhus and cancer are not the same disease, and thus tell their stories separately.

Contemporary psychiatry, however, provides us with no map of comparable stability or clarity. When the standard array of aforementioned questions are applied to a mental disorder, satisfactory answers fail to emerge. Indeed, for a given mental illness psychiatrists would be hard-pressed to point to any unambiguous anatomic markers, to describe its pathophysiological process, or to explain its cause with a model that is intuitive, testable, and conforms to prevailing biological wisdom. Lacking in these familiar desiderata of scientific medicine, a mental disorder such as paranoia simply is not granted the same level of ontological certainty that is ascribed to an "organic" disease like leukemia. Until such time as we solve the age-old conundrum of the relations between mind and body, discovering a formula that converts states of consciousness to properties of matter (or vice versa), it is likely that such barriers will persist.

Visibly unmoored to fixed biological truths, classifications of mental disease thus seem capable of infinite drift. In consequence, the task of writing a history or geography of any given psychiatric illness might be regarded as a pointless, premature exercise. What exactly are we trying to map? If we follow the development of the word *neurosis,* we find that in one century it refers to exclusively nonorganic conditions, and in a century earlier, it includes organic disorders. If we disregard this problem as one of mere wordplay and try to identify the actual conditions that were labeled to such mischievous effect, another quandary develops. It is difficult enough to establish whether a given mental disease appears in another country, let alone in a distant time. That different eras produce variant mental diseases is more than plausible. Unfortunately, there exists no assay of human experience that can bridge the past. Though the bones of a mummy may reveal to X-rays whether a pharaoh suffered from arthritis, they remain silent as to his having suffered a major depression. Finally, each of the many psychiatries has its own guide to understanding mental disease; which

filter, then, do we apply to the past? Do we look for anxiety disorders as interpreted by the behaviorist, neuropharmacologist, or psychoanalyst?

Current philosophical critics of psychiatry, such as Thomas Szasz, advise us to abandon the effort. Szasz contends that, strictly speaking, mental illnesses are not valid medical entities and thus their stories have no place in any compendium on human disease. Madness exists, to be sure, but it is a quality of personhood, not of body or disease. Problems of living are manifold and serious, but without positive evidence that an individual's condition is due to a physiological cause, the physician has no business intervening. Unless psychiatrists can meet the best standards of scientific medicine, they should be thought of as modern quacks, laughable if not for their countless victims. According to Szasz, labeling someone a schizophrenic in the late twentieth century is no different from calling someone a witch in 1680 or a communist in 1950. It means that you disapprove of them, wish them ill, and have conspired with the community to punish them.

Any critique that brings to light real and potential abuses of psychiatry is laudable. As a general historical framework, however, Szasz's approach is limited, in that it conflates a philosophical ideal of what medicine should be with what the historical record shows it in fact is. A significant portion of current — and virtually all of past — medicine fails to meet similar tests of scientific purity. Are there only a few "real" physicians? It is easy to forget that the criteria of what constitutes "good" medical science are not fixed, but evolve. For example, controlled clinical trials became the ideal only after World War II. We may be chagrined to learn, just a few decades from now, that our remaining "real" physicians were quacks, too.

A better approach is to revisit categories of mental disorder in their original historical context, to see how they fit within prevailing conceptions of disease — not to define an illness according to an abstract standard, but to derive its meaning from the actual interpretations of patients and physicians. Otherwise, we are left with the absurdity that only those doctors who employ correct therapeutics, and conceptualize in terms of true disease categories (as judged by today's knowledge), have the right to be called physicians. Rather, we might follow the lead of Donald Goodwin and Samuel Guze and simply consider as diseases those conditions linked to suffering, disability, and death, which the lay and medical community regard as the responsibility of medicine. As much recent writing in the history of medicine argues, the "existence" of a disease can be as much a matter of social convention as a question of its biological reality.

This alternative approach to the history of mental disease will also sidestep the pitfalls associated with following the story of any particular psychiatric disorder through the centuries. The goal of this essay is to reconstruct the stages and processes by which insanity came to be seen first as a medical problem and then as a matter for specialized expertise. Particular attention will be given to the interactions between lay and medical conceptions of mental illness, in which physicians become drawn to issues of social concern and, in turn, their theories are incorporated into social thought; to the fit between the specific professional agenda of physicians and the medical conceptions they espoused; and to the challenges as well as opportunities that advances in general medicine posed for psychiatric practitioners. In so doing, we might arrive at a better appreciation of what is embedded within our current categories of mental illness and a clearer perception of what is the social function of psychiatry as a medical discipline.

Early Modern Europe to the Seventeenth Century

In this period, no single approach to the problem of insanity dominated. Although categories of insanity in the Renaissance derived mainly from the classical system of mania, melancholy, and dementia, which were based on the broad medical doctrine of bodily humors, the implications were diverse in practice. Physicians and lay people alike typically depicted mad persons as wild beasts, devoid of reason. Brutal handling of the insane was commonplace. Yet a pattern of hospital care for the insane had been emerging since the late Middle Ages. The famous English hospital of St. Mary of Bethlehem, later known as "Bedlam," was founded in 1450 as an institution to care for those who had "fallen out of their wit and their health." Moreover, in that age a belief prevailed that melancholics and some mad persons held powers similar to those of saints, such as talking in tongues and prophesying. Erasmus himself wrote that Christianity is a form of madness. This tradition stemmed from the rediscovery of Plato's teachings, that human beings are compound beings, part heaven and part earth. When the organic part is disturbed, as in madness, the soul becomes partially liberated. Poets, seers, and lovers might all exhibit true mania. And because this was a time when religion infused everyday life, visions were not rejected as deformed thoughts of diseased minds. Rather,

they were embraced as tangible manifestations of a divine universe that was otherwise liminal.

More to the point, religion, magic, and medicine in this eclectic age were viewed as overlapping – not incommensurate – domains. Loss of reason was attributed to any combination of natural illnesses, grievous misfortunes, evil spirits, and deeds so sinful as to incur God's direct wrath. Insanity thus became the proper business of astrologers as well as physicians, and of clergymen as well as lay adepts. Moreover, these roles often merged. A healer of sick souls might offer counseling to assuage a spiritual affliction in combination with a therapeutic regimen to restore a humoral balance. A course of physic might be accompanied by a magic spell and implemented according to the patient's horoscope. For the Renaissance doctor, an individual instance of madness was a thorny interpretative challenge, for its meaning might be located in bodily corruption, in devilry, or even in the signs of sainthood.

These entangled threads, however, pull apart in the seventeenth century as a consequence of intellectual and social revolutions. A foundation was being constructed for a naturalistic interpretation of insanity that would eventually overshadow supernatural and religious frameworks. First, the scientific revolution that culminated in the work of Francis Bacon and Isaac Newton placed science and the experimental method at the forefront of human achievement. The universe was beheld as a clockwork whose structure and mechanism could be understood – and eventually manipulated – by rational human investigation. As the macrocosm could be found in the microcosm, such investigations explored the physiology of the human body; the most notable was William Harvey's demonstration of the function of the heart and circulatory system.

Attention was also drawn to the mechanisms by which the soul commanded the body – the search was on for the *sensorium commune,* the organ that might mediate between passions, sensations, and body humors. The pineal gland, the organ suggested by René Descartes during the first half of the seventeenth century, was one of many candidates proposed at the time. Descartes's philosophical tour de force of dualism, although known for its splitting the analysis of mind from the analysis of body, nonetheless spurred research into the somatic mechanisms that commute a volition into an action. The seventeenth-century work of Thomas Willis, who is often considered the father of neuroanatomy, stands out for its pioneering efforts to place the brain at the center of human action – and disease. For example, Willis's studies on women with hysteria led him to conclude that the disease originated in the brain, not in the uterus, as maintained in classical doctrine. His teachings, later expanded by such students as John Locke, directed investigators to uncover the role of the nervous system as the basis of human experience and knowledge. Paralleling the interest in the somatic mechanisms of self was a focus on the range and force of the passions. Of special interest were the late-sixteenth- and early-seventeenth-century physicians Thomas Wright, who discussed how patients' mental states could be critical to their recovery from illnesses, and Robert Burton, whose *Anatomy of Melancholy* (1621) stressed the psychological causes and cures of insanity.

Major social upheavals were also underway. Following the midcentury English Revolution, in which religious enthusiasts temporarily gained power, respectable people repudiated religious fanaticism in all its forms. Embracing the rationalist worldview of scientists and natural philosophers, the educated classes ridiculed astrologers and empirics, in the process abandoning therapies based on religious and magical means. The way was clear for the nascent scientific communities to construct new interpretations of health and illness. In turn, the consolidation of the naturalist model had important consequences for the cultural boundaries of insanity. During the Reformation, Puritan ministers often demonstrated the powers of their practical divinity by healing sick souls. Considering themselves "physicians of the soul," they led afflicted individuals through intense rituals of community prayer and healing fasts. Such potentially helpful ties between learned religion and popular culture were lost, however, in the rush to remove demons from psychopathology.

In addition, the naturalist model allowed for a novel form of ideological warfare. Where Anglican pamphleteers might be labeled heretics by their religious enemies, the favor was returned when they denounced these foes as sufferers of a mental disease. Madness thus emerged as a form of "counterreality," an appellation that marginalized the religious fanatics who so recently had destabilized the nation. Before the Restoration, a time when talking directly to God was still thought possible, hallucinations and delusions were not especially important signs of insanity. Afterward, however, such experiences were considered the very essence of madness. In the hierarchical world order before the Revolution, it was one's willingness to obey that determined one's insanity. In the new political order, which was constructed around innovative theories of social contract and willful association, it was the inner choices behind assent that were open to dispute and control. Not yet sorted out, however, was the exact role that physicians would play in constructing, and responding to, this new "counterreality."

The Enlightenment

The eighteenth-century period of the Enlightenment has been characterized as the Age of Reason, when the powers of mind reached out to command both nature and human affairs. The goal was the perfectibility of "man" and of "man's lot" on earth, and the means to this end was rationality tempered by direct observation. Within this context, all that held back or confounded the development of civilization – whether particular individuals or society as a whole – came under heightened scrutiny, a problem to be solved by the reasoned application of science and medicine. Madness, or, as some might put it, "unreason," stood out as a dark challenge to the light of progress. Indeed, this was the era in which physicians discovered that the insane presented a significant and distinct institutional population, one amenable to medical intervention; that society was wracked by distressing conditions composed of psychic as well as physical ailments; and that the source of most diseases was traceable to the newly dissected nervous system. Because of the numerous ties forged between medicine and the problem of insanity, many consider the modern concept of mental *illness* to have been itself an Enlightenment product.

In traditional histories, modern psychiatry dawns with the legendary moment in 1795 when Philippe Pinel, chief physician of the Salpêtrière asylum for women, struck the chains from the inmates. The mad were no longer to be considered mere brutes deprived of reason, amusing grotesqueries, but as afflicted persons in need of pity, humane care, and enlightened physic.

Applying the principle of direct clinical observation, Pinel reorganized categories of mania, melancholia, dementia, and idiocy to reflect specific, identifiable symptom clusters derived from his cases. For example, he distinguished between mania with delirium and mania without delirium – a disturbance of will without intellectual deficit. (Later, Pinel's nosological stance would revolutionize general medicine.) Mental illness resulted when persons of unfortunate hereditary stock were overwhelmed by their social environment, poor living habits, a disruption in routine, or unruly passions. Physical factors, such as brain lesions, fever, and alcoholism, were thought possible but not as common as "moral" or psychogenic factors. Asylum statistics revealed that mental illness was, surprisingly, an intermittent or temporary condition, curable if treated before it had a chance to become somatically ingrained. The physician's best weapon was discovered to be the hospital itself, for its strict regimens were the very tools by which the superintendent might instill into his charges an inner discipline, emotional harmony, and the habits of productive citizenship. In linking, in one stroke, progressive reform to medical advance and, in another stroke, the stability of a patient's inner psychic milieu to the proper management of the external hospital environment, Pinel set in motion the optimistic expansion of institutionally based psychiatry.

Recent critics, such as Michel Foucault, view Pinel's accomplishment less favorably. Physical chains were indeed removed, but only to be replaced by internal ones, more insidious for their invisibility — shame and guilt can be just as constraining as iron. Through the guise of humane treatment, patients were coerced into conforming to putative "normal," "healthy" standards of conduct. Moreover, critics like Foucault hold, it was no accident that insanity was placed under the purview of the large centralized institutions of Paris, since Pinel's model fit well with the demands of the emerging political order. The growing asylum populations were themselves only a part of a larger phenomenon. Those who, for whatever circumstances, failed to fulfill their duties as citizens within the new state became managed increasingly through civic institutions, be they almshouses, jails, workhouses, hospitals, or asylums. Physicians, in reaching out to asylum inmates through an expanded medical view of insanity, were at the same time complicit in cementing the new political realities. Pinel may indeed have rescued asylum inmates from base neglect, but the benevolent paternalism of the "clinical gaze" has had its toll. Henceforth, "modern man" is enslaved within a medicalized universe, for there can be no form of protest that cannot be interpreted, and thus dismissed, as pathological in origin.

Foucault's approach has since been shown to be not wholly satisfactory. True, it was in this period that the institutional face of insanity was dramatically revealed. The pattern is not uniform, however. The model works best in such contexts as France and Germany, where larger asylums for the poor evolved within a spirit of centralized authority and medical police. By contrast, in England, such growth occurred mostly in the small private asylums patronized by the higher classes, which were directed by lay as well as medical superintendents. The formation of relations between nascent psychiatry and its clientele remains a complicated, poorly understood story. Clearly, though, the growing institutional populations sharply focused both social and medical attention on severe madness as a problem requiring solution.

An exclusive concentration on the institutional history of psychiatry may also obscure the broader social currents that already were greatly expanding the concept of mental illness. Milder forms of insanity, such as hypochondriasis and hysteria, had by Pinel's day gained a status as the period's quintessential medical complaint. These conditions, also known as the vapors, spleen, melancholy, or later "nerves," referred to an irksome cluster of psychological and somatic (especially gastric) complaints, ranging from ennui to flatulence. Through such works as Richard Blackmore's *Treatise of the Spleen and Vapours* (1725) and George Cheyne's *The English Malady* (1733), the valetudinarian "hypochondriack," known by oppressive moodiness, oversensitive skin, and bad digestion, became enshrined as a stock Enlightenment figure.

The arrival of the "nervous" disorders coincided with the emergence of new social functions for the concept of mental illness. Woven out of the perceived interactions between psyche and soma, temperament and life-style, such conceptions offered a facile interpretative matrix for connecting to issues that stretched beyond personal health. In particular, members of polite society found in the "hypochondriack" disorders a rich social resource. Such complaints enabled one to mull endlessly over the minor discomforts of life and were also a self-replenishing well for claims on others' sympathy. But they served a more subtle function as a conspicuous indicator of social location, for those believed at risk for the ailments were only those of a truly refined and exquisite temperament. In the words of the *Encyclopedia Brittanica* (1771), hypochondriasis was a "peculiar disease of the learned." Indeed, James Boswell wrote that the suffering hypochondriacks — himself included — might console themselves with the knowledge that their very sufferings also marked their superiority.

When "furious distraction" or severe mania was the hallmark of the psychically afflicted, the designation of insanity was tantamount to banishment from normal society. In contrast, hypochondriasis was a form of social promotion. There was a collective function, too. Contemporaries explained the dramatic outcropping of the malady as a direct consequence of the unnatural circumstances imposed by the new urban, "civilized" life-style. Sedentary living, rich food, populous towns – all were thought to exact a toll, the price of progress. In short, through the innumerable discourses on hypochondriasis, the anxieties and ambivalences of a rising class found a favorite means of expression.

The new power of the disease categories did not remain for long the exclusive property of the higher classes. By the end of the eighteenth century, physicians were chagrined to find that tradesmen and domestic servants were equally likely to exhibit hypochondriack or hysteric complaints. As it happened, when elite physicians looked to the hospital infirmary for new sources of medical advance, they were confronted with the realities of the sick poor. Institutional portraits of disease thus clashed with those derived from private practice – the democratization of hysteria and hypochondriasis was but one consequence. The poor, for their part, had discovered that the nervous disorders served as entry tickets to one of the few sources of medical charity then available.

The popular appeal of the new concepts of mental illness must also be attributed to developments in medical research and theory that stressed the importance of the nervous system to all pathology and that presumed a psychosomatic model of interaction between mind and body. The trend stems from Willis, who looked to the brain as the fundamental organ; his model, though, remained humoral, based on poisonous "nervous liquors." As the extensions of the nervous system became further elaborated in the eighteenth century through the work of Giovanni Morgagni, Albrecht von Haller, and Robert Whytt, a new medical system appeared that was based on the "irritability" and "sympathy" of the muscles and nerves. The renowned Scottish physician William Cullen went so far as to declare that the majority of all diseases were caused by either too much or too little nervous "tone," a pathological condition that he termed a *neurosis*. Neuroses, as defined by Cullen, were afflictions of sense and motion that lacked fever or localized defect – a "functional" as opposed to structural condition. Subsumed within this new category were such afflictions as hysteria, epilepsy, tetanus, asthma, and colic. (Cullen's model of neuroses persisted well into the late nineteenth century.) Through Cullen and his followers, the nervous system was elevated to central importance within physiology, pathology, and nosology, laying the conceptual

groundwork by which general medicine was to break away from the neohumoral systems that had dominated since the Renaissance.

Cullen's nosology, in which diseases were classified on the basis of the patient's presenting symptoms, be they physical or mental, was essentially psychosomatic in orientation. Medical interest in the inner contents of self also followed in the wake of Lockean theorists who were building a new psychology of mental associations, and of William Battie and others of the eighteenth century who were exploring the role of the passions in determining mental and physical harmony. Perhaps the best example of the strength of the psychosomatic model can be seen in the heroic treatments of the insane, which included the notorious dunking chair. This intervention was not simply an expression of random cruelty or cultural atavism. Rather, it was a logical product of the belief that mental shocks were akin to physiological action, with effects as powerful as those induced by bleeding or purging. Terrifying the mind was a medical recourse used for a broad range of pathological conditions.

To explain the proliferation of the psychosomatic model in this period, sociologists and historians look to the nature of the patient–physician relationship. Because medical practice consisted of private consultations, where physicians were dependent on satisfying the whims as well as the needs of their wealthy patrons, medicine was patient-oriented. Treatment was formulated to satisfy the client, a tailored reading of life-style, circumstances, and habits, with heroic treatments applied in response to demands for dramatic action. Similarly, Cullen's symptom-based nosology was based not on direct physical examination – the physician's own domain – but on patients' descriptions of their complaints. Given these circumstances, it was the totality of the sick-person's experience that gave unity to the day's medical theories, a phenomenological orientation in which psychic complaints were on a level ontological footing with somatic disturbances. Medical priorities – and hence realities – were thus set by what patients considered bothersome. We must remember that physicians as professionals were only then developing an institutional base, such as the hospital, wherein they might control their patients and establish internally derived standards of research and treatment.

Finally, the ties forged between the problem of mental illness and medicine must be placed in the context of the new social meaning of health and the expansive role of physicians in the Enlightenment.

Historians have described how in this period health itself become a goal, if not an obligation, for individuals and society to pursue, a secular gauge of progress that could be accomplished in the here and now. In response to a thirst for practical knowledge, medicine was "laid open," translated from Latin texts, and popularized in an explosion of pamphlets and health guides. Health as a commodity generated a tremendous market for physicians' services and, in the age of Franz Anton Mesmer and electricity, for any treatment remotely fashionable. Psychic disorder was a particularly fertile niche for physicians to exploit. This was especially true after it was linked by the neurosis model to a broad range of everyday conditions and once its curability in even severe forms was demonstrated. (The work of Pinel and the dramatic turnabout in behavior of mad King George III was particularly effective in this regard.)

Medicine, defined as keeper of the welfare of the human race, extended far beyond matters of individual treatment and grew into an Enlightenment metaphor for broad political reforms. Guiding thinkers such as the philosophes saw themselves as nothing less than medical missionaries who cured the ills of society itself. Since the individual was a product of society and nature, the science of physiology came to signify the proper functioning of the social as well as individual body. Moral philosophy and biology joined in the new science of man; theories of the perfectibility of human society were interlaced with secular theories of health. Thus, Pinel's striking of the chains was understood to be as much an act of civic benevolence as the first step of a new "medical" approach. Medical progress and benevolent reform commingled, a shared task. Furthermore, the problem of mental illness and the proper development of mind were of special fascination in an age obsessed with how reason was self-consciously mastering nature and reconstituting society. Through a cause célèbre like the case of the Wild Boy of Aveyron, the original feral youth, and the contention of Pierre Cabanis that the brain excreted thought like the liver excreted bile, the belief was growing that the forward movement of civilization might depend on scientific forays into the darkness of human pathology.

In sum, madness during the Enlightenment became a central cultural concern. Mental afflictions were newly visible in the asylums, in the rise of hypochondriasis and related disorders, and in the investigations into the functions of the nervous system. With the expansion of the concept of mental illness to include conditions that were not drastically removed from everyday experience and that

were considered amenable to medical intervention, mental afflictions became important social resources for the expression of individual and collective anxieties. Physicians discovered in the growing popularity of these conditions not only a fresh source of patients and an institutional base, but new service roles for themselves as social critics and experts – madness became the very measure of civilization. Thomas Trotter, enlarging on the work of Cheyne, claimed that the nervous diseases resulted when citizens' life-styles and occupations did not fit their constitutions and temperament. He warned that England, owing to a combination of its peculiar climate, free government, and wealth, was the most threatened country. The survival of civilization, with its complex social differentiation of labor, depended on the decreasingly likely event of persons working within their proper stations in life – lest the nation degenerate into one of idiots and slaves. Physicians bore the responsibility for "diagnosing" the need for adjustments in the biological – and social – hierarchy.

We must not, however, overstate the extent of insanity's "medicalization." Persons were transported to asylums not so much because medical treatment was considered necessary as because these people were perceived to be dangerous or incompetent. The insanity defense had become an increasingly popular resort in criminal trials, yet the examination of a defendant's mental status was as likely to be performed by a lay authority as by a medical one. And there existed as yet no professional grouping of psychiatrists, let alone regular physicians, who had specialized knowledge of the insane. The concept thus remained a product mostly of general culture, transparent for all to read and make judgments upon.

1800 to 1850

In the first half of the nineteenth century the treatment of mental illness was marked by two trends: a wave of asylum building and the differentiation of a small band of medical professionals who claimed mental disorders as their special domain. These two developments were linked through a materialist model of mental physiology that had reformist connotations and the arrival of new categories of mental illness that advanced the value of psychiatric expertise.

Written as only a modest, local report of the way Quakers cared for their small number of lunatics, Samuel Tuke's *Description of the [York] Retreat* (1813) nevertheless launched a worldwide movement of asylum construction. In this system of care later known as "moral treatment," the asylum was envisioned as a functional microcosm of society at large where troubled persons might reconform to proper social behavior through a vigorous program of occupational therapy and moral suasion. Chains were to be replaced by admonitions, bars by comfortable furnishings, and the inmates' mania quelled by distracting amusements. In the words of John Connolly, an asylum pioneer known for his popularization of the "nonrestraint" method, the combined psychological effect of enlightened architecture and behavioral management had rendered the asylum a "special apparatus for the cure of lunacy." Originally designed for fewer than 30 patients, the new asylums were artificial family environments, heavily dependent on the talents and personality of the superintendent. His burdens included intimate contact with patients and their families; the judicious meting out of an array of mild rewards and punishments; and immediate attention to the smallest administrative problem. A commanding presence, diplomacy, boundless sympathy, worldly wisdom, moral probity, and frugality were all characteristics essential to the task. A medical background was not a necessary qualification – and by no means was it a sufficient one.

The Tuke model of moral treatment was particularly fruitful in developing asylums in the United States, a success attributed to several factors. As civic responsibilities shifted from town to county and later to state government, officials looked to the centralized asylum as the rational (albeit more expensive) site of humane care not available in local jails, almshouses, or homes. Also, it has been argued that in the troubled times of Jacksonian America the well-ordered asylum gained favor as an innovative symbol of social control. Moreover, families increasingly looked to the asylum as a solution to their terrible burdens. It is not clear whether this was due to social changes that rendered them either unwilling or unable to provide home care, or whether they had become convinced by the vaunted success of asylum cures. In either case, the unquestioned ease with which patients were shipped to asylums had prompted even Connolly to warn that the proof of an individual's sanity was quickly collapsing into the simple question of whether he or she had ever been institutionalized.

Although when first constructed the asylums were as likely to be managed by lay authorities as by medical ones, their growth nevertheless provided a base for a new breed of physicians whose practice was limited to mental problems. Such posts were often quite attractive, and an esprit de corps developed among the elite who occupied them. The origin of psychiatry as a profession is typically traced to the 1840s, when these medical superintendents, or "mental alienists," banded together to form specialized organizations and medical journals. (For example, the forerunner of today's American Psychiatric Association began in 1844 as the Association of Medical Superintendents of American Institutions for the Insane; this predated by four years the American Medical Association.)

The challenge for the first psychiatrists was to expand both their institutional base and their claim to specialized knowledge. The former goal was advanced by championing the idea that insanity was curable if its victims were removed at once from their homes to asylums, where they might receive the full advantages of moral treatment – in combination with a regular medical regimen. Moral treatment as a nonmedical practice was thus neatly coopted. In turn, the growing empire of asylums crystallized the young profession around a privileged therapy. Patients were locked in, but just as significantly, medical competitors were locked out. The alienists also made progress in advertising their expertise. In France, when the Napoleonic code made provision for a legal defense of not guilty by reason of insanity, alienists attracted national attention by their involvement in celebrated homicide trials. In advocating social if not legal justice for insanity's unfortunate victims, the alienists were advancing a political cause of liberal philanthropy (in the heat of Restoration politics) and also a professional one, the elevation of their status to that of experts.

The alienists seized on the concept of *monomania,* a term coined by Jean Etienne Esquirol around 1810, to argue that a person could be driven by delusions to perform acts for which he or she was not responsible. Descended from Pinel's *manie sans délire,* monomania referred to a nosological region intermediate between mania and melancholia. Unlike those with nervous or hypochondriack disorders, which comprised the gray zones between everyday preoccupations and total loss of mind, monomaniacs were indeed quite insane, but only in one part of their mind, and perhaps intermittently so. A morbid perversion of the emotions did not necessitate a corresponding loss of intellect. The defining characteristic of the disorder was that, save for a single delusion or disturbance of mind, an afflicted individual might appear entirely normal. Here, then, was a semiotic wall that could not be breached by lay or even nonspecialized medical knowledge. Significantly, at the trials the alienists employed neither arcane technique nor extensive jargon. Their claim to expertise was the discerning eye of a seasoned clinician, a skill that was honed on asylum populations where insanity was visible in all of its protean and elusive forms. Knowledge does not have to be exceedingly learned to be restrictive. It was a sufficient argument that only those with extensive asylum experience could reliably distinguish the true monomaniac from the false.

The term *monomania* seems to have fallen into fast decline in France after 1838, immediately following the passage of legislation that provided greatly expanded roles for alienists in France. In success, the term lost its ideological edge. Elsewhere, similar concepts of *partial insanity* and *moral insanity* (coined by J. C. Prichard in 1835) took root, which played equally vital roles in demonstrating that questions of lunacy were matters best left to experts.

Expansion of the profession depended on communities that held potentially antagonistic viewpoints, a situation that presented the alienists with a difficult balancing act. On one hand, ties were maintained to the nonmedical constituencies who were driving forward institutional reform. On the other hand, general medicine was making great strides in the Paris clinics, where the anatomopathological approach to the localization of disease was launching modern medicine. A new medical standard had to be met. These separate goals found mutual expression in the doctrine of phrenology, a powerful movement in Europe and the United States that was based on the late-eighteenth- and early-nineteenth-century work of Franz Joseph Gall and Johann Spurzheim. Holding to the twin assumptions that psychological faculties were localized in specific regions of the brain and that cranial morphology was a guide to brain structure, the doctrine popularized "reading bumps on a head" as a means of revealing an individual's innermost talents and deficits. Although later generations heaped abuse on it, phrenology has since been credited with disseminating into general culture a materialist philosophy in which the brain was the organ of the mind and with motivating researchers in several fields to explore mental physiology as a serious pursuit. For the alienists, phrenology provided a framework for considering disordered personality, one that incorporated society, the asylum, and general medicine. Through this model, alienists participated in the movement to better society through useful knowledge, explained the effectiveness of moral treatment as a program that strengthened specific mental faculties, and followed the organicists' lead in insisting that insanity could be attributed to brain lesions. Moreover, the psychological

and physiological models merged: The well-ordered asylum restored the patient by keeping the brain in a tranquil condition.

1850 to 1900

The late nineteenth century witnessed an explosion of interest in the problems of mind and mental problems, one that extended across the cultural landscape into art, literature, science, and politics. A new frontier had been opened: the human interior. Thus commenced a wave of ambitious explorations into the conscious – and later unconscious – mind, with the aim of understanding what qualities of the self within were necessary to sustain civilization without. With the formal appearance of the human sciences, fragmented into the disciplines of anthropology, sociology, psychology, economics, and history, and a similar specialization in medicine that generated the modern professions of neurology, neurophysiology, neuroanatomy, and even psychiatry, a dizzying growth occurred in the number and variety of schools of thought on the structure and function of the human mind. From this point forward, any attempt to systematize the development of psychiatric conceptions is vastly more complex and unwieldy. Indeed, any disease category that even remotely touches on human behavior would henceforth have multiple, and perhaps contradictory, meanings – depending on who employed it, and where. Hysteria meant different things to the novelist than to the alienist or general practitioner, to the French psychologist than to the German investigator, to the neurologist in Paris than to his or her colleague in Nancy.

In addition to the interest spawned by these intellectual currents, the subject of mental disorders drew impetus from "below," from powerful social concerns. On several fronts, much more now appeared to be at stake, for the individual and for society, in the realm of the troubled self.

The Asylum and Society

The once-small asylum had swelled in size and population far beyond what its creators had initially hoped – or had farsightedly dreaded. A typical public mental institution in the United States now housed hundreds of inmates, resembling more a small town than an intimate extension of a household. Simply put, the superintendents had oversold their product; patients streamed into the institutions faster than they could be cured. And through accretion, or what contemporaries referred to as "silting up," the small but significant percentage of patients who would prove untreatable now occupied a majority of the beds. The public costs of indefinitely maintaining tens of thousands of such unproductive members of society (as well as of building additional beds to treat the incoming curables) were indeed staggering.

In subtle ways, the institutions' success in attracting patients had the unintended effect of heightening fears that the problem of mental illness was somehow worsening. What was only newly visible to the public was considered but newly existent. Moreover, the simple bureaucratic act of generating institutional records itself distorted clinical perceptions. As hospital tallies began to reveal that the same patient might be released only to be readmitted years later, and that new admittees were often related to past inmates – graphic illumination of insanity's fearsome generational grip – mental disorders of the day were concluded to be far more virulent and insidious than when the institutions originally opened. Such fears were compounded by the consequences of slow but profound demographic shifts that reinforced racial stereotypes. Where asylums based on the Quaker model of moral treatment assumed a homogeneous population, in that physician, patient, and community shared similar religious and social values, the public institutions had become cultural mixing pots filled with diverse immigrant and working-class populations. Alienists, now mostly salaried employees of the state and no longer beholden to families for private fees, became even further removed from the cultural milieu of their charges. Severe mental illness thus loomed as a social problem of paramount importance, one that had become even more grave.

"Nervous" Disorders

At the same time, the public had become obsessed with ailments of a less serious but more commonplace nature, especially those conditions in which mental and physical attributes blurred together. Rapid industrialization and urbanization brought forth dramatic transformations in the family, workplace, and society. In turn, the anxieties and inner conflicts that arose from survival in the fast-changing modern world found expression in a slew of somatic complaints, ranging from dyspepsia and skin disorders to hysteria and hypochondriasis. Cullen's and Trotter's neuroses had been resuscitated – but with a twist.

Owing to the rise of the middle class, a higher level of literacy, and the formation of a consumer culture oriented to such things as the creation of markets for health remedies, such "fashionable" diseases penetrated faster and deeper into society. Moreover, the unifying metaphor – the nervous system – had metamorphosed well beyond mere "irritation." Since even Trotter's time, neurological investigators scored major accomplishments in understanding how the brain mediates between sense impressions and motive action. In the age of the telegraph and the dynamo, of centralized bureaucracy and the division of labor, the new model of the nervous system – one part wiring diagram and one part administrative flowchart – offered an intuitive, adaptable framework for explaining how human thought or action was guided, executed, and powered. Any number of confusing conditions or troubles could now be plausibly explained by the lay public and medical personnel alike as simply a case of "nerves" – which at once said everything, and nothing. Indeed, so popular was the new framework that some have referred to the late nineteenth century as the "nervous" era.

Secondary Gains

A diagnosis is never socially neutral because the "sick role" associated with an illness has practical consequences for the patient that are as real as any physical manifestations of pathology. In the Victorian world of moralism and industry, where individuals were tightly bound by standards of duty and economic performance, the role of the nervous invalid was promoted to central stage. Legitimated by the growing prestige of scientific medicine, this and other categories of disease provided one of the few socially acceptable opportunities for many persons to step away from, at least temporarily, their everyday obligations. Because of their protean nature, nervous disorders were particularly well suited for exploitation as a social resource. While virtually any mysterious symptom or combination of symptoms might indicate an underlying nervous condition, physicians had precious few criteria by which to rule out such a disorder. The presence – and departure – of a nervous ailment was decided more by the patient than by the physician, to the immense frustration of the latter. Nervous diseases, often with simple and well-known components, were thus available to all.

This is not to say that these conditions were without drawbacks. On the contrary, the distress and limitations on existence associated with a sick role are often quite drastic. For example, historians have explained the outbreak of hysteria in this period as emanating from the conflicting and impossible demands placed on women. Although such a "flight into illness" offered some measure of reprieve, even allowing the exactment of a small manner of domestic tribute, it exposed these women to painful treatments, left the underlying conflicts unresolved, and reinforced their dependency. Benefits were gained at a definite cost, but for many, such a flight nonetheless remained a viable option.

The example of hysteria is only one illustration of a pervasive trend, the appearance of medical disorders as significant resources for the indirect negotiation of social conflicts. In addition to the battleground of household or gender-related politics, a person's health status might figure heavily in such polarized issues as the responsibility of corporations to protect the public, fitness for employment or military service, and criminal trials. Thus, victims of train wrecks (a notorious hazard of the industrial world) might be awarded some compensation on the basis of their suffering from the vague syndrome of "railway spine"; mothers accused of infanticide might be judged temporarily insane rather than be sent to prison; and battle-weary soldiers might be diagnosed as suffering from irritable heart syndrome rather than face execution as deserters.

In answering the call to pronounce judgment on matters with such public consequences, physicians were expanding their authority over everyday affairs. As indicated in the examples just given, some of the more volatile health debates touched on neuropsychiatric conditions, an area of medicine in which diagnostic and explanatory models were insufficiently powerful to enable a designated "expert" to deliver a verdict that would remain uncontested. Many opportunities for professional growth were opened, but the path was uncertain.

Thus, in the second half of the nineteenth century, mental disorders gained a commanding social presence due to the perceived threat of the asylum population, the profusion of nervous disorders, and their linkage to a range of polarized issues. This social interest was mirrored by the attention of diverse groups of learned scientists and physicians who competed for the privilege of claiming the field of mental disorders as their own. Such groups varied greatly in their institutional location, professional service role, scientific orientation, and political aims. Their disparate agendas led to a jumble of theories regarding insanity; in turn, these theories both strengthened and limited the professional opportunities of their proponents. Let us visit, in turn, the asylum alienists, three types of neurologist (the researcher, the private practice consultant, and the urban clinician), and university psychiatrists.

Asylums and Their Keepers

French Alienists and Degeneration Theory. In France, the manifold problems of asylum psychiatry surfaced by midcentury, enshrouding the young profession of *alienisme* in an unexpected fatalism. Worse yet were the political circumstances of the Second Empire (1852–71), in which the materialist basis of mental physiology was linked to the suspect ideas of Republicanism and atheism. Although their institutional posts afforded some degree of protection, alienists nevertheless were under siege. In the decade of the 1860s, for example, their public lectures were suppressed by government decree. The pessimism of the profession found expression in the theory of degeneration, or morbid heredity, which derived from the publication of B. A. Morel's *Treatise on the Physical, Intellectual, and Moral Degeneracy of the Human Race* (1857) and J. J. Moreau de Tours's *Morbid Psychology and Its Relationship to the Philosophy of History* (1859). Drawing together currents in biology, medicine, and social thought, degeneration theory was perhaps the most significant influence on late-nineteenth-century psychiatry.

The degeneration model asserted that hereditary factors were the primary cause of insanity, pathology occurring when a weak disposition was overwhelmed by intoxicants (alcohol, malaria, opium, cretinous soil), social milieu, or moral sickness. Combined effects of physical and moral injuries were especially treacherous. The distinguishing feature of the degenerationist model was its *developmental* (or "genetic," in its original meaning) orientation.

Even as enthusiasm for lesion-based systems of psychiatry waned, a new intellectual foundation was emerging from the biological theories of Jean Baptists Lamarck, Herbert Spencer, and later Charles Darwin. With evolution supplanting pathological anatomy as the core biology, questions of process overshadowed those of structure. Static taxonomies of disease thus gave way to dynamic systems, in which most mental disorders were stages of a unitary disease, stratified not by anatomic location but by a defined temporal order. Simple ailments were linked to severe ones, as the seed is to the tree. Mental illness now had a plot.

For the French alienists, the degeneration model provided a way to navigate past the Scylla and Charybdis then facing the profession, the dual hazards posed by either holding to materialist positions that invited political attack or abandoning these in favor of psychological models that were insufficiently "scientific" to silence medical critics. Morel's solution was to argue that a specific case of mental illness was the expression of a "functional" lesion of the nervous system, one based on its performance as an integrated whole. Although an organic mechanism was presumed (satisfying demands for scientific rigor), its elaboration was considered unnecessary for understanding the clinical significance of mental illness. Moreover, the integrationist stance remained agnostic on the precise interaction between mind and body. Religious conservatives need not be enthusiastic supporters of the degenerationist model, but at minimum it was palatable; although the soul no longer held a perpetual lease on the body, neither was it in immediate danger of eviction. Morel himself was deeply religious, finding in the degenerationist model a biological statement of original sin.

The theory states that the development of the individual is a reenactment of that of the species as a whole, a viewpoint later encapsulated in Ernst Heinrich Haeckel's famous phrase "Ontogeny recapitulates phylogeny." Civilization's forward progress had depended on the triumph of government and order over barbarism and base desires. Individual survival depended on no less. If anarchy and mob rule were evidence of a breakdown in the social order, a reversion to an earlier – and hence evolutionarily lower – state, then madness was its equivalent in the individual, an atavism from a time when emotions ruled the intellect. Because we are biological as well as spiritual entities, the animal beneath the skin can only be controlled, never exorcised. Mental composure depended on an interminable conquest of desire by discipline.

Although heuristically powerful, the degenerationist framework offered no immediate therapeutic advantage for institutional practice. Rather, its strength lay in its expansion of psychiatric authority beyond the walls of the asylum. With overfilled institutions belying the curability of severe mental illness, alienists faced the prospect of becoming an alliance of mere custodians, should no dramatic treatment appear. Instead, alienists looked outward, recasting their medical responsibility to include prophylaxis – society would be served best by staunching the flow of inmates at its source. The new explanations of madness provided alienists with a blueprint for such extramural intervention, one that augmented and did not undermine their institutional base.

Asylums provided alienists with a unique vantage from which to observe directly countless broken lives. Every new admission was an object lesson in the fragility of normal life, of how a single path wrongly taken – perhaps a pint of gin, an act of masturbation, or a flirtation with prostitution – might set a once vigorous individual on a course of dissolution that would end in a locked asylum ward.

Such stories provided alienists a rich harvest from which to manufacture their most valued product: advice. Moreover, given the Lamarckian assumption of the day, that a person's habits over time were eventually transmitted to future generations as heritable traits, it was not just an individual's life, but the life of the nation, that was at risk. With dissolution as the key to insanity, mental illness acquired a definite moral as well as biological structure. Unless the alienists' warnings were heeded, a generation of dissolute citizens would flood the country with nervous children, and insane grandchildren in even greater numbers. Madness was the very destiny of a people unfolded.

Alienists thus trumpeted themselves as advisers on matters of social policy, alone competent to pilot civilization past hidden reefs. Their message was especially poignant in France in the 1870s, when the country was recovering from the devastating military loss to the Prussians and from the turmoil of the Paris Commune. It seemed that one had to look no further than the specter of working-class mobs to see the link between social revolution and morbid degeneracy. The model gained popular credence through the work of Cesare Lombroso, an Italian author who devised popular categories of criminal insanity. As we shall see, aspects of the degenerationist model penetrated virtually all major conceptual systems of mental illness espoused in the late nineteenth century. Indeed, the model resurfaces even today, whenever life-style is evoked as a basis for understanding disease.

Neurology

The latter half of the nineteenth century was neurology's "golden age," in research, private practice, and the urban teaching clinic. Each of these three neurological domains had significant repercussions in the medical conceptualization and treatment of madness.

British Experimental Neurology and Epilepsy.
Through the efforts of mostly British, German, and Russian investigators, the reflex became the building block of neurophysiology. In the 1830s Marshall Hall demonstrated the importance of the reflex system in maintaining all vital bodily activities. Following the British philosophical tradition of volitionalism, however, purposive acts and thought processes were left inviolate. Such dualism of mind and body came under assault by Thomas Laycock. Drawing on German science, in which a *natur-philosophie* orientation presumed a unity of man in nature and a continuous evolution from animal to man, Laycock argued for a

gradual blending of automatic acts, reflexes, instincts, emotions, and thought. Laycock's student, John Hughlings Jackson, is often described as the true originator of modern neurology. Incorporating Hall's and Laycock's ideas, Jackson went furthest in constructing a neurological basis for human action. In his classic research on the localization of epilepsy (the major epileptic syndrome long bore his name), Jackson focused on the pattern by which nervous functions disappear in the course of a fit; here was an indirect means of peering into the functional organization of the brain.

Combining Spencer's evolutionary cosmology with the degenerationist outlook, Jackson constructed a topology of self in which the nervous system was hierarchically layered according to the evolutionary scale. At the lowest or most "primitive" level was the spinal system, which was controlled by the "middle" level, the motor system; this in turn was mastered by the "highest" level, the frontal lobes – the organ of the mind and the acme of evolution. Epilepsy could now be understood as nothing less than a body caught in the visible throes of dissolution. This answered Jackson's clinical puzzle concerning why aberrations of conscious thought were the first epileptic symptoms to appear; nervous functions were lost in precisely the reverse order of their evolution.

Much of the appeal of the degenerationist model resulted from its resonance with fundamental changes then occurring in the social fabric. Issues of social differentiation and hierarchy surfaced in the wake of nationalism which pitted one country's heritage and international standing against another's; industrialism, which produced a vast laboring underclass; and imperialism, which placed whole countries of "primitives" under European stewardship. With religious authority in decline, models of scientific naturalism were expected to provide a rational social order in step with the times. Jackson's model, which dovetailed a neurological "localization of superiority" with Spencer's dictum that "separateness of duty is universally accompanied by separateness of structure," exemplifies the fact that in the Victorian era visions of the external world could be disaggregated from those applied to the internal one. Jackson's accomplishment was a paradigm that continues to influence us today, one that all too neatly converged neurological, evolutionary, and social stratifications into a spatial metaphor of unusual power.

With Jackson's model, the degenerationist model of insanity now has a firm neurological basis. As Jackson himself argued, mental illness resulted from the dissolution of the higher centers, compli-cated by overactivity in the lower centers. Empirical proof of the connection could be found in the asylums, all of which housed a significant number of epileptics. For some time to follow, the ignominy associated with the biological corruption of the epileptic would spill over into categories of mental illness. Not clearly inferable from Jackson's work, however, was the actual involvement the neurologist was to have with the problem of mental illness, for although a solution to grave mental illness might come from a cure for epilepsy, this awaited much further neurophysiological research. The divide between neurology and mental illness was a matter of professional location as well as knowledge, in that few neurologists had access to asylum patients. As for the noninstitutional population, Jackson's preference for disease models based on clear organic mechanisms led him to declare that "functional" disorders were best left to other aspiring specialties such as gynecology and obstetrics.

Neurology and Neurasthenia in the United States.
Neurology as a viable profession in the United States dates from the Civil War, which produced a larger number of soldiers with nerve injuries and severe emotional disorders requiring specialized care. After the war, neurology rode the wave of specialism that was transforming urban medicine. Physicians with graduate training in European medical science hoped to build alternative medical careers by limiting their practice to areas that might benefit from specialized knowledge. Cities provided both the requisite critical mass of varied clinical material and the pool of motivated, affluent citizens to support these ventures.

In 1869 New York neurologist George M. Beard diagnosed Americans as especially prone to nervous exhaustion. His conception of *neurasthenia* – literally weak nerves – achieved international usage as a major trope of the Victorian era. The condition referred to a cluster of distressing, often vague symptoms that ranged from simple stress to severe problems just short of certifiable insanity. Bodily complaints such as headaches and hot flashes appeared alongside psychological ones such as lack of interest in work or sex and morbid fears about trivial issues. Thus burdened, neurasthenics retreated from the fulfillment of obligations to their families, employers, or social groups. The physiological link common to all these cases, Beard suggested, was the depletion of the vital nervous forces.

Neurasthenia's prevalence in the modern era was

no mystery, Beard argued. The telegraph, railroad, daily press, crowded quarters, and financial market had rendered life simultaneously more hectic, intense, and stressful. Civilization placed demands on our nervous systems that nature had never anticipated. Reminiscent of earlier interpretations of hypochondriasis, the eighteenth-century "English malady," the presence of neurasthenia served as a marker of advanced society. Once again, mental illness was a conspicuous price of progress. Americans, world leaders in industrialization, paid dearly. Here, too, patterns of incidence were interpreted as clues to social hierarchy. Men thought most likely to succumb were those at the vanguard of social advance, such as inventors and entrepreneurs. Women, whose smaller brains were dominated by their reproductive systems, might be overcome by the daunting task of running a Victorian household or by excessive intellectual effort. The ranks of the lower classes, to be sure, did yield a significant number of neurasthenics. But since their hardier constitutions would bear up under all but the worst shocks, such as alcoholism or inveterate depravity, the condition in them was more a badge of shame than one of honor.

For practicing neurologists, the concept of neurasthenia brought order to chaos and provided a defensible base for the profession's enlargement. The bewildering array of ailments that fell under the category of "functional" disorders (all those without gross anatomic damage or known organic cause, such a hysteria and hypochondriasis) were unified into a single clinical picture that was comprehensible to both neurologist and patient. Briefly stated, nervous energy was a precious quantity that must neither be squandered nor misdirected; temporary habits eventually became fixed pathways in the brain and might even be transmited to the next generation.

The reality of the functional diseases had been an open question for the public, which was often far more skeptical than many medical experts. The neurasthenic model, although lacking a precise organic mechanism, was able to relegitimate these disorders by imparting the cachet of a state-of-the-art scientific theory. Furthermore, the emphasis on brain physiology was consistent with the growing emphasis in biology and medicine on the central nervous system as the dominant bodily system. This displaced the open-ended physiological models of the eighteenth and early nineteenth centuries in which pathogenic processes might arise from the influence of any of a number of interconnected systems that included the liver, stomach, circulation, or nerves. Previously, any

knowledgeable physician might have been able to understand the development of a mental pathology, based on a reading of the balance of the organism as a whole. Now, however, only a nerve specialist was qualified. And as an untreated cold might lead to pneumonia, so a nervous complaint not handled by a neurologist might be the portal to an asylum. In short, by establishing the principle that troubling but otherwise unremarkable mental states might produce morbid bodily changes as dramatic as any physical insult, Beard and his followers were constructing a neuropathology of everyday life.

The strength of Beard's model lay not in its originality but in its artful extension of medical and social trends. Indeed, by this time, nervous conditions represented to family physicians a significant portion of their practice and were also responsible in large measure for the booming market in health products and services. At first, neurologists followed uninventive therapeutic programs, endorsing the standard use of mild tonics and sedatives, dietary restrictions and supplements, massages, low-current electrical stimulation, and visits to water spas and other health resorts. The goal was to help patients restore their "strength" and to maintain a healthy "nervous tone." Morbid thoughts and other dangers of introspection were to be derailed through outdoor exercise and cheerful admonitions by the doctor and family.

The neurasthenic model also gained impetus as an articulation of a Victorian conception of self, one that incorporated health's new moral meaning. Character was indeed a matter of destiny, but neither heredity nor rational intent solely determined one's fortunes. Rather, it was one's *will* that mediated between what one could be and what one should be. Not all persons were created equal, nor were they forced to meet stresses and tests of comparable severity. Nevertheless, what individuals made of their lots was inescapably their responsibility. In this worldview, health became a secular measure of moral character. Although illness in general was no longer interpreted as a direct manifestation of God's wrath, conditions that resulted from a damaged constitution were read as the certain consequences of immoral or unnatural habits – a failure of will. Observers noted that unlike malaria or the pox, which might attack the weak and the strong indifferently, mental diseases fell only on those who lacked self-control. The concept of neurasthenia, which focused on activities that damaged the will itself, thus provided an adaptable matrix for the consideration of human character.

The special business of neurologists, in addition to providing the usual treatments for nervousness, was to offer individuals the expert guidance necessary to avoid permanent or worsened injury to the constitution, advice based on their putative knowledge of brain function and human affairs. Thus construed, the role of neurologists combined both intimacy and scientific objectivity. On one hand, neurologists were to be consulted by patients on an expanding variety of personal issues, ranging from major life decisions, such as the advisability of marriage, to minor points of life-style, such as the amount of fat to be included in one's diet. The role of adviser merged with that of confessor: Critical to the success of the treatment was the patient's full disclosure of all behavior, no matter how disreputable. Indeed, it was precisely on questions of damage caused by vices that medical treatment so often appeared to hinge. Medical penance, as outlined by neurologists, became the new absolution. On the other hand, in the interest of invading clinical territory already inhabited by either alienists or family physicians, neurologists were obliged to base their expertise on the emerging laboratory and clinical science of the brain. This dual obligation of scientist and counselor proved difficult to reconcile.

Neurologists learned soon enough what alienists had discovered already: Mental disorders are more managed than cured. Furthermore, such close intervention in patients' lives yielded a clinical paradox. A nervous complaint, successfully treated, might disappear only to be replaced by another; or a wide range of treatments might prove equally effective – for a time. Even as they were constructing elaborate scientific justifications for their clinical intervention, neurologists were discovering that it was not so much the specific medical treatment that mattered as it was the discipline that patients exhibited in adhering to the treatment plan. With this in mind, S. Weir Mitchell perfected his famous "rest cure," in which patients were isolated from their families and placed in the full care of a neurologist and nurse. Stripped of all power to make decisions, and consigned to a state of ultradependency (which included such things as spoon-feedings), patients were supposed to rebuild their willpower completely. Focus thus shifted away from external signs and symptoms to the dynamics of the patient–physician relationship. The resistance of the patient to being cured became a new index of pathology. Ostensibly following a somatic program, New York neurologists uneasily awakened to the reality of psychological aspects of nervous disorders.

Charcot's Parisian Teaching Clinic and Hysteroepilepsy. Although Esquirol, in the 1840s, ignored hysteria as an uncertain diagnosis of little significance, by the 1880s the condition had risen to a newfound prominence. This turnabout was directly attributable to the efforts of Jean Martin Charcot, an internationally renowned neurologist whose teaching clinic at the Salpêtrière Hospital greatly influenced a generation of students who were destined to become leaders in medicine. At the height of his clinical and pedagogic career, Charcot committed his full resources to the vexing problem of hysteria. If successful, one more trophy would be added to his collection that boasted classic descriptions of amyotrophic lateral sclerosis, multiple sclerosis, tabes, and locomotor ataxia.

Charcot insisted that hysteria was like any other neurological disorder, with a definite, even predictable, clinical course. The truth of hysteria would surely be revealed once exhaustive clinical observation was combined with the experimental method recently outlined by Claude Bernard. The Salpêtrière provided Charcot with the resources necessary for just this kind of medical campaign: a concentration of scientific equipment and trained personnel to perform exacting measurements and a reliable supply of clinical material. The clinic's social structure was an equally important factor. The rigorous program of experimental study that Charcot envisioned necessitated privileged access to human bodies, access that was of a scale and manner inconsistent with the realities of private practice, where permission would have to be negotiated case by case, if it was obtainable at all. Indeed, Charcot's experimental protocols called for the incessant monitoring of every conceivable physiological index, including hourly urinary output and vaginal secretions; these humiliations might be followed by the application of painful ovarian compresses. At the Salpêtrière, a public charity hospital, Charcot could ignore rebuffs to such requests, for its wards were filled with lower-class women over whose bodies the physician in chief held full dominion.

After some effort, Charcot announced his discovery that hysteria indeed had a definite clinical form. A true hysteric attack passed through four complex stages, beginning with hysteroepileptic spasm of tonic rigidity and ending with a resolution in grand theatrical movements. Hysteria's elusive "code" had been broken. At his celebrated clinics, which the elite of Paris attended, Charcot was able to demonstrate the disease in its full glory through hypnotic induction on patients known for their spectacular fits. Because the code was essentially visual, an iconographic reading of the outward manifestations of the body, Charcot devised the technique of making extensive drawings and photographic recordings so that clinicians not present might "see" the disease in its natural progressions.

Charcot's model of hysteria tapped into several currents that aided neurologists in the extension of their social and professional base. With hysteria mastered by science, they now had a justification for reaching outside the walls of the clinic to treat the masses afflicted with its milder forms. Since Charcot's hysteria was constructed in a degenerationist mold, neurologists would have a new basis for commenting on such worrisome social problems as crime, adultery, and mob unrest. Furthermore, in the reversal of political fortunes that followed the installation of the Third Republic, secular models of behaviors became useful in anticlerical vendettas. Charcot, for example, went so far as to identify one type of fit as "religious possession" and to denigrate past examples of stigmata and other miraculous displays as forms of hysteria. Finally, the model provided the first wave of a promised series of incursions by neurologists into a clinical domain that was still dominated by alienists. Charcot, first holder of a French chair on *nervous* diseases, was establishing the institutional precedent for such an expansion.

Academic Psychiatry

German University Psychiatry and the New Nosology. Through the creation of university chairs of psychiatry, a pattern that began in Berlin (1864) and Göttingen (1866), Germany soon took the lead in establishing the academic study of mental illness. Unique to the German approach was a psychosomatic orientation that held to a fundamental parity between mental, somatic, and even environmental forces and insisted that this parity also be reflected in the relations among academic disciplines. Thus, both psychology and neuropathology might be joined in a common medical investigation. Legitimated as an integral part of mainstream medicine, psychiatry also shared in the developments that propelled Germany to the position of world leader in medicine by the end of the nineteenth century. Led by Wilhelm Griesinger and then Emil Kraepelin, the German school of psychiatry created a lasting framework for classifying mental disorders.

Griesinger was an accomplished internist who also lectured on medical psychology at Tübingen. Believing that further medical progress in mental disease would not come from asylum managers, who lacked training in recent medical advances, or from academic psychologists, who had no direct contact with patients, Griesinger decided to bring psychiatric patients into his own general clinic. Although he was known for his promotion of the doctrine that all mental disease was in fact brain dysfunction, Griesinger's major focus was on the process by which a person's *ego*, the integrated self, disintegrated. Rejecting nosological systems based on faculty psychology, which led to a diverse array of symptom-based disease categories, Griesinger maintained that insanity was a single morbid process, differentiated by stages of degeneration. This point was reinforced by his acknowledgment of the inherent closeness between sanity and insanity and of the existence of borderline conditions.

In Griesinger's approach, a mentally ill person was someone who no longer had the same desires, habits, and opinions and thus was estranged from him- or herself (alienated). This judgment could be made only by reference to a patient's premorbid life, a history that must include family background, mode of living, emotional state, and even the nature of the patient's thoughts on world affairs. Once a full portrait of the individual was constructed (from in-depth interviews with family and friends), symptoms that at first seemed bizarre were now understandable – perhaps even predictable. Moreover, the importance of any specific contributing cause, such as alcoholism or prostitution, could not be ascertained without reference to the individual's case history. Mental illness originated as a confluence of multiple factors, psychological as well as somatic, that interacted early in life, when character was being formed. Developmental knowledge of mental illness thus was joined to a contextual reading of the patient's past.

With Kraepelin, the German clinical school of psychiatry reached its zenith. Trained as a neuroanatomist, an experimental psychologist under Wilhelm Wundt, and a mental hospital physician, Kraepelin brought a diverse background to the problem of mental illness. Insisting on a combination of neurological, neuroanatomic, psychological, and even anthropological studies, Kraepelin held that the case study was the sine qua non of psychiatric investigation. Combining Griesinger's clinical conception of a unified personality with Rudolph Virchow's new principle of diseases as separate entities, Kraepelin closed the century with a classificatory system that has been recognized as the foundation of modern psychiatry.

Where Griesinger blended one mental disorder into another, just as hues subtly progress in a single color spectrum, Kraepelin differentiated conditions on the basis of essential clinical syndromes, as revealed by their signs, course, and outcome. Drawing from published case reports as well as his own clinical work, Kraepelin grouped Morel's *dementia précoce,* Ewald Hecker's hebephrenia (1871), and Karl Kahlbaum's catatonia (1874) into a single category of mental disease termed *dementia praecox,* which began at puberty and progressed inevitably toward early senility and death. Manic-depression, which was known by its favorable prognosis, and paranoia were identified as the second and third types of major psychosis. Into separate divisions Kraepelin placed the neuroses (hysteria and epilepsy), psychopathic states (compulsive neuroses and homosexuality), and states of idiocy. Confusion as to which disease was afflicting a mental patient would not last forever, for it was only a matter of time before the disease would resolve into an endpoint that identified the underlying syndrome. For example, true neurasthenia was rare, since most diagnosed cases were simply early instances of a major psychosis or a complication of a cardiac or bowel irritation.

Clinicians worldwide celebrated the immediate applicability of Kraepelin's nosology to their practices, for cases of his major syndromes were easily recognized in any asylum. Moreover, here was a system of mental disease that was based on the highest standards of clinical medicine, one that incorporated a program for continued empirical revision. Contemporaries did recognize that Kraepelin's work, at heart a descriptive system, offered little explanation of mental illness, suggested few novel treatments, and indicated mostly fatalistic prognoses. It was a sufficient triumph, however, for Kraepelin to have liberated the study of insanity from its ancient classifications of melancholia and mania, as well as from the more recent and confusing additions of partial insanities, which continued to multiply, and of neurasthenia, which threatened to dissolve all distinctions. (In addition, by incorporating a measure of despair into the clinical diagnosis, Kraepelin to some extent relieved asylum psychiatrists of their obligation to cure, allowing attention to be concentrated on description and study.) Accurate diagnosis was to be the avatar of the new scientific psychiatry.

The Problem of the New Science.   We have thus seen how, in the second half of the nineteenth century, the great social interest in the problem of mental afflic-

tions, mild as well as severe, was met by an equally strong response from a broad array of learned disciplines. Both inside the asylums and outside, a vast terrain of clinical problems was opened for cultivation by practitioners and researchers representing diverse specialties. Since the late Victorian era was the period in which science and medicine forged their modern image as engines of power, faith grew that even problems as elusive and intractable as mental illness might be mastered by empirical investigation. Moreover, positioned at the nexus of major social and scientific concerns, the mystery of insanity gained a special poignancy. As human beings were increasingly revealed to be products of nature, and a nation's destiny a matter of its biological as well as cultural heritage, the unnatural in humans became a counterpoint to the advance of civilization. Merged together were issues of brain and behavior, willpower and productive vitality, and even national harmony and international struggle. In this context, the derangement of an individual was a sign of a larger social decay, which required immediate solution by the new hero of civilization, the scientist.

The joining of the new medical science to the problem of mental illness was extremely problematic, however, for several reasons. First, there was no one specialty that controlled the field. The profession of psychiatry is a creation of the twentieth, not the nineteenth, century. As we have seen, alienists and the various types of neurologists each brought to the subject their distinct professional agendas, resulting in the proliferation of widely varying conceptual orientations. In practice, no single model proved able to bridge the gulf between the disorders that appeared in the asylums and those that surfaced in everyday life.

Second, scientific models of brain and behavior were in transition, proving to be fickle sources of legitimation. Although a new form of scientific knowledge can confer respectability on a particular specialty, the benefit is not permanent. The alienists of the early nineteenth century, who had predicated their expertise on the presumption that lesions of the brain affected specific mental functions, found their prestige fading as neuroanatomic findings failed to confirm their theory. The introduction of the degenerationist model extended the reach of alienists outside of the asylum, but did little to allow the new medical science to peer within it.

Private-practice neurologists were all too happy to point out, soon enough, that alienists in their splendid isolation had let the latest science pass by. To bolster their own status as experts, they pointed to new theories of an integrated nervous system that supported their reading of the constitutional hazards of particular life-styles. Beard's model of neurasthenia drew strength from its equal mixing of nature and nurture, whereby a single disease category contained an expansive matrix of moral and biological elements, a framework that empowered the clinician to intervene as both counselor and scientist. In due course, however, this approach was undermined by the further elaboration of the brain's fine structure and a new emphasis on specific disease entities. Further knowledge of nature had constrained nurture's sphere of influence.

Third, science often creates or distorts the very objects it putatively observes. This simple fact led to subtle, unintended consequences in the arena of mental disorders. For example, Charcot discovered this paradox, to his misfortune, yielding one of the grand ironies in the development of the human sciences. In the rigorously controlled order of the neurological ward, Charcot's patients were indirectly cued to produce symptoms in the exact sequence and form predicted by his theory. When it became clear that only patients in the Salpetrière manifested "pure" hysteria, contemporaries soon ridiculed Charcot for perpetrating theatrical creations as true clinical syndromes. In his original act of constructing hysteria as a regular neurological syndrome, Charcot had already set in motion his own undoing.

Another example is provided by the difficulties of private-practice neurologists in confronting neurasthenia. Beard and his followers, unlike Charcot, did not create their patients' symptoms outright, but they did fall into a different kind of trap. Patients termed neurasthenics had come to these physicians with an array of mysterious, but nonetheless truly bothersome ailments. Neurologists were thus in the position of having to construct a new reality out of the material presented to them, a role that was becoming increasingly common in the nineteenth century as science-based professions were expected not only to manipulate nature, but to construct a new map of reality itself. However, the very act of legitimating the patients' complaints as a new disease transformed the delicate social balance of what was at stake in the symptoms. Indeed, as Mitchell realized, the dynamics of the patient–physician relationship was itself somehow related to the expression of the disorder. Since the organic models of disease provided no means of recognizing these secondary effects, neurologists were forced to belabor a theory whose very dissemination had changed the clinical reality under observation. How to integrate the psychological di-

mension of mental disorders within a scientific framework remained a confounding problem.

1900 to 1950
The first half of the twentieth century is marked by two somewhat opposing currents in the conception of mental illness: the entrance of the Freudian model of psychodynamics and a rash of somatically oriented theories and treatments. Furthermore, when medical schools began to offer systematic instruction in the medical treatment of insanity, they united "nervous and mental disorders" in a single curriculum as dictated by the new nosology, thus bridging the historical gap between the asylum and private practice. The modern profession of *psychiatry* was born.

Freud and the Unconscious
The realm of human activity and experience that lies outside normal consciousness was attracting considerable literary and scholarly attention in the late nineteenth and early twentieth centuries. Psychological novels shared the theme that the rational intellect had only a limited ability to shape our lives. Neurological investigators, constructing ever more complex systems of reflex integration, described as unconscious those bodily activities that did not require continuous volitional monitoring. Nonconscious mentation was also investigated by academic psychologists, although the concept was often rejected as oxymoronic. Some psychologically oriented neurologists, such as Charcot's rival Hippolyte Bernheim, became interested in the powers of the mind over body – *ideodynamism* – through the dramatic effects of hypnosis and suggestion. The work of Morton Prince, Boris Sidis, and Pierre Janet focused attention on the clinical significance of minds that have disintegrated, or even divided. Janet developed an extensive theory of *psychasthenia*, paralleling neurasthenia, that referred to the inability of a weakened mind to maintain a unified integrity. Neurotic symptoms resulted from traumatic memories, such as unfortunate sexual episodes, that had been "split off" from the main consciousness. Cathartic treatment was the cure.

Perhaps the strongest exponent of the unconscious before Freud was Frederic W. H. Myers, a nineteenth-century British psychologist known mostly for his advancement of psychicalist (paranormal) research. Myers popularized the theory of the *subliminal* self as a hidden domain that was vast and profound, providing the basis for all psychic life. Incorporating such phenomena as genius, hypnosis, and even telepathy,

Myers cast the unconscious world in a highly spiritual, positive light, establishing a rationale for the use of psychotherapy as a tool for unleashing the inner creative forces. In the United States, religious healing cults like Christian Science and the Emmanuel movement made psychotherapy synonymous with a practical means of tapping into the subconscious, the reservoir in human beings of God's spirit and power.

Sigmund Freud was a Viennese neurologist trained in neuroanatomy, neurophysiology, and neuropsychiatry, who also boasted a deep knowledge of literature and anthropology. Freud's own journey into the hidden self, an exploration that commenced with *The Interpretation of Dreams* (1900), has been generally recognized as one of the monumental intellectual achievements of our time. Only a sketch of his work can be attempted here. Although the therapeutic merit of psychoanalysis remains a controversial issue, there can be little doubt that the Freudian model of human action has had a tremendous and pervasive influence in many areas of culture. In his early publications, Freud argued for the importance of the *unconscious* in directing most of our waking activities and all of our nocturnal ones. Consciousness represented only a fraction of our true selves. In contrast to the ideas of Myers and other supporters of psychotherapy, Freud's conception of the unconscious referred to a realm of primitive, even carnal, desires that followed its own irrational inner logic of wish fulfillment. Indeed, our entire mental apparatus, even our conscious selves, depended on the energy, or libido, that derived from the unconscious. Our path to normal adulthood consisted of successfully negotiating certain developmental challenges, which included the oral, anal, and genital stages, and resolution of the notorious Oedipal conflict. Developmental aberrations could be traced to the after-effects of sexual conflicts in childhood.

In his later work, Freud developed a tripartite metapsychology of self, comprised of the *id,* the pool of unconscious desires and memories; the *ego,* the core adaptive mechanism, which was built on territory reclaimed from the unconscious as the infantile pleasure principle was superseded by the mature reality principle; and the *superego,* the ego's censor, a mostly unconscious system of rules and mores internalized from parental and societal instruction. The ego, the component of self we most identify with, is a partly conscious and partly unconscious structure that must continually mediate between the desires of the id and the restrictions of the superego. Toward the end of his career, in such publications as *Civilization and Its Discontents* (1929), Freud turned his attention to the interaction between individuals' desires and society's demands, highlighting the relation between repression and culture.

From in-depth clinical studies, Freud assembled a model of the mind as a dynamic battleground where libidinous energies surge from the unconscious through a preconscious stage and then to consciousness, but only after intensive censorship that misdirects the energy to less threatening endpoints. Internal harmony is maintained at the price of continual suppression of unwanted thoughts and memories; anxiety is the internal warning that the dynamic equilibrium is becoming unstable. Psychopathology results from the desperate attempts by the ego – weakened by childhood trauma and saddled by insecurity and guilt – to maintain control in the face of intrapsychic conflict. At low levels of stress, the ego copes through simple defense mechanisms, such as displacement, projection, and denial. Higher levels may yield full psychoneurotic symptoms such as phobias, hysteria, and compulsions. For example, a hysterical paralysis of the legs might afflict a young actor who, although feeling otherwise normal stage fright, is unable to confront his fears because of long-internalized parental demands that he not admit failure (associated with some childhood trauma). The paralysis allows the actor to sidestep the conflict and even the very fact that that is what he is doing. Such symptoms may allow psychic survival, but they exact a heavy price in inflicting a diminished level of existence. At the highest level of stress, the unconscious demands overwhelm the ego's defenses, resulting in psychotic disintegration.

A distinguishing characteristic of Freud's system was the insistence that mental disorders had meanings. Being neither random nonsense nor mere neurological defects, such symptoms were in fact creative responses to specific problems that confronted a troubled individual. (Freud thus departed from Janet's model of neurosis as a product of a weakened mind, seeing it instead as resulting from a mind that was all too vigorous.) A psychopathological symptom was like a key to an unidentified lock; the clinical challenge was to make the shape of the lock visible. Psychoanalysis was to provide the clinician with the knowledge and tools necessary for recognizing what the immediate conflict was and then tracing backward to the distant trauma that had engendered this particular symptom formation. Until the underlying conflict was disinterred, neurotics were condemned to react inappropriately to current challenges, unwittingly seeing in them replays of a past battle that could no longer be won. Therapy consisted of analyzing unconscious material, as revealed in dreams, slips of the tongue, and free associations, and a careful manipulation of the patient–physician relationship, in which patients made visible their neurotic structures by transferring onto the therapist their unresolved emotions. The couch was to become a dissecting table for the dispassionate analysis of psychic morbidity. In time, patients, liberated from externalized demands and guilt, would be free to reintegrate their desires into more authentic, stronger selves. Deprived of their function, the symptoms would simply cease to exist.

After Freud, the analysis of human behavior would never again be simple. Henceforth, the surface or manifest meaning of any action might belie multiple hidden or latent desires that would have to be decoded. The nineteenth-century hierarchical model of reason mastering desire was humbled by the realization that there existed no pure rational part of self that acted without the distorting influence of the unconscious; and every noble accomplishment of civilization was now sullied as a by-product of excess libido. The lines between sanity and insanity, and between normality and abnormality, were forever blurred, for each individual existed in a dynamic equilibrium in which unconscious forces held sway every night and at times during the day. Furthermore, in making a distinction between our instinctual aims and their objects (the aim of the sex drive was reproduction; the object was one's lover), Freud severed the connection whereby mental disease was equated with behavior contrary to instinct. Normal desires could lead to perverse acts, and vice versa. Judgments of mental illness were no longer simply statements of what was "unnatural."

Freud's immediate effect within psychiatry was to achieve for the neuroses what Kraepelin had accomplished for the psychoses. In Kraepelin's system, neuroses were an unsettled mixture of somatic and functional disorders. Freud directed psychoanalysis at the latter group, heightening the distinction by the use of the term *psychoneurosis*. Thus, certain disparate conditions, such as hysteria, obsessions, compulsions, and phobias, were united in a single category, yet each retained its own integrity as a clinical syndrome, recognizable in case histories. So successful was Freud's approach that soon the original somatic connotation of *neuroses* was entirely lost and the term *psychoneurosis* was dropped as redundant. Freud went even further than Kraepelin, however, in providing a model that was causal as well as descriptive. Although psycho-

analysis for some time remained targeted mainly on neuroses, his psychodynamic model was of sufficient heuristic strength to encompass psychotic disorders as well. The combination of Freud and Kraepelin was a nosological framework that integrated private practice and institutional systems of mental disorder – the beginning of modern psychiatry.

Psychoanalysis provided a fresh solution to the vexing problems facing neurologists who had built their practices on theories of neurasthenia, already in decline. Where psychological interactions of patient and physician were devilish problems for practitioners following organically justified systems, Freud's psychogenically based models turned a liability into a virtue. As a high technique of the mind, created by a distinguished Viennese physician, psychoanalysis co-opted religiously suspect psychotherapy, transforming it into a medically legitimate tool that office practitioners could adopt. Even better, for those physicians who relied on uncertain methods of suggestion, hypnosis, or enforced discipline, psychoanalysis provided a direct means of handling those nervous patients who undermined the doctors' competence by refusing to get better. The fault was thrown back into the patient as "resistance."

In the United States, which would become the largest supporter of Freud's theories (rejected as "Jewish psychology" in his homeland), not only psychologically oriented neurologists but many psychiatrists as well welcomed the new model. Even though psychoanalysis was irrelevant in the institutional context, which represented the majority of psychiatric care, the advent of a system that brought with it the trappings of learned study and European prestige was welcomed by many as a means of raising the status of what was widely regarded as the most backward of medical specialties. This interest was particularly strong in research institutes, which many states had created in this period to serve as catalysts for scientific advance.

The precise manner in which the Freudian doctrine rose to prominence in general culture is still not well understood. As one example, recent historical work suggests that World War I played a precipitating role in Britain when a large number of soldiers broke down in battle. That anyone might act insane, given sufficient stress, was forceful testimony of sanity's fragility. Neurologists diagnosed these soldiers as suffering from "shell shock," originally interpreted in terms of a somatic injury. Neither reflex hammer nor rest cure proved useful, however. The best success was obtained by physicians who applied a form of Freudian psychotherapy to relieve the trauma. Overnight, psychoneuroses gained national currency. Those neurologists involved in the war effort were precisely the ones who would later gain for Freudianism a solid professional footing in Britain.

Biology

In the 1920s and 1930s, virtually every branch of biomedical science sought to apply the tools of experimental medicine to the problem of psychiatry. Indeed, given the isolation of the asylum from centers of medical advance, it was an even bet whether the next scientific breakthrough would emerge from within psychiatry or from an outside field. The paradigm was syphilis, whose tertiary state, general peresis, had been responsible for up to 20 percent of mental hospital admissions. In 1897 Richard von Krafft-Ebing demonstrated the long-suspected connection between syphilis and paresis, a link soon confirmed by the Wasserman test. The culpable spirochete was identified in paretic brains by Hideyo Noguchi in 1913. Finally, in 1917 the Austrian physician Julius von Wagner-Juaregg developed a method of fever therapy to halt further paretic deterioration; in 1927 he was awarded the Nobel Prize. The success of a purely organic solution to a major psychiatric disorder suggested that other such achievements were sure to follow.

Leading researchers thus pursued metabolic, endocrine, neurophysiological, and even toxicological models for psychopathology. Constitutional theories were advanced by the German Ernst Kretschmer, who correlated body types to predispositions for specific mental illnesses. Franz Kallman investigated the genetics of mental illness by studying schizophrenic twins. I. V. Pavlov launched a model of experimental neurosis in which animals frustrated in conditioned learning tests developed forms of mental breakdowns. The introduction of a wave of somatic treatments for mental illness in the middle 1930s transformed psychiatric practice. Insulin shock, metrazole shock, electric shock, and psychosurgery had dramatic effects on patient behavior, raising hopes that the fatalism associated with severe mental illness might prove untrue. Psychosurgery in particular was believed to restore chronic schizophrenics to productive citizenship. Its inventor, Portuguese neurologist Antonio Caetano de Egas Moniz, was awarded the 1949 Nobel Prize in medicine.

Classification at Midcentury

After World War II, professional organizations such as the American Psychiatric Association became ac-

tive in the creation of standardized systems of nomenclature. Military experience and the growth of centralized reporting bureaus highlighted the need for diagnostic uniformity. The first *Diagnostic and Statistical Manual, Mental Disorders* (DSM), created in 1950, reflected the extension of the Kraepelin and Freudian systems, augmented by new theories of personality. Earlier, dementia praecox had been reconceptualized by Swiss psychiatrist Eugen Bleuler into the *schizophrenias* (hebephrenia, catatonia, paranoia), a term that referred to the splitting of thoughts from affects. Incorporating some aspects of psychoanalysis. Bleuler emphasized the development of the psychotic mental process.

In contrast to Kraepelin, Bleuler argued that favorable outcomes were possible in many cases. The DSM followed Bleuler in its description of the category of major psychoses, referring to personality disintegration and a failure to relate effectively to people or work. Included within this group were the schizophrenias, as well as paranoia, manic-depression, and involutional psychosis (depression of old age). The second major category consisted of psychoneuroses, described in Freudian terms as disorders caused by the unconscious control of anxiety through the use of defense mechanisms. These included anxiety reactions, dissociation, conversion reaction, obsessive-compulsion, and depression. The third category, comprising personality disorders, was differentiated by its stress on behavioral as opposed to emotional disturbances. Described in this category were such popular terms as *sociopath, antisocial behavior*, and *sexual deviate*.

As a shift from earlier attempts at standard psychiatric nosology, which were directed toward inpatient populations, the DSM reflected the new reality of psychiatry's burgeoning private-practice base, as well as the experiences of military psychiatrists, whose observations on broad populations revealed that the vast majority of psychopathologies did not fit the earlier classifications. Published statements of nosology do not necessarily reflect full clinical reality, however. The DSM was by no means universally adopted. It reflected more the penetration of Freudian psychiatrists into the power structure of the profession than it did any dramatic shift in the state hospitals, where niceties of diagnosis were considered superfluous to the daily choice of treatment plan.

After 1950

In the decades following World War II, psychiatry as a medical profession experienced tremendous expansion. In the United States the advent of community mental health centers and third-party payments swelled the ranks of noninstitutional practitioners. The shift away from the state hospital, the historical center of the profession, redirected momentum toward mild disorders and their treatment through counseling. Psychodynamically oriented psychiatrists found their authority further magnified as a new army of clinically trained psychologists, social workers, and guidance counselors looked to them for professional training and supervision. Psychotherapy, though not necessarily Freudian psychoanalysis, became viewed by the middle class as both useful and affordable. Psychiatrists and their proxies in the allied professions offered a colorful array of different forms of counseling, which included behavior therapy, group therapy, client-centered therapy, existential therapy, and even primal scream therapy.

At the same time, dramatic developments occurred in somatically oriented treatment and research. The introduction in the mid-1950s of the major tranquilizers, such as chlorpromazine, revolutionized hospital care. By dampening hallucinations and other florid psychotic symptoms, the new drugs quieted ward life and encouraged new "open-door" hospital policies. Also, they accelerated the process of deinstitutionalization, helping many patients to achieve a level of functioning consistent with some form of extramural existence. Tranquilizers were soon followed by other classes of psychoactive drugs, such as antidepressants and the use of lithium in the treatment of manic-depression. The growing importance of psychopharmacology spurred neurophysiological research, leading to suggestive models of neurotransmitter deficiencies as the mediating cause of severe mental disorders. Other biological research has pursued genetic interpretations of the tendency of severe mental disorders to run in families. In recent years, there has been a clear shift within psychiatry to the somatic orientation.

One of the striking developments of the postwar years in the conceptualization of mental disorders has been the influence of the social sciences, especially sociology and anthropology. Once behavior is understood to reflect the matrix of psychological, social, and cultural forces that mold an individual, it is a natural progression to assume that abnormal or impaired behavior is likewise shaped and should be investigated with these additional tools. Again, the literature is much too large to provide other than a bare outline. Sociologists have reported on such influences as social class, role conflicts, social control, life stress, social integration, family interactions,

institutional milieu, and even the very act of psychiatric labeling in determining patterns of mental disorder. Anthropologists have brought the power of cross-cultural study to the problem of mental illness, showing that what was assumed to be biologically fixed often was in fact "culture bound," a local product, specific to place and time. Within any major U.S. city are subpopulations who conceptualize – and experience – disease in incommensurate ways. Moreover, if a diagnosis of mental illness reflects a judgment as to adaptive functioning, mental disorders can no longer be held to be natural, universally true categories of illness, for what is adaptive in one local culture is maladaptive in another. These studies of health and healing have also brought to light the manifold ways in which concepts of disease and therapeutic rituals enter into the complex web of power relations we call society.

Psychiatric conditions, which touch on our most intimate concerns and relationships, are especially rich cultural resources and have embedded meanings and structures not easily seen – and often denied by the professional culture of scientific medicine. Mental illness is a fundamentally messy construct, an irreducible mixture of personal, social, cultural, and scientific beliefs.

Classification in the 1980s

In 1980, the third version of the DSM was released, signaling a new departure in psychiatric nomenclature. Responding to calls for a diagnostic system that might elevate psychiatry's status as a scientific discipline, the DSM task force pared down medical classification to its most basic elements, the description of known phenomena, usefully arranged. Without question, the most stable and powerful nosologies are those based on proven etiology. For example, identification of the culpable spirochete made it possible to distinguish paresis from senility. Because debate still surrounds the true cause of any mental disorder, the DSM argues that it is premature for psychiatry to construct etiologically based systems. At present, we find that phobic disorders can have Pavlovian, Freudian, or somatic explanations. In disagreeing about theory and treatment, however, clinicians nevertheless can reach a consensus on the identification of a disorder.

The stated goal of the DSM-III is simply to provide a set of criteria and procedures by which all camps of psychiatrists might speak a common diagnostic language. In the interest of ensuring interrater reliability, disorders were to be defined unambiguously and based on checklists of easily verified data. The diagnostic categories were themselves to be constructed in the form of statistically significant clusters of symptoms, derived from extensive field trials and empirical reports. Without etiology, psychiatric ailments can be referred to only as *syndromes* or *disorders,* not specific diseases. Indeed, it is expected that elements from several different disorders might appear in any one individual. The authors of DSM-III argue that the quest for scientific purity has not, however, negated all clinical utility. Tightly defined and empirically tested descriptions of syndromes do allow practitioners to predict a patient's course and outcome, and they provide some guidance in treatment choice. For example, the identification of a major depressive syndrome alerts the clinician to the likelihood of the patient's having a future hypochondriacal reaction.

As of 1980 the DSM outlined the following categories: disorders of childhood or infancy (hyperactivity, anorexia, retardation, autism); known organic cause (diseases of old age, drug-induced); disorders of schizophrenia (disorganized, catatonia, paranoid, undifferentiated); paranoid disorders (without schizophrenic signs); affective disorders (bipolar, major depressive); anxiety disorders (phobias, obsessive-compulsive); somatoform (conversion disorder, hypochondriasis); dissociative (fugue states, amnesia, multiple personality); and personality disorders. Perhaps the most controversial change in the new approach was the elimination of the category of psychoneuroses. In the "atheoretical" approach, disorders were grouped according to symptoms, not underlying psychic mechanism. Neurotic disorders thus resolve into various forms of anxiety states. Also removed was the heading of *psychosis,* which had included the major affective disorders; experience showed that many patients labeled psychotic did not have psychotic features. Involutional melancholia was collapsed into ordinary depression, because no evidence surfaced to show that it was unique.

It is, of course, far too early to make informed judgments about the consequences of the new DSM. However, some trends can be discerned. First, DSM-III clearly marks a loss of professional authority by psychoanalysis, one that will worsen. Much of the need for teaching Freudian theory to the mass of workers within the allied mental health professions – most of whom would never practice true psychoanalysis – was based on the need to explain the psychiatric diagnostic system.

Second, a more subtle and unpredictable effect of DSM-III concerns its diminution of the value of clinical judgment. On one hand, its "atheoretical" emphasis shifts power into the hands of the statistical researcher and away from the clinician. DSM-III sets in place procedures for the continued revision of diagnostic categories, whose organization may soon reflect more of what seems "statistically significant" than the realities of clinical practice. On the other hand, the symptom-based nosology also harkens back to the eighteenth century, when patients' subjective assessments of their problems set the pace of medical practice. In DSM-III homosexuality was eliminated from the rolls of mental disorders – except when it is considered bothersome by the patient. Squeezed between deference to patients' self-rating scales and statistical priorities, the clinician has less room to form independent diagnoses.

Mental Illness and Psychiatry: Retrospect and Prospect

From our historical survey, several themes emerge concerning the linked development of psychiatry and conceptions of mental illness. Psychiatry as a learned discipline contains no one school of thought that is sufficiently dominant to control the medical meaning of insanity. Given the administrative realities within which mental health professionals currently labor, the move to a standardized diagnostic system may nonetheless win out. It is important for the various factions to share a common language, but this is not the same as reaching a consensus on why someone is disturbed and what should be done about it – two components of illness as a cultural reality.

This difficulty reflects in part psychiatry's unique evolution as a medical specialty. Common sociological wisdom holds that the livelihood of a scientific specialty depends on its capacity to defend the perimeter of its knowledge base. This task has always been problematic for psychiatrists, for the borders between lay and learned conceptions of madness remain indistinct, a situation that also pertains to the relations between psychiatry and other disciplines, medical as well as nonmedical. To begin with, mental disorders are not restricted to the controlled environs of the analyst's couch or laboratory bench, but are manifested in the home, school, or office, as disruption in love, work, or play. When the very stuff of madness is reduced to its basic elements, we find nothing more than a tangled heap of curious speech acts and defiant gestures, odd mannerisms and perplexing countenances – surely nothing as removed from everyday experience as is the retrovirus, the quark, or the black hole. Available for all to see and interpret, psychiatric phenomena thus form an epistemological terrain that is not easily defended by a band of professionals who look to stake claims on the basis of privileged, expert knowledge.

Psychiatry's turf is also vulnerable at its flank, from adventurers in other learned disciplines who find that their own research endeavors, logically extended, encompass some aspect of mental illness. Thus, as a performance of the body, insanity has routinely been investigated by all the tools available to biomedical scientists and clinicians. Commentators have often noted that, as soon as a valid biological model is found to exist for a specific mental disorder (as in the case of syphilis and general paresis), that condition is moved out of the purview of psychiatry and is claimed by some other field — perhaps neurology or endocrinology. Over time, the condition even ceases to be considered psychiatric. And now that madness is known to have a cultural reality as well as a biological one, psychopathology has become a proper focus of most social sciences as well.

Unable to police its own borders, it is no wonder that psychiatry remains a confusing, polyglot world, one that reflects the input of myriad disciplines and sources. The surfeit of conceptual approaches to the problem of mental illness has often been cited as evidence that psychiatrists are a singularly contentious or poor-thinking lot. A popular professional response has been to invoke a "biopsychosocial" model of disease (expressed, e.g., by the multiaxial system of DSM-III), one that is interdisciplinary and multidimensional. The root of the problem is deeper, however. As mental disorders reflect the entirety of a person, so the study of insanity comes to reflect the present contradictions inherent in our universe of scholarly disciplines. Our various knowledge systems are unified more in rhetoric than in reality. The status of psychiatry and of the concept of mental illness suffers for making this situation visible.

Our historical survey provides us with another approach to the problem of mental illness, one that focuses not so much on the intellectual boundaries of knowledge as on the professional and social function of psychiatry. First, we have seen how modern psychiatry emerged not in isolation, but in relation to other areas of medicine: Psychiatry's peculiar domain is precisely those problems that baffle regular medicine. (The rise of the "nervous" disorders provides an excellent example of this phenomenon.) In the late nineteenth century, as medicine gained status as a scientific discipline, this role attained a special significance. Before, when virtually all of medicine was based on uncertain knowledge, there

was no clinical problem that could be said to lie outside the physician's grasp. But as the physiological and bacteriological terrain came into sharper focus, so too did those areas in which medicine was admittedly ignorant. Paradoxically, as our scientific knowledge becomes increasingly sure, leading to ever higher expectations, those problems that cannot be solved develop an increased capacity to threaten our faith in science. "Functional" or "nonorganic" disorders, whose explanation as well as cure remain outside the boundaries of regular medicine, thus become disturbances not only within an individual but within the system of medicine as well. It is psychiatry's intraprofessional obligation to deal with these problems, shoring up the faith that, although no precise medical answers yet exist, they are still medical problems — and not yet the business of the astrologer or faith healer. Ironically, psychiatry is despised by the rest of medicine for this lowly, but vital role.

A more fundamental service role has been that of responding to personal crisis. As a specific construct, the term *schizophrenia* may one day find its way into the dustbin that holds *neurasthenia, chlorosis,* and other long-abandoned medical concepts. But the suffering and torment felt by persons so afflicted are not as easily dismissed, nor is the distress of their families. Patients and their families look to the psychiatrist to intervene in a situation where there is often little hope, to "do everything possible" to make the person whole again.

Put simply, psychiatry is the management of despair. This is the heart of the psychiatrist's social function, to care for those whose problems have no certain cure or satisfactory explanation, problems that often place a serious burden on society. To a large extent, this function stems from psychiatry's historical ties to the asylum, an institution into which poured a new class of social dependents. But psychiatry is more than custodial care that can be supervised by hospital administrators. Apparently, we find a measure of emotional security in entrusting these special woes to a group of trained professionals who have dealt with similar matters, believing that practical wisdom comes with experience; to those who can link our seemingly unique problems with past cases and thus somehow lessen the alienation and shame. The additional value of a medical degree is the promise that with it comes a trained intellect, a calm authority in response to crisis, and access to all available medical tools that might yield even a remote possibility of benefit, even if they are not yet understood.

In sum, psychiatry is a field defined not by reference to a specific part of the human body, like podiatry, or a specific class of people, like gerontology, or even a specific disease process, like oncology. Rather, it is a field demarcated by our collective helplessness in the face of human problems that by all appearances should be solvable and understandable through medical science, but as yet are not. Hence, what comprises mental illness is fundamentally a moving target, a hazy area that is redrawn by every generation and local culture as new problems and dilemmas arise. Specific categories of mental disorder are formed at the interface of social concern and professional interests, much in the way that the pressures of tectonic plates produce new features of the physical landscape. Thus, shifts in either cultural anxieties or professional priorities can shape the clinical geography. We have also seen that this border is a dynamic one, as professionals both respond to and in turn shape these areas of concern. That a given disease, once understood, is no longer considered psychiatric is thus not so much a loss for psychiatry as it is an indication of what has been psychiatry's true function. Once a disorder is well understood, psychiatry's proper business with it has in fact come to an end.

Now we have a perspective from which to view, in retrospect and prospect, the peculiar geography of mental illness. Looking backward at the history of the conditions associated with mental illness, at such things as hypochondriasis and monomania, we see an archaeological record not to be dismissed as mere professional folly, but a record of life's tragedies, large and small. No matter how successful science will be in the future in providing additional tools to alter the mind or brain, some of us nevertheless will be overwhelmed by life's new challenges, finding our own internal resources insufficient. For some, whether because of faults of biology, environment, or will, the collapse will be complete. That is the reality of mental disorders, which is surely not soon to disappear.

What the future holds for the organization of psychiatry as a medical specialty is not easily predicted. The special task of psychiatrists, in managing the unmanageable, is increasingly difficult to perform as it becomes harder to maintain the dual role of counselor and medical scientist. As medicine in general relies on ever stricter laboratory standards of what is real or valid, the definition of what constitutes a good doctor becomes that much narrower. The decline of the status of psychoanalysis, for example, may reflect the shrinkage that already has occurred. In the past, part of a physician's medical authority stemmed from the assumption that he or she was learned in the ways of people and society, a knowledge that was seen as legitimating his or her right to intervene in intimate human affairs. Psychoanalysts, among the most scholarly of physicians, were thus looked upon as effective doctors. Now, however, such broad cultural learning is no longer considered an appropriate route to a career that demands the absorption and analysis of a tremendous volume of scientific facts. Whether psychiatry will dissolve into two separate professions, one of lay counseling and the other of purely biological treatment, remains to be seen. Yet there is also a possibility that general medicine will reintegrate the special function of the healing relationship into its list of medical priorities. Perhaps in this psychiatry might lead the way.

Jack D. Pressman

Bibliography

Ackerknecht, Erwin H. 1968. *A short history of psychiatry*, 2d edition. New York.

Armstrong, D. 1980. Madness and coping. *Sociology of Health and Illness* 2: 296–316.

Ayd, F. J., and B. Blackwell, eds. 1970. *Discoveries in biological psychiatry*. Philadelphia.

Burnham, J. 1978. The influence of psychoanalysis upon American culture. In *American psychoanalysis: Origins and development*, ed. J. Quen and E. Carlson, 52–72. New York.

Bynum, W. F. 1981. Theory and practice in British psychiatry from J. C. Prichard (1785–1848) to Henry Maudsley (1835–1918). *Nihon Ishigaku Zasshi* 27: 1–22.

  1983. Psychiatry in its historical context. In *Handbook of Psychiatry*, Vol. 1, ed. M. Shepherd and O. Zangwill, 11–38. Cambridge.

  1984. Alcoholism and degeneration in 19th-century European medicine and psychiatry. *British Journal of Addiction* 79: 59–70.

Bynum, W. F., Roy Porter, and Michael Shepherd, eds. 1985–8. *The anatomy of madness: Essays in the history of psychiatry*, 3 vols. London.

Carlson, E. T., and N. Dain. 1962. The meaning of moral insanity. *Bulletin of the History of Medicine* 36: 130–40.

Cooter, R. 1976. Phrenology and British alienists, c. 1825–1845. *Medical History*, 20: 1–21, 135–51.

Dain, N. 1964. *Concepts of insanity in the United States, 1789–1865*. New Brunswick, N.J.

Davidson, A. 1988. How to do the history of psychoanalysis: A reading of Freud's three essays on the theory of sexuality. In *The trial(s) of psychoanalysis*, ed. F. Meltzer, 39–64. Chicago.

Donnelly, M. 1983. *Managing the mind*. London.

Eisenberg, L. 1988. Editorial: The social construction of mental illness. *Psychological Medicine* 18: 1–9.

Ellenberger, H. 1970. *The discovery of the unconscious: The history and evolution of dynamic psychiatry.* New York.

Fischer-Homberger, E. 1972. Hypochondriasis of the eighteenth century – neurosis of the present century. *Bulletin of the History of Medicine* 46: 391–9.

Foucault, M. 1965. *Madness and civilization: A history of insanity in the Age of Reason,* trans. R. Howard. New York.

  1987. *Mental illness and psychology,* trans. A. Sheridan. Berkeley and Los Angeles.

Gay, P. 1988. *Freud, a life of our time.* New York.

Geyer-Kordesch, J. 1985. Cultural habits of illness: The enlightened and the pious in eighteenth-century Germany. In *Patients and practitioners,* ed. R. Porter, 177–204. Cambridge.

Goldstein, J. 1982. The hysteria diagnosis and the politics of anticlericalism in late nineteenth-century France. *Journal of Modern History* 54: 209–39.

  1987. *Console and classify: The French psychiatric profession in the nineteenth century. New York.*

Goodwin, D., and S. Guze. 1984. *Psychiatric diagnosis,* 3d edition. New York.

Gosling, F. G. 1987. *Before Freud: Neurasthenia and the American medical community.* Urbana, Ill.

Grob, G. 1973. *Mental institutions in America: Social policy to 1875.* New York.

  1983. *Mental illness and American society, 1875–1940.* Princeton, N.J.

Hale, N. G. 1971. *Freud and the Americans.* New York.

Hunter, R., and I. Macalpine. 1963. *Three hundred years of psychiatry, 1535–1860.* London.

Jacyna, L. S. 1982. Somatic theories of mind and the interests of medicine in Britain, 1850–1879. *Medical History* 26: 233–58.

Jewson, N. 1974. Medical knowledge and the patronage system in 18th-century England. *Sociology* 8: 369–85.

Jimenez, M. A. 1987. *Changing faces of madness: Early American attitudes and treatment of the insane.* Hanover, N.H.

Kleinman, Arthur. 1988. *Rethinking psychiatry.* New York.

Lawrence, C. 1979. The nervous system and society in the Scottish Enlightenment. In *Natural order: Historical studies of scientific cultures,* ed. B. Barnes and S. Shapiro, 19–40. London.

MacDonald, M. 1981. *Mystical bedlam: Madness, anxiety and healing in seventeenth-century England.* Cambridge.

  1982. Religion, social change, and psychological healing in England, 1600–1800. In *The church and healing,* ed. W. J. Shields, 101–25. Oxford.

  1986. The secularization of suicide in England, 1600–1800. *Past and Present* 111: 50–100.

McGrath, W. 1986. *Freud's discovery of psychoanalysis.* Ithaca, N.Y.

Mechanic, David. 1978. *Medical sociology,* 2d edition. New York.

Midelfort, E. 1980. Madness and civilization in early modern Europe. In *After the Reformation: Essays in honor of J. H. Hexter,* ed. B. Malament, 247–65. Philadephia.

Mora, George. 1980. Historical and theoretical trends in psychiatry. In *Comprehensive textbook of psychiatry,* 3d edition, ed. Harold Kaplan, Alfred Freedman, and Benjamin Sadock, 4–98. Baltimore.

Parry-Jones, W. L. 1972. *The trade in lunacy.* London.

Porter, R. 1979. Medicine and the Enlightenment in eighteenth-century England. *Bulletin of the Society of the Social History of Medicine* 25: 27–40.

  1981. Being mad in Georgian England. *History Today* 31: 42–8.

  1983. The rage of party: A glorious revolution in English psychiatry? *Medical History* 27: 35–70.

  1987. *Mind-forg'd manacles: A history of madness in England from the Restoration to the Regency.* Cambridge, Mass.

Powell, R. 1979. The "subliminal" versus the "subconscious" in the American acceptance of psychoanalysis, 1906–1910. *Journal of the History of Behavioral Science* 15: 155–65.

Ray, L. J. 1981. Models of madness in Victorian asylum practice. *Archives of European Sociology* 22: 229–64.

Risse, G. 1988. Hysteria at the Edinburgh infirmary: The construction and treatment of a disease, 1770–1800. *Medical History* 32: 1–22.

  (In press). *The great neurosis: Clinical constructions of hysteria, 1876–1895.*

Rosenberg, C. 1968. *The trial of the assassin Guiteau: Psychiatry and law in the Gilded Age.* Chicago.

  1989. Body and mind in the nineteenth-century medicine: Some clinical origins of the neurosis construct. *Bulletin of the History of Medicine* 63: 185–97.

Rothman, D. 1971. *The discovery of the asylum: Social order and disorder in the New Republic.* Boston.

  1980. *Conscience and convenience: The asylum and its alternatives in progressive America.* Boston.

Rousseau, G. S. 1976. Nerves, spirits and fibres: Towards defining the origins of sensibility. *Studies in the Eighteenth Century* 3: 137–57.

Scull, A. 1975. From madness to mental illness: Medical men as moral entrepreneurs. *European Journal of Sociology* 16: 218–51.

  ed. 1981. *Madhouses, mad-doctors, and madmen.* London.

  1982. *Museums of madness: The social organization of insanity in nineteenth-century England.* New York.

Shortt, S. E. D. 1986. *Victorian lunacy: Richard M. Bucke and the practice of late nineteenth-century psychiatry.* New York.

Showalter, E. 1980. Victorian women and insanity. *Victorian Studies* 23: 157–80.

Sicherman, Barbara. 1977. The uses of a diagnosis: Doctors, patients, and neurasthenia. *Journal of the History of Medicine* 32: 33–54.

Smith, R. 1973. *Trial by medicine: Insanity and responsibility in Victorian trials*. Edinburgh.

Smith-Rosenberg, C. 1972. The hysterical woman: Sex roles and conflict in nineteenth-century America. *Social Research* 39: 652–78.

Spitzer, R., and Janet Williams. 1980. Classification in psychiatry. In *Comprehensive textbook of psychiatry*, 3d edition, ed. Harold Kaplan, Alfred Freedman, and Benjamin Sadock, 1035–72. Baltimore.

Stone, L. 1982. Madness. *New York Review of Books* 16 Dec.: 128–36.

Sulloway, F. 1979. *Freud: Biologist of the mind*. New York.

Szasz, T. 1972. *The myth of mental illness*. London.

Temkin, Owsei. 1971. *The falling sickness: A history of epilepsy from the Greeks to the beginnings of modern neurology*, 2d edition. Baltimore.

Tischler, G., ed. 1987. *Diagnosis and classification in psychiatry: A critical appraisal of DSM-III*. New York.

Tomes, Nancy. 1984. *A generous confidence: Thomas Storykirkbride and the art of asylum-building, 1840–1883*. Cambridge.

Zilboorg, Gregory, and George W. Henry. 1941. *A history of medical psychology*. New York.

II.4
Sexual Deviance as a Disease

Sexual "deviance" is technically any deviation from the sexual norm. Sexual disease, a new diagnostic category in the eighteenth century, was classed as a syndrome and seems in retrospect to have been an iatrogenic one based more on philosophical and moral grounds than on any medical ones. The disease entity, however, was fitted into some of the medical theories of the time, and as these theories were challenged and undermined, modifications were made in order to justify maintaining certain forms of sex behavior in the category of disease.

In recent decades much of the sexual behavior previously classed as disease has been removed from that category. This redefinition has been based on a better understanding of sexual behavior. It has also been a result of the protests of some groups who reject being classed as ill or sick and having their behavior categorized as pathological, emphasizing the iatrogenic component of the disease. Nonetheless, efforts are being made to maintain other kinds of sexual activity under the rubric of disease. Generally, these are activities that are regarded as unacceptable by society or viewed as compulsive behavior

by behavioral psychologists. Perhaps both groups maintain the classification as a way of justifying their intervention or of promising a cure.

Medical Background

Though physicians throughout recorded history have been interested in diseases and infirmities that affect sexual performance, the concept that certain forms of sexual behavior constitute a disease in and of themselves is a modern phenomenon. It also seems to be restricted to western Europe and people and cultures descended from or influenced by western European culture.

One reason for the development of the concept of sexual "deviation" as a disease can be found in some of the early modern challenges to the humoral theory of medicine. Early in the eighteenth century, the great clinician Hermann Boerhaave, a dominant figure in medical thought, had written in his *Institutiones Medicae* (1728) that the rash expenditure of semen brought on lassitude, feebleness, a weakening of motion, fits, wasting, dryness, fevers, aching of the cerebral membranes, obscuring of the senses, particularly that of sight, decay of the spinal cord, fatuity, and similar evils. Though Boerhaave's idea undoubtedly was based on observations of the general lassitude usually afflicting men and women after orgasm, it was also an encroachment of traditional Christian teaching about sex into the medical field.

Boerhaave's observations of sex as a causal factor in some forms of illness also fit into a new medical theory known as "vitalism," based on the work of Georg Ernst Stahl as well as others. Stahl (1768) had taught that there was a unity of soul and body, a unity symbolized by the anima, which protected the body from deterioration. When the tonic movements of normal life were altered by the body or its organs, disease supervened. Disease was thus little more than the tendency of the anima (or of nature) to reestablish the normal order of these movements as quickly and efficiently as possible.

A contemporary (and rival) of Stahl, Frederich Hoffmann, equated life with movement, whereas death corresponded to the cessation of movement. The living organism was composed of fibers having a characteristic neurogenic tonus (the capacity to contract and dilate being regulated by the nervous system) centered in the brain. When tonus was normal, the body was healthy, but every modification of tonus brought a disturbance of health. Thus, a man who indulged in masturbation gradually damaged his memory because of the strain on the nervous system.

Building on this foundation were other physicians, including John Brown and Théophile de Bordeu. Brown's medical philosophy, summarized in his *Elements of Medicine* (1803), is based at least in part on his own experience with gout. In theorizing about his gout, he concluded that "debility" was the cause of his disorders and that the remedy was to be sought in "strengthening measures." To overcome his gout he had to strengthen himself, avoid debilitating foods, and treat himself with wine and opium.

Whether his gout was cured remains debatable, but from his experience he erected a medical philosophy known as "brunonianism." Basic to his belief system was the notion of excitability, defined as the essential distinction between the living and the dead. The seat of excitability was the nervous system, and all bodily states were explained by the relationship between excitability and excitement. Too little stimulation was bad, whereas excessive stimulation had the potential of being worse because it could lead to debility by exhausting the excitability. Excitability was compared to fire. If there was not enought air (insufficient excitement), the fire would smolder and die out, but under a forced draft (too much excitement), the fire would burn excessively, become exhausted, and go out.

This led Brown to conclude that there were two kinds of diseases, those arising from excessive excitement (sthenia) and those from deficient excitement (asthenia). Too much stimulation carried an asthenic ailment into a sthenic one. Contact between the sexes, through kissing and being in each other's presence, gave an impetuosity to the nerves, and intercourse itself, though it gave temporary relief, could release too much turbulent energy if carried to excess and could thus cause difficulty. Taking a somewhat different approach but ending up with a similar conclusion was de Bordeu, who maintained that the lymphatic glands as well as the muscular nervous system had vital activity. Secretions, including seminal secretion, drained the vital essences residing in every part of the body.

Onanism

At the same time these medical authors were developing new theories of medicine, concern over onanism was increasing. The concept of onanism is based on the story in Genesis 38:7–10 of Onan, who, following the Levirate custom, was supposed to take over the wife of his deceased brother Er, who had been killed by Jehovah. In addition, Onan was supposed to impregnate his sister-in-law, which he was ordered to do by his father Judah:

And Onan knew that the seed should not be his;
and it came to pass, when he went in unto his brother's wife,
that he spilled it on the ground,
lest that he should give seed to his brother.
And the thing which he did displeased the Lord;
wherefore He slew him also.

Though the story has often been interpreted as a prohibition against masturbation, the act described is coitus interruptus; the punishment seems to have been meted out not so much for Onan's having spilled the seed as for his having refused to obey the Levirate requirement that he take his brother's wife as his own.

Around 1700 an anonymous writer, perhaps in London, wrote a work in English dealing with onania. This had a wide circulation and was translated into several languages. The first U.S. edition was published in Boston in 1724 under the title of *Onania; or, the Heinous Sin of Self-Pollution, and all its Frightful Consequences, in both Sexes, Considered. With Spiritual and Physical Advice to those, who have already injur'd themselves by this Abominable Practice. And Seasonable Admonition to the Youth (of both SEXES) and those whose Tuition they are under, whether Parents, Guardians, Masters, or Mistresses. To which is Added, A Letter from a Lady (very curious) Concerning the Use and Abuse of the Marriage-Bed. With the Author's Answer thereto.* The author attributed a number of "corruptions of the body" to "self-pollution," including palsies, distempers, consumptions, gleets, fluxes, ulcers, fits, madness, childlessness, and even death itself. Some of these ideas were derived from Boerhaave, but the author went so far as to imply that onanism could affect offspring, who were likely to be born sickly and ailing.

A copy of the book eventually passed into the hands of the distinguished Swiss physician Simon André Tissot, doctor to a pope, a correspondent of François Voltaire and Jean Jacques Rousseau, and a researcher very much interested in the prevention of disease. In Lausanne, Tissot (1758) had printed his own *Tentamen de Morbis ex Manusturpatione,* which went through many editions and translations. Later editions, including Tissot's own French version, were entitled *Onanism.* The English translation by A. Hume was published in 1776. There were many printings and editions in most Western languages.

Although he considered the earlier treatise on

onania truly chaotic and the author's reflections nothing but theological and moral trivialities, Tissot did adopt some of the concepts it contained (including the association of sexual activity with insanity). More important, he put onanism into the theoretical medical framework of the day. Tissot believed that the physical body suffered from continual wastage, and unless this was periodically restored, death would result. Much could naturally be restored through nutrition, but even with an adequate diet the body could waste away through diarrhea, loss of blood, and, more important for the purposes of this chapter, seminal emission. The importance of semen to the male, Tissot observed, was documented by the effect it had on physiognomy, because semen was what caused the beard to grow and the muscles to thicken. Proof of this influence came from the fact that these physiognomic effects could be eliminated by amputation of the testicles. Though Tissot recognized that semen was lost in the process of "replenishing" the human race, he held that too great a loss (from too great a frequency) was dangerous and hence sexual intercourse had to be limited if health was to be preserved. Tissot asserted that involuntary emissions such as "wet dreams" were also weakening. Most dangerous, however, was the "unnatural loss" of semen through masturbation.

Masturbation (or onanism) comprised a broad category of sexual activities. For men, it included all seminal emissions not intended for procreation, and thus in effect every sexual activity not leading to procreation was not only a cause of illness but an illness in itself. Tissot defined the sequelae of masturbation as the following: (1) cloudiness of ideas and sometimes even madness; (2) decay of bodily powers, resulting in coughs, fevers, and consumption; (3) acute pains in the head, rheumatic pains, and an aching numbness; (4) pimples on the face, suppurating blisters on the nose, breast, and thighs, and painful itching; (5) eventual weakness of the power of generation, as indicated by impotence, premature ejaculation, gonorrhea, priapism, and tumors in the bladder; and (6) disordering of the intestines resulting in constipation, hemorrhoids, and so forth. Though Tissot recognized that not everyone addicted to onanism was so cruelly punished, he felt that most were, and that everyone was afflicted to some degree or another.

Onanism affected women even more than men because in addition to most of the male sequelae, onanism left women subject to hysterical fits, incurable jaundice, violent stomach cramps, pains in the nose, ulceration of the matrix, and uterine tremors that deprived them of decency and reason by lowering them to the level of the most lascivious and vicious brutes. Even worse than simple masturbation in women was mutual clitoral manipulation that caused them to love one another with as much fondness and jealousy as they did men. Onanism was far more pernicious than excesses in simple fornication, although both were dangerous. Onanism was particularly debilitating to those who had not yet attained puberty, because it tended to destroy the mental faculties by putting a great strain on the nervous system.

Tissot's explanation gained a number of followers not only because it fit into some of the general medical theories, but because it was consistent with general superficial observations. It also tied into the general anxiety about sexual activity that was so much a part of the Western Christian tradition.

Many of the sequelae that Tissot associated with onanism we now know derive from sexually transmitted diseases such as syphilis, gonorrhea, genital herpes, and others, all of which at that time were often explained by the concept of onanism. Moreover, it was observed that individuals in some mental institutions frequently masturbated, as did those who were developmentally disabled, and rather than being regarded as a consequence of institutionalization, it was believed to be a cause. The decline in male potency and sexual activities with age were indicative, according to Tissot's theory, of the dangers of having lost semen or vital fluids earlier in life. The neatness of Tissot's explanation was that it not only squared with current medical theory but explained so many previously unexplained illnesses and diseases.

In sum, if a syndrome can be defined as the concurrence or running together of signs and symptoms into a recognizable pattern, then onanism furnished such a pattern. As Tristam Engelhardt (1974) put it, onanism was more than a simple pattern, because a cause was attributed to the syndrome, providing an etiologic framework for a disease entity. If the development of the concept of disease is seen as a progression from a collection of signs and symptoms to their interrelation in a recognized causal mechanism, then the disease of onanism was fairly well evolved.

Once established as a disease entity, onanism had a long and varied life, adapting to new developments in medicine and in society. One of the leading exponents of Tissot's ideas was Benjamin Rush (1794–8), the dominant medical figure in the United States of the late eighteenth and early nineteenth centuries. Rush, after studying in Edinburgh, returned to the United States to introduce a variation of John Brown's medical beliefs whereby all disease was considered to be the result of either a diminution or an increase of nervous energy. Because sexual intercourse was a major cause of excitement, careless indulgence in sex inevitably led to a number of problems, including seminal weakness, impotence, dysuria, tabes dorsalis, pulmonary consumption, dyspepsia, dimness of sight, vertigo, epilepsy, hypochondriasis, loss of memory, manalgia, fatuity, and death. Rush, however, also cautioned against abnormal restraint in sexual matters because it too could produce dangers.

The syndrome of onanism was seized on by a wide variety of popularizers as well, some physicians and some not. In the United States, Sylvester Graham (1838) concluded that excessive sexual desire led to insanity, and insanity itself incited excessive sexual desire. In fact, the influence of sexual desire was so pervasive that it could disturb all the functions of the system, causing a general debility. Claude-François Lallemand, a French surgeon, was concerned with the involuntary loss of male semen, spermatorrhea, which he felt would lead to insanity. This caused his U.S. translator (1839) to report that 55 of the 407 patients in the Massachusetts State Lunatic Hospital at Worcester had become insane from the effects of masturbation.

William Acton (1871), an English physician, had a somewhat different view of the dangers of sexual activity, arguing that God had made women indifferent to sex in order to prevent men's vital energy from being totally depleted. John Harvey Kellogg (1882), another popularizer in the United States, held that the nervous shock accompanying use of the sexual organs was the most profound to which the nervous system was subject, and even those who engaged in procreation would have to place rigid limitations on themselves or else insanity would result.

Because the dangers of sexual activity were so great, one problem with the new syndrome was to explain why the human race had not died out earlier. George M. Beard (1884) believed that it had not been necessary for earlier generations to be so concerned about excessive sexual activity because their lives had been simpler. It was the growing complexity of modern civilization and evolutionary development that put so much stress on men and women. Consequently, a larger and larger number of them were suffering from nervous exhaustion. This exhaustion, he held, was particularly serious among the educated and intelligent workers in society, who represented a higher stage on the evolutionary scale than the lower social classes. In other words, as humanity advanced, it became more and more necessary to save nervous energy.

Those who were unable to control their sexuality not only would suffer physical debilities but would become homosexuals, which was a consequence of youthful masturbation according to such nineteenth-century writers as John Ware (1879), Joseph Howe (1889), James Foster Scott (1899), and Xavier Bourgeois (1873). The alleged correlation of sexual activity with nervous energy, which in turn was associated with intellectual development, led some writers such as Edward Clarke (1874) to argue that, because menstruation was a result of nerve stimulation, women should not engage in mental activity at all. Some even argued that menstruation itself was pathological.

Challenges to the Diagnosis and New Classifications

The idea of sexuality as a disease entity was undermined, in part, by a better understanding of sexually transmitted diseases and their sequelae, which came about during the last part of the nineteenth century. The discovery and acceptance of the germ theory also undermined the belief that sexual activity caused ailments such as tuberculosis. Medicine, however, did not abandon its emphasis on the disease potential of nonprocreative sex. It was simply placed in another category.

The latter is usually associated with the efforts of Carl Westphal, professor of psychiatry at the University of Berlin, who was influenced by the German homosexual movement. Led by such individuals as Karl Heinrich Ulrichs (1881) and Karoly Kertbenny (1905), that movement sought to establish that homosexuality was inborn. In 1869 Carl Westphal had published the case histories of a young woman who from her earliest years liked to dress as a boy and of a young man who liked to dress as a woman. From these cases he argued that sexual abnormality was congenital, not acquired. He called the phenomenon "contrary sexual feeling" and insisted that, although neurotic elements were present in such individuals, they were not insane (Bullough 1989).

If the "contrary sexual feeling" was inborn, was it also incurable? Jean Martin Charcot, the director of the Salpêtrière Hospital, and a colleague had attempted to cure several cases of "contrary sexual instinct" or "sexual inversion" with only modest success and concluded in an 1882 publication that inversion was a constitutional nervous weakness due to hereditary degeneration.

This concept was further developed by Paul Moreau (1887), who theorized that in addition to the usual senses of sight, hearing, touch, taste, and feeling, humans had a sixth sense, a genital sense that, like the others, could suffer physical or psychic injury without damage to the other senses. This propensity to injury stemmed from either a hereditary taint or a predisposition to perversion provoked by certain other factors such as age, proverty, constitution, temperament, and seasons of the year. The result could be sexual inversion, nymphomania, satyriasis, bestiality, rape, or profanation of corpses. The only way to deal with these individuals so afflicted was to turn them over to asylums, where they could be cared for. Not everyone agreed with this, however.

One of the early researchers who was most important in influencing public opinion was Richard von Krafft-Ebing, whose *Psychopathia Sexualis,* first published in 1886, remained in print until the 1980s. He combined several prevailing nineteenth-century theories to explain sexual "perversion": (1) the idea that disease was caused by the physical nervous system, (2) the notion that there were often hereditary defects in this system, and (3) the concept of degeneracy. Civilization, he claimed, was possible only because lust had been tempered by altruism and restraint, based on the knowledge that sexual excess weakened the body. The purpose of sex was reproduction, and sexual activities not undertaken with this ultimate purpose in mind were "unnatural practices" and a perversion of the sexual instinct. Though Krafft-Ebing distinguished between innate and acquired perversion, even acquired perversion existed only when there was hereditary weakness in the nervous system, and onanism was a causal factor in this.

Differing from Krafft-Ebing somewhat was Sigmund Freud (1913, 1922a, 1922b, 1924–50, 1938), his younger and even more influential contemporary. Freud agreed that variant sexual behavior came from misdirected sexual drives, but he held that the cause of the misdirection lay in the nervous system and the mind through which the instinctual drive operated. Though Freud himself paid comparatively little attention to most forms of variant sexual behavior, his followers seized on his concepts to emphasize environmental and accidental causes of variant sexual impulses.

Later behaviorists carried this kind of thinking to an extreme, so that the practical result of both Freudianism and the learning psychologies was to suggest that everyone had the ability to channel his or her drives. Although they differed about specific factors, followers of Freud usually agreed that deviant sexuality was caused by environmental rather than constitutional factors and was, by implication, curable. Some groups, however, still looked upon it as inborn, though treatable if not curable. In any case, variations in sexual behavior were now regarded as coming under the jurisdiction of psychiatrists, and there they have remained.

Certain forms of variant sexuality, such as homosexuality, are no longer regarded as an illness, and masturbation is considered as normal behavior. Much of this latest change in attitude grew out of challenges to the research methodologies and theories that had originally classified much of human sexual behavior as an illness.

One challenge was made by Alfred Kinsey and his colleagues (1948), whose data on what actually constituted sexual behavior resulted in a redefinition of some of the norms. A second kind of challenge was aimed at the research of earlier physicians and psychiatrists. Most of the theorizing of Tissot and his successors had been rejected as germ theory gained credence and the endocrinological forces involved in sexuality came to be understood. This left psychiatrists as the only major group to maintain the contention that deviant sexual behavior could be illness. Prominent among them were psychoanalysts, who were attacked by a number of researchers in the 1960s and 1970s for working with small samples, not using control groups, and not taking into account cultural differences.

Attitudes toward nonprocreative sex also changed with the widespread adoption of contraceptives and the acknowledgement that sex was an enjoyable activity for both men and women. The recognition that people engaged in sex for pleasure as well as for procreation also weakened hostility to forms of sexual activity other than conventional heterosexual intercourse and raised questions about medical categorization. The knowledge that other cultures and peoples had attitudes toward sex that were radically different from those of Westerners was also important in challenging the western European and U.S. notion of sexual deviation as disease. Finally, in 1974 homosexuality was eliminated from the *Diagnostic and Statistical Manual* (DSM) of the American Psychiatric Association as a category of illness.

Not all forms of "deviant" sexual behavior, however, have been removed from the DSM, and in fact there remains a strong tendency to categorize as ill individuals who are pedophiles, exhibitionists, or necrophiliacs and those who engage in numerous other more or less forbidden sexual activities. There is also a countermovement as of this writing to establish a new category – that of sexually compulsive people – perhaps to get them into the offices of behavioral psychologists to be treated through behavior modification. Thus, although theories have changed and challenges to previous categorizations have been mounted, there remains a strong belief in the helping professions that socially unacceptable sexual behavior is an illness or at least a behavior problem of one sort or another. Since the time of Tissot these professions have essentially replaced religion in determining what sexual activity is permissible and what should continue to be stigmatized.

Vern L. Bullough

Bibliography

Acton, William. 1871. *The functions and disorders of the reproductive organs in childhood, youth, adult age, and advanced life considered in their physiological, social, and moral relations*, 5th edition. London.

Bayer, Ronald. 1981. *Homosexuality and American psychiatry*. New York.

Beard, George M. 1884. *Sexual neurasthenia, its hygiene, causes, symptoms, and treatment*, ed. A. D. Rockwell. New York.

Boerhaave, H. 1728. *Institutiones medicae*. In *Opera medica universa*. Geneva.

Bourgeois, Dr. X. 1873. *The passions in their relations to health and disease*, trans. Howard F. Damon. Boston.

Brown, John. 1803. *The elements of medicine*, rev. by Thomas Beddoes. 2 vols. in 1. Portsmouth, N.H.

Bullough, Vern L. 1975. Sex and the medical model. *Journal of Sex Research* 11: 291–303.

1976. *Sexual variance in society and history*. Chicago.

1989. The physician and research into human sexual behavior in nineteenth-century Germany. *Bulletin of the History of Medicine* 63: 247–67.

Bullough, Vern L., and Bonnie Bullough. 1987. *Women and prostitution*. Buffalo, N.Y.

Bullough, Vern L., and Martha Voght. 1973a. Homosexuality and its confusion with the "Secret Sin" in nineteenth century America. *Journal of the History of Medicine and Science* 28: 143–56.

1973b. Women, menstruation, and nineteenth century medicine. *Bulletin of the History of Medicine* 47: 66–82.

Charcot, Jean Martin, and Valentin Magna. 1882. Inversion du sens genital perversions sexuelles. *Archives de neurologie* III and IV.

Clarke, Edward H. 1874. *Sex in education; or a fair chance for girls*. Boston.

Engelhardt, H. Tristram, Jr. 1974. The disease of masturbation: Values and the concept of disease. *Bulletin of the History of Medicine* 48: 234–48.

Freud, Sigmund. 1913. Die drei Grundformen der Homosexualität. *Jahrbuch für Sexuelle Zwischenstufen* 15: Parts 2, 3, 4.

1922a. *Leonardo da Vinci*, trans. A. A. Brill, London.

1922b. *Three contributions to sexual theory*. New York.

1924–50. *Collected papers*. London.

1938. *Basic writings*. New York.

Graham, Sylvester. 1838. *A lecture on epidemic diseases, generally and particularly the spasmodic cholera*. Boston.

1848. *A lecture to young men, on chastity, intended also for the serious consideration of parents and guardians*, 10th edition. Boston.

Greenberg, David. 1988. *The construction of homosexuality*. New York.

Howe, J. W. 1889. *Excessive venery, masturbation, and continence*. New York.

Kellogg, J. H. 1882. *Plain facts for old and young*. Burlington, Iowa.

Kertbenny, K. M. 1905. Section 143 des Preuszischen Strafgestzbuchs vom 14. April 1851 und seine Aufrechterhaltung, and Section 152 in Entwurfe eines Strafgesetzbuchs für den norddeutschen Bund, reprinted *Jahrbuch für Sexuelle Zwischenstufen* 7: 3–66.

King, A. F. A. 1875–6. A new basis for uterine pathology. *American Journal of Obstetrics* 8: 242–3.

Kinsey, Alfred, Wardell Pomeroy, and Clyde Martin. 1948. *Sexual behavior in the human male*. Philadelphia.

Kinsey, Alfred C., Wardell B. Pomeroy, Clyde E. Martin, and Paul H. Gebhard. 1953. *Sexual behavior in the human female*. Philadelphia.

Krafft-Ebing, R. von. 1886. *Psychopathia sexualis*. Stuttgart.

Lallemand, C.-F. 1839. *On involuntary seminal discharges*, trans. W. Wood. Philadelphia.

MacDonald, R. H. 1967. The frightful consequences of onanism. *Journal of the History of Ideas* 28: 423–31.

Moreau, Paul. 1887. *Des aberations de sens genetique*. Paris.

Onania; or, the heinous sin of self-pollution, and all its frightful consequences, in both sexes, considered. With spiritual and physical advice to those, who have already injur'd themselves by this abominable practice. And seasonable admonition to the youth (of both SEXES) and those whose tuition they are under, whether parents, guardians, masters, or mistresses. To which is added, a letter from a lady (very curious) concerning the use and abuse of the marriage-bed. With the author's answers thereto. 1724. Boston.

Rush, Benjamin. 1794–8. *Medical inquiries and observations upon the diseases of the mind*. Philadelphia.

Scott, J. F. 1899. *The sexual instinct*. New York.

Shyrock, Richard H. 1947. *The development of modern medicine*, 2d edition. New York.

Stahl, Georg Ernst. 1768. *Theoria medica vera*. Hulle.

Tissot, Simon-André. 1758. *Tentamen de morbis ex manusturpatione*. Lausanne.

1776. *Onanism: Or a treatise upon the disorders of masturbation*, trans. A. Hume. London.

Ulrichs, K. H. 1881. *Memnon: Die Geschlechsnatur des mannliebenden Urnings*. Scheliz.

Ware, John. 1879. *Hints to young men on the true relations of the sexes*. Boston.

Weinberg, Martin S., and Colin J. Williams. 1974. *Male homosexuals: Their problems and adaptations*. New York.

Westphal, C. F. O. 1869. Die kontrare Sexualempfindung. *Archiven für Psychiatrie und Nervenkrankenheit* 2: 73–108.

II.5
Concepts of Heart-Related Diseases

In 1628 William Harvey, physician to St. Bartholomew's Hospital, London, used quantitative, experimental methods to show that the blood must move in a circle, rather than being continuously regenerated as earlier theories had proposed. In addition, Harvey showed that the heart supplies the power to send the blood on its circuit around the body. Harvey's revolutionary ideas reflected ancient thought about the perfectibility of circular motion as much as they did new ideas about the value of experimental evidence. Nonetheless, in many ways and by most accounts, the year 1628 marks the beginning of current Western ways of looking at the heart and its diseases. However, although Harvey's demonstration of cardiac physiology in animals seemed logically applicable to human beings, it failed to lead immediately to any dramatic changes in the diagnosis or treatment of human heart disease. Over the next few centuries many people tried to discover what was going on within the thoraxes of patients who showed the debilitating signs of cardiac disease. Their notions about heart disease were reflected in the diagnostic techniques they thought appropriate.

Diagnosing Heart Disease

Physical Diagnosis
During the mid-eighteenth century, Leopold Auenbrugger, working in Vienna, described a new diagnostic technique. By percussing the chest – that is, by striking the chest and both listening to and feeling the reverberation – he was able to tell, to some extent, what lay within. His method enabled him to ascertain the size of the heart and to determine the presence of fluid in the chest, a common manifesta-

tion of heart failure. However, because prevailing disease theories placed little importance on the localization of lesions in the body, Auenbrugger's technique attracted little attention. His work was to gain greater attention as a result of a political upheaval in a nearby country.

The French Revolution not only reshaped the political structure of France, but also radically changed the institutions that controlled hospitals and medical schools. Physicians practicing in these institutions changed the perception of disease. Their emphasis on the importance of specific lesions in the body stimulated a desire to correlate clinical physical findings with anatomic lesions found at autopsy. Every day, Parisian physicians in the early nineteenth century went from bedside to bedside, examining patients with all manner of diseases, and all too often they had the opportunity to correlate their physical findings with those found at autopsy. In this milieu, René Laennec invented the stethoscope for listening to sounds in the chest. Auenbrugger's technique of percussion became widely used when it was discovered that lesions could be localized in the chest with Laennec's stethoscope. Although both of these techniques were used primarily to diagnose diseases of the lung, they were also used to diagnose heart problems.

Auscultation with the stethoscope was not immediately accepted. It was a skill that took time and practical experience to learn, and one that could yield misleading results. Furthermore, it was of no help in diagnosing many cardiac diseases that did not produce physical signs and could be diagnosed only by the patient's own sensations. One of these diseases was manifested by chest pain and is now understood to be caused by occlusion of the coronary arteries of the heart.

Diagnosis by History: Coronary Heart Disease
In addition to anatomic studies, eighteenth-century practitioners published descriptions of coronary heart disease based on patients' reports of characteristic symptoms. (*Coronary heart disease*, as we now use the term, encompasses such entities as angina pectoris and myocardial infarction, or "heart attack.") In 1768 William Heberden of London gave a lecture at the College of Physicians of London, published in 1772, in which he coined the term *angina pectoris* and differentiated it from other pains in the chest:

They who are afflicted with it, are seized while they are walking, (more especially if it be up hill, and soon after eating) with a painful and most disagreeable sensation in the breast, which seems as if it would extinguish life, if it were to increase or to continue; but the moment they stand still, all this uneasiness vanishes. . . . In all other respects, patients are, at the beginning of this disorder, perfectly well. . . . Males are most liable to this disease, especially such as have past their fiftieth year.

Heberden focused on the clinical manifestations of the disease, not on its cause. However, others had earlier described disease of the coronary arteries. The English surgeon John Hunter, after finding this condition during an autopsy on a person who had died in a fit of anger, declared: "My life is in the hands of any rascal who chooses to annoy me." Hunter's words proved true. He collapsed and died in 1793, presumably of a myocardial infarction, soon after leaving an acrimonious meeting.

Many different manifestations of coronary heart disease were noted over the next century. Although the first diagnosis before death was probably made in 1878, recognition of coronary heart disease did not become widespread until its diagnosis by technological means became common early in the twentieth century. That new technology was derived in some ways from one of the oldest forms of diagnosis — feeling the pulse.

Mechanical Diagnosis: The Pulse and the Electrocardiogram

People have felt the pulse to diagnose disease since antiquity. Attempts to analyze the pulse have included timing its rate and noting its pattern, particularly any abnormalities in its rhythm. John Floyer, who in 1709 constructed a portable clock with which to time the pulse, noted that the natural pulse rate varied according to a person's place of residence, age, and sex.

A very slow pulse, one of the most striking abnormalities, was often associated with intermittent loss of consciousness, or syncope. This condition has come to be known as Stokes–Adams (or occasionally Adams–Stokes) disease, after two Dublin physicians, Robert Adams and William Stokes, each of whom described characteristics of the disease in the first half of the nineteenth century. Today this condition is treated with pacemakers (described later). Early attempts to understand the cause of a slow beat led to the development of mechanical devices for analyzing heartbeat.

In 1859 the French physiologist Etienne-Jules Marey drew on the earlier work of German physiologists such as Carl Ludwig, inventor of the kymograph, to devise an instrument that could produce a permanent record of the cardiac pulsations on a drum of smoked paper. Marey used this instrument to record the pressure within the heart of a horse. He also recorded pressure tracings from the arteries that could be felt on the surface of the human body. In the 1890s the English physician James Mackenzie developed the polygraph, an instrument that recorded the pulsations of the arteries and veins directly onto a continuous strip of paper. With this device he was able to describe many abnormalities of the pulse and to identify the cardiac causes of several of these. His work was advanced by the London physician Thomas Lewis, who analyzed abnormal cardiac rhythms with the electrocardiogram (EKG), a new instrument that could record the electrical signals generated by the heart. Invented in 1902 by Willem Einthoven, the EKG earned its inventor the 1924 Nobel Prize in medicine or physiology.

Because Lewis and Mackenzie were working within a social system that placed a high value on the clinical skills of the physician and a low value on the use of technology, neither thought of the EKG machine as an instrument that could replace the senses of the skilled bedside observer. However, working in a climate in which the role of the physician was not so socially important, James Herrick of Chicago saw the value of the EKG for diagnosing diseases that could not be diagnosed with the unaided senses. Coronary artery disease was one such disease. Herrick's clinicopathological description of it in 1912 received little attention; however, after his collaboration in 1918 and 1919 with Fred Smith to describe the characteristic EKG changes, Herrick's definition of the disease entity became widely recognized. This was an early example of a pattern to be repeated throughout the twentieth century – a disease first described clinically would become more widely accepted once it was defined in terms of a laboratory technique.

Hemodynamic Diagnosis: Diagnosis by Measuring Physiology

In a sense, the development of hemodynamic diagnosis was returning full circle to the issues of pressures and volumes in the heart that Harvey was working with in 1628. Harvey had been unable to measure these parameters in human hearts. Physicians' daily use of these measurements today is in large part the result of a self-experiment performed in 1929.

During the spring of 1929, while working in the relatively unsophisticated setting of a small German country hospital, Werner Forssmann became fascinated by the work of nineteenth-century French physiologists such as Marey, and particularly by a diagram showing Marey's recorded pressures from a horse's heart. Forssmann decided to perform the procedure Marey had used on himself by passing a urethral catheter from the main vein in his arm up into his heart, hoping to provide a new, more effective means of delivering medication. Despite his supervisor's refusal to grant him permission, Forssmann was determined to perform the experiment. However, he needed the cooperation of the surgical nurse who controlled access to the necessary instruments.

Forssmann was eventually so successful in convincing her of the safety and importance of the experiment that she insisted he perform the experiment on her. Forssmann, however, persuaded the nurse to lie down on a cart, where he strapped her down, claiming the action to be a "precaution against falling off." With the nurse thus immobilized, Forssmann inserted the catheter into his own arm, pushed it through the veins into his heart, and then released the nurse. She helped him walk down the stairs into the basement, where an X-ray image confirmed that the catheter was indeed within his heart. The experiment earned Forssmann some praise, but much more hostility, and as a result, he left academic medicine and did no more work on cardiac catheterization.

But others went forward with Forssmann's method. In 1932 Dickinson Richards, Jr., and André Cournand began collaborating on studies of the heart and circulation at New York Hospital. They started with the assumption that the heart, lungs, and circulatory system form a single system for the exchange of gases between the environment and the organism. In order to calculate the cardiac output, they needed to obtain blood samples from the right atrium, the cardiac chamber that collects blood from the body before pumping it to the lungs to receive more oxygen. After practicing Forssmann's technique on laboratory animals for four years, Cournand, Richards, and their colleagues determined that the passage of catheters into animals' hearts did not significantly interfere with cardiac functioning.

Although their first attempt to perform the procedure on a patient, in 1940, was unsuccessful, they were encouraged to continue their efforts by senior investigators studying cardiac output determined by the ballistocardiogram, an instrument that recorded the motion of the body caused by the heartbeat. Cournand was eventually able to insert a catheter into a human heart and to compare the directly measured cardiac output with that determined by the ballistocardiogram. He showed that cardiac output as measured by the ballistocardiogram was too low. More important, he showed that it was practical and safe to insert a catheter routinely into the right side of the human heart.

During the next few years, Richards, Cournand, and their colleagues designed a new catheter that was easier to maneuver and constructed a measuring device that enabled them to record simultaneously four different pressure tracings along with the EKG. In 1942 they advanced the catheter into the right ventricle, and in 1944 into the pulmonary artery, thus making it possible to measure the hemodynamic pressure and the amount of oxygen present in the blood at each stage of passage through the right side of the heart. Funded by the federal government through the Committee on Medical Research, from 1942 to 1944 this group studied more than 100 critically ill patients suffering from traumatic shock, hemorrhagic shock, burn shock, and shock caused by rupture of an internal organ. They outlined the profound effects of reduced circulating blood volume on cardiac output, particularly on the flow of blood to peripheral organs and the kidneys, and described how the condition could be reversed by replacement of the appropriate volume of blood. Later, they used the same catheterization technique to diagnose congenital cardiac defects: An abnormal opening between the cardiac chambers was detected by means of pressure and oxygen measurements made with the catheter. Similarly measuring the pressure in the cardiac chambers was found to be valuable for diagnosing acquired cardiac defects, particularly diseases of the heart valves.

Richards and Cournand shared the 1956 Nobel Prize in medicine or physiology with Forssmann. Not long after the discovery that right-sided pressures could be measured, others extended the technique to measure pressures on the left side of the heart. The procedure has greatly aided our understanding of the pathophysiology underlying various forms of congestive heart failure. The invention of electronic devices for measuring pressures has enabled physicians to analyze the pulsatile pressure tracings in various disease states. Other investigators have shown how injecting dye into the heart can aid in diagnosis. Today, the passing of diagnostic catheters into the heart is such a routine procedure that patients may not even spend a night in the hospital.

These techniques for hemodynamic monitoring have come to define and dominate places in hospitals set aside for the care of critically ill patients. Some intensive care units are designed specifically for the care of patients suffering from coronary artery disease. Physicians and nurses working in coronary care units, which first became widespread in the United States in the 1960s and 1970s, utilize both hemodynamic monitoring and EKG monitoring of the pulse, the latter to detect and correct life-threatening cardiac dysrhythmias. In other intensive care units, cardiac catheters are used to monitor the cardiac function of patients suffering from a wide variety of noncardiac disorders. Although they are useful for some groups of patients, whether coronary care units are necessary for all patients with myocardial infarction remains unclear.

Western ideas about what constitutes heart disease are based increasingly in technological diagnosis and on the ability to invade the thorax in order to make diagnoses and also to intervene. Along with the increased use of technology has come the unstated but generally pervasive assumption that diagnosis has finally become objective, transcultural, and reflective of some natural, inevitable underlying diagnostic system. The validity of this assumption is doubtful. Historical analysis shows that the definition of heart disease, as well as of the specific diseases and their appropriate diagnostic tests, is a product of both biology and culture.

Changing Concepts: What Constitutes Heart Disease?

Concepts about what constitutes heart disease have changed a great deal in the past century. For example, the corresponding section of a predecessor to this work, August Hirsch's *Handbook of Geographical and Historical Pathology* (1883–6) is entitled "Diseases of the Heart and Vessels," not diseases of the heart, and one of the main topics is hemorrhoids. Anatomic linkage of the heart and vessels into a single unit was common in the nineteenth century, as is shown by such titles as *Diseases of the Heart and Aorta* and *Diseases of the Heart and Great Vessels*. Around the end of the nineteenth century, however, the conceptualization of heart disease changed fundamentally. As Christopher Lawrence has pointed out, British physicians started to think about the heart in terms of its functional capacity rather than in terms of its anatomy. This led them to regard cardiac murmurs, such as would be detected by a stethoscope, as less important than physiological measurements of function.

This conceptual change was particularly apparent in discussions of a soldier's disease described at one time as "DaCosta's syndrome" and later, at the start of the First World War, as "soldier's heart." Afflicted by breathlessness, fatigue, and a feeling of impending doom, soldiers with this syndrome were initially treated by the British military with extended hospital bedrest. The presence of a cardiac murmur was taken as ipso facto evidence of heart disease. However, as the war continued, lasting far longer than originally anticipated, heart disease became a serious military, economic, and political problem. It was, in fact, the third most common reason for military discharge. Yet heart disease held out far more hope of treatment and return to service than did the most common cause of discharge, "wounds and injuries." Nonetheless, the long convalescence strained both the military hospitals and the political fortunes of England's leaders, who were forced to institute a military draft in 1916. Given these political exigencies, physicians working for the Medical Research Council reconceptualized the disease as the "effort syndrome." They decided that heart murmurs were important only insofar as they impaired the ability of the soldier to work, and then prescribed a series of graded exercises rather than hospitalization and bedrest. The result was that many soldiers previously declared "unfit for service" were reclassified as "fit." All of this demonstrates that some notions about what constitutes heart disease are informed by social needs.

Physicians' ideas have continued to be shaped by social context. Studies of the incidence of heart disease in black Americans early in the twentieth century were influenced by the cultural context in which they were written. Many investigators concluded that coronary artery disease was rare in black people, largely because black people were considered less likely to experience stress, owing to their assumed disinclination to hurry or worry about their lot in life, and because they were presumed to be less intellectually alert than the "refined, intellectual" classes.

In the late twentieth century, culture has continued to have an impact on our definitions of heart disease. For example, Lynn Payer has pointed out that failure to appreciate that the West German concept of heart disease differs from the U.S. concept could lead to the erroneous conclusion that death rates from ischemic heart disease are lower in West Germany than in the United States. In fact, the rates are approximately the same, but that type of heart disease is more likely to be called "ischemic heart disease" in the United States and "cardiac insufficiency" in West Germany.

The Rise of Cardiac Diseases

Changes in disease classification reflect both social and biological events. Even after accounting for changes in definitions, it seems clear that there has been a significant change in the types of disease from which people die. During the twentieth century, our methods of classification have helped to make heart disease an increasingly important cause of death and disability. The predominant causes of sickness and death were once infectious diseases. In the mid-nineteenth century, for example, tuberculosis accounted for an estimated one-seventh of all deaths in western Europe. Yet the impact of infectious diseases has subsequently decreased in many parts of the world, partly because of improved living conditions and partly because of improved treatment with antibiotics.

Two major forms of heart disease related to infectious agents have undergone a dramatic shift in pattern. Rheumatic fever, a disease related to infection with a specific streptococcus that can cause heart disease, was once a major cause of heart disease in Western countries. In industrialized countries, it has now become a relatively minor cause of heart disease, with a prevalence as low as 0.6 per 1,000 school-aged children in the United States and 0.7 per 1,000 in Japan. In other parts of the world, however, rheumatic heart disease remains a serious problem; the prevalence per 1,000 school-aged children has been reported to be in the range of 15 to 20 for Algeria, Bolivia, and Thailand.

Endocarditis, an infection of the heart valves, carried an almost certain death sentence before the advent of antibiotics. At one time, endocarditis in the United States primarily afflicted people with valvular disease caused by rheumatic heart disease. The changing pattern of this illness reflects changes not only in treatment but also in life-style. Now endocarditis is far more often a disease of intravenous drug abusers.

Another result of the decline of infectious diseases has been an increase in the average life expectancy. People now live long enough to succumb to diseases that take time to develop, which is the case with many cardiac diseases, particularly coronary heart disease. And again life-styles have changed. A lack of physical activity and a change in diet may contribute to the increased incidence of coronary heart disease.

Finally, the development of cardiology as a major field of specialization in the United States is indebted in large part to the earlier campaign against tuberculosis, which prompted the development of the voluntary health movement. The first U.S. cardiology organization, the American Heart Association, drew substantial intellectual, organizational, and financial support from the antituberculosis movement, primarily the National Tuberculosis Association.

Coronary Disease

Coronary disease has become the major form of heart disease in industrialized countries. As such, it has become a major object of attention for health care workers. Much of that attention has been focused on explaining the geographic and historical changes in the pattern of disease.

Heart disease caused 979,000 deaths in the United States in 1986. Accounting for 47 percent of all deaths, it is by far the leading cause of death, with myocardial infarction the most common diagnosis. Many more people suffer from heart disease than die from it. In the United States, there were an estimated 57,700,000 people with cardiovascular disease in 1983, 21,500,000 of whom had heart disease and 7,200,000 of whom had coronary heart disease. Of those with heart disease, 12,600,000 were under age 65, as were 3,200,000 of those with coronary heart disease. The physical activity of one-quarter of those with heart disease was limited, making the condition an important cause of disability as well as death.

Declining Coronary Death Rate in the United States

At the turn of the nineteenth century, heart disease was the fourth leading cause of death in the United States, behind pneumonia and influenza (combined), tuberculosis, diarrhea, enteritis, and ulceration of the intestines. All of these produced death rates in excess of 100 per 100,000 population. A sharp upward trend in coronary disease became apparent around 1920, and coronary disease was recognized with increasing frequency throughout most of the first 50 years of the twentieth century. By 1940 only two disease categories with death rates of more than 100 per 100,000 remained: cancer and diseases of the heart. The death rate from heart diseases then began a dramatic series of changes.

As Figure II.5.1 shows, the death rate reached a peak in 1963 and has declined continuously since then. There was some initial concern about whether the decline was real or only a product of a 1968 change in disease classification. But now there is little doubt that the death rate for coronary heart disease in the United States has fallen dramatically since the 1960s. However, that decline has not been evenly distributed. The mortality rate for heart diseases in California, for example, peaked relatively early, around 1955, and the subsequent decline there

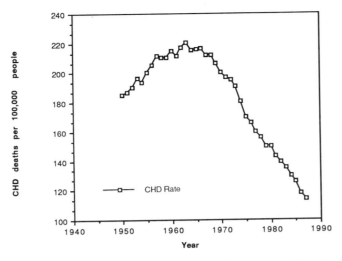

Figure II.5.1. Rate of coronary heart disease per 100,000 people in the United States (age-adjusted to 1940 age distribution). (Data from Vital Statistics of the United States, as prepared by the National Heart, Lung, and Blood Institute; data for 1987 provisional.)

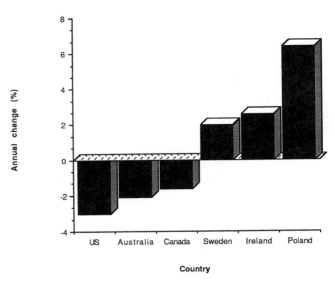

Figure II.5.2. Annual change in mortality from ischemic cardiac disease, 1968–77 (men aged 40 to 69). (Data from WHO MONICA 1988.)

was repeated in other parts of the United States throughout the 1960s and 1970s. By 1986 the death rate for coronary heart disease was 55 percent of the 1966 rate, and the decline in the death rate for all cerebrovascular diseases was proceeding three times faster than the decline for all other causes of death combined.

Worldwide Variation in Coronary Diseases

Such countries as Australia, New Zealand, and Canada have experienced similar declines in the death rate from coronary disease among men. Other countries, however, have experienced significant increases in death rates, as revealed in Figure II.5.2. These have included countries, such as Scotland and Northern Ireland, with death rates initially comparable to that of the United States, as well as countries, such as Poland and Switzerland, initially having death rates much lower than that of the United States.

Some of the increase may be due to the impact of industrialization. In China, for example, infectious diseases such as tuberculosis and nutritional deficiencies were the major causes of morbidity and mortality, with cardiovascular disease of little concern until the late 1950s. Even among industrialized countries, the rate of death from cardiovascular diseases has varied widely, from 913 per 100,000 in Finland (for men aged 40 to 69 in 1975) to 379 in Japan.

Attempts have been made to explain these differences in disease rate. The World Health Organization's Multinational Trends and Determinants in Cardiovascular Disease (MONICA) has made one such attempt. With 41 projects in 21 countries, MONICA is helping to make cardiovascular disease a focus of international and cross-cultural comparisons. Only AIDS has received similar worldwide attention.

Studies of changing patterns of cardiac disease have contributed to the invention of *risk factor,* a concept that is receiving widespread attention as a way of conceptualizing the cause of many diseases. Unlike infectious diseases, which are defined in terms of a single, specific agent, *risk factor* is conceptualized on an epidemiological and probabilistic basis.

Risk Factors for Coronary Heart Disease

Much of our current explanation for the historical and geographic differences in death rates from coronary heart disease derives from the concept of risk factor. A number of long-term prospective studies have enhanced the utility of this concept. The most widely known study is the Framingham Heart Study, in which 5,209 men and women have been carefully examined every two years since the investigation began in 1948 in Framingham, Massachusetts. Studies such as this have identified a number of factors that contribute to the likelihood of developing coronary heart disease. Some of these cannot be modified. For example, men are more likely to suffer from heart disease than women; older people are more likely to develop the disease than younger ones; and those having a family history of early cardiac disease are at greater risk than those without such a history.

However, other factors can be modified. Cigarette smoking dramatically increases the likelihood of a coronary event and represents the greatest and most preventable cause of heart disease. Once a person stops smoking, the risk rapidly declines to a level approximately the same as it would be if the person had never smoked. High blood pressure and diabetes are also important risk factors.

A positive relationship between blood cholesterol level and the development of heart disease has been clearly demonstrated. Almost no Japanese men have serum cholesterol levels above 200 mg/dl, whereas almost no Finnish men have concentrations below that level. Consistent with the hypothesis that cholesterol is associated with death from coronary heart disease, the death rate from coronary heart disease in Finland is more than 10 times that in Japan. Historical analysis has shown that the death rate from heart disease in Europe fell during the Second World War, presumably as a result of a lack of foods that elevate serum cholesterol level. Most population-based studies have shown a consistently positive relationship between increased serum cholesterol level in the form of low-density lipoprotein and the rate of heart disease. At high levels the association is particularly strong; the risk of death for persons having cholesterol values in the top 10 percent is four times the risk of persons in the bottom 10 percent. There is now good evidence that lowering cholesterol level with drug therapy will lower the death rate from coronary disease. This effect of reducing cholesterol level is most beneficial for those having the highest levels, but the value of reducing cholesterol level for those without elevated cholesterol remains unclear.

Exercise has a beneficial effect on the types of lipids circulating in the bloodstream. Although obesity is associated with hypertension, whether obesity is an independent risk factor for coronary heart disease is as yet unclear.

In the 1950s some U.S. investigators argued that people who were hard-driving, competitive, overcommitted, impatient perfectionists and who found it difficult to relax – these with the so-called type A personality – were at increased risk for coronary heart disease. These findings have been a subject of intense debate. Some studies of workers in Great Britain have identified civil service manual workers, not those with the hard-driving behavior indicated in the original research, as those at greatest risk from their behavior type. Although the exact role of type A behavior as an independent risk factor

in the development of coronary heart disease remains unclear, recent studies suggest that the type A personality may actually improve longevity after a myocardial infarction.

Alcohol intake in small quantities – two or fewer drinks per day – may diminish the risk of developing coronary disease. However, alcohol in greater amounts is clearly associated with greater morbidity and mortality from both cardiac and noncardiac disease.

Explaining Change

Many investigators have attempted to use the concept of risk factor to explain geographic and historical changes in the rate of death from coronary heart disease. The decline in the U.S. death rate may have been due partly to improved medical interventions, including the widespread establishment of coronary care units, improvements in prehospital resuscitation and care, better surgical and medical treatment of those with known heart disease, and more extensive treatment of the large proportion of the population with hypertension. The decline may also have been due in part to changes in life-style. Cholesterol consumption peaked in 1959, and the percentage of North Americans who smoke has declined steadily over the past few decades. However, a significant part of the change cannot be fully explained.

Although coronary heart disease appears to be an increasing cause of death in developing countries, accounting for 15 to 25 percent of all deaths as the mean life expectancy reaches 50 to 60 years, more is required to explain the rates of death from coronary heart disease than merely to blame increasing industrialization. People moving from one industrialized country to another tend to develop the susceptibility to heart disease prevalent in the host country, suggesting that other environmental factors play an important role in determining the incidence of heart disease. Striking confirmation of this comes from a study of 11,900 people of Japanese ancestry living in Japan, Hawaii, and California. Those living in Japan had the lowest incidence of heart disease, those living in Hawaii had an intermediate incidence, and those living in California the highest. The best predictor of the incidence of heart disease among those living in California was not the presence of known risk factors, but the extent to which those Japanese who had moved from Japan to California continued to adhere to traditional Japanese values: those who retained more of these values had a lower rate of heart disease.

Geographic Variation in Types of Heart Disease

In many parts of the world, other types of heart disease are more common than coronary heart disease. Endomyocardial fibrosis, for example, is common in the tropical rain forest belt of Africa and South America. The disease has a characteristic pathological process and leads to heart failure, accounting for up to 20 percent of patients with heart failure in Uganda, the Sudan, and northern Nigeria. It can affect people who live in the area as well as those who visit from other parts of the world. Although its precise cause is unknown, and in some instances it may be due to a parasitic infection, the underlying cause may be an increase in the number of eosinophils. In many parts of South America, the parasite *Schistosoma mansoni* is a common cause of heart disease. Also common in South America is Chagas' disease. Other heart diseases having characteristic geographic patterns include some forms of congenital heart disease that are more significant for people who live at high altitudes, where the concentration of oxygen in the inspired air is reduced.

Peripartum cardiac failure is developed by up to 1 percent of women in northern Nigeria during the postpartum period. Occurring most often in July, it seems to be caused by a combination of extreme heat, exhaustion exacerbated by the traditional custom of lying on a bed over a fire, and eating food rich in lake salt. Thus, peripartum cardiac failure appears to be largely a result of cultural patterns. In this respect it resembles coronary heart disease, which is linked to Western culture in ways that we identify as risk factors and in ways that we do not fully understand, as exemplified by the impact of Japanese cultural values on coronary disease just described.

Recent Changes

Perhaps because of the prevalence of cardiac disease as well as the symbolic significance of the heart, concern for heart-related diseases has been central to much of what we have come to identify as late-twentieth-century medicine. That includes both "high-tech" innovations and preventive medicine strategies, such as risk-factor intervention and lifestyle modifications.

The echocardiogram is a "high-tech" approach to cardiac diagnosis based on the reflection of sound waves in the body. The technique was first demonstrated in the 1950s, and recent advances have greatly increased the quality of the images, such that it is possible to diagnose heart disease even in a fetus. By bouncing sound waves off the interior of the heart, a picture can be generated that reflects the heart's anatomy, and by the use of small air bubbles to provide contrast, the passage of blood can also be traced. The echocardiogram's greatest advantages lie in its complete safety (so far as is now known) and freedom from pain.

Other imaging techniques applied to cardiac disease include tagging blood constituents with radioactive substances (which can be used to measure both function and blood flow) and both computerized axial tomography and magnetic resonance imaging. The latter two techniques make use of digital processing and imaging to provide cross-sectional images based on a computerized reconstruction of the information provided by scanning from many different directions. In addition, computerized axial tomography and positron emission tomography are now being used to measure the metabolic state of the heart muscle.

Treatment of patients with acute myocardial infarction has evolved from observing and supporting the patient to attempting to intervene in the disease process itself. Typically, patients with myocardial infarction suffer from an obstruction of one of the coronary arteries that supply blood to the heart. Two methods for relieving that obstruction are now being used, one mechanical and one in which medication dissolves the blockage. The mechanical intervention is percutaneous transluminal coronary angioplasty (PCTA), during which a catheter is directed into the coronary artery and expanded in order to clear the lumen. Since its introduction in 1977, PCTA has become widely used for the treatment of coronary disease. The number of procedures performed in the United States rose from 32,206 in 1983 to 175,680 in 1987. The procedure has also become popular in other countries, with approximately 12,000 procedures being done in the Federal Republic of Germany and 10,048 in Japan during 1987. The initial success rate approaches 95 percent at some institutions, but a significant percentage of patients experience later failure. PCTA continues to be used for people who suffer from symptoms caused by an obstruction of the coronary arteries, but who have not yet suffered death of the heart muscle. The technique has been attempted as well with patients who have recently suffered death of the heart muscle, causing myocardial infarction, but recent studies suggest that it is not as useful for urgent therapy.

Tissue-dissolving agents include products of recombinant DNA technology. These agents should be administered soon after a person suffers a heart attack in order to dissolve the clot before irreversible damage has been done to the heart muscle. Although PCTA requires rapid transportation of a heart attack patient to the hospital, often via helicopter, treatment with clot-dissolving agents can be initiated before the patient reaches the hospital. This therapy must be closely monitored, however, making hospitalization necessary for optimal treatment. This may negate studies from the 1970s that showed that hospitalization made no difference in the prognosis of patients suffering from an uncomplicated myocardial infarction. The optimum therapy for patients with myocardial infarction is being evaluated.

The first successful transplantation of a human heart into another human being was performed in South Africa by Christian Barnard in 1967. Transplantation was at first reserved for critically ill patients not likely to survive for long. However, a series of advances, primarily in the posttransplant management of patients, has led to a dramatic increase in survival after transplantation and to a tendency to carry out the procedure on patients with severe heart failure much earlier in the course of the disease. As a result, the number of transplantations performed worldwide increased from 3,000 in 1986 to more than 6,800 by January 1988. The five-year actuarial survival worldwide exceeded 70 percent and was more than 80 percent for some subgroups. Moreover, more than 80 percent of survivors were able to return to their previous occupations or comparable levels of activity. The success of cardiac transplantation prompted Medicare, the primary federal means of payment for elderly U.S. citizens receiving health care, to fund heart transplantations. It did so, however, at only a few locations, selected on the basis of results and experience, thus linking reimbursement with some measure of quality. Although not all heart transplantations are covered by Medicare, many insurance plans have indicated an intent to employ Medicare criteria in deciding which institutions will be paid for the procedure.

That some patients suffer from an abnormally slow heartbeat has been known for some time. Current treatment for many of them (perhaps too many) is provided by an artificial pacemaker. The first pacemaker was implanted in 1959, and now more than 200,000 pacemakers are implanted each year worldwide, approximately half of these in the United States. The pacemaker, which usually weighs about 40 grams, is connected to the heart by wires and is powered by lithium batteries that commonly last 7 to 10 years. At first pacemakers produced electrical pacing signals at a constant rate in order to treat

Stokes–Adams disease; more recent models can be programmed to respond to changing conditions in a variety of ways. A new device can electrically shock the heart out of an uncoordinated rhythm called ventricular fibrillation. This automatic implantable defibrillator, first used in 1982, appears to be helpful for patients who suffer from arrhythmias that are difficult to control.

Unlike the stomach or the limbs, for example, a person's heart cannot stop functioning for long or the person will die. This fact made operations on the heart difficult to contemplate during the nineteenth century, when great advances were being made in surgery on other organs. Some leading surgeons of the day flatly asserted that surgery on the heart would always be impossible. Nonetheless, early in the twentieth century, surgical treatment of valvular heart disease was attempted. From 1902 to 1928, 10 attempts were made to cure mitral stenosis (a narrowing of the valve leading to the main pumping chamber of the heart); 8 of the patients died. Because of the dismal outcomes, no one attempted another such operation until the mid-1940s. Starting in the 1950s, the availability of cardiac bypass in the form of an effective pump and oxygenator enabled surgeons to work on a still, "open" heart rather than on a beating organ. Valve replacements became relatively easy. Coronary artery bypass grafting (surgery to bypass blocked coronary arteries) is now a common means of treating coronary artery disease. Whereas at first surgeons bypassed only one or two obstructed vessels, now many more are commonly bypassed during a procedure.

Our ability to replace diseased valves has also greatly increased. Some patients suffering from abnormal heart rhythms can be helped by heart surgery designed to interrupt abnormal conduction pathways within the heart. Some centers are investigating a heterotopic prosthetic ventricle, a mechanical device designed to support a failing heart until a suitable transplant can be procured. Others have attempted to use an artificial heart for long-term support. Such a device would not be subject to the immunologic phenomena associated with transplantation and would obviate the need to locate a donor heart. However, problems with clots and hemolysis have thus far severely limited the attractiveness of this option.

Coda

The heart continues to have a central place in Western medicine. Heart diseases are common, and many of the most prominent new approaches to disease in the past few decades have been directed at heart disease. Cardiologists have become the most powerful subspecialists in internal medicine.

But the heart has long been central to the broader Western culture as well. The heart is seen as the seat of the emotions – as in the expressions a "broken heart," "crimes of the heart," a "bleeding heart," and a "change of heart." The heart is also the source of strength: "Take heart!" or "You've gotta have heart." The heart is metaphorically the site of a central issue or concern, as in the "heart of the country" or the "heart of the issue." Finally, the heart is often seen, both metaphorically and literally, as the source of life, and its failure is considered both a cause and a marker of death. Concepts of heart disease are drawn from general cultural concepts of what it means to be human, and studies of how and when they change will increase our understanding not only of the history of medicine but of history in general.

Joel D. Howell

Bibliography

Ackerknecht, Erwin H. 1967. *Medicine at the Paris hospitals, 1794–1848.* Baltimore.

Andy, J. J., F. F. Bishara, and O. O. Soyinka. 1981. Relation of severe eosinophilia and microfilariasis to chronic African endomyocardial fibrosis. *British Heart Journal* 45: 672–80.

Auenbrugger, Leopold. 1936 (orig. 1761, trans. John Forbes 1824). On percussion of the chest. *Bulletin of the History of Medicine* 4: 379–403.

Bedford, D. Evan. 1951. The ancient art of feeling the pulse. *British Heart Journal* 13: 423–37.

Biörck, Gunnar. 1956. Wartime lessons on arteriosclerotic heart disease from northern Europe. In *Cardiovascular epidemiology,* ed. Ancel Keys and Paul D. White, 8–21. New York.

Block, Peter C., et al. 1988. A prospective randomized trial of outpatient versus inpatient cardiac catheterization. *New England Journal of Medicine* 319: 1251–5.

Bourassa, Martial G., et al. 1988. Report of the joint ISFC/WHO task force on coronary angioplasty. *Circulation* 78: 780–9.

Brett, Allan S. 1989. Treating hypercholesterolemia: How should physicians interpret the published data for patients? *New England Journal of Medicine* 321: 676–80.

Burch, G. E., and N. P. de Pasquale. 1964. *A history of electrocardiography.* Chicago.

Chazov, E., R. G. Oganov, and N. V. Perova, eds. 1987. *Preventive cardiology.* Proceedings of the International Conference on Preventive Cardiology, Moscow, June 23–6, 1987. London.

Cherubin, C. E., and H. C. Neu. 1971. Infective endocarditis at the Presbyterian Hospital in New York City from 1938–1967. *American Journal of Medicine* 51: 83–96.

Criqui, Michael H. 1987. The roles of alcohol in the epidemiology of cardiovascular disease. *Acta Medica Scandanavia,* Suppl., 717: 73–85.

Davidson, N. M., and E. H. O. Parry. 1978. Peri-partum cardiac failure. *Quarterly Journal of Medicine,* New Ser., 47: 431–61.

Davies, J. N. P. 1956. Endomyocardial fibrosis. In *Cardiovascular epidemiology,* ed. Ancel Keys and Paul D. White, 106–10. New York.

DeVries, William C. 1988. The permanent artificial heart: Four case reports. *Journal of the American Medical Association* 259: 849–59.

Dimsdale, Joel E. 1988. A perspective on Type A behavior and coronary disease. *New England Journal of Medicine* 318: 110–12.

Dock, George. 1939. Historical notes on coronary occlusion: From Dock to Osler. *Journal of the American Medical Association* 113: 563–8.

Dodu, R. A. Silas. 1988. Emergence of cardiovascular disease in developing countries. *Cardiology* 75: 56–64.

Farrar, David J., et al. 1988. Heterotopic prosthetic ventricles as a bridge to cardiac transplantation: A multicenter study in 29 patients. *New England Journal of Medicine* 318: 333–40.

Fishman, Alfred P., and Dickinson W. Richards, Jr. 1964. *Circulation of the blood: Men and ideas.* New York.

Forssmann, Werner. 1974. *Experiments on myself: Memoirs of a surgeon in Germany,* trans. Hilary Davies. New York.

Fowler M. B., and John S. Schroeder 1986. Current status of cardiac transplantation. *Modern Concepts of Cardiovascular Disease* 55: 37.

Fox, Renée C., and Judith P. Swazey. 1970. The clinical moratorium: A case study of mitral valve surgery. In *Experimentation with human subjects,* ed. Paul A. Freund, 315–57. New York.

Fragomeni, Luis Sergio, and Michael P. Kaye. 1988. The Registry of the International Society for Heart Transplantation: Fifth Official Report – 1988. *Journal of Heart Transplantation* 7: 249–53.

Frank, Robert. 1988. The telltale heart: Physiological instruments, graphic methods, and clinical hopes, 1854–1914. In *The investigative enterprise: Experimental physiology in nineteenth-century medicine,* ed. William Coleman and Frederick L. Holmes, 211–90. Berkeley and Los Angeles.

Fye, W. Bruce. 1985a. Cardiology in 1885. *Circulation* 72: 21–6.

1985b. The delayed diagnosis of myocardial infarction: It took half a century! *Circulation* 72: 262–71.

Goldman, Lee, and Francis E. Cook. 1984. The decline in ischemic heart disease mortality rates: An analysis of the comparative effect of medical intervention and changes in lifestyle. *Annals of Internal Medicine* 101: 825–36.

Hall, A. Rupert. 1960. Studies on the history of the cardiovascular system. *Bulletin of the History of Medicine* 34: 391–413.

Harvey, William. 1928 (orig. 1628, trans. G. L. Keynes). *An anatomical disquitation on the motion of the heart and blood in animals (De motu cordis)*. London.

Heberden, William. 1941 (1772). Account of a disorder of the breast. In *Classics of cardiology*, Vol. 1, ed. Frederick A. Willius and Thomas E. Keys, 221–4. New York.

Hill, J. D., J. R. Hampton, and J. R. A. Mitchell. 1979. Home or hospital for myocardial infarction: Who cares? *American Heart Journal* 98: 545–7.

Hirsch, A. 1883. *Handbook of geographical and historical pathology*, Vol. 1, trans. C. Creighton. London.

Howell, Joel D. 1984. Early perceptions of the electrocardiogram: From arrhythmia to infarction. *Bulletin of the History of Medicine* 58: 83–98.

  1985. "Soldier's heart": The redefinition of heart disease and specialty formation in early twentieth-century Great Britain. *Medical History,* Suppl. No. 5: 34–52.

  1988. Hearts and minds: The invention and transformation of American cardiology. In *Grand rounds: One hundred years of internal medicine,* ed. Russell C. Maulitz and Diana E. Long, 243–75. Philadelphia.

Johnson, Stephen L. 1970. *The history of cardiac surgery, 1896–1955*. Baltimore.

Keys, Ancel. 1980. *Seven countries: A multivariate analysis of death and coronary heart disease*. Cambridge, Mass.

Laennec, R. T. H. 1821. *A treatise on diseases of the chest,* trans. John Forbes. London.

Lawrence, Christopher. 1985. Moderns and ancients: The "new cardiology" in Britain, 1880–1930. *Medical History,* Suppl. No. 5: 1–33.

Leaf, Alexander. 1989. Management of hypercholesterolemia: Are preventive interventions advisable? *New England Journal of Medicine* 321: 680–4.

Leibowitz, J. O. 1970. *The history of coronary heart disease.* London.

Lewis, Thomas. 1925. *The mechanism and graphic registration of the heart beat.* London.

Liss, Ronald Sandor. 1967. *The history of heart surgery in the United States (1938–1960).* Zurich.

McKenzie, James. 1902. *The study of the pulse, arterial, venous, and hepatic, and the movements of the heart.* Edinburgh.

MacMurray, Frank G. 1957. Stokes–Adams disease: A historical review. *New England Journal of Medicine* 256: 643–50.

Marmot, M. G., and S. L., Syme. 1976. Acculturation and coronary heart disease in Japanese-Americans. *American Journal of Epidemiology* 104: 225–47.

Mitchell, S. Weir. 1971 (orig. 1891). *The early history of instrumental precision in medicine.* New York.

National Cholesterol Education Program Expert Panel on Detection, Evaluation, and Treatment of High Blood Cholesterol in Adults. 1988. Report of the National Cholesterol Education Program Expert Panel on Detection, Evaluation, and Treatment of High Blood Cholesterol in Adults. *Archives of Internal Medicine* 148: 36–69.

National Heart, Lung, and Blood Institute: Fact Book, Fiscal Year 1987. 1987. Bethesda, Md.

Olsen, Eckhardt G. J., and Christopher J. F. Spry. 1985. Relation between eosinophilia and endomyocardial disease. *Progress in Cardiovascular Diseases* 27: 241–54.

Payer, Lynn. 1988. *Medicine and culture: Varieties of treatment in the United States, England, West Germany, and France.* New York.

Pernick, Martin S. 1988. Back from the grave: Recurring controversies over defining and diagnosing death in history. In *Death: Beyond whole-brain criteria,* ed. Richard M. Zaner, 17–74. Dordrecht.

Pisa, Z., and K. Uemura. 1982. Trends of mortality from ischaemic heart disease and other cardiovascular diseases in 27 countries, 1968–1977. *World Health Statistics Quarterly* 35: 11–47.

Ragland, David R., and Richard J. Brand. 1988. Type A behavior and mortality from coronary heart disease. *New England Journal of Medicine* 318: 65–9.

Renlund, Dale G. et al. 1987. Medicare-designated centers for cardiac transplantation. *New England Journal of Medicine* 316: 873–6.

Roberts, Stewart R. 1932. Nervous and mental influences in angina pectoris. *American Heart Journal* 7: 21–35.

Rose, G., and M. G. Marmot. 1981. Social class and coronary heart disease. *British Heart Journal* 45: 13–19.

Shaper, A. G., M. S. R. Hutt, and Z. Fejfar, eds. 1974. *Cardiovascular disease in the tropics.* London.

Shaper, A. G., Goyas Wannamethee, and Mary Walker. 1988. Alcohol and mortality in British men: Explaining the U-shaped curve. *Lancet* 2: 1267–73.

Smith, Dale C. 1978. Austin Flint and auscultation in America. *Journal of the History of Medicine* 33: 129–49.

Stallones, Reuel A. 1980. The rise and fall of ischemic heart disease. *Scientific American* 243: 53–9.

TIMI Research Group. 1988. Immediate vs delayed catheterization and angioplasty following thrombolytic therapy for acute myocardial infarction. *Journal of the American Medical Association* 260: 2849–58.

Topol, Eric J. 1988. Coronary angioplasty for acute myocardial infarction. *Annals of Internal Medicine* 109: 970–80.

Townsend, Gary L. 1967. Sir John Floyer (1649–1734) and his study of pulse and respiration. *Journal of the History of Medicine* 22: 286–316.

Weiss, Morris W. 1939. The problem of angina pectoris in the negro. *American Heart Journal* 17: 711–15.

WHO MONICA Project Principal Investigators. 1988. The World Health Organization MONICA Project (Monitoring trends and determinants in cardiovascular disease): A major international collaboration. *Journal of Clinical Epidemiology* 41: 105–14.

Williams, Richard Allen. 1987. Coronary artery disease in blacks. *Journal of Clinical Hypertension* 3: 21S–24S.

World Health Organization. 1982. *Prevention of coronary heart disease.* Technical Report Series No. 678. Geneva.

  1988. *Rheumatic fever and rheumatic heart disease.* Technical Report Series No. 764. Geneva.

Ying-kai, Wu, Wu Zhao-su, and Yao Chong-hua. 1983. Epidemiological studies of cardiovascular diseases in China. *Chinese Medical Journal* 96: 201–5.

II.6
Concepts of Cancer

In past centuries people feared epidemic diseases with their sudden onset, ghastly symptoms, agonizing death for many, and sometimes disfigurement or physical impairment for survivors. Today, especially in the developed world (with a few notable exceptions), the dread of epidemic contagion seems almost as anachronistic as the burning of witches. It has been replaced by the dread of cancer. As with the epidemics of yesterday, the basic causes of cancer remain shrouded in mystery, while its effects in terms of human suffering are all too well known.

Cancer is a process whereby a loss of control of normal cell division and multiplication produces a tumor that can invade adjacent tissues and metastasize, that is, implant cancerous cells at a site that is noncontiguous to their origin, where abnormal multiplication continues. When cancer originates in connective tissues (mainly bone or muscle), it is called *sarcoma;* when it originates in epithelial tissues (lining tissues and organs such as the breast, lungs, or stomach), it is called *carcinoma.* The latter is by far more common. Invasive tumors occur in all complex species and probably antedate the advent of vertebrates. The oldest paleopathological evidence is limited to lesions that affected bones, such as those found in dinosaurs. Tumors have been found in Egyptian mummies dating from 2000 to 3000 B.C., and physicians of that ancient land knew of and treated patients for cancers of several sites.

Certainly the ancient Greeks were familiar with this disease, or perhaps better, this group of diseases. The condition is discussed in the Hippocratic corpus, and in fact its nomenclature is dominated by Greek words. Hippocrates himself is credited with having named the disease cancer from *karcinos,* the Greek word for crab, perhaps because some cancers of the breast have a crablike appearance or perhaps because the pain that cancer can produce resembles the pinching of a crab. Similarly, *neoplasm,* meaning "new formation," and *oncology,* literally the "study of masses," are derived from the Greek, as is the word *tumor.*

Hippocratic medicine attributed tumors – which included all sorts of swellings – to an abnormal accretion of humors. Although some remedies are mentioned, aphorism VI.38 advocates conservatism: "It is better not to apply any treatment in cases of occult cancer; for, if treated, the patients die quickly; but if not treated they hold out for a long time." Galen sought to differentiate more clearly cancers from inflammatory lesions and gangrene. Cancer was held to be caused by black bile; if the cancer ulcerated, the black bile was undiluted; if there was only a tumor, the pathogenic humor had been diluted.

Carcinoma of the breast was probably the earliest actual neoplasm for which surgical eradication was attempted. Leonides of Alexandria, who slightly preceded Galen, is known to have progressively incised and cauterized, both to prevent bleeding and to destroy the neoplasm. Galen, conversely, recommended that bleeding be permitted, presumably for the pathogenic humor to be drained. Some surgeons performed a total mastectomy. Little was written about the healing of these terrible procedures, but Rhazes warned in the ninth century that those who performed surgery on a cancer generally only caused it to worsen unless it was completely removed and the incision cauterized.

Although barber-surgeons probably incised and excised boils and warts in the belief that they were curing cancer, it seems likely that few cancers were treated surgically until relatively modern times. Ambroise Paré wrote toward the end of the sixteenth century that those who pretended to cure cancer surgically only transformed a nonulcerous cancer into an ulcerated one. "I have never seen a cancer cured by incision, nor known anyone who has." Nevertheless, in the seventeenth century, Wilhelm Fabricius of Hilden described the removal of axillary nodes in a breast cancer operation and provided adequate descriptions of operations for other cancers.

The discovery of the lymphatic system by Gasparro Aselli in 1622 directed medical attention away from the black bile theory, which no one had demonstrated, toward abnormalities of the lymphatic structures in the causation of cancer. Basically, the idea was that cancer was an inflammatory reaction to extravasated lymph, the type of lesion depending on its qualities. About 150 years later John Hunter modified the lymph theory by defining "coagulating lymph" (i.e., blood serum), as opposed to true lymph, as that component of blood that clotted spontaneously when it was extravasated. It was this "lymph," when it was contaminated by a "cancerous poison" and oozed into tissues, that Hunter viewed as the cause of cancer. Quite presciently, he described metastases as "consequent cancers" that reached distant parts via lymphatic channels.

A more transitory hypothesis advocated particularly by the German Daniel Sennert and the Portuguese Zacutus Lusitanus early in the seventeenth century was that cancers, at least when ulcerated, were, like leprosy, contagious. Popular fear of the contagiousness of cancer persisted into the twentieth century. The first accurate etiologic observation about any cancer can be attributed to the London surgeon Percival Pott, who reported in 1775 that many men who had worked as chimney sweeps since boyhood and were routinely lowered into narrow chimneys suffered scrotal cancer. He linked this observation to the irritating effect of chronic contact with soot and thereby identified the first occupational cancer.

The impact of microscopy on cancer research came very slowly. Robert Hooke, the pioneering seventeenth-century microscopist who coined the term *cell,* thought that tissues were composed of fibers – a hypothesis that persisted into the nineteenth century. Not until after 1830, when Joseph J. Lister designed the first achromatic microscope lenses, did progress in histology begin, made mostly by German investigators. The first new concept, advanced by Theodor Schwann and supported by Johannes Mueller, was that all tissues were composed of microscopic cells, not fibrils. Yet the lymphatic theory was not easily abandoned, and cells were thought to derive from "blastema," which was organized from intercellular fluids. In 1854, however, Rudolph Virchow questioned the existence of the unidentified blastema, and in the following year he stated the principle that all cells originated from cells and postulated that neoplasms developed from immature cells. But even then the spread of cancer was considered to result from some sort of a humor rather than the dissemination of cells. In 1867 Edwin Klebs advanced the opinion that most cancers originated in epithelial tissues (carcinomas in modern terminology), and coincidentally, Wilhelm Waldeyer applied the old, previously unspecific term *sarcoma* to neoplasms that arose in connective tissues.

Despite these scientific developments, cancer research is usually viewed as a twentieth-century undertaking and, despite its antiquity, the disease itself is viewed as largely a twentieth-century phenomenon. As infectious ailments have receded, cancer, along with cardiovascular diseases, has been perceived to be the greatest single health problem facing the developed world. Actually, cancer presents a set of problems, because the term should be considered a collective noun. The World Health Organization has classified some 100 kinds of cancer depending on their sites of origin, a figure that may be too conservative.

It is generally estimated that some form of cancer will develop in one-third of the inhabitants of the industrialized world. Moreover, the probability is increasing. Less than two decades ago it was calculated that one in four would develop cancer – with even those odds prompting the charge that cancer represents the "failure of medicine" (Braun 1977). Certainly this seems to be the case when a comparison is made with medicine's triumphs against epidemic illnesses, which came one on top of the other after the advent of the germ theory. Although we are well into the second century since the beginnings of cell theory, cures for cancer have thus far largely eluded scientific medicine. Nor has Virchow's observation that irritants could summon forth cancerous cells proved very helpful in cancer prevention – although irritants are among the foci of cancer research today.

The concept of *autonomy* suggests that once a cell has become truly cancerous it is beyond bodily control. The concept was established around the turn of the century by Arthur Hanau, Leo Loeb, and Carl O. Jensen, who transplanted cancer cells into healthy animals and plants of the same species and observed the unrestrained growth of new cancers in the previously healthy hosts. Yet the fact that cancers, once established, can enter a stage of remission – sometimes permanently – argues that the body can rally to retard or even reverse previously uncontrolled cell proliferation.

Following these transplantations, the next advances in research were made when cancer was produced experimentally in plants and animals by the administration of various chemical, physical, and biological agents. These experiments revealed, for example, that some 150 different viruses cause tumors in living organisms, that ultraviolet light and X-rays as well as radioactive substances such as radium and uranium induce cancer, and that coal tars, dyes derived from them, and other substances can also induce the disease. Moreover, even natu-

Table II.6.1. *Ten most common invasive neoplasms and estimated new cases as percentage of all new cases in the United States, 1990*

Neoplasm	Percentage	Cases
Male		
Prostate	21.1	30,000
Lung	19.6	92,000
Colon	10.0	26,000
Bladder	6.9	6,500
Rectum	4.6	4,000
Non-Hodgkin's lymphomas	3.6	9,500
Leukemias	3.0	9,800
Kidney	2.9	6,100
Stomach	2.7	8,300
Pancreas	2.6	12,100
Total	77.0	204,300
Female		
Breast	28.8	44,000
Colon	11.1	27,300
Lung	10.6	50,000
Uterus	6.3	4,000
Rectum	4.0	3,600
Ovary	3.9	12,400
Non-Hodgkin's lymphomas	3.3	8,700
Pancreas	2.8	12,900
Cervix	2.6	6,000
Bladder	2.5	3,200
Total	75.9	172,100

Table II.6.2. *Deaths due to cancer as percentage of all deaths according to sex and age group, United States, 1986*

Age	Male (%)	Female (%)
1–14	10.0	11.6
15–34	5.9	14.0
35–54	21.4	41.0
55–74	30.2	34.6
75+	19.2	13.8
Total	22.7	21.8

Table II.6.3. *Most common cancers as causes of death from cancer, according to sex and age group, United States, 1986*

Age	Male Cancer	Percentage	Female Cancer	Percentage
1–14	Leukemia	37.0	Leukemia	35.6
15–34	Leukemia	18.5	Breast	18.8
35–54	Lung	34.4	Breast	30.8
55–74	Lung	39.2	Lung	23.3
75+	Lung	26.9	Colon and rectum	17.9

rally occurring substances in the body, such as the sex hormone estrogen, have been shown to cause cancer when given to experimental animals.

The extent to which the incidence of cancer is increasing is a complicated issue. It is predominantly an illness of middle age and, with the exception of a few forms, such as certain leukemias, it is relatively rare in children. Thus, people in the developed world, having escaped famine and epidemic disease, have had their life expectancy extended beyond 50 years of age into that age in which the frequency of cancers becomes increasingly high. Although a shift in the age distribution of a population affects the actual incidence of cancer, the statistics have also shown artifactual increases. These are due to vast improvements in the diagnostic techniques of endoscopy, imaging, and biochemistry that can now be used to detect many asymptomatic cancers and pathological techniques that facilitate the differentiation of neoplastic from inflammatory lesions, primary from secondary neoplasms, and so forth.

The following interpretation of the most recent

U.S. cancer statistics offers some quantification of the impact of the disease in relation to age, sex, and race (see Tables II.6.1 through II.6.4). The three most common cancers of men, those arising in the prostate, lung, and colon, comprise about 50 percent of new cases and 55 percent of deaths due to cancer. The three most frequently occurring cancers of women, breast, colon, and lung, also comprise about 50 percent of new cases and account for 50 percent of deaths. As a proportion of all deaths, those from cancer do not increase linearly with age. This is mainly because of the accidental deaths of children and young adults, on the one hand, and cardiovascular diseases in the elderly, on the other. Of deaths from cancer in women, the peak, 41.0 percent, occurs in the 35 to 54 age group. In contrast, men have a somewhat older average age of death with 30.2 percent in the 55 to 74 age group. Most of this difference is attributable to the difference in the age distribution of women with carcinoma of the breast and men with carcinoma of the prostate. Survival has improved variably from the 1960s to the 1980s. The

Table II.6.4. *Five-year survival rates by race in two time periods from principal malignant neoplasms in the United States*

Neoplasm	1960–5		1980–5	
	White	Black	White	Black
Lung	8	5	13	12
Breast (F)	63	46	76	64
Prostate	50	35	73	63
Colon	43	34	55	48
Bladder	53	24	78	56
Uterus	73	31	83	52
Ovary	32	32	38	38
Cervix	58	47	67	59
Rectum	38	27	53	39
Non-Hodgkin's lymphomas	31	?	51	44
Kidney	37	38	52	55
Leukemias	14	?	34	27
Stomach	11	8	16	19
Pancreas	1	1	3	5

Note: Data are percentages.
Source: Data through 1986 from state records of Connecticut, Hawaii, Iowa, New Mexico, Utah, and Atlanta, Detroit, Seattle–Puget Sound, San Francisco–Oakland.

greatest improvements have occurred in the treatment of stomach cancer in both sexes and in uterine cancer. Of the more common neoplasms, only lung cancer has increased in incidence in both sexes, as has carcinoma of the prostate in men. Survival was below 20 percent for four of the more common neoplasms in the 1960s (leukemias, stomach, lung, pancreas), and save for the leukemias, it remains below 20 percent. The explanation for the decrease in death from stomach cancer lies in a decline in its occurrence, not by a great improvement in therapeutic success. Survival generally has been and remains poorer for black than for white patients. In 1960 white patients had a 42 percent better chance than their black counterparts of survival following treatment of carcinoma of the uterus, a 29 percent better chance with carcinoma of the bladder, and a 17 percent better chance with carcinoma of the breast. In 1980 the greatest race-related survival differences were such that whites had the following better chances than blacks: carcinoma of the bladder, 22 percent; carcinoma of the uterus, 21 percent; and carcinoma of the rectum, 14 percent. These differences have often been attributed to the black population's poorer access to medical care. However, this is obscured by the fact that there do not seem to be race-related differences in survival of other relatively common carcinomas such as those of the lung, kidney, and stomach.

For the incidence of a disease to be considered meaningfully, it must be presented in age-specific terms. As the average age of a population increases and the proportion of an age group in which various cancers most commonly occur becomes larger, an increase in the number of cases is to be expected. This increase, however, can tend to blur the more important question of whether the incidence of that disease is increasing in a specific age group. The statistical analyst must also be cognizant of the impact of technological improvements on the finding of potential cases and the establishment of a diagnosis, as well as changes in interest in the disease in question and changes in access to medical care.

Moreover, the addition to or removal from the environment of a carcinogen is a convenient explanation for the waxing or waning of the occurrence of a cancer. In this regard the long latent period of most clinical cancers is often overlooked. For example, an argument used in the 1940s against the hypothesis that cigarette smoking was a major cause of lung cancer was that many more women were smoking than had previously been the case, yet no increase in lung cancer among women had occurred. Consequently, the relationship between smoking and lung cancer in men was viewed by some to be coincidental rather than causal. But of course, in retrospect we can see that most of the women in question had not yet smoked for a sufficient length of time for the result to become evident in cancer statistics. Perhaps future analysis will clarify in a similar fashion why gastric cancer is decreasing in the United States or why prostate cancer is increasing. Certainly one of the most difficult problems in identifying causes of cancer is that of cocarcinogenesis. The most flagrant example is the additive effect of the inhalation of both cigarette smoke and asbestos particles on the occurrence of lung cancer. Both of these agents are independently carcinogenic, and their combined effect greatly increases the incidence of the disease.

With regard to public health, the greatest problem of exogenous carcinogenesis today is not exposure to industrial pollutants, as many believe, but rather the use of tobacco products. Whereas cigarette smoke appears to exert the most potent carcinogenic effect, cigar smoke and chewing tobacco are also implicated. Historically, the possibility that an increase in lung cancer was related to an increase in cigarette smoking was first raised in Germany in the 1920s. In the United States interest in this question was stimulated in 1950 with the publication of three epidemiological studies, each of which showed that lung cancer patients were likely to be heavy smokers.

Although an epidemiological association cannot prove a causal relationship, the satisfaction of five criteria make such a connection highly probable: (1) The association between the suspected pathogen and the disease is observed consistently. (2) In comparison with suitable control groups, the association is strong. (3) The association is relatively specific with the disease in question. (4) The temporal relationship between exposure to the pathogen and the onset of the clinical disease is appropriate and consistent. (5) The association is consistent with a known or plausible explanation of the natural history of the disease.

Resistance to the acceptance of a causal relationship between smoking and the development of lung cancer was based initially on doubt that the incidence of lung cancer was actually increasing and then on a failure to appreciate the long preclinical phase of the disease. A massive prospective study of the effects of smoking on health published by E. C. Hammond and D. Horn in 1958 purported to show that smoking was not uniquely associated with lung cancer.

Similarly, the observation that cigarette smoking was associated with neoplasms of organs, such as the bladder, which did not come into contact with smoke, and with cardiovascular diseases was used by proponents of tobacco interests and some biostatisticians to cast doubt on a causal relationship between the inhalation of cigarette smoke and the development of lung cancer. This argument ignored the multiplicity of components of tobacco smoke, which could easily act differently on different tissues, and the clearly quantitative relationship between smoking and the increased probability of lung cancer developing. Nevertheless, lung cancer occurs in a small minority of even heavy smokers. This has been taken to indicate an intrinsic predisposition that, if identified, could be used to warn persons at risk. But investigations have thus far failed to yield useful results. Finally, there have been no reproducible experiments in which tobacco smoke has caused lung cancer in experimental animals. Although positive results would be convincing, negative results are attributable to species differences and, perhaps, insufficient duration of exposure.

Eight prospective studies of male cigarette smokers have shown an excess mortality from lung cancer in comparison with nonsmokers ranging from 3.8 to 14.2 percent (mode 11 percent). In four studies of women the excess was smaller, ranging from 2.0 to 5.0 percent. Despite the fact that no specific sufficiently potent pulmonary carcinogens have as yet been identified in tobacco smoke, a 1970s finding appears to clinch the causal relationship between smoking and the development of lung cancer. R. Doll and R. Peto (1976), in a 20-year investigation of the mortality of British physicians in relation to smoking, showed that the risk diminishes increasingly after smoking has been discontinued for several years. This obviously cannot be ascribed to genetic or psychological factors. However, even 15 years after cessation the risk among former smokers remained twice that of men of similar age who had never smoked.

Smoking has now been common among women long enough to be reflected in an alarming increase in the incidence of lung cancer. This began in the mid-1960s, and the incidence now is half that of men in the United States. As of 1986 the rate of death from lung cancer for U.S. women equaled that for breast cancer, which has remained stable. In the case of the latter disease it appears that, of the half-million women worldwide in whom breast cancer develops annually, half reside in North America and western Europe, which contain less than 20 percent of the world's population. However, it is hazardous to compare prevalence or even mortality statistics without knowing critical local circumstances. For example, why would the age-adjusted rate of death from breast cancer in Finland and Denmark be more than triple the rate in Sweden, and why would the rate in Scotland be quintuple that of England?

A daughter or sister of a woman with breast cancer has a nearly three times greater risk of developing this disease than a woman without such an association. The risk is greater if the relative's cancer was found at an early age, and a great deal more if both mother and sister have been affected. This suggests a genetically mediated predisposition, as does the increased risk of a secondary primary breast cancer as compared with the risk of a first occurrence. However, other observations indicate that environmental factors must also enter in. For example, the prevalence of breast cancer in Japan is about one-fourth that in northern Europe or North America. Nevertheless, among women of Japanese ancestry living in North America, the incidence of breast cancer by the second generation matches that of white North American women. Whether dietary or other potential cofactors are implicated remains unresolved.

Unfortunately, cancer statistics often reveal the complexities of the disease under investigation rather than causal explanations. Carcinoma of the prostate is the second most frequently occurring cancer among U.S. men; it is the fifth worldwide. This disease is more prevalent among U.S. blacks, despite their heterogeneity, than any other population that has been studied. It is about 80 percent more common in black than in white men in the United States. It is also common in black Caribbean populations, whereas sketchy information from Africa indicates much lower prevalences. Carcinoma of the prostate is 28 times as common among blacks in Atlanta as among Japanese in Osaka. Although the incidence appears to be low throughout the Orient, it is much higher among men of Chinese and Japanese extraction living in Hawaii.

The incidence of clinically evident prostate cancer is more highly correlated with increasing age above 50 than is any other neoplasm. It is six to seven times more prevalent in the 75 to 84 than the 55 to 64 age group, and the black–white difference in prevalence diminishes with increasing age. There is no convincing evidence of the pathogenicity of any industrial exposure for this neoplasm. However, an increased risk is associated with chronic cigarette smoking, and there appears to be a correlation between an above-average sexual drive and susceptibility to prostatic carcinoma. This could mean that a subtle alteration in the metabolism of sexual hormones has a predisposing role, but studies have yielded inconsistent results. Alternatively, men with a high sexual drive, particularly in a permissive culture, have an increased likelihood of exposure to multiple sexual partners. A correlation between promiscuity and prostatic carcinoma, if substantiated, would suggest an analogy to the better-documented correlation between promiscuity and carcinoma of the cervix in women and the possibility that a sexually transmitted virus is a pathogenetic agent. None of these hypotheses, however, explains the increase in the occurrence of this disease in the late 1900s.

With regard to possible roles of diet in carcinogenesis there has been particular interest in whether the presence or deficiency of certain components of food influences the development of colorectal cancer. Both diets low in fiber and high in fat have been proposed to be pathogenetic. Investigations have yielded conflicting results, but the best evidence now points to a carcinogenic effect of increased fat consumption, particularly in women. Colorectal cancer has been reported to be up to 10 times as common in central European countries as in tropical countries such as Peru, Ecuador, or Panama, but data from other countries conflict with these extreme examples.

Certainly the Westernizing of the Japanese diet has provided persuasive evidence of the carcinogenic role of fat. Nutrition surveys of 1955 and 1984 indicate that the fat intake of Japanese women increased by about 180 percent during these years and the mortality from colorectal cancer increased by about 130 percent. There was a lag of about 15 years between the beginning of the widespread dietary change and the beginning of the increase in death from this neoplasm. A recent U.S. study has also demonstrated an association between a high level of animal fat consumption and the occurrence of this neoplasm. The predominant hypothesis for this association is that, since a higher fat consumption increases the excretion of bile acids and the growth of colonic bacteria, the opportunity to convert bile acids into carcinogenic substances by bacterial metabolism is facilitated. In the United States the incidence of colorectal cancer has remained stable in white men and has decreased moderately in white women, but has increased in the black population. In addition to changes in incidence, an unexplained pathological change has been occurring: In U.S. patients the lesion is less commonly located in the rectum and more commonly found in the colon. It would be satisfying to conclude that this is a reflection of the increasingly frequent removal of premalignant lesions from the rectum, but medical intervention is an unlikely explanation.

One well-recognized environmental carcinogen is the ultraviolet component of sunlight, which is a major cause of skin cancers. Susceptibility is related to paleness and a poor ability to tan, as well as to chronic exposure to sunlight. The overall incidence of nonmelanoma skin cancers in the white U.S. population is about 165 per 100,000. However, the prevalence in Texas is about three times that in Iowa. The incidence of melanoma is only about 4 per 100,000, but 65 percent of the deaths attributed to skin cancers are caused by this disease. The lesion occurs twice as often on the legs of white women as on those of white men. It occurs nearly twice as frequently on the male trunk than the female trunk. This may reflect relative exposure to sunlight due to differences in clothing. Not only is melanoma uncommon in blacks, but its location tends to be different: It is more commonly found on palms or soles and within the mouth – less heavily pigmented areas. The incidence of melanoma has been found to be increasing wherever statistics have been kept. The highest incidence has been found in Arizona (16 per 100,000), where the disease has more than quadrupled in the brief period from 1969 to 1978. It also quadrupled in Connecticut from 1939 to 1972. The smallest increase has been observed in Sweden: 80 percent from 1957 to 1971. Consistent with the increased incidence, mortality has nearly doubled. Whether the increase of this lethal disease is attributable to changes in ultraviolet intensity due to atmospheric pollution is as yet unknown.

Turning to human cancers definitely attributable to "civilization," X-rays and related ionizing radiation are estimated to be the cause of no more than 3 percent of cancers. Exposure to radon gas has been clearly shown to be a cause of lung cancer in uranium miners. Although this is a small group at risk, if it were confirmed that the concentration of radon in some homes was sufficient to be carcinogenic, presumably the proportion of cases of cancer known to be due to radiation exposure would increase substantially. Thyroid cancer results from a small to moderate radiation exposure to the neck with a latency period of about a decade. A dose that is large enough to destroy the gland leaves no tissue to undergo neoplastic transformation. Bone marrow is another radiosensitive organ. The increased risk of developing leukemia, depending on dosage of radiation, begins as early as 2 years after exposure, reaches a peak probability after 6 to 8 years, and then diminishes. Fetuses and infants are particularly sensitive.

Suspicion of potential carcinogenesis has also fallen on synthetic food additives, such as dyes and flavoring agents, and contaminants, such as pesticides and fertilizers, either from direct spraying or from absorption of affected groundwater. Because of this suspicion, the Delaney amendment to the U.S. Food, Drug and Cosmetic Act was passed in 1958. The amendment requires the banning of food additives if they cause cancer in any species of experimental animal in any dosage. One result has been the forced withdrawal of some products based on quite dubious and unrealistic experiments. In view of the huge number of compounds, both synthetic and natural, to which people are exposed, usually in combinations having unknown interactions, deciding which ones to test and what tests are both relevant and practical is an insoluble problem.

Worldwide, stomach cancer, which has become relatively uncommon in the United States, is the most prevalent visceral cancer (second for men, fourth for women). Nevertheless, death rates have been declining since the 1930s to become only about 35 percent of what they were at that time. The de-

crease has been worldwide and for unexplained reasons. It remains the most prevalent carcinoma in East Asia, with the rate in Japan being more than seven times that in the United States, accounting for one-third of all cancer deaths on those islands. The repetitive ingestion of high concentrations of salt irritates the stomach lining, and this has been proposed as a potential cause of gastric cancer. In fact, the decline in the incidence of this disease has been correlated with the decline in the salt preservation of foods. In regions in which stomach cancer remains common, such as Japan, salted seafood has remained a dietary staple. The incidence of gastric cancer among first-generation immigrants from Japan to the West is similar to that in their communities of origin, but it declines to the incidence of the Western community in which the next generation resides. This suggests that the neoplastic process begins irreversibly during childhood, regardless of relocation or dietary changes after a certain age. Because this is not a genetically determined disease, a generation that has not been exposed to the inducing irritant of salt at a critical age presumably will not suffer inordinately from this neoplasm.

Carcinoma of the cervix appears not to be related to geography, but primarily to the sexual practices in a given region or subculture. The commencement of sexual intercourse during adolescence, multiple partners, or partners who have had numerous partners are all factors associated with an increased risk of developing the disease, as is a large number of pregnancies. Thus, carcinoma of the cervix is rare among nuns and common among prostitutes. A sexually transmitted virus is suspected to be a causative factor or cofactor. As with prostatic cancer, chronic cigarette smoking appears to increase the risk of occurrence of this neoplasm. Another peculiar difference, at least in the United States, is that carcinoma of the cervix occurs about twice as frequently among black as among white women, whereas carcinoma of the uterus occurs two to four times as often in white women.

Cancer of the liver is much more prevalent in many of the developing countries than in the industrialized world. Its incidence is highest in sub-Saharan Africa, China, southern Asia, and Japan (the exception among industrialized countries). China alone accounts for about 45 percent of the world's cases. The liver is subject to two principal types of cancer. One originates in liver cells, and a history of infection with the hepatitis B virus predisposes to this. The other originates in cells of the bile ducts. A predisposition to develop this form of cancer is caused by infestation with the liver fluke *Clonorchis sinensis* and related parasites. The geographic distribution of these parasites is reflected in the prevalence of this disease. Alcoholism has not been shown to be a major predisposing factor.

Other cancers in the developing world are associated with indigenous infectious agents and with cultural practices. Betel nut chewing, for example, is linked with high rates of oral cancer in central and southeast Asia and Kashmir; Bantu natives, who hold warming pans of charcoal against their bodies, are subject to cancers of the abdominal wall. The frequent occurrence of esophageal cancer has been related to the consumption of very hot beverages in some cultures. Burkitt's lymphoma, which occurs almost exclusively in central Africa and New Guinea, is probably caused by the Epstein–Barr virus in genetically predisposed individuals. Bladder cancer is a common problem in North Africa, and especially Egypt, because infestation with the parasite *Schistosoma haematobium* induces the disease.

In summary, the concept of cancer has evolved through the ages from that of a single disease to one of many diseases with many causes. Most prevalent are carcinomas of the stomach, lungs, breast, cervix, colon and rectum, prostate, and liver. Chief among carcinogens are irritants such as fumes of tobacco and certain metals, ionizing and ultraviolet radiation, specific chemical compounds, some helminthic parasites, and possibly viruses. Everyone is constantly bombarded by carcinogens of various potencies, but cancer develops in a minority of people. A few uncommon neoplasms clearly are genetically determined, but the degree of resistance to carcinogens also appears to have a genetic basis.

Yet even if cancer is viewed as multiple diseases with multiple causes, each disease involves the same phenomenon: an inadequately controlled division and multiplication of cells that can infiltrate adjacent tissues and, in many types, form distant secondary lesions. The factors that permit metastatic tumor cells to survive and implant remain just as mysterious as the factors that initiate the loss of control of cell division.

The available treatments are generally drastic and poorly selective of the foci of disease and, in many circumstances, not curative. Earlier diagnosis improves the cure rate of many but not all cancers. Therefore, public education about the signs of cancer and further improvements in the sensitivity of diagnostic methods should be sought. However, until our understanding of the fundamental biology of cancer improves, preventive measures, such as minimizing exposure to known carcinogens, will exert by far the greatest benefit to public health.

Thomas G. Benedek and Kenneth F. Kiple

Bibliography

Ackerknecht, Erwin H. 1965. *History and geography of the most important diseases.* New York.

Austoker, Joan. 1988. *A history of the Imperial Cancer Research Fund.* Oxford.

Boyle, P., C. S. Muir, and E. Grundmann, eds. 1989. *Cancer mapping.* New York.

Braun, Armin C. 1977. *The story of cancer: On its nature, causes, and control.* London.

Burnet, Macfarlane, and David O. White. 1972. *Natural history of infectious diseases,* 4th edition. Cambridge.

Cancer Research Campaign. 1988. Factsheet, Nos. 4–12. London.

Davis, Devra Lee. 1989. Natural anticarcinogens, carcinogens, and changing patterns in cancer: Some speculation. *Environmental Research* 50: 322–40.

Doll, R., and A. B. Hill. 1952. A study of the aetiology of carcinoma of the lung. *British Medical Journal.* 2: 1271–86.

  1954. The mortality of doctors in relation to their smoking habits. *British Medical Journal* 1: 1451–5.

Doll, R., and R. Peto. 1976. Mortality in relation to smoking: 20 years' observations on male British doctors. *British Medical Journal* 2: 1525–30.

  1981. *The causes of cancer: Quantitative estimates of avoidable risks of cancer in the United States today.* Oxford.

Elwood, J. M., and J. A. Lee. 1975. Recent data on the epidemiology of malignant melanoma. *Seminars in Oncology* 2: 149–53.

Ernster, V. L. 1988. Trends in smoking, cancer risk, and cigarette promotion. *Cancer* 62: 1702–12.

Greenberg, Michael. 1983. *Urbanization and cancer mortality: The United States experience, 1950–1975.* New York.

Haenszel, W., and M. Kurihara. 1968. Studies of Japanese migrants. I. Mortality from cancer and other diseases among Japanese in the United States. *Journal of the National Cancer Institute* 40: 43–68.

Hammond, E. C., and D. Horn. 1958. Smoking and death rates: Report on forty-four months of follow-up of 187,783 men. *Journal of the American Medical Association* 166: 1159–72.

Hirsch, August. 1886. *Handbook of geographical and historical pathology,* Vol. 3, trans. Charles Creighton. London.

Hippocrates. 1931. *Aphorisms VI,* trans. and ed. W. H. S. Jones. Cambridge.

Honda, G. D., L. Bernstein, R. K. Ross, et al. 1988. Vasectomy, cigarette smoking, and age at first sexual intercourse as risk factors for prostate cancer in middle-aged men. *British Journal of Cancer* 46: 1307–18.

Howe, G. Melvyn. 1977. *A world geography of human diseases*. London.

Jones, Lovell A., ed. 1989. *Minorities and cancer*. New York.

Luinsky, William. 1989. Environmental cancer risks – real and unreal. *Environmental Research* 50: 207–9.

McGrew, Roderick E. 1985. *Encyclopedia of medical history*. New York.

Miller, D. G. 1980. On the nature of susceptibility to cancer. *Cancer* 46: 1307–18.

Mills, P. K. et al. 1989. Cohort study of diet, lifestyle, and prostate cancer in Adventist men. *Cancer* 63: 598–604.

Muir, C. S. 1990. Epidemiology, basic science, and the prevention of cancer: Implications for the future. *Cancer Research* 50: 6441–8.

Natarajan, N., G. P. Murphy, and C. Mettlin. 1989. Prostate cancer in blacks: An update from the American College of Surgeons' patterns of care studies. *Journal of Surgical Oncology* 40: 232–6.

Parkin, D. M., E. Läärä, and C. S. Muir. 1988. Estimates of the worldwide frequency of sixteen major cancers in 1980. *International Journal of Cancer* 41: 184–97.

Patterson, James T. 1987. *The dread disease: Cancer and modern American culture*. Cambridge, Mass.

Preston-Martin, S., et al. 1990. Increased cell division as a cause of human cancer. *Cancer Research* 50: 7415–21.

Rather, L. J. 1978. *The genesis of cancer: A study in the history of ideas*. Baltimore.

Reedy, J. 1975. Galen on cancer and related diseases. *Clio Medica* 10: 227–38.

Satariano, W. A., and M. Swanson. 1988. Racial differences in cancer incidence: The significance of age-specific patterns. *Cancer* 62: 2640–53.

Silverberg, E., C. C. Boring, and T. S. Squires. 1990. Cancer statistics, 1990. *California Cancer Journal for Clinicians* 40: 9–25.

Swanson, G. M. 1988. Cancer prevention in the workplace and natural environment. *Cancer* 62: 1725–46.

Whittemore, A. S., and A. McMillan. 1983. Lung cancer mortality among U.S. uranium miners: A reappraisal. *Journal of the National Cancer Institute* 71: 489–505.

Willett, W. 1989. The search for the causes of breast and colon cancer. *Nature* 338: 389–94.

Willett, W., et al. 1990. Relation of meat, fat, and fiber intake to the risk of colon cancer in a prospective study among women. *New England Journal of Medicine* 323: 1644–72.

Wolff, Jacob. 1907. *The science of cancerous disease from earliest times to the present*, trans. Barbara Ayoub, 1989. Canton, Mass.

United States General Accounting Office. 1987. *Cancer patient survival: What progress has been made?* Washington, D.C.

Zarizde, S., and P. Boyle. 1987. Cancer of the prostate: Epidemiology and aetiology. *British Journal of Urology* 59: 493–502.

PART III

Medical Specialties and Disease Prevention

III.1
Genetic Disease

The idea that a particular physical feature, either normal or abnormal, is hereditary is probably as old as our species itself. However, as has been noted by many other writers, tracing the origins of an idea is a formidable, if not impossible, task. Clearly, the concept of "like begets like" found a practical expression in the early domestication of animals; breeding stock was chosen on the basis of favorable traits. The first tangible evidence that human beings had at least a glimmer of the notion of heredity can be found in the domestication of the dog some 10,000 years ago. Yet it is only in the past 100 years that we have begun to understand the workings of heredity.

This essay traces the development of the concept of heredity and, in particular, shows how that development has shed light on the host of hereditary and genetic diseases we have come to recognize in humans. It begins with a brief discussion of some basic concepts and terms, which is followed by an outline of the heuristic model of genetic transmission that has come to be the standard of modern medical genetics. Once this groundwork is in place, the history of the study of human genetic disease is developed from the earliest records, through the birth of medical genetics, to the molecular era. Naturally, a detailed narrative of this history would require several volumes. Therefore, some events and ideas have been omitted or treated only cursorily.

The most recent development in the study of human genetic diseases is traced through three specific examples. Each of these represents a microcosm of the development of medical genetics. Our understanding of the first of them, sickle cell anemia, represents a triumph of the molecular model of human disease. The discovery of the second, Down syndrome, reveals the role in medical genetics of the cytogeneticist, who studies chromosomes. The third, kuru, exemplifies a case in which the expectations of modern medical genetics led initially to an erroneous conclusion, although that failure led eventually to spectacular new knowledge. This essay closes with a brief assessment of the future development of medical genetics in the molecular era.

Some Operational Definitions

More often than not, when the term *hereditary* is applied to a particular trait, the natural inclination is to equate it with the term *genetic*. However, *hereditary* refers only to the sustained passage of a trait from generation to generation. Surnames, property, and titles may be hereditary by law or custom, but they are not genetic. We may regard a hereditary trait as genetic only when the passage of that trait from generation to generation is determined, at least in part, by one or more *genes*. In much the same way, the term *congenital* has often been equated with *genetic* when, in fact, this term signifies only that a trait is present at birth. A congenital trait is not necessarily genetic or even hereditary. Thus, the purview of medical genetics may be said to include those traits, both congenital and of delayed onset, whose origins lie in defects in single genes, in groups of genes, or in the size or number of the chromosomes.

A useful checklist for assessing whether a trait is genetically determined was provided by J. V. Neel and W. J. Schull (1954). A trait is genetically determined by the following:

1. It occurs *in definite proportions* among persons related by descent, when environmental causes have been ruled out.
2. It fails to appear in unrelated lines such as those of in-laws.
3. It displays a characteristic age of onset and course of development, in the absence of other known causes.
4. It shows greater concordance in monozygous (identical) twins than in dizygous (fraternal) twins.

When the role of chromosomal anomalies became fully appreciated in the 1960s, a fifth item was added to the checklist:

5. It consists of a characteristic suite of features (syndrome) coupled with a clearly demonstrated chromosomal abnormality (Thompson and Thompson 1980).

In the present era of molecular biology and recombinant DNA technology we must add yet another item to the list:

6. It is linked to a specific DNA sequence (probe) that has been mapped to a particular region of a chromosome.

Throughout the following discussions, traits that are regarded as genetic but not chromosomal, having met criteria 1 through 4 and 6 but not 5, are accompanied by a reference number. This number is the entry number of a given disorder in the catalog complied by V. A. McKusick (1986) of more than 3,000 Mendelian phenotypes in human beings. For example, the entry number for sickle cell anemia is 14190. An excellent reference for chromosomal conditions is E. Thurman (1986).

Models of Genetic Transmission

In recent years, medical geneticists have been supplied with a battery of sophisticated analytic tools to be used in conjunction with advanced laboratory techniques for determining the transmission of various traits. These analytic methods have been derived from what is now called the multifactorial (or mixed) model (see Morton 1982). According to this model the observed variation in a trait, such as the clinical presentation of a genetic disease or the liability to develop a complex disorder like heart disease, is determined by the joint effects of major gene loci and a background composed of multiple minor loci (a polygenic effect) and a nongenetic component (an environmental effect). A graphic representation of the multifactorial model is shown in Figure III.1.1. The most important difference between this model and earlier ones is that the nongenetic component is regarded as transmissible, as are genetic effects.

The impact of this model has been twofold. First, it has provided a theoretical underpinning for the field of genetic epidemiology (Morton and Chung 1978;

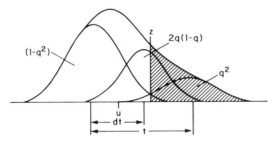

Figure III.1.1. Mixed model of liability for complex human disease. The abscissa reflects an arbitrary liability scale in which the left-most point is low risk and the right-most is high risk. Z is a threshold beyond which (shaded area) individuals will develop the disease in question. The effects of a single major locus are indicated by the frequency distributions of the alleles: $AA = (1 - q^2)$, $Aa = 2q(1 - q)$, and $aa = q^2$, where a is taken to be the disease gene. The presence of AA and Aa individuals beyond Z indicates the further effects of the multifactorial background, including nongenetic effects. The value u is the mean population liability, t the deviation in mean genotype-specific liability, and d the degree of dominance at the locus. (From Comings et al. 1984, with permission from the *American Journal of Human Genetics*.)

Morton 1982). Second, it has become a heuristic device through which clinical variation in the presentation of a disease can be assessed. After spending more than half a century studying the inheritance of complex traits, Sewall Wright (1968) concluded that there is a network of effects leading from the gene to the final outward manifestation, the *phenotype,* and that a number of basic generalizations can be made:

1. The variations of most characters are affected by a great many loci (the multiple-factor hypothesis).
2. In general, each gene replacement has effects on many characters (the principle of universal pleiotropy).
3. Each of the innumerable alleles at any locus has a unique array of differential effects in taking account of pleiotropy (uniqueness of alleles).
4. The dominance relation of two alleles is not an attribute of the alleles but of the whole genome and the environment. Dominance may differ for each pleiotropic effect and is in general easily modified (relativity of dominance).
5. The effects of multiple loci on a character in general involve much nonadditive interaction (universality of interaction effects).
6. Both ontogenetic homology and phylogenetic homology depend on calling into play similar chains of gene-controlled reactions under similar developmental conditions (homology).
7. The contributions of measurable characters to overall selective value usually involve interaction effects of the most extreme sort because of the usually intermediate position of the optimum grade, a situation that implies the existence of innumerable selective peaks (multiple selective peaks).

From this perspective one must say that no gene responsible for a human genetic disease exists in a developmental vacuum. It exists in a milieu composed of its own locus, its chromosomal position and close neighbors, the various effects of other genes elsewhere in the genome, the inter- and intracellular environment, and the external environment, both intra- and extrauterine, in which it ultimately finds expression. However, the mechanisms by which this multitude of effects operates are only just being discovered. This phase of the history of genetic disease has yet to be written.

History of the Study of Genetic Disease: From the Greeks to Garrod

As already stated, the idea that the features of parents could be transmitted to their offspring was applied very early in human history in the domestication of animals. Some of the knowledge of "good inheritance," the transmission of favorable features, undoubtedly came from observations of "bad inheritance." Thus, for some 10,000 years we have been aware to a greater or lesser degree that certain malformations and diseases are hereditary, if not genetic. However, only from the written records of ancestors can we reliably assess the state of their awareness regarding heredity.

Early History

By the time of the Greeks, ample evidence already existed that people were cognizant of heredity, both good and bad. Moreover, many Greek scholars speculated as to the mechanism of heredity. Nearly all of them had a theory of vertical transmission, but the theory promoted by Hippocrates survived until the Renaissance. Writing in the fourth century B.C., Hippocrates put forth the idea that each organ and tissue produced, in its turn, a specific component of semen. This composite semen was then transmitted to the woman through coitus, whereupon it incubated to become a human baby. This, of course, included the good *and* the bad:

... of the semen, however, I assert that it is secreted by the whole body – by the solid as well as by the smooth parts, and by the entire humid matters of the body. . . . The semen is produced by the whole body, healthy by healthy parts, sick by sick parts. Hence when as a rule, baldheaded beget baldheaded, blue-eyed beget blue-eyed, and squinting, squinting; and when for other maladies, the same law prevails, what should hinder that longheaded are begotten by longheaded. (Hippocrates in Vogel and Motulsky 1979)

Note that in this single passage Hippocrates accounts for the inheritance not only of desirable traits but of the abnormal and undesirable as well, and by the same mechanism. So powerful was the idea of heredity among the Greeks that many scholars felt the need to warn against unfavorable unions. Thus did the sixth-century B.C. scholar Theognis lament:

We seek well bred rams and sheep and horses and one wishes to breed from these. Yet a good man is willing to marry an evil wife, if she bring him wealth: nor does a woman refuse to marry an evil husband who is rich. For men reverence money, and the good marry the evil, and the evil the good. Wealth has confounded the race. (Theognis in Roper 1913)

Clearly, Theognis believed that marriage for the sake of money would cause the race to sink into mediocrity and greed.

The traits commented on by the Greeks when discussing heredity were usually abstract qualities such as good and evil or desirable normal characteristics such as eye color, strength, speed, and beauty. Of course, they also took notice of the shocking and fantastic, gross malformations, or severe illness. Empedocles suggested in the fifth century B.C. that the cause of *monsters,* as grossly malformed infants came to be called, was an excess or deficit of semen. Many other writers held similar views, which presumably became part of the hereditary theory of Hippocrates. The treatment of infants with abnormalities was roughly the same everywhere in the ancient world. They either were left to die or were killed outright. Often, the mother suffered the same fate as her offspring. The practice of destroying abnormal infants was advocated by Hippocrates, Plato, Aristotle, and virtually all others whose works on the subject have survived. Yet the practice was not universal, as evidenced by the mummy of an anencephalic (20650) infant at Hermopolis. The archaeological evidence suggests that this baby, who would have been stillborn or died shortly after birth, was an object of worship (Glenister 1964).

The physical, mechanistic interpretation of the causes of birth defects was modified by the somewhat more mystical Roman frame of mind. In the first century A.D., Pliny the Elder wrote that mental impressions resulting from gazing on likenesses of the gods during pregnancy were sufficient to produce monsters. Indeed, the root of the word *monster* is the Latin word *monere,* "to warn." Thus, such children were regarded as warnings from the gods transmitted to pregnant women. J. W. Ballantyne (1902) related the circumstances of a black queen of ancient Ethiopia who presented her husband, the black king, with a white child. It was concluded that the queen had gazed on a white statue of the goddess Andromeda during the early stages of her pregnancy. The description of the white infant, however, leads one to suspect that it was an albino (20310), particularly given the propensity for royalty to marry close relatives.

The decline of reason that marked the Middle Ages was reflected in interpretations of the birth of malformed infants. T. W. Glenister (1964) notes that such children were called "Devil's brats" and were generally believed to have been conceived in a union with Satan. As was the case with any perceived deviation from piety, the fate of both infant and mother was quickly and ruthlessly determined. Late in the Middle Ages, however, the rise of astrology sometimes made for surprising outcomes. For example, when in the beginning of the thirteenth century a deformed calf said to be half human in its appearance was born, the cowherd was immediately accused of having committed an unnatural act, the punishment for which was burning at the stake (Glenister 1964). Fortunately for the cowherd it was pointed out that a particular conjunction of the planets had recently occurred, a conjunction that was often the cause of oddities of nature. The cowherd's life was spared.

As the Renaissance dawned, reason returned to the writing of discourses on heredity and failed heredity. Scholarly works of the classical era were rediscovered, and the development of a science of heredity was once again underway. A curious episode occurred a few years after the death of Leonardo da Vinci in 1519. A half-brother of Leonardo conducted an experiment in an attempt to produce a second Leonardo. The half-brother, Bartolommeo, who was 45 years younger than the great artist and scholar, tried to recreate the exact circumstances of Leonardo's birth. Leonardo was the illegitimate son of Fiero, a notary of Vinci, and a peasant girl of the same city named Caterina. Bartolommeo, a notary by trade, moved to Vinci, whereupon he sought out a peasant girl much like Caterina. He found one and married her, and she bore him a son, whom they named Piero. One author notes the following:

Bartolommeo had scarcely known his brother whose spiritual heir he had wanted thus to produce and, by all accounts, he almost did. The boy looked liked Leonardo, and was brought up with all the encouragement to follow his footsteps. Pierino da Vinci, this experiment in heredity, became an artist and, especially, a sculptor of some talent. He died young. (Ritchie-Calder in Plomin et al. 1980)

As the foregoing passage indicates, the Rennaisance saw a revival of the principles of heredity. The writings of Hippocrates and Aristotle were translated and amplified by medical scholars such as Fabricius ab Aquapendente and his pupil William Harvey. In addition, there was a growing interest in rare and unusual medical cases. Weeks before his death in 1657, William Harvey wrote a letter of reply to a Dutch physician's inquiry about an unusual case in which he counseled, "Nature is nowhere accustomed more openly to display her secret mysteries than in cases where she shows traces of her workings apart from the beaten path" (in Garrod 1928).

For Harvey and others, rare pathology was not a source of revulsion or the workings of Satan but, rather, a subject demanding study and understanding. In 1882, Sir James Paget made a similar appeal on behalf of the study of rare disorders: "We ought not to set them aside with ideal thoughts and idle words about 'curiosities' or 'chances.' Not one of them is without meaning; not one that might not become the beginning of excellent knowledge." He went on to speak of new diseases that "are due mainly to morbid conditions changing and combining in transmission from parents to offspring."

The debt owed to scholars such as Harvey was acknowledged in the twentieth century, when medical genetics was coming into full bloom. Archibald Garrod, the father of human biochemical genetics, of whom we will hear more, paid homage to his intellectual ancestor: "It is rather, as Harvey saw so clearly, because we find in rare diseases the keys to note a few dark places of physiology and pathology, that I recommend them to you as objects of study" (Garrod 1928).

The Forgotten Origins of Medical Genetics

With the Enlightenment the floodgates to inquiry were opened for medical scientists and progress was made on nearly all fronts in understanding pathology. However, in spite of eloquent writings on heredity in general and on rare cases in particular, few references to specific genetic diseases were made before the twentieth century. Yet among those few instances are to be found brilliant insights.

Between 1745 and 1757 the French natural philosopher Pierre Louis Moreau de Maupertuis conducted studies on the heredity of polydactyly (the condition of having more than the normal number of fingers and/or toes; 26345). Maupertuis published a four-generation pedigree of polydactyly and commented, "That peculiarity of the supernumerary digits is found in the human species, extends to the entire breeds [races]; and there one sees that it is equally transmitted by the fathers and by the mothers" (Glass 1947).

He based his theory of heredity on these studies and suggested that *particles* of inheritance were *paired* in the "semens" of the father and the mother and that "there could be . . . arrangements so tenacious that from the first generation they dominate" (Glass 1947). This led him to suggest that hereditary pathologies were accidental products of the semen. In other words, he correctly predicted genes, dominance, and mutation. In addition, he estimated the probability of polydactyly at 1 per 20,000 by his own survey and noted that the chance of a joint occurrence of an affected parent and an affected offspring was 1 per 400,000,000 and that of an affected grandparent, parent, and offspring in sequence was 1 per

8,000,000,000,000 if the disorder was not hereditary. This made the probability of his four-generation family being chance so small as to be immediately dismissed. Here, then, was also the first use of statistics in a study of heredity.

Various sex-linked, or X-linked, disorders such as color blindness (30370) and hemophilia (30670) were accurately described in the late eighteenth and early nineteenth centuries. A German physician and professor of medicine, Christian F. Nasse, presented in 1820 a detailed pedigree of X-linked, recessive hemophilia and noted:

All reports on families, in which a hereditary tendency toward bleeding was found, are in agreement that bleeders are persons of male sex only in every case. . . . The women from those families transmit this tendency from their fathers to their children, even when they are married to husbands from other families who are not afflicted with this tendency. This tendency never manifests itself in women. (Vogel and Motulsky 1979)

Perhaps the most remarkable instance before the work of Gregor Johann Mendel (which although published in 1866 had to await rediscovery until the beginning of the twentieth century) was an 1814 publication by British physician Joseph Adams (Motulsky 1959). In this study, the author drew a distinction between familial diseases, which he considered to be confined to a single generation, and hereditary diseases, which he noted were passed on from generation to generation. Moreover, Adams defined congenital disorders as ones appearing at birth and regarded them to be more likely familial than hereditary. He observed that familial inherited diseases were often very severe, so much so that subsequent transmission from the affected individual was ruled out by early death. These conditions increased among the offspring because of mating between close relatives and were often to be seen in isolated districts where inbreeding was common. Clearly, from a modern perspective, Adams's familial diseases were what we term recessive and his hereditary diseases were what we term dominant.

Adams also concluded that hereditary diseases (in the modern sense) were not always to be found at birth but might have later ages of onset, that correlations existed among family members with regard to the clinical features of a hereditary disease, and that hereditary diseases might be treatable. Adams hinted at the phenomenon of mutation when he remarked that a severe disease would last only a single generation were it not for the fact that normal parents occasionally produced offspring in whom the

disease originated. Finally, he called for the establishment of hereditary disease registers that could be used for the study of these diseases: "That to lessen anxiety, as well as from a regard to the moral principle, family peculiarities, instead of being carefully concealed, should be accurately traced and faithfully recorded" (Adams 1814, in Motulsky 1959).

The Impact of Mendelism

The story of the discovery of the basic hereditary laws of segregation and independent assortment by the Austrian monk Mendel and of their subsequent independent rediscovery by Carl Correns, Hugo de Vries, and Erich von Tschermak some 35 years later has been told many times (e.g., Olby 1966; Stern and Sherwood 1966). Mendel, conducting experiments in hybridization with the common garden pea, *Pisum sativum*, in his garden at the Augustinian monastery in Brno, Czechoslovakia, demonstrated that alternative hereditary "characters" for a single trait segregated from one another each generation and that the characters for multiple traits assorted independently in each generation. Moreover, the observed distribution of characters for multiple traits followed a precise mathematical formulation – a binomial series. Mendel reported his results to the Natural Science Association of Brno in 1865. His written report was published the following year, but almost no attention was paid to it until 1899.

By that time, however, numerous investigators were pursuing experiments in heredity, and many of them had chosen simple plants as their experimental systems. Professor Hugo de Vries, a Dutch botanist, studying hybridization, came upon a reprint of Mendel's report, where he found the solution to the problems he had been working on. Thus, while he had independently derived his own formulation of the law of segregation, he reported the Mendelian results as well and stressed their importance in a 1900 publication (Olby 1966). At the same time, both the German botanist Correns and the Austrian botanist von Tschermak independently discovered the Mendelian laws and recognized their significance. All three published translations of Mendel's paper and commented on the laws therein. That these papers opened the new field of genetics and put it on a sound analytic footing from the outset is undeniable. However, as we will see, the translation by de Vries had an almost immediate impact on the study of human genetic disease.

The English biologist William Bateson was also interested in plant hybridization. However, his interest stemmed from the fact that, as an ardent advocate of evolution, he was unable to reconcile his belief that hereditary variation was discontinuous with the Darwinian model of evolution through selection on continuous variation. Bateson thus had spent years searching for a mechanism for discontinuous traits (Carlson 1966). Then in 1900 he read de Vries's account of Mendel's experiments. As E. A. Carlson (1966) notes, Bateson called the moment when he recognized the importance of Mendel's work "one of the half dozen most emotional moments of his life." In Mendel's work, Bateson believed he had found the mechanism for discontinuous variation for which he had searched. Shortly after this time, Bateson mistakenly championed Mendelism as an alternative to Darwinism, a position that haunted him the rest of his life (Sturtevant 1966). In 1901, however, Bateson, as we shall see, made an almost offhand comment that turned out to be a fundamental contribution to the study of human genetic diseases.

In 1897 Sir Archibald E. Garrod, a member of the staff of London's St. Bartholemew's Hospital, came upon and was intrigued by a case of alkaptonuria (20350). Alkaptonuria is a nonfatal disorder, present at birth, that is characterized by the excretion of homogentisic acid in the urine, which turns the urine dark upon standing. The disorder is often accompanied in later years by arthritis and a black pigmentation of cartilage and collagenous tissues. At the time that Garrod was diagnosing his first case of alkaptonuria it was believed that the condition was infectious and that the excretion of homogentisic acid was the result of bacterial action in the intestine. Garrod, however, refused to accept this view, believing instead that the condition was a form of abnormal metabolism (Harris 1963). He published this theory in 1899 along with the contention that the error of metabolism was congenital (Garrod 1899.

Less than a year later Garrod made what would prove to be his crucial observation. He noted that, among four families in which all alkaptonuric offspring had two unaffected parents, three of the parental pairs were first cousins. In 1901 he wrote in the *Lancet:*

The children of first cousins form so small a section of the community, and the number of alkaptonuric persons is so very small, that the association in no less than three out of four families can hardly be ascribed to chance, and further evidence bearing upon this point would be of great interest.

This circumstance would hardly have surprised Garrod's fellow countryman and physician Joseph Adams, who, it should be remembered, had made a similar observation about inbreeding nearly 90 years earlier. William Bateson read the paper and discussed its conclusions with Garrod. Bateson recognized that the pathology was discontinuous, all or none, affected or normal. Moreover, the high incidence of consanguinity and the characteristic familial pattern of normal, consanguinous parents having affected offspring were precisely what would be expected were the abnormality determined by a rare, recessive Mendelian character. Bateson commented on the case in a footnote in a 1902 report to the Evolution Committee of the Royal Society with E. R. Saunders:

Now there may be other accounts possible, but we note that the mating of first cousins gives exactly the conditions most likely to enable a rare and usually unseen recessive character to show itself . . . first cousins will frequently be bearers of *similar* gametes, which may in such unions meet each other, and thus lead to the manifestation of the peculiar recessive characters in the zygote.

In Bateson's interpretation of the situation, Garrod saw the solution to the problem of alkaptonuria. Garrod published the landmark paper "The Incidence of Alkaptonuria: A Study in Chemical Individuality" in 1902, adding further clinical data and incorporating the hereditary mechanism proposed by Bateson. Therein he reported on nine families of alkaptonuries and noted:

It will be noticed that among the families of parents who do not themselves exhibit the anomaly a proportion corresponding to 60 per cent are the offspring of marriages of first cousins.

However, he continued:

There is no reason to suppose that mere consanguinity of parents can originate such a condition as alkaptonuria in their offspring, and we must, rather seek an explanation in some peculiarity of the parents, which may remain latent for generations, but which has the best chance of asserting itself in the offspring of the union of two members of a family in which it is transmitted.

Garrod (1902) suggested that the laws of heredity discovered by Mendel and relayed to him by Bateson offered an explanation of the disorder as an example of a Mendelian recessive character and, thus,

there seems to be little room for doubt that the peculiarities of the incidence of alkaptonuria and of conditions which appear in a similar way are best explained by supposing that . . . a peculiarity of the gametes of both parents is necessary.

Here Garrod had already gone beyond alkapton-uria to include the possibility of other disorders sharing the same hereditary mechanism. Indeed, Garrod did go on to study cystinuria (22010), albinism (20310), and pentosuria (26080) and to put them all in the same class with alkaptonuria.

In 1908 Garrod delivered the Croonian Lectures to the Royal College of Physicians. To these lectures, and to the four disorders on which they were based, Garrod gave the name "Inborn Errors of Metabolism." The impact of Mendelism was fully felt by then, and there were few who doubted that these and other diseases were due to Mendelian characters. Garrod then went on to the next stage of the study of inborn errors, by noting in the case of alkaptonuria that

we may further conceive that the splitting of the benzene ring in normal metabolism is the work of a special enzyme, that in congenital alkaptonuria this enzyme is wanting, whilst in disease its working may be partially or even completely inhibited.

He was suggesting that the pathology of inborn errors of metabolism consisted of a blockade at some point in the normal pathway and that this blockade was caused by the congenital deficiency or absence of a specific enzyme (Harris 1963). The truth of his insight is evidenced by the metabolic pathways shown in Figure III.1.2. Clearly, Garrod believed that these deficiencies were transmitted as Mendelian characters, or determinants, and that the study of the families, particularly those in which inbreeding was known or suspected, was crucial to obtaining new insights into old disease entities.

The principal tenet of inborn errors of metabolism, that transmitted enzymic defects cause disease, eventually led to the "one gene–one enzyme" hypothesis (Beadle 1945) and to the theory of gene action. In 1950 G. W. Beadle called Garrod the "father of chemical genetics" (Harris 1963).

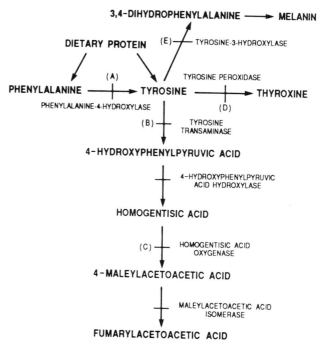

Figure III.1.2. A representation of metabolic pathways involving the amino acid tyrosine. These pathways are linked to no fewer than six genetic diseases of the type envisioned by Garrod. (A) A defect in the gene coding for phenylalanine-4-hydroxylase results in the recessive disorder phenylketonuria (26160). (B) A defect in the gene coding for tyrosine transaminase results in the rare disease tyrosinosis (27680), whereas a defect at the next step involving 4-hydroxyphenylpyruvic acid hydroxylase leads to the much more serious disorder tyrosinemia (27660). (C) The metabolic lesion suggested by Garrod for alkaptonuria is in fact a defect in the gene coding for homogentisic acid oxygenase. (D) A form of goitrous cretinism (27470) is caused when there is a lesion involving the enzyme tyrosine peroxidase. (E) Another of Garrod's original defects, albinism, arises when the gene for tyrosine-3-hydroxylase is defective. To date, more than 500 such disorders are known to exist in humans. Some are vanishingly rare, but others, such as phenylketonuria, are quite common (From McKusick 1986).

The Modern Era of Medical Genetics: Three Examples of "Excellent Knowledge"

From our contemporary perspective, the work and insights of Garrod are landmarks. There can be no doubt that the incorporation of the Mendelian laws of heredity into the study of human diseases was the turning point in the history of medical genetics. Surprisingly, however, Garrod's theories and suggestions went largely unnoticed for several decades. One reason for this slow recognition, according to H. Harris (1963), was that it was quite impossible at the time Garrod was writing for most geneticists to reduce Mendel's laws to purely chemical phenomena. Indeed, in the earliest days of the rediscovery of Mendel much of the effort being expended in formal genetics was devoted to coming to terms with a growing list of exceptions to those laws (Carlson 1966).

This is not to say that medical genetics had been put on hold until the middle of the twentieth century. In fact, progress in understanding the hereditary nature of numerous human diseases was being made, but it did not truly come together until the middle of this century. Two disorders that contributed greatly to this progress were sickle-cell anemia and Down syndrome.

The Triumph of the Molecular Model: Sickle-Cell Anemia

G. J. Brewer (1985) has commented that sickle cell anemia (14190) is one of the most fascinating diseases in medicine. And this one disease may be credited with having ushered in the era of molecular medicine.

The first case of sickle-cell anemia was reported in 1910 by a Chicago physician, J. B. Herrick. Upon his examination of a young black man from Grenada, West Indies, he found, among other features, "a secondary anemia not remarkable for the great reduction in red corpuscles or hemoglobin, but strikingly atypical in the large number of nucleated red corpuscles of the normoblastic type and in the tendency of the erythrocytes to assume a slender sickle-like shape" (Herrick 1910). Herrick had never before encountered a similar abnormality and reported:

Whether the blood picture represents merely a freakish poikilocytosis or is dependent on some peculiar physical or chemical condition of the blood, or is characteristic of some particular disease, I cannot at present answer. I report some details that may seem non-essential, thinking that if a similar blood condition is found in some other case a comparison of clinical conditions may help in solving the problem. (Herrick 1910)

Soon after, a similar case was reported, and within a very few years, the first fully scientific investigation of the sickling phenomenon was described. That study, published in 1917 by V. E. Emmel, was based on the case of a young black woman in St. Louis. The patient had an ulceration on her leg and severe anemia, and "instead of the typical rounded disk form, about one-third of the corpuscles are greatly elongated in shape. A large percentage of the latter have a rounded, rod-like shape with more or less tapered ends, and as a rule present a curved or crescentic form" (Emmel 1917). Emmel was the first to show that the sickling of the red cells was developmental, with seemingly normal, enucleate red cells undergoing the sickling change as they matured. He further showed that none of the red cells from controls or from any other type of anemia or leukemia could be induced to sickle. However, Emmel did find that a small proportion of the red cells from the patient's father, who was not anemic, did undergo sickling in cell culture conditions.

Curiously, even though the father of the patient showed traces of the sickling trait and three of the patient's siblings had died at an early age of severe anemia, Emmel made no reference to a possible hereditary component in the disorder. The first such suggestion was offered six years later by J. G. Huck (1923). In addition to reporting the first large clinical sample, 17 patients, Huck displayed the pedigrees of two sickle-cell families. In one of these families, *both* parents were affected but had produced one normal offspring in addition to two affected offspring. The significance of these families was noted: "Apparently the 'sickle cell' condition in man is inherited according to the Mendelian law for the inheritance of a single factor." Moreover, "one interesting feature of this inheritance is the fact that the sickle cell condition is dominant over the normal condition" (Huck 1923). Over the course of 13 years, reports of a unique pathological finding had led to the recognition of a hereditary disease – sickle-cell anemia.

After this good start, the study of sickle-cell anemia slowed dramatically – partly because most investigators failed to recognize a fundamental difference between sickle-cell anemia and the nonanemic sickle-cell trait. Most believed that the latter was merely the dormant stage of the former. In 1933 L. W. Diggs and his colleagues suggested that this interpretation was incorrect. They showed that the percentages of hemoglobin determinations among black schoolchildren with the sickle-cell trait were not different from those of controls. In addition, no significant pathology appeared to be associated with the sickle-cell trait. Clearly this meant that "the importance of the sickle cell trait appears to be limited to the relatively small grooup who in addition to the trait have sickle cell anemia" (Diggs et al. 1933).

As the distinction between the trait and the anemia became fully accepted, the pace of research on sickle-cell anemia quickened, and in 1949 two milestones were reached almost simultaneously. First, two investigators independently discovered the correct mechanism of inheritance of the trait and the anemia. One of these, a medical officer serving in what was then Rhodesia, compiled several large Bantu pedigrees of the sickle-cell trait. In one he observed two affected parents having a child with sickle-cell anemia. From his studies he concluded that the sickle-cell trait appears as a heterozygote with the normal allele, whereas sickle-cell anemia is the homozygous state of the sickle-cell gene, meaning that it must be inherited from both parents (Beet 1949).

Second, J. V. Neel (1949) reported precisely the same conclusion based on a more statistical analysis. These findings led to the recognition that the vast majority of dominant genetic diseases are heterozygous. The first report on the implications of an altered molecule in the pathogenesis of a human disease should probably be credited to M. Hoerlin and G. Weber, a German physician and a medical student, respectively, who wrote in 1947 that the condition known as methemoglobinemia (14170) was due to a "variant of the globin component of the hemoglobin molecule" (Heller 1969). However, the report that is celebrated is that of L. Pauling and colleagues (1949). Through a set of meticulous experiments they were able to show that the hemoglobin molecules in individuals with sickle-cell anemia and those in normal controls were fundamentally different but, "having found that the electrophoretic mobilities of sickle-cell hemoglobin and normal hemoglobin differ, we are left with the considerable problem of locating the cause of the difference" (Pauling et al. 1949).

They predicted that the abnormality would be found in the globin part of the molecule and not in the heme groups, that the sickling process involved abnormal interactions of altered molecules, and that the alteration resulted in two to four more net positive charges per molecule. Their predictions, we know, were all correct, as was shown by V. M. Ingram in 1956. Denatured sickle-cell hemoglobin (HbS), digested with trypsin, was compared with normal hemoglobin (HbA) after sequential electrophoresis and partition chromatography (Figure III.1.3). The abnormal HbS differed in only one "spot" on the filter, which had a net positive charge. Within three years it was demonstrated that the charge was caused by the alteration of a single amino acid through a mutation (Ingram 1959).

Since the moment the puzzle of sickle-cell anemia was solved, the study of mutant globins and their associated disorders has signaled nearly every major advance in molecular biology. In 1978 R. M. Lawn and colleagues and Y. W. Kan and A. M. Dozy independently demonstrated the first human restriction fragment length polymorphisms (RFLPs) in the region of the beta-chain of the hemoglobin molecule. This led to the explosion of recombinant-DNA-based studies on human genetic diseases as well as human gene mapping (Willard et al. 1985). The discovery of highly repetitive DNA sequences in globin genes has resulted in the development of the hypervariable "minisatellite" and VNTR (variable number of tandem repeat) DNA probes (Jeffreys et al. 1985, 1986; Nakamura et al. 1987). In addition, the use of other recombinant DNA techniques in the molecular

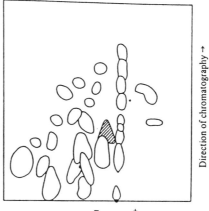

Direction of chromatography →

− +
Sickle-cell hemoglobin

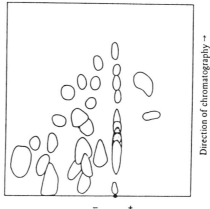

Direction of chromatography →

− +
Normal hemoglobin

Figure III.1.3. The original two-dimensional chromatographic spreads of normal and sickle-cell hemoglobins. The different "spot" having a net positive charge is seen to have moved further left in the electrophoretic field, toward the negative pole. The alteration in the pattern represents the substitution of the amino acid valine for glutamic acid. (From Ingram 1956, with permission; copyright 1956 by Macmillan Journals Limited.)

diagnosis of genetic diseases was pioneered with HbS by Kan and Dozy (1978) and is now being applied to a wide range of disorders, including cancer and acquired infectious diseases (Caskey 1987).

The Arrival of Cytogenetics: Down Syndrome

The chromosome theory of heredity, that the Mendelian characters were contained in the chromosomes, developed soon after the rediscovery of Mendel's laws and was in large measure a direct result of the precision of Mendel's own experimental observations. W. S. Sutton had observed a very high degree of organization of the chromosomes of the orthopteran genus *Brachystola*. He concluded that the parallels between the organization and behavior of the chromosomes and the laws of segregation and independent assortment could not be due to chance: "We have reason to believe that there is a definite relation between chromosomes and allelomorphs or unit characters" (Peters 1959). Sutton proposed that multiple characters would be found on a single chromosome and made a direct reference to genetic linkage: "If then, the chromosomes permanently retain their individuality, it follows that all allelomorphs represented by any one chromosome must be inherited together" (Peters 1959).

Spurred by the work of Sutton and others interested in chromosomes, T. H. Morgan and a group of his students at Columbia University began to study the inheritance of unit characters, the individual factors of Mendelian transmission (Allen 1978; Carlson 1981). Using the fruit fly *Drosophila* as their experimental model, Morgan and his students made a series of fundamental discoveries that led, by 1914, to their conclusion that the Mendelian factors, or genes, were physical entities present in the chromosomes in a *linear* manner (Sturtevant 1913; Morgan 1914).

In 1923 T. S. Painter suggested that the number of human chromosomes was 48, and this became the accepted number for the next 23 years. Improved cytological techniques eventually led to better resolution of the chromosomes, with the result that J. H. Tjio and A. Levan (1956) established that the correct number of human diploid chromosomes was $2n = 46$. So strong had been the belief in Painter's estimate that, as Tjio and Levan themselves noted, a previous study by another group had been abandoned because "the workers were unable to find all the 48 human chromosomes in their material; as a matter of fact, the number 46 was repeatedly counted in their slides" (Tjio and Levan 1956). (Clearly, an open mind is as important as good technique.)

It was not long after the number of human chromosomes was established that the solution to an old and curious medical puzzle became apparent. A condition called *furfuraceous idiocy* had been described in 1846 by the French physician E. Séguin. The traits marking the syndrome included characteristic facial features, slow and incomplete growth, and mental retardation. J. Langdon Down ascribed these traits to the Mongol type in 1867: "A very large number of congenital idiots are typical Mongols. So marked is this, that when placed side by side, it is difficult to believe that the specimens are not children of the same parents" (Down 1867).

From this publication the term *Mongolian idiot* replaced the previous name for the condition, and later the term *Down syndrome* became interchange-

able with it. For the next 92 years repeated studies of Down syndrome failed to produce a viable etiologic hypothesis. L. S. Penrose (1939) summarized the state of knowledge by noting that the disorder had failed to meet Mendelian expectations, though some had favored "irregular dominance" as an explanation, and that the only clear and stable correlate was late maternal age. Penrose (1939) ended his paper by suggesting that "Mongolism and some other malformations may have their origin in chromosome anomalies." Two decades later the improvements in cytological techniques that allowed the correct number of human diploid chromosomes to be determined also provided the solution to Down syndrome. In 1959 three French cytologists, led by J. Lejeune (1959), announced that patients with Down syndrome had an extra chromosome, which was one of the small telocentric chromosomes later designated as chromosome 21 (Figure III.1.4).

This first example of a human disorder caused by a specific chromosome anomaly in which there existed at least one triploid chromosome in an otherwise diploid set (now called trisomy) led to a spate of similar findings. These included Turner's syndrome (caused by the lack of one X-chromosome-XO), Kleinfelter's syndrome (XXY), trisomy 13, and trisomy 18 (Thurman 1986). In 1960 the first international congress was called, in Denver, Colorado, to establish a standardized cytogenetic nomenclature. Much of the impetus came from the discovery of chromosome banding techniques by which each chromosome could be identified individually. Over time these techniques have been refined to the point where subbands and regions within them can be identified (Thurman 1986). However, even with these refinements it has only recently been possible to study directly what specific regions of chromosome 21 are responsible for the Down syndrome phenotype.

As has been the case with sickle-cell anemia and many other human diseases, recombinant DNA technology has enabled researchers to study Down syndrome with greater detail and precision. Chromosome 21 contains less than 2 percent of the DNA in the human genome, yet with an estimated 50,000 genes in the genome (Shows, Sakaguchi, and Naylor 1982), it probably houses 1,000 genes. By means of recombinant DNA and related techniques, more than 20 of those genes, along with nearly 50 anonymous sequences, have been mapped (see Figure III.1.4). Among the mapped genes is one that codes for a ribosomal RNA (RNR-4, 18045). In addition, several genes of medical interest are known. These include the gene for the enzyme cystathionine beta-

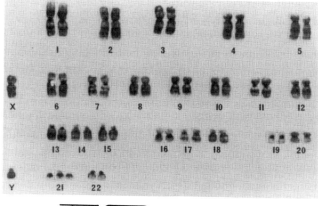

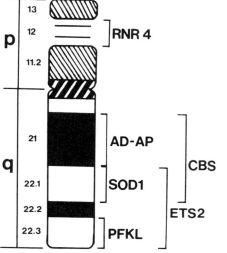

Figure III.1.4. Top: G-banded chromosome spread of a man with Down syndrome (47, XY, +21). The individual chromosome numbers are designated by convention. Bottom: ideogram of human chromosome 21 indicating the subregional localization of several genes of interest (see text). (From J. A. Fraser-Roberts and Marcus E. Pembrey 1978, with permission.)

synthase (CBS), which is implicated in the recessive metabolic disorder homocysteinuria (23620); the gene for liver-type phosphofructokinase (PFKL), which, in deficiency, leads to a type of hemolytic anemia (17186); and two oncogenes, ETS-2 (16474) and ERG (16508). The precise localization of ETS-2 to band 21q22 was a major indication that this region of chromosome 21 is the one responsible for many of the medical features of Down syndrome.

Individuals with Down syndrome have, in addition to classical facial features and mental retardation, a greatly increased risk of developing myeloid leukemia, a high incidence of cataract, and, in older patients, a neurological degeneration resembling Alzheimer's disease. The oncogene ETS-2 at 21q22 is known to be rearranged in acute myeloid leukemia

(McKusick 1986), and linked to this locus at 21q22 is the locus for the enzyme superoxide dismutase (SOD-1). Y. Groner and colleagues (1986) have reviewed molecular evidence that SOD-1 enhances lipid peroxidation, which leads to toxic neurological effects and to cataracts.

The Alzheimer's disease–like dementia of older Down syndrome patients suggested that the q22 region of chromosome 21 might be the location of the amyloid protein found in the senile plaques of Alzheimer's patients. D. Goldgaber and colleagues (1987) and R. E. Tanzi and colleagues (1987) independently reported that the amyloid-B protein gene mapped nearby at 21q21. The effect resulting from the extra copy of the amyloid-B protein gene in Down syndrome is an overproduction of amyloid and presenile plaque formation.

Finally, the advent of recombinant DNA techniques and sophisticated analytic tools for estimating genetic linkage relationships have enabled one group to focus on the cause of the trisomy. Using several well-mapped anonymous DNA sequences from chromosome 21 as well as a probe for SOD-1, A. C. Warren and colleagues (1987) have demonstrated that recombination among DNA markers on chromosomes 21 that have undergone nondisjunction, the event leading to a trisomy, occurs to a significantly lesser extent than it does in controls. Reduced recombination is indicative of *asynapsis,* or a failure of normal chromosome pairing. This result will very likely lead to the discovery of the molecular mechanism of chromosome pairing.

A Failure of Expectations: Kuru

In August 1953, an officer in an Australian government patrol working in the South Fore region of the highlands of Papua New Guinea noted a peculiar condition:

Nearing one of the dwellings [at Amusi], I observed a small girl sitting down beside a fire. She was shivering violently and her head was jerking spasmodically from side to side. I was told that she was a victim of sorcery and would continue thus, shivering and unable to eat, until death claimed her within a few weeks. (J. McArthur 1953, in Lindenbaum 1979)

The condition from which she was suffering was locally called *kuru* (trembling or fear), a progressive neurological disorder peculiar to that region of Papua New Guinea.

Because the South Fore region was relatively isolated and the villages interrelated through extensive kinship ties, it was thought that kuru was a genetic disease occurring in an isolated district where inbreeding was elevated. However, kuru required that the gene be dominant in women and recessive in men for the epidemiology of the illness to be accounted for by a genetic factor (Bennett, Rhodes, and Robson 1959). Thus, even as early as 1963 the genetic etiology that seemed plausible was being discarded (Lindenbaum 1979).

The case of kuru is mentioned here briefly because it is a good example of the sophistication achieved in medical genetics and the study of human diseases. In the early part of the twentieth century, the power of the Mendelian model was so great that the abandonment of an unwieldy genetic hypothesis, which for kuru took only a couple of years, might have required decades. The true cause of kuru was a bizarre infectious agent that S. B. Prusiner (1982) termed a *prion*, or proteinaceous infectious particle. In an odd twist, the infectious component in prions, a relatively small protein called the prion protein, PrP 27–30 (Prusiner et al. 1984), was found to have a normal homolog in mammalian genomes, including human ones. PrP produced its effect by forming rodlike structures resembling amyloid, and it was thought that not only was the PrP gene to be found on chromosome 21 but that Alzheimer's disease and even Down syndrome might be associated with prion infection (Prusiner 1982). However, Y.-C. J. Liao and colleagues (1986) and R. S. Sparkes and colleagues (1986) independently reported cloning the human PrP gene and mapping it to chromosome 20. The story of the prion and of the PrP gene is still unfolding, and although it is not technically a genetic disease, kuru and neurological disorders like it fit well within the multifactorial heuristic model that moved the study of genetic diseases from one of recording oddities to a complex, interdisciplinary enterprise making use of a full range of techniques and technologies.

Summary and Prospects

The history of the study of human genetic diseases is not unlike that of any other area of medical science. It has been marked by periods of superstition and pseudoscience as well as by flashes of brilliant insight such as those of Maupertius, Adams, and Garrod. It has also been characterized by an exponential increase in fundamental understanding coupled with technological and methodological breakthroughs, as was clearly exemplified by sickle-cell anemia and Down syndrome. The recent development of recombinant DNA technology has ushered in a revolution in the study of human genetic disease, a quickening of the pace of discovery matched only by that seen when Mendel's laws of heredity were revealed in 1900.

The future of medical genetics is very bright indeed. Systematic screening of the human genome has revealed hundreds of inherited DNA sequence variants, or RFLPs (Willard et al. 1985; O'Brien 1987). Exploitation of these markers has made it possible to establish genetic linkage and chromosome map locations for a large number of hereditary human illnesses including Duchenne muscular dystrophy (Davies et al. 1983; 31020), Huntington's disease (Gusella et al. 1983; 14310), cystic fibrosis (Tsui et al. 1985; 21970), adult polycystic kidney disease (Reeders et al. 1985; 17390), retinoblastoma (Cavenee et al. 1985; 18020), familial polyposis (Bodmer et al. 1987; 17510), manic-depressive or bipolar illness (Egeland et al. 1987; 30920), and neurofibromatosis (Barker et al. 1987; 16220). Moreover, the genes themselves have been cloned for retinoblastoma (Friend et al. 1986) and Duchenne muscular dystrophy (Monaco et al. 1986), as well as for chronic granulomatosus disease (Royer-Pokora et al. 1986; 30640). These successes have made the production of a genetic map of the entire human genome, first suggested by D. Botstein and colleagues (1980), not just a desirable goal but a feasible imperative. Much of this work has already been accomplished (see Donis-Keller et al. 1987; White 1987), but much more must be done. Clearly, the day of an exact science of molecular medical genetics has dawned and with it has come, after 10,000 years, the potential for treating and even curing genetic diseases (Anderson 1984).

Eric J. Devor

This work was supported in part by Grants MH 31302 and AA 03539 from the National Institutes of Health. Jeanette A. Sharif typed the manuscript and Roberta Rich provided the illustrations.

Bibliography

Allen, G. E. 1978. *Thomas Hunt Morgan: The man and his science*. Princeton, N. J.

Anderson, W. F. 1984. Prospects for human gene therapy. *Science* 226: 401–9.

Ballantyne, J. W. 1902. *Antenatal pathology and hygiene*. Edinburgh.

Barker, D., et al. 1987. Gene for von Recklinghausen neurofibromatosis is in the pericentromeric region of chromosome 17. *Science* 236: 1100–2.

Bateson, William, and E. R. Saunders. 1902. *Experimental studies in the physiology of heredity: Report to Evolution Committee of the Royal Society, No. 1*. London.

Beadle, G. W. 1945. Biochemical genetics. *Chemical Review* 37: 15–96.

Beet, E. A. 1949. The genetics of the sickle-cell trait in a Bantu tribe. *Annals of Eugenics* 14: 279–84.

Bennett, J. H., F. A. Rhodes, and H. N. Robson 1959. A possible genetic basis for kuru. *American Journal of Human Genetics* 11: 169–87.

Bodmer, W. F., et al. 1987. Localization of the gene for familial adenoma tous polyposis on chromosome 5. *Nature* 328: 614–16.

Botstein, D., et al. 1980. Construction of a genetic linkage map in man using restriction fragment length polymorphism. *American Journal of Human Genetics* 32: 314–31.

Brewer, G. J. 1985. Detours on the road to successful treatment of sickle cell anemia. In *Genetic perspectives in biology and medicine,* ed. E. D. Garber. Chicago.

Carlson, E. A. 1966. *The gene: A critical history.* Philadelphia.

1981. *Genes, radiation, and society: The life and work of H. J. Muller.* Ithaca, N.Y.

Caskey, C. T. 1987. Disease diagnosis by recombinant DNA methods. *Science* 236: 1223–9.

Cavenee W. K., et al. 1985. Genetic origin of mutations predisposing to retinoblas toma. *Science* 228: 501–3.

Comings, D. E., et al. 1984. Detection of a major gene for Gilles de la Tourette's syndrome. *American Journal of Human Genetics* 36: 586–600.

Davies, K. E., et al. 1983. Linkage analysis of two cloned sequences flanking the Duchenne muscular dystrophy locus on the short arm of the human X chromosome. *Nucleic Acids Research* 11: 2303–12.

Donis-Keller, et al. 1987. A genetic linkage map of the human genome. *Cell* 51: 319–37.

Diggs, L. W., C. F. Ahmann, and J. Bibb. 1933. The incidence and significance of the sickle cell trait. *Annals of Internal Medicine* 7: 769–78.

Down, J. L. H. 1867. Observations on an ethnic classification of idiots. *Journal of Mental Science* 13: 121–3.

Egeland, J. A., et al. 1987. Bipolar affective disorder linked to DNA markers on chromosome 11. *Nature* 325: 783–7.

Emmel, V. E. 1917. A study of the erythrocytes in a case of severe anemia with elongated and sickle-shaped red blood corpuscles. *Archives of Internal Medicine* 20: 586–98.

Fraser-Roberts, J. A., and M. E. Pembrey. 1978. *An introduction to medical genetics,* 7th edition. Oxford.

Friend, S. H., et al. 1986. A human DNA segment with properties of the gene that predisposes to retinoblastoma and osteosarcoma. *Nature* 323: 643–6.

Garrod, A. E. 1899. Contribution to the study of alkaptonuria. *Proceedings of the Royal Medical and Chirurgical Society* 11: 130–5.

1901. About alkaptonuria. *Lancet* 2: 1484–6.

1902. The incidence of alkaptonuria: A study in chemical individuality. *Lancet* 2, 1616–20.

1908. The Croonian Lectures on inborn errors of metabolism. *Lancet* 2: 1–7, 73–9, 147–8, 214–20.

1928. The lessons of rare maladies. *Lancet* 1: 1055–9.

Glass, B. 1947. Maupertius and the beginnings of genetics. *Quarterly Review of Biology* 22: 196–210.

Glenister, T. W. 1964. Fantasies, facts, and foetuses. *Medical History* 8: 15–30.

Goldgaber, D., et al. 1987. Characterization and chromosomal localization of a cDNA encoding brain amyloid of Alzheimer's disease. *Science* 235: 877–80.

Groner, Y., et al. 1986. Molecular genetics of Down's syndrome: Overexpression of transfected human Cu/Zn-superoxide dismutase gene and consequent physiological changes. *Cold Spring Harbor Symposium on Quantitative Biology* 51: 381–93.

Gusella, J. F., et al. 1983. A polymorphic DNA marker genetically linked to Huntington's disease. *Nature* 306: 234–8.

Harris, H. 1963. *Introduction: Garrod's inborn errors of metabolism.* London.

Heller, P. 1969. Hemoglobin M: An early chapter in the saga of molecular pathology. *Annals of Internal Medicine* 70: 1038–41.

Herrick, J. B. 1910. Peculiar elongated and sickle-shaped red blood corpuscles in a case of severe anemia. *Archives of Internal Medicine* 6: 517–21.

Huck, J. G. 1923. Sickle cell anemia. *Johns Hopkins Hospital Bulletin* 34: 335–44.

Ingram, V. M. 1956. A specific chemical difference between the globins of normal human and sickle-cell anemia hemoglobin. *Nature* 178: 792–4.

1959. Abnormal human hemoglobins: III. The chemical difference between normal and sickle cell hemoglobins. *Biochemical Biophysical Acta* 36: 402–11.

Jeffreys, A. J., V. Wilson, and S. L. Thein. 1985. Hypervariable "minisatellite" regions in human DNA. *Nature* 314: 67–73.

Jeffreys, A. J., et al. 1986. DNA "fingerprints" and segregation analysis of multiple markers in human pedigrees. *American Journal of Human Genetics* 39: 11–24.

Kan, Y. W., and A. M. Dozy. 1978. Polymorphism of the DNA sequence adjacent to the beta globin structural gene: Relationship to sickle mutation. *Proceedings of the National Academy of Sciences* 75: 5671–5.

Lawn, R. M., et al. 1978. The isolation and characterization of linked delta and beta-globin genes from a cloned library of human DNA. *Cell* 15: 1157–74.

Lejeune, J., M. Gautier, and R. Turpin. 1959. Etude des chromosomes somatiques de neuf enfants mongoliens. *Comptes Rendus* 248: 1721–2.

Liao, Y.-C. J., et al. 1986. Human prion protein cDNA: Molecular cloning, chromosome mapping, and biological implications. *Science* 233: 364–7.

Lindenbaum, S. 1979. *Kuru sorcery.* Palo Alto, Calif.

McKusick, V. A. 1986. *Mendelian inheritance in man,* 7th edition. Baltimore.

Monaco A., et al. 1986. Isolation of the candidate cDNAs for portions of the Duchenne muscular dystrophy gene. *Nature* 323: 646–50.

Morgan, T. H. 1914. The mechanism of heredity as indicated by the inheritance of linked characters. *Popular Science Monthly,* January, 1–16.

Morton, N. E. 1982. *Outline of genetic epidemiology.* Basel.

Morton, N. E., and C. S. Chung, eds. 1978. *Genetic epidemiology.* New York.

Motulsky, A. E. 1959. Joseph Adams (1756–1818): A forgotten founder of medical genetics. *Archives of Internal Medicine* 104: 490–6.

Nakamura, Y., et al. 1987. Variable number of tandem repeat (VNTR) markers for human gene mapping. *Science* 235: 1616–22.

Neel, J. V. 1949. The inheritance of sickle cell anemia. *Science* 110: 64–6.

Neel, J. V., and W. J. Schull. 1954. *Human heredity.* Chicago.

O'Brien, S. J., ed. 1987. *Genetic maps, 1987: A compilation of linkage and restriction maps of genetically studied organisms.* Cold Spring Harbor, N.Y.

Olby, R. C. 1966. *Origins of Mendelism.* New York.

Paget, J. 1882. The "Bradshawe" lecture on some rare and new diseases. *Lancet* 2: 1017–21.

Painter T. S. 1923. Studies in mammalian spermatogenesis: II. The spermatogenesis of man. *Journal Experimental Zoology* 37: 291–336.

Pauling, L., et al. 1949. Sickle cell anemia, a molecular disease. *Science* 110: 543–8.

Penrose, L. S. 1939. Maternal age, order of birth and developmental abnormalities. *Journal of Mental Science* 85: 1139–50.

Peters, J. A., ed. 1959. *Classic papers in genetics.* Englewood Cliffs, N.J.

Plomin, R., J. C. DeFries, and G. E. McClearn. 1980. *Behavior genetics: A primer.* San Francisco.

Prusiner, S. B. 1982. Novel proteinaceous infectious particles cause scrapie. *Science* 216: 136–44.

Prusiner, S. B., et al. 1984. Purification and structural studies of a major scrapie prion protein. *Cell* 38: 127–34.

Reeders, S. T., et al. 1985. A highly polymorphic DNA marker linked to adult polycystic kidney disease on chromosome 16. *Nature* 317: 542–44.

Roper, A. G. 1913. *Ancient eugenics.* Oxford.

Royer-Pokora, B., et al. 1986. Cloning the gene for an inherited human disorder: Chronic granulomatous disease on the basis of its chromosomal location. *Nature* 322: 32–8.

Shows, T., A. Y. Sakaguchi, and S. L. Naylor. 1982. Mapping the human genome, cloned genes, DNA polymorphisms, and inherited diseases. In *Advances in human genetics,* Vol. 12, ed. H. Harris and K. Hirschern. New York.

Sparkes, R. S., et al. 1986. Assignment of the human and mouse prion protein genes to homologous chromosomes. *Proceedings of the National Academy of Sciences* 83: 7358–62.

Stern, C., and E. R. Sherwood, eds. 1966. *The origin of genetics: A Mendel source book.* San Francisco.

Sturtevant, A. H. 1913. The linear arrangement of six sex-linked factors in *Drosophila,* as shown by their mode of association. *Journal of Experimental Zoology* 14: 43–59.

1966. *A history of genetics.* New York.

Tanzi, R. E., et al. 1987. Amyloid beta-protein gene: cDNA, mRNA distribution, and genetic linkage near the Alzheimer locus. *Science* 235: 880–4.

Thurman, E. 1986. *Human chromosomes: Structure, behavior, effects,* 2d edition. New York.

Thompson, J. S., and M. W. Thompson. 1980. *Genetics in medicine,* 3d edition. Philadelphia.

Tjio, J. H., and A. Levan. 1956. The chromosome number of man. *Hereditas* 42: 1–6.

Tsui, L.-C., et al. 1985. Cystic fibrosis locus defined by a genetically linked polymorphic DNA marker. *Science* 230: 1054–7.

Vogel, F., and A. G. Motulsky. 1979. *Human genetics.* New York.

Warren, A. C., A. Chakravarti, and C. Wong, 1987. Evidence for reduced recombination on the nondisjoined chromosomes 21 in Down syndrome. *Science* 237: 652–4.

White, R. L., ed. 1987. *Linkage maps of human chromosomes.* Salt Lake City, Utah.

Willard, H., et al. 1985. Report of the committee on human gene mapping by recombinant DNA techniques. *Human Gene Mapping 8, Cytogenetic Cell Genetics* 40: 360–498.

Wright, S. 1968. *Evolution and the genetics of populations,* Vol. 1. Chicago.

III.2
Immunology

The knowledge of acquired resistance to disease and the practices connected with it are very old. Ancient medical systems of both East and West offered explanations of why no one got smallpox twice and how one might be protected from getting it at all. But the history of immunology as a science began only 100 years ago with the experiments of Louis Pasteur.

This history falls into two distinct periods, roughly before and after World War II. It begins with a fanfare, with the production of protective vaccines and antisera, probably the earliest example of truly effective medical treatment. The great theoreticians of the period were biochemists, investigating the chemistry of antigen and antibody and the nature of the antigen–antibody reaction. The part played by blood cells in the body's defenses had been in the foreground of discussions before the turn of the century, but it was pushed into the shade by the discovery of the striking therapeutic effects of immune sera.

After World War II, when it became clear that antibiotics could control infections for which there was no serological treatment, interest in immunological methods of treatment waned and focused instead on the cellular biology of the immune process as a part of general biology. A single theory came to unite all of immunology, making possible the striking expansion of the field that took place in the 1970s.

Cells and Serum

The idea of cells defending the body against invaders was proposed by the Russian zoologist I. I. Mechnikov. He saw that a yeast infecting a transparent water flea was surrounded by white blood cells that stuck to the yeast and killed it. Mechnikov called the cells phagocytes (Mechnikov 1884; Besredka 1921). As Arthur Silverstein has pointed out, phagocytosis at this time was associated with the pathology of inflammation rather than immunity. The first experimental work on immunity, Pasteur's early experiments on chicken cholera, was only four years old in 1884 when Mechnikov's work appeared, and the germ theory of disease itself was hardly any older (Silverstein 1979). Mechnikov's idea attracted Pasteur's interest, and Mechnikov was invited to Paris in 1888.

In Germany, especially among the Berlin bacteriologists around Robert Koch, the chief role in defense appeared more and more clearly to belong to the blood serum rather than the cells. This group of workers had earlier mounted an all-out attack on Pasteur and the French workers, including Mechnikov. This was a transposition into scientific terms of the old nationalistic hatred between France and Germany that had resulted in the Franco-Prussian War of 1870 (Foster 1970). In this case, the Germans had some very telling ammunition. In 1890, Emil von Behring and his Japanese colleague Shibasaburo Kitasato, working at Koch's institute, diverted attention from cellular to so-called humoral immunity when they showed that animals could be made immune to the effects of the toxins produced by both the tetanus and diphtheria bacilli. Immunity could be transferred by an injection of immune serum, a finding that was quickly applied outside the laboratory. Within a year, on Christmas Eve of 1891, the serum was tried out on a child acutely ill with diphtheria. The results were sensational (Behring 1895). The production of sheep and goat serum began in 1892, and in 1894 it was introduced into the Berlin hospitals. There was an immediate fall in diphtheria mortality (Behring 1895). Meanwhile in Paris, Emile Roux and Alexandre Yersin made the large-scale production of the serum possible by using horses as a source of antitoxin. In their first 300 cases, mortality fell from 50 to 25 percent. In 1894 the Pasteur serum was taken to England by Joseph Lister, and it was equally successful there (Parish 1965).

In England, cells and serum came together in the work of the clinical bacteriologist Almroth Wright. Wright demonstrated that phagocytes could not engulf their victims without the help of a serum factor that he called an opsonin. The level of opsonic activity showed the state of his patients' defenses against bacterial infection and their response to the vaccines he prepared for them. Local infections, such as boils, acne, appendicitis, and tuberculosis, were treated with autovaccines made from the patient's own organisms and calculated, in Bernard Shaw's phrase, to stimulate the phagocytes. At the Department for Therapeutic Immunization at St. Mary's Hospital in London, he and a devoted group worked night and day at stimulating the phagocytes and determining opsonic indices. Autovaccination and injections were the treatment of the moment, especially, it seems, in the English-speaking world. From about 1945 onward, however, autovaccines were superseded by antibiotics. Among the young bacteriologists who were Wright's colleagues was Alexander Fleming, who later discovered penicillin. The department Wright founded is now the Wright–Fleming Institute.

The Age of International Serology, 1900–50

In spite of the popular appeal of the struggle of phagocytes, it was not cells but serum that set the style. The key event of this period is the discovery of the striking clinical effectiveness of diphtheria antitoxin. The production and control of this serum and others like it pointed the direction for research in theory and in practice.

Although it was the diphtheria serum and its problems that lent them much of their significance, the first of the national serum institutes was established just before the appearance of the serum. The Institut Pasteur was set up in 1888, following the national enthusiasm in France created by Pasteur's success with rabies immunization (Delaunay 1962). The institute was not, strictly speaking, a state concern, because it was independently funded, but it had national status. Its opening marked the end of Pasteur's active life; he had had a stroke the previous year, and the new institute was to be run not by Pasteur himself, but by his successors, the Pastoriens.

From its beginning, the institute offered courses on

bacteriological technique. Among the students were young bacteriologists from all over the world; many were medical officers of the French colonies, which led to the establishment of the Instituts Pasteur d'Outre-Mer. The first four of these, in Saigon, Nhatrang, Algeria, and Tunis, were founded between 1891 and 1894. Among them may also be mentioned the Haffkine Institute in Bombay, founded in 1899 and led by a Pastorien, Waldemar Haffkine. As Noël Bernard points out, the vulnerability of the whites in these new areas of colonization stimulated interest in the diseases endemic in them; the Instituts Pasteur d'Outre-Mer concentrated on plague, cholera, and malaria – and snake bite (Bernard 1960). In Europe, needs were different: Centers that had begun by working on vaccines turned their attention to the large-scale production of diphtheria antiserum. Thus, Institut Pasteur set up a special center for making horse serum at Garches, outside Paris.

A similar evolution took place in London, leading to the foundation of the British Institute of Preventive Medicine, renamed the Lister Institute in 1891 (Chick, Hume, and Macfarlane 1971). Rabies at that time was an uncommon, but fatal result of animal bites in England, as on the Continent; no one could predict which bite might be fatal. Pasteur himself suggested a Pastorien, Marc-Armand Ruffer, who had connections in England and Germany, as well as Paris, to head it. In 1893 Ruffer reported on the astonishing effectiveness of Behring's diphtheria serum, and in 1894 a serum department was created at the Lister. Soon after, the Wellcome Laboratories were founded to make the serum commercially.

In the same year Carl Salomonsen, director of the University Bacteriology Laboratory in Copenhagen, went to Paris to learn the techniques. On Salomonsen's return, he applied to his government for funding for a laboratory for serotherapeutic experiments and undertook at the same time to produce diphtheria serum in quantity for free distribution. The Statens Serum Institutet under Thorwald Madsen became independent of the University in 1901 (Salomonsen 1902). Elsewhere too, rabies vaccination led the way to the manufacture of diphtheria serum, which was not only a tremendous therapeutic success, but a commercial success as well (Defries 1968).

The most important of the problems raised by the clinical use of the serum was that of standardization. The first attempt at a biological assay was made by Behring. His method was to standardize the antiserum against the toxin. The minimum fatal dose of toxin was first established, and one unit of antitoxin was defined as the amount necessary to protect a guinea pig against 100 fatal doses of toxin. The method seemed logical, but in practice the results were unreliable.

The problem was taken up by Paul Ehrlich, head of the newly established Institut für Serumprüfung und Serumforschung in Berlin. Ehrlich's assay procedure followed Behring's quite closely, but he defined his units using a standard toxin and a standard antiserum, and new batches of either were assayed by comparison with these. The Lo dose of a new toxin was the number of lethal doses (L.D.'s) neutralized by one unit of the original antiserum, and the $L+$ dose was the number of lethal doses just not neutralized. Theoretically, as Behring had expected, $L+ - Lo = 1$ L.D. But in practice, as the toxin aged, the difference increased. The toxin's capacity to neutralize antitoxin remained constant, but the toxicity of the solution gradually declined.

Ehrlich interpreted this in terms of his side-chain theory as meaning that there were two different side chains on the toxin molecule, which he called the toxophore and the haptophore groups, responsible for the toxic property and the property of neutralizing antitoxin, respectively. The toxophore group, he thought, was labile, so that toxicity declined over time. A further difficulty lay in the fact that successive additions of antiserum had unequal effects on the toxicity: The first few additions might not diminish the toxicity at all, though antibody was being absorbed. Ehrlich thought this meant that the toxin consisted of a mixture of different components, each giving a different ratio of antigen to antibody.

The most "avid" components took up the highest proportion of antibody and took it first; the less avid, later. He illustrated this by a stepped diagram, the profile of which represented the relationship between toxicity and avidity for antiserum at each stage of neutralization. Each step represented a separate, named component, which he called toxin, toxone, and toxoid, each with named subdivisions (Ehrlich 1887–8). The development of a clearly visualized, but quite speculative chemistry, along with a new vocabulary to describe the visualized substances, was very typical of Ehrlich's thinking (Mazumdar 1976). It was the first statement of his side-chain theory, the theory of immunity around which argument raged for the next 20 years and which has never quite disappeared from immunology.

The feature of Ehrlich's assay procedure that made it so successful was his insistence on measuring all new serum samples against a standard serum. The standard was preserved desiccated, frozen, and under vacuum, at Ehrlich's own new specialized laboratory in Frankfurt, which continued to provide for international standardization up to World War I. During the war, communications with Frankfurt were cut off, and standards began to drift.

The decision to take over the regulation of serum standards was made by the League of Nations Health Committee in 1921. A series of International Conferences on the Standardization of Sera and Serological Tests was held; it was decided to keep the Ehrlich unit as the international standard, but since Germany was excluded from the League of Nations, the standard serum was to be in Copenhagen. Madsen suggested that similar agreements could be reached for other biologicals, such as hormone preparations and plant extracts. In 1924, the Permanent Commission on Biological Standardization was set up with Madsen as its chairman (Hartley 1945). Copenhagen became the center of coordination for all work on serum standards, with individual samples of diphtheria antitoxin and other antibacterial sera kept at Cophenhagen, Frankfurt, Hampstead, and Toronto, and at Paris at the Institut Pasteur (Jensen 1936).

The Nature of Specificity, 1900–50

In the nineteenth century, the startling success of the serum treatment of diphtheria had given rise not only to the practical problems of standardization and their solution, and to the international organization to coordinate the work, but also to a theoretical interest in the antigen–antibody reaction and the nature of specificity. The earliest formulation of these problems came with Ehrlich's side-chain theory. According to the theory, the antibody had a unique chemical affinity for the haptophore on the toxin. Ehrlich suggested that the union of antitoxin with its toxin tore the antibody molecule free of the cell that carried it on its surface. This trauma caused an overproduction of identical replacement molecules, rather as healing of an injury caused overproduction of new tissue (Ehrlich 1887–8; Mazumdar 1976; Silverstein 1982).

The side-chain theory had two implications that drew criticism. First, the side chains were supposed to bind to their receptors firmly and irreversibly according to the law of definite proportions, by the type of linkage now called covalent. Second, the theory required that the body be provided with pre-existing antibodies to match every conceivable antigen, even those artificial molecules that could have had no possible role in the evolution of the species.

Madsen, who had learned the technique of diphtheria serum assay from Ehrlich himself, but who had

also been in contact with Jules Bordet at the Institut Pasteur, was the first to develop an alternative interpretation of Ehrlich's stepped diagram. Working with the physical chemist Svante Arrhenius, he suggested that the antigen–antibody reaction was a reversible equilibrium like the neutralization of acid by base, a type of reaction that gave a smooth exponential curve rather than a series of steps. There was no need to postulate a whole series of different substances (Arrhenius and Madsen 1902; Rubin 1980). The theory had an indifferent reception, but Ehrlich's enemies, led by Max von Gruber in Vienna, hoped that what they saw as a splendid refutation meant the end of Ehrlich's ascendancy.

For Bordet, however, the outstanding fact was that an agglutinable substance absorbed different amounts of its agglutinin according to the relative proportions of the reacting substances: The reaction was not chemical at all, but physical. He compared the phenomenon to that of dyeing: If one dipped a series of pieces of paper in a dye solution, the first few would be strongly colored, and the later ones paler and paler as the dye was exhausted. As early as 1896, he had suggested that "serum acts on bacteria by changing the relations of molecular attraction between bacteria and the surrounding fluid" (Bordet 1896).

Bordet's physical point of view was taken up by Karl Landsteiner in Vienna, who had been trained in both medicine and structural organic chemistry. He had joined Gruber's serological laboratory in 1896 and, like other Gruber students, followed the Gruber line of anti-Ehrlich argument. Landsteiner proposed a physicochemical model for the antigen–antibody reaction: the precipitation of inorganic colloids. The model was particularly apt because the form of antigen–antibody reaction that Landsteiner usually worked with was a precipitin reaction, in which a soluble antigen was precipitated out of solution by an antibody.

Colloid chemistry dealt with the behavior of materials that formed very large particles, so large that their reactions depended on the physical properties of their surfaces rather than on their chemical nature. In the early part of the twentieth century, the physical chemistry of colloids seemed to hold great promise for explaining the reactions of living tissue and its major constituent, protein. It seemed particularly appropriate for the antigen–antibody reaction, because it was thought that only proteins were antigenic. Working with the Viennese colloid chemist Wolfgang Pauli, who was one of the most enthusiastic proponents of the "chemistry of life," Landsteiner pointed out that it was colloids with opposite charges that precipitated each other. The antigen–antibody reaction might be an electrochemical surface adsorption: Subtle surface charge effects might account for antibody specificity (Landsteiner 1909). He and Pauli developed an apparatus for comparing the charge on proteins by following their movements in an electric field. Their apparatus was adopted by Leonor Michaelis and his group in Berlin, who thought the same features might account for the activities of enzymes. Landsteiner then entered into a long program of research, aiming to define the antigenic specificity of proteins carrying known substituent groups, a project that made use of his skill in structural chemistry. The final proof of his position came in 1918, when he demonstrated that antigenic specificity was determined mainly by the charge outline of the antigen (Landsteiner and Lampl 1918). This conclusion united the colloid or physical concept of charge with the structural concept of the chemical nature of the molecule (Mazumdar 1976; Silverstein 1982).

Landsteiner's demonstration of the importance of charge outline had several implications. The first was that specificity need not be absolute, as Ehrlich's theory would have it. Cross-reactions could take place between similarly charged groups similarly placed on the antigens. A huge number of different specific antibodies was not, therefore, necessary. The second was that the antigen–antibody reaction was not a firm chemical binding; the two were linked not by valency bonds, but by the so-called short-range forces that surrounded a molecule, as in the model of a crystal lattice (Marrack 1934). The third implication, that of the generation of antibody diversity, was not made until 1930, by the Prague biochemist Felix Haurowitz.

Haurowitz's training, like that of Landsteiner, had included both colloid chemistry and structural chemistry. He spent some time with Michaelis working on the physical chemistry of charge in relation to enzyme activity. But after the war Prague had lost its links with Vienna; Haurowitz heard nothing about the work of Landsteiner until 1929, when the serologist Fritz Breinl told him about it. Breinl and Haurowitz, then working together, suggested that antibody might be assembled on the charge outline of its antigen, appropriately charged amino acids lining up by adsorption onto the antigen to form a specific antibody globulin. There was no need for Ehrlich's innumerable preformed specificities. The organism made its antibody as required. It was a simple and economical solution to the problem of antibody diversity; it made use of the most advanced

thinking in both immunology and chemistry (Mazumdar 1989). In English, it became known as the template theory, and in one form or another, it was generally accepted for the next 20 years or more.

Landsteiner had been a rather isolated theoretical thinker at a time when theory was of little interest to the practical serologist. In addition, criticism of Ehrlich was not popular in Vienna. Thus, after the political and economic collapse of Austria at the end of World War I, Landsteiner was eager to leave, and in 1922 was invited to joining the Rockefeller Institute in New York. There, in a sympathetic environment, he was able to continue his work on artificial antigens. He also turned again to the blood groups, which he had not worked on since 1901–9, when he discovered them (Landsteiner 1901). It was for this discovery, and not the work on artificial antigens, that he was given the Nobel Prize in 1932.

Landsteiner's interest in the blood groups began in 1900, when he and many others tried to explain the presence of antibodies in human blood that agglutinated the red cells of other human bloods. Most proposals linked them to some common disease, such as tuberculosis and malaria. It was Landsteiner's suggestion that these were "natural antibodies" whose presence was independent of infection. Landsteiner himself showed curiously little interest in this pregnant finding, perhaps because the "natural antibodies" and the sharply defined specificity of the different groups seemed to support Ehrlich's theory. Although Landsteiner had suggested in 1901 that a knowledge of blood groups would be useful in blood transfusion, transfusion was used very little for many years afterward. It was reported on occasionally during World War I, and although a large literature accumulated, it did not become a routine hospital procedure until the establishment of blood banks shortly before World War II. In Britain, fear of civilian casualties on a large scale stimulated the organization of a blood collection and distribution system.

Landsteiner and his colleagues at the Rockefeller Institute discovered several more sets of inherited antigens on red cells, the MN and P systems, and in 1940 the rhesus, or Rh, system. These workers found rhesus incompatibility between mother and fetus to be the cause of hemolytic disease of the newborn, a discovery that led in the 1960s to an immunologic method of specifically suppressing antibody formation in the mother and so preventing the disease.

In an era when human genetics was represented by the eugenics movement, blood groups were the only normal human trait that was clearly inherited according to Mendelian laws. They seemed to be direct products of the genes, untouched by any environmental effect. They could be analyzed mathematically as the Göttingen statistician Felix Bernstein had shown (Bernstein 1924; Mazumdar 1992), and as a model genetic system, they might come to do for human genetics what the fruit fly *Drosophila* had done for genetic theory in the 1920s. To critics of the eugenist's social biases, such as the left-wing scientists of the 1930s, blood groups represented a means of making human genetics the genuinely "value-free science" that it had so far grotesquely failed to be (Hogben 1931). In practice, the complex genetics of blood group antigens was to provide a model for the genetics of tissue types, essential in the choice of organs for grafting and for the genetics of proteins (Grubb 1989).

The Chemistry of Antibody Globulins, 1930–60

The history of protein chemistry is the history of a sequence of innovations in instrumentation and technique, each of them pointing to a new vein of knowledge to be worked. Most of these were fractionation methods; proteins could be separated in terms of charge or particle size, and biological activity correlated with the resulting serum fractions or protein fragments. For most of the period, efforts in this area were more or less independent of the work on immune specificity, but they too had their roots in colloid chemistry. Not until after World War II did protein chemists begin to feel that the high aspirations of colloid chemistry were an absurdity better forgotten.

The earliest and simplest preparative separation method for serum proteins was "salting-out," achieved by adding neutral salts to the protein solution, a technique introduced in the mid-nineteenth century. By 1930 there were still some chemists who were not convinced that the serum antibodies were actually globulins, and not some other material (Spiegel-Adolf 1930).

With their sophisticated techniques and mathematical approach, the physical chemists working at Uppsala in Sweden transformed colloid chemistry. The vitalistic enthusiasm of Pauli faded into a hardline physical science. However, both The Svedberg and Arne Tiselius thought of themselves as colloid chemists.

Svedberg's work on protein separation began to appear in 1925. Using a high-speed centrifuge, he found that proteins were forced to the bottom of a tube in order of their size. He assigned to each a sedimentation coefficient S that indicated molecular weight. The serum globulin mainly had a sedimentation coefficient of 7 S, corresponding to a molecular weight of about 15,000, but there was a small amount of heavier 18 S globulin. As in the salting-out technique, antibody activity went along with the globulin fraction. Svedberg saw ultracentrifugal analysis as a contribution to classical colloid chemistry: Particle size and dispersal of proteins in solution were central to the colloid tradition.

In 1930 Svedberg's younger colleague Tiselius developed an apparatus for the separation of protein molecules in terms of their charge, based on the work of Landsteiner and Pauli. Tiselius, too, felt that the study of electrokinetic phenomena was among the most important of the tasks of colloid chemistry (Tiselius 1938).

Svedberg's and Tiselius's earlier methods had been useful for the analysis of protein mixtures, whereas the new techniques of the 1940s made it possible to prepare the products on a large scale. The name *chromatography* was coined by the Russian botanist M. Tswett in 1910 to describe his method of separating colored plant materials. The first good chromatographic method for proteins was introduced in 1944 by A. J. P. Martin and his colleagues at St. George's Hospital in London. Martin's method was to use a filter-paper sheet as the adsorbent, with the solvent containing the test material flowing slowly up a vertical sheet by capillary action. It also incorporated the novel idea of two-dimensional separation. When separation with one solvent was complete, the paper was turned 90 degrees and another separation with another solvent, or with an electric current, was performed. This method, called "fingerprinting," was good for identifying differently charged amino acids in a mixture of peptide fragments of proteins, and it became a favorite with protein geneticists.

After the war ended, a new group of methods for the separation of charged molecules appeared. Ion exchangers are essentially insoluble acids or bases in the form of a highly cross-linked matrix, usually a resin, through which a solvent carrying the material to be analyzed can percolate. Molecules with the same charge as the solid are repelled by it to various degrees and pass more or less quickly through, whereas those with the opposite charge are entangled and delayed. In 1951 an ion-exchange resin was brilliantly applied to the separation of amino acids by Stanford Moore and William H. Stein at the Rockefeller Institute in New York (Moore and Stein 1951). They not only obtained a quantitative separation of mixtures containing an astonishing number of different substances, up to 50 in some cases, but also automated the procedure so that it could be run unattended overnight. In the morning, the researchers would find a series of tubes filled by an automatic fraction collector, ready for them to analyze. This type of method with its greatly increased productivity made possible the rapid accumulation of information on amino acids and their sequence in many different proteins.

Protein molecules, however, easily lost their biological activity with the rough handling that resins gave them. Investigators might succeed in isolating a protein peak by a preparative method, only to find that all the antibody activity had disappeared, "lost on the column." It was not long before a better way was found. Cellulose-based ion exchangers were introduced by Herbert A. Sober and Elbert A. Peterson and by Jerker Porath at Uppsala (Sober et al. 1956). The anion exchanger was diethylaminoethyl cellulose, or DEAE, and the cation, carboxymethyl (or CM) cellulose. These materials turned out to be far less destructive to the protein molecule. A second type of material developed by Porath was a dextran gel called Sephadex by its manufacturer. It was not an ion exchanger; it acted, to use Porath's (1960) expression, as a kind of molecular sieve. Large molecules, such as the 18 S globulin, passed almost unhindered through it, excluded from the finer pores of the gel; smaller ones, such as albumin and 7 S globulin, wandered more slowly, exploring the labyrinth within. All these materials were soon available commercially, many from firms centered in Uppsala. As the techniques and the rather expensive equipment for column chromatography and automatic fraction collecting spread through laboratories, protein chemistry, particularly the chemistry of antibody globulins, moved very rapidly (Morris and Morris 1964).

The range of separation methods now available made possible an attack on the structure of the immunoglobulin molecule. Rodney Porter, working at St. Mary's Hospital Medical School in London, separated out a rabbit immunoglobulin by chromatography on DEAE, and then digested it with the proteolytic enzyme papain to break it into sections small enough to be understood. The digest was first put into the ultracentrifuge. There was only one peak, at 3.5 S, showing that the 7 S globulin had broken into smaller fragments of roughly equal size. On CM cellulose, there were three peaks. Amino acid analysis by the Moore and Stein method on an ion-exchange resin showed that peaks I and II were almost identical, and III, very different from them; antibody activity was present in peaks I and II. Porter's first interpretation of his results was that the molecule was a long single chain with three sections,

supporting Linus Pauling's suggestion in 1940 of a long antibody molecule with a rigid centerpiece and two flexible ends, which folded, or molded, themselves on the antigen as a template to effect a specific match (Porter 1959). For Porter in 1959, a template theory of the generation of antibody diversity was still the most likely possibility.

In 1962 Porter tried a different dissection of the antibody globulin by opening its disulfide bonds. Separation of the result on a Sephadex column produced two peaks, one heavy and one light. He thought that these must be two chains of the globulin molecule, normally joined together by disulfide bonds. Amino acid analysis showed that there must be two of each chain. The relation of the chains to the papain pieces was determined immunologically, using goat antisera to the rabbit fragments. Porter then proposed a second model of the 7 S globulin molecule, with a pair of heavy chains joined by disulfide bonds and a light chain attached to each one, with the antibody site in fraction I, probably on the heavy chain. This model stood up satisfactorily to additional evidence, to the discovery of different types of heavy chain in different classes of immunoglobulin, and to the discovery of individual genetically determined polymorphisms of both chains (Porter 1973).

Using the fingerprinting technique, several laboratories in Britain and the United States, and Michael Sela and his group in Israel, found that the peptide maps of I and II from different antisera were very slightly different from each other. The chemists were getting nearer to finding out the amino acid sequence of an individual antibody; there was, however, still too much heterogeneity in normal antibody to make such detail possible.

The problem was solved by an accident of nature. To everyone's surprise, the fingerprints of normal light chains and the so-called Bence-Jones protein turned out to be almost identical. This material, named for its nineteenth-century discoverer, is found in the urine of patients with myeloma, a lymphoid tumor of the bone marrow. The only difference seemed to be that normal light chains were a mixture of two types, whereas the Bence-Jones chains were homogeneous, and therefore an ideal material available in large quantities for sequence studies on the amino acid analyzer. It appeared that each patient produced a different chain; each chain consisted of two sections, a variable region and a constant region. Of the 105 amino acids of the variable region, about 30 varied from case to case. In this variation lay the essence of antibody specificity.

Parallel with the detailed information that built up throughout the 1950s on amino acid sequences, evidence began to accumulate that these sequences were under genetic control. Information that specified each amino acid was found to be encoded in deoxynucleic acid, or DNA, transferred to a messenger ribonucleic acid, or RNA, and transcribed as an amino acid to be added to the growing peptide chain. The system appeared to be strictly directional. Francis Crick of Cambridge University stated what he called the "central dogma" of protein synthesis: Once genetic information has passed into protein, it cannot get out again. No protein could be formed by copying another protein (Crick 1957).

If this were so, it would make the template theory of antibody formation impossible. But the template theory had deep roots, and distinguished supporters, such as the U.S. immunochemists Pauling and Michael Heidelberger. Haurowitz, now at Indiana University, continued to hold that antigen could interfere, if not with the primary amino acid sequence of the protein, at least with its folding. In 1963 he was arguing that antibodies were normal globulins and that their amino acid sequences were shown by fingerprinting to be almost identical with one another, leaving only the folding to account for antibody specificity. By then, he knew that his theory was becoming less and less likely to be validated, and he often appeared to accept that its time had passed. But Haurowitz never laid down his arms. As he had said in 1960, he could not imagine the formation of a mold without a cast, or antibody without antigen.

Cellular Immunology and the Selection Theories

It was not, however, the argument from the central dogma that turned immunologists away from the template theory. In spite of the growth of molecular biology in the postwar period, it was the complex phenomena of immune cells and immunized animals that provided the impetus for building the new theory. The theoreticians, especially Frank Macfarlane Burnet, considered themselves biologists and drew their ideas from contemporary thinking in biology.

During the 1940s, a number of pieces of evidence accumulated that were to throw doubt on the template theory. One was the phenomenon of tolerance: Ray Owen in California had found that cattle twins that shared intrauterine circulation before birth each contained some of the other's blood cells and made no antibody to them as adults. In 1949 Burnet of the Walter and Eliza Hall Institute in Melbourne,

Australia, together with Frank Fenner of the Australian National University, suggested that an animal body had some mechanism for distinguishing "self" from "not-self." Antigens that were present before birth were accepted as "self," and an animal made no antibody to them (Burnet and Fenner 1949). Burnet's experiment failed, but a similar one that produced a tolerance to foreign skin grafts succeeded at the hands of a British group led by Peter Medawar. During the war, Medawar had served in a London hospital, treating the wounded and burned of the London blitz. He had tried to use grafts of donor skin in the same way he had used donor blood, which was then saving so many lives. But donor skin did not "take." It was Medawar's idea that graft rejection was an immunogenetic phenomenon, as it was Burnet's idea that self-tolerance was established in fetal life. In 1960 Burnet and Medawar shared a Nobel Prize.

From the early 1950s, attention focused on tolerance. Burnet, speaking at a conference at the Royal Society of London in 1956, saw the interest in this "vital" phenomenon as one of the ways in which immunology was becoming more and more biologically oriented (Burnet 1957). There was also the discovery by the U.S. investigators William Taliaferro and David Talmage that a very few cells, containing no detectable antigen, could transfer the full antibody-forming capacity of an immune animal to a new host. These findings could not be explained by the template theory. Alternative explanations began to appear.

Among the most important alternatives was the *natural selection theory* of the Danish immunologist Niels Kaj Jerne, which appeared in 1955. It was a theory that would have appealed to Paul Ehrlich: It proposed that "natural" antibodies were continuously being formed, before any antigen was presented. A given antigen would select its match from among this population of miscellaneous antibodies and would form an antigen–antibody complex. The complex would then be taken up by a phagocyte, which would trigger further production of the same antibody specificity (Jerne 1955). The theory fitted Burnet's concept of self-tolerance: There should be no antiself antibodies. Ehrlich had called this the *horror autotoxicus.*

Both Talmage and Burnet offered improvements on Jerne's idea. Talmage suggested that attention should focus on antibody-producing cells rather than on serum antibody: Certain cells might be selected for multiplication when their produce reacted with the antigen. Talmage's suggestion, however, was overshadowed by that of Burnet, which was similar in many ways but much more fully worked out. Burnet called his version the *clonal selection theory,* and it was this version that eventually obtained general acceptance.

Burnet was born and educated in Australia, where he took his medical degree in 1922. His postgraduate tour, however, took him to London's Lister Institute, where he worked on bacteriophage viruses and their serological classification. After getting his doctorate, Burnet joined the National Institute for Medical Research. Here he learned the practical techniques of limit dilution and cloning used to grow a virus in pure culture. According to his colleague Gordon Ada (1989), this work at the bench may have provided him with models for his later immunologic theories.

Burnet was always careful to give Jerne full credit as the "onlie begetter" of the selection theory (Burnet 1967). But he did not like the idea that phagocytosing an antigen–antibody complex caused a cell to produce antibody. He suggested instead that the natural antibody was not free in the serum but attached to the cell surface as a receptor, rather as Ehrlich had supposed 50 years before. Antigen then selected the cell that carried a suitable antibody, and that was the stimulus for the cell to start proliferating. Somatic cells do not mate; apart from mutations, their progeny are identical, a clone of genetically identical cells, all producing identical antibodies. Burnet suggested that each cell probably produced only one or two antibodies, because that gave a reasonable number of cell types to deal with the number of different possible antigens (Burnet and Fenner 1962).

This theory explained two biological phenomena of immunity that had not gone well with the template theory. It explained tolerance of self as the absence of "forbidden clones" of cells that would have made antiself antibody. And it matched the kinetics of antibody production: the delay following inoculation of the antigen while the first few generations of cells were produced and then the exponential rise in titer as the doubling numbers of each new generation came into being. It explained why a second exposure to antigen had a more immediate and more marked effect: A substantial number of cells of the right clones already existed, ready to begin their proliferation.

Burnet did not waste much time on the central dogma, but it supported his position, and as a biologist, he very soon accepted it as a matter of course. It had become a kind of Lamarckian heresy, he said, to believe that the environment could produce heritable changes in protein structure (Burnet and Fenner 1962).

The clonal selection theory appeared in 1957. Almost at once, evidence strongly supporting the theory was produced by Gustav Nossal and Joshua Lederberg. Using the most direct means of testing clonal selection, they isolated single lymphocytes from rabbits immunized with two antigens and found that each cell produced only one specificity of antibody. It was technically a difficult feat and not easy to reproduce (Nossal and Lederberg 1959).

Although Burnet himself had not insisted on the capacity of each cell to make only one antibody, it seems to have been this finding that provided the strongest support for his theory. *One cell, one antibody:* By 1967 Jerne could call that slogan "Burnet's dogma in its uncompromising form" (Jerne 1967), thus giving it equal status with Crick's "central dogma," mentioned earlier. At the Cold Spring Harbor Symposium that year, it began to seem as if the clonal selection theory had been accepted by the leaders in the field. In the 10 years since it had been proposed, a plethora of experiments on lymphocytes had demonstrated that antigen turned a small subpopulation on to clonal expansion and that antigen was not present in all the antibody-producing cells. As Burnet had said, the way the theory was stated made it easy to think of ways to test it.

Immune System

The growing power of the clonal selection theory during the late 1960s created a magnetic storm in the minds of immunologists. The disturbance was worldwide, but the epicenter was at the Hall Institute in Melbourne, where Burnet and his students Ada, Nossal, and Jacques Miller, all biologists, disentangled the life and work of lymphocytes. The Soviet immunologist R. V. Petrov (1987) has called this the period of the dictatorship of the lymphocyte. The consequence of the acceptance and pervasiveness of the clonal selection theory was a general reorientation of the field toward the study of cells.

The thymus was an organ whose histology was described in great detail in all the elementary textbooks, but it had never been found to have any function. Thymectomy seemed to have no effect on a normal adult. In 1961 Burnet suggested to Miller that he try to discover the effect of thymectomy not on adults, but on newborns in whom, according to his theory, self-tolerance was still being established. Experiments on mice produced a striking effect: The thymectomized mice looked ill; they had constant diarrhea and infections; foreign skin grafts, even skin grafts from rats, flourished on them, and they could hardly produce any antibody (Miller 1962).

In 1963 Australian and U.S. investigators met for a conference on the thymus. It was arranged by the U.S. pediatrician Robert Good, who had been treating children with immune deficiencies, most of whom had congenital absence of the thymus. Like Miller's mice, they suffered from endless infections, and they neither rejected grafts nor produced antibodies. In some of them, the thymus looked normal and graft rejection was normal, but no antibodies were produced. The only known experimental model of this type of deficiency was the chick from which the bursa of Fabricius, an organ rather like the mammalian appendix, had been removed. The bursa seemed to be responsible for producing the cells that made antibody, suggesting that there were two different types of lymphocyte, one mediating graft rejection and the other making antibody. During the 1960s, details accumulated on the powers of different types of cell cultured in isolation. It was left to Miller and Graham Mitchell at the Hall Institute in 1968 to add one more parameter, the behavior of thymus and bone marrow cells mixed together. The mixed culture generated 20 times more antibody-producing cells than either cell type alone: The antibody response must depend on cellular cooperation. Their next paper made the roles clear. The bone marrow, or B, cells produced antibody, but the thymus, or T, cells were needed as "helpers" (Petrov 1987). It was soon found that T cells were composed of helpers, suppressors, and cytotoxic cells.

Back in 1890, Robert Koch announced that he had found a cure for tuberculosis. He was injecting a secret substance, later admitted to be an extract of tubercle bacilli, which he called tuberculin. It produced a striking flare-up of skin lesions in an infected patient. But disappointingly, it was not a cure (Koch 1891). The Viennese pediatrician Clemens von Pirquet, working on the "serum sickness" that often followed the injection of diphtheria serum, recognized that the tuberculin reaction had some relation to his concept of "allergy," or altered reactivity, but it was independent of antibody and could not be transferred by serum. Others saw the same kind of lesion in chronic bacterial infections, and it came to be called "infectious allergy" (Schadewaldt 1979). The lesions were very characteristic: a hard red lump that often had a black, necrotic center, which developed slowly over a few days and took weeks to heal. The reaction was thought perhaps to be responsible for the tissue destruction in tuberculous lungs, and as "delayed hypersensitivity," to be quite separate from protective immunity.

In an era that concentrated on serology and protec-

tion against infection, something that had nothing to do with serum and seemed to be destructive rather than protective did not attract much interest. It was not until 1939 that Landsteiner and his colleague Merrill Chase at the Rockefeller Institute made the connection between delayed hypersensitivity and contact hypersensitivity to such things as poison ivy and to the artificial antigens that Landsteiner had been working on for the past half-century (Landsteiner and Chase 1939). In the following year, Landsteiner and Chase managed to transfer contact sensitivity by means of live cells. In addition, Jules Freund (1956), working at the New York Public Health Research Institute, found that lesions could be made much bigger by injecting antigen in an oily mixture that contained a trace of tuberculin. Because there were now techniques that could be used, research could begin.

It soon became clear that delayed hypersensitivity could take the form of autoimmune disease, and that this kind of disease could often be reproduced by injecting material from the target organ in Freund's adjuvant. During the 1950s, laboratories in Britain and the United States worked on the problem using experimental allergic encephalitis as a model. Under the microscope, all the lesions looked very much the same: There was always a cuff of cells surrounding the small blood vessels. Most of the cells were lymphocytes, with some phagocytic cells, the macrophages. The New York immunologist Sherwood Lawrence insisted that he was able to transfer specific sensitization with a cell-free extract from sensitized cells; he called his putative agent "transfer factor." Other immunologists thought that there was something wrong with his experiments. There were no known soluble factors, other than antibody, or perhaps antigen – Burnet thought it must be antigen – that could transfer a specific sensitivity.

Throughout the 1960s, under the influence of the clonal selection theory, more and more attention came to be focused on lymphocytes. Byron Waksman and his group at Yale University found that they could wipe out delayed hypersensitivity with anti-lymphocyte serum, an experimental finding that could be used clinically to prolong the life of transplants as well as to dampen autoimmune disease (Waksman, Arbouys, and Arnason 1961). Tissue culture techniques improved, so that immune lymphocytes could be watched as they responded to antigen by beginning to proliferate. The relation of the two types of cell in the lesions could be disentangled; antigen stopped the migration of macrophages away from a site, but it worked through the lymphocyte, which produced a soluble "migration inhibition factor," the first of many such factors to be described. A different group of T cells could be seen to kill the cells of foreign grafts or tumor cells. Activated macrophages, too, could kill normal cells, especially if the cells were coated with antibody. It was Wright's opsonic effect brought back to life. Attempts were made to apply this new knowledge to human pathology. Patients' lymphocytes were tested for their behavior with suspected antigens in some diseases thought to be autoimmune.

As Anne-Marie Moulin (1989) has pointed out, the Cold Spring Harbor Symposium of 1967 marked the moment at which immunologists seem to have agreed to accept the clonal selection theory. During the 1960s, different domains of immunology had evolved under the guidance of its heuristic influence. The theory suggested new questions and demanded new techniques, particularly techniques for growing and manipulating cell cultures on the microscopic scale. These new techniques in turn laid bare dozens of new phenomena and relationships. An early indicator of the crossing over between the separate areas of immunology was the change of name around 1970 of delayed hypersensitivity, first to delayed (cellular) hypersensitivity, then to cell-mediated immunity, as the barriers disappeared between the work on antibody-producing clones of lymphocytes and the work on the lymphocytes of delayed hypersensitivity.

Cell-mediated immunity in the 1970s was, as Waksman has noted, completely redefined. More than 100 descriptions of new cellular phenomena were published over the 10 years (Waksman 1989). Many experiments showed that relationships between cells were mediated by soluble factors. Some of these turned out to be capable of performing in more than one experimental scenario. The first of them was the lymphocyte-stimulating factor released by T cells that turned the B cells on to clonal proliferation. There was also a suppressor factor and a macrophage inhibitory factor, which kept the macrophage close to the active focus, and there were lymphotoxins, which were released by the "killer T cells," or "K cells," that worked directly on a foreign target cell. It became possible to define the complicated relationships that could exist among the target cell, the immunoglobulin, and the macrophage or K cell, or between antigen–antibody complexes and effector cells. Transfer factor was now in good company. As Sherwood Lawrence (1970) wrote, the spell was broken, and the ambiguity that had so long surrounded this branch of immunology was being cleared up. The diffusion of this knowledge into practical medicine was marked by the appearance of more than one textbook of clinical immunology.

Waksman has called the decade beginning in 1980 the "holocene era," the era when everything is connected to everything else. That era had already begun in the 1970s, with the work on cell–cell interactions. The end of the decade saw interaction beginning between cell biologists with their culture techniques and immunochemists and their sequence studies. The common meeting ground was now to involve not only cells and serum, but also genetics and molecular biology. The raw material was provided by the myeloma proteins, each representing a different immunoglobulin that could be studied in isolation. By 1970 it was fully accepted that antibody diversity was genetically determined. The question was still, as it had been for half a century, how such tremendous diversity could be genetically controlled.

Sequence studies had shown that the variable region on the globulin was confined to one end of each chain and that these sites were separately coded in the genome. The number of genes for the variable regions was estimated to be perhaps no more than a thousand. Were all these genes to be found in the germ line of every cell? Some immunologists, such as Jerne, argued that a small number of them were but that this number was expanded by somatic mutation in the individual after conception (Jerne 1971). The argument against this view was that the sequences within variable regions fell into distinct groups, identical in all members of a species, and these appeared to be inherited in the regular Mendelian fashion, making somatic mutation unlikely.

Yet many workers had found that the 18 S globulin formed just after immunization seemed to show less variety of variable regions than the 7 S that came later, suggesting that somatic mutation could have occurred during clonal expansion. Evidence for somatic mutation came in 1981 from Lou Hood and his group at the California Institute of Technology. They used the hybridoma technique, developed in the mid-1970s, to make a myeloma that produced antibody of a predetermined specificity. Cells from a mouse myeloma were hybridized with spleen cells from 19 different immunized mice. The variable-region sequences of the antibody globulins were compared with the germ-line sequence of mouse DNA related to the antibody binding site. Not all of the antibody sequences were identical: Half of them reflected the exact sequence as coded for in the germ line, but the others differed from one another by one to eight amino acids. The germ-line sequence was found in the 18 S globulin and the variants in the 7 S (Crews et al. 1981; Clark 1983). It appears that the variable region is encoded by the germ-line genes but that further variants can arise after birth and perhaps after stimulation by antigen. Clonal expansion seems to generate new mutants, some of which respond to the antigenic stimulus by producing a shower of new clones. Some of these clones may produce an ever closer antigen–antibody match, rather as an animal species evolves to fill an ecological niche by natural selection.

The Clonal Selection Theory and the Field

As already mentioned, the Cold Spring Harbor Symposium of 1967 was a marker for the point at which immunologists accepted the clonal selection theory. It also marked the point at which the volume of immunology research began to expand enormously. As Moulin has pointed out, the conception of the immune apparatus as a system began to appear soon after 1967. A system implied a unified body of knowledge as well as a complex mechanism with interacting parts. Significantly, it also provided a means of formulating problems in a way that attracted grants to solve them. It provided a framework for experiment, if not a guarantee of experimental success (Moulin 1989). With the acceptance of the clonal selection theory as a basis for research programs, the sudden expansion of immunology as a research field gave birth to a large number of specialist research journals. Between 1970 and the date of writing in 1988, 47 new immunological journals came into being.

As part of the same surge of growth, immunologists began to create a formal international organization for themselves. Conferences on particular problems, such as the one on tolerance in London in 1957, the Antibody Workshop, which met irregularly between 1958 and 1965, and the Cold Spring Harbor Symposium of 1967, had always been of great importance to the workers in this very international field (Porter 1986). But from 1968, with the formation of the International Union of Immunological Societies, the connections became structured and permanent. The First International Congress of Immunology was held in Washington, D.C., in 1971. One of the goals of the International Union was to demonstrate the range and power of the new immunology, as well as its applicability in medicine and industry, so as to promote the creation of independent departments of immunology in universities and medical schools (as opposed to research institutes) and to encourage the expansion and funding of teach-

ing programs (Cinader 1975). The first congress in 1971 attracted about 4,000 participants, the sixth, held in Toronto in 1986, about 12,000. An expansion was clearly taking place.

Conclusion

A historian of science brought up on Thomas Kuhn's concepts of paradigm change and discontinuity in science would probably want to ask whether the clonal selection theory and the massive expansion of the field that followed its acceptance could qualify as the kind of gestalt shift that Kuhn had in mind. Was there a profound discontinuity between the thinking of prewar serologists and that of cellular immunologists after 1957? In the author's opinion, there was not. The new theory had the effect of enormously enlarging the field, uniting its domains, and linking immunology to the broader biological sciences. But a large part of the practice and theory of the prewar years was carried over, intact, to the synthesis of the 1960s and 1970s.

The work on vaccines lost nothing in the transition, although some of it has been less generally useful since the coming of antibiotics. In some cases, it was the very success of the vaccination program that made its continuation unnecessary. In others, such as that of diphtheria, the rarity of the disease in the West has made the serum treatment a thing of the past, though diphtheria is still an important concern of the Haffkine Institute in India. Serological tests for disease are as important as they ever were.

One of the most significant continuities has been in blood grouping. As well as being directly utilized in hospital blood banking, the thinking about and techniques of blood group serology laid the conceptual foundation for human genetics in general. Blood group genetics with its complex antigens and its mathematical Mendelism provided a model on which human genetics, and the genetics of proteins and cells, could be patterned.

On the theoretical side, Landsteiner's work on the nature of specificity is probably more significant now than it was to most of his contemporaries, who were more interested in the control of infectious disease. The new findings extended rather than reinterpreted his work, and immunologists continue to use his techniques. Of the ideas based on Landsteiner's template theory, only Haurowitz's was totally discarded by clonal selectionists. Its destruction, in fact, had been essential to their program. Even if it had not been, it would have been run aground sooner or later on the changes in protein genetics and the central dogma. It was embedded in the chemistry of the 1920s and 1930s, and there it had to stay. Colloid chemistry itself evolved away from the vitalism of its original exponents, but it was the source of the physical chemistry that developed in Uppsala and of the work on the antigen–antibody reaction.

The elevated position of Ehrlich's theory in contemporary immunology is rather paradoxical. On the one hand, its basic premises of perfect one-to-one specificity of antigen and antibody and firm chemical union of the covalent type had already been outgrown by his contemporaries. His diagrams, like his terminology, seemed to pretend to a concrete knowledge that he did not really possess. In addition, the side-chain theory needed a huge diversity of preformed antibody specificities. It was this weakness that Haurowitz's instruction theory of antibody formation was meant to correct. But to our contemporaries, that was just the feature that gave Ehrlich's theory its lasting value: It was a selection theory, like the theories of the 1950s. Finally, Ehrlich's drawings of the side-chain theory are a visual metaphor; they can represent a modern receptor as well as they did the receptor of 1900. Thus, Ehrlich has been given the role of an inspired precursor by historically conscious immunologists of the 1980s (Ada and Nossal 1987).

Finally, as Burnet himself saw, the conception of the clone originates in bacteriology, and that of selection, in a Darwinistic population genetics. The theory was not a new one. Instead, it was an old one transposed to a new and fertile setting, where it developed a truly explosive heuristic power. Rather than being revolutionary, it placed immunology among the biological sciences of the twentieth century, sharing with them their most fundamental assumptions.

The history of immunology, in spite of its seeming discontinuities, is one of the evolution of a single species: There are few extinctions in the fossil record of this science. But then, it is only 100 years old.

Pauline M. H. Mazumdar

Bibliography

Ada, Gordon L. 1989. Conception and birth of the clonal selection theory. In *Immunology 1930–1980: Essays on the history of immunology,* ed. Pauline M. H. Mazumdar, 33–40. Toronto.

Adan, Gordon L., and Sir Gustav Nossal. 1987. The clonal-selection theory. *Scientific American* 257: 62–9.

Arrhenius, Svante, and Thorvald Madsen. 1902. Physical chemistry applied to toxins and antitoxins. In *Contri-* butions from the University Laboratory for Medical Bacteriology to celebrate the inauguration of the State Serum Institute, ed. Carl J. Salomonsen. Copenhagen.

Behring, Emil von. 1895. Leistungen und Ziele der Serumtherapie. *Deutsche medizinische Wochenschrift* 21: 623–34.

Bernard, Nöel. 1960. Les Instituts Pasteur d'Outre-Mer. *L'Opinion Economique et Financière* 35: 86–92.

Bernstein, Felix. 1924. Ergebnisse einer biostatistischen zusammenfassenden Betrachtung über die erblichen Blutstrukturen des Menschen. *Klinische Wochenschrift* 3: 1495–7.

Besredka, Alexandre. 1921. *Histoire d'une idée: L'oeuvre de E. Metchnikoff: Embryogène, inflammation, immunité, sénéscence, pathologie, philosophie.* Paris.

Bordet, Jules. 1896. Sur le mode d'action des sérums préventifs. *Annales de l'Institut Pasteur* 10: 193–219.

Breinl, Friedrich, and Felix Haurowitz. 1929. Chemische Untersuchungen des Präzipitates aus Hämoglobin und anti-Hämoglobin-Serum und Bemerkungen über die Natur der Antikörper. *Hoppe Seylers Zeitschrift für physiologische Chemie* 192: 45–57.

Burnet, Sir Frank Macfarlane. 1957. A discussion of immunological tolerance under the leadership of Sir Frank Macfarlane Burnet, 8 March 1956. *Proceedings of the Royal Society of London (Series B)* 146: 1–92.

1967. The impact of ideas on immunology. *Cold Spring Harbor Symposium on Quantitative Biology* 32: 1–8.

Burnet, Sir Frank Macfarlane, and Frank Fenner. 1949. *The production of antibodies.* Melbourne.

1962. *The integrity of the body.* Cambridge, Mass.

Chick, Harriette, Margaret Hume, and Marjorie Macfarlane. 1971. *War on disease: A history of the Lister Institute.* London.

Cinader, Bernhard. 1975. Six years of the International Union of Immunological Societies: Presidential Report, Brighton, 1974. *International Archives of Allergy & Applied Immunology* 48: 1–10.

Clark, William R. 1983. *The experimental foundations of modern immunology,* 2d edition. New York.

Crews, S., et al. 1981. A single VH gene segment encodes the immune response to phosphoryl choline: Somatic mutation is correlated with the class of the antibody. *Cell* 25: 59–66.

Crick, Francis H. 1957. On protein synthesis. *Symposium of the Society for Experimental Biology* 12: 138–67.

Defries, R. D. 1968. *The first forty years, 1914–1955: Connaught Medical Research Laboratories, University of Toronto.* Toronto.

Delaunay, Albert. 1962. *L'Institut Pasteur des origines à aujourd'hui.* Paris.

Ehrlich, Paul. 1887–8. Die Wertbemessung des Diphtherieheilserums. *Klinisches Jahrbuch* 6: 299–324.

Foster, W. D. 1970. *A history of medical bacteriology & immunology.* London.

Freund, Jules. 1956. The mode of action of immunological

adjuvants. *Advances in Tuberculosis Research* 7: 130–48.

Geison, G. J. 1974. Pasteur. In *Dictionary of scientific biography*, Vol. 10, ed. C. C. Gillispie, 350–416. New York.

Grubb, Rune. 1989. Interaction between immunology and genetics: Blood group systems as important early models and as tools. In *Immunology, 1930–1980*, ed. P. M. H. Mazumdar, 131–42. Toronto.

Hartley, Sir Percival. 1945. International biological standards: Prospect and retrospect. *Proceedings of the Royal Society of Medicine* 39: 45–58.

Haurowitz, Felix. 1960. Immunochemistry. *Annual Review of Biochemistry* 29: 609–34.

1963. *The chemistry and functions of proteins.* New York.

Hogben, Lancelot. 1931. *Genetic principles in medicine and social science.* London.

Jensen, Klaus. 1936. Report on international standards maintained at the Statens Serum Institutet, Copenhagen, Denmark, on behalf of the Health Organisation of the League of Nations. *League of Nations, Quarterly Bulletin of the Health Organisation.* Special number on biological standardisation, II. November 1936, 728–34.

Jerne, Nils Kaj. 1955. The natural selection theory of antibody formation. *Proceedings of the National Academy of Sciences of the U.S.A.* 41: 849–57.

1967. Summary: Waiting for the end. *Cold Spring Harbor Symposium on Quantitative Biology* 32: 591–603.

1971. The somatic generation of immune recognition. *European Journal of Immunology* 1: 1–9.

Judson, Horace. 1979. *The eighth day of creation: Makers of the revolution in biology.* New York.

Koch, Robert. 1891. Weitere Mittheilung über das Tuberculin. *Deutsche medizinische Wochenschrift* 17: 1189–92.

Landsteiner, K. L. 1901. Ueber Agglutinationserscheinungen normalen menschlichen Blutes. *Wiener klinische Wochenschrift* 37: 1132–4.

1909. Die Theorien der Antikörperbildung. *Wiener klinische Wochenschrift* 22: 1623–31.

Landsteiner, K. L., and Merrill W. Chase. 1939. Studies on the sensitisation of animals with simple chemical compounds: VI. Experiments on the sensitisation of guinea pigs to poison ivy. *Journal of Experimental Medicine* 69: 767–84.

Landsteiner, K. L., and H. Lampl. 1918. Ueber die Abhängigkeit der serologischen Spezifizität von der chemischen Struktur (Darstellung von Antigenen mit bekannter chemischer Konstitution der spezifischen Gruppen) XII Mitteilung über Antigene. *Biochemische Zeitung* 86: 343–94.

Lawrence, Sherwood H. 1970. Editorial: Cellular immunology. *Cellular Immunology* 1: 1–2.

Marrack, John R. 1934. *The chemistry of antigens and antibodies.* Privy Council: Medical Research Council Special Report Series No. 194, 82–7. London.

Mazumdar, Pauline M. H. 1974. The antigen–antibody reaction and the physics and chemistry of life. *Bulletin of the History of Medicine* 48: 1–21.

1975. The purpose of immunity: Landsteiner's interpretation of the human isoantibodies. *Journal of the History of Biology* 8: 115–33.

1989. The template theory of antibody formation. In *Immunology, 1930–1980,* ed. P. M. H. Mazumdar, 13–32. Toronto.

1990. *The eugenists and the pauper class: The genetics of human inferiority.* London.

1992. *Eugenics, human genetics, and human failings: The eugenic society, its sources and its critics.* London.

In press. *Species and specificity: An interpretation of the history of immunology.*

Mazumdar, Pauline M. H. ed. 1989. *Immunology 1930–1980: Essays on the history of immunology.* Toronto.

Mechnikov, Ilya Ilyich. 1884. Ueber eine Sprosspilzkrankheit der Daphnien: Beitrag zur Lehre über den Kampf der Phagocyten gegen Krankheitserreger. *Archiv für pathologische Anatomie und Physiologie und für klinische Medizin (Virchow)* 96: 177–95, 2 plates.

Miller, J. F. A. P. 1962. Effect of thymectomy on the immunological responsiveness of the mouse. *Proceedings of the Royal Society of London,* Ser. B, 156: 415–28.

Moore, Stanford, and William H. Stein. 1951. Chromatography of amino acids on sulfonated polystyrene resins. *Journal of Biological Chemistry* 192: 663–81.

Morris, C. J. O. R., and P. Morris. 1964. *Separation methods in biochemistry.* London.

Moulin, Anne-Marie. 1989. Immunology old and new: The beginning and the end. In *Immunology, 1930–1980,* ed. P. M. H. Mazumdar, 241–8. Toronto.

1991. *Le dernier langage de médecine: Histoire de l'immunologie de Pasteur au SIDA.* Paris.

Nossal, G. J. V., and J. Lederberg. 1959. Antibody production by single cells. *Nature* 181: 1419–20.

Parish, H. J. 1965. *A history of immunisation.* Edinburgh.

Petrov, R. V. 1987. *Me or not-me: Immunological mobiles.* Moscow.

Porath, Jerker. 1960. Gel filtration of proteins, peptides and amino acids. *Biochimica et Biophysica Acta* 39: 193–207.

Porter, R. R. 1959. The hydrolysis of rabbit gammaglobulin and antibodies with crystalline papain. *Biochemical Journal* 73: 119–27.

1973. Structural studies of immunoglobulins. *Science* 180: 713–16.

1986. Antibody structure and the Antibody Workshop. *Perspectives in Biology & Medicine* 29(3, pt. 2): S161–5.

Rubin, Lewis P. 1980. Styles in scientific explanation: Paul Ehrlich and Svante Arrhenius on immunochemistry. *Journal of the History of Medicine* 35: 397–425.

Salomonsen, Carl Julius. 1902. The rise and growth of the serum institute. In *Contributions from the University for Medical Bacteriology to celebrate the inauguration of the State Serum Institute,* 3–20. Copenhagen.

Schadewaldt, Hans. 1979. *Geschichte der Allergie,* Vol. 1. Munich.

Silverstein, Arthur M. 1979. Cellular versus humoral immunity: Determinants and consequences of an epic 19th century battle. *Cellular Immunology* 48: 208–21.
1982. Development of the concept of specificity, I and II. *Cellular Immunology* 67: 396–409; 71: 183–95.

Sober, Herbert A., F. J. Gutter, Mary M. Wyckoff, et al. 1956. Chromatography of proteins: II. Fractionation of serum protein on anion-exchange cellulose. *Journal of the American Chemical Society* 78: 756–63.

Spiegel-Adolf, Mona. 1930. *Die Globuline.* Leipzig.

Svedberg, The. 1938. Ueber die Ergebnisse der Ultracentrifugierung und Diffusion für die Eiweisschemie. *Kolloid Zeitschrift* 85: 119–28.

Tiselius, Arne. 1938. Electrophoretische Messungen am Eiweiss. *Kolloid Zeitschrift* 85: 129–36.

Waksman, Byron H. 1989. Cell-mediated immunity. In *Immunity, 1930–1980,* ed. P. M. H. Mazumdar, 143–66. Toronto.

Waksman, Byron H., S. Arbouys, and B. G. Arnason. 1961. The use of specific lymphocyte sera to inhibit hypersensitive reactions of the delayed type. *Journal of Experimental Medicine* 114: 997–1022.

III.3
Nutritional Chemistry

The idea that diet is an important factor in health is a very old one and, if anything, had greater prominence in the time of Hippocrates than it does now. However, the development of a workable system or science of nutrition had to await the development of modern chemistry with its significant advances at the end of the eighteenth century.

Before that time, the purpose of nutrition in adults was assumed to be the replacement of abraded (or worn-out) tissues. Meat, the tissues of other animals, seemed an effective food for this purpose, because it provided essentially like-for-like, but vegetable foods seemed to be made of quite different "stuff." Animal tissues allowed to decompose became putrid and alkaline, whereas most vegetables became acid and did not become putrid. When heated and dried, animal tissues became hornlike, whereas vegetables became powdery. However, Iacopo Bartolomeo Beccari of the University of Bologna pointed out in 1728 that, when sieved (i.e., debranned) wheat flour was wetted and pummeled into a dough and then kept under running water until the floury starch had been washed out, the residual gluten had all the properties of animal tissues. Similar fractions were found in other plant foods. It was thought that these were the essential nutrients, and it was the job of the digestive system to winnow away the unwanted starch, fiber, and so forth and leave the glutenlike material to be circulated in the blood, for patching and filling.

Protein

With the discovery of nitrogen as an element toward the end of the eighteenth century, and the development in France of methods for analyzing the amount of nitrogen in different materials, came the discovery that both animal tissues and the "animal-like" fractions in vegetables contained nitrogen, whereas starch, sugar, fats, and vegetable fibers contained only carbon, hydrogen, and oxygen.

After more work, mostly in Germany, it was concluded that these nitrogenous compounds were really all of one class, the *proteins,* and that they could be converted one to another by animals, but that as a class they had to come from the vegetable kingdom. Because they were considered the true nutrients, the value of a food or animal feedstuff could be judged by its nitrogen content. It was also thought that the force exerted in the contraction of muscles came from the "explosion" and destruction of some of their protein, with the subsequent breakdown of the residue to urea, a simple nitrogen compound that the kidneys diverted into the urine. It was therefore particularly important for those engaged in hard physical work to have a high-protein diet, and on a dry matter basis, the foods highest in protein were meat, cheese, and eggs.

As a corollary to this idea, carbohydrates (i.e., starch and sugars) and fats were considered "respiratory" foods. These were combusted in the body (i.e., they reacted with oxygen) and this produced heat; this reaction, by "mopping up" oxygen in the tissues, was thought to protect the valuable protein from oxidation.

Because people in affluent countries tended to eat more animal foods, and therefore more protein, it was concluded that the extra protein gave them extra energy, which, in turn, made them prosperous. The diet chosen by healthy, hard workers in the United States was found to contain, typically, some 120 grams of protein per day, and this was adopted generally as a recommended standard at the end of the nineteenth century.

Once set, however, the whole pyramid of ideas collapsed with the discovery that physical labor did not cause a significant breakdown of muscle protein. Fats and carbohydrates were the main energy sources for all forms of activity. Tests showed that 60 grams of protein per day could support health and vigor in an active man. However, in the early years of the twentieth century, it was also discovered that all proteins were *not* nutritionally equal. Whereas protein molecules themselves were very large, typically containing more than 10,000 atoms, boiling them in a solution of strong acid resulted in the production of 20 or so fairly simple crystalline compounds, all of the same chemical class – the amino acids. Later work showed that proteins had to be broken down to these constituent units in the digestive tract before absorption could take place. The body proteins were then built up anew from these units, or building blocks, with each protein having a fixed composition.

The practical significance of this is that humans, and other members of the animal kingdom, have the ability to convert some amino acids to others, but about half of the amino acids must be provided by the diet. These are called the *essential amino acids*. In general, the mix of individual proteins contained in foods, even those of plants, includes all the amino acids, but the proportions differ. It was demonstrated in 1915 that growth stopped in young rats when the only protein they received was zein, a particular protein fraction from maize containing none of the amino acids lysine and tryptophan. Ordinary growth was restored by supplementing the diet with both of these chemicals, proving that they were dietary essentials. In later experiments with bean proteins, methionine (present in beans at a low level in relation to the requirements of animals) was determined to be the limiting factor for growth.

For productive farm animals, with their high rates of growth and reproduction, it has proved economic in some circumstances to supplement commercial diets with synthetic lysine or methionine. However, in practical human diets based on mixtures of foods, there is little evidence of a single amino acid being limiting. An exception are the amino acid–deficient diets of infants given some all-vegetable-protein formulas as substitutes for milk.

Energy

We return now to the role of carbohydrates and fats. After the realization that carbon, hydrogen, oxygen, and nitrogen together make up the great bulk of food materials, and the development of reasonably good analytic methods for their determination by about 1830, attempts were made in England to assess what quantities of carbon and nitrogen were required for an adequate diet. (Hydrogen and oxygen could be supplied in the form of water.) There was a demand at this time for objective, scientific answers to the problem of providing food for prisoners and inmates of poorhouses that would support health without being superior to what was within reach of honest, working laborers. The first estimate was that the average man required at least 300 grams of carbon and 15 grams of nitrogen per day.

It had been demonstrated as early as the 1780s, by Antoine Laurent Lavoisier and others, that respiration and combustion were similar processes, with carbon dioxide being an end product of each. By 1870 it had been shown that the heat produced by the metabolism of food in the body was the same as that produced by the combustion of food in the laboratory. This made it possible to transfer the physicists' new thinking about the conservation of energy and the mechanical equivalent of heat to nutrition. The contribution of carbohydrates and fats to the diet was then expressed not as so many grams of carbon, but as so many kilocalories of energy that would be released if they were metabolized to carbon dioxide and water in the body. (The amount of heat required to raise the temperature of 1 kilogram of water by 1°C is 1 kilocalorie. This is the unit used in nutritional literature, but commonly written as Kcal, the K indicating that the unit is the kilogram rather than the gram unit.)

It was possible to estimate the energy value of foods by burning them in an atmosphere of pure oxygen (to make complete combustion more rapid), using a submerged metal casket (usually called a "bomb"), and measuring the heat released from the increase in temperature of the surrounding water. This "gross" figure needed correction for the proportion of the food that was indigestible. With ordinary human foods, this was only a small correction, and for practical purposes values of 4 Kcal per gram for carbohydrates and 9 Kcal per gram for fats have been found adequate. Protein not needed for new tissue synthesis and broken down also yields approximately 4 Kcal per gram. Energy requirements were found to vary from as few as 2,000 Kcal per day in sedentary men to as many as 4,000 Kcal in someone doing long hours of physical work. Women, in general, had lower requirements in proportion to their smaller muscular frame. In practice, more than 90 percent of the food we eat is needed as fuel, that is, as a source of energy, rather than for the replacement of worn-out tissue.

Vitamins

Although the scientific evaluation of diets at the end of the nineteenth century focused on protein and energy, some realized that there were other requirements for a healthy diet. In particular, it was known that sailors on long voyages developed scurvy unless they periodically ate fresh green vegetables or fruit. Citrus fruit juice was particularly valued. James Lind, a British naval surgeon, carried out a famous controlled trial on a group of scorbutic sailors in 1747. He found that a combination of oranges and lemons produced a rapid cure, whereas neither sulfuric acid nor vinegar had any value.

Lind believed that scurvy resulted from the debilitating effect of the moist air in ships at sea and that the antiscorbutic factor in citrus fruits was not normally needed by people living on land. Nineteenth-century experience showed that this was not so. Scurvy was a serious disease among those rushing to the California gold fields in 1849, both when they were en route by ox wagon and after they had arrived. It caused thousands of deaths in the Allied armies during the Crimean War, and even broke out during the relatively short siege of Paris in 1870–1.

A lecturer at a London medical school had said in 1830: "Scurvy is a purely *chemical* disease . . . each part of the body is ready to perform all its functions, but one of the external things necessary for its doing so is taken away." He compared the condition to the suffocation of someone deprived of fresh air. The "necessary thing" for preventing scurvy, he said, was contained in fresh animal and vegetable food. By contrast, the diet of sailors and soldiers on active duty was normally restricted to dried and preserved foods. His views were finally to be proved correct 100 years later. After a series of erroneous guesses as to the nature of the antiscorbutic factor, real progress was made when a report from Norway in 1907 indicated that the disease could be reproduced in guinea pigs. This made it practicable to test different fractions of lemon juice and other foods, to concentrate the active factor, and finally to isolate it. This work was completed in 1932, and the chemical, called ascorbic acid (or vitamin C), was synthesized in 1933. Ascorbic acid proved similar to a sugar in its structure, and a daily intake of only 10 milligrams per day was sufficient to prevent scurvy. (This corresponds to approximately one-eighth of an ounce over an entire year.)

Since the discovery of vitamin C, there has been some controversy as to how much is required for optimal health. The official recommendation in most countries is from 30 to 75 milligrams per day, levels that can be provided by an ordinary mixed diet. Others, however, have recommended megadoses of up to 1,000 milligrams per day, or even more, on the principle that "if a little is good, more must be better," especially in resisting disease. In practice, such quantities can be obtained only by consuming the synthetic chemical.

A continuing role of nutritional chemistry is that of determining whether new kinds of food processing result in the destruction of vitamin C. For example, potatoes have been important in protecting northern Europeans from scurvy since their adoption as a major food staple in the eighteenth century. However, the process whereby they are converted to "instant" mashed potato powder destroys most of their vitamin C. Manufacturers therefore add synthetic ascorbic acid, so that the consumer receives the same benefit as that obtained from traditionally cooked potatoes.

Another disease that was associated with faulty diet by the end of the nineteenth century was beriberi, a potentially fatal condition first encountered by Europeans in the Dutch East Indies and Malaysia. Statistics from prisons and elsewhere indicated that it was associated with the use of white (i.e., highly milled) rice, rather than the cruder brown rice. The initial explanation was that, with the outer protective layers removed, white rice grains became contaminated by the penetration of toxic microorganisms through their porous surface. In a period when microorganisms were found to be responsible for so many diseases, the explanation seemed plausible. However, when it was discovered that chickens that had developed the same disease when fed white rice could be cured by the addition of the "branny layer" or "rice millings" to the white rice diet, the explanation seemed less satisfactory. Next it was realized that, if other starchy foods were substituted for white rice, the disease could still occur. Finally, it was accepted that this disease, and presumably others, could be explained by a *lack* of something, rather by positive toxicity. This became a central concept in the development of nutritional views.

The first attempts to isolate and identify the antiberiberi factor, using animals to test the activity of different materials, actually came before the corresponding work on the antiscorbutic factor. In 1912 Casimir Funk suggested that the factor in rice bran was a "vital amine," or "vitamine," and that a number of diseases were caused by a dietary lack of minute amounts of this or similar organic compounds. This proved to be true except that the compounds were not all of the chemical group called *amines,* and the term was reduced to *vitamin.* At least until the chemical structures of the factors became known, they were listed as vitamins A, B, C, and so forth. And when vitamin B, the water-soluble factor in yeast, was realized to be itself a complex of factors, these factors were called B_1, B_2, B_6, and so on. These code names have now been largely replaced by the corresponding chemical names, which in this case are thiamine, riboflavin, and pyridoxine for B_1, B_2, and B_6. Altogether 13 vitamins have been discovered.

Some species need other organic compounds in addition to the vitamins required by humans; others can synthesize vitamins. Dogs, pigs, and many other animals, for example, make their own vitamin C and thus thrive on a diet that would be scorbutic for human beings.

Because the animal kingdom, as a whole, lives on the vegetable kingdom, one would expect that all of the vitamins we in the animal kingdom require would be synthesized by plants. However, there were some puzzling exceptions for investigators to unravel. The first was vitamin A (or retinol), the fat-soluble factor, the lack of which resulted first in an inability to see in dim light and then in ulceration of the cornea of the eye and permanent blindness. The richest sources of the factor were fish liver oils; it was colorless and had characteristic chemical properties. Yet green leafy foods also prevented the deficiency, but apparently did not contain the same chemical. Finally it was discovered that green leafy foods contained a group of chemicals, the carotenoids, yellow, orange or red in color, which acted as provitamins – and were converted to the actual vitamin in the body.

Another disease to be associated with the lack of a fat-soluble vitamin was rickets, and again workers engaged in studying the cause of the disease obtained apparently contradictory results. Some reported that they could cure rachitic puppies by giving them exercise, that is, taking them for walks, without changing their diet. Others reported that they could cure the condition not by giving the puppies exercise but by supplementing their diet with fish liver oil – even if the oil had been oxidized so that it had lost its vitamin A activity. This paradox was resolved by a long series of studies showing that an active factor (to be named vitamin D) was produced by the action of the sun's ultraviolet rays on sterols, such as cholesterol, which animals synthesized for themselves. Vitamin D is synthesized in animal or human skin exposed to sunlight, after which it is stored in the liver.

The function of vitamin D was next related to the absorption of calcium and its deposition in bones. Rickets, which characteristically results in bent legs, occurs when bones are soft and undermineralized. The condition so prevalent in young children in Victorian cities was caused by inadequate irradiation of the skin, because of the pall of smoke from coal-burning homes and industries *and* the use of starch-based weaning formulas that lacked the vitamin. For a given amount of irradiation, less vitamin D is synthesized in people with pigmented skins than in people with less pigmentation. At the beginning of the twentieth century, a mild case of rickets was considered almost normal in the young children of black families who had migrated to northern industrial cities in the United States. It is still a problem among children of Asian immigrants in the United Kingdom.

Cobalamin (or vitamin B_{12}), the last vitamin to date to be discovered (in 1948), is synthesized only by microorganisms. Ruminant animals obtain it from the bacteria living in their rumen (i.e., forestomach), and others from food with adhering soil bacteria. Omnivores, humans among them, obtain the vitamin from meat, fish, eggs, and milk.

As with ascorbic acid, the development of chemical analytic methods for determining the levels of each vitamin in foods and the inexpensive production of vitamins have enabled food manufacturers to fortify processed foods with them – without unduly raising their prices. Thus, margarine has vitamins A and D added at levels at least as high as those in butter, for which it is a substitute. White rice is fortified with thiamine, milk with vitamin D, and so on. In addition, many people in the more affluent countries take vitamin pills, or capsules, to ensure that they are receiving a sufficient dosage or in the hope of "superhealth," although there is no conclusive evidence that there is such a thing.

Minerals

The last class of long-recognized nutrients comprises minerals. Dried bones were known to consist mainly of calcium phosphate, and when other tissues were brought to red heat in a furnace, there was always a small residue of incombustible ash, or mineral salts. Up to about 1850 it was apparently assumed that a practical diet would always supply a sufficient quantity of these minerals in humans, and even in fast-growing farm animals. Yet deficiencies can and do occur, as can be seen from a discussion of three elements.

The fact that iron salts were an effective treatment for chlorosis ("green sickness") in young women was not at first regarded as the correction of a nutritional deficiency. Thomas Sydenham, for example, wrote in 1670 that a medicine made from steeping iron filings in wine and boiling the liquid down to a syrup had the effect in cases of chlorosis of "returning the pale and death-like face to a ruddy color and giving the pulse strength." But there was no more suggestion of this being a nutritional use of iron than there was of mercury being a nutritional factor in the treatment of syphilis.

By 1800, however, it was understood that blood contained iron, and then that the level of iron was reduced in the paler blood of chlorotics. From 1830 pills containing ferrous sulfate were in standard use for the treatment of chlorosis, or anemia as it came to be known, and were considered to be generally effective.

German workers, however, who were in the lead from 1850 in carrying out quantitative balance studies in model animals, became skeptical as to whether these pills actually contributed iron to the blood. When large doses of ferrous sulfate were given orally to dogs, the iron was recovered almost completely in their feces, with little or none appearing in the urine. This result contrasted with the results of the Germans' previous work on protein nutrition in dogs. Proteins were absorbed almost entirely from the gut, and those not immediately required were broken down, with the surplus nitrogen appearing in the form of urea in the urine. The scientists' first conclusion, therefore, was that inorganic iron salts were indigestible and therefore useless in the treatment of anemia. But realizing that this was contrary to the clinical evidence, they hypothesized that the iron in some way neutralized the harmful effects of bacteria in the gut, leading to better absorption of the natural components of the food.

Further work showed that even iron salts injected into a dog's tissues failed to appear in the urine. In fact, it appears that animals and humans have essentially no means of excreting surplus iron from tissues. The balance is maintained by carefully controlled absorption mechanisms that normally admit only as much iron through the gut wall as is required by the tissues. However, even under conditions of acute deficiency, no more than 20 percent of iron in foodstuffs can be absorbed, and normally it may be only 1 to 2 percent. Mild anemia remains a problem in many parts of the world, particularly for women on mainly vegetarian diets. They generally eat less than men but have a greater need for iron because of their loss of menstrual blood.

Animals grazing in fields where the soil is low in particular elements are unproductive because the plants they eat are also low in such elements as copper, cobalt, and phosphorus. This problem is virtually unknown in human nutrition because of the greater variety of our diets. However, iodine is one exception. This element was discovered in 1811, and by 1820 its salts were already being used in the treatment of goiter. This is a condition of gross swelling of the thyroid gland at the front of the neck. It had always been common in particular areas of the world, usually those well away from the ocean. Traditional treatments with seaweed and the ash of sponges were explained by their high content of iodine, and by the 1830s it was proposed that goiter, and the associated condition of cretinism in children, was due to a deficient iodine intake. This was followed by the widespread use of iodine compounds, often with bad effects, so that the theory became discredited. August Hirsch, in the English edition of his *Handbook of Geographical and Historical Pathology,* published in the 1880s, referred to the "short-lived opinion" that iodine deficiency explained the problem and said that the evidence compelled one to conclude that goiter and cretinism should be classed among the infective diseases.

Gradually, however, it came to be understood that relatively small excesses of iodine could be toxic, but that a minimal average intake of 50 millionths of a gram per day was needed to avoid goiter. Indeed, the swelling of the thyroid produced by iodine deficiency is apparently a feedback reaction whereby the body attempts to capture more of the element in order to use it for the synthesis of hormones. The prevention of goiter is the only known role of iodine in animal organisms, but the stimulatory effect of hormones extends to all tissues. Children born as cretins, because of a lack of iodine, have irreversible brain damage.

Extensive chemical analysis of foods and water supplies have failed to explain the existence of goiter in a few areas of the world, and it is believed that other factors may reduce either the bioavailability of the iodine consumed or the effectiveness of the thyroid hormone produced from it. Some such factors, in cabbage family plants, for example, are already known. However, even in these areas an increase in the iodine supply has greatly reduced the incidence of goiter and also of cretinism.

In most countries where the production of domestic salt is organized in fairly large-scale units, it has been found practicable to fortify it with up to 1 part in 10,000 of potassium iodide or iodate. This has proved an effective public means of preventing the disease. In areas where salt is not refined, those at risk are sometimes given an injection of iodized oil, which can remain effective for as long as two years. In many affluent countries, chemists must ascertain whether the consumption of iodine is excessive because of the increasing use of iodine-containing chemicals for the disinfection of food-processing equipment.

Another chemical element discovered in the same decade as iodine is selenium. In the 1930s it was found to be present at toxic levels in plants grown on soils rich in selenium in Wyoming and the Dakotas, and responsible for disease among grazing sheep. But not until 1957 was it recognized as an essential nutrient. Farm animals have been found to be deficient in places as far apart as Sweden and New Zealand; these animals have characteristic lesions in their muscles, including heart muscle. The major cause of keshan disease in parts of China, in which children die with characteristic changes in their heart muscle, is now suspected to be selenium deficiency.

Reassessments

By the 1960s the status of nutrition could be summarized as follows:

1. Apparently all of the chemical nutrients had been identified, so that it was possible to define an adequate diet in completely chemical terms.
2. There was still a great deal of malnutrition among the poorest people on the earth, mainly because of a lack of *quantity* of food. And the coarsest foods were too bulky for the small stomach capacities of newly weaned infants. The main problem was therefore one of economic distribution of purchasing power and of the organization of food production rather than programs aimed at supplying specific nutrients.
3. The main exceptions to this were the deficiency of vitamin A in children in developing countries and the large pockets of goiter and cretinism, also mainly in developing countries. Again, there were scientifically tested procedures for dealing with these deficiencies, and their execution was a matter for government programs of education and public health, with technical support.
4. The populations of the most affluent countries had diets that in general provided most of the recommended levels of nutrients. Yet life expectancy at age 5 in a country such as Cuba or Panama was greater than that for corresponding children in a country like the United States or Sweden, with a

much greater average income per head and far more sophisticated sanitary and medical resources. The major cause of the shorter life expectancy in the richer countries was the greater risk of cardiovascular heart disease resulting in a "heart attack." It also appeared that individuals in affluent communities were more subject to certain types of cancer.

Rich Diets

Among the factors considered to be potential contributors to this condition was the "affluent diet." Obviously, individuals' diets differed, but typical patterns in the more prosperous Western countries revealed considerably higher levels of sugar, salt, and fat than existed in diets elsewhere. Almost all recommendations up to that point had consisted of "at least so much of this" and "don't risk being short of that," particularly to encourage maximum growth in the young.

But now there is an entirely new type of research on dietary factors that could have adverse long-term effects when nutrients are consumed at high levels for long periods. One factor is total energy intake. People whose intake is not limited by a shortage of money and who burn fewer calories because they do not engage in much physical work or exercise tend to gain weight. Grossly obese people are, in general, poor health risks – for diabetes, for example, as well as for cardiovascular heart disease. One can calculate the number of calories a person needs to consume to maintain an ideal weight, but appetite can be compelling, and obesity is a problem for millions of people, in terms of both physical health and self-esteem. Nutritional science has not been able to provide a simple solution, though the dietary changes to be discussed next have been of some help in this regard. (It should be noted that health risks increase only with *severe* obesity. Many people feel compelled to become abnormally thin, and young women in particular may become seriously ill from anorexia, that is, "failure to eat.")

Cholesterol and Fat

Cardiovascular disease involves the blockage of arteries that provide oxygen within the muscular walls of the heart. The death of even a small portion of this muscle from lack of oxygen can result in the disorganization of the heartbeat and thus a failure of the heart to meet the body's oxygen needs. The plaques that build up in blood vessels and that narrow the flow of blood contain a high proportion of cholesterol. The typical diet of affluent Westerners with their high intake of animal foods (i.e., meat, eggs, and dairy products) is rich in cholesterol. One recommendation, therefore, has been to lower cholesterol intake, in particular the intake of egg yolks (even though in the past eggs were regarded as the perfect food because they contained everything the rapidly growing embryonic chicks needed).

Cholesterol, however, is a vital constituent of cell walls, and we, like other animals, synthesize it continuously, regulating that synthesis (at least to some extent) according to dietary intake. Some studies indicated that people with high blood levels of cholesterol were at greater risk from cardiovascular heart disease. But evidence mounted that cholesterol levels in the blood were affected more by the dietary intake of saturated fat than by simple cholesterol intake. "Saturated," in this context, means saturated with hydrogen. In practice, saturated fats are those, like beef or mutton fat, butter, and some types of margarine, that are solid at room temperature.

In contrast, most vegetable fats, which are called "oils" because they are normally in the liquid state – for example, corn oil and olive oil – are more unsaturated. Margarines are made from vegetable oils that are saturated by hydrogen to various extents. Soft, or "tub," margarines are the least saturated. Of current interest is whether the fat content of the "affluent diet," in which fats typically provide 40 percent of the calories, should be reduced or whether there is something about unsaturated fat that counteracts the adverse effects of animal fats. In particular, the "omega-threes" found in fish oils are under intensive study. Also, strong evidence exists that people with high blood pressure (hypertension) are at increased risk from cardiovascular heart disease, and that a high salt intake promotes this condition.

Dietary Fiber

Modern food industries have been able to process seeds and vegetables so as to extract the fat and sugar or, in the case of grains, to mill off the outer branny layers to yield white rice or white wheat flour. The public, in general, prefers sweet foods that "slip down" easily because of their fat content and contain nothing "scratchy in the mouth." The fibrous residues from the processing of foods of this type have been used to feed farm animals. Ruminants, in particular, are able to ferment and utilize cellulose.

In the past it was thought that, because "roughage" apparently passed through the gut unchanged, the fiber had no significance as long as people had just enough not to become constipated. But in recent years, a lower incidence of cancer of the colon among communities isolated from sophisticated Western food products has prompted the suggestion that these people are protected by the higher fiber content of their diets. Perhaps the greater volume of material in the colon dilutes any carcinogenic compounds present. It is thought that gut bacteria may produce such carcinogens by acting on bile acids.

Of course, differences among communities in the incidence of colon cancer can be explained by things other than diet. However, genetics does not appear to be one of them, because, in general, after two generations, emigrant groups seem to have a disease pattern similar to that of their hosts. Moreover, some studies have confirmed the importance of diet in colon cancer; there tend to be fewer cases among vegetarians than among other groups. Vegetarians obviously have a lower intake of fat and animal protein than do others, and they consume more vegetables and more fiber.

Vegetables are extremely complex mixtures of natural, "organic" chemicals. Some believe that, rather than fiber, the green and yellow vegetables that are the principal sources of carotenoids in our diet may provide protection against colon cancer. The protective factors could also be other chemicals found in some vegetables more than others. For example, there is a class of compounds, including pectins and gums, that are not digested in the small intestine along with starch, but are rapidly fermented by bacteria when they reach the colon. They are now subsumed within the overall term *dietary fiber,* though they may in some respects produce effects that differ from those of the largely unfermented cellulose.

Research in the field of nutrition is inevitably slow. Diseases appearing mainly in middle-aged humans cannot be modeled with certainty in short-term animal trials. In the meantime, nutritionists' most common advice, after the admonition to get more exercise and stop smoking, is to consume a "prudent" diet modeled on the traditional Mediterranean peasant diet, with a predominance of cereals, vegetables, and fruit, a sparing amount of meat, preference being given to fish and chicken, and a moderate amount of dairy products that are low in fat.

Summary

The first problem for nutritional science, to identify the chemicals required in a diet to support growth and maintenance, has been solved. The deficiencies involved in diseases such as scurvy and beriberi have been identified. The adequacy of diets can be determined and the deficient nutrients supplied. The problems of malnutrition are now largely political and economic. Another problem for nutritional science is to ascertain which components of our foods either enhance or reduce our resistance to chronic disease. This work is still at an early stage.

Kenneth J. Carpenter

Bibliography

Beccari, I. B. 1728. *De frumento*. (English translation in C. H. Bailey [1941], A translation of Beccari's lecture "Concerning grain," *Cereal Chemistry* 18: 555–61.)

Carpenter, K. J. 1986. *The history of scurvy and vitamin C*. New York.

Goodman, D. C. 1971. The application of chemical criteria to biological classification in the eighteenth century. *Medical History* 15: 23–44.

Greenwald, P., E. Lanza, and G. A. Eddy, 1987. Dietary fiber in the reduction of colon cancer risk. *Journal of the American Dietetics Association* 87: 1178–88.

Guggenheim, K. Y. 1981. *Nutrition and nutritional diseases: The evolution of concepts*. Lexington, Mass.

Holmes, F. L. 1964. Introduction to "Animal Chemistry by Justus Liebig." *Sources of Science* No. 4: vii–cxvi.

1975. The transformation of the science of nutrition. *Journal of the History of Biology* 8: 137–44.

Ihde, A. J., and S. L. Becker. 1971. Conflict of concepts in early vitamin studies. *Journal of the History of Biology* 4: 1–33.

McCollum, E. V. 1957. *A history of nutrition*. Boston.

National Research Council. 1980. *Recommended dietary allowances*. Washington, D.C.

Stockman, R. 1895. Observations on the causes and treatment of chlorosis. *British Medical Journal* 2: 1473–6.

Yetiv, J. Z. 1986. *Popular nutritional practices: A scientific appraisal*. Toledo, Ohio.

III.4
Diseases of Infancy and Early Childhood

In ancient times physicians wrote primarily on the care of infants, and only incidentally about children's diseases, because their concept of medicine stressed the maintenance of health rather than the diagnosis of specific disease entities (for medical perspectives on children during antiquity, see Etienne 1973). The earliest of these "pediatric" texts known to us was that of Soranus of Ephesus (active around A.D. 100), *On Gynecology,* which included 23 chapters on infant care (see Soranus 1956; also Ruhräh 1925; Still 1931; Garrison 1965; Peiper 1966). First, Soranus gave instructions on sectioning the umbilical cord, feeding, swaddling, choosing a wet nurse (if necessary), bathing the baby, and other activities essential to infant care. Then he discussed the treatment of common disorders of infancy, including teething, rashes, and "flux of the belly," or diarrhea.

Soranus was a leader of the Methodist sect at a time when Greek medicine was enlivened by various contending schools of thought. Methodism taught that disease was due to excessive relaxation or contraction of internal pores of the body, leading to immoderate secretion and moisture in the first instance and to diminished secretion and dryness in the second. The cause of disease was considered unimportant, stress being laid instead on treatment that, crudely put, consisted of inducing the contrary state, drying the moist or humidifying the dry. In his section on infant management, Soranus concentrated on the practicalities of care and treatment without slavish adherence to the tenets of Methodism. The result was a pragmatic guide uncomplicated by theoretical or speculative overtones.

During the second century, Claudius Galen inaugurated a radical change in perspective by setting out his own complex theoretical synthesis. In so doing he established humoral theory, already several hundred years old, as the main guide to understanding health and disease. He was so successful that for the next 1,500 years humoral doctrine permeated most medical writings, including those on children and their diseases (for a guide to humoral theory, see Ackerknecht 1968).

According to this doctrine, the four elements, earth, fire, air, and water, were related to four qualities, hot, dry, cold, and wet. These qualities in turn interacted with the four humors of the body, blood, phlegm, yellow bile, and black bile. Well-being depended on the humors being in balance. Illness came about when one or more humors became predominant either for internal, constitutional reasons or because of external strains, usually dietetic or climatic. To restore health required ridding the body of excess humors either actively, through drugs, purging, vomiting, or bloodletting, or passively, by maintaining the patient's strength while trusting nature to restore the natural humoral state. Hippocratic physicians had favored the latter, expectant method, whereas Galen advocated the former, more energetic course of action.

Book 1 of Galen's *Hygiene*, entitled "The Art of Preserving Health," contains five chapters on the care of the newborn and young child. Milk, according to Galen, was the ideal food for infants "since they have a moister constitution than those of other ages" (Galen 1951). Infants were also warm by nature, and "in the best constituted bodies," this quality would remain constant until adolescence, when it would increase in intensity. In contrast, the normal body would steadily dry out from infancy onward to reach desiccation in old age. In addition, there were individual differences, inborn divergences from the ideal constitution, that would require special management, but these were not specifically discussed in Galen's *Hygiene*.

However, the concept of constitutional change during growth and development, associated with that of innate differences in temperament or constitution, gave great flexibility to humoral theory and an almost limitless explanatory power. In part because the theory was so intellectually satisfying, its validity was not seriously questioned until about the sixteenth century. Even after the surfacing of doubts, humoralism survived, in various eroded forms, into the nineteenth century. In contrast to the modern ontological concept of diseases as specific entities (each with its own cause, natural history, and cure), under humoral doctrine illness was considered a personal manifestation of humoral imbalance due to environmental stress interacting with the individual's own special constitution. However, the dichotomy was not absolute, because ancient physicians recognized some diseases as specific entities and named them according to presumed anatomic site or to cause. Thus, the Hippocratic writings described phthisis (tuberculosis), pneumonia, and pleurisy, and in succeeding centuries such distinctions became more common. (For fuller discussions of histori-

cal conceptions of disease and its relation to health, see Riese 1953; Temkin 1977.)

The interplay between the humoral and ontological interpretation of disease can be illustrated by an examination of medieval and early modern descriptions of measles and smallpox. Rhazes, an Arab philosopher and physician at the turn of the tenth century, wrote a text on children, *Practica puerorum,* unusual for the times in that it dealt only with diseases and ignored infant management (for an English translation and analysis, see Radbill 1971). Rhazes also penned a treatise on smallpox and measles, which he distinguished between but considered to have the same cause: putrefaction and fermentation of the blood. Whether a person exhibited the symptoms of smallpox or those of measles depended on humoral constitutions (see Rhazes 1939).

Until about the seventeenth century, physicians followed Rhazes' example in describing the two diseases under the same heading. Thomas Phaire, a Welsh physician whose pediatric text, published in 1545, was the first to appear in the English language, began his chapter on smallpox and measles thus: "This disease is common and familiar . . . it hath obtained a distinction into two kinds: that is to say, varioli the measles, and morbilli, called of us the smallpox. They be both of one nature, and proceed of one cause, saving that the measles are engendered of the inflammation of blood, and the smallpox of the inflammation of blood mingled with choler [yellow bile]" (Phaire 1965).

In the following century an English physician, Thomas Sydenham, provided the first description of measles per se, as well as of scarlet fever and "chorea" (St. Vitus dance, Sydenham's chorea). He did so on the basis of clinical observation while retaining a humoral interpretation of cause and treatment. That Sydenham could be innovative while still adhering to humoral theory was due in part to his conviction that diseases could be classified into species, as were plants and animals. In giving advice on medical reform, he stated: "It is necessary that all diseases be reduced to definite and certain *species,* and that, with the same care which we see exhibited by botanists in their phytologies" (Sydenham 1848; Yost 1950). Sydenham himself never published a nosology, but his advice was repeatedly heeded in the eighteenth century, Carl von Linné (Linnaeus), the great plant and animal taxonomist, being one of the first to produce a classification of diseases.

Nosology did not prosper in pediatrics, where eighteenth-century physicians continued to list symptoms and diseases unsystematically. Yet it was one of Sydenham's pupils, Walter Harris, who first diverged from classical humoral theroy. In his *Treatise of the Acute Diseases of Infants* (published in 1698 in Latin) Harris insisted that the prevailing cause of illness in infancy was excess acidity. Cure involved neutralizing and absorbing the acid with "testaceous powders" such as powdered oyster shell, crab's claws, egg shell, chalk, coral, mother of pearl, and burned ivory. The residue was then removed by purgation. Harris recommended rhubarb, a mild laxative by the standards of the time.

For the next 100 years, until the early nineteenth century, Harris's acid theory was predominant. George Still (1931) has suggested that its popularity was due to its simplicity. The old humoral pathology no longer seemed a reliable guide: it had become very complex because commentators felt free to amend it to suit themselves. In contrast, Harris supplied his readers with a simple cause and remedy for most early childhood ailments.

The late eighteenth century witnessed a revolution in chemistry. Owing to experimental input from many natural scientists and to Antoine Lavoisier's deductive genius, much time-honored knowledge was discarded. This included the Aristotelean doctrine of the four elements so intimately related to humoral theory, which was replaced by propositions that became foundational to modern chemistry. The revised science had swift repercussions in medicine, including pediatrics. Previously, physicians and others had evaluated the quality of milk on sight, by tasting, or through a nail test originally credited to Soranus that involved assessing the consistency of milk by pouring a drop on the fingernail and watching the rate of spread (Soranus 1895; Still 1931). Now, both human and animal milk could be subjected to chemical analysis. In the 1799 edition of his pediatric text, the English surgeon-midwife Michael Underwood (1806) discussed and tabulated the comparative properties of human and animal milk. Early in the nineteenth century, chemists were supplying information on the nitrogenous (protein), fat, carbohydrate, and mineral content of common foodstuffs. However, vitamin detection was delayed until the twentieth century with consequences that will be discussed in the section on deficiency diseases.

In the second half of the eighteenth century some medical men, notably Giovanni Morgagni and John Hunter, stressed the need to correlate clinical signs during life with later autopsy findings. This approach was occasionally used in the eighteenth-century pediatrics, by Robert Whytt, for example, in his observations on dropsy in the brain or acute hydrocephalus (reprinted and discussed in Ruhräh 1925). Whytt gave an excellent clinical account of this condition, which, however, would not be recognized as meningitis due to tuberculosis until the early nineteenth century. The regular practice of performing autopsies began with the advent of children's hospitals, which were introduced in Paris after the French Revolution. The Enfants Malades was established in 1802 for sick children over the age of 2 years and the ancient foundling hospital, the Enfants Trouvés, was reorganized to accommodate ailing babies as well as unwanted ones.

From contemporary reports one gathers that physicians were rarely refused permission to perform autopsies (Crosse 1815). With a relatively large number of children under their care, hospital doctors could also apply the so-called numerical method, a rudimentary statistical analysis by which mortality as well as complication and recovery rates could be assessed (Ackerknecht 1967). Under this system certain diseases, such as early childhood tuberculosis, could now be recognized and reported. Whytt's "dropsy of the brain" was classified as a manifestation of tuberculosis when it was discovered that the disease was associated with granular tubercular deposits on the membranes covering the brain (Papavoine 1830).

French pediatricians attempted to classify children's diseases, whereas, as already mentioned, earlier authors had dedicated chapters with complete impartiality to symptoms (e.g., nightmares, sneezing, hiccoughs) and to specific morbid conditions (e.g., mumps, measles, smallpox). In 1828 Charles M. Billard published a text exclusively on infant diseases, which he classified according to the site of the main lesion: skin infections, those of cellular tissue, of the digestive tract, of the respiratory and cardiac systems, of nervous or cerebrospinal origin, of the locomotor and generative systems, and finally congenital disorders. Frédéric Rilliet and Antoine Barthez, authors of a general pediatric treatise first published in 1843, used a different method. Diseases were classified primarily according to underlying pathology: phlegmasias (inflammations), hydropsies (accumulation of watery fluid), hemorrhages, gangrenes, neuroses, acute specific diseases, the various kinds of tuberculosis, and finally entozoan (parasitic, caused by various worms) diseases. Under these headings, further subdivisions were made according to the site affected (Barthez and Rilliet 1853).

In early-nineteenth-century Paris, with children's hospitals growing in number and size, pediatrics emerged as a specialty inasmuch as physicians there could engage full time in the care of children. They published extensively, stimulating interest in pediatric research abroad, although in the United States and in Britain physicians continued throughout the nineteenth century to be generalists rather than specialists (for the history of pediatrics in the United States, see Cone 1979). At first, the concept of pediatric hospitals did not gain approval in English-speaking countries for a variety of reasons, some of which are remarkably consonant with modern opinion. It was said that children, especially babies, should not be separated from their parents and would have a better chance of recovering at home than in hospitals, where, as evident from the Parisian reports, cross-infection was rife (Anon. 1843). On Malthusian and moral grounds, Henry Brougham held that "the gratuitous maintenance of poor children, may safely be pronounced dangerous to society, in proportion as it directly relieves the parent from his burthen. It removes the only check upon improvident marriages, and one of the principal guards of chastity" (Brougham 1823). With Brougham, foundling hospitals were the prime but not the exclusive subject of contention. Nevertheless, by the 1850s opinion had changed sufficiently to allow for the establishment of pediatric hospitals, albeit small ones initially, in the United States and Britain. One reason for the change was pressure from physicians who argued that the intensive investigation of pediatric disease required a hospital base (Anon. 1849).

For the next hundred years, pediatric hospitals and clinics served as sites of further investigation and treatment of disease. After World War II, however, the earlier concept that babies and small children should not be separated from their mothers surfaced again with renewed intensity. Psychoanalysts in particular drew attention to the long-term emotional effects of maternal deprivation, most evident in children reared in orphanages but also demonstrable in babies hospitalized for acute disease or for surgery. Most influential perhaps was the 1951 report prepared by John Bowlby (1951) for the United Nations program on the welfare of homeless children, but as early as 1942 Harry Bakwin, a pediatrician, had drawn attention to apathy in babies confined to hospitals. Indeed, from the mid-nineteenth century onward some physicians had opposed the isolation of infants, but the dictates of hospital organization and fears of cross-infection severely restricted parental access to their children until the psychoanalytic concept of maternal deprivation was elaborated in the 1950s.

Cross-infection had frequently ravaged pediatric wards in the early nineteenth century; hence, with the discovery that microorganisms caused contagious diseases, the isolation of potentially infective patients seemed an obvious solution. As Harry Dowling (1977) points out, between 1880 and 1900, 21 microorganisms were identified as the causes of specific diseases, including the bacilii responsible for tuberculosis, typhoid fever, and diphtheria. Also discovered were the pneumococcus and meningococcus associated with the common forms of pneumonia and meningitis, and the streptococcus whose hemolytic form produced scarlet fever and rheumatic fever. Yet knowing the causes of these illnesses was not immediately helpful. More obvious benefits would have to await specific vaccines and antibiotics.

Babies continued to die at a steady rate. As historians have frequently indicated, in England the infant mortality rate did not decline during the nineteenth century, hovering between about 140 and 160 per 1,000 from 1839, when national vital statistics were first recorded, until 1900, even though all other age groups exhibited a falling death rate from midcentury onward (Logan 1950; McKeown 1976; F. B. Smith 1979; Winter 1982; Wohl 1983; Dwork 1987).

Most other countries that kept vital statistics were looking at similar trends. In Massachusetts, the earliest state to keep continuous records, the infant mortality rate was similar to that of England. During the second half of the nineteenth century, Massachusetts reported the highest infant mortality rate of 170 for the years 1870 to 1874 and the lowest of 123 for the years 1855 to 1859; for 1895 to 1899 the rate was 153 (U.S. Bureau of the Census 1960). The French and Germans reported even higher infant death rates; in 1895 the French infant mortality rate was 177, the German one 230 (Mitchell 1975). However, the Scandinavian countries and Ireland were doing much better, with lower and falling infant death rates during the second half of the century, demonstrating that much loss of life elsewhere was unnecessary. In 1895 the infant mortality rate in Norway was 96, in Sweden 95, in Denmark 137, and in Ireland 104 (Mitchell 1975). In England, regional statistics showed that infant mortality was often twice as high in industrial areas as in rural ones, which, together with the Scandinavian experience, suggested that predominantly agricultural societies exhibited conditions most favorable to infant survival (for contemporary discussions, see Jones 1894; Newman 1907). Industrial areas were more lethal, it was often concluded, because so many mothers went out to work, abandoning their babies to casual care and bottle feeding. Dirt and environmental pollution, including food contamination, were seen as secondary to the damage caused primarily by a lack of breast feeding.

According to English vital statistics, the main killers of infants were "atrophy" and debility, pulmonary diseases (bronchitis and pneumonia), convulsions and meningitis, diarrheal diseases, and tuberculosis (Newman 1907). In the United States the picture was similar, except that diarrheal diseases accounted for a larger porportion of deaths, while pulmonary diseases were less prominent than in England (Cone 1976). By the last third of the nineteenth century, smallpox, which formerly had been particularly hazardous to babies, no longer accounted for many deaths, probably owing to widespread vaccination in the first months of life. But otherwise, medical progress, including the recognition of microorganisms as the cause of infectious diseases, seems to have had little relevance to the plight of infants. The diarrheal diseases, for example, included a variety of conditions that defied simple classification. Job Lewis Smith, a noted New York pediatrician, discussed simple diarrhea, intestinal catarrh or enterocolitis, the dreaded cholera infantum, enteritis, and colitis in the 1890 edition of his *Treatise on the Diseases of Infancy and Childhood*. Infantile cholera, the most acute and severe type, was so called because its symptoms were so similar to those of epidemic cholera. Diarrheal diseases were more common and fatal in the hot summer months, but the hot weather alone could not be responsible because summer diarrhea caused less harm in rural areas. Smith therefore subscribed to the time-honored view that the cause was related "to the state of the atmosphere engendered by heat where unsanitary conditions exist, as in large cities." Once, out of deference to germ theorists, he sent intestines from a child who had died of cholera infantum for examination by William H. Welch. The report was inconclusive because all kinds of bacteria were found on the surface of the intestines. Still, Victor C. Vaughan, professor of hygiene and physiological chemistry at the University of Michigan, was confident that the diarrheas were caused by toxin-producing bacteria. In his opinion, "there is not a specific micro-organism, as there is in tuberculosis, but any one or more of a large class of germs, the individual members of which differ from one another sufficiently morphologically to be regarded as distinct species, may be present and may produce the symptoms" (Vaughan 1897).

Recent historians, particularly Anthony S. Wohl (1983), have pointed out that maternal malnutrition probably contributed significantly to the high infant mortality. Chronically undernourished women gave birth to puny, sickly babies ill-equipped to withstand exposure to infection and the other hazards prevailing in a working-class environment, such as cold and damp housing and an inadequate diet. On the whole, however, Victorian physicians did not consider poverty and its consequences to be responsible for the unacceptably high infant mortality rate. Instead, they focused on the dangers of artificial feeding; influenced by middle-class expectations and standards, they berated women for going out to work, leaving their infants to be bottle-fed and possibly drugged by ignorant baby minders. It apparently did not occur to them that a mother's earnings might be essential for family survival, probably because a working mother was so contrary to the general Victorian image of womanhood.

By the onset of the First World War, infant mortality had fallen significantly in most European countries and in the United States. The infant mortality rate for Massachusetts dropped from 141 in 1900 to 116 in 1914 (Woodbury 1926). In England and Wales the reduction was from 154 in 1900 to 105 in 1914. Some of this abrupt change must be attributed to factors that had emerged in the nineteenth century but had taken time to prove beneficial, for example, better nutrition for the population at large leading to the birth of healthier babies (for discussions of the reasons for the decline of mortality at the turn of the century, see Woodbury 1926; McKeown 1976; Dyhouse 1978; F. B. Smith 1979; Dwork 1987). The contribution of direct medical intervention to the initial decline in mortality remains debatable, but progress in the understanding of disease began to exert observable effects on infant survival after World War I.

So numerous were the twentieth-century breakthroughs in understanding pediatric disease that only a brief summary can be attempted here. A listing of important disease categories is accompanied by a short discussion of how changes in traditional thinking gradually provided a new basis for remedial action.

Diseases Related to Infant Feeding

Infant nutrition is intimately connected with health. Breast feeding was always recognized as the ideal method of nourishing infants but was not always practicable. If a mother was unable or unwilling to suckle her baby, wet nursing was a socially acceptable alternative until the beginning of this century. In poorer families, however, nursing could be replaced only by artificial feeding. A fourth option, direct suckling from an animal, commonly the goat, was sometimes adopted on the European continent.

The literature on infant feeding is enormous (for comprehensive historical studies, see Wickes 1953; Cone 1976; Fildes 1986). By the nineteenth century, physicians in the United States and Britain tended to discourage wet nursing because of the adverse effects on the nurse's own infant, who was usually abandoned to foster care and the bottle. Efforts were directed toward increasing the safety of bottle feeding, perceived as the most important cause of high infant mortality. In 1867 Justus von Liebig, the renowned German chemist, marketed an infant food prepared on scientific principles (Drummond and Wilbraham 1958). It was not as perfect as he assumed (vitamins were then undreamed of), but it was the forerunner of an endless variety of proprietary infant foods. Many contained only powdered carbohydrates and thus, if not made up with milk and supplemented with other foods, could not begin to nourish an infant (for a discussion of interactions between physicians, infant food companies, and mothers, see Apple 1981).

A somewhat different situation prevailed in France, where it had become common practice by the eighteenth century for infants to be sent into the countryside to be wet-nursed together with the foster mother's own baby (Sussman 1982). Infant mortality was even higher than in English-speaking countries, the fertility rate was lower, and in part because of the threat of depopulation, concerned French physicians finally introduced novel methods for improving infant survival. In 1892 Pierre Budin, professor of obstetrics, organized a "Consultation de Nourrisons" at the Charité Hospital in Paris. Women who had been delivered at the hospital were advised on breast feeding and infant care; after discharge, the babies were examined and weighed weekly until weaned, then less frequently until they were 2 years of age. Great emphasis was placed on breast feeding, as well as on weight and height. Also in 1892 Gaston Variot, a pediatrician, organized the distribution of sterilized milk, at reduced prices, at the Belleville dispensary. Two years later, Léon Dufour, a medical practitioner in Normandy, opened a milk station, called the "Goutte de Lait," at Fécamp. Here also babies' growth was carefully supervised, and when breast feeding proved impracticable, sterilized milk was provided free or at reduced prices (McCleary 1935; Blake 1953).

At first there was friction between Budin and Dufour because the former felt that the Gouttes de Lait, rapidly being established all over France, encouraged artificial feeding. But soon the two men compromised and together organized the first international conference on infant welfare (Congrés International des Gouttes de Lait, 1905) held in Paris. Similar movements were developing in other countries. As early as 1893, the philanthropist Nathan Straus began organizing the distribution of pasteurized milk for children under 5 years of age in New York City (Straus 1917). At about the same time, Henry L. Coit arranged for the production of certified milk in Newark, New Jersey (Blake 1953). These pilot schemes demonstrated the possibility of ensuring a clean milk supply, although because of the expense involved city authorities only gradually adopted similar methods to ensure safe milk for all inhabitants. Rapidly disappearing, however, was the nineteenth-century conviction that breast feeding was the only safe way of nourishing infants. The new century ushered in greater professional acceptance of bottle feeding, spurred on by the availability of methods of checking the purity of milk and its bacterial content and of sterilization and pasteurization. Also novel was the awareness that incipient illness was often indicated by the failure of a baby's height and weight to increase, measures that were easy to monitor on a regular basis.

However, as will be discussed in the next section, not until the 1920s was it understood why infants fed sterilized milk, or proprietary foods, might not thrive unless also given supplements such as orange juice.

Deficiency Diseases

According to J. C. Drummond and Anne Wilbraham (1958), the earliest mention of rickets as a disease entity was made in a 1634 Bill of Mortality for the city of London. Between 1645 and 1650, at least three physicians, including Francis Glisson, gave accounts of the disease. Glisson's work, *De rachitide*, published in 1650, not only was the most extensive but also made reference to scurvy as a disease that could be associated with rickets in infants. Subsequently, most European pediatric texts discussed rickets, but no clear reference to infantile scurvy reappeared until the late nineteenth century. It would seem that rickets was commonplace in northern Europe, particularly in England, whereas infantile scurvy was rare until the advent of proprietary foods and the use of boiled or sterilized milk. In the United States, however, rickets was either unrecognized or had a low incidence until the late nineteenth century, for it was rarely discussed in the earlier pediatric textbooks or, if mentioned, was dismissed as of rare occurrence (for the first North American monograph on rickets, see Parry 1872).

Thomas Cone and others have pointed out the lack of consensus on the cause of rickets by the end of the nineteenth century (Hess 1929; Cone 1979). Some believed it was due to an improper diet, others to a lack of sunshine or exposure to polluted air. Yet others regarded it as a degenerative disease. In this view, fortified by perceived similarities in the microscopic bony lesions of syphilis and rickets, parental syphilis could be expressed in offspring as rickets or as an increased liability to rickets (for a discussion of "hereditary" syphilis as the cause of other diseases in the offspring of syphilitics, see Lomax 1979).

As indicated by Kenneth Carpenter (1986) ideas about the cause of scurvy were just as confused. In 1883 Thomas Barlow described the clinical and pathological signs of infantile scurvy, a disease entity rarely recognized in babies. He also indicated that the best remedy was orange juice. Soon physicians in other countries were recognizing "Barlow's disease," but they could not agree as to the cause or even the cure. In 1898 the American Pediatric Society reported an investigation of infantile scurvy. Most physicians who had been consulted thought that proprietary foods, and perhaps sterilized milk, were responsible for the condition. One dissenter, August Caillé, considered the illness to be a form of ptomaine poisoning caused by the absorption of toxins (Cone 1979; Carpenter 1986). Epidemiology and clinical medicine could not produce decisive evidence in favor of any particular theory (see Wilson 1975).

Early in the twentieth century, researchers using animal models to establish dietary requirements came to the rescue. Administering modified diets to animals was not a new technique, but with improvements in chemical analysis it was becoming more precise. In 1907 scurvy was produced experimentally in guinea pigs, and further experiments led Casimir Funk to propose, in 1912, that scurvy, pellagra, rickets, and beriberi were caused by a dietary lack of essential factors, which he called "vitamines." The hypothesis was received with enthusiasm, deficiency diseases were induced in animals, and between 1928 and 1938, vitamins A, B_1, C, D, and E were isolated and chemically defined (Harris 1970).

Another type of deficiency was recognized when Cicely Williams (1933) drew attention to kwashiorkor, a disorder brought on by malnutrition in previously healthy West African toddlers after weaning.

Since then, physicians and nutritionists have sought to understand, prevent, and cure this and similar disorders and syndromes, collectively known as protein–energy malnutrition (PEM) and most commonly found in developing countries. (The research literature is very large; see, e.g., Trowell, Davies, and Dean 1954; Jellife 1969; Olson 1975.) At one extreme are marasmic infants, in whom growth failure is combined with wasting from starvation, as a result of a diet deficient in both calories and protein. At the other extreme is kwashiorkor, thought to be due to a diet with an adequate caloric content but deficient in usable protein. In between are less obvious forms of PEM, characterized by growth retardation and associated with a greater liability to infection than is found in well-nourished children. Infectious disease interferes with a child's appetite, thereby provoking or worsening malnutrition, and the latter state decreases resistance to infection. In former centuries, protein–calorie deficiency syndromes were probably responsible for much wasting, infection, and diarrhea in American and European babies, but the incidence would be difficult to estimate retrospectively because illness was perceived and described so differently at that time.

Congenital Abnormalities

In the past, a great deal of ingenuity was applied to explaining the occurrence of birth defects. In the sixteenth century the French surgeon Ambroise Paré suggested no fewer than 13 possible causes, including the wrath of God, imperfections in "the seed," the imagination of the pregnant mother, and injuries to the uterus during gestation (Paré 1982). The notion that maternal impressions during pregnancy could influence the developing fetus was very persistent. As indicated by Joseph Warkany (1977), a chapter entitled "Maternal Impressions" in J. M. Keating's 1889 *Cyclopedia of the Diseases of Children* recorded 90 cases of congenital defects, blaming mental trauma suffered by the mother during pregnancy for the abnormalities. Explanations of this sort were advanced in the late nineteenth century because the mechanism of inheritance remained a mystery. Most physicians and biologists, such as Charles Darwin, continued to believe that acquired parental characteristics could be transmitted to offspring under appropriate circumstances. This age-old concept was the basis not only of Jean Baptiste de Lamarck's theory of evolution but also of Darwin's theory of pangenesis (Zirkle 1946; Churchill 1976).

Change came in 1900 with the dramatic rediscovery of Gregor Mendel's work on the laws of inheritance in peas. In 1902 an English physician, Archibald Garrod, voiced his suspicion that a rare disease in babies called alkaptonuria was hereditary and surmised that this "inborn error of metabolism" (Garrod's term) was due to the lack of a necessary enzyme and that genes (the Mendelian hereditary factors) produced enzymes (Garrod 1908). However, his hypothesis was not taken seriously until it was confirmed in 1941 by George Beadle and E. L. Tatum, who had investigated the genetic control of biochemical reactions in a mold – neurospora.

Apart from genetic anomalies, birth defects can be caused by chromosomal abnormalities, by a deleterious environment, or by a multiplicity of factors (Chudley 1985). Definite evidence of environmental action was not adduced until 1941, when N. M. Gregg reviewed 78 cases of congenital cataract, finding a history of maternal rubella infection during pregnancy in all but 10 cases. Twenty years later the "thalidomide scandal" concentrated attention on the teratogenic risk associated with drugs taken during pregnancy. This was followed by the equally dramatic recognition that specific congenital malformations, Kenneth Jones's "fetal alcohol syndrome," could result from maternal alcoholism during pregnancy (Jones and Smith 1973).

Since antiquity, maternal alcoholism had been associated with injury to offspring. But as indicated by Rebecca Warner and Henry Rosett (1975), concern about and research into the potential hazards of maternal alcoholism "virtually disappeared" between about 1920 and 1940. Many reasons can be adduced for this rather sudden change, including the effects of prohibition in the United States and the discrediting of the ancient belief in the inheritance of acquired characteristics. Especially in the nineteenth century, the latter concept was exploited to explain the appearance of many congenital diseases, including damage to an infant born to an inebriate woman. Alcohol was presumed to damage the germ cells, male or female, and hence to have an adverse effect on the offspring. To the nineteenth-century mind, this was an example of the hereditary transmission of disease leading to familial degeneration. By the 1920s such Lamarckian-type hereditary transmission had been largely discredited, and the phenomena it had allegedly explained were now usually ascribed to social and economic disadvantage. Furthermore, the uterine environment was not perceived to be a potential site of teratogenic action until the maternal rubella findings were published in the early 1940s.

Infectious Diseases

Although their cause was uncertain until the last third of the nineteenth century, childhood exanthemata and whooping cough were recognized by a majority of physicians as contagious. The responsible agent was thought to be a specific virus, or morbid poison, often undetectable by the senses. However, physicians who subscribed wholeheartedly to the miasmic theory of transmission did not accept the notion of a causal virus or physicochemical agent of infection. Instead, they believed that polluted air, or miasma, could excite a variety of fevers, the specific nature of any epidemic being determined by the geography of the locality, the season of the year, or the personal constitution. For example, William P. Dewees, author of the first U.S. pediatric textbook (1826), doubted that whooping cough, mumps, and measles were contagious. In his view they were epidemic diseases, that is, dependent on some condition of the atmosphere. In his words: "It is a rule, with few or no exceptions, that, where a disease can be traced to atmospherical influence, it does not prove contagious. Nature indeed can hardly employ two such opposite causes to produce the same effect" (Dewees 1829).

In 1798 Edward Jenner had advocated the use of cowpox (vaccination) as protection against smallpox, a disease particularly fatal to infants. In a remarkably short time, vaccination replaced inoculation as the means of providing immunity to smallpox (Edwardes 1902; Hopkins 1983). However, because the mechanism of protection was not understood, confirmed miasmatists continued until the end of the nineteenth century to protest vaccination, which contradicted their epidemic, nonspecific theory of disease (for antivaccinationist views, see Crookshank 1889; Creighton 1894; Tebb 1898). In their opinion, the decreased incidence of smallpox after mass vaccination was due not to protection afforded by vaccination, but to a natural decline in smallpox epidemics counterbalanced by an increase in other diseases such as measles and whooping cough.

Immunity began to be understood when Louis Pasteur discovered that the injection of an attenuated culture of chicken cholera protected laboratory birds from the effects of a subsequent inoculation of virulent culture (for a discussion of Pasteur's work on attenuation, see Bulloch 1938). Strategies of attenuation were enlarged to include dead organisms and prepared extracts; at the same time immunity began to be explained by the production of specific serum antibodies to bacterial antigens and of antitoxins that neutralized toxins. Scientists undertook the preparation of specific protective sera with striking success in 1894, when Pierre P. E. Roux demonstrated the value of diphtheria antitoxin, which had been discovered earlier by Emil von Behring and Shibasaburo Kitasato.

Diphtheria antitoxin, although frequently life-saving, conferred only passive, temporary immunity and could not prevent the spread of disease. Gradually a safe attenuated toxin (toxoid) was developed so that by the 1930s children could be actively immunized against diphtheria. By this time, a vaccine against pertussis had also been discovered, and passive immunization against tetanus, as well as certain types of pneumococci and meningococci, was possible. Research continued apace during the Second World War, when a safe tetanus toxoid was discovered (Dowling 1977). This was followed by the discovery of poliomyelitis vaccine in 1956 and, more recently, of vaccines for rubella, measles, and mumps. Today, a full immunization program during infancy eliminates, in large measure, the ill health, chronic disability, and mortality that were once associated with the common infectious diseases of childhood.

Conclusion

Unfortunately, it is impossible in the space allotted to discuss all of the novel concepts of early childhood illness that evolved during the twentieth century. Among these was an appreciation of the rapid debility and death that result whenever fluid is quickly lost and not replaced; this led to the development of methods for maintaining or restoring acid–base balance during rehydration. Also in the twentieth century were the recognition and treatment of hormonal disorders, of hemolytic disease of the newborn, and of numerous neurological and viral disorders.

In 1906 George Newman had already indicated that prematurity and immaturity at birth were among the largest contributors to infant mortality and were on the increase (Newman 1907). Today infection and malnutrition, the chief causes of infant death between the ages of 1 month and 1 year in Newman's time, are well understood and are rarely fatal, thus allowing pediatric medicine and research to concentrate on improving the premature infant's chance of survival during the neonatal period. Newman and his contemporaries would be gratified, perhaps amazed, that the current infant mortality rate in developed countries is one-fifteenth to one-twentieth the rate in their time. Even in Third World countries, where many more babies are subject to malnutrition and vulnerable to infection, the infant mortality rate is usually much lower than that which prevailed in western Europe and the United States at the turn of the century.

Elizabeth Lomax

Bibliography

Ackerknecht, Erwin H. 1967. *Medicine at the Paris hospital, 1794–1848*. Baltimore.

1968. *A short history of medicine*. New York.

Anon. 1843. On the diseases of children. *British and Foreign Medical Review* 15: 320–8.

1849. On the diseases of children. *British and Foreign Medico-Chirurgical Review* 3: 406–32.

Apple, Rima. 1981. "How shall I feed my baby?" Infant feeding in the United States, 1870–1940. Ph.D. dissertation, University of Wisconsin.

Bakwin, Harry. 1942. Loneliness in infants. *American Journal of Diseases of Childhood* 63: 30–40.

Barthez, A.-C.-E., and F. Rilliet. 1853. *Traité clinique et pratique des maladies des enfants*, 3 vols. Paris.

Billard, Charles M. 1835. *Traité des maladies des enfants nouveau-nés et à la mamelle*, 3d edition. Brussels.

Blake, John B. 1953. *Origins of maternal and child health programs*. New Haven, Conn.

Bowlby, John. 1951. *Maternal care and mental health*. World Health Organization Monograph No. 2. Geneva.

Brougham, Henry. 1823. Early moral education. *Edinburgh Review* 38: 437–53.

Bulloch, William. 1938. *The history of bacteriology*. London.

Carpenter, Kenneth J. 1986. *The history of scurvy and vitamin C*. Cambridge.

Chudley, A. E. 1985. Genetic contributions to human malformations. In *Basic concepts in teratology*, ed. T. V. N. Persaud, A. E. Chudley, and R. G. Shalko, 31–66. New York.

Churchill, Frederick B. 1976. Rudolf Virchow and the pathologist's criteria for the inheritance of acquired characteristics. *Journal of the History of Medicine* 31: 115–48.

Cone, Thomas E. 1976. *200 years of feeding infants in America*. Columbus, Ohio.

1979. *History of American pediatrics*. Boston.

Creighton, Charles. 1894. *History of epidemics in Britain*, Vol. 2. Cambridge.

Crookshank, Edgar M. 1889. *History and pathology of vaccination*, 2 vols. London.

Crosse, John. 1815. *Sketches of the medical schools of Paris*. London.

Dewees, William P. 1829. *Treatise on the physical and medical treatment of children*, 3d edition. Philadelphia.

Dowling, Harry F. 1977. *Fighting infection: Conquests of the twentieth century*. Cambridge, Mass.

Drummond, J. C., and Anne Wilbraham. 1958. *The Englishman's food: A history of five centuries of English diet*. London.

Dwork, Deborah. 1987. *War is good for babies and other young children*. London.

Dyhouse, Carol. 1978. Working class mothers and infant mortality in England, 1895–1914. *Journal of Social History* 12: 248–62.

Edwardes, Edward J. 1902. *A concise history of small-pox and vaccination in Europe.* London.

Etienne, R. 1973. La conscience médicale antique et la vie des enfants. In *Annales de démographie historique,* ed. J. Dupaquier, 15–46. Paris.

Fildes, Valerie. 1986. *Breasts, bottles and babies.* Edinburgh.

Galen, 1951. *Galen's hygiene (De sanitate tuenda),* trans. Robert Montraville Green. Springfield, Ill.

Garrison, Fielding H. 1965. In *Abt–Garrison history of pediatrics,* 1–170. Philadelphia.

Garrod, A. E. 1908. Inborn errors of metabolism. *Lancet* 2: 107, 73–9, 142–8, 214–20.

Gregg, N. McAlister. 1941. Congenital cataract following German measles in the mother. *Transactions of the Ophthalmological Society of Australia* 3: 35–46.

Harris, Leslie J. 1970. The discovery of vitamins. In *The chemistry of life,* ed. Joseph Needham, 156–70. Cambridge.

Hess, Alfred F. 1929. *Rickets including osteomalacia and tetany.* Philadelphia.

Hopkins, Donald R. 1983. *Princes and peasants: Smallpox in history.* Chicago.

Jelliffe, Derrick B. 1969. *Child nutrition in developing countries.* Washington, D.C.

Jenner, Edward. 1798. *An inquiry into the causes and effects of the variolae vaccinae.* London.

Jones, Hugh R. 1894. The perils and protection of infant life. *Journal of the Royal Statistical Society* 58: 1–98.

Jones, Kenneth L., and David W. Smith. 1973. Recognition of the fetal alcohol syndrome in early infancy. *Lancet* 2: 999–1001.

Logan, W. P. D. 1950. Mortality in England and Wales from 1848 to 1947. *Population Studies* 4: 132–78.

Lomax, Elizabeth. 1979. Infantile syphilis as an example of nineteenth century belief in the inheritance of acquired characteristics. *Journal of the History of Medicine* 34: 23–39.

McCleary, G. F. 1935. *The maternity and child welfare movement.* London.

McKeown, Thomas. 1976. *The modern rise of population.* London.

Mitchell, B. R. 1965. *European historical statistics.* New York.

Newman, George. 1907. *Infant mortality: A social problem.* New York.

Olson, R. E., ed. 1975. *Protein calorie malnutrition.* New York.

Papavoine, Jean Nicholas. 1830. Arachnitis tuberculeuses. *Journal Hebdomadaire* 4: 113.

Paré, Ambroise. 1982. *Ambroise Paré, on monsters and marvels,* trans. and ed. Janis L. Pallister. Chicago.

Parry, John S. 1872. Observations on the frequency and symptoms of rachitis with the results of the author's clinical experience. *American Journal of the Medical Sciences* 63: 17–52, 305–29.

Peiper, Albrecht. 1966. *Chronik der Kinderheilkunde.* Leipzig.

Phaire, Thomas. 1965. *The boke of children.* Reprint. London.

Radbill, Samuel X. 1971. The first treatise on pediatrics. *American Journal of Diseases of Children* 122: 369–76.

Rhazes. 1939. Rhazes' treatise on the small-pox and measles, trans. Williams A. Greenhill; reprinted in *Medical Classics* 4: 19–84.

Riese, Walther. 1953. *The conception of disease.* New York.

Ruhräh, John. 1925. *Pediatrics of the past.* New York.

Smith, F. B. 1979. *The people's health, 1830–1910.* London.

Smith, Job Lewis. 1890. *Treatise on the diseases of infancy and childhood,* 7th edition. Philadelphia.

Soranus. 1895. *Soranus d'Ephese, "Traité des maladies des femmes,"* trans. into Franch by F.-J. Herrgott. Nancy. 1956. *On gynecology,* trans. Owswi Temkin. Baltimore.

Still, George F. 1931. *The history of paediatrics.* London.

Straus, Lina Gutherz. 1917. *Disease in milk, the remedy pasteurization: The life work of Nathan Straus.* New York.

Sussman, George D. 1982. *Selling mother's milk: The wet-nursing business in France, 1715–1914.* Urbana, Ill.

Sydenham, Thomas. 1848. *The works of Thomas Sydenham, M.D.,* Vol. 1, trans. from the Latin by R. G. Latham. London.

Tebb, William S. 1898. *A century of vaccination and what it teaches.* London.

Temkin, Owsei. 1977. *The double face of Janus.* Baltimore.

Trowell, H. C., J. P. N. Davies, and R. F. A. Dean. 1954. *Kwashiorkor.* London.

Underwood, Michael. 1806. *Treatise on the diseases of children.* Boston.

U. S. Bureau of the Census. 1960. *Historical statistics of the United States: Colonial times to 1957.* Washington, D.C.

Vaughan, Victor. 1897. Diarrheal diseases. In *An American textbook of the diseases of children,* ed. Louis Starr, 479–500. Philadelphia.

Warkany, Joseph. 1977. Congenital malformations of the past. In *Problems of birth defects,* ed. T. V. N. Persaud, 5–17. Baltimore.

Warner, Rebecca H., and Henry Rosett. 1975. The effects of drinking on offspring: An historical survey of the American and British literature. *Journal of the Studies of Alcohol* 36: 1395–420.

Wickes, I. G. 1953. A history of infant feeding. *Archives of Diseases of Childhood* 28: 151–8, 232–40, 416–22, 495–502.

Williams, Cicely D. 1933. A nutritional disease of childhood associated with a maize diet. *Archives of Diseases of Childhood* 8: 423–33.

Wilson, Leonard G. 1975. The clinical description of scurvy and the discovery of vitamin C. *Journal of the History of Medicine* 30: 40–60.

Winter, J. M. 1982. The decline of mortality in Britain, 1870–1950. In *Population and society in Britain, 1850–1980,* ed. Theo Baker and Michael Drake, 100–20. London.

Wohl, Anthony S. 1983. *Endangered lives: Public health in Victorian Britain.* London.

Woodbury, Robert M. 1926. *Infant mortality and its causes.* Baltimore.

Yost, R. M. 1950. Sydenham's philosophy of science. *Osiris* 9: 84–105.

Zirkle, Conway. 1946. The early history of the idea of the inheritance of acquired characters and of pangenesis. *Transactions of the American Philosophical Society,* 2d Ser., 35: 91–151.

III.5
Famine and Disease

Famine can be defined as a failure of food production or distribution resulting in dramatically increased mortality. This increase is attributable to two, and very often three, orders of disease. First, there is the disease of general starvation characterized by wasting and inanition. Second, there are behavioral disorders and social disruptions, some a direct consequence of energy deficiency, others linked to mental disturbance. These can be lethal in their own right while at the same time contributing to the general starvation and to the spread of contagious illness. Third, there is epidemic infection, which is not always seen in mass starvation but which is frequent enough to be considered a classic concomitant. Facilitated by impaired individual and community resistance to pathogenic agents, contagions tend to run an exceedingly rapid course through famished populations, contributing in large measure to overall mortality.

General Starvation

Starvation, a condition in which the body draws on its own internal reserves for energy, arises from normal processes essential to survival. These processes lead to the disease of general starvation, or undernutrition, only after progressing beyond a threshold where damage resulting in functional incompetencies is done to active tissue. If starvation is not acute, that is, not rapidly induced, dysfunctions incompatible with heavy work are not apparent in nonobese people before the loss of 10 percent of prestarvation weight.

Ordinary starvation may be said to begin some 4 or 5 hours after a meal. It is then that the liver begins to release as glucose its store of glycogen. As this process continues, muscle and adipose (fatty) tissue, which otherwise rely on free glucose for fuel, gradually revert to the oxidation of fatty acids. This allows circulating glucose to be consumed primarily by the brain.

Liver glycogen alone in the absence of any food intake supplies glucose to the blood for roughly 12 to 16 hours before a number of metabolic changes begin shifting liver activity to gluconeogenesis, the conversion of muscle protein into glucose. Within 24 hours or longer, depending on the level of food intake, liver glucose output is fully dependent on imported protein. With the onset of gluconeogenesis, the liver itself burns fatty acids delivered from adipose tissue. As these arrive in increasing amounts, only partial oxidation occurs. This results in the liver sending ketones (incompletely burned fatty acids) into circulation. These become fuel for both muscle and brain as their level in the blood increases. In the case of rapidly induced starvation, keto acid concentrations can reach dangerous levels, resulting in dehydration and, eventually, in coma. This, however, can be avoided by the intake of small amounts of carbohydrate.

Gluconeogenesis continues for about a week before ketone production levels off. Muscle gradually ceases to be reliant on keto acids, making ever greater use of free fatty acids liberated from adipose tissue. The brain now takes ketone bodies over glucose for nourishment. This allows gluconeogenesis to shut down, eliminating the demands of this process on muscle protein. At this point, the body's metabolism is fully adjusted to draw on fat for almost all of its energy needs.

Protein catabolism and the destruction of active tissue is never totally eliminated, however. Wasting, loss of weight or body mass, the most obvious external manifestation of general starvation, is most precipitous during the first few days. It becomes less so over a longer period. If semistarvation extends over weeks or months, the rate of wasting will continue to decline. Fat accounts for the greatest portion of wastage after the first several days, but to the end there is a relatively slight but slowly increasing usage of protein.

This continuing attrition of protein, even as fat remains available, is not borne equally by all organs of the body. Heart and kidney tissue sustain slightly less loss than would be expected given their proportion of total body mass. The liver, intestines, and skin incur more than their share of the loss. Postmortem examinations of starvation victims reveal no part of the body immune to atrophy except the brain.

During famine, starvation initially affects those who are physiologically the most vulnerable. Different forms of protein–energy malnutrition, kwashiorkor and marasmus, show up early in young children. Before gross weight loss is seen in older children and adults, there is a loss of endurance. Those who are afflicted require frequent rests from work. As general starvation becomes more advanced, there are complaints of weakness and muscle pains. Movement becomes sluggish. Individuals sit or lie down whenever possible. A slow, shuffling gait develops. Nocturnal sleep is interrupted, but total sleep progressively increases. An acute sensitivity to noise develops; the skin becomes extremely sensitive and bruises easily. There are complaints about feeling cold. Blood pressure and heart rate decline. A diarrhea attributed to visceral atrophy and malfunction occurs in individuals who are free of intestinal infection. Edema often appears, first in the face, then in the extremities, later in the abdominal and thoracic cavities.

Whereas the intellect remains largely unimpaired, the emotions are greatly affected. Victims' moods alternate between apathy and extreme irritability. The starving become discouraged and depressed but also display an exaggerated ill temper. Critical ability seems to fail. There is lack of concentration and lapse of memory. Speech becomes slow. Appearance and manners become matters of indifference. Interest in sex disappears. Women experience amenorreah; spermatogenesis declines in men. An inversion takes place: Light hair appears on women's faces, whereas men's beards stop growing. Both sexes lose hair from the top of the head and around the genitals. Victims think only of their diseased condition and food. But when starvation becomes acute, even appetite disappears.

The length of time a starving individual can survive on endogenous sources of energy varies, depending on fat reserves, the magnitude of caloric deficit (determined by energy intake and level of physical activity), and ambient temperature. Inactive individuals with normal weight for height can endure nearly total starvation for about 2 months. Semistarvation in active subjects consuming between 1,300 and 1,600 kilocalories per day has been studied under controlled conditions for up to six months. During a famine food intake may fall below this level but often for only brief periods of time at first. Hence, victims can endure for months. Once a 30

percent weight loss is incurred, however, the chances of survival are virtually nil without medical intervention. A 40 percent wastage during famine is almost certainly fatal.

Individuals suffering from advanced undernutrition can survive for prolonged periods owing to two remarkable means of accommodation that allow the energy budget to reach near equilibrium and permit weight loss to slow dramatically despite a very low level of caloric intake. The first is a decline in basal metabolism, which occurs because wasting reduces the number of metabolically active cells, accompanied by a decrease in the metabolic rate of the surviving biomass. The second is a decline in spontaneous movements and a decreased cost of movement. In other words, starving people reduce their actions to a minimum. Moreover, any activity that cannot be avoided becomes less expensive energywise because of reduced weight. Of these two factors, curtailed activity accounts for the greatest savings. In experiments conducted during World War II, volunteers restricted to a semistarvation diet for 6 months were observed to reduce movement-related energy expenditures by 71 percent. Approximately 60 percent of this was achieved by elective curtailment of activity. A reduction of anywhere near this magnitude during a famine is bound to have profound social implications.

Behavioral Disturbances and Social Disorders

People suffering inanition obviously find it impossible to maintain normal social relations. No matter what their cultural definition, ordinary interactions are also affected by the emotional correlates of starvation and by individual and collective efforts to survive under extreme conditions. Famine, as a net result, gives rise to a series of social transformations. Seen as variously altered patterns of interaction, these transformations progressively unfold under deteriorating conditions. For this reason, they have been viewed as broadly diagnostic of the prevailing level of want. This view is most certainly justified with respect to two dimensions of interaction, its frequency and the extent to which it involves positive reciprocities. Both of these indicators disclose the characteristic rise and fall of a stress–response curve as famine progresses from threat to full-fledged reality. Figure III.5.1 illustrates this in terms of the relationship between food supply and generosity.

Social responses to famine develop through three phases. The first, the alarm phase, marked by general hyperactivity and intensified feelings of attach-

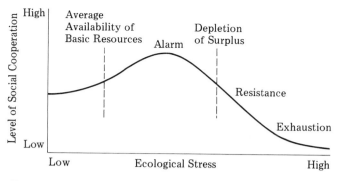

Figure III.5.1. Relation of social cooperation to ecological stress in a social action system. (Adapted from Laughlin and Brady 1978.)

ment, is triggered by the onset of an emergency. This reaction, also reported in the wake of sudden catastrophes such as floods and tornadoes, can create on the community level what has been called a "disaster utopia," a social environment of extraordinarily intense mutual care and assistance. Thus, the sharing of food and other resources among friends and neighbors actually increases, apparently irrespective of whether there is any prospect of outside assistance. Although accounts of local-level responses to this earliest phase of famine are relatively few, this phenomenon has been documented in a variety of cultural settings, including diverse urban and rural locations in Africa, western Europe (Ireland and the Netherlands), South Asia (India and Nepal), and Oceania (Yap and Tikopia). Hoarding at this stage does occur, but it appears to be limited to market economies and, more particularly, to those individuals least threatened by starvation.

Intensification affects virtually every sphere of life during the alarm stage. Market activity increases and, under certain conditions, may become chaotic. Food prices soar. Population movement increases, as individuals and families seek to relieve their mounting plight. Mystical efforts to find relief intensify; religious congregations swell. Political activity increases. Violence erupts, both spontaneous and concerted, frequently at sites where food and other commodities are in storage or transit.

As starvation begins to exact a physical toll and individuals become weaker and more easily fatigued, famine progresses beyond the stage of alarm and into a protracted phase of resistance. The question of available energy becomes paramount at this point. People turn to unusual sources, including foods known to be edible but normally ignored and species ordinarily regarded as inedible or abhorrent. Items of no nutritional value may be consumed

merely to assuage hunger. To conserve supplies, expenditures other than those immediately related to obtaining food are pared to a minimum. The extent of active social relations as indexed by food sharing shrinks considerably as a result.

This "social atomization" is the hallmark of the resistance phase. Essentially, it entails the closure of the household as a food-sharing unit. Generosity disappears; supplies are hidden; food preparation and consumption take place in secret. Visits from relatives and friends arouse suspicion and may be regarded as unfriendly acts.

Lawlessness, including physical aggression, continues to increase, but during the resistance phase of famine there tends to be less concerted and sustained violence, particularly after the average level of weight loss in a community begins to exceed 20 percent. The physical wherewithal for rioting or other active expressions of political unrest becomes practically nil beyond this point. Active expressions of any sort gradually disappear. Ritual observances are put off; religious attendance declines. People congregate only where there is promise of receiving food.

Exhaustion, the final phase of famine, comes with the disintegration of the household, the social bulwark of resistance. Its collapse is foreshadowed as food sharing within the household becomes increasingly discriminatory during the resistance phase. There is a distinct tendency to see the elderly as a drain on provisions. Tolerance toward younger dependents does not erode as quickly, but generally there comes a point when children too receive disproportionately small amounts of food. These types of discrimination – arguably adaptive insofar as they favor principal providers, those on whom eventual recovery will depend – show up in age-specific mortality rates. In the Punjab, for example, where in 1939 famine resulted in an overall increase in mortality of more than 52 percent, the elderly sustained a 288 percent increase in their rate of death and mortality among children under 10 rose by 192 percent. By contrast, among individuals between 10 and 60 years of age, mortality actually declined to a level 14 percent less than the average for the preceding 4 years.

Although exhaustion does not sweep over a famished population all at once, the appearance of neglected, wandering children is a certain sign that pockets of it exist within a region. The same holds for the abandonment and sale of children. Parents may take such drastic steps out of concern for their own survival or out of the hope that being in some other individual's or agency's custody will save their offsprings' lives. But in either instance, as well as in the case of infanticide or parental suicide, an underlying cause is almost certainly the mental fatigue that comes from hearing ceaseless cries for food that cannot be stilled.

The final vestiges of cooperation in the worst famines are found only in the most instrumental relationships. Anyone promising to put a bite of food in one's mouth is a friend. The fact that people sometimes kill ruthlessly to acquire scraps of food suggests that anyone standing in the way of eating is an enemy. Cannibalism may occur during extreme famine, though its extent is impossible to gauge. Suicide, even in cultures where it is otherwise unheard of, becomes very common.

Exhaustion leaves an indelible mark on survivors. A significant incidence of gross stress reaction (acute situational maladjustment), a disease category that originally comprised the mental depressions of combat personnel whose disturbances could not be described accurately by existing psychiatric labels, has been documented among both European famine victims and Australian aborigines. Gross stress reaction is thought to arise from a severely disturbed interpersonal environment.

Relief-induced agonism is another postfamine syndrome worthy of note. It consists of a varied pattern of aggressive, exigent, and quarrelsome behavior, both verbal and nonverbal. It is seen during the course of relief operations, particularly after the refeeding of victims. Relief-induced agonism appears to be nonspecific in the sense that it is not directed at any particular target. The agonism expresses itself as a general irritability and a remonstrative or combative attitude toward anyone at hand, including relief personnel. What sometimes causes people who were heretofore wasted, inactive, and emotionally apathetic to become suddenly quite animated, clamorous, and contentious upon receiving ample nourishment is not known.

Famine and Infectious Disease

General starvation increases susceptibility to numerous pathogens. Conversely, infection accelerates the course of general starvation. This process is enhanced as declining health and increased mortality add to social disorder, creating greater impediments to the acquisition of food, increased undernutrition, and conditions ripe for the spread of disease.

This vicious circle can originate on the side of either pathogenic illness or undernutrition. Epidemic disease has the potential for ushering in general starvation, especially if infections debilitate or kill a large number of food producers. This is most liable to occur when a new disease is introduced into a region whose inhabitants have no acquired immunity. Many native American populations suffered severe famine upon first exposure to such commonplace Old World illnesses as measles and smallpox. Generally speaking, however, it is more often the case that infectious epidemics follow in the wake of starvation. The diseases that become epidemic tend to be familiar ones, long endemic to a region. Virtually any endemic illness has epidemic potential during famine, but certain of them have become notorious.

In the Western world, those diseases most disposed to reach epidemic proportions have been typhus, relapsing fever, smallpox, dysentery, tuberculosis, bubonic plague, influenza, and pneumonia. Changes affecting public health have altered the epidemic potential of these diseases at various points in history. Thus, typhus (famine fever, spotted fever), a louseborne infection that for centuries had been Europe's most dreaded famine disease, ceased to be a concern among most undernourished groups during World War II owing to the widespread use of DDT. However, with the disappearance of typhus, epidemic tuberculosis, which almost certainly had been present but undetected in previous famines, became a major problem.

As for the East, experience with famine-related epidemics has been much the same as that of Europe, with some exceptions. Typhus has not been seen in well-watered tropical and semitropical regions where people are accustomed to bathing daily. In contrast, waterborne disease such as dysentery and cholera have become virtually synonymous with mass starvation in such climates. Typhoid epidemics have been associated with famines in China. Acute malaria and heavy hookworm infestations have been observed in famished populations of India.

In Africa the effects of malaria do not appear to be aggravated by general starvation. However, contrary to experience in the rest of the Old World, including India, recent episodes of general starvation in Ethiopia, Nigeria, and the Sahel have been accompanied by epidemics of measles extremely lethal to children. Yet judging from records of the Great Ethiopian Famine of 1888–92, the greatest of all African famines, epidemic measles has not always been a problem in Africa in times of dearth. More common have been epidemics of cholera, smallpox, meningitis, dysentery, and pneumonia, and typhus outbreaks have also been reported in Ethiopia.

Two factors, often working together, facilitate the occurrence of epidemics under famine conditions.

The first is loss of community resistance to the spread of infection, and the second is loss of individual immune competence.

Loss of community resistance can be accounted for by a number of phenomena. These include population dislocations and the overcrowding of public facilities, both of which destroy barriers to the spread of infections. Transmission is further abetted by the behavioral economies that accompany inanition and undermine domestic hygiene and public sanitation.

Loss of community resistance is clearly illustrated in the case of typhus. Normally confined to isolated pockets of stark poverty, typhus often broke out over vast areas of Europe during starvation winters when a massive number of people, lacking energy and wrapped in thick layers of clothing to combat hypothermia, found it increasingly difficult to bathe or wash their clothes. This lapse opened the way to heavy louse infestations. Since dessicated louse feces clinging to unwashed garments were readily inhaled or rubbed into the eyes, the disease spread rapidly by casual contact wherever famished wanderers passed through a region or clustered to find relief from cold and hunger. During the Russian famine of 1919–22, the incidence of typhus in Leningrad showed a negative relationship not only with energy intake but with frequency of bathing. The death of nearly 193,000 people was attributed to typhus and relapsing fever, also louseborne, during Ireland's Great Hunger (1845–52). By comparison, approximately 20,000 died of starvation.

Starvation can undermine individual resistance at virtually every line of bodily defense. As protein is lost, protective anatomic surfaces such as skin and mucous membranes lose integrity as barriers against the invasion of pathogens. Flaky skin lesions, intestinal atrophy, and a reduction in tissue-healing capacity, frequently observed in children suffering from chronic protein–energy malnutrition, facilitate infection.

Once inside the body, infective agents encounter an impaired immune system. On the cellular side of this system, starvation has ill effects on both phagocytes and T-lymphocytes as the former lose efficiency as bacteria killers and the formation of the latter is depressed. On the humoral side, the complement system, a group of proteins that interact to form substances for the destruction of bacteria and viruses, functions poorly in undernourished children. Immunoglobulins, protein molecules secreted by B-lymphocyte-derived plasma cells and a principal element of the humoral immune system, are often found in serum at high levels among mal-nourished populations. Reflecting the high incidence of infection that such populations experience even in the best of times, the buildup of immunoglobulin levels in children is especially rapid. Despite this, when confronted with certain antigens, including the pathogens of typhoid, influenza, mumps, diphtheria, and yellow fever, the immunoglobulins appear hypoactive. Secretory immunoglobulin A (IgA), which prevents bacteria from adhering to mucosal surfaces, is found at abnormally low levels in the undernourished, which helps to explain why starvation is generally associated with high rates of respiratory and gastrointestinal infection. What remains unknown, and this applies to all of the foregoing functional impairments, is the degree of depression of immunoglobulin levels that can be withstood before the onset of clinical disease.

Nutritional balance is adversely affected by a number of reactions to infection. These include higher caloric expenditure resulting from greater mobilization of protein due to increased stress and adrenocortical activity; decreased food intake owing to general malaise, increased secretion of mucus, and appetite loss; and intestinal changes leading to reduced absorption of ingested foods. With regard to energy expenditure, relatively little is known beyond the fact that, if infection involves fever, basal metabolism increases. Nevertheless, it is suspected that even in the absence of fever virtually all infections increase the demand on energy sources. The effects of illness on protein nutrition have received a great deal of attention. Protozoal and helminthic diseases such as malaria and hookworm have adverse affects on nitrogen balance proportional to parasitic load. Most bacterial and viral infections have negative effects on nitrogen balance. Bacterial and viral infections of the intestinal tract are of major significance in most developing countries where diarrhea constitutes a major disease, particularly in infants and young children. Intestinal infections impair the absorption of nitrogen, but more significant in creating a nitrogen imbalance is an abnormally high excretion of that element in urine, much of this coming from an increased breakdown of muscle tissue. Considerable nitrogen is also lost through fever-induced sweating. Making up for nitrogen loss is difficult given the decline in appetite that typically accompanies intestinal illness.

History and Geography

Food production and distribution in every society are enmeshed in human ecologies of great complexity. Because of this, untoward conditions and events of many sorts can lead to famine. These include natural disasters such as drought, flood, volcanic eruption, frost, and pestilence. In addition, there are social factors such as war, revolution, political policy, general economic collapse, speculation in food commodities, administrative decision or indecision, inadequate transportation, runaway population growth, and gross social inequality. Despite the popular inclination throughout history to blame food disasters on one or another of these phenomena, close analysis of specific cases invariably reveals multiple causes. Efforts to untangle general factors have led to the creation of various classification schemes and models of famine development. They have also resulted in regional studies of outstanding quality. To date, however, little headway has been made in explaining famine in a way that would account for its historical and geographic incidence on a global scale.

One large-scale pattern awaiting explanation is seen in the proportional number of famines suffered in regions of the Old World over the past 6,000 years. Beginning about 4000 B.C. and until 500 B.C., existing records point to the Middle East and northeast Africa, especially the valleys of the Tigris and Euphrates rivers and the Nile, as extraordinarily famine prone. Over the next 1,000 years, the region of disproportional incidence shifted to Rome and the eastern parts of its empire, including Greece, Asia Minor, Syria, and Judea. Western Europe became the major locus about A.D. 500. Eastern Europe assumed this grim distinction after 1500, but about 1700 the high frequency of famine moved further eastward. From that year until 1974, periods of dearth occurred with greatest frequency among peoples residing within a huge belt extending from regions of Russia south of Moscow, across the southern Asian steppes, into India and China. More recently, African regions, especially the East and the Sahel, have been the scene of a disproportionate share of food emergencies.

The several published lists of the world's major famines, all compiled before the 1970s, contain little mention of catastrophic food shortages among the peoples of sub-Saharan Africa, Oceania, and the New World. These omissions grossly underrepresent the experiences of "peoples without history," leaving vast sectors of the world a blank map and much of the information required to chart the occurrence of famine beyond Eurasia unassembled. What truly universal patterns might be discovered once the temporal and spatial distribution of famine has been more broadly mapped can be glimpsed from a preliminary analysis of unpublished data drawn from the Standard Cross-Cultural Sample (SCCS), a representative, worldwide sample of the world's known and well-described societies. The SCCS, developed by George P. Murdock and Douglas R. White, includes 186 communities dependent on a wide variety of subsistence systems. Each community is precisely located at a point in time, the sample as a whole spanning history from ancient civilization to the twentieth century. The incidence of famine recorded in SCCS bibliographic sources reveals no remarkable differences in the frequency of unexpected food shortages among the world's major geographic regions. Climatically, data show no more than a mildly positive relationship between the incidence of starvation and aridity. With respect to persistent famine (i.e., its occurrence more than once per generation) the sample does show, as many would predict, a rather strong association with endemic hunger. Finally, statistics indicate a global tendency for the severity of food shortages to increase with both increased societal complexity and dependence on food importation.

Detection of Famine

Possibly throughout history, most certainly in the nineteenth and twentieth centuries, the term *famine* has been used loosely. Hungry seasons, annual periods of dearth afflicting societies just before harvest, have been called famines. To add to the semantic confusion, there have been allegedly deliberate misapplications of the term by some governments in order to elicit aid when it was not warranted. Moreover, some governments have avoided using the term when it ought to have been used. The concept of famine has clearly been politicized. Nevertheless, one must admit that famines, unlike sudden physical catastrophes such as earthquakes and hurricanes, are not always easy to detect. Often unannounced by any violent event, famine can develop insidiously, remaining invisible for a protracted period to members of the privileged classes, especially if they are inured to the sight of poverty, endemic undernutrition, and disease. One can perhaps better comprehend the tendency for famine to escape notice by reflecting on the fact that during the Ethiopian famine of 1973–5 it was estimated that at any one time not more than 8 percent of that country's population was starving to death. In a nation where as many as 20 million people are perpetually hungry, the threshold at which suffering becomes perceived as an emergency stands relatively high.

For this reason, historical sources bearing on the study of famine, whether official, academic, or popular, must be read with caution. A rigorous historical detection of famine should include the following:

1. evidence of a dramatic increase in mortality;
2. evidence that such an increase occurred in several adjacent communities at once;
3. consideration of the possibility that lethal disease unrelated to general starvation bears responsibility for increased mortality;
4. data showing a correlation between mortality curves and the price of food;
5. information indicating disproportional mortality among the economically marginal;
6. evidence of a depression in live births; and
7. statements contained in contemporary accounts referring to dearth, misery, or death owing to want.

Robert Dirks

Bibliography

Appleby, Andrew. 1973. Disease or famine? Mortality in Cumberland and Westmoreland, 1580–1640. *Economic History Review*, 2d Ser., 26: 403–31.

Blix, Gunnar, et al., eds. 1971. *Famine: A symposium dealing with nutrition and relief operations in time of disaster.* Upsala.

Burger, G. C. E., et al. 1948. *Malnutrition and starvation in western Netherlands, September 1944–July 1945,* 2 parts. The Hague.

Cawte, John. 1978. Gross stress in small islands: A study in macro-psychiatry. In *Extinction and survival in human populations,* ed. Charles Laughlin, Jr., and Ivan Brady, 95–121. New York.

Cepede, M., and M. Lengelle. 1953. *Economique alimentaire du globe.* Paris.

Chandra, R. K. 1976. Nutrition as a critical determinant in susceptibility to infection. *World Review of Nutrition and Dietetics* 25: 167–89.

Colson, Elizabeth. 1979. In good years and bad: Food strategies of self-reliant societies. *Journal of Anthropological Research* 35: 18–29.

Dando, William A. 1980. *The geography of famine.* New York.

Dirks, Robert. 1979. Relief induced agonism. *Disasters* 3: 195–8.

1980. Social responses during severe food shortages and famine. *Current Anthropology* 21: 21–44.

Gopalan, C., and S. G. Srikantia. 1973. Nutrition and disease. *World Review of Nutrition and Dietetics* 16: 98–141.

Goure, L. 1962. *The siege of Leningrad.* Stanford, Calif.

Grande, Francisco. 1964. Man under caloric deficiency. In *Handbook of physiology,* Sec. 4, ed. D. B. Dill, 911–38. Washington, D.C.

Greenough, Paul R. 1982. *Prosperity and misery in modern Bengal: The famine of 1943–1944.* New York.

Helwig-Larsen, Per, et al. 1952. *Famine disease in German concentration camps, complications and sequels.* Copenhagen.

Hocking, Frederick. 1969. *Starvation.* Melbourne.

Keys, Ancel. et al. 1950. *The biology of human starvation,* 2 vols. Minneapolis.

Laughlin, Charles D., Jr., and Ivan A. Brady. 1978. Introduction: Diaphasis and change in human populations. In *Extinction and survival in human populations,* ed. Charles D. Laughlin, Jr., and Ivan A. Brady, 1–48. New York.

MacArthur, Sir William P. 1957. Medical history of the famine. In *The great famine,* ed. Edward R. Dudley and T. Desmond Williams, 263–316. New York.

Murdock, G. P., and D. R. White. 1969. Standard cross-cultural sample. *Ethnology* 8: 329–69.

Pankhurst, Richard. 1966. The great Ethiopian famine of 1888–1892: A new assessment. *Journal of the History of Medicine and Allied Sciences* 21(2, 3): 95–124, 271–94.

Post, John D. 1976. Famine, mortality and epidemic disease in the process of modernization. *Economic History Review* 29: 14–37.

Robson, John R. K., ed. 1981. *Famine: Its causes, effects and management.* New York.

Scrimshaw, N. S., et al. 1968. *Interactions of nutrition and infection.* World Health Organization Monograph Series No. 57. Geneva.

Smith, Dean A., and Michael F. A. Woodruff. 1951. *Deficiency diseases in Japanese prison camps.* Medical Research Council Special Report Series No. 274. London.

Taylor, C. E., and Cecile DeSweemer. 1973. Nutrition and infection. *World Review of Nutrition and Dietetics* 16: 204–26.

Turnbull, Colin. 1972. *The mountain people.* New York.

Tushnet, L. 1966. *The uses of adversity.* New York.

Woodham-Smith, Cecil. 1962. *The great hunger, Ireland, 1845–1849.* New York.

III.6
A History of Chiropractic

Chiropractic is a system of healing that holds that disease results from a lack of normal nervous function caused by a disordered relationship between the musculoskeletal and nervous systems. Controversial from its inception, chiropractic has grown into the largest nonallopathic healing profession in the United States, with nearly 35,000 active practitioners. Although considered by many a "marginal" group, chiropractors are licensed in all 50 states, are reimbursed by Medicare, Medicaid, and many third-party payers, and in 1984 earned an average yearly net income of $55,000. The recent defeat of the American Medical Association (AMA) by chiropractors in a major lawsuit dramatically emphasizes chiropractic's current strength. The public image of chiropractic has significantly improved, and opposition from medical organizations has abated. Chiropractic has successfully established itself as an alternative healing profession.

At first glance, it seems an unlikely system to have achieved such success. Chiropractic was founded in 1895, just as medicine was being transformed into a dominant profession. Successfully uniting disparate elements of the medical community, the AMA reorganized in the early 1900s and developed into a powerful force, influencing nearly every aspect of the U.S. health care system. The homeopathic and eclectic sects, important mid-nineteenth-century competitors, virtually disappeared during the first decades of the twentieth century. Physicians actively and effectively suppressed competition from patent medicine vendors with pure food and drug legislation. Yet despite the impressive strength of the medical profession, chiropractic thrived. Whereas nearly every other form of unorthodox healing was being suppressed, banned, or co-opted, this system of healing established itself as an independent profession. By 1930 it was already the largest nonallopathic sect in the United States, with nearly 16,000 practitioners.

This extraordinary development does not fit easily into current historiographic models. Broadly speaking, two models have been offered to explain medicine's enormous growth during the late nineteenth and early twentieth centuries. According to the first, medicine benefited from scientific developments, which provided a new rational basis for medical practice and offered effective treatments. Proponents of this model point to the establishment of the germ theory of disease, the development of diphtheria antitoxin, the creation of salvarsan (for use against syphilis) and the discovery of insulin as evidence of how scientific progress fueled medicine's expansion. According to the second model, political organization and lobbying were the critical factors behind medicine's new strength. Proponents of this model point to demographic data suggesting that medical practice had little impact on morbidity and mortality and to the aggressive political maneuvering of the AMA to support their argument.

Despite their differences, these two schools share the assumption that allopathic medicine established hegemony over health care during the early twentieth century. Neither approach provides a particularly useful framework for discussing chiropractic, because each virtually ignores unorthodox medicine. Although medicine clearly wielded the greatest influence on the U.S. health care system, the success of chiropractic demonstrates that there are important limits to medicine's authority. A close examination of chiropractic history helps identify those limits and the forces that define them.

The Critical Early Years, 1895–1924

In 1895 Harvey Lillard visited the offices of Daniel David Palmer. "D.D.," as he is nearly always referred to, had recently opened his practice in Davenport, Iowa, after a varied career that included stints as a schoolmaster and grocery clerk. Lillard, a janitor, complained that ever since he had received a blow to his neck 17 years ago he had been deaf. Palmer examined the patient and noted a lump in the cervical region. He manipulated Lillard's spine and, much to the delight of both patient and practitioner, restored his hearing. Chiropractic was born.

Therapeutic manipulation was not unknown to late-nineteenth-century North Americans. They were aware of the long tradition of massage as a healing modality. Bohemian immigrants to the Midwest practiced a special form of massage, napravit. Bonesetting, a form of manipulation involved primarily in treating orthopedic problems, had flourished in some areas. Finally, in Kirksville, Missouri, in 1874, Andrew Taylor Still had founded osteopathy, a school of healing that utilized spinal manipulation.

These diverse healing techniques shared more than their emphasis on manual manipulation. Drugless healing was an important theme in many nonallopathic systems in the mid-nineteenth century. It was part of a larger response to the excesses of "heroic" therapies (i.e., vigorous cathartics, emetics, and bloodletting) and in fact, mid- and late-nineteenth-century healers, both inside and outside the medical profession, increasingly began to emphasize milder interventions. They shared a growing recognition that the worth of many conventional remedies had never been scientifically proved and placed a new emphasis on the healing power of nature. Their skepticism about heroic medicine was epitomized by the words of Oliver Wendell Holmes when he proclaimed in 1860 that, with the exception of a few specific remedies, "if the whole materia medica, *as now used,* could be sunk to the bottom of the sea, it would be all the better for mankind and all the worse for the fishes."

Nonallopathic healers took advantage of this climate arguing against any pharmacological therapy, and host of drugless alternatives developed, among them hydropathy, osteopathy, and magnetic healing. As a drugless system that emphasized the body's natural healing powers, chiropractic fit easily into this important nineteenth-century trend.

Briefly stated, Palmer's chiropractic fused magnetic healing with therapeutic manipulation. Palmer believed that subluxations of the spinal column caused disease by impinging on the nervous system and inhibiting the flow of the body's vital "fluid," which Palmer called "innate intelligence"; disease resulted from either a deficiency or an excess of this fluid. By examining the patient's spine, a chiropractic could detect the malalignment responsible for the patient's ailment, manually manipulate the vertebrae, and restore normal alignment, allowing the return of proper nervous function. Once the normal flow of "innate intelligence" resumed, the body's inner healing powers ensured a return to health.

Palmer argued that his chiropractic approach offered the world an important new philosophy. He believed that God had created a balanced, ordered universe and that equilibrium was the fundamental organizing principle of life. "Innate intelligence" represented God's presence in human beings. Subluxations created disequilibrium, and the inevitable sequela of this violation of natural law was disease.

Palmer's vision was consonant with cultural and intellectual assumptions that were prevalent in the United States at the turn of the century. It linked health care to a worldview in which God was benevolent and ruled the universe through natural laws. It emphasized that there should be no conflict between religion and science; science served religion by demonstrating the Creator's natural laws.

This view of science was a critical component of chiropractic and contrasted sharply with the view of medicine's new research elite. Increasingly secular, the science of medicine was located in university laboratories, required special training, and was based on a reductionist philosophy. Deductive reasoning and the manipulation of nature in an experimental setting were its hallmarks. In contrast, chiropractors emphasized a different scientific approach. A scientist observed nature, collected facts, classified these facts, and thereby gained insights into the laws of nature. Furthermore, science linked the physical and spiritual worlds and reemphasized the perfection of the Creator. In his seminal 1910 work, *Textbook of the Science, Art and Philosophy of Chiropractic,* Palmer explained:

Chiropractic is the name of a systematized knowledge of the science of life . . . an explanation of the methods used to relieve humanity of suffering and the prolonging of life, thereby making this stage of existence much more efficient in its preparation for the next step, a life beyond.

Palmer believed that science ought to serve a subordinate and supportive role in relation to religion. A significant portion of U.S. society shared that view as the popularity of fundamentalism in the 1920s and the Scopes monkey trial dramatically demonstrated. Thus, the chiropractic approach to science remained a powerful model well into the twentieth century, with its legitimacy resting heavily on the assumption that science should reflect God's grandeur.

Ironically, chiropractors also sought to benefit from the growing prestige of science. They deflected allopathic attacks on chiropractic as quackery by arguing that their system of healing was a truly scientific way of dealing with disease. In fact, they even launched their own offensive by ridiculing physicians for adopting a scientific approach that epitomized the corrupt "atheistic materialism" that was destroying the United States.

Their efforts to reconcile science and religion by emphasizing the primacy of God attracted support at a time when the appropriate relationship between science and religion was hotly contested. They argued that by using drugs and surgery as therapies, and by failing to appreciate the importance of the spiritual in health and disease, physicians rejected the healing power of nature, and implicitly rejected the beneficence and wisdom of God Himself. When surgeons began to perform an increasing number of appendectomies in the early twentieth century, chiropractors sarcastically noted that it seemed odd that the creator of the universe had made the mistake of giving humans a useless appendix. By focusing on the appendix, an organ presumed to be a vestigial remnant of the evolutionary process, chiropractors highlighted their allegiance with antievolutionists.

Chiropractic's appeal extended beyond the scientific and philosophical. Important turn-of-the-century social and political themes also reverberated in the chiropractic literature. Chiropractors repeatedly characterized the AMA as a trust, invoking a familiar and powerful image central to this era of reform. They pointed to the growing public health movement as an indication that medicine, like all trusts, manipulated government to its own profit. Compulsory allopathic examination of schoolchildren and the armed forces' refusal to use nonallopathic healers, they contended, demonstrated the power of medicine over government.

Like all trusts, medicine was ruled by a narrow circle of conspirators. It was not the trustworthy, rural general practitioners who were responsible for medicine's monopolistic excesses; they too were being duped by a small group of eastern, elite intellectuals. This argument sought to capitalize on the disgruntlement of those physicians who resented the AMA's increasing emphasis on research science. Furthermore, it allowed individuals to condemn the medical profession but to retain confidence in their personal physician.

Chiropractors accused medicine of dominating the media, another characteristic of monopolies. They cited AMA boycotts of newspapers that contained "quack" advertisements and the explosive increase in the number of press releases by physicians' organizations.

The chiropractic solution to the problem of the medical trust was simple: open competition. The United States was built on rugged individualism. The merit of each practitioner and each healing profession should be established solely by a jury of patients. Individuals should determine whether their health care was adequate; government regulation was unnecessary and demeaned the "common man" by suggesting that he was incapable of assessing the quality of his health care. Physicians had no right to expect governmental protection or to hold themselves up as elite members of the healing profession. Rather, they were a wealthy aristocracy attempting selfishly to protect their interests. AMA efforts at educational and licensing reform were guaranteed to exclude the honest poor from the medical profession. By requiring collegiate training before medical school and the use of Latin prescriptions, the AMA had erected artificial barriers designed to elevate the physician and intimidate the patient. In contrast, chiropractic colleges required no formal educational background and no foreign languages. Anyone with common sense who was willing to apply himself or herself could become a chiropractor.

Although necessary, the congruence of chiropractic's social, political, cultural, and scientific appeals with early-twentieth-century beliefs was not sufficient to ensure the system's survival. To be successful, chiropractic needed more than a coherent message; it needed a leader. The man who responded to this need was Bartlett Joshua Palmer.

B.J., as he is invariably referred to, was D. D. Palmer's son. When the elder Palmer was jailed in 1906 for violating the medical practice law, B.J. took over the reigns of the Palmer School of Chiropractic (P.S.C.). Under his charismatic leadership both the school in Davenport, Iowa, and the general focus of chiropractic expanded enormously. B.J. began to market this system of healing aggressively, and enrollment at the P.S.C. increased from a trickle, to a stream, to a flood. There had been a total of 15 graduates in the decade before B.J. inherited the school. Starting in 1921 the P.S.C. graduated more than 1,000 students per year. Although the number of graduates soon declined into the hundreds, the Palmer School remained a major chiropractic institution throughout B.J.'s career.

B.J. did not limit his efforts to the development of the P.S.C. He tirelessly proselytized for all of chiropractic. Establishing a printing office at the Palmer School, he turned out a flood of chiropractic literature. He opened one of the first radio stations in Iowa, over whose powerful airways he proclaimed the benefits of chiropractic healing. B.J. went on lecture tours, organized the Universal Chiropractors Association, lobbied legislators, and appeared at trials. A nearly cultlike atmosphere developed around him and few could be neutral about the man. Nonetheless, B.J.'s forceful advocacy of chiropractic created more publicity, which was necessary to the development of the field. Indeed, it began to flourish as his efforts combined this system of healing with a philosophy of health and disease that resonated with important concerns for many North Americans. The growing influence of chiropractic arguments and chiropractors is suggested by their ability to convince legislators that chiropractors deserved licensure. In 1913 Kansas passed the first law recognizing chiropractors, and several other states in the Midwest soon did the same. By the 1930s, despite vigorous medical opposition, chiropractors had obtained some form of legal recognition in 32 states. Despite the skepticism and outright hostility of physicians, millions of North Americans were consulting chiropractors.

Parallel Evolution, 1920–60

The rapidly changing medical, social, and political landscape of the 1920s to the 1960s challenged chiropractic's ability to adapt and thus to survive. On the one hand, an excessive reliance on beliefs and theories developed in the 1890s might render this system anachronistic. On the other, chiropractic risked losing its distinctive character if it underwent radical reform and became "medicalized." An examination of the changing role of technology in chiropractic, the modification of its criticisms of the germ theory, and the stiffening of chiropractic educational standards will demonstrate how it successfully responded to the challenge.

Mixers versus Straights: Technology in Chiropractic

At the 1924 annual homecoming of the P.S.C., B. J. Palmer made a startling announcement: Henceforth the "neurocalometer" would be a vital component of the chiropractic system. Touted as a breakthrough for scientific chiropractic, the neurocalometer was a machine designed to help diagnose subluxations by registering differences in heat alongside the spinal column. It could be obtained only from the Palmer School for $500 and a $1.00 per month service charge.

Chiropractors were stunned, and with good reason. Since chiropractic's earliest years, the use of technology had engendered enormous controversy. B. J. Palmer himself had argued strenuously that diagnosis and treatment should be performed only by manual manipulation. In fact, he claimed that the Palmer School taught chiropractic "P, S, and U" – pure, straight, and unadulterated – and scornfully labeled any practitioners who utilized other modalities as "mixers."

For "straight" practitioners, chiropractic was a natural system of healing that allowed the body to manifest its intrinsic restorative powers. The use of machines implied that natural methods of diagnosis and treatment were inadequate. By avoiding the use of machines, chiropractic buttressed its argument that it was fundamentally different from medicine, which relied increasingly on new technologies during the early years of the twentieth century. By rejecting technology, chiropractic also avoided regulation under medical practice laws.

On a deeper level, the rejection of technology reflected the ambivalence of many Americans toward machines. Machines created change, and although change could be positive, it also caused uncertainty and upheaval. As industrialization proceeded during the late nineteenth and early twentieth centuries, many were uncertain whether the changes induced by modern technology were improvements, and straight chiropractors were able to tap into this wellspring of concern.

Conversely, the "mixers" utilized the positive image of technology to foster their growth. Machines were new and exciting, the wave of the future, and chiropractic needed to take advantage of modern technology in order to see that future. Many mixer schools, led by the National School of Chiropractic of Chicago, advocated using diagnostic and therapeutic adjuncts. As if to emphasize its differences with the straight chiropractors, the National School of Chiropractic had several physician-chiropractors on its faculty by 1916.

As the leader of straight chiropractic, B. J. Palmer had rarely declined an opportunity to ridicule the mixers. When he suddenly declared that the neurocalometer was not only acceptable but central to chiropractic practice, many ardent supporters were outraged. Four key members of the Palmer School faculty resigned. Palmer was accused of betraying his colleagues, and because the neurocalometer could be obtained only from Palmer, many thought he had been motivated by greed. The neurocalometer debate signaled an important change in chiropractic. Although advocates of straight practice continued to play an important role, their strength waned and gradually most chiropractors incorporated adjuncts into their practice. The introduction of the neurocalometer in 1924 reflected a shift in U.S. attitudes toward technology, for the prosperity of the 1920s had eased earlier fears about it while highlighting its economic benefits. B. J. Palmer's acceptance of machines is best seen in this light. As machines became firmly enmeshed in the fabric of U.S. life, it became untenable for this system of healing to reject them, although the distinction between straights and mixers, while increasingly blurred, would endure for some time.

The Germ Theory and Chiropractic

Another milestone in the evolution of chiropractic was an increasing acceptance of the germ theory of disease. At first many chiropractors had rejected the notion that bacteria could cause disease. However, as germ theory achieved widespread acceptance, they realized that rejection of the association between bacteria and disease would make chiropractic seem retrogressive. Accordingly, chiropractors no longer insisted that bacteria could not cause disease but instead argued that bacterial infection was a secondary phenomenon that occurred only in persons whose ability to resist disease had been vitiated by a spinal subluxation. This stance allowed chiropractors to highlight a major problem with germ theory: If the key to disease was simply infection with pathogenic organisms, why didn't everyone exposed to a germ become ill? Or why did some people infected with the same organism die and others experience only a mild illness? By emphasizing resistance as the key to health and disease, chiropractors retained their explanatory model while continuing to challenge formal medicine.

Educational Reform in Chiropractic

Education provides another window on the development of this system of healing. During the earliest years of chiropractic, disagreements developed over what, if any, formal education should be required. One group of practitioners, commonly referred to as "field-men," opposed any formal training, arguing that it was elitist. They felt that chiropractors should reject the medical model of education with its emphasis on "book-learning" and instead rely on the practical training that an apprenticeship provided. Although the field-men's arguments were heavily influenced by their concern that licensing legislation would exclude practitioners who lacked a chiropractic diploma, their stance also highlighted the ideological commitment to egalitarianism that many chiropractors felt their field should embody.

Competition among chiropractic colleges also inhibited the adoption of educational standards. Each institution vied for students and wanted to be recognized as the "true" standard bearer of the profession. Each had a slightly different definition of chiropractic, typically dividing along the "mixer–straight" axis. Each wanted its own diploma to be the exclusive prerequisite for a chiropractic license. Attempts to block the legislative recognition of rivals occasionally resulted in open warfare among the schools.

Despite this contentious beginning, the conviction that there was a need for minimal educational standards gradually gained wider acceptance. Exposés of mail-order chiropractic "colleges" had tarnished the reputation of the entire profession, and the dramatic reform of medical education in the early twentieth century had opened a wide gap between the training standards of regular physicians and those of chiropractors. Physicians exploited this difference by frequently ridiculing the standards of chiropractic schools, many of which had curricula that required only 18 months of schooling.

Chiropractors responded by gradually embracing a professional model of training and reducing 79 schools in 1920 to only 21 by 1932. Those that remained increased the period of training and strengthened their faculties, and schools that had previously emphasized how rapidly one could become a chiropractor increasingly stressed the advantages of their clinical facilities, eminent faculty, and comprehensive curricula. In 1935 the National Chiropractic Association (NCA), the mixers' professional organization, established a Commission on Educational Standards. This led to the adoption of formal accrediting procedures, and the International Chiropractors Association, the straight chiropractics' representative, followed suit. Spurred by the tireless efforts of John Nugent, director of education of the NCA, a continual strengthening of educational standards occurred in the 1940s and 1950s.

The adoption of technology, reconceptualization of the relationship between bacteria and disease, and educational reform were all ways in which chiropractors responded to a changing environment. Chiropractic's ability to retain its distinct identity while undergoing this evolution helps explain how it has avoided the fate of other alternative healing sects. The evolutionary trajectories of medicine and chiropractic can be conceived of as two parallel lines, and the ability of the latter to maintain a constant distance from medicine is perhaps the most remarkable quality in its historical development. If the distance between the two professions had narrowed, as in the case of homeopathy and osteopathy, chiropractic would have risked losing its identity. If the distance had widened, chiropractic would have risked becoming anachronistic. Instead, it flourished as it adroitly maneuvered between the Scylla of convergence and the Charybdis of divergence.

From Marginally Acceptable to the Acceptable Margin: The 1960s through the 1980s

The 1950s and 1960s were a golden age for medicine. Federal support for biomedical science expanded enormously after World War II, and impressive diagnostic and therapeutic advances aided medicine's emergence as the most highly regarded profession in the United States. Federal subsidies for hospital construction helped create an enormous health care industry.

Simultaneously, chiropractic seemed to stagnate. It received no significant federal support, and indirect subsidies, in the form of support to veterans under the G.I. bill to finance their chiropractic education, were small indeed in comparison with the massive investment in orthodox medicine. Perhaps more than ever before, medicine dwarfed chiropractic, and in the early 1960s the AMA set out to destroy it. The motives for its assault ranged from concern that chiropractic was gradually achieving acceptance to the conviction that chiropractors were unscientific cultists who were detrimental to the public health. The assault was launched by the AMA Committee on Quackery, created in 1963.

The committee mounted an intensive campaign. Under its direction, the AMA adopted a resolution calling chiropractic an unscientific cult, distributed publications critical of its practice, and discouraged medical organizations from condoning interactions between physicians and chiropractors, even declaring consultation with chiropractors unethical.

Despite this remarkable onslaught, chiropractic not only survived but thrived. During the tenure of the committee (1963–74), chiropractic greatly expanded as schools opened, the number of chiropractors grew, and licensing was granted in the few states that had withheld it. Chiropractic achieved federal recognition when it became incorporated into the Medicare and Medicaid programs.

The ability of chiropractic to resist AMA's assault rested on four important developments: (1) a new social climate, (2) improved intraprofessional cohesion, (3) shrewd political maneuvering, and (4) jettisoning of its one cause–one cure hypothesis. A new social climate had come about with the extraordinary upheavals of the 1960s. The civil rights movement, the women's movement, the antiwar movement, and the environment movement, among others, rejected the status quo. What had previously been held to be authoritative was now condemned as authoritarian. Science and technology were no longer accepted as unalloyed good, critics argued that physicians had lost touch with the art of medicine, and conventional health care came to be viewed as impersonal, costly, and inefficient. Long critical of organized medicine, chiropractors began to find an increasingly receptive audience as tolerance for, and interest in, alternative medicine expanded enormously. Chiropractic benefited greatly from this new openness and yet, as a well-established profession, simultaneously avoided the appearance of being a fad. The criticism that medicine was too reliant on technology led chiropractors to reemphasize their reliance on "natural" healing. (Ironically, the use of technologies like diathermy

again became controversial in chiropractic, and a new "superstraight" faction emerged that eschewed nearly all machinery.) The AMA's antichiropractic efforts may have paradoxically created new support for this system of healing.

Chiropractic witnessed much more cohesion among its practitioners, for efforts by the medical profession to eradicate it had the effect, despite the persistent argument between mixers and straights, of unifying chiropractors. Certainly, the tangible manifestation of chiropractic unity was adept political maneuvering. From their earliest struggles to obtain state licensure at the beginning of the twentieth century, chiropractors have demonstrated a considerable mastery of the U.S. political process and thus, despite opposition from the vaunted AMA lobby, they have shrewdly combined personal appeals, mass mailings, and the efforts of paid lobbyists to promote their goals.

Finally, chiropractic began explicitly to limit its claim of effectiveness and increasingly emphasized its role in the management of musculoskeletal disorders. In 1969 both major chiropractic associations rejected the "one cause–one cure" tenet of chiropractic. This freed chiropractors from having to respond to medical hecklers who ridiculed them for believing that cancer, diabetes, and other ills were caused by spinal subluxations. Growing evidence supported chiropractic's contention that it was an effective therapeutic modality for low back pain. The prevalence of this condition combined with orthodox medicine's paucity of effective treatments for back problems helped chiropractors define a niche for themselves in the U.S. health care system.

By the mid-1970s chiropractic occupied a new and greatly strengthened position. In the face of a changing social climate and numerous antitrust lawsuits instituted by chiropractors, opposition from organized medicine began to abate. The AMA and other medical organizations grudgingly recognized that there might be some benefits from spinal manipulation, and of course the inclusion of chiropractic in the Medicare and Medicaid programs helped legitimize the profession. In 1979 a conference sponsored by the National Institute of Neurological and Communicative Disorders and Stroke of the National Institutes of Health addressed the research status of spinal manipulative therapy. At this meeting, medical doctors, osteopaths, scientists, and chiropractors exchanged information. Although the scientific basis for manipulative therapy remained a subject of debate, a consensus emerged that this therapy was of clinical value in the treatment of back pain. The fact that chiropractic was seriously discussed by a branch of the National Institutes of Health – one of the cathedrals of scientific medicine – symbolizes how far chiropractic had traveled.

Although, as this essay has shown, chiropractic has become more acceptable to the mainstream of U.S. society, it has not become widely accepted as a conventional therapy. The majority of Americans have never visited a chiropractor, and considerable confusion exists about what chiropractors do. However, the number of people who have been treated by a chiropractor is gradually increasing, and chiropractic's public image is improving. The periphery of the U.S. health care system is perhaps the ideal position for chiropractic. It provides legitimacy while allowing for the distance from conventional medicine that is fundamental to chiropractic's identity.

Steven C. Martin

Bibliography

Baer, Hans A. 1987. Divergence and convergence in two systems of manual medicine: Osteopathy and chiropractic in the United States. *Medical Anthropology Quarterly* 1: 176–93.

Brennan, Matthew J. 1987. *Demographic and professional characteristics of ACA membership: 1987 annual survey and statistical study.* Arlington, Va.

Cooper, Gregory S. 1985. The attitude of organized medicine toward chiropractic: A sociohistorical perspective. *Chiropractic History* 5: 19–25.

Dye, A. Augustus. 1939. *The evolution of chiropractic: Its discovery and development.* Philadelphia.

Gibbons, Russell W. 1980. The evolution of chiropractic: Medical and social protest in America. In *Modern development in the principles and practice of chiropractic,* ed. Scott Haldemann, 3–24. New York.

  1985. Chiropractic's Abraham Flexner: The lonely journey of John J. Nugent, 1935–1963. *Chiropractic History* 5: 44–51.

Palmer, Bartlett J. 1917. *The science of chiropractic,* 3d edition. Davenport, Iowa.

Palmer, Daniel D. 1910. *Textbook of the science, art, and philosophy of chiropractic.* Portland, Ore.

Reed, Louis. 1932. *The healing cults.* Chicago.

Turner, Chittendon. 1931. *The rise of chiropractic.* Los Angeles.

Wardwell, Walter I. 1972. Limited, marginal, and quasi-practitioners. In *Handbook of medical sociology,* 2d edition, ed. Howard E. Freeman, Sol Levine, and Les G. Reeder, 250–73. Englewood Cliffs, N.J.

  1988. Chiropractors: Evolution to acceptance. In *Other healers: Unorthodox medicine in America,* ed. Norman Gevitz, 157–91. Baltimore.

Wilk v. American Medical Association. 1987. 671 F. Supp. 1465 (N.D. Ill.).

III.7
Concepts of Addiction: The U.S. Experience

Addiction has remained a vague concept in spite of efforts to define it with physiological and psychological precision. The word's Latin root refers to a legal judgment whereby a person is given over to the control of another. In recent centuries the meaning has ranged from a simple inclination toward an activity or interest to an uncontrollable desire to take opium, which historically was viewed as the most addictive of drugs. Opiate addiction is characterized chiefly by the repeated use of the drug to prevent withdrawal symptoms, which include muscle and joint pains, sweating, and nausea. The extreme discomfort of withdrawal passes away after one to three days, although a yearning for the drug may last for a very long time. Some attempts to define addiction in medical terms (e.g., restricting it to opiate withdrawal phenomena) have led to confusion among members of the public because cocaine, according to that restricted definition, would be considered nonaddictive and, by implication, safer than the opiates.

For the sake of brevity, this essay considers chiefly opium and coca and their constituents and derivatives. The chemicals that could be discussed range from the barbiturates to lysergic acid diethylamide (LSD), but the models of control and therapy commonly applied to these other substances evolved in the past two centuries from experience with the coca bush, opium poppies, and their powerful alkaloids.

Opium

The opium poppy appears to be indigenous to the eastern Mediterranean area. The manner of producing crude opium is to scratch the surface of the poppy pod and scrape off the juice that exudes, collecting and drying the material until it is solid. This crude opium can be taken alone or in combination with other substances. Mithradatum, theriac, and philonium are three ancient and renowned medicines that contained opium, among other substances, when compounded during the early centuries of the Roman Empire, although in subsequent eras opium was not invariably a constituent.

The smoking of opium, so closely associated with China in the nineteenth and early twentieth centuries, appears to have been introduced to the Chinese in the seventeenth century by Dutch traders who had earlier supplied tobacco for smoking. The Chinese government attempted to outlaw the practice as early as 1729, but through much of the nineteenth century, as supplies came from the region of Turkey and Persia and later mostly from India, the attraction of smoking opium grew. The attempts of some Chinese administrators to cut off foreign opium importation were frustrated by the defeat of China in the so-called Opium War of 1839–42. Near the close of the century, young reformers blamed widespread addiction to opium and consequent lethargy and inefficiency for China's defeat by Japan in 1895. In response to a growing antagonism to opium use, the dowager empress Tzu Hsi instituted a program to eliminate domestic opium production and to seek a reduction in the importation of opium from India. This action was one of three crucial events in 1906 that led to a worldwide effort to control the production and distribution of opium and the opiates.

The second event was the Liberal Party's victory in the British parliamentary elections. The Liberal Party had long taken a stand against sending opium from India to China against the will of the Chinese people and government, although treaty rights to do so had been established by the British military. Complicity in facilitating Chinese addiction to opium deeply offended many Britons, especially those who promoted Christian missionary efforts in China. Previous British governments had argued that opium was not particularly harmful, being the equivalent of distilled spirits among Westerners, and that the opium trade was needed to pay for the British administration in India. After 1906, however, cooperation between the British and Chinese governments in curbing opium production was theoretically possible.

The third major antiopium event of 1906 was the U.S. decision to convene the Shanghai Opium Commission, a decision that reached fruition in 1909, as is discussed in the section on the origin of international control.

Morphine and the Hypodermic Syringe

The isolation of morphine from opium by F. W. A. Sertuener in 1805 marked the beginning of a new era in opium use. Physicians now had access to a purified active ingredient; hence, they were no longer uncertain of the strength of a dose and could investigate the effect of a specific amount. Commercial production followed the isolation of morphine and by the 1830s morphine was commonly available in any area touched by pharmaceutical trade with Europe and the United States. Morphine was administered by mouth, clysis, or absorption through denuded skin, as after blistering. The refinement of the hypodermic syringe and needle at midcentury created a mode of delivery as revolutionary in the history of addiction as had been the isolation of morphine.

Hollow needles and syringes had been employed long before the appearance of the familiar syringe and needle in the nineteenth century, but the growing number of purified chemicals, such as morphine, that could be directly injected into the body stimulated the pace of development and production. At first, injected morphine was considered less likely to be addictive than oral morphine because a smaller amount was required for equivalent pain relief. But by the 1870s this assumption was found to be erroneous, although many physicians continued to use injected morphine for chronic ailments, such as arthritis.

Restrictions

In most European nations, the central government controlled the practice of medicine and the availability of dangerous drugs through legislation. In addition, by the mid-nineteenth century, European physicians and pharmacists had organized themselves on a national level. By contrast, in the United States the federal government relegated to the individual states control over the health professions, and the professions themselves were poorly organized nationally. No laws controlled the sale of, contents of, or claims for "patent medicines," and there were few local laws restricting the availability of opium, morphine, and, later, cocaine. The result was a thriving and open market in these substances until late in the century, when some states began to enact laws preventing the acquisition of opiates and cocaine except with a physician's prescription. The U.S. Constitution grants the regulation of commerce among the states to the federal government, so no state law could affect the sale of drugs or products across state lines. The consequence was a higher per capita consumption of opium and opiates in the United States than in other Western nations and even, a government official claimed in 1910, more than the legendary consumption of opium in China.

Addiction and Its Treatment

The model of addiction to opium and opiates is the one to which addiction to other substances has been compared. Such addiction has long been viewed in moral terms, with the addict seen as "vicious" or "degenerate," driven by a "sinful" desire for pleasure. But as drugs were increasingly used to treat illnesses it was also understood that an individual could inadvertently become addicted to them – an understanding that has helped to give rise to the biological concept of addiction as an illness.

The investigation of addiction has experienced a decided shift over the past two centuries or so from the moral view of addiction as "sin" to the biological concept of addiction as disease, prompting some to argue that the "disease" in question was invented rather than discovered. Yet as more and more have adopted the view of addiction as a disease, the question of susceptibility has arisen, with biologists oscillating between the conviction that everyone is equally susceptible and the belief that only some are susceptible for psychological as well as physiological reasons.

Such ambivalence can also be found in legal systems that attempt to distinguish between morally "superior" and morally "inferior" addicts and in the medical profession, where physicians for a century have tried to find among their patients signs that would warn of addictive liability. These questions are still relevant to contemporary addiction research.

During the nineteenth century, once opiate addiction became familiar to physicians, a debate ensued over whether the continuous use of opium was a habit or a disease over which the patient had little control. The debate was complicated by a belief that abrupt withdrawal from opium could cause death. Three options were proposed and vigorously defended. The first was abrupt withdrawal, recommended almost exclusively as a hospital procedure. The addict was considered to be ingenious in obtaining drugs and to have a will so weakened by addiction and craving for opium that, unless he or she was securely confined, withdrawal would not be successful. It could be assisted by the administration of belladonna-like drugs that counteracted withdrawal symptoms such as sweating. These drugs also caused delirium, which, it was hoped, would have the effect of erasing the addict's memory of the withdrawal. (Scopalamine is given today just before general anesthesia for a similar reason.) The high rate of relapse in the weeks after treatment brought into question the value of detoxification.

The second option was gradual withdrawal, recommended because of the presumed ease of the treatment as well as the fear that sudden termination of the opiate would result in death. The idea that abrupt withdrawal could cause death was not widely refuted in the United States until about 1920. Gradual withdrawal was a technique that favored outpatient care and self-treatment by over-the-counter addiction "cures." Critics of this method argued that many addicts could lower their opiate intake only to a certain level below which they could not comfortably descend. An example of this threshold is the case of William Steward Halsted, a physician at Johns Hopkins Medical School who had to take a daily amount of morphine, about two to three grains, for the last 30 years of his life.

Halsted's experience suggests the third option, indefinite opiate maintenance. Of course, the strong, and for some the invincible, hold that opiates had over a user is what led to popular and professional fear of narcotics. Perpetuating addiction was the opposite of curing it, and initially the reason for doing it was simply the difficulty of stopping. Early in the twentieth century, however, scientific reasons for maintenance were advanced. Influenced by the rise of immunology, some researchers theorized that the body produced antibodies to morphine. If the level of morphine dropped below that required to "balance" the antibodies, the antibodies would produce withdrawal symptoms. Thus, unless the antibodies and every vestige of morphine could be removed from the individual, maintenance would be required to create a normal physiological balance.

Research produced no evidence of antibodies to morphine, but a less specific claim found adherents around the time of World War I. The hypothesis was that continued exposure to a substance like morphine caused a pathological change in the body's physiology that could not be altered by any known treatment, but required indefinite maintenance for normal functioning. This hypothesis was rejected in the antiaddiction fervor just after World War I in the United States, although it was revived by Vincent Dole and Marie Nyswander in the 1960s as a justification for maintenance by methadone, a synthetic, long-acting opiate.

A treatment for addiction that found wide acceptance in the first two decades of the twentieth century, especially in the United States, was described by Charles B. Towns, the lay proprietor of a hospital for drug and alcohol abusers, and Alexander Lambert, a respected professor of medicine at Cornell Medical School and later president of the American Medical Association. An insurance salesman and stockbroker, Towns purchased from an anonymous person a general treatment for addictions. Lambert became convinced of the treatment's efficacy, and he and Towns published it jointly in the *Journal of the American Medical Association* in 1909. The reputation of the Towns–Lambert treatment can be gauged by the fact that the U.S. delegation attempted to persuade the Shanghai Opium Commission to approve the treatment formally. The commission declined to do so.

The treatment, which combined various medical theories of the time, was based on the belief that morphine or other addicting substances had to be eradicated from the body. Therefore, a powerful mercury-containing laxative, called "blue mass," was administered several times, culminating in the passing of a characteristic stool that brought a profound sense of comfort. During the latter part of the therapy a formula, chiefly belladonna and hyoscine, which presumably counteracted the symptoms of withdrawal, was given at half-hour intervals. In the early years of this treatment, prominent physicians such as Richard C. Cabot of Boston allowed their names to be closely associated with that of Towns. In the years immediately after World War I, however, Lambert rejected the treatment as worthless and adopted the position then becoming popular that there was no specific treatment for addiction. Towns, by contrast, continued to operate his hospital in New York, applying the same treatment to alcohol addiction. "Bill W." received the inspiration to found Alcoholics Anonymous while undergoing treatment at the Towns Hospital in 1934.

In subsequent years, the treatment of opiate addiction has focused on achieving abstinence following detoxification, or maintenance using heroin, morphine, or methadone. Even when abstinence is achieved, however, relapses are common. In the 1970s pharmacological research led to the development of naltrexone, which blocks the effects of opiates, and several new drugs, most prominently clonidine, that lessen the discomfort of withdrawal.

The popularity of treatment and the growing emphasis on law enforcement to curb supply and punish users reflect social attitudes toward drug use. These attitudes have, in the course of a long span of drug consumption, evolved from toleration of use during the decades immediately following the introduction of new substances, such as cocaine, to extreme hostility toward drugs and drug users as the "epidemic" wears on. In the United States, medical and therapeutic approaches initially found favor but have since given way to law enforcement in response to the public's belated fearful reaction to the effect of drugs on individuals and society. Some countries, such as Indonesia, employ the death penalty against drug suppliers, whereas others rely on less stringent controls.

Cocaine

Cocaine, a central nervous system stimulant, offers a contrast to the opiates, although both have been subject to extreme praise and condemnation. Coca bushes are native to South America, and the leaves have been chewed there for millennia. The amount of cocaine extracted by chewing was increased by the addition of an alkaline substance to the wad of leaves, but the tissue level of cocaine obtained in this way was small compared with that obtained from the purified alkaloid cocaine, identified and named by Albert Niemann in 1860. Cocaine was not commercially available until the early 1880s. Before it was introduced to the market, extracts of coca leaves, often in a wine solution such as Vin Marianni, found favor as a tonic both with physicians and with the public.

Pure cocaine proved extraordinarily popular. Within a year of its introduction in the United States in 1884, Parke, Davis & Co. offered cocaine and coca in 14 forms. Cocaine was expensive, but soon became an ingredient in the new drink Coca-Cola and was found to be a specific remedy for hay fever and sinusitis. Within a few years, reports appeared in medical journals and the popular press telling of ruined careers and bizarre behavior among some users, but eminent experts such as William A. Hammond, a professor of neurology in New York medical schools and a former surgeon-general of the U.S. army, reassured the profession and the public that cocaine was harmless and the habit no more severe than that of drinking coffee.

Within 10 years, however, observers raised serious doubts that cocaine was as safe as had been asserted by Hammond and by cocaine's chief advocate in Europe, Sigmund Freud. By the first decade of the twentieth century, cocaine was no longer considered an ideal tonic but an extremely dangerous substance. In the United States, this new image, now associated with uncontrolled consumption, violence, and distorted thinking, provided powerful impetus to establish a national antinarcotic law, despite constitutional restrictions. In most other nations cocaine production and distribution was already regulated by national pharmacy laws. Through a complex series of events, the United States placed a national prohibition on narcotics use except for medical purposes and initiated an international campaign to control the production and distribution of opiates and cocaine.

The U.S. Response to Addiction

The per capita consumption of narcotics in the United States was officially described in the late nineteenth century as much higher than that of any comparable Western nation, perhaps even that of China. This may well have been the case, but reliable comparisons are often difficult to make, partly because drug use and addiction have been topics relatively neglected by historians.

Concern in the United States over opiate addiction and the rise in consumption, which reached a peak in the 1890s, led to state laws that in most instances made morphine available only by a physician's prescription, although there was no restriction on interstate commerce. Cocaine use increasingly worried the public, who associated it with the underworld and assumed that its use by blacks was a cause of unrest among them in the South. The latter association exemplifies the linkages so easily made by the public between drugs and social problems.

Some of the unusual factors associated with extensive narcotics use in the United States (i.e., late professionalization of medicine, an open drug market, and constitutional restrictions on national legislation) began to change in the late nineteenth century. A domestic movement to control dangerous drugs, especially patent medicines, led to passage of the Pure Food and Drug Act of 1906, which required accurate labeling of the narcotic contents of products sold in interstate commerce. The acquisition of the Philippine Islands in 1898 and the necessity of dealing with the opium problem there spurred the most important decision making on narcotics by the federal government. The Philippine experience not only accelerated the passage of national laws but, of broader significance, led directly to a U.S.-inspired treaty to control narcotics worldwide, as well as to the international antiaddiction effort that persists to this day.

Origin of International Control

Under Spanish rule, there had been an opium monopoly in the Philippines from which opium smokers could obtain supplies. The newly arrived U.S. government decided to reinstitute the monopoly and use the profits to help support universal education there. However, U.S. missionary and political leaders strongly rejected the proposal. The impasse led to the creation of an investigating committee appointed by the Philippine government that included Charles Henry Brent, Protestant Episcopal bishop of the Philippines, who would become the key figure in establishing an international campaign against narcotics. The committee examined control measures used in other areas of the Orient and recommended a gradual reduction approach for opium users in the

Philippine Islands. The U.S. Congress took a more severe stance, mandating total prohibition of opium and derivatives, except for medical purposes, for Filipinos in 1905 and all other groups (mainly Chinese) in the Islands in 1908.

It was obvious to the U.S. government that its meager enforcement could not prevent the smuggling of opium into the Philippines. Conflict with China over the treatment of Chinese aliens in the United States along with the crucial events of 1906 in China and the United Kingdom provided Bishop Brent with a rare opportunity. He wrote President Theodore Roosevelt urging that the United States convene a meeting of relevant nations to assist China with its antiopium crusade. Successful control of narcotics traffic would aid the Philippines and the United States, and might also placate China. The acceptance of Brent's idea resulted in a survey of the U.S. domestic drug problem and the convening of the International Opium Commission at Shanghai in February 1909. Brent was chosen to preside over the 13 nations that gathered there. The commission's rather noncontroversial resolutions were used by the United States to convene the International Opium Conference, a treaty-making body, at the Hague in December 1911. The dozen nations represented at the conference, again chaired by Brent, adopted an International Opium Convention in January 1912. This treaty also included provisions for the control of cocaine. Control would be enforced primarily through the domestic legislation of several nations: However, the treaty would not come into force until every nation on earth had ratified. This difficult requirement arose out of the fear of some producing and manufacturing nations that, without universal adoption, the nonadhering nations would be able to dominate a lucrative market.

At a conference in June 1914, it was decided that any nation ratifying the treaty could put it into effect without waiting for unanimity. The United States chose to do so, and enacted the Harrison Narcotic Act in December 1914. World War I slowed ratification, but when the fighting ended, several of the victorious nations, including the United Kingdom and the United States, added the Hague Convention to the Versailles Treaty, mandating that ratification of the Peace Treaty include the Opium Convention. It was as a result of this requirement, and not of any domestic drug crisis, that the United Kingdom enacted the Dangerous Drugs Act of 1920. In later decades, especially in the United States, the origins of this act were forgotten, and the provision of opiates to some addicts allowed under the act was claimed to have solved a serious addiction problem in the United Kingdom. This is an example, common in the area of drug policy, of trying to base solutions to an addiction problem on the laws or practices of another nation without taking into consideration differences in history and culture.

The Establishment of an International Bureaucracy

The League of Nations assumed responsibility for the Hague Convention in 1920. In 1924 the First Geneva Opium Conference addressed the gradual suppression of opium smoking. This was soon followed by the Second Geneva Opium Conference, which expanded international control over drugs by establishing a system of import and export certificates, creating the Permanent Central Opium Board (PCOB) to oversee the new provisions, and adding coca leaves and cannabis to the list of controlled substances. The United States, because it did not recognize the League, relinquished leadership of the international movement, and went so far as to walk out of the Second Geneva Opium Conference because, in its view, the other nations were unwilling to take meaningful steps to curb opium production and refused to ban the manufacture of diacetyl-morphine, more commonly known by its generic name, heroin. Heroin had been introduced by the Bayer Company in 1898 as a cough suppressant and within two decades had replaced morphine as the drug of choice among youth gangs in New York City. Heroin had an advantage over morphine in that it could be sniffed as well as injected and became the most feared of the opiates in the United States. In 1924 the United States banned domestic production of heroin.

In 1931 a conference was held in Geneva on limiting the manufacture of narcotic drugs, and in 1936 another Geneva conference dealt with suppressing the illicit traffic in dangerous drugs. After World War II the United Nations accepted responsibility for narcotics control, and in 1961 the various treaties were combined into the Single Convention on Narcotics. A significant addition to the older treaties was the prohibition of cannabis production.

The United Nations placed drug control under the Economic and Social Council (ECOSOC). The UN Commission on Narcotic Drugs meets annually to review the drug problem and make recommendations on policy to ECOSOC. The commission is the successor to the League's Advisory Committee on Traffic in Opium and Other Dangerous Drugs (1921–40). Also under ECOSOC is the International Narcotic Control Board (INCB), which oversees the ongoing functioning of treaty obligations and provides technical assistance in the form of statistics and chemical analyses. INCB, established by the Single Convention, succeeds the League's PCOB (1929–67) and the Drug Supervisory Board (1933–67).

The appearance in the 1960s of problems with newer drugs, such as LSD, barbiturates, amphetamines, and tranquilizers, prompted a new treaty, the Convention on Psychotropic Drugs (1971), which aims to expand international supervision beyond the traditional substances linked to opium, coca, and cannabis. In 1988 a convention intended to improve criminal sanctions against international traffickers was submitted to members of the United Nations for ratification.

Recent Responses to Drug Use

Research into the mechanisms of drug addiction and dependence has greatly increased in the past quarter-century. In the nineteenth century, research centered on modes of delivery, the development of the hypodermic syringe, and the nature of opiate addiction. The pattern of withdrawal was described and treatment for opiate addiction sought. Cocaine was offered, for example, as a cure for morphinism and alcoholism. Other cures were drawn from popular medical theories of the time, autointoxication, and other aspects of immunological response.

Confidence in treatment was equaled only by enthusiasm for research, until after World War I when, especially in the United States, a powerful reaction against drug use caused both professionals and the public to reject current treatments – which, in fact, were of little value – and to lose interest in research. The battle against drug abuse came to rely primarily on law enforcement. Research again found support in the late 1960s and the 1970s when consumption rose and there was a certain toleration of "recreational" or "experimental" drug use among youth. However, as fear of drugs and drug users increased, the public grew impatient with treatment and toleration of any drug use and, again, funding for research fell. In recent decades, significant advances have included the discovery of opiate receptor sites in the brain, of the existence of naturally produced opiates, endorphins, and of the existence of chemicals that block opiate receptor sites. Specific treatment for cocaine dependence has eluded investigators.

On an international level, attempts have been made to interdict drugs coming from producing areas; persuade local growers of poppies, coca bushes,

and marijuana to grow other crops; arrest local dealers; and spray illicit crops with herbicides. Crop substitution as an international policy dates to the
1920s, when the League of Nations sought to persuade opium growers in Persia to grow other crops,
and continues today in major opium-producing areas, such as the "Golden Triangle" in northern
Burma. This scheme has not yet cut into the world
supply of opium and coca and, of course, is irrelevant
to the control of manufactured drugs such as synthetic opiates and stimulants like amphetamine.
Spraying the crops of producing nations and other
policies advocated by consuming nations raise sensitive questions of sovereignty. Furthermore, producing nations claim, as they did during the first U.S.
campaign to control production before World War I,
that the problem is not production but the consuming nations' demand for drugs.

In its worldwide campaign against addiction, the
United States early in this century asserted that the
use of narcotics for anything other than strictly medical treatment was dangerous and morally wrong.
This attitude represented the thinking of most
North Americans at the time, but it was not a universal view and is not a view always held by the United
States. The vicissitudes of moral attitude toward
addiction over the past two centuries illustrate that
the response to addiction is intimately bound to the
social history and mores of a nation or region at any
given time. The history of addiction has a medical
element, but it is also a reflection of nations' characteristic approaches to individual and social problems. Integration of the history of addictive substances with the social history of nations and regions
remains a fertile area for research.

David F. Musto

Bibliography

Bonnie, Richard J., and Charles H. Whitebread II. 1974.
   *The marihuana conviction: A history of marihuana
   prohibition in the United States*. Charlottesville, Va.
Clark, Norman H. 1976. *Deliver us from evil: An interpretation of American prohibition*. New York.
Courtwright, David T. 1982. *Dark paradise: Opiate addiction in America before 1940*. Cambridge, Mass.
Lowes, Peter D. 1966. *The genesis of international narcotics control*. Geneva.
Morgan, H. Wayne. 1981. *Drugs in America: A social history, 1800–1980*. Syracuse, N.Y.
Musto, David F. 1987. *The American disease: Origins of
   narcotic control*. New York.
Parssinen, Terry M., and Karen Kerner. 1980. Development of the disease model of drug addiction in Britain,
   1870–1926. *Medical History* 24: 275–96.
Taylor, Arnold H. 1969. *American diplomacy and the narcotics traffic, 1900–1939*. Durham, N.C.
Terry, Charles E., and Mildred Pellens. 1928. *The opium
   problem*. New York.

III.8
Tobaccosis

The term *tobaccosis* in this essay denotes, collectively, all diseases resulting from the smoking,
chewing, and snuffing of tobacco and from the
breathing of tobacco smoke. They include cancers of
the mouth, nasopharynx, larynx, trachea, bronchi,
lungs, esophagus, stomach, liver, pancreas, kidney,
bladder, prostate, and cervix, as well as leukemia.
They also include atherosclerosis of the cardiovascular system – coronary heart disease (with ischemia
and infarction), cardiomyopathy, aortic and other
aneurysms, cerebrovascular hemorrhages and blockages; renal failure and peripheral vascular disease;
emphysema and chronic obstructive pulmonary diseases; peptic ulcer disease and regional ileitis; cirrhosis of the liver; immunological deficiencies and
failures of endocrine and metabolic functions; and
fetal diseases and perinatal disabilities.

Tobaccosis is the foremost plague of the twentieth
century and thus joins the most fearsome plagues
that devastated humanity during this millennium
such as the Black Death, smallpox, malaria, yellow
fever, Asiatic cholera, and tuberculosis. But unlike
microparasitic plagues, whose victims experienced
pathognomonic disease manifestations within days
or weeks of exposure, tobaccosis is an extraordinarily
insidious disease entity of long latency resulting from
exposure to tobacco for many years or decades and
manifested by increased occurrence of any of a broad
spectrum of neoplastic and degenerative diseases ordinarily associated with advanced age. Thus, the powerfully malignant nature and magnitude of the tobaccosis pandemic went largely undetected during the
first four centuries of its global march; and it is only
late in the fifth century of the post-Columbian world's
exposure to tobacco that the extent of tobacco's depredations is being fully revealed. Because of its leadership in the production, marketing, and use of tobacco,
the United States has borne much of the brunt of the
tobaccosis pandemic. Hence, this historical account
deals mainly with the U.S. experience.

Origin and Peregrinations of Tobacco

Tobacco is native to the Americas and was extensively cultivated and smoked by the aborigines there. The addictive weed was first encountered by Christopher Columbus and crew on the island of Cuba in November 1492. For some years it was known as *paetun* and by other names before it was given its common name, *tobacco,* from the pipes in which it was smoked on the island of Santo Domingo.

Increasingly cultivated and used by Spaniards and blacks in the West Indies and by Portuguese and blacks in Brazil during the early decades of the sixteenth century, tobacco was introduced to many European countries during the latter decades of that century. In 1559 tobacco seeds obtained in Lisbon by Jean Nicot, the French ambassador, from a Dutch trader just returned from the New World were sent as a medicinal to Queen Catherine de Medici and the House of Lorraine, thereby initiating tobacco cultivation and use in France and gaining lasting fame for Nicot.

Tobacco was brought to England in 1565 by John Hawkins, returning from a second voyage to Florida, but it did not gain immediate popular use. Two decades later, Walter Raleigh established a colony on Roanoke Island in Virginia. When Francis Drake visited the ill-fated colony in June 1586, the governor and others returned with him to England, bringing with them the tobacco and pipe-smoking practices soon popularized by Raleigh and others at Queen Elizabeth's court. By 1600 tobacco was widely used in all the maritime nations of Europe.

Meanwhile Portuguese traders carried tobacco in the latter 1500s to African ports and to India, the Spice Islands, Japan, Macao, China, and elsewhere in the Orient; and Spanish traders carried it to the Philippines. Other European merchants trading in the Levant took the weed with them throughout the East. Thus, by the end of the seventeenth century, tobacco was widely available and used in virtually all trading nations of the world.

Tobacco in Europe

Among American Indians, from Canada to Brazil, tobacco was widely smoked for its intoxicating effects, as a medicinal, and for ceremonial purposes. The spread of tobacco use from the New World gave rise to the first great drug controversy of global dimensions. From the onset, opinions regarding tobacco differed radically. Used by Indians as a remedy for aches and pains, snake bite, abdominal and chest pains, chills, fatigue, hunger and thirst, tobacco was extolled by European purveyors for its miraculous curative powers.

Yet the popularity of tobacco in England was challenged by James I, who became monarch of the British Isles after the death of Queen Elizabeth in 1603. His "Counterblaste to Tobacco," published anonymously in 1604 and considered extreme and rather quaint during intervening centuries, can now be appreciated as somewhat prescient:

And now good countrey men let us (I pray you) consider, what honour or policie can move us to imitate the barbarous and beastly manners of the wild, godlesse, and slavish Indians, especially in so vile and stinking a coustome? . . . A custome lothesome to the eye, hatefull to the nose, harmfull to the braine, dangerous to the lungs, and in the black stinking fume thereof neerest resembling the horrible stigian smoke of the pit that is bottomless. (Quoted in Austin 1978)

The following year he organized, at Oxford, the first public debate on the effects of tobacco, at which – to get his point across – he displayed black brains and black viscera allegedly obtained from the bodies of smokers. To discourage tobacco sales and use, James I increased the tax thereupon 40-fold; but when use and smuggling increased, he reduced the tax in 1608 to one shilling per pound of tobacco and sold the monopoly right to collect it. With the establishment in 1607 of his namesake colony on the James River in Virginia and on the initiative of John Rolfe, tobacco quickly became its principal crop and export. In 1615, 2,300 pounds were exported, in 1618, 20,000 pounds, and by 1620, 40,000 pounds.

An outbreak of plague in London in 1614 gave further impetus to smoking, in that doctors declared that steady smokers were not as subject to infection as others and recommended tobacco as a disinfectant. At that time, 7,000 shops were selling tobacco in London, with use spreading among the poor despite high prices. By 1615 tobacco imports had risen to such an extent that James revoked his 1608 monopoly grant and reassigned it at a higher price. In 1620 he ordered that all tobacco bear the government seal, and in 1624 he decreed that only Virginia tobacco be imported. Thus, despite the high costs and discomfort of smoking, chewing, and snuffing and despite intense repressive actions of such sovereigns as King James I of England, King Christian IV of Denmark, Tsar Michael Romanov of Russia, and Sultan Murâd of Turkey, tobacco continued to increase in popularity.

Snuffing Cancer

Among the lower classes, pipe smoking was the common method of tobacco consumption; among the European upper classes during the 1700s, pipe smoking was largely supplanted by snuffing (the practice of sniffing tobacco dust). Within a few decades the widespread practice of snuffing generated the first clinical reports of cancer caused by tobacco – cancer of the nasal passages, as described by an English physician, John Hill, in 1761:

This unfortunate gentleman, after a long and immoderate use of snuff, perceived that he breathed with difficulty through one of his nostrils; the complaint gradually encreased 'till he perceived a swelling within. . . . It grew slowly, till in the end, it filled up the whole nostril, and swelled the nose so as to obstruct the breathing . . . he found it necessary to then apply for assistance. The swelling was quite black and it adhered by a broad base, so that it was impossible to attempt to the getting it away . . . and the consequences was the discharge of a thick sharp humor with dreadful pain, and all the frightful symptoms of cancer . . . and he seemed without hope when I last saw him. (Quoted in Whelan 1984)

Also in 1761, the Italian anatomist Giovanni Battista Morgagni described lung cancer at postmortem without identifying its cause. A few years later, in 1775, Percival Pott described a scrotal cancer epidemic among London chimney sweeps, documenting the carcinogenicity of chimney *smoke,* which should have alerted many to the pathogenic implications of chronic exposure of respiratory tissues to tobacco smoke.

Although tobacco-induced lung cancer must have produced many thousands of deaths from the sixteenth to the nineteenth century, all such progressive chest diseases were lumped under the rubric of *phthisis* or *consumption* until the late-nineteenth-century scientific advances of histology, bacteriology, and X-ray. At that time, because of the often obvious relationships between snuffing and nasal cancer, pipe smoking and lip cancer, tobacco chewing and cancer of the mouth, cigar smoking and cancer of the mouth and larynx, there was a growing realization that tobacco use produced cancers of directly exposed topical tissues.

Nineteenth-Century Wars and Tobaccosis

British soldiers returning from campaigns on the Iberian Peninsula during the years 1808–14 introduced cigarettes to England. Likewise, veterans returning from the Crimean War (1853–6) increased cigarette smoking in Britain – a practice soon brought to the United States by returning tourists, including New York society women.

During the U.S. Civil War (1861–5) the use of all kinds of tobacco, including that of cigarettes, in-

creased, and after the war tobacco factories mushroomed. By 1880, with a population of 50 million people, the United States consumed 1.3 billion cigarettes annually, 500 million made locally and the rest imported. Nonetheless, chewing tobacco – a U.S. concoction of tobacco and molasses – remained the leading form of tobacco in the United States throughout the nineteenth century. Along with a great increase in tobacco consumption during the nineteenth century came increasing reports of tobaccosis, especially cancers of directly exposed tissues. Although medical science was still in its infancy in the nineteenth century, occasional astute clinical observations gradually increased people's awareness of the pathogenicity of tobacco.

In 1851, for example, James Paget saw a patient with leukoplakia ("smoker's patch") on the tongue where he always rested the end of his pipe, and "told him he certainly would have cancer of the tongue if he went on smoking" (quoted in Whelan 1984). And in 1857 *Lancet* commented:

Tobacco . . . acts by causing consumption, haemoptysis and inflammatory condition of the mucous membrane of the larynx, trachea and branchae, ulceration of the larynx; short, irritable cough, hurried breathing. The circulating organs are affected by irritable heart circulation. (Quoted in Whelan 1984)

In 1859 a French physician reported a remarkably thorough study of 68 cases of cancer of the oral cavity in a French hospital. Ascertaining the habits of 67 of these patients, he found that 66 smoked tobacco and the other chewed tobacco. He also noted that cancer of the lip ordinarily occurred at the spot where the pipe or cigar was held.

In 1882 the *Boston Medical and Surgical Journal* offered this prescient view of cigarettes:

The dangers, then, which are incident to cigarette smoking are, first, the early age at which it is taken up; second, the liability to excess; and, third, the bad custom of inhaling the smoke. These are dangers super-added to those attendant upon the ordinary use of tobacco, and should be considered by all medical men.

Despite such examples, however, leading physicians of the late nineteenth century were generally oblivious to the hazards of tobacco. In the monumentally detailed *Medical and Surgical History of the War of the Rebellion,* prepared under the direction of Surgeon General of the Army Joseph K. Barnes by J. J. Woodward and colleagues and published in six huge volumes from 1875 to 1888 under the authority of the U.S. Congress, there are only two comments about tobacco: that tobacco clyster may be used for the treatment of zymotic disease and that abuse of tobacco may cause "irritable heart." Nor was tobaccosis frequently mentioned by John Shaw Billings, founder of the *Index Medicus,* the National Library of Medicine, and author of voluminous analyses of late-nineteenth-century U.S. mortality. William Osler in his classic 1892 text, *The Principles and Practice of Medicine,* devoted only three sentences in 1,000 pages to the effects of tobacco.

With the advent of cigarette-making machines, which made possible the nearly unlimited production of cigarettes, and portable "safety" matches (introduced at the turn of the century), which enabled smokers to light up whenever and wherever they wished, the stage was set for a vast increase in cigarette consumption. However, as tobacco companies intensified promotional activities, a powerful antitobacco movement developed, led by Lucy Page Gaston and the Women's Christian Temperance Movement, which substantially curbed cigarette sales during the 1890s and early 1900s.

Twentieth-Century Cigarette Tobaccosis

A comprehensive view of evolving tobacco use patterns in the United States during this century is presented in Table III.8.1, which documents the progressive trend from cigar smoking and the use of "manufactured tobacco" (pipe tobacco, chewing tobacco, and snuff) to cigarette smoking. Annual production of manufactured tobacco increased from 301 million pounds in 1900 to a peak of 497 million pounds in 1918 and subsequently decreased to 142 million pounds (1988). During the twentieth century, cigar production oscillated between 4 and 10 billion annually, with more cigars produced in 1900 (5.6 billion) than in 1988 (3.2 billion).

Meanwhile, cigarette production and consumption increased more than 100-fold, with consumption increasing from 2.5 billion cigarettes in 1900 to 640 billion in 1981, then decreasing to 562 billion in 1988. On a per capita basis in the United States, annual cigarette consumption increased from 54 per adult in 1900 to a peak of 4,345 per adult in 1963. Since then it has decreased to 3,096 cigarettes per adult in 1988.

The foremost determinants of national cigarette consumption can be inferred from the trend changes seen in Figure III.8.1. Cigarette consumption doubled during World War I, when cigarettes were included in soldiers' rations sent to France. It doubled again during the 1920s, propelled by innovative advertising campaigns and augmented by radio and cinema. But then it decreased during the early years

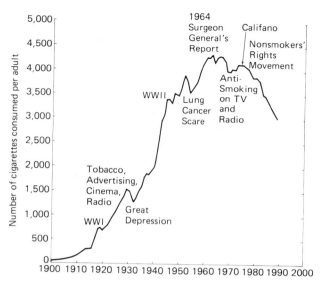

Figure III.8.1. Annual consumption of cigarettes by U.S. adults (18 years of age and older), 1900–88. (Data from the Economic Research Service, U.S. Department of Agriculture.)

of the depression of the 1930s, only to increase during the latter part of the decade, presumably in response to intensified advertising in magazines, on billboards, and on radio as well as in response to the incessant smoking of popular film stars and other famous personalities.

During World War II, when cigarettes were made freely available to many military and some civilian groups, consumption almost doubled again – from 1,976 cigarettes per adult in 1940 to 3,449 in 1945. After the war, cigarette consumption continued upward until 1950, when scientific findings showed smoking to be the principal cause of a rapidly increasing epidemic of lung cancer. However, tobacco sales soon recovered.

Intense wrangling over the validity of research findings on the harmful effects of tobacco generated so much confusion that in 1962 Surgeon General Luther Terry established the Advisory Committee of Experts, whose landmark report on 11 January 1964 rendered an authoritative verdict: "Cigarette smoking is causally related to lung cancer in men; the magnitude of the effect of cigarette smoking far outweighs all other factors. The data for women, though less extensive, point in the same direction."

Again the tobacco industry took vigorous defensive action with intensified advertising; but when a fairness doctrine required that advertising messages on radio and television be balanced by antismoking messages, tobacco advertising was discontinued in the broadcast media.

Table III.8.1. *U.S. tobacco production and consumption, 1900–88*

| Year | Mfg. tobacco (lbs. × 10⁶) | Tobacco products produced | | Cigarette consumption | |
| | | Total in billions | | | |
		Cigars	Cigarettes	Total in billions	Per adult (18+ years)
1900	301	5.6	3.9	2.5	54
1901	314	6.1	3.5	2.5	53
1902	348	6.3	3.6	2.8	60
1903	351	6.8	4.0	3.1	64
1904	354	6.6	4.2	3.3	66
1905	368	6.7	4.5	3.6	70
1906	391	7.1	5.5	4.5	86
1907	388	7.3	6.3	5.3	99
1908	408	6.5	6.8	5.7	108
1909	431	6.7	7.9	7.0	125
1910	447	6.8	9.8	8.6	151
1911	424	7.0	11.7	10.1	173
1912	435	7.0	14.2	13.2	223
1913	444	7.6	16.5	15.8	260
1914	441	7.2	17.9	16.5	267
1915	442	6.6	18.9	17.9	285
1916	466	7.0	26.2	25.2	395
1917	483	7.6	36.3	35.7	551
1918	497	7.6	47.5	45.6	697
1919	424	7.1	53.9	48.0	727
1920	413	8.1	48.1	44.6	665
1921	387	6.7	52.8	50.7	742
1922	420	6.7	56.4	53.4	770
1923	413	7.0	67.2	64.4	911
1924	414	6.6	73.2	71.0	982
1925	414	6.5	82.7	79.8	1,085
1926	411	6.5	92.5	89.1	1,191
1927	396	6.5	100.2	97.5	1,279
1928	386	6.4	109.1	106.0	1,366
1929	381	6.5	122.8	118.6	1,504
1930	372	5.9	124.2	119.3	1,485
1931	371	5.3	117.4	114.0	1,399
1932	347	4.4	106.9	102.8	1,245
1933	342	4.3	115.1	111.6	1,334
1934	346	4.5	130.3	125.7	1,483
1935	343	4.7	140.1	134.4	1,564
1936	348	5.2	159.1	152.7	1,754
1937	341	5.3	170.2	162.8	1,847
1938	345	5.0	171.8	163.4	1,830
1939	343	5.2	180.8	172.1	1,900
1940	344	5.4	189.4	181.9	1,976
1941	342	5.6	218.1	208.9	2,236
1942	330	5.8	257.7	245.0	2,585
1943	327	5.9	296.3	284.3	2,956
1944	307	5.2	323.7	296.3	3,030
1945	331	5.3	332.3	340.6	3,449
1946	253	5.6	350.1	344.3	3,446
1947	242	5.5	369.8	345.4	3,416
1948	245	5.6	386.9	358.9	3,505
1949	239	5.4	385.0	360.9	3,480
1950	235	5.5	392.0	369.8	3,522
1951	227	5.7	418.8	397.1	3,744
1952	220	5.9	435.5	416.0	3,886
1953	209	6.0	423.1	408.2	3,778
1954	204	5.9	401.8	387.0	3,546
1955	199	5.8	412.3	396.4	3,597
1956	185	5.8	424.2	406.5	3,650
1957	179	5.9	442.3	422.5	3,755
1958	180	6.4	470.1	448.9	3,953
1959	176	7.3	489.9	467.5	4,037
1960	173	6.9	506.1	484.4	4,174
1961	173	6.6	518.0	502.5	4,266
1962	169	6.8	529.9	508.4	4,265
1963	168	6.6	543.7	523.9	4,345
1964	180	8.6	535.0	511.3	4,195
1965	167	8.9	562.4	528.8	4,259
1966	162	8.0	562.7	541.3	4,287
1967	158	7.3	572.8	549.3	4,280
1968	159	7.7	570.7	545.6	4,186
1969	161	7.5	573.0	528.9	3,993
1970	165	8.0	562.2	536.5	3,985
1971	158	7.8	576.4	555.1	4,037
1972	154	10.0	599.1	566.8	4,043
1973	152	8.8	644.2	589.7	4,148
1974	153	8.3	635.0	599.0	4,141
1975	155	7.4	625.0	607.2	4,123
1976	153	6.7	688.0	613.5	4,092
1977	155	5.8	673.0	617.0	4,051
1978	156	5.6	688.0	616.0	3,967
1979	156	5.1	707.0	621.5	3,861
1980	163	4.9	702.0	631.5	3,851
1981	162	5.0	744.0	640.0	3,840
1982	160	4.5	711.0	634.0	3,753
1983	159	4.3	668.0	600.0	3,502
1984	159	4.5	657.0	600.4	3,446
1985	158	4.0	665.3	594.0	3,370
1986	148	3.9	658.0	583.8	3,274
1987	143	3.2	689.4	575.0	3,197
1988	142	3.2	694.5	562.5	3,096
Total	25,285	555.9	28,004.7	26,366.1	2,387 av.

Source: Economic Research Services, U.S. Department of Agriculture.

Despite these setbacks for the tobacco industry, sales ascended during the early 1970s. During the late 1970s, however, consumption began to decline under Joseph Califano as Secretary of Health, Education, and Welfare, a trend that fortunately has continued, for several reasons. Among these are increasing evidence of the harm to persons who are chronically

Table III.8.2. *Per capita adult consumption of manufactured cigarettes by country, 1985*

Cyprus	4,050	Netherlands	1,690
Cuba	3,920	Sweden	1,660
Greece	3,640	Suriname	1,660
Poland	3,300	Trinidad and	
United States	3,270	Tobago	1,600
Japan	3,270	Algeria	1,590
Hungary	3,260	China	1,590
Canada	3,180	Hong Kong	1,580
Iceland	3,100	South Africa	1,550
Yugoslavia	3,000	Tunisia	1,470
Switzerland	2,960	Barbados	1,380
Lebanon	2,880	Nicaragua	1,380
Libyan Arab		Costa Rica	1,340
Jamahiriya	2,850	Fiji	1,320
Kuwait	2,760	Mexico	1,190
Spain	2,740	Democratic Peo-	
Australia	2,720	ple's Republic	
Republic of		of Korea	1,180
Korea	2,660	Guadeloupe	1,080
Austria	2,560	Morocco	1,070
Ireland	2,560	Indonesia	1,050
Czechoslovakia	2,550	Honduras	1,010
New Zealand	2,510	Chile	1,000
Italy	2,460	Paraguay	1,000
Bulgaria	2,410	Guyana	1,000
France	2,400	Iraq	980
Germany, Fed-		Dominican	
eral Republic	2,380	Republic	980
Germany, Demo-		Reunion	940
cratic Republic	2,340	Congo	920
Israel	2,310	Thailand	900
Singapore	2,280	Ecuador	880
USSR	2,120	Panama	850
United Kingdom	2,120	Sierra Leone	830
Denmark	2,110	Jamaica	820
Saudi Arabia	2,110	El Salvador	750
Romania	2,110	Benin	740
Syrian Arab		Côte d'Ivoire	710
Republic	2,050	Vietnam	670
Belgium	1,990	Pakistan	660
Turkey	1,970	Iran	620
Norway	1,920	Senegal	610
Colombia	1,920	Cameroon	610
Philippines	1,910	Guatemala	550
Venezuela	1,890	Kenya	550
Egypt	1,860	Angola	530
Malaysia	1,840	Zimbabwe	500
Argentina	1,780	Sri Lanka	500
Uruguay	1,760	Lao People's	
Portugal	1,730	Democratic	
Finland	1,720	Republic	490
Jordan	1,700	Togo	460
Brazil	1,700	Madagascar	450
Mauritius	1,700	Liberia	450

Mozambique	430	Cape Verde	210
Zambia	400	Zaire	210
Malawi	390	India	160
Ghana	380	Chad	150
Nigeria	370	Burma	150
Peru	350	Nepal	150
Bolivia	330	Sudan	130
United Republic		Niger	100
of Tanzania	330	Ethiopia	60
Central African		Afghanistan	50
Republic	280	Papua New	
Bangladesh	270	Guinea	30
Uganda	260	Guinea	30
Haiti	240	Burkina Faso	30

Note: An adult is defined as someone 15 years of age and over.
Source: WHO Program on Smoking and Health.

exposed to smoke generated by others and stronger antitobacco activities by official and voluntary agencies at national, state, and local levels, as well as the vigorous campaign mounted by Surgeon General C. Everett Koop.

World Tobacco Trends

During recent decades, as antitobacco movements have hobbled tobacco promotion and sales in some of the affluent countries and as income levels have risen in many less developed countries, the multinational tobacco companies have intensified their advertising efforts in the less developed world, resulting in the global tobacco consumption pattern seen in Table III.8.2.

The leading countries in the production and consumption of tobacco are China, the United States, the Soviet Union, Japan, the Federal Republic of Germany, the United Kingdom, Brazil, India, Spain, France, and Italy. World production and consumption of cigarettes now exceed 5 trillion annually – more than enough to raise the world tobaccosis death toll substantially above the current level of about 3 million annually. Fortunately, during the 1980s the World Health Organization began to exercise forthright leadership in supplying information on this difficult issue, though it had not yet applied financial and personal resources commensurate with the nature and magnitude of the tobaccosis pandemic.

Nature of the Tobacco Hazard

Addictive Pleasures

Although it has always been obvious that tobacco contains a substance (nicotine) that yields psychic

Table III.8.3. *Percentage of U.S. adults who smoked regularly, 1945–85*

Year	Men (%)	Women (%)	Combined (%)
1945	48	36	42
1950	54	33	44
1955	54	25	40
1960	52	34	42
1965	52	34	42
1970	44	31	38
1975	42	32	37
1980	38	30	34
1985	33	28	30
40-year average	46	31	39

Source: Estimated from survey data by Gallup Poll, National Center for Health Statistics, and Centers for Disease Control.

pleasures not obtained by the smoking of other plant leaves, only during the 1980s did a strong scientific and societal consensus emerge that nicotine is truly addictive – just as addictive as heroin or cocaine and much more addictive than alcohol.

Indeed, cigarette smoking is now the most serious and widespread form of addiction in the world. The proportion of adult men and women who have smoked cigarettes in the United States during the past half-century is indicated in Table III.8.3. Half of adult men smoked at midcentury, this proportion decreasing to 33 percent in 1985 and 30 percent in 1987. Likewise, smoking by adult women decreased from 34 percent in 1965 to 28 percent in 1985 and 27 percent in 1987.

Lethal Poisons

The smoke of burning tobacco contains several thousand chemicals and a number of radioisotopes, including hydrogen cyanide, nitriles, aldehydes, ketones, nicotine, carbon monoxide, benzopyrenes, aza-arenes, and polonium 210, an alpha-particle emitter and therefore *the* most powerful contact mutagen, more than 100 times more mutagenic than equivalent RADs of gamma radiation. The combination of an addictive substance (nicotine) and more than 50 potent mutagens (especially polonium 210) has made tobacco the foremost human poison of the twentieth century.

Pathogenic Mechanisms

When tobacco smoke is inhaled deeply into the lungs, most of the tars contained therein are cap-

tured and retained by the respiratory mucous blanket. Soluble components are then promptly absorbed into the pulmonary circulation and conveyed by the systemic circulation throughout the body. Less soluble tars trapped by the mucous blanket are raised by ciliary action and coughing to the pharynx, then swallowed; thereafter, they pass to the esophagus, stomach, small intestine, portal circulation, and liver. Hence, chronic inhalation of tobacco smoke exposes the entire body – every tissue and cell – to powerful mutagens and carcinogens, thus hastening the malignant cellular evolutionary process and accelerating the development of the broad spectrum of neoplastic and degenerative diseases constituting tobaccosis (Table III.8.4).

The differences in mortality among smoking and nonsmoking U.S. veterans amply confirm the pioneering findings of Raymond Pearl, published in 1938, showing a great decrease in the longevity of smokers. In fact, the life-shortening effects of smoking are now so obvious that it seems incredible that they were generally overlooked for four centuries. Among persons who start smoking in adolescence and continue to smoke a pack of cigarettes daily, the *average* loss of life is roughly 8 years – approximately equal to the cumulative time actually spent smoking.

The most surprising finding of prospective and pathological studies – that the *majority* of tobaccosis deaths are caused by diseases of the cardiovascular system – initially generated incredulity, and indeed the phenomenon is still not well understood or fully believed by many. It nonetheless deserves full credence and is central to understanding the nature and magnitude of tobaccosis.

The fabric of evidence that cigarette smoking is a major cause of atherosclerosis is woven of these evidential threads:

1. The epidemic increase in ischemic heart disease in the United States during the twentieth century followed the rise in cigarette smoking and occurred particularly among those age–sex subgroups most exposed.
2. Individual studies document a close relationship between heavy cigarette smoking and early coronary disease.
3. There is a plausible pathogenic mechanism by which tobacco smoke could damage vascular tissue: The absorption of inhaled tobacco smoke results in the circulation of polonium 210 and other toxins, with injury to endothelial and other cells, causing cellular damage, clonal proliferation, intramural hemorrhage, lipid deposition, fibrosis,

Table III.8.4 *Deaths and mortality ratios among smoking U.S. veterans, 1980*

Cause of death	Observed deaths	Expected deaths	Mortality ratio (O ÷ E)
All causes	36,143	20,857	1.73
Respiratory diseases	2,139	483	4.43
Emphysema and bronchitis	1,364	113	12.07
Influenza and pneumonia	460	259	1.78
Pulmonary fibrosis and bronchiectasis	144	48	3.02
Pulmonary tuberculosis	81	36	2.27
Asthma	90	27	3.28
Cancer of directly exposed tissue	3,061	296	10.34
Buccal cavity, pharynx	202	33	6.12
Larynx	94	8	11.75
Lung and bronchus	2,609	231	11.29
Esophagus	156	24	6.50
Cancer of indirectly exposed tissue	4,547	3,292	1.38
Stomach	390	257	1.53
Intestines	662	597	1.11
Rectum	239	215	1.11
Liver and biliary passages	176	75	2.35
Pancreas	459	256	1.79
Kidney	175	124	1.41
Bladder	326	151	2.16
Prostate	660	504	1.31
Brain	160	152	1.05
Malignant lymphomas	370	347	1.07
Leukemias	333	207	1.61
All other cancers	597	407	1.47
All cardiovascular diseases	21,413	13,572	1.58
Coronary heart disease	13,845	8,787	1.58
Aortic aneurysm	900	172	5.23
Cor pulmonale	44	8	5.57
Hypertensive disease	1,107	724	1.53
Cerebral vascular disease	2,728	2,075	1.32
Peripheral vascular disease	20	6	3.52
Phlebitis and pulmonary embolism	214	175	1.22
Other diseases	1,333	724	1.84
Ulcer of stomach, duodenum, jejunum	365	92	3.97
Cirrhosis of the liver	404	150	2.69
Nephritis, nephrosis, other kidney disease	349	261	1.34
Diabetes	315	221	.97
All other diseases	2,801	2,100	1.33
No death certificate found	849	390	2.18

Source: Data from Rogot and Murray (1980).

and calcification. Though often overlooked, ionizing radiation is a powerful cause of atherosclerosis and premature death from cardiovascular disease.

4. Prospective studies of heavy smokers matched with nonsmokers for numerous confounding variables have consistently shown the relative risk of death from atherosclerosis to be much higher for smokers and directly related to the number of cigarettes smoked.

5. Members of certain religious groups that eschew the use of tobacco, such as Seventh-Day Adventists and Latter-Day Saints, have markedly lower morbidity and mortality rates from atherosclerotic disease.

6. Quitting smoking is ordinarily followed by a reduced incidence of coronary heart disease, among specific groups and for the entire population.

7. Experimental studies in animals have demonstrated that tobacco constituents are potent causes of atherosclerotic disease.

The evidence is clear, consistent, and compelling that tobacco smoke is a major cause of atherosclerotic disease and death.

Epidemic Curves

Temporal relationships between twentieth-century epidemic curves for cigarette smoking and death from coronary heart disease, lung cancer, and emphysema/COPD (chronic obstructive pulmonary disease) are presented in Figure III.8.2. The figure shows the massive epidemic of coronary heart disease beginning in the 1920s – a few years after the World War I doubling of cigarette smoking; followed by epidemic lung cancer beginning in the 1930s – 20 "pack years" or 150,000 cigarettes after World War I; followed by epidemic emphysema/COPD beginning in the 1940s – the third decade after World War I. Furthermore, as tar content and per capita cigarette smoking decreased during the last 2.5 years, mortality from coronary heart disease and cerebrovascular disease decreased.

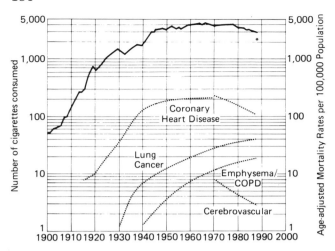

Figure III.8.2. Cigarette consumption and tobaccosis mortality in the United States, 1900–87. The asterisk indicates that the population exposure to tobacco tars is decreasing faster than the cigarette curve. (From Economic Research Service, U.S. Department of Agriculture; Vital Statistics of the United States; WCHSA Archives [personal communication]; Ravenholt 1962; Walker and Brin 1988; U.S. Department of Health and Human Services.)

Magnitude of the Hazard

Although some astute observers attributed lung cancer to smoking during the 1920s, 1930s, and 1940s, there was little general awareness of this relationship until the publication of case-control studies in 1950 showing that almost all (more than 90 percent) of lung cancer patients were smokers. The association of smoking with cancer of the lung was so obvious, consistent, and understandable that many scientists were readily convinced that smoking was the main cause of that disease. But when a number of prominent statisticians (who were themselves smokers) criticized these studies because of possible biases inherent in retrospective studies, massive prospective studies of morbidity and mortality differentials among smokers and nonsmokers were launched about the same time by the British Medical Association, the American Cancer Society, and the American Veterans Administration. (Among the many publications resulting from these studies were those by Doll and Hill [1952], Hammond and Horn [1958], Dorn [1959], and Rogot and Murray [1980].) The studies showed that smokers not only died from cancers of directly exposed tissues of the mouth, larynx, and lungs, but also died at a greatly accelerated rate from a bodywide spectrum of diseases, especially cardiovascular diseases (Table III.8.4) – thus confirming the finding of Raymond Pearl in 1938 that smoking exerted a profound life-shortening effect.

Furthermore, a matched-pair analysis of American Cancer Society prospective data by E. C. Hammond (1964) enabled this author to construct a Lung Cancer Index to total tobaccosis mortality and the estimate of *a quarter million U.S. tobaccosis deaths in 1962* – equal to the sum of all deaths from accidents, infection, suicide, homicide, and alcohol. Truly, for those who smoke a pack or more of cigarettes daily, tobacco is an environmental hazard equal to all other hazards to life combined. In 1967 this estimate was updated to 300,000 deaths for 1966.

During two ensuing decades, U.S. lung cancer deaths alone more than doubled from 48,483 in 1965 to 137,000 in 1987. In 1984, with the help of the Multi-Agency Working Group at the National Institute on Drug Abuse, seeking to achieve an updated, realistic estimate of U.S. tobaccosis mortality during the 1980s, this author applied proportionate analytic methods to 1980 U.S. mortality data; 485,000 tobaccosis deaths from cigarette smoking were estimated that year (Table III.8.5), as were

Table III.8.5 *Estimated number of deaths caused by cigarette smoking in the United States, 1980*

Anatomic site or nature of disease or injury (ICD number)	No. of deaths
Malignant neoplasms (140–209, 230–9)	147,000
Diseases of the circulatory system (390–459)	240,000
Ischemic heart disease (410–14)	170,000
Other vascular diseases	70,000
Diseases of the respiratory system other than cancer (460–519)	61,000
Emphysema (492)	13,000
Chronic bronchitis and other respiratory diseases	48,000
Diseases of the digestive system (520–79)	14,000
Diseases of the esophagus, stomach, and duodenum (530–7)	2,000
Cirrhosis and other diseases of digestive system	12,000
Certain conditions originating in perinatal period (760–79) (caused by maternal smoking, low birth weight, and other congenital disabilities)	4,000
External causes of injury (E800–E999)	4,000
Injuries caused by fire and flames (E890–E899)	2,500
Other accidental injuries	1,500
Miscellaneous and ill-defined diseases	15,000
Total	485,000

Source: Ravenholt (1984).

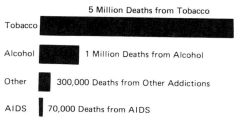

Figure III.8.3. The price of pleasure: deaths from addictive substances and AIDS in the United States, 1980s. (From Ravenholt 1984 and Centers for Disease Control.)

more than 500,000 tobaccosis deaths from all forms of tobacco use.

This estimate was accepted and used by the American Council on Science and Health and the World Health Organization, but not by the U.S. Office of Smoking and Health (OSH), which preferred a more "conservative" estimate of 320,000 tobacco deaths in 1987, raised to 390,000 in 1988.

Suffice it to say that the annual tobaccosis death toll – whether the OSH "conservative" estimate of 390,000 or the more complete estimate of 500,000 tobaccosis deaths – is far greater than mortality from any other preventable cause of death in our time and more than 25 times greater than current mortality from the acquired immune deficiency syndrome (AIDS), which emerged during the 1980s as a newly recognized and formidable disease entity (Figure III.8.3).

Conclusion

Tobacco owes much of its destructive power to the fact that its lethal effects are not immediately discernible. Initial reactions to smoking like nausea and respiratory distress usually subside, and many persons continue smoking, chewing, or snuffing tobacco for several decades without apparent serious injury or death. When serious illness does occur, it assumes such diverse forms that few comprehend the common cause.

Only recently, during the fifth century of post-Columbian tobacco experience, has medical and epidemiological science advanced sufficiently that the diffuse nature and great magnitude of tobacco's depredations have become fully evident. In the twentieth century alone, we tally these numbers:

In the United States the smoking of 26 trillion cigarettes and 556 billion cigars and the consumption of 25 billion pounds of "manufactured tobacco" (pipe tobacco, chewing tobacco, and snuff) have produced:

more than 2.9 million deaths from lung cancer,

more than 7 million deaths from cardiovascular disease, and

more than 14 million deaths from all forms of tobaccosis.

During the 1980s, the U.S. tobaccosis death toll was roughly 500,000 annually, for a total of 5 million deaths in the decade. Moreover, even if all tobacco use ceased immediately, many millions would still die of tobaccosis in ensuing decades.

In 1989 the world's inhabitants were smoking 5 trillion cigarettes annually and consuming millions of tons of tobacco as cigars, bidis, chewing tobacco, and snuff, as well as in pipes and hookas. The tobaccosis death toll was more than 2.5 million, and that in the twentieth century more than 50 million.

Considered a global entity with an extraordinarily diffuse, subtle nature and with lifetime latencies, tobaccosis poses the ultimate challenge to epidemiology and to world public health and political leadership.

R. T. Ravenholt

Excerpted and reprinted with the permission of the Population Council from R.T. Ravenholt. 1990. Tobacco's global death march. *Population and Development Review* 16(2):213–40.

Bibliography

Anon. 1882. Editorial. *Boston Medical and Surgical Journal* 107: 501.

Auerback, O., et al. 1957. Changes in the bronchial epithelium in relation to smoking and cancer of the lung. *New England Journal of Medicine* 256: 97–104.

Austin, G. A. 1978. *Perspectives on the history of psychoactive substance abuse.* Rockville, Md.

Berkson, J. 1959. The statistical investigation of smoking and cancer of the lung. *Proceedings of the Mayo Clinic* 34: 206–24.

Billings, J. S. 1885–6. *Report on the mortality and vital statistics of the United States as returned at the tenth census (June 1, 1880),* 3 vols. Washington, D.C.

Chandler, W. U. 1986. *Banishing tobacco.* World Watch Paper 68. Washington, D.C.

Coleman S., P. T. Piotrow, and W. Rinehart. 1979. Tobacco: Hazards to health and human reproduction. *Population Reports,* Ser. L, No. 1. Baltimore.

Diehl, H. L. 1969. *Tobacco and your health: The smoking controversy.* New York.

Doll, R., and A. B. Hill. 1952. A study of the aetiology of carcinoma of the lung. *British Medical Journal* 2: 1271–86.

Dorn, H. F. 1959. Tobacco consumption and mortality from cancer and other disease. *Public Health Reports* 74: 581–8.

Fisher, R. A. 1957. *Smoking: The cancer controversy, some attempts to assess the evidence.* Edinburgh.

Hammond, E. C. 1964. Smoking in relation to mortality and morbidity: Findings in first 34 months of follow-up in a prospective study started in 1959. *Journal of National Cancer Institute* 32: 115–24.

Hammond, E. C., and D. Horn. 1958. Smoking and death rates: Report on forty-four months of follow-up of 187,783 men. *Journal of the American Medical Association* 166: 1194–308.

Harris, J. E. 1983. Cigarette smoking among successive birth cohorts of men and women in the United States during 1900–80. *JNCI* 71: 473–9.

Hiryama, T. 1983. Passive smoking and lung cancer: Consistency of the association. *Lancet* 2: 1425–6.

Klebba, A. J. 1982. Mortality from diseases associated with smoking. *Vital and Health Statistics,* Ser. 20, No. 17. Hyattsville, Mo.

National Center of Health Statistics. 1950–86. *Vital Statistics of the United States.* Annual volumes. Washington, D.C.

Ochsner, A. 1941. Carcinoma of the lung. *Archives of Surgery* 42: 209.

Osler, W. 1892. *The principles and practice of medicine.* New York.

Pearl, R. 1938. Tobacco smoking and longevity. *Science* 87: 216–17.

Plenge, K. 1930. Tabakabusus und Koronarsklerose. *Deutsche medizinische Wochenschrift* 56: 1947.

Pollin, W., and R. T. Ravenholt. 1984. Tobacco addiction and tobacco mortality: Implications for death certification. *Journal of the American Medical Association* 252: 2849–54.

Radford, E. P., and V. R. Hunt. 1964. Polonium 210: A volatile radioelement in cigarettes. *Science* 143: 247–9.

Ravenholt, R. T. 1962. Historical epidemiology and grid analysis of epidemiological data. *American Journal of Public Health* 52: 776–90.

1964. Cigarette smoking: Magnitude of the hazard. *American Journal of Public Health* 54: 1923–5.

1966. Malignant cellular evolution: An analysis of the causation and prevention of cancer. *Lancet* 1: 523–6.

1982. Circulating mutagens from smoking. *New England Journal of Medicine* 307: 312.

1984. Addiction mortality in the United States, 1980: Tobacco, alcohol, and other substances. *Population and Development Review* 10: 697–724.

1985. Tobacco's impact on twentieth-century US mortality patterns. *American Journal of Preventive Medicine* 1: 4–17.

Ravenholt, R. T., and W. H. Foege. 1963. Epidemiology and treatment of lung cancer in Seattle. *Journal of Diseases of the Chest* 44: 174–85.

Ravenholt, R. T., et al. 1966. Effects of smoking upon reproduction. *American Journal of Obstetrics and Gynecology* 96: 267–81.

Ravenholt, R. T., and W. Pollin. 1983. Tobacco addiction and other drug abuse among American youth. *Proceedings of the 5th World Conference on Smoking and Health.* Winnipeg.

Reducing the health consequences of smoking – 25 years of progress: A report of the Surgeon General. 1989. Rockville, Md.

Report of the Surgeon General: The health consequences of smoking. 1964. Washington, D.C.

Rogot, E., and J. L. Murray. 1980. Smoking and causes of death among American veterans: 16 years of observation. *Public Health Reports* 95: 213–22.

Smoking and health: A report of the Surgeon General. 1979. Washington, D.C.

Tabor, S. J. W. 1843. A series of nine historical sketches of tobacco from 1492 to 1800. *Boston Medical and Surgical Journal* 27: 396–9.

Walker, W. J., and B. N. Brin. 1988. U.S. lung cancer mortality and declining cigarette tobacco consumption. *Journal of Clinical Epidemiology* 41: 179–85.

Warren, S. 1942. Effects of radiation on the cardiovascular system. *Archives of Pathology* 34: 1070–9.

Whelan, E.M. 1984. *A smoking gun: How the tobacco industry gets away with murder.* Philadelphia.

WHO programme on tobacco or health, 15 November 1985. Report by the Director-General, World Health Organization, to the Executive Board, 77th Session.

Woodward, J. J., et al. 1875–88. *The medical and surgical history of the War of the Rebellion,* 6 vols. Washington, D.C.

Wynder, E. L., and E. A. Graham. 1950. Tobacco smoking as a possible etiologic factor in bronchogenic carcinoma: A study of six hundred and eighty-four proved cases. *Journal of the American Medical Association* 143: 329–36.

III.9
Occupational Diseases

In recent years, occupational diseases have become an area of intense interest to medicine, public health, industry, and labor. Whole new areas of medical and public health specialization have developed since the end of World War II, partly in response to the detection of carcinogens in the workplace, dust in the air that workers breathe, and human-made chemicals that workers touch, taste, or inhale. Black lung (coal workers' pneumoconiosis), brown lung (byssinosis), and white lung (asbestosis) are three industry-specific diseases that have gained international attention and highlighted the role of occupation in the creation of illness. Laborers as well as physicians have become acutely aware of the dangers posed by substances and materials at work in a host of industries from steel to petrochemicals.

The growing attention to the hazards of the industrial workplace has alerted workers even in "clean" worksites to occupational disease. Physical dangers are posed to office workers by video display terminals, poorly designed furniture, noise, and vibrations. Stress at the workplace is now seen as important in the creation of the modern epidemics of high blood pressure, heart disease, and stroke. The very definition of disease has been altered by a rising popular and professional consciousness of the importance of occupation as a source of illness.

Occupational Diseases through the Industrial Revolution

Despite the recent concern, however, attention to the worksite as a source of disease is not new. Even the ancients recognized that certain occupations presented special risks of disease and injury. Hippocrates described lead poisoning among metal miners. Pliny the Elder was the first to describe the dangers that dust posed to tradesmen. Decimus Junius Juvenalis (Juvenal) wrote of the dangers that blacksmiths faced from the soot of "glowing ore." Over the course of the next two millennia a variety of observers remarked on the health hazards faced by specific tradesmen, artisans, and common laborers. But it was not until 1700 that Bernardino Ramazzini wrote his classic text, *De Morbus Artificum Diatriba* (Diseases of workers). This manuscript, the result of a lifetime of study and observation, was the first systematic treatment of the relationship between the workplace and the occurrence of disease. Ramazzini wrote of the health problems of common laborers and skilled artisans as well as of scribes, scholars, tradesmen, and others in the growing commercial classes. He alerted physicians to the significance of the workplace in identifying the sources of a patient's illness.

The Industrial Revolution fundamentally changed the methods of production and work relationships throughout the world. The factory system, which displaced workers from their land and homes, created new dangers. In addition to accidents caused by machinery, a faster pace of production, and long hours, new diseases plagued the working classes. Because England was the first industrial nation, English reformers and physicians quantified, measured, and documented the effects of industrialism and urbanization on the lives of the English working classes. Edwin Chadwick, Thomas Percival, and William Farr were among a group of Benthamites, Tories, and social reformers who sought to use statistical and quantitative analyses to impose order and expose the horrible working and living conditions that were closely linked to the development of the factory system. Charles Turner Thackrah, a physician in Leeds, paid particular attention to the diseases of various trades and, in 1832, wrote *The Effects of Arts, Trades, and Professions on Health and Longevity*. Thackrah organized his text by occupation, listing the diseases and disabilities associated with each trade. Diseases of operatives, dealers, merchants and master manufacturers, and professional men were itemized. Among the operatives who were exposed to harmful substances at work were cornsillers, maltsters, coffee roasters, snuff makers, rag sorters, papermakers, flock dressers, and feather dressers. Dangers listed in the section on merchants and manufacturers were "anxiety of mind" and "lack of exercise." Despite the obvious impact of new industrial and urban conditions on the life of the workers and their families, much of this early work is remarkable for its emphasis on the responsibility of individual workers to both remedy and control those forces destroying their lives.

The growing European socialist movements interpreted the disintegration of workers' health as confirmation of the unacceptable social costs of industrial capitalism. In the mid-nineteenth century, Frederick Engels wrote his classic treatise, *The Condition of the Working-Class in England*. In this work he devoted two chapters to the conditions of work in a variety of industries, specifically noting the effects of these conditions on the health of workers. He was especially concerned with the impact of child labor on the health of children pointing to its relationship with child mortality and disablement:

In the manufacture of glass, too, work occurs which seems little injurious to men but cannot be endured by children. The hard labor, the irregularity of the hours, the frequent night-work, and especially the great heat of the working place (100 to 190 Fahrenheit), engender in children general debility and disease, stunted growth, and especially affections of the eye, bowel complaint, and rheumatic and bronchial affections. Many of the children are pale, have red eyes, often blind for weeks at a time, suffer from violent nausea, vomiting, coughs, colds, and rheumatism. . . . The glass-blowers usually die young of debility of chest infections. (Engels 1980, reprint 1892 publication)

By the mid-nineteenth century, physicians, sanitary and social reformers, and radicals recognized a wide variety of occupational diseases that afflicted industrial populations. The medical literature was filled with articles about dust diseases and heavy-metal poisonings closely linked to the high temperature, poor ventilation, and bad lighting of the early factories. Consonant with much medical theory that associated disease with the social and moral environment of different populations, the medical literature noted the explicit relationship between disease and the work environment. Health was understood to be a reflection of the balance between people and nature. Disease was seen as a reflection of the imbalance between humans and the unnatural environments that they created for themselves. Cities, factories, slums, and other manifestations of industrialism were creating this imbalance. Hence, physicians and public health workers writing about treatments, diagnoses, and cures for disease often framed their arguments in the personal, moral, and social terms that infused medical theory. For example, throughout most of the nineteenth century, impure air, "miasmas," and dust were considered sources of disease; industrial dust was seen as the source of one form of "phthisis" or consumption, a chronic condition that affected broad cross sections of western European and U.S. populations. Popular and medical opinion coincided in that both used the terms *phthisis* and *consumption* to denote a set of symptoms of diverse social origins. The symptoms of wasting away, coughing, spitting, and weakening appeared in victims from various classes and social strata. The root of a worker's disease could be found by looking at a host of variables including race, ethnicity, personal characteristics, home life, and work.

By the last third of the nineteenth century, however, the growing acceptance of germ theory moved the medical and public health communities away from this social explanation of disease. This was illustrated most directly by the effect of Robert Koch's discovery of the tubercle bacillus on the history of industrial lung disease. By the time of Koch's discovery in 1882 an enormous literature about the effect of dust on the health of workers had developed, especially in Europe. But with the discovery of the bacillus, the study of its relation to industry ceased, according to Ludwig Teleky (1948), a noted industrial physician and author of the first modern history of industrial hygiene. In Europe, researchers "mocked at all those 'curiosities' of quartz lungs, coal lungs, and iron lungs, 'all of which belong in a cabinet of curiosities.' " Until the beginning of the twentieth century all consumption or phthisis came to be understood as tuberculosis, caused by a specific organism and spread like other infectious diseases.

The United States in the Early Twentieth Century

In the United States the medical community also narrowed its focus, which set back the study of occupational disease for a generation. Others outside of the medical community developed a broader conception of the relationship between the work environment and health. In the late nineteenth and early twentieth centuries, reformers concerned with the plight of the urban poor saw that the terrible conditions of their lives and their work could not be separated. Charity and settlement-house workers, for example, documented that in nearly one of every four dwellings in New York City in 1890 there was a death from consumption. In the poorer neighborhoods, it was clear, the toll was much higher, leaving those communities devastated by the disease. The Progressive Era (1890–1920) analysis that intimately linked social conditions and disease led reformers and public health workers to emphasize the connection between work and disease as well.

In industrial sections of the United States, individual physicians and state public health officials participated in reform movements for workmen's compensation legislation, and John B. Andrews and the American Association for Labor Legislation led campaigns against such problems as lead poisoning and "phossy jaw" (necrosis of the jaw caused by exposure to phosphorus, as in the making of matches). But occupational disease was not yet seen as an intrinsic part of the mandate of public health.

It was only in 1915 that the U.S. Public Health Service was granted authority to investigate "occupational diseases and the relation of occupations to disease." It organized an Industrial Hygiene and Sanitation section, and shortly thereafter the American Public Health Association also formed its own Industrial Hygiene section. In addition, a few of the state departments of health took an active and sustained interest in occupational diseases, most notably in Ohio under the leadership of Emery R. Hayhurst.

Even those reformers and physicians who were concerned with diseases of occupation focused mostly on acute poisonings, especially heavy-metal and phosphorus exposure. In the early years of the twentieth century, such investigators as Alice Hamilton, Florence Kelley, Andrews, and Hayhurst carried out detailed studies of lead, phosphorus, and mercury in such states as New York, Illinois, and Ohio. In 1911, following the tragic Triangle Shirtwaist fire in New York, in which scores of immigrant women were killed, the state sponsored a massive study of factory conditions led by Robert Wagner and Frances Perkins, among others. In the 1920s and after, industrial hygienists and occupational physicians investigated chronic diseases in workers in a number of occupations, especially painters and battery workers exposed to lead, watch-dial makers exposed to radium, and miners exposed to coal, silica, asbestos, and other dusts. The problem of lead had been known since antiquity, but the widespread introduction of lead into paint and gasoline and the increased smelting of ores associated with the Industrial Revolution heightened the awareness of the danger of lead to workers and the public alike.

During the early 1920s, workers in various petrochemical plants and research centers developed signs of acute lead poisoning. This alerted the public health community to the potential environmental damage that the recently introduced leaded gasoline posed. The Workers' Health Bureau argued that oil refinery workers were being "used like canaries in the coal mines" to test for the presence of poisonous substances. A major national conference was convened by the U.S. Public Health Service to discuss public policy regarding the use of organic lead in gasolines. However, it was not until the late 1960s and early 1970s that systematic efforts were made to eliminate lead from both indoor paint and gasoline.

It was also in the 1920s that women who worked in factories producing luminous watch dials in New Jersey were found to have symptoms of chronic radiation poisoning. This prompted occupational disease researchers and local physicians to undertake one of the first studies on the dangers of radium exposure. But again, it took until well after World War II for the U.S. government to act on their warnings about the deleterious effects of radiation.

Medical and public health interest in occupational diseases gave rise to new professions, such as that of industrial hygienist, and new specialties, such as occupational medicine. They were dominated in the 1920s by private companies, which supplied financial support, research facilities, and even patients. Indeed, in the United States hundreds of corporations hired their own physicians, nurses, and engineering and medical personnel as part of company welfare and health plans. But there were very few industrial agencies that were concerned with industrial health and only a few universities, such as Harvard, Yale, and New York University, organized departments that addressed industrial hygiene specifically. Thus, the control of workplace hazards was in the hands of professionals associated largely with private industry and therefore was not really associated with the broader perspectives of the Progressives and labor reformers.

The Problem of Dust and the Emergence of Chronic Disease

While a host of investigators began to study particular acute diseases caused by specific industrial toxins, the problem of dust in the closed environments of factories and mines galvanized the attention of the health community and work force. Dust was a potential problem in virtually every industrial setting. There were mineral and metal dusts in coal and metal mines, foundries, steel mills, and rubber factories, and vegetable and animal dusts in granaries, bakeries, textile mills, and boot and shoe factories. In the early twentieth century, the work of Thomas Oliver and a series of British governmental studies were instrumental in revitalizing interest in the industrial etiology of lung disease and the problem of chronic occupational diseases in general. In 1902, in his famous treatise *Dangerous Trades,* Oliver cited four specific dust diseases: chalicosis or silicosis, siderosis, anthracosis, and byssinosis.

In the first half of the twentieth century, labor and business focused mostly on silica dust, and though this diverted attention from the other dust diseases, it did lead to the formulation of general public policies that were applicable to other chronic industrial diseases. Politicians, labor, management, insurance company representatives, physicians, and lawyers all raised questions of responsibility for risk in the new industrial workplaces.

The central questions of the debate were: What was an industrial disease? How could occupational and environmental diseases be distinguished? How should responsibility for risk be assigned? Should a worker be compensated for impairments or for loss of wages due to occupational diseases and disabilities? Should industry be held accountable for chronic illnesses whose symptoms appeared years and sometimes decades after exposure? At what point in the progress of a disease should compensation be paid? Was diagnosis sufficient for compensation claims, or was inability to work the criterion? Who was to define inability to work – the employee, the government, the physician, or the company? In short, the questions and arguments addressed the problem of who defined what today we would call latency, time of onset, and the very process of disease.

Shortly after the Boer War, silicosis gained wider public notice, as English miners who had worked in the South African gold mines returned to Great Britain. Oliver described the fate of "young miners in the bloom of health" who, after working in the gold fields for only a few years, "returned to Northumberland and elsewhere broken in health." Because of the hardness of the rock from which gold was extracted, dry drilling and blasting created special hazards both for native workers and for their English overseers. In 1902 a British governmental commission was appointed to study the nature and prevalence of lung diseases in these mines. Investigators such as Edgar Collis, H. S. Haldane, and the Miners' Phthisis Commission demonstrated clearly that victims of "Rand Miners' phthisis" were primarily suffering not from tuberculosis, but from silicosis. This was the first systematic study of the hazard of exposure to silica dust.

In the United States, the British findings were employed by Frederick L. Hoffman in his study *The Mortality from Consumption in Dusty Trades* (1908). It began with the observation that "no extended consideration [was required] to prove that human health was much influenced by the character of the air breathed and that its purity is a matter of very considerable sanitary and economic importance."

The study built on the clinical evidence presented in the British material as well as on progressive social analysis. But it was also significant because Hoffman used statistical data drawn from insurance company records and census materials from both Great Britain and the United States. Although the British (especially Thomas Oliver) had also used statistical and epidemiological data in their investigations, Hoffman was the first American to use such methods. In so doing he documented the prevalence and scope of industrially created lung diseases and also used the statistical materials for their implications about the work environment. Although the case for the significance of dust as a cause of pneumoconiosis was building, Hoffman's focus in this 1908 report remained on industrial dusts and tuberculosis.

The dust hazards for metal miners and other workers had become sufficiently apparent that, in 1911, the U.S. Public Health Service and the Bureau of Mines were asked by the National Association for the Study of Tuberculosis to conduct a thorough investigation of lung diseases of metal miners. In 1914 the two federal agencies initiated the first such epidemiological study in the tristate lead- and zinc-mining region of Missouri, Kansas, and Oklahoma. The study exposed the horrendous toll that metal dusts were taking on miners in the area and graphically described the suffering that many of the miners experienced as the disease progressed: "If we can imagine a man with his chest bound with transparent adhesive plaster, we can form a mental picture of how useless were the efforts at deep inhalation made by these patients" (Lanza 1917a).

In Europe, as well as in the United States, the introduction of power hammers, grinders, cutting instruments, and sand blasters at the turn of the century had exposed large numbers of industrial workers to massive quantities of fine silica dust, which could penetrate deeply into their lungs. By the time of the Great Depression, many of these workers had developed symptoms of silicosis and, under the financial strains created by massive unemployment, began to bring their claims for disability benefits into the workers' compensation and court systems of the industrialized nations. Thus, silicosis emerged as a major political, social, and economic issue in the mid-1930s.

In the United States this produced a massive number of lawsuits which ultimately led to the convening of national conferences and the revision of workers' compensation systems. In this process, the issue of chronic industrial disease was forced onto the agendas of the medical and public health communities, and the debate began over responsibility for risk as well as over definitions of the technical and medical means of distinguishing and diagnosing chronic conditions. In the ensuing years the problem of noninfectious chronic diseases created by industrial work processes would become the centerpiece of industrial medicine.

Although the relationship of dust exposure to cancer was noted by the 1930s, it was only during the 1950s and 1960s that the medical and public health communities acknowledged its significance and such investigators as Wilhelm Heuper, Harriet Hardy, Irving Selikoff, and Lorin Kerr began to link exposure to dusts and toxins at the workplace to a variety of cancers. The investigations by Irving Selikoff of asbestosis, mesothelioma, and lung cancer were particularly effective in galvanizing popular and professional attention; the widespread dispersal of asbestos throughout the general environment caused profound awareness of the dangers of industrial production to the nation's health.

Occupational health was also a matter of concern for many social, labor, and political movements and this concern focused on industrial hazards. During the Progressive Era, for example, such unions as the Bakers' and Confectioners' Union, the International Ladies Garment Workers Union, and the Amalgamated Clothing Workers joined middle-class reform groups such as the National Consumers' League to press for reform of working conditions. During the 1920s, activist organizations like the Workers' Health Bureau of America sought to aid labor unions in investigations of workplace hazards and joined painters, hatters, and petrochemical workers to demand reform of factory conditions. During the 1930s various unions within the Congress of Industrial Organizations used deplorable health and safety conditions as a focal point for organizing workers in heavy industry. In the next two decades, other unions, such as the International Union of Mine, Mill and Smelter Workers, pressed for national legislation to protect their members from dust hazards. In the 1960s safety and health became major activities for such unions as the Oil, Chemical and Atomic Workers' Union (OCAW) and the United Mine Workers (UMW). Leaders like Lorin Kerr of the UMW and Anthony Mazzochi of the OCAW were involved in lobbying for national legislation to protect miners and other workers, and the UMW was also active in urging special legislation to compensate victims of coal workers' pneumoconiosis.

All of these activities culminated in the Coal Mine Health and Safety Act of 1969 and the Occupational Safety and Health Act of 1970. The latter act mandated the creation of both the Occupational Safety and Health Administration (OSHA) in the U.S. Department of Labor and the National Institute of Occupational Safety and Health (NIOSH) in the Department of Health and Human Services (previously Health, Education and Welfare). OSHA was to set and enforce national standards of safety and health on the job, and NIOSH, the research arm, was to determine safe levels of industrial pollutants.

With the decline of heavy industry after 1960 and the rise of white collar and service industries, many people argued that occupational disease was a legacy of the industrial era. Yet the problem of occupational diseases has merely taken on a new form. The emergence of a strong environmental movement has once again focused attention on the dangers of industrial production at the same time that it has broadened the scope of what was once seen as a problem for the industrial work force alone. The emergence, for example, of a nuclear power industry – whose domain ranges from the production of atomic weapons to nuclear medicine – has heightened awareness about the danger that radiation poses for workers even in the most highly technical professions. Furthermore, the problems of industrial and atomic waste disposal have forged a link between those who are concerned primarily about protecting workers and environmentalists.

Moreover, as international economic competition intensifies and workers and professionals alike experience intense pressure to increase the speed of production and improve the quality of products, the scope of the definition of occupational disease continues to broaden. Stress, for example, which was once considered a problem of executives, is now a major reason for compensating claims in California. And some miscarriages have been linked with exposure to low-level radiation from video display terminals.

In conclusion, the history of occupational diseases reflects the broad history of industrial production and changing relationships between capital, labor, and the state. Professionals such as physicians, industrial hygienists, and engineers, who have addressed the problem of industrial disease, have often also played auxiliary roles in the political and social conflict over the value of workers' lives. But control of industrial diseases has been accomplished largely through political activities and changing economic conditions rather than through medical or engineering interventions. Professionals have usually played an important technical role after an issue has been forced upon the public's agenda because of an industrial or environmental catastrophe or because of concerted political activity.

Until the 1950s, the history of medicine was often understood to be the history of infectious disease. However, with the evolution of chronic, noninfectious disease as a major public health problem, industrial illnesses have taken on a new importance and are no longer mere oddities in a "cabinet of curiosities." Indeed, industrial disease may prove to be a model for understanding all noninfectious illness, for those physicians, government agencies, and professionals who study it will be forced to address a host of questions regarding social and political responsibility for society's health. In fact, ultimately, industrialized countries will be forced to ask what level of risk is acceptable for industrial progress and who should bear the cost.

Gerald Markowitz and David Rosner

Bibliography

Chernick, Martin. 1986. *The hawk's nest incident.* New Haven, Conn.

Derickson, Alan. 1988. *Workers' health, workers' democracy.* Ithaca, N.Y.

Engels, Frederick. 1980. *The condition of the working-class in England.* Moscow. (Reprint of 1892 ed. London.)

Hoffman, Frederick L. 1908. *The mortality from consumption in dusty trades.* U.S. Bureau of Labor Bulletin No. 79. Washington, D.C.

Lanza, Anthony. 1917a. *Miners' consumption.* Public Health Bulletin No. 85. Washington, D.C.

 1917b. *Physiological effects of siliceous dust on the miners of the Joplin district.* U.S. Bureau of Mines Bulletin No. 132. Washington, D.C.

Markowitz, Gerald, and David Rosner. 1987. *Slaves of the depression: Workers' letters about life on the job.* Ithaca, N.Y.

Oliver, Thomas. 1908. *Diseases of occupation.* London.

Rosner, David, and Gerald Markowitz. 1987. *Dying for work: Occupational safety and health in twentieth century America.* Bloomington, Ind.

 1991. *Dusted: Silicosis and the politics of industrial disease.* Princeton, N.J.

Stellman, Jeanne, and Susan Daum. 1973. *Work is dangerous to your health.* New York.

Stern, Bernhard J. 1946. *Medicine in industry.* New York.

Teleky, Ludwig. 1948. *History of factory and mine hygiene.* New York.

Thackrah, Charles Turner. 1985. *The effects of arts, trades and professions on health and longevity* (1832), ed. Saul Benison. Canton, Mass.

Weindling, Paul. 1985. *The social history of occupational health.* London.

III.10
History of Public Health and Sanitation in the West before 1700

Throughout most of the past, ideas about the means and necessity of providing for the health of the general community were based on notions of what ensured an individual's well-being. At this personal level, measures that we might consider motivated by aesthetic choices (rather than fully developed ideals of cleanliness and the health necessities of personal hygiene) were interwoven with practices designed to minimize exposure to disease and injury. In a narrow sense, public health practices refer only to the organization of care for the sick of a community and the implementation of epidemic controls. Public sanitation includes all collective measures taken to protect the healthy from disease. Yet even today many believe that what ensures the health of an individual should be reflected in the rules for maintaining the public's health.

Through much of the past and present, the view of "public" health has involved a compromise between available community resources and the ideals of health maintenance at the individual level. Thus, in order to examine the history of public health and sanitation before the 1700s, it is necessary to include some discussion of the ideas and ideals of personal hygiene along with the development of concepts that led to genuine public health practices. "Basic" sanitary organization largely comprised rudimentary sanitation and sanitary law, care of the sick poor, provision for public physicians, and epidemic controls.

Sanitation

Archaeological records testify to the antiquity of communal efforts to provide clean water and dispose of human and animal wastes. The engineering achievements of some peoples, such as the ancient Peruvians in the Western Hemisphere and the Etruscans in Europe, were most impressive. They managed extensive systems for refuse drainage and clear water conveyance. However sophisticated the outcome, the motivation for these projects probably lay in fears common among tribal societies – for example, the fear of pollution offending a god or gods, who in turn could send disease and disorder. Reflecting these aboriginal values, natural springs and wells were sites of religious activity for millennia. But independently of the health benefits, the maintenance of a reliable water supply and efficient drainage of agricultural lands permitted larger human settlements, and thus, whether or not the health benefits were perceived, these practices were copied or reinvented in all the early civilizations of the Mediterranean, in the valleys of the Yellow, Indus, Tigris, Euphrates, and Nile rivers, and in the Incan and Mayan civilizations.

The most celebrated early sanitary engineering achievements were those of republican and imperial Rome, c. 300 B.C. to A.D. 200. In fact, many of the conduits built by the Romans remained in use until the twentieth century. Basing drainage projects on the successes of Etruscan predecessors, who were able to construct extensive underground drainage channels because the loose, volcanic soil of southern Italy was easily worked, early Romans developed systems of wells, rainwater cisterns, and irrigation ditches that promoted rural, agricultural development. Before 300 B.C., the Romans seem to have associated the assurance of clean and abundant water with ordinary life, an ideal never specifically related to the maintenance of health, public or private. But when they began to build cities, aqueducts became a public symbol of the Roman way of life, as well as a symbol of Roman power and sensitivity to the general welfare. Frontinus, in *On Aqueducts* (c. A.D. 100), says that the first one was constructed in Rome in 312 B.C.

In rural areas, the prosperity of the "farm" or villa seems to have been the inspiration for securing a reliable water supply, a favorite topic for the pragmatic and aristocratic authors of treatises on Roman agriculture and medicine (Scarborough 1981). These authors fastidiously detailed the benefits and drawbacks of using plants and drugs, differentiated harmful from benign bugs, and analyzed myriad substances that promoted or undermined the well-being of the farm and the farmer. For Cato, Columella, Frontinus, Vitruvius, Varro, and Celsus, health benefits were the natural harvest of the well-managed farm, a pastoral ideal of Roman life that survived through the urban, imperial centuries.

Although Romans generally welcomed practical advice, the adoption of the Greek ideals of personal hygiene was delayed until after the period of early republican growth – a time of rapid development of architectural and administrative models for aqueducts, cisterns, cloacae, drains, and wells. Greeks and Romans, however, shared a passion for the details of personal hygiene, including a fondness for baths,

cleansing agents for the skin, and oils, soaps, unguents, and other cosmetics used to maintain a good personal appearance and skin tone. Moreover, concern for personal hygiene went far beyond the realm of attracting sexual partners or performing religious cleansing rituals. Greeks and Romans worshiped health and consequently elevated in importance to their life-style the technical knowledge they believed would promote individual health and longevity.

Galen's *Hygiene,* written shortly after the death of Emperor Marcus Aurelius in A.D. 180, represents the acme of professional health theory and advice through which Greek medical thought and pragmatic Roman farm hygiene were united in late Mediterranean antiquity (Sigerist 1956). The Hippocratic theory of the four humors, describing health as a balance of the humors, which in turn represented the four elements of all material substance, dictated the fundamental ways of preserving equilibrium through an individual's natural changes in age, diet, season, and exposure to noxious influences. The emphasis was on prevention, and the health seeker needed to learn which foods were right for his or her constitution, when baths promoted or jeopardized health, what exercise was appropriate, when purgation was needed, and what substances and influences were lethal. Attention was to be focused on the fine details and management of the individual's environment.

Nonetheless, despite the foregoing, which seems an idealistic portrayal of health practices in antiquity, the stark reality is that 25 years was the average life expectation for most Greeks, Romans, Egyptians, and others in the vast ancient Greco-Roman Empire. Roman elites recognized the importance of effective disposal of human wastes and so constructed miles of sewers and cloacae, as well as public and private latrines, and collected the waste for use as fertilizer in rural areas (Scarborough 1981). However, an enormous gulf separated the privileged and the poor. The hovels and lean-to shacks of the destitute, homelessness, and severe crowding (all of which mimic life in modern Western and Third World slums) dominated Roman life (Scobie 1986). The ideals promoted by the wealthiest citizens apparently had little impact on the public's health. De facto, the drainage systems installed in individual homes were seldom connected to street drains and sewers, as archeology at Pompeii has shown, and latrines were not provided with running water. Alex Scobie (1986) has detailed the multiple health problems attending the practical aspects of Roman public hygiene, observing that a city the size of Rome with a population of approximately 8 to 10 million in early imperial times would have produced about 40,000 to 50,000 kilograms of body waste per day. Arguing that only a fraction of that output reached the "public" collection sites, he shows that the emphasis in Roman public hygiene was the maintenance of the farm and an aristocratic life-style, whatever the adverse health costs to the general population. The emptying of public and private facilities enhanced agricultural productivity and provided a livelihood for armies of unskilled workers. The collection of urine aided the cloth industry, because fullers used urine as a mordant for certain dyestuffs. Roman literature does not adequately testify to the horrors of Roman cesspits "nauseating mixture(s) of the corpses of the poor, animal carcasses, sewage, and other garbage" (Scobie 1986).

Nor have the marvels of the aqueducts fared well under recent historical scrutiny. Frontinus sang the praises of the nine aqueducts that daily supplied the city of Rome (scholars have calculated that they provided about 992,000 cubic meters of water each day), but he tells us little about the distribution of water and whether there were any mechanisms to stem the flow of water into basins and tanks. Because of their malleability, lead pipes were commonly used in the plumbing of aristocratic homes, but we do not know whether the water they carried was soft or hard. (Hard water would have prevented much of the lead from seeping into the drinking water.) Ancient pastoral fondness for rainwater probably protected many Romans outside the great city from the multiple health hazards attending advanced urban sanitary technology.

The best and worst features of Roman public health, and of the Greek traditions and theories of personal hygiene, were passed along in the books and physical artifacts that survived the piecemeal dismantling of the Roman Empire. Thus, the strong aristocratic voice that determined the ideals of public and private health and their implementation remained relatively unchanged in the societies that inherited Roman custom, such as the Byzantine and Islamic empires. But in western Europe, retreat to a rural economic base, the effective disappearance of cities and market economies, and the introduction of Germanic customs interrupted the Greco-Roman public health tradition. It is true that in Benedictine monasteries upper-class monks constructed infirmaries, baths, latrines, *caldaria,* or steam rooms, and cold rooms in the best of Roman aristocratic tradition. (St. Gallen monastery in Switzerland, built in the eighth century, is one of the best surviving examples of this tradition.) But most Roman sanitary

practices were adopted and gradually transformed only as Christian Mediterranean cities began to grow again in the eleventh and twelfth centuries.

In the European Middle Ages, cities grew to a maximum of 100,000 to 150,000 individuals by the early fourteenth century, only one-tenth the size of ancient Rome. The Roman legal principles holding individual property owners responsible for cleaning the streets in front of their homes dominated "public" sanitary intervention. Medieval Italians were far more willing than the Romans to specify what individual behaviors put others at risk and therefore to write new legislation prohibiting the pollution of public streets with animal carcasses, human refuse, and other noisome substances. Yet we do not know to what extent laws were actually enforced, and it is probable that medieval cities were even more squalid than those of antiquity. Nonetheless, there seems to have been a new ethic of communal, collective responsibility for public health. Some of the change may have come about with the Christianization of Europe, which among other things emphasized the physical and spiritual dangers of evil. Roman baths were used in common by the wealthier classes, but medieval laws dictated strict segregation of the sexes, treating as prostitutes, for example, women who strayed near the baths on a day when only men could use the facilities.

During the Middle Ages, urban dwellers could empty chamber pots into the streets as liberally as aristocratic Romans might have done, but medieval lawmakers often prescribed the times at which such wastes could or could not be evacuated or ordered that words of warning be shouted to passersby below. For example, thirteenth-century residents of Siena were enjoined to cry "Look out!" three times before tossing the contents of a pot onto the street, and fines were specified for those who were found noncompliant. Medieval city governments, like their Roman predecessors, hired laborers to clean streets, cisterns, and sewers and to evacuate garbage. But unlike Roman officials, who appear to have adopted a laissez-faire attitude toward enforcement, they elected or appointed district supervisors to patrol both these employees and citizen behavior, and to report infractions to judicial authorities. The medieval belief that humans were sources of pollution (by the fourteenth century, lepers were forced to wear yellow to symbolize their danger to the community) had profound consequences for the development of epidemic controls, as will be discussed in a later section.

Leading the way for the rest of Europe, Italian and

probably Spanish cities appropriated detailed Roman law and customs regulating the trappings of public sanitation – baths, sewers, fountains – as well as sanitary personnel and marketplace regulations, leaving most of these features unchanged, at least on paper, for hundreds of years. Public hygiene laws in 1700 strongly resembled those of 1300, with even the fines little changed. Those who could afford to follow all the recommendations of Galenic personal hygiene did so without questioning the basic premises of health maintenance, public or private. Only the creation of boards of public health, a very important late-medieval contribution to public health, and, late in the seventeenth century, medical attention to occupational disease represented significant advances in modern public health philosophy and practice.

Care of the Indigent and Public Physicians

The organization of basic health services within a community involves the provision of medical care to all members of that community and a conscious attempt to prevent or minimize disease. A relatively recent innovation is the appropriation of communal resources for hospitals devoted principally to *medical* intervention, that is, to hospitals that are something other than a refuge for the sick, the poor, or pilgrims. The earliest hospital in the modern Western sense was probably the Ospedale Maggiore of Milan. It was built in the mid-fifteenth century, funded by church properties, and managed by a lay board of governors, who in turn were appointed by state officials. Most medieval cities acknowledged the need for city hospitals, symbols of good Christian governance, and thus hospitals became as characteristic of this society as the aqueducts had been of Rome.

The public employment of physicians was another significant development in the history of public health before 1700. Even ancient Greece, where many physicians were itinerant healers forced to wander in search of patients, established political and economic centers and provided salaries and other privileges to individuals who would agree to minister to their populations (Nutton 1981). Yet wherever a settlement grew large enough to support ethnic, linguistic, or even economic diversity, it was more difficult to ensure a sufficient number of healers.

In some places, such as Mesopotamia, the provision of physicians could extend the power of rulers or of a religion if people were assured that the proper gods would be summoned when intervention was necessary. With politically or religiously less important illnesses, a patient's family could post the pa-

tient at their doorway or in the marketplace, giving passersby the opportunity to make a diagnosis or offer therapeutic suggestions.

In Egypt, India, and China where political upheaval was not as common as in Mesopotamia and Greece, highly individualized solutions to the communal responsibility for providing physicians were devised. Thus, Egypt may have developed a state system for the use of doctors as expert witnesses and provided a living allowance to all physicians, and by the period of the New Kingdom had established a formal hierarchy of doctors, the chief palace physician at its pinnacle. Similarly, in ancient India the king and other extremely wealthy individuals were obliged to provide medical care for their people by underwriting the services of priestlike Ayurvedic physicians (Basham 1976).

It was the Greek tradition that was ultimately transmitted to western Europe. From as early as the fourth century B.C., the Greeks had established a network of salaried physicians throughout the Hellenistic world. The terms of their contracts to individual communities varied widely, but the arrangement assured healers of some measure of personal stability. Unlike physicians in the more monolithic Egyptian society, who were natives subject to the same legal privileges and restrictions as their patients, physicians in the mobile Greek world were often foreigners who received salaries as well as tax immunities and special privileges (e.g., citizenship, the right to own land, rent-free housing, or even choice theater tickets) in return for contractual service to a community. This "system" – if indeed one can so call a functional solution to the provision of medical care – was adopted by the Romans in the designation of *archiatri,* or public physicians, whose duties were extended and to some extent redefined over the centuries. Later Renaissance European elaborations of the concept of public health mediated by public physicians was a rediscovery of ancient practices lost during the Middle Ages.

By the second century of the common era, large Roman cities designated up to 10 *archiatri,* their salaries set by municipal councilors, to minister to the poor. Physicians often competed for these communal posts, suggesting that there were financial rewards beyond the salary itself – most likely access to a wealthy patient population. Public physicians seem to have been selected by laymen. Sources are largely silent on how their performance was assessed or how they typically sought access to their clientele. It is unlikely that they had any responsibility for the maintenance of public health in other respects, such as epidemic control or sanitation. Other salaried physicians in the Roman Empire included physicians to gladiators (Galen began his professional career in such an assignment), to baths, and to courts or large households.

The financial privileges and immunities granted to public physicians may have ensured the survival of the office well into the early Middle Ages, for with inflation and the heavy fiscal demands on Roman citizens around A.D. 200, these inducements were considerable. In the early fourth century, the emperor Constantine the Great extended state salaries to teaching doctors irrespective of their medical services to the community, thus linking the interests of public physicians to those of local medical personnel. That association would become paramount in the later Middle Ages, leading to the monitoring and licensing of medical practice, ostensibly for the public good but equally obviously for the financial benefit of particular groups of healers. Under Emperor Theodoric, in the early sixth century, Roman doctors were given an overseer, an imperial physician called "count of the *archiatri*," who may have formed the first formal link between lay interests and medical elites because he could nominate and appoint physicians to a college of medicine. Specialized medical services, such as those of official public midwives, may also date from this period. The Islamic state, which replaced most of the Roman Empire in the Middle East, brought regulatory power over physicians under the control of the state, which paid the salaries of physicians appointed to hospitals and even administered licensing examinations (Karmi 1981).

The medical institutions of late Rome did not persist through the early Middle Ages, even in relatively urbanized Italy and Spain. The practice of community hiring of salaried physicians was not reestablished until the twelfth and thirteenth centuries. Vivian Nutton (1981) argues persuasively that early Italian interest in jurisprudence and their editions of Roman law texts led to the reestablishment of public physicians in Italy. Thus, the office acquired legal responsibilities not typical of the ancient world. Perugia's first medicus vulnerum (before 1222) probably had to provide expert testimony in cases of assault and battery. Public physicians in succeeding centuries typically had to judge whether a wound or injury had caused death. By the end of the fifteenth century, the system of hiring physicians was almost universal in Mediterranean western Europe, a system undoubtedly reinforced by the recurrence of plagues, which necessitated state intervention to ensure medical care. Yet public physicians were not true public health physicians or medical officers of health, positions that Renaissance Italians seem to have invented. The institutions addressing communal medical responsibility for health surveillance arose instead from epidemic controls.

Richard Palmer (1981) has demonstrated that in large metropolitan areas the system of *medici condotti*, the Italian medieval name for *archiatri*, fell into disuse by the sixteenth century. But in small towns the system continued or even increased in popularity because it was a means of securing quality medical care without being at the mercy of itinerant quacks or "specialists."

The system of rural public physicians was able to absorb the late medieval expansion in the number of medical professionals, which brought about a more equal distribution of medical goods and services. Cities no longer needed to import physicians. The financial benefits they offered, the opportunities they provided for other, similarly trained practitioners, and often the presence of a university provided ample inducements for urban medical practice.

The major cities of Italy and Spain provided the prototype in medicine for the northern European cities of the seventeenth and eighteenth centuries: They developed local medical colleges dedicated to defending professional standards, restricting practice to the "qualified," regulating pharmacies, and mediating the state's charitable obligations to the poor in areas the church had abandoned (Lopez Piñero 1981; Palmer 1981). Tightening the restrictions on membership became common in Italy, foreshadowing the mercantilistic objectives of state medicine.

Epidemic Controls

Refuse disposal and the provision of clean water were regarded as aesthetic problems for growing cities as much as they were means to improve health. Nevertheless, by the thirteenth century, all Italian cities with statutes of laws had incorporated a system of sanitary provision modeled on ancient Roman patterns. The hallmarks of this system were maintenance of clean water sources, patrolling refuse disposal, and the posting of gatemen to identify potential sources of infection in the city. Two explanatory models underlay this approach to public health. The first was based on the assumption that polluted air caused disease by altering the humoral balance of humans and animals. The second was based on the knowledge that some diseases, such as leprosy, could be transmitted from one person to another.

The first of these two models was influential among public physicians when boards or offices of public health were created. The second model of contagion was not widely accepted during antiquity and the Middle Ages, at least among the educated elite. One exception, the practice of isolating lepers in special hospitals (*leprosaria*), is noteworthy because the custom was later adapted and justified as a means of epidemic control. Strict social isolation of individuals designated as lepers, whatever conditions may have been responsible for cases of advanced skin infection and/or physical deformities, was a practice derived from the Jews of antiquity. In biblical times priests identified those suffering from "leprosy" and used their authority to cast these people out of a settlement. Drawing on this practice, medieval Christian communities permitted priests to identify lepers and, at least in northern Europe, subject them to a ritual burial and banish them from the community.

Unlike Jews, medieval Christians accepted a communal responsibility for providing lepers with organized care – food, clothing, shelter, and religious services – but rarely medical care. The church and state cooperated in the construction and maintenance of residential hospitals for lepers. The peak of this building activity occurred in the period from 1150 to 1300.

Nonetheless, lepers were ostracized. Guards often kept them outside city gates. Those formally identified as lepers were made to wear symbols of their infection and perhaps to carry a bell or clapper to warn those who might get too near them. They could shop at markets only on designated days and hours, and could touch things only with a long pole. Moreover, practices such as these survived throughout the early modern period even when *leprosaria* were turned to other uses.

In other societies (e.g., Chinese and Muslim) in which leprosy was considered to be a communicable disease, social restrictions were often linked to legal restraints on lepers' activities. In Muslim lands, "mortal" illnesses, including both leprosy and mental illness, cast their victims into a state of dependency, somewhat like that of a child or slave. They lost the right to make and maintain contracts, including the right to continue a contract of marriage. Though a wide variety of behavioral responses to lepers existed across Islamic society, ranging from pity, to aggressive medical assistance, to isolation of the sufferers in leper hospitals, Michael Dols (1983) emphasizes the distinctiveness of Western Judeo-Christian tradition. In Europe, but not in the Middle East, lepers were considered diseased in soul as well as body, were ritually separated from the community, were deemed fiercely contagious to others, and were subjected to religious penance and other punishments even after diagnosis and isolation.

Apart from exaggerated responses in the West to lepers (as well as to prostitutes, homosexuals, heretics, and Jews), collective action to protect public health was, as a rule, crisis-oriented. Plague and other epidemics may not have been the most important manifestations of disease in earlier societies in terms of mortality, but they were certainly the most visible. Recurrent bubonic plague epidemics evoked the greatest response, making plague what Charles-Edward Winslow (1943) called the "great teacher." Beginning with the wave now called the Black Death, plague appeared in Europe at least once every generation between 1348 and 1720. At the first outbreak of the disease, fourteenth-century government officials in Florence, Venice, Perugia, and Lerida called on medical authorities to provide advice on plague control and containment. Of these, only Lerida's adviser, Jacme d'Agramont, seems to have articulated a contagion model for the spread of disease. The Florentine and Venetian approaches to epidemic control may have been the most sophisticated: aggressive cleanup of refuse, filth, offal, and other sources of corruption and putrefaction on the city streets. They applied traditional health practices to meet an emergency, but created a novel bureaucratic unit to orchestrate public efforts. In these two republican city-states, small committees of wealthy citizens were appointed to oversee the administration of ordinary sanitary laws, to hire physicians, gravediggers, and other necessary personnel, to maintain public order and respect for property, and to make emergency legislation. These communities saw no need for the direct intervention of the medical guilds. By contrast, in Paris, which lacked a tradition of lay involvement in public health control, members of the university medical faculty collectively offered advice about surviving pestilence, a practice individual doctors elsewhere followed in providing counsel to their patients.

For whatever reason, during the following century there seems to have been no deliberate reappraisal of the sanitary methods used in the earliest plague epidemic, and no temporary re-creation of boards of health other than in Milan, the only northern Italian city not stricken during the 1348 epidemic. Most cities relied instead on maintaining order, particularly in the burial of bodies, acquiring information about cities that were havens from disease (or, conversely, cities that were stricken with plague), providing physicians and other service personnel, and transferring property and goods after the plague to heirs or to the state. Rarely, however, did cities specifically address the technical problems of public or community-level measures for containing plague even though the "corruption of the air" theory presumably should have dictated intervention. Purifying bonfires, the disinfection or destruction of the goods and clothing of plague victims, and fumigation or other cleansing of infected dwellings were practices first employed aggressively in Milan in the late fourteenth century. Elsewhere and later, antiplague measures based on either the contagion or the corruption model of plague were adopted. *Cito, longe, tarde* – "Flee quickly, go far, and return slowly" – was the advice most wealthy city dwellers followed during the first century of plague experience, thereby eschewing costlier and more direct measures against the disease.

The tiny Dalmatian colony of Venice, Ragusa (now Dubrovnik), invented the quarantine in 1377. This was a response to impending plague whereby a temporary moratorium on travel and trade with the town was decreed. The Ragusan practice, actually then a *trentino,* or 30-day waiting period, became standard maritime practice by the sixteenth and seventeenth centuries. Although the quarantine in common parlance has acquired a more aggressive meaning, in the maritime context it was a passive measure designed to prevent incursions of plague rather than to segregate active cases. Through reproduction of a typographical error in the early nineteenth century, many surveys of quarantine and public health have credited Marseilles with the use of the quarantine by 1483. In reality the Ragusan maritime quarantine was not widely used until the sixteenth century.

Another feature of what was to become regular plague control, the pest house, or *lazaretto,* was used during the first plague century, 1350 to 1450, but chiefly as a means of delivering medical care to the poor. After the 1450s both quarantine (passive, preventive isolation of the healthy) and active hospital isolation of the ill became more popular antiplague measures in city-states, which can be taken as evidence for the increasing acceptance of a contagion theory of plague. Finally, official boards of health were reestablished. Throughout the early modern period, these bureaucracies identified and handled human cases of plague and acted as arbiters of standard public health controls (Cipolla 1976; Carmichael 1986).

Only during the fourteenth century do descriptions of plague note the loss of many principal citizens. After that period, elites seem to have worked out effective patterns of flight, so that only those who remained in the cities were exposed to danger. Unfortunately, in urban areas, plague control measures may have inadvertently augmented the death tolls. Standard practices developed in Italian cities during the fifteenth century – practices that would be followed by northern Europeans during the late sixteenth and seventeenth centuries – included the house arrest or hospital confinement of all family members of plague victims as well as others who may have had contact with them, whether or not the others were sick. This led to the construction of ramshackle buildings, *lazarettos,* that could segregate as many as 5,000 to 10,000 individuals at a time. By the sixteenth century, larger urban areas were quarantining the still-healthy contacts of plague victims in one place, isolating the ill together with immediate family members in a medically oriented hospital, and placing those who recovered in houses or hospices for a second period of quarantine.

By 1500 many of the principal Italian city-states had created permanent boards of health to monitor urban sanitation and disease threats even when no crisis arose. Rarely were physicians members of these aristocratic boards, though in many cities the lay directors employed medical officers of health. Nevertheless, local colleges of medicine and university medical faculties assumed the responsibility of providing diagnostic and therapeutic advice when crises threatened. By the second half of the sixteenth century, boards of health routinely consulted members of the medical establishment, one group helping the other in publication efforts to dispense both health advice and sanitary legislation and in the provision of public "debriefings" after a plague had passed. During the sixteenth and seventeenth centuries, these basic principles of public health surveillance and epidemic control were adopted by states north of the Alps.

In Italy and the Mediterranean, generally, the boards of health developed into tremendously powerful bureaucracies, commanding sizable portions of state resources and the cooperation of diplomats in securing information about the health conditions in other states. Carlo Cipolla (1976) identifies both vertical and horizontal paths of transmitting such information, emphasizing the aristocratic character of health boards and their successes in superseding any authority that merchants might claim from the state. Detailed information about plague or other diseases thought to be contagious was gathered from the reports of ambassadors as well as from broad networks of informants and spies at home. Armed with these data, health magistracies could impose quarantine at will, confiscate goods, and impound, fumigate, disinfect, or burn them. Though they usually agreed to reimburse the owners at half to two-thirds the value of their property, dire necessity and heavy expenditures during great epidemics left many boards of health bankrupt in all but their broad judicial authority. In fact, despite all efforts and a rigorous interpretation of the contagion theory of plague, the plagues of the late sixteenth and seventeenth centuries were catastrophic in the Mediterranean countries, in terms of both human and financial losses.

Not surprisingly, with the sweeping powers Italian boards of health were given, permanent magistracies required greater justification for their existence and their policies than the control of plague. They could argue that plagues would have been even worse without their efforts, but the economic costs of quarantine and isolation policies were more than early modern populations could bear without the creation of widescale human misery. Yet as strong monarchies emerged, legislators, physicians, and concerned aristocrats of the seventeenth and early eighteenth centuries were able to weave some public health controls into the evolving theories of mercantilism. Apart from epidemic surveillance, medical "police" extended state medicine into the licensure of midwives, the control of drugs and markets for drugs, stricter control of nonlicensed practitioners, and a variety of other matters. The results were optimistically summarized at the end of the eighteenth century by an Austrian state physician working in Lombardy, Johann Peter Frank (Sigerist 1956).

Outside the Italian sphere, where state medicine and public health carried the longest and strongest tradition, public health boards and epidemic controls did not evolve into permanent magistracies concerned with all aspects of public health. As Caroline Hannaway (1981) has indicated, at the beginning of the eighteenth century, the French, British, German, and, ultimately, U.S. traditions of public health relied mainly on the traditional Galenic–Hippocratic discourse about what ensured an individual's good health. Superimposed on those interests was makeshift machinery of epidemic control borrowed from the Italians. Concern for the health of "the people," however, spurred by general mercantilist goals and the early Enlightenment passion for

order and reason, was pan-European. During the eighteenth century, the impetus for change and reform in public health thus moved northward. Rejecting the political bases for state medicine that had led to the Italian boards of health, northern Europeans turned their energies to the production and consumption of health information: popular handbooks and manuals, such as those by William Buchann and S. A. Tissot; the proliferation of foundling homes, hospitals, and infirmaries; and the earliest efforts at systematic information gathering. As we move closer to the modern world, the rhetoric and rationale on which sanitation, care for the indigent, provision of public physicians, and epidemic controls were based before 1700 are blended into a new campaign for cleanliness and order, public and private.

Ann G. Carmichael

Bibliography

Basham, A. L. 1976. The practice of medicine in ancient and medieval India. In *Asian medical systems,* ed. Charles Leslie, 18–43. Berkeley and Los Angeles.

Brody, Saul Nathan. 1974. *The disease of the soul: A study in the moral association of leprosy in medieval literature.* Ithaca, N.Y.

Carmichael, Ann G. 1986. *Plague and the poor in Renaissance Florence.* New York.

Cipolla, Carlo M. 1976. *Public health and the medical profession in the Renaissance.* New York.

Dols, Michael. 1983. The leper in medieval Islamic society. *Speculum* 58: 891–916.

Hannaway, Caroline. 1981. From private hygiene to public health: A transformation in Western medicine in the eighteenth and nineteenth centuries. In *Public health: Proceedings of the 5th International Symposium on the Comparative History of Medicine – East and West,* ed. Teizo Ogawa, 108–28. Tokyo.

Karmi, Ghada. 1981. State control of the physicians in the Middle Ages: An Islamic model. In *The town and state physician,* ed. A. W. Russell, 63–84.

Lopez-Piñero, José María. 1981. The medical profession in sixteenth-century Spain. In *The town and state physician,* ed. A. W. Russell, 85–98.

Nutton, Vivian. 1981. Continuity or rediscovery? The city physician in classical antiquity and medieval Italy. In *The town and state physician,* ed. A. W. Russell, 9–46.

Palmer, Richard J. 1981. Physicians and the state in post-medieval Italy. In *The town and state physician,* ed. A. W. Russell, 47–62.

Rosen, George. 1958. *A history of public health.* New York.

Russell, Andrew W., ed. 1981. *The town and state physician in Europe from the Middle Ages to the Enlightenment.* Wolfenbüttel.

Scarborough, John S. 1981. Roman medicine and public health. In *Public health: Proceedings of the 5th Inter-*

national Symposium on the Comparative History of Medicine – East and West, ed. Teizo Ogawa, 33–74. Tokyo.

Scobie, Alex. 1986. Slums, sanitation and mortality in the Roman world. *Klio* 68: 399–433.

Sigerist, Henry E. 1956. *Landmarks in the history of hygiene.* New York.

Sun Tz'u. 1981. The washing away of wrongs. *Science, medicine and technology in East Asia,* Vol. 1, trans. Brian E. McKnight. Ann Arbor, Mich.

Temkin, Owsei. 1977. An historical analysis of the concept of infection. In *The double face of Janus and other essays,* 469–70. Baltimore.

Varron, A. G. 1939. Hygiene in the medieval city. *Ciba Symposia* 1: 205–14.

Winslow, Charles-Edward Amory. 1943. *The conquest of epidemic disease: A chapter in the history of ideas.* Princeton, N.J.

III.11 History of Public Health and Sanitation in the West since 1700

The nature and role of public health are constantly changing, and its definition has been a major preoccupation of public health leaders in the twentieth century. Essentially, public health is and always has been community action undertaken to avoid disease and other threats to the health and welfare of individuals and the community at large. The precise form that this action takes depends on what the community perceives as dangers to health, the structure of government, the existing medical knowledge, and a variety of social and cultural factors. From the beginning, communities, consciously or not, have recognized a correlation between filth and sickness, and a measure of personal and community hygiene characterized even the earliest societies.

By the eighteenth century, personal and community hygiene were becoming institutionalized. A wide variety of local regulations governed the food markets, the baking of bread, the slaughtering of animals, and the sale of meat and fish. These regulations were motivated by a concern for the poor, a desire for food of a reasonable quality, and commercial considerations. Bread was always a staple of the poor, and regulations in the Western world invariably set the weight, price, and quality of loaves. For economic reasons, merchants shipping food abroad promoted regulations on meat and grains in order to protect their markets and save themselves from dishonest competition.

The American colonial laws and regulations, which were patterned after those of English towns and cities, illustrate the ways in which communities protected their food. Most of the regulations were enacted in the first century of colonization and strengthened in the second. For example, when New York City received a new charter in 1731, the old bread laws were promptly reenacted. Bakers were required to stamp their initials on loaves, the mayor and aldermen determined the price and quality of bread every three months, and bread inspectors were appointed to enforce the regulations. Butchers could be penalized for selling putrid or "blowne" meat, and a series of regulations governed the town markets, with special attention to the sale of fish and meat.

Slaughterhouses, which could be both public nuisances and potential sources of bad meat, were among the earliest businesses brought under town control. The term *public nuisance* in the eighteenth and nineteenth centuries embraced a great many sources of filth and vile odors. Wastes, rubbish, and garbage were simply dumped into the nearest stream or body of water, except in major cities, which generally had one or more covered sewers. Some foul-smelling open sewers characterized all cities and towns. The water closet was rare until the late nineteenth century, and the vast majority of residents relied on privies. In the poorer areas they were rarely emptied, with the result that their contents overflowed into the gutters. The work of emptying privies was handled by scavengers, sometimes employees of the municipality, but more often private contractors. They slopped human wastes in open, leaking carts through the streets to the nearest dock, wharf, or empty piece of land.

Street cleaning and garbage collection were left largely to private enterprise and were haphazard at best. The malodorous mounds of manure in the dairies and stables and the equally foul-smelling entrails, hides, and other materials processed by the so-called nuisance industries attracted myriad flies in addition to offending the nostrils of neighboring residents. The putrefying odors from these accumulations of entrails and hides, particularly in summer, must have been almost overwhelming.

Early U.S. towns were spared the worst of these problems because they were smaller and their residents more affluent. The small size of communities and the cheapness of land made it easier for the town fathers to order the slaughterers and other nuisance industries to move to the outskirts. By 1800, however, the growing U.S. cities were beginning to experience the major sanitary problems faced by their British and European counterparts. The great bubonic plagues beginning in the fourteenth century had taught Europeans the value of quarantine and isolation, but by the eighteenth century, the major killer diseases had become endemic. Smallpox, one of the most deadly, was largely a children's disease by the second half of the eighteenth century, and no longer aroused alarm. On the Continent, occasional resurgences of bubonic plague led governments to establish quarantines on their eastern borders, but even this threat diminished toward the close of the century.

The one area where quarantines were applied with some consistency was the North American colonies. Because of the colonies' sparse population and geographic separation from Europe and one another, great epidemic diseases could not establish themselves permanently until late in the colonial period. The two most feared disorders were smallpox, brought from Europe or by slaves from Africa, and yellow fever, usually introduced from the West Indies. Smallpox appeared only occasionally in the seventeenth century, but it struck the colonials with devastating effect. By 1700 all of the colonies had enacted quarantine laws of various degrees of effectiveness and most of the port towns had established "pesthouses" in which to isolate smallpox patients.

Yellow fever did not enter the colonies until the end of the seventeenth century. Unlike smallpox, which was obviously spread from one individual to another, yellow fever was a strange and unaccountable pestilence that brought death in a horrible fashion to its victims. It struck the colonies only occasionally, but news of its presence in the West Indies led authorities in every coastal town to institute quarantines against vessels from that area. A series of epidemics, which struck the entire eastern coast beginning in 1793, led to the establishment of permanent quarantine officers and temporary health boards in nearly every major port. The limited sanitary and quarantine laws of the eighteenth century, many of which dated back several hundred years, were to prove inadequate under the impact of rapid urbanism and industrialism after 1750. Fortunately, that eighteenth-century period of intellectual ferment, the Age of Enlightenment, created a new awareness of the need for a healthy population. The earlier theory of mercantilism had argued that population represented wealth, and the emergence of political arithmetic or population statistics in the seventeenth century provided a crude means of measuring the health of a given population. John Locke's *Essay on Human Understanding,* emphasizing the role of environment, encouraged intellectuals, particularly in France, to advocate improving the lot of human beings through social reform. In his *Encyclopedia,* Denis Diderot discussed medical care, hospitals, and a wide range of topics related to health.

Economic changes led to a population explosion in Europe beginning in the mid-eighteenth century, and one result was an enormous infant mortality rate in the crowded cities and towns. A second result was the emergence of a socially conscious middle class out of which grew the British humanitarian movement. An important aspect of the movement was a concern for infant welfare, a concern that stimulated the rise of voluntary hospitals in Great Britain and ultimately led to an awareness of the deplorable health conditions of all workers. The eighteenth century, too, saw the publication of Bernardino Ramazzini's classic study on the diseases of workers, *De Morbus Artificum Diatriba.*

Even more significant than the writings of Ramazzini, the French philosophers, and other intellectuals in bringing government action was the work of Johann Peter Frank. In 1779 he published the first volume of a comprehensive nine-volume study instructing government officials on how to maintain the health of the people. Stimulated by the prevailing intellectual ferment, the enlightened despots of Prussia, Austria, Russia, and other states made tentative attempts to impose health regulations on their subjects. At that time, however, the governing structures were inadequate for the task, and the upheavals of the French Revolution and Napoleonic Wars temporarily ended efforts at health reform.

In Great Britain the seventeenth century had seen the execution of one king and the deposing of a second in the course of the Glorious Revolution of 1688. The resulting distrust of the central government meant that, for the next century and a half, a high degree of authority remained at the local level. Hence, until the mid-nineteenth century, efforts to improve public health were the work of voluntary groups or of local governments. Although some progress was made at the local level – most notably in terms of infant care, the mentally ill, and the construction of hospitals – public health was of little concern to the national government. Probably the most significant development was the rapid increase in hospitals and asylums and the appearance of dispensaries or outpatient clinics. In England the majority of these were funded by private charity, whereas on the Continent they were largely municipal or state-supported.

It was no accident that England, which was in the vanguard of the Industrial Revolution, took the first effective steps toward establishing a national public health program. The original charters of most English towns and cities gave the municipal government only limited powers, and these proved totally inadequate to meet the needs of their increasing populations. The first local health board in Great Britain came into existence in Manchester in 1796. A series of typhus epidemics among the overworked cotton mill employees, who lived and worked in crowded, filthy conditions, led Thomas Percival, John Ferriar, and other physicians to organize a voluntary board of health. In Liverpool, James Currie and a small group of other physicians assumed the same responsibility. Owing to the haphazard structure of English local government and the prevailing laissez-faire sentiment, little was accomplished in the following half-century.

Atrocious factory conditions, particularly as they affected child and female workers, provided the next stimulus to public health. Through the agitation of socially minded physicians, and in particular the work of Sir Robert Peel, a socially responsible textile manufacturer, the first English factory law, the Pauper Apprentice Act of 1802, was pushed through Parliament. Changing circumstances made the law meaningless, and it took years of agitation by Peel, Robert Owen, and numerous others before a relatively effective factory act in 1833 limited the working hours of children in textile mills. The most significant feature of the act was a provision for four officers to inspect, report on, and enforce the law. This measure marked the first time that the central government broke away from a laissez-faire policy and assumed a limited responsibility for health and welfare. Equally important, the reports of the factory inspectors proved invaluable to Edwin Chadwick, Southwood Smith, Lord Ashley, and other reformers seeking to make the public aware of the brutal and degrading conditions in which workers labored and lived.

At least as important as the horrible factory conditions in promoting government action on behalf of health was the first of the three great pandemics of Asiatic cholera to strike the Western world in the nineteenth century. This disease, which devastated the poor, who were crowded in filthy, miserable slums, convinced public health pioneers that sanitary programs were the solution to the problems of disease and ill health. Consequently, in the prevailing argument over the value of quarantine versus sanitation, the sanitationists, represented by Chadwick in England, won out. The panic and disruption in Great Britain caused by the first epidemic in 1831 undoubtedly contributed to the general unrest in England and, indirectly, was responsible for a number of major reforms. Among the significant legislative measures enacted in these years were the Parliamentary Reform Bill of 1832, the Factory Act of 1833, the Poor Law Amendment of 1834, and the Municipal Corporations Act of 1835. The last act was particularly important because it strengthened the authority of town officials and gave them wider powers in the areas of health and social services.

In 1834 Chadwick was made secretary of the new Poor Law Board, and the board's investigations under his direction laid the basis for his great *Report on the Sanitary Condition of the Labouring Classes.* Its publication in 1842 led to the appointment of a Royal Commission on the Health of Towns, and the grim reports of this commission eventually forced Parliament to enact the first major national health law, the Public Health Act of 1848, which created the General Board of Health. This board ran into immediate difficulties, since the medical profession was strongly opposed to it, and local officials were still reluctant to surrender any of their authority to a central board. In 1858 the board was dismissed, and its public health responsibilities were transferred to the Privy Council. Despite its weakness, the board was successful in spreading the gospel of cleanliness and sanitation.

During these years a series of sanitary laws, such as the Nuisances Removal Act, Common Lodging House Act, and the Adulteration of Food Act, were shepherded through Parliament. In addition, beginning in 1847, medical officers were appointed in a number of cities. The culmination of almost half a century of health education was the passage (helped along by the third cholera pandemic) of the Sanitary Act of 1866. This measure broadened the health and sanitary areas under the jurisdiction of the national government and authorized its officials to compel municipalities and counties to meet minimum sanitary standards. Within the next nine years successive legislative action gradually strengthened the 1866 law. In 1875 a comprehensive health law consolidated the many pieces of legislation relating to health and sanitation and gave Great Britain the best national health program of any country in the world.

The Industrial Revolution was much slower in coming to France and other countries, and the energy devoted to improving social conditions in England was dissipated on the Continent in wars and struggles for political freedom and national independence. Yet the French Revolution and the Napoleonic Wars gave France leadership in medicine and public health by destroying much of the old order and releasing the energy of the lower classes. Among its contributions in these years was the publication of the first public health journal, the *Annales d'hygiéne publique et médecine legale,* which appeared in 1829. The outstanding public health figure in France during these years was René Louis Villermé, whose studies in the 1820s clearly demonstrated the relationship between poverty and disease. His major report in 1840 on the health conditions of textile workers led to the enactment the following year of a limited child labor law.

Continued appeals for reform by Villermé and health reformers achieved a measure of success following the Revolution of 1848. The new French government under the Second Republic established a system of local health councils (*conseils de salubrité*). Despite the hopes of public health leaders, these councils, which met every three months, were purely advisory and exercised no real authority. Any further chance of immediate health reform was dashed in 1851 when Napoleon III overturned the Second Republic. The system of weak advisory health councils remained in effect until the end of the nineteenth century, and public health in France continued to lag far behind that of Britain.

On paper, the public health regulations of the Russian imperial government seemed quite advanced, and because the government was autocratic, it had the power to enforce its laws. Unfortunately, as the successive Asiatic cholera epidemics revealed, these regulations were seldom exercised with any degree of effectiveness. Quarantine measures against cholera were belated, haphazard, and applied too ruthlessly. The widespread poverty and ignorance of the Russian people made many of them resent even the most well intentioned government actions. Whereas the cholera outbreaks in the West aroused demands for health reform, particularly in Britain and the United States, the autocratic government in Russia and the lack of a socially conscious middle class prevented any meaningful reform before the twentieth century. The development of public health in the United States closely followed that of Great Britain, although the sheer expanse of the nation reinforced the belief in local control and delayed action by the federal government. Spurred on by epidemics of Asiatic cholera and yellow fever, U.S. cities began appointing permanent quarantine officers at the beginning of the nineteenth century. New York City, which tended to assume leaderhsip in public health, created the Office of City Inspector in 1804. The office was designed to gather statistics and other information relating to the city, but under the leadership of such men as John Pintard and John H. Griscom, it became a significant force for social change. Their annual reports as city inspectors were damning indictments of the poverty, misery, and squalor that characterized the life of so many New Yorkers.

Nonetheless, the prevailing spirit in the nineteenth century was laissez-faire, and except when epidemics threatened, government officials felt little responsibility for health. The threat of an epidemic or its presence usually aroused the quarantine officials from their lethargy and stimulated the city council to appoint a health board, open temporary hospitals, and initiate a campaign to clean up the worst sanitary abuses. Once the epidemic was over, the quarantine was relaxed and city hall returned to politics as usual. When a particular abuse, such as an unusual number of putrefying dead animals in the streets or a particularly odorous canal or sewer down the main street, became an outrage, public opinion would demand action, but the relief was usually temporary.

While the public worried about the two great epidemic diseases of the nineteenth century, yellow fever and Asiatic cholera, and to a lesser extent about smallpox, the major causes of morbidity and mortality in both Europe and the United States were pulmonary tuberculosis and other respiratory infections, enteric disorders, malaria, typhoid, typhus, and such perennials as measles, diphtheria, scarlet fever, and whooping cough. These were familiar disorders that killed young and old alike, and in an age when almost half of the children died before the age of 5 and sickness and death were omnipresent, the public attitude was one of quiet resignation.

One explanation of this passive acceptance of endemic disorders was that before the bacteriological revolution little could be done about them. Another is that, until the accumulation of reasonably accurate statistics, it was impossible to gauge the significance of these diseases. Beginning in the 1830s, individuals in Great Britain, on the Continent, and in the United States began collecting a wide range of statistical information. The studies of William Farr in England and Villermé and Pierre Laplace in

France were duplicated in the United States by Lemuel Shattuck, Edward Jarvis, and others. These early statistics, however, brought few immediate results in the United States. The same can be said of three classic public health studies published in the years before the Civil War – Griscom's *Sanitary Condition of the Laboring Population of New York City,* Shattuck's *Report of a general plan for the promotion of public and personal health* (1850), and McCready's essay (1837) on occupational diseases. Nonetheless, these men laid the basis for substantial progress in the post–Civil War years.

Their work also contributed to arousing an interest in public health and sanitation in the United States during the 1850s. Devastating yellow fever outbreaks from 1853 to 1855 raised fears throughout the country and led to a series of National Quarantine and Sanitary Conventions from 1856 to 1860. The major issue at these meetings was whether yellow fever could be kept at bay by quarantine or by sanitation. The sanitationists won the day. By 1860 they were preparing to turn the conventions into a national organization of health officers and sanitary reformers, but the outbreak of civil war brought the project to a sharp halt.

All was not lost, however, because the hygienic problems engendered by crowding thousands of men into army camps and the movements of troops throughout the country stimulated the public health movement. As evidence of this, in 1866 the Metropolitan Board of Health was established in New York City, the first permanent municipal health department. It was followed in 1869 by the first effective state board of health in Massachusetts. By the end of the nineteenth century, most major cities had established some type of health agency. Many of them, particularly the state boards, were only nominal, but the principle of governmental responsibility for public health was firmly established.

In the meantime the work of Joseph Lister, Robert Koch, Louis Pasteur, and a host of scientists working in microbiology was changing the whole basis for public health. Sanitation and drainage, the chief preoccupation of health officials in the nineteenth century, were replaced in the twentieth century by specific methods of diagnosis, prevention, and cure. Yet the sanitary movement had brought remarkable advances in life expectancy and general health. A higher standard of living, the introduction of ample and better city water, and large-scale drainage and sanitary programs all contributed to a sharp reduction in the incidence of urban disorders. Although the basis for the sanitary movement, the miasmic theory, was invalid, the movement itself achieved notable success in improving the public's health.

The major drive in all Western countries during the early twentieth century was to reduce or eliminate the major contagious diseases. With the aid of new diagnostic techniques, antitoxins, and vaccines, the major killer diseases of former times gradually were brought under control. Tuberculosis, probably the most fatal disease in the West during the nineteenth century, was greatly reduced, in part by improved living conditions and in part through concerted action by voluntary associations and governments to identify, isolate, and cure all cases. In addition, large-scale educational campaigns informed the public about the disease, and visiting nurses and social workers helped families of victims. As was true of drives against other contagious disorders, large-scale screening programs were used for the early identification of cases. Recognition of the role of vectors made it possible to drive malaria and yellow fever virtually from the Western world through antimosquito campaigns. The greatest success against disease has been with smallpox. With the help of the World Health Organization and massive vaccination programs, the disorder literally has been eliminated from the world.

Even as the fight against contagious diseases was getting underway, health officials began moving into other health areas. Among the more obvious social problems in the late nineteenth century was the enormous infant death toll. In western Europe, where nationalism was the real religion and the military power to defend that religion was equated with population, the birthrate was falling, increasing pressure to improve maternal and child care. The movement to do so began in England and France, where voluntary organizations began promoting dispensaries for child care. In the United States a New York philanthropist, Nathan Straus, opened a pure-milk station in 1893 to provide free or low-cost milk to the poor. The idea was picked up in other U.S. cities and soon spread to western Europe. Over the years, these stations gradually evolved into well-baby clinics and maternal and child health centers.

A major step forward in the movement for child care was taken in 1908 when New York City, in response to the urging of Sara Josephine Baker, became the first municipality to establish a Division of Child Hygiene. The success of Baker's program in New York encouraged Lillian Wald and Florence Kelley, who had long been advocating a children's bureau at the national level, to redouble their efforts. Four years later, in 1912, President Theodore Roosevelt signed a bill establishing the Federal Children's Bureau. The next action at the national level was the passage of the Sheppard–Towner Act of 1921, a measure that provided matching federal grants for states to encourage maternal and child health programs. Although this act was allowed to lapse in 1929, the New Deal Program of Franklin Roosevelt in the 1930s firmly established a role for the national government, not only in maternal and child care, but in all aspects of public health.

Another important health area that had its origins in Europe in the late nineteenth century was school health. Smallpox vaccination appears to have been the entering wedge, because compulsory vaccination of school children was relatively easy to enforce. The discovery of so many other contagious disorders among children led to the introduction of school inspectors and school nurses around the turn of the century. The early twentieth century saw the beginning of physical examinations for school children, and these in turn created a need for school clinics and other remedial measures. As living standards were raised, particularly after World War II, school health programs declined in importance.

The discovery of vitamins (so named by Casimir Funk in 1912) opened up the field of nutrition, and a substantial effort has been made by health officials to educate the public on matters of diet. Commercial firms, capitalizing on public ignorance of scientific matters and the popularity of food fads, have managed to confuse the issue of what constitutes a well-balanced diet, thus negating much of the educational work. Despite this, however, food and drug regulations have generally improved the quality of the food supply.

An effective autocracy can mandate public health, but health officials in the Western democracies have been forced to rely largely on health education. The United States, which has the oldest tradition of mass education, was the first to recognize the value of information and persuasion in changing people's way of life. By the 1890s, a number of state and municipal health boards were publishing weekly or monthly reports and bulletins. Originally, these publications were intended for physicians and other professionals serving as health officers, but by the early twentieth century a variety of pamphlets and bulletins were being distributed to the general public. By this time, too, health education was given a formal status in the organization of health departments. Lacking the U.S. penchant for public relations, European health departments have not given as much emphasis to health education, relying much more on private groups to perform this task.

The education of public health workers originated in Great Britain in the second half of the nineteenth century. It was essentially a practical course to train food and sanitary inspectors. Early in the twentieth century, courses in public health were offered by the University of Michigan, Columbia, Harvard, and the Massachusetts Institute of Technology, and in 1913 Tulane University established a School of Hygiene and Tropical Medicine. The latter survived only briefly, and the first permanent school of public health was opened by Johns Hopkins University in 1918. Rather than an institution designed to train general health workers, it was essentially a research organization intended to educate the highest echelon of public health professionals. This pattern has been followed by all subsequent U.S. public health schools.

Although the term *public health* implies government action on behalf of the community, from the beginning voluntary work by individuals, groups of citizens, and philanthropic foundations has played a major role in promoting the general health. Citizens' sanitary organizations were very active in the late nineteenth century, and their counterparts in the twentieth have been voluntary groups fighting against particular disease and medical problems. These associations are found in nearly all Western countries, but they are most active in the United States. One of the best examples is the National Tuberculosis Association, founded in 1904, which had an active part in reducing the incidence of this disorder in the United States. Of the many foundations working in the health area, the Rockefeller Foundation is the best known. Along with the Carnegie Foundation, it has given major support to medical education. It is equally well known for its contributions to public health, particularly with respect to the drive against hookworm in the southern United States, the Caribbean, and Brazil and yellow fever in Latin America and Africa. The efforts of the Rockefeller Foundation also helped lay the basis for the Pan American Health Organization and the World Health Organization.

Since World War II, public health agencies, having won control over most of the contagious infections that formerly plagued the Western world, have turned their attention to chronic and degenerative disorders and to the problems of aging. Veneral diseases appeared to have been relegated to a position of minor significance with the success of antibiotics in the 1950s, but resistant strains and the appearance of genital herpes and AIDS have drastically changed the picture. An area where some success has been achieved is that of community mental health, but progress has been slow.

With the success of the sanitary movement and the emergence of bacteriology in the early twentieth century, health departments tended to assume that care for the environment was largely an administrative matter. Since the 1950s, they have come to recognize many subtle, and not so subtle, forms of air and water pollution and dangers from pesticides, harmful factory wastes, and radiation. They have also sought to deal with problems of alcoholism, drug addiction, occupational hazards and diseases, and a major source of death and disability, automobile accidents.

The twentieth century has seen public health shift from an emphasis on the control of contagious diseases to the broader view that public health should concern itself with all factors affecting health and well-being. Whereas an original aim was to increase life expectancy, today public health also seeks to improve the quality of life. The current view of public health is that it should actively promote health rather than simply maintain it. Achieving a longer life expectancy is still a major aim, but it is equally important to improve the quality of life.

John Duffy

Bibliography

Blake, John B. 1959. *Public health in the town of Boston.* Cambridge, Mass.

Brand, Jeanne L. 1965. *Doctors and the state: The British medical profession and government action in public health, 1870–1912.* Baltimore.

Duffy, John. 1950. Early English factory legislation: A neglected aspect of British humanitarianism. In *Brit-ish humanitarianism,* ed. Samuel C. McCulloch. Philadelphia.

1968. *A history of public health in New York City, 1826–1866.* New York.

1974. *A history of public health in New York City, 1866–1966.* New York.

Frank, Johann Peter. 1779–1827. *System einer Vollständigen medizinischen Polizey,* 9 vols. Mannheim Tübingen, Vienna.

Galishoff, Stuart. 1975. *Safeguarding the public health, Newark, 1895–1918.* Westport, Conn.

Jordan, Philip D. 1953. *The people's health: A history of public health in Minnesota to 1948.* St. Paul, Minn.

Katz, Alfred H., and Jean S. Felton. 1965. *Health and the community: Readings in the philosophy and sciences of public health.* New York.

Leavitt, Judith W. 1982. *The healthiest city, Milwaukee and the politics of reform.* Princeton, N.J.

Lerner, Monroe, and Odin W. Anderson. 1963. *Health progress in the United States, 1900–1960.* Chicago.

Mazyck, Ravenel, ed. 1921. *A half century of public health reform.* New York.

McCready, Benjamine W. 1837. On the influence of trades, professions and occupations in the United States, on the production of disease. *Transactions of the medical society of the state of New York,* vol. 3. Reprinted 1943, Baltimore.

McGrew, Roderick E. 1965. *Russia and the cholera, 1823–1832.* Madison, Wis.

Pelling, Margaret. 1978. *Cholera, fever and English medicine, 1825–1865.* Oxford.

Rosen, George. 1958. *A history of public health.* New York.

Rosenkrantz, Barbara G. 1972. *Public health and the state: Changing views in Massachusetts, 1842–1936.* Cambridge, Mass.

Shattuck, Lemuel, et al. 1850. *Report of a general plan for the promotion of public and personal health.* Boston.

PART IV

Measuring Health

The subject of early (for our purposes, pre–World War II) data on mortality is a vast one, and thus this treatment is quite broad. The emphasis is on identifying classes of data, sources of ambiguity, and general approaches to problems of interpretation. Wherever possible, citations are made to critical surveys of the literature, rather than to the literature itself. Some of the points discussed here can be extended, with appropriate caution and revision, to the equally important, but much less tractable area of early morbidity data.

Protostatistical Populations

There are rich opportunities for studying death and disease in populations for which vital statistics in the modern sense are nonexistent. Primary data sources include faunal evidence obtained by archaeological excavation, epigraphic evidence from funerary monuments, and information contained in parish records and family genealogies. In most cases, however, although these data allow inferences to be made regarding overall mortality among specific and highly localized populations, they contain little information on national-level populations and, with the exception of some faunal evidence, on causes of death. We can address the first shortcoming merely by assuming that the population studied accurately represents the total population, an assumption that is probably robust in very high mortality populations. The second difficulty – the lack of information on causes of death – is irremediable in the main. Furthermore, these data are rarely complemented by accurate population statistics, which are essential for computing rates and probabilities. Because of the dearth of early census data, genealogies and parish records, which provide a link between birth and death records, are especially important for estimating life expectancy (e.g., Henry 1956; Hollingsworth 1964; Wrigley 1968).

Early Statistical Populations

A key date in historical demography is 1532, when it was mandated that London parish priests compile weekly "Bills of Mortality," which were in turn the primary source of the first known life table (Graunt 1662). As this ecclesiastical registration system expanded, it provided the basis for Thomas Short's early study (1750) of geographic variation in British mortality. Not until 1837, however, was a national civil vital registration system established in England, and not until 1875 did registration of vital events become mandatory.

The English system was antedated by compulsory national civil vital registration systems in Scandinavia: Finland (1628), Denmark (1646), Norway (1685), and Sweden (1686). In Sweden the ecclesiastical registration system dates from 1608, slightly antedating the English Bills of Mortality. By the end of the nineteenth century, civil registration was compulsory in virtually all European countries, North America, Japan, and a host of other countries such as Egypt (1839), Mexico (1859), and Brazil (1885). Unfortunately, not all of these early registration systems, enumerated by Henry Shryock and Jacob Siegal (1980), contain cause-of-death data.

In addition to the registration systems, a number of important compilations and secondary sources exist. The International Statistical Institute of the League of Nations published its *Annuaire international de statistique* in 1916, 1917, 1919, 1920, and 1921 and its *Aperçu de la demographie des divers pays du monde* in 1922, 1925, 1927, 1929, and 1931. Publication of the latter series was suspended until 1939, when a volume covering 1929–36 was published. The U.S. Bureau of the Census and Library of Congress collaborated on a compilation of interwar European demographic statistics (U.S. Bureau of the Census and Library of Congress 1946), and to this may be added an earlier effort of the U.S. Bureau of the Census and Library of Congress (1943a,b). The standard compilation of historical mortality statistics for Latin America is that of Eduardo Arriaga (1968). Other national and international data compilations, as well as secondary studies of pre–World War II (mostly European) vital rates, are cited by Shryock and Siegal (1980) and, in the European case, by E. A. Wrigley (1969).

In the United States, although the availability of early church records, genealogies, and epigraphic evidence is impressive, particularly in New England (Vinovkis 1972) and Mormon Utah, vital registration got off to a late start. Beginning with the seventh census of the United States in 1850, questions regarding deaths in the household during the previous year were included in the compilation (a similar system was adopted in nineteenth-century Canada). The decennial U.S. Censuses of Mortality are the main source of nationwide mortality data from 1850 to

1890, but they are seriously incomplete (Condran and Crimmins 1979). This is in contrast to the situation in the United Kingdom, where civil registration data, including cause-of-death and limited socioeconomic data, are quite accurate from the mid-nineteenth century forward. A few states, such as statistically precocious Massachusetts, initiated state registration systems during the nineteenth century, and some cities published local mortuary records. In 1900 the federal government began collecting and publishing mortality data from a Death Registration Area consisting of the 10 states (plus the District of Columbia) in which it was judged that at least 90 percent of all deaths were registered. Under federal urging, more and more states initiated and improved compulsory registration systems, until by 1933 all of the present states except Alaska were included in a national vital registration system.

Among a number of compilations of U.S. vital statistics, the most noteworthy are volumes prepared by the U.S. Bureau of the Census (1933, 1943a,b); the U.S. Public Health Service (1961) has also published in a single volume comparable U.S. life tables for 1900–59. The fifteen volumes of the Vital and Health Statistics Monograph Series of the American Public Health Association, together with the final summary volume, *Mortality and Morbidity in the United States* (Erhardt and Berlin 1974), present a comprehensive view of the U.S. case. The emphasis of the series is on the 1960s, but a wealth of twentieth-century statistics, as well as some comparative international data, are presented in many of the volumes.

Statistics collected and special studies prepared by life insurance companies represent an underutilized body of data for nineteenth-century mortality in the United States and Europe. Because of the financial incentive to maintain accurate death records, these data may be quite accurate, and they contain considerable cause-of-death detail. The greatest drawback is that, because such data deal with only the insured population, they may underestimate the true extent of mortality among the broader population. To these data sources should be added the life tables calculated by eighteenth- and nineteenth-century actuaries such as Edward Wigglesworth, the accuracy of which has been the subject of intense scrutiny (Vinovkis 1971; Haines and Avery 1980).

One straightforward approach to setting a lower bound on the availability of early mortality data is simply to enumerate the pre–World War II multiple-decrement life tables in the work of Samuel Preston, Nathan Keyfitz, and Robert Schoen (1972). The criteria for inclusion in this authoritative compilation were stringent: Only populations for which accurate mortality statistics, including cause-of-death detail, and accompanied by reliable population data, are represented. These are daunting barriers to entry, but nevertheless the number of pre–World War II populations included is quite large: Australia (1911, 1921, 1933, 1940); Canada (1921, 1931); Chile (1909, 1920, 1930, 1940); Czechoslovakia (1934); Denmark (1921, 1930, 1940); England and Wales (1861, 1871, 1881, 1891, 1901, 1911, 1921, 1931, 1940); France (1926, 1931, 1936); Greece (1928); Italy (1881, 1891, 1901, 1910, 1921, 1931); Japan (1899, 1908, 1940); the Netherlands (1931, 1940); New Zealand (1881, 1901, 1911, 1921, 1926, 1936); Norway (1910, 1920, 1930); Portugal (1920, 1930, 1940); Spain (1930, 1940); Sweden (1911, 1920, 1930, 1940); Switzerland (1930); Taiwan (1920, 1930, 1936); and the United States (1900, 1910, 1920, 1930, 1940).

Problems of Interpreting Early Mortality Data

As already mentioned, relatively few sources of early mortality statistics can satisfy the Preston–Keyfitz–Schoen criteria. The deficiencies of such data are easily enumerated (Shryock and Siegal 1980):

1. *Definition of death.* This is an issue mainly in the case of stillbirths and neonatal deaths.
2. *Misallocation of deaths by place of occurrence.* In cases where large hospitals serve an extended catchment area, it is common for death notices to be listed incorrectly, indicating the residence of the deceased to be the metropolitan area in which the hospital is located rather than the outlying areas.
3. *Misallocation of deaths by time of occurrence.* Deaths are commonly tabulated on a year-of-occurrence basis, and mistakes in reporting are inevitable.
4. *Age misreporting.* This is a problem mostly at the older end of the age spectrum, where there is a tendency for reported ages to exceed actual ages significantly. It is also a problem in the case of children.
5. *Completeness of registration.* This is a problem involving both the *extent* and the *accuracy* of registration. In many countries, national registration systems were not in fact national, as in the United States with its original 10-state Death Registration Area. In other countries, certain populations were explicitly excluded from early registration

systems, such as Maoris of New Zealand and persons residing in the Yukon and the Northwest Territories of Canada. Even assuming that the entire population of a nation was included in the registration process, some degree of undercounting was inevitable. This tends to be the most serious problem in the case of infants, children under 5, and persons over 65.

6. *Cause misreporting.* Preston, Keyfitz, and Schoen (1972) have categorized problems in this area into errors in diagnosing cause of death and errors in translating an accurate diagnosis into an entry on the death registration form. The latter include errors in categorizing deaths according to international vital statistics convention (e.g., brain tumors were once classified under diseases of the nervous system, but are now grouped with neoplasms) and, more important, errors arising from complex issues in the case of multiple causes of death. To these two areas of difficulty should be added biases arising from the extent and accuracy of registration. Even an incomplete death registration system can, in theory, reflect accurately the population's cause-of-death structure. Unfortunately, differential completeness of registration can skew the cause-of-death structure. For example, if deaths among the elderly are systematically underreported, the resulting cause-of-death structure will understate the role of chronic and degenerative diseases, among them neoplasms and cardiovascular disease.

Among these problems, the fifth and sixth typically are of greatest concern, and it is to these that the remaining pages of this essay are devoted.

Estimating Completeness of Death Registration

Direct Approaches

There are two broad approaches to estimating completeness of death registration: direct and indirect. In the direct approach, the true level of mortality is independently estimated and compared with the level reported in the registration system. Household surveys of child survival, often performed in conjunction with census enumeration, are examples of the direct approach, but few such surveys are available for the pre–World War II era. Of more interest to social scientists are "matching" studies, in which deaths appearing in one tabulation (e.g., a parish register) are matched with deaths tabulated in the civil registration system during the same period (Marks, Seltzer, and Krotki 1974). It can be shown

that, if inclusion in the civil registration system and inclusion in the alternative tabulation are statistically independent, then completeness of civil registration, say C, is equal to the ratio of deaths recorded in both systems, say D(Both), to deaths recorded in the alternative system, say D(Alt):

$$C = D(\text{Both})/D)\text{Alt}). \qquad (1)$$

It is important to note that, given statistical independence, it is unnecessary to assume that the alternative recording system is complete. The main advantage of matching studies, which have had extensive historical application (e.g., Crimmins 1980), is their conceptual simplicity. They are also well suited to the study of highly disaggregated mortality data, such as deaths in a given city from a given cause among a given segment of the population. The main difficulties, in addition to violations of the independence assumption, are empirical, particularly in deciding what constitutes a true match. It should be added that the matching-study approach is inherently labor intensive.

Indirect Approaches

Most indirect approaches to estimating completeness of civil registration are of comparatively recent development. The basic data requirement for all such methods is a reported age distribution of deaths in a given year. Other requirements, depending on the method employed, include population by age in the study year and age-specific population growth rates (calculated from two censuses, neither of which need have been taken during the study year). Most indirect methods require either the assumption of a stable population (i.e., one that is closed to migration and in which rates of birth and death have been constant for a long period of time) or, at a minimum, the assumption of no migration. In some cases, the methods are fairly robust to violations of these assumptions.

Some notion of the indirect approach can be gained by looking briefly at one of the earliest and simplest of these methods developed by William Brass. (The present section is based on the discussion in MacKellar 1987.) The Brass method is based on the fundamental population change accounting identity:

$$r(x+) = b(x+) - d(x+) + m(x+). \qquad (2)$$

Here $r(x+)$ is the actual growth rate of the population aged over x, and $b(x+)$ is the actual birthrate of the population aged over x; that is, the number of xth birthdays celebrated in a given year divided by the number of person-years lived in a state of being aged over x in that year. $d(x+)$ is the actual death rate of the population aged over x, analogously defined; and $m(x+)$ is the actual net migration rate of the population aged over x, analogously defined.

Setting x equal to zero, we find that (2) reduces to the familiar identity whereby the growth rate of the total population equals the crude birthrate minus the crude death rate plus the crude rate of net migration.

The population is assumed to be stable, and since the age distribution of a stable population is invariant, $r(x+)$ is constant for all x. Let this constant growth rate be r. Since there is, by assumption, no net migration, we have $m(x+) = 0$ for all x. The completeness of death registration is assumed to be constant with age over age x. Let the proportion of actual deaths enumerated be C. Then (2) can be rearranged to yield the following:

$$b(x+) = r + (1/C)\, d'(x+), \qquad (3)$$

where $d'(x+)$ is the *recorded* death rate over age x.

If $N(x+)$ is the recorded population aged over x and $N(x, x + n)$ is defined as the population aged between x and $x + n$, $b(x+)$ can be estimated by a statistic such as the following:

$$b(x+) = (N(x - n, x) + N(x, x + n))/2nN(x+). \qquad (4)$$

Thus, given a set of observed age-specific death rates and a single population census for the calculation of $b(x+)$, linear regression or any other curve-fitting procedure can be used to estimate the population growth rate and the completeness of death registration (see United Nations 1983 for a discussion of estimation issues).

The primary advantages of indirect approaches are, first, that their data requirements are modest, and second, that as a result, they are much less labor intensive than direct methods. However, indirect methods are applicable almost exclusively to national-level populations and allow no disaggregation by cause of death, residence, socioeconomic status, and so on.

The Accuracy of Cause-of-Death Data

Errors in ascertaining true cause of death may arise from inaccurate diagnosis by the attending physician (if any), failure to perform an autopsy, inaccurate autopsy results, including inability of the pathologist to specify multiple causes of death, and failure of the death certifier to take into account the results of autopsy. In the last case, problems arise from changing vital statistics conventions and the

inevitable resulting misassignments of correctly diagnosed deaths. There is a large volume of postwar research on the accuracy of reported cause of death (Preston et al. 1972; Manton and Stallard 1984). This literature is useful not only for isolating principal themes in the misdiagnosis of cause of death, but also in setting upper bounds on the accuracy of prewar statistics.

Prewar populations present special problems. Specific clinical problems of diagnosis and pathology are outside the scope of this essay, but several general points are important. First, because of intracategory misassignment (e.g., strokes due to cerebral hemorrhage being misassigned to strokes due to cerebral thrombosis), there are significant gains in accuracy from aggregating individual causes of death into broader categories (Preston et al. 1972). The more fine-grained the category, the higher the likely degree of error.

Second, any death wrongly excluded from the correct category, if it does not escape the registration system entirely, represents an incorrect addition to another category; problems of overattribution, in other words, may be as serious as problems of underattribution.

Third, as death has increasingly occurred at older ages from chronic and degenerative diseases, researchers have been forced to replace the traditional underlying-cause model, in which one disease or condition is assumed to have resulted in death, with more complex multiple cause-of-death approaches (Manton and Stallard 1984). In the case of historical populations of low life expectancy, however, use of the simple underlying-cause model is more defensible than in the case of modern populations. Of course, it is frequently inappropriate for the case of aged persons, and the contributory role of chronic conditions such as nutritional deficiency and low-level diarrheal disease may be significant.

Finally, because of the improving state of medical knowledge, increasing presence of an attending physician, and increasing frequency of competent autopsy, the overriding problem of the proportion of deaths attributed to unknown, ill-defined, and bizarre or nonsensical causes in cause-of-death statistics has been in steady decline (Preston et al. 1972). Among ill-defined causes, we include old age, senility, debility, fever, teething, dropsy, and so on. However, even in compilations as early as the 1850 U.S. Census of Mortality, the proportion of deaths assigned to bizarre causes is tiny, and attributions to unknown and ill-defined causes are confined largely to deaths of persons over 65.

Moreover, we are not totally ignorant of the underlying nature of many deaths assigned to unknown and ill-defined causes. There is an a priori reason to believe that historical cause-of-death data systematically underreport causes of death most common in old age because of the inherent difficulty of correctly diagnosing chronic and degenerative conditions. The most likely scenario is that these deaths ended up in the *unknown* and *ill-defined* categories, a hypothesis in support of which Preston (1976) has adduced strong statistical evidence. In particular, most deaths attributed to old age and senility can, with some confidence, be attributed to cardiovascular disease and cancer.

Thus, there are further compositional advantages, in addition to the enhanced validity of the underlying-cause mortality model, to dealing with low-life-expectancy historical populations. Calculations indicate that in a population with a life expectancy of 30, of the men 52.9 percent eventually die from causes falling into fairly robust categories: respiratory tuberculosis, other infectious and parasitic diseases, diarrheal disease, the influenza–pneumonia–bronchitis complex, and violence. In a population with a life expectancy of 70, by contrast, the corresponding figure is only 14.6 percent (Preston et al. 1972; Preston 1976). Partially vitiating this compositional advantage of low-life-expectancy populations is the relatively large proportion of deaths from diseases of infancy and early childhood that are difficult to diagnose. Nevertheless, it appears that nineteenth- and early-twentieth-century mortality statistics give a fairly accurate picture (excluding problems related to chronic and degenerative disease) of the actual cause-of-death structure.

F. Landis MacKellar

Bibliography

Arriaga, Eduardo. 1968. *New life tables for Latin American populations in the nineteenth and twentieth centuries.* University of California, Institute of International Studies, Population Monograph Ser. No. 3. Berkeley.

Condran, Gretchen, and Eileen Crimmins. 1979. A description and evaluation of mortality data in the federal census: 1850–1900. *Historical Methods* 12: 1–22.

Crimmins, Eileen. 1980. The completeness of 1900 mortality data collected by registration and enumeration for rural and urban parts of states: Estimates using the Chandra Sekar–Deming technique. *Historical Methods* 13: 163–9.

Erhardt, Carl, and Joyce Berlin, eds. 1974. *Mortality and morbidity in the United States.* Cambridge, Mass.

Graunt, John. 1662. *Natural and political observations mentioned in a following index, and made upon the bills of mortality.* London.

Haines, Michael, and Roger Avery. 1980. The American life table of 1830–1860: An evaluation. *Journal of Interdisciplinary History* 11: 71–95.

Henry, Louis. 1956. *Anciennes familles génèvoises.* Paris.

Hollingsworth, T. H. 1964. The demography of the British peerage. *Population Studies,* suppl. 18(2).

MacKellar, Landis. 1987. U.S. adult white crude death and net migration rates, by state, in 1850. In *Proceedings of the Middle States Division of the Association of American Geographers, New York, New York, October 17–18, 1986,* ed. Cathy Kelly and George Rengert, 66–72. Philadelphia.

Manton, Kenneth, and Eric Stallard. 1984. *Recent trends in mortality analysis.* New York.

Marks, E., W. Seltzer, and K. Krotki. 1974. *Population growth estimation: A handbook of vital statistics measurement.* New York.

Preston, Samuel. 1976. *Mortality patterns in national populations, with special reference to recorded causes of death.* New York.

Preston, Samuel, Nathan Keyfitz, and Robert Schoen. 1972. *Causes of death: Life tables for national populations.* New York.

Short, Thomas. 1750. *New observations on city, town, and country bills of mortality.* London.

Shryock, Henry, and Jacob Siegal. 1980. *The methods and materials of demography.* Washington, D.C.

United Nations, 1983. *Manual on indirect methods of demographic estimation.* New York.

U.S. Bureau of the Census. 1923. *Mortality rates: 1910–20.* Washington, D.C.

1933. *Introduction to vital statistics of the United States: 1900–1930.* Washington, D.C.

U.S. Bureau of the Census and Library of Congress. 1943a. *Vital statistics rates in the United States: 1900–40.* Washington, D.C.

1943b. *General censuses and vital statistics in the Americas.* Washington, D.C.

1946. *National censuses and vital statistics in Europe: 1918–1939.* Washington, D.C.

U.S. Public Health Service. 1961. *Guide to United States life tables: 1900–1959.* Public Health Service Publication No. 1086, Public Health Bibliography Ser. No. 42. Washington, D.C.

Vinovkis, Maris. 1971. The 1789 life table of Edward Wigglesworth. *Journal of Economic History* 31: 570–91.

1972. Mortality rates and trends in Massachusetts before 1860. *Journal of Economic History* 32: 184–213.

Wrigley, E.A. 1968. Mortality in pre-industrial England: The case of Colyton, Devon, over three centuries. *Daedalus* 97: 246–80.

1969. *Population and history.* New York.

IV.2
Maternal Mortality: Definition and Secular Trends in England and Wales, 1850–1970

Maternal mortality signifies the deaths of women that take place during pregnancy, labor, or the puerperium, once frequently referred to as "deaths in childbirth." Despite past claims, in the context of total deliveries, maternal death was a rare event compared with death from disease. Even in the worst periods of the eighteenth and nineteenth centuries, the mother survived in at least 98 percent of deliveries. Nonetheless, a death rate of 1 to 2 percent is high when the average number of deliveries *per day* is about 2,000, as it was in England and Wales by the end of the nineteenth century. In the United States during the 1920s, for example, death in childbirth claimed some 15,000 to 20,000 lives a year, and it was second only to tuberculosis as a cause of death in women of childbearing age.

This essay is about the historical epidemiology of maternal mortality – the distribution and determinants of maternal mortality in different populations at different periods. The epidemiological approach to the history of maternal mortality is not, of course, the only one, but it is the method that makes the greatest use of statistics to attempt to discover why the mortality rate changed at different periods, and why one region or one country suffered more maternal deaths than another. It is necessary to examine a broad range of clinical, social, political, economic, and geographic factors, all of which affected childbirth in different countries and at different times. Although this is a historical exercise, some of the answers are undoubtedly relevant to obstetric problems in certain parts of the Third World today.

To illustrate how maternal mortality is determined, the trend in England and Wales will be examined first. Maternal deaths and other data are shown in Table IV.2.1 for certain selected decennia and in Figure IV.2.1 for successive decennia from the 1850s through the 1970s.

In England and Wales the population of women of childbearing age more than doubled between the 1850s and the 1970s, but the birthrate more than halved, so that the average number of births per day (or per decade) was almost exactly the same in the 1850s and the 1970s. But the risk of childbirth had been enormously reduced. Total maternal deaths, as shown in Table IV.2.1, rose from an average of 8.5 per day in the 1850s to a peak of 12 per day in the 1890s before descending to the present level of about 1 per week. In the nineteenth century, a woman would most likely have known of at least one death in childbirth among her friends or neighbors, if not her own family. Today, maternal deaths are so rare that very few people have personal knowledge of such a tragedy.

There is a certain pattern of mortality with which historians and epidemiologists are familiar. It consists of a general decline in deaths dating either from the mid-nineteenth century or from the beginning of the twentieth. This decline was seen, for instance, in death rates from all causes, deaths from the common infectious diseases, and infant mortal-

Table IV.2.1. *Birthrates and maternal deaths in England and Wales, 1851–1980*

Decennium	Population of women aged 15–44 (millions)	Birthrate[a]	Average number of births per day[b]	Average number of maternal deaths per day[b]	Average annual maternal deaths per million women aged 15–44	Maternal deaths per 10,000 births
1851–60	4.60	144.8	1,775	8.5	675	47.0
1891–1900	7.50	122.9	2,507	12.0	621	50.9
1951–60	9.27	77.1	1,938	1.1	43	5.6
1971–80	9.77	67.3	1,772	0.23	8	1.2

Note: For all three quantities, the value for the 1850s is expressed as 100; subsequent values are shown as the percentage above or below the level of the 1850s.
[a]Birthrate expressed as births per 1,000 women aged 15–44.
[b]Average daily births and maternal deaths for the decade.

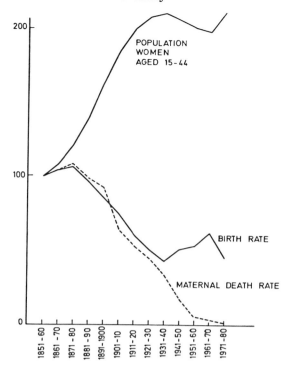

Figure IV.2.1. Birthrates and maternal mortality rates for England and Wales, 1851–1980. Values for 1850 = 100. (From Annual reports, Decennial Supplements and Statistical Reviews of the Registrar General for England and Wales.)

with a general improvement in health and hygiene associated with a rising standard of living.

Figure IV.2.1 shows maternal deaths per million women of childbearing age. The graph appears at first sight to conform to the general pattern, because it shows that maternal deaths declined from the 1870s onward. However, this decline is seen only when the birthrate is ignored and maternal mortality is measured solely in terms of the total number of women of childbearing age. In fact, the population at risk is not *all* women of childbearing age; it is only women during pregnancy, labor, or the puerperium. Maternal mortality has to be measured in terms of births, not total population, and Figure IV.2.1 shows clearly that the birthrate was declining alongside deaths in childbirth.

The maternal mortality rate (henceforth, the MMR) is therefore calculated by dividing the total number of registered maternal deaths (the numerator) by the total number of registered births (the denominator). The quotient is then multiplied by 1,000, 10,000, or, as is usual today, 100,000. Deaths per 10,000 births is the most convenient when one is working with historical data and is used here. The ideal denominator for the calculation of maternal mortality would, of course, be pregnancies rather than births; but total pregnancies cannot be recorded when there are no statistics on abortions or multiple births from single pregnancies. Total births (or live births before stillbirths were registered) are therefore used instead.

When the MMR is calculated in terms of births rather than women of childbearing age, the graph is very different (Figure IV.2.2). Between the 1850s and

ity. The reasons for the decline have been debated for a number of years. In the past it was attributed to advances in scientific medicine. It is now generally accepted that the decline in mortality rates before the Second World War had little to do with advances in medical or surgical therapy, but a great deal to do

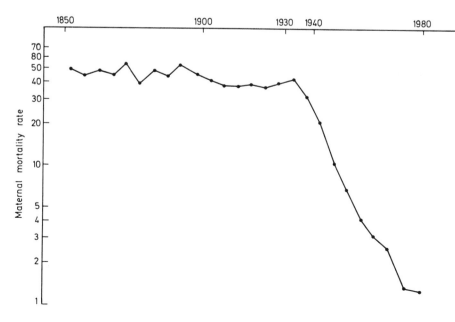

Figure IV.2.2. Maternal mortality rates for England and Wales, 1851–1980 (logarithmic scale). Maternal mortality rates expressed as maternal deaths per 10,000 births. (From Annual reports, Decennial Supplements and Statistical Reviews of the Registrar General for England and Wales.)

1930s the MMR, far from declining, remained on a plateau while other major causes of death were declining. This plateau, and the steep and sustained decline that started in the mid-1930s, are the two prominent features of the graph. The plateau suggests that the factors that caused a general decline in death rates between the 1870s and the mid-1930s had no effect on the MMR. This is especially surprising when one recalls that obstetrics differed from the use of medicine in surgery in that, starting in the 1880s, certain measures were introduced into obstetric practice that should have reduced mortality. These included antisepsis and asepsis, the compulsory regulation and training of midwives, and the growing importance of antenatal care. But it appears that at the national level they had no effect. There is yet another unusual feature of maternal mortality: the correlation with social class. For most of the common causes of death in the past, social-class gradients existed, with the highest mortality rates among the poor and lowest among the well-to-do. In the case of the MMR, the gradient was reversed.

From the mid-1930s, the abrupt and sustained decline in mortality is as striking as the previous absence of any decline. Maternal mortality is puzzling and fascinating because of these unexpected features. Were England and Wales, however, unusual in these respects, or were similar trends found in other countries?

International Comparisons of Maternal Mortality

Few countries published vital statistics before the mid-nineteenth century. The exception was Sweden, where, as Ulf Högberg (1985) has shown, the MMR fell from about 100 per 10,000 births in 1750 to about 50 in the mid-nineteenth century, followed by a rise to about 63 in the 1870s. Work by R. Schofield (1986) suggests that the MMR in England probably fell from about 100 per 10,000 births during 1700–50 to around 80 during 1750–1800 and to between 50 and 60 in the first half of the nineteenth century. The MMR in Europe in the late eighteenth and early nineteenth centuries may have been about 100 deaths per 10,000 births, but this is speculative.

Data on maternal deaths were not always included in early lists of causes of death, but they were usually included in vital statistics (with various degrees of reliability) from the 1850s in European countries, from about the 1880s in Australia and New Zealand, and from 1900 in the United States (except for the state of Massachusetts, where statistics on maternal mortality can be obtained from 1850).

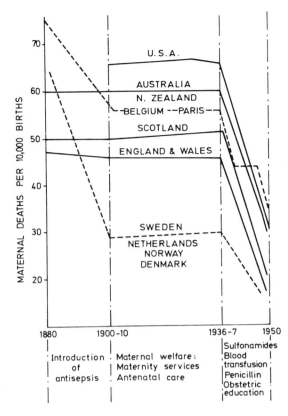

Figure IV.2.3. Changes in maternal mortality rates in different countries, 1880–1950. (Based on the vital statistics of the countries shown.)

Data from the United States as a unit present a special problem because they were based on the expanding Death Registration Area, established in 1880. Initially this consisted of the states of New Jersey and Massachusetts, the District of Columbia, and nineteen cities. Other states were added year by year. The process was completed by 1933 with those states that recorded the highest MMRs coming last and to some extent accounting for the rising MMR in the United States between 1900 and 1933. In spite of this complication, however, there is little doubt that the United States experienced one of the highest MMRs in the developed world during the first four decades of the twentieth century.

Figure IV.2.3 is a schematic representation of the secular trend in the MMR in various countries between 1880 and 1950. In 1880 the MMR in most developed countries lay somewhere in the range of 50 to 100 deaths per 10,000 births. Between 1880 and 1910, some countries (e.g., Sweden and Belgium) showed a substantial reduction in the MMR, which Högberg (1985) has suggested was almost certainly the result of the effective use of antisepsis and asepsis. (Although different, both techniques are de-

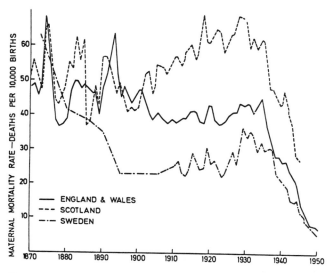

Figure IV.2.4. Maternal mortality rates in Scotland, England, Wales, and Sweden, 1870–1950. (From Annual Reports of the Registrar General for England, Wales, and Scotland. For Sweden, 1860–1910: Ulf Högberg, Maternal mortality in Sweden, Umeå University Medical Dissertations, New Ser. 156 [Umeå, 1985], 1911–1950: *Sveriges officiella Statistik,* Stockholm.)

noted by the term *antisepsis* in this essay). However, other countries (e.g., Britain and Australia) failed to reduce mortality significantly, a difference that is hard to explain but one that suggests poor antiseptic practice. An example of this difference can be seen in Figure IV.2.4, which shows the secular trends in the MMR in Scotland, England and Wales, and Sweden.

That antiseptic techniques, rigorously employed, could be very effective in reducing maternal mortality was beyond doubt. Before 1880, the experiences of lying-in hospitals all over the world were appalling and MMRs of 200 or more were common. By 1900 such hospitals as the Rotunda Hospital in Dublin, the York Road Lying-in Hospital in London, the Maternity Hospital in Basle, and the Women's Hospital in Sydney reported very low MMRs and a virtual absence of deaths from puerperal sepsis. Such success, however, seems to have been confined to a minority of hospitals, the implication being that those standards of care were the exception before the twentieth century. This was certainly the belief of the Australian Committee on Maternal Mortality of 1917, which said in no uncertain terms:

Puerperal septicaemia is probably the gravest reproach which any civilised nation can by its own negligence offer to itself. It can be prevented by a degree of care which is not excessive or meticulous, requiring only ordinary intelligence and some careful training. It has been abolished in hospitals and it should cease to exist in the community. It should be as rare as sepsis after a surgical operation.

From 1900 to the late 1930s, almost everywhere the MMR stayed level or rose slightly, although there were wide differences among national MMRs. The United States showed the highest and the Netherlands and Scandinavia the lowest. Between 1929 and 1935, the MMR declined slightly in the United States and New Zealand. Elsewhere the trend was level or rising.

When it became obvious that maternal deaths, and especially those from puerperal sepsis, were not being prevented, concern about maternal mortality increased. In many countries, including Britain, Australia, New Zealand, and North America, radical reforms were suggested. These eventually led to improvements in the education and regulation of midwives (except in the United States, where abolition of the midwife was recommended), to better obstetric training for physicians (although in practice little improvement occurred), and an increasing number of specialist obstetricians (with the inevitable tendency for obstetrics to become a branch of operative surgery). Also suggested were the encouragement of routine antenatal care (which seems to have had little effect before the 1940s) and the establishment of new obstetric institutions (clinics, maternity hospitals, and maternity departments in general hospitals in spite of the danger of cross-infection). There were repeated exhortations to use antisepsis properly (which were largely ignored), and local and national governments were urged to improve both the quality and availability of maternal care to women at all levels of society (their actions were usually weak but occasionally effective).

Some medical authorities were optimistic. Maternal mortality, it was felt, was not a difficult problem. Methods of preventing maternal death were known, and reforms based on them would reduce the tragic and unnecessary loss of so many young women in the prime of their lives. Yet national MMRs showed an obstinate refusal to fall, and a number of studies revealed wide and disturbing regional differences within nations.

Map IV.2.1 shows regional variations for England and Wales, and Map IV.2.2 the same for the United States. In England and Wales there was a well-marked northwest and southeast divide along a line from the Severn to the Wash, which persisted from the late nineteenth century until the 1930s. Most counties above the line suffered an above-average,

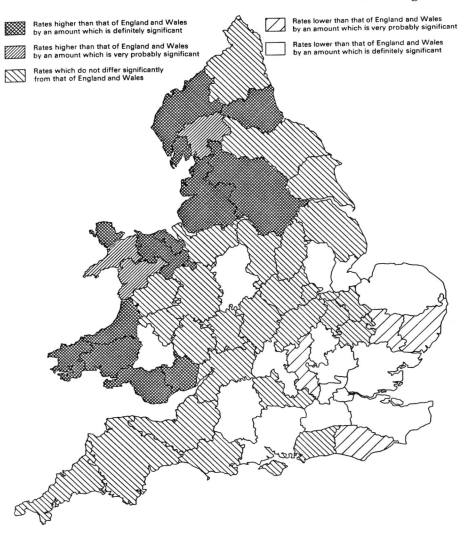

Map IV.2.1. Differences in maternal mortality rates in England and Wales, 1924–33. (From Ministry of Health 1937.)

and those below the line a lower-than-average, MMR. The explanation is neither simple nor certain, but it probably lies in the standards of obstetric care rather than standards of living (see the section on determinants).

In the United States the divide was geographically the opposite. Maternal mortality was highest in the South. The states with a high MMR lay along the curve stretching down from Wyoming, Colorado, New Mexico, and Arizona across to the states of the Deep South – Louisiana, Mississippi, Alabama, Florida, Georgia, North and South Carolina, Tennessee, and Virginia. In the Northeast, only Maine showed a persistently high MMR.

The secular trend for the United States as a whole can be seen in Figure IV.2.5. The striking features are the high MMRs and the very large difference between white and all mothers, a difference that persisted at least to the 1970s. The high MMR in the South was due largely, but not entirely, to the concentration of the black population. For white mothers as

well as black, the MMR was highest in the southern states, but the differential was relatively slight.

In the United States before the Second World War, maternal mortality was usually lower in rural than in urban areas. By the 1960s this situation had been reversed. Remote rural areas, however, often experienced special problems, and wide variations in the provision of maternal care in different parts of the same state were not uncommon. In mountainous areas with deep ravines and few roads, often no trained birth attendants of any kind were available. In other areas, low mortality might be achieved by small homogeneous populations of European origin, which included midwives trained in Europe. Yet other remote areas might possess small local hospitals where nearly all deliveries would be performed by physicians. In many developed countries, a lack of uniformity was the rule rather than the exception as far as factors affecting the MMR were concerned. It was true of Britain, for instance, but most extreme in the United States. In the years 1938–40, when the

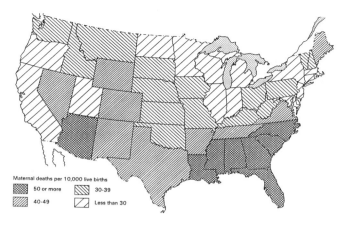

Map IV.2.2. Differences in maternal mortality rates in the United States, 1938–40. (From *Changes in infant childhood and maternal mortality over the decade 1939–1948: A graphic analysis,* Children's Bureau Statistical Series, No. 6, Federal Security Agency, Social Security Administration, Children's Bureau, Washington, D.C.; *Infant, fetal and maternal mortality, United States, 1963,* National Center for Health Statistics, Series 20, No. 3, U.S. Department of Health, Education and Welfare, Washington, D.C.)

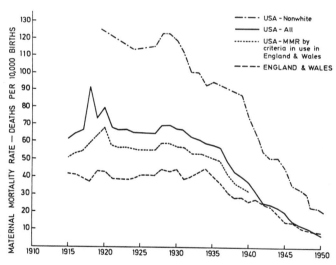

Figure IV.2.5. Maternal mortality rates in England, Wales, and the United States, 1910–50. (From Annual Reports of the Registrar General for England, Wales, and Scotland. For Sweden, 1860–1910: Ulf Högberg, Maternal mortality in Sweden, Umeå University Medical Dissertations, New Ser. 156 [Umeå 1985], 1911–50: *Sveriges officiella Statistik,* Stockholm. Children's Bureau Publication. U.S. Dept. of Labor. Washington, D.C., U.S. Govt. Printing Office; R.M. Woodbury, *Maternal mortality: The risk of death in childbirth and from all the diseases caused by pregnancy and confinement,* Rept. no. 152 [1921]; Elizabeth Tandy, *Comparability of maternal mortality rates in the United States and certain foreign countries,* Rept. No. 229 [1935].)

average MMR for the United States as a whole was 37.6 per 10,000 births, it ranged from 17.5 per 10,000 in North Dakota to 67.8 in South Carolina, a ratio of lowest to highest of 1 to 3.9. In England and Wales in the same period, the average MMR was about 28 per 10,000 and the range between regions was probably about 17 to 38, a ratio of 1 to 2.2.

All this was known to the authorities who made policy in Britain and the United States. Both countries were concerned about their unacceptable MMRs and the obstinately persistent regional differences. But they devised quite different policies. In the United States it was thought that maternal mortality could be defeated by an increase in the proportion of hospital deliveries performed by specialist obstetricians. The midwife and the general practitioner with her or his "kitchen-table midwifery" should be abolished except in remote rural areas.

In Britain it was felt that the backbone of obstetric care should continue to be home deliveries by midwives and general practitioners. Hospital care should increase, but on the whole it should be reserved for complications of labor and high-risk cases. New Zealand tended to follow the U.S. pattern, Australia, the British, and the Netherlands and Scandinavia also pursued a successful policy of home deliveries by midwives backed up by a minimum of hospital deliveries. It is interesting that, in spite of such divergent policies, none of these countries experienced a significant fall in the MMR between 1910 and the mid-1930s.

The Causes and Determinants of Maternal Mortality

Three conditions – puerperal sepsis, toxemia, and hemorrhage – caused the majority of maternal deaths throughout the developed world from the mid-nineteenth century until the mid-1930s, and the proportion of total deaths contributed by each was remarkably constant in different countries during this period.

Puerperal sepsis usually accounted for about 40 percent of deaths. At first, the term *puerperal sepsis* was synonymous with puerperal fever ("childbed fever"), an infection that appeared after delivery. Later, it included septic abortion as well, but in most countries the two were not distinguished until the late 1920s, when deaths from septic abortion were increasing, although to a widely different extent in different countries. By the early 1930s, the death rate from septic abortion had reached a high level in the United States. In New Zealand, deaths from septic abortion actually exceeded those from full-term sepsis. The contribution of septic abortion to maternal mortality in different countries is an extremely complex subject. But it is likely that the increase in the MMR in the Netherlands and Sweden in the late 1920s and early 1930s was the result of an increase in deaths from septic abortion superimposed on a more or less constant rate of deaths from puerperal fever.

Unlike deaths from septic abortion, those from puerperal fever were largely preventable. The risk of puerperal infection, however, was much greater in the past than it is today because of the prevalence and virulence of the organism known as the B-hemolytic streptococcus, Lancefield group A (*Streptococcus pyogenes*), which was responsible for the vast majority of deaths from puerperal fever. Before the Second World War, this organism was frequently carried in the nose or throat of a large proportion of the healthy population ("asymptomatic carriers"). It was also common not only as the cause of scarlet fever and erysipelas, but as an infection in people suffering from such minor complaints as sore throats, whitlows, and minor abrasions, so that the risk of cross-infection was high. The prevalence of the virulent streptococcus and the inadequacy of antiseptic procedures contributed to the high MMR. Today, asymptomatic carriers are rare, scarlet fever has become a minor disease, and rheumatic fever and acute nephritis have virtually disappeared. The reasons for the change are uncertain.

Deaths from toxemia (eclampsia and preeclampsia) accounted for about 20 to 25 percent of total maternal deaths and hemorrhage (antepartum and postpartum) for about 20 percent. Each of the remaining causes, such as "white leg" (deep-vein thrombosis) and embolism, ruptured uterus, ectopic pregnancy, hyperemesis gravidarum, puerperal mania, and so on, contributed 5 percent or less to the total.

Determinants of Maternal Mortality

Although the immediate causes of maternal deaths are not disputed, the factors that determined MMRs are much more debatable. They fall broadly into two groups: clinical factors and socioeconomic, political, and geographic factors.

Clinical factors were associated with the type and standards of obstetric care provided by the birth attendant. Standards of obstetric care were determined by a number of factors, including the status of obstetrics and thus the quality of education and training, the type of birth attendant (specialist obstetrician, general practitioner, trained or untrained midwife, etc.), the place of delivery (home or hospi-

tal), and current fashions in the management of normal and abnormal pregnancies and labors.

Nonclinical factors included the attitudes and expectations of women about the conduct of childbirth, together with socioeconomic considerations: family income, nutrition, housing and hygiene, the ability to command and pay for obstetric care where private care predominated, and the provision of maternal welfare schemes by local and national government or charities where they existed.

Some historians have suggested that high MMRs in the past were due largely to social and economic deprivation. Others have asserted that the responsibility lay not with poverty per se, but with the standards of obstetric care available to the poor. Poor standards of care might result from ignorance and lack of training. Poor practice might also, and often was, caused by negligence, laziness, hurrying, and dangerous, unnecessary surgical intervention by trained practitioners. Poor practice, therefore, was not confined to untrained midwives or even to the often-maligned general practitioners; it was often found among specialist obstetricians following the procedural fashions of their time.

Clinical and nonclinical factors were not mutually exclusive. They overlapped, and both could affect the outcome of childbirth. In any particular case, maternal risk was a reflection of the complex interplay of traditional, social, economic, and clinical features that surrounded the birth of a baby and where the baby was born. Obviously, the risks of a mother giving birth in midwinter in Montana or Maine, North Wales or the Highlands of Scotland were different from the risks experienced in the middle of London, Paris, or Boston.

Yet in spite of bewildering variety, it is the task of the historian to generalize, and to try to assess the relative importance of all such factors in different populations at different times, allowing for differences in the ways that populations are described. Europeans tend to describe populations in terms of social class; North Americans in terms of nationality, race, and color. One can suggest with reasonable confidence, however, that black mothers as a whole in the United States would have shared with the lower social classes in Britain a greater than average likelihood of suffering from malnutrition, chronic disease, and the general ill-effects of poverty. Did they suffer a high MMR as a consequence? Two lines of evidence suggest that social and economic factors were much less important determinants of maternal mortality than might be expected.

A series of reports from cities in Britain, dating

from the 1850s to the 1930s, revealed that MMRs were higher among the upper classes than the lower. These findings were confirmed by the Registrar General's analysis of maternal mortality by social class for England and Wales for the years 1930–2. This showed that the MMR for social classes I and II (professional and managerial) was 44.4, while for social class V (unskilled workers) it was 38.9.

In the United States there was no doubt that the MMR was much higher (usually by a ratio of 3 to 1) among black women than white. A few investigations were carried out on the relationship between income and maternal mortality. Most showed a higher MMR among the lowest income groups, but they generally concluded (the Massachusetts report of 1924 is an example) that inability to pay for obstetric care, not poverty per se, was the explanation.

The second line of evidence might be called experimental. It came from programs in which a high standard of obstetric care was provided in regions of social and economic deprivation. The classic example was the *Rochdale experiment*. In 1929 Rochdale (a town in Lancashire) had an exceptionally high MMR of slightly more than 90 deaths per 10,000 births. Andrew Topping, a physician serving as the new officer of health, undertook a vigorous reform of obstetric care during a period of severe economic depression. The MMR was reduced in a few years from one of the highest in England to one of the lowest. There was no change in the social and economic environment during the experiment.

A similar experiment was the establishment of the Kentucky Frontier Nursing Service by Mary Breckinridge in the 1920s. Highly trained nurse-midwives, traveling on horseback, delivered babies of women who lived in great poverty in isolated mountain terrain and suffered from a high rate of chronic illness and malnutrition. An astonishingly low MMR was achieved solely by good obstetric practice – about one-tenth of the rate among women delivered by physicians as private patients in the hospital in Lexington, the nearest town.

The countries showing the lowest MMRs – the Netherlands and Scandinavia – ran maternity services based on a strong tradition of home deliveries by highly trained midwives. In Britain a very low MMR was achieved by a similar group, the Queen's Institute Midwives. The records of outpatient charities in Britain and the United States showed repeatedly that the establishment of a free or low-cost obstetric outpatient service in areas of severe socioeconomic deprivation could result in low MMRs, even when deliveries took place under appalling conditions. Therefore, although there were maternal deaths in which anemia, malnutrition, and chronic ill-health must have been contributory factors (and it seems likely that they contributed to the high MMR in the Deep South of the United States), the weight of evidence suggests that the standard of obstetric care was usually the most important determinant of the MMR. Because hospital delivery carried the danger of cross-infection as well as the likelihood of surgical interference in normal labor, it was usually safest before the mid-1930s to be delivered at home by a trained midwife or by a medical practitioner who was conservative in his or her attitudes toward obstetrics and meticulous in antiseptic practice. The irony is that the rich often sought what they considered the "best" obstetric care in plush private hospitals and paid for it with the added risk of iatrogenic maternal mortality.

Conclusion

The fall in MMR that began in the late 1930s was due to a number of factors, which followed one another but at slightly different rates in different countries. In England and Wales these were, in succession, the sulfonamides, blood transfusion, better obstetric care (in part associated with wartime organization), penicillin in 1944, and after the war a marked improvement in obstetric education. The National Health Service hastened the adoption of a standard of obstetric care for everyone, which was available only to a minority before the war. The fact that this decline in MMR occurred throughout the developed world at much the same pace is a strong endorsement of the notion that clinical care is the main determinant of MMR. Some, however, would still maintain that the low maternal mortality today is due to good health, not medical technology. In this respect the experience of a religious group in Indiana in the 1970s is informative. This group rejected all orthodox medical care while engaging in the same middle-class occupations and earning the same incomes as their orthodox neighbors. Mothers received no prenatal care and were delivered without trained assistance. Their MMR was 100 times higher than the statewide rate.

We have noted the high MMRs between 1900 and 1935. We may ask with the benefit of hindsight whether it would have been possible for countries such as Britain and the United States to have reduced their MMRs significantly. The answer is almost certainly yes, although it is probable that the MMRs seen in the 1950s would have been out of reach in the 1930s, because of the virulence of streptococcus and the absence of sulfonamides and penicillin.

A significant reduction in maternal mortality might have been achieved, however, through education. The medical curriculum should have attached as much importance to obstetrics as to anatomy, physiology, and biochemistry. It would have been essential to demonstrate the need for a very high standard of antiseptic practice at every delivery. It would have been wise for every developed country to have established a national or regional maternity service based largely on the work of trained midwives undertaking the majority of normal deliveries at home. Maternity hospitals were necessary, of course, for the management of dangerous complications and high-risk cases, but they were not the best place for normal deliveries. The work of hospitals, general practitioners, and midwives should have been monitored by local maternal mortality committees, and care taken to establish close cooperation between all parts of the maternity service. Some of these reforms were beginning to be implemented by the late 1930s in Britain. None required knowledge that was not then available. The examples of the Kentucky Nursing Service, the Rochdale experiment, and the numerous successful outpatient charities and services were well known. The success of Scandinavia and the Netherlands, where most of the principles just outlined were in operation, was no secret.

If such simple but potentially effective changes were not adopted, it was partly because no clear consensus existed as to the way obstetric care should be delivered. Even if there had been a consensus, it would have been impossible to compel medical personnel to change their ways.

Appendix

The Problems of Comparative Statistics

Certain statistical problems surround the interpretation of the statistics on maternal mortality and international comparisons. In England and Wales before the compulsory registration of stillbirths in 1927, the denominator *births* meant *live births* only. After 1927, stillbirths were included and the term *total births* replaced *live births* in the calculation of the MMR. The difference was relatively small. In 1933, for example, the MMR was 45.2 per 10,000 live births and 43.2 per 10,000 live births plus stillbirths. The failure to take multiple births into account produces a slight distortion in the other direction, because births rather than deliveries are used as the denominator. Again, the distortion is slight. The use of the classification based on the Interna-

tional List of Diseases was important when it was adopted by England and Wales in 1911. Previously, deaths due to toxemia of pregnancy (but not deaths from eclampsia) were entered under diseases of the kidney; after 1911 they were entered as maternal deaths. Subsequent revisions of the international list made little difference to the calculation of total maternal mortality, but an appreciable difference in the way maternal deaths were classified.

A major problem in international comparisons was that of *associated,* or, to use the modern term, *indirect* deaths. Simply stated, should the death of every pregnant woman be recorded as a maternal death, regardless of the cause? There was no difficulty in identifying "true" maternal deaths such as those due to postpartum hemorrhage, puerperal fever, or ectopic gestation; and deaths that had nothing to do with the pregnancy or general health (e.g., the death of a pregnant woman in a road or railway accident) were generally excluded. Difficulties arose, however, when a woman died in the course of an otherwise normal pregnancy or labor from influenza, or some preexisting condition such as heart disease, tuberculosis, or nephritis. It was argued that such deaths were due to the combination of general disease and the strain of pregnancy or labor; if the woman had not been pregnant, she might have survived. Should such deaths be entered under maternal or general causes of death? Different opinions were held. In the United States, Australia (but not New Zealand), Denmark (but not Norway or Sweden), and Scotland (but not England and Wales), indirect deaths were usually included in the estimation of maternal mortality. There were always borderline cases, and the way they were treated could also differ, but these differences were statistically negligible. Those countries that included associated deaths often believed that they were more honest and commented angrily that, if their MMRs seemed high, it was due solely to this difference in method. This was understandable, but wrong. Elizabeth Tandy of the Children's Bureau showed in 1935 that, although some differences could be attributed to differences in method, they were only slight in comparison with the wide international differences that existed. An example can be found in Figure IV.2.5, where the MMR for the United States as a whole is shown twice: once with associated deaths included in the U.S. manner and once with associated deaths excluded in the English manner.

Perhaps the most difficult problem is that of "hidden" deaths – deaths from puerperal fever and abortion that are hidden because of the opprobrium surrounding them. A death from puerperal fever was, above all other deaths, one for which the physician or nurse was likely to be blamed. There were therefore strong motives for a physician to register a death like this in such a way that the authorities would not know it was a maternal death. In the late nineteenth and early twentieth centuries, it was not unusual for doctors to certify a death from puerperal sepsis as being due to peritonitis or septicemia without mention of childbirth. These conditions were cited because they were, in fact, the immediate causes of death in puerperal sepsis.

The true cause of death in cases such as these could be determined, however, both by asking the offending doctor outright whether childbirth had been involved or by searching the death records for an excess of deaths from peritonitis or septicemia among women of childbearing age. Deaths from both causes ("peritonitis of unstated origin" and "septicemia") were more common in men than women once deaths from puerperal sepsis were excluded. This complicated statistical exercise was carried out by government statisticians in Britain and the United States in the 1920s. Indeed, this author has carried out in some detail the same exercise using the lists of causes of death from the 1880s to the 1950s. In England and Wales, in the period from 1900 to 1930, apparently incorrect certification led to an underestimation of the true number of deaths from puerperal sepsis by about 12 percent. The MMRs described by this essay for the period up to the mid-1930s are therefore likely to be an underestimation; they are certainly not an exaggeration of the true figures. Needless to say, the exact MMRs of the past can never be known. Nevertheless, the extent of statistical distortion can to a large extent be estimated. It is then reasonable to believe that a generally correct picture of MMRs in most developed countries since the 1880s can be obtained and that the picture becomes increasingly accurate through the present century.

Irvine Loudon

Bibliography

Australia. 1917. *Report on maternal mortality in childbirth.* Commonwealth of Australia, Department of Trades and Customs, Committee concerning causes of Death and Invalidity in the Commonwealth. Melbourne.

Breckinridge, Mary. 1952. *Wide neighborhoods: A story of the Frontier Nursing Service.* New York.

Campbell, Janet. 1924. *Maternal mortality.* Reports of Public Health and Medical Subjects No. 25. London.

Campbell, Janet, Isabella D. Cameron, and Dilwys M. Jones. 1932. *High maternal mortality in certain areas.* Reports on Public Health and Medical Subjects No. 68. London.

Campbell, Dame Janet. 1935. *Maternity services.* London.

Cullingworth, C. J. 1898. On the undiminished mortality from puerperal fever in England and Wales. *Transactions of the Obstetrical Society of London* 40: 91–114.

Dart, Helen. 1921. *Maternity and child care in selected areas of Mississippi.* U.S. Department of Health, Children's Bureau, Publ. No. 88. Washington, D.C.

DePorte, J. V. 1928. *Maternal mortality and stillbirths in New York State: 1921–1925.* New York.

Galdston, Iago. 1937. *Maternal deaths: The way to prevention.* New York.

Högberg, Ulf. 1985. Maternal mortality in Sweden. Umeå University Medical Dissertations, New Ser. 156.

Jellett, Henry. 1929. *The causes and prevention of maternal mortality.* London.

Kaunitz, A.M., et al. 1984. Perinatal and maternal mortality in a religious group avoiding obstetric care. *American Journal of Obstetrics and Gynecology* 150: 826–32.

Leavitt, Judith. 1986. *Brought to bed: Child-bearing in America, 1750–1950.* New York.

Local Government Board (England and Wales). 1914–16. *44th Annual Report of the Local Government Board* 6 (supplement on maternal mortality).

Loudon, Irvine. 1986a. Deaths in childbed from the eighteenth century to 1935. *Medical History* 30: 1–41.

  1986b. Obstetric care, social class and maternal mortality. *British Medical Journal* 2: 606–8.

  1987. Puerperal fever, the streptococcus and the sulphonamides, 1911–1945. *British Medical Journal* 2: 485–90.

  1988. Maternal mortality: Some regional and international comparisons. *Social History of Medicine.* 1: 2.

Macfarlane, A., and M. Mugford. 1984. *Birth counts: Statistics of pregnancy and childbirth.* London.

Meigs, G. L. 1916. Rural obstetrics. *Transactions of the American Association for the Study and Prevention of Infant Mortality* 7: 46–61.

  1917. *Maternal mortality from all conditions connected with childbirth in the United States and certain other countries.* U.S. Department of Labor, Children's Bureau, Publ. No. 19. Washington, D.C.

Ministry of Health (England and Wales). 1937. *Report of an investigation into maternal mortality,* Cmd. 5422. London.

  1937. *Report on maternal mortality in Wales,* Cmd. 5423. London.

Moore, Elizabeth. 1917. *Maternity and infant care in a rural county in Kansas.* U.S. Department of Labor, Children's Bureau, Publ. No. 26. Washington, D.C.

Munro Kerr, J. M. 1939. *Maternal mortality and morbidity.* Edinburgh.

New York City Public Health Committee and New York Academy of Medicine. 1933. *Maternal mortality in*

New York, 1930, 1931, 1932. (Abstract in *Journal of the American Medical Association* 101: 1826–8.)

Paradise, Violet. 1919. *Maternity care and the welfare of young children in a homestead county in Montana.* U.S. Department of Labor, Children's Bureau, Publ. No. 34. Washington, D.C.

Philadelphia County Medical Society, Committee on Maternal Welfare. 1934. *Maternal mortality in Philadelphia.* Philadelphia.

Sandelowski, M. 1984. *Pain and pleasure in American childbirth: From twilight sleep to the Read method, 1914–1960.* Westport, Conn.

Schofield, R. 1986. Did the mothers really die? Three centuries of maternal mortality in the world we have lost. In *The world we have gained: Histories of population and social structure,* ed. L. Bonfield, R. Smith, and K. Wrightson. Cambridge.

Sherborne, F. B., and E. Moore. 1919. *Maternity and infant care in two rural counties in Wisconsin.* U.S. Department of Labor, Children's Bureau, Publ. No. 46. Washington, D.C.

Smith, P. M. 1986. *Maternity in dispute, New Zealand, 1920–1939.* Wellington.

Steele, Glen. 1923. *Maternity and child care in a mountain county in Georgia.* U.S. Department of Labor, Children's Bureau, Publ. No. 120. Washington, D.C.

Topping, A. 1936a. Maternal mortality and public opinion. *Public Health* 49: 342–9.

   1936b. Prevention of maternal mortality: The Rochdale experiment. *Lancet* 1: 545–7.

U.S. Department of Health, Education and Welfare. 1966. *Infant, fetal and maternal mortality.* National Center for Health Statistics, Ser. 20, No. 3. Washington, D.C.

U.S. Department of Labor, Children's Bureau. 1933. *Maternal deaths: A brief report of a study made in fifteen states.* Publ. No. 221, Washington, D.C.

   1934. *Maternal mortality in fifteen states.* Publ. 223. Washington, D.C.

Wertz, R. W., and D. C. Wertz. 1977. *Lying-in: A history of childbirth in America.* New York.

White House Conference on Child and Health Protection. 1933. *Fetal, newborn and maternal morbidity and mortality.* New York.

Williams, W. 1895–6. Puerperal mortality. *Transactions of the Epidemiological Society of London,* 100–33.

   1904. *Deaths in childbed* (being the Milroy Lectures delivered at the Royal College of Physicians of London, 1904; W. Williams was Medical Officer of Health at Cardiff). London.

Williams, J. Whitridge. 1912. Medical education and the midwife problem in the United States. *Journal of the American Medical Association* 58: 1–76.

   1922. Criticism of certain tendencies in American obstetrics. *New York State Journal of Medicine* 22: 493–9.

Woodbury, R. M. 1926. *Maternal mortality: The risk of death in childbirth and from all the diseases caused by pregnancy and confinement.* U.S. Department of La-bor, Children's Bureau, Publ. No. 158. Washington, D.C.

Young, James. 1936. Maternal mortality and maternal mortality rates. *American Journal of Obstetrics and Gynaecology* 31: 198–212.

IV.3
Infant Mortality

The infant mortality rate (which is commonly calculated as the number of deaths among infants under 1 year of age in a calendar year per 1,000 live births in that year) measures the probability that a newborn baby will survive the hazards of infancy and live to celebrate his or her first birthday. Whether a given infant survives this crucial first year of life is influenced in part by certain biological characteristics (e.g., genetic makeup, nature of the birth outcome, susceptibility to particular diseases). But a voluminous body of research over the past century has clearly identified the major determinants of the overall infant mortality rate to be, first, the nature of the physical environment, especially the state of sanitation, and, second, the nature and availability of health care facilities. Although the health of persons of all ages is affected by these conditions, the newborn infant is most susceptible and most likely to be adversely affected by the absence of appropriate sanitary and health care facilities.

It has also been solidly established that within any society infant mortality rates are strongly related to family income, which in turn is an indicator of both the nature of the environment in which an infant is born and raised and the family's ability to provide the infant with optimal health care. The basic aim of this essay is to review briefly some of the relevant research and to present empirical justification for designating the infant mortality rate as the most sensitive indicator of the overall health status of any population group.

Historical Evidence

Although precise statistical data are lacking, the little that scientists have been able to compile from various anthropological and archaeological sources clearly indicates that throughout most of its existence humankind has had to contend with an extremely high death rate. At least 20 percent and probably more of all newborn babies died before their first birthdays, and for most there was no more than a 50 percent chance of surviving to adulthood. More specific estimates of mortality in antiquity are limited to occasional estimates of *average life expectancy,* the number of years lived, on the average, by the members of a given population. This average life expectancy, or average age at death as it is sometimes crudely defined, is influenced most strongly by the mortality rate in infancy (Shryock et al. 1976); hence, where conventional birth and death statistics are not available, this measure can be used as something of a proxy for the infant mortality rate. Available historical estimates indicate that, while some of our primitive ancestors surely attained extremely old ages, the average life expectancy in ancient times among most groups was probably not much more than 25 or 30 years, and in some populations it was even lower (Russell 1958).

Although overall survival improved somewhat over the years, average life expectancy had not greatly improved as recently as the start of the present century. Estimates for England and Wales, for example, indicate that average life expectancy for the period 1891–1900 was only about 45 years (44 for men and 48 for women) (Dublin, Lotka, and Spiegelman 1949), and in the United States in 1900 it was only about 50 years (48 for men and 51 for women) (U.S. Bureau of the Census 1960). Moreover, it was still common at that time for as many as 15 percent or more of all newborn babies to die before their first birthdays. Data for the United States, for example, indicate an infant mortality rate for 1900–2 of 162 per 1,000 live births (U.S. Bureau of the Census 1960); and rates of comparable magnitude (between 150 and 170) have been estimated for this period in a number of other western European countries (Woods, Watterson, and Woodward 1988).

Contemporary scholars, concerned with the high levels of infant and childhood mortality, were clearly aware of their causes. Some were environmental factors, such as foul air, contaminated water, and poorly ventilated, overcrowded housing, which contributed to the high incidence of a variety of infectious, respiratory, and parasitic diseases. Other causes were related to poor child care, including inadequate and unsanitary delivery conditions and improper feeding practices, notably a lack of breast feeding and the associated consumption of contaminated milk, all of which led to high rates of mortality from diarrheal diseases (Woods, Watterson, and Woodward 1989). Moreover, it had generally been known since at least the mid-nineteenth century

that these detrimental health conditions were differentially distributed among the population and that the lower social classes experienced much higher infant death rates than the middle and upper classes (Woods et al. 1989). As previously mentioned, research over the years has clearly established that family income is the most significant determinant of the physical well-being of all family members, and particularly that of infants and young children. Arthur Newsholme, for example, one of the best-known investigators of this topic in the late nineteenth and early twentieth centuries, identified poverty as a major corollary of poor sanitation and high infant mortality. In England nearly 80 years ago he wrote, "No fact is better established than that the death rate, and especially the death rate among children, is high in inverse proportion to the social status of the population" (Newsholme 1910).

Similarly, in summing up his classic study of infant mortality in the United States during the first quarter of this century, Robert Woodbury (1925) noted that infant death rates were "highest when the father's earnings were low and lowest when the father's earnings were relatively high." Although Woodbury's findings suggested that several other variables bore a causal relation to infant mortality (e.g., race, physical condition of the mother, age of mother, type of feeding, length of interval between pregnancies), all of these were highly correlated with the earnings of the father. Thus, in summing up the interrelationship between infant mortality, father's income, and the other causative factors, he concluded:

The analysis indicated that low earnings of the father exerted a potent influence over the prevalence of these factors and therefore must be regarded as primarily responsible for the greater mortality associated with them. The presence of intermediate factors in the chain of causation does not lessen the responsibility of low earnings as a primary cause. (Woodbury 1925)

Twentieth-Century Mortality Declines

Mortality rates have fallen dramatically in much of the world since the early days of the twentieth century, although life expectancy values are still lower than 50 years in a number of the lesser developed countries, particularly in Africa. Recent estimates for the more developed countries of North America and Europe place the average life expectancy between a low of 73 years for Ireland and a high of 77 to 78 years for Iceland, the Netherlands, Sweden, and Switzerland (Population Reference Bureau 1989). The primary causes of this enormous mortality decline in the Western world lie in the unprecedented measure of control gained over those infectious and parasitic diseases that until quite recently took such a heavy toll, especially among the younger elements of the population (Stockwell and Groat 1984). Indeed, the most significant mortality trend of the twentieth century has been an extremely pronounced decline in the death rate among children under 1 year of age. In the United States, for example, there has been a 50 percent reduction in the total death rate since 1900 (from 17.2 to 8.6), but the infant mortality rate during the same period declined by approximately 94 percent (from 162 to 10 per 1,000). Moreover, there is evidence that declines of a similar or even greater magnitude have occurred in a number of western European countries since the beginning of the twentieth century (Woods et al. 1988). In contrast to the situation at the turn of the century, when infant mortality rates were of the order of 150 or more, a number of western European countries today have single-digit infant mortality rates; and in three countries (Finland, Iceland, and Sweden), out of every 1,000 babies born only 6 fail to survive until their first birthdays (Population Reference Bureau 1989). In addition, an infant mortality rate of less than 6 per 1,000 is found in Japan, the first non-European country to achieve a high level of modernization.

In sharp contrast to these single-digit infant mortality rates, or even those approaching 15 throughout more or less developed regions of the globe, infant mortality rates of the order of 100 or more per 1,000 live births are still fairly common in the less developed countries of the Third World. Today they are highest in the least developed countries of Africa: 18 countries on that continent have rates of 125 or more, and in at least 4 countries (Ethiopia, Guinea, Mali, and Sierra Leone) the infant mortality rate continues to exceed 150 per 1,000 live births (Population Reference Bureau 1989).

The high life expectancy values and corresponding low infant mortality rates of the more developed countries stand as an impressive testimony to the success of those countries in improving the quality of life of their populations. Conversely, the low life expectancies and corresponding high infant mortality rates in the less developed countries are, as was the case in Europe a century ago, a reflection of the poor quality of life available to the bulk of the population. In particular, they reflect the inability of existing public health programs to deal with evolving health problems, many of which are related to widespread malnutrition resulting, at least in part, from a decline in social and economic progress

(Gwatkin 1980). In other words, on an international level there remains a clear and strong association between level of modernization and the infant mortality rate. In fact, the association is so strong that the infant mortality rate is generally regarded as a much more accurate indicator of the level of socioeconomic well-being of a people than is its per capita gross national product or any of the other more conventional indices of economic development.

Family Income and Infant Mortality in Modern Societies

The infant mortality decline in the Western world described in the preceding section represents one of the truly outstanding achievements of the twentieth century. At the same time, however, it is very clear that this decline has not altered the nature of the traditional socioeconomic differential. Rather, the findings of a wide variety of studies have consistently shown that the lower income groups in all societies have been and continue to be extremely disadvantaged in the probability that their newborn infants will survive to adulthood. According to a recent effort directed by the present author, the existence of a general inverse association between infant mortality and socioeconomic status has been documented by a great many studies based on widely different population groups, covering different points in time, and using a variety of methods, not only in the United States but in a number of western European countries (Stockwell and Wicks 1981). Moreover, a follow-up investigation documented the existence of such a relationship for all race–sex groups and for all major causes of death (Stockwell, Swanson, and Wicks 1986).

This later study entailed an analysis of infant mortality differentials in a metropolitan aggregate comprising eight of the larger cities in the state of Ohio covering the years 1979–81. The general design of the research was an ecological one in which the primary analytic unit was the census tract of the mother's usual residence. (Census tracts are small geographic areas used in the United States to delimit neighborhoods composed of people possessing relatively homogeneous characteristics. They have no political basis, but are merely statistical aggregates that are used primarily for various planning programs and for research.) The independent variable was defined as the percentage of low-income families in each census tract at the time of the 1980 decennial census. An annual income of $10,000, or roughly 50 percent of the median family income, was selected as the low-income cutoff point.

Table IV.3.1. *Infant mortality rates for income areas in metropolitan Ohio, 1979–81*

| | Infant mortality rate | | |
Income area	Total	Neonatal	Postnatal
All areas	16.6	10.6	6.0
I (high income)	8.9	6.3	2.6
II	14.3	9.2	5.1
III	16.4	10.8	5.6
IV	19.7	12.6	7.1
V (low income)	24.3	14.4	9.9

Source: Stockwell, Swanson, and Wicks (1986, 74).

The dependent-variable data consisted of the number of live births in each census tract during 1980 and the number of infant deaths, by age, in the three years centering on the census date (1979–81). The analysis first used the income variable to aggregate the census tracts of the study cities into five broad groups in such a way that an approximately equal number of tracts fell into each income status group. The resulting aggregates were then ranked and compared in terms of infant deaths – total, neonatal (under 1 month), and postneonatal (1 month to 1 year). The results of these comparisons are presented in Table IV.3.1. Inspection of the data clearly reveals the existence of a consistent and pronounced inverse association between infant mortality and family income, with the differential being especially marked for postneonatal mortality, or for those deaths generally considered to be most influenced by the nature of the environment.

Similar observations can be made with respect to both men and women and for both whites and nonwhites (Stockwell et al. 1986). There are occasional deviations from a consistent linear pattern, but they are not sufficient to detract from the validity of the overall conclusion of the research: The traditional inverse association between infant mortality and family income, first documented in the United States in 1925 (Woodbury 1925), continues to be very pronounced; and it characterizes both the neonatal and postneonatal components of infant mortality, for both sexes and for both major racial groups.

Cause of Death

To understand more fully the association between income status and levels of infant mortality it is necessary to undertake a cause-specific analysis to see if the general inverse nature of the relationship can be explained largely in terms of a few selected causes or groups of causes, or if it more or less characterizes all the major causes of death. In this analysis, the census tracts were grouped into three rather than five income aggregates. A preliminary examination of the data indicated that a larger number of groupings would introduce a serious problem of rate instability because of smaller cell frequencies in the more detailed cross-tabulations. Even with only three areas, small frequencies became a problem when specific causes of death were considered; hence, this analysis was confined to the total population, and most of the comparisons were limited to two broad categories of causes of death. These are *exogenous* causes of death (those whose origin is farthest removed from the actual birth process) and *endogenous* causes of death (those whose origin is most closely associated with the physiological processes of gestation and birth). The specific cause groups, along with their identification codes from the ninth revised edition of the *International Statistical Classification of Diseases and Causes of Death,* are as follows:

Exogenous causes
Infectious and parasitic causes (001–139, 320–3, 460–6, 480–7, 500–8, 771)
Injury or poisoning (800–999)

Endogenous causes
Congenital anomalies (740–59)
Conditions originating in the perinatal period (760–70, 772–9)
Residual endogenous conditions (390–459, 470–8, 490–6, and all causes not elsewhere classified)

The overall exogenous and endogenous death rates for the three income areas, by broad age category, are shown in Table IV.3.2. As is conventional with cause-specific rates, the rates in the table are expressed in terms of 100,000 rather than 1,000 live births. Two conclusions are immediately suggested by these data. First, the vast majority of infant deaths today are caused by the endogenous conditions that are most closely associated with the physiological processes of gestation and birth. Second, both the exogenous and endogenous cause-specific death rates are inversely associated with family income. Not surprisingly, perhaps, the strength of the relationship, as measured by the difference between the death rates of the highest and lowest areas, is much greater for the environmentally related exogenous causes such as infections, accidents, and poisonings. The exogenous death rate in Area III is nearly three times greater than that in Area I. By contrast,

Table IV.3.2. *Infant mortality rates (per 100,000 live births) by broad cause-of-death group for income areas in metropolitan Ohio, 1979–81*

Income area	Exogenous causes			Endogenous causes		
	Total	Neonatal	Postneonatal	Total	Neonatal	Postneonatal
All areas	227	69	158	1,432	990	443
I (high)	129	57	72	998	703	295
II (medium)	201	61	140	1,453	1,023	429
III (low)	363	92	271	1,881	1,262	618

Source: Stockwell, Swanson, and Wicks (1986, 87–93).

the Area III endogenous death rate is only twice as great as that of Area I.

There is a tendency for the exogenous causes to account for an increasing proportion of total deaths as income decreases: 11 percent of the infant deaths in Area I compared with 16 percent in Area III were due to exogenous causes. Thus, it is clear that, despite the much lower absolute death rate, the increased risk of an infant dying as the economic status of its parents declines is relatively much greater from environmentally related exogenous causes than it is from endogenous causes. It is true that the inverse association between infant mortality and economic status seems largely due to conditions that can generally be regarded as amenable to societal control. However, this should not lead one to minimize the significance of a consistent and pronounced inverse relationship for those endogenous conditions less resistant to control, which account for the vast majority of infant deaths.

Inspection of the exogenous–endogenous rates for the neonatal and postneonatal ages reveals that the pronounced inverse association with economic status characterizes both of the causal groups for both segments of infant mortality. The more interesting point here, however, is perhaps the challenge these data pose to the traditional distinction between neonatal–endogenous as opposed to postneonatal–exogenous mortality. In the past, demographers and other epidemiological researchers have commonly used the neonatal and postneonatal death rates as proxies for endogenous and exogenous mortality (Bourgeois-Pichat 1952). Yet while the Ohio data show a clear preponderance of endogenous causes in the neonatal period (93 percent), they also reveal a preponderance of endogenous causes among postneonatal deaths (74 percent). The increasing importance of the endogenous causes in the latter period likely reflects the nature of the technological progress made in recent years in enhancing the surviv-

ability of high-risk births. In other words, many infants who a generation ago would have died within a few days or weeks after birth now have a much greater chance of surviving. For some, this change will mean a chance to survive infancy and grow to adulthood leading relatively normal lives. For others, however, it will mean surviving the neonatal period only to succumb later in infancy; the frequency of deaths due to endogenous causes in the postneonatal period thus increases (Miller 1985). In any case, these findings indicate that there is no longer any basis for assuming an age–cause proxy relationship in infancy such as may have existed in the past (Stockwell, Swanson, and Wicks 1987).

Our results demonstrated that the same general conclusions apply to both sexes as well as to the two racial groups: Endogenous causes clearly predominate in all categories, and both cause-specific rates are inversely related to income status for all sex–color groups (Stockwell, Swanson, and Wicks 1988). Moreover, this pattern was also strongly apparent in those few instances where the numbers were sufficiently large to permit a comparison based on more specific causes of death (Stockwell et al. 1988).

Overall, the results of our research show that the basic inverse relationship between infant mortality and socioeconomic status cannot be attributed solely, or even largely, to either group of causes. Although more deaths are due to endogenous than to exogenous causes, and more deaths occur in the neonatal period regardless of cause, the variations in the death rates for both broad cause groups are characterized by a similar marked inverse differential for all major subgroups in the society.

Conclusion

In spite of significant progress in maternal and infant care and an associated substantial decline in infant mortality in this century, our research, as well as that of many other contemporary scholars, points to the persistence of a strong inverse association between economic status and the probability that a newborn infant will survive the first year of life. Although there are occasional exceptions or various degrees of deviation from a perfectly linear pattern, the overriding conclusion is that infant mortality rates among lower income groups continue to be substantially above those of higher income groups.

This conclusion implicitly assumes that causality runs solely from low income to high infant mortality. But though such an assumption can be justified on the grounds that we are dealing with infants rather than adults, we cannot rule out the possibility that the general inverse relationship reflects two-way causality. That is, the poor health of parents may contribute to lower income, which is such a potent determinant of infant life chances. This possibility does not detract, however, from the validity of the overall conclusion, namely that the infant mortality rate is a powerful indicator of the general health status of a population group.

The fact that infant mortality rates have declined at all income levels obviously indicates that the benefits of new and improved infant health care programs do reach all segments of the population eventually. However, the persistence of the strong inverse association between infant mortality and income status points to the existence of a social class differential in access to health care services and facilities. The first to benefit from advances in medical technology and other health care improvements are those in the highest income classes, and only gradually do the fruits of such progress filter down to the economically deprived groups. This is indicative of an elitist approach to the delivery of health care, and in the Western world, where it is supposed that adequate health care is a basic right for all citizens, and not just an expensive privilege for those who can afford it, this situation presents a major challenge to society.

Efforts to meet this challenge must, of course, be guided by the knowledge that a wide variety of factors associated with a low economic status contribute to the observed differences in mortality, and that each of these factors will require very different kinds of programs to bring them under control. In the past, major efforts focused on those factors that exerted a direct influence on the survival chances of infants, including the adequacy of their diet; the quality of housing, water, and home sanitary facilities; and their immunization status.

These factors, which directly influence exogenous causes (e.g., parasitic diseases and respiratory infections), have already been brought fairly well under control by various public health programs, and what were once the major killers of infants and young children now account for a very small fraction of the total deaths under 1 year of age. Nevertheless, because the exogenous-disease death rates continue to vary inversely with economic status, it is clear that the progress made in the prevention and treatment of these diseases has not benefited all groups equally. There is an obvious need to continue and even accelerate efforts to extend the full benefits of advances in medical knowledge and health care practices to the more economically deprived segments of the population.

By far the biggest challenge today, however, concerns endogenous conditions, which account for about 80 percent of all infant deaths in the United States. These causes, which have traditionally been regarded as less amenable to societal control, reflect such things as social class differences in reproductive behavior (age at childbearing, length of interval between pregnancies), differences in the amount and quality of prenatal care (timing of first prenatal examination, frequency of visits), and other maternal characteristics such as adequacy of diet during pregnancy, amount of weight gain, smoking habits, and the use of drugs or alcohol. These factors generally have an indirect impact on infant mortality through their effect on pregnancy outcome – particularly on birth weight.

It has recently been recognized that a low birth weight seriously impairs an infant's chances for survival. A major policy goal, therefore, should be the prevention of low birth weights. Evidence suggests that efforts to do this must go beyond simply providing more and better prenatal care and concentrate on enhancing the overall quality of life and general health status of low-income mothers (Wise et al. 1985). A similar conclusion applies to less developed countries, where it is also recognized that reducing high infant mortality rates will depend more on general socioeconomic development than on the implementation of conventional health strategies (Gwatkin 1980). In the meantime, we will continue to live in a world where the level of infant mortality serves as a major barometer of the quality of life in any given environmental setting and the overall health status of the population.

Edward G. Stockwell

Bibliography

Bourgeois-Pichat, Jean. 1952. Essai sur la mortalité biologique de l'homme. *Population* 7: 381–94.
Dublin, Louis I., Alfred J. Lotka, and Mortimer Spiegelman. 1949. *Length of life*. New York.

Gwatkin, Davidson. 1980. Indications of change in developing country mortality trends: The end of an era? *Population and Development Review* 6: 615–44.

Miller, C. Arden. 1985. Infant mortality in the U.S. *Scientific American* 253: 31–7.

Newsholme, Arthur. 1910. *Thirty-ninth annual report of the local government board,* Report C d 5312. London.

Population Reference Bureau. 1989. *World population data sheet: 1989*. Washington, D.C.

Russell, J. C. 1958. *Late ancient and medieval populations.* Philadelphia.

Shryock, Henry S., et al. 1976. *The methods and materials of demography,* condensed ed. by Edward G. Stockwell. New York.

Stockwell, Edward G., and Jerry W. Wicks. 1981. *Socioeconomic differentials in infant mortality*. Rockville, Md.

Stockwell, Edward G., and H. Theodore Groat. 1984. *World population: An introduction to demography.* New York.

Stockwell, Edward G., David A. Swanson, and Jerry W. Wicks. 1986. *Socioeconomic correlates of infant mortality: Ohio, 1980*. Rockville, Md.

  1987. The age–cause proxy relationship in infant mortality. *Social Biology* 34: 249–53.

  1988. Economic status differences in infant mortality by cause of death. *Public Health Reports* 103: 135–42.

U.S. Bureau of the Census. 1960. *Historical statistics of the United States: Colonial times to 1957*. Washington, D.C.

Wise, Paul H., et al. 1985. Racial and socioeconomic disparities in childhood mortality in Boston. *New England Journal of Medicine* 313: 360–6.

Woodbury, Robert M. 1925. *Causal factors in infant mortality*. Washington, D.C.

Woods, R. I., P. A. Watterson, and J. H. Woodward. 1988. The cause of rapid infant mortality decline in England and Wales, 1861–1921, Part 1. *Population Studies* 42: 343–66.

  1989. The cause of rapid infant mortality decline in England and Wales, 1861–1921, Part 2. *Population Studies* 43: 113–32.

IV.4
Measuring Morbidity and Mortality

Sickness and death are individual- and population-level phenomena. At the individual level, they are best understood in terms of their causes. In illness the best prognosis derives from what is known about the cause and about the individual. At the population level, sickness and death can also be understood in terms of incidence. Future rates of sickness and death can be forecast from experience, taking into account the trend and likely variations from it. Population-level statements about sickness and death – morbidity and mortality rates – can be considered statements of comparison. As such, they underlie many judgments about health and health care.

Morbidity and mortality are also structural phenomena, which is to say that, considered for a sizable number of people, they display certain regularities. The most important of these relate to age and appear as curves or schedules when morbidity and mortality data are arranged by age. Age-specific sickness and death rates should not be expected to be identical in any two populations, but their structure – their distribution by age – should be similar. This makes it possible to make estimates for missing data and to compare individual- and population-level experience with sickness and death over time. This essay summarizes the basic method of analysis, which employs a life table, and suggests some ways in which the problem of incomplete information can be overcome with various estimation procedures.

Quantity of Life

Like other life forms, humans have a characteristic life span, a maximum number of years over which individuals might survive if protected from all hazards. The span is currently unknown. Our only direct evidence about it derives from the age at death of exceptionally long-lived people, and the reliability of this evidence is often marred by poor memory, poor records, and misrepresentation. A few people have lived longer than 110 years, and the number of people surviving to extreme ages has increased over time. But it is not clear – because the evidence is inadequate – whether there has been a change in the maximum age to which individual members of the species survive. Given the very small number of

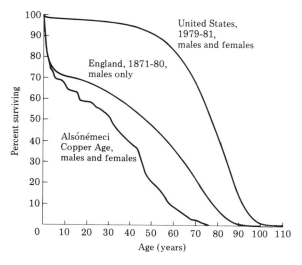

Figure IV.4.1. Survival curves. (From Acsádi and Nemeskéri 1970; Commons Sessional Papers 1884–5; U.S. Decennial Life Tables for 1979–81.)

people who survive to even older ages, the life span is often estimated at 110 and sometimes at a lower round number, 100 (Preston 1982).

An alternative procedure for estimating longevity is based on the attempt to measure the most advanced age to which people survive in significant numbers. It can safely be suggested that over most of human existence the modal age at death – the age at which more individuals died than at any other – was during the first year. Among people surviving early childhood, however, the modal age at death occurred in adulthood. Apparently it has advanced over time. A life table based on skeletal evidence for a Copper Age population indicates that the number of postinfant deaths peaked at age 46, but late-twentieth-century life tables show a much later peak. For example, a U.S. life table for 1979–81 indicates a postinfant modal age at death of 83 (Acsádi and Nemeskéri 1970; U.S. National Center for Health Statistics 1985). Estimates of the species-specific life span or values for the modal age at death are used to show capacity for survival. Often expressed as a rectangle, this capacity is a statement about how many years of life individuals born at the same time might accumulate if they avoided hazards.

These estimates have been less important in measuring and comparing health experience than they will become. The transition can be attributed to a major change in the pattern of human survival. For most of the history of the species, the space of life – the area represented by the survival rectangle – contained more years of life lost to premature death than years survived. Figure IV.4.1 illustrates this

history with survival curves for some populations, the curves showing the number of individuals who lived at each age.

For most of human history most deaths were premature, and the survival curve remained concave. It first became convex in a few advantaged societies in the nineteenth century. Since then, it has bowed out in these and some other societies, approaching a rectangular form. The concave curve can be identified with the traditional mortality regime, a regime in which the risk of death was high at every age. The convex curve is a characteristic of the modern mortality regime. And the convexity itself indicates how the transition from one mortality regime to the other has altered the problems associated with measuring mortality. For most of human history, expectations or hopes about survival have been expressed by reference to birth. The rectangularized survival curve directs attention instead toward life span, modal age at death, or another value intended to represent a survival goal. In other words, how many of the people living at the same time can be protected from premature death, and how long can they be protected?

The survival curve captures the concepts needed to compare mortality experiences. The data necessary to plot it are drawn from the life table, initially developed as a way to set insurance premiums, but subsequently put to use in epidemiology, biology, and demography. The estimation of survival curves and other elements of the life table are commonplace in historical discussion, although they are more often implicit than explicit because historians seldom work with periods and populations for which life tables exist.

One useful estimate of mortality experience is the crude death rate, the ratio of deaths in a given year to the mean population during that year. This rate is a function of the age distribution as well as the number of deaths at each age. Consider, for example, the crude death rates for the United States and Costa Rica in 1977 – 8.6 and 4.3, respectively. The lower rate for Costa Rica means a lower probability of death, but it is lower because the age structure was different in the United States rather than because the risk of death was lower at each age. In fact, Costa Ricans faced a higher mortality risk at most ages, but the younger average age offset the difference in risk of death.

The crude death rate is also influenced by migration. For example, populations receiving immigrants of a certain age group, say young adults, will appear to have higher life expectancies based on the record

Table IV.4.1. *Abridged life table for Sweden, 1751–90*

Age interval, x to $x + 1$	Proportion dying in interval, q_x	Number living at beginning of age interval, l_x	Number dying in age interval, d_x	Years lived in age interval, L_x	Accumulated years lived, T_x	Life expectation, e_x
0	0.20825	10,000	2,082	8,314	351,935	35.19
1	0.10406	7,918	824	14,884	343,621	43.40
3	0.05642	7,094	400	13,788	328,737	46.34
5	0.06700	6,694	448	32,350	314,949	47.05
10	0.03621	6,246	226	30,663	282,599	45.24
15	0.03527	6,020	213	29,567	251,936	41.85
20	0.04270	5,807	248	28,417	222,369	38.29
25	0.05065	5,559	281	27,092	193,952	34.89
30	0.05957	5,278	315	25,605	166,860	31.61
35	0.06056	4,963	300	24,065	141,255	28.46
40	0.07947	4,663	371	22,387	117,190	25.13
45	0.08611	4,292	369	20,537	94,803	22.09
50	0.10820	3,923	425	18,552	74,266	18.93
55	0.12935	3,498	452	16,359	55,714	15.93
60	0.18615	3,046	567	13,811	39,355	12.92
65	0.25879	2,479	642	10,790	25,544	10.30
70	0.36860	1,837	677	7,463	14,754	8.03
75	0.47839	1,160	555	4,443	7,291	6.29
80	0.63916	605	387	2,059	2,848	4.71
85	0.77971	218	170	789	789	3.62
90+	1.0	48	48	(123)[a]	(123)[a]	2.56

[a]The adaptation supplies the sum of years lived at 90 and higher ages.
Source: Adapted from Fritzell (1953).

of deaths than will more stable societies. Although there is often no more than fragmentary information about age structure or migration, the effects of these variables may require that the crude death rate be qualified by a statement concerning its possible distortion. In addition to reasons already mentioned, the crude rate may be misleading if, in a regime prone to epidemics, it is not averaged over several years.

Age-specific death rates can be compared (over time and space) in the form of the survival curves in Figure IV.4.1. Comparisons can also be made on the basis of age-standardized death rates, which adjust age-specific rates for a standardized population (this procedure and others are explained by Shryock et al. 1973). The reason for making these calculations of death rates is to compare two or more populations on the same terms, eliminating the effects of differences in age structure. (This procedure can also be applied to other characteristics according to which mortality or morbidity rates may differ, such as sex, residence, occupation, and marital status.)

With information about the size of a population,

the age of its members, and the number who die at each age – or plausible estimates of these quantities – it is possible to build a life table such as the one for Sweden during 1751–90 presented in Table IV.4.1. The table begins with a radix, or base population – in this case 10,000. The probabilities of death at each age, the basic quantities of the life table, are derived from age-specific death rates. Both the death rate and the probability of death at an age have the same numerator – the number of deaths at that age within a specific time period. But their denominators differ. For the death rate, the denominator is the mean population at that age over the period studied, and for the probability of dying, it is the population at that age at the beginning of the period under study. This difference is usually minor, except when one is considering the probability of death between two ages that are separated by a number of years (e.g., from 5 to 10) and except for infants.

A current, or period, life table makes use of death rates for all ages at a given time to provide a cross-sectional picture of a stationary population. Its values for life expectancy and other quantities are termed hypothetical because the death rates used to construct it apply to people at each age in the current population; the history it relates refers to a hypothetical cohort, because the people alive at this time may have been subject to different death rates in past years and may be subject to differences again in the future. A cohort, or generation, life table follows the experience of one cohort from birth to death. Its values are not hypothetical, but a cohort table cannot be constructed until all members of a cohort have died. Thus, a current table, like that in Table IV.4.1, is preferred for many uses.

When populations are small, as Sweden's population was in the eighteenth century, and when death rates fluctuate from year to year, it is customary to average experience over several years. Table IV.4.1 is also an abridged table, meaning that it provides values only for benchmark ages. Those in between can be interpolated. Because the number of years lived by the cohort at high ages is so small, the custom is to close the life table at an age that is lower than that of the oldest survivor and to sum the years lived at all higher ages. The accumulated years lived by the actual or hypothetical cohort, which is the sum of years lived in each interval, provides the information necessary to calculate life expectancy. From Table IV.4.1 life expectancy at birth (35.2) is the sum of all years lived by the hypothetical cohort (351,935) divided by the radix population (10,000); life expectancy at age 20 (38.3) is the sum of years lived after 20 (222,369) divided by the number surviving to 20 (5,807).

What makes the life table so useful for historical investigation is its capacity to represent a sequence of events over a long span. Thus, the life table has been used to estimate changes in the prevalence of specific diseases over time. Although the events of interest in this essay are mortality and episodes of morbidity, other events, such as marriage and divorce, can also be followed, as can conditional events, such as deaths among people already ill. Age-specific death rates are conditional because they depend on survival to each age. The population whose experience is followed over time may be select in the sense that its members differ in significant ways from the general population. The life table need not begin at birth or be limited to single events. More complex models treat contingent events that occur in stages, such as the evolution of cancer, with its various outcomes and probabilities at each stage. The concept can also be applied to the longevity of political regimes or credit instruments.

Because historians often know or can reliably estimate the death rate at a few ages but not throughout the life course, it is helpful to employ model life tables to make inferences about other ages or to estimate the overall structure of mortality. Model tables are based on the observation that mortality risks show some regularities over time. Populations that have low death rates at one age are likely to have low death rates at other ages, and vice versa. The regularities can be seen by plotting the mortality schedule, which consists of a line linking age-specific probabilities of death. (When the change from one benchmark to another is high, it is convenient to plot values on paper with a vertical logarithmic scale. On this scale an exponential rate of change appears as a straight line.) Figure IV.4.2 shows that the form of the mortality schedule resembles a misshapen W across the survival rectangle. Over time the W-curve has usually shifted down, so that at each age lower mortality rates are reported for recent, as opposed to past, populations.

Close scrutiny of life tables from a variety of populations shows that the W-shape is preserved across time, but that it displays some irregularities. In some populations the risk of death is greater at some ages than it is in other populations. In Figure IV.4.2, for instance, the angle of change in the mortality risk varies among the three populations, most evidently at adult ages. As can be seen, the U.S. 1979–81 schedule is lower than the other two, yet its rate of increase between ages 40 and 80 is steeper. But for these variations, model life tables would suggest all other age-specific mortality rates when only one was known. Because of these variations, demographers have fashioned groups or "families" of model life tables, each representing a variation on the basic form. One widely used collection of model tables provides four families, styled West, North, South, and East, and a variety of mortality schedules or levels (Coale and Demeny 1966; McCann 1976). With model tables, which are most readily conceived from their survival curves, incomplete information about mortality experience in a given population can provide the basis for a plausible estimate of complete experience.

Life expectancy, which incorporates age-specific death risks, is a convenient value for making historical comparisons. Over time, life expectancy at birth has advanced, and the story of that advance is part of the history of mortality and the mortality revolution. Whereas life expectancy is most commonly used as an estimate of the average remaining lifetime at birth, it also captures changes in death rates

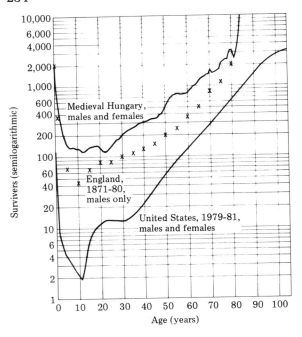

Figure IV.4.2. Mortality risk for medieval Hungary, England (1871–80), and the United States (1979–81). (From Acsádi and Nemeskéri 1970; Commons Sessional Papers 1884–5; U.S. Decennial Life Tables for 1979–81.)

at different ages. During the modern period of mortality decline, which began in the eighteenth century and has not yet ended, the risk of death did not decline in a uniform way across the age spectrum (Perrenoud 1979, 1985; Imhof 1985). In northwestern Europe, for example, the decline during the eighteenth century was concentrated among infants, youths, and young adults. Other age groups joined the shift toward declining risks later.

Life expectancy commonly appears to increase to a greater extent when measured at birth than when measured at higher ages. That is, the risk of death has declined more in infancy (up to age 1) than at any later age. It is often reported that life expectancy at higher ages, especially in adulthood, has changed relatively little over time. In some ways this is misleading. Thinking once more in terms of the survival rectangle, a disproportion is apparent in the time at risk. At birth some members of a population might be expected to live 110 years. But at each higher age their potential survival time is bounded by the human life span; it diminishes as age rises. In short, life expectancy can also be construed as an indication of how much of the available space of life has been used.

By turning our attention toward both birth and

some representation of maximum survival and by reporting an age-specific measure of mortality at several points within the life course, we obtain means of detecting more subtle changes in mortality experience. Whereas life expectancy represents the average remaining lifetime, another measure, years of potential life lost (YPLL), compares the average span achieved with the number of years that it can plausibly be supposed a population might survive. Because that value is indefinite, no convention yet exists for measuring YPLL. The U.S. National Center for Health Statistics presently uses a base of 65 years. That gauge assigns greater weight to causes of death the earlier those causes intervene, and no weight to causes that intervene at ages above 65.

Although not yet applied extensively to historical investigations, the YPLL provides a way to think about the degree to which different societies succeed in controlling mortality. If the YPLL is not adjusted for changes over time, more modern societies will systematically appear more successful than earlier societies because they have higher life expectancies. But judgments about success need not depend on the assumption implicit in this comparison, the assumption that all societies have the same potential for increasing the years its members can expect, on average, to live. If the ceiling is adjusted – perhaps using changing modal age at death – different interpretations of changes in survival may emerge. If the ceiling is adjusted with an eye on one or a few causes of death of particular interest, societies can be compared according to the efficacy of their control over leading diseases (see Preston, Keyfitz, and Schoen 1971).

Quality of Life

Mortality rates and other statistics derived from them imply that we have measures for the number of years survived. Yet equally measured mortality levels may represent quite different qualitative experiences. In search of ways to capture the quality of life, researchers have selected mortality indexes believed to be more revealing, such as infant or maternal mortality, and have combined vital and economic statistics. One index, used widely to compare the quality of life in Third World countries, is the Physical Quality of Life Index, which uses a weighted average of several demographic and economic statistics (Morris 1979). It has some possibilities for application to historical societies for which equivalent data are available.

A more promising approach to the quality of life draws on health statistics. Unlike mortality, ill health – morbidity – is not an unambiguous quantity. Individuals and societies make different decisions about the threshold between health and ill health, and these decisions raise problems concerning definitions and measurements of ill health. Some standard gauges rely on diagnostic evidence; these are encountered in reports of the number of cases of specific diseases identified in a given region and period. Other gauges are based on contact with health institutions or personnel (hospitalizations, physician visits). Still others depend on evidence about individual performance, such as restricted activity, bed disability, or work time lost; these measures are often encountered in insurance records and health surveys. Because different sources provide different forms of evidence, the important point is to find a gauge whose definition is consistent (Riley 1989).

Morbidity also differs from mortality in its complexity. Different questions are at issue. A morbidity rate may express the number of times members of a population fall ill during a period (incidence), the proportion of the population ill at a given time (prevalence), or the amount of time spent in illness by a population during a given period (duration). To take only the two extreme cases – incidence and duration – the age-specific risk of falling sick (incidence) is concave and resembles the inside of a shallow bowl, and that of being sick (duration) looks like the misshapen W identified earlier. Figure IV.4.3 provides examples of these morbidity curves, using Friendly Society records from nineteenth-century Britain (Riley 1987). Like the mortality schedule, the morbidity schedule may move up or down over time, a factor influenced by objective health experience and by subjective decisions about the threshold between health and ill health. Individual curves are likely to vary from these forms, especially when the characteristics of the population under observation change over time. For example, the National Health Interview Survey shows a morbidity schedule with a slower rate of increase at higher ages, a factor attributable in part to the exclusion of institutionalized members of the population from the survey (National Center for Health Statistics). More investigations of health experience in historical societies will help identify the causes of variation (Larsen 1979; Beier 1985; Pelling 1985).

Morbidity rates in turn can be used in association

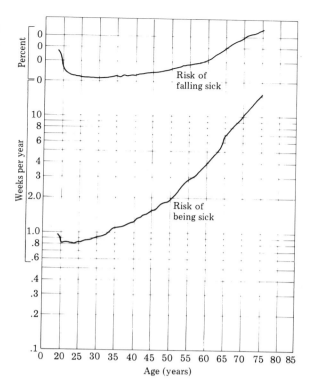

Figure IV.4.3. Morbidity rates for nineteenth-century Britain. (From Nelson 1982.)

with mortality rates to estimate the number of ill-health episodes to be expected in the average remaining lifetime or, alternatively, the proportion of lifetime remaining to be spent in ill or good health. The technique makes use of age-specific morbidity rates in combination with mortality risks in the life table. The health expectation, sometimes called the active life expectation, uses the age-specific risks of mortality and being sick to estimate the remaining lifetime and the portion of that time to be spent in good health (Riley 1989).

If changes in ill-health rates paralleled those in mortality rates, the two rising or falling together, then morbidity risks and health expectation could be estimated from mortality risks. But investigation of the association between mortality and morbidity suggests that the straightforward form of this tie – deaths are attributed to ill health – belies the statistical and population-level associations. Rates of falling sick and being sick change independently of mortality rates, which is to say that the risk of dying once one is sick changes over time. The association is conditioned by environmental forces, such as therapeutic regime or standard of living, and by changes in the composition of the population that can be attributed to mortality. For example, insurance records and health surveys show that the mortality decline of the twentieth century has been accompanied by increased duration of ill health at each age (Alter and Riley 1989).

In other words, the proportion of people dying from a given disease or injury – the case fatality rate – has shifted. Changes have occurred in the percentage of people surviving, a concept dramatically illustrated by the history of diseases that vary in virulence or that cause death much more often among people with no prior contact with them than among people relatively resistant to them, and familiar also in terms of changes in the efficacy of therapies. The case fatality rate is a useful way to measure the severity of diseases that have a short course. For chronic diseases, however, it is necessary to consider the prolonged duration of an ailment and the likelihood of death from another cause during its course. A related notion, which might be termed case duration, is the time between onset and resolution. That period may change as diagnostic practices shift or as a population's view of the ill-health threshold or its recognition of ill-health episodes changes. And it may also shift when new therapies are introduced. Because, with notable exceptions, case fatality rates as high as 50 percent have been rare, it is apparent that most ill-health episodes are resolved in recovery. Even in acute diseases, duration has been an important element in the disabling effects of illness, injury, and collective violence.

Variations

Some leading causes of variations in mortality and morbidity include sex, income, residence, season, and disease profile. Separate tables are usually calculated for each sex because of differences in male and female experience, which are partly biological and partly environmental in origin. Figure IV.4.4 shows two forms of this variation by exhibiting mortality curves for men and women in Sweden during 1816–40 and 1979–83. In recent centuries male mortality has exceeded female mortality at most ages, a characteristic that seems to suggest a biological advantage for the latter (Verbrugge 1985).

Socioeconomic status is another well-recognized cause of variation in mortality. Wealthier members of a population, in the aggregate, face lower health risks, although the causation appears to operate in

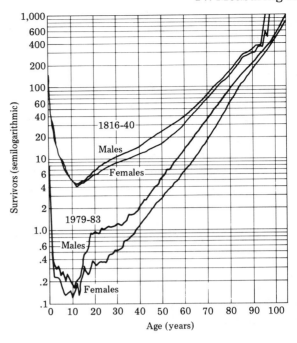

Figure IV.4.4. Mortality schedules for Sweden, 1816–40 and 1979–83. (From Sundbarg 1970; *Statistisk ärsbok för Sverige* 1986.)

both directions: Greater wealth is partly an effect of lower health risks and partly a cause.

Disease-Specific Measurements

Mortality records identifying cause of death lend themselves to disease-specific measurements and to analyses of trends of individual diseases and disease profiles (Preston et al. 1971; McKeown 1976). Although the size of the population at risk of death is often unknown for periods before the twentieth century, the annual number of deaths constitutes a denominator.

Heterogeneity

Average experience within a group can be a useful indicator, but there are many instances in which the average, and variations on it, are misleading. These occur when the distribution of vital events within a population is uneven. Thus, life expectancy at birth is a misleading measure of survival in seventeenth-century Europe because deaths occurred with two modes, infancy and late adulthood. This example is well known, and authorities regularly point to the rapid increase in life expectancy among people who survived infancy and early childhood. Irregular distributions – those taking a form other than the normal or bell curve – are often encountered. They signal something called heterogeneity – incompatible or nonproportionate elements. For example, future health is in part a function of prior health, so that some authorities suggest that a cohort divides itself into two modes, one with a high and the other with a low propensity to be sick. Thus, an average figure – such as the average age for retirement, 65 – may misstate cohort experience in such circumstances.

Members of the same cohort may have disparate health experiences, in ways just suggested, but the likelihood of disparity is greater still when different cohorts are compared. The health experiences of a cohort are shaped by the circumstances encountered at each stage in life, so that each cohort accumulates a unique health history. In modern advantaged societies these differences remain, but their magnitudes are such that they have little measured effect on basic vital statistics. Thus, life expectancy at a given age varies little in the short run. But in historical populations the disparity may be marked. In seventeenth-century England, life expectancy at birth shifted dramatically from cohort to cohort. The population alive in 1750, for example, included individuals who had survived such disparate events as the plague of 1665 and the as yet incompletely identified forces of the mid-eighteenth century favoring mortality decline. Sporadic epidemics caused the number of deaths and the death rate to fluctuate, with the result that the number of years lived by each cohort varied between wide boundaries (Wrigley and Schofield 1981). This shifting cohort pattern is a historical rhythm that deserves recognition.

James C. Riley

Bibliography

Acsádi, Gy., and J. Nemeskéri. 1970. *History of human life span and mortality*, trans. K. Balás. Budapest.

Alter, George, and James C. Riley. 1989. Frailty, sickness, and death: Models of morbidity and mortality in historical populations. *Population Studies* 43: 25–45.

Beier, Lucinda McCray. 1985. In sickness and in health: A seventeenth-century family's experience. In *Patients and practitioners: Lay perceptions of medicine in pre-industrial society,* ed. Roy Porter, 101–28. Cambridge.

Benjamin, B., and H. W. Haycocks. 1970. *The analysis of mortality and other actuarial statistics.* Cambridge.

Chiang, Chin Long. 1984. *The life table and its applications.* Malabar, Fla.

Coale, Ansley J., and Paul Demeny. 1966. *Regional model life tables and stable populations.* Princeton, N.J.

Curtin, Philip D. 1986. African health at home and abroad. *Social Science History* 10: 369–98.

Dublin, Louis I., Alfred J. Lotka, and Mortimer Spiegelman. 1949. *Length of life: A study of the life table.* New York.

Fritzell, Yngve. 1953. Overlevelsetabeller för Sverige för 1751–1815. *Statistisk tidskrift,* New Ser., 2: 406–10.

Great Britain, House of Commons. 1884–5. Sessional Papers. *Supplement to the 45th annual report of the Registrar-General of Births, Deaths and Marriages in England* 17(365): vii–viii.

Imhof, Arthur E. 1985. From the old mortality pattern to the new: Implications of a radical change from the sixteenth century to the twentieth century. *Bulletin of the History of Medicine* 59: 1–29.

Larsen, Øivind. 1979. Eighteenth-century diseases, diagnostic trends, and mortality. Paper presented at the Fifth Scandinavian Demographic Symposium.

Manton, Kenneth G., and Eric Stallard. 1984. *Recent trends in mortality analysis.* Orlando, Fla.

McCann, James C. 1976. A technique for estimating life expectancy with crude vital rates. *Demography* 13: 259–72.

McKeown, Thomas. 1976. *The modern rise of population.* London.

Morris, Morris David. 1979. *Measuring the condition of the world's poor: The physical quality of life index.* New York.

Neilson, Francis G. P. 1882. *The rates of mortality and sickness according to the experience of the five years, 1871–1875, of the Ancient Order of Foresters Friendly Society.* London.

Palmore, James A., and Robert W. Gardner. 1983. *Measuring mortality, fertility, and natural increase: A self-teaching guide to elementary measures.* Honolulu.

Pelling, Margaret. 1985. Healing the sick poor: Social policy and disability in Norwich, 1550–1640. *Medical History* 29: 115–37.

Perrenoud, Alfred. 1979. *La population de Genève du seizième au début du dix-neuvième siècle: Etude démographique.* Geneva.

1985. Le biologique et l'humain dans le déclin seculaire de la mortalité. *Annales: Economies, sociétés, civilisations* 40: 113–35.

Pressat, Roland. 1978. *Statistical demography,* trans. Damien A. Courtney. New York.

Preston, Samuel H., ed. 1982. *Biological and social aspects of mortality and the length of life.* Liege.

Preston, Samuel H., Nathan Keyfitz, and Robert Schoen. 1971. *Causes of death: Life tables for national populations.* New York.

Riley, James C. 1987. Ill health during the English mortality decline: The Friendly Societies' experience. *Bulletin of the History of Medicine* 61: 563–88.

1989. *Sickness, recovery and death.* London.

Shryock, Henry S., et. al. 1973. *The methods and materials of demography*. Washington, D.C.

Sundbärg, Gustav. 1970. *Bevölkerungsstatistik Schwedens, 1750–1900*. Stockholm.

Sweden, Statistiska Centralbyrärn. 1986. *Statistisk ärrsbok för Sverige: 1986*. Stockholm.

U.S. National Center for Health Statistics. [Annual] Current estimates from the national health interview survey. *Vital and health statistics*, Ser. 10. Washington, D.C.

————. 1985. *U.S. decennial life tables for 1979–81*. Vol. 1, No. 1. Department of Health and Human Services Publ. No. (PHS) 85-1150-1. Washington, D.C.

Vallin, Jacques, John H. Pollard, and Larry Heligman, eds. 1984. *Methodologies for the collection and analysis of mortality data*. Liege.

Verbrugge, Lois M. 1985. Gender and health: An update on hypotheses and evidence. *Journal of Health and Social Behavior* 26: 156–82.

Wrigley, E. A., and R. S. Schofield. 1981. *The population history of England, 1541–1871*. Cambridge, Mass.

IV.5
Stature and Health

In conventional terms the standard of living has become practically synonymous with a material standard, and consequently the concept has most often been equated with and measured by per capita income. Yet it can be interpreted much more broadly to encompass the psychological and biological dimensions of human existence (i.e., the quality of life in all of its manifestations). Distinguishing among these components of well-being would not add much that is conceptually meaningful to our understanding of the past if they all correlated positively and perfectly with one another. But recent empirical evidence has tended to show the importance of not conflating them into one concept.

Historians have begun to explore ways to illuminate this issue from another perspective, namely by considering the biological standard of living as an equally valid measurement of human well-being (Komlos 1989). One approach has been to study the health of historical populations, though this avenue is obviously limited by the scanty systematic evidence at our disposal (Riley and Alter 1986). Another approach has been to consider mortality an integral component of welfare and, in fact, to incorporate mortality into the conventional index of the material standard of living (Williamson 1981, 1982; Davin 1988). Yet this attempt to collapse the biological and material standards of living into a single index is vexed by the inherent difficulty of gauging the monetary value of human life.

Still another promising approach, and one with an abundant evidential basis from the seventeenth century onward, is anthropometric history, meaning the analysis of secular changes in human height, weight, and weight for height (Tanner 1981; Fogel 1987; Komlos 1987; Ward 1987; Riggs 1988; Cuff 1989; Floud and Wachter 1989). This way of looking at the issue acknowledges outright the inherent multidimensionality of the standard of living, and furthermore assumes that the several dimensions might be orthogonal to one another, which is to say that they generally cannot be collapsed into one indicator. The agenda of this research program is to construct indexes of the biological standard of living of various populations over time, by social class and gender if possible, and to ascertain how this indicator correlates with the material standard of life conventionally conceived.

Anthropometric measures are an important part of this research program, because they enable one to quantify nutritional status, which hitherto has eluded historians. This line of reasoning is based on medical research, which has established beyond doubt that the net cumulative nutritional intake of a population has a major influence on its average height, with maternal nutrition also playing a significant role (Fogel, Engerman, and Trussel 1982; Falkner and Tanner 1986). Thus, height at a particular age, as well as the terminal height attained by a population, is a measure of cumulative net nutrition: the food consumed during the growing years minus the claims on the nutrients of basal metabolism, of energy expenditure, and of encounters with disease (Tanner 1978). As nutritional status increases, more calories and protein are available for physical growth, and the closer individuals and populations come to reaching their genetic potentials of height.

The terminal height an individual reaches in a given population is also influenced by genetic factors, but this consideration does not affect studies of the evolution of human height as long as the genetic composition of the population is not dramatically altered by large-scale migration.

Holding the genetic composition of the population constant, nutritional status, measured by height, is at once an indicator of exposure to disease and of health in general. It correlates positively with food consumption and with life expectancy, and consequently shows how well the human organism thrives in its particular economic, epidemiological, and social environment (Friedman 1982). Consequently, height is a much more encompassing variable than are real wages and has the advantage in a historical context of being available for groups, such as subsistence peasants and aristocrats, for whom real wages are not pertinent.

Food consumption in prior centuries was the major component of total expenditure (Cipolla 1980), and therefore height can also be used as a proxy for real income. The positive relationship between height and income has been amply documented for twentieth-century populations, for which both variables are available (Steckel 1983; Brinkman, Drukker, and Slot 1988). Yet some caveats are in order. The distribution of income has been found to affect the mean stature of a population. Furthermore, the composition of the food consumed is also of some consequence, because the mix of calorie and protein intake is important to the growth process. This question of mix is complicated by the fact that protein is made up of many amino acids, and it is the combination of amino acids, not only their absolute quantity, that ultimately influences growth and physical well-being. Finally, food consumption obviously depends not only on real income, but also on the price of food relative to all other products. In a society in which commercialization has not proceeded very far, the availability of industrial products might be limited and therefore their prices are high. Once the availability of industrial goods increases through market integration, the structure of food consumption might change discontinuously and rapidly as a consequence of substitution. Economic development might also lead to the introduction of new products, such as coffee, tea, or sugar, that could be perceived as substitutes for some nutritious food items. This, in turn, may lead to shifts in the demand for food independently of any changes in income per capita. These constrictions indicate clearly that the analysis of the stature of a population is not a mechanical exercise.

In spite of these caveats, the results of anthropometric research have been quite revealing. Height has been shown to correlate positively with socioeconomic variables. For instance, the height of French recruits born in the late 1840s depended on their education and wealth. Illiterates averaged 164.3 cm, whereas those able to read and write were 1.2 cm taller. Presumably literate men were wealthier and spent more time at education and less at labor than did illiterate men (Le Roy Ladurie and Bernageau 1971). Another interesting finding is that by the early eighteenth century the height of the colonial North American population was already well above European norms, which implies that the ecological (and nutritional) environment of the New World was especially favorable from the human–biological point of view (Sokoloff and Villaflor 1982). Although slaves appear to have been neglected as children, even they benefited from the abundance of food in colonial North America, because as adults their height was close to that of the white population and above that of the European peasantry (Steckel 1986). In contrast to that of early North Americans, the nutritional status of the poor boys of London seems to have been truly miserable at the end of the eighteenth century. They were shorter than practically all modern populations, with the possible exception of such groups as the Lume of New Guinea (Eveleth and Tanner 1976; Floud and Wachter 1982).

Yet there were several instances in which the trends in heights and in per capita incomes diverged from one another. They occurred during the early stages of rapid economic growth: in east central Europe during the second half of the eighteenth century, in late-nineteenth-century Montreal, and in the antebellum United States. In the United States, the stature of army recruits declined by more than 2 centimeters beginning with the birth cohorts of the 1830s, even though according to conventional indicators the economy was expanding rapidly during these decades. Between 1840 and 1870 per capita net national product increased by more than 40 percent (Gallman 1972; Fogel 1986; Komlos 1987). In the Habsburg monarchy the decline in stature during the course of the second half of the eighteenth century was at least 3 but more nearly 4 centimeters. A similar pattern was found for industrializing Montreal. The birth weight of infants there fell after the 1870s, indicating that the nutritional status of the mothers was declining. Such anthropometric cycles were not known to exist previously (Ward and Ward 1984; Komlos 1985).

Determining the extent to which these episodes were accompanied by a deterioration in the epidemiological environment requires further study, but it is already clear that all three were, in fact, characterized by a decline in per capita nutrient intake. In the New World, periods of nutritional stress were accompanied by rapid economic growth, during which, by conventional measures, the material standard of living was rising. This might be considered an anomaly because an increase in per capita income normally implies that food consumption, too, is rising. It becomes less anomalous, however, once one notes that although income determines the position of the demand curve for food, an individual who purchases food at higher market prices might consume less of it than a self-sufficient peasant isolated from the market by high transport and information costs, even if the measured income of the former is larger than that of the latter. Moreover, contemporaneously with the decline in human stature in the antebellum United States, the crude death rate was increasing even as per capita income was rising, supporting the notion that the biological standard of living was declining (Pope 1986).

The divergence in biological and conventional indicators of well-being can be explained by several other factors. The examples of economic growth already provided were accompanied by rapid population growth and by urbanization. This increased the demand for food at a time when the agricultural labor force was growing more slowly than the industrial labor force and the gains in labor productivity in agriculture were still small. Hence, supply did not generally match the increased demand for food, and food prices rose relative to those of all other goods.

The relative price of food also rose because rapid technological change in the industrial sector brought with it a decline in all other prices. The rise in the relative price of food was greatest in areas that had previously been isolated from industrial centers. Early stages of growth were generally accompanied by market integration, and this meant that in some regions the price of food, relative to that of all other goods, rose sharply. This brought with it the potential for large movements along the demand curve for food in these regions. In addition, new products changed consumers' tastes and might also have been seen as substitutes for traditional food products. Thus, although the real wage might have risen in the industrial sector, it did not rise as fast as food prices. Even farm operators whose income rose as fast as food prices decreased their food consumption because the price elasticity of demand for food was greater than the income elasticity.

In east central Europe the fall in nutritional levels was initiated not by sectoral shifts from the agricultural to the industrial sector, but by rapid population growth pressing on scarce resources. In contrast to the situation in the United States, in Europe the quantity of land was fixed, and therefore population growth ran into Malthusian ceilings (Komlos 1985). The subsequent limited quantity and the rise in food prices meant a fall in consumption, particularly of meat products, because the price of a calorie is much greater if purchased through meat than if purchased through grain. This fall in the intake of animal protein, an important component of nutritional status, made it more difficult for the body to fight off nutrition-sensitive diseases. Of course, during the early stages of economic growth, individuals were usually not well informed about the importance of a balanced diet and therefore were unaware that changing their food habits would impinge on their nutritional status and health.

To be sure, not all members of the society experienced nutritional stress during the early stages of economic development. In the United States the income of the urban middle class rose sufficiently in the 1830s and 1840s to keep pace with the rise in the price of foodstuffs and, at least initially, to permit that group to maintain its nutritional status. Not until the Civil War disrupted the flow of nutrients did their biological well-being begin to suffer as well. In a similar fashion, Habsburg and German aristocrats were not affected by the Malthusian crisis of the eighteenth century, but rather increased their height advantage considerably compared with the lower classes (Komlos 1986, 1990).

Height therefore correlates positively with social class. In Germany, aristocrats were 3 to 7 centimeters taller than middle-class boys throughout adolescence. The latter in turn were about 8 centimeters taller than boys with lower social standing of the same age. Boys attending prestigious military schools in Austria, England, France, and Germany were all much taller than the population at large. For instance, adolescents of the English gentry were at least 20 centimeters taller than the nutritionally deprived slum boys of London (Floud and Wachter 1982; Komlos 1990).

Yet another pattern is that propinquity to nutrients is a crucial determinant of nutritional status in preindustrial societies and in societies caught in the early stages of economic development. In such circumstances per capita income is not as important a determinant of human stature as is the availability of food. In the eighteenth-century Habsburg monarchy, recruits from areas with a large agricultural sector, even if the economy was relatively underdeveloped, were well nourished by the standards of the time compared with those from industrially more advanced provinces. Being isolated from markets by high transportation and transactions costs had its advantages as long as population density did not exceed the carrying capacity of the land, because the subsistence peasant families had little choice but to consume all of their own food output. Once they became integrated into a larger market, however, rising food prices and their sales of agricultural commodities tended to impinge on their own food intake.

Similarly in the antebellum United States, white southern men were 1.5 centimeters taller than their counterparts in the more industrial North, even though per capita income was greater in the latter region (Margo and Steckel 1983). The same pattern held between England and its colonies. Although in the eighteenth century England had a higher per capita income, perhaps by as much as 25 percent, its soldiers were considerably shorter than their counterparts in the British colonies of North America. A century later, Irish-born recruits into the Union army during the Civil War were also taller than soldiers born in England, although English per capita income was certainly higher than that of the Irish (Mokyr and O'Gràda 1988).

Indeed, the importance of remoteness for nutritional status can be seen from the fact that in 1850 the tallest population in Europe was probably found in Dalmatia, one of the least developed areas of the Continent. This relationship reappears in an astounding form at the end of the century: Although Bosnia-Herzegovina was certainly among the least developed parts of the Habsburg monarchy, its population was nonetheless the tallest (Austrian Bureau of Health 1910).

All of this evidence corroborates the notion that being close to the supply of food during the early stages of industrialization had a positive effect on nutritional status, possibly because the costs of obtaining food were lower. In addition, rural populations doubtless benefited from a lower exposure to disease than those crowded into an urban en-

vironment. Another probable reason for the difficulty of maintaining nutritional status during the initial phase of economic development is that income distribution is more uneven during such phases than at other times. The changes in entitlement to goods, with the rise in food prices, cause many to lose their ability to "command food" (Sen 1981).

In summary, because height is a good proxy for nutritional status, it is employed to measure the biological well-being of populations of the past. The biological standard of living indicates the extent to which ecological circumstances are favorable to the functioning of the human organism. The concept encompasses such aspects of human biology as life expectancy, morbidity, and public health. Moreover, in the developed economies of the twentieth century, height correlates positively with per capita income not only because of the rise in food intake, but also because of improvements in public health and medical technology.

Yet the evidence presented here also implies that economic growth can be accompanied by a fall in nutritional status. Hence, the biological standard of living can diverge from real incomes during the early stages of industrialization. This pattern is not anomalous, because gross national product has generally grown more rapidly than the agricultural sector, and in some cases per capita food consumption has fallen. But it does mean that per capita income can be an ambiguous measure of welfare during the early stages of economic development. A rise in average per capita income is of ambiguous benefit if it is distributed unevenly and if some members of the population lead less healthy lives as a by-product of economic change. Of course, in the long run the ambiguity disappears, because the productivity of the agricultural sector improves and relative food prices decline. Hence, the share of food in consumer budgets fell in Europe from about 75 percent to about 25 percent, or even less, of income. Yet for the early stages of industrialization recent anthropometric research indicates that the conventional indicators of welfare are incomplete; they must be supplemented with a measure, such as human stature, that illuminates the biological well-being of a population.

John Komlos

Bibliography

Austrian Bureau of Health. 1910. *Militär-Statistisches Jahrbuch für das Jahr 1871*. Vienna.

Brinkman, Henk Jan, J. W. Drukker, and Brigitte Slot. 1988. Height and income: A new method for the estimation of historical national income series. *Explorations in Economic History* 25: 227–64.

Cipolla, Carlo. 1980. *Before the industrial revolution, European society and economy, 1000–1700*, 2d edition. New York.

Cuff, Timothy. 1989. Body mass index of West Point cadets in the nineteenth century. Unpublished manuscript, University of Pittsburgh, Department of History.

Davin, Eric. 1988. The era of the common child: Infant and child mortality in mid-nineteenth century Pittsburgh. Unpublished manuscript, University of Pittsburgh, Department of History.

Eveleth, Phyllis B., and James M. Tanner. 1976. *Worldwide variation in human growth*. Cambridge.

Falkner, Frank, and James M. Tanner, eds. 1986. *Human growth, a comprehensive treatise*, 2d edition. New York.

Flinn, Michael. 1984. English workers' living standards during the industrial revolution: A comment. *Economic History Review* 37: 88–92.

Floud, Roderick. 1990. *The heights of the British*. Cambridge.

Floud, Roderick, and Kenneth Wachter. 1982. Poverty and physical stature, evidence on the standard of living of London boys, 1770–1870. *Social Science History* 6: 422–52.

Fogel, Robert W. 1986. Nutrition and the decline in mortality since 1700: Some preliminary findings. In *Long term factors in American economic growth*, ed. Stanley L. Engerman and Robert E. Gallman, 439–555. Chicago.

Fogel, Robert W., Stanley L. Engerman, and James Trussel. 1982. Exploring the uses of data on height: The analysis of long-term trends in nutrition, labor welfare, and labor productivity. *Social Science History* 6: 401–21.

Friedman, Gerald C. 1982. The heights of slaves in Trinidad. *Social Science History* 6: 482–515.

Gallman, Robert E. 1972. The pace and pattern of American economic growth. In *American economic growth: An economist's history of the United States*, ed. Lance E. Davis, Richard A. Easterlin, and William Parker, 15–60. New York.

Komlos, John. 1985. Stature and nutrition in the Habsburg monarchy: The standard of living and economic development in the eighteenth century. *American Historical Review* 90: 1149–61.

1986. Patterns of children's growth in east central Europe in the eighteenth century. *Annals of Human Biology* 13: 33–48.

1987. The height and weight of West Point cadets: Dietary change in antebellum America. *Journal of Economic History* 47: 897–927.

1989. *Nutrition and economic development in the eigh-*

teenth century Habsburg monarchy: An anthropometric history. Princeton, N.J.

1990. Height and social status in eighteenth-century Germany. *Journal of Interdisciplinary History* 20: 607–22.

Le Roy Ladurie, Emmanuel, and N. Bernageau. 1971. Etude sur un contingent militaire (1868): Mobilité géographique, délinquance et stature, mises en rapport avec d'autres aspects de la situation des conscrits. *Annales de démographie historique*, 311–37.

Lindert, Peter, and Jeffrey Williamson. 1983. English workers' living standards during the industrial revolution. *Economic History Review*, 2d Ser., 36: 1–25.

Margo, Robert, and Richard H. Steckel. 1983. Heights of native born northern whites during the antebellum period. *Journal of Economic History* 43: 167–74.

McMahon, Sarah. 1981. Provisions laid up for the family: Toward a history of diet in New England, 1650–1850. *Historical Methods* 14: 4–21.

Mokyr, Joel, and Cormac O'Gráda. 1988. Poor and getting poorer? Living standards in Ireland before the Famine. *Economic History Review*, 2d Ser., 41: 209–35.

Pope, Clayne L. 1986. Native adult mortality in the U.S.: 1770–1870. In *Long-term changes in nutrition and the standard of living*, Eighth Congress of the International Economic History Association, ed. Robert W. Fogel, 76–88. Berne.

Riggs, Paul. 1988. The standard of living in Britain's Celtic fringe, c. 1800–1850: Evidence from Glaswegian prisoners. Unpublished manuscript, University of Pittsburgh, Department of History.

Riley, James, and George Alter. 1986. Mortality and morbidity: Measuring ill health across time. In *Long-term changes in nutrition and the standard of living*, Eighth Congress of the International Economic History Association, ed. Robert W. Fogel, 97–106. Berne.

Rule, John. 1986. *The laboring classes in early industrial England, 1750–1850*. London.

Schwartz, L. D. 1985. The standard of living in the long run: London, 1700–1860. *Economic History Review*, 2d Ser., 38: 24–41.

Sen, Amartya. 1981. *Poverty and famines: An essay on entitlement and deprivation*. Oxford.

1987. *The standard of living*. Cambridge.

Sokoloff, Kenneth, and Georgia C. Villaflor. 1982. The early achievement of modern stature in America. *Social Science History* 6: 453–81.

Steckel, Richard. 1983. Height and per capita income. *Historical Methods* 16: 1–7.

1986. A peculiar population: The nutrition, health and mortality of American slaves from childhood to maturity. *Journal of Economic History* 46: 721–42.

Tanner, James M. 1978. *Fetus into man: Physical growth from conception to maturity*. Cambridge.

1981. *A history of the study of human growth*. Cambridge.

Thirsk, Joan. 1983. The horticultural revolution: A cautionary note on prices. *Journal of Interdisciplinary History* 14: 299–302.

Tunzelmann, G. N., von. 1985. The standard of living debate and optimal economic growth. In *The economics of the Industrial Revolution,* ed. Joel Mokyr, 207–26. Totowa, N.J.

Ward, Peter W. 1987. Weight at birth in Vienna, Austria, 1865–1930. *Annals of Human Biology* 14: 495–506.

Ward, Peter W., and Patricia C. Ward. 1984. Infant birth weight and nutrition in industrializing Montreal. *American Historical Review* 89: 324–45.

Williamson, Jeffrey G. 1981. Urban disamenities, dark satanic mills and the British standard of living debate. *Journal of Economic History* 44: 75–84.

1982. Was the industrial revolution worth it? Disamenities and death in 19th century British towns. *Explorations in Economic History* 19: 221–45.

PART V

The History of Human Disease in the World Outside Asia

V.1
Diseases in the Pre-Roman World

In the past 15,000 years, epochal social and cultural changes have created fundamentally different relationships between humankind and the environment. One of the most important innovations has been the domestication of plants and animals, a major factor in the gradual establishment of agriculture as the world's predominant economic base. The development of agriculture brought an increase in sedentism, in which human groups lived in more or less permanent communities.

Associated with farming was the domestication of animals and, in some societies, nomadic pastoralism. By about 6000 B.C., animal husbandry provided a relatively widespread and stable source of high-quality protein in the Near East. Moreover, the protein was typically produced in ways that did not compete directly for agricultural land resources. Domestic herds grazed on agricultural land after the harvest (Bentley 1987) or on land that was fallow, marginal, or inadequate for farming.

The greater control that agriculture and the domestication of animals gave people over food production resulted in food surpluses. Surplus food created the potential for the emergence of specialists such as craftsmen, merchants, and a ruler class, which are essential components of urban society, another major social change. Urbanism began in the Near East during the Chalcolithic Age (c. 4000–3200 B.C.) but had its major efflorescence during the Early Bronze Age (c. 3200–2000 B.C.)

The advent of agriculture, the domestication of animals, and the development of urbanism had a significant impact on human health. Although agriculture dramatically increased the calories that could be produced by a given individual, the emphasis on a few cultigens increased the vulnerability of agricultural societies to famine and malnutrition (Cohen 1984a). Innovations associated with agriculture, such as irrigation, greatly heightened exposure to some infectious diseases. Plowing the soil itself probably increased the risk of acquiring fungal diseases. Sedentary communities, unlike hunting and gathering societies, which usually changed their living areas often, lived amid their own detritus with its inherent risk of causing disease (Wells 1978). The domestication of animals brought the

potential of contracting animalborne diseases (zoonoses). Urbanism brought increased population sizes and densities and a greater likelihood of exposure to dropletborne infectious agents. Extended trade and commerce, activities associated with urban society, enhanced the spread of infectious organisms between geographic areas (Cockburn 1963).

However significant these changes were, direct evidence of their having caused disease is difficult to obtain. Paleopathology, the study of ancient disease, is hampered by several limitations. Two of the most important of these are the nature of our sources and the way in which we study and interpret the data.

Our current sources of data on disease in the pre-Roman world include ancient texts that describe disease, archeological cultural artifacts that portray the effects of disease on the human body, and human skeletal and mummy remains recovered from archeological sites. There are many difficulties in utilizing some of these sources.

Although skeletal and mummy remains would appear to be a promising source of information, most diseases suffered by individuals in antiquity, and many that caused death, leave no evidence in soft-tissue remains or in bone as observed by gross or microscopic methods. In addition, attributing the relatively few conditions that do occur in the skeleton to a specific morbid syndrome is often difficult. These problems make the interpretation of the biological significance of skeletal disease difficult. However, although our sources may have limitations, much can be learned if these restrictions are kept in mind. Even tentative observations can provide the basis for further clarification and/or debate. We are hopeful that current avenues of research will provide new data and stimulate the development of new methods. For example, the work of M. Y. El-Najjar and colleagues (1980) and that of N. Tuross (1991) suggest the possibility of recovering immunoglobulins from archeological tissues, including bone.

The second and perhaps most serious limitation to the study of prehistoric human disease is that imposed by the methodological and theoretical inadequacies of current research. There is no universally accepted descriptive methodology that ensures comparability between published sources, which hampers any attempt to integrate the data presented in the literature. In addition, as will be discussed in relation to infectious diseases, paleopathology has not yet reached a theoretical consensus on the significance of many skeletal diseases.

In spite of the limitations and problems in the field of paleopathology, we have attempted some interpretation of the data. In addition, we have included findings of other researchers who have sought evidence of trends of certain conditions for sites in specific geographic regions. However, we strongly emphasize the tentative nature of these findings and the need for greater methodological rigor in future research.

In this essay, we focus on research involving human physical remains from the Old World, beginning with the Mesolithic period (about 10,000 B.C. in the Near East) and ending with the emergence of the Roman Empire. Because of the considerable chronological and geographic scope of the essay, and because of the complexity of understanding disease in antiquity, particularly in relation to modern medical experience, we briefly discuss some relevant concepts, trends, and factors.

First, it must be emphasized that the transitions between hunter-gatherer, agricultural, and urban societies occurred at various times in different areas of the Old World. For example, while the Near East was in the early stages of farming with some town life (c. 8000–5000 B.C.), Europe was still at a hunter-gatherer subsistence level. Therefore, at a specific point in time the health problems encountered by the human populations in these two areas were different.

Second, the relationship between humans and disease is continually evolving. Over time, the virulence of infectious organisms tends to become attenuated, while the human host population tends to evolve a more effective immune response to infectious organisms (Cockburn 1963). The implication of these two trends is that with the passage of time a given infectious disease is likely to become a less serious threat to life and develop a more chronic pathogenesis.

Third, the expression of disease can be influenced by many factors (e.g., age and environment). In general, the risk of disease increases with the age of the individual. With the exception of many Third World countries, people today live 30 to 40 years longer than they did in antiquity. This greatly increased longevity is a very recent development in human history and means that the prevalence of many diseases common among modern Western peoples, such as cancer and heart disease, is probably much greater than it was in antiquity. Environmental conditions, both geographic and cultural, can also influence the expression of disease. For example, exposure to smoke from wood-burning fires may be a factor in the prevalence of nasopharyngeal tumors in archeological skeletons (Wells 1977).

Finally, a helpful distinction can be made between specific and nonspecific disease (Buikstra 1976). *Specific disease* refers to those conditions in a skeleton that can be attributed to one of a fairly limited number of disease syndromes (e.g., anemia or leprosy). *Nonspecific disease* is an abnormal condition of a skeleton (e.g., periostitis, dental hypoplasia, and Harris's lines) that cannot be attributed to a discrete morbid syndrome. In a sense, specific and nonspecific diseases represent the polar extremes of a conceptual gradient.

In samples of archeological human skeletons, approximately 15 percent show evidence of significant disease. The incidence of specific disease syndromes varies among geographic areas and cultures, as does the expression of diseases, but generally the most common pathological conditions seen in archeological human skeletons include trauma, infection, arthritis, and dental disease. These conditions will be the focus of our discussion. In addition, because of current interest, we will briefly discuss anemias and tumors. Most of the other general categories of disease (e.g., dysplasias and metabolic diseases) are represented by at least one syndrome that affects the skeleton, but archeological evidence for these syndromes tends to be rare. Differential diagnosis is often difficult, and low frequencies create severe limitations in reaching paleoepidemiological conclusions.

Trauma

Trauma is a pathological condition that varies in type and frequency depending on culture and physical environment. Trauma to the skeleton can be divided into two categories: (1) accidental or unintentional trauma, such as fracture that results from a fall, and (2) intentional trauma or injury purposefully caused by another human being. Intentional trauma includes injury resulting from violence (Figure V.1.1) in warfare or interpersonal conflict, which may result in broken long bones or a fractured skull, as well as trauma induced by a therapeutic procedure.

One of the most remarkable forms of trauma in antiquity was a surgical procedure known as trephination, whereby a portion of the skull was removed, great care being taken to avoid penetration of the underlying dura. Trephination was first reported for Paleolithic Poland (Gladykowska-Rzeczycka 1981). The procedure apparently became more common in the Neolithic period, in France, England, Denmark, Germany, Italy, and Russia, and it continued into the Middle Ages (Steinbock 1976). Trephined skulls have also been reported from the Near East for the Neolithic period through

Figure V.1.1. Probable unhealed ax wound in an adult male skull from a rock tomb at Lisht in Upper Egypt dated between the Twentieth and Twenty-fifth Dynasty (c. 1100–655 B.C.). Bone fragment produced by the blow at the time of death is reflected to the right. Note the lack of remodeling on the cut surface indicative of death at the time of or shortly after the trauma. (From Catalog no. 256384, National Museum of Natural History, Washington, D.C.)

the Iron Age (Wells 1964a; Lisowski 1967; Ortner and Putschar 1981; Rathbun 1984) and from the eastern Mediterranean for the Bronze and Iron ages (Ortner and Putschar 1981; Grmek 1989); however, in the Near East and eastern Mediterranean the practice apparently was not common.

Evidence of healing, as indicated by antemortem remodeling of cut edges in trephined skulls, is common. But even when there is no evidence of healing, death may have been caused by factors other than the surgical procedure, such as a blow to the head, to which the trephination was a therapeutic response (Lisowski 1967; Ortner and Putschar 1981).

Although it may not be possible to determine all the reasons that trephination was performed, among some populations treatment for trauma seems to have been a common objective. Perhaps mental illness and epilepsy served as additional reasons. In Danish skulls trephination is found almost exclusively in male specimens, with the left side being the one most commonly operated on (Bennike 1985). This pattern suggests that trephination was the therapeutic procedure for a blow to the cranium, resulting from violence among men and usually inflicted by a right-handed opponent.

Other types of trauma found in archeological skeletal remains reveal information about early lifestyles. In general, male skeletons show a higher rate of trauma, especially violent trauma, than do female skeletons. In the eastern Mediterranean, from the Early Neolithic (c. 6500 B.C.) to the Roman period (A.D. 120), the frequency of skull wounds in men ranged from a high of 20 percent in the Early Neolithic to a low of 3 percent in the Classic period (650 B.C.). For women, the frequencies were 3 to zero percent for the same periods (Angel 1974). In Iran between 5000 and 500 B.C., there was a much higher rate of head wounds among men than among women (Rathbun 1984). At the site of Hissar in Iran, occupied from the Chalcolithic through the Early Bronze Age (4000–2000 B.C.), W. M. Krogman (1940) noted that men suffered three times more head wounds than women. In contrast, for the same time period in neighboring Iraq, T. A. Rathbun (1984) found no difference in rates of head trauma between the sexes. In fact, the postcranial material he studied for both Iran and Iraq revealed no differences between the sexes. Yet a Late Period site (664–323 B.C.) in Egypt revealed cranial trauma in 20 percent of the adult males and 8.3 percent of the adult females (Strouhal 1986).

Another pattern in the early skeletal material is the rarity of evidence of fracture or trauma in children (Grmek 1989). Specifically, this has been noted for Bronze Age Greece (Angel 1957), Denmark from the Mesolithic period through the Middle Ages (Bennike 1985), Mesolithic western Europe (Meiklejohn et al. 1984), and Late Period Egypt (Strouhal 1986). These observations, however, pose a potential methodological problem. Remodeling associated with growth generally obliterates any evidence of fracture in children, particularly if it occurs in early childhood. Thus, evidence of fracture or other trauma in children is often not seen in skeletal remains unless the child died shortly after the traumatic event.

One of the fractures most frequently seen in the pre-Roman world was caused when an individual, in attempting to protect the head, absorbed a blow with the forearm. This injury, called a *parry fracture,* most often involved the left ulna.

There have been several surveys of the incidence of forearm fractures. J. Angel (1974) found that, in prehistoric Greece and Turkey, forearm fracture was the most common form of injury. F. Wood-Jones (1910a) reported that, in pre-Dynastic through Byzantine Nubia, 31 percent of all fractures occurred in the forearm, with the ulna being broken more often than the radius and the left side more often damaged. In a British Neolithic to Anglo-Saxon series (c. 3500 B.C. to A.D. 600) fracture of the forearm bones (radius and ulna) was the most common form of postcranial injury, representing almost 49 percent of all fracture cases (Brothwell 1967).

In the eastern Mediterranean the next most common fracture site was the lower thoracic vertebrae. Fracture of the vertebral region also showed the least amount of difference between men and women (Angel 1974).

Fractures of the lower extremity are uncommon in the eastern Mediterranean (Angel 1974). In Nubian skeletons from the pre-Dynastic to Byzantine periods fractures of the foot are rare, and those of the leg are less frequent than those of the arm (Wood-Jones 1910a). In Mesolithic to medieval Danish skeletal material, fracture of the lower extremities is rare (Bennike 1985).

A review of the literature on trauma reveals several chronological trends. For the Mesolithic period through Iron Age, the rate of trauma generally seems to decrease. However, this decrease is related primarily to accidental trauma; the incidence of violent trauma appears to remain the same. For example, Angel observed that, in the eastern Mediterranean, the general rate of fracture decreased with the development of civilization but the rate of violent injury to the head remained the same (Angel 1974). Although P. Bennike (1985) did not find any time-related pattern for the postcranial Danish material, her data reveal that cranial trauma decreased over time. She also found that trauma to the skull was more common in the Mesolithic (8300–4200 B.C.) than in the Neolithic (3200–1800 B.C.), and more common in the Neolithic than in the pre-Viking Iron Age (c. 500 B.C. to A.D. 800). Bennike did not differentiate between accidental and intentional trauma.

The tendency for the incidence of trauma to decrease through time was also noted for western Europe (Meiklejohn et at. 1984) and for Iran and Iraq (Rathbun 1984). C. Meiklejohn and colleagues (1984) tentatively hypothesize that the reduction in trauma, in Mesolithic and Neolithic Europe, which in their sample was a reduction in overall accidental trauma, was due to a more sedentary existence. Rathbun (1984) observed an apparent tendency for trauma in material from Iran and Iraq to decline from the preagricultural to the urban phases several thousand years later. Although he could not differentiate between accidental and intentional trauma in the earlier skeletal material, he noted that much of the trauma of the later periods appeared to be due to human violence.

Infection

Infectious diseases are caused by bacteria, fungi, viruses, and multicellular parasites (e.g., worms). The health significance of each of these agents is affected by many variables, some of which were important factors during the history of human disease. For example, parasites may have become a greater problem for human groups after the domestication of animals, which are common vectors of diseases associated with these organisms. Airborne viruses, which require fairly large host populations (Fiennes 1978), may have become a significant health problem with the rise of urbanism. Fungi may have become a more serious problem with the advent of agriculture, particularly among groups who were under- or malnourished. Because fungi tend to be opportunistic, they are a greater problem in individuals who are immunologically compromised.

Perhaps the most interesting observation about infectious disease during the Mesolithic through the Metal Ages is its apparent low incidence in skeletal samples from most geographic areas (e.g., Wood-Jones 1910b; Martin et al. 1984; Rathbun 1984; Strouhal 1986). This low frequency has been observed both for localized infection resulting from trauma in general (Domurad 1986) and fracture in particular (Wood-Jones 1910b; Bennike 1985) and for skeletal lesions (Martin et al. 1984), which may develop as a result of systemic disease. In fact, skeletal evidence of systemic infection appears to be quite rare, and differential diagnosis often poses a great challenge even to experienced paleopathologists or orthopedic specialists.

Even though skeletal studies report a low incidence of infection, interpreting this observation requires caution and reflects some of the theoretical problems involved in paleopathology. Most serious, acute infectious diseases leave no evidence in gross skeletal remains. The lack of skeletal evidence of infection may mean that the population was healthy, but it may also mean that people were dying from acute infectious disease before the skeleton could be affected (Ortner and Putschar 1981; Rathbun 1984; Ortner 1991).

Several surveys have detected possible trends in infection rates. Rathbun (1984) notes that in Iraq and Iran there appears to have been an increased frequency of infectious-type lesions in the Neolithic and Chalcolithic periods. These rates declined significantly in the later Bronze and Iron ages. Although these trends may be real, they may also reflect stochastic effects of inadequate samples. As Rathbun (1984) suggests, however, the decline in percentage of cases exhibiting infectious lesions from the Chalcolithic to the later Bronze and Iron Age periods may be the result of people dying before bone was involved. Elsewhere in a study of European skeletal material, Meiklejohn and colleagues (1984) noted an increase in cranial infections from the Mesolithic to the Neolithic period. Dental evidence of disease in the eastern Mediterranean suggests to Angel (1984) that new diseases, including epidemics, emerged with the increased population sizes of the Middle Bronze Age.

Evidence from surveys of archeological skeletal material, site reports, and individual case reports has pointed to the existence of a number of infectious diseases in the pre-Roman era – specifically, tuberculosis, leprosy (in Egypt), osteomyelitis, and periostitis.

There is strong evidence that tuberculosis may have developed and/or become a problem with the beginning of farming. Although no unequivocal cases of destructive lesions of the spine have been reported thus far for the prefarming Mesolithic, there are numerous descriptions of lesions of the spine for Neolithic Europe (c. 4200–1500 B.C.; Bartels 1907; Patte 1971; Sager et al. 1972; Dastugue and de Lumley 1976; Formicola, Milanesi, and Scarsini 1987) and pre-Dynastic Egypt (c. 4800–3100 B.C.; Strouhal 1991), for which one possible diagnosis is tuberculosis. However, one must caution that several disease conditions other than tuberculosis produce destructive lesions of the spine, including infection by staphylococcus bacteria and fungi.

There were several cultural changes during the Neolithic that would have influenced the development of diseases affecting the spine. In the Near East the use of domestic animals became an important part of the economy. Proximity to domestic animals, particularly bovids, was likely to have been a significant factor in the development of tuberculosis (Manchester 1983). In addition, a more sedentary life-style and increased population density in the Neolithic and subsequent periods would have been likely to increase its incidence. However, farming was also likely to have increased the incidence of fungal diseases. It is thus probable that spinal lesions attributable to both bacterial and fungal infection increased in the Neolithic period. The current skeletal evidence supports this expectation, although the specific etiology for the destructive lesions remains problematic.

Reported cases of tuberculosis show wide geographic distribution. K. Manchester (1984), basing his opinion on iconographic as well as on skeletal evidence, believes that the earliest undisputed evidence for human tuberculosis comes from Egypt and that the disease spread out from a near eastern center (Manchester 1983, 1984). Although there is considerable controversy regarding the exact dating

Figure V.1.2. Partial antemortem destruction of the fourth lumbar vertebral bone from the skeleton of a young adult from the Early Bronze Age cemetery (c. 3100 B.C.) at Bab edh-Dhra', Jordan (Tomb A100E). Note the reactive bone formation on adjacent vertebral bodies, particularly the fifth lumbar vertebra. (Unaccessioned specimen, National Museum of Natural History, Washington, D.C.)

and diagnosis of the purported cases of spinal tuberculosis in Egypt (Morse 1967; Grmek 1989; Strouhal 1991), it appears that skeletal samples from this region contain at least 32 possible cases in the pre-Christian era (Strouhal 1991). Donald Ortner (1979) reports two possible cases of tuberculosis in Jordan (Figure V.1.2) in a sample of about 300 from the Early Bronze IA (c. 3100 B.C.) tombs at Bab edh-Dhra'. In central and southern Europe, in addition to the Neolithic cases already cited, five cases have been reported between the Bronze Age and 100 B.C. (Dastugue and de Lumley 1976; Steinbock 1976; Angel 1984). Manchester (1984) believes that in Britain the disease was present by the Roman period. Evidence of tuberculosis is also reported for northern Europe, where it may have begun later than the rest of Europe; most skeletal evidence is post-Roman (Brothwell, as cited in Manchester 1984).

Leprosy is another infectious disease for which there is skeletal evidence. In a review of the history of leprosy, Manchester (1984) cites the earliest evidence as that from Ptolemaic Egypt (second century B.C.). Skeletal evidence for leprosy occurs later in Europe. D. Brothwell (1961) argues that leprosy was probably not established there before the first or second century A.D. and did not become a serious problem until after the seventh century. By the Mid-

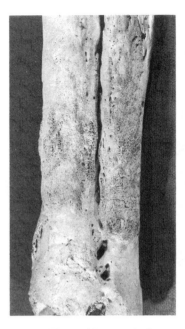

Figure V.1.3. Chronic inflammation of the left tibia and fibula resulting from an overlying ulcer in a skeleton of an adult woman probably over 50 years of age at the time of death. Specimen is from Tomb A100E in the Early Bronze Age cemetery at Bab edh-Dhra', Jordan. Note the large, oval, circumscribed area of reactive bone associated with the ulcer. Chronic inflammation involves all bone tissue and resulted in fusion of the tibia and fibula. (Unaccessioned specimen, National Museum of Natural History, Washington, D.C.)

dle Ages, the disease had become a serious problem but virtually disappeared by the end of the fifteenth century. Manchester (1991) notes that the reduced frequency of leprosy is associated with an increase in the prevalence of tuberculosis. He speculates that a factor in the decline of leprosy may have been cross-immunity induced by the closely related disease of tuberculosis.

Both osteomyelitis and periostitis have been reported in ancient skeletal material. Although their frequencies show some degree of variability (e.g., Wells, as cited in Sandison 1980; Strouhal 1986), these conditions generally are not common. Descriptions of cases are encountered in the literature. For example, Wood-Jones (1910b) describes a humerus from ancient Nubia with evidence of inflammatory bone formation. He attributes the inflammation to an infectious complication of an injury. Ortner (1979) reports a case of reactive bone formation on the tibia and fibula of a skeleton (Figure V.1.3) dated to about 3100 B.C. The specimen is of an old woman with an overlying skin ulcer of the lower leg that stimulated the inflammatory bone reaction.

Research on mummy remains has provided useful information on the antiquity of many other infectious diseases. An early case of poliomyelitis was reported in a pre-Dynastic mummy from Egypt (Mitchell 1900) dated to 3700 B.C. The leg deformity in the mummy of Pharaoh Siptah from the Nineteenth Dynasty (c. 1200 B.C.) has also recently been recognized as having been caused by polio (Fleming et al. 1980; Whitehouse 1980). Further possible evidence of this disease has been reported in Middle Bronze Age Greece (Angel 1971b) and sixth- to second-century B.C. Italy (Mallegni, Fornaciari, and Tarabella 1979).

Mummy material has also provided information on parasites (Tapp 1986). Schistosomiasis is documented in two mummies of the Twentieth Dynasty (c. 1100 B.C.) in Egypt (Sandison 1973) but probably became a problem much earlier. The practice of irrigation, which may have begun in the Near East as early as the Neolithic, would have facilitated the spread of this disease. The roundworm, *Ascaris,* was found in an Egyptian mummy dating to around 170 B.C. (Fleming et al. 1980), as well as in coprolite material from Bronze Age Britain (Jones and Nicholson 1988) and Iron Age Europe (800–350 B.C.; Aspöck, Flamm, and Picher 1973). The liver fluke was found in two mummies of the Twelfth Dynasty (Fleming et al. 1980). The tapeworm *Echinococcus granulosus* is associated with the mummy Asru dated to about 700 B.C. (Tapp and Wildsmith 1986).

Arthritis

Arthritis is a disease of the joints that includes many syndromes. The term *arthritis* implies an inflammatory condition of the joints, and inflammation is a major factor in several syndromes. One general category of arthritis, and its most common syndrome, is osteoarthritis. Inflammation may occur in osteoarthritis, but it is usually neither the initial nor the most significant factor. Although genetics, physiology, trauma, and other factors appear to play a role, the most important condition contributing to osteoarthritis is mechanical stress. Furthermore, the effect of stress in stimulating arthritic change is cumulative and thus the presence of osteoarthritis is highly correlated with age. There is also a strong association between the type and degree of physical stress and the severity of osteoarthritis. For example, relatively frequent but low-level stress over a long period of time probably has a different effect than severe intermittent stress (Ortner 1968; Jurmain 1977).

Because evidence of osteoarthritis is so common in

archeological human skeletons, the potential for discerning different patterns of joint stress that may be linked to variation in culture exists. However, the current descriptive methodology for conducting such research is poorly developed, and most of the published observations on osteoarthritis do not permit any comparative anaylsis. In addition, mean age of population is often not carefully controlled. Because of the strong association between age and development of osteoarthritis, mean age is crucial to any comparison among populations.

Osteoarthritis of the spine has received the most systematic attention in paleopathological reports. Many surveys have found that the spine is more frequently affected than any other area of the skeleton (Brothwell 1960; Gray 1967; Gejvall 1974; Meiklejohn et al. 1984; Rathbun 1984). Other surveys, although offering no comparisons among areas of the skeleton, have noted the very frequent occurrence of spinal osteoarthritis (Meiklejohn et al. 1984; Bennike 1985), particularly among Egyptians and Nubians (Wells 1964a; Dawson and Gray 1968; Vagn Nielsen 1970).

A variant of spinal degenerative arthritis known as spondylosis (spondylitis) deformans is reported among some populations, such as the Late Stone Age inhabitants of the Baltic Coast (V. Y. Derums 1964), as well as those of Neolithic Jericho (Kurth and Röhrer-Ertl 1981), Neolithic Greece (Dastugue 1974), Third Dynasty Egypt (c. 2750–2680 B.C.; Ruffer and Rietti 1912; Ruffer 1918), and Bronze Age Latvia, USSR (c. 2000–1000 B.C.; V. J. Derums 1987).

Detecting time related trends from the many surveys of vertebral osteoarthritis remains problematic. Reports for Denmark (Bennike 1985) and Egypt (Wells 1964a) indicate no significant changes in the frequency and severity of the condition. Angel (1971a) reported that evidence of osteoarthritis of the spine in the eastern Mediterranean changed little from the Upper Paleolithic (c. 60 percent) until the Classic period, when there may have been a decline (47 percent). In a later paper, however, the estimated frequency of the disease during the Classic period (76 percent) was as high as or higher than that at previous time periods (Bisel and Angel 1985). The incidence of vertebral osteoarthritis in western Europe was reported to be higher in the Neolithic than in the Mesolithic (Meiklejohn et al. 1984).

The mixed conclusions of these surveys may be reflective of methodological problems. However, the importance of physical stress as a factor in vertebral osteoarthitis means that variability in sex roles, type of subsistence, and environmental factors is likely to be great. Perhaps a better understanding can be obtained with a detailed comparative study at the site level such as was undertaken by E. Strouhal and J. Jungwirth (as cited in Aufderheide 1985). They found that in two contemporary Nubian skeletal populations dating to c. 1784–1570 B.C., agriculturists had more spinal osteoarthritis than did hunter-gatherers.

In surveys of the incidence of osteoarthritis in other areas of the skeleton or of the overall rate of general osteoarthritis, the same methodological problems exist. However, some tentative trends have been reported. Meiklejohn and colleagues (1984) found that the overall rate of arthritis in western Europe was higher in the Mesolithic than in the Neolithic, suggesting greater biomechanical stress in the earlier period.

Cultural factors and differences in physical environment have been proposed as explanations for changes in the incidence of the disease. Rathbun (1984) found an overall decrease in osteoarthritis in Iran and Iraq from the earlier periods to the later Metal Ages, which he related to the change in economic activities accompanying urban life. He also found that the Iranian material typically showed more osteoarthritis than the Mesopotamian samples – a difference that may be related to terrain. Brothwell (1961) found that in Great Britain the joints of the upper extremities exhibited more osteoarthritis in the Neolithic period through the Iron Ages than they did in modern times. Manchester (1983) attributes this difference to much greater physical stress in the earlier periods.

Sex-related roles also seem to affect the frequency and severity of osteoarthritis. Male skeletons tend to have a higher rate of the disease than female skeletons. Bennike (1985) found this to be true for the spinal column in an Iron Age sample from Denmark. Similar findings of male skeletons were reported for Bronze Age Greece (Angel 1971b), the eastern Mediterranean during the Chalcolithic through the Hellenistic period (Bisel 1980), Egypt during the Dynastic period (Gray 1967), and Sudanese Nubia during the Second Intermediate period (Strouhal and J. Jungwirth, as cited in Aufderheide 1985).

Although greater male involvement is common, there are exceptions. In the Chalcolithic–Early Bronze Age (4000–2000 B.C.) material from Kalinkaya in Anatolia, osteoarthritis was more common in women according to S. Bisel (1980), who attributes this to greater physical stress from hard work. Female skeletons also show more arthritis at Early Neolithic Nikomedeia in Greece (Angel 1973).

A second general category of arthritis is that of the inflammatory erosive joint diseases. This category includes such syndromes as Reither's syndrome, psoriatic arthritis, and three that are examined in this paper: rheumatoid arthritis, ankylosing spondylitis, and gout. Some syndromes of inflammatory erosive joint disease have a known association with bacterial infection of the bowel or genitourinary track. Lyme disease, for example, is initiated by a tick bite that introduces a bacteria (spirochete) into the host. If untreated, the disease produces severe erosive joint destruction in some patients. The prevailing theory is that other erosive arthropathies are probably initiated by infectious agents as well. Inflammatory erosive joint disease occurs in some people when an infectious triggering agent operates in combination with an individual's defective immune response. The major problem in inflammatory erosive joint disease is that the immune response to the infectious agent is not turned off after the triggering organisms are eliminated. Because of both the infectious and genetic/immune components in inflammatory erosive joint disease syndromes, their time depth and geographic range are of particular interest in the context of human adaptation and microevolutionary biology.

Differential diagnosis of some syndromes of inflammatory erosive joint disease in dry bone specimens is likely to be difficult. Statements in the literature attributing inflammatory erosive joint disease in an archaeological specimen to a specific syndrome should be treated with caution. Even distinguishing these syndromes from septic arthritis and osteoarthritis can be problematic in some cases.

There is currently a debate in the medical and anthropological literature on the antiquity of rheumatoid arthritis. B. Rothschild, K. R. Turner, and M. A. Deluca (1988) have argued that, in the New World, the disease has a history extending back at least 5,000 years. They further argue that rheumatoid arthritis may have been derived from New World pathogens or allergens. However, reports in the anthropological literature indicate that rheumatoid arthritis may have begun as early as the Neolithic in the Old World. Brothwell (1973) suggests the possibility of its presence in Neolithic skeletal material from Great Britain. Rheumatoid arthritis has also been reported in skeletal material from Neolithic Sweden (2500–1900 B.C.; Leden, Persson, and Persson 1985–6), Bronze Age Denmark (c. 1800–100 B.C.; Bennike 1985; Kilgore 1989), Fifth Dynasty Egypt (2544–2470 B.C.; May 1897), and Iron Age Lebanon (500–300 B.C.; Kunter 1977). A

specimen from Iron Age Sicily (300–210 B.C.; Klepinger 1979) may represent a case of erosive joint disease with skeletal manifestations including features of both ankylosing spondylitis and rheumatoid arthritis. More recently, L. Kilgore (1989) has suggested a diagnosis of rheumatoid arthritis for a case of erosive joint disease from Sudanese Nubia dated to between A.D. 700 and 1450.

As mentioned earlier, a diagnosis of rheumatoid arthritis should be viewed with caution. However, given the number of cases mentioned by different authors, it does seem that rheumatoid arthritis may be of some antiquity in the Old World. Although the assignment to a specific syndrome of inflammatory erosive joint disease may be incorrect, it seems likely that erosive joint disease was present by at least the Neolithic period. Further clarification of the antiquity of rheumatoid arthritis will have to await additional study of Old World archeological skeletons.

Another syndrome of inflammatory joint disease that occurs in archeological skeletal samples is ankylosing spondylitis. There is general agreement that this syndrome has a history extending for several thousand years (e.g., Resnick and Niwayama 1988). Skeletal evidence is reported in material from Neolithic France (Pales 1930; Torre and Dastugue 1976), Neolithic Sweden (Zorab 1961), and pre-Roman Germany (Zorab 1961). C. Short (1974) has concluded that there were 18 recorded cases in Egypt dating between 2900 B.C. and A.D. 200. G. Morlock (1986) has noted that cases of ankylosing spondylitis (as well as some severe forms of vertebral osteophytosis) have been misdiagnosed. He contends that some cases represent a syndrome of hypertrophic arthritis called DISH, whose antiquity therefore dates to pre-Roman Egypt, Greece, and Europe.

A third syndrome of inflammatory erosive joint disease, gout, is well known in ancient historical accounts. The Old Testament, in a passage dated to between 915 and 875 B.C., provides a graphic description of the painful symptoms of this disease (Resnick and Niwayama 1988). There are few good descriptions, however, of gout in ancient human remains. A mummy from a Christian cemetery in Egypt exhibits erosive destruction of the first metatarsals. Substance removed from the lesions produced a reaction typical of uric acid crystals (Elliot-Smith and Dawson 1924; Rowling 1961). In addition, C. Wells (1973) has reported a possible case of gout in a Roman period skeleton from a site in Gloucester, England.

Other syndromes of inflammatory erosive joint

Figure V.1.4. Dental caries of the upper left second molar in an adult male skull from Tomb A100N in the Early Bronze Age cemetery at Bab edh-Dhra', Jordan. (Unaccessioned specimen, National Museum of Natural History, Washington, D.C.)

disease may exist in ancient Old World human remains. The diagnostic criteria for evaluating the presence of these syndromes are now being developed and refined. We should have a better understanding of the historical dimension of these syndromes in the near future.

Dental Disease

Teeth and supporting tissues can be affected by many disease conditions. The size and shape of teeth can be affected by systemic diseases (e.g., infection and malnutrition) that occur during fetal, infant, and childhood dental development. Systemic diseases can also leave observable defects (hypoplasia) in the enamel. Tooth surfaces can be destroyed by bacteria, a process resulting in caries (Figure V.1.4). Caries can destroy the tooth to the point where the pulp cavity is exposed to infectious agents that can invade the bone and produce inflammation and abscess. Finally, teeth can be traumatized by gritty materials in food, by violence, and by the use of teeth as tools.

Other areas of the mouth can be affected by disease. Gums may become inflamed due to irritation from plaque or infection, resulting in periodontal disease and resorption of alveolar bone. The subsequent exposure of tooth roots with alveolar recession can result in root caries and tooth loss. Supporting bony tissues of the jaw are subject to inflammation just as bone is in other parts of the body.

In an archeological context, the dental pathologies most commonly seen are caries, periodontal disease, dental abscess, antemortem tooth loss, dental attrition, and enamel hypoplasia. Unfortunately, there are two major difficulties in extracting meaningful data from dental remains. First, like bone, teeth and their supporting tissues react to different disease conditions in similar ways, so that one may be unable to attribute an abnormal condition to a specific disease. Second, the methodology for analyzing these dental pathologies is inexact, often making comparisons among observations hazardous. For these reasons, we will examine in detail only enamel hypoplasia, a condition that has been carefully studied (e.g., Goodman, Martin, and Armelagos 1984; Molnar and Molnar 1985; Rose, Condon, and Goodman 1985; Goodman 1991). Although there is a considerable body of data on caries, methodological problems hinder interpretation. Basically, variation in caries rate appears to be attributable to two dietary factors: presence of carbohydrates and sugar, and presence of gritty food. (Gritty substances remove the crevices in the dental crown, thereby eliminating the locations for bacterial activity.)

Enamel hypoplasias can reveal a number of aspects about the health of an individual or population during childhood. If tooth surfaces have not been worn away, enamel hypoplasias can be used to estimate both the timing and severity of stress. The presence of enamel hypoplasias in the deciduous teeth indicates the occurrence of stress during the last 5 months in utero through the first year of postnatal life (Goodman et al. 1984). In the permanent incisors and canines, the teeth most commonly studied for enamel defects in adult dentitions, enamel hypoplasias reflect stress between birth and 7 years (Goodman 1991). The onset of stress can be determined in half-year intervals (Goodman 1991).

Enamel hypoplasias represent a disturbance lasting from several weeks to 2 months (Rose et al. 1985). Many sources attribute these disturbances to infection or nutritional deficiencies (y'Edynak and Fleisch 1983; Goodman et al. 1984) such as those that can occur with weaning (Rathbun 1984; Smith, Bar-Yosef, and Sillen 1984).

A general survey of the literature on enamel hypoplasia reveals several interrelated patterns. First, there seems to be a general rise in the frequency of hypoplasia from the Mesolithic to Roman period in many areas of the Old World (y'Edynak and Fleisch 1983; Rathbun 1984; Smith et al. 1984; Molnar and Molnar 1985; Formicola 1986–7; Angel and Bisel 1987). This rise seems to be related to general changes in the human environment.

P. Smith and colleagues (1984) found that in Palestine the frequency of enamel hypoplasias increased from the Natufian period (c. 10,000 to 8500 B.C.) to the Neolithic, and rose again in the later Chalcolithic and Bronze ages. They postulate that the slight rise in dental pathology in the Neolithic may have been due to changes in diet. However, they attribute the more definite increase in frequencies in the later periods to a marked decline in health due to chronic disease (Smith et al. 1984).

The Palestinian material also revealed interesting changes in the onset of childhood stress. In the Natufian period enamel hypoplasias indicate that a major period of stress occurred between 3 and 4 years of age and was probably associated with weaning (Smith et al. 1984). However, during the later Chalcolithic and Early Bronze Age periods, stress appears to have occurred earlier in life with deciduous teeth commonly affected. This suggests to Smith and co-workers (1984) that weaning took place earlier in life in these later time periods – a pattern that reflects a presumed decrease in birth spacing.

Angel's findings in the eastern Mediterranean also reflect changes in the human environment. He linked the increased frequency of hypoplasia in the Middle Bronze Age (c. 2000–1500 B.C.) skeletal samples of that area to the beginning of childhood epidemics. Epidemics were not a significant problem until that time period because human population sizes were not large enough to support the disease organisms (Angel and Bisel 1986).

A second pattern in enamel hypoplasia research is the often wide variation in frequencies within a specific time period. For example, in Neolithic skeletal samples from Hungary (Molnar and Molnar 1985) and Sweden (Gejvall 1974), there was no evidence of enamel hypoplasia. Enamel hypoplasia was found to be relatively rare in Neolithic samples from West Germany (Schaefer 1978), whereas Brothwell (1973) reports that enamel hypoplasia in Great Britain occurred in 37 percent of Neolithic skeletons. V. Formicola and colleagues (1987) reported the frequency to be high for one Italian sample.

Inadequacies in the samples raise questions about the results, but it does seem that variation among sites within a period can be interpreted to mean that specific local conditions such as parasite load may be more important than the general economic subsistence base.

There is other evidence that differences in rates of enamel hypoplasia may be related to specific geographic factors, although it is not always clear what these factors may be. Rathbun (1984) found that skeletal samples from Iran dated during the period from the Neolithic through the Metal Ages had a significantly higher rate of enamel hypoplasia than did analogous samples from Iraq. These differences were generally limited to male skeletons, and Rathbun (1984) suggests that the greater frequency in males supports the contention that growing males are more vulnerable to stress than are females.

Finally, there is some indication that the severity of hypoplasia in subadult populations is inversely associated with age of death. Some researchers have suggested that stress, producing hypoplasia, may be linked with the factors resulting in the death of the individual (Rathbun 1984; Goodman 1991). In contrast, Smith and colleagues (1984) suggest that hypoplasia is indicative of individuals who survive stress, unlike individuals who die before their teeth can be affected.

Anemia

In archeological skeletal remains, evidence of two types of anemia, although not common, are well known and of considerable biological consequence. Genetic anemias, the less common of the two, are restricted to a few geographic areas of the world. Anemia resulting from malnutrition can occur anywhere. Because of the pitfalls in diagnosing anemia in skeletal material, an understanding of the biological processes involved in this condition is helpful.

In anemia there is an abnormal increase in the need for blood formation. This may be the result of several conditions, including excessive blood loss through chronic bleeding from intestinal parasites. In the genetic anemias, the hemoglobin in red blood cells is defective. This reduces the normal life span of the cells, which in turn creates an increased demand for new blood formation. Dietary iron deficiency can also result in abnormal hemoglobin with results similar to those that exist in the genetic anemias.

Because of the increased demand for blood formation, tissues that create blood occupy more space. The bone marrow spaces that in an infant or young child are normally required for blood formation are now inadequate, and hematopoietic marrow tends to expand at the expense of cortical bone. In the postcranial skeleton the marrow volume of the long bones increases at the expense of that of the cortex, which decreases in thickness (Ortner and Putschar 1981). In the skull the diploe enlarges primarily at the expense of the outer table; the skull becomes thicker, and the external appearance of the skull becomes porous. Although many descriptive terms have been applied to this condition in the skull, currently the most commonly accepted one is *porotic hyperostosis,* introduced by Angel (1966).

Unfortunately, there are other conditions that may be associated with porous lesions of the skull, including infection and metabolic diseases such as scurvy and rickets (Ortner and Putschar 1981; Ortner 1984, 1986). Thus, unless there is unambiguous evidence of an expansion of marrow space in at least some of the cases in the skeletal sample exhibiting porous lesions of the skull, a diagnosis of anemia should be offered with caution.

Angel (1966, 1972, 1977) proposed an intriguing connection between falciparum malaria and porotic hyperostosis in the eastern Mediterranean. He hypothesized that this condition in the skeletal remains of the region is indicative of thalassemia, one of the genetic anemias that may provide some immunity against malaria, and further proposed an association between the incidence of porotic hyperostosis and the cycles of malarial severity throughout the past 10,000 years. Malaria, he argues, did not become endemic until the population settlement and increase of the Neolithic period, when the frequency of porotic hyperostosis reached 50 percent (Angel 1972). After the Neolithic, porotic hyperostosis declined to 12 percent in the Bronze Age and 2 percent in the City State period (650–300 B.C.; Angel 1972). Angel attributes this decline in anemia, and presumably malaria, to changes in environment, including lowered sea levels and drained marshes. In a book of readings edited by M. Cohen and G. Armelagos (1984b), Cohen concludes, while reviewing data presented during a symposium, that porous lesions of the skull vault and eye orbit either appeared or increased in frequency with the advent of agriculture. He cautiously argues that this trend is indicative of an increase in anemia at that time.

Tumors

Tumors of the skeleton are classified on the basis of whether they arise in bone (primary) or invade bone from another tissue (secondary, malignant, or metastatic). Most of the primary bone tumors seen in archeological human skeletons are benign. Some primary benign tumors of bone, such as osteomas, are well known in archeological skeletons; other benign tumors, such as cartilaginous exostoses (Figure V.1.5), are less common but have been reported (e.g., Ortner and Putschar 1981). These benign tumors generally have minimal medical or biological significance.

Primary malignant tumors are uncommon in archeological skeletons and tend to occur in children and adolescents. The Celtic warrior (800–600 B.C.) from Switzerland with osteosarcoma or chondro-

Figure V.1.5. Benign tumor (cartilaginous exostosis) in the area of fusion between the pubic and iliac bones of a right innominate bone. Adult female from the Twelfth Dynasty (c. 1990 B.C.) Rock Tombs, Lisht, Egypt. (Catalog no. 256474, National Museum of Natural History, Washington, D.C.)

sarcoma of the humerus (Figure V.1.6) has been reported in several publications (e.g., Ortner and Putschar 1981). Secondary (metastatic) tumors of bone are more common than primary malignant tumors. However, because this type of tumor occurs most frequently in people over 50 years of age, it is also an archeological rarity. Until very recently in human history, few people lived long enough to acquire secondary tumors of bone.

Because tumors are so rare in archeological specimens, any statement on prevalence associated with geographic areas or time periods is likely to be

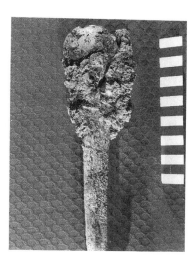

Figure V.1.6. Malignant tumor (osteosarcoma or chondrosarcoma) of the proximal left humerus of a Celtic warrior (c. 800–600 B.C.) from an archeological site near Münsingen, Bern, Switzerland. Each alternating band equals 1 centimeter. (Catalog no. A95, Natural History Museum, Bern, Switzerland.)

highly problematic. At present our data consist of case reports and surveys such as that provided by J. Gladykowska-Rzeczycka (1991) for tumors in European material. However, it seems reasonable to assume that carcinogens have been a problem for a long time. As previously mentioned, Wells (1964b) suggests that nasopharyngeal tumors seen in archeological human skeletons are associated with the open fires that have existed in human societies for millennia.

Conclusion

In this essay we have presented a broad overview of the specific diseases that may have existed in the pre-Roman Old World and outlined general patterns of health that may have been present as human society became increasingly complex. But because of the limitations imposed by the sources and the research methods used, the picture is incomplete.

From skeletal and mummy material we are fairly certain that, depending on geographic location, pre-Roman populations suffered from a number of infectious diseases (i.e., multicellular parasites, tuberculosis, poliomyelitis, periostitis, osteomyelitis, and, late in the pre-Roman era, leprosy). Most of these populations were also exposed to trauma, particularly in the form of head wounds and forearm fractures. Osteoarthritis, particularly of the spine, was prevalent, and some groups suffered from erosive joint disease. Anemia was present and apparently fairly common in some geographic locations and time periods. Tumors were rare. Determining the frequencies and geographic site of origin of some of these abnormal conditions will have to await future research.

One of the most intriguing ideas that has emerged from our review of infectious diseases is the possibility that tuberculosis became a problem in the Neolithic period. Greater population densities, sedentism, and close contact with domestic animals are all factors that, in theory, could have led to the emergence of tuberculosis as a serious health problem in the Neolithic. J. McGrath (1986) argues that large populations may not be needed for mycobacterial infections. This may be true, but it is equally true that some types of bacteria are more likely to be maintained in a host population when the population is large. A careful restudy of spines in Old World archeological skeletal samples would be most useful in clarifying this point.

Outlining general patterns of health has been equally elusive. With respect to nonspecific disease conditions (e.g., periostitis, osteitis, dental hypo-

plasia), the data seem inconsistent; there is variation among sites within the same time period, as well as among different time periods. In general, however, from the Mesolithic to the Neolithic there seems to be a trend toward increased frequencies of nonspecific disease conditions. Whether this trend is indicative of a decline in population health in the Neolithic is a question that remains, in our opinion, problematic. As we have suggested, an increased frequency of nonspecific lesions of bone may indicate a more effective immune response; individuals with nonspecific lesions of bone usually must have survived an acute phase to enter the chronic phase of a disease process.

For the urban periods, the same theoretical difficulties exist. In several areas the frequencies of enamel hypoplasias continue to increase from the Neolithic, indicating increasing childhood stress. However, the frequencies for nonspecific infectious skeletal lesions do not always increase.

Ascertaining the relation between skeletal disease and morbidity in antiquity requires great care. For example, is dental hypoplasia representative of an acute phase of a disease process occurring during late fetal life and childhood? Is periostitis indicative of chronic disease reflecting a good immune response? Issues of this type will have to be clarified before generalizations about population health can be made.

The epochal nature of the cultural change that took place between the Mesolithic and Roman periods offers an opportunity to study several important problems in human biocultural adaptation. Further research will require a much more effective descriptive and research methodology. We also need to give more careful thought to the meaning of our observations in a skeletal sample relative to the health of the living parent population.

Donald J. Ortner and Gretchen Theobald

Bibliography

Angel, J. L. 1957. Human biological changes in ancient Greece, with special reference to Lerna. In *Year Book of the American Philosophical Society*, 226–70. Philadelphia.

1966. Porotic hyperostosis, anemias, malarias and marshes in the prehistoric eastern Mediterranean. *Science* 153: 760–3.

1971a. Disease and culture in the ancient East Mediterranean. In *Proceedings of the 10th Congress of the Czechoslovak Anthropological Society at Humpolec, 1969*, 503–8. Prague.

1971b. *The people of Lerna*. Washington, D.C.

1972. Biological relations of Egyptian and eastern Mediterranean populations during pre-Dynastic and Dynastic times. *Journal of Human Evolution* 1: 307–13.

1973. Early Neolithic people of Nea Nikomedeia. In *Die Anfänge des Neolithikums vom Orient bis Nordeuropa*, ed. I. Schwidetzky, 103–12. Cologne.

1974. Patterns of fractures from Neolithic to modern times. *Anthropologiai Közlemenyek* 18: 9–18.

1977. Anemias of antiquity in the eastern Mediterranean. In *Paleopathology Association Monograph No. 2*, 1–5.

1984. Health as a crucial factor in the changes from hunting to developed farming in the eastern Mediterranean. In *Paleopathology at the origins of agriculture*, ed. M. N. Cohen and G. J. Armelagos, 51–73. Orlando, Fla.

Angel, J. L., and S. C. Bisel. 1986. Health and stress in an Early Bronze Age population. In *Ancient Anatolia: Aspects of change and cultural development*, ed. J. V. Canby et al., 12–30. Madison, Wis.

Aspöck, H., H. Flamm, and O. Picher. 1973. Intestinal parasites in human excrements from prehistoric salt-mines of the Hallstatt period (800–350 B.C.). *Zentralblatt für Bakteriologie, Parasitenkunde, Infektionskrankheiten und Hygiene* 223: 549–58.

Aufherheide, A. C. 1985. Review of *Die Anthropologische Untersuchung der C-Gruppen- und Pan-Gräber-Skelette aus Sayala, Ägyptisch-Nubien*, by E. Strouhal and J. Jungwirth. *Paleopathology Newsletter* 52: 19–20.

Bartels, P. 1907. Tuberkulose (wirbelkaries) in der jüngeren Steinzeit. *Archiv für Anthropologie* 6: 243–55.

Bennike, P. 1985. *Palaeopathology of Danish skeletons*. Copenhagen.

Bentley, G. R. 1987. Kinship and social structure at Early Bronze IA Bab edh-Dhra', Jordan. Ph.D. dissertation, University of Chicago.

Bisel, S. C. 1980. A pilot study in aspects of human nutrition in the ancient eastern Mediterranean, with particular attention to trace minerals in several populations from different time periods. Ph.D. dissertation, University of Minnesota.

Bisel, S. C., and J. L. Angel. 1985. Health and nutrition in Mycenaean Greece: A study in human skeletal remains. In *Contributions to Aegean archaeology: Studies in honor of William A. McDonald*, ed. N. C. Wilkie and W. D. E. Coulson, 197–209. Dubuque, Iowa.

Brothwell, D. R. 1960. The Bronze Age people of Yorkshire: A general survey. *Advancement of Science* 16: 311–22.

1961. The palaeopathology of early British man: An essay on the problems of diagnosis and analysis. *Journal of the Royal Anthropological Institute* 91: 318–44.

1967. The bio-cultural background to disease. In *Diseases in antiquity*, ed. D. Brothwell and A. T. Sandison, 56–68. Springfield, Ill.

1973. The human biology of the Neolithic population in Britain. In *Die Anfänge des Neolithikums vom Orient bis Nordeuropa*, ed. I. Schwidetzky, 280–99. Cologne.

Buikstra, J. E. 1976. The Caribou Eskimo: General and specific disease. *American Journal of Physical Anthropology* 45: 351–67.

Cockburn, A. 1963. *The evolution and eradication of infectious diseases*. Baltimore.

Cohen, M. N. 1984a. An introduction to the symposium. In *Paleopathology at the origins of agriculture*, ed. M. N. Cohen and G. J. Armelagos, 1–11. Orlando, Fla.

1984b. Paleopathology at the origins of agriculture: Editor's summation. In *Paleopathology at the origins of agriculture*, ed. M. N. Cohen and G. J. Armelagos, 585–601. Orlando, Fla.

Dastugue, J. 1974. Les ossements humains pathologiques. *Bulletin de la Correspondance Hellenique* 98: 749–54.

Dastugue, J., and M.-A. de Lumley. 1976. Les maladies des hommes pre-historiques. In *La Pré–historie française*, Vol. 2., ed J. Guilaine, 153–64. Paris.

Dawson, W. R., and P. H. K. Gray 1968. *Catalogue of Egyptian antiquities in the British Museum. Vol. 1: Mummies and human remains*. London.

Derums, V. J. 1987. Paleopathology of Bronze Age population in Latvia. *Anthropologie* 25: 57–61.

Derums, V. Y. 1964. Some paleopathologic data on Baltic Coast inhabitants. *Arkhiv Anatomii, Gistologii i Embriologii* 46: 225–30.

Domurad, M. R. 1986. The populations of ancient Cyprus. Ph.D. dissertation, University of Cincinnati.

Elliot-Smith, G., and W. R. Dawson. 1924. *Egyptian mummies*. New York.

Elliot-Smith, G., and F. Wood-Jones. 1910. *The archaeological survey of Nubia report for 1907–1908. Vol. 2: Report on the human remains*. Cairo.

El-Najjar, M. Y., et al. 1980. Autopsies on two native American mummies. *American Journal of Physical Anthropology* 53: 197–202.

Fiennes, R. N. 1978. *Zoonoses and the origins and ecology of human disease*. New York.

Fleming, S., et al. 1980. *The Egyptian mummy: Secrets and science*. Philadelphia.

Formicola, V. 1986. Anthropologie dentaire des restes de l'Epi gravettien final retrouvés dans la grotte des Arene Candide (Ligurie). *Bulletin et Mémoires de la Société d'Anthropologie de Paris* 3: 37–46.

1986–7. The dentition of the Neolithic sample from Western Liguria (Italy). *Ossa* 13: 97–107.

Formicola, V., Q. Milanesi, and C. Scarsini. 1987. Evidence of spinal tuberculosis at the beginning of the 4th millennium B.C. from Arene Candide Cave (Liguria, Italy). *American Journal of Physical Anthropology* 72: 1–6.

Gejvall, N.-G. 1974. Description of the human skeletons from the graves and some associated animal bones. In *Gotlands Mellanneolitiska Gravar* (The Middle Neolithic graves of Gotland), ed. O. Janzon, 141–67. Stockholm.

Gladykowska-Rzeczycka, J. 1981. A short review of paleo-pathological research in Poland. *Homo* 32: 125–30.

1991. Tumors in antiquity in East and Middle Europe. In *Human paleopathology: Current syntheses and future options,* ed. D. J. Ortner and A. C. Aufderheide, 251–6. Washington, D.C.

Goodman, A. H. 1991. Stress, adaptation and enamel developmental defects. In *Human paleopathology: Current syntheses and future options,* ed. D. J. Ortner and A. C. Aufderheide. Washington, D.C.

Goodman, A. H., D. L. Martin, and G. J. Armelagos. 1984. Indications of stress from bone and teeth. In *Paleopathology at the origins of agriculture,* ed. M. N. Cohen and G. J. Armelagos, 13–49. Orlando, Fla.

Gray, P. H. K. 1967. Radiography of ancient Egyptian mummies. *Medical Radiography and Photography* 43: 34–44.

Grmek, M. D. 1989. *Diseases in the ancient Greek world.* Baltimore.

Jones, A. K. G., and C. Nicholson 1988. Recent finds of *Trichuris* and *Ascaris* ova from Britain. *Paleopathology Newsletter* 63: 5–6.

Jurmain, R. D. 1977. Stress and the etiology of osteoarthritis. *American Journal of Physical Anthropology* 45: 353–66.

Kilgore, L. 1989. Possible case of rheumatoid arthritis from Sudanese Nubia. *American Journal of Physical Anthropology* 79: 177–83.

Klepinger, L. L. 1979. Paleopathologic evidence for the evolution of rheumatoid arthritis. *American Journal of Physical Anthropology* 50: 119–22.

Krogman, W. M. 1940. The skeletal and dental pathology of an early Iranian site. *Bulletin of the History of Medicine* 8: 28–48.

Kunter, M. 1977. *Kâmid el-Lôz.* Bonn.

Kurth, G., and O. Röhrer-Ertl. 1981. On the anthropology of the Mesolithic to the Chalcolithic: Human remains from the Tell es-Sultan in Jericho, Jordan. In *Excavations at Jericho,* Vol. 3, ed. K. M. Kenyon, 407–49. London.

Leden, O., E. Persson, and O. Persson. 1985–6. Peripheral polyarthritis in two Neolithic skeletons. *Ossa* 12: 79–88.

Lisowski, F. P. 1967. Prehistoric and early historic trepanation. In *Diseases in antiquity,* ed. D. Brothwell and A. T. Sandison, 651–72. Springfield, Ill.

Mallegni, F., G. Fornaciari, and N. Tarabella. 1979. Studio antropologico dei resti scheletrici della necropoli dei Monterozzi (Torquina). *Atti della Società Toscana di Scienze Naturali, Serie B.* 86: 185–221.

Manchester, K. 1983. *The archaeology of disease.* Bradford.

1984. Tuberculosis and leprosy in antiquity: An interpretation. *Medical History* 28: 162–73.

1991. Tuberculosis and leprosy: Evidence for the interaction of disease. In *Human paleopathology: Current syntheses and future options,* ed. D. J. Ortner and A. C. Aufderheide, 23–35. Washington, D.C.

Martin, D. L., et al. 1984. The effects of socioeconomic change in prehistoric Africa: Sudanese Nubia as a case study. In *Paleopathology at the origins of agriculture,* ed. M. N. Cohen and G. J. Armelagos, 193–214. Orlando, Fla.

May, W. P. 1897. Rheumatoid arthritis (osteitis deformans) affecting bones 5,500 years old. *British Medical Journal* 2: 1631–2.

McGrath, J. W. 1986. A computer simulation of the spread of tuberculosis in prehistoric populations of the lower Illinois River Valley. Ph.D. dissertation, Northwestern University.

Meiklejohn, C., et al. 1984. Socioeconomic change and patterns of pathology and variation in the Mesolithic and Neolithic of western Europe: Some suggestions. In *Paleopathology at the origins of agriculture,* ed. M. N. Cohen and G. J. Armelagos, 75–100. Orlando, Fla.

Mitchell, J. K. 1900. Study of a mummy affected with anterior poliomyelitis. *Transactions of the Association of American Physicians* 15: 134–6.

Molnar, S., and I. Molnar. 1985. Observations of dental diseases among prehistoric populations in Hungary. *American Journal of Physical Anthropology* 67: 51–63.

Morlock, G. 1986. Paleopathological identification of the hyperostosic disease. In *VI European Meeting of the Paleopathology Association, Proceedings,* ed. F. G. Bellard and J. A. Sanchez, 161–8. Madrid.

Morse, D. 1967. Tuberculosis. In *Diseases in antiquity,* ed. D. Brothwell and A. T. Sandison, 249–71. Springfield, Ill.

Ortner, D. J. 1968. Description and classification of degenerative bone changes in the distal joint surfaces of the humerus. *American Journal of Physical Anthropology* 28: 139–55.

1979. Disease and mortality in the Early Bronze Age people of Bab edh-Dhra, Jordan. *American Journal of Physical Anthropology* 51: 589–98.

1984. Bone lesions in a probable case of scurvy from Metlatavik, Alaska. *Journal of the Museum of Applied Science, Center for Archaeology* [*MASCA Journal*] 3: 79–81.

1986. Metabolic and endocrine disorders in human skeletal paleopathology. In *VI European Meeting of the Paleopathology Association, Proceedings,* ed. F. G. Bellard and J. A. Sanchez, 17–24. Madrid.

1991. Theoretical and methodological issues in paleopathology. In *Human paleopathology: Current syntheses and future options,* ed. D. J. Ortner and A. C. Aufderheide, 5–11. Washington, D.C.

Ortner, D. J., and W. G. J. Putschar. 1981. *Identification of pathological conditions in human skeletal remains.* Smithsonian Contributions to Anthropology No. 28. Washington, D.C.

Pales, L. 1930. *Paléopathologie et pathologie comparative.* Paris.

Patte, E. 1971. Les restes humains de la grotte sépulcrale

du Laris Goguet à Feigneux (Oise). *Bulletins et Mémoires de la Société d'Anthropologie de Paris* 7: 381–452.

Rathbun, T. A. 1984. Skeletal pathology from the Paleolithic through the Metal Ages in Iran and Iraq. In *Paleopathology at the origins of agriculture,* ed. M. N. Cohen and G. J. Armelagos, 137–67. Orlando, Fla.

Resnick, D., and G. Niwayama. 1988. *Diagnosis of bone and joint disorders,* 2d edition. Philadelphia.

Rose, J. C., K. W. Condon, and A. H. Goodman. 1984. Diet and dentition: Developmental disturbances. In *The analysis of prehistoric diets,* ed. R. I. Gilbert, Jr., and J. H. Mielke, 281–305. New York.

Rothschild, B. M., K. R. Turner, and M. A. DeLuca. 1988. Symmetrical erosive peripheral polyarthritis in the Late Archaic period of Alabama. *Science* 241: 1498–1501.

Rowling, J. T. 1961. Pathological changes in mummies. *Proceedings of the Royal Society of Medicine* 54: 409–15.

Ruffer, M. A. 1918. Studies in palaeopathology: Arthritis deformans and spondylitis in ancient Egypt. *Journal of Pathology and Bacteriology* 22: 152–96.

Ruffer, M. A., and A. Rietti. 1912. On osseous lesions in ancient Egyptians. *Journal of Pathology and Bacteriology* 16: 439–65.

Sager, P., M. Schalimtzek, and V. Møller-Christensen. 1972. A case of spondylitis tuberculosa in the Danish Neolithic Age. *Danish Medical Bulletin* 19: 176–80.

Sandison, A. T. 1973. Evidence of infective disease. In *Population biology of the ancient Egyptians,* ed. D. R. Brothwell and B. A. Chiarelli, 213–24. New York.

   1980. Diseases in ancient Egypt. In *Mummies, disease and ancient cultures,* ed. A. Cockburn and E. Cockburn, 29–44. New York.

Schaefer, U. 1978. Menschliche Skelettfunde aus dem Neolithikum im Gebiet der Länder Schleswig-Holstein, Niedersachsen, Nordrhein-Westfalen und Hessen (BRD). In *Die Anfänge des Neolithikums vom Orient bis Nordeuropa,* ed. I. Schwidetzky, 66–92. Cologne.

Short, C. L. 1974. The antiquity of rheumatoid arthritis. *Arthritis and Rheumatism* 17: 193–205.

Smith, P., O. Bar-Yosef, and A. Sillen. 1984. Archaeological and skeletal evidence for dietary change during the Late Pleistocene/Early Holocene in the Levant. In *Paleopathology at the origins of agriculture,* ed. M. N. Cohen and G. J. Armelagos, 101–36. Orlando, Fla.

Steinbock, R. T. 1976. *Paleopathological diagnosis and interpretation.* Springfield, Ill.

Strouhal, E. 1986. Anthropology of the Late Period cemetery in the tomb of King Horemheb ad Saqqara (Egypt) (preliminary report). *International Journal of Anthropology* 1: 215–24.

   1991. Vertebral tuberculosis in ancient Egypt and Nubia. In *Human paleopathology: Current syntheses and future options,* ed. D. J. Ortner and A. C. Aufderheide, 181–94. Washington, D.C.

Strouhal, E., and J. Jungwirth. 1984. *Die Anthropologische*

Untersuchung der C-Gruppen- und Pan-Gräber-Skelette aus Sayala, Agyptische-Nubien. Vienna

Tapp, E. 1986. Histology and histopathology of the Manchester mummies. In *Science in Egyptology,* ed. R. A. David, 347–50. Manchester.

Tapp, E., and K. Wildsmith. 1986. Endoscopy of Egyptian mummies. In *Science in Egyptology,* ed. R. A. David, 351–4. Manchester.

Torre, S., and J. Dastugue, 1976. Néolithiques de Basse Normandie: Le Deuxième tumulus de Fontenay-le-Marmion (Pathologie). *l'Anthropologie* 80: 625–53.

Tuross, N. 1991. Recovery of bone and serum proteins from human skeletal tissue: IgG, osteonectin and albumin. In *Human paleopathology: Current syntheses and future options,* ed. D. J. Ortner and A. C. Aufderheide, 51–4. Washington, D.C.

Vagn Nielsen, O. 1970. *The Nubian skeleton through 4000 years.* Denmark.

Wells, C. 1964a. *Bones, bodies and disease.* New York.

   1964b. Two Mediaeval cases of malignant disease. *British Medical Journal* 1: 1611–21.

   1973. A paleopathological rarity in a skeleton of Roman date. *Medical History* 17: 399–400.

   1977. Disease of the maxillary sinus in antiquity. *Medical and Biological Illustration* 27: 173–8.

   1978. Disease and evolution. *Biology and Human Affairs* 43: 5–13.

Whitehouse, W. M. 1980. Radiologic findings in the Royal mummies. In *An x-ray atlas of the royal mummies,* ed. J. E. Harris and E. F. Wente, 286–327. Chicago.

Wood-Jones, F. 1910a. Fractured bones and dislocations. In *The archaeological survey of Nubia report for 1907–1908. Vol. 2: Report on the human remains,* ed. G. Elliot-Smith and F. Wood-Jones, 293–342. Cairo.

   1910b. General pathology (including diseases of the teeth). In *The archaeological survey of Nubia report for 1907–1908. Vol. 2: Report on the human remains,* ed. G. Elliot-Smith and F. Wood-Jones, 263–92. Cairo.

y'Edynak, G., and S. Fleisch. 1983. Microevolution and biological adaptability in the transition from food-collecting to food-producing in the Iron Gates of Yugoslavia. *Journal of Human Evolution* 12: 279–96.

Zorab, P. A. 1961. The historical and prehistorical background of ankylosing spondylitis. *Proceedings of the Royal Society of Medicine* 54: 415–20.

V.2
Diseases of Western Antiquity

There are good reasons for believing that diseases and complaints of various kinds and degrees of severity were as much a part of everyday life in classical antiquity as were the assorted battle wounds and injuries so dramatically portrayed from Homer onward. This is indicated not only by the surviving Greek and Latin medical texts and the fragments preserved in Greco-Egyptian papyri, but also by the large corpus of nonmedical Greek and Latin texts, some of which are still being read today. In poetry, tragedy, and comedy, in history and annals, in philosophy and theology, as well as in botanical, agricultural, and pharmacological texts, illness and health and life and death constitute distinctive motifs.

To be certain, the evidence, both written and nonwritten, has survived in different states of preservation. It permits us, nonetheless, to reconstruct in part the intellectual and technological achievements of our past. Large gaps, however, exist in our knowledge of that past, and the absence of crucial details has led to hypotheses and inferences that cannot be tested directly.

Our knowledge of the diseases of classical antiquity stands somewhere between demonstrative certainty and complete ignorance. There is, after all, a sizable body of Greek and Latin medical texts, and it, in turn, has generated an even larger body of secondary literature. But for all that, our knowledge of the diseases of classical antiquity is far from complete. There are several reasons for its incompleteness, but it is important to keep in mind the enormous differences between the conceptual bases of the modern medical sciences and those of antiquity. These differences have important consequences in any attempt to identify the diseases of classical antiquity and to understand their effects.

One significant consequence is primarily philological: Many Greek and Latin medical terms cannot be rendered adequately by any single term in most modern languages. A case in point is the specialized vocabulary denoting diseases, used primarily though not exclusively by the ancient medical writers. Obviously this has a bearing on the study of disease. Some ancient medical terms appear to cover an indeterminately wider range of meaning than is expressed by their modern equivalents. For example, *lepra* (λεπρα)

and *gonorrhea* (γονορρηια), mean something more than the modern clinical entities whose names they bear; in fact, it is not altogether certain that *lepra* denoted Hansen's disease or that *gonorrhea* denoted the disease that today is positively diagnosed only by the presence of gonococcus.

A second consequence, far more formidable than the philological one just noted, concerns the very foundations of classical medicine. Beginning with Hippocrates, and accepted by the better medical writers throughout classical antiquity, was the notion of disease as a process. Regardless of the philosophical theory that supported the etiology, whether humoralism or solidism, a disease, theoretically, could be described as a series of stages with a predictable outcome. Each of those stages normally occupied a narrowly circumscribed period of time, such as 7, 14, or 20 days. Associated with the chronological development was a series of changes in the condition of the patient, each of which was described in specific, though not necessarily unique, terms representing the symptom or symptoms associated with that specific stage of the disease. It is with respect to the latter point that grave difficulties are encountered in an attempt to identify some of the diseases of classical antiquity. First of all, it was widely believed that some diseases were capable of passing into or changing into another disease. The latter was then characterized by its distinctive symptom or symptoms, which often were similar to the principal symptom or symptoms that characterized the original disease process. The newly arisen disease was then regarded as a species of the disease from which it originated at a certain stage in the morbid process. Then it too ran its predictable course, although therapeutic intervention (drug therapy, regiminary therapy, or surgery) might alter its course.

There was considerable discussion in antiquity concerning the proper nomenclature and, of course, therapy of these so-called species or varieties of a disease; and as one might guess, there was little agreement concerning details, especially with regard to their classification. On one issue, however, there was agreement and that was the widely adopted classification of diseases as acute or chronic. In the main, acute diseases were characterized by a sudden onset, a clearly circumscribed febrile stage, and the involvement of a specific localized area, frequently the respiratory or digestive system. As such, most of our infectious diseases were regarded as acute diseases in classical antiquity. Those disease processes in which a clearly demarcated febrile stage was absent and whose outcome could not be predicted on the basis of a specified sequence of stages fell into the larger, less organized category of chronic disease (e.g., gout, lead poisoning, and scurvy).

Because it was not possible to base an etiology on specific microscopic, pathological organisms, close attention was paid to the description of symptoms at each stage of the disease process, from onset to outcome. Thus, many of the so-called species or varieties of a disease acquired distinctive names; these were based on a few of the salient symptoms or on a consistent clinical pattern, the latter resembling what later came to be called a syndrome (literally, a "running together" of symptoms).

It must be stressed, finally, that ancient therapeutics was almost wholly symptomatic. Consequently, the large body of literature surviving from classical antiquity must be used with due recognition of the fact that the illnesses for which the many hundreds of recipes and remedies were designed must be considered, in the main, to be symptoms and syndromes.

These caveats notwithstanding, some of the diseases of classical antiquity can be identified with assurance and others can be identified with degrees of confidence that vary in proportion to both the quality and the quantity of the evidence at our disposal. In either case, however, efforts have been made to summarize the etiologic, epidemiological, and pathological evidence in such a fashion that the diseases of classical antiquity can be correlated historically with the same diseases viewed in later terms.

Apoplexy

Apoplexy (Greek *apoplexia*) is sometimes also called paraplexia or paralysis. The name *apoplexia*, according to Caelius Aurelianus, is derived "from the fact that it involves a sudden collapse, as if from a deadly blow. It is a sudden seizure (*oppressio*), in general without fever, and it deprives the body of all sensation; it is always acute and never chronic."

The etiology of apoplexy was stated in different ways by the ancient medical authors. The earliest account is from the Hippocratic corpus: It is caused by winds or breaths (φυσας), "so, if copious breaths rush through the whole body, the whole patient is affected with apoplexy. If the breaths go away, the disease comes to an end; if they remain, the disease also remains." Centuries later, Celsus wrote that the relaxation of the sinews (*resolutio nervorum*) was a common disease everywhere. "It attacks at times the whole body, at times part of it. Ancient writers named the former, apoplexia, the latter, paralysis."

Elsewhere a humoralistic etiology was advanced: black bile (melancholy) by Hippocrates, or cold, vis-

cous phlegm by Paul of Aegina (see also Galen). Finally, a solidist etiology was proposed by the Methodist sect – for example, by Soranus, whose last work was translated into Latin by Caelius Aurelianus. The latter states that apoplexy is a disease caused by strictures (*passio stricturae*) of the tube and pore structure of the human body. Isidore of Seville suggests quite a different theory, but offers no evidence or source. In fact, Isidore's entire entry for apoplexy consists of one sentence: "Apoplexia is a sudden effusion of blood, by which those who die are suffocated."

In addition to the clinical relationship between apoplexy and paralysis, there is evidence of a more primitive distinction between apoplexy and temporary mental confusion (e.g., the state of being dumbfounded, astounded, speechless), which is translated as ʼαποπλγκος and/or απυπλγκτικος in the non-medical literature, such as that by Herodotus, Aristophanes, and Sophocles.

It is difficult to separate neatly the classical beliefs regarding the incidence and epidemiology of apoplexy because of the ignorance surrounding its etiology. A few brief passages, here and there, suggest, however, that its incidence in particular must have been a subject of some discussion. Thus, there are two Hippocratic aphorisms concerned with age incidence: The first contains a short list of complaints common to old men, including apoplexy. The meaning of *old* is specific in another: "Apoplexy occurs chiefly between the ages of forty and sixty." (See also Caelius Aurelianus, who notes that old women have special therapeutic problems.) Data on seasonal incidence are also scarce. Hippocrates simply stated that apoplexy was one of several diseases that frequently occurred in rainy weather. Caelius Aurelianus, however, thought it most prevalent at the end of autumn or in the winter.

With regard to the pathology of apoplexy, detailed, clinical descriptions are provided by Celsus, Caelius Aurelianus, Galen, and Paul of Aegina. Though their descriptions do not agree verbatim, we can summarize them by noting the major areas of consensus:

1. Sudden onset (with no or few antecedent indications)
2. Lack of fever
3. Feeble pulse and shallow respiration following the stroke
4. Lack of sensation
5. Impairment of muscular control, sometimes accompanied by tremors
6. Comatose state

If there is recovery, the victim may show evidence of mental impairment, especially in his or her speech and uncontrolled muscular action. This catalogue of signs was important to the physician not only for making a diagnosis but also for differentiating apoplexy from other diseases, especially epilepsy, lethargy, and some forms of paralysis.

Asthma

"The disease called orthopnoia," wrote Aretaeus, "is also called asthma because those who have paroxysms pant for breath (*asthmainousi*)." The Greek term *asthma,* used by Homer for a gasping, painful breathing, had acquired a distinct medical sense by the time of Hippocrates.

The two terms *asthma* and *orthopnoia* are not uncommon in ancient literature, but on the basis of the adjectival form, *asthmatikos,* a nonmedical usage (e.g., the labored panting of an athlete) may be suspected.

Like many diseases, the etiology of asthma was explained in humoralistic terms. "The cause," Aretaeus states, "is the coldness and moistness of the pneuma but the matter is moist, cold, and glutinous." Airborne pollen and dust do not seem to have been implicated in the sometimes sudden onset of an allergic reaction, the latter a concept not explicitly associated with asthma in classical texts. It may be significant, however, that Hippocrates notes that asthmatic attacks are frequent in the autumn.

Aretaeus's account of the symptoms, the best single description in classical antiquity, refers in unmistakable terms to the overt characteristics of asthma and emphasizes the dry wheezing, often unproductive cough, inability to sleep in a prone position, and labored efforts to breathe leading to gulping or gasping. He seems not to have recognized, however, the constriction of the lumen of the bronchi or the possibility of neurological or hereditary factors.

Bubonic Plague

In the large, sometimes uncritical literature in the history of bubonic plague, the earliest, unimpeachable reference to the plague in classical antiquity is that provided by Rufus of Ephesus. There are also a considerable number of Greco-Roman descriptions of and references to epidemics in our sense of the term (or, in Greek and Latin, λογος [whence our word *plague*] and *pestis pestilentia*). These were of various kinds, usually unidentifiable, with various degrees of morbidity and mortality, and not always chronologically or geographically positioned. The most famous were those of the *Iliad*, the "plague of Athens,"

and the "plague of Justinian." Many different communicable diseases have been proposed for these "epidemics" (a term that in Hippocrates' *Epidemics* does not always mean what we mean by an *epidemic disease;* see Deichgraber 1933). Likewise, many different diseases have been proposed for the less well known, but equally sporadic and frightening epidemics whose echoes frequently resound in classical texts, such as those of Karl Jax, Jürgen Grimm, and Jean-Marie André. Some of those epidemic diseases may have been bubonic plague but, save for the description by Rufus and the acknowledged existence of the plague of Justinian (sixth century A.D.), the evidence is inconclusive. The likelihood of bubonic plague cannot be dismissed totally, however, because there is good evidence, first, that the plague was endemic in the Near East in the preclassical period and, second, that the Greeks and Romans had frequent contact with the people of the Near East from the sixth century B.C. onward and could easily have contracted diseases thereby. It is, finally, almost certain that bubonic plague was not unknown in late antiquity, as Byzantine reports by Paul of Aegina and Arabic and early Western medieval reports testify.

It is, then, in the context of the later stages of Greco-Roman civilization that one must consider the passage from Rufus noted at the beginning of this section. Rufus of Ephesus, a highly regarded physician and medical writer, lived during the reign of the emperor Trajan (A.D. 98–117). He is known to have been active in Rome and to have spent some time in Egypt. A short passage referring to the buboes typical in a case of plague was preserved, presumably because of its unusual interest, by the later (fourth-century) Greek physician Oribasius in his chapter on buboes. Because of its historical importance, I have translated the passage from Rufus:

The buboes termed pestilential are the most fatal and the most acute, especially those that are seen in Libya, Egypt, and Syria, as reported by Dionysius the Kyrtos. Dioscorides and Poseidonius have studied especially the plague (λοιηος) which occurred in Libya in their time. They have said that [it was characterized by] high fever, pain, disturbance (συστασις) of the entire body and the formation of large buboes, hard and non-suppurating. They develop not only in the ordinary places but also in the groins and the neck. (Translated from Oribasius.)

It may be noted that buboes had been mentioned many centuries earlier by Hippocrates. Sometimes they meant glands, but in other cases they seemed to refer to the large lymphatic swellings associated with the plague. Because Hippocrates does not assign a name to the disease of which the buboes are one of the most dramatic signs, it is difficult to decide whether bubonic plague was known to him.

Before Oribasius, Aretaeus referred to pestilential buboes of the liver, whereas Pliny the Elder referred to a plant, *bubonium*, whose name derived from the fact that it was considered especially beneficial for swellings of the groin (*inguinum*). These bits and pieces of information (and undoubtedly others exist), especially when coupled with references to "pestilential times" by Marcus Aurelius and Aristides, suggest that bubonic plague may have been implicated, more often than we have recorded, in the numerous outbreaks and epidemics, though not recognized as a discrete clinical entity.

Cancer

The term *cancer* derives from the Latin *cancer*, which in turn derives from the Greek καεκινοω both originally meaning a crab. Other medical terms used in classical antiquity derive from the same root. These terms, however, do not necessarily mean or refer to a neoplastic growth or malignant lesion. There is some evidence, in fact, that ulcers and lesions associated with other diseases (e.g., erysipelas and gangrene) were not always distinguished from malignancies.

As a medical term, καεκινοω first appears in Hippocrates but in contexts that only suggest what is meant today by cancer. Later uses of the term by Galen and his followers were similar to the medical and clinical uses that prevailed up to the time of Rudolph Virchow. In the same way, the more restricted term *carcinoma* might have denoted a malignant condition, especially when the condition terminated fatally as, for example, in Hippocrates, Caelius Aurelianus, and Cassius Felix. The most extended account of cancer, next to Galen's, was that of Celsus, who attempted to distinguish a variety of swellings (tumors). He gave special names (e.g., *atheroma, steatoma,* and *therioma*) to some of these – probably not the malignant ones. However, he also described certain, more serious conditions, perhaps complications of erysipelas and gangrene, and these he likened to cancer. He reserved the term *carcinoma* or *carcinode* for other tumors that, when they did not appear to have been the result of another, antecedent disease, may have been malignant.

The terms just noted and other Greco-Roman cognates such as *cancroma* are not as common in the medical literature as one might expect and are even rarer in the nonmedical literature. Instead, there

developed an elaborate taxonomy, with corresponding names, for a wide range of conditions that are reproduced in English by the nonspecific, generic term *swellings*. Celsus's distinctions were carried further by Galen, who distinguished among a wide range of diseases, localized morbid conditions, and various dermatological complaints. But Galen introduced one important improvement: He identified as malignant only those ογκοι (tumor[s]) that most closely resemble our concept of malignant neoplasms and called them κακογδγ.

The large amount of space devoted to recipes and other therapeutic forms for "swellings" and abscesses (e.g., by Cato, Paul of Aegina, Pliny, and Hippocrates) strongly suggests that malignant, often fatal, conditions were not uncommon, despite the lack of consensus on signs and symptoms and the equally obvious lack of a standardized nomenclature. Slightly more certain to have involved cancer is a series of inoperable, incurable, or fatal conditions of specific organs or bodily parts that were, more or less, amenable to examination, such as the breast, testicles, nose, and throat. It is even more problematic that neoplastic growths of internal organs were recognized, but perhaps it was to these that Hippocrates was referring by the phrase κευπτοι καεχιωοι (hidden cancers).

Reflecting the uncertainties in the diagnosis and therapy of what Galen called "swellings contrary to nature," their etiology was equally uncertain. Galen, however, twice explicitly stated that black bile was the cause of cancers. A hint of another, not necessarily incompatible etiology is contained in Celsus's statement that, whereas some ulcers arise from an external cause, carcinomata and the like "arise from within, from some part of the body which has been corrupted."

Diphtheria

The term *diphtheria*, introduced by Pierre Bretonneau to replace his earlier term *diphtheritis*, derives from the Greek, literally "skin, hide," referring to the characteristic tough, white pseudomembrane of the trachea and other respiratory organs in advanced cases. There do not appear to be any classical Greek or Latin terms to designate this once-dreaded infectious disease. Aretaeus's terms (Egyptian and Syriac ulcers) were not adopted by later writers. Diphtheria seemingly was not always differentiated from other infectious diseases, and it was not unambiguously described until many centuries later.

The two best accounts of diphtheria in classical antiquity are those of Aretaeus and Aetius of

Amida. These two passages, supplemented by the more vague accounts of Hippocrates, described the principal signs and symptoms on the basis of which classical diagnoses were made before Friedrich Löffler's identification and isolation in 1884 of *Bacillus diphtheriae,* now *Corynebacterium diphtheriae.* The Hippocratic passages alluded to and a remotely possible reference by Soranus describe a condition that is not incompatible with diphtheria, but the absence of crucial data make a more positive identification impossible.

At any rate, these passages together provide a clinical picture similar to the early modern accounts of *angina maligna,* one of the many names in use before Bretonneau. Signs and symptoms as reported by Aretaeus and Aetius of Amida (Hirsch 1886) include the development of a phlegmatic, whitish film in the mouth and throat, rapidly spreading to the trachea, accompanied by a foul odor. The disease, often accompanied by fever, is rapidly fatal, especially among juveniles. Death is caused by suffocation, but weakness due to an aversion to food and drink may be a contributing factor. The voice is hoarse and strangely modulated; respiration is rapid but shallow; and liquids are sometimes passed out through the nose (due to a paralytic destruction of the soft palate, though not explicitly so stated by the classical authors).

As is well known, diphtheria epidemics have occurred, and both morbidity and mortality rates can be high, especially for children. For those reasons one would expect prima facie a larger number of classical references to diphtheria. There are perhaps two reasons for the paucity of data. First, diphtheria might have been confused with other diseases (e.g., aphthae, tonsilitis, candidasis). Second, the rapid course of fatal diphtheria did not permit the ancient physicians sufficient time to examine the patient with an eye on prognosis.

The source material at our disposal suggests that the etiology of diphtheria was somewhat uncertain. An overabundance of phlegm easily accounted for the development of the characteristic pseudomembrane. A further explanation is provided by Aretaeus's remark that the natural heat of young children is cooled by the rapid respiration and inspiration of cold air (apparently thus hastening the development of the phlegmatic pellicle). Finally, a dietetic cause is subjoined by Aretaeus: The thick and impure food and drink of the Egyptians lead to morbid changes, the so-called Egyptian ulcers.

Only the barest facts on incidence are available, but they highlight two important facts: Children, especially infants, were highly susceptible, and the season of highest incidence was winter. There seems to be no evidence for a disproportionate sexual incidence.

Dysentery

The word *dysentery* (Latin *dysenteria*) derives from the Greek *dys* (bad) plus *enteria* (intestine), thereby indicating the system involved, though not, of course, the causative agent.

Although explicit references are not common, it is probable that dysentery was widespread in antiquity. Some evidence is provided by a series of four aphorisms in Hippocrates, as well as the explicit statement that dysentery was common in the summer and autumn. Elsewhere, in an attempt to establish the disease pattern and age incidence, it is written that men (beyond the age of young men, i.e., 30 years and older) commonly suffer from 11 diseases, 2 of which are chronic diarrhea and dysentery. This fits the pattern of men of military age and the conditions of crowding and lack of proper sanitation facilitating local outbreaks, if not small epidemics.

Various philosophical and medical theories were advanced to explain the sudden outbreak, its spread, and the distinctions, not always clear, between acute and chronic dysentery, on the one hand, and between dysentery and diarrhea, on the other. Roughly, there were two different kinds of etiologic proposals, each of which had its adherents, some of whom tried to combine the salient features of the two competing theories. Whether the humoral explanation came earlier is difficult to judge; at any rate, Hippocrates seems to have been the earliest exponent of the theory that one of the humors, in this case black bile, was the causative agent. Other writers (e.g., Plato, Timaeus, and Cassius Felix) selected other humors as the causative agent. The other theory, equally reasonable at that stage of medical inquiry, was that unconcocted or undigested food, not necessarily "bad" food, was the cause. This theory is represented by Aristotle and Aretaeus. At the end of the classical period, Paul of Aegina suggested that the mucus found in the feces indicated undigested food, although he opted for black bile as the principal cause. We may note here, before discussing the pathology of dysentery, that no evidence is available at present as to whether the dysentery of the classical writers was bacillary (shigellosis) or amebic.

The literature on the signs and symptoms of dysentery corroborate the belief that dysentery was both widespread and common. All authorities are in agreement that a compelling need to defecate, the frequency of which is proportionate to severity, quickly becomes unproductive and that the production of well-formed stools, within 48 to 72 hours, changes to the production of watery stools. Such watery stools, from ones tinged reddish to ones highly colored with blood, were often thought to contain fleshlike shreds of undigested food (i.e., mucus or pus). In addition, the gripings in the lower abdomen, so ran the prevailing theory, led to typical straining – *tenesmoi* – that both physically evacuated the inadequately concocted food products and dehydrated and physically enervated the victims.

There was less agreement regarding other signs. Celsus, for example, asked whether the patient was always fevered, and Alexander of Tralles tried to determine the extent to which the liver was involved. Galen has left us the best account of the typical ulcerated lower intestine. Finally, Hippocrates seems to have regarded dysentery following an enlarged spleen (perhaps of malarial origin) as a favorable condition, doubtless with the thought in mind that a natural catharsis would help to reduce a swollen organ by removing impurities.

Erysipelas

Erysipelas is a direct transliteration of the Greek, literally "red skin," referring to its most obvious characteristic. It was usually termed *ignis sacer* (holy fire) in classical Latin, and the synonym is confirmed by Celsus and Cassius Felix. It is important to note that the erysipelas termed ignis sacer is distinct from ergotism, sometimes also called ignis sacer or St. Anthony's Fire.

Although noted several times by Hippocrates, erysipelas was not given much attention in classical medical writings and is very rare in nonmedical writings (but see Lucretius and possibly Virgil). It was considered to be serious, however, and an epidemic was reported by Hippocrates. Fatalities were reported by Hippocrates and Paul of Aegina. It is clear that the erysipelas of classical texts is not always restricted to the streptococcal infection known by that name today, for apparently sometimes it was confused with gangrene and herpes, as, for example, by Scribonius Largus.

Despite the relatively slight attention paid to the etiology and incidence of erysipelas by classical writers, there are reasons for believing that, in fact, it was far from rare. First, the disproportionately large amount of space devoted to a host of different therapeutic forms by Caelius Aurelianus, Scribonius, Pliny, and Oribasius strongly suggests it was not uncommon. Second, the prevalence of wounds, abra-

sions, and contusions must have provided easy access to the pathogens. Third, even without therapeutic intervention, many cases of self-limiting erysipelas ran their courses with little lasting trauma to the patient.

The symptoms of erysipelas are so clearly described by the classical medical writers as to leave little doubt about the accuracy of the identification. These include redness and swelling with a spreading painful lesion (Celsus), usually accompanied by fever (Hippocrates). In agreement with modern symptomatology, erysipelas was described on most of the more exposed portions of the body; specifically, it was noted as involving the face and the mucous membranes of the mouth and throat (Hippocrates), thus perhaps as being one of the causes of noninfantile aphthae. Celsus and Hippocrates noted appearance of erysipelas soon after the infliction of a wound, and Celsus made the distinction, though not with complete understanding, between idiopathic and traumatic erysipelas. It is more difficult to understand what is meant by erysipelas of specific, usually internal, organs, for example, uterus and lungs (Hippocrates) and brain (Paul of Aegina). A Hippocratic aphorism suggests that the phrase *inward-turning erysipelas* (regarded as a dangerous sign) is simply a way of expressing the fact that other, more serious symptoms accompanied the external, reddened areas.

The etiology of erysipelas was not altogether clear but, as was frequently the case with infectious diseases of rapid onset, a humoralistic explanation was advanced by Galen and Paul of Aegina.

Hippocrates noted that "early in the spring" was the season of highest incidence and that "those of about sixty years" were especially prone; however, his detailed case history in *Epidemics* describes the nonfatal case of an 11-year-old boy.

Malaria

In the opinion of most scholars, malaria was common in classical antiquity. Moreover, it seemed to be widespread geographically, as references to both local malarious and malaria-free regions indicate. Malaria, in fact, may have been endemic in some regions; if so, it undoubtedly colored the clinical findings of some chronically ill patients and may have been responsible for infant deaths not otherwise indicated. Less certain are the socioeconomic consequences of endemic malaria, although work efficiency must certainly have been impaired in malarious regions and among those who suffered from chronic malaria.

Despite the large literature on the history of malaria and the innumerable surveys undertaken in conjunction with malaria eradication programs (in which patients were examined before or in the absence of chemotherapy, and hence were clinically analogous to patients of classical times), it is not easy to document the early history of malaria.

There are many reasons for our lack of certainty regarding malaria in classical antiquity, and since they are so intimately bound up with our interpretations of classical sources, it is worth listing some of them. This will help us to do what the ancient physicians tried to do, namely to distinguish malaria from a host of other diseases and pathological conditions.

First, until the late nineteenth century, there was no knowledge of the pathogenic organisms (the *Plasmodia*) involved. Thus, any diagnosis of malaria (or of one of the diseases with which it was often confused) depended, to a great extent, on the accurate recording of the signs and symptoms exhibited by a patient. Second, and perhaps as a function of its widespread distribution, malaria was often confused with other febrile conditions (e.g., phrenitis). On this matter, we have the explicit testimony of Galen's works, as well as smaller texts such as that of Alexander of Aphrodisias. Diocles and Crasistratus both wrote books entitled *On Fevers,* which have been lost. Third, and as a consequence of the first two points, the nomenclature was confused and inconsistent. Until the postclassical term, literally meaning "shivering fever," came into use, other terms were commonly employed. None of them were completely satisfactory because they had other conflicting definitions such as "nightmare" or the shivers that accompanied the disease. The term *febris* was too broad, and hence although the root meanings of fire, heat, and burning were applicable to malaria fever, they could and did apply to other febrile conditions; καυσος, or *febris ardens,* also signified intense, burning heat, though, of course, there was no way of translating the subjective sensations of a feverish patient into thermometric terms. Other, more restricted terms existed, but they will be examined later. Fourth, the different types of *Plasmodium* infection, best exemplified by the well-known terms *tertian* and *quartan* malaria, were so well recognized that they were regarded as separate diseases; moreover, other diseases (e.g., phrenitis and lethargy), which may have had a malarial basis, were regarded as capable of passing or changing into other febrile conditions and hence confounded diagnosis, prognosis, and therapy alike.

These difficulties notwithstanding, a close reading of the chapters devoted to "fever" and so forth in the classical medical texts and a comparison of those texts with the numerous but scattered references to "fever" in the nonmedical texts leaves little doubt that malaria was indeed common and well known. The best evidence for this claim is provided by the conjunction of signs and symptoms that would be recognized as malarial today, in the absence of any chemotherapy. Principally, three signs, when associated with other data (e.g., cachexia or habitation in an area known to be "unhealthful," especially when situated near a marsh or estuary), established diagnoses until the advent of blood smears. First was splenomegaly. In routine physical examinations of the sort that Hippocrates advocated, palpation of the hypochondrium would often reveal an enlarged, tender spleen according to Celsus and Hippocrates. Second was the invariable sequence of chills, fever, and sweats, which was noted in many texts, among them those of Celsus, Pliny, and Hesychius. Third was the periodic nature of the disease, usually indicated in Latin by *accessia*. This is a more complex issue because of the nosological tendencies of medical writers who divided and classified fever into various forms: cottidian (daily); tertian (every third day; counting day of onset and day of crisis = every 48 hours); quartan (every fourth day; counting day of onset and day of crisis = every 72 hours). To these may be added the more puzzling quintans, septans, nonans, semitertians, and other mathematical, though not necessarily clinical, entities.

It was presumably through a long period of noting and recording the constellation of such signs, and patients' symptoms, that a "malarial constitution" was defined, according to Hippocrates. This, in turn, led to the establishment of the typical malaria cachexia and its common occurrence in classical Rome, as indicated by Martialis, Juvenal, Horace, and Livy.

The same wide range of opinion covering the differential diagnosis of malaria applies equally well to its etiology. There are hints of a very ancient belief in a supernatural origin. Sophocles, when describing an epidemic (of unknown origin) at Thebes, refers to a "fever-bringing god." This does not prove that malaria was the cause of the epidemic any more than the presence of a temple dedicated to the goddess or numen Febris in Rome (according to Cicero and Pliny) proves that malarial fevers could always be distinguished from other fevers.

In Hippocrates, the etiology of four types of fever was explained in humoralistic terms. Three of the fevers are clearly malarial: cottidian, tertian, and quartan. The first two of these were caused by various amounts of surplus yellow bile; quartan was caused by a mixture of yellow and black bile. It was the "mixed humoral state" that was responsible for the longer cycle, which explained why quartan was more recalcitrant to therapy.

In addition to a humoralistic etiology, Galen wrote of a "feverish constitution" being due to a pestilential air, which could also be described as a "pestilential constitution." It was also observed, for example by Celsus, that fatigue and hot weather led to fever; elsewhere he states, however, that therapy is difficult because fever can have both evident and hidden causes.

Both medical and nonmedical writers (e.g., Hippocrates, Horace, and Juvenal) agreed that late summer and autumn were the most likely seasons to be characterized by fever – a vestige of which survived until recently in the phrase *estivoautumnal fever* for falciparum malaria.

Jerry Stannard

Bibliography

André, Jean-Marie, and Alain Hus. 1974. *L'Histoire à Rome: Historiens et biographes dans la littérature latine*. Paris.

Aretaeus of Cappadocia. 1828. *Aretaei Cappadocis opera omnia*, ed. C. G. Kühn. Leipzig.

Aristides, Aelius. 1958. *Aelii Aristidis Smyrnaei quae supersunt omnia*, ed. Bruno Keil. Berlin.

Aristophanes. 1988. *The wasps*, ed. Douglas M. McDowell. Oxford.

Aristotle. 1908–52. *The works of Aristotle translated into English*, 12 vols., ed. J. A. Smith and W. D. Ross. Oxford.

Aurelianus, Caelius. 1950. *On acute diseases and on chronic diseases*, trans. Israel Edward Drabkin. Chicago.

Blass, Fredrich Wilhelm. 1895. *Acta apostolorum: Sive, lucae and theophilum liber alter*. Göttingen.

Bretonneau, Pierre Fidèle. 1826. *Des inflammations spéciales du tissu muqueux et en particulier de la diphthérite, ou imflammation pelliculaire*. Paris.

Cassius, Felix. 1879. *Casii Felicis de medicina: Ex graecis logicae sectae auctoribus liber, translatus sub Artabure et Calepio consulibus*, ed. Valentin Rose. Leipzig.

Cato, Marcus Porcius. 1966. *De agricultura*, trans. Ernest Brehaut. New York.

Celsus, Aulus Cornelius. 1938. *De medicina*, trans. Walter George Spencer. Cambridge.

Deichgräber, Karl. 1933. *Die epidemien und das corpus Hippocraticum: Voruntersuchungen zu einer Geschichte der Koischen Artzeschule*. Berlin.

Dioscorides, Pedanius. 1906–14. *De materia medica*, 3 vols., ed. Max Wellmann. Berlin.

Galen. 1821–33. *Opera omnia*, 22 vols., ed. C. G. Kühn. Leipzig.

Grimm, Jürgen. 1965. *Die literarische darstellung der pest in der antike und in der Romania*. Munich.

Herodotus of Halicarnassus. 1958. *The histories of Herodotus of Halicarnassus*, trans. Harry Carter. New York.

Hesychius of Alexandria. 1965. *Hesychii Alexandrini Lexicon*, ed. Moriz Wilhelm Constantin Schmidt and Rudolph Menge. Leipzig.

Hippocrates. 1894–1902. *Opera*, 2 vols., ed. H. Kuehlewein. Leipzig.

Hirsch, August. 1883–6. *Handbook of geographical and historical pathology*, 3 vols., trans. Charles Creighton. London.

Homer. 1950. *The Iliad*, trans. A. H. Chase and W. G. Perry, Jr. Boston.

Horace. 1936. *The complete works of Horace*, ed. Casper J. Kraemer, Jr., trans. Hubert Wetmore Wells. New York.

Isidore of Seville, Saint. 1964. *Etymologiae*, trans. William D. Sharpe. Philadelphia.

Jax, Karl. 1932. *Aegypten in Hellenistischer und Römischer zeit nach antiken papyris*. Münster.

Juvenal. 1965. *Juvenal: Satires*, trans. Jerome Mazzaro. Ann Arbor, Mich.

Livy. 1976. *Livy: In fourteen volumes*, ed. G. P. Goold and T. E. Page, trans. B. O. Foster et al. Cambridge, Mass.

Löffler, Friedrich. 1884. Untersuchungen über die bedeutung der mikroorganismen für die Entstehung der *Diphtherie beim Menschen, bei der Taube und beim Kalbe: Mittheilung kaiserlichen Gesundhante* 2: 421–99.

Lucretius Carus, Titus. 1937. *Der rerum natura*, trans. R. C. Trevelyan. Cambridge.

Marcellus Empiricus. 1567. Writings. In *Medicae artis principes post Hippocraticum et Galenum, Graeci Latinitate donati*, ed. H. Stephanus. Geneva.

Marcus Aurelius. 1983. *The meditations*, trans. G. M. A. Grube. Indianapolis.

Martialis, Marcus Valerius. 1947–50. *Epigrams*, trans. W. C. A. Ker. Cambridge.

Oribasius. 1964. *Oribasii collectionum medicarum reliquiae*, 4 vols., ed. Johann Raeder. Amsterdam.

Ovidius Naso, Publius. 1933. *Ovid's Metamorphoses*, 2 vols., ed. and trans. Brookes More. Boston.

Paul of Aegina. 1844–7. *The seven books of Paulus Aegineta*, 3 vols., trans. Francis Adams. London.

Pliny the Elder. 1855–87. *The natural history of Pliny*, trans. John Bostock and H. T. Riley. London.

Rufus of Ephesus. 1726. *De vesicae renumque morbis. De purgantibus medicamentis. De partibus corporis humani*, ed. William Clinch. London.

Scribonius Largus. 1887. *De compositionibus medicamentorum liber unus*, ed. G. Helmreich. Berlin.

Sophocles. 1970. *Philoctetes*, ed. T. E. L. Webster. Cambridge.

Soranus of Ephesus. 1927. *Sorani Gynaeciorum libri IV, De signis fracturarum, De faciis, Vita Hippocratis secundum Soranum*, ed. Johannes Ilberg. Leipzig.

Thucydides. 1921–30. *History of the Peloponnesian War*, 4 vols., trans. Charles Forster Smith. London.

Trallanius, Alexander. 1963. *Alexander von Tralles: Original-text und Uebersetzung nebst einer einleitenden Abhandlung: Ein Beitrag zur Geschichte der Medizin*, 2 vols., ed. and trans. Theodor Puschmann. Amsterdam.

V.3
Diseases of the Middle Ages

During the Middle Ages (roughly A.D. 500–1500), Europe changed from an agrarian society composed of relatively small and isolated communities to an increasingly commercial and urban world, though still predominantly agricultural. After centuries of static or declining growth in late antiquity, the population of Europe increased approximately threefold between 800 and 1300. Generally, the history of medieval diseases reflects these demographic and economic facts. While the ancient diseases of pneumonia, tuberculosis, and smallpox, and others including typhoid, diphtheria, cholera, malaria, typhus, anthrax, scarlet fever, measles, epilepsy, trachoma, gonorrehea, and amebiasis persisted throughout our period, many diseases of Europeans during the early Middle Ages were related to deficient diet.

Improved nutrition in the later Middle Ages led to a relatively larger population. As Fernand Braudel (1979) has emphasized, an increase in population alters all aspects of life, bringing advantages but at the same time threatening the existing standard of living and hope of improving that standard. In addition, it can bring disease. Ironically, the improved nutrition that made possible the growth of population, towns, and trade in the Middle Ages in turn created fertile opportunities for the contagious diseases that ultimately changed the face of Europe.

Nutrition and Disease

A revolution in agricultural techniques in northern Europe has been credited with this remarkable population growth (e.g., White, Jr. 1962). Agrarian methods inherited from the Roman Empire were suitable for the warm, dry lands of the Mediterranean and Near East, but proved inadequate on the broad, fertile plains of northern Europe. The old scratch plow that required the double labor of cross-plowing to turn the soil, plodding oxen, and two-field rotation

(half of the fields sown in the autumn to take advantage of winter rains in the south, half left fallow to restore fertility) were ultimately replaced by the heavy plow, the horse, and a three-field rotation system. A new plow, usually mounted on wheels and heavy enough to require eight animals to pull it, turned the soil so thoroughly that no cross-plowing was required and produced long, narrow fields instead of the square plots of the south. The moldboard of the new plow, which could turn the turf in either direction to assist drainage of the fields, was ideal for the opening of alluvial bottomland, the richest land of all. After the development of nailed horseshoes and a padded horse collar with harness attached (the old oxen neckstrap tightened across the jugular vein and windpipe of the horse), horses gained greater speed and staying power, which not only increased the amount of land a peasant could farm but also the distance he could travel to reach his outermost strips.

But horses eat more than oxen do and prefer oats, which are planted in the spring; therefore, the widespread use of the horse had to await the food surpluses of the three-field rotation system. Spreading outward from the Frankish lands between the Rhine and the Seine, this system faced great practical obstacles in the creation of the third field and was firmly established only in the wake of the devastation caused by raids of Vikings and Magyar horsemen in the ninth and tenth centuries. By approximately 1200, most of northern Europe had accepted the three-field system, whereby one-third of arable land was planted in spring to catch the abundant summer rains, one-third was planted in autumn, and one-third was left fallow. The system meant an overall increase in production of 50 percent.

Before this revolution, the peasantry, which comprised 98 percent of the European population, had subsisted on a high-carbohydrate diet ingested as bread, porridge, and beer, whether derived from barley, as in some parts of the north, or from rye and wheat. When a peasant's principal crop failed, he and his family might well starve. Moreover, even with optimal harvests, they very likely experienced severe protein deprivation. The agricultural revolution brought them not only greater yields, but a diversity of crops, including legumes and peas, which served as a protection against famine and provided more vegetable protein. These nutrients were to be of far-reaching nutritional consequence, for the peasant seems to have received little animal protein in the early Middle Ages.

It is true that abundant meats – domestic and

game – as well as poultry and fish covered the tables of the rich. But the peasants are believed to have consumed what very little animal protein they received in the form of what was known, with unmistakable irony, as "white meat," that is, dairy products – milk, cheese, and eggs (Drummond and Wilbraham 1959). Peasants might own some livestock and poultry, which wandered freely in the village; however, early medieval animals were subject to the frequent hazards of disastrous epidemics, winter starvation, and sacrifice in time of famine, and consequently they could not be regarded as a dependable source of food (Drummond and Wilbraham 1959). Seemingly conflicting evidence has been obtained from excavations of several ports and other emporia of the ninth century (Dorestad, Holland; Southampton, England; and others) that reveals that not only prosperous merchants, but humble citizens with small houses and farm plots within the town, consumed a considerable amount of meat and seafood, judging by bones and shells found in pits (Hodges 1982, 1984). However, town dwellers, especially in coastline communities, were not representative of the great portion of the population that was tied to the land, and as a general rule, early medieval peasants can be assumed to have seldom eaten meat – usually what they could obtain by hunting or poaching on the manor lord's land (Drummond and Wilbraham 1959).

Hunting diminished as population increased and the forests yielded to the plow. Presumably, as the forest dwindled, poaching penalties became more severe, though the trapping of small animals must have remained common. Freshwater fish filled mill ponds, of which England had 5,624 in 1086 according to the Domesday Book, and ocean fish became far more available after the salting of herring was introduced in the thirteenth century or soon after. Rabbits spread northward slowly across northern Europe from Spain in the early Middle Ages, reaching England by 1186 at least (White 1976). Nevertheless, it was only after the agricultural revolution produced food surpluses that could sustain food livestock, as well as humans and horses, that animal protein became readily available. That this was the case by the early fourteenth century is evidenced by the fact that the church saw fit to urge abstinence from eating flesh on fast days, indicating that regular meat consumption must have become an ordinary practice (Bullough and Campbell 1980). In addition, protests against the enclosure movement of the sixteenth century, in which country people complained that they could no longer afford beef, mut-

ton, or veal, suggest that by then these meats had become the food of ordinary people (Drummond and Wilbraham 1959). Finally, the agricultural revolution brought surpluses in a variety of crops, so that there was less risk of starving when one crop failed. The result was better nutrition for all, which preserved the lives of those less fit, especially children.

Women are believed to have suffered more than men from the deficient diet of antiquity and the early Middle Ages. Many sources from the ancient world indicate that men outlived women, and an examination of French and Italian records from the ninth century shows that, whereas more female childern than male reached the age of 15, males nonetheless enjoyed a greater life expectancy than females (Herlihy 1975). Numerous explanations of this paradox have been offered, including the underreporting of women because they were living in concubinage and death in childbirth (for a survey of theories, see Siegfried 1986).

In the thirteenth and fourteenth centuries, however, writers begin to indicate a surplus of women. Rheims had an excess in 1422, Fribourg in 1444, and Nuremberg in 1449 (Herlihy 1975). Some scholars explain this reversal by the greater iron content of the average diet of the later Middle Ages that accompanied the greater consumption of meat and legumes. Until the onset of menstruation at 12 to 14 (the average age mentioned in ancient and medieval medical treatises; see Bullough and Campbell 1980), young girls need no more iron than boys, but after menarche, they require replacement iron of 1 to 2 milligrams per day.

In the early Middle Ages women probably received no more than 0.25 to 0.75 milligram and consequently must have become progressively iron deficient. Cooking in iron pots can increase iron intake, but pottery probably was in common use until the twelfth or thirteenth centuries. During pregnancy and lactation, a woman's iron requirements are considerably greater, rising to as much as 7.5 milligrams per day in late pregnancy. Severe anemia predisposed women to death from other causes – respiratory, coronary, or hemorrhagic – and by the third pregnancy, a woman's life must have been at severe risk (Bullough and Campbell 1980).

Unfortunately for historians, few medieval records exist to document protein or iron deficiency or the other numerous deficiency diseases recognized by modern science. Still, rickets, known since ancient times, can be assumed to have existed in regions where neither ample sunshine nor a diet containing substantial amounts of seafood or dairy products was available. Ophthalmia, caused by vitamin A deficiency, would have been a problem wherever famine or severe poverty was found. Scurvy may be assumed to have been prevented by the inclusion of cabbage or other vegetables or fruits in the diet, though fruits were expensive, available only for a limited season, and widely regarded with suspicion (Drummond and Wilbraham 1959; Talbot 1967). Pellagra, however, was not a problem in Europe until maize, which is deficient in niacin, was brought from the New World in the sixteenth century and became the staple crop in some areas.

Although malnutrition or undernutrition can produce higher infection rates, history shows us that epidemics by no means regularly follow famines. It is true that in the process known to biologists as the synergism of infection, victims cease to eat well, even though they have greater metabolic needs and are exhausting their protein reserves in the fight against infection. But the host's immune system fails only when actual starvation exists. Indeed, chronic malnutrition may actually assist the host in withholding nutrients necessary for a microorganism, in the natural defense mechanism known as nutritional immunity, and many virulent infections appear without any synergism in victims of poor nutrition (Carmichael 1983).

Although not a deficiency disease, ergotism, called ignis sacer or St. Anthony's fire, is associated with such diseases because it attacked whole communities that had consumed rye grain infected with the ergot fungus. Because the fungus grows in damp conditions, contamination of the crop occurred most frequently after a severely cold winter (which reduced the resistance of the grain) and a rainy spring, or when rye had been planted in marshy land, such as land newly cultivated because of the pressures of population growth. Figuring prominently in the history of French epidemics in the Middle Ages, ergotism can be traced as far back as 857, with five outbreaks in the tenth century and several in each successive century. It occurred most frequently in the Loire and eastern French provinces. Its cause was not then recognized, and miraculous cures were claimed through the intercession of St. Anthony the Hermit, who was generally associated with ignis sacer. It was in his name that an order of hospitallers was founded at La Motte, in a mountainous region of France (inhabitants of alpine areas were particularly vulnerable to ergotism because of cool weather), which became a pilgrimage center for those who suffered from the disease (Talbot 1967). Victims – frequently children and teenagers, who,

because they were growing, ingested more ergot per unit of body weight – exhibited dramatic symptoms, writhing and screaming from burning pains in their limbs. In fact, a close correlation has been made between the growing of rye, cold and damp weather, and the persecution of what was regarded as witchlike behavior in sixteenth- and seventeenth-century England (Matossian 1983).

Infectious Disease

As the agricultural revolution progressed, it promoted population growth and a much greater population density – indeed, a density not known since the decline of Rome in the late empire. This density in turn became the new enemy of population growth in the West. The Near East had long been characterized by a relatively high density of population and urban centers, and consequently the peoples of the region had long been developing resistance to the disease generated in such dense populations. Thus, Europeans who came in contact with the old centers of civilization were at serious risk of developing infection.

Nonetheless, travel to these centers increased throughout the Middle Ages. Simple pilgrimages drew Europeans to the Holy Land as early as the fourth century. Wars of Christian reconquest in Sardinia, Spain, and Sicily reopened the Mediterranean Sea in the eleventh century, and from 1096 to 1271 Crusaders struck out for the Holy Land. Contact with the East stimulated a taste for its products, especially textiles, furs, and spices, and led to the establishment of permanent trade routes, with caravans regularly traveling as far as the Mongol Empire.

This trade contributed to the widespread growth of European cities and the birth of new towns. Overcrowding in poorly ventilated dwellings with thatched roofs and dirt floors, and infested with rats and fleas, provided fertile ground for the spread of communicable diseases inevitably brought in, often from afar.

The water supply in these urban areas was usually dependent on a river, which underwent seasonal variation in volume and was subject to contamination from sewage and refuse. Brewers, dyers, tanners, and other trades people dumped waste into waterways, as did butchers and fishmongers; in 1369 London butchers were ordered to stop polluting the Thames (Talbot 1967). Perhaps the greatest pollution was found in the streets: Household waste was thrown from windows, dead animals were left to decay where they fell, and the entire contents of stables were swept outside.

The absence of good personal hygiene also predisposed the populace to contagious disease. Although physicians prescribed steam, cold, or herb baths, and bathing had a role in rituals such as those performed upon induction into knighthood or on certain feast days (Talbot 1967), baths, partly because of limited water supplies, could not have been as common as they are today, even for the well-to-do. Urban dwellers were undoubtedly better served: Public baths were available in many towns, even for the less wealthy. Country people surely bathed less than town dwellers, and had few changes of clothing. Apparel, predominantly woolen in northern Europe, was relatively expensive and difficult to launder. For rich and poor alike, clothing and hair sheltered lice and fleas, according to medical treatises of the time (Talbot 1967). All of these conditions greatly assisted the spread of contagious diseases.

With population density at a critical level, the last few centuries of the Middle Ages saw the unique social, intellectual, economic, and demographic influence of four contagious diseases – plague, influenza, leprosy, and tuberculosis. The dramatic impact of the Black Death in 1347–50 inspired contemporary accounts as well as subsequent studies, now literally in the thousands. Leprosy has also been a favorite subject for historians. The study of influenza, however, has long suffered from problems of correct identification. And the presence and importance of medieval tuberculosis must be largely inferred.

Tuberculosis

The incidence of tuberculosis, an age-old malady, is believed to have increased greatly during the Middle Ages, although this is difficult to document. Although excavation of medieval graves has disclosed only a few skeletons showing tuberculosis of the bone, this tells us very little since the disease is known today to affect the bone in only 5 to 7 percent of untreated cases (Steinbock 1976; Manchester 1984).

Tuberculosis is a population-density-dependent illness, and the growth of towns may well have been accompanied by an increase in the disease. Relying on the assumption that a high death rate in the years from 20 to 40 is evidence of widespread tuberculosis, (historically it has ravaged this age group the most), investigators examining skeletons dating from the years 1000 to 1348 in Germany and other areas have concluded that an increase in the disease did indeed parallel urbanization (Russell 1985). Evidence for the importance of tuberculosis in the Middle Ages is provided by the ancient custom among French and English kings of attempting to cure vic-

tims of scrofula (tuberculosis of the cervical lymph nodes) by touching them. Called the king's evil or the royal disease, this form of tuberculosis was sufficiently widespread to have attracted the attention of the court. According to English records of the king's pence given as alms to the sick, Edward I touched 1,736 victims during 1289–90, 983 during 1299–1300, and 1,219 during 1303–4 (Bloch 1973). In part because of the natural remissions of scrofula (if, indeed, these cases were correctly diagnosed), which were thought to be effected by the God-given powered of the monarch, the practice persisted, in some form at least, into the nineteenth century in France.

No doubt, the design of medieval farm homes, in which cattle and humans were housed under the same roof, contributed to the spread of the bovine tuberculosis bacillus to humans, and thus spread of tuberculosis in Europe. Bovine tuberculosis existed in Po Valley dairy cattle before their introduction to northern Europe in the thirteenth century (Manchester 1984). Crowded conditions in the new towns also increased the diffusion of the disease, for it can spread by droplets produced by sneezing, coughing, and the like.

Tuberculosis is caused by *Mycobacterium tuberculosis,* which is of the same genus as *Mycobacterium leprae,* the causative agent of Hansen's disease, termed leprosy by commentators in the Middle Ages.

Exposure to tuberculosis confers an immunity to leprosy. Because tuberculosis was often transmitted to small children by human or cow milk, early immunity to both tuberculosis and leprosy might have been acquired by those who survived the first few years of life. One factor in the late medieval decline of leprosy may have been the concurrent increase in tuberculosis in the densely populated urban centers. Unfortunately, leprosy does not confer an immunity to tuberculosis (Manchester 1984).

Leprosy

Leprosy flourished in Europe during the twelfth and thirteenth centuries, afflicting as much as 1 percent of the populace, according to some authorities. Possibly brought to the West from India with the returning army of Alexander in 327–6 B.C., leprosy traveled across Europe with Roman colonization. Skeletons from fifth-, sixth-, and seventh-century England display clear evidence of lepromatous leprosy in the skull or limbs, with loss of phalanges. Anglo-Saxon England apparently did not segregate lepers, because the bones of victims have been found in general cemeteries (Manchester 1984), but a few lazar houses were established as early as the eleventh century. The disease seems to have reached a high point in England during the first half of the thirteenth century, when 53 hospitals were constructed. In all, some 200 such institutions are known to have been established. By the fifteenth century no new ones had been built, and by the sixteenth century the disease had nearly disappeared from England.

The pattern in other European countries was similar. In the twelfth and thirteenth centuries almost every Italian town had a leper house outside its walls. France was said to have had 2,000 leprosaria in the thirteenth century. Medieval Denmark had 31, and in the cemetery of the leprosarium of St. Jorgens in Naestved, Denmark, 650 patients were buried between 1250 and 1550 (Møller-Christensen 1969).

The Third Lateran Council in 1179 directed that lepers be segregated from the rest of society, and that separate churches and burial places be provided for them. Great differences in the stringency of rules among communities existed, varying from clement care to the burning of live victims. Typically, a ceremony was conducted over a male leper in which he was declared to be "dead unto the world, but alive unto Christ." As the leper stood in a grave, a priest threw earth over him (Brody 1974). He, in fact, lived on, but he was dead in the eyes of the law, and his heirs inherited his possessions, though divorce was usually not permitted. Bishops or abbots endowed leprosaria with income from tithes, rents, and tolls; and in parts of Europe – northern Italy, for example – lepers were under civic control. A leper house usually lodged 6 to 12 people, but might be built for one victim alone. Such community efforts to prevent the spread of the disease were no doubt motivated by terror of the dire symptoms of leprosy, despite widespread ecclesiastical declarations that the illness was caused not by mere exposure to the disease but by divine punishment for lechery and other sins. Though the mechanism of contagion might be unclear, medieval Europe was ready to be empirical. Lepers were provided with cloaks and bells and ordered to keep their distance on penalty of death, and lazar houses were built downwind from towns.

Historians long believed that "leprosy" in the Middle Ages actually included a range of skin disorders, perhaps including syphilis. However, the excavation of medieval leper cemeteries, principally in Naestved, Denmark, has demonstrated that diagnosis by medieval doctors was actually conservative. Approximately 80 percent of the 650 skeletons at Naestved showed evidence of advanced lepromatous leprosy, whereas only a small percentage of modern cases, even untreated, are known to involve bones. Therefore, it can be speculated that only those most severely affected by the disease were confined there (Møller-Christensen 1969). As John of Gaddesden advised in the fourteenth century, "No man is to be adjudged a leper and isolated from all his fellows until the appearance and shape of his face be destroyed" (as cited by Cholmeley 1912). This was a merciful criterion in view of the grief and penalties of banishment, but one that allowed the population to contract the disease from those with early or less apparent forms.

Medieval physicians had repeatedly observed that the blood of lepers was thick, greasy, or gritty (Bernard of Gordon 1496; Guy de Chauliac 1890; John of Gaddesden, cited in Cholmeley 1912). Recently, laboratory tests have substantiated these descriptions. Blood samples show two or three times normal platelet adhesiveness, among other qualities (Parvez et al. 1979; Ell 1984a). The age-old claims that lepers were unusually sexually active and that leprosy was sexually transmitted have been harder to explain. It has been demonstrated, first, that subclinical leprosy may become overt during pregnancy (Duncan et al. 1981), thereby giving the impression that the disease has sexual origin, and second that remissions of leprosy in men might heighten sensitivity to testosterone. In addition, confinement in a leper house could have released the sexual inhibitions of both sexes (Ell 1984a). Yet because of the similarities of the early stages of leprosy and syphilis, syphilis may in fact have been present in medieval Europe and mislabeled leprosy. Modern lepers show an unusually high incidence of syphilis, suggesting an unknown affinity (Murray 1982; Ell 1984a). V. Møller-Christensen (1969), however, found no skeletal evidence of syphilis in the 650 leprosy victims at Naestved.

Historians have long believed that the Black Death greatly diminished the incidence of leprosy during the second half of the fourteenth century, attacking the weakened victims in their leper houses, which were found virtually empty at the end of the plague. However, it has recently been recognized that leprosy was already in decline when the plague began. The immune defect in the lepromatous patient is specific; it is not a generalized immune deficiency until the disease becomes advanced. In many ways, leprosy represents a hyperimmune state (Ell 1987). Leprosaria were probably found empty because members of the religious orders serving as keepers suffered a high death rate (Biraben 1975; Russell 1985), and the lepers fled to find food, escape the plague, or run from persecution as scapegoats. Alternatively, leprosy has been claimed to confer an immunity to plague, because leper houses consistently served meals very sparse in meat, whereas the plague bacillus requires a high serum iron level (Richards 1977; Ell 1984b, 1987). For all these reasons some medieval scourge other than plague may have hastened the end of leprosy. Tuberculosis, as noted earlier, confers an immunity to leprosy (only one leper with tuberculosis was found among the victims at Naestved; Møller-Christensen 1969), though leprosy does not confer immunity to tuberculosis (Manchester 1984). Thus, tuberculosis itself may have promoted the end of the leprosy epidemic in the late thirteenth and fourteenth centuries as tuberculosis increased among the new urban population.

Influenza

Believed in the Middle Ages to be a singularly English disease, "sweating sickness" (now widely accepted as influenza) first appeared in the very month in 1485 in which Richard III was defeated at Bosworth Field. Four other outbreaks – in 1508, 1517, 1528, and 1551 – occurred in the first half of the sixteenth century, before, according to the theory that prevailed until recent times, the disease vanished forever. After the eminent Tudor physician John Caius had treated victims in 1551, he described the disease as a sweat and fever with pains in the back, extremities, head, with "grief in the liver and the nigh stomacke," killing "some in one hour, many in two," but lasting only 24 hours if the patient survived (Caius 1912).

Even though an epidemic of fever and sweats was known to have devastated much of northern Europe in 1529 at approximately the same time as an English outbreak of the sweating sickness, no relationship between the two phenomena was seen at the time. In keeping with the prevailing doctrine of humoral pathology, which accounted for all disease as an imbalance of the four natural humors – blood, phlegm, black bile, and yellow bile – the English sweating sickness was believed to be drawn to a constitution predisposed by an excess of one of the humors and possibly by an immoderate life-style. The immediate cause was believed to be, in the words of Caius, "evel mists and exhalations drawn out of the grounde by the sune in the heate of the yeare." Explanations of the causation and character of the disease remained localist and miasmatic into the nineteenth century, when in 1844 German historian J. F. C. Hecker (1844) called it a "spirit of the mist" and said that epidemics were inevitable if "rain be excessive . . . so that the ground is completely saturated, and the mists attract baneful exhalations out of the earth."

Even August Hirsch (1883) accepted the unique nature of the English sweating sickness, and not until the twentieth century were the five British epidemics recognized to be influenza, an illness known to be caused by an unstable microorganism having variable disease patterns.

Traditionally, the first influenza epidemic, as identified by Hirsch (1883), occurred in 1173 in Italy, Germany, and England, during which the monk Godefridus described an intolerable cough as a symptom. There were major bouts of influenza in France and Italy in 1323, when nearly all of the citizens of Florence fell ill with chills and fever, and again in 1387, when the disease was described as *ex influentia coelesti*, giving rise to the use in Italy of the term *una influenza*. When the disease struck Paris in 1411, one of the symptoms was a cough so severe that it caused women to abort. Influenza returned in 1414 to Italy and to Paris, where some 100,000 cases were claimed, and again in 1427. Following this, Hirsch (1883) described no more epidemics until the great 1510 outbreak, with general diffusion all over Europe, starting in Sicily in July and reaching northern Italy in August, France in September, and the Netherlands and Spain in October. But even as the visitations of influenza in Europe were increasing and the incidence of leprosy diminishing, a greater scourge than either was about to strike.

Bubonic Plague

Bubonic plague (Black Death or the Black Plague) was commonly known as the Great Mortality or the Great Pestilence. Probably in the majority of cases, certain symptoms were characterized as "black." In the words of Giovanni Boccaccio (1978), an eyewitness: "There appeared . . . certain swellings, either on the groin or under the armpits . . . of the bigness of a common apple . . . [or] an egg. From these . . . after awhile . . . the contagion began to change into black or livid blotches . . . in some large and sparse and in others small and thick-sown." Other sources describe small black blisters spread widely over the body, swollen glands and boils surrounded by black streaks, or the throat and tongue black and swollen with blood. But many victims experienced no "black" symptoms. As a consequence, many believe that the *black* in the name of the disease derives from a too-literal translation in sixteenth-century Scandinavia of a common fourteenth-century Latin phrase, *atra mors* meaning "terrible death," as "black death."

In 542, during the reign of Justinian, bubonic plague was reported to have taken the lives of 25 percent of the population of the Roman Empire, in what has been called the first European epidemic. Though the exact nature of this outbreak has been debated, plague is now believed, on the basis of literary and cemetery evidence, to have spread across Europe, reaching the British Isles in 544 and returning there in 664 (when, significantly, the Venerable Bede described St. Cuthbert as having a tumor [or bubo] on the thigh) and again in 682 (Russell 1976). Probably, episodes of plague attacked Rome in 1167 and 1230, Florence in 1244, and Spain and southern France in 1320 and 1333. It was during the last outbreak that Roch of Languedoc, who was on a pilgrimage to Rome, contracted the disease, was cured, began to nurse plague victims, and subsequently became the patron saint of plague.

In 1331 civil war and plague struck Hopei, China, and both soon raged throughout that nation; chronicles report that two-thirds of the population perished. The disease moved west along the caravan routes through Tashkent, Astrakhan, and other cities of southern Russia, transmitted by rats and fleas perhaps lodged in the grain supplies of the caravans (for a discussion of caravan transportation, see McNeill 1976). It reached the Crimea in 1346, where Genoese merchants were being attacked in their fortified trading post of Caffa by a Mongol army. The attackers were suffering from plague, and before they withdrew they transmitted their affliction to the besieged town by catapulting corpses of victims over the walls.

Fleeing Caffa, the ships of the now-diseased Genoese were driven away from Messina, Sicily, and the disease was carried to North Africa and the western Mediterranean. Soon Corsica and Sardinia, Spain and southern Italy were affected, then all of Italy, Austria, Hungary, Yugoslavia, and Bavaria. Marseilles was the destination of one of the ships, and the disease quickly spread up the Rhone and then throughout France. By 1348 most of France and Switzerland were under siege by the plague, which soon reached the southern coast of England, Germany, Sweden, and Poland. The plague's assault on Russia was delayed until 1351, good evidence that the disease traveled by the international trade routes and not by river transport, or it might have reached Russia from the Crimea several years earlier.

Plague was transported by armies and ships, merchants, pilgrims, fair goers, transient laborers, and other human travelers. Traders hauling grain, fodder, forage, hides, furs, and bolts of cloth also transported rats, fleas, and other vermin. Pilgrimage routes and trade routes to fairs were natural paths of the disease, which first broke out in London at the time of the Bartholomew Fair. When Edward III began the construction of Windsor Castle in 1359, plague attacked the workforce (Shrewsbury 1970).

Plague is a millennia-old disease of wild rodents. In a cycle widely believed to be the method of transmission of the Black Death, rat fleas (*Xenopsylla cheopis*) carry the *Yersinia pestis* bacillus to the black or house rat, *Rattus rattus*. When the host rat dies, its fleas leave to find another living rat, but failing that, they may jump temporarily to less favored hosts, human beings, and by biting them transmit the disease.

In humans, plague has three major forms: bubonic, septicemic, and pneumonic. The first form results from an insect bite, with the bacillus moving through the lymphatic system to the nearest lymph node, frequently in the groin, where it forms a palpable swelling, the characteristic "bubo," from the Greek word for groin. Other possible sites for buboes are the armpits and the neck, depending on the location of the bite. In the septicemic form, the insect injects the bacillus directly into the bloodstream of the victim, where it multiplies quickly. Blood seeps from the mouth and the nose, and death results in a few hours. Septicemic plague is virtually always fatal. Nevertheless, the most menacing form is pneumonic plague. A modern outbreak in Manchuria in 1921, for example, was 100 percent lethal (McNeill 1976). Because the pneumonic form is a lung infection, it can be transferred directly from human to human by airborne sputum or by fomites (clothing and other articles contaminated by victims).

All three forms of the disease were found in the fourteenth-century pandemic, and judging by a study of 300 contemporary literary sources, the relative importance of the three types may have been 77 percent bubonic, 19 percent septicemic with secondary pneumonia, and 4 percent pneumonic (Ell 1980).

Because of the entrenched medieval belief in the humoral pathology inherited from the Greeks, which had not been seriously challenged in more than a thousand years, therapeutic measures were based on correction of the imbalance of humors. The imbalance might be precipitated by an immoderate intake of food or drink or by meteorological or astronomical phenomena. Because plague was of a short incubation period and therefore could readily be seen to be transferred from person to person, the best etiologic explanation consistent with the traditional pathology was that corrupt air emanated from the ill person or a corpse, or even from someone still not ill but coming from a place of sickness. Standing only a few feet away from such a source might be enough to contract the disease. Belief in the vital role of air was so strong that the clergy of Avignon imagined that mountain dwellers had been immunized against the plague by their own pure air and so imported them as gravediggers in 1348. Unfortunately, they died of the infection as soon as they arrived (Biraben 1975).

Medieval physician and surgeon Guy de Chauliac (1890) wrote the most accurate and complete medical account of the 1348 plague epidemic of any contemporary observer. In it he described both the pneumonic and bubonic types of the disease, and may also have recognized the septicemic type with a reference of blood spitting. His first counsel was the traditional injunction *"Fuge cito, vade longe, rede tarde"* – "Flee quickly, go far, and come back slowly." But he also advised such surgical and medical measures as reducing blood volume by phlebotomy, purifying the air by fire and incense, and opening or cauterizing buboes. Most of the medical texts of the time echo the treatments Guy de Chauliac advocated. Surgical intervention, baths, and apothecary cures were recommended. Physicians visiting the sick were accompanied by boys carrying incense burners to purify the air, and all held before their noses a sponge soaked in vinegar and spices. When Philip VI of France ordered the Paris medical faculty to ascertain the cause of the disease, a confident report came back that the pestilence was caused by the conjunction of Saturn, Jupiter, and Mars, which had occurred at 1 P.M. on March 20, 1345 (Campbell 1931).

Those who could afford to, including physicians, fled the infected towns. Orvieto, for example, had to offer a doctor 100 livres per year to stay and treat the poor. The Catalonian Cortés fled Barcelona, and all the inhabitants of Agrigento, Sicily, ran away in 1347. Citizens of Marseilles burned the La Rousselle quarter to contain the plague (Biraben 1975). Perhaps because both cities forbade entry by travelers, Milan and Parma remained largely free of the disease during its first outbreak in 1347–50. In Milan early victims were also heartlessly walled up in their houses (Ziegler 1970; Ell 1984b). At Ragusa (now Dubrovnik, Yugoslavia), ships were isolated for 40 (*quaranta*) days, in a first effort at quarantine.

The first great outbreak of the Black Death was followed by three waves in the same century, in 1360,

1369, and 1375. It has been estimated that the death rate in Britain decreased with each successive wave, starting with 25 percent in 1348 and becoming 22.7 percent in 1360, 13.1 percent in 1369, and 12.7 percent in 1375. It is assumed that the disease lost its virulence at the same time that people's immunity increased (Russell 1948; Carpentier 1978).

Persistent questions about the Black Death perplex modern historians. Was bubonic plague the sole disease, or where there others? Why was no unusual black rat mortality mentioned by contemporary writers? Why is the black rat unknown today in Europe except in a few port cities? Was a sylvatic, or wild, home for the plague ever created in Europe – either at the time of the sixth-century eruption or in the fourteenth century? If so, what eradicated it? Modern sylvatic foci, in the southwestern United States and Russia, are almost impossible to eradicate (McNeill 1976).

It has been suggested that more than one disease was active during the fourteenth-century epidemics, with typhus, smallpox, and anthrax as candidates. Scholars have been puzzled by records of high infection rates during the winter months, since plague is a warm-weather disease. This and other contradictory factors support the case for anthrax, which is caused by a much hardier organism, is characterized by pustules with a jet-black center, often precipitates the voiding of black blood, and also has a pulmonary form (Twigg 1984).

Doubts about the classical explanation of plague transmission derive partly from the present-day absence of *R. rattus* in northern Europe, except in a few port cities. Moreover, no medieval record exists of the explosive black rat mortality that would have been expected. Finally, *R. rattus* is timid and not normally migratory (Shrewsbury 1970; Ell 1980).

As already mentioned, spring and summer are the seasons of ratborne plague in cities (infection occurs most commonly when both Fahrenheit temperature and humidity are between 68 and 80; Russell 1976), yet the Black Death occurred throughout the year. The explanation may lie in two possible forms of interhuman transmission: Respiratory infection, which produces pneumonic plague, would explain the winter occurrences, and transmission by the human flea, *Pulex irritans,* would account for the undoubted majority of bubonic cases (Ell 1980). *P. irritans,* which can transmit plague, would have needed no rat host and could have lodged in long, loose clothing, traveling from person to person. Lice, ticks, and bedbugs, which can also transmit plague, may have been vectors as well (Biraben 1975; Ell 1980).

As for the sylvatic foci in rodents, an alternative explanation would be that multiple human and animal reservoirs, based on complete and partial immunities, perhaps constantly shifting, propagated the plague bacillus without a sylvatic home. Plague immunity is known or suspected to be conferred by salmonella infections, *Yersinia enterocolitica*, tularemia, and typhus, as well as leprosy (Ell 1984b).

Explanations for the final disappearance of plague from Europe in the eighteenth century included speculations that the bacillus mutated to a less virulent form, that *R. rattus* was replaced by *Rattus norvegicus*, and that new practices of housing construction, shipping, personal hygiene, nutrition, and public health finally brought the disease to an end (for reviews of theories see Appleby 1980; Ell 1984b). In addition, the rats themselves may have become immune. Communities of immune rats are known to have existed in India in the twentieth century. The reason the rats did not become immune in northern Europe until the seventeenth century (and a few decades later in the south) may be that a certain high density of population would have been required for all remaining susceptible rats to be infected and finally killed (Appleby 1980).

Historians have long accepted a type of Malthusian theory to account for the appearance of plague in 1348. According to this theory, a too rapid population expansion led to the clearing of all arable land and crowding into already overpopulated cities. The populace then suffered a series of crop failures and famines when the weather turned unusually cold early in the fourteenth century. As rats fled empty granaries to find food in human dwellings, the human population, weakened by starvation, fell victim to a chance epidemic. Critics of this Malthusian position have objected that the weakest members of society were not eliminated by the plague; men between 20 and 40 died in larger proportion than women, children, the aged, or even lepers. The *Y. pestis* organism requires exogenous iron for growth and replication, and young men were the least iron-deficient group in the medieval population (Ell 1984b, 1987).

Believed to have left in its wake some 20 million dead in Europe in the four years from 1346 to 1350, the Black Death brought about critical social and ideological changes. Considering the medical world alone, we find that the public health tradition, inherited from the care of lepers, was strengthened – even though social efforts to clean streets, collect garbage, empty sewers, remove bodies, regulate the sale of food, and enforce quarantines of ships did little to stop the spread of plague. A new charitable impulse, encouraged by the religious revival after the plague, led to the building of hospitals, both religious and civic. New religious orders were devoted to the care of the sick. Owing to the heavy loss among scholars, physicians, and other educated men, Latin ceased to be the sole language of important texts, and medical as well as other books began to be written in the vernacular (Campbell 1931).

A widespread interest in disease prevention became current, and many works on diet, hygiene, proper clothing, and other topics of health care were published. Because surgeons had made heroic efforts to lance or cauterize buboes during the plague, the status of this profession was considerably enhanced, rising relative to that of physicians, too many of whom had fled. The growth of surgery as a discipline and desire to ascertain the causes of the pandemic led to an increased sanctioning of postmortem examinations, a practice that was to contribute directly to the growth of academic anatomic dissections in the following century.

Finally, humoral pathology suffered a serious blow – from which it would ultimately expire in centuries to come – because of its complete failure to palliate suffering and effect cures, not only for plague but for the other contagious illnesses of leprosy, tuberculosis, and influenza that ravaged the late Middle Ages.

Ynez Violé O'Neill

Bibliography

Appleby, Andrew B. 1980. The disappearance of plague: A continuing puzzle. *Economic History Review* 33: 161–73.

Bernard of Gordon. 1496. *Tabula practice Gordonii dicte lilium medicine*. Venice.

Biraben, Jean-Noël. 1975. *Les hommes et la peste en France et dans les pays européens et méditerranéens*, 2 vols. Paris.

Bloch, Marc. 1973. *The royal touch: Sacred monarchy and scrofula in England and France*, trans. J. E. Anderson. London.

Boccaccio, Giovanni. 1978. Plague in Florence: A literary description. In *The Black Death: A turning point in history?* ed. William M. Bowsky, 7–12. Huntington, N.Y.

Braudel, Fernand. 1979. *The structures of everyday life*, trans. Sian Reynolds. New York.

Brody, Saul Nathaniel. 1974. *The disease of the soul: Leprosy in medieval literature*. Ithaca, N.Y.

Bullough, Vern, and Cameron Campbell. 1980. Female longevity and diet in the Middle Ages. *Speculum* 55: 317–25.

Caius, John. 1912. A boke or counseill against the disease commonly called the sweate or sweatyng sicknesse. In *The works of John Caius, M.D*, ed. E. S. Roberts, 3–36. Cambridge.

Campbell, Anna Montgomery. 1931. *The Black Death and men of learning*. New York.

Carmichael, Ann G. 1983. Infection, hidden hunger, and history. *Journal of Interdisciplinary History* 14: 249–64.

Carpentier, Elisabeth. 1978. The plague as a recurrent phenomenon. In *The Black Death: A turning point in history?* ed. William M. Bowsky, 35–37. Huntington, N.Y.

Cholmeley, H. P. 1912. *John of Gaddesden and the Rosa Medicinae*. Oxford.

Drummond, J. C., and Anne Wilbraham. 1959. *The Englishman's food: A history of five centuries of English diet*. London.

Duncan, M., 1981. The association of leprosy and pregnancy. *Leprosy Review* 52: 245–62.

Ell, Stephen R. 1980. Interhuman transmission of medieval plague. *Bulletin of the History of Medicine* 54: 497–510.

1984a. Blood and sexuality in medieval leprosy. *Janus* 71: 153–64.

1984b. Immunity as a factor in the epidemiology of medieval plague. *Reviews of Infectious Diseases* 6: 866–79.

1987. Plague and leprosy in the Middle Ages: A paradoxical cross-immunity? *International Journal of Leprosy and Other Mycobacterial Diseases* 55: 345–50.

Guy de Chauliac. 1890. *La grande chirurgie*, ed. E. Nicaise. Paris.

Hecker, J. F. C. 1844. *The epidemics of the Middle Ages*, trans. B. G. Babington. London.

Herlihy, David. 1975. Life expectancies for women in medieval society. In *The role of woman in the Middle Ages*, ed. Rosmarie Thee Morewedge, 1–22. Albany, N.Y.

Hirsch, August. 1883–6. *Handbook of geographical and historical pathology*, 3 vols., trans. Charles Creighton. London.

Hodges, Richard. 1982. *Dark age economics: The origins of towns and trade, A.D. 600–1000*. London.

1984. Diet in the dark ages. *Nature* 310: 726–7.

Manchester, Keith. 1984. Tuberculosis and leprosy in antiquity: An interpretation. *Medical History* 28: 162–73.

Matossian, Mary Kilbourne. 1983. Bewitched or intoxicated? The etiology of witch persecution in early modern England. *Medizin Historisches Journal* 18: 33–42.

McNeill, William H. 1976. *Plagues and peoples*. Garden City, N.J.

Møller-Christensen, V. 1969. Provisional results of the examination of the whole Naestved leprosy hospital churchyard – ab. 1250–1550 A.D. *Nordisk medicinhistorisk årsbok* 29–41.

Murray, Katherine A. 1982. Syphilis and leprosy. *Journal of the American Medical Association* 247: 2097.

Parvez, M., et at. 1979. A study of platelet adhesiveness in leprosy. *Leprosy in India* 51: 363–8.

Richards, Peter. 1977. *The medieval leper and his northern heirs*. Cambridge.

Russell, Josiah Cox. 1948. *British medieval population*. Albuquerque, N.M.

1976. The earlier medieval plague in the British Isles. *Viator* 7: 65–78.

1985. *The control of late ancient and medieval population*. Philadelphia.

Shrewsbury, J. F. D. 1970. *A history of bubonic plague in the British Isles*. Cambridge.

Siegfried, Michael. 1986. The skewed sex ratio in a medieval population: A reinterpretation. *Social Science History* 10: 195–204.

Steinbock, R. Ted. 1976. *Paleopathological diagnosis and interpretation: Bone diseases in ancient human populations*. Springfield, Ill.

Talbot, C. H. 1967. *Medicine in medieval England*. London.

Twigg, Graham. 1984. *The Black Death: A biological reappraisal*. London.

White, Lynn, Jr. 1962. *Medieval technology and social change*. Oxford.

1976. Food and history. In *Food, man, and society*, ed. Dwain N. Walcher, Norman Kretchmer, and Henry L. Barnett, 12–30. New York.

Ziegler, Philip. 1970. *The Black Death*. London.

V.4
Diseases of the Renaissance and Early Modern Europe

The Renaissance in European history was a time of political, intellectual, and cultural change that had its origins in Italy during the fourteenth century. Beginning roughly during the lifetime of the poet Francesco Petrarch, who died in 1374, literati began to look to classical Greece and Rome for models of human political behavior and stylistic models of discourse and artistic representation. This humanistic quest involved the energies of philosophers and artists throughout the fifteenth, sixteenth, and seventeen centuries, as Renaissance ideas spread northward. Though narrowly conceived in scholarly and artistic circles, the Renaissance matured in urban settings. Because this time period coincides with technological innovations and the subsequent exploration and conquest of new worlds, we are inclined to associate the issue of Renaissance diseases with both the growth of cities and the age of European discovery. The period also frames the era of recurrent epidemics of bubonic plague in Europe.

Population growth in Europe was steady during the central, or "High," Middle Ages but did not lead to the growth of large metropolitan centers. Urbanization was earliest and most dramatic in the Mediterranean lands, where city cultures had also been the basis of ancient Roman hegemony. By the late thirteenth century, Florence and Venice, as successful commercial centers, had populations of more than 100,000. Rome, Milan, and Barcelona may have been equally large. Smaller urban areas of 50,000 to 80,000 individuals existed throughout northern Italy and Spain. These cities were roughly twice as large as the "urban" areas of England, including London. Uniformly dense, mixed urban and village networks were also characteristic of the Low Countries at the end of the Middle Ages, and the Seine valley could boast of at least one true city, Paris.

Outside the urban Mediterranean, the period of the Renaissance is better labeled the late Middle Ages. Most people lived in small villages and market towns, where goods, information, and epidemic disease passed through at a more leisurely rate. The British Isles, for example, had no town larger than 50,000 people until after 1600. But by the late sixteenth century, France, Germany, and England began to grow in population and in number of cities. The Thirty Years' War effectively eclipsed growth in Germanic Europe during the early seventeenth century. London and Paris, however, became the largest cities of Europe. By the eighteenth century, Scotland and Scandinavia began the processes of urbanization, commercialization, and protoindustrialization. A general improvement in health and longevity accompanied economic growth, even though the prevalence of infectious diseases remained high.

The "Black Death" epidemic of bubonic plague in 1348–50 caused up to 40 percent overall mortality in large cities, and as much as 60 percent mortality in smaller Italian cities such as Siena. Nevertheless, the greatest proportional destruction of the plague and subsequent periodic epidemics of disease in the fourteenth century seems to have fallen on villages and towns of western Europe, necessitating changes in landholding and land usage, and forcing individuals to migrate to cities in search of nonagricultural work. From 1350 to 1500, recovery was slow and uneven, but as early as the 1450s the great cities of Italy, Spain, and the Low Countries began to wrestle with the sanitary pressures brought about by new growth. These cities grew at the expense of the surrounding countryside, and market economies responded to this growth with the development of local industries, particularly in cloth, and with the development of trading networks that would facilitate further urban growth. During the sixteenth century, an impressive demographic recovery of rural populations seems to have fueled still more urban growth as more and more individuals migrated steadily, even relentlessly, to the cities from the countryside. Thus, even though struck by epidemics of plague, the populations of Venice, Florence, Milan, and Rome all exceeded pre-1348 levels. During the sixteenth century, Madrid expanded 10-fold in population while increasing only 4-fold in size, a dramatic example of the problems of crowding that the growth of Renaissance cities created.

In both Renaissance and early modern Europe, social and economic conditions help to identify and define the diseases then common. Naturally the disease experience of urban settlements differed significantly from that of rural town networks. City administrators were forced to deal with increasingly serious health threats, particularly with problems of refuse disposal and the provision of clean water, and of course with recurrent epidemic diseases.

At a time when at least one-third of all babies born died before their fifth birthdays, chronic infections mediated the lives of most adults, and two-thirds of rural residents did not survive to reproductive age, the acute crises of plague and other epidemics may not have been the most important diseases of the Renaissance. But they were certainly the most visible disease threats, and this shapes modern-day perceptions of the period as a dark age of plagues and other acute infections.

In early modern Europe the specter of famine loomed over the rural landscape. Although the adage "First famine, then fever" did not hold true for all periods of food shortage, periodic subsistence crises tended to provoke mortality crises. Normal annual mortality was as high as 3 percent of a population. But these crises generally carried away 6 to 10 percent of the population, and when very acute could claim as much as 30 to 40 percent. This short-run instability of mortality rates, what Michael Flinn (1981) has described as the demographic system of the ancien régime, was also nonuniform, so that neighboring towns could be affected quite differently during any given crisis. Across a community, the highest death rates occurred among those less than 10 years of age, with most deaths occurring within the first 2 years of life.

The basic problem, then, is to identify the cause or

causes of such high mortality. Famine, epidemics, or war could singly or in combination precipitate a mortality crisis, though infectious disease usually became the proximate cause of death. Yet rural populations often made up the losses quickly through reproduction, and years immediately before and after a period of crisis were times of lower than average mortality. Certainly it would seem that the most vulnerable members of a population were systematically pruned away during a mortality crisis, a classic Malthusian picture.

Plague

Beginning with the wave now called the Black Death, plague appeared in Europe at least once every generation between 1350 and 1720. During the late fourteenth century, smaller communities may have been disproportionately affected, for depopulation and deserted villages were uniform phenomena throughout Europe. Indeed, smaller centers may not have remained economically or demographically viable settlements after an episode of plague, leading to the reaggregation of people in villages, towns, and cities. By the fifteenth century, however, no matter how uniform the distribution of rodent vectors responsible for conveying plague to smaller human settlements and however sophisticated the development of trade networks to supply food to nonagricultural centers, the written records of plague recurrence suggest that the human plague epidemics were largely confined to urban areas. O. J. Benedictow (1987), however, has argued that a knowledge of the ecology and epidemiology of plague allows us to infer that there were heavy losses in the rural areas surrounding affected cities.

Bubonic plague epidemics were principally summer infections, no doubt augmented in severity by diarrheal diseases. Most surviving records of these epidemics suggest that overall mortality rates of 10 percent were common among the people who could not escape the city. Nevertheless, devastating population losses from plague epidemics, comparable to those from the Black Death, occurred in the sixteenth and seventeenth centuries in the heavily urbanized areas of north central Italy and Castille and may have led to the economic decline of the Mediterranean areas by the seventeenth century. During the seventeenth and eighteenth centuries, northern European countries witnessed the growth of cities and large towns, whereas Mediterranean centers slipped into a period of stagnation, probably because the epidemic waves of 1575–7, 1596, and 1630 were particularly severe in southern Europe.

Only during the fourteenth century do descriptions of plague note the loss of many principal citizens. After that period elites seem to have established effective patterns of flight. For those who did not flee, plague controls may have increased the risk of death, because both sufferers and their healthy contacts were isolated for weeks in pesthouses, temporary shacks, or, if they were lucky, their own homes. The maintenance of normal standards of hygiene and alimentation was difficult in such circumstances, and many undoubtedly died from less extraordinary causes than plague.

Whatever the individual causes of death in these mixed epidemics, for more than 300 years bubonic plague recurred in Europe at least every quarter-century. Then it disappeared during the late seventeenth and early eighteenth centuries, a phenomenon that has prompted two vexing, unsettled questions about diseases of the Renaissance and early modern Europe. First, why did plague disappear? Second, was its disappearance in any way responsible for the early phases of the modern rise of population? The first of these two questions has rather clearer options, if not firm answers. Some scholars argue that quarantine and other efforts to interrupt the spread of plague from town to town, region to region, or country to country effectively localized the outbreak of the plague. Admittedly these sanitary measures were designed to thwart a disease spread by human-to-human contact and did little to disturb rodent colonies that harbored the plague. But because rodents are commensal, rarely traveling far from human settlements, it is felt by some that the dispersal of plague ultimately depended on human actions. The proponents of this "quarantine-worked" model argue that humans inadvertently carried rodents and infected fleas in containers ranging from satchels to ships. This explanation has much to recommend it, but depends on the assumption that plague was always imported to Europe and that efforts to intercept and deter such importation ultimately succeeded even when quarantine stations were poorly maintained and were, at best, sieves straining out only gross contaminants.

Others argue that either climatic changes or changes in trade patterns led to the retreat of plague from Europe. The disease hit northern Europe for the last time in the 1660s and southern Europe (Marseilles and Provence only) in 1720. The interval between these last European plagues corresponds roughly to the "Maunder minimum" of sunspot activity and to the peak phases of the "little ice age." Insofar as global climate changes could have affected rodent colonies in central Asia, where bubonic plague has a perennial home, the number of infected fleas and rodents reaching Europe could have declined independently of efforts to control plague. Alternatively, the fact that northern Europeans turned to an Atlantic-based trade, shifting markets away from the Mediterranean to colonies in the Western Hemisphere and to the Far East, may be related to the decline of plague first in Great Britain, Scandinavia, and the Low Countries. The plague was always conveyed east to west across the Mediterranean and principally by sea. The relatively later survival of plague in Italy and Spain, where plague surveillance and quarantines had long been used, adds some weight to these latter explanations.

Whether the retreat of plague had any measurable effect on subsequent population growth is more difficult to answer, for there is no easy way to frame a model showing what would have happened had plague continued its assaults. Urban population growth in northern Europe was well underway before the two great plagues of 1630 and 1665–6. Even if Benedictow is right in stating that bubonic plague epidemics claimed horrifying percentages, on the order of 40 to 85 percent, of both the urban and rural populations exposed, net European population growth was not reversed during the sixteenth and seventeenth centuries.

John Hatcher (1977) and others have claimed that the profound demographic depression of the late fourteenth and fifteenth centuries was due in part to the combination of plague with other lethal epidemics, often staggered in such a way that few children reached reproductive age. Nonetheless, the frequency of *recorded* epidemics of diseases other than plague increased during the later centuries, and yet did not bring on population stagnation, as may have been the case in the late Middle Ages.

Thus, the economic expansion of Europe, with some improvements in travel, trade, and communication and dramatic improvements in regional and interregional markets, seems to best account for the beginnning of the European mortality decline in early modern times. The Europeans found themselves increasingly insulated from local famines, periodic harvest shortfalls, and other crises that evoked great fear of accompanying plague and pestilence, and were gradually able to overcome the hemorrhagic demographic impact of recurrent epidemic plague. To understand how this could have happened, it is necessary to assess what other infections threatened human survival at this time and to ask whether improved nutrition because of regularly available food has a positive influence on human survival even in the presence of serious infectious diseases.

Other Epidemics

During the Renaissance period, influenza pandemics recurred frequently enough to be well described by the fifteenth century. At least three influenza epidemics were quite severe during the sixteenth century, those of 1510, 1557–8, and 1580. The last in particular resembled the devastating influenza of 1918, in that the first wave occurred in the summer and early fall, and morbidity and mortality were high among young adults. The periodic influenza in the seventeenth century has not been a subject of scholarly study, though the epidemics of 1627 and 1663 seem to have been quite lethal. In contrast, epidemics of the eighteenth century have received considerable attention. K. David Patterson (1986) points to two epidemic periods in particular, from 1729 to 1733 and from 1781 to 1782, that mirror sixteenth-century pandemic influenza, suggesting that worldwide distribution of this common infectious disease antedated advances in global transportation.

Virulent smallpox, by contrast, may have appeared in Renaissance Europe only in the mid-sixteenth century (Carmichael and Silverstein 1987). Before that time measles and smallpox were described as relatively mild infections of childhood, an observation resting on those of ninth- and tenth-century Muslim physicians, Rhazes and Avicenna. Unless many of the fourteenth- and fifteenth-century epidemics of plague were in fact mixed epidemics of plague and smallpox, with the latter masked by the horror of the plague, records of epidemics of smallpox were sparse before the 1560s and 1570s. More likely a milder strain of smallpox prevailed before virulent smallpox entered England in the seventeenth century. Smallpox has a much more prominent – if not preeminent – place among the diseases of the seventeenth and eighteenth centuries and will thus be discussed later in more detail.

The history of other infections transmitted by airborne droplets is a patchy one during the Renaissance. Diphtheria was certainly described well in epidemics of malignant sore throat, as was whooping cough, the earliest examples dating from the sixteenth-century epidemiologist Guillaume de Baillou. In Spain, accounts of epidemics of *garoffilo* appeared during the early seventeenth century, depicting what was presumably a considerable threat to young children. Yet diphtheria was confused with epidemics of streptococcal sore throat as late as the mid-nineteenth century.

The German physician Daniel Sennert is credited with having written the first unambiguous description of scarlet fever. Rheumatic fever, another manifestation of severe streptococcal infection, was described well by Baillou in the sixteenth century and by the English physician Thomas Sydenham in the seventeenth century. Epidemic typhus fever seems to have been a new disease in Renaissance and early modern Europe.

One of the great problems facing historians of Renaissance diseases is the difficulty of discerning the precise cause of an epidemic much before 1500. For example, the following account from a Parisian chronicler in 1414 suggests both whooping cough and influenza:

And it pleased God that a foul corrupt air should fall upon the world, an air which reduced more than a hundred thousand people in Paris to such a state that they could neither eat, drink, nor sleep. They had very sharp attacks of fever two or three times each day, especially whenever they ate anything. Everything seemed very bitter to them, very rotten and stinking, and all the time, where ever they were, they shook and trembled. Even worse, besides all this they lost all bodily strength so that no one who had this disease could bear to touch any part of his body, so wretchedly did he feel. It continued without stopping three weeks or more; it had begun in early March of the same year and was called the tac or herion. . . . As well as all the misery described above, people had with it such a fearful cough, cattarh, and hoarseness that nothing like a high mass could be sung anywhere in Paris. The cough was so much worse, night and day, than all the other evils that some men suffered permanent rupture of the genitals through it and some pregnant women gave birth prematurely because of this coughing, alone and without help, and died, mother and child, in great distress. When people began to get better they passed a lot of clotted blood through nose, mouth and below, which frightened them very much. Yet no one died of it. But it was with great difficulty that people managed to recover from it, even after the appetite came back it was still more than six weeks before they were really cured. No physician could say what this disease was. (Shirley 1968)

This vivid description is echoed by a brief mention of a contemporary catarrhal illness in the other urban areas of Europe, suggesting that the disease was influenza. The cough and low case fatality, however, indicate whooping cough (the chronicler is unlikely to have noted the deaths of babies). But if either whooping cough or influenza was a truly new disease in the early fifteenth century, then the implications for changing disease patterns in the later Renaissance would be considerable. It is more likely that the criteria for diagnosis and the medical theories governing the description of disease changed during the Renaissance, making difficult a retrospective assessment of what was new and different then.

In others words, evidence for the sudden appearance of many common diseases in the sixteenth and seventeenth centuries is somewhat artifactual – a "reporting phenomenon." During the Renaissance, physicians increasingly turned to models of contagion to explain (and, hence, control) the spread of plagues and pestilences, and were aided considerably by adoption of ontological theories of disease. That is, physicians crafted new medical definitions of diseases, which had long possessed common lay names, describing them as individual entities with unique and distinguishing characteristics. Though chronic "diseases," such as fevers, consumption, arthritis, gout, cancer, ulcers, and fistulae, were still best explained and treated only by a thorough understanding of the Galenic–Hippocratic humoral system that dominated medicine until the nineteenth century, medical accounts from the sixteenth century onward tended to identify acute health problems in terms of specific diseases. These new ways of looking at illness had a profound effect on the recognition and description of diseases known today. Moreover, the spread of medical information through the medium of print accelerated and normalized the understanding of many diseases as specific and individual.

In the sixteenth and seventeenth centuries, dozens of "new" diseases seemed to demand or defy medical explanation, which resulted in some of the earliest medical descriptions we possess for scurvy, rickets, typhus, syphilis, scarlet fever, the "English sweate" (whatever that was), and even anorexia nervosa. Thus, one of the fundamental problems for historical epidemiologists is determining which of these, if any, were indeed new or newly important during the period from 1400 to 1800. And by "newly important," we mean diseases that changed in incidence and prevalence in a society rather than those that became important to some groups within these societies. For example, was gout "important" to Renaissance and early modern elites because it became a noble form of suffering – in contrast, for example, to the ignominy of syphilis – or because meat consumption among the upper classes, together with a heavy consumption of dehydrating alcohol, increased the clinical expression of gout? In many cases we will never know the answer, and thus must make some assumptions based on those data that did not change over the reporting period while considering significant shifts in the criteria for definition and diagnosis. In this respect, much scholarly attention has been devoted to smallpox and syphilis, which thus form two illustrative case studies of the problems involved in tracing the history of diseases of early modern Europe.

Smallpox and the Modern Rise of Population

Smallpox was long recognized as a contagious disease with a pustular rash. Distinctive clinical features, such as the simultaneous maturation of pustules (this distinguishes it from chickenpox) and the centripetal distribution of pustules over the body, were not noted. Oddly, the residual facial scarring among recovered variola major victims, was rarely mentioned. Nevertheless, by the early seventeenth century, smallpox was recognized by both lay and medical observers as a distinctive disease.

Even if many cases were missed because the victim was severely infected, or was very young, and died before the rash appeared, mortality records from England, Italy, Sweden, and elsewhere testify to the accelerating intensity of smallpox over the course of the seventeenth and eighteenth centuries. Epidemic years of smallpox in Italian cities of the eighteenth century could account for up to 30 percent of the annual mortality, and recurrences swept urban areas at least once a decade (Panta 1980). In London, the largest city of Europe by the eighteenth century, there were no gaps between major outbreaks of smallpox. Annual mortality in the metropolis averaged 10 percent of all deaths. Thus, there is much agreement that smallpox was one of the principal causes of morbidity and mortality after plague disappeared. The residual questions are: Why was smallpox increasing in incidence and prevalence, and what effect on population and other diseases did inoculation and vaccination against smallpox have? Finally, can the stepwise retreat of smallpox with the introduction of innovative therapies explain any part of the modern rise of population, which began in the eighteenth century?

The answers to these questions depend in part on the assumptions demographers and epidemiologists make about the principal causes of death in early modern cities. Many view cities as death traps, their highly unsanitary environments containing a rich variety of gastrointestinal pathogens that tipped the balance between births and deaths and necessitated in-migration to maintain populations. Nonrespiratory tuberculosis, water- and foodborne infections, and, to a somewhat more limited extent, midwinter respiratory infections complete the list of pathogens that plagued the cities. However, Allan Sharlin and Roger Finlay (1981; see also Sharlin 1978) have chal-

lenged this picture with an even broader equilibrium model, arguing that the reason the difference between deaths and births was quite large in the cities was that many adult migrants temporarily resided in the city, without marrying or contributing to the replenishment of the population. Thus, an excess of nonreproductive adults in the cities accounts for a good part of the difference between rural and urban mortality statistics.

William H. McNeill (1976) portrays cities as the frontlines of the human battle against microbes that entered these cities through commerce and migration. City residents were usually the first group to be hard hit by a novel infection, but over the long run city populations were, on the whole, immunized earlier in life to viral diseases, which produced lifelong immunity. Young adults migrating into the city from the countryside might add to the pool of individuals susceptible to common infections. Unhealthy-appearing, impoverished urban dwellers would better survive an epidemic of measles than a comparable group of strapping young adults from the provinces.

McNeill's view would make smallpox an excellent example of the long-term advantages, largely immunological, to city dwellers, and John Landers and Anastasia Mouzas (1988) have found robust empirical support for this view in the records of London mortality. Moreover, Landers (1987) has found the beginning of a decline in the summer peaks of deaths from gastrointestinal infections by the late seventeenth century. Thus, he doubts the view of an endogenously unhealthy city, with its citizens at the mercy of microbes. Moreover, with the immunity of survivors of exogenous killer diseases, such as smallpox, urban mortality changed significantly during the "long" eighteenth century, 1670–1830. Hidden in those changes, he believes, are the reasons for the initial modern rise of population.

In addition, A. J. Mercer (1985) argues that smallpox may have been uniquely important in a demographic sense not only because it killed a large number of young children, but because its survivors often succumbed to other infections, once "weakened" by smallpox. Although general crisis mortality, in city or countryside, cannot be linked to famine or to weather conditions, statistically it can, in the eighteenth century, be linked to epidemic waves of smallpox. Mercer is not willing to ascribe a determinant role to smallpox among the diseases of the eighteenth century, but he is convinced that vaccination, where adopted even halfway, contributed significantly to the survival of children to adulthood, accelerating population growth in the early nineteenth century.

Other scholars consider typhus and tuberculosis to have been as important as smallpox. There is once again an artifactual aspect to the high prevalence of typhus, for it was only during the eighteenth century that physicians first described its clinical and epidemiological features well and differentiated typhus from a miscellany of other fevers – nervous, biliary, inflammatory, continuous, hectic, and intermittent.

Most have accepted Hans Zinsser's (1935) argument in his celebrated *Rats, Lice and History* that epidemic typhus fever was a new disease in the late fifteenth century, brought to Spain and Italy during the battles against Turkish expansion in the Mediterranean. The dramatic urbanization of northern Europe (London grew from c. 400,000 in 1650 to more than 1 million by the early nineteenth century) accelerated crowding and poverty, optimal social conditions for the spread of typhus by body lice. Crowding and poverty also supported the transmission of respiratory tuberculosis, which many have argued was at a peak at about 1800.

It was during this era of earliest industrialization that population began to swell, and thus the model of the city as a death dispensary or as a provider of immunity may not be especially relevant. Indeed, Thomas McKeown (1976) has been the principal spokesperson for a view that credits improving nutrition rather than declining disease with that growth. According to McKeown, whether an individual survives a disease, be it an acute viral infection such as measles or a chronic infection such as tuberculosis, depends on the individual's state of nutrition. Yet this argument is based more on experiential data generated by physicians treating well-nourished and undernourished mothers and children than on laboratory studies of human nutrition and specific infectious diseases. With many diseases, there is little direct relationship between the outcome of infection and the prior nutritional state of the host. Yet the ability to outlast several serious infections does depend on steady access to food and, obviously, to protection from further health insults. In a few diseases, such as measles and tuberculosis, there is, moreover, a positive association between poor nutrition and severity of infection. Insofar as these two were among the most common diseases of the early modern period, nutritional security and the generally improved standards of living this implies may have permitted the survival of more children to reproductive age. When smallpox, the last great killer

of little children, came under control, population growth was dramatic, even though exposure to multiple infections and specific medical measures did not change the features of disease experience for nineteenth-century Europeans.

At just the time McKeown finds general improvements in human nutrition, the appearance of widespread deficiency diseases marked further change in the European disease experience. The prevalence of scurvy increased, including that of "land scurvy" suffered by the most impoverished city dwellers. Pellagra was described first in the eighteenth century among the desperately poor farmers of northern Italy and Spain, who became dependent on American maize. Potato and squash cultivation eased the lives of many northern Europeans, helping them to avoid famine crises that had been common before the eighteenth century, but well into the nineteenth century the dependence on single crops or foodstuffs often gave the poor no relief from a miserable nutritional regimen. Thus, in many instances, the benefits of improvements in nutrition may have largely accrued to upper- and middle-class urban dwellers. It would seem that the disappearance first of plague – a relentless killer of young adults – and then smallpox permitted the survival of a greater number of reproductive adults, well nourished or not.

Chronic Infectious Diseases

The attention of demographers and others trying to explain the modern rise of population has seldom turned to the chronic infectious diseases. Thus, the steady silent killer, tuberculosis, and the flashy new infection of Renaissance Europe, syphilis, are seldom discussed in this context. Yet there exists a reciprocal relationship between copathogens, acute and chronic. For example, survivors of smallpox might have been weakened by this disease and thus succumbed to tuberculosis. Conversely, an underlying tuberculosis infection should have weakened the ability of individuals to fight off smallpox and other epidemic illnesses. A reduction in the morbidity of chronic infectious disease may play an important role in the decline of mortality from acute infectious disease. Thus, Stephen Kunitz (1983) has argued that the cause of the modern rise of population was stabilization of mortality from all causes.

Those historians, such as Alfred Crosby (1972), William McNeill (1976), Emmanuel Le Roy Ladurie (1981), Kenneth Kiple (1984), and others, who have taken very grand perspectives of the period from 1400 to 1800 have seen Europeans participating in a saga of unprecedented success because of their outward migration and colonization. European population expanded externally far beyond the bounds of a modest modern rise of population. They unintentionally exported both chronic and acute infectious diseases, which had disastrous consequences for the native populations of the Western Hemisphere and Australasia. In return, Europeans brought back home only a few infections that caused serious concern.

Foremost among these may have been syphilis. Imported, at some time during the late fifteenth century, possibly with the Spanish colonization of the Americas, possibly with earlier Portuguese conquests in western Africa, syphilis suddenly appeared in the mid-1490s, uncharacteristically as a pustular rash, a large pox in contrast to the small pox. Within half a century, however, syphilitic patients suffered the same general pathology that untreated victims would in the twentieth century, including long, chronic bouts with ulcers and fistulae. The records of both the initial pandemic wave and individual cases of syphilis from 1550 to 1800 are intertwined with heightened moral concerns and fears of stigmatization, so that it is difficult to assess the prevalence of syphilis during this period. Police and public health officers of the nineteenth century took an aggressive interest in the control of syphilis, especially in the control of prostitution. They thereby generated our earliest numerical surveys of syphilis, comparable to earlier records of plague and smallpox.

Because of European contacts with Africa and the tropical world, mosquitoborne diseases also traversed Europe increasingly after 1500. Malaria may have increased in prevalence, partially from increased contact with Africans and partly from increased rice cultivation. A more alarming mosquitoborne disease, however, was yellow fever, epidemics of which increased in frequency through the seventeenth and eighteenth centuries and culminated in the catastrophic Barcelona outbreak of 1821. The eighteenth-century expansion of urban environments, especially of port cities and other trade centers, along with the construction of irrigation ditches for agriculture and canals for transport between markets, increased the number of breeding places for mosquitoes.

Finally, we should mention again tuberculosis, as John Bunyan called it in *Pilgrim's Progress,* "captain of all these men of death." Scourge of the wealthiest Renaissance families and a persistent problem in Renaissance Italian cities, tuberculosis followed the pulse of European urbanization, moving northward as cities appeared, to peak in the eighteenth century. Most city children were infected early in life, recovered, and lived a normal life span, then 40 to 55 years. The heaviest mortality from tuberculosis occurred in infancy, the heaviest morbidity probably in the middle adult years. A small percentage of older children died of pulmonary tuberculosis, chronic diarrhea, or any of the many varieties of extrapulmonary infection. A slightly larger percentage of the once-infected succumbed as young adults.

Thus far we have concentrated mainly on mortality. But the biography of Alexander Pope by Marjorie Nicholson and George Rousseau, *This Long Disease, My Life* (1968), provides a classic illustration of the process of chronic disease in individuals who escaped plague and the ravages of smallpox. Pope was struck by a tubercular infection that left him disabled. He labored to keep up his correspondence and wrote poetry between visits to the baths and visits from physicians. Throughout his life, he valiantly bore the great pain of travel by coach, a harrowing experience for a body as gnarled as his, bravely sampled the latest remedies, and occasionally confessed his trials to his numerous invalid friends: "I am grown so tender as not to be able to feel the air, or get out of a multitude of Wastcotes. I live like an Insect, in hope of reviving with the Spring." One of the last visitors to Pope's deathbed observed, "He dyed on Wednesday, about the Middle of the Night, without a Pang, or a Convulsion, unperceived of those that watched him, who imagined he was only in a sounder Sleep than ordinary."

One suspects that the gradual recession of both acute and chronic infectious diseases also went unperceived even among those who were watching. But the human costs of epidemic diseases as well as chronic infections lessened as people gained greater access to food, as well as more nutritional variety, and developed means of distancing their exposure to acute infectious diseases during the economic expansion of the eighteenth century.

Ann G. Carmichael

Bibliography

Appleby, Andrew B. 1975. Nutrition and disease: The case of London, 1550–1750. *Journal of Interdisciplinary History* 6: 1–22.

1980. The disappearance of the plague: A continuing puzzle. *Economic History Review* 33: 161–73.

Benedictow, O. J. 1987. Morbidity with historical plague epidemics. *Population Studies* 41: 401–31.

Carmichael, Ann G., and Arthur M. Silverstein. 1987. Smallpox in Europe before the seventeenth century: Virulent killer or benign disease? *Journal of the History of Medicine and Allied Sciences* 42: 147–68.

Crosby, Alfred W. 1972. *The Columbian exchange: Biological and cultural consequences of 1492*. Westport, Conn.

Flinn, Michael W. 1981. *The European demographic system, 1500–1820*. Baltimore.

Hatcher, John. 1977. *Plague, population and the English economy, 1348–1530*. London.

Kiple, Kenneth F. 1984. *The Caribbean slave: A biological history*. Cambridge.

Kunitz, Stephen J. 1983. Speculations on the European mortality decline. *Economic History Review*, Ser. 2, 36: 349–64.

Landers, John. 1987. Mortality and metropolis: The case of London, 1675–1825. *Population Studies* 41: 59–76.

Landers, John, and Anastasia Mouzas. 1988. Burial seasonality and causes of death in London, 1670–1819. *Population Studies* 42: 59–83.

Le Roy Ladurie, Emmanuel. 1981. A concept: The unification of the globe by disease, fourteenth to seventeenth centuries. In *The mind and method of the historian*, ed. Emmanuel Le Roy Ladurie, 28–83. Chicago.

Major, Ralph H. 1945. *Classic description of disease*, 3d edition. Springfield, Ill.

McKeown, Thomes. 1976. *The modern rise of population*. New York.

McNeill, William H. 1976. *Plagues and peoples*. Garden City, N.Y.

Mercer, A. J. 1985. Smallpox and epidemiological-demographic change in Europe: The role of vaccination. *Population Studies* 39: 287–307.

Nicholson, Marjorie, and George S. Rousseau. 1968. A medical case history of Alexander Pope. In *This long disease, my life: Alexander Pope and the sciences*, 7–82. Princeton, N.J.

Panta, Lorenzo del. 1980. *La epidemie nella storia demografica italiana*. Turin.

Patterson, K. David. 1986. *Pandemic influenza, 1700–1900: A study in historical epidemiology*. Totowa, N.J.

Sharlin, Allan. 1978. Natural decrease in early modern cities: A reconsideration. *Past and Present* 79: 126–38.

Sharlin, Allan, and Roger Finlay. 1981. Debate: Natural decrease in early modern cities. *Past and Present* 92: 169–80.

Shirley, Janet, trans. and ed. 1968. *A Parisian journal, 1405–1449*. London.

Slack, Paul. 1979. Mortality crises and epidemic disease in England, 1485–1610. In *Health, medicine and mortality in the sixteenth century*, ed. Charles Webster, 9–59. New York.

1981. The disappearance of plague: An alternative view. *Economic History Review*, 2d Ser., 34: 409–76.

Stevenson, Lloyd. 1965. "New diseases" in the seventeenth century. *Bulletin of the History of Medicine* 39: 1–21.

Walter, John, and Roger Schofield. 1989. *Famine, disease and the social order in early modern society*. New York.

Zinsser, Hans. 1935. *Rats, lice and history*. Boston.

V.5
Diseases and the European Mortality Decline, 1700–1900

In his study of world population published more than 50 years ago, A. M. Carr-Saunders (1936) observed that the population of western Europe had begun to increase by the early eighteenth century, if not earlier, as a result of a growing gap between births and deaths. The gap was accounted for primarily by the fact that mortality was declining whereas fertility was high and in some countries was even growing. Addressing the reasons for the decline in mortality, he, like others both before and since, classified the causes into several categories:

For the purposes of this discussion the conditions, of which note must be taken, may be classified into four groups, though the boundaries between them are indefinite and though there is much overlapping: (1) political, that is conditions in relation to the maintenance of external and internal order; (2) social, including the state of knowledge in relation to the production and use of food, and to the making and use of clothing; (3) sanitary, that is conditions relating to housing, drainage, and water-supply; (4) medical, including both the state of knowledge concerning the prevention and cure of disease and its application to the public at large.

Because Carr-Saunders was dealing with the period after 1700, he thought that the first category – social order – no longer applied because conditions in England and the rest of northwestern Europe were by that time comparatively stable and orderly. Thus, the other three categories were of most value in explaining the mortality decline in northwestern Europe in the eighteenth and nineteenth centuries. Under (2) he included the adoption of root crops, the improvement of gardening, and the use of cotton for clothing, which improved personal cleanliness. Under (3) he included the improvement of towns and their water supplies, the paving and cleaning of streets, and the substitution of brick for timber. Category (4) included increased scientific knowledge, practical applications even when the theory was not understood, a profession of practitioners (apothecaries in England), and the construction of hospitals (Carr-Saunders 1936). He did not attempt to determine which category was most significant.

He then pointed out that in the countries of southwestern Europe (excluding France) mortality did not begin to decline until the 1890s, probably as a result of the late introduction of improvements in categories (2), (3), and (4). Finally, in eastern Europe the course of mortality showed some resemblance to that of southwestern Europe, but began to decline even later, when the same three causal categories were first introduced.

In general, writers before Carr-Saunders had taken a similarly broad approach. After World War II, however, the situation changed. In an article on a century of international mortality trends, George Stolnitz (1955) observed the following:

> Increasing life chances are almost always explained by reference to two broad categories of causes: rising levels of living on the one hand (income, nutrition, housing, literacy), and on the other technological advances (medical science, public health, sanitation). The usual approach has been to regard these sets of factors as more or less coordinate, with little attempt to assess their relative importance. At the same time there has been considerable emphasis on their interdependence, a common observation being that the developing and application of disease control techniques would have been very different in the absence of widespread social change. Both of these views, which evolved largely on the basis of Western mortality experience, have also been traditional explanations of the contrasting patterns found in other parts of the world. Only recently has their adequacy been seriously questioned, mainly as a result of developments in Latin America–Africa–Asia. The introduction of new disease-control methods in this region, usually unaccompanied by any important shifts in socio-economic conditions, has led to drastic mortality declines in the last few years. It is worth noting, therefore, that a similar causal process may have been operative in the acceleration of Western survivorship a good deal earlier.

The measurable reduction in mortality rates following the introduction of antibiotics and pesticides led not only to revisionist views of the past accomplishments of medical technology. It led as well to a major reshaping of the biomedical research and education establishment in the United States in the decades following World War II, at a time when the United States had emerged as the dominant force in scientific research in the West.

Both the intellectual and institutional changes evoked a response from others with different ways of explaining historical and contemporary disease patterns. We may call theirs a "holistic" approach, for it emphasized the significance of the social context, economic forces, and modes of life, and placed less weight on medical factors. For example, in 1955 Thomas McKeown and R. G. Brown wrote that the medical interventions usually invoked to explain declining mortality in eighteenth-century England could not possibly have had the effect attributed to them. In fact, some may have done more harm than good, as R. Dubos (1959) also pointed out.

Others have argued that, at worst, hospitals and dispensaries, inoculations for smallpox, and "man-midwives" had no discernible effect and may have been beneficial. McKeown (1976), in *The Modern Rise of Population,* has suggested that improved nutrition in the eighteenth century initiated the decline. Others have their favorite "first causes" as well: J. Riley (1987) has suggested environmental improvements, and W. H. McNeill (1976), among others, has advanced the increasing genetic resistance to infectious diseases of European populations.

It is likely that the mortality decline proceeded in stages, with certain classes of diseases being reduced in sequence (Omran 1971). The first to be reduced were pandemic and epidemic diseases not responsive to the nutritional status of the host. Next were diseases that caused lifelong immunity after an infection. Last to decline were diseases that were either identifiable nosological entities or clusters of signs and symptoms (i.e., the so-called pneumonia-diarrhea complex), all of which were made especially lethal by the malnourished state of the host. Different conditions were causally associated with the decline of each disease.

By the early 1700s the great pandemics of plague, as well as subsistence crises, had receded from western Europe. As Carr-Saunders (1936) had suggested, this was largely the result of the growing stability of governments. More recently M. W. Flinn (1981) has elaborated this point, suggesting that a number of factors were responsible for the diminution of mortality from wars, famines, and plague. There was, he suggests, a change in warfare: a shift to naval and colonial wars, the development of a science of military hygiene, greater discipline of armies, and increasing isolation of armies from civilian populations (all of which would have contributed to a decline in typhus, among other causes of death). There was also a diminution of subsistence crises, attributable to the spread of new crops, the opening (in eastern Europe especially) of new lands, improved transportation, and more sophisticated "social administration" and famine relief. There was, finally, a diminution of plague in western Europe, which a number of observers have attributed to increasingly effective quarantine procedures, for example, the Hapsburgs' *cordon sanitaire* along the boundary of their empire with the Ottoman Empire. All of these measures were a reflection of growing efficiency in the administration of increasingly large states (Flinn 1981).

Thus, by 1700, the start of the period under consideration, a major transformation in mortality was well underway. The great waves of mortality were ebbing and, by the mid-eighteenth century, death rates were stabilizing – albeit at high levels. Not until about the turn of the nineteenth century, however, did they begin a definite decline.

These observations refer primarily to northwestern Europe. Eastern Europe and the Balkans, and to a lesser degree southern Europe, still suffered from high and fluctuating mortality rates, as can be seen in the devastating plague epidemic that afflicted Moscow in the 1770s (Alexander 1980). Indeed, it was in the eighteenth century that mortality in northwestern Europe began to diverge from that of the rest of Europe. These large regional differences will be dealt with first, followed by mortality in northwestern Europe.

It is beyond the limits of this essay to account for the rise of urban industrial societies in northwest Europe during the eighteenth century, and more rural, agricultural societies elsewhere. That both processes were somehow related is generally agreed, though precisely how is much less clear. Certainly as cities grow, they must draw on a hinterland of increasing size for agricultural produce. Just why rings of production within nations or across Europe (and the globe) acquired the characteristics they did in the eighteenth and nineteenth centuries is a subject of disagreement. Clearly, ease of transport and magnitude of demand are important variables (Dodgshon 1977).

Whatever the cause, it appears that in the eighteenth century agricultural production was differentiated across Europe such that the east central, eastern, and southern areas were devoted largely to the production of staples on large estates, worked by an impoverished peasantry. In contrast, agriculture in northwest Europe was characterized largely by mixed dairy and arable activities on farms of 20 to 50 hectares (Abel 1980), usually worked by individual families and servants.

Family organization and household size differed significantly among regions of Europe as well, again for reasons that are poorly understood. Northwest European family organization tended to be neolocal, and household size to be smaller than elsewhere in Europe, where households were large and complex in organization. In northwest Europe, too, marriage tended to occur at an older age than elsewhere, and it was not universal (Laslett 1983). Even to attempt to explain the genesis of these differences, or their association with differences in

agricultural patterns and industrial and urban development, is not appropriate here. It is sufficient to note simply that, even before industrialization occurred, northwestern Europe differed significantly from the rest of Europe with respect to land use, the organization of work, and household size and composition. However, it is also appropriate to suggest some of the ways in which these differences may contribute to an explanation of the differences in mortality rates and patterns across Europe in the eighteenth and nineteenth centuries after the recession of great pandemics. Indeed, distinctions remained even into the twentieth century.

It has been said that mortality stabilized in northwestern Europe during the eighteenth century as a result of growth of stable states, and that elsewhere rates tended to fluctuate widely as epidemics persisted into the nineteenth century. Nonetheless, even in the more peripheral regions of Europe, there seems to have been a diminution of pandemics and famines as compared with their occurrence in previous centuries. The diseases that remained were endemic. They included named diseases such as tuberculosis, typhoid, scarlet fever, measles, as well as various forms of pneumonia, enteric infections, and, in children, the so-called pneumonia–diarrhea complex. Even smallpox, which in the past had caused such fearsome epidemics, became in the course of the eighteenth century and even more in the nineteenth, increasingly a disease of children rather than of young adults, a result of both the growth and integration of populations and inoculation and vaccination. Most of these diseases were made more lethal by the malnourished state of the host, although smallpox seems to have been an exception.

There were several ways in which agricultural and household organization affected this constellation of airborne, foodborne, and waterborne diseases. For example, early marriage associated with early childbearing increased the risk of infant death. Large households were likely to be crowded, and density increased the risk of contracting airborne infections as well as the opportunity of spreading body lice (vectors of typhus) in particularly unsanitary conditions. Indeed, typhus continued to be common in the civilian populations of Russia and the Balkans well into the nineteenth century.

The pattern of agriculture that persisted in the peripheral regions of Europe throughout the nineteenth century – agricultural wage laborers or serfs working on large estates devoted to monocropping – required the exploitation of female labor. In addition to imposing physiological stress on women, it prevented them from breast feeding for as long as might have been desirable. Moreover, the fact that dairying was not common probably meant that, when infants were weaned, they were put on a very modified adult diet rather than one that included a large amount of nonhuman milk. Under such circumstances, so-called weanling diarrhea was probably very common. Weanling diarrhea is a lethal syndrome in which a malnourished child develops diarrhea and in which diarrhea may precipitate malnutrition. Diarrhea may or may not be caused by malnutrition, but malnutrition increases the likelihood that an episode of diarrhea will be fatal.

Studies in Russia at the end of the nineteenth century showed that infant mortality increased during the summer, when mothers often worked long hours in the fields, generally leaving their children at home, where they could not be nursed. In addition, the practice of using a pacifier rather than breast feeding increased the chances both of malnutrition and of the acquisition of infections, since the pacifier was "a rag covering crumbled bread or rolls, wet dough, or milk kasha – a device ripe with bacteria, especially when combined with milk or, as was the custom, prechewed by an adult" (Frieden 1978). Medical reformers who attempted to change these practices frequently met resistance from people for whom domestic arrangements within an extended family reinforced traditional beliefs and child-rearing practices.

Germany provides another example of the association between peasant life on large estates and mortality. In eastern Prussia the growth of Junker estates devoted to grain monoculture gave rise to a peasant class that needed to exploit women in order to subsist, the result being, as in Russia, an inability to breast feed properly and a high rate of infant mortality. In western Prussia, by contrast, land reforms in the early nineteenth century led to a wider distribution of peasant landownership, a greater variety of crops, and greater ownership of livestock by more people. Thus, spontaneous abortions and infant, perinatal, and maternal mortality were all lower in the West than in the East (Kunitz 1983).

Similar regional differences were observed in Italy, where the south was distinguished from the north by a high proportion of latifundia and high crude mortality rates. Interestingly, however, in this case infant mortality did not differ from one region to another. No explanation for the lack of difference is available; rates all over Italy continued to be among the highest in Europe right to the present century. Indeed, in one particularly poor "latifondo"

region in Calabria, the crude mortality rate averaged about 50 per 1,000 in the latter part of the nineteenth century. In one commune of this area between 1861 and 1875, the average annual crude mortality rate had been about 60 per 1,000 and the infant mortality rate averaged about 500 per 1,000 live births. There was no natural increase in the population (Kunitz 1983).

There are no available data from nineteenth-century Spain that permit a distinction to be made between areas of latifundia and areas where peasants owned their own land. Similarly, nineteenth-century data from the Balkans are somewhat sparse. Crude mortality rates in Croatia were almost 40 per 1,000 between 1800 and 1870 and began to decline significantly only in the 1870s. Rates were lower in Slovenia, probably reflecting the greater influence of Austria. Data from Serbia are available from 1860, with rates ranging from 27 to 33 per 1,000 between 1860 and 1890 (Gelo 1982–3). It is likely that mortality stabilized gradually over the century as the Ottoman Empire instituted reforms modeled on those of Western governments, including efforts to control plague. The fact that it stabilized at high rates was undoubtedly due to continuing backwardness, for throughout the area feudal or semifeudal relations persisted for much of the nineteenth century. In the Hapsburg lands, where servile obligations were formally revoked in 1848, the state developed semifeudal relationships between members of its bureaucracy and the peasantry, but in Bosnia-Herzegovina, under Hapsburg domination from 1878, and in Macedonia, feudalism persisted until 1918. In Serbia the state and money lenders were the chief forces dominating the peasantry (Kunitz 1983).

Turning now to a consideration of mortality patterns within northwestern Europe during the eighteenth and nineteenth centuries, we have already observed that mortality had stabilized and even begun to decline in the eighteenth century. This was primarily a rural phenomenon. Urban mortality remained high well into the nineteenth century, though a widely shared definition of *urban* is sometimes difficult to arrive at.

The points made about the consequences for mortality rates of agricultural and household organization in the peripheral regions of Europe suggest, by way of contrast, why mortality in the rural parts of northwestern Europe declined more rapidly. Households were smaller and presumably less crowded; marriage and therefore childbirth occurred at later ages; dairying became increasingly common and was practiced year round beginning in the eighteenth century; there seems to have been less exploitation of female labor; increasing emphasis was placed on breast feeding of infants and young children; and when weaning occurred, infants were likely to be given cows milk rather than a watered-down version of adult table foods. The result was lower rates of infant, child, and crude mortality in rural northwestern Europe than elsewhere.

In contrast, urban mortality in northwestern Europe throughout most of the nineteenth century was often as high as in the high-mortality countries of Europe; rates in some cities seem actually to have increased in the first part of the nineteenth century. The issue of whether urban mortality did in fact increase is bound up with the so-called standard of living debate (Woods and Woodward 1984). On one side are the "pessimists" – usually to the left of the political spectrum – who claim with Friedrich Engels that industrial development resulted in a deterioration of living conditions of the working class. On the other side are the "optimists," who claim that development made life better for all and that in some regions of Europe industrial development averted a subsistence crisis, so severe was rural poverty (Komlos 1985). As almost always happens, there is a middle position, whose advocates in this case claim that urban mortality did increase but that it was never as high as it had been in the seventeenth and eighteenth centuries, when epidemics could run amok (e.g., Armstrong 1981).

In both England and France, urban mortality seems to have begun to decline in the second half of the nineteenth century. The diseases that declined were spread in different ways: through the air (e.g., respiratory tuberculosis), food, or water (e.g., typhoid and gastroenteritis of all sorts). Many of them seem to be more lethal if the host is malnourished. Indeed, McKeown (1976) has argued that the decline in deaths from tuberculosis in England was the result of improved host resistance resulting from better nutrition, whereas the decline of foodborne and particularly waterborne diseases was the result of improvements in public health measures, such as protected water supplies and sewage disposal, which seem to have been introduced with increasing frequency in the second half of the nineteenth century. Some diseases such as scarlet fever may have decreased in virulence as a result of genetic shifts in the microorganism itself. Others, such as diphtheria, may have increased in virulence for the same reason. There seems little doubt that, in both urban and rural places, the incidence of smallpox declined

dramatically throughout the century as a result of vaccination. And unquestionably the pneumonia–diarrhea complex of childhood declined significantly as well.

It will never be possible to apportion credit with total accuracy to the many preventive measures that contributed to the decline in urban mortality. Public health interventions, changing standards of individual behavior, and improved housing and diets presumably played more or less important roles. Efforts to sort through all of these factors will doubtless raise more questions.

For example, because it has proved difficult to get good direct measures of the standard of living in past times, individual stature, an ingenious indirect measure, has increasingly been relied on (Fogel, Engerman, and Trussell 1982). It is generally assumed that height is a good reflection of nutritional status. Thus, if better diets were responsible for the stabilization of or increase in life expectancy, there should have been an accompanying increase in stature. Unfortunately, the association is complicated by the fact that height also reflects the impact of disease, particularly gastrointestinal afflictions. Permanent stunting may not occur if the intervals between bouts of childhood sickness are sufficiently long that catch-up growth can take place. In developing countries this is often not the case, however, and it has been said that "infections are as important a cause of malnutrition as is the limited availability of food" (Martorell and Ho 1984).

The same may have been true in eighteenth- and nineteenth-century Europe. Thus, the findings regarding variations in height among European populations (Floud 1984), between urban and rural populations (Sandberg and Steckel 1987), and within populations over the course of 100 or 200 years (Fogel et al. 1982) are difficult to interpret if one wants to use them as a measure of the availability of food. This is important because an increase in height (which began in most western European countries in the nineteenth century) could be interpreted as a reflection of the increased availability of food or a reflection of declining sickness resulting from public health measures and from changes in personal behavior, or – what is more likely – both.

In England, at least, fluctuations in life expectancy diminished by the mid-eighteenth century, stabilized at relatively low levels, and then began to increase in the first decades of the nineteenth century. Height also began to increase in the early nineteenth century. Unfortunately, regional data on height are not yet available. But these observations can be interpreted tentatively to mean that the stabilization of mortality was not caused by improved nutritional status and that, when both height and life expectancy began to increase in the nineteenth century, the effects could have been reciprocal: reduced sickness contributing to increased height, improved nutrition (partially reflected in increased height) making people less susceptible to the lethal effects of the most prevalent infectious diseases. In other words, height is a good measure of the standard of living, but it is difficult to determine whether more food or less disease was responsible for the height increase.

There are several points on which most observers seem to agree. First, the initial recession of pandemics seems to have been a result of the growth of nation-states. Second, specific curative measures applied by individual physicians to individual patients had little if any impact on mortality, regardless of the comfort or distress they may have caused patients and their families. Third, the recession of a variety of endemic diseases had a mix of causes: environmental cleansing and active public health interventions; changes in personal behavior (more frequent bathing, handwashing, the cessation of spitting in public, the covering of one's mouth and nose when sneezing and coughing); and improvements in living conditions. Fourth, urban mortality in western Europe increased for a generation or two in the early nineteenth century.

There are also significant areas of disagreement. One, the standard-of-living debate, has already been mentioned. Another, which has received less attention, is the degree to which individual behavior, as opposed to collective measures, affected mortality. McKeown (1976) has argued that, in developed nations, individual behavior is now more significant than environmental conditions in determining health status whereas in the past environmental conditions were more important than individual behavior. There is certainly disagreement with regard to the truth of this assertion. It has been argued, for example, that attitudes toward breast feeding and personal cleanliness had a measurable impact on mortality in the eighteenth and nineteenth centuries (Razzell 1974; Fildes 1986).

Another subject of disagreement has to do with the notion that European populations were selected for resistance to a wide variety of infectious diseases. Some claim that this was an important determinant of declining mortality, whereas others deny that it was. What is clear is that the European mortality decline was a momentous phenomenon, not simply for Europeans but for all peoples. Its causes were bound up with the very creation of the world as we now know it and will continue to be a topic of debate for as long as we disagree about why the world is as it is.

Stephen J. Kunitz

Bibliography

Abel, W. 1980. *Agricultural fluctuations in Europe from the thirteenth to the twentieth centuries*. London.

Alexander, J. T. 1980. *Bubonic plague in early modern Russia*. Baltimore.

Armstrong, W. A. 1981. The trend of mortality in Carlisle between the 1780s and the 1840s: A demographic contribution to the standard of living debate. *Economic History Review* 34: 94–114.

Carr-Saunders, A. M. 1936. *World population: Past growth and present trends*. Oxford.

Dodgshon, R. A. 1977. The modern world system: A spatial perspective. *Peasant Studies* 6: 8–19.

Dubos, R. 1959. *The mirage of health*. New York.

Fildes, V. 1986. *Breasts, bottles and babies: A history of infant feeding*. Edinburgh.

Flinn, M. W. 1981. *The European demographic system, 1500–1820*. Brighton.

Floud, R. 1984. Measuring the transformation of the European economies: Income, health and welfare. Discussion paper series, No. 33, Centre for Economic Policy Research, London (2d Ser.) 34: 94–114.

Fogel, R. W., S. L. Engerman, and J. Trussell. 1982. Exploring the uses of data on height: The analysis of long-term trends in nutrition, labor welfare, and labor productivity. *Social Science History* 6: 401–21.

Fogel, R. W., S. L. Engerman, and R. Floud. 1983. Secular changes in American and British stature and nutrition. *Journal of Interdisciplinary History* 14: 445–81.

Frieden, N. M. 1978. Child care: Medical reform in a traditionalist culture. In *The family in imperial Russia*, ed. D. L. Ransets, 236–59. Urbana, Ill.

Gelo, J. 1982–3. Usporedna slika demografshih promjena Hrvatske i odabranih zemalja od 1780. do 1980. godine (Demographic change in Croatia and selected countries between 1780 and 1980: A comparative picture). *Stanovnistvo* 20–1: 85–98.

Komlos, J. 1985. Stature and nutrition in the Habsburg monarchy: The standard of living and economic development in the eighteenth century. *American Historical Review* 90: 1149–61.

Kunitz, S. J. 1983. Speculations on the European mortality decline. *Economic History Review*, 2d Ser., 36: 349–64.

Laslett, P. 1983. Family and household as work group and kin group: Areas of traditional Europe compared. In *Family forms in historical Europe*, ed. R. Wall, J. Robin, and P. Laslett, 412–20. Cambridge.

Martorell, R., and T. J. Ho. 1984. Malnutrition, morbidity,

and mortality. In *Child survival: Strategies for research,* ed. W. H. Mosley and L. C. Chen, 49–68. Cambridge.

McKeown, T. 1976. *The modern rise of population.* New York.

McKeown, T., and R. G. Brown. 1955. Medical evidence related to English population changes in the eighteenth century. *Population Studies* 9: 119–41.

McNeill, W. H. 1976. *Plagues and peoples.* New York.

Omran, A. R. 1971. The epidemiologic transition: A theory of the epidemiology of population change. *Millbank Memorial Fund Quarterly* 49: 509–38.

Razzell, P. E. 1974. An interpretation of the modern rise of population: A critique. *Population Studies* 28: 5–17.

Riley, J. C. 1987. *The eighteenth-century campaign to avoid disease.* London.

Sandberg, L., and R. H. Steckel. 1987. Heights and economic history: The Swedish case. *Annals of Human Biology* 14: 101–10.

Stolnitz, G. 1955. A century of international mortality trends: I. *Population Studies* 9: 24–55.

Woods, R., and J. Woodward, eds. 1984. *Urban disease and mortality in nineteenth-century England.* London.

V.6
Diseases of Sub-Saharan Africa to 1860

Disease in Africa, as elsewhere, has been and continues to be intimately linked with the ways that human populations have fed themselves. Throughout most of the evolutionary journey of *Homo sapiens* on the African continent (again, as elsewhere), the species existed in small bands of hunter-gatherers with generally fewer than 100 members. As such, individuals were constantly on the move, seldom pausing in one place long enough to foul their water supplies or let their garbage and excrement pile up. They were, as a consequence, spared a host of waterborne parasites and insect disease vectors. Because hunter-gatherers did not have domesticated animals, they were also spared the incredible number of ailments that animals pass along to human masters. Moreover, their numbers were too small to support directly transmitted microparasitic diseases such as smallpox and measles. Finally, evidence suggests that hunter-gatherers were essentially free from the predominant noncommunicable diseases of today, such as cancer, heart-related diseases, and diabetes.

This does not mean that they enjoyed perfect health. They were tormented by a variety of arthritic conditions and suffered from accidents connected with hunting and warfare. Those living within the line of 40-inch rainfall would have been infected from time to time by the trypanosome, which is presumably a very ancient parasite of wild animals. When it is transmitted to humans and large animals by the tsetse fly, it causes often-deadly sleeping sickness. Indeed, as William McNeill points out, the disease probably set some limits on the territory in which early humans were able to hunt and gather. Those living close to the forest would also have been infected on occasion by arboviruses (carried by primates) such as dengue and yellow fever, and it would appear that vivax malaria was ubiquitous at some stage of human development in sub-Saharan Africa. *Plasmodium vivax* is thought to be the oldest of the malaria types that presumably were passed along to humans by their primate cousins. That this occurred quite some time ago is suggested by the fact that the blood of most (95 percent or more) black Africans and those of African descent scattered around the globe lack Duffy antigen, which makes them absolutely refractory to this malarial parasite. Indeed, vivax malaria has died out in Africa, presumably for a lack of hosts.

It is perhaps ironic that, by domesticating plants and animals in the first gigantic effort of humans to control their environment, they created a disease environment over which they had no control, one over which even today only a small measure of control has been gained. We will probably never know with certainty what prompted hunter-gatherers to become sedentary agriculturalists. A good guess, however (for Africa as elsewhere), is that the relatively disease-free environment contributed to population growth, that slowly a band of fewer than a hundred individuals became more than a hundred and divided, and that these bands grew too large and divided again, until at some point there were simply too many people for even the huge expanse of Africa to support in their hunting and gathering.

If this is true, then another factor was the expansion of the Sahara desert, which meant the shrinking of resources. The concept of sub-Saharan Africa is a relatively recent one. Some 50,000 years ago that desert was no desert at all, but rather a region covered by Mediterranean flora, and as late as 4,000 years ago farmers and pastoralists inhabited many regions that are dry and barren today. The effect of the desiccating desert was to split the continent into two subcontinents, cut off most intercourse between the two, and leave the lower subcontinent in relative isolation from the rest of the world. The isolation of eastern Africa, which fronted on the Indian Ocean, was less severe than that of the West, where a hostile Atlantic Ocean formed still another barrier to the rest of the world.

They were Stone Age peoples who found themselves slowly pressed south by the expanding Sahara. At first they lived by harvesting the seeds of wild grasses on its fringes. Then, gradually, they learned how to sow those seeds, which, with repeated effort, would become domesticated sorghums and millets. To the south, on the edge of the forest, dwelled other Stone Age peoples, who fed themselves by trapping small animals and collecting the roots and fruits of the forest, which they also learned to domesticate. To the east, however, hunting and gathering continued, although some cattle were apparently herded in the northern regions.

It was in the south on the eve of the Iron Age, which is to say, the first millennium B.C., probably in the Congo basin, that there developed an agriculturally oriented people who would soon spread over much of sub-Saharan Africa. These were the Bantu. Their language, proto-Bantu, was not a language of hunters, but rather of farmers with words for domesticated animals and plants. It would seem, however, that at first they were not the cereal agriculturalists that most later became, but rather yam and palm oil cultivators who had discovered that these plants grew best in the wetness of cleared-forest areas. While the language was still in a formative stage, it incorporated words for ax and knife and iron and bellows. These agricultural people with a knowledge of ironworking made up the groups that began to expand southward and eastward from their nuclear area to absorb, conquer, and supplant other peoples until the Bantu culture (and agriculture) predominated in almost all of sub-Saharan Africa save for West Africa.

The latter region was, in the meantime, filling up as the expanding desert continued to nudge people, as well as the forest itself, farther and farther south, with the densest populations staying just to the north of the retreating forest. Many of these peoples were perhaps slower than the Bantu to become accomplished agriculturalists, but by the end of the first millennium A.D. most had done so. By this time the region had achieved a good deal of urbanization on the savannas of Sudan, Mali, northern Ghana, and Nigeria, and obviously a well-developed agricultural base was necessary to support the cities.

It is likely that this political consolidation on the savannas, coupled with the advent of the Iron Age, hastened the occupation of the West African forest. For one thing, the forest was a place of refuge from that consolidation, which was based to some extent on slavery, and from mounted slave hunters who were frustrated by the lack of mobility in the forest and whose horses were vulnerable to the tsetse fly and sleeping sickness in many forest areas. Another reason that people gravitated to the forest had to do with both the development of iron tools that were used to clear it and the efficient cultivation of newly imported Southeast Asian food plants such as the Asian and coco yams: These yams were considerably higher yielding than any African food plant and grew well in forest clearings.

Accompanying this conversion to sedentary agriculture for most sub-Saharan Africans were parasite proliferations. They came from herds of domestic animals in the north, they arrived via caravan across the desert as people from the northern subcontinent came to trade, and they developed internally. The hot, rainy, humid portions of Africa harbor a vast and nasty collection of disease-bearing insects, among them some 60 of the world's species of *Anopheles* mosquitoes. The creation of clearings and slash-and-burn agriculture made fine breeding places for many of them, including *Anopheles gambiae,* the most efficient vector for malaria. With stationary humans acting as reservoirs for the disease, human being to mosquito to human being malaria cycles began. Vivax malaria was in recession but was replaced by the new and much more deadly falciparum malaria, which forced populations to build genetic defenses against it, such as sickle trait, glucose-6-dehydrogenese deficiency, and thalassemia traits. In addition, the less lethal but nonetheless debilitating *Plasmodium malariae* became widespread, and genetic defenses notwithstanding, immunity acquired by suffering a few bouts of malaria and surviving them was doubtless the first line of defense.

With the development of sickle trait, however, African youngsters probably began to develop deadly sickle cell anemia. Although sickle-shaped cells somehow limit the extent of parasitization in the case of *Plasmodium falciparum,* that protection comes at a very dear price. When both parents of a child have the trait, the odds are 1 in 4 that the child will be born with sickle cell anemia. In the past, an afflicted child would most likely have died. Thus, in the more malaria-ridden regions of Africa, where the frequency of sickle trait reached 40 percent or more, sickle-cell anemia must have been an important killer of the African young.

Permanent villages in and near the forest accumulated human junk, such as broken pottery, which encouraged the breeding of another disease vector, the *Aedes aegypti* mosquito. As the latter came to depend on closely packed human populations for blood meals, it began to spread yellow fever among them. Depending on location, villages were cursed with dracunculiasis (guinea worm infection), schistosomiasis, and filariasis (elephantiasis) including onchocerciasis (river blindness, craw craw), and loiasis (loa loa). Individuals now living in close proximity to one another in large numbers passed yaws and leprosy back and forth. Fouled water supplies supported endless rounds of typhoid fever and amebic and bacillary dysentery. In addition, the blood of the animals that were domesticated and lived cheek to jowl with their masters attracted the tsetse fly, which infected humans as well with sleeping sickness (sleepy distemper). They also attracted disease-bearing insects with their dung and passed along parasites like tapeworm, ascaris, and trichuris worms. These and other worms, such as the hookworm, became ubiquitous in towns and villages where fecal material was disposed of casually, if at all, and individuals went barefoot. Indeed, for reasons yet to be explained, West Africans, at least, had so much experience with hookworm infection that they developed a natural resistance to hookworm anemia.

If the forest offered protection from human predators, a price of that protection was frequently isolation: Self-sustaining village-states were remote from one another as well as from the larger world outside the forest. One consequence of this was the development of a rigid social structure that guaranteed the social stability so necessary for survival, but at the expense of innovation and change. Another likely consequence was frequently sufficient isolation from the disease pools of the outside world that when epidemics did strike they proved to be of exceptional virulence.

It is important to stress that the shift to sedentary agriculture among both cereal farmers and yam and palm oil cultivators was not an overnight phenomenon (and indeed, Africa today has hunter-gatherers). Rather, the shift was the result of a process in which expanding food supplies created expanding populations, which in turn sought new areas to bring under cultivation. However, as the diet narrowed from the variety of foodstuffs enjoyed by hunter-gatherers to

the single crop generally produced by sedentary agriculturalists, nutritional illnesses must have joined the list of new diseases in Africa. A diet that is essentially vegetable in nature and limited to a very few nutriments is low in iron, the vitamin B complex, and essential amino acids. In these circumstances it is the young, just weaned from the high-quality protein in breast milk to a vegetable pap, who suffer the most from protein–energy malnutrition with kwasiorkor and marasmus as its symptomatic poles. Animal milk would have prevented the disease, but as hinted at previously those within the line of 40-inch rainfall could not develop a dairying industry because of the blood-sucking tsetse fly, which seeks out large animals and infects them with African trypanosomiasis. This explains, in large part, the high frequency of lactose intolerance among those of West African descent. If they did not drink milk after infancy, there was no reason to maintain the lactose enzyme.

Most West Africans, in particular, were limited to raising a few animals such as goats, chickens, dogs, and perhaps a pig or two. But because these animals were slaughtered only on festive occasions, and because of taboos against drinking goats milk and eating eggs, animal protein figured very little in the diet. Moreover, African soils in the tropical belt are heavily acidic, nitrogen deficient, and leached by rains of their mineral content, especially calcium and phosphorus. As a result, crops that grow on them, as well as animals that graze on them, are protein and mineral deficient. That the West African diet was extraordinarily low in high-quality protein is suggested by the fact that slaves from Africa reaching the Caribbean Islands were significantly shorter than island-born counterparts, despite the miserable quality of the slave diet in the West Indies.

In addition to deficiency diseases, sedentary agriculture led to a reliance on crops that could and did fail because of insects, drought, and warfare. Thus, periodic famine, famine-related diseases, and starvation thinned populations that had swelled during good times, and this synergism became another unpleasant fact of African life. In short, in the switch from hunting and gathering to sedentary agriculture, Africans became what Thomas Malthus called a "forced population," meaning that although the population grew, this growth was managed only at a decreased level of subsistence for everybody.

Contact with Europeans and, through them, their American empires brought a second agricultural revolution to sub-Saharan Africa. Cassava (manioc), maize, peanuts, and sweet potatoes, high-yielding plants imported from America, spread throughout Africa until they became much more important than indigenous crops and further stimulated population growth. Ironically, much of that growth was drained off to America via the slave trade. In addition to population growth, however, the new plants stimulated disease. It has been discovered that those Africans whose diets centered on maize very often suffered from pellagra, and those who consumed cassava were assaulted by beriberi. Also, given the vegetable nature of their diets coupled with the parasites that infected them, most sub-Saharan Africans were anemic. Moreover, the tell-tale spongy and bleeding gums of scurvy were not uncommon.

With the Europeans, and with more contact with the outer world, also came increased exposure to contagious diseases. The earliest European report of smallpox in sub-Saharan Africa dates from Angola in the 1620s, but the strong probability exists that it had been present there for several preceding centuries. In fact, August Hirsch pinpointed regions of central Africa along with India as the "native foci" of the disease, and others have also reported that smallpox was a very old disease on the African continent. This was very likely true of measles, chickenpox, and most other Eurasian diseases as well. Evidence for this assumption derives from the fact that, unlike the American Indians or the Pacific Islanders, sub-Saharan Africans did not die in wholesale fashion after contact with the Europeans. The Europeans, however, were extremely susceptible to African illnesses, especially to the African fevers – yellow fever and malaria. Indeed, white sailors on slaving vessels, and especially soldiers stationed in Africa, suffered such horrendous levels of mortality (in some instances soldiers died at a rate of 500 to 700 per 1,000 per annum) as to earn West Africa the sobriquet "the white man's grave." Thus, it was not until the advent of modern medicine that Europeans were able to colonize much of sub-Saharan Africa.

One Eurasian disease that was slow to make inroads in Africa was tuberculosis. There seems no doubt that whereas tuberculosis was a disease of many ancient civilizations and even prehistoric people in Europe, it was unknown in sub-Saharan Africa until the arrival of the Europeans. Because a long experience with this disease appears to confer some ability to resist it, and conversely, because it falls on "virgin-soil" peoples with considerable fury, one might have expected tuberculosis to have become a severe health problem in Africa long before it did in the nineteenth and twentieth centuries. In the latter part of the nineteenth century, Hirsch pronounced the disease "very malignant" in sub-Saharan Africa. Yet eighteenth-century European observers saw little of it and called it rare.

It may be that the observers in question simply did not recognize the disease, because tuberculosis can have atypical symptoms. Certainly the isolation of many African groups and the relative lack of urban life probably also help to account for the phenomenon. Another possibility, however, deserves some attention.

Leprosy and tuberculosis are both caused by bacilli from the genus *Mycobacterium* and an inverse relationship between the two diseases has been noticed (e.g., where leprosy is prevalent, tuberculosis is not and vice versa). It is generally thought that, although tuberculosis protects against leprosy, the converse is not the case. Yet in Nigeria, in the heart of the leprosy belt, where it is assumed that the disease has been endemic for many centuries, tuberculosis was very slow to take hold. As late as 1936, for example, a British physician reported much leprosy in Nigeria, but made no mention of tuberculosis.

Bacillary pneumonia, like tuberculosis, was brought to Africa by the Europeans, and like tuberculosis it would prove to be of extraordinary virulence among the Africans, at least by the nineteenth century. Observers reported much lung disease around the Bight of Benin; the disease was viewed as one of the most serious to torment the people of Angola; and Hirsch reported pneumonia as "common" on most of the African West Coast and the East Coast as well.

Syphilis was also a late arrival in sub-Saharan Africa and, like tuberculosis, was slow to spread. But here we are on more solid ground in explaining its slow diffusion. The causative agents of both syphilis and yaws are of the same family (the two diseases may be only one illness with different symptoms and means of transmission) and thus provide cross-immunity. Because yaws was endemic to much of sub-Saharan Africa, it would seem that syphilis had much difficulty finding hosts – so much so that David Livingstone was convinced that "pure Africans" could not develop the disease. Earlier, Mungo Park, the great explorer of the Niger River at the turn of the nineteenth century, saw a great deal of yaws but no syphilis. In contrast, Father Giovanni Cavazzi, in his classic treatment of the diseases of the Congo and Angola, writes of the "mal Frances," called "bubas" by the Portuguese, as the most common disease of the region. Though incomplete, his description suggests syphilis racing through a virgin-soil people, which may well have been the case, for the padre was describing people who had been in contact with Europeans longer than had most others. Yet the disease he reported could also have been leprosy, because until well into the twentieth century, physicians have had difficulty differentiating between syphilis and leprosy in Africa.

To the extent that they were successful in making this distinction, reporters indicate that the disease had apparently overcome the resistance of yaws to become common at least in the port cities of West and West Central Africa during the nineteenth century, although it remained rare in Mozambique until the early twentieth century. From the reports of Livingstone and Park, however, the disease was slow to spread inland.

Gonorrhea, the other major sexually transmitted disease of yesterday, was present much earlier in sub-Saharan Africa and probably had been acquired from the Arabs. Unlike syphilis, gonorrhea had no yawslike disease to hinder its spread and quickly became ubiquitous. The disease is usually not life threatening. But it may cause ophthalmia neonatorum, which along with onchocerciasis was probably responsible for much of the blindness reported among the African natives.

Other nonlethal ailments that tormented sub-Saharan Africans include still more eye ailments, which must have been caused by an absence of vitamin A, since night blindness was regularly seen. The skin complaints that seemed to plague almost everyone resulted from riboflavin deficiency as well as from pellagra, yaws, syphilis, onchocerciasis, and a variety of insect pests including the mites that produce scabies, which were widely reported. Ainhum, sometimes called the "dry gangrene of the little toe" by European observers, which involved the constriction and eventual loss of that digit, was another ailment reported with some frequency; and rheumatism and arthritis were rife across the continent. Finally, women and children often ate dirt and clay, presumably in response to mineral deficiencies.

By 1860, then, sub-Saharan Africans were being born into a world teeming with pathogens. Almost all of the major diseases of the rest of the world had been introduced, including cholera, which had already paid visits to East Africa in 1821, 1836–7, and 1858–9, to enrich a disease pool already brimming with tropical ailments that much of the rest of the world had been spared (cerebrospinal meningitis and plague were yet to arrive). The reasons for

the abundance of tropical diseases – helminthic, viral, microbial, and protozoal – in sub-Saharan Africa are diverse. The existence of numerous populations of primates that could harbor diseases and pass them on to humans is obviously one. Another has to do with the high average temperatures and humidity that, along with lush vegetation, make tropical Africa a paradise for the myriad insects that are free from the seasonal controls of more temperate climates and thus can abuse humans on a year-round basis. The same, of course, is true of the many helminthic parasites that find the ecology of the African tropics ideal. As a result, Africans were seldom free of disease, and most likely suffered from more than one at the same time.

Moreover, those born into this world were not provided with much good nutrition to combat their illnesses, and in fact illness often worked synergistically with malnutrition. The chief sufferers of both the disease and nutritional environments were, of course, the young. Infants died at horrendous rates, as did children, and it is likely that 50 percent of those born in sub-Saharan Africa did not live until age 5. Yet such high infant and child mortality constitutes a powerful selective mechanism, and it seems clear that, in the face of sickness and malnutrition, Africans adapted to both in ways we know and in ways we have yet to discover.

Kenneth F. Kiple

Bibliography

Curtin, Philip. 1967. Epidemiology and the slave trade. *Political Science Quarterly* 83: 190–216.

Daniell, William F. 1849. *Sketches of the medical topography and native diseases of the Gulf of Guinea, Western Africa.* London.

Ford, John. 1971. *The role of the trypanosomiasis in African ecology: A study of the tsetse fly problem.* Oxford.

Hartwig, G. W., and K. David Patterson, eds. 1978. *Disease in African history.* Durham, N.C.

Hoeppli, R. 1969. *Parasitic diseases in Africa and the Western Hemisphere: Early documentation and transmission by the slave trade.* Basel.

Kiple, Kenneth F. 1984. *The Caribbean slave: A biological history.* Cambridge.

Kiple, Kenneth F., ed. 1987. *The African exchange: Toward a biological history of black people.* Durham, N.C.

Kiple, Kenneth F., and Virginia H. King. 1981. *Another dimension to the black diaspora: Diet, disease and racism.* Cambridge.

Latham, Michael. 1965. *Human nutrition in tropical Africa.* Rome.

Lewiki, Tadeuz. 1976. *West African foods in the Middle Ages.* London.

McKeown, Thomas. 1988. *The origins of human disease.* London.

McNeill, William H. 1976. *Plagues and peoples.* Garden City, N.Y.

Miller, Joseph C. 1988. *Way of death: Merchant capitalism and the Angolan slave trade, 1730–1830.* Madison, Wis.

Ransford, Oliver. 1984. *"Bid the sickness cease": Disease in the history of black Africa.* London.

Shaw, Thurstan. 1977. Hunters, gatherers, and first farmers in West Africa. In *Hunters, gatherers, and first farmers beyond Europe: An archaeological survey,* ed. J. V. S. Megaw, 69–125. Leicester.

V.7
Diseases of Sub-Saharan Africa since 1860

Africa was long characterized as the "dark continent," impenetrable, disease-ridden, and dangerous. To many Europeans, Africans personified degeneracy and suffering, and their environment seemed a hothouse of fever and affliction. Europeans had good reason to connect sub-Saharan Africa with disease. For centuries, their attempts to penetrate the coastal fringes of the continent had been effectively frustrated by diseases against which they had little or no resistance (Carlson 1984). In the early nineteenth century, Europeans arriving in West Africa suffered appalling mortality from disease (most often yellow fever and hyperendemic malaria) at rates of between 350 and 800 per 1,000 per annum (Curtin 1968), and the West African coast became known as the "white man's grave." With such mortality rates, it is no surprise that Europeans believed that Africa was more disease-ridden than other parts of the world.

In fact, many continue to believe that tropical Africa has a well-deserved reputation as a vast breeding ground and dispersal center for dozens of diseases and thus would subscribe to the recent assertion that "Africa is a sick continent, full of sick and . . . starving people" (Prins 1989). This view has been reinforced by scientific speculation concerning the appearance of so-called exotic new diseases like Ebola, Marburg, and Lassa fevers in the 1960s and 1970s (Westwood 1980; Vella 1985). The HIV viruses that cause the acquired immune deficiency syndrome (AIDS) are the most recent additions to this list.

Recent technological advances, especially in electron microscopy, coupled with the rapidly expanding specialties of molecular biology, genetics, and immunology, have given rise to an equally rapid expansion of virology. Scientists are now on the threshold of making important new discoveries that it is hoped will lead to cures for viral infections to equal those available for many bacterial, fungal, and parasitical infections. Unfortunately, however, the identification of Africa as the home of "exotic new diseases" has reinforced the widespread view of that continent as a major source of disease-causing germs.

Disease has been an important factor in the history of sub-Saharan Africa since 1860. Across the continent people have been under constant attack by endemic diseases in their struggle for survival, and epidemic diseases have decimated millions. In 21 countries, life expectancy today ranges from only about 44 to 56 years according to I. Timaeus (personal communication). In some countries, mortality rates have grown recently, and in most regions they remain high. Increases have occurred in Angola, Ethiopia, Mozambique, Niger, Nigeria, and Rwanda. In the first three there were 250 to 299 deaths per 1,000 live births, and in Gambia, Sierra Leone, Mali, and Malawi child mortality rates were more than 300 per 1,000 (United Nations 1987). The direct causes of this mortality in most developing countries are the following: diarrhea, malnutrition, malaria, measles, acute respiratory infections, tetanus, and other neonatal causes. Now AIDS reminds us of the potential havoc of an epidemic disease in Africa.

Nevertheless, other countries have experienced an appreciable decline in infant and child mortality in the past 20 years. In Kenya in the late 1950s, the child mortality rate (for children less than 5 years of age) was 265 deaths per 1,000 live births, whereas in 1989 it had declined to 150 per 1,000 (Blacker 1989). It must be made clear that in some regions of Africa there have been significant increases in population growth, whereas other regions such as Kivu in eastern Zaire have been densely populated for many decades. African demography is a rapidly expanding field of study among social scientists and members of the medical and scientific communities, and there is a continuing debate concerning the relationship between biomedical provision and morbidity and mortality rates in sub-Saharan Africa. Some observers contend that over the past century, medical provision has been the major factor in lower morbidity and mortality, whereas others believe that improved socioeconomic conditions, more than medical provision, have resulted in less illness and death among

Africans. Proponents of this view refer to the apparent paradoxical situation in some regions of the continent in which populations have increased in spite of the quite dramatic disintegration of health care delivery systems that were inherited from the colonial period. We shall probably have to await the twenty-first century for satisfactory explanations of the dynamics of African demography and its history.

An analysis of disease environments can be made in terms of both natural factors and socioeconomic considerations. Natural factors, crucial to proponents of the "determinist" school of disease causation, include such items as altitude, temperature, rainfall, humidity, and soil, as well as the proliferation of potential disease hosts and vectors like animals, birds, insects, and parasites. Epidemiologists describe three major disease patterns in sub-Saharan Africa roughly akin to the three main climatic zones: damp uplands, damp lowlands, and savanna regions with a long dry season. Damp uplands include the Kenyan highlands, southwestern Uganda, mountain slopes of eastern and western Africa (mounts Elgon and Kilimanjaro), and parts of Rwanda and Burundi. The much vaster damp lowlands include coastal West Africa and the massive Congo basin, which are the regions of Africa that most readily fit the popular notion of "the tropics." The third and most extensive climatic pattern is identified by a limited rainy season and a longer dry season. At one extreme in this climatic pattern is the Sahel, where the dry season dominates, but the pattern pertains to savanna regions as well (Bradley 1980).

Disease patterns vary immensely throughout these three zones, yet generalizations can be made. In the damp uplands, including the Kenya highlands, the southwestern tip of Uganda, parts of Rwanda and Burundi, and the southern Kivu district of eastern Zaire, population densities are high and the predominant infections are respiratory and diarrheal, both largely diseases of poverty and poor sanitation. In the damp lowlands with their prolific insect vectors, malaria dominates the disease pattern, with almost every person infected within the first year of life. Yaws, hookworm, the diarrheas, typhoid, infective hepatitis, and numerous viruses are also common. The third disease pattern, that of the savannas, is again dominated by malaria, with diarrheal diseases and waterborne diseases predominating. The latter include schistosomiasis and dracunculiasis (guinea worm), whereas another devastating disease, sleeping sickness, is especially prevalent along waterways, the haunt of many tsetse flies, which transmit the disease. Another im-

portant disease of this environment is cerebrospinal meningitis.

Analyses of disease patterns that focus more on the role of social, cultural, political, and economic factors emphasize the dynamic relationships that exist between humans and their total environment. This is the approach of those concerned with the "social production of health and disease" (Turshen 1984). Only rarely do analyses of disease patterns combine both the deterministic and the socioeconomic approaches and thus reveal the complex interrelations between natural and socioeconomic factors (Blacker 1989). John Ford's (1971) brilliant study of the tsetse problem is an example of a successful combining of the two.

Yet in the case of Africa, climate and geography are less important determinants of health than are the social, economic, and political factors. (The majority of sub-Saharan Africa is not the sweltering, humid tropics of popular imagination but is rather temperate savanna or forest.) Medicine has only a limited role in ameliorating the health of populations (McKeown 1979), and upon closer examination, it can usually be shown that the *root causes* of ill health are embedded in social and economic structures. Indeed, in much of sub-Saharan Africa, it is precisely because of social and economic upheaval that we have recently seen a rapid increase in morbidity and mortality, and medical services in some regions have deteriorated so seriously as to be nonexistent (Dodge and Wiebe 1985).

Overview of Disease in Africa Since 1860

Most of the written sources for the history of diseases in Africa since 1860 derive from Europeans, who had very specific interests in health. Their first concern was for their own health and that of fellow Europeans, whereas concern for the health of Africans was extended mainly to those people the Europeans needed as laborers or producers. It was clear from the outset that Africans were human capital. Medical opinion of the mid-nineteenth century set the pattern for most of the colonial period when it expounded the view that only blacks could labor in the tropical regions of Africa, and in this, science allegedly corroborated the imperialist view that the physical constitution of the African was different from that of the European.

Certainly it must have seemed so. Early European accounts describe the devastating morbidity and mortality they suffered, but we learn very little about the impact of disease on African populations apart from those employed as porters and soldiers.

Non-Eurocentric accounts of diseases and health conditions among African populations are rare for the earlier period, and those dating from World War II are also limited in number and scope. Nearly all Europeans in Africa – explorers, traders, missionaries, or colonials – were concerned primarily with the diseases that threatened their own health, and this must be borne in mind by anyone looking at early accounts of diseases of Africa.

Between 1860 and 1885 European exploration and trade along with coasts of Africa increased and finally culminated in the full expression of foreign imperialism with formal colonization; by 1920 most of equatorial, eastern, and central Africa had been taken over by Europeans. The result for much of the region was a series of catastrophes in the form of wars of conquest and the initial consolidation of colonial rule. The primary motive for colonization was economic exploitation of natural resources and human populations. In their rush for profit, Europeans often employed roughshod, even brutal, methods that greatly affected disease patterns.

Some African societies, like those located along the west coast of the continent, had long been in contact with outsiders and thus did not seem to be as immediately affected by new pathogens and other stresses as were populations in eastern and central Africa, which had been more isolated. For many societies of eastern, central, and southern Africa, however, the period 1890–1920 was so traumatic as to have been described as a time of tumultuous "ecological disaster" (Ford 1971; Kjekshus 1977). New diseases were spread to nonimmune populations, and previously endemic diseases became epidemic. It is clear that the great epidemics of human sleeping sickness throughout the Congo basin beginning in the late nineteenth century, which in Uganda produced an estimated 300,000 deaths between 1901 and 1905, were a result of violent disruptions to those regions. In fact, the history of sleeping sickness illustrates well the effects of upheavals in large parts of sub-Saharan Africa around the turn of the century. Increased stresses accompanied by reduced nutritional and immune status led to greatly increased morbidity and mortality for millions of Africans.

During the four decades between 1920 and 1960, colonial rule and economic exploitation of the land and people were refined and greatly extended. Ever-increasing numbers of Africans were drawn, often unwillingly, into colonial economies as laborers and tax payers. Others were forced into an "informal" economy earning cash as prostitutes or petty traders and by providing other services. Highly mobile and most often poorly nourished, these Africans often attracted the attention of colonial authorities, who considered them an important source of disease, especially venereal disease. Military leaders commonly complained about the threat to public health posed by prostitutes and female "camp followers."

In all colonies, there was constant fear among European colonizers that the new "detribalized" individuals gravitating toward the new urban centers were spreading disease, which in turn contributed to the development of powerful stereotypic images of Africans. Technologically inferior, Africans were thought to be less "civilized" (Comaroff and Comaroff 1991), and because civilization was equated with hygiene, many believed that Africans were by nature unhygienic. Consequently, all colonies by the early decades of the twentieth century had implemented a public health policy of racial segregation in order to protect the health of whites (Spitzer 1968; Swanson 1977).

By 1940 many African societies had been literally "restructured" as a result of the need to meet the increasing demands of European industries and markets. Throughout the continent, millions of Africans were forced to migrate annually to labor in unsafe and unsanitary conditions in mines, on plantations, and in public works projects such as road and rail building. In addition to the more apparent effects of heavy labor in harsh conditions on African health were those that attended the proletarianization and urbanization of millions of Africans across the continent. This had the important effect of disrupting and often destroying African forms of social organization, which also had an adverse effect on the health of Africans.

Migrant laborers, who were usually malnourished, poorly clothed, crowded into miserable dwellings, and overworked, were victims of a wide range of infectious and contagious diseases. Similarly, men and women left behind in the rural sector were burdened with the crushing labor of agricultural production, which was required by the colonial administrators to feed the migrant labor force as well as the rapidly expanding urban populations. The result was that nutrition declined everywhere in Africa, and given the complex interaction of disease and malnutrition we can guess the result.

Large parts of sub-Saharan Africa experience a "hungry" season, which takes place after the long dry season, just as the rains start and food stores are low or depleted. This period is the point in the agricultural calendar when intense labor is required, but it is also the time when people are ill. Recent studies have revealed that it is at the end of the dry season when measles and pneumonia deaths peak for a combination of reasons. Among them are lower standards of child care because mothers have to labor in the fields and suppressed immune responses exacerbated by malnutrition, both of which must have played a major role in disease incidence during the colonial period. Other contributing factors were the widespread colonial practice of implementing cash crop economies, which were often based on monoculture. In Ghana, for example, where cocoa production formed the basis of the colonial economy, when prices were high, staple food production fell off and people suffered accordingly.

The two world wars compounded the burden of colonial labor and production for African populations. The wars were also periods of nutritional deprivation for millions of people. Thousands of men were recruited into military service, and disease and death were rife. Mass recruitment programs during the First World War revealed the poor state of African health to colonial authorities, and as a consequence plans were launched to provide medical services to the masses. The emphasis remained, however, on the curative as opposed to the preventive approach.

Since the 1960s, when most African colonies gained political independence, there has been a considerable increase in population throughout much of the subcontinent. This is a subject that in the last part of the twentieth century has become the focus of much study and debate and that in all likelihood will have to wait the next century for an in-depth explanation. While population has increased in many regions, in many African states economic decay has been accompanied by a reduction in the immune and nutritional status of large segments of the population. An important cause has been protracted wars of independence such as those in Angola, Mozambique, Zimbabwe, and Namibia and civil wars such as those in Nigeria, Sudan, and Uganda. These political upheavals have caused the widespread destruction of human lives, a decline in agricultural production, the disruption of civil society, and the creation of hundreds of thousands of displaced persons and refugees. Closely related to the political upheavals have been a series of droughts, famines, and epidemics that have further increased the toll on human life. If current World Health Organization projections are even only partially correct, mortality from AIDS in sub-Saharan Africa can be expected to devastate parts of the continent, where it threatens to strike down young adults in their productive and reproductive prime.

A number of accounts of the overall health of Africans since 1860 have stressed the point that biomedicine and improved public health were the most valuable legacies of the colonial powers. Certainly there were some notable successes starting in the 1920s with the introduction of the sulfa drugs. Yaws, a widespread endemic disease, responded almost miraculously to sulfonamides; Africans by the thousands eagerly sought injections, and in many regions yaws was almost eradicated. Similarly, sleeping sickness, endemic throughout much of eastern, central, and western Africa, was by the 1950s and 1960s under control as a result of sometimes enormous campaigns aimed at this one disease. In the Belgian Congo and French Equatorial Africa, the systematic examination and medication of the entire population was the goal, and at the same time all affected colonies practiced some degree of mass removal and resettlement of populations thought to be at risk of infection.

Yet even where biomedical solutions have proved effective, the serious problem of their costs remains. Large-scale medical campaigns launched against single diseases like those aimed at sleeping sickness, yaws, malaria, and more recently smallpox are called "vertical" campaigns and are expensive. More general, or "horizontal," health programs address a broad spectrum of public health issues such as control of endemic and epidemic diseases, infant and mother care, vaccinations, and primary health clinics and are usually far more cost effective in their use of personnel, infrastructure, and supplies. Unfortunately, throughout much of the colonial period in sub-Saharan Africa, medical services tended to be more vertical than horizontal. The huge and costly campaigns launched against single diseases absorbed scarce resources and drew money away from other crucial areas of health provision. For Africans, closely related to this problem of health economics is another: Most pharmaceutical companies have been and remain reluctant to invest heavily in the research and development of medicines for diseases that afflict mainly impoverished, often rural populations in underdeveloped regions of the world. Since the late 1800s, the combination of vertical medical campaigns and the reluctance of pharmaceutical companies to invest in research has had profoundly adverse affects on the health of millions of sub-Saharan Africans.

Nonetheless, by the time of their independence in the 1960s the health of many African populations was considerably better than that of preceding generations. Vaccination campaigns in many countries had become routine. In some regions, more often urban centers, public health programs had imposed a degree of control over malaria. Maternal and child health programs were also well established in many colonies. Large-scale employers such as mines and plantations had expressed some concern for the well-being of their labor forces, and in some regions working conditions were improved. Mortality and morbidity rates were lower than ever, and major epidemics occurred far less frequently than before.

Departing colonial administrations took credit for these improvements, which were seen as stemming from the ameliorating effects of those medical services that, as we noted, many believed to be the most valuable colonial legacy. In other words, it was believed that the incidence of disease had been decreased through the beneficial effects of Western biomedical staff, infrastructure, and techniques. At that time few would have credited improvements in the standard of living of many millions of Africans for the decreased incidence. Yet as Thomas McKeown has argued convincingly, it was improved socioeconomic conditions, rather than medical therapies, that accounted for the overall improvements in the health of Western populations. Doubtless this also played a substantial if not well-recognized role in ameliorating the health of Africans as well.

Science and Disease in Africa

The last quarter of the nineteenth century was an exciting chapter in the history of science and medicine. It was also the period when much of sub-Saharan Africa was formally colonized by Europeans and, indeed, the two phenomena were not unrelated. By the late nineteenth century, important developments in the areas of scientific, statistical, and epidemiological thought had combined with the development of specificity in disease etiologies and therapies to enable Europeans to penetrate and permanently settle the interior regions of the continent.

Late Victorians had great confidence that Cartesian science and new, rapidly evolving technology would provide humans with the means to reshape their environment to suit themselves. In fact, medical advances seemed to be elegant proof of this ability to overcome the dangers of the environment. During the 1854 expedition along the Niger, for example, the successful prophylactic use of quinine demonstrated that it was at last possible for Europeans to survive the onslaughts of malaria. Then around the turn of the century, new concepts of what constituted disease rapidly evolved, as did the role of the new expert health professionals – both develop-

ments having serious implications for the new African colonies.

Most important in the new science was the role of the laboratory, which became the real battlefield on which questions of life and death would be settled. Laboratories could be mobile, as they were soon to be in the new specialty of tropical medicine. Between 1860 and 1900, Joseph Lister, Louis Pasteur, and Robert Koch transformed forever our understanding of the relationships of humans and their disease-causing pathogens. The new sciences gave specificity to diseases whose etiologies could now be ascertained. With more concrete understanding of the pathology of a specific disease and knowledge of its particular cause, the pathogen or germ, scientists could think in terms of equally specific therapies (e.g., Paul Ehrlich's "magic bullet").

There was an unfortunate consequence, however, for these exciting developments prompted scientists involved in tropical health in Africa to cast aside most of the earlier theories of disease causation. Earlier ideas concerning the influences of environment on health, a view that stressed the relationships between humans and their environment, were overshadowed by the empiricism of the new laboratory science with its method of verifiable experiment. Thus, budding theories of the "social construction of diseases" were, by the turn of the century, almost entirely superseded by powerful theories of the "biological determinism of disease." The latter approach would dominate most medical and public health thinking throughout the colonial period.

The Disease Environment

In addition, Africans had their own tropical illnesses: malaria, blackwater fever, yellow fever, trypanosomiasis (sleeping sickness), filariases, leishmaniasis (kala-azar), schistosomiasis (bilharziasis), onchocerciasis (river blindness), leprosy, yaws, guinea worm, helminthiasis, relapsing fever (louse- and tickborne), and tropical ulcer. A number of these are caused by parasites that are transmitted to humans by insects. Because both the parasites and the insects require very specific conditions of temperature and moisture and because many of the other diseases are waterborne, the emphasis on "tropical" is understandable. Also understandably, diseases that had such complex and fascinating etiologies and that required the combined expertise of zoologists, protozoologists, epidemiologists, chemists, and biologists overwhelmingly attracted the attention of early investigators in Africa. Unfortunately, other important causes of morbidity and mortality, such as respiratory diseases, childhood diseases, and malnutrition, were not given research priority. "Tropical" diseases were mistakenly conceptualized as distinct from other communicable diseases. In this way, tropical medicine evolved as a specialty outside of mainstream medicine.

By the mid-nineteenth century, tropical Africans were afflicted by most of the diseases of the temperate Old World, such as brucellosis (Malta fever), undulant fever, cerebrospinal meningitis, cholera, diphtheria, influenza, measles, plague, pneumonia, poliomyelitis, smallpox, tuberculosis, typhoid fever (enteric fever), typhus and other rickettsial infections, venereal diseases, and whooping cough. The causes of 50 to 90 percent of illness and death among the poor in the underdeveloped world, including Africa, fall into two main groups: nutritional deficiencies and communicable diseases (Sanders 1985). The major causes of adult mortality are infectious and parasitic diseases, acute respiratory infections, cardiovascular disease, and accidents and violence. Most childhood mortality is caused by a limited number of infectious diseases: diarrheal diseases, acute respiratory infections, malaria, measles, and neonatal tetanus (I. Timaeus, personal communication). Moreover, there is evidence that in recent years the incidence of noninfectious and degenerative diseases is increasing.

What constitutes a disease environment and what causes it to change? Every human community coexists with specific microorganisms that contribute to the disease environment of the group. Many diseases represent the failure of one organism, in this case human beings, to cope successfully with competing organisms, in this case microorganisms, in the ceaseless struggle for survival. A disease environment contains many elements: humans, animals, various other forms of flora and fauna, microorganisms, climate, and geographic features. Many disease environments are often located close to one another, and these undergo frequent and sometimes rapid change. For instance, after a period of interaction with a stable human population, disease-causing pathogens can adapt and produce new strains in response to the immune defenses produced by that population. In recent decades this has been demonstrated in parts of the world by the appearance of new strains of chloroquinine-resistant *Plasmodium falciparum,* the cause of the most deadly of the malarial diseases.

Conversely, human host communities develop immunity to endemic diseases. In other words, humans who survive the diseases of their environment often acquire some resistance to further infection. Epidemics of disease occasionally flare up when nonimmune members of the community are exposed to pathogens or when newcomers in large enough numbers reach a disease environment containing pathogens against which they have no immune protection. Poor hygiene resulting from ignorance of disease causation coupled with the widespread lack of safe water supplies and sewage disposal also profoundly affect a society's disease environment.

As stated previously, disease environments are affected by both natural and sociocultural factors. A natural factor of much importance in Africa is the proliferation of insects, many of which serve as vectors of disease-causing pathogens. Another factor is climate, which can be a major determinant of those diseases that have specific requirements of temperature, humidity, or aridity. An equally important factor encompasses the sociocultural practices of communities. For instance, ritual practices may bring humans into regular and intimate contact with certain features of the physical environment that results in contact with disease-causing pathogens. Shrines hidden deep in forested regions may bring humans into contact with pathogen-bearing insects such as the tsetse fly and anopheles mosquito. In addition, agricultural practices, such as the cultivation of certain crops close to homesteads, often bring humans into contact with pathogens. And changes in crops or techniques often provide new ecological niches in which disease-bearing pathogens flourish. An example of this is the introduction by a British colonial officer of a new variety of hedge, the lantana, from India into Uganda in the 1940s. The lantana flourished in its new environment, gradually spreading northward toward the southern Sudan. Unfortunately, it provided an excellent habitat for a species of tsetse fly, *Glossina pallidipes,* which in turn introduced new strains of trypanosomes, the cause of human sleeping sickness.

Perhaps the most important factors in disease environments are water supply and human excreta. Waterborne diseases include typhoid fever, poliomyelitis, infectious hepatitis, cholera, schistosomiasis, dracunculiasis, and leishmaniasis. Water supplies and sewage disposal are complex subjects of much concern to health planners in the late twentieth century. But during much of the nineteenth century these two vitally important areas of public health were given very little serious attention and even less investment. Indeed, despite John Snow's brilliant 1849 analysis of the epidemiology of cholera in London when he revealed that a water pump was responsible for the spread of the disease, the supply of safe water and the disposal of sewage remained for more than a century conceptually separate from the concerns of medicine with its focus on cure.

Rather, clean water supplies and sanitary sewage disposal, as means of disease prevention, were, until very recently, solely the concern of the engineer. Thus, a major source of much human disease was neglected by medical people. The colonial legacy included very little in the way of safe/water supplies and effective sewage disposal systems, except in a few of the urban areas where the Europeans themselves resided. And Africans are suffering the effects to the present day.

Last but hardly least among the African "pathogenic factors" is protein–energy malnutrition, for the excessive mortality of African children under 5 years of age is due largely to the synergism between protein–energy malnutrition and infectious and parasitic diseases. Until fairly recently, nutrition has been largely ignored in relation to morbidity, yet it is a vitally important key to understanding the widespread perception of Africa as a "disease-ridden" continent.

Earlier theories of epidemiology held that exposure to new pathogens was sufficient cause for epidemic outbreaks, and much emphasis was laid on the increased interactions of African populations, witnessed by Europeans from the mid-nineteenth century on, as an explanation for apparently increased rates of morbidity and mortality. More recently, however, it has been argued that more than mere exposure is needed to explain why humans fall ill and why epidemics flare. Thomas McKeown (1979) argued convincingly that, for almost the whole of human existence, disease and early death have resulted from basic deficiencies or from hazards related to them and that the role of nutrition is of paramount importance.

Thus, medical services, specific remedies, and the increasingly complex technology of biomedicine may not provide the best solutions to African health problems; rather, the total ecology of health and disease may be a more fruitful area of study for future health planners.

Maryinez Lyons

The author thanks Ian Timaeus for his help.

Bibliography

Blacker, J. G. C. 1991. Infant and child mortality: Development, environment and custom. In *Disease and mortality in sub-Saharan Africa*, ed. R. G. Feachem and D. T. Jamison, 75–86. Washington, D.C.

Bradley, David J. 1980. The situation and the response. In *Health in tropical Africa during the colonial period*, ed. E. E. Sabben-Clare, D. J. Bradley, and K. Kirkwood, 6–12. Oxford.

Carlson, Dennis, G. 1984. *African fever: A study of British science, technology, and politics in West Africa, 1787–1864*. Canton, Mass.

Chirimuuta, R. C., and R. J. Chirimuuta. 1987. *AIDS, Africa and racism*. London.

Comaroff, Jean and John. 1991. *Of revelation and revolution: Christianity, colonialism, and consciousness in South Africa*, vol. 1. Chicago and London.

Crosby, A. 1986. *Ecological imperialism: The biological expansion of Europe, 900–1900*. Cambridge.

Curtin, P. 1961. The white man's grave: Image and reality, 1780–1850. *Journal of British Studies* 1: 94–110.

1968. Epidemiology and the slave trade. *Political Science Quarterly* 83: 190–216.

Dodge, Cole P., and Paul D. Wiebe. 1985. *Crisis in Uganda: The breakdown of health services*. Oxford.

Ford, John. 1971. *The role of the trypanosomiases in African ecology*. Oxford.

Hartwig, G., and K. D. Patterson. 1978. *Disease in African history: An introductory survey and case studies*. Durham, N.C.

Headrick, Rita. 1987. The impact of colonialism on health in French Equatorial Africa, 1880–1934. Ph.D. dissertation, University of Chicago. University Microfilms DA 48A: 2955.

Kjekshus, Helge. 1977. *Ecology control and economic development in East African history: The case of Tanganyika*. London.

McKeown, Thomas. 1979. *The role of medicine: Dream, mirage or nemesis?* Oxford.

1988. *The origins of human disease*. Oxford.

Packard, Randall. 1989. *White plague, black labor: Tuberculosis and the political economy of health and disease in South Africa*. Berkeley and Los Angeles.

Prins, Gwyn. 1989. But what was the disease? The present state of health and healing in African studies. *Past and Present* 124: 159–79.

Sanders, David, with Richard Carver. 1985. *The struggle for health: Medicine and the politics of underdevelopment*. London.

Spitzer, Leo. 1968. The mosquito and segregation in Sierra Leone. *Canadian Journal of African Studies* 2: 49–62.

Swanson, Maynard. 1977. The sanitation syndrome: Bubonic plague and urban native policy in the Cape Colony, 1900–1909. *Journal of African History* 18: 387–410.

Turshen, Meredeth. 1984. *The political ecology of disease in Tanzania*. New Brunswick, N.J.

United Nations. 1987. *Mortality of children under age 5: World estimates and projections, 1950–2025*. Department of International Economic and Social Affairs, 1987 (ST/ESA/SER A/105). New York.

Vella, Ethelwald E. 1985. *Exotic new diseases: A review of the emergent African viral haemorrhagic fevers.* London.

Westwood, John C. N. 1980. *The hazard from dangerous exotic diseases.* London.

V.8
Diseases of the Pre-Columbian Americas

Although the antiquity of the earliest colonists in the Americas remains a controversial subject, human presence is well established by the close of the Pleistocene, approximately 10,000 B.P. (before the present) (Bryan 1978, 1986; Shutler 1983; Fagan 1987). Kill sites and habitation areas, in conjunction with lithic tools and a few human remains, provide convincing evidence for the presence of highly mobile, small groups whose subsistence was based on hunting and gathering of naturally available "wild" resources.

The health of these most ancient American populations, poorly documented owing to a paucity of human remains (Hrdlicka 1907, 1912; Stewart 1946, 1973; Young 1988), can best be inferred by analogy with recent hunting and gathering peoples. In making inferences we must keep in mind that such groups today tend to occupy marginal environments, unlike the often resource-rich ecosystems that attracted early human populations. If we use contemporary hunter-gatherers for our model, then parasitic infections, infections for which insects and animals serve as the primary vectors or intermediate hosts, and traumatic episodes would have been among the primary sources of ill health among the earliest Americans (Dunn 1968; Truswell and Hansen 1976; Howell 1979; Lee 1979; Cohen 1989). Degenerative diseases, neoplasms, and epidemic diseases would have been extremely rare, as would have been chronic undernutrition. Seasonal periods of nutritional stress would, however, have been expected. Thus, health status would have reflected the exceptionally close relationship between hunter-gatherers and their environment.

We must be careful, however, not to overgeneralize and thus simplify our picture of hunter-gatherer adaptations, which were undoubtedly complex and rich with the knowledge gained through intimate acquaintance with the landscape (Cohen 1989). Given the wide variety of settings available for human occupation in the Americas, ranging from stark Arctic polar environments to lush tropical forests, we should anticipate that human cultural and biological adaptions ranged widely within the context of changing cultural systems and environmental regimes. The quality of life, as measured by health status, would have depended on the nature of these interactions as well as those among the human groups themselves.

Beginning with the earliest colonists – the Americans who entered this continent before the end of the Pleistocene – we find a rich fabric of evolving relationships between people and their natural and cultural environments that held strong implications for both health and the history of disease. Although certain groups maintained life-styles without plant and animal domestication (or management) throughout their history, the Americas also saw the development of complex civilizations. The Maya, the Aztec, the Inca, and – on a smaller scale – the eastern North American agriculturalists, known to archeologists as Mississippian peoples, all developed cities where thousands of people lived together in permanent settlements. Problems of health, sanitation, and nutrition common to such large agglomerations of humans throughout the world emerged in each of these situations.

Although animal husbandry never assumed the importance that it did in the Old World, the dog was one of several domesticated New World animals, along with the turkey, the Muscovy duck, the guinea pig, the alpaca, and the llama (Crosby 1972). These animals, living close to humans, could have served as vectors or intermediate hosts of disease. Similarly, the nutritional adequacy of ancient diets depended on these as well as wild animal resources.

Inedible, but economically important plants, such as cotton and tobacco, along with many comestibles including maize, manioc, squash, beans, cocoa, sunflower, potatoes, chiles, chenoa, and tomatoes, were domesticated (Crosby 1972). These crops attracted the attention of Europeans and are presently part of Western cuisine (Crosby 1972, 1986). Other indigenous plants were also cultivated prehistorically, with some being truly domesticated, that is, showing distinctive morphological changes due to human intervention or growing beyond their natural range. In eastern North America, for example, a group of cultivated indigenous plants, termed the eastern horticultural complex, included sumpweed (*Iva annua*), goosefoot (*Chenopodium berlandieri*), knotweed (*Polygonum erectum*), and little barley (*Phalaris carolin-*

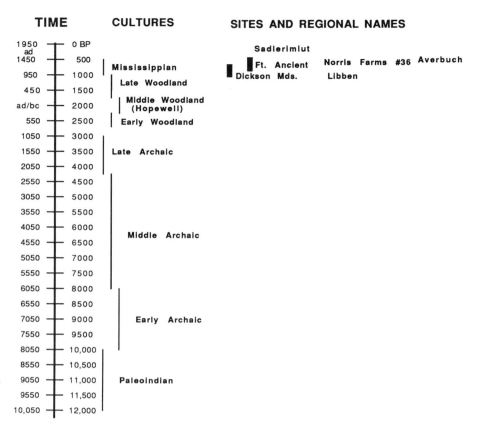

TIME   **CULTURES**   **SITES AND REGIONAL NAMES**

Figure V.8.1. Model time line for prehistoric eastern North America. (Based on Buikstra 1988.)

iana), as well as sunflower (*Heliantus annuus*) and various cucurbits (Asch and Asch 1985; Smith 1987). In that nutritional adequacy is closely linked to health status, these components of ancient diets must also be mapped when one is investigating paleopathological conditions.

This review of health conditions in the pre-Columbian Americas focuses primarily on the evidence gained through the study of skeletal material. Mummified remains, a very rich data source, are unfortunately found only in a few settings favoring soft-tissue preservation, especially the arid North American Southwest and coastal Peru and Ecuador. Dry caves, such as those of the Mammoth Cave system in North America, also yield mummified human remains, but only in small numbers (Watson 1974). Other sources of information concerning disease and medical treatments, such as the Mochica and Mexican figures, and various pictographs will not be considered here. These renderings are notoriously ambiguous, frequently charged with symbolic meanings that relate to ritual life rather than accurate representations of maladies and deformities.

Figures V. 8.1 and V. 8.2 present model chronologies for eastern North America and coastal Peru and Ecuador, two regions frequently referenced in the following text. The chronological basis for Figure

V. 8.1 follows J. Buikstra (1988); Figure V. 8.2 is based on the sequences presented in R. Keatinge (1988) and B. Fagan (1972). Sites discussed in this text are placed appropriately on these time lines. This brief chronological review is developed in order to establish a broad time scale against which to display disease patterning. In general, North American materials are emphasized, given that the majority of the relevant literature is based on North American collections.

We first focus on trephination, distinctly South American and an enormously successful form of ancient surgery. Following this we consider the expression of two forms of trauma in human skeletal materials, fractures and osteoarthritis. A discussion of fractures and true degenerative joint disease centers on North American materials, as does a consideration of rheumatoid arthritis in adults. Brief mention, however, is made of an example of juvenile rheumatoid arthritis that was recovered from a c. 1000 B.P. Peruvian grave. The subsequent discussion of two forms of infectious pathology, treponematosis and tuberculosis, ranges widely across the hemisphere, as does the description of techniques for inferring diet from bones and teeth. We close with a consideration of parameters used to estimate population health, dealing primarily with North American

TIME **PERIOD (CULTURE)** **SITES**

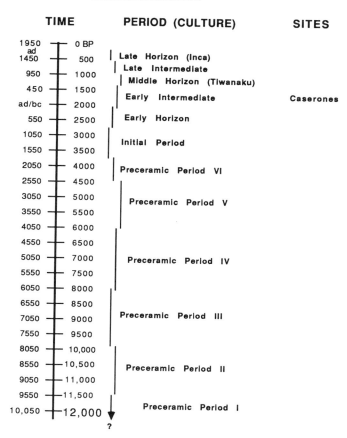

Figure V.8.2. Model time line for prehistoric Peru and Chile. (Based on Keatinge 1988 and Fagan 1972.)

skeletal samples that chronicle the development and intensification of maize agriculture.

Trephination (Trepanation)

Trephination, one of the earliest surgical procedures involving the skull, was first reported in prehistoric skeletal remains during the nineteenth century (Squier 1877; Rytel 1956; Lisowski 1967; Steinbock 1976; Ortner and Putschar 1981). E. Squier's early description of trephination in Peruvian remains led to the recognition that this procedure was frequently practiced in pre-Columbian South America (Stewart 1958; Steinbock 1976). The success rate of this surgery, which exceeded 50 percent in the South American examples (Stewart 1958), is particularly significant for the history of medicine. It far exceeded recovery predictions for individuals subjected to brain surgery in eighteenth- and nineteenth-century Europe, where death was the expected result (Schröder 1957, cited in Lisowski 1967).

The removal of a segment of skull without injuring the underlying meninges and brain is an exceedingly delicate operation. Commonly practiced in South America during the millennium between

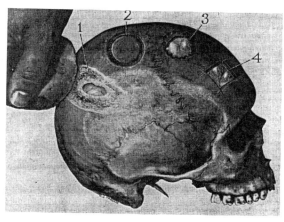

Figure V.8.3. Different methods of trepanation. 1, Scraping; 2, grooving; 3, boring and cutting; 4, rectangular intersecting incisions. (After Lisowski 1967, with permission, Charles C. Thomas, Publisher.)

1500 and 2500 B.P., trephination encompassed several distinctive techniques with various results. One of the most extensive descriptions is that of M. Meyer (1979), who reports 10 different types of surgical method in his study of 374 trephined crania from Peru. Most common were the scraping and grooving procedures (Figure V. 8.3, after Lisowski 1967), which had been performed on more than 61 percent of this sample. Meyer (1979) attributes the popularity of the scraping technique to its high success rate (85 percent). Given that the key problem in surgery of this type is the removal of bone without penetrating the dura, the finer control afforded by the scraping technique rendered it maximally effective (Ortner and Putschar 1981).

The overall recovery frequency reported by Meyer (1979) is 61.9 percent, which compares quite favorably with the rate of 62.5 percent reported by J. Tello (1913) in a sample of 400 Peruvian skulls. Meyer also reports similar figures for researchers dealing with smaller series. Thus, fewer than half of these ancient Peruvian patients died as a result of skull surgery.

Various motives have been attributed to those who performed trephination, ranging from the utilitarian to the spiritual. Meyer (1979) observed cranial pathology, due either to infection or to trauma, in association with 42.0 percent of his trephined sample. As he notes, the rate would undoubtedly have been higher, given the fact that either the operation itself or subsequent healing would have obliterated symptoms visible at the time of surgery. He also reports that fractures were more commonly, but by no means exclusively, associated with men in his sample, with infection appearing more frequently in trephined women. There tended to be a larger number of healed trephinations among men than among women, which contributes to Meyer's observation that relatively few young men appear in his trephined sample. He attributes "ritual practice" to this pattern, but male survival rates must also be considered.

Meyer also suggests, on the basis of observation of stains and osteoporotic pitting in the trephined region, that Peruvian surgeons used antiseptics. Unlike earlier observations by T. Stewart (1958) on a less extensive series, Meyer's (1979) observations revealed that most trephinations in his sample occurred on the parietal bone. The left side of the skull was more commonly trephined than the right, which may reflect the agonistic origins of many cranial fractures.

Contemporary examples of trephination using primitive technology include the African cases cited by E. Margetts (1967) and Bolivian examples reported by K. Oakley and colleagues (1959). The African techniques were similar to prehistoric methods, whereas in Bolivia a young man was operated on with "a rusty nail and a stone" (as cited in Meyer 1979). The African operations were quite successful; in one instance of multiple trephinations, for example, the subject continued to live a "normal" life. Clearly, ancient peoples had discovered a surgical strategy that was remarkably successful, even in the absence of modern antibiotics.

Fractures

Evidence of healed fractures has been reported for numerous skeletal series throughout the Americas. Few workers, however, have attempted to develop a biobehavioral model for interpreting etiology, through either a rigorous diachronic approach or the development of an epidemiological viewpoint. Exceptional perspectives have been developed by R. Steinbock (1976), who surveys temporally sequential North America samples, and by C. Lovejoy and K. Heiple (1981) in an intensive investigation of the Libben site (900–1200 B.P.).

Using the individual as the basis for comparison, Steinbock reports postcranial fracture frequencies for 12 skeletal series from North America (V.8.1). The highest fracture frequency occurred in Middle and Late Archaic populations – those considered to be hunters and gatherers. Given our previous model derived from ethnographically documented groups, this observation is not unexpected. As an aside, G. Steele (personal communication) noted that the only pathological condition in a survey of Paleo-

Table V.8.1. *Healed fracture frequencies for North American prehistoric remains*

Population	Percent
Middle Archaic	
Indian Knoll, Ky. No. 1	10.7
Indian Knoll, Ky. No. 2	9.8
Late Archaic	
Robinson site, Tenn.	9.6
Morse site, Ill.	9.7
Woodland	
Tollifero site, Va.	5.4
Steuben site, Ill.	5.5
Klunk site, Ill.	5.0
Mississippian	
Clarksville site, Va.	3.9
Dickson Mounds, Ill.	3.3
Emmons site, Ill.	1.2

Source: After Steinbock (1976, 23).

Indian remains that pre-dates 8500 B.P. is a healed fracture in the right eighth rib of a skeleton from the Pelican Rapids site, Minnesota.

As noted by Steinbock (1976), and emphasized by Lovejoy and Heiple (1981), Steinbock's frequencies may be unreasonably low, due to his method of reporting. Steinbock's use of the individual as the unit for analysis led him to include incomplete remains whose missing elements might have presented healed fractures. Also, as pointed out by this author (1981a), Middle Archaic cemetery samples can be segregated by health status. Thus, archeological recovery may have emphasized those areas where individuals with fractures were more likely to be buried.

Lovejoy and Heiple (1981), basing their analysis on the Late Woodland Libben site of northern Ohio, report that each individual within this series had a 45 percent chance of fracturing a major limb long bone. The clavicle was most frequently broken, with the humerus showing the fewest healed fractures. The rather high rate of forearm fractures is attributed to falls rather than to conflict owing to the low prevalence ($n = 2$) of classic "parry fractures." That only two cranial fractures were observed in the series also supports this conclusion. Although these data have undoubtedly been affected by the ease of reduction for each of the elements surveyed, it is very clear that the Libben series represents a sample for which there is little evidence of conflict.

After developing a years-at-risk analysis, Lovejoy and Heiple (1981) concluded that there were two periods within the Libben life span in which the risk of fracture was greatest: 10 to 25 years years and 45 plus years. Youthful activity and senescence undoubtedly explain this pattern.

A contrasting picture is presented by the Norris Farms No. 36 sample described by G. Milner, V. Smith, and E. Anderson (1991). Slightly more recent than the Libben sample, this Oneota series is derived from a late prehistoric population that lived near major Mississippian settlements. Healed fractures within the Norris Farms No. 36 series include many in the trunk and upper limb, with the skull also heavily involved. In addition, 33 individuals, approximately 12.5 percent (33/264), show evidence of mutilation, including scalping, decapitation and postcranial dismemberment, actual injuries, such as projectile points in bone and spiral fractures, or both forms of damage to bone. Many of these skeletons, as well as 10 others for a total of 43, exhibit carnivore gnawing that is thought to have occurred after death but before the recovery of the body for burial in the village cemetery. Those who were older than 15 years at the time of death are evenly divided between men (18) and women (18). This represents about 33 percent of the total male subset of the population and 29 percent of the female subset. The male proportion is not unexpected in tribal-level societies; however, the female frequency is extremely high, suggesting the presence of intensive raiding and social conflict.

The contrasting patterns presented by the Libben and Norris Farms No. 36 series underscore the impact that life-style and living conditions can have on the expression of trauma in prehistoric remains. Just as there appears to be no typical late prehistoric pattern, it would be foolhardy to generalize concerning any other temporal or chronological unit without contextual data.

Arthritis

As pointed out by D. Ortner and G. Theobald in their examination of the diseases of prehistory in the West in this volume, a great many conditions can lead to inflammation of the joints. In the Americas, most diagnostic attention has been paid to articular changes that may be characteristic of tuberculosis, treponematosis, rheumatoid arthritis, and osteoarthritis due to mechanical stress. Our current knowledge of the first two conditions is discussed in the relevant sections of this essay. Here we will focus on recent studies of osteoarthritis (degenerative joint disease) and rheumatoid arthritis.

Daily activities produce stresses that over time promote degeneration of joint surfaces in the human skeleton. Thus, the "wear and tear" of ancient lifestyles can be read through an analysis of the porosity, eburnation, and lipping characteristic of arthritic joints. One of the most careful studies of extensive degenerative joint changes is that of Ortner (1968), who details the patterning discovered in Alaskan Eskimo and Peruvian skeletons. Ortner's work is reminiscent of the methods pioneered by J. Angel (1966) and T. Stewart (1932). Stewart's careful investigation of intraindividual patterning established the standard of comparison of vertebral osteophytosis, whereas Angel's creative inferences concerning behavior (e.g., atlatl [spear or dart throwing stick] elbow) are oft-cited attempts to link individual activities to bone pathology.

R. Jurmain (1977) has compared arthritic patterns characterizing the Alaskan Eskimo shoulder, elbow, knee, and hip with those of Pueblo Indians and modern skeletons. Jurmain emphasizes the multifactorial nature of osteoarthritis, although he believes that functional stress is of paramount importance.

After an extensive survey of degenerative joint disease among the Native Point Sadlerimiut Eskimo from Southampton Island, Canada, C. Merbs (1969, 1983) identified distinctive male and female activity patterns that yielded arthritic change. Typical male activities that produced upper-limb arthritis included harpoon throwing and kayak paddling. Female skeletons bore evidence of activities related to the processing of skins.

Following the recording strategy developed by Ortner (1968) and Merbs (1969), J. Tainter (1980) observed distinctive arthritic patterning across status groups of Middle Woodland men from Illinois. He interpreted these patterns to mean that the day-to-day activities differed significantly across socially defined segments of Hopewell communities.

A more recent study (Pickering 1984) has extended Tainter's earlier synchronic investigation to an analysis of diachronic changes associated with the development of maize agriculture. Also embedded in this work is an attempt to isolate patterns in the male upper limb that were associated with the documented shift in hunting technology between the spear, characteristic of Middle Woodland groups, and the bow and arrow, used by Late Woodland and Mississippian populations.

Although an altered hunting technology was indeed documented within west-central Illinois during the period in question, no significant difference in symmetry, timing of onset, patterning, or degree of arthritic expression in the upper limb was discovered in the male subsample. The arthritic costs of agricultural intensification are clearly written, however, in age-corrected severity scores for the female upper back. The demands of repetitive food production activities associated with maize agriculture and larger family size are implicated in the apparent differences in degenerative joint disease.

In provocative new work based on observations in two large prehistoric North American skeletal populations, B. Rothschild and colleagues argue that rheumatoid arthritis "is a New World disease that subsequently spread to the Old World" (Rothschild, Woods, and Turner 1987; Rothschild, Turner, and DeLuca 1988; Woods and Rothschild 1988). Their conclusions are based on the form and distribution of erosive lesions in several series of skeletons, including the Libben Late Woodland sample (900–1200 B.P.) and Archaic skeletons from Alabama that are at least 5,000 years old (Rothschild et al. 1987, 1988; Woods and Rothschild 1988). A convincing case of juvenile rheumatoid arthritis in an adolescent from the Tiwanaku period (c. 1100 B.P.) in Peru has also been described (Buikstra 1991).

Treponematosis

Evidence of inflammatory response, usually appearing as symmetric periostitic expressions on the surfaces of the limb long bones, is common in North American skeletal series. South American materials are said to present similar symptoms (Williams 1932; Goff 1967). At times accompanied by evidence of osteomyelitic changes, as well as occasional stellate scarring of the external table of the skull, these lesions are the basis of a long-standing controversy concerning the possible New World origin of venereal syphilis (e.g., Jones 1876; Whitney 1883; Williams 1932; Goldstein 1957; Bullen 1972; Cook 1976; Brothwell 1981). Theoretical articles by medical historians enrich this literature (e.g., Cockburn 1963; Hudson 1965; Hackett 1967; Crosby 1969, 1972).

The cause of these lesions, which are characteristic of many cemetery samples from throughout eastern North America, has been a matter of debate for more than a century. In 1876 J. Jones argued that the "erosions" he observed in burials from stone box graves and mounds in Tennessee and Kentucky were syphilitic, a conclusion cautiously supported by W. F. Whitney (1883), curator of the Warren Anatomical Museum of the Harvard Medical School, a decade later. Such notables as the anatomist R. Virchow have disputed this conclusion, thus fueling an argument that continues today (Jarcho 1966).

The nature of the debate has changed, however. Today few would disagree with the notion that the skeletal lesions presented by these prehistoric remains resemble most closely the constellation of related diseases collectively known as the treponematoses. Included within this group are venereal syphilis, yaws, and endemic syphilis. In her rigorous consideration of clinical and epidemiological patterning from recent medical literature, D. Cook (1976) argues compellingly that either nonvenereal syphilis or yaws is the best modern model for the observed prehistoric pathology. Her thesis is based on the high prevalence of lesions observed in American prehistoric series, the age-accumulative patterning of incidence, and the total absence of dental changes diagnostic of congenital syphilis, such as Hutchinson's incisors or mulberry molars.

Yet it is clear that, in isolated examples, venereal transmission of this disease occurred. The most convincing cases are two prehistoric burials that include both adults and juveniles with the stigmata of venereal syphilis. In one of these, a mulberry molar was found in juvenile remains in a burial site that also included adult skeletons having treponemal long-bone lesions (Clabeaux Geise 1988). A second example is represented by the remains of a prehistoric achondroplastic dwarf recovered from a Middle Woodland burial mound in Illinois (Charles, Leigh, and Buikstra 1988; Burgess 1988). This adult woman, whose left lower limb is heavily remodeled, died in childbirth. Her fetus presents evidence of periostitic changes, as well as dwarfing. Although the data are scant, they suggest that at least some prehistoric American women acquired treponemal infections as adults, presumably through sexual intercourse. The infection thus acquired would have been in an acute stage during the childbearing years, which would have facilitated transplacental infection (Grin 1956; Powell 1988).

The most recent overview of theoretical and empirical arguments concerning the origin of venereal syphilis is that of B. Baker and G. Armelagos (1988). After extensively reviewing current evidence, these authors conclude that pre-Columbian American skeletal materials reflect a treponematosis that spread to the Old World through nonvenereal contact. European social and environmental conditions favored the development of venereal transmission, and thus originated the "French disease."

Doubtless the question of treponematosis and the development of venereal forms will remain controversial for some time. Eagerly awaited is further skeletal evidence from Europe, as well as the development of an immunological technique that will make it possible to identify treponemal antigens in ancient materials (Baker and Armelagos 1988).

Even though there is little evidence for venereal transmission of treponematosis in pre-Columbian American skeletons, it is important to underscore the presence on this continent of a chronic treponemal disease that affected a significant number of individuals. Beginning in childhood and progressing throughout life, inflammations produced by the illness doubtless created a considerable health burden for prehistoric peoples of the Americas.

Tuberculosis

A form of pathology distinctly different from the treponematosis syndrome also affected prehistoric peoples from North and South America (Allison, Mendoza, and Pezzia 1973; Buikstra 1981b). Expressed most commonly as erosive spinal lesions, less frequently affecting joint surfaces of the limb long bones, this disease is found in North American populations postdating 1100 B.P. The Chilean materials reported by M. Allison and colleagues (1981) predate the North American examples by over a millennium. Pulmonary involvement is reported for three individuals from the Caserones site (c. 1660 B.P.), as well as an isolated case of Potts's disease dating to c. 2110 B.P.

Epidemiological patterning considered with lesion location suggests that the most closely analogous modern disease is tuberculosis rather than blastomycosis, a fungal infection. Both blastomycosis and tuberculosis present similar skeletal lesions, but their expected age-specific mortality patterns differ. Young adults are disproportionately represented among those dying with clinically documented bone tuberculosis, whereas blastomycosis tends to present an age-accumulative profile. The age-specific disease pattern observed in large series, including those from west-central Illinois, resembles tuberculosis more closely than blastomycosis (Buikstra and Cook 1981; Buikstra 1991).

The tuberculosis diagnosis developed from modern clinical literature does not, however, provide a perfect diagnostic fit for our prehistoric example. Through simulation analysis, J. McGrath (1986) has modeled the course of a tuberculosislike disease in Middle Woodland, Late Woodland, and Mississippian populations from west-central Illinois. She concludes that a disease resembling modern tuberculosis would have rendered our prehistoric peoples extinct or would have itself ceased to exist. Thus, either our estimates of group size and interaction

frequency are misspecified, or the modern tuberculosis model is not fully transferable to prehistoric contexts. The important role of effective population size in the spread of disease is emphasized in McGrath's conclusions, underscoring the importance of relatively brief periods of contact involving a large number of individuals. Thus, the role of socially important economic and religious collective activities that encourage population aggregation – however brief – must be considered in explaining patterns of disease spread and maintenance in prehistoric groups.

Diet

Although paleobotanic and paleofaunal residues are the most accurate indicators of resources available to prehistoric peoples, estimates of ancient diets are best derived from the actual physical remains of the consumers. Dental health, for example, can assist in dietary determinations. Caries rates in adults are widely recognized as an indication of maize in the diet of native North Americans (Cohen and Armelagos 1984; Powell 1985). One must postulate such an association with care, however, because it appears that an intake of high-carbohydrate seeds from the eastern horticultural complex can also lead to an elevated frequency of caries (Rose, Marks, and Tieszen 1990). Circular caries in Late Woodland juvenile dentitions have been used by Cook and Buikstra (1979) to argue for a significant proportion of carbohydrates in the weaning diet, most likely a disadvantageous circumstance.

More sensitive to dietary differences, however, are the chemical constituents of the skeleton. The composition of both the mineral and the organic phases of bone is to some degree influenced by diet. Trace elements, such as stable strontium and barium, are carried from the soil to an herbivore's bones through plant consumption. Because both strontium and barium tend to concentrate in osseous rather than soft tissue, primary and secondary carnivores receive relatively little dietary strontium. Thus, within a region, the relative herbivory of an omnivorous species such as *Homo sapiens* can be estimated. Zinc tends to concentrate in flesh and is thus a dietary marker for animal protein consumption.

The strontium content of bones has been used by M. Schoeninger (1979) in her investigation of status clusters of graves from the Chalcatzingo site, Morelos, Mexico. Her careful argument concludes that diet varied by status group at this prehistoric Meso-American site dating from 2900 to 3100 B.P.

Zinc and strontium have been used to investigate dietary differences within and between Middle and

Late Woodland groups in west-central Illinois (Lambert, Spzunar, and Buikstra 1979; Buikstra et al. 1989). Although other elements such as vanadium co-vary with diet and would thus be desirable dietary markers, most are subject to postdepositional enrichment or depletion (diagenesis) and are thus contextual signatures rather than dietary signals. Focused on intrasite variation, the earliest Illinois studies examined patterning across status groups in Middle Woodland mounds and sought gender-related differences within Middle and Late Woodland samples. The nonrandom distribution of trace elements across burial groups in Hopewell mounds suggests the presence of status-related dietary habits within Middle Woodland communities. Although no gender differences were observable in Middle Woodland data, bones of Late Woodland men contained significantly more zinc and less strontium than those of women. This may reflect either a true gender-based dietary difference or the increased metabolic demands that Late Woodland women faced owing to closer birth spacing (Buikstra et al. 1987).

Diachronic study of Illinois Middle and Late Woodland samples indicates that, although zinc values do not vary chronologically, strontium levels do decrease during Late Woodland times. This decrease may seem enigmatic, given the development of maize agriculture during this period. Maize, however, is relatively poor in elements, and thus the observed pattern is expected. The values for zinc suggest that the proportion of animal protein in the diet did not vary significantly across Woodland groups. Similar patterning has been reported for a temporally sequential series of skeletal samples from Ontario (Katzenberg and Schwarcz 1986; Katzenberg 1988).

A second form of chemical study has focused on the collagen fraction of bone. The results of studies based on stable carbon isotope ratios derived from bone collagen make it possible to predict the presence of maize in diets with a precision far beyond estimates based on the paleobotanic record or dental health. Maize, a tropical grass, fixes carbon through the Hatch–Slack, or C_4 pathway. This contrasts with the usual pattern for temperate-climate vegetation in which the common pathway is Calvin, or C_3. As partial differential carbon-13 values – the standard transformation used in such studies – become more positive, the presence of maize in the diet is more likely. Values derived from human collagen that are more positive than −20 or −21 are considered evidence of C_4 plant consumption.

The association of maize agriculture with Missis-

sippian cultures is well known. Debate has centered, however, on the degree to which the timing of maize intensification was directly associated with the development of Mississippian lifeways and the relative importance of maize to Mississippian peoples. The carbon isotope technique has provided a means of resolving these and related issues concerning agricultural intensification in the eastern United States. This significant methodological advance, developed only within the past 10 years, has facilitated the resolution of century-old arguments about the role of corn in North American prehistory.

Partial differential carbon-13 values from across eastern North America clearly document the fact that maize consumption predates the Mississippian period (Lynott et al. 1986; Buikstra et al. 1988). In the central Mississippi valley, these values suggest a rather gradual increase during the terminal phases of Late Woodland, including a highly variable period of experimentation. Values stabilize during Mississippian times, indicating that corn was a significant component of the diet for the late prehistoric peoples. Of special interest is the fact that corn consumption was apparently higher in the "farmstead" communities of the lower and central Illinois valley than it was at the major ceremonial center of Cahokia during the early, expansive phase of the Mississippian period (Buikstra and Milner 1988). Also significant is the fact that the partial differential carbon-13 values from Illinois never reach the extremely positive figures (−7.8 to −8.0 o/oo) that characterize the Mississippian peoples of the Ohio Valley and the Nashville Basin of Tennessee. These very positive values are currently a source of debate, with suggested causal factors ranging from true dietary contrasts to varietal differences in corn (Buikstra et al. 1988). Certain of these late prehistoric populations present evidence of severe ill health (Cassidy 1984; Eisenberg 1986). The degree to which nutritional deficiencies are implicated remains a point of controversy (Buikstra et al. 1988).

Ratios of nitrogen-15 to nitrogen-14 have been used to identify the presence of legumes in prehistoric diets, as well as to distinguish between marine and terrestrial resource utilization (DeNiro, Schoeninger, and Tauber 1983; Schoeninger and DeNiro 1984; DeNiro 1987). A bivariate plot of partial differential carbon-13 and nitrogen-15 values enables the researcher to distinguish the effects of marine enrichment from those of maize utilization. Diets composed of marine resources derived from coral-reef habitats appear to present an anomalous pattern (Schoeninger et al. 1983; Keegan and DeNiro 1988).

At present, most studies of coastal series using both carbon and nitrogen ratios are limited to small samples. Expanded applications of these promising techniques are anticipated.

Nonspecific Indicators of Stress

Within the past two decades there has been an explosion of interest in applying the so-called nonspecific indicators of stress to questions of community health. These indicators range from those that apparently mark episodes of acute stress and recovery, such as Harris lines and dental defects, to those that are associated with chronic mal- or undernutrition. Each type of change has been observed to be associated with disadvantaged health status in modern clinical examples, with predisposing factors including nutritional inadequacy, infectious disease, and even severe emotional episodes. Working with ancient materials, the observer cannot precisely determine the cause of a specific condition, but instead assumes that a sample with more evidence of nonspecific stress is less advantaged than one with fewer indicators of poor health. The popularity of this approach has been influenced by an emphasis on population biology in physical anthropology, as well as by archaeological interest in human ecology (Buikstra and Cook 1980; Cohen and Armelagos 1984).

Harris lines, observed as radiopaque lines perpendicular to the cortex of limb long bones, result from episodic stress. Because the lines, which can also be visualized as disks in the affected diaphyses, can remodel, they are less satisfactory indicators of poor health than are dental defects that include both hypoplastic bands and microdefects such as Wilson's bands (Rose, Condon, and Goodman 1985). Even so, Harris lines have proved useful in documenting the presence of annual periods of growth arrest, which appear to be characteristic of archaic peoples in Illinois, Kentucky, and California (McHenry 1968; Buikstra 1981a; Cassidy 1984). Such repetitive patterning is not characteristic of sedentary groups, whose storage facilities may have buffered them from seasonal stress.

A number of North American studies have focused on the biological costs and benefits of increased dependence on maize agriculture. As noted at the beginning of this essay, maize cultivation represented a late prehistoric intensification of a trend in plant utilization begun many centuries before. Estimates of relative maize dependence suggest that maize comprised a very significant part of the diet for certain late prehistoric peoples, including the Fort Ancient Late Mississippian communities of Ohio and Kentucky.

These studies have employed various markers of health status, including stature attainment rates in juveniles, adult stature, sexual dimorphism, cortical thickness, demographic patterning, and porotic hyperostosis, as well as the Harris lines and dental defects mentioned previously (Lallo 1973; Lallo, Armelagos, and Rose 1978; Rose, Armelagos, and Lallo 1978; Cook 1979, 1981, 1984; Lallo, Rose, and Armelagos 1980; Buikstra 1984; Cassidy 1984; Goodman et al. 1984; Larsen 1984; Perzigian, Tench, and Braun 1984; Goodman and Armelagos 1985). In general, it is assumed that populations with disadvantaged health status will exhibit slower growth, depressed adult stature, less sexual dimorphism, reduced cortical thickness, elevated death rates, and increased frequencies of porotic hyperostosis when compared with closely related groups in advantaged situations. In this context, it should be noted that the cranial porosities termed porotic hyperostosis and cribra orbitalia are usually considered to be evidence for nutritional anemias in the New World. No convincing arguments have been made for the existence of anemias of genetic origin, such as sickle-cell anemia and thalassemia, in the prehistoric Americas.

The regional studies cited earlier generally support the notion that a certain health risk was associated with the development of maize agriculture. Late Woodland agriculturalists in West-Central Illinois, for example, present evidence of disadvantaged health status in juveniles, including such features as depressed growth curves, elevated weaning age, elevated death rates, and decreased cortical thickness (in juveniles). However, as Cook (1984) pointed out, the more recent and increasingly maize-dependent Mississippian peoples in the same region show less evidence of nonspecific stress. Their only liability appears to have been a tuberculosislike pathology (Buikstra and Cook 1981), a density-dependent disease, which is most closely linked to effective population size and only indirectly reflects subsistence base.

A. Goodman and co-workers (1984; see also Lallo 1973; Lallo et al. 1978, 1980; Rose et al. 1978; Goodman and Armelagos 1985) report deteriorating health for Mississippian peoples from Dickson Mounds, located in the central Illinois River valley. It is clear, however, that the shift to maize intensification in this region does not correlate tightly with the periods of extreme ill health (Buikstra and Milner 1988). The residential sites associated with Dickson Mounds are fortified during the Mississippian period, which suggests that socially mediated stresses may have been at least as important as diet in explaining the health status of the skeletal sample excavated from the Dickson Mounds cemeteries.

Farther to the east, there is evidence of extreme maize dependence among late prehistoric populations from Ohio, Kentucky, and Tennessee (Broida 1983, 1984; Buikstra et al. 1988). Disadvantaged health status is clear for many of these same groups (Cassidy 1984; Eisenberg 1986). In fact, the population profile for the Averbuch site (Eisenberg 1986) is consistent with the presence of disease epidemics (Buikstra et al. 1988). Thus, however probable it is that Western diseases caused severe depopulation during protohistoric times (Ramenofsky 1987), there is also convincing evidence for severe ill health in at least some American native populations that clearly predates Columbian contact.

Summary

This essay has presented an overview of recent research on ancient disease in the Americas. Materials from North America and the west coast of South America have been emphasized, as they have been in studies of pathology. Our survey highlights the success of ancient Peruvian surgeons, and as well illustrates the frequency of healed fractures and osteoarthritis in North American materials. North American remains also dominate the recent investigations of nonspecific indicators of population health, as they do studies of bone chemistry designed to reveal the approximate content of ancient diets. Recent studies emphasizing the biological costs and benefits of maize agriculture, as summarized in this essay, illustrate synergism between diet and health status, as well as the importance of cultural and environmental contexts in explaining disease in the past.

Several of the subjects addressed here are a source of debate in the 1990s. The antiquity of rheumatoid arthritis in the New World has received recent attention, as has the long-standing question of venereal syphilis and its origins. In the 1950s the prevailing opinion was that no tuberculosislike pathology existed in the prehistoric New World (Morse 1961), a view that has been reversed. Even so, the conditions under which this tuberculosislike pathology developed remain obscure and controversial.

As noted by Buikstra and Cook (1980) in their review of paleopathology in the Americas, there has been increased emphasis on the study of ancient disease since 1970. Frequent collaboration between medical and social scientists, with input from chemists, is producing remarkable new insights concerning the quality of life of peoples who left few clues other than their tissues. This productive trend is vital to the full appreciation of America's unwritten past, as it is to research concerning the history of disease.

Jane E. Buikstra

Bibliography

Allison, M. J., et al. 1981. Tuberculosis in pre-Columbian Andean populations. In *Prehistoric tuberculosis in the Americas*, ed. J. E. Buikstra, 49–61. Evanston, Ill.

Allison, M. J., D. Mendoza, and A. Pezzia. 1973. Documentation of a case of tuberculosis in pre-Columbian America. *American Review of Respiratory Disease* 107: 985–91.

Angel, J. L. 1966. Early skeletons from Tranquility, California. *Smithsonian Contributions to Anthropology* 2(1): 1–19.

Asch, D., and N. Asch. 1985. Prehistoric plant cultivation in West-Central Illinois. In *Prehistoric food production in North America*, No. 75, ed. R. I. Ford, 149–203. Ann Arbor, Mich.

Baker, B. M., and G. J. Armelagos. 1988. The origin and antiquity of syphilis. *Current Anthropology* 29: 703–37.

Broida, M. O. 1983. Maize in Kentucky Fort Ancient diets: An analysis of carbon isotope ratios in human bone. Master's thesis, University of Kentucky.

  1984. An estimate of the percents of maize in the diets of two Kentucky Fort Ancient villages. In *Late prehistoric research in Kentucky*, ed. K. Pollack, C. Hockensmith, and T. Sanders, 68–82. Frankfurt, Ky.

Brothwell, D. R. 1981. Microevolutionary change in the human pathogenic treponemes: An alternative hypothesis. *International Journal of Systematic Bacteriology* 31: 82–7.

Bryan, A. L. 1986. *New evidence for the Pleistocene peopling of the Americas*. Orono, Me.

Bryan, A. L., ed. 1978. *Early man in America*. Occasional Paper No. 1 of the Department of Anthropology, University of Alberta.

Buikstra, J. E. 1981a. Mortuary practices, palaeodemography and palaeopathology: A case study from the Koster site (Illinois). In *The archaeology of death*, ed. R. Chapman, I. Kinnes, and K. Randsborg, 123–31. New York.

  ed. 1981b. *Prehistoric tuberculosis in the Americas*. Scientific Paper No. 5, Northwestern University Archeological Program.

  1984. The lower Illinois River region: A prehistoric context for the study of ancient diet and health. In *Paleopathology at the origins of agriculture*, ed. M. N. Cohen and G. J. Armelagos, 215–34. New York.

  1988. *The mound-builders of Eastern North America: A regional perspective*. Amsterdam.

Buikstra, J., and D. C. Cook. 1980. Paleopathology: An American account. *Annual Review of Anthropology* 9: 433–70.

1981. Pre-Columbian tuberculosis in West-Central Illinois: Prehistoric disease in biocultural perspective. In *Prehistoric tuberculosis in the Americas,* ed. J. E. Buikstra, 115–39. Scientific Paper No. 5, Northwestern University Archeological Program.

Buikstra, J. E., and G. R. Milner. 1988. Isotopic and archaeological interpretations of diet in the Central Mississippi valley. Paper presented at the 2nd Conference on Diet and Human Evolution, Capetown.

Buikstra, J. E., and S. Williams. 1991. Tuberculosis in the Americas: Current perspectives. In *Human paleopathology: Current syntheses and future options,* ed. D. J. Ortner and A. C. Aufderheide, 161–72. Washington, D.C.

Buikstra, J., et al. 1987. Diet, demography, and the development of horticulture. In *Emergent horticultural economies of the Eastern Woodlands,* ed. W. Keegan, 67–85. Occasional Papers of the Center for Archaeological Investigations, Southern Illinois University.

Buikstra, J. E., et al. 1988. Diet and health in the Nashville Basin: Human adaptation and maize agriculture in Middle Tennessee. In *Diet and subsistence: Current archaeological perspectives,* ed. B. V. Kennedy and G. M. LeMoine, 243–59.

Buikstra, J. E., et al. 1989. Multiple elements: Multiple expectation. In *The chemistry of prehistoric human bone,* ed. T. D. Price, 155–210. Cambridge.

Buikstra, J. E., et al. 1991. A case of juvenile rheumatoid arthritis from pre-Columbian Peru. In *In honor of J. Lawrence Angel,* ed. J. E. Buikstra. Washington, D.C.

Bullen, A. K. 1972. Paleoepidemiology and distribution of prehistoric treponemiasis (syphilis) in Florida. *Florida Anthropologist* 25: 133–74.

Burgess, S. 1988. The Achondroplastic Dwarf from the Elizabeth site. M. A. thesis, University of Chicago.

Cassidy, C. M. 1984. Skeletal evidence for prehistoric subsistence adaptation in the central Ohio River valley. In *Paleopathology at the origins of agriculture,* ed. M. N. Cohen and G. J. Armelagos, 307–45. New York.

Charles, D. K., S. R. Leigh, and J. E. Buikstra, eds. 1988. *The Archaic and Woodland cemeteries at the Elizabeth site in the Lower Illinois Valley.* Kampsville, Ill.

Clabeaux Geise, M. 1988. Comment. *Current Anthropology* 29: 722–3.

Cockburn, A. 1963. *The evolution and eradication of infectious diseases.* Baltimore.

Cohen, M. N. 1989. *Health and the rise of civilization.* New Haven, Conn.

Cohen, M. N., and G. J. Armelagos, eds. 1984. *Paleopathology at the origins of agriculture.* New York.

Cook, D. C. 1976. Pathologic states and disease process in Illinois Woodland Populations: An epidemiologic approach. Ph.D. dissertation, University of Chicago.

1979. Subsistence base and health in prehistoric Illinois Valley: Evidence from the human skeleton. *Medical Anthropology* 3: 109–24.

1981. Mortality, age structure and status in the interpretation of stress indicators in prehistoric skeletons: A dental example from the Lower Illinois Valley. In *The archaeology of death,* ed. R. Chapman, I. Kinnes, and K. Randsborg, 133–44. New York.

1984. Subsistence and health in the Lower Illinois Valley: Osteological evidence. In *Paleopathology at the origins of agriculture,* ed. M. N. Cohen and G. J. Armelagos, 235–69. New York.

Cook, D. C., and J. E. Buikstra. 1979. Health and differential survival in prehistoric populations: Prenatal dental defects. *American Journal of Physical Anthropology* 51: 649–64.

Crosby, A. W. 1969. The early history of syphilis: A reappraisal. *American Anthropology* 71: 218–27.

1972. *The Columbian exchange.* Westport, Conn.

1986. *Ecological imperialism: The biological expansion of Europe, 900–1900.* Cambridge.

DeNiro, M. J. 1987. Stable isotopy and archaeology. *American Scientist* 75: 182–91.

Dunn, F. L. 1968. Epidemiological factors: Health and disease in hunter-gatherers. In *Man the hunter,* ed. R. B. Lee and I. DeVore, 221–40. Chicago.

Eisenberg, L. E. 1986. Adaptation in a "marginal" Mississippian population from Middle Tennessee: Biocultural insights from paleopathology. Ph.D. dissertation, New York University.

Fagan, B. 1972. *In the beginning,* 2d edition. Boston.

1987. *The great journal.* London.

Goff, C. W. 1967. Syphilis. In *Diseases in antiquity,* ed. D. R. Brothwell and A. T. Sandison, 279–93. Springfield, Ill.

Goldstein, M. S. 1957. Skeletal pathology of early Indians in Texas. *American Journal of Physical Anthropology* 15: 299–311.

Goodman, A. H., and G. J. Armelagos. 1985. Disease and death at Dr. Dickson's mounds. *Natural History* 94: 12–18.

Goodman, A. H., et al. 1984. Health changes at Dickson Mounds, Illinois (A.D. 950–1300). In *Paleopathology at the origins of agriculture,* ed. M. N. Cohen and G. J. Armelagos, 271–305. New York.

Grin, E. T. 1956. Endemic syphilis and yaws. *Bulletin of the World Health Organization* 15: 959–73.

Hackett, C. 1967. The human treponematoses. In *Diseases in antiquity,* ed. D. R. Brothwell and A. T. Sandison, 152–69. Springfield, Ill.

Howell, N. 1979. *Demography of the Dobe !Kung.* New York.

Hrdlicka, A. 1907. Skeletal remains suggesting or attributed to early man in North America. *Bulletin of the Bureau of American Ethnology* Vol. 33.

1912. Early man in South America. *Bulletin of the Bureau of American Ethnology* Vol. 52.

Hudson, E. H. 1965. Treponematosis and man's social evolution. *American Anthropologist* 67: 885–901.

Jarcho, S. 1966. *Human palaeopathology.* New Haven, Conn.

Jones, J. 1876. *Explorations of the aboriginal remains of Tennessee.* Smithsonian Contributions to Knowledge No. 259. Washington, D.C.

Jurmain, R. D. 1977. Stress and the etiology of osteoarthritis. *American Journal of Physical Anthropology* 46: 353–65.

Katzenberg, M. A. 1988. Changing diet and health in pre- and protohistoric Ontario. *Social Science and Medicine.*

Katzenberg, M. A., and H. P. Schwarcz. 1986. Paleonutrition in southern Ontario: Evidence from strontium and stable isotopes. *Canadian Review of Physical Anthropology* 5: 15–21.

Keatinge, R. W., ed. 1988. *Peruvian Prehistory.* Cambridge.

Keegan, W. F., and M. J. DeNiro. 1988. Stable carbon- and nitrogen-isotope ratios of bone collagen used to study coral-reef and terrestrial components of prehistoric Bahamian diet. *American Antiquity* 53: 320–36.

Lallo, J. 1973. The skeletal biology of three prehistoric American Indian societies from Dickson Mounds. Ph.D. dissertation, University of Massachusetts.

Lallo, J., G. J. Armelagos, and J. C. Rose. 1978. Paleoepidemiology of infectious disease in the Dickson Mounds population. *Medical College of Virginia Quarterly* 14: 17–23.

Lallo, J. W., J. C. Rose, and G. J. Armelagos. 1980. An ecological interpretation of variation in mortality within three prehistoric American Indian populations from Dickson Mounds. In *Early native Americans: Prehistoric demography, economy, and technology,* ed. D. Browman, 203–38. The Hague.

Lambert, J. B., C. B. Spzunar, and J. E. Buikstra. 1979. Chemical analyses of excavated bone from Middle and Late Woodland sites. *Archaeometry* 21: 115–29.

Larsen, C. S. 1984. Health and disease in prehistoric Georgia: The transition to agriculture. In *Paleopathology at the origins of agriculture,* ed. M. N. Cohen and G. J. Armelagos, 367–92. New York.

Lee, R. B. 1979. *The !Kung San.* Cambridge.

Lisowski, F. P. 1967. Prehistoric and early historic trepanation. In *Diseases in antiquity,* ed. D. R. Brothwell and A. T. Sandison, 651–72. Springfield, Ill.

Lovejoy, C. O., and K. G. Heiple. 1981. The analysis of fractures in skeletal populations with an example from the Libben site, Ottawa County, Ohio. *American Journal of Physical Anthropology* 55: 529–41.

Lynott, M. J., et al. 1986. Stable carbon isotopic evidence for maize agriculture in Southeast Missouri and Northeast Arkansas. *American Antiquity* 51:51–65.

Margetts, E. L. 1967. Trepanation of the skull by the medicine-men of primitive cultures, with particular reference to present-day native East African practice. In *Diseases in antiquity,* ed. D. R. Brothwell and A. T. Sandison, 673–701. Springfield, Ill.

McGrath, J. W. 1986. A computer simulation of the spread of tuberculosis in prehistoric populations of the Lower Illinois River valley. Ph.D. dissertation, Northwestern University.

McHenry, H. 1968. Transverse lines in long bones in prehistoric California Indians. *American Journal of Physical Anthropology* 29: 1–17.

Merbs, C. F. 1969. Patterns of activity-induced pathology in a Canadian Eskimo isolate. Ph.D. dissertation, University of Wisconsin.

  1983. *Patterns of activity-induced pathology in a Canadian Eskimo population.* National Museum of Man Mercury Series, No. 119. Ottawa.

Meyer, M. 1979. Trephination in Pre-Columbian Peru. B.A. honors thesis, Harvard University.

Milner G. R., V. G. Smith, and E. Anderson. 1991. Conflict, mortality, and community health in an Illinois Oneota population. In *Between bands and states,* ed. S. Gregg. Carbondale, Ill.

Morse, D. 1961. Prehistoric tuberculosis in America. *Review of Respiratory Diseases* 83: 489–504.

Oakley, K. P., et al. 1959. Contributions on trepanning or trephination in ancient and modern times. *Man* 59: 287–9.

Ortner, D. J. 1968. Description and classification of degenerative bone changes in the distal joint surface of the humerus. *American Journal of Physical Anthropology* 28: 139–55.

Ortner, D. J., and W. G. J. Putschar. 1981. *Identification of pathological conditions in human skeletal remains.* Smithsonian Contributions to Anthropology No. 28. Washington, D.C.

Perzigian, A. J., P. A. Tench, and D. J. Braun. 1984. Prehistoric health in the Ohio River valley. In *Paleopathology at the origins of agriculture,* ed. M. N. Cohen and G. J. Armelagos, 347–66. New York.

Pickering, R. B. 1984. Patterns of degenerative joint disease in Middle Woodland, Late Woodland, and Mississippian skeletal series from the Lower Illinois Valley, Ph.D. dissertation, Northwestern University.

Powell, M. L. 1985. The analysis of dental wear and caries for dietary reconstruction. In *The analysis of prehistoric diets,* ed. R. I. Gilbert and J. H. Mielke, 307–38. New York.

  1988. *Status and health in prehistory.* Washington, D.C.

Ramenofsky, A. 1987. *Vectors of death.* Albuquerque, N.M.

Rose, J. C., G. J. Armelagos, and J. W. Lallo. 1978. Histological enamel indicators of childhood stress in prehistoric skeletal samples. *American Journal of Physical Anthropology* 49: 511–16.

Rose, J. C., K. W. Condon, and A. H. Goodman. 1985. Diet and dentition: developmental disturbances. In *The analysis of prehistoric diets,* ed. R. I. Gilbert and J. H. Mielke, 281–305. New York.

Rose, J. C., M. K. Marks, and L. L. Tieszen. 1990. Bioarcheology and subsistence in the central and lower portions of the Mississippi valley. In *What mean these bones? The dynamic integration of physical anthropology and archaeology in the Southeast,* ed. M. L. Powell,

A. M. Mires, and P. Bridges. University of Georgia Press.

Rothschild, B. M., K. R. Turner, and M. A. DeLuca. 1988. Symmetrical erosive peripheral polyarthritis in the Late Archaic period of Alabama. *Science* 241: 1498–1501.

Rothschild, B. M., R. J. Woods, and K. R. Turner. 1987. New World origins of rheumatoid arthritis. *Arthritis and Rheumatism* (Suppl.) 30: S61.

Rytel. M. M. 1956. Trephinations in Ancient Peru. *Quarterly Bulletin of the Northwestern Medical School* 30: 365–9.

Schoeninger, M. J. 1979. Diet and status at Chalcatzingo: Some empirical and technical aspects of strontium analysis. *American Journal of Physical Anthropology* 51: 295–309.

Schoeninger, M. J., and M. J. DeNiro. 1984. Nitrogen and carbon isotopic composition of bone collagen from marine and terrestrial animals. *Geochimica et Cosmochimica Acta* 48: 625–39.

Schoeninger, M. J., M. J. DeNiro, and H. Tauber. 1983. $^{15}N/^{14}N$ ratios of bone collagen reflect marine and terrestrial components of prehistoric human diet. *Science* 220: 1381–3.

Schröder, G. 1957. Radiologische Untersuchungen an trepanieten Schädeln (Neolithikum-Mittelalter). *Zeitschrift für Morphologie und Anthropologic* 48: 298–306.

Shutler, R., Jr., ed. 1983. *Early man in the new world.* Beverly Hills, Calif.

Smith, B. D. 1987. The independent domestication of indigenous seed-bearing plants in eastern North America. In *Emergent horticultural economies of the Eastern Woodlands,* ed. W. F. Keegan, 3–47. Carbondale, Ill.

Squier, E. G. 1877. *Peru: Incidents of travel and exploration in the land of the Incas.* New York.

Steinbock, R. T. 1976. *Paleopathological diagnosis and interpretation.* Springfield, Ill.

Stewart, T. D. 1932. Vertebral column of the Eskimo. *American Journal of Physical Anthropology* 17: 123–36.

  1946. A reexamination of the fossil human skeletal remains from Melbourne, Florida. *Smithsonian Miscellaneous Collections* 106: 1–28.

  1958. Stone age skull surgery. *Annual Report of the Board of Regents of the Smithsonian Institution for 1957* 53: 469–91.

  1973. *The people of America.* New York.

Stout, S. D. 1978. Histological structure and its preservation in ancient bone. *Current Anthropology* 19: 601–4.

Tainter, J. A. 1980. Behavior and status in a Middle Woodland mortuary population from the Illinois valley. *American Antiquity* 45: 308–13.

Tello, J. C. 1913. Prehistoric trephining among the Yauyos of Peru. In *International Congress of Americanists, 1912,* 75–83. London.

Truswell, A. S., and D. L. Hansen. 1976. Medical research among the !Kung. In *Kalahari hunter-gatherers,* ed. R. B. Lee and I. DeVore, 166–94. Cambridge, Mass.

Watson, P. J., ed. 1974. *Archeology of the Mammoth Cave area.* New York.

Whitney, W. F. 1883. On the existence of syphilis in America before the discovery by Columbus. *Boston Medical and Surgical Journal* 108: 365–6.

Williams, H. U. 1932. The origin and antiquity of syphilis: The evidence from diseased bones, as reviewed, with some new material from America. *Archives of Pathology* 13: 799–813, 931–83.

Woods, R. J., and B. M. Rothschild. 1988. Population analysis of symmetrical erosive arthritis in Ohio Woodland Indians (1200 years ago). *Journal of Rheumatology* 15: 1258–63.

Young, D. 1988. An osteological analysis of the Paleoindian double burial from the Horn Shelter, No. 2. *Central Texas Archaeologist* 11: 13–115.

V.9
Diseases of the Americas, 1492–1700

During the first 200 years of European exploration and settlement of the Americas, native populations experienced catastrophic die-offs from the introduction of acute infectious diseases. Pinpointing which parasites were responsible for this decimation is not a simple matter. European knowledge of the infectious disease process was primitive in the sixteenth and seventeenth centuries, with the result that conquerors, settlers, and clergy were ill-prepared to describe the illnesses they witnessed. Statements that simply describe the death experience of native peoples are the most common. In the Roanoke documents of 1588, for instance, T. Hariot described native death from disease, but he attributed the outbreaks to witchcraft:

There was no towne where he had any subtile devise practiced against us, we leaving it unpunished or not revenged (because we sought by all meanes possible to win them by gentlenesse) but that within a fewe dayes after our departure from every such town, the people began to die very fast, and many in short space, in some townes about twentie, in some fourtie, and in one six score, which in trueth was very many in respect to their nombers. This happened in no place that we could learne, but where we had bene, where they used a practice against us, and after such a time. The disease, also strange, that they neither knew what is was, not how to cure it. (Hariot 1973)

The quality of disease descriptions in the Americas greatly improved during the eighteenth century. A description of the frequency of colds among the Natchez stands in stark contrast to Hariot's sixteenth-century description of disease:

Colds, which are very common in winter, likewise destroy great numbers of natives. In that season they keep fires in their huts day and night; and as there is no other opening but the door, the air within the hut is kept excessively warm without any free circulation; so that when they have occasion to go out, the cold seizes them, and the consequences are almost always fatal. (Le Page du Pratz 1975)

Because of epidemiological advances, it is easier for historical epidemiologists to reconstruct disease etiology in the Americas from the eighteenth century to the present. Unfortunately, focusing epidemiological reconstructions on later centuries to the exclusion of the sixteenth and seventeenth centuries is comparable to measuring the destruction of a hurricane that strikes the Gulf Coast by its effect in St. Paul, Minnesota. As has been stressed (Burnet and White 1972), the earliest epidemics among virgin-soil populations are the most severe.

Although new pathogens, such as cholera (Benenson 1976a), reached America's shores in later centuries, they operated at reduced scales, affecting only those who had survived a microbial war of 200 years. Thus, this essay attempts to reconstruct the group of diseases that spread to the Americas between A.D. 1492 and 1700. Although multicellular organisms, including round- and pinworms, undoubtedly reached the Americas during the sixteenth and seventeenth centuries, this discussion focuses largely on unicellular or subcellular organisms, viruses, bacteria, and protozoa, that are defined as acute and infectious and that periodically erupt as epidemics.

Disease Source Material

Whether explicitly stated or not, the identification of parasites responsible for past epidemics is always indirect. The truth of this statement is dramatized by the 1918 influenza pandemic that killed millions of people in less than a year and a half (Jordan 1927). Despite early-twentieth-century advances in public health, microbiology, and immunology, an understanding of the variations of the influenza viruses was not attained until the 1970s (Mackenzie 1980; Stuart-Harris 1981). In 1918 and 1919 suggestions regarding the source of the disease ranged from Pheiffer's bacillus to swine influenza (Crosby 1976).

At least four methods are employed to reconstruct disease agents in historical epidemics: (1) evolutionary theory; (2) disease loads in nonimmune populations; (3) historical documents; and (4) skeletal biology. Typically, researchers rely on one or, at the most, two of these methods. To determine the strengths and weaknesses of any epidemiological reconstruction, the assumptions of each method must be evaluated.

Parasite Evolution and Ecology

Darwinian evolution is the theoretical framework for explaining the differential persistence of variation. Variation and natural selection are the principles that account for this persistence. Variation arises through such processes as mutation and genetic drift. Mechanisms of selection determine which variations persist or become extinct (Lewontin 1974; Levins and Lewontin 1985).

In the disease drama, individual variation between parasites and hosts determines, in part, which parasites become fixed in the disease load of the population. Parasites are predators seeking to maximize their reproductive fitness by colonizing hosts (Burnet and White 1972; Youmans, Paterson, and Sommers 1980). Not all predators are successful. Those that are take over cell machinery; cells then produce parasites at the expense of host cells.

The host's defenses, including skin, cilia, mucous membranes, and antibodies or immunoglobins, are the primary selective agents working to repel parasites. If the host's defense mechanisms are successful, there will be no predatory invasion. If they are not, illness and death of the host may ensue.

Besides explaining the relationship between predator and prey, Darwinian principles focus attention on how and why the relationship changes through time. If the parasite is specific in its reproductive requirements and kills the host before a new generation of parasites is released, the parasite faces death. A more successful strategy for the parasite is to inhibit or neutralize host defenses without causing the death of the host. As suggested by the European experience with epidemic or venereal syphilis (C. J. Hackett 1963; Hudson 1968; Crosby 1972), over time a kind of symbiosis evolves in which the host works for the parasite, but both host and parasite survive.

The pattern from initial virulence to relative quiescence has implications for the reconstruction of past infections. Quite simply, as I have stated elsewhere

(Ramenofsky 1987), present diseases cannot be accepted as analogs for diseases of antiquity. New parasites have become fixed by human populations; older parasites have evolved less destructive adaptive strategies; still other parasites, most likely unidentifiable, have died out. Although present processes of infection and transmission may be comparable to those of the past, the present human disease load does not mirror the past.

Epidemiologists with an interest in understanding past diseases are well aware of this problem of analogs. To overcome it, they have focused on reconstructing the human ecological settings most conducive to the fixing and persistence of human infectious parasites (Cockburn 1963, 1971; Black 1966, 1980; Fenner 1971, 1980). Immunology, population size and density, and population mobility are the key variables considered in this approach.

Most of the diseases considered in this essay have one trait in common: Recovery from the infection confers long-term or permanent immunity. Because of this protection, parasites require a continual pool of susceptible hosts to survive.

Large nucleated populations, such as those of cities, meet the criterion for such a pool. As documented archeologically, nucleated populations of any magnitude did not become a consistent feature of the human landscape until after the evolution of agricultural systems. Cities developed shortly thereafter, having a temporal depth in western Asia of approximately 5,000 years (Wenke 1984). Although it is likely that acute, infectious parasites periodically colonized individuals or populations before 5000 B.P., natural selection fixed these parasites only when population density passed a threshold necessary for parasitic survival. Even after 5000 B.P., the distribution of acute infections probably was uneven across Asia and Europe simply because population distribution was uneven.

Smaller nucleated populations that are sedentary or consist of those who practice a mobile settlement strategy are likely to be infected by other types of parasites. The list of potential parasites varies, depending on the degree of mobility, the presence or absence of herd animals or pets, and the size of the population. Both F. Fenner (1980) and F. L. Black (1980) think chronic or latent infections, including chickenpox (*Varicella zoster*) and *Herpes simplex,* are probable candidates for persistence in small populations. Zoonotic infections, including yellow fever (arbovirus) and tetanus (*Clostridium tetani*), that are transferred from animal reservoirs to humans by accidents of proximity are also likely.

On a global scale, these abstract treatments suggest that a variable set of diseases have infected human populations through time. Small mobile or sedentary populations are expected to have chronic or latent microbial flora. As population size or density of movement between populations increases, human groups are subject to acute infectious parasites that periodically erupt as epidemics. To determine whether these expectations hold on a local scale requires the use of other data sets.

In summary, Darwinism is crucial for any discussion of historical epidemics. Variability and selection explain the evolution and differential persistence of human diseases under differing environmental conditions. These simple principles account for the extinction of older diseases and the sudden onset of new ones. Ecological factors, including population distribution, nature of settlement, and immunology, are useful for stipulating the global distribution of chronic and acute infections.

Although important, Darwinian theory is also subject to limitations. Because of evolutionary changes in hosts and parasites, present diseases cannot be accepted as analogs for past diseases. In addition, theory, by definition, is ideational. Without testing ideas against the complexity of empirical variability, ideas about how evolution, persistence, or extinction occurred are empty.

Infectious Diseases in Population Isolates

The second method of reconstructing historical epidemics is to study the effects of introduced acute infections on living population isolates. Because of population size, distribution, or geography, these isolates, or virgin-soil populations, do not maintain acute infections endemically. These infections must be introduced from external sources. The temporal lapse between introductions of the same parasite coupled with the immunological responses of previously infected individuals determine whether the foreign parasite will have a minimal or maximal effect. Whereas temporal isolation of one year may be sufficient to cause an epidemic of the common cold (Burnet and White 1972), a six- to eight-year lapse may be necessary to cause a smallpox epidemic (Pitkanen and Eriksson 1984).

There are two approaches to the study of acute infectious outbreaks in nonimmune populations. During an epidemic, surveillance teams may continuously monitor the appearance of new victims and the recovery or death of older victims (e.g., Paul and Freeze 1933; Nagler, Van Rooyen, and Sturdy 1949; Christensen et al. 1953a,b; Peart and Nagler

1954; Phillip et al. 1959; Monrath et al. 1980; Brenneman, Silimperi, and Ward 1987; Gerber et al. 1989). Alternatively, antibody reactions can be measured in sputum or serological samples (Black and Rosen 1962; Adels and Gajdusek 1963; Brown, Gajdusek, and Morris 1966; Black et al. 1970; Brown and Gajdusek 1970; Neel et al. 1970).

Although both attack and mortality rates can be determined from disease notifications, the accuracy of the rates varies according to the severity of the outbreaks, the rapidity of spread, and the number of surveillance teams. In severe disease episodes, it is likely that both morbidity and mortality are greatly underestimated (Crosby 1976).

Because of immunological memory, antibody testing can be done at any time. Consequently, an entire population can be surveyed for the presence of measles antibody 15 years after the epidemic. Unfortunately, the resulting trends apply only to the survivors. Without independent evidence (e.g., death certificates, disease notifications), trends in mortality cannot be measured.

In addition to incomplete reporting, contemporary studies of epidemics in virgin-soil populations are subject to the problem of analogs. Although it is tempting to use modern morbidity and mortality data to account for what might have occurred 500 years ago, such an approach is erroneous for two reasons. First, as previously described, less deadly symbioses between parasites and hosts evolve through time. Second, where present, medical intervention will curtail the course of a disease outbreak. Because of these factors, contemporary responses of virgin-soil populations to acute infectious parasites are likely to be rather pale reflections of sixteenth- or seventeenth-century disease events.

Despite these limitations, knowledge of contemporary epidemics is crucial for understanding the infectious process. As demonstrated by the accidental introductions of measles to southern Greenlanders in 1951, stochastic contacts between infected and susceptible individuals still occur (Christensen et al. 1953a,b). In addition, these contemporary studies detail the complex interactions between the health of the hosts and primary and secondary invasions. Between 1942 and 1943 in the Yukon, a small band of Tlingit experienced six epidemics, including measles, malaria, whooping cough, diarrhea, and meningitis. With each episode, the health of the population deteriorated, allowing for the invasion of other parasites (Marchand 1943).

In summary, contemporary studies of the infectious process and disease loads of nonimmune populations are useful guides to understanding epidemic conditions in the past. These studies document the ease with which infectious parasites spread and the trauma that follows in the wake of epidemics. Rather than single epidemic events, it is likely that native Americans in the sixteenth and seventeenth centuries experienced waves of infections. The deterioration of health following an initial disease event established conditions appropriate for the invasion of other, allochthenous and autochthenous, parasites.

Historical Descriptions of Epidemics

Consulting historical documents is the third method of reconstructing past epidemics. Although lumped within a single heading, these sources vary from casual references to disease outbreaks to detailed descriptions of a single epidemic. Finding these documents demands great investments of time. Rarely are medical data indexed or otherwise distinguished in archives. Consequently, researchers may search assiduously through primary documents before coming across a single description of a disease event.

Descriptions of epidemics among native Americans during the Columbian period are subject to three sources of error. First, because contacts during the period were irregular, descriptions of any sort, including references to disease, are also irregular. Consequently, the first reference to a disease event may not mark the onset of introduced parasites. As late as 1800 contact between Europeans and native groups of the North American plains was still irregular. When Meriwether Lewis and William Clark visited the Upper Missouri tribes, the Mandan described a smallpox epidemic that had occurred 20 years earlier (Thwaites 1904).

Second, as discussed previously, the crudeness of European knowledge during the Columbian period affected the nature of early disease descriptions. For one thing, it is likely that observers failed to record many outbreaks. Moreover, a lack of familiarity with the people being described made it difficult for even the most conscientious explorers to estimate the number of deaths that diseases wrought. The Gentleman of Elvas (Bourne 1904), for instance, simply described the abandonment of villages visited by the expedition of Hernando DeSoto. Similarly, Daniel Gookin (1806) described an epidemic event from hearsay evidence that had decimated native groups of New England seven or eight years before the English established New Plymouth.

Third, there is confusion over disease names. Because Europeans were writing about native disease experiences, knowledge of what was known in Europe is crucial for understanding this ambiguity. C. Creighton's (1894) sourcebook on epidemics in Britain continues to be one of the finest and most readily available compendiums of evolving medical knowledge.

Before 1743, influenza was frequently confused with other agues or catarral fevers. Diphtheria was not defined as a separate illness until the eighteenth century. Before that time, it was lumped with scarletina or the purples. Because measles and smallpox both produced rashes, the two terms were used interchangeably until 1593. By 1629, however, when the Bills of Mortality were established, smallpox and measles were consistently differentiated. Smallpox was noted as "flox or smallpox."

Because smallpox, measles, influenza, and diphtheria are acute and infectious, they all could have been introduced to the Americas at the time of first contact. Whether they were requires careful reading of documents informed by contemporary epidemiological knowledge. Historical documents by themselves are of marginal utility. The confusion over names, which they reflect, coupled with medical naïveté and unfamiliarity with the populations being described by observers, has led one microbiologist to state that documentary evidence "provides, at best, an accumulation of suppositions, since most accounts give insufficient details of symptoms or of epidemiological patterns for us to impute an aetiological agent" (Mackenzie 1980).

Despite these limitations, historical descriptions are crucial sources of information and must be integrated into any disease reconstruction. Documents not only highlight the presence of some infectious parasite, but force the historical epidemiologist to investigate what and why the disease event occurred.

Burial Populations

Irregularity of initial contact and the limitations of medical knowledge among observers during the Columbian period have been recognized as sources of error for some time. To compensate for these problems, other types of data have been deployed in reconstructing historical epidemics. Human skeletal remains are of some importance here (Milner 1980; Blakely 1989). G. R. Milner (1980) has argued that the analysis of mortuary populations from the earliest period of contact is of central importance in unraveling the timing and magnitude of aboriginal population loss from introduced infectious diseases.

Skeletal populations are employed in two ways. Analysis of the age–sex structure of a population can suggest whether its demographic profile reflects an epidemic episode (Blakely 1989; Blakely and Detweiler-Blakely 1989). Moreover, the frequency and type of skeletal pathologies can provide information on the presence, absence, and, perhaps, type of acute infectious agent (Steinbock 1976).

The use of reconstructed demographic profiles to infer past epidemics requires two assumptions, however. First, the mortuary population represents a single temporal interval comparable to an epidemic interval. Second, the burial sample is representative of those who lived. Both assumptions are difficult to support archeologically.

Although archeologists are skilled in controlling for time, the temporal resolution obtainable from the archeological record is rarely comparable to a single epidemic event. Only in unique depositional settings, such as the Tathum burial mound in west Florida (Mitchem 1989; Hutchinson 1990), does the weight of evidence suggest that the burial population represents an epidemic episode. Mortuary settings that incorporate 50 to 100 years are far more common.

Even if the temporal dimension is controlled for, the problem of the representativeness of the burial sample remains. Skeletal populations are typically biased samples of those who lived. Some age–sex classes are underrepresented; others may be overrepresented (Buikstra and Cook 1980). Controlling for these biases is challenging, especially under epidemic conditions. As suggested by historical descriptions and rarity of burial populations during the Columbian period (Ramenofsky 1987), native populations may have ceased interment in some areas. This practice raises serious questions about the nature of available burial samples: Do they represent the victims or survivors of epidemics? Without controlling for sampling biases, accurate reconstruction of demographic profiles from cemetery data is, at best, difficult.

As with skeletal analyses, the investigation of osteological evidence of epidemic mortality has serious shortcomings. First, not all acute infections are expressed osteologically. In illnesses such as venereal syphilis, or tuberculosis, bone cells become involved only when the disease has progressed to a severe stage. If the individual dies before that point, the disease will not be reflected osteologically.

Second, bone cells have limited ways of responding to infectious agents: tissue loss, tissue gain, both loss and gain, or abnormal morphology (Ortner and Putschar 1981). The remodeling may be variously expressed, but different causative agents can result in the same osteological expression (Steinbock 1976;

Ortner and Putschar 1981). Although osteological remodeling may suggest the presence of an acute infection, stipulating the causative agent responsible for the remodeling is frequently impossible. Even in those rare instances where a specific acute infectious parasite is implicated as causing osteological remodeling (Jackes 1983), it is unlikely that the individual died from the infection. The process of osteological remodeling is of longer duration than the illness.

Because of inherent difficulties in isolating causative agents, bioarcheologists have begun to consider nonspecific stress indicators, especially osteomylitis and periostitus (Detweiler-Blakely 1989). If the health of native populations deteriorated after contact, the frequency or intensity of stress responses should have increased. To determine whether the suggested association holds requires the analysis of burial populations through time. Even if such a series were available and the appropriate pattern were documented, the cause or causes of the stress responses would remain elusive (Buikstra and Cook 1980). Periosteal responses, for instance, can be caused by anemia, treponemal infections, scurvy, trauma, or osteomylitis (Ortner and Putschar 1981).

In summary, inadequate control of the temporal dimension, biases present in cemetery populations, and nonspecific skeletal responses to disease limit the utility of skeletal populations as primary sources of data for reconstructing epidemic mortality in the Americas during the Columbian period. As a secondary resource, these investigations may provide information unobtainable through other sets of data.

The reconstruction of past epidemics is challenging because it is elusive. Instead of a single infallible method, historical epidemiologists must employ a suite of methods. Results of one investigation can then be weighed against those obtained from other inquiries. Even then, we can never be certain whether smallpox or malaria was the biggest killer of native Americans in the sixteenth century. At the same time, the integration of evidence from Darwinian theory, contemporary disease investigations of nonimmune populations, historical documents, and skeletal analyses can suggest the magnitude of the parasitic invasion that faced native peoples during the earliest centuries of European contact.

Allochthonous Parasites in the Americas

Previous Syntheses
Some researchers have investigated the introduction of specific diseases to the Americas in general

Table V.9.1. *Diseases suggested to have been introduced to the Americas*

Disease	Crosby (1972)	Crosby (1986)	Dobyns (1983)	Ramenofsky (1987)
Chickenpox		X		X
Dengue fever		X		
Influenza	X	X	X	X
Measles	X	X	X	X
Mumps			X	X
Rubella				X
Smallpox	X	X	X	X
Cholera		X	X	
Diphtheria		X	X	
Pneumonia				X
Pertussis		X		X
Scarlet fever		X	X	X
Typhoid fever		X	X	
Anthrax				X
Bubonic plague			X	X
Malaria			X	X
Typhus			X	X
Yellow fever		X	X	X
Total	3	11	12	14

(e.g., Stearn and Stearn 1945), whereas others have studied the introduction of all diseases to a specific region (e.g., Cook 1982). Few have attempted a comprehensive treatment of the introduction of all diseases to both continents. Table V.9.1 summarizes the conclusions of three scholars regarding the introduction of acute infectious agents to the Americas.

It will be noted that none of the lists includes epidemic (venereal) syphilis or tuberculosis. The omission of these two major diseases should not be interpreted as supporting the notion that either disease originated in the Americas. Controversies over their origins are extensive (regarding syphilis: Crosby 1972; Ramenofsky 1987; Baker and Armelagos 1988; regarding tuberculosis: Black 1980; Clark et al. 1987; Ramenofsky 1987). Until this question is resolved, these diseases cannot be considered to be either allochthonous or autochthonous to the New World.

There are some disagreements about specific introductions that stem from the temporal or intellectual focus of the work. In 1972 A. Crosby considered only sixteenth-century introductions. In 1986 he adopted a much larger temporal framework; his suggested introductions reflect that change. Although in 1983 H. Dobyns described more introduced infections than those listed in Table V.9.1, the summary is limited to those diseases that arrived during the sixteenth and seventeenth centuries. My own list (1987) is also limited to the first two centuries of European contact.

In developing that list, I weighed evidence from all sources described previously. Although my total was greater than either Crosby's or Dobyns's, several diseases were excluded; other diseases were included. Cholera was excluded because according to current opinion (Creighton 1894; Benenson 1976a) it spread to the Americas in the eighteenth century. Diphtheria was excluded because of the ambiguity of the name (Creighton 1894).

Typhoid (enteric) fever was excluded for several reasons. Although native populations of the Americas certainly suffered from diarrheal infections in the postcontact period, the question becomes whether these infections were new and whether *Salmonella typhi* caused some of the infections. The first question cannot be answered; the second can be addressed indirectly. The disease was not isolated from typhus or other nonspecific childhood fevers until the nineteenth century (Creighton 1894; Overturf and Underman 1981). In addition, although rare, typhoid fever can take a chronic form and can spread to humans from nonhuman reservoirs including turtles (Youmans et al. 1980). The combination of a chronic state and the indisputable presence of turtles in precontact America suggested that *S. typhi* could have been present in the Americas before 1492.

The diseases that I listed as introductions, but not treated by Crosby or Dobyns, include anthrax, rubella, and pneumonia. Anthrax is typically a relatively minor infection in humans. Domestic stock, cattle, sheep, horses, and goats are the primary source of the infection; humans become ill through accidents of proximity (Whiteford 1979). In those areas, such as the Southwest or the pampas of South America, where domestic stock were part of the cultural baggage of European colonists, anthrax could have been a source of infection.

Rubella was added to the list for two reasons. First, although a relatively mild disease in adults, it can seriously affect the reproductive fitness of a population. If a woman develops German measles during the first trimester of pregnancy, the fetus may be born with major congenital defects, including cataracts, heart disease, microcephaly, and mental retardation (Top 1976). Second, although rubella was confused with measles and smallpox until the eighteenth century, the presence of measles and smallpox in America during the sixteenth and seventeenth centuries suggested that rubella could have been introduced at the same time.

The bacterial pneumonias are caused by a group of unrelated organisms. Some of these (*Streptococcus pneumoniae*) are part of the normal flora of the human upper respiratory tract. Thus, some causative agents of severe lung infections in humans had to have been present in the Americas before European contact. In contrast, contemporary studies (Brenneman et al. 1987) suggest that some native American populations are at higher risk from other agents of pneumonia (*Hemophilis influenzae*). This elevated risk may indicate that not all causative bacteria of pneumonia were present before Europeans arrived in the Americas. Moreover, because pneumonias are major secondary invaders that follow such viral infections as measles and influenza, and because both measles and smallpox were allochthonous to the Americas, it is likely that at least some types of lung infection spread to the Americas with Europeans. As health deteriorated from viral infections, bacterial agents could invade and cause death.

Although both Dobyns and I view epidemic typhus as an Old World introduction to the Americas, H. Zinsser (1947) thought that it predated European contact. The vector of typhus is the human body louse. The current worldwide distribution of people means that epidemic typhus is also worldwide (Wisseman 1976). Although it is likely that body lice predated Europeans in the Americas, I think it unlikely that typhus-infected lice were present. The disease thrives under conditions of intense crowding, poor sanitation, and social or economic upheaval associated with war. Despite the archeological evidence of warfare in the Americas, the distribution of human populations was inappropriate for fixing epidemic typhus as part of the disease load of native populations. Dense concentrations of people were simply too rare.

In summary, a minimum of 11 and a maximum of 14 viral, bacterial, or protozoal diseases are suggested in Table V.9.1 as having diffused to the Americas during the first two centuries of European contact. There is unanimous agreement on five disease introductions (influenza, measles, smallpox, scarlet fever, and yellow fever). I have increased the total introductions from 11 to 14 by adding anthrax, rubella, and pneumonia.

Current Synthesis

After reexamining the evidence for and against the introduction of diseases listed in Table V.9.1, I have removed one disease. Chickenpox is omitted from Table V.9.2 because it is present in small nucleated populations that lack antibodies for acute, infectious

Table V.9.2. *Viral, bacterial, and protozoal agents introduced to the Americas*

Mode of transmission	Viral	Bacterial	Protozoal
Direct	Influenza Measles Mumps Rubella Smallpox	Pneumonia Scarlet fever Pertussis	
Zoonotic	Yellow Fever	Anthrax Bubonic plague Typhus	Malaria

microbes (Black 1980). In addition, *Varicella zoster* can follow a chronic course, expressing itself as chickenpox in children and as shingles in adults (Brunell 1976).

Table V.9.2 lists viral, bacterial, and protozoal agents, characterized by two modes of transmission. Eight of the 13 viruses (influenza, measles, mumps, rubella, smallpox) and bacteria (pneumonia, scarlet fever, pertussis) colonize humans only and are transmitted by them only. Of the remaining 5 diseases, yellow fever is viral; anthrax, plague, and typhus are bacterial; and malaria is protozoal. All 5 of these agents are classified as zoonoses, meaning that the primary reservoir is a nonhuman, invertebrate or vertebrate species (except in rare cases, e.g., pneumonic plague [Benenson 1976b]).

Previously discussed difficulties of reconstructing past epidemics by a single method have direct implications for the current synthesis. I will not attempt to reconstruct the precise date or port of entry of each disease introduction. My goal is to build general expectations about the postcontact spatial persistence of parasites, and to accomplish this I will use data on transmission cycles, evolution, ecology, and history.

For those viruses and bacteria that colonize and reproduce only in humans, density of human populations, regularity of communication, and incubation period of the parasite determined the size of spatial epidemic waves. As population density decreased or communication became irregular relative to the incubation period of the parasite, the parasite died out. Whether a second introduction of the same parasite caused another epidemic outbreak varied according to the number of reproductively active survivors and time. Although individuals who escaped infection during the first disease event could be subsequently infected at any time, the size of the susceptible pool determined whether any new outbreak would be local or regional in scale (Bartlett 1956; Black 1966; Cockburn 1971).

Recently, the 1520 introduction of smallpox to the Americas has been a subject of some interest. It is a classic example of disease transmission and spatial diffusion. On the basis of information drawn from historical documents, Dobyns (1983) has argued that the virus became the initial New World pandemic, spreading as far south as Chile and as far north as the Canadian border. The Caribbean islands were the initial focus of infection in 1518. The virus was then carried to Mexico by a crew member of Panfilo de Narvaez's expedition. The large size and extreme density of aboriginal populations in the valley of Mexico encouraged the rapid dissemination of the virus.

The question of spatial diffusion beyond the valley of Mexico has been investigated by historians and archeologists. Noble Cook (1981), historian, has not found evidence of spatial diffusion into the Peruvian Empire. A second introduction of smallpox to Panama in 1524 did, however, spread down the Andean chain (Cook 1982). Using climatic data to explain the persistence of smallpox, S. Upham (1986) argued that the smallpox epidemic did spread to southwestern groups. Other archeologists (Ramenofsky 1987; Campbell 1989) have relied on archeological indicators of population change and time. Although generally supportive of an early-sixteenth-century introduction of the parasite to North America, the archeological evidence of catastrophic population loss was ambiguous. Evidence of a sixteenth-century disease introduction was not documented in central New York or the Middle Missouri (Ramenofsky 1987). S. Campbell (1989) documented a large population decline in the Chief Joseph Reservoir during the early sixteenth century. I discovered a comparable population decline in the Lower Mississippi valley between 1540 and 1600. The magnitude and rapidity of the loss argued in favor of some acute, infectious parasite. Neither the 1520 nor the 1524 smallpox epidemic could be implicated directly.

In summary, for directly transmitted viruses and bacteria, the distribution of susceptible populations, communication systems, and incubation periods of the parasite determined whether local disease events became regional or multiregional. Even with detailed historical records, it is difficult to define the spatial extent of a specific parasite. Although the scale of resolution currently obtainable from regional archeological data bases may be sufficient for concluding that acute infectious microbes caused catastrophic die-offs, current knowledge is simply insufficient for stipulating whether one or another epidemic event was causal.

Transmission cycles of zoonotic infections are fundamentally different from infections transmitted solely between humans. Because vertebrate or invertebrate species other than humans are the primary reservoir of the parasite, niche requirements of the reservoir and microbe determined the postcontact spatial pattern across the American continents. Humans became infected through accidental interactions with the reservoir and causative agent. The following focuses on those aspects of reservoir or microbial niches pertinent to reconstructing the postcontact spatial patterning of these infections.

Temperature severely curtails the distribution of yellow fever. The viral disease is transmitted to humans or other nonhuman primates by several mosquito vectors, including *Aedes* and *Haemagogus* (Taylor 1951). The optimal temperature for incubation of the arbovirus and the transmission ability of the vectors is approximately 30°C (Whitman 1951). At temperatures less than 24°C *Haemagogus,* for instance, cannot transmit the disease, and the incubation period of the virus lengthens. In addition, the vectors have preferred breeding habitats. *Aedes aegypti* breeds in clay-bottomed containers; other species of *Aedes* and *Haemagogus* prefer breeding in trees of climax rain forests (Carter 1931).

Like yellow fever, malaria is a vectorborne disease that is transmitted to humans by numerous species of *Anopheles*. The temperature limitations and elevational preferences of these species vary greatly. Whereas *Anopheles maculipennis* can reproduce in cold pools along lake margins at elevations greater than 4,000 feet in the western United States, *Anopheles quadramaculatis* prefers breeding in swampy nonbrackish pools or bayous typified by the Lower Mississippi valley (Hackett 1941; Watson and Hewitt 1941). In addition, the body temperature of the vector affects the reproductive potential of the protozoans. *Plasmodium vivax* and *Plasmodium malariae* will not develop in anophelines if the body temperature is less than 15°C; *Plasmodium falciparum* requires an anopheline body temperature of greater than 18°C for reproduction (Zulueta 1980).

Epidemic typhus is an acute infectious disease for both vector and human populations. The human body louse, *Pediculus humanus,* is the vector; the causative agent is a bacterium, *Rickettsia prowazekii*. After ingesting the agent, the typhus-infected louse dies within 7 to 10 days. When the louse feeds on human blood, the rickettsial agent is transmitted to humans (Zinsser 1947; Wisseman 1976).

Plague and anthrax are bacterial infections transmitted to humans from nonhuman mammalian reservoirs. The distribution of the reservoir largely determines the distribution of the disease. Wild rodent populations in wooded or desert areas are the true reservoir of the plague bacterium: In these settings, the disease is endemic (Meyer 1963; Benenson 1976b). In urban areas, the causative agent, *Yersinia pestis,* is transmitted to humans through a secondary vector, the rat flea, *Xenopsylla cheopis*. The proximity of humans to rats and their fleas creates a tertiary focus of the disease.

As previously mentioned, anthrax is a bacterial disease of domestic ungulates. The causative agent, *Bacillus anthracis,* is transmitted to humans through the ingestion of contaminated meat or milk products, contact with infected animals, or the inhalation of viable airborne spores (Brachman 1976; Whiteford 1979).

Because not all New World habitats were appropriate for the reproduction of reservoirs, vectors, and parasites, it is likely that zoonotic infections were more limited spatially than were directly transmitted viruses and bacteria. Yellow fever became fixed in tropical climates; malaria survived between 60° north latitude and 40° south latitude (Watson and Hewitt 1941); epidemic typhus survived where human groups were concentrated; herds of domestic ungulates became the focus of anthrax; bubonic plague was fixed as a disease of ports. As rats migrated away from ports, plague also migrated.

The variability in reproductive requirements and, therefore, transmission cycles of parasites has implications for the postcontact spatial patterning in the Americas. Because all native populations were virgin soil, the accidental introduction of any parasite could decimate a single population aggregate. Whether the parasite diffused spatially and acquired an endemic status in the rich American environment depended on a number of factors.

The probability of fade-outs of directly transmitted viruses and bacteria varied according to stochastic contacts between infected and susceptible hosts, the overall distribution of population, and the time separating introductions of the same parasite. As just described, the spatial pattern of zoonoses depended on reproduction requirements of reservoirs, vectors, and parasites. Certainly by the seventeenth century, natural selection had fixed the spatial variability of all introduced parasites. Like threads joining patches of a quilt, communication mechanisms linked sources of infection to potential recipients. Each epidemic wave further reduced survivors of previous disease outbreaks.

Conclusions

As demonstrated by this synthesis, simple questions are frequently the most difficult to answer. Determining which diseases were allochthonous in the Americas before A.D. 1700 requires the expertise of numerous disciplines, including the study of evolution, ecology, microbiology, history, archeology, and geography. The integration of diverse and sometimes contradictory sets of information provides a means of evaluating past and present assumptions and of suggesting future directions. Although skeptical of the possibility of reconstructing the exact number of introductions, or dates and places of entry during the Columbian period, I support serious interdisciplinary efforts aimed at establishing the nature of the parasitic environment that confronted native populations during the sixteenth and seventeenth centuries. I hope that this preliminary synthesis will promote such efforts.

Ann Ramenofsky

Bibliography

Adels, B. R., and D. C. Gajdusek. 1963. Survey of measles patterns in New Guinea, Micronesia, and Australia. *American Journal of Hygiene* 77: 317–43.

Baker, B. J., and G. J. Armelagos. 1988. The origin and antiquity of syphilis: Paleopathological diagnosis and interpretation. *Current Anthropology* 29: 703–36.

Bartlett, M. S. 1956. Deterministic and stochastic models for recurrent epidemics. *Proceedings of the Third Berkeley Symposium on Mathematical Statistics and Probability* 4: 81–109.

Benenson, A. S. 1976a. Cholera. In *Communicable and infectious diseases,* 8th edition, ed. F. H. Top, Sr., and P. F. Wehrle, 174–83. St. Louis, Mo.

  1976b. Plague. In *Communicable and infectious diseases,* 8th edition, ed. F. H. Top, Sr., and P. F. Wehrle, 502–7. St. Louis, Mo.

Black, F. L. 1966. Measles endemicity in insular populations: Critical community size and its evolutionary implication. *Journal of Theoretical Biology* 11: 207–11.

  1980. Modern isolated pre-agricultural populations as a source of information on prehistoric epidemic patterns. In *Changing disease patterns and human behavior,* ed. N. F. Stanley and R. A. Joske, 37–54. London.

Black, F. L., and L. Rosen. 1962. Patterns of measles antibody in residents of Tahiti and their stability in the absence of reexposure. *Journal of Immunology* 88: 727–31.

Black, F. L., et al. 1970. Prevalence of antibody against viruses in the Tiriyo, an isolated Amazon tribe. *American Journal of Epidemiology* 91: 430–8.

Blakely, R. L. 1989. The life cycle and social organization. In *The King site: Continuity and contact in sixteenth-century Georgia,* ed. R. L. Blakely, 17–34. Athens, Ga.

Blakely, R. L., and B. Detweiler-Blakely. 1989. The impact of European diseases in sixteenth-century Southeast: A case study. *Midcontinental Journal of Archaeology* 14: 62–89.

Bourne, E. G., ed. 1904. *Narratives of the career of Hernando De Soto,* 2 vols. New York.

Brachman, P. S. 1976. Anthrax. In *Communicable and infectious diseases,* 8th edition, ed. F. H. Top, Sr., and P. F. Wehrle, 137–42. St. Louis, Mo.

Brenneman, G., D. Silimperi, and J. Ward. 1987. Recurrent invasive *Haemophilis influenzae* type b disease in Alaskan natives. *Journal of Pediatric Infectious Diseases* 6: 388–92.

Brown, P., and D. C. Gajdusek. 1970. Disease patterns and vaccine response studies in isolated Micronesian populations. *American Journal of Tropical Medicine and Hygiene* 19: 170–5.

Brown, P., D. C. Gajdusek, and J. A. Morris. 1966. Epidemic A2 influenza in isolated Pacific island populations without pre-epidemic antibody to influenza types A and B, and the discovery of other still unexplored populations. *American Journal of Epidemiology* 83: 176–88.

Brunell, P. A. 1976. Chickenpox. In *Communicable and infectious diseases,* 8th edition, ed. F. H. Top, Sr., and P. F. Wehrle, 165–73. St. Louis, Mo.

Buikstra, J. E., and D. C. Cook. 1980. Paleopathology: An American account. *Annual Review of Anthropology* 9: 433–70.

Burnet, Macfarlane Sir, and D. O. White. 1972. *Natural history of infectious disease,* 4th ed. Cambridge.

Campbell, S. K. 1989. Postcolumbian culture history in the northern Columbian Plateau: A.D. 1500–1900 Ph.D. dissertation, University of Washington.

Carter, H. R. 1931. *Yellow fever: An epidemiological and historical study of its place of origin,* ed. L. A. Carter and W. H. Frost. Baltimore.

Christensen, P. E., et al. 1953a. An epidemic of measles in southern Greenland, 1951:II. Measles in virgin soil. *Acta Medica Scandinavica* 144: 430–49.

  1953b. An epidemic of measles in southern Greenland, 1951: III. Measles in virgin soil. *Acta Medica Scandinavica* 144: 450–4.

Clark, G. A., et al. 1987. The evolution of mycobacterial disease in human populations: A reevaluation. *Current Anthropology* 28: 45–62.

Cockburn, A. 1963. *The evolution and eradication of infectious diseases.* Baltimore.

  1971. Infectious diseases in ancient populations. *Current Anthropology* 12: 45–62.

Cook, N. D. 1982. *Demographic collapse: Indian Peru, 1520–1620.* Cambridge.

Creighton, C. 1894. *History of epidemics in Britain,* 2 vols. Cambridge.

Crosby, A. 1972. *The Columbian exchange: Biocultural consequences of 1492.* Westport, Conn.

1976. *Epidemic and peace 1918.* Westport, Conn.

1986. *Ecological imperialism: The biological expansion of Europe, 900–1900.* Cambridge.

Detweiler-Blakely, B. 1989. Stress and the battle casualties. In *The Kino site: Continuity and contact in sixteenth-century Georgia,* ed. R. L. Blakely, 87–100. Athens, Ga.

Dobyns, H. F. 1963. An outline of Andean epidemic history to 1720. *Bulletin of the History of Medicine* 37: 493–515.

1983. *Their number became thinned.* Knoxville, Tenn.

Fenner, F. 1971. Infectious diseases and social change. *Medical Journal of Australia* 1: 1043–7, 1099–201.

1980. Sociocultural change and environmental diseases. In *Changing disease patterns and human behavior,* ed. N. F. Stanley and R. A. Joske, 7–26. London.

Gerber, A. R., et al. 1989. An outbreak of syphilis on an Indian reservation: Descriptive epidemiology and disease-control measures. *American Journal of Public Health* 79: 83–5.

Gookin, D. 1806. Historical collections of Indians of New England, 1674. *Collections of the Massachusetts Historical Society,* Ser. 1 (1792), 1: 141–227.

Hackett, C. J. 1963. On the origin of the human treponematoses. *Bulletin of the World Health Organization* 29: 1–41.

Hackett, L. W. 1941. Malaria and community. In *A Symposium on human malaria with special reference to North America and the Caribbean region,* ed. F. R. Moulton, 148–56. Washington, D.C.

Hariot, T. 1973. A brief and true report of the new found land of Virginia (1588). In *Virginia voyages from Hakluyt* (1589), ed. D. B. Quinn and A. M. Quinn, 46–76. Oxford.

Hudson, E. H. 1968. Treponematosis and human social evolution. *American Anthropologist* 67: 885–92.

Hutchinson, D. L. 1990. Postcontact biocultural change and mortuary site evidence. In *Columbian consequences 2. Archaeological and historical perspectives on the Spanish borderlands east,* ed. D. H. Thomas. Washington, D.C.

Jackes, M. K. 1983. Osteological evidence for smallpox: A possible case from seventeenth-century Ontario. *American Journal of Physical Anthropology* 60: 75–81.

Jordan, E. O. 1927. *Epidemic influenza.* Chicago.

Le Page du Pratz, A. S. 1975. *The history of Louisiana* (1758), ed. J. G. Tregle. Baton Rouge, La.

Levins, R., and R. C. Lewontin. 1985. *The dialectical biologist.* Cambridge.

Lewontin, R. C. 1974. *The genetic basis of evolutionary change.* New York.

Mackenzie, J. S. 1980. Possible future changes in the epidemiology and pathogenesis of human influenza A virus infections. In *Changing disease patterns and human behavior,* ed. N. F. Stanley and R. A. Joske, 129–49. London.

Marchand, J. F. 1943. Tribal epidemics in the Yukon. *Journal of the American Medical Association* 123: 1019–20.

Meyer, K. F. 1963. Plague. In *Diseases transmitted from animals to man,* ed. T. G. Hull, 527–87. Springfield, Ill.

Milner, G. R. 1980. Epidemic disease in the post-contact Southeast: A reappraisal. *Mid Continental Journal of Archeology* 5: 39–56.

Mitchem, J. M. 1989. Redefining Safety Harbor: Late prehistoric/protohistoric archaeology in west peninsular Florida. Ph.D. dissertation, University of Florida.

Monrath, T. P., et al. 1980. Yellow fever in Gambia, 1978–1979. Epidemiological aspects with observations on the occurrence of orungo virus infections. *American Journal of Tropical Medicine and Hygiene* 29: 912–28.

Nagler, F. P., C. E. Van Rooyen, and J. H. Sturdy. 1949. An influenza virus epidemic at Victoria Island, N.W.T., Canada. *Canadian Journal of Public Health* 40: 457–65.

Neel, J. V., et al. 1970. Notes on the effect of measles and measles vaccine in a virgin-soil population of South American Indians. *American Journal of Epidemiology* 91: 418–29.

Ortner, D., and W. G. Putschar. 1981. *Identification of pathological conditions in human skeletal remains.* Smithsonian Contributions to Anthropology 28. Washington, D.C.

Overturf, G. D., and A. E. Underman. 1981. Typhoid and enteric fevers. In *Communicable and infectious diseases,* 9th edition, ed. P. F. Wehrle and F. H. Top, Sr., 736–45. St. Louis, Mo.

Paul, J. H., and H. L. Freeze. 1933. An epidemiological and bacteriological study of the "common cold" in an isolated arctic community (Spitzbergen). *American Journal of Hygiene* 17: 517–35.

Peart, A. F., and F. P. Nagler. 1954. Measles in the Canadian arctic. *Canadian Journal of Public Health* 45: 146–56.

Phillip, R. N., et al. 1959. Observations on Asian influenza on two Alaskan islands. *Public Health Reports* 74: 737–45.

Pitkanen, K., and A. W. Eriksson. 1984. Historical epidemiology of smallpox in Aland, Finland: 1751–1890. *Demography* 21: 271–95.

Ramenofsky, A. F. 1987. *Vectors of death: The archaeology of European contact.* Albuquerque, N.M.

Stearn, E. W., and A. E. Stearn. 1945. *The effects of smallpox on the destiny of the Amerindian.* Boston.

Steinbock, R. T. 1976. *Paleopathological diagnoses and interpretations.* Springfield, Ill.

Stuart-Harris, C. 1981. The epidemiology and prevention of influenza. *American Scientist* 69: 166–72.

Taylor, R. M. 1951. Epidemiology. In *Yellow fever,* ed. G. K. Strode, 427–538. New York.

Thwaites, R. G., ed. 1904. *Original journals of Lewis and Clark, 1804–1806,* vols. 1, 5. New York.

Top, F. H., Sr. 1976. Rubella. In *Communicable and infectious diseases,* 8th edition, ed. F. H. Top, Sr., and P. F. Wehrle, 589–97. St. Louis, Mo.

Upham, S. 1986. Smallpox and climate in the American Southwest. *American Anthropologist* 88: 115–28.

Watson, R. B., and R. Hewitt. 1941. Topographic and related factors in the epidemiology of malaria in North America, Central America, and the West Indies. In *A symposium on human malaria with special reference to North America and the Caribbean region,* ed. F. R. Moulton, 135–47. Washington, D.C.

Wenke, R. J. 1984. *Patterns in prehistory: Man's first three million years,* 2d edition. New York.

Whiteford, H. H. 1979. Anthrax. In *Bacterial, rickettsial and mycotic diseases,* Handbook Series in Zoonoses, vol. 1, ed. J. H. Steele, 31–66. Boca Raton, Fla.

Whitman, L. 1951. The arthropod vectors of yellow fever. In *Yellow fever,* ed. G. K. Strode, 228–98. New York.

Wisseman, C. L. 1976. Rickettsial diseases. In *Communicable and infectious diseases,* 8th edition, ed. F. H. Top, Sr., and P. F. Wehrle, 567–84. St. Louis, Mo.

Youmans, G. P., P. Y. Paterson, and H. M. Sommers. 1980. *The biologic and clinical basis of infectious disease.* 2d edition. Philadelphia.

Zinsser, H. 1947. *Rats, lice, and history.* New York.

Zulueta, J. de. 1980. Man and malaria. In *Changing disease patterns and human behavior,* ed. N. F. Stanley and R. A. Joske, 175–86. London.

V.10
Diseases and Mortality in the Americas since 1700

It has been clear to virtually every observer of demographic patterns in the Americas that the differences between Anglo and Latin America are traceable to the differences between the nations that colonized each region, as well as to the characteristics of the indigenous populations of each region. The settlement of North America by the British was a commercial venture, the numerous settlements reflecting the economic and religious diversity of the English Reformation and the growing economic complexity of Britain itself. By contrast, "in Spanish America, the diverse conditions of an entire continent had to find expression in the same set of standard institutions" (Lang 1975).

Moreover, by the sixteenth century the Iberian Peninsula was becoming "underdeveloped" in contrast to the countries of northwestern Europe, including England. Like eastern Europe, it was characterized by large estates worked by a servile peasantry. This pattern was replicated in the Americas, where the Spanish encountered an extensive indigenous agricultural population with whom they established a semifeudal relationship. There was no such indigenous population in the north, and the British either pushed aside or killed those they did encounter. As a result, socioeconomic and settlement patterns differed. With the exception of the southeast, family-owned and -operated farms became the dominant pattern in English America. In most of Latin America, haciendas and plantations became the dominant pattern. In the areas where an extensive agricultural society was conquered, Indians provided the servile labor force. Elsewhere, primarily in the Caribbean islands and in what became Brazil, slaves imported from Africa provided the servile labor force on plantations originally devoted to sugar growing. Only in the southeastern part of English America were there plantations worked by slaves.

Upon achieving independence, these two former colonial regions continued to develop in entirely different ways. The former Iberian colonies remained producers of raw materials for export (Stein and Stein 1970), whereas within a century the former English colony became one of the leading manufacturing nations in the world. It is beyond the bounds of this chapter to offer an explanation for these differences save to suggest the following: (1) In the new Latin American nations there persisted local landowning elites with an interest in perpetuating the former colonial system, complete with its dependence on a servile, illiterate population for the extraction of staples and raw materials. (2) The settlers in English America came from a society "which generally treated literacy, toleration, individual rights, economic liberty, saving and investment as inseparable elements of the process of change and growth" (Stein and Stein 1970).

Latin America

Not all Iberian settlement in the Americas took place in areas in which Indians or black slaves formed a servile labor force. Grassland sections of what became Argentina, Uruguay, and southern Brazil were without a sedentary indigenous agricultural population and did not attract extensive European immigration until the latter part of the nineteenth and the twentieth centuries. The areas in which there were sedentary agricultural populations attracted the most attention and as a result suffered devastating pandemics. The magnitude of the resulting population collapse is a matter of debate, but that it was catastrophic is beyond question. Though crisis mortality caused by pandemics and famines receded over the three centuries following first European contact, mortality remained high enough that there was essentially no population growth during the eighteenth century (McGovern-Bowen 1983). Indeed, significant growth did not begin until the early decades of the nineteenth century (McEvedy and Jones 1978). The increase resulted partially from the importation of African slaves (particularly to Brazil and the Caribbean) and European immigration from Mediterranean countries (particularly to Brazil and Argentina) and partly from changes in mortality patterns.

Data on mortality are sparse until about the mid-nineteenth century. Some scattered estimates of crude mortality rates from the early years of the century are as follows: between 21.2 and 28.9 per 1,000 in São Paulo, Brazil, during the years 1777–1836; between 36 and 46 per 1,000 in Havana between 1801 and 1830; 44 per 1,000 in the town of San Pedro in Guatemala in 1810–16 (the most valid of several estimates from a series of neighboring towns); and probably never fewer than 30 to 35 per 1,000 in Mexico City at any time until the mid-nineteenth century. In São Paulo at the end of the eighteenth century, infant mortality is estimated to have been 288 per 1,000 live births and life expectancy at birth about 38 years (Kunitz 1986).

Judging by population estimates and scattered estimates of mortality as well as fertility, it was in the first half of the nineteenth century that births began to outnumber deaths with sufficient consistency for population to begin to grow. This presumed stabilization of mortality, albeit at a high level, coincides with the period when independence was achieved by most Latin American nations. The two are not unrelated, for the result of independence was that the monopoly on trade long held by Spain and Portugal was broken, and the new nations began to trade openly with the industrial nations, particularly England. Moreover, relative social stability characterized most of the new nations during the nineteenth century. "In sum, in Latin America the colonial heritages reinforced by external and internal factors produced economic growth without appreciable sociopolitical change during the nineteenth century" (Stein and Stein 1970). Thus, political and social stability and economic improvements – still within a neocolonial context characterized by an illiterate and servile labor force working on plantations and haciendas producing raw materials for export –

seem to have resulted in a stabilization of mortality at levels that were high but nonetheless low enough for population to grow.

It appears that among the most important identifiable endemic diseases or syndromes were the following: the pneumonia–diarrhea complex of infancy and childhood, the severity of which is exacerbated by protein–energy malnutrition; in some regions malaria; and tuberculosis, which was widespread. Among black troops serving in British West Indian regiments in the West Indies, for instance, the average annual death rate from tuberculosis was 6 per 1,000 in the 1860s, 8.5 in the 1870s, 5 in the 1880s, 3 in the 1890s, and less than 1 in the 1900s. Diseases of the respiratory tract, including tuberculosis, were the leading cause of death. Over the same period black deaths from malaria ranged between 1 and 2.5 per 1,000 per year (Curtin 1987). Life table estimates are available from the middle of the nineteenth century for all of Latin America, except Argentina, Uruguay, and Cuba. From 1860 to 1900, life expectancy at birth increased from 24.4 to 27.2 years. These average figures mask differences among countries. The Dominican Republic, Guatemala, and Nicaragua had a lower life expectancy in 1900 than Brazil, Chile, Colombia, Costa Rica, Mexico, and Panama had had in 1860 (Kunitz 1986). Diversity within some of the large nations, such as Mexico, was probably every bit as great as it was among nations.

The differences in mortality among nations, as well as in the rate at which it declined in the latter half of the nineteenth century and the first several decades of the present century, were primarily reflections of their economic development. These in turn were a reflection of the degree to which countries were dependent on a servile labor force or had, like Argentina and Uruguay, attracted a large European population. Starting in the 1930s, however, the rapidity with which mortality declined increased substantially, particularly in the high-mortality countries, and the rate at which improvement occurred became essentially the same among all of them. Eduardo Arriaga and Kingsley Davis (1969) attribute this to the widespread availability of public health programs that were imported from the industrial nations beginning at about this time or somewhat earlier. This interpretation is supported by the observation that among Latin American nations with the lowest crude mortality rates at the turn of the twentieth century were Cuba and Panama, both places in which the U.S. government had important interests and in which major public health activities had been established (Kunitz 1986).

Thus, crisis mortality seems to have been reduced by the development of relatively stable societies with a slowly improving standard of living. But because living conditions did not improve dramatically due to the neocolonial structure of most of these nations, mortality rates remained high. Dramatic improvements began to occur in the twentieth century when public health measures were introduced. These measures were aimed primarily at controlling the vectors of the most lethal and most prevalent infectious diseases, most notably perhaps malaria and yellow fever (Mandle 1970; Soper 1970; Giglioli 1972), and were not especially concerned with changing either the living conditions or the socioeconomic status of the bulk of the population. Thus, up to a point, technical interventions could play the same role in reducing mortality that economic and social development played in western Europe and North America. The question remains, where is that point? In other words, at what point can technical interventions no longer take the place of socioeconomic development?

Mortality continued to decline after World War II, although to the present there has been a strong positive association between life expectancy and per capita gross national product, along with adult literacy, and an inverse relationship with the proportion of the labor force involved in agriculture. These ecological data as well as individual-level studies (Kunitz 1986) suggest that in much of Latin America, the relationships persist between agricultural production for the international market, low levels of economic development, and high mortality.

Between 1950–5 and 1980–5 there were substantial increases in life expectancy in most Latin American nations, the rate of improvement being inversely associated with the life expectancy in 1950–5, which is to say, the greater the life expectancy at the beginning of the period, the less was the proportionate increase over the following 30 years (PAHO 1986). The reason for this seems to be that populations with greater life expectancy to begin with were those in the economically more developed nations, in which a relatively large proportion of deaths were due to noninfectious diseases. Low life expectancy was associated with high death rates, particularly at young ages, for those infectious diseases most responsive to public health interventions. Thus, the diminution in the rate at which life expectancy has improved over the past two decades has been associated with a shift in the proportionate contribution to mortality of infectious and noninfectious diseases. Noninfectious diseases are accounting for an increasing share of mortality, and they have continued to be less responsive

to public health and medical measures than the infectious diseases (Arriaga 1981).

It appears that what differentiates the contemporary mortality experience of most Latin American nations is mortality rates among infants and young children rather than rates and patterns at older ages. That is to say, mortality at all ages beyond about age 5 is due primarily to violence, accidents, and noninfectious diseases such as cancers and cardiovascular diseases. It is the magnitude of the contribution of infectious diseases to deaths among children during the first 5 years of life that accounts for most of the international differences, and these rates are highest in the poorest countries. The explanation that has been offered for these observations by the United Nations (1982) is as follows:

The departure of Latin American countries from the European experience is related to a disequilibrium between improvements in socio-economic conditions and health interventions. While the latter may have a significant influence on adult mortality in the complete absence of the former, the connexions between one and the other are more subtle at the beginning of life. The longer the population is exposed to health interventions in the absence or under conditions of precarious improvements in standards of living the greater will be the disparity between child and adult mortality.

This is so, it is argued by some, because neither therapy (including oral rehydration) nor public health measures are likely to have a profound impact on infant and child mortality caused by the interaction of malnutrition, pneumonia, and diarrhea in the absence of significant economic development. Others disagree, claiming that, rather than economic development, relatively simple interventions such as equitable distribution of food, increased literacy, and a few simple primary health care measures are all that are required (Halstead, Walsh, and Warren 1985). How easily achieved even such "minor" measures are is a question that will undoubtedly engender debate.

In either case, to the degree that reductions in infant and child mortality are dependent on increased spending for health and social services, as well as on improving standards of living, the current economic crisis and international indebtedness may make such improvements difficult to achieve. The evidence for an association between international indebtedness and a diminution in the rate of improvement of life expectancy has been suggestive but not overwhelmingly persuasive, however, largely because changes in domestic policies may mitigate the worst effects of the economic crisis, at least in the short term (Musgrove 1987).

Thus, there are two observations about contemporary mortality changes in Latin America that, though not necessarily at odds with each other, place emphasis on different elements of the process. One emphasizes that continuing improvements in life expectancy will result from continuing socioeconomic improvements, which will have their most profound impact on the health of infants and children. The other suggests that the pattern of causes of death now reflects the overwhelming significance of human-made and noninfectious conditions among adults and that behavioral change at the individual level is likely to contribute most to further significant declines in the future (Litvak et al. 1987).

North America

The indigenous peoples of North America suffered as catastrophic a population decline as did those in what became Latin America. As already suggested, the North American Indians did not live in the same sort of extensive agricultural societies as existed to the south, nor did the new settlers come from a society like those of the Iberian Peninsula. Settlement patterns therefore tended to differ, with family-owned and -operated farms predominating in most of the region except the southeast.

Endemic diseases such as dysentery and malaria, and epidemic diseases such as measles, smallpox, and yellow fever, were prevalent throughout the colonial period, but their severity seems to have differed substantially from North to South. Life expectancy was lower in Maryland than in New England in the seventeenth century, for example, and crude mortality rates were higher and epidemic diseases more severe in the South than the North throughout the eighteenth and nineteenth centuries.

In the eighteenth century, crude death rates in New England ranged from 6 to 20 per 1,000 population, depending on the location of a given community as well as its age structure (Meindl and Swedlund 1977; Dobson 1987). In French Canada during the eighteenth century, the crude mortality rate varied from 23 to 39 per 1,000, again probably depending on the changing age structure of the population (Henripen 1954).

In the early nineteenth century, crude mortality rates varied widely as well. In northern U.S. cities they tended to be in the range of 18 to 25 per 1,000, increasing as one moved south to 80 or 90 per 1,000 in such cities as Savannah and New Orleans (Dobson 1987). Though there is some disagreement, evidence now exists that mortality rates increased in the course of the first half of the nineteenth century (Meindl and Swedlund 1977; Kunitz 1984; Fogel 1986). This coincided with the first great wave of Irish immigration to the United States, and it is likely that the new settlers were poorer than their predecessors, lived in more squalid circumstances, and spread new diseases to the rest of the population while suffering disproportionately from diseases themselves. Nonetheless, in the North at least, mortality rates remained remarkably low.

Though mortality crises seem not to have been frequent in New England during the colonial period, regular epidemics of measles and smallpox did sweep the population. They seem to have diminished by the end of the period as both diseases increasingly afflicted children, a sign that the population was becoming sufficiently large to convert the diseases into endemic diseases (Kunitz 1984). In general, however, the curve of mortality from year to year retained the jagged, saw-toothed shape characteristic of the presence of epidemics (Omran 1975), although these were never of sufficient magnitude or frequency to keep populations from growing.

Mortality began to decline after the Civil War, though whether this occurred in the 1870s or 1880s is still a matter of disagreement (Kunitz 1984). Robert Higgs (1973) has estimated that the crude mortality rate declined from between 23 and 29 per 1,000 in the 1870s to 15 to 17 per 1,000 in the 1910s in urban areas; and from 21 to 23 per 1,000 to 14 to 15 per 1,000 in rural areas over the same period. These rates are roughly comparable to those observed among Catholics in Canada in the 1860s: 20.9 per 1,000 (Kalbach and McVey 1971). Among the most important of the identifiable syndromes and diseases were the pneumonia–diarrhea complex of infancy and childhood and tuberculosis. Both afflicted Amerindians, blacks, and immigrants more than native-born whites, and both declined in the late nineteenth and twentieth centuries.

Yet even at their zenith in the middle decades of the nineteenth century, mortality rates in North America were low compared with the rates in most of Latin America half a century later, with the exceptions noted previously: Uruguay and Argentina, with no indigenous Indian populations and a high proportion of European settlers, and Cuba and Panama, which both benefited and suffered from the presence of the U.S. army (Sanchez-Albornoz 1974).

The significance of the decline in mortality from midcentury onward is enhanced by the fact that these were the very years during which masses of immigrants from poverty-stricken regions of eastern and southern Europe flocked to the United States and Canada. Although, in general, immigrants had higher mortality rates than native-born people, they tended to have lower mortality rates than were observed in their countries of origin (Kunitz 1984).

The very low mortality observed during the colonial period is explicable in terms of the dispersed nature of settlement and the fact, supported by data on heights, that the population tended to be well nourished. With the exception of blacks brought as slaves to work on plantations in the South, there was not a large servile class such as existed in much of Latin America. The increase in mortality that seems to have occurred after the colonial period has been attributed to the influx of a large and impoverished immigrant population living in unsanitary and rapidly growing cities.

What, then, explains the decline in mortality after the Civil War, when an even larger influx of immigrants every bit as poor as those who had preceded them flooded the cities? It seems likely that the sources of the change were the remarkable productivity of the industrializing U.S. economy and the reform movements that resulted in sanitary improvements in many cities, as well as in small towns and villages (Levison, Hastings and Harrison 1981).

There were, of course, differences in the mortality rates of different cities. By the end of the nineteenth century, these were attributable largely to differences in deaths of infants and young children caused by endemic conditions such as the pneumonia–diarrhea complex. Variations in death rates among cities were explainable by differences in socioeconomic measures, except among southern cities, in which the proportion of blacks living in extreme poverty was an important variable (Crimmins and Condran 1983).

In the course of the eighteenth and nineteenth centuries, then, there was a shift from epidemics afflicting people of all ages to endemic infectious diseases afflicting primarily infants and children. The change occurred earlier in the North than the South, although by the 1920s and 1930s, malaria was in decline south of the Mason–Dixon line. In the course of the twentieth century, the pneumonia–diarrhea complex continued to decline as economic conditions continued to improve, literacy increased, and public health measures were strengthened. By the 1930s tuberculosis and other infectious diseases caused fewer deaths than cardiovascular diseases and cancer. This change was unrelated to medical therapy, for until the late 1930s such therapy had no discernible effect

on mortality (Omran 1977). At that time, however, first sulfonamides and then antibiotics were introduced. The result was a small but measurable impact on mortality rates. In the last seven years of the pre-chemotherapy era (1930–7) the age-adjusted mortality rate declined an average of 4.28 deaths per 100,000 population per year. From 1937 through 1954, when antibiotics became widely available, the age-adjusted rate declined on average 19.4 deaths per 100,000 population. From 1955 through 1968 the decline all but ceased, averaging 2.1 deaths per 100,000 population per year. At the time many people argued that the decline had ceased because infectious diseases had ceased to be a significant cause of death, and the noninfectious and human-made causes of death were refractory to any intervention. It will be recalled that the same explanation was given for the diminution in the mortality decline in Latin America. Beginning in the late 1960s, however, the decline resumed. From 1968 to 1978 the average annual decline was 11.8 deaths per 100,000 population, and this decline has continued to persist (McDermott 1981).

The decline in mortality since the late 1960s has been accompanied by a shift to later and later ages at death, a pattern sufficiently unusual that some observers have claimed it represents a new and previously undescribed stage of epidemiological history (Olshansky and Ault 1986). The debates generated have been about several issues. First, what has caused the decline in mortality since the late 1960s: medical care, changes in behavior, or environmental changes? There is no doubt that early, widespread, and vigorous treatment of hypertension has had a measurable impact on the prevalence of that condition. Presumably that is reflected in a decreasing number of deaths from cardiovascular disease. There have also been changes in smoking patterns, the consumption of meat, and the degree to which people exercise.

Second, is survival to older and older ages accompanied by improvements in morbidity and level of function? On one hand are those who argue that there is a finite life span of about 85 years; that more and more people are living that long in a healthy state; and that they will then die of "natural causes" without lingering illnesses. This has been called the "rectangularization" of the mortality and morbidity curves (Fries and Crapo 1981). On the other hand are those who argue that 85 does not seem to be the upper limit to the human life span; that the survival of more and more people to older and older ages will be accompanied by a disproportionate increase in disability and morbidity; and that the presence of lingering chronic conditions will impose an enormous cost on the health care system (Schneider and Brody 1983).

Finally, what causes of death have been responsible for most of the decline in mortality at older ages? Although cardiovascular conditions are generally implicated, sorting out causes among chronically ill people with multiple health problems is often difficult.

Conclusions

Whether one is considering mortality in highly developed or less developed countries, similar questions frequently emerge: To what degree have public health and therapeutic interventions made a difference? To what degree has economic development been responsible for increasing life expectancy? And to what degree are changes in individual behavior important?

It is generally agreed that in the developed countries development itself has been responsible for most of the change. In contrast, much of the improvement in mortality in less developed countries is said to have been caused by imported public health measures, especially those that could be widely and inexpensively applied in the absence of fundamental changes in the socioeconomic characteristics of the population itself.

More evident disagreement surrounds the question of what is required to reduce mortality further in less developed countries: relatively modest technical assistance from abroad and a domestic policy of literacy and equitable food availability or major socioeconomic change. In developed countries, disagreement has to do with the degree to which individual behavioral changes, on one hand, and environmental changes, on the other, have been important, as well as what will be the future role of biomedical research and health care in addressing the health care problems of the very old. The questions are fraught with political implications and the answers are by no means obvious.

Stephen J. Kunitz

Bibliography

Arriaga, Eduardo E. 1981. The deceleration of the decline of mortality in LDCs: The case of Latin America. *IUSSP International Population Conference, Manila 1981*. Liege.

Arriaga, Eduardo E., and Kingsley Davis. 1969. The pattern of mortality change in Latin America. *Demography* 6: 223–42.

Crimmins, Eileen M., and Gretchan A. Condran. 1983. Mortality variation in U.S. cities in 1900. *Social Science History* 7: 31–59.

Curtin, Philip D. 1987. African health at home and abroad. In *The African exchange,* ed. Kenneth F. Kiple, 110–39. Durham, N.C.

Dobson, Mary J. 1987. From old England to New England: Changing patterns of mortality, Research paper 38, Oxford: Oxford University, School of Geography.

Early, John D. 1982. *The demographic structure and evolution of a peasant system: The Guatemalan population.* Gainesville, Fla.

Fogel, R. W. 1986. Nutrition and the decline in mortality since 1700: Some preliminary findings. In *Long-term factors in American economic growth,* ed. S. L. Engerman and R. E. Gallman, 439–555. Chicago.

Fries, J. F., and L. M. Crapo. 1981. *Vitality and aging.* San Francisco.

Giglioli, G. 1972. Changes in the pattern of mortality following the eradication of hyperendemic malaria from a highly susceptible community. *Bulletin of the World Health Organization* 46: 181–202.

Halstead, Scott B., Judith A. Walsh, and Kenneth S. Warren. 1985. *Good health at low cost.* New York.

Henripen, J. 1954. *La population canadienne au debut du XVIII$_e$ siècle.* Paris.

Higgs, Robert. 1973. Mortality in rural America, 1879–1920: Estimates and conjectures. *Explorations in Economic History* 10: 177–95.

Kalbach, W. E., and W. W. McVey. 1971. *The demographic bases of Canadian society.* Toronto.

Kunitz, Stephen J. 1984. Mortality change in America, 1620–1920. *Human Biology* 56: 559–82.

1986. Mortality since Malthus. In *The state of population theory,* ed. D. Coleman and R. Schofield, 279–302. Oxford.

1987. Explanations and ideologies of mortality patterns. *Population and Development Review* 13: 379–408.

Lang, J. 1975. *Conquest and commerce: Spain and England in the Americas.* New York.

Levison, C. H., D. W. Hastings, and J. N. Harrison. 1981. The epidemiologic transition in a frontier town – Manti, Utah: 1849–1977. *American Journal of Physical Anthropology* 56: 83–93.

Litvak, J., et al. 1987. The growing noncommunicable disease burden, a challenge for the countries of the Americas. *PAHO Bulletin* 2: 156–71.

Mandle, J. R. 1970. The decline of mortality in British Guiana, 1911–1960. *Demography* 7: 301–15.

McDermott, Walsh. 1981. Absence of indicators of the influence of its physicians on a society's health. *American Journal of Medicine* 70: 833–43.

McEvedy, C., and R. Jones. 1978. *Atlas of world population history.* New York.

McGovern-Bowen, C. G. 1983. *Mortality and crisis mortality in eighteenth century Mexico: The case of Patzcuaro, Michoacan.* Syracuse, N.Y.

Meindl, Richard S., and Alan C. Swedlund. 1977. Secular trends in mortality in the Connecticut valley, 1700–1850. *Human Biology* 49: 389–414.

Musgrove, P. 1987. The economic crisis and its impact on health and health care in Latin America and the Caribbean. *International Journal of Health Services* 17: 411–41.

Olshansky, S. J., and A. B. Ault. 1986. The fourth stage of the epidemiologic transition: The age of delayed degenerative diseases. *Milbank Memorial Fund Quarterly* 64: 355–91.

Omran, Abdel R. 1975. The epidemiologic transition in North Carolina during the last 50 to 90 years: I. The mortality transition. *North Carolina Medical Journal* 36: 23–8.

1977. A century of epidemiologic transition in the United States. *Preventive Medicine* 6: 30–51.

PAHO. 1986. *Health conditions in the Americas, 1981–1984*, Vol. 1, Scientific Publication No. 500. Washington, D.C.

Sanchez-Albornoz, N. 1974. *The population of Latin America: A history*. Berkeley and Los Angeles.

Schneider, E., and J. Brody. 1983. Aging, natural death, and the compression of morbidity: Another view. *New England Journal of Medicine* 309: 854–6.

Soper, Fred L. 1970. *Building the health bridge*. Bloomington, Ind.

Stein, S. J., and B. H. Stein. 1970. *The colonial heritage of Latin America*. New York.

United Nations. 1982. *Levels and trends of mortality since 1950*. New York.

V.11
Diseases of the Islamic World

The advent of Islamic culture is well defined by the life of the founder of Islam, Muhammad (c. 570 to 632). Shortly after his death, Muslim Arabs began a series of dramatic conquests of the Middle East and North Africa, so that by A.D. 750 their hegemony stretched from Andalusia (southern Spain) to the Sind (modern Pakistan). Islam was gradually established as the predominant religion in these areas, and Arabic became the preeminent language in most of them. In the later Middle Ages, Islam spread appreciably in sub-Saharan Africa, Turkey, eastern Europe, the Indian subcontinent, and Southeast Asia; the only areas in which it retreated were the Iberian Peninsula and eastern Europe.

Most of our information about disease has been derived from literary sources, including Muslim hagiography and medical texts. The former are biased toward urban conditions, although the majority of the population lived in the countryside at a subsistence level and often at the mercy of nomadic depredations. The medical works have the serious disadvantage of being largely nonclinical and highly derivative of classical medical texts, and the anecdotes of renowned physicians are frequently apocryphal. Yet major features of a "pathological tableau" do emerge, in which illness is inextricably tied to poverty as both cause and effect. Blindness is conspicuous, particularly in Egypt; the result of a number of diseases, blindness seems to have afflicted a large percentage of the population, and the blind were traditionally employed as Koran reciters in mosques. Deafness was often congenital, and mutism was associated with nervous disorders. Paralysis, epilepsy, and mental disorders are frequently described in the medical and nonmedical texts, which include surviving magical incantations and prayers directed against demonic possession.

Among internal maladies, digestive and excretory complaints are commonly referred to; the descriptions suggest dysentery, internal parasites, typhoid-paratyphoid, and cancer. In Moghul India, cholera and dysentery were clearly the major diseases from the sixteenth century; Asiatic cholera does not appear to have afflicted the Middle East until the early nineteenth century. Schistosomiasis (bilharzia) has been present in Egypt since pharaonic times, but it attracted no special interest in the medieval period. Dropsy and elephantiasis are often mentioned in the medical texts. Along with these conditions are observations of muscular problems, fatigue, and general malaise; the last-named might be attributed to malaria, but its endemic and chronic forms were not always recognized as a specific illness and were accepted as a natural state of health.

Some of the most common complaints were dermatological disorders, which are particularly difficult to distinguish in the historical sources but appear to have aroused considerable apprehension. Skin ulceration, infections, and bleeding disorders appear to have been due to nutritional deficiencies. There is also some evidence of an endemic, nonvenereal form of syphilis in the rural population. More certain are the existence and recognition of smallpox and measles. In the tenth century, Rhazes (al-Razi), who was atypical of Muslim medical writers in giving detailed clinical descriptions of diseases, was the first to provide a complete description of the symptoms of both diseases and their treatment.

Plague (*tâ'ûn*), leprosy, and syphilis are given special attention here. They seriously endangered personal and public life, and consequently illustrate well Muslim cultural responses to life-threatening diseases. These three diseases were also generally distinguishable in the past because of their distinctive symptoms and, therefore, are amenable to historical investigation.

Plague

There have been three major plague pandemics in recorded history: the plague of Justinian in the mid-sixth century, the Black Death in the mid-fourteenth century, and the Bombay plague in the late nineteenth century. Apart from the high mortality rates and the social dislocation caused by these pandemics, each initiated a long series of plague epidemics with significant cumulative effects.

Before the Arab conquests in the seventh century, plague had recurred cyclically in the Near East following the plague of Justinian, but it apparently had little effect on the Arabian Peninsula, where environmental conditions for plague were unfavorable. In 638–9, however, a plague epidemic struck the Arab army after its conquest of Syria and it spread to Iraq; the disease killed many soldiers of the conquering army as well as the native population. During the Umayyad caliphate (661–749), plague reappeared a number of times in Syria, Iraq, Egypt, and North Africa. Inexplicably, however, the disease disappeared after 749 and did not reappear again until 913, when it struck Baghdad. There were occasional outbreaks of "pestilence" until the fourteenth century, but they cannot be clearly identified as plague because of the imprecision of the Arabic sources and the lack of any distinct epidemic pattern.

In 1347 plague dramatically reappeared in the Middle East, being carried overland from central Asia to the Crimea in 1346. From the Black Sea region, it was transported by Italian merchants to Constantinople and from there to the major Mediterranean ports. Egypt was infected by the autumn of 1347 and Syria by the following spring. In addition, the plague spread inland; the central Middle East may have been infected from southern Russia as well. There is, incidentally, no evidence for the theory that the pandemic was transmitted from India via the Persian Gulf and the Red Sea to the Middle East and Mediterranean littoral. In 1348–9 plague attacked Arabia for the first time and infected Mecca. This pandemic was the same one that struck medieval Europe and is known familiarly as the "Black Death." From all indications, the effects of the Black Death in Muslim lands were as devastating as they were in Europe.

In both regions the Black Death also established a cycle of plague recurrences, but the reappearances in the Middle East (roughly about every nine years) were far more damaging because of the nature of the epidemics and their persistence. In the Near East, recurrences until the end of the fifteenth century included pneumonic plague (the form of plague that is most infectious and almost always fatal) as well as the other two forms, bubonic and septicemic; all three forms had been present in the Black Death. The result of these plague recurrences was clearly a sustained decline in population in the late fourteenth and fifteenth centuries. This decrease in population was the essential phenomenon of the social and economic life of Egypt and Syria in the later Middle Ages.

There is little evidence for pneumonic plague in Europe after the Black Death, except in isolated Russian epidemics. The recurrent epidemics in the Near East were frequent and lasted until the end of the nineteenth century, whereas epidemics of plague disappeared from most parts of Europe in the seventeenth century. Generally, the Middle East was at the crossroads of a number of endemic foci of plague, which accounts for the numerous and seemingly chaotic occurrences of the disease since the Black Death. By land and sea, the movements of men and their cargoes promiscuously carried the disease over the entire region, giving the appearance of endemicity throughout the Middle East. The endemic foci, however, that were the generators of recurrent plague before the twentieth century in the Middle East appear to have been the following: central Asia, western Arabia (Assîr), western Asia with its center in Kurdistan, central Africa, and northwestern India.

Plague was a well-recognized disease in Muslim society after its first appearances in early Islamic history. Drawing on classical Greek medical works, physicians adequately described the disease, and although it had not been discussed by Hippocrates and Galen, they interpreted it according to humoral theory, attributing it to a pestilential miasma. Not until the Black Death, however, do we have relatively accurate medical observations of plague and historically reliable accounts in the Arabic sources, which are primarily plague treatises and chronicles.

Three of the treatises at the time of the Black Death in Andalusia were mainly medical works. Comparable medical tracts devoted to plague do not seem to have been written in the Middle East, but it was discussed in most of the standard medical compendia written both before and after the Black Death. Following the Black Death, Muslim scholars in the Middle East composed treatises of a largely legal nature that interpreted the disease according to the pious traditions of the Prophet, instructed the reader on proper conduct during an epidemic, and gave some peripheral medical advice. In addition, these works usually ended with a chronology of plague occurrences from early Islam until the writer's own time. These treatises virtually form a genre of religiolegal literature, inspired by the constant reappearances of plague from the time of the Black Death until the end of the nineteenth century.

The treatises are obviously important for their chronicling of plague epidemics but also for the evidence they provide of an ongoing concern of a religious elite that was split on the issue of the religious tenets regarding plague, some arguing for them and some against them. The tenets in question were the following: Plague is a mercy and a source of martyrdom for the faithful Muslim and a punishment for the infidel; a Muslim should neither enter nor flee a plague-stricken region; and plague is noncontagious.

There must have been serious doubts about the soundness of these precepts. The treatises are repetitive concerning this conflict between martyrdom and health, although they often supply original observations of the symptomatology of contemporary plague epidemics. In one respect, the series of tracts show an increasing interest in pseudomedical or magical methods of plague prevention and treatment. It would be hazardous, however, to conclude that this is evidence for the decline of medical practice in the Islamic world, because the discussion of magical practices may indicate merely a greater recognition by legal scholars of common folk practices, which had always existed side by side with professional medical practices. In any event, the treatises explain to a great extent the Muslim attitudes toward plague.

The historical chronicles are relatively abundant for the Black Death and the recurrences of plague during the latter half of the Mamluk period in Egypt and Syria (1250–1517), although we have only one complete eyewitness account of the Black Death itself. These chronicles diminish sharply in quality and quantity in the last half of the fifteenth century, and we are no longer supplied with the kind of specific descriptions of epidemics that enable us to determine with a fair degree of accuracy the duration and nature of the various epidemics.

From the late fifteenth century, the Arabic sources can be supplemented by information from European observers, including merchants and pilgrims, physicians and diplomats, whose reports increase in number with an increasing Western involvement in the Muslim world. The subject of plague in that world alone inspired a large European literature, especially among physicians, who gave conflicting interpretations and advocated conflicting prophylaxes. By and large, this literature is surprisingly uninformative despite some interesting accounts, such as those of the English physicians Alexander Russell and his brother Patrick Russell on plague in Aleppo in the mid-eighteenth century.

The immediate and long-term consequences of plague epidemics are difficult to judge, but in the cities of Egypt and Syria at the time of the Black Death and later plague recurrences, no serious breakdown of urban life was noted, although there were certainly disruptions in food supplies. The organization of large processions, funerals, and burials would suggest the maintenance, if not a heightening, of public order. There is evidence that, despite religious proscription, people did flee from infected regions – both to and from the cities – which doubtless aggravated the situation, because they would often have carried the disease to unaffected areas while exposing themselves to other illnesses and to starvation.

In the Egyptian countryside, by contrast, considerable evidence exists of depopulation through either death or flight from the land, and thus the most disruptive, long-term effect of plague epidemics appears to have been the changes that were wrought in rural areas. Reduced cultivation led to a decrease in the amount of food available for the cities, which depended on surplus rural production, as well as in tax revenues. The first consequence was less important than the second because (based on evidence suggesting that there was no long-term price inflation for agricultural products in Egypt in the aftermath of the Black Death) reduced agricultural production was apparently feeding a diminishing population. The government's attempts to maintain tax revenues, however, were disastrous because a larger share of taxes was imposed on a smaller rural population, which in turn encouraged peasant indebtedness and flight to the cities. Symptomatic of the social and economic plight caused by plague epidemics in Egypt was the virtual disappearance of Christian monasticism, which had begun in Egypt and thrived there for more than a millennium.

Leprosy

Unlike plague, leprosy (Hansen's disease) was often a disfiguring, lifelong disease, and it posed very different social problems. Leprosy appears to have existed in the Middle East from the early Christian Era. The earliest proof of the presence of leprosy in the Middle East has been found in the bone lesions of two skeletons from Aswân (Egypt) that date from about A.D. 500. Therefore, there can be little doubt that genuine leprosy was present from the early Islamic period and that physicians had sufficient opportunity to observe it. Practically every Arabic medical writer discussed leprosy to some degree. The pathology and therapeutics of the disease in these accounts are largely consistent with earlier Greek medical texts. The Arabic medical works said that leprosy was both contagious and hereditary; yet it was not viewed as fiercely contagious, and those sources lack any element of moral censorship of the diseased. Moreover, the medical texts did not recommend flight from lepers or their isolation from the community.

The Arabic terminology for leprosy was created on the basis of its symptomatology. Yet aside from the distinctive signs of advanced lepromatous leprosy, these terms were not restricted to leprosy and were applied to other skin disorders as well. No clinical case descriptions of leprosy have survived in the medieval Arabic medical literature that might clarify the terminology. (The best clinical description in the medieval Near East is, curiously, the early-thirteenth-century description by William, bishop of Tyre, of the condition of Baldwin IV, king of the Latin Kingdom of Jerusalem. This description contains incontrovertible evidence of the anesthetic symptoms of leprosy.) The difficulty is certainly due to the numerous forms that leprosy can take, particularly in its early stages, and its mimicry of other skin diseases.

The Arabs in pre-Islamic Arabia were afflicted by leprosy, along with a large number of other communicable diseases. Leprosy is mentioned by the famous Arabic poets of the period. The Koran mentions in two places the healing of lepers by Jesus. More important for Muslims were the pious traditions of the Prophet concerning the disease, which were in contradiction to the medical texts. For example, the best known of these traditions is the statement that a Muslim should flee from the leper as he would flee from the lion. Similarly, another familiar tradition asserts that a healthy person should not associate with lepers for a prolonged period and should keep a spear's distance from them. The two traditions are prescriptions for social behavior and appear to deal with both moral and medical difficulties posed by the leper. The traditions may have strengthened the desire of those who wished to avoid individuals who were conspicuously afflicted by the disease because it was morally as well as physically offensive.

Atypically, leprosy was believed by some to be a punishment by God for immorality and thus was sometimes invoked as a curse for immoral behavior. But there were also traditions of the Prophet that recommended supplication to God for relief from leprosy, for the matter should not be left entirely to fate. Medically, both traditions seem to express an implicit belief in contagion, which is incompatible with the predominant Muslim view of noncontagion. The pious legend of the Prophet advising flight from the leper is, in fact, preceded by a complete denial of contagion in the canonical collection of such traditions by al-Bukhari, which was made in the ninth century. Certainly those who argued in favor of noncontagion would have been able to make a good case, because leprosy is only moderately contagious and some people are not susceptible to it at all.

The legal status of the leper was directly related to the pious traditions. Leprosy is not discussed in the Arabic legal texts as a separate subject, but it is treated as a disability within such broad areas as marriage, divorce, inheritance, guardianship, and interdiction of one's legal capacity. Because leprosy was considered a moral illness, the leper was limited in his legal rights and obligations – along with minors, the bankrupt, the insane, and slaves. In fact, the leper's status seems to have been particularly close to that of the insane in legal matters, especially with regard to marriage and divorce: A marriage could be dissolved by either person because of the disease. In Maliki law, a man in an advanced state of leprosy was to be prevented from cohabiting with his slave wives and even more so with his free wives. In addition, whereas Maliki law allowed an automatic guarantee of three days against any "faults" in a slave, that guarantee was extended to one year in the case of leprosy. Moreover, the development of the disease could be cause for his or her manumission.

The differing religiolegal traditions served as the bases for various interpretations of leprosy, and underlie a wide spectrum of behavior by and toward the leper, from total freedom of action to segregation in leprosaria. The range of popular responses to the leper is reflected in the early Arabic literature that deals with the disease and other skin irregularities. The famous Arab prose writer al-Jahiz, in the ninth century, collected poetry and narrative accounts on this subject. One of his works is devoted to physical infirmities and personal idiosyncrasies. His objective was to show that they did not hinder an individual from being a fully active member of the Muslim community or bar him from important offices. Al-Jahiz maintained that such ailments were not social stigmas but were what could be called signs of divine blessing or favor. The afflicted were spiritually compensated by God, and special merit was to be attached to their lives. He also cited numerous references to leprosy in early Arabic poetry and mentioned those poets who were themselves leprous.

Nonetheless, there are indications of discrimination against lepers. According to a late-medieval Egyptian handbook for urban market inspectors, they were not supposed to allow people suffering from leprosy to visit the baths. Lepers were also excluded from employment in endowment works. Such discrimination shows that the theological proscription of contagion might have had very little practical effect.

Leprosy certainly existed throughout the Islamic world in the medieval period, but there is no way of determining its extent. Individual cases of leprosy are occasionally mentioned in the historical literature. The most important political figure in early Islam who was afflicted by leprosy was Abd al-Aziz ibn Marwan, an early governor of Egypt who died in 704. It is reported that he suffered from "lion sickness," that is, leprosy. He was given many medications for the ailment, but they were ineffective. Therefore, his physicians advised him to move to Hulwân because of its sulfurous springs, and he built his residence there. Hot springs were a popular treatment for skin disorders in the medieval period and especially for leprosy. It is known, for example, that the Jews commonly sought healing for leprosy in the hot springs and salubrious air of Tiberias.

Shortly after the time of Abd al-Aziz, the caliph al-Walid I conferred a number of benefits on the people of Damascus, the capital, in 707. The chronicles say that "he awarded the lepers and said: 'Do not beg from the people.' And he awarded every invalid a servant and every blind man a leader." As he did with the invalids and the blind, the caliph apparently made provisions for the lepers. The passage seems to imply that he had the lepers separated from the rest of the population. Al-Walid's unusual act is traditionally considered by Arab historians to be the institution of the first hospital in Islam. One may well imagine that the caliph created a hospice for the afflicted in the city, comparable to Byzantine practice. The later well-known hospitals of the Abbasid period appear to have treated lepers and those with other chronic ailments in special quarters.

Still, lepers commonly begged in the streets of the medieval cities, despite the pious endowments on their behalf and laws against mendicancy. Though many must have been genuinely leprous, it was not unusual for men and women to feign the disease by intentional disfigurement in order to receive public charity. Deception of the opposite kind was also common in the slave market, where (despite guarantees) a buyer had to be on his guard against the concealment of leprous sores on the bodies of slaves. Moreover, during the late Middle Ages, the reappearances of plague must have destroyed a large number of lepers because debility increased their vulnerability to other infections.

In the Islamic West, leprosaria were established and special quarters were designated for lepers. The quarters seem generally to have been located outside the walls of many Muslim cities, often in conjunction with leper cemeteries. In Anatolia the Ottomans built leper houses as well as hospitals. A leper asylum was built at Edirne in the time of Murad II, the first half of the fifteenth century, and functioned for almost two centuries. In 1514 the sultan Selim I established a leprosarium near Istanbul and in 1530 Sulayman II built one in Scutari, and both survived until modern times. Lepers and leprosaria were increasingly noticed by Western travelers, and their accounts add to our knowledge about the plight of the diseased. There is, however, no reliable observation of true leprosy by these travelers in the Middle East during the medieval and early modern periods, except for the report of leprosy in Egypt by Prosper Alpin in the late sixteenth century. The disease seems to have been as common in the countryside as in the cities, and leprosy, syphilis, and elephantiasis are all reported to have occurred frequently in Egyptian villages in the nineteenth century.

Syphilis

Syphilis presents us with a new disease, or what was believed to be a new disease when it first appeared in Muslim societies, beginning in the late fifteenth century. Syphilis and other European diseases were introduced into the Middle East in the early modern period by Europeans, who also brought their own methods of treatment. Western medicine was disseminated by missionaries and merchants, travelers, and consular doctors. Before the era of translating Western medical textbooks into oriental languages, the extent of the transmission of Western medicine can be gauged, in some degree, by the recommendation by native physicians of Western treatments for the new Western diseases.

In the early sixteenth century, whooping cough and syphilis were reported, for example, by the Persian Baha ad-Dawla. In one of his works he describes, in considerable detail, "the Armenian sore" that had spread from Europe to Constantinople and Arabia. Reportedly, syphilis had appeared in 1498 in Azerbaijan, and then in Iraq and Persia. Because of some symptomatic similarities with smallpox, it was known as "European pox" or "little fire." It was also confused with anthrax or ignis persicus. Baha ad-Dawla observed the rash, sore throat, and neural involvement of the disease. He recommended purges, venesection, and appropriate foods and drugs, and he referred to European physicians, whom he did not mention by name. He recommended a salve known as the "European pox medicine," which he believed could restore health if properly employed. Baha ad-Dawla did not say what the salve contained, but he mentioned a few lines later that mercury could be given in an electuary. Another of his recipes and one of the European physicians also contained mercury.

According to Leo Africanus, who wrote in the first half of the sixteenth century, syphilis was brought to North Africa by Jews driven out of Spain, and it spread rapidly among the Berber population. In Fez "the first to be contaminated were regarded as lepers, driven from their homes, and obliged to live with the lepers." The first mention of the appearance of syphilis in Egypt was made by Ibn Iyas in his contemporary chronicle of Egypt for the year 1497–8. Among the unhappy events of that year, an evil known as "the French pox had appeared among the people . . . the doctors were powerless in the face of this disease that had never appeared in Egypt before the beginning of this century; countless people died of it."

Naturally, the indigenous physicians took cognizance of the new disease, and it is discussed in the medical textbook of Dawud ibn Umar al-Antaki, who wrote in the later sixteenth century and was perhaps the last great Arabic medical author in the Greek tradition. His textbook displays an intriguing mixture of hallowed Greco-Arabic medicine and the first indications of exposure to European learning, even in matters as small as the Western names for the months of the year.

More important, al-Antaki gives the earliest medical description of syphilis in Egypt in his chapter on carbuncles. He says that syphilis was popularly called "the blessed" in Egypt as a way of avoiding a mental association with the disease and contamination. As for treatment:

If one mixes mercury with frankincense, resin, wax, and oil and uses it as an ointment and if the patient is covered warmly for a week and eats proper and unsalted food, he recovers after suffering gangrene of the mouth, salivation, and tumefaction of the throat. If he becomes cold, he will feel pain in the joints. The ointment should be used three times a week. It is a well-known treatment in the hospital of Cairo. Sometimes one begins by applying the ointment to the extremities and the neck and only after a purge.

Interestingly, al-Antaki provides the entire mercury treatment for syphilis in his textbook as it was practiced in Europe until the eighteenth century.

The broader context in which al-Antaki worked is presented by Prosper Alpin in his description of medical practices in sixteenth-century Egypt. His account, first published in 1591, is surely one of the earliest studies of non-European medicine, and Alpin himself well represents the means whereby Western medicine most effectively reached Egypt. He was an Italian physician-botanist; in 1580 he became physician to the Venetian consul in Cairo, where he spent three and a half years. Alpin did not confine himself to the closed European community in Cairo. He sought the widest possible contacts with Egyptians of all classes and religions. He treated their illnesses in collaboration with Egyptian doctors, and profited from the experience of these native physicians. Alpin watched them operate, observed their instruments, and talked at length with them since they shared the same Galenic tradition; he often criticized their knowledge of Galen but admired their empirical knowledge, which he believed went back to ancient Egyptian practice. He remarked particularly on the indigence and malnutrition of the poor and their medications. The habits of the ordinary people and the women's remedies drew his attention, so that he returned to Italy with a large number of recipes for dishes, medicaments, clysters, and refreshments, including coffee. Alpin also observed the widespread and dangerous use of bloodletting as a panacea for all ills, as well as the common resort to baths for their therapeutic effects and the employment of numerous drugs and medications. These methods had been adopted, according to Alpin, for the new Western diseases, especially syphilis.

In the long term, the appearance of these new diseases, in addition to periodic reappearances of plague, and the measures taken against these diseases by all the foreign European communities helped to diminish traditional Muslim opposition to the notion of contagion. Thus, in the seventeenth century, Evliya Chelebi, a renowned Turkish traveler, described the contagion of syphilis in Cairo quite matter-of-factly. The seventeenth century also witnessed clear evidence of the new age of European medicine, when Ibn Sallum, physician to the midcentury Ottoman sultan Mehmet IV, wrote his medical textbook. In this work Ibn Sallum not only described the new illnesses – for example, chlorosis, syphilis, scurvy, and Polish plait (plica polonica) – but an altogether new system of medicine, namely the "chemical medicine of Paracelsus." Although the Paracelsian system was erroneous and Ibn Sallum's influence may have been slight, the work clearly marks the advent of European medicine in the Middle East. With the introduction of Western-style medical schools in Cairo and Istanbul in the second quarter of the nineteenth century, the ascendancy of Western medicine was assured. All of this, however, was to the detriment of many traditional values and native forms of healing.

Michael W. Dols

Bibliography

Africanus, Leo. 1956. *Description de l'Afrique,* 2 vols., ed. and trans. A. Epaulard. Paris.

Alpin, Prosper. 1980. *La médecine des Egyptiens. 1581–1584,* trans. R. de Fenoyl. Cairo.

al-Razi, Abu Bakr Muhammad Ibn Zakariya. 1939. *A treatise on the smallpox and measles,* trans. W. A. Greenhill. Reprinted in *Medical classics,* Vol. 4. Baltimore.

Browne, E. G. 1962. *Arabian medicine.* Reprint, Cambridge.

Conrad, L. I. 1982. *Tâ'ûn* and *Wabâ:* Conceptions of plague and pestilence in early Islam. *Journal of the Economic and Social History of the Orient* 25: 268–307.

Dols, M. W. 1974a. Ibn al-Wardî's *Risâlah al-naba' 'an al-waba':* A translation of a major source for the history of the black death in the Middle East. In *Near Eastern numismatics, iconography, epigraphy and history: Studies in honor of George C. Miles,* ed. Dickran K. Kouymjian, 443–55. Beirut.

1974b. Plague in early Islamic history. *Journal of the American Oriental Society* 94: 371–83.

1977. *The black death in the Middle East.* Princeton, N.J.

1979a. Leprosy in medieval Arabic medicine. *Journal of the History of Medicine and Allied Sciences* 34: 314–33.

1979b. The second plague pandemic and its recurrences in the Middle East: 1347–1894. *Journal of the Economic and Social History of the Orient* 22: 162–89.

1983. The leper in medieval Islamic society. *Speculum* 58: 891–916.

1986. Malâryâ [malaria], in *The encyclopaedia of Islam* 5: 229–30. London.

1987a. Insanity and its treatment in Islamic society. *Medical History* 31: 1–14.

1987b. The origins of the Islamic hospital: Myth and reality. *Bulletin of the History of Medicine* 61: 367–90.

Dols, M. W., and A. S. Gamal, eds. and trans. 1984. *Medi-*

eval Islamic medicine: Ibn Ridwân's treatise "On the prevention of bodily ills in Egypt." Berkeley and Los Angeles.

Ebied, R. Y., ed. 1971. *Bibliography of medieval Arabic and Jewish medicine and allied sciences.* London.

Elgood, C. 1951. *A medical history of Persia and the Eastern Caliphate.* Cambridge.

1970. *Safavid medical practice.* London. *The encyclopedia of Islam.* 1908–38. 1st edition. Leidon-London.

1960–. 2d edition. Leiden-London.

Gallagher, N. E. 1983. *Medicine and power in Tunisia, 1780–1900.* Cambridge.

Goitein, S. D. 1967–83. *A Mediterranean society,* 4 vols. Berkeley and Los Angeles.

Guliamov, A. G. 1958. Consumption (pulmonary tuberculosis) in the "Canon of Medical Science" of Abu Ali Ibn Sina [in Russian]. *Meditssinskii Zhurnal Uzbekistana* 1: 69–72.

Hamarneh, S. M. 1978a. Ibn al-'Ayni Zarbi and his definition of diseases and their diagnoses. *Proceedings of the First International Symposium for the History of Arabic Science* 2: 305–23.

1978b. Ar-Razi's independent treatise on gout. *Physis, Rivista Internationale di Storia della Scienza* 20: 31–48.

Hau, F. R. 1975. Razis Gutachten über Rosenschnupfen. *Medizin Historisches Journal* 10: 94–102.

Ibn Sina. 1983. *Avicenna's tract on cardiac drugs and essays on Arab cardiotherapy,* 2 vols., trans. H. M. Said, ed. H. A. Hameed. New Delhi.

Iskandar, A. Z. 1960. Rhazes on smallpox and measles. *Hamdard Medical Digest* 4: 29–32.

Izzeddine, C. 1909. *Le choléra et l'hygiène à la Mecque.* Paris.

Judaeus, Isaac. 1980. *On fevers (The third discourse: On consumption),* ed. and trans. J. D. Latham and H. D. Isaccs. Arabic Technical and Scientific Texts No. 8. Cambridge.

Klein-Franke, Felix. 1982. *Vorlesungen über die Medizin im Islam.* In *Sudhoffs Archiv,* Supplement 23. Wiesbaden.

Leiser, Gary, and M. W. Dols. 1987. Evliyâ Chelebi's description of medicine in seventeenth-century Egypt, part 1. *Sudhoffs Archiv* 71: 197–216.

1988. Evliyâ Chelebi's description of medicine in seventeenth-century Egypt, part 2. *Sudhoffs Archiv* 72: 49–68.

Maimonides, Moses. 1963. *Treatise on asthma,* trans. by S. Muntner, Vol. 1 of *The medical writings of Moses Maimonides.* Philadelphia.

Meyerhof, Max. 1941. An early mention of sleeping sickness in Arabic chronicles. *Journal of the Royal Egyptian Medical Association* 24: 284–6.

Meyerhof, Max, and M. Monnerot-Dumaine. 1942. Quelques maladies d'Europe dans une encyclopédie médicale arabe du XVIIe siècle. *Bulletin de l'Institut d'Egypte* 24: 33–44.

1984. *Studies in medieval Arabic medicine: Theory and practice,* ed. Penelope Johnstone. London.

Panzac, Daniel. 1985. *La Peste dans l'Empire Ottoman, 1700–1850,* Collection Turcica No. 5. Leuven.

Pearson, J. D., ed. 1958–. *Index Islamicus.* Cambridge.

Pringle, G. 1957. Oriental sore in Iraq: Historical and epidemiological problems. *Bulletin of Endemic Diseases* 2: 41–76.

Qusta ibn Luqa. 1987. *Abhandlung über die Ansteckung.* In *Abhandlung für die Kunde des Morgenlandes,* Vol. 48, ed. and trans. Harmut Fahndrich. Stuttgart.

Rahman, Fazlur. 1987. *Health and medicine in the Islamic tradition.* New York.

Raymond, André. 1973. Les grandes épidémies de peste au Caire aux XVIIe et XVIIIe siècles. *Bulletin d'Etudes Orientales* 25: 203–10.

Reddy, D. V. S. 1940. Medicine in India in the middle of the XVI century. *Bulletin of the History of Medicine* 8: 49–67.

Renaud, H. P. J. 1934. Les maladies pestilentielles dans l'orthodoxie islamique. *Bulletin de l'Institut d'Hygiène du Maroc* 3: 5–16.

Richter P. 1913. Uber die allgemeine dermatologie des ʿAlî Ibn al-ʿAbbâs (Haly Abbas) aus dem 10 jahrhundert unserer zeit rechnung. *Archiv für Dermatologie und Syphilis* 118: 199–208.

Schacht, J. 1950. Max Meyerhof [Obituary with bibliography of Meyerhof's numerous works on ophthalmology]. *Osiris* 9: 6–32.

Seidel, E. 1913. Die Lehre von der Kontagion bei den Arabern. *Archiv für Geschichte der Medizin* 6: 81–93.

Serjeant, R. B. 1965. Notes on the 'Frankish chancre' (syphilis) in Yemen, Egypt and Persia. *Journal of Semitic Studies* 10: 241–52.

Spies, O. 1966. Zur geschichte der pocken in der arabischen literatur. *Medizingeschichte Spektrum* 7: 187–200.

Théodoridès, J. 1955. La Parasitologie et la zoologie dans l'oeuvre d'Avenzoar. *Revue d'Historie des Sciences et de Leurs Applications* 8: 137–45.

Thies, Hans-Jürgen. 1971. *Der diabetestraktat ʿAbd al-Latîf al-Baghdâdî's. Untersuchungen zur geschichte des krankheitsbildes in der arabischen medizin.* Bonner Orientalistischen Studien, N.S., 21.

Ullmann, Manfred. 1970. *Die Medizin im Islam.* In *Handbuch der Orientalistik,* ed. B. Spuler. Leiden.

1978. *Islamic medicine,* Islamic Surveys no. 11. Edinburgh.

Watson, A. M. 1983. *Agricultural innovation in the early Islamic world: The diffusion of crops and farming techniques, 700–1100.* Cambridge.

Yar-Shater, Ehsan, ed. 1985–. *Encyclopedia Iranica.* London.

PART VI

The History of Human Disease in Asia

VI.1
Diseases of Antiquity
in China

Only because of a great movement in China that has been going on for about 70 years have we been able to review the records of diseases in ancient China and publish them in a Western language. This movement has been closely allied with a revaluation of the practice of traditional Chinese medicine by those who have taken a special training in it. Many valuable works have been written in Chinese on the history of Chinese medical art and science. So far, however, all this material has remained practically unassimilated by sinologists and other Western students of Chinese culture. Thus, for example, most of the dictionary definitions in common use are quite out of date. Among the works that we have used in preparing the present contribution is the brilliant monograph of Yü Yün-hsiu on ancient nosology, or what might be called *pathognostics* – the recognition and classification of individual disease entities. Western historians of medicine should be aware that the treatise of Wu Lien-te and Wang Chi-min (K. C. Wong and Wu Lien-teh 1932) on Chinese medicine (nearly always the only one they know) may be described as the very small exposed piece of an iceberg, 90 percent of which is "below the surface" (i.e., in the Chinese language and therefore inaccessible to most historians of medicine). Since about the mid-1950s, the study of Chinese medicine has been revitalized; a great number of rare medical books from ancient and medieval times have been republished in photographic form, and some ancient texts have been reproduced in the modern colloquial (*pai-hua*) style, "translated" as it were from the ancient (*ku-wen*) style, either abridged or complete. For this reason, we feel no need to apologize for departing from former translations and identifications. Limitations of space in the present work will prevent us from providing extensive documentation for our statements, but the reader can consult our more expansive work, *Science and Civilisation in China*, Volume 6 (Needham et al. 1954).

Overview

There are three sources of information concerning diseases prevalent among the people of ancient China during the 1½ millennia before the beginning of the present era: These include (1) the oracle-bone writings of the second half of the second millennium B.C.; (2) epigraphical (especially sphragistic) evidence in the form of seals and other objects found in tombs during the first millennium B.C.; and (3) texts of the various classical writings ranging from the *Shu Ching* and the *Shih Ching* not long after 1000 B.C.; to the first of the great dynastic histories, the *Shih Chi,* completed in 90 B.C.; to the great medical classic, the *Nei Ching,* which took its present form probably about the first century B.C. This material provides, all told, a quite astonishing wealth of technical terminology. Although its analysis is not yet complete, it still provides a firm basis for our conclusions as to the diseases known during this period. The imprecise definitions of some of the terms present perhaps the greatest difficulty, but in fact they are much clearer than one might anticipate before undertaking such an investigation. Moreover, the great continuity of Chinese civilization should not be ignored. Almost unique among the cultures, China possesses continuous traditions of interpretation in this field, directly linking the "sorcerer-physicians" of the second millennium B.C. with the profoundly learned and enlightened medical exponents of the Ming dynasty (sixteenth century A.D.).

It would be possible to organize our material in several ways: purely chronologically, listing texts and their content; or purely nosologically, listing diseases and the terminology relating to them. Both of these approaches would, however, produce extremely dull reading, and therefore we shall adopt a combination of approaches. Moreover, we can provide only a limited number of examples. We propose to bring the story down to the end of the first century B.C., but in so doing we intend to utilize the *Nei Ching* only in part; we cannot mention all the diseases that are described in that fundamental medical classic. It will be convenient also to consider diseases in the light of the macrocosm–microcosm theories current in early Chinese medicine. The physicians of the Chou period, which lasted most of the first millennium B.C., were extremely conscious of the relation of diseases to geography, to the prevailing climate, and to the seasonal changes of the year. They therefore very markedly shared the Hippocratic conception of "airs, waters and places."

Oracle-Bone and Bronze Inscriptions

The oldest form of Chinese writing is that found on the scapulae and tortoise-shells used for divination in the Shang Kingdom (fifteenth to eleventh centuries B.C.). From this was derived the scripts found on bronze vessels recovered from tombs of the Chou

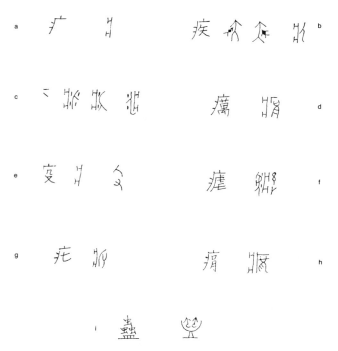

Figure VI.1.1. Oracle-bone and bronze terms specifying disease entities: (a) *ni* – sickness (radical); a bed. (b) *chi* – epidemic disease; a man with arrows of disease attacking him, or lying on a bed. (c) *chieh* – "itching scabies-like epidemic"; a man with spots of rash lying on a bed. (d) *li*[1] – epidemic fever; man, bed, and scorpion. (e) *i* – epidemic fever; bed, and hand holding stick; the patient belabored by the disease. (f) *nio* – fever (later more specifically malarial); man, bed, and spots, with other pictographic components of unknown significance. (g) *pi* – thin scabs or lesions on the head; bed, and unknown pictographic components. (h) *yuan* – arthritic pains; bed, and other pictographic components of unclear significance. (i) *ku* – poison or disease; insects or worms within a vessel. (From Yü 1953.)

period (first eight centuries of the first millennium B.C.). Chinese writing was stylized into approximately its modern form after the first unification of the empire under the Chhin dynasty in the third century B.C.

The radical *ni,* under which the great majority of diseases were later classified, is revealed by the oracle bones to have been the pictogram of a bed (Figure VI.1.1a). Of the 20 or more medical terms that are found on bronze inscriptions, some four of these are clearly recognizable already on the oracle bones. For example, *chi,* which subsequently invariably meant "epidemic disease in general," shows a man alone or lying on a bed with the arrow of the disease shooting into him (Figure VI.1.1b). The word *chieh,* in great use afterward to designate an "itching scabieslike epidemic" (i.e., infectious fever preceded by rash),

shows again a man lying on a bed, but the spots are actually indicated (Figure VI.1.1c). *Li*[1] also means an epidemic fever, and in this case the oracle-bone form seems to show a scorpion (for that is the meaning of the phonetic in this case) occupying the bed alone, with little remaining of the patient; or, perhaps the maggotlike object is the patient, and the scorpion is represented by the little numeral "1" (Figure VI.1.1d). Another term for epidemic disease, *i,* combines the disease radical with a phonetic that is a pictogram of a hand holding a stick (Figure VI.1.1e). This, however, has been found only on bronzes. The last of these oracle-bone terms is the word *nio,* which combines the disease radical with pictograms for tiger and hand; the drawing in Figure VI.1.1f is complex, and the significance of it is not clear. In later ages, this word came to be confined to fevers of malarial type, but in ancient times it was used to indicate all kinds of fevers.

Among the bronze forms we find the word *pi* (Figure VI.1.1g), which means "thin scabs" or "lesions on the head," suggesting eczema and lichen or alopecia or psoriasis, for which there were other words used later on. On the bronze we also find *yuan* (Figure VI.1.1h), which signified arthritic pains in the joints.

The medical content of the oracle bones is, of course, far from exhausted by mere consideration of the few technical terms that had been developed at that early time. Many inscriptions show that illnesses were defined without relying on technical terms. From these we know that there were diseases of the special sense-organs such as eyes and ears; dental problems; speech defects; abdominal diseases; dysuria; diseases of the extremities, including beriberilike syndromes; and pregnancy abnormalities and diseases of women and children. We also know of epidemic diseases coming at a particular time of year and causing death. All these they mention without recourse to a technical phraseology. There is one other oracle-bone term of great interest, however, and that is the poison or disease *ku* (Figure VI.1.1i): This pictogram indicates insects or worms within a vessel. Although we know that in later ages *ku* did indicate particular poisons prepared artificially by humans, there is also reason to think that it referred to a particular disease. This has been identified by Fan Hsing-chun and others as schistosomiasis, partly because the term *ku* occurs so often in combination with the term *chang* (*ku*[1] *chang,* *ku*[2] *chang*) and hence indicates without any doubt edematous conditions of various kinds – in particular, ascites. And the *Nei Ching* describes similar syndromes; certainly in schistosomiasis the liver and spleen become enlarged, and ascites occurs when the disease is chronic.

Seals of Excavated Tombs

Another valuable source of information about the diseases of the late Chou period (the Warring States period, i.e., the fifth to third centuries B.C.) is the seals that have been discovered in excavated tombs. These are important also because they demonstrate an early development of specialization in medical practice. Thus, for example, we have the seal of physician Wang, who specialized in speech defects (*yin*); physician Chang, who claimed to be able to cure external lesions (*yang*); physician Kao, who specialized in the care of ulcers (*yung*); physician Kuo, who dealt with edematous conditions (*tso*), very likely beriberi; physician Thu, who specialized in removing nasal polypi (*hsi*); and physician Chao, who was expert in psychological diseases (*yü¹*). These are only a few examples taken from those that Chhen Chih has collected. From the Warring States period also there are a large number of records written with ink on strips of wood or bamboo, but these have not so far yielded much of medical interest. Medical material on this medium indeed exists, but it derives largely from the army records of the later Han dynasty (first and second centuries A.D.), which is later than the period we are discussing here.

Classical Writings

Diseases and the Seasons

Yüeh Ling. The *Yüeh Ling* (Monthly Ordinances) is admittedly an ancient text, but opinions differ as to its date; some would put it as late as the third century B.C., when it was incorporated in the *Lü Shih Chhun Chhiu,* or also later in the *Li Chi;* but internal astronomical evidence tends to place it earlier (seventh to fifth centuries B.C.). In the course of its description of the activities proper to the different seasons, information is given about what is likely to occur if the weather is entirely unseasonable. Thus if autumn or summer weather comes in the spring, or autumn weather in the summer, or spring weather in the winter, there will be great epidemics (*ta i, ping i, chi i, yang yü i*). In one of these cases the word *li¹* is used; here it is taken as standing for another word, *li²,* and not for *lai,* which it often could do later on, for *lai* specifically refers to leprosy. As we shall see later in this chapter, the first indication of leprosy occurred just about the sixth century B.C. Now *chieh* refers to one of the evils of spring weather

coming in winter; although from early times this meant scabies, it must be translated here as an "itching, scabieslike epidemic." Under any winter conditions, exanthematic typhus is perhaps to be suspected, but the descriptions of *chieh* also sometimes include convulsions, with arched back, and speechless "lockjaw," so that the word sometimes may have been used for tetanus. We shall suggest immediately below a more satisfactory meaning for it.

The *Yüeh Ling* text has other interesting features: It says, for example, that if cool spring weather comes in what would normally be a very hot summer, there will be much *feng kho* (i.e., tonsillitis, bronchitis, pneumonia, etc.). It also says that if hot summer weather comes in autumn, there will be many cases of fever (*nio chi*). This is the word later appropriated to malarial fevers, but in the ancient times of which we are now speaking, it was simply associated with rapid alterations of shivering cold and hot fever. The text also says that if the hot rainy season continues into the autumn, there will be many cases of *chhou chih* (i.e., diseases involving sneezing, such as colds and catarrhs with some fever). The last part of the text says that if spring weather occurs in the last month of winter, there will be many problems of pregnancy, especially miscarriages and stillbirths (*thai yao to shang*). A possible explanation for this association might be shocks to the body caused by going out without sufficient clothing.

Another feature of this particular kind of unseasonableness was described as a high incidence of *kü³ ping. Kü³ ping* – literally, "obstinate diseases" or "enfeebling diseases" (*fei*) – might be described as those in which the patient is enfeebled and cannot easily help him- or herself; such "handicapped" people were not considered fit to participate in social affairs. The *Kuliang chuan,* one of the three great commentaries on the *Chhun Chhiu* (Spring and Autumn Annals) of the State of Lu (722–481 B.C.), defines four forms of handicap that prevented social competency: (1) *thu,* a skin disease of the scalp; (2) *miao,* an eye defect, possibly ankyloblepharon or Horner's syndrome but more probably trachoma; (3) *po,* lameness, often congenital; and (4) *lu,* meaning "hunchback" or "a person with arthritic limbs," the descriptions also covering rickets in advanced form, and osteomalacia. We shall mention this again.

Texts of the centuries just subsequent to the *Yüeh Ling* (if we may regard it as of the late seventh century B.C.) began to differentiate clearly between tertian and quartan malaria, the former being generally termed *hsien* or *tien* and the latter *kai* or *chiai*. There is considerable reason, however, for believing that at some of these periods *chiai nio* was a joint expression used for a disease of slow development ending in hemoptysis, which we can identify as tuberculosis.

Chou Li.   Another interesting description of the seasonal incidence of disease occurs in the *Chou Li* (Record of Institutions of the Chou Dynasty). Although much of the material in this book may well date from the Chou period, its compilation must undoubtedly be considered a work of the early Han (second century B.C.). It gives a detailed account of what the people of that time considered the ideal democratic organization of the state. Here in Chapter 2 we read as follows:

Each of the four seasons has its characteristic epidemics (*li*[1] *chi*). In spring there comes feverish aches and head-aches (*hsiao shou chi*); in summer there are "itching scabies-like epidemics" (*yang chieh chi*); in autumn there are malarial and other fevers (*nio han chi*); in winter there are respiratory diseases (*sou shang chhi chi*).

How is one to interpret these technical terms? No doubt the feverish aches and headaches of the spring refer to influenza, catarrhs, and so forth, but the "itching, scabieslike epidemics" of the summer were certainly far more serious. In the light of the passage that we have just studied in the *Yüeh Ling*, it would seem that cerebrospinal fever (menin-gococcal meningitis, spotted fever) may have been one of the important components of these epidemics, for the course of the disease links together severe rash, fever, and convulsions. Here epidemic encepha-litis is less likely, though it certainly occurred widely in North China down to our own times, and one must also leave a place for scarlet fever and other less important infectious diseases. In the au-tumn, apart from malaria, one would naturally also think of dysentery of both kinds and gastroenteritis (enteric fever caused by *Salmonella*, etc.) as consti-tuting the meaning of the words *nio han chi* (i.e., epidemics caused by a cold, internal or external). The winter picture almost certainly involved pneu-monia, acute and chronic bronchitis, and similar pulmonary afflictions. This is obviously indicated by the words used, which suggest the rising of the *pneuma* into the region of the lungs, with coughing and difficulty in breathing. Among the epidemics of summer and autumn, one would obviously also want to leave a place for typhoid-type diseases and perhaps staphylococcal bacteremia, though tubercu-losis would hardly have been classified as an epi-

demic. The word that later would be universally used to denote diarrhea and dysentery, *li*[3], does not seem to occur much in texts of this date earlier than the *Nei Ching* itself.

Diseases and "Airs, Waters, and Places"

In the *Lü Shih Chhun Chhiu*, Chapter 12, we read as follows:

In places where there is too much "light" (*chhing*, clear) water, disease of the scalp (*thu*; alopecia, ringworm, psoria-sis, etc.) and goitre (*ying*) are commonly found. In places where there is too much "heavy" (*chung*, turbid) water, people suffering from swellings and oedematous ulcers of the lower leg (*thung*[1]) are commonly found and there are many seriously affected who are unable to walk at all (*pi*). Where sweet (*kan*) water abounds, men and women will be health[y] and handsome. Where acrid (*hsin*) water abounds there will be many skin lesions, such as abscesses (*chü*) and smaller boils (*tso*); where bitter (*khu*) water abounds there will be many people with bent bones (*wang yü*).

These technical terms are of much interest. The scalp diseases (*thu*) we have already encountered, but this is the first time that we have seen goiter, for which the term *ying* is characteristic and indubitable. In the next sentence the term *thung*[1] (more correctly written in medical usage *thung*[2]) associated with *pi*, which means lame in both feet, and bedridden, strongly suggests beriberi, indeed the wet form. This term occurs again in a much older text, in one of the poems in the *Shih Ching* (approximately eighth cen-tury B.C.) where it is associated with another word, *wei*, both meaning ulceration of the lower leg. The commentators of the Book of Odes describe it as a disease of swampy places, where, no doubt, the vitamin in the stored grain was destroyed by moulds. The word *wang* resembles that for edema in general (*chung*), which is to be distinguished from the terms for ulcers: *yung* if edematous and unbroken; and *chü* if open, much worse and generally fatal. The probable identification of beriberi in the *Shih Ching* as well as in the *Lü Shih Chhun Chhiu* is accepted by Hu Hou-hsüan and Chhen Pang-hsien, who indeed find evidence of it as far back as the oracle bones them-selves, but there only with reference to disease of the feet. It is pleasant to hear of one place at least where people were healthy and handsome, but immediately afterwards we learn of places where *chü* were plenti-ful; *chü* means carbuncles, furuncles, and perhaps also cancer, whereas *tso* refers to smaller skin lesions such as acne. Rickets and osteomalacia are certainly to be recognized in the last sentence. The bronze script form of *wang* is a pictogram of a person with a crooked back, and many famous people of antiquity are said to have been deformed in this way, even the great Duke of Chou himself. *Yü²* undoubtedly means hunchback; it occurs in the expression *yÿu² lu*, which we find in Chapter 7 of the *Huai Nan Tzu* book (approximately 120 B.C.). There Tzu-Chhiu at 54 years of age "had an illness which left his body deformed. He was so bent that his coccyx was higher than his head and his sternum was so lowered that his chin was bent below the level of his spleen." There can be no doubt that rickets and osteomalacia were widespread in ancient China. There are a number of other valuable texts of the "airs, waters, and places" type, such as those found in the *Huai Nan Tzu* book (Chapter 4) and in the *Nei Ching, Su Wen* itself (Chapter 12).

Shih Ching

Nosological data in the *Shih Ching* (Book of Odes, about eighth century B.C.) have been analyzed in detail by Yü Yün-hsiu, but there is a special difficulty here because these ancient folksongs naturally took advantage of poetic license and it is sometimes difficult to determine whether the disease terms are being used in their proper medical sense; some of them may have been used to indicate malaise or depression in general. Nevertheless, *shou chi* (feverish headaches), *shu* (enlarged neck glands, perhaps goiter, tuberculosis, or Hodgkin's disease) and *meng, sou* (various forms of blindness) are all of interest. Nosological data derived from the *Tso Chuan*, the greatest of the three commentaries on the *Chhun Chhiu* already mentioned, are more reliable and also much more abundant. More than 55 consultations or descriptions of diseases occur in these celebrated annals. Perhaps the most important is the consultation dated 540 B.C. which the Prince of Chin had with an eminent physician, Ho, who had been sent to him by the Prince of Chhin. Physician Ho, as part of his bedside discourse, included a short lecture on the fundamental principles of medicine that enables us now to gain great insight into the earliest beginnings of the science in China. Especially important is his division of all disease into six classes derived from excess of one or other of six fundamental, almost meteorological, *pneumata* (*chhi*). Excess of Yin, he says, causes *han chi*; excess of Yang, *je chi*; excess of wind, *mo chi*; excess of rain, *fu chi*; excess of twilight influence, *huo chi*; and excess of the brightness of day, *hsin chi*. The first four of these are subsumed in the *Nei Ching* classification under *je ping*, diseases involving fever; the fifth implies psychological disease;

and the sixth, cardiac disease. The classification into six divisions is of extreme importance, because it shows how ancient Chinese medical science was independent of the theories of the Naturalists, who classified all natural phenomena into five groups associated with the Five Elements. Chinese medicine never entirely lost its 6-fold classification; but that is a long story, which cannot be told here. Physician Ho diagnosed the illness of the Prince of Chin as *ku¹*, by which he did not mean the artificial poison nor, so far as we can see, schistosomiasis, but rather some kind of physical exhaustion and melancholia arising from excessive commerce with the women of his inner compartments.

Tso Chuan

There is something of interest in every one of the medical passages of the *Tso Chuan*. For example, in 638 B.C. a deformed (*wang*) sorceress, doubtless suffering from rickets or osteomalacia, was to be burnt as a remedy for drought, but a skeptical statesman, Tsang Wen-chung, intervened and said that other means would be much more efficient, so this method was not used. Two years later, we hear of Chhung Erh, the son of Prince Hsien of Chin State, who suffered from *phien hsieh* (i.e., his ribs were so distorted and deformed as almost to meet in front of the sternum). Moved by scientific curiosity perhaps, the Prince of Tshao succeeded in getting a view of him while in the bathhouse. In an episode of 584 B.C., a certain country was described as dangerous for giving people a disease named *o*, although in this particular case the disease endemic there seems to have been beriberi, because there is talk of edematous leg swellings and waterlogged feet (*chui*). We encounter the same term again (*o ping*) in the *Lun Yü*, the discourses of Confucius, dating from about a century later. One of his disciples, Po Niu, suffered from *o ping*, and the universal interpretation of all the commentators since that time has been that this disease was leprosy. We do not find the term *lai* at such an early date, but there seems no reason to reject so old and continuous a tradition that this was the first mention of leprosy in Chinese literature.

Another case relating to the date 569 B.C. was death by heart disease (*hsin chi, hsin ping*); it happened to a general, Tzu-Chung (Kung tzu Ying-chhi of Chhu), who was greatly distressed after a military failure, and we may regard it as angina pectoris brought on by anxiety. Soon afterward, the term *shan* came into use to denote this disease, the symptoms and psychosomatic nature of which are so characteristic. We find this word in the *Nei Ching*, used instead of the term just mentioned for the parallel *hsin thung* of the *Shan Hai Ching,* an ancient geographical text that belongs to the middle of the Chou period. In 565 B.C., the *Tso Chuan* notes another case of *fei chi,* some kind of chronic disability that prevented the normal life of a minister's son. Hydrophobia is also fairly clearly indicated in an entry connected with 555 B.C., where a mad dog (*chi kou* or *hsia kou*) entered into the house of Hua Chhen, a minister of Sung State. The word *khuang* was used indiscriminately for the mad dog itself and for the disease that it caused. Toward the end of the *Tso Chuan* we have a story dated 497 B.C., in the latter part of the life of Confucius, which includes the famous remark that "only he who has thrice broken his arm can make a good leech."

Shan Hai Ching

We have already mentioned the *Shan Hai Ching.* This is a strange book, full of legendary material, which reached its present form probably about the second century B.C., but which contains much far older material. Many legendary and mythological elements pervade its descriptions of the mountains and forests of the Chinese culture area, the spirits proper to be worshiped by travelers in any particular region, and also the peculiar plants and animals and their virtues. More than 30 herbs, beasts, and stones are recommended to ward off various diseases, and this is where the nosological interest comes in. Many terms we have already met with, such as epidemic fevers (*i, li*[1]), epidemics with rash (*chieh*), edematous swellings (*chung*), goiter (*ying*), rodent ulcers (*chü*), and eye defects, probably trachoma (*mi*). *Ku*[1] disease is also mentioned. *Yu*[1] we have not encountered previously; it means both swellings in the neck and also torticollis or palsy. If equivalent to *yu*[2] or *chan,* the commentators interpret it as paralysis agitans or senile tremor, but it may also refer to an affliction called *yu*[3] *chui.* This consists not only of large swollen lymph glands or the parotitis of mumps, but also small, wartlike tumors on the head, neck, and extremities which recall verruca, the multiple warts produced by a rickettsia. Another of the disease terms met with in the *Shan Hai Ching* is *chia,* which undoubtedly refers to a massive infestation with intestinal worms (ascariasis or oxyuriasis). This brings us to the great period of Han case-histories, and so to the work of Shunyü I.

Han Period: Shunyü I

During the Warring States, Chhin, and early Han periods, there were two great schools of medicine:

The earliest grew up in the western state of Chhin; the other was located in the eastern seaboard state of Chhi. From Chhin came the physician Huan, whose attendance on the Prince of Chin in 580 B.C. long remained famous; the physician Ho, already mentioned as examining another Prince of Chin 40 years later, also came from there. More celebrated than either of them was Pien Chhio, about whom there is much to be said, but as the records concerning him do not give us very much in the field of disease nomenclature, we mention him only in passing. But Shunyü I is a different persona entirely. Born in 216 B.C. in Chhi, he studied under Kungsun Kuang and Yang Chhing, practicing medicine successfully from about 180 B.C. on. In 167 B.C., he was accused of some crime and taken to court, but he was acquitted after the supplication of his youngest daughter. As he had been attending on the Prince and lords of Chhi, he was summoned to answer an inquiry from the imperial court some time between 164 and 154 B.C., then released again, and he continued in practice until his death about 145 B.C. It is owing to this perquisition by the imperial authority that we possess today the records of some 25 detailed case histories which Shunyü I reported. For every one we have the name of the patient, the circumstances in which the disease was contracted, the details of the attendance of Shunyü I, the treatment that he prescribed, the explanations that he gave of his diagnostic reasoning, in which the pulse played a very prominent part, and finally the ultimate result. We also have the answers that Shunyü I gave to eight general questions, answers that throw a flood of light upon the general conditions of medical education and practice in the second century B.C. R. F. Bridgman (1955), who had given us a pioneer study of Shunyü I and his times, has concluded that the general level of Chinese medicine thus revealed was in no way inferior to that of the contemporary Greeks, and in this judgment we concur. For the present purpose the point is that the clinical descriptions are so detailed that we can see exactly what Shunyü I meant by his own technical terminology.

Let us first look at some of the less severe cases that Shunyü I was able to cure — or at least relieve for a time. In a child, *chhi ko ping* was clearly difficulty in breathing, probably influenza or catarrh, perhaps acute laryngitis; some fever is implicit in the explanation. In a palace superintendent, *yung shan* was evidently vesical schistosomiasis, accompanied by hematuria, urinary retention, vesicular calculi, perhaps prostatorrhea. Other similar cases, however, were too far gone to recover — for example, a police chief who seems to have had bladder cancer accompanied by intestinal obstruction due to heavy ascaris infestation (*chia*). The Chief Eunuch of the Palace of Chhi fell into a river and got very cold and wet, so his *je ping* due to *han* was surely bronchitis or pneumonia; Shunyü I gave antipyretic drugs and pulled him through. Then the Queen Mother of Chhi had *feng tan,* which is clearly interpretable as acute cystitis, probably connected with nephritis. She had hematuria, but she got better under Shunyü's treatment. An old nurse of the princely family had *je chüeh,* with hot and swollen feet; this may have been gout accompanied by chronic alcoholism, or possibly simply a traumatic infection of the extremities. *Chhiu chih* was clearly dental caries, and one of the grand prefects of Chhi had it. One of the concubines of the Prince of Tzu-chhuan had a difficult childbirth; Shunyü I gave nitrate and obtained the rejection of postpartum blood clots. A young courtier had *shen pi* – traumatic lumbago or muscular strain caused by trying to lift a heavy stone, together with dysuria, perhaps caused by compression of the hypogastric plexus; he also got better. By means of a vermifuge prepared from the gingko tree, a girl was cured of an intense *Enterobius* infestation (oxyuriasis). Here the description is particularly precise because the term used was *jao chia,* and already by this time there were several other terms (*hui, chiao, pa,* etc.) for other types of intestinal parasites. Another case of *pi* was that of a young prince who had acute lobar pneumonia but recovered.

One of the more striking features of Shunyü I's practice was the way in which he was able to give a long-term diagnosis. For example, on one occasion he was asked to give a general health checkup of the serving maids of the Prince of Northern Chhi, and among these he found one who was certainly not ill but in his opinion was going to be. She was, he said, suffering from *shang phi,* and this must have been tuberculosis because it ended in a sudden and fatal hemoptysis some 6 months later. No one would believe that Shunyü I was right in saying that she was ill, but events confirmed his opinion. On another occasion he was alarmed by the appearance of a slave of the client of the Prime Minister of Chhi, who again, in his view, had a *shang phi chhi,* although the man himself did not feel particularly ill. Shunyü I said that he would not last through the following spring, and he did not. Here the clinical description suggests hepatic cirrhosis, almost certainly of parasitic origin, caused by liver flukes (hepatic distomiasis); jaundice was apparent, and the case might also have been one of acute yellow atrophy of the liver.

One of the most extraordinary cases reported by Shunyü I was that of another royal physician, by name Sui. He must have been interested in Taoist arts, for he had himself prepared elixirs from the "five mineral substances," and when Shunyü I saw him he was suffering from *chung je,* apparently in this case a pulmonary abscess, presumably brought on by arsenical or mercury poisoning. Shunyü I warned him that it would be hard to avoid a fatal result, and in fact some months later the abscess burst through under the clavicle, and Sui died. Another man had what Shunyü I described as *ping khu tho feng* (i.e., some progressive paralysis), possibly disseminated sclerosis or possibly progressive muscular dystrophy.

More rapidly fatal in termination were other cases. A palace chamberlain had a peritoneal abscess, perhaps a perforating ulcer (*chü,* leading to *chung je*); perhaps the perforation was due to heavy ascarid infestation. Another man died of *fei hsiao tan* with delirious fever (*han je*). This would have been acute hepatic cirrhosis, probably caused by liver and blood flukes. In this case, the royal physician of Chhi had diagnosed and treated it quite wrongly. It is curious that up to this time we have not found the characteristic term for cholera (*ho luan*), but it seems that Shunyü I may well have had a case of it among his records, for a minister of the Lord of Yang-hsü died of "penetrating pneuma" (*tung feng*), the description of which suggests total failure of digestion, intense diarrhea, possibly due to enteric fever, perhaps to cholera. The word *shan* appears again in a combination *mu shan,* where it clearly refers to an aortic aneurism that caused the death of a general. The last case we shall mention was that of a Court Gentleman of Chhi who had a fall from his horse onto stones; the resulting traumatic abdominal contusion followed by intestinal perforation of a gut probably already weakened by parasitic infestations of one sort or another was termed *fei shang,* that is, injury not to the lung but to the tract (*ching*) of the lung. This brings us to the last subject that we can touch upon here, namely the medical system of the *Nei Ching.*

The *Nei Ching*

The *Nei Ching* was, we think, approximately already in its present form by the first century B.C. The full title under which it is commonly known is the *Huang Ti Nei Ching* (The Yellow Emperor's Manual of Esoteric Medicine), consisting of two parts, the *Su Wen* (Pure Questions and Answers) and the *Ling Shu* (Spiritual Pivot). This was the recension that came from the editorship of Wang Ping in the Thang dynasty, but it is probable that this was not the recension that the Han people had. Another one, known as the *Huang Ti Nei Ching, Thai Su,* which was edited 100 years or so earlier than Wang Ping, by Yang Shang-shan in the Sui period, and which has only come to light in very recent times, may be considered nearer the original text of the Han. The *Nei Ching* system of diagnosis classified disease symptoms into six groups in accordance with their relation to the six (n.b., not five) tracts (*ching*) which were pursued by the pneuma (*chhi*) as it coursed through and around the body. Three of these tracts were allotted to Yang (Thai-Yang, Yang-Ming, Shao-Yang) and three to Yin (Thai-Yin, Shao-Yin, and Chüeh-Yin). Each of them was considered to preside over a "day," one of six "days" – actually stages – following the first appearance of the feverish illness. In this way, differential diagnosis was achieved and appropriate treatment decided upon. These tracts were essentially similar to the tracts of the acupuncture specialists, though the acupuncture tracts were composed of two 6-fold systems, one relating to the hands and the other to the feet, and crossing each other like the cardinal (*ching*) and decumane (*lo*) streets of a city laid out in rectangular grid arrangement. Moreover, by the time of the *Nei Ching* the physicians had achieved full recognition of the fact that diseases could arise from purely internal as well as purely external causes; the ancient "meteorological" system explained by physician Ho had therefore been developed into a more sophisticated 6-fold series, namely *feng, shu, shih, han, sao, huo.* As external factors, they could be translated as wind, humid heat, damp, cold, aridity, and dry heat; but as internal causes we could name them blast (cf. van Helmont's *blas*), fotive *chhi,* humid *chhi,* algid *chhi,* exsiccant *chhi,* and exudative *chhi.* It is interesting to notice the partial parallelism with the Aristotelian–Galenic qualities, which were part of a quite different, 4-fold, system.

In the brief remaining space of this contribution, it would be impossible for us even to sketch the etiologic and diagnostic system of the *Nei Ching,* but it is fair to say that the system provided an elaborate classificatory framework into which the results of keen clinical observation could be fitted. A rather comprehensive theory of medicine, both diagnostic and therapeutic, was now available. Interpreting a whole millennium of clinical tradition, the physicians of the former Han dynasty were able to combine into one science the influences of external factors on health, the abnormal functioning of internal organs whether by excess or by defect, and

the manifestation and interrelationship of symptoms; using the concepts of Yin Yang (the two fundamental forces in the universe), Wu Hsing (the five elements), Pa Kang (the eight diagnostic principles), and Ching Lo (the circulatory system of the *chhi*). The five elements had not been part of the most ancient Chinese medical speculations; they derived from another school, that of the Naturalists (Yin–Yang chia) whose greatest exponent and systematizer had been Tsou Yen (c. 350–270 B.C.) Five-element theory (a lengthy discussion of which can be found in *Science and Civilisation in China,* Volume 2 [Needham et al. 1954]) was so influential and so widespread in all the nonmedical sciences and protosciences of ancient (and medieval) China that the physicians could not remain unaffected by it, but in incorporating it into their theoretical disciplines they added a sixth unit or entity to conform with their 6-fold categories. Thus there were five Yin viscera (liver, heart, spleen, lungs, and urinogenital organs) and five Yang viscera (gallbladder, stomach, larger and small intestines, and bladder) recognized by all schools. To these the physicians added a further entity in each category, the *hsin pao lo* (pericardial function) and the *san chiao* (three coctive regions); and the particular interest of this lies in the fact that these additions represented physiological operations rather than morphologically identifiable structures. The six "viscera" could thus correspond readily with the six *chhi,* the six tracts, and so on. It must not be supposed that the state of Chinese medicine at the time of the *Nei Ching* synthesis was destined to remain unchanged through the following nearly two millennia of autochthonous practice; on the contrary, there were great developments, many elaborations, and a proliferation of diverging schools. However, if we are to think of any presentation of Chinese medicine as classical, this is what deserves the name.

The ancient Chinese physicians were extremely conscious of the temperature-regulating and -perceiving systems of the human body, so that although they had no means of measuring temperature accurately, the observation of subjective chill or fever, together with algophobia or algophilia, was extremely important for them. By this time also the study of the pulse and its modifications had advanced to a highly developed state.

All fevers were placed in a category of *shanghan* diseases and termed diseases of temperature (*je ping*). Every sign that is still examined today (pain, perspiration, nausea, etc.), short of the results of modern physicochemical texts, was studied by them and meant something to them. For example *fu man*, or abdominal fullness, was an important sign. This could mean edema (*chung*). The *Nei Ching* actually says that "fluid passing into the skin and tissues by overflow from above and below the diaphragm forms oedema." It could also mean ascites occurring in liver cirrhosis, heart failure, and especially schistosomiasis, undoubtedly so common in ancient China. *Fu man* was also accompanied by the excretion of watery feces with undigested food (*shih i*) found in gastroenteritis, cholera, and the like. *Fu man* was also called *fu chang* and *tien*. This latter word is a good example of a word that can be pronounced in two ways; pronounced *tien,* it meant abdominal distension; but pronounced *chen,* it meant various forms of madness and, in the *binome chen hsien,* epilepsy. It is clear from the clinical description that from Han times onward the terms *lao feng* and *lao chung* referred to tuberculosis. The term *feng* by itself always had the connotation of convulsion or paralysis; it might be regarded as a violent *pneuma,* in distinction from the mild *pneuma* (*chhi*), which was part of the physiology of the normal body. Other forms of *chung feng,* therefore, were hemiplegia (*phien khu*) and cerebral hemorrhage giving full apoplexy (*fi*). Among the fevers (*wen ping*) we now find fairly clear descriptions of diphtheria, as *she pen lan* (lesions at the root of the tongue), doubtless complicated by streptococcal infections. Diphtheria is also clearly denoted by *meng chü,* "fierce ulcer" (of the throat). Hepatic cirrhosis caused by liver and blood flukes was now called *kan je ping;* tuberculosis, *phi je ping;* pneumonia, *fei je ping.*

It does not always follow that the organs referred to in descriptions (in the three preceding cases: liver, spleen, and lungs, respectively) were those to which we might refer the diseases today. Rather these were the organs concerned with the six tracts already spoken of, each one of which was connected with an organ. Of the malarial types of fever (*chiai nio*) we have already spoken. The terminology now continued with little change, but one disease, *tan nio,* may be identified with relapsing fever caused by *Borrelia* spirochetes as Sung Ta-jen has suggested.

One last word on diabetes. Polyuria was recognized as the sign of a special disease in the *Nei Ching,* where it is called *fei hsiao.* Han ideas about this illustrate the principle of successive involvement or shifting (*i*) when some pathological influence spreads from organ to organ in the body. Thus in *fei hsiao* the cold *chhi* in the heart passes over into the lungs and the patient excretes twice as much as what he drinks. Though the characteristic name for

diabetes (*hsiao kho, hsiao chung*) had not been developed by the end of this period, there can be little doubt that diabetes was here in question. The sweetness of the urine was discovered a good deal later, indeed in the seventh century A.D.

The fact that mummification was not practiced in ancient Chinese civilization has no doubt militated against the acquisition of a mass of concrete evidence concerning many of the diseases from which people suffered in those times, such as has been developed for ancient Egypt. As far as we know, almost nothing has been done on the pathological anatomy of the skeletons that have been excavated from ancient tombs in China, whether in the Neolithic or in the Chou, Chhin, and Han periods. Since there must be a mass of skeletal material in the Chinese museums, it may be that this task could still be accomplished with valuable results by Chinese archeological pathologists. However, the study of the written records of ancient China, from the middle of the first millennium B.C. down to the beginning of our era, shows that they have preserved a veritable mass of information concerning the diseases prevalent in those times, and although the study of human remains themselves may bring precious confirmation of what the writings reveal, it may well be that on balance the written records, when fully analyzed, will present a broader picture than the study of the skeletal remains themselves alone could ever give us.

Lu Gwei-Djen and Joseph Needham

We acknowledge with thanks an earlier version of this essay printed under the title "Records of Diseases in Ancient China" in the *American Journal of Chinese Medicine* (1976, 4 [1]: 3–16), published by the Institute for Advanced Research in Asian Science and Medicine, Inc., which was previously printed in Don Brothwell and A. T. Sandison's *Diseases in Antiquity,* 1967, published by Charles C. Thomas.

Bibliography

Bridgman, R. F. 1955. La médecine dans la Chine antique. *Mélanges Chinois et Bouddhiques* 10: 1–20.

Chhen Chih. 1958. Hsi Yin Mu Chien chung Fa-hsien-ti Ku-Tai I-Hsüeh Shih-Liao (Ancient Chinese medicine as recorded in seals and on wooden tablets). *Kho-Hsüeh Shih Chi-Khan* 1: 68–87.

Chhen Pang-hsien. 1957. *Chung-Kuo I-Hsüeh Shih* (History of Chinese medicine). Shanghai.

Fan Hsing-chun. 1954. *Chung Kuo Yü Fang I-Hsüeh Ssu-Hsiang Shih* (History of the conceptions of hygiene and preventative medicine in China). Peking.

Hu Hou-hsüan. 1943. Yin Jen Ping Khao (A study of the

diseases of the Shang (Yin) people (as recorded on the oracle-bones). *Hsüeh Ssu,* No. 3, 73; No. 4, 83.

Needham, J., and Lu Gwei-djen. 1978. *Proto-endocrinology in medieval China.* Bucharest.

Needham, J., et al. 1954. *Science and Civilisation in China,* 7 vols. Cambridge.

Sung Ta-jen. 1948. Chung-Kuo Ku-Tai Jen Thi Chi-Sheng-Chhung Ping Shih (On the history of parasitic diseases in ancient China). *J-Hsüeh Tsa Chih* 2 (3–4): 44.

Wang Chi-min, and Wu Lien-te (K. C. Wong and Wu Lien-teh). 1932. *History of Chinese medicine.* Shanghai.

Yü Yün-hsiu. 1953. *Ku-Tai Chi-Ping Ming Hou Su I* (Explanations of the nomenclature of diseases in ancient times). Shanghai.

VI.2
Diseases of the Premodern Period in China

Old Diseases

It is very difficult to trace precisely the historical development of particular epidemic diseases in China. First, traditional Chinese medical terminology is based on a system hardly translatable into modern Western terms. Second, not only the concepts of disease, but the diseases themselves have changed, so much so that it is impossible to determine whether an ancient classical term meant the same thing when used in premodern texts, or to find the exact modern counterpart of a disease discussed in old texts.

Only during the second half of the nineteenth century did diseases in China begin to be scrutinized by Western medical practitioners, and as late as the early twentieth century, it was difficult to construct a complete picture because "there were classes of disease that were rarely brought for treatment to modern doctors" (Polunin 1976).

One principal feature of the traditional Chinese medical system (a system that achieved classical form by the second century) that makes it difficult to identify individual epidemic diseases in premodern China is the ancient categorization of both epidemic and endemic diseases along with other afflictions into a large group labeled *shanghan* ("affection by cold," although today it is the modern term for typhoid fever). Ge Hong, one of China's most impor-

tant early medical thinkers, specified in the early fourth century A.D. that the *Shanghan* diseases included not only those caused by winter cold but also those caused by spring warmth and by seasonal *liqi* (epidemic "breath"). However, he conceded that differences among the origins of the three types of diseases were slight and they should therefore be grouped into a single category. This ambiguous conception of epidemic "fevers" as part of a more general category of "cold fevers," despite some minor modifications, remained relatively unshaken in Chinese medical thought until the seventeenth century (late Ming and early Qing dynasties).

Widespread epidemics during the late Ming dynasty (Dunstan 1975) induced certain medical thinkers to reject the entire *shanghan* theory because most of the diseases they were called on to treat were found not to be caused by winter cold. The most representative of these pioneer thinkers was Wu Youxing, a seventeenth-century native of the epidemic-stricken eastern Jiangsu region. His work *Treatise on Warmth Epidemic Disease,* written in 1642, put forward the theory that seasonal epidemics were caused by deviant *qi* ("ether") in the atmosphere (Dunstan 1975). The "warm factor" was now favored over the "cold factor" as cause for the disease. Even diseases such as smallpox that had traditionally been considered manifestations of the body's internal "fire" or "poison" were now grouped with communicable diseases caused by external *qi*.

Even this important development in understanding the etiology of epidemic diseases in premodern China does not help us understand all diseases in this period in Western terms. Insufficient descriptions of the symptoms of diseases in medical texts as well as in local gazettes and dynastic histories where most of the information on epidemics can be found constitute the main obstacle to such understanding. Moreover, China's vast size implies regional differences in disease history that are still grossly unappreciated. At the present stage of research, with the exception of a few diseases that are easily identifiable, the best guesses as to the identity of most remain highly hypothetical.

Old and New Diseases

The sixteenth century can be considered a watershed in China's disease history. With the coming of European traders to China's southeast coast and the intensification of international commercial activities in South and Southeast Asia, China entered the world community and a few new epidemic illnesses entered China. Scarlet fever, cholera, diphtheria, and syphilis are the more important ones to be added to the reservoir of older diseases that had been ravaging China for centuries. Among the latter were smallpox, pulmonary diseases, malarial-types of fevers, other febrile illnesses, dysentery, and possibly plague. However, the social and demographic impact of the new diseases on China after the sixteenth century is a field largely unexplored despite its important historical implications.

Smallpox is one of the oldest diseases known to China. An early sixth-century medical work claimed that the malady (then called *luchuang*, "barbarian boils") was introduced around A.D. 495 during a war with the "barbarians" in northern China (Fan 1953; Hopkins 1983). Little is known of the development of smallpox thereafter, until the late eleventh century (Northern Song period) when treatises on the disease written by pediatricians first appeared.

That pediatricians wrote of smallpox suggests that by this time it had developed into a childhood illness among the Chinese population (Leung 1987b). The technique of variation using human pox was first practiced in the lower Yangtze region not later than the second half of the sixteenth century, and vaccination became popular in the early nineteenth century, when Jennerian vaccination techniques were introduced through Canton. Yet, despite the early practice of variation, smallpox was rampant in China, especially in the north (the Manchus and the Mongolians were the most vulnerable, and two of the Manchu emperors died of the disease) where variation was much less practiced than in the south (Leung 1987b).

Malarial-types of fevers (*nue* or *zhang*) first appeared in medical texts in the seventh century, when the economy of the subtropical regions south of the Qinling Mountains became of great importance to the northern central government. From the twelfth century on, after northern China was occupied by the Jurchens and the Song government fled to the south, specialized medical books on malarial fevers and other subtropical diseases believed to be caused by the "miasma" (*zhangqi*) of these regions appeared in increasing number (Fan 1986). Some scholars believe that temperatures during the Tang period (A.D. 618–907) were probably higher than those of today, which suggests that the northern limits of diseases associated with the southern climates (malaria, schistosomiasis, and dengue fever) were further north than they are today (Twitchett 1979). The number of victims of these diseases was therefore likely to be larger than previously thought. In fact, malaria was still a major killer in South and South-

east China during the early twentieth century (Chen 1982).

The history of plague in China is a controversial subject. Some believed that it arrived in China in the early seventh century (Twitchett 1979), whereas others date the first appearance in the 1130s in Canton (Fan 1986). Yet both of these views are based at least in part on simple descriptions of symptoms (appearance of *he*, "nodes"; or *houbi*, "congestion of the throat"), which is far from conclusive evidence. By tracing the development of plague epidemics in the Roman Orient, and in Iraq and Iran from the mid-sixth century to the late eighth century, D. Twitchett (1979) has argued that at least some of the epidemics that struck China from the seventh and eighth centuries were those of bubonic plague. By contrast, those who feel that plague burst out as devastating epidemics only in the early thirteenth or fourteenth century (McNeill 1976; Fan 1986) suggest a possible relationship to the European Black Death of the same period.

Unfortunately, there is no direct evidence to support either of the above hypotheses. Even as late as the seventeenth century, when China was again struck by a series of epidemics, it is impossible to prove that these were outbreaks of plague (Dunstan 1975). The first epidemic in China, which we have substantial reason to believe was plague, was that first striking Yunnan in 1792. It then spread to the southeastern provinces of Guangdong and Guangxi, up the Chinese coastline to Fujian and to the northern part of China (Benedict 1988). But it was only in the late nineteenth century that medical works on the "rat epidemic" (*shuyi*) began to be published (Fan 1986).

In addition to the epidemic diseases discussed above, several endemic ailments were likely to be equally devastating. Among these were pulmonary diseases (probably pneumonia and tuberculosis), dysentery, various fevers (the *shanghan* category of fevers), which probably included typhoid fever, typhus, and possibly meningitis, cerebrospinal fever, influenzas, and the like. Most popular almanacs and family encyclopedias of the Ming–Qing period that contained chapters on common illnesses and their treatment mentioned dysentery, the *shanghan* diseases, and coughs. Skin diseases, *huoluan* (prostrating fever with diarrhea), beriberi, and *nue* (malarial-type fever) were also frequently discussed (Leung 1987a).

Perhaps some notion of the relative importance of these endemic diseases, especially in southern China, can be gleaned from surveys done in Taiwan during the Japanese occupation period (1895–1945). The disease that caused the highest mortality in Taiwan from 1899 to 1916 was malaria. In 1902, it accounted for 17.59 percent of mortality among the native Taiwanese, causing 4.62 deaths per 1,000. Malaria was followed by dysentery and enteritis until 1917, after which "pneumonia" became the region's biggest killer (4.42 deaths per 1,000 in 1935). Next in importance was dysentery (2.55 deaths per 1,000 in 1935), whereas other contagious diseases including parasitic ailments accounted for 1.5 deaths per 1,000 in 1935 (Chen 1982).

That pulmonary diseases and dysentery persisted as the major fatal diseases among southern Chinese from the premodern period to the early twentieth century seems obvious. The secondary place that Ming–Qing almanacs accorded to the malarial-type fevers, despite the fact that malaria was the principal killer in nineteenth-century Taiwan, can be explained by the fact that few, if any, of these almanacs were written by authors from subtropical and frontier regions. It is also possible that malaria was confused with some of the *shanghan* diseases in almanacs.

Parasitic diseases, which ranked third on the list of high-mortality diseases in Taiwan in the 1930s and 1940s, were rarely mentioned in the almanacs. But their importance was emphasized by Western scientists who came to China in the early twentieth century. Thus G. F. Winfield claimed that feces-borne diseases caused about 25 percent of all deaths in China, especially among peasants in the rice and silk regions of the south (Winfield 1948).

Syphilis was one of the first "new diseases" that reached China. It was probably first introduced to Guangdong through Portuguese traders in the early sixteenth century, as a 1502 medical work recorded that syphilis was called the "boils of Guangdong" (*guangchuang*) or "plum boils" by the people of the lower Yangtze region. The disease was already much discussed in sixteenth- and seventeenth-century medical texts, some of which clearly stated that it was transmitted through sexual intercourse (B. Chen 1981; Fan 1986). Along with gonorrhea, syphilis probably accounted for 2 to 5 percent of all Chinese deaths in the 1930s (Winfield 1948).

Cholera probably arrived after syphilis. The modern term for the disease – *huoluan* – was in the past a name for any disease that caused sudden and drastic vomiting and diarrhea. Reliable records date the first real cholera epidemics in China from the 1820s. Like syphilis it also was first introduced in Guangdong and spread from there along the south-

eastern coast up to Fujian and Taiwan. It usually struck in the months of August and September.

Some scholars suspect that an epidemic in 1564, which had reportedly killed "10 million people," may have been cholera. But regardless of the possibility of cholera's presence at an earlier date, there is no question about the devastating effects of cholera in nineteenth-century and early twentieth-century China, especially in crowded urban centers (B. Chen 1981; S. Chen 1981; Fan 1986).

Scarlet fever and diphtheria came to China in the early and late eighteenth century, respectively. Scarlet fever was epidemic in the lower Yangtze region in the 1730s during the winter–spring transition and was then called "rotten-throat fever" (*lanhousha*). The contemporary epidemiologist Ye Gui (1665–1745) noticed that the illness struck all age groups and that the victims were covered with dense red spots and had red sore throats. The disease seemed to be more devastating in the north. In the Peking area of the 1930s, the estimated mortality of scarlet fever was 80 per 100,000 (S. Chen 1981).

Diphtheria was confused with scarlet fever when it first reached China in the late eighteenth century. It became widespread and epidemic in the decades of the 1820s through the 1850s, spreading from the lower Yangtze region to southwestern China and to the northeastern regions before it reached the northwest in the late nineteenth century. The first medical work on diphtheria (then called "white-throat disease," *baihoulong* or *baichanhou*) was also published in the mid-nineteenth century (Fan 1986).

It is difficult to estimate quantitatively the mortality caused by the new diseases. Their older counterparts seemed to remain on the top of the list of high-mortality diseases into the early twentieth century. However, as scarlet fever was the tenth leading cause of mortality in the Peking area between 1926 and 1932 (S. Chen 1981), and as syphilis (with gonorrhea) accounted for 2 to 5 percent of all deaths in China, their roles cannot be underestimated. Perhaps the reason why the impact of cholera and diphtheria epidemics in the premodern period was not quantified was that the former was too seasonal and the latter basically a childhood disease.

According to local gazetteers of the southern provinces, epidemics usually struck during the spring–summer and the summer–autumn transitions. This seasonability of disease prevalence was confirmed by the 1909 Foochow Missionary Hospital Report, which recorded 2,004 patients treated in May, 1,943 in June, and 1,850 in October – equaling about one third of the 17,456 patients treated during the entire year (Kinnear 1909). Dysentery was generally the biggest killer in the summer, whereas cholera did its most important damage in October.

Unlike Japan whose isolation from the important world trade routes kept major diseases away from its shores during premodern times (Jannetta 1987), China was always exposed to epidemic disease. Trade through the old silk route, war with the northern "barbarians," travel to and from India and Indochina – all brought the "old" diseases to China, whereas the coming of the Europeans by sea from the sixteenth century onward brought a few "new" ones.

The low mortality rate resulting from diseases in premodern Japan preceded a period of low fertility, all of which shaped Japan's demographic development (Jannetta 1987). Comparison with Japan in turn raises the question of the extent to which epidemic diseases in China may have been an important factor in its population growth. For example, did China ever experience something similar to the Black Death, which struck Europe in the fourteenth and fifteenth centuries, or the smallpox epidemics that paralyzed the Amerindian communities in the sixteenth century?

Population and Disease

Questions such as those above have always intrigued historians of China because the Chinese population has experienced mysterious declines that were *possibly* caused by widespread epidemics. One such decline of population occurred in north China in the late seventh century, whereas another was a decline in the lower Yangtze region during the ninth century. Other examples are the drastic depopulation of north China during the Mongol dynasty in the fourteenth century, and the decline during the Ming–Qing transition in the mid-seventeenth century (Cartier and Will 1971; Zhou 1983; Wu 1988). Indeed, despite the nature of Chinese sources that do not permit any precise demographic reconstruction, it is generally conceded that China's population in the tenth century remained very much the same as it had been nine centuries earlier. A significant growth, however, took place during the three centuries following the tenth century and in the early thirteenth century, when the population was estimated to have reached an unprecedented high of between 100 million and 120 million people (Cartier and Will 1971). Yet the fourteenth century was one of demographic disaster. Ho Ping-ti estimates the population level at the end of the fourteenth century to have been around 65 million, although it exceeded

130 million by the turn of the following century and soared to 150 million by 1600 (Ho 1959). Another drastic decline seems to have occurred in the mid-seventeenth century, which may have reduced the population to 83 million in 1651 (Wu 1988). Momentum was regained during the eighteenth century by the end of which the population had tripled, reaching 313.2 million in 1795. By comparison, China's population in 1686 was only 101.7 million.

Scholars have attributed some of these drastic population declines to epidemics. Twitchett (1979), for example, argues that epidemics had some effect upon demographic trends in the seventh, eighth, and ninth centuries, and might have been one major reason for population stagnation before the tenth century. It is also tempting to attribute the mysterious but real decline of population in north China during the fourteenth century to plague, as does William McNeill (1976). Some scholars would go even further by hypothesizing that plague was ravaging northern China as early as the thirteenth century. The beginning of the century saw a series of epidemics in Hebei and Shanxi, and then an epidemic struck Kaifeng (Henan) in 1232, reportedly killing nearly 1 million people within 50 or 60 days (Fan 1986).

Moving to the late Ming period, of the sixteenth and seventeenth centuries, H. Dunstan's (1975) preliminary survey of epidemics suggests that these catastrophes also had long-term effects on population growth and that the prosperity of the ensuing early and middle Qing dynasty was the result of an easing of pressure on land resources brought about by huge die-offs from disease, as well as from war and famine around the middle of the seventeenth century.

Yet the question of the impact of disease on China's population remains controversial because of different interpretations of demographic sources (Cartier and Will 1971; Bielenstein 1975; Wang 1988). Also remaining is the question of how regional differences in population development can be related to local epidemics. Natural catastrophes like epidemics or famines were usually local rather than widespread occurrences and of smaller magnitude and shorter duration than impressionistic accounts have led many to believe. In fact, it could be argued that they were unlikely to have had long-term demographic impact (Watkins and Menken 1985).

Thus, it is perhaps most reasonable to see the presence or absence of epidemic disease in China as just one of the determining factors in long-term population growth. The unprecedented upsurge in population during the Song period (eleventh to thirteenth centuries) is generally believed to be closely related to a series of revolutionary changes in agriculture in the more developed southern regions, especially with rice growing. The period witnessed the introduction of early-ripening rice as well as improvements in irrigation and other agricultural technologies all of which greatly increased land productivity (Ho 1959, 1969; Bray 1984). The next upsurge in population, however, was from the eighteenth century onward, a period in which there was no comparable technological revolution. Could the "stagnation" between the two upsurges be explained by differing mortality rates in which infectious diseases had a role?

Stagnations in "preindustrialized" populations occurred when high or moderately high fertility rates were balanced by similarly high mortality rates resulting from uncertain food supplies and unavoidable diseases. It is generally agreed that in Asia, where marriage was early and nearly universal, fertility was higher than in preindustrialized western and northern Europe, where women married late and forced celibacy was more common (Coale 1986). Therefore, a stagnation in population development in China can best be explained by high "normal" mortality rates.

Subsistence crises were always a constant threat to the Chinese, which, by causing undernutrition (if not death from starvation), reduced their resistance to disease. The prevalence of dysenteries, *shanghan* (discussed earlier), and respiratory diseases might be an indication of general dietary deficiencies (Polunin 1976). Certainly, beriberi, which was often discussed in the family encyclopedias, could cause death directly or indirectly by leaving the individual less able to resist diseases, whereas infantile beriberi has proven to be a major killer of nursing infants in thiamine-deficient populations.

In addition, parasitic diseases probably killed millions of peasants because the use of human feces as fertilizer was a universal practice for centuries. Flooded rice fields were also breeding grounds of mosquitoes – the carriers of malaria and other infections. In addition to malnutrition and agricultural practices, poor hygienic conditions, especially in some of the southern provinces and frontier regions, must also have been an important factor in encouraging insect-borne diseases like malaria and plague. Other important factors that could account for high morbidity rates, especially in urban centers in the late Ming period, were the absence of sewage and water control, and the inflow of masses of vagrants from poorer areas to the centers who were most likely carriers of contagious diseases (Liang 1986; Leung 1987a).

Thus, with fertility rates already high, the demographic upsurge of the eighteenth century is best explained by a remarkable decline in mortality. At least the initial stage of the upsurge can be explained in terms of mortality decline, although subsequent increases in populations were likely to have been generated largely by the internal dynamics of an already huge population. The industrialization of the period was neither important nor modern enough to cause a significant rise in tuberculosis.

Ann Jannetta (1987) suggests that the practice of infanticide and abortion in Tokugawa Japan was a sign of attempts to control fertility because of an already slowly declining mortality. This may also have been the cause in China, for it was the case from the late seventeenth century onward that foundling homes were widely established, possibly reflecting increasing infanticide and child abandonment. Interestingly, the only precursor to this movement was in the thirteenth century when China experienced its first population boom (Leung 1985).

Decline in Chinese Mortality

Why then did mortality decline? Ho Ping-ti's (1959, 1978) findings on the introduction of new crops from the Americas during the sixteenth century provide us with one of the more persuasive answers. These easy-to-grow crops – for example, sweet and white potatoes and maize – may well have substantially stabilized food supplies for the poor in less fertile and mountainous regions. D. H. Perkins (1969), however, suggests that changing cropping patterns and rising traditional capital inputs increased crop yields per acre. Either way an improved food supply was certain to have reduced the chances of starvation for the people and consequently their susceptibility to various diseases.

Some would argue that long-term climatological evolution was the main factor: the post–fifteenth-century population growth, its decline in the mid-seventeenth century, as well as the explosion in the eighteenth century, all corresponded to climate changes of the time (Eastman 1988). Here even the changes in food production and the disease factor can be considered as affected by the climate.

Another important factor that should be considered is that in its earliest stages, a mortality decline is the result of lowered mortality rates for the young. This was the case in modern Europe and in Japanese-occupied Taiwan (Chen 1982; Riley 1986).

The health of the mother is an important variable in infant mortality, whereas better resistance to childhood diseases typically explains a reduced mortality in children over one year of age. Surely mother's education and infant mortality are directly related; however, the relationship is impossible to verify in this period. In addition, the lowering of mortality in children in modern Europe and early twentieth-century Taiwan was closely linked to the improvement in general hygiene (Chen 1982; Riley 1986). Unfortunately, it would be mere speculation to say anything about the improvement in the hygienic conditions (especially the provision of clean water for drinking, washing, and bathing) in premodern China at this stage, and in any event, there must have been enormous regional differences.

However, the early practice of variolation against smallpox is a possible factor in explaining the decline in Chinese mortality. An eighteenth-century smallpox specialist, for example, claimed that over 80 percent of the children of wealthy families in China had been inoculated (Leung 1987b). On the other hand, the majority of children were not inoculated, and clearly, no single factor is likely to serve as an explanation. Avenues of research that may prove fruitful in examining the question of reduced infant and child mortality include changing concepts of pregnancy, childbirth, and infancy (Leung 1984; Furth 1987); the attitudes behind the nationwide establishment of foundling homes; improved hygiene and immunization; and traditional diet therapy based on the humoral dimensions, and the whole folk nutritional science built largely on empirical observation (Anderson 1988).

If we are uncertain of the positive effects of new developments in agriculture, new crops, or variolation on reducing mortality, we can at least be confident that diseases no longer hindered long-term population growth, and that the contribution of disease to the mortality rate was no longer as great as it had been in the past, despite the introduction of some new diseases from the sixteenth century onward. Improved therapy and medication may have played a limited role in reducing the importance of disease, as, for example, the increasing use of herbal-based drugs (before the introduction of quinine in the eighteenth century) to fight malaria instead of the more dangerous arsenicals used in the Ming–Qing period (Miyasita 1979). But like variolation, the effects of herbal-based drugs, probably only used by small sections of the population, are difficult to estimate.

Certain institutional changes may have had some indirect effects on mortality rates. The Song state in the twelfth and thirteenth centuries took responsibility for providing medical help to the poor through public pharmacies. The Mongol dynasty continued this tradition by creating a nationwide system of "medical schools" to train local doctors. Yet, the tradition began to decline in the late fourteenth century, and by the late sixteenth century such institutions had largely disappeared. To some extent, this void was filled by local philanthropists who took responsibility for providing regular medical help to the needy from the seventeenth century on. They organized charitable dispensaries that provided the local people with medical care and medicines, and sometimes decent burials for the dead. These public but nonstate medical organizations could be found in many urban centers in the eighteenth and nineteenth centuries (Leung 1987a), and the free or very cheap medical treatment offered must have provided at least a minimum of necessary care to the urban poor. Moreover, the burying of dead bodies collected from the streets also helped to upgrade the sanitary conditions of these urban centers. According to an 1860 report by the American Presbyterian missionary in Shanghai, John Kerr, the local charitable dispensary, which was staffed by eight or nine Chinese physicians, was visited daily by 300 to 500 individuals "of all classes" (Kerr 1861).

After weighing the many changes that together brought about the mortality decline in China, we find it probable that an improved supply of food, which strengthened the nutritional status of the general population, was the most important factor from the late seventeenth century onward. The spread of variolation and an increasingly denser network of charitable dispensaries in the same period may also have contributed to a reduction in mortality, especially in southern China. Improved hygiene and child care practices were also probably important factors in bringing about what seems to have been a decline in infant mortality rates, but this has yet to be demonstrated.

Chinese Medicine

Discussion of some prominent features of Chinese medicine and the traditional reaction of the people toward disease will help us understand the Chinese system and allow us to gauge its relative effectiveness from the modern point of view. Quarantine, which was a common practice in Europe from the fifteenth century onward, was never widely practiced in China. There were, however, instances of isolation of individuals for certain diseases such as smallpox and especially leprosy.

Apparently, lepers were put into "lazaretto"-type hospices as early as the Qin dynasty (221–207 B.C.), and examples of such institutions are also found in sixth-century sources (Xie 1983). Unfortunately, there is no systematic documentation relating to hospices, and there is only sporadic mention of them in later sources. In the mid-nineteenth century, for example, we know that leper hospices existed in eastern Guangdong, where interned lepers were allowed to marry only among themselves. Moreover, their offspring were freed only after the third generation, when the genetic "poison" was believed to be exhausted (Liang 1982). In the same period, leper hospices were also organized by overseas Chinese communities in Batavia (Yang 1842).

As for smallpox-quarantine measures, there is at least one instance on record. In 1645, when the Manchus had just conquered Peking, they decreed that all smallpox victims and their families be banished 40 *li* (about 3 miles) from the city wall. The policy was still in force in 1655 (Hopkins 1983; Leung 1987a). Yet, as noted above, these were exceptional instances, and it is difficult to understand the Chinese lack of interest in quarantine (Leung 1987a). Ethics, however, probably had something to do with it. Moralists like Zhu Xi of the twelfth century, for example, condemned the "abandoning" of one's relatives and friends who fell victim to contagious diseases. Rather, one should risk infection by remaining behind to care for the sick, and there existed some conviction that moral power thus manifested would somehow keep the epidemic spirit away (*Huizhoufu zhi* 1502). On the other hand, the concept that diseases were caused by broad environmental influences – ether or vital energy (*qi*), wind (*feng*), fire or heat (*huo*), and water (Xie 1983) – would also seem to have discouraged quarantine measures.

Chinese medicine as a body of knowledge to fight disease never developed into a "science" as it did in Europe from the seventeenth century onward. For the scholar, medicine was a respectable field of study linked to philosophy, although the practicing physician was not accorded a high social status (Hymes 1987; Leung 1987a). Medical skills were transmitted within families and not by government-authorized institutions. The Imperial Academy of Medicine (*taiyiyuan*) trained doctors only for government service and for the imperial family, and had no obligation to standardize medical knowledge or control the medical profession. Under such circumstances, medicine had a tendency to become "democratized," because all educated people had access to medical literature.

Popular Ming–Qing almanacs and encyclopedias must also have reinforced this trend (Leung 1987a).

As in premodern Europe, peddler-doctors, self-trained midwives, women-pharmacists and other "heterodox" healers flourished especially in the countryside. Women and children were often treated by female healers exclusively (Leung 1987a). In 1759, a book on the principles and practices of peddler-doctors, *A Collection of Proper Methods* (*Chuanya*), was published by the scholar-pharmaceutist Zhao Xuemin. The work was based on his interviews with a peddler-doctor and reveals a long tradition of popular healing that relied heavily on acupuncture, purging either through *ding* (provoked vomiting) or *chuan* (provoked diarrhea), and other methods (*jie*) that aimed at stopping symptoms instantly. Yet healers who practiced these "violent" methods were the lowest stratum in a system that emphasized memorization of abstract theories from the medical classics, subtle diagnosis, and a long and respectable family tradition of medical practice.

More often than not during epidemics, state financial aid was used for buying coffins to bury the dead (Leung 1987a), and people, high and low alike, commonly resorted to rituals and shamanistic practices when illness struck. Indeed, healing by charms and amulets (*zhuyou ke*), which had its roots in antiquity, was part of the curriculum of the Imperial Academy of Medicine since Tang times. Diseases and especially epidemic diseases were firmly believed to be caused by unpacified ghosts and spirits of the locality; thus rituals were essential in disease avoidance (*Huangchao jingshi wenbian* 1897). Individuals afflicted by illness were likely to ask help from various deities, or to correct moral faults that were believed to be the source of the physical corruption (Leung 1987a).

Such fatalistic attitudes toward illness and lack of total confidence in medicine should not be cause for surprise. To a certain extent, this behavior is still prevalent among the Chinese populace today.

Angela Ki Che Leung

Bibliography

Anderson, E. N. 1988. *The food of China*. New Haven, Conn.

Benedict, C. 1988. Bubonic plague in nineteenth-century China. *Modern China* 14.2: 107–55.

Bielenstein, H. 1975. Review on the article of Cartier & Will. *T'oung Pao* 61: 181–5.

Bois, G. 1984. *The crisis of feudalism: Economy and society in eastern Normandy c. 1300–1550*. Cambridge.

Bray, F. 1984. *Agriculture*. Vol. 6 of Part II of *Science and civilisation in China*, ed. J. Needham. Cambridge.

Cartier, M., and P.-E. Will. 1971. Démographie et institutions en Chine: Contribution à l'analyse des recensements de l'époque impériale (2 ap. J.-C. – 1750). *Annales de Démographie Historique* 1: 162–245.

Chen B.-x. 1981. *Zhongguo yixue shi* (History of Chinese medicine). Taipei.

Chen S.-k. 1981. *Zhogguo jibing shi* (History of Chinese diseases). Taipei.

Chen S.-x. 1982. *Taiwan di renkou bianqian yu shehui bianqian* (Population and social change in Taiwan). Taipei.

Coale, A. J. 1986. The decline of fertility in Europe since the eighteenth century as a chapter in human demographic history. In *The decline of fertility in Europe,* ed. A. J. Coale & S. C. Watkins, 1–30. Princeton.

Dunstan, H. 1975. The late Ming epidemics: A preliminary survey. *Ch'ing-shih wen-t'i* 3.3: 1–59.

Eastman, L. E. 1988. *Family, fields and ancestors: Constancy and change in China's social and economic history, 1550–1949.* Oxford.

Fan X.-z. 1953. *Zhongguo yufang yixue sixian shi* (History of immunization in China). Shanghai.

—— 1986. *Zhongguo yixue shilue* (A brief history of Chinese medicine). Peking.

Furth, C. 1987. Concepts of pregnancy, childbirth, and infancy in Ch'ing dynasty China. *Journal of Asian Studies* 46.1: 7–35.

Ho P.-t. 1959. *Studies on the population of China, 1368–1900.* Cambridge.

—— 1969. *Huangtu yu Zhongguo nongye di qiyuan* (The Loess and the origin of Chinese agriculture). Hong Kong.

—— 1978. Meizhou zuowu di yinjin, chuanbo ji qi dui Zhongguo liangshi shengchan di yingxiang (The introduction of American crops and their impact on Chinese food productivity). In *Dagong Bao zai Gang fukan sanshi zhounian jinian wenji* (Volume to celebrate the 30th anniversary of the re-publication of the Dagong Bao in Hong Kong), 673–731. Hong Kong.

Hopkins, D. 1983. *Princes and peasants: Smallpox in history.* Chicago.

Huangchao jingshi wenbian (Collection of works on practical administration of the country). 1897. 1972 facsimile edition (Taipei) of the original.

Huizhoufu zhi (Gazetteer of Huizhou prefecture). 1502. 1987 facsimile edition (Taipei) of the original Huizhou edition.

Hymes, R. 1987. Not quite gentlemen? Doctors in Sung and Yuan. *Chinese Science* 8: 9–76.

Jannetta, A. B. 1987. *Epidemics and mortality in early modern Japan.* Princeton.

Kerr, J. 1861. *Report of the medical missionary for the year 1860.* (Pamphlet). Report for Canton hospital. Canton.

Kinnear, H. N. 1909. *The annual report of Ponasang Missionary Hospital.* Foochow.

Leung, K. C. 1984. Autour de la naissance: la mère et l'enfant en Chine aux XVIe et XVIIe siècles. *Cahiers Internationaux de Sociologie* 74: 51–69.

—— 1985. L'Accueil des enfants abandonnés dans la Chine du bas-Yangzi aux XVIIe et XVIIIe siècles. *Etudes chinoises* 4.1: 15–54.

—— 1987a. Organized medicine in Ming–Qing China: State and private medical institutions in the lower Yangzi region. *Late Imperial China* 8.1: 134–66.

—— 1987b. Mingqing yufang tianhua cuoshi zhi yanbian (Smallpox prevention in the Ming and Qing dynasties). In *Guoshi shilun* (Collection of essays on Chinese history), 239–54. Taipei.

Liang Q.-z. (Leung, K. C.) 1986. Mingmo Qingchu minjian cishan huodong di xingqi (Rise of private charitable activities during the late Ming and early Qing period). *Shih-huo Monthly* 15.7/8: 52–79.

Liang S.-r. 1982. *Liang ban qiuyu an suibi* (Notes of the Two Autumn Rains Study). Shanghai (original edition, 1837).

McNeill, W. 1976. *Plagues and peoples.* New York.

Miyasita, S. 1979. Malaria (*yao*) in Chinese medicine during the Chin and Yuan periods. *Acta Asiatica* 36: 90–112.

Perkins, D. H. 1969. *Agricultural development in China 1368–1968.* Chicago.

Peter, J.-P. 1972. Malades et maladies à la fin du XVIIIe siècle. In *Médicins, climat et épidemies à la fin du XVIIIe siècle,* ed. Jean-Paul Desaive et al., 135–70. Paris.

Polunin, I. 1976. Disease, morbidity, and mortality in China, India, and the Arab world. In *Asian medical systems: A comparative study,* ed. C. Leslie, 120–32. California.

Riley, J.C. 1986. Insects and the European mortality decline. *The American Historical Review* 91(4): 833–58.

Twitchett, D. 1979. Population and pestilence in T'ang China. In *Studia Sino-Mongolica: Festschrift für Herbert Franke,* ed. Wolfgang Bauer, 42–53. Wiesbaden.

Wang Q.-j. 1988. Ming chu quan guo renkou kao (Survey on the national population at the beginning of the Ming dynasty). *Lishi yanjiu* (Historical research) I: 181–90.

Watkins, S. C., and J. Menken. 1985. Famines in historical perspective. *Population and Development Review* 11.4: 647–75.

Winfield, G.F. 1948. *China: The land and the people.* New York.

Wu, H. 1988. Qing dai renkou di jiliang wenti (Quantitative problems in Qing demography). *Zhongguo shehui jingji shi yanjiu* (Research on Chinese social and economic history) I: 46–52.

Xie X.-a. 1983. Zhongguo gudai dui jibing chuanran xing di renshi (Concepts of disease contagion in old China). *Zhonghua yishi zazhi* (Journal of Chinese Medical History) 13(4): 193–203.

Yang B.-n. 1842. *Hailu* (Record of the seas). 1984 facsimile edition (Taipei) of the original edition.

Zhou Y.-h. 1983. A study of China's population during the Qing dynasty. *Social Sciences in China*, 61–105.

VI.3
Diseases of the Modern Period in China

Overview

Modern China, with a 1985 population of 1.04 billion (*World Development Report* 1987), is by far the most populous country on earth, though its surface area of 9.56 million square kilometers ranks it third in size (behind the former Soviet Union and Canada). Ninety-five percent of the population live on less than 50 percent of the total area, primarily along the great river systems of the east and southeast, and only 22 percent of those in the population are classified as urban residents. The climate covers a broad range of patterns, extending from the hot, humid, and wet provinces in the south and southeast to those provinces in the north and northwest, which are for the most part dry and subject to hot summers and cold winters. By 1985 China's per capita gross national product in current dollars was estimated at U.S. $310 (*World Development Report* 1987). Approximately 33 percent of the gross domestic product was derived from agriculture, down from about 39 percent in 1965. An estimated 74 percent of the labor force was in agriculture, 14 percent in industry, and 12 percent in services in 1980 (*World Development Report* 1987).

China's population growth has slowed dramatically. In 1956, Ma Yin-chu, China's well-known economic expert, urged the government to introduce population control, and to slow down population growth. But China's leader, Mao Zedong (Mao Tsetung) rejected this advice vehemently. In 1965, however, the slogan was "*yige bushao, liangge zhenghao, sange duole*" ("One [child] is not too few, two [children] are just right, three are many"). By 1972, population control was justified by eugenic arguments: "quality instead of quantity." The slogan was (and still continues) *shaosheng yousheng* ("few births but superior births"; or "few lives but superior lives"). A policy announced in 1978 was designed to achieve a stable population at the 1.13 billion level by the year 2000, and in 1979 the one-

child policy was introduced. From 1965 to 1980, the annual population growth rate averaged 2.2 percent; and from 1980 to 1985, 1.2 percent. Owing to a slower rate of decline in the birth rate it is now estimated that China's population may stabilize at 1.6 billion by around the middle of the twenty-first century.

By 1985, life expectancy at birth was estimated to reach 69 years, and infant mortality had dropped to about 35 per 1,000 according to the World Bank (1987). In specific regions, however, the rates were quite different. In the *People's Daily* of April 26, 1989, the government admits that in about 300 of the poorer regions infant mortality averages 100 per 1,000. UNICEF estimates infant mortality rates at 190 per 1,000 for Tibet.

Despite a large number of small nationality groups who speak many different languages, China has a relatively homogeneous population. Approximately 93 percent of the population are Han, or ethnic Chinese. Most of China's peoples speak one of the two major spoken languages, which, though quite different, share the same written characters.

Patterns of Disease

China has been witness to one of the most rapid and profound changes in health patterns that has ever occurred in recorded history. This chapter gives primary consideration to the disease patterns present in China in the 1980s; however, to place current events in context, one must start with a brief description of the social, economic, and health situations that prevailed in 1949, the year the People's Republic was proclaimed.

Midcentury China emerged from yet another of what must seem to the Chinese a near endless cycle of natural and human-made disasters, in this case, more than two decades of foreign invasion, occupation, and civil war. The country was completely exhausted. The World Bank estimated that in 1950 the Chinese population was 603 million; the birth rate, 42 per 1,000; the death rate, 33.5; the infant mortality rate, 252; and life expectancy at birth, 32 years (*World Development Report* 1987). With a very low per capita income and an extremely limited health-care system, the predominant diseases were those associated with malnutrition and communicable disease.

China's disease patterns have changed so rapidly since the 1950s that it is helpful to compare the present situation with that estimated, by much less complete statistics, at around the time of the declaration of the People's Republic in 1949. The first two sections look at the causes of mortality and morbidity, with a brief consideration of regional variations, and the last section looks at selected causes of disease, especially those that are unusually prevalent in China. Unless otherwise indicated, disease-specific data are from the 1984 World Bank report entitled *China: The Health Sector.* This source, as well as the 1986 publication *Public Health in the People's Republic of China,* relies primarily on official Ministry of Public Health data sources, which are still subject to numerous limitations in both coverage and quality despite many improvements since the 1950s. The reader will therefore need to interpret the reported findings with caution.

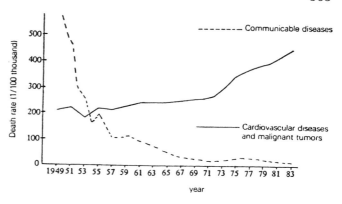

Figure VI.3.1. Mortality rates for the urban population of Shanghai, 1949–83. (From *Public Health in the People's Republic of China* (1986), p. 86.)

Mortality

Good historical data on mortality for all of China are not available. Figure VI.3.1, based on data from the urban population of Shanghai, China's largest city, dramatically depicts the shift from mortality due largely to communicable disease, to a situation in which cardiovascular disease and malignant tumors predominate. The 10 leading causes of death in selected cities in 1957 and in both urban and rural areas in 1984 are listed in Table VI.3.1. The top three causes of death in 1957, all communicable diseases, accounted for

32.3 percent of all deaths, whereas by 1984 they amounted to less than 10 percent. By 1984 the top three causes – heart disease, cancer, and stroke – accounted for 64.9 percent of urban deaths and 54.9 percent of those in rural areas. Collectively, the top 10 causes accounted for almost 90 percent of all deaths in 1984, as compared with only two-thirds of those in 1957.

Wide interprovincial variations exist in the death rates due to the top three causes (see Table VI.3.2). Although these are likely explained in part by reporting errors and age differences, they are probably

Table VI.3.1. *Leading causes of death, selected cities and counties of Shanghai, 1957 and 1984*

13 cities (1957)			28 cities (1984)			70 counties (1984)		
Cause	Rate[a]	Percent[b]	Cause	Rate[a]	Percent[b]	Cause	Rate[a]	Percent[b]
Respiratory disease	120.3	16.9	Heart disease	124.6	22.7	Heart disease	158.5	24.6
Communicable disease	56.6	7.9	Cerebrovascular disease	116.3	21.1	Cerebrovascular disease	98.8	15.3
Pulmonary TB	54.6	7.5	Malignant tumors	116.2	21.1	Malignant tumors	97.0	15.0
Digestive disease	52.1	7.3	Respiratory disease	48.4	8.8	Respiratory disease	78.5	12.2
Heart disease	47.2	6.6	Digestive disease	23.8	4.3	Digestive disease	36.4	5.6
Cerebrovascular disease	39.0	5.5	Trauma	19.4	3.5	Trauma	27.6	4.3
Malignant tumors	36.9	5.2	Pulmonary TB	10.2	1.9	Pulmonary TB	26.9	4.2
Nervous disease	29.1	4.1	Intoxication	10.2	1.9	Intoxication	20.8	3.2
Trauma/intoxication	19.0	2.7	Urinary disease	9.5	1.7	Communicable disease	15.3	2.4
Other TB	14.1	2.0	Communicable disease	8.1	1.5	Neonatal disease[c]	79.5	.2
Total	468.9	65.7	Total	486.7	88.5	Total	639.3	87.0

[a]Deaths per 100,000 population.

[b]Percent of total deaths.

[c]Deaths per 1,000 newborns.

Source: Adapted from *Public Health in the People's Republic of China* (1986), table 4, p. 86.

Table VI.3.2. *Leading provincial causes of death in China, 1985*

	Cause #1	Cause #2	Cause #3
East China			
Anhui Province	Accidents (90)[a]	Respiratory (85)	Heart (83)
Fujian Province	Cancer (91)	Heart (83)	Respiratory (82)
Jiangsu Province	Cancer (122)	Respiratory (98)	Heart (85)
Shandong Province	Respiratory (128)	Cancer (77)	Heart (73)
Shanghai Municipality	Cancer (105)	Stroke (101)	Heart (97)
Zhejiang Province	Cancer (102)	Respiratory (99)	Heart (97)
West China			
Gansu Province	Communicable (96)	Respiratory (93)	Digestive (77)
Ningxia Aut. Region	Respiratory (13)	Communicable (116)	Congenital (101)
Qinghai Province	Communicable (157)	Respiratory (152)	Heart (101)
Xinjiang Aut. Region	Respiratory (164)	Communicable (129)	Heart (116)
Xizang (Tibet) Aut. Region	Respiratory (153)	Heart (152)	Digestive (100)
Northeast China			
Heilongjiang Province	Heart (148)	Respiratory (67)	Stroke (57)
Jilin Province	Heart (188)	Respiratory (83)	Stroke (78)
Liaoning Province	Heart (131)	Respiratory (81)	Cancer (72)
North Central China			
Beijing Municipality	Heart (165)	Stroke (137)	Cancer (76)
Hebei Province	Heart (182)	Stroke (101)	Cancer (98)
Henan Province	Heart (120)	Respiratory (115)	Cancer (93)
Nei Mongol (Inner Mongolia) Aut. Region	Heart (162)	Respiratory (101)	Cancer (68)
Shaanxi Province	Respiratory (125)	Heart (125)	Cancer (83)
Shanxi Province	Heart (168)	Respiratory (107)	Cancer (106)
Tianjin Municipality	Heart (147)	Stroke (129)	Cancer (79)
South Central China			
Hubei Province	Respiratory (115)	Accidents (106)	Heart (93)
Hunan Province	Respiratory (138)	Heart (112)	Accidents (90)
Jiangxi Province	Respiratory (125)	Heart (113)	Accidents (90)
Southwest China			
Sichuan Province	Heart (162)	Respiratory (153)	Accidents (101)
Yunan Province	Respiratory (200)	Heart (147)	Communicable (113)
South China			
Guizhou Province	Respiratory (258)	Communicable (168)	Digestive (137)
Guangdong Province	Respiratory (74)	Cancer (57)	TB (18)
Guangxi Aut. Region	— [b]	Respiratory (79)	TB (57)

[a]The numbers in parentheses refer to the death rate per 100,000.
[b]The classification of causes of death in Guangxi differs from that in other regions; the leading cause of death in Guangxi in 1985 was "aging and feebleness," and the deaths attributed to this cause were omitted from the source table.
Source: Based on data in *Public Health in the People's Republic of China* (1986), table 3, p. 94.

also due to regional differences in environmental, nutritional, and other factors. Heart disease death rates are highest in the northern provinces, ranging from a high of 188 per 100,000 population in Jilin Province down to 73 in Shandong. Cancer rates are highest in the east, ranging from 122 in Jiangsu to 57 in Guangdong.

Morbidity

Communicable diseases reported for 1985 are given in Table VI.3.3. Though these estimates, especially for the less serious illnesses, are likely very much underreported, they do give some notion of the relative frequency with which the various conditions are reported to the authorities.

Table VI.3.3. *Communicable diseases in China, 1985*

	Number of cases	Number of deaths
Cholera	6	2
Cerebrospinal fever	654	7
Diphtheria	1,423	184
Dysentery	3,280,596	2,352
Encephalitis B	29,065	2,433
Epidemic hemorrhagic fever	103,778	3,111
Forest tick-borne encephalitis	270	15
Influenza	3,407,383	361
Leishmaniasis	145	1
Leptospirosis	26,632	544
Malaria	563,400	44
Measles	418,159	2,654
Pertussis	147,298	237
Plague	6	1
Poliomyelitis	1,537	95
Scarlet fever	61,591	17
Tsutsugamushi disease	1,695	6
Typhoid and paratyphoid fever	86,482	251
Viral hepatitis	794,269	2,313

Source: Excerpted from *Public Health in the People's Republic of China* (1986), table 13, p. 218.

No national data exist on causes of morbidity or reasons for seeking health care, but a 1981 study of 737 households in Shanghai County (Parker et al. 1982) provides some indication of what illness patterns may be like. On the basis of a 2-week recall it was estimated that area residents annually averaged 6.0 days of restricted activity, 2.4 days in bed, 7.6 days lost from work, and 2.6 days lost from school. There were 44 hospitalizations per 1,000 respondents per year, and every 2 weeks there were 156 morbidity conditions, 49 cases of acute disability, and 187 primary care visits. In a survey of 3,122 people, 499 ill persons experienced 487 conditions. The percentages reporting the five leading conditions were as follows: respiratory, 27.3; gastrointestinal, 14.4; cardiovascular, 13.3; musculoskeletal, 7.8; and nervous system, 5.1.

Communicable Diseases

Parasitic Diseases

Ancylostomiasis and Ascariasis. Estimates of the 1945–59 period suggest that up to 100 million people in China have had intestinal infestation with parasites causing ancylostomiasis (the hookworm) or ascariasis (the roundworm). Ancylostomiasis remains prevalent in 14 southern provinces, and ascariasis is widespread in most of China. Improved environmental sanitation and night soil management have reduced the prevalence of both parasites, but the limited information available indicates that both remain a public health concern.

Filariasis. In the 1950s, filariasis, transmitted by a mosquito vector, was said to have affected between 20 million and 30 million people. By 1958, more than 700,000 patients had been treated, and the Patriotic Health Movement led to major improvement of environmental sanitation in many localities and to widespread extermination of mosquitoes. Shandong Province, with a population of 75 million, had eradicated the disease by 1983, and by 1985 about 76 percent of China's endemic areas were essentially disease free. In the mid-1980s filariasis was prevalent in 864 counties and cities in 14 provinces, autonomous regions, and municipalities. Slightly over half of the jurisdictions were endemic with Bancroftian filariasis, about one-fourth were endemic with Malayan filariasis, and the rest had mixed infections.

Leishmaniasis (Kala-Azar). A 1951 survey showed the area of China endemic for visceral leishmaniasis to be entirely north of the Yangtze River, covering 1.2 million square kilometers. Prevalence was 1 to 5 per 1,000, with an estimated 530,000 cases, most of whom were children. Destruction of dogs and treatment of human cases with a specially produced antimony drug played a major role in decreasing transmission. Reduction in incidence may also have resulted from a decline in the sandfly vector due to insecticide spraying for both sandflies and malarial mosquitoes. Since 1958, kala-azar outbreaks have become sporadic, with fewer than 100 cases reported every year.

Malaria. Prior to 1949, malaria incidence in China was estimated at more than 30,000,000 new cases annually (5 per 100 people), with 300,000 deaths (a 1 percent case-fatality rate). Seventy percent of China's counties were endemic for malaria in the early 1950s. Surveys in 1957 reported 70 percent prevalence among children in Guangdong and 48 percent in counties in Yunnan. Vigorous efforts to control mosquito breeding sites – consisting of environmental management, mass chemoprophylaxis during the transmission period, and mass treatment – caused disease rates to fall rapidly in the 1950s.

Since 1974, the five provinces of Jiangsu, Shandong, Henan, Anhui, and Hubei, which together account for about 80 percent of the national total of malaria cases and which represent the main tertian malaria areas, have worked jointly to bring the disease under control. In 1985, the number of new cases in the five provinces was 350,000, compared to the 14 million cases recorded in 1973 before the joint prevention and control measures were taken. Overall, approximately one third of China's population is now living in malaria-free areas, another third in areas with minimum risk, and the remaining third in endemic areas. The 563,400 cases reported for all of China in 1985 represent an incidence of approximately 5 per 10,000 population, close to the goal of under 1 per 10,000 by the year 2000.

Schistosomiasis. Schistosomiasis japonica, the form of the disease found in China, is prevalent in the provinces of Shanghai, Jiangsu, Zhejiang, Anhui, Fujian, Guangdong, Guangxi, Hunan, Hubei, Yunnan, Sichuan, and Jiangxi. It is carried by snails and is endemic in three types of environments: water courses, hilly regions, and lakes and marshlands. Water courses account for 8 percent of the endemic areas and 33 percent of the patients; comparable values are 10 and 26 percent for hilly regions, and 82 and 41 percent for the lake and marshlands areas.

Control efforts have been deployed on a large scale. In December 1955, China set up prevention and control stations in epidemic areas, and by 1958, 197 stations were staffed by more than 1,200 medical teams and 17,000 specialized personnel (Chien 1958). By 1985, there were only 371 endemic counties with a total of 11.6 million cases and 14,000 square kilometers of snail-infested areas. During the early stage of the nationwide prevention and control program, infestation rates typically ranged from 20 to 30 percent and in some areas reached 40 percent. Of those affected, about 40 percent were symptomatic and about 5 percent evidenced advanced illness. Cattle and other domestic animals were also seriously afflicted by the disease.

The elimination of snails has been a key objective of the program through such measures as draining marshlands, digging new ditches and filling up old ones, changing paddies into dry crops, tractor ploughing, field rolling, building snail trenches, and killing snails by chemical methods. The construction of dikes and the use of chemicals have proved very effective along the banks of the Yangtze River in Jiangsu Province.

Efforts to reduce the source of infection have included early detection and treatment of patients at all stages of the disease, with emphasis on those who handle diseased animals. People in snail-infested areas are encouraged to wear protective gear and take prophylactic medicines when coming into contact with water. Measures are also taken to ensure the safe collection and use of feces, and to encourage the use of safe water supplies.

By the end of 1985, schistosomiasis was declared officially eradicated in Shanghai and Guangdong, while Fujian, Jiangsu, and Guangxi have virtually eradicated the disease with more than 98 percent of the endemic areas cleared of snails and over 90 percent of the known patients cured. Among the 371 endemic counties and cities, 110 have been declared eradicated and 161 have almost eradicated the disease. In the remaining 100 counties and cities, more than 50 percent of the townships and about two-thirds of the villages have eradicated or almost eradicated the disease. Accomplishments by 1985 included the following: 95 percent of the 11.6 million patients were treated; 77 percent of the infested area was cleared of snails; and 92 percent of the 1.2 million head of afflicted cattle were treated or disposed of.

Despite these gains, concerns are being expressed by Chinese and foreign schistosomiasis experts about the future. UNICEF's Situation Analysis for China of 1989 estimated that schistosomiasis was still present in 12 provinces with a combined population of 50,000,000 and that the total of old cases approached 1,000,000 to which several thousand new cases were added annually (UNICEF 1989). The schistosomiasis control problem seems to have shifted over the decades from that of devising methods to control a major endemic parasitic disease to that of identifying the few lightly infected individuals in a sea of negatives, and ensuring that past gains are maintained without backsliding (Basch 1986).

Nonparasitic Diseases

Acquired Immune Deficiency Syndrome (AIDS). As of August 1989, China had reported only 22 human immunodeficiency virus (HIV)-infected individuals and three cases of AIDS. All were foreigners except for four Chinese who were infected through contaminated blood products (*China Daily,* Sept. 7, 1989). The first indigenous case acquired through homosexual contact with a foreigner was reported in late 1989 (*China Daily,* Nov. 2, 1989). Persons from areas of high endemicity who wish to extend their visa stay beyond a limited period of time are required to have a test for HIV antibodies performed in China, and must leave China immediately if the test is positive. By December 1990 (*China Daily,* Dec. 31, 1990), China had identified a total of 446 HIV-positive cases, since it started monitoring the epidemic in 1985, including 68 persons "from overseas."

Cholera. Cholera was said to be "virtually eliminated" by 1960 (Lampton 1977), and in 1985 only six cases and two fatalities were reported. More recent data from the Ministry of Public Health suggest that the disease is again of some importance, perhaps in part owing to better reporting. In 1989, the Ministry of Public Health reported that cholera still threatens residents of Hainan, Zhejiang, and Guandong provinces, a part of suburban Shanghai, and Guangxi Zhuang Autonomous Region. In 1988 more than 3,000 cholera cases were reported, but cases dropped to about 1,000 by the end of 1989 (*China Daily* 1989).

Dengue. The first recognized dengue epidemic since 1949 occurred in Guangdong Province between June and September 1978, with an estimated 20,000 cases affecting persons of all ages. Approximately 25 percent had hemorrhagic manifestations. Because the usual vector, the *Aedes aegypti* mosquito, is thought to be absent from this area of China, suspicion has focused on the *Aedes albopictus.* Epidemiologists who investigated this epidemic assumed that refugees from Vietnam (estimated to exceed 200,000) imported the virus. Another dengue outbreak occurred on Hainan Island in 1980, and sporadic cases continued until 1982. Transmitted by the *A. aegypti* mosquito, the epidemic resulted in a peak morbidity rate of 2,146 per 10,000 and caused 64 deaths (Qiu Fu-xi and Zhao Zhi-guo 1988). Dengue has been added to the list of officially notifiable diseases, and no cases were reported in 1985.

Epidemic Hemorrhagic Fever. Epidemic hemorrhagic fever was first found in Heilongjiang province in the 1930s and then in the construction sites of the northeast China forest zones and the Baoji-Chengdu Railway. The disease became more common in later years as the population increased in endemic areas as a result of water conservation, land reclamation, and other construction projects.

China has three types of epidemic foci: house mouse, field mouse, and the "mixed type." Gamasid and Trombiculid mites may also carry the virus. Measures directed primarily at reducing mouse

populations have been found to be effective in controlling the disease. Early diagnosis, rest, and hospital care in order to reduce the incidence of coma and renal failure have lowered the case fatality rate to about 3.2 percent in 1984 (*Public Health in the PRC* 1986).

Influenza. Influenza is the most frequently reported disease in China. Surveillance has been under way since 1968, yielding an epidemic pattern in south China that peaks in the summer and early fall, and an epidemic pattern in north China that peaks in the winter. As China's population ages and grows more vulnerable to influenza because of other serious chronic diseases, influenza will become more important as an immediate cause of death. An extensive immunization campaign has been carried out in recent years, resulting in a reduction from 8 million cases in 1975 to about 500,000 in 1980 and 1981. An unknown part of this decline may simply reflect the cyclic nature of the disease.

Japanese B Encephalitis. Japanese B encephalitis is a mosquito-transmitted viral disease seen throughout much of East Asia and is thought to be present in all of China except Tibet and Xinjiang. The case-fatality rate in 1949 was estimated at about 30 percent, and large epidemics were frequently seen near Shanghai, where the annual incidence was over 50 per 100,000. Since 1965 the incidence in the Shanghai area has been only 2 to 3 per 100,000. Mosquito vector control and vaccination of children have been priorities. Human cases peak at 4 to 5 years of age. About 100,000 cases are reported annually in China.

Leprosy. Leprosy has been present in China for more than 1,000 years. High prevalence areas are in southeast and southwest China; low prevalence areas are in the northeast and north. The official estimate for prevalence in China in 1951 was 1.2 million, although some international estimates placed the prevalence as high as 3 million.

Since the 1950s about 500,000 cases have been found, and more than 400,000 have been successfully treated. Methods used included specialized training for health personnel, prevention and control networks, early diagnosis and treatment, and infection control. In Shandong, the average annual incidence declined from 5.1 in the late 1950s to 0.14 per 100,000 in the early 1980s; the prevalence declined from 91 in 1950 to 2.3 per 100,000 in 1984. In 1958, 17,535 villages reported leprosy cases, this number dropping to only 1,500 villages by 1984.

Current estimates suggest a total of 100,000 to 200,000 patients and a prevalence of less than 20 per 100,000. China has recently embarked on a campaign to eliminate most leprosy by the year 2000 through intensified efforts of education, research, and early diagnosis and treatment (*Pubic Health in the PRC* 1986).

Measles. In 1950 the measles case-fatality rate was 6.5 percent, declining to 1.7 percent in 1956 with improved nutrition. When mass vaccination began in 1969, the incidence was estimated at about 3,000 per 100,000, but it now has dropped to below 20 per 100,000 for most big cities. The 1989 Ministry of Public Health epidemiologic report gave a time series estimate of 2.4 million cases in 1978, and 418,000, 199,000, 105,000, and 96,000 cases in 1985 through 1988, respectively. During the years 1986–8, the proportion of infants under 1 year immunized for measles rose steadily from 63 percent to 78 and 95 percent. The total annual reported deaths from measles since 1985 has been less than 1,000.

Neonatal Tetanus. Although data for pre-1949 are unavailable, it is likely that neonatal tetanus accounted for as much as 20 percent of infant mortality, a percentage similar to that reported in the early 1980s in rural Thailand. Maternal and child health services in China now monitor more than 90 percent of deliveries in most provinces, and neonatal tetanus is now said to be a rarity. Sample surveys have detected neonatal tetanus in some of the more remote counties, with an average death rate of approximately 3 per 1,000, ranging from 0.3 to over 13. By using very fragmentary data from various sources, UNICEF has estimated that there are perhaps 10,000 neonatal tetanus deaths per year, or a rate of about 0.5 per 1,000 live births.

Plague. The earliest known outbreak of plague in China was in Lu'an County, Shanxi Province in 1644 (*Public Health in the PRC* 1986). A well-documented massive outbreak of pneumonic plague occurred in 1911 in Manchuria. This epidemic, in which 60,000 people were affected, led to the first international medical conference in China and to the establishment of the Manchurian Plague Preventive Service. The failure of traditional Chinese medicine to control the outbreak (practitioners of traditional medicine experienced a 50 percent case-fatality rate) and the success of Western methods (a case fatality rate of 2 percent) were important factors in the rise of Western medicine in China (Bowers 1972).

During the early phase of the antiplague campaign, the state encouraged and subsidized rat-killing drives by agricultural collectives along with programs to reduce other potential host animals. Measures were also taken to destroy the ecological environment of major hosts in the course of planting trees or in carrying out farmland improvement and water conservation projects. As a result, rodent plague has been virtually eliminated from most heretofore endemic foci, and the ground squirrel, marmot, and other host populations have been sharply reduced.

By the end of the 1950s, the annual incidence of plague in China had declined to about 30 per 100,000, and by the end of the following decade it was under 12. The number of counties reporting plague cases annually ranged from 26 to 61 in 1950–4, 6 to 15 in 1955–60, and 0 to 8 after 1961 (*Public Health in the PRC* 1986). There were only 6 cases of plague in 1985, and the case fatality rate in recent years has been less than 8 percent.

Poliomyelitis. Prior to 1955, epidemics of poliomyelitis were common in China. In 1959 in Nanning the incidence was 151 per 100,000, and incomplete statistics for 17 administrative jurisdictions showed an overall incidence of 5 per 100,000. There were polio epidemics early in the Cultural Revolution (1968–70), during which all immunizations were said to have been neglected. The generation of those 10 to 20 years old at that time was most affected. As a result of a vigorous live-vaccine immunization campaign, the incidence had declined to around 0.5 to 0.75 per 100,000 by the mid-1980s. About 3,600 polio cases were reported from January to September 1989 – up substantially from the approximately 700 cases during the previous year (*China Daily* 1989).

Smallpox. The incidence of smallpox may have been as high as 200 per 100,000 population before 1949. A massive immunization campaign was started, and by 1953 over 50 percent of China's then 600 million population had been vaccinated. The last cases, in Tibet and Yunnan, were seen in 1960 (Kung 1953).

Trachoma. Trachoma, an infectious eye disease that can cause blindness, was a major public health problem in China. Half of the population was estimated to have been affected in the mid-1950s, and in some areas the prevalence may have reached 90 percent. Trachoma was estimated to have caused 45 percent of the visual impairment and between 25 and 40 percent of the blindness in China. Although the current prevalence is unknown, trachoma is no longer a public health problem. Education against towel sharing ("one person one towel, running water for washing face") had been very important as a control mechanism.

Tuberculosis. Tuberculosis was a leading cause of death in China in the late 1940s, with a death rate of 200 per 100,000 and a morbidity rate of 5,000 per 100,000 in major cities. At that time there were only 13 prevention and control institutions and five small prevention and control stations in the country, and only 7,500 people in all of China received bacillus Calmette-Guérin (BCG) vaccine as immunization between 1937 and 1949 (*Public Health in the PRC* 1986).

Government control efforts resulted in the creation of a tuberculosis prevention and control network to find, register, and treat patients at the earliest disease stage possible. In addition, BCG immunization campaigns were launched, with emphasis on newborns and on the reinoculation of primary school students. The BCG immunization campaign began in 1950, and by 1979 an estimated 500 million immunizations had been given. A sample survey in the latter year indicated that prevalence had been reduced to 717 per 100,000, with sputum-positive cases averaging only 187 per 100,000.

Since 1984, the Ministry of Public Health has promoted the creation of tuberculosis prevention and control in existing antiepidemic stations. By the end of 1985, 1,686 such institutions had been established at the county level, and there were 117 tuberculosis hospitals throughout the country. A sample survey of nine provinces and cities in 1984 found a prevalence of less than 500 per 100,000. The incidence remains high, however, in remote areas and those inhabited by minority nationalities (*Public Health in the PRC* 1986).

Typhoid and Paratyphoid Fevers. National data on typhoid and paratyphoid fevers were not available until recently. In 1975, Shanghai registered an estimated 600 cases of typhoid fever (Lampton 1977), and in 1985 there were an estimated 86,000 cases of typhoid and paratyphoid nationwide.

Venereal Disease. In the early 1950s, the prevalence of venereal disease in China was estimated at 3 to 5 percent in the cities, and as high as 10 percent among those who lived in the frontier areas (Lampton 1977). Extraordinary efforts were mounted to combat these diseases and were reported to have successfully "eradicated" them in China by the mid-1960s.

Patients with venereal disease, however, began to be seen again in 1984, and by 1988 "tens of thousands" of such cases had been reported. Preliminary reports from the country's 16 venereal disease inspection stations for the first 9 months of 1989 showed a 61 percent rise in new VD patients over the 1988 figure, bringing the cumulative total for the period to more than 220,000 (*China Daily* 1989). The highest incidence has been in coastal areas, such as Guangdong, Guangxi, and Fujian provinces, though cases have also been reported in Beijing, Shanghai, Tienjin, Harbin, and Xinjiang. More than 70 percent of the patients are male, and the most common diseases are gonorrhea, syphilis, and condyloma. According to the head of a national venereal disease prevention committee, the renewed spread "arises from the reemergence of prostitutes, the increased activities of 'sex gangs,' as well as changing attitudes toward sex on the part of some young people seeking sexual freedom" (*Beijing Review* 1988). In response, the State Council has issued a "strict ban" on prostitution; sex education courses have been widely introduced in middle schools; courses on venereal disease are being reintroduced at medical colleges; a national center for prevention and treatment of venereal disease has been established; and monitoring and treatment stations have been set up around the country.

Viral Hepatitis. Since the 1950s hepatitis has been increasing in many countries. In China, outbreaks have occurred in the northeast and north, with fluctuation in the incidence. In 1979–80 an extensive nationwide survey of the disease was conducted covering 277,186 people in 88 large, medium-sized, and small cities and 121 rural counties. Positive seroreactivity to anti-HBV averaged 71.4 percent and to hepatitis B surface antigen (HBsAg), 88 percent. Infection appeared predominantly in two peak age groups, those under 10 and those between 30 and 40 years; rates for males were higher than for females. HBsAg seropositivity was higher in family groups and did not seem to be particularly correlated with occupation (*Public Health in the PRC* 1986).

Viral hepatitis research became a priority under the sixth five-year plan (1981–5), with particular emphasis directed toward development of a low-cost vaccine and on the improvement of prevention and control measures. Research and development of a hepatitis B hemogenetic vaccine began in 1978 and was completed in 1983. Confirmatory tests in 1985 showed that the vaccine was safe and effective, and mass production is planned.

Responsibility for hepatitis prevention and control is vested in the sanitation and antiepidemic stations at all administrative levels. Stations collect and analyze morbidity data, conduct epidemiologic studies, and provide assistance to medical units, to patients' families, and to organizations on such matters as patient isolation, sterilization, food and water management, environmental sanitation, and personal hygiene. They also provide regular medical examinations to food industry and nursery personnel.

Strengthened hygienic legislation, standards, and administrative guidelines have also contributed to a reduction in the spread of both hepatitis A and B. For example, many hospitals have set up hepatitis wards to prevent hepatitis B from spreading. Special attention has been given to screening blood donors and to the strict management of blood products. Most health facilities now use disposable needles and syringes and have tightened the control and disposal methods of blood stained water and objects.

Chronic Diseases

Chronic diseases now account for almost two-thirds of all mortality in China and are expected to become even more significant in the future, owing to an aging population and to changing environmental and life-style factors. This section considers briefly the three main chronic disease categories: heart disease, stroke, and cancer.

Heart Disease.   Heart disease is now the leading cause of death in China. Among the deaths from heart disease the causes are, in declining order of frequency, hypertensive heart disease, cor pulmonale, rheumatic heart disease, and coronary heart disease. The importance of coronary heart disease is, however, increasing rapidly.

Hypertension's contribution to stroke and renal disease as well as to hypertensive heart disease probably makes this condition the largest single risk factor for death in China. Based on age-specific hypertension rates observed in a 1979 national hypertension sample survey, by 2010 China could have more than 110 million cases of hypertension. With rising incomes, however, and a probable parallel rise in age-specific rates, this may be a low estimate.

Cor pulmonale, manifested by right ventricular hypertrophy and decreased output, appears to be linked to the high prevalence of chronic obstructive lung disease (COLD). This condition is most often the end result of pneumoconiosis secondary to air pollution from factories, transport, home cooking over open stoves, and, with increasing frequency, cigarette smoking. Although national statistics are still inadequate to distinguish between cor pulmonale and COLD, data from the Disease Surveillance Point (DSP) system covering a population of about 10 million will soon be able to provide better estimates of the magnitude of these and other health problems. COLD morbidity has been estimated at 20 times COLD mortality and appears to affect rural residents substantially more than those in urban areas.

Rheumatic heart disease has accounted for a major portion of heart disease morbidity and mortality in the past, but today, with the widespread use of antibiotics, its significance is on the decline. In 1986, an estimated 50,000 deaths resulted from this disease, with perhaps some 1 million infected.

Coronary heart disease, the main form of heart disease in the industrialized countries, is in fourth place in China but is expected to gain rapidly in importance as a result of the delayed effects of richer diets and more cigarette smoking. In four urban districts of Beijing, for example, the coronary heart disease death rate doubled from 71 per 100,000 in 1958 (10.8 percent of all deaths), to 141 per 100,000 in 1979 (25 percent of all deaths).

Cerebrovascular Disease.   More commonly known as stroke, cerebrovascular disease is most often a complication of hypertension and is currently the third leading cause of death in China. In the same four urban districts of Beijing mentioned above, stroke was responsible for 152 deaths per 100,000 population in 1979 (27.3 percent of all deaths), as compared to 107 per 100,000 in 1958. The ratio of stroke to coronary heart disease mortality (a relatively small part of all heart disease mortality) in China is about 4:1 as compared with about 1:3 in the United States, though this is expected to change rapidly as the effects of dietary and smoking habits come to be fully manifest.

Cancer.   Cancer has become one of China's top three causes of death. According to 1986 Disease Surveillance Point mortality data, the five leading cancers in men were, in rank order, lung, stomach, liver, esophagus, and colorectal, while for women cervix cancer replaced colorectal in fifth place. Those who live in urban areas have a 50 percent higher cancer mortality rate than do rural residents, and men are about 50 percent more at risk than are women, regardless of location. When compared with the results of a retrospective survey of all deaths in mainland China for the years 1973–5, these data suggest that overall cancer mortality rates are rising, lung cancer is gaining in relative importance, and esophageal cancer may be declining.

Three examples from the 1973–5 survey illustrate the wide regional variations that can be observed in cancer mortality according to site, variations that have recently been mapped by the government's National Cancer Control Office. Nasopharyngeal cancer is virtually limited to south China, with the highest incidence in Guangdong Province, from which it decreases in concentric bands. Mortality due to cancer of the esophagus varies more than sixfold across China's counties, with higher prevalence locations often separated by long distances. Liver cancer tends to be concentrated in coastal plains in the southeast.

The diverse patterns in the geographic distribution of cancer have led to epidemiological research on selected cancers (see, e.g., Armstrong 1982). With 60 percent of all fatal cancers originating in the upper alimentary tract, particular attention has been given to the role of diet and food hygiene. Cancer epidemiology has also focused on trend analysis. Through such studies it has been found that whereas the incidence of stomach cancer in China has been decreasing in recent years, that of lung cancer has increased rapidly. This latter trend had been especially pronounced in urban areas and is presumably associated with rising levels of smoking, as shown by studies such as that by Y. T. Gao and colleagues (1988). High lung cancer rates have also been found in rural areas subject to serious problems of indoor air pollution (Chapman, Mumford, and Harris 1988).

Chinese authorities have recently begun to address the public health hazards of smoking. Surveys have found that some 69 percent of Chinese men and 7 percent of women above the age of 20 smoke, and, although the rate for women is still low, this is likely to increase rapidly in the future. Antismoking measures – including education, cigarette price increases, limits on tobacco production, and banning of smoking in certain locations – have not had much effect thus far. Rather, cigarette production increased 9-fold between 1949 and 1980. Chinese cigarettes have about double the world average of tar, and now with the government deriving significant revenues from the sale of cigarettes, and the sudden increase in the importation of foreign brands, the potential for a rapid increase in tobacco consumption is great indeed.

Occupational Diseases

The safety of the workplace has received increasing attention since the first industrial health organization was established in 1950. By 1985 there were more than 170 such organizations and industrial health sections at more than 3,300 sanitation and antiepidemic stations, and about 25,000 persons were employed in this field. Starting with the promulgation of regulations on the control of silicon dust at the workplace in 1956, health authorities have extended industrial health regulations until by 1985 there were 122 industrial health standards and 16 standards for diagnosing occupational diseases. The decline in the incidence of silicosis documents both what has been accomplished and what remains to be done. According to a recent study of silicosis in 26,603 dust-exposed workers at seven mines and industrial plants, the 8-year cumulative incidence of silicosis declined from 36.1 percent among workers employed before 1950 to 1.5 percent for those employed after 1960 (Lou and Zhou 1989). During the same period, the cumulative incidence of tuberculosis decreased from 54.7 to 16.7 percent, and the silicosis case-fatality rate declined from 53.9 to 18.3 percent. The average age at the detection of silicosis increased from 41.3 to 52.7 years from the 1950s to the 1970s, while the average survival times of silicosis patients increased from 2.0 to 12.2 years.

Nutritional Diseases

Endemic Fluorine Poisoning.   Endemic fluorine poisoning is a chronic disease caused by an excess in intake of fluorine. On the basis of epidemiological surveys, it is currently estimated that in all areas of endemicity there are some 21 million people suffering from fluoride-caused mottled enamel and 1 million from bone disease caused by fluorine poisoning (*Public Health in the PRC* 1986). Efforts to control the disease include the use of rainwater, along with wells and other low-fluorine water sources, for drinking purposes, and treating water supplies to reduce the fluorine content. The provision of fluorine-free drinking water became one of China's projects in a 10-year world program for attaining a safe drinking-water supply and environmental hygiene.

Endemic Goiter and Endemic Cretinism.   Endemic goiter is caused by lack of iodine in the diet. Surveys suggest that about 35,000,000 people in China suffered from endemic goiter and another 250,000 from endemic cretinism. However, over the past three decades more than 2,500 monitoring stations have been set up to supervise the production, marketing, and use of iodized salt. By 1985 this salt was available to about 85 percent of the counties in the endemic areas, and as a result of these and other measures, over 22,000,000 endemic goiter patients have been successfully treated. The average incidence of the disease has been reduced to under 4 percent, and few patients with endemic cretinism are now found (*Public Health in the PRC* 1986).

Kaschin–Beck Disease. This disease is a chronic degenerative osteoarthropathy of unknown cause. The major pathological changes include degenerative necrosis of leg and arm joints and of epiphyseal plate cartilage. The earliest written record of the disease was made in 1934, but it is believed to have existed in China for a long time.

Surveys conducted since the early 1950s show that Kaschin–Beck disease prevails in a wide area from the northeast to the southwest, covering 287 counties and cities in 15 provinces, autonomous regions, and municipalities. It is estimated that 1.6 million people suffer from the disease, 65 percent of whom are youths and teenagers. Disease incidence fluctuates substantially, and a rainy autumn usually results in an increased incidence the next year. There are three views as to the etiology of Kaschin–Beck disease: poisonous organic matter in water, the fusarium tox in grain, and excessive or insufficient trace elements in water, soil, and grain (*Public Health in the PRC* 1986).

Several methods have been used to prevent and treat Kaschin–Beck disease. One includes the use of deep wells, alternate water sources, or water treatment with active carbon and magnesium sulfate to improve its quality. A study done in Fusong County of Jilin Province from 1972 to 1977 showed that disease incidence for people drinking water diverted from nearby springs was 1.2 percent, as compared with 13.5 percent for those who continued to drink from old sources (*Public Health in the PRC* 1986).

Another method is to provide grain from non-affected areas to people in affected areas. Meanwhile, efforts are made to prevent grain in storage from becoming mildewed. A 7-year study in Shuang-yashan City which compared two areas using the same water sources found no new cases in an area where outside grain was available. By contrast, the incidence continued to rise in the area using indigenous grain (*Public Health in the PRC* 1986).

More recent studies have demonstrated a relationship between selenium intake and Kaschin–Beck disease. Between 1974 and 1976, Gansu Province

used sodium selenite and vitamin E to treat 224 children suffering from the early-stage Kaschin–Beck disease. In areas where the disease is present, the lower the ambient selenium levels, the greater the prevalence. From 1981 to 1985, Shaanxi Province experimented with use of seleniumized table salt to prevent the disease. Measures to increase selenium intake, now used among more than 8 million people, are considered a major approach to the prevention of Kaschin–Beck disease (*Public Health in the PRC* 1986).

Keshan Disease. Keshan disease is a myocardial disease found in a long, narrow strip of land covering 309 counties from northeast to southwest China. The disease is sudden in onset and often acute, with a high case-fatality rate of around 20 percent. Housewives and teenagers are at particular risk. Keshan disease has been endemic in China for about 100 years, and a 1935 outbreak of the disease in Keshan County, Heilongjiang Province, led to its name. Endemic areas have been found to have low selenium levels in the water, earth, grain, and vegetables, and residents suffer from a deficiency of selenium. Considerable success in reducing disease incidence has been achieved with oral sodium selenite, but selenium deficiency may not be the only cause.

Effective measures to prevent and control Keshan disease include keeping homes warm, dry, and free of smoke, ensuring safe drinking water, improved eating habits, early diagnosis, and treatment. The principal treatment methods are intravenous injection of high doses of vitamin C and blood expanders; oral selenite is used to prevent acute and subacute Keshan disease. There have been no widespread outbreaks of the disease for 15 years. In 1985, only 374 cases of acute and subacute Keshan disease were found, with 92 deaths, the lowest rates ever. The number of chronic patients has decreased from 220,000 in the early 1970s to 76,500 by the mid-1980s. A total of 4.1 million people now take oral selenite, contributing to the falling incidence (*Public Health of the PRC* 1986).

Summary

China has undergone a remarkably rapid epidemiological transition over the past 40 years, from a preponderance of deaths due to communicable disease to a preponderance of deaths due to chronic disease. As China looks ahead to the twenty-first century, with its reduced birth rate and longer life expectancy, it faces the prospect of ever higher percentages of older people. According to World Bank estimates, by 2025 China could have 185 million people aged 65 and over or about 12 percent of its projected 1.5 billion population, and the burden of chronic disease will be great. With the 2025 per capita gross national product unlikely to exceed U.S. $2,000, China will find it very difficult to provide the high technology, institution-based care for chronic disease that has become the dominant pattern in industrialized countries. Innovative and inexpensive methods for the prevention of and care for chronic illnesses, for providing continuing patient care, and for maintaining past gains in the control of communicable disease, are therefore even more important in China than in the economically developed countries. These challenges will be all the greater as China undergoes major social, economic, and political changes that have reduced its ability to mobilize mass patriotic campaigns and to provide organized rural health care.

Thomas L. Hall and Victor W. Sidel

The authors gratefully acknowledge the assistance of Mr. Gu Dezhang of the Chinese Medical Association, Beijing, in obtaining and verifying some of the data used in this chapter.

Bibliography

Armstrong, Bruce. 1982. The epidemiology of cancer in China. *World Health Forum* 3: 95–101.

Basch, Paul F. 1986. Schistosomiasis in China: An update. *American Journal of Chinese Medicine* 14(1–2): 17–25.

Beijing Review. May 30, 1988. VD spread causes public concern.

Bowers, John Z. 1972. *Western medicine in a Chinese palace.* New York.

Chapman, R. S., J. L. Mumford, and D. B. Harris. 1988. The epidemiology of lung cancer in Xuan Wei, China: Current progress, issues, and research strategies. *Archives of Environmental Health* 43: 180–5.

Cheng Tien-hsi. 1973. Disease control and prevention. In *Public health in the People's Republic of China,* ed. Myron E. Wegman, Tsung-yi Lin, and Elizabeth F. Purcell, 185–207. New York.

Chien Hsin-chung. 1958. Summing up of mass technical experience with a view to expediting eradication of the five major parasitic diseases. *Chinese Medical Journal* 77: 521–32.

China Daily. 1989. Science and medicine. Sept. 7, Nov. 2, and Dec. 12.

China: The health sector. 1984. The World Bank. Washington, D.C.

Gao, Y. T., et al. 1988. Lung cancer and smoking in Shanghai. *International Journal of Epidemiology* 17: 277–80.

Kung, N. C. 1953. New China's achievements in health work. *Chinese Medical Journal* 71: 87–92.

Lampton, David M. 1977. *The politics of medicine in China.* Boulder, Co.

Lou, Jiezhi, and Chen Zhou. 1989. The prevention of silicosis and prediction of its future prevalence in China. *American Journal of Public Health* 79: 1613–16.

Nathan, Carl F. 1967. *Plague prevention and politics in Manchuria, 1910–1931.* Cambridge.

The National Cancer Control Office of the Ministry of Health. 1980. *Investigation of cancer mortality in China.* Beijing.

Parker, R. L., et al. 1982. The sample household health interview survey. *American Journal of Public Health* 72 (Suppl., Sept.): 65–70.

People's Daily. 1989. April 26.

Public health in the People's Republic of China. 1986. Beijing.

Qiu Fu-xi, and Zhao Zhi-guo. 1988. A pandemic of dengue fever on the Hainan Island: Epidemiologic investigations. *Chinese Medical Journal* 101: 463–7.

Sidel, Ruth, and Victor W. Sidel. 1982. *The health of China.* Boston.

UNICEF. 1987. *UNICEF in China.*

1989. *Children and women of China – A UNICEF situation analysis.* Beijing.

World Development Report. 1987. Published for the World Bank.

Worth, Robert. 1973. New China's accomplishments in the control of diseases. In *Public Health in the People's Republic of China,* ed. Myron E. Wegman, Tsung-yi Lin, and Elizabeth F. Purcell, 173–84. New York.

VI.4
Diseases of Antiquity in Japan

Our knowledge about diseases in the prehistoric era of Japan is extremely limited because not much paleopathological research has been done thus far. For the little information we have about the occurrence of diseases during the early historic period we have to rely on a small number of literary sources. One general assumption, however, may be made from the geographic situation of the Japanese islands: Prior to more extensive contact with the Asian continent, Japan may have been free from regular epidemics of certain contagious diseases such as smallpox and plague.

The most important sources on the early history of Japan are the *Kojiki* (The Ancient Chronicle), completed in A.D. 712, and the *Nihonshoki* (The Chronicles of Japan), completed in A.D. 720. Both these chronicles include references to diseases that affected individuals, as well as to epidemics. The *Kojiki* informs us that there "raged many plagues" at the time of Emperor Sujin, who was supposed to be the first Emperor and to have reigned around the end of the third century A.D. The *Nihonshoki* confirms that "plagues spread out everywhere in Japan." These epidemics may have been caused by climatic irregularities at that period; one passage in this source states: "Because the winter and the summer exchanged their places and the cold and heat occurred in irregular order, the plagues spread and the people suffered." Considering the influence of these climatic changes on the crops, one may speculate that these epidemics were famine-related dysenteries. A passage in the *Nihonshoki* describes the symptoms of a princess at the court who had fallen ill, by stating that she "lost her hair and became very thin" – symptoms suggestive of high fever and dehydration that might accompany such forms of dysentery. On the other hand, it would appear unlikely that famine would have reached the immediate environment of the emperor. Hence, with so little information a diagnosis can hardly be made with any degree of probability.

Undoubtedly, poor sanitation and a lack of hygiene must have been responsible for epidemics of dysentery; these were recorded as *ribyō* or *kakuran*. The epidemic recorded for the year 861 was identified as *sekiri*, possibly meaning bacillary dysentery. From the first mention of this illness onward, it appears to have reappeared frequently. One of the representations on the *Yamai-no-Sōshi* (Scrolls of Disease) made during the twelfth century, at the end of the Heian Era, carries a caption stating that a woman "has a sharp pain in the bowels, vomits water, has diarrhea and stumbles around to create a strange spectacle"; these symptoms suggest bacillary dysentery.

Diaries written by members of the gentry of the same period refer to the occurrence of malaria. The *Anopheles* mosquito, the host of various types of plasmodia, seems to have been present in Japan at all times. Malaria was called either *okori* or *warawa-yami*, the latter meaning high fever and chills. Another name, also found in the scrolls, was *gyaku-shitsu*: According to this source, illness was characterized by fever and chills that recurred throughout an individual's life.

Tuberculosis, especially pulmonary tuberculosis, may also have been present in ancient Japan. Possible references to pulmonary tuberculosis are contained in certain passages in the *Genji-Monogatari* and in the *Makura-no-Sōshi*, the two greatest literary works of ancient Japan. In these passages, persons are said to "suffer from the chest." The *Ishinpō*, a collection of excerpts from Chinese medical books, compiled by the Japanese scholar Tamba Yasuyori in 984, records a disease called *denshibyō*. The symptoms of this illness were similar to those of tuberculosis.

The *Ishinpō* also lists nine helminthic parasites, among which the tapeworm, roundworm, and pinworm can be identified; in ancient Japan all three were called *suhaku*. With the understanding that the Japanese compiler of this book selected subjects from Chinese medical literature that were applicable to the situation in Japan at the end of the first millennium, it seems safe to assume the existence of a wide array of parasitosis there as well. Another text of the period describes a woman suffering from *suhaku*, who was pale and had dropsical swellings. A physician drew from her body a white worm, 12 to 14 meters in length.

Although there are some indications of the existence of lice in ancient Japan, there is no proof for the occurrence of exanthematous typhus. Nor is there any source prior to the nineteenth century suggesting an outbreak of the bubonic plague, a disease that raged in China for decades around the turn of the eighth to the ninth century.

Beriberi, a disease caused by thiamine deficiency and often associated with cultures that relied on rice as staple food, was endemic in Japan. It was called, alternatively, *kakke*, *kakubyō*, or *ashinoke*, the latter meaning "illness of the legs." The oldest record of beriberi in Japan refers to the son of the Emperor Shōmu, who died of this disease in A.D. 744, at the age of 17 years. The *Ishinpō*, compiled one and a half centuries later, contains a detailed description of the symptoms, such as pain, paralysis of the legs, anasarca, and palpitations.

In A.D. 733, Yamanoueno Okura, the famous poet of the *Manyōshu* (the oldest existing anthology of poetry), died at the age of 74. According to his poem he had suffered from a disease for 10 years that caused him considerable discomfort: "The hands and feet do not move, every joint aches, the body is like a heavy stone and walking is difficult." Hattori Toshirō (1945) has concluded that this disease was rheumatoid arthritis. Others believe that arthritis deformans is a more likely possibility. Both conditions must have tormented ancient Japanese, whereas neuralgia of the hands and feet must have been quite common because of agricultural labor.

The oldest Japanese statutory law, the *Yōro-ryō*, enacted in 718, classified diseases of laborers and military men into three grades, ranging from severe to relatively mild. Among the most severe of diseases was leprosy. In this text it is described as follows: "The intestines are eaten by worms, the eyebrows fall down, the nose is out of shape, the voice changes, the body bends over, and it is contagious." Leprosy was called *rai* or *rei* or else *tenkei-byō,* which means literally "disease of heavenly punishment." Although lepers were regarded as untouchables and had to be strictly separated from the healthy population, a Buddhist legend has it that Empress Kōmyō (701–60), while cleaning pus from a leper's body, discovered that the man was Buddha.

As in all premodern societies, skin diseases, particularly inflammatory afflictions, were known among the Japanese. The *Ishinpō* includes chapters on afflictions that can be identified as scabies, pustular and other forms of suppurative dermatitis, carbuncles, scrofula, felon, and erysipelas. Some sources indicate that gonorrhea and soft chancre occurred in ancient Japan, under the names *rin-shitsu, bendoku,* and *genkan.* However, these terms appear in medical books only from the fifteenth century onward. Similarly, syphilis is encountered for the first time during this period. Japanese pirates apparently brought the bacterium into the islands from European ports in China.

Among the diseases of the nervous system, we have an illustration of cerebral apoplexy in the *Yami-no-Sōshi.* Not unfrequently, diaries and literary works describe instances of mental disorders that can be identified as schizophrenia, or other neurological conditions such as epilepsy.

A well-documented and typical case of diabetes mellitus may be found in the medical history of Fujiwara no Michinaga, a very powerful nobleman of the Heian Era. In 1016, at the age of 62 years, he began suffering from thirst, weakness, and emaciation. His disease was diagnosed as *insui-byō.* As the illness advanced, he suffered from carbuncles, developed cataracts, and finally died from a myocardial infarction. As a matter of fact, this disease was hereditary in this branch of the Fujiwara family: Michinaga's elder brother, his uncle, and his nephew all died of diabetes at fairly young ages.

The relative isolation of Japan long protected it from the great epidemics, such as smallpox, plague, and influenza, which raged in other areas of Asia. This isolation was, however, as William McNeill (1976) has pointed out, a "mixed blessing." As Buddhism flourished, and contacts with Korea and China increased, diseases that were endemic in these countries began to strike the dense and immu-

nologically defenseless population of the Japanese archipelago. Smallpox, most probably originating from India, reached China in the wake of Indian Buddhist missionaries via the Silk Road. It was first described by a Daoist, Ge Hong, in his *Zhou-hou bei-ji fang.* The first record of a smallpox epidemic in China appeared in the Jianwu Era (around A.D. 495), when it was called *hu-dou,* "barbarian pox." It spread to Korea, and eventually reached Japan with the first Buddhist missionaries, arriving there in 552. In the same year a series of epidemics started ravaging the country and continued periodically until 582. There is no proof as to whether the disease was smallpox in every instance; measles or influenza could have been similarly devastating. Since the relationship between the opening of the country and the arrival of these diseases was apparently understood, there is little wonder that opinions about the question of whether Buddhism should or should not be introduced to Japan divided society and the influential feudal families.

Shōji Tatsukawa

Bibliography

Cloudsley-Thompson, J. L. 1976. *Insects and history.* London

Dohi, K. 1921. *Sekai baidoku-shi* (History of syphilis). Tokyo.

Fujikawa, Yū. 1912. *Nihon shippei-shi* (History of diseases in Japan). Tokyo.

Hattori, Toshirō. 1945. *Nara-jidai igaku no Kenkyū* (Medicine in Nara-Era). Tokyo.

 1955. *Heian jidai igaku no kenkyū* (Medicine in Heian period, 784–1185). Tokyo.

Henschen, Folke. 1966. *The history and geography of diseases,* trans. Joan Tate. New York.

McNeill, W. 1976. *Plagues and peoples.* New York.

Tatsukawa, Shōji 1976. *Nihonjin no byōreki* (History of diseases in Japan). Tokyo.

VI.5
Diseases of the Premodern Period in Japan

The role of disease in Japanese history is a topic that has attracted the interest of Western historians only recently. The strongest stimulus for the study of disease and its effects on Japan's premodern society was the publication of a new edition of Fujikawa Yū's classic *Nihon shippei shi* in 1969 with a foreword by Matsuda Michio (*A History of Disease in Japan,* originally published in 1912). Along with his *History of Japanese Medicine* (*Nihon igaku shi,* 1904), *A History of Disease in Japan* provided historians with a detailed list of many of the epidemics that ravaged the Japanese population in the premodern era, including original sources of information and a diagnosis of many diseases in terms of Western medicine. Hattori Toshirō supplemented and updated Fujikawa's work in the postwar era with a series of books on Japanese medicine from the eighth through the sixteenth century.

William McNeill also kindled interest with *Plagues and Peoples* (1976), a book that fit the disease history of East Asia into the context of world history. Both William Wayne Farris (1985) and Ann Bowman Jannetta (1987) have investigated pestilence in premodern Japan in detail, but the field is still relatively undeveloped, as compared to work on Western history. The influence of the *Annales* school of France on Japanese scholars, which began in the late 1970s, may draw more scholars into work on disease, especially for the well-reported but unstudied period between 1300 and 1600.

Data for the study of disease in Japan present both opportunities and frustrations. The quantity of information on disease, especially epidemic afflictions, is better than for most other civilizations, including possibly western Europe. The reason for this is that the Japanese imported the Chinese practice of reporting diseases among the common people around 700. Many of these reports were included in court chronicles in abbreviated form. The custom of reporting epidemics suffered, however, as the links between the provinces and the capital waned after 900, and many outbreaks of pestilence undoubtedly went unnoticed by the aristocrats at court who did the recording of disease. Moreover, even when the reporting system was operating at its best, the sources often do not provide important facts such as the nature of the

disease, the regions afflicted, or levels of mortality inflicted. In addition, local records that would enhance our knowledge of diseases that prevailed are largely lacking before 1100, and the job of ferreting through village and town documents for signs of pestilence after 1100 has yet to be attempted.

About the time that the Japanese government borrowed the Chinese custom of recording outbreaks of pestilence, it also borrowed their medical theory. The description, diagnosis, and treatment of disease in premodern Japan almost always derive from Chinese texts. Buddhist scriptures from India also influenced how disease and medicine were perceived in early Japan. It is unclear how much the Japanese knew about disease and its treatment before Chinese and Indian influences. Some medical practices reported during early epidemics may well derive from native roots, as during the Great Smallpox Epidemic of 735–7 (Farris 1985). For the most part, however, the native Japanese view of disease was that it was demonic possession to be exorcised by shamans and witch doctors.

It is important to distinguish between infectious diseases, which can create epidemics, and other afflictions, which, to use McNeill's terminology (1976), form the "background noise" to history. Japanese sources provide information on a wide variety of diseases, especially when they attacked a statesman, artist, or priest. However, it is often difficult to classify the illness in Western terms. For this reason, the focus of this essay will be chiefly on epidemic outbreaks, with occasional reference to identifiable, noninfectious ailments.

The relationship between disease and Japan's geography is significant in two respects. First, Japan presents a good case of "island epidemiology" (McNeill 1976). Because of its comparative isolation, Japan remained relatively free of epidemic outbreaks as long as communication with the continent was infrequent. Consequently, the populations grew dense. However, once an infectious disease was introduced to the archipelago, it ravaged those dense populations that had had virtually no opportunity to develop resistance to it. Thus, immunities were built up only slowly in a process that took centuries.

Second, because of Japan's mountainous terrain, one cannot always assume that an epidemic reached the entire Japanese populace at once. Severe outbreaks undoubtedly afflicted isolated villages and regions even in the Edo period (1600–1868). Certainly, more study of the important relationship between Japan's topography and transportation routes and disease transmission is needed.

The history of epidemics in Japan until 1600 (when Japan banned travel and trade with most nations) falls into four periods: (1) from earliest times to 700, when little is known about disease; (2) 700–1050, an age of severe epidemics; (3) 1050–1260, a transitional stage when some killer diseases of the past became endemic in the population; and (4) 1260–1600, a time of lessening disease influence despite the introduction of some new ailments from the West.

Pre–A.D. 700

The record of disease in Japan's prehistory is a matter of guesswork. In the earliest times, the Paleolithic (150,000 B.C. to 10,000 B.C.) and Neolithic (10,000 B.C. to 200 B.C.) periods, population was too sparse to sustain many afflictions. Evidence indicates that there was a Malthusian crisis in the late Neolithic epoch, about 1000 B.C., but archaeologists have not been able to discern any signs of infectious diseases in the skeletons of Neolithic peoples (Kitō 1983). The bronze and iron ages (200 B.C. to A.D. 300), when rice agriculture was imported from the Asian mainland, would seen to have been an age of great population increase and therefore of potential disease outbreak as well. However, again the archaeological record gives no indication of illnesses in those few skeletons that remain. Similarly, there is little evidence on disease for the era from 300 to 500.

700–1050

Most scholars of Japan agree that the historical age begins with the sixth century, and hard evidence of disease in the region also originates with this time. Japan's first court history, *The Chronicles of Japan,* records that in 552 many were stricken with disease. It is no accident that this epidemic occurred at the same time that the gifts of a statue of the Buddha along with sutras arrived at the Japanese court from Korea (Aston 1972). Disease doubtless also arrived with the carriers, although the court blamed the outbreak on the introduction of a foreign religion and destroyed the gifts.

In 585, the court again banned the worship of the Buddha, and this time chroniclers noted that many people were afflicted with sores. *The Chronicles of Japan* states that those attacked by the sores were "as if they were burnt," a condition suggesting fever. According to Hattori Toshirō (1943), the 585 epidemic was the first outbreak of smallpox in Japanese history, although it should be noted that some sources from later centuries record that the 585 epidemic was measles.

The 552 and 585 (*not* 587, as some have reported) outbreaks are the only signs of pestilence between 500 and the end of the seventh century. There are two ways to interpret the absence of data on disease for this epoch. First, the sixth and seventh centuries may have been relatively disease-free, in which case the era must have seen a population boom – a boom that would have coincided with the introduction of Chinese institutions into Japan. A second and more likely answer is that the chroniclers simply did not record epidemics. Sources from the period 500 to 700 are notoriously scarce and inaccurate. Moreover, during these two centuries Japan sent 11 embassies to China, received 7 from China, and had about 80 exchanges with Korea (Farris 1985). Given these contacts with the outside world, it is therefore conceivable that disease was an important feature of Japanese demographic history for the era 500 to 700.

Beginning in 698, it definitely was. Historical sources disclose an alarming number of epidemic outbreaks. There are 34 epidemics for the eighth century, 35 for the ninth century, 26 for the tenth century (despite a marked decline in the number of records), and 24 for the eleventh century, 16 of which occur between the year 1000 and 1052 (*SZKT* 1933 and 1966; Hattori 1945; Tsuchida 1965; Fujikawa 1969; and Farris 1985).

Because of this spate of pestilential outbreaks, the period from about 700 to about 1050 stands out as Japan's age of plagues. Records suggest that the diseases were imported from the Asian mainland as the Japanese traveled to China and Korea to learn of superior continental political and cultural systems and to trade. Disease became a major influence on Japanese society, shaping tax structure, local government, land tenure, labor, technology, religion, literature, education, and many other aspects of life. Certainly, the epidemics in these centuries held back economic development of the islands. On the other hand, by undergoing such trauma early in their history, the Japanese people built immunities at a relatively early date and thus escaped the onslaught of diseases that came to the civilizations of the Incas, Aztecs, and others with Western contact in the sixteenth century.

Unfortunately, historical documents do not often reveal the nature of the diseases in question. Historians can identify only five of them: smallpox, measles, influenza, mumps, and dysentery. In addition, McNeill (1976) has suggested that plague may have found its way to Japan in 808, and his argument has a great deal to recommend it. Plague was then afflicting the Mediterranean and the Middle East, and

Arabic traders and sailors frequented Chinese, Korean, and Japanese ports. Denis Twitchett (1979) has shown that China received many diseases from the West via the Silk Route. The presence of plague in Japan would also go a long way in explaining several severe epidemics that have yet to be identified. Yet because there is no description of symptoms by the Japanese sources, the existence of plague in Japan during this period remains in doubt.

Smallpox

The most deadly killer among the five diseases that are known to have assaulted early Japan was smallpox (mogasa, "funeral pox"). Epidemics of the pestilence are listed for the years 735–7, 790, 812–14, 853, 915, 947, 974, 993–5, 1020, and 1036 (compiled from data in SZKT 1933; Hattori 1955; Fujikawa 1969; Farris 1985). During this era, especially in the eighth and ninth centuries, smallpox was primarily a killer of adults. According to Jannetta (1987), smallpox had become endemic in the population by 1100 or even earlier, but the basis for this belief is not clear.

The best example of a smallpox, and indeed of any epidemic in this period, is the Great Smallpox Epidemic of 735–7, the earliest well-reported smallpox epidemic in world history (Farris 1985). It began in northern Kyushu, transported there by a Korean fisherman. The foreign port of Dazaifu was the first to feel the effects of the disease, a sure sign that the affliction was imported. Kyushu suffered throughout the summer and fall of 735, and the disease raged again in 736. Just as the epidemic was burning itself out in western Japan, a group of official emissaries to Korea passing through northern Kyushu encountered the ailment and carried it to the capital and eastern Japan. The epidemic assaulted all levels of Japanese society, killing peasant and aristocrat alike. One record reads that "in recent times, there has been nothing like this" (Farris 1985).

Two remarkable records survive that describe the symptoms and treatment of smallpox. The disease began as a fever, with the patient suffering in bed for from 3 to 6 days. Blotches then began to appear, and the limbs and internal organs became fevered. After the fever diminished and the blotches started to disappear, diarrhea became common. Patients also suffered from coughs, vomiting, nosebleeds, and the regurgitation of blood.

The prescribed remedies are as fascinating as the descriptions of the symptoms. Government doctors trained in Chinese, Indian, and native medicine advocated a variety of palliatives, including wrapping the patient in warm covers, drinking rice gruel, eating boiled scallions to stop the diarrhea, and forcing patients with no appetite to eat. Medicines were seen as of little use against the disease. After the illness, those who recovered were admonished not to eat raw fish or fresh fruit or vegetables, drink water, take a bath, have sex, or walk in the wind or rain. Doctors also advocated mixing flour from red beans and the white of an egg, and applying the mixture to the skin to eliminate the pox. Bathing in a woman's menstrual flow or wrapping a baby in a menstrual cloth to wipe out the blotches; and applying honey, powdered silkworm cocoons, white lead, or powdered falcon feathers and lard was also suggested.

Tax records extant from the time of the epidemic provide a glimpse of the mortality inflicted by the Great Smallpox Epidemic of 735–7. In the year 737 alone, the province of Izumi near the capital lost 44 percent of its adult populace, while Bungo in northern Kyushu and Suruga in eastern Japan sustained death rates of about 30 percent. The average mortality for all known areas was about 25 percent in 737 alone. Population depletion for the 3 years probably amounted to between 25 and 35 percent, making the Great Smallpox Epidemic of 735–7 comparable in its death toll to the European Black Death of the fourteenth century.

Disastrous as it may have been, one great outbreak of pestilence would not have halted demographic growth for long. But harsh epidemics continued to follow on its heels. In 790, smallpox struck again, borne from Chinese ports and afflicting those aged 30 or less. The historical record is fragmentary and difficult to read for the epidemic of 812–14, but it seems likely that the dread killer entered Japan via its foreign port in northern Kyushu as early as 807 and spread across the archipelago to the east. According to the records, "almost half" of the population died. In 853, the disease seems to have focused on the capital, Heian (modern Kyoto), but the epidemic also spread to the countryside.

The disease, however, still seems to have been primarily an ailment of adults. In 925, for example, the Emperor Daigo contracted smallpox at the age of 41. The smallpox outbreak of 993–5 was particularly severe. In 993, the Emperor Ichijō was a victim at the age of 15, but the disease was probably not yet endemic, as smallpox appeared in Kyushu the next spring, suggesting a foreign source. The disease was so bad in the capital that 70 officials of the fifth court rank or higher died; the roads were littered with corpses serving as food for dogs and vultures. In

1020 smallpox returned to Kyushu again, possibly reaching Japan with one of the continental invaders the year before. A diary states that those aged 28 and under were especially afflicted (Tsuchida 1965; Farris 1985).

Measles

The second killer disease that attacked the Japanese populace in the era between 700 and 1050 was measles (akamogasa, "red pox"). Two epidemics are known, in 998 and 1025, although it is not clear that Japanese doctors were always able to distinguish between measles and smallpox in this early age. Nonetheless, A Tale of Flowering Fortunes, a chronicle of the tenth and eleventh centuries, clearly differentiates the 998 affliction from smallpox, stating that the disease caused a "heavy rash of bright red spots" (McCullough and McCullough 1980). The pestilence began in the early summer in the capital, where the wives of high officials were the first affected. Foreigners did not die from the disease, a clue that reinforces McNeill's (1976) thesis about Japan's island epidemiology. Later in the year, the ailment attacked the rest of Japan, killing more people than any other in recent memory.

In 1025, measles once again returned to Japan. The disease afflicted people of all classes who had not suffered from the disease in the 998 epidemic. The diaries of aristocrats indicate that several noble houses suffered from the illness. The focus of the disease seems to have been the capital, although one source states that "all under heaven" caught the malady.

Influenza

A third ailment was influenza (gai byō or gaigyaku byō, "coughing sickness"), which struck in 862–4, 872, 920, 923, 993, and 1015 (Hattori 1955; Fujikawa 1969). Unlike smallpox and measles, which were most active in the spring, summer, and fall, influenza generally struck in the late winter and early spring. The epidemics of 862–4 and 872 were particularly severe, killing many people in the capital region. In general, however, the death toll from influenza probably did not match the mortality from smallpox or measles.

Mumps

Mumps (fukurai byō, "swelling sickness") was the fourth epidemic illness encountered by the Japanese in this period. Records state that the disease flourished in 959 and 1029, mainly in Heian, the populous capital of the era. In both epidemics, historians

indicated that the sickness was marked by a swelling of the neck.

The final pestilence of the age of plagues was dysentery (sekiri, "red diarrhea"). Epidemics are documented for 861, 915, and 947 (Hattori 1955). The season for dysentery was the late summer and fall. Often dysentery appeared in tandem with other afflictions, as in the Great Smallpox Epidemic of 735–7. The dysentery epidemic of 861 was followed by influenza in 862 and 863. In 915 and 947, smallpox was again an accompanying malady. The measles epidemic of 1025 was also probably related to dysentery infections among the Heian nobility. Their diaries indicate that when patients caught dysentery they quickly lost their appetites and suffered from fever.

Other Maladies

In addition to these five epidemic afflictions, other illnesses were common among the populace. According to The Pillow Book, a series of essays written by a lady at court (Sei Shōnagon) about the year 1000, the three diseases most feared by the tiny coterie of aristocrats at the Heian court were chest trouble (munenoke), evil spirits (mononoke), and beriberi (ashinoke). Chest trouble undoubtedly refers to tuberculosis, although Hattori (1975) suspects that heart-related afflictions were also common. Tuberculosis is one of the oldest diseases known to humanity, and it may have been that because the tuberculosis bacillus is often transmitted via unpasteurized milk, the aristocracy contracted the malady by eating a yogurtlike food product of which they were fond. Evil spirits suggest mental illnesses, and Hattori (1975) has found evidence of schizophrenia, autism, and manic-depressive behavior in the imperial line. Beriberi, a disease caused by a deficiency of thiamine (probably due to a lack of fats in aristocratic diets), is noted in several sources for the early period (Hattori 1964).

Some diseases were never diagnosed by court doctors who were trained only in Chinese medicine. Japanese records tell of a "water-drinking illness" (mizu nomi yami) common to the Fujiwara family, the mating line for the imperial house (Hattori 1975). According to Hattori, this disease was diabetes, and was hereditary in that family. Several prominent Fujiwara statesmen, including the great Michinaga (the model for Prince Genji in The Tale of Genji), complained of the malady and its related afflictions such as glaucoma and impotence (Hurst 1979).

Another malady that did not kill many victims

but had a great effect on all levels of society was malaria (*warawayami, furuiyami,* or *okori,* "the chills"). Even Prince Genji himself suffered from the malady (Seidenstecker 1985). Doctors of this era were unaware that the disease could be carried by mosquitoes, although a court lady seemed to believe that butterflies were common where the disease broke out. Japan is a land with many swamps; it is interesting to speculate about the effects of malaria on a peasantry trying to convert these low-lying lands into productive rice paddies.

In addition to the plentiful information on diseases supplied by court histories, literature, and other records, medical texts and an encyclopedia called the *Wamyō ruijū shō* also list medical terminology (Hattori 1945). Among the infections included are idiopathic cholera (*shiri yori kuchi yori koku yamai, kakuran*), leprosy (*raibyō*), elephantiasis (*gejū*), bronchitis (*shiwabuki yami*), hepatitis (*kibamu yamai*), dropsy (*harafukuru yamai*), ascarids (*kaichū*), threadworms (*gyōchū*), meningitis (*fubyō*), infantile dysentery (*shōji kakuran*), diphtheria (*bahi*), bronchial asthma (*zensoku*), epilepsy (*tenkan*), chronic nephritis (*shōkatsu*), tonsilitis (*kōhi*), osteomyelitis (*fukotsuso*), thyroiditis (*ei*), erysipelas (*tandokusō*), ringworm (*sensō*), gastritis (*iso*), palsy (*kuchi yugamu*), and scabies (*kaisō*). Records from the era 700–1050 also have led scholars to infer the existence of cancer, pneumonia, tapeworms, rheumatoid arthritis, and hookworms.

Effects of Plagues on Japanese Society

The effects of the age of plagues (700–1050) on Japanese society and culture were many and varied. Parallels with the Black Death pandemic that struck western Europe in the fourteenth and fifteenth centuries are tempting to draw, and it may be true that pestilence stimulates the same human responses in widely disparate societies. In the social and economic realm, the epidemics were responsible for several phenomena. First, disease caused population stagnation. Sawada Goichi estimated the population of Japan at 6 million in the eighth century, and it is unlikely that population grew significantly through the year 1050 (Kitō 1983).

Second, plagues caused the desertion of villages. After the Great Smallpox Epidemic of 735–7, an entire layer of village administration was abolished. Later, after the epidemics of 990–1030, the court once again abandoned the current village system in favor of new laws.

Third, pestilence inhibited agriculture, especially rice monoculture, because it became difficult to culti-

vate lands continuously. In 743, after the 735–7 outbreak, the aristocracy attempted to stimulate farming by enacting a policy giving permanent private tenure to anyone who would take up a hoe. In 1045, lawgivers countered unparalleled field abandonment by recognizing all previously banned estates.

Fourth, outbreaks of pestilence stimulated migration and made for a shortage of laborers. The court enacted legislation to bind peasants to their land throughout the eighth and ninth centuries, but to little effect. Labor shortages often made it difficult to finish temple construction or rice planting on time, and by the year 800, the court had given up capital construction and the conscription army.

Fifth, disease was responsible for a growing maldistribution of income. A new class of regional strongmen, called the "rich" in the documents, came into being by capitalizing on opportunities arising from famines and epidemics. The "rich" often resorted to violence to resist provincial tax collectors and exploit the peasantry.

Sixth, the stagnation of population growth resulting from disease reduced the demand for manufactured goods. At the same time, because epidemics kill people but do not destroy wealth, survivors of the pandemic among the aristocracy were left with great riches. Reduced overall demand and the increased opulence of a few gave rise to industry that produced luxury goods for a tiny elite.

In the political realm, epidemics brought several alterations in tax structure. After the Great Smallpox Epidemic, provincial governors were converted into tax farmers, which put them into competition for revenues with the leaders of the smaller district units that comprised the province. The competition for taxes among local officials while the tax base was shrinking helped engender a society that looked to violence to solve its problems. By 1050, the district had disappeared as a unit of administration, primarily because it could not compete with the larger province. Moreover, epidemics provided political opportunities. After the 735–7 epidemic, for example, all four of the Fujiwara brothers from a powerful aristocratic family had passed away, and Tachibana no Moroe, a bitter rival, became the new head of the government. Or again in 994, when smallpox raged in the capital and many aristocrats fell victim, a beneficiary of the deaths was Fujiwara no Michinaga, who became perhaps the greatest of all Fujiwara leaders.

In addition, disease influenced inheritance. To cope with the horrendous number of deaths of family members from plagues, the aristocracy practiced polygamy. Often property and children were retained in the woman's line against the advent of an untimely demise by her husband. Survivors inherited unparalleled wealth and political power.

Finally, plagues reduced the size of administration. In the early eighth century, the government bureaucracy numbered about 10,000 persons. By the early ninth century, leaders were already cutting back the size of government, and although hard figures are difficult to come by, the bureaucracy did not again reach that size until the fourteenth century.

The age of plagues also influenced religion and culture. Unquestionably, the epidemics played a role in both the adoption of Chinese culture in the eighth century and a return to the native culture in the tenth and eleventh centuries. It is unlikely that the Japanese of the 700s borrowed Chinese civilization simply because it seemed superior to their own. Only coercion, such as military force or epidemic disease, would have inspired the Japanese to adopt such an obviously foreign culture. On the other hand, disease played a role in the demise of Chinese culture in Japan because the constant plagues killed off experts in Chinese language and the classics, thus making these subjects harder to learn. Disease was also a factor in the development of a major motif in Japanese literature, *mono no aware,* the ephemeral nature of all living things. Disease is a constant presence in the classic *The Tale of Genji,* which includes reference to an epidemic (Seidenstecker 1985). Many of Genji's friends and lovers pass away after the briefest time, and in most cases the villain was disease. To have reached one's forties was considered to have lived a long life (Hattori 1975).

The repeated outbreaks of pestilence also influenced Japanese religion profoundly. The introduction of Buddhism occurred amidst a plague of smallpox. As a transcendental religion, Buddhism was perfectly adapted for an environment in which disease outbreaks were common. Early believers reached out to Buddhism because of the promise of protection from illness. After the Great Smallpox Epidemic of 735-7, the Emperor Shōmu increased state support of the religion by ordering the construction of the great state temple Tōdaiji and branch temples throughout the countryside. By the tenth and eleventh centuries, Buddhism had become a faith of good works, as Christianity was during the plague pandemic in the fourteenth and fifteenth centuries. The frequency of pilgrimage in both religions is another striking parallel. By the eleventh century, Japanese religious thought was characterized by pessimism and a flight from the intellect. Millennialism, symbolized by "the latter day of the law"

(*mappō*), dominated Japanese thought. According to this doctrine, three ages of 500 years each followed the death of the Buddha: the first era, when salvation was simple; the second, when it was more difficult; and the latter day, when delivery from hell would come to just a few. Ironically, the latter day was believed to begin in 1052, just as the epoch of plagues drew to a close.

Popular culture also reflected a concern for disease. The Gion Festival, today celebrated from the July 17 to July 24 (the 14th of the sixth month according to the old lunar calendar) began as an attempt to rid the capital of Heian of epidemics. The festival was first conducted by Gion Shrine (later Yasaka Shrine) in eastern Heian in 869, just after an epidemic. Sixty-six spears, one for each province in Japan, were placed on end and marched through the city to chase the disease away. In 970 the festival became an annual affair, suggesting the growing endemicity of disease in the capital.

The smallpox pestilence of 993–5 gives another rare glimpse of popular reaction to epidemics. Late in the sixth month of 993, a festival to drive away disease gods was held in the Kitano section of the capital. Two palanquins were built by the government, Buddhist monks recited a sutra, and music was provided. Several thousand persons gathered and offered prayers to the gods. The palanquins, invested with the gods of the epidemic, were then borne by the populace several miles to the ocean to wash the smallpox affliction away (Tsuchida 1965; Fujikawa 1969).

1050–1260

The era from 1050 to 1260 marks a time of declining importance of disease in Japan. There were 50 epidemics over 210 years, an average of one outbreak every 4.2 years, compared to one epidemic every 2.9 years in the 700s and one every 3.8 years in the poorly documented 900s (cf. Hattori 1955, 1964; Fujikawa 1969). The killers of the former age retreated into endemicity. As always, the record is most complete for smallpox. Epidemics broke out in 1072, 1085, 1093–4, 1113, 1126, 1143, 1161, 1175, 1177, 1188, 1192, 1206–7, 1225, 1235, and 1243 (cf. Hattori 1955, 1964; Fujikawa 1969). Although some plagues of smallpox appear to have been severe, especially those in 1072 and 1175, the disease showed clear signs of becoming an affliction of childhood. A letter of 1085 records a mother's concern for her infant who had contracted smallpox (Hattori 1975). In the late twelfth century, Minamoto no Yoriie, the eldest son of the great warrior leader Yoritōmō, had smallpox as a boy. His sickness seems to suggest the growing significance of the disease in eastern Japan, away from the greatest centers of population. The record of the 1243 epidemic of smallpox specifically states that the disease afflicted young children, which led McNeill (1976) to assert that the ailment was endemic by that date.

In the case of measles, epidemics struck in 1077, 1093–4, 1113, 1127, 1163, 1206, 1224, 1227, and 1256 (Fujikawa 1969). In the plague of 1077, young children were afflicted, although the record also reveals that many adults died. That the 1224 affliction seems to have attacked mainly young children, however, suggests to McNeill (1976) that, like smallpox, measles was probably endemic by that time. On the other hand, Jannetta (1987) has found evidence that the disease was still a foreign-borne plague as late as the nineteenth century. Analysis of additional records between 1200 and 1600 is still required to determine the precise status of measles in Japanese history, but it is important to note that at least Jannetta agrees with McNeill that the disease was not a major factor in the region's demographic history by 1200.

Influenza, a disease for which no permanent immunity is conferred, took a devastating toll in the era 1050–1260. According to the records, epidemics occurred in 1150, 1228, 1233, 1244, and 1248. The outbreak in 1150 was extremely severe, carrying off many elderly persons. The epidemic of 1244 was also harsh, afflicting all those aged 10 and above. An important reason for the grave plagues of influenza was undoubtedly the weather, which turned much colder and damper after 1150 (Kitō 1983).

Dysentery also continued to attack the populace. There is evidence of a dysentery outbreak in the year 1077, and prominent individuals contracted the malady in 1144, 1240, and 1243 (Fujikawa 1969). As during the age of plagues, the malady usually accompanied other diseases; the 1077 affliction of dysentery coincided with a measles epidemic.

In addition to diseases from the previous era, the period 1050–1260 also witnessed the first accounts of a new ailment. Fujikawa (1969) argues that in 1180 the Japanese first became aware of the existence of a smallpox-like affliction that may have been chickenpox. Eventually, doctors in Japan came to call the disease "water pox" (suitō or henamo), and chronicled an epidemic in 1200. It is unlikely that the disease had a great demographic impact, and may well have existed in Japan long before the Japanese medical establishment became aware of it.

A disease that gained new prominence in the era from 1050 to 1260 was leprosy (raibyō). Although this affliction appears in records as early as the eighth century, Hansen's disease seems to have become a serious social problem in the thirteenth century. The colder climate probably caused people to huddle together, thereby facilitating the transmission of the malady as in western Europe. Healthy commoners spurned lepers and treated them as outcasts. The Buddhist monk Ninshō became renowned for his treatment of lepers in a sanatorium at Kuwagatani. The Portuguese missionary Luis de Almeida would gain a similar reputation for his work in the 1500s (Hattori 1964, 1971).

Medical texts and other sources list other ailments as well; they include cirrhosis of the liver (daifuku suichō), bronchitis, dropsy, idiopathic cholera, hepatitis, worms, malaria, furunculosis (ōryō shi), diabetes, and tuberculosis (denshi byō). The Hanazono Emperor and Fujiwara no Kanezane were afflicted with beriberi (kakke), whereas the poet Fujiwara Teika suffered from repeated bouts with bronchial asthma (Hattori 1964).

Because the effects of disease in the age 1050–1260 were limited, especially during the period 1050–1150, decreasing mortality from both old and new afflictions possibly spurred some population growth. Demographic expansion was particularly evident in the Kantō region (modern Tokyo and vicinity), as the warriors cleared lands for cultivation. The land clearance of this epoch was the basis for the estate (shōen) system adopted in the late eleventh century. The extent of population growth, however, remains undetermined.

Yet, no matter how much the impact of pestilence on Japanese society decreased during the years 1050–1150, there is little doubt that disease combined with unusually harsh weather in the following century to restrict population growth. Temperatures turned much colder and the amount of moisture increased dramatically, especially in eastern Japan where there was the greatest potential for growth. In three years – 1182, 1230, and 1259 – the inclement weather induced widespread famine and accompanying sicknesses. The Great Famine of 1230 was said to have killed one-third of the population. In all three cases, epidemics assisted famine as Grim Reapers of the peasantry. Thus, despite the growing endemicity of many formerly severe diseases, the poor performance of the agricultural sector greatly restricted Japan's potential for population growth.

1260–1600

The final era in the history of disease in Japan before 1600 encompasses the years 1260–1600, which are critical for any real comprehension of the role of pestilence in Japanese history. Yet this period has not been investigated in detail by historians, although they have access to thousands of unpublished records from this era. Fujikawa (1969) has listed some of the epidemics for this epoch, but, as Jannetta (1987) and Hattori (1971) have pointed out, it is likely that he has missed some. A major difficulty is that reporting mechanisms of disease were hindered by warfare, especially in the periods 1333–65 and 1460–1550. Thus, records kept at the capital in Kyoto are simply inadequate for the systematic analysis of disease in this period.

Despite problems with the sources, however, broad contours can be sketched if this age is broken down into three subperiods: 1260–1420, 1420–1540, and 1540–1600. In the first subperiod, harsh weather and war assisted disease in limiting population growth from 1261 to 1365. There were 29 epidemics over this 105-year span, or one every 3.6 years. From 1366 to 1420, there were 16 epidemics, or one every 3.4 years. The era included smallpox outbreaks in 1314, 1342, 1361, 1365, and 1374, with that of 1365 appearing to have been the only harsh epidemic. Measles is recorded for 1306–7, 1320, 1362, 1380, and 1405 and afflicted mainly children in 1306–7. Influenza struck in 1264, 1329, 1345, 1365, 1371, 1378, and 1407–8, with the attacks of 1365 and 1371 being particularly widespread; Hattori finds strong evidence that, beginning in the 1300s, more people suffered and died from respiratory diseases than smallpox or measles. No epidemics of dysentery or chickenpox are documented (Hattori 1964; Fujikawa 1969).

Perhaps the most important event in the disease history of Japan during the years 1260–1365 was one that did not occur. In 1274 and 1281, the Mongols attempted to invade the archipelago, but failed both times; in the last invasion, Japan was saved by the intervention of the "divine winds" of a typhoon. As McNeill (1976) has argued, the Mongols carried the plague bacillus from southern China, where it was endemic, to new territories such as China proper and western Europe. If the Mongols had succeeded in their invasion of the islands, then Japan, too, undoubtedly would have suffered from the plague. But Japan remained plague-free, population continued to grow, and the country moved toward an agrocentric society, a condition western Europe avoided in the plague pandemic of 1350–1450.

Although the historical record is difficult to read for the era 1421–1540, it appears that disease remained an important factor in demographic change.

The period contains 45 epidemics of various descriptions, or one outbreak of pestilence for every 2.7 years, representing an increase over the previous era. Smallpox was particularly active, coming in 1452–3, 1477, 1495, 1523, 1525, 1531, and 1537. In all years excepting 1495 and 1525, however, the disease struck only children. The Portuguese missionary Luis Frois wrote that nearly all Japanese bore pockmarks from smallpox, and he believed that the ailment was more severe among the Japanese than the Europeans (Fujikawa 1969; Hattori 1971).

Measles appeared more frequently, as well, attacking the populace in 1441, 1471, 1484, 1489, 1506, and 1513. The outbreaks of 1471, 1484, and 1512 were harsh, killing many people of all ages. Influenza is recorded as epidemic in 1428 and 1535. Dysentery and chickenpox are not documented. The era 1460–1550 was a period of chronic warfare in Japan, which leads one to suspect a link between the increased social strife and the higher incidence of pestilence (Fujikawa 1969; Hattori 1971).

The period from 1540 to 1600 was an era of great population growth in Japan, which represents the beginning of the Edo demographic explosion. Evidence of 14 epidemics has survived in the records, or one for every 4.3 years (Fujikawa 1969; Hattori 1971). An epidemic of 1593–4 should probably be linked to Hideyoshi's invasion of Korea. Smallpox was present only in 1550, and measles struck only in 1578 and 1587. Influenza was reported in 1556, when many children died, but, again, dysentery and chickenpox are not noted in the historical record.

In 1543, the first Westerners visited Japan, but unlike notable other areas, Japan did not suffer unduly from this new contact. Only two new diseases entered the archipelago at this time. The first was syphilis, which may also have been a new ailment in western Europe. The first appearance of syphilis in Japan, however, predates contact with Westerners, for it arrived in 1512 (Hattori 1971, citing Fujikawa). The Japanese immediately dubbed syphilis the "Chinese pox" (tōgasa), and often confused it with both leprosy and smallpox. Frois wrote that syphilis did not cause the embarrassment to the Japanese that it did to the Europeans (Hattori 1971). Its demographic impact was probably small.

The second new disease was introduced directly by the West, specifically by the Portuguese (Boston Globe 1984). Robert Gallo, chief of the Laboratory of Tumor Cell Biology at the National Cancer Institute, has discovered an AIDS (acquired immune deficiency syndrome) virus in the blood of many Japanese living in the southern islands. The virus is called human T-cell leukemia/lymphoma virus (HTLV) I and II, and is somewhat different from the AIDS virus found in the United States, which is named HTLV-III. Of the southern Japanese people who are infected with the virus, only 1 person in 80 develops cancer. The rest suffer from a viral disease, characterized by fever, rash, and malaise. Gallo surmises that Portuguese sailors coming to Japan in the 1500s brought infected monkeys and African slaves, who transmitted the disease to the Japanese population. Historical records betray no evidence of this malady.

The other diseases of the early modern period in the West, such as typhus, do not appear to have been transported to Japan until the Edo period. Thus the Japanese were extraordinarily fortunate when compared to the natives of the New World or the southern Pacific, who were subjected to the onslaught of unfamiliar Western parasites. Many inveterate afflictions, such as malaria, beriberi, dysentery, asthma, pneumonia, worms, idiopathic cholera, dropsy, hepatitis, diabetes, chickenpox, rheumatoid arthritis, tuberculosis, and stomach cancer, continued to leave their mark on Japanese culture. Musō Kokushi, the Zen prelate, died of malaria, whereas several Ashikaga shoguns probably had diabetes.

Recapitulation

The history of disease in Japan over the era 500 to 1600 can be divided into four subperiods. During the first, 500 to 700, evidence indicates the importation of maladies such as smallpox, and frequent communication between the Japanese and their continental neighbors would suggest that epidemics were more common than the sources indicate.

In the second subperiod, from 700 to about 1050, the population suffered from repeated devastating epidemics of killer diseases including smallpox, measles, influenza, dysentery, and mumps. These important infections attacked a population that by and large had no immunities and killed great numbers of adults. The epidemics resulted in population loss, agricultural stagnation, a shortage of labor, revisions in laws dealing with land tenure, tax structure, and local government, a growing maldistribution of income, the rise of a transcendental religion (Buddhism) and millennialism, as well as a sensitivity to the evanescence of life in literature. Other important diseases of this age of plagues included beriberi, malaria, diabetes, and tuberculosis.

The third subperiod, 1050–1260, saw the killer infections of the former period transformed into endemicity and thus to childhood illnesses. It is fairly clear that smallpox and measles were attacking primarily children by the mid-thirteenth century, and probably even earlier. Influenza, however, may have grown in virulence, especially after 1150, when the climate turned colder and wetter. Other serious maladies included leprosy and chickenpox. The period from 1050 to 1260 may have seen some demographic expansion, notably in the east, but disastrous weather patterns and ensuing famine and pestilence began to close this "window of opportunity" around 1150.

The last subperiod, 1260–1600, represented an epoch when disease had a decidedly decreased impact on the archipelago. The Japanese escaped importation of the plague by defeating the Mongols in the 1200s, and by 1365 neither infection nor famine nor war was restricting the growth of Japan's population. The era 1420–1540 may have seen some increased virulence of disease, accompanied by civil war, but the second half of the sixteenth century was remarkably disease-free. Two new infections, syphilis and a relatively harmless variant of the AIDS virus, were brought to Japan from the West, but the effect of these ailments seems to have been limited.

Examination of the sweep of 1,100 years of disease history suggests that demographic trends in Japan were almost the mirror opposite of western Europe. Only in the eras 1050–1150 and 1500–1600 did Japan and the West both experience population growth. To the extent that one equates population growth with economic growth, it seems clear that Japan and western Europe were each led along substantially different paths by a differing biological past.

W. Wayne Farris

Bibliography

Aston, Williams, trans. 1972. *Nihongi*, Vol. 2. Tokyo.
Boston Globe. 1984. May 7.
Farris, Wayne, 1985. *Population, disease, and land in early Japan: 645–900*. Cambridge.
Fujikawa, Yū. 1904. *Nihon igaku shi* (History of Japanese medicine). Tokyo.
  1969. *Nihon shippei shi* (A history of disease in Japan). Tokyo.
Gottfried, Robert. 1983. *The black death*. New York.
Hattori, Toshirō. 1943. Jōko shi iji kō. *Nihon Ishi Gaku Zasshi* 1312: 64–76.
  1945. *Nara jidai igaku no kenkyū* (Medicine in the Nara period, 710–784). Tokyo.
  1955. *Heian jidai igaku no kenkyū* (Medicine in the Heian period, 784–1185). Tokyo.
  1964. *Kamakura jidai igaku shi no kenkyū* (A history of medicine in the Kanakura period, 1185–1333). Tokyo.
  1971. *Muromachi Azuchi Momoyama jidai igaku shi no*

kenkyū (A history of medicine in the Muromachi Azuchi and Momoyama periods, 1333–1600). Tokyo. 1975. *Ōchō kizoku no byōjō shindan.* Tokyo.

Hurst, Cameron. 1979. Michinaga's maladies. *Monumenta Nipponica* 34: 101–12.

Jannetta, Ann B. 1987. *Epidemics and mortality in early modern Japan.* Princeton, N.J.

Kitō, Hiroshi. 1983. *Nihon nisen nen no jinkō shi.* Tokyo.

McCullough, William, and Helen McCullough, trans. 1980. *A tale of flowering fortunes,* Vol. 1. Stamford, Conn.

McNeill, William. 1976. *Plagues and peoples.* New York.

Seidenstecker, Edward, trans. 1985. *The tale of Genji.* New York.

SZKT (*Shintei zōho kokushi taikei*), 1933. *Ruijū fusen shō.* Tokyo.

——— 1966. *Nihon Montoku tennō jitsuroku.* Tokyo.

Takeuchi, Rizō, et al., eds. 1979. The tale of the Masakado. In *Nihon shisō taikei; Kodai seiji shakai shisō,* Vol. 8. Tokyo.

Tsuchida, Naoshige. 1965. *Nihon no rekishi: Ōchō no kizoku.* Tokyo.

Twitchett, Denis. 1979. Population and pestilence in T'ang China. In *Studia Sino-Mongolica: Festschrift für Herbert Franke,* ed. Wolfgang Bauer, 42–53. Wiesbaden.

VI.6 Diseases of the Early Modern Period in Japan

The diseases of early modern Japan (the Tokugawa period) are of particular interest to the history and geography of disease. The Japanese Islands, situated as they are at the far eastern periphery of East Asia, had relatively little contact with the people of other world regions until the late nineteenth century. Historically Japan's isolation afforded the people some measure of protection from exposure to certain of the world's diseases, and in the early seventeenth century, the Tokugawa shoguns reinforced this natural protection when they imposed severe restrictions on foreign contacts. They limited official foreign trade to the port of Nagasaki, restricted the number and the nationality of ships that could enter that port, denied mobility beyond the port to the crews of foreign ships, and prohibited the Japanese from going abroad and returning to Japan. These policies were a response, in part, to the unwelcome activities of Westerners who had begun to reach the islands in the second half of the sixteenth century. They remained in effect until a

U.S. fleet forced Japan to open its ports to international commerce in the 1850s.

Elsewhere explorers, adventurers, traders, and settlers were circumnavigating the globe, carrying new diseases to previously unexposed peoples, and causing waves of high mortality among the populations of many world regions. By 1850 the increasing volume of international contacts had produced a worldwide system of disease dissemination, but Japan, remaining aloof from world affairs, had also remained largely unaffected by the epidemiological events of the early modern world. The diseases of Tokugawa Japan were, for the most part, diseases that had reached the islands centuries earlier.

Japan was part of an East Asian disease dissemination system that differed in certain respects from that of western Eurasia. Human populations in East Asia were larger and more dense than those in the West, and many human disease organisms were able to establish permanent reservoirs of infection with little difficulty. In earlier times, epidemic diseases were disseminated outward from the large population centers of China to the less densely settled regions of the periphery. Occasionally these epidemics would reach Japan, and Japan's population, which was heavily concentrated along the coastal plains, provided an environment highly conducive to disease propagation and dissemination. By 1600, Japan's population was large enough to support many disease organisms in endemic fashion that in earlier times had been imported as epidemics from China.

The most important changes in the disease environment of early modern Japan, relative to earlier periods, were brought about by domestic rather than international developments. Japan's population grew from about 18 million to approximately 30 million people during the seventeenth century, and Edo (present-day Tokyo) became one of the world's largest cities with a population of around 1 million inhabitants. Economic development, which included the commercialization of agriculture, regional specialization, and interregional trade, accompanied population growth. All these developments served to intensify disease transmission within Japan, and by 1850 few communities were remote enough to avoid either the indigenous diseases of Japan or the imported diseases that sometimes managed to penetrate the *cordon sanitaire* that served to protect the country from the international traffic in pathogens.

Sources on Diseases of Japan

Japanese sources that contain information about the diseases of Japan are abundant and of excellent quality. The most important are contemporary reports of epidemics, medical books with descriptions of the symptoms and treatment of important diseases, government documents that issued warnings or commissioned relief measures, temple registers that recorded causes of death, and general writings of the period. Early in the twentieth century, two pioneering Japanese medical historians, Fujikawa Yū and Yamazaki Tasuku, compiled references to disease from many Japanese sources. Their works still stand as basic references on the history of disease in Japan.

Some Western sources also contain references to disease in Japan, but most of these were written before or after the Tokugawa period because during that period there were few Western visitors. Thus Portuguese, Spanish, English, and Dutch adventurers who lived in Japan in the late sixteenth and early seventeenth centuries wrote of illnesses that were observed among the Japanese as well as diseases that seemed to be absent. And two and one-half centuries later, in the late nineteenth century, when Westerners again arrived in Japan, they, too, wrote of the diseases they noticed. Western observations reported at the beginning and the end of the Tokugawa period are of value as benchmarks that help to identify the illnesses that were prevalent during this period.

The diseases of early modern Japan can be divided into two general categories: those that are easily identified on the basis of their symptoms and epidemiological characteristics, and those that are not. Ailments in the first category are primarily acute infectious diseases that have distinctive symptoms, affect many people within a short period of time, and are therefore highly visible. These infections, which have well-established histories, are easily recognized in Japanese sources. Diseases in the second category present symptoms that are vague or general. They may have been very important in causing illness or death, but they cannot be subsumed under any modern disease classification.

Infectious Diseases

Smallpox

Among the acute infectious diseases that can be clearly identified from the sources, smallpox emerges as the major killer and the most common cause of premature death. Certainly, more medical books were written about this illness than any other. An old disease in Japan, smallpox was endemic in the large cities well before 1600, and by the late eighteenth and early nineteenth centuries, epidemics struck even remote parts of Japan every 3 or 4 years. Smallpox

was almost entirely an illness of children under the age of 5 years, with few escaping it and many dying of it. As late as 1850, at least 10 percent of the population died of smallpox, and Western observers wrote in the 1860s that smallpox in Japan was so common that virtually every countenance was pockmarked. The introduction of smallpox vaccine in 1849 would reduce the importance of the disease as a cause of death by the late nineteenth century.

Measles

The history of measles in Japan is unlike that of western Europe. In the parts of Europe for which there are good records, measles epidemics were reported frequently. At the end of the eighteenth century, for example, epidemics were occurring regularly in England in about one of every 3 years, and in Germany at regular intervals of about 4 to 5 years. But in Japan, only 11 measles epidemics were reported between 1616 and 1862, and contemporary accounts also provide evidence that epidemics were very rare. Consequently, measles was regarded as a dread disease because unlike smallpox, which was omnipresent, measles seemed to come out of nowhere, and infected young and old alike.

The different epidemiological patterns of measles epidemics in Japan on the one hand and in western Europe on the other seem to be related to different patterns of contact between populations in which the virus circulated. Frequent contact between the many trading centers of western Europe promoted the dissemination of the virulent measles virus and caused frequent epidemics. By contrast, the restriction of trade and the infrequent and seasonal pattern of maritime trade between Japan and other countries of East Asia may have prevented the measles virus from being imported very often.

In Japan the measles virus invariably spread from the port of Nagasaki in the southeast to the major cities of Kyoto, Osaka, and Edo to the northeast, and from there to the more remote parts of central and northern Japan. Moreover, it spread very rapidly because the population was densely concentrated along internal trade routes, and because, with infrequent epidemics, an unusually large segment of the population was susceptible to infection. In these circumstances, the measles virus quickly ran out of new hosts to infect and thus died out, which meant that a new importation of the virus was required for another epidemic to occur.

Unusually good records of measles epidemics were kept during the Tokugawa period, presumably because they infected so many people. These records document epidemics in 1616, 1649, 1690, 1708, 1730, 1753, 1776, 1803, 1824, 1836, and 1862. The geographic pattern of dissemination, the age distribution of the cases, and other contemporary evidence suggest that measles remained an imported disease that caused infrequent but severe epidemics in Japan until after 1850.

Measles was clearly distinguished from smallpox in the Japanese records because of its very different epidemiological pattern. A person was most likely to get smallpox as a young child because the virus was always circulating through the population, whereas a person would get measles only when the virus happened to sweep through the country. Morbidity and mortality rates were high in measles epidemics because of the large proportion of the population that became ill at once. However, measles mortality over the long term was much lower than smallpox mortality.

Other Airborne Infections

Other well-known airborne infections that cause skin rashes or eruptions are also described in Tokugawa sources. Chickenpox, for example, seems to have been common. In fact, in the shogun's palace, special ceremonies were held to celebrate a child's recovery from smallpox, measles, and chickenpox, indicating that all of these diseases were considered a threat to life in Tokugawa Japan.

Influenza is also prominently mentioned in the Japanese sources from early times, and 27 influenza epidemics are described in contemporary accounts of the Tokugawa period. The Japanese accounts are similar to accounts of influenza epidemics elsewhere: They describe a coughing epidemic that spread extremely rapidly, infecting everyone – young and old, male and female. As is typical of influenza, the mortality rate was highest among the very young and the very old. Influenza epidemics, like other imported epidemics, were said to enter Japan through the port of Nagasaki. In the seventeenth and eighteenth centuries, the timing of epidemics was different from those reported in Europe; but by the nineteenth century, influenza epidemics were noted in both regions at very nearly the same time. It appears that two distinct regional dissemination systems for influenza may have merged during the early modern period as the frequency of contact and speed of transport between East and West increased.

Diarrheal Diseases

In Japan, epidemics of diarrheal diseases were reported as early as the ninth century, but severe, large-scale epidemics seem to have been fairly rare in the early modern period. Fujikawa mentions only seven epidemics of diarrheal diseases for the Tokugawa period in his chronology of epidemics in Japan. It is impossible to distinguish between the different kinds of enteric diseases known today, because the symptoms of diarrheal infections are much the same regardless of the infecting agent. Such infections were most likely to be reported in Japanese historical sources when a large city or an important person was stricken, and these occasions were quite rare.

The absence of major dysentery-type epidemics is not too surprising. Because enteric diseases are caused by contaminated water or food, they normally have a local or at most a regional distribution. Local records, however, suggest that in certain localities, diarrheal diseases were fairly common. For example, a temple death register from Hida province that recorded causes of death in the late eighteenth and early nineteenth centuries documents a fairly severe epidemic in the autumn of 1826. Dysentery claimed 59 lives within a 6-week period; the victims were mostly children under 10 years of age. But such epidemics were unusual. It was more common for diarrheal diseases to claim a few lives each year in the later summer or autumn than to erupt in major epidemics.

An enteric disease that did attract national attention in the late Tokugawa period was "Asiatic" cholera. The first cholera pandemic, which began to spread outside of India in 1817, reached Japan toward the end of 1822. It followed the pattern typical of imported diseases in Japan by breaking out first in the port of Nagasaki, where it ws heralded as a new disease. It spread from there in a northeasterly direction to Kyoto and Osaka, but died out, presumably because of the cold weather, before reaching the capital at Edo. Ironically, the disease that was known in the West as "Asiatic" cholera was known in Japan as "the disease of the Western barbarians."

There is no further evidence of cholera in Japan until 1858, when it once again arrived in Nagasaki, this time on the American ship *Mississippi*. The fact that there were no outbreaks of cholera in Japan between 1822 and 1858 is remarkable, because it was during this period that the disease became a major threat to cities of the West. But Japan's political *cordon sanitaire* seems to have been effective in keeping cholera out. By the late 1850s, however, after its ports had beeen opened to international trade by American gunboats, Japan was stricken by the same pandemics that affected other world regions.

Chronic Diseases

It is much more difficult to identify the nonepidemic or chronic diseases of the early modern period, but there is no doubt that venereal diseases were common. Gonorrhea was an old disease in Japan and presumably had a wide distribution. However, a new venereal disease that was probably syphilis reached Japan around 1513. The Japanese called it "the great pox" – the same name that Europeans had given to syphilis a short time before. The Japanese later claimed that syphilis had been brought to them by the Portuguese, but as the Portuguese did not reach Japan until 1543, this conclusion is questionable. Syphilis probably spread from Portuguese to Japanese or Ryukyuan traders in the East Indies in the early sixteenth century, and then subsequently entered Japan on East Asian ships.

By 1600 syphilis was a major health problem in Japan's large cities. Sixteenth-century European observers had reported that it was widespread among the Japanese population, and contemporary Japanese writers claimed that in Edo more doctors treated syphilis than any other disease. Fully 9.64 percent of the human skulls that have been excavated from several Edo period sites in and around Tokyo show cranial lesions caused by tertiary syphilis (8.8 percent male; 5.9 percent female). This rate seems quite high, especially when one considers that the incidence of earlier stage syphilis in the population would have been much higher than the incidence of tertiary syphilis. However, when one considers the high proportion of males in the population of Edo and the numerous licensed pleasure quarters and widespread prostitution, perhaps a high rate of syphilis morbidity and mortality was to be expected.

Other Diseases

Bubonic plague and epidemic typhus, the two most important vector-borne diseases in early modern Europe, seem not to have afflicted early modern Japan. Rather plague was first reported in Japan at the end of the nineteenth century and believed to have arrived on ships from China that carried plague-infested rats. Typhus probably arrived somewhat earlier, but typhus and typhoid were confused in Japan as they were in Europe, so it is difficult to determine which disease is being referred to in the Japanese sources. A Japanese variant of typhus, called *tsutsugamushi* disease, is fairly common in the Shinano River Valley. It is carried by a mite, and although the illness can be fatal, it has a much more benign history than European typhus.

The popular literature of the Tokugawa period mentions other common illnesses, but, as noted earlier, it is usually impossible to identify them within modern nosology. The kinds of diseases referred to, however, were those experienced by many early modern societies. Ailments of the eye were apparently very common, as they were featured in medical books and in general accounts of the period. Pompe van Meerdervoort, a Dutch physician who arrived in Japan in the 1850s, writes that he was struck by the number of Japanese people who were visibly afflicted, often blinded, by eye diseases. These people probably suffered from trachoma, a disease that was common in Japan in the late nineteenth century, and presumably in earlier times as well.

Other health problems frequently mentioned in contemporary literature include beriberi, toothaches, hemorrhoids, ringworm, coughing disease, kidney problems, and food poisoning. In addition to these common ailments, there are two others, which are called *senki* and *shaku*. These two terms, used in Japan as early as the tenth century, appear to refer to a host of diseases that cause stomach, intestinal, or back pain. *Senki* seems to refer to chronic disease, and *shaku* to more acute problems.

The various treatments recommended for these two illnesses suggest that they may have been caused by worms or other intestinal parasites, tumors, diseases of the stomach or gallbladder, ulcers, kidney disease, and various problems involving the lower back. In other words, these were catch-all terms that covered many of the different diseases that afflict humanity. The various manifestations of *senki* and *shaku* were featured in Tokugawa medical books, and, depending upon the symptoms, it was the task of the physician to recommend appropriate treatment.

There are few surprises in the kinds of disease described in the Tokugawa sources. Of greater interest is the failure to find evidence of certain diseases that were common in the West. Plague and epidemic typhus, already mentioned, are conspicuous by their absence. And Westerners who arrived in Japan in the late nineteenth century commented on the rarity of scarlet fever, diphtheria, tuberculosis, typhoid, cholera infantum, epidemic dysentery, and severe forms of malaria. Even tuberculosis seemed much less prevalent in Japan in the 1860s than in contemporary Europe, but tuberculosis death rates were rising sharply by the end of the century. The differences in the disease histories of Japan and the West suggest again that Japan's isolation from world trade gave the islands a measure of protection from some of the major diseases of the early modern period.

Ann Bowman Jannetta

Bibliography

Fujikawa, Yū. 1939. *Nihon shippei shi*, 3d edition. Tokyo.

Jannetta, Ann B. 1987. *Epidemics and mortality in early modern Japan.* Princeton, N.J.

Maekawa, Kyūtarō. 1976. Sasuyu kiroku yori mita Tōsō, mashin, suitō. No Ōoku e no denpa. *Nihon ishigaku zasshi* 22: 157–68.

Matsuda, Takeshi. 1971. Edo jidai no mashin ryūkō. *Nihon Ishigaku Zasshi* 17: 206–12.

Morse, Edward. 1917. *Japan, day by day, 1877, 1878–79, 1882–83.* Vol. 1. New York.

Suda, Keizō. 1973 *Hida "Ō" jiin kakochō no kenkyū.* Takayama.

Suzuki, Takao. 1984. *Paleopathological and paleoepidemiological study of osseous syphilis in the Edo period.* Tokyo.

Tatsukawa, Shōji. 1974. Shomin shiryō ni miru Edo jidai no shippei. *Nihon ishigaku zasshi* 20: 313–35.

1976. *Nihonjin no byōreki.* Tokyo.

Yamazaki, Tasuku. 1931. *Nihon ekishi oyobi bōeki shi.* Tokyo.

VI.7
Diseases of Antiquity in Korea

The history of diseases in Korea, especially the diseases of the early historic period, constitutes a still largely unexplored area, save for the efforts of a few pioneering scholars whose findings are not yet available in English translations (Miki 1962; Kim 1966). However, this field should be of considerable interest to students of Asian history as well as those concerned with the history of medicine.

Geography, History, and Background

Much of Korea's epidemiological past has been shaped by its geography. The country occupies a peninsula south of Manchuria that is separated from the Chinese mainland to the west by the Yellow Sea, and from nearby Japan to the east by the Korean and the Tsushima Straits. Forming a land bridge between northern Asia and the islands of Japan, Korea has time and again been subjected to invasions by armies from the Asian mainland intending to attack Japan, or by Japanese armies establishing a base from which to attack the Asian mainland. Undoubtedly, these contacts must have brought infectious diseases to Korea.

To discuss diseases of antiquity in Korea means to discuss those illnesses that occurred during the Old Choson Period (traditionally dated 2333 B.C. to A.D. 562), and the Three Kingdoms Era encompassing the Kingdoms of Koguryo (37 B.C. to A.D. 688), Paekche (18 B.C. to A.D. 660), and Silla (57 B.C. to A.D. 935), as well as the Koryo Era (918–1392). By the ninth century B.C., rice-cultivating Bronze Age cultures had been established on the Korean peninsula. During the Three Kingdoms Era, the Chinese writing system was adopted by the courts in order to ensure the writing down of state chronicles. Only fragments of these texts have survived by being incorporated in the *Samguk sagi* (History of the Three Kingdoms), which was compiled in 1145 and constitutes the oldest preserved history of Korea.

The introduction of Buddhism to Korea from China during the fourth century A.D. increased contacts with the Asian mainland. Particularly during the Three Kingdoms Era, many Korean Buddhist monks studied in China and were responsible for the influx of many aspects of Chinese culture to the peninsula. When, after long periods of warfare, the Three Kingdoms were unified in 661, the resulting Kingdom of Unified Silla extended cultural and economic contacts with China. Besides an increasing number of Buddhist monks, students interested in Confucian learning went to China. Some Buddhists even reached India, endeavoring to study their religion at its source. This period also saw increasing cultural and economic exchange with Japan, and commercial intercourse with Arab traders.

Although Korea was epidemiologically not as isolated as Japan, and the development of immunities within the population must have set in earlier and more intensively, the long periods of unrest, poverty, and famine during the wars of unification must have favored the outbreak of epidemics and famine-related diseases. Social reforms during the Koryo Era (918–1392) may have improved this situation. Relief programs, sponsored by the government and by the Buddhist church, were implemented; granaries were built as a precaution against years of drought; infirmaries were created; and a system of medical care in the countryside was established. Despite all these efforts, however, the vast majority of the population stayed in poverty and, consequently, remained particularly vulnerable to contagious diseases.

Diseases

Textual sources relevant to the study of diseases in the early history of Korea are scarce. The *Shin Jip Ban* (Anthology of Paekche Prescriptions) and the *Bup Sa Ban* (Prescriptions of the Masters of Silla), medical texts compiled in the states of Paekche and Silla, respectively, are lost. Only some passages and prescriptions have survived by being incorporated into Chinese and Japanese texts. The *Ishinpō,* a collection of mainly Chinese medical texts, compiled by the Japanese scholar Tamba Yasuyori in 984, refers to the *Shin Jip Ban* in a discussion concerning abscesses.

Korean physicians were very much influenced by Chinese medical thinking, and adopted Chinese medical terminology. But they also reinterpreted Chinese material in their own way and added information obtained from Indian sources.

Owing to the lack of genuine medical literature of that period, we have to rely on historical literature for information regarding diseases. The *Samguk sagi* mentions a first occurrence of an epidemic during the reign of Onjo, king of Paekche, in 15 B.C. There are a great number of different terms for epidemic diseases in ancient Korean writings such as "poison epidemic," "evil epidemic," "epidemic of the time," "epidemic of disease," and others. Identifications of these terms are, however, difficult. Thus, the Chinese character that could be translated "leprosy epidemic" might simply refer to a widespread disease of a very severe nature.

Diseases were discussed in terms of their major symptoms. However, often no clear distinctions were made, and death from famine was recorded with the same wording as death from an epidemic. No need for precision may have been felt in a society that attributed misfortune, disease, and death to the action of ghosts, devils, and demons. Although the more rational principles of Chinese medicine were known to the physicians, they rarely made distinctions solely based on these criteria.

The only complete extant medical book of the Koryo Era is the *Hyang-yak kugup pang* (Emergency remedies of folk medicine). This collection of simple relief measures and preparations was compiled during the reign of King Kojong, in 1236. It deals mainly with emergency measures such as employed in accidents; injuries; bites by insects, reptiles, and other animals; drowning; sunstroke; food poisoning; drunkenness; and toothache. It describes, however, also symptoms of diseases and their treatment. This book may be considered to reflect the scholarly attitude toward health care because it leans strongly on the tradition of Chinese medicine. Thus, symptoms such as hemorrhages, blockages of the throat, loss of consciousness, and sudden death from various infectious diseases are discussed. A combined study of the *Hyang-yak kugup pang* and official annals such as the *History of Koryo* would provide more insights into the epidemiology of that period. It must be noted, however, that the official historical writings expressed little awareness of medical problems in the country except in case of extended and devastating epidemics, those that involved the capital city or its environs, or cases of illness within the royal family.

The following represents a survey of diseases or groups of diseases, endemic or epidemic, the occurrence of which can be inferred from miscellaneous textual sources:

Smallpox

Historians generally agree that smallpox originated from India. According to the *Tongui pogam* (Exemplar of Korean Medicine 1610), smallpox had appeared in China already at the end of the Zhou dynasty and the beginning of the Han dynasty (i.e., during the late third century B.C.). A first mentioning of smallpox in a Chinese source suggests a later date (*Zhou-hou bei-ji fang* by Ge Hong, first half of the fourth century A.D.), whereas a first documented smallpox epidemic can be dated A.D. 495.

A terminus antequem for the arrival of smallpox to Korea may be deduced from the fact that Korean envoys of King Song (523–54) of Paekche, who brought Buddhist scriptures and statues to Japan, transmitted the disease to that country in 552. Shortly after Emperor Kimmei legalized Buddhism, an epidemic of smallpox broke out, and led to the immediate abolition of the new religion. In 584, Japanese officials visited Korea and brought back to Japan the disease together with two images of Buddha. Emperor Bidatsu himself became a victim of the ensuing epidemic the following year. Two years later, with the epidemic still raging, Emperor Yomeī (585–7) died of the disease, too. Also the epidemics of 735–7 and of 763 are supposed to have been transmitted to Japan from the Korean peninsula. At any rate, during the Three Kingdoms Era, Korea was a frequent victim of the disease; two kings, Sondock (780–5) and Munjong (839–57), died of smallpox.

For the Koryo Era there is no evidence for the occurrence of smallpox epidemics. Yet, the *Hyang-yak kugup pang* refers to eruptive diseases in the chapter "Various Childhood Diseases"; the text speaks of "pea-sized boils" and "bean-sized boils in the child." This could well be a reference to small-pox. If we correctly interpret this passage, and if smallpox had become one of the common children's diseases, then it would have been firmly established in Korea at this period. It should, however, be noted that measles was apparently not distinguished from smallpox until the beginning of the Yi dynasty (1392–1910).

Other Febrile Illnesses

There can be little doubt that malaria was epidemic on the Korean peninsula from time immemorial. A first mentioning of the disease, however, is as late as the *History of Koryo*. The *Hyang-yak kugup pang* contains a passage on "malaria disease" and its therapy. Although not always strictly differentiated from other febrile illnesses, the symptoms of the "3-day fever," as it was usually called, are sufficiently distinct to recognize it with some degree of certainty; various drugs were employed to obtain relief during the attacks (Miki 1962). Although typhoid fever may have been subsumed under and classified together with other febrile diseases, when one considers the social and hygienic conditions of the period, there can be little doubt of its role in Korean medical history. The same may apply to diphtheria; perhaps the term "blockage of the throat" refers to this disease.

Respiratory Diseases

The *Hyang-yak kugup pang* refers to illnesses that, in modern terms, would be classified as respiratory diseases. In fact, there seem to be references to asthma, pleurisy, and hydrothorax. Whether or not pulmonary tuberculosis and pneumonia, frequent diseases in many premodern societies, were recognized as individual diseases cannot be ascertained from the text.

Parasitic Infestations

The texts mention a disease with bloody saliva. This symptom is characteristic of pulmonary distomatosis, an infestation with *Paragonimus westermani*, which is still prevalent in East Asia, particularly in Korea.

Diarrhea and Dysentery

Taking the minute categorization of diseases accompanied by diarrhea, as found in the *Hyang-yak kugup pang*, as an indicator, this group of illnesses appears to have been common and well known. Whereas the official chronicles omitted these, the *Hyang-yak kugup pang* gives a description of an epidemic with precise details of its symptomatology, including the twisting stomachache and bloody stools. Besides, this book mentions "cold dysentery," "dysentery with blue color," "hot dysentery with reddish-yellow color," "red dysentery with stomachache," and others.

Venereal Diseases

One of the main symptoms of advanced gonorrhea, difficult urination, is mentioned in the *Hyang-yak kugup pang*. Besides this book distinguishes five types of gonorrhea. That the nature of contagion of this disease was understood is implied in the following passage in the *History of Koryo*:

One night Mr. Hong took the previous King Chunghye (1330–1332) to his house and they feasted. The King ordered a priest-doctor to cure Mr. Hong's gonorrhea. The King always took a fever drug and visited many ladies. As a result he had disease. The King and Mr. Hong received curing methods from the priest. The King . . . used the fever medicine to increase his stamina. (Miki 1962)

Diseases due to Nutritional Deficiencies

In a largely agricultural society, only sufficient local harvests could avert famine and famine-related diseases. In the early Three Kingdoms period, the king of Paekche was held responsible for crop failure and, in such cases, removed from the throne or even killed (Lee 1984). One of the most common nutritional diseases in rice-growing societies up to recent times has been beriberi, that is, thiamine or vitamin B deficiency. Although there is no description of the symptoms in Korean sources prior to the Yi dynasty (1392–1910), we may assume that this disease was common, whenever rice was polished and the husk, which contains this vitamin, was stripped from the grain.

Skin Diseases, Tumors, and Leprosy

The *Hyang-yak kugup pang* contains a section on tumors. However, whether these refer to abscesses, carbuncles, and other inflammatory swelling remains uncertain, particularly because these descriptions are mixed with those of other skin diseases such as furunculosis, dermatitis, scabies, and erysipelas; erysipelas of the head and face is emphasized in the text. Another skin disease marked by boils that is mentioned in this text most probably refers to leprosy. The *History of Koryo* frequently refers to leprosy as the "bad disease" which is widespread, malignant, and hard to cure. That persons stricken with this disease not only spread horror to the healthy population but also tended to elicit pity and gave rise to benevolent deeds is shown by a passage from the *History of Koryo* in which a devoted son cut off a piece of his own flesh in order to cure his father's disease.

Miscellaneous Diseases and Conditions

The Hyang-yak kugup pang gives a clear-cut definition of tetanus by stating that a spear wound will be fatal if it has caused lockjaw and spasms. Similarly, brief descriptions are given for rabies, stroke, epilepsy, hemorrhoids, prolapsed anus, and diabetes mellitus. The latter is defined as causing much urine, being unrelated to gonorrhea, and resulting in very thin patients. Somewhat obscure is the category of "water-swelling" diseases. Obviously referring to edemas, this term may include not only primary heart or kidney disease but also edemas of wet beriberi; consequently, the symptoms of "water-swelling" diseases are also listed in this book under the heading of "paralysis," this being one of the cardinal symptoms of dry beriberi.

Finally, the *Hyang-yak kugup pang* has a section on insanity, termed "uneasiness of mind," "unusualness of mind," or, in the case of psychosis, "true madness." However, insanity was a health problem that was considered outside the confines of scholarly medicine; treatment called for the *mudang* (shaman) rather than the physician.

Lois N. Magner

Bibliography

Ackerknecht, Erwin H. 1965. *History and geography of the most important diseases.* New York.

Fujikawa, Yū 1934. *Japanese medicine,* trans. John Ruhrah. New York.

Han Woo-keun. 1970. *The history of Korea,* trans. Lee Kyung-shik, ed. Grafton K. Mintz. Seoul, Korea.

Henschen, Folke. 1966. *The history and geography of diseases,* trans. Joan Tate. New York.

Huard, Pierre, and Ming Wong. 1972. *Chinese medicine,* trans. Bernard Fielding. New York.

Kim Tu-jong. 1966. *Han'guk uihaksa* (A history of Korean medicine). Seoul, Korea.

Lee Ki-baik. 1984. *A new history of Korea,* trans. Edward W. Wagner. Cambridge, Mass.

Miki, Sakae. 1962. *History of Korean medicine and of disease in Korea.* Japan. [In Japanese]

Ponsonby Fane, R. A. B. 1959. *The Imperial House of Japan.* Japan.

VI.8
Diseases of the Premodern Period in Korea

Medical Literature

In 1392 Yi Songgye assumed the throne as King T'aejo and the Yi Dynasty (1392–1910) began. His supporters initiated a sweeping land reform program that began with a cadastral survey of landholding throughout the country and the destruction of previous registers of public and private landholdings. New developments in agriculture as well as in science, technology, and medicine followed, stimulating inventions and publications. For example, the agricultural manual called *The Art of Farming,* compiled in 1430, was based on the reasonable but novel premise that because Korean climate and soil differed from those of China, agricultural methods should be designed to meet the specific conditions found in the peninsula. Improvements in agricultural techniques produced increased yields, and the spread of cotton cultivation provided improved clothing for the common people.

Important developments in medical knowledge took place in the early years of the Yi dynasty, as the government encouraged its study and created two specialized institutions for medical care. One served the royal family and elite officials, and the other was to serve the general population. Candidates who scored well on the "Miscellaneous Examinations" could be employed in the Palace Medical Office, which trained regional medical officials.

The concept that indigenous conditions must be considered was increasingly incorporated into medical as well as agricultural writings. China's influence on medical philosophy remained strong, but interest in the study and exploitation of Korea's own traditional folk remedies stimulated the development of independent medical scholarship as may be seen in the *Hyang-yak kugup pang* (Emergency Remedies of Folk Medicine 1236).

A major milestone in the development of Korean medical science was the publication of a medical encyclopedia in 85 volumes entitled the *Hyangyak chipsong pang* (Compilation of Native Korean Prescriptions 1433). A similar format was followed by the compilers of the *Uibang yuch'wi* (Classified Collection of Medical Prescriptions), which was completed in 1445. In an attempt to include all known theories of medicine, the compilers assembled 264 volumes. Unfortunately, this resulted in a massive collection unsuited for general use, and only a few copies were ever produced. In 1596 the King ordered Ho Chun to prepare a more useful text. The project took Ho Chun and his group more than 10 years to complete. It resulted in the highly respected 25 volumes of *Tongui pogam* (Exemplar of Korean Medicine 1610), which were still being reprinted in Korea, China, and Japan during the eighteenth century. The work's preparation was, at least in part, a response to the devastation caused throughout almost all of Korea during the 7-year struggle of the Hideyoshi Invasion (1592–8). In the most severely affected provinces some villages were totally destroyed, population was markedly decreased, and famine and epidemic disease inevitably compounded the misery of the people (Lee 1984).

The *Hyangyak chipsong pang* and the *Tongui pogam* served as the models for many other medical books of this era. Ho Chun, the author of the *Tongui pogam,* was a Taoist, and his medical philosophy rested on the three Taoist essences: mind, sense, and spiritual power. His classification of disease was based on causes as well as symptomatology and the physical location of disorders. The view of disease initiated by the *Tongui pogam* exerted a profound influence on the Korean medical world during the second half of the Yi Dynasty. Epidemics were collectively referred to as "bad disease" in the ancient period, but as medical knowledge developed, references to epidemic diseases became more specific. Generally, the epidemic diseases recorded as "bad disease" in the *Yijo Sillok* (True History of the Yi Dynasty) constituted those other than the eruptive fevers, among them influenza, epidemic meningitis, typhoid and typhuslike diseases, and other diseases that have no particularly well-marked external manifestations.

Typhus and Typhoid Fever Group

Clear descriptions of typhus begin to appear only in modern times, but epidemic occurrences of typhuslike diseases in ancient times can be recognized in China and Korea. For example, an epidemic that started in P'yongan Province in July 1524, and spread continuously until it reached the middle provinces of the peninsula, seems suspiciously typhuslike. The epidemic lasted until the spring of 1527, and contemporary accounts emphasized the high fever and contagious nature of the ailment. Another typhuslike epidemic seems to have occurred in 1543, and still another in 1612 in the province of Hamgyong and then spread to the south. It was

because of this latter epidemic that Ho Chun was ordered to compile a new book of detailed curing methods, and certainly his account leaves the impression that this disease was a member of the typhus fever group.

As with typhus, little historical evidence of major epidemics of typhoid fever in Korea exists. Yet occasionally whole villages contracted a disease with symptoms suggestive of typhoid. It is likely that typhoid fever was endemic and epidemic during the Yi Dynasty, but few local outbreaks were noted in official records. Until recent times, typhus and typhoid were not distinguished from each other. Typhoid fever remained endemic in modern Korea, but many people viewed typhoid as a rather minor disease of about the same severity as "red dysentery."

Relapsing fever, a tick-borne disease that was considered one of the forms of typhus, may have appeared in Korea during the sixteenth century when epidemics occurred in China and Manchuria, but the evidence from the early Yi Dynasty is obscure. Two other diseases that might have existed in Korea during this time period are *leptospirosis* (Weil's disease or leptospiral jaundice) and *rat-bite fever.* Most Korean therapeutic texts included a brief account of certain curing methods that suggest knowledge of rat-bite fever.

Bubonic Plague

Although waves of devastating epidemics of bubonic plague have been recorded in China since 1331, the surviving literature from Korea does not seem to contain specific descriptions of similar epidemics (Miki 1962).

Influenza

The *Hyangyak chipsong pang,* the *Tongui pogam,* and other medical texts of the Yi Dynasty discuss symptoms of epidemic disease best explained as influenza. Although large and small epidemics of influenza probably occurred many times during this period, the historical records are ambiguous; perhaps the outbreaks were not sufficiently striking or widespread to be separated from other epidemic diseases. However, major influenza epidemics occurred in Japan during this period, and it seems reasonable to assume that there were comparable epidemics in Korea. Moreover, given the nature of influenza, epidemics could have ricocheted back and forth between Korea and Japan (Fujikawa 1934).

Smallpox

Smallpox was the most feared disease on the peninsula because epidemics were extensive and mortality rates were high. Before the practice of vaccination was established, few people avoided an encounter with smallpox.

Most references to the epidemiology of smallpox during this era are found in the *Yijo Sillok,* historical records of the Yi Dynasty. Thus, the records are biased toward epidemics that occurred near the capital and affected the royal family. For example, in 1418 the Prince died of the "disease with bean-sized eruptions." In 1424, King Sejong's son died of an eruptive disease. In 1675, King Sukchong contracted smallpox. In 1680, an epidemic broke out in the capital city, and the Queen contracted the disease (the King had previously moved to another palace). During the seventeenth and eighteenth centuries, Western science and technology were coming into Korea and stimulating progress in science and medicine. An example of this trend was the *Makwa hoet'ong* (Comprehensive Treatise on Smallpox), a specialized medical treatise published in 1798 (Lee 1984).

Chickenpox

Although chickenpox was confused with smallpox until very recent times, the history of the reign of King Myongjong (1545–67) refers to "big" and "small" eruptive diseases. The big eruptive disease probably corresponds to smallpox; however, whether the small eruptive disease corresponds to chickenpox or measles is uncertain. In the *Sukchong Sillok* (Sukchong reigned from 1674 to 1720), a description of eruptive diseases with big and small efflorescences survives that suggests a slightly different meaning from previous records of these eruptive diseases. At this time, measles was generally distinguished from smallpox, so the small eruptive disease could have been chickenpox. In the records of the period 1724–76, references to episodes of illness and recovery of the Queen and the Prince included all the symptoms of chickenpox. Similar examples can be found following the middle period of the Yi Dynasty.

Measles

During the early period of the Yi Dynasty, medical texts such as the *Hyangyak chipsong pang* indicate a dawning recognition that measles was a disease that could be separated from smallpox. Seventeenth-century Korean texts described a "dot-eruption disease" that appears to be measles. However, doctors seemed to have had difficulty securing knowledge of this eruptive disease, suggesting that epidemics of measles were rare. It is worth noting that Ho Chun suggested that the "poisonous epidemic of the T'ang"

that occurred in 1613 was similar to measles, but was a separate disease. This epidemic may have been scarlatina, as doctors were unable to differentiate between scarlatina and measles.

Subsequent medical books say nothing significant or new about the "dot-eruptive disease" until the eighteenth century, when doctors influenced by the "School of Positivism" began to write specialized medical texts based on their own experiences and case studies. A measles outbreak that occurred in 1707 stimulated interest in the disease, and several specialized books on measles were written in response to the epidemics of 1752 and 1775. Such texts provided comprehensive discussions of the symptoms and treatment of measles and smallpox, and made it possible for doctors to differentiate the eruptive diseases.

Rubella

It is difficult to determine whether physicians of this period were familiar with rubella, for even the most specialized eighteenth-century books on smallpox and measles do not seem to describe it. In the chronicles of King Yongjo (1724–76), however, there are entries noting that the 9-year-old Prince had measles in 1743. Then, when the Prince was 18 years old, he had measles again, and two years later he had "dot-measles." There was a major epidemic of measles when the Prince was 18 years old, so presumably the Prince really had measles at that time. Because an individual has measles only once, the other episodes could have been rubella and scarlatina. There are several other examples of such cases.

Scarlatina, or Scarlet Fever

Scarlatina was not described as an independent disease in Korea at this time, but a disease that might be scarlatina occurred in 1613 under the name "poisonous epidemic of the T'ang." A detailed study of the epidemic, symptoms of the disease, and curing methods was prepared by Ho Chun.

Dysentery

Diseases with the characteristic symptoms of dysentery existed in ancient times in China, Korea, and Japan. Dysentery-like diseases were given many descriptive names, such as red dysentery, bloody dysentery, red-white dysentery, thick-blood dysentery, and so forth. The major symptoms common to the entire group were fever, stomachache, bloody excretions, spasms, and frequent diarrhea. Major epidemics are generally associated with true *Shigella* dysentery, but both bacillary and amebic dysentery were endemic in Korea. Compared to other epidemic diseases, dysentery was not considered very grave, and therefore, it was often omitted from official chronologies of epidemics.

The *Hyangyak chipsong pang* divided all diarrheas into 23 different forms, including red dysentery. The text also describes various diarrheas that affect children and lists 10 different forms based on the symptoms that predominated under different conditions. Medical books written during the middle and late years of the Yi Dynasty also describe dysentery symptoms.

Diphtheria

In Korea, as in China and Japan, there are no clear descriptions of a disease corresponding to diphtheria until the modern age. Differential diagnosis of sore throat diseases, such as diphtheria, scarlet fever, and tonsillitis, is just as difficult as sorting out the eruptive fevers and the typhuslike diseases. Moreover, diphtheria is not strongly associated with dramatic epidemics of high mortality. Indeed, mild cases are not unusual, and immunity is often quietly acquired at an early age. Since ancient times, however, many different names have been applied to various diseases of the throat. It therefore appears probable that diphtheria was recognized as a particular disease marked by a characteristic symptomatology.

Two diseases consistent with a diagnosis of diphtheria are listed in the *Hyangyak chipsong pang* under the heading "Throat." The *Tongui pogam* lists several different forms of throat disease, including a contagious disease that might correspond to diphtheria. Korean medical treatises of the eighteenth century also described throat diseases with symptoms similar to those of diphtheria.

Whooping Cough or Pertussis

Symptoms similar to those of pertussis appear in the *Hyangyak chipsong pang*. A list of various "coughing diseases" includes symptoms suggesting pertussis, and the section on pediatrics describes symptoms similar to pertussis under the heading "Children's Coughing." The *Tongui pogam* and texts from the eighteenth century also describe symptoms that suggest whooping cough.

Epidemic Meningitis

A disease that might have been epidemic cerebrospinal meningitis is described in the annals of the reign of King Songjong (1469–94). According to these records, in November 1471, an epidemic disease appeared in Hwanghae Province. It died out by March of the following year, but the unusual nature of the epidemic attracted the attention of the central government. Medical officials were dispatched to the province to dispense medicines and report on the causes and symptoms. According to the official observer, the disease occurred mainly within Hwanghae Province. In comparison to other epidemic diseases, its ability to spread was weak, and thus the number of individuals affected was not very large. The disease had probably occurred previously in the same province as early as 1434. Outbreaks continued into 1458, but the number and dates of outbreaks cannot be ascertained.

The first symptoms of the disease included blurred vision, loss of vision, delirium and babbling, frenzy, and finally prostration and collapse. Other symptoms were difficulty of movement of the whole body, paralysis below the waist, swelling of the lower abdomen, pains, blackening of the teeth, weakness in the extremities, coughing, and gasping. If one member of the family fell ill, the whole family might sicken and die. When all the symptoms are considered, a tentative diagnosis of epidemic cerebrospinal meningitis seems reasonable (Miki 1962).

Malaria

Malaria was the most common of the infectious diseases in Korea, where it almost always appeared as the "3-day fever" and where knowledge about it developed relatively early. The relief methods in the *Hyangyak chipsong pang* are based on a combination of Chinese remedies and those in the *Hyang-yak kugup pang*.

Sexually Transmitted Diseases

Syphilis probably came to Korea from China between 1506 and 1521, and by the seventeenth century had spread among all classes of people throughout the country. Venereal diseases were known in the Orient long before syphilis spread throughout the world. Korean texts contain descriptions of such diseases, but the venereal diseases described in the older texts were not associated with skin lesions; their main symptoms were increased frequency and urgency of urination. Other symptoms were rather ambiguous. However, references to a disease allegedly occurring only in males, involving the "bad nature of eruptions on the genitals related to consorting with women," found in the *Yijo Sillok* probably indicate syphilis.

Japan and the continent were the two possible routes for the transmission of syphilis to Korea.

Yet trade between foreign countries and the peninsula during the first half of the sixteenth century was rather limited, especially with Japan. In fact, the only contacts with the Japanese during this period would have been invasions by those marauders who had been attacking the Korean coast since the thirteenth century. Thus, the possibility that syphilis could have been brought from Japan to Korea cannot be absolutely ruled out, but it is more likely that the primary route was from the continent, for trade between Korea and Ming China occurred many times per year through special emissaries, including numerous officials and merchants. Moreover, the first Korean medical texts to discuss the new disease suggest that syphilis came from China.

At the time, it was thought that the immoral and illegal use of medicines made of human flesh and gallbladder were linked to the arrival of syphilis in Korea. Thus, the following was reported in February 1566:

There were many people in Seoul who killed people to take the gallbladder and this was said to be for the use of very promiscuous people. Many beggars disappeared from the street. After several years there were no longer any beggars and the killers turned to child murder. Officials and other people who consorted with prostitutes got the disease. They tried to cure it with human gallbladder and used up all the beggars. (Miki 1962, author's translation)

Whatever the authenticity of this story, it reflects the desperation of the sick and their willingness to resort to murder as well as superstition to procure remedies for their ailments. The exact origin of this aberration is unknown, but throughout the world there are many accounts of the use of human blood and organs against diseases such as leprosy, syphilis, and tuberculosis; Korean and Chinese pharmacopoeias included a wide range of human parts and products under the general category "human medicine" (Cooper and Sivin 1973).

The *Hyangyak chipsong pang* refers to eight kinds of gonorrhea, and the descriptions are quite detailed. The *Tongui pogam* also describes various symptoms of the eight different kinds of gonorrhea. Although the relationship between the disease and sexual intercourse was apparently recognized, the contagious nature of disease does not seem to have been understood.

The writings of the Yi Dynasty suggest the existence of chancroid, but it is difficult to separate this ancient venereal disease from gonorrhea and syphilis.

Tuberculosis and Other Respiratory Diseases

During the Yi Dynasty, medical knowledge of tuberculosis became more abundant and precise. The *Hyangyak chipsong pang* describes pulmonary tuberculosis and recognizes the contagious nature of the disease as well as the relationship between the most common form, pulmonary tuberculosis, and its other forms (Miki 1962). The *Tongui pogam* also contains a good description of pulmonary tuberculosis and the symptoms of other forms of the disease. Moreover, it describes symptoms suggesting scrofula, which was considered primarily childhood tuberculosis.

The *Hyangyak chipsong pang* discusses the symptoms of asthma clearly, and the *Tongui pogam* has a discussion of asthma under the heading of "coughing." Asthma was divided into eight different forms; asthmatic attacks were attributed to excess eating, fear, and shock. Further, under the column dealing with symptoms of "lung swelling," there is a discussion of a condition that may be related to emphysema.

Ailments that appear to correspond to modern pleurisy and hydrothorax also appear in the medical literature of this period in discussions of "heart pain" and "waist pain." The *Hyangyak chipsong pang* and the *Tongui pogam* describe symptoms that suggest hydrothorax in a discussion of conditions attributed to the accumulation of "chest water," which indicate observations of both the accumulation of water in the chest and swelling of the whole body.

Lobar pneumonia is probably one of the illnesses included in the "harm caused by cold" category of fever diseases. Within this category, the *Hyangyak chipsong pang* and the *Tongui pogam* discuss diseases marked by high fever, coughing, and bloody mucus.

Heart Disease

The precise diagnosis of various forms of heart disease was achieved only after the development of pathological anatomy, auscultation, and the stethoscope. Under Chinese medical philosophy, abstract arguments concerning the pulse, combined with heart pain and shortness of breath, were used for diagnosis of heart diseases. Under the heading "heart pain," the *Hyangyak chipsong pang* lists nine different kinds. These entries and similar discussions in other texts composed during the later years of the Yi Dynasty suggest knowledge of angina pectoris as well as other symptoms of heart disease.

Digestive Disorders

Gastritis seems to be the major disease in the category of stomach diseases. The *Hyangyak chipsong pang* and the *Tongui pogam* described symptoms that suggest gastritis. Gastric ulcer might be the modern diagnosis for the disorder associated with a "wound of the stomach spilling blood" accompanied by severe stomach pains.

A precise diagnosis of peritonitis, intestinal tumors, or obstructions was very difficult in both the East and West in ancient times, but some of the symptoms discussed in the *Tongui pogam* suggest intestinal tumors. Tumors behind the intestine that were not movable were called "cancer," whereas a kind of tumor that moved was ascribed to parasites. Stomach cancer, liver cancer, tuberculous peritonitis, uterine cancer, and probably many other forms of cancer were included in this category. Still, other intestinal disorders, such as acute appendicitis, enteritis, acute enteritis, and enterostenosis are also discussed.

Acute enteritis, in which the symptoms are similar to those of food poisoning and cholera, was treated in the medical texts composed in the later Yi Dynasty. Ascites and meteorism (tympanites) might be indicated in the category that contained diseases in which the abdomen swelled. Disorders of the rectum, such as hemorrhoids and prolapse of the anus, were described in detail, along with methods of treatment and dietary restrictions.

Liver Disease

The *Hyangyak chipsong pang* lists 25 forms of jaundice, but these conditions were not linked to problems of the liver and gallbladder. By contrast, the *Tongui pogam* reduced all the subdivisions simply to jaundice. Its cause was explained in terms of "damp fever," in which the blood evaporates and becomes hot and dark in color. This dark color first appears in the eyes and face, but as it spreads, the whole body becomes yellow. Causes of jaundice included alcohol poisoning, lack of appetite, excessive sexual indulgence, and yellow sweat. Some texts apparently described gallstones along with colic, but all the painful "stone diseases" were essentially indistinguishable.

Although cirrhosis of the liver was not uncommon, this disorder was not specifically ascribed to the liver. The symptoms of cirrhosis were probably considered along with ascites, meteorismus, and other disorders involving abdominal swelling.

Parasitic Infestations

Paragonimiasis or pulmonary distomiasis is caused by infection with a worm of the genus *Paragonimus*, especially *Paragonimus westermani*. In Korea the disease was usually acquired by eating raw crab meat, and references to a disorder characterized by rusty-brown mucus in the ancient texts probably reflect paragonimiasis.

In the *Hyangyak chipsong pang* under the heading "pediatrics" are descriptions if infestations of roundworms and pinworms. The section on "worms" in the *Tongui pogam* describes various disease symptoms attributed to nine different worms. Many plant remedies were used to remove these parasites. Ancylostomiasis (hookworm disease) and secondary anemia are not specifically described, but symptoms of anemia due to ancylostomiasis seem to be described among the forms of jaundice.

Kidney Disease, Urinary Disease, and Diseases of the Reproductive Organs

Clinically, the main symptom of nephropathy is swelling; thus, the "water-swelling diseases" of the ancient texts probably included symptoms due to disorders of the cardiovascular system as well as kidney diseases. Kidney disease might be found in the ancient texts under the headings of swelling, water disease, or water-"cancer" disease (ascites). "Water-swelling diseases" associated with irregular pulse probably indicated disorders due to heart disease, rather than kidney disorders. The section on "water-swelling disease" in the *Hyangyak chipsong pang* lists ten different forms.

Because symptoms of diseases of the urinary bladder are conspicuous and painful, they were the subject of considerable medical interest. The *Hyangyak chipsong pang* discusses dysuria, ischuria, pollakiuria, urinary incontinence, hematuria, gross hematuria associated with high-fever diseases, and enuresis. Various symptoms of urinary problems are also discussed in connection with gonorrhea. Some of the "disorders of urine" might have been caused by tuberculosis of the urogenital system.

The *Tongui pogam* discusses the urinary bladder and diseases of urination in detail. The five colors of urine were said to provide diagnostic clues to the origin of illness. Diseases related to difficult urination were followed by a discussion of various forms of gonorrhea symptoms.

Diabetes Mellitus

According to the *Tongui pogam* the thirst associated with diabetes mellitus was due to "heart fever." The symptoms of diabetes included intense thirst and hunger, increased eating and drinking, frequent urination, weakness, and wasting. Although the patient ate and drank large quantities, all the food consumed turned to urine, and the patient became very thin. In advanced cases the disease was accompanied by "bad boils," usually referring to ulcera cruris.

To prevent or treat diabetes mellitus, it was said that one must abstain from three things: alcohol, sex, and salty food. In patients with the disease, acupuncture and moxibustion should not be performed for more than 100 days because inflammation of the wound could lead to death. The sudden formation of bad boils in such patients could signal imminent death.

Beriberi

Several conditions described in the Korean medical texts suggest a long familiarity with beriberi, also known as "kakke." Symptoms described under this heading included swelling of the lower limbs, followed by swelling of the heart and stomach and difficulty in urination, weakness in the feet, dizziness in the head and eyes, and so forth.

Although it is likely that beriberi existed in Korea since very ancient times, true beriberi was probably not distinguished from the various forms of neuritis, heart disease, rheumatism, and other forms of malnutrition. According to the *Hyangyak chipsong pang*, beriberi was due to the "wind poison" generated by wind, cold, hot, and dampness. Later medical texts attributed the disease to "water dampness." Beriberi was most likely to have appeared during times of famine, but otherwise the disease was probably somewhat rare in Korea, even during the latter Yi period, because few people depended on polished white rice.

Stroke

The *Hyangyak chipsong pang* and the *Tongui pogam* describe the main symptoms of stroke, including collapse, loss of speech, paralysis, loss of faculties, and inability to move the extremities. Fat people over 50 were said to be most susceptible to strokes. Numbness in the thumb and fingers, weakness in the hands and feet, and a numb or tingling sensation were considered warning symptoms that a severe stroke might occur within 3 years. Treatment was provided even if the patient was unconscious. When the person could not talk or swallow, medicine could be boiled so that the patient would inhale the steam. Medicine could also be blown directly into the nose, but if the patient could not inhale, the case was judged incurable.

Skin Diseases and Leprosy

The texts describe many interesting and important skin diseases, but the most dreaded was certainly leprosy. In ancient Korea leprosy was nonspecifically referred to as "bad disease." Although various conditions that were included under this rubric were considered malignant and hard to cure, leprosy was probably the major disease. Medical texts of the Yi Dynasty referred to leprosy as "big-wind-lepra" or "big-wind-boil."

Leprosy was said to result when a "bad wind" got into the body, but the disease was also said to be transmitted from person to person. Records for 1445 in the *Yijo Sillok* describe outbreaks of leprosy in Cheju Island. According to the chronicler, the people of Cheju Island abandoned lepers in uninhabited areas along the coast because they feared them as sources of contagion. Another folk belief found in the historical records for 1613 was based on the idea that when lepers washed their boils, the fish in the river or the chickens in the house would acquire the leprosy. Then when city people ate the contaminated fish or chicken, they would be infected (Miki 1962). Leprosy was also seen as Heaven's punishment for criminal acts in this life or past lives.

The historical literature also indicates a tradition of relief work and quarantine for leprosy, especially on Cheju Island where the disease was most prevalent. However, people greatly feared infection, and so lepers were abandoned on uninhabited islands and there were also many "accidents" in which lepers fell from the cliffs. Officials did establish "relief places" and "cure places" and tried to help lepers by appointing priests and medical students to give them medicine and help them bathe in the ocean. An entry in the historical records for 1612 states: "Leprosy is the worst disease under the sky" (Miki 1962).

The ancient medical texts also describe erysipelas, carbuncles, dermatitis, furunculosis, inflammations, abscesses, tumors, pustules, lymphagitis, and gangrene, as well as scabies, which probably existed in Korea and China from ancient times. Texts from the Yi Dynasty described this condition and useful methods of cure, including sulfur poultices. The *Tongui pogam* says that there are five kinds of scabies: dry, damp, sand, insect, and pus.

Eye, Ear, Nose, and Throat Diseases

Many forms of deafness and their supposed causes are discussed in the *Tongui pogam*. The condition referred to as earache accompanied by "purulent ear" was probably otitis media. A section on major and minor nose disease includes symptoms suggesting rhinorrhea, hypertrophic rhinitis, and maxillary sinusitis. There are also many diseases discussed that were associated with inflammation of the throat and mouth. Symptoms in the *Tongui pogam* are consistent with tonsillitis, diphtheria, uvulitis, tongue cancer, ranula (sublingual cyst), and various forms of tooth disease.

Because of their debilitating effect and their direct influence on daily life activities, eye diseases were readily observed and described. Although eye disorders caused by problems within the body or peculiar diseases inside the eyeballs were hard to detect, conditions affecting the surface were described in detail. The *Tongui pogam* described eye diseases, including pterygium and trachoma, in terms of more than 20 symptoms. Liver diseases were thought to cause problems behind the eyeball, which led to incurable loss of vision.

Women's Diseases

Diseases of women discussed in the texts of this era include problems of pregnancy and childbirth, amenorrhea, dysmenorrhea, hypomenorrhea, hypermenorrhea, oligomenorrhea, prolapsed and inverted uterus, cancers, and hysteria. Breast cancer is listed in the *Tongui pogam* in a discussion of lactation.

Abnormal conditions in pregnant women seem to have included eclampsia, unusual mental conditions, pyelonephritis, dysentery, malaria, and pain due to expansion of the heart and chest. After childbirth, women were susceptible to five kinds of fever due to the following: (1) excessive loss of blood leading to anemic fever; (2) uterine fever; (3) high fever caused by food poisoning; (4) high fever due to wind and cold; and (5) fever caused by inflammation of the mammary glands.

Other symptoms associated with diseases of women suggest painful disorders of the bladder and urethra, hernia, ovarian varicocele, and elephantiasis vulvae. A condition associated with inflammation, pus, and pain in the urethra and the surrounding muscles, said to come from "perverted" sexual acts, was probably due to gonorrhea. A condition called "poisonous urine" was associated with the discharge of pus and blood.

Convulsions in Children

According to the pediatric sections of the medical texts of this era, convulsions were second only to smallpox as a medical problem characteristic of childhood. Childhood convulsions included all kinds of diseases of a nervous nature, such as nervousness, spasms associated with high fever, epilepsy, spasmo-

philia, infantile tetany, night terrors, chorea minor, tics, and fits.

Insanity and Psychosis

The relationship between Ho Chun's Taoist philosophy and his medical theories are most apparent in his consideration of mental illness. He based his medical philosophy on the three essences of the Taoist religion: spirit, air, and god. To simplify, we may say that Ho Chun spoke of seven aspects of "mind": happiness, anger, melancholy, thought, sadness, fear, and fright. Injury to these seven "minds" results in disease and mental illness.

The *Tongui pogam*'s section on insanity covers symptoms that suggest epilepsy as well as insanity. Psychosis was considered "true madness," and was thought to be caused by devils. The discussion in the *Tongui pogam* makes it clear that mental disease was thought to be of two main kinds. The first was epilepsy and insanity; the other was psychosis or "true madness." In ancient times, however, insanity was outside the domain of scholarly medicine; treatment called for the *mudang* (Korean shaman) rather than the physician.

Miscellaneous

The Chinese character for epilepsy used in the Korean texts implies both seizure with loss of consciousness and insanity. The *Tongui pogam* discusses a similar condition known as "God disease," which is probably equivalent to epilepsy.

Both the *Hyangyak chipsong pang* and *Tongui pogam* discussed tetanus in connection with strokes. However, since the Koryo era, physicians had been well aware of the relationship between tetanus and wounds.

The medical texts discussed ordinary dog bites, mad-dog bites, and rabies. Treatment began with washing the bite and cleaning it to remove dirt, wood splinters, and so forth. The wound was washed with water or hot human urine to remove the poison. Medicines that had cats as their main ingredient were prescribed. Presumably, the cat in the medicine would scare away the dog poison.

A condition that appears to be polyarthritis was called "white tiger disease" because the pain was as severe as that of having been bitten by a tiger. The *Tongui pogam* also emphasizes the varying levels of pain associated with arthritis. A condition referred to as "wind pain" might have been gout, whereas another description suggests the modern diagnosis of osteomyelitis or periostitis. A condition described as a disease caused by a worm eating the synovial fluid might have been osteomyelitis of a tuberculous nature.

Symptoms associated with rickets, including a condition referred to as "turtle chest," appear in the pediatric section of the *Hyangyak chipsong pang.* Osteomalacia, a form of adult rickets, which is far more common in women than in men, was called "gentle wind" disease.

Lois N. Magner

This publication was supported in part by NIH Grant RO1 LM 04175 from the National Library of Medicine.

Bibliography

Ackerknecht, Erwin H. 1965. *History and geography of the most important diseases.* New York.

Cooper, William, and Nathan Sivin. 1973. Man as a medicine: Pharmacological and ritual aspects of traditional therapy using drugs derived from the human body. In *Chinese science: Explorations of an ancient tradition,* ed. Shigeru Nakayama and Nathan Sivin, 203–72. Cambridge, Mass.

Fujikawa, Yū 1934. *Japanese medicine,* trans. John Ruhran. New York.

Han Woo-keun. 1970. *The history of Korea,* trans. Lee Kyung-shik, ed. Grafton K. Mintz. Seoul, Korea.

Henschen, Folke. 1966. *The history and geography of diseases,* trans. Joan Tate. New York.

Kim Tu-jong. 1966. *Han'guk uihaksa* (A history of Korean medicine). Seoul, Korea.

Lee Ki-baik. 1984. *A new history of Korea,* trans. Edward W. Wagner. Cambridge, Mass.

Miki, Sakae. 1962. *History of Korean medicine and of disease in Korea.* Japan. [In Japanese]

VI.9
Diseases of the Modern Period in Korea

Medical Missionaries

Except for the addition of cholera, the diseases of Korea of the nineteenth century and the first half of the twentieth century differed little from the ones prevailing in earlier times. In fact, Westerners who came to Korea in the 1880s and 1890s thought that the illnesses found in Korea were generally the same as those in North America. George W. Woods, for example, a surgeon aboard the U.S.S. *Juniata* of America's Asiatic Squadron, reported that he knew of no diseases peculiar to Korea, but he was struck by the almost universal presence of smallpox and malaria. Woods, who spent almost 3 months of 1884 in Korea, was one of the first Americans to visit the peninsula (Bohm and Swartout, Jr. 1984).

Medical missionaries, upon whose observations we rely for much of this essay, tended to believe that Korean medical knowledge was entirely borrowed from China and that the history of real medical work in Korea began in September 1884, when Horace N. Allen of the Presbyterian Mission came to Seoul. Medical missionaries soon realized that foreign doctors could best establish a claim to medical superiority through surgery. Among the operations Allen performed were excision of the ankle, knee, shoulder, and wrist; amputation of fingers, arms, legs, cancers, and tumors; dissection of scrofulous glands; enucleation of the eyeball; treatment of cataract and pterygium; and closure of harelip. One of the most frequently performed minor surgical operations was for fistula. One Western physician, Oliver R. Avison, blamed this apparently common condition on the Korean custom of sitting on the floor instead of on chairs (Avison 1897).

After a little more than 3 years of medical work in Korea, Avison concluded that the kinds of diseases seen in Seoul were about the same as those seen in Canada, but also that the relative frequency was different. Avison, founder of Severance Union Medical College and Hospital, had come to Korea in 1893 in response to H. G. Underwood's call for medical missionaries. His Korean patients suffered from all the usual diseases of the major organs, eye diseases, conjunctivitis, ulceration of the cornea, hernias, various forms of heart disease, hysteria, epilepsy, paralysis, Bright's disease, asthma, bronchitis, tuberculosis, whooping cough, diphtheria, ulcerative tonsillitis, skin diseases, scabies, diarrhea, dysentery, intestinal worms, leprosy, syphilis, smallpox, malaria, typhus, and fevers of various sorts. Although he usually wrote with immense confidence in his own opinions, Avison admitted that "as we do not have the privilege of making autopsies to correct our diagnoses in case of death, many of our suppositions . . . may not be correct" (Avison 1897).

Among the cases seen in the 1920s by Sherwood Hall were the following: gangrene, enlarged spleen due to chronic malaria, enlarged liver due to liver abscess, ascites, pleural effusion, edema, distomiasis due to lung flukes, and many forms of tuberculosis, often advanced cases. Hall thought that the use of unsterilized needles in acupuncture and moxa often led to infection and painful inflammation. Among women patients, Marian Hall encountered abdomens swollen from enlarged uterine fibroids, tumors, and ovarian cysts (Hall 1978).

The early missionaries often fell victim themselves to endemic diseases such as malaria, typhus, and dysentery. Some of these deaths were obviously unnecessary even with nineteenth-century medical techniques, such as the missionary from Australia who contracted smallpox after only a few months in Pusan, apparently because he had placed his faith in Providence instead of vaccination.

Despite the obvious effectiveness of quinine, vaccination, and various surgical operations, the medical missionaries found that Western medicine was quite powerless before "continued fevers" or, put another way, that the *mudang* (Korean shaman) was equally as effective as they were. Indeed, the missionaries admitted that in the treatment of many ailments, the results obtained by Korean doctors were comparable to those of the Western doctor (Busteed 1895).

Studies of Korean village life in the 1940s found that although people died from many different diseases, no adequate accounts of morbidity and mortality patterns were available. Practitioners noted that many children died of tuberculosis, whereas many adults died of uncertain maladies of the stomach or intestines, which probably included bacillary dysentery. Among the diseases common in the villages were smallpox, typhoid, typhus, cholera, malaria, and parasitic worms. Quinine and preventive vaccines did make inroads on malaria, and some of the other diseases and health examinations were conducted in the schools where inoculations were given to students if infectious diseases were found (Osgood 1951).

Population

According to the *Korean Repository* of 1892, the only honest answer to the question "What is the population of Korea?" was that "a definite figure cannot be reached at present." Estimates varied from 5 million to 29 million. The Korean census printed under government auspices in 1885 reported the population (probably a sizable overestimate) as about 28 million (15,004,292 males and 13,003,109 females). According to Woods, the population of Seoul in 1884 was about 500,000 inhabitants, but Percival Lowell suggested that about 250,000 people lived within the 10 square miles of the city (Bohm and Swartout, Jr. 1984).

In 1944, the population was estimated at about 23 million Koreans and about 630,000 Japanese, but by this time epidemic diseases were being tamed by public health work, quarantine regulations, and vaccinations against smallpox, typhoid fever, and cholera. Nevertheless, tuberculosis, intestinal diseases, venereal diseases, and leprosy (despite isolation of lepers) remained as public health problems (Simmons et al. 1944).

Water Supply

As in most nineteenth-century cities, the streets of Seoul were "filthy, dirty lanes" flanked by ditches that drained house privies and sewage. Refuse was poured into the ditches with the hope that it would eventually disappear into the river. Wells were dug conveniently close to major city lanes, which unfortunately meant inevitable contamination with sewage from the nearby ditches and, thus, intestinal diseases such as diarrhea and dysentery. The situation was similar in small towns and rural communities using water from wells, springs, creeks, and rivers. Both produce and water were generally contaminated because of the use of night soil as fertilizer.

It follows then that much sickness and death could be attributed to contaminated water, although most adults were partially immune because of constant infection. In addition, the custom of drinking tea or water boiled in the rice kettle provided some safety.

In the twentieth century, the problem began to abate somewhat, and by 1944, the larger cities and towns had modern water facilities, and public health laboratories were involved in testing food and water (Simmons et al. 1944). The conditions that had prevailed in the nineteenth century, however, created fertile soil for not only dysentery but also cholera and typhoid.

Cholera

After escaping its original home in India in 1817, cholera began a global migration; by 1820 it had advanced into China and shortly afterward into Korea and Japan as well. According to Korean records, the first major cholera epidemic occurred in 1821, and observers were sure that the devastating disease, which reached P'yongyang by the end of July 1821, had begun in China. Within 10 days more than 1,000 people had died. The epidemic reached Seoul in August, and by the end of September was in the southern part of the peninsula and all the cities of Kyongsang Province.

Physicians could neither cure nor prevent the spread of this disease, which terrified observers claimed would kill 9 out of every 10 people stricken. Once the first cases of cholera developed, it appeared to spread instantly to surrounding areas, killing countless numbers of people. Stunned by its virulence, the King appealed to the gods, and the people held feasts and ceremonies to propitiate disease devils. Gradually as winter arrived, cholera seemed to disappear, but in April of the following year it reappeared around Seoul and once again spread throughout the country. By mid-August, the epidemic had reached Japan (Miki 1962).

Between 1822 and the 1870s, epidemic cholera made several more invasions, but the records are not precise. There are indications of several cholera interchanges between Korea and Japan during this period, and sometimes the disease spread from Japan to Korea; however, it usually followed the northern land route from Manchuria along the western coast or across the Yellow Sea. Following the 1870s, cholera epidemics were recorded for the years 1881, 1885, 1886, 1890, and 1891.

Modern cholera prevention practices began in 1880 when the illness spread from Japan to Pusan. Emergency policies included established of Disinfection Stations and Cholera Refugee Hospitals. In 1895, during the Sino-Japanese War, cholera broke out in Manchuria. The epidemic slowly but inexorably crept into Korea, finally attacking Seoul with great virulence: At the peak of the epidemic, over 300 were dying per day. During the 6 weeks of the epidemic, over 5,000 deaths in Seoul and vicinity were counted out of a population of about 220,000. The exact number of cases throughout the country is unknown, but it is estimated that some 300,000 people died (Clark 1979). The first cholera hospital organized by Avison in Seoul was closed after the mortality rate of the first 135 patients reached 75 percent.

A second hospital treated 173 cases with a mortality rate of 35 percent (Avison 1895).

In 1902 when cholera epidemics were reported on the continent, all the harbor towns in Korea established Quarantine Stations; nevertheless, epidemic cholera once again attacked Seoul, and deaths reached about 10,000. In 1907 it claimed hundreds of victims in outbreaks around Seoul, Pusan, Inchon, and P'yangyong. It appeared again in 1908, and in 1909 reached Seoul and Inchon from Manchuria. In the latter epidemic, 1,775 contracted cholera and 137 died. During still another outbreak in 1910, which also seems to have originated in China, 456 Koreans contracted the disease and 367 died, along with 722 Japanese in the country who suffered from the illness (Miki 1962). During the epidemic of 1919–20 there were some 44,000 cases, and then for several years no cases were reported. In 1929, only 18 cases were reported, but 15 were fatal, and in 1933, 70 cases were reported with 37 deaths.

One must consider that official reports may have underestimated or deliberately concealed cholera outbreaks. For example, the League of Nations listed Korea as a country in which cholera was epidemic in 1937, while the official reports noted only one case (Simmons et al. 1944). Indeed, some claimed that cholera was never endemic in Korea and always came from outside the country, but this was disputed by other authorities.

Dysentery

Diseases with the characteristic symptoms of dysentery existed in ancient times in China, Korea, and Japan, and in modern Korea both bacillary and amebic dysentery were quite prevalent. Noting that Korean patients recovered from amebic dysentery better than Japanese patients, Hall concluded that dietary habits created different intestinal environments. He advised his Japanese patients to include kimchee in their diet and thought that this improved recovery during later outbreaks (Hall 1978).

Adults probably acquired some immunity as a result of repeated infections in childhood, whereas dysentery in children was probably confused with common "summer complaints." Nevertheless, fatality rates during the 1930s were estimated at about 20 percent of those attacked. Between 1929 and 1937 the number of cases reported annually varied from about 2,000 to almost 5,000. Amebic dysentery was more common than the bacillary type (Simmons et al. 1944).

Typhoid and Paratyphoid Fevers

In Korea many people considered typhoid a rather minor disease, perhaps because most adults had been exposed during childhood. Woods's informants thought typhoid a rare disease, but he was sure that it could not be, given the poor sanitary state of Seoul (Bohm and Swartout, Jr. 1984). Avison also considered Korea to have all the conditions needed for typhoid fever to flourish, but at the same time he stated that he had never seen a case he could definitely identify as typhoid.

Nevertheless, as diagnostic procedures improved, it became apparent that typhoid fever was the most frequent of the enteric diseases in Korea. Between 1929 and 1937 about 6,000 cases were reported annually, with a fatality rate about 17 percent. During the same period, between 300 and 700 cases of paratyphoid fever were reported annually, with a fatality rate of about 7 percent (Simmons et al. 1944).

Parasitic Infestations

Intestinal infestations with parasitic worms were so widespread in early twentieth-century Korea that some public health authorities believed at least 95 percent of the people were affected. Avison (1897) noted a great demand for worm medicine and reported seeing round worms and tapeworms of prodigious size.

Infestation with flukes was also widespread because of the preference for eating raw fish and crustacea which were often contaminated with the lung fluke (*Paragonimus westermani*), the liver fluke (*Clonorchis sinensis*), or the intestinal fluke (*Metagonimus yokogawai*). Paragonimiasis or pulmonary distomiasis was most common; it was generally acquired by eating raw crab meat. The developing parasites lodge in the lungs and cause an intense inflammatory reaction that results in the production of rusty-brown sputum. Before the etiology and transmission of the disease was understood, cases of paragonimiasis numbered as many as 40,000 per year. Metagonimiasis was also quite frequent, but this disorder was considered mild. Clonorchiasis was rare, but it did cause severe damage in affected individuals (Miki 1962).

Ancylostomiasis, or hookworm disease, caused by *Necator americanus* and *Ancylostoma duodenale*, was common during the nineteenth and early twentieth centuries in Korea. Such infestations probably affected 25 to 30 percent of the people and were the cause of much malnutrition and secondary anemia. In addition, *Ascaris lumbricoides*, the roundworm, was said to infect about 95 percent of the people. By contrast, the pinworm or threadworm, *Enterobius yermicularis*, and the whipworm, *Iricouris trichiura*, seemed to have been comparatively uncommon (Simmons et al. 1944).

Tuberculosis and Pneumonias

Tuberculosis was "the great enemy of health" in Korea, as in much of the world in the 1890s. Pulmonary tuberculosis was the major form, but physicians also saw cases of bone and joint disease, scrofula, and abscesses of the lymph nodes. Avison (1897) argued that consumption was even more difficult to treat in Korea than in Canada, and in fact regarded such cases as hopeless, unless they were discovered very early and the patient was given good food and attention.

The disease remained highly prevalent in the 1940s, with pulmonary tuberculosis still the most common form, but all forms – such as nodular, cutaneous, intestinal, bone, and joint – could be found. Lobar and bronchopneumonia were also common (Simmons et al. 1944).

According to Hall (1978), who founded the first tuberculosis sanatorium in Korea, the disease affected about one out of five Koreans. Almost all adults produced a positive reaction to the tuberculin test. Unsanitary, crowded conditions among factory workers in the city contributed heavily to the spread of tuberculosis from big cities to rural villages and back again along new lines of travel. As elsewhere, an increase in tuberculosis in Korea was part of the toll of modernization and communication with the outside world.

Smallpox

Smallpox was one of the most feared diseases on the peninsula, and almost every person past the age of 10 years had smallpox scars (Hirsch 1883). In fact, children were hardly considered members of the family until they survived their bout with this illness. One woman told Avison that she had given birth to 11 children, but that all of them had died of smallpox before reaching the age of 2 years.

It is interesting that most medical missionaries never mentioned the practice of inoculation and asserted that in Korea there were no methods of prevention or treatment other than magical ceremonies to propitiate the evil spirit that supposedly caused the disease. On the other hand, Woods had no difficulty in learning about the Korean method of smallpox inoculation during his 3-month visit. In a meeting with an elderly Korean physician the subject of smallpox was the major topic of discussion. According to Woods, smallpox was so common and "apparently so mild in type" that it was considered no more dangerous than measles. Perhaps he misinterpreted a situation in which mortality from measles made it almost as dangerous as smallpox. In any case, Woods noted that Koreans had practiced inoculation for centuries and that vaccination was beginning to displace the ancient methods.

Inoculation was commonly performed by powdering the smallpox scab, placing it on cotton, and introducing it into the nostrils. Alternatively, the scab was mixed with candy and given to the child. That these methods were not very effective, however, can be seen by the fact that the disease seemed to leave its characteristic sign on so many. On one occasion, when surrounded by a crowd of men and boys in Seoul, Woods amused himself by counting those who were pock-marked; he counted 40 with scarred faces among 70 people (Bohm and Swartout, Jr. 1984).

The question of smallpox scars was said to have determined Queen Min's survival in the palace intrigues of 1882. When King Kojong's father seized power, he condemned the Queen to death. Disguised as a peasant, the Queen tried to escape to the countryside, but she was stopped by guards at the city gate. Because the guards did not know the Queen, one of them suggested that they examine the woman's face, knowing other members of her family to be pock-marked. The Queen's face was perfectly smooth. Sure that a woman of good complexion could not be a member of the Min family, the guards let her go free. Eventually the King and Queen were restored, and the King's father became a state prisoner in Peking (Bohm and Swartout, Jr. 1984).

Vaccination was increasingly accepted during the early twentieth century. Hall, who was born in Korea in 1893, noted that smallpox had been very prevalent when he was a boy, but had been practically eradicated in the late 1920s (Hall 1978). In 1909, as many as 4,540 people suffered from the disease. In the following year, of the 2,425 Koreans who contracted smallpox, 445 died; 36 out of 455 Japanese who also contracted the disease died (Miki 1962). In 1921, there were 8,321 reported cases, but by 1936 this had been reduced to 1,400, with 371 deaths. In 1937, there were only 205 cases with 44 deaths, but the number of deaths rose again in 1940, which was reported to have been an epidemic year. The fatality rate estimated during the first 40 years of the twentieth century was about 20 to 27 percent (Simmons et al. 1944).

Mosquito-Borne Illnesses

Malaria seems to have been the most common, widely distributed disease in Korea. On the Korean peninsula, malaria almost always appeared as the "3-day fever" and was most prevalent in areas with numerous rice fields, which Avison thought "constitute a suitable home for the development of the malarial poison." He assumed that all the varieties of malaria would be found in Korea, but most cases were of the tertian or quartan type. The people were familiar with quinine, and there was a great demand for it, especially during the fall and winter months. Unfortunately, bogus products were often sold as quinine (Avison 1897). Malaria was still common in the 1940s, especially in the southern provinces.

Filiariasis due to *Wunchereria bancrofti* was also found in the southern provinces of Korea in the 1940s. The principal vectors of this disease were *Anopheles hyrcanus sinensis* and *Culex fatigans*.

It is interesting to note, however, that dengue fever and yellow fever were not found in Korea despite the presence of dengue fever in areas that had frequent intercourse with Korea. This is particularly remarkable because the principal vectors of dengue fever, *Aedes aegypti* (also the principal vector of yellow fever) and *Aedes albopictus,* are found in Korea.

Bubonic Plague

Although devastating epidemics of bubonic plague were recorded in China since 1331, the surviving Korean literature does not seem to reflect similar episodes. The bubonic plague outbreaks that occurred in Asia from the 1890s to the 1920s were, of course, watched with great interest by bacteriologists and public health workers. Of special concern to Korea was the epidemic that occurred in northwestern Manchuria and spread along the newly constructed railroad lines to various cities of northern China, killing 600,000 people in 1911–12. As the 1911 epidemic spread through China, Korea organized preventive teams of personnel and established a quarantine line along the northern frontier. Later plague epidemics in Manchuria, Mongolia, and northern China also failed to reach Korea.

Human plague was reported in Korea in 1919, but there were no official reports of the disease between that year and 1944. Nevertheless, sporadic cases may have occurred and some cases may have been imported during World War II. In 1939, Hall was summoned to the military hospital wing of the Haiju Government Hospital for a consultation about a mysterious condition spreading among wounded soldiers returning from Manchuria. It was apparently a type of lung disease that had also attacked medical attendants. The Japanese physician in charge had ruled out bubonic plague because the sick had no swelling or tenderness of the lymphatic glands in the groin or axilla; however, a sudden severe headache was followed by nausea and vomiting. Other symptoms were high fever; extreme prostration; rapidly labored breathing; cough; and expectoration of a watery, frothy sputum: The afflicted died within hours, almost black with cyanosis. Hall suspected plague and found *Pasteurella pestis* in sputum from the sick. Sworn to secrecy by the Medical Officer, Hall suggested increased precautions to protect the staff and an all-out war on rats. Yet, no new cases appeared among hospital patients or staff, and the Chief Medical Officer decided that it was not necessary to alarm the public by instituting rodent control measures (Hall 1978).

Relapsing Fever

Relapsing fever, once considered one of the forms of typhus, may have appeared in Korea during the sixteenth century, when epidemics occurred in China and Manchuria. In addition, the epidemic fever that appeared in 1886 might well have been relapsing fever (Miki 1962). Reports from the 1940s indicated that this disease was very rare in Korea, although ticks that serve as vectors of relapsing fever are present.

Typhus Fever

Typhus fever was fairly prevalent in the 1890s in Korea, especially among the poor. By the 1940s observers had detected three types of typhus fever in Korea: the epidemic, or louse-borne type (*Rickettsia prowazeki*); the endemic, or flea-borne type; and the mite-borne type caused by *Rickettsia orientalis*, known as tsutsugamushi disease or Japanese river fever. The forms of typhus transmitted by mites and lice have the highest fatality rates, but endemic typhus, sometimes called "Honan fever," was the most common form in Korea. Several types of mite existed in Korea, including *Trombicula akamushi*, the chief vector of *R. orientalis*. All three varieties of human lice were prevalent in Korea.

Between 1929 and 1937 the annual number of typhus cases reported varied from 890 to 1,683. The fatality rate was estimated as 11 to 13 percent. Tsutsugamushi disease was the least frequently reported. Body lice were also found to carry *Rickettsia quintana*, which causes trench fever.

Venereal Diseases

According to Avison, veneral diseases were about as common in Korea as they had been in England, but the syphilitic patients who came to the hospital were all in the third stage of the disease. During the earlier stages the usual method of Korean treatment was exposure to the fumes of a mixture containing mercury. Similar remedies had long been popular in Europe, although the benefits were dubious and side effects of mercury poisoning included excessive salivation, ulceration of the gums, and loss of teeth (Avison 1897).

Venereal diseases were still prevalent in the 1940s. The most significant venereal diseases were syphilis, gonorrhea, and chancroid. Lymphogranuloma venereum was occasionally reported, and granuloma inguinale was quite rare.

Nutritional Diseases

Several conditions described in classical Korean medical texts suggest long familiarity with beriberi, especially in association with times of famine. However, beriberi was rare in Korea as compared to other areas in Asia. In the early modern period the disease almost never appeared in rural Korea, but it was observed among Japanese students in Korean cities. In the 1940s the disease was still more prevalent among the Japanese than Koreans, because the Japanese were more likely to consume polished rice. During World War II, however, eating white rice became more common, and beriberi was sometimes observed even in villages.

Osteomalacia, or adult rickets, a gradual deformation of improperly calcified bones caused by lack of vitamin D, was fairly common in older women. Scurvy and pellagra were very rare, but nutritional anemia and anemia secondary to hookworm infestation were not uncommon.

Leprosy

Since ancient times, leprosy has been one of the most abhorred diseases. According to Korean medical folklore, the disease could be transmitted directly by the sick or through "intermediate hosts" such as fish or chicken. It was also seen, however, as heaven's punishment for sins in this life or in previous lives. Even in the modern era, when leprosy appeared, superstitious people would say "an evil spirit remained in that house and caused disease in the descendants."

In the 1890s a few isolated cases of leprosy could be found in the general area of Seoul, but most patients came from the southern provinces. The disease generally progressed slowly, but according to

Avison (1897) it appeared in all the forms described in the textbooks.

Segregation laws were passed in the early twentieth century, but were not strictly enforced, primarily because facilities for isolation were not available. According to statistics gathered in the 1930s and 1940s, relief stations of an official and a private nature housed about 7,000 lepers, and medical workers estimated the number of lepers living outside these institutions to be another 7,000. These numbers, however, are probably grossly inaccurate, with the total number perhaps closer to 20,000. In the 1940s about 5,000 lepers lived in the government leper colony on Little Deer Island off the southern coast, and another 1,500 or so lived in mission-operated colonies. Gradually, public health policies, relief agencies, and improved living standards have reduced the number of lepers.

Scabies

Scabies probably existed in Korea and China from ancient times. Since the fifteenth century, Korean doctors treated scabies with remedies that included sulfur poultices and arsenic sulfide. Avison reported that scabies was very common among his patients, as were scalp eruptions from head lice, and various forms of suppurating sores on other parts of the body (Avison 1897). The itch-mite, *Sarcoptes scabiei,* which causes scabies, is only one of the varieties of mites found in Korea. During the 1940s, scabies, trichophytous infections, and impetigo were quite common.

Eyes, Ears, Noses, Teeth

According to Woods and Avison, eye diseases were quite common. Eye disorders included purulent conjunctivitis, ulceration of the cornea, and complete destruction of the eyeball. Often severe eye disease began with simple conjunctivitis following measles or smallpox. Surgical operations for cataract and pterygium were often successful (Avison 1897). During the 1940s, trachoma was frequently the cause of the pannus, entropion, trichiasis, and corneal ulcerations that caused loss of vision. Other causes of blindness were gonorrheal ophthalmia and smallpox. *Hemophilus influenzae* (Koch–Weeks bacillus) was one of the causes of purulent conjunctivitis reported in the 1940s (Simmons et al. 1944).

Ear diseases were quite common: Most cases were the result of smallpox in childhood. Suppuration of the middle ear often led to destruction of the drum, and sometimes there was growth of polypi. Nasal polypi were quite common, but surgical removal produced good results. The need for tooth extraction was quite low, because most people, except for those with congenital syphilis, had very good teeth (Avison 1897).

Miscellaneous Diseases

In Korea, as in China and Japan, there is no clear historical description of a disease corresponding to diphtheria until the modern age, perhaps because diphtheria is not strongly associated with dramatic epidemics of high mortality. Indeed, mild cases are not unusual, and immunity is often quietly acquired at an early age. Avison (1897) thought it very strange that diphtheria was so rare in Korea. He had seen a few cases that he was certain were diphtheria, but some physicians claimed that the disease was not found in Korea.

By contrast, twentieth-century physicians found diphtheria to be rather common in Korea. In 1937 there were 2,361 cases, with 608 deaths. The fatality rates varied from 21 to 29 percent over a 12-year period.

Scarlet fever was also quite common in the 1940s. Between 1929 and 1937 reported cases varied from 937 to 2,190 per year, with fatality rates from 10 to 15 percent. Mumps, whooping cough, poliomyelitis, and encephalitis were also reported in the 1940s (Simmons et al. 1944).

Outbreaks of cerebrospinal meningitis continued to occur in the modern period, with a major epidemic taking place in 1934–5. The disease remained endemic in the 1940s, with about 50 to 500 cases reported annually between the years 1929 and 1937. The fatality rate varied from about 50 to 60 percent (Simmons et al. 1944).

Leptospirosis, also known as Weil's disease, or infectious jaundice, was endemic in Korea. The disease is spread via food or water contaminated by the urine and feces of infected rats. Rat-bite fever, caused by *Spirillum minus,* was transmitted by the bite of infected rats.

While visiting a drugstore in Seoul with his interpreter, Woods (see the first section of this chapter) examined many roots and herbs that were all said to be "good for the stomach!" This suggests, of course, that digestive disorders were common. Gastritis seemed to be the major disease in the category of stomach diseases, although Avison thought that common complaints of chronic indigestion included many cases of stomach ulcers.

The Avison family learned that rabies was a fairly common threat when two of the children were bitten by a rabid dog. Rabies was still a problem in the 1940s because of the large numbers of stray dogs.

And finally, according to Woods's informants, midwifery was practiced by old women, who consulted physicians in difficult cases. Many of the midwives were reportedly skillful and able to perform the manipulations necessary in correcting unnatural presentations (Bohm and Swartout, Jr. 1984). Lack of cleanliness in the instruments used to cut the umbilical cord was responsible for many cases of neonatal tetanus in infants, even in the 1940s (Simmons et al. 1944).

Diseases in the 1940s

Epidemic and endemic diseases were carefully monitored by the U.S. Army Military Government after World War II. Among the communicable diseases reported in 1946 and 1947 were typhus, smallpox, relapsing fever, cholera, meningitis, encephalitis, malaria, diphtheria, typhoid, and bacillary dysentery. The Institute for the Prevention of Infectious Diseases stocked and dispensed diagnostic tests and vaccines for many of these as well as other diseases. Although there were no cases of human plague reported in South Korea, antiplague measures, including port quarantine stations and rat control, were instituted when a case was reported in North Korea near the Manchurian border (Summation 1946, 1947).

By the end of 1947, the communicable disease picture was relatively stable. The incidences of many diseases, especially typhus, typhoid, and smallpox, were substantially decreased. In 1946, 117 cases of typhus had been reported, but only 4 were reported in 1947. Typhoid fever cases were reduced from 239 to 24 cases, and smallpox cases decreased from 41 to 2. When cholera appeared immediately after World War II, the American occupation forces were involved in managing the outbreak. Nevertheless, in the 1946 cholera epidemic there were 15,748 cases with 10,191 deaths. By 1947, however, there were only 14 cholera cases, with 10 deaths (Summation 1947).

The general decrease in communicable diseases was attributed to (1) disease control programs; (2) educational prevention programs; (3) increased availability of preventive inoculations and therapeutic drugs; and (4) establishment of clinics and health centers.

By 1948, diphtheria, typhus, and typhoid were about the only major communicable diseases still reported in South Korea. Typhus was generally the louse-borne form, but relapsing fever was often mistaken for typhus. A few sporadic cases of relapsing fever, bacillary dysentery, and smallpox were reported and gonorrhea and syphilis were not uncommon among prostitutes in Seoul and other cities (Summation 1948). However, leprosy remained a public health problem. There were only six leper clinics in South Korea, and the authorities conceded that it would be impossible to institutionalize all of the approximately 31,000 lepers in the country (Summation 1948).

A study of mortality in children revealed that from April to December 1946, 36 percent of all deaths were of children under 5 years of age. Measles, complicated by bronchopneumonia, accounted for 18 percent of the child deaths; pneumonia for 14 percent; and meningitis for 8 percent. Influenza and dysenteries followed meningitis in order of importance. An epidemic of smallpox was the cause of another 4 percent of the deaths. Therefore, 40 percent of the deaths in children under 5 years could have been prevented by use of penicillin, sulfonamides, and vaccination (Summation 1948).

Korea in the 1980s

The history of disease in twentieth-century Korea illustrates the remarkable effect of improved sanitary conditions and public health measures. Despite the devastation caused by World War II and the Korean War and the repatriation of millions of Koreans from Manchuria, China, and Japan, many of the epidemic and endemic diseases discussed have been virtually eliminated. Moreover, Korea's traditional agrarian Confucian society has been transformed into one that is highly mobile, urbanized, and well educated. The percentage of South Korean citizens attending colleges ranks among the highest in the world.

The population of the Republic of Korea was about 32 million in 1971, giving it a population density ranking about fourth in the world. With improvements in sanitation, public health, and medical facilities, the population had been increasing at a rate of 2.4 percent per year as infant mortality fell, life expectancy was extended, and endemic and epidemic diseases were brought under control. In the 1980s the population of South Korea was about 42,643,000; one in four Koreans lives in Seoul, the capital city (Gibbons 1988).

Lois N. Magner

This publication was supported in part by NIH Grant RO1 LM 04175 from the National Library of Medicine.

Bibliography

Avison, Oliver R. 1895. Cholera in Seoul. *Korean Reposi-tory* II: 339–44.

1897. Disease in Korea. *Korea Repository* IV: 90–4, 207–11.

Bohm, Fred C., and Robert R. Swartout, Jr. 1984. *Naval surgeon in Yi Korea: The journal of George W. Woods.* Berkeley, Cal.

Busteed, J. B. 1895. The Korean doctor and his methods. *Korean Repository* II: 189–93.

Centennial of modern medicine in Korea (1884–1983), ed. Medical News Co. Seoul, Korea. [In Korean]

Clark, Allen DeGray. 1979. *Avison of Korea: The life of Oliver R. Avison, M.D.* Seoul, Korea.

Gibbons, Boyd. 1988. The South Koreans. *National Geographic* 174: 232–57.

Hall, Sherwood. 1978. *With stethoscope in Asia: Korea.* McLean, Va.

Hay, Woo-keun. 1970. *The history of Korea,* trans. Lee Kyung-shik, ed. Grafton K. Mintz. Seoul, Korea.

Henschen, Folke. 1966. *The history and geography of diseases,* trans. Joan Tate. New York.

Hirsch, August. 1883. *Geographical and historical pathology,* Vol. I, trans. Charles Creighton. London.

Kim Tu-jong. 1966. *Han'guk uihaksa* (A history of Korean medicine). Seoul, Korea.

Korean Repository, Vols. I–V. 1964. Reprint. New York. [First edition published in Seoul, 1892–8.]

Lee, Ki-baik. 1984. *A new history of Korea,* trans. Edward W. Wagner. Cambridge, Mass.

Miki, Sakae. 1962. *History of Korean medicine and of disease in Korea.* Japan. [In Japanese]

Osgood, Cornelius. 1951. *The Koreans and their culture.* New York.

Simmons, James Stevens, et al. 1944. *Global epidemiology: A geography of disease and sanitation.* Philadelphia.

Summation of the United States Army military government activities in Korea. 1946–1948. Commander-in-Chief, U.S. Army Forces, Pacific.

VI.10
Diseases of Antiquity in South Asia

South Asia, also known as the Indian subcontinent, extends from the Himalayas south to form a huge triangle that juts into the Indian Ocean with the Arabian Sea on one side and the Bay of Bengal on the other. India, Bangladesh, Afghanistan, Sri Lanka, the Maldives, and the small Himalayan countries of Nepal and Bhutan are included in this area. South Asia can be divided roughly into three parts, beginning with the triangle-shaped Deccan Plateau, moving north to the fertile plain along the Ganges and Indus rivers, and finally extending to the north-ernmost section at the foot of the Himalayas.

Background: The Ancient Indian Texts

The Ayurvedic Texts

Ancient Indian Medicine had close ties with philosophy and religion. The basic texts of Hinduism are the four Vedas: *Rg, Sam, Yajur,* and *Atharva. Ayurveda,* meaning the "science of life," is considered to be the fifth of these texts and as important as the other four. All of the first four Vedas have sections that deal with healing and the prevention and cure of sickness. Yet the approach is usually magical or by prayer to the deities of the Vedic pantheon.

The Ayurvedic texts, by contrast, are of later origin and tend to attribute disease to divine causes less frequently. The codification of Ayurveda probably occurred around the sixth century B.C., and the texts presumably took their defined forms, in which they are still available, by the sixth or seventh century A.D. They were compiled in the northwestern part of India and in areas that today include Pakistan and Afghanistan, although, with the spread of the Aryans and their culture, Ayurveda came to be practiced over much of the country. Among other things this meant that the texts were modified to take account of the impact on health of geographic location, climate, water, seasonal variations, and diet. Indeed, many sections mention diseases due to these external factors, and one even suggests that geographic variations cause a difference in general health, and that certain locations favor epidemic disease.

The texts are known as the *Samhitas* – a Sanskrit term meaning "any systematically arranged informational collection of texts or verses." The five known Ayurvedic Samhitas are the *Sushruta*, the *Caraka*, the *Astangahrdaya*, the *Bhela*, and the *Kashyapa*. Some doubt exists about the authenticity of a sixth and incomplete text: the *Harita*.

Ayurveda deals with life (human and animal) in all its aspects including hygiene, ethics, medical education, and rules of behavior. Dietetics, geographic pathology, and even the philosophical basis of existence are also treated. Both the Sushruta and the Caraka divide medicine into eight broad areas: (1) Surgery (*Salya*); (2) Diseases of the Ear, Nose, Throat, and Eye (*Salakya*); (3) Internal Medicine (*Kayachikitsa*); (4) Mental Diseases (*Bhutavidya*); (5) Pediatrics Including Pregnancy and Its Complications (*Kaumarabhrtya*); (6) Chemicals Used in Treatment (*Rasayana*); (7) Rejuvenation; and (8) Aphrodisiacs (*Vajikarana*). The *Astangahrdaya* also mentions eight divisions of the Ayurveda, which are similar but not identical to the previous sections.

Caraka and Sushruta

Any discussion of diseases recognized during the period under scrutiny must rely heavily on the two major Ayurvedic texts – Caraka and Sushruta – because they are the most comprehensive and the least altered by later authors. These texts constitute a massive compendium that describes more than 360 separate diseases. This essay will concentrate on only the more clearly defined of these and, when possible, attempt to equate them with modern disease entities. The detailed observations of the ancient Ayurvedic physicians make available a body of information in which we can find something of a reflection of many of the diseases affecting the Indian subcontinent today.

In discussing the human being in health and disease, the Caraka mentions the necessity of examining the following facets: structure, function, causation, symptoms, methods of treatment, objectives of treatment, the influence of seasons and age, the capabilities of the physician, the nature of the meditations and appliances used in treatment, and the procedures to be used and their sequences.

Concepts of Disease

Ackerknecht (1982) summarized the ancient Indians' concern for disease and health thusly:

The ancient Indians put great emphasis on hygiene and prevention. They recommended toothbrushing, chewing of betel leaves, anointing, combing, exercise, massage, bathing, piety, taking the proper food, sitting idle, sexual inter-

course (once in four days), politeness, not being witness or guarantor, not going to crossroads, not urinating in the presence of superiors, cows, or against the wind, not sleeping during the daytime, and not eating fly-infested food. During epidemics one should not drink water or eat raw vegetables; one should run away and pray. Lest we smile at this strange mixture of Indian hygienic measures, we might remember that the Indians knew for thousands of years a technique for preventing smallpox, which the Europeans learned from the Turks only during the eighteenth century: inoculation.

In the Ayurveda, the balance of bodily health is viewed as being maintained by the healthy functioning of three *dosas* – *Vayu*, *Pitta*, and *Kapha* or *Sleshma* – which are somewhat akin to the Greek notion of bodily humors. Disturbances of one or more of the *dosas* caused by indiscretions in eating or by bad personal habits, such as suppression of the desire to defecate or excessive sexual intercourse or male intercourse with a menstruating woman, were seen as causes of illness. A few diseases could be triggered by riding on a horse, mule, or camel in an ungainly fashion. Others could arise because of external influences, such as injuries, whereas still others were due to heredity.

After being disturbed, the *dosas* were believed to lodge in a system of the body in an attempt to be excreted. While there, however, they produced disease. Thus specific symptoms or signs were generally viewed as disease, and consequently, the descriptions of many conditions are quite similar.

Wounds, Abscesses, Lymphadenopathies, and Superficial Neoplasms

The descriptions of wounds and abscesses in the texts are detailed and quite complete. The term *brana*, which is often used in the literature and is generally taken to mean an ulcer, has to be interpreted more liberally as a surgical or traumatic wound or even an abscess. A swelling that (1) is localized to one part of the body, (2) is hard, and (3) affects the skin and soft tissues in a particular manner is an inflammatory swelling or *shofa*. These swellings were thought to arise from various causes and were associated with manifestations of imbalance of the particular humors producing the disease.

Such inflammatory swellings were described as red, yellow, or black in color and increased in size at different rates. They produced local heat, burning, and other abnormal sensations and were said to pass through the phases of *Ama* (cellulitis), *Pacchyamana* (localization), and *Pakka* (localized abscess).

The clinical features specifically diagnostic of an

abscess or a wound are also discussed in detail in various chapters; for example, an abscess in connection with a broken bone discharges a mixture of marrow, blood, and often small spicules of bone in a fluid resembling clarified butter. Similar diagnostic features of abscesses at various sites are also given as prognostic signs of danger and curability. The exact timing for the incision of an abscess was thought to be critical, and dependent upon the clinical findings.

Deep-seated spherical or irregular swellings were called *Vidradhi*. Four types were thought to arise from the three disturbed *dosas* individually or in combination. Two other types mentioned are *Agantuka* (due to external trauma) and *Raktaja* (*Rakta* means "blood"). The descriptions of the various *Vidradhis* are often similar. They could develop anywhere in the body, and the overlying skin would have shallow ulcers of varying colors with discharges of differing natures – characteristics that identified the *dosa* responsible.

None of the *Vidradhi* involving the three *dosas* were attended with fever, which makes it difficult to accept them as being abscesses (the usual belief). The *Sannipataja* type – the most serious – resembles the description of a squamous carcinoma more than anything else, and other *dosaja Vidradhis* could quite well have been the same.

Vidradhi arising in the marrow of a bone was termed *Asthividradhi*. This seems clearly to have been acute osteomyelitis, as the bone was swollen with acute pain, and the patient had high fever. Finally the abscess discharged outside through the skin and muscles.

The two types of *Vidradhi* where high fever and thirst were prominent, suggesting an infectious origin, are the *Agantuka* type (caused by a deep wound due to an external agent) and the *Rakta Vidradhi*, arising in the pelvis of pregnant women following parturition, doubtless in many cases puerperal fever.

A variant is the *Antarvidradhi* or internal *Vidradhi*, a situation in which one developed on an internal organ such as the bladder, spleen, liver, or heart. Rectal examination and the passage of sounds into the bladder were common diagnostic techniques in these cases. A *Vidradhi* in the rectum caused symptoms suggestive of large intestinal obstructions, and one on the bladder neck probably indicated obstruction of the passage of urine. However, these symptoms also suggest neoplastic obstruction rather than abscess.

Disturbed *dosas* were also thought to produce slowly growing, cold, round swellings in the tissues,

termed *Arbuda*, which never suppurated and were probably neoplasms. A variant called the *Raktarbuda* reportedly grew rapidly and produced both a discharge and heaped flesh. Because patients suffering from *Raktarbuda* quickly become emaciated and the disease was viewed as incurable, the strong suspicion is that they were suffering from a malignant neoplasm.

Cancer, however, as a specific type of illness was not recognized in the Ayurveda, and the process of metastasis seems not to have been appreciated. Nonetheless some *Arbudas* were known to produce satellite *Arbudas* close by.

Fevers (*Jvara*)

Seven types of fevers were viewed as due to various combinations of the *dosas*, and an eighth was seen as the result of external causes. *Abhinyasajvara* and *Ojoniruddhajvara* are fevers, both of which were thought to occur when all *dosas* were defective. Their symptoms suggest typhoid fever and typhoid fever with delirium as well as cerebral malaria. The *Visamajvaras* were recurrent fevers with intermissions of normal temperature and thus seem to fit the cycles of some of the various types of malaria.

Poisons

The texts make it clear that the specialty of toxicology (*Agadatantra*) was well developed in India. Poisons from plants and minerals are discussed, as well as the symptoms and effects of insect, reptile, and animal bites and methods of treatment. In fact, 10 types of poisonous snakes and the effects of their venom are discussed together with the appropriate antidotes.

Skin Diseases

A disturbed Vayu driving Pitta and Kapha *dosas* into the skin was thought to bring on some skin diseases, whereas other skin diseases were viewed as the work of parasites. As a group, skin ailments were generally termed *Kustha*. The 7 *Maha* (or major) *Kusthas* appear to be variants of leprosy, a disease existing in India from ancient times. The 11 minor *Kusthas* were other skin diseases that are more difficult to equate with current cutaneous orders. However, it would seem that pityriasis versicolor, pemphigus, chilblains, moist eczema, dermatitis, scabies, and leukoderma were all represented.

Leprosy or *mahakushtha*, as it was known in the texts, was understood to be contagious, although it was also thought to be inherited by offspring of affected parents.

Head and Neck Diseases

Some Ayurvedic diseases of the mouth would seem to have a recognizably modern counterpart, among them (1) neoplasms of the lip (when the latter is described with raised areas of flesh that ultimately ulcerate); and (2) herpes labialis, with varicolored multiple small swellings. A condition in which the gums became spongy, retreated, and bled easily may have indicated scurvy, whereas another in which the gums and dental roots bled easily and gave off a purulent exudate may have been pyorrhea or periodontitis. *Mahashaushira* was a grave and painful condition in which teeth became loose in the gums, and the palate and the cheek were ulcerated. This seems to have been either cancrum oris or buccal carcinoma.

Impacted wisdom teeth, dental caries, and a situation in which the teeth were so sensitive that even touch was painful were also described, as were "gravel in the teeth" (tartar), and a condition in which destroyed teeth took on a blue-black color.

The diseases of the tongue discussed in the texts cannot be clearly divided into glossitis and epitheliomata, and many symptoms were taken to be disease entities in themselves. Diseases of the throat are generally termed *Kantharoga*. Among those that appear to be discussed are diphtheria, peritonsillar abscess, carcinoma of the base of the tongue, laryngeal and pharyngeal cancer, acute stomatitis, and chronic laryngitis.

Specific recognizable afflictions of the nose include nasal tumors and nasal polypi, whereas those of the ear embraced deafness, otalgia, otorrhea, and tinnitus.

In the region of the neck it was thought that Vayu and Kapha can become vitiated and lodge in the muscles and fat. The result would be a swelling called *Galaganda,* which did not suppurate, enlarged slowly, and might produce a vague noise in the throat. This disease was clearly goiter. The vague noise mentioned may be the stridor of tracheal compression, though associated difficulty in breathing is not mentioned.

In the hot, dry climate of northwestern India, eye diseases have always been common, and thus the sections on eye diseases are among the most detailed and remarkable of the Ayurveda. These diseases are divided into two broad groups: *Netrarogas,* or diseases of the eyeball; and *Drshtirogas,* or disturbances of vision. Seventy-three *Netrarogas* are described, although some seem to be different manifestations of the same disease. Four of these, for example, seem to be forms of trachoma and two more forms of blepharitis. Various types of corneal ulcers are discussed, as is conjunctivitis and glaucoma. The Ayurvedic variants of a disease called *Adhimantha* are actually the progressive stages of glaucoma, producing a swift loss of vision if untreated.

The section on diseases of vision describes cataract and various forms of another disease that resulted in disturbed vision – possibly symptomatic of glaucoma. Other disturbances of vision included day blindness and night blindness.

Neurological Disorders

Disturbances of Vayu were thought to create many neurological diseases. These included *Dhanustambha* (literally a pillar curved like a bow) or tetanus. Other conditions caused by disturbed Vayu included convulsions, the two types of which may well have been descriptions of petit mal and grand mal epilepsy; paralysis of one lower extremity; paraplegia; sciatica; brachial palsy; and facial palsy. Other diseases that we now do not think of as being neurogenic are also ascribed to disturbed Vayu. These include one that appears to be synovitis of the knee joint, another that seems suggestive of paresthesias of the feet, and still another that seems to have been bowel obstruction. Dumbness, nasal speech, and indistinct speech were also seen to stem from the same cause.

Heart Disease

Examination of the pulse played an important role in diagnosis and prognosis in Hindu medicine. But the nature of circulation and cardiac function was not well understood, which helps to explain the sketchy nature of the descriptions of cardiac diseases in the texts. Moreover, the descriptions in the Sushruta and the Caraka do not exactly correspond. Heart disease due to disturbed Vayu that caused palpitations, pain, slowing of the heart rate, fainting fits, and murmuring sounds in the heart constitutes the only condition that truly suggests a cardiac disorder. Other diseases of the "heart" seem more like gastrointestinal disorders in that they could be caused by bad eating habits, and their symptoms included a sense of heaviness in the precordium, a bitter or acid taste in the mouth, tiredness, and belching. Another type of "heart disease" was due to parasites arising in putrefied food. Here, the parasites were thought to invade one portion of the heart and gradually destroy the rest.

Respiratory Disorders

Respiratory problems are discussed under two major sections of the texts: disorders of breathing and of cough. Hiccough was thought to be a precursor of respiratory disease which, if left untreated, could help to bring on tuberculosis. Certainly tuberculosis was as common in the past as it now is in the Indian subcontinent. Also apparently described are pulmonary edema, bronchiectasis, and a number of chronic pneumonia types.

Abdominal and Intestinal Disorders

Udara is the anatomical name used in the texts for the abdomen. The term also signifies generalized abdominal disease manifested by enlargement. Most of the Udara disorders are ascribed to bad eating habits or to eating spoiled or poisonous food. A few conditions, however, can be understood by modern medicine. Among them is enlargement of the left side of the abdomen because of a large spleen. The symptoms associated with this condition suggest splenomegaly resulting from malaria or filariasis. Enlargement of the right side of the abdomen was the result of involvement of the liver and at times must have indicated cirrhosis. A particularly ominous situation resulted when all three *dosas* were disturbed: The patient turned yellow and suffered from pain, ascites, and emaciation. This could have been either advanced hepatic cirrhosis with liver failure or liver or pancreatic cancer.

A disease called *Dakodara* was clearly ascites. The abdomen enlarged with fluid that could be palpated, the umbilicus was flattened out or everted, and there were enlarged blue veins in the thin abdominal wall. Another abdominal distension arose from obstruction of the large bowel, and was manifested by progressive constipation, gaseous swelling of the abdomen, and crampy pains, all of which provides a picture of left colonic cancer or, less commonly, progressive anal stenosis. The latter was ascribed to sharp pieces of food perforating the gut and causing continuous thin and liquid anal discharge associated with vomiting, anorexia, abdominal distension, and pain. The condition could well have been acute gastroenteritis, which was, and is still, a common disease in the Indian subcontinent.

Among the discernible intestinal disorders are dyspepsia, acute diarrhea, and dysentery with some symptoms of the latter suggestive of amebic dysentery. Clearly discernible is cholera, or *Vishuchika* – the Ayurvedic term for cholera. The patient vomits, trembles, has continuous watery diarrhea, severe abdominal pain, and hiccoughs. In agonal stages there is tingling all over the body, and the patient loses consciousness and becomes cyanotic. The voice becomes weak, the muscles and joints become lax, and the eyes retract into the orbital cavity. In a variant termed *Alashaka,* diarrhea is not prominent, the abdomen distends, the patient has severe cramps and is very thirsty and nauseated. These symptoms parallel those of cholera sicca.

Miscellaneous

Hemorrhoids were clearly distinguished in the text, and were associated with or seen to be aggravated by excessive horseback riding, sitting on hard wooden seats, and friction with clothes or skin. By contrast, because the anatomy and functions of the kidneys were not well known, specific diseases due to disorder of renal function are difficult to spy. Tasting the urine, however, was an important element in diagnosis, and diabetes mellitus appears to have been understood as a disease.

Another disease, *Pishta,* which translates as "water containing ground rice" and which caused the patient to shiver as he or she urinated, may well have been *Chyluria;* this disease, which arises from filariasis, is common in India today, and probably was in the past as well. In this vein, *Shleepada,* which means "elephantiasis," the most prominent symptom of filariasis, was reported to occur most commonly in areas where stagnant water was plentiful – a desirable breeding ground for the mosquitoes that spread the disease. *Schleepada* was a progressive swelling, generally of the legs and less commonly of the hands, lips, ears, nose, and face, and in its late stages produced irregularities and vesicles on the surface of the skin.

The *dosas* could be disturbed by sexual practices that included too much abstinence or too much intercourse. Syphilis was introduced to India by the Portuguese, and thus there is no mention of syphilitic chancres in the older Ayurvedic texts. But at least soft chancre seems to be discussed under diseases of males and various forms of vaginitis under the female heading. In addition, ailments of women such as amenorrhea and possibly eclampsia can be discerned.

The above sections contain only a fraction of the immense corpus of the Ayurveda. Because of the lack of systematic dissection as well as ignorance of physiological principles, the descriptions of internal disorders in the Ayurveda are vague. However, diseases of the superficial organs and viscera are very well described and generally can be recognized for their modern-day counterparts. The detailed observations of the ancient Ayurvedic physicians have left a body of information in which we can see a reflection of many of the diseases affecting the Indian subcontinent today.

Ranes C. Chakravorty

Bibliography

Ackerknecht, Erwin H. 1982. *A short history of medicine.* Baltimore.

Bhisagratna, K. K., ed. 1963. *Sushruta Samhita,* 3 vols., 2d edition. Varanasi, India.

Cockburn, T. Aidan. 1971. Infectious diseases in ancient populations. *Current Anthropology* 12: 45–62.

Filliozat, J. 1949. *La Doctrine classique de la médecine indienne: Ses origines et ses parallèles grecs.* Paris.

Leslie, Charles, ed. 1976. *Asian medical systems: A comparative study.* London.

Sastri, K., and G. Chaturvedi, eds. 1979. *The Charaka Samhita,* 7th edition. Varanasi, India.

Shastri, K. A., ed. 1972. *Sushruta Samhita,* 2 vols., 3d edition. Varanasi, India.

VI.11
Diseases of the Premodern Period in South Asia

Overview

A geographic notion of South Asia generally includes India, Pakistan, Bangladesh, Sri Lanka (Ceylon), and Nepal. But although these countries may be thought of as constituting a single region, they contain a multitude of ethnic groups. Nonetheless, during the medieval ages, they had a common medical heritage rooted in the Greco-Roman world. At the extremities of the system, in northern or northwestern Europe and along the Russian river system, the Greco-Roman medical inheritance was thin. But in southern Europe and throughout the Muslim–Byzantine world, that heritage was rich. The geographic position of the Arabs in Asia Minor close to Greek sources had provided them with the opportunity to know the old Greek authors, especially in philosophy and medicine; therefore, the Arabs became the channels through which Greek influences were carried back into the West once more. Many new observations about diseases and a vast materia medica of the available drugs and medicaments in central Asian countries traveled through channels containing contributions by the eminent physicians of the Christian, Jewish, Muslim, and Hindu religions. Building on Hippocrates and Galen, they all wrote in the common Arabic language, the official language of the Caliphate.

By the beginning of the ninth century, some of the most famous medical men from the East and the West were meeting in Baghdad and ushering in a Renaissance. Indian physicians learned the examination of pulse at Baghdad from Greek and Arab physicians, who were expert in this sort of diagnosis. Knowledge of and interest in alchemy, along with the use of opium and many metallic compounds for treatment of various diseases, were also acquired from contact with the Greeks and the Arabs.

The concept of the modern hospital is a Persian contribution. When the Muslims conquered large parts of the Indian subcontinent, they introduced the concept of hospitals along with other institutions and traditions, and since then hospitals have been a part of city life. One of the 12 commandments issued by the Emperor Jehangir on ascending the throne in the seventeenth century was for the establishment of a hospital in all the larger cities in his domain. Allauddin II was the earliest Muslim king of the Deccan to build a hospital, *Dar-ul-Shifa,* at Bidar, his capital during the fifteenth century where food and drugs were provided to patients free of charge.

The hospitals were mainly staffed by Muslim physicians well versed in Greek and Arabic (now called *Unani*) systems of medicine. Many of them had Ayurvedic physicians on the staff as well. From the ninth century, this tradition of having both Hindu and Muslim physicians in the hospitals continued, particularly in India.

Diseases and Epidemics

The first important Arabic medical treatise that elaborately discussed and summarized the Indian system of medicine of this age is *Firdaus-al-Hikmat,* by Ali ibn Sahl Rabban al-Tabari, who died about A.D. 855.

The work of Rhazes, written in this period, deals systematically with head, eye, lungs, and digestive and circulatory systems, along with diseases of women and midwifery. The contents of the author's studies demonstrate his competence and skill in recognizing various diseases, in differentiating similar diseases symptomatically, in making their classifications, and in adopting methods to treat them.

Appearing early in the eleventh century, *Al-Qanun fi al-Tibb* by Avicenna is by far the largest and most famous medical work of this period. The work is divided into five major books. The first book treats general principles; the second treats simple drugs arranged alphabetically; the third deals with diseases of particular organs and members of the body from head to toe; the fourth deals with diseases that, though local and partial in their inception, tend to spread to other parts of the body; and the fifth deals with compound medicines.

The *Madanul-Shifa i-Sikandar Shahi* (Sikandar Shah's Mine of Medicine), written in 1512 by Mian Bhowa, discusses the symptoms and treatments of many diseases, including fevers, diarrhea, whooping cough, dropsy, epilepsy, rheumatism, erysipelas, heart diseases, gonorrhea, scrofula, elephantiasis, leprosy, smallpox, measles, and afflictions of children. In all, it discusses 1,167 diseases and the effects of various medicaments.

Smallpox

Inoculation for smallpox seems to have been known to the Hindus from a very early age. Long before Edward Jenner, certain classes in India, especially cow herders, shepherds, charans, and the like, had been in the habit of collecting and preserving the dry scabs of the pustules. They would place a little of this material on the forearm, and puncture the skin with a needle. As a result of this inoculation, these classes are purported to have enjoyed a certain amount of immunity from the disease.

In India, temples in which a deity of smallpox was worshiped hint at its presence prior to 1160 B.C. In ancient India, smallpox was, therefore, apparently regarded by the Hindus as a manifestation of a Hindu goddess called *Maria-tal, Mari-amma Devi, Mata,* or *Sitala.* According to W. A. Jayne (1979), "Sitala (the 'Cool-Lady' with a euphemistic allusion to the burning fever) was small-pox." The goddess was worshiped regularly so that she would not circulate among the villages. One could probably find shrines to her in any village or town in ancient India, according to O. P. Jaggi (1980).

So it seems that the Indian civilization has faced smallpox epidemics on numerous occasions, yet details regarding the complete history of the illness in South Asia remain obscure. The first clinical account of the disease appears in the Middle Ages, by the most competent physician of his age, Rhazes. Although brief mention of smallpox is made in two medical treatises of the period, the work of Rhazes is the first in which the illness is fully treated and in which its symptoms are described. Bhowa's medical treatise appearing in 1512 mentioned the disease smallpox-measles, along with its treatment. Around 1700, Hakim Mohammed Akbar bin Mohammad Muqin Arzani wrote *Mufarreh ul-Qulub,* in which he recorded his own experiments with treatments he adopted to relive the burning and throbbing sensation of the vesicles of smallpox.

The disease attacked the rich and the poor alike. A civil surgeon of Dacca, for example, found that in the history of the Tipperah family, between the fifteenth and eighteenth centuries, 5 out of 16 Maharajahs died from smallpox. According to S. P. James (1909), an observer writing in 1767 about the prevalence of smallpox in Bengal, said:

Every seventh year with scarcely any exception, the small-pox rages epidemically in these provinces during the months of March, April and May, until the annual returning rains about the middle of June put a stop to its fury. On these periodical returns, the disease proves universally of the most malignant confluent kind, from which few either of the Indians or the Europeans escaped that took the distemper in the natural way, commonly dying on the first, second or third day of eruption.

Inoculation against smallpox has been practiced in the subcontinent since ancient times, and accounts of the procedure are available in the writings of several British writers. O. Coult has given an account of smallpox inoculation (*tikah*) as he observed it in Bengal in the year 1731. Edward Ives, who was a naval surgeon on the flagship *Kent* and who was in India in 1754–7, has given further details of the method. In Calcutta inoculation was practiced among certain classes of Europeans as early as 1785, and apparently in 1787 the government established a hospital for smallpox inoculation at Dum Dum. In 1798, after much experimentation, Edward Jenner established that prior cowpox inoculation (i.e., vaccination; the Latin word for "cow" being *Vacca* and for "cowpox," *Vaccinia*) protected the person from getting smallpox, even though he or she was exposed to it. The practice of vaccination was accepted quickly in England, western Europe, and Russia, and by 1802, only 4 years after this discovery, vaccination was introduced in India.

Cholera

The history of cholera began on the subcontinent of India. Both literary records and religious practices suggest that cholera was endemic to the South Asian region for at least 2,000 years, but it was not until the sixteenth century that European travelers, explorers, traders, and officials provided detailed descriptions of a terrible plague whose symptoms were those of cholera and which was reported to reach epidemic proportions. One authority has identified 64 separate accounts of cholera in India between 1503 and 1817, and no less than 10 of those refer specifically to epidemics. The areas of cholera's historic endemicity were in South Asia, and especially in the delta regions of east and west Bengal.

It is said that the first pandemic of the early nineteenth century remained geographically in Asia, though it approached Europe, and it may have touched Africa at Zanzibar. The following second, third, and fourth pandemics affected the entire world, though with considerable regional variations; the areas of incidence receded significantly in the fifth and sixth pandemics.

During the medieval period, court chronicles described the occurrence of pestilences, though it is difficult to identify their correct nature in terms of diseases we now recognize. G. Gaskoin (1867) refers to *Lendas da India,* a publication by a Portuguese named Gaspar Correia, who in the spring of 1543 witnessed cholera in an epidemic form at Goa. The local people called it *moryxy,* and the mortality was so great that burying the dead was difficult. In 1563, Garcia da Orta wrote a vivid description of cholera as he saw it at Goa, adding that the disease was most severe in June and July. In the 1600s, more reports of epidemic cholera appeared in Madura (1609), Jakarta (1629), and Goa (1683). Cholera was next reported in 1783, when it broke out at Hardwar and, in less than 8 days, killed approximately 20,000 pilgrims. At the same time, the Maratha armies, engaged in war with Tipu Sultan (the Sultan of Mysore), suffered severely from the disease. In 1787, there was another account of the disease in India given by an English physician (a Dr. Paisley). Again in 1796, Fra Paolino de S. Bartolomeo penned an account of cholera in India.

The appearance of the disease at Fort William in 1814 was reported by R. Tytler, Civil Surgeon of Jessore. However, the first full and accurate account of epidemic cholera dates from 1817 to 1823. The earliest notice of this epidemic was given by Tytler in a letter dated August 1817: "An epidemic has broke out in the bazaars, the disorder commencing with pain or uneasiness in different parts of the body, presently succeeded by giddiness of the head, sickness, vomiting, griping in the belly and frequent stools."

While the cholera epidemic spread in the countries to the west of India, it was also transported to the east. In 1819, Burma and Ceylon were under its influence. The next year Siam was afflicted, as was Malacca, where the disease was said to have been brought by a vessel from the coast. Shortly after some persons with cholera-like symptoms landed from a vessel, the outbreak began. This outbreak occurred after Dutch vessels coming from Calcutta had anchored at Malacca. China and the islands of the Mauritius were also overwhelmed by the disease.

The cholera epidemic of 1817–23 gradually disappeared from the countries over which it had spread, and in Bengal little was heard of the disease throughout the years 1823–5, except in the endemic areas. But during the first quarter of 1826, cholera again erupted throughout the lower Bengal. From there it spread to Banaras and extended as far as the Kanpur Division, reaching the stations on the right bank of the Jamna. It was heard of at Hardwar in April and throughout the northwestern frontier provinces and along the Himalayas before the middle of June. Bombay Presidency, Sind, and the Punjab were assaulted by the disease which reached there from the east during the year 1827. It entered Khiva and Herat via Kabul in 1829. The epidemic from Kabul, Herat, and Persia spread to Russia and Poland in 1830, to England in 1821–32, to France in 1832, and in the same year to America, where it made its first appearance, to Cuba and Mexico in 1833, again to Europe from 1835–7, and finally to Africa in 1837. Subsequent cholera epidemics were observed in Europe and America (1848–53), in Punjab (1855), in Persia (1857), and in Arabia (1858–9). It appeared again in Punjab (1861), and traveled from Bengal to Africa, Arabia, Europe, and America (1863–5).

Plague

There is uncertainty in attempting to trace the historical background of plague in South Asian territories. According to Jaggi, extant references in Indian history for some pestilences that raged from time to time could indicate epidemics of plague. One probable epidemic attacked the army of Muhammad Tughlaq in the twelfth century. Again in the year 1443, a pestilence caused great loss of life in the army of Sultan Ahmad I. Farishta, a contemporary of the Mogul emperor Akbar, mentioned the occurrence of a fatal epidemic similar to that of bubonic plague in Bihar in 1548. A very devastating plague-like pestilence raged in Gaur, the medieval capital of Bengal, in 1573. The great famine of 1590 was followed by a severe epidemic, which may or may not have been plague. Tuzuk-i-Jahangiri described the occurrence of plague near Agra in 1618.

The Gujarat plague epidemic of 1812–61 was the first in India for which a detailed account is available. It broke out in 1812 in Kutch and is said to have destroyed half of the population before spreading to Kathiawar and Gujarat. According to a statement given by D. V. Gilder in the *Indian Medical Gazette* near the turn of the century (Nathan 1898):

In tracing the origin of disease in question the natives agree in referring the period of its first introduction to the

Hindoo year or *Sumwat* 1873 (A.D. 1817) three years subsequent to the dreadful famine, which raged with such destructive fury over Gujarat and Kathiawar. The disease extended to several other areas such as Kutch, Dholera, Peeplee, and Limree, etc., and people roughly distinguished it by the term *Ghaut no roque* possessing the following symptoms: great and general uneasiness of the frame, pains in the head, lumbar region and joints on the day of attack, hard, knotty and highly painful swellings of the inguinal or axillary glands (whence the name appears) in some instances; the parotids are affected in 4 or 5 hours, fever supervenes; these symptoms go on increasing in violence, attended with great thirst and delirium until the third day of the attack, when death closes the scene.

Another British physician also gave an interesting account of disease spread from Kathiawar, according to R. Nathan (1898):

In 1813 the plague was present in Central India and Rajputana, Kutch and Kathiawar and was first noticed at Kumtakale, and spread throughout Wagar during January, February and March 1816, and by the end of that year had extended to Sunde where the mortality was great. The disease was still prevalent in Central India in 1819, and disappeared in 1821. Nothing more was heard of the disease in Central India till July 1836, when it broke out at Pali, a town of Marwar, whence it spread to Jodhpur. It prevailed at Deoghur, in Meywar, in March 1837, and thereafter extended to Jalia and Ramghat in the district of Ajmere. The disease disappeared toward the end of 1837, but in November of that year, it again broke out in epidemic form at Pali, and continued till February the following year.

The same physician also wrote of *mahamari* (*gola* or *phutkiya rog*), an endemic disease of Kumaun and Garhwal in the Himalayas. The first record of the disease is dated 1823 at Kedarnath, Garhwal. From 1834, outbreaks in these districts occurred every few years, except for a long interval between 1860 and 1875, when it appeared to remain quiescent. After 1878, the outbreaks were not severe. The disease descended to the plains in 1853. In that year it appeared in an epidemic form in towns in the district Moradabad. According to Nathan (1898), a physician there concluded that *mahamari* was identical with the uncomplicated form of glandular plague of Egypt and that it could be conveyed by contagion and spread by endemic causes such as filth, poverty, and unclean habits of the inhabitants. In 1875, the disease was prevalent in certain villages in Kumaun where C. Planck (Jaggi 1980) recorded about 277 deaths and confirmed the opinion that it was the pestis or plague in medical terminology; he also recorded the first local history of *mahamari* in 40 vil-

lages attacked. This disease continued to be reported in the surrounding regions until 1893.

In 1896 plague broke out in Bombay, and its diagnosis was confirmed by W. M. Haffkine (Nathan 1898) in October of that year. The mortality rate in Jains at that time was significant, reaching a peak of over 100,000 persons. A Plague Research Commission was formed in Bombay in 1905, which worked under an advisory committee that was constituted in India and included representation of the Royal Society, the Lister Institute, and the India Office. This commission continued to work until 1913, and their studies have formed the basis of our present knowledge of the epidemiology of bubonic plague.

Malaria

Malaria is a parasitic disease that probably tormented primates long before humankind walked the Earth. The Indian art and medical classics make it clear that malaria had a long history on the subcontinent area, a history that has been illuminated at various points in the classical medical texts of ancient Hindu medicine. Susruta established a vague relationship between malaria and mosquito bites. This mythical savant classified the relevant types of fevers, and linked these with specific types of mosquitoes. As in Egypt and Mesopotamia, in the tropical dampness of the Indian river valleys, malaria reaped a deadly harvest, as it had probably done for millennia (1.4 million deaths in British India in 1939 alone) (Thorwald 1963).

The existence of a great many diseases in ancient South Asia is reflected in the Vedic books. As might be expected, fevers predominate because India is still probably the most malarial country on Earth, as well as the breeding ground for plague and cholera. But no clear statistics on the early history of malaria are available.

The nineteenth-century British medical statistics give some clear indications of the intensity of the infection. In Bengal, Bombay, and Madras, over the periods 1847–54 and 1860–75, of 1,110,820 British soldiers, 457,088 (or 41.1 percent) were reported as malarial cases (McGrew and McGrew 1985). Two other nineteenth-century investigations are worthy of mention: (1) In 1845, a surgeon major introduced the spleen rate as a measure of malarial endemicity and used it to map out the incidence of malaria in villages in the Punjab lying along the course of the old Jammu canal. (2) A great advance in malaria therapy was made in 1877 when a method of manufacturing pure quinine sulfate was discovered at the government's Sikkim plantation, which resulted in a great reduction in the cost of quinine production all over the world.

Kala-Azar or Visceral Leishmaniasis

In India kala-azar has been recognized as a distinct clinical entity for over 150 years. A number of epidemics occurred in Bengal in the mid-nineteenth century, and, although it was undoubtedly confused with malaria, the high treatment failure and mortality rates made the physicians of those days realize that they were dealing with a different illness. More attention was paid to the disease when in 1875 it began to invade Assam; kala-azar swept up the Brahmaputra Valley in three distinct epidemic waves between 1875 and 1917. The nature of the disease was clarified in 1903 when the causal organism now classified as *Leishmania donovani* was discovered by William Leishman in the spleen of a soldier who died in England from kala-azar, which he had contracted at Dum Dum, a military post just outside Calcutta.

Cutaneous leishmaniasis – or "oriental sore" or Delhi boil – is prevalent in the northern and western parts of India, especially in the United Provinces and the Punjab. It is caused by *Leishmania tropica,* which is transmitted by *Phlebotomus papatasii* in the subcontinent.

Other Diseases

Typhoid, influenza, dysentery, hepatitis, tuberculosis, as well as illnesses associated with malnutrition, are comparatively new diseases in South Asia in the sense that they are newly identified. However, leprosy and the venereal diseases are quite old, and ancient Vedic texts include descriptions of these diseases although they are not well sorted out from other diseases of the same classes.

Hakim Mohammed Said

Bibliography

Ackerknecht, Erwin. 1982. *A short history of medicine.* Baltimore.

Balfour, Edward. 1982. *Encyclopaedia Asiatica,* Vol. 8. New Delhi, India.

Browne, E. G. 1921. *Arabian medicine.* Cambridge. 1962. *Arabian medicine,* 2d edition. Cambridge.

Burrows, T. W. 1963. Virulence of *Pasteurella pestis* and immunity to plague. *Ergebnisse der Mikrobiologie Immunitaetsforschung und Experimentelle Therapie* 37: 54–113.

Chakraberty, Chandra. 1983. *An interpretation of ancient Hindu medicine.* Reprint of 1923. Delhi.

Curtis, C. 1807. *An account of the diseases of India.* Edinburgh.

Elgood, Cyrill. 1951. *A medical history of Persia.* Cambridge.

Gaskoin, G. 1867. Contribution to literature of cholera. *Medico-Chirurgical Review* 50: 220–38. London.

Gordon, Benjamin Lee. 1949. *Medicine throughout antiquity.* Philadelphia.

Hamdard Medical Digest. 1962. Karachi.

Horder, Lord, ed. 1951. *The British encyclopaedia of medical practice,* Vol. 7.

Jaggi, O. P. 1980–1. *History of science, technology and medicine in India,* Vols. 4, 8, 12, and 14. Delhi.

James, S. P. 1909. *Small pox and vaccination in India.* Calcutta.

Jayne, Walter Addison. 1979. *The healing gods of ancient civilizations.* First AMS edition. New Haven.

Keswani, NandKumar H. 1970. Medical education in India since ancient times. In *The history of medical education,* ed. C. D. O'Malley. Berkeley and Los Angeles.

Learmont, A. T. A. 1965. Health in the Indian subcontinent 1955–64. A geographer's review of some medical literature. Occasional papers 2. Canberra, Australia.

Leslie, Charles, ed. 1976. *Asian medical systems: A comparative study.* London.

Macnamara, C. 1876. *A history of Asiatic cholera.* London.

Major, Ralph H. 1954. *A history of medicine,* Vol. 1. Springfield, Ill.

McGrew, Roderick E., and Margaret P. McGrew. 1985. *Encyclopaedia of medical history.* London.

Nathan, R. 1898. *The plague in India, 1896, 1897.* Simla, India.

Rabban al-Tahari. 1981. *Firdaws al-Hikmat Fi al-Tibb,* trans. Rasheed Ashraf Nadvi. Pakistan.

Said, Mohammed, ed. 1966. *Hamdard pharmacopeia of Eastern medicine.* Karachi.

Siddiqi, Mohammad Zubayr. 1959. *Studies in Arabic and Persian medical literature.* Calcutta.

Sinhjee, Bhagvat. 1927. *A short history of Aryan medical science,* 11th edition. Gondal.

Thorwald, Jurgen. 1963. *Science and secrets of early medicine,* trans. Richard and Clara Winston. New York.

Transactions of the Medical and Physical Society. 1842. Calcutta.

Tytler, R. 1817. *District of Jessore.* Calcutta.

Ullmann, Manfred. 1978. *Islamic medicine.* Islamic surveys, Vol. 11. Edinburgh.

Walsh, James J. 1920. *Medieval medicine.* London.

Wriggins, W. Howard, and James F. Guyot, eds. 1973. *Population, politics, and the future of southern Asia.* New York and London.

VI.12
Diseases of the Modern Period in South Asia

The history of disease in modern South Asia has been dominated by epidemic diseases. Smallpox, cholera, and malaria, along with plague and influenza, figured prominently among the leading causes of sickness and mortality in the region for much of the period from the eighteenth to the mid-twentieth centuries. The recent decline or disappearance of several of these diseases has correspondingly resulted in a marked fall in overall levels of mortality.

Although the statistics are unreliable in detail (with perhaps a quarter or more of all deaths passing unrecorded), the broad trend is clear. From a peak mortality of nearly 50 deaths per 1,000 inhabitants in British India in the late nineteenth and early twentieth centuries, mortality rates were roughly halved by the 1950s, declining from 42.6 per 1,000 in 1901–10 and 48.6 in 1911–20, to 36.3 in 1921–30, 31.2 in 1931–40, and 27.4 in 1941–50 and 22.8 in 1951–60. In 1966–70, the figure was 15.3 per 1,000. The fall in infant mortality over the same period further confirms this trend. From an annual average of 212 deaths per 1,000 live births between 1911 and 1920, infant mortality in India fell to 176 in 1921–30, 168 in 1931–40, 148 in 1941–50, and 113 in 1966–70 (Davis 1951; Chandrasekhar 1972).

Mortality Levels

The reasons underlying this fall in mortality (and the earlier high levels of mortality) have been much debated. Kingsley Davis (1951) argued that India became "the home of great epidemics" only during the period of British rule (1757–1947), when it was "exposed to foreign contact for the first time on such a great scale." India's "medieval stagnation" was broken down later than that of Europe and so the region fell prey to pathogenic invasions, such as plague, at a later date. But, as in Europe earlier, India's population gradually developed an immunity to these diseases. Thus, Davis argued, even without medical and sanitary intervention, India's epidemic diseases began to lose much of their initial virulence. However, as Ira Klein (1973) has pointed out, some of the most destructive epidemics of the colonial period were not exotics but rather diseases long established in the region. Although India suffered very severely from invasions of plague and influenza between 1896 and 1918, diseases native to the region (notably smallpox, cholera, and malaria) also contributed substantially to the period's heavy mortality.

Davis probably exaggerates India's precolonial isolation. He also neglects its importance as a disseminator as well as a recipient of epidemic disease. The five pandemics of "Asiatic cholera" that raged between 1817 and 1923 all had their sources in India, as did the smallpox epidemics that caused such devastation at the Cape of Good Hope in the eighteenth century. Through extensive trading links developed long before the advent of British rule, as later through the exodus of its laborers and soldiers, South Asia acted as a source of several major diseases. Ancient ties of commerce and conquest with the rest of the Eurasian landmass saved the Indian subcontinent from many of the "virgin soil epidemics" that wrought such human havoc in the Americas and Oceania: Even plague had visited India several times before 1896. The critical factor was thus not so much the arrival of Europeans or the establishment of British rule as the greater degree of external contact that resulted from expanding trade and improved communications during the nineteenth and early twentieth centuries and the consequent social, economic, and environmental changes that facilitated the spread of epidemic diseases, whether exotic or indigenous in origin, throughout the region.

A second explanation for the twentieth-century decline in epidemic mortality focuses on the role of medical and sanitary intervention. Measures to protect South Asia from epidemic disease began early in the colonial period with the introduction of smallpox vaccination in 1802, and it has been claimed that this dramatically reduced the incidence of what had formerly been one of the region's greatest afflictions. Later measures against cholera, plague, and malaria – from mass immunization to chemical spraying – have likewise been identified as decisive factors in the eradication or control of these diseases. Davis (1956) claimed that by the mid-twentieth century, medical technology had the capacity to reduce mortality without waiting for supporting advances in socioeconomic conditions. But the limits of therapeutic intervention have since become apparent (especially with the resurgence of malaria since the 1960s), and recent writers are more skeptical about its effectiveness as an explanation for earlier falls in mortality. The low level of colonial (and postcolonial) expenditure on medicine and public health; the paucity of doctors, hospitals, and medical supplies relative to the size of the population; and the enormous technical, social, and cultural obstacles in the way of effective medical action – all have been cited as evidence of the limited human capacity to master epidemic disease in South Asia.

A third hypothesis draws close parallels with the European experience. It has been argued that the fall in mortality in eighteenth- and nineteenth-century England owed little to medical advances (apart, latterly, from vaccination) and derived instead from improved living conditions and diet. A comparable development has been suggested for South Asia, albeit at a somewhat later date. Despite massive famines that resulted in some 20 million deaths in British India during the second half of the nineteenth century, it is claimed that there was a significant improvement in economic conditions by 1900. The food supply became more dependable, helped by the construction of an extensive rail network and the expansion of irrigated agriculture; famine relief grew more effective in saving lives, and there was a rise in rural incomes through the stimulus of an expanding market economy. Those epidemic diseases most closely associated with famine – smallpox and cholera – declined with the disappearance of severe famines from India after 1908 (apart from the Bengal famine of 1943–4, which significantly saw a marked recurrence of epidemic mortality). The high death rate was sustained into the 1920s only by epidemics of plague and influenza, diseases that (it is claimed) had little connection with rural poverty and hunger (McAlpin 1983).

This argument has the virtue of singling out famine as a critical determinant of mortality trends in South Asia and hence provides a nonmedical explanation for the decline of two of the greatest killer diseases, smallpox and cholera. But although famine as such may have disappeared from most of the region after 1908, South Asia remained (and remains) afflicted by chronic poverty, with half the population below the poverty line. Malnutrition and overcrowded and unsanitary living conditions have remained fertile ground for disease and have kept mortality and morbidity at levels far above the norm in Western countries. Economic gains have failed to reach most of the people, and per capita foodgrain availability may even have fallen during the course of the twentieth century. There thus seems little basis for claiming that socioeconomic change has resulted in a healthier population. It would be more realistic to argue instead that although the cessation of major famines and the medical targeting of specific diseases like smallpox and cholera have been responsible for reducing or eliminating some of the earlier and most conspicuous causes of high mortality, other "competing" causes of debility and death have taken over or have remained largely unaffected. Mortality has declined since 1900, but sickness and death remain all too common.

Diseases

In view of the diverse characteristics of the main diseases of South Asia and of the various factors affecting them, it will be helpful to consider the recent history of the most important of them in turn.

Smallpox

Smallpox was held by nineteenth-century medical opinion to be "the scourge of India," responsible for more deaths than all other diseases combined. Endemic throughout much of the region, smallpox returned in epidemic strength every 5 to 7 years. So prevalent was the disease between February and May that it was known in eastern India as *basanta roga,* the "spring disease." With the onset of the monsoon season, however, smallpox abated, reaching its lowest ebb in October and November. Climate might provide a partial explanation for this marked seasonality, but social and cultural factors were influential, too. In India the dry spring months, a slack period in the agricultural year, were traditionally a time for congregation and travel, for religious fairs, pilgrimages, and marriages, all activities that provided the close social contact needed for transmission of the *Variola* virus.

In driving large numbers of destitute and undernourished villagers to seek food in relief camps and cities, famines also created conditions favorable to the dissemination of the disease. So, too, did the dislocation caused by warfare. Just as Maratha invasions may have contributed to an upsurge in smallpox mortality in eighteenth-century Bengal, so did the displacement of millions of refugees in the same area during Partition in 1947. Bangladesh's war of independence in 1971–2 also occasioned major outbreaks of the disease (Chen 1973).

In the absence of reliable statistics it is impossible to gauge the full extent of smallpox mortality before the late nineteenth century. One demonstration of the disease's long-standing importance was the reverence paid throughout South Asia to the Hindu goddess Sitala (or her counterparts) as the deity credited with the power to either cause or withhold the disease. A nineteenth-century writer further attested to the prevalence of smallpox when he speculated that as many as 95 percent of the 9 million inhabitants of the north Indian Doab had experienced the disease. So common was it, he claimed, that "it has become quite a saying among the agricultural and even wealthier classes never to count children as permanent members of the family . . . until they have been attacked with and recovered from smallpox" (Pringle 1869).

As these remarks suggest, smallpox was mainly a childhood disease, the chronology of smallpox epidemics being largely determined by the creation of a pool of susceptible infants born since the previous outbreak. Between 60 and 70 percent of fatalities occurred among children under 10 years of age, and of these half died before they were even one year old, although one of the consequences of the spread of childhood vaccination was to increase the proportion of adult victims.

Smallpox mortality probably reached a peak in British India in the middle and later decades of the nineteenth century before entering a period of sustained decline. From 1.4 million deaths recorded for the decade 1868–77, and 1.5 million for 1878–87, smallpox mortality fell to barely 1 million in 1888–97 and 800,000 in 1898–1907. From 0.8 smallpox deaths per 1,000 inhabitants in 1878–87, the ratio fell to 0.4 in 1908–17 and down to 0.2 in 1937–43, before the Bengal famine and Partition fueled a partial resurgence. Although in epidemic years in the 1870s the number of smallpox deaths soared as high as 2 per 1,000, by the 1930s there were fewer than 0.5 fatalities per 1,000 of the population (James 1909; Hopkins 1983).

Significantly, smallpox mortality began to decline even before the worst famines of the period were over, and exactly when medical intervention began to have an effect on smallpox mortality is unclear. In Sri Lanka, an island with a small population, vaccination may have eliminated endemic smallpox early in the nineteenth century; but because of constant reinfection from India, the disease was not finally eradicated until 1972.

Although vaccination was introduced into India in 1802–3, its impact there at first was slight. Imported lymph was unreliable, and local sources of supply were not adequately developed until late in the century. The arm-to-arm method of vaccination was extremely unpopular, and the bovine origin of vaccinia provoked strong Hindu hostility. Vaccination had, moreover, a popular and well-established rival in variolation (smallpox inoculation), which was considered more effective and culturally acceptable. Faced with such opposition, the colonial regime was disinclined to commit substantial resources to vaccination, and during the nineteenth century it was practiced mainly among Europeans and those

Indians, especially of the middle classes, most closely associated with them. Compulsory vaccination and the outlawing of variolation began in Bombay city in 1877 and was followed by the Government of India's Vaccination Act in 1880. However, the implementation of the acts was piecemeal and deficient. As late as 1945, primary vaccination was compulsory in only 83 percent of towns in British India and a mere 47 percent of rural circles. Compulsory revaccination was even rarer (Arnold 1988). Nevertheless, the evidence suggests that vaccination did contribute to the relatively low levels of smallpox mortality achieved by the early twentieth century. The number of vaccinations in India rose from approximately 4.5 million a year in the 1870s to twice that number in the 1900s and exceeded 40 million (nearly three-quarters of them revaccinations) by 1950. Given the heavy death toll smallpox had formerly levied among those under 10 years of age, vaccination significantly reduced mortality among infants and children.

Existing methods of smallpox control were, however, inadequate to secure the final eradication of the disease. In 1962, the year in which India launched its eradication program, the country reported 55,595 cases of smallpox and 15,048 deaths from the disease. There were a further 4,094 cases and 1,189 deaths in Pakistan (mainly East Pakistan). Five years later, the World Health Organization began its own eradication campaign, which concentrated upon early recognition and reporting of the disease, the isolation of cases, and the vaccination of contacts. The Bangladesh war of 1971–2 delayed eradication and enabled a fresh epidemic to flare up. In 1974 India again suffered a severe outbreak (showing that *Variola major* had lost none of its former destructiveness), with 188,003 cases and 31,262 deaths. South Asia was finally freed of smallpox in 1975.

Cholera

Like smallpox, cholera has had a long history in South Asia. Reliable accounts of the disease date back to at least the sixteenth century, and it was reported from several parts of India during the late eighteenth century (MacPherson 1872). But the cholera epidemic that erupted in the Jessore district of Bengal in August of 1817 assumed an unprecedented malevolence and in barely 2 years it penetrated to almost every part of the subcontinent, including Sri Lanka, before setting out shortly afterward on the first of its "global peregrinations." Epidemics of cholera repeatedly swept through South Asia during the nineteenth century, and the disease was undoubtedly a leading cause of high mortality and (relatively) low population growth in India before 1914. Perhaps from the absence of any existing immunity, mortality rates were particularly high during the 1817–19 epidemic (though not as high as an alarmed Europe was willing to believe).

The incidence of epidemic cholera in India can be related to a number of factors: The emergence of Calcutta, the most populous city of British India and an important regional center for trade and administration, during the eighteenth and nineteenth centuries favored the wide dissemination of the disease from its endemic home in the Ganges–Brahmaputra delta. As elsewhere in the world, cholera often moved in the wake of advancing armies. Soldiers unwittingly helped spread the disease in northern and central India in 1817–18 and again during the Mutiny campaigns of 1857–8. The seasonal migration of laborers and plantation workers may also have had a comparable effect. They passed through endemic areas, lived in primitive accommodation at the site of their employment, and drew water from contaminated sources.

Of even greater significance was the close association, much remarked upon during the nineteenth century, between epidemic cholera and Hindu pilgrimage. Pilgrims traveled long distances, mainly on foot (before the railway age); they were ill-clothed and ill-fed, and crowded in their thousands into insanitary towns or into makeshift camps at the main fairs and festivals. Cholera not only spread easily and rapidly among the pilgrims themselves but also was carried far afield as they dispersed to their homes. Several of the largest epidemics of the nineteenth century were traced to the festival of Rath Jatra, held annually at Puri in Orissa, close to the Bengal cholera zone, and the 12 yearly bathing festivals, the Kumbh melas at Hardwar and Allahabad on the Ganges (Pollitzer 1959).

As a mainly waterborne disease, cholera was endemic in low-lying areas, such as lower Bengal, where the cholera vibrio flourished in village reservoirs ("tanks") and irrigation channels that were also used for drinking water. But epidemic cholera occurred, too, in conjunction with famine. Although major epidemics could occur (as in 1817–19) in the absence of famine conditions, the scale of cholera morbidity and mortality was greatly magnified by the migrations of the famine-struck, by their lack of physical resistance to the disease, and by their dependence upon scant sources of water and food that quickly became contaminated.

Whereas in times of good harvests cholera tended to retreat to the low-lying areas where it was endemic, many of the worst epidemics between the 1860s and the early 1900s bore some relation with concurrent famine. The disease thus exhibited even more violent fluctuations than smallpox, dying away in some years, only to return in devastating strength once or twice in a decade. In 1874, for example, cholera mortality in India sank to 0.16 per 1,000 of the population; only 3 years later (with famine widespread), it reached 3.39 per thousand, before ebbing away again to 0.64 in 1880.

In 1900 cholera soared to its highest recorded peak with 797,222 deaths in British India, a ratio of 3.70 per 1,000: In this year of sickness and starvation, cholera accounted for a tenth of all mortality (Rogers 1928). But, having hovered at around 4 million deaths each decade between 1889 and 1919, cholera mortality finally began to fall, dropping to 2.2 million in 1920–9, and 1.7 million in 1930–9, although there was a partial resurgence during the 1940s (the decade of the Bengal famine and Partition) to just over 2 million deaths with 500,000 cholera deaths in 1943 alone, nearly 50 percent of them in Bengal. From a death rate of 0.74 per 1,000 in 1925–47, and 0.17 in 1948–63, the ratio continued to fall to 0.0017 in 1964–8. Epidemic cholera did not disappear entirely, however. In 1974, for instance, there were 30,997 reported cases in India with 2,189 deaths. In the same year Bangladesh suffered 5,614 cases and 177 deaths, while Sri Lanka, long the recipient of epidemics originating on the Indian mainland, had 4,578 cases and 343 deaths.

Although various theories were advanced during the nineteenth century to explain cholera's origins and spread, it was only in 1883 that Robert Koch finally identified cholera vibrios in a Calcutta tank. Even without this knowledge, sanitary measures (as taken in Europe and North America) had had some earlier effect, helping in particular to reduce mortality among European soldiers who, until the 1870s, suffered a high proportion of casualties from the disease. Improved sewers and filtered water lessened cholera mortality in several major cities (including Calcutta from 1869); the long-term decline in the disease has also been identified with the creation of public health departments in the provinces from the early 1920s. But the latter were poorly funded, and in India, with a predominantly rural society and a large and growing slum population, sanitary reform had a more limited impact than in the West.

Cholera inoculation proved a less effective form of

prophylaxis than smallpox vaccination, and the connection between cholera and Hindu India's pilgrimages and sacred sites made the colonial authorities wary for a long time of provoking a religious backlash. But, for all this, anticholera inoculation is likely to have had some success in curbing the explosions of mortality formerly associated with pilgrimages and melas. For many years a voluntary practice, inoculation for pilgrims became compulsory in 1954 in time for the Allahabad Kumbh mela, when nearly a quarter of a million pilgrims were inoculated. Combined with intensive medical surveillance and prompt reporting, inoculation contributed to the decline of epidemic mortality, although, again, the absence of major famines after 1908 (apart from that of 1943–4 in Bengal) must also have been a contributory factor.

In addition, the virulence of the disease may have been on the wane by 1914 (or human resistance may have been increasing). The El Tor biotype, which invaded the region from Southeast Asia in 1964–5, proved less fatal than the "classical" form it largely displaced. Immunity acquired early in life, rather than inoculation or improved sanitation, possibly contributed most to cholera's long-term decline. But, despite this, cholera remains a recurrent threat to human health in South Asia.

Other Enteric Diseases

The reasons for the persistence of cholera – insanitary living conditions and contaminated water supplies – are also reasons for the continuing importance of other enteric diseases. *Dysentery* and *diarrhea* have long been significant among the major causes of sickness and death in South Asia, and, like cholera, greatly swelled mortality during times of famine. Alexander Porter (1889), in his pioneering study, reckoned dysentery and diarrhea the chief cause of death among famine sufferers in Madras in 1877–8. In the high wave of mortality at the turn of the century, one death in every seven in British India was attributed to dysentery and diarrhea, placing these diseases in third place behind malaria and plague as major killers. But they also accounted for a great deal of the mortality even in nonfamine times, particularly among children. In 1962 in India they were responsible for 179,714 deaths (equivalent to 0.4 per 1,000 population). In 1974, along with 846,858 cases of gastroenteritis and 333,687 of typhoid (with 3,623 and 924 deaths, respectively), dysentery, with 4.5 million cases and 2,182 deaths, stood high among the most commonly reported illnesses.

Malaria

Although malaria has undoubtedly been present in South Asia for a very long time, it was not recorded separately from other "fevers" until late in the nineteenth century and so is even more difficult than are smallpox and cholera to trace in recent times. But, once identified as a distinct disease, malaria was soon recognized as a primary cause of much ill health and death. Almost a fifth of the mortality that occurred between the 1890s and the 1920s (amounting to some 20 million deaths) was attributed to malaria. As plague, smallpox, and cholera abated, so malaria gained prominence as the greatest single threat to health in South Asia. J. A. Sinton estimated in the 1930s that malaria was responsbile for 3 or 4 times as many deaths as the 3 other diseases combined. Of 6.3 million deaths in British India between 1924 and 1933, at least 1 million, he believed, were directly attributable to malaria, while millions more, weakened by the disease, fell ready prey to other ailments and afflictions. In addition, the disease was a frequent cause of abortions and stillbirths.

As elsewhere, malaria in South Asia has had a close relationship with the environment and with environmental change. During the nineteenth century, the expansion of irrigation canals and the building of railway embankments and other major construction works that interfered with the natural lines of drainage or left patches of stagnant water created human-made environments in which malaria-bearing *Anopheles* mosquitoes could breed (Klein 1972). South Asia thus failed to experience the beneficial side-effects of the draining of marshlands and swamps that contributed so significantly to malaria's decline in Europe. The extension of irrigated cultivation and the dense settlement it commonly sustained in South Asia, combined with the development of new networks of labor migration and mobility, have also tended to create conditions favorable for human transmission of the disease.

Until recently, malaria infestation largely prevented agricultural colonization of areas like the Terai in the Himalayan foothills and the hill tracts along the Andhra–Orissa border. The partial eradication of malaria in the 1950s and 1960s facilitated the penetration and settlement of these areas, but its return severely affected immigrant farmers (e.g., in the Chittagong Hill tracts of Bangladesh) with no inherited or acquired immunity to the disease.

Like the other diseases so far discussed, malaria has some connections with human hunger. S. R. Christophers (1911) showed a close correlation between peaks of malaria mortality and morbidity in the Punjab between 1869 and 1908, and periods of high food prices, a basic index of widespread poverty and incipient famine. But in this instance the decline of famine was apparently not matched by any corresponding downturn in malaria morbidity and death.

Around 1950 malaria was still killing 500 out of every 100,000 of the population in South Asia, with India alone suffering 800,000 deaths a year. Although quinine prophylaxis and the mosquito nets and screens have provided limited protection to a small minority (mainly Europeans), the advent of DDT from the end of World War II made a comprehensive assault on malaria possible for the first time. India launched a National Malaria Eradication Campaign in 1958, and such was the apparent success of DDT spraying there and in Sri Lanka that Davis (1956) was prompted to write of the "amazing decline" in Third World mortality modern medicine made possible. But the triumph soon proved short-lived. Increasing anopheline resistance to DDT and the diminishing effectiveness of the drug chloroquine resulted in a startling recrudescence of malaria during the 1960s and 1970s. From a low point of 50,000 cases in India in 1961, the number rose to 1.4 million in 1972 and 1.9 million in 1973. It then shot up to 3.2 million in 1974 and 5.2 million in 1975. Two years later, in 1977, an estimated 30 million people in India were suffering from malaria.

Plague

Although not unknown to the subcontinent in previous centuries, plague arrived in epidemic force in 1896, when the disease broke out in Bombay city and then gradually spread to other parts of western and northern India. By 1907 close to 2 million plague deaths had been recorded, and at its peak in 1904–5 the number of deaths reached 1.3 million in a single year. By 1907–8 plague accounted for more than 14 percent of all mortality in British India, and its heavy toll swelled India's great mortality between the 1890s and the 1920s. In this third plague pandemic, India was exceptionally hard-hit. Of 13.2 million deaths recorded worldwide between 1894 and 1938, 12.5 million occurred in India: Nearly half of the deaths in India fell in the period from 1898 to 1908, with a further third between 1909 and 1918 (Hirst 1953). At first mainly a disease of the cities, plague moved steadily into the countryside. The Punjab was worst affected, with nearly 3 million fatalities between 1901 and 1921; in 1906–7 alone there were 675,307 deaths in the province, equivalent to 27.3 per 1,000 inhabitants.

But for all the severity of the disease, plague in modern India never took as heavy a toll of human life as in Europe during the Black Death of 1347–9, partly because the deadly pneumonic form of the disease was absent. Several areas escaped largely unscathed. Northern and western India bore the brunt of the epidemic, whereas Bengal, the south, and Sri Lanka were far less affected. One possible explanation for this, favored by L. Fabian Hirst, was that the type of flea found on the rats in western and northern areas, *Xenopsylla cheopis,* was a more efficient vector of the plague bacillus than *Xenopsylla astia,* which was more common in southern regions.

At the start of the epidemic, in part responding to international pressure and the threat of commercial sanctions by other European powers, the British adopted measures of far greater severity than previously employed against cholera and smallpox. Suspects and victims of the disease were hospitalized or put in segregation camps; house searches were made to discover concealed cases and corpses; many thousands of travelers were examined, and walls and roofs pulled down to allow sunlight and fresh air into dark interiors. At this early stage the role of rat fleas in the transmission of the bacillus was not understood, and the assumption was that plague was a disease of "filth" or an "acute infectious fever" spread through close human contact.

But medical intervention on such a scale proved singularly ineffective. It failed to extirpate the disease, which continued to spread (in part through people fleeing from such drastic measures), and it led to evasion and even open defiance in several cities. In consequence, the British administration soon settled for a less interventionist policy, turning down W. M. Haffkine's suggestion of compulsory inoculation with the antiplague serum he had recently developed. Reliance was placed instead upon voluntary segregation and hospitalization, greater use of indigenous medical practitioners, and latterly (once the rat flea connection had been established) on the trapping and poisoning of rats.

These measures may have contributed to the decline of the disease, already marked by 1917; so also may the extensive use made of voluntary inoculation (in the long term). It is possible that just as the prevalence of famine in the early years of the epidemic aided the spread of plague, so the later absence of famine contributed indirectly to its decline. The bulk movement of grain (and with it *X. cheopis*) in times of food shortages may have facilitated the spread of the disease: There is some evidence for this connection in its partial resurgence as a result of the massive movements of grain triggered by the Bengal famine of 1943–4. Another possibility is that whereas human susceptibility remained unchanged, rats developed a growing immunity to the plague bacillus. For whatever reason, plague was in decline in India from the early 1920s and, since 1950, has been rare, confined to a few isolated pockets, mainly in the southern Deccan.

Influenza

Influenza had a much shorter but more devastating career than did plague. As with plague, India was one of the areas of the globe hardest hit by the influenza pandemic of 1918–19. In the space of barely 3 months it lost between 12 million and 20 million lives, equivalent to nearly 5 percent of the total population of British India, and up to twice as many as had fallen victim to plague during the whole of the previous decade. As with plague, influenza entered India through international ports like Bombay, but then moved with lightning speed from one city to the next along the main lines of transport and communication. Southern and eastern India were again the areas least affected (Davis 1951; Mills 1986).

The greatest number of deaths occurred during October, November, and December 1918, with the major casualties being young adults between the ages of 20 and 40. Connections between influenza and famine have often been denied, but because the epidemic struck at a time of high prices and food shortages in several parts of India and caused disproportionate mortality among the poorer classes, grounds exist for arguing that one reason why India suffered so severely from the epidemic was precisely because so large a part of its population was at the time hungry or malnourished (Klein 1973; Mills 1986). As elsewhere influenza died away almost as quickly as it had come, and though influenza has remained a common affliction in the region, it has been responsible for few deaths. In 1974, for example, 1,700,000 cases of influenza were reported for India, but there were only 87 deaths.

Tuberculosis

Tuberculosis was not a disease that attracted much medical attention before 1945, but it has increased in importance as other diseases have declined and as the crowded, especially slum, conditions in South Asian cities have grown. Already at the start of the century, TB and the other respiratory diseases accounted for at least one-seventh of all deaths. Fully 342,391 deaths from the disease were reported in

India in 1961–2 (equivalent to 0.85 per 1,000), and between 100 and 150 out of every 100,000 city-dwellers died from this cause. By 1981 an estimated 1.5 percent of the total population of India was affected, placing TB among the leaders of India's many competing causes of death.

Miscellaneous

Several other diseases warrant mention, however briefly. *Tetanus* in India has been particularly associated with childbirth through the use of unsterilized implements to cut the umbilical cord. Cases numbered 32,825 in India in 1974, with 4,400 reported deaths. *Hepatitis* was widespread, too, with 126,071 cases and just over 1,000 deaths in 1974. In that year there were also 206,386 cases of *whooping cough* (300 deaths) and 333,697 (924 deaths) from *typhoid,* making these, along with malaria, dysentery, gastroenteritis, and influenza, two of the main identifiable causes of morbidity.

Leprosy remains strongly entrenched in South Asia. Whereas the census of 1881 counted only 131,618 lepers in British India (surely a gross undernumeration), the census of India 90 years later, in 1971, put the figure at 3.2 million. Some experts, however, estimate at least 4 million cases of leprosy in the country. Not only is this a high figure in national terms, with 5 to 6 per 10,000 of the population affected, but it also makes India home to one-third of the world's leper population. Despite the availability of modern drug therapies, the socioeconomic conditions in which leprosy is transmitted (and perpetuated) have so far prevented its effective eradication.

Conclusions

Several major epidemic diseases of the recent past have been brought under control (or have largely disappeared through reasons that may have little to do with human intervention). But, so long as poverty remains endemic in the region and levels of public health expenditure and provisioning remain low even by Third World standards, there seems little likelihood that the high levels of morbidity and mortality that continue to afflict the region will effectively disappear.

David Arnold

Bibliography

Arnold, David. 1988. Smallpox and colonial medicine in India. In *Imperial medicine and indigenous societies,* ed. David Arnold, 45–65. Manchester.

Chandrasekhar, S. 1972. *Infant mortality, population growth and family planning in India.* London.

Chen, Lincoln C., ed. 1973. *Disaster in Bangladesh.* New York.

Christophers, S. R. 1911. *Malaria in the Punjab.* Calcutta.

Davis, Kingsley. 1951. *The population of India and Pakistan.* Princeton, N.J.

1956. The amazing decline of mortality in underdeveloped areas. *American Economic Review* 46: 305–18.

Hirst, L. Fabian. 1953. *The conquest of plague.* Oxford.

Hopkins, Donald R. 1983. *Princes and peasants: Smallpox in history.* Chicago.

James, S. P. 1909. *Smallpox and vaccination in British India.* Calcutta.

Klein, Ira. 1972. Malaria and mortality in Bengal, 1840–1921. *Indian Economic and Social History Review* 9: 132–60.

1973. Death in India, 1871–1921. *Journal of Asian Studies* 32: 639–59.

MacPherson, John. 1872. *Annals of cholera from the earliest periods to the year 1817.* London.

McAlpin, Michelle Burge. 1983. *Subject to famine: Food crises and economic change in western India, 1860–1920.* Princeton, N.J.

Mills, I. D. 1986. The 1918–1919 influenza pandemic: The Indian experience. *The Indian Economic and Social History Review* 23: 1–40.

Pollitzer, R. 1959. *Cholera.* Geneva.

Porter, Alexander. 1889. *The diseases of the Madras famine of 1877–78.* Madras.

Pringle, R. 1869. On smallpox and vaccination in India. *Lancet* I: 44–5.

Rogers, Leonard. 1928. *The incidence and spread of cholera in India: Forecasting and control of epidemics.* Calcutta.

Sinton, J. A. n.d. *What malaria costs India.* Delhi.

VI.13
Diseases of Antiquity and the Premodern Period in Southeast Asia

In the imaginations of commentators, both Asian and European alike, disease and Southeast Asia have long held a close association. For Chinese officials posted to the southernmost regions of the T'ang empire, it was a fearful place of miasmas and malarial fevers. To many Europeans, Southeast Asia was, like tropical Africa, a "white man's grave." In the chronicles of the inhabitants of the region, the reality of disease merged with that of other calamities, in a world populated with spirits that held sway over human life. Aside from biomedical considerations, there are clearly important political and cultural dimensions to these links between region and disease. This essay will examine some of the factors that have given disease such a prominent place in Southeast Asian history.

The Region

Following Anthony Reid (1988), Southeast Asia will here be taken to refer to the area of Asia lying between the southern regions of China and the northwestern extremities of New Guinea. This region encompasses both the land areas of mainland Asia draining the eastern Himalayas, characterized by large rivers and plains, and the many volcanic islands lying between the Pacific and Indian oceans. A feature of the region is its high temperatures and monsoonal rainfalls, which, prior to recent times, supported an abundant flora and fauna.

Human settlement also flourished in this environment from around 18,000 B.C., when the earliest hunter-gatherers are thought to have existed in the region (Higham 1989). Evidence suggests that village settlements developed from around the third or fourth millennium B.C., and more complex, centralized polities from the first century A.D. (Coedès 1975; Higham 1989). The larger "city-states" of mainland Southeast Asia developed from the sixth and seventh centuries A.D. It is from the time of the development of these complex polities that the earliest written records of Southeast Asian peoples date.

Prior to the nineteenth century, the region was, as a whole, sparsely populated, the inhabitants concentrated mainly in large trading cities and areas of wet rice cultivation (Reid 1988). With the development of "city-states" and an increase in commerce and trade both within the region, and with China, India, and the Middle East, important changes occurred in Southeast Asia. These changes, which affected the size and distribution of Southeast Asian populations, their occupations, living conditions, and diet, were further enhanced by the contact with the West, via both Africa and the Americas, which developed from the sixteenth century. This culminated in the colonization of much of Southeast Asia by European powers, beginning with the establishment of a Portuguese colony at Malacca in 1511.

The development of the region was, however, confined to certain sections of the region and its population. Until very recently, a considerable proportion of the people of Southeast Asia lived much as they had hundreds of years ago. There remain, for example, hunter-gatherer communities in remote areas of Borneo and Northern Thailand. Even for villagers living in rural areas, and the urban poor, many aspects of thought and culture continue to reflect traditional concepts and values. For this reason it is difficult to make a general distinction between "antiquity" on the one hand, and the "premodern" and "modern" periods on the other. For the sake of convenience, however, in this essay "antiquity" will be used to refer to the period prior to the entry of Europeans into the Southeast Asian region. The period following the entry of Europeans into the region, up until the beginning of the present century, will be termed the "premodern era" of Southeast Asian history.

The peoples who inhabited the region in antiquity spoke languages representing a diversity of families, including Austronesian, Austro-Asiatic, and Tai. However, though there were considerable regional variations in their customs and rituals, a good many of the peoples of the region were unified by some basic cultural features. Thus, throughout much of Southeast Asia, transport was (until recent times) mainly by water, dwellings were of wood and bamboo, and rice and fish formed the basis of the diet. Similarly, the custom of betel chewing, and sports such as cockfighting and *takraw,* played with a rattan ball, were common to many peoples. Trade, and the ease of maritime access within the region, probably facilitated the process of acculturation (Reid 1988).

Beliefs regarding the soul and the spirit world were also widely shared throughout Southeast Asia. It was believed that if the soul, or life-force, contained within the human body were weakened or disturbed in some way, then health could be impaired. The outside world was believed to be populated by spirits that had the potential to inflict harm on humans (Anuman 1962; Endicott 1970; Terwiel 1978). Practices performed in order to strengthen the soul, or to propitiate the spirit world, were thus common to the region as a whole (Reid 1988).

The natural wealth of Southeast Asia, together with its intermediary position between the East and West, has ensured that contact with some of the world's major civilizations has taken place over a long period of time. Early contacts with China and India were later followed by Arabs and then Europeans. Many features of these civilizations – in particular, religion and writing – were to become important in Southeast Asian life. However, at least up to the premodern period, as Reid points out, ties within the region were generally more important than those with peoples beyond it (Reid 1988).

This "distancing" from civilizations outside the region is reflected in the pattern of the adoption of cultural features. There is strong evidence to suggest that aspects of other civilizations were restated in terms of the indigenous cultures concerned (the phenomenon termed "localization" by Owen Wolters in 1982) in many of the areas where such borrowing occurred. It will be argued here that this process of adaptation was also prominent in the classification of, and response to, disease.

Disease in the Southeast Asian Past

Knowledge of disease in the Southeast Asian past is severely constrained by some of the same features that give the region its uniqueness. Human remains, and written records of disease, deteriorate rapidly in the acid soils, heat, and humidity that are characteristic of this part of the world. This lack of sources would, in itself, constitute a major difficulty in the study of the history of disease in Southeast Asia. However, the cultural diversity of the region also raises other issues fundamental to the interpretation of the past. For our purposes, paramount among these is the question of differing perceptions of disease.

Following Arthur Kleinman (1987), the term "disease" will be used here to include a wide range of explanations or perceptions of illness. Unlike plants and animals, most diseases are not so readily distinguishable by common features. Not only do peoples differ in the ways in which they group the various symptoms of illness into diseases, but there may be considerable variation in the types of bodily phenomena that constitute symptoms. Conditions such as the enlarged spleen associated with malaria may, among some populations, be regarded as nonpathological (Ackerknecht 1946). With other peoples, much emphasis is placed on whether symptoms are located in the upper or lower part of the body and the time of their onset in relation to the phases of the moon (Ohnuki-Tierney 1981; Mulholland 1987). In some cases there may even be little distinction made between disease and the agent that causes it (Schafer 1967). As a consequence, available descriptions of illness often do not provide the type of information that is necessary for biomedical diagnoses to be made.

Information on illness in the Southeast Asian past comes in several forms: In addition to what may be regarded as indigenous classifications, there are Indic, Chinese, and early Western systems of classification. It is possible, for example, that a case of diarrhea might be seen as "internal heat," "an expansion of the heat element," "fluxes," or as a "normal" phenomenon, depending on the source of the description. Furthermore, as Norman Owen (1987) has indicated, a feature of the Southeast Asians' response to disease was their syncretism. An appropriate diagnosis and treatment was selected from among the various systems available. For this reason, a history of disease in Southeast Asia is, in part, a history of the ways in which illness has been classified in this region of the world.

This is not to say that biomedical interpretations are not possible. In past accounts one can recognize many of the diseases that were known in the region until quite recent times and, in a large number of cases, are still prevalent in the region today. Malaria, smallpox, dysentery, cholera, typhoid, typhus, plague, leprosy, beriberi, goiter, trachoma, respiratory diseases, tuberculosis, and parasitic and helminthic infestations are but a few examples. However, although it is often possible to interpret accounts of illness in terms of our modern understanding of pathology, this approach reveals only one aspect of the history of disease in Southeast Asia. Neglected is the place of disease in the context of extra- and intraregional dynamics involving trade, warfare, politics, and culture. In short, biomedical interpretations do not show how Southeast Asians perceived disease and what it meant to them.

Another difficulty in treating the history of diseases in Southeast Asia as a whole is posed by the number of different ethnic groups and languages in the region. This problem is further exacerbated by the diversity of languages and methodologies of the available secondary sources on the subject. For this reason, although the general features described will relate, in the main, to the history of diseases in the whole of Southeast Asia, the specific illustrations given in this essay will be taken mainly from mainland Southeast Asia. In particular, a good many examples will be drawn from the Thai peoples.

There are several reasons for this narrow focus. In part it reflects this writer's own area of specialization, a situation that is unavoidable in approaching such a topic. In addition, however, the history of disease among the Thai peoples is an appropriate focal point for a study of the disease in Southeast Asia. The region of mainland Southeast Asia where the Thai kingdoms developed in many ways represented a meeting place for the major civilizations of Asia, lying between China to the north, India to the west, and the Austronesian peoples to the south and east. Originating in the north, the Thai, who were "syncretizers" par excellence, moved into a region already occupied by Mon and Khmer peoples. Furthermore, although the kingdom of Siam came to dominate the other Thai "city-states," it was alone among Southeast Asian countries in remaining uncolonized by Europeans. On the other hand, it may be argued that, though not directly colonized, Siam was a de facto colony, in that its development during the late nineteenth and early twentieth centuries was mainly in the hands of European and American advisors.

Previous historical studies have not, in general, taken advantage of the opportunities that mainland Southeast Asia presents for the examination of disease. The processes of adaptation, perception, and response to illness have, for the most part, been examined in the context of the colonized regions of insular Southeast Asia. This is to be expected, in view of the ready availability of information on disease, and the size of the populations in these areas, with their concomitant health problems. But in using illustrations from uncolonized mainland Southeast Asia, this chapter seeks to redirect some of the emphasis in the study of the history of disease.

Diseases in the Prehistoric Period

Our knowledge of the types of diseases suffered by the prehistoric inhabitants of Southeast Asia is, of necessity, based on the examination of a very limited range of human remains unearthed in a few sites in present-day Thailand, the Malay Peninsula, and Sulawesi. The remains represent only the most durable of the body's hard tissues, primarily the skull, mandible, and teeth. Despite such limitations, however, they nevertheless reveal a good deal of information regarding the diseases suffered by the ancient inhabitants of the region.

Skeletal remains, for example, recovered from sites at Ban Chiang, Non Nok Tha, and Ban Na Di in northeastern Thailand suggest that the prehistoric inhabitants of these villages suffered many of the same diseases found in these areas today. As might be expected from the nature of the source materials, these included a range of diseases primarily affecting the skeleton, such as osteoarthritis (or degenerative joint diseases), and bone infections, possibly including osteomyelitis and tuberculosis of the spine.

There is also evidence for a range of dental pathology, including caries, periodontal disease, abscesses (periapical and alveolar), and excessive tooth wear, sometimes with pulpal involvement (Pietrusewsky 1974, 1982, 1982–3; Houghton and Warrachai 1984). Evidence for caries, periodontal disease, and abscesses has also been found in human remains from sites at Talaud Island in North Sulawesi, and Gua Cha in the Central Malay Peninsula (Bulbeck 1982).

In addition, examination of skeletal remains provides evidence of diseases affecting other organs of the body. These include tumors, or tumorlike defects (in a child's cranium from Ban Chiang), and blood disorders. Evidence for the latter comes from a number of skeletons found in northeastern Thailand, which, it has been argued, may indicate thalassemia or elevated hemoglobin B levels (Pietrusewsky 1982, 1982–3).

These conditions, both of which are widespread in the region today, may be associated with resistance to malaria, which is common in the area. Indeed the evidence from the pathology observed in skeletal remains has thus been used to argue for the antiquity of malaria (Pietrusewsky 1982). More recently, however, iron deficiency anemia has been put forward as an alternative explanation (Houghton and Warrachai 1984). This explanation is consistent with the effects of parasitic infestations of the body, which are also prevalent today in this region of Southeast Asia.

Diseases in Antiquity

Apart from evidence derived from archeological research, the earliest available sources of information on disease in Southeast Asia are references in inscriptions and accounts appearing in traditional texts. Khmer inscriptions of the seventh and eighth centuries A.D., for example, make reference to lice, eye impairments, and "dermatitis" or "ringworm" (Jenner 1981). It is difficult to date some of these sources, especially texts, but it is clear that by the time of their appearance there had already been considerable contact between Southeast Asia and

civilizations in other parts of Asia. Much of the language used, and the means of recording itself, were exotic in origin. Originally these descriptions were made using techniques probably borrowed from India or China. Inscriptions were made on stone, or on palm leaves trimmed and bound together with cord, or else written on paper. The scripts employed were similarly of Indic or Chinese origin (Guy 1982; Marr 1987).

Traditional Medical Texts

In addition to short references to disease in chronicles, or other official records, certain works were devoted solely to medicine. These appear to have been a feature of almost every major civilization in the region, including those of the Burmese, Thai, Lao, Khmer, Vietnamese, Malay, Javanese, and Balinese (La Loubère 1691; Sangermano 1833; Macey 1910; Pigeaud 1967; Pham Dinh Ho 1973; Martin 1983; Social Research Institute 1986; Lovric 1987; Reid 1988). Commonly, the contents of these books consisted of passages relating to theories of illness, lists, and descriptions of diseases, and details of the methods used in their treatment.

It is likely, however, that such texts provide incomplete accounts. One reason for this is their perishability. Being sensitive to decay and insect attack, traditional texts had to be continually recopied in order to preserve their contents. Not only did this introduce the possibility of human error through mistakes in transcription, but, more importantly, there was always the threat that disruptions caused by warfare or other adversity would result in the loss of large numbers of texts. For example, in 1767 the Siamese capital of Ayuthaya was sacked by the Burmese, an event which, in itself, resulted in the destruction of much of the court's medical library (Koenig 1894). Moreover, the loss was compounded by the slowness of the subsequent recompilation process, which was not completed until some 40 years later, around 1816.

Another difficulty in the use of traditional texts as source materials is in determining the extent to which their contents reflected diseases actually occurring in Southeast Asia, and their prevalence. It is quite possible that accounts of diseases contained in texts may be largely based on Indic, Chinese, or, later, Arabic medical treatises. This is certainly the case with other types of texts, such as literary or astrological works (Quaritch Wales 1983; Reid 1988). On the other hand, evidence suggests that, although Southeast Asian medical texts may incorporate disease terms and concepts derived from traditions outside the region, they are not simply translations of texts belonging to those medical systems. It appears that in the area of disease, as with other aspects of Southeast Asian culture, a process of localization took place, resulting in the selective emphasis of certain concepts of parts of theories, and changes in the meanings of words borrowed from languages outside the region. Some examples of these processes will be considered later in this essay.

Travelers' Accounts

A further important source of information on disease in Southeast Asia consists of the accounts written by early travelers to the region. These included the Chinese Buddhist monk Yi Jing, who passed through the region on his way to India toward the end of the seventh century A.D. (I Tsing 1896), Chou Ta-kuan (1951), who accompanied a Chinese ambassador to Cambodia in the thirteenth century, and the later European travelers such as S. de La Loubère (1691), and E. Kaempfer (1906). Kaempfer's account is of particular interest, because he represented a class of scholarly voyagers whose interests often extended to a number of disciplines. As a physician and botanist, he took care to record accurately what he saw and heard, including indigenous terms and descriptions. When compared with accounts obtained from indigenous texts, such information is extremely useful.

Ethnomedical Studies

Modern-day studies of indigenous perceptions of disease in the Southeast Asian region constitute another important kind of available information. As well as information on disease appearing in the context of more general anthropological or linguistic studies, a number of specific examinations of indigenous medical systems in Southeast Asia have been conducted. These include those of insular peoples, as well as those of mainland Southeast Asia (see, e.g., Frake 1961; Martin 1983; Boutin and Boutin 1987; Brun and Schumacher 1987; Gumpodo, Miller, and Moguil 1988; Bamber 1989). Although there have been far-reaching changes in Southeast Asian life, it is probable that, until quite recently, for a large number of people in the region, life was lived in much the same manner as it had been centuries ago (Hall 1981). It is thus likely that, for certain sections of the Southeast Asian population, present-day perceptions and treatment of disease bear a strong resemblance to those of the past. An analysis of such contemporary "folk" medical beliefs and disease classifications, made in conjunction with information

derived from the other sources discussed above, may thus make an important contribution toward our understanding of disease in Southeast Asia in ancient times.

Indigenous Views of Disease

It is clear from the information contained in the various sources described above that in the past, Southeast Asian peoples recognized a large number of diseases, and classified them in ways that were, in many cases, quite complex. One feature, which is immediately striking to an observer familiar with Western concepts, is that conditions that are understood to be diseases in modern medicine were not necessarily viewed as such by Southeast Asians. This is especially evident in the area of diseases affecting the gastrointestinal tract which, along with "fevers," occupy perhaps the most prominent place in accounts of illness in the region (see Dampier 1927; Chou Ta-kuan 1951; Schafer 1967; Cook 1968).

A number of severe gastrointestinal diseases were well differentiated by Southeast Asians and elicited treatment responses. Symptoms and treatments for conditions such as cholera, dysentery, severe diarrhea, and certain types of parasitic infestations were, for example, described in traditional texts (Mulholland 1979; Lovric 1987; Terwiel 1987). However, certain other conditions that biomedicine would recognize as diarrhea were apparently not always considered to be diseases. Recent studies indicate, for example, that in certain areas of Southeast Asia infant diarrhea is not necessarily viewed as pathological. Thus, among some Northeast Thais one type of diarrhea (su) may be regarded as a normal phenomenon, common to all infants (Earmporn, Pramote, and Stoeckel 1987). This would also appear to be the case for people in parts of northern Thailand and Laos. Similar findings have been reported for the Acehnese and other Indonesian peoples (Raharjo and Corner 1989).

It is likely that such poorly defined boundaries between pathological conditions and "normal" bodily states are also to be found for other types of disease. Included in these are a number of Southeast Asian disease categories that are unrepresented in modern medicine. Examples of these that are better known because of their dramatic expression are the conditions of amok and latah, Malay behavioral syndromes that appear to have counterparts in other parts of Southeast Asia (Westermeyer 1973; Simons 1985).

Other conditions, lacking such overt behavioral symptoms, reflect classifications of illness that are equally different from those of modern medicine. One such disease is the Thai category *saang* (children's disease), which includes a range of symptoms mainly affecting the mouth and skin of young children (Mulholland 1987). The onset of this disease has strong links with Thai beliefs regarding "soul loss" (Hanks and Hanks 1955; Hanks 1963).

Shared Disease Terms

It is apparent from a comparison of disease terms in a number of Southeast Asian languages that certain categories were widely shared throughout the region. One explanation for this situation is the contact that resulted from the movement of large populations within the region, such as occurred with the establishment of the Tai peoples in the Chaophraya River valley and the Malay Peninsula from the mid-eleventh century A.D. (Wyatt 1984). Contact with peoples already established in the region, such as the Malay, Mon, and Khmer, was reflected in the adoption of disease terms from these languages. Thus, for example, the Malay disease *sawan* (convulsions), which affects small children (Wilson 1985), also appears, as *saphan* or *taphan,* in traditional Thai medical texts (Mulholland 1987).

A similar though more complex process seems to have taken place with respect to terms for certain types of skin diseases. This may be seen in the case of the ancient Mon–Khmer term *mren,* which probably referred to skin afflictions in general. This term appears to have undergone a change in meaning at some stage, possibly prior to contact with the Thai, to signify ulcer in Khmer, and superficial skin conditions in Mon (Shorto 1971).

Following contact with the Mon and Khmer, the term *mren* was adopted by the Thai, cognates appearing in traditional medical texts as *mareng* and *baheng.* In this case, however, because in Thai skin diseases appear to have been well differentiated prior to contact with the Mon and Khmer, there is evidence of an accommodation with existing terms (Li 1977). Thus in central Thai, which was in close contact with Khmer, *mareng* came to mean "deep-seated ulcer" (McFarland 1944). However, in northern Thai *baheng* refers to superficial skin diseases, indicating that the term was adopted from the neighboring Mon peoples (Brun and Schumacher 1987).

These examples also point to the existence of more complex processes within the Southeast Asian region which contributed to the sharing and interchange of terms and concepts related to disease. Medicine was an area of culture that was particularly amenable, for a number of reasons, to trade

and exchange (Golomb 1985). These processes would have involved not only concepts and terms indigenous to the region but also those originating from outside Southeast Asia – in Chinese, Indic, or Islamic medicine. Perhaps the most well-known example of the integration and adaptation of foreign concepts of disease into the Southeast Asian framework is that of the so-called wind illness.

"Wind Illness," Humoral Theories, and Therapeutic Practices

A type of illness common to most of the peoples of Southeast Asia has been termed wind illness (Hart 1969). The disease has been reported among Indonesian and Malay peoples, where it is referred to as *masuk angin,* literally "wind enters" (Gimlette 1939), among Filipinos (Hart 1969), Burmese (Sangermano 1833), Khmer (Headley 1977), Vietnamese (Eisenbruch 1983), and a number of Thai groups. The conditions represented by wind illness vary widely through the region, ranging from symptoms of the common cold among Indonesians and Malays, to fainting, dizziness, and, more rarely, leprosy, among mainland Southeast Asian peoples.

Most explanations for the phenomenon have been made in terms of theories derived from the major medical systems with which Southeast Asian peoples have come into contact. In Chinese medicine, for example, wind illness figures as part of a theory that sees disease arising through the entry of wind into the body (Unschuld 1982). Wind illness is similarly important in the humoral theories of Indic and Islamic medicine. Here, however, it refers to diseases of the wind element, one of the four elements (the others being earth, fire, and water) of which the body is said to be composed (Hart 1969; Ullmann 1978). According to the Indic version of this theory, the wind element denotes the quality of bodily movement, or sensation. Any disease that involves an impairment or abnormality in these faculties would thus be designated as a wind illness. Following from this rationale, wind illness includes a number of diseases or conditions, such as paralysis, epilepsy, and leprosy, which are considered in modern medicine to constitute quite separate disease entities (Caraka 1949).

Versions of both these theories are to be found in the Southeast Asian region. The Indic theory of the four elements is expounded, for example, in Thai medical texts (Mulholland 1979); Islamic humoral theory is widely known in peninsular Malaysia and Indonesia (Manderson 1986); and beliefs regarding the ill effects of the entry of wind into the body accompanied Chinese who settled in the region (Kwa Tjoan Sioe 1936). However, the wind illness of Southeast Asia does not always fit neatly with these theories. Early writers on Thai medicine commented, for example, on the prevalence of wind illness in comparison to diseases affecting the other three elements (Pallegoix 1854; Bradley 1967). Thai wind illnesses also appear to have encompassed a far wider range of diseases than one would expect on the basis of Indic theory (Muecke 1979).

Discounting the unlikely possibility that Thais, or other Southeast Asian peoples, are predisposed to diseases affecting bodily sensation or movement, it would seem that the Indic concept of wind illness has been reinterpreted to accord with indigenous concepts relating to the cause of illness. These concepts probably have more to do with beliefs linking disease to soul loss, or the spirit world, than they do with humoral theories (Laderman 1987). The resulting concept of wind illness represents a complex, incorporating elements derived from both within the Southeast Asian region and outside of it.

Similar interactions may be seen throughout the region in relation to other aspects of disease. For example, the etiological concept of hot and cold physical states is also widespread in Southeast Asia. Accordingly, certain diseases, foods, and treatment practices are regarded as heating or cooling (Hart 1969; Manderson 1981). As with wind illness, this concept appears to be the result of an integration of indigenous beliefs with Indic, Islamic, or Chinese theories (Manderson 1981; Marr 1987).

Therapeutic practices were also shared throughout the region. One well-known example is in the ritual ridding of a person, or community, of disease. Among the central Thai this was termed *sia kabaan,* and consisted of the symbolic transference of the disease to inanimate objects, such as dolls or animal images, which were subsequently floated away on streams, or otherwise removed from the locale of the patient (Anuman 1958). Similar rituals have been described for most other Thai groups (Terwiel 1980–1), and in several other regions of Southeast Asia, with variations according to the local culture (Snouck Hurgronje 1893; Skeat 1900; Reid 1988). Often these local variants included elements derived from Indic or Islamic tradition.

The picture that emerges from this brief look at some of the features of Southeast Asian views of disease prior to increased contact with the West is one of a dynamic state. Close contact among peoples within the region ensured that conceptions of disease and its treatment were frequently shared. The development of links with the major civilizations outside of the region meant that different perceptions of disease and therapeutic techniques continued to be introduced to Southeast Asia, and incorporated into indigenous systems (Owen 1987). The result was a matrix of classifications and strategies that could be brought to bear on the experience of illness.

Disease in the Premodern Period

As noted earlier, from around the beginning of the sixteenth century, a marked economic and social development occurred in most Southeast Asian states. The development of the region had significant effects in relation to disease. These included changes in the types of disease suffered by Southeast Asians, their susceptibility, and the ways in which they viewed and treated disease. One important feature of this period was the large-scale intervention of the state in the control and prevention of disease. This period saw the initiation of public health measures, the establishment of hospitals, and the commencement of vaccination campaigns. It also saw Southeast Asia come to play an important role in the development of Western science. In this section of the chapter, some of these features will be examined against the background of the cultural and socioeconomic changes that came about at this time.

Changes in the Types of Disease

From the medical historian's point of view, one important legacy of the European colonization of Southeast Asia was the propensity of the colonizers to collect statistics, compile reports, and make detailed observations on illness. These range from simple parish records, as in the Philippines (Owen 1987), to colonial office records such as those that exist for Java and Malaya (see Gardiner and Oey 1987; Manderson 1987). Moreover, European interest in Southeast Asia was not limited to administrative concerns; the region was visited by a good number of scholars, encompassing a diversity of disciplines, and their accounts contain detailed descriptions of the region, its peoples, and history.

Nonetheless, considerable care must be taken in the interpretation of the sources because they generally reflect European preconceptions, regarding both Southeast Asia and disease. Thus whereas figures are generally good for foreign communities, the reliability of statistics for the indigenous populations is often questionable (Boomgaard 1987; Gardiner and Oey 1987). As has been noted by a number of commentators, there was a strong tendency in Western sources to emphasize dramatic events such as epidemics (Boomgaard 1987; Owen 1987). Epidemics of "plague," smallpox, and a number of other diseases were indeed a frightening and regular feature of Southeast Asian life during this period. However, insofar as they posed no threat to the health or commercial interests of the European community, other less dramatic diseases of the region tended to be neglected in accounts. Yet, in the long run, the toll they took of human life was probably considerably greater.

It is true that references to disease in certain types of indigenous sources, such as chronicles, are also often concerned with epidemics. However, these references, which occur mainly in connection with accounts of crises, and the performance of state ceremonies, reflect the political or religious function of such sources, rather than an attempt to provide balanced descriptions of disease. In other indigenous sources, such as medical treatises, much space is often devoted to the description of diseases that do not figure significantly in either European or official indigenous accounts.

A further difficulty in the interpretation of European and indigenous sources alike is that both the systems of classification and the illnesses they sought to classify were changing. In the indigenous languages of the region it was not uncommon, at different times and in different contexts, for a disease to be known under several names. Similarly, early European accounts often differentiated poorly between illnesses, references frequently being confined to such general terms as fluxes, or fevers (see Dampier 1927; Cook 1968).

The difficulties thus posed for the identification of illness in modern terms are illustrated by the case of the history of cholera in Siam (Terwiel 1987). It is generally agreed that the first major epidemics of cholera in Southeast Asia occurred in the early nineteenth century as the result of the spread of the disease from India. Yet in earlier Thai sources cholera was known under several names, including *ahiwaat, khai puang yai,* and *rook long raak.* Thus, owing to both the difficulties in interpreting indigenous accounts, and the lack of sophistication of early Western classifications of the illness, it remains unclear whether a less virulent strain of cholera had previously existed in the region (Boomgaard 1987; Owen 1987; Terwiel 1987).

Similar difficulties are encountered in the identification of other diseases, as seen in the case of leprosy, another condition with a long history in Southeast Asia. Human figures with features consistent with leprosy are depicted in Khmer bas-reliefs on the Bayon at Angkor, and at Ta Keo (Coedès 1941). The disease was also noted by a Chinese traveler during his stay in Cambodia in 1296 and 1297 (Chou Ta-kuan 1951). Legend also has it that in ancient times, there was a Khmer "leper king" (Coedès 1941; Chou Ta-kuan 1951). But other written accounts do not always permit a fine distinction to be made between leprosy and other skin afflictions. In traditional Thai medical texts, for example, the term that today is used to denote leprosy, *ru'an,* also includes a range of other skin conditions such as tinea. This is also the case in some early European accounts. Thus the leprosy which William Dampier reported to be widespread in Mindanao and Guam during his 1686 visit was probably the same fungal skin disease, possibly *tinea imbricata,* later reported by John Crawfurd in Java (Crawfurd 1820; Dampier 1927).

Some of the difficulties mentioned above may be attributed to the complexities of indigenous disease naming, as in the Thai examples, or to the lack of diagnostic expertise of the individual observer, as was perhaps the case with Dampier. More importantly, however, the examples above point to the fact that diseases, their incidence, and the ways in which they were classified, were continually changing. Thus as diseases were changing in virulence, the susceptibility of the population to disease was also changing. Moreover, new diseases were being introduced into the region, and, largely due to the development of Western medical science, changes were occurring in the understanding of disease. Here, we look at some of the factors that were central to these changes.

The Development of Cities

The most important factor concerning disease during this period was probably the redistribution of populations, associated in particular with the development of large cities. Whereas in the past the location of cities was primarily determined by strategic considerations, which almost certainly would have included the provision of secure food and water supplies, trade and industry now became a major determinant.

In Southeast Asia major cities, such as Batavia, Singapore, Manila, and Bangkok, developed in coastal or estuarine areas as port cities with their associated commercial activities. In these areas, which were usually low-lying or marshy, drainage, the removal of wastes, and the supply of clean household water quickly became a problem. The poor, on whose labor the operation of ports and commerce depended, were faced with the additional problems of crowded housing and a diet that was often barely adequate. In addition to the dangers these conditions posed for health, the constant port traffic and the linking of Southeast Asia with the rest of the world meant that the region was increasingly open to the entry of communicable diseases.

Of the Southeast Asian port cities that emerged during this period, Batavia probably had the greatest reputation for unhealthiness. The city was reported to be relatively free from disease for some years following its establishment in 1619. But its growth and the development of an adjacent hinterland placed such demands on the city's drainage systems and water sources that from the early eighteenth century onward disease became a major problem (Blussé 1985). By the time the explorer James Cook called at Batavia in late 1770 to take on supplies and prepare his ship for the journey back to England, conditions were extremely bad. After a long voyage heretofore notable for the good health of its crew, Cook wrote that his ship, the *Endeavour*, left Batavia "in the condition of an Hospital Ship."

European residents of Batavia were able to insulate themselves to a large degree from the disease prevalent in the city by moving away from the old areas within the city walls. But the Chinese and Indonesian inhabitants, unable to move, continued to suffer illness at rates that were higher than most other towns in Java (Abeyasekere 1987). Although Batavia provides just one example, this pattern of disease, related to overcrowded and unsanitary living conditions, existed in most other Southeast Asian coastal cities (Lord 1969; Worth 1985; Manderson 1987).

The growth of cities was, of course, not the only stimulant to disease. Labor, often immigrant, was also required to work plantations and mines, under conditions that also posed considerable risks to health (Cohen and Purcal 1989). Changes in the exploitation of the rural environment also created circumstances that led to the spread of disease, as seen in the association between wet rice cultivation and the spread of malaria in Java (Boomgaard 1987). Similarly, plantation agriculture was instrumental in the spread of malaria and dengue as well, by providing opportunities for mosquitoes to breed, such as in the water trapped in Latex cups and coconut shells or husks (Wisseman and Sweet 1961).

Economic changes in Southeast Asia also contributed to changes in disease by the creation of a landless and impoverished class. In part, this class was brought about by the disruption of traditional forms of agriculture, particularly by the development of plantations, the introduction of money economies, and wage labor (Robison 1986). Thus under colonial administrations, the imposition of taxes, to be paid in cash rather than by goods or labor, has been pointed to as a significant factor in the impoverishment of many (Worth 1985). On the other hand, as Lysa Hong (1984) has pointed out, taxation systems did not necessarily serve to impoverish populations. But when combined with crises such as droughts, they could produce extreme hardship. Such was the situation in Siam in 1844, when farmers in Suphanburi, already affected by successive rice crop failures, were faced with the added burden of taxes (Terwiel 1989).

The many economic changes that produced widespread poverty meant, of course, that large sections of the population were placed in situations where they were more susceptible to disease, through either direct exposure or poor resistance. Individuals were also less able to afford the medical care that might have promoted recovery from disease. Thus, in addition to famines, and problems directly related to nutritional deficiencies such as beriberi and rickets, the effects of poverty showed up in a range of other diseases. These included chronic respiratory disease, tuberculosis, and eye ailments. Infant children were one group particularly at risk, and this was reflected in high infant mortality rates, as in Malaya in the early part of the twentieth century (Manderson 1987). The conditions of poverty also meant that the effects of epidemic diseases, as in the influenza pandemic of 1918, were considerably more pronounced among the non-European population of Southeast Asia (Brown 1987).

Changes in Susceptibility

Balancing the deleterious effects of the development of the region on health were a number of other factors. It was, after all, in the interests of colonists and Southeast Asian rulers alike to ensure a supply of productive labor. By the same token, these economic interests also meant that they often did not do much more than they had to. As Owen (1987) has put it, the colonial system "forced the poorest to the brink," but it "kept most . . . from toppling over." Yet the things that kept the majority of the population from "toppling over the brink" with regard to health were not all attributable to the direct intervention of the state in the treatment and prevention of disease. A number of the changes affecting the susceptibility of individuals to disease occurred at this time, following from increased contact with the rest of the world. Indeed one consequence of prolonged contact between Southeast Asian populations and the rest of the world was the development of disease resistance. Thus although initial exposure to diseases previously unknown to the region resulted in a high mortality, long-term exposure produced resistance to them. Indeed the openness of the region to trade, it has been argued, meant that immunity to most serious epidemic diseases was already developed in much of Southeast Asia prior to contact with Europe (Reid 1988). Moreover, the existence of some diseases in the region prior to contact may also have had some effect in minimizing the impact of introduced diseases. Thus it has been suggested that the prior existence of yaws in Southeast Asia was a factor in limiting the spread of syphilis introduced by the Europeans (Boomgaard 1987).

Probably of even greater significance in keeping people away from the brink was the introduction of new foods, habits, and customs which followed the European presence in the region. A number of food plants, such as the papaya, potato, tomato, and chilli pepper, which originated in the New World, came to Southeast Asia with the Spanish and Portuguese and rapidly became an important part of the region's cuisine. Footwear also came to be adopted by sections of the population that would have prevented entry through the skin of parasites such as hookworm. Traditional unhygienic practices relating to the cutting and treatment of the umbilical cord of the newborn child, which often produced tetanus, also lost favor during this period (Hanks 1963; Manderson 1987).

The Adoption of Western Medicine

Contact with the West also meant contact with Western medical practices, although it is doubtful that such medicine had any favorable impact on health prior to the late nineteenth century, when the first major benefits of medical science came to be felt. In fact, even then progress was slow. Colonial doctors and administrators were not, in general, representative of the most advanced thinking of the age (Owen 1987). Furthermore, the medical and health services introduced were based on European models and were mainly directed at the European populations, and at the labor force upon whom they depended.

European efforts directed at improving the health of indigenous populations were often carried out without regard for local beliefs and customs. In its extreme this was seen in measures such as the burning of homes and the desecration of the dead, which took place in Java following the outbreak of plague in the early years of the twentieth century (Hull 1987). Where more sensitive attempts were made to

use Western medicine to treat the non-European population, ulterior motives such as religious conversion were often at work (Hutchinson 1933; Worth 1985). Besides the suspect attitudes and methods of colonists and missionaries, there were other important reasons why Western approaches to the diagnosis, treatment, and prevention of disease were not readily adopted by Southeast Asians. For most, language and finances also presented practically insurmountable barriers to the acquisition of Western medical knowledge. Prominent, too, were indigenous beliefs regarding illness and the working of the body, and negative perceptions of the efficacy of Western methods. In the latter case although the value of certain aspects of Western medicine, such as the medicinal use of opium, had long been recognized in Southeast Asia, the efficacy of other features was not apparent. Many of the practices introduced by Europeans in the prevention and treatment of illness were hardly any better than local ones they replaced. These included "cholera drinks," "cholera belts" (a broad band of flannel worn while sleeping at night to protect the abdominal organs from chill), and dutch wives (cylindrical cushions used to support or protect the body from chills while sleeping at night) (Bangkok Times 1904; Bangkok Times Weekly Mail 1906; Abeyasekere 1987; Owen 1987). Indeed, some European practices, such as bloodletting, ran quite counter to local beliefs (Reid 1988; Bamber 1989).

Nevertheless, there were occasions when features of Western medicine appear to have been well accepted. In some cases, such as in the use of quinine to treat malaria, which became available from the late eighteenth century, acceptance came as a result of the demonstrable pharmacological value of the drug. In other cases it appears that Western medical practices were adopted because of a fortuitous coincidence with existing Southeast Asian beliefs. This seems to have been responsible in part for the acceptance of the treatment of smallpox by vaccination, which fitted well with local beliefs that substances inserted beneath the skin could confer magical power (Reid 1988; Terwiel 1988).

Smallpox Vaccination

Smallpox, at least from the time it was recorded in seventeenth-century accounts, was one of the most feared diseases in Southeast Asia (La Loubère 1691; Lovric 1987; Reid 1988). Traditional methods of treatment, such as herbal medicines and bathing, were largely ineffective against epidemics that occurred regularly throughout the region. Little could be done by the local inhabitants except to limit the spread of the disease (Reid 1988). But with increased contact with peoples outside the region, different methods of prevention became available. One of these was inoculation (variolation), involving the deliberate introduction of smallpox matter into the body, usually via the nose, first practiced by the Chinese and Indian populations in the region (Terwiel 1988). This technique was also later employed by the Dutch in Java around 1780, and appears to have been practiced by Europeans in Siam from 1833 (Boomgaard 1987; Terwiel 1988). At the request of the Siamese king, inoculation campaigns were begun in Bangkok in 1838 (Terwiel 1988).

Vaccination, a less dangerous and unpleasant form of smallpox prevention, began in Java in 1804, although its spread was limited until the introduction of mass immunization programs (Boomgaard 1987). The Dutch also introduced regulations in 1820 that ensured that outbreaks were reported and contained, which may in fact have contributed more to the control of the disease than did the immunization program (Boomgaard 1987). In Siam, largely because of problems in obtaining viable vaccine, vaccination programs against smallpox did not succeed until late in the nineteenth century (Terwiel 1988). In Vietnam, smallpox vaccination appears to have been initiated in order to protect the French military and settlers: Free smallpox vaccination campaigns were introduced among French troops in 1867, and compulsory vaccination of villagers took place in 1871 when a major epidemic occurred. Further mass vaccination campaigns, mainly in the south and center of the country, were conducted in 1895 and 1896 (Worth 1985; Marr 1987).

It may have been the case that methods adopted by the colonial administrations in the introduction of vaccination were at times heavy-handed. However, the practice does not, in general, seen to have met with resistance from the local inhabitants of the region. This is suggested by the active interest taken by the Siamese, for example, in the pursuit of knowledge about vaccination. Where there was reluctance to employ the technique, it appears to have arisen from doubts regarding the viability of the vaccine, rather than from the method itself. This was not always the case in the introduction of other Western practices used in the management of disease, particularly in regard to the establishment of hospitals.

Hospitals and Public Health

State involvement in public health care was not new to Southeast Asia. Departments of physicians were a feature of the courts of a number of Southeast Asian rulers (Worth 1985; Marr 1987; Bamber 1989). It is likely, however, that the services of such "hospitals" were largely confined to the elite (Marr 1987; Reid 1988). By the same token, it is unclear whether the hospitals that existed in Cambodia during the twelfth century under the reign of Jayavarman VII were in fact "open to all" as their inscriptions suggested, and whether they can be regarded as "hospitals" in the Western sense. On this point the inscriptions are not clear, and could simply mean dispensaries (Coedès 1941). That this may have been the case is supported by later accounts which comment on a reluctance by Southeast Asian peoples to build or enter hospitals (Hutchinson 1933) because of an association of hospitals with death. For many Southeast Asians, hospitals were seen as places where one went to die, and in all likelihood harbored the spirits of those who had already died there (Chai 1967; Thompson 1967; Abeyasekere 1987). The fact that a number of hospitals were originally founded by missionaries as hospices for the care of the victims of epidemics, or those suffering incurable illnesses, would have done little to change this view (Yuwadee 1979; Worth 1985).

Hospitals created by colonial governments were generally not intended for the use of most non-European Southeast Asians but, rather, for the military and civilian personnel serving the colonial administrations. Thus, the health care service provided by the Dutch East India Company was for company servants, as was the hospital system introduced by the British in the Malay states from 1878 (Chai 1967). In Vietnam hospital facilities were introduced in the late nineteenth century, largely for the care of the colonial army and administration (Worth 1985).

Where hospitals were established specifically for the benefit of workers, the funding appears to have come mainly from the groups concerned. For example, the Chinese Hospital established by the Dutch in Java was financed by taxes on Chinese residents (Abeyasekere 1987). The "paupers" hospitals associated with mining centers, which were established by the British in Malaya, were also funded by taxing the Chinese workers (Chai 1967).

The impetus to establish hospitals in Southeast Asia did not come solely from colonialists. In the case of Siam, for example, the monarch played an important role in introducing the hospital system. On a temporary basis, hospitals had been established in Siam, from the early nineteenth century, in order to care for the victims of epidemics (Yuwadee

1979; Muecke and Wichit 1989). In 1855 an offer of land and materials for the building of a hospital was made by the King to an American missionary doctor, but was not taken up (Terwiel 1983). The first state-financed hospital, Siriraj (Wang Lang), was established at the order of the King following the cholera epidemic of 1881, and officially opened in 1888 (Sanguan 1973). Although it is probable that he was counseled by the European and American doctors in Siam at the time, the Siamese monarch was well acquainted with Western medicine, having previously traveled to Singapore and Batavia, and there is no reason to doubt that the initiative came from the Court (Yuwadee 1979).

Medical services were initially staffed, in both colonial and noncolonial Southeast Asia, by European or American doctors. Some attempts were made to train local people in medical procedures, for example, the *dokter-djawa* of Java, who carried out some basic treatments (Boomgaard 1987; Gardiner and Oey 1987). In general, however, access to a full Western medical education was beyond the reach of most Southeast Asians, and even where entry to medical schools was possible, problems remained. For example, for some years after its opening in 1890, the Western medical school established in Bangkok suffered a shortage of Siamese students, probably because of the long, difficult nature of the course, its expense, and the uncertain prospects facing graduates (Yuwadee 1979). In Malaya, positions in the Civil Service were closed to non-Europeans and non-Malays, thus denying Chinese doctors employment, regardless of their qualifications (Chai 1967).

Southeast Asian Disease and the Development of Western Medical Science

Closely linked to the development of colonial medical services was the establishment of research institutes for the study of "tropical diseases." From the standpoint of scientific inquiry, Southeast Asia had long played an important role in Western medicine. The region was an important source of Western materia medica such as cloves, menthol, camphor, benzoin, and, after 1850, quinine. Southeast Asia also figured prominently in the development of botanical and pathological taxonomy, and a number of influential figures in the development of Western natural science traveled to the East Indies as doctors in the employ of the Dutch.

The first research institute concerned with tropical medicine, later to become known as the Pasteur Institute, was set up by the French in Saigon in 1890, and a further three branches were established in other parts of the colony (Morin 1938; Worth 1985). Their purpose was initially military, being intended to carry out research on the diseases – in particular, dysentery and malaria – which severely affected French troops stationed in Vietnam.

The British also founded research institutes. The London School of Tropical Medicine was opened in 1899 in order to undertake scientific inquiry into tropical diseases, and to prepare medical officers for service in the Crown Colonies (Chai 1967). In 1901, in response to a request from the Resident-General of the Federated Malay States, a Pathological Institute, which later became the Institute for Medical Research, was opened in Malaya (Chai 1967).

In the context of the development of the specialty of tropical medicine, the establishment of these institutes has been viewed by some writers as "imperial arrogance" (Owen 1987). Certainly, by their focus on scientific research into diseases, rather than public health measures, they served imperialist ends in several ways (Worboys 1976; Owen 1987). In the short term, it might therefore be argued that Southeast Asia did far more for Western medicine than Western medicine did for Southeast Asia. Nevertheless, in the long term, Southeast Asians came to benefit substantially from the knowledge of disease that was generated by these research institutes. The French laboratories in Vietnam were, for example, the site for important research on plague, smallpox, rabies vaccine. The Malayan Institute was largely responsible for undertaking the research that established the nutritional basis of beriberi, a discovery that was given wide publicity at the first biennial meeting of the Far Eastern Association of Tropical Medicine. This conference, held in Manila in 1910, was attended by medical officers from most of the countries of the region (*Bangkok Times Weekly Mail* 1904; Chai 1967). The findings were subsequently disseminated into areas of Southeast Asia that were outside direct colonial control, and otherwise unlikely to benefit from the work of the research institutes.

The Impact of Western Medicine on Traditional Perceptions of Disease

Indigenous views of disease were largely disregarded in the introduction of Western medical systems (Owen 1987). Even in Siam, where there was a degree of freedom in the adoption of Western-style medical education, traditional medicine was officially neglected. In fact, it was originally omitted from the curriculum of the medical school when that curriculum was set up under the direction of Western doctors in 1889. Later, however, at the request of the king, traditional medicine was included, but only as an optional subject; because of differences between the Siamese and Western doctors engaged to teach in the school, it was only in 1907 that courses in Siamese medicine became a compulsory part of the curriculum (Yuwadee 1979). Tellingly, one reason for the pressure to introduce traditional medicine into the medical curriculum in Siam came from doctors who had completed the course and gone to work in provincial areas. They complained that they were unable to make use of indigenous medicines to treat patients when the scarce supplies of Western medicines and equipment were exhausted. The doctors argued that if only they had had some basic training in traditional medicine, they could be of greater value to the provincial population (Yuwadee 1979).

Although Western medicine may have been beyond the reach of most Southeast Asians, it nevertheless produced changes in the ways in which those without direct access perceived disease (Owen 1987). The germ theory of disease, for example, was integrated into indigenous beliefs regarding illness causation. For example, among the Agusan Manobo of Mindanao there is a belief that disease may result from germs carried by supernatural agents (Montillo-Burton 1982). However, in applying germ theory, a distinction may be made by Southeast Asians between diseases endemic to the region and those that are "foreign." In this case, it is only the foreign diseases that are caused by germs (Montillo-Burton 1982).

In other cases, there appear to have been semantic changes in traditional terms for illness in order to accommodate Western disease categories. An example is the Thai term *mareng,* which (as discussed earlier) in the past signified a "deep-seated ulcer" and came to refer to cancer. Similarly, *wannarok,* the currently employed Thai term for tuberculosis, formerly referred to "illnesses involving infections or abscesses" (Bamber 1989). In both these cases, the effect has been to emphasize one part of a wide semantic range, so that the resultant meaning conforms more closely to that of disease categories in Western medicine.

Conclusions

Just as Southeast Asia is not unique in terms of its geography, so are its diseases, as seen in biomedical terms, not unique to this part of the world. The distinctive profile of disease in the region is more the result of a complex interaction among the Southeast Asian

environment, its inhabitants, and the world outside. In this essay this interaction was examined over two broad periods of time, the division of which was marked by the arrival of Europeans in the region.

How Southeast Asian peoples perceived and responded to disease prior to contact with the West reflects the processes of localization seen in other aspects of their culture. Perceptions of disease were dynamic, integrating features deriving from other regions of Southeast Asia, as well as from Chinese, Indic, and Islamic civilizations. These processes (which were evident in the naming of diseases), theories of causation, and therapy continued after contact with the West.

With the development of large, more concentrated, populations in the region, different types of disease became prevalent, most notably epidemics. The prominence of these diseases in accounts probably served to enhance the notoriety of the region for unhealthiness, among both Asians and Europeans (Schafer 1967). However, underlying these diseases and the many others that were less dramatic in their effects and that did not figure prominently in accounts were widespread poverty and poor nutrition. These, rather than miasmas and steaming swamps, were the reasons for the prevalence of numerous diseases in the region. Thus, despite the introduction of public health measures, hospitals, vaccination, and eventually some of the other advances made by medical science, what could have the greatest effect on the prevalence of disease in the region was the relief of poverty. This is still the case.

Scott Bamber

Bibliography

Abeyasekere, Susan. 1987. Death and disease in nineteenth century Batavia. In *Death and disease in Southeast Asia: Explorations in social, medical and demographic history,* ed. Norman G. Owen, 189–209. Oxford.

Ackerknecht, E. H. 1946. Natural diseases and rational treatment in primitive medicine. *Bulletin of the History of Medicine* 19: 467–97.

Anuman Rajadhon. 1958. The expulsion of evil spirits. In *Five papers on Thai custom,* 5–8. Ithaca.

  1962. The khwan and its ceremonies. *Journal of the Siam Society* 50: 119–64.

Bamber, S. 1989. Trope and taxonomy: An examination of the classification and treatment of illness in traditional Thai medicine. Ph.D. thesis, Australian National University. Canberra.

Bangkok Times. Daily newspaper. Bangkok.

Bangkok Times Weekly Mail. Weekly news summary. Bangkok.

Blussé, Leonard. 1985. An insane administration and an unsanitary town: The Dutch East India Company and Batavia (1619–1799). In *Colonial cities,* ed. Robert J. Ross and Gerard J. Telkamp, 65–85. Dordrecht.

Boomgaard, Peter. 1987. Morbidity and mortality in Java, 1820–1880: Changing patterns of disease and death. In *Death and disease in Southeast Asia: Exploration in social, medical and demographic history,* ed. Norman G. Owen, 33–69. Oxford.

Boutin, Michael E., and Alanna Y. Boutin. 1987. Classification of disease among the Banggi of Sabah. *Anthropological Linguistics* 29: 157–69.

Bradley, Dan B. 1967. Siamese theory and practice of medicine. reprint. *Sangkhomsat Parithat* 5: 103–19.

Brown, C. 1987. The influenza pandemic of 1918. In *Death and disease in Southeast Asia: Exploration in social, medical and demographic history,* ed. Norman G. Owen, 235–56. Oxford.

Brun, Viggo, and Trond Schumacher. 1987. *Traditional herbal medicine in Thailand.* Berkeley.

Bulbeck, F. David. 1982. Continuities in Southeast Asian evolution since the Late Pleistocene. M.A. thesis, Australian National University. Canberra.

Caraka. 1949. *Caraka samhita.* Jamnagar.

Chai Hon-chan. 1967. *The development of British Malaya 1896–1909.* Kuala Lumpur.

Chou Ta-kuan. 1951. *Mémoires sur les coutumes du Cambodge,* trans. Paul Pelliot. Paris.

Coedès, G. 1941. L'Assistance médicale au Cambodge à la fin du XIIᵉ siècle. *Revue Médicale Francaise d'Extrême-orient* 19: 405–15.

1975. *The Indianized states of Southeast Asia.* Canberra.

Cohen, Paul, and John Purcal. 1989. The political economy of primary health care in Southeast Asia: Problems and prospects. In *The political economy of primary health care in Southeast Asia,* ed. Paul Cohen and John Purcal, 159–76. Canberra.

Cook, James. 1968. *Captain Cook's journal (1768–71).* Library Board of South Australia.

Crawfurd, John. 1820. *History of the Indian archipelago.* Edinburgh.

Dampier, William. 1927. *A new voyage around the world,* ed. Sir Albert Gray. London.

Earmporn Thongkrajai, Pramote Thongkrajai, and J. E. Stoeckel. 1987. Socioeconomic and health program effects upon the behavioral management of diarrhoeal disease in northeast Thailand. Paper presented at the Department of Demography, Research School of Social Science, Australian National University.

Eisenbruch, M. 1983. "Wind illness" or somatic depression? A case study in psychiatric anthropology. *British Journal of Psychiatry* 143: 323–6.

Endicott, K. M. 1970. *An analysis of Malay magic.* Oxford.

Frake, Charles O. 1961. The diagnosis of disease among the Subanun of Mindanao. *American Anthropologist* 63: 113–32.

Gardiner, Peter, and Mayling Oey. 1987. Morbidity and mortality in Java, 1880–1940: The evidence of the colonial reports. In *Death and disease in Southeast Asia: Explorations in social, medical and demographic history,* ed. Norman G. Owen, 70–90. Oxford.

Gimlette, J. D. 1939. *A dictionary of Malayan medicine.* London.

Golomb, Louis. 1985. *An anthropology of curing in multiethnic Thailand.* Urbana.

Gumpodo, Theresa, John D. Miller, and Aloysia Moguil. 1988. Village medical treatment among the coastal Kadazan. *The Sarawak Museum Journal* 39: 149–67.

Guy, J. 1982. *Palm-leaf and paper. Melbourne.*

Hall, D. G. E. 1981. *The making of Southeast Asia.* New York.

Hanks, Jane R. 1963. *Maternity and its rituals in Bang Chan.* Ithaca.

Hanks, Lucien M., and Jane R. Hanks. 1955. Diphtheria immunisation in a Thai community. In *Health, culture, and community,* ed. B. D. Paul, 155–85. New York.

Hart, Donn V. 1969. *Bisayan Filipino and Malayan humoral pathologies: Folk medicine and ethnohistory in Southeast Asia.* Ithaca.

Headley, R. K. 1977. *Cambodian–English dictionary.* Washington, D.C.

Higham, Charles. 1989. *The archaeology of mainland Southeast Asia.* Cambridge.

Hong, Lysa. 1984. *Thailand in the nineteenth century: Evolution of the economy and society.* Singapore.

Houghton, P., and Warrachai Wiriyaromp. 1984. The people of Ban Na Di. In *Prehistoric investigations in northeastern Thailand,* ed. C. Higham and Amphan Kijngam, 391–412. Oxford.

Hutchinson, E. W. 1933. The French Mission in Siam. *Journal of the Siam Society* 26: 1–72.

Hull, Terence H. 1987. Plague in Java. In *Death and disease in Southeast Asia; Explorations in social, medical and demographic history,* ed. Norman G. Owen, 210–34. Oxford.

I Tsing. 1896. *A record of the Buddhist religion as practised in India and the Malay archipelago (A.D. 671–695) by I Tsing,* trans. Junjiro Takakusu. Taipei.

Jenner, Philip N. 1981. *A chrestomathy of pre-Angkorian Khmer,* Vol. 2: *Lexicons of the dated inscriptions.* Honolulu.

Kaempfer, E. 1906. *The history of Japan, together with a description of the history of the kingdom of Siam,* trans. J. G. Scheuchzer. Glasgow.

Kleinman, Arthur M. 1987. Symptoms of relevance, signs of suffering: The search for a theory of illness meanings. *Semiotica* 65: 163–71.

Koenig, J. G. 1894. Journal of a voyage from India to Siam and Malacca in 1779. *Journal of the Royal Asiatic Society* 26: 58–201.

Kwa Tjoan Sioe. 1936. De gerzondheidstoestand der Chineezen in Nederlandsch-Indie. *Koloniale Studien* 20(5): 64–77.

Laderman, Carol. 1987. The ambiguity of symbols in the structure of healing. *Social Science and Medicine* 24: 293–301.

La Loubère, S. de. 1691. *Du royaume de Siam*. Amsterdam.

Li, Fang-kuei. 1977. *A handbook of comparative Tai*. Honolulu.

Lord, Donald C. 1969. *Mo Bradley and Thailand*. Grand Rapids.

Lovric, Barbara. 1987. Bali: Myth, magic and morbidity. In *Death and disease in Southeast Asia: Explorations in social, medical and demographic history,* ed. Norman G. Owen, 117–41. Oxford.

Macey, Paul. 1910. L'Art de guérir au Laos. *Revue Indochinoise* 13: 489–502.

Manderson, Lenore. 1981. Roasting, smoking and dieting in cross-cultural perspective. *Social Science and Medicine* 15B: 509–20.

1986. Food classification and restriction in peninsular Malaysia: Nature, culture, hot and cold? In *Shared wealth and symbol,* ed. Lenore Manderson, 127–43. Cambridge.

1987. Blame, responsibility and remedial action: Death, disease and the infant in early twentieth century Malaya. In *Death and disease in Southeast Asia: Explorations in social, medical and demographic history,* ed. Norman G. Owen, 257–82. Oxford.

Marr, David G. 1987. Vietnamese attitudes regarding illness and healing. In *Death and disease in Southeast Asia: Explorations in social, medical and demographic history,* ed. Norman G. Owen, 162–86. Oxford.

Martin, Marie A. 1983. Eléments de médicine traditionelle khmère. *Seksa Khmer* 6: 135–70.

McFarland, George B. 1944. *Thai–English dictionary*. Stanford.

Montillo-Burton, Erlinda. 1982. The impact of modern medical intervention on the Agusan Manobo medical system of the Philippines. Ph.D. thesis. University of Pittsburgh.

Morin, M. 1938. Les Instituts Pasteur d'Indochine. In *L'Indochine Française: Recueil de notices rédigées à l'occasion du Xe congrès de la Far Eastern Association of Tropical Medicine,* 289–413. Hanoi.

Muecke, Marjorie A. 1979. An explication of "wind illness" in Northern Thailand. *Culture, Medicine and Psychiatry* 3: 267–300.

Muecke, Marjorie A., and Wichit Srisuphan. 1989. Born female: The development of nursing in Thailand. *Social Science and Medicine* 29: 643–52.

Mulholland, J. 1979. Thai traditional medicine: Ancient thought and practice in a Thai context. *Journal of the Siam Society* 67: 80–115.

1987. *Medicine, magic and evil spirits*. Canberra.

Ohnuki-Tierney, Emiko. 1981. *Illness and healing amongst the Sakhalin Ainu: A symbolic interpretation*. Cambridge.

Owen, Norman G. 1987. Towards a history of health in Southeast Asia. In *Death and disease in Southeast Asia: Explorations in social, medical and demographic history,* ed. Norman G. Owen, 3–30. Oxford.

Pallegoix, Jean-Baptiste. 1854. *Description du royaume Thai ou Siam*. Paris.

Pham, Dinh Ho. 1973. La Médecine vietnamienne au XVIIIe siècle, trans. Nguyen Tran Huan. *Bulletin de l'école française d'extrême-orient* 60: 375–84.

Pietrusewsky, M. 1974. *Non Nok Tha: The human skeletal remains from the 1966 excavations at Non Nok Tha, N.E. Thailand*. Dunedin.

1982. The ancient inhabitants of Ban Chiang. *Expedition* 24: 42–50.

1982–3. Pioneers on the Khorat Plateau: The prehistoric inhabitants of Ban Chiang. *Journal of the Hong Kong Archaeological Society* 10: 90–106.

Pigeaud, T. G. T. 1967. *Literature of Java*. The Hague.

Quaritch Wales, H. G. 1983. *Divination in Thailand*. London.

Raharjo, Yulfita, and Lorraine Corner. 1989. Cultural attitudes to health and sickness in public health programmes: A demand-creation approach using data from West Aceh, Indonesia. Paper presented at the Health Transition Workshop, National Centre for Epidemiology and Population Health, Australian National University, May 15–19.

Reid, Anthony. 1988. *Southeast Asia in the age of commerce, 1450–1680*, Vol. 1. New Haven.

Robison, Richard. 1986. *Indonesia: The rise of capital*. Sydney.

Sangermano, Vincentius. 1883. *A description of the Burmese empire,* trans. William Tandy. London.

Sanguan Ankhong. 1973. *Sing raek nai Mu'ang Thai*. Bangkok.

Schafer, Edward H. 1967. *The vermilion bird: T'ang images of the south*. Berkeley.

Shorto, H. L. 1971. *A dictionary of the Mon inscriptions*. London.

Simons, R. C. 1985. The resolution of the latah paradox. In *The culture-bound syndromes,* ed. R. C. Simons and C. C. Hughes, 43–62. Baltimore.

Skeat, W. W. 1900. *Malay magic: Being an introduction to the folklore and popular religion of the Malay peninsula*. London.

Snouck Hurgronje, C. 1893. *The Acehnese,* trans A. W. S. O'Sullivan. Leiden.

Social Research Institute. 1986. *Lanna literature: Catalogue of palmleaf texts on microfilm*. Chiangmai.

Terwiel, B. J. 1978. The Tais and their belief in khwans. *The South East Asian Review* 3: 1–16.

1980–1. *The Tai of Assam*, Vol. 1. Gaya.

1983. *A history of modern Thailand, 1767–1942*. St. Lucia.

1987. Asiatic cholera in Siam: Its first occurrence and the 1820 epidemic. In *Death and disease in Southeast Asia: Explorations in social, medical and demographic history,* ed. Norman G. Owen, 142–61. Oxford.

1988. Acceptance and rejection: The first inoculation

and vaccination campaigns in Thailand. *Journal of the Siam Society* 76: 183–201.

    1989. *Through travellers' eyes: An approach to early nineteenth century Thai history.* Bangkok.

Thompson, V. 1967. *Thailand: The new Siam.* New York.

Ullmann, M. 1978. *Islamic medicine.* Edinburgh.

Unschuld, Paul U. 1982. Der wind als ursache des krankseins. *T'oung pao* 68: 91–131.

Westermeyer, J. 1973. On the epidemicity of amok violence. *Archives of General Psychiatry* 28: 873–6.

Wilson, Christine S. 1985. Malay medicinal use of plants. *Journal of Ethnobiology* 5: 123–33.

Wisseman, Charles L., and Benjamin H. Sweet. 1961. The ecology of dengue. In *Studies in disease ecology,* ed. Jacques M. May, 15–43. New York.

Wolters, Owen W. 1982. *History, culture and region in Southeast Asian perspectives.* Singapore.

Worboys, Michael. 1976. The emergence of tropical medicine: A study in the establishment of a scientific specialty. In *Perspectives on the emergence of scientific disciplines,* ed. Gerard Lemaine et al., 75–98. The Hague.

Worth, Dooley, 1985. Health as a political decision: Primary health care in the Democratic Republic of Vietnam. Ph.D. thesis, New School for Social Research. New York.

Wyatt, David K. 1984. *Thailand: A short history.* Bangkok.

Yuwadee Tapaneeyakorn. 1979. Wiwatthanakan khong kanphaet Thai tangtae samai roemton chonthu'ng sinsut rachakan Phrabatsomdet Phrachunlachom-klawchawyuhua. M.A. thesis, Department of History, Chulalongkorn University, Bangkok.

VI.14
Diseases and Disease Ecology of the Modern Period in Southeast Asia

Southeast Asia can be visualized as the part of Asia that spills into the sea, comprised of long coasts, tidal plains, peninsulas, and islands. There are high mountains, inland plains, plateaus, and upland valleys; nonetheless, to a very large degree, human culture has developed with an acute awareness of water, from the sea, the rivers, and the monsoon rains. It is therefore not surprising that many of the endemic health problems in the region are related to water; indeed, since prehistoric times, nearly all major areas of habitation have been exposed to global contact by water transport.

Maritime routes linking the littoral civilizations of the Eurasian landmass have passed through Southeast Asia for more than two millennia. We can accordingly assume that from early times the region experienced all of the epidemic diseases familiar to the ancient world. What inhibits discussion of diseases in the earlier historical periods of Southeast Asia is the lack of data. Because of the prevailing tropical–equatorial climate, the preservation of written records has, until recently, required greater effort than most human societies were prepared to make. Our first information comes from the observations of Chinese annalists, whose works survived in the temperate climate of northern China. As the Chinese moved southward into what is today northern Vietnam, they recorded perceptions of disease associated with what for them were southern lands.

Most prominent among the health problems encountered by ancient Chinese armies in Vietnam were malaria and other "fevers" associated with the monsoon rain season. Chinese generals timed their expeditions into Vietnam to coincide with the dry season, from November to May. When, in 542, ill-informed imperial officials ordered a reluctant army to move into Vietnam during the rainy season, 60 to 70 percent of the army was soon reported dead from fevers (Taylor 1983). Earlier, the general of a Chinese army encamped in Vietnam during the rainy season of A.D. 42 described the scene as a kind of exotic hell: "Rain fell, vapors rose, there were pestilential emanations, and the heat was unbearable; I even saw a sparrowhawk fall into the water and drown!" (Taylor 1983).

It became customary for Chinese generals to explain their failures in Vietnam in terms of "miasmal exhalations" by which they associated the heat and humidity of the area with disease. One of the most famous episodes of disease among soldiers was in 605 after a Chinese army successfully plundered a Cham city in the vicinity of modern Da Nang, on what is today the central coast of Vietnam: The army nearly disappeared when it was struck by an epidemic on its return northward (Taylor 1983). This disease was not malaria, but may have been cholera, smallpox, or possibly even plague. In 627, a prominent Chinese official refused an imperial order to serve as governor of the Vietnamese territories on the grounds that in Vietnam "there is much malaria; if I go there I shall never return." He ultimately chose to be beheaded for insubordination rather than accept the assignment (Taylor 1983). Previously in 136, a Chinese official had argued against sending an army to Vietnam because, among other reasons, the anticipated losses to disease would require the sending of reinforcements who would be disaffected at being ordered into a pestilential region (Taylor 1983). The failures of Chinese invasions against Vietnam in 980–1 and 1176–7 were accompanied by large losses of manpower to malaria.

Generally, malaria has never been a serious problem in preurban lowland areas where waterworks are kept in good repair and the population is at peace (Fisher 1964). Those species of anopheline mosquitoes that breed in the swamps, irrigation canals, and ricefields of the lowlands tend to prefer the blood of animals; and since animals are not susceptible to human malaria and therefore do not provide a reservoir for the disease, these mosquitoes normally do not carry malaria (Stuttard 1943). On the other hand, those species of *Anopheles* that breed in the shady, cool water of streams in the foothills and mountainous areas are strongly attracted to human blood and are dangerous vectors of malaria (Stuttard 1943; Fisher 1964).

Chinese armies entering Vietnam by land must pass through upland areas where malaria is endemic. This fact, along with the desire to achieve the advantage of surprise, explains why Chinese generals, having had the luxury of water transport and enough time to lay plans without haste, preferred to invade Vietnam by sea (Taylor 1983). Malaria became a threat in populated lowlands only when warfare or other disorders led to large-scale slaughtering of animals, a scattered population, and a breakdown of the water control system (Murphy 1957).

Beginning in the late nineteenth century, malaria became a problem on a larger scale than had been previously known because of circumstances associated with the development of colonial and semicolonial economies. These included the improvement of communication systems, large-scale population movements, the opening of new ricelands, and the extension of urban settlement. All of these changes required relatively large-scale construction and engineering projects that opened new areas congenial to certain mosquito species and to epidemics that decimated cattle populations, thereby turning mosquitoes toward human beings (Boomgaard 1987).

In the early 1950s, when the Malayan emergency resulted in the resettling of large numbers of people into crowded lowland camps, an observer noted that the health of the population improved the farther upriver one went; the same observer argued that upland peoples who had been resettled in more densely populated areas near the sea experienced an "accentuation of an already existing pattern of disease" as a consequence of "the loss of interest in life due to the breakdown of the old culture" (Polunin 1952). It may be that any disease ecology must also take into account the political and psychological conditions of a population.

Another observer has claimed that cultural factors can be important in the experience of disease and illness, that there is a relationship between disease and social marginality, and that the incidence of disease can operate as a mechanism of social control enforcing respect for authority. In fact, he has written that "the social system tends to precipitate events which validate the medical beliefs, and this in turn affirms the principles upon which the social structure is based" (Feinberg 1979). It is relatively easy to discuss this approach in relation to the practice of medicine in premodern societies (Lan-Ong 1972), but contemporary attitudes toward modern medicine tend to resist this line of analysis.

Beginning in the tenth century, Southeast Asians began to record observations and write annals that provide local information, first in Vietnam and eventually in Thailand, Burma, Cambodia, and Java. Epidemics are mentioned regularly, particularly in times of warfare, though it is very difficult to determine with certainty what diseases were being observed. Some modern researchers believe that cholera was absent from Southeast Asia until the 1820s, and bubonic plague was likewise absent until 1911. The evidence, however, is ambiguous (Boomgaard 1987; Hull 1987; Terwiel 1987; Reid 1988). The great outbreaks of cholera and bubonic plague in the nineteenth and twentieth centuries were apparently related to the circumstances of European colonial expansion in the region and represented a more virulent experience of these diseases than can today be imagined for earlier times. Southeast Asia's historic openness to maritime trade and the global contacts that went with it surely resulted in a measure of immunity being built up in the population against the diseases common to international entrepots.

A relatively dispersed village settlement pattern and the Southeast Asian habit of bathing frequently are two other factors that appear to account for what has been called the "relatively mild epidemic cyle" in premodern times (Reid 1988). The most serious epidemic disease, according to Siamese chronicles from the fourteenth century and European observers in the sixteenth and seventeenth centuries, was smallpox (Terwiel 1987; Reid 1988). Leprosy and yaws also figured prominently in early European perceptions of disease in Southeast Asia, probably because of their disfiguring effects (Reid 1988). Plague, according to French observers in Indochina, was found only where there were large numbers of Chinese, namely port cities with a concentration of ships, large stores of grain, and consequently an abundance of rats (Stuttard 1943). In the 1960s, by which time plague had been eradicated in most of Southeast Asia, outbreaks still occurred in Vietnam as a result of wartime conditions (South East Asian Regional Centre for Tropical Medicine 1967).

From the 1960s, there has been a growing literature enumerating and analyzing diseases in Southeast Asian countries, particularly Thailand. The category of "tropical diseases" is sometimes used to emphasize that most of the health problems encountered in the region are now seldom seen in temperate climates. The 1967 syllabus of the "tropical medicine" course at Bangkok's University of Medical Science, Faculty of Tropical Medicine, covered the following illnesses, all identified as "common diseases": (1) viral, such as smallpox, rabies, dengue, hemorrhagic fever; (2) rickettsial, such as typhus fever; (3) bacterial, such as typhoid fever, bacillary dysentery, food poisoning, cholera, leprosy, and plague; (4) spirochetal, such as amebiasis, malaria, kala-azar, and giardiasis; (5) helminthic, such as hookworm infection, ascariasis, trichuriasis, enterobiasis, strongyloidiasis, gnathostomiasis, filariasis, fasciolopsiasis, and paragonimiasis; (6) nutritional, such as protein–calorie deficiencies, mineral and vitamin deficiencies, and food toxicants; and (7) miscellaneous, such as effects of heat, heat exhaus-

tion, blood diseases of the tropics, hemoglobinopathies and other genetic factors, as well as snake and other venomous bites (South East Asian Regional Centre for Tropical Medicine 1967).

In the same year, South Vietnamese disease specialists identified malaria and plague as their greatest problems and categorized "endemic infections" as follows: bacteriological (cholera, salmonellosis, bacillary dysentery, and typhoid), parasitic (amebiasis, ascariasis, hookworm infections, gnathostomiasis, strongyloidiasis, diphyllobothriasis, sparganosis, and taeniasis), viral (hemorrhagic fever and dengue fever, smallpox, infectious hepatitis, Japanese B encephalitis, and rabies), bacterial (leprosy and venereal diseases), and mycotic (cutaneous mycoses) (South East Asian Centre for Tropical Medicine 1967).

What can be emphasized is that a very large percentage of these diseases are waterborne or are transmitted by a parasite that depends upon a water-dwelling host such as the snail. In a region where a large part of the population is involved in paddy agriculture requiring barefoot work in fields covered with water, where sanitation depends upon the common use of rivers and ponds, and where nearly half of each year is a time of heavy rainfall, such diseases account for much of the burden of unhealthiness. Dysentery, amebic infections, intestinal worms, and skin afflictions are endemic. The linkage between health and seasonality is obvious to any observer and has been an object of study in recent years. The wet season, in addition to providing an environment in which many disease vectors thrive, is also a time of food shortages and of a consequent relative increase in poverty and decrease in physical well-being. Women and children are particularly at risk during this time (Charles 1979). This writer was in Hanoi in May 1986 during the onset of the rainy season and saw that within a few days a large part of the population had become ill with fevers and other "flu" symptoms; local people considered this a normal phenomenon.

Medically trained observers in Southeast Asia have difficulty in determining mortality statistics. Such compilation efforts are complicated by the fact that although death may be occasioned by the onset of a particular disease, such as malaria, the person's inability to resist the disease is generally due to prior debilitation from a combination of other afflictions, such as intestinal parasites and nutritional deficiencies (Institute for Population and Social Research 1985).

Beriberi, caused by vitamin B deficiency, was in

premodern times largely confined to the islands of eastern Indonesia where sago rather than rice was the main dietary staple (Reid 1988); recently, however, it has become a more general regional phenomenon as a result of the increasing use of polished rather than whole-grain rice (Fisher 1964). Beriberi was first reported by the Portuguese in Southeast Asia during the sixteenth century, and the term is of Malay derivation (Reid 1988).

The ecology of disease in Southeast Asia is currently in a period of rapid and significant change, the beginning of which is usually dated around 1970. For one thing, except for infants and children under 5 years, infectious diseases are no longer a significant threat to health. Tuberculosis remains a hazard for the aged population (which has grown), and malaria remains endemic in many areas, but, in general, tuberculosis, pneumonia, malaria, diarrheal diseases, and nutritional deficiencies, along with other infectious diseases, have declined. On the other hand, death rates for heart-related diseases, cancer, and accidents along with violent deaths have significantly increased (Institute for Population and Social Research 1985). Increasing attention is being given to the problem of infant mortality, for persons under 5 years have benefited least from the overall improvement in health. Diseases of pregnancy, delivery, and puerperium have also become more prominent of late. In addition, cirrhosis of the liver and hepatitis have appeared as significant health problems (Institute for Population and Social Research 1988).

The rise in noninfectious diseases, namely coronary–cerebrovascular diseases and malignant neoplasm (cancer), is primarily a phenomenon of the large urban centers such as Bangkok. It is believed to come not only from improvements in diagnosis but also, in the words of a Thai government report, from "real increases in the incidence rate due to various environmental hazards of the present living conditions" (Kanchanaraksa 1987).

Larger proportions of the populations of the Southeast Asian countries are increasingly concentrating in major urban centers. Living conditions in these places are increasingly exposed to the chemical environment of modern industry and to the emotional pressures of modern business activity. As Southeast Asia is integrated into a global system of manufacturing and markets, we can expect that its disease ecology will begin to display characteristics already familiar to areas where this system has been in place for several decades.

Keith W. Taylor

Bibliography

Abeyasekere, Susan. 1987. Death and disease in nineteenth century Batavia. In *Death and disease in Southeast Asia,* ed. Norman G. Owen, 189–209. Singapore.

Boomgaard, Peter. 1987. Morbidity and mortality in Java, 1820–1880: Changing patterns of disease and death. In *Death and disease in Southeast Asia,* ed. Norman G. Owen, 48–69. Singapore.

Brown, Colin. 1987. The influenza pandemic of 1918 in Indonesia. In *Death and disease in Southeast Asia,* ed. Norman G. Owen, 235–56. Singapore.

Charles, Robert. 1979. *Health, agriculture, and rural poverty: Why seasons matter.* Brighton.

Feinberg, Richard. 1979. *Anutan concepts of disease.* Honolulu.

Fisher, C. A. 1964. *South-east Asia.* London.

Gardiner, Peter, and Mayling Oey. 1987. Morbidity and mortality in Java, 1880–1940: The evidence of the colonial reports. In *Death and disease in Southeast Asia,* ed. Norman G. Owen, 70–90. Singapore.

Hull, Terence H. 1987. Plague in Java. In *Death and disease in Southeast Asia,* ed. Norman G. Owen, 210–34. Singapore.

Institute for Population and Social Research. 1985. *The morbidity and mortality differentials. ASEAN Population Programme Phase III, Thailand: A report on the secondary data analysis.* Bangkok.

1988. *The morbidity and mortality differentials. ASEAN Population Programme Phase III, Thailand, country study report.* Bangkok.

Kanchanaraksa, Sukon, ed. 1987. *Review of the health situation in Thailand, priority ranking of diseases.* Bangkok.

Lan-Ong. 1972. *Thuong Kinh-Ky-Su.* Paris.

Lovric, Barbara. 1987. Bali: Myth, magic and morbidity. In *Death and disease in Southeast Asia,* ed. Norman G. Owen, 117–41. Singapore.

Manderson, Lenore. 1987. Blame, responsibility and remedial action: Death, disease and the infant in early twentieth century Malaya. In *Death and disease in Southeast Asia,* ed. Norman G. Owen, 257–82. Singapore.

Marr, David G. 1987. Vietnamese attitudes regarding illness and healing. In *Death and disease in Southeast Asia,* ed. Norman G. Owen, 162–86. Singapore.

Murphy, Rhoads. 1957. The ruin of ancient Ceylon. *Journal of Asian Studies* 16: 181–200.

Owen, Norman G. 1987a. Toward a history of health in Southeast Asia. In *Death and disease in Southeast Asia,* ed. Norman G. Owen, 3–30. Singapore.

1987b. Measuring mortality in the nineteenth century Philippines. In *Death and disease in Southeast Asia,* ed. Norman G. Owen, 91–114. Singapore.

Polunin, Ivan. 1952. Studies on the diseases of the aborigines and other peoples of the Malay Peninsula. Doctor of Medicine thesis, University of Oxford, The Queen's College.

Reid, Anthony. 1987. Low population growth and its causes in pre-colonial Southeast Asia. In *Death and disease in Southeast Asia,* ed. Norman G. Owen, 33–47. Oxford and Singapore.

    1988. *Southeast Asia in the age of commerce 1450–1680,* Vol. 1: The lands below the winds. New Haven.

Stuttard, J. C., ed. 1943. *Indo-China.* London.

South East Asian Regional Centre for Tropical Medicine. 1967. *Report of the first meeting of the Central Coordinating Board convened by the government of Thailand with the cooperation of the Southeast Asian Ministries of Education Secretariat at the Faculty of Tropical Medicine, University of Medical Science.* Bangkok.

Taylor, K. W. 1983. *The birth of Vietnam.* Berkeley.

Terwiel, B. J. 1987. Asiatic cholera in Siam: Its first occurrence and the 1820 epidemic. In *Death and disease in Southeast Asia,* ed. Norman G. Owen, 142–61. Singapore.

PART VII

The Geography of Human Disease

VII.1
Disease Ecologies of
Sub-Saharan Africa

Disease Patterns Before A.D. 1000

The prevalence and distribution of diseases in sub-Saharan Africa have been determined by the natural environment, indigenous living patterns, and the interrelationships between African peoples and newcomers from other continents. The spread of agriculture since about 3000 B.C.; the extensive commercial contacts with the Moslem world from about A.D. 1000, and with Europe since the fifteenth century; and the establishment of colonial rule in the late nineteenth century – all have had important consequences for health conditions in Africa.

There is little evidence about the disease environment confronting Africans until fairly recent times. Literacy dates back to only about A.D. 1000, and then only in Ethiopia and some areas of the savanna zone just south of the Sahara desert. Written accounts of conditions on parts of the western and eastern coasts begin with the Portuguese voyages of the fifteenth and sixteenth centuries, but literary information on most of the vast interior is not available until well into the nineteenth century. Serious medical data collection really began with the colonial period, but even today knowledge of disease incidence and prevalence is far from adequate.

Africa south of the Sahara is a vast area with many different ecological zones. Besides the Sahara itself, there are extensive desert regions in the Horn of northeastern Africa, and the Kalahari in Namibia and Botswana in the southwestern part of the continent. Tropical rain forest prevails along most of the west coast, in the Zambezi valley of Mozambique, and in large areas of western equatorial Africa, including much of Gabon, Congo–Brazzaville, and northern Zaire. Forest, however, covers only about 10 percent of the land area. Rolling grassland, often called savanna or sudan, predominates between the desert-edge lands and the forest, both north and south of the equator. The desert and the equatorial forest have always been relatively sparsely populated; most Africans have always lived in coastal West Africa or the savanna areas north and south of the equatorial forest.

Paleontological studies indicate that hominids almost certainly evolved in Africa, and our species, *Homo sapiens,* probably was widely distributed over the continent by at least 40,000 years ago. Scattered bands of stone-age hunter-gatherers spread lightly over the entire continent. Signs of permanent settlement by fishermen around lakes and rivers are evident in eastern Africa and places that are now in the Sahara from about 7000 B.C. Knowledge of stock-raising diffused from southwest Asia from about 5500 B.C., and agriculture followed the same course shortly afterward. The Sahara region did not begin to become a desert until about 2500 B.C., so these developments first reached peoples in and just south of the present Sahara. Here the new ways of life allowed the gradual development of settled village life, population growth, the rise of political and economic specialization, and, in general, the more complex societies associated with the Neolithic "Revolution." Iron technology diffused from the North African coast to what is now the West African savanna by about 300 B.C., giving peoples in the belt south of the desert, the ancestors of most modern black Africans, an additional advantage over more isolated populations further south.

As of the first or second century B.C., demographic growth among these iron-age, agricultural groups was encouraging them to expand southward against weaker, less numerous hunting and gathering peoples. Peoples ancestral to the modern pygmies probably dominated much of the forest. Further south were the ancestors of the Khoisans, who once inhabited most of the southern third of Africa, but are now restricted to parts of the Kalahari and bordering regions. In the west the farming peoples soon reached a barrier, the Gulf of Guinea, but members of one linguistic group in the borderlands of modern Nigeria and Cameroun had a continent before them. For roughly 2,000 years these technologically superior peoples have been gradually colonizing half a continent, driving away, killing, or absorbing most of the indigenous groups. The descendants of these people, speakers of languages of the Bantu family, now dominate most of the continent from the equatorial forest almost to the southern tip.

Disease Patterns from A.D. 1000 to 1500

By about A.D. 1000, most of the better agricultural lands had been settled by village farmers. There was still a frontier in the extreme south, and pastoral groups were important in and near the deserts and in parts of the East African interior, but the pygmy and Khoisan peoples were increasingly being pushed into pockets of marginal jungle or desert – a process that has continued until the present. Farming was often of a slash-and-burn type, with villages moving to seek new lands at intervals of several years to a generation or more, but hundreds of people often lived close together in compact, relatively permanent settlements. Small cities began to develop in response to long-distance trade in parts of the western Sudan and along the east coast.

These long, complex processes must have had important implications for health conditions. Hunting-gathering populations were too sparse to support many acute diseases, especially smallpox, measles, poliomyelitis, chickenpox, and other viral infections that produce long-lasting immunities. They were mobile enough to avoid living for long in close proximity to accumulations of their own wastes.

Village life, on the other hand, whether based on fishing and intensive collecting or on agriculture, put much larger numbers of people in close, continuous contact in fixed places. Diseases of crowds, like many of those caused by respiratory transmission of common bacterial and viral infections, could be readily transmitted. Disposal of wastes and contamination of water became problems, and failure to solve them resulted in much greater opportunities for the spread of gastrointestinal infections, such as dysentery and diarrhea of various etiologies, as well as *Ascaris, Trichuris,* and other parasitic worms. Hookworm, transmitted by fecal contamination of soil, was also common in many places. Villages and land cleared for agriculture helped provide breeding sites for the mosquito vectors of malaria, yellow fever, and filariasis. Animal husbandry also provided enhanced opportunities for transmission of beef and pork tapeworms, anthrax, and other diseases. Animal manure attracted disease-carrying flies. In Africa, as elsewhere, the price for the advantages of village life and a more reliable and abundant food supply was a dramatic increase in the variety and frequency of infectious diseases.

Africans gradually developed immunologic and cultural defenses against many of these diseases, and population grew, although much more slowly than in recent decades. Although direct evidence is lacking, it is likely that the pool of diseases afflicting sedentary populations was especially deadly for indigenous hunting-gathering groups beyond the expanding agricultural frontier. As in the Americas, Australia, New Zealand, and probably also Siberia, diseases from what William McNeill has called "civilized disease pools" helped to pave the way for newcomers by killing large numbers of the aboriginal populations.

By about A.D. 1000 the more densely inhabited portions of Africa, or at least those north of the equatorial forest, probably had had at least limited experience with most of the infectious diseases common to the Eurasian land mass. There was some attenuation, however, due to distance and relative isolation, as well as modifications from the tropical environment and the fairly low average population density. The disease mixture would be enriched and the frequency of outbreaks increased in later centuries as a result of more intensive commercial and other contacts with the Moslem world and with western Europe.

We have little direct knowledge of health conditions before about 1500, but scattered data and inferences from more recent times allow some general, if somewhat speculative, comments. Many Africans suffered from a wide range of intestinal parasites spread by the fecal–oral route, and from dysentery and other bacterial and viral diseases associated with poor sanitation, although cholera did not exist here until it was imported from Asia in the nineteenth century.

Some have argued that there is an old focus of plague in central Africa, but the evidence for this is not compelling, and it is not clear that plague had any real importance in Africa before the late nineteenth century. Smallpox was known in Egypt by the sixteenth century B.C., and may have been epidemic in Ethiopia as early as 570. South of the Sahara, smallpox and perhaps also measles were probably uncommon and tended to occur in epidemic form at long intervals. Respiratory infections like pneumonia were uncommon, and tuberculosis was rare or absent, except perhaps in trading towns. Cerebrospinal meningitis probably did not appear until the late nineteenth century. Guinea worm and schistosomiasis were, then as now, focal waterborne infections with high prevalence rates in some localities.

Except in the deserts, malaria was ubiquitous. It tended to spread in the forest as land clearance for farming created better breeding sites for *Anopheles* mosquito vectors. The antiquity of falciparum malaria is indicated by the widespread prevalence of sickle cell trait, a costly but effective genetic defense. Most African groups lack Duffy antigen, probably another old genetic adaptation, which protects them against vivax malaria. Yellow fever existed in forest areas, but attacked mainly children and may have caused relatively little harm. Yaws and leprosy were especially prevalent in moister climates. Trachoma was more common in arid regions. Gonorrhea probably had been established by the first century A.D., at least in the towns of the western Sudan, but syphilis was a post-Columbian import via Europe and North Africa. Human and animal trypanosomiasis occurred in places where tsetse flies lived. Then, as now, animal trypanosomiasis prevented stock raising in forest areas. Pockets of savanna bush were infested with flies carrying both human and animal pathogens; these places were generally known and avoided.

Disease Patterns of 1500–1900

More intensive trade and political contacts with the outside world, especially Europe, developed from the sixteenth to mid-nineteenth centuries. These contacts, accompanied by more extensive long-distance trade within Africa and by widespread patterns of political centralization, helped to spread many infectious diseases.

Europeans and Africans began a long commercial relationship with the arrival of the Portuguese in the fifteenth century. Trade grew rapidly over the centuries, and came to involve most of the states of western Europe and the Americas and, directly and indirectly, most African groups living within a few hundred miles of the sea. Coastal African merchants sold slaves, ivory, gold, dyewood, and other commodities for cloth, guns, metal goods, tobacco, alcoholic beverages, and other manufactured items. African products were obtained by trade networks extending far into the interior. Negotiations between the coastal middlemen and foreigners were often long and complex, providing ample opportunities for exchanges of pathogens; the trade routes provided paths for diseases to spread into the interior.

Among the most important and best documented diseases in early African history was smallpox. Although it was widespread in North Africa by the seventh century, and had almost certainly reached the western Sudan as a by-product of the trans-Saharan caravan trade by about A.D. 1000, smallpox may not have been indigenous to the western coast or the southern half of the continent until the seventeenth century. Ships brought infection from abroad or carried it from place to place along the coast at irregular intervals, after enough time had passed to allow the appearance of a new generation of susceptibles. An epidemic caused great loss of life along the Gold Coast in the 1680s, and by at least 1700 some West African peoples had adopted or invented variolation techniques. Smallpox epidemics were frequent in the eighteenth and nineteenth centuries, and a major shipborne outbreak swept the whole coast as far south as Gabon and Angola in the early 1860s. In South Africa, where the Dutch East India Company had established a colony at Cape

Town in 1652, smallpox epidemics introduced by sea in 1713, 1755, and 1767 had serious demographic consequences for the colonists and were devastating for the indigenous and already hard-pressed Khoi pastoralists. On the east coast, it is likely that smallpox was an early accompaniment of the Indian Ocean trade, but there is little evidence for it in the pre-European period. The Portuguese recorded a major epidemic in 1589. Smallpox diffusion into the East African interior probably occurred later than in West Africa because of weaker trade networks; it may date back only to about 1800.

Measles and chickenpox were probably also introduced by traders from time to time, but there is little documentation. Tuberculosis probably reached coastal West Africa in the early days of contact, but it did not become widespread until after 1900. Venereal diseases were a different story; syphilis and gonorrhea were common among coastal groups by the eighteenth century, and these diseases must have spread inland as well. Gonorrhea may well have been an indigenous disease whose diffusion was facilitated by new conditions; syphilis almost certainly arrived from the outside world.

Trans-Saharan trade had existed for centuries prior to 1000, and no doubt the caravans, like the sailing ships, sometimes were accompanied by infectious diseases. Smallpox could well have reached the Sudanese market towns, either with infected merchants or in goods. Tuberculosis, measles, and gonorrhea no doubt diffused from North Africa with trade, although they may have already existed in the savanna. Similarly, the extensive pre-European trade along the east coast, between the Swahili towns and merchants from India, Persia, and Arabia, must have resulted in some disease transmission.

It is clear, despite the weakness of the data, that contacts with Europeans and other foreigners had serious disease consequences for many African peoples in the precolonial period, especially those along the west and east coasts and in the market centers for the Sudan. However, although some small groups may have suffered heavily, there was no postcontact pattern of mass death in Africa similar to what occurred in parts of the Americas or the Pacific. Africans shared enough of the Old World disease pool to avoid major demographic disaster. Stronger social systems of African peoples may also have played a role in their enduring and recovering from great epidemics. Even with the drain of the Atlantic, trans-Saharan, and Indian Ocean slave traders, Africa was not depopulated. Disease resistance, strong local social and political systems, and the introduction of new food crops like maize and manioc helped to sustain populations.

The African disease environment did have very serious consequences for foreigners. We still know relatively little about how Moslem traders fared, but North African visitors to the Sudan did try to finish their business before the rainy season brought malarial fevers, and Omani Arabs suffered severely from falciparum malaria on the Swahili coast.

The fate of Europeans on the west coast is much better documented. "Fevers" and "fluxes" – especially malaria, yellow fever, and the dysenteries – took a frightful toll among sailors, soldiers, traders, missionaries, explorers, and slavers. Studies of British, Dutch, and French experiences have shown that death rates of 50 percent in a year were not uncommon. It is possible that Portuguese death rates were somewhat lower, but they too paid a heavy price for their African commerce. Mortality prevented any serious European military activity in most of West Africa; maintaining weak, sickly garrisons in a few coastal forts was all that they could normally do. Disease not only helped save West Africans from European encroachment, but also gave them a considerable commercial advantage. African merchants could, and frequently did, drag out trade negotiations, knowing that the Europeans were anxious to complete a deal and leave before the fevers began to reduce their numbers. The limited Portuguese expansion in northern Angola, although hampered by disease, took place in a drier area where malaria was not as serious as elsewhere on the western coast. European colonization at the Cape was possible only because the Dutch were operating south of the tropical disease environment.

Africa was more important as a donor than as a recipient in the post-Columbian exchange of diseases. Falciparum malaria and yellow fever reached Europe from time to time, but probably did not have major demographic consequences there. Much more significant was the transfer of African diseases to the New World, mostly as a by-product of the slave trade. Falciparum malaria and yellow fever played a major role in the population history of the warmer parts of the Americas, from the southern United States to southern Brazil. Whites suffered severely, and these diseases were leading causes of deaths among the American Indians, especially in the Caribbean basin. The African hookworm, misnamed *Necator americanus,* came over in the bodies of enslaved Africans, and was a very serious cause of sickness and death in the southern United States and in much of the West Indies and Brazil well into

the twentieth century. Other African diseases, including onchocerciasis, filariasis, *Schistosoma mansoni* infection, and yaws, also became established in American foci.

Cosmopolitan diseases like dysentery and smallpox were frequently introduced into ports along with cargoes of slaves. In Brazil, slave imports often rose when there was drought and famine in Angola. Drought conditions caused people to migrate in search of food; they tended to congregate, often as defenseless, disorganized refugees, in areas where they could find sustenance. Such aggregations encouraged flare-ups of endemic smallpox as well as the depredations of slavers. The virus was often transported by captives, and there is a strong correlation between smallpox epidemics in Brazil and in its Angolan slave supply territory.

In sum, the biological consequences of the African slave trade included millions of deaths in the Americas, among both Europeans and Indians. African labor was crucial in many New World economies, but the demographic costs were enormous for inhabitants of North and South America and for European sailors on slave ships, as well as for sub-Saharan Africa. Indeed, at least in the United States, the demographic balance was almost certainly unfavorable. About 300,000 Africans were imported, probably far fewer than the number of whites who died of falciparum malaria, yellow fever, and hookworm infection from the eighteenth to the early twentieth centuries. The period of the European conquest of Africa and the consolidation of colonial rule, roughly from 1880 to 1920, was the most deadly period in history for much of the continent. West Africa, perhaps because of its earlier experience with introduced epidemics, did not suffer as severely as portions of equatorial, East, and central Africa. Intensified long-distance trade, warfare, labor demands, and famine characterized this era, as many African peoples found their relative isolation shattered. People, pathogens, and vectors all moved, and there were radical changes in living conditions. Smallpox spread widely, especially in East Africa, where coastal Moslem merchant caravans had begun to operate in the interior from the 1830s. Cholera was introduced several times into East Africa and diffused over the trade routes, with an especially destructive epidemic occurring in the 1850s. Cerebrospinal meningitis epidemics appeared, probably for the first time, in the western Sudan in the 1880s; there were several great epidemics there and in parts of the Anglo-Egyptian Sudan and East Africa during the twentieth century. On a less spectacular but still important level, even short-distance moves might bring people into contact with antigenically novel strains of familiar organisms, such as the protozoa that caused malaria and amebic dysentery.

Tuberculosis, noted in the coastal towns of West Africa around the turn of the century, spread slowly inland. In the Cape Verde Islands migrants returning from the United States facilitated the spread of infection by the 1880s. The rise of the mining industry in South Africa and the Rhodesias was dependent on migrant labor. Poor conditions in the mines in the early twentieth century led to extremely high tuberculosis rates and explosion of the disease among the rural African population as infected miners returned to their homes.

Besides mining, other development efforts of the colonial era often had unexpected and deleterious health consequences. Major infrastructure projects usually depended on migrant labor and sometimes took a heavy toll in lives. For example, thousands of workers conscripted in the savanna country of southern Chad and Ubangui-Chari died from dysentery, respiratory ailments, and other diseases during the construction of the Congo–Océan railroad in French Equatorial Africa in the 1920s. Water projects frequently facilitate disease transmission in tropical climates. The Gezira irrigation scheme in Sudan, for example, as well as the massive Volta Lake in Ghana, has resulted in hyperendemic schistosomiasis. On a smaller scale, dam ponds may also become foci for malaria and guinea worm infection, and, in parts of northern Ghana, dam spillways and bridge pilings provided breeding sites for the vector of onchocerciasis, a worm disease that often causes blindness.

Venereal diseases also diffused rapidly in the late nineteenth and early twentieth centuries, as labor migration and urbanization disrupted social patterns. Equatorial Africa experienced a very destructive gonorrhea epidemic as a direct result of harsh Belgian and French colonial policies; this resulted in widespread sterility, which is believed to be largely responsible for the very low fertility rates in the region even today. Movements associated with the early colonial period were also apparently responsible for great outbreaks of human trypanosomiasis in French Equatorial Africa and the Lake Victoria region of East Africa in the first decade of the 1900s. At least 250,000 died in East Africa alone.

On a more trivial but still significant level was the rapid spread of the burrowing flea *Tunga penetrans* (chigoes). This insect invades tissues under the nails and may result in secondary infections that cause

disability, or a loss of digits or limbs. Native to Brazil, the fleas were introduced into the Senegambia region about 1800, and to the Angolan coast about 1850. From Angola they spread over central and East Africa in a few decades, causing great misery in any given place, until people learned how to remove them.

Disease Patterns of 1900–60

The most explosive and most destructive epidemic ever to strike Africa was the influenza pandemic of 1918–19. Introduced at Sierra Leone in late August 1918, and to ports around the continent in the next several weeks, the disease spread rapidly inland over the newly constructed colonial roads, railroads, and river transport systems. Diffusion was especially rapid on the southern African rail system and on the river steamers in the Belgian Congo. Indeed, so quickly did the disease move by these means, that places in the Congo only 100 miles from the coast were first attacked by way of the Union of South Africa. Almost every inhabited spot on the continent was struck in a matter of 6 or 7 months, graphic proof that the old isolation was gone forever and that the continent was an epidemiological unit closely linked to the rest of the world. Approximately 2 million people – about 2 percent of the population – died during the epidemic.

The demographic balance began to shift by the 1920s in much of West and South Africa, and by the 1930s elsewhere. The harsher aspects of colonial rule were being mitigated, famine relief was made more effective with better transportation, and medical measures began to have some effect. Progress was most rapid in the Belgian and British colonies and in French West Africa; medical services were slower to develop in Portuguese territories and in French Equatorial Africa.

Colonial medicine had little to offer Africans for many years, except for surgery, yaws therapy, and smallpox vaccination. But by the 1930s, efforts to control smallpox, cerebrospinal meningitis, tuberculosis, louse- and tick-borne relapsing fever, and other epidemic diseases were beginning to have some impact. Plague broke out in several territories in the early twentieth century, but public health measures prevented serious loss of life. Extensive efforts to contain trypanosomiasis, primarily by vector control in the British colonies and by chemical treatment and prophylaxis in the French territories, had considerable success. The growing cities continued to function as nodes for the diffusion of infectious diseases into the countryside, but measures to improve water supplies and waste disposal, control malarial mosquitoes, provide vaccinations, and treat patients began to have a positive impact in almost all urban areas by 1940. Ironically, improved water supplies meant that fewer people were exposed to polio virus as small children when they were most likely to have mild or asymptomatic cases. Postponement of infection until adolescence created an increase in the number of paralytic cases in the post–World War II period – an unintended by-product of incomplete sanitary reform.

The advent of sulfa drugs in the late 1930s and especially the antibiotics in the 1940s provided a revolution in the effectiveness and, consequently, the popularity of the colonial medical services. Africa's rapid demographic growth dates from the late 1940s and is partially the result of the success of most colonial medical services in lowering death rates from bacterial diseases. Populations are growing at rates that will double the numbers of people in most countries in around 20 years, a situation that is already placing grave strains on medical services and food supplies.

Disease Patterns Since 1960

Most African states became independent after 1960, but they have not been able to effect radical improvements in health conditions. Colonial medical services and their successors in sovereign African countries have tended to stress therapy over prevention, and to favor cities over the rural areas. There has been some real progress. Smallpox has been eradicated, thanks to a concerted worldwide campaign. Vaccines, many developed only after 1960, have begun to make inroads against measles, diphtheria, polio, cerebrospinal meningitis, and other common infections, but new vaccines are urgently needed for other diseases, including malaria and the bacterial and viral agents of childhood diarrheas. The most urgent need is to improve rural water supplies and sanitation, which would greatly reduce the incidence of a host of infections. Greater attention to nutrition and to infant and child health is also essential.

Malaria and schistosomiasis are still major causes of morbidity and mortality, and almost no progress has been made against the common intestinal parasites. Even yaws, which is readily treated with penicillin, has reemerged in areas such as Ghana where economic distress has curtailed medical services. Similarly, internal strife and misgovernment in Uganda have disrupted trypanosomiasis control, with predictable results. Campaigns sponsored by the World Health Organization and other groups against such major scourges as malaria, onchocerciasis, schistosomiasis, trypanosomiasis, and leprosy are promising, but high death rates, weak and sometimes declining economic and political systems, and the AIDS epidemic show that grave problems remain. More than ever, Africa's disease environment is determined by its poverty.

K. David Patterson

Bibliography

Alden, Dauril, and Joseph C. Miller, 1987. Out of Africa: The slave trade and the transmission of smallpox to Brazil. *Journal of Interdisciplinary History* 18: 195–224.

Curtin, Philip D. 1968. Epidemiology and the slave trade. *Political Science Quarterly* 88: 190–216.

Curtin, Philip D., et al. 1978. *African history.* Boston.

Domergue-Cloarec, Danielle. 1986. *Politique coloniale française et réalités coloniales: La santé en Côte d'Ivoire, 1905–1958.* Toulouse.

Ford, John. 1971. *The role of the trypanosomiases in African ecology: A study of the tsetse fly problem.* Oxford.

Hartwig, Gerald W., and K. David Patterson. 1984. *Schistosomiasis in twentieth century Africa: Historical studies in West Africa and Sudan.* Los Angeles.

  eds. 1978. *Disease in African history: An introductory survey and case studies.* Durham, N.C.

Hoeppli, R. 1969. *Parasitic diseases in Africa and the Western Hemisphere: Early documentation and transmission by the slave trade.* Basel.

Hopkins, Donald R. 1983. *Princes and peasants: Smallpox in history.* Chicago.

Hughes, Charles C., and John M. Hunter. 1970. Disease and development in Africa. *Social Science and Medicine* 3: 443–93.

McNeill, William H. 1976. *Plagues and peoples.* Garden City, N.Y.

Patterson, K. David. 1979. *Infectious diseases in twentieth-century Africa: A bibliography of their distribution and consequences.* Waltham, Mass.

  1981. *Health in colonial Ghana: Disease, medicine, and socio-economic change, 1900–1955.* Waltham, Mass.

Patterson, K. David, and Gerald F. Pyle. 1983. The diffusion of influenza in sub-Saharan Africa during the 1918–1919 pandemic. *Social Science and Medicine* 17: 1299–1307.

Patterson, K. David, and Gerald W. Hartwig. 1984. *Cerebrospinal meningitis in West Africa and Sudan in the twentieth century.* Los Angeles.

Wiesenfeld, Stephen L. 1967. Sickle-cell trait in human biological and cultural evolution. *Science* 157: 1134–40.

VII.2
Disease Ecologies of the Middle East and North Africa

This study of disease ecologies of the Middle East and North Africa aims to demonstrate the interrelationships of environmental and etiologic factors in the diseases endemic to that region. In so doing, the essay surveys the area between Morocco in the west and the Iranian border in the east, including the Anatolian Peninsula in the north and the Arabian Peninsula to the south.

Conditions before the mid-twentieth century are generally emphasized in this study. The population data and some obviously changing current conditions are, however, pertinent to conditions in the late twentieth century. The State of Israel is not included in the discussion because of the general time frame and for other reasons. Israel does not fit into most generalizations about the region because of its diversified economy and the comprehensive health-care system created by preindependence settlers. The chapter also will not deal with the region's emerging pattern of the degenerative, metabolic, and genetic disease concerns of industrialized societies. Many of the data are derived from the accumulation of information assembled by the attempt of European nations to deal with epidemics and exotic diseases encountered during the nineteenth century in Africa and Asia. This material is sufficient to sketch a tentative disease profile, stressing infectious diseases. Moreover, twentieth-century investigations in nutrition have been used to supplement and qualify this information.

Geography, Topography, and Climate

The Middle East and North Africa occupy that part of the Earth's crust where three tectonic plates converge, causing great ranges of high-fold mountains to be thrust up, notably in western North Africa and in the northern tier states of Turkey and Iran. Peaks in the high Atlas Mountains of Morocco and the Taurus range in Turkey exceed 12,000 feet, whereas Mount Damavand, in Iran's Elburz mountains, exceeds 18,000 feet. Running north and south, the Hijaz, Asir, and Yemen ranges are high escarpments in the southwestern Arabian Peninsula, paralleling the anticlinal highlands that form the Lebanon and Anti-Lebanon mountains and the Judean Hills of Palestine.

The Middle East and North Africa lie roughly between latitudes 20° and 40° north in a transitional climatic zone between equatorial and mid-latitude climates. Because of general atmospheric circulation patterns, a characteristic of these latitudes is prevailing aridity – the "Mediterranean Rhythm" of winter rain and summer drought. Only westward-facing coasts and mountain ranges receive the 250 millimeters (about 10 inches) rainfall considered the minimum necessary for cultivation. The lack of cloud cover is a major factor influencing temperature, for clear skies and intense solar heating of the land cause very high temperatures during the day although temperatures fall considerably at night. Another characteristic of the region is scanty water supply. Except for the Nile, Tigris, and Euphrates, the majority of rivers are short streams with a rapid and intermittent course down rugged mountain sides. The lack of wooded land is another serious deficiency. Long occupation has meant prolonged exploitation of the land over millennia, almost total deforestation, and removal of ground cover, resulting in uncontrolled water runoff and soil erosion. Aggravated by overcultivation and unrestrained grazing, especially by goats, soil erosion has led to extensive desiccation and desertification. Hence, at mid-twentieth century, it was estimated that only 5 to 7 percent of the total area is cultivable naturally.

The implications of prevailing aridity and great expanses of mountainous or desert terrain have been significant for human survival: Population has been relatively sparse and discontinuous in distribution; until recently, nomadism was widespread; and settled argiculture most often has required irrigation and complex infrastructures to govern the allocation of scarce water resources.

Population

The total population in 1984 of countries under consideration in the region, estimated at 257 million, was about 5.6 percent of the world population, in an area occupying about 10 percent of the Earth's surface. The largest populations were in Egypt, Turkey, and Iran, which comprised 52 percent of the inhabitants of the region.

Turkey was the only country in which population was distributed relatively evenly. Even at the mid-twentieth century, about 75 percent of the inhabitants lived in small villages scattered over the Anatolian Peninsula, whereas in other states, the population had already been concentrated along the seacoast or river banks, on oases, or around the countries' metropolitan centers. Since midcentury, population pressure on the land has reduced the percentage of people in agriculture and accelerated the move to urban centers. By 1984, it was estimated that 42 percent of the population of North Africa and 53 percent in the Middle East had gravitated to towns or cities. At the same time, 40 to 45 percent of the populations surveyed were under 15 years. (An overall annual growth rate of 2.8 percent means almost doubling the population in 25 years.)

About 93 percent of the people of the region are Muslim and about 57 percent speak Arabic; other important languages are Turkish, Persian, Hebrew, Kurdish, and Berber (Fisher 1971; Drysdale and Blake 1975).

Economic Life
Until very recently, about 60 percent of the population cultivated the traditional crops of the Mediterranean – cereals and olive and fig trees – whereas date palms and sugar cane predominated in the southern deserts. Antiquated and inequitable land-holding and tenancy systems have discouraged long-term development by individual farmers, and the traditional but excessive subdivision of land has worked against cost-effective production. This region still must remain vigilant for periodic swarms of destructive locusts, both Saharan and Arabian types, in addition to the pests that damage crops in other parts of the world.

Whereas most lands capable of cultivation have been planted with cereals, areas where water and good soil are lacking have been left to herders. Sheep are preponderant in all areas; goats also are kept in large numbers, especially in steppe and mountainous areas; and water buffalo have provided most animal power in the marshes of Iran and Iraq and the irrigated fields of Egypt. As transport has become increasingly mechanized, the use of the camel has declined, but the donkey still carries people and commodities everywhere. Neither cattle nor horses are important economically because of lack of pasturage. Mineral resources are limited, with the exception of petroleum in some states, and large-scale extraction has begun only relatively recently. Good-quality coal exists only in northwestern Turkey, but hydroelectric power and petroleum have been supplying energy for industrialization in recent decades.

The traditional handicrafts and manufactures of the Middle East and North Africa – metal working, glassware, textiles for articles of clothing, and woolen carpet-making – have suffered from the competition of foreign imports, but many countries are now promoting them for export. Four countries –

Egypt, Israel, Syria, and Turkey – no longer conform to the typical Third World economic pattern, in that one-fifth or more of their gross domestic product is derived from the manufacturing industry. Generally, however, the countries of the Middle East and North Africa belong to the Third World, being still heavily dependent upon the export of primary products and the import of food, consumer goods, equipment, and technology (*Oxford Regional Economic Atlas* 1964; Fisher 1971; Drysdale and Blake 1985).

Disease Patterns
The foregoing sketch suggests a distinctive ecological disease pattern for the Middle East and North Africa. Pastoralism and the farmers' reliance on animals for transport, power, fertilizer, and dung fuel have made these occupational groups, living in close proximity to their livestock, vulnerable to zoonoses and to insect-borne diseases, some of which infest domestic or wild animals. Another important disease complex has developed out of the necessity for irrigation: the widespread incidence of parasitism due to favorable conditions for proliferation of the insect carrier and an intermediate host where required. At an agricultural conference in 1944, it was reported that expanding irrigation in one area of Egypt had raised the incidence of both malaria and schistosomiasis from 5 to 45 or even 75 percent of the population in that area (Fisher 1971). This survey, therefore, will begin with those ailments most closely related to the rural environment: arthropod-borne diseases and parasitic infestations. Next it shall consider the "crowd diseases," most characteristic of urban societies, but also found in crowded villages and oases. Last it shall sketch the diseases caused by nutritional deficiencies among rural and city people. Within those categories, diseases are listed in descending order of their prevalence or importance as death- or disability-threatening experiences.

Major Arthropod-Borne Diseases
Because the many species of anopheline mosquitoes have adapted to breeding in the widest variety of hydrological conditions – from swamps and stagnant irrigation pools to fast-moving mountain streams, and from freshwater springs to brackish marshland – they are found throughout the region except in stretches of desert lacking any surface collection of water. From 9 to 19 species of anopheline mosquitoes exist in each Middle Eastern and North African country, of which 3 or 4 have been identified as vectors of *malaria*.

Although mosquitoes cannot survive dry, hot

weather, their proliferation in oases in Libya's Fezzan Desert and in the Arabian Peninsula demonstrates their tenacity. One species of *Anopheles* endemic in southwestern Arabia has caused recurrent epidemics of malaria under favorable rainfall conditions. The last such epidemic was reported in 1950–1, when this species spread inland from Jidda along the road to Mecca, carried by the increased traffic of the Muslims' annual pilgrimage.

Malaria has been reported in all the countries of the Middle East and North Africa. Since World War II the World Health Organization (WHO) has carried out extensive mosquito eradication projects. Nonetheless, malaria continues to break out periodically, and in 1950 a public health survey in Morocco reported that it was still the most prevalent disease in the country (Simmons et al. 1954; *Nosologie marocaine* 1955; Kanter 1967; Benenson 1975).

The *Aedes Aegypti* mosquito that transmits *dengue fever* also is a potential vector of yellow fever, but that infection has not been reported in the Middle East and North Africa. Dengue is endemic in the eastern Mediterranean area but has not been observed at heights exceeding 600 meters (2,000 feet) and has been largely confined to coastal areas. Most countries in the Middle East have sporadic outbreaks of dengue fever, and a few cases are reported in Libya every year; whereas in Morocco, Algeria, and Tunisia, the infection has remained only a potential threat (Simmons et al. 1954; Kanter 1967; Benenson 1975).

Because early symptoms of *Bancroftian filariasis* may be simply fever and lymphadenitis, the disease was not reported historically until prolonged and repeated infection caused elephantiasis of the limbs or outer genitalia. Today, although the most common mosquito vector of filariasis is abundant throughout the region, the threat of the disease has remained potential. In Lebanon, filariasis appears occasionally. There is one focus of infection in the southwestern Arabian Peninsula and another in Egypt, where the mosquito vector proliferates in numerous brackish wells in Rosetta (Simmons et al. 1954; Benenson 1975).

Bubonic plague is transmitted by the bite of an infective flea, usually *Xenopsylla cheopis,* and marked by acute lymphadenitis forming buboes, at the site of the infection; *septicemic plague* occurs in severe and advanced bubonic plague, causing petechial hemorrhages; *pneumonic plague,* the most infectious and fatal form, is airborne, spread by inhalation of exhaled droplets from infected patients.

The Middle East and North Africa suffered se-

verely in the sixth-century plague of Justinian, and repeatedly thereafter. Because Procopius had placed the origin of that pandemic in Egypt, the Nile Valley became identified in Europe's popular and professional imagination as "the cradle of plague." However, the recurring epidemics of bubonic plague in this region were initially imported. Infected fleas on rats infesting the holds of cargo ships transmitted the infection to domestic rats in Mediterranean port cities and established endemic loci for the disease. Only the coast is naturally vulnerable to plague. Inland areas are too hot or too cold, and above all too dry to be susceptible to enzootic plague. However, irrigation systems acted as networks for transmitting infective fleas by providing harborage for rats in the embankments of canals. Epidemics flared periodically whenever optimum weather conditions – high humidity and moderate temperatures – coincided with an adequate rat–flea density. After the adoption of quarantine measures in the southern and eastern Mediterranean in the nineteenth century, followed by the discovery of the rat–flea nexus, most areas of the world including the Middle East and North Africa managed to bring plague under control until the epidemic of 1894, which originated in northern China.

Plague, however, continues to be a potential danger in the Middle East and North Africa. A reservoir of sylvatic (wild rodent) plague in the mountains of southwestern Arabia and the Kurdish highlands, shared by Iran, Iraq, and Turkey, may spread infection by contact with domestic rats. In Libya sporadic cases transmitted by steppe rodent fleas broke out almost annually from the time of World War I until 1940. In Morocco as well, plague recurred sporadically until 1946, and it was also reported in Tunisia, Algeria, and Egypt up to the early 1950s (Hirsch 1883; Hirst 1953; Pollitzer 1954; Simmons et al. 1954; *Nosologie marocaine* 1955; Kanter 1967; Benenson 1975; Gallagher 1983).

Characteristic of colder climates, *typhus* is not common in this region and has occurred chiefly during the winter among nomads who wear the same heavy clothing day and night. The human body's humid microclimate provides a favorable environment for the louse to deposit eggs (*nits*) that hatch into young lice in a few days. Warm dry weather is unfavorable for breeding because humans dress more lightly, exposing the lice to high temperatures and sunlight. Displacement of people and crowding during World War II contributed to a series of epidemic outbreaks of typhus in North Africa, but delousing campaigns appeared to eliminate the disease. Nonetheless, occasional outbreaks have been reported in Iran, Iraq, Syria, and Jordan, from congested villages and town quarters as well as from refugee camps (Rodenwaldt 1952; Simmons et al. 1954; *Nosologie marocaine* 1955; Kanter 1967; Benenson 1975).

Other Arthropod-Borne Diseases

Although foci for endemic *tick-borne relapsing fever* (alternating febrile and afebrile periods) exist throughout the region, the disease is rare. Epidemic *louse-borne relapsing fever* is more common; between 1942 and 1945 a series of epidemics spread throughout North Africa from Morocco through Egypt and extended into Turkey, but it has occurred only sporadically since then. *Boutonneuse fever* is a mild to moderately severe febrile illness widely distributed in countries adjacent to the Mediterranean, Caspian, and Black seas. The disease, which is transmitted by the bite of an infected dog tick, occurs occasionally in Morocco, Algeria, Tunisia, Libya, and Turkey, and rarely in Israel and Lebanon. Also, another tick-borne disease, *tularemia,* a plaguelike infection of wild and domestic animals, especially rodents and rabbits, is found only in Turkey (Rodenwaldt 1952; Simmons et al. 1954; Benenson 1975).

Of the three types of *leishmaniasis,* only *cutaneous leishmaniasis (Leishmania tropica)* is common in the Middle East and North Africa. In 1756 Patrick Russell named the affliction the "Aleppo boil," and today it is also known as "Baghdad boil" in Iraq and "Jericho boil" in Jordan. In Israel it is most common in the Haifa area. It also occurs sporadically in the Arabian Peninsula and in southeastern Turkey, where it is known as "Urfa sore." In North Africa cutaneous leishmaniasis is endemic and prevalent in Algeria and Morocco, widespread in Tunisia and Egypt, but rare in Libya (Russell 1794; Rodenwaldt 1952; Omran 1961; Kanter 1967; Benenson 1975).

Kala-azar, or *visceral leishmaniasis,* is a chronic systemic infection disease characterized by fever, enlargement of the liver and spleen, anemia, and progressive emaciation and weakness. Untreated, it is a highly fatal disease. Although the vectors of kala-azar are not common in this region, three species of sandflies are suspected of transmitting visceral leishmaniasis that appears sporadically in the northern and western coastal provinces of Turkey, and the littoral of Algeria and Morocco (Simmons et al. 1954; Benenson 1975).

Sandfly fever or *pappataci fever* (phlebotomus fever) is a viral 3- or 4-day fever that resembles influenza and is carried by the same phlebotome – *Phlebotomus papatasii* – transmits cutaneous leishmaniasis. Sandfly fever reportedly is endemic in Syria, Lebanon, Israel, Iraq, Iran, and sporadic in Jordan and Saudi Arabia (Simmons et al. 1954; Benenson 1975).

Finally, numerous species of flies are abundant throughout the Middle East and North Africa; among the most common of these are species of the *Muscidae* family, thought to be implicated in the mechanical transmission of intestinal and eye infections. For example, *gastroenteritis* causing infantile diarrhea and dehydration, which has been held responsible for more than half the infant deaths in Egypt, shows a striking peak of incidence during the hot, dry, fly season (Labib 1971). Several species cause myiasis in livestock and occasionally in humans, but cases of these invasions are rare (Simmons et al. 1954).

Helminth-Transmitted Diseases

Of the four species of blood flukes infecting humans – *Schistosoma haematobium, Schistosoma mansoni, Schistosoma intercalatum,* and *Schistosoma japonicum* – only the first two are endemic in the Middle East and North Africa. Persistence of the disease depends upon the presence of freshwater snails as the intermediate hosts.

The evolution of schistosomiasis probably occurred during the period when human populations were shifting from hunter-gathering economies to societies based on settled agriculture. Parasitism requires a stable relationship between host and parasite, such as is available in settlements close to slow-moving water in which snail hosts of the disease dwell. Vesical or urinary schistosomiasis probably existed in both ancient Mesopotamia and Egypt. Babylonian inscriptions and Egyptian papyri (Ebers, Kahun) refer to hematuria and prescribe remedies. In 1910 Marc Ruffer discovered ova in Egyptian mummies dating from 1200 B.C., and J. V. Kinnear-Wilson considers the finding of shells of the most common host snail, *Bulinus truncatus,* in the mud brick walls of Babylon evidence that *S. haematobium* was the cause of hematuria described in Babylonian texts. French soldiers suffered with hematuria during the occupation of Egypt in 1798–1801, but the causative parasite was not identified until 1851 when Theodor Bilharz recovered adult worms from the portal system during an autopsy in Cairo. The life cycles of the intermediate molluscan hosts were demonstrated early in the twentieth century.

Studies and clinical records between 1931 and 1961 reported schistosomiasis in all the countries of the Middle East and North Africa. However, because of prevailing desert conditions, North Africa, except for Egypt, has not harbored parasites that require surface water or moist soil for survival. A notable exception is the Fezzan in Libya, where in some oases with shallow wells, up to 86 percent of the inhabitants have been infected. However, outside a relatively small radius the groundwater available to oases has too high a salt content to support the host snail. The highest incidence, up to 100 percent in some villages, has occurred in Iraq and especially in Egypt where the inhabitants of the Nile Valley have maintained irrigation systems for millennia.

The widespread species has been *S. haematobium;* infection with *S. mansoni* has appeared only in Egypt and among Yemeni and Iraqi immigrants to Israel, although the host snail exists in the Arabian Peninsula and North Africa (Ruffer 1910; Simmons et al. 1954; *Nosologie marocaine* 1955; Malek 1961; Farooq 1964; Kanter 1967; Kinnear-Wilson 1967; Benenson 1975; Sandbach 1976; Sandison 1980).

Ancylostomiasis, or hookworm disease, is probably quite old. A chronic disease of the digestive system described in the Ebers Papyrus of 1550 B.C. has been interpreted as hookworm disease. In 1838 Angelo Dubini discovered a worm that he called *Ancylostoma duodenale,* during autopsies in Egypt, and a colleague found the same parasite during autopsies in 1845, but neither related them to specific diseases. In 1853, Wilhelm Griesinger identified ancylostomiasis as the cause of the endemic anemia, called "Egyptian chlorosis," and observed that 25 percent of the causes of death were traceable to the effects of this infestation.

Ancylostomiasis occurs in all Mediterranean countries, but the Nile Valley has been a particular locus of the infection (Khalil 1932; Simmons et al. 1954; *Nosologie marocaine* 1955; Benenson 1975).

Ascariasis (infection of the small intestine caused by *Ascaris lumbricoides,* the large intestinal roundworm) may cause digestive and nutritional disturbances. Pictorial evidence demonstrates the presence of *Ascaris* in ancient Mesopotamia, and numerous prescriptions for roundworm in the Ebers Papyrus indicate that the ancient Egyptians complained of this parasite as well. In the twentieth century, ascariasis has been most common among school children, who may suffer anemia and eosinophilia from high infestation. Serious complications among children may include bowel obstruction and occasionally death due to the migration of adult worms into liver

or gallbladder (Simmons et al. 1954; Kanter 1967; Kinnear-Wilson 1967; Benenson 1975; Sandison 1980).

Other worm-related diseases include *trichinosis,* which, because of the Muslim and Jewish prohibition against pork, is rare in the Middle East and North Africa, and has been reported only in Lebanon. *Taeniasis,* an infection with the beef tapeworm, *Taenia saginata* – causing anorexia, digestive disturbances, abdominal pain, and insomnia – occurs where the larvae are ingested with raw beef. It is particularly frequent among herding peoples whose sheep, cattle, and dogs have a high rate of infection, which may be passed to humans. In Libya, for example, the government hospital at Benghazi reported the existence of the larval form of tapeworm in 20 to 28 percent of the patients annually between 1960 and 1963 (Kanter 1967; Benenson 1975).

Zoonoses

The zoonoses that occur in the Middle East – brucellosis, anthrax, and Q fever – are all occupational diseases of herders, farm workers, veterinarians, abattoir workers, and industrial workers who process hides, wool, or other animal products. *Brucellosis,* which causes a generalized infection, also known as *undulant fever,* has been reported in Morocco, Algeria, Tunisia, Iran, Turkey, Syria, and Lebanon. *Anthrax,* an infectious disease of ruminants, occurs only in Turkey. *Q fever* rarely infects humans in areas where the disease exists enzootically in animals. Occasional cases, however, have been reported in Morocco that were suspected of having been transmitted by tick vectors.

Also increasingly rare is *rabies* or hydrophobia, an acute, almost invariably fatal viral infection of the central nervous system, transmitted to humans by the bite of a rabid animal. At mid-twentieth century, James Simmons and colleagues (1954) reported rabies in Iran, Syria, and Jordan; however, most countries in this region have controlled rabies by quarantining and licensing pets and by destroying stray animals (Benenson 1975).

Food- and Waterborne Enteric Diseases

Acute diarrheal disease in early childhood, most prevalent after weaning, is important in the Middle East and North Africa as in all developing countries. Although it may include specific infections, *infantile diarrhea* frequently is a clinical syndrome of unidentifiable etiology caused by bacteria, viruses, helminths, or protozoa. Common in areas of poor sanitation and prevailing malnutrition, infant diarrhea may produce as many as 275 attacks per 100 children per year, more than 50 deaths per 1,000 per year in preschool children. Protein–calorie malnutrition is commonly associated with acute diarrheal episodes, which may precipitate kwashiorkor. The highest incidence tends to occur in hot, dry periods, calling for *oral rehydration therapy,* which has become a high priority program for the WHO in recent years (Simmons et al. 1954; Benenson 1975).

At mid-twentieth century, Simmons reported "dysenteries" for all Middle Eastern countries, but provided no data. All North African countries, including Egypt, reported higher incidence rates for *shigellosis* then *amebiasis,* except in Morocco and Libya, where amebiasis was reported more prevalent. Between 1900 and 1950 comparative mortality rates were 8.7 percent for amebic dysentery and 11.8 percent for bacillary dysentery (Rodenwaldt 1952; Simmons et al. 1954; Kanter 1967).

In the Middle East and North Africa, raw fruits and vegetables handled by infected persons are important vehicles of the transmission of *typhoid fever,* and flies are often vectors for spreading contamination. At mid-twentieth century, the disease was reported in all countries considered in this survey but was reported as rare in Libya (Rodenwaldt 1952; Simmons et al. 1954). *Paratyphoid* infection due to *Salmonella* of all groups except *S. typhosa* is a generalized bacterial enteric infection, clinically similar to but with a lower fatality rate than typhoid fever; it occurs only sporadically in this region.

Cholera did not appear in the Middle East and North Africa until the great pandemics of the nineteenth century that were caused by troop movements in the lands bordering India, Afghanistan, and Iran, and by accelerated sea transport linking Asia with the rest of the world. Six pandemic waves of cholera swept around the world between 1817 and 1923, invading all settled communities in Asia, Africa, Europe, and the Americas. Middle Eastern and North African countries were vulnerable to invasion by the disease because returning Muslim pilgrims carried the infection from the holy cities of Arabia, where it was introduced by Muslims from South Asia. After discovery of the cholera vibrio and the rationalization of quarantine practices, as well as nineteenth-century sanitary reform programs, cholera receded as a major threat. The adoption of efficient control techniques, particularly since the Second World War, has effectively neutralized the danger of dissemination from the Muslim pilgrimage sites. The last major outbreak, which occurred in Egypt in 1947, was due to relaxation of quarantine regulations during the Second World War. However, since 1961 a new strain of cholera, El Tor, has spread extensively from a focus in Sulawesi in Indonesia, through most of Asia and the Middle East into Eastern Europe and Africa, and from North Africa into the Iberian Peninsula and Italy (Hirsch 1883; Simmons et al. 1954; Pollitzer 1959; Kanter 1967; Benenson 1975).

Diseases Transmitted Through the Respiratory Tract

Tuberculosis is widespread in the Middle East in the pulmonary form that was known earlier as phthisis or consumption. Egyptian wall paintings depict humpbacks typical of bone tuberculosis of the spine, known as Pott's disease, and tuberculous bones have been found in tombs dating to 3000 B.C. In modern times, tuberculosis appeared to accompany the rise of industrialization and urbanization in the nineteenth century, succeeding smallpox as the most common affliction in city life. In congested slums tuberculosis assumed epidemic proportions because the infection is transmitted by exposure to the bacilli in airborne droplet nuclei from the sputum of infected persons. In the mid-twentieth century, tuberculosis was reported in all Middle Eastern and North African states. Wartime displacement had caused a steep rise in incidence. In Libya, for example, many uprooted nomads from the Fezzan emigrated to shanty towns on the coast. Because food was scarce and sanitary installations were nonexistent, tuberculosis spread rapidly among these desert people in a severe form that was often fatal. In the 1950s, the WHO and UNICEF supported immunization programs with the result that tuberculosis in the Middle East has become similar to the European type, milder and chronic (Simmons et al. 1954; *Nosologie marocaine* 1955; Kanter 1967; Benenson 1975; Sandison 1980).

By contrast, *pneuomococcal pneumonia* was reported to have a significant mid-twentieth-century incidence only in Egypt and Turkey. This may suggest susceptibility among the ill-housed, undernourished poor inhabiting the overcrowded metropolises, as well as an above-average involvement among the coal miners in Turkey (Simmons et al. 1954; Benenson 1975).

Diphtheria typically has been a disease of colder months in temperate zones. It was reported in Egypt, Israel, Jordan, and Iraq in the mid-twentieth century; in Morocco it was identified as one of several diseases that accompanied an influx of Europeans during the Second World War (Simmons et al. 1954; *Nosologie marocaine* 1955; Benenson 1975).

Meningitis occurs more frequently in children and young adults and more commonly in crowded living conditions. In the mid-twentieth century, meningococcal infection was reported in Turkey, Iraq, Lebanon, and Egypt (Simmons et al. 1954; Benenson 1975).

Smallpox had been a recognized scourge in the Middle East since the sixth-century epidemic struck Ethiopian invaders threatening Mecca. The Islamic scholar-physician Rhazes, in the tenth century, wrote the classic clinical description of the disease, implying that smallpox was very common and endemic to the entire Islamic world from Spain to Persia at that time. It is true that plague overshadowed smallpox in the Mediterranean for several centuries, but the latter remained widespread and continued to claim great numbers of victims until the early nineteenth century when Europeans began introducing Edward Jenner's vaccination into their colonies in Africa and Asia. Nevertheless, although most countries in the Middle East adopted immunization procedures during the nineteenth and early twentieth centuries, smallpox continued to break out in all of them until systematic vaccination campaigns coordinated by WHO eradicated the disease in Libya by 1949 and elsewhere in the region by 1977 (Simmons et al. 1954; Kanter 1967; Hopkins 1983; Fenner et al. 1988).

At about midcentury, measles was recorded only in Egypt, Algeria, and Morocco (Simmons et al. 1944; Benenson 1975).

Diseases Transmitted by Human Contact

Eye diseases are widespread in the Middle East and along the Mediterranean littoral. The most serious, trachoma (earlier called "Egyptian ophthalmia"), is a bacterial infection that progresses clinically from tiny follicles on the eyelid conjunctiva to invasion of the cornea, with scarring and contraction that may lead to deformity of the eyelids and blindness. It is often accompanied by *acute bacterial conjunctivitis,* a highly contagious form of conjunctivitis, most often caused by the Koch–Weeks bacillus, characterized by inflammation, lacrimation, and irritation, followed by photophobia, purulence, and edema of the eyelids.

Both trachoma and conjunctivitis are transmitted through contact with fingers or articles contaminated by discharges of infected persons. Flies or eye gnats often spread the infection, and lack of water and exposure to dry winds, dust, and sandstorms are thought to aggravate the problem.

Between 1928 and 1936, trachoma morbidity was very high in the Middle East. Egypt was considered the principal focus, where about 90 percent of the population was reported to have suffered trachoma, often combined with acute bacterial conjunctivitis or occasionally gonococcal conjunctivitis. In Syria, Lebanon, and Palestine, about 60 percent of the Arab schoolchildren and 10 percent of the Jewish children from rural areas were infected with trachoma. In Turkey, 60 percent of the population in the southeast steppe area with no forestation was reported affected. In Iran, the highest incidence also was reported in steppe and desert areas near the Persian Gulf and in the interior south of Isfahan. In Iraq, the high incidence of trachoma in Baghdad – 80 percent – was attributed to susceptibility to infection from exposure to the loess dust from the Tigris and Euphrates flood areas during the hot dry season.

In Algeria and Morocco about 10 percent, and in Tunisia 40 percent, of the population were infected with trachoma. According to practitioners in Morocco, trachoma was not an independent nosological entity; bacterial conjunctivitis accompanied 80 percent of the cases. In Libya trachoma was most common in the Fezzan oases, where morbidity was estimated at 60 percent of the inhabitants. In the post–World War II migration of desert people to the coastal cities, incidence ranged from 30 percent to 70 percent in the shanty towns outside Tripoli. In spite of preventive programs, the disease was still widespread in 1963, when 4,126 cases were recorded in Tripolitania Province (Rodenwaldt 1952; Simmons et al. 1954; *Nosologie marocaine* 1955; Kanter 1967; Benenson 1975).

Among North Africans, *leprosy* was believed to have been imported from the eastern Mediterranean by many peoples. In the ninth century B.C., Phoenicians were blamed for it. Jews driven from Jerusalem in A.D. 135 were believed to have reintroduced it, as were Arab invaders in the eighth century. In addition, it was probably periodically reintroduced by Saharan caravans as well. By mid-twentieth century, however, leprosy had effectively disappeared in North Africa, except among the Berbers, where there were an estimated 8,000 cases, and in Egypt where 30,000 cases were reported (Rodenwaldt 1952; Simmons et al. 1954; *Nosologie marocaine* 1955; Kanter 1967; Benenson 1975).

Finally, in the mid-twentieth century, *scabies* was reported in Egypt, Morocco, Iran, Syria, and Jordan, perhaps aggravated by wartime displacement and crowding, as in refugee camps, with consequent lack of water for bathing (Simmons et al. 1954; Benenson 1975).

Venereal Diseases

Because leprosy was often confused with venereal diseases in antiquity, it is not clear when *syphilis* first appeared in the Middle East and North Africa. Following the Crusades, however, when all Europeans were referred to generically as "Franks," syphilis was associated definitively with Europeans as *"il-franji"* – that is, the Franks' disease. *Gonorrhea* reportedly is relatively rare, but occurs fairly frequently as blennorrhea or gonococcal conjunctivitis among infants or very young children. In the mid-twentieth century, nevertheless, venereal diseases were acknowledged public health problems in all the countries of the Middle East and North Africa (Rodenwaldt 1952; Simmons et al. 1954; Kanter 1967; Benenson 1975).

Nutritional Deficiencies and Disorders

The traditional diet of North Africa reflects the geographic divisions of the area. Each country from the Senegal River to the Nile has a littoral and a desert region that are separated from each other by fertile plateaus and arid mountains. Commonly, the littoral food pattern has been based on cereals and fruit; the plateau diet, on cereals, olives, sheep's milk, and meat; and the desert diet, on dates and camel's milk.

The dietary patterns of Middle Eastern countries also reflect geographic and economic conditions. Except for Israel and Lebanon, where vegetables and fruits abound, cereals provide the major portion of both the caloric and protein intake in the average diet. Wheat is the most widely consumed cereal in all countries; maize is the chief staple in the delta region of Egypt and the Black Sea coast of Turkey; rice is also popular, but its high cost limits its consumption to producing areas (mainly Egypt) and the well-to-do; burghul (parboiled wheat sundried and crushed) is eaten in Turkey, Syria, and Lebanon as a substitute for rice. Lentils and other legumes are consumed widely.

Vegetables such as onions, tomatoes, eggplant, cucumbers, peppers, squash, and cabbages are universally popular but are consumed in inadequate amounts. Consumption of fruits shows wide seasonal variations, except for dates, raisins, grapes, and apricots, which can be preserved by drying. The difficulty of transporting and preserving fresh milk has led to the widespread use of fermented milk, yogurt, and, to a lesser extent, sheep and goat cheese.

Throughout the Middle East, meat is consumed at a low level, mainly because of its relatively high cost. Although the animal population in this region is among the highest in the world, livestock repre-

sent capital to the herdsmen that is not to be wasted by slaughter. Thus, meat contributes only about 2 percent of the total caloric intake, compared with 21 percent in the United States. Mutton is the principal meat consumed in Muslim countries, and to some extent beef and goat are also eaten. Like the nomads' herds, poultry and eggs provide a livelihood for villagers; they are sold and eaten mainly in towns. Fish as food has been important only among the inhabitants of the Black Sea area in Turkey, the delta lakes region in Egypt, and the marsh dwellers of southern Iraq.

Certain cultural and environmental features restrict diet in both the Middle East and North Africa. Both Muslims and Jews, for example, are enjoined from eating meat not slaughtered according to their religious codes, and this ritual slaughter adds to the cost. More generally, climatic conditions and the lack of efficient means of food preservation, refrigeration, and transport drastically restrict consumption of fruits, vegetables, milk products, fish, and meat. The scanty and irregular distribution of rainfall has been a constant factor retarding the development of agriculture. Although production has increased in all areas since the Second World War, the low purchasing power of the population, especially in rural areas, as well as the lack of transport and distribution facilities, has kept consumption of food low. The result of the foregoing is that a significant segment of the population is afflicted with nutritional diseases.

In Egypt, Iraq, and to a lesser extent in Syria, hypochromic microcytic *anemia* has been attributed to the prevalence of hookworm infestation in irrigated farm areas, but there is evidence that parasitic infestation also contributes to the high morbidity of nutritional anemia (May and Jarcho 1961).

One investigation in Algeria found that macrocytic nutritional anemia was common among various population groups in the capital, mainly inhabitants of the city slums or rural areas whose diets were unusually low in protein, fats, fresh fruits, and vegetables. Another survey (May 1967) revealed that a large percentage of children under 1 year of age in Tunisian cities showed signs of nutritional anemia. And in Morocco it was reported that women, especially those pregnant or lactating, showed gross evidence of iron deficiency anemia.

Kwashiorkor is not as common in the Middle East and North Africa as in sub-Sahara Africa, but it has been reported among the poorest classes in Egypt and Israel. In Morocco, Algeria, and Tunisia, it reportedly has been common following weaning of children between 1 and 3 years of age (May and Jarcho 1961; May 1967).

Xerophthalmia or night blindness due to vitamin A deficiency is common in the Middle East and North Africa. Lack of vitamin A also lowers resistance to infection. For example, keratoconjunctivitis occurring in a child deficient in vitamin A increases that child's susceptibility to chronic trachoma. Also, in Libya bacterial infections rise during the autumn date harvest when flies proliferate; combined with vitamin A deficiency, an eye infection may lead to serious complications – rupture of the cornea and prolapse of the iris – and blindness (Kanter 1967). Night blindness has been reported in Iran and among sedentary communities of the northern Sahara in North Africa (May and Jarcho 1961; May 1967; Benenson 1975).

Pellagra, by contrast, has been reported only in the Black Sea area of Turkey and the delta of Egypt where maize is the staple grain, and in North Africa during periods of wheat or barley shortage when consumption of corn has become necessary.

Scurvy is rare in the Middle East and North Africa, where citrus fruits are usually available, except in Erzerum in northeastern Turkey, which is isolated from food supply lines during winter months.

Rickets, on the other hand, has been observed in large towns of Iran, Syria, and Egypt where infants were swaddled and therefore not exposed to the sun. In North Africa rickets was reported in the sunless slums of coastal cities in Morocco, Algeria, and Tunisia and among sedentary communities in the northern Sahara. Southern nomads appeared to escape this disease as well as scurvy and xerophthalmia perhaps because of greater exposure to sunlight and higher milk consumption. Erzerum in northeastern Turkey has reported seasonal incidence of rickets as well as scurvy during long, severe, sunless winters (May and Jarcho 1961; May 1967; Benenson 1975).

General Observations on Nutrition

Although malnutrition (overreliance on starch in the diet, with little fat or protein) has been observed, undernutrition (calorie as well as protein-deficient diet) has been far more common in the Middle East and North Africa. In most countries, the population rise has consistently exceeded the increase in cultivated land. The most dramatic example is Egypt, where population is increasing by about a million people each year.

In extensively irrigated countries like Egypt and Iraq, and to a lesser extent Syria, there is a synergistic interaction between inadequate diet and parasitic infestation, particularly hookworm, causing severe anemia and threatening retardation of the physical and mental development of children. Investigators also have suggested that an interaction between poor diet and schistosomiasis may cause pellagra.

In North African countries and the states of the Arabian Peninsula, protein and vitamin deficiencies are reported predominantly among women and children, and are not common among men. This observation is valid as well for other countries in the region that share the patriarchal custom of serving the father and older sons of the family first, leaving what remains for women and children, which may not include meat, fruits, and vegetables.

In North Africa where the child between 1 and 3 years old is weaned abruptly and then given a diet of carbohydrates familiar in family fare, the young may not be able to tolerate the change, which may then cause dyspepsia, infantile diarrhea, lowered resistance to infectious diseases, and kwashiorkor. Nomadic tribespeople of the Sahara south of the Atlas mountains, however, wean the infant over a 6-month period, introducing it gradually first to camel's milk and then to cereals.

On the positive side, the high consumption of whole wheat and other cereal products may explain the comparative absence of vitamin B complex deficiencies. Also, traditional dishes that combine cereals with legumes such as beans, chickpeas, and lentils have been demonstrated to be a good source of protein.

In addition, there are some naturally occurring foods that compensate the inhabitants of unproductive areas for the lack of more common foods. In Iraq, for example, an herb called *khoubbaz* (*Malus rotundifolia*), which is eaten raw by both rural and nomadic peoples, has been found to have a high ascorbic acid content. And in Libya's Fezzan, two naturally occurring foods have been found to be rich in beta-carotene and riboflavin. One, *danga,* is prepared from an alga growing on salt lakes; the other, *duda,* consists of small crustaceans from the salt lakes. Both are kneaded, formed into small cakes, dried in the sun, and later mixed with barley, millet flour, or dates, and eaten as a main dish in a meal. Lastly, dates, an important food among nomadic and seminomadic peoples, are ideal for desert dwellers in that they have a high sugar content, are relatively resistant to contamination with pathological bacteria, and show long-keeping qualities.

Conclusions

In examining these data on the Middle East and North Africa, I have attempted to connect spatial patterns of disease incidence with characteristic features of the local environments. The study has indicated how the geography, topography, and resulting climates have been used and misused by humankind over time. The negative aspects of all these factors led to low populations in this region until very recently. With the introduction of hydroelectric power and petroleum, the ensuing industrialization has enabled even greater proportions of the populations to live on the seacoast or river banks, and to develop urban centers.

The disease ecologies resulting from the peculiar rural environment, mainly with insufficient water; the specific problems of overcrowded, spatially limited living areas near water; and the general nutritional deficiencies of poor economies have now been augmented by increasing population. This phenomenal population rise following the establishment of post–World War II stability has especially aggravated conditions of overcrowding, substandard housing, and sanitation and poor nutrition in the urban communities. Although the economic and political patterns of the region vary among the countries, the interrelationships of many of the other factors remain similar.

LaVerne Kuhnke

Bibliography

Benenson, Abram S., ed. 1975. *Control of communicable diseases in man*. Washington, D.C.

Brothwell, Don, and A. T. Sandison, eds. 1967. *Diseases in antiquity: A survey of the diseases, injuries and surgery of early populations*. Springfield, Ill.

Cockburn, Aidan, and Eve Cockburn, eds. 1980. *Mummies, disease and ancient cultures*. Cambridge, U.K.

Dols, Michael. 1977. *The black death in the Middle East*. Princeton, N.J.

Dorland's illustrated medical dictionary. 1988. Philadelphia.

Drysdale, Alasdair, and Gerald H. Blake. 1985. *The Middle East and North Africa: A political geography*. New York and Oxford.

Farooq, M. 1964. New partnerships in schistosomiasis control. *Journal of Tropical Medicine and Hygiene* 67: 265–70.

Fenner, Frank, et al. 1988. *Small pox and its eradication*. Geneva.

Fisher, William B. 1971. *The Middle East: A physical, social and regional geography*. London.

Gallagher, Nancy E. 1983. *Medicine and power in Tunisia, 1780–1900*. Cambridge, U.K.

Hirsch, August. 1883–6. *Handbook of geographical and historical pathology*, 3 vols., trans. Charles Creighton. London.

Hirst, L. Fabian. 1953. *The conquest of plague: A study of the evolution of epidemiology*. Oxford.

Hopkins, Donald R. 1983. *Princes and peasants: Smallpox in history*. Chicago and London.

Johnson, R. H. 1965. The health of Israel. *Lancet* 2: 842–5.

Kanter, Helmuth. 1967. Libya: A geomedical monograph. In *Studies in geographical medicine*, ed. Helmuth Jusatz, 1–139. Berlin and Heidelberg.

Khalil, Mohamed. 1932. A century of helminthology in the Cairo Medical School. *Comptes rendus du congrès international de médecine tropicale et d'hygiène* 4: 3–25.

Kinnear-Wilson, J. V. 1967. Organic diseases of ancient Mesopotamia. In *Diseases in antiquity,* ed. Don Brothwell and A. T. Sandison, 191–208. Springfield, Ill.

Labib, Ferdos M. 1971. *Principles of public health*. Cairo.

Malek, Emile A. 1961. The ecology of schistosomiasis. In *Studies in disease ecology,* ed. J. M. May, 261–313. New York.

May, Jacques M., ed. 1961. *Studies in disease ecology*. Studies in medical geography, Vol. 2. New York.

May, J. M. 1967. *The ecology of malnutrition in Northern Africa*. Studies in medical geography, Vol. 7. New York.

May, Jacques M., and Irma S. Jarcho. 1961. *The ecology of malnutrition in the Far and Near East*. Studies in medical geography, Vol. 3. New York.

News from the Eastern Mediterranean: Health activities, 1979–80. *WHO Chronicle* 34: 322–4.

Nosologie marocaine. 1955. *Maroc Medical* 34: 365–7, 1165–646.

Omran, Abdel Rahim. 1961. The ecology of leishmaniasis. In *Studies in disease ecology,* ed. J. M. May, 331–88. New York.

Oxford regional economic atlas: The Middle East and North Africa. 1964. Oxford.

Pollitzer, Robert. 1954. *Plague*. Geneva.
    1959. *Cholera*. Geneva.

Rodenwaldt, Ernst, ed. 1952. *World atlas of epidemic diseases*. Hamburg.

Ruffer, Marc A. 1910. Note on the presence of bilharzia maematobia in Egyptian mummies of the 20th dynasty (1250–1000 B.C.). *British Medical Journal* 16: 177.

Russell, Alexander. 1794. *The natural history of Aleppo, containing . . . an account of the climate, inhabitants and diseases*. London.

Sandbach, F. R. 1976. The history of schistosomiasis research and policy for its control. *Medical History* 20: 259–75.

Sandison, A. T. 1980. Diseases in ancient Egypt. In *Mummies, disease and ancient cultures*, ed. Aidan Cockburn and Eve Cockburn, 29–44. Cambridge, U.K.

Simmons, James S., et al. 1954. *Global epidemiology: A geography of disease and sanitation*, Vol. 2: *Africa;* and Vol. 3: *Near and Middle East*. Philadelphia.

Disease ecology refers to the intricate human and environmental relationships that form the context of one or a group of diseases. Diseases are not simply biomedical entities; rather, they have their physical, environmental, sociocultural, psychological, and even political parameters. Distinctive human and biophysical environmental webs form the context of distinctive groups of human diseases. Major changes in this web, whether brought about by human intervention, environmental catastrophes, or a combination thereof, can result in a new context and possibly a new group of diseases. In developing countries, human control of the environment is limited, basic needs of a healthful life are not met, and, therefore, infectious and communicable diseases are the major cause of death. Improvements in health conditions will no doubt reduce the incidence of mortality resulting from infectious diseases and, in turn, bring about the prominence of chronic diseases more closely related to life-styles and life stages than to environmental parameters. South Asia as a geographic region still remains a region of poverty within which there is a marked contrast between the rural and urban *genre de vie*. Morbidity and mortality patterns in the rural and urban areas are, therefore, likely to be somewhat different, although paucity and quality of data make generalizations hazardous.

Ecologically, South Asia is one of the most distinctive regions of the world. Physiographically well demarcated, and climatically distinguished by the monsoonal rainfall regime, South Asian life has a rhythm marked by seasonality. Although agriculture is still the dominant occupation, rapidly swelling cities create air pollution, overcrowding, social stress, and the immense problem of waste disposal. The dominantly agrarian economic base is being increasingly supplemented by the diversity of urban occupations and modern life-styles. Rapidly increasing populations on a large numerical base create an environment of overcrowding, an acute housing shortage, substandard living conditions, and an ever present danger of recurring epidemics. Inadequacy of potable drinking water has meant an endemicity of various gastroenteric diseases. Undernutrition of pregnant mothers and inadequacy of

neonatal and postneonatal infant care result in very high infant mortality rates and a host of nutritional disorders. Under such living conditions, and the highly inadequate nature of the data, discussion of disease ecology of South Asia must remain broad. In order to understand South Asia's health context, it is necessary to keep in mind an outline of some of the essential facts of its physical and human environments.

The Physical Environment

Topography

The Himalaya and its associated mountain ranges form a physical and cultural divide between South Asia and the lands to the north and east. They rise in a series of roughly parallel ranges northward from the plains of Bangladesh, India, and Nepal, with each range progressively higher. The much lower Sulaiman and Kirthar ranges of western Pakistan, with their many passes, have permitted intercourse with other parts of Asia. Mountains closest to the plains have been heavily denuded of their forest cover, and are subject to intense soil erosion.

South of the world's highest mountain system is the densely populated alluvial plain of Ganga in India and Bangladesh, and the Indus Plain, mostly in Pakistan. Both these plains have extensively developed systems of irrigation. Canal irrigation is particularly well developed in the Indus Plain and the western Ganga Plain. These plains are subject to periodic flooding that is especially heavy and periodically devastating in the eastern part of India and Bangladesh.

The Thar Desert, south of the Indus Plain, is shared by India and Pakistan. Here is a vast arid region hemmed in from the east by the low Aravalli Range. This thinly populated desert region is characterized by shifting sand dunes, large playa lakes, salt pans, and, to the southwest, marshlands.

South of the Ganga Plain is peninsular India. Composed of several plateaus, this region, except for the black soils of the Deccan Plateau and the river deltas, is primarily an area of thin, reddish soils of medium to poor quality. Part of the peninsula that is still forested and of marginal quality for agriculture is home to many tribal people. Skirting the peninsula on the west is the narrow but intensively cultivated and densely populated Malabar coast. On the east the coastal plain is broader. The island nation of Sri Lanka is composed of central highlands surrounded by a coastal plain.

Climate

South Asia is very hot during the summer; the highest temperatures are found in the Thar Desert. Hot desiccating winds in May and June are frequent in the entire Indus–Ganga Plain and cause substantial problems of heat stress (Planalp 1971). Temperatures of over 90°F are commonplace. In the mountainous regions elevation modifies the temperatures. During winter there is a general temperature gradient from north to south. Temperatures are in the 40°F range in the north, reaching well over 75°F in the south.

South Asia is characterized by a high degree of rainfall seasonality, with very uneven geographic distribution, and great variability from year to year. In much of India, Bangladesh, Nepal, Bhutan, and Pakistan, most of the rainfall is received from June through September. Over the southern part of peninsular India, autumn rainfall is significant. On the southeastern coastal area the predominant season of rains is autumn. Most of peninsular India and the Thar region suffer from high variability of rainfall. In general, the seasonality of rainfall in the predominantly agrarian societies of South Asia has meant that farming is very dependent upon rainfall despite major developments in irrigation during the twentieth century. Variability of rainfall, therefore, means that farming communities may suffer from frequent seasonal food shortages, undernutrition, lowered resistance, and higher morbidity.

Convincing arguments have been made about the relationship of climatic seasonality to seasonal morbidity, especially among the poor. Evidence from diverse regions of the world, including India and Bangladesh, shows that seasonal fluctuations bear more heavily on the poor than on other social groups (Chambers, Longhurst, and Pacey 1981). High-rainfall regions, especially where humidity is also high (e.g., the Malabar coast, Eastern India, and Bangladesh) are the major endemic areas of infectious diseases such as cholera, typhoid, filariasis, and malaria.

The Sociocultural Environment

The Demographic Aspect

The South Asian nations are characterized by high birthrates, rapidly declining overall death rates, and consequently high natural increases to their already large population bases. For example, Bangladesh, at current rates, will double its population in 25 years, Pakistan in 24, and India in 32 years. The immediate reality is that in spite of much lowered crude death rates in the 1980s, infant mortality rates are very high: 112 per 1,000 live births in Nepal, about 120 in Pakistan, and 138 in Bangladesh. A large proportion – nearly 40 percent – of the population of South Asia is composed of children under 15 years of age. Maternal and child health must therefore consume a large part of the national health budgets. Large families, especially of the poor, lead to a high incidence of protein–energy malnutrition (PEM). Migration to urban areas, and life in overcrowded houses and hutments mean constant exposure to pathogens.

Social Realities

In South Asia, irrespective of religious beliefs, most of which are expressed in Hinduism, there is a strong concept of social groupings or castes. The most important aspect of this system that concerns us here is that the lowest caste groups ("scheduled castes") constitute about 15 percent of India's population. They have not only been socially disadvantaged but also tend to be the poorest. They have traditional occupations such as sweeping, cleaning of human waste, skinning animals, and leather working, and are spatially segregated in the villages and cities. Although they are not ethnically different from the majority population, the hamlets of these predominantly landless workers are located separately from the main villages, and their densely populated clusters of huts are found on the outskirts of cities along major roads and railway lines. Living conditions in their settlements are extremely unhygienic because they lack waste disposal systems. Proximity to urban dumps, and pools of stagnant water in construction pits create ideal conditions for a very high density of flies and mosquitoes in their settlements.

Tribal cultural groups, collectively termed "scheduled tribes," who make up about 3 percent of India's population, live mostly in forested, agriculturally marginal areas of the eastern states, the northeastern part of peninsular India, and the degraded forests in Madhya Pradesh, Maharashtra, Rajasthan, and Gujarat. Many of these groups practice *jhumming,* or slash-and-burn agriculture, but others have migrated to cities and mining areas in search of employment. Because virtually all of their traditional habitat has been isolated, health programs have rarely been extended effectively to them.

Differential gender valuation is common in South Asia. Male children are valued more than females. This tendency is reflected in the actual share of food and health care that is available to female children, who may get a less nutritious diet. When sick, the males are more likely than females to receive medical attention. In general, it would appear that female morbidity is underreported.

General Health Conditions in South Asia

South Asia is home to most diseases of humankind; surprisingly, yellow fever and some others are absent. The major causes of death include infectious and parasitic diseases such as tuberculosis, diarrhea, malaria, typhoid, gastrointestinal disorders, and a variety of childhood diseases such as tetanus, pneumonia, whooping cough, diphtheria, measles, and other preventable diseases (Nyrop 1984). A health survey in Pakistan during the mid-1970s revealed that nearly 30 percent of the people had malaria, and almost 100 percent had worm or parasitic afflictions (Nyrop 1984). Although published data on many health indicators are lacking or woefully deficient, some indication of health conditions may be obtained from life expectancy, crude death rates, and infant mortality rates. Death rates in South Asia, as in most developing regions of the world, have declined markedly since the 1970s, although they are still above the world average. Within South Asia, Sri Lanka has the lowest death rate (about 6 per 1,000), which is lower than most of the European countries and the United States (9 per 1,000). Death rates are higher for India (10 per 1,000) and even higher for Pakistan (14), Bangladesh (15), Nepal and Bhutan (17 each). Infant mortality rates, however, reveal a grimmer picture of the prevalent health conditions. Despite official claims to the contrary, infant mortality rates are very high, except in Sri Lanka, thanks largely to a very high female literacy rate compared with other South Asian countries. Considering Sri Lanka as the exception, South Asia as a whole shows clear signs of environmentally related causes of death, especially of infants.

Sanitation conditions in South Asia are appalling, made worse by the monsoon rains. Most rural inhabitants and those living on the outskirts of the cities use fields and any open space as a latrine. Although the new "Sulabh" (semiflushing) latrine is gaining ground in Indian cities, human waste disposal remains a serious problem, leading to a variety of gastrointestinal diseases. Contamination of municipal drinking water during the rainy season, including cities such as Delhi, results in periodic outbreaks of hepatitis epidemics.

The process of urbanization in South Asia is bringing vast numbers of rural unemployed workers to the cities. Those unable to find relatives, or who are too poor to rent, must live wherever they can. Thus, many semipermanent urban accretions have developed. Health conditions in these periurban slums are very poor. In fact, these settlements form a virtual ring of high morbidity around growing cities. Engulfed by rapidly growing suburban housing, these shanties are frequently found in close proximity to outward developing metropolitan areas. City governments are constantly trying to "clear" these semipermanent worker settlements (in India called *jhuggies* and *jhonparies,* or simply *JJ*'s), often with great difficulty. In the meantime, they remain as centers of high morbidity and infant mortality.

Expanding cities are also engulfing preexisting villages, thus juxtaposing two very different ways of life. Demand for milk and meat in the burgeoning urban populations has spurred these farming communities to intensify their farming by growing vegetables, and by keeping dairy cows, buffaloes, and chickens. The lower castes raise goats and pigs in these periurban locations. One effect of this urban agriculture is that the density of flies and mosquitoes in these areas is very high, thus helping to maintain endemicity of gastroenteric diseases.

Ecology of Selected Diseases in South Asia

In the space of this essay, it is possible to focus on only a few selected prevalent diseases in South Asia. Thus, smallpox, in spite of the fact that it was once a major killer disease in India, has been omitted because it has been eradicated. Likewise, although plague has some endemicity, its incidence is now very limited. Instead the focus is on diseases of high endemicity or prevalence.

Cholera

Although cholera, an acute communicable disease, is not peculiar to South Asia, there are endemic areas of cholera in this region from which periodic outbreaks have occurred (see Map VII.3.1). Cholera etiology is relatively simple, since this disease is caused by the ingestion of *Vibrio cholerae.* Two distinct modes of cholera transmission are usually recognized (Craig 1986). In the "primary" transmission, the vibrio is ingested through vegetables and fish raised in water that is contaminated with the vibrio. The "secondary" mode is the fecal–oral transmission. In nonimmunized persons with relatively lowered stomach acidity, symptoms of cholera develop rapidly, marked by frequent watery stools, vomiting, and fever. Since the vibrio is present in great quantities in the characteristic watery stools, flies may carry the germ from them to human food. Consumption of this contami-

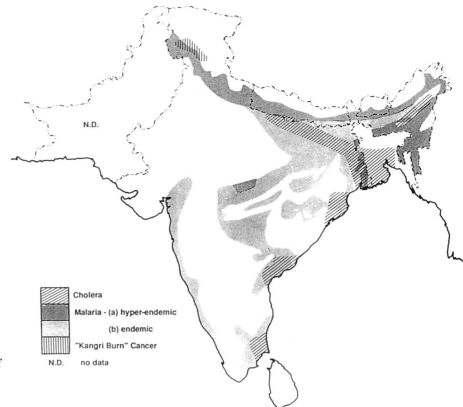

Map VII.3.1. General endemicity of cholera, malaria, and "kangri burn" cancer. (Based on Misra 1970; Hutt and Burkitt 1986.)

Cholera
Malaria - (a) hyper-endemic
            (b) endemic
"Kangri Burn" Cancer
N.D.   no data

nated food results in the ingestion of the vibrio, thus creating a fecal–oral link, resulting in manifestation of the disease. Death occurs as a result of excessive dehydration, electrolyte imbalance, and the pyrogenic endotoxins of *V. cholerae*.

Cholera remains endemic in the delta lands of Ganga in West Bengal and Bangladesh. Indeed, the "cholera pandemic that scourged the world in the first half of the nineteenth century began in the Bengali basin and spread as far and as rapidly as man was then able to travel" (Cahill 1976). The reasons for cholera's endemicity have to do with a combination of physical, environmental, and human conditions. The deltaic region is characterized by heavy monsoon rainfall from June through September, resulting in frequent and often disastrous flooding. In the aftermath of rains, slow-moving water in the maze of Ganga's distributaries and stagnant water in numerous shallow pools characterize the landscape. Tanks and wells used as a resource for drinking water are filled with surface flow. Algal infestations of these ponds and tanks greatly increase the alkalinity of stagnant water, and create favorable conditions for the multiplication of *V. cholerae* (Jusatz 1977). Most people defecate outdoors and seek proximity to water for cleaning themselves. Thus, chances for the accu-

mulation of cholera germs in pools of water increase, putting at risk individuals who use this water for drinking. During the dry season, shrinking pools and tanks, owing to intense heat, become even more concentrated with the vibrio. Fish taken from these sources, and vegetables washed with this water, can transmit cholera. Since most drinking water is neither filtered nor boiled, chances for vibrio ingestion remain high. During the monsoon season, when heat and humidity are high, people tend to lose large amounts of moisture with sweating. Drinking large quantities of water greatly dilutes the stomach acidity. If vibrio-infected food or water is taken under this condition, the chances for disease manifestation multiply. This situation happens usually at village fairs, periodic markets, or other big gatherings in the open. Because the disease has a very rapid course, causing vomiting, fever, and passage of watery stools, vibrio from such body wastes can be easily conveyed by the ubiquitous flies to food items being consumed by other participants at the fair. Cholera epidemics are therefore notorious for their speed and virulence during the summer monsoon season.

From the delta region of the Ganges, cholera has often spread in epidemic forms (May 1958; Ackerknecht 1972), although today the death rate is quite low because of widespread immunization in South Asia. In the past, cholera has also been spread through the agency of pilgrims, both Hindu and Muslim (Misra 1970; Dutta 1985). Hindus visiting their sacred places in different parts of India have been exposed to cholera. The massive Kumbha bathing festivals that attract pilgrims from all over India have been the scene of cholera epidemics. Pilgrims from the endemic areas have inadvertently carried the cholera germ to sacred centers, where sanitation breakdowns have occurred, leading to the exposure of pilgrims from nonendemic areas. Muslim pilgrims on *hajj* to Mecca from Bengal in the past may also have been both carriers of and affected by cholera. Although these religious convergences remain a potential mechanism for the diffusion of cholera, large-scale immunization efforts and improved water supplies at these religious centers have prevented epidemics of cholera. At large pilgrimage congregations in India, pilgrims are routinely checked for certification of cholera immunization at points of entry to the designated area of religious fairs. Those without a valid certificate are inoculated on the spot before proceeding further on their religious journey.

Dysentery and Diarrheal Disease

Intestinal infections of various types are widely prevalent in South Asia. Cholera has been the focus of much attention because of its notorious epidemics and pandemics; however, it is dysentery (both amebic and bacillary) that generally leads in morbidity in most normal years. Unfortunately, dysentery and diarrhea (due to a variety of diseases of the alimentary canal) have not been accorded the attention they deserve because they are predominant among poor rural children. Perhaps as many as 80 percent of rural India's children are infected by parasitic worms (Nyrop 1986). Tropical diarrhea, mostly a traveler's disease, has attracted far more attention in the literature than the killer infantile diarrhea, which is linked to high infant mortality throughout India, Pakistan, Nepal, Bhutan, and Bangladesh.

The causative agent of bacillary dysentery is bacteria of the *Shigella* group, whereas amebic dysentery is produced by protozoa. However, both diseases manifest after ingestion of the pathogen whether by food infected by flies carrying the pathogen, by one's own infected hands, or by infected vessels, such as food containers. Thus, cultural practices, personal cleanliness, and the nature of the food available determine whether the disease will actually develop in an individual or family. The practice of using water on bare hands for cleaning the anal area after defecation increases the chances that the pathogen could be carried under the fingernails, and conveyed to food. Many middle-class South Asian families employ servants as cooks who come from poor families. Dysentery pathogens may be inadvertently conveyed to the food of these families, even though the latter may have a high standard of personal hygiene. Many edible items in stores and shops are exposed to flies and dust in spite of public health regulations. It is virtually inevitable that such items when consumed (without cooking) will carry pathogens with them. In cities, where it is easier to enforce environmental hygiene regulations, and where the modernizing consumers themselves exert sufficient pressure, store owners do respond by adopting strict hygienic practices. But most of the population of South Asia is rural, and therefore the enforcement of public health measures is highly problematic. In addition, the population – especially the adult rural population – of South Asian countries (Sri Lanka is again the exception) is mostly illiterate, and does not effectively demand hygienic practices from food vendors. Thus, dysentery, a highly preventable disease, persists.

As expected, dysentery shows marked seasonality in South Asia, because conditions for the multiplication of flies, a major carrier of dysentery pathogens, become ideal during and soon after the rainy season, through summer and early autumn. This is also the season when many types of melons, other fruits, and vegetables are sold in the open. Thus, even the more literate urban populations are placed at risk. Poor sections of the cities – the slums and the shanties – are particularly vulnerable because of the virtual lack of sanitation facilities that lead to a very high density of fly population. Many sanitary systems break down, and wells get polluted. The diffusion of tube wells as sources for irrigation and drinking water in the rural areas may have had some impact on the incidence of dysentery. The prevalence of dysentery in South Asia illustrates the fallacy of considering disease as only a biomedical entity. It forces us to recognize the significance of looking at the web of ecological relationships between people and their total environment.

Malaria

Fevers of many types have been described in the ancient Vedic literature of India. Vedic hymns speak of fevers that cause chills and high body temperature, and torment the sufferer during summer and autumn (Filliozat 1964). An intermittent fever, *takman,* seems to have been particularly feared by the Aryans living in the Indus Basin. Their descriptions indicate characteristics of the fever much resembling malaria in its seasonality and symptoms.

Unlike cholera, malaria ecology is complex, since this infection depends upon the life cycles of the parasite *Plasmodium* and the vector *Anopheles* mosquito on the one hand, and human contact with the infected vector on the other. This contact has to be close enough for the infected vector to take a human blood meal and, in the process, to inject the pathogen parasite into the human bloodstream. Repeated infections are not uncommon, and once the plasmodium parasite is in human blood, fever relapse can occur. Characterized by chills, high fever, splenomegaly, and debilitation, malaria fever has had a serious impact on economic development by affecting millions of people. Between 1947, India's year of Independence, and 1953, the year the Malaria Control Program was first launched, malaria incidence was about 75 million, of which nearly 800,000 lives were lost to this disease annually (India 1987).

Distribution. Geographic distribution of malaria, as indeed of several other diseases, has been affected by socioeconomic changes in South Asian countries since the 1950s. Before Independence, the major hyperendemic areas (spleen rates over 75 percent) included the following:

1. The narrow *tarai* belt along southern Nepal and northern Uttar Pradesh. Lying at the foot of the Himalaya Mountain system, this strip was characterized by tall thick grass and *sal* forest on a relatively thin stony soil. Rainfall in this region decreases toward the west but is generally over 60 inches per annum.
2. The hills of eastern India up to a height of about 5,000 feet. These forested and poorly accessible areas have been thinly populated by tribal people who practiced considerable slash-and-burn agriculture. Rainfall in these areas is very heavy and is highly concentrated during the months of June through September.
3. The Chota Nagpur Plateau and the Eastern Hills region of the Indian Peninsula. Covered by forests, these regions have poor reddish soils and marginal agriculture carried on by tribal people. Rainfall is well over 40 inches and occurs mostly in the months of June through September.
4. A narrow forested strip along the crest of the western Ghats. This region receives heavy rainfall during the monsoon season, but the rest of the year is quite dry.
5. The western part of the Ganges Delta, and parts of the Coromandel coastal region of peninsular India. The Ganges Delta, of course, has the typical monsoon rainfall regime, but the Coromandel coastal region is an area of mostly autumn rainfall. These are densely populated, dominantly agricultural areas.

In addition to these areas of hyperendemicity, most of India, with over 40 inches of rainfall, was considered endemic for malaria. Moderate malaria endemicity also was found in the plains of Punjab, especially along the rivers and the irrigation canals. The rest of India, with rainfall of less than 40 inches, suffered from periodic, but severe, epidemics of malaria. Especially intense "fulminant" epidemics occurred in the western Ganga Plains and the adjoining Punjab Plains.

Malaria Resurgence. A. T. Learmonth (1957, 1958), A. K. Dutt, R. Akhtar, and H. Dutta (1980), and later Learmonth and Akhtar (1984) have added significantly to our knowledge of malaria ecology in India. In a series of maps, they bring out the story of malaria resurgence from 1965 to 1976. Through the efforts of the government of India, aided by the World Health Organization (WHO), and the active support of the state governments, malaria seemed to have been brought under control. The success of the Malaria Control Program, consisting mostly of the spraying of DDT, encouraged the government of India to convert this program to malaria eradication, which showed spectacular success until about 1965. In that year, malaria incidence had declined to 100,000 as compared to 70 million in 1947. But two India–Pakistan wars (1965 and 1970–1), the war of Bangladesh's liberation, and later the oil crisis resulted in massive disruption of the campaign against malaria. In addition, both the *Anopheles* vector species and the pathogen *Plasmodium* have developed resistance to antivector and anti-*Plasmodium* chemicals and drugs, respectively. Thus, hopes of malaria eradication were replaced by the stark reality of its recrudescence. From a low of about 100,000 cases in 1965, a resurgence of malaria developed, with over 5 million cases in 1975. In spite of further malaria control efforts, there were still 2 million cases in 1979, only marginally declining to about 1.6 million by 1985. A similar resurgence has occurred in several other countries (*Development Forum* 1988).

Geographically, as Learmonth and Akhtar (1984) have showed, by 1965 most of India had a low annual parasite index (API) (see Map VII.3.2). An API of

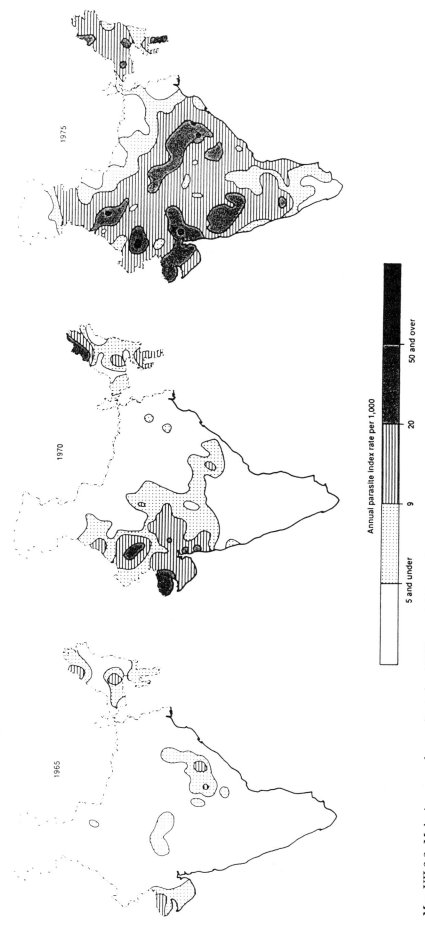

Map VII.3.2. Malaria: annual parasite index (API), per 1,000 population, for selected years. (Based on Learmonth and Akhtar 1984.)

over 5 per 1,000 existed in the hyperendemic region of Eastern Hills, parts of Chota Nagpur Plateau and northeastern peninsular India, western Vindhyan Range, the marshlands of Kachch and western Gujarat, and the foothill zone of western Uttar Pradesh. Relative inaccessibility is a major common attribute of all these areas. Their rainfall and soil characteristics vary widely, but all these areas have a high proportion of "scheduled tribes." It needs to be stressed that these people have a somewhat different *genre de vie* than do the nontribal populations of India. Formerly much more widespread, the tribal peoples now occupy "refuge areas" of marginal agricultural productivity. Malaria control – eradication programs of the government of India – seemed to have been ineffective in these poorly accessible areas. Thus, these areas remained highly endemic malarial time bombs. Slackening of the eradication programs, due to diversion of the national resources to two major wars in the subcontinent, in 1965 and again in 1971, meant a partial reassertion of the pre–Malaria Control Program pattern of malaria epidemics. From these focal points, malaria spread again to virtually all parts of India, although as a result of antimalarial drugs and greater availability of medical facilities, mortality is now minimal. A virtually similar process of malaria resurgence occurred in Bangladesh (Paul 1984). Malaria had been beaten back to the remote tribal areas of Chittagong Hills, from which it has reasserted itself.

The history of malaria control holds a major lesson for all concerned. That lesson is that a disease with a complex ecology deserves a multipronged approach. It is necessary to have a well-orchestrated plan of action by specialists in various pertinent fields of science and bureaucracy, but it is imperative that the political leadership exercise wisdom. Malaria control, let alone eradication, is possible only under conditions of political stability, permitting an uninterrupted commitment of national resources. Current interethnic conflicts in Punjab, eastern Indian states, Bangladesh, and Sri Lanka will surely affect malaria control programs adversely.

Leprosy

Leprosy (Hansen's disease) has been known in South Asian countries since antiquity. Called *kustha* in the Hindu medical literature, it was considered to be transmittable to the child from parents "when a woman and a man have (respectively) the blood and sperm vitiated by leprosy" (Filliozat 1964). During the British rule in India, the Census of India (1913) collected data on four types of disabilities for each

decade since 1881: insanity, deaf-muteness, blindness, and leprosy. The last disease is usually of two types – tuberculoid and lepromatous. Tuberculoid leprosy is usually self-limiting, whereas the lepromatous form is progressive. The causative pathogen of leprosy is the bacillus *Mycobacterium leprae*. Lepromatous leprosy is the classic dreaded disease in which, in advanced cases, loss of digits and other deformities occur. The pathogen is usually thought to enter the body through the mucous membrane of the upper respiratory tract, or through repeated and close skin contact, but there is controversy among leprologists as to the exact mode of transmission (Cahill 1976; Sutherland 1977). The incubation period is long – 1 to 5 years – making research, early detection, and understanding of the diffusion process very difficult.

Persons with advanced stages of leprosy are frequently found begging at the railway stations, at the bus stations, and especially at the holy places all over South Asia. Even though legislation against begging has been frequent, the problem is far from solved. Likewise, the stigma attached to leprosy has made early treatment very difficult by discouraging patients to seek appropriate treatment. Since the disease is considered the greatest misfortune, sufferers from it arouse pity rather than understanding. In general, leprosy sufferers are isolated from the society either because of their own voluntary response or as a result of government policy. India has in place a national leprosy control program under which 434 leprosy control units along with 6,784 survey, education, and treatment centers, 721 urban leprosy centers, and 46 leprosy training centers have been developed (India 1987). In neighboring Nepal, the National Leprosy Control Program was established in 1975; now the Leprosy Service Development Board, it provides treatment and rehabilitative services for leprosy patients.

Geographic Distribution. South Asian countries have a medium rate of leprosy, but the very large total population base results in a correspondingly large absolute number of sufferers. In India alone, the prevalence rate of 5.7 per 1,000 population in 1986 suggests that the number of leprosy patients exceeds 4 million, according to government data (India 1987). Areas of high leprosy prevalence in India (over 10 per 1,000) include the following: (1) a belt of coastal districts of Tamil Nadu, Andhra Pradesh, and Orissa, which continues into most of West Bengal and adjoining southern Bihar; (2) western Maharashtra and the adjoining eastern Andhra Pradesh,

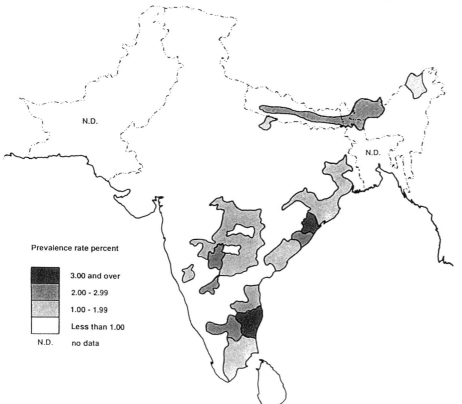

Map VII.3.3. Leprosy: prevalence rate percentage, 1974–5. (Based on Pearson 1984, 1988.)

Prevalence rate percent

3.00 and over

2.00 - 2.99

1.00 - 1.99

Less than 1.00

N.D.   no data

a substantial part of which was once the princely state of Hyderabad (all of this area lies in the interior section of the Deccan Plateau); (3) isolated areas in other parts of India, including the *tarai* region of Uttar Pradesh and the far eastern parts of India. Surprisingly, Bangladesh reported only 110 cases of leprosy in 1979; Pakistan, 3,269; and Sri Lanka, 751 (WHO 1981). The longitudinal river valleys of Nepal apparently show a high prevalence of endemic leprosy – over 10 per 1,000 population.

Problems of Leprosy Control. Because leprosy is prevalent in both flat coastal areas and hills and valleys, and in areas of low and high rainfall, any relationship with broad physical environmental factors seems only tenuous at best (see Map VII.3.3). Secrecy surrounding earlier phases of the disease and the victims' fear of social ostracism in the latter stages make control and curative efforts difficult to implement. Slow progression of the disease and the necessity for prolonged treatment compound both the preventive and curative problems. It has been found in Nepal that people do not necessarily use the treatment facilities located nearest to them, for fear of being stigmatized in their local community. Patients seem deliberately to seek treatment at distant facilities (Pearson 1988). This trend has major implica-

tions for the diffusion of leprosy. With increasing mobility, the disease could spread without notice. As Kevin Cahill (1976) observed, in the "meagerness of our knowledge of the clinical, the bacteriological and the pathological course in the incubational phase of leprosy lies the primary reason for the failure of international control and eradication programmes." Peoples along traditional routes of commerce – for example, the river valleys in Nepal – could be especially at risk (Pearson 1984). In spite of the argument that leprosy is not easily communicable, intrusive tourism does place the visitors at risk of carrying the disease from the traditional endemic areas to other parts of the world.

At one time it was hoped that the disease could be eradicated because human beings are known to be the only significant reservoirs of the leprosy pathogen (Lechat 1988). That this has not occurred seems reason for less optimism, at least in the foreseeable future. However, "multidrug therapy" (MDP), early identification of cases and at-risk populations, social and cultural sensitivity toward the patient, long-term commitment of the governments, and immunologic and epidemiological research, can together make a major impact. Immunologic advances, based upon the cultivation of large quantities of *M. leprae* bacilli in armadillos, and advances in molecular

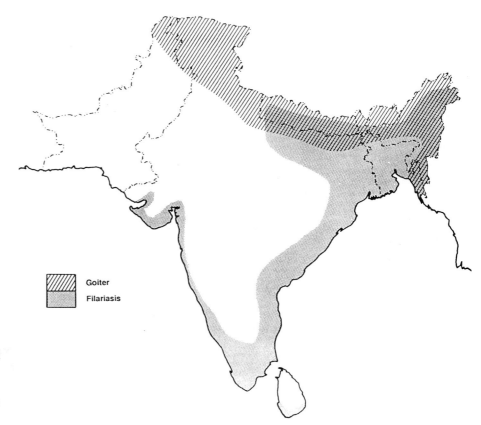

Map VII.3.4. General distribution
of filariasis and goiter. (Based on
May 1961; Misra 1970; Schweinfurth 1983; and *India, a reference
annual* 1987.)

Filariasis

Filarial infections, caused by worms such as *Wuchereria bancrofti* and *Brugi malayi,* are widespread in
the tropical climates of Africa, Southeast and South
Asia, and the Caribbean. In India alone, over 15
million people suffer from filariasis, and over 300
million are at risk (India 1987) (see Map VII.3.4).

Filariasis is endemic in the entire Konkan and
Malabar coastal areas of western India, the coastal
areas of Tamil Nadu, Andhra Pradesh, and Orissa.
Its incidence declines rapidly toward the interior
and the northwestern parts of India. The lowest incidence is found in the Himalaya region. Sri Lanka's
major endemic area of filariasis is in the hot, humid,
and high rainfall areas of the coastal southwest
(Schweinfurth 1983). Filariasis is found in both the
rural and urban areas of this coastal region, although there are significant differences in the implicated pathogen of the two settings.

Microfilariae of the worm pathogens entering the
human bloodstream through mosquito bites, circulate in blood, develop into larvae and, under suitable
conditions, into adult worms. Filariasis leads to fever, lymphadenitis of the groin, and epididymitis. As
the worms multiply, reach adulthood, and die, conditions such as hanging groins and elephantiasis of
the legs develop. The high prevalence rate of elephantiasis of legs on the Malabar coast of India has
led to the nomenclature "Malabar legs."

The essential components of the filaria ecology in
South Asia are the pathogens *W. bancrofti* and *B.
malayi,* several species of the mosquito vectors
(*Culex, Anopheles, Aedes*), a hot and wet climate
with high humidity, moist and warm soil, availability of stagnant pools of water, and a population of
predominantly poor people. *Culex* and *Anopheles*
mosquitoes, both abundant in all parts of South
Asia, but especially in the high rainfall regions, pick
up microfilaria through a blood meal from infected
human beings, which reach the larva stage in the
mosquito. These larvae are then introduced to other
human beings through repeated mosquito bites.
Filarial larvae reach adulthood in from 1 to 3 years,
and may produce swarms of microfilariae. Most of
the pathological symptoms are due to larvae and
adult worms (Cahill 1976).

More than women, men are susceptible victims
because of their outdoor agricultural activities and
relatively less protective clothing. There is increasing concern that filariasis is becoming an urban

disease as well. This is happening primarily as a result of the migration of rural males to large cities in search of jobs. Many of these poor migrants must live on the outskirts of the cities, where there is an abundance of stagnant water pools as a result of construction activity. These pools serve as breeding grounds for the urban mosquitoes, which, in turn, become intermediate hosts of the pathogen between new immigrants and the established city populations. Thus, a disease that at one time was thought to be primarily rural is on its way to becoming an urban phenomenon as well. U. Schweinfurth (1983) provides a very interesting case study of filariasis infections at the University of Peradenya in Sri Lanka. The beautification of the campus also provided a very good habitat for the breeding of *Culex* vector. Students attending this university from infected areas were the carriers of *W. bancrofti* in their blood. In the beautified university campus, they became the source of the pathogen for the mosquito that also found the university campus environment conducive for breeding. The vector mosquitoes in turn introduced the disease to students from non-endemic areas as well.

Difficulty of detection of the disease (microfilariae show no pathogenic symptoms) at the early stage makes preventive measures difficult as well. Sadly, filaricidal and larvicidal treatment is available to only about 10 percent of the population in the endemic areas of India (WHO 1984). Efforts to introduce larvivorous fish in pools of water where mosquitoes breed may be helpful as part of a comprehensive filaria control program. This strategy, however, may be ineffective in the periurban areas where pools of water quickly become polluted and filled with urban waste. These pools are useless for fish culture, but do invite mosquitoes to breed.

Ecology of Nutritional Deficiency Diseases

Attention to communicable diseases may tend to mask the prevalence of a great variety of diseases that are the result of undernutrition as well as malnutrition. With a very large number of people living in extreme poverty in South Asia, dietary deficiencies are to be expected. Although "diseases of poverty" do not constitute a special category in the official *International List of Disease Classification,* the international medical community is increasingly cognizant of such a class (Prost 1988). M. S. R. Hutt and D. P. Burkitt (1986) go so far as to say that "most so-called tropical diseases are, in fact, diseases of poverty, rather than of geography." On the basis of his field studies on the nutrition of children in

Haryana, S. K. Aggarwal (1986) found that "no other factor seems to affect the nutritional status of the children as much as family income." The scientific concept of balanced diet in South Asia is only of academic importance; the real concern is dietary sufficiency.

The Indian Council of Medical Research found in its surveys that about 35 percent of children have protein–calorie malnutrition (Mitra 1985). Earlier emphasis on protein deficiency has given way to the more widely acceptable concept of protein–calorie malnutrition (PCM) or protein–energy malnutrition (PEM) (Learmonth 1988). India, Bangladesh, and Nepal together have a serious problem of malnutrition and hunger, even though in recent years agricultural production has been rising, especially in India. The situation in Pakistan and Sri Lanka is, on the average, "adequate," but in India, Bangladesh, and Nepal, less than 90 percent of the average daily energy requirements are met.

The relationship between food in the market and its availability to an individual for actual consumption depends on a host of intervening factors (Aggarwal 1986). Among these factors are family income, gender, age, season of the year, government regulations, and cultural factors such as dietary restrictions, taboos, and preferences. Addressing the role of cultural dietary preferences in disease ecology, A. K. Chakravarti (1982) provides evidence to show that existing regional differences do translate into a significantly higher incidence of diet-related diseases. These facts were earlier noted by J. M. May (1961). In predominantly rice-eating areas, where highly polished rice is preferred, beriberi is preeminent, because of thiamine deficiency, which results from the polishing process. Where parboiled rice is widely employed, however, the incidence of beriberi is claimed to be significantly lower. Consumption of *khesari* as the basic pulse in eastern Madhya Pradesh has been associated (Chakravarti 1982) with the incidence of lathyrism, which is characterized by muscular atrophy, causing the typical "scissors gait," incontinence of urine, and sexual impotence (Manson-Bahr 1966).

The impact of malnutrition is not easily measured, but some of the effects are well known and include anemia, goiter, night blindness, rickets, beriberi, and probably permanent damage to the nervous system, resulting in mental disorders. The long-term economic, social, and personal impact of these dietary deficiencies can only be imagined. In addition, undernutrition of pregnant mothers has adverse consequences both for them and for their babies, who are often of low-birthweight. It is a well-established fact that low-birthweight is a major correlate of infant mortality. Thus low-income, undernourished mothers are likely to have a higher frequency of low-birthweight babies, and thus contribute disproportionately to higher infant mortality. Even in the same village infant mortality among the poor is twice that of the privileged people (Mitra 1985).

Some of the nutritional deficiency diseases have a clear regional prevalence. Goiter, for example, has a high rate of endemicity in a sub-Himalayan belt extending from Arunachal Pradesh and other states in northeast India through Bhutan, West Bengal, Sikkim, Bihar, Nepal, Uttar Pradesh, Himachal Pradesh, Jammu, and Kashmir. Goiter is also found in parts of Gujarat, Madhya Pradesh, and Maharashtra (India 1987). Endemic goiter is primarily due to a dietary iodine deficiency, resulting in enlargement of the thyroid gland. At one time considered only an unsightly inconvenience, goiter is now known to be a possible precursor of cancer of the thyroid, and is associated with below normal mental and physical development. It is also possible that very high infant mortality in these regions is related to regional iodine deficiency (Hutt and Burkitt 1986). The government of India in 1983 launched a major program, through both private and public channels, of iodizing salt, in an effort to combat iodine deficiency and decrease goiter incidence.

Every culture has some distinctive practices that may be associated with culture-specific diseases. For example, only in Kashmir do people use an earthen pot (*kangri*) containing live coal, nestled in a wicker basket, that hangs by a thread around their neck during the winter season, as a portable personal body warmer. Heat and irritation from this *kangri* practice is significantly associated with the kangri-burn cancer, especially among the elderly (Manson-Bahr 1966). Similarly, cancer of the buccal cavity is found to be associated with the long-term habit of chewing betel. This habit is common in eastern Ganga Plain and southwestern India.

Economic Development and Disease Ecology

In his influential book, *Man, Medicine, and Environment* (1968), Rene Dubos makes a poignant observation about disease and development:

Disease presents itself simultaneously with so many different faces in any given area that it is usually impossible to attribute one particular expression of it to one particular set of environmental circumstances. Nevertheless, some generalizations appear justified. Without question, nutritional and infectious diseases account for the largest percentage of mortality and morbidity in most underprivileged countries, especially in those just becoming industrialized. . . . In contrast, the toll taken by malnutrition and infection decreases rapidly wherever and whenever the living standards improve, but other diseases then become more prevalent.

South Asian societies are in the process of major change, since economic development has become the goal of all the nations (except perhaps Bhutan). In pursuit of this goal, national governments have become deeply involved in directing the nature and pace of change. Against heavy odds, the processes of social and economic change are beginning to show their impact. Even in some rural areas of India, a major reduction in seasonal morbidity of communicable diseases has been observed concomitant with agricultural prosperity (Bhardwaj and Rao 1988), suggesting that Western-style development is not a *sine qua non* for better health conditions. Sri Lanka, which placed great emphasis on education, has achieved a high female literacy rate (over 80 percent). This has had a major impact on the reduction of the birthrate and has helped greatly to reduce the infant mortality rate, even though Sri Lanka has not become an economically well-developed country. Nepal, India, Pakistan, and Bangladesh have not been able to accomplish the same for their female population, and consequently their infant mortality rates are still very high. Female literacy in India varies widely between social groups and regions. Where female literacy is high – for example, in the urban areas and in the southwest (Kerala) – birthrates and infant mortality have come down.

One of the results of the Green Revolution has been an increased labor demand in the highly irrigated areas of western U.P., Punjab, Haryana, and Rajasthan. Long-distance agricultural labor migrations from Bihar and eastern U.P. to the above areas have now become commonplace. This means that *Plasmodium* from the eastern part of India has a greater chance of establishing itself in the farming communities of northwestern India. Increased availability of water in the irrigated areas provides an expanded habitat for the *Anopheles* mosquito vector as well.

International migration and tourism, which are intensifying in South Asia, have been implicated in the importation of newer diseases; AIDS is only one example (*India Abroad*, October 26, 1990). When the first few cases of AIDS were reported in India, the

Indian government was alarmed enough to enforce serotesting of foreign students, especially coming from AIDS endemic areas of sub-Saharan African countries. This action immediately aroused the anger of exchange students and strong reactions from several African governments. According to a WHO warning, there may be already over 250,000 HIV-positive cases in India with an expectancy of over 60,000 AIDS patients by 1995 (*India Abroad,* October 26, 1990). The incidence of AIDS is, as yet, reported primarily from the major metropolitan areas such as Bombay, Madras, Calcutta, and Delhi, and is currently associated mostly with prostitution. Precisely because of this association, however, AIDS will very likely spread into the general population. Since migration to cities is large, and rural–urban interaction is intensifying, the vast rural areas will not be immune from AIDS for long. Existing models of AIDS diffusion strongly suggest this possibility (Shanon and Pyle 1989). Thus, the context of health is becoming much wider than imagined under the older health paradigm in which the physician was considered the final health authority. L. Eisenberg and N. Sartorius (1988) have rightly asserted that "health will have to be seen as a state of balance between human beings and their environment. Human ecology can help to develop this approach to health and its promotion." South Asian countries have already started to prove the efficacy of such an approach.

Surinder M. Bhardwaj

Bibliography

Ackerknecht, Erwin H. 1972. *History and geography of the most important diseases.* New York.

Aggarwal, Surinder K. 1986. *Geo-ecology of malnutrition: A study of the Haryana children.* New Delhi.

Akhtar, Rais. 1985. Goitre zonation in the Kumaon region. *Social Science and Medicine* 12D: 152–63.

Akhtar, Rais, and Andrew T. A. Learmonth. 1985. The resurgence of malaria in India. In *Geographical aspects of health and disease in India,* ed. Rais Akhtar and A. T. A. Learmonth, 107–23. New Delhi.

Bhardwaj, Surinder M., and Bimal K. Paul. 1986. Medical pluralism and infant mortality in a rural area of Bangladesh. *Social Science and Medicine* 23: 1003–10.

Bhardwaj, Surinder M., and Madhusudana N. Rao. 1988. Regional development and seasonality of communicable diseases in rural Andhra Pradesh, India. *Social Science and Medicine* 26: 15–24.

Cahill, Kevin M. 1976. *Tropical diseases: A handbook for practitioners.* Westport, Conn.

Census of India. 1913. *Census of India, 1911, India,* part 1: *Report.* Calcutta.

Chakravarti, Aninda K. 1982. Diet and disease: Some cultural aspects of food use in India. In *India: Cultural patterns and processes,* ed. Allen G. Noble and Ashok K. Dutt, 301–23. Boulder, Colo.

Chambers, R., Richard Longhurst, and Arnold Pacey, eds. 1981. *Seasonal dimensions to rural poverty.* London.

Craig, Marian. 1988. Time–space clustering of *Vibrio cholerae* 01 in Matlab, Bangladesh, 1970–1982. *Social Science and Medicine* 26: 5–13.

Development Forum. 1988. The malaria comeback. *Development Forum* 16(2): 16.

Dubos, Rene. 1968. *Man, medicine, and environment.* New York.

Dutt, A. K., Rais Akhtar, and Hiran M. Dutta. 1980. Malaria in India with particular reference to west-central states. *Social Science and Medicine* 14D: 317–30.

Dutta, M. K. 1985. The diffusion and ecology of cholera in India. In *Geographical aspects of health and disease in India,* ed. Rais Akhtar and A. T. A. Learmonth, 91–106. New Delhi.

Eisenberg, Leon, and Norman Sartorius. 1988. Human ecology in the repertoire of health development. *World Health Forum* 9: 564–8.

Filliozat, J. 1964. *The classical doctrine of Indian medicine: Its origins and its Greek parallels.* Delhi.

Gopalan, C., et al. 1971. *Diet atlas of India.* Hyderabad.

Hasan, Arif. 1988. Low cost sanitation for a squatter community. *World Health Forum* 9: 361–4.

Hazara, Jayati. 1989. The changing pattern of diseases in West Bengal, India. *Singapore Journal of Tropical Geography* 10: 144–59.

Hutt, M. S. R., and D. P. Burkitt. 1986. *The geography of non-infectious diseases.* Oxford.

Hyma, B., and A. Ramesh. 1985. The geographic distribution and trend in cholera incidence in Tamil Nadu. In *Geographical aspects of health and disease in India,* ed. Rais Akhtar and A. T. A. Learmonth, 169–219. New Delhi.

India Abroad (weekly). October 26, 1990, 19.

India, Government of. 1987. *India: A reference annual 1986.* New Delhi.

Jusatz, H. 1977. Cholera. In *A world geography of human diseases,* ed. G. Melvyn Howe, 131–43. London.

Learmonth, Andrew T. A. 1957. Some contrasts in the regional geography of malaria in India and Pakistan. *Transactions of the Institute of British Geographers* 23: 37–59.

1958. Medical geography in Indo-Pakistan: A study of twenty years' data. *Indian Geographical Journal* 33: 1–59.

1988. *Disease ecology: An introduction.* Oxford.

Learmonth, Andrew T. A., and Rais Akhtar. 1984. The malaria resurgence in India 1965–76. *Annals, National Association of Geographers, India* 4: 23–69.

Lechat, M. F. 1988. Leprosy: The long hard road. *World Health Forum* 9: 69–71.

Manson-Bahr, Philip H. 1966. *Manson's tropical diseases: A manual of the diseases of warm climates.* London.

May, Jaques M. 1958. *The ecology of human disease.* New York.

   1961. *The ecology of malnutrition in the Far and Near East.* New York.

Misra, R. P. 1970. *Medical geography of India.* New Delhi.

Mitra, Asok. 1985. The nutrition status in India. In *Nutrition and development,* ed. Margaret Biswas and Per Pinstrup-Andersen, 142–62. Oxford.

Nag, Moni. 1988. The Kerala formula. *World Health Forum* 9: 258–62.

Nyrop, Richard F., ed. 1984. *Pakistan: A country study.* Washington, D.C.

   1986. *India: A country study.* Washington, D.C.

Paul, Bimal K. 1984. Malaria in Bangladesh. *Geographical Review* 74: 63–75.

Pearson, Maggie. 1984. Leprosy moves along the Nepalese valleys. *Geographical Magazine* 54: 504–9.

   1988. What does distance matter? Leprosy control in west Nepal. *Social Science and Medicine* 26: 25–36.

Planalp, Jack M. 1971. *Heat stress and culture in North India.* Alexandria, Va.

Prost, A. 1988. When the rains fail. . . . *World Health Forum* 9: 98–103.

Schwartzberg, Joseph E., ed. 1978. *A historical atlas of South Asia.* Chicago.

Schweinfurth, U. 1983. Filarial diseases in Ceylon: A geographic and historical analysis. *Ecology of Disease* 2: 309–19.

Shanon, Gary W., and Gerald F. Pyle. 1989. The origin and diffusion of AIDS: A view from medical geography. *Annals of the Association of American Geographers* 79: 1–24.

Sri Lanka, Survey Department. 1988. *The national atlas of Sri Lanka.* Colombo.

Sutherland, Ian. 1977. Tuberculosis and leprosy. In *A world geography of human disease,* ed. G. Melvyn Howe, 175–96. London.

WHO. 1981. *World health statistics annual.* Geneva.

   1984. *Lymphatic filariasis; Fourth report of the WHO Expert Committee on Filariasis.* Geneva.

   1985. Vaccination trials against leprosy. *WHO Research and Training in Tropical Diseases* 85.3: 1–15.

   1986. *WHO Expert Committee on Malaria; Eighteenth report.* Geneva.

   1987. Multidrug therapy in leprosy control. In *World health statistics annual,* 23–4. Geneva.

   1988. Malaria control activities in the last 40 years. In *World health statistics annual,* 28–9. Geneva.

VII.4 Disease Ecologies of East Asia

East Asian scholars have begun only recently to examine Chinese, Korean, and Japanese sources for evidence of the history of disease in East Asia. Research is at a very early stage: There is much that we do not know, and some of what we think we know may turn out to be wrong. At present, scholars disagree about basic facts as well as about how to interpret them. It is possible, however, to discuss how disease ecologies changed as East Asian civilization developed, and this essay will consider how longterm historical change in East Asia altered the disease ecologies of this major world region.

East Asia is a large ecological niche bounded on all sides by less hospitable terrain. To the north and northwest lie the vast steppe lands of Central Asia and the virtually impossible Takla Makan Desert. To the west lie the high Tibetan Plateau and the Himalayan Range with the world's highest mountains. To the south is the mountainous terrain of southwest China and the jungles of Southeast Asia. And to the east lies the Pacific Ocean. These formidable barriers and the great distances between eastern and western Eurasia long separated East Asia from the ancient civilizations of the West, and permitted a distinctive culture to develop and to spread throughout the region with relatively little influence from the outside.

East Asia can be divided into two major ecological zones. The northern zone encompasses the steppe and forest lands that lie north of China's Great Wall and today includes the modern regions of Inner Mongolia and Manchuria. This vast territory is unsuitable for agriculture, and it has long been the homeland of nomadic tribes who migrate with the seasons seeking grazing lands for their livestock. The steppe supports relatively few people, and thus has been sparsely settled throughout human history. Low population density and a pastoral, nomadic way of life have prevented the buildup of endemic foci of disease organisms in any one place.

Ecological conditions south of the Great Wall are altogether different. North China, which includes the areas drained by the Yellow River and its tributaries, as well as the northern tributaries of the Yangtze River, has a temperate, semiarid climate with hot summers and cold winters. Rainfall is limited and uncertain – about 400 to 800 millimeters per year. North China is most suitable for growing millet, wheat, and beans, and one or two crops a year can be grown in a growing season that lasts from 4 to 6 months.

South China, generally the region from the Yangtze Valley to the coast of southern China, has a subtropical climate, abundant rainfall (approximately 800 to 1,600 mm per year), and temperatures that are less extreme than those of North China. Rice is the dominant crop in the south, and two or three crops can be grown during 9 to 12 months of the year. Despite these differences in climate, North and South China have been bound together historically by a dominant, distinctive culture common to them both. And in historic times both regions have supported far greater population densities than the frontier regions north of China's Great Wall.

In prehistoric times Paleolithic humans roamed over all of East Asia. Early hunters and gatherers inhabited the forests and steppes of northeastern Asia, the highlands and plains of North China, the semitropical and tropical regions of South China, the Korean peninsula, and the Japanese islands. As long as primitive humans moved from place to place in search of food, the disease ecologies of East Asia must have been essentially unchanging. Although early humans may have been afflicted with maladies caused by microparasites indigenous to the different regions of East Asia, they did not suffer from many of the diseases with which we are familiar today, because the microparasites that cause them require large and concentrated host populations that did not yet exist.

The history of changing disease ecologies in East Asia begins with the emergence of Chinese civilization in late Neolithic times. In East Asia, as in other parts of the world, human society underwent a fundamental change in the late Neolithic period when the ancestors of the Chinese people began to engage in agriculture and to live in permanent communities. This transition from shifting to permanent places of residence occurred in at least two and possibly several regions of China about 6,000 years ago. The best known Neolithic sites are found in the loess region of North China near the juncture of the Wei and Yellow rivers; however, recent excavations in the Yangtze River delta have turned up evidence of Neolithic communities that may be even earlier than those of North China. The historic relationship between these cultures is not clear, but it was from these core regions that the culture we regard as distinctively East Asian evolved.

The Neolithic Revolution in China was clearly successful. Archeological evidence and early forms of Chinese ideographic script reveal an advanced society based on labor-intensive agriculture from the time of the Shang dynasty (1765–1122 B.C.). The need for labor led to dense concentrations of people and the need for protection to walled cities where grain could be stored and defended. These fundamental changes altered the size, density, and distribution of populations on the East Asian mainland. The growth of cities brought new problems: Human and animal wastes accumulated, drinking water became contaminated, parasites that thrive in stagnant water flourished, and people who now lived close together in permanent settlements became a reservoir for microparasites that cause human disease.

The range of Chinese expansion to the south and east was virtually unlimited. As indigenous peoples took up an agrarian way of life, more land was brought under cultivation and China's population grew. From the time of the Shang dynasty to the unification of China in 221 B.C., the Chinese people were ruled by great regional lords who controlled large territories in North and South China. There are no census statistics to serve as benchmarks, but other kinds of evidence indicate that even before unification China had produced a large population. The size of armies increased 10-fold during the Warring States period (421 to 403 B.C.), and by the fourth century B.C. each of the leading states of China was able to support a standing army of about 1 million men.

In 221 B.C., Shih Huang-t'i, ruler of the state of Ch'in, conquered all of China, unifying the states and regions of North and South China. He ordered the construction of large-scale public works designed to consolidate political control and to unify China economically. These projects, which included the construction of a national network of roads and the completion of the Great Wall on China's northern frontier, offer further evidence of an abundant labor force. The latter project alone required an estimated 700,000 laborers to build.

Long periods of warfare and large public works projects helped to homogenize the disease environment. The amassing of soldiers for battle and the concentration of many thousands of workers provided an ideal environment for disease organisms to propagate. And when the participants returned home, they carried diseases to the towns and villages through which they passed. Hence, the construction of roads and canals, whose function was to strengthen centralized control, promoted the spread of disease throughout the empire.

The Ch'in dynasty was short-lived, but the consolidation of political power under centralized imperial rule continued under the dynasties that followed. The four centuries of Han rule (202 B.C. to A.D. 220) were a period of expansion in which the Chinese way of life based upon labor-intensive, irrigated agriculture became the dominant culture on the mainland. And during the Sui (581–618) and T'ang (618–907) dynasties, the completion of the Grand Canal that connected the Yangtze and Yellow rivers reinforced the links between north and south China.

Urbanization was another prominent feature of social development in the early empire. By T'ang times, China had 21 cities with more than a half-million inhabitants. The largest urban concentration was at the T'ang capital of Ch'ang-an, which had 2 million registered inhabitants. Even smaller cities like the southern port of Canton and the bustling economic center at Yangchow, where the Grand Canal joined the Yangtze River, were centers of human density large enough to serve as reservoirs for many human disease pathogens.

In short, from very early times China had one of the world's largest populations and conditions of life that could support many of the density-dependent diseases of civilization with which we are familiar today. Indeed social, demographic, and environmental conditions in the early empire were such that China must have had a full range of indigenous diseases that varied by region according to the climate, the available host and vector populations, the density and distribution of human host populations, and the sanitary conditions in those regions. But for the most part, we do not know what diseases were present in the early empire.

We do know, however, that many different kinds of human disease existed in China from very early times, because they were written about on the Shang oracle bones that were used for divination (as indicated in Lu and Needham, in this volume, VI.1). According to these ancient writings, the diseases prevalent at the time exhibited many different symptoms and were called by many different names. But whether they were caused by pathogenic agents that exist today, by related pathogens, or by unrelated pathogens is uncertain.

Introduction of New Diseases

The introduction of new diseases to a virgin population can be calamitous. The most celebrated case is known as the "great dying" that followed the introduction of Old World diseases to the New World in the sixteenth century. But contact between virulent disease-causing organisms and nonimmune populations must have been repeated over and over again in the course of human history as civilizations with different disease ecologies came into contact with one another. Thus it is appropriate to ask whether East Asian populations also suffered major demographic catastrophes as a result of the introduction of unfamiliar disease organisms.

Undoubtedly there was such a time, but Chinese historians have not defined it as such. A likely time for such an occurrence was around the beginning of the Christian era, when growth and expansion of the early empire brought China into more frequent contact with neighboring peoples to the south. By the first century B.C., a string of populous communities stretched from South China to Bengal, and by the first century A.D., traders and Buddhist missionaries were traveling overland from northern India to China through Central Asia and by way of Vietnam. Chinese scholars also traveled to India to study at Buddhist monasteries, and they returned with foreign diseases as well as foreign philosophies.

One of these foreign diseases, possibly the first to be reported in Chinese sources, was smallpox. Smallpox, a prominent, density-dependent disease of the past, is used here as a paradigm for disease in general, because it was highly visible and because changes in its incidence and distribution reflect changing disease ecologies.

It is not clear exactly when smallpox first reached China, but at least two early references to it are known. Donald Hopkins (1983) suggests that a disease called "Hun pox" that came to China from the north around 250 B.C. may have been smallpox. He also suggests a second introduction of smallpox from the south about A.D. 48, when a Chinese general and half his troops lost their lives to a "barbarian" disease as they were putting down a rebellion in southwest China. The first unmistakable description of smallpox comes from an account written in the fourth century A.D. (Leung, in this volume, VI.2). However, given the extent of earlier Chinese contact with India – where it is believed this disease was known before 400 B.C. – smallpox must have reached China earlier than the fourth century.

We do not need to know precisely when smallpox first reached China to understand that early smallpox epidemics would have been very costly in terms of human life. Smallpox normally produced a 25 percent case-fatality rate, and in virgin-soil epidemics the rate would have been much higher. Thus given China's population size and the links between many centers of density, we can be certain that the introduction of smallpox to China caused a demographic crisis of considerable magnitude.

Population trends for the early empire suggest that there were several demographic crises that might have been caused by unfamiliar diseases. Periods of population growth alternated with periods of population decline: From the Warring States period through the T'ang dynasty, China's population fluctuated, reaching and then retreating from a maximum of about 60 million people. The periods of decline during these centuries have been associated with natural disasters and China's periodic wars, but high mortality from disease, undoubtedly exacerbated by war and famine, certainly contributed to population decline.

After the initial shock waves subsided, however, the demographic characteristics of China's population would have ensured that smallpox became an endemic disease rather quickly. Hopkins estimates that a population of less than 300,000 people was sufficient to maintain smallpox as an endemic disease, because enough new susceptibles would have been borne each year to sustain the chain of smallpox infection indefinitely. As an endemic disease, smallpox would have circulated throughout the empire, appearing most frequently in the larger cities and least often in the sparse populations of the hinterlands. We know that smallpox continued to claim numerous lives in China for many centuries; however, once smallpox and other infectious diseases became endemic, the risk of a catastrophic demographic crisis would have been sharply reduced.

The history of smallpox in East Asia reveals a curious chronology in the transmission of this disease. Of particular interest is the fact that smallpox is documented much earlier in the ancient civilizations of the West. Egyptian mummies 3,000 years old have been found with scars that resemble the typical pockmarks left by smallpox; and the people of ancient Greece, as well as the people of India, are believed to have been afflicted with this disease before 400 B.C. The much later documentation of smallpox in China suggests that smallpox spread to eastern Asia from the West – a journey, if estimates of when smallpox reached China are even close to being correct, that took more than a thousand years.

The Dissemination of Disease Within East Asia

By late Han times Chinese culture began to spread to the other regions of East Asia. As the indigenous peoples of Korea and Japan began to adopt irrigated, wet-rice agriculture, their numbers increased, cities were built, and these countries began to be afflicted with the civilized diseases of China. Contact between China, Korea, and Japan increased after the sixth century, and smallpox and other epidemic diseases were spread along with Buddhism and other cultural exports.

Japanese accounts of smallpox epidemics in A.D. 585 and 735–7 provide excellent early descriptions of this disease. The smallpox epidemic of 735 came from the kingdom of Silla in southern Korea. It began in the part of Kyushu nearest to Korea, and it spread toward the major population centers in the region around the capital at Nara. Although this was not Japan's first smallpox epidemic, it caused high mortality among all age groups in the population, indicating that smallpox epidemics did not reach Japan very frequently. Wayne Farris believes that high mortality from virulent, imported diseases between 645 and 900 caused Japan to suffer a demographic setback that had a major impact on Japan's political, economic, and social development in this early period.

Once imported epidemics reached Japan, the direction of spread was invariably from the southwest – where ports of entry for foreign ships were located – to the northeast along routes where Japan's population was concentrated. Japan had a high population density very early in its history, and as in China, most diseases became endemic with little difficulty. Smallpox was clearly endemic in Japan by the twelfth century and probably well before (Jannetta 1987).

The more sparsely settled and remote areas of East Asia could still be seriously threatened by severe epidemics as late as the seventeenth century. In Japan, offshore islands, villages in the northeast, and mountainous regions remained vulnerable. In China it was the dispersed, low-density populations that lived in semiautonomous areas along the enormous northern and western frontier that were at greatest risk of suffering highly disruptive mortality from epidemics.

During the seventeenth and eighteenth centuries, the dissemination of disease intensified as these peripheral regions were gradually incorporated into the main networks that operated in East Asia. Several factors contributed to this intensification process: East Asian populations increased in size and density, urbanization accelerated in both China and Japan, contact between core and periphery increased, and activity on China's frontier intensified.

Changes in tribute relations accompanied the consolidation of Tokugawa and Ch'ing power in the seventeenth century, and promoted the dissemination of disease within East Asia. Between 1637 and 1765, contacts between China and Korea increased: An average of 3.8 tribute missions a year traveled from Korea to Peking, and in fact Korea and the Ryukyu Islands sent tribute missions to Japan as well. The King of the Ryukyus was regularly required to pay his respects to the daimyo of Satsuma and on occasion to the Tokugawa shogun in Edo (Sakai 1968). In Japan, the shogunate institutionalized contact between core and periphery with the creation of the *sankin–kotai* system. This system required that large numbers of retainers travel to Edo from each of the provinces in alternate years to pay attendance upon the shogun. All of these activities would have increased the rate of disease dissemination in Japan.

The development of interregional trade in Japan also served to disseminate density-dependent diseases throughout the islands. As outlying regions were drawn into a more widespread market network, they were also incorporated into a wider network of disease dissemination. Local records show that epidemics became more frequent in the hinterlands of Japan during the Tokugawa period. By the end of the seventeenth century, smallpox epidemics were occurring every few years in outlying villages; by the end of the eighteenth century, smallpox epidemics had become increasingly frequent on the island of Tanegashima, and in the Ryukyu Islands. Even the most isolated islands of the Izu chain south of Chiba Prefecture were stricken by smallpox – reportedly for the first time – in the late eighteenth century. By the late 1700s density-dependent diseases common to the urban centers were afflicting even the most remote regions of Japan (Jannetta 1987).

On the East Asian mainland, the disease ecology of China began to expand across the northern frontier. To the north and northwest the range of Chinese expansion had been sharply limited. The steppes of Mongolia and Manchuria and the high Tibetan wastes had no great river systems from which water could be drawn to support intensive, irrigated agriculture, and a pastoral society that stood in stark contrast to that of China had developed on China's northern frontier. The steppe had become the home of nomadic tribes whose wealth was moveable herds of livestock, not land or grain. The Great Wall of China, built to keep out the "barbarian" peoples who raided Chinese settlements, marked the frontier between two fundamentally different cultures.

The Great Wall also marks the frontier between the two major disease ecologies of East Asia. The dispersed and mobile populations north of the Great Wall had much less exposure to human pathogens than did the densely settled populations to the south. And because of infrequent exposure they were extremely vulnerable to the civilized diseases of China.

During the late Ming (1368–1644) and early Ch'ing (1644–1911) dynasties, Chinese civilization began to encroach on territories to the north, and there was increasing contact between northern Chinese and the nomadic peoples of the steppe. China's traditional policy had been to forbid trade with these barbarian enemies. But as this policy simply encouraged invasion raids and seizure of whatever goods were available, at times the Chinese government reluctantly set up official markets to facilitate the exchange of goods.

The numerous military campaigns of the late Ming period required large supplies of horses. In the second half of the sixteenth century, the Chinese set up official horse markets on China's northern frontier, where cloth and grain were exchanged for Mongol cattle, sheep, mules, and horses. Initially there were four market locations – at Tatung, Hsuan-fu, Yen-sui, and Ningsia – where horse fairs were held during the spring and summer months. In time, smaller markets were added at other places along the Great Wall where forts were situated. These small markets permitted Mongols who lived near the frontier to come to trade once or twice a month, and the regularization of these markets provided a more dependable supply of goods for Chinese and Mongol alike (Hou 1956). At the same time, more frequent contact between Mongols and Chinese permitted the dissemination of the density-dependent diseases of China to the tribal peoples of the steppe.

The disease problems that followed the growth of fairs and the border trade in the second half of the sixteenth century are documented in both Chinese and Mongol sources. The Mongols were most fearful of smallpox, which was rare in Mongolia. The biography of Tu T'ung, a military commander in Shensi, tells of an incident in which men returning from the border caught smallpox and died. The incident resulted in several border clashes, because the Mongols, who were unfamiliar with smallpox, thought that the men had been poisoned by the Chinese.

Chinese contacts constituted the gravest danger from smallpox for the Mongols, who recognized that danger and did what they could to contain the disease and prevent further contamination. It was customary strictly to avoid the stricken person, whether a parent, brother, wife, or child:

They provide [the sick] with a Chinese to take care of him; and if there is no Chinese available, they prepare his food and other necessities in a place other than their own and let the person stricken with smallpox take care of himself. . . . [T]hey regard China as a house on fire, and they refuse to stay there long for fear of contracting smallpox. (Serruys 1980)

For the Mongols the danger of exposure to smallpox and other diseases increased during the sixteenth century because of increasing contact with the Chinese. Not only did they encounter them during invasion raids and at the border markets and fairs, but also after midcentury many Chinese immigrants settled north of the Great Wall and lived intermingled with the Mongols. These communities were particularly vulnerable to high mortality from epidemic diseases. One Chinese observer claimed that the border communities had grown to 100,000 by the 1590s, but "luckily" a great epidemic had cut their numbers down by half (Serruys 1980).

The Manchus, too, had increasing problems with the civilized diseases of China. In Manchuria, as in Mongolia, smallpox was a relatively rare disease. The widely scattered populations, often on the move, had prevented the virus from gaining a foothold. However, in the late Ming as Chinese began to settle in Manchuria and as contacts between Manchus and Chinese increased, the diseases of China – smallpox in particular – became a serious threat.

An observation relating to the year 1633, when the Manchu armies were ready to invade China, indicates their awareness of this threat: "Order *beiles* who have already once contracted smallpox to lead an army from I-p'ien-shih to take Shan-hai-kuan" (Serruys 1980). The order to pick only immunized troops for an extended stay in China shows that they understood the great risk of contracting smallpox there, and they knew that those who had once had the disease would not get it again.

Even after China was conquered by the Manchus, Ch'ing legislation for the Mongol bannermen indicates that the Manchu rulers continued to take the problem of smallpox seriously. Proscriptions against going to the capital when one had not been already infected with the disease were incorporated into the Ch'ing codes. Two expressions – "those who have already had smallpox" and "those who have not yet had smallpox" – became almost technical terms in the Li-fan-yuan code, which was translated into Mongolian. Mongols who inherited a rank within the administration, and who would normally go to Peking to receive their succession, were excused if they had not yet contracted smallpox. They would go instead to Jehol for the ceremony. Although some scholars have thought that the code was designed to protect the Chinese from Mongol infections, it is clear that its intent was to protect the Mongols who would needlessly be exposed to a grave danger.

These examples illustrate the changes that took place in East Asia in the early modern period. There were real differences between the disease ecologies of the East and West, and these differences continued to be important. Unlike Africa, the Americas, and many of the more sparsely settled countries of Europe, many density-dependent diseases were already endemic in East Asia before the sixteenth century. Disease ecologies in the West were completely transformed by the discovery of the New World. The high level of epidemic mortality in the early modern West may well be related to the unusual disease exchange that took place between the urban centers of Europe and the peripheral primitive societies with relatively low-density populations with which they came in contact.

No such transformation took place in East Asia. There was much greater stability in the high-density populations of China and Japan where many diseases were endemic and circulated regularly within a relatively closed system. Thus the arrival of the Europeans in the sixteenth century changed the disease ecology of East Asia very little.

The disease environment of early modern East Asia did change, but the reason for change was totally unrelated to new foreign contacts. In East Asia the dissemination of disease intensified because of population growth, increasing urbanization, an increase in the volume of trade within the region, and the integration of more sparsely populated frontier regions into the network of civilized diseases. This process was affected very little by outside developments. In the modern period, however, when rapid transport began to connect all of the world regions, East Asia's large, high-density population emerged as a disease center that could disseminate diseases to the rest of the world.

Ann Bowman Jannetta

Bibliography

Chun Hae-jong. 1968. Sino-Korean tributary relations in the Ch'ing Period. In *The Chinese world order,* ed. J. K. Fairbank, 90–111. Cambridge, Mass.

Farris, W. W. 1985. *Population, disease, and land in early Japan, 645–900.* Cambridge, Mass.

Fujikawa, Y. 1969. *Nihon shippei shi.* Tokyo.

Hsu Cho-yun. 1980. *Han agriculture.* Seattle.

Hopkins, D. R. 1983. *Princes and peasants: Smallpox in history.* Chicago.

Hou Jen-chih. 1956. Frontier horse markets in the Ming dynasty. In *Chinese social history: Translations of selected studies,* American Council of Learned Societies.

Hucker, C. O. 1975. *China's imperial past.* Stanford.

Jannetta, A. B. 1987. *Epidemics and mortality in early modern Japan.* Princeton.

Sakai, R. K. 1968. The Ryukyu (Liu Ch'iu) Islands as a fief of Satsuma. In *The Chinese world order,* ed. J. K. Fairbank, 112–34. Cambridge, Mass.

Serruys, H. 1980. Smallpox in Mongolia during the Ming and Ch'ing dynasties. *Zentralasiatische Studien* 14: 41–63.

VII.5
Disease Ecologies of Australia and Oceania

Geography and Demography

The islands of Oceania are divided into three large geographic areas. Polynesia occupies an enormous triangle in the eastern and central Pacific, stretching from Hawaii in the north, to French Polynesia and Easter Island in the east, to New Zealand in the west. Melanesia encompasses the western island chains that lie south of the equator and extend from New Guinea to New Caledonia and Fiji. Micronesia includes the groups of islands that lie west of Polynesia and north of Melanesia. Although Polynesia is spread widely across the Pacific, the physical environments – whether volcanic high islands or coral atolls – are all quite similar in being lushly vegetated and almost all rich in food resources from land and sea. Melanesia has the greatest variety of physical environments: mountain rain forests, grassy plateaus, gorges and valleys, low jungles and alluvial plains, mosquito-ridden riverine and coastal swamps, sandy beaches, volcanic fields, and earthquake-prone rifts. In western Micronesia, weathered volcanic islands are interspersed among small, lush coral atolls. Farther to the east (Marshall Islands and Kiribati), the Micronesian atolls are generally much drier and larger. Except for temperate New Zealand and arid or temperate Australia, the climate of Oceania remains generally hot and humid year-round. It is generally accepted that Oceania and Australia were populated by waves of immigrants initially from Southeast Asia (Oliver 1962; Howe 1984; Marshall 1984). In fact, it was over

30,000 years ago that Southeast Asian hunter-gatherers crossed land bridges and narrow channels into New Guinea, Australia, and Tasmania. Intermigration among these landmasses was curtailed around 8,000 years ago, when New Guinea and Tasmania became separate islands.

A later wave of Malay-type horticulturalists from islands of Southeast Asia invaded the coasts and rivers of New Guinea about 6,000 years ago, bringing root crops, pigs, chickens, dogs, and polished tools. These agriculturalists then spread out through the islands of Melanesia around 3,000 to 4,000 years ago in their sailing canoes. At this same time, other Southeast Asian agriculturalists migrated from the Philippine Islands to Yap and the Mariana Islands and from Sulawesi to Palau, thus settling the high islands of western Micronesia. After the voyagers had settled the major islands of Melanesia, they pushed north from Vanuatu into Kiribati, thence into the Marshall Islands, and finally into the Caroline Islands about 2,000 years ago. As Micronesia was thus being settled, other voyagers advanced from Fiji east to Samoa and Tonga around 3,000 years ago. From this cradle, they moved out through the rest of eastern Polynesia – to the Marquesas 2,000 years ago and from there to the Society, Cook, and Hawaiian Islands around A.D. 600, New Zealand around A.D. 750, and Tokelau and Tuvalu and assorted scattered outliers after A.D. 1000.

With rare exception, these Pacific Basin island people were gardeners and fisherfolk, supplementing their diet with various parts of wild plants, small animals of the beach or bush, or pigs and chickens that they raised. Most lived in small hamlets of close relatives, although sizable villages were to be found especially on the coasts of the larger islands. The Australian aborigines were nomadic within circumscribed territories. Like the aboriginal Australians, the New Zealand Maori were hunters and gatherers without pigs or chickens, yams or taro. Unlike the Australians, the Maori lived in large settlements and had sweet potato and fern root as well as a rich variety of birds, reptiles, and fish to eat (Oliver 1962).

Water supplies were often limited throughout most of the region (Henderson et al. 1971). Atoll dwellers were without rivers or lakes, and had to rely on rain catchment or brackish pools. The volcanic islands generally had freshwater sources, but settlements near them caused pollution, and people living on ridgetops above them had to transport the water over long distances. Water kept near shelters was easily contaminated. Lack of abundant fresh-water for washing resulted in poor hygiene.

Indigenous Diseases

Those European explorers who commented upon the health of the indigenous people they contacted described them as strong, well-shaped, clean, noble, and generally healthy (Moodie 1973; Howe 1984). Because the weak, ill, or deformed were unlikely to be among the greeting party, such an appearance might be made even if endemic diseases were present. Although geographic isolation had protected Pacific peoples from the epidemic diseases that had swept Europe, Africa, and the New World, their continued if infrequent contacts with Southeast Asia, ever since the initial migrations to Australia and New Guinea, exposed them to some of the diseases extant there (Ramenofsky 1989). Diseases known (from explorers' journals or dated skeletal remains) to be present in the region before first contact with Europeans include malaria (restricted to Melanesia as far south as Vanuatu), respiratory infections, enteritis, rheumatism and degenerative arthritis, dental wear and decay, eye infections, filariasis, ringworm, boils, tropical ulcers, yaws, and a disfiguring ulceration of the skin. Infant mortality rates were high, and those who survived could expect to live into their thirties (Howe 1984; Denoon, with Dugan and Marshall 1989).

Contact with the Outside World

Early in the sixteenth century, the first Europeans ventured into the Pacific, beginning the waves of foreigners who reached this region carrying assorted new infectious diseases (Oliver 1962). Magellan's ships crossed the Pacific from the Americas to Southeast Asia, making the initial contact with the Marianas Islanders. Within a few decades, Guam was a regular port of call on the Spanish trade route between Mexico and the Philippines, and Spanish missionaries were proselytizing the Marianas. In the latter part of the century, Spanish explorers sailed from Peru to the Marquesas and to the islands of Melanesia before reaching the Philippines.

In the seventeenth century, Dutch traders explored the northern, western, and southern coasts of Australia, coastal New Guinea and New Ireland, and island groups in eastern and western Polynesia. British parties during this time period harried the Spanish galleons in the Pacific Basin and along the New Guinea coast, calling in at islands as fresh food and water were needed. In the latter half of the eighteenth century, British explorers first contacted most of the islands of Polynesia, including New Zealand, as well as the Marianas and the east coast of Australia. At this time, the French were charting some of the same islands in Polynesia plus groups of islands off the east coast of New Guinea.

British, French, and American missionaries; British, French, German, and American merchants; and British and American whalers began to move into the Pacific in the late eighteenth century. The British established their first permanent settlement in eastern Australia in 1788, and claimed sovereignty over Australia and New Zealand by 1840. Whaling peaked in the 1850s, but the missionaries and merchants had become a continuing feature of Pacific island life in the nineteenth century. In the latter half of that century, coconut and sugar plantations were developed on many of the islands, and "blackbirding" sailing ships raided islands in Micronesia and Melanesia for indentured laborers to work on plantations in the islands, in Peru, and in northeastern Australia. By the late nineteenth century, only residents of the interior highlands of a few large Melanesian islands had escaped extensive experience with Westerners.

In addition, Chinese, Japanese, and Filipino laborers were brought to the plantations of Hawaii, South Asian laborers to Fiji, Southeast Asian laborers to Vanuatu and New Caledonia, and Chinese traders were prevalent on many of the large islands. Gold mining operations in the late 1800s led to the importation of Southeast Asian workers who lived in overcrowded camps and towns in Melanesia under worse living conditions than laborers residing on plantations.

Commerce and communication were somewhat disrupted in the region by World War I, but the main effects of that war were the shuffling of colonial powers and the major influx into Micronesia and Melanesia of Japanese, Korean, and Okinawan businessmen, fishermen, miners, and military. Hong Kong laborers flocked to the phosphate mines of Nauru and Banaba after the war. The discovery of large deposits of gold in northeastern New Guinea, Fiji, and the Solomons in the 1920s triggered new interest in these areas and encouraged the exploration of New Guinea's central highlands by airplane. This opening up of previously impenetrable landscape by air allowed the first contact between the large populations of highlanders and Europeans. Contact among all the islands of the Pacific and between the islands and the continents bordering the Pacific was greatly facilitated by the establishment of transpacific and Australia–New Guinea air routes in the decades before World War II.

Pacific islanders suffered greatly during the Second World War. When peace finally returned, the United States replaced Japan as the colonial presence (U.N.-mandated trustee) in much of Micronesia, and joined Britain, France, Australia, and New Zealand in major disease-eradication projects in the region, made possible by the advent of new drug therapies. In the subsequent years, towns and cities have grown up, opportunities for formal education and for travel abroad have increased markedly, tourism has replaced plantation produce, and even the small islands of the Pacific Basin have become integrated into the world economy and communication network. Yet the diversity in environments and cultures remains. As in any Third World situation, many indigenous people in the urban centers face overcrowding, unemployment, poverty, poor sanitation, and easy availability of all sorts of imported foods and drugs, while their relatives in the hinterlands have poor access to any services (including health care) or often even to clean water. Mortality rates and malnutrition are often higher in remote areas than near the centers, and in most cases the indigenous people in this entire region have inadequate housing, poor screening, less pure water, inadequate food storage facilities, poor diet, inadequate waste removal, inadequate health services, and high birthrates. The greatest value this region now has to major political powers is a strategic one. In addition to hosting a few military bases, some of the islands have been sites for controversial weapons storage and nuclear testing by the United States, England, and France.

Imported Diseases

The European explorers and missionaries who first contacted the indigenes brought with them diseases common in their own homelands or in the ports they had been visiting. However, in the small isolated communities common throughout this region, most diseases could not be maintained indefinitely and needed to be reintroduced through outside contact after a new pool of susceptibles had developed. Such reintroductions were accomplished by interisland voyaging, trade among different tribal groups, explorers, merchants, whalers, missionaries, soldiers, "blackbirders," Asian laborers on plantations and in mines, and soldiers from afar. Lacking the immunity that develops after centuries of coexisting with pathogens, Pacific populations provided a "virgin

soil" for these epidemics from the rest of the world or even – in the case of malaria in the Papua New Guinea highlands – from circumscribed areas of endemicity within the region.

Because it involved translocating large numbers of people around the Pacific and concentrating them in crowded unhygienic quarters, the labor trade had a particularly devastating effect on health (Saunders 1876; Schlomowitz 1987). Laborers not properly screened or in a preclinical phase of a disease when recruited could infect the entire ship during the journey. If the pathogen survived in new susceptibles until the ship landed, the disease rapidly spread throughout the labor camp. Moreover, in addition to introducing infections, the new recruits were particularly susceptible to any diseases present in the camps. Excessively heavy work, poor shelter, lack of sanitation, poor diet, impure water, and lack of health care meant that many did not survive the first year.

Along with internecine warfare and the usual natural disasters that led to famine and water shortages, diseases in this region caused extensive loss of life before preventive or curative methods were successful. Endemic diseases regulated fertility and mortality over time; epidemics of new diseases often caused severe depopulation in all age groups when first introduced. The latter were devastating not just because of their initial toll but also because the loss of mature adults reduced the group's ability to provide food, shelter, and nursing care for itself or to reproduce itself. Pneumonia, diarrheal diseases, and – if present – malaria are still major causes of severe morbidity and mortality for infants and toddlers in the region (Prior 1968; Moodie 1973; Marshall and Marshall 1980; Townsend 1985).

However, as in other regions of the world, infectious diseases have not constituted all of the health problems in Oceania and Australia. Nutritional deficits or excesses, either alone or in concert with infectious agents or predisposing genotypes, have caused a number of important diseases, as have environmental toxins. Hemorrhage, obstructed labor, and sepsis in childbirth have had fatal consequences in the many areas where specialized care is relatively inaccessible (Marshall and Lakin 1984). The same has been true for any trauma leading to hemorrhage or sepsis. In addition, since the post–World War II years, the chronic life-style diseases (obesity, diabetes, cardiovascular disorders, cancers, substance abuse) have become common throughout most of the Pacific.

Diseases of the Region in Time and Space

Arthropod-Borne Diseases

Malaria. Malaria has been a major cause of morbidity and mortality at least in the historical period throughout Melanesia, except Fiji, New Caledonia, and certain coral atolls. Although the anopheline mosquito vector is present in Micronesia, the *Plasmodium* parasite has not been introduced. Malaria is also absent from Polynesia (Norman-Taylor et al. 1964; Gurd 1967; Willis 1970; Henderson et al. 1971). The disease was endemic in the aboriginal lands of northern Australia before its eradication in 1962. Because of the continued presence of *Anopheles* in Australia, reintroduction from New Guinea or southeast Asia remains a threat (Moodie 1973).

In New Guinea, malaria is hyperendemic in the hot, wet lowlands. As the indigenous people were "pacified" by colonial administrations and forced to live in larger village units, the resultant proximity of large groups of people and numerous small pools of mosquito-breeding water facilitated the spread of malaria (Vines 1970). It did not reach the highlands, however, until the 1930s, as a result of European road building, airstrip construction, pond and ditch digging, along with increased migration of contract workers between coastal plantations and highland homes (Riley 1983). In some remote mountain valleys, the unstable parasite pool has become nearly self-sustaining in the 1970s. *Plasmodium* cannot, however, complete its life cycle in *Anopheles* at altitudes above 2,000 meters, where temperatures are below 16°C, even though its vector can survive higher up (Nelson 1971; Sharp 1982).

Although the Polynesian outlier atolls in Papua New Guinea and the Solomon Islands were initially free from malaria, it was introduced within a decade of first European contact in the nineteenth century to Ontong Java and Sikiana (Bayliss-Smith 1975). Malaria control efforts in the 1950s–70s have had varying degrees of success (Moodie 1973; Bayliss-Smith 1975; Taufa 1978). The Institute for Medical Research in Papua New Guinea has initiated clinical trials of a malaria vaccine.

In areas of endemic malaria, the disease has its greatest effect on children from 6 months to 5 years of age. Before 6 months they are protected by maternal antibodies, and after 5 years they have generally acquired some immunity of their own from repeated infections (Burnet and White 1972). However, increased incidence of malaria in Melanesia is not necessarily associated with increased infant mortality (Van de Kaa 1967). Low-protein diets for children under 3 years of age in some New Guinea communities may increase resistance to or decrease severity of the symptoms of malaria (Lepowsky 1985).

Malaria may have indirect effects on child health as well. Decreased maternal immunity to malaria during pregnancy poses problems for fetal oxygenation and growth – and consequent infant health – in that the unchecked plasmodia clog the placenta, disrupt red blood cells, and induce high fever. Thus, birth weights in the Solomon Islands increased a few months after initiation of a malaria control program (Taufa 1978).

Malaria has been a scourge of settlers, colonists, missionaries, laborers, soldiers, and tourists in Melanesia, just as it has been of the indigenous people. Symptoms are worse for those adults who have not acquired some immunity in childhood or are malnourished. Nineteenth-century Samoan missionaries for the London Mission Society died of malaria at various stations in Vanuatu (Howe 1984). In World War II, it caused considerable mortality among the Australian, American, and presumably Japanese forces, as well as among Melanesians from regions other than the coastal lowlands (Burnet and White 1972). Tourists, anthropologists, and Peace Corps volunteers in Melanesia today regularly take their weekly antimalarial doses, which are generally available over the counter in local pharmacies.

Filariasis. Filariasis was indigenous throughout the tropical Pacific. Different strains of *Wuchereria bancrofti* are transmitted by different mosquito vectors in different regions. *Culex* in Micronesia and *Anopheles* in some of the Papua New Guinea islands as well as the Solomon Islands and Vanuatu carry nocturnally periodic strains, whereas daybiting *Aedes* transmit nonperiodic strains in Polynesia, Tuvalu, Kiribati, Fiji, and New Caledonia (Norman-Taylor et al. 1964; Iyengar 1965; Gurd 1967; Vines 1970; Henderson et al. 1971; Chowning 1989). In the first half of the twentieth century, filariasis was highly prevalent in Polynesia except New Zealand (Iyengar 1965; Henderson et al. 1971; Montgomerie 1988). In the Cook Islands in 1946, 75 percent of the school children were infected (Beaglehole 1957), as was nearly half the Tahitian population in 1949 (McArthur 1967). However, in the same time period, the disease was much less common in Papua New Guinea, the Carolines, Marshalls, Marianas, and Kiribati (Kraemer 1908; Hetzel 1959; Maddocks 1973), and the progression to elephantiasis was rare. In Fiji, adult male plantation workers generally have the highest rates of infection, although equally high rates are found in women who work near mosquito-breeding areas in pandanus and coconut groves. Filariasis is more common on the less developed islands, where screens on windows are often absent and mosquito-breeding puddles are plentiful near houses; yet it does not exist on the very small islands in this archipelago. Major mosquito eradication campaigns in the middle of this century were fairly successful in Micronesia (Henderson et al. 1971), Marquesas, Tahiti, Samoa, Tonga (Iyengar 1965), and Torres Straits islands.

Dengue. Dengue epidemics have occurred for at least a century in Oceania in places where the *Aedes* mosquito has been present, generally on lush wet islands where unscreened rain catchment is close to houses. The 1885–6 epidemics in Fiji and New Caledonia spread eastward into Tahiti, causing miscarriages and excessive mortality in children in southern French Polynesia (McArthur 1967). Wallis and Futuna experienced an epidemic in 1907, as did Torres Straits islands in the early twentieth century, the northern Cook Islands in 1930–1 (McArthur 1967), Kiribati in the 1950s, and Fiji in 1943–4 and 1953 (Wilkinson et al. 1973). Epidemics occurred infrequently in aboriginal lands in tropical northern Australia, probably arriving from nearby southeast Asia (Moodie 1973).

Dengue hemorrhagic fever, which is frequently fatal in children, appears to be a post–World War II phenomenon along major transport routes in southeast Asia and the Pacific islands. It has appeared in Tahiti and elsewhere when at least one other strain of the virus co-occurred with the type 2 strain (Chastel and Fourquet 1972; Hammon 1973). In 1971–2, major outbreaks of dengue of varying severity occurred in coastal Papua New Guinea, Vanuatu, New Caledonia, Fiji, Nauru, Kiribati, Tuvalu, Western Samoa, Tonga, Niue, and Tahiti (Pichon 1973; Wilkinson et al. 1973; Zigas and Doherty 1973). The symptoms were relatively mild in most areas, with a type 2 strain as the sole causative agent. In Rabaul, the clinical features of the type 2 infection were more severe, but hemorrhage and shock were not seen (Zigas and Doherty 1973). Over half the population of Tahiti was affected, some of whom developed hemorrhagic fever. Severe hemorrhagic symptoms and high mortality characterized the Niue outbreak that struck one-third of the population (Pichon 1973).

Although dengue had ceased to exist in Micronesia by 1948 (Hetzel 1959), it was reintroduced into Palau in the late 1980s by Indonesian drift voyagers who landed on the southwestern outer islands. Since then, cases have appeared in neighboring Yap and in Guam. *Aedes* was thought to have been eradicated in Palau, but seems to have been reintroduced from southeast Asia. Signs in an eastern Micronesian airport in 1988 warned visitors of the danger of dengue spreading from Palau.

Respiratory Diseases

Respiratory infections, which are extremely common in hot humid climates, still constitute a major cause of mortality everywhere in the Pacific region. Upper respiratory infections routinely spread throughout villages or whole island populations soon after the arrival of a ship. Transfer is rapid in the generally crowded conditions where handwashing is far less frequent than personal touching, coughs and sneezes are rarely covered, and flies are plentiful.

Influenza. Influenza epidemics followed quickly upon first contact with Europeans and continued almost annually thereafter. The disease was first reported in Tahiti in 1772, Fiji in 1791–2, Samoa in 1830, the Cook Islands in 1837 (McArthur 1967), Pohnpei before 1841, Yap in 1843, the Marshall Islands in 1859, Pingelap in 1871 (Hezel 1983), Papua New Guinea in 1889 (Allen 1989), and remote Australia before 1890 (Moorehead 1966). The first epidemic in Fiji indirectly brought on a famine because of the depletion of food resources by the excessive number of funerary feasts prompted by the heavy mortality (McArthur 1967).

Adult mortality was high in the early influenza epidemics in each location. Later, given the wide-based population pyramid, the very young began to account for the greater share of mortality, although lessened immune responsiveness at both ends of the age spectrum has made influenza a special threat to the elderly as well. Certain of the subsequent epidemics were particularly severe in the mortality they generated. Among them were those that struck New Zealand in 1838 (Owens 1972), Fiji in 1839, Tahiti in 1843, Samoa in 1837 (McArthur 1967), Pohnpei in the 1840s, Kosrae in 1856–7, Palau in 1872 (Hezel 1983), Vanuatu in 1863 (Howe 1984), Wallis and Futuna in 1870 from Fiji, Polynesian outliers in Melanesia around 1900 (Bayliss-Smith 1975), Caroline Islands in 1877, 1927, and 1937 (Marshall 1975; Nason 1975), Kiribati in 1915, 1935, and 1956, Papua New Guinea in 1957 and 1965 from eastern Australia (Warburton 1973), and Kiribati and Tuvalu in the 1960s (Henderson et al. 1971).

The influenza pandemic of 1918–19 swept across

most of the Pacific, but spared Papua New Guinea, the Marquesas, and Australia, and some remote islands in every group. Although the highest mortality rate in the world for that epidemic was in Western Samoa (25 percent), neighboring American Samoa escaped altogether by quarantining all ships in its harbor. A single ship from Auckland carried the disease to Fiji, Tonga, and Western Samoa. However, the New Zealand-dependent Cook Islands major port was infected from Tahiti, where mortality was similar to that in Western Samoa. The highest mortality throughout the region was among 15- to 40-year olds and was generally caused by secondary bacterial pneumonia (McArthur 1967; Burnet and White 1972).

Diphtheria and Pertussis. Epidemics of diphtheria and pertussis (whooping cough) have been reported in various parts of the region since colonial times. The first diphtheria outbreaks in Australia occurred at a time when the disease had intensified in England and Europe. The disease appeared in southeast Australia and Tasmania in 1858–9 and in small scattered settlements in the far west in 1864 (Burnet and White 1972). Vanuatu experienced an epidemic in the 1860s (Howe 1984). It has since been rare in isolated aboriginal Australian communities (Moodie 1973) and in Papua New Guinea, although epidemics did occur in the 1950s and 1960s in the highlands of the latter. After the construction of their jet airport in 1965, Easter Islanders experienced a diphtheria epidemic.

Pertussis has caused high mortality in the nineteenth and twentieth centuries among infants and children in the highlands and islands of Papua New Guinea (Vines 1970; Paine 1973; Lindenbaum 1979), Vanuatu (Howe 1984), Australian aborigines (Moorehead, 1966; Moodie 1973), Kiribati, Fiji, Tonga, Western Samoa, Tahiti, Leeward and Cook Islands (McArthur 1967), and New Zealand Maori (Prior 1968).

Pneumonia. Secondary pneumonia usually causes the respiratory infection fatalities in this region. Pneumonia epidemics have occurred following influenza epidemics since first European contact (Maddocks 1973). Mortality has been highest among the very young, the very old, and those in remote areas (Allen 1989). Pneumonia was rife in the goldfield labor camps in the mountains, perhaps because of the chilly nights with close contact among the workers around smokey fires and the scanty food rations which had to be carried in on workers' backs (Vines

1970; Riley 1973; Schlomowitz 1988). Because pneumonia is a particular problem for everyone in the highlands, a vaccine for the common pneumococci has been tested there recently (Riley 1973). In Papua New Guinea, pneumonia is endemic in rural areas and prevalent among young men who have recently migrated to towns (Hocking 1974). In highland Papua New Guinea domiciliary smoke has also been implicated in the *chronic obstructive pulmonary disease* (COPD), which is so common there (Vines 1970), although its high prevalence on the coast as well suggests repeated acute infections as a more likely cause (Woolcock, Colman, and Blackburn 1973).

Streptococcal Infections. Sequelae of repeated untreated *streptococcal throat infections* have also been a problem in many areas of Oceania. *Rheumatic carditis* is prevalent in Fiji (Gurd 1967), in French Polynesia, where it occurs frequently in children under 5 years of age (Houssiaux, Porter, and Fournie 1972), and among Australian aborigines (Moodie 1973) and New Zealand Maori (Prior 1968). *Poststreptococcal glomerulonephritis* is one of the most common causes of death among adult Australian part-aborigines in south Australia (Moodie 1973).

Tuberculosis. Tuberculosis, or "wasting sickness" as it was called, was introduced into Fiji in 1791 by a British ship (McArthur 1967). Reports of "consumption" among the Maori living near missionaries and sawyers from England began to increase in the 1820s (Owens 1972). Tuberculosis became common in much of Polynesia and some of Melanesia and aboriginal Australian lands by the mid-1800s, and was a major health problem for Australian aborigines by the turn of the century (Kuykendall 1966; Moorehead 1966; McArthur 1967; Moodie 1973; Bayliss-Smith 1975; Howe 1984). Interisland migration as well as ships from outside spread it widely throughout the Pacific during the nineteenth century. Although present in even remote areas of the New Guinea islands by the early 1900s (Chowning 1989), it reached the highlands only decades later. Travelers from the eastern highlands avoided overnight stays in the nearby lowland valleys because they feared tuberculosis; this custom also protected them from night-biting anophelines (Riley 1983). Tuberculosis was first introduced into certain populous areas of the highlands in 1970, and has occurred only sporadically since (Pust 1983).

The disease remains an important health problem in the modern Pacific, where crowded households and extensive sharing of personal articles facilitate spread, and intercurrent infections decrease resistance. The 1960s campaigns with screening, immunization, and chemotherapy have been at least somewhat successful in most island groups (Henderson et al. 1971).

Scrofula, characterized by tumors, wasting, neck swellings, and spinal curvature, was widespread in Polynesia in the early nineteenth century. A number of authors have equated it with tubercular adrenitis. Said to have been brought to Tahiti by British and Spanish explorers in the eighteenth century, scrofula was carried by Tahitian teachers to the Cook Islands in the 1830s, where it spread throughout the group in a time of famine, causing many deaths over the next 15 to 20 years (McArthur 1967).

Other Infectious Diseases

Leprosy.   Leprosy was introduced into the region by Asian workers and immigrants in the nineteenth century, then spread with interisland migration. Although called the "Chinese disease" in Hawaii, the actual circumstances of introduction to those islands are unknown. It was present in the 1830s, and numerous cases were reported in 1863, a few years before the Molokai leper colony was established to isolate the afflicted. Hundreds were sent to Molokai over the years, yet many remained in their own communities. Hawaiian islanders did not fear the disease and therefore resisted this internment (Kuykendall 1966). Leprosy appears to have entered New Zealand in the 1850s, perhaps with Asian travelers, but was rare until the 1900s (Montgomerie 1988). Australian aborigines in the northeast acquired the disease from infected Chinese and Melanesian laborers in the nineteenth century (Moodie 1973). It was present in New Guinea in 1875 (Maddocks 1973) and was brought into the northern Cook Islands in 1885 by a native son who had spent several years in Samoa with a leprosy sufferer from Hawaii (McArthur 1967). The disease spread to Easter Island (where it is still greatly feared) from Tahiti, and although widespread in Polynesia in 1900, it still had not reached the Caroline Islands (Kraemer 1908).

After World War II, leprosy also become widespread in Micronesia west of the Marshall Islands (Hetzel 1959), but was brought under control – even in a spot of high incidence – by 1970 (Sloan et al. 1972). In the 1970s, it was still sufficiently prevalent in Polynesia (including outliers), Fiji, and Kiribati, that immigrants to New Zealand from these islands

reintroduced the disease every year (Gurd 1967; *Leprosy Review* 1973). Shared sleeping mats have been suspect in areas of increasing incidence. Leprosy is present throughout Melanesia as well (Gurd 1967; Willis 1970; *Leprosy Review* 1973; *WHO Weekly* 1973). In Papua New Guinea, the highest incidence is in the highlands, although it is also prevalent along the New Guinea coast (Vines 1970; Russell 1973). There are endemic foci among the northern Australian aborigines, but it is rare in other aboriginal communities (Moodie 1973). Many cases in rural areas remain undetected, so rates all over the region may actually be much higher. Outpatient treatment has largely replaced the leprosy hospitals built earlier this century (Henderson et al. 1971).

Measles.   Measles, although present in much of the Pacific Rim in 1800, did not reach eastern Australia until 1828 and Hawaii until 1848. In the 1850s, it spread throughout Australia, to New Zealand, and into the islands (McArthur 1967; Cliff and Hagget 1985). In 1875, a London Mission Society ship carried measles along the Papuan coast of New Guinea. In the same year, a ship carrying Fijian royalty home from a visit with the governor of Sydney transported the virus to Norfolk Island, the Solomon Islands, and Vanuatu as well. The effect on Fiji was particularly devastating, as over a thousand representatives from most of the individual islands had gathered to greet the ill prince and to celebrate for 2 weeks Fiji as a new Crown Colony before dispersing home. The sudden loss of so many adults in Fiji, Tahiti, and Vanuatu contributed to the heavy mortality, as few remained able to provide food or care (Cliff and Haggett 1985).

Similar epidemics struck Kiribati in 1890 (Lambert 1975), and Tonga and Western Samoa in 1893 (McArthur 1967). Quarantine kept Fiji from all but local port outbreaks until 1903, when measles again swept through the group. The 1911 outbreak was mild on most islands, but severe in those few remote islands that had escaped earlier. Every epidemic thereafter came at shorter intervals, caused fewer deaths, and affected ever younger children only (Cliff and Haggett 1985). The same pattern – sporadic epidemics that become more frequent and less severe – has occurred everywhere in the region with regular outside contact or large populations. Small remote islands still have rare epidemics with variable mortality (McArthur 1967; Van de Kaa 1967; Brown and Gajdusek 1970; Vines 1970; Willis 1970; Henderson et al. 1971; Moodie 1973; Lindenbaum 1979; Cliff and Haggett 1985).

Rubella. Rubella epidemics have been recently documented for Guam, remote Micronesian atolls, Western New Guinea, and Papua New Guinea and have been associated with excessive hearing impairment from in utero exposure (Brown and Gajdusek 1970; Stewart 1971; Allen 1989).

Mumps. Mumps was already present in the Cook Islands when it reached Samoa on a ship from California in 1851 (McArthur 1967). The disease subsequently spread over much of the region, although it did not appear in the New Guinea highlands until the 1940s (Lindenbaum 1979).

Scarlet Fever. Scarlet fever caused deaths among foreigners in French Polynesia and the Cook Islands in 1846–7, but remained mild among the islanders (McArthur 1967). Symptoms are similarly mild among Australian aborigines in recent times (Moodie 1973).

Chickenpox. In the twentieth century, chickenpox became more common and is now widespread in the region. High prevalence was reported from numerous island groups, New Guinea, and Australia in the 1930s (Moodie 1973; Allen 1989). In fact, it has been suggested that some of the smallpox reported for Australia and Papua was actually chickenpox (Maddocks 1973; Moodie 1973).

Smallpox. Smallpox epidemics in the Pacific region resulted primarily from contact with outsiders. The first reported epidemic was in the Spanish colony of Guam in 1688 (Carano and Sanchez 1964). A century later, within a year of the founding of Port Jackson (now Sydney) in 1788, smallpox erupted among the aborigines camped nearby. The immune settlers were relatively unaffected, but large numbers of aborigines died (Moorehead 1966).

Trade ships and whalers brought the disease to many islands: Gambier in 1834, Tahiti in 1841, Pohnpei in the 1840s and in 1854, Hawaii in 1853–4, the Maori, Palau, and Polynesian outliers in Melanesia in midcentury, Papua in 1865, and the New Guinea coast in 1870–90. In many of these cases, sick passengers or crew were put ashore and died on the island, passing the disease to any who helped them. Islanders visiting the port spread the virus to their home communities nearby (McArthur 1967; Kuykendall 1968; Owens 1972; Maddocks 1973; Bayliss-Smith 1975; Nason 1975; Allen 1983, 1989; Hezel 1983).

The labor trade also introduced smallpox from Asia and South America. In the 1860s, Polynesians returning to their homes after years of involuntary servitude in the mines of Peru contracted smallpox on board the ships (McArthur 1967). The first shipload of plantation workers from India introduced smallpox and cholera to Fiji in 1879. The need to train vaccinators locally led to the construction of the Suva Medical School in 1885 (Lander 1989). Cantonese laborers reintroduced the disease as they slipped undetected into Hawaii in 1881 (Kuykendall 1967). Before 1900, Javanese laborers for the plantations along the New Guinea coast introduced smallpox as they arrived. It spread into the nearby coastal mountains, up the Sepik River and across the channel to New Britain to remote areas not yet contacted by Europeans (Allen 1989; Chowning 1989).

Yaws. Yaws was present in the Pacific region prior to outside contact. Before the eradication campaigns of the mid-twentieth century, yaws was found among Australian aborigines, and in all of Melanesia, western Polynesia, Micronesia, French Polynesia, and Hawaii. Conversely, it was not present in New Zealand, Gambier, Easter, or Pitcairn Islands (Hetzel 1959; Pirie 1971–2; Moodie 1973). It occurred less commonly in particularly dry, cool, or high-altitude areas or in islands settled late.

Yaws was usually acquired by children from regular playmates. After recovery from the debilitating skin lesions, solid immunity to treponeme-caused yaws and to syphilis as well is attained. Incidence of yaws decreased as people washed with soap and covered their bodies with clothes (Pirie 1971–2). After World War II, the disease was virtually eradicated by penicillin injections, although antibodies remained in those who had been infected (Norman-Taylor et al. 1964; Fischman and Mundt 1971; Henderson et al. 1971; Davenport 1975). Some pockets of infection remained after the campaigns in the Marshall Islands (Hetzel 1959) and tropical northern Australia (Moodie 1973).

Hepatitis. *Hepatitis B* has been highly prevalent in the 1980s in Micronesia and in American Samoa, where public health posters announce "Hep is not hip." The Australia antigen for identifying the virus was isolated in 1967 from the blood of an anemic Australian aborigine who had received numerous transfusions. In the Solomon Islands, the antigen was commonly present in those with no clinical symptoms or predisposing history (Burnet and White 1972).

Hepatitis A is endemic in much of island Oceania

and tropical Australia, subclinically infecting most of the indigenous population under age five (Moodie 1973), as might be expected in view of the warm climate and casual hygiene among children.

Poliomyelitis.   Poliomyelitis, being epidemiologically similar to infectious hepatitis in unvaccinated populations, was endemic in tropical Australia and the Solomon Islands before World War II, but provided only rare instances of paralysis (Cross 1971; Moodie 1973). Before the massive vaccination campaigns of the 1960s, most Guamanian under 3 years of age were already immune (Burnet and White 1972). Western and American Samoa experienced an epidemic in 1935 with highest mortality and morbidity among young adults rather than children. New Guinea and Guam had also been "virgin soil" for earlier polio epidemics (Burnet and White 1972). After World War II and before vaccination, epidemics occurred across the South Pacific (Peterson et al. 1966; Cross 1971). Vaccination and quarantine finally limited the spread (Peterson et al. 1966).

Acquired Immunodeficiency Syndrome (AIDS).   AIDS has surfaced in various indigenous Pacific population in 1988–9. It is now present among urban-dwelling Australian aborigines, as well as among the people of Papua New Guinea, French Polynesia, Tonga, Marshall Islands, Guam (Karel and Robey 1988), Fiji (*Pacific Island Monthly* 1988), Northern Marianas, American Samoa (but not Western Samoa), and Hawaii (information received at the Hawaii exhibit, Fifth International Conference on AIDS, Montreal). On the other hand, extensive screening in the Solomon Islands and Papua New Guinea found no individuals with the virus (HIV) in 1985–6.

Venereal Diseases
Syphilis and *gonorrhea* were brought into the Pacific by early explorers and whalers. Because syphilis might have been mistaken for yaws, tropical ulcer, scrofula, leprosy, or gonorrhea, confusion exists about the circumstances of introduction even though early ships' logs did comment on the presence of venereal diseases. In tropical Australia and the wet islands of the southwestern Pacific, where yaws was highly prevalent and promiscuity was not customary, syphilis has been a relative newcomer; in cooler New Zealand and drier or more recently settled islands of Micronesia and eastern Polynesia where yaws was less common and Europeans and island women often mixed more freely, syphilis was re-

corded soon after regular contact. British and French explorers in 1767–9 gave each other credit for the syphilis in Tahiti reported by Captain James Cook in 1769 and spread elsewhere in French Polynesia by explorers over the next few decades. Cook's surgeon wrote that the ship's crew introduced syphilis accidentally to Tonga in 1777 and knowingly to Hawaii in 1779, although other observers stated that the disease was present earlier in Hawaii (Moorehead 1966; McArthur 1967; Pirie 1971–2; Smith 1975; Stannard 1989). Venereal syphilis was found among the Maori before 1840 and became more prevalent but with milder symptoms by 1855 (Pirie 1971–2; Owens 1972). Pohnpei, Kosrae, the Marshall Islands, and Kiribati were also infected by whalers and traders in the 1840s and 1850s, but a century later the disease there had become almost nonexistent (Hezel 1983). Syphilis was unknown in northern Australia before 1939, but since then has spread among the aborigines around the country (Moodie 1973). Papua New Guinea highlands, where yaws had never existed, experienced an epidemic of syphilis in 1969, after the new highway opened up access. It was first reported in 1960 and has remained largely confined to the highlands (Lindenbaum 1979; Lombange 1984).

Gonorrhea, often referred to in the region as "venereal disease," was first noted in 1769 in Polynesia and 1791 in Palau. Whalers, traders, and beachcombers passed gonorrhea back and forth with islanders in the 1830s through 1850s in the Caroline and Marshall islands, French Polynesia, and Hawaii, which were popular ports of call with more relaxed sexual attitudes than in most of western Polynesia or Melanesia (Pirie 1971–2; Hezel 1983). Venereal disease did reach one frequently visited Polynesian outlier by the 1850s, but has never been present on its more remote neighbors (Willis 1970; Bayliss-Smith 1975). The first reports of venereal disease on Papua New Guinea coasts were in 1902–8, but it has since become prevalent throughout the country (Pirie 1971–2; Lombange 1984). Thus with rare exceptions, the disease has become ubiquitous in Oceania, as it has in Australia in the same time period (Moorehead 1966; Moodie 1973).

Food- and Waterborne Diseases
Enteric infections flourish in conditions commonly found throughout this region (Marshall and Marshall 1980; Allen 1983; Burton 1983; Reid 1983). They are often fatal in the very young or in those who for any reason quickly become dehydrated in the hot climate. Gastroenteritis is ubiquitous, al-

though less common in nomadic or low-density populations (Willis 1970; Reid 1983).

Cholera. Discrete epidemics of cholera have occasionally occurred. It was reported in Kiribati in 1841, among the Maori in 1838 and after 1840 (Owens 1972), and carried into Fiji by new South Asian plantation laborers (Lander 1989). Cholera has not been documented for either Papua New Guinea or Australia, even though the easily spread El Tor strain was present in neighboring western New Guinea and Sulawesi in 1962 (Moodie 1973; Riley 1983). Still a threat in modern times, cholera broke out in Kiribati in the late 1970s. An infected crewmember on a Japanese fishing vessel debarked in Truk, causing a major epidemic in 1982–3 which, until recently, devastated the tourist trade.

Diarrhea, Dysentery, and Clostridial Diseases. Epidemics of the "bloody flux," or *bacillary dysentery,* have plagued Pacific islanders at least since 1792, when a British explorer brought it to Tahiti. Unlike measles, these epidemics did not become more frequent and less severe with repetition in a given population. Severe epidemics of bacillary dysentery were often associated with concurrent civil wars, famines, typhoons, droughts, measles, incarceration on labor vessels, employment on the goldfields in Papua New Guinea, or ship visitations (McArthur 1967; Prior 1968; Bayliss-Smith 1975; Allen 1983; Burton 1983; Howe 1984; Schlomowitz 1988). Two notable epidemics of bacillary dysentery occurred in Papua New Guinea during World War II: one introduced by Japanese in the course of building an airstrip on the north coast using indigenous labor, and one introduced by members of an American military team in the central highlands. Australian soldiers also brought dysentery that they had earlier picked up in North Africa (Allen 1983; Burton 1983). The Marshall Islands have had epidemics of dysentery in recent years soon after imported chicken has been off-loaded and sold in local stores. It is endemic in most groups of aborigines (Moodie 1973). *Typhoid fever* and *amebic dysentery* have appeared throughout the islands and Australia as well (Hetzel 1959; Gurd 1967; McArthur 1967; Burnet and White 1972; Moodie 1973).

The third leading cause of death in the Papua New Guinea highlands is *enteritis necroticans,* known locally as *pigbel.* Peak incidence of this syndrome of bloody diarrhea, stomach pain, nausea, and vomiting occurs at 4 years of age. Those over 40 years old generally have developed immunity to the causative agent, *Clostridium perfringens* beta toxin. Feasts with literally heaps of pork occasionally punctuate the usual highland low-protein, largely sweet potato diet. *Clostridia* enter the slaughtered pork as it sits in the dirt and is handled regularly for about 4 days before the feast. It is ingested with the meat, colonizes the gut, and produces a toxin that should be inactivated by intestinal trypsin. However, protein deprivation or the presence of trypsin inhibitor from sweet potato (or from the ubiquitous *Ascaris*) prevents the enzyme from doing so. A vaccine for the toxin became available in the 1980s (Lindenbaum 1979; Murrell 1983).

Another clostridial disease, *tetanus,* occurs widely in the Pacific islands and Australia, even in areas without domestic animals (Gurd 1967; Moodie 1973; Lindenbaum 1979). The disease is not found on Easter Island, however, even though horses, cattle, goats, sheep, *Clostridium tetani,* and bare feet are common. Immunization as part of prenatal care in Papua New Guinea has reduced mortality from neonatal tetanus, which was once very high in rural areas where umbilical cords were cut with contaminated objects (Townsend 1985).

Helminth-Transmitted Diseases

Intestinal-dwelling *nematodes* have been very common in the Pacific region wherever the soil is moist enough to keep their eggs alive. Generally prevalence of *Ascaris* and *Trichuris* is lower on dry atolls (e.g., Marshall and northern Cook islands) or in lowland rainforests (as on the New Guinea coast). However, the southern Cook and Caroline islands rainforests have had very high rates, whereas *Ascaris* is rare in Vanuatu (Hetzel 1959; Norman-Taylor et al. 1964; Vines 1967, 1970). *Ascaris* is widely distributed in aboriginal lands in Australia, but is more common in the cooler drier south (Moodie 1973). *Enterobius* is ubiquitous (Vines 1967). Hookworms have had a low prevalence in Kiribati and isolated Pitcairn and Easter islands but are plentiful on wet lowlands. *Necator* has been far the more common parasite, although *Ankylostoma* has replaced it in Vanuatu. They have been highly prevalent in aboriginal lands in Australia, except in the Central Desert. They spread out from the tropical north with cattleherders. Eradication campaigns in many islands and among the Australian aborigines have had no enduring effect (Hetzel 1959; Norman-Taylor et al. 1964; Vines 1967, 1970; Willis 1970; Moodie 1973).

Zoonoses

Other health problems have arisen as well from the close association between humans and various animals in this region. The disabling or even fatal dog tapeworm is common among Australian aborigines who keep dogs closeby in their camps (Moodie 1973). *Cysticercosis,* from pig tapeworm, was first introduced into the densely populated pig-raising highlands of Western New Guinea via a gift of infected pigs from nearby Bali in 1971. Within 4 years it had spread to the border with Papua New Guinea, and within 10 years had become a major cause of morbidity and mortality in that region, which has been a hotbed of rebellion against the alienation of Papuan lands by Indonesian settlers (Hyndman 1988).

Since 1948, epidemics of *eosinophilic meningitis* generally attributed to ingestion of rat lungworm, *Angiostrongylus,* have been reported in small areas dotted across the Pacific: New Caledonia, Pohnpei, Cook Islands, Tahiti, and Hawaii. In some of these cases, shellfish eaten raw were the intermediaries (Rosen et al. 1967).

Toxoplasmosis is endemic in much of Oceania and Australia, where cats appear to play a critical role in transmission (Wallace, Marshall, and Marshall 1972; Moodie 1973). Contact through breaks in the skin with water or mud contaminated with the urine of rats, pigs, or cattle has been responsible for *leptospirosis* among Australian aborigines working in sugarcane fields, as swineherds, or as stockmen in tropical northeastern Australia. This infection causes intermittent fever and meningitis (Burnet and White 1972). *Bubonic plague* persisted for 10 years in seaport rats in southeastern Australia before eradication efforts succeeded (Burnet and White 1972). *Scrub typhus* mites flourished in grassy clearings away from human villages in Papua New Guinea and northeastern Australia, causing minimal problems for indigenes but becoming the second leading cause of death – after malaria – among the foreign soldiers cutting through the Bush there in World War II (Burnet and White 1972).

Diet-Related Diseases

Anemia. Anemia is widespread among women in Oceania, especially at sea level. The proportion of women having hemoglobin levels below 12 grams-percent is higher than in any other region of the world (Wood and Gans 1981; Royston 1982). Anemia is especially common among children in Vanuatu and among New Zealand Maori (Norman-Taylor et al. 1964; Prior 1968). It has been documented occasionally for Micronesia, less in the western Carolines than in the Marianas or Marshalls (Hetzel 1959). Diet and malabsorption problems are respon-

sible for the high prevalence of iron-deficiency anemia among Australian aborigines (Moodie 1973).

Protein–calorie deficiency does occur, mostly in poor remote areas of the New Guinea mainland. Diet on the smaller islands, while simple, is usually sufficient (Vines 1970).

Goiter and *cretinism* have been problems in patches in inland Melanesia, where highland people have had to trade with coastal people for their sea salt. In 1955, colonial patrols worsened the situation in the Papua New Guinea highlands by trading in noniodized salt, which the highlanders preferred to their traditional supply. A campaign in the 1960s to reverse the deficiency with injections of iodized poppyseed oil was successful (Henderson et al. 1971; Lindenbaum 1979).

Diabetes and Obesity.   Chronic diseases have increasingly become primary causes of morbidity and mortality in industrialized societies since the 1950s as immunization and chemoprophylaxis have reduced infectious diseases, as sedentary wage employment has become available, and as imported foods constitute an ever-growing share of people's diets. These diseases are distributed unevenly, occurring far less regularly in remote rural areas.

Non-insulin-dependent *diabetes mellitus* (NIDDM) is unusually prevalent among certain Pacific societies: Australian aborigines (Moodie 1973), New Zealand Maori (Prior 1968), Cook Islanders (Prior 1968), American Samoans (Baker and Crews 1986; Hanna and Baker 1986), Marshall Islanders and I-Kiribati (King et al. 1984), Nauruans (Patel 1984; Taylor and Thoma 1985), Torres Straits islanders (Patel 1984), Fijian women (King et al. 1984), and residents of Papua New Guinea's most acculturated urban but not rural or highland areas (Savige 1982; Patel 1984). The disease is more common among the wealthy (34 percent prevalence in affluent Nauru), the more acculturated, the urban, and perhaps the female. Its meteoric rise in the mortality statistics has paralleled increases in dietary refined carbohydrates and calories and decreases in exercise and dietary fiber.

Obesity even beyond the cultural ideal has also accompanied these changes in all of these areas as well as in the Marquesas and Solomons (Friedlaender and Rhoads 1982; Darlu, Couilliot, and Drupt 1984). Yet similar dietary changes and decreased activity level have not led to obesity or NIDDM on Easter Island. The familial tendency apparent within these populations and the extremely high rates among certain related island groups suggest a partial genetic basis. According to J. M.

Hanna and P. T. Baker (1986), the metabolic ability to gain weight rapidly and hold it may have given a selective advantage for long interisland voyaging with limited space to transport food. Crowding and psychosocial stress in acculturated urban areas may also play a role in the etiology. Compliance with treatment regimes (diet, exercise, daily insulin) in the absence of frank clinical symptoms has been low, especially among men who avoid seeking help unless their problem is evident and severe.

Surveys of blood pressure after World War II indicated that for most Pacific people, adult blood pressures averaged lower than for equivalent age groups in industrialized societies and did not rise with age (Norman-Taylor et al. 1964; Vines 1970; Shaper 1972; Moodie 1973; Gee 1983; Patrick et al. 1983; Ward 1983). However, in recent years *hypertension* and age-related increases have become much more common in areas where modern wage-earners are concentrated, obesity is obvious, and imported salt intake is high (Prior 1968; Henderson et al. 1971; Moodie 1973; Gee 1983; Patrick et al. 1983; Ward 1983; Taylor and Thoma 1985; Hanna and Baker 1986; Prior 1986). Coronary artery disease is also becoming more common in these same situations (Hanna and Baker 1986).

Chronic Degenerative Neurological Diseases

Certain chronic degenerative neurological diseases that have close parallels in the industrialized world have been highly prevalent in very restricted locations in Oceania. *Kuru*, a subacute spongiform cerebellar encephalopathy caused by an unconventional slow virus, has been present in the Fore area of the eastern highlands of Papua New Guinea since 1920. In the 1950s, it was the most common cause of death in adult women and in children 5 to 16 years old in that area. The unusual age distribution was due to the local practice – extant from 1910 to 1955 – of cannibalism. The dead were consumed by female kin and young children of either sex. The virus entered via cuts in the skin as the flesh and brain were prepared. Two to 20 years later, symptoms appeared: ataxia, tremoring, pain, slurred speech, loss of smooth and voluntary muscle control, and pathological laughter. Death followed within nine months. The number of cases declined progressively after cannibalism was discontinued (Burnet and White 1972; Gajdusek 1977; Lindenbaum 1979).

Since before World War II, the indigenous Chamorro of the Marianas Islands have had an extremely high incidence of a syndrome with varying combinations of *Alzheimer-like dementia, amyotro-phic lateral sclerosis,* and *Parkinsonism.* Occasional cases with similar symptoms have also been found among Caroline Islanders, Filipinos, and Caucasians resident in the Marianas. The syndrome has also appeared in Chamorros 30 years after leaving Guam. Until recently, the Chamorro ate great quantities of the false sago plant seeds, which contain a toxin that causes degeneration of the same motor neurons that disappear in amyotrophic lateral sclerosis and Parkinsonism. On the other hand, a genetic susceptibility to the effects of such a toxin in this population has not been ruled out (Mathai 1970; Lewin 1987).

High incidence of an autosomal recessive *congenital blindness* (tapetoretinal degeneration with cataracts) on a single Carolinian atoll has been attributed to the fact that the island was almost isolated in the 2 centuries following the 1780 typhoon that killed all but nine of the men on the island (Brody et al. 1970).

Ciguatera, a frequently fatal fish poisoning caused by a curare-like toxin present in certain fish throughout the region, has been of grave concern in the Pacific islands where fish is the major protein food. The source of the toxin appears to be algae that grow on submerged World War II equipment or nuclear testing apparatus and are consumed by the fish. It has been reported in French Polynesia, Guam, Marshall Islands, and Hawaii, all of which provide appropriate surfaces for the algal growth (Banner et al. 1963; Henderson et al. 1971; Bagnis 1972).

Afterword

Oceania and Australia have been spared many of the major scourges of the tropical Third World: schistosomiasis, trypanosomiasis, onchocerciasis, and leishmaniasis. Yet they have coexisted for millennia with malaria, filariasis, and other troublesome diseases. Through contact with Asia and the New World in the past several centuries, they were exposed to all of the major epidemic diseases, which have largely become preventable childhood illnesses. The continued lack of comprehensive public health programs for basic sanitation, hygiene, and home screening in the region means that the threat of fatal epidemics as in the past still remains. Lack of refrigeration and transportation problems make it difficult to deliver antibiotics and vaccines to those in need.

In the more affluent areas, decreasing infant mortality rates, a sedentary life-style, and a change in diet have permitted an increasing number of people who reach adulthood, and who may be particularly genetically susceptible, to experience chronic diseases generally more common in industrialized areas. Although the recreational drugs of the West became available only after first contact and were often prohibited to indigenes until recently, substance abuse has become a major problem. In recent years the islanders and Australian aborigines exposed to experimental radioactive fallout have shown the world some of the minor health complications of nuclear warfare, which would be – for all – the final epidemic.

Leslie B. Marshall

The author is deeply grateful to M. Marshall, D. Denoon, H. Hethcote, and G. Rushton for providing essential bibliographic resources. The author also wishes to thank J. Armstrong, J. Boutilier, L. Carrucci, J. Fitzpatrick, D. Hrdy, B. Lambert, D. Lewis, M. Maifield, C. Murry, K. Nero, N. Pollock, U. Prasad, M. Scott, B. Zzferio, and a Hawaii public health representative for providing valuable information.

Bibliography

Allen, B. J. 1983. A bomb, a bullet or the bloody flux? *Journal of Pacific History* 18: 218–35.

　1989. Infection, innovation and residence. In *A continuing trial of treatment,* ed. S. Frankel and G. Lewis, 35–68. Dordrecht.

Bagnis, R. 1972. La Ciguatera: Un problème original d'oceanographic médicale. Nouvelle tentative d'explication de sa cause. *Médicine de l'Afrique Noire* 19: 27–34.

Baker, P. T., and D. E. Crews. 1986. Mortality patterns and some biological predictors. In *The changing Samoans,* ed. P. T. Baker, J. M. Hanna, and T. S. Baker, 93–122. Oxford.

Banner, A. H., et al. 1963. Fish intoxication: Notes on ciguatera, its mode of action and a suggested therapy. SPC Technical Paper No. 141.

Bayliss-Smith, T. P. 1975. The central Polynesian outlier populations since European contact. In *Pacific atoll populations,* ed. V. Carroll, 286–343. Honolulu.

Beaglehole, E. 1957. *Social changes in the South Pacific.* London.

Brody, J. A., et al. 1970. Hereditary blindness among Pingelapese people of Eastern Caroline Islands. *Lancet* 1: 1253–7.

Brown, P., and D. C. Gajdusek. 1970. Disease patterns and vaccine-response studies in isolated Micronesian populations. *American Journal of Tropical Medicine and Hygiene* 19: 170–5.

Burnet, M., and D. O. White. 1972. *Natural history of infectious disease,* 4th edition. London.

Burton, J. 1983. A dysentery epidemic in New Guinea and its mortality. *Journal of Pacific History* 18: 236–61.

Carano, P., and P. C. Sanchez. 1964. *A complete history of Guam.* Rutland.

Carroll, V. 1975. The population of Nukuoro in historical perspective. In *Pacific atoll populations,* ed. V. Carroll, 344–416. Honolulu.

Chastel, C., and R. Fourquet. 1972. Responsabilité du virus dengue type 2 dans l'épidémie de dengue de Taihiti en 1971. *Review of Epidemiology* 20: 499–508.

Chowning, A. 1989. The doctor and the curer. In *A continuing trial of treatment,* ed. S. Frankel and G. Lewis, 217–47. Dordrecht.

Cliff, A. D., and P. Haggett. 1985. *The spread of measles in Fiji and the Pacific.* Canberra.

Crane, G. G., R. W. Hornabrook, and A. Kelly. 1972. Anaemia on the coast and highlands of New Guinea. *Human Biology in Oceania* 1: 234–41.

Cross, A. B. 1971. The rehabilitation of poliomyelitis cripples in the Solomons. *South Pacific Bulletin* 21: 32–3.

Darlu, P., M. F. Couilliot, and F. Drupt. 1984. Ecological and cultural differences in the relationships between diet, obesity and serum lipid concentrations in a Polynesian population. *Ecology of Food and Nutrition* 14: 169–83.

Davenport, W. 1975. The population of the outer reef islands, British Solomon Islands Protectorate. In *Pacific atoll populations,* ed. V. Carroll, 64–116. Honolulu.

Denoon, D., with K. Dugan and L. Marshall. 1989. *Public health in Papua New Guinea.* Cambridge.

Dompmartin, D., E. Drouhet, and L. Improvisi. 1970. Aspects cliniques et mycologiques de "tinea imbricata" (Tokelau). *Bulletin de la Société Française de Dermatologie et de Syphiligraphie* 77: 186–90.

Firth, S. 1987. *Nuclear playground.* Honolulu.

Fischman, A., and H. Mundt. 1971. Test patterns of yaws and antibodies in New Zealand. *British Journal of Venereal Disease* 47: 91–4.

Friedlaender, J. S., and J. G. Rhoads. 1982. Patterns of adult weight and fat change in six Solomon Island societies: A semilongitudinal study. *Social Science and Medicine* 16: 205–15.

Gajdusek, D. C. 1977. Unconventional viruses and the origin and disappearance of kuru. *Science* 197: 943–60.

Gee, R. W. K. 1983. The epidemiology of hypertension in the South Pacific. *Papua New Guinea Medical Journal* 26: 55–61.

Gurd, C. H. 1967. Health problems in the Pacific Islands. *New Zealand Medical Journal* 66: 211–13.

Hamblett, E. P. 1968. Tuberculosis in the British Solomon Islands Protectorate (1958–1965). SPC Technical Paper No. 157.

　1969. Tuberculosis in the Gilbert and Ellice islands colony (1964–1968). SPC Technical Paper No. 161.

Hammon, W. McD. 1973. Dengue hemorrhagic fever: Do we know its cause? *American Journal of Tropical Medicine and Hygiene* 22: 82–91.

Hanna, J. M., and P. T. Baker. 1986. Perspectives on health and behavior of Samoans. In *The changing Samoans,* ed. P. T. Baker, J. M. Hanna, and T. J. Baker, 419–84. Oxford.

Henderson, J. W., et al. 1971. *Area handbook for Oceania.*

Hetzel, A. M. 1959. Health survey of the Trust Territory of the Pacific Islands. *U.S. Armed Forces Medical Journal* 10: 1199–222.

Hezel, F. X. 1983. *The first taint of civilization.* Honolulu.

Hocking, B. 1974. Health problems and medical care in Papua New Guinea. *International Journal of Epidemiology* 3: 9–13.

Houssiaux, J. P., J. Porte, and L. J. Fournie. 1972. Où est le rhumatisme articulaire aigue en Polynésie française? *Médecine de l'Afrique Noire* 19: 93–101.

Howe, K. R. 1984. *Where the waves fall.* Honolulu.

Hyndman, D. 1988. How the west was won. *Pacific Islands Monthly* 58: 32–4.

Iyengar, M. O. T. 1965. Epidemiology of filariasis in the South Pacific. SPC Technical Paper No. 148, November.

Karel, S. G., and B. Robey 1988. AIDS in Asia and the Pacific. *Asian and Pacific Population Forum* 2: 1–30.

Kerr, A. R. 1972. TB and Polynesians. *New Zealand Medical Journal* 76: 295.

King, H., et al. 1984. Risk factors for diabetes in three Pacific populations. *American Journal of Epidemiology* 119: 396–409.

Kraemer, A. 1908. Die Medizin der Truker. *Archiv für Schiffs- und Tropen-Hygiene* 12: 456–64.

Kuykendall, R. S. 1966. *The Hawaiian kingdom (1854–1874),* Vol. II. Honolulu.

1967. *The Hawaiian kingdom (1874–1893),* Vol. III. Honolulu.

1968. *The Hawaiian kingdom (1778–1854),* Vol. I. Honolulu.

Lambert, B. 1975. Makin and the outside world. In *Pacific atoll populations,* ed. V. Carroll, 212–85. Honolulu.

Lander, H. 1989. A century of service. *Pacific Islands Monthly* 59: 20–2.

Lepowsky, M. A. 1985. Food taboos, malaria and dietary change: Infant feeding and cultural adaptation on a Papua New Guinea island. In *Infant care and feeding in the South Pacific,* ed. L. B. Marshall, 58–81. New York.

Leprosy Review. 1973. Leprosy in the South Pacific. 44: 7.

Leproux, P., and P. R. Lande. 1972. Profil physiologique de Tahiti et de ses archipels. *Médecine de l'Afrique Noire* 19: 103–10.

Lewin, R. 1987. Environmental hypothesis for brain disease strengthened by new data. *Science* 237: 483–4.

Lindenbaum, S. 1979. *Kuru sorcery,* Chaps. 2–3. Palo Alto.

Lombange, C. K. 1984. Trends in sexually transmitted disease incidence in Papua New Guinea. *Papua New Guinea Medical Journal* 27: 145–57.

Maddocks, I. 1973. History of disease in Papua New Guinea. In *The diseases and health services of Papua New Guinea,* ed. C. O. Bell, 70–4. Port Moresby.

Marshall, L. B., and J. A. Lakin. 1984. Antenatal health care policy, services, and clients in urban Papua New Guinea. *International Journal of Nursing Studies* 21: 19–34.

Marshall, L. B., and M. Marshall. 1980. Infant feeding and infant illness in a Micronesian village. *Social Science and Medicine* 14B: 33–8.

Marshall, M. 1975. Changing patterns of marriage and migration on Namoluk atoll. In *Pacific atoll populations,* ed. V. Carroll, 160–211. Honolulu.

Marshall, M., ed. 1982. *Through a glass darkly: Beer and modernization in Papua New Guinea.* Boroko.

Marshall, M. 1984. Structural patterns of sibling classification in island Oceania: Implications for culture history. *Current Anthropology* 25: 597–637.

1987. An overview of drugs in Oceania. In *Drugs in western Pacific societies,* ed. L. Lindstrom, 13–50. Lanham.

Marshall, M., and L. B. Marshall. 1975. Opening Pandora's bottle: Reconstructing Micronesians' early contacts with alcoholic beverages. *Journal of the Polynesian Society* 84: 441–65.

Mathai, K. V. 1970. Amyothrophic lateral sclerosis and Parkinsonism dementia in the Marianas. *American Journal of Tropical Medicine and Hygiene* 19: 151–4.

McArthur, N. 1967. *Island populations of the Pacific.* Canberra.

Miles, J. A., et al. 1973. A serological study on the occurrence of some respiratory infections in Fiji. *Human Biology in Oceania* 2: 79–96.

Montgomerie, J. Z. 1988. Leprosy in New Zealand. *Journal of the Polynesian Society* 97: 115–52.

Moodie, P. M. 1973. *Aboriginal health.* Canberra.

Moorehead, A. 1966. *The fatal impact: An account of the invasion of the South Pacific (1767–1840).* New York.

Murrell, T. G. C. 1983. Pigbel in Papua New Guinea: An ancient disease rediscovered? *International Journal of Epidemiology* 12: 211–14.

Nason, J. D. 1975. The strength of the land: Community perception of population on Etal atoll. In *Pacific atoll populations,* ed. V. Carroll, 117–59. Honolulu.

Nelson, H. E. 1971. Disease, demography and the evolution of social structure in highland New Guinea. *Journal of the Polynesian Society* 80: 204–16.

Norman-Taylor, W., et al. 1964. A health survey in the New Hebrides. SPC Technical Paper No. 143.

Oliver, D. O. 1962. *The Pacific islands,* revised edition. Cambridge.

Owens, J. M. R. 1972. Missionary medicine and Maori health: The record of the Wesleyan mission to New Zealand before 1840. *Journal of the Polynesian Society* 81: 418–36.

Pacific Islands Monthly (PIM). 1988. AIDS in the islands. 59: 30.

Paine, B. G. 1973. Pertussis in the highlands: A clinical review. *Papua New Guinea Medical Journal* 16: 36–41.

Patel, M. S. 1984. Diabetes, the emerging problem in Papua New Guinea. *Papua New Guinea Medical Journal* 27: 1–3.

Patrick, R. C., et al. 1983. Relationship between blood pressure and modernity among Ponapeans. *International Journal of Epidemiology* 12: 36–44.

Peterson, C. R., et al. 1966. Poliomyelitis in an isolated population: Report of a type 1 epidemic in the Marshall Islands, 1963. *American Journal of Epidemiology* 82: 273–96.

Pichon, G. 1973. Lutte contre la dengue dans le Pacifique Sud. Institut de Recherches Médicales Louis Malarde et Service des Endémies. Report No. 167/IRM/J.5.

Pirie, P. 1971–2. The effects of treponematosis and gonorrhea on the populations of the Pacific Islands. *Human Biology in Oceania* 1: 187–206.

Prior, I. 1968. Health. In *Maori people in the 1960s,* ed. E. E. Schwimmer, 270–87. New York.

Pust, R. E. 1983. Clinical epidemiology of tuberculosis in the Papua New Guinea highlands. *Papua New Guinea Medical Journal* 26: 131–5.

Radford, A. J. 1973. Balantidiasis in Papua New Guinea. *Medical Journal of Australia* 1: 238–41.

Ramenofsky, A. F. 1989. Another perspective on acculturation and health in highland New Guinea. *Current Anthropology* 30: 67–8.

Reid, J. 1983. *Sorcerers and healing spirits.* Canberra.

Riley, I. D. 1973. Pneumonia in Papua New Guinea. *Papua New Guinea Medical Journal* 16: 9–14.

    1983. Population change and distribution in Papua New Guinea: An epidemiological approach. *Journal of Human Evolution* 12: 125–32.

Rosen, L., et al. 1967. Studies on eosinophilic meningitis: Epidemiologic and clinical observations on Pacific islands and the possible etiologic role of *Angiostrongylus cantonensis. American Journal of Epidemiology* 85: 17–44.

Royston, E. 1982. The prevalence of nutritional anemia in women in developing countries. *World Health Statistics Quarterly* 2: 52–91.

Russell, D. A. 1973. Leprosy in Papua New Guinea. *Papua New Guinea Medical Journal* 16: 83–5.

Saunders, K. 1976. The Pacific Islander hospitals in colonial Queensland. *Journal of Pacific History* 11: 28–50.

Savige, J. 1982. Diabetes mellitus in the Tolais of the Gazelle Peninsula, New Britain. *Papua New Guinea Medical Journal* 25: 89–96.

Schlomowitz, R. 1987. Mortality and the Pacific labor trade. *Journal of Pacific History* 22: 34–55.

    1988. Mortality and indentured labor in Papua (1885–1941) and New Guinea (1920–1941). *Journal of Pacific History* 23: 70–9.

Shaper, A. G. 1972. Cardiovascular disease in the tropics: Blood pressure and hypertension. *British Medical Journal* 3: 805–7.

Sharp, P. T. 1982. Highlands malaria: Malaria in Enga Province of Papua New Guinea. *Papua New Guinea Medical Journal* 25: 253–60.

Sloan, N. R., et al. 1972. Acedapsone in leprosy chemopro-

phylaxis: Field trial in three high-prevalence villages in Micronesia. *International Journal of Leprosy* 40: 40–7.

Smith, H. M. 1975. The introduction of venereal disease into Tahiti: A re-examination. *Journal of Pacific History* 10: 38–45.

Stannard, D. E. 1989. *Before the horror: The population of Hawaii on the eve of Western contact.* Honolulu.

Stewart, J. L. 1971. Rubella-deafened children in Guam. *South Pacific Bulletin* 21: 15–17.

Taufa, T. 1978. Malaria and pregnancy. *Papua New Guinea Medical Journal* 21: 197–206.

Taylor, R., and K. Thoma. 1985. Mortality patterns in the modernized Pacific island nation of Nauru. *American Journal of the Public Health* 75: 149–55.

Townsend, P. K. 1985. *The situation of children in Papua New Guinea.* Boroko.

Van de Kaa, D. J. 1967. Medical work and changes in infant mortality in Western New Guinea. *Papua New Guinea Medical Journal* 10: 89–94.

Vines, A. P. 1967. Intestinal helminthiases in the South Pacific area. South Pacific Commission Seminar on Helminthiases and Eosinophilic Meningitis, Noumea, New Caledonia. June, SPC/SHEM/WP.3.

    1970. *An epidemiological sample survey of the highlands, mainland, and islands regions of the Territory of Papua and New Guinea.* Port Moresby.

Wallace, G. D., L. Marshall, and M. Marshall. 1972. Cats, rats, and toxoplasmosis on a small Pacific island. *American Journal of Epidemiology* 95: 475–82.

Walzer, P. D., et al. 1973. Balantidiasis outbreak in Truk. *American Journal of Tropical Medicine and Hygiene* 22: 33–41.

Warburton, M. F. 1973. Epidemiology of influenza in Australia and Papua New Guinea. *Medical Journal of Australia* 1 (special supplement): 14–18.

Ward, R. H. 1983. Genetic and sociocultural components of high blood pressure. *American Journal of Physical Anthropology* 62: 91–105.

WHO Weekly Epidemiology Record. 1973. Leprosy (B.S.I.P.). 48: 229–30.

Wilkinson, P. J., et al. 1973. *The 1971–1972 dengue epidemic in Fiji.* Otago, N.Z.

Willis, M. F. 1970. The Takuu islanders: Health and social change in an atoll population. *South Pacific Bulletin* 20: 39–42.

Wood, C. S., and L. P. Gans. 1981. Hematological status of reproductive women in Western Samoa. *Human Biology* 53: 268–79.

Woolcock, A. J., M. H. Colman, and C. R. B. Blackburn. 1973. Chronic lung disease in Papua New Guinea and Australian populations. *Papua New Guinea Medical Journal* 16: 29–35.

Zigas, V., and R. L. Doherty. 1973. An outbreak of dengue in the Rabaul community. *Papua New Guinea Medical Journal* 16: 42–5.

VII.6
Disease Ecologies of the Caribbean

The Pre-Columbian Period

The belief that the American Indians were indigenous persisted until relatively recently. But today it is generally accepted that the first Americans were actually wandering Asians who took advantage of the prevailing ice age to cross the Bering Straits from Siberia to Alaska and enter a continent devoid of human life. Then, perhaps 10,000 years ago most of the large ice caps melted and seas rose, inundating the land bridge and sealing off the Asian pioneers in what would later be called the New World.

They were hunter-gatherers, these pioneers, with a nomadic way of life, which meant that when a band became too numerous to function efficiently, a part would break off and move on to new lands. Gradually this hiving out took them southward, and archeological remains tentatively suggest that some 9,000 years ago the southerly thrust finally came to an end as they reached the southern tip of South America.

It seems to have been much later, however, that the first humans settled the islands of the Caribbean, although there is neither a firm date nor agreement on the mainland from which those first to arrive came. For example, the northern Antilles, Cuba, is a short sailing distance from both southern Florida and the Yucatan Peninsula, whereas on the other end of the island chain, to the southeast, lies Trinidad, just off the South American continent.

When the first Spaniards reached the Caribbean, they found at least four Indian cultures whose bearers had apparently arrived at different times, with the levels of those cultures reflecting the stage of human development on the mainlands when the migrations occurred. There is some evidence to indicate that one of these peoples may have come from Florida, although this is in dispute. Most, however, came from the northeast of South America. Because of these various migrations it is probably safe to assume that the Caribbean Indians carried most of the same kinds of pathogens as their mainland counterparts, meaning that they too were blessed with a freedom from illnesses that had been denied to most of the rest of the world's peoples for millennia. The pioneers who had crossed into the Americas made that crossing before the Old World was caught up in its Neolithic revolution. This was before Old World hunter-gatherers with stone tools (which the pioneers were) became sedentary farmers with metal tools, and settled down to domesticate plants and animals and, not incidentally, to propagate disease.

The animals that gave these Old World farmers milk, eggs, meat, and hides also passed on bacteria and viruses and helminthic parasites that flourished in the new environment, which humans were creating for them. Unlike hunter-gatherers who were always on the move, sedentary farmers stayed put to pass those pathogens back and forth among themselves through fouled water supplies, mounting human garbage, and filthy housing that harbored insects, rodents, and other assorted pests adept at spreading illness. Moreover, no sooner did one group develop immunities to local ailments than human migration and trade brought them into contact with another group and new diseases, or new and deadly strains of old diseases.

The later construction of cities also saw the construction of a near perfect pathogenic paradise to provide a last crucial step in the immunologic tempering of Old World peoples. Crowded together as they were, spitting, coughing, and breathing on one another, surrounded by the excrement of humans and animals alike to contaminate all they consumed with the aid of swarms of flies buzzing about, the city peoples were natural targets for epidemic disease. But their growing numbers meant that diseases once epidemic soon became endemic and thus became childhood diseases to be endured as a kind of a rite of passage that would ensure immunity against them as adults.

By extreme contrast, New World populations experienced very little of this sort of immunologic preparation. Rather, their pioneering ancestors had left home before the Old World Neolithic Revolution had begun. Thus, they came without animals with whom to share diseases, while those humans who were sick or weak would have been summarily weeded out by the hardship and cold inflicted on them in their passage to Alaska. The result was that the salubrious environment of the Americas remained relatively disease-free despite human invasion.

One says "relatively," because by 1492 a New World Neolithic Revolution had been under way for some time. Many had settled into sedentary agriculture, some animals had been domesticated, and some complex civilizations such as the Mayas, Incas, and Aztecs had long before constructed large cities. Thus, some kinds of tuberculosis had developed, at least among the city dwellers, and they were tormented by ailments that derived from their water and food such as intestinal parasites and hepatitis. In addition, pinta seems to have been endemic among those in warmer climates whose dress was sufficiently scanty to permit ready skin-to-skin transmission. Whether they had venereal syphilis has long been a matter of dispute, with one of the reasons for that dispute being that pinta would have provided some cross-immunity against syphilis.

There is little question, however, that the New World Indians were "virgin soil" peoples for the host of diseases about to descend on them from Eurasian and African Old Worlds. In the words of Alfred Crosby (1986), "They seem to have been without any experience with such Old World maladies as smallpox, measles, diphtheria, trachoma, whooping cough, chicken pox, bubonic plague, malaria, typhoid fever, cholera, yellow fever, dengue fever, scarlet fever, amebic dysentery, influenza and a number of helminthic infestations."

The diet of the Indians of the hemisphere, in contrast, was apparently considerably more varied than their diseases. In the Caribbean, the principal nutriment of those engaged in sedentary agriculture came from manioc (yucca), which they grew in cultivated fields and processed into a bread, which the Spaniards called "cassava." Corn was not the important staple that it was elsewhere in the Americas, but it did supplement some West Indian diets as did white and sweet potatoes, beans, pumpkins, and peanuts. With no domesticated animals save for a kind of dog (sometimes eaten), animal protein was served up mostly in the form of fish along with certain reptiles and insects.

Fishing, however, appears to have been more a leisurely activity than an industry, and it would seem that animal protein played a fairly minor role in the diet. This essentially vegetable diet based largely on manioc, which is notorious for its lack of important nutrients, coupled with the Spanish observation that the Indians ate very sparingly, suggests that they probably suffered from some nutritional deficiencies, and these, in combination with the Indians' lack of disease immunities, would have rendered them even less able to ward off the Old World illnesses about to arrive.

European Diseases

Perhaps no other region on the globe has ever experienced such a sudden and devastating ecological assault as the islands of the Caribbean with the arrival of the Europeans. Ship after ship arrived to disgorge humans bearing Old World pathogens in their blood, bowels, and hair, and on their breaths and skin. Disease-bearing insects and rodents winged their way and scampered ashore, while cattle, horses, and especially hogs wobbled down gangplanks on stiff legs to begin munching and trampling their way across the fragile flora of the islands, reproducing wildly as they went with no natural predators to thin their numbers.

The long-run consequence of this Old World invasion is that today the islands are truly artificial; only their limestone, volcanic rock, coral, and the underlying mountain ranges upon which they rest are of this hemisphere. The plants that grow on them, along with the animals and humans that inhabit them, are practically all Old World immigrants.

Of the pre-Columbian island inhabitants, the humans were the first to depart, and their disappearance unfortunately was accomplished very quickly. They left behind them little more than a few artifacts and the unanswered question of how numerous they were prior to the arrival of Columbus so that the magnitude of the demographic disaster that befell them can be measured. There has been a tendency to disregard early Spanish estimates as excessive and to portray the West Indies as sparsely populated. More recently, however, considerably more respect has been accorded the earlier estimates, and the size of pre-Columbian populations is being revised sharply upward. For example, S. F. Cook and W. W. Borah (1971, 1974, 1979) have calculated that the island of Hispaniola (today the Dominican Republic and Haiti) contained close to 4 million Indians; they suggest that by 1508 that population had dwindled to less than 100,000, thereby providing us with at least a glimpse of the holocaust of disease the islands had become.

Another glimpse comes from Cuba, which was conquered in 1511. Just a few short years later, Francisco López de Gomara could write that this island "was once heavily populated with Indians: today there are only Spaniards." This of course was an impression only, and the Cook and Borah estimate, although based on an array of evidence and informed demographic reasoning, remains an estimate only. Yet knowledge of what specific diseases have done to immunologically defenseless peoples lends a good deal of plausibility to theories that urge the existence of much larger pre-Columbian populations than previously believed.

Francisco Guerra (1988) argues convincingly that the first epidemic disease unleashed on the Indians was swine influenza; it reached the West Indies in 1493 with swine brought by Columbus from the Canary islands on his second voyage. Certainly some disease began sweeping the islands shortly after the discovery and long before smallpox apparently made its Caribbean debut. There were reports of massive die-offs not just in Hispaniola but in Cuba and the Bahamas as well.

Typhus had surfaced in Spain during the war with Granada and doubtless also reached the islands (and the Indians) even before smallpox began its relentless assault on Hispaniola in 1518, and on Cuba the following year. There ensued a decade during which dozens of other diseases were probably introduced, before the next reported epidemic, measles, which struck in 1529.

Swine influenza has been known on occasion to precipitate mortality levels as high as 20 to 25 percent of a population, and smallpox has killed upward of 40 percent of a people experiencing it for the first time; measles, a relatively benign disease for Europeans, has thinned the ranks of "virgin soil" peoples by 25 percent; whereas typhus has historically produced mortality for between 10 and 40 percent of those ill with the disease.

Clearly then, with maladies capable of producing these high levels of mortality, conceivably the pre-Columbian populations of the Caribbean could have been much larger than heretofore believed. This also ignores mortality generated by other illness such as chickenpox, diphtheria, scarlet fever, typhoid, whooping cough, and bubonic plague, all of which were also introduced from Spain. No wonder then, that by 1570 most of the Indians of the region had vanished. Only the Caribs still survived in the eastern Caribbean – an area not yet much frequented by the Europeans.

It is important to note, however, that all of these maladies struck equally hard at mainland populations. But although they also experienced massive die-offs, the survivors slowly built immunities, and after a century or two those populations began to grow once again. But this was not the case in the West Indies. Part of the reason was that the Caribbean was a corridor through which all Europeans had to pass to reach various parts of the mainland; therefore, those in the corridor had more exposure to disease than those outside it. But the main reason was that the West Indian Islands became the target of still another wave of disease – this time from Africa. The most deadly of these diseases were mosquito-borne and seldom reached up into the cooler elevated regions of the mainlands, which were home for so many Indians, but they turned the low-lying areas of the West Indies into one huge death

trap for the remaining original Americans as well as for the white newcomers who up to this point had found the islands reasonably healthful.

African Diseases

Vivax malaria probably arrived in the blood of the first Europeans and, although a relatively benign form of the disease, nonetheless joined in the slaughter by claiming its share of Indian lives. As the Indian die-off progressed, the Spaniards found themselves forced to look elsewhere for hands to put to work colonizing the Americas, and they chose the black African. By 1518 the transatlantic slave trade was under way, which almost immediately opened a conduit for the transatlantic flow of a much more deadly form of the disease: falciparum malaria.

The circumstances surrounding the introduction of yellow fever from Africa are less clear: Although it is now generally accepted that the anopheline mosquitoes that spread malaria were on hand in the New World to do just that, the *Aedes aegypti* vector of yellow fever most probably was not. Thus both vector and virus had to be imported and to reach human populations dense enough to support them. A case has been made that all of these conditions were met by 1598 at San Juan, Puerto Rico, and there is absolutely no question that they were met by 1647 when yellow fever launched assaults on Barbados and Guadeloupe, before continuing on to Cuba and the Gulf coasts of Mexico and Central America.

The slaves had lived with both of these tropical killers for eons and in the process had developed a relative resistance to them. But in addition, they were also accustomed to most of the other Old World illnesses that had proven so devastating to the Indians. The ironic result of this ability to resist disease was that it made blacks even more valuable as slaves. The Indians died of European and African diseases, the whites died of African diseases, but the blacks were able to survive both, and it did not take the Europeans long to conclude that Africans were especially designed for hard work in hot places.

This view was not limited to the Spaniards, although they had been the first to discover the blacks' durability. Other Europeans had begun trickling into the Caribbean, impelled from their mother countries because of wars, religion, politics, crimes committed, or just outright lust for adventure and riches. They settled first on the islands of the eastern Caribbean, which had been left relatively untouched by the Spaniards, and brought disease to, and ultimately an end to, the surviving Caribs.

If at first these new arrivals grew any "cash

crops," they grew tobacco in small plots, which the Dutch, by then ubiquitous in West Indian waters, marketed for them. All this changed abruptly, however, when the Dutch, who had moved into Brazil, were driven out, taking with them the secrets of sugar production. These they gave to the small planters of the eastern Caribbean along with financial assistance, and the sugar revolution was under way. Tobacco growers became sugar planters, small tobacco plots were consolidated into large sugar plantations, and the demand for black labor soared. The Dutch met that demand with their slave ships, which brought African pathogens as well as Africans, both of which had heretofore only trickled into the Caribbean and now began to pour in.

In addition to yellow fever and falciparum malaria came the filarial worm, also carried by mosquitoes, to create the infamous disease "Barbados leg." It seems to have broken out on that island first, but soon was widespread throughout much of the Caribbean, although always strangely absent in Jamaica. The Africans also carried with them the misnamed hookworm *Necator americanus,* which found the West Indian sugarcane fields an especially favorable habitat. That dracunculiasis was rife among them could be noted as Guinea worms poked their heads out of slave legs to be patiently wound on a stick by the victim until all of the worm was removed. In addition, yaws blossomed on the bodies of slave youngsters, leprosy assaulted the adults, and onchocerciasis invaded the eyes of both. Indeed, even smallpox began arriving from African rather than European reservoirs, and the Caribbean was transformed practically overnight into an extension of an African, as opposed to a European, disease environment.

Paradoxically, the increasing dangers of such an environment paralleled the increasing value of the West Indian Islands in the eyes of the capitals of Europe. As colonies that sustained a slave trade, purchased products from mother countries, and supplied sugar for processing to those countries, the islands fit marvelously into – indeed helped to shape – the prevailing mercantilist philosophy, a part of which prescribed grabbing as many more islands as possible from European competitors.

The political consequence was that Europe's wars of the seventeenth and eighteenth centuries were fought out in the islands as well as on the continent. The epidemiological consequence was the slaughter of tens of thousands of nonimmune soldiers and sailors sent to do that fighting who died, not from battle, but from yellow fever and malaria. During the years 1793–6, for example, the British lost 80,000 troops

in the West Indies, the bulk of them to this pair of tropical killers. Much of that mortality had been sustained during the British invasion of San Domingue, where the slaves were revolting against French masters. Because of their ability to resist the disease, the ex-slaves had a strong ally in yellow fever, as the disease counterattacked the British with deadly effect.

Next came the French attempt to retake San Domingue. Briefly they met with success. Then they met with yellow fever and within 10 months of landing had lost some 40,000 men including 1,500 officers and their commander, Napoleon's brother-in-law.

Yellow fever flourished in the Caribbean wherever the virus discovered a sufficient number of nonimmune persons to host it, for the *A. aegypti* is a domesticated mosquito that lives close to and feeds on humans and breeds in rain-filled gouges humans have made in the earth or in any of the discarded accoutrements of civilization that hold water. Anopheline mosquitoes that carry malaria, however, are not so tied to humankind and consequently are not spread evenly across the Caribbean. Thus August Hirsch (1883–6) identified Cuba, Jamaica, Santo Domingo, Guadeloupe, Dominica, Martinique, St. Lucia, Grenada, Trinidad, and Tobago as the places where the disease was most prevalent. He termed malaria "rare" in the Bahamas, Antigua, St. Vincent, and Barbados, where today we know that for a variety of reasons anopheline mosquitoes had difficulty in breeding successfully.

It should be stressed that, although yellow fever and malaria were the chief killers of whites in the West Indies, the victims were generally newcomers. Old residents, by contrast, usually suffered from yellow fever while quite young, at an age when the malady is relatively gentle with its victims, and in the process earned a lifetime of immunity against another visitation. Similarly, resistance to malaria was gained by repeated bouts with the disease although this was not so perfect an immunity as that acquired against yellow fever.

Blacks, on the other hand, although remarkably resistant to these diseases, suffered greatly from other illnesses that generally bypassed whites, and their resulting experience with disease was so different from that of whites that physicians were moved to write whole books on the subject. They identified one of the most fearful diseases of slave infants as the "9-day fits," which today would be diagnosed as neonatal tetanus triggered by an infected umbilical stump. Another example of a presumed black disease came from the same source. Plantations were littered with the droppings of horses and oxen containing tetanus spores, so the almost always fatal illness struck hard at slaves with open wounds resulting from frequent accidents with machinery, and because almost all went barefoot.

Poor nutrition, however, was probably the biggest destroyer of slave life, either directly because of nutritional diseases or indirectly because it left slaves less able to combat other ailments. Their basic diets of very little salted fish (jerked beef in Cuba) and lots of manioc and other root crops, plantains, rice, and corn produced symptoms of frank beriberi (related to thiamine deficiency) and pellagra (related to niacin deficiency) among slaves all across the Caribbean. Of the two, beriberi had the greatest demographic impact because thiamine deficiency is passed along from mother to infant in her milk, and infantile beriberi has proved historically to be almost invariably fatal.

Another major disease of the slave young was protein–energy malnutrition (PEM) brought on by a lack of whole protein in the diet. Slave infants were nursed by their mothers for about 3 years and were thus safe from the disease, which struck after they were weaned to a diet of pap almost totally devoid of good-quality protein. Some developed marasmus, a symptomatic pole of PEM in which the child simply wastes away. More often, however, they developed the swollen bellies of kwashiorkor, which are evident in physicians' descriptions of slave children. The prevalence of PEM in Barbados can be assumed from the conclusions of an investigation of the teeth of excavated slave skeletons, which revealed considerable nutritional stress at the time of weaning (Handler and Corruccini 1986).

The term *dropsy* was very frequently recorded as the cause of slave deaths, and doubtless when a child died of kwashiorkor, this was called dropsy. Similarly, the fluid accumulations of wet beriberi would have been called dropsy. Other dropsy cases were probably the work of hypertensive heart disease. Apparently in the largely salt-free environment of sub-Saharan Africa, black bodies had developed an ability to retain the mineral that is crucial to life itself (Wilson 1986). In the West Indies, however, slaves received an abundance of the mineral in their salted fish or beef, and in addition, were issued a great deal more as a condiment. For a people with the knack for retaining salt, this must have provoked much fluid accumulation and frequently proved deadly.

Dry beriberi's symptoms are remarkably similar to those of a mysterious illness of the slaves called the *mal d'estomac* in some islands and *hatiweri* or *cachexia Africana* in others. Physicians first thought that the lack of energy, breathlessness, and nerve problems including an unsteady, high-stepping gait – the symptom constellation of *mal d'estomac* – were caused by dirt eating; later investigators have suspected that the cause was hookworm disease. But because, as will be discussed shortly, blacks of West African origin are very resistant to the ravages of hookworm infection, dry beriberi remains the best explanation for this particular ailment.

Another disease that remained a mystery at least until recently, and which struck white troops as well as slaves, was the "dry belly ache." But research by Jerome Handler, Arthur Aufderheide, and others (1986) has made it clear that this ailment was actually lead poisoning; the lead being ingested in non-aged rum made with distilling equipment containing the metal and from molasses and sugar whose production also involved the leaching of lead from some of the equipment.

The successful slave revolution in San Domingo brought ruin to one major sugar-producing area of the Caribbean, whereas the abolition of the British slave trade in 1807, and then of British slavery in 1833, severely damaged most other sugar islands. This left the field to Cuba, which developed a flourishing contraband slave trade, and became the new focus of such African diseases as filariasis, leprosy, and yaws while at the same time achieving the unhappy distinction of becoming the nineteenth-century yellow fever capital of the hemisphere.

Other diseases also became prevalent during this period. Typhoid, for example, was an increasingly serious health problem in the West Indies throughout the century, although in part this trend doubtless reflects nothing more than better diagnosis as physicians learned to untangle typhus and typhoid from each other and both from the whole bundle of fevers that bedeviled the region. Because the fouled water supplies that brought typhoid were serious problems everywhere, it was predictable that the islands would pay a steep price for this condition when the pandemics of Asiatic cholera reached them. This first occurred in Cuba where, during the years 1833–6, the disease wiped out at least 8 percent of the slave population.

The 1850s, however, were the real cholera years for the Caribbean during which as many as 34,000 slaves in Cuba perished, between 40,000 and 50,000 individuals died in Jamaica, another 20,000 to 25,000 lives were lost in Barbados, and at least 26,000 succumbed in Puerto Rico. Cholera returned a final time to Cuba in 1867, where it claimed a few thousand more lives before leaving the region forever. In its wake, however, it left a far greater percentage of black than white victims. Because there is no racial predisposition to cholera, the best explanation for this lies in the impoverished circumstances of blacks on the one hand and lesions of nutrition that deprived them of gastric acid to fight cholera vibrios on the other (Kiple 1985).

The fact that tuberculosis waited until the nineteenth century to fall on blacks with the fury that it did is less easy to explain. Tuberculosis was not one of the Euroasian diseases that blacks had experienced in Africa, and they proved to be extraordinarily susceptible to it when exposed. That such exposure was so long delayed suggests that the plantation probably served as a kind of quarantining device. After slavery, however, the disease exploded among them as many impoverished blacks crowded into the cities. In Havana, for example, the disease generated mortality rates approaching 1,000 per 100,000 population.

Nonetheless, although tuberculosis continued to rage, it was during the last half of the nineteenth century that much of the region began to experience a significant decline in mortality. Certainly some of the decline was due to nothing more than the end of slavery. But empirical observation also played a considerable role. Cholera had drawn attention to the dangers of bad water, and the last decades of the century witnessed important efforts to improve water supplies, with a resulting decrease in the prevalence of typhoid and dysentery. Empirical observation had also established once and for all the efficacy of quinine against malaria, and its regular use also brought important mortality reductions.

Cuba, however, was largely exempted from the mortality decline enjoyed elsewhere during this period. No sooner had the contraband slave trade come to an end, capping the pipeline of disease from Africa, and no sooner had cholera receded than the Ten Years' War (1868–78) erupted. Soldiers arrived from Spain to extinguish the rebellion only to introduce smallpox and be extinguished themselves by that disease in tandem with yellow fever and malaria. A few years later, this pattern was repeated as Spain once more sent soldiers to Cuba to quell the rebellion that began in 1895. In both instances, yellow fever and malaria claimed far more lives than did bullets, with war and disease slashing Cuba's population from about 1.8 million in 1895 to 1.5 million in 1899 – fully a 15 percent reduction in less than 5 years.

The Twentieth Century

The twentieth century has been a time of a tremendous mortality decline in the Caribbean as it has in much of the rest of the underdeveloped world. Improved nutrition, great strides in public health and sanitation, and the increasing sophistication of modern medicine have all played significant roles.

Yellow fever's Caribbean career came to a close during the occupation of Cuba by the United States when the theory of Cuban physician Carlos Finlay that the disease was mosquito-borne was proved correct by a Yellow Fever Commission headed by Walter Reed. Ensuing mosquito control measures were successful in throttling the long-dreaded malady in Cuba, and, armed with this new epidemiological understanding of the disease, William Gorgas was able to eliminate yellow fever in Panama where the canal was under construction. The disease flared up one last time in Cuba in 1905 but, after that, retreated from the whole of the Caribbean.

The public health activities of the U.S. Army also brought sweeping sanitary reforms to Cuba, which in Havana resulted in a decrease of "close to 30 percent in the crude death rate in that city by 1902" (Diaz-Briquets 1983). Similarly the annexation of Puerto Rico, and the occupation of the Dominican Republic and Haiti by the United States, although deplorable, nonetheless brought important health benefits to these countries in the form of cleaner water supplies, adequate sewage disposal systems, mosquito control, and medical treatment.

Just at the time when one African disease, yellow fever, was conquered, however, another African malady was revealed. In Puerto Rico, the Puerto Rico Anemia Commission discovered a hookworm problem estimated to be causing one third of all deaths on the island. War was declared on this disease, as well as on malaria and yaws, in much of the Caribbean by the Rockefeller Sanitary Commission and later by the Rockefeller International Health Board. The Rockefeller physicians in the West Indies and in the southern United States discovered that black people were resistant to hookworm disease although not to hookworm infection, whereas pockets of poor whites and Asians in the West Indies living side by side with blacks suffered severely from the disease.

Tuberculosis receded among Caribbean blacks as mysteriously as it had appeared, and it had ceased to be much of a health problem long before the end of World War II when medicine finally got its "magic bullet" against the malady. Yet the greatest gains in reduced mortality have taken place among the very young. Infant mortality rates, which were as high as

303 per 1,000 live births in Barbados earlier in the century, have plummeted in most places to rates of 20 per 1,000 or below. Exceptions are the Dominican Republic and especially Haiti, where age-old problems of neonatal tetanus, malaria, yaws, and other African diseases still linger.

Less satisfactory have been improvements in the nutrition of the young, and it is quite possible that fully half the deaths that have taken place among the age group 1 to 4 years in Hispaniola and Jamaica in recent years are the result of PEM – the same disease that proved so devastating to the slave young of yesterday. Other problems or potential problems left over from the disease ecology of that period also remain. Yellow fever is still very much alive in its jungle form in the treetops of South America and, with the present lax mosquito control measures, could easily return to the Caribbean as it in fact attempted to do in Trinidad during 1954. Indeed the ever increasing number of dengue epidemics that have taken place of late in the region show just how vulnerable the West Indies are to yellow fever, because the same mosquito spreads both diseases.

Similarly the pockets of falciparum malaria that still exist may also suddenly expand, as happened in Cuba during the 1920s when tens of thousands of Haitian and Jamaican laborers entered the country bringing the illnesses with them. Haiti, in particular, remains a focus of the infection, as an epidemic there in 1963 so vividly demonstrated by assaulting some 75,000 individuals.

Filariasis has not been completely eradicated. In fact, the people of Puerto Rico were found to have a surprisingly high rate of infection during a survey in the 1960s. In Barbados, however, where the disease was once notorious, the malady (or at least its most notable symptoms) has become rare. Schistosomiasis may still be found in some of the Lesser Antilles, and small endemic foci have been located in the Dominican Republic as well, and intestinal parasites remain widespread across the Caribbean region. In addition, another new, seemingly African disease – AIDS – has surfaced in Haiti, although the extent to which this threatens the rest of the Caribbean remains to be seen.

One of the greatest assaults of late mounted on remaining health problems in the region has taken place in Cuba, where the government of Fidel Castro has made improved health a top priority. The extension of health services to the countryside, mass vaccination campaigns, and important advances in sanitation have allowed the Cuban people to attain a life expectancy considerably more favor- able than that enjoyed by those in most other developing nations.

Yet it is ironic that today the greatest threat to the health of West Indian people is their own relatively good health. With the tremendous strides made in reducing infant and child mortality, populations have mushroomed in alarming fashion. In the past, much of the excess population of the region migrated to Great Britain or to the United States; that safety valve has been shut down by the recent restrictions both of these countries have placed on immigration from the islands. And they are islands, which by definition means a limited area of land. If, as is the case in so many of them, land is put into sugar instead of foodstuffs, then the latter must be imported. Thus, swelling populations can only threaten the level of their nutrition while placing perhaps impossible pressures on the ability of governments to continue to deliver essential medical and sanitary services.

Kenneth F. Kiple

Bibliography

Ashburn, P. M. 1947. *The ranks of death: A medical history of the conquest of America.* New York.

Ashcroft, M. T. 1965. A history and general survey of the helminth and protozoal infections of the West Indies. *Annals of Tropical Medicine and Parasitology* 59: 479–93.

Cook, S. F., and W. W. Borah. 1971, 1974, 1979. *Essays in population history: Mexico and the Caribbean,* 3 vols. Berkeley.

Crosby, A. W. 1972. *The Columbian exchange: Biological and cultural consequences of 1492.* Westport, Conn.

1986. *Ecological imperialism: The biological expansion of Europe, 900–1900.* New York.

Curtin, P. D. 1989. *Death by migration: Europe's encounter with the tropical world in the nineteenth century.* New York.

Dobyns, H. F. 1983. *Their numbers become thinned: Native American population dynamics in eastern North America.* Knoxville.

Diaz-Briquets, S. 1983. *The health revolution in Cuba.* Austin.

Dirks, R. 1978. Resource fluctuations and competitive transformations in West Indian slave societies. In *Extinction and survival in human populations,* ed. C. Laughlin and I. Brady. New York.

Guerra, F. 1988. The earliest American epidemic: The influenza of 1493. *Social Science History* 12: 305–25.

Handler, J., and R. S. Corruccini. 1986. Weaning among West Indian slaves: Historical and bioanthropological evidence from Barbados. *William and Mary Quarterly,* 3d ser., 43: 111–17.

Handler, J., et al. 1986. Lead contact and poisoning in

Barbados slaves: Historical, chemical, and biological evidence. *Social Science History* 10: 399–425.

Hirsch, A. 1883–6. *Handbook of geographical and historical pathology*, 3 vols., trans. C. Creighton. London.

Hoeppli, R. 1969. *Parasitic diseases in Africa and the Western Hemisphere: Early documentation and transmission by the slave trade.* Basel.

Kiple, K. F. 1976. *Blacks in colonial Cuba.* Gainesville, Fla.

  1984. *The Caribbean slave: A biological history.* New York.

  1985. Cholera and race in the Caribbean. *Journal of Latin American Studies* 17: 157–77.

Sheridan, R. B. 1985. *Doctors and slaves: A medical and demographic history of slavery in the West Indian Islands, 1680–1834.* New York.

Wilson, T. W. 1986. Africa, Afro-Americans, and hypertension: An hypothesis. *Social Science History* 10: 489–500.

VII.7
Disease Ecologies of Europe

We can consider the ecology of disease to be the sum total of all the influences on pathogens and their hosts and, because of the interdependence of the two for disease expression, the internal structures and systems of both that bear upon a disease question. Thus we are clearly considering a structure of relations whose complexity surpasses all comprehension. Such may also be said of a single disease. No one has yet fully defined all that constitutes the expression of even one disease, and such an explanation would be its ecology. To describe the disease ecology of Europe is a task at first so daunting as to admit no possibility. Still, there are a few aspects of the ecology of disease in Europe that can be described, if without claim to completeness or ultimate value, at least with an eye to creating a target for more detailed studies and criticism.

With such cautions in mind, I should like to offer a few general comments on human disease and its expression, and then set forth a very limited number of aspects of the totality of my subject, which I feel can be discussed. For most of the sojourn of humankind on Earth, we have only skeletal remains upon which to build any concept of disease in the past. Even after the advent of agriculture and the earliest civilizations, we have little upon which to develop a coherent view. General trends are perceptible in classical times, and very sketchy numbers can be offered for population in the late medieval period. Modern times have, of course, brought masses of statistics, but these as often confuse as enlighten. Still, it is possible, at least, to discern some of the impact of disease upon demography and to infer some aspects of the influences that played upon certain diseases. Because it is so difficult to identify diseases in the past, I confine myself largely to the specific diseases of plague, leprosy, tuberculosis, and smallpox. Otherwise, the influence of epidemic disease of unknown type will be the other main consideration, along with some presumed diseases of childhood. There is at least some reason to feel that the four specific diseases may be identified as factors in human demography in the past, as can epidemic and endemic diseases whose exact nature is unidentifiable.

All human populations share some common features, and European populations carry some particular features, which can help us at least conjecture about factors influencing the expression of disease. For example, about 105 males are born per 100 females (Russell 1977). Although malnutrition can cause disease, major population losses do not necessarily reflect malnourishment (Wilson 1957; Wrigley 1962; Rotberg and Rabb 1983). Certainly the diseases of postindustrial society are those of an abundance of food. Despite the fascination since ancient times with food as a cause, predisposing factor, and therapeutic agent in disease, very little is actually known about the relationship between food and health beyond the effects of some vitamin-deficient states, and full-blown protein–energy malnutrition.

The ability of human populations to replenish themselves is limited. A birthrate above 50 per 1,000 population per year is truly exceptional, and above 30 is quite uncommon (Wrigley 1962). There are well-known age and sex predilections for a variety of diseases, but they are as etiologically obscure as they are epidemiologically well documented (Wilson 1957). For example, although infants are extremely susceptible to tuberculosis, children between the ages of 5 and 15 exhibit a relative immunity to the disease. Then a sex predilection occurs, with women much more commonly the victims from about 25 years up to around age 45, at which time men are the predominant victims of the disease until late in life (Wilson 1957). These observations are based on data gathered mainly in the British Isles during the nineteenth century, but no one knows the extent to which they represent the result of metabolic versus environmental factors in pathogen and host. It is also generally felt that societies tended to have more males than females among adults because more women than men die between the ages of 25 and 45 (Russell 1977). This generalization, however, is based to a very great extent on the perceived epidemiology of tuberculosis, a disease neither universal nor of equal importance in all societies.

In Europe, several generalizations are usually accepted regarding human populations. Since classical times until the Industrial Revolution, cities have harbored more women than men. Cities have also been unable to replenish their own populations, at least from medieval times until the nineteenth century, because of the unfavorable disease climate of urban life (McNeill 1976; Russell 1977). Before the nineteenth century, the vast majority of humans in Europe lived in villages or on farms, with only a very small fraction residing in cities (Guillaume and Poussou 1970; Russell 1977). The total population of preindustrial societies contained at least one-third children, of whom less than half lived to adulthood from medieval until modern times (Flinn 1985).

Humans also affect their environment and in turn affect their own disease ecology. Practices we take for granted, such as the domestication of animals, change another species' disease environment, and the interaction of domesticated animals with humans has often led to human disease (Lovell 1957). An example of a disease that became of at least minor importance among humans primarily in this way is *brucellosis,* usually introduced to humans through goats. During the Crimean War, for example, Malta became an endemic area for brucellosis; in 1906 the means of human infection was described (Alausa 1983).

Disease in turn may alter the character of human populations. After major epidemics of infectious disease associated with high mortality, a period of markedly reduced mortality generally begins. It is felt that such epidemics "weed out," at least in some cases, the weaker elements in a population, leaving a healthier one behind (Wrigley 1962). On the other hand, diseases such as plague and some rickettsial infections often kill the healthy.

If we limit our generalizations about humans in Europe, our knowledge of their pathogens is even sketchier. The whole question of virulence among various bacteria is extremely complicated, and, since it is not well understood in modern infections and since organisms can mutate, virulence can be assessed only by effect. The effect of an organism in turn is related to host, pathogen, and environment, so that any comments about organisms in the past is unrealistic. Host–parasite relations vary from nonspecific, in which multiple species support the organism, to those in which the organism is dependent upon a single host. In the second case, it is felt that the organism has lost the ability to synthesize its own essential nutrients to an extreme degree (Lovell 1957). Leprosy is an example of an organism that cannot be cultured in an ordinary fashion and is highly host dependent (and even specific to certain cells in the host). This characteristic suggests that the susceptible tissues contain some chemical or provide some enzymatic function (or possibly something entirely different) that cannot be provided in culture media (Wilson 1957). If we consider virulence to be the property that permits an organism to cause death or damage to the body parts invaded, we are left with a multitude of factors to consider. An increase in virulence toward one species may decrease that strain's virulence to others (Wilson 1957), indicating the intimacy of the relationship to a given host. The same strain of *Mycobacterium tuberculosis* is generally much more virulent when entering the host via the respiratory route as opposed to the gastrointestinal tract, but with bovine tuberculosis the situation is the opposite. Such information, however, offers little practical guidance in the history of diseases, for the specificity of an organism toward humans (e.g., organisms causing leprosy, meningococcal meningitis, typhoid fever, and smallpox) only tells us that if the disease is present, so are humans, which is rarely in question.

In general, organisms are tissue specific. *Clostridium tetani,* for example, is harmless to intact skin, but can be deadly when in contact with abraided or necrotic tissue (Wilson 1957). The longer an organism is in contact with the environment and outside a host, the likelier it will be damaged. Organisms that affect the gastrointestinal tract, such as *Salmonella typhi,* are able to withstand environmental pressures longer than those not waterborne or foodborne (as a generalization) (Wilson 1957). Insect vectors may result in significant effects on the expression of disease. Arthropod vectors are more important, generally, in parasitic infections than in bacterial ones (Wilson 1957), but plague and typhus are notable exceptions.

Despite the staggering complexity of host–pathogen relationships, the presence of certain diseases can reveal important aspects of human populations. Measles is a human disease only and requires at least a population of some hundred thousands in some contact to remain endemic (Bailey 1954, 1957; Bartlett 1957, 1960; Becker 1979; Smith 1983). Diseases such as measles and smallpox (another human disease whose pathogen needs a fairly large population to remain active) tend to become childhood diseases (Mc-Neill 1976; Smith 1983). Thus the first observation of measles would tell us when a communicating population of humans reached a certain level. Unfortunately, we do not know when this occurred in Europe because we do not know when measles first appeared. The clinical expression of a given disease can also tell us about genetic factors in a population. Susceptibility to leprosy, in both its polar forms (although more in tuberculoid leprosy), is in part genetically mediated (Smith 1979; Eden et al. 1980; Keyu et al. 1985). When measles and TB have fulminant courses with high and dramatic mortality, they are present in a previously unexposed population (Wilson 1957; Mc-Neill 1976). The same may have been the case when syphilis appeared in Europe at the end of the fifteenth century, but this is hardly an undisputed subject. It is also becoming apparent that some resistance to particular diseases reflects prior exposure to others that confer cross-immunity (Ell 1984a).

Characteristics of childhood diseases, especially measles, have become the subject of mathematical modeling. Birthrate has been shown to be an important factor in determining whether or not a disease like measles can remain endemic and in predicting interepidemic periods (Bailey 1957; Bartlett 1957; Becker 1979). Unfortunately, such models, although of great theoretical and some practical interest, cannot explain much of what occurs in a given epidemic. They are based on populations of constant size and without immigrants – factors from which deviation has been crucial in many other epidemics (Siegried 1960; Biraben 1975). This mathematical modeling is of very limited value in considering the disease ecology of Europe in the past. Too many of the factors are unknown (population size, birthrate), and the effect of social customs has not proved very susceptible to quantification. Further, in this chapter we perceive childhood mortality as a nearly constant background factor for much of the time period discussed, with major epidemics, which have proved resistant to neat equations, the more influential factors.

In the following pages, I try to discern, within what is known about the demographic history of Europe, the effects of disease on that history. Partly because war has been an invariable aspect of human behavior, and partly because it reflects so much else about a society, I focus often on military strategy, on the composition and size of armies, as well as on the direct effects of disease upon armies. The time frame considered extends from the hunter-gatherers of prehistoric Europe to late twentieth-century society. I have very little to say about medicine, because I do not believe it has had a significant effect on the ecology of disease except in very limited circumstances.

Geographically, I define "Europe" as extending as far east as western Poland down through Greece, as far north as Scandinavia (but excluding Iceland), as far west as the British Isles, France, and Spain, and as far south as Greece, Italy, and Malta.

Prehistoric Europe

Hunting-Gathering Societies and the Neolithic Revolution

It is often observed that hunter-gatherers are healthier than their supposedly more "civilized" contemporaries. This anthropological observation of the still-extant human groupings that practice hunting-gathering has been extrapolated into the past to suggest that, because of a meat-rich diet, very low population density, natural birth control through lactation, and a variety of other factors, hunter-gatherers innately enjoyed more healthful circumstances than did other preindustrial societies. There is, however, little evidence of any kind to support such claims. Skeletal remains have been used to claim a life expectancy similar to that of the rural poor of the nineteenth century (Birdsell 1957; McNeill 1976). (What is less obvious is that skeletal remains from the very distant past will tend to support this hypothesis because the skeletons of children and infants neither weather as well nor were often buried as carefully as those of adults.) Although it is true that hunter-gatherer groups do not have enough population to support measles, they do have diseases exquisitely adapted to their circumstances. An example of this phenomenon is *kuru,* a slow virus that afflicts cannibal aborigines. There is no reason to imagine that hunting-gathering peoples of the past did not experience diseases equally consonant with their particular patterns of life. There is no real foundation for the claim that the hunter-gatherers of prehistoric Europe were healthier than people from the Neolithic and pre-Industrial periods. We simply lack any evidence to support a conclusion of any type.

Likewise, we do not know much about the changes in disease ecology occasioned by the development of agriculture and the first numerically more substantial groupings of persons. Observations about remaining societies that mirror Neolithic times, or even about remaining hunting-gathering peoples, are suspect simply because the groups' mere survival indicates something not generalizable about them. Of the population of Europe before historical times, it would be difficult to frame a convincing argument for a number with an order of magnitude error included.

It is felt that parasitic, especially helminthic infestations are among the oldest of diseases (Smith 1983), but beyond noting the claim, we can do nothing to confirm it. The prehistory of Europe is just that; to impose a demographic and disease structure upon it is folly.

Bronze Age Civilizations

The civilizations of Mycenaean Greece and of Minoan Crete are discoveries of the last century. Before excavations at the site of Troy and among the Greek cities of Homeric renown, along with Crete, the period covered by the Homeric epics was an unknown. Scholarship has translated much, inferred much, and given us striking impressions of these lost societies. From the point of view of disease, we have little to offer. Mycenaean civilization seems to have fallen to outside invaders. There is no evidence to support disease as a major factor in the decline of either mainland Greek or Minoan civilization. The latter may plausibly be linked to a natural disaster. The disease history of these fascinating cultures remains beyond our grasp.

Classical Antiquity

The Golden Age

The time limits of classical antiquity are as protean as all artificial periodization. For the purposes of this discussion, I shall concentrate on Greece from the sixth century B.C. through the Western Roman world into the second century A.D. Overall, the disease picture here suggests societies with significant overpopulation expanding into new territories and experiencing few major epidemics, until a point was reached when exposure to infectious epidemic disease began a process of demographic decline and cultural retraction.

If one considers classical Greece, the former part of this process can be seen in full swing. The settlement of Magna Graecia by colonists from the Greek mainland speaks clearly of population pressure. The Greeks also colonized the coast of what is now Turkey. The Italian and Sicilian settlements became major sources of grain for mainland Greece, and the need for reliable grain sources has been linked plausibly to the Athenian military debacle in Sicily during the Peloponnesian War (Guillaume and Poussou 1970).

The Peloponnesian War also saw the famous Plague of Athens. In Thucydides' description of this plague, there is no sense of epidemic disease on this scale being any part of ordinary Greek life. To that author, the epidemic was one of the main factors in Athens' ultimate loss because it bore away Pericles whom Thucydides clearly felt could have led his people to victory (Thucydides 1958).

The exploits of Alexander the Great resulted in the Hellenization of parts of Asia and Africa. The army of Alexander was able to campaign for 12 years in Asia without suffering a significant loss to disease. Fresh recruits from Macedonia and Greece arrived mainly to replace those retiring or lost in battle. The whole concept of a campaign like that of Alexander, which lacked temporal and spatial goals, would be either unthinkable or pure folly in an environment similar to that found in Renaissance Europe wherein plague could easily defeat both opposing armies. The size of the armies of the Persian king, Darius III, although beyond the scope of the ecology of Europe, also bespeaks a very heavily populated realm (Bosworth 1988).

Although no social custom so complex and deeply rooted in Greek society as the exposure of infants (Veyne 1987) can admit an easy explanation, the practice still argues for significant population pressure. In response to most severe epidemics, the birthrate rises, probably partly consciously to repopulate, but also because many epidemics remove weaker elements from the population (Wrigley 1962; Neraudau 1984). The deliberate abandonment of infants in places where their survival would depend on some other adult's desire for a child being strong enough to rescue them presents a picture of children as an apparently significant economic liability. This is rarely the perception when epidemic disease makes day-to-day life totally unpredictable and when an outbreak can destroy entire family lines. The Greek myths are filled with tales that bear on the abandonment of infants, of which the story of Oedipus is but the most famous. Many others involve the abandonment of children by the poor.

There is reason to believe that children were an economic liability in fact as well as in perception. A worker in Periclean Athens could earn enough to live comfortably, if he did not marry. Once married, he could still afford food and shelter. But each child added significant strain to that ability (Austin and Vidal-Naquet 1977; Finley 1981). The mindset of past societies cannot reliably be reconstructed, but it seems reasonable to imagine that persons exposing children had little reason to suppose that the family was at significant risk of being decimated by disease. Classical Greece seems to offer the picture of a society at the limits of its population potential, but which perceived and experienced minimal risk of epidemic disease altering the tenor of life.

The Hellenistic Age shows little difference in this regard. Greek became the *lingua franca* of much of the Mediterranean world, and Alexandria, an Egyptian city founded by Alexander, became one of the intellectual (and population) centers of the world. Greek influence is clearly to be found in sculpture native to India during this period, a measure of how extensive Greek expansion and culture became.

It is said that as he spent his last months of life in Babylon, Alexander the Great considered the conquest of Rome, a state just then beginning to become prominent in Mediterranean affairs (Bosworth 1988). Alexander died short of his thirty-third birthday without having affected Rome other than through the latter culture's admiration of him. Rome then began perhaps the most impressive expansion in all of world history. In order to gain some insight into the disease ecology of the Roman world, it is instructive to consider the Second Punic War, which established Rome as the most important power in the western Mediterranean. This war, fought at the end of the third century B.C. (ending in 202 B.C.), gives glimpses of both a very highly populated Italy and a military strategy that excluded any significant impact secondary to epidemic disease.

Hannibal invaded Italy (with his elephants, as every Western schoolchild used to know), commanding an army of around 40,000 mercenaries. These men had marched through Spain, across southern France (for convenience, I refer to places by their modern names, insofar as is possible), over the Alps and into northern Italy. According to contemporary sources, Rome could have put an army in the field 20 times the size of that of Hannibal. Rome could call upon a reserve of 700,000 foot and 70,000 cavalry (figures sometimes adjusted to 580,000 and around 60,000) (Caven 1980). Rome replied more cautiously but, using smaller armies, lost 15,000 and 5,000 men in the first two major encounters with Hannibal. At Cannae, a larger Roman force left around 25,000 men on the field and a similar number prisoner (Caven 1980). Yet Rome refused to ransom the prisoners, even though Hannibal offered. (It may have also been good strategy to keep Hannibal's soldiers busy guarding prisoners.)

The Roman reserve of soldiers, the losses sustained, and the disdain for ransoming prisoners in one of the darkest hours of Republican Roman history are impressive. No army of medieval or Renaissance Europe could have approached the size of the army Rome could have mustered from its Italian population alone. Losses such as those sustained at Trasimeno and Cannae would likewise have left even many early modern states without the manpower even to consider continuing a war. The Roman Senate judged that a similar number of men were not worth ransoming to help fend off an incredibly skilled opponent; rather, the image of what a Roman soldier should be was more important.

If the early course of the war argues for abundant population and little risk or heed of epidemic disease, the remainder of the conflict shows the same features. Hannibal was able to campaign in Italy for nearly 2 decades, with only minimal reinforcements. He was never defeated on Italian soil. When Rome finally produced a general capable of opposing the Carthaginian commander, the strategy employed again indicates the same picture with regard to epidemic disease.

Scipio Africanus the Younger took his army to Africa to threaten Carthage, reasoning that Hannibal would be obliged to return and defend his homeland. This he did, and Scipio defeated the Carthaginian master at the battle of Zama in 202 B.C. Once again, in moving the most important Roman army to Africa as a strategic ploy, we see no fear of an epidemic destroying Rome's greatest chance to end the war. Indeed, the relative ease with which armies traversed great distances during this war argues for a relatively uniform environment in terms of disease and one that had little to frighten an adult. Hannibal's army operated on two continents, yet never experienced significant loss to disease. In 1630, the Venetian army met that of the Hapsburgs at Mantua. At a fraction of the distance from home traversed by the armies of the Second Punic War, plague caused so much mortality that neither the victorious Hapsburgs nor the beaten Venetians could even reorganize their forces (Lane 1973).

The Mediterranean world in the centuries before the first emperor of Rome appears to have been an environment abundantly populated, but relatively free of at least major epidemic disease. Of the fate of children, we know much less. The Romans continued the practice of exposure or abandonment of infants. The head of a Roman household decided on the fate of any infant born into that household. Once again, there are complex cultural phenomena at work, but children were definitely an expendable commodity (Veyne 1987).

All of this speaks of the great classical civilization

being largely spared devastating epidemics of infectious disease. Of the disease background we know little. The writings of the Hippocratic corpus, in particular, describe many illnesses (it is felt by some that brucellosis is described therein), but putting modern names to them is another matter. No one has successfully identified the disease that caused the Plague of Athens. Background causes of morbidity and mortality are simply beyond reach. At a time when fever was considered a disease and not a symptom or sign, there is no realistic way to translate most diseases from Ancient Greek or Latin into a modern equivalent.

Some generalizations seem reasonable, nonetheless. There was probably a surplus of men among the adult population because more women died in the 25- to 45-year age group. Much of this is probably attributable to death associated with childbirth. If this period had the attributes common to most preindustrial societies, about 30 to 40 percent of the total population was composed of children. What is singularly lacking is a sense of what the probability of a child at birth growing to adulthood was. This is both the most important factor in determining life expectancy at birth (much of the spectacular change in this parameter in modern times is the result of decreasing childhood mortality).

The Tide Begins to Turn

As we have seen, military strategy in the early Roman Empire again depended upon abundant manpower and low risk of epidemics. A controversial but compelling reassessment of Roman strategy over time has divided the military strategy of the empire into three phases (Luttwak 1976): First was the use of client or buffer states to separate Rome from potential enemies. These states, such as those along the Asian border of the empire, could be paid or otherwise induced to mediate or simply physically separate Rome from potential enemies. If attacked, such states also buffered the conflict to give Rome the time necessary to concentrate forces and plan a campaign against the opponent. Such a strategy could operate only when the empire could confront any enemy on the battlefield with an army that might be gathered from many regions and transported a long distance, while the buffer state was itself strong and populous enough to hold off the enemy at least for enough time for the Romans to make their military reply.

The second strategy was that of fixed frontiers. Perhaps here is the first inkling that the population situation was not so favorable. Even though this strategy had in position soldiers in the hundreds of thousands, the soldiers over time also became colonists and were defending their own land. Hadrian's Wall across England is an example of this phase of strategy. Its sophistication and effectiveness speak for themselves. It was perhaps no longer so safe to move armies to strange countries. Recall that Marcus Aurelius died near Vienna while on a frontier campaign. In fact, the "plague" epidemic of the end of the second century has been seen by Robert Lopez (1967) as perhaps the most important of the myriad of factors in the subsequent decline of the empire. In any case, after the second century, the empire was obliged to develop new and increasingly risky military strategies to maintain itself.

A.D. 200–1000: The West Reaches Its Nadir

The Barbarians, c. A.D. 200–600

When it was no longer feasible for Rome to defend the frontiers from the barbarians who lurked upon the eastern side of the Rhine–Danube frontier, the empire enlisted them to defend what they coveted. Given land in the empire, the barbarians were partially Romanized and, in return for their land, were asked to defend the frontier. At this point, the third phase of the tripartite strategy comes into play. Because armies were not available in sufficient size to guarantee the immense frontier of the empire, and because the colonized barbarians themselves might decide to sack a nearby town or two, a "defense in depth" approach was developed. Strongly fortified positions were built, which could be supplied and manned to hold out for a long time in the rear of an enemy encroachment. These fortifications gave the Romans a foothold in areas that could only too easily be overrun. These strongholds could shelter and defend the frontier population until adequate military strength could be massed to counter the incursion. A strategy of this type clearly depends upon a much smaller population. For a stronghold to house more than a token population, the frontier population had to be small in the first place. This is further attested by the fact that the forts were victualed for long campaigns. Generally such fortifications were set upon natural defensive positions, minimizing the manpower necessary to defend them.

Even if this picture of the strategy of the empire is incorrect, there are too many other signs of population decline and of the increasing importance of local environments to deny convincingly that the demographic and disease picture had not changed immensely. The empire itself, which had dominated the

Mediterranean world, divided itself up into two main units, with a "second Rome" emerging in the form of Constantinople. By the fourth century it had become two major territories, each usually with its own emperor. No longer could armies feasibly be moved around so effortlessly as in the Punic Wars. The Greek and Latin empires drifted apart. The Latin Empire was increasingly the prey of barbarians. Peoples on the borders of the empire in the West, whether under population pressure of their own or because of pressure from more remote peoples, invaded and often settled in the lands that had comprised the empire. Often, they tried to revive Roman government and customs, as with the Ostrogoths, only to fall prey to more aggressive and less civilized peoples such as the Lombards. Matters were further complicated by the advent of Christianity, as if the empire was not experiencing enough travails.

The Christian religion arose (and was seen so to arise by divine plan by Augustine) in the empire. Its appeal was undeniably greatest to people who found the world they lived in unsatisfactory. Again so complex a subject as the change in the overall concept of the cosmos cannot be related to something as simple as disease, but there is little question that Christianity denigrated the world, as human beings lived in it, in favor of a life that would come after death. St. Augustine died while the Vandals besieged the city of which he was bishop. It would be an incredible oversimplification to attribute the fact that the City of God could not exist in this world, to the world Augustine lived in, but the religions of classical antiquity with few exceptions (and those exceptions became the rule as the situation of the empire worsened) saw this life as real life and what came after as a shadow thereof.

What diseases weakened the empire? Did the Romans come in contact with a distant disease pool, as has been suggested by William McNeill (1976)? We have essentially no hope of knowing the details. Nonetheless, epidemic diseases played an increasing role in the fate of the empire. In the sixth century, Justinian made a supreme effort to reunite the two halves of the empire. He might have succeeded had not a monstrous epidemic (in this case identifiable as plague) wreaked such mortality that the prospect was not entertained again for centuries.

The barbarians who occupied Roman lands first were almost invariably displaced by others who obviously had the manpower and freedom from epidemics to oust their rivals, who in their turn seem to have suffered much the fate of the Romans them-

selves. The first wave of barbarian invasions ended with western Europe in the hands of barbarian kingdoms and the East still a state with considerable territory and the ability to defend itself.

Cities, the cornerstones of classical antiquity, declined. In a famous example, the inhabitants of one city declined to the point where they lived in the city stadium. Effective government collapsed and local strongmen became the only powers that affected most of the population. In this decline of cities in particular, plague may have had a major role. In general, plague favors city over rural populations. Barbarians came from nonurban civilizations, but typically settled in the Roman cities they conquered. As epidemic followed epidemic (or, in the case of the Plague of Justinian, continued well into the seventh century), succeeding waves of barbarians probably profited from their predecessors' disease experience. Certainly there is reason to believe that the Huns were displaced by another tribe that was experiencing overpopulation.

Aside from the Plague of Justinian, we can identify few of the epidemics that afflicted Europe. The practical knowledge that permitted the Romans to drain swamps to lessen malaria was replaced by superstition and senseless violence. When an epidemic threatened the lives of the children of one of the Frankish kings, he decided that he was being punished by God for taxing the people. He burned the tax rolls, Gregory of Tours (1905) tells us, and his children survived. Again a single incident has much to tell us. First, unlike the societies that exposed children, we see a king terrified that his children will die. Partly this is a difference in religion and culture – barbarian Christian versus classical Greek – but partly there is a background of epidemic diseases that pose terrifying threats. There is also a population on the edge of disaster, low in number, and barely managing to subsist. There are enemies everywhere in the form of humans, diseases, and the supernatural (the term dates from the fourteenth century).

Among the myriad factors that have been argued to have contributed to Rome's fall, the unfavorable epidemic disease picture, as opposed to the threat of the barbarians, is a factor that cannot be discounted.

The Early Middle Ages, c. A.D. 500–1000

However influential the Plague of Justinian was, once its century-long devastation of Europe ended, plague did not recur in western Europe again until 1347. Why this is so is totally obscure. Even if cities and overall population density declined, plague is primarily a zoonosis and, once established, counts humans as incidental victims. It seems likely that the plague never established an enzootic focus in Europe, or if it did, that focus died out quickly. This pattern has been documented in recent years for Hawaii (Ell 1984a; Tomich et al. 1984). In such places, a few susceptible animal strains allowed the disease an enzootic foothold, but could not sustain it indefinitely.

Despite the temporary absence of plague, the Early Middle Ages saw its share of disease. Chronicles rarely covered more than a few years before noting some outbreak of epidemic disease.

Although charges of abandoning children, suffocating them in their sleep, and so forth, remained part and parcel of medieval lore, children were certainly not subjected to a formal decision on survival at birth. We can read little or nothing into this as regards population dynamics, however, because we are in the world of Christianity and Germanic custom rather than classical practice.

If the barbarians started their careers in a favorable demographic position relative to the Romans, this situation seems to have lasted a very short time, as suggested above. Despite the influx of barbarians into western Europe, cities contracted further, and secondary waves of barbarians overwhelmed earlier arrivals. The best example of this phenomenon is the primacy of the previously obscure Franks, who were the only barbarian tribe that by chance had not converted to what was rapidly perceived as a heretical form of Christianity.

There was certainly little enough to favor population growth. The Roman governmental apparatus was among the most elaborate the world has ever seen and certainly surpassed anything to be seen in Europe at least until the Renaissance (and then on a much smaller scale). When the barbarians tried to take over this system, the results were indeed barbaric. Roads were not repaired. Tax rolls were not updated, so that someone living in a given place might legally be someone long dead and owe the latter's taxes. The newly risen landowners might live a life unencumbered with taxes, while identifiable units from the past were asked for money they could not pay. War, which was the king's truest business and accounted for much of his revenue, contributed little to this already bleak picture. Every spring, the Frankish kings reviewed their armies and went off to war. Since war generally increases epidemic disease, the annual royal endeavor again would be likely to worsen the disease situation.

As if political ineptitude, gratuitous violence, and an unfavorable disease climate were not enough, the experience of the Romans was about to be mimicked by their inheritors. The comparatively settled barbarian kingdoms had by 800 coalesced (largely by force of arms, to be sure) into the Empire of Charlemagne. What the future of this empire left to itself might have been, we will never know. A storm of new invaders fell mercilessly on western Europe, and a near parody of what had gone before occurred.

Evidence from Scandinavia suggests that that region was overpopulated (Musset 1971). Again, for unclear reasons, peoples outside what was left of the Roman Empire seem to have enjoyed a much more favorable disease ecology and significant population growth. In 796, the first Viking raid sacked the monastery at Lindisfarne. A little over two centuries later, a Dane ruled England. Until very recently, the English Book of Common Prayer contained the phrase "God protect us from the fury of the Northmen." William the Conqueror was the descendant of the Viking conquerors of Normandy.

The north was not the only battleground. For more obscure reasons, the Magyars, fierce horsemen from central Europe, began to press the eastern borders of the old Carolingian domains. Their depredations destabilized the precarious hold of the young German monarchy, which finally crushed them at the Battle of Lechfeld in 955.

In the south, Islam entered one of its periodic expansionist phases and threatened Europe. Pirates and small armies made every locale anywhere near the Mediterranean coast unsafe. No single engagement or event ended this incursion, but it ebbed away almost completely by the year 1000.

The wave of barbarian invasions ended differently from the first. Despite high cost, the existing institutions proved capable of driving off or absorbing the invaders. More importantly, the second wave of barbarian invasions was the last. By 1066, Europe was free to develop politically without outside threat. The weak had begun to grow strong again.

The High Middle Ages, 1000–1348

Renewal

A marginal agricultural surplus began to be produced by at least the tenth century, and by the year 1000 the demographic profile of western Europe began to improve dramatically. Whenever the actual improvements in agricultural techniques began is unclear, but so long as Europe was under the siege of the second wave of barbarians, such improvements were unlikely to have a significant effect. Once a period of relative peace ensued, the small agricultural surplus then available provided the basis for one of the great periods of population growth in European history (Duby 1981). Other factors were also at work, including better government and probably the abatement of a now unidentifiable series of epidemics. In any case, for the next 300 years, western Europe enjoyed very favorable demographic circumstances. Indeed by the year 1300, parts of rural Italy enjoyed population densities that would not be reached again until the nineteenth century (Herlihy 1968). The results of this growth in population were spectacular.

Huge amounts of land were brought under cultivation for the first time. Improvements in plows and crop rotations boosted agricultural yields (White 1962; Duby 1968). Gothic architecture arose at the hands of Suger of St. Denis and cast its magic light over Europe (Duby 1981). Partly because less effort was required for daily life, persons of means turned hungrily toward knowledge and found it on the interface of Christianity and Islam, mainly in Spain and Sicily. The vast storehouse of classical literature, along with the brilliant commentaries and original works of the great minds of Islam, was translated for the Latin world (Southern 1966; Lindberg 1978; Stock 1978). This fueled one of the most exciting intellectual flowerings in Western history. The university, which arose from the cathedral school, dates from the High Middle Ages and remains a foundation of intellectual life.

For the first time, western Europe began to expand against its neighbors. In Urban II's call for the First Crusade, there is an overt reference to an overpopulation of knights, who were creating internal violence. Thus aside from its religious content, the First Crusade was seen as a partial solution to overpopulation. This adventure involved not only knights but also thousands of peasants, who attempted to make their way to the Holy Land, only to perish en route. The Germanic kingdom began to expand to the East, and in Spain the *reconquista* to drive out the Moors was accelerated.

The recovery of classical and Islamic medical writings permits, along with contemporary Western works, the identification of at least a few diseases. Smallpox and chickenpox were separated, and smallpox can occasionally be identified. Like most endemic diseases of humans that require direct contact, smallpox was a major killer of children (Hopkins 1983). Plague made its reappearance only to mark the end of the High Middle Ages, but leprosy was a near obsession in western Europe.

Leprosy in medieval Europe has produced an immense literature. (Probably the most complete and the most extensive bibliography to date is Brody 1974.) In recent years, it has become possible to speak of medieval leprosy as the same disease we know today, at least from around the year 1200 on (arguments summarized in Ell 1986). This statement is based mainly on the results of excavations of skeletal remains from the cemeteries of leprosaria (after the Fourth Lateran Council of 1215, a leprosy patient could not be buried in the same cemetery as a person not suffering from the disease), coupled with the writings of contemporary physicians (Ell 1986, 1989b). In particular, the works of Theodoric of Cervia in the thirteenth century and Guy de Chauliac in the fourteenth show a clear acquaintance with a disease that is readily recognizable as leprosy (usually the lepromatous, or low-immunity type). Many claims made by these authors and dismissed by several generations of more modern commentators can be shown to have a basis in fact, often fact that has only recently been rediscovered (Ell 1984b, 1986, 1989b).

It has been claimed that leprosy was the most common disease in Europe before plague. Unfortunately, there is absolutely no ground for supporting such a claim. Very tentative and speculative work using skeletal remains, and a regression analysis of bone loss in the anterior maxilla as related to duration of lepromatous leprosy, have suggested that part of southern Denmark experienced an incidence of 20 cases per 1,000 population between the years 1250 and 1550 (Ell 1988). It is unrealistic at the current time to extrapolate any aspect of this study to the rest of Europe, and it is well to remember that Scandinavia was probably the highest-incidence area in Europe, and clearly the area in which the disease persisted longest.

If the study cited above is correct, however, the incidence in that region of Denmark was in the highest range classified today (Sansaarico 1981). Not only is it risky to extrapolate the proposed incidence in this part of Denmark to the rest of Europe, but it is well known that the incidence of the disease may vary significantly within a small geographic region. This pale glimpse of the possible prevalence of one disease in a small region is both speculative and isolated, for we have no information at all on other diseases. Tuberculosis, frequently mentioned in discussions of medieval disease history, cannot readily be identified beyond the point of stating that the disease was present in medieval Europe, but at what level and significance we have no idea.

Premonitions of Disaster

Thomas Aquinas, the greatest philosopher of the High Middle Ages and one of the greatest synthesizing authors of all time, when asked who would carry on to completion his reconciliation of classical and Christian sources, is reputed to have replied, on his deathbed, that the work could not be done. Aquinas died on the eve of one of the greatest demographic disasters in the history of Europe, the Plague of 1348, but his remark, apocryphal or not, shows a changing mood in western Europe.

High medieval thought and activity abound with optimism. Intoxicated with new knowledge and increasing material abundance, the prevailing expectations of the future were very high. Around 1300, this mood began to change, and it changed in many areas. Major defaults by important Italian banks, famines reappearing in a population freed from them for two centuries, overcrowded and overworked farmland – all these reverses changed the mood of the fourteenth century to one of anxiety and foreboding. Although Dante would die in 1330, 18 years before plague struck the city in exile from which he composed the greatest work of the Middle Ages, he wrote, "Io non averei creduto che morte tanta n'avesse disfatta" ("I would not have believed death had undone so many" – author's translation of a 1981 edition of Dante). This line might stand as the motto for what was to come. Whatever stance historians may take regarding an economic depression in the fourteenth century, it is clear that Europe was in demographic decline before the plague struck.

The Later Middle Ages

In 1347, the plague began its journey through Europe. When the pandemic ended in 1350, a third of the population of Europe was dead. The population of Europe on the eve of the epidemic has been estimated at 75 million. Although life expectancy at birth was only around 30 years, the very high infant mortality rate artificially lowered this relative to the life expectancy of a person who reached adulthood. Women tended to fare worse, probably as a result of childbirth, although some authors also cite tuberculosis and malaria (Russell 1977). Before the year 1000, no city in medieval Europe had a population exceeding 20,000. In 1340, the largest European cities were Venice, Paris, Florence, and Genoa, each with populations around 100,000. Closely behind were cities such as London, Barcelona, Bologna, Brescia, Ghent, and Cordoba, each of which had populations over 50,000 (Beloch 1937, 1940, 1961;

Keyser 1938; Mols 1954–6; Baratier 1961; Herlihy 1967; Acsadi and Nemeskevi 1970; Russell 1971, 1977). It has been suggested that infant mortality was lower in medieval Europe than in early industrial Europe, because there was less crowding and somewhat superior living conditions (Russell 1977). This is a reasonable argument, but no more than that; there is not a shred of evidence to support this.

Plague left Europe, indeed most of the world, in a catastrophic state. In Venice 75 percent of the nobility was dead (Archivio 1348; Ell 1980). Cities routinely lost over 50 percent of their populations (Carpentier 1962a, 1962b). Strange heresies arose, such as the Flagellants, who traveled about, beating themselves unconscious with whips to repent the sins that had brought the epidemic. Medicine, as usual, was powerless to do anything to stop the disease. More damning, the Church failed to offer much real comfort or practical relief. Infant mortality and the loss of elderly adults are most easily absorbed by any society; however, plague tends to affect young adults and children over 5 years old (Ell 1984a, 1985). Yet careful local studies have not always borne out such a pattern in European plague epidemics of this period. The exact epidemiology remains unclear, or perhaps varied from place to place. When plague left infants and the elderly relatively untouched, but decimated the rest, it could destroy the productive and reproductive present and future of whole societies. This phenomenon has been well documented for Orvieto (Carpentier 1962b). Plague did not visit Europe once and then disappear, as did the Plague of Justinian. Rather, Europe became a site of recurrent epidemics, none as ghastly as the first, but even in 1630–1 Venice still lost a third of its population to the disease (Ell 1989a). It is difficult to give a sense of what this level of loss is like. The worst-hit countries in World War II lost 10 percent of their population. Venice lost 7.5 times that percentage in about one-twentieth the time.

No argument can be made for a hypothesis that the epidemic was triggered by population density. As noted, population was already in decline, and plague returned many times after the population density had plummeted. It is also clear that the pattern these epidemics took does not fit the classical rat–flea model of transmission. In fact, the European experience of plague does not fit the general model derived from India and China by the British Plague Commission around the turn of the century. According to that model, animal foci or reservoirs of plague are established among wild rodents, which can harbor the infection indefinitely, either only among themselves or, as is now more often recognized, among multiple species. The natural history of such foci is that they enlarge. For example, the focus in the United States, which was established in the first decade of the twentieth century, now extends over almost the entire western half of the country (Ell 1980). It is considerably more reasonable to postulate that there was never an enzootic focus of plague in Europe but, rather, that the disease was repeatedly reintroduced, most likely through trade or travelers. The observed epidemiology is much more compatible with interhuman transmission via the human flea than with either rat–flea or pneumonic spread (Ell 1984).

Whatever historiographic stance one takes with regard to the points discussed above, the recurrent plague epidemics undeniably mark a major change in the ecology of disease in Europe. For the first time, in an institutionalized way, European governments began to try to alter disease ecology. In 1486 Venice made permanent the *Provveditori alla Sanità,* a public health board that had first been established in 1348 and was re-formed in response to each epidemic. The invention of the quarantine is credited to Venice, which first tested it in the Venetian colony of Ragusa in 1379. Measures such as quarantine are not always useful against plague, with its complicated transmission pattern, but were valuable against other infectious diseases. More importantly, such measures introduced the concept that human and particularly governmental actions could modify the expression of disease. When plague appeared, city-states, which traditionally were at odds with one another, exhibited a high degree of cooperation, as elegantly documented by Carlo Cipolla (1981). Much of the future of European disease ecology would follow from this none too successful attempt to control plague, and humans would begin increasingly to modify disease. Yet much of what plague brought was considerably less positive.

Artistic and literary styles in the immediate wake of the epidemic of 1348 were profoundly world-weary and pessimistic. The concept of the macabre arose in this period. The so-called transit tomb style, in which the deceased is sculpted both in his well-dressed idealized appearance and as a rotting corpse, being devoured by vermin, is one of the most striking elements of this deep cultural pessimism. This was a society in which the young and healthy adult could die in a few hours without warning or reason. It is likely that such an atmosphere could produce behavior of so careless or dangerous a nature that mortality from other diseases increased, but we have no real evidence to back up such an argument.

The conventional pillars of Christian faith and doctrine began to change to new, more startling views. People turned away from the belief that reason could lead them to God. Radical nominalism developed, and left an indelible mark upon subsequent philosophy. The Doctrine of Double Truth also emerged. According to this view, individuals could by reason arrive at certain conclusions, but only revelation was the source of ultimate truth. Aquinas had tried to keep the comprehension of truth in this world and available to reason. Postplague Europe made truth something separate from and unattainable from this world.

For totally unclear reasons, leprosy had begun to decline in much of western Europe by 1300 and definitely before plague struck. There is no known explanation. It is claimed that the climate of Europe became colder. It is indeed true that climate can affect the epidemiology of disease as well as much else in human society. A change of 1°C average temperature over a year can change the growing season by 2 weeks in England, for example. It is known that figs were grown in England in the time of Charlemagne. The climatic cooling of the fourteenth and fifteenth centuries has been called the "Little Ice Age" (Russell 1977). Such a shift in climate would certainly affect crops and food supplies, as well as some diseases (e.g., influenza is largely a disease of cold weather, whereas enteric fevers tend to occur in summer). Although climatic cooling has been credited for the decline of leprosy, the fact that the disease thrived in Scandinavia renders this argument at best incomplete and probably irrelevant. Whatever the cause, half the previously occupied beds in leprosaria in England were empty in 1300 (Richards 1977). The argument that plague killed an inordinate number of leprosy victims is not supportable in a direct way because leprosy is considered to confer immunity to plague. Indirectly, through the deaths of those who looked after leprosaria patients, plague may have hastened the decline of leprosy in much of Europe, but it neither initiated nor finished the change (Ell 1987).

Although it itself is highly speculative, let us consider another possible cause of leprosy's decline in much of Europe. The elaborate rituals and merciless rules by which leprosy patients were excluded from contact with normal society have been described extensively (Brody 1974; Richards 1977). If we consider the fact that Japan completely rid itself of leprosy early in this century by strictly separating contagious cases from the population (Saikawa 1981), it seems possible that the less scientific, but still powerful apparatus of medieval Europe may have produced the same end. This hypothesis, however, like so many others, cannot explain the persistence of the disease in Scandinavia. One difference, however, lies in the possibility that the organism is found in parts of Scandinavia outside a human host (in fact, in a type of moss), which would provide a reservoir of the organism able to survive irrespective of what happened to patients with the disease (Huang 1980; Job 1981).

It is often argued (e.g., by Russell 1977) that tuberculosis became the most important infectious disease during this period. Tuberculosis is simply too protean to be identifiable in the Middle Ages and Renaissance, except in rare instances. Its perceived effects on human demography are reasonable, but again real evidence is lacking.

The Renaissance

No two dates for the Renaissance ever seem to coincide. If we judge from art and literature, Giotto and Dante would place the starting date in the fourteenth century. If we follow the reasoning of Hans Baron that the Renaissance is a reflection of a civic image, the date shifts to 1405. Probably everyone would agree that Michelangelo and Leonardo da Vinci belong in the Renaissance, but if we turn to science the greatest change comes with Galileo, who lived after the Reformation! Very artificially, let us put this period at 1400 to 1550.

Two changes in European disease ecology stand out strongly. Both result from the new trade and exploration involving the Far East and the Americas. On the one hand, Europe became a major exporter of its endemic diseases to the Americas and appears to have acquired two diseases in return.

It has become increasingly apparent in recent years that the role of the introduction of European diseases such as smallpox into the Americas was a factor in the ability of the tiny European armies to conquer empires inhabited by millions of persons. Since it appears that the native American population had no previous exposure to such pathogens, the results were disastrous, and estimates have gone so far as to suggest that in the century after the establishment of contact with the Americas, up to 95 percent of the population of the major centers of American civilizations had perished. In part, the shift from ruler to ruled (or, in effect, enslaved) probably worsened the situation, as did the forced adoption of European religion, language, and customs. Europe's extensive prior experience with infectious diseases was to prove catastrophic later when,

for example, the Polynesian peoples were exposed to measles. Smallpox was probably the most disastrous disease for the post-Columbian Indians.

Within a few years of Columbus's discoveries, Europe perceived itself to be plagued by two new diseases, namely syphilis and typhus. The debate over syphilis has raged for many years, with some claiming that it was an import from the Americas, and others claiming that it was either first recognized as a disease entity at the end of the fifteenth century or was a new disease – the result of a mutation. When one considers the fact that skeletal evidence may show the existence of syphilis in pre-Columbian America, whereas no skeleton from Europe before 1495 has ever shown osseous changes, the first hypothesis seems more reasonable.

Typhus was also seen as new. Here the question is more difficult. First, it is not clear at this time whether recognition of typhus preceded the discovery of the New World. In any case, Europe's ties with new trading partners very likely caused typhus to appear in western Europe. Furthermore, typhus was not conclusively differentiated from typhoid fever until the nineteenth century, and thus the question of recognizing a new disease is extremely difficult. Nonetheless, it was perceived as new, and that in itself is of some importance.

In the case of syphilis and typhus, the perception of new diseases helped to end the rather static medical models of the time. They stimulated considerable written discussion and, of course, the poem from which the name syphilis comes. The perception of these diseases as "new" aspects of the human disease experience is perhaps most significant, but it is not clear at what point this perception began. Plague was known, at least in writing, from centuries past when it struck again in 1347, but syphilis and typhus were perceived as new. Probably the most important aspect of the diseases in Europe is the fact that the quality of Renaissance thought permitted observation to allow what mindset would have prohibited in the past.

Syphilis seems to have had a much more fulminant course than would be expected now. This again suggests a new disease in a previously unexposed society. As time passed, the pressure of the disease probably altered European population genetics toward genetic makeups capable, in most cases, of staving off the organism or coexisting with it.

From the point of view of disease ecology, the Renaissance marks the era of new diseases in two senses. The following years would see more and more precise and, to modern physicians, identifiable descriptions of diseases that had no doubt been extant for many years. Medicine did not, except in exceedingly rare instances, prove capable of combatting them, but at least it differentiated them.

The second sense of new diseases lies in the European export of diseases to previously unexposed peoples. F. Braudel (1979) has argued convincingly that, of the great civilizations of around the year 1500, Europe excelled only in its shipping. That shipping made it richer and more powerful, and permitted it to devastate the Americas and, later, other lands with its own combination of infectious diseases. Although the appearance of cycles of epidemic diseases, often from elsewhere, mark the history of ancient Greece, Rome, and the medieval world, the Europe of the Renaissance and later tended to be a potent exporter of disease.

Early Modern Europe, 1550–1800

What began in the Renaissance continued and accelerated in Early Modern Europe, except that new diseases were not a significant factor within Europe. The population recovered surprisingly quickly from plague epidemics. Some of the Italian city-states made grants of citizenship easier to obtain, so as to repopulate. Plague gradually became less common. Venice enjoyed more than half a century without an epidemic before the outbreak of 1630. By the eighteenth century, plague was rare indeed.

Cities remained unhealthy places, however. It is unclear if major cities could maintain their own population or continued to demand an influx from the countryside. Smallpox was probably the single worst childhood killer, although a variety of unidentifiable diseases took their toll. Among adults, it is assumed that tuberculosis was on the rise, although again evidence to support this contention is precarious. Many diseases can imitate tuberculosis, and tuberculosis can imitate many other diseases. Because the diagnosis became very reliable in the nineteenth century and because tuberculosis was then a severe problem, it is assumed that the same was the case in Early Modern Europe. It may well have been.

The countryside remained healthier than the city. Country homes for the wealthy city noble or merchant probably owe much to this fact. It is interesting to speculate how many of the magnificent villas along the Brenta near Venice would be there if plague had not so often threatened their owners' lives in the city. The population remained predominantly rural, and there are clear signs of population pressure for the first time since before 1300.

Although the first voyages to the Americas were primarily searches for trade routes and later for indigenous wealth to be returned to Europe, more and more colonists left Europe for the New World. At first, the settlers were primarily Spanish and Portuguese, but the British and French soon followed. Behind this one assumes a favorable turn in the disease ecology of Europe, allowing populations to increase. The gradual cessation of plague epidemics cannot have been the only factor. Leprosy maintained a foothold primarily in Scandinavia. What had been a European disease became a largely regional one. Plague pandemics gave way to much more local epidemics, with those more widely spaced in time.

Even medicine, in a practical way, began to offer some help. The discovery of quinine for use against malaria made life less risky in the tropics and even in those parts of Europe where malaria remained. The discovery of the use of citrus fruit to prevent scurvy allowed sea voyages to be longer without the risk of that peculiar ailment, only understood in near completeness in the twentieth century. Variolation and later vaccination began to bring the long reign of smallpox to an end. Smallpox was a perfect disease to attack by vaccination. The causative virus is not known to mutate, and is antigenically similar to the much less virulent virus that produces cowpox. This explanation was beyond the state of medical knowledge of the time, but many other positive contributions in medicine also have arisen pragmatically, whereas theory has often led to adverse treatments. In actual fact, medicine had only a very small impact on disease overall. The hospital, a medieval invention, remained for the most part a charitable rather than medical institution. In eighteenth-century France, 63 percent of all hospital beds were used to look after the needy, not to treat disease (Joerger 1980). In this period, those engaged in childbirthing care in Provence, France, underwent a change from older women serving simply as midwives, to younger, stronger women who could exert the strength sometimes necessary in dealing with difficult labor. An eighteenth-century tract on obstetrics comments on 600 difficult cases, in which 78 mothers and 230 infants died (Laget 1980), hardly a testimony to medical progress in this vital area.

Even the combination of all these effects seems inadequate to explain the growth of Europe's populations. Still, demographic balance is often precarious. Slight shifts in even a small number of diseases can mean the difference between population growth and decline. Clearly the population of Europe was increasing and had been since some point, not clearly identified, when plague no longer killed off as many as had been born and survived childhood.

It was during this period that Europe as an exporter of diseases proved spectacularly lethal. Measles, introduced into some of the South Pacific islands, resulted in essentially 100 percent mortality. In one sense, there is nothing more fittingly symbolic of the growing power and influence of Europe than the ability accidentally to kill off an entire population.

Just as the greatest generals of the ancient world gave insights into disease demography, so also does the career of Napoleon Bonaparte, with which we may end this brief discussion of the eve of the Industrial Revolution. At the time of Napoleon, we again see armies in the field numbering in the hundreds of thousands of men. Rome also produced armies of such magnitude (even if they were not concentrated in one place), but a very long interval elapsed before this phenomenon repeated itself.

Industrial and Post-Industrial Civilization

The most characteristic change in disease ecology relating to the Industrial Revolution and post-Industrial society is an almost complete exchange of the diseases of importance. Although medicine has claimed credit for the eradication of infectious diseases, it has been convincingly demonstrated that every major infectious disease of earlier times was already sharply in decline when medical cure became available, with only very few exceptions. Tuberculosis is an excellent example. The tuberculosis epidemic in England and Wales can be seen to have become very significant in the eighteenth century. It peaked around 1810 and then began to decline (Lovell 1957). Effective antibiotic therapy was well over a century away. T. McKeown (1976) has shown that the introduction of antibiotic therapy lies in the asymptotic portion of the curve of incidence.

The impact of the Industrial Revolution is difficult to overestimate. It produced profound changes in a nation's gross national product, patterns of raw material usage and consumption, and real incomes that in turn led to improved living standards. All of these helped to permit explosive population growth (Wrigley 1962). For example, the population of England and Wales was under 10 million in 1800, but in 1990 is approaching 50 million; world population took until 1830 to reach one billion and had quadrupled by 1975 (McKeown 1988). Yet another unique feature of the Industrial Revolution is that explosive population growth, which the exponential increase in wealth probably could have supported for a long time,

was replaced in Europe by a demography of indolent growth. This change seems to have been a directly voluntary effect. Contraception – however primitive the means – became the rule rather than the exception. Although the explosive growth begun in Europe during the Industrial Revolution continues, it does so primarily in the Third World, where agricultural progress and decreases in infant mortality allow impoverished populations to expand continuously.

Europe avoided this fate, and proceeded with a relatively stable population. Decreases in infant mortality caused average life expectancy to double, and more sanitary living conditions coupled with abundant food added still more years to the average life-span. Medicine played a major role in decreasing infant mortality, once the germ theory of disease had been accepted and infants were delivered under conditions conducive to their survival. But at the other end of the life spectrum, medicine has not contributed much. The diseases of modern societies are not primarily infectious. Atherosclerosis, interestingly enough the commonest radiographic finding when the royal mummies of ancient Egypt were X-rayed, has come to the fore as the most significant cause of adult mortality. Myocardial infarctions, fatal arrhythmias, and cerebrovascular accidents, respectively, are some of the major causes of death in modern society. This is a strikingly post-Industrial phenomenon. As late as the end of the nineteenth century, upper-class Englishmen ate a diet as rich in fats and cholesterol as the world has known. Obesity was the rule, not the exception. Yet myocardial infarction was almost unknown. For all the pretensions of modern medicine, the ecology of disease is still wrapped in mystery, particularly when it comes to the appearance and disappearance of individual diseases.

Cancer, certainly known for as long as there have been medical writings, but a rare cause of death in antiquity, has also become one of the commonest causes of death in modern society. Genetics plays some role. Some carcinogens have been convincingly identified, such as tobacco and asbestos. Yet the incidence of some cancers continues to rise, whereas the incidence of a commoner cancer of early industrial times (and still common today in parts of the Orient), namely adenocarcinoma of the stomach, is in decline. Diet is assumed to play a major role, but it is sobering to recall that diet has historically been implicated whenever it was unclear why a disease behaved as it did.

If we examine the length of the disease history of Europe, it is striking that patterns of disease experience, once identifiable, did not change significantly until the Industrial Revolution. In these terms, it is probably appropriate to divide history into post-Neolithic and post-Industrial only. In any case it is clear that the Industrial Revolution changed the disease ecology of Europe almost totally. Medicine has perfected the cure of the diseases that were in the process of disappearing anyway, but has grappled with only very limited success with the diseases of the new age (McKeown 1988). It remains for future historians to determine whether or not humans will be able to alter the disease ecology they have produced by industrialization.

Stephen R. Ell

Bibliography

Acsadi, Gy., and J. Nemeskevi. 1970. *History of human life span and mortality.* Budapest.

Alausa, O. K. 1983. Brucellosis in Nigeria: Epidemiology and practical problems of control. In *Human ecology and infectious diseases,* ed. N. A. Croll and J. H. Cross, 312–31. New York and London.

Archivio de Stato di Venezia. 1348. *Provveditori alla Sanità: Rubbrica delle Leggi,* Vol. 2, Folio 194.

Austin, M. M., and P. Vidal-Naquet. 1977. *Economic and social history of ancient Greece,* trans. M. M. Austin. Berkeley.

Bailey, N. T. J. 1954. A statistical method of estimating the periods of incubation and infection of an infectious disease. *Nature* 154: 139–40.

1957. *The mathematical theory of epidemics.* London.

Baratier, E. 1961. *La Démographie provençale du XIIIe au XIVe siècle.* Paris.

Bartlett, M. S. 1957. Measles periodicity and community size. *Journal of the Royal Statistical Society,* Ser. A, 120: 48–70.

1960. The critical community size for measles in the United States. *Journal of the Royal Statistical Society,* Ser. A, 123: 37–44.

Becker, N. G. 1979. The uses of the epidemic models. *Biometrics* 35: 295–305.

Beloch, J. 1937, 1940, 1961. *Bevölkerungsgeschichte Italiens.* Berlin.

Biraben, J.-N. 1975. *Les Hommes et la peste en France et dans les pays européens et méditerranéens,* Vol. 1. Paris.

Birdsell, J. B. 1957. Some population problems involving Pleistocene man. *Cold Spring Harbor Symposium of Quantitative Biology* 20: 47–69.

Bosworth, A. B. 1988. *Conquest and empire: The reign of Alexander the Great.* Cambridge and New York.

Braudel, F. 1979. *The structures of everyday life: Civilization and capitalism, 15th–18th century,* Vol. 1, 402–7. New York.

Brody, S. N. 1974. *The disease of the soul: Leprosy in medieval literature.* Ithaca and London.

Carpentier, E. 1962a. Autour de la peste noire: Famines et épidémies dans l'histoire du XIVe siècle. *Annales: Economies, Sociétés, Civilizations* 17: 1062–92.

1962b. *Une Ville devant la peste: Orvieto et la peste noire de 1348.* Paris.

Caven, B. 1980. *The Punic Wars.* New York.

Cipolla, C. M. 1981. *Fighting the plague in seventeenth century Italy.* Madison, Wis.

Duby, G. 1968. *Rural economy and country life in the medieval West,* trans. C. Postan. Columbia, S.C.

1981. *The age of the cathedrals,* trans. E. Levieux and B. Thompson. Chicago and London.

Eden, W. van, et al. 1980. HLA segregation of tuberculoid leprosy: Confirmation of the DR2 marker. *Journal of Infectious Diseases* 141: 693–701.

Ell, S. R. 1980. Interhuman transmission of medieval plague. *Bulletin of the History of Medicine* 54: 497–510.

1984a. Immunity as a factor in the epidemiology of medieval plague. *Reviews of Infectious Diseases* 6: 866–79.

1984b. Blood and sexuality in medieval leprosy. *Janus* 71: 153–64.

1985. Iron in two seventeenth-century plague epidemics. *Journal of Interdisciplinary History* 15: 445–57.

1986. Leprosy and social class in the Middle Ages. *International Journal of Leprosy* 54: 300–5.

1987. Plague and leprosy in the middle ages: A paradoxical cross-immunity? *International Journal of Leprosy* 55: 345–50.

1988. Reconstructing the epidemiology of medieval leprosy: Preliminary efforts with regard to Scandinavia. *Perspectives in Biology and Medicine* 31: 496–506.

1989a. Three days in October of 1630: Detailed examination of mortality during an early modern plague in Venice. *Reviews of Infectious Diseases* 11: 128–39.

1989b. Three times, three places, three authors, and one perspective on leprosy in Medieval and Early Modern Europe. *International Journal of Leprosy* 57: 823–33.

Finley, M. I. 1981. *Economy and society in ancient Greece.* London.

Flinn, M. W. 1985. *The European demographic system, 1500–1800.* Baltimore.

Gregory of Tours. 1905. *Historia francorum.* Monumenta Germaniae historica. Scriptores rerum merovingicarum, Book 5, Chapter 34.

Guillaume, P., and J.-P. Poussou. 1970. *Démographie historique.* Paris.

Herlihy, D. 1967. *Medieval and Renaissance pistoia.* New Haven, Conn.

1968. Santa Maria impruneta: A rural commune in the late middle ages. In *Florentine studies,* ed. N. Rubinstein, 242–71. Evanston, Ill.

Hopkins, D. R. 1983. *Peasants and princes: Smallpox in history.* Chicago and London.

Huang, C. L.-H. 1980. The transmission of leprosy in man. *International Journal of Leprosy* 48: 309–18.

Job, C. K. 1981. Leprosy – the source of infection and its

mode of transmission. *Leprosy Review* 52 (Suppl. 1): 69–76.

Joerger, M. 1980. The structure of the hospital system in France in the *ancien regime,* trans. E. Forster. In *Medicine and society in France,* ed. R. Forster and O. Ranum, 104–36. Baltimore.

Keyser, E. 1938. *Bevolkerungsgeschichte Deutschlands.* Leipzig.

Keyu, X., et al. 1985. HLA-linked control of predisposition to lepromatous leprosy. *International Journal of Leprosy* 53: 56–63.

Laget, M. 1980. Childbirth in seventeenth and eighteenth century France: Obstetrical practices and collective attitudes. In *Medicine and society in France,* ed. R. Forster and O. Ranum, 137–76. Baltimore.

Lane, F. 1973. *Venice: A maritime republic.* Baltimore.

Lindberg, D. 1978. The transmission of Greek and Arabic learning to the West. In *Science in the Middle Ages,* ed. D. Lindberg, 52–90. Chicago.

Lopez, R. 1967. *The birth of Europe.* New York and Philadelphia.

Lovell, R. 1957. The biological influences of man and animals on microbial ecology. In *Microbial ecology,* 315–27. Cambridge.

Luttwak, E. N. 1976. *The grand strategy of the Roman Empire.* Baltimore.

McKeown, T. 1976. *The modern rise of population.* New York.

1988. *The origins of human disease.* Oxford.

McNeill, W. H. 1976. *Plagues and peoples.* Garden City, N.Y.

Mols, R. J. 1954–6. *Introduction à la démographie historique des villes de l'Europe du XIVe au XVIIIe siècle.* Gembloux.

Musset, L. 1971. *Les Invasions: Le second assaut contre l'Europe chrétienne VIe–XIe siècles.* Paris.

Neraudau, J.-P. 1984. *Etre enfant à Rome.* Paris.

Richards, P. 1977. *The medieval leper and his northern heirs.* Totowa, N.J.

Rotberg, R. I., and T. K. Rabb. 1983. *Hunger and history: The impact of changing food production and consumption patterns on society.* Cambridge.

Russell, J. C. 1971. *Medieval regions and their cities.* Newton Abbot.

1977. Population in Europe. 500–1500. In *The Fontana economic history of Europe,* Vol. 1: *The Middle Ages,* ed. Carlo Cipolla, 25–70. London and Glasgow.

Saikawa, K. 1981. The effect of rapid sosio[*sic*]-economic development of the frequency of leprosy in a population. *Leprosy Review* 52 (Suppl. 1): 167–75.

Sansaarico, H. 1981. Leprosy in the world today. *Leprosy Review* 51 (Suppl. 1): 1–15.

Siegried, A. 1960. *Itinéraires des contagions: Epidémies et idéologies.* Paris.

Smith, D. G. 1979. The genetic hypothesis of susceptibility to lepromatous leprosy. *Human Genetics* 50: 163–77.

Smith, D. M. 1983. Epidemiology patterns in directly transmitted human infections. In *Human ecology and infectious diseases,* ed. N. A. Croll and J. H. Cross, 332–52. New York and London.

Southern, R. 1966. *The making of the Middle Ages.* New Haven, Conn.

Stock, B. 1978. Science, technology, and economic progress in the Early Middle Ages. In *Science in the Middle Ages,* ed. D. Lindberg, 1–51. Chicago and London.

Thucydides. 1958. *The Peloponnesian war,* trans. R. Crawley. Garden City, N.Y.

Tomich, P. Q., et al. 1984. Evidence for the extinction of plague in Hawaii. *American Journal of Epidemiology* 119: 261–73.

Veyne, P. ed. 1987. *A history of private life: From Rome to Byzantium,* trans. A. Goldhammer. Cambridge, Mass., and London.

White, L. 1962. *Medieval technology and social change.* Oxford.

Wilson, G. S. 1957. The selective action on bacteria of various factors inside and outside the body, with particular reference to their effect on virulence. In *Microbial ecology,* 338–59. Cambridge.

Wrigley, E. A. 1962. *Population and history.* New York and Toronto.

VII.8
Disease Ecologies of North America

America north of the Rio Grande, that life zone sometimes referred to as the Nearctic region, presents the scholar of history and geography of disease with numerous challenges. These include such questions as the following: What potential disease-causing agents existed in the hemisphere before the comparatively recent arrival of human beings? How effective was the "cold screen" (Stewart 1960) in ensuring the health of the migrants crossing the link from Eurasia to the New World? Given the isolation of this population, how varied was it in a genetic sense, and how well adapted did it become to North American ecologies? Were native North Americans indeed "far more healthy than any others of whom we know" (Ashburn 1980)? Just what was the impact of the "Columbian exchange" (Crosby 1972)? Did these invaders receive the country "from the hands of nature pure and healthy" (Rush 1786)? What relative contribution to ill health and disease did the European group provide compared to that of the enslaved African populations? What were the dimensions and timing of the "epidemiologic transition" in North America (Omran 1977)? How real have urban and rural differences in health experience been through time? How serious is the threat today of "life-style" diseases?

Clearly all of these and other equally intriguing questions arise. This brief discussion can only hope to touch on some of them and to review a portion of the work by persons from biochemists to medical historians, from archaeologists to medical geographers, who have applied their learning to the fascinating question of human well-being through the ages in North America.

The Ecological Region

North America, which is separated from the Old World by major oceans (apart from the Bering Strait, now a mere 85 kilometers wide), encompasses an area of just over 19 million square kilometers. It stretches across 136° of longitude, from 52° west at Cape Spear in Newfoundland to 172° east longitude at Attu Island in the western extremity of the Aleutians, but its latitudinal extent of 64°, from 83° north at Ellesmere Island to the Florida Keys, is all north of the Tropic of Cancer. Nevertheless, tropical influence is not unknown in the region, as the continent is open to climatic incursions along the Gulf coast penetrating across the interior Mississippian lowlands northward to the Great Lakes. In essence, this means that extratropical cyclones develop along the jet stream and migrate from west to east and, in so doing, draw up hot humid air in summer, and lead to incursions of freezing air masses as far south as Florida in winter.

Throughout the eastern and central sections then, seasonal contrasts are marked, especially when compared to those of northwestern Europe. The mountains of the West modify these conditions, giving rise to wet Pacific coastlands in the north and semiarid rainshadow valleys on the eastern lee with subhumid areas extending over more and more extensive areas toward the southwest. The natural vegetation mirrors the climatic conditions. It ranges from luxuriant forests of the Northwest through scrub and grasses of the semiarid plains and the evergreen boreal forests of the northlands, to the deciduous forests of the East fringed on the southeast coast by marshlands, with each presenting its own niches for life forms from buffalo to mosquito.

Indigenous Disease Agents of North America

Within this varied habitat a myriad of organisms lived and died with the usual range of interrelationships ecologists have led us to expect. Birds and mammals must have had their parasites, and, it is assumed, sylvan cycles of infection and death took place. To identify these in the lack of any, as yet, human presence is difficult, but insofar as today's known zoonoses cycles in North America have been elucidated, some endemic conditions can be postulated.

These would include the bacteria known to cause tularemia, botulism, relapsing fever, anthrax, and pasteurellosis (Cockburn 1971; Meade, Florin, and Gesler 1988) as well as the highly localized *Babesia microtia* of ticks infesting rodents on Nantucket Island. Additionally, *Rickettsia rickettsii* of the tick *Ixodes* infested small mammals, and possibly *Rickettsia typhii* was carried by the fleas on native rodent species already present (Newman 1976). More certainly, the viral encephalitis group is nidal in the region (MacLean 1975), as are a number of helminthic conditions such as the tapeworm *Diphyllobothrium pacificum,* whose definitive host is the Pacific seal (Patrucco, Tello, and Bonavia 1983), the pinworm *Enterobius vermicularis,* and the thorny-headed worm *Acanthocephala;* all are parasites of wild animals (Fry, Moore, and Englert 1969; Fry and Moore 1970). The parasitic flatworm of migratory waterfowl, whose intermediate host is the snail, is endemic among the bird populations of the North American flyways, and has probably been so for eons before unfortunate humans encountered the cercariae and experienced "swimmers' itch" (Du-Four 1986).

Other organisms associated with water and the faunal population include *Leptospira* (although the agent of Weil's disease was not present until the introduction of its natural host, the brown rat – *Rattus norvegicus*) and a number of *Salmonella* organisms carried by seagulls and other sea-living animals including oysters and fish (Ffrench 1976). Furthermore, the free-living ameba *Naegleria flowleri,* inhabiting soil, water, and decaying vegetation (but only entering medical literature as a disease agent in 1965), along with other similar organisms, has long been in the environmental complex of Nearctica (Craun 1986).

Still another group of organisms associated (in at least 27 cases) with a free-living existence in soil and water is the mycobacteria (Runyon 1971). As is well known, some species of the genus *Mycobacterium* are associated with human tuberculosis and leprosy. Others, however, called "environmental," vary in frequency, depending upon locale, soil conditions, and climate; and modern American studies have shown that human exposure to these is quite common (Steinbock 1987). Furthermore, *Mycobacterium bovis* and occasionally *Mycobacterium avium* produce disease in humans that is clinically identical to that caused by *Mycobacterium tuberculosis*. Native Nearctic guinea pigs, mice, bison, and birds may well have harbored these varieties. Thus organisms capable of causing human tubercular lesions were almost certainly in the New World before the advent of humans (Anderson et al. 1975).

Prehistoric Incidence of Disease

According to L. E. St. Hoyme (1969): "[I]t is easy enough to explain why few diseases entered the New World with man; it is far harder to explain the origin of those diseases that man acquired in the New World before the coming of Columbus." The entry of humans into the Nearctic realm through the land bridge of the Bering Straits area up to 35,000 years ago (Yi and Clark 1985) has been assumed to have been sporadic, small scale, and across a harsh environment. More recently, the founding groups have been seen as limited to between 300 and 500 and possibly associated with but three waves of migration – the so-called Amerind, Na-Dene, and the Aleut-Eskimo – none older than 15,000 B.C.; the order of chronology, however, remains uncertain (Greenberg, Turner, and Zegura 1986). Given this general scenario, it is claimed that the numbers would be far too small to sustain a human-to-human mode of infection (Cockburn 1963; St. Hoyme 1969). However:

As man wandered around the world, he would take many of his parasites with him. Those such as the louse, the pinworm, herpes virus, typhoid bacillus, and others that were closely attached to him would not have great trouble in travelling in this fashion. Others that required transmission by a specific intermediate host would die out once the territory of the necessary intermediate hosts was left behind. (Cockburn 1963)

Moreover, it now seems possible that human tuberculosis made the voyage as well, in that one or more of the Bering Strait migrants may have had a childhood primary infection that, like 5 percent of cases today, developed into chronic destructive tuberculosis (Myers 1965; Steinbock 1987). The predisposing factors for this transformation (any condition that impairs acquired cell-mediated immunity) include poor nutrition, diabetes, or an acute infection possibly from a traumatic incident. All of these could have occurred in a band of hunter-gatherer adventurers in spite of the "cold screen." At least one scholar (Klepinger 1987), however, denies that there is any evidence of the disease being carried

over by the Beringia transmigrants, and claims that it would be more likely to arise de novo in the Western Hemisphere.

But what of the "cold screen" or, perhaps more correctly, the cold filter? T. D. Stewart (1960), arguing that New World populations were relatively free of Old World pathogens, stated that "the cold of the Far North has been characterized as a screen serving in past times to prevent the flow of many pathological germs along with the movements of their human hosts," a position that has become widely accepted in the literature (Jarcho 1964; Hare 1967; Dunn 1968; St. Hoyme 1969; Crosby 1972, 1986; Newman 1976; Martin 1978; Dobyns 1983). Thus it has been claimed that

[n]ot only did very few people of any origin cross the great oceans, but those who did must have been healthy or they would have died on the way, taking their pathogens with them. The indigenes were not without their own infections, of course. The Amerindians had at least pinta, yaws, venereal syphilis, hepatitis, encephalitis, polio, some varieties of tuberculosis (not those usually associated with pulmonary disease), and intestinal parasites, but they seem to have been without any experience with such Old World maladies as smallpox, measles, diphtheria, trachoma, whooping cough, chicken pox, bubonic plague, malaria, typhoid fever, cholera, yellow fever, dengue fever, scarlet fever, amebic dysentery, influenza, and a number of helminthic infestations. (Crosby 1986)

The aborigines, then, seem to have been relatively disease-free, as a result of their isolated and limited populations initially, and the harsh climate. Moreover, given the nature of the immigrant economy, and the paucity of animal domesticates, only the guinea pig, turkey, and South American cameloids served along with the dog in the New World as reservoirs for horizontal transfer of disease (Newman 1976). Thus we have an image of human beings in a nearly ideal state of physical health, removed from the main channels of human disease (Dubos 1968). However, B. Trigger (1985) has rightly warned:

Scholars should not succumb to the temptation of believing that in prehistoric times illnesses had not been prevalent or of concern to native people [for] [t]he extraordinary levels of mortality and other misfortunes that followed European contact must have caused them to idealize earlier times as a halcyon age of physical health, economic prosperity, and social harmony.

Alfred Crosby (1986) maintains that the spirochetal diseases of pinta, yaws, and venereal syphilis were present in pre-Columbian America. A great deal has been written regarding *Treponema pallidum* (the organism causing venereal syphilis) and its virulent expression in Europe following the discovery of Nearctica (Cockburn 1971; Crosby 1972). However, it appears now that like many other organisms this one spirochete has adapted over time to present different clinical patterns under different climatic and sociological regimes (Hudson 1963, 1965, 1968). Moreover, C. J. Hackett (1963, 1967) has argued that pinta was brought into the Americas by the founding groups and has "a long duration of infectiousness which would maintain it in small population groups, even in families, which suggests that it is the early human treponematosis."

Additionally, there is some suggestion that the treponematosis that causes yaws produced depressions in some prehistoric Indian crania, which may indicate a northern extension of yaws in earlier times up the Mississippi into the Midwest (St. Hoyme 1969). On the other hand, as recently as 1967, it was argued that there was no osteological proof of pre-Columbian yaws and that the traditional view that it had been introduced by African slaves was still acceptable (Stewart and Spoehr 1967). In addition, recent reports (Rothschild and Turnbull 1987) of syphilis in a Pleistocene bear skeleton in Nebraska have been discounted, as no authenticated treponemal infections have been found in a nonprimate (Neiburger 1988).

In summary, sparse populations of indigenes would be fairly free of diseases transmitted from other humans, although their contact with game, and especially their ingestion of raw meat and of water, would bring them into contact with some invasive pathogens (Fenner 1970). Their necessarily mobile hunting-and-gathering life-style would protect them from a degree of self-contamination, but failure of the hunt would periodically stress them and accidents would traumatize some.

As the sedentary maize-based cultures spread north from Mexico, villages appearing after 7000 B.C. and, later, larger settlements (possibly as large as 40,000 as at Cohokia, Illinois) created other health problems, among them those of sanitation (Heidenreich 1971; Crosby 1986). Furthermore, the invasion of settlements by rodents and fleas would have led to human contact with the illnesses of native animals (Dobyns 1983). One can only speculate as to the impact of these concomitant aspects of agriculture; but while the carrying capacity of local areas, and hence their population densities, grew, there is no firm evidence that morbidity declined. Rather, there may well have been a shift in the

causes of death, reflecting the new relationship between human and land (Martin 1978; Dobyns 1983).

The Native American and Disease Ecology

The long-term result of the development of North American peoples in the absence of contact with others was a healthy population adjusted to its environmental niches. Humankind had multiplied from the founding stock and by the late fifteenth century numbered somewhere between 4.4 million (Ubelaker 1976) and 9.8 million (Dobyns 1966). Within this total, a degree of variety had arisen in the human populations of Nearctica in the course of some 600 generations, reflecting the historical and environmental conditions (Brues 1954; Szathmary 1984).

The genetic characteristics of American Indian populations are sufficiently similar to one another and different from those of other continental groups to permit (as a first approximation) of their description as a "distinct" subgroup of the human species. . . . Closer analysis of genetic affinities reveals that over larger areas the genetic continuity takes the modified form of gradients or clines. Thus the frequency of the gene for blood group A decreases from north to south, that for the allele for the Diego factor and the M gene increases from north to south. (Weiner 1971; see also Suarez, Crouse, and O'Rourke 1985)

Throughout the region the B gene is singularly lacking, with almost all Amerindian groups belonging to the O blood group. This situation may explain a particular susceptibility to smallpox on its introduction (Mourant, Kopec, and Domaniewska-Sobczak 1958). Not all scholars agree even on this point, however:

The role of the blood groups in the resistance of certain infections or parasites has been controversial. If it was demonstrated, its importance would be significant in accounting for the repetition of certain factors . . . [I]n the region of pestilential or variolic endemic diseases, the plague would be worse and more frequent among people with type O, and smallpox, among those with type A. (Bernard and Ruffie 1966, trans. Graham)

This interpretation is based on the discovery that *Pasteurella pestis* possesses an antigen similar to the H antigen, whereas the variola virus has an antigen similar to the A antigen. As people with blood group O are not able to produce any anti-H antibody (which corresponds to the H antigen of *P. pestis*), they have a very poor prognosis when infected (Vogel, Pettenkofer, and Helmbold 1960; Matsunage 1962, 1982). Although anthropologists and others have used these studies to support theories of genetic distance and purity of Amerindian stock (Post,

Neel, and Schull 1968; Roberts 1976; Szathmary 1984), the consensus on the theory of genetic susceptibility to disease is that the case is unproven in the context of the exposure of these peoples to the imported Old World infections (Newman 1976; Ward 1980; Joralemon 1982).

There is, however, increasing evidence in genetic epidemiology that certain conditions are related to genotype–environment interactions. In the case of contemporary North American native peoples, these conditions include inflammation of the inner ear (Gregg, Steele, and Holzheuter 1965), gallbladder disease (Burch, Comess, and Bennett 1968), diabetes (Miller, Bennett, and Burch 1968), and alcoholism (Broudy and May 1983; *Social Biology* 1985). Indeed, it has been claimed that at the present time

Many Amerindian peoples are experiencing a major epidemic of a series of diseases which include a tendency to become obese at an early adult age, adult onset of *diabetes mellitus,* the formation of cholesterol gallstones. [T]his epidemic . . . seems to be due to an interaction between susceptible Amerindian genotype(s) and some recently changed aspect of the environment, probably involving dietary components. (Weiss, Ferrell, and Hania 1984)

It would seem, then, that there is evidence of an ecology of disease specifically associated with the continent's native peoples, one of the three major human stocks presently inhabiting the region.

The Columbian Impact

Although evidence of varying quality exists for human penetration of Nearctica prior to the arrival of Columbus in 1492 (Boland 1961), that event and the almost simultaneous arrival of Africans were to be catastrophic in terms of the disease ecology of the continent (Ashburn 1947; Crosby 1972, 1976; McNeill 1976). Europeans and Africans represented a totally different set of disease foci and introduced pathogens that initially devastated the native Americans. The age of contagious or infectious disease had dawned in America. There were two basic reasons for this, beyond the obvious one of disease importation. The first involved the zoonoses introduced as a result of the transfer of animals previously unknown to the continent; the second related to the colonization that led to communities having threshold populations that could sustain infection.

In the initial period, European diseases spread rapidly into the interior, outdistancing the newcomers who had brought them, while decimating native populations (Dobyns 1983). This fact, in turn, gave rise to the realization that Europeans – and in the south, Africans – entered what Francis Jennings (1975) has called a "widowed" land. This interpretation, in contradistinction to that of the "Black Legend" (Newman 1976), which blamed the decline of native populations on the cruelty and warfare of the invading peoples, views the role of accidentally introduced disease as critical. "Virgin soil" disease ecologists argue that persons having no previous contact with the larger pathogen pool of humanity are immunologically defenseless. And so the Amerindians who had not before encountered Old World bacteria and viruses succumbed in large numbers to ailments that scarcely touched the immune Europeans (Hauptman 1979; Joralemon 1982; Dobyns 1983; Curtin 1985; Hader 1986). M. T. Newman (1976), however, warns:

There is mounting evidence that American Indians were no more susceptible to most of these infectious disease imports than other populations where these diseases had not struck within the lifetime of the people – none of whom therefore had acquired specific immunities.

For this reason Newman quotes W. R. Centerwall (1968), who called for "a reevaluation . . . with respect to the primary susceptibility of the Indian to . . . diseases of civilization, such as pertussis (whooping cough), smallpox, and tuberculosis"; and Centerwall concluded that "during the conquest, cultural disruption should be added to the impacts of the new pathogens, compounded by the force of European arms and the later ill-treatment of slavery."

Numerous other scholars have also implicated psychological, economic, and social factors stemming from introduced disease in the high mortality and even decimation of Amerindian populations (Crosby 1976; Dobyns 1976, 1983; Meister 1976; Miller 1976; Trigger 1985). In any event, the indigenes went into decline as their battle with disease resulted generally in high death rates – up to 90 percent has been mentioned in some smallpox outbreaks, with case fatalities of 74 percent in others (see Fenner 1970; Joralemon 1982; Hader 1986).

This kind of die-off, of course, did not occur simultaneously or uniformly across the continent (Meister 1976). Pertussis, smallpox, pulmonary tuberculosis, measles, diphtheria, trachoma, chickenpox, bubonic plague, malaria, typhus, typhoid fever, cholera, scarlet fever, influenza, and a number of intestinal infections arrived with the Europeans at various times over 5 centuries. Of these, smallpox has generally been seen as the most dramatic (Ashburn 1947) and was one of the earliest to arrive. In Española it made

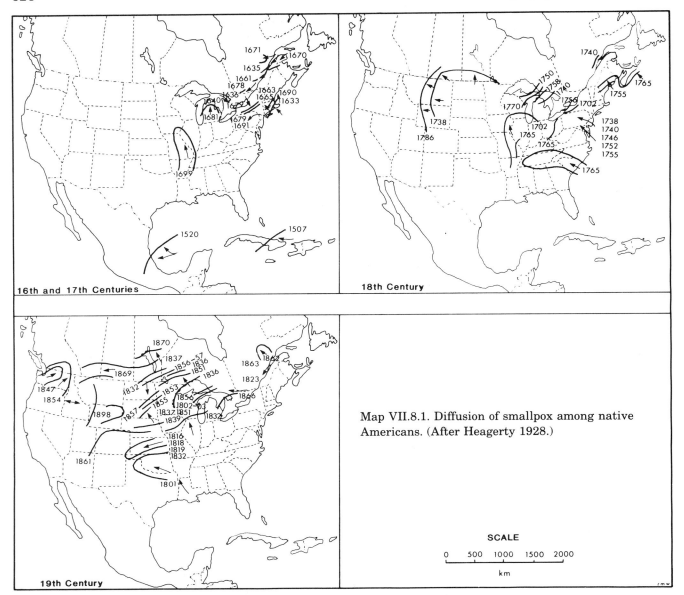

Map VII.8.1. Diffusion of smallpox among native Americans. (After Heagerty 1928.)

its appearance by 1519 (Crosby 1986), and was present in North America prior to the middle of the century, spreading northward from Mexico (Dobyns 1983; Trigger 1985). As a new disease moving without an intermediary vector, from person to person, it hit those of all ages, although the mortality of young males in many populations was especially devastating (Ray 1974).

Most Europeans had experienced smallpox in childhood, and hence were protected, but this was not true for the Amerindians or, for that matter, many of the blacks in America. Repeated introductions along the East Coast and up the St. Lawrence led to further outbreaks from the seventeenth to the nineteenth century, including an outbreak that dramatically influenced the population decline in Huronia in 1639–40 (Trigger 1985), and the 1837 epi-

demic on the Great Plains, which decimated about half the remaining natives there (Hearne 1782, quoted in Innis 1962; Crosby 1976).

Maps VII.8.1 and VII.8.2, based on J. J. Heagerty (1928) and H. F. Dobyns (1983), respectively, summarize in a stylistic manner the history and geography of these outbreaks and illustrate that full elucidation of these events awaits an in-depth study based on original accounts, documents, and interpretations. Thus the hypothesized lower susceptibility, of those with a dominance of blood group O, noted above, is not borne out by the historical evidence. On the other hand, the anomalous group of the Blackfoot Indians, with their A blood group, certainly suffered very severely; over two-thirds or some 6,000 Blackfoot were decimated in the smallpox outbreak of 1837 (Bradley 1900; Ewers 1958).

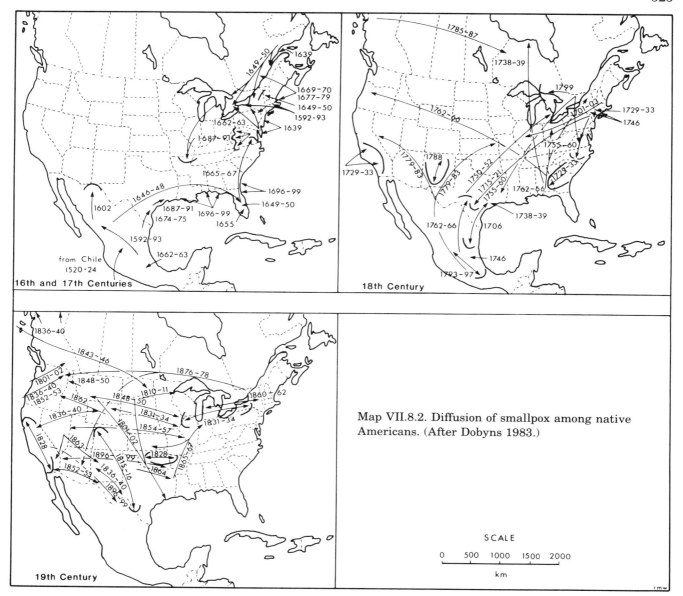

Map VII.8.2. Diffusion of smallpox among native Americans. (After Dobyns 1983.)

SCALE

0   500   1000   1500   2000

km

The Europeans, however, were not all immune to smallpox, as population growth in the colonies increased the number of susceptibles. Thus, in Boston a 10 percent death rate from this scourge was recorded for 1721, and in each of the years 1702, 1730, and 1752 over 6 percent of the population of that city died from this one disease (Dobson 1987).

Measles was also introduced in the seventeenth century from Europe, and as early as 1635 the Jesuits reported an outbreak among the French and Indians (Duffy 1972). The disease was very contagious, and a series of epidemics such as those of 1713–15 spread inland from the seaports. Indeed, in 1772 measles was a leading cause of death in Boston (Duffy 1972) and was claimed to be more often fatal in America than in England as in the former it took the form of a series of introduced epidemics and affected a larger number of adults in the New World. Only late in the colonial period, with population clusters in excess of 500,000, could measles or, for that matter, smallpox become established as endemic in America (Black 1966; Fenner 1970; Cliff et al. 1981). When and where this first occurred is not known, but it was probably not until the nineteenth century (Cartwright 1972). The fact that the pair of diseases was confused in the records does not help in establishing this important turning point.

Unlike the two diseases just discussed (and other purely human diseases such as scarlet fever and diphtheria), vectored diseases and zoonoses required infective agents to become established in the New World. Just two of these – plague and malaria – will be discussed. Plague was one of the earliest diseases to be introduced from Europe (Williams 1909; Posey 1976). Rats infested every ship that crossed the Atlantic, though only occasionally was the rat–human relationship as close as that described by Colonel H. Norwood (n.d.) in the mid-seventeenth century. "The infinite number of rats that all the voyage had been our plague, we now were glad to make our prey to feed on." No doubt, however, those that survived landed and by 1612–19 in Florida and New England, these newcomers and their fleas had given rise to human plague (Dobyns 1983). As D. A. Posey (1976) explains, "Once the rodent carriers were transported to this virgin territory, the plague would have spread as wild native rodent populations became reservoirs of the dreaded disease . . . and few, if any, animals, except the louse were more common in Indian and colonial camps."

Thus, the conditions were present for plague long before the first fully documented case was recorded in 1899 as having come from Japan into San Francisco (Link 1953; Schiel and Jameson 1973). Three views of plague in the hemisphere can be sustained on the basis of present knowledge. One view is that it has long existed, even from prehistoric times as a sylvatic cycle disease in rodents. The remaining two, more probable, views entail its introduction from Europe, followed by possible extinction in eastern locations, and the documented transpacific reintroduction in the late nineteenth century. Certainly this third route has given rise to endemic plague from the Mexican border to Alberta primarily among ground squirrels and their fleas (Hubbard 1947). Unfortunately, domestic animals from time to time pick up these fleas and transport them into Western homes where occasional human infections are contracted, the annual incidence rate being 3.4 cases per year, 1927–69 (Canby 1977).

Falciparum malaria, dysentery, smallpox, intestinal worms, yaws, guinea worm, schistosomiasis, and yellow fever were contributed by the African slave (Ashburn 1980; Dunn 1965). Of these African diseases, malaria and yellow fever were the most significant (McNeill 1976), but their impact differed among the major population groups involved (Postell 1951; Duffy 1972; Kiple and Kiple 1977). In the case of malaria, the African slaves usually had been previously exposed, or had blood anomalies to protect them. Malaria among this group was generally a childhood disease in terms of mortality, though recurrence in later years was debilitating. On the other hand, among native Amerindians mortality from malaria could be as high as 75 percent (Dobyns 1983),

but malaria was more often a predisposing condition rather than a fatal disease once the milder vivax malaria (introduced from Europe) became established in the Mississippian west. For Europeans (who may have been exposed to the vivax variety in England), falciparum malaria was deadly wherever it had been introduced to the local mosquitoes by slaves along the marshlands of the Atlantic and Gulf coasts (Childs 1940; Savitt 1978).

Although a variety of strains and perhaps even both major species may have been introduced by diverse carriers at a fairly early date, a more probable model, given the flow of immigration and the prevalence of *vivax* in Europe and *falciparum* in Africa, would have strains of the former entering during the first half of the [seventeenth] century, followed by the gradual establishment of areas of stable, low-level endemicity. The shattering of this picture would occur as blacks in numbers began arriving from a variety of African areas, bringing with them new strains of . . . *falciparum*. . . . [A] qualitative change occurred sometime in the second half of the century as *falciparum* entered the colony. . . . [T]he benign *vivax* was prevalent in the 1670's but was supplanted by the more virulent *falciparum* in the 1680's. (Rutman and Rutman 1976)

Further vivax introductions from African sources would be strictly limited because of the absence of the Duffy blood group determinants Fy^a and Fy^b in most individuals of African descent, which prevents them from hosting the disease (Mourant, Kopec, and Domaniewska-Sobczak 1976).

The transmission, of course, depended on the transmission of infection to *Anopheles* mosquitoes from those suffering with malaria parasites. Unfortunately, Nearctica was already amply provided with potential vectors (Freeborn 1949), and these mosquitoes became instrumental in spreading the infection from the south and east right up the Mississippi Valley as far as Canada, where seasonal transmission took place among the native peoples and settlers locally into the 1940s (Drake 1850/1954; Moulton 1941; Ackerknecht 1945). Furthermore, malaria was widespread in the nineteenth century in the Pacific Northwest of the continent (Boyd 1985; see also Map VII.8.3). Indeed, infection and even death from this imported disease still take place in North America, although changed environmental and social conditions led to its retreat to the South. By the 1950s, malaria – "*the* United States disease of the late 19th century" (Meade, Florin, and Gesler 1988) – had been eradicated. Much of the resurgence of the South and its development as the "Sun Belt" are related to this aspect of disease ecology.

The nineteenth-century social and economic condi-

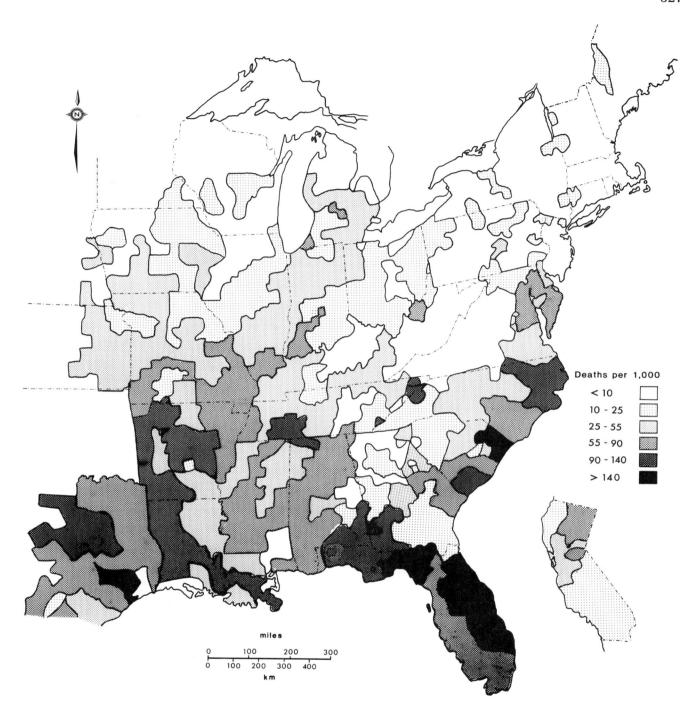

Map VII.8.3. Malarial disease deaths per 1,000 population, 1870. (Based on Ninth U.S. Census; assembled by author.)

tions, together with improved communication and ever increasing flows of immigrants, opened the continent to further invasions of disease. Indeed, immigrants, poverty, and disease were almost synonymous in many circles in this period. Most dramatic of these imported epidemics were those of cholera, with its ability to kill an estimated 40 to 60 percent of its victims within hours (Morris 1976) and an etiology that was unknown until Robert Koch discov-

ered the microorganism *Vibrio cholerae* in 1883. In the pandemics of 1831–2, 1848–50, 1853–4, and 1866, North America was not spared. Entering at port cities such as New York, Quebec, and New Orleans, the disease spread with the migrants and created terror but eventually catalyzed the development of meaningful public health reporting and treatment networks (Bilson 1980). This result would perhaps have taken much longer to achieve than it

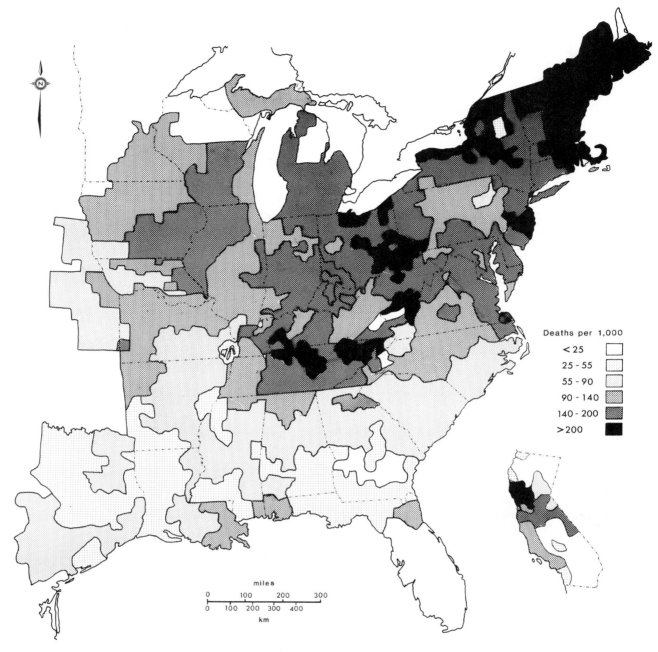

Map VII.8.4. "Consumption" deaths per 1,000 population, 1870. (Based on Ninth U.S. Census; assembled by author.)

actually did had not this one condition had such a powerful effect on the population as a whole.

The other great scourge of the nineteenth century was pulmonary tuberculosis, also known as the "white plague." As previously noted, mycobacteria had long been present in the Western Hemisphere, but it was only in the nineteenth century, with urbanization (crowding of masses of people, often in poor-quality housing and lacking good nutrition), that this person-to-person infection assumed epidemic proportions (Ashburn 1947; Cockburn 1963).

It came to "transcend all maladies in the total number of its victims and the cost to society" (Ashburn 1947; see also Map VII.8.4).

That Amerindians had little experience with epidemic tuberculosis prior to contact with Europeans (Clark et al. 1987) is borne out by the dramatic susceptibility of Indians after exposure. For example, R. G. Ferguson (1934) wrote:

A most disastrous epidemic appeared among the tribes settled on the reservations and within a few years [after

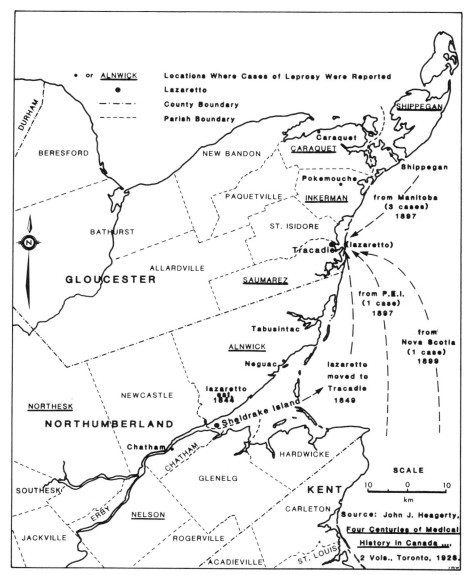

Map VII.8.5. Leprosy area of New Brunswick, predominantly in the nineteenth century. (From Heagerty 1928.)

1879] the general death rate among them was varying from 90 to 140 deaths per 1,000, two-thirds of these due to tuberculosis.

In 1928 the U.S. Bureau of the Census reported that 11.6 percent of Amerindian deaths were due to tuberculosis, as compared to 5.5 percent of Negro deaths and 5.6 percent of all white deaths (Ashburn 1947).

As far as blacks are concerned, some suggest that tuberculosis was rare among slaves (Postell 1951), though all agree that during Reconstruction it became a major cause of ill health and mortality, as social and economic conditions for most blacks declined markedly (Savitt 1978). As for other mycobacteria, leprosy is said to have been introduced with the slave population (Ashburn 1947) and remained an endemic disease in small numbers into

modern times. (Among Europeans, it had been introduced [Heagerty 1928] but never became established, except for a brief period in the Florida Keys. Only a handful of persons – for instance, in New Brunswick – are recorded as having had the disease; see Map VII.8.5; Losier and Pinet 1984).

The Present and the Past

Writing in 1963, A. Cockburn claimed that "tuberculosis had not displaced malaria as the world's number one problem in infectious disease," but like malaria, it has become rare and under control in Nearctica.

Like other so-called developed areas, North America has undergone both demographic and epidemiological transitions (Omran 1977): from high birth and death rates to low birth and death rates, and from the predominance of infectious diseases in causing death, to a preeminence of degenerative diseases (heart disease and cancers) in causing death (Dubos 1968). Genes replace "germs" as the significant variables in these societies (Ward 1980). Having said that, one can question just how and when these transitions took place. Almost certainly they did not occur simultaneously for each of the three groups discussed here. The Amerindians survived an initial period of adjustment on entering the continent, when adaptation would bring great stress but infections as such would be rare. They then grew in numbers and, with the development of agriculture and sedentary villages, attained densities that gave rise to self-contamination, in addition to the hazards of the field and hunt. However, as St. Hoyme (1969) observed, "At the time of the conquest, Indians suffered less from contagious diseases than from arthritis, nutritional and metabolic disturbances, and nonspecific infections associated with traumata."

At this point, the era of exotic contagions dawned, with death rates threatening extinction. This did not happen uniformly or necessarily (Meister 1976). Thus, some areas experienced rapid population decline, and others growth. Gradually white newcomers and, to a lesser extent, blacks, as well as Amerindians, all adjusted to the new disease environment, and populations recovered, only to encounter new hazards as a result of environmental moves from traditional homelands.

Today, however, most Amerindian groups continue to have high infant mortality rates and high rates of infectious disease. The blacks, too, like the Amerindians prior to contact, were in a state of health homeostasis when rudely plucked from Africa and transported to the New World, with a terrible toll being paid en route (Pope-Hennessy 1967; Kiple 1984). Once in America they suffered a large number of infections that, according to William Postell (1951),

may have been caused by dietary deficiency. The great number of dental caries, sore eyes, sore mouths, sore feet and legs, and skin lesions is suggestive of pellagra . . . for it is suspected that the slave received an improperly balanced diet, particularly during the winter months [and] suffered greatly from cholera, pneumonia, dysentery . . . and probably to a lesser extent than his white master, from yellow fever and malaria.

Respiratory complaints or "pleuretical disorders" were particularly fatal to them (Duffy 1972). Since the days of slavery, conditions have improved for black Americans, but much more slowly than for the white segment of the population. Thus there are now fewer deaths from fevers and tuberculosis and infant mortality is declining, but both are still much higher among blacks than among white Americans (Bouvier and Van der Tak 1976). The result is that the national mortality rates for the United States for many ages and causes are inflated by inclusion of the relatively disadvantaged black minority, and the full impact of lower birth and death rates has not yet been seen for this group.

White Americans, like the blacks, experienced an initial seasoning period upon arriving in Nearctica. Thereafter they grew rapidly in numbers, experiencing more healthful conditions than those currently prevailing in Europe (Duffy 1972; Dobson 1987). They did, however, have higher mortality rates in the southern colonies and continually in the coastal towns into which disease was constantly brought from overseas. Thus, urban areas acted as reservoirs of infection that periodically broke out to cause sudden devastation in the new generation of susceptibles in the smaller settlements and countryside (Dobson 1987). Prophylactic measures, notably improved sanitation and standard of living, enabled this group to enjoy the full benefits of the transition model. Thus,

as a result of the ensuing rise in economic standards, diseases associated with toiling for food and coping with natural disasters have been supplanted by those which spring from the complexities of our technological age, in which man's connection with the soil has become less direct. (Furness 1970)

The Present and the Future

Although all three population groups have seen dramatic improvements in their health, disease ecologies continue to evolve. Today virus infections remain as serious public health problems, acting differentially on the genetic variation present on the continent. Often forgotten in this context is that perplexing virus, influenza. It is perplexing because of its mutational history, with each strain – "Asian," "Hong Kong," "swine," and so forth – being distinct immunologically, and ever dangerous in light of the still readily recalled devastation caused by the 1918–20 pandemic. Recent work by Gerald Pyle, a medical geographer, epitomizes the promise of the application of geographic modeling to public health problems of tracing the diffusion of diseases such as this (Pyle 1986). The acquired immune deficiency syndrome (AIDS) has established itself as of prime concern and appears to be following much the same pattern of spread as the earlier urban-centered epi-

Table VII.8.1. *Incidents of serious contamination in U.S. work sites and residential areas*

Location	Chemicals	Health effects	Cause of incident
Southern United States[a]	mirex	Causes cancer in mice. Toxic to crabs and shrimp. Detected mirex in fatty tissue of 25% of people living in area sprayed.	Mirex was sprayed over several of the southern states in order to control fire ants. Its use was phased out in 1978 owing to health effects. Mirex stays in the environment longer than DDT.
St. Louis Park, Minn.[b]	creosote	Severe skin reaction from handling creosote-bearing soil.	Reilly Tar and Creosote Manufacturer had an 80-acre site where waste was dumped. Nearby wells were contaminated by the site.
Hopewell, Va.[c]	kepone	June 1975: A worker became ill with dizziness and trembling due to high concentration of kepone in his blood. State official investigations found 7 workers ill enough to require immediate hospitalization. Over 100 people, including wives and children, had kepone in their blood, and 30 more people were hospitalized with tremors and visual problems. Some people may be permanently sterile, and all are threatened with possible development of liver cancer.	The Life Science Products Corporation produced the pesticide kepone and employed the people affected.
Tyler, Tex.[c]	asbestos	25–40 of 900 workers have died from breathing asbestos. The death toll is expected to reach 200 workers.	The asbestos plant closed in 1972.
Chattanooga, Tenn.[c]	nitrogen dioxide	Exposed persons are more susceptible to respiratory disease, colds, bronchitis, croup, and pneumonia.	TNT plant located nearby. Levels of exposure up to 500 grains/billion have been shown.
Times Beach, Mo.[c]	dioxin [TCDD] (300 ppb) and others	Effects of dioxin exposure appeared almost immediately. In 10 days hundreds of birds and small animals died; kittens were stillborn, and many horses died.	Man was hired to spread oil on dirt roads; oil residues plus other wastes that remained in the containers were mixed into the oil. Dioxin in the form TCDD as high as 300 ppb (1 part per billion is the maximum dose deemed safe).
Times Beach, Mo.[c]	dioxin [TCDD]	Miscarriages, seizure disorders, liver impairment, and kidney cancer.	EPA purchased every piece of property in the town and ordered its evacuation.

Sources: [a]Gould (1986, 28–9); [b]Epstein, Brown, and Pope (1987, 75); [c]Getis, Getis, and Feldman (1981).

demics of alien origin. Immigrants continue to introduce new potential pathogens and are the source of reintroduction of others to which the resident population may have lost herd immunity (Kliewau 1979). Urban wastes as well as technologies constantly tend to poison the environment (Greenberg 1978), and through disposal efforts and acid rain, virtually the whole population is exposed. The health effects of contamination are not always dramatic, but as Table VII.8.1 shows, the results can be very real.

Perhaps because of the shorter time lapse involved, the monitoring of birth defects and infant mortality provides an important measure of these new hazards (Puffers and Serrano 1973). Although improvements in infant survival rates encourage the belief that a new homeostasis is being reached, any marked change for the worse and any increase in congenital anomalies need to be treated very seriously.

Much remains to be learned about the natural history of health and disease in the Americas. . . . We do not know why diseases occur or do not occur at a given time and place. Even less do we know what conditions and circumstances cause them to spread within a country and between countries in the Hemisphere. Indeed, accurate knowledge of the etiology of a specific disease does not tell us about the sequence of events that produce it. Today we accept the fact that multiple causes are involved in the development of disease. (Horwitz 1973)

These causes include those of nature, inherited in infancy from the genetic stream, predisposing in all probability to a number of conditions from hypertension in black North Americans to schizophrenia and beyond. The triggers creating recognizable diseased individuals, however, often appear to remain environmental and related to poverty. The comprehensive evaluation of these links of nature and nurture remains the challenge of a historically based medical geography of the Americas.

Frank C. Innes

The support, advice, and editorial assistance of Dr. Robert Doyle, Department of Biology, was invaluable. Student assistance of Lydia Stam-Fox and Amanda James and cartography by Ron Welch together with a grant from University of Windsor Research Board made this contribution possible.

Bibliography

Ackerknecht, G. H. 1945. Malaria in the Upper Mississippi Valley 1760–1900. *Bulletin of the History of Medicine,* Suppl. No. 4. Baltimore.

Anderson, D. H., et al. 1975. Pulmonary lesions due to opportunistic mycobacteria. *Clinical Radiology* 26: 261–9.

Ashburn, P. M. 1980. *The ranks of death: A medical history of the conquest of America,* 4. Philadelphia.

Bernard, J., and J. Ruffie. 1966. *Hématologie géographique écologie humaine caractères héréditaires du sang,* Vol. 1: 333. Paris.

Bilson, G. 1980. *A darkened house.* Toronto.

Black, F. L. 1966. Measles endemicity in insular populations: Critical community size and its evolutionary implications. *Journal of Theoretical Biology* 11: 207–11.

Boland, C. M. 1961. *They all discovered America.* New York.

Bourque, B. J., and R. H. Whitehead. 1985. Torrentines and the introduction of European trade goods in the Gulf of Maine. *Ethnohistory* 32: 327–41.

Bouvier, L. F., and J. Van der Tak. 1976. Infant mortality – progress and problems. *Population Bulletin* 31: 3032.

Boyd, R. T. 1985. Infections among the Northwest Coast Indians 1770–1870. Ph.D. dissertation, University of Washington, Seattle.

Bradley, J. H. 1900. Affairs at Fort Benton 1831–69. *Montana Historical Society Contributions,* Vol. 3. Helena.

Broudy, D. W., and P. A. May. 1983. Demographic and epidemiologic transition among the Navajo Indians. *Social Biology* 30: 1–16.

Brues, A. M. 1954. Selection and polymorphism in the A–B–O blood groups. *American Journal of Physical Anthropology* 12: 559–97.

Burch, T. A., L. J. Comess, and P. H. Bennett. 1968. The problem of gall bladder disease among Pina Indians. In *Biological challenges presented by the American Indian.* Pan American Health Organization. Scientific Publication No. 165. Washington, D.C.

Canby, T. Y. 1977. The rat: Lapdog of the devil. *National Geographic* 152: 20–87.

Cartwright, F. F. 1972. *Disease and history.* New York.

Centerwall, W. R. 1968. A recent experience with measles in a "virgin-soil" population. In *Biological challenges presented by the American Indian.* Pan American Health Organization, Scientific Publication No. 165, 77–81. Washington, D.C.

Childs, St. J. R. 1940. Malaria and colonization in the Carolina low country 1526–1696. *Johns Hopkins University Studies in Historical and Political Science,* Ser. LVIII: 1.

Clark, G. A., et al. 1987. The evolution of mycobacterial disease in human populations. *Current Anthropology* 28: 45–62.

Cliff, A. D., et al. 1981. *Spatial diffusion: An historical geography of epidemics in an island community.* Cambridge.

Cockburn, A. 1963. *The evolution and eradication of infectious diseases.* Baltimore.

   1971. Infectious diseases in ancient populations. *Current Anthropology* 12: 45–62.

Craun, G. F., ed. 1986. *Waterborne diseases in the United States.* Boca Raton, Fla.

Crosby, A. W. 1972. *The Columbian exchange: Biological and cultural consequences of 1492.* Westport, Conn.

   1976. Virgin soil epidemics as a factor in the aboriginal depopulation in America. *William and Mary Quarterly,* 3d ser., 23: 289–99.

   1986. *Ecological imperialism: The biological expansion of Europe, 900–1900.* Cambridge.

Curtin, P. D. 1985. *Cross cultural trade in world history.* Cambridge.

Dobson, M. J. 1987. From old England to New England: Changing patterns of mortality. Research Paper No. 38, School of Geography, Oxford.

Dobyns, H. F. 1966. Estimating aboriginal American population: An appraisal of techniques with a new hemisphere estimate. *Current Anthropology* 7: 395–416, 425–45.

1976. Brief perspective on a scholarly transformation: widowing the "virgin" land. *Ethnohistory* 23: 95–104.

1983. *Their numbers became thinned: Native American population dynamics in eastern North America.* Knoxville.

Drake, D. 1850/1954. *A systematic treatise on the principal diseases of the interior valley of North America,* Vols. 1–2. Cincinnati.

Dubos, R. 1968. *Man, medicine and environment.* New York.

Duffy, J. 1972. *Epidemics in colonial America.* Port Washington, N.Y.

DuFour, A. P. 1986. Diseases caused by water contact. In *Waterborne diseases in the United States,* ed. G. F. Craun, 23–42. Boca Raton, Fla.

Dunn, F. L. 1965. On the antiquity of malaria in the Western Hemisphere. *Human Biology* 4: 241–81.

1968. Epidemiological factors: Health and disease in hunter-gatherers. In *Man and hunter,* ed. R. B. Lee and I. DeVore, 221–8. Chicago.

Epstein, S., L. Brown, and C. Pope. 1987. *Hazardous waste in America.* San Francisco.

Ewers, J. D. 1958. *The Blackfoot, raiders of the Northwestern Plains.* Norman, Okla.

Fenner, F. 1970. The effects of changing social organization on the infectious diseases of man. In *The impact of civilization on the biology of man,* ed. S. V. Boyden, 49–68. Canberra.

Ferguson, R. G. 1934. A study of tuberculosis among Indians. *Transactions of the American Clinical and Climatological Association,* 1–9.

Ferguson, R. G. 1934. Some light thrown on infection, resistance and segregation by a study of tuberculosis among Indians. *Transactions of the American Clinical and Climatological Association,* 18–26.

Ffrench, G. 1976. Water in relation to human disease. In *Environmental medicine,* ed. G. M. Howe and J. A. Lorraine, 40–71. London.

Freeborn, S. B. 1949. Anophelines of the Nearctic region. In *Malariology,* ed. M. F. Boyd, 379–98. London.

Fry, G. F., and J. G. Moore. 1970. *Enterobius vermicularis:* 10,000-year-old infection. *Science* 166: 1620.

Fry, G. F., J. G. Moore, and J. Englert. 1969. Thorny-headed worm infections in North American prehistoric man. *Science* 163: 1324–5.

Furness, S. B. 1970. Changes in non-infectious diseases associated with the processes of civilization. In *Impact of civilization on the biology of man,* ed. S. V. Boyden. Canberra.

Getis, A., J. Getis, and J. Feldman. 1981. *The Earth science tradition.* Dubuque.

Gould, Jay, M. A. 1986. *Quality of life in American neighborhoods,* ed. A. T. Marlin, Boulder, Colo.

Greenberg, J. H., C. G. Turner, II, and S. L. Zegura. 1986. The settlement of the Americas: A comparison of the linguistic, dental and genetic evidence. *Current Anthropology* 27: 477–97.

Greenberg, M. R. 1978. *Public health and the environment: The United States experience.* New York.

Gregg, J. B., J. P. Steele, and A. M. Holzheuter. 1965. Roentgenographic evaluation of temporal bones from South Dakota Indian burials. *American Journal of Physical Anthropology* 23: 51–61.

Hackett, C. J. 1963. On the origin of the human treponematoses. *Bulletin of the World Health Organization* 29: 7–41.

1967. The human treponematoses. In *Disease in antiquity: A survey of the diseases, injuries and surgery of early populations,* ed. D. Brothwell and A. T. Sandison, 152–69. Springfield, Ill.

Hader, J. M. 1986. The effects of epidemic illnesses on the American Indians. *Western Canadian Anthropologist* 3: 19–34.

Hare, R. 1967. The antiquity of disease caused by bacteria and viruses: A review of the problem from a bacteriologist's point of view. In *Diseases in antiquity: A survey of the diseases, injuries and surgery of early populations,* ed. D. Brothwell and A. T. Sandison, 115–31. Springfield, Ill.

Hauptman, L. M. 1979. Smallpox and the American Indian. *New York State Journal of Medicine* 79: 1945–9.

Heagerty, J. J. 1928. *Four centuries of medical history in Canada and a sketch of the medical history of Newfoundland,* 2 vols. Toronto.

Heidenreich, C. G. 1971. *Huronia: A history and geography of the Huron Indians, 1600–1650.* Toronto.

Horwitz, A. 1973. Foreword to *Patterns of mortality in childhood: Report of the inter-American investigation of mortality in childhood,* ed. R. R. Puffer and C. V. Serrano. Pan American Health Organization, Scientific Publication No. 262. Washington, D.C.

Hrdlicka, A. 1909. Tuberculosis among certain Indian tribes. *Bureau of American Ethnology Bulletin* 42: 1–48.

Hubbard, C. A. 1947. *Fleas of western North America.* Ames.

Hudson, E. H. 1963. Treponematosis and anthropology. *Annals of International Medicine* 58: 1037–48.

1965. Treponematosis and man's social evolution. *American Anthropology* 67: 885–901.

1968. Christopher Columbus and the history of syphilis. *Acta Tropica* 25: 1–15.

Innis, H. A. 1962. *The fur trade in Canada.* Toronto.

Jarcho, S. 1964. Some observations on disease in prehistoric North America. *Bulletin of the History of Medicine* 38: 1–19.

Jennings, F. 1975. *The invasion of America: Indians, colonialism, and the cant of conquest.* Chapel Hill, N.C.

Joralemon, D. 1982. New world depopulation and the case of disease. *Journal of Anthropological Research* 38: 108–27.

Kiple, K. F. 1984. *The Caribbean slave: A biological history.* Cambridge.

Kiple, K. F., and V. H. Kiple. 1977. Black yellow fever

immunities, innate and acquired, as revealed in the American South. *Social Science History* 1: 419–36.

Klepinger, L. A. 1987. Comment on *The evolution of mycobacterial disease in human populations,* by G. A. Clark, M. A. Kelley, J. M. Grange, and M. C. Hill. *Current Anthropology* 28: 45–62.

Kliewau, E. W. 1979. Factors influencing the life expectancy of immigrants in Canada and Australia. PhD. dissertation, University of British Columbia, Vancouver.

Link, V. B. 1953. A history of plague in the United States. *Public Health Monographs* No. 26. Washington, D.C.

Losier, M. J., and G. Pinet. 1984. *Children of Lazarus.* Fredericton, N.B.

MacLean, D. M. 1975. Group A mosquito-borne arboviruses, primarily in the Western Hemisphere. In *Diseases transmitted from animals to man,* ed. W. T. Hubbert, W. F. McCulloch, and P. R. Schnurrenberger, 968–83. Springfield, Ill.

Martin, C. 1978. *Keepers of the game: Indian–animal relationships and the fur trade.* Berkeley.

Matsunaga, E. 1962, 1982. Selection mechanisms operating on ABO and MN blood groups with special reference for prezygotic selection. *Social Biology* 29: 291–8.

McNeill, W. H. 1976. *Plagues and peoples.* Oxford.

Meade, M., J. Florin, and W. Gesler. 1988. *Medical geography.* New York.

Meister, C. W. 1976. Demographic consequences of Euro-American contact on selected American Indian populations and their relationship to the demographic transition. *Ethnohistory* 23: 161–72.

Miller, M., P. H. Bennett, and T. A. Burch. 1968. Hyperglycemia in Pima Indians: A preliminary appraisal of its significance. In *Biomedical challenges presented by the American Indian.* Pan American Health Organization Scientific Publication No. 165, 89–93. Washington, D.C.

Miller, V. 1976. Aboriginal Micmac population: A review of the evidence. *Ethnohistory* 23: 117–27.

Morris, R. J. 1976. *Cholera 1832: The social response to an epidemic.* London.

Moulton, F. R., ed. 1941. *A symposium on human malaria.* American Association for the Advancement of Science No. 15.

Mourant, A. E., A. C. Kopec, and K. Domaniewska-Sobczak. 1958. *The ABO blood groups.* Oxford.
   1976. *The distribution of the human blood groups and other biochemical polymorphisms,* 2d edition. Oxford.

Myers, J. A. 1965. The natural history of tuberculosis in the human body: 45 years of observation. *Journal of American Medical Association* 194: 184–90.

Neiburger, E. J. 1988. Syphilis in a Pleistocene bear? *Nature* 333: 603.

Newman, M. T. 1976. Aboriginal new world epidemiology. *American Journal of Physical Anthropology* 45: 667–72.

Norwood, Col. H. n.d. [ca. 1650]. A voyage to Virginia. In *Force, Tracts* III: 10.

Omran, A. R. 1977. Epidemiologic transition in the United States. The health factor in population change. *Population Bulletin* 32: 1–42.

Patrucco, R., R. Tello, and D. Bonavia. 1983. Parasitological studies of pre-Hispanic Peruvian populations. *Current Anthropology* 24: 393–4.

Pope-Hennessy, J. 1967. *Sins of the fathers.* London.

Posey, D. A. 1976. Entomological considerations in southeastern aboriginal demography. *Ethnohistory* 23: 147–60.

Post, R. H., J. V. Neel, and W. J. Schull. 1968. Tabulations of phenotype and gene frequencies for 11 different genetic systems studied in the American Indian. In *Biomedical challenges presented by the American Indian.* Pan American Health Organization Scientific Publication No. 165, 131–3, Washington, D.C.

Postell, W. D. 1951. *The health of slaves on southern plantations.* Baton Rouge.

Puffers, R. R., and C. V. Serrano. 1973. Patterns of mortality in childhood. In *Reports of the inter-American investigation of mortality in childhood.* Pan American Health Organization Scientific Publication No. 262. Washington, D.C.

Pyle, G. 1986. *The diffusion of influenza: Patterns and paradigms.* Totowa, N.J.

Ray, A. J. 1974. *Indians in the fur trade: Their role as trappers, hunters, and middlemen in the lands southwest of Hudson Bay, 1660–1870.* Toronto.

Roberts, D. F. 1976. The geography of genes. In *Environmental medicine,* ed. G. M. Howe and J. A. Lottaire, 238–53. London.

Rothschild, B. M., and W. Turnbull. 1987. *Nature* 329: 61–2.

Runyon, E. H. 1971. Whence mycobacteria and mycobacterioses? *Annals of Internal Medicine* 72: 467–8.

Rush, B. 1786. An enquiry into the cause of the increase of bilious and intermitting fevers in Pennsylvania with hints for preventing them. *Transactions of the American Philosophical Society* 2.25: 206–12.

Rutman, D. B., and A. H. Rutman. 1976. Of agues and fevers: Malaria in the early Chesapeake. *William and Mary Quarterly,* 3d ser., 23: 31–60.

St. Hoyme, L. E. 1969. On the origins of New World paleopathology. *American Journal of Physical Anthropology* 31: 295–302.

Savitt, T. C. 1978. *Medicine and slavery, the diseases and health care of blacks in antebellum Virginia.* Chicago.

Schiel, J. B., and W. C. Jameson. 1973. The biogeography of plague in western United States. In *Proceedings of the American Association of Geographers,* 240–5. Washington, D.C.

Social Biology [special issue]. 1985. Genetics and the human encounter with alcohol. 32: 3, 4.

Steinbock, R. T. 1987. Commentary on *The evolution of mycobacterial disease in human populations* by G. A. Clark et al. *Current Anthropology* 28: 56.

Stewart, T. D. 1960. A physical anthropologist's view of

the peopling of the New World. *Southwest Journal of Anthropology* 16: 259–73.

Stewart, T. D., and A. Spoehr. 1967. Evidence on the paleopathology of yaws. In *Diseases in antiquity: A survey of the diseases, injuries and surgery of early populations*, ed. D. Bothwell and A. T. Sandison, 307–19. Springfield, Ill.

Suarez, B. K., J. D. Crouse, and D. H. O'Rourke. 1985. Genetic variation in North American populations: The geography of gene frequencies. *American Journal of Physical Anthropology* 67: 217–32.

Szathmary, E. J. E. 1984. Peopling of northern North America: Clues from genetic studies. *Acta Anthropogenetica* 8: 79–109.

Trigger, B. 1985. *Natives and newcomers: Canada's "Heroic Age" reconsidered.* Kingston and Montreal.

Ubelaker, D. H. 1976. Prehistoric New World population size: Historical review and current appraisal of North American estimates. *American Journal of Physical Anthropology* 45: 661–5.

Vogel, F., H. J. Pettenkofer, and W. Helmbold. 1960. Ueber die populationsgenetik der ABO blutgruppen. II. *Acta Genetica* 1.00: 267–94.

Ward, R. H. 1980. Genetic epidemiology: Promise or compromise? *Social Biology* 27.2: 87–100.

Weiner, J. S. 1971. *The natural history of man.* New York.

Weiss, K. M., R. E. Ferrell, and C. L. Hania. 1984. A New World syndrome of metabolic disease with a genetic and evolutionary basis. *Yearbook of Physical Anthropology* 27: 153–78.

Williams, H. V. 1909. The epidemic of the Indians of New England, 1616–1620, with remarks on native American infections. *Johns Hopkins Hospital Bulletin* 20: 340–9.

Yi, S., and G. Clark. 1985. The "Dyuktai culture" and New World origins. *Current Anthropology* 26: 1–13.

VII.9
Disease Ecologies of South America

Pre-Columbian Peoples

The natural environment of the continent of South America is overwhelmingly diverse and thus has posed special problems of physiological adaptation to its indigenous populations, as well as later to European, African, and Asian intruders. Indeed, because of the harsh environments of much of the continent, there are but few places in which people can flourish without great effort and skillful labor. In much of the continent's vast interior, even communication and transportation would be impossible without the river systems of the Amazon and the Paraná–Paraguay along with the smaller rivers of Colombia and Venezuela, the Magdalena and the Orinoco, and the São Francisco of northeastern Brazil.

One of the most formidable environments is that of the Andes Mountains, which range from western Venezuela to the tip of the continent, with snow-capped peaks at more than 20,000 feet in altitude and with populations perched at 10,000 and 13,000 feet. At such altitudes, scarcity of oxygen has led to physiological adaptations in the bodies of the indigenous peoples of Peru and Bolivia that permit them to perform hard physical labor in the thin air.

The Andes break the westerly movement of rainfall from the Amazon basin, and rain falls in profusion on the eastern slopes, where lush tropical forests shelter the people of the Upper Amazon from outside invaders. On the opposite side of the Andes, a lack of rainfall creates the semiarid coastal lowlands intersected by small rivers flowing through the desert to the ocean.

As early as 13,000 B.C., people settled in camps along the coast of Peru and Chile. They fished and hunted the marine life of the Humboldt current that sweeps up from Antarctica, and planted crops along the rivers. Some 3,000 to 5,000 years ago, they built temples and monumental structures in "U" shapes along the northern coast (Stevens 1989). They would later construct massive irrigation complexes, cities, and states, the greatest of which was the Kingdom of Chimu, conquered first by the Incas and then by the Spaniards.

From these earliest beginnings in the coastal deserts, civilizations evolved and spread to the highlands at Chavín de Huantar in the Andes and the great grasslands around Lake Titicaca in the high plain (*altiplano*) of Peru and Bolivia, where stone monoliths recall the civilization of Tiwanaku, whose wealth was based on enormous herds of llamas, alpacas, and vicuñas. In Colombia the golden chiefs of "El Dorado" ruled confederations of chiefdoms from their towns and villages, while the powerful empire of the Incas governed large cities from Ecuador to northern Argentina and Chile, and embraced both coastal deserts and mountain valleys. Great armies swept along the Inca roads, sometimes spreading a mysterious disease, which may have been typhus (Guerra 1979).

While large cities and empires evolved in the Andean world, large towns also arose along the Amazon River and its tributaries, where many people lived before 1500. In fact, Donald Lathrup views the central Amazon and its chiefdoms as the "cradle" of civilization in South America (Stevens 1989). They were in touch with the Andean world. They traded with it, and their armies (along with "fevers") repelled Incan armies that tried to conquer them. When the Spanish under Francisco de Orellana penetrated the Amazon in the 1540s, they encountered "very large cities" whose armies attacked them as they explored the river to its mouth. Civilization thus extended all the way to Santarém at the Tapajós river (where mound builders sculpted fanciful ceramics) and to Marajó Island at the mouth of the Amazon (where another group of mound builders, the Marajoara, buried their ancestors in large funeral urns) until about A.D. 1300, when the people there mysteriously disappeared (Roosevelt 1989). Those who lived along the Amazon River raised maize on the floodplain of the river, or root crops such as manioc on marginal soils. They traded with one another, held large fiestas in which maize beer was drunk, and worshiped their ancestors. In other words, the Amazon region was populated and even "civilized" on the eve of the conquest.

Between the rivers, nomadic hunters and gatherers roamed as far south as the semiarid savanna region (the *cerrado*) of central Brazil or occupied the great swampland (the *pantanal*) of western Mato Grosso and Bolivia. Either too little water for 6 months in the *cerrado* or too much in the *pantanal* during the rainy season forced people to migrate with the changing seasons.

Further south more propitious conditions for settlement existed along the floodplains of the Paraná–Paraguay rivers, where the Guaraní lived a settled agricultural life-style in small towns and villages. Linguistically related to them were the Tupí, who had migrated to the Brazilian coast and farmed in the tropical forests along coastal rivers. The vast grassland of the *pampas* housed nomads who hunted a "humpless camel" and large flightless birds. Other hunters and gatherers followed their prey to the barren, windswept lands on the edge of Antarctica, where they occupied the rocky outcrops of the Straits of Magellan.

The Spanish, who, following Columbus, landed at Trinidad off the coast of Venezuela in 1498, would confront sophisticated civilizations that had mastered difficult environments from lowland tropical rain forests and deserts without rainfall to high mountain valleys. As settled agriculturalists living in villages, towns, and cities, they raised a variety of foodstuffs, giving many of them an excellent diet, and traded surpluses to neighbors in different localities. Only nomadic hunters and gatherers had uncertain food supplies by 1500. On the eve of the conquest, the pre-Columbian populations of South America were among the best-fed peoples of the fifteenth century, which in turn had an impact on the quality of their health and nutritional status, and hence resistance to disease.

In the Andean highlands, the staples were maize, white potatoes (often stored as freeze-dried chuñu), and the "Andean rice" *quinoa*, which were supplemented by guinea pigs and llama meat. Warehouses built as early as 3,800 years ago stored food against times of famine. In the coastal deserts, farmers raised corn, beans, squashes, peanuts, and sweet potatoes, and caught fish, hunted birds, or raised *guanacos* in Chile. The peoples of the Amazon specialized in the root crops, such as manioc, peanuts, and sweet potatoes, as well as maize, and hunted deer and tapirs, fished in the great rivers, and gathered nutritious wild fruits and nuts. Only away from the rivers were food resources precarious for nomadic hunters and gatherers. Some of these populations, as well as the coastal Tupí of Brazil, supplemented their diet with human victims acquired in wars and eaten in religious rituals.

On the whole, diets were largely vegetarian – low in animal fats but rich in vitamins and vegetable protein from beans, peanuts, and amaranth – with some animal protein from fish, birds, and animals. The lack of dairy cattle and goats, however, often meant calcium deprivation in weaned babies and children and osteomalacia in adult women who had multiple pregnancies. In fact, ceramic figurines from western Mexico and the west coast of South America that depict bed-ridden females with "deformities and bowing of the lower extremities" may document calcium deprivation in pre-Columbian women (Weisman 1966). Otherwise, limited skeletal analysis from Peru suggests that the pre-Columbian people as a group were healthy and died from accidents and war injuries, old age, and ritual sacrifices rather than from frequent epidemic diseases. There is, however, some evidence from bone scars for a severe childhood febrile illness among the coastal cultures of Paracas, Nazca, and Ica (Allison, Mendoza, and Pezzia 1974). All this would change with the arrival of the Europeans and their African slaves, who would alter both the diet and disease environment of South America.

Pre-Columbian Diseases

On the eve of the European arrival, there are only a limited number of diseases that can be documented for South America. The best evidence survives for Peru in the ceramics of the Moche and Chimu, who accurately depicted diseases, ulcers, tumors, and congenital or acquired deformities in their portrait pots, and in the remains of mummies and skeletons preserved in the coastal deserts and at high altitudes in the Andes (Perera Prast 1970; Horne and Kawasaki 1984).

Because so many ancient Peruvians lived in crowded towns and cities, it is hardly surprising that paleopathologists have found evidence for tuberculosis, a disease so often associated with urban populations (Cabieses 1979). In a study of 11 mummies from Chile and Peru, two dating from A.D. 290 had "cavitary pulmonary lesions from the walls of which acidfast bacilli were recovered." According to William Sharpe, two of these mummies have "diagnoses of tuberculosis about as solidly established as paleopathologic techniques will permit" (Sharpe 1983).

A second disease for which convincing evidence survives is arthritis. According to Fernando Cabieses (1979), Peruvian museums have many vertebrae and bones that reveal "typically rheumatic injuries." While examining these remains, A. Hrdlicka discovered a type of arthritis of the hip in adolescents, which modern experts identify as Calvé–Perthes disease (Cabieses 1979). Another specific study on bone lesions in skeletons from Chancay, in coastal Peru, documents osteoarthritis in the skeletal remains (Berg 1972), and Jane Buikstra (in this volume, V.8) reports a "convincing case of juvenile rheumatoid arthritis in an adolescent from the Tiwanaku period." A mummy of a young girl of the Huari culture exhibits "one of the earliest known cases of collagen disease" with "many aspects compatible with SLE" (systemic lupus erythematosus) (Allison et al. 1977).

Evidence for the presence of treponematoses (venereal syphilis, yaws, endemic syphilis, and pinta) also exists for Peru and northern South America. Although the debate on the origin of venereal syphilis continues unabated, skeletal remains suggest that some type of treponemal disease existed in South America before 1500 (see Buikstra in this volume, V.8). Some deformations in bone surfaces in skeletons and a skull from Paracas in coastal Peru suggest venereal syphilis (Cabieses 1979). Sixteenth-century chroniclers in Peru also described *bubas* (a word used for syphilis and yaws) in Spanish conquistadores, such as Diego de Almagro, who had had sexual intercourse with Indian women. Furthermore, in sixteenth-century Chile more Spaniards than Indians suffered from *bubas* (Costa-Casaretto 1980), which may suggest that the Indians had a longer experience with a treponemal disease than did the Spaniards. At that time it was a "seemingly venereal ailment that produced genital secretions" (Cabieses 1979). According to Francisco López de Gomara, "all Peruvians" suffered from *bubas* (Cabieses 1979). The problem, however, is that *bubas* is such a vague term used for skin sores or ulcers that it could refer to verruga (Carrión's disease) and yaws, whereas Cabieses (1979) believes that *bubas* descriptions resemble Nicolas–Favre disease (lymphogranuloma).

Another treponemal disease, pinta (also *carate*), was called *ccara* by the Incas (Guerra 1979) and is now endemic in Colombia. Descriptions of pinta in Colombia date from the arrival of the Spanish, who adopted the Indian name for the disease: *carate*. The Jesuit Juan de Velasco often observed the disease, and it seems to have been a common skin disease in slaves (Chandler 1972). Colombia is also one of the few countries in which yaws, pinta, and venereal syphilis occur together (Hopkins and Flórez 1977).

Possibly confused with treponemal diseases that cause skin changes was bartonellosis (Carrión's disease, Oroya fever, Peruvian verruga). Characterized by high fever, anemia, and a warty eruption on the skin, it severely afflicted Francisco Pizarro's soldiers when they invaded Peru (Hirsch 1885). In one area of Ecuador, Spanish soldiers died of it within 24 hours or suffered from warts "as large as hazelnuts," whereas the Indians experienced less severe forms of the disease (Cabieses 1979). Pre-Columbian ceramics depict the warty eruptions of the disease, whereas a case of Carrión's disease in the warty phase has been documented in a mummy of the Tiwanaku culture (Allison et al. 1974b). On the basis of this evidence, as well as the high Spanish mortality in verruga areas in the Andes, there is little doubt that this endemic disease was of great antiquity in the Peruvian Andes (Herrer and Christensen 1975).

Another old Peruvian disease is *uta,* a type of leishmaniasis (Herrer and Christensen 1975). The Spanish called it the "cancer of the Andes," since it left ulcers on the nose and lips and often destroyed the septum. Pedro Pizarro may have described it when he reported that "those who entered the jungle contracted a 'disease of the nose' very similar to leprosy for which there was no cure" (Cabieses 1979). Ceramic evidence of mutilated noses and lips also documents the existence of uta in the pre-Columbian period for Colombia and Peru. A pre-Columbian ceramic from Cundinamarca, Colombia, where leishmaniasis is now endemic, depicted "mutilated nasal tissue" on an Indian's face (Werner and Barreto 1981).

In contrast to uta and Carrión's disease, American trypanosomiasis (Chagas' disease) is difficult to document before the sixteenth century. It is, however, unquestionably of New World origin, because the vectors and the disease do not exist outside of the Americas. Now one of the most important vector-borne diseases in South America, Chagas' disease extends throughout much of the interior of South America, but especially from northeastern Brazil to north central Argentina in a wide savanna corridor sandwiched between the coastal forests and the tropical rain forests of the Amazon (Bucher and Schofield 1981; Schofield, Apt, and Miles 1982). Because this region was remote from the Incas or coastal European settlements, historians know little about the disease before 1500. The earliest descriptions of Chagas' disease symptoms were made in sixteenth-century Brazil, whereas those for the vectors (triatomine bugs) date from the sixteenth century for Chile, Argentina, and Peru and the seventeenth century for Bolivia, where the illness is still endemic (Buck, Sasaki, and Anderson 1968; Guerra 1970; Schofield et al. 1982). Charles Darwin was attacked by triatomine bugs – what he termed "Benchuca" – when he traveled through endemic areas in 1835 (Schofield et al. 1982). Because of the way in which Chagas' disease causes facial edema, it was sometimes confused with endemic goiter, which often occurred in the same regions because of the lack of salt in the diet (Guerra 1970). The Incas identified goiter as *coto* (Guerra 1979).

Another disease of the Brazilian interior that may have existed among "the aborigines of Brazil" (Silva 1971) is *fogo selvagem* (endemic pemphigus foliaceus), which means wild fire in English and is endemic in central Brazil along the Tocantins and Paraná rivers and their tributaries. In 1902–3, Caramuru Paes Leme reported it among the Indians living along the Araguaia River of central Brazil, whereas another good description of the disease from 1900 dates from Bahia, a state near the Tocantins River. Apparently, *fogo selvagem* was limited in incidence as long as the Brazilian interior was sparsely settled or people avoided living along the rivers. Since the construction of Brasília and the opening of the interior to the landless poor, the disease has spread to Acre, Amazonas, and Rondonia, where it was once unknown, as well as to neighboring countries (Diaz et al. 1989).

Since many of the pre-Columbian peoples in the Andes raised animals for food and wool or kept them as pets, intestinal parasites may have been common. Some parasite remains have been recovered in autopsies on mummies from Chile and Peru. An examination of the body of a young boy revealed *Trichuris trichiura* ova as well as those for head lice (Horne and Kawasaki 1984). According to chroniclers, the poor in the Inca Empire had to "pay tribute in the form of small containers of lice." Not surprisingly, typhus was "a very common disease in ancient Peru" (Cabieses 1979). Evidence of pinworms from Chile and hookworm from Brazil has been collected in fossilized feces (Parasitologista 1986), whereas a mummy of the Tiwanaku culture yielded hookworms from around A.D. 900 (Allison et al. 1974a). *Tunga penetrans,* the chigger that burrows into the feet where it lays its eggs and causes painful foot ulcers, was native to Brazil. In the nineteenth century it spread to Africa (Crosby 1986) and thus was one of the few New World vectors to migrate to the Old World.

On the eve of the conquest, the people of South America had a limited number of diseases: tuberculosis, arthritis, and one or more treponemal diseases – Carrión's disease, uta, Chagas' disease, endemic goiter, and hookworm infestation. In addition, many doubtless suffered from nonlethal diarrheas caused by other worms and parasites as well as from foot ulcers caused by the chigger. Unspecified fevers, such as typhus, also caused ill health; and viruses have even been found in a well-preserved mummy from near Santiago, Chile (Horne and Kawasaki 1984). Not all diseases existed everywhere, however, because of known environmental limitations, particularly of the vectors. Carrión's disease, for example, occurs only where the sandfly lives, whereas Chagas' disease follows the range of the triatomine insects. Thus, prior to 1500, diseases were limited to specific environments (tuberculosis in the cities and towns) or vectors, and few deadly epidemics decimated populations.

Old World Diseases

Which of the new diseases brought to the New World by the Europeans first touched South America is unknown, but the best documented disease in terms of its progression is smallpox. In 1514 smallpox may have arrived in Panamá with a group of Spanish colonists (Hopkins 1983). Because of frequent trade and communication between the isthmus and Peru, smallpox preceded the Spanish into the Inca Empire. A devastating illness of the mid-1520s, characterized by "fever, rash, and high mortality," struck the Inca and his imperial court in Quito and killed the Inca, Huayna Capac; it also killed many in the capital of Cuzco. Henceforth, smallpox would sweep ahead of the Spanish *conquistadores* and claim thousands of victims before they arrived. By 1554 it had reached as far south as Chile, where it attacked the Araucanians. A year later it appeared at Rio de Janeiro among a group of French Huguenots, who spread it to the coastal Indians. They in turn fled into the interior, where they passed it on to others living far from the coast. By the 1590s it was decimating the Indians of Paraguay (Luque 1941). Jesuit missionaries unwittingly took the contagion as far inland as the Upper Amazon, and from the seventeenth century on, smallpox epidemics reappeared in even the most remote parts of the interior. The continuous arrival of ships from Portugal, Spain, and Africa would renew the epidemics, and, because control measures were often ineffective, smallpox would continue to ravage South America until it was finally eradicated in Brazil in 1971 (Hopkins 1983; Ruffié and Sournia 1984; Lanning 1985; Alden and Miller 1987).

Less easily traced but often as virulent in its impact on the Indians was measles, which often accompanied smallpox epidemics or was confused with the disease. It arrived in Peru in 1530–1 (Ruffié and Sournia 1984), settled in among all population groups, exacted a high cost in lives among mission Indians and Africans in the slave trade, and reappeared in frequent epidemics throughout the centuries (Luque 1941). It continued to attack isolated Indians as late as the 1980s, as road builders and settlers opened up the Amazon region to migrants and their children from endemic-measles areas.

Next to smallpox and measles, possibly the major killers of the Indians, past and present, were the respiratory diseases, which early missionaries and miners inadvertently encouraged by gathering Indians into mission villages and mines, where influenza and the common cold could sweep from person to person with lethal impact. Pneumonia, tuberculosis, and bronchitis also preyed on the survivors. Peruvian Indians forced to work in the mines died of pneumoconiosis and silicosis (Munizaga et al. 1975); only by fleeing the missions, mines, and European settlements could Indians survive. In the 1990s, their descendants still confront, and die of, the same diseases.

Because so many Indians could and did flee into the interior, the impact of European diseases in sixteenth-century South America was uneven and possibly less catastrophic in some regions than in Mexico. Population decline in the southern highlands of Peru, for example, was not as precipitous as in coastal Peru (Cook 1981) or central Mexico. Nonetheless, all peoples would eventually suffer depopulation as a result of flight, disease, forced labor, warfare, and the massive disruptions in indigenous food supply and consumption that accompanied the European conquests. In other words, although environmental diversity blunted the catastrophe that so quickly overtook the Caribbean and Mexican populations in the sixteenth century, it also prolonged the trauma of the impact of disease through the centuries until the present.

On the other hand, much of South America's environment facilitated the establishment of new mosquito-borne diseases in the tropical lowlands of northern South America, the Amazon basin, and coastal Brazil. These diseases came from Europe and from Africa aboard slave ships and in the bodies of the African slaves forcibly imported into South America.

The first of these great killers was malaria; when and where and in what form its parasites and vectors entered the continent has long been debated (Dunn 1965). Malaria may have been indigenous and hence may have been the reason ancient Peruvians built their houses far from the rivers (Cabieses 1979); it also might have been one of the "fevers" that attacked the Inca armies as they invaded the Upper Amazon (Cabieses 1979). On the other hand, this seems unlikely, given population densities achieved in the Upper Amazon before the conquest.

Prevailing opinion is that malaria was an imported disease, and one or more strains of malarial parasites were undoubtedly introduced into the Americas in the sixteenth century from endemic areas in Europe and Africa (and, as a matter of fact, as late as 1930 when an epidemic spread by *A. gambiae* erupted with particular virulence in Brazil) (Marks and Beatty 1976). Sixteenth-century Jesuits recorded attacks of fever throughout the tropics; and a century later Europeans discovered the treatment for these fevers, cinchona bark (the source of *quina* or quinine), but did not use it very effectively (Luque 1941; Dunn 1965; McCosh 1977). In the eighteenth century, malaria was known as *sezões* in the Brazilian interior, and by the nineteenth century as intermittent or pernicious fever (Documentos 1942; Karasch 1987). More recently, scientists identified and classified the parasites and vectors as causal agents, and widespread spraying with insecticides followed, retarding malarial incidence until the 1980s, when it once again became a serious problem of health. A chloroquinine-resistant strain of parasite, and massive deforestations in Rondonia and other parts of the Amazon have led to significant outbreaks of malaria among miners, Indians, and settlers in the region.

Urban yellow fever is more easily traced than malaria in historical sources, owing to the distinctive bloody (black) vomit and high mortality with which it is associated (Goodyear 1978). One of the first unmistakable descriptions of the disease dates from 1623, when Aleixo de Abreu, who had served in Brazil and Africa, wrote his *Treatise of the Seven Diseases* in which he described a "disease of the worm" marked by blood vomit. The disease, henceforth to be called *bicha* or *os males* (the evils), took epidemic form in Pernambuco in the northeast of Brazil between 1685 and 1694 (Rosa and Franco 1971) and then apparently disappeared until it attacked Salvador and Rio de Janeiro in 1849 (Ward 1972; Cooper 1975).

The first good descriptions of sylvan or jungle yellow fever date from 1898–9 from the interior of São Paulo when the authorities encountered cases of yellow fever "in full virgin forest" (Franco 1969). Since the mid-nineteenth century, yellow fever (in both its urban and sylvan forms) has swept through tropical and subtropical South America (Henschen 1966). Because of successful twentieth-century eradication programs that began with the efforts of Osvaldo Cruz in Brazil in 1903, yellow fever was eliminated from many parts of the continent. It has, however, resumed the offensive in the 1980s as settlers have moved into areas of sylvan yellow fever or built towns in the Amazon region that created optimal breeding conditions for *A. aegypti*, the most prominent vector of the disease, and thus for the transmission of urban yellow fever. Indeed, the breakdown in

public health programs in coastal cities of South America has led to the reappearance of the vector *A. aegypti* in cities such as Rio de Janeiro and sporadic outbreaks of yellow fever. Most cases continue to be reported in the Amazon region or other parts of rural, tropical South America. As James Ward concluded in 1972, "Yellow fever is not a disease of the past" but rather "a disease of the present" in South America.

A third tropical fever is dengue, which attacked Lima, Peru, in 1818 and northern South America in the 1820s. By the 1840s it had reached Rio de Janeiro (Hirsch 1883). Since that time, dengue is often difficult to trace because of its confusion with other fevers. With the eradication of its vector, *A. aegypti* (which also carries yellow fever), in twentieth-century coastal cities, dengue retreated until the 1980s, when it again swept urban, southeastern Brazil – wherever the vector had reestablished itself owing to faltering public health campaigns. By 1990 it was in the Amazon region as far inland as Iquitos, Peru.

Next to the tropical fevers in virulence were other diseases that reached South America from Africa. As long as the slave trade with Africa existed, so too did epidemics associated with Africans and the trade (Karasch 1987). Thus, until the effective abolition of the slave trade to Brazil in 1850, smallpox and measles attacked slave ships and port cities or wherever infected Africans were unloaded for sale. Dysentery (Hirsch 1886; Karasch 1987) preyed on those confined to slave ships and the great slave markets of Cartagena, Salvador, Buenos Aires, and Rio de Janeiro. From the markets it often spread to kill untold victims in the coastal cities and neighboring Indian missions. Intestinal parasites infested most slaves, and sometimes led to wormy ulcers in the rectum, the malady known as *bicho* or *maculo* in Brazil and Africa (Guerra 1970). Schistosomiasis (*S. mansoni*) settled into coastal Brazil (Silva 1983), Suriname, and Venezuela (WHO 1985), whereas leprosy reached into the interior of the continent to as far as Goiás in the eighteenth century and the tropical lowlands of Colombia. Filarial worms (filariasis) found congenial breeding grounds in the swampy lowlands of Brazil and northern South America, and soon the bodies of their human hosts swelled to "elephantine size." The African disease *ainhum*, which led to the loss of toes, was observed in slaves in Brazil (Peixoto 1909). Blinding eye diseases of conjunctivitis and trachoma (ophthalmia) accompanied slave ships and attacked coastal cities and plantation areas. Onchocerciasis found new vectors in northern South America and settled into the river valleys of Colombia's Pacific lowlands (Trapido, D'Alessandro, and Little 1971), Venezuela, and northern Brazil (Pan American 1974). The Guinea worm arrived in the bodies of Africans, along with a variety of other worms and parasites. The *sarna*, or "itch," caused epidemics of itching on ships and in ports, whereas scurvy, pellagra, and beriberi, as well as other nutritional diseases, affected slaves fed manioc or corn with beans and a little dried beef. Yaws swept through slave quarters and settled down among blacks in coastal Colombia, where it is still endemic (Chandler 1972). In blacks it was often confused with syphilis. Once the slave trade ended, the most lasting legacy of these waves of epidemics was the establishment of the African diseases as endemic diseases in tropical South America.

The diseases of the slave trade were followed by a new wave of diseases in the nineteenth century, as European and Asian immigrants replaced the Africans. German colonists brought epidemics of typhus to southern Brazil, whereas severe outbreaks of diphtheria and scarlet fever, probably accompanying the Europeans, attacked southern South America (Hirsch 1883; Karasch 1987). This was, however, not the first time diphtheria had appeared in South America. In 1614 it struck Cuzco, Peru, and reportedly touched every household (Marks and Beatty 1976; Cook 1981). As once small towns grew into densely crowded cities with slums lacking clean water or sewer systems, the incidence of typhoid fever increased and hepatitis worsened.

Tuberculosis attacked the black slaves and the poor of the growing cities with exceptional virulence. Indeed after the late nineteenth century, possibly more died of tuberculosis in cities like Rio de Janeiro than of the "great tropical killers" as a result of swamp removals and public health campaigns against mosquito habitats. As so many rural migrants crowded into urban slums with precarious food, water, and health care, the frequency and virulence of these "urban" diseases increased dramatically.

These urban slum populations would be among those to fall prey to a new disease that appeared in South America for the first time in the nineteenth century: Asiatic cholera. This Asian import was first reported among sailors coming from Europe to Brazil in 1855. The first Brazilian case occurred in Belém in 1855 with the next in Salvador about a month later, followed by cases in Rio de Janeiro. This first great epidemic of 1855–6 may have claimed up to 200,000 lives in Brazil alone (Cooper 1986). It also attacked Argentina and appeared in a major epidemic during the Paraguayan War (1864–70), where it claimed both civilian and military lives (Reber 1988). Cholera continued to reappear in epidemics throughout the continent until twentieth-century public health campaigns brought it under control.

Another Asiatic disease that has settled into South America is the bubonic plague. How it came to survive in countries as far distant as Brazil and Ecuador is still uncertain. In 1899 the plague broke out in Rio de Janeiro and Santos (Vianna 1975). About 9 years later, in 1908, merchant ships introduced the plague into the port of Guayaquil and coastal Ecuador, from which it spread to the highland populations, among whom it was still endemic in the 1930s (Jervis 1967). Most cases of plague, however, occurred in Brazil, especially in the region of the Northeast. In 1903 an epidemic of plague broke out in Maranhão and Pará, and the disease was well established in the interior of Pernambuco by the 1920s (Oliveira 1975; Vianna 1975). In 1973 Brazil registered 35 percent of the cases of plague reported to the World Health Organization (Marks and Beatty 1976). Over 10 years later, from 1984 to 1986, epidemics of bubonic plague erupted in Paraíba and Minas Gerais, but isolated cases occur every year in the states of Ceará and Bahia. Only rapid medical intervention prevents a high mortality (Peste 1986).

In most of the twentieth century, public health programs and massive immunization projects, combined with the removal of mosquitoes and their habitats, led to the control of many epidemic diseases. Exceptions are the great influenza epidemic of 1918–19, which exacted the same high cost in lives in South America as elsewhere in the world, and the AIDS epidemic of the 1980s, which rages unchecked in the heterosexual population of Brazil. In the 1960s modern medicine and scientific technology had seemed to be victorious over epidemic disease, but in the 1980s the deteriorating economies of South America have stifled public health and immunization programs. Children's diseases such as measles, chickenpox, and pertussis once more prey on the nonvaccinated, whereas polio cripples children and meningitis sweeps through the slums of Brazil. Diarrhea and dehydration kill infants, and intestinal parasites plague the poor. Schistosomiasis saps their strength, and Chagas' disease extends its range as deforestation changes habitats and people continue to live in thatched-roof houses, where the vector hides. Malaria, yellow fever, and dengue have once more resumed the offensive as a result of the environmental changes in the Amazon region and the reestablishment of vectors in the towns and cities. While the ancient Peruvian fevers still attack and disfigure the rural poor, unknown but deadly fevers have erupted in settlers along the Trans-Amazon Highway. Viral hemorrhagic fevers, for example, whose victims died of massive bloody hemorrhages, erupted in the 1970s and 1980s. Even cholera reappeared in South America in the early 1990s.

The combination of population growth, environmental devastation, and deteriorating public health services due to a debt crisis and capital outflows have led to severe setbacks in the modern campaigns to contain epidemic disease in South America. As the number of rural and urban poor increase, so too does the frequency of disease, since so many diseases, such as Chagas', hepatitis, and typhoid, are often linked to low socioeconomic standards of living. Thus, although once isolated from the onslaught of Old World diseases, the South American continent now suffers from all those illnesses that international travelers carry with them from the urban coastal cities to the most remote parts of the Amazon region. Unless economic and political strategies are developed to improve public health in the 1990s, the diseases of both the Old and the New World will continue to flourish and grow in virulence in South America.

Mary C. Karasch

Bibliography

Ackerknecht, Erwin H. 1965. *History and geography of the most important diseases.* New York and London.

Alden, Dauril, and Joseph C. Miller. 1987. Unwanted cargoes: The origins and dissemination of smallpox via the slave trade from Africa to Brazil, c. 1560–1830. In *The African exchange: Toward a biological history of black people,* ed. Kenneth F. Kiple, 35–109. Durham and London.

Allison, Marvin J., et al. 1974a. A case of hookworm infestation in a Precolumbian American. *American Journal of Anthropology* 41: 103–6.

　1974b. A case of Carrion's disease associated with human sacrifice from the Huari culture of southern Peru. *American Journal of Physical Anthropology* 41: 295–300.

Allison, Marvin J., Daniel Mendoza, and Alejandro Pezzia. 1974. A radiographic approach to childhood illness in Precolumbian inhabitants of southern Peru. *American Journal of Physical Anthropology* 40: 409–15.

Allison, Marvin J., et al. 1977. Generalized connective tissue disease in a mummy from the Huari culture (Peru). *Bulletin of the New York Academy of Medicine* 53: 292–301.

Berg, Ed. 1972. Paleopathology: Bone lesions in ancient peoples. *Clinical Orthopaedics and Related Research* 82: 263–7.

Bowers, John Z., and Elizabeth F. Purcell, eds. 1979. *Aspects of the history of medicine in Latin America.* New York.

Bucher, E. H., and C. J. Schofield. 1981. Economic assault on Chagas' disease. *New Scientist,* October 29, 321–4.

Buck, Alfred A., Tom T. Sasaki, and Robert I. Anderson. 1968. *Health and disease in four Peruvian villages: Contrasts in epidemiology.* Baltimore, Md.

Cabieses, Fernando. 1979. Diseases and the concept of disease in ancient Peru. In *Aspects of the history of medicine in Latin America,* ed. John Z. Bowers and Elizabeth F. Purcell, 16–53. New York.

Campos, Hermenegildo Lopes de. 1909. *Climatologia medica do estado do Amazonas,* 2d edition. Manaus.

Chandler, David L. 1972. Health and slavery: A study of health conditions among Negro slaves in the viceroyalty of New Granada and its associated slave trade, 1600–1810. Ph.D. dissertation, Tulane University, New Orleans.

Cook, Noble David. 1981. *Demographic collapse: Indian Peru, 1520–1620.* Cambridge.

Cooper, Donald B. 1975. Brazil's long fight against epidemic disease, 1849–1917, with special emphasis on yellow fever. *Bulletin of the History of New York Academy of Medicine* 51: 672–96.

　1986. The new "Black Death": Cholera in Brazil, 1855–1856. *Social Science History* 10: 467–88.

Costa-Casaretto, Claudio. 1980. Las enfermedades venereas en Chile desde el descubrimiento hasta la colonia. *Revista Médica de Chile* 108: 969–76.

Crosby, Alfred W. 1986. *Ecological imperialism: The biological expansion of Europe, 900–1900.* Cambridge.

Diaz, Luis A., et al. 1989. Endemic pemphigus foliaceus (Fogo Selvagem): II. Current and historic epidemiologic studies. *Journal of Investigative Dermatology* 92: 4–12.

Documentos relativos ao Brasil. 1942. *Boletim do Arquivo Histórico Militar* 12: 232.

Dunn, Frederick L. 1965. On the antiquity of malaria in the Western Hemisphere. *Human Biology* 37: 385–93.

Franco, Odair. 1969. História da Febre-Amarela no Brasil. *Revista Brasileira de Malariologia e Doenças Tropicais* 21: 315–511.

Gache, Samuel. 1895. *Climatologie médicale de la République Argentine at des principales villes d'Amérique.* Buenos Aires.

Gajardo Tobar, Roberto. 1979. Las enfermedades de los aborigenes y el cataclismo que siguio a la conquista. *Revista Médica de Chile* 107: 182–4.

Goodyear, James D. 1978. The sugar connection: A new perspective on the history of yellow fever. *Bulletin of the History of Medicine* 52: 5–21.

Guerra, F. 1970. American trypanosomiasis: An historical

and a human lesson. *Journal of Tropical Medicine and Hygiene* 72: 83–104; and 73: 105–18.

Guerra, Francisco. 1979. Pre-Columbian medicine: Its influence on medicine in Latin America today. In *Aspects of the history of medicine in Latin America,* ed. John Z. Bowers and Elizabeth F. Purcell, 1–15. New York.

Henschen, Folke. 1966. *The history and geography of diseases,* trans. Joan Tate. New York.

Herrer, Aristides, and Howard A. Christensen. 1975. Implication of *Phlebotomus* sand flies as vectors of bartonellosis and leishmaniasis as early as 1764. *Science* 190: 154–5.

Hirsch, August. 1883–6. *Handbook of geographical and historical pathology,* 3 vols., trans. Charles Creighton. London.

Hopkins, Donald R. 1983. *Princes and peasants: Smallpox in history.* Chicago.

Hopkins, Donald R., and Daniel Flórez. 1977. Pinta, yaws, and venereal syphilis in Colombia. *International Journal of Epidemiology* 6: 349–55.

Horne, Patrick D., and Silvia Quevedo Kawasaki. 1984. The prince of El Plomo: A paleopathological study. *Bulletin of the New York Academy of Medicine* 60: 925–31.

Jervis, Oswaldo. 1967. La peste en el Ecuador de 1908 a [*sic*] 1965. *Boletín de la Oficina Sanitaria Panamericana* 62: 418–27.

Karasch, Mary C. 1987. *Slave life in Rio de Janeiro, 1808–1850.* Princeton, N.J.

Lanning, John Tate. 1985. *The royal protomedicato: The regulation of the medical professions in the Spanish Empire,* ed. John Jay TePaske. Durham, N.C.

Luque, Pedro Leon. 1941. *Apuntes históricos sobre epidemiologia Americana con especial referencia al Río de la Plata.* Cordoba.

Marks, Geoffrey, and William K. Beatty. 1976. *Epidemics.* New York.

McCosh, Fred. 1977. Malaria and goitre in South America one hundred and fifty years ago. *Central African Journal of Medicine* 23: 254–8.

Munizaga, Juan, et al. 1975. Pneumoconiosis in Chilean miners of the 16th century. *Bulletin of the New York Academy of Medicine* 51: 1281–93.

Oliveira, Valdemar de. 1975. *No tempo de Amaury.* Recife.

Pan American Health Organization. 1974. *Research and control of onchocerciasis in the Western Hemisphere.* Proceedings of an international symposium. Scientific Publication No. 298. Washington, D.C.

Parasitologista estuda doenças pré-colombianas. 1986. *Jornal do Brasil,* August 17.

Peixoto, Afranio. 1909. *Climat et maladies du Brésil.* Rio de Janeiro.

Perera Prast, D. Arturo. 1970. Las representaciones patológicas en la cerámica precolombiana del Perú. *Anales de la Real Academia Nacional de Medicina* 87: 403–8.

Peste bubônica mata dois de uma mesma família na Paraíba. 1986. *Jornal do Brasil,* October 16.

Reber, Vera Blinn. 1988. The demographics of Paraguay: A reinterpretation of the Great War, 1864–70. *Hispanic American Historical Review* 68: 289–319.

Rodrigues, Bichat A. 1975. Smallpox eradication in the Americas. *Pan American Health Organization Bulletin* 9: 53–68.

Roosevelt, Anna. 1989. Lost civilizations of the lower Amazon. *Natural History* 2: 76–82.

Rosa, João Ferreira da, and Odair Franco. 1971. *A febre amarela no século XVII no Brasil.* Rio de Janeiro.

Ruffié, Jacques, and Jean-Charles Sournia. 1984. *Les épidémies dans l'histoire de l'homme.* Paris.

Salterain, Joaquin de. 1884. *Contribucion al estudio del desarrollo y profilaxia: Epidémicas en Montevideo.* Montevideo.

Sasa, Manabu. 1976. *Human filariasis: A global survey of epidemiology and control.* Baltimore.

Schofield, C. J., W. Apt, and M. A. Miles. 1982. The ecology of Chagas' disease in Chile. *Ecology of Disease* 1: 117–29.

Sharpe, William D. 1983. Essay-Review. *Transactions and Studies of the College of Physicians of Philadelphia,* Ser. 5(5): 278–81.

Silva, J. Ramos e. 1971. Idéias gerais sôbre o pênfigo sul-americano; Seu histórico no Brasil; Conceituação atual do grupo pênfigo. *Revista Brasileira de Medicina* 28: 611–15.

Silva, Luiz Jacintho da. 1983. Sobre a antigüidade de alguns focos de esquistossomose do estado de São Paulo. *Revista Brasileira de Malariologia e Doenças Tropicais* 35: 73–8. Rio de Janeiro.

Stevens, William K. 1989. Andean culture found to be as old as the great pyramids. *New York Times,* October 3.

Strong, Richard P., et al. 1915. *Report of first expedition to South America 1913.* Cambridge.

Trapido, H., A. D'Alessandro, and M. D. Little. 1971. Onchocerciasis in Colombia: Historical background and ecologic observations. *American Journal of Tropical Medicine and Hygiene* 20: 104–8.

Van Thiel, P. H. 1971. History of the control of endemic diseases in the Netherlands Overseas Territories. *Annales de la Société Belge de Médecine Tropicale* 51: 443–57. Antwerpen.

Vianna, Arthur. 1975. *As epidemias no Pará,* 2d edition. Belém.

Ward, James S. 1972. *Yellow fever in Latin America: A geographical study.* Liverpool.

Weisman, Abner I. 1966. Pre-Columbian artifacts portraying illness. *Bulletin of the Menninger Clinic* 30: 39–44.

Werner, J. Kirwin, and Pablo Barreto. 1981. Leishmaniasis in Colombia, a review. *American Journal of Tropical Medicine and Hygiene* 30: 751–61.

WHO Expert Committee. 1985. *The control of schistosomiasis.* WHO Technical Report Series No. 728. Geneva.

PART VIII

Major Human Diseases
Past and Present

VIII.1
Acquired Immune Deficiency Syndrome (AIDS)

Acquired immune deficiency syndrome (AIDS), first identified in 1981, is an infectious disease characterized by a failure of the body's immunologic system. As a result, affected individuals become increasingly vulnerable to many normally harmless microorganisms, eventually leading to severe morbidity and high mortality. The infection, spread sexually and through blood, has a high fatality rate, approaching 100 percent. Caused by a human retrovirus known as HIV-1, AIDS can now be found throughout the world – in both Western industrialized countries and also the developing nations of Africa and Latin America.

Although precise epidemiological data remain unknown, public health officials throughout the world have focused attention on this pandemic and its potentially catastrophic impact on health, resources, and social structure. Treatments for the disease have been developed, but there is currently no cure or vaccine.

Etiology and Epidemiology

Beginning in the late 1970s, physicians in New York and California reported the increasing occurrence of a rare type of cancer, Kaposi's sarcoma, and a variety of infections including pneumocystis pneumonia among previously healthy young homosexual men. Because of the unusual character of these diseases, which are typically associated with a failure of the immune system, epidemiologists began to search for characteristics that might link these cases. AIDS was first formally described in 1981, although it now appears that the virus that causes the disease must have been silently spreading in a number of populations during the previous decade. Early epidemiological studies suggested that homosexual men, recipients of blood transfusions and blood products (especially hemophiliacs), and intravenous drug users were at greatest risk for the disease. For this reason, research focused on a search for a common infectious agent that could be transmitted sexually or through blood. This research led to the identification in 1983, in French and American laboratories, of a previously undescribed human retrovirus. Officially named HIV-1 for *human immunodeficiency virus,* this organism is an RNA retrovirus. Although the biological and geographic origins of the organism remain obscure, the AIDS epidemic appears to mark the first time this organism has spread widely in human populations. There is no evidence for casual transmission of HIV.

Following the identification of HIV-1, tests to detect antiviral antibodies to the virus were devised in 1984. Although these tests do not detect the virus itself, they are generally effective in identifying infection because high levels of antibody are produced in most infected individuals. The enzyme-linked immunosorbant assay (ELISA), followed by Western blot testing, has made possible the screening of donated blood to protect the blood supply from HIV, as well as testing for epidemiological and diagnostic purposes.

Distribution and Incidence

Although identified only in 1981, AIDS can now be found throughout the world. Spread by sexual contact, by infected blood and blood products, and perinatally from mother to infant, AIDS had been reported in 138 countries by July 1988, according to the World Health Organization. Since HIV infection precedes the development of AIDS, often by as many as 7 to 11 years, the precise parameters of the epidemic have been difficult to define. Estimates suggest that worldwide between 5 and 10 million individuals were infected with the virus by the end of 1988. At that time, in the United States more than 80,000 cases of AIDS had occurred, and nearly 50,000 of these individuals had died. Projections by the U.S. Public Health Service Centers for Disease Control estimate that between 1.5 and 2.0 million Americans are infected with HIV but are currently asymptomatic. Although the "cofactors" that may determine the onset of symptoms remain unknown, all current evidence suggests that HIV-infected individuals will eventually develop AIDS.

Researchers have identified three epidemiological patterns of HIV transmission, which roughly follow geographic boundaries. Pattern I includes North America, Western Europe, Australia, New Zealand, and many urban centers in Latin America. In these industrial, highly developed areas, transmission has been predominantly among homosexual and bisexual men. Since the introduction of widespread blood screening, transmission via blood now occurs principally among intravenous drug users who share injection equipment in these areas. Although there is no evidence of widespread infection among the heterosexual population in these countries, heterosexual transmission of the virus from those infected via intravenous drug use has increased, leading to a rise in pediatric cases resulting from perinatal transmission.

Within the United States the distribution of AIDS cases has been marked by a disproportionate representation of the poor and minorities. As the principal mode of transmission has shifted to intravenous drug use, AIDS has increasingly become an affliction of the urban underclass, those at greatest risk for drug addiction. Serum surveys reveal that 50 percent or more of the intravenous drug users in New York City are infected with HIV. Blacks and Hispanics, who comprise 20 percent of the U.S. population, accounted in 1988 for more than 40 percent of all AIDS cases. Women, who account for more than 10 percent of new AIDS cases, are typically infected by intravenous drug use or by sexual contact with a drug user; in 70 percent of all infected newborns, transmission can be traced to drug use. By 1991, between 10,000 and 20,000 children in the United States are expected to have symptomatic HIV infections.

In pattern II countries, comprised of sub-Saharan Africa and, increasingly, Latin America, transmission of HIV occurs predominantly through heterosexual contact. In some urban areas in these countries, up to 25 percent of all sexually active adults are reported to be infected, and a majority of female prostitutes are seropositive. In addition, transfusion continues to be a mode of transmission because universal screening of blood is not routine. Unsterile injections and medical procedures may also be contributing to the spread of infection. In these areas, perinatal transmission is an important aspect of the epidemic; in some urban centers at least 5 to 15 percent of pregnant women have been found to be infected.

Pattern III countries, which include North Africa, the Middle East, Eastern Europe, Asia, and the Pacific, have thus far experienced less morbidity and mortality from the pandemic. Apparently, HIV-1 was not present in these areas until the mid-1980s; therefore, fewer than 1 percent of all cases have been found in pattern III countries. Infection in these areas has been the result of contact with infected individuals from pattern I and II countries, or importation of infected blood. The nature of world travel, however, has diminished the significance of geographic isolation as a means of protecting a population from contact with a pathogen.

In 1985, a related virus, HIV-2, was discovered in West Africa. Although early reports have suggested that HIV-2 may be less pathogenic, the natural history of infection with this agent remains unclear, as does its prevalence.

Immunology

HIV cripples the body's immunologic system, making an infected individual vulnerable to other disease-causing agents in the environment. The most common of these opportunistic infections in AIDS patients has been pneumocystis pneumonia, an infection previously seen principally among patients receiving immunosuppressive drugs. In addition to pneumocystis, AIDS patients are prone to other infectious agents such as cytomegalovirus (CMV), *Candida albicans* (a yeastlike fungus), and *Toxoplasma gondii* (a protozoan parasite). There is also evidence that infection with HIV makes individuals more vulnerable to infection with tuberculosis. A resurgence of tuberculosis has been reported in nations with a high incidence of AIDS.

Immunologic damage occurs by depletion of a specific type of immune cell, a white blood cell known as a helper T4 lymphocyte. Destruction of these cells accounts for the vulnerability to many normally harmless infectious agents. In some cases, infection of the central nervous system with HIV may cause damage to the brain and spinal column, resulting in severe cognitive and motor dysfunction. In its late manifestations, AIDS causes severe wasting. Death may occur from infection, functional failure of the central nervous system, or starvation.

Clinical Manifestations and Treatment

HIV infection has a wide spectrum of clinical manifestations and pathological abnormalities. After infection, an individual may remain free of any symptoms for years, perhaps even a decade or longer. Some individuals do experience fever, rash, and malaise at the time of infection when antibodies are first produced. Patients commonly present with general lymphadenopathy, weight loss, diarrhea, or an opportunistic infection. Diagnosis may be confirmed by the presence of antibodies for HIV or by a decline in T4 helper cells. Most experts now agree that HIV infection itself should be considered a disease regardless of symptoms.

Research efforts to develop effective therapies have centered on antiviral drugs that directly attack HIV, as well as drugs likely to enhance the functioning of the immune system. Because the virus becomes encoded within the genetic material of the host cell and is highly mutable, the problem of finding safe and effective therapies has been extremely difficult, requiring considerable basic science and clinical knowledge. Studies are currently being conducted to determine the anti-HIV properties of many drugs, but the ethical and economic obstacles to clinical trials with experimental drugs are formidable. Given the immediacy of the epidemic, it is difficult to structure appropriate randomized clinical trials, which often take considerable time, to assess the safety and efficacy of a drug. At present, the U.S. Food and Drug Administration has licensed only one drug for the treatment of HIV infection, AZT (azidothymidine) which, according to clinical studies, delays but does not prevent death. Since the beginning of the epidemic, clinical reasearch has refined the treatment of opportunistic infections. Recent studies, for example, have demonstrated the effectiveness of aerosolized pentamidine, an antibiotic, in preventing the development of pneumocystis pneumonia. Despite these advances, expected survival currently (as of 1988) averages 2 years after the onset of symptoms. With anticipated improvements in antiviral treatments, length of survival is likely to increase.

History and Geography

In its first decade, AIDS has created considerable suffering and has generated an ongoing worldwide health crisis. During this brief period, the epidemic has been identified and characterized epidemiologically, the basic modes of transmission have been specified, a causal organism has been isolated, and effective tests for the presence of infection have been developed. In spite of this remarkable progress, which required the application of sophisticated epidemiological, clinical, and scientific research, the barriers to controlling AIDS are imposing and relate to the most complex biomedical and political questions. AIDS has already sorely tested the capabilities of research, clinical, and public health institutions throughout the world.

Because HIV is related to other recently isolated primate retroviruses such as simian T lymphotropic virus (STLV)-III, which has been isolated in wild African green monkeys, there has been considerable speculation that HIV originated in Africa. Antibodies to HIV were discovered in stored blood in Zaire dating back to 1959, and it seems likely that evidence of the organism will be identified in even earlier specimens. According to Robert Gallo and Luc Montagnier, who have been credited with the identification of HIV, it is likely that the virus has been present for many years in isolated groups in central Africa. Because outside contacts were minimal, the virus was rarely spread, and an epidemic

could not be sustained. Once a sizable reservoir of infection was established, however, HIV became pandemic. As with other sexually transmitted diseases, such as syphilis, no country wished to be associated with the stigma of the "origin" of the virus.

The epidemic began at a moment of relative complacency, especially in the developed world, concerning epidemic infectious disease. Not since the influenza epidemic of 1918–20 had an epidemic appeared with such devastating potential. The Western, developed world had experienced a health transition from the predominance of infectious to chronic disease and had come to focus its resources and attention on systemic, noninfectious diseases. Thus AIDS appeared at a historical moment in which there was little social or political experience in confronting a public health crisis of this dimension. The epidemic fractured a widely held belief in medical security.

Not surprisingly, early sociopolitical responses were characterized by denial. Early theories, when few cases had been reported, centered on identifying particular aspects of "fast track" gay sexual culture that might explain the outbreak of cases of immune-compromised men. Additional cases among individuals who had received blood transfusions or blood products, however, soon led the U.S. Centers for Disease Control to the conclusion that an infectious agent was the likely link among these individuals. Nevertheless, in the earliest years of the epidemic, few wished to confront openly the possibility of spread beyond these specified "high-risk" groups. During this period, when federal and state interest and funding lagged, grassroots organizations, especially in the homosexual community, were created to meet the growing needs for education, counseling, patient services, and in some instances, clinical research. Agencies such as the Gay Men's Health Crisis, founded in New York City in 1982, and the Shanti Project, established in San Francisco in 1983, worked to overcome the denial, prejudice, and bureaucratic inertia that limited governmental response.

As the nature and extent of the epidemic became clearer, however, hysteria sometimes replaced denial. Because the disease was so powerfully associated with behaviors characteristically identified as either immoral or illegal (or both), the stigma of those infected was heightened. Victims of disease were often divided into categories: those who acquired their infections through transfusions or perinatally, the "innocent victims"; and those who engaged in high-risk, morally condemnable behaviors, the "guilty perpetrators" of disease. Since the early recognition of behavioral risks for infection, there has been a tendency to blame those who became infected through drug use or homosexuality, behaviors viewed as "voluntary." Some religious groups in the United States and elsewhere saw the epidemic as an occasion to reiterate particular moral views about sexual behavior, drug use, sin, and disease. AIDS was viewed as "proof" of a certain moral order.

People with AIDS have been subjected to a range of discriminatory behavior including loss of job, housing, and insurance. Since the onset of the epidemic, incidents of violence against gays in the United States have risen. Despite the well-documented modes of HIV transmission, fears of casual transmission persist. In some communities, parents protested when HIV-infected schoolchildren were permitted to attend school. In one instance, a family with an HIV-infected child was driven from a town by having their home burned down.

By 1983, as the potential ramifications of the epidemic became evident, national and international scientific and public health institutions began to mobilize. In the United States, congressional appropriations for research and education began to rise significantly. The National Academy of Sciences issued a consensus report on the epidemic in 1986. A presidential commission held public hearings and eventually issued a report calling for protection of people with AIDS against discrimination and a more extensive federal commitment to drug treatment. The World Health Organization established a Global Program on AIDS in 1986 to coordinate international efforts in epidemiological surveillance, education, prevention, and research.

Despite the growing recognition of the significance of the epidemic, considerable debate continues regarding the most effective public health responses to the epidemic. Although some nations such as Cuba have experimented with programs mandating the isolation of HIV-infected individuals, the World Health Organization has lobbied against the use of coercive measures in response to the epidemic. Given the lifelong nature of HIV infection, effective isolation would require lifetime incarceration. With the available variety of less restrictive measures to control the spread of infection, most nations have rejected quarantine as both unduly coercive and unlikely to achieve control, given current estimates of prevalence. Traditional public health approaches to communicable disease including contact tracing and mandatory treatment have less potential to control infection because there are currently no means of rendering an infected individual noninfectious.

Because biomedical technologies to prevent trans-

mission appear to be some years away, the principal public health approaches to controlling the pandemic rest upon education and behavior modification. Heightened awareness of the dangers of unprotected anal intercourse among gay men, for example, has led to a significant decline in new infections among this population. Nevertheless, as many public health officials have been quick to note, encouraging the modification of risk behaviors, especially those relating to sexuality and drug use, present no simple task, even in the face of a dread disease.

The burden of AIDS, in both human suffering and its demands on resources, is likely to grow in the years ahead. Projections now estimate expenditures totaling nearly $70 billion per year in the United States by 1991. Ensuring quality care for those infected will become even more difficult, especially in the epidemic's epicenters, where those infected are increasingly among the minorities and poor. In the developing world, AIDS threatens to reverse advances in infant and child survival in recent decades. The epidemic is likely to have a substantial impact on demographic patterns. Because the disease principally affects young and middle-aged adults, 20 to 49 years of age, it has already had tragic social and cultural repercussions. Transmitted both horizontally (via sexual contact) and vertically (from mother to infant), the epidemic has the potential to depress the growth rate of human populations, especially in areas of the developing world. In this respect, the disease could destabilize the work force and depress local economies.

AIDS has clearly demonstrated the complex relationship of biological and behavioral forces in determining patterns of health and disease. Altering the course of the epidemic by human design has already proved to be no easy matter. The lifelong infectiousness of carriers; the private, biopsychosocial nature of sexual behavior and drug use; and the fact that those at greatest risk are already stigmatized – all have made effective public policy interventions even more difficult. Finally, the very nature of the virus itself – its complex and mutagenic nature – makes a short-term technological breakthrough unlikely.

The remarkable progress in understanding AIDS is testimony to the sophistication of contemporary bioscience; the epidemic, however, is also a sobering reminder of the limits of that very biotechnology. Any historical assessment of the AIDS epidemic must be considered provisionary. Nevertheless, it already has become clear that this epidemic has forced the world to confront a new set of biological imperatives.

Allan M. Brandt

Bibliography

Anderson, R. M., R. M. May, and A. R. McLean. 1988. Possible demographic consequences of AIDS in developing countries. *Nature* 332: 228–34.

Bayer, Ronald. 1989. AIDS, privacy, and responsibility. *Daedalus* 118: 79–99.

Bloom, David E., and Geoffrey Carliner. 1988. The economic impact of AIDS in the United States. *Science* 239: 604–10.

Christakis, Nicholas A. 1989. Responding to a pandemic: International interests in AIDS control. *Daedalus* 118: 113–34.

Cotton, Deborah. 1988. The impact of AIDS on the medical care system. *Journal of the American Medical Association* 260: 519–23.

Curran, James W., et al. 1988. Epidemiology HIV infection and AIDS in the United States. *Science* 239: 610–16.

Fauci, Anthony S. 1983. The acquired immune deficiency syndrome: The ever broadening clinical spectrum. *Journal of the American Medical Association* 249: 2375–6.

1988. The human immunodeficiency virus: Infectivity and mechanisms of pathogenesis. *Science* 239: 617–22.

Fineberg, Harvey V. 1988. Education to prevent AIDS: Prospects and obstacles. *Science* 239: 592–6.

1988. The social dimensions of AIDS. *Scientific American* 259: 128–34.

Fox, Daniel M. 1986. AIDS and the American health policy: The history and prospects of a crisis of authority. *Milbank Quarterly* 64: 7–33.

Fox, Daniel M., Patricia Day, and Rudolf Klein. 1989. The power of professionalism: Policies for AIDS in Britain, Sweden, and the United States. *Daedalus* 118: 93–112.

Friedland, Gerald H. 1989. Clinical care in the AIDS epidemic. *Daedalus* 118: 59–83.

Friedland, G. H., and R. S. Klein. 1987. Transmission of the human immunodeficiency virus. *New England Journal of Medicine* 317: 1125–35.

Friedman, Samuel, et al. 1987. The AIDS epidemic among blacks and Hispanics. *Milbank Quarterly* 65 (Suppl. 2): 455–99.

Gallo, Robert, and Luc Montagnier. 1988. AIDS in 1989. *Scientific American* 259: 48.

Gostin, Larry. 1986. The future of communicable disease control: Toward a new concept in public health law. *Milbank Quarterly* 64: 79–96.

Hamburg, Margaret A., and Anthony S. Fauci. 1989. AIDS: The challenge to biomedical research. *Daedalus* 118: 19–58.

Haseltine, William A. 1989. Prospects for the medical control of the AIDS epidemic. *Daedalus* 118: 1–21.

Heyward, William L., and James W. Curran. 1988. The epidemiology of AIDS in the U.S. *Scientific American* 259: 72–81.

Institute of Medicine. National Academy of Sciences. 1988. *Confronting AIDS*. Washington, D.C.

Keniston, Kenneth. 1989. Introduction to the issue. *Daedalus* 118: IX–XXXII.

Macklin, R., and G. H. Friedland. 1986. AIDS research: The ethics of clinical trials. *Law, Medicine, and Health-Care* 14: 273–80.

Mann, Jonathan M., et al. 1988. The international epidemiology of AIDS. *Scientific American* 259: 82–9.

May, Robert M., Roy M. Anderson, and Sally M. Blower. 1989. The epidemiology and transmission dynamics of HIV AIDS. *Daedalus* 118: 163–201.

Nelkin, Dorothy, and Stephen Hilgartner. 1986. Disputed dimensions of risk: A public school controversy over AIDS. *Milbank Quarterly* 64: 118–42.

Nicholas, Eve K. 1989. *Mobilizing against AIDS*. Cambridge, Mass.

Osborn, June E. 1988. AIDS: Politics and science. *New England Journal of Medicine* 318: 444–7.

1989. Public health and the politics of AIDS prevention. *Daedalus* 118: 123–44.

Panos Institute. 1988. *AIDS and the Third World: Update*. Washington, D.C.

Piot, Peter, et al. 1988. AIDS: An international perspective. *Science* 239: 573–9.

Presidential Commission on the Human Immunodeficiency Virus Epidemic. *Report*. 1988. Washington, D.C.

Ron, Aran, and David E. Rogers. 1989. AIDS in the United States: Patient care and politics. *Daedalus* 118: 41–58.

Rosenberg, Charles E. 1989. What is an epidemic? *Daedalus* 118: 1–17.

Shilts, Randy. 1987. *And the band played on*. New York.

U.S. Office of Technology Assessment. 1985. *Review of the public health services response to AIDS: A technical memorandum*. Washington, D.C.

Winkenwerder, William, Austin R. Kessler, and Rhonda M. Stolec. 1989. Federal spending for illness caused by the human immunodeficiency virus. *New England Journal of Medicine* 320: 1598–603.

Zalduondo, Barbara O. de, Gernard Iddi Msamanga, and Lincoln C. Chen. 1989. AIDS in Africa: Diversity in the global pandemic. *Daedalus* 118: 165–204.

VIII.2 African Trypanosomiasis (Sleeping Sickness)

African trypanosomiasis, or sleeping sickness, is a fatal disease caused by a protozoan hemoflagellate parasite, the trypanosome. It is transmitted through the bite of a tsetse fly, a member of the genus *Glossina*. Sleeping sickness is endemic, sometimes epidemic, across a wide band of sub-Saharan Africa, the so-called tsetse belt that covers some 11 million square kilometers. Although the disease was not scientifically understood until the first decade of the twentieth century, it had been recognized in West Africa from the fourteenth century.

The chemotherapy to combat trypanosomiasis has remained archaic, with no significant advances made and, indeed, very little research done between the 1930s and the 1980s. Most of the victims are poor, rural Africans, which has meant that there is little or no economic incentive for pharmaceutical firms to devote research resources to the disease (Goodwin 1987). However, in the mid-1980s field trials of a promising new drug, D1-alpha-difluoro-methylornithine (DFMO), demonstrated the drug's efficacy in late-stage disease when there is central nervous system involvement. In addition, there have been exciting recent developments in the field of tsetse eradication with the combined use of fly traps and odor attractants (Hall et al. 1984). And, the World Health Organization's Special Program on Tropical Disease is trying to overcome the research problem resulting from the reluctance of pharmaceutical firms to get involved.

Etiology

There are two forms of human sleeping sickness in Africa. An acute form caused by *Trypanosoma brucei rhodesiense* with a short incubation period of 5 to 7 days occurs in eastern and southern Africa. The chronic form, *Trypanosoma brucei gambiense,* of western and central Africa can take from several weeks to months or even years to manifest itself. Both diseases are transmitted by tsetse flies. There are many species of *Glossina,* but only six act as vectors for the human disease. The *palpalis* group, or riverine tsetse, is responsible for the transmission of *T. b. gambiense* disease. Riverine tsetse include *Glossina palpalis* (see Figure VIII.2.1), *Glossina fuscipes,* and *Glossina tachinoides;* these inhabit the

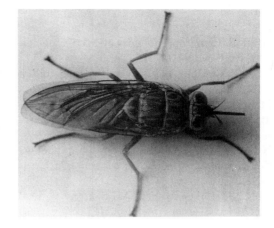

Figure VIII.2.1. *Glossina palpalis.*

two large blocks of lowland rain forest in western and central Africa as well as the fringing gallery forests along waterways, which extend into neighboring savanna regions. The *morsitans* group, or savanna tsetse, is the vector for *T. b. rhodesiense,* the cause of the rhodesiense form of sleeping sickness; it includes *Glossina morsitans* (see Figure VIII.2.2), *Glossina pallidipes,* and *Glossina swynnertoni,* which live in the savanna woodlands of eastern and southern Africa (see Maps VIII.2.1 and VIII.2.2). Although tsetse flies are not easily infected with trypanosomes, once infected they remain vectors of the disease for life.

After being bitten by an infected fly, most victims experience local inflammation, or the trypanosomal chancre; and parasites migrate from this site to multiply in blood, lymph, tissue fluids, and eventually the cerebrospinal fluid. The blood trypanosome count oscillates cyclically, with each successive wave, or *parasitemia,* manifesting different surface antigens. In this manner, trypanosomes evade antibodies raised by the host to their previous surface coats. (This antigenic variability has helped to make

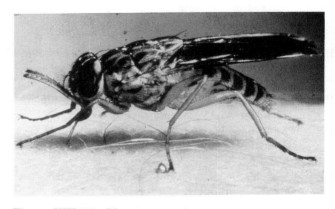

Figure VIII.2.2. *Glossina morsitans.*

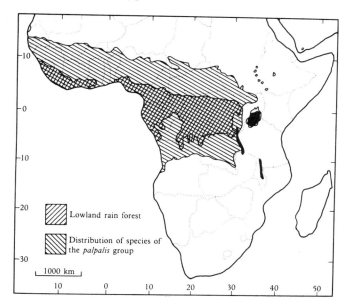

Map VIII.2.1 Distribution of African sleeping sickness (*palpalis* group). (From A. M. Jordan. 1986. *Trypanosomiasis control and African rural development.* Essex: Longman House, by permission of the publisher.)

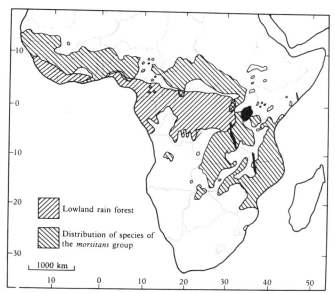

Map VIII.2.2 Distribution of African sleeping sickness (*morsitans* group). (From A. M. Jordan. 1986. *Trypanosomiasis control and African rural development.* Essex: Longman House, by permission of the publisher.)

the trypanosome one of the most researched pathogenic parasites and a particular favorite with molecular biologists today [Warren, personal communication].) Eventually, all organs are invaded, with central nervous system involvement ultimately leading to death.

Epidemiology

The epidemiology of African sleeping sickness is far from being fully understood (Jordan 1986). A complex epidemiology makes it most difficult to analyze and predict, thereby necessitating analysis of the total context of the disease pattern. In addition, the epidemiological pattern varies considerably from place to place. Nevertheless, two features are well-recognized. First, trypanosomiasis is exceptionally focal, occurring at or around specific geographic locations; and second, the number of tsetse flies is apparently not as important for disease incidence as is the nature of the human–fly contact.

The focal nature of sleeping sickness means that the ecological settings in which it occurs are of vital importance for understanding its epidemiology. Seemingly impossible to destroy, many historical foci tend to flare up in spite of concentrated efforts since the 1930s on the part of surveillance and prevention personnel (Duggan 1970; Janssens, personal communication). This means that very often the villages and regions that were affected decades ago remain problem areas today. The disease involves humans, parasites, tsetse flies, wild and domesticated animals, and the ecological setting that they share. Although foci remain at varying levels of endemicity, increasing population movements have complicated the epidemiology (Lucasse 1964; Ruppol and Libala 1977). Moreover, disease incidence is not necessarily related to fly density. Research has shown that a small number of flies with good human–fly contact can sustain an endemic, even as epidemic, incidence.

The average life-span of tsetse flies is 1 to 6 months, during which they require shade, humidity, and a temperature range between 20° and 30°C. Tsetse species have varying food preferences, ranging from the blood of wild and domestic animals to that of humans, but they require a daily blood meal, thereby making a single fly potentially highly infective.

Gambiense sleeping sickness is classically a disease of the frontier of human environment, where human-created habitat meets sylvan biotope. Humans are the principal reservoir of *T. b. gambiense*, and they maintain the typical endemic cycle of the disease. It is now known, however, that some animals, including domestic pigs, cattle, sheep, and even chickens, can act as reservoirs. The key to understanding the *gambiense* form is its chronicity and the fact that there are usually very low numbers of parasites present in the lymph and other tissue fluids. *Gambiense* disease can be maintained by a mere handful of *peridomestic* flies – that is, those that have invaded bush or cultivations near human settlements. This is known as close human–fly contact. Cultivation practices such as the introduction of banana groves, shade trees, new crops like tobacco and lantana hedges, or the creation of new farms can provide fresh ecological niches into which tsetse flies may spread, introducing sleeping sickness through peridomestic transmission.

Riverine *G. palpalis* are most commonly found near the low-level brush bordering smaller waterways and pools; during dry seasons, when humans and flies are brought together through their shared need for water, the flies become particularly infective. Activities such as fishing, bathing, water collection, and travel bring humans into daily contact with the insects, and in this way an endemic level of the disease can be maintained over long periods. Other common foci for the disease are sacred groves, which are often small clearings in the forest where the high humidity allows the flies to venture farther from water sources.

The virulent *rhodesiense* form of the disease is a true zoonosis maintained in wild animal reservoirs in the eastern African savannas. In the case of *T. b. gambiense,* humans are probably the normal mammalian hosts, with wild and domestic animals as adventitious hosts, whereas in the case of *T. b. rhodesiense* the usual mammalian hosts are wild ungulates, with humans as adventitious hosts. Transmission of *rhodesiense* disease is more haphazard and directly relates to occupations such as searching for firewood, hunting, fishing, honey gathering, poaching, cultivation, cattle keeping, and being a game warden or a tourist. Whereas the *gambiense* form of the disease is site related, the *rhodesiense* form is occupation related, which helps to explain why the latter characteristically affects many more men and boys than women and girls. However, when a community moves near bush infested with infected flies, the entire population is at risk.

The wild and domestic animal reservoir of trypanosomes is an important factor in the epidemiology and history of sleeping sickness. The paleogenesis of human trypanosomiasis has been much studied, and it is well established that the trypanosomiases are ancient in Africa. Indeed, it is conjectured that the presence of sleeping sickness may explain why the ungulate herds of the African savanna have survived human predators for so long; the wild-animal reservoir of trypanosomes firmly restricted the boundaries of early human settlement (McNeill 1977). Although the wild ungulate herds became trypo-tolerant, with few exceptions domestic cattle still succumb to the disease, and the vast majority of research and funding has been aimed at solving the problem of animal – *not* human – sleeping sickness.

In evolutionary terms, the presence of trypanosomes in Africa may perhaps have precluded the development of some ground-dwelling faunas, thus encouraging certain more resistant primates, including the early ancestors of humankind, to fill the empty ecological niches (Lambrecht 1964). If so, then humans were exposed to the possibility of trypanosomal infection at the time of their very remote origin. The parasites are, on the whole, poorly adapted to humans, which accounts for the variety of clinical symptoms and ever-changing epidemiological patterns. The fact that the parasitism of human beings is still evolving helps us to understand the unpredictable nature of the disease. A perfectly adapted parasite does not kill its host – at least in the short run.

Distribution and Incidence

An estimated 50 million people in 42 countries are at risk for trypanosomal infection (Molyneux and Smith, personal communication), while it is estimated that only about 5 to 10 million people have access to some form of protection against or treatment for the disease (World Health Organization 1985). Sleeping sickness is endemic across the wide band of sub-Saharan Africa known as the "tsetse belt" lying roughly between 20° north and 20° south of the equator (see Maps VIII.2.1 and VIII.2.2), where it can attain epidemic proportions for a variety of natural and sociopolitical reasons.

The actual numbers of cases will never be known, as it is a disease of remote rural areas, and even today people in such places often die undiagnosed and uncounted. Most national statistics are grossly underreported, with the World Health Organization being notified of about only 10 percent of the new cases. Based upon data from reporting countries, the current estimate of incidence is 20,000 to 25,000 cases annually, which is alarming because most of the victims are concentrated in Zaire, Uganda, and southern Sudan, the most important foci of the disease in the 1980s. In 1987, Busoga (Uganda) reported around 7,000 new cases, whereas the same region reported 8,500 to 9,000 cases in 1979–80. Some villages had infection rates of up to 25 percent (Smith, personal communication). In the late 1970s and 1980s, severe outbreaks occurred in Cameroon, Angola, Central African Republic, the Ivory Coast,

Tanzania, as well as the Sudan, Zambia, Uganda, and Zaire.

Clinical Manifestations and Pathology

Although trypanosomiasis has been studied for over 80 years, much is still unknown about the pathology of the disease. Three phases follow the bite of an infected fly: first the chancre itself; then the hemolymphatic or "primary stage"; and finally the meningocephalitic or "secondary stage." On average, people infected with *T. b. gambiense* live 2 or 3 years before succumbing, although there are recorded cases of infection spanning as much as 2 decades. In contrast, infection with the more virulent *T. b. rhodesiense,* if untreated, usually leads to death within 6 to 18 weeks.

The disease manifests a bewildering, sometimes startling, array of clinical symptoms, which can vary from place to place. Progressing through the two stages, there is increasing parasitemia with eventual involvement of the central nervous system. Clinical symptoms can include fever, headache, and psychiatric disorders such as nervousness, irascibility, emotionalism, melancholia, and insomnia, which reflect neuronal degeneration. Other symptoms include loss of appetite, gross emaciation, sleep abnormalities, stupor, and the characteristic coma from which sleeping sickness derives its name. Some of the initial symptoms of sleeping sickness are also characteristic of early malaria, which can make differentiation between the two diseases difficult in the field. A common, easily recognizable symptom is swelling of lymph nodes, especially those of the cervical, subclavicular, and inguinal regions. Another common symptom is called "moon face," an edema caused by leaking of small blood vessels. A most common complication during trypanosomiasis is pneumonia, which is a frequent cause of death. A disturbing aspect of the chronic *gambiense* form can be its long period of development, sometimes as long as 15 years after the victim has left an endemic area.

Immunology

The prospect of a vaccine for human trypanosomiasis is bleak. This pessimism is occasioned in part by the trypanosome's ability to alter rapidly surface antigens, apparently to evade the host's humoral immunity. Nevertheless, immune mechanisms may be involved in several aspects of the disease. This is probably the case for endemic *gambiense* disease in western and central Africa, where sleeping sickness is known to be an ancient disease, and where early field workers sometimes observed the phenomenon of asymptomatic carriers. During *gambiense* infection, trypanosomes multiply, and, with increased parasitemia, the victim suffers fever after which the parasitemia recedes in apparent response to the production of antibodies. Soon the parasites again multiply, but this generation produces antigenic material against which the previous antibodies are ineffective. It is this phenomenon of "antigenic variation" that greatly reduces the prospect of producing an effective vaccine, and at present very little research is underway on vaccine development (Boothroyd 1985).

History and Geography

The history of sleeping sickness in Africa is long and complex, stretching across millennia to threaten millions today. The complicated ecology of the trypanosomiasis, involving the human host, trypanosome, tsetse fly, wild and/or domestic animal reservoir, climate, and geography has dramatically affected demographic patterns in sub-Saharan Africa. The parameters and density of human settlement have been limited in many regions until the present time, while the trypanosomiasis have prevented cattle-keeping across vast regions of the continent, thereby seriously affecting the nutrition of entire populations.

The "African lethargy," or "sleepy distemper," was well known to Europeans in West Africa from as early as the fourteenth century, through good descriptions given by Portuguese and Arab writers. For centuries slave traders rejected Africans with the characteristic swollen cervical glands, for it was common knowledge that those with this symptom sooner or later died in the New World or North Africa (Hoeppli 1969). In 1734 an English naval surgeon described the disease along the Guinea coast, and in 1803 another English doctor described the symptom of swollen cervical glands, which came to be called "Winterbottom's sign" (Atkins 1735; Winterbottom 1803). As European exploration and trade along the West African coast increased between 1785 and 1840, the disease was reported in Gambia, Sierra Leone, and western Liberia, whereas between 1820 and 1870, it was also commonly noted along the Liberian coast.

Colonial Period

Certainly the disease was an important factor in the history of colonial Africa. In the beginning, colonial administrators were concerned mainly with the health of Europeans and those few Africans in their service. But the threat of epidemics of sleeping sickness eventually forced colonial authorities to take much more seriously the health of entire African populations.

For many Africans the disease occasioned their first, often traumatic, encounters with their new political masters, while epidemics enabled many colonial authorities to increase their political hegemony through public health measures. In those colonies affected by sleeping sickness, medical services often developed in direct response to this one disease, which resulted in the development of "vertical" health services – programs aimed at controlling a specific disease, while neglecting other crucial public health issues. Although the colonial powers have departed, as recently as the 1970s the World Health Organization urged developing countries to move toward "horizontal" health services that take into account the multifactoral nature of disease and health.

Research in Parasitology and Tropical Medicine.
Sleeping sickness, along with malaria and yellow fever, played an important role in the development of the new specialties of parasitology and tropical medicine. In 1898, Patrick Manson, the "father of tropical medicine," published the first cogent discussion of the new scientific discipline. He explained that tropical diseases, those present in warm climates, were very often insect-borne parasitical diseases, the chief example being trypanosomiasis (Manson 1898).

Trypanosomiasis at the time was very much on the minds of colonial officials. In the decade between 1896 and 1906, devastating epidemics killed over 250,000 Africans in the new British protectorate of Uganda, as well as an estimated 500,000 residents of the Congo basin. Understandably, the new colonial powers, including Britain, France, Germany, Portugal, and King Léopold's Congo Free State, perceived sleeping sickness to be a grave threat to African laborers and taxpayers, which in turn could dramatically reduce the utility of the new territories. Moreover, the fears were not limited to the continent of Africa; the British also speculated that sleeping sickness might spread to India, the "jewel" of their empire (Leishman 1903).

Thus ensued one of the most dramatic campaigns in the history of medicine, as scientific research teams were dispatched to study sleeping sickness. They began with the Liverpool School of Tropical Medicine's expedition to Senegambia in 1901 and the Royal Society's expedition to Uganda in 1902; other expeditions followed until World War II.

Many of these were sent by new institutions especially designed to investigate the exotic diseases of warm climates. The British, for example, opened schools of tropical medicine at Liverpool and London in 1899, while other such schools came into being in Germany, Belgium, France, Portugal, and the United States. This new field of scientific endeavor, tropical medicine ("colonial medicine" for the French), offered the opportunity for bright young men to gain international acclaim and a place in the history of medicine. According to John L. Todd of the Liverpool School of Tropical Medicine in 1903, "Tryps are a big thing and if we have luck, I may make a name yet!" (Lyons 1987).

It should be noted that sleeping sickness was not the only disease to receive such attention as Europeans sought to establish themselves permanently in regions of the globe where health conditions were difficult and mortality was high (Carlson 1984; Bradley 1986). There were major discoveries by Manson, who was the first to demonstrate insects as vectors of human disease (filariasis); and by Ronald Ross, who found that the malaria parasite was transmitted by the *Anopheles* mosquito. Yet, despite the fact that endemic malaria was probably the cause of far more morbidity, the trypanosome and trypanosomiases attracted much attention in the new field of tropical medicine for the next 2 or 3 decades. Indeed, obsession with it dominated the first issue of the *Transactions of the Society of Tropical Medicine and Hygiene* in 1907.

Quite literally, sleeping sickness captured the colonial imagination (Martin 1923). International meetings were convened to discuss sleeping sickness, beginning with one at the British Foreign Office in 1907. As the number of "tryps" specialists increased, sleeping sickness became a key factor in the international exchange of research findings in tropical medicine. The Sleeping Sickness Bureau was opened in London in 1908 to facilitate communication of research findings on all aspects of the disease. Its work continues to the present time as the important *Tropical Diseases Bulletin*.

After World War I and the formation of the League of Nations' Health Organization (the antecedent of the World Health Organization), two major conferences in 1925 and 1928 were convened to focus on African sleeping sickness. These conferences, following the pattern of the nineteenth-century sanitation and hygiene conferences, sought international collaboration and cooperation in implementing public health solutions. In Africa, special research centers on tsetse flies and sleeping sickness appeared in many colonies including Uganda, Kenya, Tanganyika (now Tanzania), Belgian Congo (Zaire), Nigeria, Ghana, and French Equatorial Africa (Chad, Central Africa Republic, Congo-Brazzaville, and Gabon). Sleeping sickness thus became an important catalyst for cooperation among the colonial powers in Africa, which in turn aided the rapid growth of tropical medicine as a field. In fact, sleeping sickness early in the twentieth century attracted international attention to Africa with an urgency that was repeated in the early 1980s with AIDS (Kolata 1984).

Response to the disease occurred within the private sector as well. Concerned at the possible loss of increasingly important African markets, the European business and commercial community encouraged and sometimes initiated research into tropical diseases. For example, the principal founder of the Liverpool School of Tropical Medicine in 1899 was the influential and powerful capitalist Alfred Lewis Jones, chairman of a Liverpool-based shipping line that plied a lucrative trade along the West African coast (Morel 1968). He was also a personal friend of the notorious King Léopold of the Congo Free State. The businessman shared the imperialist's dismay at the potential devastation that could be caused by sleeping sickness, and together they were keen to support attempts to prevent the decimation of African populations.

Politics and Epidemiology.   The politics of colonialism often reflected contemporaneous perceptions of the epidemiology of sleeping sickness. By 1900, for example it was widely accepted that the disease had been endemic in West Africa for centuries but had only recently begun spreading into the Congo basin and eastward. H. H. Johnston, the English colonial expert, popularized this view by arguing that sleeping sickness had been spread eastward across the Congo basin in 1888–9 by H. M. Stanley's Emin Pasha Relief Expedition (Morris 1963; Lyons 1987).

From the earliest days of colonial settlement, it was not uncommon to blame sleeping sickness for the abandoned villages and depopulated regions that Europeans encountered during their push into the interior. It usually did not occur to the intruders that in many cases Africans were withdrawing from areas because of the brutal nature of colonial conquest, and half a century would pass before researchers began to examine the deeper socioeconomic and political causes of the dramatic changes in the African disease environment that had resulted in the spread and increased incidence of sleeping sickness.

The word "epidemic" is a relative term that involves many factors. The declaration of an epidemic is most often made by an authority with the sanction of the state. Epidemics are social and political, as well as medical, events and their declaration can serve a variety of needs (Stark 1977). Early in the twentieth century, the declaration of an epidemic could provide a pretext by which to control unruly populations suffering the traumas of colonial conquest. For example, in response to threatened epidemics of disease, African populations could be recognized and relocated for ease of political control and administration. On the other hand, declarations of sleeping sickness epidemics also enabled public health and medical service personnel to implement measures designed to contain the incidence and spread of the disease.

Medical experts at the turn of the nineteenth century tended to favor the theory of circumstantial epidemiology, which held that diseases were spread mainly through human agency within specific sets of circumstances. Lacking effective treatments, the principal methods of control of epidemic disease consisted of segregation or isolation and disinfection with acrid smoke or strong fumes such as sulfur and vinegar. Disease was perceived as an invader to be demolished. This view accounts for much of the imagery and idiom of war used in early public health campaigns. A major adjunct to this theory was the belief that once the circumstances had been identified, most diseases in Africa could and would be controlled, even eliminated, with techniques and technology developed in Europe. The European colonials assumed that they would succeed where Africans had failed and that they would transform the continent by conquering the problems of tsetse and the trypanosome, among others. Most colonists believed that much of the backwardness they saw in African society was attributable, at least in part, to endemic diseases such as sleeping sickness that could, they thought, help to explain the lack of the use of the wheel and the attendant need for human porterage, as well as the lack of animal-powered plows, mills, and the like.

Powerful notions of the potential of Western technology for solving health problems in Africa, sleeping sickness among them, have survived until quite recently. Rarely, if ever, did colonial authorities consider the possibility that Africans not only possessed some ideas about the ecology of sleeping sickness but had gained fairly effective control of their environment. An example of one such African strategy was the warnings to early European travelers not to travel through certain regions during daylight hours when tsetse flies were active and might infect their transport animals. Moreover, throughout the tsetse-infested regions, there were instances of African residence patterns that allowed coexistence with the ubiquitous tsetse flies yet avoided population concentrations conducive to epidemic outbreaks. It was, according to John Ford (1971),

a curious comment to make upon the efforts of colonial scientists to control the trypanosomiases, that they almost entirely overlooked the very considerable achievements of the indigenous peoples in overcoming the obstacle of trypanosomiasis to tame and exploit the natural ecosystem of tropical Africa by cultural and physiological adjustment both in themselves and [in] their domestic animals.

European colonizers, by contrast, often disrupted – or destroyed – indigenous practices and survival strategies with the result that endemic sleeping sickness spread and sometimes became epidemic with disastrous effects. For example, from the late 1880s through the 1920s, the Belgians forced Congolese individuals to spend ever-increasing amounts of time searching farther and farther afield for sources of wild rubber with which to meet tax demands. In northern Zaire, rubber vines proliferated in the gallery forests, and such galleries were, and remain, superb ecological niches for the vector of *gambiense* sleeping sickness, *G. palpalis*.

The colonial powers, however, held their own version of the history of sleeping sickness and its evolution (Morris 1963; Burke 1971). Prior to their arrival, ancient, intractable foci of the disease had existed in West Africa and in the Congo basin around which, from time to time, the disease would flare into epidemic proportions. Colonials believed that it really began to spread only after the European newcomers had suppressed local wars and slave raiding among African peoples and established law and order. This in turn allowed many Africans, for the first time ever, to move freely and safely away from their home regions. Protected by Pax Brittannica, Belgica, and the like, the increased movements of Africans carried sleeping sickness from old endemic foci to new populations. There was some basis for this hypothesis, especially in West Africa such as in Ghana and Rukuber of Nigeria (cf. Duggan 1970). This widely accepted notion of the spread of sleeping sickness had an important consequence in the enormous effect expended by the Europeans in trying to regulate African life at every level, and especially to limit strictly any freedom of movement.

Ford, the British entomologist who spent over 25

years researching sleeping sickness, was one of the first to challenge this "classical view" of the pacification of Africa and the spread of the disease. He argued that it was not the pacific character of European colonization but, on the contrary, its brutal nature, that greatly disrupted and stressed African populations (Kjekshus 1977). In particular, the balanced ecological relationships among humans, tsetse flies, and trypanosomes were disrupted by European activities with the result that endemic sleeping sickness flared into epidemic proportions. Vivid examples of the results of such ecological upheaval were the sleeping sickness epidemics in Uganda and the Congo basin that had killed hundreds of thousands.

Public Health Initiatives. Epidemics continued throughout much of the colonial period, especially prior to World War II when there were serious outbreaks in both West and East Africa, which occasioned a great deal of morbidity and mortality (Duggan 1970). Public health regulations proliferated to control the disease that affected other areas of administration such as taxation, labor supply, and freedom of movement across international frontiers. In some colonies, sleeping sickness programs became so extensive and bureaucratic that they came into conflict with other colonial departments, exacerbating competition for scarce staffing and financial resources within colonial administrations. In addition, sleeping sickness regulations were often responsible for confrontations between the private and state sector as members of the former found themselves increasingly hindered in their attempts to exploit the people and resources of Africa.

Two major patterns emerged in the colonial campaigns against sleeping sickness. In one, the focus was on tsetse eradication, whereas in the other, the focus was on the medicalization of victims. Both approaches, however, involved varying degrees of brush clearance as a prophylactic measure, and in reality, most campaigns were a combination of features from each approach. For instance, it was pointless to think of successfully destroying tsetse habitat in the rainforest conditions of the Congo basin or much of French Equatorial Africa. Nevertheless, in some areas combined campaigns of brush clearance, resettlement, and medicalization were carried out.

Within this framework, national variations emerged in the colonial campaigns. The British took a more broadly ecological approach to control of the disease, whereas the French and the Belgians took a more "medical" approach to the problem of human infection. British policy was to break the chain of sleeping sickness transmission by separating people from flies. Thus, while British administrators implemented social policies aimed to protect people from disease, the scientific community, especially the new entomologists, searched for solutions to the "tsetse fly problem" in Africa (Ford 1971). The compulsory mass resettlement of Ugandans, which probably helped save lives, from lakeshore communities in Buganda and Busoga in 1908, and the huge Anchau (northern Nigeria) scheme begun in 1936 are good examples of breaking transmission chains. Likewise, in some regions where it was ecologically feasible, Belgians resettled groups of people such as those along the Semliki River in eastern Congo.

Unfortunately, in the context of recently conquered and colonized Africans, who had rural subsistence economies, and whose culture and tradition were intricately linked to locale, compulsory relocation sometimes had calamitous effects on those it was meant to protect. In the Belgian Congo an extraordinary amount of legislation and effort was directed at the control of populations in relation to sleeping sickness. In some places people found themselves forbidden to go near rivers that were designated "infected" with the disease. They could not fish, cross the rivers, use their rivercraft, or even attend to cultivations along the banks. It is not surprising that many Africans regarded sleeping sickness as *the colonial disease* because of the sometimes overwhelming amount of administrative presence it elicited (Duggan, personal communication; Lyons 1985).

French and Belgian efforts were directed chiefly at "sterilizing the human reservoir" of trypanosomes through mass campaigns of medicalization, or injections. To achieve this, they conducted systematic surveys of entire populations, hoping to locate, isolate, and treat all victims. Eugène Jamot, a French parasitologist, developed this method in Ubangui-Chari (French Equatorial Africa), and later introduced it to affected parts of Cameroon and French West Africa (Jamot 1920). In 1916, he organized an ambitious sleeping sickness campaign based upon mobile teams, which systematically scoured the country for victims of the disease to be injected.

A grid system was devised to ensure complete surveys, and the mobile teams worked with true military efficiency. Between July 1917 and August 1919, over 90,000 individuals had been examined, and 5,347 victims were identified and treated. Jamot's design for a sleeping sickness service was soon adopted by the Belgians in the Congo, and by 1932 there were five such teams operating annually in northern Congo alone. Admirable as it was for its sheer scale of organization, the policy of mass medicalization did not affect the fundamental ecology of the parasites; indeed, this approach had the effect of removing the store of antibodies from humans that had been built up through long contact with the parasites (Lyons 1987).

Sterilization of the human reservoir was made possible in 1905 when the first trypanocidal drug became available in the form of an arsenical compound, atoxyl. Discovered by the German chemist Paul Ehrlich, and adapted for use with sleeping sickness by Wolferstan Thomas of the Liverpool School of Tropical Medicine, atoxyl, alone or in combination with other compounds, remained the only chemotherapy for 2 decades. Atoxyl was toxic for 38 percent of patients, with dreadful side effects suffered by those whom it did not kill outright, among them the blinding of 30 percent of those injected. By the early 1920s, new drugs – suramin (1916–20) and tryparsamide (1919–25), and later in the early 1940s, pentamidine – were in use for early-stage *rhodesiense* and *gambiense* disease. Melarsoprol, a most problematic arsenical with serious side effects, including up to 5 percent mortality, was and is used for second-stage disease. Together with suramin and pentamidine, these three have remained the drugs of choice since the 1940s.

Postcolonial Period

In the early 1960s, which saw independence for many African territories, colonial rulers concurred that human sleeping sickness was under control in Africa. But political upheavals in many countries following independence, accompanied by the breakdown of medical infrastructures and large-scale population displacements, once again seriously affected the epidemiology of sleeping sickness. Some countries – Zaire, Uganda, Sudan, and Ivory Coast, for instance – witnessed epidemics of sleeping sickness, and it has been estimated that by 1969 there were up to 1 million sleeping sickness victims in the Congo alone (Mulligan 1970).

Sleeping sickness continues to afflict unknown numbers of Africans. Epidemics occurred in the 1980s in old, well-known foci located in those regions of Africa experiencing disorder and decay of public service brought about by socioeconomic and political conditions. In fact, some areas are experiencing a disheartening replay of events earlier this century, while other areas are experiencing the introduction of the disease for the first time.

Tsetse flies and the trypanosomes that cause sleeping sickness will continue actively to shape the future of humankind in Africa. Because the most effective means of control is continual and thorough surveillance and treatment with available chemotherapy, present-day health planners and administrators must be aware of the history of this disease and the ease with which that history can repeat itself.

Maryinez Lyons

Bibliography

Atkins, John. 1735. *Voyage to Guinea, Brasil, and the West-Indies: In His Majesty's ships, the Swallow and the Weymouth.* London.

Balfour, Andrew, et al. 1923. *Interim report on tuberculosis and sleeping sickness in equatorial Africa.* Geneva.

Behrman, Jack N. 1980. *Tropical diseases: Responses of pharmaceutic companies.* Washington, D.C. and London.

Boothroyd, John C. 1985. Antigenic variation in African trypanosomiasis. *Annual Review of Microbiology* 39: 475–502.

Bradley, David J. 1986. Tropical medicine. In *The Oxford companion to medicine,* Vol. 2, ed. John Walton, Paul B. Beeson, and Ronald Bodley Scott, 1393–9.

Burke, Jean. 1971. Historique de la lutte contre la maladie du sommeil au Congo. *Annales de la Société Belge du Médecine Tropicale* 51: 65–482.

Carlson, Dennis. 1984. *African fever: A study in British science, technology, and politics in West Africa, 1787–1864.* New York.

Domergue, D. 1981. La Lutte contre la trypanosomiase en Côte d'Ivoire, 1900–1945. *Journal of African History* 22: 63–72.

Duggan, Anthony J. 1970. An historical perspective. In *The African trypanosomiases,* ed. Hugh W. Mulligan, xli–lxxxviii, London.

Eyidi, Marcel Beby. 1950. *Le Vainqueur de la maladie du sommeil: Le Docteur Eugène Jamot, 1879–1937.* Paris.

Ford, John. 1971. *The role of the trypanosomiases in African ecology.* Oxford.

Goodwin, Leonard G. 1987. Chemotherapy and tropical disease: The problem and the challenge. In *Chemotherapy of tropical diseases,* ed. M. Hooper, 1–18. Chichester.

Hall, D. R., et al. 1984. A potent olfactory stimulant and attractant for tsetse isolated from cattle odors. *Insect Science and Its Application* 5: 335–9.

Hoeppli, R. 1969. *Parasitic diseases in Africa and the Western Hemisphere.* Basel.

Jamot, Eugène. 1920. Essai de prophylaxie médicale de la maladie du sommeil dans l'Oubangui-Chari. *Bulletin de la Société de Pathologie Exotique et de Ses Filales* 13: 340–76.

Jordan, Anthony M. 1986. *Trypanosomiasis control and African rural development.* London.

Kjekshus, Helge. 1977. *Ecology control and economic development in East African history: The case of Tanganyika, 1850–1950.* London.

Kolata, Gina. 1984. Scrutinizing sleeping sickness. *Science* 226: 956–9.

Lambrecht, Frank. 1964. Aspects of evolution and ecology of tsetse flies and trypanosomiasis in prehistoric African environment. *Journal of African History* 5: 1–23.

Leishman, W. B. 1903. On the possibility of trypanosomiasis in India. *British Medical Journal* 2: 1252–4.

Lucasse, C. 1964. Control of human sleeping sickness at present times. *Annales de la Société Belge du Médecine Tropicale* 44: 285–94.

Lyons, Maryinez. 1985. From "death camps" to cordon sanitaire: The development of sleeping sickness policy in the Uele district of the Belgian Congo, 1903–1914. *Journal of African History* 26: 69–91.

  1987. The colonial disease: Sleeping sickness in the social history of northern Zaire, 1903–1930. Ph.D. thesis, University of California, Los Angeles.

  1988a. Sleeping sickness policy and public health in the early Belgian Congo. In *Imperial medicine and indigenous societies,* ed. David Arnold, 105–24. Manchester.

  1988b. Sleeping sickness, colonial medicine and imperialism: Some connections in the Belgian Congo. In *Disease, medicine and empire,* ed. Roy M. McLeod and Milton Lewis, 242–56. London.

McKelvey, John M. 1973. *Man against tsetse: Struggle for Africa.* Ithaca, N.Y.

McNeill, William. 1977. *Plagues and people.* Oxford.

Manson, Patrick. 1898. *Tropical diseases: A manual of the diseases of warm climates.* London.

Martin, Gustave. 1923. *Interim report on tuberculosis and sleeping sickness in equatorial Africa.* Expert Committee of the League of Nations. Health Committee.

Matzke, G. E. 1988. Sleeping sickness control strategies in Tanzania. In *Health and disease in tropical Africa: Geographical and medical viewpoints,* ed. Rais Akhar, 359–72. London.

Maurice, G. K. 1930. The history of sleeping sickness in the Sudan. *Journal of Royal Army Medical Corps* 55: 161–241.

Molyneux, D. H., and R. W. Ashford. 1983. *The biology of Trypanosoma and Leishmania, parasites of man and domestic animals.* London.

Morel, E. D. 1968. *E. D. Morel's history of the Congo reform movement,* ed. William R. Louis and Jean Stengers. Oxford.

Morris, K. R. S. 1963. The movement of sleeping sickness across Central Africa. *Journal of Tropical Medicine and Hygiene* 66: 159–76.

Mulligan, Colonel H. W. 1970. *The African trypanosomiases.* London.

Musambachime, Mwelwa. 1981. The social and economic effects of sleeping sickness in Mweru–Luapula, 1906–1922. *African Economic History* 10: 151–73.

Ruppol, J. F., and K. Libala. 1977. Situation actuelle de la lutte contre la maladie du sommeil au Zaire. *Annales de la Sociéte Belge du Médecine Tropicale* 57: 299–314.

Stark, E. 1977. Epidemic as a social event. *International Journal of the Health Sciences* 74: 681–705.

Winterbottom, Thomas. 1803. *An account of the native Africans in the neighbourhood of Sierra Leone to which is added an account of the present state of medicine among them.* London.

World Health Organization. 1985. African trypanosomiases. In *Tropical disease research,* 7th Programme Report. Geneva.

1986. *Trypanosomiasis control manual.* Geneva.

VIII.3
Ainhum

The name *ainhum* is derived from a word in the Nagos language of East Africa meaning "to saw." It describes the development of constricting bands about digits, almost always the fifth, or smallest, toe, which ultimately undergoes self-amputation. Typically the disease is bilateral (i.e., affecting both small toes).

Ainhum is ordinarily a disease of middle-aged black Africans of both sexes accustomed to going barefoot. The disease is common in Nigeria and East Africa, and has been reported less frequently in other tropical areas, including India, Burma, Panama, the Antilles, and Brazil (Burgdorf and Goltz 1987).

Ainhum was noticed frequently among slaves in Brazil and was first described in detail in 1867 by Brazilian doctor J. F. da Silva Lima who also named the disease. Silva Lima's description is outstandingly accurate, and has not been bettered. In one case he wrote that the toe had taken the shape of a small oval potato; the covering skin had become coarse and scabrous, and very tender to touch. As the disease progressed, wrote Silva Lima, a strong constriction appeared at the base of the toe, and, as the blood flow to the toe was impeded, the bones ceased to exist. In time, spontaneous amputation of the toe occurred (Cole 1965; Silva Lima 1867).

The cause of ainhum is unknown. According to Walter Burgdorf and Robert Boltz, chronic trauma, infection, hyperkeratosis, decreased vascular supply, and impaired sensation may alone or in combination produce excessive fibroplasia, and lead to ainhum. It is an acquired condition, although a hereditary pre-

disposition has not been ruled out (Curban and Moura 1965). Surgery is the mainstay of therapy, for in most cases prompt amputation may allow the patient to escape pain and infection.

Donald B. Cooper

Bibliography

Browne, S. G. 1965. True ainhum: Its distinctive and differentiating features. *Journal of Bone and Joint Surgery* 47B(1): 52–5.

Burgdorf, Walter H. C., and Robert W. Goltz. 1987. Ainhum and other forms of constricting bands (pseudo-ainhum). In *Dermatology in general medicine,* 3d edition, ed. Thomas Fitzpatrick et al., 1031–2. New York.

Cole, C. J. 1965. Ainhum: An account of fifty-four patients with special reference to etiology and treatment. *Journal of Bone and Joint Surgery* 47B(1): 43–51.

Curban, Guilherme V., and J. B. Athayde Moura. 1965. Ainhum: Considerações sobre o conceito nosologico. *Revista do Hospital das Clinícas: Faculdade de Medicina da Universidade do São Paulo* 20: 225–34.

Silva Lima, J. F. da. 1867. Estudo sobre o "Ainhum" – moléstia ainda não descrita, peculiar a ráça ethiópica, e afetando os dedos mínimo dos pés. *Gazeta Médica da Bahia* 1: 146–51, 172–6.

VIII.4
Alzheimer's Disease

In 1906, Alois Alzheimer first described a neurological disorder of the brain associated with global deterioration of cognitive functioning and resulting in severe social impairment. Once thought rare, senile dementia of the Alzheimer's type is the most commonly acquired progressive brain syndrome. Alzheimer's disease begins with insidious intellectual and memory loss as the brain becomes shrunken from nerve cell loss and advances over 5 to 15 years to a chronic vegetative state. Progressive cognitive, psychological, and social dysfunction has a profound effect on family and friends. Alzheimer's disease is associated with significant morbidity, and it may be the fourth leading cause of death in the United States (Katzman 1976). D. K. Kay and colleagues (1964) showed the average survival for demented men to be 2.6 years after the diagnosis of illness, whereas the survival period for nondemented men of the same age was 8.7 years. However, there is great variability in survival statistics from different studies.

Although Alzheimer's disease is the leading cause of dementia, its etiology remains unknown, and treatment is supportive. The illness is a major problem among the elderly. Approximately 4 percent of the population over the age of 65 is affected, and by age 80, prevalence reaches 20 percent (Brodie 1982). As the elderly population of the United States increases, the number of persons with Alzheimer-type dementia will also increase. Alzheimer's disease exists in the presenium, but it has been difficult to document a bimodal distribution with regard to age. Even though pathological changes in presenile and senile forms of the illness are similar, there is evidence that early- and late-onset Alzheimer-type dementia differ clinically (Seltzer and Sherwin 1983).

Clinical Manifestations and Diagnosis

Clinical Manifestations

Alzheimer-type senile dementia is associated with behavioral signs and symptoms that divide into corresponding stages. In the early stage, subjective memory deficit may be difficult to differentiate from benign senile forgetfulness. However, elderly persons with benign forgetfulness are unable to recall unimportant details, whereas patients with Alzheimer-type senile dementia forget important and unimportant information randomly (Kral 1962).

Typically, patients with Alzheimer's disease forget where things are placed, become lost easily, and have difficulty remembering appointments. Both recent and remote memory are affected, which may be documented by neuropsychological testing. When patients recognize their cognitive and social losses, many develop feelings of hopelessness and despondency. As Alzheimer-type senile dementia progresses, the patient enters a confusional phase with more global impairment of cognitive functioning (Schenk, Reisberg, and Ferris 1982). Changes in higher cortical functions, such as language, spatial relationships, and problem solving, become more apparent.

During the confusional phase, obvious denial begins to replace anxiety, and cognitive deficits are noticeable to family and friends. In the final phase, the patient becomes aimless and may hallucinate or be restless and agitated. Language disorders such as aphasia occur in late stages. Abnormal neurological reflexes, indicative of loss of higher neural inhibition, are common. Not all patients with Alzheimer-type senile dementia demonstrate the classic evolution of symptoms. Although almost all patients have some memory impairment, other focal cortical defi-

cits may predominate initially. Spatial relationship impairment is common early. The patient may also complain of word-finding difficulty or demonstrate mild problems in speaking and understanding. In cases where damage to the frontal lobes of the brain predominates, the patient presents with judgment problems.

Diagnosis

Diagnosis of Alzheimer's disease remains a diagnosis of exclusion. In the absence of biological markers for the illness, it is not surprising that clinical diagnosis may be less than accurate and, in fact, may be correct in as few as one-half of Alzheimer-type senile dementia cases (Alafuzoff et al. 1987). Not only do cognitive changes associated with normal aging overlap those found in the early stages of dementia, but also a wide spectrum of conditions may produce dementia. In any given patient, several conditions leading to progressive cognitive decline may occur simultaneously. Even neuropathologists may encounter diagnostic difficulty and may be reluctant to make the diagnosis without the proper clinicopathological correlation (Khachaturian 1985).

The clinical diagnosis of Alzheimer-type senile dementia always requires documentation of progression (McKhann et al. 1984). Reports from family and friends provide the most valid measures of cognitive decline in elderly persons and support the clinician's judgment that global intellectual deterioration has occurred.

Clinical Staging and Evaluation

Progression is usually gradual but with fluctuation of symptom severity. The patient may react very dramatically to changes in the living situation, to losses of friends or relatives, or even to admission to the hospital for evaluation. These acute changes probably represent withdrawal of orienting stimuli and emotional distress rather than progression of the disease process.

A number of clinical staging strategies have been developed, but there is no entirely satisfactory technique as yet. Simplified rating scales (such as the Folstein Mini-Mental) may be efficiently administered, but only identify the presence or absence of cognitive impairment. Other cognitive scales are more accurate, but they are also more complex and may take an hour to administer. The Blessed Scale (Blessed, Tomlinson, and Roth 1968) obtains information from collateral sources and has the advantage of documented correlation with pathological lesions at autopsy. Unfortunately, it provides little information about cognitive performance. Other behavioral scales rely solely on the interviewer's interpretation of the patient's performance on several activities (Salzman, Kochansky, and Shader 1972).

Psychometric tests may be useful in delineating patterns of cognitive deficit at various stages of severity and in identifying the qualitative aspects of performance deficit. Although laboratory tests are sometimes used to support the diagnosis of Alzheimer's disease, the laboratory is actually more useful in excluding other causes of cognitive deterioration. Atrophy of the cerebral cortex is often seen on computed tomography, but it is frequently overinterpreted. There is a poor correlation between size of the brain ventricles, widened cerebral sulci, and severity of dementia (Fox, Topel, and Huckman 1975). Attempts have been made to correlate dementia with brain density (Albert et al. 1984). Unfortunately, results have been inconsistent, and there is a pressing need for quantitative computed tomographic studies that correlate the scanning images with clinical and pathological findings.

Differential Diagnosis

Alzheimer's disease may be difficult to distinguish from other untreatable progressive dementias, which include Pick's disease, demyelinating diseases, slowly progressive brain tumors, inflammatory diseases, arteriosclerotic vascular diseases, toxic exposures, repeated metabolic insults, deficiency diseases, late sequelae of head trauma, Creutzfeldt–Jakob disease, and viral and fungal infections. Dementia is common in patients with terminal cancer and may result from a variety of causes.

The evaluation of a patient presenting with dementia often reveals untreatable causes, but treatable dementia is discovered in 20 to 25 percent of such patients (Wells 1977).

Treatable causes of dementia include pernicious anemia, thyroid disorders, chronic central nervous system infections, toxic exposures, surgically correctable mass lesions, inflammatory vascular disease, certain forms of arteriosclerotic vascular disease, and normal-pressure hydrocephalus. Occasionally, iatrogenic dementia, related to the inappropriate use of medication or to idiosyncratic drug effects, is identified. Multi-infarct dementia may be the most difficult progressive dementia to differentiate from Alzheimer's disease despite the fact that specific diagnostic criteria for each have been promulgated in the official nomenclature. There is an obvious need for a valid and reliable set of clinical criteria to distinguish the two conditions. Nonetheless, risk fac-

tors for stroke should be evaluated and controlled when possible in every patient with early dementia.

J. L. Cummings and D. F. Benson (1983) suggest that all forms of dementia other than Alzheimer's and Pick's disease show signs of subcortical dysfunction in addition to more obvious cortical signs. This is especially true of dementia associated with basal ganglia disease, which regularly produces the characteristic subcortical pattern of slowed thinking, attention deficit, memory impairment, and apathy. Subcortical dementia occurs in 20 to 40 percent of patients with Parkinson's disease (Marttila and Rinne 1976) and is also observed in progressive supranuclear palsy, Huntington's chorea, and Wilson's disease. Symptomatic treatment of basal ganglia disease occasionally improves the associated dementia. Antidepressants may improve cognition as well as any associated depression (Albert, Feldman, and Willis 1974).

Depression is the most common treatable illness that may masquerade as Alzheimer-type senile dementia. Cognitive abilities return to baseline levels when depression is treated. Because some patients with early dementia have secondary depression, dementia and pseudodementia may be difficult to differentiate. The depression that occurs in the early stages of Alzheimer-type senile dementia tends to resolve as the disease progresses. Pseudodemented, depressed patients are apt to have poor attention, inconsistent cognitive changes, absence of cortical signs, weight loss, sleep disturbance, guilt, poor self-esteem, a past personal family psychiatric history, and a more rapid onset.

In contrast, patients with cortical dementia of Alzheimer-type often show insidious onset, slow progression, early loss of insight, amnesia for remote and recent events, spatial disorientation, reduction in spontaneous speech, and occasionally aphasia. Agnosia, apraxia, increased muscular tension, and abnormal neurological reflexes may also be present (Gustafson and Nilsson 1982).

Epidemiology and Etiology

Alzheimer's disease is ultimately a neuropathological diagnosis. A wide variety of gross morphological and microscopic changes occur in the brain of patients with Alzheimer's disease. Unfortunately, many of these changes are difficult to distinguish from alterations that occur in the brain of normal elderly persons, who also show some atrophy of white matter and, to a lesser extent, gray matter.

Neurochemically, Alzheimer's disease has been associated with a decrease in the activity of the enzyme choline acetyltransferase, which synthesizes acetylcholine (Coyle, Price, and DeLong 1983). Acetylcholine is the neurotransmitter most involved in memory circuits. Levels naturally decrease with age, but in patients with Alzheimer-type dementia, choline acetyltransferase may decline to 20 percent of that in age-matched control subjects. Other neurochemical changes associated with Alzheimer's disease include a decrease in gamma-aminobutyric acid, substance P, and somatostatin-like activity in the brain of patients with Alzheimer-type dementia. The significance of these findings is unclear.

Although it is generally recognized that genetic influences are important in Alzheimer's disease, the exact nature of these genetic influences also remains unclear. There are some families that have a large number of members with the clinical or pathological diagnosis of Alzheimer's disease (Cook et al. 1979). The most important practical point regarding these kindreds is that most of them meet criteria for autosomal dominant inheritance. Penetrance of the gene exceeds 90 percent in most of these families. As a result, the children of an affected person have a 50 percent risk of developing dementia if they survive to the age at which dementia begins in that family. The exact proportion of familial cases is unknown, but they may account for as many as 10 percent of all cases of Alzheimer-type dementia (Kokmen 1984). There is some familial clustering in families without dominant inheritance. It would appear that concordance for dementia is somewhat higher in monozygotic versus dizygotic twins, suggesting genetic factors. On the other hand, concordance is not 100 percent, so environmental factors must have a role. Since age of onset varies within a twin pair, it may be difficult to be certain whether a given pair is truly discordant.

An association has been shown also between Alzheimer's disease and families that produce children with Down syndrome (Heston and Masri 1966). Further support for a link between Down syndrome and Alzheimer's disease is provided by the fact that patients with Down syndrome tend to demonstrate neuropathological findings consistent with Alzheimer-type senile dementia if they live to adult life. Since Down syndrome represents a disorder of chromosome 21, a point of origin for the search for the genetic determinants of Alzheimer's disease is suggested. The amino acid sequence for the amyloid that accumulates in the brains of patients with Alzheimer's disease is called the *A4 beta-pleated amyloid*. The gene for the precursor has been identified, cloned, and mapped to the proximal long arm of chromosome 21 (St. George-Hyslop et al., 1987). Recent data favor the hypothesis of a genetically induced overproduction of amyloid protein as a factor in the cause of Alzheimer's disease.

When families request genetic counseling, one can only explain what is known about the genetic factors. In a family with a single Alzheimer victim, the lifetime risk for a close relative also to develop dementia is approximately 10 percent. Since most dementia develops over the age of 70, this is a relatively small probability. In families with dementia occurring over several generations, an autosomal dominant inheritance is probable, and the risk for children of an affected parent may approach 50 percent. In these families, optimum health management indicates the suspicion of dementia in every elderly person with altered environmental–social interactional skills, multiple physical complaints in the absence of objective disease, or vague and unclear history. Autopsy can be suggested to confirm diagnosis to trace the pedigree more accurately.

Environmental causes for Alzheimer's disease have also been suggested. Some investigators have linked focal intranuclear accumulation of aluminum to the presence of neurofibrillary degeneration in hippocampal neurons. The relationship of aluminum to Alzheimer-type senile dementia, however, is not well accepted (Markesbery et al. 1981). General decline of immunologic competence with aging suggests an autoimmune mechanism. Although elevated levels of brain antibody have been demonstrated in Alzheimer's disease, antineuronal antibodies have not been demonstrated in the central nervous system (Watts, Kennedy, and Thomas 1981). Serum protein abnormalities have been demonstrated, notably changes in haptoglobin functions. Finally, a viral cause has been proposed but not substantiated (Wisniewski 1978).

Treatment

Although the cause of this disease remains unclear, good clinical management is nonetheless critical. Every effort should be made to maintain the patient's independence within the limits of safety. Measures to maintain orientation, such as memory aids, eyeglasses, hearing aids, calendars, diaries, adequate lighting, and organization of the patient's personal items, are helpful (Eisdorfer and Cohen 1981). Appropriate locks to prevent unsafe wandering, and suitable safeguards on dangerous household appliances must be utilized. Of course, the patient should not be permitted to drive.

Providing quality care, however, requires an understanding of the health care delivery system in which physicians and patients find themselves. Psychosocial management is based on enhancing the function of the care system that surrounds the patient. This usually involves several family caregivers, who should receive accurate information concerning the disease and the prognosis. Caregivers must take care of themselves and may benefit substantially from referral to a support group of the Alzheimer's Disease and Related Disorders Association. Caregivers should be made aware of the factor that most insurance does not cover either community services or long-term care in nursing homes. A competent legal adviser and appropriate financial counselor can be of substantial help. Even though many families want to keep elderly individuals in the home, in-home support services are expensive and often not available.

Alzheimer's disease remains a major challenge not only to modern medicine but also to the health care delivery system, and to society at large. Not only is further research necessary in the diagnosis and management of the disease itself, but also major changes are necessary in the health care delivery system if patients afflicted with this illness are to get the care that they need.

History

Although Alzheimer's disease only recently "has exploded into public and scientific consciousness" (Rabins 1988), it doubtlessly has a long history under such rubrics as "senility," "hardening of the arteries," and "dementia," to name but a few. Certainly senility and dementia are conditions that have been recognized for millennia. The Assyrians, Greeks, and Romans all knew and described them. Peter V. Rabins (1988) credits J. E. D. Esquirol, however, for the first modern description, in 1838, of what seems to have been Alzheimer's disease. Esquirol wrote of a "senile dementia" that increases with age (Beach 1987). Seven years later, Wilhelm Griesinger published a textbook on mental disease that clearly recognized the condition of "presenile dementia" caused by brain atrophy found at autopsy. Neither of these reports, however, seems to have had much influence on investigators at the time (Wisniewski 1989).

It was during the latter half of the nineteenth century that public as well as scientific concern for problems of the elderly increased considerably. With that concern came the birth of the field of geriatrics and increasing attention paid to dementia in the elderly (Beach 1987). Much of the effort during these decades focused on whether it was an inevitable product of aging, or rather an actual disease. Emil Kraepelin, one of the founders of modern psychiatry, pointed out the difficulty in separating normal senility from senile dementia. In applying the new technique of silver staining, Alzheimer, his student, identified a new neuropathological marker of dementia in the brain of a patient who had died at age 55 after a 4-year illness. This marker was the neurofibrillary tangle, which he speculated was the marker of a dead cell. Alzheimer thus made the first correlation between clinical characteristics of dementia in a patient and pathological lesions in the brain. Kraepelin later named the illness Alzheimer's disease in honor of his former pupil.

The question then became one of determining if this disease was the same as senile dementia. It revolved around the ancient problem of what pathological changes can be attributed to aging as opposed to other causes. Kraepelin had emphasized the presenile nature of Alzheimer's disease, yet because of its similarity to senile dementia some investigators suggested that Alzheimer's disease might be caused by "a premature onset of the aging process" (Beach 1987). Also confusing the picture was the nineteenth-century notion which extended also into the twentieth century: that cerebral arteriosclerosis might be the cause of senile dementia. By the late 1920s, there had been a sufficient accumulation of case descriptions of dementia among the elderly that statistical analysis could be brought to bear on the problem. It was found that most of the cases did in fact occur between the ages of 50 and 60, sustaining the notion of its presenile nature. In 1955 Martin Roth showed that mental changes could be triggered by a variety of both "functional" and "organic" diseases, and by the 1960s two major groups of researchers were at work on Alzheimer's disease. One, headed by Robert Terry, was based at Albert Einstein University, and the other, headed by Bernard Tomlinson, Gary Blessed, and Roth, was located at Newcastle-upon-Tyne. From their work and from other studies, it became apparent, among other things, that the changes in the brain found in cases of presenile dementia were the same as those in senile dementia (Katzman 1986; Vannoy and Greene 1989).

The discovery broadened the definition of Alzheimer's disease and thereby increased enormously the number of individuals viewed as victims of it. It also created major semantic problems. Previously the *presenile* nature of Alzheimer's disease was a defining factor. Now the illness shown to be a major affliction of the elderly population was called *senile dementia of the Alzheimer type* (SDAT), which psychiatrists call "primary degenerative dementia." *Senile dementia* (SD) has been used to mean either SDAT or Alzheimer's disease (AD), but it may also refer to other forms of dementia in the elderly (Reisberg 1983). In addition, Alzheimer's disease and senile dementia were often lumped together as senility or as cerebral arteriosclerosis. This latter concept proved to be so tenacious that even as late as the middle 1970s it was called "probably the most common medical misdiagnosis" of the cause of mental deterioration in the elderly (Beach 1987).

In the early 1980s, Alzheimer's disease was defined as an "age-associated cognitive decline of gradual onset and course, accompanied by Alzheimer-type neuropathologic brain changes" with "no distinction with respect to age of onset" (Reisberg 1983), and was thought to be responsible for 50 percent or more of all dementias (Vannoy and Greene 1989).

This definition is essentially the working one as we enter the last decade of the twentieth century. Experts at a 1990 conference on the illness believe that Alzheimer's disease is being diagnosed correctly in about 80 percent of cases, even though such diagnoses can be confirmed only after death, and even though the etiology and epidemiology of the disease remain obscure.

It may well be determined that Alzheimer's disease is not a single disease but, rather, many different diseases with multiple causes ranging from genetics to exogenous toxins. The extent to which age and aging will rank among those causes remains a subject of debate. Reports of the condition among individuals in their 30s have been used to support the contention that the disease is unrelated to aging. On the other hand, there is a rising prevalence with age, such that by age 85 and over, some 20 percent or more are demented. If, of course, Alzheimer's disease is a specific disease or diseases (as opposed to an inevitable product of the aging process for some 5 to 7 percent of the population over age 65), then, of course, there is hope for a cure.

The question, however, of why Alzheimer's disease has been called the disease of this century – one that has only recently burst upon the developed world in epidemic proportions – is certainly bound up with advancing age for many and with the demographic changes that this has wrought. In 1900, there were only 3 million Americans aged 65 or older. Today there are 27 million, and it has been estimated that in the year 2030 there will be 50 million. Given the fact that an individual who lives to be 80 has an almost 1:4 chance of developing Alzheimer's disease or a related disorder, estimates suggest that the number of these victims will increase from some 2.5 million in the late 1980s to about 4 million by the turn of the century. As the 1990s began, it was further estimated that fully half of all nursing home patients in the United States are Alzheimer victims.

The implications of the growing number of these victims for health care delivery systems are staggering. In 1967 a White House conference on aging resulted in the creation of the National Institute on Aging, which greatly facilitated research on Alzheimer's disease. In 1983, a Task Force on Alzheimer's Disease was created by the Department of Health and Human Services, which has emphasized the need for increased research and increased research funding, and in 1987 the journal *Alzheimer's Disease and Associated Disorders – An International Journal* was founded to report such research. As more and more resources are brought to bear, the outlook for breakthroughs in understanding the causes of Alzheimer's disease and treating it are more optimistic than in former times. But at the time of writing, it remains a devastating disease whose etiology is unknown.

Joseph A. Kwentus

Bibliography

Alafuzoff, I., et al. 1987. Histopathological criteria for progressive dementia disorders: Clinical pathological correlation and classification by multivariate data analysis. *Acta Neuropathologica* 74: 209–25.

Albert, M. T., R. G. Feldman, and A. L. Willis. 1974. The subcortical dementia of progressive supranuclear palsy. *Journal of Neurology, Neurosurgery and Psychiatry* 37: 121–50.

Albert, M. T., et al. 1984. CT density numbers in patients with senile dementia of the Alzheimer type. *Archives of Neurology* 41: 1264–9.

Bartus, R. T., et al. 1982. The cholinergic hypothesis of geriatric memory dysfunction. *Science* 217: 408–17.

Beach, Thomas G. 1987. The history of Alzheimer's disease: The debates. *Journal of the History of Medicine and Allied Sciences* 42: 327–49.

Blessed, G., B. E. Tomlinson, and M. Roth. 1968. The association between quantitative measures of dementia and of senile change in the cerebral grey matter of elderly subjects. *British Journal of Psychiatry* 114: 797–811.

Brodie, J. A. 1982. An epidemiologist views senile dementia facts and fragments. *American Journal of Epidemiology* 115: 115–62.

Christie, J. E., et al. 1981. Physostigmine and arecoline: Effects of intravenous infusions in Alzheimer presenile dementia. *British Journal of Psychiatry* 138: 46–50.

Cohen, E. L., and R. J. Wurtman. 1976. Brain acetylcholine: Control by dietary choline. *Science* 191: 561–2.

Cook, R. H., et al. 1979. Studies in aging of the brain: IV. Familial Alzheimer disease: relation of transmissible dementia, aneuploidy, and microtubular defects. *Neurology* 29: 1404–12.

Coyle, J. T., D. Price, and M. R. DeLong. 1983. Alzheimer's disease: A disorder of central cholinergic innervation. *Science* 219: 1184–9.

Cummings, J. L., and D. F. Benson. 1983. *Dementia: A clinical approach.* London.

Devanand, D. P., H. A. Sackeim, and R. Mayeux. 1988. Psychosis, behavioral disturbance, and the use of neuroleptics in dementia. *Comprehensive Psychiatry* 29: 387–401.

Eisdorfer, C., and D. Cohen. 1981. Management of the patient and family coping with dementing illness. *Journal of Family Practice* 12: 831–7.

Folstein, M. F., S. E. Folstein, and P. R. McHugh. 1975. Mini-mental state: A practical method for grading the cognitive state of patients for the clinician. *Journal of Psychiatric Research* 12: 189–98.

Fox, T. H., J. L. Topel, and M. S. Huckman. 1975. Use of computerized tomography in senile dementia. *Journal of Neurology, Neurosurgery and Psychiatry* 38: 948–53.

Gustafson, L., and L. Nilsson. 1982. Differential diagnosis of presenile dementia on clinical grounds. *Acta Psychiatrica Scandinavica* 65: 194–209.

Harner, R. N. 1975. EEG evaluation of the patient with dementia. In *Psychiatric aspects of neurologic disease,* ed. D. F. Benson and D. Blumer, 63–82. New York.

Haxby, J. V., et al. 1986. Neocortical metabolic abnormalities precede nonmemory cognitive defects in early Alzheimer's-type dementia. *Archives of Neurology* 43: 882–5.

Hersch, E. L. 1979. Development and application of the extended scale for dementia. *Journal of the American Geriatrics Society* 27: 348–54.

Heston, L. L., and A. R. Masri. 1966. The genetics of Alzheimer's disease: Associations with hematologic malignancy and Down's syndrome. *Archives of General Psychiatry* 34: 976–81.

Hughes, C. P., et al. 1982. A new clinical scale for the staging of dementia. *British Journal of Psychiatry* 140: 566–72.

Johnson, K. A., et al. 1987. Comparison of magnetic resonance and roentgen ray computed tomography in dementia. *Archives of Neurology* 44: 1075–80.

1988. Single photon emission computed tomography in Alzheimer's disease: Abnormal iofetamine I¹²³ uptake reflects dementia severity. *Archives of Neurology* 45: 392–6.

Katzman, R. 1976. The prevalence in malignancy of Alzheimer's disease: A major killer (editorial). *Archives of General Psychiatry* 33: 217–18.

1986. Alzheimer's disease. *New England Journal of Medicine* 314: 964–73.

Kay, D. W. K., P. Beamish, and M. Roth. 1964. Old age mental disorders in Newcastle-upon-Tyne. *British Journal of Psychiatry* 110: 146–8.

Khachaturian, Z. S. 1985. Diagnosis of Alzheimer's disease. *Archives of Neurology* 42: 1097–105.

Kokmen, E. 1984. Dementia: Alzheimer type. *Mayo Clinic Proceedings* 59: 35–42.

Kral, B. A. 1962. Forgetfulness: Benign and malignant. *Canadian Medical Association Journal.* 86: 257–60.

Markesbery, W. R., et al. 1981. Instrumental neutron activation analysis of brain aluminum in Alzheimer's disease and aging. *Annals of Neurology* 10: 511–16.

Marttila, R. J., and U. K. Rinne. 1976. Dementia in Parkinson's Disease. *Acta Neurologica Scandinavica* 54: 431–41.

Mayeux, R., Y. Stern, and S. Spanton. 1985. Clinical heterogeneity in patients with dementia of the Alzheimer type: Evidence for subgroups. *Neurology* 35: 453–61.

McKhann, G., et al. 1984. Clinical diagnosis of Alzheimer's disease: Report of the NINCDS–ADRDA ADRDA Work Group under the auspices of Department of Health and Human Services Task Force on Alzheimer's disease. *Neurology* 34: 939–44.

Morris, J. C., et al. 1988. Consortium to establish a registry for Alzheimer's disease. *Psychopharmacology Bulletin* 24: 641–52.

Mundy-Castle, A. C., et al. 1953. The electroencephalogram in the senile psychosis. *Electroencephalography and Clinical Neurophysiology* 6: 245–52.

Nuwer, M. R. 1988. Quantitative EEG: II. Frequency analysis and topographic mapping in clinical settings. *Journal of Clinical Neurophysiology* 5: 45–85.

Rabins, Peter V. 1988. Science and medicine in the spotlight: Alzheimer's disease as an example. *Perspectives in Biology and Medicine* 31: 161–9.

Reisberg, Barry. 1983. *Alzheimer's disease.* New York and London.

Reisberg, B., et al. 1982. The Global Deterioration Scale (GDS): An instrument for the assessment of primary degenerative dementia. *American Journal of Psychiatry* 139: 1136–9.

Reisberg, B., et al. 1983. The Brief Cognitive Rating Scale (BCRS): Findings in primary degenerative dementia. *Psychopharmacology Bulletin* 19: 47–50.

Reynolds, C. F., et al. 1983. Electroencephalographic sleep aging, and psychopathology: New data and state of art. *Biological Psychiatry* 18: 139–55.

Salzman, C., G. E. Kochansky, and R. I. Shader. 1972. Rating scales for geriatric psychopharmacology – a review. *Psychopharmacology Bulletin* 8: 3–50.

Schenk, N. K., B. Reisberg, and S. H. Ferris. 1982. An overview of current concepts of Alzheimer's disease. *American Journal of Psychiatry* 139: 165–73.

Seltzer, B., and I. Sherwin. 1983. A comparison of clinical

features in early and late-onset primary degenerative dementia: One entity or two? *Archives of Neurology* 40: 143–6.

Sharp, P., et al. 1986. Application of iodine-I^{123} labeled isopropylamphetamine imaging to the study of dementia. *Journal of Nuclear Medicine* 27: 761–8.

Sojdel-Sulkhowska, E. M., and C. A. Marotta. 1984. Alzheimer's disease brain: Alterations in RNA levels and in a ribonuclease–inhibitor complex. *Science* 225: 947–9.

Spor, J. E., and R. Gerner. 1982. Does the dexamethasone suppression test distinguish dementia from depression? *American Journal of Psychiatry* 139: 238–40.

St. George-Hyslop, P. H., et al. 1987. The genetic defect causing familial Alzheimer's disease maps on chromosome 21. *Science* 235: 885–90.

Stern, Y., M. Sano, and R. Mayeux. 1988. Long-term administration of oral physostigmine in Alzheimer's disease. *Neurology* 38: 1837–41.

Summers, W. K., et al. 1986. Oral tetrahydroaminoacridine in long-term treatment of senile dementia Alzheimer's disease. *New England Journal of Medicine* 315: 1241–5.

Terry, R. D., et al. 1981. Some morphometric aspects of the brain in senile dementia of the Alzheimer type. *Annals of Neurology* 10: 184–92.

Thal, L. J., et al. 1983. Oral physostigmine and lecithin improve memory in Alzheimer's disease. *Annals of Neurology* 13: 491–6.

Tierney, M. C., et al. 1988. The NINCDS–ADRDA Work Group criteria for the clinical diagnosis of probable Alzheimer's disease: A clinicopathologic study of 57 cases. *Neurology* 38: 359–64.

Tomilson, D. E., G. Blessed, and M. Roth. 1968. Observations on the brains of non-demented old people. *Journal of the Neurological Sciences* 7: 331–56.

  1970. Observations on the brains of demented old people. *Journal of the Neurological Sciences* 11: 205–32.

Vannoy, John F., and James A. Greene. 1989. Alzheimer's disease: A brief history. *Journal of the Tennessee Medical Association* 82: 15–17.

Visser, S. L., et al. 1976. Visual evoked response in senile and presenile dementia. *Electroencephalography and Clinical Neurophysiology* 40: 385–92.

Volicer L., and L. R. Herz. 1985. Pharmacologic management of Alzheimer-type dementia. *American Family Physician* 32: 123–8.

Watts, H., P. G. E. Kennedy, and M. Thomas. 1981. The significance of antineuronal antibodies in Alzheimer's disease. *Journal of Neuroimmunology* 1: 107–16.

Wells, C. E. 1977. *Dementia*. Philadelphia.

  1979. Pseudodementia. *American Journal of Psychiatry* 136: 895–900.

Wettstein, A., and R. Spiegel. 1984. Clinical trials with the cholinergic drug RS86 in Alzheimer's disease (AD) and senile dementia of the Alzheimer's type (SDAT). *Psychopharmacology* 84: 572–3.

Wisniewski, H. M. 1978. Possible viral etiology of neurofibrillary changes and neuritic plagues. In *Alzheimer's disease: senile dementia and related disorders,* ed. R. Katzman, R. D. Terry, and K. L. Beck, 355–8. New York.

  1989. *Alzheimer's disease and related disorders*. New York.

Wurtman, R. J., M, J. Hirsch, and J. Growdon. 1977. Lecithin consumption raises serum free-choline levels. *Lancet* 2: 68–9.

VIII.5
Amebic Dysentery

Amebiasis is an infection of the colon caused by a parasitic protozoan, the ameba *Entamoeba histolytica*. Several species of ameba inhabit the large intestine. Most are harmless commensals or minor parasites, usually causing little or no clinical damage. The closely related species *Entamoeba coli* and *Entamoeba hartmanni* are commensals, and infection with *E. histolytica* is also often asymptomatic. *E. histolytica* is probably a species complex, with a number of morphologically similar forms with varying degrees of invasiveness. *E. hartmanni*, formerly believed to be a "small race" of *E. histolytica*, is now recognized as a separate nonpathogenic species. Pathogenic amebas cause light to severe intestinal damage (amebic dysentery) and sometimes spread to the liver, lungs, brain, and other organs.

Etiology

The parasite exists in two forms during its life cycle. Active adults, trophozoites, multiply in the lumen of the colon. They frequently live there harmlessly, feeding on the contents of the intestine. Some strains are generally commensal; others are highly pathogenic. Under conditions of stress, lowered host resistance, or when a particularly pathogenic strain is involved, amebas invade the intestinal wall and cause abscesses. As they pass lower into the large intestine, the drier environment stimulates them to form a cyst wall. The original cell nucleus divides twice, producing four daughter nuclei. Cysts are passed with the feces and are infective when swallowed. Excystation takes place in the small intestine, and the young trophozoites, four from each cyst, are carried in the fecal stream to the large intestine. When dysentery occurs, trophozoites are swept out too rapidly to encyst. Even though huge numbers of amebas may be passed, they die quickly and are not infective. Persons with mild or no symptoms produce infective cysts, and it is they, not the patients with dysentery, who spread the disease.

Epidemiology

Infection is by the fecal–oral route. Direct infection can take place in circumstances of extreme crowding among children, as well as inmates of institutions for the mentally retarded and insane, and among male homosexuals. Indirect spread, however, by fecal contamination of food and water, is more common. Waterborne epidemics of amebic dysentery are not so frequent as those of bacillary dysentery, but the former do occur when sewage contaminates wells or water pipes. Fruits and vegetables can become covered with cysts when human feces are used as fertilizer, or when fruits are washed in contaminated water or are handled by a symptomatic or asymptomatic carrier. Flies and cockroaches can mechanically transmit cysts from feces to food. The disease thus flourishes in poor sanitary conditions but is rare where good personal hygiene is practiced and where water and sewer systems function properly. Dogs, cats, and monkeys can be infected in the laboratory, but there is no evidence that animal reservoirs have an epidemiological significance.

Distribution and Incidence

Infection with *E. histolytica* occurs around the world, although both commensal and pathological amebiasis is more common in poor, tropical countries. Prevalence rates vary greatly, as does the proportion of infections that result in clinical disease.

Amebiasis, especially clinical disease, is rare today in developed countries and is confined largely to specific groups such as residents of institutions, male homosexuals, travelers, and immigrants. In the United States from 3,000 to 4,000 cases were reported annually in the 1960s through the late 1970s. However, a spurt to roughly twice that level occurred in 1979–84. The disease was concentrated in Texas and California and was probably due to increased immigration from Mexico and Southeast Asia.

On the other hand, cases may be significantly underreported. One recent estimate suggests that the real annual total probably exceeds 100,000, and, in a 1970 study, 4 percent of military recruits had positive serologic tests. As recently as the early 1950s, infection rates of 10 to 20 percent were found in some rural southern counties. In Britain the car-

rier rate is between 2 and 5 percent; 31 amebiasis deaths were recorded from 1962 to 1971.

Asymptomatic and clinical amebiasis is much more common in Third World countries. Surveys have shown prevalence rates of from 2 to 60 percent, reflecting real differences as well as technical difficulties. It is clearly a major public health problem in much of South and Southeast Asia, China, Africa, and parts of Latin America. Mexico appears to have an unusually high prevalence. In the early 1980s it was estimated that 5 to 6 million clinical cases and 10,000 to 30,000 deaths took place annually in a population of some 70 million. Men in their 20s and 30s were most likely to die. In 1981, it was estimated that there were about 480 million infected people in the world: 290 million in Asia, 80 million in Africa, 90 million in the Americas, and remarkably, 20 million in Europe. Serious disease struck 10 million in the Americas, 15 to 30 million Asians, 10 million Africans, and few if any Europeans. The global death toll was between 40,000 and 110,000.

Diagnosis, Clinical Manifestations, and Pathology

Diagnosis depends on microscopic examination of stools, serologic tests, and clinical symptoms. The classic method, discovery of trophozoites or cysts in stools, is tedious and requires considerable skill, even with modern equipment and staining techniques. Trophozoites remain active only in fresh specimens and must be distinguished from commensal species and white blood cells. Preserved fecal specimens may be concentrated and stained, but detecting the adults and cysts and identifying them accurately are still difficult procedures. Furthermore, since trophozoites and cysts are not continually passed, more than one sample must be examined. Three or more specimens collected on separate days will find 80 to 90 percent of infections; fewer will be needed in symptomatic cases, as trophozoites are most readily detected in bloody patches in stools. Serologic tests also have limitations. Antibodies do not form unless amebas reach the bloodstream. It has been estimated that antibodies circulate in 85 to 90 percent of patients with liver abscess but in only 50 to 80 percent of those with severe dysentery. Serologic tests detect antibodies from recovered as well as active cases, which further limits the use of such methods in prevalence surveys.

Amebas cause disease when they invade the mucosal and submucosal layers of the large intestine, producing characteristic flask-shaped lesions. In severe cases the lesions become large and confluent, resulting in substantial tissue destruction, bleeding, loss of fluids, and sloughing of patches of mucosa. Damage to the intestinal wall reduces water absorption, and loose stools with blood and mucous are passed. In addition to severe and perhaps fatal damage to the gut, amebas sometimes penetrate through the muscular coat of the bowel, where they enter the bloodstream and are carried to other organs, especially the liver. Intestinal perforation may result in fatal peritonitis. Large abscesses may form in the liver, with grave and sometimes fatal consequences. Amebas may also migrate from the liver through the diaphragm to the lungs and cause new abscesses there. Brain abscesses are rare, but lethal. Very destructive skin ulcerations can also occur, especially around the anus.

Clinical symptoms of intestinal amebiasis range from mild diarrhea and abdominal discomfort to frequent loose stools with blood mucus, severe pain, emaciation, and prostration. Onset is generally insidious. Liver involvement may develop without evidence of intestinal disease. Symptoms include severe, continuous pain, enlarged and tender liver, fever, and weakness. Diagnosis is by biopsy or serology. Chronic amebiasis, both intestinal and hepatic, is sometimes very difficult to identify.

Differential diagnosis must rule out bacillary dysentery. Amebic dysentery tends to be a chronic disease with a gradual onset and little or no fever. The stools tend to be more abundant but less frequent and not to be bright red with blood, as is common in bacillary dysentery. Amebic dysentery has a longer incubation period, 20 to 90 days or more, compared to 7 days or less for the bacillary form. Finally, with its shorter incubation period and greater probability of water transmission, bacillary dysentery is more likely to occur in dramatic epidemics.

Prevention

Prevention is achieved with improved sanitation, especially good water and sewer systems and proper washing of fruits, vegetables, and hands. Routine chlorination of water does not destroy cysts. A Brazilian root, ipecacuanha, and its active ingredient, emetine, have been given orally to treat dysentery since the seventeenth century. It was first given by injection in 1912 and, despite its toxicity, is sometimes still employed for both intestinal and extraintestinal amebiasis. Safer drugs, such as metronidazole, are usually employed but must be given over 10- to 20-day periods and relapses are frequent. Infection does not produce immunologic protection against reinfection with the same or another strain.

History

Little is known of the early history of amebiasis. The disease probably did not become a serious problem until people began to adopt a sedentary, agricultural way of life. Dysentery has been described in the early medical writings of Europe and Asia, and outbreaks were frequent in military units, on slave ships, and in prisons. It is generally impossible, however, to determine whether amebic or bacillary dysentery was involved in any particular outbreak of the "flux."

British doctors in India provided good clinical accounts of amebiasis in the early nineteenth century. In 1828 James Annesley published an important study, based on clinical and pathological work, which clearly linked the intestinal and hepatic aspects of the disease. The pathogen was described in 1875 by a Russian physician, Fedor A. Lösch. Lösch, working in St. Petersburg with a patient from northern Russia, noted the clinical course of the disease, identified the ameba, and was able to produce similar lesions in dogs by feeding them ameba-rich stools from his patient. Lösch, however, believed that something else initially caused the disease and that the ameba merely "sustained" it. Technical problems, especially in identifying amebas and determining which were pathogenic and which were harmless, greatly impeded further research.

Stephanos Kartulis kept interest in the subject alive in the 1880s. Working in Cairo, he established that an ameba was the probable cause of tropical dysentery and managed to transmit infection to kittens. Then in 1890, a Canadian, Henri Lafleur, and an American, William Councilman of Johns Hopkins, published a definitive study of the pathology of the disease. Two German investigators, H. Quincke and E. Roos, distinguished between a pathogenic and a commensal ameba of humans, on clinical and morphological grounds, as well as by infection experiments on kittens. Still, the situation remained confused, as ameba identification and taxonomy was controversial and many research results could not be replicated. Doubts about the significance of pathogenic amebas were widespread in the early 1900s, despite painstaking studies like those of Leonard Rogers in Calcutta. Even Sir Patrick Manson, perhaps the single most important figure in tropical medicine, expressed skepticism about the role of amebas in dysentery as late as 1909. Ernest L. Walker (1913), an American scientist working in the Philippines, established the basic outline of the life cycle of *E. histolytica* and cleared some of the confusion about nonpathogenic forms with a series of feeding experiments on volunteer Filipino convicts. The discovery of methods to raise amebas in culture in 1925 has contributed to further clarification. Many mysteries still remain, however, as to distinctions between pathogenic and nonpathogenic strains, and factors such as diet, stress, and concomitant infections that trigger invasiveness in longstanding, asymptomatic infections.

K. David Patterson

Bibliography

Foster, W. D. 1965. *A history of parasitology.* Edinburgh.

Kean, B. H., Kenneth E. Mott, and Adair J. Russell, eds. 1978. *Tropical medicine and parasitology: Classic investigations,* Vol. I, 71–168. Ithaca and London.

Parasitic Diseases Programme, World Health Organization. 1986. Major parasitic infections: A global review. *World Health Statistical Quarterly* 39: 145–60.

U.S. Public Health Service. Centers for Disease Control. 1986. *Summary of notifiable diseases, United States, 1986.* Athens.

Walker, E. L. 1913. Experimental entamoebic dysentery. *Philippine Journal of Science* 8: 253–371.

Walsh, Julia A. 1986. Problems in recognition and diagnosis of amebiasis: Estimation of the global magnitude of morbidity and mortality. *Reviews of Infectious Diseases* 8: 228–38.

Wilcocks, Charles, and P. E. C. Manson-Bahr. 1972. *Manson's tropical diseases.* London.

World Health Organization. 1980. Parasite-related diarrheas. *Bulletin of the World Health Organization* 58: 819–30.

Wright, Willard H. 1955. Current status of parasitic diseases. *Public Health Reviews* 70: 966–75.

VIII.6
Anemia

Anemia, an insufficiency of red blood cells (RBC) and hemoglobin for oxygen-carrying needs, results from a variety of disease processes, some of which must have existed since ancient times. It was defined in quantitative terms in the mid-nineteenth century, but before that the evidence of anemia is found in the descriptions of pallor or in the occurrence of diseases that we now know cause anemia. For example, lead poisoning decreases RBC production and was apparently widespread in Rome. Intestinal parasites cause iron deficiency anemia and were known to exist in ancient times. Parasites found in paleopathological specimens include *Ascaris lumbricoides, Trichiuris trichiuria,* and various species of *Taenia (ovis, globosa, solium,* and *saginata),* all of which can cause intestinal blood loss and anemia. *Diphyllobothrium latum,* which leads to malabsorption of vitamin B_{12} and a megaloblastic anemia, has been found in mummies in Prussia and Peru.

Congenital abnormalities in RBC metabolism, including glucose 6-phosphate dehydrogenase (G6PD) deficiency and various forms of thalassemia and sickle-cell disease, were probably present also in ancient times. Thalassemia protects against malaria, and the incidence of the relatively mild, heterozygotic form of thalassemia (thalassemia minor) probably increased in the Mediterranean region after the appearance of falciparum malaria, the most fatal form of the disease.

Iatrogenic anemia was also common throughout most of recorded history, because bleeding was considered therapeutic from Greek and Roman times until the mid-nineteenth century.

Quantitation of Hemoglobin

The first quantitation of blood elements is attributed to Karl Vierordt of Tübingen, who published his method for counting RBC in 1852. The method was laborious, however, requiring some 3 hours, and other methods for diluting the blood and the use of pipets and counting chambers were subsequently developed. George Hayem of the University of Paris introduced a diluting solution in 1875. (It was the same saline solution he used intravenously to treat cholera.) Hayem observed that the average size of erythrocytes in chlorosis was smaller than normal (6 μm vs. 7.5 μm in diameter) and that the amount of hemoglobin per RBC was decreased in chlorosis (Wintrobe 1985).

The quantitation of hemoglobin specifically was introduced in 1899 by Theodur W. Tallquist of Finland. The results, reported as percentages of "normal," had a wide margin of error, but the method was used well into the mid-twentieth century. Other physicians had measured the hematocrit in centrifuged, anticoagulated blood, or had used the size of red blood cells and a color index as measures of hemoglobin concentration. In 1903 the "volume index" was introduced. It was clear that in various forms of anemia, the red cell size and concentration of hemoglobin in the red blood cells varied (Wintrobe 1985).

Classification

There are many conditions or deficiencies that result in anemia. This section will identify several types of anemia prevalent today.

Pernicious Anemia (PA)

Awareness of this type of anemia appears in the second half of the nineteenth century. Thomas Addison of Guy's Hospital described a severe, usually fatal form of anemia in 1855. Macrocytes were recognized by Hayem in 1877; he also noted a greater reduction of hemoglobin than of red blood cells in pernicious anemia. In 1880, Paul Ehrlich found large nucleated RBC in the peripheral blood containing dispersed nuclear chromatin; he called them *megaloblasts*, correctly concluding that they were precursors of Hayem's giant red cells that had escaped from the marrow (Castle 1980).

In 1894, T. R. Fraser of Edinburgh became the first physician reported to have fed liver to patients with PA. Although he achieved a remission in one patient, others could not immediately repeat his success (Castle 1980). But in 1918, George H. Whipple bled dogs and then fed them canned salmon and bread. After the dogs became anemic, he needed to remove very little blood to keep the hemoglobin low, although when the basal diet was supplemented, he found that he needed to bleed them more often. It turned out that liver was the most potent supplement, but it was not until 1936 that hematologists realized that the potency of liver was due to its iron content (Whipple and Robsheit-Robbins 1925).

George Richards Minot of Harvard University became interested in the dietary history of his patients following the first reported syndromes due to deficiency of micronutrients. He focused attention on liver after Whipple's observations in dogs; in trying to increase the iron and purines in the diet of patients with pernicious anemia, he fed them 100 to 240 grams of liver a day. He observed that the reticulocytes (an index of bone marrow activity) started to rise 4 to 5 days after the liver diet was begun. In fact, patients showed a consistent rise in RBC count and hemoglobin levels whenever they consumed liver in adequate amounts. In the attempt to purify the protein in liver, it was found that extracts were effective, and subsequently, cyanocobalamin – vitamin B_{12} – was identified. It was purified in 1948 and synthesized in 1973 (Castle 1980; Wintrobe 1985).

The possible role of the stomach in PA was pointed out by Austin Flint in 1860, only 5 years after Addison's description of the ailment appeared. In 1921, P. Levine and W. S. Ladd established that there was a lack of gastric acid in patients with PA even after stimulation. William B. Castle established that gastric juice plus beef muscle was effective in treating pernicious anemia, although either alone was not. An autoimmune basis for development of pernicious anemia has been established in recent years (Doniach, Roitt, Taylor 1963; Castle 1980).

Iron-Deficiency Anemia

Iron-deficiency anemia is by far the most common cause of anemia in every part of the world today (Davidson and Passmore 1969). It undoubtedly existed in ancient times as well. In this condition, fingernails develop double concave curvature, giving them a spoon shape (*koilonychia*). A Celtic temple at Nodens, in Gloucestershire, England, built in Ascelpian style after the Romans had left Britain in the fourth century A.D., contains a votive offering of an arm fashioned crudely proximally but with increasing detail distally; it shows characteristic koilonychia (Hart 1980).

Pallor, the hallmark or cardinal sign of anemia, is seen especially in the face, lips, and nails, often imparting a greenish tint to Caucasians, a presenting sign that led to the diagnosis of *chlorosis* or the "green sickness" in the sixteenth century. In the seventeenth century, pallor became associated in the popular mind with purity and femininity, and chlorosis became known as the "virgin's disease" (Hart 1980). Constantius I, father of Constantine the Great, was called Constantius Chlorus, because of his pale complexion (Hart 1980), and it seems most likely that he had a congenital form of chronic anemia. (He came from an area known today to have a relatively high frequency of thalassemia.)

Preparations containing iron were used therapeutically in Egypt around 1500 B.C. and later in Rome, suggesting the existence of iron deficiency. In 1681, Thomas Sydenham mentioned "the effect of steel upon chlorosis. The pulse gains in strength and frequency, the surface warmth, the face (no longer pale and death like) a fresh ruddy coulour. . . . Next to steel in substance I prefer a syrup . . . made by steeping iron or steel filings in cold Rhenish wine. . . ." In 1832 P. Blaud described treatment of chlorosis by use of pills of ferrous sulfate and potassium carbonate that "returns to the blood the exciting principle which it has lost, that is to say the coloring substance" (London 1980).

Children have increased needs for iron during growth, as do females during menstruation, pregnancy, and lactation. Chronic diarrhea, common in the tropics where it is often associated with parasitism, decreases iron absorption whereas parasitism increases iron losses. Estimates indicate that the needs of pregnant and lactating women in tropical climates are about twice those of women in temperate zones. In the tropics high-maize, low-iron diets are common, and soils are iron deficient in many areas (Davidson and Passmore 1969).

Glucose 6-Phosphate Dehydrogenase (G6PD) Deficiency

Favism, or hemolytic anemia due to ingestion of fava beans, is now known to occur in individuals deficient in G6PD. The Mediterranean type of G6PD deficiency is found in an area extending from the Mediterranean basin to northern India, an area corresponding to Alexander's empire. Sickness resulting from ingestion of beans was probably recognized in ancient Greece, forming the basis for the myth that Demeter, Greek goddess of harvest, forbade members of her cult to eat beans. Pythagoras, physician and mathematician of the fifth century B.C. who had a great following among the Greek colonists in southern Italy, also seems to have recognized the disorder, since he, too, forbade his followers to eat beans. It is in that area of southern Italy that the incidence of G6PD deficiency is highest (Hart 1980).

In 1956, the basis for many instances of this type of anemia was recognized as to a hereditary deficiency of the enzyme glucose-6-phosphate dehydrogenase within the red cell. Inheritance of G6PD is now recognized to be a sex-linked characteristic with the gene locus residing on the X chromosome.

It is estimated that currently over 100 million people in the world are affected by this deficiency. Nearly 3 million Americans carry the trait for G6PD deficiency; about 10 to 14 percent of black American males are deficient in G6PD. The defect is not lim-ited to blacks; it is found among Sephardic and Kurdish Jews, Sardinians, Italians, Greeks, Arabs, and in the Orient among Filipinos, Chinese, Thais, Asiatic Indians, and Punjabis. It has not been found among North American Indians, Peruvians, Japanese, or Alaskan Eskimos.

The first documented report of drug-induced (as opposed to fava bean-induced) hemolytic anemia appeared in 1926 following the administration of the antimalarial drug pamaquine (Plasmoquine). During World War II, after the world's primary sources of quinine were captured by the Japanese, about 16,000 drugs were tested for antimalarial effectiveness. In 1944, an Army Medical Research Unit at the University of Chicago studying these potential antimalarial drugs encountered the problem of drug-induced anemia. Research by this group over the next decade elucidated the basic information on G6PD deficiency (Keller 1971).

Pamaquine was found to cause hemolysis in 5 to 10 percent of American blacks but only rarely in Caucasians, and the severity of the hemolysis was observed to be dependent on the dose of the drug (Keller 1971; Beutler 1980). Although similar sensitivity to the related drug primaquine and many other related drugs was demonstrated, the term "primaquine sensitivity" came to be used to designate this form of hemolytic anemia. It was subsequently demonstrated that the hemolysis was due to an abnormality in the erythrocytes of susceptible individuals and that it was self-limited even if administration of primaquine was continued (Dern et al. 1954). Several biochemical abnormalities of the sensitive red cells, including glutathione instability, were described. In 1956, Paul E. Carson and colleagues reported that G6PD deficiency of red cells was the common denominator in individuals who developed hemolysis after one of these drugs was administered, and the term G6PD deficiency became synonymous with primaquine sensitivity (Carson et al. 1956). It was soon found that this deficiency was genetically transmitted (Beutler 1980).

Sickle-Cell Disorders

Sickle-cell disorders have existed in human populations for thousands of years. However, the discovery of human sickle cells and of sickle-cell anemia was first announced in the form of a case report by James Herrick at the Association of American Physicians in 1910. In 1904, Herrick had examined a young black student from Grenada who was anemic; in the blood film he observed elongated and sickle-cell-shaped RBC (Herrick 1910).

By 1922 there had only been three cases of this type of anemia reported. But in that year Verne R. Mason, a resident physician at Johns Hopkins Hospital, described the first patient recognized to have that disease at that institution. He entitled his report "Sickle Cell Anemia," thus introducing the term that would become the standard designation (Mason 1922).

In 1923 C. G. Guthrie and John Huck performed the first genetic investigation of this disease and developed a technique that became an indispensable tool for the identification of sickle trait in later investigations, population surveys, and genetic studies (Guthrie and Huck 1923).

Virgil P. Sidenstricker, of Georgia, recorded many of the clinical and hematologic features of sickle-cell disease. He introduced the term "crisis," was the first to suggest that the anemia was hemolytic, and reported the first autopsy describing the typical lesions of the illness including a scarred, atrophic spleen. He was also the first to describe sickle-cell anemia in childhood, noting the peculiar susceptibility of victims to infection with a high mortality rate (Sidenstricker et al. 1923).

The first case of sickle-cell anemia to be reported from Africa was described in 1925 in a 10-year-old Arab boy in Omdurman, and the first survey of the frequency of sickle-cell trait in the African population was reported in 1944 by R. Winston Evans, a pathologist in the West African Military Hospital. In a study of almost 600 men of Gambia, the Gold Coast, Nigeria, and the Cameroons, he found approximately 20 percent to have the trait, a sickling rate about three times that in the United States (Evans 1943–4).

In East Africa, E. A. Beet found a positive test for sickling in 12.9 percent of patients in the Balovale district of Northern Rhodesia. He also reported striking tribal differences in the prevalence of sickle-cell trait. By 1945 H. C. Trowell had concluded that sickle-cell anemia was probably the most common and yet the least frequently diagnosed disease in Africa. He noted that in his own clinic in Uganda no cases had been recognized before 1940, but 21 cases were seen within the first 6 months of 1944 when he began routine testing for sickling (Trowell 1945; Beet 1946).

For many years, it was thought that sickle-cell anemia was rare in Africa in contrast to the greater prevalence observed in America, and some thought that interbreeding with white persons brought out the hemolytic aspect of the disease. It was not until the mid-1950s that it was understood that few homozygous sickle-cell cases came to medical attention because of a high infant mortality rate from that disease. This was demonstrated in Léopoldville when J. and C. Lambotte-Legrand found that only two cases of sickle-cell anemia had been reported among adults in the Belgian Congo although sickling occurred in about 25 percent of the black population. They subsequently followed 300 infants with sickle-cell anemia. They found that 72 died before the end of the first year of life, and 144 had perished by the age of 5 (Lambotte-Legrand and Lambotte-Legrand 1955).

Subsequent research by others, however, established the fact that sickle-cell anemia patients who did survive to adolescence came from the higher social groups, and that the standard of living, the prevalence of infection and nutritional deficiency, and the level of general health care were the principal factors affecting the mortality rate from sickle-cell anemia in young children. By 1971, as improved health care became available, the course of the disease was altered; and, at the Sickle Cell-Hemoglobinopathy Clinic of the University of Ghana, it was reported that 50 percent of the patients with sickle-cell anemia survived past age 10 (Conley 1980).

Geographic distribution of sickle-cell gene frequency was mainly charted by the mid-twentieth century. The prevalence of sickling in black populations of the United States was well established by 1950. Numerous studies performed in central and South Africa also revealed that although the frequency of sickling varied, the occurrence of the gene that caused it was confined mostly to black populations.

In Africa, after World War II, surveys established that across a broad belt of tropical Africa, more than 20 percent of some populations were carriers of the sickle-cell trait. Significantly, a high frequency of sickle trait was also found among whites in some areas of Sicily, southern Italy, Greece, Turkey, Arabia, and southern India. Yet by contrast, sickling was virtually absent in a large segment of the world extending from northern Europe to Australia. These observations led to several hypotheses about where the mutant gene had had its origin and how such high frequencies of a deleterious gene are maintained (Conley 1980).

Hermann Lehmann presented evidence that sickling arose in Neolithic times in Arabia, and that the gene was then distributed by migrations eastward to India and westward to Africa. He and others have speculated that the frequency of the gene increased significantly in the hyperendemic malarial areas of Africa and spread northward across the Sahara along ancient trade routes, particularly along the routes that led to Mecca in Arabia. Since the eastern and western Arabian types of sickle-cell disease are different, spread must have occurred along sea trade routes, accounting for similarities in sickle-cell anemia in eastern Africa, eastern Arabia, and southern India (Lehmann and Huntsman 1974).

Obviously then, there was much interest generated in the cause of the very high frequency of the sickle-cell gene in Africa. In 1946, Beet in Rhodesia noted that only 9.8 percent of sicklers had malaria, whereas 15.3 percent of nonsicklers were affected (Beet 1946). P. Brain, of Southern Rhodesia, suggested that RBC of sicklers might offer a less favorable environment for survival of malarial parasites (Brain 1952). In 1954, J. P. Mackey and F. Vivarelli suggested that "the survival value [of the trait] may lie in there being some advantage to the heterozygous sickle cell individual in respect of decreased susceptibility of a proportion of his RBC to parasitization by P. falciparum" (Mackey and Vivarelli 1954).

A relationship between sickle-cell trait and falciparum malaria was reported by A. C. Allison in 1954. He noted that the frequency of heterozygous sickle-cell trait was as high as 40 percent in some African tribes, suggesting some selective advantage or else the gene would be rapidly eliminated because most homozygotes die without reproducing. He decided that a high spontaneous mutation rate could not account for the high but varying frequencies of the gene, and postulated that sickle-cell trait occurs as a true polymorphism and that the gene is maintained by selective advantage to the heterozygous. Comparing the distribution of falciparum malaria and sickling, Allison found that high frequencies of the trait were invariably found in hyperendemic malarial areas. He also found that people with sickle-cell trait suffer from malaria not only less frequently but also less severely than other persons, and concluded that where malaria is hyperendemic, children with the sickle-cell trait have a survival advantage (Allison 1954).

Previously in 1979, Linus Pauling and Harvey Itano had reported the aberrant electrophoretic mobility of sickle hemoglobin, and ascribed the altered hemoglobin of patients with sickle-cell anemia to a change in the globin portion of the molecule. It was shown that the red cells of sickle-cell anemia patients contain the abnormal hemoglobin almost exclusively, whereas those with sickle-cell trait contain other normal and abnormal components. These findings supported the theory of the genetic basis of sickle-cell anemia, proposed earlier by James Neel – that the person with sickle-cell trait is a heterozygous carrier of the sickling gene – and supplied a direct link between defective hemoglobin and molecules and the pathological consequences (Pauling et al. 1949).

Thalassemia

Thalassemia, an inherited form of anemia, results from the deficient synthesis of a portion of the globin molecule and is thought by some also to have stabilized in the face of malaria. A variety of forms exist, based on the chain and site within a specific chain at which the genetically determined defect exists. It has been suggested that thalassemia originated in Greece and spread to Italy when it was colonized by Greeks between the eighth and sixth century B.C. At present, it is most frequent in areas where ancient Greek immigration was most intense: Sicily, Sardinia, Calabria, Lucania, Apulia, and the mouth of the Po (Ascenzi and Balistreri 1977).

Skeletal Changes in Anemia: Porotic Hyperostosis

Chronic anemia from any cause results in bone changes, which can be recognized in archaeological specimens. These changes, called porotic or symmetrical hyperostosis, result from an overgrowth of bone marrow tissue, which is apparently a compensatory process. The cancellous zone between the cortical layers or tables of the skull is enlarged and the trabeculae become oriented perpendicular to the inner table, giving a radial pattern described as "hair standing on end." The inner table is unchanged, but the outer table is displaced externally and may be thinned or completely atrophied and often has a spongy appearance. The process varies in location in different individuals; frontal, parietal, temporal, occipital, and maxillary bones can be affected. A similar process is also seen in the metaphysical ends of long bones and anterior superior and acetabular areas of the ilium.

Today porotic hyperostosis is seen classically in X-rays of patients with congenital hemolytic anemias, as well as in children with chronic iron deficiency anemia. This is especially the case when the iron deficiency occurs in premature infants or is associated with protein malnutrition or rickets (Lanzkowksy 1968).

Porotic hyperostosis has been observed in archaeological specimens from a variety of sites, including areas of Greece, Turkey, Peru, Mexico, the United

States, and Canada. In most areas, the findings are considered evidence of iron-deficiency anemia, although thalassemia was apparently responsible in some areas. Around the shores of the Mediterranean, malaria was probably the most frequent cause of chronic anemia at certain times.

Archaeological specimens from the Near East show an incidence of anemia of only 2 percent in early hunters (15,000–8000 B.C.) who ingested a lot of animal protein and thus took in reasonable amounts of dietary iron. By contrast, farming populations of 6500 to 2000 B.C. showed an anemia incidence of 50 percent.

Many New World natives whose diet consisted primarily of corn (maize) and beans had a diet deficient in iron and protein. Moreover, when cooked in water for long periods of time, the food in the diet was also low in ascorbate and folate. Ascorbate helps convert dietary ferric to ferrous iron, which is more easily absorbed; therefore, deficiency of this vitamin increased the problem of deficient dietary iron. A high incidence of iron deficiency has been demonstrated by modern studies of infants and children in populations living on a diet consisting mostly of maize and beans (El-Najjar and Robertson 1976). It is not surprising then, in North America, that porotic hyperostosis was found in 54 percent of skeletons in the canyons of northern Arizona and northern New Mexico, among a population that ate little meat and subsisted mainly on maize. By contrast, plains dwellers in southern Arizona and southern New Mexico, who used more animal foods, had an incidence of only 14.5 percent. Absence of evidence for malaria or hemoglobinopathies in the New World before the arrival of the Europeans argues against these possible causes of porotic hyperostosis (Hart 1980).

Alfred Jay Bollet and Audrey K. Brown

Bibliography

Allison, Anthony C. 1954. Protection afforded by sickle-cell trait against subtertian malarial infection. *British Medical Journal* 1: 290–4.

Angel, J. Lawrence. 1975. Paleoecology, paleodemography and health. In *Population, ecology and social evolution,* World Anthropology Series, 167–90. Chicago.

1977. Anemias of antiquity: Eastern Mediterranean. In *Porotic hyperostosis: An enquiry,* ed. E. Cockburn, Paleopathology Associates Monograph No. 2, 1–5. Detroit.

Ascenzi, A., and P. Balistreri. 1977. Porotic hyperostosis and the problem of the origin of thalassemia in Italy. In *Porotic hyperostosis: An enquiry,* ed. E. Cockburn. Paleopathology Associates Monograph No. 2, 5–9. Detroit.

Beet, E. A. 1946. Sickle cell disease in the Balovale district of Northern Rhodesia. *East African Medical Journal* 23: 75–86.

Beutler, E. 1980. The red cell: A tiny dynamo. In *Blood pure and eloquent,* ed. M. W. Wintrobe, 141–68. New York.

Brain, P. 1952. Sickle cell anemia in Africa. *British Medical Journal* 2: 880.

Carson, Paul E., et al. 1956. Enzymatic deficiency in primaquin-sensitive erthrocytes. *Science* 124: 484–5.

Castle, W. B. 1980. The conquest of pernicious anemia. In *Blood pure and eloquent,* ed. M. W. Wintrobe, 171–208. New York.

Conley, C. Lockhart. 1980. Sickle-cell anemia. In *Blood pure and eloquent,* ed. M. W. Wintrobe, 319–71. New York.

Davidson, S., and R. Passmore. 1969. *Human nutrition and dietetics.* Baltimore.

Dern, R. C., et al. 1954. The hemolytic effect of primaquin. I. The localization of the drug-induced hemolytic defect in primaquin-sensitive individuals. *Journal of Laboratory and Clinical Medicine* 43: 303–9.

Doniach D., I. M. Roitt, and K. B. Taylor. 1963. Autoimmune phenomena in pernicious anemia: Serologic overlap with thyroiditis, thyrotoxicosis and systemic lupus erythematosus. *British Medical Journal* 1: 1374–9.

El-Najjar, M. Y., and A. Robertson. 1976. Spongy bones in prehistoric America. *Science* 193: 141–3.

Evans, R. W. 1943–4. The sickling phenomenon in the blood of West African natives. *Transactions of the Royal Society of Tropical Medicine and Hygiene* 37: 281–6.

Guthrie, C. G., and J. G. Huck. 1923. On the existence of more than four isoagglutinin groups in human blood. *Bulletin of the Johns Hopkins Hospital* 34: 37–48.

Hart, Gerald D. 1980. Ancient diseases of the blood. In *Blood pure and eloquent,* ed. M. W. Wintrobe, 33–56. New York.

Herrick, J. B. 1910. Peculiar elongated and sickle-shaped red blood corpuscles in a case of severe anemia. *Archives of Internal Medicine* 6: 517–21.

Keller, Dan. 1871. *G-6-PD deficiency.* Cleveland.

Lambotte-Legrand, J., and C. Lambotte-Legrand. 1955. Le Prognostic de l'anemie drapanocytaire au Congo Belge (A propos de cas de 150 décédés). *Annales de la Société Belgique de Médecine Tropicale* 35: 53–7.

Lanzkowsky, Philip. 1968. Radiological features of iron deficiency anemia. *American Journal of Diseases of Children* 116: 16–29.

Lehmann, Hermann, and R. G. Huntsman. 1974. *Man's hemoglobin.* Oxford.

London, Irving. 1980. Iron and heme: Crucial carriers and catalysts. In *Blood pure and eloquent,* ed. M. W. Wintrobe, 171–208. New York.

Mackey, J. P., and F. Vivarelli. 1954. Sickle cell anemia. *British Medical Journal* 1: 276.

Mason, Verne, R. 1922. Sickle cell anemia. *Journal of the American Medical Association* 29: 1318–20.

Pauling, Linus H., et al. 1949. Sickle cell anemia, a molecular disease. *Science* 110: 543–8.

Sidenstricker, Virgil P., W. A. Mulherin, and R. W. Houseal. 1923. Sickle cell anemia. Report of 2 cases in children with necropsy in one case. *American Journal of Diseases of Children* 26: 132–54.

Trowell, H. C. 1945. Sickle cell anemia. *East African Medical Journal* 22: 34–45.

Whipple, George H., and F. S. Robsheit-Robbins. 1925. Blood regeneration in severe anemia. II. Favorable influence of liver, heart and skeletal muscle in diet. *American Journal of Physiology* 72: 408–18.

Wintrobe, M. W. 1985. *Hematology, the blossoming of a science.* Philadelphia.

VIII.7
Anorexia Nervosa

Anorexia nervosa is a psychophysiological disorder especially prevalent among young women and is characterized by prolonged refusal to eat or to maintain normal body weight, an intense fear of becoming obese, a disturbed body image in which the emaciated patient feels overweight, and the absence of any physical illness that would account for extreme weight loss. The term *anorexia* is actually a misnomer, because genuine loss of appetite is rare, and usually does not occur until late in the illness. In reality, most anorectics are obsessed with food and constantly struggle to deny natural hunger.

Clinical Manifestations and Pathology

In anorexia nervosa, normal dieting escalates into a preoccupation with being thin, profound changes in eating patterns, and a weight loss of at least 25 percent of the original body weight. Weight loss is usually accomplished by a severe restriction of caloric intake, with patients subsisting on fewer than 600 calories per day. Contemporary anorectics may couple fasting with self-induced vomiting, use of laxatives and diuretics, and strenuous exercise.

The most consistent medical consequences of anorexia nervosa are amenorrhea (ceasing or irregularity of menstruation) and estrogen deficiency. In most cases amenorrhea follows weight loss, but it is not unusual for amenorrhea to appear before noticeable weight loss has occurred. The decrease in estrogens causes many anorectics to develop osteoporosis, a loss of bone density that is usually seen only in postmenopausal women (Garfinkel and Garner 1982).

By the time the anorectic is profoundly underweight, other physical complications due to severe malnutrition begin to appear. These include bradycardia (slowing of the heartbeat), hypotension (loss of normal blood pressure), lethargy, hypothermia, constipation, the appearance of "lanugo" or fine silky hair covering the body, and a variety of other metabolic and systemic changes.

In addition to the physical symptoms associated with chronic starvation, anorectics also display a relatively consistent cluster of emotional and behavioral characteristics, the most prominent of which grows out of the anorectic's distorted perception of food and eating. Unusual eating habits may include monotonous or eccentric diets, hoarding or hiding food, and obsessive preoccupation with food and cooking for others.

Emotionally, anorexic patients are often described as being perfectionistic, dependent, introverted, and overly compliant. Although studies have failed to find a consistent psychiatric symptom pattern for the disorder, frequently reported neurotic traits include obsessive compulsive, hysterical, hypochondriacal, and depressive symptoms. A decrease in or disappearance of sexual interest is also a frequent concomitant of anorexia nervosa, according to the 1987 *Diagnostic and Statistical Manual (DSM)* of the American Psychiatric Association.

A distorted body image is an almost universal characteristic of anorectics, with many patients insisting that they are overweight even when their bodies are extremely emaciated. As a result, most individuals with anorexia nervosa deny or minimize the severity of their illness and are thus resistant to therapy. The anorectic's refusal to acknowledge her nutritional needs, and her steadfast insistence that nothing is wrong, make anorexia nervosa one of the most recalcitrant disorders in contemporary medicine.

Distribution and Incidence

Once considered to be extremely rare, the reported incidence of anorexia nervosa has more than doubled during the 1970s and 1980s (Herzog and Copeland 1985). The disorder is especially prevalent among adolescent and young adult women. Indeed 90 to 95 percent of anorectics are young and female, and as many as one in 250 females between 12 and 18 years of age may develop the disorder. Onset of anorexia nervosa occurs almost exclusively during the teens, although some patients have become anorectic as early as age 11 and others as late as the sixth decade of life. Patients are typically from middle- or upper-class families.

Anorexia nervosa is comparatively rare in men: Approximately 5 to 10 percent of anorectics are male. The clinical picture for male anorectics is also much different from that for women. In general, male anorectics tend to display a greater degree of psychopathology, are often massively obese before acquiring the disorder, are less likely to be affluent, and are even more resistant to therapy than their female counterparts (Garfinkel and Garner 1982).

Among American blacks, Chicanos, and first- and second-generation ethnic immigrants, there are few reported cases. However, this racial and ethnic distribution reflects socioeconomic status rather than racial characteristics (Herzog and Copeland 1985). Similarly, anorexia nervosa is confined to the United States, Canada, Western Europe, Japan, and other highly industrialized areas. The absence of the disorder in developing nations, and its high incidence among affluent social groups in Westernized countries have led many clinicians to classify anorexia nervosa as a "culture-bound" syndrome (i.e., a disorder that is restricted to certain cultures primarily because of their distinctive psychosocial features) (Prince 1985).

Etiology and Epidemiology

Although the etiology of anorexia nervosa is an area of intense investigation, researchers have yet to reach a consensus about the origin of the disorder. The most sophisticated thinking on the subject regards anorexia nervosa as a disorder that involves an interplay of biological, psychological, and cultural factors. Advocates of this model view these three etiologic factors as reciprocal and interactive, and believe that it is simplistic to isolate one component as the single underlying cause of the disorder (Garfinkel and Garner 1982; Brumberg 1988a; Brumberg and Striegel-Moore 1988).

Joan Brumberg (1988a) has developed a multi-determined etiologic model based on a two-staged conceptualization of anorexia nervosa, which delineates the relative impact of sociocultural influences and individual biological and psychological variables in precipitating the disorder. In the first stage – the "recruitment" phase of the illness – sociocultural factors play the dominant role. During this period, cultural assumptions that associate thinness with female beauty lead certain women into a pattern of chronic dieting. Indeed, research on the

sociocultural causes of anorexia nervosa has linked the increased incidence of anorexia nervosa and other eating disorders with the tremendous cultural attention given to dieting and food, standards of beauty increasingly based on thinness, and the fitness movement (Chernin 1985; Schwartz, Thompson, and Johnson 1982; Orbach 1986). Yet sociocultural variables alone cannot explain why some women but not others move from chronic dieting to anorexia nervosa. Therefore, other individual factors must be implicated in the final development of the illness.

Brumberg's model of anorexia nervosa relies on a second stage – career or acclimation – to correct the shortcomings of sociocultural explanations of the disorder. During the career phase, specific biological and psychological features determine which individuals develop the full-blown psychopathology of anorexia nervosa. In order to explain the transition between the recruitment and career phases of anorexia nervosa, Brumberg relies on recent research in the biological and social sciences that has sought to uncover the unique physiological and psychological characteristics of anorexic patients.

Since the early 1900s, a number of different endocrinological and neurological abnormalities have been postulated as underlying biological causes of anorexia nervosa: hormonal imbalance, dysfunction in the satiety center of the hypothalamus, lesions in the limbic system of the brain, and irregular output of vasopressin and gonadotropin (Herzog and Copeland 1985). The search for a biomedical cause of anorexia nervosa is made difficult, however, by the fact that chronic starvation itself produces extensive changes in hypothalamic and metabolic function. Researchers in this area have yet to find a common biological characteristic of the anorectic population that is unmistakably a cause rather than a consequence of extreme weight loss and malnutrition (Brumberg 1988a).

A more satisfactory explanation of the biological factors that contribute to the "career" phase of anorexia nervosa is the "addiction to starvation" model proffered by the British psychiatrists George I. Szmukler and Digby Tantum (1984). According to Szmukler and Tantum, patients with fully developed anorexia nervosa are physically and psychologically dependent on the state of starvation. Much like alcoholics and other substance abusers, anorectics find something gratifying or tension-relieving about the state of starvation, and possess a specific physiological substrate that makes them more susceptible to starvation dependence than individuals who merely engage in chronic dieting. Szmukler and Tantum add, however, that starvation dependence is not the total explanation of anorexia nervosa. Rather, they believe that starvation dependence acts in conjunction with a range of sociocultural, psychological, and familial factors that encourage certain individuals to use anorexic behavior as a means of expressing personal anguish.

Current psychological models of anorexia nervosa fall into three basic categories: psychoanalytic, family systems, and social psychology. In both the psychoanalytic and family systems models, anorexia nervosa is seen as a pathological response to the development crisis of adolescence. Orthodox psychoanalysts, drawing on the work of Sigmund Freud, view the anorectic as a girl who fears adult womanhood, and who associates eating with oral impregnation (Brumberg 1988a). Family systems theory, however, offers a more complex explanation of the relationship between adolescence and anorexia nervosa. On the basis of clinical work with anorectics and their families, family systems therapists have found that the majority of anorexic patients are "enmeshed," meaning that the normal process of individuation is blocked by extreme parental overprotectiveness, control, and rigidity. Anorexia nervosa is therefore seen as a form of adolescent rebellion against parental authority (Minuchin, Rosman, and Baker 1978; Bruch 1988).

Research in social psychology and the field of personality has devised several psychological tests to distinguish the psychological characteristics of anorectics from others in their age group. One study has shown that whereas many of the psychological traits of anorectics and other women are indistinguishable, anorectics display a markedly higher degree of ineffectiveness and self-esteem. Other studies have proposed that anorectics have actual cognitive problems with body imaging, whereas others suggest a relationship between anorexia nervosa and sex-role socialization (Garfinkel and Garner 1982).

Finally some researchers have attempted to fit anorexia nervosa within other established psychiatric categories such as affective disorders and obsessional neurosis. Many anorectics in fact display behavior patterns associated with obsessive-compulsive disorders: perfectionism, excessive orderliness and cleanliness, meticulous attention to detail, and self-righteousness. This correlation has led a number of researchers to suggest that anorexia nervosa is itself a form of obsessive-compulsive behavior (Rothenberg 1986). Depressive symptoms are also commonly seen in many patients with anorexia nervosa. Various family, genetic, and endocrine studies have found a corre-

lation between eating disorders and depression. However, the association between anorexia nervosa and other psychiatric disorders remains controversial (Garfinkel and Garner 1982; Herzog and Copeland 1985).

History

Pre–Eighteenth Century

The existence of anorexia nervosa in the past has been a subject of much historical debate. Some clinicians and medical historians have postulated that anorexia nervosa was first identified in 1689 by the British doctor Richard Morton, physician to James II (Bliss and Branch 1960; Silverman 1983). The medieval historian Rudolph Bell has dated the origins of anorexia nervosa even earlier, claiming that certain medieval female saints, who were reputed to live without eating anything except the eucharist, actually suffered from anorexia nervosa (Bell 1985).

Other historians, however, have argued that attempts to label all historical instances of food refusal and appetite loss as anorexia nervosa are simplistic, and maintain that the historical record is insufficient to make conclusive diagnoses of individual cases (Bynum 1987; Brumberg 1988a). Although these historians agree that the final physiological stage of acute starvation may be the same in contemporary anorectics and medieval ascetics, the cultural and psychological reasons behind the refusal to eat are quite different. Thus, to reduce both to a single biomedical cause is to overlook the variety of social and cultural contexts in which certain individuals have chosen to refuse food.

Nineteenth Century

The modern disease classification of anorexia nervosa emerged during the 1860s and 1870s, when the work of public asylum keepers, elite British physicians, and early French neurologists partially distinguished anorexia nervosa from other diseases involving loss of appetite (Brumberg 1988a). In 1859, the American asylum physician William Stout Chipley published the first American description of *sitomania,* a type of insanity characterized by an intense dread or loathing of food (Chipley 1859). Although Chipley found sitomania in patients from a broad range of social and age groups, he identified a special form of the disease that afflicted adolescent girls. Chipley's work was ignored by his contemporaries, however, and it was not until the 1870s, when two influential case studies by the British physician William Withey Gull (1874) and the French alienist

Charles Lasègue (1873) were published, that physicians began to pay significant attention to anorexia in girlhood. Gull's primary accomplishment was to name and establish anorexia nervosa as a coherent disease entity distinct from either mental illnesses in which appetite loss was a secondary feature, or physical "wasting" diseases such as tuberculosis, diabetes, or cancer. Despite widespread acclaim for Gull's work with anorectic patients, however, clinicians during the late nineteenth century generally rejected the conception of anorexia nervosa as an independent disease. Instead, they conceptualized it either as a variant of hysteria that affected the gastrointestinal system, or as a juvenile form of neurasthenia (Brumberg 1988a).

Nineteenth-century physicians also tended to focus on the physical symptom of not eating, and ignored the anorectic patient's psychological reasons for refusing food. An important exception was Lasègue, who was the first to suggest the significance of family dynamics in the genesis and perpetuation of anorexia nervosa. Because of the somatic emphasis of nineteenth-century medicine, however, most nineteenth-century medical practitioners disregarded Lasègue's therapeutic perspective. Instead, they directed medical intervention toward restoring the anorectic to a reasonable weight and pattern of eating rather than exploring the underlying emotional causes of the patient's alleged lack of appetite (Brumberg 1988a).

Early Twentieth Century

In the twentieth century, the treatment of anorexia nervosa changed to incorporate new developments within medical and psychiatric practice. Before World War II, two distinct and isolated models dominated medical thinking on anorexia nervosa. The first approach was rooted in late-nineteenth-century research in organotherapy, a form of treatment based on the principle that disease resulted from the removal or dysfunction of secreting organs and glands (Brumberg 1988a). Between 1900 and 1940, a variety of different endocrinologic deficiencies were proposed as the cause of anorexia nervosa. In 1914, Morris Simmonds, a pathologist at the University of Hamburg, published a clinical description of an extreme cachexia due to destruction of the anterior lobe of the pituitary. Because patients with anorexia nervosa and those with Simmonds' disease shared a set of common symptoms, many clinicians assumed that a deficiency in pituitary hormone was the cause of both conditions (Brumberg 1988a).

Other researchers implicated thyroid insuffi-

ciency as the cause of anorexia nervosa. Research conducted at the Mayo Clinic in Rochester, Minnesota, during the period between the two world wars established a relationship between thyroid function and body weight, and led many physicians to regard anorexia nervosa as a metabolic disorder caused by a deficiency in thyroid hormone. Throughout the 1920s and 1930s, insulin, antuitrin, estrogen, and a host of other hormones were also employed in the treatment of anorexia nervosa (Brumberg 1988a).

The second major approach to anorexia nervosa in the early twentieth century grew out of the field of dynamic psychiatry, which emerged during the 1890s and early 1900s. Beginning in the last decade of the nineteenth century, practitioners in dynamic psychiatry increasingly focused on the life history of individual patients and the emotional sources of nervous disease. Two of the leading pioneers in this new field – Freud and Pierre Janet – were the first to suggest a link between the etiology of anorexia nervosa and the issue of psychosexual development. According to Freud, all appetites were expressions of libido or sexual drive. Thus, not eating represented a repression of normal sexual appetite (Freud 1918–59). Similarly, Janet asserted that anorectic girls refused food in order to retard normal sexual development and forestall adult sexuality (Janet 1903; Brumberg 1988a).

Because of the enormous popularity of endocrinologic explanations of disease, the idea of anorexia nervosa as a psychosexual disturbance was generally overlooked for more than 30 years. By the 1930s, however, the failure of endocrinologic models to establish either a predictable cure or a definitive cause of anorexia nervosa, the growing reputation of the Freudian psychoanalytic movement, and increased attention to the role of emotions in disease led a number of practitioners to assert the value and importance of psychotherapy in the treatment of anorexia nervosa. Although biomedical treatment of the disorder continued, most clinicians realized that successful, permanent recovery depended on uncovering the psychological basis for the anorectic's behavior. Following on the work of Freud and Janet, orthodox psychiatrists during this time postulated that refusal to eat was related to suppression of the sexual appetite, and claimed that anorectic women regarded eating as oral impregnation and obesity as pregnancy (Brumberg 1988a).

Post–World War II

After World War II, a new psychiatric view of eating disorders, shaped largely by the work of Hilde

Bruch, encouraged a more complex interpretation of the psychological underpinnings of anorexia nervosa. Although Bruch agreed that the anorectic was unprepared to cope with the psychological and social consequences of adulthood and sexuality, she also stressed the importance of individual personality formation and factors within the family to the psychogenesis of anorexia nervosa. Here, Bruch revived Lasègue's work on the role of family dynamics in anorexia nervosa. According to Bruch, the families of most anorectic patients were engaged in a dysfunctional style of familial interaction known as "enmeshment": Such families are characterized by extreme parental overprotectiveness, lack of privacy of individual members, and reluctance or inability to confront intrafamilial conflicts. Although superficially these families appeared to be congenial, said Bruch, this harmony was achieved through excessive conformity on the part of the child, and undermined the child's development of an autonomous self. Anorexia nervosa, according to Bruch, was therefore a young woman's attempt to exert control and self-direction in a family environment in which she otherwise felt powerless (Bruch 1973, 1988).

Bruch was also primarily responsible for the tremendous growth in the popular awareness of anorexia nervosa and other eating disorders in the 1970s and 1980s. Through her book, *The Golden Cage: The Enigma of Anorexia Nervosa* (1978), which sold over 150,000 copies, and numerous articles in popular magazines, Bruch brought anorexia nervosa into common American parlance (Brumberg 1988b).

At the same time that the American public was becoming increasingly aware of anorexia nervosa, the number of reported cases of the disorder grew tremendously. This phenomenon has led some clinicians and social commentators to suggest that the popularization process itself may promote a "sympathetic host environment" for the disorder (Striegel-Moore, Silberstein, and Rodin 1986; Brumberg 1988b). As Bruch (1988) herself observed:

Once the discovery of isolated tormented women, it [anorexia nervosa] has now acquired a fashionable reputation, of being something to be competitive about. . . . This is a far cry from the twenty-years-ago anorexic [*sic*] whose goal was to be unique and suggests that social factors may impact the prevalence of the disorder.

Heather Munro Prescott

Bibliography

Bell, Rudolph. 1985. *Holy anorexia.* Chicago.

Bliss, Eugene L., and C. H. Hardin Branch. 1960. *Anorexia nervosa: Its history, psychology, and biology.*
New York.

Bruch, Hilde. 1973. *Eating Disorders: Obesity, anorexia
nervosa, and the person within.* New York.

1978. *The golden cage: The enigma of anorexia nervosa.*
New York.

1988. *Conversations with anorexics,* ed. Danita Czyzew-
ski and Melanie A. Suhr. New York.

Brumberg, Joan Jacobs. 1988a. *Fasting girls: The emergence of anorexia nervosa as a modern disease.* Cambridge, Mass.

1988b. From fat boys to skinny girls: Hilde Bruch and
the popularization of anorexia nervosa in the 1970s.
Paper presented at the 1988 American Association for
the History of Medicine meetings.

Brumberg, Joan Jacobs, and Ruth Striegel-Moore. 1988.
Continuity and change in the symptom choice: Anorexia nervosa in historical and psychological perspective. Unpublished paper available from authors.

Bynum, Caroline Walker. 1987. *Holy feast and holy fast:
The religious significance of food and medieval
women.* Berkeley, Cal.

Chernin, Kim. 1985. *The hungry self: Women, eating and
identity.* New York.

Chipley, William S. 1859. Sitomania: Its causes and treatment. *American Journal of Insanity* 26: 1–42.

Freud, Sigmund. 1918–59. From the history of an infantile neurosis. In *Collected papers,* Vol. 3. New York.

Garfinkel, Paul E., and David M. Garner. 1982. *Anorexia
nervosa: A multidimensional perspective.* New York.

Gull, William. 1874. Anorexia nervosa (apepsia hysterica,
anorexia hysterica). *Transactions of the Clinical Society of London* 7: 22–8.

Herzog, David B., and Paul M. Copeland. 1985. Eating
disorders. *New England Journal of Medicine* 313:
295–303.

Janet, Pierre. 1903. *Les Obsessions et la psychasthénie.*
New York.

Kaye, W. H., et al. 1986. Caloric consumption and activity
levels after weight recovery in anorexia nervosa: A
prolonged delay in normalization. *International Journal of Eating Disorders* 5: 489–502.

Lasègue, Charles. 1873. De L'Anorexie hystérique. *Archives générales de médecine* 1: 385–7.

Minuchin, Salvador, Bernice L. Rosman, and Lesley
Baker. 1978. *Psychosomatic families: Anorexia nervosa in context.* Cambridge, Mass.

Morton, Richard. 1689. *Phthisiologia, seu exercitationes de
phthisi.* London.

Orbach, Susie. 1986. *Hunger strike: The anorectic's struggle as a metaphor for our age.* New York.

Prince, Raymond. 1985. The concept of culture-bound syndrome: Anorexia nervosa and brain-fag. *Social Science and Medicine* 21: 197–203.

Rothenberg, Albert. 1986. Eating disorder as a modern
obsessive-compulsive syndrome. *Psychiatry* 49: 45–53.

Schwartz, Donald M., Michael G. Thompson, and Craig L.

Johnson. 1982. Anorexia nervosa and bulimia: The socio-cultural context. *International Journal of Eating Disorders* 1: 20–36.

Silverman, Joseph. 1983. Richard Morton, 1637–1698: Limner of anorexia nervosa: His life and times. *Journal of the American Medical Association* 250: 2830–2.

Striegel-Moore, Ruth, Lisa R. Silberstein, and Judith Rodin. 1986. Toward an understanding of risk factors in bulimia. *American Psychologist* 41: 246–63.

Szmukler, George I., and Digby Tantum. 1984. Anorexia nervosa: Starvation dependence. *British Journal of Medical Psychology* 57: 303–10.

VIII.8
Anthrax

Anthrax is an acute zoonotic disease, primarily of herbivorous animals, which is transmissible to human beings. The causative organism is *Bacillus anthracis,* often referred to in earlier, and especially in French, texts as *bactéridie,* the name first bestowed on it by Casimir Davaine in 1863. Humans are infected only secondarily through contact with animals or animal products, and thus the disease in human beings must be considered in relation to anthrax in animals.

The species of domestic animals most commonly affected are cattle, sheep, and goats; pigs, dogs, and cats are less susceptible. Since an enlarged spleen is a classic observation in animals with anthrax, the disease has also been known as *splenic fever* or *splenic apoplexy.* In humans the cutaneous form is known as *malignant pustule,* and the pulmonary or intestinal, industrial type, as *woolsorters' disease* or *industrial anthrax.* In French the equivalent of splenic fever is *sang de rate,* in German *Milzbrand;* other French synonyms include *charbon* and *pustule maligne.*

Etiology and Epidemiology

Because *B. anthracis* produces resistant spores in suitable soils, the disease has long been endemic in many areas throughout the world, with a majority of the outbreaks occurring in Europe and Asia. The Americas, Africa, and Australasia are less affected. Once contaminated with anthrax spores, an area can be extremely difficult to clear, as has been demonstrated on the island of Gruinard off the west coast of Scotland, which was experimentally contaminated during World War II. This is of prime importance for the eipdemiology of the disease because it is rarely spread directly from animal to animal, but almost always through ingestion of contaminated food, either by grazing or, in cooler climates, through imported winter foodstuffs. Humans are accidentally infected either by contact with infected animals or by contaminated animal products. The infectivity of the anthrax bacillus for people is low, and therefore, even where large numbers of spores and bacilli are found in an industrial environment, only relatively few cases occur.

The nonindustrial type of anthrax in humans affects those in professions such as veterinary surgery, pathology, farming, butchery, and the like and takes the form of malignant pustule – a lesion due to contamination of the skin with material from infected animals. The industrial type may present as either malignant pustule or pulmonary disease and is acquired in the woolen industries especially through contaminated air. The disease approached an epidemic situation in the late eighteenth and nineteenth centuries in France and in England in factories processing imported horsehair and sheep's wool.

Distribution and Incidence

Anthrax is widely distributed throughout the world, but there are distinct differences in incidence and in species affected among the various continents and countries. Outbreaks in animals in Europe (mainly cattle) and in Asia (sheep and goats) heavily outweigh those in the United States and Africa, whereas Australia and Canada are rarely affected. Extensive enzootic areas with a constant presence of infection include China, Ethiopia, and Iran, and, in the Americas, Mexico and some South American countries. Available data suggest an annual average total of some 10,000 outbreaks throughout the world; for Great Britain the annual total between the two world wars ranged from 400 to 700, mostly very minor outbreaks. Since then there appears to have been a gradual reduction in incidence, helped in Great Britain by the introduction in 1919 of the Anthrax Prevention Act, forbidding importation of certain types of potentially contaminated material. Since World War II the number of fatal cases in human beings has been substantially reduced following the introduction of antibiotic therapy.

In countries such as Italy and Russia, a close correlation has existed between the seasonal incidence of the disease in people and in animals, with a rise during the hot summer months reflecting the seasonal changes in temperature, humidity, and vegetation favoring spread and reproduction of the bacillus.

Immunology

The immunogenic behavior of the anthrax bacillus is complex, and it is not certain whether or to what extent immunity develops in cases of recovery from infection. The existence of an extracellular toxin produced by *B. anthracis,* which in part determines its virulence was demonstrated only during the 1980s. Certain strains of certain animal species possess a high degree of natural resistance, a fact that introduced confusion and fed much of the controversy surrounding the early work on the etiology of and immunity in anthrax. The live attenuated vaccines used by Louis Pasteur have undergone continued development and improvement over the years, but early results claiming reductions in incidence and fatality rates following their use were not readily sustained. Thus, the early vaccines have gradually been replaced by spore-based vaccines and methods combining active and passive immunization using prepared antiserum. Until recently, vaccines have not been considered safe for use in human beings, but serum treatment has been used extensively for prophylactic and therapeutic purposes.

For occupational reasons women are less liable to exposure than men, but the disease, when established, is more commonly fatal in females.

Clinical Manifestations and Pathology

In its principal animal hosts, anthrax may take one of three forms: (1) a *peracute* type (*splenic apoplexy*), where sudden death occurs almost simultaneously with the first symptoms; (2) an *acute* type characterized by an acute fever, usually followed by death after 2 to 12 days; and (3) a *subacute* type often followed by recovery. Classical signs include fever, stupor, spasms, convulsions, intestinal disturbances, and respiratory or cardiac distress. Death follows septicemia and accompanying severe toxic manifestations. Characteristic enlargement of the spleen is reflected in the name of splenic fever.

Anthrax in people may take the form of a malignant pustule (cutaneous anthrax), where the bacilli enter through the skin, producing a primary lesion developing into a characteristic area of inflammation surrounding a dark necrotic center; or it may take the form of the pulmonary or – less commonly – the intestinal type, which follows inhalation of dust containing anthrax spores, as has occurred in the woolen industries. Monkeys exposed to artificially generated aerosols of anthrax spores develop symptoms mimicking woolsorters' disease. Postmortem findings include hemorrhages in the lung, hemorrhagic mediastinitis and lymphadenitis, and sometimes hemorrhagic meningitis.

History and Geography

In the past, outbreaks of anthrax (along with other epizootic diseases) among animals have undoubtedly helped to prepare the way for major outbreaks of epidemic disease in human beings. When anthrax has decimated herds of cattle or sheep, for example, human populations have faced starvation which, in turn, has lowered their ability to resist those epidemics. Anthrax has been known from antiquity, although until relatively recently it was not clearly separated from other diseases with similar manifestations. Possibly sudden death of animals at pasture, blamed by Aristotle (and subsequently by his followers over the centuries) on the shrewmouse and its "poisonous bite," may in many cases have been due to the peracute form of anthrax commonly referred to as *splenic apoplexy*.

Nineteenth-century authors speculated that the fifth and sixth plagues of the Egyptians as described in *Exodus,* which struck their herds and the Egyptians themselves, might have been anthrax. Evidence that this may have been the case centers on the Israelites, who were installed on sandy ground above the level of the Nile. They escaped the plagues, whereas those who did not lived in areas subject to flooding by the rising of the Nile, which could have provided perfect conditions for growth of the anthrax bacillus. Three decades before the birth of Christ, Virgil, in the *Georgics,* vividly described an animal plague that had much in common with anthrax, and warned against its transmission to people through contact with infected hides.

Through the centuries since Biblical times there are many records of animal plagues that almost certainly were anthrax but were often confused with a number of other complaints. By 1769, when identification of epidemic diseases of animals and human beings had become more precise, Jean Fournier in Dijon classified a number of different lesions as a single disease entity (anthrax), which he called *charbon malin.* More importantly, he recognized the transmission of the disease to people, and drew attention to cases occurring in workers who handled raw hair and wool, a theme developed in several accounts published in France during the following decade. These were all concerned with workers who had contracted anthrax while opening and sorting bales of horsehair imported from Russia. From the mid-nineteenth century, the disease became a problem in English factories as well, and subsequently in those of Scotland. At about the same time, the woolen industries began experiencing the problem as wool and hair from the East were introduced to the British trade. Wool-sorting, until then considered a particularly healthful occupation, suddenly began to show an alarming increase in the number of deaths and the extent of disease among the workers. The workers themselves suspected an association between the disease and the growing proportion of wool and hair imported from the East. By the late 1870s, concern in the Yorkshire factories was acute, but by then the new bacteriology had led to the identification of the cause of anthrax. J. H. Bell in Bradford had demonstrated that both woolsorters' disease and malignant pustule in humans derived from anthrax in animals.

Bell's work had been made possible by the work of Davaine and that by Robert Koch in the 1860s and 1870s. During the nineteenth century, the study of anthrax and the use of animal models in its pursuit had become an important part of the framework for the emergence of bacteriology as an academic discipline. In France, Eloy Barthélemy established the transmissibility of anthrax in feeding experiments with horses in 1823. From 1850 onward, study of the putative agent was pursued by workers in Germany and in France, beginning with the results obtained by Aloys Pollender, then by Pierre Rayer, and finally by Davaine who, during extensive work with guinea pigs in the 1860s, bestowed on it the name of *bactéridie,* which survived in the literature for a long time. From 1876 onward, the anthrax bacillus became a cornerstone of both Koch's theories and his development of pure culture methods; in the late 1870s, W. S. Greenfield at London's Brown Institution and H. Toussaint in Lyons published the first studies of acquired immunity against anthrax in animals, before Pasteur took over the field and was able to demonstrate, at Pouilly-le-Fort in 1881, that immunity could be produced through vaccination of sheep.

In Great Britain, industrially acquired anthrax became a notifiable disease in the Factory and Workshops Act of 1895; the incidence was reduced when the Anthrax Prevention Act of 1919 prohibited importation of certain types of potentially contaminated material. Since World War II, following the introduction of antibiotic therapy, the number of fatal human cases has been substantially reduced.

Lise Wilkinson

Bibliography

Brachman, Philip S. 1980. Inhalation anthrax. *Annals of the New York Academy of Science* 353: 83–93.

Cunningham, William. 1976. The work of two Scottish medical graduates in the control of woolsorters' disease. *Medical History* 20: 169–73.

Fleming, George. 1871. *Animal plagues: Their history, nature and prevention.* London.

Lincoln, Ralph E., et al. 1964. Anthrax. *Advances in Veterinary Science* 9: 327–68.

Page, Cecil H. W. 1909. British industrial anthrax. *Journal of Hygiene* 9: 279–315; 357–98.

Théordorides, Jean. 1968. Un grand médecin et biologiste: Casimir-Joseph Davaine (1812–82). In *Analecta medico-historica,* 4. Oxford.

Wilson, Graham, and Geoffrey Smith. 1983–4. Anthrax. In *Principles of bacteriology, virology and immunity,* 7th edition, Vol. 3, Chap. 54, 102–12. London.

Wyatt, Vivian. 1978. Maladie de Bradford – after 100 years. *New Scientist* 79: 192–4.

VIII.9
Apoplexy and Stroke

Apoplexy

The old, very popular and quite international term *apoplexy* (or its equivalents *apoplectic attack, attack, apoplectic ictus* or *ictus*) today generally means stroke. The word "apoplexy" comes from the Greek *apoplexia,* which is derived from the verb *apoplessein,* meaning, respectively, "stroke" and "to strike." To define apoplexy is therefore to relate the history of the word and of its different successive significations. The history of apoplexy, from the Greeks to the twentieth century, will be presented first, followed by the medical details of stroke.

History

In the Hippocratic corpus, "apoplexy" appears as an obviously clinical term. For many centuries after Galen's writings of the second century A.D., it was thought that apoplexy involved brain matter, whereas epilepsy represented a disturbance of brain function. From the invention of the printing press to the late nineteenth century, several hundred monographs were devoted to apoplexy. Indeed the medical history of A. Dechambre (1866) listed some 150 such references between 1611 and 1865.

The first autopsies involving postmortem examinations of the brain were performed in the seventeenth century. Many more were done, however, after the publication of *De Sedibus, et Causis Morborum per*

Anatomen Indagatis, Libri Quinque by Giovanni Battista Morgagni in 1761. Morgagni reported numerous cases of postmortem examinations of apoplexy cases, which he separated into serous apoplexy (*apoplexia serosa*) and sanguineous apoplexy (*apoplexia sanguinea*).

In his 1820 treatise *On Apoplexy,* John Cooke considered that hemorrhagic lesions were commonest and that the other types of lesions (e.g., tumors, suppuration, cysts) were questionable cases of apoplexy. In his volume *Cases of Apoplexy and Lethargy with Observations upon the Comatose Diseases* published in 1812, John Cheyne thought that apoplexy might be "serous" or "sanguineous," but he was skeptical of the former entity. The periodic apnea, now known as the Cheyne–Stokes respiration, was first described by Cheyne in an 1818 article. "A case of apoplexy in which the fleshy part of the heart was converted into fat." For John Abercrombie, writing on *Pathological and Practical Research on Diseases on the Brain and Spinal Cord* in 1828, the cerebral lesion of apoplexy might be either a hemorrhage or a serous effusion, but sometimes there seemed to be no apparent anatomic lesions.

In his well-known *L'Anatomie pathologique du corps humain . . .,* Jean Cruveilhier, professor of morbid anatomy in Paris, used the word "apoplexy" as a synonym for "hemorrhage" (in its anatomic, pathological meaning). He distinguished "apoplexy without loss of consciousness" from "apoplexy with loss of consciousness" and wrote of pontine or spinal apoplexies as well as cerebral ones. This pathological point of view was strengthened by Richard Bright who, in his book *Diseases of the Brain and Nervous System* (1831), described and illustrated under the term "apoplexy" several cases of cerebral hemorrhage.

This association of apoplexy with hemorrhage in the central nervous system led gradually to the use of apoplexy as a synonym for hemorrhage and to the creation of expressions such as "spinal apoplexy" (in place of "spinal hemorrhage"), "pulmonary apoplexy" (in place of "hemorrhagic pulmonary infarct"), "abdominal apoplexy" (in place of "massive abdominal hemorrhage"), "renal apoplexy" (in place of "renal hemorrhage"), "splenic apoplexy" (in place of "hemorrhage of the spleen"), and so forth.

From the second half of the nineteenth century to the beginning of the twentieth century, the semantic confusion between apoplexy and hemorrhage continued. J. Russell Reynolds, for example, in his *Diagnosis of Diseases of the Brain, Spinal Cord, Nerves and Their Appendages* (1866), stated that an apoplectic attack could result from congestion, hemorrhage, tumor, uremia, or vascular obstruction. A. Trousseau, a professor in Paris, however, had attacked this problem of confusion in his famous *Clinique médicale de l'Hôtel-Dieu de Paris* (1865), and the French neurologist J. M. Charcot later (1881) emphasized that apoplexy was a clinical syndrome that unfortunately had often been used synonymously with cerebral hemorrhage.

Thus, Trousseau and Charcot, along with individuals such as Dechambre (1866), E. Bouchut and A. Desprès (1889), and J. Déjerine (1914), concluded that apoplexy could arise from conditions other than intracerebral hemorrhage, and that the use of the term should be restricted to the clinical syndrome that involved a "sudden and simultaneous loss of all the brain functions, consciousness, feeling and movement, without conscpicuous change of respiration and blood circulation" (Déjerine 1914). Surprisingly, in 1921, J. Lhermitte, in his well-known *Traité de pathologie médicale,* nonetheless persisted in the use of apoplexy as a synonym for hemorrhage and opposed the "hemiplegy of the apoplexy" and "the hemiplegy of the infarctus."

The term "apoplexy" has since become obsolete and disappeared from the indices of most contemporary textbooks of neurology and neuropathology and from the usual vocabulary of the modern physician. Nevertheless, it remains widely used in popular language and literature. Its proper use, however should be restricted to the field of the history of medicine, from Hippocrates to the beginning of the twentieth century. In the present medical vocabulary, the term "apoplexy" must be replaced either by "stroke" or by "hemorrhage" according to the context.

Stroke

According to World Health Organization diagnostic criteria, a stroke consists of "rapidly developing clinical signs of focal (at times global) disturbance of cerebral function, lasting more than 24 hours or leading to death with no apparent causes other than that of vascular origin." "Global" refers to patients in deep coma and those with subarachnoid hemorrhage (SAH). This definition excludes transient ischemic attacks (TIA), a condition in which signs last less than 24 hours.

Distribution and Incidence

Strokes are the most common life-threatening neurological disease and the third leading cause of death, after heart disease and cancer, in Europe and the United States. Death rates from strokes vary with age and sex; for example, in the United States, the rates for males are 11.9 per 100,000 for those aged 40 to 44, and 1,217 per 100,000 for those aged 80 to 84. For females the rates are 10.9 (aged 40 to 44) and 1,067 (aged 80 to 84). In France, in the 30- to 34-year-old group, fully $2\frac{1}{2}$ times more men than women die of the disease. The differential, however, declines progressively with increasing age so that at over age 84 the sex ratio is equal. Large differences in cerebrovascular disease (CVD) mortality have been noted among races. For example, in the United States, mortality is 344 per 100,000 for nonwhites but just 124 per 100,000 for whites. Among countries differences in mortality due to stroke ranged from 70 in Switzerland to 519 per 100,000 in Japan. Within the same region, mortality from stroke is higher in Scotland than it is in England and Wales.

Decline in CVD deaths has occurred in all developed countries since 1915, and the decline has accelerated during the last two decades. The acceleration seems related to decline in incidence, because 30-day case fatality rates were unchanged over this 20-year period. Interestingly, this decrease in incidence was demonstrated in a Rochester study (Schoenberg 1978).

The incidence in Rochester, New York, in 1983 was 103 per 100,000. The 3-week mortality rate was within the range of 25 to 35 percent. But strokes are more disabling than lethal: 20 to 30 percent of survivors became permanently and severely handicapped. Moreover, recurrent strokes have been observed in 15 to 40 percent of stroke survivors.

Risk Factors

Apart from age, the most important risk factor for CVD is arterial hypertension. Control of severe and moderate, and even mild, hypertension has been shown to reduce stroke occurrence and stroke fatality. Cardiac impairment ranks third, following age and hypertensive disease. At any level of blood pressure, people with cardiac disease, occult or overt, have more than twice the risk of stroke. Other risk factors are cigarette smoking, increased total serum cholesterol, blood hemoglobin concentration, obesity, and use of oral contraceptives.

Etiology and Pathology

Strokes are a heterogeneous entity caused by cerebral infarction or, less commonly, cerebral hemorrhage. Cerebral infarction accounts for the majority of strokes (63 percent, as documented by the New York Neurological Institute, in 1983–4). When perfusion pressure falls in a cerebral artery below critical levels, brain ischemia (deficiency of blood) develops, progressing to infarction if the effect per-

sists long enough. In most cases, ischemia is caused by occlusion of an intracerebral artery by a thrombus or an embolus arising from extracranial artery disease or cardiac source. The main cause of ischemic strokes (40 to 56 percent of the cases) is atherosclerotic brain infarction, the result of either intracerebral artery thrombosis or embolism arising from stenosed (narrowed or restricted) or occluded extracranial arteries. Lacunar infarction (14 percent of the ischemic strokes) is a small, deep infarct in the territory of a single penetrating artery, occluded by the parietal changes caused by hypertensive disease. Cerebral embolism from a cardiac source accounts for 15 to 30 percent of ischemic strokes. The main cause is atrial fibrillation related to valvular disease or ischemic heart disease. Other causes of cerebral infarction are multiple, resulting from various arterial diseases (fibromuscular dysplasia, arterial dissections, arteritis), hemopathies, systemic diseases, or coagulation abnormalities. However in 20 percent of the cases, the cause of cerebral infarction, despite efforts to arrive at a diagnosis, remains undetermined.

Intracranial hemorrhages (ICH) account for 37 percent of strokes. The main cause of ICH is the rupture of miliary aneurysms that have developed in the walls of interior arteries because of hypertensive disease (72 to 81 percent of the ICH). Nonhypertensive causes of ICH are numerous and include substance abuse, cerebral amyloid angiopathy, intracerebral tumors, and coagulation abnormalities.

Clinical Manifestations and Classification

Clinical manifestations of strokes depend on both the nature of the lesion (ischemic or hemorrhagic) and the part of the brain involved. In the early 1960s, a classification of strokes according to their temporal profile was proposed to promote the use of common terminology in discussion of natural history and treatment programs.

The term *incipient stroke* (TIA) was defined as brief (less than 24 hours), intermittent and focal neurological deficits due to cerebral ischemia, with the patient normal between attacks. The term "reversible ischemic neurological deficit" (RIND) was coined for entirely reversible deficits occurring over more than 24 hours.

The term *progressing stroke* (stroke-in-evolution) is applied to focal cerebral deficits observed by the physician to progress in the severity of the neurological deficit over a period of hours or, occasionally, over a few days.

The term *completed stroke* is used when the neurological signs are stable and no progression has been noted for 18 to 72 hours. *Major stroke* is a term applied when immediate coma or massive neurological deficit occurs. In these cases, hope of recovery and of effective treatment are minimal. *Minor stroke,* by contrast, is a term applied to cases where the deficits relate to only a restricted area of a cerebral hemisphere, or where the symptoms experienced are of only moderate intensity. With minor strokes, diagnosis and institution of treatment should be rapidly combined to avoid further deterioration and, if possible, facilitate the regression of deficit.

These definitions contain some obvious uncertainties, particularly in categorizing a stroke during the early hours. However, they underscore the fact that the management of a stroke often depends more on its temporal profile and on the severity of the neurological deficit than on the nature of the lesion.

Jacques Poirier and Christian Derouesné

Bibliography

Alperovitch, A., et al. 1986. Mortality from stroke in France. *Neuroepidemiology* 5: 80–7.

Barnett, H. J. M., et al., eds. 1986. *Stroke: Pathophysiology, diagnosis, and management,* 2 vols. New York.

Bouchut, E., and A. Després. 1889. *Dictionnaire de médecine et de thérapeutique médicale et chirurgicale,* ed. Félix Alcan. Paris.

Charcot, J. M. 1881. *Clinical lectures on senile and chronic diseases.* London.

Dechambre, A. 1866. *Dictionnaire encyclopédique des sciences médicales,* Vol. V. Paris.

Déjerine, J. 1914. *Sémiologie des affections du système nerveux.* Paris.

Derousné, C. 1983. *Pratique neurologique.* Paris.

Escourolle, R., and J. Poirier. 1978. *Manual of basic neuropathology,* 2d edition. Philadelphia.

Jaccoud, ed. 1865. *Nouveau dictionnaire de médecine et de chirurgie pratiques.* Paris.

Lhermitte, J. 1921. Les Lésions vasculaires de l' encéphale et de la moëlle épinière. In *Traité de pathologie médicale et de thérapeutique appliquée,* Vol. VI, ed. E. Sergent, L. Ribadeau Dumas, and L. Babonneix, 195. Paris.

Malmgren, R., et al. 1987. Geographical and secular trends in stroke incidence. *Lancet* 2: 1196–9.

Schoenberg, B. S., ed. 1978. *Neurological epidemiology.* New York.

Spillane, John D. 1981. *The doctrine of the nerves: Chapters in the history of neurology.* Oxford.

Stehbens, W. E. 1972. *Pathology of the cerebral blood vessels.* St. Louis.

Trousseau, A. 1865. *Clinique médicale de l'Hôtel-Dieu de Paris,* Vol. 2, 2d edition. Paris.

VIII.10
Arboviruses

Arbovirus is a truncated term for arthropod-borne viruses, all of which require multiplication in their vectors for transmission. Arboviruses diseases may be simpler to understand when viewed solely from the position of the end product, which is disease in humans or other vertebrates. The diseases fall into a few recognizable sets: (1) encephalitides; (2) diseases with fever and rash, often fairly benign; (3) diseases with hemorrhagic manifestations, often fatal; and (4) mild fevers, quite undiagnosable except through laboratory study. A common feature of all of these is periodic outbreaks, with dozens, hundreds, or thousands of cases. A second common feature is lack of specific treatment. In addition, only for very few of the diseases do vaccines exist. Possibility of disease control is real, however, and is based on a knowledge of the epidemiology of arbovirus infections in general, the role that vectors play, and the particular features in regard to the transmission of the specific disease in question.

Etiology

Arboviruses, numbering at latest count 512 separate and identifiable agents, are placed in 11 families, with a few as yet unclassified agents. Table VIII.10.1 presents a listing of family and subfamily groupings, limited to those viruses of major importance in human and veterinary diseases.

It is evident from the table that there is no simple delimiting definition of an arbovirus on a taxonomic basis, or even on a biochemical basis. There are 511 RNA viruses, and then there is African swine fever virus (ASF), a DNA virus. ASF belongs to the Iridoviridae and is the only Iridovirus (so far as is yet known) with an arthropod vector and a vertebrate host. There are numerous Iridoviridae, incidentally, with arthropod vectors and plant or arthropod hosts.

Viruses must qualify in several important points in order to be considered as arboviruses. The life cycle of an arbovirus involves an arthropod (usually insect, tick, or mite) that is capable of becoming infected itself when it imbibes the virus from an infected host. The arthropods serve as vectors of the virus, from an infected vertebrate host to an uninfected one. The virus must multiply in the arthropod, a process requiring several days, and reach a concentration suffi-

Table VIII.10.1. *512 recognized arboviruses listed by family and subcategories, with totals*

Virus family	Genus	Antigenic groups within genus	No. of viruses in groupings	Total no. arbovs. in family
Bunyaviridae				251
	Bunyavirus	17	128	
	Nairovirus	6	24	
	Phlebovirus	1	38	
	Uukuvirus	1	6	
	Hantavirus	1	4	
	Bunyavirus-"like"	10	25	
	Ungrouped "bunya"		26	
Reoviridae				72
	Orbivirus	14	61	
	Ungrouped		11	
Rhabdoviridae				64
	Lyssavirus	1	2	
	Other groupings	9	39	
	Ungrouped		23	
Togaviridae				98
	Alphavirus	1	28	
	Ungrouped alpha		1	
	Flavivirus	1	68	
	Ungrouped flavi		1	
	Rubivirus–measles	1	not arboviruses	
Coronaviridae				2
	Coronavirus	1	2	
Herpesviridae				1
	Ungrouped		1	
Nodaviridae				1
	Nodavirus	1	1	
Orthomyxoviridae				2
	Thogoto	1	1	
	Ungrouped		1	
Paramyxoviridae				2
	Paramyxovirus	1	1	
Poxviridae				4
	Salanga	1	1	
	Ungrouped		3	
Iridoviridae				1
	African swine fever	1	1	
Unclassified to family				14
	Nyamanini	1	1	
	Somone	1	1	
	Ungrouped		12	
Grand total				512

Source: Modified from U.S.P.H.S. Centers for Disease Control, Center for Infectious Diseases (1988)

cient to be passed, in a later feeding, to the host, and to induce an infection in that host. The host, in turn, must have a viremic phase in order to pass the virus back to a biting or sucking arthropod.

This rigid definition gives rise to confusion (e.g., recent misconceptions about putative arthropod vectors of measles, hepatitis B virus, and human immunodeficiency (HIV) virus), but the definitions are uncompromising. The confusion is compounded when it is realized that although an arthropod, with mouth parts freshly contaminated by feeding on an infected host, may possibly transmit virus mechanically, a defined vector must be capable of multiplying the virus internally over a period of several days and of transmitting it by then biting a susceptible host in later feedings. This is referred to as the *biological transmission cycle*. Mechanical transmission must be quite unusual and with respect to arboviruses has never been observed in nature, but has been achieved in the laboratory under controlled conditions. In the case of HIV (not an arbovirus), mechanical transmission by needle is thought to be a dominant mode of transmission in the subset of drug users in some societies. The malaria parasite similarly can be transmitted by infected needle.

Again, from the point of view of the virus, it must be capable of multiplying in one or more vertebrate hosts, usually over a period of several days, reaching a level in the bloodstream adequate to infect a foraging vector.

The above considerations define (1) the interval between the arthropod ingestion of infected blood and the ability to transmit virus biologically, again by biting, to a susceptible host (the *extrinsic incubation period*), and (2) the period, in the host, before the viremia level rises to a height necessary to infect the biting arthropod (the *intrinsic incubation period*). The minimum interval between infection in one vertebrate host and acquisition of infection by the next vertebrate host is the sum of the extrinsic and intrinsic incubation periods. It is frequently about a week or more, and the maximum interval from one infection to the next may be weeks or months.

Virus Morphology, Size, Structure, and Characteristics

Arboviruses from selected families or subgroupings that contain viruses of importance to humans or other vertebrates are compared in Table VIII.10.2. Size varies considerably; shapes range from spherical to rhabdoform (bullet-shaped) to icosahedral.

Structurally, some entire groupings of viruses are enveloped, some are not. There are other differential characteristics, as indicated in the table. Again, the common bond is biological transmission by arthropod to vertebrate. How, in the evolution of viruses, this ability to exploit two phyla of living creatures arose again and again in such widely different taxa, is not known.

Virus morphology is not totally explicated by reference to arboviruses subsumed in such groups as alphaviruses, flaviviruses, bunyaviruses, rhabdoviruses, orbivirus (see Table VIII.10.1). More detailed references (e.g., Theiler and Downs 1973; Field 1985) must be consulted for further information. Almost the entire grouping of arboviruses consists of RNA viruses that are readily degradable by lipid solvents, ribonucleases, or heat and freezing (at temperatures above $-70°C$). The viral agents can be vacuum-desiccated satisfactorily, permitting greatly lengthened periods of storage with minimal loss in titer. Wet or desiccated material in glass-sealed ampoules can be stored in dry-ice containers or, better yet, in liquid nitrogen containers for long periods of time.

Epidemiology

When the science of epidemiology of the nineteenth century was applied to the study of yellow fever, the epidemiologist was hampered by a lack of knowledge of infectious agents and of vector arthropods in the transmission cycle. Consequently, there was great confusion and an endless diatribe surrounding various hypotheses on how infection could travel so mysteriously from place to place, with infections occurring in people who apparently never had had contact with a case. With Theobald Smith's demonstration in cattle of transmission of the Texas redwater fever organism by ticks, Ronald Ross's demonstration of transmission of the parasite of malaria by mosquitoes, and Walter Reed's demonstration of transmission of the virus of yellow fever by mosquitoes, came the dawn of modern epidemiological studies on arthropod-transmitted diseases.

As can be seen in Table VIII.10.3, a mysterious specificity exists between certain feeding arthropods and certain viruses; furthermore, a preferential feeding of certain arthropods (mosquitoes, for example) on certain food sources is shown. Some vertebrates react to a specific virus with severe disease. Yellow fever, for example, produces severe illness in humans, laboratory white mice, rhesus monkeys, and *Alouatta* monkeys. On the other hand, yellow fever

Table VIII.10.2. *Size, morphology, structure, and composition of selected virus families or genera that contain arboviruses*

Family	Genus	Size	Morphology	Composition	Structure
Bunyaviridae		80–120 nm	spherical	RNA	Lipid bilayer or envelope that anchors external surface projections of 5–10 nm, arranged regularly Uukuniemi has hexagonal arrays of surface structure
Togaviridae					
	Alphavirus	60–65 nm	spherical	RNA	Enveloped; symmetrical surface filaments, 6–10 nm; icosahedral with 42-subunit symmetry
	Flavivirus	43 nm (mean diam.)	spherical	RNA	Enveloped with surface projections
Reoviridae					
	Orbivirus	50–65 nm (inner core)	spherical	RNA	Double-protein capsid shell; nonenveloped; icosahedral symmetry
Rhabdoviridae		60–85 nm wide; approx. 180 nm long (animal rhabs)	"bullet shape"	RNA	Enveloped; intricate internal structure
Coronaviridae		100–150 nm	spherical	RNA	No envelope; 20-nm surface projections
Iridoviridae					
	African swine fever	175–215 nm	icosahedral	DNA	Capsid has dense outer shell; central nucleoid, 72–80 nm

Source: In part based on Theiler and Downs (1973); Field (1985); and Monath (1988).

may infect dogs, cats, *Cebus* monkeys, cows, and horses without producing overt disease. Among the encephalitides, eastern equine encephalitis (EEE) virus (endemic strains) can produce severe disease and death in human beings, laboratory mice, certain other vertebrates, and very specifically equines. But cattle do not develop illness with this agent, nor do sheep, goats, dogs, or cats. By contrast, the South American EEE strain that kills horses produces no illness in human beings but does produce detectable antibodies.

The resistance of various vertebrates to various arboviruses can be of use to the investigator because it permits the production of large quantities of immune sera in such vertebrates. Such immune sera are of minimal importance in treating disease in human beings, but are of cardinal importance in the design of specific serologic tests for virus identification. With the advent of cell culture techniques, leading to the preparation of monoclonal antibodies to specific portions of a virus genome, identification work has been greatly broadened in scope and much narrowed in specificity, often providing in a matter of hours identification of a virus that would have required days or weeks for identification using older techniques.

Modern techniques, founded on studies carried out over a period of half a century, involving basic laboratory techniques of complement fixation, precipitation, electrophoresis, centrifugation, hemagglutination inhibition, and virus neutralization, have been extended by later advances such as "tagged"

Table VIII.10.3. *Twenty-nine selected arboviruses important in causing human and/or animal diseases, with data on vectors, hosts, and geographic distributions*

Family	Subfamily or group	Virus (abbr.)	Vector(s)	Principal host(s) involvement	Geographic range
Togaviridae	Alphaviridae	EEE	mosquito	equines, birds, humans	Americas
		WEE	mosquito	equines, birds, humans	Americas
		VEE	mosquito	equines, small mammals, humans	Americas
		CHIK	mosquito	humans	Africa, Asia
		RR	mosquito	humans	Australasia, Pacific
		MID	mosquito	large vertebrates, humans	Africa
	Flaviviridae	YF	mosquito	monkeys, humans	tropical, Americas and Africa
		DENs	mosquito	humans, monkeys	pantropical and subtropical
		SLE	mosquito	birds, humans, horses, dogs	Americas
		JBE	mosquito	birds, humans, pigs, horses	Asia, Southeast Asia
		MVE	mosquito	birds, humans	Australia, New Guinea
		ROC	mosquito	humans	Brazil
		RSSE	tick	small mammals, humans	northern Eurasia
		KFD	tick	monkeys, humans	India (Mysore State)
		POW	tick	small mammals, humans	USA, Canada
Bunyaviridae	California gp	LAC	mosquito	small mammals, humans	midwest USA
	Phlebovirus gp	SFS	*Phlebotomus*	humans	Mediterranean region
		SFN	*Phlebotomus*	humans	Mediterranean region
		RVF	mosquito	sheep, cattle, humans	tropical Africa, Egypt, RSA
	Simbu serogroup	ORO	*Culicoides*	humans	Trinidad, South America
	Nairovirus gp	CHF	tick	cattle, humans	Middle East, Africa, s. Russia
		NSD	tick, *Culicoides*	sheep, humans	Africa
	Hantaan gp	HAN	mites	small animals, humans	worldwide, seaports
Rhabdoviridae	Rabies (not an arbovirus)				
	Vesiculovirus gp	VSI	mosquito	bovines, humans	
		PIRY		marsupials, humans	Brazil
		CHP	*Phlebotomus*	humans	Asia, Africa

Table VIII.10.3. *(cont.)*

Family	Subfamily or group	Virus (abbr.)	Vector(s)	Principal host(s) involvement	Geographic range
Orbiviridae	Colorado tick fever gp	CTF	tick	small mammals, humans	western USA
	Changuinola gp	CHAN	*Phlebotomus*	humans	Panama, South America
Iridoviridae	African swine fever	ASF	tick	swine, warthog	Africa, Europe, Cuba

Abbreviations: ASF = African swine fever; CHP = Chandipura; CGL = Changuinola; CHIK = Chikungunya; CTF = Colorado tick fever; CHF = Crimean hemorrhagic fever; DENs = dengues (1,2,3,4); EEE = eastern equine encephalitis; HAN = Hantaan (Korean hemorrhagic fever); JBE = Japanese encephalitis; KFD = Kyasanur Forest disease; LAC = LaCrosse; MID = Middelburg; MVE = Murray Valley encephalitis; NSD = Nairobi sheep disease; ORO = Oropouche; PIRY = Piry; POW = Powassan; RVF = Rift Valley fever; ROC = Rocio; RR = Ross River; RSSE = Russian spring/summer encephalitis; SFN = Naples sandfly fever; SFS = Sicilian sandfly fever; SLE = St. Louis encephalitis; VEE = Venezuelan equine encephalitis; VSI = Vesicular stomatitis (Indiana); WEE = Western equine encephalitis; YF = yellow fever.

Sources: Based in part on Calisher and Thompson (1985); Evans (1984); and Karabatsos (1975), among others.

antibodies – that is, the use of monoclonal antibodies in combination with "tagged probes" in electron microscopy. Such new techniques, involving the use of specific "probes," are presently a fertile area of research, from which is emerging a more rational and complete knowledge of the virus particle itself and its interactions with vertebrate and invertebrate hosts.

Dengue

Geographic distribution of viruses and disease is determined by the characteristics of the vectors, rather than by the characteristics of the viruses. Taking dengue viruses (*Flavivirus* genus) as an example, the limits of their distribution are defined by the limits of the distribution of the principal vector, *Aedes aegypti*. This mosquito, originally found in Southeast Asia, spread worldwide, traveling wherever humans traveled and established itself in tropical and subtropical and often temperate regions, but not in Arctic and Antarctic polar extremes. The dengue viruses moved with the vectors and became established worldwide, particularly in tropical and subtropical regions. The viruses may have had, in their original territories of Southeast Asia, cycles involving *A. aegypti* and/or *Aedes albopictus* and subhuman forest primates, but as the virus left their original home, they adapted to a vector–human–vector cycle, allowing them to exist in endemic form wherever humans exist, and to appear in epidemic form at intervals.

The other Southeast Asian vector, *A. albopictus*,

has of recent years established itself in other countries such as the United States, with as yet unknown potential for involvement in the life cycles of still other viruses such as yellow fever. There are also other aedine vectors of dengue in Polynesia. The dengues are placed in four serotypes, one or more of which are associated with often fatal manifestations of dengue hemorrhagic fever and dengue shock syndrome. These are important causes of mortality in small children in countries of Southeast Asia, scattered cases being seen elsewhere. It is hypothesized that sequential infections in the same individual by different serotypes of dengue may lead to these serious complications.

Yellow Fever

Yellow fever, a *Flavivirus* serologically related to the dengues, is also capable of being transmitted from human to human by *A. aegypti* and can maintain itself endemically in a human population by such means. This mode of transmission occurred a century and more ago but has not been observed recently. The virus is found in Africa, south of the Sahara, and in the equatorial South American jungle regions. In both Africa and South America (here including Central America, and the West Indies), and even in the United States, Spain, France, Gibraltar, and England, periodic outbreaks of the disease, often explosive and devastating, have been observed since *A. aegypti* may establish itself in subtropical and even temperate locales. Although *A. aegypti* (and *A. albopictus*) is prevalent in Asia and

Australia, yellow fever has never established itself in these regions. With vectors present, as well as millions of nonimmune humans, there is a continuing threat of its introduction.

A reason yellow fever has been able to maintain itself in tropical South America and Africa is that the virus can utilize a different set of vectors: the forest canopy-frequenting *Haemagogus* mosquitoes of the New World, as well as *A. aegypti* and *Aedes africanus, Aedes simpsoni, Aedes taylori, Aedes furcifer,* and other aedines in Africa, often with and often without *A. aegypti.* Using the endemic *Haemagogus* or *Aedes* species, the virus remains established as an endemic virosis in various subhuman primates of these regions. This maintenance cycle is referred to as "sylvan" or "jungle" yellow fever. The sylvan *Haemagogus* or *Aedes* can and often does bite humans, and thus can transfer the virus out of the mosquito–monkey–mosquito cycle into a mosquito–human–mosquito cycle. An infected forest worker in the early stage of illness (and circulating virus in high titer) can migrate to an urban setting infested with *A. aegypti* and establish the dreaded urban mosquito–human–mosquito cycle. Recently, several large outbreaks of this type have occurred in Africa and in South America, some of them involving the deaths of thousands of people such as in the Nigeria epidemic in 1986.

A completely effective attenuated yellow-fever vaccine (17D) has been available since 1935, but governments in regions where yellow fever is endemic have as yet failed to react adequately in getting the population at risk immunized. The blame for this rests not on technical failure (the vaccine itself), nor on difficulties in administration of same, but in the inability of governments to establish adequate bureaucratic–administrative procedures to protect the health of the people. *Aedes* control projects, often employed for disease control, again suffer from a bureaucratic inability to maintain effective programs at a high level of efficiency over periods of years.

Encephalitides

Another group of the arboviruses, the encephalitides (Venezuelan, eastern, western, St. Louis, Japanese, Murray Valley, Russian spring–summer encephalitis), present mechanisms quite different from the dengue or yellow fever models. The vectors in question – mosquitoes or ticks – are of themselves geographically delimited, and therefore, the specific viruses associated with specific vectors are geographically delimited, with little chance of spread beyond natural ecological barriers. The viruses themselves have a basic vertebrate cycle in birds or small mammals. Certain of the viruses, such as Venezuelan equine encephalitis, eastern equine encephalitis, and western equine encephalitis, can escape from the mosquite–small vertebrate–mosquito cycle and spread like wildfire in one or another of the larger vertebrates, causing widespread mortality, and humans may be thus involved. These epidemics are sporadic and unpredictable. The endemic cycles are present continuously, but unobserved unless specifically sought for. Others of the viruses are associated particularly with birds and mosquitoes. These viruses include St. Louis encephalitis virus of the Americas, Japanese encephalitis virus of the Orient, Murray Valley encephalitis of Australia and New Guinea, Ilheus virus of South America and Trinidad, Rocio virus of southeast Brazil, and West Nile virus of Africa, the Middle East, and India. The viruses are often very prevalent in a region, in birds, with the disease usually being uncommon in human beings, but sometimes occurring in large epidemics. Heron rookeries and pig farms in the Orient have been shown to be Japanese encephalitis virus-amplifying localities, providing opportunities for infection of large numbers of mosquito vectors and thus facilitating large-scale transmission of virus to human beings. Immunity rates in populations are often high (bespeaking inapparent infections), and encephalitis rates low.

In the central United States, a recent arrival on the virus scene, La Crosse virus, a member of the California virus group, has established its position as the commonest arboviral cause of encephalitis. This endemic disease has some unusual features. It is transmitted by woodland aedine mosquitoes, and has as vertebrate hosts certain small mammals of the region. It has been further established that the virus can be transmitted transovarially (TOT) from mosquito to mosquito, vertically, through the egg, and laterally, from female to male or from male to female during copulation. This mechanism has been hypothesized to explain the long persistence of virus in a vector, serving to carry it over periods of inclement weather or drought. Similar TOT has been shown for dengue, Japanese encephalitis, and yellow fever.

Tick-borne encephalitis (Russian spring–summer encephalitis, RSSE) in the Eurasian continent and Powassan virus encephalitis in America are delimited by the range of specific tick vectors; these viruses are endemic in small mammals and present themselves in humans as sporadic cases, often not distinguished from encephalitis caused by other viruses or of unknown etiology except by special laboratory studies.

Epidemiology of arboviruses can be conceptualized as a huge, multidimensional matrix, involving many viruses on one axis, many vectors on another, many vertebrate hosts on another, and yet another axis for ecological, ethological, meteorological, cultural, and edaphic influences impinging on vectors and hosts.

Clinical Manifestations and Diagnosis

The early days of onset of most arboviral infections are usually accompanied by fevers, aching, and general malaise, and cannot be distinguished from early stages of other very common diseases such as influenza, malaria, measles, pneumonias, meningitis, other respiratory afflictions, and even Lassa fever and smallpox. As diseases progress in their course, specific later manifestations may provide aid in differential diagnosis. Such specific manifestations include rashes, eruptions, nausea and vomiting, diarrhea, cough, and encephalitis.

Sporadic cases in a population may be quite impossible to diagnose specifically. But as epidemics progress, specific features may appear and provide the clue to diagnosis. Malaria in the tropics and influenza in temperate regions and the tropics serve as "coverup" or "umbrella" diagnoses that often block out recognition of arbovirus illness.

Definitive diagnosis demands the assistance of experienced virologists working in adequate laboratory diagnostic facilities. There exist only a few dozen such facilities in the world, supported by the World Health Organization, governments, armed forces military establishments, and, in a few instances, private philanthropy. Such laboratories usually combine laboratory diagnostic methodology and facilities for carrying out field epidemiological studies.

Specific diagnosis can only rarely benefit the patient, but is of vital importance in alerting health departments of the presence of a potentially threatening epidemic. Appropriate control procedures directed at the vectors can then be applied on an emergency basis. In the special case of yellow fever, mass immunization of exposed populations can successfully halt an epidemic in its tracks. Such an immunization campaign is usually combined with emergency mosquito control.

Treatment and Control

Aside from provision of nursing care, and maintaining nutrition and fluid balance, there are no specific remedies for infections. Nonspecific measures, particularly treatment of shock (maintaining fluid and electrolyte balance) may be life-saving in dengue-shock syndrome cases.

Vector control is applicable in certain situations. Fred Soper and co-workers in the 1930s eradicated *A. aegypti* from all of Brazil, thus eliminating the risk of urban yellow fever. The mosquito has reinvaded much of the territory formerly freed, and the threat of yellow fever has returned. Short-term vector control is widely practiced, particularly when epidemics threaten. This may include airplane spraying of insecticides, treatment of interior walls of buildings with residual insecticides, insecticide treatment of mosquito breeding places, destruction or drainage of mosquito breeding places, screening of dwellings, use of insecticidal fogs in and around dwellings, use of insect repellents, and wearing of protective clothing.

The attenuated live yellow fever virus vaccine (17D) has been used for over 50 years in the successful immunization of millions of people. A live attenuated dengue virus vaccine is being tried. A killed Japanese encephalitis virus vaccine is given to millions of people in the Orient. A killed RSSE virus vaccine is used extensively in parts of the former Soviet Union. Killed virus vaccines against eastern equine encephalitis, western equine encephalitis, Venezuelan equine encephalitis, and Rift Valley fever virus are used primarily to protect livestock. Laboratory workers studying these viruses are routinely immunized.

Wilbur G. Downs

Bibliography

Barber, T. L., and N. M. Jochim, eds. 1985. *Bluetongue and related Orbiviruses*. New York.

Beneson, A. S., ed. 1985. *Control of communicable diseases in man*, 14th edition. New York.

Calisher, C. H., and W. H. Thompson, eds. 1985. *California serogroup viruses*. New York.

Evans, A. S., ed. 1984. *Viral infections of humans*, 2d edition. New York.

Fenner, F., and A. Gibbs. 1988. *Portraits of viruses*. New York.

Field, B. N., ed. 1985. *Virology*. New York.

Fraenkel-Conrat, H., and R. R. Wagner, eds. 1979. *Comparative virology*. New York.

1987. *The viruses*. New York.

Gear, J. H. S., ed. 1988. *Handbook of viral and rickettsial hemorrhagic fevers*. Boca Raton, Fla.

Karabatsos, N., ed. 1975. *International catalogue of arboviruses including certain other viruses of vertebrates*. Washington, D.C.

Klingberg, M. A., ed. 1979. *Contributions to epidemiology and biostatistics*, Vol. 3. New York.

Lennette, E. H., and N. J. Schmidt, eds. 1979. *Diagnostic procedures for viral, rickettsial and chlamydial infection.* New York.

Lennette, E. H., E. H. Spaulding, and J. P. Truant, eds. 1974. *Manual of clinical microbiology,* 2d edition. Washington, D.C.

Monath, T. P., ed. 1980. *St. Louis encephalitis.* New York.
    1988. *Arboviruses: Epidemiology and ecology,* 5 vols. Boca Raton, Fla.

Pan American Health Organization. 1985. *Proceedings of an international conference on vesicular stomatitis.* New York.

Schlesinger, R. W., ed. 1980. *The togaviruses: Biology, structure, replication.* New York.

Scott, H. H. 1939. *A history of tropical medicine,* 2 vols. Baltimore.

Strode, G. K., ed. 1951. *Yellow fever.* New York.

Theiler, Max K., and Wilbur G. Downs. 1973. *The arthropod-borne viruses of vertebrates: An account of the Rockefeller Foundation virus program.* New Haven.

U.S. Public Health Services Centers for Disease Control. Center for Infectious Diseases. 1988. *Arthropod-borne virus information exchange,* June 14. Atlanta.

World Health Organization. 1986. *Prevention and control of yellow fever in Africa.* Geneva.

Yunkers, Conrad., ed. 1987. *Arboviruses in arthropod cells in vitro,* 2 vols. Boca Raton, Fla.

VIII.11
Arenaviruses

The Arenaviridae are a small group of viruses, containing several of considerable importance as human disease agents. They are listed in the *Catalogue of Arthropod-Borne Viruses,* not because they are arboviruses but because they have been discovered in large part by arbovirologists, working on details of arthropod-transmitted viruses. Most of the 14 members of the group have rodents as reservoir hosts, but they occasionally infect humans who imbibe or ingest the virus when accidentally consuming rodent-contaminated food and drink, or are otherwise in contact with an environment contaminated by rodent excreta. At least one of the viruses, however, Lassa virus, can pass directly from person to person. This happens particularly in hospital settings. Other Arenaviruses important in human disease are Junin (Argentine hemorrhagic fever), Machupo (Bolivian hemorrhagic fever) from South America, and the virus causing lymphocytic chorio-

meningitis (LCM). Six of the viruses – Junin, Machupo, Pichinde, Tacaribe, Lassa, and LCMs – have infected laboratory workers. (Because Lassa fever is covered elsewhere in this work, it will not be treated here in any detail.)

Virus Morphology, Size, and Structure

Electron micrographic studies of infected cells reveal round, oval, or pleomorphic budding particles with mean diameters of 110 to 130 nanometers. The envelopes, which have spikes, are derived from the plasma membranes of the host cell by budding. The interior contains variable numbers of electron-dense granules measuring 20 to 25 nanometers and resembling ribosomes. These sandy grains gave rise to the name *Arenavirus* because *arena* means "sand" (Rowe et al. 1970). The exact composition of this core material and its derivation are as yet uncertain. The virions are enveloped RNA-containing nucleocapsids. The genome consists of two single-stranded RNA molecules (Lehmann-Grube 1988).

History

The first arenavirus to be discovered was the one causing LCM in mice and monkeys; it was reported in 1934 by C. Armstrong and R. D. Lillie. Later studies showed that the virus was present in feral *Mus musculus* (the common house mouse) and accounted for a scattering of human cases annually in Europe and America. More commonly, those cases were seen in personnel who were handling laboratory animals, particularly white mice and hamsters. The agent itself was characterized morphologically by electron microscopy, and later investigated in serologic, biochemical, and biophysical studies. No serologic relatives were found, and over several decades, only scattered cases and outbreaks have been reported in America and Europe.

In 1957, a virus named Tacaribe was recovered from a fruit-eating bat in Trinidad, West Indies (Downs et al. 1963). This agent remained unclassified. Meanwhile a disease was observed among field workers in the northern provinces of Argentina that occurred at harvest time and caused considerable mortality. A virus subsequently named Junin (Parodi et al. 1958) was recovered from these patients, and the disease was named Argentinian hemorrhagic fever (AHF). Cases occur annually, and there have been epidemics of the disease over the past 30 years.

A particularly virulent infection broke out in the small town of San Joaquin, Beni Department, in the Amazonian lowlands of Bolivia. In due course it was called Bolivian hemorrhagic fever (Johnson et al. 1965). The outbreak was checked, however, once the rodent host of the Machupo virus that caused the disease was implicated and rodent control mechanisms were instituted. Since then Machupo virus has "gone underground"; no further outbreaks have been reported and little further epidemiological work is being done on the disease.

In January 1969, another of the arenaviruses was forcefully brought to the attention of Western medicine, with an outbreak among medical personnel in Lassa, northeastern Nigeria (Buckley, Casals, and Downs 1970). At least seven more outbreaks of the disease subsequently named Lassa fever have taken place since then, involving about 450 patients and almost 125 deaths. The virus appears to have a natural cycle of transmission in rodents but, as previously mentioned, can spread from human to human.

Epidemiology (and Phylogenetic Considerations)

Table VIII.11.1 lists the 16 members of the Arenaviridae, their known vertebrate hosts' geographic distribution, date of first finding, and author(s) and dates of first description. Four of these are important agents in human disease: LCM, Junin, Machupo, and Lassa. In addition, 10 other members of the group are apparently nonpathogenic (for human beings). Epidemiological information about these is scanty, although several – particularly Tacaribe and Pichinde – have been studied intensively in the laboratory.

Table VIII.11.1. *History and natural occurrence of arenaviruses*

Virus	First finding	Natural Occurrence		First description
		Principal host	Geographic distribution	
LCM	1933	*Mus musculus*	America, Europe	Armstrong and Lillie 1934
Quaranfil	1953	*Bubulcus ibis:* pigeon *Argas* ticks	Egypt, S. Africa, Afghanistan, Nigeria	Taylor et al. 1966
Tacaribe[a]	1956	*Artibeus literatus* *Artibeus jamaicensis*	Trinidad, West Indies	Downs et al. 1963
Junin	1958	*Calomys laucha* *Akodon azarae*	Argentina	Parodi et al. 1958
Amapari	1964	*Oryzomys* sp. *Neacomys guianae*	Brazil (Amazonas)	Pinheiro et al. 1966
Araguari	1964	opossums	Brazil	USPHS 1988
Johnston Atoll	1964	*Ornithodorus capensis*	Johnston Atoll (Pacific)	Taylor et al. 1966
Machupo	1965	*Calomys callosus*	lowland Bolivia	Johnson et al. 1965
Parana	1965	*Oryzomys buccinatus*	Paraguay	Webb et al. 1970
Tamiami	1965	*Sigmodon hispidus*	Florida (U.S.A.)	Calisher et al. 1970
Pichinde	1965	*Oryzomys albigularis* *Thomasomys lugens*	Colombia	Trapido and Sanmartin 1974
Latino	1965	*Calomys callosus*	Brazil, Bolivia	Webb et al. 1973
Lassa	1969	*Praomys natalensis*	Nigeria, Liberia Sierra Leone	Buckley et al. 1970
Flexal	1975	*Oryzomys bicolor*	Edo. de Para, Brazil	Pinheiro et al. 1977
Mopeia	ca.1976	*Praomys natalensis*	Southeast Africa	Wulff et al. 1977
Mobala	ca.1982	*Praomys jacksoni*	Central African Republic	Gonzalez et al. 1983

Note: Three of these viruses are already named in the International Catalogue of Arboviruses (1975 and 1988 update): Araguari, Quaranfil, and Johnston Atoll are considered possible Arenaviridae, the latter two on basis of electron microscopic studies (Zeller, personal communication, 1989). None of these three viruses has rodent hosts.
[a]The isolation of Tacaribe from mosquitoes is considered doubtful, and due to a possible laboratory numbering error (Downs et al. 1963).

In regard to the Tacaribe group viruses, beginning with LCM, and continuing with other members of the group, a rodent association is usually found. Exceptions are Tacaribe, a virus isolated several times from bats in Trinidad in 1957 (and never reisolated there or elsewhere), and the two recently associated agents, Quaranfil and Johnston Atoll, found in birds and tick ectoparasites of birds (learned from personal communication with wife of H. Zeller in 1989).

A fascinating feature is the geographic–ecological–natural host range of the Arenaviridae. Each rodent species involved with an individual virus has its ecologically determined range, and thus delimits the territory of distribution of the virus. As can be seen in Table VIII.11.1, the exception to the limited-host-range rule is the house mouse, *M. musculus*. The genus *Mus* is an Asiatic and European genus. *Mus musculus* is well adapted to the human environment and now has worldwide distribution but is found particularly in the temperate regions of America, Europe, and Asia. It moves where humans move, and communication by sea has opened the world to it, although in the tropics it has remained more restricted to coastal or riverine settlements.

Praomys natalensis, the multimammate mouse, is also very common; commensal with humans, it is widely distributed in Africa, and is associated with Lassa virus and Mopeia virus. *Praomys jacksoni,* another member of the genus, which holds 14 species, is associated with Mobala virus in the Central African Republic. The literature is confusing because *Praomys* is often referred to as *Mastomys*. Currently, however, *Mastomys, Myomys,* and *Myomyscus* are all considered to be synonymous with *Praomys* (Honacki, Kinman, and Koeppl 1982). *Praomys* is placed in the rodent family Muridae.

The New World rodents associated with arenaviruses are all placed in the family Cricetidae, with several genera involved. It is likely that there have been many opportunities for virus dispersal as well as adaptation of viruses to new rodent hosts, when one considers (1) the number of viruses, such as LCM, Lassa, Junin, Machupo, and others; (2) the diversity of rodents; and (3) the rise (and later enormous development) of intracontinental and intercontinental traffic; and (4) the recently recognized pair of viruses Quaranfil and Johnston Atoll (provisionally placed in the Arenaviridae on the basis of electron microscopic studies), which are associated with birds that disperse widely. Thus it seems evident that the whole world is at risk for species radiation of Arenaviridae.

Immunology

The various arenaviruses have been shown to be related principally via complement fixation reactions to the glycoprotein gp44 in the viral envelopes. The nucleoproteins of the viruses demonstrate relationships through virus neutralization tests. The fatal infection induced in adult mice experimentally inoculated with LCM has been shown to be associated with a T cell-mediated immune response. Studies of the several viruses of the Tacaribe group have extended knowledge of this phenomenon. When newborn mice are infected intracerebrally with LCM, their immune response is deficient, and they go into a lifetime chronic carrier state. This same response can be induced in adult mice that have been immunosuppressed.

Clinical Manifestations, Diagnosis, Treatment, and Control

Lymphocytic Choriomeningitis (LCM)

LCM has been found in the Americas, Europe, and Asia, but not in Africa or Australia. Outbreaks are sporadic and often associated with experimental animal colonies. The disease in humans is usually benign, with symptoms resembling influenza. Inapparent cases (determined by serologic changes) are frequent during outbreaks. Meningitis (with 90 to 95 percent lymphocytes in the cerebrospinal fluid) may occur as a primary symptom of disease, or more usually as a relapse several days after apparent recovery from the acute illness. In some cases there may be meningoencephalitic signs and symptoms, with reflex changes, paralyses, cutaneous anesthesias, and somnolence. Fatal cases are rare. When infections occur in pregnancy, complications of encephalitis, hydrocephaly, and chorioretinitis in the fetus and the newborn may be seen. Treatment is limited to supportive care. Control is limited to control of mouse populations in houses and to vigilant supervision of laboratory colonies of mice and hamsters.

Argentine Hemorrhagic Fever (Junin)

The disease occurs in the heavily agricultural moist pampas provinces to the west of Buenos Aires. It is seen in the rural regions, mostly in farm workers, including migrant workers. Several hundred cases are seen annually, occurring mainly in the harvest season between April and July. Infection in humans results from contact with field rodents. The incubation period is from 10 to 14 days, with an insidious onset beginning with malaise, fever, chills, head and back pains, nausea, vomiting, and diarrhea or constipation.

In progressive cases, hemorrhagic manifestations begin about the fourth day of illness, and may proceed to death (in about 10 percent of confirmed cases). In some cases, neurological symptoms may predominate.

Laboratory findings include leukopenia, thrombocytopenia, albuminuria, and cylindruria. Serologic testing is an aid to diagnosis, but as is the case with many virus diseases, virus isolation and identification are recommended. Convalescence lasts several weeks after severe illness, and recovery is then usually complete. There are no proven specific antiviral agents; but there are recent reports of successful treatment with immune plasma. When it has been given before the eighth day of illness, marked reduction in mortality has been observed. Rodent control would appear to be an obvious prevention measure, but it is not practical, given the vast areas where the virus is endemic. Much attention has been given to development of a vaccine, and at present a live attenuated vaccine shows promise of becoming useful in preventing disease in human beings. Another vaccine possibility being explored utilizes the avirulent Tacaribe virus to induce immunity against Junin.

Bolivian Hemorrhagic Fever (Machupo)

This disease is localized to several provinces of the Department of Beni, in the Amazonian lowlands, and is endemic in the local rodent (*Calomys*) populations. Exposed human beings have an incubation period of about 2 weeks. Patients have a high fever for at least 5 days; myalgia, headache, conjunctivitis, cutaneous hyperesthesia, nausea, and vomiting are features of the illness. Hemorrhagic manifestations occur in some 30 percent of patients, and there may be serious bleeding. Hypotension in the second week of illness is seen in about 50 percent of patients, and in many patients it proceeds to hypovolemic shock and death. Symptoms indicative of central nervous system involvement, among the tremors of tongue and extremities, convulsions, and coma, appear in almost half the patients. The death rate in several epidemics has been about 25 percent. Convalescence is protracted. Laboratory findings include leukopenia, hemoconcentration, and proteinuria. Pathological findings include generalized adenopathy and focal hemorrhages in various organs. No specific therapy is known. Treatment is limited to supportive measures. Rodent control in homes and villages has proven to be an effective means of controlling epidemics, and also of preventing sporadic cases of disease.

Wilbur G. Downs

Bibliography

Acha, Pedro N., and Boris Szyfres. 1987. *Zoonoses and communicable diseases common to man and animals,* 2d edition, 289–97, 297–301, 392–6. Pan American Health Organization Scientific Publication No. 503.

Armstrong, C., and R. D. Lillie. 1934. Experimental lymphocytic choriomeningitis of monkeys and mice produced by a virus encountered in studies of the 1933 St. Louis encephalitis epidemic. Public Health Reports, Washington 49: 1019–27.

Auperin, D. D., and J. B. McCormick. 1989. Nucleotide sequence of the Lassa virus (Josiah strain) genome RNA and amino acid sequence of the N and GPC proteins to other arenaviruses. *Virology* 168: 421–5.

Benenson, A. S., ed. 1985. *Control of communicable diseases in man,* 14th edition, 16–18. American Public Health Association. Chicago.

Buckley, S. M., J. Casals, and W. G. Downs. 1970. Isolation and antigenic characterization of Lassa virus. *Nature* 227: 174.

Calisher, C. H., et al. 1970. Tamiami virus, a new member of the Tacaribe group. *American Journal of Tropical Medicine and Hygiene* 19: 520–6.

Casals, Jordi. 1979. Arenaviruses. In *Diagnostic procedures for viral and rickettsial and chlymadial infections,* eds. E. H. Lennette and N. J. Sather, 5th edition, 815–41. American Public Health Association. Chicago.

Compans, R. W., and D. H. L. Bishop. 1984. *Segmented negative strand viruses: Arenaviruses, bunyaviruses and orthomyxoviruses,* 51–64, 109–16, 193–216, 341–7. New York.

Downs, W. G., et al. 1963. Tacaribe virus, a new agent isolated from *Artibeus* bats and mosquitoes in Trinidad, West Indies. *American Journal of Tropical Medicine and Hygiene* 12: 640–6.

Fuller, J. G. 1974. *Fever.* New York.

Gear, J. H. S., ed. 1988. *Handbook of viral and rickettsial hemorrhagic fevers.* Boca Raton, Fla.

Gonzalez, J. P., et al. 1983. An arenavirus isolated from wild-caught rodents (*Praomys* sp.) (*Praomys jacksoni,* sic) in the Central African Republic (Mobala). *Intervirology* 19: 105–12.

Honacki, J. H., K. E. Kinman, and J. W. Koeppl. 1982. *Mammal species of the world: a taxonomic and geographic reference,* 542–4. Lawrence, Kans.

Johnson, K. M., et al. 1965. Virus isolations (Machupo) from human cases of hemorrhagic fever in Bolivia. *Proceedings of the Society of Experimental Biology and Medicine* 118: 113–18.

Karabastos, N., ed. 1985. *International catalogue of arenaviruses, including certain other viruses of vertebrates.* American Society of Tropical Medicine and Hygiene, Subcommittee on Information. (Looseleaf)

Lehmann-Grube, F. 1988. Arenaviruses. In *Portraits of viruses,* ed. F. Fenner and A. Gibbs. Basel, Switzerland.

Oldstone, M. B. A. 1987. Arenaviruses. *Current Topics in*

Microbiology and Immunology 134: 5–130, 145–84, 211–39.

Parodi, A. S., et al. 1958. Sobre la etiologia del brote epidémico de Junin. *Dia Médica* 30: 2300–2.

Pinheiro, F. P., et al. 1966. A new virus of the Tacaribe group from rodents and mice of the Amapa Territory, Brazil. *Proceedings of the Society of Experimental Biology and Medicine* 122: 531–5.

1977. Studies on arenaviruses in Brazil (Flexal). *Medecina* (Buenos Aires) 37: 175–81.

Rowe, W. P., et al. 1970. Arenaviruses: Proposed name for a newly described virus group. *Journal of Virology* 5: 651–2.

Taylor, R. M., et al. 1966. Arboviruses isolated from Argas ticks in Egypt: Quaranfil, Chenuda and Nyamanini. *American Journal of Tropical Medicine and Hygiene* 15: 75–86.

Trapido, H., and C. Sanmartin. 1974. Pichinde virus, a new virus of the Tacaribe group from Colombia. *American Journal of Tropical Medicine and Hygiene* 20: 631–41.

U.S. Public Health Service. Centers for Disease Control. Center of Infectious Diseases. 1988. Arthropod-borne virus information exchange. June 24.

Webb, P. A., et al. 1970. Paraná, a new Tacaribe complex virus from Paraguay. *Archives für die gesammte Virusforschung* 32: 379–88.

1973. Behavior of Machupo and Latino viruses in *Calomys callosus* from two geographic areas of Bolivia. In *Lymphocytic choriomeningitis virus and other arenaviruses,* ed. F. Lehmann-Grube, 313–22. Berlin.

World Health Organization. 1975. International Symposium on Arenaviral Infections, 14–16 July 1975. *Bulletin of the World Health Organization* 52: 381–766.

Wulff, H., et al. 1977. Isolation of an arenavirus closely related to Lassa virus. *Bulletin of the World Health Organization* 55: 441–4.

VIII.12
Arthritis (Rheumatoid)

Rheumatoid arthritis, the major crippling illness among chronic rheumatic disorders, is a systemic disease that affects many joints with an inflammatory reaction lasting months or years. Frequently, the small joints of the hands and feet are affected first, although often the larger peripheral joints of the wrists, hips, knees, elbows, and shoulders are involved as well. Some remissions do occur, but the illness progresses to produce damage and deformity. There is no known etiology.

In 1961, the American Rheumatism Association developed a set of eight diagnostic criteria for rheumatoid arthritis suitable for epidemiological surveys. They are as follows:

1. Morning stiffness
2. Pain on motion or tenderness in at least one joint
3. Swelling (soft tissue) of at least one joint
4. Swelling of at least one other joint
5. Symmetrical joint swelling
6. Nodules under the skin, typically on the surface of muscles that extend or stretch the limbs
7. Observable changes identified by X-rays, typically erosions of bone
8. Positive serologic test for rheumatoid factor

In a given patient, a definite diagnosis of rheumatoid arthritis would depend on the presence of at least five of these criteria and the absence of evidence for other rheumatic conditions.

Distribution and Incidence

When using the above definition, a number of researchers have indicated that rheumatoid arthritis is worldwide, affecting all ethnic groups. A summary of prevalence data in rheumatoid arthritis has been provided by P. D. Utsinger, N. J. Zvaifler, and E. G. Ehrlich (1985). Fifteen studies were cited from countries such as the United States, United Kingdom, Finland, Puerto Rico, Canada, Japan, Bulgaria, and Jamaica. The authors have concluded that the prevalence of rheumatoid arthritis, as defined above, is consistently between 1 and 2 percent of the adult population in all parts of the world. In general, females suffer the illness about two and a half times more frequently than males; however, prevalence increases for both females and males over age 35, making it normally a disease of the middle years. The number of new cases per 1,000 population per year ranges from 0.68 to 2.9. The prevalence of chronic arthritis in children among Caucasians is 5 percent that of adults. The mode of onset in children may vary more than that in adults, in that the simultaneous involvement of four or more joints – seen in 93 percent of the adult cases – occurs in only 30 percent of those children in whom diagnosis of rheumatoid arthritis is subsequently established.

Epidemiology and Etiology

Despite the years of intensive study of endocrine, metabolic, and nutritional factors as well as geographic, occupational, and psychological variables, the etiology of rheumatoid arthritis has not been elucidated. A genetic predisposition is suspected (because certain histocompatibility markers are found frequently); however, bacterial and viral infections are often associated with acute polyarthritis in humans, and thus an infection followed by an altered or sustained immunologic response could be instrumental for development of the disease. Certainly, immunologic abnormalities appear to play a role in both the aggravation and perpetuation of the inflammatory process. Cellular and humoral immunologic reactions occur at the local site (joints) and often systemically. The production of antiimmunoglobulins or rheumatoid factors occurs initially in the inflammatory tissue of the joint and can subsequently be detected in the serum of 80 percent of the patients treated for the condition. Those patients with rheumatoid arthritis who are seropositive for rheumatoid factor show a more marked progression of the disease than do those who are seronegative.

Clinical Manifestations and Diagnosis

The onset and course of rheumatoid arthritis are particularly variable. Usually, fatigue, weight loss, and generalized aching and stiffness, especially on awakening in the morning, precedes localization of symptoms and the development of joint swelling. These symptoms at times develop explosively in one or more joints, but more often there is progression to multiple joint involvement. The disease may remit spontaneously in the first year or diminish in intensity, only to recur in the same or additional joints at intervals. The more troublesome cases usually continue to affect many joints with sustained inflammatory reactions for months or years. In these latter cases, marked bone and joint damage often develop, with drift of the ulna (outer bone of the forearm) and consequent deviation of the fingers, leading to lim-

ited function and instability. Signs of systemic involvement may also be seen, for example, nodules at the elbows, cutaneous degeneration at the fingertips (which appear as small, 1- to 2-millimeter infarcts in the nail fold) or at the elbow tip, pulmonary fibrosis, inflammation of the sac enclosing the heart, anemia, fever, rash and peripheral ulcers in the lower limbs, disease of the nervous system, and wrist weakness occasioned by the carpal tunnel syndrome. In addition, there is usually a gradual weight loss as well as the loss of muscle volume and power.

Treatment

Although there is no cure, the principles of treatment are, first, to minimize the swelling, pain, and damage; and second, to maintain joint function as closely to normal as possible. To this end, a number of medical and surgical modalities are available to manage patients over the course of their disease. Drug therapy is an important part of this management as it is directed toward controlling the destructive inflammatory processes within the joint.

The antiinflammatory agents commonly used for this control include aspirin and similar compounds referred to as nonsteroidal antiinflammatory agents. Whereas some symptoms and signs of the disease can be improved by these drugs, additional agents may be required for those patients who have continuing progressive damage. This treatment might include gold salts and antimalarial, antitumor, and immunosuppressive agents. Corticosteroid derivatives are recognized to be potent antiinflammatory agents with some immunomodulating effect. Although they may dramatically improve the most troublesome symptoms, they have not been proven to alter significantly the progression of the disease. Moreover, the side effects of these drugs may be hazardous over the many years needed to treat chronic conditions such as rheumatoid arthritis.

History and Geography

The clinical term "rheumatoid arthritis" was first introduced in the medical literature by A. B. Garrod in 1859. It was not in common usage until "officially recognized" in the United Kingdom by the Department of Health in 1922 and by the American Rheumatism Association in 1941. Until recent times many names were used to describe what we currently recognize as rheumatoid arthritis: rheumatic gout, chronic rheumatic arthritis, goutte asthenique primative, rheumatismus nodosus, and rheumatoid osteoarthritis. Broader terms such as gout, arthritis, and rheumatism would also have encompassed rheumatoid arthritis as well as numerous other conditions.

Evidence for the existence of rheumatoid arthritis in earlier times, however, must be gleaned from literature, from art, and from paleopathological studies of ancient bones, and to date that evidence has been far from overwhelming. Indeed the lack of early descriptions of this disease led authors such as E. Snorrason (1952) to suggest that the disease is recent in origin (i.e., since the seventeenth century) and is evolving to develop a peak incidence during the twentieth century before ultimately disappearing (Buchanan and Murdoch 1979).

By contrast, other arthritic disorders such as ankylosing spondylitis, osteoarthritis, and spinal hyperostosis have been recognized in skeletons thousands of years old and appear to be unchanged from the present condition. In fact, given the lack of evidence of the existence of rheumatoid arthritis until relatively recent times, L. Klepinger (1979) and others have suggested that rheumatoid arthritis has evolved from ankylosing spondylitis. Suffice it to say that the uncertainty about the antiquity of rheumatoid arthritis is at least partly due to the methods by which we have examined the evidence of a disease whose current definition includes a combination of clinical, radiological, and serologic criteria. Nonetheless, a search for evidence of rheumatoid arthritis in the literature, art, and bones of the past is an intriguing one.

Literature

In 1800, A. J. Landré-Beauvais wrote an account of a disease that is today universally accepted as representing rheumatoid arthritis. Earlier European descriptions of rheumatoid arthritis, which C. L. Short (1974) and the present authors find convincing, were written by Thomas Sydenham in 1676, W. Heberden in 1770, and B. Brodie in 1818. These observers each described long-term, chronic, debilitating diseases affecting multiple joints, which included descriptions of typical hyperextension deformity of the interphalangeal joints of the fingers. Before these dates, there are several descriptions of disease that *could* represent certain phases of rheumatoid arthritis, ranging from the acute explosive attack to one of chronic sustained disability. This is particularly so in the case of the Emperor Constantine IX (ca. 980–1055) who, at the age of 63, suffered from polyarthritis in the feet, and subsequently the hands, shoulders, and knees, leading to a nodularity and residual deformity in the fingers, and flexion and swelling of the knees. However, the absence of currently applied diagnostic criteria based on skeletal X-rays and serologic information does not absolutely exclude a diagnosis of polyarticular gout or some other erosive joint disease in an otherwise very suggestive report.

In the thirteenth century, a less complete description was written in Britain by Bartolemeus Anglicus who, after describing several types of arthritis, stated that "one form of the disease is worse for it draws together tissues and makes the fingers shrink and shrivels the toes and sinews of the feet and of the hands."

Perhaps the earliest known description suggestive of rheumatoid arthritis is in the Eastern literature (India) and discussed in the *Caraka Samhita*, written about A.D. 123. In this work, the disease in question was said to manifest itself as swollen, painful joints initially in the hands and feet and then affecting the whole body. The ailment was reported to be protracted, difficult to cure, and associated with anorexia. Although ultimate proof is lacking, these descriptions may represent the earliest written record of rheumatoid arthritis.

Art

Although there is no unequivocal illustration of symmetrical polyarthritis, attention has been drawn to some presentations of deformities of the hands in the Flemish painters (1400–1700) who otherwise painted the ideal, unaffected limb with considerable accuracy (Klepinger 1979). Some works of Peter Paul Rubens show changes typical of rheumatoid arthritis, suggesting to T. Appelbloom and colleagues (1981) that Rubens, who himself suffered from rheumatoid arthritis, painted the progressive phases of his own disease in the hands of his subjects during the years 1609–38.

Paleopathology

Of the thousands of mummies and whole skeletons from the distant past that have been observed, there are surprisingly few specimens that show features compatible with rheumatoid arthritis. The reader will recall that the definition of the disease requires a symmetrical pattern commonly affecting the small joints. This poses a problem when the determination of symmetry is not possible because one or more long bones are absent or because the small bones of the hands and feet are frequently lost.

Although rheumatoid arthritis, at the present time, is a major cause of symmetrical erosive polyarthritis, other causes do exist, and thus it seems appropriate to employ the term "erosive joint disease," which may or may not have been rheumatoid arthritis when describing the arthritis seen in ancient bones.

The description by W. P. May (1897) of an Egyptian mummy 5,500 years old indicates a case of possible rheumatoid arthritis: a male, 50 or 60 years of age with hands, wrists, elbows, and knees, and feet affected. Particular note was made of the fingers – "small joints of the hands are swollen and fusiform" – while the metatarsophalangeal joints were markedly involved with some peripheral fusion. The author emphasized the unequal symmetry, and no erosions were described. Studies by J. Rogers and colleagues (1981) and A. K. Thould and B. T. Thould (1983) in the United Kingdom have identified only two or three cases of erosive arthritis compatible with rheumatoid arthritis in some 816 skeletons dating from the Saxon to Roman and British medieval times.

A detailed analysis of a well-preserved 34-year-old female Eskimo mummy from the Kodiak Islands is described by D. Ortner and C. S. Utermohle (1981); in this instance evidence of erosive inflammatory polyarthritis compatible with juvenile rheumatoid arthritis is clearly presented. More recently, reports of erosive polyarthritis occurring in ancient bones ranging from 5,000 years to 1,000 years old in North America have been identified by B. M. Rothschild's group (1987). In fact, Rothschild and colleagues have speculated that rheumatoid arthritis could have had a viral origin in North America and then migrated to Europe in the post-Columbian period, where it manifested itself as a more severe disease in subsequent centuries. This, they argue, might account for the apparent relative infrequency of the disease in Europe prior to the seventeenth century.

Today the disease is identified in most ethnic groups and in all parts of the world. Thus only detailed studies and precise reports on skeletal remains can establish whether erosive arthritis, which may have been rheumatoid arthritis, was more prevalent in the past than it is presently. These findings could impact considerably upon our understanding of the pathogenesis of the disease and perhaps also suggest whether it is likely to disappear as some have argued.

Howard Duncan and James C. C. Leisen

Bibliography

Appelbloom, T., et al. 1981. Rubens and the question of the antiquity of rheumatoid arthritis. *Journal of the American Medical Association* 245: 483–6.

Badui, E., et al. 1987. El corazón y la artritis reumatoide.
Estudio prospective de 100 casos. *Archivos del Instituto de Cardiologia de Mexico* 57: 159–67.

Buchanan, W. W., and R. M. Murdoch. 1979. Hypothesis: That rheumatoid arthritis will disappear. *Journal of Rheumatology* 6: 324–9.

Caughey, D. E. 1974. The arthritis of Constantine IX. *Annals of the Rheumatic Diseases* 33: 77–80.

Garrod, A. B. 1859. *The nature and treatment of gout and rheumatic gout.* London.

Klepinger, L. 1979. Paleopathological evidence for the evolution of rheumatoid arthritis. *American Journal of Physical Anthropology* 50: 119–22.

May, W. P. 1897. Rheumatoid arthritis (osteitis deformans) affecting bones 5,500 years old. *British Medical Journal* 2: 1631–2.

Ortner, D., and C. S. Utermohle. 1981. Polyarticular inflammatory arthritis in a pre-Columbian skeleton from Kodiak Island, Alaska. *American Journal of Physical Anthropology* 56: 23–31.

Rogers, J., P. Dieppe, and I. Watt. 1981. Arthritis in Saxon and medieval skeletons. *British Medical Journal* 283: 1668–70.

Rothschild, B. M., R. J. Woods, and K. Turner. 1987. New World origins of rheumatoid arthritis (abstr.). *Arthritis and Rheumatism* 30 (Suppl.) S61: B29.

Short, C. L. 1974. The antiquity of rheumatoid arthritis. *Arthritis and Rheumatism* 17: 193–205.

Snorrason, E. 1952. Landré-Deauvais and his goutte asthenique primative. *Acta Medica Scandinavica* 142 (Suppl.): 115–18.

Thould, A. K., and B. T. Thould. 1983. Arthritis in Roman Britain. *British Medical Journal* 287: 1909–11.

Utsinger, P. D., N. J. Zvaifler, and E. G. Ehrlich, eds. 1985. *Rheumatoid arthritis.* Philadelphia.

VIII.13
Ascariasis

The giant intestinal roundworm, *Ascaris lumbricoides,* is a very common parasite with a worldwide distribution. The adult worms are 15 to 35 cm (6 to 14 inches) long and reside in the lumen of the small intestine. Sometimes, however, they are passed in the feces and, if vomited into the oral cavity, may exit from the host's mouth or nostrils; thus they have been known to medical observers for millennia. Female worms produce up to 200,000 fertilized eggs daily, which are passed in the feces. Eggs incubate in the soil for at least 2 to 3 weeks to produce an infective larval stage within them. The eggs are very resistant to chemicals, desiccation, and extreme temperatures, but they mature or "embryonate" most rapidly in warm, moist, shady conditions in clay soils. People become infected by eating embryonated eggs in food or water contaminated with feces; or, in the case of toddlers, infection occurs by direct ingestion of eggs with dirt. Poor rural sanitation and the use of human feces for fertilizer obviously favor transmission. Mature eggs hatch in the small intestine, and the larvae then undergo a remarkable series of migrations in the host. They penetrate the intestinal wall and are carried in blood or lymph vessels to the liver and heart, and then the lungs. Here they break out into the air sacs, develop, and molt for about 3 weeks, and then climb up the trachea to the throat, where they are subsequently swallowed to establish themselves as adults in the small intestine.

Distribution and Incidence

This nematode was known to ancient writers in China, India, Mesopotamia, and Europe, and was present in pre-Columbian America. The World Health Organization estimated in the early 1980s that between 800 and 1,300 million people harbored an average of six worms each. The true figure may be even higher. Surveys have demonstrated infection in more than 50 percent of sampled populations in such countries as Bangladesh, Brazil, China, Colombia, India, Iran, Kenya, Mexico, Tanzania, and Vietnam, and the rate approaches 100 percent in many rural areas. In China, it was estimated that the 1947 *Ascaris* population produced 18,000 tons of eggs a year; they may be even more productive today. The worm is also common in developed countries, although improved sanitation has greatly reduced prevalence in recent decades. During the 1960s, surveys conducted in school children and other groups showed infection rates of 2.5 to 75 percent in Italy, 21 percent in Spain, 40 to 80 percent in Portugal, 18 percent in Romania, 2 to 5 percent in urban Japan, and up to 20 percent in the Japanese countryside. Foci still exist in some rural areas in the southern United States.

Clinical Manifestations, Diagnosis, Treatment, and Control

Symptoms of ascariasis vary widely. As is often true for helminthic infections, low worm loads may cause few or no symptoms. Large numbers of larvae in the lungs may produce ascaris pneumonitis, with symptoms resembling pneumonia. Allergic reactions can cause asthma attacks. Larvae can reach atypical (ectopic) sites such as the brain, eye, or kidney, where they may produce grave, life-threatening conditions, but such events are fortunately rare. Adult worms in the intestine can cause fever, abdominal discomfort, diarrhea, and allergic reactions to their proteins. Fever may induce worms to wander to the larynx, where they can cause suffocation, or to exit the mouth or nostrils. Heavy infections rob the host of nutrients, and tangled masses of worms can result in fatal intestinal obstruction if not treated promptly. Intestinal ascariasis is especially serious in young children. A study in Kenya showed that ascariasis produced signs of protein–energy malnutrition in many children and often retarded their growth; similar results have been reported from other Third World countries. Even if severe effects occur in only a small percentage of cases, the ubiquity of the worm makes it an important cause of morbidity in many countries.

Diagnosis is made by detecting eggs in microscopic examination of the feces. Drug treatment is usually safe and effective, but care must be taken to keep the adult worms from wandering about in response to therapy. Intestinal obstruction is treated by inducing vomiting or by surgery. Preventive measures include sanitary latrines, composting feces to be used as fertilizer, and careful washing of fruits and vegetables that are eaten raw. Mass treatment may also reduce the danger of continued reinfection.

K. David Patterson

Bibliography

Jeffery, G. M., et al. 1963. Study of intestinal helminth infections in a coastal South Carolina area. *Public Health Reports* 78: 45–55.

Kean, B. H., Kenneth E. Mott, and Adair J. Russell, eds.

1978. *Tropical medicine and parasitology: Classic investigations*, Vol. II, 346–59. Ithaca and London.

Latham, L., M. Latham, and S. S. Basta. 1977. The nutritional and economic implications of ascaris infection in Kenya. *World Bank Staff Working Paper* No. 277 (September). Washington, D.C.

Pawlowski, Z. S. 1984. Strategies for the control of ascariasis. *Annales de la Société Belge de Médecine Tropicale* 64: 380–5.

Stoll, N. R. 1947. This wormy world. *Journal of Parasitology* 33: 1–18.

World Health Organization. Parasitic Diseases Programme. 1986. Major parasitic infections: A global review. *World Health Statistics Quarterly* 39: 145–60.

VIII.14
Bacillary Dysentery

Bacteria from several genera, including *Campylobacter, Salmonelle,* and *Yersinia,* as well as some strains of the common intestinal bacillus *Escherichia coli,* can invade the mucosa of the large intestine and cause dysentery, but members of the genus *Shigella* are by far the most important agents. Shigellosis is a common disease that occurs worldwide and afflicts persons of all races and age groups. In addition, *Campylobacter* appears to be an emerging pathogen, at least in the United States. It lives in the small intestine and produces a dysentery-like condition that is usually self-limiting.

Etiology and Epidemiology

Four species or subgroups of *Shigella* cause human disease. *Shigella dysenteriae* (subgroup A), the first to be discovered, is the most virulent. *Shigella flexneri* (B), *Shigella boydii* (C), and *Shigella sonnei* are less dangerous. More than 40 serotypes are recognized and are useful in tracing the spread of outbreaks.

Shigella organisms are passed in the feces and spread from person to person by the fecal–oral route. Bacteria are excreted during the illness and for about 4 weeks after recovery, but some asymptomatic individuals may act as carriers for a year or more. Contaminated food and water are the most common modes of transmission. Direct fecal contamination or mechanical carriage by flies can introduce bacteria into food, milk, or water. Sick, convalescent, or even healthy food handlers who have poor hygienic practices are especially dangerous; proper handwashing after defecation is a simple but effective preventive measure. Crowding and poor sanitation favor transmission, and outbreaks are common in jails and institutions for the retarded and mentally ill.

Epizootics have been reported in colonies of captive primates, and two species have been isolated from dogs, but animal reservoirs have no known epidemiological significance.

Distribution and Incidence

Shigellosis occurs worldwide, but is especially common in countries with poor water and sewage systems. The virulent *S. dysenteriae* is mostly confined to the tropics and East Asia; a much less pathogenic form, *S. sonnei,* is the most abundant species in the United States. All age groups are vulnerable, but severe disease is most common in children and among the elderly. There appears to be no racial or ethnic immunity, although populations can acquire considerable resistance to locally prevalent strains. Travelers may become ill when they encounter unfamiliar strains. Accurate incidence rates are impossible to obtain, but shigellosis is a serious health problem in most underdeveloped countries and a major cause of infant and child mortality. The disease is commonly endemic in poor countries, but great epidemics can also take place. During World War II, acute dysentery, apparently introduced by Japanese and/or Allied troops, attacked many indigenous groups in western New Guinea, causing thousands of deaths despite the efforts of Australian authorities. In 1969 an epidemic of *S. dysenteriae* caused 110,000 cases and 8,000 deaths in Guatemala.

Shigellosis is also a constant threat in developed countries, especially when sanitary standards are weakened. For example, two important *S. sonnei* outbreaks occurred in the United States in 1987. One took place among Orthodox Jews in New York, New Jersey, Ohio, and Maryland, with the majority of cases occurring among small children in religious schools. Patterns of spread were consistent with person-to-person transmission among religious communities in the four states. The first outbreak was in New York City, where 132 cases were reported and at least 13,000 were suspected. Smaller epidemics in upstate New York and other states appeared to be linked with Passover visits to relatives in the city. The second epidemic began with the annual meeting of a counter-culture group, the Rainbow Family, in a national forest in North Carolina in early July. Poor hygiene and inadequate latrines allowed infection to spread among the campers, who caused at least four clusters of cases in Missouri and Pennsylvania when they dispersed. Shigellosis rates in the United States ranged from about 5 to 11 per 100,000 from 1955 to 1986; the disease is almost certainly seriously underreported.

Diagnosis, Clincial Manifestations, and Pathology

Diagnosis is by clinical signs, cultivation of *Shigella* or other bacteria from tissue swabs and feces, and serologic tests to determine species and strains. Differential diagnosis must exclude other agents of dysentery, including other bacteria, viruses, and amebas.

Bacteria invade the mucosa of the large intestine, where they cause mucus secretion, edema, and, usually, superficial ulceration and bleeding. The watery diarrhea is probably caused by a toxin that increases the secretions of the cells of the intestinal wall.

The incubation period is from 1 to 4 days. Onset is sudden in children, with fever, drowsiness or irritability, anorexia, nausea, abdominal pain, tenesmus, and diarrhea. Blood, pus, and mucus appear in the diarrheal stools within 3 days. Increasingly frequent watery stools cause dehydration, and death can occur as early as 12 days. If the patient survives, recovery usually begins after about 2 weeks. In adults, there is usually no fever, and the disease generally resolves itself after 1 to 6 weeks. Symptoms in both children and adults may vary from simple, transient diarrhea to acute dysentery and death.

It is not always possible to differentiate amebic and bacillary dysentery on clinical grounds, but shigellosis generally has a more sudden onset and more acute course, is more likely to occur in explosive epidemics, and is not a chronic disease. Tenesmus is a much more common symptom in shigellosis, and the stools are generally less abundant and contain more bright red blood than in typical cases of amebic dysentery.

Control and Treatment

Sanitary measures are crucial for the prevention of bacillary dysentery and other diseases that are spread by fecal–oral route. Proper waste disposal, postdefecation handwashing, and safe water supplies are essential. Chlorination of water kills *Shigella* and other bacterial agents of dysentery. Sanitary food preparation, control of flies, and pasteurization of milk are also important. In areas with inadequate sanitation, avoidance of raw foods and use of bottled water can help to protect the traveler.

Patients may require rehydration and replacement of lost electrolytes, as well as symptomatic care for cramps and discomfort. Bed rest is important. After a day or two of fasting, soft, easily digestible food should be given in small, frequent meals. In most cases, such supportive therapy is sufficient. A variety of antibiotics can be effective against various *Shigella* species, but drug resistance is a growing problem. Many strains of *S. sonnei* in the United States have developed resistance to ampicillin and tetracycline; thus, in cases where drug therapy is essential, newer agents must be employed.

History

Medical writers have described dysentery or "the flux" since ancient times, but the bacterial form of the disease was not clearly distinguished until late in the nineteenth century. Dysentery ravaged Persian armies invading Greece in 480 B.C., and the disease has always been a companion of armies, often proving much more destructive than enemy action. This disease was, and remains, common among both rural and urban poor people around the world. An epidemic of what must have been shigellosis swept France in 1779, causing especially severe damage in some rural areas of the western part of the country. Troop movements for a planned invasion of England helped spread the disease. At least 175,000 people died, with some 45,000 deaths in Brittany alone. Children constituted the majority of the fatalities. During the U.S. Civil War, Union soldiers had annual morbidity rates of 876 per 1,000 from dysentery, and annual mortality rates of 10 per 1,000. Dysentery outbreaks were problems for all belligerents in World War I, especially in the Gallipoli and Mesopotamian campaigns.

Bacterial dysenteries took a heavy toll among infants and young children in Western countries until very recent times. During the late nineteenth and early twentieth centuries, the decline in breast feeding and the growing use of cows' milk in European and American cities exposed infants and toddlers to a variety of bacterial and other agents of dysentery and diarrhea. As milk is an excellent growth medium for *Shigella* and many other pathogens, contaminated milk and lack of refrigeration led to especially high death rates in hot weather. Milk-borne shigellosis was a significant contributor to the "summer complaint," which took thousands of young lives annually in cities like Paris and New York. Infant health movements, public health education, and pasteurization of milk largely eliminated the problem in western Europe and North America by about 1920. Shigellosis, however, still contributes to the "weanling diarrhea," which afflicts tens of millions of Third World children every year.

The Japanese bacteriologist Kiyoshi Shiga isolated *S. dysenteriae* in 1898, and confirmed its role as a pathogen by showing that the organism reacted with sera of convalescing patients. The other species were discovered early in the twentieth century, and much research has been directed to immunologic studies of various strains. The role of *Campylobacter* species as common human pathogens has been recognized only since the 1970s.

K. David Patterson

Bibliography

Bulloch, William. 1938. *The history of bacteriology.* Oxford.

Burton, John. 1984. A dysentery epidemic in New Guinea and its mortality. *Journal of Pacific History* 18: 336–61.

Lebrun, François. 1981. La Grande dysenterie de 1779. *L'Histoire* 39: 17–24.

Rosen, George. 1958. *A history of public health.* New York.

Smith, David T., and Norman F. Conant. 1960. *Zinsser microbiology,* 12th edition. New York.

U.S. Public Health Service. Centers for Disease Control. 1987. *Morbidity and Mortality Weekly Report* 36 (July 17): 440–2, 448–50; (October 2): 633–4.

   1988. *Campylobacter* isolates in the United States, 1982–1986. In *CDC Surveillance Summaries* (June), 1–13.

<hr>

VIII.15
Beriberi

Beriberi is a disease caused by a deficiency of thiamine, or vitamin B_1, that is expressed in three major clusters of symptoms, which vary from person to person. It involves edema, or swelling, of the legs, arms, and face. The nerves may be affected, causing, first, a loss of sensation in the peripheral nerves and, later, paralysis. The cardiovascular system may be involved, evidenced by enlargement of the heart and extremely low diastolic blood pressure. Beriberi may be chronic and so low-grade that it cannot be detected by clinical examination; in its chronic form, it may alternatively result in disability for months or years; or it may be acute and result in death in a few weeks. Until major tissue damage occurs, it is curable and reversible by consumption of thiamine.

The name "beriberi" derives from a Sinhalese word, meaning weakness. As *kakke,* it has been known in Japan since antiquity and is described in the earliest Chinese medical treatises. The several forms of beriberi have often been considered as separate diseases. In "wet" beriberi, swelling and heart complications occurred, although often with loss of the sense of touch, pain, or temperature. In "dry" beriberi, there was little swelling, but instead a progressive loss of those senses and then of motor control followed by atrophy of the muscles of the paralyzed limbs and a general wasting syndrome. Today it is thought that dry beriberi was partly due to a deficiency of vitamin B_2. *Shoshin* beriberi was a term used to denote a fulminating, or acute form with severe heart complications. "Infantile" beriberi was the last form to be recognized; in addition to swelling, heart enlargement, and other cardiovascular complications, indicative of beriberi, suckling infants also had such symptoms as loss of voice and gastrointestinal disturbances, neither of which occurred in adults.

The discovery that beriberi was caused by a nutritional deficiency led to the identification and study of vitamins. The isolation and later synthesis of thiamine led to the enrichment of key foods as a public health intervention. Beriberi was not only a cause of enormous human suffering and death, but also one of the most important diseases in the development of medical science.

Etiology and Epidemiology

Thiamine is vital to every living thing, both plant and animal. It is an essential component of dozens of enzymes that metabolize food. In particular, thiamine is necessary to derive energy from glucose, the preferred food of nerve cells, and from other carbohydrates. It is more indirectly involved in the metabolism of the amino acids isoleucine, leucine, and valine.

An enzyme is a catalyst for chemical reactions. It consists of a protein and a coenzyme that attaches to the target substance, activates the chemical change, and then detaches to be ready again for the target substance. In its most important role, thiamine, as thiamine pyrophosphate, is the coenzyme of carboxylase. Among other things, it causes carboxyl (COOH) groups to be oxidized into carbon dioxide and water, releasing energy to body cells. Because it functions as part of a reusable enzyme catalysis system and is not an integral part of tissue structure itself, thiamine is needed in only small amounts of 1 to 3 micrograms a day.

Thiamine is a water-soluble vitamin that is found widely in foods. It is most concentrated in whole grains, yeast, and legumes; in liver, heart, and kidneys of most mammals; and in oysters. It is available also in most green vegetables and pork. An antagonistic enzyme produced by bacteria – *thiaminase* – is found in a few diverse foods such as raw fish and tea. The symptoms of beriberi are caused by a deficiency of thiamine, which may be slight or severe, temporary or long term. The deficiency usually results from the shortage of thiamine in a restricted and monotonous diet, but it can sometimes be exacerbated by the consumption of large amounts of foods high in thiaminase.

The epidemiology of beriberi follows from the role of thiamine in energy metabolism and its deficiency in restricted diets. The population at highest risk for beriberi have been (1) people engaged in heavy labor, such as farmers plowing their fields and soldiers and construction workers; (2) pregnant women; and subsequently, (3) their nursing infants. The populations in which beriberi has been most prevalent have been of two kinds: people confined to institutions, such as prisons, asylums, and naval ships, who are limited to monotonous and restricted diets such as bread and water or fish and rice; and people who derive a large portion of their calories from rice from which milling has removed most of the bran in which the thiamine is found.

Rice Cultures

Beriberi is in large part a disease of rice culture. When rice is the staple food, it is eaten in very large quantities and commonly provides 80 percent or more of the caloric energy. When the hull is removed with a mortar and pestle at home, enough bran remains on the rice to provide the necessary thiamine. When the rice is milled efficiently in modern plants, however, it is polished into white rice and thiamine is almost entirely eliminated.

Cooking methods are also important in the etiology of the disease. In northern China, Korea, and Japan, the rice hulls were traditionally removed before shipment in order to reduce bulk. When the rice reached the cities, it was so crawling with weevils that the subsequently highly-milled rice was covered in weevil juices and thus often treated with talc. Cooking procedures called for the rice to be thoroughly washed several times. The first washing alone removed half of the thiamine. In Burma and other parts of Southeast Asia, the custom has been to cook rice with excess water and throw away the water that is not absorbed, which contains most of the thiamine. Other peoples either cook the rice so as to absorb all the water, or use the extra water for drinking purposes or for other cooking. In the lower Ganges Valley in India, in Bihar and Bengal, the custom has been to parboil rice. Steaming the rice for partial cooking before drying it and then milling it for distribution preserves most of the thiamine in white rice, and is protective against beriberi. However, the labor or costs required in the process and the different taste and texture produced have not been widely acceptable among other peoples in Asia.

Numerous cultural beliefs and practices are involved in the regional etiology of beriberi. In northeastern Thailand and Laos, for example, people usually steam their glutinous variety of rice – a protective behavior. But, unlike other people in Thailand, they have very limited supplies of fresh fruit or vegetables or of meat for consumption. They eat fish, most of which is in the form of a fermented raw paste and is high in thiaminase, the destroyer of thiamine. Throughout the region, rice is so central to the cultures that it is synonymous with food itself. One result is that invalids, weanlings, and other susceptible people may eat nothing except rice. As milling spreads throughout the region, beriberi has resulted.

Other At-Risk Groups

There is now indication that in eighteenth- and nineteenth-century Brazil, the disease was endemic among slaves and members of the working classes. The deficiency was usually the result of diets consisting mainly of manioc flour and a little dried meat. This flour actually contains less thiamine than does milled rice, and the preparation of the lean dried meat not only eliminated most of its natural thiamine but also increased the body's need for the vitamin (Kiple 1989).

A new population at risk has recently been recognized. In urbanized and industrial countries, beriberi occurs most frequently among alcoholics. At the same time that chronic alcohol consumption impairs the absorption of thiamine by the intestine and its storage and utilization in the liver, it increases the metabolic rate and requires relatively enormous amounts of thiamine for metabolism of the alcohol. When the alcoholic substitutes alcohol for other foods in his or her diet and curtails consumption of thiamine, Wernicke's encephalopathy and other neuropsychiatric disorders may occur, involving loss of motor coordination, loss of feeling in the hands and feet, and inability to remember or learn.

There are a few other specific groups of individuals at risk of beriberi. These include people suffering from renal failure and under long-term dialysis, and people under long-term intravenous feeding.

Because beriberi is a deficiency disease, it is entirely preventable by the consumption of adequate amounts of thiamine. In the United States, enrichment of white bread — replacing the thiamine that had been removed in the milling and bleaching of wheat — caused clinical disease virtually to disappear except among alcoholics. More recently, rice enrichment has also proved beneficial.

Distribution and Incidence

Within recent centuries, beriberi has occurred among institutionalized populations and military forces all over the world. Although the disease has afflicted poor Americans subsisting mainly on white bread and poor Europeans consuming a monotonous diet of potatoes without meat or vegetables, beriberi is and has been most prevalent among the large Asian populations who consume white rice. In the first decade of the twentieth century, mortality from beriberi in Japan averaged 20 per 100,000, and in 1920 reached 70 per 100,000 among the urban population (Shimazono and Katsura 1965). In that same first decade, an estimated 120 per 1,000 people in the Straits Settlements (what is now Malaysia and Singapore) had beriberi, and in the Philippines, 120 per 1,000 of Filipino military scouts were admitted to a hospital for the disease (Williams 1961). Jacques May (1977) reported that in recent times beriberi still occurred in southern China, Vietnam, the Philippines, Indonesia, parts of Burma, southern India, Sri Lanka, Madagasgar, central Africa, local areas in west Africa, and Venezuela, northwestern Argentina, and Brazil.

The true contemporary incidence of beriberi cannot be determined. Since it is so easily treated upon detection by the administration of thiamine, it has almost ceased to be fatal. As a nutritional deficiency, it is rarely reportable at any governmental statistical level. At the subclinical level, however, it probably still occurs widely. In a study in Australia, one in five healthy blood donors and one in three alcoholics at a hospital were found by biochemical assay to be deficient in thiamine (Wood and Breen 1980).

There was an epidemic of beriberi in the decades following World War II. Before the war, hand milling of rice was universal except for the largest cities. With independence and economic development, power milling spread along the railroads and, via new highways, to the rural hinterland and eventually even to the remote hill country. In the late 1950s, beriberi was thought to be responsible for a quarter or more of the infant mortality in parts of Burma and the Philippines (Postumus 1958) and to be the tenth highest cause of overall mortality in Thailand (May 1961). Enrichment of rice at the mills has greatly reduced clinical beriberi, but even in southern China it still occurs (Chen, Ge, and Liu 1984).

Clinical Manifestations and Pathology

The beriberi clinical triad consists of edema and neurological and cardiovascular manifestations. The complex of symptoms resulting from thiamine deficiency, however, has often been confused by the common occurrence of other vitamin deficiencies at the same time. Thus, some of the symptoms that distinguished "dry" beriberi were indicative of riboflavin deficiency. A diet deficient in thiamine would usually be deficient in other B vitamins as well. Some of the differences in the manifestation of thiamine deficiency disease among laboring adults, suckling infants, and alcoholics are due to such complications.

A person with beriberi classically entered the medical system when he or she developed symptoms of the weakness that gave the disease its name. There was malaise, a heaviness in the lower limbs, loss of strength in the knee joint and wrist, and usually some loss of sensation. There was tightness in the chest, palpitations, restlessness, loss of appetite, and often a full feeling in the epigastrium. Infants also vomited, had diarrhea, and had difficulty breathing.

Edema is one of the important signs and is always present in the early stages. Edema, or dropsy, commonly progresses until the lower extremities and the face are swollen. Pain and sensitivity in the calf muscles is an early sign as muscles begin to swell, degenerate, and atrophy. Swelling of the lining of the intestines can also congest them. Edema of the lungs often causes sudden respiratory distress and, with heart failure, death.

Heart palpitations, even at rest, and a diastolic blood pressure below 60 millimeters of mercury are usually diagnostic. There is enlargement of the heart, particularly the right ventricle. A heart murmur may be heard. An EKG may be normal in a mild case but shows abnormal waves of sinus origin in advanced ones.

First the autonomic, then the sensory, and finally the motor nerves are affected. On autopsy, there is proliferation of Schwann's cells in the sciatic nerves. In chronic beriberi, there is progressive degeneration of nerve fibers. There is loss of coordination, sometimes even of the eyes. Sensibility to tactile stimulation, then to pain, and finally to temperature is lost. The motor nerves are next affected, with paralysis beginning in the lower extremities. Then the fingers are affected, the hand drops limp at the wrist, and the fingers contract into a claw hand. Eventually, even the intercostal muscles, diaphragm, and speech control muscles are affected.

Other symptoms that commonly occur include a full sensation or cramping of the epigastrium, heartburn, constipation, and mental confusion. B. Wood and K. J. Breen (1980) define clinical thiamine deficiency to consist of beriberi heart failure and Wernicke's encephalopathy. The latter is a dysfunction of the brain that is characterized by confusion and by a loss of coordination and independent movement of the eyes that is commonly found in alcoholics. Thiamine reverses most of the symptoms, but many patients are left permanently with an inability to form new memories (Korsakoff's psychosis).

In classic beriberi, death results eventually from severe disturbances of the circulatory system and paralysis of the respiratory muscles ending in heart failure.

History and Geography

Most historical studies of beriberi have been concerned not with its occurrence or impact, but with the developments in medical science that led to an understanding of its etiology, treatment, and prevention. The geography of the disease has been closely bound to the rice-eating peoples of Asia, although the disease has never been limited to them.

In the nineteenth century, beriberi was common among troops and institutionalized people around the globe. What appeared to be epidemics occurred on British ships in the Bay of Bengal, Dutch ships in the East Indies, Norwegian whalers, ships plying the China trade in the Sea of Japan, and ships bringing "coolies" home to India from labor in the French Antilles (Hirsch 1885). The broader epidemiology was very puzzling.

The Search for the Etiology

August Hirsch (1885) noted many contradictions as he described the changing pattern of beriberi in the latter half of the nineteenth century. In a few places, notably Japan and the Malay archipelago and the state of Minas Gerais in Brazil, the disease was endemic. The disease had first appeared in Bahia in Brazil in 1866, and then had spread to São Paulo and Rio Grande do Sul by 1874, along the Brazilian seacoast, and into the interior provinces and on into Paraguay. Similarly, the disease had been known on the coast of Japan, but had now spread into interior towns. Earlier opinion had held that a distance of 40 to 60 miles from a seacoast or great river was enough to give immunity, but the disease now occurred hundreds of miles into the interior of Burma and India as well as Brazil. Its appearance in new places showed that it was not caused by climate, which had not changed, and yet it was associated with the rainy season and hot, humid weather. It seemed associated with a period of acclimatization, since people from the interior who moved to the coast as well as new troops usually did not develop the disease for 8 months to a year. It afflicted people in the prime of life, and wealth and high position did not grant immunity. People who led sedentary lives, such as scholars and teachers, were prone to the disease but so were soldiers and laborers. Tainted water was contraindicated. Clearly people who lived in crowded and poorly ventilated quarters were at risk. The evidence for a dietary cause was confusing. There seemed to be an association with insufficient diet, especially lack of fat and albumin, and with preponderance of rice and dried fish in the diet. Rice, however, was eaten widely in places where beriberi did not occur, and cases had been observed in Borneo where troops eating beef and eggs contracted the disease whereas laborers on a diet of rice and fish did not. Hirsch concluded from the global evidence that the cause of beriberi was *sui generis,* a peculiar and specific poison and not the climate, weather, soil, manner of living, or diet. It is instructive to contemplate the complexity of the disease, which was not clarified until the concept of a nutritional *deficiency,* lack of a vitamin, (or mineral) was developed and replaced the idea of a positive poison, in the twentieth century. Then three factors could explain Hirsch's observations quite simply: the monotonous, restrictive diets of certain populations such as prisoners, troops, and coolies; the metabolic needs of heavy labor; and, notably, the spread of steam-driven milling to supply the urban grain needs. The power mills, first established along coasts and at great ports, then spread along transportation routes through the urban system. They intensified and spread an ancient problem in East Asian populations, and introduced it to plantation societies and booming cities in Latin America and Africa. Power milling practices continued to widen and to cause beriberi in Asia especially until into the 1970s.

Ship beriberi was serious among the fishing fleets of New England, Norway, Great Britain, and Canada. There were epidemics in the asylums of Arkansas, and among convicts in South Carolina. It was reported along the entire coast of South America from Venezuela to Argentina, but was especially serious in Panama City and among the Brazilian navy. In Africa, where there was little rice consumption, it affected troops in Senegal, Sierra Leone, Gabon, the Congo, and Angola. Seven epidemics along the Ivory Coast killed 80 percent of 1,100 known afflicted. It afflicted especially those who ate diets based on bananas, corn, and yams.

Robert R. Williams (1961) has best described the importance of the disease as he first encountered it in the Philippines in 1910 (25 years after Hirsch's description) by summarizing some of the numerous papers and presentations of Edward B. Vedder. In Asia, beriberi was one of the leading causes of death. In what is now Malaysia, British doctors estimated that in 20 years they had treated 150,000 hospitalized cases, of whom 30,000 had died out of a total population of 1,250,000. In the hospitals of Kuala Lumpur between 1895 and 1910, 8,422 admissions out of 33,735 were for beriberi; 20 percent died (Williams 1961). In Japan, where white rice was popular, mortality increased from 20 per 100,000 to over 30 per 100,000 in the early 1920s (Shimazono and Katsura 1965). General morbidity among the Japanese population is not known, but in the Russo-Japanese War of 1904–5 more than 20,000 cases among the troops made beriberi "the only ravaging epidemic."

There were early suspicions that diet was responsible. K. Takaki observed as a student in Europe the low incidence of beriberi among European navies. In 1885, as surgeon general of the Japanese navy, he altered the diet on the ship where sailors had previously been much afflicted with beriberi, and in so doing provided convincing evidence of beriberi's nutritional etiology. He subsequently ordered the protein ration increased for all naval personnel, and barley was added to their diet.

By the late nineteenth century, the Dutch in Indonesia had also become convinced that diet was somehow to blame for beriberi. Experiments were carried out among the penitentiaries of Java in which locally hand-milled rice was substituted for white rice, and beriberi almost disappeared among the prisoners. In 1890, Christian Eijkman, a Dutch officer in Java, discovered that a paralytic disease with nerve damage characteristic of beriberi could be induced in chickens fed polished rice. He and his successor, Gerrit Grijns, demonstrated in 1900 that this condition could be prevented or cured by feeding rice bran. Later Grijns extracted the water-soluble factor from the bran and used it to treat people.

These Dutch efforts were the first experimental characterization of nutritional deficiencies, and they developed an animal model that was essential for later nutritional work. Their immediate impact was limited, however, because American and Japanese physicians did not read Dutch. The belief continued across much of the globe that beriberi must be due to some toxin or microbe, although none could be found, or to food spoilage. After the work of Louis Pasteur, the assumption was that every disease must have a positive etiology, an active cause.

Isolation of the Active Factor

In 1910 in the Philippines, Vedder, a U.S. Army captain, began treating beriberi cases with an extract from rice bran, and enrolled the efforts of Williams, a new scientist at the Bureau of Science in Manila, to isolate the active factor. A Filipino doctor, Jose Albert, was then able to identify infantile beriberi: Recognizing that in Europe, breast feeding was protective compared to artificial feeding of babies, but that in the Philippines two-thirds of the mortality occurred in breast-fed infants, he made the connection linking the mothers' eating habits to the disease.

In 1911, Casimir Funk at the Lister Institute in London isolated a crystalline substance, which he erroneously thought was the active antiberiberi factor and called it a "vitamine" after its amine function. In 1926, two Dutch chemists in Java, B.C.P. Jansen and W. F. Donath, succeeded in isolating and crystallizing the active substance from rice bran.

They mischaracterized it, however, by missing its sulfur atom, and other scientists were unable to repeat the isolation.

Williams, now a chemist at Bell Laboratories working on marine cables, continued on his own time and money at home to isolate the active factor and succeeded in 1933. He and those working with him characterized it chemically, and finally, in 1936, completely synthesized it and proved their active synthetic material to be biologically and chemically identical to the antiberiberi factor. Williams named it *thiamin,* to which research councils later added a final *e.* Taking out a patent whose royalties funded the Williams–Waterman Fund for the Combat of Dietary Disease, Williams interested Merck & Company in developing a commercial process. Production of thiamine increased from 100 kilograms in 1937 to 200,000 in 1967 (Gubler 1984) until, as Williams remarked with satisfaction, synthetic thiamine was cheaper than that which could be extracted from any natural source (Williams 1961).

Prevention of Beriberi

In the final stage, from his position on the Food and Nutrition Board of the National Academy of Science's National Research Council, Williams pioneered and supported the enrichment of grain with synthetic thiamine. Russell M. Wilder led the effort to enrich flour, which General Mills supported, and in 1941, the first definitions and standards for enrichment were established. The principle espoused was to raise thiamine to "high natural levels" in the milled flour. Because it was a standard and not a requirement, enrichment of bread in the United States was not fully accomplished until a popular movement was organized during World War II.

Other methods of preventing beriberi had been practiced for decades in Asia. There was considerable success in both Japan and Indonesia in limiting the extent of milling so that bran remained on the rice. These efforts involved the large, central mills of major cities rather than isolated rural enforcement. Professionals involved in public health generally believed in the importance of educating the public and improving diet to prevent beriberi. Williams, who repeatedly traveled to Asian countries campaigning for the prevention of beriberi, noted that there was opposition on the part of British nutritionists and their Asian pupils to any artificial enrichment of cereals because of a viewpoint that "any commercial intent is suspect with respect to any public health measure" (Williams 1961). The result was that even as beriberi spread through the Southeast Asian countryside as an epidemic following the spread of power rice milling and development, the United Nations and its Food and Agriculture Organization continued to ignore efforts at rice enrichment. Finally, in the 1970s the government of Thailand undertook heavy investments, and others followed their example until the agencies of the United Nations became supportive. It was difficult to treat rice grains with synthesized vitamins (locally deficient) and seal them with a protective coating against washing and excess cooking water, let alone to distribute tons of the enriched rice to be mixed with deficient rice at thousands of small mills extending into the most remote areas, and then to regulate and enforce the system. Nonetheless the success of recent efforts portends that, although marginal and subclinical beriberi may persist forever, the scourge of beriberi is ended.

Melinda S. Meade

Bibliography

Chen, Xue-Cun, Ke-you Ge, and Ling-Fen Liu. 1984. Studies in beriberi and its prevention. *Journal of Applied Nutrition* 36: 20–6.

Gubler, Clark J. 1984. Thiamin. In *Handbook of vitamins,* ed. Lawrence J. Machlin, 245–97. New York.

Hirsch, August. 1885. *Handbook of geographical and historical pathology,* Vol. II, trans. Charles Creighton, 569–603. London.

Kiple, Kenneth K. 1989. The nutritional link between slave infant and child mortality in Brazil. *Hispanic American Historical Review* 69: 677–90.

Leevy, Carroll M., and Herman Baker. 1968. Vitamins and alcoholism. *American Journal of Clinical Nutrition* 21: 1325–8.

May, Jacques M. 1961. *The ecology of malnutrition in the Far and Near East.* New York.

    1977. Deficiency diseases. In *A world geography of human diseases,* ed. G. Melvyn Howe, 535–75. New York.

Postumus, S. 1958. Beriberi of mother and child in Burma. *Tropical and Geographical Medicine* 10: 363–70.

Shimazono, Norio, and Eisuke Katsura, eds. 1965. *Review of Japanese literature on beriberi and thiamine.* Tokyo.

Thomson, A. D., M. D. Jeyasingham, and D. E. Pratt. 1987. Possible role of toxins in nutritional deficiency. *American Journal of Clinical Nutrition* 45: 1351–60.

Wilcocks, C. 1944a. Medical organization and disease of Burma before the Japanese invasion. *Tropical Disease Bulletin* 41: 621–30.

    1944b. Medical organization and disease of Indochina before the Japanese invasion. *Tropical Disease Bulletin* 41: 887–98.

    1944c. Medical organization and disease in the Netherland East Indies before the Japanese invasion. *Tropical Disease Bulletin* 41: 983–96.

1944d. Medical organization and disease of Thailand before the Japanese invasion. *Tropical Disease Bulletin* 41: 791–802.

Williams, Robert R. 1961. *Toward the conquest of beriberi.* Cambridge, Mass.

Wood, B., and K. J. Breen. 1980. Clinical thiamine deficiency in Australia: The size of the problem and approaches to prevention. *Medical Journal of Australia* 1: 461–4.

World Health Organization. 1958. *Fifth report of the Joint FAO/WHO Expert Committee on Nutrition.* Geneva.

1980. *Peripheral neuropathologies.* W.H.O. Technical Report Series No. 654, Geneva.

VIII.16
Black Death

The "Black Death" is the name given by modern historians to the great pandemic of plague that ravaged parts of Asia, the Middle East, North Africa, and Europe in the middle of the fourteenth century. Contemporaries knew it by many names, including the "Great Pestilence," the "Great Mortality," and the "Universal Plague." This epidemic was the first and most devastating of the second known cycle of widespread human plague, which recurred in waves, sometimes of great severity, through the eighteenth century. Some of the later and milder "plagues" in this period seem to have also involved other diseases, including influenza, smallpox, and dysentery. Nonetheless almost all historians agree, on the basis of contemporary descriptions of its symptoms, that the Black Death should be identified as a massive epidemic of plague, a disease of rodents, caused by the bacillus *Yersinia pestis,* that can in the case of massive epizootics be transmitted to human beings by fleas. Although the Black Death manifested itself most commonly as bubonic plague, it also appeared at various times and places in its primary pneumonic and septicemic forms.

History and Geography

The geographic origins and full extent of the Black Death are still unclear. The earliest indisputable evidence locates it in 1346 in the cities of the Kipchak Khanate of the Golden Horde, north and west of the Caspian Sea. Until recently, most historians have claimed, based on Arabic sources, that the epidemic originated somewhere to the east of the Caspian, in eastern Mongolia or Yunnan or Tibet, where

plague is enzootic in various populations of wild rodents. From there it was supposed to have spread along the Mongol trade routes east to China, south to India, and west to the Kipchak Khanate, the Crimea, and Mediterranean. Recently, however, John Norris (1977) has contested this account, pointing out that the sources describing Chinese epidemics of the 1330s and 1340s and the inscriptions on the graves at Issyk Kul (1388–9), south of the Aral Sea, are too vague to allow us to identify the disease(s) in question as plague, and that there are no reliable records of Indian epidemics in the mid-fourteenth century. Although Norris's own theory that the Black Death originated to the south of the Caspian in Kurdistan or Iraq is highly speculative (Dols 1978; Norris 1978), he is certainly correct that much more work needs to be done with Chinese and Mongol sources before we can say anything definite about the course of the Black Death before 1346 and its eastern geography and chronology after that date.

The epidemic's westward trajectory, however, is well established. It reached the Crimea in the winter of 1346–7 and Constantinople shortly afterward. From there it followed two great, roughly circular paths. The first swirled counterclockwise south and east through the eastern Mediterranean and the Middle East. The Black Death reached lower Egypt in the autumn of 1347 and moved slowly up the Nile over the next 2 years. By early 1348, it had also hit Cyprus and Rhodes, and during the late spring and summer it moved through the cities of the Mediterranean littoral and Palestine – Gaza, Jerusalem, Damascus, Aleppo – and then east to Mecca, Armenia, and Baghdad, where it appeared in 1349.

The second circle described by the plague was greater in length and duration and moved clockwise, west and north and finally east again, through the western Mediterranean and Europe. According to Italian chroniclers, Genoese ships brought the disease to Sicily from the Black Sea in the autumn of 1347, at about the same time it appeared in Alexandria. From there it spread to Tunisia, the Italian mainland, and Provence. By the summer of 1348 it had moved westward into the Iberian peninsula and as far north as Paris and the ports of southern England. During 1349 it ravaged the rest of the British Isles and northern France, parts of the Low Countries and Norway, and southern and western Germany. In 1350 it was in northern and eastern Germany, Sweden, and the Baltics, and in 1351, in the eastern Baltics and northern Poland. During the following 2 years, it attacked Russia, reaching as far east as Moscow in the summer of 1353.

Although the Black Death lasted in all at least 7 years, from its first clearly recorded appearance in the Caspian area to its final devastation of Moscow, no single city or region suffered for more than a small fraction of that period. The plague moved like a wave through the Middle East and Europe, and the average duration of the epidemic in any given place seems to have been about 5 to 6 months. The reasons for this are complicated. The ecology of plague means that it is a seasonal phenomenon; in its dominant, bubonic form, it flourishes in warm weather, whereas its rarer, primary pneumonic form is most common in winter. Thus the Black Death was above all a disease of spring, summer, and early autumn, typically receding in the last months of the year. For this reason, areas first affected in early spring, like Tunis or the cities of central Italy, in general suffered longer and more severely than those, like northern France and Flanders, affected in August or September. The most unfortunate regions were those such as Lower Egypt, the Veneto, Provence, or Ireland, which experienced successive pneumonic and bubonic epidemics (lasting as long as 9 or 10 months, spanning both winter and summer) or were reinfected in successive years.

Transmission and Mortality

There is considerable debate over the ways in which the Black Death was transmitted from person to person and place to place. Plague is an ecologically complex disease, depending on the mutual interaction of bacilli, rodents, fleas, and humans; the lack of detailed evidence about the experience and behavior of animals and insects in the mid-fourteenth century forces us to rely on indirect and therefore ambiguous evidence derived from the speed and pattern of the epidemic's spread.

The disease was clearly propagated by humans; rather than moving slowly across fields and forests from one group of rodents to another, it progressed quickly along major routes of trade and communication, traveling faster by sea than by land. Thus in virtually every area in which its trajectory is known (the Black Sea, the Mediterranean, the North Sea, the Baltic), it appeared first in ports and then spread more slowly along roads and rivers to inland cities and from there into the surrounding countryside. A number of extremely remote areas, including parts of the Pyrenees, the central Balkans, and the sub-Atlas region, seem to have escaped largely or entirely.

Historians differ, however, about the ways in which humans acted to spread the plague. Virtually all agree that ships carried colonies of diseased rodents from port to port, where they could infect the local rat population, and that sick rats also traveled overland hidden in shipments of cloth and grain. Some also emphasize the autonomous role of the oriental rat flea, *Xenopsylla cheopis,* which could survive independently and be transported in cloth and bedding. Others add to that the role of the human flea, *Pulex irritans,* arguing that in severe epidemics such as the Black Death with a high incidence of septicemic plague, fleas could transmit the disease between humans with no need for a rodent intermediary (Biraben 1975; Ell 1980). In addition, on the basis of detailed contemporary descriptions, it is now almost universally accepted that in both Europe and the Middle East, the Black Death also included numerous pockets of primary pneumonic plague, a highly contagious airborne disease. It seems likely that all of these forms of transmission were involved, although their relative importance varied according to local conditions.

It is difficult to judge mortality rates during the Black Death with any precision, except in a few areas. Contemporary chroniclers tended to give impossibly high estimates, whereas other records – necrologies, testaments, hearth taxes, and so forth – are incomplete or reflect only the experience of particular groups or require extensive interpretation. Nonetheless, historians generally agree that death rates most commonly ranged between about 30 and 50 percent in both Europe and the Middle East, with the best records indicating a mortality in the upper end of that range. Some areas are known to have suffered more than others. It is frequently claimed that central Italy, southern France, East Anglia, and Scandinavia were most severely affected, although the evidence for this claim is uneven. Clearly, however, certain regions were relatively fortunate; Milan, for example, Bohemia, and parts of the Low Countries seem to have experienced losses of less than 20 percent, whereas Nuremberg, for some reason, escaped entirely. In general, however, the trend in recent research is to move the estimated mortality rates upward. It now appears that many remote and rural areas suffered as much as the larger cities and that a number of regions previously thought largely to have escaped the epidemic, such as parts of the Low Countries, were in fact clearly affected. The Black Death seems to have been more universal and more virulent than many historians a generation ago believed.

Some groups also suffered more than others, even within a single city or region. A number of contemporary observers in various parts of Europe commented on the relatively high death rates among the poor. These assertions are plausible; the poor lived in crowded and flimsy houses, which would have allowed the easy transmission of plague from rats to humans and from person to person, and they did not have the luxury of fleeing, like the rich, to plague-free areas or to their country estates. Conversely, death rates seem to have been somewhat lower than average among the high European aristocracy and royalty, who lived in stone buildings and were relatively mobile. People whose occupations brought them into contact with the sick, such as doctors, notaries, and hospital nurses, appear to have suffered disproportionately, at least in some areas, as did people who lived in large communal institutions, such as the Mamluks of Egypt and Syria or members of Christian religious orders. For all these groups, the main factor seems to have been increased exposure rather than susceptibility.

Attempts at Control and Prevention

The Black Death was in many ways a completely unprecedented experience for those who suffered through it. Plague had virtually disappeared from the Middle East and Europe during the centuries between the end of the first pandemic in the eighth century and the beginning of the second pandemic, and although the first half of the fourteenth century had been marked by a number of epidemics of other diseases, none approached the Black Death in destructiveness and universality. Contemporaries reacted vigorously against the disease, attempting to halt its spread, mitigate its virulence, and alleviate the suffering it provoked. For the most part, however, their responses took traditional forms: Rather than developing new strategies for managing the crisis, they fell back on established measures, though in many cases they applied these with unprecedented rigor.

For those who could afford it, the most common reaction sanctioned by established medical authorities was flight; even in the Islamic world, where religious authorities inveighed against the practice and exhorted believers to accept the mortality as a martyrdom and a mark of divine mercy, people abandoned infected cities in search of more healthful territory. Those who remained sought spiritual remedies. In both Islamic and Christian countries, religious leaders organized prayers, processions, and special religious services, supplicating God to lift the epidemic. The European reaction, however, had a unique perspective, which was lacking for the most part among Muslims for whom the epidemic was a morally neutral event: Drawing on traditional teachings concerning sin and penance, Christians on every level of society interpreted the plague as a mark of divine wrath and punishment for sin and, in some cases, even as a sign of the approaching apocalypse.

In many Italian cities, private individuals engaged in acts of piety and charity in an attempt to ensure the safety and salvation of themselves and their communities, while public authorities released poor prisoners and passed temporary laws against concubinage, swearing, sabbath-breaking, and games of chance. But public reaction often took more extreme forms – among them, groups of flagellants, who professed publicly, whipping themselves and preaching repentance, in order to ward off God's wrath and the Black Death. This movement seems to have begun in Italy, where it drew on thirteenth-century precedents, but it reached its height in northern and central Europe, in Austria, Thuringia, Franconia, the Rhineland, and the Low Countries. In Thuringia it was associated with a radical critique of ecclesiastical authorities, which led Pope Clement VI to condemn the practice as heretical.

The most extreme and shocking example of Christian religious reaction to the Black Death, however, was directed against Jewish communities in Provence, Catalonia, Aragon, Switzerland, southern Germany, and the Rhineland. Jews in these areas were accused of spreading the plague by poisoning Christian springs and wells. This kind of scapegoating was not unprecedented – earlier fourteenth-century epidemics had provoked similar accusations against lepers, foreigners, and beggars as well as Jews – but the violence of the popular reaction was extraordinary, in some places resisted and in some places abetted by rulers and municipal governments.

Despite the protests of the pope, hundreds of Jewish communities were completely destroyed in 1348 and 1349, their members exiled or burned en masse, while the residents of many others were imprisoned and tortured, with their property confiscated. The destruction was great enough to shift the center of gravity of the entire European Jewish population significantly eastward. Like the flagellant processions, with which they were occasionally associated, many of these pogroms had a prophylactic intent; some of the most violent episodes took place before the plague had actually reached the areas in question. There is no evidence for practices of this sort in Islamic communities, which could boast both a long tradition of religious pluralism and tolerance and a less morally loaded theological interpretation of the epidemic.

A second set of defensive reactions belonged to the realm of medicine and public health. Although both Muslims and Christians identified Divine Will as the ultimate cause of plague, most accepted that God worked through secondary causes belonging to the natural world, and this allowed them to interpret the epidemic within the framework of contemporary medical learning. Both societies shared a common medical tradition based on the works of Greek writers such as Hippocrates and Galen, which explained epidemics as the result of air corrupted by humid weather, decaying corpses, fumes generated by poor sanitation, and particular astrological events. Thus both Muslim and Christian doctors recommended (with some differences in emphasis) a similar set of preventive and curative practices that included a fortifying diet, rest, clean air, and moderate bloodletting for the healthy, together with salves, internal medication, and minor surgery for the sick.

Where Europe and the Islamic world clearly diverged was in their attitudes toward public health. There is little evidence that Islamic communities (where theological teachings combined with the classical medical tradition to deemphasize contagion as a cause of infection) engaged in large-scale social measures to prevent plague, beyond religious ceremonies and occasional public bonfires to purify the air. From the very beginning of the epidemic, however, the populations of a number of European cities – above all, in central and northern Italy, which boasted a highly developed order of municipal and medical institutions – reacted aggressively in a largely futile attempt to protect themselves from the disease. Initially they fell back on existing sanitary legislation, most of it dating from the thirteenth and early fourteenth centuries; this emphasized street cleaning and the control of particularly odoriferous practices like butchery, tannery, dyeing, and the emptying of privies. As the plague moved closer, however, a number of Italian governments instituted novel measures to fight contagion as well as corrupt and fetid air. They imposed restrictions on travel to and from plague-stricken cities and on the import and sale of cloth from infected regions and individuals. They passed laws against public assemblies and regulated the burial of the dead. They hired doctors to study the disease and treat its victims (many physicians had fled the cities along with others of their class), and they appointed temporary boards of officials to administer these measures. In Milan the ducal government boarded up the houses of plague victims, and in Avignon, the pope created a settlement of wooden huts outside the city walls to receive the sick and isolate them from the rest of the community.

These measures against contagion were unprecedented in the context of both contemporary medical theory and municipal practice; they seem initially to have been a response to the experience of pneumonic plague, which ravaged the cities of Italy and southern France in the winter and spring of 1347–8. The ecology of plague and problems of enforcement made such measures largely ineffective, although it is striking that Milan, which applied anticontagion practices most drastically, was the least affected of all major Italian cities. Nonetheless, such measures represent the beginnings of large-scale public health organizations in Europe; succeeding epidemics saw their elaboration and their spread to other parts of the continent, where they eventually became the basis for widespread practices such as quarantines and cordons sanitaires.

Katharine Park

Bibliography

Biraben, Jean-Noell. 1975. *Les Hommes et la peste en France et dans les pays européens et méditerranéens*, 2 vols. Paris.

Bowsky, William, ed. 1971. *The Black Death: A turning point in history?* New York.

Bulst, Neithard. 1979. Der Schwarze Tod: Demographische, wirtschafts- und kulturgeschichtliche Aspekte der Pestkatastrophe von 1347–1352. Bilanz der neueren Forschung. *Saeculum* 30: 45–47.

Callicó, Jaime Sobrequés. 1970–1. La peste negra en la península ibérica. *Anuario de Estudios Medievales* 7: 67–101.

Campbell, Anna Montgomery. 1931. *The Black Death and men of learning*. New York.

Carabellese, F. 1897. *La peste del 1348 e le condizioni della sanità pubblica in Toscana*. Rocca San Casciano.

Carpentier, Elisabeth. 1962a. Autour de la Peste Noire: Famines et épidémies dans l'histoire du XIVe siècle. *Annales: Economies, Sociétés, Civilisations* 17: 1062–92.

1962b. *Une ville devant la peste: Orvieto et la Peste Noire de 1348*. Paris.

Dols, Michael W. 1977. *The Black Death in the Middle East*. Princeton.

1978. Geographical origin of the Black Death: Comment. *Bulletin of the History of Medicine* 52: 112–13.

Ell, Stephen R. 1980. Interhuman transmission of medieval plague. *Bulletin of the History of Medicine* 54: 497–510.

Hatcher, John. 1977. *Plague, population and the English economy, 1348–1530*. London.

Kieckhefer, Richard. 1974. Radical tendencies in the Flagellant movement of the mid-fourteenth century. *Journal of Medieval and Renaissance Studies* 4: 157–76.

Lerner, Robert E. 1981. The Black Death and western European eschatological mentalities. *American Historical Review* 86: 533–52.

Meiss, Millard. 1951. *Painting in Florence and Siena after the Black Death.* Princeton.

Norris, John. 1977. East or West? The geographic origin of the Black Death. *Bulletin of the History of Medicine* 51: 1–24.

       1978. Response to Michael W. Dols. *Bulletin of the History of Medicine* 52: 114–20.

Williman, Daniel, ed. 1982. *The Black Death: The impact of the fourteenth-century plague.* Binghamton, N.Y.

Ziegler, Philip. 1969. *The Black Death.* New York.

VIII.17
Black and Brown Lung Disease

Black and brown lung are the names given by workers in the coal and textile industries, respectively, and by some physicians and public officials, to symptoms of respiratory distress associated with dusty work. Most physicians and epidemiologists have, however, preferred to categorize these symptoms as they relate to findings at autopsy and studies of pulmonary function and to name their appearance in particular patients as, respectively, *coal workers' pneumoconiosis* and *byssinosis.* The terms "black lung" and "brown lung" are historical legacies of intense negotiations about the causes of respiratory distress and mortality among workers in the coal and textile industries of Europe and North America, especially since the nineteenth century. (For the conventional medical definitions of the pathology subsumed under the terms black lung and brown lung, see the extensive bibliographies in papers by Fox and Stone [1981] and Corn [1980]).

History and Geography

For many centuries, medical observers, and workers and their employers, have recognized respiratory distress and its consequences as an occupational hazard among underground miners and employees of industries that generate considerable dust (notably refineries, foundries, and the manufacturing of cotton, flax, and hemp). Pliny described the inhalation of "fatal dust" in the first century. In the sixteenth century, Agricola observed that miners, physicians, and engineers were aware of shortness of breath and premature death. In the early nineteenth century, pathologists observed that some miners in Scotland had black lesions on the lung at autopsy. The term *pneumoconiosis* appears to have been invented in 1867. *Brown lung* seems to have been named by analogy with *black lung,* apparently in the 1960s.

The contemporary, imprecise medical synonym for black lung is *coal workers' pneumoconiosis* (CWP). CWP occurs in two forms: simple CWP and progressive massive fibrosis. Both forms have characteristic lesions. Agencies awarding compensation for disability usually use the designation "black lung" as a rough synonym for pathologically defined CWP and for obstructive airways disease among coal miners.

Most medical authors, epidemiologists, and agencies awarding compensation usually use "brown lung" as a popular synonym for byssinosis or *chronic dust-induced respiratory disease* (CDIRD). The pathology in these descriptions resembles that of chronic bronchitis.

The rich literature on the history and geography of black and brown lung cannot be summarized in conventional terms. Many authors have attempted to describe the history of these conditions, but they have almost invariably done so on the basis of the precise definition of symptomatology accepted at the time they were writing. The reported geography of the conditions is consistent with the distribution of industries in which dust is a by-product, but the perception of the conditions in particular places (and by later observers) has determined what is said, in retrospect, about their geography.

Distribution and Incidence

Each condition has been described among workers exposed to coal dust (CWP) and cotton dust (byssinosis). Perhaps 1 million workers worldwide are currently exposed to both coal and cotton dust. The most reliable statistical accounts of the conditions, both contemporary and historical, are available in British and American sources. The historical and geographic incidence of each condition (and of the particular diseases defined at each time of writing) has been influenced by public policy and regulations for dust suppression, by the characteristics of the mining and manufacturing process (and, for black lung, by the type of coal itself), by the workers' general state of health, and by their exposure to other causes of respiratory disease, notably cigarette smoke, and by the availability of publicly supported programs of disability compensation and medical care.

Opinions about the distribution and incidence of the conditions have been linked to competing views about their clinical manifestations and pathology. For many years and in many communities, physicians did not differentiate the symptoms of black and brown lung from those of other common respiratory disorders. In the early stages of both diseases, workers are frequently asymptomatic and without functional impairment. For black lung defined medically as CWP, the progression of symptoms often includes chronic cough and phlegm, shortness of breath, and then functional impairment; but some workers with lesions of CWP at autopsy remained free of symptoms. The initial symptoms of byssinosis are tightness in the chest, dyspnea, and a cough following a return to work after a weekend or holiday. Later symptoms extend to other workdays and include a chronic stage, with severe continuous dyspnea, chronic cough, and permanent ventilatory insufficiency.

Epidemiology and Etiology

Both black and brown lung (and their medically named partial synonyms) have been the focus of many studies – and are highly controversial. Early epidemiological studies established an association between occupation and respiratory disease. Studies of both conditions in the United States were, in general, initiated later than those in Britain for reasons that include the political roles of manufacturers and unions and the structure of public regulation as well as different perceptions of the relative importance of silica and coal dust and the amount of dust that constituted a dangerous exposure in textile manufacturing. Moreover, many epidemiological, clinical, and pathological investigations have yielded uncertain results.

Aspects of coal miners' lung distress that remain controversial include the following: (1) the mechanisms by which coal dust acts on the lungs; (2) the significance of the correlation, or lack of it, between clinical evidence of respiratory impairment and X-ray findings; and (3) the absence, in some studies, of strong, independent correlations between respiratory disorders in mining communities and work in the mines. Caplan's syndrome is an example of the complexity and controversy surrounding coal miners' lung conditions. This syndrome, first described among Welsh coal miners in 1953, appears to be a consequence of the interaction of characteristics of rheumatoid arthritis with a residue of silica in the lungs; yet the syndrome seems extremely rare in the United States, dispite the high incidence of both dust exposure and arthritis among miners.

For byssinosis, areas of uncertainty include the following: (1) the substance in cotton dust that causes respiratory distress; (2) lack of clear evidence linking levels of dust exposure to findings indicative of clinically defined disease; and (3) the absence of widely agreed upon findings from clinical and pathological examinations that are sufficiently specific to permit a diagnosis of disease.

Nevertheless, the contemporary literature on both conditions is widely regarded as offering considerable guidance for public action. Most investigators agree that the relatively high incidence of respiratory distress in mining and textile workers is evidence of exposure to toxic agents in industrial dust. Many authors have hypothesized mechanisms by which these agents could operate in the lung. There is considerable agreement about clinical manifestations and pathology. And there is overwhelming consensus that reducing dust levels in the workplace contributes to reducing the incidence of both black and brown lung and the symptoms, signs, and findings defined by medical scientists as diseases among workers in dusty industries.

Throughout their histories, black and brown lung have been matters of controversy involving people and institutions beyond the medical profession. The definitions of the conditions have been matters of intense political concern. Generalizations about their incidence and distribution depend on how they are defined, and defining them has long been controversial. Etiology and epidemiology remain in dispute in part because of scientific uncertainty but also because involved as well are significant amounts of money and fundamental issues about the relationship between employers and employees and the public interest in workplace health and safety. Laws and regulations are often more important sources than medical texts for understanding what clinical manifestations and pathological findings mean for treatment, compensation, and control of the environment of the workplace.

Daniel M. Fox

Bibliography

Benedek, Thomas G. 1973. Rheumatoid pneumoconiosis: Documentation of onset and pathogenic considerations. *American Journal of Medicine* 55: 515–24.

Corn, Jacqueline Karnell. 1981. Byssinosis – an historical perspective. *American Journal of Industrial Medicine* 2: 331–52.

Elwood, P. C., et al. 1986. Respiratory disability in ex-cotton workers. *British Journal of Industrial Medicine* 43: 580–6.

Fox, Daniel M., and J. F. Stone. 1980. Black lung: Miners' militancy and medical uncertainty, 1968–72. *Bulletin of the History of Medicine* 54: 43–63.

Judkins, Bennett M. 1986. *We offer ourselves as evidence: Toward workers' control of occupational health.* Westport, Conn.

Kilburn, Kaye H. 1986. Byssinosis. In *Maxcy–Rosenau public health and preventive medicine,* ed. John M. Last et al., 12th edition. Norwalk, Conn.

Merchant, James A. 1986. Coal workers' pneumoconiosis. In *Maxcy–Rosenau public health and preventive medicine,* 12th edition, ed. John M. Last et al. Norwalk, Conn.

Salvaggion, John E., et al. 1986. Immunologic responses to inhaled cotton dust. *Environmental Health Perspectives* 66: 17–23.

Smith, Barbara Ellen. 1987. *Digging our graves: Coal miners and the struggle over black lung disease.* Philadelphia.

Wegman, David H., et al. 1983. Byssinosis: A role for public health in the face of scientific uncertainty. *American Journal of Public Health* 73: 188–92.

VIII.18
Bleeding Disorders

The existence of a hereditary tendency to excessive bleeding was recognized in the second century A.D. by Rabbi Judah, who exempted from circumcision the son of a woman whose earlier sons had bled to death after this rite. But only in this century has expanding knowledge of the physiology of *hemostasis* – the arrest of bleeding – made evident the diverse nature of inherited bleeding disorders. In addition, only recently has it been recognized that a tendency to thrombosis might likewise be due to an inherited hemostatic defect.

Physiology of Hemostasis

The mechanisms by which blood loss in mammals is stopped after vascular disruption are complex. Small vascular injuries are sealed by platelets that adhere to the site of damage, where they attract other circulating platelets, so as to form an occlusive aggregate or plug that can close small gaps. Larger defects in vessel walls are occluded by coagu-lation of blood – that is, by its transformation from a fluid to a gel-like state. Uncontrolled bleeding and its antithesis, thrombosis (the formation of a clot within a blood vessel), are important pathogenetic factors for human disease, including a large variety of hereditary disorders.

The basic structure of both the occlusive clots that halt blood loss and pathological intravascular clots (or *thrombi*) is a meshwork of fibrous protein (*fibrin*) that entraps blood cells. Plato and Aristotle both described the fibers found in shed blood. When the blood vessel wall is disrupted, whether by trauma or disease, a soluble plasma protein, *fibrinogen (factor I)*, is transformed into the insoluble strand of fibrin. Fibrin formation takes place through three steps: First, a plasma proteolytic enzyme, *thrombin,* cleaves several small peptides from each molecule of fibrinogen. Molecules of the residue, called *fibrin monomers,* polymerize to form the fibrin strands. Finally, these strands are bonded covalently by a plasma transamidase, *fibrin-stabilizing factor (factor XIII)*, itself activated by thrombin, increasing their tensile strength.

Thrombin is not found in normal circulating plasma, but evolves after vascular injury from its plasma precursor, *prothrombin (factor II)*, via either or both of two interlocking series of enzymatic events, the extrinsic and intrinsic pathways of thrombin formation. The steps of the extrinsic pathway begin when blood comes into contact with injured tissues (such as the disrupted vascular wall). The tissues furnish a lipoprotein – *tissue thromboplastin* or *tissue factor (factor III)* – that reacts with a plasma protein, *factor VII*. Factor VII then converts a plasma proenzyme, *Stuart factor (factor X)*, to its active form. Thus activated, *Stuart factor (factor Xa)*, acting in conjunction with a nonenzymatic plasma protein, *proaccelerin (factor V)*, releases thrombin from prothrombin, and in this way initiates the formation of fibrin.

The intrinsic pathway of thrombin formation is launched when vascular disruption brings plasma into contact with certain negatively charged substances, such as subendothelial structures or the oily sebum layer of skin. Exposure to negative charges changes a plasma protein, *Hageman factor (factor XII)*, to an enzymatic form, *activated Hageman factor (factor XIIa)*, that participates in both clotting and inflammatory reactions. In the latter role, activated Hageman factor converts a plasma proenzyme, *prekallikrein,* to *kallikrein,* an enzyme that releases small peptides from a plasma protein, high molecular weight *kininogen.* These peptides, notably *bradykinin,* increase vascular permeability, dilate small blood vessels, and induce pain.

The role of activated Hageman factor in the intrinsic pathway is to initiate a series of proteolytic reactions that lead ultimately to the release of thrombin from prothrombin. These reactions involve the sequential participation of several plasma proteins, including *plasma thromboplastin antecedent* (PTA, *factor XI*), high molecular weight kininogen, plasma prekallikrein, *Christmas factor (factor IX)*, *antihemophilic factor (factor VIII)*, Stuart factor (factor X), and proaccelerin (factor V). Of these various proteins, PTA, plasma prekallikrein, Christmas factor, and Stuart factor are the precursors of proteolytic enzymes, whereas high molecular weight kininogen, antihemophilic factor, and proaccelerin serve as nonenzymatic cofactors. The ultimate product, activated Stuart factor (factor Xa), releases thrombin from prothrombin through the same steps as those of the extrinsic pathway. Hageman factor also enhances clotting via the extrinsic pathway by augmenting the activity of factor VII, whereas factor VII in turn can directly activate Christmas factor. Thus, the steps of the extrinsic and intrinsic pathways are intertwined.

Certain steps of both the extrinsic and intrinsic pathways require the presence of calcium ions and phospholipids, the latter furnished, in the extrinsic pathway, by tissue thromboplastin and, in the intrinsic pathway, by platelets and by plasma itself.

Antihemophilic factor (factor VIII) is of peculiar interest as it circulates in plasma loosely bound to another plasma protein, *von Willebrand factor* (vWf), which fosters hemostasis by promoting adhesion of platelets to injured vascular walls. The plasma proteins participating in coagulation are synthesized at least in part by the liver, except for von Willebrand factor, which is synthesized in vascular endothelial cells and megakaryocytes.

Synthesis of certain of the plasma clotting factors – namely prothrombin, factor VII, Stuart factor (factor X), and Christmas factor (factor IX) – is completed only in the presence of *vitamin K,* furnished by leafy vegetables and by bacterial flora in the gut.

The clotting process is modulated by inhibitory proteins present in normal plasma. *Plasmin,* a proteolytic enzyme that can be generated from its plasma precursor, *plasminogen,* can digest fibrin clots as well as certain other plasma proteins. *Antithrombin III* inhibits all of the plasma proteases of the clotting mechanism, an action enhanced by *heparin,* a glycosaminoglycan found in various tissues but not in plasma. *Heparin cofactor II,* a protein distinct from antithrombin III, also inhibits clotting in the presence of heparin. *C1 esterase inhibitor* (C$\overline{1}$-INH) originally detected as an inhibitor of the activated form of the first component of the immune complement system (C1), also blocks the activated forms of Hageman factor and PTA as well as plasmin. *Alpha-1-antiproteinase (alpha-1-antitrypsin)* is an inhibitor of activated PTA. *Protein C,* when activated by thrombin, blocks the coagulant properties of antihemophilic factor (factor VIII) and proaccelerin (factor V), an action enhanced by *protein S;* proteins C and S both require vitamin K for their synthesis. Activated protein C also enhances the conversion of plasminogen to plasmin. *Alpha-2-macroglobulin* is an inhibitor of plasma kallikrein, and plasmin can be inhibited by several plasma proteins, notably by *alpha-2-plasmin inhibitor.*

Human disorders due to the functional deficiency of each of the factors needed for the formation of a clot have been recognized and extensively studied. In some instances, the patient's plasma appears to be deficient or totally lacking in a specific clotting factor or inhibitor. In others, plasma contains a nonfunctional variant of the normal plasma protein.

Classic Hemophilia

Clinical Manifestations

The best known of all the bleeding disorders is classic hemophilia (hemophilia A, the hereditary functional deficiency of factor VIII), which is the prototype of an X chromosome-linked disease, limited to males but transmitted by female carriers. Necessarily, all daughters of those with the disease are carriers, as are half the daughters of carriers. In turn, half the sons of carriers inherit the disease. A typical family history of bleeding inherited in the manner described is found in about two-thirds of cases; in the rest, the disorder appears to arise de novo, either because a fresh mutation has occurred or because cases were unrecognized in earlier generations.

Classic hemophilia varies in severity from family to family. In the most severe cases, in which plasma is essentially devoid of factor VIII, the patients may bruise readily and bleed apparently spontaneously into soft tissues and joints, with the latter resulting in crippling joint disease. Trauma, surgical procedures, and dental extractions may lead to lethal bleeding. The life expectancy of those with severe classic hemophilia is foreshortened, death coming from exsanguination, bleeding into a vital area, or infection. The prognosis of classic hemophilia has been greatly improved by modern therapy in which episodes of bleeding are controlled by transfusion of fractions of normal plasma containing the functionally missing proteins. This therapy is not without hazard, for transfusion of concentrates of factor VIII derived from normal plasma has been complicated by transmission of the viruses of hepatitis and the acquired immunodeficiency syndrome (AIDS).

In those families in which classic hemophilia is milder, bleeding occurs only after injury, surgery, or dental extraction. The severity of clinical symptoms is paralleled by the degree of the deficiency of antihemophilic factor (factor VIII), as measured in tests of its coagulant function.

Geography

Classic hemophilia appears to be distributed worldwide but geographic differences in its incidence have been described. In the United States, Great Britain, and Sweden, estimates of the prevalence of classic hemophilia range from about 1 in 4,000 to 1 in 10,000 males; a somewhat lower prevalence has been estimated in Finland. Whether classic hemophilia is less prevalent in blacks than in other groups, as has been suggested, is uncertain since milder cases may not be brought to medical attention for socioeconomic reasons.

Christmas Disease

Clinical Manifestations

Christmas disease (hemophilia B), the hereditary functional deficiency of Christmas factor (factor IX), is clinically indistinguishable from classic hemophilia, and can be differentiated only by laboratory tests. It is inherited in the same way as an X chromosome-linked disorder and is therefore virtually limited to males. As is true of classic hemophilia, the disorder varies in severity from family to family in proportion to the degree of the clotting factor deficiency. Christmas disease is heterogeneous in nature, for in some families the plasma is deficient in Christmas factor, whereas in others the plasma contains one or another of several nonfunctional variants of this clotting factor. Therapy for hemorrhagic episodes in Christmas disease is currently best carried out by transfusion of normal plasma, which contains the factor deficient in the patient's plasma. An alternative therapy, infusion of concentrates of Christmas factor separated from normal plasma, may be needed in some situations, but its use may be complicated by the transmission of viral diseases as well as by other problems.

Geography

Worldwide, Christmas disease is perhaps one-eighth to one-fifth as prevalent as classic hemophilia. Most reported cases have been in individuals of European origin, but in South Africa and in the United States, as reflected by Ohio data, Christmas disease is relatively as common in blacks as in whites. Christmas disease of moderate severity is particularly prevalent among inhabitants of the village of Tenna, in Switzerland, and among Ohio Amish. This disorder is said to be rare in Japan.

Von Willebrand's Disease

Clinical Manifestations

Classic hemophilia is not the only hereditary deficiency of antihemophilic factor. Von Willebrand's disease is a bleeding disorder of both sexes which in its usual form is present in successive generations; thus, it is inherited as an autosomal dominant trait. The plasma of affected individuals is deficient in both parts of the *antihemophilic factor complex* – that is, the coagulant portion (factor VIII) and von Willebrand factor (vWf). The *bleeding time* – the duration of bleeding from a deliberately incised wound – is abnormally long, distinguishing von Willebrand's disease from classic hemophilia or Christmas disease. The disorder is usually mild, although variants have been observed in which severe bleeding episodes are frequent. Inheritance in these cases is probably recessive in nature.

Geography

The prevalence of von Willebrand's disease is uncertain because mild cases are easily overlooked. Using Ohio as something of a proxy for the United States, von Willebrand's disease is about one-fourth as prevalent as classic hemophilia, meaning about 2 or 3 cases per 100,000 individuals. Estimates of 3 to 6 cases per 100,000 have been made in the United Kingdom and Switzerland, whereas the prevalence is somewhat higher in Sweden, about 12 per 100,000. A study conducted in northern Italy on a population of school children revealed that 10 of 1,218 had laboratory evidence of the disease as well as a family history of hemorrhagic problems. By contrast, the disorder is relatively uncommon in blacks. Similarly, although the severe, autosomal recessive form of von Willebrand's disease is unusual in most individuals of European extraction (perhaps 1 per 1 million), it is particularly prevalent among Israeli Arabs, in whom it can be detected in about 5 individuals per 100,000, and in Scandinavia.

Unusual Disorders of Hemostasis

Functional deficiencies of Hageman factor (Hageman trait), plasma prekallikrein (Fletcher trait), and high molecular weight kininogen (Fitzgerald, Flaujeac, or Willimas trait) are all asymptomatic, although in each case a major defect in clotting is found in the laboratory. These disorders occur with equal frequency in both sexes, and are recessive traits, meaning that they must be inherited from both parents. Hageman trait and deficiencies of plasma prekallikrein and high molecular weight kininogen are all rare, and data concerning their prevalence are available only for Hageman trait, which, in Ohio, occurs in about 1 in 500,000 individuals. By contrast, a disproportionately high number of cases of Hageman trait have been reported from the Netherlands. No racial predilection for Hageman trait or deficiency of high molecular weight kininogen had been described, but deficiency of plasma prekallikrein appears to be more frequent in blacks and in individuals of Mediterranean extraction.

Hageman trait is a heterogeneous disorder; in most families, the plasma appears to be deficient in Hageman factor, but plasma in a few contains a nonfunctional variant of this clotting factor. A similar heterogeneity had been observed in plasma prekallikrein deficiency, with the plasma of those patients of Mediterranean origin containing a nonfunctional variant of plasma prekallikrein.

The hereditary deficiency of plasma thromboplastin antecedent (PTA or factor XI deficiency) is also inherited in an autosomal recessive manner. The hemorrhagic symptoms are usually mild; in women, excessive menstrual bleeding may be troublesome. Nearly all reported cases have been those of Ashkenazi (i.e., eastern European) Jews or Japanese, although cases in individuals of American black, Arabic, Italian, German, Yugoslav, Dutch, Scandinavian, English, Korean, and Asiatic Indian heritage have also been recognized. In Israel, as many as 0.1 to 0.3 percent of Ashkenazi Jews may be affected, and 5.5 to 11 percent may be heterozygous carriers. Similarly, in Ohio, at least 0.3 percent of Ashkenazi Jews have PTA deficiency, and at least 3.4 percent are heterozygotes.

Hereditary deficiencies of factor VII, Stuart factor (factor X), proaccelerin (factor V), and prothrombin are rare, and no racial or geographic distribution is yet apparent. An estimate of one case of factor VII deficiency per 100,000 has been made. A still rarer syndrome, the combination of factor VII deficiency and Dubin–Johnson syndrome (the latter a disorder of billirubin metabolism) has been described in Is-

raeli Jews of Sephardic origin, the patients coming from Iran, Iraq, and Morocco.

In each of these disorders, the deficiency appears in both sexes and is inherited as a recessive trait, and in a number of instances the parents have been consanguineous. In general, the basic nature of these functional deficiencies is variable. In some instances, the plasma of the affected individuals appears to be deficient in the factors, as shown in functional assays. In others, the plasma contains an incompetent variant of the supposedly missing factor. For example, patients functionally deficient in prothrombin may either be truly deficient in this protein, or their plasma may contain one or another variant, nonfunctional form of prothrombin (congenital dysprothrombinemia). A similar variability in the nature of functional deficiencies of factor VII and Stuart factor (factor X) has been detected. In one variant of factor X deficiency, first observed in patients in the village of Friuli in northeast Italy, Stuart factor could not be detected in the usual functional assays, but behaved normally when the venom of Russell's viper was added to the patients' plasma.

The symptoms of deficiencies of factor VII, Stuart factor, and proaccelerin (the last called parahemophilia) are variable, some individuals having hemorrhagic episodes comparable to those of severe hemophilia, whereas others are spared except in the event of severe trauma. In women, excessive menstrual bleeding may be a serious problem.

Disorders of fibrin formation are of peculiar interest. Patients with congenital afibrinogenemia (who have no detectable fibrinogen in plasma) may bleed excessively from the umbilicus at birth, and thereafter from injuries or surgical procedures. In addition, they may exsanguinate from relatively minor vascular injuries, and menorrhagia may be disastrous; yet they may have little in the way of spontaneous bleeding. Fortunately, cogenital afibrinogenemia is a rare recessive disorder, detected in both sexes, and only about 150 cases have been recorded to date. Often the parents are consanguineous. A milder form, congenital hypofibrinogenemia (in which the plasma contains small but measurable amounts of fibrinogen), has also been described in about 30 families, and some investigators believe that this is the heterozygous state for congenital afibrinogenemia, meaning that these individuals have inherited the abnormality from but one parent. In still other families, the concentration of fibrinogen in plasma is normal or only moderately decreased, but the fibrinogen is qualitatively abnormal. This disorder, congenital dysfibrinogenemia, occurs in both sexes and in successive generations; that is, it is inherited as a dominant trait. The affected individuals may be asymptomatic, detected only by chance, or they may suffer mild bleeding problems. Paradoxically, they may also sustain thrombosis. Over 100 families with dysfibrinogenemia have been described, and the molecular defect in each family is almost always unique.

Fibrin-stabilizing factor (factor XIII) deficiency is similarly rare; perhaps 100 cases have been described thus far. In some, plasma appears to be deficient in fibrin-stabilizing factor, and in others, plasma contains a nonfunctional variant of this agent. Patients with fibrin-stabilizing factor deficiency have severe bleeding problems beginning with the umbilicus at birth. The patients may die of central nervous system hemorrhage, and in women spontaneous abortion is frequent. Some evidence suggests that affected males are sterile.

Little information is available concerning a racial or geographic predilection for any of these disorders of fibrin formation, but the prevalence of fibrin-stabilizing factor deficiency in the United Kingdom is said to be 1 in 5 million.

Another disorder of great interest is the hereditary deficiency of alpha-2-antiplasmin. In this disease, which is inherited as a recessive trait, patients may have symptoms suggestive of severe classic hemophilia. Bleeding apparently results from the rapid dissolution of clots by plasmin, whose proteolytic activity is unchecked because of the deficiency of alpha-2-plasma inhibitor. Too few cases have been recognized to determine whether there is a geographic predilection for this disorder, but it has been reported in Japan, the Netherlands, Norway, the United States, and Argentina.

Hereditary Thrombotic Disorders

In contrast to the deficiency states described to this point, a hereditary deficiency of certain of the inhibitors of clotting results in an increased tendency to thrombosis. Thus, familial recurrent thrombosis has been observed in individuals of both sexes, with inherited partial deficiencies of antithrombin III, protein C, protein S, or heparin cofactor II. The affected individuals, most of whom are heterozygotes (i.e., they have inherited an abnormal gene from but one parent), have about half the concentration of the inhibitory proteins of normal individuals. Only a handful of cases of deficiencies of heparin cofactor II, protein C, or protein S have been recorded, but a deficiency of antithrombin III is relatively common.

In Massachusetts, the prevalence is said to be about 50 per 100,000. No geographic or racial predilection has been reported.

Most of the reported cases of deficiencies of these several inhibitors have been in individuals of European origin. Additional instances of antithrombin III deficiency have been recognized in Japanese, Algerians, and American blacks; protein C deficiency has been seen in Jordanian and Israeli Arabs, and in Japanese; and protein S deficiency has been reported in Japan.

History

The earliest record of the existence of hereditary hemorrhagic disease is in the Babylonian *Talmud*. Recurrent descriptions of what was probably hemophilia were recorded thereafter, but it was only in 1803 that John Otto, a Philadelphia physician, recognized that this disorder was limited to males and transmitted by certain of their asymptomatic female relatives. During the nineteenth century, the mode of inheritance of hemophilia was delineated, and in their 1911 review of all the published cases of hemophilia, W. Bulloch and P. Fildes were unable to find a single authentic case of hemophilia in a female.

The mechanism underlying the defect in classic hemophilia was elucidated by A. J. Patek, Jr., and R. H. Stetson in 1936, who determined that the patients were functionally deficient in what is now called antihemophilic factor (factor VIII). Only later was it realized independently by P. N. Aggeler, I. Schulman, and R. Biggs that an essentially identical disorder, inherited in the same way, resulted from a deficiency of Christmas factor (factor IX). In 1926, E. A. von Willebrand recognized the disease that now bears his name among inhabitants of the Åland Islands in the Gulf of Rothnia. This hereditary hemorrhagic disorder affects both sexes and was detected in succeeding generations; these characteristics, along with the presence of a prolonged bleeding time, distinguishes von Willebrand's disease from hemophilia. In 1953, several independent groups of investigators found that the titer of antihemophilic factor (factor VIII) was abnormally low in patients with von Willebrand's disease, and some years later T. S. Zimmerman reported a deficiency also in the concentration of what is now called von Willebrand factor.

With few exceptions, the existence of the various clotting factors required for normal coagulation of blood was detected by the study of patients with unusual hemorrhagic disorders. In each instance, a protein extracted from normal plasma corrected the specific defect in the patient's plasma. Thus, current knowledge about the physiology of blood clotting has been derived from the interplay between the clinic and the laboratory.

Oscar D. Ratnoff

Bibliography

Bulloch, W., and P. Fildes. 1911. Hemophilia. In *Treasury of human inheritance,* Parts V and VI, Sect. XIVa: 169–347. London.

Colman, R. W., et al. 1987. *Hemostasis and thrombosia,* 2d edition. Philadelphia.

Jandl, J. H. 1987. *Blood: Textbook of hematology.* Boston.

Mammen, E. F. 1983. Congenital coagulation disorders. *Seminars in Thrombosis and Hemostasis* 9: 1–72.

Ratnoff, O. D. 1980. Why do people bleed? In *Blood, pure and eloquent,* ed. M. M. Wintrobe, 601–57. New York.

Ratnoff, O. D., and C. D. Forbes. 1984. *Disorders of hemostasis.* Orlando, Fl.

Stamatoyannopoulos, G., et al. 1987. *The molecular basis of blood diseases.* Philadelphia.

Table VIII.19.1. *Types of* Clostridium botulinum, *susceptible species, and sites of outbreaks*

Type	Species	Site of outbreaks
A	Humans	U.S., former U.S.S.R.
B	Humans, horses	Northern Europe, U.S., former U.S.S.R.
C	Birds, turtles, cattle, sheep, horses	Worldwide
D	Cattle, sheep	Australia, South Africa
E	Humans, birds	Canada, Northern Europe, Japan, U.S., former U.S.S.R.
F	Humans	Denmark, U.S.
G	No outbreaks recognized	

Source: L. Smith (1977), *Botulism: The Organism, Its Toxins, the Disease.* By courtesy of Charles C. Thomas, Publisher, Springfield, Ill.

VIII.19
Botulism

Botulism is an uncommon, potentially fatal paralytic disease caused by a protein neurotoxin that is produced by the bacterium *Clostridium botulinum.* The disease is most frequently seen as a foodborne intoxication first clearly documented in the early nineteenth century; however, two other forms of the disease have been identified in the latter part of the twentieth century: wound botulism and infant botulism.

Etiology

Botulism is caused by very powerful neurotoxins that are elaborated during the growth and multiplication of the bacterium *C. botulinum.* The bacterium, which exists in nature as a spore, multiplies and produces its toxin in oxygen-deprived or anaerobic conditions, such as may occur in canned or hermetically sealed foods or unclean wounds. Spores of *C. botulinum* are found naturally in soil and marine sediments, and thus may readily occur as normal contaminants of many vegetable and animal sources of food. The spores and their toxins are inactivated by boiling canned foods according to food industry specifications.

To date, seven immunologically distinct forms of botulinum toxins, labeled A through G, have been identified. Botulism in humans has generally been associated with A, B, E, or F toxins, whereas the C and D toxins have been identified in botulism outbreaks among various animal species, as shown in Table VIII.19.1.

Clinical Manifestation and Pathology

The onset of disease usually occurs within 12 to 36 hours of ingestion of food contaminated with botulinum toxin. Botulism typically presents with an array of distressing signs of motor nerve dysfunction, including double or blurred vision and difficulty with speech and swallowing. The unabated disease progresses to generalized paralysis and death from respiratory muscle involvement.

Diagnosis is confirmed by detecting botulinum toxin in the blood, feces, or wound site of the patient. Depending on the dose of toxin, untreated botulism carries a high fatality rate. Early treatment with antitoxin accompanied by respiratory assistance and other supportive intensive care may be life-saving.

The pathophysiology involves inhibition of release of the neurotransmitter substance acetylcholine at the neuromuscular junction, thus preventing the initiation of the electrical impulse needed for muscle contraction. Electromyography shows a characteristic decrease in amplitude of the evoked muscle action potential in response to an electrical stimulus.

Infant botulism, a condition confined to babies between 2 weeks and 9 months of age, typically presents with listlessness and generalized weakness ("floppy baby") and has been shown to cause some cases of sudden infant death syndrome (SIDS). It has been associated with ingestion of various processed infant foods – honey in particular – that contain botulinum spores. First described in the United States in 1976, where the majority of cases have been reported, infant botulism has also been documented in Europe, Australia, Asia, and South America.

History

Botulism derives its name from the Latin word, *botulus* (sausage), based upon observations in the late 1700s and early 1800s by physicians in southern Germany who noted the occurrence of an unusual but frequently fatal disease following ingestion of spoiled sausage. Justinius Kerner, a district health officer in Württemberg, compiled these reports in official documents, with the result that botulism has at times been called "Kerner's disease." A similar illness seen in nineteenth-century Russia in association with eating smoked or pickled fish was labeled "ichthiosismus."

In 1896, Emile von Ermengem, student of Robert Koch and professor of bacteriology at the University of Ghent, established that the disease was caused by a neurotoxin produced by an anaerobic bacterium. This discovery emerged from his laboratory investigation of the cause of a dramatic outbreak of the disease that occurred at a gathering of musicians in a small Belgian village.

Following initial recognition of the disease in the United States in 1899, the repeated occurrence of botulism outbreaks associated with commercially canned foods led to extensive applied research in the 1920s. Sponsored by the National Canners Association, these studies established the safe food processing practices that are now in widespread use by the industry.

Geographic Distribution

A low incidence and sporadically occurring disease, botulism has been well documented in many parts of the world, as indicated in Table VIII.19.2. Although completeness of official reporting varies among countries, hence preventing reliable estimates of true distribution and incidence, it is clear that botulism is a disease with significant case fatality rates wherever reported.

Table VIII.19.2. *Reports of botulism from various countries in recent years*

Country	Average cases (per year)	Average deaths (per year)	Case fatality rate (%)
Poland (1959–69)	310	31	10
Germany (1962–71)	66	3	5
U.S.S.R. (1958–64)	47	14	29
United States (1950–73)	21	7	31
Japan (1951–9)	19	5	27
France (1956–70)	9	1	5
China (Sinkiang) (1949–57)	9	4	44
Canada (1961–7)	8	3	35
Belgium (1946–71)	4	NA[a]	–
Norway (1957–71)	4	NA[a]	–
Denmark (1958–72)	1	NA[a]	–
Hungary (1950–65)	1	1	9

Source: Smith (1977), *Botulism: The Organism, Its Toxins, the Disease.* By courtesy of Charles C. Thomas, Publisher, Springfield, Ill.

[a]NA = not available.

Foods primarily responsible for botulism vary considerably among countries, reflecting differing dietary and food preservation practices. In Poland, Germany, and France, canned meats have accounted for the vast majority of outbreaks, whereas in Japan and Russia home-preserved and pickled fish have been most commonly incriminated. In the United States, low-acid canned vegetables, particularly beans, peppers, and mushrooms, have been the most common sources of botulism, with relatively few outbreaks traced to meat or fish. Most instances in all parts of the world are associated with improper home canning or pickling, though the far more serious public health problem of botulism associated with faulty commercial canning does continue to occur.

William H. Barker

Bibliography

Arnon, Stephen S., Damus Karla, and James Chin. 1981. Infant botulism: Epidemiology and relation to sudden infant death syndrome. *Epidemiologic Reviews* 3: 45–66.

Barker, William H., et al. 1977. Type B botulism outbreak caused by a commercial food product. *Journal of the American Medical Association* 237: 456–9.

Merson, Michael H., and V. R. Dowell. 1973. Epidemiologic, clinical and laboratory aspects of wound botulism. *New England Journal of Medicine* 289: 1005–10.

Meyer, K. F. 1956. The status of botulism as a world health problem. *Bulletin of the World Health Organization* 15: 281–98.

Smith, Louis. 1977. *Botulism: The organism, its toxins, the disease*. Springfield, Ill.

U.S. Public Health Service. Centers for Disease Control. 1979. *Botulism and the United States, 1899–1977: Handbook for epidemiologists, clinicians and laboratory workers*. Atlanta.

VIII.20
Brucellosis

Brucellosis, or *undulant fever,* is a zoonotic infection caused in humans by organisms of three main species of the genus *Brucella: Brucella melitensis,* whose natural host is the goat; *Brucella abortus,* transmitted largely from cattle; and *Brucella suis,* transmitted from pigs. Clinically, all three types cause similar infections in humans characterized by intermittent waves of fever that may persist for weeks, often with subsequent relapses and prolonged periods of ill health. The causal relationship between organism and disease was first recorded by David Bruce in Malta in 1887; the name *Malta fever,* which reflects its prevalence among civilians and British troops in that island in the nineteenth century, has been in general use for most of the present century. More recently, other *Brucella* species have been found to be implicated in the human disease, which has been shown to be widespread around the globe. The terms "Malta fever" and "Mediterranean fever" have been gradually replaced by undulant fever, or brucellosis.

Etiology and Epidemiology

The type of brucellosis originally studied in Malta and described by Bruce in 1887 is caused by *B.*
melitensis. It is transmitted to human beings by consumption of milk from infected goats; occasional cases due to contamination of skin with infective material have also been observed. The mode of transmission became established only during the first decade of the twentieth century. In Malta and elsewhere around the Mediterranean littoral, the disease was endemic rather than epidemic during the nineteenth century, its highest incidence occurring during the summer months. Officers of the services, and their wives and children, appeared to be more susceptible than the lower ranks; and likewise among civilians, the professional classes suffered more than the laborers. Records going back to the mid-nineteenth century show very high annual morbidity rates, but low case-fatality rates.

Other areas traditionally affected by undulant fever due to *B. melitensis* show variations in epidemiological patterns. For example, in southeast France where sheep and goats also vastly outnumber cattle, the disease was still widespread in the 1930s. There it had more the character of an occupational disease than of a consumers' disease. The majority of cases occurred in the farming communities and resulted from direct contact with infected animals and manure, although consumption of goats' milk and of fresh cheese prepared from goats' or ewes' milk also played some part.

Present in all countries around the Mediterranean, brucellosis, caused by *B. melitensis,* is also known in India, China, South Africa, and South America. In 1918 Alice Evans suggested that the agent of the cattle disease known as contagious abortion was very similar to *B. melitensis* and might be capable of causing a similar disease in human populations. This was soon confirmed, and cases of brucellosis caused by *B. abortus* transmitted to human beings by consumption of raw cows' milk have occurred worldwide, especially in areas of high incidence of epizootic abortion in cattle.

The third major type of undulant fever is due to *B. suis.* As the name suggests, its natural host is the pig, and the human variety of the disease attacks mainly slaughterers and packers infected by handling contaminated carcasses. In most cases, *B. suis* invades the human host through skin lesions, although airborne infection is also thought to be possible. The disease in pigs, and in human beings, is far less common than its counterparts in goats and in cattle, and therefore, undulant fever in human beings due to *B. suis* has been observed mainly in hog-raising areas of the American Midwest, Brazil, and the Argentine. Sporadic cases of undulant fever in

Alaskan Eskimos have resulted from a type of *B. suis* infecting wild reindeer.

Distribution and Incidence

The three main types of *Brucella* infection in human populations are widespread around the globe in areas dependent in one way or another on those domestic animals that are the main hosts of the respective organisms. Undulant fever caused by *B. melitensis* follows the distribution of goats all along the Mediterranean littoral (Malta or Mediterranean fever) as well as in parts of China, India, South Africa, and South America, although pasteurization of milk has substantially reduced its incidence during the second half of the twentieth century. The same applies to *B. abortus* infections. Contagious abortion of cattle, and with it the disease in humans, has been almost completely eradicated from several countries in northern Europe where the incidence is now very low. The true incidence of *B. abortus* is difficult to assess because it has low pathogenicity and often causes latent infections.

In the United States, brucellosis is still not uncommon, the causative organism being, in order of importance, *B. abortus*, *B. suis*, and lastly *B. melitensis*. Most cases occur sporadically, although occasional minor outbreaks have been reported. Also, the situation is constantly changing as a result, in part, to various eradication programs.

Bruce's discovery of the causal agent had no immediate impact on the incidence of Malta fever; only after identification of the mode of transmission was there a dramatic fall in number of cases, first in the British armed services in Malta where supplies of goats' milk to the troops were curtailed by 1906. In an island where goats are the almost exclusive source of milk, control of the disease in the civilian population was a much greater problem. It was achieved, in Malta and elsewhere, only after World War II, when pasteurization became generally accepted.

Immunology

The failure of the immune systems of both animals and humans to deal quickly and decisively with *B. melitensis* and *B. abortus* accounts for the persistence of infection and thus frequent cases of long duration. Evans, who first drew attention to the similarities between the two organisms, contracted a laboratory infection with the disease in 1922 and suffered recurring episodes of debilitating undulant fever, alternative with periods of apparent recovery, for more than 20 years (in spite of this she lived, after final recovery, until the age of 94).

B. abortus, in particular, can give rise to latent infection, leading to latent immunity, which occurs more frequently in persons exposed to milk infection over a period of time than in those suddenly exposed to heavy doses of infective material. This may help to explain the low rate of clinical disease in veterinarians, who as a group show immunologic evidence of exceptionally high levels of response to erstwhile infection.

Vaccination is possible against *B. abortus* in cattle and against *B. melitensis* in sheep and goats, but in human beings it is still at an experimental stage. Some knowledge of the immunogenic constituents of the bacillus has become available since the 1960s, but the animal vaccines developed thus far are too toxic for use in humans. In Britain a free calf vaccination service was introduced by the Ministry of Agriculture in 1962.

Clinical Manifestations and Pathology

Undulant fever due to *B. melitensis* is essentially a septicemia or blood poisoning characterized by an irregular temperature curve with intermittent waves of fever, usually lasting for 10 to 30 days. Although case fatality rates are low, the protracted character of many cases makes it a serious and debilitating illness. Its duration varies; it may be only a few days, or it may last as long as a year. Subsequent relapses may occur over a period of several years, accompanied by general ill health alternating with periods of apparent recovery. Symptoms included weakness, muscular pain, nocturnal sweats, anorexia, chills, and nervous irritability. Recorded postmortem appearances include congestion and enlargement of the liver and hypertrophy of the spleen; cultures taken from both these organs have been found to be positive for *B. melitensis* in 100 percent of cases.

B. abortus appears to be less capable than *B. melitensis* of producing clinical cases in humans, but more likely to give rise to latent infection, especially in veterinarians. Once established, however, the clinical disease seems to develop in similar fashion. It lasts an average of 13 weeks and may become chronic. *B. abortus* can also cause a short influenza-like illness, and sometimes a persistent low intermittent fever. In rare cases, infection in pregnant women has been followed by abortion.

Undulant fever caused by *B. suis* is clinically similar to the above types.

History and Geography

Among the fevers plaguing the Mediterranean peoples since antiquity, a low type with regular remissions or intermissions has been recorded since the time of the Hippocratic writings. Its geographic origins are indicated by many synonyms of which the best known are Malta fever and Mediterranean fever, although other variants involve Naples, Constantinople, Crete, and Gibraltar. A differential description of Malta fever as distinct from other fevers was first given by J. A. Marston in 1863; he called it "gastric remittent fever" and described several cases including his own ("a mild case of gastric remittent fever"). In 1887, Bruce, a surgeon attached to the Malta garrison like Marston before him, recorded his discovery of a small microorganism in the spleen of fatal cases. He proceeded to establish its causal role and called it *Micrococcus melitensis,* although in the 1920s it was changed to *Brucella melitensis* in his honor. Returning from duty in Malta, Bruce taught at the Army Medical College at Netley; among his students was Matthew Louis Hughes who, posted to Malta in 1890, enthusiastically embraced Bruce's interest in the prevailing fever. He wrote, both alone and in collaboration with Bruce, several papers dealing with the disease during the next decade, until he died under enemy fire while tending casualties in South Africa at Ladysmith in December 1899. It was Hughes (1897) who published a definitive clinical description of Malta fever, which is still quoted today as a model of its kind.

Since the time of Bruce, and because of the presence of British troops in the island, the disease and its epidemiology have received particular attention in Malta, culminating in the work of the British Mediterranean Fever Commission, which began reporting in 1905. During this work, Themistocles Zammit was able to establish the presence of the disease in local goats and the role of goats' milk in transmitting the disease to the human population. The results of his research caused the British army and navy to prevent troops from drinking goats' milk; within a year the disease had all but disappeared from the British forces in Malta (see Figure VIII.20.1). As already mentioned, for social and economic reasons control of the disease in the civilian population proved far more difficult to achieve; only the advent of pasteurization could eventually solve this problem, although it should be noted that the disease in goats is still resisting control.

B. melitensis infections had been observed and described in the late 1800s, following Robert Koch's epoch-making demonstration of the methods for isolating and identifying specific disease agents. It was Bruce, however, who isolated the causal microorganism in 1887. Nearly two more decades were to elapse

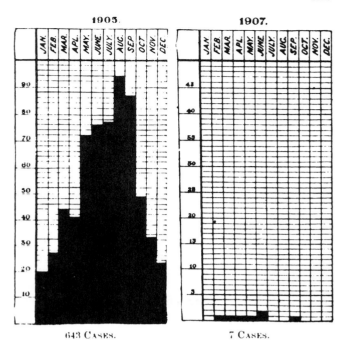

Figure VIII.20.1. Graphs illustrating the dramatic reduction in the incidence of brucellosis in the British garrison in Malta from 1905 to 1907, following the ban on the use of goat's milk. (From D. Bruce 1908.)

before the goat was identified as the natural host of *B. melitensis* and the mechanism of transmission to humans became clear. In the case of *B. abortus* infections, the historical sequence of events was rather different. The disease in cattle had been described by several authors during the first half of the nineteenth century. In the context of the times some considered it contagious, others not. Its transmissibility was demonstrated in pregnant cattle in 1878; and just before the turn of the century Bernhard Bang in Copenhagen was able to isolate and identify the causal agent. It was only in 1918, however, that Evans noted a close morphological and biochemical similarity between *B. melitensis* and *B. abortus;* within a few years *B. abortus* had been shown to be pathogenic for human beings and to give rise to cases of undulant fever in many areas around the world where raw cows' milk rather than goats' milk was consumed, and where epizootic abortion of cattle was a common occurrence.

Last of the major types of undulant fever to attract attention was that caused by *B. suis.* The first case to be diagnosed appears to have been in the United States in 1922, although even then the identity of the agent was not immediately recognized. Clinically (and bacteriologically) the disease is similar to the two other major types although it is less extensively distributed in either pigs or humans. *B. suis* infection of swine first began to cause concern in the large hog-raising areas of the midwestern United States in the 1930s. The disease has since been reported to be present in a number of other countries, but cases appear to be mostly sporadic, with only a few recognized outbreaks in the United States, and one in Denmark in 1929.

Lise Wilkinson

Bibliography

Bruce, David. 1908. *The extinction of Malta fever.* London.

Dudley, S. F. 1931. Some lessons of the distribution of infectious diseases in the Royal Navy. Lecture III. The history of undulant fever in the Royal Navy. *Lancet* i: 683–91.

Duguid, J. P., B. P. Marmion, and R. H. A. Swain. 1978. *Mackie and McCartney's medical microbiology.* Edinburgh.

Evans, Alice. 1918. Further studies on *Bacterium abortus* and related bacteria II. A comparison of *Bacterium abortus* with *Bacterium bronchisepticus* and with the organism which causes Malta fever. *Journal of Infectious Diseases* 22:580–93.

Hughes, G. W. G., and M. H. Hughes. 1969. Matthew Louis Hughes and undulant fever. *Journal of the Royal Army Medical Corps* 115: 198–203.

Hughes, M. L. 1897. *Mediterranean, Malta or undulant fever.* London.

Huntley, B. E., R. N. Philip, and J. E. Maynard. 1963. Survey of brucellosis in Alaska. *Journal of Infectious Diseases* 112: 100–6.

Hutyra, Franz, J. Marek, and R. Manninger. 1938. *Special pathology and therapeutics of the diseases of domestic animals.* London.

Marston, Jeffery Allen. 1863. Report on fever (Malta). *Army Medical Department Statistical Report* 3: 486–521.

Meyer, M. E. 1964. Species identity and epidemiology of *Brucella* strains isolated from Alaskan Eskimos. *Journal of Infectious Diseases* 114: 169–73.

Roux, J. 1972. Les Vaccinations dans les brucelloses humaines et animales. *Bulletin de l'Institut Pasteur* 70: 145–202.

Thomsen, Axel. 1934. *Brucella infection in swine: Studies from an epizootic in Denmark 1929–1932.* Copenhagen.

Wilson, Graham, and Geoffrey Smith. 1983–4. Brucella infections of man and animals. In *Bacterial diseases,* Vol. 3 of *Principles of bacteriology, virology and immunity,* ed. G. R. Smith, W. W. C. Topley, and G. S. Wilson, 141–69. London.

World Health Organization. 1964. Expert committee on brucellosis. World Health Organization Technical Report Series, No. 289.

VIII.21
Bubonic Plague

Plague has often been used as a synonym for *pestilence,* which refers nonspecifically to any acute epidemic accompanied by high mortality. But the term also refers to the recurrent waves of bubonic plague punctuating European history from 1348 to 1720. Bubonic plague epidemics occurred when *Yersinia pestis,* a rodent disease, was communicated to humans through the bite of infected fleas. Humans have exceedingly poor immune defenses to this organism, and within 6 days of infection most victims develop a grossly swollen lymph node, a bubo, signifying the body's attempt to contain and arrest multiplication of *Y. pestis.* On the average, around 60 percent of those infected died within a week after the appearance of the bubo. Thus bubonic plague brought high and dramatic rates of mortality when it extended into human communities.

Distribution and Incidence

With the historically ironic exception of western Europe, *Y. pestis* today occurs naturally throughout the world among the wide variety of rodents and lagomorphs (i.e., rabbits and related species). Some of the more than 300 rodent species affected are relatively resistant to disease from *Y. pestis* and can survive and reproduce while technically infected by the organism. *Y. pestis* infects new animals either because fleas transmit it or because the microbe is shed and survives in the protective microclimate of warm rodent burrows. Some literature refers to this part of the plague cycle as "sylvatic" plague, or "enzootic" plague.

The "disease," then, is not always a disease, and it is ecologically very complex. Indeed, it is occasional ecological change or disturbance that brings susceptible rodents into contact with *Y. pestis.* Historically the most important of these rodents is considered to be *Rattus rattus,* the common, commensal black or brown house rat, that literally "shares man's table." When infected by *Y. pestis* these susceptible animals die quickly of an overwhelming infection, with blood levels of the microbe so high that their rat fleas imbibe large numbers of organisms.

The oriental rat flea *Xenopsylla cheopis* and the human flea *Pulex irritans* are thought to be historically important arthropod vectors transmitting "epizootic" plague to humans. *X. cheopis* is an efficient vector because a bend in its feeding tube, or proventriculus, creates a location for growth of *Y. pestis,* such that the flea becomes "blocked," unable to swallow a full blood meal. Attempting to dislodge this bolus or wad, the flea infects new mammalian hosts. Other fleas clear *Y. pestis* more quickly, so that only the excreta of the flea, or the crushing of its body, will infect. *P. irritans* had an important historical role because it is a flea that feeds indifferently upon both humans and the common house rat.

Human plague usually arises after an epizootic plague has produced high mortality among susceptible rodents, when infected fleas, deprived of rodent hosts, begin to feed on humans. Although some historians speak of "endemic plague," no such phenomenon can exist. Humans do not normally carry the *Y. pestis* organism, and thus cannot infect fleas or otherwise pass the disease to new hosts. For human communities, plague is an acute infection ultimately derived from infected rodents.

In areas of the world today where plague routinely infects resistant rodents, ecologists and public health officials try to monitor the passage of the disease to susceptible species. In these regions – the American southwest, south central Eurasia, and Southeast Asia – humans who are likely to encounter infected animals or their fleas must be revaccinated often, for human immunity to *Y. pestis* is short-lived.

Immunity

Yersinia pestis was once called *Pasturella pestis,* a name that has persisted because it was used in much of the older, widely consulted, historical literature about European plagues. In 1971, the name was changed in part to honor Alexandre Yersin, a French microbiologist and student of Louis Pasteur, who, working in Southeast Asia during the late nineteenth century outbreak of plague, successfully cultured the microorganism.

Other members of the *Pasturella* family are rarely pathogenic in humans and do not provide cross-immunization with *Y. pestis.* Two organisms, however, have been added to the *Yersinia* group: *Yersinia pseudotuberculosis,* which causes a mild respiratory infection, and *Yersinia enterocolitica,* which causes a gastroenteritis that can be life-threatening in very young children. Infection with either of the other *Yersinia* species establishes some cross-immunity with *Y. pestis,* because they have shared antigens.

The antigens, or components of the organism, which stimulate an immune response, can vary in virulence, such that vaccines can be created that are very mild plague strains. *Y. pestis* causes severe human disease when it contains an envelope protein facilitating its entry into cells and other antigens that impede the body's white blood cells' attempt to kill infected cells. *Y. pestis* can liberate both endotoxins and exotoxins, leading to circulatory collapse. These combined activities stimulate, and can defeat, both cellular and humoral immunity to plague, and explain why the disease can carry extremely high-case fatality rates. With a typical virulent strain of the bacterium, over 60 percent of all infected humans untreated will die within 10 days of infection. If the organism reaches the lungs, there is even less chance the person will survive. A victim whose lungs become infected during the course of bubonic plague can cough out highly virulent, encapsulated organisms, which are rapidly absorbed on the mucous membranes of any nearby, susceptible person. This can lead to "primary" pneumonic plague in which the bubonic plague of disease is bypassed and spreads directly from human to human. When this has occurred, case fatality rates have been close to 100 percent.

Clinical Manifestations and Diagnosis

Once a human is infected with *Y. pestis,* the organism rapidly replicates at the site of the flea bite. This area can subsequently become necrotic, where dead tissue blackens to produce a carbuncle or necrotic pustule often called a "carbone" in many historical accounts. But in many cases the progress of infection is too rapid for this to happen. The lymphatic system attempts to drain the infection to the regional lymph node, where organisms and infected cells can be phagocytized (ingested by macrophages and white blood cells). That node becomes engorged with blood and cellular debris, creating the grossly swollen bubo. Because infected fleas usually bite an exposed area of the body, often a limb or the face, the location of the subsequent bubo is often visible. Frequent sites are the groin, the axilla, or the cervical lymph nodes.

But drainage can occur to an internal lymph node, or the infection can proceed too rapidly for the lymphatic system to effect a defense. In the latter case, "septicemic" or blood-borne plague has occurred, seeding the organism quickly in many organs. Victims of septicemic plague become rapidly moribund and often develop neither eschar nor bubos, although the more usual clinical course is the formation of a bubo, described in historical accounts as reaching the size of an egg, orange, or even grapefruit. The area is inflamed, boggy or doughy to the touch, and exquisitely painful. Patients often demanded that a physician or surgeon incise and drain the bubo, a process that could have liberated infective organisms.

The bubo often appears within 4 to 6 days after infection, and because of the multiple ways in which *Y. pestis* is virulent to humans, disease progresses quickly after this point. In about 5 to 15 percent of the cases the lungs are infected, but more often a high fever with headache and mental disorientation are characteristic symptoms. Occasionally circulatory collapse and hemorrhagic sepsis occurs, blackening the surface of the body. Death typically occurs within 4 to 6 days after the onset of symptoms. In the past, a diagnosis of plague might have been made on the basis of this rapid clinical progression from health to death alone, although clearly this could have been caused by countless other conditions. But the acute formation of a bubo, visible in 60 percent of bubonic plague victims, is pathognomonic of plague, meaning that no other disease commonly causes this reaction.

History and Geography

Most of the historical literature of plague identifies three lengthy time periods when bubonic plague repeatedly assaulted human communities. The first known cycle of widespread human plague occurred during late Greco-Roman antiquity. Byzantine historian Procopius of Caesarea described the acute lymphadenopathy well: "Those in whom the bubo grew to the largest size and suppurated while ripening usually survived, no doubt because the malignant property of the already weakened boil was annihilated" (quoted in Biraben and Le Goff 1975). Procopius described the devastating epidemic of 542 in Constantinople, which was dubbed the "Plague of Justinian" because of his dramatic account. The wave of epidemic reached western Europe by 547, which was also powerfully described by Bishop Gregory of Tours. Virulent, epidemic plague recurred throughout the Mediterranean for the next 200 years.

The second cycle of plague, at least in its early stages, is often referred to as the Black Death and is treated in this work as a separate entry, for certainly it is the most heavily studied of the plague cycles. Beginning about 1300, the cycle is generally considered to have ended at about 1800, although the ending date can be disputed. This manifestation of the disease took a very heavy toll in the Middle East as well as in Europe and appears to have also invaded Asia. It has held a special fascination for Europeans,

however, and any bibliography assembled on important European works dealing with this second cycle would contain several hundred listings.

This is the case because the plague has been viewed as pivotal in so many areas of historical inquiry. Surely it was to some significant extent responsible for the stagnant demographic performance in Europe prior to the mid-eighteenth century, and surely, too, the plague stimulated new and important public health efforts in the great urban centers of Europe. In addition, the continued presence of the disease in Europe presents a mystery because at no other time in history was the disease able to survive in northern Europe without constant reintroduction from the Middle East. Finally, over the course of a half millennium the plague was the source of inspiration for numerous literary works, and more than a few on medicine.

Historians frequently credit public health measures devised during the fifteenth through the seventeenth centuries to combat the plague with some mitigation of the disease and its ultimate disappearance. However, in the light of modern medical knowledge of bubonic plague, it is clear that such measures – quarantine of well individuals, isolation of the sick and their household contacts, large pesthouses or lazarettoes, and even the elaboration of a theory of contagion – would have little effect on its course.

Certainly the most important questions about these 500 years of plague in Europe have to do with its disappearance and demographic consequences. In the latter case, it is important to realize that much of the mortality credited to the plague was due to its indirect impact, rather than infection. When an epidemic struck, panic ensued and this alone, by bringing an end to normal sanitary and social services while precipitating headlong flight, would have taken a significant number of lives, as would isolating both ill and well in hospitals and pesthouses. Chief among these victims would have been the very young, the very old, and the economically disadvantaged.

Beginning in the early eighteenth century, Europe was increasingly protected from plague invasions from Ottoman lands by a staunch Austrian barrier. Manned by over 100,000 men and featuring numerous quarantine and checkpoint stations, this famous sanitary cordon limited both trade and human traffic, which may have helped to spare Europe from the third or most recent cycle of the plague that seems to have had its beginning in central Asia about the middle of the eighteenth century (Benedict 1988).

From there the plague spread to the Yunnan region of China and simultaneously to northern India and, then, aided by rapid sea transportation, radiated globally from Hong Kong, Bombay, and Calcutta.

But if Europe was bypassed, the Americas were not. Rather, along with Australia and eastern Africa, North and South America were infected for the first time, and by the early years of the nineteenth century some regions of the Western Hemisphere were experiencing relatively minor, but nonetheless panic-inspiring, epidemics. Those that struck San Francisco are among the best documented in this pandemic cycle, although the disease killed millions in India and in African countries.

If the Americas and Australia did not suffer greatly from this third cycle of the plague, one consequence was that the disease did establish itself among the rodents and lagomorphs of these New Worlds. In North America the geographic extent of the plague has subsequently widened each year, and sporadic cases of human plague claim 8 to 15 victims annually despite the effectiveness of therapy with antibiotics such as tetracycline and streptomycin. In the Americas, as elsewhere, smoldering enzootic foci of plague demand a constant global effort in surveillance and control.

Ann G. Carmichael

Bibliography

Appleby, Andrew B. 1980. The disappearance of plague: A continuing puzzle. *Economic History Review* 33: 161–73.

Benedict, Carol. 1988. Bubonic plague in nineteenth-century China. *Modern China* 14: 107–55.

Biraben, Jean-Noël. 1975–6. *Les Hommes et la peste*, 2 vols. Paris.

Biraben, Jean-Noël, and Jacques Le Goff. 1975. The plague in the early Middle Ages, trans. E. Forster and P. M. Ranum. In *Biology of man in history: Selections from the Annales; Economies, Sociétés, Civilisations.* Baltimore.

Carmichael, Ann G. 1986. *Plague and the poor in Renaissance Florence.* New York.

Ell, Stephen R. 1980. Interhuman transmission of medieval plague. *Bulletin of the History of Medicine* 54: 497–510.

Hirst, L. Fabian. 1953. *The conquest of plague: A study of the evolution of epidemiology.* Oxford.

Link, Vernon. 1953. *A history of plague in the United States of America.* U.S.P.H.S. Public Health Monograph No. 26. Washington, D.C.

1977. *The plague reconsidered: A new look at its origins and effects in 16th and 17th century England.* Local Population Studies Supplement. Derbyshire.

Pollitzer, R. 1954. *Plague.* Geneva, WHO.

Rothenberg, Gunther E. 1973. The Austrian sanitary cordon and the control of the bubonic plague: 1710–1871. *Journal of the History of Medicine and Allied Sciences* 28: 15–23.

Shadwell, Arthur, and Harriet L. Hennessy. 1910. Plague. In *Encyclopedia Britannica*, 11th edition.

Shrewsbury, J. F. D. 1970. *A history of bubonic plague in the British Isles.* Cambridge.

Slack, Paul. 1985. *The impact of plague in Tudor and Stuart England.* London.

Winslow, Charles-Edward Amory. 1980. *The conquest of epidemic disease.* Reprint of 1943 edition. Madison, Wis.

VIII.22
Carrión's Disease

Carrión's disease is an infectious disease caused by a microorganism of the genus *Bartonella*. Two species have been described, the *bacilliformis* type and the *verrugiformis* type. These bacteria are parasites of human red blood and histiocytic cells. The *bacilliformis* type produces two stages of the disease, a febrile acute hemolytic anemia known as "Oroya fever," followed by a granulomatous mucocutaneous eruption known as "Verruga Peruana." The *verrugiformis* type produces only the verrucose stage.

Etiology and Epidemiology

B. bacilliformis are pleomorphic bacteria, well stained with the Romanovsky stain. In the red blood cells and in the histiocytic cells, the bartonella assumes a rodlike (bacillus) or coccoid shape, 1 to 3 microns in size (Figure VIII.22.1). The electron microscope shows the flagella of the bartonella. It grows well in liquid and in semisolid blood media. The human bartonella is closely related to the animal bacteria *Hemobartonella*, *Eperythrozoon*, and *Grahamella*.

In 1913 Charles Townsend identified the sandfly *Phlebotomus verrucarum* as the insect vector of the disease. The female is the only transmitter, and the transmission occurs during the night. Carrión's disease is a rural disease, and, like yellow fever, it does not need a human reservoir because the bartonella lives in the small animals in the area.

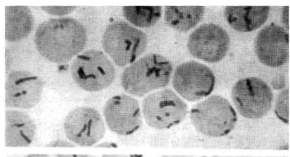

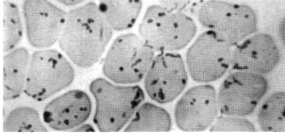

Figure VIII.22.1. *Bartonella bacilliformis* within red blood cells stained by Giemsa and Romanovsky stains. (From O. Urteaga-Ballón and J. Calderón. 1972. *Dermatología Clínica,* by permission of the author.)

Immunology (Experimental Transmission)

Between 1948 and 1950, the author and collaborators conducted a series of experimental transmission on human volunteers. Thirty healthy men were inoculated with parasitic blood through subcutaneous, intramuscular, and intravenous routes. None of the volunteers developed the disease, and the blood culture remained negative after more than 120 days. Another four volunteers who had been splenectomized for other reasons were infected with the same inoculum. All of them developed the disease, with bartonellas evident in the erythrocytes and blood cultures positive. Antibiotics halted the parasitism, and the volunteers recovered immediately.

After our experiments, three of the former healthy volunteers were exposed to the bite of the insect in the verrucogenous zone. None of them developed the disease. They appeared to have developed immunity as a result of the previous live inoculation. Later on, 10 workers out of a group of 100 were inoculated with attenuated live bartonellas in order to test a vaccine against the disease. None of them developed any symptoms, and the blood cultures remained negative. Meanwhile 45 of their companions who were not vaccinated developed the disease.

Our conclusions were as follows: First, the natural infection of the bartonellosis occurs only through the sandfly vector. Second, the inoculation from a sick person to a healthy person does not effect transmission of the disease. Rather the inoculation of a live germ appears to produce immunity. Third and last, direct inoculation of the *B. baciliformis* into a splenectomized patient produces the disease, with bartonellas evident within the erythrocytes and blood cultures testing positive.

Clinical Manifestations

There are two stages in Carrión's disease: the "anemic stage," characterized by an acute febrile anemia with bartonellas in the red blood cells; and the "verrucose stage," characterized by a disseminated verrucous eruption in the skin and mucous membranes. The anemia is of the macrocytic and hypochromic types, and, in severe infection, erythrocyte levels plummet to less than a million in a few days. The parasitic index in these cells reaches 80 to 100 percent.

The onset is abrupt, with fever, chills, and generalized osteal pain. Bone marrow hyperplasia, reticulocytosis, and jaundice are observed, with an increase of bilirubin in the blood and urine. The blood culture is positive, even in the earliest days of the anemia. The verrucose stage is characterized by a diffuse generalized granulomatous eruption on the mucocutaneous integument. Usually this phase is separated from the anemic stage by an asymptomatic interval of several months to a year or more. There are several types of eruption. The first, called the "miliary form," is a profuse, homogeneous, small intradermic eruption, which resembles multiple disseminated hemangioma. In the second, the "nodular form," nodules appear primarily on the arms and the legs; they can be deep in the dermis or prominent on the surface of skin; some are ulcerated and bloody. The third type, the "mular form," has pseudotumoral lesions 1/2 to 1 inch in diameter which are seated in the deep tissue. The eruption become painful only when a secondary infection develops or with increased bleeding (Figure VIII.22.2A–C).

In the *verrugiformis* type, the clinical picture is that of a diffuse granulomatous eruption similar to the *bacilliformis* type, but less intense. One special feature of the *verrugiformis* type is that the eruption can recur two or more times during a lifetime; some of these patients of endemic areas become latently infected.

Pathology

The main pathogenic feature is the intracellular reproduction of the bartonella inside the cytoplasm of

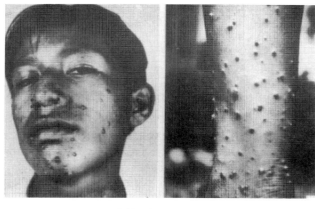

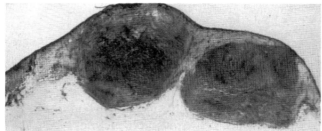

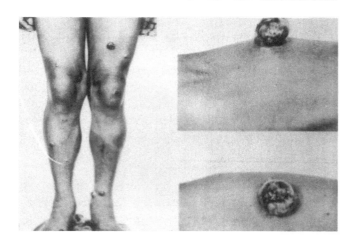

Figure VIII.22.2. Verrucose eruptions: (top) miliary form, diffuse and generalized; (middle) nodular form, two intradermic nodules; (bottom) mular form. In the pseudotumoral eruption (bottom), the granulomatous lesions are seated in the deep tissue; sometimes the eruption becomes painful when a secondary infection develops or when bleeding increases. (From O. Urteaga-Ballón and J. Calderón. 1972. *Dermatología Clínica,* by permission of the author.)

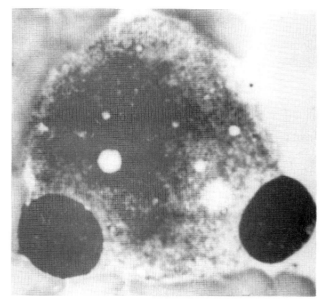

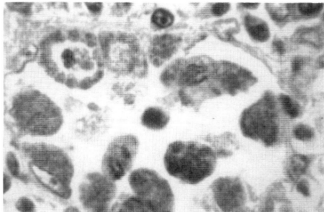

Figure VIII.22.3. Intracellular reproduction cycle of the *Bartonella bacilliformis* (top) the cytoplasm of a histiocytic bone marrow cell, and (bottom) the endothelial cells of a lymph node. (From O. Urteaga-Ballón and J. Calderón. 1972. *Dermatología Clínica,* by permission of the author.)

the endothelial cell. Microscopically these cells are swollen with tremendous numbers of bacteria, which push the nucleus of the cell eccentrically (Figure VIII.22.3A,B). The pressure resulting from the multiplication of the bartonellas causes the cell membrane to rupture, releasing millions of bacteria,

which then start a new intracellular colonization in other endothelial cells. Also, the bartonellas act as parasites on the peripheral erythrocytes, inducing the anemia syndrome.

Histopathological study of the anemia of Carrión's disease reveals massive hyperplasia of the phagocytic reticuloendothelial cells in the spleen, lymph nodes, liver, and bone marrow. Erythrophagocytosis is responsible for the anemia. The macrophages initiate the destruction of the parasitized erythrocytes. The extraordinary phagocytic hyperplasia characterizes the cellular immunoresponse of this disease. The macrophages contain, in their cytoplasm, 2 to 10

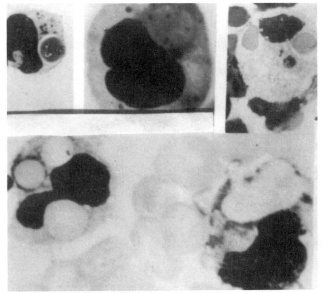

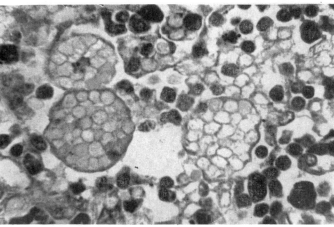

Figure VIII.22.4. Erythrophagocytosis of parasitized erythrocytes in (top) peripheral blood; and (bottom) spleen. Bottom panel, showing extraordinary phagocytic hyperplasia, and macrophages containing more than 10 erythrocytes, illustrates the mechanism responsible for the anemia. (From O. Urteaga-Ballón and J. Calderón. 1972. *Dermatología Clínica,* by permission of the author.)

erythrocytes with bartonellas (Figures VIII.22.4 A,B). Severe cases show thrombosis and infarction in the spleen, centrolobular necrosis of the liver, and lung congestion.

At the end of the anemia stage, an immunoresponse is mounted against the active basilar bartonellas, which then are converted to the resistant coccoid stage. This is the most dangerous period of the disease. The "anoxemia" is extremely severe, with the red blood cell count falling to below 1 million. In at least 30 percent of the cases, the untreated patient dies after physical collapse. Another 40 percent die from secondary complications. The nonspecific immunoreaction decreases to the "anergic stages," but some quiescent chronic infection in the patient will exacerbate to an acute stage. The most frequent complications are salmonellosis, tuberculosis, malaria, and amebiasis in carrier cases.

From the clinical point of view, the patient has recovered. He or she appears to be normal, but the bartonellas still live in the adventitial cells surrounding the subcutaneous capillaries. Blood and bone marrow cultures are still positive. There is an unstable balance between the intracellular bacteria and the immune response. In time, when this equilibrium breaks down, the bartonellas start a new cycle of reproduction in the histiocytes. The second stage of the disease appears as a disseminated verrucose eruption. This histiocytic proliferation, with the in situ presence of the microorganism, is a clear example of cellular immunity. Sometimes the histiocytic proliferation is so great that the lesion appears like a tumor, a histiocytic lymphoma.

The histopathology of the granulomatous phase shows an angioblastic proliferation with large, pale histiocytes and endothelial cells, some filled with coccobacillus bartonellas. The rupture of these cells results in the dissemination of the bartonellas through the skin, with the appearance of new verrucose eruptions. The eruptive phase tends to heal spontaneously without scars.

Diagnosis and Treatment

The diagnosis is made upon a finding of bartonellas within the red blood cells in acutely anemic patients. Blood and bone marrow cultures are the most useful diagnostic test for carrier cases in the endemic zones. The eruptive phase is easily identified with some clinical experience, but surgical biopsy is required to show the bartonella inside the histiocytes in the Giemsa stain. The cultured tissue is positive.

Before the advent of antibiotics the mortality rate from Carrión's disease was very high. In acute severe cases, 30 to 70 percent of patients died in the anemic phase, either directly from the bartonella infection or from secondary complications. Antibiotics have a powerful antibactericidal effect; the anemia is arrested, and blood regeneration starts immediately. Until now, chloromycetin has been the most effective antibiotic in the anemic stage, because it is also specific for salmonellosis, the most serious complication. Streptomycin is the ideal antibiotic during the eruptive phase. In 4 to 5 days, the eruption shrinks and the verrucose nodes subside without any scar.

According to our experiments a specific vaccine must be prepared with attenuated live bartonellas. However, it must be kept in mind that the live germ vaccine will produce the acute anemic phase in splenectomized patients.

History and Geography

Carrión's disease was probably depicted thousands of years ago in the pottery of the ancient Peruvian civilization. The disease flourished jointly with malaria and cutaneous leishmaniasis in the inter-Andean valleys of western South America. The focus of the endemic transmission is in Peru, although some cases exist in Colombia and Ecuador. The endemic areas of the disease are confined to rural areas in narrow valleys where the elevation is 2,100 to 7,500 feet.

The disease in both its forms was probably noticed and described during the Spanish Conquest. It attracted worldwide attention only in 1870, when an epidemic of the acute febrile form of the disease killed thousands of workers during the construction of a railroad from Lima to Oroya. In 1885, Daniel Carrión, a Peruvian medical student, contracted the disease by self-inoculation with verruga and died of Oroya fever, thus establishing the connection between the two conditions. In 1909 Alberto Barton, a Peruvian physician, described the presence of live organisms in the red blood corpuscles of victims of Oroya fever, and a decade later these findings were confirmed by R. P. Strong and his colleagues (1913). They, however, felt that despite the work of Carrión, Oroya fever and verruga peruana were caused by two distinct agents. The controversy was resolved by H. Noguchi and T. Battistine (1926), who reported the pair to be different manifestations of the same disease. M. Hertig in 1942 definitively described both the disease and its vector.

Oscar Urteaga-Ballón

Bibliography

Aldana, L., and O. Urteaga-Ballón. 1947. Bartonellosis post-esplenectomia. *Archivos Peruanos de Patologia y Clínica* 1: 289–312.

Barton, A. 1909. Descripción de elementos endo globulares hallados en los enfermos de fiebre verrucosa. *La Crónica Médica Lima* 26: 7–17.

Noguchi, H., and T. Battistine. 1926. The etiology of Oroya fever. I. Cultivation of *"Bartonella baciliformis."* *Journal of Experimental Medicine* 49: 851–64.

Strong, R., et al. 1913. *Report of the first expedition to South America*. Cambridge.

Townsend, Charles. 1913. La titira es transmisora de la verruga. *La Crónica Médica Lima* 30: 588–600.

Urteaga-Ballón, O., and J. Calderón. 1965. Ciclo biológico de reproducción de la *"Bartonella baciliformis"* en los tejidos de los pacientes de verruga peruana o enfermedad de Carrión. *Archivos Peruanos de Patología y Clínica* 19: 1–77.

1972. Verruga Peruana o enfermedad de Carrión. In *Dermatología Clínica*, ed. José Luis Cortés, Cap. 54, 2d edition. Tlacotalpan, México.

VIII.23
Catarrh

Catarrh is now regarded as inflammation of the mucous membranes, especially of the air passages, together with the production of a mucoid exudate. Simple though this definition is, it bears evident traces of the history of the disease.

History

The name derives from Hippocrates' use of *katarrhoos,* "a flowing down" of humors from the head. In that use, the term was probably not yet technical, and so akin to such a Latin word as *defluxio*. In commenting on Hippocrates, however, Galen distinguishes from a general "downflowing" a more precise meaning of "catarrh" – that is, a defluxion from the head *to the lungs,* producing a hoarseness of voice and coughing.

The Greek word became *catarrhus* in Latin and a technical term with, increasingly, Galen's meaning attached to it. Although it is tempting to identify *catarrhus* and catarrh, we have to remember that for Galen and doctors down to the seventeenth century, *catarrhus* could not be defined without reference to Galenic pathology. *Catarrhus* was a process in which the brain, preternaturally affected by cold, produced a qualitatively unbalanced humor in excessive quantity that passed down through the pores in the palate and by way of the trachea to the lungs. This unspoken assumption behind the name is paralleled by that behind the modern definition: We make the assumption that the "inflammation" of the definition is due to infection by an organism. It is the identity of the organism that gives us the ontology of the disease. A similar situation existed in all historical periods; that is to say, definitions of disease have always carried with them some part of a theory of causation. (Purely empirical accounts of disease are descriptions of symptoms.) To put it another way, disease in Western medicine has traditionally been seen as disordered function. But function is a process, and knowledge of it depends on knowledge of how the body works.

In the eighteenth and nineteenth centuries, there were a number of different so-called systems of physiological knowledge, in each of which what was indicated by a single disease-name was seen differently. For example Franciscus de Le Boë (F. Sylvius), as an iatrochemist, divided catarrhs into groups distinguished by the chemical qualities of the humor produced. As a hydraulically inclined mechanist, Hermann Boerhaave thought of catarrh in terms of obstruction of the small vessels, which caused swelling. Indeed, his most frequent use of the term was as an adjective to describe angina. "Angina" was any difficulty in breathing, and catarrhous angina was the result of swollen membranes. Although membranes also played an important part in the new tissue-pathology of early nineteenth-century Paris, the Parisian view of the body, and therefore disease, was again different. Marie François Bichat had stressed the sympathies between membranes and their ability to secrete and imbibe the fluids of the cavity they lined. To this were added the new techniques of physical diagnosis by percussion and stethoscope.

Catarrh again became a disease of membranes, of excessive secretion, and of fluids moving audibly in their cavities. Some Bichatian sympathy of membranes seems to lie behind the early nineteenth-century notion of a catarrh of the urinary bladder. This opinion is recorded in R. Hooper's *Lexicon Medicum,* which also distinguishes sharply common catarrh, which is a cold and particularly a cold in the head, from epidemic catarrh, which is identified with influenza. The modern meaning is derived from the former.

Roger K. French

Bibliography

Blakiston's Gould medical dictionary. 1972. 3d edition. New York.

Boerhaave, H. 1728. *Aphorismi de cognoscendis et curandis morbis.* Paris.

Hooper, R. 1848. *Lexicon medicum, or medical dictionary.* London.

Le Boë, Franciscus de (F. Sylvius). 1693. *Opera medica.* Geneva.

Maulitz, R. 1987. *Morbid appearances.* Cambridge.

Sweiten, G. van. 1792. *Indicis in swieteni commentariorum tomos undecim supplementum.* Wurtzburg.

VIII.24
Cestode Infections

Cestodes or tapeworms are a class of flatworms in the phylum Platyhelminthes. The adult stages of four species and the larval stages of two are important parasites of humankind. Several other species, most of which normally parasitize other vertebrates, can also cause human disease.

K. David Patterson

VIII.25
Chagas' Disease

Chagas' disease (American; trypanosomiasis, trypanosomiasis cruzi) is an illness of the Americas which can take the form of either an acute, febrile, generalized infection or a chronic process. The cause is a protozoan, *Trypanosoma cruzi,* which is harbored by both domesticated and wild animals. When it is transmitted to humans by insects, this essentially untreatable disease is associated with fever, edemas, and enlargement of the lymph nodes and can cause dilation of parts of the digestive tract leading to megacolon and megaesophagus as well as cardiac enlargement and failure. In fact, Chagas' disease is the leading cause of cardiac death of young adults in parts of South America.

Distribution and Incidence

The disease, which probably had its origins in Brazil, is limited to the Western Hemisphere, with heavy concentrations in Brazil, Argentina, Chile, and Venezuela. Cases are also reported in Peru, Mexico, and most other Central and South American countries along with the Caribbean islands and the United States.

Epidemiology and Etiology

T. cruzi, a member of the class Mastigophora, family Trypanisomidae, has over 100 vertebrate hosts including dogs, cats, armadillos, opossums, monkeys, and humans. Unlike other trypanosomes it does not multiply in the bloodstream, but rather lives within various tissues of the host and multiplies by binary fission. It is transmitted by reduvid bugs that ingest the trypanosome during a blood meal from a vertebrate host. The trypanosomes in turn develop in the intestines of the bug, and, while they neither enter its saliva nor are injected when the bug bites, they do pass out in its feces.

Thus the infection is transmitted when the infected insect breaks the skin to draw blood and then defecates following its meal, thereby contaminating the site of the bite. Infection can also occur when the feces is rubbed into the eyes or reaches the mucosa of the mouth, and possibly through contaminated foods as well. The trypanosomes can also be transmitted via the placenta, maternal milk, and blood transfusions.

The insect vector, which is the principal means of transmission, flourishes in huts in poor rural areas where it lives in cracks in the walls and in thatching and mats used as roofing. Cases may be few in spite of large numbers of infected bugs, if the bugs are not domesticated – that is, adapted to living in houses.

Clinical Manifestations and Pathology

There are a number of different forms of the disease, which will be considered separately. In all cases, however, the prognosis is poor because there is no effective treatment. The acute form ends in death in 10 percent of the cases, and although the chronic form may last from 10 to as long as 40 years, few individuals remain asymptomatic for life. Chronic cardiac disease as well as megacolon and megaesophagus all can shorten life.

The acute form, occurring primarily in young children, is most commonly a febrile illness; other symptoms are normally those of generalized lymph node enlargement as well as enlargement of the liver and spleen, and edema of the face. When death occurs, it is generally due to acute inflammation of the muscular walls of the heart (myocarditis) or to a complicating bronchopneumonia.

The latent form of the disease is seen in patients who have recovered from the acute form, as well as others who have harbored the parasite but have not displayed symptoms of the illness. Multiple examinations, however, often reveal changes in esophageal and peristaltic motility as well as electrocardiographic changes.

The subacute form of Chagas' disease is normally seen in young adults who suffer a rapidly progressive cardiac failure.

The chronic form of the illness is the leading cause of death in endemic areas. The heart becomes tremendously enlarged, and in about 30 percent of the cases, parasites may be found within pseudocysts in muscle fibers. Although survival may be as long as 5 years, death usually intervenes within 6 to 12 months.

The digestive form of Chagas' disease presents as megacolon or megaesophagus in endemic areas. The afflicted suffer the degeneration and diminution of nerve cells in the muscular layers of these organs, leading to their enlargement. The condition by itself is normally not fatal, but patients often experience difficulty in swallowing because of the enlarged esophagus, and constipation that normally accompanies megacolon. These difficulties in turn can promote other illnesses that are life-threatening.

The congenital form of the disease has long been known. The fetus is infected transplacentally, and the result can be premature fetal death or a newborn with Chagas' disease in its acute stage.

History and Geography

Chagas' disease is unusual in that its etiological agent, vector, and the major features of its epidemiology were described before the first human case was ever reported. All this was done by Carlos Chagas, a Brazilian physician, in a series of publications beginning in 1909, with the result that the disease appropriately bears his name.

The illness, however, is not new. Studies undertaken of mummies from the Tarapaca Valley in northern Chile have revealed megacardia, megacolon, and megaesophagus in a number of individuals who lived more than 2,000 years ago, and although the etiological agent was not discovered, the valley today is an endemic area of Chagas' disease (see Figure VIII.25.1).

According to L. J. da Silva (1985), nineteenth-century visitors to Brazil reported instances of megaesophagus and the presence of the cone-nosed bug vectors of Chagas' disease. Most interesting is the case of Charles Darwin, who wrote that he was bitten by a huge *Triatoma* carrier of the infection while in South America. Frank Burnet (1962) reported that Darwin's mysterious chronic illness, from which he always suffered, dated from this time, and cited a distinguished protozoologist who believed that Darwin was infected with Chagas' disease.

The disease, although similar to the African form

Figure VIII.25.1. Megaesophagus from a case of possible Chagas' disease from the Tarapaca Valley in northern Chile (c. third century A.D.). (From author's original slide.)

of trypanosome disease (sleeping sickness), most likely had an independent evolutionary journey. Its cradle is believed to be the Bahia–Minas–Gerais area of Brazil, although as noted previously it has subsequently spread throughout the Americas and has a notable presence in Argentina. In fact, it was in that country that a systematic study carried out by S. Mazza and colleagues (1941) established that the disease was much more widespread than previously believed and stimulated other such studies, all of which led to the recognition that Chagas' disease was a serious health threat to South America. It would seem to be a growing threat as well. Since the 1950s, the illness has become increasingly common in the Arequipa area of southern Peru, although the vector (called "chirimacha") is known throughout all of Peru.

Marvin J. Allison

Bibliography

Burnet, Frank MacFarlane. 1962. *Natural history of infectious disease.* 3d edition. Cambridge.

Chagas, C. 1909. Nova tripanozomaize humana. Estudos sobre a morfolojia e o ciclo evolutivo do *Schizotrypanum cruzi* n. gen., n. sp., ajente etiolojico de nova entidade morbida do homen. *Memorias do Instituto Oswaldo Cruz* 1: 159–218.

Crowell, B. C. 1923. The acute form of American trypanosomiasis: Notes on its pathology with autopsy reports and observations on trypanosomiasis cruzi in animals. *American Journal of Tropical Medicine* 3: 425–54.

Goldsmith, R. S., et al. 1985. Clinical and epidemiological studies of Chagas' disease in rural communities in Oaxaca State, Mexico, and a seven-year follow-up: I. Cerro del Aire. *Pan American Health Organization Bulletin* 19: 120–38.

Mazza, S., et al. 1941. *Primer quinquenio de la investigacion por la M.E.P.R.A de la enfermedad de Chagas en la provincia de Mendoza, Mission de estudios de patologia regional Argentina.* Buenos Aires.

Rothamer, F., et al. 1985. Chagas' disease in pre-Columbian South America. *American Journal of Physical Anthropology* 68: 495–507.

Silva, L. J. da. 1985. A doença de Chagas no Brasil. Indícios de sua ocurrência e distribuição até 1909. *Revista do Instituto de Medicina Tropical de São Paulo* 27: 219–34.

VIII.26
Chlorosis

In current nosology, diseases are categorized as degenerative, malignant, genetic, endocrine, and so on. For purposes of the history of diseases we must add a category that we might term ephemeral. This requires a bit of literary license, because many conditions that fall in the class of ephemeral diseases had a longer existence than that word usually implies. Ephemeral diseases comprise a large number of entities that carried working diagnostic names for earlier physicians (see, e.g., typhomalarial fever), but that are no longer recognized, at least by their previous names (Straus 1970; Hudson 1977a; Jarcho 1980).

Clinical Manifestations

A historical example of a disease that died only to leave behind a host of sprightly ghosts is the "green sickness" or chlorosis. Although noted in two Hippocratic treatises, *Prorrhetic* and *The Diseases of Girls,* the condition received its now classic description by Johann Lange in 1554 (Hippocrates 1853, 1861). He called the condition *morbus virgineus.* His description contains many of the elements found in the Hippocratic texts, as does the account by Ambroise Paré in 1561. Also reflecting the Hippocratic corpus is the work of Jean Varandal who is credited with first using the word "chlorosis" in 1615 (Starobinski 1981). For Varandal, chlorosis was a class of syndromes.

Reflecting a different approach, Thomas Sydenham's description in 1683 embodied many of the clinical features relied upon at least two centuries later:

The face and body lose colour, the face also swells; so do the eyelids and ankles. The body feels heavy; there is tension and lassitude in the legs and feet, dyspnoea, palpitation of the heart, headache, febrile pulse, somnolence, pica, and suppression of the menses. (Sydenham 1850)

The actual clinical entity was only defined later, by Friedrich Hoffmann in 1731.

After centuries of nosologic confusion, chlorosis was associated almost entirely with Caucasian girls encountering puberty. Still, from clinical observations alone, the etiology remained obscure. Inconsistencies abounded. Not all young women developed the disease at the age of menarche. It struck the rich as well as the poor. Some, but not all, suffered a morbid appetite termed pica (the consumption of stones, clay, chalk, and other substances of no nutritional value). Even into the nineteenth century, confusion permeated medical thinking about chlorosis. The ailment has been likened to a lion in elephant grass; all physicians heard its roar, but none could delineate it with absolute certainty. S. Ashwell opened his lengthy analysis in 1836 by saying. "Disease of menstruation, *especially chlorosis and amenorrhea*, are, in this country, of very frequent occurrence. . . . They are too *greatly neglected in their early stages, when they are most curable; and lastly, there is by no means an agreement of professional opinion as to their exact nature.*"

By the time of William Osler later in the century, medical opinion was far more confident. The clinical features of chlorosis had been distilled to the point that in many instances the condition could be "recognized at a glance" (Osler 1893).

Etiology and Treatment

Developments in laboratory medicine brought physicians to something approaching consensus regarding the pathophysiology of chlorosis. By the mid-nineteenth century, reasonably accurate methods were available to determine the number of red blood cells and their hemoglobin content. With this it became apparent that the *sine qua non* of chlorosis was an iron deficiency anemia. In the minds of many physicians, chlorosis could now be separated from earlier mimics such as love-sickness, hypochondriasis, and neurasthenia.

The natural history of chlorosis, whether treated with iron or not, remained a matter of dispute. In part, this undoubtedly related to frequent misdiagnoses. Using iron, some physicians reported that a single cure was lasting (Thomson 1886; Faber and Gram 1924). For others the disease progressed to phthisis, many cases of which probably were tuberculosis as such, rather than chlorosis. After iron be-

came a standard treatment, there was general agreement that the disease recurred when treatment was stopped, but responded when iron was reinstituted and continued.

Ralph Stockman wrote the most comprehensive and effective accounts of the nature and treatment of chlorosis (Stockman 1893, 1895a, 1895b). In his series of 63 cases, 27 were suffering their first attack, 11 their second, and 22 several attacks. Of the last group, some were chronically anemic. If patients remained on the prescribed iron long enough, the chronic cases responded as well as the newly diagnosed (Stockman 1895c). From what we now know of iron deficiency anemia, those receiving proper doses of iron should have done well, whereas the improperly or untreated cases would have ended badly, even fatally.

Some observers might look on the use of iron in treating chlorosis before an iron deficiency had been demonstrated as sheer luck, and one more example in the history of medicine where physicians did the right thing for the wrong reason. Yet although there are many examples of right thing—wrong reason in medicine's past, iron for chlorosis probably is not one of them. For when physicians employed proper iron compounds in correct doses, the clinical results were dramatic and altogether convincing. The failures, when iron was used, might more properly be thought of as doing the right thing with the wrong regimen.

Even if it was correct that the central feature of chlorosis was an iron deficiency anemia, a good deal of confusion remained. Still to be elucidated were a host of diseases marked by pallor, wasting, and lassitude, some of which had anemia as a secondary manifestation. These included nephritis, hypothyroidism, subacute bacterial endocarditis, mitral stenosis, and tuberculosis. What did subside was the focus on many factors once thought of as central, but which were now relegated to a contributory role at most. These included lack of fresh air and exercise, corsets, love sickness with its related sexual frustration, Rudolph Virchow's notion of hypoplasia of the arterial system, and a variety of uterine disorders.

Chlorosis reminds us of the complex interaction between physiology and social elements in the genesis of human disease. This interplay is better understood in light of our current notions of iron metabolism. To protect the body against the destructive effects of excessive iron, intestinal absorption is fixed at a rate that barely replaces the small amount lost normally. This balance is so exquisite that the prolonged loss of 2 teaspoons of blood daily will exceed the body's ability to absorb iron from a normal diet, and anemia follows. Iron deficiency anemia can result from a decrease in dietary iron, an increase in bodily demand for iron, or a loss of blood.

In chlorosis the decrease in iron intake came about either from poverty that precluded the intake of iron-rich foods or from cultural influences that led young women to avoid meat, eggs, and even milk because of the belief that animal foods increased the sexual drive, a very undesirable state of affairs in Victorian times. The increase in bodily demands for iron, for our purposes, resulted simply from the rapid growth associated with adolescence. For the historian of disease seeking physiological explanations for chlorosis, these factors would combine to produce an iron deficiency anemia.

Historical Interpretations

Clinical Manifestations and Diagnosis

The green skin color of chlorosis, from which it may have derived its name, remains, like the origin of syphilis, one of the more fascinating problems in the history of disease. The conundrum appeared when chlorosis was equated with iron deficiency; yet greenish skin in Caucasians was rarely observed in the many cases of hypochromic anemia then being diagnosed. Some of these cases undoubtedly related to the conditions just mentioned in which a hypochromic anemia appeared secondarily. Another possibility is that chlorosis was a misnomer, that the word "green" was used metaphorically. In this sense the word can be traced back to the *Oxford English Dictionary* to mean "of tender age, youthful . . . immature, raw, inexperienced."

Significantly, the green skin was included only sporadically in clinical descriptions of chlorosis over the years. Lange made no mention of it in his original description. In one study, of 27 authors who listed the usual signs of chlorosis, only 16 mentioned greenish skin as characteristic of the disease (Hudson 1977b). In another analysis, of 19 descriptions only 3 were considered definitely green, 3 possibly so, and 2 yellowish green (Loudon 1980). In 1915 Richard Cabot, author of a popular textbook of physical diagnosis, concluded that "it takes the eye of faith to see any justification for the title of the disease." On the other hand, the 1975 edition of a prominent textbook of dermatology averred that "the skin may have a green or brown tint in the iron deficiency syndrome" (Siddall 1982). Yet recent work on the nature of chlorosis has done nothing to alter this author's conclusion of a decade ago: "In the question

of the green skin of chlorosis, the available historical evidence permits us to go no further than a suspension of judgment" (Hudson 1977b). At the very least, it is now reasonable to remove green skin as the outstanding characteristic that the designation chlorosis implied.

Distribution and Incidence

The incidence of chlorosis in earlier times is impossible to determine. From the attention it received in medical and other literature as well as in art, one may infer that the condition was not rare. By the end of the nineteenth century, it was viewed as extremely common. Clifford Allbutt (1909) observed, for example, that "the chlorotic girl is well-known in every consulting room, public or private." This conclusion is all the more striking in light of the rapid exit of chlorosis from center stage. By 1915 medical observers were commenting on the disappearance of the green disease (Osler and McCrae 1915; Campbell 1923). Between 1924 and 1930 only seven cases of chlorosis were diagnosed in Guy's Hospital (Witts 1930). By 1936 W. M. Fowler was asking "What disease . . . can compare with chlorosis in having occupied such a prominent place in medical practice only to disappear spontaneously while we are speculating as to its etiology?"

He was premature, in his use of the words "disappear" and "spontaneously," but he was not alone. Others concluded that chlorosis had never been anything but a simple iron deficiency anemia brought on by an inadequate diet and a loss of menstrual blood (Patek and Heath 1936). With this understanding another physician wrote that "this disease about which so much has been written and disputed has finally ended its stormy career" (Bloomfield 1960). Again the optimism was premature. Physicians continued to find chlorosis very much alive. In 1969 it was listed as one of the five major categories of hypochromic anemia that were considered diseases *sui generis* (Witts 1969). In 1980 Irvine Loudon concluded that chlorosis was a functional disease intimately related to anorexia nervosa; that although chlorosis, like the Cheshire cat, "faded from sight, it is, in this story, still there under another name." Current medical dictionaries still carry the term and define it as an iron deficiency anemia of young women.

Owing perhaps to its ephemeral nature, chlorosis has been particularly alluring to revisionist historians. Recent work has emphasized the importance of the general perception of women and their role in what physicians thought and did about disease, although there is surprisingly little about chlorosis as such in this literature (Hartman and Banner 1974).

Marxist and social historians have also become interested in chlorosis. These revisionist approaches, to varying degrees, tend generally to diminish the importance of pathological physiology in explaining the rise and decline of chlorosis. The more committed the revisionists are to their historical biases, the more difficulty they have squaring their interpretations with those of others as well as with more purely medical explanations. The Marxist, for example, must construct social and political conditions that produced chlorosis in young women of the capitalist class as well as the oppressed poor, because the evidence is incontrovertible that the condition affected both, as one of them readily acknowledges (Figlio 1978).

The feminists who would argue that nineteenth-century physicians mistreated women consciously on the basis of gender must account for the fact that many of the treatments accorded women by male physicians at the time derived from an inadequate understanding of reproductive physiology, and that masculine sexual conditions were also mistreated. The historian who argues that chlorosis was nothing more than a cultural construction of Victorian family life, that physicians diagnosed the condition simply because they expected to encounter it, and that young women simply learned to manifest the clinical picture of chlorosis (Brumberg 1982) must explain the well-documented existence of the disease in young men as well (Fox 1839; Evans 1845; Witts 1930).

Enthusiasm for new historical approaches to disease should not obscure the importance of the final common pathway of social, political, and cultural forces. And that common denominator for chlorosis in the nineteenth and early twentieth centuries was an iron deficiency anemia. Social and cultural factors certainly predisposed individuals to chlorosis, but persons became patients ultimately because they had red blood cells that were too small and lacked the normal amount of hemoglobin. Poor nutrition — whether due to poverty or cultural preferences — certainly contributed. Physicians, with their heavy reliance on blood-letting, even prophylactically in pregnant women, undoubtedly played a part as well (Siddall 1980). Chlorotic women gave birth to iron-deficient children — "larval chlorotics" they were called. Chlorosis, at bottom, was a deficiency disease. Explaining it historically demands an eclectic historiography. The biopsychosocial model emerging as the proper paradigm for health professionals dealing with disease in our time has always operated historically. Ockham's razor may be useful in logic, but it may slice too narrowly in history. Plethora rather than parsimony more often illuminates the complexities of humanity's interaction with society at any given time and place. Chlorosis is a case in point. There remains ample reason to recall L. J. Witt's remark (1969) that "however one looks at it, one is left with the uneasy feeling that the mystery of chlorosis, like that of Edwin Drood, remains unsolved."

Robert P. Hudson

Bibliography

Allbutt, Clifford. 1909. *System of medicine by many medical writers,* Vol. 5. London.

Ashwell, S. 1836. Observations on chlorosis and its complications. *Guy's Hospital Reports* 1: 529–79.

Bloomfield, Arthur L. 1960. Chlorosis. In *A bibliography of internal medicine: Selected diseases.* Chicago.

Brumberg, J. J. 1982. Chlorotic girls, 1870–1920: A historical perspective on female adolescence. *Child Development* 53: 1468–77.

Cabot, Richard. 1915. Chlorosis. In *Modern medicine: Its theory and practice,* ed. William Osler and Thomas McCrae. Philadelphia.

Campbell, J. M. H. 1923. Chlorosis: A study of the Guy's Hospital cases during the last thirty years with some remarks on its etiology and causes of its diminished frequency. *Guy's Hospital Reports* 73: 247–97.

Evans, J. T. 1845. Cases of chlorosis in the male, with clinical remarks by Dr. Evans. *Dublin Hospital Gazette* 1: 79–81, 98–101.

Faber, Knud, and H. C. Gram. 1924. Relations between gastric achylia and simple and pernicious anemia. *Archives of Internal Medicine* 34: 658–68.

Figlio, Karl. 1978. Chlorosis and chronic disease in nineteenth-century Britain: The social constitution of somatic illness in a capitalistic society. *Social History* 3: 167–97.

Fowler, W. M. 1936. Chlorosis – an obituary. *Annals of Medical History,* new ser., 8: 168–77.

Fox, Samuel. 1839. *Observations on the disorder of the general health of females called chlorosis.* London.

Hartman, Mary J., and Lois Banner, eds. 1974. *Clio's consciousness raised: New perspectives on the history of women.* New York.

Hippocrates. 1853, 1861. *Oeuvres complètes,* Vols. 8 and 9, trans. Emile Littré. Paris.

Hudson, Robert P. 1977a. How diseases birth and die. *Transactions and Studies of the College of Physicians of Philadelphia* 45: 18–27.

   1977b. The biography of disease: Lessons from chlorosis. *Bulletin of the History of Medicine* 51: 448–63.

Jarcho, Saul. 1980. Some lost, obsolete, or discontinued

diseases: Serpus apoplexy, incubus, and retrocedent ailments. *Transactions and Studies of the College of Physicians of Philadelphia* 4: 241–66.

Loudon, I. S. L. 1980. Chlorosis, anaemia, and anorexia nervosa. *British Medical Journal* 281: 1669–75.

Osler, William, 1893. *The principles and practice of medicine*. New York.

Osler, William, and Thomas McCrae. 1915. *Modern medicine*. Philadelphia.

Patek, Arthur, and Clark Heath. 1936. Chlorosis. *Journal of the American Medical Association* 106: 1463–6.

Siddall, A. Clair. 1980. Bloodletting in American obstetric practice, 1800–1945. *Bulletin of the History of Medicine* 54: 101–10.

  1982. Chlorosis – etiology reconsidered. *Bulletin of the History of Medicine* 56: 254–60.

Starobinski, Jean. 1981. Chlorosis – the "green sickness." *Psychological Medicine* 11: 459–68.

Stockman, Ralph. 1893. The treatment of chlorosis by iron and some other drugs. *British Medical Journal* 1: 881–5, 942–4.

  1895a. Observations on the causes and treatment of chlorosis. *British Medical Journal* 2: 1473–6.

  1895b. On the amount of iron in ordinary dietaries and in some articles of food. *Journal of Physiology (London)* 18: 484–9.

  1895c. A summary of sixty-three cases of chlorosis. *Edinburgh Medical Journal* 41: 413–17.

Straus, Bernard. 1970. Defunct and dying diseases. *Bulletin of the New York Academy of Medicine* 46: 686–705.

Sydenham, Thomas. 1850 *The works of Thomas Sydenham,* Vol. 2, trans. W. Greenhill. London.

Thomson, William H. 1886. Chlorosis. In *A reference handbook of the medical sciences,* Vol. 2, ed. Albert H. Buck. New York.

Witts, L. J. 1930. Chlorosis in males. *Guy's Hospital Reports* 10: 417–20.

  1969. *Hypochromic anemia*. Philadelphia.

VIII.27
Cholera

Cholera is an acute diarrheal disease usually accompanied by vomiting and resulting in severe dehydration or water loss and its consequences. The disease, in the strict sense of the term cholera, is caused by a specific, comma-shaped bacterium, *Vibrio cholerae,* first isolated in Egypt and Calcutta by Robert Koch and colleagues in 1883. Mortality rates have reached up to 50 percent and even 70 percent of those with the disease during epidemics. It has apparently been long endemic in the Ganges Delta of India and Bangladesh from which it has spread in periodic epidemics to other parts of India, the East, and eventually to much of the rest of the world. Most of this spread has occurred since 1817, when the modern history of the disease outside India begins; it is now generally agreed that some seven pandemics have occurred since its initial spread. The most recent began in 1961 and is only now receding. The bacterium is disseminated by the so-called fecal–oral route as a consequence of sewage and fecal contamination of water supplies and foodstuffs. This indirect transmission long made its spread difficult to understand.

In the course of history, the term "cholera" has been variously applied. In order to understand the literature of cholera in the past, the reader must also understand these varying usages. The word "cholera" appears first in the Hippocratic corpus and there refers to sporadic diarrheal disease. It has been suggested that it derives from the Greek word for "bile" and for "flow" (difficult to accept since cholera excreta are singularly free of bile), or from a Greek work for "spout" or "gutter." Later classical writers including Celsus, Aretaeus, and Caelius Aurelianus described a condition under the same name. By late 1669, Thomas Sydenham employed the term in describing an epidemic in London. The term was also widely used to describe endemic or sporadic diarrhea throughout the nineteenth century and earlier in western Europe and the Americas. This is sometimes specifically designated as *cholera nostras.*

The term *cholera morbus* has also been widely used in a manner that can cause confusion because it has been applied to indicate both epidemic and sporadic or endemic forms of illness marked by diarrhea. Today the term is applied as defined above and thus is limited to the disease caused by *V. cholerae.* Synonyms have included *Asiatic cholera* or *cholera asiatica, epidemic cholera* or *cholera epidemica, malignant cholera, cholera asphyxia,* and *cholera spasmodica.* It is now generally accepted that all cholera in the West prior to the nineteenth-century epidemics was endemic or sporadic – and not caused by *V. cholerae.* It is also generally accepted that the cholera of India prior to 1817 was an earlier expression of the epidemic cholera, with the first reference appearing in Western literature in the *Lendas da India,* published in 1543 by the Portuguese explorer Gaspar Correia. He describes an outbreak occurring in 1503 in the army of the Sovereign of Calicut. Cholera was also described in 1563 by Garcia da Orta in one of the earliest books printed in Goa. Its Portuguese name was *mordexim,* from which the French *mort de chien* is derived. Other Eastern terms were *hyza* (Arabic and Hindustani), *tokhmu* (Persian), *bisoochtau* (Sanskrit), and *fural* (Mahratta). That the differentiation is not universally accepted can be seen in the 1961 writings of the Indian bacteriologist S. N. De, who includes all types of conditions under one disease entry and therefore objects to the implications of the term "Asiatic" cholera. Nonetheless, this survey will be limited to the epidemic of Asiatic cholera, unless specifically indicated to the contrary.

Etiology

As noted already the etiologic agent of Asiatic or epidemic cholera is a comma-shaped bacterium, *V. cholerae.* It is gram-negative, made motile by means of a single terminal or polar *flagellum* – or motility organ. This bacterium was seen in the excreta and intestinal contents of cholera victims by Filippo Pacini and described by him so accurately in a report he published in Florence in 1854 that it still carries the name he gave it, although the finding made little impact at the time.

The bacterium can be grown in the laboratory in simple media and in an alkalinity greater than that tolerated by most other bacteria. This latter characteristic is of significance for its growth in the human small intestine, as will be duly noted. On the other hand, it is more sensitive to acidity. This bacterium survives and multiplies in the environment outside the human body, notably in any relatively uncontaminated alkaline environment. It does not regularly infect animals; its host range is limited to humans. And it can be carried and spread by humans, especially convalescents, in the absence of overt disease. The bacteria produce and secrete a toxin, which is the actual cause of the symptoms that constitute the disease.

Control and Distribution

The infection is spread solely by infected humans, whose excreta may contaminate drinking water and food. This is not the direct contact that contagionists in earlier generations expected from experience with readily transmittable infections such as smallpox. Thus communicability was a highly controversial matter until its bacterial etiology was established. With this in mind one can state that the appearance and spread of cholera in a community or country depend first on the appearance of a person, either ill or well, who is discharging the cholera vibrio from his or her intestinal tract, and second on the state of hygiene, water supply, and sewage disposal in promoting or impeding the transmission of the bacterium to a potential victim. In endemic areas such as the Ganges Delta, a water table hardly below the surface of the ground has posed almost insurmountable problems. In the past, unsatisfactory sanitary facilities have been necessary conditions for cholera outbreaks in Europe and the Americas. Indeed, the history of the control of cholera is the history of improved sanitation.

Current distribution of epidemic cholera is largely limited to areas in the Indian continent and the tropical Far East, where it persists and occasionally breaks out in low-lying wet areas of contaminated water supply and sewage disposal. Since the Second World War, it has made sporadic forays into the Middle East and Far East, often associated with social disruption. In the early 1970s, cholera appeared briefly in Europe, with outbreaks in Mediterranean ports especially Naples (over 30 deaths), Barcelona, and the Atlantic port of Lisbon with over 2,000 cases. Some cases were carried by rapid transportation to the north, but resulted in no further extension of the disease. One small area of persistent infection appears to be the lower bayou country outside of New Orleans, the origin of these recurring cases.

Immunology

A natural immunity or resistance to cholera seems to exist because not all persons ingesting infected material contract the infection. C. Macnamara (1870) noted that of 19 persons accidentally drinking infected water on shipboard in 1861, only 5 contracted the infection. This resistance might well be nonspecific; the natural acidity of the stomach could act as a barrier to infection (a possibility well appreciated by Macnamara). On the other hand, one infection does not produce the solid immunity against repeated infections in survivors as in other infections such as smallpox and measles. When post-infection immunity does arise, it is of relatively short duration. Extensive experimental and clinical trials with immunization against cholera have not been convincing. Such measures have been mandated at times for travelers, nevertheless. The weakness of postinfection immunity is consistent with the weakness of the case for immunization.

Clinical Manifestations and Pathology

The bacterial infection is limited to the intestinal tract; no microbes are found to invade the body tissues. The low bacterial population normally in the small intestine as well as its high alkalinity contribute to the cholera vibrio's ability to survive and grow there, usually in massive numbers. They adhere to the intestinal wall and secrete a toxin that inhibits the absorption of water and electrolytes (salts) from the intestine into the circulation. Since the blood delivers large amounts of water and salts into the intestinal tract, which are then normally reabsorbed back into the bloodstream, failure of this reabsorption results in the loss and excretion of many liters of fluid in the course of a single day. This loss presents as a massive, debilitating diarrhea, which is the major clinical feature of cholera. All other symptoms of the disease are attributable to this water and salt depletion. These symptoms and clinical findings include weakening and finally loss of palpable pulse, thickening of the circulating blood, suppression of urination, loss of tissue fluids giving the face a sunken appearance, cyanosis, muscular spasms, and a disastrous fall in blood pressure leading to profound shock, which represents the fatal conclusion of the disease. The mind is ordinarily clear throughout the course of the disease. Recovery, when it occurs, is marked by the return of the capacity to reabsorb and retain fluids and salts, and a reversal of the signs and symptoms discussed above.

Pathological changes observed in the past on examination of the body at autopsy can now be attributed to postmortem changes. Early reports describe an erosion of the intestinal wall leading to the fluid loss mentioned, with the intestinal lining being found shed into the excreta. But in 1960, Eugene J. Gangarosa of the Walter Reed Hospital was able to observe the intestinal walls of cholera patients directly and found no evidence of any structural damage to cells in this area. Thus was research directed toward damage at an enzymatic or molecular level, pathologically caused by the cholera toxin already discovered by De in 1959.

Treatment

Norman Howard-Jones (1972) described the earlier treatment of cholera as follows: "In the whole of the history of therapeutics before the twentieth century there is no more grotesque chapter than that on the treatment of cholera, which is largely a form of benevolent homicide."

Modern therapy consists simply of replacing the lost water and salts. This may be done by intravenous therapy, or by oral administration in milder cases or as an adjunct to the intravenous therapy in more serious cases. This has greatly facilitated the treatment of diarrhea patients, especially in resource-poor countries. Thus cholera is essentially curable. Antibiotics play only a minor role, in that they may shorten the duration of disease and reduce the massive amounts of necessary fluid replacement.

History and Geography

Consideration of the historical literature under the rubric "cholera" requires appreciation of what disease is being treated. Literature on cholera in western Europe and the Americas that was written prior to about 1830 and that described an endemic or sporadic disease called "cholera" is excluded from the following account. There is a relatively sparse literature on the disease in India, which serves as a prelude to the modern history of true cholera. The modern literature on cholera starts slowly in 1817 and accelerates with its appearance in Russia in 1829, eastern Europe in 1831, and western Europe and North America in 1832.

Antiquity

There have been conflicting opinions concerning the possible references to cholera in the early Hindu literature. James Annesley (1825) stated: "I have not been able to obtain any information from those acquainted with the writings of the Hindoos, favouring the inference that cholera has prevailed in former ages as a wide-spreading epidemic." Robert Pollitzer (1959) makes only a brief and doubtful reference to the matter. Jan Semmelink (1885), formerly principal physician of the army of the Netherlands East Indies, in the French translation and condensation of his much more heavily documented Dutch edition of the same year, reviewed available English, French, and German translations very critically and rejected all references to possible early epidemic cholera in the Far East.

Sixteenth Through Eighteenth Century

Reference has already been made to the explorer Correia, who stated that in the spring of the year 1503, 20,000 men died in the army of the Sovereign of Calicut, some of a "disease, sudden-like, which struck with pain in the belly, so that a man did not last out eight hours time." Correia also met cholera in an epidemic form in Goa in the spring of 1543, called by the natives *moryx,* where the mortality was so great that it was very difficult to bury all of the dead. The disease was marked "by vomiting, with drought of water accompanying it, as if the stomach were parched up, and cramps that fixed the sinews of the joints" (Macnamara 1870). Garcia da Orta's report from Goa in 1563 called the disease *hachaiza* or *haiza* as the Arabs did, and also *colerica passio* and *morxi.*

The Netherlander Jan Huygen van Linscoten described what he called *mordexijn* in Goa in 1584, as did the Frenchman Vincent Le Blanc also in Goa in 1585. Reports followed through the rest of the 1500s and 1600s, including that of the well-known Jacobus Bontius in the earlier 1600s, who extended his observations to Batavia, now Indonesia. Notices of the disease continued to appear into the eighteenth century when they were joined by those of Englishmen. Thomas Percival in 1788 reported that a ship surgeon from Chester was treating cholera morbus with *radix Columbo* in the East Indies during the 1750s, and provided a fair description of the disease. The Scotsman James Lind described cholera throughout the East Indies and in India in the 1760s as a "constant vomiting of a tough white pellucid phlegm, accompanied by a constant diarrhea, [which] was deemed the most mortal symptom." He used the term *mordechin.*

Macnamara (1870) recorded that the "earliest account of the occurrence of cholera in India, from the pen of an English physician (Dr. Paisley), is dated Madras, February 1774, and is to be found in Curtis's *Works on Diseases of India,* published in Edinburgh in 1807." Although nothing further seems to be known of this Paisley, his letter forms a cornerstone in the history of the disease in British India. Annesley (1825), in an early English classic on cholera, quotes the following passage: "Thus," Paisley wrote from Madras, in 1774, "there can be no doubt that their (the troops') situation contributed to the frequency and violence of this dangerous disease, which is, as you have observed, a true cholera morbus." In 1781, it ravaged the troops in the district of Ganjam, requiring the admission to the hospi-

tal on March 22 alone of no less than 500 men of a division of 5,000. It is curious to note that the report cited calls the disease a "pestilential disorder" and does not name it cholera, although later writers (including Macnamara) assumed that it was.

This outbreak is reported to have reached Calcutta. In April of 1783, "cholera burst out at Hurdwar, and in less than eight days is supposed to have cut off 20,000 pilgrims." Fragmentary observations continued to appear, some from travelers, describing the following:

[D]isease broke out with terrible ferocity, and destroyed an enormous number of people. During the month of October, 1787, epidemic cholera committed terrible ravages at Arcot and Vellore. With regard to this outbreak, Mr. Davis, a member of the Madras Hospital Board, remarks: "I found in what was called the Epidemic Hospital, three different diseases, viz., patients labouring under cholera morbus; an inflammatory fever with universal cramps; and a spasmodic affection of the nervous system, distinct from cholera morbus. I understood, from the Regimental Surgeon, that the last disease had proved fatal to all who had been attacked with it, and that he had already lost twenty-seven men of the regiment in a few days. Five patients were then shown to me with scarce any circulation whatever to be discovered; with their eyes sunk within the orbits; jaws set, bodies cold, and extremities livid."

Nineteenth Century: The Pandemics

Cholera, or cholera-like disease, continued to be observed during the rest of the eighteenth and into the nineteenth century. Then, in the year 1814, outbreaks of cholera occurred in a number of Indian provinces, including the crowded barracks of Fort William at Calcutta among recruits just arrived from England.

Macnamara, who evaluated all these many reports of the appearance of the disease, concluded that "we are, . . . I think justified in arriving at the conclusion that it was nothing new for cholera to spread over India in an epidemic form prior to 1817 and 1819." At this point, something drastically "new" did occur, as cholera escaped the bounds of India and initiated the waves of pandemics that were to engulf the world. This change in cholera's pattern of activity has led a few to conclude that a new disease arose in Bengal in 1817, a contention Pollitzer (1959) regards as untenable, observing the following:

Incomplete or even fragmentary though the evidence brought forward . . . often is, it leaves no room for doubt that cholera, present in India since ancient times, not only continued to exist but was apt to manifest itself periodically in wide spread conflagrations.

Dissenting views do, however, exist, including those of Annesley (1825) who, writing within a decade of the 1817 outbreak, states "[t]hat we have no proof of the prevalence of cholera in India, as a widespreading epidemic in former times." Again the skeptical Semmelink devotes a whole work to the observations of cholera in the East before 1817, providing detailed criticism of what must be essentially every report in the European literature. And again he is vehement in his judgment that the accounts refer to other than the epidemic cholera of 1817 and after, although his nosology is sometimes archaic and difficult to follow. It has also been suggested in this age of genetic engineering that a genetic modification in the microbe was responsible for this supposed change in cholera's nature.

The First Pandemic. In any event, in March 1817, a death from cholera took place in Fort William, but because it was a solitary case no notice was taken of it. By July, however, outbreaks occurred in several districts in the Province of Bengal. The first notice of this in the *Proceedings of the Bengal Medical Board* was a letter from Robert Tytler, civil surgeon of Jessore, dated August 23, 1817. He wrote:

An epidemic has broken out in the bazaar, the disorder commencing with pain or uneasiness in different parts of the body, presently succeeded by giddiness of the head, sickness, vomiting, griping in the belly, and frequent stools. The countenance exhibits much anxiety, the body becomes emaciated, the pulse rapidly sinks, and the patient, if not speedily relieved with large doses of calomel, followed by one of opium, . . . [is carried off] within four and twenty hours.

In July and the following months, Calcutta was affected; 25,000 of its inhabitants were under medical treatment for the disease of whom 4,000 died. Thus begins the modern history of Asiatic or epidemic cholera, although none of the documents immediately surrounding the event make reference to the name "cholera," until a letter dated September 16 specifically refers to "cholera morbus."

Within 3 months the disease had spread throughout the Province of Bengal, and in November it reached the camp of the Marquis of Hastings in Bundelcund. During 1818, it moved over the greater part of India including Delhi and Bombay, with estimated attack rates of up to 7.5 percent of the exposed population. It continued to rage through 1819 and 1820, extending into Ceylon and Burma, Siam, Malacca and Singapore, and the Philippines. By 1821, it had invaded Java, Batavia, and China to the east and Persia to the west, reaching Baghdad with a besieging Persian army, and extending from there to Aleppo. By 1823, it was in Egypt, Astrakhan, and the Caspian shores and throughout Syria along the shores of the Mediterranean. But it receded for a number of years, thereby terminating the First Pandemic.

The Second Pandemic. By 1824, cholera had retreated to its endemic area in Bengal, where it remained active in the Ganges Delta through 1826. But in 1827, it spread out again in the so-called Second Pandemic into the Punjab, and by 1829 extended through Persia to the shores of the Caspian Sea. In Orenburg in 1829 (August 26), it soon expanded north and west into Russia. By September of 1830, cholera was in Kharkov and Moscow, and began spreading west into Bulgaria. During the winter of 1830–1, it persisted in the Russian army in Poland, and then in the spring it invaded Warsaw and soon after, Riga. Meanwhile, cholera was also raging through Mecca and Turkey, reaching Constantinople and Alexandria by July and August. On August 3, it entered Berlin and Vienna, and reached Hamburg by the beginning of October. Around the end of October, if not before, it appeared in England at Sunderland, supposedly imported from Hamburg or Riga. Late fall and early winter brought a brief respite, during which teams of observers were sent to infected areas from as yet unaffected areas, while commissions at home were trying to prepare for the coming onslaught and arguments about such matters of quarantine, sanitation, contagiousness, and treatment.

The opening of the year 1832 was soon followed by a reawakening of cholera. In February, it appeared in Newcastle, Edinburgh, and London, as well as places in between. Next it reached France, bursting on Paris on March 24, and soon engulfing all districts of the city. Within 18 days no fewer than 7,000 persons were dead. Next, cholera hurdled the Atlantic Ocean to appear on June 8 in Quebec and on June 19 in Montreal. Presumably, it arrived with emigrants on the brig "Carricks," which left infected Dublin in April and lost 42 of its 173 passengers before reaching Quebec on June 3. On June 23, cholera invaded the United States, appearing in New York on that date and in Philadelphia on July 5. From these ports of entry, it marched westward across both North American countries.

Entry into Spain, Portugal, and the Caribbean and Latin America was delayed until 1833, and into Italy until 1835. Havana lost 8,253 persons in a population of 65,000 between February 26 and April 20, 1833, and by August no less than 15,000 had perished in Mexico.

Yet by 1834, the disease was beginning to recede, and while it persisted in a number of Mediterranean and Central American areas for a few more years, it retreated once again in 1837 to its Indian homeland. This pandemic has been described in detail, as it was the first modern experience with the disease for much of the world and because subsequent epidemics or pandemics were to follow much the same route. In addition, a great deal of popular and governmental response to subsequent appearances was based on experience gained during this pandemic.

The Third Pandemic.   During the following decade, cholera continued to plague India, and it entered Afghanistan with British troops in 1839, and China in 1840 – again with troops from India – where it remained into 1841 and 1842. In 1844–5, it extended into Persia and Central Asia, reaching the Arabian coast as well as the Caspian and Black seas in 1846–7. Constantinople was attacked on October 24, 1847. In the spring of 1848, it broke out with renewed vigor, advancing as far as a line drawn through Arabia, Poland, and Sweden, reaching Berlin in July and Hamburg and Holland by September, and then London and Edinburgh in short order. After a short period of comparative rest, it renewed its activity in the spring, reaching Paris in March and by now was covering much the same ground of the earlier epidemic. Meanwhile, in December 1848 cholera had crossed the Atlantic to invade New York and New Orleans, and spread rapidly across the continent from these centers. In 1850, it reached California with the wagon trains as well as by ships from Panama. In that year it was reported in North Africa, Europe, and both North and South Americas. In many of these regions, it continued through 1851 and 1852.

There is some debate over the dates of the second and third pandemics. Most accept the worldwide spread of cholera during the decades of the 1840s and 1850s as constituting the Third Pandemic. However, Pollitzer (1959) and a few others date the Third Pandemic at 1852 or 1853, and place the Second Pandemic within the mid-1840s to 1851, in spite of the obvious lull from the mid-1830s to the mid-1840s, at least outside the Indian subcontinent. It is true that cholera was present in eastern Europe in 1852, either because of persistent infection in these areas (i.e., continuation of the earlier pandemic) or because of a fresh wave of infection starting in India in 1849 (Pollitzer 1959). But in either case, it seems fairly unlikely that what for all appearances seems to have been a pandemic would break at mid-point.

The year 1854 found cholera widely spread in Europe, England, Greece, Turkey, and North and South America. It was one of the worst cholera years on record. It was during this pandemic that John Snow made his observations in London that in 1855 led to the publication of his critical, if not immediately appreciated, study on cholera transmission by contaminated water. In 1855 and after, the disease died down in much of the West, but it continued in a few spots there as well as in much of the East.

The Fourth Pandemic   Pollitzer dates the Fourth Pandemic from 1863; it was to last about 10 to 12 years. In 1865, Macnamara estimated that a third of 90,000 pilgrims at Mecca succumbed. As before, it reached Constantinople and spread around the Mediterranean, reaching northern Europe in 1866 and 1867, and the United States and the Latin Americas in 1866. It raged over its old grounds until 1874.

The Fifth Pandemic.   According to Pollitzer, the Fifth Pandemic began in 1881, and lasted until 1896. It was during this epidemic that the studies of Koch in Alexandria and Calcutta in 1883–4 led to the isolation and identification of the causative microbe. In addition to Egypt, the epidemic was at first largely limited to the Mediterranean shores of Africa and Europe, although it later became widespread in Russia, and in Germany where it was marked by the explosive outbreak in Hamburg in 1892. Importation into New York in 1887 was arrested, but outbreaks did occur in Latin America. The disease was also widely prevalent in the Far East – in China and Japan.

The Sixth Pandemic.   The Sixth Pandemic ran from 1899 through 1923. It followed much the pattern of the fifth – largely affecting India, the Near and Far East, Egypt, western Russia, and the Balkan Peninsula. Sporadic outbreaks occurred in southern Europe and Hungary in the West and China, Japan, Korea, and the Philippines in the East. But this time cholera did not reach the Western Hemisphere.

The Seventh Pandemic.   The Seventh Pandemic dates from about 1961 to the mid-1970s and followed much the pattern of the previous epidemic. It is particularly important in providing an opportunity for the significant advances in studies of cholera pathogenicity and therapy extensively described by W. E. Van Heyningen and John Seal (1983), studies carried out in Egypt, India, Bangladesh, and the Philippines by several U.S. teams.

This brief sketch can provide only the barest outline of the nineteenth-century history of this significant disease. Pollitzer's numbering of the pandemics is utilized here for the later ones, although, as has been mentioned, historians of the disease have not always agreed on this numbering. In fact, it is sometimes not entirely clear *why* or *when* one pandemic is said to have terminated and another to have begun.

Historical Considerations of Etiology, Control and Prevention, and Treatment

In addition to the history of the pandemics themselves, the history of several other aspects of the disease seems significant to the overall history of medicine. Among these are the discovery of the etiology of the disease, concepts of contagion, developments in sanitation and public health institutions, and developments in therapy.

Earlier thoughts on the causes of cholera were embedded in notions of disease causation going back to Hippocrates: weather, seasons, geographic environment, bad air and miasmas, and dietary indiscretions. If an infecting agent was referred to at all, it was likely to indicate an "infection" by a poison or miasma.

By the middle of the nineteenth century, however, ideas of a microbial etiology were gaining ground with the writings of such individuals as F. G. Jakob Henle. In 1849, William Budd and two associates described microscopic bodies in cholera excreta and published their findings with illustrations. The French botanist Charles Robin reproduced these illustrations in 1853, denying their "vegetal nature." These were seen by the German botanist Ernst Hallier, who rejected Robin's rejection and set out to grow microbes from cholera excreta using bacteriological techniques that could not have produced success. He published his findings in *Die Cholera-Contagium* in 1867.

T. R. Lewis tried to confirm Hallier's work in Calcutta in 1870, and in failing, became somewhat of an anticontagionist. In the meantime, as already described, Pacini made his correct but at the time largely ignored observations of the actual *V. cholerae* in 1854. Thus it was left to the genius, persistence,

and technical elegance of Koch in 1883 to isolate and identify the microbe and to introduce the modern phase of the understanding of the disease. It was not, however, until 1959 that the toxin produced by the microbe was discovered along with its role in disease causation.

The question of the "contagiousness" of cholera was a matter of heated debate throughout most of the nineteenth century. It can be generally observed that the contagionists were viewed by contemporaries as archaic, conservative, and even antisocial, whereas the anticontagionists were seen as modern, bourgeois, mercantile, and socially responsible. Most of the debate focused on the question of quarantine which, of course, was anathema to mercantile interests, and the anticontagionists gained ground as the nineteenth century progressed. The demonstration of Snow of the waterborne nature of cholera was slow to gain acceptance, but this development, coupled with the discovery by Koch of the infective nature of the disease, finally proved the "contagion" of the disease, providing, of course, that one allows for the intermediary role of infected excreta and water or food, and that some individuals can act as carriers but do not develop the disease.

Sanitation has always played a major role in the thinking and in the efforts of those aiming to understand and control the propagation of cholera. As a consequence, a large body of literature has been generated on the role and influences of cholera epidemics on the development of public health policies, public health organizations, and the development of sanitation procedures and techniques.

The earlier history of the treatment of cholera has been thoroughly treated by Norman Howard-Jones (1972) and Michael Durey (1979). Most of the therapeutics employed were representative of the practice of medicine generally in and before the nineteenth century. Emetics, purgatives, and bleeding seem in retrospect to have been worse than ineffective. Calomel and opium were the standard drugs administered, beginning with British physicians in India. Castor and croton oils, antimony, mustard, bismuth, arsenic, camphor, and quinine were among other drugs administered. A red-hot iron to the heel was widely employed in India, to the spine in Paris. Water hot or cold orally, per rectum, or as baths was sometimes recommended.

The definitive treatment – intravenous fluid and salt replacement – was a long time in developing. As early as 1830, the German chemist R. Hermann demonstrated in Moscow that the change in the blood's fluid balance was reflected in the contents of the cholera excreta. A German colleague on one occasion injected 6 ounces of water into the terminally ill patients, a treatment that produced a quick, temporary return of the pulse, although death nonetheless occurred 2 hours later. In October 1831, the Berlin surgeon J. F. Dieffenback took the premature step of injecting several ounces of whole blood into three patients. They died 6 minutes, 2 hours, and 6 hours later, respectively, the first during violent convulsions. In Great Britain in late 1831 and early 1832, W. B. O'Shaughnessy published papers suggesting the intravenous replacement of salt and water. These suggestions led Thomas Latta of Leith, Scotland, and two associates to try the treatment on patients. They reported that 5 of 15 patients survived. Other sporadic attempts followed, with some but not convincing success during the 1830s. Sporadic trials continued through the century in Britain and France, and in Calcutta in the 1890s, but the treatment was not successful until Leonard Rogers perfected it in Calcutta in the early 1900s. There were a number of technical problems to be solved first, not the least being sterility. But with these difficulties resolved, the definitive treatment of cholera was established.

Reinhard S. Speck

Bibliography

Ackerknecht, Erwin H. 1948. Anticontagionism between 1821 and 1867. *Bulletin of the History of Medicine* 22: 562–93.

Annesley, James. 1825. *Sketches of the most prevalent diseases of India.* London.

Chambers, J. S. 1938. *The conquest of cholera: America's greatest scourge.* New York.

Chevalier, Louis, 1958. *Le Cholera: La Première épidémie du XIX siècle.* La Roche-sur-Yon.

De, Sambhunath N. 1961. *Cholera: Its pathology and pathogenesis.* Edinburgh and London.

Delaporte, Francois. 1987. *Diseases and civilization: The cholera in Paris.* Cambridge.

Dieffenbach, Johann Friedrich. 1832. Physiologisch-chirirgische Beobachtungen bei Cholera-Kranken. *Cholera-Archiv* 1: 86–105.

Durey, Michael. 1979. *The return of the plague: British society and the cholera, 1831–2.* Dublin.

Evans, Richard J. 1987. *Death in Hamburg: Society and politics in the cholera years, 1830–1910.* Oxford.

Howard-Jones, Norman. 1972. Cholera therapy in the nineteenth century. *Journal of the History of Medicine and Allied Sciences* 27: 373–95.

Longmate, Norman. 1966. *King cholera: The biography of a disease.* London.

Macnamara, C. 1870. *A treatise on Asiatic cholera.* London. 1876. *A history of Asiatic cholera.* London.

McGrew, Roderick E. 1965. *Russia and the cholera, 1823–1832.* Madison and Milwaukee.

Morris, R. J. 1976. *Cholera, 1832: The social response to an epidemic.* London.

Pollitzer, Robert, 1959. *Cholera.* Geneva.

Rosenberg, Charles E. 1962. *The cholera years: The United States in 1832, 1849, and 1866.* Chicago.

Semmelink, Jan. 1985. *Histoire du cholera aux Indies Orientales avant 1817.* Utrecht.

Sticker, Georg. 1912. *Abhandlungen aus der Seuchengeschichte und Seuchenlehre. II. Band: Die Cholera.* Giessen.

Van Heyningen, W. E., and John R. Seal. 1983. *Cholera: The American scientific experience.* Boulder.

Wendt, Edmund Charles. 1885. *A treatise on Asiatic cholera.* New York.

VIII.28
Cirrhosis

Cirrhosis is a chronic hepatic disorder, anatomically characterized by diffuse liver fibrosis and nodule formation. These pathological changes produce the clinical features of portal hypertension and hepatocellular failure. Cirrhosis is the end product of progressive liver injury resulting from many diverse causes including toxins, drugs, viruses, and parasites. The clinical manifestations of cirrhosis vary according to the severity and duration of the underlying disease. In the West, cirrhosis is a major cause of disability and death among middle-aged alcoholic males. In the East and Africa, cirrhosis is predominantly an intermediate lesion in the evolution from chronic hepatitis B infection to primary hepatocellular carcinoma.

Classification

Cirrhosis is classified on the basis of morphology and etiology. The morphological classification recognizes three types based on the size of the nodules:

1. *Macronodular cirrhosis.* The liver is firm, large or small in size, with bulging irregular nodules greater than 3 millimeters in diameter.
2. *Micronodular cirrhosis.* The liver is usually enlarged, and very firm or hard in consistency. The nodules on cut sections appear small and uniform, less than 3 millimeters wide.
3. *Mixed micro/macronodular cirrhosis.* The liver

shows groups of small nodules interspersed with fields of large nodules.

The terms "micronodular" and "macronodular" cirrhosis replace the older terminology, *Laennec's* and *postnecrotic cirrhosis.*

Neither the gross nor the microscopic appearance of the liver can alone differentiate among the many causes (see Table VIII.28.1). In individual cases, the etiology is often unknown. Alcohol injury is most frequently associated with the pattern of micronodu-

Table VIII.28.1. *Etiology and incidence of cirrhosis*

Etiology	Incidence
Toxins and drugs Alcohol	5–15% of chronic alcoholics
Methotrexate, methyldopa, and isoniazid	
Infections Hepatitis (non-A, non-B virus)	1–2% of acute infection 5–15% of chronic disease
Hepatitis (delta virus) Schistosomiasis japonicum	20–60% of chronic disease
Disturbed immunity Chronic active hepatitis	30–50% of chronic type B viral hepatitis
Primary biliary cirrhosis	6–15 per 1 million population (incidence) 4–14 per 100,000 (prevalence)
Chronic cholestasis Gallstone, biliary tumor, stricture, biliary atresia	1 per 8,000–15,000 live births
Mucoviscidosis	2–20% of patients (1 per 2,000 live births)
Metabolic disorders Primary hemochromatosis	2–3 per 1,000 (prevalence)
Wilson's disease	30 per 1 million population (prevalence)
Alpha-1-antitrypsin deficiency	1 per 15,000 Scandinavian adults
Vascular diseases Veno-occlusive disease Budd–Chiari syndrome Chronic right heart failure	
Others Indian childhood cirrhosis Intestinal bypass	
Cryptogenic causes	

lar cirrhosis, and other causes in this category include primary biliary cirrhosis, primary hemochromatosis, and chronic right heart failure. The macronodular deformation is seen in the cirrhosis due to viral, drug, and cryptogenic origins, and in the end-stage cirrhosis of any etiology.

Distribution and Incidence

Cirrhosis is distributed worldwide, affecting all races, nationalities, ages, and both sexes. Well over 300,000 persons die of the disease annually. This figure, based on World Health Organization statistics of the 1960s, is an underestimate because countries such as mainland China and the former Soviet Union are not included. In the United States in 1983, cirrhosis ranked as the ninth leading cause of mortality, accounting for 27,000 deaths.

The worldwide incidence of cirrhosis is determined chiefly by the per capita consumption of alcohol and the prevalence of the hepatitis viruses. The rise in the number of cases of cirrhosis is attributable to an increase in one or both of these factors. Based on mortality statistics (WHO data, 1983 or 1984), the incidence of cirrhosis in various countries can be grouped as follows:

1. Low incidence (less than 10 cirrhotic deaths per 100,000 population): Canada, Venezuela, England, Scotland, Sweden, Netherlands, Australia, Hong Kong, and the United Arab Republic.
2. Intermediate incidence (11–23 per 100,000): Mexico, United States, Denmark, and Japan.
3. High incidence (greater than 24 per 100,000): Chile, Austria, Italy, France, West Germany, and Portugal.

Occurrence rates for the different types of cirrhosis are presented in Table VIII.28.1.

Epidemiology

The statistics on cirrhosis suffer from the uncertainty of diagnosis, which can be confirmed only on autopsy or by liver biopsy. Nevertheless, the figures generated from many sources are sufficiently consistent to establish that geography, race, age, sex, economic and social class and occupation; the amount, duration, and pattern of alcohol consumption; and prevalence of hepatitis viruses all modify the occurrence of cirrhosis. The prevalence rate of cirrhosis in autopsies averages 3 to 4 percent for most countries in Europe, 5 to 8 percent for North and South Americas, and 1 to 2 percent for Japan. Among selected populations of patients, the prevalence rate of cirrhosis ranges from 0.7 percent in Copenhagen, to 1.3

percent in Wurzburg (Germany), 1.5 percent in Athens, and 3.8 percent in Abidjan (Ivory Coast).

The older epidemiological studies, discussed by John Galambos (1979), disclosed a rising incidence of cirrhosis, especially among women. Recent investigations have confirmed this trend. In the United States, deaths from cirrhosis rose 71.7 percent from 1950 to 1974, while those due to cardiovascular disease fell 2 percent. The age-adjusted death rates from cirrhosis in the United States in the period 1960–74 by race and sex showed that the increase was marked for nonwhite males, moderate for non-white females, and only slight for white males and females. For blacks in the United States, mortality rates for cirrhosis were similar to or slightly lower than those of the white population before 1955. The pattern changed rapidly after that, with American blacks experiencing an epidemic of cirrhosis compared to the increase in whites. The rise in cirrhosis deaths followed a geographic pattern. Rates among the blacks quadrupled in urbanized coastal and northern regions and remained low in the southern rural areas of the United States. Among whites the pattern was reversed, with the death rates increasing more in the southern than in the northern industrial areas. For urban America, both male and female mortality rates for cirrhosis in the nonwhite population are at least double those of the white population. The overall cirrhosis mortality in the United States dropped in the late 1970s and, with the exception of 1979, declined further in the early 1980s.

Elsewhere, in Birmingham, England, the annual incidence of cirrhosis rose from 5.6 per 100,000 population in 1959 to reach a peak of 15.3 in 1974, and then fell slightly. The annual death rate for cirrhosis in Denmark climbed from 7.5 per 100,000 population in 1963 to 9.7 in 1978. When analyzed according to sex and age, the increase in mortality rate was 3-fold among young and middle-aged men, but fell by 50 percent among older women. In western Australia cirrhosis mortality for males over age 30 increased from 14.1 per 100,000 in 1971 to 21.0 in 1982. Deaths from alcoholic cirrhosis increased in Finland and Denmark 10-and 5-fold, respectively, from 1961 to 1974. During the same period, males in Sweden and Norway had, respectively, a 3-fold and 2-fold increase in mortality due to alcoholic cirrhosis.

The steady rise in cirrhosis death rates in industrialized nations is linked to the increased per capita consumption of alcohol. Mortality figures from the United States, England, and France have dropped whenever the sale of alcohol has been prohibited or restricted during the twentieth century. A doubling of alcohol intake in a country is followed by a 4-fold increase in alcohol-induced disease. The association between alcohol and cirrhosis has been further strengthened by the confirmation of a dose–response relation. The relative risk (RR) for cirrhosis among the French has been defined as follows:

	20–39 g alcohol/day	40–59	60–79	80–99
Men	3.6 (RR)	4.56	13.47	21.60
Women	4.13	21.60	32.17	–

The risk of cirrhosis increases with the daily intake of alcohol much faster in females than in males. Similar trends in cirrhotic risks also occur in Canadian men and women for comparable levels of alcohol consumption. Although progression to severe liver injury is accelerated in women, the male/female ratio remains at least 2:1 for most groups. There are some notable exceptions, such as American Indian women – who account for 50 percent of the cirrhosis deaths of this ethnic group.

In the West, alcoholic cirrhosis comprises the major share of all cirrhosis. An estimated 75 percent of cirrhosis in the United States is alcoholic in origin; 15 percent is viral, and 10 percent is cryptogenic. A different distribution pertains in Great Britain, where 50 percent is alcoholic, 25 percent is cryptogenic, and 25 percent is viral. In Asia and Africa, where the prevalence of hepatitis B virus is high and the per capita consumption of alcohol is low, the proportion of virus-related cirrhosis to the alcoholic type is the reverse of that seen in the West. Past literature written on the disease from data gathered from east European countries suggests no association between cirrhosis and viral hepatitis. The studies were done, however, before the introduction of serologic markers for hepatitis, and thus, the type of viral heptatitis was not identified. The occurrence rate of hepatitis B virus cirrhosis is uncertain (see Table VIII.28.1). Epidemiological studies strongly support the association between chronic hepatitis B infection and the development of primary hepatocellular carcinoma. Infection at birth results in chronic hepatitis, cirrhosis, and carcinoma 2 to 3 decades later. How the virus causes the carcinoma is not understood, but the process involves cirrhosis, especially among males. Cirrhosis, like its sequela, hepatocellular carcinoma, is common in countries where hepatitis B virus is endemic.

Clinical Manifestations and Diagnosis

Clinically cirrhosis may be latent (5 to 10 percent of cases), well compensated, or active and decompensated. The clinical features depend on the underlying etiology and the appearance of the two cardinal manifestations, portal hypertension and hepatocellular failure. As cirrhosis usually evolves over a period of several years, the course may be intermittent with therapeutic intervention such as with corticosteroids or with temporary cessation of injury. During the early phase of disease, patients often present with nonspecific symptoms and signs including malaise, lethargy, *anorexia,* loss of libido, and weight gain. Incidental laboratory findings of abnormal liver function tests, positive hepatitis B serology and hypergammaglobulinemia, and incidental physical findings such as icterus, hepatomegaly, gynecomastia, and spider nevi may point to the presence of cirrhosis. With the progression of disease, portal hypertension and hepatocellular failure invariably supervene. These two complications are interrelated in their pathogenesis, and often represent the initial presentation of many cirrhotics. Esophageal varices, ascites, splenomegaly, and gastrointestinal hemorrhage indicate elevated pressure in the portal venous system. Jaundice and abnormal liver function tests may occur in early and mild hepatocellular failure, which in its severe state is manifested as hepatic encephalopathy and hepatorenal syndrome.

Prognosis need not be poor, as cirrhosis can be checked, for example, in the alcoholic who abstains from alcohol abuse. Treatment can reverse the hepatic fibrosis and improve the outlook of patients with chronic active hepatitis, primary hemochromatosis, or Wilson's disease. On the other hand, after ascites has developed, the 5-year survival rate falls to below 50 percent.

History and Geography

The ancient Greeks recognized the clinical features of cirrhosis. In about 300 B.C., Erasistratus associated ascites with liver disease. Galen, in the third century A.D., commented on the physical diagnosis, and noted that heavy wine consumption "will increase the damage to the liver when inflammation and scirrhus already existed." His contemporary, Aretaeus the Cappadocian, suggested that cirrhosis may evolve from hepatitis, and carcinoma, from cirrhosis. The clinical descriptions left by the Greeks remained unexcelled until recent times.

In the sixteenth century, Vesalius described rupture of the portal vein in a lawyer with an indurated nodular liver. When pathological anatomy became a discipline in the seventeenth century, sporadic reports of the cirrhotic liver appeared. Among the earliest illustrations of cirrhosis was that by Frederik Ruysch in his atlas of normal and abnormal anatomy (1701–16). In his massive tome on pathology, Giovanni B. Morgagni (1716) introduced the term "tubercle" to denote any nodule of the liver. This covered a variety of lesions, and sowed the confusion between carcinoma and cirrhosis of the liver for decades afterward. Among the English, William Harvey in 1616 reported on two cases of cirrhosis. He antedated John Browne, whose description in 1685 has been regarded by historians as the first in English. Matthew Baillie's accurate description in 1793 established cirrhosis as a nosological entity in pathology. He also noted the strong association between the disease and alcohol intake. During the eighteenth century, a surplus of corn led Parliament to promote distilling and consumption of spirits as a way of stabilizing the price. The excessive consumption of cheap spirits gave rise to an epidemic of cirrhosis, which became popularly known as "gin liver" in England and "brandy liver" in other countries.

Twenty-five years after Baillie, René Laennec, who invented the stethoscope, introduced the name cirrhosis in a brief footnote appended to a case discussion. Subsequently, clinicians on the Continent began to speculate on the morphogenesis of the lesion. In 1829, Gabriel Andral formulated the idea that hypertrophy of the yellow substance of the liver that normally secretes bile accounted for the nodules, whereas atrophy of the red substance containing the vessels represented the depressed areas of cirrhosis. This concept, relating cirrhogenesis to the dual substance of the liver, influenced thinking on this subject for the next two decades. In 1838, Robert Carswell in England conjectured that cirrhosis depended on the growth of interlobular connective tissue. The speculations acquired a more solid foundation when microscopes with good resolving power became available. Also in the early nineteenth century, Gottlieb Gluge and Dominique Lereboullet saw hepatic fat and argued that this was the basic lesion of cirrhosis, whereas Karl von Rokitansky attributed the "granulations" of cirrhosis to the result of chronic inflammation.

During the mid-nineteenth century, interest in vascular studies gathered momentum after improvements were made in cast corrosion techniques. The vascular alterations in cirrhosis also came under scrutiny during the latter half of that century and the first decades of this century, as researchers from Lionel S. Beale writing in 1857–9, through the work of A. H. McIndoe in 1928, revealed the vascular damage that occurs with cirrhosis. Some, such as Karl von Liebermeister in 1864 and J. M. Legg in 1872, continued to focus on the interlobular connective tissue as the seat of the cirrhotic process. Others emphasized the regenerative aspects of cirrhosis which represented the end product of many injurious episodes. In 1911, Frank B. Mallory summarized the clinicopathological features in an important paper that introduced the entity of alcoholic hepatitis. He regarded it as a precursor lesion of cirrhosis. Mallory's concept was recently revived after a dormancy of 50 years.

While pathologists debated the issue of morphogenesis, speculations on etiology also abounded. Earlier it had been suggested that alcoholic fatty liver was the precursor of cirrhosis. By the second half of the nineteenth century, most physicians accepted this thesis, believing that alcohol intake increased hepatic fat, which in turn was converted into cirrhosis. However, experiments by P. Ruge in 1870 and G. de Rechter in 1892, among others, failed to demonstrate the cirrhogenic effect of alcohol in animals. This result led to the notion that it was not alcohol but some contaminant in the alcohol, such as copper, which damaged the liver, whereas another set of theories stressed that gastric malfunction was the underlying cause in that disturbed gastric function produced or allowed the absorption of hepatotoxins. The hypothesis of nutritional deficiency came to the foreground when experimenters such as J. M. Hershey and Samuel Soskin in 1931 and D. L. McLean and Charles H. Best in 1934 showed that the fatty liver condition caused by insulin deficiency could be prevented by choline and other lipotropic agents. Other dietary models of cirrhosis soon followed, including lipotroph deficiency, a low-fat diet, and vitamin E deficiency. It remained for Harold P. Himsworth and L. E. Glynn in 1944 to correlate the two pathways of cirrhogenesis: (1) a diffuse fatty liver developing into a finely nodular cirrhosis seen in the animal model with lipotroph deficiency; and (2) massive hepatic necrosis proceeding to the coarsely nodular liver created experimentally by cystine deficiency. The nutritional theory declined in popularity when careful experiments by Charles S. Lieber and colleagues, among others, showed in 1968 that alcohol was directly hepatotoxic in humans, and cirrhogenic in baboons.

Another technical innovation has advanced our understanding of cirrhosis. Introduced by Paul Ehrlich in 1884, and popularized by P. Iversen and K. Roholm in 1939, the liver biopsy achieved wide use as a routine method of diagnosis. The accumulated histologic studies clarified the relationship of hepatitis to cirrhosis, and cirrhosis to hepatocellular carcinoma. They also helped to consolidate the various classifications of cirrhosis proposed in the past. The recent standardization of nomenclature (see Table VIII.28.1) was proposed by the Fogarty International Center in 1976 and the World Health Organization in 1977.

Thomas S. N. Chen and Peter S. Y. Chen

Bibliography

Chen, Thomas, S., and Peter S. Chen. 1984. *Understanding the liver: A history.* Westport, Conn.

Conn, Harold O., and Colin E. Attenbury. 1987. Cirrhosis. In *Diseases of the liver,* 6th edition, ed. Leon Schiff and Eugene R. Schiff. Philadelphia.

Galambos, John T. *Cirrhosis.* 1979. Philadelphia.

Garagliano, Cederic F., Abraham M. Lilienfeld, and Albert I. Mendeldoff. 1979. Incidence rates of liver cirrhosis and related diseases in Baltimore and selected areas of the United States. *Journal of Chronic Disease* 32: 543–54.

Herd, Denise. 1985. Migration, cultural transformation and the rise of black liver cirrhosis mortality. *British Journal of Addiction* 80: 397–410.

Jorke, D., and M. Reinhardt. 1982. Contributions to the epidemiology of liver cirrhosis and chronic hepatitis. *Deutsche Zeitschrift für Verdauungs-und Stoffwechselkrankheiten* 42: 129–37.

Millward-Sadler, G. H., E. G. Hahn, and Ralph Wright. 1985. Cirrhosis: An appraisal. In *Liver and biliary disease,* 2d edition, ed. Ralph Wright et al. Philadelphia.

Tuyns, A. J., and G. Pequignot. 1984. Greater risk of ascitic cirrhosis in females in relation to alcohol consumption. *Internationsl Journal of Epidemiology* 13: 53–7.

VIII.29
Clonorchiasis

The Chinese liver fluke is a small worm that parasitizes the bile ducts and livers of humans, dogs, cats, pigs, and several wild animals in China, Japan, Korea, and Indochina. It was discovered in 1875, and recently, it was estimated that 20 million individuals in China alone are infected. Eggs are laid in the bile ducts, pass in the feces, and if they reach the proper freshwater snail, undergo a series of stages in this intermediate host. Eventually, free-swimming larvae are formed, which penetrate and encyst the skin or muscles of fish, expecially those of the carp family. Human beings and other definitive hosts become infected by eating the cysts (*metacercaria*) in raw or poorly cooked fish. Raw fish are a delicacy in many Asian countries, and fish are sometimes raised in ponds fertilized with human feces. Encysted metacercaria larvae are resistant to smoking, pickling, salting, and drying. Imported fish have caused human cases in Hawaii, and the popularity of Asian cuisine poses a potential danger to gourmets far beyond Asia.

Light infections are often asymptomatic. Heavy infections may produce diarrhea, fever, jaundice, and abdominal pain. Bile duct blockage and liver abscesses occur in chronic cases, and *Clonorchis sinensis* has been tentatively linked to liver cancer. Diagnosis is made by microscopic examination of the feces to discover the characteristic eggs. Drug therapy is sometimes successful. Preventive measures include rural sanitation, regulation of fish-farming methods, and cooking fish thoroughly. It is unlikely, however, that long-established culinary practices can be changed.

K. David Patterson

Bibliography

Hou, P. C. 1965. The relationship between primary carcinoma of the liver and infestation with *Clonorchis sinensis*. *Journal of Pathological Bacteriology* 72: 239–46.

Kean, B. H., Kenneth E. Mott, and Adair J. Russell, eds. 1978. *Tropical medicine and parasitology: Classic investigations*, Vol. II, 546–60. Ithaca and London.

Kim, D. C., and R. E. Kuntz. 1964. Epidemiology of helminth diseases: *Clonorchis sinensis* (Cobbold, 1875; Looss, 1907 on Taiwan, Formosa). *Chinese Medical Journal* 11: 29–47.

Komiya, Y. 1966. *Clonorchis* and clonorchiasis. In *Advances in parasitology*, ed. B. Dawes, 53–106. New York.

VIII.30
Croup

The term *croup* is used in an inclusive way to identify several different respiratory illnesses of children manifested by varying degrees of inspiratory stridor, cough, and hoarseness due to upper-airway obstruction. Classically croup was a manifestation of diphtheria. In the twentieth century, many other infectious causes of croup syndromes are recognized, and in addition, similar illnesses can be caused by noninfectious processes.

A classification of crouplike illnesses is presented in Table VIII.30.1. Although long-term obstruction in the glottic and subglottic regions can lead to chronic illnesses, croup syndromes are described here as acute self-limited or fatal illnesses. Most cases of croup today are either laryngotracheitis or spasmodic croup.

Etiology

Acute epiglottitis (inflammation of the epiglottis) is virtually always caused by *Haemophilus influenzae* type B; rare cases have been due to *Streptococcus pneumoniae* and *Staphylococcus aureus*. Laryngitis is usually due to the common respiratory viral agents, the most important of which are adenoviruses and influenza viruses.

Laryngotracheitis and spasmodic croup are common illnesses in children and are due to viruses or *Mycoplasma pneumoniae*. The most important agent is parainfluenza virus type 1. This virus, as well as parainfluenza type 2 and influenza A and B viruses, results in outbreaks of disease. In areas of the world

Table VIII.30.1. *Classification of crouplike illnesses*

Infectious
Epiglottitis
Laryngitis
Laryngotracheitis and spasmodic croup
Laryngotracheobronchitis
Laryngotracheobronchiopneumonitis
Mechanical
Foreign body
Postintubation trauma
Allergic
Acute angioneurotic edema

where diphtheria toxoid immunization is not carried out, laryngotracheitis is also caused by *Corynebacterium diphtheria*.

Laryngotracheobronchitis and laryngotracheobronchiopneumonitis are frequently caused by the same viruses that cause laryngotracheitis. These two illnesses are caused also by *S. aureus*, *Streptococcus pyogenes*, *S. pneumoniae*, and *H. influenzae*.

Epidemiology

Croup syndromes occur worldwide. Most illnesses are due to the common croup viruses: parainfluenza types 1 and 2 and influenza viruses. Outbreaks occur every year during the cold-weather months; in the tropics croup is more common during the rainy season. The highest attack rate occurs in children 7 to 36 months of age; few cases occur in children after the sixth birthday. During the second year of life, about 5 percent of children experience an episode of croup. Croup is more common in boys than in girls and also tends to be more severe in boys.

The viruses that cause croup are present in the nasal secretions of adults and children with colds and other upper and lower respiratory tract illnesses. Virus is transmitted from infected persons by sneezing, nose blowing, and the general contamination of external surfaces (including the hands) with nasal secretions. A susceptible child can become infected either by inhaling virus in droplet nuclei (small particles) or by a direct nasal hit of virus-containing large droplets from a sneeze or nose blowing. Infection can also occur indirectly as a result of contamination of the fingers of the recipient. It is important to emphasize that parainfluenza virus infections in adults are manifested by colds; older persons with relatively trivial illnesses may be the source of severe croup in young children.

Clinical Manifestations

Acute Epiglottitis

Acute epiglottitis is a disease of relatively abrupt onset and rapid progression which, if untreated, results in death due to airway obstruction. Illness is characterized by fever, severe sore throat, dysphasia, and drooling. Airway obstruction is rapidly progressive and is associated with inspiratory distress, a choking sensation, irritability, restlessness, and anxiety. In contrast to viral croup, the patient is not hoarse and does not have the typical "croupy cough," but the speech is muffled or thick-sounding. The child with epiglottitis insists on sitting up and

will become worse and exhibit great anxiety if forced to lie down.

Patients with epiglottitis will have leukocytosis with neutrophilia and positive blood cultures for *H. influenzae* type B. The epiglottis is swollen and cherry red. Therapy depends upon rapid diagnosis, the establishment of an airway, and the administration of antibiotics appropriate for the treatment of *H. influenzae* type B.

Acute Laryngotracheitis

In this section, only viral causes of croup are discussed. Initial symptoms in laryngotracheitis are usually not alarming and include nasal dryness, irritation, and coryza (profuse nasal discharge). Cough, sore throat, and fever occur. After 12 to 48 hours, signs and symptoms of upper-airway obstruction develop. The cough becomes "croupy" (sounding like a sea lion), and there is increasing respiratory stridor (difficulty associated with inspiration). The degree of airway obstruction is variable. Most severe disease is manifested by marked respiratory distress with supra- and infraclavicular and sternal retractions, cyanosis, and apprehension. Hypoxia can occur, and if there is no intervention, asphyxial death will occur in some children.

In laryngotracheitis the walls of the trachea just below the vocal cords are red and swollen. As the disease progresses, the tracheal lumen will contain fibrinous exudate, and its surface will be covered by pseudomembranes made up of exudative material. Because the subglottic trachea is surrounded by a firm cartilaginous ring, the inflammatory swelling results in encroachment on the size of the airway; it is often reduced to a slit 1 to 2 millimeters in diameter.

The treatment of laryngotracheitis includes the following: oxygen for hypoxia, fluids (locally via aerosol and systemically) to liquefy secretions, racemic epinephrine by aerosol to decrease inflammatory edema, and rarely the establishment of the mechanical airway. Corticosteroids are also frequently administered to decrease inflammation, but their use is controversial.

Spasmodic Croup

This croup is a distinct clinical syndrome, which in some instances is difficult to distinguish from mild laryngotracheitis. In contrast to laryngotracheitis in which the obstruction is due to inflammatory exudate and cellular damage, the obstruction in spasmodic croup is due to noninflammatory edema. Illness always has its onset at night, and it occurs in children thought to be well or to have a mild cold with coryza. The child awakens from sleep with sudden dyspnea, croupy cough, and inspiratory stridor. There is no fever.

Spasmodic croup tends to run in families, and affected children often have repeated attacks. Treatment relies upon the administration of moist air and reassurance by the parents.

Acute Laryngotracheobronchitis and Laryngotracheobronchiopneumonitis

These illnesses are less common than laryngotracheitis and spasmodic croup but are more serious. Initial symptoms and signs are similar to those of laryngotracheitis. Usually the signs of lower respiratory involvement develop 2 to 7 days into the illness; occasionally both upper- and lower-airway obstructions occur simultaneously. In addition to the usual findings in croup, patients with laryngotracheobronchiopneumonitis will have rales, air trapping, wheezing, and an increased respiratory rate.

The illness is due to a more generalized infection with parainfluenza or influenza viruses or to secondary bacterial infection of the trachea, bronchi, and lungs. Exudate, pseudomembrane, and respiratory epithelial damage occur. Care involves appropriate antibiotics in addition to conventional treatment for laryngotracheitis.

History

The word *croup* is derived from the Anglo-Saxon word *kropan,* meaning "to cry aloud." Croup was first used in medical writing in 1765 by Francis Home, a Scottish physician. Until this century virtually all croup-like illnesses were confused with diphtheria.

Daniel Slade in 1864 traced the clinical history of diphtheria to the time of Homer, and A. Sanné in 1887 believed that the writings of Hippocrates demonstrate knowledge of diphtheria. Aretaeus of Cappadocia, in the second century A.D., noted extension of the disease to the lower respiratory tract, which resulted in death by suffocation. Galen noted the expectoration of the pseudomembrane. At this time, the disease was common in Syria and Egypt and was called *ulcus Syriacum* or *Egyptiacum* by Aretaeus. Aetius of Amidu, in the fifth century, added his experiences to the previous descriptions of Aretaeus. Although both Aretaeus and Aetius were describing diphtheritic croup, it is clear that there was confusion with other illnesses such as Ludwig's angina and streptococcal tonsillitis.

The historical trail of diphtheria disappeared in the fifth century and did not reappear until the sixteenth century: First, in 1557, Peter Forest described an epidemic in Alkuaer, Holland. Then in 1576, Guillaume de Baillou described an epidemic in Paris and specifically commented on false membrane. In 1771 Samuel Bard published the first U.S. report on the nature, causes, and treatment of suffocative angina. Pierre Bretonneau named diphtheria in 1826 and recognized its infectious nature. T. A. Edwin Klebs in 1883 noted the diphtheria bacillus in smears from pseudomembranes, and a year later Friedrich Löffler established the organism as the etiologic agent.

From 1920 to 1940 the incidence of diphtheria in the United States fell from approximately 200 cases to 20 cases per 100,000 population as a result of the use, first, of toxin-antitoxin and then of toxoid. In association with this decline in diphtheria, and also predating it, there was a general realization of other cases of croup in this century. Prior to 1900, only occasional notations of illnesses suggesting nondiphtheritic croup appeared. For example, E. Bouchut in 1852 described false croup, *Stridalous laryngitis,* which seems to have been spasmodic croup. In his treatise (1887), Sanné referred to an epidemic of simple croup in Germany, and Home (1765) noted two forms of croup. Bretonneau differentiated diphtheria from spasmodic croup in 1826.

In the United States during the first half of the twentieth century, severe croup was called laryngotracheal-bronchitis. It was recognized that it was caused by *C. diphtheria* bacteria and by other bacteria as well. In 1948, Edward Rabe described three types of croup infections: diphtheritic croup, *H. influenzae* type B croup (epiglottitis), and "virus" croup. Shortly thereafter, with the widespread use of tissue culture techniques, the viral etiology of croup was confirmed. During a period of approximately 30 years (1950–79), croup due to bacteria other than *C. diphtheria* was overlooked in medical papers and textbooks. In 1976, nondiphtheria/bacterial croup was rediscovered, and since then it has received considerable attention in the literature.

The history of spasmodic croup is not clear because the clinical and pathological aspects of the entity are poorly defined. In the 1940s spasmodic croup was separated from other more severe forms of croup by Francis Davison; however, since then the pathogenesis of this entity has received little attention.

James D. Cherry

Bibliography

Bouchut, E. 1859. Bouchut on croup. In *Memoirs on diphtheria,* ed. Robert Hunter Semple, 271–97. London.
Cherry, James D. 1981. Acute epiglottitis, laryngitis, and croup. In *Current clinical topics in infectious diseases,*

ed. J. S. Remington and M. N. Swartz, 1–29. New York.

1987. Croup (laryngitis, laryngotracheitis, spasmodic croup, and laryngotracheobronchitis). In *Textbook of pediatric infectious diseases,* Vol. II, ed. R. D. Feigin and J. D. Cherry, 237–50. Philadelphia.

Cramblett, Henry G. 1960. Croup – present day concept. *Pediatrics 25: 1071–6.*

Davison, Francis W. 1950. Acute obstructive laryngitis in children. *Pennsylvania Medical Journal* 53: 250–4.

Gittins, T. R. 1932. Laryngitis and tracheobronchitis in children: Special reference to non-diphtheritic infections. *Annals of Otology, Rhinology and Laryngology* 41: 422–38.

Guersant. 1959. Guersant on croup. In *Memoirs on diphtheria,* ed. Robert Hunter Semple, 207–32. London.

Home, Francis. 1765. *An inquiry into the nature, cause and cure of the croup.* Edinburgh.

Jacobi, A. 1880. *A treatise on diphtheria.* New York.

Mortimer, Edward A. 1988. Diphtheria toxoid. In *Vaccines,* ed. S. A. Plotkin and E. A. Mortimer, 31–44. Philadelphia.

Nelson, Waldo E. 1950. Acute spasmodic laryngitis. In *Textbook of pediatrics,* ed. Waldo E. Nelson, 951. Philadelphia.

1959. Acute laryngotracheobronchitis. In *Textbook of pediatrics,* ed. Waldo E. Nelson, 778–80. Philadelphia.

1984. Bacterial croup: A historical perspective. *Journal of Pediatrics* 105: 52–5.

Rabe, Edward F. 1948a. Infectious croup: I. Etiology. *Pediatrics* 2: 255–65.

1948b. Infectious croup: II. "Virus" croup. *Pediatrics* 2: 415–27.

Sanné, A. 1887. *A treatise on diphtheria.* St. Louis.

Slade, Daniel D. 1864. *Diphtheria: Its nature and treatment.* Philadelphia.

Top, Franklin H. 1964. Diphtheria. In *Communicable and infectious diseases,* ed. F. H. Top, 217–35. Saint Louis.

VIII.31
Cystic Fibrosis

Cystic fibrosis, also called fibrocystic disease of the pancreas, and mucoviscidosis, is a genetically determined disease of infants, children, and young adults. Most of its many manifestations result from the abnormally viscous mucus, which interferes with pulmonary function, and the insufficient production of pancreatic digestive enzymes, which causes nutritional deficiencies and developmental retardation.

Etiology

Among Caucasians, cystic fibrosis (CF) is the most common fatal disease having an autosomal recessive inheritance. Despite the primary involvement of several organs, the disease is caused by a single defective gene that is located on chromosome 7 and is carried by about 4 percent of the Caucasian population. Its expression is similar in both sexes.

Clinical Manifestations

CF manifests itself at birth in about 8 percent of cases through mechanical obstruction of the small intestine by the secretion of abnormally viscous mucus (meconium ileus). Symptoms of insufficient secretion of exocrine (noninsulin) digestive enzymes by the pancreas appear during the first year of life in 90 percent of cases. The development of such symptoms indicates that pancreatic function is less than 10 percent of normal; and the more severe the deficiency of pancreatic enzymes, the more severe the fecal excretion of undigested fat, usually as diarrhea. As much as 80 percent of dietary fat may be lost, thus partially explaining malnutrition. Loss of undigested nutrients can be corrected only partially by treatment with pancreatic enzyme tablets. Pulmonary disease is responsible for most of the debility and mortality. Onset occurs in the first 2 years of life in at least 75 percent of cases, and by the age of 6 years in most of the remaining cases. The initial pulmonary abnormality is obstruction of the small bronchi by abnormally thick mucus. Structural deterioration of the lungs results in part from this and is exacerbated by an increased susceptibility to infections. A small number of patients retain sufficient pancreatic function to maintain nearly normal digestion; such patients also tend to have fewer respiratory difficulties. The variability in severity is explained by the occurrence of several different mutations on the pathogenetic gene.

The sweat of a child with CF contains a concentration of sodium and chloride that is about five times greater than normal, although salt is not lost excessively by other routes. Determining the salt content of perspiration has become a basic diagnostic test. The propensity to become salt-depleted makes persons with CF particularly intolerant to heat. As a result of pulmonary and metabolic therapy, many CF patients are now living into reproductive age, and thus it has been found that CF men, but not CF women, are sterile. In spite of all efforts, few patients survive to age 40.

History and Geography

According to a medieval German saying, "The infant who when kissed leaves a taste of salt will not reach the first year of life." Hence, CF was probably recognized many centuries ago. However, it was first identified in 1936 by the Swiss pediatrician Guido Fanconi and associates, and further delineated by Dorothy H. Andersen of New York in 1938. The diagnostic perspirational salt loss was quantified by Paul di Sant'Agnese and associates (New York) in 1953.

CF is most prevalent among people of central European ancestry (1 in 2,000 to 3,000 births) and is somewhat less common in Scandinavia. Inbreeding explains incidences of greater than 1 per 1,000 in small areas. For example, the prevalence of CF among nearly 11,000 Amish in one Ohio county was more than 1 per 600, with all cases within six families, whereas there were no cases in another Amish community in a nearby county. Similar results of inbreeding have been reported from Brittany and from Afrikaners in Namibia. CF has been reported in about 1 in 17,000 black Americans, and in 1 in 90,000 Orientals (mainly Japanese) in Hawaii. The prevalence of CF has not been investigated adequately in Asia or Africa. It is possible that its true prevalence is masked by high infant mortality in large portions of these continents.

The CF gene was identified in 1989. With the rapid advances in gene transfer therapy, it may soon become possible to correct the defect from which the multiple pathological processes of this disease result. Then, instead of merely prolonging life by treating the symptoms, physicians may give CF infants a normal future.

Thomas G. Benedek

Bibliography

Andersen, D. H. 1938. Cystic fibrosis of the pancreas and its relation to celiac disease: A clinical and pathological study. *American Journal of Diseases of Childhood* 56: 344–99.

Boat, T. F., M. J. Welsh, and A. L. Beaudet. 1989. Cystic fibrosis. In *The metabolic basis of inherited disease*, 6th edition, ed. C. R. Scriver, et al., 2649–80. New York.

Dean, M., et al. 1990. Multiple mutations in highly conserved residues are found in mildly affected cystic fibrosis patients. *Cell* 61: 863–70.

Denning, C. R., S. C. Sommers, and H. R. Quigley. 1968. Infertility in male patients with cystic fibrosis. *Pediatrics* 41: 7–17.

Fanconi, G., E. Uehlinger, and C. Knauer. 1936. The coeliac syndrome in congenital cystic fibrosis of the pancreas and bronchiectasis. *Wiener Medizinische Wochenschrift* 86: 753–6.

Gaskin, K., et al. 1982. Improved respiratory prognosis in patients with cystic fibrosis with normal fat absorption. *Journal of Pediatrics* 100: 857–62.

Kerem, B., et al. 1989. Identification of the cystic fibrosis gene: Genetic analysis. *Science* 45: 1073–80.

Klinger, K. W. 1983. Cystic fibrosis in the Ohio Amish: Gene frequency and founder effect. *Human Genetics* 68: 94–8.

Kulczycki, L., and V. Schauf. 1974. Cystic fibrosis in blacks in Washington, D.C.: Incidence and characteristics. *American Journal of Diseases of Childhood* 127: 64–7.

Sant'Agnese, P. A. di, R. C. Darling, and G. A. Perea. 1953. Abnormal electrolyte composition of sweat in cystic fibrosis of the pancreas. *Pediatrics* 12: 549–63.

Sant'Agnese, P. A. di, and P. B. Davis. 1979. Cystic fibrosis in adults. *American Journal of Medicine* 66: 121–32.

Selander, P. 1965. The frequency of cystic fibrosis of the pancreas in Sweden. *Acta Paediatrica Scandinavica* 51: 65–7.

Wright, S. W., and N. E. Morton. 1968. Genetic studies on cystic fibrosis in Hawaii. *American Journal of Human Genetics* 10: 157–68.

VIII.32
Cytomegalovirus Infection

Cytomegalic inclusion disease (CID) usually occurs as a subclinical infection followed by periodic reactivation revealed by shedding of the virus. It may be serious in the neonate when infection is transmitted to the fetus in utero.

Clinical Manifestations and Pathology

Cytomegalic infection is characterized histologically by the presence of large cells containing inclusion bodies in the midst of an infiltration of mononuclear cells that may be present in any of the body organs.

In prenatal infections most infants are born without clinical evidence of disease, although some 10 to 15 percent may show microcephaly, retardation of growth or mental development, hepatosplenomegaly, jaundice, and calcifications in the brain. There may be abnormalities in liver function tests and in hematopoiesis. Some 10 to 30 percent of infants with symptomatic disease die in early life. Evidence of involvement of the central nervous system can develop in the early years of life, even though the child may appear normal. The evidence is manifested as impaired intellect, neuromuscular abnormalities, chorioretinitis, optic atrophy, or hearing loss.

Neonatal infection acquired at birth from an infected cervix or later from the mother's milk usually goes unnoticed but can be identified by the development of antibodies. In addition, respiratory symptoms including pneumonia, as well as petechial rash and enlargement of the liver and the spleen, may occur. In these cases, however, acute involvement of the central nervous system is rare.

Infection in children is generally asymptomatic and is evidenced only by the development of antibodies and the shedding of virus. Occasionally hepatosplenomegaly and abnormal liver function are found. There is no proof that pharyngitis occurs at the presumed portal of entry.

When infection occurs in adults the clinical picture is similar to infectious mononucleosis, with pharyngitis; lymphadenopathy; systemic symptoms of fever, chills, and headaches, and occasionally a maculopapular rash being the primary symptoms. Atypical lymphocytosis is usual, and there may be abnormal liver function.

In instances where the disease is transmitted by transfusion of blood or its products, the infectious mononucleosis syndrome usually appears as a post-transfusion episode at 2 to 4 weeks. Immunocompromised patients are at special risk of exogenous infection by transplanted organs or by transfusions, or of activation of the latent state. Death may occur from interstitial pneumonia, often complicated by superinfection with gram-negative organisms, fungi, or other unusual invaders.

Distribution and Incidence

Serologic studies show that cytomegalic inclusion disease has a worldwide distribution. It remains asymptomatic despite prolonged shedding of the virus at periodic reactivation but is not highly communicable. Presumably the virus is spread mainly by contact with oral secretions because it is shed from the salivary glands, and cultures from pharyngeal lymphoid structures commonly are positive. The virus has been isolated from urine, breast milk, semen, and cervix uteri, and consequently the infection may be a sexually transmitted disease.

The most serious aspect of CID is its role as a prenatal disease. Even though the mother is asymptomatic and immune, transmission of the virus to the fetus does occur. Recurrence of infection is the most probable explanation for prenatal infection although, of course, primary infection may occur during pregnancy, and there is evidence suggesting that infection in the offspring is more serious under such circumstances than when infection takes place because of recurrence in a mother protected by antibodies. A recent study has shown that children infected in a day-care center may be the source of infection for pregnant mothers.

With a disease spread mainly by oral secretions, a higher incidence is to be anticipated in those living in crowded and unhygienic surroundings. For example, 100 percent of the women in Tanzania have antibodies by the time they reach childbearing age. Other studies show seropositivity in 50 to 80 percent of children in boarding schools and orphanages in England as compared to 10 percent to 20 percent in children of the same age attending day schools. In Puerto Rico, between 70 and 80 percent of adults have the antibodies, whereas in London the figure is only 50 to 60 percent. J. A. Hanshaw has pointed out that studies in the United States and the United Kingdom show that from 0.2 to 7.5 percent of newborns are virus positive, making this disease the most common fetal infection. In the United States, the complement-fixing antibody is present in 5 to 25 percent of infants 8 to 24 months of age. In a study of the prevalence of cytomegalovirus excretion in 244 children aged from less than 1 year to 4 years in five day-care centers of a southern city of the United States, each child was tested for viral isolation by mouth swab and urine sample. It was found that 49 percent, 40 percent, 32 percent, 13 percent, or 9 percent of children, depending on the center, were excreting virus. Of the workers at the centers, 50 to 100 percent had antibodies to the virus, as did 56 to 88 percent of the parents.

Immunology

Antibodies develop upon infection to last for life. Nevertheless, as in other diseases caused by the herpesviridae, the presence of circulating antibodies even in high titer does not forestall recrudescences of infection.

History and Geography

Early in this century, pathologists noted the enlarged cells with inclusion bodies in organs of children dying of presumed congenital syphilis. The inclusions were thought to be amebae. In 1921 E. W. Goodpasture and F. B. Talbot noted their similarity to changes found in varicella and guessed they represented viral infection and described the cellular enlargement as "cytomegaly." The virus was isolated in 1956 by investigators working independently in St. Louis, Boston, and Bethesda. Epidemiological studies became feasible with the recognition of antibodies to the virus in 1968. A rapid expansion of knowledge concerning epidemiology, incidence, and clinical manifestations continues from the late 1960s.

R. H. Kampmeier

Bibliography

Anon. 1985. Epidemiologic Note. Prevalence of cytomegalovirus excretion from children in five day care centers – Alabama. *Morbidity and Mortality Weekly Report.* Centers for Disease Control. U.S. Public Health Service 34: 49–51.

Diosi, P. L., et al. 1967. Cytomegalovirus infection associated with pregnancy. *Lancet* 2: 1063–6.

Goodpasture, E. W., and F. B. Talbot. 1921. Concerning the nature of "protozoan-like cells" in certain lesions of infancy. *American Journal Diseases of Children* 21: 415–25.

Hanshaw, J. A. 1971. Congenital cytomegalovirus infection: A fifteen year perspective. *Journal of Infectious Disease* 123: 555–61.

Harris, J. R. 1975. Cytomegalovirus infection. In *Recent advances in sexually transmitted diseases,* ed. R. S. Morton and J. R. W. Harris, Chap. 42. London.

Jordan, M. Colin. 1983. Cytomegalovirus infections. In *Infectious diseases,* ed. Paul D. Hoeprich, Chap. 75, 3d edition. Philadelphia.

Lang, David J. 1924. Cytomegalovirus infections. In *Sexually transmitted diseases,* ed. King K. Holmes et al., Chap. 44. New York.

Pass, R. F., et al. 1987. Young children as probable source of maternal and congenital cytomegalovirus infection. *New England Journal of Medicine* 316: 1366–70.

Weller, Thomas H. 1971. The cytomegaloviruses: Ubiquitous agents with protean clinical manifestation. *New England Journal of Medicine* 185: 203–14.

1981. Clinical spectrum of cytomegalovirus infection. In *The human herpesviruses: An interdisciplinary perspective,* ed. Andrew J. Nahmias et al. New York.

VIII.33
Dengue

Dengue is an acute febrile disease caused by infection with a group B arbovirus of four serotypes, transmitted by the bite of infected *Aedes aegypti* and *Aedes albopictus* mosquitoes. Endemic throughout the tropics and subtropics, uncomplicated dengue is rarely fatal, although return to normal health after an attack may take several weeks. It does not always have a benign course, however, and can be complicated by hemorrhagic manifestations (hemorrhagic dengue) and circulatory collapse (dengue shock syndrome) with a potentially fatal outcome unless facilities are available for the urgent medical treatment of those affected.

Typical uncomplicated dengue has an incubation period of 3 to 15 days and is characterized by abrupt onset of chills, headache, lumbar backache, and severe prostration. Body temperature rises rapidly, perhaps reaching as high as 40°C; bradycardia (slow heart rate) and hypotension (low blood pressure) accompany the high fever. Conjunctival injection, lymph node enlargement, and a pale, pink rash, especially noticeable on the face, are usually present during this first phase of the disease. In classical dengue, the fever lasts for 48 to 96 hours initially, subsides for 24 hours or so, and then returns (*saddleback fever*), although the peak of temperature is usually lower in the second phase than in the first. A characteristic red rash appears in the second phase, usually covering the trunk and extremities, but sparing the face. The fever, rash, and headache, together with the other pains, are known as the *dengue triad*. The acute illness ends in 8 to 10 days, and one attack confers immunity to the particular dengue subtype.

Hemorrhagic dengue usually strikes children under the age of 10 and has its highest mortality rate in infants under the age of 1 year. It is more likely to occur when type 2 dengue virus infection follows an earlier type 1 infection in the same individual or when subgroup-specific antibodies have been acquired transplacentally from an immune mother, a phenomenon known as *enhancement*. Signs of this ominous complication usually occur between the second and the sixth day of the illness and include sudden collapse with a rapid pulse of low volume; cyanosis (blue discoloration) of lips, ears, and nail beds; and cold, clammy extremities while the trunk remains warm. Nosebleeds, the appearance of spontaneous bruising, prolonged bleeding from injection sites, and bleeding from both the upper and lower gastrointestinal tract signal the gross disturbances of blood coagulation mechanisms that occur in this form of the disease.

The world *dengue* comes from the Spanish, a homonym for the Swahili *Ki denga pepo* (a sudden cramplike seizure caused by an evil spirit); it was introduced into English medical usage during the Spanish West Indies epidemic of 1827 and 1828. The synonym *breakbone fever* dates from Philadelphia in 1780, and the term *knokkel-koorts* comes from Batavia about the same year. All of these terms refer to some characteristic of the disease, either its sudden onset or the severity of its musculoskeletal pain, or both.

Etiology and Epidemiology

Dengue viruses belong to the family of flaviviridae, the prefix of the family name being derived from *flavus* (Latin: "yellow") and referring to the yellow fever virus. The family consists of the genus *Flavivirus,* which has 65 related species and two possible members – cell fusing agent (CFA) virus and simian hemorrhagic fever virus.

Most flaviviruses are arboviruses, and all are serologically interrelated. They infect a wide range of vertebrate hosts, causing asymptomatic infections and diseases such as yellow fever, dengue, and numerous encephalitides. *A. aegypti* and *A. albopictus* are responsible for dengue transmission in Asia. *A. albopictus* has recently been discovered in the United States and in Brazil, but it has not yet been implicated in the transmission of disease. It is an aggressive, human-biting mosquito with both urban and rural habitats and transmits dengue viruses

transovarially (from female mosquitoes to their offspring through infection of the eggs) and from person to person. Populations of *A. albopictus* found in the United States are capable of overwinter survival in northern latitudes because they are capable of diapause, and thus the spread of this particular mosquito represents a major public health concern. Although recent outbreaks of dengue in Brazil have been atrributed to *A. aegypti,* the presence of *A. albopictus* gives rise to serious concern that it may become an important vector for the introduction of flaviviruses into areas previously free of them.

A. albopictus is primarily a sylvan species that has become adapted to the urban environment, although it is not as strongly dependent on humans as is *A. aegypti*. It breeds in tree holes, bamboo stumps, coconut husks, and other naturally occurring containers in Asia, as well as in tires and discarded water containers. It has apparently been established in Hawaii for many years, although Hawaii seems to be free from dengue.

Dengue outbreaks are particularly likely in endemic areas when there has been a heavy rainfall. Monthly rainfall exceeding 300 mm is associated with a 120 percent increase in the number of cases of dengue, and the lag time between the onset of heavy rain and the outbreak of dengue is between 2 and 3 months. Any condition that increases the number of mosquito breeding sites, or the number of susceptible persons, in dengue endemic areas automatically facilitates the transmission of dengue.

Immunology

Infection with one dengue serotype confers long-lasting type-specific protection, a benefit that may be more apparent than real because the type-specific protection also brings a greatly increased susceptibility to severe dengue disease in the event of infection with dengue virus of another serotype. Epidemiological studies clearly link the severe forms of dengue disease to previous dengue infection and to transplacental acquisition of maternal dengue antibody.

Dengue virus infects mononuclear phagocytes, and there is both in vitro and in vivo evidence that the interaction is facilitated and severe infection more likely when antibody to another dengue serotype is present. This phenomenon alone has important implications for the development of dengue vaccines. Administration of monovalent or polyvalent vaccines, even if they were now available for human use, carries with it serious risk of predisposing partially immune populations to further and more serious dengue virus disease.

Secondary dengue infections that carry no risk of dengue hemorrhagic fever or dengue shock syndrome can occur when sequential dengue infections occur at intervals of 5 or more years, when sequential infections do not end with dengue type 2, and when two or more dengue viruses, including type 2, are endemic in the same area. Malnourished children and alpha-thalassemia patients have a greatly reduced risk of dengue hemorrhagic fever and dengue shock syndrome.

Clinical Manifestations and Pathology

Dengue is characterized by sudden onset of high fever, headache, prostration, joint and muscle pain, lymphadenopathy, and a rash that appears simultaneously with a second temperature rise following an afebrile period (saddle-back fever). However, classical saddle-back fever occurs in only 50 percent of cases; lymphadenopathy is not an invariable finding; and the rash may either never develop at all or else not develop until the fourth or fifth day, or during the second phase if the fever is saddle-backed.

An outbreak of dengue fever occurred at Clark Air Force Base, a large U.S. military installation located about 70 kilometers north of Manila on Luzon Island, Republic of the Philippines, between June and September 1984. Of 119 persons suspected of having dengue, 42 cases were confirmed by hemagglutination-inhibition (HI) antibody seroconversion or by virus isolation. Seroconversion implies that HI antibody was lacking in the serum of patients at an early stage of their illness, but could be detected subsequently, usually during convalescence, providing indirect evidence of the cause of the illness. Virus isolation from the blood of dengue-infected persons is the most accurate diagnostic test for dengue, but it is impracticable for widespread use because the vast majority of cases of dengue infection occur in parts of the world where sophisticated medical facilities are simply not available. A further nine cases were considered to be probable dengue, as HI antibody was detectable in serum obtained from patients during the acute phase of their illness.

The most frequent clinical findings were fever (97 percent), headache (80 percent), and muscle and joint pain (80 percent). Other signs and symptoms frequently reported were malaise, chills, anorexia, nausea, vomiting, diarrhea, and maculopapular skin eruption (blotchy, raised, red rash). Dizziness, unusual taste sensation, and itching/scaling of the palms were less frequently reported. Hemorrhagic signs occurred in 18 patients and consisted of petechiae (pinpoint hemorrhages into skin and mucous membranes) in 13 patients, gastrointestinal bleeding in 4 patients, and gum bleeding in 1 patient.

Common laboratory findings in 29 patients admitted to hospitals were low white blood cell count, relative lymphocytosis (71 percent), and a reduced platelet count. All four dengue serotypes were isolated (12 cases of dengue 1, 4 cases of dengue 2, 5 of dengue 3, and 1 of dengue 4). All patients survived their illness and returned to normal health. This outbreak of mixed classical benign dengue fever and dengue hemorrhagic fever of multiple serotype is typical of current dengue epidemics.

Severe dengue disease – dengue hemorrhagic fever and dengue shock syndrome – proceeds through two stages. The first is similar to that of benign dengue; however, patients deteriorate during or shortly after the fall in temperature. If hypovolemic shock supervenes (because of a greatly reduced volume of plasma), untreated patients may expire within 6 hours. The clinical evidence of disturbances of blood coagulation is accompanied by abnormal laboratory tests. Hemoconcentration and reduced platelet count are invariable findings. Reduced levels of serum albumin, elevations of serum transaminases and blood urea nitrogen, prolonged prothrombin time, and reduced serum levels of factors II, V, VI, IX, and XII are common. Hypofibrinogenemia is a frequent finding, and the condition is best described as an acute vascular permeability syndrome accompanied by activation of the blood clotting and complement systems.

The World Health Organization has developed diagnostic criteria for dengue hemorrhagic fever and dengue shock syndrome:

Clinical

a. Fever – acute onset, high, continuous, and lasting for 2 to 7 days
b. Hemorrhagic manifestations including at least a positive tourniquet test and any of:
   petechiae, purpura, ecchymosis (skin eruptions) nose or gum bleeding
   hematemesis and/or melena (passing of black stools)
c. Enlargement of liver
d. Shock – manifested by rapid and weak pulse with narrowing of the range of pulse pressure (20 mmHg/2.7 kPa or less) or hypotension, with cold, clammy skin, and restlessness

Laboratory

a. Thrombocytopenia (0.10×1012/L or less)
b. Hemoconcentration – hematocrit increased by 20 percent or more

Distribution and Incidence

Dengue literally girdles the globe, with a distribution approximately equal to that of its principal vector, *A. aegypti*. Areas of dengue endemicity include tropical and subtropical regions of the Americas, Africa, Asia, and Australia. There are areas of *A. aegypti* infestation in Europe and in the southern United States, where dengue has caused epidemics in the fairly distant past, but which have no current dengue activity although they remain susceptible to its reintroduction. The example of the 1927–8 outbreak of dengue in Athens and adjacent areas of Greece illustrates such a situation, for, although type 1 dengue virus caused an epidemic with a high incidence of hemorrhagic manifestations and a high death rate in the region, that region today is not considered to be one of significant dengue prevalence.

Types 1, 2, 3, and 4 dengue viruses are endemic in Asia. Types 1, 2, and 3 are prevalent in Africa, where type 3 is the most recent arrival, first identified in Mozambique during the 1984–5 epidemic. Types 1, 2, 3, and 4 are now present in the Americas, where type 1 made its first appearance in 1977; in the Caribbean, type 4 appeared in the same region in 1981. Type 1 dengue virus was found to be responsible for the 1981–2 Australia epidemic in northern Queensland.

Dengue fever epidemics typically involve large numbers of people and have a high attack rate. As many as 75 percent of the susceptible persons exposed to dengue virus will acquire the disease. Mosquitoes take between 8 and 11 days to become infectious after ingesting infected blood, and remain infectious for life; therefore, a single mosquito can infect a number of members of a household. The 1977 Puerto Rican dengue epidemic resulted in the infection of an estimated 355,000 persons with types 1, 2, and 3 virus; the 1986 Rio de Janeiro type 1 epidemic affected 100,00 persons between March and May alone.

Recurrent outbreaks of dengue in the same geographic region indicate either that new dengue virus types have been introduced or that endemic types are now affecting groups of the population lacking immunity – generally those born since the last epidemic.

Dengue hemorrhagic fever is especially frequent in Southeast Asia, where it is among the leading causes of hospital admissions in children and the commonest cause of death from communicable disease at any age. Dengue hemorrhagic fever's first reported appearance in epidemic form in the Western Hemisphere came during the 1981 Cuban epidemic. Several cases of dengue hemorrhagic fever with shock and death were reported during the 1984–5 Mozambique epidemic. Review of data from the 1897 epidemic of dengue in north Queensland suggests that the deaths of 30 children were the result of dengue shock syndrome.

A. aegypti is primarily a domestic mosquito, breeding around areas of human habitation in discarded tires, cans, and other containers that can act as receptacles for the water necessary for the mosquitoes' breeding places. Worldwide increase in dengue activity appears to be directly related to a failure to control mosquito populations effectively, to overpopulation, to progressive urbanization, and to the social and political disruptions caused by wars. Although a jungle cycle involving forest mosquitoes and wild monkeys, in a fashion similar to that of yellow fever, has been demonstrated, zoonotic acquisition of dengue does not appear to be a factor in the general pattern of increasing dengue prevalence.

The current pattern of dengue epidemiology in the Americas resembles that of Southeast Asia in the 1950s, before it changed from a benign flulike illness to the leading cause of morbidity and mortality in children.

History and Geography

Dengue has been known as a distinct disease entity for at least several centuries. Benjamin Rush is traditionally given credit for historical priority with his account of breakbone fever, the epidemic that afflicted Philadelphia in 1780. Although his 1789 *Account of the Bilious, Remitting Fever* is generally accepted as the first modern medical account of dengue, claims have also been made on behalf of David Bylon, a Dutch physician who described an epidemic of knokkel-koorts (knuckle-fever), which appeared in the Dutch East Indies in 1779.

The disease discussed by Bylon (1780) superficially resembles dengue (sudden onset of high fever, severe musculoskeletal pain, facial rash, and swelling, benign outcome), but appears atypical in that the severe joint pain suggested by the name is more characteristic of Chikungunya (CHIK) fever, a group A arbovirus infection with a mosquito vector. Bylon, state surgeon to the city of Batavia, treated 89 patients for knokkel-koorts and then caught it himself. His illness began with pain in the joints of his right hand and arm, and rapidly progressed to include a high fever within a few hours. He concluded his account of the epidemic by remarking that the disease was well known in Batavia, but had never before reached epidemic proportions. That alone would serve to distinguish knokkel-koorts from dengue, given what we know of the epidemiology of the latter disease.

Patrick Macdowall was a Scot who participated in the Darien Scheme, which was an attempt to found a Scottish colony in 1699 on the Isthmus of Panama, then known as Darien. The plan was the brainchild of William Paterson, the founder of the Bank of England, and was intended to gain for Scotland a share of the riches of the New World from Darien's advantageous position astride the Atlantic and Pacific trade routes. The colonists were ravaged by disease, and Macdowall, who kept a journal still preserved in the National Library of Scotland, gave an excellent description of his own illness, which could well have been dengue. Macdowall survived an acute febrile illness lasting 4 or 5 days that was characterized by nausea, vomiting, prostration, severe retro-orbital headache, disordered sensation of taste, bone and joint pain, generalized rash, and faintness. His convalescence was prolonged and marked by general weakness and a continual tendency to faintness.

Was Macdowall's illness dengue? Classical saddle-back fever occurs in only 50 percent of cases of dengue, and even lymphadenopathy is not an invariable finding. Macdowall's personal case history may well be the earliest recorded description of dengue.

The importance of the mosquito in the transmission of dengue was recognized early this century when T. L. Bancroft, using human volunteers, proved that dengue could be transmitted via the bite of infected *Stegomyia fasciata* (*A. aegypti*) mosquitoes and that the infecting agent was neither an intracorpuscular parasite nor a bacterium, but an ultramicroscopic organism. His observations also incriminated *A. aegypti*, of all the possible culprits, as the actual disease vector. However, he erroneously concluded that the dengue organism lives only for a few days in infected mosquitoes, because his attempts to transmit the disease were unsuccessful when he used mosquitoes that had been infected 15 or more days previously. The most likely reason for this error is the inadvertent inclusion of immune subjects in the study population. This, however, should not detract from the credit due him as the person who recognized the viral etiology and mosquito transmission of dengue long before Albert Sabin was able to cultivate the virus in the laboratory in the late 1940s.

Proof that *A. albopictus* is a vector of dengue came in 1931 when James S. Simmons and co-workers published an account of their experimental studies on dengue in the Philippines.

The general pattern of dengue activity since World War II has been one of increasing prevalence and severity within the context of unrestrained proliferation of its vectors. Today those vectors that spread yellow fever as well as dengue pose a very real threat to humanity.

James McSherry

Bibliography

Anderson, C. R., W. G. Downs, and A. E. Hill. 1956. Isolation of dengue virus from a human being in Trinidad. *Science* 124: 224–5.

Bancroft, T. L. 1906. On the etiology of dengue fever. *Australian Medical Gazette* 25: 17–18.

Bylon D. 1780. Korte Aantekening Wegens Eene Algemeene Ziekte, Doorgaans Genaamd Knokkel-Koorts. *Verhandelungen van het Bataviaasch Genootschop der Konsten en Wetenschappen. Batavia* 2: 17–30.

Carey, D. E. 1971. Chikungunya and dengue: A case of mistaken identity. *History of Medicine and Allied Sciences* 26: 243–62.

Carey, D. E., R. N. Myers, and P. M. Rodriguez. 1965. Two episodes of dengue fever caused by type 4 and type 1 viruses in an individual previously immunized against yellow fever. *American Journal of Tropical Medicine and Hygiene* 14: 448–50.

Carey, D. E., et al. 1971. Dengue viruses from febrile patients in Nigeria, 1964–1968. *Lancet* 1: 105–6.

Darien Papers. MS. DP 49/353–60. The National Library of Scotland. [Cited in J. Preble. 1970. *The Darien disaster*. Harmondsworth.]

Halstead, S. B. 1984. Selective primary health care: Strategies for control of disease in the developing world. XI. Dengue. *Review of Infectious Diseases* 6 (2): 251–64.

Pepper O. H. P. 1941. A note on David Bylon and dengue. *Annals of Medical History*, 3d ser. 3: 363–8.

Robin, Y., et al. 1971. Les Arbovirus au Senegal: Étude dans la population humaine du village de Bandia. *African Medicine* 10: 739–46.

Simmons, James Steven, et al. 1931. Experimental studies of dengue. *Philippine Journal of Science* 44: 1–251.

U.S. Public Health Service. Centers for Disease Control. 1986. Dengue in the Americas, 1985. *Mortality and Morbidity Weekly Reports* 35: 141–42.

  1986. Dengue Fever in U.S. military personnel – Republic of the Philippines. *Mortality and Morbidity Weekly Reports* 34: 495–501.

  1986. *Aedes albopictus* infestation United States, Brazil. *Mortality and Morbidity Weekly Reports* 35: 493–5.

Westaway, E. G., et al. 1985. Flaviviridae. *Intervirology* 24: 183–92.

World Health Organization. 1986. *Dengue haemorrhagic fever: Diagnosis, treatment and control.* Geneva.

VIII.34
Diabetes

Diabetes mellitus (DM) is an endocrine disorder characterized by the lack or insufficient production of insulin by the pancreas. DM has been recognized as a disease for at least two millennia, but only since the mid-1970s has there been a consensus on its classification and diagnosis.

The primary diagnostic criterion for DM is elevation of blood glucose levels during fasting or at 2 hours following a meal. Normal plasma glucose values for adults in the fasting state are 80 to 120 milligrams per deciliter (mg/dL) or 4.4 to 6.7 millimoles per liter (mmol/L). Definition of unequivocal DM requires a 2-hour postingestion plasma glucose level equal to or greater than 200 mg/dL (11.1 mmol/L) for the appearance of classical symptoms of diabetes. These symptoms, which include excessive urination, urine containing sugar, hunger, thirst, fatigue, and weight loss, are common to all types of DM.

Classification

Today the designation *type I DM*, or *insulin-dependent diabetes*, has replaced terms such as ketosis-prone, juvenile-onset, brittle, and so forth, whereas *type II DM*, or *non–insulin-dependent diabetes*, has replaced the terms ketosis-resistant, maturity-onset, and mild diabetes. Many terms were also used for impaired glucose tolerance, a condition that may be a precursor to overt diabetes. Some of these earlier terms include latent, subclinical, and chemical diabetes, or prediabetes. Other variants of DM include maturity-onset diabetes of youth (MODY), tropical or J-type diabetes, which shows characteristics of both insulin dependence and non–insulin dependence, and gestational diabetes, which occurs during the latter part of pregnancy.

Approximately 90 to 95 percent of all individuals with DM may be classified as non–insulin-dependent, and about 5 percent as classically insulin-dependent. Diabetes may also be secondary to certain conditions or syndromes that result in the permanent or temporary destruction of the insulin-producing pancreatic islet cells. Some 2 percent of diabetes have DM secondary to disease, genetic syndromes, drugs, chemicals, or traumatic injury.

History of the Classification

As early as the sixth century, Hindu physicians recognized the clinical symptoms of diabetes and attributed them to dietary indiscretion. Early descriptions were based on the classic symptoms of diabetes, including its most salient sign of excessive urination. The term *diabetes*, meaning "to run through," was first used in the second century by Aretaeus.

In 1679 Thomas Willis noted the sweet taste of urine from diabetics, and in 1776 Matthew Dobson of Manchester was able to demonstrate that one could assay the amount of sugar in the urine by evaporating it and weighing the dried residue. Dobson stated that this residue looked and tasted like "ground sugar." It was by the absence of this sweet taste that DM was distinguished from *diabetes insipidus*. The thirst and excessive urination of the latter uncommon unrelated disease is caused either by a lack of the antidiuretic hormone from the posterior pituitary gland or by the unresponsiveness of the renal tubules to this hormone. Therefore, glycosuria (sugar in the urine) became diagnostically important and later was used to measure the effectiveness of treatment of DM. In 1815 M. D. Eugène Chevreul published his discovery that glucose is present also in the blood of diabetics.

From the mid-1700s until the 1970s, many types of diabetes were described. Observations by Apollinaire Bouchardat, culminating in his 1875 book on glycosuria, clearly distinguished two types of diabetes: In type I, the patients were relatively young; the onset was acute, weight loss was striking, and death ensued rapidly from *ketoacidosis* – the buildup of poisonous ketones from excessive fat metabolism. In type II, the patients were older and tended to be overweight, and the onset was slower. Some of these individuals could control their glycosuria with a low carbohydrate diet.

Much of the early work focused on elucidating the causes of polyuria. John Rollo, in the late 1790s, did an extended metabolic study of an obese diabetic patient at the Greenwich Naval Hospital. He noted that the amount of urine excreted depended upon the type of food that was eaten. Urinary production increased after ingestion of vegetables and decreased when the diet was high in animal fat and protein. These findings shifted the focus from the kidneys to the gastrointestinal tract and provided a scientific basis for therapeutic diets high in fat and protein and low in carbohydrates.

The gross autopsies that were performed in the 1850s and 1860s revealed no abnormalities of the pancreas of diabetics. In 1855 the French physiologist Claude Bernard discovered that the liver secretes glucose from the "animal starch" stored in it. Bernard and Moritz Schiff, furthermore, found that the apparent destruction of the pancreas in experimental animals did not result in the onset of diabetes. These findings led some to believe that a liver disease was the source of diabetes. Attention was redirected to the pancreas in 1889 when Josef von Mering and Oscar Minkowski demonstrated that complete removal of the pancreas did cause diabetes in dogs.

Specialized "heaps of cells" had been identified in the pancreas by Paul Langerhans in 1869. Continued research by Minkowski and others in the 1890s demonstrated that these "islets of Langerhans" were the source of an "internal secretion" that regulated glycosuria. This work suggested convincingly that DM is caused by a disorder of the endocrine portion of the pancreas. In 1921 Charles Best and Frederick Banting (Toronto) were able to isolate the internal secretion and named it *insulin*. They realized that insulin is responsible for the control of blood glucose levels and the appearance of clinical symptoms associated with diabetes. During the 1920s, other hormonal secretions of the pituitary and adrenals were discovered, which indicated that glucose control is more complex. However, insulin alone constituted the antidiabetes hormone used in therapy.

Although insulin was first used in 1922, it was not until the 1950s that appropriate bioassays of human insulin were developed. These definitive measurements clearly showed that individuals with juvenile-onset, or type I, diabetes produced no insulin at all, whereas individuals with maturity-onset, or type II, diabetes had varying amounts of insulin produced by the pancreas. This discovery provided a clear rationale for insulin therapy in those individuals with type I DM, and for diet, exercise, and, after 1955, oral hypoglycemic agents in those with type II diabetes.

The first major epidemiological study of DM, by Haven Emerson and Louise D. Larimore (1924), attempted to explain the increases in diabetes mortality in New York City from 1866 to 1923. A number of factors were considered influential, including race, affluence, lack of physical activity, and changes in dietary habits, which emphasized the increasing abundance of all foods. These authors also noted an increasing prevalence of DM among females over the age of 45. It is, however, the famous American diabetologist Elliott P. Joslin whose studies in the 1930s concerning the "epidemic" of diabetes (Joslin, Dublin, and Marks 1933; Joslin 1935) demonstrated the utility of the epidemiological approach.

Etiology and Epidemiology

Insulin-Dependent Diabetes Mellitus (Type I)

Insulin-dependent DM is characterized by clinically acute onset, usually at an early age, lymphoid infiltration of the islets of Langerhans, reduction in the functioning and production of their betacells, reduction in the production and excretion of insulin, increases in islet cell antibodies, weight loss, thirst, frequent urination, and high levels of blood sugar. After the acute onset of type I diabetes, a clinical remission may occur in 25 to 100 percent of the reported cases for periods ranging from 1.8 to 15 months. After this initial period, all patients require insulin therapy to prevent severe symptoms and profound biochemical aberrations that can lead to ketosis, coma, and death.

Typical type I diabetes is uncommon. The prevalence of insulin-dependent diabetes mellitus is less than 0.5 percent of the world's population. The reported prevalence of type I diabetes ranges from 0.1 to nearly 4.0 per 1,000 children under 20 years of age. There are 18 registries evaluating geographic patterns of type I diabetes, many in northern Europe and North America, and as much as a 35-fold difference in prevalence has been reported among populations around the world.

Genetic Markers.   The etiology of type I diabetes is multifactorial. There is strong evidence for a genetic susceptibility associated with the antigens of the major histocompatibility complex, the human leukocyte antigens (HLA). Among individuals in whom DM occurs before the age of 16 years, 90 to 96 percent carry either HLA DR3 or HLA DR4. These are present in about 22 percent and 25 percent of the white population, respectively. The presence of one of these antigens increases the risk of the occurrence of DM 3- to 4-fold. Since only 30 to 50 percent of even these individuals develop DM, environmental factors also appear to have an etiologic role.

Infectious Diseases and Immune Responses.   The role of infectious diseases, particularly viruses, coupled with the appropriate HLA type, has been investigated in a number of populations. Although there is ample experimental and clinical evidence to implicate the role of Coxsackie B4, mumps, rubella, and other viruses in the destruction of the betacells of the pancreas, the epidemiological data are not definitive. There were early reports of mumps-induced pancreatitis. In 1927 E. Gunderson observed that mortality rates from diabetes increased 2 to 4 years after epidemics of mumps. More recently, other viruses have been under investigation. For example, investigators in Poland discovered increases in antibodies against enteroviral meningitis and Coxsackie A and B viruses in newly diagnosed diabetics. The meningitis epidemics regularly preceded periods of increased incidence of diabetes by 4 to 6 months.

Many studies have attempted to link infectious diseases to seasonal patterns in the onset of diabetes. The results have not demonstrated a consistent picture. Furthermore, seasonal variation may be linked to factors other than infectious diseases. Worldwide, there is apparently no "peak season" for the appearance of type I diabetes.

Recent work indicates that there is an autoimmune factor in the destruction of the beta cells of the pancreas. Circulating immune complexes have been found in 30 to 90 percent of all newly diagnosed type I diabetics. Antibodies against islet cells are the most common, but antibodies against gastric parietal cells, thyroid, and adrenal tissue have also been detected in some diabetics. A strong association exists between the presence of autoimmune antibodies and HLA DR3.

Other Population Genetic Factors. Genetic factors at the population level may play a role in the etiology of type I diabetes. The relative risk of HLA DR3 is lowest for African blacks and is approximately the same for Caucasians, African-Americans, and Japanese (relative risk: 3.3–3.5). On the other hand HLA DR4 shows a 3-fold higher risk (9.6) for American blacks than for the other three groups.

Low rates of type I DM are found among New World Asian-derived native populations (Eskimos, Aleuts, and Amerindians), as well as Old World Asian populations, including the Japanese and Chinese. Prevalence rates vary considerably on the Indian subcontinent. Rates are lower in the southern part of India (i.e., Bombay) than in northern India (i.e., New Delhi). K. M. West (1978) cites a number of studies indicating an increased prevalence of type I diabetes among populations that previously showed low rates. Increases are particularly marked among Japanese, black Africans, and black Americans. In general, these increases are associated with a "Westernization" in life-style since World War II.

Biological Factors. Sex and age also play roles in the onset of type I diabetes. In most populations, the number of boys and girls afflicted with the disease is nearly equal. However, in children under 5 years of age, the incidence is slightly higher for boys. Age of onset of type I diabetes peaks at the beginning of puberty and during the adolescent growth spurt for both girls and boys.

Nutritional Factors. Some nutritional factors have been suspected of being involved in the etiology of type I diabetes, although again there is no consistent epidemiological picture. Excess caloric intake does not seem to be the important etiologic factor it is in type II diabetes. A Danish study has reported a negative correlation between breast-feeding and type I DM, and finally T. Helgason and M. R. Jonasson (1981) suspect that N-nitroso compounds from smoked mutton may be responsible for the seasonal incidence of type I diabetes found in Iceland, where this meat is traditionally consumed at Christmas time. The range of nutritional factors implicated in type II diabetes is much greater and is discussed below.

Other Factors. A further risk factor in type I DM is urbanization with accompanying changes in life-style and a greater risk of infection due to increased population density. Thus there is generally a higher prevalence of type I diabetes among urban as opposed to rural populations within a given country.

Non–Insulin-Dependent Diabetes (Type II)

Between 90 and 95 percent of all individuals with diabetes have type II diabetes and are over the age of 35 years. In contrast to type I diabetes cases, there are many cases (up to 50 percent) that remain undiagnosed. Type II diabetics produce insulin but may require more of it in order to manage their glucose levels. The majority of all patients are treated with dietary modifications, often with caloric reductions for weight loss, and with oral hypoglycemic tablets. Type II diabetics are ketosis resistant but may suffer from the macrovascular and microvascular complications of ketosis (see Table VIII.34.1).

Many factors have been implicated in the etiology and pathogenesis of type II diabetes. Not only are they numerous but also their interactions are complex.

Genetic Factors. The numerous problems in discovering a genetic mechanism responsible for diabetes have been outlined in works by W. Creutzfeldt, J. Kobberling, and J. V. Neel (e.g., 1976), and K. M. West (1978). Unlike type I DM, type II DM (the more common non–insulin-dependent DM) has no associated genetic markers. However, genetic mechanisms

Table VIII.34.1. *Causes and suspected causes of, and risk factors for, diabetes*

Generally accepted
Obesity
  Caloric excess, indolence
Heredity
Destruction or damage of beta cells
  Cancer
  Pancreatectomy
  Pancreatitis from many causes
  Viral infections
  Coxsackie viruses, measles
  Beta cytotoxic drugs
Diabetogenic hormones (exogenous or endogenous)
  Growth hormone
  Epinephrine
  ACTH or glucocorticoids
Hemochromatosis
Disorders of insulin receptors
Factors of immunity and autoimmunity
Human leukocyte antigens (HLA)

Widely suspected of causing or precipitating diabetes
Pregnancy
Excessive serum iron
Cassava (manioc or tapioca) consumption
Some drugs
Cirrhosis
Potassium deficiency
Certain brain lesions
Affluence in some circumstances and poverty in others
Myotonic dystrophy

Suspected by some scientists but doubted by others
Dietary fat
Dietary sugars
Refined carbohydrates
Insufficient dietary fiber
Contraceptive steroids
Deficiency states
  Chromium, iron, zinc, pyroxidine
Severe protein malnutrition
Psychological stress
Stress of prolonged or severe illness
Temperate climate
Hypertriglyceridemia
Specific racial susceptibility
  (e.g., Jews, Indians, American Indians, Polynesians)

Source: Adapted from K. M. West (1978: 34).

interacting in complex ways with environmental factors are involved in the risk for type II diabetes.

Type II DM occurs more frequently in families in which one or more members have DM than in the general population. Yet family studies have not sup-

ported a simple mode of inheritance. A 40-fold risk of DM occurs for children of fathers who had an age of onset of diabetes under 20 years. Risks are somewhat less for children of type I mothers, and are increased only one to three times for offspring of parents who had an age of diagnosis of diabetes over the age of 40.

Biological Factors. Both age and sex are risk factors for type II diabetes. In most affluent societies, the rate of diagnosed type II diabetes increases steadily from 30 to 60 years of age. The decline in the rate in old age may be the result of the smaller number of individuals at risk. The extent to which physiological aging is a risk factor is unknown. However, H. Silwer (1978) showed that for Swedish populations the proportion of cases that were "severe" declined sharply in old age, from 28 percent in the sixth decade to 4 percent in the ninth decade.

Many observations have been made on sex differences in the frequency of type II diabetes. Before 1900, diabetes was observed to be more frequent in men in both Europe and the United States. Indeed R. Lepine cited seven different studies from Europe in which women constituted 17 to 43 percent of the cases, whereas Emerson and Larimore found that in England and Wales the male/female ratios were typically 2:1 before 1910. Since 1930, however, clinicians in both America and Europe have repeatedly observed a greater frequency in female diabetics.

Nonetheless, many developing nations show a male predominance. Populations with a high male/female ratio include rural Africans, Hong Kong Chinese, and populations in Iraq, Jordan, Japan, Korea, India, and Pakistan. Populations with a predominance of females include the United States, the Caribbean countries, Sweden, Belgium, the former Soviet Union, Thailand, and South Pacific countries.

Parity has also been considered a risk factor. In 1924, Emerson and Larimore reported that married women in New York City had a rate of mortality from diabetes about four times higher than that of single women. Joslin and his associates, however, found that married diabetic women weighed on the average about 20 pounds more than single diabetic women, and in well-controlled studies no relationship was found between parity and diabetes in Pima Indians. On the other hand, it is true that pregnancy can have a physiological effect that is diabetogenic, and women who suffer from gestational diabetes are at greater risk for type II diabetes in their nonpregnant state. In summary, it appears that parity is not a major risk factor for diabetes, and that the association is confounded by both obesity and age.

Exercise. Exercise would seem to be a potent protective factor in diabetes. It enhances both carbohydrate metabolism and the efficient use of insulin. As early as 1893, B.C. Sen noted that active men in India had a lower rate of diabetes than their more sedentary counterparts. Overall, a decrease in energy expenditure has been related to changes in lifestyle, a relationship that has been particularly well-documented in the South Pacific. Unfortunately, quantitative data on exercise are limited, and the short- and long-term effects of exercise on carbohydrate metabolism are incompletely understood.

Obesity. There is abundant worldwide evidence associating obesity with type II diabetes, and the 1980 World Health Organization Expert Committee on Diabetes has concluded that it is the most powerful risk factor for non–insulin-dependent DM. Many studies have shown that between two-thirds and nine-tenths of individuals may be classified as obese at the time of diagnosis of DM.

This association between obesity and diabetes is an old one, first noted by Indian physicians. Modern concern with obesity began with Joslin's landmark paper in 1921, in which he assembled overwhelming data showing obesity as the major risk factor for type II diabetes. Diabetes rates were 6 to 12 times greater in obese than in lean individuals. More recently, West (1978) documented high frequencies of both obesity and diabetes among a number of Amerindian tribes in Oklahoma. Later works on native American groups have corroborated these findings. The positive relationship of diabetes with obesity is also found in Latin American populations. Yet it does not hold true for all peoples; in some populations with high levels of both conditions – for example, the Pima Indians and Mexican-Americans – for specific age and sex groups diabetics are not more obese than nondiabetics.

The distribution of body fat presents an additional risk factor. A centripetal distribution of fat around the chest, waist, and abdomen presents a greater risk than an increase in fat in the lower portion of the torso, hips, and thighs. This central or android distribution of fat has been correlated with risk for diabetes in a number of ethnic and racial groups. The duration of the diabetes and other hormonal factors may be additional risks related to the amount of fat tissue or degree of obesity.

Dietary Factors. Calories are units of energy derived from food, and high caloric intake and low caloric expenditure are both related to obesity. Diabetes rates appear to have increased markedly in a number of countries wher caloric consumption per capita has also increased. These countries include Japan, Taiwan, Haiti (among the wealthy), New Guinea, and many parts of Africa. A number of authors have noted that during World War I and II in Europe and during World War II in Japan, when caloric intake was markedly decreased, the rate of obesity and diabetes both declined. On the other hand, recent work in 1975 by J. H. Medalie and his colleagues indicate no significant differences in caloric intake among diabetic and nondiabetic Israeli men.

Many dietary components have been investigated as potential risk factors for type II diabetes. Most researchers agree that there is no convincing evidence that a single dietary component increases the risk of diabetes. For example, West reported 21 studies indicating that table sugar or sucrose consumption was a risk factor for diabetes and another 22 studies suggesting that it was not. Furthermore, the distinction between simple and complex carbohydrates has been called into question in recent years. A number of researchers focusing on previously designated complex carbohydrates (starches such as potato and wheat bread) have shown that these starches can lead to the production of high levels of insulin and glucose in nondiabetics and type II diabetics. In fact, the glucose response to white potatoes and dextrose sugar was approximately the same.

H. C. Trowell, D. P. Burkitt, and colleagues suggest that dietary fiber favorably alters absorption patterns to decrease the risk for diabetes, and currently many different forms of dietary fiber are being investigated in this connection. In most of the epidemiological work, however, it is difficult to disentangle the effects of decreased fiber consumption from increased sugar and refined carbohydrate intake, increased total calories, total fat, decreased caloric expenditure, and stresses associated with rapid dietary change and modernization. Thus, there remain many unanswered questions concerning the role of refined and unprocessed carbohydrates and dietary fiber in the risk and treatment of DM.

Dietary fats have also been viewed as dietary risk factors, although studies investigating fat intake are often confounded because of the higher caloric density of fat compared to carbohydrates and proteins (ratio = 9:4:4). Furthermore, high fat intake is generally associated with low fiber intake. Historically, one of the more important works on the matter is that of Harold P. Himsworth (1935–6), in which he presented evidence positively linking fat and negatively linking carbohydrate consumption to diabetes. Yet other epidemiological observations have not supported the relationship between high fat consumption and high diabetes rates when diet is controlled for caloric intake. Furthermore, evidence that challenges any such relationship is found among Eskimos living a traditional life-style with diets high in fat and protein yet suffering little from DM. Alternatively, protein deficiency in the tropics has been implicated in certain types of diabetes, particularly those secondary to pancreatic disease.

Finally, deficiencies in micronutrients – in particular, chromium – have been postulated as potential factors for diabetes. However, there are few epidemiological data and the clinical data are conflicting.

Other Factors. Other life-style factors such as urbanization and psychosocial stress have been implicated in the etiology of type II diabetes. As populations become more "developed," there is an increase in diabetes. The populations of the South Pacific, for example, provide a natural laboratory in which the degree of modernization has been correlated with increases in chronic diseases including diabetes. Many other factors associated with diabetes are listed in Table VIII.34.1.

Tropical Diabetes. A third type of diabetes found primarily in developing countries in tropical areas has clinical characteristics of both type I and type II diabetes. Tropical diabetes has been described in many areas of the world including the South Pacific, the West Indies, Africa, Southeast Asia, and India. Thus, the disease has been referred to variously as phasic insulin-dependent diabetes, J-type diabetes for Jamaica, K-type diabetes for Kenya, malnutrition diabetes, and tropical pancreatic diabetes. The clinical profile involves the following: (1) a different genetic pattern of diabetes than in temperate regions; (2) a low prevalence rate of type I DM; (3) a younger age on onset of type II; (4) a sex ratio with male predominance in India and Africa, but female predominance in the West Indies; (5) an association of low calorie and protein intake during childhood and adulthood with the presentation of lean or underweight diabetic individuals in Old World tropical areas, but overweight diabetic individuals in the Western Hemisphere; (6) the predominance of diabetes in urban areas in most countries, with the excep-

tion of rural sugar-cane farming populations in the West Indies; (7) ketosis resistance; and (8) intermittent need for insulin therapy.

Information is relatively sparse on the genetics of diabetes in tropical countries. Recent studies on the human leukocyte antigens (HLA) and properdin (factor B, BF) system have shown that there is great population variability in the association of particular HLA haplotypes and increased susceptibility to diabetes. Genetic studies of Indian populations suggest a stronger familial or genetic factor among Indian diabetics compared to diabetics in other populations.

Environmental risk factors for tropical diabetes involve unique dietary items. In 1979, D. E. McMillan and P. J. Geevarghese suggested that the cyanide-containing glycosides of some types of cassava (manioc) may be toxic to the beta cells of the pancreas and thus produce pancreatic damage. Abnormal changes in pancreatic tissue give support to the cassava-cyanide hypothesis in the pathogenesis of diabetes. However, many tropical areas show high rates of diabetes in populations that do not consume cassava, and conversely, some populations have high cassava consumption and low rates of diabetes. In Kenyan (K type) diabetes, a local alcohol called *changaa* is implicated in causing the disease. Finally, in most tropical areas carbohydrates constitute 70 to 80 percent of the total calories of the diet, which is considerably higher than the percentage of carbohydrates in diets of many developing countries. Indeed, such a diet is implicated in classic "malnutrition diabetes" because of the relatively low nutrient density and high fiber content.

Gestational Diabetes. In 1882, J. M. Duncan noted a type of diabetes present only during pregnancy. However, it was not until the 1940s that the term "gestational diabetes" appeared in the English language medical literature. D. R. Haddon found that from 1975 to 1984, 165 studies on gestational diabetes were published, representing investigations in 25 countries. The majority (69 percent) were from the United States and Europe, although 16 were reported from Australia. One important difficulty in evaluating the incidence of gestational diabetes is that the frequency of type II diabetes among women of childbearing age is unknown for many countries. Therefore, a woman could have diabetes prior to pregnancy, but not have it diagnosed until pregnancy. Babies born to diabetic mothers usually are large (over 9 pounds), but may have organ systems that are not mature, in which case they may not survive.

The prevalence of gestational diabetes varied from 0.15 percent in Newcastle, United Kingdom, to 12.2 percent in Los Angeles, California. In general, cities in the United States report a higher prevalence of gestational diabetes then do European cities. The one African report from Nairobi, Kenya, indicates a prevalence of 1.8 percent. The highest reported rate of gestational diabetes occurs among the Pima Indians of Arizona, who also have the highest prevalence of type II diabetes of any known population.

Distribution and Incidence

Many methods have been used to ascertain the prevalence of DM. Methods have ranged from telephone and household surveys, reviews of hospital records, to screenings using urine and blood determinations of glucose concentrations. Because of its acute onset and obvious symptoms, type I diabetes is readily identified and, therefore, permits a more accurate picture of worldwide prevalence. Data from the 1960s through the 1980s indicated that populations with prevalence rates of insulin-dependent DM of at least 1.0 per 1,000 include Finland, Sweden, the United States, England, France, and Australia. Intermediate prevalence rates of 0.5 to 0.9 per 1,000 are found in Scotland, Switzerland, East Germany, and Denmark. Rates below 0.5 per 1,000 occur in Italy, Japan, India, Taiwan, Vietnam, Libya, China, the South Pacific, Ethiopia, and the West Indies. Type II DM is a chronic disease with generalized symptoms; therefore, many cases are not diagnosed. The American Diabetes Association estimates that 40 to 50 percent of Americans with type II DM have not been diagnosed. On the whole, however, rates of type II do appear to be increasing in developing nations. Table VIII.34.2 lists the prevalence rates of diabetes in 1960–85 for 28 countries.

Most surveys on the annual incidence of insulin-dependent DM include individuals in the age range 0 to 14 or 0 to 16 years. High rates of 15 to 30 per 100,000 are reported for Finland, Sweden, Scotland, Norway, and Yugoslavia; intermediate rates of 10 to 14.9 per 100,000 for Denmark, the United States, the Netherlands, and New Zealand; and low rates of 0 to 9.9 per 100,000 for Israel, Japan, Great Britain, France, Canada, India, Italy, Ghana, and Nigeria. The incidence data from Sweden also indicate an increase in the number of cases of type I diabetes from 19.6 per 100,000 (1970–5) to 24.9 per 100,000 (1980–2) for children age 0 to 14 years. Generally, investigators have been cautious in interpreting the rates as an actual increase in the incidence of insulin-dependent DM. Prevalence rates continue to

Table VIII.34.2. *Prevalence of diagnosed diabetes in representative populations, 1960–85*

Country	Population description	Rate (%)
United States	American Indians (multitribal adults)	10.0
United States	>20	6.2
Canada	all ages	2.0
Argentina	adults	2.9
Costa Rica	>30 years	5.4
El Salvador	>30 years	3.2
Guatemala	>30 years	4.2
Jamaica	≤25 years	8.0
Panama	>30 years	2.5
Trinidad	≥20 years	4.5
Uruguay	>30 years	6.9
Venezuela	>30 years	7.0
England	all ages	0.6
Germany	all ages	1.3
Italy	all ages	2.5
Scotland	all ages	0.6
Spain	all ages	1.3
Sweden	all ages	2.0
Yugoslavia	≥15 years	1.1
Australia	adults	0.9
India	rural≥15 years	1.3
India	urban≥15 years	3.0
Japan	all ages	0.4
Malaysia	≥30 years	4.2
Singapore	≥15 years	6.1
South Africa	whites≥15 years	3.6
South Africa	Bantu≥15 years	4.1
Zambia	urban all ages	0.3
Fiji	≥20 years	11.8
Samoa	urban≥20 years	10.1
Tonga	urban≥20 years	9.9

Sources: Hamman (1983), Bennett (1983), Taylor and Zimmet (1983), West (1978: 132–4).

rise because of increased longevity of individuals with type I diabetes.

The incidence rates for type II diabetes vary extensively by age and sex for different populations. In general, the incidence increases with age for both males and females until the sixth or seventh decade of life. The incidence of diabetes in the United States, or the number of newly diagnosed cases per 10,000 population per year, has risen 7-fold since the first large-scale survey in 1935–6, when the rate was 3.8 per 10,000. The highest incidence was reported in 1973 (29.7 per 10,000) and the information from 1979 to 1981 reveals a rate of 22.7 per 10,000. Approximately 95 percent of these cases are type II diabetes.

Incidence rates of greater than 200 per 100,000 population of adults or total population are found in the United States, Israel, Finland, England, Denmark, Saudi Arabia, the South Pacific islands, and Australia. Intermediate rates between 100 and 200 per 100,000 population per year have been found in Scotland, Germany, Spain, Yugoslavia, Czechoslovakia, and Romania, and lower rates have been found in Canada, India, Southeast Asia, and some African countries.

Clinical Manifestations

There are five stages in the natural history of DM:

First stage: susceptibility based on a combination of (1) genetic risk factors; (2) physiological states such as obesity for type II diabetes; (3) and environmental factors including diet, climate, activity, and other life-style patterns.

Second stage: glucose intolerance, which is recognized as a phase preceding both insulin-dependent and non–insulin-dependent diabetes. Not all individuals having impaired glucose tolerance progress to symptomatic diabetes.

Third stage: chronic hyperglycemia without complications.

Fourth stage: frank diabetes with complications but without disability.

Fifth stage: disability due to functional impairment from the complications of diabetes, which involve primarily the vascular system. Common complications include renal disease, blindness due to retinopathy, neuropathy, cerebral vascular disease, cardiac disease, and peripheral vascular disease often leading to lower limb amputation.

Mortality

Diabetes represents an underlying and contributing cause of death that places it among the top 10 causes of death in developed countries. In Western countries, DM ranks seventh as a cause of death. In the United States from 1976 to 1983, diabetes was listed as the cause of death in 14.8 per 100,000 population. This rate was considerably higher in Mexico and in the Caribbean, with rates as high as 45 deaths per 100,000 for Trinidad and Tobago. In Africa the mortality rates are generally below 10 per 100,000. In

Table VIII.34.3. *Diabetes mortality trends by country and geographic area, 1970–2 and 1976–83 (rates per 100,000 population)*

Area and country	1970–2	1976–83	Increase/Decrease
Africa			
Egypt	6.0	7.1	↑
Mauritius	12.9	17.1	↑
Americas			
Canada	8.9	13.0	↑
United States	18.8	14.8	↓
Mexico	19.8	18.8	↓
Venezuela	8.9	11.4	↑
Asia			
Singapore	9.6	15.1	↑
Hong Kong	7.2	5.1	↓
Japan	7.4	7.1	↓
Europe			
England and Wales	10.8	9.3	↓
Malta	76.3	21.7	↓
Sweden	11.9	19.4	↑

Source: World Health Organization (1972, 1984).

Asia rates range from 5.1 per 100,000 for Hong Kong to 15.1 per 100,000 for Singapore. In Europe, the rate ranges from a high of 21.7 per 100,000 for Malta to a low of 9.4 per 100,000 for England and Wales.

The best early data on mortality are reported by Joslin and his associates in the 11 editions of Joslin's book, *Treatment of Diabetes Mellitus,* the first of which was published in 1916. These volumes document a trend toward a decrease in early mortality from diabetes, due to increasing sophistication in therapeutic approaches, particularly with the advent and wide-scale use of insulin. Table VIII.34.3 reports comparative statistics for changes in diabetes mortality rates by geographic region for both developed and developing nations.

History and Geography

One of the best accounts on the geography of DM, published in the *British Medical Journal* in 1907, was a symposium on diabetes in the tropics, which was chaired by Richard Havelock-Charles. The authors reviewed within- and between-country differences in the prevalence of diabetes. It was noted, for example, that diabetes was more common in Bengal than in upper India, and was less common in Sudan and the Cameroons than in Europe. Papers also indicated the rarity of diabetes in Japan and China. In 1908 Robert Saundby reviewed differences in the prevalence of diabetes in Europe. Richard T. Williamson in 1909 reported high rates of DM in Malta, which were substantiated in later works. He also noted that there were low rates in Cyprus, Hong Kong, Malaya, Aden, Sierra Leone, British Honduras, Cuba, Labrador (Eskimos), Fiji, and certain populations of Asian Indians and Chinese. In addition, he summarized available evidence on rates by time and place in many European populations. In 1922 Fredrick L. Hoffman published data on mortality rates due to DM for 15 countries or regions for persons over the age of 20. These rates ranged from 67.8 per 100,000 in Malta to 8.6 in Italy. The extensive data on the epidemiology of diabetes of Emerson and Larimore published in 1924 included mortality statistics by geographic region. Comparative mortality data were also published in the many editions of Joslin's *Treatment of Diabetes Mellitus*. In the 1930s, there were many reports showing very low rates of diabetes among Eskimos and American Indians. Other pioneering studies on the prevalence in other European populations between 1916 and 1952 have been summarized by Silwer (1958).

Modern observations of geographic differences began with the publication of S. M. Cohen's (1954) paper showing marked differences in diabetes rates among Amerindian tribes. This was followed shortly by J. G. Cosnett's (1957) work describing very high rates of diabetes in Asian Indian immigrants to South Africa. These rates were 30 to 40 times higher than among black South Africans. *Diabetes Mellitus in the Tropics* (1962), by J. A. Tulloch, summarized much of the evidence on the prevalence of diabetes in developing and developed countries.

Attempts to standardize definitions and criteria began when the International Diabetes Federation held its first conference in 1952. The National Diabetes Data Group published the presently used classification of diabetes in 1979, and in 1980 the World Health Organization Expert Committee on Diabetes Mellitus published a second report standardizing definitions and criteria for DM and imparied glucose tolerance. One good example of these international efforts is the work edited by J. I. Mann, K. Pyorala, and A. Teuschner in 1983 covering epidemiology, etiology, clinical practice, and health services throughout the world. In 1985, the National Diabetes Data Group published *Diabetes in America*.

Data in Tables VIII.34.2 and VIII.34.3 show contemporary prevalence figures for different countries and, in some cases, distinguish between urban and rural populations. Virtually all of these figures were derived from actual determination of the concentration of blood glucose, either fasting or after an oral glucose challenge.

Many migrant populations have been especially prone to high rates of diabetes. For example, Jews have shown an increased susceptibility to diabetes in native European enclaves as well as in various migrant groups. It was noted that Jews in New York City had rates 10 times higher than other U.S. ethnic groups. A number of studies from the early 1900s show high rates of diabetes among Jews in Budapest, Bengal, Boston, and Cairo. More recently, studies have shown that Sephardic Jews in Zimbabwe and Turkey have high rates of diabetes. Migration of Jewish people to and from Israel has produced many different ethnic subgroups. Newly immigrant Yemenites and Kurds to Israel show lower rates than long-time residents of the same ethnic groups. A. M. Cohen and colleagues, publishing in 1979, found that in a 20-year period there was an increase from 0.06 percent to 11.8 percent in the prevalence of diabetes found among Israeli Yemenites. Medalie and co-workers, studying various ethnic groups in 1975 in Israel, found that European-born Jews had a lower incidence of diabetes than those born in Africa, Asia, or Israel. They found that obesity was a significant predictor of the prevalence of diabetes among these Israeli ethnic groups.

Early reports for Chinese populations indicate a very low prevalence of diabetes, and in fact, Saundby in 1908 observed that none of his colleagues had ever seen a case of diabetes in a Chinese patient. In modern China, the rates remain very low, ranging from 0.2 percent to 1.2 percent. Most authors conclude that the Chinese have a reduced susceptibility to diabetes, although rates are somewhat higher in immigrant Chinese populations in Hawaii (1.8 percent), Singapore (1.6 percent), and Malaya (7.4 percent). The Japanese, like the Chinese, also show a very low prevalence of diabetes in their native countries. However, with migration, the Japanese in Hawaii and California have also showed increased rates of DM.

Amerindians, in particular, have very high rates of diabetes. The highest rates occur among the southwestern Indian groups, with the Pima Indians exhibiting the highest rate (35 percent) of DM. Yet the high rates among Amerindians appear to be recent. Early reports (using different testing methods, of course) indicated very low prevalence of diabetes among North American Indian groups at the turn of this century. Moreover, rates among South American Indian groups still tend to be low.

Other aboriginal groups also seem to be particularly prone to diabetes, among them Polynesians and Micronesians. Rates are somewhat lower among Melanesians. Hawaiians have a diabetes rate seven times higher than Caucasians in Hawaii. Among New World black populations in the West Indies and in the United States, there is a high prevalence of type II diabetes, particularly among women. Michael Stern and other researchers have documented high rates of diabetes among Mexican Americans.

One explanation of the high frequency of type II DM among certain of these populations is that they developed a highly efficient carbohydrate metabolism under traditional life-styles of a feast and famine cycle. The thrifty mechanisms of carbohydrate metabolism, however, became detrimental with rapidly changing life-styles associated with a decrease in physical activity, an increase in energy in the diet, a reduction of dietary fiber, an increase of refined carbohydrates, and an increase in psychosocial stress.

Among Asian Indians, diabetes rates are low. The overall prevalence of diabetes in India is approximately 2 percent. Diabetes is more prevalent among urban populations, the rich, and the professional classes. In Indian men there also is a north-to-south gradient of diabetes prevalence, with thrice the prevalence in the south.

Yet like other migrant groups, Asian Indian migrants to other countries show high prevalence rates compared to those of indigenous populations. For example, in South Africa only 1 to 4 percent of blacks had DM compared to 17 to 32 percent of Asian Indians. High rates have also been reported from East Indian populations in Fiji, Trinidad, and Singapore. The Indians in South Africa, in particular, were brought over as indentured servants and had a life-style not dissimilar to those of New World black populations. A diabetes-thrifty genotype may have been selected for in these populations as well.

Among black Africans DM is still comparatively rare. Nevertheless, increased prevalence has been noted by Tulloch for urban Africans in a number of nations. Apparently, for susceptible genotypes, the life-style changes associated with rural-to-urban migration result in higher relative risks for type II diabetes.

It is important to note that there is a great deal of genetic heterogeneity among socially designated racial and ethnic groups. This heterogeneity should not be ignored when looking at the environmental or geographic factors that lead to increases in the relative risks for type II diabetes.

The foregoing historical and geographic data indicate that we may anticipate an increase in the worldwide prevalence of DM. The focus has been and remains on treatment of hyperglycemia and the vascular complications of long-term diabetes. Using the epidemiological data and historical perspectives, we are now beginning to develop better programs aimed at early intervention and prevention.

Leslie Sue Lieberman

Bibliography

Ahuja, M. M. S., et al. 1976. National collaborative study on epidemiology of diabetes in India. *Excerpta Medica* 400: 183.

Allen, C., M. Palta, and D. J. D'Alessio. 1986. Incidence and differences in urban–rural seasonal variation of type I (insulin-dependent) diabetes in Wisconsin. *Diabetologia* 29: 629–33.

Bennett, P. H., et al. 1976. Epidemiologic studies in diabetes in the Pima Indians. *Recent Progress in Hormone Research* 32: 333–76.

Bennett, P. H. 1983. Diabetes in developing countries and unusual populations. In *Diabetes in epidemiological perspective*, ed. J. J. Mann, K. Pyoralas, and A. Teuscher, 43–57. Edinburgh.

Berger, M., W. A. Muller, and A. E. Renold. 1978. Relationship of obesity to diabetes: Some facts, many questions. In *Advances in modern nutrition*, Vol. 2: *Diabetes, obesity, and vascular disease*, ed. H. Katzen and R. Mahler, 211–22. New York.

Bernard, Claude. 1855. Sur le mécanisme de la formation du sucre dans le foie. *Centre de la Recherche de l'Academie de Science* 41: 46–9.

Blom, L., and G. Dahlquist. 1985. Epidemiological aspects of the natural history of childhood diabetes. *Acta Paediatrica Scandinavica [Supplement]* 320: 20–5.

Bonham, G. S., and D. W. Brock. 1985. The relationship of diabetes with race, sex and obesity. *American Journal of Clinical Nutrition* 41: 776–83.

Bornstein, J., and R. D. Lawrence. 1951. Plasma insulin in human diabetes mellitus. *British Medical Journal* 2: 1541.

Bouchard, C., and F. E. Jonston, eds. 1987. *Fat distribution during growth and later health outcomes: Current topics in nutrition and disease*, Vol. 17. New York.

Bouchardat, A. 1875. *De la Glycosurie ou diabète sucré.* Paris.

Chevreul, M. D. Eugène 1815. Note sur le sucre de diabètes. *Annuaires de la Chimie* 95: 319–20.

Cohen, A. M., et al. 1979. Diabetes, blood lipids, lipoproteins and change of environment: Restudy of "New immigrant Yemenites in Israel." *Metabolism* 28: 716–28.

Cohen, S. M. 1954. Diabetes mellitus among Indians of the American Southwest: Its prevalence and clinical characteristics in a hospitalized population. *Annals of Internal Medicine* 40: 588–99.

Cosnett, J. G. 1957. Illness among Natal Indians. *South African Medical Journal* 31: 1109.

Creutzfeldt, W., J. Kobberling, and J. V. Neel. 1976. *The genetics of diabetes mellitus.* New York.

Diabetes 1951–   . (Journal)

Diabetes Care 1977–   . (Journal)

Diaz, O. D., and O. F. Cepero. 1987. The diabetic foot and peripheral vascular complications. *International Diabetes Federation Bulletin* 32: 134–7.

Duncan, J. N. M. 1882. On puerperal diabetes. *Transactions of the Obstetrical Society of London* 24: 256–85.

Ekoe, J. M. 1987. Diabetic complications in Africa. *International Diabetes Foundation Bulletin* 32: 138–41.

Emerson, H., and L. D. Larimore. 1924. Diabetes mellitus: A contribution to its epidemiology based chiefly on mortality statistics. *Archives of Internal Medicine* 34: 585–630.

Everhart, J., W. C. Knowler, and P. H. Bennett. 1985. Incidence and risk factors in non–insulin-dependent diabetes. In *Diabetes in America,* ed. National Diabetes Data Group, 1–35. Washington, D.C.

Flack, J. F., and D. K. Yue. 1987. Diabetes neuropathy: Recent developments and future trends. *International Diabetes Foundation Bulletin* 32: 132–4.

Freiherr, Greg. 1982. Pattern of body fat may predict occurrence of diabetes. *Research Resources Reporter* 6: 1–4.

Gundersen E. 1927. Is diabetes of infectious origins? *Journal of Infectious Disease* 41: 197.

Hamman, Richard S. 1983. Diabetes in affluent societies. In *Diabetes in epidemiological perspective,* ed. J. I. Mann, K. Pyorala, and A. Teuscher, 7–42. Edinburgh.

Havelock-Charles, R. 1907. Discussion on diabetes in the tropics. *British Medical Journal* 2: 1051–64.

Helgason, T., and M. R. Jonasson. 1981. Evidence for a food additive as a course of ketosis-prone diabetes. *Lancet* ii: 716–20.

Himsworth, H. P. 1935–6. Diet and the incidence of diabetes mellitus. *Clinical Science and Molecular Medicine* 2: 117–48.

Hirsch, A. 1885. Diabetes. *Handbook of Geographical and Historical Pathology* 112: 642–7.

Hoffman, F. L. 1922. The mortality from diabetes. *Boston Medical and Surgical Journal* 187: 135–7.

Jackson, W. P. U. 1967. Diabetes and pregnancy. *Acta Diabetologica Latina* 4: 1–528.

Joslin, E. P. 1916. *Treatment of diabetes mellitus.* Philadelphia.

1921. The prevention of diabetes mellitus. *Journal of the American Medical Association* 76: 79–84.

Joslin, E. P., L. I. Dublin, and H. H. Marks. 1933. Studies on diabetes mellitus: 1. Characteristics and trends of diabetes mortality throughout the world. *American Journal of Medical Sciences* 186: 753–73.

1935. Studies in diabetes mellitus: 3. Interpretation of the variations in diabetes incidence. *American Journal of Medical Sciences* 189: 163–92.

Keen, H., and H. Rifkin. 1987. Complications of diabetes: A soluble problem. *International Diabetes Federation Bulletin* 32: 121–2.

Klein, R. 1987. Management of diabetic eye disease. *International Diabetes Federation Bulletin* 32: 123–8.

Knowler, W. C., et al. 1981. Diabetes incidence in Pima Indians: Contributions of obesity and parental diabetes. *American Journal of Epidemiology* 113: 144–56.

Kobberling, J., and R. B. Tattersall, eds. 1982. *The genetics of diabetes mellitus.* London.

Lepine, R. 1909. *Le Diabète sucré,* ed. F. Alcan. Paris.

Levine, R. 1986. Historical view of the classification of diabetes. *Clinical Chemistry* 32: 84–6.

Liebermann, L. S. 1988. Diabetes and obesity in elderly black Americans. In *Research on aging black populations,* ed. J. Jackson, 150–89. New York.

Mann, J. I., K. Pyorala, and A. Teuschner, eds. 1983. *Diabetes in epidemiological perspective.* Edinburgh.

Medalie, J. H., et al. 1974. Diabetes mellitus among 10,000 adult men: 1. Five year incidence and associated variables. *Israeli Journal of Medical Science* 10: 681–97.

1975. Major factors in the development of diabetes mellitus in 10,000 men. *Archives of Internal Medicine* 135: 811–18.

Miki, E. 1987. Renal disease in diabetes mellitus. *International Diabetes Federation Bulletin* 32: 127–9.

Mohan, V., A. Ramachandran, and M. Viswanathan. 1985. Tropical diabetes. In *The diabetes annual,* ed. K. G. M. M. Alberti and L. P. Krall, 82–92. New York.

Morse, J. L. 1913. Diabetes in infancy and childhood. *Boston Medical and Surgical Journal* 168: 530–5.

National Diabetes Advisory Board, eds. 1983. *The prevention and treatment of five complications of diabetes.* Washington, D.C.

National Diabetes Data Group. 1985. *Diabetes in America.* Washington, D.C.

Neel, J. V. 1962. Diabetes mellitus: a "thrifty" genotype rendered detrimental by "progress." *American Journal of Human Genetics* 14: 353–62.

Omar, M., et al. 1985. The prevalence of diabetes mellitus in a large group of South African Indians. *South African Medical Journal* 67: 924–6.

Panzram, G. 1987. Mortality and survival in type 2 (non-insulin-dependent) diabetes mellitus. *Diabetologia* 30: 123–31.

Rollo, J. 1798. The history, nature and treatment of diabetes mellitus. In *Causes of the diabetes mellitus,* ed. T. Gillet and C. Dilley. London.

Rosenbloom, A. L. 1977. Nature and nurture in the expression of diabetes mellitus and its vascular manifestations. *American Journal of Diseases of Children* 131: 1154–8.

Rosenbloom, A. L., et al. 1985. Screening for diabetes

mellitus. *Journal of the Florida Medical Association* 72: 1033–7.

Samanta, A., et al. 1985. Prevalence of known diabetes in Asians and Europeans. *British Medical Journal* 291: 1571–2.

Saundby, R. 1908. Diabetes mellitus. In *A system of medicine by many writers,* ed. C. Allbutt and H. D. Rolleston, 167–212. London.

Schiff, Moritz. 1857. Mitteilungen von Herrn Professor Schiff in Bern. *Archiv für Physiolgische Heilkunde* 1: 263–6.

Sen, B. C. 1893. Diabetes mellitus. *Indian Medical Gazette,* July, 241–8.

Silwer, H. 1958. Incidence of diabetes mellitus in the Swedish county of Kristianstad. Incidence and coincidence of diabetes mellitus and pulmonary tuberculosis in a Swedish county. *Acta Medica Scandinavica* [*Supplement*] 335: 5–22.

Simpson, N. E. 1968. Diabetes in the families of diabetics. *Canadian Medical Association Journal* 98: 427–32.

Sinha, Denesh. 1984. Obesity and related diseases in the Caribbean. *Cajanus* 17: 79–106.

Stern, Michael. 1983. Epidemiology of diabetes and coronary heart disease among Mexican-Americans. *Association of Life Insurance Medical Directors of America* 67: 79–90.

Striker, Cecil. 1961. *Famous faces in diabetes.* Boston.

Tauscher, T., et al. 1987. Absence of diabetes in a rural West African population with a high carbohydrate/cassava diet. *Lancet* i: 765–8.

Taylor, R., and P. Zimmet. 1983. Migrant studies and diabetes epidemiology. In *Diabetes in epidemiological perspective,* ed. J. I. Mann, K. Pyorala, and A. Teuscher, 58–77. Edinburgh.

Tiwari, J. L., and P. I. Terasaki. 1985. *PI: HLA and disease associations.* New York.

Trowell, H., D. P. Burkitt, and K. Heaton. 1985. *Dietary fiber, fiber-depleted foods and disease.* London.

Tulloch, J. A. 1962. *Diabetes mellitus in the tropics.* Edinburgh.

  1966. Diabetes in Africa. In *Diabetes mellitus,* ed. L. J. Duncan, 115–24. Edinburgh.

Viveros, M. G. 1980. Research on diabetes mellitus. In *Biomedical research in Latin America: Background studies,* ed. U.S. Department of Health, Education and Welfare, 165–78. Washington, D.C.

Von Mering, J., and O. Minkowski, 1889. Diabetes mellitus nach Pankrease stirpation. *Zentrablatt für klinische Medizin* 10: 393–4.

Walker, A. R. P. 1966. Prevalence of diabetes mellitus. *Lancet* i: 1163.

Waugh, N. R. 1986. Insulin-dependent diabetes in a Scottish region: Incidence and urban/rural differences. *Journal of Epidemiology and Community Health* 40: 240–3.

West, K. M. 1978. *Epidemiology of diabetes and its vascular lesions.* New York.

Wilcox, H. B. 1908. Diabetes in infants and young children. *Archives of Pediatrics* 25: 655–68.

Williamson, R. T. 1909. Geographic distribution of diabetes mellitus. *Medical Chronicle* 1: 234–52.

Willis, Thomas. 1697. Of the diabetes or pissing evil. In *Pharmaceutics rationalis,* Chap. 3. London.

World Health Organization. 1964. *Statistical yearbook: epidemiology and vital statistics report* 17: 40, 51, 307–30. Geneva.

  1972. *World health statistics annual, 1970–1972.* Geneva.

  1980. *Expert committee on diabetes mellitus,* 2d Report. Technical Report Series No. 646. Geneva.

  1984. *World health statistics annual, 1978–1983.* Geneva.

  1985. Multinational study of vascular diseases in diabetes: Prevalence of small vessel and large vessel disease in diabetic patients from 4 countries. *Diabetologia* 28: 616–40.

VIII.35
Diarrheal Diseases (Acute)

Acute diarrheal illness can be defined as the sudden onset of the passage of a greater number of stools than usual that show a decrease in form. It is generally accompanied by other clinical symptoms such as fecal urgency, tenesmus, abdominal cramps, pain, nausea, and vomiting. In most cases the symptom complex is a result of intestinal infection by a viral, bacterial, or parasitic enteropathogen; occasionally it is secondary to ingestion of a microbial exotoxin.

Distribution and Incidence

Acute diarrhea is often hyperendemic in certain populations: infants and young children in developing tropical countries of Latin America, Africa, and southern Asia; persons traveling from industrialized to developing regions; military populations stationed in or deployed to tropical areas; and toddlers who are not toilet trained and are attending day-care centers. Diarrhea rates in children less than 5 years of age in developing countries range from between three and seven episodes per child each year. The rate of diarrhea for non-toilet-trained infants in day-care centers in urban areas of the United States is comparable to the rate of illness seen in Third World countries. Travelers' diarrhea occurs in 20 to 40 percent of persons visiting high-risk areas from regions showing low disease endemicity. The rate of diarrhea occurrence in infants and young children under 5 years of age in the United States is approximately 0.8 to 1.0 episode per child each year. In all populations, acute diarrhea occurs less commonly in older children and adults than in infants.

Etiology and Epidemiology

The ultimate source of most of the enteric pathogens is infected humans, although for selected pathogenic organisms (i.e., *Salmonella*, *Giardia*), animals may serve as a reservoir. Environmental factors play an important role in disease endemicity. Both water quality and water quantity are important. Although the degree of microbial contamination of water may be responsible for exposure to diarrhea-producing organisms, the availability of adequate amounts of water for personal and environmental cleansing, even if it is contaminated, may be beneficial. Sewage removal is a prerequisite for clean water and a healthful environment.

Personal and food hygiene standards in a population are important to enteric infectious disease occurrence. Effective handwashing as a routine practice is practically unheard of in many areas of the developing world. Food all too often is improperly handled. Vegetables and fruits rarely are washed properly when reaching the house prior to preparation, despite the fact that they may have been exposed to human excreta used as fertilizer. Foods may be contaminated by unclean kitchen surfaces or hands. One of the most important errors in food hygiene is the storage of foods containing moisture at ambient temperatures between meals, which encourages microbial replication. This problem is especially severe during the warmer months. Medical care is often inadequate so that intestinal carriage of microbial pathogens and continued dissemination of the agents continue. Finally, underlying medical conditions can contribute both to the occurrence of diarrhea and to the severity of the resultant disease; measles and malnutrition are two important examples.

In most countries where acute diarrhea is a serious medical problem, it tends to be most prevalent during the warmer months. The reason is probably that bacteria grow rapidly in warm, moist conditions. Flies also can play a role in the transmission of enteric infections.

In day-care centers, when a non–toilet-trained child develops diarrhea, a variety of fecal organisms may spread to the hands of teachers and children, and to the toys shared by the children. Because of the efficient interchange of organisms during outbreaks, several pathogenic organisms are often identified during the same time period.

By employing optimal enteric microbiological techniques, an etiologic agent can be detected in approximately 50 percent of cases of acute diarrhea. The specific agent responsible for acute diarrhea will generally depend upon the age of the host, the geographic location, and the season. Table VIII.35.1 summarizes the most important etiologic agents in diarrhea, and Table VIII.35.2 indicates the microorganisms most frequently associated with diarrhea in certain settings.

Immunology

When an enteric infectious microorganism is highly endemic and there is a high degree of antigenic homogeneity among the implicated strains, immunity tends to develop with age. The infectious enteric organisms that fit this description and to which immunity is known to increase with age in endemic areas are the following: *Vibrio cholerae*, *Salmonella typhi*, enterotoxigenic *Escherichia coli*, *Shigella*, Norwalk virus, and *Rotavirus*. There is great hope that effective immunizing agents against these organisms will be developed for use in high-risk populations.

Clinical Manifestations

For most of the enteric infections, a characteristic clinical illness is not produced by a given etiologic agent. When patients acquire enteric infection, a variety of symptoms other than diarrhea may result, including abdominal cramps and pain, nausea, vomiting, and fecal urgency and incontinence or the urge but inability to defecate. When patients experience fever as a predominant finding, invasive bacterial pathogens should be suspected (*Salmonella*, *Shigella*, and *Campylobacter*). Vomiting is the primary complaint in viral gastroenteritis (often due to rotavirus in an infant or Norwalk-like viruses in older children or adults), staphylococcal food poisoning, or foodborne illness due to *Bacillus cereus*. When dysentery (the passage of small-volume stools that contain gross blood and mucus) occurs, amebic *Shigella* or *Campylobacter enteritis* should be suspected. In salmonellosis, gatroenteritis stools are grossly bloody in just under 10 percent of cases. Other less common causes of dysentery are inflammatory bowel disease, *Aeromonas*, *Vibrio parahemolyticus*, *Yersinia enterocolitica*, *Clostridium difficile*, and *Entamoeba histolytica*.

Table VIII.35.1. *Commonly identified etiologic agents in diarrheal disease*

Agent	Comment
Bacterial	
Escherichia coli	
Enteropathogenic *E. coli* (EPEC)	Causes infantile diarrhea; may cause chronic diarrhea
Enterotoxigenic *E. coli* (ETEC)	Major cause of infant and childhood diarrhea in developing tropical countries, and travelers' diarrhea
Enteroinvasive *E. coli* (EIEC)	Occasionally causes foodborne febrile diarrhea
Enterohemorrhagic colitis (EHEC)	Causes colitis, low-grade fever associated with hamburger consumption; may result in hemolytic uremic syndrome
Shigella, Salmonella, Campylobacter jejuni	Common in all areas, especially during the summertime
Aeromonas	Of uncertain importance
Plesiomonas shigelloides	Causes diarrhea in travelers and those exposed to seafood
Vibrio parahemolyticus, other nonagglutinable vibrios	Causes diarrhea in those exposed to seafood
Staphylococcus aureus, Bacillus cereus	Associated with foodborne outbreaks of vomiting ($\pm$ diarrhea)
Viral	
Rotavirus	Found in infants <2 years age; shows wintertime propensity in temperate climates; occurs in all seasons in tropical areas
Norwalk viruses	Major cause of waterborne and shellfish-associated gastroenteritis
Caliciviruses and enteric adenoviruses	Of uncertain importance
Parasitologic	
Giardia lamblia	Causes protracted diarrhea commonly in those exposed to mountainous areas or day-care centers
Entamoeba histolytica	Commonly causes recurrent diarrhea in persons living in tropical countries
Cryptosporidium	Causes diarrhea in patients with AIDS, those in day-care centers, and in travelers to Leningrad

Table VIII.35.2. *Etiologic agents of diarrhea, characteristically identified in special settings*

Setting	Commonly identified agents
Day-care centers	Rotavirus, *Giardia, Shigella,* Cryptosporidium
Person traveling from industrial to developing countries	Enterotoxigenic *Escherichia coli, Shigella, Salmonella, Campylobacter, Plesiomonas, Giardia*
Male homosexuals	*Herpes simplex, Chlamydia trachomatis, Treponema pallidum, Neisseria gonorrhoeae, Shigella, Salmonella, Campylobacter, Clostridium difficile, Giardia*
Acquired immune deficiency syndrome	Cryptosporidium, *Isospora belli, Herpes simplex,* cytomegalovirus, *Salmonella, Mycobacterium avium–intracellulare*

Pathology

A basic prerequisite for infection by enteric pathogens is attachment to the intestinal lining by the pathogenic microorganism. The mechanism of the attachment varies from a highly specific receptor–ligand interaction, as seen for enterotoxigenic *E. coli,* to a nonspecific type of attachment, as is seen for the protozoan *Giardia,* which possess sucking disks for intestinal adherence. Variable degrees of intestinal damage can be seen in enteric infection. No anatomic or structural alterations are found in infection by enterotoxigenic *E. coli* or *V. cholerae,* where intestinal secretion and watery diarrhea occur secondary to cyclic nucleotide stimulation.

In shigellosis and campylobacteriosis, extensive inflammation with microabscess formation is seen. Small bowel pathogens (rotavirus, Norwalk viruses, and *Giardia*) may lead to depletions of intestinal disaccharidases and lactose (milk) intolerance. Malnutrition, which is common in areas where diarrhea is highly endemic, leads to a more prolonged disease of greater severity, although malnutrition does not predispose to the occurrence of diarrhea.

The synergy between the effects of malnutrition and diarrhea is an important reason why death from diarrhea is so common in Third World countries. Diarrheal illnesses have adverse effects on growth and contribute to malnutrition. There is a 20 to 60 percent decrease in body caloric intake during a bout of diarrhea. Ways in which malnutrition contributes to more severe or prolonged diarrhea may include decreased gastric acidity, impaired intestinal immunity, greater exposure to a contaminated environment, delayed recovery of intestinal mucosa, and persistent lactase deficiency. The agents producing the greatest frequency of dehydration are *V. cholerae*, enterotoxigenic *E. coli,* and rotavirus. Rotavirus is the major cause of death in infants with diarrhea.

History

Diarrheal diseases have been important to all societies since the beginning of recorded history. Hippocrates used the term "dysentery" to denote a condition wherein the affected person, experiencing straining and painful defecation, passed many stools containing blood and mucus. Through the First World War, outbreaks of diarrhea and dysentery were as important to deciding the outcome of many military campaigns as were war-related injuries.

The modern era of diarrheal diseases began, as was the case with other infectious disorders, with the identification of the causative agents involved. During the mid-1800s, *Giardia lamblia* and *Entamoeba histolytica* were first identified. Then during the latter part of the nineteenth century, *Shigella* and *Salmonella* organisms were characterized, and the two forms of dysentery – bacillary and amebic – were distinguished.

During the 1960s, a series of landmark studies helped to elucidate the mechanisms of disease production when cholera toxin was purified. As an extension of research with *V. cholerae* during the 1970s, enterotoxigenic *E. coli* were identified as important causes of diarrhea. Soon thereafter, other enterotoxin- or cytotoxin-producing bacteria were discovered: *Salmonella, Aeromonas, Yersinia, Clostridium perfrigens, C. difficile,* enterohemorrhagic *E. coli,* noncholera vibrios, and *Staphylococcus aureus.*

Also during the early 1970s, viruses were clearly implicated as causes of diarrhea in humans. Initially, Norwalk virus was shown to produce gastroenteritis in volunteers fed bacteria-free stool filtrates derived from an elementary school outbreak in Norwalk, Ohio, and the 27-millimeter viral particle was visualized by electron microscopy. Soon thereafter, larger viral particles were observed in the duodenal mucosa of infants with diarrhea, and within a few years rotaviruses were established as a major cause of infantile gastroenteritis. Additional pathogens are being identified in cases of diarrheal disease as the research laboratory discovers novel mechanisms of pathogenesis or as new microbiological techniques for isolation and identification are developed. The future will bring studies of organism-specific epidemiology, therapy, and disease prevention.

Prevention and Treatment

The factors contributing to the problem of acute diarrhea are well known. However, their modification will not be easy because of cost and required changes in behavior. The important variables that will require attention include the following: availability of plentiful potable water; adequate systems of sewage removal; improved personal and food hygiene; improved nutrition through food supplementation programs; discontinuance of the practice of using night soil as fertilizer; promotion of breast feeding; effective measles vaccine programs; availability of adequate health care to administer oral rehydration therapy and selected antimicrobial therapy; family planning; insect control; vaccine development and implementation for certain enteric infections such as cholera, enterotoxigenic *E. coli* diarrhea, rotavirus gastroenteritis, shigellosis, and typhoid fever. Because achieving all of these activities will initially be too costly in developing areas, research in developed countries will be essential to devising cost-effective prevention and treatment methods.

Currently there are three forms of therapy for acute diarrhea. The first and most fundamental form of treatment is fluid and electrolyte replacement. Nearly all forms of acute diarrhea can be successfully managed by administering oral rehydration solution. For dehydrating choleralike illnesses, the solution should have optimal electrolyte–glucose concentrations to facilitate intestinal absorption. The major problems with this solution are that it does not provide the caloric requirements of infants with diarrhea, and it may actually increase stool fluid losses. Newer "super solutions" are being evaluated that are better absorbed and furnish more calories at no osmotic expense. For nondehydrating forms of diarrhea, solutions with lower sodium concentrations are useful. The second form of therapy involves drugs that reduce the symptoms of diarrhea by inhibiting secretion or by binding to luminal water. The final form is antimicrobial therapy directed against a bacterial or parasitic agent, which is of value in the treatment of enterotoxigenic *E. coli* diarrhea, shigellosis, and travelers' diarrhea.

Herbert L. DuPont

Bibliography

Davison, W.C. 1922. A bacteriological and clinical consideration of bacillary dysentery in adults and children. *Medicine* 1: 389–510.

DuPont, H. L., and L. K. Pickering. 1980. *Infections of the gastrointestinal tract, microbiology, pathophysiology, and clinical features.* New York.

DuPont, H. L., et al. 1971. Pathogenesis of *Escherichia coli* diarrhea. *New England Journal of Medicine* 285: 1–9.

Gorbach, S. L. 1978. *Infectious diarrhea*. Boston.

Mata, L. J., 1978. *The children of Santa Maria Cauque: A prospective field study of health and growth*. Cambridge, Mass.

Nalin, D. R., et al. 1968. Oral maintenance therapy for cholera in adults. *Lancet* ii: 370–3.

Puffer, R. R., and C. V. Serrano. 1973. *Patterns of mortality in childhood*. Pan American Health Organization Scientific Publication No. 262. Washington, D.C.

VIII.36
Diphtheria

Diphtheria is a human disease caused by *Corynebacterium diphtheriae,* so named for its clubbed shape (Greek: *koryne,* or "club") and for the hidelike pseudomembrane (Greek: *diphtheria,* for "shield" or "membrane") that forms on the tonsils, palate, or pharynx in severe cases of infection. Although this bacillus may cause no more than an innocent, subclinical infection and can be transmitted via well carriers, during diphtheria epidemics more virulent strains are responsible for case fatality rates ranging from 30 to 50 percent of affected young children. In such circumstances the bacterium itself is infected by a phage virus responsible for the elaboration of a potent exotoxin. Even though the exotoxin can cause rapid fatty degeneration of the heart muscle and peripheral nervous system damage resulting in paralysis, young children often die because the airway is occluded. Both the suddenness of suffocation in children and the capricious emergence of virulent epidemics of diphtheria are important features of historical interest in the disease.

Also called the Klebs–Löffler bacillus in early twentieth-century medical literature, this gram-positive organism is usually spread by respiratory secretions and droplet infection. After a brief incubation period of 2 to 4 days, the bacillus multiplies in the upper respiratory tract, creating a membranous exudate on pharyngeal tissues. The bacillus invades the local tissues and kills cells, causing necrosis and, often, discoloration of the membrane. The foul breath associated with necrosis and the greenish or blackened membrane are hallmarks of the disease to most clinical observers differentiating diphtheria from streptococcal sore throat and from croup. The

organism rarely causes a systemic infection, however, although skin infections are common in tropical regions. Most damage to the infected individual is produced by the powerful toxin disseminated through the bloodstream.

Distribution, Incidence, and Immunity

Corynebacteria are distributed throughout the world, but *C. diphtheriae* occurs naturally only in humans. Farm animals can be infected through human cases, and many laboratory animals are susceptible to deliberate infection. Indeed, diphtheria's wide host range accounts for part of the success in studying this organism during the early bacteriologic revolution.

In historical accounts, it is often described as a malignant sore throat, and one of the most puzzling features is the sudden appearance of an epidemic. In the "throat distemper" epidemic of colonial New England, Boston was spared the high childhood mortality and morbidity experience elsewhere in Massachusetts and New Hampshire, illustrating the patchy geographic distribution of severe cases that one could observe even during an epidemic. Peter English (1985) describes how a phage virus is associated with the virulence of the diphtheria bacilli in that the "tox" gene can either elaborate toxin (tox$^+$) or not (tox$^-$). But in both cases the presence of this gene incorporated into the bacterial DNA stimulates immunity to virulent diphtheria. Because a low-iron environment or medium tends to stimulate or facilitate the production of toxin, English further speculates that the nutritional poverty of many premodern populations helped to discourage the frequent recurrence of epidemic diphtheria. Many other researchers, including Ernest Caulfield (1939), point to a mixture of organisms during epidemics of sore throat, diphtheritic and pseudodiphtheritic. In the Boston epidemic of sore throat in 1735, for example, a rash accompanied clinical cases, suggesting coinfection with streptococcal organisms. Suprainfection with streptococcus is common even for true diphtheria, but it is not known what influence, if any, the presence of a copathogen has in the elaboration of toxin.

The phage carrying the tox$^+$ genome does enhance iron binding, permitting the microorganism to acquire this essential metabolite for its reproduction. Normally the human immune system is able to withhold iron and "starve" a pathogen (Weinberg 1978). Thus the production of toxin and the emergence of virulent strains should not depend upon an individual host's nutritional status. Epidemiologically the appearance of virulent diphtheria epidemics should reflect increased opportunities for transmitting the bacillus to susceptible hosts, as through crowding or urbanization. Historically diphtheria epidemics were recorded only after medical theories supported recognition of the clinical specificity of this disease.

Epidemiology

The ultimate sources of diphtheritic contagion are humans. In addition to respiratory transmission of the bacillus through cutaneous diphtheritic lesions, the disease can be spread by touch and by fomites – such as schoolchildren's pencils. Thus, an infection can be transmitted to a cow's udders from an infected milker's fingers. Milk, if unpasteurized, can also transmit the infection. Even dust around the bed of a diphtheria patient can remain infective for weeks (Christie 1974).

The experience with diphtheria in England and Wales, from 1915 to 1942, is probably typical of industrialized countries in the twentieth century. Early in this period, over 50,000 cases were reported each year, and it was the leading cause of death for children aged 4 to 10 years. Over this time period, however, case fatality rates declined by 40 percent as a result of more rapid diagnosis and therapeutic interventions in the form of antitoxin and tracheostomy (surgically providing a way to breathe when the upper pharynx is occluded).

After World War II, mass immunization efforts effected a rapid decline in the overall number of cases, and the age of incidence rose. In virulent cases of diphtheria, mortality remains today around 5 percent, a fact that leads A. B. Christie (1974) to assert that we do not possess convincing proof that antitoxin alone reverses the clinical course of diphtheria. The organism itself is sensitive to penicillin.

Unlike measles, the common early springtime viral disease of childhood, diphtheria in temperate climates usually peaks in incidence in autumn and early winter. Most cases during the last 200 years have occurred among individuals under 15 years of age. Crowded conditions to which the poor are subjected facilitate passage of the organism, and so accounts of diphtheria before the germ theory of disease was widely accepted often described it as a filth disease naturally favoring the poor (Ziporyn 1988). In tropical regions cutaneous diphtheria is much more common, resulting in "punched," weeping ulcers sometimes called "desert sores." Contact with these lesions, usually on the extremities, is probably an important means of spreading the disease in such regions.

Clinical Manifestations and Pathology

Even virulent diphtheria begins quietly, after a brief incubation period. Its victims rarely suffer the high fever, vomiting, or myalgias common in acute viral illnesses, and the sore throat is much less pronounced than it is in streptococcal pharyngitis. As the organism multiplies and invades pharyngeal tissues, however, the area around the neck can swell dramatically, and internally the passage of air becomes difficult. The "bullneck" appearance of a diphtheria sufferer differs from the streptococcus victim because there is little enlargement of the regional lymphatic nodes. If the victim can open his or her mouth, an observer usually will see a membrane 1 to 3 millimeters thick, its rough edge curling away from the tonsils, palate, uvula, or pharynx. Depending upon the amount of destruction of local blood vessels, this "shield" can range in color from a more benign-appearing yellowish white, to green or even black. An exudate that remains white, whether or not it looks like a membrane, is usually not due to diphtheria.

The German pathologist Edwin Klebs first identified the *C. diphtheriae* in 1883 by peeling off this membrane and culturing the bleeding surface underneath. The following year Friedrich Löffler developed an enriched medium on which to grow the delicate bacillus, which could be rapidly overgrown by other organisms cultured from the mouth and pharynx. Both noted the absence of other affected organs at autopsy of diphtheria victims. The bacillus is not distributed through the body, but the toxin alone seems to have the lethal effects described above. Most perplexing is the peripheral nervous system involvement, contributing to a characteristic progression of paralysis in diphtheria victims: first the palate, then the eyes, then the heart, pharynx, and larynx (with respiratory muscles), and finally the limbs. In virulent diphtheria, patients appear quite toxic, and, although the fever is not usually high, the pulse is elevated.

Diagnosis and Treatment

The "Schick test" can help to identify diphtheria sufferers in that it depends upon a patient's failure to react to a small amount of purified toxin injected subcutaneously, thus signaling the absence of antitoxin in the body, in turn indicating an absence of previous diphtheria infection. Because many factors can influence the accurate reading and interpretation of such a test, most laboratory diagnosis depends upon culture of the organism itself on enriched "blood agar" or the "Löffler slant" tellurite medium developed over a century ago. Penicillin, antitoxin, and maintenance of an open airway are the usual means of clinical intervention.

History

It is impossible to determine whether diphtheria was at any point a "new" disease in recorded human history, though it is so described during the early modern period. Diseases resembling diphtheria are also described in Greek medical literature of antiquity (English 1985) and during the sixteenth through eighteenth century. Historical interest in this particular disease has nevertheless been confined largely to the role diphtheria played in the emergence and confirmation of the germ theory of disease. As Terra Ziporyn (1988) points out, diphtheria was to a considerable extent "the darling of the bacteriological revolution."

A clinician of Tours trained during the French Revolution, Pierre Bretonneau was the first to describe the specific clinical features of diphtheria and to give the disease its name. Witnessing relatively severe epidemics in the mid-1820s, Bretonneau carefully noted the appearance of a pseudomembrane as a hallmark of the disease and used this particular infection to elaborate his concepts of disease specificity, based on uniform clinical and postmortem findings. Nevertheless, diphtheria was usually viewed as a disease of poverty, rather than as an exceptionally severe threat to human survival, as were epidemics of cholera and yellow fever. Periodic peaks in diphtheria mortality received no attention among clinicians.

Immediately after Robert Koch articulated a germ theory of disease based on his 1882 work with tuberculosis, Klebs and Löffler clearly demonstrated the precise causal connection between diphtheritic organisms and membranous sore throat. Löffler especially provided an elegant summary of the isolation and culture of *C. diphtheriae* together with a description of Koch's principles as "postulates" proving the germ theory (Lechevalier and Solotorovsky 1974). Löffler's classic paper in 1884 also introduced some of the most basic and innovative research problems for germ theorists. Speculating upon the reasons why diphtheria bacilli, unlike *Mycobacterium tuberculosis,* failed to invade areas of the body other than the nasopharynx, Löffler ventured that an "extraordinarily deleterious" poison was disseminated through the bloodstream. Moreover, his careful work illustrated that the organism could not always be cultured from the throats of clinically "typical" cases and that healthy individuals could carry diphtheria bacilli. The latter

phenomenon led Löffler in 1887 to a description of nonvirulent strains of diphtheria.

Filtering cultures of bacilli in Louis Pasteur's laboratory, P. P. Emile Roux and Alexandre Yersin demonstrated the probability of Löffler's hypothesis that a toxin was involved in lethal cases of diphtheria. In 1888 they showed that bacteria-free filtrates reproduced all features of the disease in experimental animals except the formation of a membrane, and they tried unsuccessfully to apply Pasteur's rabies method in habituating animals to the toxin. Soon afterward, in 1890, Emil Behring and Shibasaburo Kitasato, working in Koch's laboratory, explored the use of serum from convalescing individuals to treat diphtheria patients (and experimental animals). Thus before the beginning of the twentieth century, diphtheria had provided the best single model for proving the germ theory of disease, and suggested the concept of the healthy carrier, the possibility of filterable (nonbacterial) disease agents, and the general usefulness of serology in diagnosis and treatment of infectious disease.

After a legendary, dramatic, Christmas eve rescue of a diphtheritic child with the Kitasato–Behring serum, Behring personally escalated his study and production of "antitoxin," standardizing and popularizing his procedures for harvesting immune serum from horses inoculated with filtered toxin. Diphtheria rapidly became a largely curable disease, and Behring was honored as the "children's savior" and elevated to the hereditary nobility of Germany. Simultaneously, however, diphtheria was depicted as a classic, feared contagious disease and, unlike so many diseases in this category, as a widespread, merciless killer of innocent children. Indiana physician Thurman Rice, for example, vividly recalled that his father "drove two miles out of his way to avoid passing in front of a house where there was a case of diphtheria, and yet this house stood at least one hundred yards back from the road; he had children and was taking no chances" (Rice 1927). Diphtheria also frames the plot for one of the most famous physician stories in the English language, William Carlos Williams's "The Use of Force" (1933).

Finally, the study of diphtheria was involved in two further stages of twentieth-century research on the germ theory and its applications. First, the Schick test helped to identify individuals who had no immune response to small doses of toxin injected just under the skin. In the testing of immunity and the anaphylactic responses of individuals with "serum sickness" in response to foreign sera (a considerable problem with Behring's method), clinicians used

Table VIII.36.1. *Diphtheria mortality rate per 100,000 population*

	New York	Chicago	Boston	Pittsburgh	Washington
1890–4	134.4	117.3	112.2	86.4	77.9
1895–9	85.8	69.7	83.9	32.9	50.9
1900–4	58.0	33.9	53.7	36.9	23.5
1905–9	40.0	27.0	26.2	20.4	11.2
1910–14	28.0	37.9	20.0	29.3	6.9
1915–19	21.8	31.2	26.3	22.3	11.9
1920–4	14.0	17.5	20.2	20.1	10.5
1925–9	10.7	11.7	8.3	11.5	7.1
1930–4	2.2	4.5	3.2	5.1	3.7
1935–9	0.6	2.2	0.7	1.3	2.8
1940–4	0.1	0.8	0.4	0.5	0.2

Source: Diphtheria mortality in large cities of the United States in 1947 (1948).

diphtheria throughout the early part of the century to delineate the research problems in human immunity (Levy 1975). (See Table VIII.36.1 for trends in large U.S. cities.) Second, in the early 1950s, identification and isolation of the phage virus that infected diphtheria bacilli greatly aided early research establishing phage–bacterial chromosome relationships and, in the process, the fields of bacterial genetics and molecular biology (Berksdale 1971).

Ann G. Carmichael

Bibliography

Berksdale, Lane. 1971. The gene tox⁺ of *Corynebacterium diphtheriae.* In *Of microbes and life,* ed. Jacques Monod and Ernest Borek. New York.

Biggs, H. M. 1899. The serum-treatment and its results. *Medical News* 75: 97.

Billings, J. S. 1905. Ten years' experience with diphtheria antitoxin. *New York Medical Journal* 82: 1310.

Caulfield, Ernest. 1939. *The throat distemper of 1735–1740.* New Haven.

Christie, A. B. 1974. *Infectious diseases: Epidemiology and clinical practice,* 2d edition. London.

Diphtheria mortality in large cities of the United States in 1947. 1948. *Journal of the American Medical Association* 137: 1525.

Dolman, Claude. 1973. Landmarks and pioneers in the control of diphtheria. *Canadian Journal of Public Health* 64: 317–36.

English, Peter C. 1985. Diphtheria and theories of infectious disease: Centennial appreciation of the critical role of diphtheria in the history of medicine. *Pediatrics* 76: 1–9.

Lechevalier, H. A., and M. Solotorovsky. 1974. *Three centuries of microbiology.* New York.

Levy, F. M. 1975. The fiftieth anniversary of diphtheria and tetanus immunization. *Preventive Medicine* 4: 226–37.

Major, Ralph H. 1965. *Classic descriptions of disease,* 3d edition. Springfield, Ill.

Rice, Thurman B. 1927. *The conquest of disease.* New York.

Weinberg, Eugene D. 1978. Iron and infection. *Microbiological Reviews* 42: 45–66.

Williams, William C. 1984. The use of force. In *The doctor stories,* ed. Robert Coles. New York.

Ziporyn, Terra. 1988. *Disease in the popular American press: The case of diphtheria, typhoid fever, and syphilis, 1870–1920.* Westport, Conn.

VIII.37
Down Syndrome

Down syndrome, previously called "mongolism," is a relatively common condition resulting from the presence of an extra chromosome, number 21, in all the cells of the body. In each human cell, there are 23 chromosome pairs containing basic genetic material that organizes the body's development and physiological functioning. Each pair has a distinctive size and conformation and can be readily identified on microscopic examination. Chromosome pair number 21 is one of the smaller chromosomes. In Down syndrome there are usually three (*trisomy*) rather than two number 21 chromosomes (*trisomy 21:* found in 95 to 98 percent of all cases). In a small number of children with Down syndrome, the extra number 21 chromosome is attached to a chromosome of a larger pair (numbers 13 to 15; *translocation Down syndrome* – about 2 percent of all cases). In some children with the features of Down syndrome, the extra chromosome is present in less than 90 percent of the cells (*mosaic Down syndrome* – about 2 to 4 percent of all cases). Down syndrome is the most frequently occurring chromosome abnormality in live-born humans, and is also among the most frequently identified chromosomal abnormalities, representing about 4 percent of all aborted fetuses (Lilienfeld 1969). Down syndrome is usually recognizable at birth as a cluster of physical and neurological abnormalities (see Clinical Manifestations), which develop in a characteristic fashion during the life cycle.

Distribution and Incidence

Recent estimates of overall worldwide incidence of Down syndrome are around 0.8 per 1,000 live births (Janerich and Bracken 1986). In the United States, the 1983 Birth Defects Monitoring Program indicated an incidence of 0.82 per 1,000 live births. These figures evidence a decline from those reported 20 years ago in Western countries, where incidence was about 1.7 per 1,000. This change is thought to be the result of the use of prenatal diagnosis.

Down syndrome occurs in all races and ethnic groups, though good documentation of specific incidence in many groups and geographic areas is lacking (Lilienfeld 1969). There is some evidence for spatial aggregation, such as in northern Finland and British Columbia (Janerich and Bracken 1986), but these instances appear to be sporadic, and are probably related to environmental sources.

Epidemiology and Etiology

The presence of the additional number 21 chromosome in all cells of the individual with Down syndrome is usually the result of an error in cell division called *nondisjunction*. In normal cell division, the two members of each of the 23 chromosome pairs separate and move into one of the two resulting cells, whereas in nondisjunction, both members of the chromosome pair end up in a single cell. In Down syndrome, the nondisjunction has usually occurred during meiosis (sex cell division) usually of the female sex cell (the ovum). Thus, when an ovum with two number 21 chromosomes is fertilized, three number 21 chromosomes (two from the mother and one from the father) will be passed on to all the cells in the developing fetus. The occurrence of Down syndrome is most consistently associated with advanced maternal age, with incidence rising from 0.45 per 1,000 live births in women 20 to 24 years of age (8 studies) to 9.4 per 1,000 live births for women 40 to 44 years (7 studies). The largest risk increase occurs between the age groups 30 to 34 and 34 to 39 years (Lilienfeld 1969).

Four potential reasons for the maternal age association have been suggested:

1. Whereas the prenatal incidence of Down syndrome is constant across all ages, the older uterus is less selective in rejecting the Down syndrome conceptus.
2. Longer delays between intercourse result in a relatively "aged ovum," more likely to experience nondisjunction.
3. In older women, the ova themselves have aged longer and have an increased rate of nondisjunction.
4. Long-term exposure to environmental agents has resulted in damage to the spindle mechanism that in turn produces meiotic nondisjunction.

Because the additional chromosome can be traced to the father in 20 percent of the cases of Down syndrome, studies have also evaluated a paternal age effect on incidence. However, such an effect cannot be conclusively demonstrated (Janerich and Bracken 1986).

About 30 to 60 percent of all Down syndrome births, however, are not age dependent, meaning that they occur in mothers of ages under 30 years. Indeed, a high incidence of infants with Down syndrome has recently been reported in women less than 15 years of age. In both younger and older sibs of index patients, the risk of having offspring with Down syndrome is increased 2- to 10-fold. Younger mothers are more likely to have a second offspring with Down syndrome than are older mothers. The recurrence risk is 1 in 3 for mothers who are translocation carriers.

A number of environmental and metabolic mechanisms for Down syndrome have been evaluated, among them maternal drug, tobacco, alcohol, and caffeine use; use of hormonal and nonhormonal contraceptives; fluoridated water; and radiation exposure. However, findings from these studies have been inconsistent. Some investigators have suggested that a possible recessive gene producing nondisjunction might explain up to 10 percent of the cases. However, studies in consanguineous marriages do not support this suggestion. Dwight Janerich and Michael Bracken (1986) indicate that the association with elevated maternal age is undoubtedly a surrogate variable for other underlying associated factors, the most important of which are probably endocrine changes associated with aging.

Clinical Manifestations

The most easily recognizable features of Down syndrome derive from abnormalities in growth of the cranium and face. These include a short, relatively broad head (brachycephaly), hypoplastic maxilla, upslanting palpebral fissures, epicanthal folds, increased neck skin, small ears, and flattened nasal bridge. Common postcranial anomalies include a wide space between the first and second toe, abnormal finger and palm dermatoglyphs (in particular, the occurrence of single palmar creases), and shortened distal long bones. About 80 percent of children with Down syndrome are hypotonic and 90 percent are hyperflexible. There are also variably associated major organ anomalies, the most important being congenital heart disease (CHD), which occurs in 30 to 50 percent of all children with Down syndrome. In addition, metabolic and hormonal systems are variably affected and include, among others, carbohydrate metabolism, deficient absorption of vitamin A, elevated serum uric acid, and abnormal serotonin metabolism.

In an extensive recent survey of 1,341 children with Down syndrome born between 1952 and 1981 in British Columbia, Patricia Baird and Adel Sadovnick (1987) reported survival rates up to 30 years of age in 50 percent for those with CHD, but nearly 80 percent for those without CHD. The survival rate for the latter group, however, was less than that for a comparison group of mentally retarded individuals without Down syndrome.

Children with Down syndrome experience abnormal physical and cognitive development. Birth weight and length are near normal, but the growth rate in the first 3 years of life is significantly slower than normal, and most children are less than the fifth percentile in height by the time they are 3 years of age. Growth rate during childhood is near normal, but the adolescent growth spurt is often absent (Cronk et al. 1988). Deficient growth differentially affects distal segments of the long bones. Whereas some early developmental milestones are normal, more marked delays in walking, talking, and other motor and cognitive skills usually become apparent by the end of the first year of life. Mild to moderate mental retardation (IQ: 30 to 67) is commonly present by childhood. Recent innovations in early intervention and new special education programing allow individuals with Down syndrome to hold jobs as adults in sheltered work situations.

History and Geography
Probably the earliest record of Down syndrome was a Saxon skull excavated in the seventh century showing osteological changes consistent with the condition. There are also accounts of sixteenth-century paintings of children having the features of the syndrome. The first accounts of Down syndrome, however, did not appear until the nineteenth century. In 1846 E. Sequin wrote of a specific type of mental retardation case, which he described as a "furfuraceous cretin with its white, rosy, and peeling skin, with its shortcomings of all the integuments, which give an unfinished aspect to the truncated fingers and nose; with its cracked lips and tongue; with its

red ectropic conjunctiva, coming to supply the curtailed skin at the margin of the lids" (quoted in Brousseau and Brainerd 1928). The first formal description was given in a report by J. Langdon Down in 1866. He described a type of congenital defect bearing resemblance to the Tartar race which he called Kalmuc or Mongolian. Down, who had been influenced by the racial hypothesis and the writings of Charles Darwin, suggested that the entity represented a reversion to an earlier phylogenetic type. This hypothesis never gained wide acceptance, and in fact, Down's own son, also a doctor, disagreed with it, suggesting that the features of the syndrome were accidental and superficial (Brain 1967).

The next important reports were presented by John Fraser and Arthur Mitchell in 1875 at the Royal College of Physicians in Edinburgh. Mitchell pointed out the similarities between the syndrome and "cretinism" (congenital hypothyroidism). Reports by W. W. Ireland and G. E. Shuttleworth followed during the 1870s and 1880s. Shuttleworth suggested that children with the condition were actually "unfinished," representing the persistence of anatomy characteristic of a particular phase in fetal development. He specifically cited the already recognized association between the syndrome and advanced maternal age, pointing out the large number of children with Down syndrome who were the last-born in large families. During the end of the nineteenth and beginning of the twentieth centuries, many reports appeared, expanding the description of the syndrome's phenotypic manifestations. Important among these were the extensive neuropathological descriptions by A. W. Wilmarth presented in reports from 1885 to 1890.

From the initial description in the mid-nineteenth century to 1959, a large number of etiologic hypotheses were advanced for the syndrome, including maternal syphilis, familial tuberculosis, familial incidence of epilepsy, insanity, instability, and mental retardation. Once the increased incidence of congenital heart disease in the syndrome was recognized by John Thomson and A. E. Garrod in 1898, a cause in early fetal existence was sought. Among theories advanced were maternal alcoholism, fetal hyperthyroidism, maternal dysthyroidism, hypoplasia of the adrenals, dysfunction of the pituitary, abnormality of the thymus, chemical contraceptives, curettage, faulty implantation, degeneration of the ovum, and emotional shock in early pregnancy.

As early as 1932, a chromosomal anomaly was suggested as a possible cause of the disorder (Bleyer 1934). In 1959, shortly after the correct diploid number of chromosomes in the human cell was established, a small sample of children with Down syndrome were demonstrated to have an extra acrocentric chromosome and a total chromosome number of 47 in cultures of fibroblasts. This finding was verified by subsequent studies. Later in the same year, J. A. Book and co-workers (Book, Fraccaro, and Lindsten 1959) concluded that the extra chromosome was most similar to number 21 in the Denver classification. In 1960, other investigators reported the case of a girl with Down syndrome having only 46 chromosomes, and postulated a reciprocal translocation occurring between two chromosome groups (Polani et al. 1960).

Initially, Down syndrome was thought to occur only in the Caucasian race. Subsequently, however, reports have shown that it occurs in every racial group and country although thorough, well-designed studies have not allowed an accurate picture of its true distribution across racial and ethnic groups. Early reports indicated a low incidence in African and black American groups. However, recent investigations in Ibadan, Nigeria, and in Memphis, Tennessee, found black incidence rates much the same as those of white populations (Janerich and Bracken 1986). Similarly, although detection in Oriental populations is thought to be inhibited by sameness of features, recent studies in Japan reveal rates much like those in the United States. An extensive study from the World Health Organization in 1966 indicated that a low incidence of Down syndrome is reported in India, Malaysia, and Egypt (Lilienfeld 1969), whereas by contrast a high incidence was reported in Yugoslavia, Czechoslovakia, and at least one location in Melbourne, Australia.

A. M. Lilienfeld (1969) summarized 11 studies that attempted to indicate the spatial and temporal clustering of the syndrome. However, even the most sophisticated of these, carried out in Melbourne, Australia (Collman and Stoller 1962), failed to give satisfactory statistical proof for clustering. A 1983 report by P. M. Sheehan and I. B. Hillary describes a cluster of children with Down syndrome born to women who attended the same boarding school in their youth. This suggests that in some instances, an environmental agent may influence the incidence of Down syndrome.

Christine E. Cronk

Bibliography

Baird, P. A., and A. D. Sadovnick. 1987. Life expectancy in Down syndrome. *Journal of Pediatrics* 110: 849–54.
Bleyer, A. 1934. Indications that mongoloid imbecility is a gametic mutation of degressive type. *American Journal of Diseases of Children* 17: 342–8.
Book, M. A., M. Fraccaro, and J. Lindsten. 1959. Cytogenetical observations in mongolism. *Acta Paediatrica* 48: 453–68.
Brain, L. 1967. Historical introduction. In *Mongolism,* CIBA Foundation Study Group No. 25, 1–5. London.
Brousseau, K., and H. G. Brainerd. 1928. *Mongolism: A study of the physical and mental characteristics of mongolian imbeciles.* Baltimore.
Collman, R. D., and A. Stoller. 1962. Epidemiology of congenital anomalies of the central nervous system with special reference to patterns in the State of Victoria, Australia. *Journal of Mental Deficiency Research* 7: 60–8.
Cronk, C. E., et al. 1988. Growth charts for children with Down syndrome, one month to 18 years. *Pediatrics* 81: 102–110.
Down, J. Langdon. 1867. Observations on ethnic classification of idiots. *Journal of Mental Science* 13: 121–3.
Janerich, D. T., and M. B. Bracken. 1986. Epidemiology of trisomy 21: A review and theoretical analysis. *Journal of Chronic Disease* 39: 1079–93.
Lilienfeld, A. M. 1969. *Epidemiology of mongolism.* Baltimore.
Penrose, L. S. 1954. Observations on the aetiology of mongolism. *Lancet* 2: 505–9.
Polani, P. E., et al. 1960. A mongol girl with 46 chromosomes. *Lancet* 1: 721–4.
Pueschel, S. M. 1984. *The young child with Down syndrome.* New York.
Pueschel, S. M., and L. S. Steinberg. 1980. *Down syndrome: A comprehensive bibliography.* New York.
Sheehan, P. M., and I. B. Hillary. 1983. An unusual cluster of babies with Down's syndrome born to former pupils of an Irish boarding school. *British Journal of Medicine (Clinical Research)* 287: 1428–9.

VIII.38
Dracunculiasis

This disease is a pathological condition resulting from infection with the parasite *Dracunculus medinensis*. In most instances, the adult worms, which are about 1 meter long, are quite evident as they emerge slowly through the skin of their victims.

Distribution and Incidence

In the 1980s and 1990s, Dracunculiasis is found mainly in India, in Pakistan, and in a band of 19 African countries between the Sahara Desert and the equator, from Senegal in the west to Ethiopia in the east (see Map VIII.38.1). Formerly this disease was much more widespread in the Middle East and Africa, and it occurred for some years in the Americas after it was introduced there by infected Africans during the slave trade.

In general, the incidence of dracunculiasis is significantly higher in endemic rural Africa communities than in endemic Asian villages. In West Africa especially, for example, rates of infection in affected areas often reach 20 to 40 percent, and sometimes exceed 50 percent, whereas in Asia, the rates usually are below 20 percent. In rural areas, the disease occurs sporadically, with adjacent villages sometimes differing greatly in the percentage of those infected. Susan Watts (1987), a medical geographer, has estimated that the number of persons at risk of this infection in Africa is about 120 million, with another 20 million at risk in India and Pakistan, based on the assumption that everyone is at risk who is living in a rural district where a minimum of one case of dracunculiasis has occurred.

The number of persons affected annually by this infection is not known. Although diseases are often underreported in the countries affected, the reporting of dracunculiasis is especially poor because the infection generally is found only in impoverished rural communities where medical facilities are rare, and where many victims cannot walk and have little incentive to seek treatment because there is no drug that can cure the infection. The best estimate is that probably between 5 and 15 million persons contract dracunculiasis each year.

Epidemiology and Etiology

Dracunculiasis is a seasonal infection, usually occurring at the precise time of year when rural villagers must plant or harvest their crops. People are infected when they drink water containing a tiny crustacean of the genus *Cyclops*, called a copepod, which harbors the infective larvae of the parasite. About a year later, the adult worms emerge through the skin to discharge larvae into freshwater, to be ingested by an appropriate copepod, thus continuing the cycle. In drier ecological areas, such as the Sahelian zone in Africa, the infection appears during the brief rainy season (summer), when surface water is available. In areas that receive more rainfall, such as the coastal regions along the Bight of Benin, the infection appears, and is transmitted, during the dry season (winter), when stagnant surface water sources are scarcest and most polluted.

The most commonly affected age groups are generally persons 15 to 45 years of age – that is, working adults. Younger children are affected, but not infants under 1 year, and generally not many children under 5 years. Often farmers are particularly liable to infection, apparently because they drink large volumes of contaminated water while laboring on their farms. School children also suffer high rates of infection in some areas. Male or female victims may predominate in any given area, depending on their relative exposures.

There is no drug suitable for effective mass treatment of dracunculiasis, and from time immemorial, the disease has been treated by slowly winding the emerging worm around a stick. The disease can, however, be prevented by teaching villagers to boil their drinking water or filter it through a cloth, by treating contaminated sources of water with a chemical (temephos), or by providing protected sources of

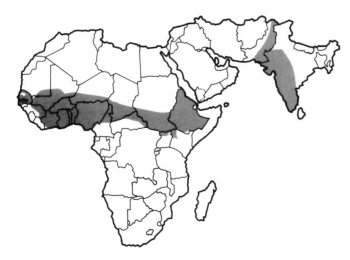

Map VIII.38.1. Areas in which dracunculiasis is reported or probably exists.

drinking water, such as tube wells or draw wells (rather than ponds or open "step wells").

Clinical Manifestations and Pathology

Usually the first clinical sign of infection is a blister, which the adult worm produces, accompanied by severe burning of the skin, at the site where the worm is about to start emerging. This begins about 1 year after the contaminated water has been drunk. The blister ruptures when the affected part of the body is immersed in water, leaving a small ulcer, at the center of which is the worm. Most worms emerge on the foot, ankle, or lower leg, but they can emerge through the skin on any part of the body. Sometimes the worm first appears as a curvy line beneath the skin, or at the center of a painful abscess or nodule.

Worms that do not emerge from the body die and are then absorbed, or calcify, in which case they appear as characteristic curled lines on X-ray. The worms may invade a major joint, the brain or spinal cord, or other vital area, producing more serious manifestations, although this is rare. Much more common are secondary infections of the local wound that give rise to abscesses, local arthritis, and sometimes tetanus. In most patients, only one worm emerges at a time, though as many as two dozen or more may present themselves simultaneously in one person.

Affected persons may be crippled for several weeks or even months, by the pain associated with the worm's slow emergence and secondary infections. Because the infection appears at such a critical time of year for food production and cripples large numbers of persons simultaneously, it has an enormous economic impact. Moreover, people who are infected develop no immunity, so they may be and often are infected year after year.

History and Geography

This is a very old infection, which many believe to have been the "fiery serpent" said by Moses to have attacked the Israelites when they were on the shores of the Red Sea. At least one calcified *Dracunculus* worm has been discovered in the mummy of a 13-year-old Egyptian girl who died around 1000 B.C., and a treatment for this condition may be described in the *Ebers Papyrus*.

Some Greek and Roman writers described the infection, and it was Galen who named it "dracontiasis." The ancient medical practice of treating infections by winding the worm slowly around a stick is thought by some historians to have been the origin of the Staff of Aesculapius. Several medieval Ara-

bian physicians described dracunculiasis. Of these, Avicenna gave the first detailed clinical description of what he called "medina sickness," because the infection was then so common in Medina. Shortly before, Rhazes showed that the swelling caused by the infection was due to a parasite.

Sixteenth-century European travelers mentioned having encountered cases of the disease in Persia and the Congo. It is said to have been called "Guinea worm" for the first time by another European who saw persons suffering from the infection on the Guinea Coast (West Africa) early in the seventeenth century. The disease is also mentioned in the traditional legend by which the Dahomeyans explained the founding of their ancestral cult. Although G. H. Velschius described the parasite clearly in his monograph, published in 1674, it was left for Linnaeus (Carl von Linné) to give the worm its modern scientific name of *Dracunculus medinensis* in 1758.

British army medical officers reported seeing cases of dracunculiasis among British military personnel serving in India in the nineteenth century, and a large punitive English expedition sent to invade Ethiopia in 1868 also suffered greatly from the same disease. The role of the copepod intermediate host in the life cycle of the parasite was discovered only in the 1870s, by a Russian, Aleksei Fedchenko.

The geographic extent of dracunculiasis shrank considerably during the first half of the twentieth century, largely, it appears, because of gradually improving standards of living, and especially standards that have produced better water supplies. The disease was eliminated from the southern area of the Soviet Union in the 1930s by means of a deliberate campaign, and from Iran in the 1970s. With the advent of the United Nations-sponsored International Drinking Water Supply and Sanitation Decade in the 1980s, India and several other endemic countries began national campaigns to eradicate dracunculiasis. In 1986, the World Health Assembly adopted a resolution calling for the elimination of this disease country by country. It appears likely that this ancient disease will not plague humankind much longer.

Donald R. Hopkins

Bibliography

Foster, William C. 1965. *A history of parasitology*. London.
Hopkins, Donald R. 1983. Dracunculiasis: An eradicable scourge. *Epidemiologic Reviews* 5: 208–19.
  1987. Dracunculiasis eradication: A mid-decade status report. *American Journal of Tropical Medicine and Hygiene* 37: 115–18.

Muller, Ralph. 1971. Dracunculus and dracunculiasis. *Advances in Parasitology* 9: 73–151.

Watts, Susan J. 1987. Dracunculiasis in Africa: Its geographical extent, incidence, and at risk population. *American Journal of Tropical Medicine and Hygiene* 33: 121–7.

World Health Organization. 1989. Dracunculiasis: Global surveillance summary – 1988. *Weekly Epidemiological Record* 64: 297–300.

VIII.39
Dropsy

The historical diagnosis of dropsy – which is now obsolete – indicated simply an abnormal accumulation of fluid; the word derives from the Greek *hydrops* (water). Alternative or supplementary terms included *hydrothorax* (fluid in the chest cavity), *ascites* (which still indicates excess free fluid in the abdominal cavity), *anasarca* (still used to describe generalized edema throughout the body), *hydrocephalus* (used until the nineteenth century to indicate excess fluid within the skull), and *ovarian dropsy* (large ovarian cysts filled with fluid). Edema was often a synonym for dropsy, but it now has additional connotations, and pulmonary edema has been differentiated from hydrothorax. Since the mid-nineteenth century, dropsy has been recognized as a sign of underlying disease of the heart, liver, or kidneys, or of malnutrition. Untreated dropsy was, eventually, always fatal.

Etiology and Epidemiology

The major underlying causes of dropsy are congestive heart failure, liver failure, kidney failure, and malnutrition. Because they were not clearly differentiated before the nineteenth century, a historical diagnosis of dropsy cannot be taken to indicate any one of these alone in the absence of unequivocal supporting evidence, as from an autopsy. However, heart failure was probably the most frequent of the four.

The etiologies of dropsy can be explained most conveniently in terms of fluid balance. One principal force in the maintenance of normal fluid balance is the hydrostatic (or hydraulic) pressure within capillaries. The other major force is oncotic pressure, the normal tendency for sodium or large particles (e.g., proteins) in capillary blood to draw water out of tissues, much as salt draws water to the cut surface of a raw potato. Thus, fluid accumulates in tissues when either intracapillary pressure increases or the blood's ability to remove water from tissues decreases. In both cases, fluid that has moved out of the capillaries is poorly reabsorbed. Most hydrostatic defects are primary heart diseases, whereas most oncotic defects result from renal and hepatic disease.

Congestive heart failure produces dropsy, or edema, when the heart becomes too weak to maintain the normal pressure head behind blood flow in the capillaries, so that even the normal resistance to flow through them facilitates the leakage of water from capillary blood into surrounding tissues. The adjective "congestive" refers to the accumulation and stagnation – congestion – of blood in organs, especially the lungs, when they are not adequately emptied because of backward pressure from obstructions distal to them.

The other major causes of dropsy, which appear chiefly as edema of the foot (pedal edema) and ankle, ascites, and occasionally anasarca, are listed below for the sake of completeness, but will be discussed further only in relation to heart failure:

1. *Liver failure* capable of producing ascites most often occurs in advanced cirrhosis because the diseased liver cannot manufacture sufficient protein (albumin) to maintain the oncotic pressure of the blood. Right ventricular failure (see below) can also produce hepatic congestion and failure.
2. *Renal failure* causes dropsy when the glomerular filtering units become so diseased (e.g., in glomerulonephritis, first known as Bright's disease) that albumin and other large molecules are lost from the blood into the urine, resulting in decreased oncotic pressure.
3. *Malnutrition* results in ascites when protein intake is so low that the liver is unable to manufacture adequate amounts of albumin. Beriberi, the result of insufficient dietary thiamine, can also weaken the heart.

The epidemiology of dropsy is that of its underlying causes. For instance, elevated serum cholesterol levels and smoking both predispose to hypertension and myocardial infarction ("heart attack"), which are major causes of heart failure. Beriberi heart disease is associated with diets consisting chiefly of highly polished rice, and with alcoholism. Similarly, the epidemiology of streptococcal infections governs the appearance of the inflammatory reactions that can eventuate in glomerulonephritis or in cardiac valve distortions.

However, the epidemiology of some forms of dropsy has changed in recent years. The introduction of penicillin for the treatment of streptococcal infections after World War II, for example, has reduced the occurrence of their cardiac and renal sequelae. On the other hand, the increasing life expectancy of Americans in the twentieth century for many years meant an increased incidence of heart disease. Now, however, recent data suggest that the incidence of coronary artery disease and myocardial infarction has been falling, perhaps as a result of factors such as changes in diet and exercise level.

Heart failure occurs more often in men than women, inasmuch as men are at greater risk for most forms of cardiovascular disease. The risk is greater for older than younger patients: Three quarters of heart failure patients are over 50 years of age. Risk factors for hepatic cirrhosis include chronic alcoholism and hepatitis, just as renal causes of dropsy may be associated with rheumatic fever or the nephrotic syndrome.

Distribution and Incidence

The distribution of dropsy within or among populations parallels the distributions of its underlying causes, such as hypertension, myocardial and coronary artery insufficiency, hypercholesterolemia, valvular disease, streptococcal infection, cirrhosis, and renal glomerular disease. Risk factors for these conditions are still being identified and their clinical implications evaluated. Only for malnutrition are geographic distinctions clear-cut (e.g., in drought-stricken areas of Africa, or countries where diet centers too closely on polished rice).

Historically, a diagnosis of dropsy was based simply on abnormal accumulations of fluid in the legs, abdomen, or chest. The diagnosis was so easy that artists such as Thomas Rowlandson (in his 1810 print "Dropsy Courting Consumption") could portray it in popular prints with the expectation that their customers would recognize it immediately. Consequently, it is not surprising that the reported incidence of dropsy has not changed substantially over the 400 years for which comparable records are available. That is, dropsy has been diagnosed in about 3 to 5 percent of deaths, hospital admissions, or adult patients in London in 1583–1849, and in American villages and cities in 1735–1839. Typical modern incidences of congestive heart failure include 7 percent of patients discharged from a Baltimore hospital medical service in 1969–70, 2.31 percent of outpatients who had prescriptions filled in a San Francisco hospital in 1971, and 3.05 percent of persons over 30 years of age in the

Framingham (Mass.) Heart Study in 1971. In 1985, 3 of every 1,000 Americans were reported to develop heart failure annually, producing an overall incidence of about 1 percent of the population, regardless of age; 34 to 58 percent of heart failure patients die each year.

Clinical Manifestations and Pathology

This discussion focuses only on congestive heart failure because it was probably the major underlying cause of dropsy. The heart is able to compensate, up to a point, for diminished strength of contraction, for increased resistance to arterial outflow (resulting in "pressure overload"), and for accumulations of blood that cannot be completely removed from the ventricles at each contraction (resulting in "volume overload"). The usual responses to these stresses include the following: (1) reflexly increased heart rate (tachycardia), to speed blood flow (actually, oxygen delivery) into the arteries; (2) hypertrophy (increased mass) of ventricular muscle, in response to pressure overloads; and (3) dilation and thinning of ventricular walls, in response to volume overloads, although hypertrophy can be expected to follow as a further adjustment.

Symptoms of heart failure begin to occur when no further compensations can be made. "Forward failure" symptoms occur when the heart can no longer empty the left ventricle completely because of reasons such as myocardial weakness or obstruction to aortic outflow. Normally the ventricles eject 60 to 66 percent of the blood in them at each beat. But when only 40 percent of the blood in the left ventricle can be expelled, symptoms begin to appear, and they become severe when only 20 percent can be expelled. Symptoms of "backward failure" occur when the heart chambers become incapable of complete filling, due to incomplete relaxation of the heart between beats, or to obstructions to venous inflow into the right atrium.

Heart failure can be produced by several underlying pathological causes, although seldom does any one of them occur alone:

1. *Myocardial insufficiency,* in which the heart is too weak to maintain normal blood flow, occurs acutely when a substantial portion of the muscle is incapacitated by infarction, or in association with gradual left ventricular failure. Both dilation and hypertrophy are likely adaptations.
2. *Left ventricular failure* may occur suddenly, after a myocardial infarction, or slowly, owing to pressure overload, most often imposed by increasing

resistance (hypertension) to blood expelled into the aorta. Other causes include stenosis (narrowing) of the aortic valve, which increases the pressure against which the heart must pump, and aortic insufficiency, also called regurgitation, which occurs when an incompetent valve that cannot close permits a volume overload to build up as blood flows back into the left ventricle instead of forward into the aorta.

3. *Right ventricular failure* usually follows when the pressure head built up as a result of left ventricular failure is transmitted backward through the pulmonary vessels to the right ventricle. Other causes of right heart failure include stenosis of the mitral valve, cor pulmonale (see below), and insufficiency of the tricuspid valve.

4. *Failure of both ventricles* simultaneously usually accompanies a strain common to both sides of the heart, as in constrictive pericarditis, beriberi, hypothyroidism, or anemia so severe that the heart rate increases markedly to compensate for the reduced number of red blood cells delivering oxygen to the tissue.

5. *Chronic cor pulmonale* (pulmonary heart disease) occurs when chronic obstructive pulmonary disease (e.g., emphysema) increases resistance to outflow from the right ventricle, resulting in right ventricular failure.

6. *Acute cor pulmonale* is caused by sudden massive obstruction of the pulmonary circulation, almost always by a clot that has formed as a result of thrombophlebitis in a leg vein, and has dislodged (embolized) so that it follows the venous pathway to the right heart and thence into the lungs, where it becomes wedged so as to obstruct blood flow distal to it. The results include infarction of the affected lung, impaired venous return, and dilation of the right ventricle.

7. Less frequent causes of congestive heart failure include, among others, diminished arterial blood flow to both kidneys, resulting in decreased sodium excretion.

Whatever the underlying cause, the major manifestation of heart failure is reduced cardiac output, measured as the liters of blood ejected from the left ventricle per unit time. The associated symptoms and signs are usually clearly recognizable.

For instance, the first symptoms of *left heart failure* are those of being quick to tire and having shortness of breath (*dyspnea*), due to insufficient delivery of oxygen to the body's tissues, followed by rapid breathing (*tachypnea*) as the respiratory system attempts to compensate for the lack of oxygen. Both dyspnea and tachypnea increase as fluid from the pulmonary capillaries begins to flood the lungs. When the lungs become sufficiently congested (*pulmonary edema*), the patient coughs up copious sputum, which is characteristically rust-colored (with small amounts of blood) if mitral stenosis is present. *Stertor* (noisy inspirations) often accompanies the dyspnea. A more serious form of dyspnea is *orthopnea*. This term is applied to shortness of breath that prevents the patient from sleeping horizontally because venous blood, which remains in the lower part of the body as a result of gravity during waking hours, further congests the lungs, causing dyspnea. An exaggerated form of orthopnea called *paroxysmal nocturnal dyspnea* may waken the patient suddenly at night; it is sometimes called "cardiac asthma" because it produces wheezing and labored breathing.

Physical examination and X-rays reveal cardiac enlargement and fluid in the lungs and chest; other tests can confirm that cardiac output is low. Further symptoms of left heart failure as it worsens include pale dusky skin, sweating, cold hands and feet, and tachycardia, all reflex responses to diminished cardiac output, and decreased urine output (oliguria) secondary to diminished blood flow through the kidneys.

Although *right heart failure* is far more likely to occur as a sequela of left heart failure than by itself, it does produce distinctive symptoms in addition to the usual dyspnea and tachypnea, both of which may be more pronounced in right than left heart failure. Pedal edema occurs, accompanied by hydrothorax. Ascites is a late sign of right heart failure, and may be followed by anasarca and oliguria. The skin becomes bluish (cyanosis), because the sluggishly moving red cells are not adequately oxygenated in the lungs. The jugular veins in the neck distend because the increased pressure in the right heart prevents them from emptying completely into the superior vena cava. Other evidence of increased venous pressure includes congestive enlargement of the liver (hepatomegaly) and sometimes the spleen (splenomegaly).

History and Geography

Dropsy is not much different from one geographic area to the next, except when it accompanies localized famines or beriberi induced by local dietary habits, and the symptoms of dropsy have not changed over the centuries. Its history is the story of evolving interpretations of its clinical features over 2,000 years as the relationships of dyspnea, "suffocative catarrh," pulmonary edema, hydrothorax, ascites, syncope, and "fever" to heart failure were elucidated.

Antiquity Through the Fifteenth Century

The first known mention of dropsy is in an Egyptian medical text of about 1550 B.C., the *Ebers Papyrus*. It associates dropsy with increased abdominal girth, and hints that it is accompanied by a weak pulse. The Hippocratic *Aphorism* VII, 47, correctly prognosticates that "[t]here is no hope when a patient suffering from dropsy develops a cough." And Jesus defied the lawyers and Pharisees by healing a man with dropsy on the Sabbath (Luke 14), although no symptoms are recounted. Soon after, Aulus Cornelius Celsus described two forms of dropsy: (1) generalized edema (*aqua inter cutem*), which could be drained through small skin incisions above the ankle; and (2) ascites, in which the excess fluid detectable by observing fluid waves in the abdominal wall could be removed by *paracentesis,* or *tapping* (i.e., drainage through a metal tube inserted through an incision in the abdominal wall).

Galen of Pergamum listed several causes of dropsy in the first century A.D., including a hardened liver, as well as inadequate blood formation (which he thought occurred in the liver), hemorrhoids, and both amenorrhea and uterine hemorrhage. Virtually all writers on dropsy until the mid-seventeenth century cited the teachings of Hippocrates, Celsus, and Galen. Their ideas were also relayed in the eleventh century by Avicenna of Baghdad, who thought that the tachycardia, palpitations, pulmonary edema, dyspnea, and syncope (fainting or shock, which he postulated was a sign of a weak heart) that accompanied dropsy were related to one another.

Sixteenth and Seventeenth Century

Five centuries later, the French surgeon Ambroise Paré described dropsy in identical terms. His countryman Jean Fernel relied on the same theories when he associated heart disease, but not dropsy specifically, with palpitations, syncope, and the pallor, cold sweat, and weak pulse often observed in cardiogenic shock. Also in the sixteenth century, Paracelsus theorized that dropsy (*wassersucht*) occurred when the body's tissues dissolved. He associated it with dyspnea, cough, and oliguria. Following his usual mystical chemical reasoning, he recommended that dropsy be treated with mercuric oxide to remove superfluous water, with other metallic oxides to dry the patient's body, and with sulfur,

because its drying action was analogous to that of the sun in dispelling rain.

Like his contemporaries, Girolamo Capivaccio of Italy agreed with Galen that dropsy was due to liver disease and impaired blood formation, so that fluid was released into the abdominal cavity to form ascites, which he detected by percussion, as Celsus had. Capivaccio also attributed dropsy to disease in other organs, such as obstruction of the pathways to the kidneys, but he did not mention the heart or even hydrothorax; he surmised that dyspnea was caused by upward pressure from a pathologically enlarged liver on the diaphragm.

The sixteenth-century physician Ludovicus Mercatus of Valladolid defined dyspnea as rapid, difficult breathing, sometimes accompanied by stertor, caused by constricted airways or by excess heat in the heart and lungs; he thought the chief function of respiration was to cool the heart. He followed Galen's classification of dyspnea into three stages of increasing severity: tachypnea, asthma (by which he meant convulsive gasping for breath), and orthopnea. Mercatus thought that hydrothorax fluid descended from the brain to produce the "suffocative catarrh" described by Galen as suffocation in the absence of inflammation, and that its associated dyspnea was caused by fluid in the lungs, or even by heart disease. He theorized that hydrothorax fluid was overflow from ascites or from obstructed urinary passages.

Throughout the seventeenth century, it became increasingly clear that dropsy was associated with altered fluid dynamics as postmortem dissections and experimentation were exploited more frequently. For instance, Carolus Piso (Charles le Pois) of Lorraine detected hydrothorax as "bubbling" when he applied his ear to the chest. Coupling clinical observations with autopsy findings, he attributed paroxysmal nocturnal dyspnea to fluid in the chest cavity. Fabrizio Bartoletti of Italy disagreed with Mercatus and Capivaccio in some of their interpretations, but he used observations like Piso's to hypothesize that hydrothorax fluid came from the lungs. He noted that the first clue to its presence was dyspnea on exertion, followed by "fever" (which he probably detected as modest tachycardia), tachypnea, orthopnea, dry cough, thirst, syncope, leg and scrotal edema, and, finally, ascites. Bartoletti thought that although hydrothorax was not rare, it was always fatal because it suffocated its victims.

In 1616 William Harvey found that edema accumulated behind ligated veins. Later he postulated that if the entire venous system were maximally distended, the heart would stop and suffocation would follow. In *De Motu Cordis* (1628), he described the heart and lungs as "storehouses" for the blood, the metaphor that Saul Jarcho, the leading student of dropsy, thinks led to the concepts of pulmonary engorgement and passive congestion – concepts that would prove to be critical to further understanding of dropsy in the chest.

In his *Tractatus de Corde* (1669), Richard Lower of Oxford and London described how he had produced edema and ascites in dogs by ligating the jugular veins and the superior vena cava. He also found that excess fluid in the pericardial sac could restrict cardiac expansion sufficiently to diminish venous return, resulting in bradycardia, syncope, and death. Lower went on to postulate that the right and left sides of the heart should be of equal strength in order to maintain the circulation, while noting that the left side alone may be weakened, an early expression of the notion of forward failure. He also perceived that excessive amount, pressure, or flow rate of blood might adversely affect health. Finally, he recognized Galen's "suffocative catarrh" as pulmonary edema, although they were considered to be separate clinical entities for many years afterward.

In 1681 Marcello Malpighi of Bologna carried Harvey's quantitative approach to experimental physiology an important step further when he noted the increased weight of dyspneic lungs (attributable to the stagnant blood within them). Because he had discovered capillaries 20 years earlier, he could hypothesize that blood escaped from them into the lungs. Malpighi thought that stagnant blood in the pulmonary vessels produced palpitations and irregular pulses because it precluded an orderly blood supply to the heart. He reasoned that an imbalance between arterial outflow and venous resorption of water from the blood caused dropsy, but he attributed the imbalance to chemicals that constricted blood vessels or irritated and thus stimulated the nerves that controlled the heart and the respiratory muscles. One of Malpighi's students, Giorgio Baglivi, described the symptoms of suffocative catarrh so that it finally became clearly recognizable as acute pulmonary edema (not the result of fluid falling from the head): dyspnea, cough, stertor, sensitivity to cold, chest pain, thirst, anxiety, and, one of his major original observations, foaming at the mouth.

Eighteenth Century to Modern Times

Physicians were slow to understand that the heart *could* be diseased, probably because it was thought to be absolutely essential to life, but in the early eighteenth century two students of dropsy provided the first clues that cardiac disease might not be incompatible with life. One of them, Raymond Vieussens of Montpellier, correlated the work of Harvey, Lower, and Malpighi with his own postmortem dissections of dropsy patients. By 1705, he had concluded that structural disease of the heart could result in dropsy, after showing how mitral or pulmonary stenosis, or aortic insufficiency, could produce the clinical signs of what is now called backward failure. At almost the same time, Giovanni Maria Lancisi was dissecting victims of sudden death in Rome. Although among the last to cite Fernel, his own observations permitted him to recognize that edema, hydrothorax, and ascites could be related to failure of the heart's propulsive force (i.e., forward failure), to aortic regurgitation, and to obstructions in the right heart. Explicitly recognizing the importance of hydrostatic principles in cardiovascular physiology, Lancisi went on to explain how stagnation of blood within the pulmonary vasculature could result in dyspnea, and he learned how to diagnose hydrothorax ante mortem. He cited Lower's experiments to support his conclusion that right heart failure could produce engorgement and pulsation of the jugular vein. Thus together Lancisi and Vieussens uncovered the cardiac basis of dropsies of the lungs and thorax.

Their work was expanded a few years later by another of Malpighi's pupils, Ippolito Francesco Albertini, also of Bologna. He echoed his mentor's conclusion that sluggish circulation through the lungs leads to dyspnea. A frequent dissector, Albertini emphasized the time course of dyspnea when he pointed out that it comes on rapidly when obstructions occur in the pulmonary vein of the left heart, resulting in delayed removal of blood from the lungs, erosion of the pulmonary vessels, hemoptysis, and hydrothorax.

Another interpretation of dropsy arose from Harvey's demonstration that the blood circulates within a closed system. In this case, dropsy came to be seen as a febrile disease, because it was usually accompanied by a fast pulse, regarded as a cardinal clinical sign of fever over the centuries before clinical thermometers became widely available in the 1870s. Thus Thomas Willis, Lower's mentor and colleague, defined fever as an "intestine motion or commotion of the blood" arising in chemical disturbances like those described over a century earlier by Paracelsus.

Hermann Boerhaave of Leyden was a major proponent of the idea that dropsy was a fever, which should be treated accordingly. He based much of his teaching on the work of Friedrich Hoffmann of Prussia, who saw the body as a machine, subject to the effects of mechanical forces. This led Boerhaave to argue that in dropsy, fever is the result of increased cardiac work and increased vascular resistance to blood flow – in short, of friction. Therefore, by his reasoning, dropsy was a fever because it was associated with a fast pulse. At the same time, he postulated that dropsical fluid accumulated because defective veins released more fluid into body tissues than those weakened vessels could reabsorb. In Italy, Luca Tozzi, who adopted the newer ideas of Paracelsus, Lower, Malpighi, and Hoffmann, was among the first to differentiate hydrothorax, pulmonary edema, and pneumonia at autopsy, which permitted him (and, later, Albertini) to differentiate pulmonary and thoracic dropsies ante mortem by palpating the chest and apical impulse of the heart.

A new method for detecting hydrothorax appeared in 1761, when Leopold Auenbrugger of Vienna described how to strike the chest with the fingers to estimate, by the resonance they produced, the amount and nature of fluid in the pleural cavity and lungs. However, his discovery of percussion added no new information about the pathology of dropsy, and was neglected until it was reintroduced in France in 1808.

The first book devoted to dropsy alone was published in 1706 by the Leopoldine Academy of Sciences in Breslau; its principal author was probably Christianus Helwich. The Academicians described the clinical features of dropsy much as previous authors (especially Piso) had done, but they attributed the escape of fluid from the vessels to diminished blood viscosity and to defective vessel walls, as Boerhaave, too, was suggesting.

In 1733, Stephen Hales, a rural English clergyman, concluded from his experiments in animals that dropsy could be caused by decreased numbers of red blood cells. However, he did not reason that the paucity of red cells would decrease blood viscosity, much less oncotic pressure. Rather, he thought that the body would compensate for the lack of "red Globules" by heating the blood into a feverish state that resulted in dropsy. He was perhaps the first to recognize that inadequate venous return to the heart in dropsy could lead to compensatory (reflex) tachycardia.

Donald Monro of Edinburgh published the second book devoted to dropsy in 1755. He followed Boerhaave in ascribing it to "a weakness and laxity of the fibers . . . when the vessels do not act with sufficient force," and listed several factors that would tend to weaken blood vessels: a watery diet, "any great evacuation," kidney disease, obstruction of small or large vessels, or any debilitating disease. Neither Monro nor later writers mentioned the blood viscosity hypothesis.

In 1763 Samuel Clossey of Dublin and New York applied the principles governing the relationship between pressure and flow velocity, outlined 35 years earlier by Daniel Bernoulli of Basel, to his own studies of the hydrostatic properties of the cardiovascular system. Clossey realized that the development of hydrothorax is a long process, when he computed that it would take about 2 years for 3 pints of hydrothorax fluid to accumulate. He followed Lancisi in associating dropsy with weakness of the heart, but postulated that cardiac strength derived from that of the blood vessels.

Thus, regardless of how they were interpreted, the major clinical manifestations of dropsy had been identified by the mid-eighteenth century. Some physicians followed Boerhaave's dictum that dropsy was caused by weak blood vessel fibers, whereas others attributed the omnipresent dyspnea to weakened cardiac contraction, as did the medical encyclopedist Robert James of London in his *Medicinal Dictionary* of 1745. But by the turn of the century, unproven – and unprovable – theories of dropsy based on fever, chemical disturbances, blood viscosity, and fiber tone began to fade, and the role of the diseased heart came into sharper focus.

In 1806, Jean-Nicholas Corvisart, who would soon popularize Auenbrugger's discovery of percussion in French translation, showed how heart disease could produce dropsy, dyspnea, and orthopnea when venous return was slowed. Three years later Allan Burns of Glasgow demonstrated that ossification of the mitral and pulmonary valves leads to right heart dilation and dropsy, although it is not clear whether he was aware of Vieussens's pioneering observations along the same lines. And in 1835 James Hope of Cheshire showed how myocardial failure results in dyspnea.

In 1813 John Blackall of London was among the first to suggest that dropsy can result from noncardiac conditions such as liver and kidney disease, when he demonstrated that the albumin content of urine can help differentiate among the underlying causes of dropsy. Blackall's thesis about renal causes of dropsy was confirmed by Richard Bright, whose careful autopsies at Guy's Hospital in London led him to report, in 1827, that albumin could be found in the urine of patients with glomerulonephritis who died of dropsy. A few years later, Bright showed that renal disease could also be associated with left ventricular hypertrophy, presumably because hypertension is often associated with renal disease. In 1909 C. J. Rothberger and H. Winterberg in Austria, and Thomas Lewis in London, independently showed that a nonanatomic cardiac condition, atrial fibrillation, could produce heart failure, and in 1935 Paul Dudley White and Sylvester McGinn of Boston described acute cor pulmonale.

Although many details of the pathophysiology of congestive heart failure are still being ascertained, all investigators continue to exploit the relationships discovered by Ernest Henry Starling at University College, London. He noted in 1897 that the strength of heart muscle fiber contraction is proportional to fiber length – up to a point. But it was not until 1920 that he adduced experimental evidence to demonstrate the relevance of the rate of blood flow from the veins into the heart, and of the arteries' resistance to outflow, to his basic "Law of the Heart." In 1936 Tinsley R. Harrison of Vanderbilt University consolidated Starling's and other surviving concepts of heart failure to explain the phenomenon more or less as we understand it today, although heart failure remains the subject of many increasingly detailed investigations.

Historical Treatments

The earliest measures for treating dropsy were chiefly attempts to correct humoral imbalances. Celsus, for example, recommended drugs he regarded as diuretics, as well as a wide variety of other medicines with different physiological effects. (One of his diuretics, squill, was finally abandoned only after White demonstrated its lack of dependability in 1920.) During the Renaissance, Capivaccio, Mercatus, and Piso were still recommending Galenic drugs to carry away dropsical fluid, especially cathartics, emetics, diaphoretics, expectorants, and diuretics like squill. In addition, Capivaccio pointed out that blistering with cantharides ("Spanish flies") and paracentesis would remove dropsical fluid, but he recommended bleeding only if the patient's blood had been diseased because of disturbed liver function.

The number of drugs recommended for dropsy diminished during the course of the seventeenth century. The Leopoldine Academicians described some they thought would increase blood viscosity by removing excess fluid from the body, such as diuretics, cathartics, and diaphoretics. Baglivi and Lancisi favored diuretics almost exclusively. Malpighi and his student, Albertini, on the other hand, who based their treatments on the teachings of Hoffmann, recommended tonic drugs to strengthen the tone of the weakened resorbing veins, so that fluid that had

leaked into the tissues could be removed more readily. So did Clossey and Monro, who said that dropsy should be treated with tonic drugs, "which by their stimulus force the sensible [i.e., excitable] organs into contractions."

In 1785, there appeared the single most influential – and perhaps most widely read and immediately accepted – book in the history of dropsy, *An Account of the Foxglove,* by William Withering of Birmingham, England. His was the first prospective study of the clinical efficacy and safety of any drug, for the treatment of any disease. Using historical controls as negative controls, Withering clearly demonstrated the therapeutic benefit of digitalis in patients with dropsies that were not related to primary disease in other organs, such as the ovaries. Because increased urine production usually followed the administration of digitalis, he thought it was a diuretic. Although he noted that the pulse rate fell in patients whose symptoms were ameliorated by the new drug, he did not recognize the drug's tonic effect on the heart.

Because dropsy had been seen since the mid-eighteenth century as a "weakness and laxity of the fibers," some physicians who followed Withering concluded that digitalis stimulated the "system," whereas others concluded that it was a depressant because it reduced fast heart rates. In 1813 Blackall (not John Ferriar, as some have supposed) first suggested that digitalis actually strengthens the heart. This concept resurfaced in papers published in 1905–11 by James Mackenzie of London and Karel Frederik Wenckebach of Holland and Vienna, but it was only verified in 1938–44, by H. J. Stewart and John McMichael. Wenckebach also demonstrated the efficacy of digitalis in atrial fibrillation.

The two major clinical goals of treatment in congestive heart failure today are improved oxygenation of the tissues by increasing cardiac output, and reduction of hydrostatic pressures in the veins. Digitalis glycosides (chiefly digoxin and digitoxin, both of which must still be extracted from the purple foxglove, *Digitalis purpurea,* or the white species, *Digitalis lanata*) increase cardiac output by strengthening the force with which the heart contracts; diuresis occurs secondarily, because the resulting increase in the amount of blood that can then be circulated to the kidneys permits increased removal of water into the urine. True diuretics, which act on the kidneys alone, relieve pressure in the venous system by removing excess fluid from the body via the urine.

Other drugs now used in the treatment of heart

failure include dopamine, dobutamine, hydrala-zine, nitroprusside, and enalapril; although all of these agents reduce hydrostatic pressures by dilat-ing blood vessels, they act on the vessels in different ways. Enalapril is unusual in that it can also facili-tate reversal of left ventricular hypertrophy. In addi-tion, amrinone and milrinone both dilate vessels and increase the force of cardiac contraction. Oxygen and rest, which may have to be induced with sedatives, are important adjuncts to drug therapy. Paracentesis and thoracentesis may occasionally still be required, but the subcutaneous leg drainage tubes described by R. Southey of London in 1871 were abandoned with the advent of true diuretics. Patients with acute pulmonary edema (as in acute cor pulmonale) are often treated with morphine, which reduces not only their anxiety and their tachycardia but also their hydrostatic pressures against blood flow (via an effect in the central nervous system).

J. Worth Estes

Bibliography

Blackall, John. 1813. *Observations on the nature and cure of dropsies,* 3d edition. London.

Estes, J. Worth. 1979. *Hall Jackson and the purple fox-glove: Medical practice and research in revolutionary America, 1760–1820.* Hanover, N.H.

Fye, W. Bruce. 1983. Ernest Henry Starling, his law and its growing significance in the practice of medicine. *Circulation* 68: 1145–8.

Jarcho, Saul. 1980. *The concept of heart failure from Avicenna to Albertini.* New York.

Jarcho, Saul, trans. and ed. 1971. *Practical observations on dropsy of the chest* [Breslau, 1706]. *Transactions of the American Philosophical Society* 61 (n.s.): 3–46.

McKee, P. A., et al. 1971. The natural history of congestive heart failure: The Framingham study. *New England Journal of Medicine* 285: 1441–6.

Monro, Donald. 1755. *An essay on the dropsy.* London.

Temkin, Owsei. 1952. The elusiveness of Paracelsus. *Bulletin of the History of Medicine* 26: 201–17.

White, Paul Dudley. 1951. *Heart disease,* 4th edition. New York.

Withering, William. 1785. *An account of the foxglove, and some of its medical uses; with practical remarks on dropsy and other diseases.* Birmingham. [See, espe-cially, the edition annotated by J. K. Aronson (Lon-don, 1985).]

VIII.40
Dysentery

Dysentery is an inflammation of the large intestine characterized by loose stools containing blood and mucus, and by tenesmus – painful and unproductive attempts to defecate. Diarrhea, marked by the fre-quent production of watery stools, may be confused with dysentery in historical accounts, but references to "bloody flux" refer to true dysentery. The condi-tion may be caused by an ameba, *Entamoeba histo-lytica,* or by several species of bacteria, especially in the genus *Shigella.* See Amebic Dysentery, Bacillary Dysentery, and Diarrheal Diseases (Acute), Chap-ters VIII.5, VIII.14, and VIII.35, this volume.

K. David Patterson

VIII.41
Dyspepsia

Derived from Greek roots meaning "difficult diges-tion," dyspepsia has long served as a synonym for indigestion, one of the most common – and etiologi-cally varied – of human miseries. It has thus been as regularly employed to label the symptoms of diverse organic disorders as to identify a distinct disease, with the result that some gastroenterologists find the word uselessly elastic: "This is really a meaning-less term because it has so many meanings." The majority of practitioners, however, have reached a consensus to use dyspepsia to denote either the ail-ment of functional indigestion or the symptoms of peptic ulcer.

Distribution and Incidence

Peptic ulcer dyspepsia is rare in people under the age of 20, but by age 30, 2 percent of the males and 0.5 percent of the females in a population have devel-oped the condition. For men, the incidence increases steadily with age, reaching a peak of around 20 percent in the sixth decade of life. The incidence for women remains low, about 1 percent, until meno-pause, after which it climbs as rapidly as in men. A morbidity rate of nearly 14 percent has been reported in women in the age group 70 to 79. Death from peptic ulcer occurs three times as often in men as women.

The prevalence of functional dyspepsia, by contrast, is uncertain. Having no distinct pathology, being neither communicable nor reportable, and only occasionally motivating its victims to seek medical help, it does not generate statistics. The widely shared clinical impression is that women are affected more than men, and people under the age of 40 more than those over age 40. Functional dyspepsia is also believed to be more prevalent in developed countries.

Epidemiology and Etiology

Although the most common, peptic ulcer is hardly the only organic source of dyspepsia. Esophagitis; hiatus hernia; gastritis; carcinoma of the stomach, colon, or pancreas; Crohn's disease; disease of the biliary tract; chronic nephritis; or any of several other conditions, including pregnancy, can produce indigestion. In approximately half of the cases of dyspepsia, however, no lesion can be found, and symptoms arise from derangements of motor, secretory, or absorptive functions, especially delayed gastric motility, esophageal reflux, and hyperacidity. This functional indigestion has been related to physical stress (aerophagia, fatigue, dietary indiscretion) and, more commonly, to nervous stress. Anxiety, anger, frustration, and other indications of emotional turmoil can significantly impair digestive function in sensitive or tense individuals (a similar psychic component – chronic tension and repression of emotion – has been implicated in peptic ulcer). Because the symptoms of functional dyspepsia are virtually identical to those of peptic ulceration, the condition has also been termed *X-ray negative* dyspepsia and *nonulcerative* dyspepsia; the term *endoscopy-negative* dyspepsia has been proposed as well in recent years.

Clinical Manifestations

That most eminent of Victorian dyspeptics, Thomas Carlyle, likened his torment to "a rat gnawing at the pit of the stomach." Dyspepsia's victims still complain of gastric pain, along with fullness or heaviness in the stomach, nausea and vomiting, belching, flatulence, and/or acid eructations. Finally, dyspeptics may suffer heartburn, a caustic pain behind the sternum that sometimes climbs into the throat, resulting from esophageal reflux. Heartburn is the special affliction of those with sliding hiatus hernia when they bend or lie down.

History and Geography

Great suppers do the stomach much offend,
Sup light if quiet you to sleep intend.

So advised the author of the medieval *Regimen Sanitatis Salernitanum,* and no doubt his words were already age-old wisdom. Yet if indigestion has plagued the human race for as long as it has eaten, and no less hoary an expert than Hippocrates described its tortures, it was not until the nineteenth century that dyspepsia attained a prominent standing in pathology. Previously it was regarded as a too common but predictable and temporary discomfort brought on by immoderacy in diet. Alexander Pope's scolding couplets characterized pre-Victorian views (Davis 1966):

[T]he stomach cramm'd from every dish,
A tomb of roast and boil'd, of flesh and fish,
Where *bile* and *wind,* and *phlegm* and *acid* jar.
And all the man is one intestine war.

The sources of intestinal turbulence came to appear more numerous during the early nineteenth century. The distrust of sensuality that marked the Victorian ethos more than once expressed itself in the blaming of physical decline on moral perversion. And because dyspepsia was so often found in patients guilty of some excess and just as often lacked any apparent organic basis, physicians found it easy to explain the condition on the basis of any aberrant behavior that might plausibly have upset the patient's system. Gluttony, of course, was still a sin, and doctors had no quarrel with Ambrose Bierce's (1911) definition of a glutton as "a person who escapes the evils of moderation by committing dyspepsia." They generally added to gluttony the bolting of inadequately chewed food, a practice that many charged was epidemic in the dining rooms of ever-in-a-hurry America. Nevertheless, a nineteenth-century attack of dyspepsia was just as likely to be blamed on the abuse of spirits or tobacco, to the reading of French novels, or to masturbation or "excessive venery."

The nineteenth century's list of dyspepsia's causes was also lengthened by examples of fast living of a second type, that of the mental and emotional excitation accompanying the bustling anxiety-filled life of the industrial city. A. P. W. Philip's *Treatise on Indigestion* (1825), which recommended against excessive venery, also warned, in the same breath, of the dangers of "too long application to business [and] severe study." Such caveats would appear with increasing regularity in medical texts and home health guides alike until finally becoming mandatory with the ascension of neurasthenia, or nervous exhaustion, to the position of *the* disease of modern society during the last quarter of the century. George Beard, neurasthenia's prophet, declared "delicacy of digestion" to be "one of the best known and first observed effects of civilization upon the nervous system," and his message that dyspepsia was on the rise as the special complaint of the modern brainworker and risk-taker met with universal acceptance. The 1873 proclamation of *The Household Physician* by Ira Warren and A. E. Small was not hyperbole for the time:

Dyspepsia is a disease of civilization. Savages know nothing of it. It is the costly price we pay for luxuries. All civilized nations suffer from it, more or less, but none so much as the people of the United States. It is here, in the new world, that the disease has become domesticated, and we, as a people, who have threatened to monopolize its miseries.

The neurasthenia era, furthermore, defined "modern dyspepsia" as a nervous complaint that gave as good as it got, one that having originated in anxiety, then generated more anxiety, as well as irritability, depression, and other neurotic suffering in addition to mundane heartburn. This virtual equation of dyspepsia with nervousness led to its being defined almost exclusively as a functional condition produced by stress.

During the first half of the twentieth century, that same stress of coping with civilization seems to have brought about an abrupt increase in dyspepsia of organic origin as well. Between the two world wars, peptic (particularly duodenal) ulcer grew from a rarely encountered condition to a significant cause of disability, reaching a high point in the 1950s, then declining sharply to the present. This pattern has suggested that ulcer dyspepsia is less a disease of civilization than a condition of adjustment to civilization; the first generations to confront the pressures of urban-industrial life are buffeted more heavily than those born after the turbulent transition period. Functional dyspepsia, of course, might be expected to decrease for the same reason, yet its domain has been diminished still more rapidly by the X-ray and the endoscope, improved diagnostic techniques having transferred many cases of "nervous indigestion" to peptic ulcer's column. Advances in understanding of the neurohumoral mechanisms that regulate the digestive tract and the biochemical basis of emotion, furthermore, promise to provide organic interpretations for the dyspepsias now identified as functional. As a consequence, the very term "dyspepsia," historically associated with nervous, nonorganic illness, is becoming antiquated. In the last decades, medical writers have taken to encapsulating the word in quotation marks to call attention to its quaintness, and inserting it into the index only to be followed with "see indigestion."

James Whorton

Bibliography

Bierce, Ambrose. 1911. *The devil's dictionary.* Cleveland.

Coghill, N. F. 1969. Dyspepsia. In *Diseases of the digestive system,* ed. Martin Ware, 1–7. London.

Davis, Herbert, ed. 1966. *Pope. Poetical works.* Oxford.

Horrocks, J. W., and F. T. DeDombal. 1978. Clinical presentation of patients with "dyspepsia." *Gut* 19: 19–26.

Jones, F. Avery, J. W. P. Gummer, and J. E. Lennard-Jones. 1968. *Clinical gastroenterology,* 2d edition. Oxford.

Mendeloff, Albert. 1983. Epidemiology of functional gastrointestinal disorders. In *Functional disorders of the digestive tract,* ed. William Chey, 13–19. New York.

Philip, A. P. W. 1825. *A treatise on indigestion and its consequences,* 5th edition. Philadelphia.

Sleisinger, Marvin, and John Fordtran. 1973. *Gastrointestinal disease.* Philadelphia.

Spiro, Howard. 1977. *Clinical gastroenterology,* 2d edition, New York.

Susser, Mervyn, and Zeno Stein. 1962. Civilization and peptic ulcer. *Lancet* 1: 115–19.

Warren, Ira, and A. E. Small. 1873. *The household physician.* Boston.

Wightman, K. J. R., and K. N. Jeejeebhoy. 1973. Assessment of symptoms. In *Gastroenterology,* ed. Abraham Bogoch, 9–41. New York.

VIII.42
Ebola Virus Disease

Textbooks on tropical diseases in Africa are well out of date. With the recognition of new and deadly viral infections – Lassa, Marburg, Ebola, Congo–Crimean Hemorrhagic Fever, Rift Valley Fever, and AIDS – the classical descriptions of major diseases such as malaria and yellow fever must be thoroughly revised, and to the roster of more minor ailments can be added dengue, Chikungunya, O'Nyong Nyong, West Nile fever, and others. One must be ready to challenge earlier descriptions of African fevers in general. Malaria in particular has been an "umbrella" diagnosis, which obscured and still obscures the diagnosis of other, sometimes dangerous concomitant illnesses in regions where malaria itself is endemic to hyperendemic. The absolute need for laboratory confirmation to support the clinical impression is slowly being recognized. This must extend beyond the simple demonstration of presence of malaria parasites in the blood. Malaria parasites in the blood certainly prove that the individual in question harbors the parasite. But it is not necessarily proof that the actual immediate infection from which the individual is suffering is related to the existing chronic malarial position. Treatment of the malarial infection is indicated, and is followed almost universally in tropical Africa, with or without confirmation of the presence of malaria parasites. The first diagnosis entertained for all of the viral infections listed above is almost always "malaria."

It is when the patient does not respond to the antimalarial therapy exhibited that other possible diagnoses are considered. In addition to the viral possibilities, the list should also include influenza, typhoid fever, various rickettsioses, leptospiral infections, bacterial and viral enteropathogenic agents – indeed the range of infections capable of inducing a febrile response.

After the appearance of the Marburg virus in 1967 and the Lassa virus in 1969 had given a jolt to complacency, the Ebola virus in 1976 provoked a convulsive shudder. The Ebola story began with almost simultaneous outbreaks of a deadly infection in the Maridi region of southern Sudan and in the Bumba Zone of the equator region of north central Zaire, neighboring on the Sudan, and in towns along the course of the Ebola River. The Sudan and Zaire foci are about 150 kilometers distant from each other, and people are continually passing back and forth between these regions.

Epidemiology, Distribution, and Incidence

The epidemic of a highly fatal disease (later named Ebola virus disease) began in June 1976, with an index case in Nzara, southern Sudan, among workers in a cotton factory. This patient went to a large hospital in Maridi, where the disease spread rapidly among hospital patients and staff. The epidemic ran its course by November 1976. There were 148 deaths in 284 detected cases (52 percent mortality). In 1979 a further outbreak occurred in southern Sudan, with fewer cases and a small number of deaths.

The epidemic in Zaire was traced to an index case seen on September 1, 1976. The individual in question had received an intravenous injection of chloroquine for presumptive malaria with fever at the outpatient clinic of Yambuku Mission Hospital, Bumba District. He recovered, but within a week a large epidemic of fever began in hospital patients and staff. A total of 318 cases occurred, with 288 deaths (90.5 percent mortality). A number of inpatients and members of the hospital staff, physicians, and attendants also died. The epidemic had terminated by November 5, 1976. The diagnosis of the first epidemiological team sent to the area was "a fulminating epidemic of typhoid fever in a non-vaccinated population." Fatalities, however, occurred in a hospital in Kinshasa in the cases of three nurses who had been transferred from the infected area, and it became clear, as investigations continued, that passage of the virus from human to human had occurred through the medium of contaminated needles and syringes. Whereas formerly rigidly enforced isolation and barrier procedures had been somewhat relaxed, strict syringe and needle discipline and isolation of patients were reestablished and maintained as a permanent part of hospital operations protocol.

The epidemics in the Sudan and Zaire terminated as abruptly as they had started. However, in 1979 another hospital-centered outbreak occurred in Tandala, Zaire, 300 kilometers distant from the original Bumba outbreak. In total, 33 patients were diagnosed, of whom 22 died (66 percent mortality). Through the 1980s no further outbreaks have been reported in Sudan or Zaire or elsewhere in Africa, with the exception of a probable case from Kenya reported in 1983.

Complacency was shattered in the United States and internationally in early November 1989 when an epidemic, confirmed to be caused by Ebola virus, erupted in a shipment of 100 *Macaca cynomolgus* monkeys originating in the Philippines and shipped to a laboratory in Virginia, in the United States, via Amsterdam and J. F. Kennedy airports. Sixty of the 100 monkeys died. A second shipment received 2 to 3 weeks later in Virginia had two infected monkeys therein.

Extensive epidemiological explorations internationally have focused on this frightening episode. No human cases have been reported. At the time of writing (February 14, 1990), no satisfactory explanations have been advanced. All exposed individuals are being monitored.

This demonstration of the danger of transmission of virus by use and reuse of inadequately sterilized needles and syringes has important implications for medical practice, not just in underdeveloped countries but also in developed cultures because of AIDS. Excessive parenteral administration of many drugs, which could be equally efficacious given by mouth, constitutes bad medical practice. Parenteral administration of drugs in medical emergencies is understandable and desirable. But such a practice for the "typical" patients seen at the clinic for undiagnosed fevers that are not immediately life-threatening is indefensible.

Unsophisticated patients unfortunately cherish an intuitive feeling that drugs, from vitamin preparations up the scale to specific therapeutic agents, are much more effective when given intradermally, subcutaneously, intramuscularly, or intravenously. Indeed, patients often demand parenteral administration of drugs and think poorly of a physician who does not oblige them. This view unfortunately is not discouraged by some practitioners of the medical arts, both licensed and unlicensed, and the practice also greatly increases the bill for pharmaceuticals benefiting drug companies and pharmacists. The poorer countries can ill afford the increased cost.

Epidemiologists have been active in trying to trace the origins of the Ebola virus and the distribution of the infection throughout Africa, locate host vertebrates other than humans, as well as learn methods of transmission to humans and the ways the virus is maintained and propagated in nature. Table VIII.42.1 summarizes these data. Although it may appear that much has been done, actually efforts have been limited to a handful of dedicated investigators, and to a scattered, spotty sampling of the vast expanse of Africa south of the Sahara.

Primates have been sampled (see Table VIII.42.1) and have revealed no involvement, or at best mini-

Table VIII.42.1. *Ebola serosurveys*

Study area	Date	No. examined	No. positive	Percent positive	Remarks
Humans					
Northern Senegal	1977	273	5	1.8	semidesert region
Zaire, Bumba province	1979	251	43	17	region of 1967 outbreak
Cent. African Republic	1980	499	17	3.4	several regions
Zaire, Tandala	1980	?	?	7	region of 1969 outbreak
Liberia	1982	400+	24	6	several regions
Zaire, Tandala	1982	138	7	5.1	
Cameroons	1982	1517	–	3.2–23.5	several regions
Kenya	1983	52	2	4	
Kenya	1983	741	8	1.1	
Kenya	1986	471	46	10	in fever cases
Northern Sudan	1986	% of 2000	?	v. few pos	desert region, north of outbreak
Southern Sudan	1986	% of 2000	?	15–30	in Maridi region; agricultural
Nigeria	1988	1677	30	1.8	several regions
Primates					
Kenya	1982	136	0	0	monkeys of 3 species
Kenya	1982	184	3	1.6	baboons
Zaire	1981	200+	0	0	monkeys
Guinea pigs					
Zaire, Tandala	1982	138	36	26.1	region of 1979 epidemic

mal involvement. In connection with the 1979 Tandala, Zaire, outbreak is the unexpected finding of guinea pig immunes. Guinea pigs are South American rodents, inquilines in human habitations in the high Andes. The inhabitants raise them for pets and for food. They were introduced to Africa decades ago and in some regions have established themselves as inquilines in houses. In this respect, their behavior resembles that of the abundant multimammate rat (*Mastomys natalensis*), already known to be involved in Lassa virus maintenance and spread to human beings. Guinea pig immune rates as high as 26.1 percent were found in these animals in some houses in Tandala. Study of the background of those who were positive, however, failed to indicate guinea pig-to-guinea pig transmission, guinea pig-to-human spread, or human-to-guinea pig spread.

Etiology

The Ebola agent was demonstrated by electron microscopy to consist of long filamentous rods, sometimes branched, often intertwined. The virion contains one molecule of single-stranded RNA and is not of itself infectious.

The infectious virus particle is inactivated by ultraviolet (UV)-irradiation, gamma-ray irradiation, 1 percent formalin, beta-propiolactone, and lipid solvents. The particles closely resemble those of the Marburg agent, but there are some distinguishing characteristics. The Ebola agent, for example, has more branching than the Marburg agent. Oligonucleotide patterns are distinctive. Seven nucleoproteins have been described. Serologically no relationship has been demonstrated, either to Marburg or to Lassa or to any other of a long list of arbo and nonarbo viruses. Another distinguishing characteristic of Ebola–Sudan and Ebola–Zaire is pathogenicity. Both cause excessive mortality, but mortality is lower for the Sudan strain than for the Zaire strain. *Cercopithecus* monkeys infected with and recovered from Ebola–Sudan virus, and therefore resistant to superinfection by the homologous virus, nonetheless succumbed when inoculated with Ebola–Zaire virus. A new family, Filoviridae, has been created for the agents Marburg and Ebola. As of 1988, no further agents have been proposed.

Clinical Manifestations

Onset of illness was usually sudden, with progressively more severe frontal headache of a type frequently seen with *P. falciparum* malaria infection, spreading occipitally. Fever and weakness were al-

ways present. Myalgia appeared early. Arthralgia of the large joints was very common from the onset. Severe generalized disease followed in a matter of a day or two. Patients were lethargic, their faces expressionless with deep set eyes. Loss of appetite, sometimes accompanied by vomiting and rapid weight loss, was a nearly constant feature. In 2 to 3 days, gastrointestinal symptoms developed, frequently accompanied by cramping.

In later stages, particularly in patients with hemorrhagic manifestations, red blood was seen in the stools. Vomiting was common, being seen in nearly half of the patients with hemorrhagic signs; vomitus was often of red blood or changed blood (cf. the *vomitusniger* of yellow fever). Other common manifestations included sore throat and dysphagia, fissures and open sores on the lips, conjunctivitis sometimes accompanied by subconjunctival bleeding, and coughing. Jaundice occurred in some. Pancreatitis (clinical diagnosis) was also seen frequently, and abortion occurred in 23 percent of 82 infected pregnant women. Hemorrhagic manifestations, seen in many patients and in over half of those who died, probably resulted from disseminated intravascular coagulation. Death occurred as early as the fourth day, but more usually on the fifth or sixth day and in occasional cases as late as the twentieth day.

Pathology and Diagnosis

Very few specimens were obtained for histological study. In three adequately preserved liver specimens available, fatty changes and necrosis of hepatocytes and Kupffer cells were noted, necrosis being of the focal type, distributed throughout the liver lobules. Intact cells with hyalinized cytoplasm and ghostlike nuclei (Councilman bodies of yellow fever fame) were seen, as were large amounts of karyorrhectic debris. Inflammatory changes were minimal in the liver and other organs.

Comparisons were made with Marburg disease, for which there was a large amount of pathological material available, both from human beings and from experimental animals. Here, in addition to the focal necrotic centers in the liver, was evidence of hemorrhagic diathesis in many organs and of panencephalitis in the brain, with glial nodule formation, perivascular lymphocyte cuffing, and interstitial edema.

Several pathologists deemed the differential diagnosis of Ebola infection to be extremely difficult in settings where there might be malaria, Lassa fever, Marburg disease, yellow fever, Congo–Crimean hemorrhagic fever, typhoid fever, infectious hepatitis, leptospirosis, brucellosis, and other fevers. Some other pathologists felt the lesions observed to be adequately specific to permit an Ebola diagnosis.

Clinical pathological data are extremely limited. A few white blood cell counts were normal to slightly elevated. No differential counts were made. Proteinuria occurred frequently.

Treatment and Prevention

Plasmapheresis with plasma from recovered patients has been tried as treatment. Interpretation of limited trials (at the tail end of the epidemics) indicates little hope of an effective therapy. No drugs have been effective. A hospital staff member attending an Ebola patient (from Africa) in a hospital in England became ill and soon was gravely ill. Interferon and immune plasma were both given and the patient recovered. A possible vaccine remains a dream.

Interestingly, 11 of 11 blood donors for plasmapheresis had microfilariae, although no protozoa, in their blood. It should be emphasized that most of the Ebola patients who came to a clinic or a hospital had had several days of treatment with an antimalarial drug, often followed by typhoid treatment or antibiotics of whatever kind available. Malarial parasites could hardly be expected to be found under such circumstances.

Wilbur G. Downs

Bibliography

Baskerville, A., et al. 1985. Ultrastructural pathology of experimental Ebola hemorrhagic fever virus infection. *Journal of Pathology* 147: 199–209.

Bowen, E. T. W., et al. 1977. Virological studies in a case of Ebola virus infection in man and in monkeys. In WHO–PLITM Colloquium, 78–85.

Cox, N. J., et al. 1983. Evidence for two subtypes of Ebola virus based on oligonucleotide sequences. *Journal of Infectious Diseases* 147: 272–5.

Downs, W. G. 1975. Malaria, the great umbrella. *Bulletin of the New York Academy of Medicine* 51: 984–90.

El Mekki, A., and G. van der Groen. 1977. Attempts to classify ungrouped arboviruses by electron microscopy. In WHO–PLITM Colloquium, 281–8.

El Tahir, B. M. 1977. The hemorrhagic fever outbreak: Maridi–Western Equatoria, southern Sudan. In WHO–PLITM Colloquium, 131–4.

Elliot, L. H., M. P. Kiley, and J. B. McCormick. 1985. Descriptive analysis of Ebola virus proteins. *Virology* 147: 169–76.

Germain, M. 1977. Collections of mammals and arthropods, Zaire. In WHO–PLITM Colloquium, 38–9.

Groen, G. van der, et al. 1977. Growth of Lassa and Ebola in different cell lines. In WHO–PLITM Colloquium, 157–67.

Heymann, D. L., et al. 1980. Ebola hemorrahgic fever: Tandala, Zaire, 1977–1978. *Journal of Infectious Diseases* 142: 372–6.

Isaacson, M. 1977. Containment and surveillance of a hospital outbreak of African hemorrhagic fever due to Ebola virus in Kinshasa, Zaire. In WHO–PLITM Colloquium, 117–30.

Johnson, K. M., P. A. Webb, and D. L. Heymann. 1977. Evaluation of the plasmapheresis program in Zaire. In WHO–PLITM Colloquium, 157–60.

Kiley, M. P. et al. 1982. Filoviridae: A taxonomic home for Marburg and Ebola viruses. *Intervirology* 18: 24–32.

Murphy, F. 1977a. Pathology of Ebola virus infection. In WHO–PLITM Colloquium, 38–9.

1977b. Ebola and Marburg virus morphology and taxonomy. In WHO–PLITM Colloquium, 40–60.

Pattyn, S. R. 1977. Virological diagnosis of Ebola virus infection. In WHO–PLITM Colloquium, 61–8.

Piot, P., and P. Sureau. 1977. Clinical aspects of Ebola virus infection in Yambuku Area, Zaire. In WHO–PLITM Colloquium, 9–25.

Regnery, R. L., K. M. Johnson, and M. Kiley. 1980. Virion nucleic acid of Ebola virus. *Journal of Virology* 36: 465–9.

Robin, Y., et al. 1971. Les Arbovirus au Sénégal: Etude dans la population humaine du village de Bandia. *Africain Médicale* 10: 739–45.

Sanchez, A., and M. P. Kiley. 1987. Identification and analysis of Ebola virus messenger RNA. *Virology* 157: 414–20.

Sareau, P., and P. Piot. 1977. Containment and surveillance of an epidemic of Ebola virus infection in Yambudu Area, Zaire. In WHO–PLITM Colloquium, 91–116.

WHO Weekly Epidemiological Record. 1989. No. 49, December 8, and No. 50, December 15. Geneva.

World Health Organization and Prince Leopold Institute of Tropical Medicine. 1977. *International colloquium on Ebola virus infection and other hemorrhagic fevers*. Antwerp, Belgium.

VIII.43
Echinococcosis (Hydatidosis)

The larval stages of three tapeworms of the genus *Echinococcus* can cause severe disease in humans. All three normally become adults in the intestines of dogs or other canids. Eggs are passed in the feces and, if ingested by a herbivore, develop in the liver or other organs into a saclike container of larvae, the hydatid cyst. Carnivores become infected by eating cysts with the flesh of the herbivore. *Echinococcus granulosus*, which commonly has a sheep–dog cycle, but which may also infect goats, cattle, swine, and camels, is the most likely to infect human beings. Human echinococcosis occurs primarily in sheep-rearing areas. Dogs ingest cysts in the offal of dead sheep and pass eggs in their feces. Humans acquire the eggs from a dog's fur or from contaminated food or water. Cysts holding 2 or more liters of fluid and larvae can grow for years in the liver, lungs, brain, or other organs and exert enough mechanical pressure to cause grave or fatal consequences. Rupture of a cyst by trauma or surgery releases daughter cysts, which may grow elsewhere in the victim; the hydatid fluid can cause fatal anaphylactic shock.

Hydatid cysts in humans and animals have been known since Roman times, but, as was true for the other tapeworms, the relationship between the larval cyst and the adult worm was not suspected until the eighteenth century. *E. granulosus* was described as a separate species in 1850, and its life cycle was worked out with feeding experiments in 1863.

The parasite first became a serious danger to humans when animals were domesticated. The expansion of European settlement spread infection to the Americas and Australasia. Echinococcosis is also found in North Africa, Cyprus, the Middle East, northern and central Asia, and most of sub-Saharan Africa. Iceland was a major focus in the mid-nineteenth century, but education, dog control, and sanitary slaughtering have eliminated the disease. Similar methods, including the mass treatment of dogs, have greatly reduced its incidence in Australia and New Zealand. The highest known prevalence of echinococcosis is among the Turkana, a stock-raising people in northwestern Kenya. Colonial medical authorities in Kenya did not recognize the disease until the 1950s, and an incidence rate of 96 per 100,000 was estimated in 1976, more than seven times the previous record rate in Cyprus. The Turkana problem is linked to a very close association between children and dogs.

Echinococcosis is often difficult to diagnose. Cysts can be detected by X-rays or surgery; several serologic tests are also used. Surgery was the only effective therapy until the early 1980s, when the drug mebendazole was employed with at least some success.

K. David Patterson

Bibliography

Araujo, F. P., et al. 1975. Hydatid disease transmission in California: A study of the Basque connection. *American Journal of Epidemiology* 102, 4: 291–302.

Beard, Trevor C. 1973. The elimination of echinococcosis from Iceland. *Bulletin of the World Health Organization* 48: 653–60.

Foster, W. D. 1965. *A short history of parasitology*. Edinburgh and London.

Gemmel, M. A., J. R. Lawson, and M. G. Roberts. 1986. Control of echinococcosis/hydatidosis: Present state of worldwide progress. *Bulletin of the World Health Organization* 64: 333–9.

Kean, B. H., Kenneth E. Mott, and Adair J. Russell, eds. 1978. *Tropical medicine and parasitology: Classic investigations*. Vol. II, 636–52. Ithaca and London.

Leuckart, Rudolph. 1886. *Parasites of man and the diseases which proceed from them*. Edinburgh.

Nelson, G. S. 1986. Hydatid diseases: Research and control in Turkana, Kenya 1. Epidemiological observations. *Transactions of the Royal Society of Tropical Medicine and Hygiene* 80: 177–82.

Nelson, George S., and Robert L. Rausch. 1963. Echinococcus infections in man and animals in Kenya. *Annals of Tropical Medicine and Parasitology* 57: 136–49.

O'Leary, Patricia. 1976. A five-year review of human hydatid cyst disease in Turkana district, Kenya. *East African Medical Journal* 53: 540–4.

Schantz, Peter M., and Calvin Schwabe. 1969. World-wide status of hydatid disease control. *Journal of the American Veterinary Medical Association* 155: 2104–21.

Stallbaumer, M. F., et al. 1986. The epidemiology of hydatid disease in England and Wales. *Journal of Hygiene (Cambridge)* 96: 121–7.

Eclampsia is a puzzling hypertensive disorder affecting only women. Associated solely with pregnancy and childbirth, it is an epileptic form of convulsions that develops during the second half of pregnancy and disappears after conception. The severity depends upon the degree and timing of the illness as well as the characteristics of the patient. Eclampsia is associated with hypertension, edema, and toxemia, and all three can cause the symptoms of the disease to vary widely. *Preeclampsia* refers to hypertension, abnormal edema, or proteinuria during pregnancy, whereas eclampsia is the disease's most extreme form, manifested by severe convulsions, coma, and even death. Eclampsia is a leading cause of maternal and fetal mortality and can cause stillbirths or premature labor. Medical experts remain confused about the cause of this disorder and have no effective way to cure the disease other than to terminate pregnancy by delivering the baby. Through careful prenatal care, however, physicians can usually control the problem, and it is now relatively rare in the United States and Europe.

Not only is the disease difficult to define, but also accurate records of its existence are rare, especially in Third World countries where prenatal care by a medical attendant is uncommon. Although eclampsia is one of the diseases most troubling to obstetricians, research on the illness is difficult because it is found only in human beings. Its etiology remains unknown but may be multifactorial.

Distribution and Incidence

For reasons not understood, eclampsia seems to be more common among the economically underprivileged. The typical patient is a young woman in her first pregnancy, who is of low socioeconomic status and has had little or no prenatal care. It is more common among women who (1) are diabetic; (2) have high blood pressure or suffer from renal or vascular diseases; (3) suffer from poor nutrition or hydatiform moles; (4) are on the age extremes of their childbearing years; and (5) bear twins. It occurs more frequently in the spring and summer and in certain locations. It also evinces a familial tendency, suggesting some kind of genetic disorder.

Eclampsia is less likely to occur in women who have experienced a previous case. There are few conclusive studies indicating that race is a factor, though it has been suggested that black women in the United States are more likely to suffer from eclampsia than their white counterparts because of greater tendency to develop chronic hypertension on the one hand, and less opportunity for proper maternal care on the other. The disorder occurs in 6 to 8 percent of all pregnancies. Statistics show that it is more common in urban areas, though this association may reflect only the fact that urban women who experience eclampsia or preeclampsia receive more medical assistance in giving birth than rural women, and thus the condition is more frequently noted and reported. Indeed, it is difficult to determine the frequency of eclampsia in rural areas or Third World nations because women there seldom seek, have access to, or can afford regular prenatal care and a hospital delivery. In the United States it has been estimated that the incidence of toxemia is between 5 and 7 percent of all deliveries, and that of eclampsia between 0.12 and 0.26 percent of all deliveries. On the other hand, the incidence figures from several Navajo studies soar to as high as 15.2 and .41, respectively, yet hypertension does not seem to be a predisposing factor (Slocomb and Kunitz 1977). Afro-Americans also have a much higher incidence of toxemia and eclampsia than the general U.S. population, but in this case hypertension does seem to predispose to the disease (Williams, ed. 1975).

Clinical Manifestations

Symptoms of eclampsia and preeclampsia include excessive and sudden weight gain, edema, hypertension, and proteinuria. Patients may also suffer from headache, dizziness, visual disturbances, anorexia, nausea, vomiting, upper abdominal pain, and swelling of the face and extremities. In severe cases, women experience visual and neurological disturbances, oliguria (a deficiency of urine excretion), and, of course, convulsions. In addition, cardiac output increases and the kidneys (which seem to be the target organ for the disease) are affected. Eclampsia can lead to lethal complications affecting the liver, kidney, uterus, and brain, such as *abruptio placentae,* acute renal failure, cerebral hemorrhage, disseminated intravascular coagulation, and circulatory collapse. Preeclampsia does not occur before the twentieth week of pregnancy, and eclampsia rarely before the thirty-second week. Doctors carefully monitor blood pressure and weight gain to prevent its occurrence, although the disease's progress can be rapid and sudden.

History and Geography

It is difficult to determine how common or serious eclampsia was in ancient times. The writings of Egyptian, Chinese, Indian, and Greek scholars do not convincingly note cases, other than an occasional remark describing a pregnant woman's convulsion, fit, or headache. For centuries eclampsia was commonly mistaken for epilepsy. If discussed at all, writers generally attributed the disease to uterine suffocation, believing that the uterus had wandered into the abdominal region. Therapy focused on encouraging a retrograde motion of the uterus to relieve pressure on the upper body and brain. Medieval writings only hint at the disease, but perhaps the reason for this paucity of information was that midwives had a monopoly on assisting births and did not provide written descriptions of problems they encountered. In the second century, Galen noted that epilepsy could be fatal to pregnant women, and Eucharius Rösslin in the sixteenth century stated that convulsions and unconsciousness were ominous signs in pregnant women. Jacques Guillimeau in 1612 concluded that convulsions occurred because the fetus was striving to come forth or that improper positioning extended the womb, thus fostering convulsions. François Mauriceau in 1688 was the first physician systematically to describe eclampsia, thereby indicating a new concern with the disorder as men began entering the field of obstetrics. He also was the first to note that primogravids were at greater risk that multigravids. Mauriceau suggested several causes, including excessive hot blood flowing from the uterus and malignant vapors from a dead fetus. In 1694, he recommended that two or three phlebotomies be performed routinely during pregnancy should a woman exhibit eclamptic tendencies. All early medical experts agreed that it was a dangerous disease.

During the nineteenth century, speculation about the disease was widespread, and physicians considered it to be the most dreaded disorder associated with pregnancy. Doctors speculated on numerous possible causes of eclampsia, including a woman's rapidly changing emotions, a sanguine or plethoric state, excessive hemorrhaging, blood to the brain, nutritional deficiency, excessive protein in the system, albuminuria, renal deficiency, retention of urinary constituents, nerve irritation, high blood pressure, seasonal changes, lethargy, melancholia, wealth, improper positioning of the womb, corrupt menstrual flow, a bad seed, an unstable personality, passions of the mind, and interrupted circulation.

Therapy was generally "heroic." Solutions included warm baths, doses of opium, extensive bleeding from the jugular vein or a temporal artery, depletion to rid the body of toxins, removal of meat or milk from the diet, mustard poultices, ice or cold water on the head, snuff, clysters, emollients to dilate the cervix, and plasters to the lower body to draw the uterus downward. Doctors disagreed on whether it was wise to deliver the baby immediately. Heroic cures, especially those emphasizing depletion, doubtlessly contributed to maternal deaths.

In 1768 Thomas Denman wrote one of the earliest monographs on the disease in English. John Lever and James Young Simpson in 1843 simultaneously discovered the consistent occurrence of proteinuria in preeclamptic patients by finding albumin in their urine. This was a major breakthrough, for the disease could now be considered a toxemia rather than one caused by mechanical pressure. Until the twentieth century, eclampsia was associated with wealthy women, probably because they used male doctors who wrote about the disorder. Not until the 1930s were poor women viewed as susceptible. Unwed mothers were also seen as vulnerable, perhaps because their infants were more likely to be primogravids. Early in the twentieth century, eclampsia was usually associated with hypertension and elevated blood pressure, though speculation as to its origin was still common.

Today physicians depend upon careful monitoring of blood pressure and proteinuria during pregnancy, while watching for edema and excessive weight gain. Early detection is essential. If a woman should suffer preeclampsia, physicians recommend rest and constant monitoring. If a patient suffers from convulsions, attendants take immediate measures to prevent physical injury by suctioning her air passage, providing oxygen, and employing magnesium sulfate to control the seizures. Should the convulsions persist, in rare cases sodium amorbarbital, a barbituate, is administered. Seizures can cause fetal death because the convulsive woman is not breathing and thus the baby is cut off from its oxygen supply. If the baby is near term, doctors make every effort to deliver it once the convulsions have subsided and the patient is conscious. Eclampsia remains one of the greatest puzzles in the list of human diseases and fosters much debate and concern. Doctors have developed better means to manage the disease but still lack an understanding of its etiology.

Sally McMillen

Bibliography

Brewer, Thomas H. 1966. *Metabolic toxemia of late pregnancy: A disease of malnutrition.* Springfield, Ill.

Chesley, Leon C. 1981. *Hypertensive disorders in pregnancy.* New York.

Coudon, James. 1813. *An inaugural essay on eclampsia or puerperal convulsions.* Baltimore.

Davies, A. Michael. 1971. *Geographical epidemiology of the toxemias of pregnancy.* Springfield, Ill.

Denman, Thomas. 1768. *Essays on the puerperal fever and on puerperal convulsions.* London.

Dieckmann, William Joseph. 1952. *The toxemias of pregnancy,* 2d edition. St. Louis.

International Society for the Study of Hypertension in Pregnancy and Pregnancy Hypertension. 1980. *Proceedings of the First Congress of the International Society,* ed. John Bonner, Ian Macgillivray, and Malcolm Symond. Baltimore.

Kitzmiller, John. 1977. Immunologic approaches to the study of preeclampsia. *Clinical Obstetrics and Gynecology* 20, 3: 717–35.

MacGillivrary, Ian. 1983. *Pre-eclampsia: The hypertensive disease of pregnancy.* New York.

Pritchard, J. A., ed. 1985. Hypertensive disorders in pregnancy. In *Williams' obstetrics,* 17th edition, 525–60. Norwalk, Conn.

Slocomb, John C., and Stephen J. Kunitz. 1977. Factors affecting maternal mortality and morbidity among American Indians. Public Health Reports No. 92. Washington, D.C.

Williams, Richard Allen, ed. 1975. *Textbook of black-related diseases.* New York.

VIII.45
Emphysema

Pulmonary emphysema is defined in morphological rather than clinical terms. The 1958 Ciba Symposium defined emphysema as an "increase beyond the normal of air spaces, distal to the terminal bronchiole, either from dilation or from destruction of their walls." The subsequent American Thoracic Society statement in 1962 made anatomic destruction a part of the definition: "Emphysema is an anatomic alteration of the lung characterized by an abnormal enlargement of the air spaces distal to the terminal, nonrespiratory bronchiole, accompanied by destructive changes of the alveolar walls."

The definition was refined in 1985 in a workshop report of the National Heart, Lung, and Blood Institute: "Emphysema is defined as a condition of the lung characterized by abnormal, permanent enlargement of airspaces distal to the terminal bronchiole, accompanied by the destruction of their walls, and without obvious fibrosis."

Emphysema can also be subclassified in anatomic terms. The *acinus* is the gas-exchanging unit of the lung served by a single terminal bronchiole. Within the acinus, the terminal bronchiole is succeeded by three orders of branching respiratory bronchioles that are subsequently succeeded by alveolar ducts and terminal alveolar sacs, all of which bear alveoli. If emphysematous changes predominate in the region of respiratory bronchioles, the condition is termed *centriacinar* or *centrilobular* emphysema. More uniform involvement constitutes *panacinar* or *panlobular* emphysema. Emphysema located predominantly in the periphery of the acinus along lobular septa is *paraseptal* emphysema. Occasionally, emphysema may occur adjacent to a scar or fibrotic process and is called *paracicatricial* emphysema.

Distribution and Incidence

Because emphysema is, by definition, a morphological diagnosis, its presence and prevalence depend on the interpretation of an examination of the lungs during an autopsy. Obvious emphysema is likely to be found in at least 50 percent of an average autopsy population, with a frequency of about 65 percent in men and 15 percent in women. Incidence increases with age, reaching 30 percent by the fourth decade and 60 percent by the seventh decade of life. It has been suggested that at least some emphysema may be a universal finding in elderly adults if properly prepared lungs are carefully examined.

Epidemiology

Whereas most epidemiological studies are based on information elicited by questionnaires or physiological tests, emphysema is a morphological diagnosis and epidemiological studies must be confined to autopsy data. Furthermore, the lungs must be properly fixed on inflation and examined using comparable techniques and emphysema grading methods. Perhaps because of a younger average age of the population examined and a lower prevalence of cigarette smoking, studies from Africa reveal a lower frequency of emphysema than elsewhere. Yet even when populations are of the same age, and the lungs are examined by the same investigators, there appear to be some national and even regional differences. For example, the frequency of emphysema is greater in parts of the United Kingdom than in Sweden or some parts of North America, and lower in some North American cities than in others. The frequency differences may reflect different patterns of cigarette smoking or levels of air pollution, or the selection of people autopsied. The various studies do agree that the amount and severity of emphysema increase with advancing age, and cigarette smoking is a primary cause of the disease. In the various studies, emphysema is found, and in more severe form, at least twice as often in men as in women. The greater incidence of emphysema in males may reflect the greater prevalence of smoking in men; if that is the case, then as more women take up cigarette smoking, this sex preference may change. Although emphysema is remarkably common, it is a cause of, or contributes to, death in only a small percentage of cases.

Etiology

The disruption of alveolar architecture characteristic of emphysema appears to be the result of tissue destruction caused by elastolytic proteases derived from polymorphonuclear leukocytes and alveolar macrophages. Uninhibited digestion of tissue is observed in patients with alpha-1-antitrypsin deficiency. This genetically determined *protease inhibitor phenotype Z* (PiZ) occurs in no more than 1 in 1,000 individuals in a general population, however, and thus can account for only a small proportion of emphysema cases. Evidence suggests that cigarette smoke can enhance accumulation of leukocytes and macrophages in the lung with release of elastolytic enzymes, and can also inhibit antiprotease activity by mechanisms still under study. Although some forms of mild emphysema are quite common and can occur in nonsmokers, there is nonetheless a strong association between cigarette smoking and emphysema. Thus, although the precise mechanisms remain to be elucidated, cigarette smoking is the most important cause of the moderate to severe forms of emphysema, causing clinical symptoms, respiratory impairment, disability, and death.

Clinical Manifestations

The patient with clinically significant emphysema is typically an older male smoker who gives a history of breathing difficulties that increase in severity over time. On physical examination, he is usually thin, with a thoracic configuration (barrel chested) suggesting hyperinflation, and has markedly diminished breath sounds when listened to on auscultation. Airflow obstruction can be demonstrated by slowing of forced expiration. The chest radiograph confirms hyperinflation with a relatively small heart and decreased peripheral lung markings. However, this "typical" clinical picture is more often the exception than the rule. In several reported series of autopsies, moderate to severe forms of emphysema were found in a significant proportion of individuals who did not exhibit clinical evidence of the disease. In addition, chest radiographs are not reliable in either diagnosing or ruling out emphysema. Most often, emphysema occurs in conjunction with chronic bronchitis and is accompanied by a chronic productive cough.

The presumptive diagnosis of emphysema cannot be made without pulmonary function tests. Chronic airflow obstruction manifested by slowing of forced expiration is characteristic of moderate to severe emphysema, although even this finding may not be universal. When emphysema increases in severity, hyperinflation is reflected by an increase in total lung capacity and residual volume, and the carbon monoxide diffusing capacity is reduced. Loss of lung elastic recoil is commonly associated with emphysema. Such physiological data provide more sensitive indicators of the presence of emphysema than do clinical signs and symptoms or radiological findings.

History

In a postscript to his 1698 *Treatise of the Asthma,* John Floyer described bullous emphysema, together with hyperinflation and loss of lung elastic recoil, from his dissection of a broken winded mare. In his 1793 book on *Morbid Anatomy,* Matthew Baillie described the morphology of human emphysema with tissue destruction leading to airspace enlargement. There is good evidence that the lung used as an illustration in Baillie's book was that of Samuel Johnson, whose lungs, at autopsy, were found to be permanently distended and failed to collapse on opening the chest. René Laennec's classic *Treatise on the Diseases of the Chest* first appeared in 1819 and was expanded in a subsequent edition in 1826, the year of his death. In it, Laennec provided the first description of pulmonary emphysema, the destructive nature of the disease, and its association with chronic bronchitis. James Jackson, Jr., accumulated a series of cases of emphysema and noted that the disease exhibited a familial predisposition. Though he died in 1834, his work was published in a paper by his mentor Pierre Louis in 1837. It was not until 1963 that the genetically determined alpha-1-antitrypsin deficiency associated with emphysema was described. The physiological changes associated with emphysema have attracted the attention of many investigators over the years. The loss of lung recoil associated with emphysema was inferred from early observations. It was noted by Fritz Rohrer in 1916 and studied by K. von Neergaard and K. Wirz in 1927 and Ronald Christie in 1934 among others. Recent advances in the pathological anatomy of emphysema stem from the work of J. Gough in 1952 using techniques developed by him and by J. E. Wentworth. The precise mechanisms leading to the lung destruction characteristic of emphysema are under current investigation.

Ronald J. Knudson

Bibliography

American Thoracic Society. 1962. Definitions and classifications of chronic bronchitis, asthma, and pulmonary emphysema: A statement by the American Thoracic Society. *American Review of Respiratory Diseases* 85: 762–8.

Ciba Symposium. 1959. Terminology, definitions, and classification of chronic pulmonary emphysema and related conditions: A report of the conclusions of a Ciba guest symposium. *Thorax* 14: 289–99.

Report of a National Heart, Lung, and Blood Institute, Division of Lung Diseases Workshop. 1985. The definition of emphysema. *American Review of Respiratory Diseases* 132: 182–5.

Snider, Gordon L., ed. 1983. *Clinics in chest medicine,* Vol. 4, No. 3.

Thurlbeck, William M. 1976. *Chronic airflow obstruction in lung disease.* Philadelphia.

    1982. The anatomical pathology of chronic airflow obstruction. In *Current pulmonology,* ed. D. H. Simmons, 1–24. New York.

VIII.46
Encephalitis Lethargica

Foremost among recorded encephalitis epidemics was the global pandemic of encephalitis lethargica that emerged in and from Europe during the last years of the Great War and occurred in successive waves throughout the world during the following decade. Although the diagnosis of encephalitis lethargica is sometimes applied to sporadically occurring cases of inflammation of the brain having a strong lethargic or stuporous aspect, this discussion focuses upon the encephalitis pandemic that accompanied and followed the 1918 influenza pandemic.

Clinical Manifestations and Pathology

Clinically, encephalitis lethargica was characterized by diffuse involvement of the brain and spinal cord, producing practically the entire range of the signs and symptoms of neurological disease. Sometimes occurring in close conjunction with respiratory-spread influenza, but more often after a long interval, encephalitis patients developed an illness usually characterized by the triad signs of fever, lethargy, and disturbances of eye movement, along with a broad range of other signs and symptoms. These included headache, tremor, weakness, depression, delirium, convulsions, the inability to articulate ideas, coordinate movements, or recognize the importance of sensory stimuli, as well as psychosis and stupor. Oculogyric crisis (eyeballs fixed in one position for a period of time) and other disorders of eye movement, the most frequent sign of localized damage to the nervous system, were present in three-fourths of the cases. Lethargy, another common symptom, in some patients lasted only a few days, but in others it persisted for weeks and months or until death from comatose respiratory failure. Not infrequently, spasmodic twitching and severe psychic and behavior changes persisted long after the acute illness. Approximately a third of encephalitis lethargica patients died of their acute illness, and a large proportion (80 percent) of survivors developed parkinsonism during ensuing decades.

The main pathological findings during the acute encephalitic illness were a diffuse inflammatory reaction in the meninges and around the blood vessels of the brain and the spinal cord; degenerative changes were found in the neurones, especially in the brainstem, basal ganglia, and cerebellum, but

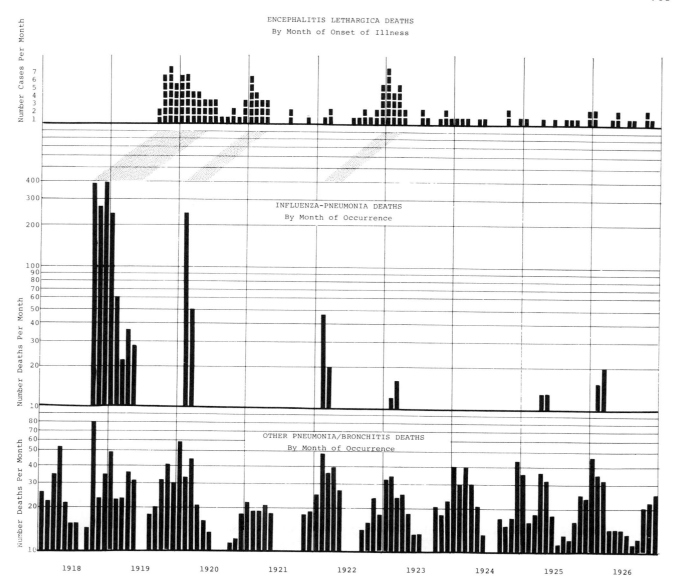

Figure VIII.46.1. Encephalitis lethargica, influenza-pneumonia, other pneumonia/bronchitis deaths in Seattle–King County, Washington, 1918–26. (From Ravenholt and Foege. 1981. 1918 influenza, encephalitis lethargica, parkinsonism. *Lancet* 2: 860-4, by permission of *The Lancet.)*

also including the cortex and the subcortical white matter. In the spinal cord, both the white and gray matter were involved in the inflammatory, degenerative disease process.

Epidemiology

The dominant epidemiological feature of encephalitis lethargica was its unique time distribution. Although epidemics of encephalitic disease had occurred in conjunction with many previous influenza epidemics – 1580, 1658, 1673–5, 1711–2, 1729, 1767, 1780–2, 1830–3, 1847–8, and especially 1889–92 – the global pandemic of encephalitis accompanying and following the 1918 influenza pandemic was in a

class by itself with respect to virulence and sequelae. Along with its unique time distribution, 1917–26, the encephalitis lethargica epidemic, as Figure VIII.46.1 indicates, also had a pronounced seasonal predilection for the winter months. Encephalitis cases often occurred in such close conjunction with individual and community attacks of influenza that many professional and laypersons initially believed the disease to be caused by the devastatingly virulent influenza. But the fact that many cases and epidemics of encephalitis subsequently occurred at times when, and in places where, there was no discernible influenza activity generated confusion and skepticism that influenza could be the principal cause. Long latent intervals and slow viruses were not well recognized in 1918; hence encephalitis epidemics occurring a year and more after attacks of influenza were perceived as evidence against rather than supportive of influenza as the cause. Likewise, the fact that influenza was highly contagious and encephalitis was not was misinterpreted as indicating that these were unrelated diseases rather than being different manifestations of the same viral agent.

Earliest reports of epidemic encephalitis in 1917 by Constantin Economo in Vienna and by French observers differed little in substance; but Economo's provocative title, encephalitis lethargica – giving unique emphasis to one sign in the broad spectrum of clinical manifestations – gained him lasting recognition while generating ongoing diagnostic confusion.

Although these reports of encephalitis preceded the explosive general global dissemination of influenza in 1918, influenza was active in war-torn Europe during the winter of 1916–17. In 1918, in close association with the initial massive waves of influenza, encephalitis was reported in Britain, Scandinavia, Germany, the United States, and many other countries; but the greatest epidemic peaks of encephalitis occurred in 1919–20 and during subsequent winters – as shown for Seattle in Figure VIII.46.1.

Typically, encephalitis lethargica was generally distributed by age, sex, race, occupation, education, economic status, and geographic location. Ages of cases ranged from infancy to old age, with the highest attack rates among young adults; and the sexes were equally represented. Rarely was there discernible clustering of encephalitic cases within families and neighborhoods; and where such was reported, it is retrospectively apparent that the clustering arose as a result of diagnostic confusion with other causes of central nervous system disease – for example, botulism.

Attack rates for encephalitis lethargica during the pandemic years 1918–26 approached 1 case per 1,000 general population in the United States and in European countries where fairly complete records were maintained. Of those afflicted, roughly one third died during their acute illness. Extensive but less precise reports from throughout the world indicate that attack rates for encephalitis lethargica may have been similar worldwide, except in those few small populations, most notably American Samoa, where neither influenza nor encephalitis occurred during the pandemic years. Hence, the world total of encephalitis lethargica cases was probably more than 1.5 million – of whom about 500,000 died of acute illness and more died from parkinsonism and other complications following the acute illness stage.

Etiology

Despite the assertions of F. G. Crookshank (1919), Rudolf von Jaksch (1923), and others that 1918 influenza was the principal cause of encephalitis lethargica, leading researchers of the 1920s, such as E. O. Jordan (1927) and A. J. Hall (1924), judged the relationship between influenza and encephalitis to be so inconsistent and confusing that they stated the etiology of encephalitis lethargica to be "unknown." But now, 60 and more years after the pandemic, from research done in Seattle and Samoa by R. T. Ravenholt and W. H. Foege (1982), the etiology of encephalitis lethargica seems clear. Death records in Seattle show a characteristic modal lag of approximately a year from influenza-pneumonia death peaks to onset of encephalitis lethargica clusters terminating in death (Figure VIII.46.1), providing strong evidence that encephalitis cases previously thought to have occurred independently of influenza were actually late sequelae.

The Samoan Islands were chosen as another site for study because the sharply contrasting experience of Western and American Samoa with respect to the 1918 influenza epidemic provided a unique basis for study of its pathological effects. As stated by Jordan:

In no part of the world did influenza exact a more crushing toll than in the islands of the South Sea. In Western Samoa the steamer Talune from Auckland introduced the disease on November 7, 1918, into the islands of Upolu and Savaii. As a result there were nearly 8,000 deaths, the population during the two months ended December 31, 1918, being reduced from 38,178 to 30,636.

Meanwhile, American Samoa, just 70 kilometers away, and inhabited by the same racial stock, managed to exclude the infection with strict quarantine measures and good fortune.

During May 1982, American Samoa records stored in the National Archives and Records, in San Bruno, California, along with death records for American Samoa maintained by the Lyndon B. Johnson Tropical Medicine Center on Tutuila, and death records for Western Samoa available in the Registrar's Office at Apia were analyzed. Although the rudimentary nature of the death records in Western Samoa limited the comparative studies that could be made of mortality patterns in American and Western Samoa during the 1920s, it was clear that whereas Western Samoa suffered heavily from both influenza-pneumonia and encephalitis lethargica during the years 1918–22, American Samoa was remarkably free of both these diseases during those years. The evidence, then, is compelling that the pandemic of influenza beginning in 1918 and the pandemic of encephalitis lethargica generally beginning the following year had a common etiology. Both pandemics were globally distributed and were closely related in time, and only one etiologic agent (swine influenza virus) has been reliably identified.

Local, regional, and national influenza-pneumonia epidemics ordinarily (perhaps invariably) preceded local, regional, and national epidemics of encephalitis lethargica. A large proportion of individual encephalitis lethargica cases during the early years of the pandemic had had clinical influenza. Later, as influenza and encephalitis occurrence patterns shifted from massive epidemic to sporadic endemic, the relationship between these two diseases became progressively obscured.

Seasonal and global occurrence patterns of encephalitis lethargica rule out the possibility that this pandemic was caused by an arbovirus or any known nonrespiratorily spread infection. Moreover, although influenza-pneumonia was highly communicable from person to person, encephalitis lethargica was remarkably noncommunicable from person to person by any known route.

Analogous pandemics of encephalitis have been recorded in close association with other influenza epidemics, although none as severe as that in association with the 1918 influenza pandemic. Guillain–Barré's disease following inoculation with swine influenza antigen suggests a neurotoxic effect of this organism, even in the killed state. Likewise occurrence of parkinsonism during convalescence from influenza and/or encephalitis and during many years and decades thereafter demonstrates the extraordinary neuropathogenic qualities of the causative agent – now identified as the 1918 (swine) influenza virus.

Immunology

The immunologic findings of E. T. Gamboa and colleagues in 1974 support the contention that the 1918 influenza (swine, type A) and encephalitis lethargica epidemics had a common etiology: They found deceased patients with well-documented postencephalitic parkinsonism to have intranuclear fluorescent antibody to neurotropic influenza A strain antigen in hypothalamic and midbrain sections, whereas no such fluorescence was observed in similar sections

Table VIII.46.1. *Time interval from encephalitis to parkinsonism to death in six patients*

Patient	Year of encephalitic illness	Years from encephalitic illness to parkinsonism	Years from encephalitic illness to death
1	1925	1	47
2	1927	13	45
3	1924	2	48
4	1926	17	46
5	1921	12	51
6	1918	30	54

Source: Gamboa et al. (1974).

from brains of persons with idiopathic (not postencephalitic) parkinsonism. The long intervals between the several manifestations of 1918 (swine) influenza virus – pneumonia, encephalitis lethargica, parkinsonism – must be kept in mind when seeking to understand the interrelated epidemiology of these diseases (see Table VIII.46.1).

History

From among all causes of encephalitis – structural, chemical, and microbiological – it was a difficult task sorting out the many infectious causes of encephalitis by specific causative organism and route of transmission. But with the explosion of scientific knowledge in the late nineteenth and twentieth centuries, many important agents and vectors of encephalitis were identified, among them, the spirochete of syphilis, and the trypanosome of African sleeping sickness, transmitted by sexual contact and tsetse flies, repectively; the bacterial toxin of botulism, from ingested food; the viruses of yellow fever, Japanese B encephalitis, equine encephalitis, transmitted by mosquitoes; the virus of rabies, transmitted by the bite of rabid animals; the viruses of influenza, mumps, and measles, transmitted by the respiratory route; the enteroviruses, transmitted by the fecal–oral route; and, most recently, the human immunodeficiency virus, transmitted by sexual contact and blood.

Adding to the diagnostic confusion generated by these numerous encephalitic microorganisms were the many cases and deaths from stuporous encephalitic reactions to various toxins and drugs, especially Reye's syndrome following the use of aspirin (introduced in 1899) to control the fever and discomfort of influenza, varicella, and other childhood diseases. The role of aspirin in the production of Reye's syndrome has become known only in the last decade.

But the main causative agent of epidemic encephalitis during the pandemic years 1917–26 was the respiratorily spread influenza virus. Successive peaks of encephalitis occurred in European, Asian, African, and American countries from 1918 to about 1926. In the United States, encephalitis lethargica progressed across the country from the east to the west in 1919, just as influenza had the previous year, reaching peak occurrence in New York during January 1919, in Virginia during February, and in Illinois, Louisiana, and Texas during March; whereas in California more cases were reported in April than in any other month, and in Seattle the first encephalitis lethargica cases were reported in October 1919. Although Britain reported its peak number of cases in 1924, this was apparently a reporting artifact – as judged from the mortality pattern during the 1920s.

For too long, medical science has tended to relegate the 1918 influenza–encephalitis lethargica–parkinsonism puzzle to an intellectual ash heap, apparently on the assumption that these epidemics are past history and of little or at least dwindling importance to current and future health. But failure to identify influenza virus as the cause of encephalitis lethargica and parkinsonism has crippled progress toward the understanding of influenza pathology and epidemiology needed to fuel and guide prevention of these elusive but exceedingly important diseases.

According to William Osler, Karl Menninger, and August Wimmer, almost every disease of the central nervous system (CNS) may follow influenza. Thus we should look to the diminutions of CNS structures caused by influenza attacks during earlier life when seeking the keys to prevention of much serious CNS disease, especially senile dementia (Alzheimer's disease).

R. T. Ravenholt

Bibliography

Collins, S. D., and J. Lehmann. 1953. *Excess deaths from important chronic diseases during epidemic periods, 1918–51.* Public Health Monographs. U.S.P.H.S. Publication No. 213.

Crosby, A. W. 1976. *Epidemic and peace: 1918.* Westport, Conn.

Crookshank, F. G. 1919. Epidemic encephalomyelitis and influenza. *Lancet* 1: 79–80.

Economo, C. 1931. *Encephalitis lethargica: Its sequelae and treatment,* trans. K. O. Newman. London.

Gamboa, E. T., et al. 1974. Influenza virus antigen in postencephalitic parkinsonism brain. *Archives of Neurology* 31: 228–32.

Hall, A. J. 1924. *Epidemic encephalitis (encephalitis lethargica).* New York.

Jaksch, Rudolf von. 1923. Influenza encephalitis. *Acta Medica Scandinavica* 58: 557–84.

Jordan, E. O. 1927. *Epidemic influenza: A survey.* Chicago.

Matheson Commission Reports I, II, III. 1929, 1932, 1939. *Epidemic encephalitis: Etiology, epidemiology, and treatment.* New York.

Menninger, K. A. 1926. Influenza and schizophrenia: An analysis of post-influenzal "dementia praecox" as of 1918, and five years later: Further studies of the psychiatric aspects of influenza. *American Journal of Psychiatry* 5: 469–529.

Merritt, H. H. 1967. *A textbook of neurology,* 4th edition. Philadelphia.

Ministry of Health. 1924. Memorandum on encephalitis lethargica. HMSO, London.

Ravenholt, R. T., and W. H. Foege. 1982. 1918 influenza, encephalitis lethargica, parkinsonism. *Lancet* 2: 860–4.

Shope, R. E. 1931. Swine influenza I: Experimental transmission and pathology. *Journal of Experimental Biology* 54: 373–85.

Wimmer, A. 1924. *Chronic epidemic encephalitis.* London.

Winternitz, M. D., L. M. Wasson, and F. P. McNamara. 1920. *The pathology of influenza.* New Haven.

VIII.47
Enterobiasis

The pinworm *Enterobius vermicularis* (formerly *Oxyuris*) is a common parasite around the world and is the most prevalent parasitic helminth in developed countries today. Enterobiasis has afflicted and annoyed humans from ancient times; it was known to ancient Chinese, classical, and Islamic writers and was present in pre-Columbian America. Humans are the only hosts. Mature worms, ranging from 2 to 13 millimeters in length, inhabit the cecum and adjacent regions of the large and small intestines. Gravid females migrate out the host's anus and deposit thousands of eggs on the skin of the perianal region. The eggs mature quickly and are infectious in several hours. Infection by ingestion of eggs from the hands is common, as the worms induce itching and scratching. Eggs are frequently eaten with contaminated food, and, because they are light, they are easily inhaled in household dust. Eggs hatch in the small intestine and develop into mature adults in as short a time as 4 weeks. Retroinfection, when the eggs hatch on the perianal skin and the larvae crawl back into the rectum, is possible but rare. Pinworms are especially prevalent among small children and often become a family affair.

Enterobiasis is rarely a serious disease. Intestinal disturbances, if any, are minor, but pinworms can cause great discomfort, and scratching can lead to secondary infections. Migrating worms occasionally reach the vagina or appendix, but rarely cause serious harm. Rectal itching and consequently insomnia, especially in children, are suggestive of pinworm infection.

Diagnosis is made by microscopic examination of perianal swabs to detect eggs. The condition normally is self-limiting in the absence of continuing reinfection. Drug treatment is safe and effective, but often the whole family or institutional living group must be treated simultaneously, and bedding and clothing must be thoroughly cleaned. Even the most fastidious housekeepers may find it very difficult to rid a home of airborne eggs. Personal hygiene is the best preventive measure.

K. David Patterson

Bibliography

Kean, B. H., Kenneth E. Mott, and Adair J. Russell, eds. 1978. *Tropical medicine and parasitology: Classic investigations*, Vol. II, 363–4. Ithaca and London.

Stoll, Norman R. 1947. This wormy world. *Journal of Parasitology* 33: 1–19.

VIII.48
Epilepsy

Epilepsy is characterized by the repeated occurrence of seizures that result from recurrent, abnormal, excessive, synchronous discharges of populations of cerebral neurons (Epilepsy Foundation of America 1981). It has a worldwide distribution and probably has been in existence since the dawn of human history. The condition is chronic but rarely fatal, and most types of epilepsy do not disturb the affected individual's desire or ability to lead a normal life. Modern antiepileptic medications most often control seizures, and the limitations imposed by the disorder may be negligible. Unfortunately, epileptics are all too frequently stigmatized and excluded from many activities of daily life. Outdated beliefs and misconceptions about epilepsy have only recently shown signs of lessening in the United States and other industrialized societies.

It is misleading to think of epilepsy as one disease. There are many causes of this symptom cluster, just as there are for the symptom cluster of nausea and vomiting. A better term would be "the epilepsies." The epilepsies do, however, share certain physiological characteristics. Clusters of neurons in some parts of the brain begin to discharge impulses in a disorganized fashion. The parts of the body controlled by the affected neurons respond with disorganized activity such as convulsions or tremors, or by loss of normal function such as loss of consciousness, paralysis of a limb, or localized numbness. The condition is also chronic, marked by the recurrence of seizures. By monitoring the brain with electrodes, an electroencephalographer can often detect abnormal brain waves, either localized in one part of the brain or coming from all parts at once.

Etiology

Although epilepsy can begin at any age, the majority of patients have their first seizure before the age of 20. In fact, the age of onset is often related to the cause. Perinatal injuries, severe hypoxia, developmental brain defects, and genetic metabolic defects are common causes of epilepsy among infants and the newborn. Brain infections such as meningitis and encephalitis often result in damage to some brain cells with subsequent development of epilepsy. Many children experience seizures during periods of high fever caused by infection in parts of the body other than the brain. Only a very small percentage of these febrile seizures persist after the age of 4, however. Head trauma is one of the most common causes of seizures among adults, although brain tumor must also be suspected, as about 40 percent of all patients with brain tumors have seizures. Later in life, seizures may be caused by cerebrovascular attacks.

Despite medicine's increased ability to determine the various causes of epilepsy, no known cause can be found or reasonably presumed for a large proportion of seizures. Until a very few years ago, genetic predisposition was thought to be the cause of what was called "idiopathic" epilepsy. Today, most experts do not believe that heritability plays as large a role as the proportion of patients whose seizures have been diagnosed as idiopathic might suggest. That genetic factors are involved, however, is indicated by the fact that people with a family history of epilepsy have a higher incidence of seizures than the population in general. In addition, the electroencephalogram (EEG) tracings of asymptomatic relatives of patients with some forms of epilepsy show a higher incidence of abnormal discharge than is found among the rest of the population.

Epilepsy is characterized by *recurrent* seizures; therefore, an individual's first seizure does not, of itself, indicate its presence. Nervous system infections, metabolic imbalance, and transient reactions to head injury may all result in a seizure episode without putting the individual at risk for further seizures. Among epileptics an almost infinite number of stimuli may trigger seizure activity. Fatigue, alcohol abuse, and infection, for example, commonly precipitate attacks in people whose epilepsy is otherwise well controlled. Despite the great variability in thresholds and types of seizures and in the unpredictability of its course during the patient's lifetime, some features appear with striking frequency, and some attacks are remarkably similar for many people.

Epileptics as well as nonepileptics may experience seizures that are not associated with abnormal brain wave activity and that have no known physiological cause. These *pseudoseizures* are often called *hysterical seizures* or *conversion reactions*. Like epileptic seizures, pseudoseizures have characteristics that appear repeatedly. Epileptics with pseudoseizures tend to exhibit the same signs and symptoms in the same sequence with each episode. Nonepileptics' symptoms may vary in site and nature if there are many episodes. Despite the fact that pseudoseizures are responsive to the social environment and appear to

vary among cultures, they are often very difficult to distinguish from epileptic seizures. Between 8 and 20 percent of epileptics are thought to experience pseudoseizures in addition to their epileptic seizures, and it has been estimated that even experienced neurologists can identify pseudoseizures only 75 percent of the time (Lechtenberg 1984).

Epidemiology

Because epilepsy is a nonreportable disease, it is difficult to arrive at reasonable estimates of its incidence. Perhaps half the cases in the United States are preventable in the sense that they are the sequelae of trauma, infections, birth injury, and so forth, with clear damage to the brain, the seizures appearing as a secondary symptom of the underlying brain damage. In cases of cerebral palsy or mental deficiency, epileptic seizures are often the least dramatic of the symptoms. These secondary cases are more frequent when there is poor prenatal and perinatal care and in populations suffering from poverty with its attendant overcrowding, malnutrition, neglect, and violence. From a world health point of view, epilepsy is a very common and disabling condition, particularly in regions where there is a high incidence of low virulence central nervous system infections causing secondary cases, and where traumas, particularly the subdural hematomas of infancy and early childhood, are neglected.

Distribution and Incidence

In the United States the incidence of epilepsy is about 0.3 to 0.4 percent per year, or roughly one tenth the incidence of mental deficiency and perhaps one half the incidence of schizophrenia. The rate for males is slightly higher than that for females for all types of seizures combined, and is highest for ages 0 to 4 years, reaches a low level after adolescence, and peaks again after 70 years as the result of late cerebral disease (Kurland 1949).

Since the early 1970s, several good epidemiological surveys of epilepsy have been made in Iceland, England, and the United States, which report crude prevalence rates between 3.6 and 5.5 per 1,000 population (Kurland, Kurtzke, and Goldberg 1973). Epidemiological studies of epilepsy, however, are plagued by a variety of problems. Of prime importance in this regard is the lack of agreement on the definition of epilepsy itself as well as what constitutes an active or an inactive case. In addition, there are difficulties involved in estimating the size of the population universe and the number of cases not identified by the case finding procedures. The most rigorous survey conducted in a community in the United States was done in Rochester, Minnesota (Hauser and Kurland 1975). The crude rate for all types of epilepsy was 5.7 per 1,000 population. Seventy-five percent of the patients' seizures were of undetermined cause, and approximately 70 percent had generalized seizures. A prevalence rate of 2.8 per 1,000 population has been reported for Tokyo (Tsuboi 1988) and of 2.47 for rural Kashmir, India (Koul, Razdan, and Motta 1988).

Crude prevalence rates between 7.6 and 8.4 per 1,000 population have been reported for four North American Indian tribes (Levy, Neutra, and Parker 1987). Environmental factors account for the difference between Indians and the non-Indians of Rochester. The former have significantly more epilepsy attributed to trauma, postencephalopathy, and inflammatory disease. Even higher rates are found in urban ghettos, where lead poisoning and drug addiction are among the leading causes of epilepsy (Hauser, personal communication).

Classification, Clinical Manifestations, and Pathology

The growing emphasis on physiological mechanisms and electroclinical correlations has led to a classification of the epilepsies by the localization of the electrical abnormality in the brain. The major division is between *generalized (centrencephalic) seizures,* where the brain activity is spread over the entire cerebral cortex; and *partial (focal) seizures,* which occur when only one part of the brain is involved. Generalized seizures demonstrate bilateral motor activity and involve a loss of consciousness, which may or may not occur in partial seizures depending upon the part of the brain initially affected and the subsequent involvement of other structures. There is an approximate correspondence between the sites of the brain where electrical abnormality occurs and the clinical manifestation of the seizure.

Generalized Seizures

The term "epilepsy" was first used to denote the symptoms of *major,* or *grand mal seizure,* currently referred to as a *tonic-clonic seizure.* To this day, over 60 percent of all individuals diagnosed as epileptic have tonic-clonic seizures. A sudden burst of discharges involving the whole brain occurs without warning. The patient falls to the ground unconscious. Then, in the tonic phase, the patient goes rigid and often gives a short cry, due to the contraction of the diaphragm and chest muscles. The eyes may roll up or turn to one side, and the tongue may be bitten. After this, a period of jerky, clonic, spasms alternately flex and extend the muscles of the head, face, and extremities. During this phase, the patient may injure him- or herself as well as be incontinent. Cyanosis is generally marked. Breathing is deep, and there is sweating and salivation. Subsequent to the seizure, the patient may wake in a confused state (*postictal twilight state*) and even display some bizarre behavior. Sometimes patients are hard to arouse, sleep for hours, and awaken with headache or sore muscles. Although most tonic-clonic seizures last for only a few minutes, some patients develop a series of seizures with no letup, or a continuous prolonged seizure. This is a serious condition known as *status epilepticus,* which may lead to death if immediate care is not provided.

A variety of other generalized seizures have also been recognized. Sometimes patients exhibit only the tonic or clonic aspects of the seizure. Between the ages of 4 and 12 years, *absence seizures* often occur. These have been known as *petit mal* because they are of such brief duration, no more than a few seconds, that they often go unrecognized and untreated. During the brief lapse of consciousness, the child stares vacantly and neither speaks nor hears. Subsequently, activity is resumed with no period of stupor. Equally brief are *atonic seizures,* during which the child simply falls to the ground; *myoclonic seizures,* which are sudden, brief, and massive, involving either the entire body or confined to the extremities, face, or trunk; and *infantile spasms,* during which the child is jerked into a fetal position with the knees drawn up. Many children with infantile spasms are also mentally retarded.

Partial Seizures

All partial seizures begin in one part of the brain, and, because different parts of the brain control different parts of the body as well as mental and sensory functions, their signs and symptoms are varied and, often, quite complex. Many patients exhibit behaviors easily mistaken as psychiatric problems which can make accurate diagnosis difficult. It is also among victims of partial seizures that one is most likely to observe displays of bizarre, learned, culturally conditioned behavior.

Simple partial seizures have been variously called *focal, focal motor,* or *focal sensory seizures.* Although the symptoms may be motor, autonomic, psychic, sensory, or a combination, they are all linked to the affected area of the brain. The patient does not lose consciousness as a general rule, and the attacks last no more than 30 seconds. One type of simple partial seizure has been called the *Jacksonian.* It characteristically begins with the twitching of one foot or hand, and the patient retains consciousness. Until very recently, seizures were classed as Jacksonian even if the activity subsequently spread to both sides of the body and involved loss of consciousness. Today, however, such seizures are classed as partial but secondarily generalized.

Complex partial seizures are characterized by complex symptoms and, unlike simple partial seizures, by impairment of consciousness. Often the patient appears to be conscious but later has no recollection of the episode. These seizures are usually associated with the temporal or frontal lobe and often begin with an aura that warns of the impending attack. Auras may include any of a large variety of sensations. Some of those most commonly reported are nausea; faintness; dizziness; numbness of the hands, lips, and tongue; choking sensations; and chest pain. Less often, patients have reported visions, palpitation, or disturbances of smell or hearing. Some patients have sensations that may begin hours or even days before the seizure. These symptoms are called the *prodrome* and most often involve irritability or feelings of uneasiness. When psychomotor symptoms appear during a seizure, they are generally semipurposeful and inappropriate actions such as clumsy attempts to disrobe. Patients often stagger about uttering guttural sounds. Such behavior is often confused with psychiatric disorder and is often alarming to those present.

Secondarily generalized partial seizures occur when seizures with a focal onset spread throughout the brain and produce generalized tonic-clonic seizures. Because the generalized phase is so dramatic, patients and their families often overlook the focal onset. The presence of an aura indicates the presence of the focal onset and the need to observe the initial phase more closely.

The diagnosis of epilepsy and the classification of the type of seizure depend primarily on information obtained from the medical history. The first task is to determine whether the patient has epilepsy or has experienced another kind of brief, reversible alteration of consciousness or behavior. Subsequently, specifying the type of epileptic seizure is important for confirming the diagnosis and as a major guide in choosing the initial antiepileptic medication. Because the physician is most often unable to observe the patient or obtain an EEG reading during a seizure, an accurate medical history is of crucial impor-

tance. EEGs administered between seizures may or may not reveal patterns suggestive of epilepsy. Nevertheless, because they often do reveal abnormal discharges, routine administration of EEGs is of significant value in the evaluation of any patient with a history suggestive of epilepsy.

By conservative estimates, some 50 percent of patients can have their recurrent seizures controlled without side effects when optimal medical treatment is available. Another 30 percent can achieve seizure control but experience some side effects of the medication. For some patients whose seizures cannot be controlled by medication, surgery may be an option if a distinct piece of brain tissue that is causing the seizures can be identified, and if its removal will not cause unacceptable neurological deficits such as speech difficulty or memory loss.

History

Antiquity

The antiquity of epilepsy is attested to by an ancient Akkadian text that speaks of a person whose neck turns left, whose hands and feet are tense and eyes wide open, from whose mouth froth flowed, and who lost consciousness. The Greeks referred to it as "the sacred disease" as well as "epilepsy," which means seizure and which may derive from the idea that all diseases represented attacks by supernatural beings. The term "sacred disease" is found first in the writings of Heraclitus and Herodotus, but its identification with epilepsy is made explicit in the book *On the Sacred Disease,* part of the Hippocratic collection of medical writings from about the year 400 B.C. and the first monograph on epilepsy we possess.

Underlying the great variety of explanations offered by the ancients lies the basic belief that epilepsy is an affliction or possession by a higher power and that its cure must be supernatural. The Romans called epilepsy *morbus comitalis* because the attack spoiled the day of the comitia, the assembly of the people. There was also the idea that the disease was contagious: The epileptic was unclean and whoever touched him or her might become prey to the demon. The idea that epilepsy was contagious was one of the factors that made the epileptic's life miserable and gave him or her a social stigma. To the ancients the epileptic was an object of horror and disgust and not a saint or prophet as has sometimes been contended. Wherever the physicians of antiquity wrote of the sacred disease, they meant epilepsy and differentiated it from hysterical attacks as well as from madness.

In the struggle between supernatural and scientific explanations of disease, science has gradually emerged victorious in the Western world. The fight, however, has been long and eventful, and in it epilepsy held one of the key positions. Showing both physical and psychic symptoms, epilepsy more than any other disease was open to interpretation both as a physiological process and as the effect of supernatural influences. The first record we have of the battle is in *On the Sacred Disease,* an attack on popular superstition that called epilepsy the "sacred" disease. It maintained that epilepsy was hereditary, that its cause lay in the brain, and its treatment was to be by diet and drugs as long as it had not yet become chronic. It is here we first find the fundamental statement that the seat of the disease is in the brain and that the brain is the organ of all psychic processes both normal and pathological. Moreover, according to the author of this work, not only epilepsy but all mental diseases were to be explained by disturbances in the brain.

Middle Ages Through the Eighteenth Century

During the Middle Ages, the literature on epilepsy propounded two contrasting views. On the one hand, the "falling evil" was bound to demoniac beliefs and theological speculations; on the other, physicians clung to the idea of a definite natural disease. Little effort was made to force the issue, however; physicians rarely discussed the theological aspects and seem, moreover, to have been unable to rid themselves of traditional definitions and explanations. By the end of the sixteenth century, this appears to have changed, the debate became open, involving the role of the devil, witchcraft, and various types of magical treatment. Despite many efforts to define epilepsy and classify types of seizures, little progress was made medically, although, gradually, the idea that epilepsy was a natural disease did gain more credence, especially after the Age of Enlightenment.

Nineteenth Century

By the beginning of the nineteenth century, epileptics were hospitalized, but unlike the insane, were allowed to go to mass on Sundays. Confined epileptics, however, became the object of systematic medical attention only in the early nineteenth century. The care of epileptics, especially children, progressed slowly. Only in 1838 were epileptic children in Paris transferred from the Hospital of the Incurably Ill to the Bicêtre, where some kind of education was provided for them. The separation of hospitalized epileptics from the insane was motivated less from solicitude for the epileptics who might suffer from contact with the insane than from the belief that epilepsy was an infectious disease that would affect the insane even more than it did the healthy. The confinement of epileptics in separate wards of lunatic asylums became established procedure in Europe around 1850 and was soon followed by requests for special institutions for epileptics.

During the early part of the nineteenth century, the most valuable contributions to the medical history of epilepsy were made by physicians associated with hospitals and lunatic asylums, and it was then that new terminology, increased use of statistics, and interest in the psychiatric side of epilepsy developed. The terms grand and petit mal, absence, status epilepticus, and aura, for example, were in common usage and survive to this day. The growing use of statistics fostered investigations into the inheritability of epilepsy and determination of the various causes of the illness, prominent among which were fright, sorrow, and masturbation. Despite the increased attention paid to epilepsy, however, modern medicine's understanding is usually said to have begun around 1880, when the impact of John Hughlings Jackson's work in England and that of Jean Charcot in France began to be felt. Jackson outlined a neurological theory of epilepsy, while Charcot separated epilepsy from hysteria more emphatically than any of his predecessors. Jackson's principles were publicly demonstrated in 1888, by William Macewan, who was "probably the first surgeon to localize the cerebral focus by inference from the motor or sensory signs of the epileptic seizure" (Temkin 1971).

Jerrold E. Levy

Bibliography

Epilepsy Foundations of America. 1981. How to recognize and classify seizures. Landover, Maryland: Epilepsy Foundation of America.

Ervin, Frank R. 1967. Brain disorders. IV: Associated with convulsions (epilepsy). In *Comprehensive textbook of psychiatry,* ed. Alfred M. Freedman and Harold I. Kaplan, 795–816. Baltimore.

Hauser, W. Allen, and Leonard T. Kurland. 1975. The epidemiology of epilepsy in Rochester, Minnesota, 1935 through 1967. *Epilepsia* 16: 1–66.

Koul, Roshan, S. Razdan, and Anil Motta. 1988. Prevalence and pattern of epilepsy (Lath/Mirgi/Laran) in rural Kashmir, India. *Epilepsia* 29: 116–22.

Kurland, Leonard T. 1949. The incidence and prevalence of convulsive disorders in a small urban community. *Epilepsia* 1: 143.

Kurland, Leonard T., John F. Kurtzke, and Irving D. Goldberg. 1973. *Epidemiology of neurologic and sense organ disorders.* Cambridge.

Lechtenberg, Richard. 1984. *Epilepsy and the family.* Cambridge.

Levy, Jerrold E., Raymond Neutra, and Dennis Parker. 1987. *Hand trembling, frenzy witchcraft, and moth madness: A study of Navajo seizure disorders.* Tucson.

Temkin, Owsei. 1971. *The falling sickness: A history of epilepsy from the Greeks to the beginnings of modern neurology,* 2d edition. Baltimore.

Tsuboi, Takayuki 1988. Prevalence and incidence of epilepsy in Tokyo. *Epilepsia* 29: 103–10.

VIII.49
Ergotism

Ergotism is a disease condition acquired by eating cereal grains infected with ergot fungus. Known since the time of Galen, it was prevalent in medieval Europe, particularly among the poor who, during famine, consumed bread made from spoiled rye. Ergot (*secale cornutum,* spur of the corn, horned rye, womb grain), the dried sclerotium of *Claviceps purpurea,* develops on the ovary of common rye, or on corn, where it was previously known as corn smut. The actual cause of ergot in grasses was hotly debated by early naturalists, some of whom thought it occurred in rainy weather and was attributable to fog or impure atmosphere. Others believed it to be the work of worms or butterflies, whereas still others regarded it as the product of improper fecundation or perhaps the cooking of the sexual parts of the plants.

Classification

Ergotism has two forms: (1) *convulsive,* or *spasmodic,* also known as *creeping,* which affects the central nervous system; and (2) *gangrenous,* which affects the blood vessels and blood supply to the extremities. Common names for the gangrenous form are *St. Anthony's fire* (after the patron saint of the disease), hidden fire, saint's fire, evil fire, devil's fire, and holy fire. As a result of early imprecision in disease specificity and diagnosis, physicians confused ergotism with the plague and a variety of other diseases including leprosy, anthrax, typhus, smallpox, and scurvy.

Clinical Manifestations and Pathology

Convulsive or spasmodic ergotism affects the central nervous system, causing areas of degeneration in the spinal cord. Early German accounts mentioned tingling and mortification in the fingers and toes, with occasional extension to the rest of the body, and vomiting, diarrhea, intense hunger, anxiety, unrest, headache, vertigo, noises in the ear, stupor, and insomnia as symptoms. Often the limbs became stiff, accompanied by convulsive contractions of the muscles which led to staggering and awkward movements, often aggravated by being touched. Although many victims recovered, symptoms sometimes remained for long periods, resulting in permanent stiffness of the joints, muscular weakness, optic disorders, and occasional imbecility. In the 1930s, Ralph Stockman demonstrated that convulsive ergotism was "caused by poisons (phytates) normally present in rye and other grains" which, unless broken down in the bowel, were absorbed, creating lesions in the nervous system.

Midwives and empirics discovered that spasmodic ergotism caused abortion or miscarriage in pregnant women, the drying up of milk in lactating mothers, and amenhorrea in young girls. This abortifacient or oxytocic effect was later noted by orthodox medicine and led to the widespread use of ergot to accelerate uterine action. Before long, doctors began distinguishing ergot with such sobriquets as *poudre obstetrical, forcing powders,* or more commonly, *forcing drops.* Not surprisingly, it also played a major role among quacks, charlatans, and "private specialists" who promised a quick and painless cure for women desiring to "regulate" their menstrual cycles. The term "regulation" was euphemistically used to mean the termination of a pregnancy. For some, ergot substituted for the more common borax, cinnamon, and turpentine as an abortifacient.

Gangrenous ergotism often began with itching and formications in the feet, or sensations of extreme coldness, followed by burning pain, or a crop of blisters. A dark spot usually appeared on the nose or affected extremity, leading to loss of sensibility in the part. Early nineteenth-century accounts mentioned headache, dizziness, nausea, vomiting, diarrhea, and spreading erysipelatous redness. The epidermis was raised by serous exudation, and the surface assumed the appearance of gangrene with the extremities becoming withered and blackened. Usually the gangrene was dry, but the moist variety was not unknown. The patient suffered from a continual low fever and phthisical symptoms, and faced eventual death from exhaustion or septicemia. Often, however, recovery followed loss of the affected limb. When gangrene attacked the viscera, however, death occurred quickly. Matthias Grunewald's Isenheim Altarpiece, commissioned between 1508 and 1516 at the Antonite monastery, and currently displayed in the Musée d'Unterlinden in Colmar, testifies to the outbreak of St. Anthony's fire in France and its gruesome impact on those afflicted.

History and Geography

First allusions to ergotism are concurrent with the French monastic hospices, which cared for the common people and which took special note of the disease. Along with these observations came the designation of patron saints for ergotism, including St. Benedict of Umbria, St. Martial of Limoges, St. Geneviève of Paris, St. Martin of Tours, and St. Anthony of Egypt whose remains were carried to France in the eleventh century. From this last saint the name St. Anthony's fire was derived.

In his *Handbook of Geographical and Historical Pathology* (1883–6), August Hirsch recorded 132 epidemics of ergotism between 591 and 1789. Accounts of ergotism are also found in the *Annals* of the Convent at Xanten, near the Rhine, detailing an outbreak in 857, and are described by François Eudes de Mézeray in the seventeenth century as St. Anthony's fire. Later French epidemics of the gangrenous type reportedly killed 40,000 in 922 and 14,000 in Paris alone during 1128–9. The spasmodic form occurred in Spain in 1581 and 1590 and in Germany in 1595; epidemics in the Sologne district of France, in Germany, and in Switzerland recurred throughout the seventeenth century. The French districts of Sologne and Dauphiné, frequently subject to flooding, suffered continuously from outbreaks of ergotism, as did Artois, Lorraine, and the Limousin. The disease also affected the Netherlands, Sweden, Majorca, Italy, Poland, and central Russia, where outbreaks were reported as late as 1926. Hirsch noted three epidemics in the British Isles, and during the American Revolutionary War soldiers stationed in upper New York State reportedly sickened on ergotted flour shipped from Ohio. A later American outbreak reportedly occurred at a New York prison in 1825.

More recent research has suggested that ergotism can explain the convulsions and hallucinations that attended religious revivals, including the Salem witchcraft affair, as well as the time of "The Great Fear" (between July 20 and August 6, 1789), which swept through the rural countryside prior to the French Revolution, and even the seasonability of mortality and conception patterns in Europe.

Epidemiology and Etiology

Research in the 1930s suggested that the distribution of convulsive and gangrenous ergotism was a function of the presence or absence of vitamin A in the diet. An analysis of the 1770 epidemic of gangrenous ergotism in Sologne and of convulsive ergotism in Hanover indicated that Sologne, on the left bank of the Rhine, was a dairy district that provided a diet rich in vitamin A, whereas Hanover, on the right bank, was unable to sustain a dairy economy. The striking difference in the effects of ergot on the two communities in close proximity caused researchers to study their differing experiences in a laboratory by feeding ergot to dogs along with different levels of vitamin A. The results confirmed the efficacy of vitamin A in mitigating the effects of ergotism.

Similarly, while some researchers believed that England's relative freedom from ergotism was due to the abundant ingestion of meat and potatoes, others demonstrated that the English diet, which was rich in milk and butter products, had enabled its inhabitants to remain relatively free from the convulsive effects of ergotized grain. In areas rich in dairy products, the phytase and the bowel bacteria broke down the poisonous phytates of the grain into the comparatively innocuous inorganic phosphates. Thus, the convulsive ergotism which had been common to nondairy areas was virtually absent in England and certain sections of France.

John S. Haller, Jr.

Bibliography

Barger, George. 1931. *Ergot and ergotism*. London.

Berde, B., and H. O. Schild, eds. 1978. *Ergot alkaloids and related compounds*. Berlin.

Bové, Frank J. 1970. *The story of ergot*. Basel.

Caporael, L. R. 1976. Ergotism: The Satan loosed in Salem? *Science* 192: 21–6.

Haller, John S., Jr. 1981. Smut's dark poison: Ergot in history and medicine. *Transactions and Studies, College of Physicians of Philadelphia*, Ser. 5, III: 62–79.

Hirsch, August. 1883–6. *Handbook of geographical and historical pathology*, 3 vols. London.

Matossian, Mary. 1982a. Ergot and the Salem witchcraft affair. *American Scientist* 70: 355–7.

1982b. Religious revivals and ergotism in America. *Clio Medica* 16: 185–92.

Stockman, Ralph. 1934. The cause of convulsive ergotism. *Journal of Hygiene* 34: 235–41.

VIII.50
Erysipelas

The term erysipelas (*erythros* = red, *pella* = skin) was used in Hippocratic times (often but not always) to describe classic cellulitis. For the past century or so, however, erysipelas has commonly referred to infection of the derma with a streptococcal organism, usually *Streptococcus pyogenes*. Infection with a group A, beta-hemolytic streptococcus can produce a painful, red, edematous indurated skin lesion called *peau d'orange* for its resemblance to the texture of an orange skin. Sharp borders of the infection extend rapidly, dissecting the underlying dermis from the epidermis. Erysipelas usually appears on the face, producing a butterfly rash over the cheeks and nose. The same streptococci that cause erysipelas can also cause scarlet fever, giving both diseases a fairly distinctive age pattern: Erysipelas is much more common among adults who generally escape scarlet fever, which normally attacks the young. The prognosis for untreated erysipelas is especially serious when this infection is secondary to some other insult such as laryngeal infection, or puerperal sepsis. Indeed distinctions are still made among gangrenous erysipelas, erysipelas grave internum (a form of puerperal fever), surgical erysipelas (which occurs after a surgical procedure), and traumatic erysipelas (which begins in a wound).

History

Antiquity Through the Eighteenth Century

Early accounts of erysipelas are often confusing because they lumped purulent and gangrenous afflictions under this rubric. Thus Hippocrates distinguished between "traumatic" erysipelas, which accompanied wounds, and a myriad of other skin lesions that had no known external cause. Galen in turn distinguished between "phlegmon," including suppurative ulcers and gangrene, and nonnecrotic cellulitis – but viewed both as forms of erysipelas. Celsus, in the first century A.D., considered septic ulcers, "canker," erythematous wound infections, and *Ignes Sacer* to all be types of erysipelas.

Such confusion has continued into the modern period, with some historians interpreting epidemics of *Ignes Sacer* (sacred fire) or Saint Anthony's fire as ergotism, whereas others have viewed these scourges as recurrent erysipelas. Before the modern period, however, physicians tended to embrace the distinc-

tions made by Galen, and consequently included a wide variety of ailments including diseases of the uterus and lungs among the varieties of erysipelas.

Nineteenth Century

During the nineteenth century, physicians began giving greater attention to the causes and prevalence of erysipelas because, on the one hand, the disease seemed connected to wound infection, and, on the other hand, because epidemics of erysipelas were occurring simultaneously with peak years of puerperal sepsis, or "childbed fever." Their investigations eventually led to the discovery of streptococci and the distinctions that have provided us with our current definitions of erysipelas.

In 1795 Alexander Gordon of Aberdeen became the first clinician formally to associate erysipelas with puerperal fever (Loudon 1987). Then around the middle of the nineteenth century, two seminal studies appeared. In 1842, Oliver Wendell Holmes published an essay on the contagiousness of puerperal fever, and in 1861 Philip Ignaz Semmelweis published his classic study of *The Etiology, Concept, and Prophylaxis of Childbed Fever*. Both men blamed physicians for carrying infective particles to the bedsides of parturient women. Holmes stated specifically that puerperal sepsis could be caused "by an infection originating in the matter or effluvia of erysipelas" (Carter ed. 1983). The great French clinician Armand Trousseau, writing during this same period, regarded even trivial skin injuries as precursors to erysipelas.

In 1882 following the discovery of streptococci, Friedrich Fehleisen published a study of the etiology of erysipelas, which he associated with *S. pyogenes*. In addition, he reported using his cultures on human subjects, justifying the production of iatrogenic infection as a means of combatting some forms of cancer – a procedure in vogue in Germany at the time. In follow-up studies, another German surgeon, Friedrich Julius Rosenbach, described the ability of the erysipelas-causing streptococci to spread through host tissues without causing suppuration. This research was of paramount interest to surgeons concerned with controlling the omnipresent infections – occasionally called "hospitalism" – that killed survivors of otherwise "successful" operations.

Twentieth Century

Although the use of aseptic and antiseptic techniques led to dramatic reductions in postsurgical mortality rates, maternal mortality still remained high. During the 1920s and 1930s, the research of Leonard and

Dora Cook and others permitted the identification and typing of strains of streptococci. This, in turn, led to irrefutable evidence that puerperal fever was an exogenous infection, usually transmitted from a physician, midwife, or nurse attending a parturient woman (Loudon 1987). Yet even family and friends could communicate the streptococci that caused puerperal sepsis in women in labor, for these were the same streptococci that caused erysipelas. Consequently, maternal mortality from puerperal fever declined only some time after effective antibiotics became available. Indeed, Irvine Loudon (1987) has shown that despite well-known changes in the virulence of streptococcal organisms historically, no sudden and spontaneous decline in the virulence of the organism can account for the abrupt decline in mortality from erysipelas, scarlet fever, and puerperal fever. Instead, credit for moderating these ancient scourges belongs to the beginning of the antibiotic era and, in particular, to the use of sulfonamides.

Ann G. Carmichael

Bibliography

Carter, Codell, ed. and trans. 1983. Translator's Introduction to Ignaz Semmelweis, *The etiology, concept, and prophylaxis of childbed fever.* Madison, Wis.

Celsus. 1938. *De medicina,* Vols. 3 and 5, trans. W. G. Spencer. London.

Lenhartz, Hermann. 1902. Erysipelas and erysipeloid. In *Nothnagel's encyclopedia of practical medicine,* ed. John W. Moore, trans. Alfred Stengel. Philadelphia.

Loudon, Irvine. 1987. Puerperal fever, the streptococcus, and the sulphonamides, 1911–1945. *British Medical Journal* 295: 485–90.

Wilson, Leonard. 1987. The early recognition of streptococci as causes of disease. *Medical History* 31: 3–14.

VIII.51
Fascioliasis

The liver fluke *Fasciola hepatica* is usually a parasite of sheep and cattle. "Liver rot" in sheep was described in a French work in 1379, and the first human case was described in 1760. The fluke's life cycle was discovered in 1881. Fascioliasis is a significant veterinary problem, but human infection is also fairly common. The fluke's life cycle is much like that of *Fasciolopsis buski* (see Fasciolopsiasis), with people or herbivores infected by eating raw watercress or other plants contaminated by the cysts of the fluke. Adult worms settle down in the bile ducts after a period of wandering in the liver. Mild infestations may cause little damage, but fever, jaundice, and right upper quadrant abdominal pain radiating to the shoulder blade are common symptoms. Bile ducts may become partially or totally obstructed, and liver destruction can be severe.

F. hepatica is cosmopolitan in distribution, with important foci of human infection in southern France, in Algeria, and in South America. Diagnosis is made by examining the feces of symptomatic patients with a microscope to find the eggs. Treatment is generally effective. Prevention is by treating sheep to keep them from perpetuating the cycle, controlling snail intermediate hosts, and keeping domestic animals away from ponds where watercress is grown.

K. David Patterson

Bibliography

Deschiens, R., Y. LeCorroller, and R. Mandoul. 1961. Enquête sur les foyers de distomatose hépéatique de la Vallée de Lot. *Annales de l'Institut Pasteur* 10: 5–12.

Foster, W. D. 1965. *A short history of parasitology.* Edinburgh.

Kean, B. H., Kenneth E. Mott, and Adair J. Russell, eds. 1978. *Tropical medicine and parasitology: Classic investigations,* Vol. II, 561–83. Ithaca and London. [Nine important accounts, including two from the sixteenth century.]

Reinhard, Edward G. 1957. The discovery of the life cycle of the liver fluke. *Experimental Parasitology* 6: 208–32.

VIII.52
Fasciolopsiasis

VIII.53
Favism

Fasciolopsiasis is caused by the giant intestinal fluke, *Fasciolopsis buski*. Discovered in 1843, the organism occurs in China, Korea, Southeast Asia, and parts of India and Indonesia. The adult worm, which has a life-span of only 6 months, attaches itself to the wall of the small intestine of humans. Pigs and dogs can also be infected, and sometimes are important reservoir hosts. Eggs produced by the hermaphroditic adults pass out in the feces and, if they reach fresh water, produce motile larvae that penetrate into the tissues of certain planorbid snails. After two generations of reproduction, another motile form leaves the snail, finds a plant like the water chestnut, water caltrop, or water bamboo, and encysts on it. Humans become infected with cysts by peeling raw fruits of plants with their teeth or eating them uncooked. The disease can become very prevalent in areas where these plants are cultivated with human feces as fertilizer.

Mild infections are often asymptomatic, but flukes can irritate and even ulcerate the intestinal mucosa. Abdominal pain, diarrhea, anemia, and fluid accumulation in the abdomen are common symptoms. Extreme cases can be fatal. Diagnosis is made by discovery of the eggs in the feces. Drug therapy is usually effective. Prevention includes better rural sanitation and control of swine reservoir hosts. Cooking vegetables would also be very beneficial, but drastic changes in long-established culinary habits are unlikely.

K. David Patterson

Bibliography

Kean, B. H., Kenneth E. Mott, and Adair J. Russell, eds. 1978. *Tropical medicine and parasitology: Classic investigations,* Vol. II, 584–99. Ithaca and London.

Sadun, E. H., and C. Maiphoom. 1953. Studies on the epidemiology of the human intestinal fluke. *Fasciolopsis buski* (Lankester) in central Thailand. *American Journal of Tropical Medicine and Hygiene* 2: 1070–84.

Favism is an acute hemolytic reaction triggered by exposure either to fava beans (*Vicia faba*) or to certain drugs (e.g., sulfa-based antibiotics and the antimalarial primaquine) in people with an inherited deficiency of the enzyme *glucose-6-phosphate dehydrogenase* (G6PD). In favism, the patient can suffer from destruction of red blood cells, severe anemia, and possibly death. There are two necessary conditions for the disease: (1) genetic inheritance of the "Mediterranean" variant of the abnormal gene trait for G6PD deficiency; and (2) ingestion of fava beans, usually fresh, or exposure to some drugs. The bean is a dietary staple in areas where favism is reported. Only an estimated 20 percent of those with the genetic trait for G6PD are likely to experience episodes of favism. Under modern medical conditions the hemolytic anemia caused by favism is only rarely fatal. Strong evidence suggests that both the gene for G6PD deficiency and the cultural practice of fava bean consumption are evolutionarily adaptive traits that protect against death from all types of malaria. Favism, then, could be described as a negative outcome of the interaction of the positive adaptive qualities of both the gene and the bean.

Distribution and Incidence

Favism is found primarily in the Mediterranean and Middle East regions where fava beans are a staple food and the Mediterranean variant of G6PD deficiency gene is relatively common. Mark Belsey (1973) reports that it is frequently encountered in Greece, Sardinia, Italy, Cyprus, Egypt, Lebanon, Israel, Iran, Iraq, Algeria, and Bulgaria, and is particularly common among Sephardic Jews. Favism has also been sporadically reported in China, Germany, France, Poland, Romania, Yugoslavia, Great Britain, and the United States. The disease is considered a serious public health problem in contemporary Greece (Trakas 1981).

The incidence of favism has been estimated for few areas. The most complete study in two Iranian provinces on the Caspian coast found an annual incidence that ranged between 0.65 and 6.39 cases per 10,000 population, with some areas reporting incidences as high as 9.27 cases per 10,000 (Lapeyssonnie and Keyhan 1966). William Crosby (1956), on the other hand, estimated 50 cases per 10,000 for Sardinia. Mortality is generally rare, with rates ranging between 1 and 4 percent of the reported cases.

Epidemiology and Etiology

Favism is generally a pediatric illness in which the majority of victims are between 2 and 5 years of age, although cases as young as 6 months and as old as 65 years have been reliably reported. The disease has a marked seasonal cycle corresponding to the harvest of fresh fava beans, a 4- to 5-week period between April and July, although in areas where the bean is dried for later consumption, cases can occur all year. There is evidence that the toxic factor that induces the favism crisis has four characteristics:

1. It is located in the skin of the bean.
2. It is heat stable.
3. It is able to enter the breast milk of lactating women.
4. Its toxicity decreases when the beans are dried and the skin changes color.

Active biochemical agents in the skin of the bean — the pyrimidine oxidant compounds vicine, isouramil, divicine, and L-dopa — are probably responsible. These same biochemical agents are believed to provide some protection against malaria for people with normal genotypes when they eat fresh fava beans. Although it is widely believed that inhalation of pollen of the *V. faba* can trigger cases of favism, recent studies indicate that this is not true.

Boys are much more likely to suffer favism attacks than girls, with male/female case ratios varying from 2.1:1 to 2.7:1. The reason for the increased risk for males is that G6PD deficiency is a sex-linked trait; the gene is located on the X chromosome. Only carrier males (hemizygotes) and homozygous females can suffer from favism. Heterozygote females appear to be at an evolutionary advantage because they have no risk of favism and also enjoy a degree of protection against the malaria protozoa *Plasmodium*.

The G6PD enzyme, found in all tissues, plays important housekeeping functions in red blood cell metabolism. The cells of enzyme-deficient individuals tend to become oxidant-sensitive, and any exogenous sources of increased oxidants (malaria parasites, antimalaria drugs, or fava beans) can result in the lysis (explosion) of the cell (Katz and Schall 1979). In enzyme-deficient individuals, this process can result in either favism or protection from a severe malaria infection, depending on the context.

The geographic distribution of the many varieties of G6PD-deficient genes has been exceptionally well studied by population biologists. Over 200 varieties

of the gene have been identified. Both population genetic data and in vitro studies indicate that the distribution of these genes is correlated with the historical distribution of malaria. Favism occurs in only a small proportion of individuals with the Mediterranean variant of G6PD deficiency, and within that population it follows familial lines. It has been recently recognized that there is substantial genetic variation within the Mediterranean variant (Luzzatto and Battistuzzi 1985).

Clinical Manifestations

Favism is characterized by five general symptoms: weakness, fatigue, pallor, jaundice, and hemoglobinuria (blood in the urine). The anemia caused by hemolysis is severe. In a clinical study in Greece, one-third of favism cases had hemocrit levels below 4 grams of hemoglobin per 100 milliliters of blood (Kattamis, Kyriazakov, and Chidas 1969). In populations at risk, this set of symptoms is recognized as a distinct illness, often referred to as "fava bean poisoning."

History and Geography

The historical puzzle of favism is that peoples of Mediterranean and Middle Eastern societies would continue to eat a food that regularly causes illness and even death. From an evolutionary perspective, both fava bean consumption and G6PD deficiency appear to be retained in populations because they provide some protection from malaria. The correlation between the geographic distribution of these traits and malaria is one line of evidence for this relationship. Fava bean cultivation dates back to the Neolithic period in areas that have favism. Ancient Indo-European culture, and particularly Greek culture, placed remarkable emphasis on the symbolic rather than nutritional qualities of the fava bean. Alfred Andrews (1949) argues that "no plant or animal known to the Indo-Europeans has produced a more luxuriant growth of benefits than fava beans."

Fava beans have had three primary symbolic associations: the life principle, the souls of the dead, and the generative powers of male sexuality, and they are ritualistically eaten at certain times of the year, a practice that continues in European folk cultures. On the other hand, taboos against the consumption of fava beans for certain groups, particularly priests, have been reported in ancient Greece, Egypt, India, and Africa. The most famous case of such a taboo was among the Pythagoreans, who had the maxim, "It is an equal crime to eat beans and the heads of one's parents." Although many historical analyses for this taboo have been suggested, a medically informed hypothesis based on the risk of favism appears most reasonable (Brumbaugh and Schwartz 1979).

In the history of medicine, the early clinical descriptions by the Italian physician Antonio Gasbarrini were a landmark for the diagnosis and treatment of favism attacks of varying severity. Within the tradition of Galenic medicine, treatment, although not always for favism attacks, emphasized the reinforcement of the blood with red wine among other things. Understanding the evolutionary history of favism has been a recent development that paralleled the discovery of the malaria connection with other genetic polymorphisms like thalassemia and sickle-cell anemia. The analytical connection with G6PD deficiency was first suggested in 1956, by Crosby, and the development of a genetic screening technique for the trait created a wealth of population genetic data during the 1960s. Such data on genetic markers in populations – for example, the variants of G6PD deficiency – have a potential for historical reconstruction of population movements and culture contact (Brown 1981).

Peter J. Brown

Bibliography

Andrews, Alfred C. 1949. The bean and Indo-European totemism. *American Anthropologist* 51: 274–92.

Belsey, Mark A. 1973. The epidemiology of favism. *Bulletin of the World Health Organization* 48: 1–13.

Brown, Peter J. 1981. New considerations on the distribution of thalassemia, glucose-6-phosphate dehydrogenase deficiency and malaria in Sardinia. *Human Biology* 53: 367–82.

Brumbaugh, Robert, and Jessica Schwartz. 1979. Pythagoras and beans: A medical explanation. *Classical World* 73: 421–2.

Crosby, William H. 1956. Favism in Sardinia. *Blood* 11: 91–2.

Kattamis, C. A., M. Kyriazakov, and S. Chidas. 1969. Favism: Clinical and biochemical data. *Journal of Medical Genetics* 6: 34–41.

Katz, Solomon, and Jean Schall. 1979. Fava bean consumption and biocultural evolution. *Medical Anthropology* 3: 459–76.

Lapeyssonnie, L., and R. Keyhan. 1966. Favism in the Caspian littoral area. In *Proceedings of the first seminar on favism in Iran.* Teheran.

Luzzatto, L. 1969. Glucose-6-phosphate dehydrogenase deficient red cells: Resistance to infection by malarial parasites. *Science* 164: 839–42.

Luzzatto, L., and G. Battistuzzi. 1985. Glucose-6-phosphate dehydrogenase. *Advances in Human Genetics* 14: 217–327.

Trakas, Deanna. 1981. Favism and G6PD deficiency in Rhodes, Greece. Ph.D. thesis, Michigan State University.

VIII.54
Filariasis

The term "filariasis" refers to several diseases of both humans and animals caused by infection with a specific group of parasitic nematodes called *filarial worms* (named for the hairlike appearance of the adult form). Those worms that affect humans belong to the Order Filarioidea, Family Dipetalonematidae. They include (1) *Wuchereria bancrofti* and *Brugia malayi,* which are common causes of *elephantiasis* (extreme swelling and skin thickening of the legs, scrotum, labia, or arms) and *chyluria* (lymph and emulsified fat globules in the urine); (2) *Loa loa,* the "eye worm"; and (3) *Onchocerca volvulus,* the cause of *onchocerciasis.* Depending upon their species, adult filarial worms of both sexes reside in the lymphatic system, subcutaneous tissues, or peritoneal and pleural cavities. Sexual reproduction results in embryos (microfilariae) that enter blood or skin, where they are ingested by a particular intermediate host (certain species of mosquitoes, horse fly, black fly, or other arthropods). The microfilariae develop into larvae in their intermediate hosts and then reenter vertebrate hosts (humans or animals) through bites in the skin made by the intermediate host arthropods. Loa Loa is endemic in West and central Africa, whereas onchocerciasis is found in Mexico, Central America, and West Africa. Discussion of human lymphatic filariasis in the remainder of this entry will be limited to the most prevalent form (90 percent of infections), that caused by *W. bancrofti* (Sasa 1976; Beaver, Jung, and Cupp 1984; Mak 1987; Manson-Bahr and Bell 1987).

Distribution and Incidence

Bancroftian filariasis is widely distributed throughout the tropics. Though it no longer exists in areas such as North America (most notably the Charleston, S.C. area), southern Europe, Australia, and some Caribbean islands, and is decreasing in prevalence in other Caribbean islands, Central America, and South America, *W. bancrofti* is becoming more prevalent in parts of Asia. At some time nearly every nonarid region of the tropics or subtropics as well as temperate parts of China and Japan has experienced *W. bancrofti* infection (Sasa 1976; Beaver et al. 1984; Mak 1987; Manson-Bahr and Bell 1987).

Although no precise count of the number of people infected with *W. bancrofti* exists, in 1984 the World Health Organization estimated that number at more than 81 million. Prevalence is highest in Asia (especially China, India, and Indonesia) and Africa. The disease affects primarily the rural and urban poor of working age living in areas of poor sanitation where mosquitoes abound (Mak 1987; Partono 1987).

Etiology and Epidemiology

The threadlike, white, adult *W. bancrofti* (males: 40 mm long × 0.1 mm in diameter; females: 65–100 mm × 0.2–0.3 mm) lie coiled together in human lymphatic vessels and lymph glands, where they can live for 10 to 18 years. Within 6 months to 1 year of infection, tiny larvae called *microfilariae* leave the adult female and enter the host's peripheral blood and lymph channels. Microfilariae move freely through the lymph or blood and, depending on the strain, show nocturnal or diurnal periodicity in the blood. Nocturnal microfilariae (the most common infective form) reside in the arterioles of the lungs during the day, whereas the diurnal (also called subperiodic) strain appears in the peripheral blood continuously, although in reduced numbers at night. Geographically, nocturnally periodic microfilariae are generally found west of 140° east longitude, and diurnal microfilariae are present east of 180° east longitude. Both types may be found between these two meridians. The largest concentrations of diurnal microfilariae exist in the Polynesian and New Caledonian regions of the Pacific Ocean (Sasa 1976; Beaver et al. 1984; Manson-Bahr and Bell 1987).

Bancroftian filariasis is transmitted only by mosquito. There is no known animal reservoir of *W. bancrofti*. Microfilariae may be transmitted to another human through blood transfusion, and from the maternal to the fetal circulation, but in both situations the microfilariae never develop into adults (Beaver et al. 1984; Manson-Bahr and Bell 1987).

Microfilariae have adapted their daily cycles to either day- or night-feeding mosquitoes, depending on the species and activity of these insects in a particular geographic area. The mosquito becomes an intermediate host of microfilariae after taking a blood meal. Microfilariae develop into infective larvae within the insect host in less than 2 weeks, and escape from its proboscis onto the skin of the mosquito's next human host during feeding. The larvae burrow into the human's skin through the tiny puncture wound and find their way to lymph vessels where they mature within a year and mate, producing more microfilariae (Beaver et al. 1984; Manson-Bahr and Bell 1987).

In a given geographic area, the *microfilaria rate* (percentage of a given population carrying mi-

crofilariae in the peripheral blood), the density of the intermediate host mosquito population, and the presence of a susceptible human population available for repeated bites by infected mosquitoes are key factors in the epidemiology of bancroftian filariasis. The significance of filariasis in an area may be measured by either the microfilaria rate or the *actual disease rate* (percentage of the population displaying symptoms of filarial infection) (Beaver et al. 1984; Manson-Bahr and Bell 1987).

Clinical Manifestations and Pathology

In nature, only humans develop elephantiasis from filarial infection of the lymphatics, so scientists could not easily study the pathogenesis of bancroftian filariasis until the recent development of a cat model. As a result of this and other work, researchers have described the pathogenesis and pathology of bancroftian filariasis more accurately. Filarial disease may not manifest itself for many years despite the presence of microfilaremia. If reexposure to larvae does not occur, infection usually disappears within 8 years. Repeated exposure over many years generally results in clinical disease during adulthood. Newly exposed adults display a different disease pattern and a stronger reaction than do persons who are exposed from childhood. In both cases clinical symptoms occur throughout the body because of widespread disruption of the lymphatics (Beaver et al. 1984).

Once the filarial larva settles in a human lymph channel and begins to mature, it provokes a localized response consisting of lymph vessel dilation and a slowing of lymph flow through that worm-occupied channel. With time the host body responds immunologically, sending eosinophils, plasma cells, and macrophages to the sites of infection. Lymphangitis (inflammation of lymph channels) usually results in swelling, redness, and pain, and, when the lymph vessels become hypertrophied, in varices. Fibrosis of the vessel occurs, trapping and killing the adult worm, which is absorbed or calcified. Obliteration of the lymph vessel forces extravasation of lymph into the tissue space, where it accumulates and causes the typical lymphedema of filarial elephantiasis. The swelling can become quite large, consisting of lymph, fat, and fibrotic tissue under tightly stretched and thickened skin (Beaver et al. 1984; Manson-Bahr and Bell 1987).

The clinical course of bancroftian filariasis can follow one of two paths: In highly endemic areas, people are exposed to repeated filarial infections from a very young age. The microfilariae provoke only a weak local tissue response, and the children show little effect of infection. When the larvae move to and then reside in lymph vessels, their hosts in these highly endemic areas do not react with a strong immunologic response (or display severe symptoms), thus allowing new microfilariae to be discharged through the now dilated lymph channels into the blood. The living worms survive for years, producing microfilariae that circulate in their hosts' blood. These microfilariae soon become part of mosquitoes' meals and are passed on in their larval stage to other human hosts. As the adult worms eventually die in their tolerant human hosts' lymphatics, fibrosis and calcification of these channels disrupt the lymph system. In this chronic phase of filarial infection, as lymph channels become obstructed, typical elephantoid manifestations develop, especially in the groin and lower extremity. People in highly endemic areas are repeatedly infected over the years and so will manifest various stages of filariasis simultaneously.

Uninfected adults newly arrived in an endemic region generally show an inflammatory response to filarial infection. American troops in the Pacific during World War II experienced this problem. Their immune systems reacted quite strongly to the presence of microfilariae in lymphatics, sending a variety of cellular defenders to the affected areas. They surrounded the worms, ultimately causing stenosis of the lymphatics. Many soldiers developed very painful swelling of the scrotum, spermatic cord, and arms or legs, as well as orchitis, lymphangitis, and *filarial fever* (acute fever with headache and symptoms resembling malaria, recurring sometimes for years). Such a powerful response generally kills the worm, making it impossible for microfilariae to develop and circulate in the blood, but also causing disruption of the lymphatic system and the early development of elephantiasis. Some researchers believe that extreme elephantiasis occurs as a result of secondary infection with streptococcus or other bacteria.

Chronic obstructive filariasis can result in lymph gland enlargement, chyluria (due to obstructed lymph flow to the thoracic duct above the lymphatic branches of the kidney), lymph scrotum (scrotal thickening with lymphatic varicosities), hydrocele, and elephantiasis of the legs, scrotum, labia, arms, or (rarely) breasts (Beaver et al. 1984; Manson-Bahr and Bell 1987; Partono 1987).

Treatment and Control

Several microfilaricidal drugs exist; the most effective is diethylcarbamazine citrate (DEC), first used in 1947. This drug also kills adult worms. When DEC is used in conjunction with a comprehensive mosquito control plan, the rate of *W. bancrofti* infection in an area declines dramatically. Mosquito control alone is not highly effective because of the long reproductive life of the adult worms in human lymphatics. Behavioral measures, such as wearing clothes that leave little of the body exposed to mosquitoes, avoiding outdoor gatherings at night, and avoiding outdoor work at peak mosquito biting times, also help to reduce transmission of the disease, but these measures are difficult to implement (Beaver et al. 1984; Mak 1987; Manson-Bahr and Bell 1987).

Surgical treatment of elephantiasis does not permanently cure the problem, though removal of thickened skin and extra tissue from the affected area generally relieves the patient's burden. Pressure bandaging of affected lower limbs helps reduce swelling.

Once a person is infected with *W. bancrofti*, prognosis depends on the extent and nature of the infection, reexposures to the parasite, and the body's reaction to the infection. Chronic cases have a poor prognosis.

History and Geography

Antiquity Through the Eighteenth Century

The preponderance of evidence indicates that bancroftian filariasis existed in the ancient tropical world. One can find discussions of something called elephantiasis in the works of many ancient Greek and Roman authors, including Celsus, Galen, Aretaeus, Caelius, Aurelianus, Pliny, and Plutarch. The disease many of them were describing, however, was probably leprosy, which came to be known as *elephantiasis graecorum,* to distinguish it from another form of elephantiasis with a different appearance, *elephantiasis arabum,* probably bancroftian filariasis. Leprosy can cause affected parts of the skin to resemble that of an elephant, but does not cause the scrotal or leg swelling so characteristic of filarial infection.

Bancroftian filariasis was probably not endemic in ancient Italy, Greece, or the Mediterranean region in general, except for certain parts of the Nile Delta. Traders and travelers brought knowledge of the condition to residents of the region, and an occasional newcomer undoubtedly carried the disease from his or her home country and suffered from its various manifestations in the Mediterranean region. Ancient descriptions of a medical condition resembling bancroftian filariasis exist not only from Greco-Roman writers but also from people in the Nile

Delta, Polynesian islands such as Fiji and the Society Islands, and India. Late Roman and medieval Arab writers also discussed elephantiasis, the former primarily describing leprosy, and the latter, including Rhazes, Avicenna, and Albucasis, filariasis (Adams 1844, 1846, 1847; Bhishagratna, ed. 1911; Castellani 1919; Hoeppli 1959; Foster 1965; Laurence 1967; Sasa 1976).

The historian B. R. Laurence argues that bancroftian filariasis actually originated in Southeast Asia and spread with the migration of people from that region to the South Pacific islands (especially Polynesia) and to Africa. To survive, the filarial worm adapted its life cycle to the mosquito vectors available in these new areas, thus explaining why *W. bancrofti* shows both diurnal (i.e., microfilariae present in peripheral blood during the daytime) and nocturnal periodic strains. The elephantiasis described by early Indian writers, Laurence argues, was actually caused by *B. malayi* (another filarial worm, much more limited in its distribution) rather than by *W. bancrofti*. The continued migration of tropical peoples and the opening of the tropical world to trade over the past 300 to 400 years, plus the adaptability of *W. bancrofti* to a variety of mosquito vectors, resulted in the spread of the parasite throughout the tropics, including China and India (Laurence 1968, 1977). Filariasis came to the New World, most likely as a result of the African slave trade. That trade, conducted by white Europeans, brought concentrations of infected black Africans to slave depots on West Indian islands like Barbados, where they were sold and redistributed to other West Indian islands, or to the North and South American mainlands. A legacy of this black African slave trade in the United States was the establishment of a focus of bancroftian filariasis at Charleston, South Carolina, and the surrounding "Low Country," which survived until the early twentieth century (Savitt 1977; Chernin 1987; Reynolds and Sy 1989).

Seventeenth Through Nineteenth Century

Seventeenth-, eighteenth-, and nineteenth-century European observers in tropical lands described numerous cases of leg and scrotal elephantiasis, and some of endemic hydrocele and of lymph scrotum. A few even recognized and traced the development of elephantiasis from fever through lymphangitis and lymphadenitis, to gradual swelling of a limb or scrotum. Though these writers located the seat of the disease in the lymphatics, none could identify the cause (Castellani 1919; Laurence 1970). That discovery had to await refinements to, and physicians'

acceptance of, the microscope in the latter half of the nineteenth century. Between 1863 and 1900, researchers uncovered the basic etiology and epidemiology of bancroftian filariasis (Manson-Bahr 1959; Foster 1965; Sasa 1976; Chernin 1983).

The first breakthrough in understanding the cause of elephantiasis occurred in 1863 when a French physician, Jean-Nicolas Demarquay, described microfilariae (Demarquay 1863). Demarquay withdrew a milky fluid from the swollen scrotal sac of an 18-year-old Cuban in 1862 and then again a year later. This latter time, viewing the substance under a microscope, he reported: "Attention was drawn above all to a little elongated and cylindrical creature" that "had extremely rapid movements of coiling and uncoiling" (Demarquay 1863). Demarquay and his colleagues found these worms and their eggs in five successive preparations but found none once the scrotal fluid had cooled down. He could not explain the worms' presence in the microscopic preparation, but hoped that there would be some scientific value for others in publishing the case.

Exactly 4 years after Demarquay's discovery, Otto Eduard Heinrich Wucherer, a Portuguese-born physician of German parentage who practiced in Bahia, Brazil, found "some threadlike worms" in a urinary blood clot of a woman suffering from hematuria (Wucherer 1868). Theodor Bilharz had discovered a worm in Egypt in 1852 that caused hematuria (*Schistosoma haematobium*); Wucherer was investigating the urine of Brazilian hematuria patients to learn whether the cause of the disease was the same in the New World. What he saw under the microscope differed greatly from the schistosomes Bilharz had described. Two years later, after seeing these worms in two more hematuric patients and finding that he could not identify their species from the books on human parasites that he possessed, Wucherer published his story "as an incentive for some of my colleagues, better qualified and more fortunate than I, to attempt to shed light on a disease, the etiology of which is still enigmatic today" (Wucherer 1868).

In March of 1870, in a different part of the tropical world, India, Timothy Richards Lewis found worms like those Wucherer had described. An 1867 medical graduate of the University of Aberdeen, Scotland, Lewis was treating a 25-year-old East Indian male suffering with chyluria. That patient left the hospital before Lewis could study his condition further, but a second patient, a woman with hematuria and chylous urine, entered the hospital a few days later. Lewis now took a step beyond Demarquay and Wucherer and removed blood from the patient's finger and studied it microscopically. He found what he called filariae in this blood, just as he found them in the urine. Lewis's report of these and other patients, published in 1872, documented for the first time both the presence of microfilariae and the presence of any microorganism in human peripheral blood. He also described, but could not explain, the disappearance of microfilariae from the blood. Lewis (1872) named the organism *Filaria hominis sanguinis*.

All three of these filarial researchers knew they had identified an immature form of the filarial worm. Nor were they the only ones who saw the microfilariae in chylous urine. Both T. Spencer Cobbold of London and M. Robin of Reunion Island reported similar findings in the early 1870s.

The man who brought together the various bits of knowledge published about human filarial infection and produced a useful theory was Patrick Manson. Born in Aberdeenshire and an 1866 medical graduate of Aberdeen University, Scotland, Manson spent much of his early professional life, beginning in 1866, as a medical officer in the Chinese Imperial Maritime Customs Service. He treated many Chinese elephantiasis patients, recognized and named the condition called "lymph scrotum," and devised an operation to remove scrotal tumors. During a 1-year leave in England in 1875, he read the available literature on the conditions he had been treating, including descriptions of lymph scrotum in India, the relation of lymph scrotum to elephantiasis, and Lewis's papers on filarial worms in the blood and lymph of patients with tropical chyluria (Foster 1965). In articles published in 1876 and 1877 in the *China Imperial Maritime Customs Medical Reports*, Manson presented case studies to show that lymph scrotum, elephantiasis, and tropical chyluria were etiologically related, all caused by the filarial worm described by Lewis, seated in lymphatics (Manson 1876–7). He apparently knew nothing of Demarquay's or Wucherer's articles, published in journals as poorly circulated as the one in which he himself published.

Manson tried in vain to obtain an adult filarial worm from newly deceased patients. Thwarted by the Chinese people's reluctance to allow autopsies of humans, Manson suggested in print that physicians in India, where the prejudice against dissection was much less, seek out adult worms in patients who had died with these conditions (Foster 1965). The first person to demonstrate the presence of adult filariae in humans practiced, not in India, but in Australia. Joseph Bancroft, an 1859 medical graduate of St.

Andrews University in Scotland, moved to Queensland in 1864 and found a number of patients with lymphatic conditions, though none with elephantiasis. His first adult worm came from a patient with a lymphatic abscess of the arm. He obtained another four from a hydrocele of the spermatic cord. He forwarded these specimens in 1877 to Cobbold in London, the leading British helminthologist of the time. The latter published Bancroft's cover letter with his own commentary in the *Lancet* (Cobbold 1877). Cobbold had previously encouraged Bancroft to look for the adults after Bancroft sent him, through a former teacher, immature filariae obtained from these patients. It was Cobbold who suggested naming the filarial worm for Bancroft. A co-worker of Wucherer wrote to the *Lancet* shortly after Cobbold's article appeared, suggesting that Wucherer deserved credit for discovering the parasite. Both physicians were so honored, and the filaria is known as *Wuchereria bancrofti* (Foster 1965).

How did the worm find its way into humans? Manson continued his work in China and made a key suggestion in an 1877 essay (not published until 1878), the same year Cobbold announced the discovery of the adult worm in human lymphatics (Manson 1877). The *Filaria sanguinis hominis* embryos, Manson argued, could not develop, mature, and enter the bloodstream without overwhelming their human host by their sheer number. Using his knowledge of the known life cycles of animal parasites and of certain human parasites, Manson suggested and then demonstrated that the mosquito was the "nurse" of the filarial embryo. The insect ingested filariae in its blood meal and the young worm developed in the body of this second host. When the mosquito died, usually on stagnant water a few days after feeding, Manson continued, the filariae escaped into the water and were ingested by humans drinking the now contaminated liquid. The need for a certain mosquito host, in addition to the human host, Manson concluded, explained "the limitation of the distribution of elephantoid diseases to certain districts and zones of the earth's surface . . . where the mosquito flourishes" (Manson 1877).

Another filarial mystery remained to be solved: the unpredictable disappearance and reappearance of worm embryos from the blood of patients known to harbor the parasite. Manson employed two assistants to take blood around the clock from a filariasis patient. He discovered that the number of microfilariae grew and shrunk in a regular diurnal pattern, the embryos reaching their peak presence in blood in the hours just before and after midnight. He concluded, in his 1879 article (published in 1880), that "[t]he nocturnal habits of the *Filaria sanguinis-hominis* are adapted to the nocturnal habits of the mosquito, its intermediary host, and is only another of the many wonderful instances of adaptation so constantly met with in nature" (Manson 1879).

What happened to the filariae during the rest of the day? Manson asked that question in his 1879 article but could not answer it for almost another 20 years. In February 1897, Manson, now in London, had the opportunity to study the organs of a patient with filariasis who had committed suicide at 8:30 in the morning, presumably just after the worms would have left the peripheral blood for the day. Postmortem examination revealed huge numbers of the embryo parasites in the small blood vessels of the lungs and others in the large pulmonary blood vessels (Manson 1899).

Over the next few years, Manson helped revise the answer to a question he had asked in 1877: How did the filariae pass from mosquitoes to humans? Manson's earlier answer, that humans ingested them with contaminated drinking water, was challenged shortly after it was suggested. The work of Thomas Bancroft, Joseph Bancroft's son in Australia, and of Manson's protégé, George C. Low, who used the mosquito specimens Bancroft sent to Manson, published in 1900, suggested that filarial embryos exited from the mosquito's proboscis and entered human skin when the insect was in the act of biting (Low 1900). That idea was confirmed by B. Grassi and G. Noe (1900) later that year.

British physicians working in various tropical colonies of the empire had made almost every breakthrough in uncovering the mystery of filarial infection during the previous 40 years. By 1900 the medical world had a basic understanding of a disease that had plagued and puzzled people since ancient times.

Todd L. Savitt

Bibliography

Adams, Francis. 1844, 1846, 1847. *The seven books of Paulus Aegineta,* 3 vols., II, 6–15. London.

Beaver, Paul Chester, Rodney Clifton Jung, and Eddie Wayne Cupp. 1984. *Clinical parasitology,* 9th edition. Philadelphia.

Bhishagratna, Kaviraj Kunjalal, trans. and ed. 1911. *An English translation of the Sushruta Samhita,* 3 vols., II, 79–84. Calcutta.

Castellani, Aldo. 1919. *Manual of tropical disease,* 3d edition, 1595–1618. London.

Chernin, Eli. 1983. Sir Patrick Manson's studies on the transmission and biology of filariasis. *Reviews of Infectious Diseases* 5: 148–66.

1987. The disappearance of bancroftian filariasis from Charleston, South Carolina. *American Journal of Tropical Medicine and Hygiene* 37: 111–14.

Cobbold, T. S. 1877. Discovery of the adult representative of microscopic filariae. *Lancet* 2: 70–1. [Includes letter from Joseph Bancroft reporting discovery of adult filarial worms in man.] [In *Tropical medicine and parasitology: Classic investigations,* 2 vols. B. H. Kean, Kenneth E. Mott, and Adair J. Russell, eds. 1978. Vol. 2, 392–4. Ithaca and London.]

Demarquay, Jean-Nicolas. 1863. Note on a tumor of the scrotal sac containing a milky fluid (galactocele of Vidal) and enclosing small wormlike beings that can be considered as hematoid helminthes in the embryo stage. *Gazette Médicale de Paris* 18: 665–7. [Trans. from French in Kean et al., eds., 1978. *Tropical medicine and parasitology,* Vol. 2, 374–7.]

Foster, W. D. 1965. *A history of parasitology.* Edinburgh and London.

Grassi, B., and G. Noe. 1900. The propagation of the filariae of the blood exclusively by means of the puncture of peculiar mosquitoes. *British Medical Journal* 2: 1306–7.

Hoeppli, R. 1959. *Parasites and parasitic infections in early medicine and science.* Singapore.

Laurence, B. R. 1967. Elephantiasis in Greece and Rome and the Queen of Punt. *Transactions of the Royal Society of Tropical Medicine and Hygiene* 61: 612–13.

1968. Elephantiasis and Polynesian origins. *Nature* 219: 561–3.

1970. The curse of Saint Thomas. *Medical History* 14: 352–63.

1977. The evolution of filarial infection. In *Medicine in a tropical environment,* ed. J. H. S. Gear, 644–56. Cape Town and Rotterdam.

Lewis, Timothy Richards. 1872. On a hematozoon inhabiting human blood, its relation to chyluria and other diseases. *Appendix to the eighth annual report of the sanitary commissioner with the government of India,* 1–50. [In Kean et al., eds., 1978. *Tropical medicine and parasitology,* Vol. 2, 379–85.]

Low, George Carmichael. 1900. A recent observation on *filaria nocturna* in *Culex:* Probable mode of infection of man. *British Medical Journal* 1: 1456–7. [In Kean et al., eds., 1978. *Tropical medicine and parasitology,* Vol. 2, 402–5.]

Mak, J. W. 1987. Epidemiology of lymphatic filariasis. In *Filariasis* (Ciba Foundation Symposium No. 127), 5–14. Chichester, U.K.

Manson, Patrick. 1876–77. *Filaria sanguinis hominis. Medical Reports, China Imperial Maritime Customs* 13: 30–8. [In Kean et al., eds., 1978. *Tropical medicine and parasitology,* Vol. 2, 385–7.]

1877. Further observations on *Filaria sanguinis homi-*

nis. Medical Reports, China Imperial Maritime Customs 14: 1–26. [In Kean et al., eds., 1978. *Tropical medicine and parasitology*, Vol. 2, 387–92.]

1879. Additional notes on *Filaria sanguinis hominis* and filaria disease. *Medical Repots, China Imperial Maritime Customs* 18: 36–9. [In Kean et al., eds., 1978. *Tropical medicine and parasitology*, Vol. 2, 394–5.]

1899. On filarial periodicity. *British Medical Journal* 2: 644–6. [In Kean et al., eds., 1978. *Tropical medicine and parasitology*, Vol. 2, 400–2.]

Manson-Bahr, P. E. C. 1959. The story of *Filaria bancrofti. Journal of Tropical Medicine and Hygiene* 62: 53–61, 85–94, 106–17, 138–45, 160–73. [Note: Be sure to read Chernin 1983, for corrections to these Manson-Bahr articles.]

Manson-Bahr, P. E. C., and D. R. Bell. 1987. *Manson's tropical diseases*, 19th edition. London.

Partono, Felix. 1987. The spectrum of disease in lymphatic filariasis. In *Filariasis* (Ciba Foundation Symposium No. 127), 15–31. Chichester, U.K.

Reynolds, Wade D., and Francisco S. Sy. 1989. Eradication of filariasis in South Carolina: A historical perspective. *Journal of the South Carolina Medical Association* 85: 331–5.

Sasa, Manabu. 1976. *Human filariasis: A global survey of epidemiology and control*. Tokyo.

Savitt, Todd L. 1977. Filariasis in the United States. *Journal of the History of Medicine and Allied Sciences* 23: 140–50.

Wucherer, Otto Eduard Heinrich. 1868. Preliminary report on a species of worm, as yet undescribed, found in the urine of patients with tropical hematuria in Brazil. *Gazeta Medica de Bahia* 3: 97–9 (trans. from Portuguese). [In Kean et al., eds., 1978. *Tropical medicine and parasitology*, Vol. 2, 377–9.]

VIII.55
Fungus Infections (Mycoses)

Although today, some 200 fungi are established as pathogenic for humans, causing a wide range of diverse mycoses (with an incidence measured in millions and a worldwide distribution), through the mid-nineteenth century, only two human diseases (or rather disease complexes) caused by fungi were generally recognized. These were ringworm and thrush, known since Roman times. Two important additions came at the end of the century: mycetoma of the foot (Carter 1874) and aspergillosis (Lucet 1897; Rénon 1897).

Fungi were the first pathogenic microorganisms to be recognized. Toward the end of the eighteenth century and the opening years of the nineteenth, they had been shown experimentally to cause disease in plants and insects, and during the 1840s both ringworm and thrush were shown to be mycotic in origin. For a short period, fungi were blamed for causing many diseases. Cholera, for example, was attributed to fungi. But with the recognition of the major role played by bacteria (and later, viruses) in the etiology of human disease, fungi were neglected and medical mycology became very confused. It has been only since the 1930s, with the deployment of trained mycologists to work in conjunction with clinicians, that the identity of the pathogenic fungi has been clarified, and studies on their ecology have done much to elucidate epidemiological problems. In general, the geographic distribution of mycoses (which at first tended to coincide with that of medical mycologists) has been established, and the relation of mycoses to other human diseases has been brought into perspective.

Some of the fungi causing human disease show clear adaptations for the pathogenic state, whereas others do not, and it is probable that none is dependent on a human or animal host for survival. Most are also pathogenic for animals, both domesticated and wild, which are also subject to mycoses caused by related species able to induce human infections. Many fungi pathogenic for humans are apparently members of the normal fungus flora of the environment, and their pathogenicity is regarded as "opportunistic" or "iatrogenic" when infection is rendered possible by the side effects of therapy.

Classification

Mycoses (which exhibit a wide range of symptoms) have often been named according to the part of the body affected (e.g., bronchomycosis, dermatomycosis, tinea capitis, ringworm of the scalp, athlete's foot) or the name of the pathogen (e.g., aspergillosis, cryptococcosis, dermatophytosis, rhinosporidiosis), and they have been categorized as cutaneous, subcutaneous, systemic, opportunistic, and iatrogenic, although these divisions are not mutually exclusive. In this study, for convenience, mycoses are considered under ringworm, candidiasis (including thrush, which is oral candidiasis), systemic mycoses, and opportunistic and iatrogenic mycoses.

Ringworm (Tinea, Dermatophytosis)

History

Favus (Latin for "honeycomb"), a distinctive type of ringworm because of the characteristic scutula, was described by Celsus in the first century, A.D., in his *De Medicina*. He called it *porrigo,* a term also used by Pliny in his *Historia Naturalis* of the same century and by dermatologists up to the nineteenth century. It is now, however, obsolete, having been replaced by tinea (derived from *Tineola,* the generic name of the clothes moth). Celsus also described the inflammatory lesion of some forms of ringworm, which has been known ever since as the "kerion of Celsus."

Not until the mid-1840s was the mycotic nature of favus recognized by three independent workers: J. L. Schoenlein and Robert Remak in Berlin, and David Gruby in Paris. The latter also differentiated microsporosis and the ectothrix and endothrix trichophytosis, which he showed to be caused by distinct fungi.

A period of mycologic confusion followed, complicated by the difficulty of determining the life histories of the pathogens (largely due to deficiencies in culture technique) and settling the question as to whether there was one ringworm fungus or many. Gruby's findings had been forgotten and had to be rediscovered during the 1890s by Raymond Sabouraud, a famous Parisian dermatologist, who consolidated his researches in an impressive monograph published in 1910. Many ringworm fungi were described and classified variously according to the degree of emphasis placed by different workers on mycologic and clinical features. Some thousand different names had been proposed up to 1934 when C. W. Emmons, a mycologist by training, in the United States showed that, mycologically, the many species

could be accommodated in the three genera: *Microsporum, Trichophyton,* and *Epidermophyton.* Today the number of ringworm fungi accepted is of the order of 30. At first, only asexual spore states of these pathogens were known, but later sexual states were obtained, and evidence provided that dermatophytes are closely related to a group of predominantly soil fungi.

Two historical landmarks in the treatment of ringworm were the introduction of X-ray epilation for the therapy of head ringworm in the opening years of this century and the introduction of the antibiotic griseofulvin in 1958 as an orally administered antimycotic drug.

Distribution and Incidence

The geographic distribution of the ringworm fungi is interesting. In Sabouraud's time the distribution corresponded to that of interested dermatologists. Now the ringworm fungi of most countries have been surveyed, or at least sampled, so that a more accurate knowledge of their geographic distribution is available. Some, such as *Trichophyton mentagrophytes* (causing tinea pedis and so forth) and *Epidermophyton floccosum* (tinea cruris), occur worldwide.

Microsporum audouinii (tinea capitis; the classical cause of ringworm in children), which appears to have originated in Europe, is now endemic in North America. Although frequently introduced by European children to the tropics, it has never established itself there in the indigenous population. Likewise *Trichophyton concentricum* (tinea imbricata) is endemic in Southwest Asia and the South Sea islands, where it was first recorded by William Dampier in 1686 when circumnavigating the globe. It has other minor endemic centers in South America, and, although frequently seen in Europe on returning travelers, it has never become endemic there. By contrast, *Trichophyton rubrum,* believed to have been introduced into the United Kingdom by troops returning from the Boer War, is now widespread in north temperate regions.

In similar fashion, *Trichophyton ferrugineum* established itself in western parts of the Soviet Union, after being introduced by soldiers returning from the Far East. Classical favus in western Europe is caused by *Trichophyton schoenleinii,* but typically by *Trichophyton violaceum* in North Africa and the Mediterranean basin. *Microsporum canis* (tinea canis [cat and dog ringworm], tinea capitis, and tinea corporis), coextensive with cats and dogs as pets, has become endemic in New Zealand in feral cats. Human infections are also contracted by contact with ringworm in cattle (*Trichophyton verrucosum*), horses, and other farm animals. *Microsporum gypseum* (which could be considered as an opportunistic dermatophyte) has a worldwide distribution, the outbreaks in humans usually being sporadic, short-lived, and sometimes traceable to a group of people having access to the same soil in which the pathogen is an inhabitant.

Candidiasis (including "Thrush")

Reports and studies of the many and diverse manifestations of candidiasis caused by *Candida albicans* and other species of *Candida* (e.g., *Candida guilliermondii, Candida krusei, Candida stellatoidea, Candida tropicalis*) have made a major contribution to the literature of medical mycology, as they still do. As for ringworm, a stable taxonomic base was necessary to underpin both clinical and microbiological observations and research on this mycotic complex because *C. albicans* was described as new on a number of occasions and acquired some 90 specific names distributed among a dozen genera. Much confusion resulted. One taxonomic error that the reader must still remember when consulting the earlier literature is the assignment back in 1890 of the thrush fungus to the genus *Monilia* because "moniliasis" became the generally accepted, worldwide name for candidiasis. It was mainly a group of yeast specialists working in the Netherlands who clarified the taxonomy; the genus *Candida* was proposed in 1923.

Thrush (Oral Candidiasis)

This disease (infection of the mucous membrane, especially of the mouth) in infants was referred to in the Hippocratic corpus (400 B.C.) and later by Galen and other classical writers under the heading "aphthae." Over the centuries, references to thrush in the young, as a feature of terminal illness and as a vaginal infection in women, continued, with the clinical descriptions being given increasing precision (see Higgs 1972). Candidiasis, like ringworm, was demonstrated to be mycotic by three independent workers in the 1840s: B. Langenbeck in Berlin, F. T. Berg in Stockholm, and Gruby in Paris. Berg, who had studied under Gruby, subsequently published on thrush in infants and in 1844, J. H. Bennett described in Edinburgh what was probably *C. albicans* from the human lung.

A wide range of pathological conditions attributed to *Candida* were subsequently recorded; virtually all parts of the body, with the notable exception of the hair, were susceptible to such infection under favorable conditions. Numerous surveys have shown that many apparently normal individuals carry *C. albicans:* 10 percent, in the mouth; about the same proportion of women, in the vagina (with higher values in pregnant women); and 25 percent, in the feces and gut. Although *C. albicans* has occasionally been isolated from soil, from hospital bedding (the incidence of *Candida* in hospital patients is often high), and from a wide range of animals (especially domestic animals and birds), it is clear that most human infections have an endogenous origin. Infection (clinical candidiasis) seems always to be determined by predisposing factors that may be environmental: For example, having the hands frequently wet favors paronychia (candidiasis of the nail fold). Age, debility, dentures, and drug therapy also can predispose one to infection.

The patenting of the orally administered antibiotic nystatin in 1956 was a notable contribution to the therapy of candidiasis, which has been the subject of several monographs.

Systemic Mycoses

The pathogens of the five systemic mycoses to be considered all show specialization for parasitism. All are *dimorphic* – that is, the saprobic state is mycelial (filamentous) and the pathogenic phase is unicellular and yeastlike. It is possible to effect the mycelial-to-yeast conversion in vitro. For *Blastomyces dermatitidis* (blastomycosis), the transformation is temperature dependent; for the others, nutritional adjustments are also necessary. On first description there was a tendency to assign these pathogens to the Protozoa.

Coccidioidomycosis

The first case of this disease was described from Argentina by Alejandro Posadas in 1892. About the same time a case was also studied in California by E. Rixford and T. C. Gilchrist, who attributed the cause to a protozoan, which, in 1896, they named *Coccidioides immitis*. In 1905, however, a fellow American, W. Opuls, established its mycotic nature. It was known only as a rather rare, acute, or chronic disseminating and often fatal disease. In 1938, Myrnie A. Grifford and E. Dickson, independently, and then in collaboration, established that "valley fever," prevalent in the San Joaquin Valley of California, was a mild form of coccidioidomycosis. Further investigations showed mild, often subclinical, respiratory *Coccidioides* infection to be widespread in arid parts of California and neighboring states and to induce lifelong immunity to subsequent attack. This immunity is demonstrable by a positive skin test with an antigen (*coccidioidin*) prepared from cultures of the pathogen.

C. immitis was isolated from soil, and when Emmons showed desert rodents to be infected, they were at first thought perhaps to constitute an animal reservoir of infection. But it soon became clear that these rodents, like humans, were subject to infection by this soil-inhabiting fungus. It also became clear that the dry, airborne (or dustborne) spores of the pathogen were extremely infectious (there have been many accidental laboratory infections) and that coccidioidomycosis could be contracted, for example, by servicing automobiles that had been driven through areas where the mycosis was endemic. In addition, dust storms were found to increase the rate of conversion from negative to positive skin tests with coccidioidin in local inhabitants and their domestic animals. It may be noted, that although light- and dark-skinned peoples appear to be equally susceptible to *C. immitis* infection, the disease is more likely to be systemic in those with pigmented skin. Filipinos and blacks, along with the Portuguese, are those chiefly employed in agriculture in the districts where coccidioidomycosis is endemic.

Coccidioidomycosis is endemic and of high incidence in warm dry regions (the Lower Sonoran Life Zone) of the United States and Mexico and also in parts of Central and South America where the climatic conditions are similar. Records from other parts of the world are of doubtful validity.

Histoplasmosis
This disease (*Histoplasma capsulatum*) shows many parallels with coccidioidomycosis and may be viewed as the humid region equivalent. At first considered a rare protozoan disease, it has been shown to be mycotic, and to have a mild form affecting millions of the inhabitants of the midwestern United States. The pathogen shows a predilection for bird (chicken, starling) and bat droppings.

Blastomycosis and Paracoccidioidomycosis
The former (North American blastomycosis), caused by *B. dermatitidis,* and the latter (South American blastomycosis), caused by *Paracoccidioides brasiliensis,* are both chronic granulomatous diseases of the skin and internal organs, characterized by budding cells of the pathogen in the infected tissues. The two were at first confused both with each other and with cryptococcosis (called "European blastomycosis" or "torulosis" and caused by *Cryptococcus neoformans*), but these three mycoses are now well differentiated.

Blastomycosis was first described by Gilchrist in the United States in 1894, and paracoccidioidomycosis, by Adolfo Lutz in Brazil during 1908. Neither has a mild form such as that characteristic of coccidioidomycosis and histoplasmosis, and though there have been a few records of both pathogens from soil, the natural habitats of both these fungi have not been established with certainty.

Paracoccidioidomycosis is confined to Central and South America, where it has been the subject of intensive study. Blastomycosis is endemic to the western and southeastern states of the United States, where epidemics occur; there are also records of the disease from a number of tropical African countries.

Sporotrichosis
This disease shows certain parallels with mycetoma but is included here because the causal pathogen is dimorphic. It is a cutaneous and subcutaneous infection characterized by the development of nodular lesions, often in a series affecting successive lymph nodes. Infection is frequently initiated by a lesion, often of the hand. It is caused by *Sporothrix schenckii* and was first described in the United States by B. R. Schenck in 1898. Subsequently many cases were reported from Europe, especially France, where the disease was the subject of a massive monograph, *Les Sporotrichoses,* by C. L. de Beurmann and H. Gougerot in 1912. Sporotrichosis, which is sporadic in north temperate regions, has also been recorded in Central and South America. In Uruguay, J. E. Mackinnon (1949) attempted to correlate incidence of the disease with the weather, and obtained evidence that infection occurred during periods of moist warm weather, which he suggested encouraged growth of the pathogen on plant material from which humans are infected. *S. schenckii* is one of the rare fungus pathogens of humans that has been shown experimentally to cause disease in plants (carnations). The largest outbreak of sporotrichosis ever recorded was in the Witwatersrand gold mines in South Africa during 1941–3, when approximately 3,000 miners were infected. The epidemic was brought under control by potassium iodide therapy for the men affected and fungicidal treatment of the mine timbers from which the infection was contracted.

Opportunistic and Iatrogenic Infections
To categorize some fungal infections as opportunistic is convenient, if artificial. Most fungi pathogenic for humans, even those causing such significant mycoses as coccidioidomycosis and histoplasmosis, seem to

have some natural habitat in the environment and infect humans only incidentally. Candida infections are different in that they are endogenous, and some types of ringworm are also to some extent opportunistic. The mycoses to be considered next include examples of infection resulting from the exposure of a susceptible individual to the *normal* fungus flora of the environment, and attention is drawn to the increased risk shown by compromised patients.

Mycetoma

This disease is a well-defined clinical entity characterized by swelling that affects the subcutaneous tissues, with sinuses discharging grains or granules of the pathogen, which vary in color from white through yellow, red, and brown to black. The foot is most frequently involved ("Madura foot"), but the hand or other part may be infected. Its geographic distribution is mainly tropical.

The condition was first recorded in the Indian Vedic Medical treatises (c. 2000–1000 B.C.) as *padaaval-mika* ("foot ant-hill") and first described in modern times from southern India by members of the Indian Medical Service during the mid-nineteenth century. H. Vandyke Carter, who coined the designation "mycetoma," wrote a monograph on the disease in 1874. Carter suspected the disease to be mycotic and submitted material to the Rev. M. J. Berkeley, the leading British mycologist of the time, who described a now unidentifiable fungus he obtained from the material as a new species. From the turn of the century onward, more than 25 diverse fungi (including representatives of the genera *Acremonium, Aspergillus, Curvularia, Leptosphaeria, Madurella,* and *Pseudallescheria*) and actinomycetes (aerobic species of *Actinomadura, Nocardia,* and *Streptomyces*), responsible for the condition, were identified by workers in North Africa and elsewhere, with the color of the grains often providing a clue to the identity of the pathogen.

Carter distinguished "melanoid" and "ochroid" mycetoma, and, as his illustrations show, his black-grained form was caused by the fungus that E. Brumpt in 1905 taxonomized as *Madurella mycetomatis,* which is the most important cause of mycetoma. In 1894, H. Vincent had described and named the actinomycete that he had isolated from yellow-grained mycetoma from Algeria as *Streptothrix madurae* (now designated *Actinomadura madurae*). Later, when differentiating the two classes, researchers A. J. Chalmers and R. G. Archibald at the Wellcome Laboratory for Tropical Medicine at Khartoum in the Sudan introduced the term "madura mycosis" for mycetoma caused by actinomycetes. Today the terms "Eumycetoma" (or "Eumycotic mycetoma") and "Actinomycetoma" (or "Actinomycotic mycetoma") are preferred. Classical actinomycosis caused by the anaerobic *Actinomyces israeli,* which gives rise to yellow grains ("sulfur granules"), is excluded from the complex.

There have been many publications on the incidence and etiology of mycetoma, which occurs most frequently in a band of the tropics north of the equator extending from India, across Africa, to Central and South America. Incidence is particularly high in India, the Sudan, and Senegal (where *M. mycetomatis* predominates) and Mexico (where actinomycetoma predominates). All these regions are hot and arid. *Pseudallescheria boydii* seems to favor more humid conditions, with species of *Nocardia* responsible for mycetoma in temperate Europe and North America. *Madurella grisea* is limited to South America, whereas *Cephalosporium* infections are cosmopolitan.

It was early thought probable that infection was initiated by injury, and a correlation between mycetoma and injury from plant thorns has frequently been made. Sometimes the pathogen may have been growing as a saprobe on the thorns (*Leptosphaeria senegalensis* and *Pyrenochaeta romeroi* have been isolated from such sites, and *M. mycetomatis* will grow on dead wood in sterile water); or the thorn may provide the point of entry for an organism present in the environment (dry granules from mycetoma have a long survival time), especially in soil from which pathogenic species of *Nocardia* and *P. boydii* have been isolated. All this evidence points to mycetoma being a typical opportunistic infection.

Cryptococcosis

This disease is a subacute or chronic infection of the lungs, skin, or other parts, especially the central nervous system, caused by the yeast *Cryptococcus neoformans,* which is widely distributed in nature and is sometimes the dominant organism in the droppings and debris of pigeon roosts. Although the pigeon is not infected and the yeast survives passage through the bird, human cases have frequently been associated with inhalation of the pathogen when clearing out old pigeon roosts. The most frequent infections are subclinical and self-limiting, with fatal and more generalized infection occurring mostly in debilitated patients or in those "compromised" by drug treatment.

First recorded in Europe in 1894, human cryptococcosis has a worldwide distribution. In 1946, L. B. Cox and Jean C. Tolhurst published a monograph, based on 13 Australian cases termed "torulosis" caused by *Torula histolytica;* later a very comprehensive study of the disease was published by M. L. Littman and L. E. Zimmerman (1956).

Rhinosporidiosis

This disease, an infection of mucous tissue, especially of the nose, results in the development of large polyps and is exceptional among mycoses in that the causal agent, *Rhinosporidium seeberi,* has not been cultured and its taxonomic position is uncertain. Outbreaks of the disease, which attacks both humans and animals (especially bullocks set to the plough), have been associated with water and the soil. Rhinosporidiosis was first reported from Argentina in 1900, but it occurs sporadically throughout the tropics, the highest incidence being in southern India and Sri Lanka. A monograph was published by J. H. Ashworth (1923) in Edinburgh from a case involving an Indian student at the university.

Aspergillosis and Mucormycosis

Species of *Aspergillus* and mucoraceous fungi are a conspicuous and ubiquitous component of what has been called "common mold." They are therefore not infrequently found as contaminants of cultures from morbid material and may be mistaken for pathogens. On the other hand, human infections by these and similar molds do occur sporadically and have been reported worldwide.

The pathogenicity of *Aspergillus fumigatus* is well established. It is widespread in the environment; found on decaying vegetation, it has spores that are readily airborne. Because its growth is favored by high temperatures, and it is customary to incubate bacterial cultures at 37° C (a temperature detrimental to many common molds); *A. fumigatus* frequently occurs as a contaminant of cultures from sputum and other pathological material. Thus, its significance, when it is detected, is often uncertain, and clinical and other evidence must be considered in its detection.

A. fumigatus is able to cause fatal infections, particularly in birds in which it was first recorded early in the nineteenth century, lining the airsacs with a profuse sporulating growth. J. B. G. W. Fresenius in 1850 proposed the name *Aspergillus fumigatus* based on an isolate from a bustard (*Otis tarda*). Rudolf Virchow in Germany in 1856 described human pulmonary aspergillosis caused by the same species. The classical cases of human pulmonary aspergil-

losis were those of French pigeon squab feeders in the late 1890s, who chewed in their own mouths the grain used for fattening the birds. Interest in aspergillosis in France was then at its height.

Several other species of *Aspergillus* are pathogenic. *Aspergillus niger* is often associated with infection of the ear, whereas aspergillomas or "fungus balls" sporulating growths of the pathogen in lung tissues or cavities are not uncommonly associated with pulmonary disease.

Diverse mucoraceous fungi are regularly, if sporadically, recorded in north temperate countries as responsible for human infections, especially of the rhino-facial-cerebral region when the outcome is fatal. Debility is a predisposing factor.

Dependent Mycoses

The attribution of disease to the human "constitution" has a long history. Even at the beginning of the nineteenth century, dermatologists, unable to accept the concept of pathogenicity, were attributing ringworm in children to constitutional factors, and nutrition does apparently affect symptom expression. During World War II, for example, ringworm symptoms disappeared in European prisoners held under starvation conditions by the Japanese, only to reappear on the restoration of a full diet. Also, tinea capitis (*M. audouinii*) in children, although a persistent infection, resolves spontaneously at puberty for reasons not yet fully understood. Tinea pedis has been claimed as an occupational disease of coal miners and soldiers who wear heavy boots. It is well established that *Candida* infection is affected by pregnancy, and that metabolic disorders such as diabetes are also frequently associated with the disease.

Recently, iatrogenic mycoses have been aggravated by or have resulted from the use (or abuse) of antibacterials, which can cause a change in oral conditions whereby bacterial competition is eliminated and candidosis is thus induced. In addition, the introduction of heart surgery and organ transplantation following the use of immunosuppressive drugs has resulted in *Candida* endocarditis and mycotic septicemia so that antimycotic therapy is now a routine supplementary practice.

Geoffrey C. Ainsworth

Bibliography

Ainsworth, G. C. 1987. *Introduction to the history of medical and veterinary mycology.* Cambridge.

Ashworth, J. H. 1923. On *Rhinosporidium seeberi* (Wernicke, 1903) with special reference to sporulation and affinities. *Transactions of the Royal Society, Edinburgh* 53: 301–38.

Austwick, P. K. C. 1965. Pathogenicity. In *The genus Aspergillus*, ed. K. B. Raper and D. I. Fennell, 82–126. Baltimore.

Carter, H. V. 1874. *On mycetoma or the fungus disease of India*. London.

Connant, N. F., et al. 1971. *Manual of clinical mycology*, 3d edition. Philadelphia.

Emmons, C. W. 1934. Dermatophytes: Natural grouping based on the form of the spores and accessory organs. *Archives of Dermatology and Syphilology* 30: 337–62.

Emmons, C. W., C. H. Binford, and J. P. Utz. 1971. *Medical mycology*. 3rd ed. Philadelphia.

Fiese, M. J. 1958. *Coccidioidomycosis*. Springfield, Ill.

Higgs, J. M. 1972. Muco-cutaneous candidiasis: Historical aspects. *Transactions of the St. John's Hospital Dermatological Society* 59: 175–94.

Howard, D. H., ed. 1982. *Fungi pathogenic for humans and animals*, 3 vols. New York and Basel.

Littman, M. L., and L. E. Zimmerman. 1956. *Cryptococcosis*. New York.

Lucet, A. 1897. *De l'Aspergillus fumigatus chez animaux domestiques et dans les oeufs en incubation*. Paris.

Mackinnon, J. E. 1949. The dependence on the weather of the incidence of sporotrichosis. *Mycopathologia* 4: 367–74.

Mahgoub, El L., and I. C. Murray. 1973. *Mycetoma*. London.

Odds, F. C. 1979. *Candida and candidosis*. Leicester University Press.

Rénon, L. 1897. *Etude sur l'aspergillose chez les animaux et chez l'homme*. Paris.

Stevens, D. 1981. *Coccidioidomycosis: A text*. New York.

Warnock, D. W., and M. D. Richardson, eds. 1982. *Fungal infection of the compromised patient*. Chichester, U.K.

VIII.56
Fungus Poisoning

Two categories of fungus poisoning may be distinguished: (1) *mycetism,* the result of eating poisonous fungi mistaken for the edible variety (which has a long history and a worldwide incidence), and (2) *mycotoxicoses,* the result of inadvertent ingestion of food containing toxins produced by fungi. The latter, although also of worldwide incidence, has (with the exception of ergotism) been generally recognized only during the twentieth century.

Mycetism

Calamities tend to impress, and the first reference to fungi in the Greek classics is an epigram by Euripides writing about 450 B.C. He was commemorating the death of a woman and her two children, in one day, after eating poisonous fungi. During Roman times, edible fungi were a delicacy, and diverse advice regarding them was offered by several authors such as Horace, Celsus, Dioscorides, Galen, and Pliny. The advice consisted of how to avoid poisonous species, how to render poisonous forms harmless, and how to treat fungus poisoning.

Much of this ancient folklore on precautions to ensure edibility was compiled by the authors of the first printed herbals in the fourteenth and fifteenth centuries, and some has even survived to the present day. It is, however, invariably unreliable because the distribution of poisonous and edible species seems to be random. For example, the esteemed esculents *Amanita caesarea* ("Caesar's mushroom," a Roman favorite) and *Amanita rubescens* ("the blusher") are congeneric with *Amanita phalloides* ("death cap") and several related species (*Amanita pantherina, Amanita verna, Amanita virosa*) that have been, and still are, responsible for most fatalities from fungus poisoning in north temperate regions. The only reliable guide is correct identification.

The most frequent effect of fungus poisoning is gastroenteric disturbance of greater or lesser severity. *Amanita phalloides* toxins, symptoms of which occur 4 to 6 hours or more after ingestion, also cause severe damage to the liver and kidneys. Other *Amanita* toxins have a hemolytic effect, whereas hallucinogenic species cause psychosomatic symptoms. Fever is unusual.

The chemistry of toxic fungi has been under investigation since muscarine was isolated in Germany in

1869. That name came from the "fly agaric" (*Amanita muscaria*) which has been equated by R. G. Wasson (1971) with the Indian soma. T. Wieland (1986), together with his father, brother, and other collaborators, has made extensive studies of the *Amanita* toxins (amatoxins, phallotoxins, virotoxins).

As already indicated, mycetism is of worldwide distribution, the species of fungi implicated depending on the locality, but there are variations in its reported incidence. In western Europe, for example, there are more published records of mycetism in France, where edible forms of fungi are widely collected from the wild for sale, than in the United Kingdom, where eating wild forms is still regarded with suspicion. Most poisonous fungi are larger basidiomycetes, but a few ascomycetes with large fruit bodies are poisonous (e.g., *Gynmitra esculenta*, which is, however, edible if dried or if the cooking water is discarded).

A recent development that has led to increased incidence of fungus poisoning originated from the ethnomycological studies of Wasson (1971). These studies drew attention to the hallucinogenic properties of some larger fungi, particularly species of *Psilocybe* containing the compound *psilocin* – which is able to induce psychotropic effects similar to lysergic acid and mescalin. Collection of such forms in the wild for self-administration or illegal sale has resulted in misidentifications or overdoses and the need for medical attention.

Mycotoxicoses

Until the twentieth century, the only mycotoxicosis of human beings generally recognized in the West was ergotism, although serious outbreaks of human mycotoxicoses had occurred in Russia and Japan. *Kaschin–Beck* (or Urov) *disease* of children is characterized by generalized osteoarthritis caused by eating moldy grain. It was prevalent among the Cossacks and endemic in both Asiatic and European Russia and in northern Korea and China in the 1860s. A similar mycotoxicosis (the "drunken [or intoxicating] bread syndrome") was also prevalent in Russia. But the most extensively documented mycotoxicosis in Russia is *alimentary toxic aleukia* (or septic angina); it was known before World War I and became epidemic during World War II in the Russian grain belt, when some 10 percent of the population was affected and suffered high death rates (Mayer 1953). The problem was that in affected districts it was the practice to allow the ripe cereal crop to go through the winter under the snow. When the snow cover was so heavy that the underlying soil did not freeze deeply, and the spring was mild with frequent thawing and freezing, the grain was molded by *Fusarium* species and other fungi that produced toxins (mostly trichothecines).

Known in Japan from the seventeenth century, a form of cardiac beriberi (*Shoshin–Kakke*) was shown in 1891 to be caused by eating moldy rice. In 1940 the toxin involved was identified as citreoviridin, produced by *Penicillium citreo-viride*. After World War II, a severe outbreak of a similar but different mycotoxicosis due to eating rice that had deteriorated in storage ("yellowed rice") was recorded in Japan.

Several major mycotoxicoses of farm animals have been documented in Russia, and a few more have been reported elsewhere. Significant attention was focused on mycotoxicoses after the summer of 1960, when more than 100,000 young turkeys and other poultry died in the United Kingdom after being fed a ration containing ground peanut (*Arachis hypogea*) meal imported from Brazil. Cattle and pigs were also affected, and feeding experiments induced cancer of the liver in the rat. The toxin, found to be produced by strains of *Aspergillus flavus*, was designated *aflatoxin*. At first, testing for aflatoxin was limited to animal tests using 1-day-old ducklings, which are particularlly sensitive to the toxin, but a sensitive chemical test was soon developed.

Aflatoxin was shown to be widespread in foods containing peanuts, and in parts of Africa and Asia the incidence of human liver cancer has been correlated with the intake of aflatoxin. It has not been possible, however, to legislate for aflatoxin-free peanut products because the methods of harvest and storage of peanuts in the primary peanut-producing countries are such that the introduction of the necessary changes could be effected only in the long term. The U.S. Food and Drug Administration, therefore, has set an aflatoxin tolerance of 20 parts per billion (ppb) for finished peanuts products. Interest in *aflatoxicosis,* because of its carcinogenic potential, is still intense. The literature on this subject is very extensive, and includes two major monographs (Goldblatt 1969; Heathcote and Hibbert 1978) and numerous reviews.

Geoffrey C. Ainsworth

Bibliography

Ainsworth, G. C. 1976. *Introduction to the history of mycology*. Cambridge.

    1987. *Introduction to the history of medical and veterinary mycology*. Cambridge.

Ammirati, J. F., J. A. Traquair, and P. A. Horgen. 1985.

Poisonous mushrooms of the northern United States and Canada. Minneapolis.

Bresinsky, A., and H. Bresl. 1985. *Giftpilz mit einer Einführung in die Pilzbestimmung.* Stuttgart.

Goldblatt, L. A., ed. 1969. *Aflatoxin: Scientific background, control and implications.* New York and London.

Heathcote, J. G., and J. R. Hibbert. 1978. *Aflatoxins: Chemical and biological aspects.* Amsterdam.

Lincoff, G., and D. H. Mitchell. 1977. *Toxic and hallucinogenic mushroom poisoning: A handbook for physicians and mushroom hunters.* New York.

Mayer, C. F. 1953. Endemic panmyelotoxicosis in the Russian grain belt. *Military Surgeon* 113: 173–89, 295–315.

Rumack, B. H., and E. Salzman. 1978. *Mushroom poisoning: Diagnosis and treatment.* West Palm Beach, Fla.

Wasson, R. G. 1971. *Soma: Divine mushroom of immortality.* Octavo, New York (first issued as a folio, limited edition, 1968).

Wieland, T. 1986. *Peptides of poisonous Amanita mushrooms.* New York.

Wyllie, T. D., and L. G. Morehouse, eds. 1977–8. *Mycotoxic fungi, mycotoxins, mycotoxicoses: An encyclopedic handbook,* 2 vols. New York and Basel.

VIII.57
Gallstones (Cholelithiasis)

Classification

Gallstones are quite common in modern populations, occurring in nearly 20 percent of autopsies. Though often asymptomatic, they can produce significant morbidity, leading to cholecystitis, cholangitis, biliary cirrhosis, and pancreatitis.

The chief constituents of gallstones are cholesterol, bilirubin, and calcium. Other components may include fatty acids, triglycerides, protein, and polysaccharides. Descriptively, there are four major types of gallstones: (1) pure cholesterol stones; (2) mixed stones composed of cholesterol, bilirubin, and calcium; (3) combined stones having a cholesterol center and laminated exterior of cholesterol, bilirubin, and calcium; and (4) black or brown pigmented stones composed of calcium bilirubinate.

The first three types comprise the vast majority of gallstones and may be grouped together as *cholesterol-based stones,* pathogenetically related to abnormal cholesterol and bile salt metabolism. *Black pigmented stones* are commonly associated with chronic hemolysis, particularly sickle-cell disease. Gallstones occur in 40 to 60 percent of patients with sickle-cell disease. Brown pigmented stones are associated with infection. These were historically more common in China and Japan, perhaps related to bile stasis and infection caused by *Ascaris lumbricoides* (roundworm) and *Clonorchis sinensis.*

Etiology and Epidemiology

Though incompletely understood, the three major factors in gallstone formation are abnormality in bile composition, biliary stasis, and gallbladder infection. These factors are interrelated, but current thinking ascribes the primary role to abnormal bile composition, related to cholesterol and bile acid metabolism. This in turn is affected by dietary, genetic, and hormonal factors.

A common medical maxim describes a typical patient with gallstones as "fat, fair, female, and forty." Obesity is associated with increased cholesterol secretion, producing a supersaturated or lithogenic bile. Overconsumption of calories, particularly through refined sugar and flour, appears to be the major factor accounting for the high incidence in Western countries (Heaton 1973). It also explains the increasing prevalence of cholesterol and mixed gallstones among Japanese, Eskimo, and certain African populations adopting a more Western diet. A diet high in cholesterol-rich foods may have a secondary role.

Gallstones are two to four times more common in females than in males. Estrogen causes increased secretion of cholesterol as well as decreased production of bile salts required to form soluble micelles with cholesterol. In addition, childbearing results in further elevation of estrogen in the third trimester and also promotes biliary stasis; thus multiparity is a risk factor.

There is a steady increase in gallstone prevalence with advancing age. Clinically, the symptoms of gallbladder disease related to gallstones most commonly present between the ages of 40 and 60 years.

Distribution and Incidence

Conclusions regarding the geographic distribution of gallstones are based on a variety of autopsy, hospital admission, and population survey data. The large Framingham, Massachusetts, study showed a prevalence of documented gallbladder disease among adult males (30 to 62 years old) of 1.3 percent and among adult females of 5.9 percent (Friedman, Kannel, and Dawber 1966). Many studies have shown a higher prevalence among American Indian groups, particularly in the Southwest (Brown and

Christensen 1967; Comess, Bennett, and Burch 1967; Heaton 1973). For example, a study of the Pima Indians using identical criteria and age groups as the Framingham study showed a prevalence of 5.9 percent among adult males and 36 percent among females (Comess et al. 1967).

Gallstones are usually asymptomatic. This feature, in combination with the increased prevalence with age, explains the much higher incidence of gallstones at autopsy. A large autopsy series from Philadelphia spanning the years 1920 to 1949 demonstrated gallstones in 7.8 percent of males and 16.8 percent of females. The incidence among blacks was less than half that for whites (Lieber 1952). An autopsy series of adult whites in New York City found gallstones in 16.0 percent of males and 32.5 percent of females (Newman and Northup 1959).

A similar prevalence of gallstones has been demonstrated in autopsy series from Europe, including England, France, and Germany, as well as Western-style societies such as Israel, South Africa, and Australia (Brett and Barker 1976). Sweden appears to be second only to certain American Indian groups in the frequency of gallstones. An autopsy survey from Malmo found stones in 32 percent of men and 57 percent of women over 20 years old. The prevalence rose to peaks of 70 percent in women by age 70, and 50 percent in men by age 90.

Gallstones are relatively uncommon in oriental countries; prevalence rates as low as 1.8 percent among adult men and 3.9 percent of adult women are found in Thailand. Prevalence remains low in Japan; however, there has been a shift from the infection-related pigmented stones to the Western diet-related cholesterol stones.

Most African populations demonstrate an extremely low prevalence of gallstones. Only 1.3 percent of autopsied adults in Uganda had gallstones. Many of these were black pigmented stones related to chronic hemolysis (Owor 1964). No gallstones were found in a series of 4,395 autopsies in Ghana. The disease is virtually unknown among the Masai of East Africa.

There is a general impression that gallstones are increasing in frequency in industrialized countries as well as in countries undergoing rapid development. A recent review of pre- and post-1940 autopsy series shows increasing prevalence of gallstones in Europe, North America, Japan, Chile, and Australia (Brett and Barker 1976).

A genetic tendency to develop gallstones under certain dietary conditions may account for the high rates of gallstones noted in various American Indian

groups, including Pima, Navajo, and Chippewa as well as in groups with significant Indian admixture from Mexico, Bolivia, Chile, and Peru (Weiss et al. 1984). It has been postulated that a genetic defect in conversion of cholesterol to bile acid results in lithogenic bile (Grundy, Metzger, and Adler 1972).

The geographic epidemiology of gallstones indicates a susceptibility in New World populations that is not shared, however, by their Asian ancestral relatives. The Americas were settled by crossing via the Bering land bridge formed during glacial epochs. Survival under the harsh climatic conditions depended on hunting and gathering strategies with unpredictable periods of near starvation. Individuals who could rapidly store excess calories as fat would have had a pronounced survival advantage over individuals lacking this trait. This is the "thrifty gene" theory postulated to explain the prevalence of diabetes among American Indians (Neel 1962, 1982) and possibly accounting for the association of obesity, parity, and puberty, with the formation of gallstones in American Indian females and to a lesser degree in males now exposed to a perpetual "feast" of calories and sedentary living (Weiss et al. 1984). Indeed, the worldwide distribution of other populations with high risk of gallstones corresponds closely to the area covered by the last glacial epoch (Lowenfels 1988).

History and Paleopathology

Hippocrates and Aristotle were familiar with the clinical findings of jaundice and biliary disease, but their writings do not specifically mention gallstones. Hippocrates differentiated four types of jaundice due to disease of the liver, but he did not describe any cause related to obstruction. Diocles of Carystus referred to possible mechanical obstruction of the flow of bile. Accounts of Alexander the Great's illness prior to his death in 323 B.C. are quite suggestive of gallstones and cholecystitis (Gordon-Taylor 1937).

Galen described various types of jaundice, including obstructive jaundice. He stated that small foreign bodies such as grain or fig and pomegranate seeds could obstruct the common bile duct. Given the close similarity of small gallstones to certain seeds, Galen may in fact be referring to gallstones. Gallstones in lower animals had been recognized for centuries, and crushed gallstones were an important ingredient in yellow pigment. The codified Talmudic law of the fourth century A.D. considered animals with sharp-edged gallstones unfit to eat (terefah), but kosher to eat if the gallstones were smooth like a date pit.

Alexander of Tralles of the sixth century was a Byzantine physician with wide clinical experience but scanty knowledge of anatomy and physiology. He described both gallstones and renal calculi. Haly Abbas, a tenth-century Persian physician often quoted in early Renaissance medicine, recorded the presence of calculi in the gallbladder and liver (Wilkie 1934).

Mundinus was professor of anatomy and surgery at the University of Bologna from 1295 to 1326. His manuscript on anatomy was based on the writings of Hippocrates, Galen, and Arabic authors and was widely used for nearly 250 years. He also mentions stones formed within the gallbladder and kidneys. Gentile da Foligno was a graduate of Bologna and professor at Padua, who died of the plague in 1348. In 1341 he carried out one of the earliest autopsies on record, and an account of that autopsy states that a gallstone was found embedded in the cystic duct of the gallbladder.

Antonio Benivieni wrote the first book devoted to pathological anatomy, which was published posthumously by his brother in 1507. This work, *De Adbitis,* contains 111 observations based on 20 autopsies, including two descriptions of gallstones found within the gallbladder and liver. Numerous other Renaissance physicians were familiar with gallstones encountered in clinical practice or more often at autopsy (Steinbock 1990).

Giovanni Battista Morgagni profoundly altered medicine in 1761 with the publication of *On the Sites and Causes of Disease.* He provided a vast array of pathological findings related to the clinical picture for a large number of diseases, including gallstones. Morgagni noted the increased frequency of gallstones with age, the greater preponderance of women suffering from them, the variation by locale, and an association with a very sedentary life. Bile stasis again figured as a prominent factor in gallstone formation. He also considered irritation or inflammation of the glands within the gallbladder wall as a cause of stones.

Gallstones have been recovered in burial excavations, and this evidence greatly extends the known antiquity of the disease. Given their frequency, more such examples should be expected. The earliest case comes from Mycenae, Greece, dating 1600 to 1500 B.C. Several gallstones were found between the right lower costal margin and right iliac crest of the skeleton of a 45- to 55-year-old man (Angel 1973). The stones are reddish brown in color with green patches and have several facets.

The mummy of a priestess of Amen, who died 945

B.C., revealed an intact gallbladder filled with stones. A radiograph of an intact mummy from the late Dynastic period (525 to 343 B.C.) shows a cluster of gallstones in the gallbladder. Subsequent analysis showed these to be the mixed variety (Gray 1967).

An extremely well preserved body of a 50-year-old female from the Hunan province of central China demonstrated multiple gallstones, including one obstructing the common bile duct. This example dates to the Han Dynasty (206 B.C. to A.D. 220) (Wei 1973).

In Europe, gallstones were recovered along with skeletal remains in a wooden coffin dating to Merovingian times or about A.D. 750. The coffin was found in Mainfranken, Germany. In Herault, France, the remains of an older adult buried in the ninth century also yielded gallstones. A single gallstone was recovered from 234 graves in a London cemetery dating from A.D. 1000 to 1200 (Steinbock in press).

In the New World, 16 individuals from the Libben site in Ohio exhibited gallstones (Lovejoy 1979). This Late Woodland site dates from A.D. 1000 to 1200. In northern Chile, at a site dating from A.D. 100 to 300, 2 of 75 mummies had gallstones (Munizaga, Allison, and Paredes 1978). Both individuals had pure cholesterol stones.

The frequency of cholesterol-based gallstones is affected by age, sex, parity, diet, genetics, and other factors. Infection and hemolysis are important in the formation of pigmented stones. A variable frequency in ancient human populations is to be expected, and because of dietary factors they may have been quite rare in many instances.

R. Ted Steinbock

Bibliography

Angel, L. 1973. Human skeletons from grave circles at Mycenae. Appendix in *The grave circle B of Mycenae,* G. E. Mylonas, 379–97. Archaeological Society of Athens.

Bennion, L. J., and S. M. Grundy. 1978. Risk factors for the development of cholelithiasis in man. *New England Journal of Medicine* 299: 1161–7.

Brett, M., and D. J. P. Barker. 1976. The world distribution of gallstones. *International Journal of Epidemiology* 5: 335–41.

Brown, J. E., and C. Christensen. 1967. Biliary tract disease among the Navajos. *Journal of the American Medical Association* 202: 1050–2.

Comess, L. J., P. H. Bennett, and T. A. Burch. 1967. Clinical gallbladder disease in Pima Indians. *New England Journal of Medicine* 277: 894–8.

Friedman, G. D., W. B. Kannel, and T. R. Dawber. 1966.

The epidemiology of gallbladder disease: Observations in the Framingham study. *Journal of Chronic Disease* 19: 273–92.

Gordon-Taylor, G. 1937. Gallstones and their sufferers. *British Journal of Surgery* 25: 241–51.

Gray, P. H. K. 1967. Radiography of ancient Egyptian mummies. *Medical Radiography and Photography* 43: 34–44.

Grundy, S. M., A. L. Metzger, and R. Adler. 1972. Pathogenesis of lithogenic bile in American Indian women with cholesterol gallstones. *Journal of Clinical Investigation* 51: 3026–31.

Heaton, K. W. 1973. The epidemiology of gallstones and suggested etiology. *Clinical Gastroenterology* 2: 67–83.

Lieber, M. M. 1952. The incidence of gallstones and their correlation with other diseases. *Archives of Surgery* 135: 394–405.

Lovejoy, C. O. 1979. Referred to in December *Paleopathology Association Newsletter* 28: 7.

Lowenfels, A. B. 1988. Gallstones and glaciers: The stone that came in from the cold. *Lancet* 1: 1385–6.

Munizaga, A., M. J. Allison, and C. Paredes. 1978. Cholelithiasis and cholecystitis in pre-Columbian Chileans. *American Journal of Physical Anthropology* 48: 209–12.

Neel, J. V. 1962. Diabetes mellitus: A "thrifty" genotype rendered detrimental by "progress"? *American Journal of Human Genetics* 14: 353–62.

1982. The thrifty genotype revisited. In *The genetics of diabetes mellitus*, ed. J. Kobberling and R. Tattersall, 283–93. New York.

Newman, H. F., and J. D. Northup. 1959. Collective review: The autopsy incidence of gallstones. *International Abstracts of Surgery* 109: 1–12.

Owor, R. 1964. Gallstones in the autopsy population at Mulago Hospital, Kampala. *East African Medical Journal* 41: 251–3.

Steinbock, R. T. 1990. Studies in ancient calcified soft tissues and organic concretions. III. Gallstones (cholelithiasis). *Journal of Paleopathology*.

Wei, O. 1973. Internal organs of a 2100 year old female corpse. *Lancet* 2: 1198.

Weiss, K. M., et al. 1984. Genetics and epidemiology of gallbladder disease in New World native peoples. *American Journal of Human Genetics* 36: 1259–78.

Wilkie, D. P. D. 1934. Gallstones. In *A short history of some common diseases,* ed. W. R. Brett, 146–53. London.

VIII.58
Gangrene

Gangrene is the term used by the clinician to describe local death of tissue (*necrosis*) occurring in the living body. Gangrene implies a fairly rapid process (developing in days) extending over a large visible area (a few to many centimeters) with an obvious inability of the tissues to repair or replace the gangrenous part. Although gangrene can occur in internal organs (e.g., large intestine), it generally refers to a process occurring on the surface of the body. It may involve only the skin, or it may extend into deeper tissues such as muscle or nerves.

Gangrene may be either dry or moist. Dry gangrene describes necrosis of the tissues of the extremities resulting from vascular occlusion, such as occurs in severe arteriosclerosis of the legs. Wet or moist gangrene occurs when bacteria invades dead tissue, producing putrefaction. When the gas-forming group of bacteria is involved, gas gangrene occurs. A gangrene may be dry at first, and be converted to the moist type by invading bacteria.

Clinical Manifestations

In dry gangrene, the arterial supply is gradually cut off and a drying or mummification of the tissues results. There is frequently an absence of inflammation, but pain of varying degree may precede the color changes. The soft tissue slowly and progressively shrinks and the color gradually deepens until the whole area is coal black. Constitutional symptoms may occur but are less severe than in moist gangrene.

Moist gangrene may be preceded by inflammation or trauma. The part is initially swollen and painful. The color is at first red then blue and finally turns to a green black. There is boggy swelling and putrid odor. If the moist gangrene is extensive, constitutional symptoms, such as fever, may be present.

A vivid description of hospital gangrene illustrates well the clinical aspect of moist gangrene:

A wound attacked by gangrene in its most concentrated and active form presents a horrible aspect after the first forty-eight hours. The whole surface has become of a dark-red color, of a ragged appearance, with blood partly coagulated, and apparently half putrid, adhering at every point. The edges are everted, the cuticle separating from half to three-fourths of an inch around, with a concentric circle of inflammation extending an inch or two beyond it; the limb is usually swollen for some distance, of a white, shining color, not peculiarly sensible except in spots, the whole of it being oedematous and pasty. The pain is burning and unbearable in the part itself, while the extension of the disease, generally in a circular direction, may be marked from hour to hour; so that in from another twenty-four to forty-eight hours nearly the whole of a calf of a leg, or the muscle of a buttock, or even the wall of the abdomen may disappear, leaving a deep great hollow or hiatus of the most destructive character, exhaling a peculiar stench which can never be mistaken, and spreading with a rapidity quite awful to contemplate. The great nerves and arteries appear to resist its influence longer than the muscular structures, but these at last yield; the largest nerves are destroyed, and the arteries give way, frequently closing the scene, after repeated hemorrhages, by one which proves the last solace of the unfortunate sufferer. . . . The joints offer little resistance; the capsular and synovial membranes are soon invaded, and the ends of the bones laid bare. The extension of this disease is in the first instance through the cellular structures. The skin is undermined and falls in, or a painful red and soon black patch is perceived at some distance from the original mischief, preparatory to the whole becoming one mass of putridity, while the sufferings of the patient are extreme. (Buck 1902)

Etiology

Gangrene can have many causes; Table VIII.58.1 indicates the major ones. Some are now quite rare but at one time were common. Using this table as a guide, we shall discuss the various causes, highlighting those that have been of major consequence throughout recorded history.

Vascular Causes

Historically, *ergotism* resulted from ingesting rye bread contaminated by the fungus *Claviceps purpurea*. It led to a permanent decrease in the caliber of arterioles and, eventually, to dry gangrene of the fingers and toes and, less commonly, of the ears and nose. Ergotism was responsible for many epidemics of gangrene during the Middle Ages in Europe. Along with erysipelas it was known as St. Anthony's fire. Although rare, ergotism may still occur today, as ergot preparations are often used in the treatment of migraine headaches.

Raynaud's Syndrome. This syndrome is characterized by marked episodic vascular spasms of the extremities. During a typical attack, one or more digits initially turn white. After a few minutes, the color changes to a bluish red. Slowly, the normal color returns. These episodes are often triggered by cold or emotional stress. In severe cases, gangrene may ensue, which is characteristically symmetrical and con-

Table VIII.58.1. *Causes of gangrene*

Vascular disease
Vascular spasm
    Ergotism (St. Anthony's fire)
    Raynaud's syndrome
Embolism
    Arteriosclerosis
    Organisms
    Fat and gases
    Dysproteinemias
    Abnormalities of coagulation
Primary vascular disease (peripheral vascular disease)
    Arteriosclerosis
    Thromboangiitis obliterans (Buerger's disease)
    Diabetes
Vasculitis of the so-called collagen diseases
    Rheumatoid arthritis
    Systemic lupus erythematosus
    Hypersensitivity to certain drugs

Physical agents
Burns
Cold
Trauma
Pressure
Ionizing radiation
Electrical burns

Chemical agents
Caustics
Venoms
Certain drugs
    Coumadin
    Heparin
    Chemotherapeutic agents

Microbiological agents
Bacterial infections
    Anthrax
    Streptococci (necrotizing fasciitis, Fournier's gangrene)
    Mixed (postoperative synergistic gangrene)
    Leprosy
    Pseudomonas aeruginosa
    Mycobacterial organisms (tuberculosis, Buruli ulcer)
Viral infections
    Herpes (simplex and zoster)
    Smallpox
    Chickenpox
Treponemal infections
    Syphilis
    Yaws
    Bejel
Rickettsial infections
    Rocky Mountain spotted fever
    Typhus
Protozoal infections
    Amebiasis cutis
    Schistosomiasis cutis

Table VIII.58.1 *(cont.)*

Fungal infections
Histoplasmosis
Mucormycosis (phycomycosis)
Actinomycosis/nocardiosis
Cryptococcosis
Blastomycosis (North and South American)

fined to the fingers and toes. It was once known as relapsing gangrene. Raynaud's syndrome may occur alone (*Raynaud's disease*) or in association with another condition usually of the collagen group of diseases (*scleroderma, systemic lupus erythematosus, rheumatoid arthritis*). It has also been seen as an occupational hazard in people who manipulate vibratory instruments such as jackhammers or chainsaws.

Embolism. Embolism is the sudden occlusion of an artery by blood-borne particles. These may be atheromatous material dislodged from a vascular plaque upstream; vegetations from an infected heart valve; or other unusual particles such as fat (after extensive bony fractures), gas (decompression sickness), abnormal blood proteins (dysproteinemias), or blood clots. The acute vascular compromise can lead to gangrene of the extremities, usually of the dry type.

Arteriosclerosis. Arteriosclerosis may be an underlying cause of embolism, and can also lead to gradual local vascular occlusion (*thrombosis*) of large and medium-sized arteries. It is common in the elderly and therefore has been called *senile gangrene*. A dry gangrene, it occurs mainly in the foot and was therefore previously called *Pott's disease of the toe*. It is generally preceded by severe pain and discomfort in the lower leg and foot. A special form of arteriosclerosis is *thromboangiitis obliterans* or Buerger's disease. It commonly occurs in young and middle-aged men who are heavy smokers. Finally, *diabetes* can predispose to arteriosclerosis of smaller vessels with eventual gangrene of the feet and toes. Diabetic gangrene is usually of the moist type. There are multiple other factors that may predispose to arteriosclerosis. They include hereditary factors and general life-style habits such as overeating of animal fats, lack of exercise, and smoking. With recent changes in these habits and better control of diabetes, arteriosclerosis and its resultant gangrene are now becoming less common. Surgical techniques are also available for replacing or recanalizing occluded arteries

of the legs, so that blood supply to the feet can be restored.

Physical Agents
Various types of injuries such as frostbite, compound bony fractures of the legs, contusions, gunshot wounds, and burns, if serious enough, may be the initial factor that triggers production of gangrene. However, this complication was more prevalent before effective medical care became widely available.

Chemical Agents
Tissue can also be destroyed by chemicals either of exogenous or endogenous origin. Caustics such as carbolic acid (previously used as an antiseptic solution) have been known to cause gangrene. Venoms of certain snakes (i.e., water moccasin), spiders (i.e., brown recluse spider), and jellyfish (i.e., Portuguese man-of-war) can cause local necrosis at the site of the sting or bite. Many chemotherapeutic agents (such as those used to treat malignancies) may also lead to local tissue destruction when they inadvertently seep into the surrounding area during intravenous administration. Some systemically administered drugs may rarely cause gangrene (i.e., some anticoagulants such as coumadin).

Microbiological Agents
Many organisms produce a toxin that will directly cause cell death. Other toxins have vascular effects such as spasm or vasculitis. Some organisms produce enzymes that can break down tissue locally. Other organisms – in particular, viruses – can directly destroy cells by invasion. Only a few of the most important infections will be discussed here. Many can be found elsewhere in this work.

Various streptococci, including *Streptococcus pyogenes* (group A beta hemolytic strep.), have been found to be the cause of certain varieties of gangrene. Of historical importance is *hospital gangrene,* also known as necrotizing fasciitis and *pourriture des hôpitaux.* This form of gangrene was the scourge of hospitals in the preantiseptic era. Today it is almost never seen. Trauma is usually the initiating factor, whereas predisposing factors are diabetes, alcoholism, and a generally debilitated state. Within 48 to 96 hours, gangrene would set into a wound and characteristically was rapidly progressive and deeply destructive. The patient would become febrile and eventually succumb. Although some authorities feel that this type of gangrene was due solely to *S. pyogenes,* there is now more evidence to suggest that other organisms (alone or in combination) may give a similar clinical picture. Another streptococcal gangrene, called *Fournier's gangrene,* is an acute gangrene localized to the scrotum. Finally, anaerobic streptococci in combination with other bacteria such as *Staphylococcus aureus* are the cause of postoperative synergistic gangrene. After a few days or weeks, gangrene develops around an abdominal or thoracic surgical wound site. The process is rapidly progressive and may, if left untreated, lead to the death of the patient.

History and Geography

Ergotism has long been an important cause of certain epidemics of gangrene in humankind. Gangrene of the limbs has been recognized since ancient times, and a description of gangrene following trauma appears in Hippocrates. It is probable that gangrene in ancient Greece and Rome was due mainly to infections initiated by trauma of either accidental or military origin.

In temperate and Arctic zones of the world, cold injuries causing frostbite that led to gangrene have always occurred. Explorers of cold regions were often affected, and gangrene produced by cold injury has also been a tremendous problem in troops engaged in wartime activities. Gangrene, for example, was quite prevalent among soldiers during Napoleon Bonaparte's invasion of Russia. Yet frostbite was only one of the causes of gangrene associated with military activity. Trauma from penetrating wounds, contusion of soft tissues, and compound bony fractures were often the initial insult. The introduction of gunpowder in Europe in the sixteenth century produced a tremendous loss of life and limbs from gangrene that developed in these traumatic wounds. Poor hygienic conditions and overcrowding in hospitals led to epidemic wound infections. Because hospital gangrene was rapidly progressive and lethal, many lives were lost, particularly during the Napoleonic Wars, the Crimean War, and the American Civil War. In many cases, there were almost as many soldiers killed from wounds and gangrene as were killed in action.

By the time of World War I, hospital gangrene was much less prevalent. The art of amputation and setting of fractures was advanced by the important contributions of such surgeons as Ambroise Paré in the sixteenth century, Pierre-Joseph Desault in the eighteenth, and John Bell at the turn of the nineteenth, among others. Their work significantly contributed to decreased mortality from gangrene. The concept of antisepsis and asepsis was introduced in the late nineteenth century with the work of Louis Pasteur. This concept, when applied to management of wounds, is known as *Listerism,* in honor of Lord Joseph Lister, who was the first to recognize the value and clinical application of Pasteur's discovery. Finally, the introduction of penicillin in the early 1940s totally eradicated hospital gangrene.

Arteriosclerosis is probably as old as humankind. Leonardo da Vinci, in the fifteenth century, illustrated the arteries of a subject with senile arteriosclerosis in one of his anatomic sketches. Along with prolonged life expectancy has come a greater susceptibility to degenerative diseases such as arteriosclerosis and other vascular disorders. In the early nineteenth century, it gradually became clear that organic occlusion of the arteries could cause dry gangrene. Maurice Raynaud, in his now famous 1862 thesis, *On Local Asphyxia and Symmetrical Gangrene of the Extremities,* attempted to prove that there was a disease of the arterial system that might produce gangrene, but in which arterial obliteration was not present. Only recently have the roles of life-style, diabetes, and hypertension been recognized as contributing factors in the production of arteriosclerosis. Fortunately, widespread public education is now contributing to the decline of severe peripheral vascular disease and its associated gangrene.

In advanced countries of the world today, gangrene is much less common. Infectious gangrenes are easily treated or avoided by the appropriate antiinfective agents. However, there are now a growing number of individuals who are immunosuppressed from chemotherapeutic agents and corticosteroids, which are used to prevent rejection in transplant patients, and to treat various cancers and autoimmune diseases such as rheumatoid arthritis. In such an immunocompromised state, these patients are at increased risk of developing unusual infectious gangrenes whose etiologic agents may not be easily recognized or be readily treatable.

Diane Quintal and Robert Jackson

Bibliography

Brooks, Stewart. 1966. *Civil war medicine.* Springfield, Ill.
Buck, Albert, ed. 1902. *A reference handbook of the medical sciences,* Vol. IV, 300–8. New York.
Buerger, Leo. 1924. *The circulatory disturbances of the extremities.* Philadelphia.
  1983. Thrombo-angiitis: A study of the vascular lesions leading to presenile spontaneous gangrene. *American Journal of Medical Sciences* 266: 278–91. [Reprint of Buerger's 1908 article in same journal.]
Enjalbert, Lise. 1978. De la pourriture d'hôpital à l'infection nosocomiale. *Mémoires de l'Académie des Sciences (Toulouse)* 140: 67–73.

Moschella, Samuel L. 1969. The clinical significance of necrosis of the skin. *Medical Clinic of North America* 53: 259–74.

Tanner, J. R. 1987. St. Anthony's fire, then and now: A case report and historical review. *Canadian Journal of Surgery* 30: 291–3.

U.S. Army. 1884. Index catalogue of the Library of the Surgeon-General's Office. 1263–80.

VIII.59
Giardiasis

Infection with the small flagellate *Giardia lamblia* is found around the world. This protozoan inhabits the small intestine of humans and is especially common in children. Other mammals, including beavers and muskrats, also harbor *Giardia* and are important reservoir hosts. The parasite was first seen by Anton van Leeuwenhoek in 1681 and described scientifically in 1859.

Adult parasites, the trophozoites, attach to the intestinal wall with sucking disks. As trophozoites detach and pass down the intestinal tract, they transform themselves into cysts that are able to resist many environmental pressures, including water filtration and chlorination. Humans almost always acquire infection by swallowing fecally contaminated food or water. In developed countries, many cases of giardiasis have been traced to campers who have drunk from what appeared to be pure wilderness streams, but that had been contaminated by animals. Because the cysts are surprisingly resistant to normal water purification methods, public water supplies can become infected by faulty sewer lines, as happened in two fashionable Colorado ski resorts in 1964 and 1978. Giardiasis is a frequent cause of "traveler's diarrhea," and tourist groups in Leningrad have suffered well-publicized outbreaks. In 1983, 22 of New York City's 55 police and fire department scuba divers had *Giardia*, presumably from the heavily polluted waters of the harbor. Four percent of 1 million stool samples submitted to state laboratories in the United States from 1977 to 1981 were positive for *Giardia*. Prevalence rates in developing countries range from 8 to 20 percent and higher. In poor countries like Bangladesh, where water and sanitation standards are often very favorable for transmission, a majority of the children and many adults repeatedly acquire infection.

There has been considerable dispute in the past about the clinical importance of *Giardia* infection. Although many cases are in fact asymptomatic, it is now clear that the flagellates damage the intestinal wall and that heavy infestations can cause nutritionally significant malabsorption of food. Symptoms include diarrhea, flatulence, abdominal discomfort, and light-colored, fatty stools. The classic method for detecting *Giardia* infections is to find the trophozoites in the feces with a microscope, but surveys that depend on this technique will generally underestimate prevalence because trophozoites do not appear consistently in the stools. Repeated examinations and use of serologic techniques developed in the 1980s give more accurate results for either an individual patient or an entire population. Most infections are self-limiting and treatment is effective, but reinfestation must be avoided. There is some evidence that mothers' milk helps protect infants against infection.

K. David Patterson

Bibliography

Dykes, A. C., et al. 1980. Municipal waterborne giardiasis: An epidemiological investigation. Beavers implicated as a possible reservoir. *Annals of Internal Medicine* 92: 165–70.

Gilman, R. H., et al. 1985. Epidemiology and serology of *Giardia lamblia* in a developing country: Bangladesh. *Transactions of the Royal Society of Tropical Medicine and Hygiene* 79: 469–73.

Goodman, A., et al. 1983. Gastrointestinal illness among scuba divers—New York City. *Morbidity and Mortality Weekly Report* 32: 576–7.

Kean, B. H., Kenneth E. Mott, and Adair J. Russell, eds. 1978. *Tropical medicine and parasitology: Classic investigations,* Vol. I, 169–70. Ithaca and London.

Markell, E. K., et al. 1984. Intestinal protozoa in homosexual men of the San Francisco Bay area: Prevalence and correlates of infection. *American Journal of Tropical Medicine and Hygiene* 33: 239–45.

World Health Organization. Parasitic Diseases Programme. 1986. Major parasitic infections: A global review. *World Health Statistics Quarterly* 39: 145–60.

VIII.60
Glomerulonephritis (Bright's Disease)

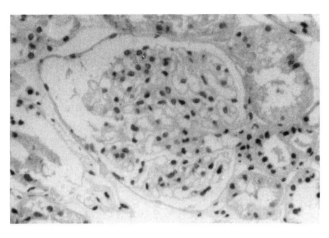

Figure VIII.60.2. Normal glomerulus. It consists largely of a tangle of tiny blood vessels (capillaries), many of which have been cut in a cross-sectional plane. They appear as spherical or oval empty spaces surrounded by a thin membrane. Many contain a nucleus (dark-stained spots) of the capillary lining (endothelial) cells.

Glomerulonephritis, an immunologic disease of the kidneys, affects the *glomerulus*. This structure, a cluster of capillaries, is the filter in the functioning unit of the kidney, the *nephron*. Inflammation, initiated by immune complexes (defined below), injures the glomerulus. Often the disease is acute, but it may be silent and completely undetected until signs and symptoms of chronic kidney failure prompt a biopsy, leading to diagnosis. Alternatively, this silent disease may prove fatal, and the diagnosis is made at autopsy.

The urine-secreting structure (nephron) (Figure VIII.60.1) consists of the glomerulus and its tubular system. Each glomerulus consists of a tangle of interconnecting capillaries branching between two tiny arteries (arterioles). A glomerular cross section shows these capillary loops (Figure VIII.60.2). The glomerulus is a blood filter that controls passage of molecules through the basement membrane, depend-

ing on their size and charge. Normally red blood cells and albumin are not permitted to pass through the membrane. The tubules reabsorb, secrete, synthesize, and excrete solutes and metabolites, thereby maintaining physiological equilibrium.

This article will deal only with poststreptococcal glomerulonephritis. This disease, described by Richard Bright in the early part of the nineteenth century, still bears his name. Other forms of glomerulonephritis, which he also described, and the glomerular diseases termed *glomerulopathies,* seen in diabetes or amyloidosis, are not discussed.

Distribution and Incidence

Glomerulonephritis occurs worldwide. The disease was seen frequently in Europe during the eighteenth and nineteenth centuries as a complication of scarlet fever during epidemics. Today glomerulonephritis occurs sporadically. Several epidemics have occurred since the 1950s in the United States, Trinidad, and Venezuela. The disease would seem to be more prevalent in the Western world, probably only because modern diagnostic aids are available. Children contract it more commonly than adults, but it occurs in all age groups. Because the disease is often silent, the exact incidence of glomerulonephritis remains unknown.

Epidemiology, Etiology, and Immunology

For more than 200 years, physicians have known that swelling of the face and extremities (dropsy) occurred

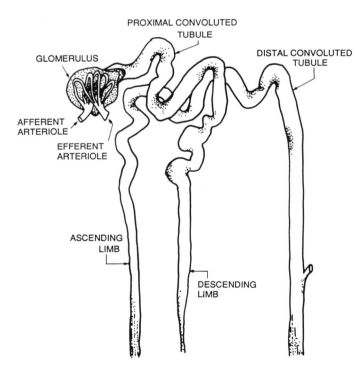

Figure VIII.60.1. Urine-secreting structure (nephron). (Modified from Arthur C. Allen. 1962. *The Kidney: Medical and Surgical Diseases,* 2d edition, 27, plate 13A. New York.)

in some individuals 10 to 14 days after bouts of scarlet fever (scarlatina). Early physicians believed that toxins, released during the fever, caused the dropsy, and long after Bright discovered the association of post-scarlatina dropsy with changes in the kidney, the role played by scarlet fever still remained a mystery. These earlier beliefs were afforded credibility with the discovery, in the latter part of the nineteenth century, that the scarlatina rash resulted from streptococcal toxins.

It was only in the latter half of the twentieth century that F. G. Germuth (1953) and F. J. Dixon and others (1961) found that rabbits developed glomerulonephritis when given injections of a foreign protein (bovine albumin). About 2 weeks after these injections, the glomerulus sustained injury from immune complexes. An *immune complex* consists of an *antigen* (the protein), an *antibody* (produced by the rabbit), and a *complement* (humoral component). Immune complexes localize in the glomerulus and damage the basement membrane. The damaged membrane leaks protein and red blood cells into the urine; swollen cells lining the capillary block the glomerular capillaries.

In humans, events mimicking this model follow certain streptococcal infections caused by "nephritogenic" strains. Before the advent of antibiotics, glomerulonephritis usually followed an attack of scarlet fever. Today, in the Western world it more often follows streptococcal infections of the throat and skin, since scarlet fever is quite uncommon. Some part (still not identified) of the streptococcus serves as the stimulus for antibody formation.

Clinical Manifestations and Pathology

Signs of kidney disease usually follow infection, but not all patients have such a history. Many have no known or recognized antecedent illness. Generalized edema is often an early symptom. Red-brown or frankly bloody urine, reduced urine volume, hypertension, and headache from fluid accumulation are other common symptoms.

In children, poststreptococcal glomerulonephritis is usually a mild disease, and most children recover without permanent kidney damage. In adults, in contrast, permanent kidney damage occurs more often. The reasons for this difference are unknown.

The main pathological changes in glomerulonephritis are an increase in glomerular cellularity (Figure VIII.60.3) and red blood cells in the tubules. With special studies, one can detect immune complexes in the glomeruli on the basement membranes. In an occasional individual, masses of cells, called *epithe-*

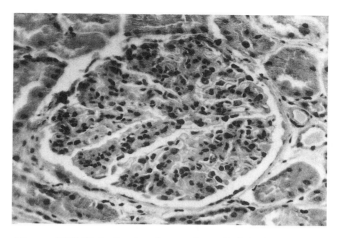

Figure VIII.60.3. Acute glomerulonephritis. As compared with Figure VIII.60.2, the glomerulus is larger and the nuclei (dark-stained spots) are both more numerous and swollen to the point of obliterating the capillary lumens, rendering them indistinguishable.

lial crescents, surround the glomeruli, and strangle blood flow to the capillaries, causing kidney failure and death to the patient unless hemodialysis is undertaken.

History and Geography

Early Accounts Through the Eighteenth Century

Dropsy, a clinical finding, occurs not only in glomerulonephritis, but also in a number of other conditions and diseases including heart failure and end-stage liver disease. There are early accounts of dropsy, and some of these certainly refer to glomerulonephritis. Glomerulonephritis also causes bloody urine, but other common causes of this symptom include urinary tract stones, tumors, and parasitic diseases.

In the writings of Rufus of Ephesus, of about A.D. 100, we read of "hardening of the kidneys." This was noted in patients who had only small amounts of urine, were free of pain, and who sometimes developed dropsy. This description could certainly be chronic glomerulonephritis. Ancient Hindu writings refer to dropsy attributed to heart disease. Avicenna, an Arabian physician and author of the *Canon*, perhaps the most famous medical text ever written, referred to patients with "chronic nephritis" around A.D. 1000.

The treatise on surgery written by Gulielmus de Saliceto of Bologna about the middle of the thirteenth century but not published until 1476, has a reference to dropsy, scanty urine, and hardened kidneys. This is chronic kidney disease, and was very likely glomerulonephritis.

In another surgical text, Peter Lowe, a Scottish physician, wrote that "hydropsie" is a "Tumor against nature, engendered of great quantitie of Water, Winde, or Flegme, which sometimes is dispersed through the whole bodie, and is called Universall," and "The cause interne of hydropsie . . . cometh . . . through the vice of the . . . kidneyes."

Scientific urinalysis, representing a major step forward from the "looking and tasting" era of the Pisse Prophets, commenced with Frederick Dekkers, who discovered in 1695 that some urine samples, like serum, would coagulate with the application of heat or the addition of acetic acid. Today we know such a coagulum as *albumin*.

In the next century, Domenico Cotugno, an anatomy professor at Naples University, was attending a young soldier with a febrile illness, who "on the fifth day had a wonderful eruption of intercutaneous water." This fluid and the urine each "contained a coagulable matter . . . over the fire." There is no indication that he knew of Dekkers' observation, and Cotugno may be the first to have noted albumin in the urine, associated with dropsy.

About this same time, Nils Rosén von Rosenstein, a Swedish physician, wrote an account of observations made during the scarlatina epidemic in Upsala in 1741:

But others . . . between the eighteenth and twenty second days, when the disease was to supposed to be quite cured . . . complained of weakness . . . and then the body began to swell, as in a dropsy [anasarca]; and upon this came on a fever, anxiety, uneasiness, oppression and asthma. Very little was discharged, and it is said to have been bloody in some patients, or appeared as water in which fresh meat has been washed.

This is an early, accurate account of post-streptococcal glomerulonephritis.

Nineteenth-Century Writings

The relationship between scarlet fever and dropsy was well recognized over the next 50 years. Thomas Bateman described eight patients with post-scarlatina dropsy seen between 1804 and 1816 in the public dispensary in London. At St. Thomas Hospital, William Charles Wells observed in 1811 that the urine in patients with dropsy after scarlet fever "contains almost always the serous, and sometimes the red matter of blood." Unaware of Cotugno's writings, he credits another with first noting, in 1798, "serum" in the urine of patients with dropsy. He

looked for serum in the urine of 130 persons who had dropsy and found it present in 78 of the samples. He also noted that "urine in dropsy, when it contains serum, is often more abundant than in health." (The increased urine volumes probably compensate for the loss of urine concentration in patients with failing kidneys.) He observed altered kidneys in one dropsical patient at autopsy who had serum in his urine, but with this limited observation did not feel justified in associating the findings with the kidney abnormalities, and wrote that "the morbid appearances in the kidneys might be altogether unconnected with morbid secretion. . . ."

In 1818 John Blackall also observed dropsy, albuminuria, and bloody urine in patients after scarlatina. Sometimes these patients at autopsy had "kidneys firmer than the ordinary, in one of them very strikingly so, approaching the scirrhus; but whether this is merely accidental, or the effect of such a course and what relation it bears to the discharge of serum must be left for future observations."

Those observations were soon to be made by Bright, a giant of medicine, who was conducting his landmark studies as a staff physician at Guy's Hospital in London, on patients with post-scarlatina dropsy and albuminuria. In 1827, he first reported his findings and wrote, "The observations which I have made respecting the condition of the urine in dropsy, are in a great degree in accordance with what had been laid down by Dr. Blackall in his most valuable treatise." Bright's meticulously recorded accounts of the clinical features of the disease, and his colored illustrations of the pathological changes in the kidneys, remain a model for us today. He firmly established that dropsy was accompanied by pathological changes in the kidneys. His studies, however, did not address the question of how albumin enters the urine. This question could not be answered until nephron structure was further defined.

Marcello Malpighi had tried to answer the question in 1666 at Bologna. He knew of the glomeruli, and that they could be filled by injected dye into the blood vessels, but his frustration in being unable to establish their function is indicated in his writing:

I worked a long time in order that I might subject to the eye this evident connection [between "glands" and tubules] *which reason sufficiently attests. For I have never been able* to observe liquids perfused through the arteries penetrating the urinary vessels, even though they fill the glands, and the same is true when the veins are filled. . . . So that, in spite of many attempts (but in vain) I could not demonstrate the connection of the glands and the urinary vessels. (Italics mine)

In the early nineteenth century, the Berlin school, led by Johannes Peter Mueller, dominated anatomy and physiology in Europe. Mueller knew of Malpighi's descriptions of the glomeruli, but he considered them to be simply receptacles of blood. He believed that urine was secreted by the epithelium of the proximal tubules.

But William Bowman in 1842 (then just 26 years old) wondered, as Malpighi had, why the glomerulus would end blindly in a space opening into the tubules. He wrote:

It would indeed be difficult to conceive a disposition of parts more calculated to favour the escape of water from the blood than that of the Malpighian body.... Why is so wonderful an apparatus placed at the extremity of each uriniferous tube, if not to furnish water, to aid in the separation and solution of the urinous products from the epithelium of the tube? This abundance of water is apparently intended to serve chiefly as a menstruum for the proximate principles and salts which this secretion contains, and which, in speaking generally, are far less soluble than those of any other animal product.

Bowman suggested that protein and red cells might pass through the glomerulus under abnormal circumstances!

A German physiologist, Carl Ludwig, followed up on Bowman's anatomic observations just a few years later, with the view that the glomerulus was a semipermeable filter. Hydrostatic pressure pushed fluids through the capillaries that held back the proteins. In 1861 Thomas Graham showed that membranes could hold back colloids but permit the passage of crystalloids. The glomerulus was established as the source of urine, but albuminuria was still thought to come from tubular epithelium. For many years the term *nephrosis* was used to express this belief and define proteinuric states.

Through the rest of the nineteenth century, pathologists adhered to this view, even as microscopic studies advanced. The source of urinary albumin in dropsy was not determined for more than a century.

Bright's descriptions of the kidney contained no records of microscopic examination. Rudolph Virchow established the cellular basis for pathology in 1858, and classified Bright's disease into three categories – involving the tubules, the connective tissue, and the blood vessels. In some of his later writings, he referred to glomerular changes, but he continued to believe the main changes were in the tubules. The first pathologist to use the word "glomerulonephritis" was Edwin Klebs in 1879. The term became synonymous with Bright's disease after F. Volhard and T. Fahr (1914, in Heptinstall 1983, Vol. 1) intro-

duced it into their classification. That classification remained in use with little modification for nearly a half century.

The active use of biopsy to evaluate the nature of the kidney disorder in the patient was also an important clinical contribution. As biopsy experiences accumulated in the 1950s, 1960s, and 1970s, clinical and pathological classifications of Bright's disease appeared in large numbers. Basic science investigators gave us an understanding of the important role of the immune system in glomerulonephritis, and they established the glomerular basement membrane as the site of leakage in albuminuric states. The tubule is *not* the source of the urine protein, but altered tubular reabsorption possibly plays a lesser role in albuminuria. The major contributions of pathology in the twentieth century are the use of thin sections, immunofluorescent techniques, and electron microscopy in biopsy interpretation.

Thus, today Bright's disease consists of many different disorders, all of which can be considered glomerulonephritis. The diagnosis and management of these disorders will continue to challenge clinicians, pathologists, and basic science investigators into the twenty-first century.

Donald M. Larson

Bibliography

Bright, Richard. 1827. *Reports of medical cases, selected with a view of illustrating the symptoms of cure of diseases by a reference to morbid anatomy.* London.

1836. Cases and observations illustrative of renal disease accompanied with the secretion of albuminous urine. *Guy's Hospital Reports* I: 338–400.

Castiglioni, Arturo. 1975. *A history of medicine,* trans. E. B. Krumbhaar. New York.

Dixon, F. J., J. D. Feldman, and J. J. Vazquez. 1961. Experimental glomerulonephritis: The pathogenesis of a laboratory model resembling the spectrum of human glomerulonephritis. *Journal of Experimental Medicine* 113: 899–920.

Germuth, F. G., Jr. 1953. A comparative histologic and immunologic study in rabbits of induced hypersensitivity of the serum sickness type. *Journal of Experimental Medicine* 97: 257–82.

Heptinstall, Robert H. 1983. *Pathology of the kidney,* 2 vols. Boston and Toronto.

Major, Ralph H. 1932. *Classic descriptions of disease.* Springfield, Ill.

1954. *A history of medicine,* Vols. I and II. Springfield, Ill.

Talbott, John H. 1970. *A biographical history of medicine.* New York.

VIII.61
Goiter

Quis tumidum guttur miratur in Alpibus?
Juvenal, *Satire 13,* c. A.D. 127

Goiter is an ancient disease that has always been more common in some places than in others. Chinese writings show that goiter was known at least by the third century B.C. (Lee 1941) and possibly earlier (Needham et al. 1970). When Juvenal (Decimus Junius Juvenalis), the Roman satirist, wrote, about A.D. 127, "Who is amazed at a swollen neck in the Alps?" he knew that goiter was so much more common there than elsewhere that it should be no surprise.

Terminology

The word "goiter" (or *goitre* in Europe) derives from the Latin *gutter,* but the meaning has shifted from "throat" or "neck" to mean specifically an enlarged thyroid gland. An ancient Greek synonym was *bronchocele,* a term actually used to describe any enlargement in the neck, although it meant literally a swelling or an outpouching of the trachea. Over time this term also came to mean an enlarged thyroid (e.g., the English "bronchocele" of the eighteenth and nineteenth centuries). Modern synonyms are the Spanish *bocio* (from Latin, *botium*), the Italian *gozzo,* and the German *Kropf.* The ancient Latin word *struma* was probably originally used to describe inflamed lymph nodes in the neck, most likely tuberculous, but was later used to denote the normal thyroid gland, and is still so used although it is almost obsolete.

Confusion over names is understandable, as the thyroid gland itself was unknown until the sixteenth century. Leonardo da Vinci may have drawn the thyroid about the year 1500, but the drawing was not published until much later. Andreas Vesalius did note "laryngeal glands" in 1543, but not in humans. Nevertheless, by the end of the sixteenth century, Vesalius's contemporaries and successors had clearly identified the human thyroid gland as a discrete structure: Bartolomeo Eustachi in 1552, Realdo Colombo in 1558, and Giulio Casserio in 1600. In 1619, Hieronymus Fabricius ab Aquapendente realized that goiter arises from an enlargement of this gland, and in 1656 Thomas Wharfton named the gland by virtue of its proximity to the thyroid ("shield-shaped") cartilage.

Classification and Diagnosis

Although shown on an occasional autopsy or dissection, the connection between goiter and the thyroid gland was not clear as a concept. Other diseases of the neck confounded the connection in a living patient. The main confounder was *scrofula,* which in medieval Latin meant "swelling of the glands" and today is still used to connote tuberculous lymph glands (or nodes) in the neck.

Because obvious and severe goiter affecting large portions of a population occurred only in certain regions, the disease in these areas was called *endemic.* In these instances the connection to the thyroid gland was fairly clear. But where only a few individuals in a population had a mass in the neck, it might be called *sporadic* goiter – because not endemic – or something else. If the mass was not too large, it might move with swallowing and so was called an *enlarged* thyroid. But if the mass were nodular, firm, and immovable, then it was considered to be probably characterized by tuberculous nodes. This diagnostic confusion persisted until the mid-nineteenth century. Jean Louis Alibert, for example, classified endemic goiter as a type of scrofula ("endemic scrofula") found in rural areas (Alibert 1835). Today endemic goiter is arbitrarily defined; it is present, according to some, if more than 10 percent of a population is goitrous.

Besides the occasional large and disfiguring goiters that were cosmetically distressing and sometimes blocked breathing, endemic goiter areas also produced a much smaller number of people who were retarded from birth, both mentally and physically, whose faces were disfigured, and who were sometimes deaf and mute. Most but not all had goiter, which was also common in their mothers. They were called *cretins,* and their disease, *endemic cretinism.* The word "cretin" probably derives from the French *crétien,* and thence from the Latin *christianus* (or Christian); the term was probably used to make clear that these persons were truly human.

Cretinism is probably as ancient a disease as goiter, but descriptions are not as old. Travelers' observations, again in the Alps, go back to the early thirteenth century, but clinical allusions begin with Paracelsus (Theophrastus Bombastus von Hohenheim), lecturing about 1527, who connected cretinism (or at least "fools") with goiter. Good descriptions begin with Felix Platter, who probably observed it in 1562 and who also made the association of cretinism with goiter (Cranefield 1962).

Thus, by the seventeenth century, the concept of

goiter as an abnormally enlarged thyroid gland was reasonably well established as was its association with cretinism and with the mountainous alpine areas of Europe. Yet, cretinism in particular was rare outside densely goitrous sites in the Alps, and thus most European physicians never saw it. Just as goiter could be confounded with other neck diseases, so could cretinism with any sort of mental retardation. Thus a certain amount of diagnostic "fuzziness" persisted into the nineteenth and twentieth centuries.

Today goiter means only an enlarged thyroid, and any large thyroid is a goiter. The goiter may be uniformly and diffusely enlarged ("simple" or diffuse goiter), have several lumps in it (multinodular goiter), or be only a single nodule, although on closer study many of the latter prove to be multinodular. The standard screening method of the World Health Organization in endemic areas is to assign gradations to the disorder. Grade O is no goiter, grade 1 is a goiter that is palpable but not visible, grade 2 is an easily visible goiter, and grade 3 is a very large goiter visible 30 meters away (Stanbury and Hetzel, eds. 1980).

Some goiters are malignant (e.g., thyroid cancer or lymphoma), but the vast majority are benign. Some are associated with specific thyroid diseases such as *hyperthyroidism* (an overactive thyroid); its opposite, *hypothyroidism* (an underactive thyroid; such as in goitrous cretinism); and *thyroiditis* (an inflammation of the thyroid that can be acute or chronic). The taxonomies (geographic, clinical, and etiologic) persist today, derived from different types of data with different historical origins. They overlap considerably and continue to give rise to confusion in diagnosis and treatment.

Cretinism is called *endemic* if it is found in an area of endemic goiter, but is called *sporadic* if not found in an endemic area; the latter is almost always nongoitrous. Again, entirely different causes underlie the two types. Both goiter and cretinism, whether endemic or sporadic, can be associated with hypothyroidism, although the notion that cretinism is synonymous with childhood hypothyroidism is false. Hypothyroidism is common but not universal in cretinism, and it occurs only occasionally with goiter.

Early Treatment

Goiter of itself is not particularly harmful unless it grows to compress the trachea or causes emotional upset. But when therapy for a large goiter was required, the only solution until the twentieth century was to remove it, or at least part of it, surgically. The problem was that surgery commonly killed the patient, and some surgeons said that such an operation should simply not be done. Others persisted, and by the 1880s were able to remove all or most of a goitrous thyroid with death rates under 1 percent.

E. Theodor Kocher in Berne and the cousins Jacques-Louis and Auguste Reverdin in Geneva were pioneers in this surgery. In 1882–3, however, these Swiss surgeons realized that removing the entire thyroid caused symptoms resembling cretinism, but that this did not happen when only part of the thyroid was taken out. Simultaneously in London, Felix Semon proposed that cretins, patients after total thyroid removal, and adults with a mysterious disorder called *myxedema* (described by William Withey Gull in 1873) all suffered because they lacked thyroid glands. He was ridiculed, but 5 years later a committee appointed to investigate this theory found Semon to be correct (Ord 1888). Thyroid deficiency or myxedema, now called *hypothyroidism,* is a synonym for decreased thyroid function or a lack of thyroid hormone secretion.

Etiology

Early Theories

Many theories were generated over the centuries to explain goiter. An ancient idea was that goiter is due to an excess of phlegm descending from the head to the throat. An excessive flexing of the head was seen as the cause by many, including Michelangelo (Michelagniolo Buonarroti), who suggested it in 1509. Geographic peculiarities were frequently blamed as well, such as high altitude or narrow valleys, as were climatic features such as high humidity, too much sun, and polluted air, proposed by physicians such as Horatio-Bénédict de Saussure in 1779 and F. E. Fodéré in 1789. Differences in drinking water were also viewed with suspicion, especially cold water, water made from snow, and water from streams or springs believed to be tainted. Finally, hereditary or constitutional factors were thought important; that idea is attributed to Jacques de Vitry about A.D. 1220.

Nineteenth-Century Theories

During the nineteenth century, the major theories of the etiology of goiter focused at least in part on some peculiarity of the drinking water, a lack of iodine, an infection of some sort, or some combination of these.

Climatic factors had been dismissed when it turned out that goiter can occur in almost any climate, dry or wet, from the Arctic to the equator (Hirsch 1885). High altitude had been rejected as well, for the disease was not limited to mountainous regions; flatlands had endemic goiter as well.

The long process of linking endemic goiter and cretinism to iodine deficiency began in 1811, when Bernard Courtois discovered the element while making saltpeter for gunpowder during the Napoleonic Wars. He noticed it as a violet vapor released from the residue of burnt seaweed by sulfuric acid. It was subsequently named iodine by Joseph Louis Gay-Lussac from the Greek word for "violet." The key was the seaweed. For hundreds of years, dating at least from the twelfth and thirteenth centuries in Europe, and from the third century A.D. in China, seaweed and marine sponge had been placed among the many animal and vegetable remedies for goiter, sometimes burned before use. Within a few years after Courtois' discovery, iodine was detected in various seaweeds by Humphry Davy, Gay-Lussac, and Andrew Fyfe.

In 1818, Jean-François Coindet, a Geneva physician, suggested that because some seaweeds were effective in treating goiter, iodine might be the active principle. He asked Jean-Baptiste Dumas (then aged 18 and later to become one of France's most famous chemists) to look for iodine in marine sponge; Dumas did and found it (Thorpe 1902). Coindet then gave iodine, mostly as potassium iodide, to goitrous patients, with good results that were almost immediately confirmed by other Swiss physicians.

An effective therapy, however, does not necessarily mean that a disease is due to a deficiency of the therapeutic agent. (Few would suggest, for example, that pneumococcal pneumonia results from penicillin deficiency.) Thus although the chemist Jean Baptiste Boussingault suggested as early as 1825 that iodine deficiency might be the cause of goiter and recommended the addition of iodine to table salt to prevent it, little came of this suggestion.

A generation later, Jean-Louis Prévost, another Geneva physician, made the same suggestion as Boussingault. But iodine had fallen into disfavor as therapy for goiter because of toxic side effects when given in excess, including (in retrospect) iodine-induced hyperthyroidism. Coindet himself had seen this (he used a dose of 1 to 2 grains of iodine per day) and had cautioned against too high a dose, but to no avail.

In the 1850s, Adolphe Chatin, a French pharma-cist and botanist, using a somewhat better assay for iodine, found the element in *freshwater* plants and suggested these plants be used to prevent goiter (Chatin 1850a). He went on to measure iodine in water samples from all over France, and in some foods as well, and concluded that a lack of iodine in drinking water in certain areas appeared to be the principal cause of goiter (Chatin 1850b). The following year, the French Academy of Sciences appointed a committee to study Chatin's results; its report (Thénard et al. 1852) congratulated Chatin for his work, but viewed the association between a lack of iodine and goiter as unproven.

There were successful trials of iodine prophylaxis of endemic goiter in the nineteenth century, notably in South America in 1835 (Dumas et al. 1851) and in Savoy in the 1840s. Yet success did not encourage further trials, and the question of iodine as a goiter preventive was not pursued.

The rise of the "new pathology" with Rudolph Virchow as its leader in the mid-nineteenth century also interfered with the idea of iodine deficiency as the cause of endemic goiter. During the 1860s Virchow himself felt that excessive growth of a tissue, in this case goiter, must be due to some irritation that stemmed from a "positive substance" and not a deficiency (Follis 1960). In France the view persisted that goiter and cretinism were serious problems but that the cause was not iodine deficiency. Rather, an *agent toxique spécial* was thought to be responsible (Baillarger 1873).

The reluctance to accept iodine deficiency as a cause of goiter is understandable: There was then no good example of a disease known to be caused by a deficiency. Further, the theory did not explain why only some people in low-iodine areas got goiter while others did not. This problem remains unresolved today.

Later in the nineteenth century, after the discovery of the bacterial cause of many diseases, it was postulated that goiter was caused by either a bacterium or a bacterial toxin, perhaps in the water. Edwin Klebs, a pioneer microbiologist, believed he had found such an agent in 1877, and August Hirsch (1885) stated flatly that "endemic goitre and cretinism have to be reckoned among the infective diseases." Indeed, the notion that goiter has an infectious cause had its twentieth-century adherents at least until mid-century, although the evidence put forth has never been convincing. But while the infectious hypothesis has faded, the parallel notion of a toxin in the water, possibly of bacterial origin, is still alive (Gaitan et al. 1983) and warrants serious consideration, particularly in areas where there is much goiter despite adequate iodine intake.

Iodine as a therapy in medicine, in contrast to its use solely to treat goiter, caught on rapidly in the decade after its discovery. Beginning in the late 1820s, for example, Jean-G. A. Lugol, another Geneva physician whose name is memorialized in the still-used Lugol's solution of iodide–iodine, employed it against any scrofulous disease (Lugol 1829). Its use spread rapidly to include treatment of other conditions, among them rheumatic diseases, almost any pulmonary condition, any disease that involved swelling of a part of the body, and syphilis. Late-nineteenth-century texts on medicine and pharmacology indicate its continued wide use while recognizing the hazards of overdosage (Wood 1881; Pepper 1894; Osler 1892). Iodine as therapy for goiter did persist (Inglis 1838; Wood 1881) but only as one of several possible treatments (Pepper 1894; Osler 1896) and was employed without much enthusiasm.

In sum, up to the 1890s there was no resolution of the problem of the cause of endemic goiter or cretinism. No clear choice could be made among the drinking water, iodine deficiency, or toxic-infective hypotheses. Prophylaxis of goiter with iodine on a mass scale was not popular and hence not done. Fear of inducing serious side effects if everyone took iodine in salt or food was widespread since, after all, iodine was a known poison. Social and political issues frequently arose, similar to those that surround questions of the chlorination or fluoridation of water.

It was in the 1890s, however, that substantial advances began to be made in goiter research. George R. Murray (1891) discovered that a glycerin extract of sheep thyroid cured myxedema (hypothyroidism). After this, investigators began to look for iodine in the thyroid gland itself. Eugen Baumann (1895), for example, in looking for the active compound in the thyroid, made a fairly potent extract. When analyzing that extract, he routinely looked for iodine, not expecting to find it; to his surprise it was there.

Twentieth-Century Theories

From this point research diverged: One path led to the isolation of a specific thyroid hormone, *thyroxine,* by Edward C. Kendall in 1914 (Kendall 1915) at the Mayo Clinic; and another led to studies relating goiter to the iodine content of the thyroid rather than to that of the environment.

David Marine came to Cleveland, Ohio, an area of endemic goiter, in 1905. He was aware of the importance of *hyperplasia* – the process that leads to

goiter – through William Halsted, his teacher at Johns Hopkins Medical School. By 1910, he showed that iodine prevented goiter in brook trout (Marine 1910), and therefore gave it to patients at Cleveland's Lakeside Hospital and to children of friends to prevent goiter. In fact, he tried to give it to all schoolchildren in Cleveland, but the school board, led by a goiter surgeon, said it would poison the children. (At the time there was also a controversy over compulsory smallpox vaccination.) Not until several years later was Marine able to carry out a large-scale study of iodine prophylaxis for goiter. The results were clear-cut: Sixty-five percent of goiters became smaller, whereas this happened in only 14 percent of the control group, and new goiter was largely prevented (0.2 percent got new goiter among those treated versus 21 percent for those untreated) (Marine and Kimball 1920). This study provided the impetus, in the United States, for the use of iodized salt, which now contains 0.01 percent potassium iodide.

Even though Marine showed iodine to be both a treatment and a preventive for endemic goiter, he had not proven that these patients were iodine deficient. It remained for J. F. McClendon, a nutrition officer in the U.S. Army during World War I, to measure accurately iodine in water and food. He showed not only that there was a correlation between lower iodine in food or water and the presence of human goiter, but also that rats on a low-iodine diet got goiter (McClendon and Williams 1923). He later put together worldwide data to support his thesis that low iodine in the water causes goiter (McClendon 1939); although the data in general did support the idea, close reading shows many exceptions.

By 1924, Michigan, a state with endemic goiter, offered iodized salt to the public after an intense public education campaign; within 12 years goiter prevalence fell from 37 percent to 8 percent and, by 1951, to 2 percent. Ohio, Marine's own state, never acted. Still, Marine's statement that "endemic goiter is the easiest known disease to prevent," though a bit hyperbolic, was finally shown to be reasonably correct.

Over the years since Marine's study, the average daily iodine intake in the United States has increased several times not only because of iodized salt (the label now says that iodine is "a necessary nutrient"), but because of the widespread use of purchased foods that contain iodine, such as bread and milk. Thus, in the United States, few can today develop iodine deficiency, and, as in countries with similar food sources, goiter is mostly sporadic and occurs either spontaneously or as a result of factors other than iodine deficiency, such as exposure to therapeutic X-rays (DeGroot et al. 1983) or radiation from atomic fallout (Hamilton et al. 1987; Morimoto et al. 1987). Sporadic goiter is also called *nontoxic goiter,* meaning that the patient is not hyperthyroid. Sporadic goiter can be any of the clinical types (i.e., diffuse or nodular). Yet, some areas of endemic goiter persist in the United States, especially in parts of Appalachia, and may be caused by a *goitrogen* (a substance that causes goiter). Goitrogens certainly exist, but how much they contribute to human goiter is unclear (Delange and Ermans 1976).

Prevention and Treatment

In many other parts of the world, both rich (Scriba et al. 1985) and poor (Prevention 1986), goiter remains endemic (World Health Organization 1960; Stanbury and Hetzel 1980) with its attendant disfigurement, cretinism, and hypothyroidism. It is worth noting that persons in an endemic area could have any of the diseases that cause sporadic goiter, which is one reason why goiter prevalence never falls to zero even with iodine repletion. For some areas this endemia is a major public health problem, and millions of people remain at risk. The disease, when endemic, is almost always associated with low iodine intake and iodine deficiency, and while there remains no good explanation as to why some do not develop goiter in areas of low dietary iodine, iodine does prevent the disease. The issue then becomes a social and political one of providing iodine to those in deficient areas and then getting them to take it. As Marine wrote, "Endemic goiter will be prevented only when society decides to do it."

If a large goiter already exists, however, iodine will likely not be of help and surgery may be needed. On the other hand, thyroid therapy alone can shrink some goiters, as was shown as early as 1894 (Bruns 1894; Reinhold 1894), and prevent recurrence of others after surgery even if the goiter is cancerous (Mazzaferri and Young 1981). Thus thyroid hormone can be the initial treatment for goiter and should be used after any goiter surgery.

Therapies for endemic and sporadic goiter and cretinism are fairly straightforward, although some disagree on details of testing or timing. In developed countries they are easy to apply in principle; the major problems are societal and relate to detection and prevention. In less developed countries the public health aspects are paramount, especially where budgets are limited; prevention of endemic goiter and cretinism is an effective use of funds.

Conclusions

Overall, changes in how goiter was defined progressed erratically. As theories and techniques employed in anatomy and pathology were developed, the concept of "goiter" shifted from the simplistic idea of a swollen neck, to an enlarged thyroid of several types, to a range of different thyroid diseases. However, early taxonomies did not disappear but persisted along with the new.

Along with these changes in taxonomy came parallel changes in purported causes and the possibilities of prevention. Focusing for the moment only on *iodine,* one can demonstrate a continuous link from the Chinese use of seaweed through the European Middle Ages and folk medicine, to the discovery and use of the element in the nineteenth and twentieth centuries. In actuality, however, although empirical "folk" medicines containing iodine were effective against goiter, they were used along with many others that seem to have had no benefit. Nineteenth-century French physicians may have been "right" in proposing iodine as a treatment for endemic goiter, but they did not convince their colleagues. That iodine deficiency might cause goiter was confounded by iodine's use in goiter treatment and prophylaxis; furthermore, the technical inability to measure consistently and accurately small amounts of iodine led to persistent and valid controversy. Improvements in the iodine assay in the late nineteenth and early twentieth centuries provided a solid basis for resurrecting earlier beliefs in its effectiveness; moreover, because it was thought that iodine *ought* to prevent endemic goiter, the studies were done that proved it. But the pendulum then swung to the other extreme, with many researchers believing that iodine was the answer to all endemic goiter. It was not, however, and we now face the scientific challenge of teasing out several probable factors in addition to iodine deficiency that can produce endemic goiter, as well as the political challenge involved in iodine prophylaxis on a worldwide basis.

In conclusion, *sporadic goiter* is usually not due to iodine deficiency but is mainly the result of an intrinsic thyroid disease, often related to genetic, immunologic, or enzymatic factors; it is apparently influenced by gender, as it is more common in women. *Sporadic cretinism* (or *neonatal hypothyroidism*) is almost never caused by iodine deficiency, but is usually the result of failure of the thyroid gland to develop; thus there is no goiter. For this condition, a public health approach, with testing of all newborns, is mandatory to prevent irreversible brain damage. On the other hand, *endemic goiter* and *cretinism* are usually related to a low dietary iodine, although goitrogens, genetic, and immunologic factors may be operative in some locales. Taking iodine cures some and prevents almost all; again a public health approach is essential.

Clark T. Sawin

Bibliography

Alibert, J.-L. 1835. *Monographie des dermatoses ou précis théorique et pratique des maladies de la peau*, 2d edition. Paris.

Baillarger, J. G. F. 1873. Enquête sur le goitre et le crétinisme. Reviewed in: *Gazette Hebdomadaire de Médicine et de Chirurgie*, 2d ser., 10: 807.

Baumann, E. 1895. Ueber das normale Vorkommen von Jod im Thierkörper. *Hoppe-Seyler's Zeitschrift für Physiologische Chemie* 21: 319–30.

Bruns, P. 1894. Ueber die Kropfbehandlung mit Schildrüsenfütterung. *Deutsche Medizinische Wochenschrift* 41: 785–6.

Chatin, A. 1850a. Existence de l'iode dans les plantes d'eau douce: Consequences de ce fait pour la géognosie, la physiologie végétale, la thérapeutique et peut-être pour l'industrie. *Comtes Rendus Hebdomadaires de l'Académie des Sciences* 30: 352–4.

 1850b. Recherches sur l'iode des eaux douce (suite): De la présence de ce corps dans les plantes et les animaux terrestres. *Comtes Rendus Hebdomadaires de l'Académie des Sciences* 31: 280–3.

Cranefield, P. F. 1962. The discovery of cretinism. *Bulletin of the History of Medicine* 36: 489–511.

DeGroot, L. J., et al. 1983. Retrospective and prospective study of radiation-induced thyroid disease. *American Journal of Medicine* 74: 852–62.

Delange, F. M., and A. M. Ermans. 1976. Endemic goiter and cretinism: Naturally occurring goitrogens. *Pharmacology and therapy [C]* 1: 57–93.

Dumas, (J.-B.), et al. 1851. Rapport sur les recherches de M. le Dr. Grange, relatives aux causes du crétinisme et du goître, et aux moyens d'en préserver les populations. *Comtes Rendus Hebdomadaires de l'Académie des Sciences* 32: 611–18.

Follis, R. H., Jr. 1960. Cellular pathology and the development of the deficiency disease concept. *Bulletin of the History of Medicine* 34: 291–317.

Gaitan, E., et al. 1983. In vitro measurement of antithyroid compounds and environmental goitrogens. *Journal of Clinical Endocrinology and Metabolism* 56: 767–73.

Hamilton, T. E., et al. 1987. Thyroid neoplasia in Marshall Islanders exposed to nuclear fallout. *Journal of the American Medical Association* 258: 629–366.

Harington, C. R. 1933. *The thyroid gland: Its chemistry and physiology*. London. [A historical chapter on goiter and cretinism.]

Hirsch, A. 1885. *Handbook of geographical and historical pathology*, Vol. II. *Chronic infective, toxic, parasitic, septic and constitutional diseases,* trans. C. Creighton, from the 2nd German edition. London.

Inglis, J. 1838. *Treatise on English bronchocele with a few remarks on the use of iodine and its compounds*. London.

Kendall, E. C. 1915. The isolation in crystalline form of the compound which occurs in the thyroid: Its chemical nature and physiologic activity. *Journal of the American Medical Association* 64: 2042–3.

Lee, T. 1941. A brief history of the endocrine disorders in China. *Chinese Medical Journal* 59: 379–86.

Lugol, J.-G.-A. 1829. *Mémoire sur l'emploi de l'iode dans les maladies scrophuleuses*. Paris.

Marine, D., and C. H. Lenhart. 1910. On the occurrence of goitre (active thyroid hyperplasia) in fish. *Bulletin of Johns Hopkins Hospital* 21: 95–8.

Marine, D., and O. P. Kimball. 1920. Prevention of simple goiter in man. *Archives of Internal Medicine* 25: 661–72.

Matovinovic, J. 1983. Endemic goiter and cretinism at the dawn of the third millennium. *Annual Review of Nutrition* 3: 341–412.

Mazzaferri, E. L., and R. L. Young. 1981. Papillary thyroid carcinoma: A 10-year follow-up report of the impact of therapy in 576 patients. *American Journal of Medicine* 70: 511–18.

McClendon, J. F. 1939. *Iodine and the incidence of goiter*. Minneapolis.

McClendon, J. F., and A. Williams. 1923. Experimental goitre and iodine in natural waters in relation to distribution of goitre. *Proceedings of the Society for Experimental Biology and Medicine* 20: 286–7.

Merke, F. 1984. *History and iconography of endemic goitre and cretinism*. Berne-Hingham. [An excellent guide to older works.]

Morimoto, T., et al. 1987. Serum TSH, thyroglobulin, and thyroidal disorders in atomic bomb survivors exposed in youth: 30-year follow-up study. *Journal of Nuclear Medicine* 28: 1115–22.

Murray, G. R. 1891. Note on the treatment of myxoedema by hypodermic injections of an extract of the thyroid gland of a sheep. *British Medical Journal* 2: 796–7.

Needham, J., et al. 1970. Proto-endocrinology in medieval China. In *Clerks and craftsmen in China and the West*. Cambridge.

Ord, W. M. (chairman). 1888. Report of a committee of the Clinical Society of London nominated December 14, 1883, to investigate the subject of myxoedema. *Transactions of the Clinical Society of London* 21 (Supplement): 1–215.

Osler, W. 1892. *The principles and practice of medicine*, 1st edition. New York.

 1896. *The principles and practice of medicine*, 2d edition. New York.

Pepper, W., ed. 1894. *A textbook of the theory and practice of medicine by American teachers*, Vol. 2, 1021–2. Philadelphia.

Prevention and control of iodine deficiency disorders. 1986. *Lancet* 2: 433–4.

Reinhold, G. 1894. Ueber Schilddrüsen Therapie bei kropf-leidenden Geisteskranken. *Münchener medizinische Wochenschrift* 41: 613–14.

Rolleston, H. D. 1936. *The endocrine organs in health and disease with an historical review.* London. [See especially pp. 192–207.]

Scriba, P. C., et al. 1985. Goitre and iodine deficiency in Europe. *Lancet* 1: 1289–93.

Stanbury, J. B., and B. S. Hetzel, eds., 1980. *Endemic goiter and endemic cretinism: Iodine nutrition in health and disease.* New York. [A modern detailed text.]

Thénard, L. J., et al. 1852. Rapport sur les travaux de M. Chatin, relatifs à la recherche de l'iode, et sur différentes notes ou mémoires présentés sur le même sujet, par MM. Marchand, Nièpce, Meyrac. *Comtes Rendus Hebdomadaires de l'Académie des Sciences* 35: 505–17.

Thorpe, T. E. 1902. *Essays on historical chemistry.* London.

Wood, H. C., Jr. 1881. *A treatise on therapeutics,* 3d edition. Philadelphia.

World Health Organization (WHO). 1960. *Endemic goitre.* Geneva. [Strong on epidemiology with good maps and a short historical chapter.]

VIII.62
Gonorrhea

The name *gonorrhea,* which means "flow of seed," and its vernacular counterparts ("clap," "dose," "strain"), reflect a hazy comprehension of the disease. The only accurate term in common use is "drip," which acknowledges the white-to-yellowish milky discharge from the male penis. But even this more honest description includes only the male urethral portion of a broader syndrome.

Gonorrhea is an infection of mucosal surfaces caused by a small gram-negative bacterium – the gonococcus – whose only reservoir in nature is human. Its presence in the lower male or female genital tract defines the condition gonorrhea; otherwise, the adjective "gonococcal" is used to precede a generic infective syndrome (as in "gonococcal endocarditis"). Though gonorrhea is transmitted primarily to genital mucosa through sexual contact, it may cause localized abscesses or generalized dissemination, with infection of the skin, heart valves, joints, and central nervous system. It is rarely the cause of death, but, if untreated, it produces serious sequelae in both men and women.

The gonococcus, *Neisseria gonorrhoeae,* shares an ecological niche with other sexually transmitted pathogens such as *Chlamydia trachomatis, Ureaplasma ureslyticum,* and *T-mycoplasmas.* It depends for its survival on variable virulence, sufficient numbers of asymptomatic infectees, an ability to produce a rapid genomic response to antibiotic pressure, a symbiotic relationship with new pieces of genetic material (called *plasmids*), and propitious set of social and sexual mores among its hosts. As history demonstrates, this seemingly delicate balance has been universally available.

Etiology and Diagnosis

The causative agent of gonorrhea is the gonococcus (*N. gonorrhoeae*) – a small, diplococcus whose flattened apposing surfaces, tinctorial properties (when stained by Gram's method), and association with polymorphonuclear leukocytes provide a typical microscopic picture. In certain sites (e.g., urethra, joint, cerebrospinal fluid, ocular conjunctiva), demonstration of the typical morphology is virtually diagnostic. From other sites (rectum, pharynx), however, the possible presence of other gonorrhea types renders the Gram-stained smear less sensitive. For all sites, culture of the organism on artificial media is required for diagnostic assurance. Confirmation requires typical morphology, demonstration of indophenol oxidase production, and the ability of the organism to metabolize glucose, but not fructose, maltose, sucrose, or mannitol.

Clinical Manifestations

Genital Site Infections in Men and Women

Pus issuing from the penile opening, often accompanied by discomfort, pain, or burning on urination, is the most frequently recognized clinical manifestation of gonorrhea. The gonococcus adheres to cells that line the distal urethra, establishing – in the symptomatic individual – an inflammatory reaction and the subsequent outpouring of polymorphonuclear leukocytes. (This primary pathological process is basically the same at all mucosal sites of infection.) Though the majority of men will become symptomatic 3 to 5 days after adequate exposure, the clinical spectrum varies. In perhaps one-quarter of patients, pain or discharge will be attenuated or subsymptomatic (i.e., insufficient to cause the patient to seek medical care). In addition, a substantial proportion of men with gonorrhea will be asymptomatic. Before the advent of antibiotics, the major sequelae of male urethral infection were postinflammatory fibrosis and stricture of the urethra. Such complications are now rare.

Though women have long been known to harbor the organism, only recently have distinct clinical syndromes been identified. Part of the delay is due to the fact that asymptomatic infection probably occurs more frequently in women, and little clinical attention is paid to the "normal" vaginal discharge. Infection of the female urethra occurs in 70 to 90 percent of women with gonorrhea, but rarely in the absence of concomitant infection of the endocervix. The more important lower tract manifestation of gonorrhea in women is infection of the uterine cervix. A syndrome of purulent or mucopurulent endocervical discharge characterizes the infection. Though the clinical diagnosis may be complicated by the coexistence of infection with other pathogenic organisms, cervical mucopus is clearly not "normal" and requires systematic bacteriologic investigation.

Both sexes contract anal and throat infection from direct exposure to infected penile secretions. Both are associated with symptoms in a minority of cases. Asymptomatic rectal infection probably plays a major role in transmission. Throat infection is of minor importance, except as a site for dissemination of the gonococcus into the bloodstream.

Pelvic Inflammatory Disease (PID)

Perhaps the major modern concern about gonorrhea is its potential for destruction of female reproductive organs. The gonococcus may spread upward from the cervix to inflame the uterine lining of the fallopian tubes (salpingitis) and ultimately cause peritonitis. Once established, PID becomes chronic, of long duration, and with serious consequences. Approximately 20 percent of women will have a recurrence after treatment for a primary episode of gonococcal PID. The syndrome of chronic pain, lower abdominal discomfort, and dyspareunia reflects insidious scarring and closure of the fallopian tubes, which may cause ectopic pregnancy and lead ultimately to involuntary infertility. Studies in Sweden indicate that the risk of sterility is 12 to 16 percent after a single episode of salpingitis and rises to 60 percent after three episodes.

Disseminated Gonococcal Infection (DGI)

An uncommon but distinctive picture appears when the gonococcus is spread via the bloodstream. The classic picture includes (often) asymptomatic infection of the pharynx, penis, vagina, or rectum in association with characteristic skin lesions and arthritis. The skin lesions are small, hemorrhagic areas with necrotic centers, and generally number fewer than 20. The infected joint(s) usually exhibit(s) the four classic features of arthritis: swelling, redness, pain, and heat. The knee is most frequently involved, followed by elbows, ankles, wrists, and small joints of the hand. Patients with DGI usually respond well to routine treatment and rarely suffer long-term musculoskeletal complications.

Other Clinical Manifestations

A variety of other rare infections with the gonococcus have been documented. Adults occasionally develop gonococcal conjunctivitis, with a potential for more serious ocular involvement, through direct (i.e., hand-to-eye) contact with infected secretions. Gonococcal endocarditis, myocarditis, hepatitis, and meningitis may occur as part of the disseminated syndrome. *Perihepatitis* (termed the *Fitz–Hugh–Curtis syndrome*) has traditionally been attributed to gonococcal infection in the upper right quadrant, usually in association with classic PID. Recent evidence, however, indicates that the syndrome is more often associated with chlamydial, rather than gonococcal, infection.

Gonococcal Infection in Children

The other major mode of transmission of the gonococcus is from mother to child. A newborn may become infected during passage through an infected birth canal, and the most common clinical manifestation is gonococcal ophthalmia. The typical syndrome includes the development of purulent discharge from one or both eyes with relatively rapid progression, in the untreated child, to more generalized ocular involvement, scarring, and blindness. The use of routine eye prophylaxis with silver nitrate (see discussion under History, below) was a landmark in preventive medicine and greatly reduced the occurrence of this syndrome. Children may develop gonorrhea in sexual sites as well. It has become apparent, in recent years, that the majority of infected children have suffered sexual abuse. In boys, symptomatic or asymptomatic anogenital infection may occur. In girls, the primary manifestation is a vulvitis, because the prepubertal cervix is not an adequate milieu for survival of the gonococcus.

Classification, Immunology, and Pathology

The importance of gonorrhea is measured not only by its considerable burden of acute disease and long-term consequences, but also by some of its extraordinary biological characteristics. The virulence of the gonococcus rests in its ability to adhere to muscosal surfaces, to resist immunological defenses, to cause asymptomatic infection, and to resist antibiotic killing. These qualities have been important in the development of four major classification schemes based upon the following:

1. The presence or absence of *pili* (long, filamentous projections on the surface of the gonococcus), which determine adherence to mucosal cells. Their presence is, in turn, reflected in the size, shape, and opacity of gonococcal bacterial colonies, and forms the basis for the earliest classification scheme used.
2. The nutritional requirements of the gonococci. Typing of organisms based on their need for certain amino acids (*auxotyping*) has determined the presence of special strains that are more or less sensitive to antiobiotics, and that have a greater propensity to cause disseminated infection.
3. The antigenic structure of the gonococcal cell envelope, which provides a mechanism for classification (*serovars*). Serovars have been used, in conjunction with auxotyping, to show patterns of distribution and to link cases epidemiologically.
4. Susceptibility to antibiotics. Four transferable pieces of genetic material (*plasmids*) have been identified, which have helped in geographic localization of cases.

These systems for classification reflect the considerable pathogenetic repertoire available to the gonococcus. In contrast, the immunologic armamentarium of the host seems inadequate. Genital secretions may have some inhibitory effect on gonococci in vitro, but are not protective. Local immunoglobulin production has been demonstrated but may be counteracted by protease produced by the gonococcus. Serum antibody is usually demonstrable in previously infected persons, but resistance to serum killing is a typical feature of freshly isolated gonococci. Indeed the net result of studies to date simply reflects the time-honored observation that people may contract gonorrhea again and again. There is no apparent protective human immunity. The existence of asymptomatic infection, and the apparent immunologic tolerance of the host, may account in part for the ecological success of the gonococcus.

Distribution and Incidence

Gonorrhea is found worldwide, but documentation of its true extent is lacking. Direct comparisons of incidence among nations are difficult to make because of the wide variation in clinical and diagnostic facilities, the extent of disease reporting, and the degree of care given to case finding. The disease is widespread in both the industrialized and the developing world, but it is likely that the burden on developing nations is greater. It is estimated that the incidence in some large African cities may be as high as 3,000 to 10,000 per 100,000 population. Because gonorrhea is, in principle, a disease of high incidence and low prevalence, it is noteworthy that surveys of women attending prenatal and family planning clinics in Africa disclose a prevalence as high as 17 percent. Among prostitutes in Latin America, Asia, and Africa, the prevalence of gonorrhea may be 30 to 50 percent. These are, of course, occasional surveys of selected populations, but, in the absence of systematic information, they provide some sense of the magnitude of the problem.

A number of industrialized nations, on the other hand, do have systematic reporting of gonorrhea. Routinely collected statistics have permitted documentation of the major epidemiological event in the history of gonorrhea: a worldwide pandemic that began in the late 1950s and peaked in the mid-1970s.

A comparison of disease rates in the United States, the United Kingdom, Sweden, and Canada (Figure VIII.62.1), all of which have advanced

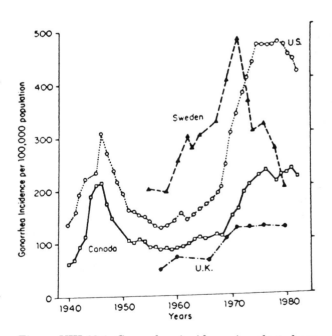

Figure VIII.62.1. Gonorrhea incidence in selected countries, 1940–83. (From R. C. Barnes and K. K. Holmes. 1984. Epidemiology of gonorrhea: Current perspectives. *Epidemiological Reviews* 6: 1–30; 3, fig. 1, by courtesy of *Epidemiological Reviews* and the *American Journal of Epidemiology*.)

health care systems, indicates a rise in gonorrhea occurrences after World War II, with a subsequent fall to a nadir in the mid-1950s. Though varying in size and timing, an increase in gonorrhea throughout the 1960s, with termination of the accelerated rise by the mid-1970s, was experienced by each nation. The graph is representative of the situation for most industrialized countries during the interval, and conveys the disparity with which nations were apparently affected. At the peak, in the mid-1970s, rates among industrialized nations differed by as much as 10-fold. (By contrast, rates among developing nations during the interval differed even more wildly, but here the variation in reporting clearly plays an important role.)

The impact and specific features of the pandemic may be demonstrated by examining the history of the disease in the United States during this period. Between 1956 and 1985, rates of gonorrhea increased in all age groups for both men and women (Figure VIII.62.2). Rates for females are higher at younger ages, and peak at ages 15 to 19 years. Rates for males peak at ages 20 to 24, producing a crossover pattern (Figure VIII.62.3). The origin of this increase, and of the pandemic in general, is not fully understood. It is often attributed to changes in sexual mores during the 1960s and 1970s, with major increases reported in the frequency of premarital sexual experiences by both men and women, a greater availability of contraceptive technology, and an increase in the number of individuals entering the age of sexual activity (the so-called baby boom generation).

It is likely that the pandemic has not yet had its full impact on the developing world, though the peak in industrialized nations seems to have passed. If so, the burden of morbidity, long-term sequelae, and mortality will continue to have a major influence on

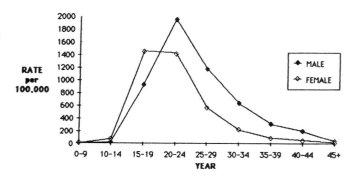

Figure VIII.62.3. Gonorrhea: age-specific rates for men and women, United States, 1985.

80 percent of the world's population in the coming years.

History

Gonorrhea is the oldest, as well as the most common, of the venereal diseases. An Egyptian papyrus from approximately 3500 B.C. prescribes plant extracts to soothe painful urination. The Hebrew *Bible* makes reference to treatment of genital exudates, which may well refer to gonorrhea. Hippocrates recognized the venereal nature of transmission at about the beginning of the fourth century B.C., and Galen, in the second century A.D., is believed to have coined the name. In the fourteenth century, a description of the ailment that stressed a major symptom, *chaude pisse,* or "hot piss," led to the disease's receiving this appellation from the French.

By 1500 or so, interest centered on the distinction between syphilis and gonorrhea. The majority opinion appeared to favor the notion that they were different manifestations of the same disease, particularly because syphilis was so clearly protean in its manifestations. However, in the middle of the sixteenth century, a French physician, Jean Fernel, wrote of gonorrhea as a separate disease from syphilis in his *Medicina*. The British physician Francis Balfour, writing two centuries later, has also been credited with the belief that syphilis and gonorrhea were distinct.

Confusion set in, however, following John Hunter's argument that the cause of both diseases was the same and that gonorrhea was a manifestation of the disease on a secreting surface (mucosa) whereas syphilis was its manifestation on a nonsecreting surface (skin). To prove this, he infected himself with pustular discharge from a patient he thought had gonorrhea, and developed syphilis instead. The patient may have been dually infected, but at any rate,

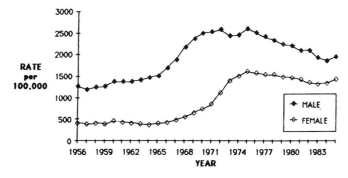

Figure VIII.62.2. Gonorrhea rates in men and women, aged 20–4, United States, 1956–85.

this was an unfortunate instance of a brilliant and heroic use of the scientific method gone wrong, and it postponed scientific understanding of the two diseases for decades.

It was during this same period (1760–90) that the most lucid literary account of gonorrhea appeared. James Boswell, the biographer of Samuel Johnson, kept a meticulous diary of his own repeated encounters with gonorrhea. The diary details the clinical manifestations and psychological effects of 19 episodes. There is little question of the impact of gonorrhea on his life, and, by extension, on the life of countless others in the era. He is believed to have died of gonorrheal complications.

In the 1790s, Benjamin Bell of Edinburgh, who was in disagreement with Hunter, published several tracts that explored the clinical and epidemiological evidence for gonorrhea and syphilis as separate disease entities. He posed a number of simple questions: Why is gonorrhea more common when the skin of the penis is at greater risk of exposure than the urethra? Why are there geographic differences in the distribution of the two diseases? Why have their manifestations appeared in the same populations at different points in time?

It remained, however, for Philippe Ricord, in a series of clinical observations and direct experiments in the mid-1800s, to provide a definitive distinction between the two diseases. It is of interest that Ricord commented that there is no justification for experimentation with grave diseases in human beings, although he inoculated 17 prisoners with gonorrheal pus, producing occasional ulcers with prompt healing, but no evidence of syphilis.

In 1879, Albert Neisser, an assistant in dermatology at the University of Breslau, Germany, published his preliminary findings which confirmed the conclusions of Ricord by describing the organism that now bears his name. This was probably the second description of a major human pathogen (after Koch's identification of the anthrax bacillus 3 years earlier). In 1882, the organism was first grown in vitro by Ernst von Bumm. The first major preventive action was taken in the following year when Karl Siegmund Credé, at the Lying-In Hospital in Leipsig, recognized the benefit of instillation of 2 percent silver nitrate solution (later reduced to 1 percent) in the eyes of newborns. The occurrence of gonococcal ophthalmia diminished rapidly with the widespread adoption of this procedure.

Unfortunately, advances did not follow in rapid succession. In fact, after the initial diagnostic procedures were established, there were no major improvements in the understanding of gonorrhea until the sulfonamides (e.g., sulfamidochrysoidine, Prontosil) were introduced in 1937. This success was short-lived, and true antibiosis for gonorrhea appeared only in the 1950s with the general availability of penicillin. The next critical breakthroughs were the description of the different colonial morphologies by Douglas S. Kellogg et al. in 1963 and the development of a selective medium for culturing the gonococcus by James D. Thayer and John E. Martin in 1964. Subsequent events, including the worldwide pandemic of the 1960s and 1970s, and the major advances in immunology and molecular biology, were alluded to earlier. Clearly, it is only in recent times that gonorrhea's effect on us, and in turn, our ability to alter its course, have dramatically changed.

Geography

Through gonorrhea is found worldwide, the lack of systematic data precludes meaningful global mapping. But even if national rates were universally available, a local approach might be more informative. In its transmission, its endemicity, and its continued propagation, gonorrhea is a neighborhood disease. An understanding of the local geography is predicated on a coherent theory for transmission.

Epidemiology

The clinical epidemiology of the classic gonorrhea syndromes forms the basis for the population epidemiology of the disease. Gonorrhea is transmitted by sexual contact. The probability of transmission from male to female after a single contact is approximately 50 percent; from female to male, 22 percent. The incubation period is 3 to 5 days in men and slightly longer in women. A significant proportion of both sexes never becomes symptomatic. The incidence of disease in a given community, then, is a function of two major parameters: (1) the degree of sexual interaction, which includes the frequency of new partners, as well as the duration, intensity, frequency, and logistics of sexual contact; and (2) the duration of infectiousness, which takes into account the proportion of asymptomatic infection, the proportion of a population that will seek health care, the adequacy of therapy, and the extent to which sex partners are apprised of their risk. Clearly, the final epidemiological picture will be a complex interaction of biological, social, and individual events. In general, however, gonorrhea is a disease of high incidence but short duration and, hence, of low prevalence.

Transmission Dynamics

Beginning in the early 1970s, mathematicians Herbert Hethcote and James Yorke constructed a theoretical framework for the transmission dynamics of gonorrhea. Using some of the concepts of population ecology, they noted that the reproduction rate for gonorrhea (i.e., the ability of an infected person to replace him- or herself) must be determined when the disease is at endemic equilibrium. In the steady state, therefore, each infected person must have two "adequate" contacts for transmission on average ("adequate" means that the gonococcus is transmitted). There must be a "source" contact and a "spread" contact for disease propagation. Because not all sexual contacts are "adequate," it follows that the average number of total contacts must be greater than 2.

In constructing a model of transmission dynamics, several key epidemiological observations must be considered:

1. Gonococcal infection does not confer protective immunity; thus an individual is "immune" only when infected.

2. Individuals become infectious soon after exposure; there is, then, no "exposed, incubating" group to be considered in a model.

3. Seasonal variation of gonorrhea is well defined, with a peak in late summer in temperate climates, but the variation is small (about 10 percent) in comparison with other diseases. This implies that the parameters used in the model can be constant.

4. Data derived from interviewing gonorrhea patients about their sex partners suggest that the average number of "adequate" contacts is well below 2. In 1985, there were only 0.3 infected contacts found for each person with gonorrhea interviewed. Even with allowances for slippage in the system of interviewing cases, finding contacts, and bringing them to medical examination, this is far below the two infected contacts per case needed to maintain a reproduction rate of 1 and to preserve endemic equilibrium.

It was reasoned, then, that the observed number of infected contacts per case is a weight average of two groups: (1) those for whom one or no contacts were identified (*nontransmitters*); (2) those with two or more contacts identified (*transmitters*). Those in the first group – the vast majority of gonorrhea infectees – were unlikely to pass the infection to another person. Hethcote and Yorke hypothesized that the transmitters – those who actually maintain the endemicity of gonorrhea – were drawn from so-called *core groups*. These groups were defined as persons with stable sociodemographic and geographic characteristics who constituted a small minority of cases (under 5 percent), but who accounted – either directly or indirectly – for most gonorrhea transmission. It is within such groups that the epidemiological features of gonorrhea (no immunity, immediate infectiousness, year-round transmission) were fully operative. The limit to gonorrhea spread within a core group was termed the *saturation effect*: that is, sexual contact between infected persons.

In a series of elegant mathematical discussions, Hethcote and Yorke developed a model for the dynamics of transmission based on population compartments that included core and noncore groups. They were able to demonstrate the plausibility of an equilibrium state in which most cases were attributable to small groups of active transmitters. Parallel with this theoretical development, some empirical evidence for the physical existence of core geographic areas and definable core groups emerged.

It was shown in 1979, based on the routine reporting of gonorrhea morbidity data, that the city of Denver contained four different areas with high concentrations of infectees (see Figure VIII.62.4). Each geographic area housed a distinct population subgroup: black heterosexuals, Hispanic heterosexuals, white homosexual men, and military recruits.

Through analysis of over 120,000 geocoded cases

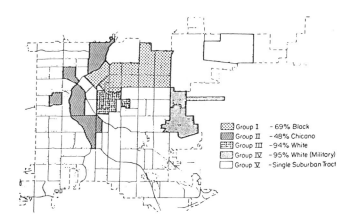

Figure VIII.62.4. Distribution of gonorrhea in Denver, Colorado, 1974–6. [From R. B. Rothenberg. 1979. Analysis of routine data describing morbidity from gonorrhea. *Sexually Transmitted Diseases* 6(1): 5–9; 6, fig. 1, by courtesy of Lippincott/Harper & Row, Philadelphia, Penna.]

of gonorrhea in upstate New York from 1975 to 1980, a general geographic pattern emerged. Within all 12 Standard Metropolitan Statistical Areas (SMSAs, the urban centers), there was intense concentration of gonorrhea in a small number of contiguous census tracts (core areas) within the inner cities. In a concentric circle surrounding the core were a group of census tracts with somewhat lessened gonorrhea rates (adjacent areas). The rest of the SMSA constitutes the peripheral area, with a markedly diminished gonorrhea burden. The concentration of gonorrhea in the core area was 20-fold higher than that for New York State in general, and several of the census tracts in the core had rates that were 40-fold higher. Not only was this pattern repeated in all SMSAs, but all the core areas were similarly characterized by high population density and low socioeconomic status. The geographic configuration for Buffalo, New York, is typical (Figure VIII.62.5).

This pattern was also documented in Colorado Springs, Colorado, using data collected from inter-

views of 97 percent of the cases that occurred during a 6-month interval. Again, clustering of over 50 percent of the cases was demonstrated in about 5 percent of census tracts. Social aggregation of cases was demonstrated by the consistent use of six drinking establishments by a major proportion of infectees, and by the aggregation of patients and their sexual partners in the same census tracts. Contrary to commonly held belief, the majority of sexual partners had known each other socially prior to sexual contact. The interconnection of individuals in networks could be demonstrated through linkage provided by the interview process. Further analysis demonstrated that the core groups in Colorado Springs generated a high *force of infectivity* (i.e., days of potential transmission in infected exposed partners),

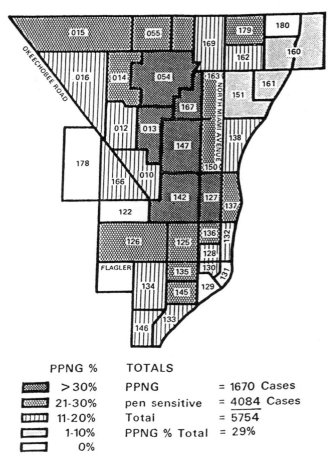

PPNG %   TOTALS
>30%   PPNG   = 1670 Cases
21-30%   pen sensitive = 4084 Cases
11-20%   Total   = 5754
1-10%   PPNG % Total = 29%
0%

Figure VIII.62.6. Penicillinase-producing *Neisseria* gonorrhea (PPNG) as percentage of total gonorrhea, by zip code analysis in Miami, Florida, March 1985 to February 1986. (From J. M. Zenilman et al. 1988. Penicillinase-producing *Neisseria gonorrhoeae* in Dade County, Florida: Evidence of core-group transmitters and the impact of illicit antibiotics. *Sexually Transmitted Diseases* 15: 45–50; 47, fig. 2, by courtesy of Lippincott/Harper & Row, Philadelphia, Penna.)

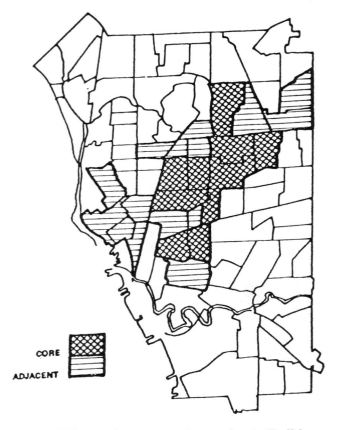

CORE

ADJACENT

Figure VIII.62.5. Occurrence of gonorrhea in Buffalo, New York, 1975–80; distribution of core and adjacent tracts. (From R. B. Rothenberg. 1983. The geography of gonorrhea: Empirical demonstration of core group transmission. *American Journal of Epidemiology* 117(6): 688–94; 691, fig. 1.)

and had a heightened degree of sexual interaction both inside and outside their core groups.

Similar geographic clustering was documented in Seville, Spain, where it was noted that all the STD syndromes appeared to exhibit a similar geographic pattern. The presence of penicillin-resistant *N. gonorrhoeae* has provided a convenient marker for the demonstration of core-group aggregation as well. In an initial outbreak reported from Liverpool in 1976, clustering of cases occurred within two small inner-city districts. In Miami, a major endemic area for resistant gonorrhea in the United States, the clustering of resistant cases within presumed core-group areas paralleled that for all of gonorrhea (Figure VIII.62.6).

It cannot be assumed that the geographic characteristics displayed in these examples are universal. In particular, differences in human ecology and sexuality in developing countries may dictate a different pattern, and data are not yet available. It might tentatively be concluded, however, that a concentric pattern of gonorrhea risk, which diminishes outward from the central inner city, exists in many major urban areas. The potential for use of geographic patterns in the development of disease control strategies, and in the understanding of other sexually transmitted syndromes, is an area for further development.

Richard B. Rothenberg

This chapter was written in the author's private capacity. No official support or endorsement by the Centers for Disease Control is intended or should be inferred.

Bibliography

Alvarez-Dardet, C., S. Marquez, and D. J. Peres. 1985. Urban clusters of sexually transmitted disease in the city of Seville, Spain. *Sexually Transmitted Diseases* 12(3): 166–8.

Barnes, R. C., and K. K. Holmes. 1984. Epidemiology of gonorrhea: Current perspectives. *Epidemiologic Reviews* 6: 1–30.

Britigan, B. E., M. S. Cohen, and P. F. Sparling. 1985. Gonococcal infection: A model of molecular pathogenesis. *New England Journal of Medicine* 312(26): 1683–94.

Hethcote, H. W., and J. A. Yorke. 1984. Gonorrhea transmission dynamics and control. *Lecture Notes in Biomathematics.* New York.

Holmes, K. K. (Chairman). 1986. WHO Expert Committee on Venereal Diseases and Treponematoses. *Technical Report Series* No. 736. Geneva.

Holmes, K. K., et al. 1984. *Sexually transmitted diseases.* New York.

Hook, E. Q., and K. K. Holmes. 1985. Gonococcal infections. *Annals of Internal Medicine* 102: 229–43.

Kampmeier, R. H. 1977. John Hunter – a man of conviction. *Sexually Transmitted Diseases* 4(3): 114–5.

  1978. Identification of the gonococcus by Albert Neisser. *Sexually Transmitted Diseases* 5(2): 71–2.

  1979. The early identification of several venereal infections. *Sexually Transmitted Diseases* 6(2): 79–81.

Kellogg, D. S., et al. 1963. *Neisseria gonorrhoeae:* I. Virulence genetically linked to clonal variations. *Journal of Bacteriology* 85: 1274–9.

Ober, W. B. 1969. Boswell's gonorrhea. *Bulletin of the New York Academy of Medicine* 45(6): 587–636.

Potterat, B. A., et al. 1985. Gonorrhea as a social disease. *Sexually Transmitted Diseases* 12(1): 25–32.

Rice, R. J., et al. 1987. Gonorrhea in the United States 1975–1984: Is the giant only sleeping? *Sexually Transmitted Diseases* 14(2): 83–7.

Rothenberg, R. B. 1979. Analysis of routine data describing morbidity from gonorrhea. *Sexually Transmitted Diseases* 6(1): 5–9.

  1983. The geography of gonorrhea: Empirical demonstration of core group transmission. *American Journal of Epidemiology* 117(6): 688–94.

Thayer, J. D., and J. E. Martin. 1964. A selective medium for the cultivation of *Neisseria gonorrhoeae* and *Neisseria meningitidis. Public Health Report* 79: 49–57.

Zenilman, J. M., et al. 1988. Penicillinase-producing *Neisseria gonorrhoeae* in Dade County, Florida: Evidence of core-group transmitters and the impact of illicit antibiotics. *Sexually Transmitted Diseases* 15: 45–50.

VIII.63
Gout

Gout is a chronic, intermittently symptomatic disease. It is manifested primarily by small numbers of acutely painful swollen joints that result from an inflammatory reaction to the precipitation of crystals of monosodium urate.

Etiology

The predisposing metabolic factor for *primary gout* is an abnormally high or rapidly changing concentration of uric acid in the blood. *Hyperuricemia* may result from an accelerated synthesis of uric acid, or decreased excretory capacity for uric acid in otherwise normal kidneys as a result of unidentified but probably heritable causes. Hyperuricemia leading to *secondary gout* occurs particularly (1) in diseases of the blood-forming tissues that increase the availability of precursors of uric acid; (2) in kidney failure, which limits the excretion of uric acid; or (3) as a result of medications that either accelerate the breakdown of purine-rich cells (e.g., antineoplastic drugs) or interfere with the renal excretory mechanism (e.g., some diuretics). Dissolved in the serum, uric acid is harmless. However, because of unidentified local circumstances it may leak from capillaries and crystallize. The crystals of monosodium urate elicit the inflammatory reaction, which is the *gouty attack,* and the microscopic identification of the crystals in synovial fluid confirms the diagnosis. Why this inflammation occurs predominantly in joints, and why much more commonly in some joints (such as those of the feet or in the knee) than in others (such as the hip or those of the vertebral column) are unexplained characteristics. Unexplained as well is the question why *tophi,* which are urate deposits that form beneath the skin, are usually painless and the antiuricemic effect of estrogens.

Clinical Manifestations

Fully 90 to 95 percent of patients are male, and gout rarely develops in women before menopause. The first attack most often occurs in the fifth decade in men and in the sixth decade in women. The rate of production of uric acid and, related thereto, the onset of primary gout, thereafter diminishes.

The normal uric acid content, the "miscible pool," in men is about 1.2 grams, and in women, 0.6 grams (Seegmiller, Laster, and Howell 1963). Because of an imbalance between synthesis and excretion, uric acid accumulates in part as the subcutaneous deposits called tophi. About 50 percent of untreated patients have tophi 10 years after their first attack of gout. Thus 53 percent of the cases seen in the Mount Sinai Hospital (New York) Gout Clinic during 1948–53 had tophi, whereas tophi were found in only 14 percent of the cases of gout first seen at the Mayo Clinic in 1949. The difference presumably was the result of referral bias. However, the incidence of tophaceous gout has decreased steadily in both institutions: In New York during 1969–73, it was 17 percent of all gout patients, and at the Mayo Clinic in 1972 it was only 3 percent (Yu 1984). Statistics of cases gathered in London during 1958–67 revealed that 21 percent had tophi, whereas 28 percent of cases seen at a German health resort during 1955–64 had tophaceous gout.

Next to tophi the most common uratic manifestation of gout is kidney stones (*nephrolithiasis*). This association has been noted since at least the sixteenth century. Uric acid stones constitute no more than 5 percent of all kidney stones, but about 80 percent of calculi in cases of gout. How close the relationship between gout and urate nephrolithiasis may be is uncertain. Although 22 percent of the 1,258 New York gout patients studied by T.-F. Yu and A. B. Gutman (1967) had renal calculi at some time, this condition antedated the first attack of gout in 40 percent, and in 14 percent the delay was from 11 to 39 years. The probability of nephrolithiasis is correlated with the serum urate content. Thus, 15 percent of their total cases of gout had serum urate of less than 8 milligrams per 100 grams of blood (mg%) without treatment, and nephrolithiasis developed in 15 percent of these; in 32 percent of the gout patients the urate concentration exceeded 10 mg%, and 43 percent of these had nephrolithiasis. In other large series of cases of gout, nephrolithiasis has ranged from 28 percent (German spa) to 4 percent (San Francisco private practice) (Table VIII.63.1).

Allopurinol therapy, which reduces the uric acid pool, decreases the incidence of uratic kidney stones and has the same effect in nongouty urate hyperexcretors who have a history of calcium stone formation.

History

For many centuries the term *gout* and *podagra* were as nonspecific as *arthritis* is in modern usage. The clinical differentiation of the disease was begun in the late seventeenth-century works of Thomas Sydenham, although his contemporary, Anton van Leeuwenhoek, using his simple microscope, described the appearance of crystals from a tophus. Nearly a century later, in 1776, Karl W. Scheele, a Swedish pharmacist, discovered an organic acid in urinary concretions which for that reason he called lithic acid. In 1797, at Cambridge, William H. Wollaston analyzed tophi and found that they contained "lithic acid." In 1798, this substance was renamed *acide ourique* by the French chemist Antoine F. de Fourcroy because he also found it to be present in normal urine.

Another half century passed before uric acid was shown to be even more intimately related to gout. In 1847 and in 1854, London physician Alfred B. Garrod devised two tests whereby uric acid could be detected in blood in hyperuricemic states such as gout and uremia. He also demonstrated urate in subcutaneous tissues and articular cartilage in cases of gout. Garrod hypothesized that gout might result either from a loss of renal excretory capacity or from increased formation of uric acid. A century after the publication of his 1859 monograph on gout, both concepts were proved to be correct. In 1876 Garrod

Table VIII.63.1. *Occurrence of nephrolithiasis with gout*

Author	Year	Location	Cases of gout			% Nephrolithiasis		
			Male	Female	Total	Male	Female	Total
Bartels	1954	Boston			450			3
Kuzell	1955	San Francisco	373	131	504	5.4	0.7	3.9
Nishioka	1980	Tokyo			2,455			5.5
Grahame	1970	London	311	43	354			9.0
Ruiz-Moreno	1959	Buenos Aires	593	44	637	10.0	2.3	9.4
Hench	1928	Rochester, Minn.			100			12.0
Kittredge	1952	New Orleans			324			13.9
Brøchner-Mortensen	1941	Copenhagen			100			15.0
Hall	1967	Framingham, Mass.	271	34	306	15.4	11.8	15.0
Talbott	1960	Buffalo	184	7	191[a]	15.8	28.5	16.2
Yu	1967	New York	1,207	51	1,258	22.4	19.6	22.2
Gamp	1965	Bad Kreuznach			200			28.0
Serane	1954	Paris	136		136	33.1		33.1

[a]Autopsied cases.

also postulated that acute gout results from the precipitation of sodium urate in a joint or adjacent tissue. This was proven in 1962 by the elicitation of gouty inflammation following the injection of suspensions of sodium urate crystals into human and canine knee joints (Rodnan 1965).

Beginning in 1871 numerous gravimetric assays of urinary uric acid were devised, but none was sensitive enough to be applicable to the much smaller concentration in the blood. The wide variations of uric acid excretion and the lack of understanding of uric acid metabolism cast doubt on the causative relationship of uric acid to gout. Two paradoxical effects on clinical practice resulted. One was that the old belief in "retrocedent" or "anomalous" gout – the idea that a wide variety of symptoms or diseases are caused by a "gouty poison" – gained new adherents. The other was that clinicians virtually ceased making the diagnosis of gout. For example, at the Johns Hopkins Hospital (Baltimore), only 42 cases were admitted with this diagnosis during 1889–1903. At the Massachusetts General Hospital, only 9 cases of gout were found among 1,033 medical admissions for rheumatic diseases during 1893–1903 (Benedek 1987). Likewise, at a hospital in Cologne the diagnosis of gout was made only 14 times among 23,870 medical admissions (0.06 percent) during 1895–1900. However, in that hospital the diagnosis was made in 10 cases or 0.35 percent of the admissions during the first year that Oscar Minkowski, who was interested in this disease, was in charge of a medical service.

The Devonshire Royal Hospital in England represented the other extreme. During 1896–1900, gout was diagnosed in 2.42 percent of 14,224 admissions (324 male, 20 female); during the next 5-year period, with changes in the physician staff, the frequency of the diagnosis more than doubled to 5.26 percent of 15,836 admissions (743 male, 91 female) (Hill 1938). Clearly, such data do not prove the traditional impression that gout was peculiarly prevalent in England but, rather, suggest that the diagnosis was being made or missed very subjectively.

The first practical colorimetric technique sensitive enough to detect normal concentrations of uric acid in blood was devised by Otto Folin at Harvard University in 1912. Its sensitivity was gradually improved so that in 1938 the uric acid content of the blood was shown to be greater in men than in women, thereby correlating with the rarity of gout in women. However, physicians continued to be poorly aware of true gout. Philip Hench (1936) commented on this as follows:

If more than 50–70% of his patients have tophi he is too exclusive and is probably omitting cases of bona fide (even if pretophaceous) gout. If less than 35–40% have tophi or if more than 2–5% are females he is too inclusive, diagnosing gout where it does not exist.

Methodological specificity in uric acid determination was achieved in 1953 with a technique that employs the enzyme uricase. Nevertheless, most laboratories continue to use less specific methods that lend themselves to automation and give some-what higher than "true" values (Benedek 1987).

Treatment

Therapy of gout has two components: (1) treatment of the acute attack and (2) prophylaxis, which seeks to decrease the uric acid pool of the body. The former has always been predominantly medicinal, whereas the latter has been both dietetic and medicinal. Colchicum in the form of various alcoholic or aqueous extracts from the bulb, stem, or seeds of the meadow saffron came into use in the second decade of the nineteenth century in France and England. It was included in the *Dispensatory of the United States of America* in 1836, although its use was advocated somewhat earlier. Hesitation about using colchicum was due to recognition of its toxicity, as manifested by severe diarrhea, which also was believed to be the mechanism of its therapeutic effect. The active component, colchicine, was isolated in 1820. Colchicine was available in pill form by 1900, but crude tinctures were still in use in the 1950s (Rodnan and Benedek 1970).

Until about 1910, when cinchophen was introduced, colchicine was the only remedy for acute gout. Cinchophen not only was effective in the acute gouty attack but, in contrast to colchicine, also was an analgesic. Because of its chemical resemblance to salicylate, cinchophen was presumed to be tolerated better than colchicine, which it virtually replaced in the treatment of acute gout. However, by the 1930s it became evident that cinchophen may cause severe and even fatal liver damage. Hence, its use faded out over a decade, and colchicine again became the standard treatment.

The fact that both cinchophen and salicylates increased the renal excretion of uric acid and thereby reduced the uric acid content of the blood was discovered in 1913 and 1915, respectively, but was not adapted to therapy. Two pharmaceutical breakthroughs occurred in 1951. Probenecid, a drug that had been developed to retard the excretion of penicillin, was found to accelerate the excretion of uric acid. Although it has no analgesic or antiinflammatory effect, it was well tolerated and convenient to take. As it reduced the serum uric acid concentration, the frequency of gouty attacks diminished and tophi shrank. The other discovery was phenylbutazone, which proved to have therapeutic effects similar to cinchophen. Like probenecid, it increased the excretion of uric acid, but also like colchicine, it counteracted the acute attack, and it was a nonspecific analgesic as well. However, it proved to be toxic,

particularly to blood cell formation in elderly persons, and it has therefore fallen into disfavor.

Another pair of important pharmaceutical discoveries was introduced in 1963. Indomethacin effectively counteracts the acute gouty attack, and, although it does not alter the excretion of uric acid, it also does not depress blood formation; therefore, it gradually superseded phenylbutazone. Since then many other "nonsteroidal antiinflammatory drugs" have been found to be similarly effective. Allopurinol lowers the uric acid pool like probenecid, but by a different mechanism. It diminishes the synthesis of uric acid by inhibiting the activity of an enzyme (xanthine oxidase). Like probenecid, allopurinol is of no value in an acute gouty attack, but it has the advantages of effectiveness in the presence of renal failure, and the convenience of once per day dosage (Benedek 1987).

Dietetic attempts to treat or prevent gout are ancient. They were based on beliefs in the virtue of moderation in all things and, more specifically, in the belief that gout is caused in large measure by excesses in the consumption of food and alcoholic beverages. Aside from the demonstration in 1924 that starvation results in an increased blood uric acid concentration, scientific investigations of gout have been done only since the 1960s. The most important finding has been that circumstances that result in the formation of certain organic acids, particularly lactate and beta-hydroxybutyrate, block the excretion of uric acid and thereby increase the possibility that a gouty attack may occur. Starvation, substantial alcohol ingestion, especially without eating, and uncontrolled diabetes mellitus are such conditions.

Uric acid found in the body is not absorbed as such, but is synthesized from breakdown products of various foodstuffs, particularly those that are rich in nucleoproteins (Seegmiller, Laster, and Howell 1963). A low-fat, largely vegetarian (60 g/day protein) diet reduces the serum uric acid concentration by 1 to 2 milligrams below that found in a more typical American diet (Gutman and Yu 1955). The effect such diets have on reducing gouty attacks is equivocal. Since the advent of urate-depleting drugs such as probenecid and allopurinol, however, dietetic therapy has become irrelevant except for the general advantages of weight reduction for the obese gout patient.

Gout rarely is a direct cause of death, although premature death due to diseases with which gout is associated (principally hypertensive or arteriosclerotic cardiovascular disease) is fairly common. For reasons that are unclear, untreated hypertension with grossly normal renal function is frequently associated with hyperuricemia. Because treatment of hypertension usually includes drugs that interfere with the excretion of uric acid, hyperuricemia is greater and more prevalent in treated than in untreated hypertensive patients. Thus, according to a survey in London, 31 percent of untreated hypertensive men and 23 percent of untreated hypertensive women had hyperuricemia, 12 percent having had attacks of gout, whereas 59 percent and 57 percent, respectively, of hypertensive men and women under treatment were hyperuricemic (Breckenridge 1966). Conversely, in a series of 354 gout patients in London, 52 percent had a diastolic blood pressure in excess of 90 millimeters (Grahame and Scott 1970), and of the cases studied by Yu (1984) in New York, 30 percent were considered hypertensive. Hyperlipidemia appears not to be correlated directly with hyperuricemia. Rather, both are associated with hypertension and obesity. According to the Framingham study, angina pectoris is twice as frequent among gouty as among nongouty men (Abbott et al. 1988), and Yu found that the causes of death among 427 gout patients were cardiovascular in 66 percent of the cases (Yu 1984).

Epidemiology

When considering the epidemiology of primary gout, one must focus separately on hyperuricemia and the factors that influence it. Although a rough correlation does exist between the level of hyperuricemia and the likelihood of an attack of gouty arthritis, the predictive value is poor and appears to be worse in certain groups than in others. Of the measurable factors that affect the serum uric acid concentration, the most important are the protein content of the diet and overweight. Weight and the rate of uric acid metabolism are to some extent genetically predetermined. However, the immediate cause of a gouty attack remains unknown.

Worldwide the severity and prevalence of gout have changed paradoxically since the 1940s. In the highly developed countries, as a result of the advent of effective prophylactic drug therapy, the disease is now rarely disabling. Elsewhere, however, it has become more prevalent, predominantly as a result of "improved" diets. Unfortunately, there were no epidemiological surveys of serum uric acid or gout in primitive societies before the 1960s, so that hypotheses about whether ethnic differences are genetic or the result of recent environmental changes are weakened by a lack of baseline data. The different biochemical techniques that have been used intro-

duce another obstacle to any comparison of data from various surveys.

The prevalence of gout that is reported depends on the diagnostic criteria used; on the population from which the cohort is drawn; and on whether the diagnosis is based on questionnaires or on single or repetitive examinations. For example, a predominantly younger population can be expected to have a lower prevalence of gout than one with a higher mean age; a workforce may have a lower prevalence than a random sample that may include persons who are disabled by gout and associated diseases. Secondary gout, in which the disease results from (1) accelerated purine metabolism inherent in another disease, usually of the blood, (2) diminished excretion of uric acid resulting from renal failure, or (3) effects of toxins such as lead, is not an epidemiological confounder because these circumstances are readily identified and uncommon. At present, secondary gout arises most frequently as an incidental effect of certain antihypertensive medications.

United States and Europe

Only a few of the larger American and European surveys of serum uric acid values will be cited. In a survey in Tecumseh, Michigan, 9.2 percent of men over 20 years of age had uric acid values greater than 7.0 mg%, and 8.7 percent of the women had values greater than 6.0 mg% (Mikkelsen, Dodge, and Valkenburg 1965). In Framingham, Massachusetts, 4.8 percent of men and 3.3 percent of women met this criterion (Hall et al. 1967). Racial comparisons in rural Georgia (31 percent black men, 35 percent black women) revealed no racial differences in mean uric acid values. However, the prevalence of hyperuricemia was high, ranging from 13.6 percent for white men to 21.1 percent for black women. This was attributed largely to the association between hypertension and hyperuricemia and the use of antihypertensive medications (Klein et al. 1973). A comparison of uric acid values between white U.S. and Brazilian male military recruits showed Americans to have higher uric acid concentrations: mean 4.87 mg% versus 4.05 mg%, with 3.26 percent versus 0.35 percent having a value above 7.0 mg%. The difference correlated best with the 17 percent greater mean weight of the Americans (Florey and Acheson 1968).

Several American surveys have compared the serum uric acid levels of executives and either lower-level employees or age-matched general population samples. The executives have consistently been found to have higher mean urate concentrations and a larger proportion of cases of hyperuricemia (Montoye et al. 1967). This finding, which has been inconsistently confirmed in Europe, has not been explained by differences in physiognomy, blood pressure, or medications.

In a survey of nearly 24,000 men in Paris, 17.5 percent were found to have a uric acid value of 7.0 mg%, and 9.9 percent with a value of 7.5 mg% (Zalokar et al. 1972). Two English studies gave results more consistent with U.S. findings, with 7.2 percent and 10.8 percent of men having concentrations of 7.0 mg%. In Finland, 5.2 percent of men and 3.5 percent of women had uric acid values of 7.0 mg% and 6.0 mg%, respectively (see Table VIII.63.2). The relation of uric acid values to nutrition was demonstrated epidemiologically by an investigation conducted in East Germany from 1969 until 1980 with samples of 726 to 1,199 adults. During these 12 years the mean serum urate content increased by about 50 percent (4.2 mg% to 6.3 mg% in men; 3.4 mg% to 5.2 mg% in women), and the percentage with hyperuricemia increased from 2.4 to 29.0 in men and from 1.8 to 19.7 in women. These changes correlated well with increases in the meat consumption of 37 percent and

alcohol consumption of 68 percent (Thiele and Schroeder 1982).

A study based on the records of general practitioners in Great Britain showed the prevalence of gout over the age of 15 years to be 7.3 per 1,000 males in England, but only 2.8 per 1,000 in Scotland. Among females the prevalence was 1.3 and 0.7 per 1,000 in England and Scotland, respectively (Currie 1979). A survey among men between the ages of 45 and 74 in three English towns demonstrates that not only sex and age distribution but also how data are obtained influence the results. A simple questionnaire was mailed to over 15,000 men, of whom two-thirds completed it. In the three communities, 3.9 percent, 4.5 percent, and 4.8 percent (average 4.4 percent) claimed to have gout, which was more than three times the prevalence for age-matched English men obtained from physicians' records (Gardner et al. 1982).

In the Framingham investigation, gout was diagnosed in 2.8 percent of the men and 0.4 percent of the women (Hall et al. 1967). The biennial incidence has been 3.2 per 1,000 men and 0.5 per 1,000 women (Mikkelsen, Dodge, and Valkenburg 1965). A survey

Table VIII.63.2. *Prevalence of hyperuricemia*

Location	Year	Males		Females	
		Cases	Percent >7 mg%	Cases	Percent >6 mg%
England	1962	436	2.3	475	2.3
Japan (Osaka)	1966	378	4.0	434	2.5
U.S. (Mass.)	1967	2,283	4.8	2,844	3.3
Bulgaria	1966	188	4.8	232	7.0
Finland	1969	737	5.2	1,048	3.5
England	1977	512	7.2	254	0.4
Scotland (Glasgow)	1977	337	8.0		
U.S. (Mich.)	1965	2,987	9.2	3,013	8.7
England (Liverpool)	1966	331	10.8		
U.S. (New York)	1971	984	12.3		
France (Paris)	1972	23,923	17.5		
New Zealand (white)	1966	202	23.3	228	16.7
Palau Islands	1972	219	36	291	24
Samoa (urban)	1981	319	36	415	23
Samoa (rural)	1981	356	43	384	29
Rarotonga	1966	243	44	227	43
Mariana Islands	1966	160	45	175	28
Mariana Islands	1972	395	49	504	30
Tokelau Islands	1966	191	48	188	49
New Zealand (Maori)	1966	388	49	378	42
Nauru	1978	217	64	238	60

Table VIII.63.3. *Prevalence of gout in relation to serum uric acid content in men*

Uric acid (mg%)	Framingham, Mass.[a]		Paris, France[b]	
	Subjects	% Gout	Subjects	% Gout
<6.0	1,615	1.1	2,099	1.3
6.0–7.9	432	8.6	1,852	3.2
>8.0	22	36.3	306	17.6
Total	2,069	3.0	4,257	3.3

[a]Hall et al. (1967). [b]Zalokar et al. (1972).

of more than 4,000 employed men in Paris found that 3.5 percent reported a history of gout and 3.0 percent had been treated for this disease (Zalokar et al. 1972) (Table VIII.63.3). However, most investigations of adult male Caucasian populations have identified gout in less than 1 percent. A large survey of industrial workers in New York, for example, revealed no cases among women or among men under the age of 40, and a prevalence of only 0.12 percent above that age (Brown and Lingg 1961). No instances of gout were detected among nearly 3,400 persons above age 15 in Holland in 1954, or among 4,300 persons in Sofia, Bulgaria. In a small Finnish town, one case was found among 787 men and none in 1,048 women.

Non-Caucasian Populations

Reports of gout in non-Caucasian populations are relatively recent. The first case report pertained to a 31-year-old African servant who died of an infection in Edinburgh in 1807, where he had often been subject to severe pains that occurred about midnight in one or the other of his great toes. A medical missionary in Hawaii in the early 1830s reported that rheumatism frequently occurred there, and, although gout might also be expected to be common because of indulgent eating habits, the mild quality of the food suggested otherwise and was unlikely to promote

the disease. Similarly, a military surgeon in New Zealand in the 1850s found that although "rheumatic affections" were much more frequent among New Zealanders than among the English, gout was unknown. Hench, a leading expert, wrote in the 1948 edition of Cecil's *Textbook of Medicine* that gout "is common in England and France, less common but increasing in North America. Hebrews are affected, prosperous American Negroes occasionally." Eugene Traut, in his textbook on rheumatic diseases, stated similarly in 1952 that gout "is unknown in China, Japan, and the tropics. . . . It is rare in Negroes."

The extent to which such statements reflected either ignorance or changing circumstances cannot be ascertained. They clearly are incorrect now. The most ubiquitous factor to account for an increased prevalence of gout is the increased proportion of proteins in many diets, which increases the amount of uric acid that is synthesized. Comparisons of mean serum uric acid values of most adequately nourished populations worldwide give similar values. The exceptions remind us that there are unidentified, presumably genetic factors that result in differences among groups that would be assumed not to differ empirically. A comparative study between Blackfeet Indians in Arizona and Pima Indians in Montana provides an example (Table VIII.63.4). The mean urate concentration and the prevalence of hyperuricemia of the Blackfeet of both sexes were significantly higher than among the Pima. Furthermore, although a high degree of correlation between obesity and hyperuricemia generally is found, more of the Pima, especially the women, were obese.

It was noted coincidentally in Honolulu and Seattle in 1957–8 that an unusually high proportion of Filipino men who visited outpatient clinics had gout or hyperuricemia. In Honolulu, remarkably, in a study of 100 men over 40 years of age, fully half were found to be hyperuricemic, and 32 had clinical gout. Among admissions to the county hospital in Seattle during 64 months, new cases of gout were diagnosed in 2.5 percent of Filipinos and in 0.13 percent of all

Table VIII.63.4. *Serum uric acid in two American Indian tribes*

Tribe	Subjects	Total	Mean urate (mg%)	Percent >7 mg%	Percent >6 mg%	Percent gout
Blackfeet	M	587	5.21 ± 1.12	5.4		0
	F	435	4.47 ± 1.16		9.2	0
Pima	M	473	4.56 ± 1.20	2.5		0.4
	F	475	3.85 ± 1.05		1.0	0

Source: O'Brien et al. (1966)

other patients. The high prevalence of gout among Filipinos living in Hawaii was confirmed by other data, such as the fact that, in a 16-month period, 20 of 24 health insurance claims for treatment of gout were submitted by Filipinos. The mean serum uric acid of Filipino men in Seattle, as in Honolulu, was significantly higher than that of other ethnic groups. This contrasted with a diagnosis of gout in 0.004 percent of admissions to the general hospital of Manila and a normal mean serum uric acid among Filipino men sampled at four sites in the Philippine Islands. This difference could not be attributed entirely to the larger mean body mass of the Filipinos who lived in Hawaii or Washington State (Healey et al. 1967).

Although the ability of gouty individuals to excrete uric acid generally is normal, when this function is challenged by administering a purine (urate precursor) load, individual differences in the maximum excretory capacity can be identified. In such a study, 4 of 13 nongouty Filipino men were unable to increase their excretion of uric acid. The other 9 Filipino and all 10 Caucasian men exhibited the normal response of approximately doubling the quantity excreted (Healey and Bayani-Sioson 1971). This observation led to the hypothesis that some ethnic groups, such as Filipinos, include an unusually large proportion of persons who have a relatively low genetically determined limit to their renal excretory capacity for urate. As long as such individuals consume a low-protein diet, such as many of the Asian rice-based diets, or diets based on yams, their excretory mechanism is not saturated, serum urate remains in the normal range of Caucasians, and gout rarely occurs. When the protein consumption of persons with this latent defect increases – that is, as their diet becomes "Westernized" – the excretory capacity is overwhelmed, urate accumulates, and gout becomes more frequent.

There is a marked difference in the prevalence of hyperuricemia between Caucasian and various Pacific island populations. When 7.0 mg% and 6.0 mg% are used as the upper limits of normal for men and women, respectively, less than 10 percent of most unselected Caucasian populations, but more than 40 percent of many Pacific populations, exceed these values (Table VIII.63.2). Many surveys have been conducted since the 1960s: among Maoris in New Zealand, Polynesians on Rarotonga (south of Samoa) and in the Cook Islands, Micronesians in the Marianas and Nauru, Melanesians in Samoa, among others. The hyperuricemia cannot be attributed entirely to dietary changes, as discussed in regard

to Filipinos, nor is alcohol consumption necessarily a contributory factor. The highest prevalence of hyperuricemia has been found on the Micronesian island of Nauru (64 percent of men, 60 percent of women). The diet here, as among the Rarotongans and Samoans, had largely become Westernized by the time these surveys were conducted. However, disparate groups such as aborigines in northern Australia and natives of New Guinea and of the Tokelau Islands (north of Samoa) were hyperuricemic on their traditional diets. The complexity of the uricemia–gout relationship is illustrated by the unexplained observation that, although the New Zealand Maoris, Tokelauans, and Rarotongans have the same high prevalence of hyperuricemia, a fourfold difference exists in the prevalence of gout: 10.4 percent, 5.3 percent, and 2.5 percent, respectively (Prior 1981).

Nevertheless, a prospective study of gout in Maoris has shown a high correlation between the occurrence of acute gout and the level of uricemia (Brauer and Prior 1978). In 11 years, gout developed in 31 percent of men and 36 percent of women with a serum uric acid greater than 8 mg%, versus 2.8 percent and 0.6 percent, respectively, of subjects having uric acid concentrations below 6 mg% (Yu 1984). These data closely resemble the findings in Framingham, Massachusetts. In the larger sample of that community, clinical gout had developed in 36 percent of men with serum uric acid levels greater than 8 mg% and in 25 percent of women with a value greater than 7 mg% (Hall et al. 1967). The difference between these two cohorts lies in the 2 mg% greater mean serum uric acid content of the Maoris, and probably not in any other predisposing factor for the occurrence of gout.

Surveys in the early 1960s in the Osaka district of Japan showed a very low prevalence of hyperuricemia. Gout was diagnosed in 0.3 percent of men and in no women. With the continued Westernization of the diet, however, an anticipated increase in the prevalence of gout is occurring. Studies in Tokyo in the 1970s have shown mean uric acid levels to be the same as in Caucasian populations (males: 5.64 ± 1.45 mg%; females: 4.40 ± 1.09 mg%). The prevalence of gout in men has increased to 1.2 percent, but the proportion of gouty women was still much lower (0.9 percent of all cases) than in Caucasians. The clinical characteristics of gout are the same and occur in similar frequencies as in Caucasian populations (Nishioka and Mikanagi 1980).

A Chinese author claimed that the first case of gout to be described in China occurred in 1948, and that by 1959 he could collect only 12 cases, 10 with tophi. This almost certainly reflects socioeconomic rather than biological circumstances. The general prevalence of gout may indeed have been low because of the widespread, inadequately low protein diet, but this would have pertained particularly to the large segment of the population that lacked medical care. In regard to the well-nourished upper classes, a lack of diagnostic acumen may have been at least partially responsible.

In the Taiwanese literature, only 19 cases of gout were reported between 1903 and 1964, according to one author. However, in 1963 another author reported 61 cases – 5 percent of the clientele of a rheumatology clinic. Of these, 35 were immigrants from the Chinese mainland.

A study of serum uric acid of 100 Chinese men who lived in British Columbia showed a higher mean value (5.44 ± 1.08 mg%) than that of 200 Caucasian men (4.55 ± 1.02 mg%) (Ford and de Mos 1964). The difficulty of interpreting such data is shown by a comparison of serum uric acid of Chinese living on Taiwan and in Malaya, using the same analytic technique. The mean concentration on Taiwan was 4.99 ± 0.91 mg% for men and 3.87 ± 0.78 mg% for women, whereas in Malaya these values were, respectively, 6.11 ± 1.29 mg% and 4.52 ± 0.9 8 mg% – significantly higher (Duff et al. 1968). At a hospital in New York, 13 cases of gout were seen among Chinese patients in 11 years, an incidence similar to that of other races. Only 1.9 percent of the 2,145 primary gout patients of the Mount Sinai Hospital of New York were Chinese. Yu (1984) interpreted this as evidence of the infrequency of gout among this racial group.

Aside from South Africa, there is little relevant information from the African continent, and most is derived from hospital admissions. Seven cases of gout (five "upper class") were seen at the principal Ugandan hospital in 6 years (1962–7). During 30 months (1960–2) 3 cases were diagnosed at a hospital in Nairobi, Kenya, which represented 11 per 100,000 admissions, whereas during the 5 years 1977–81, 19 cases were seen at the University Hospital in Durban, South Africa, which represented 4.7 per 100,000. Fifteen of these patients were male, and most were poor city dwellers (Mody and Naidoo 1984). A survey in a Nigerian village showed uric acid levels above 6 mg% in 34 percent of men and 13 percent of women. A more extensive investigation in rural south Africa revealed a normal Caucasian distribution of uric acid values, but no cases of gout among more than 1,000 adults.

Table VIII.63.5. *Serum uric acid in South African black and white populations*

Population	Age range	Subjects	Mean uric acid (mg%)
African males			
Tribal	18–75+	80	4.7 ± 1.03
Rural	14–84	128	5.0 ± 1.11
Urban	15–90	144	6.1 ± 1.45
White urban	16–95	213	6.2 ± 1.27
African females			
Tribal	15–75+	399	3.9 ± 0.85
Rural	14–96	242	4.6 ± 1.44
Urban	15–90	280	5.2 ± 1.34
White urban	16–88	298	5.0 ± 1.20

Source: Beighton et al. (1977).

The effect on uricemia of the urbanization of primitive people has been well illustrated by studies in South Africa that showed the lowest mean serum values in a tribal population, higher values in a village, and the highest levels, equal to those of urban whites, in urban (Soweto) blacks (Table VIII.63.5). The combined three black populations (621 men, 1,364 women) contained no cases of gout, whereas 3 of 240 white men and 1 of 332 white women had this disease (Beighton et al. 1977). A survey in Ethiopia in 1961–3 similarly showed the lowest values among rural Ethiopians, intermediate values among urban Ethiopians, and the normal, highest value among Caucasian and Indian urban professionals.

Data from Israel are analogous. Desert Bedouins were found to have lower serum uric acid values than villagers of the same Arabic stock, and the latter results were the same as were obtained from a nearby Jewish population in Haifa. These variations are presumed to be related to changes in nutrition associated with changes in life-style (Dreyfuss, Yaron, and Balogh 1964).

Thomas G. Benedek

Bibliography

Abbott, R. D., et al. 1988. Gout and coronary heart disease: The Framingham study. *Journal of Clinical Epidemiology* 41: 237–42.

Beighton, P., et al. 1977. Rheumatic disorders in the South African Negro. Part IV. Gout and hyperuricemia. *South African Medical Journal* 51: 969–72.

Benedek, T. G. 1987. A century of American rheumatology. *Annals of Internal Medicine* 106: 304–12.

Brauer, G. W., and I. A. Prior. 1978. A prospective study of gout in New Zealand Maoris. *Annals of the Rheumatic Diseases* 37: 466–72.

Breckenridge, A. 1966. Hypertension and hyperuricemia. *Lancet* 1: 15–18.

Brown, R., and C. Lingg. 1961. Musculoskeletal complaints in an industry. *Arthritis and Rheumatism* 4: 283–302.

Currie, W. J. 1979. Prevalence and incidence of the diagnosis of gout in Great Britain. *Annals of the Rheumatic Diseases* 38: 101–6.

Dreyfuss, F., E. Yaron, and M. Balogh. 1964. Blood uric acid levels in various ethnic groups in Israel. *American Journal of the Medical Sciences* 247: 438–44.

Duff, I. F., et al. 1968. Comparison of uric acid levels in some Oriental and Caucasian groups unselected as to gout or hyperuricemia. *Arthritis and Rheumatism* 11: 184–90.

Florey, C. D., and R. M. Acheson. 1968. Serum uric acid in United States and Brazilian military recruits, with a note on ABO blood groups. *American Journal of Epidemiology* 88: 178–88.

Ford, D. K., and A. M. de Mos. 1964. Serum uric acid levels of healthy Caucasian, Chinese and Haida Indian males in British Columbia. *Canadian Medical Association Journal* 90: 1295–7.

Gardner, M. J., et al. 1982. The prevalence of gout in three English towns. *International Journal of Epidemiology* 11: 71–5.

Grahame, R., and J. T. Scott. 1970. Clinical survey of 354 patients with gout. *Annals of the Rheumatic Diseases* 29: 461–8.

Gutman, A. B., and T.-F. Yu. 1955. Prevention and treatment of chronic gouty arthritis. *Journal of the American Medical Association* 157: 1096–102.

Hall, A. P., et al. 1967. Epidemiology of gout and hyperuricemia. A long-term population study. *American Journal of Medicine* 42: 27–37.

Healey, L. A., and P. S. Bayani-Sioson. 1971. A defect in the renal excretion of uric acid in Filipinos. *Arthritis and Rheumatism* 14: 721–6.

Healey, L. A., et al. 1967. Hyperuricemia in Filipinos: Interaction of heredity and environment. *American Journal of Human Genetics* 19: 81–5.

Hench, P. S., et al. 1936. The problem of rheumatism and arthritis (third rheumatism review). *Annals of Internal Medicine* 10: 754–909.

Hill, L. C. 1938. Gout. *Lancet* 1: 826–31.

Klein, R., et al. 1973. Serum uric acid: Its relationship to coronary heart disease risk factors and cardiovascular disease, Evans County, Georgia. *Archives of Internal Medicine* 132: 401–10.

Mikkelsen, W. M., H. J. Dodge, and H. Valkenburg. 1965. The distribution of serum uric acid values in a population unselected as to gout or hyperuricemia. *American Journal of Medicine* 39: 242–51.

Mody, G. M., and P. D. Naidoo. 1984. Gout in South African blacks. *Annals of Rheumatic Diseases* 43: 394–7.

Montoye, H. J., et al. 1967. Serum uric acid concentration among business executives. *Annals of Internal Medicine* 66: 838–49.

Nishioka, K., and K. Mikanagi. 1980. Hereditary and environmental factors influencing on the serum uric acid throughout ten years' population study in Japan. *Advances in Experimental Medicine and Biology* 122A: 155–9.

O'Brien, J. B., T. A. Burch, and J. J. Bunim. 1966. Genetics of hyperuricaemia in Blackfeet and Pima Indians. *Annals of the Rheumatic Diseases* 25: 117.

Prior, I. 1981. Epidemiology of rheumatic disorders in the Pacific with particular emphasis on hyperuricemia and gout. *Seminars in Arthritis and Rheumatism* 13: 145–65.

Rodnan, G. P. 1965. Early theories concerning etiology and pathogenesis of gout. *Arthritis and Rheumatism* 8: 599–609.

Rodnan, G. P., and T. Benedek. 1970. The early history of antirheumatic drugs. *Arthritis and Rheumatism* 13: 145–65.

Seegmiller, J. E., L. Laster, and R. R. Howell. 1963. Biochemistry of uric acid and its relation to gout. *New England Journal of Medicine* 268: 712–6, 764–73, 821–7.

Thiele, P., and H.-E. Schroeder. 1982. Epidemiologie der Hyperurikämie und Gicht. *Zeitschrift für die Gesamte Innere Medizin und ihre Grenzgebiete* 37: 406–10.

Yu, T.-F. 1984. Diversity of clinical features in gouty arthritis. *Seminars in Arthritis and Rheumatism* 13: 360–8.

Yu, T.-F., and A. B. Gutman. 1967. Uric acid nephrolithiasis in gout: Predisposing factors. *Annals of Internal Medicine* 67: 1133–48.

Zalokar, J., et al. 1972. Serum uric acid in 23,923 men and gout in a subsample of 4257 men in France. *Journal of Chronic Disease* 25: 305–12.

Herpes simplex is caused by *Herpes virus hominis,* of which there are two distinct serologic types designated as HSV-1 and HSV-2. The first mainly causes disease above the waist, such as cold sores; the second most commonly causes disease below the waist, especially genital herpes. Exceptions to this generalization occur especially among the newborn. The initial active phase is followed by prolonged latency. But the virus can be reactivated by another infection, stress, exposure to sunshine, or any number of other bodily changes.

Etiology and Epidemiology

The herpes viruses are visible in infected cells by electron microscopy and may be grown in the chick embryo, in tissue cultures, and in laboratory animals that react differently to types HSV-1 and HSV-2.

HSV-1 is shed from cells in the lacrimal and salivary glands, and both types are shed from the primary and recurrent lesions of the mucous membranes and skin. Samples of infected adults show that 2 to 4 percent are excreting the virus at a given time.

Infection with the herpes simplex virus results from person-to-person contact. HSV-1 infections commonly are transmitted by oral secretions through kissing or the sharing of eating utensils, and thus herpetic infection can easily be spread within a family. Normally HSV-1 infections are painful and bothersome but have no serious consequences. An exception can be when the virus invades the cornea of the eye. Conjunctival or corneal herpes may produce scars that impair vision. It may occur among wrestlers from skin-to-skin contact. Another form of HSV-1 infection, called *herpetic paronychia,* may occur in dentists and in hospital personnel.

HSV-2 infections are generally the result of sexual transmission at a time the virus is being shed. Lesions appear on the penis, vulva, buttocks, and adjacent areas, and the mucosa of the vagina and cervix.

The prevalence of HSV-2 infection during pregnancy and its incidence in neonates are related to the socioeconomic level, age, and sexual activity of a population. In one urban population study, 35.7 percent of women attending an obstetrical clinic had serologic evidence of past HSV-2 infections. Moreover, of these women in a study of a lower socioeconomic sample, the antepartum infection rate was 1.02 percent. The infant was safe from infection if the mother's infection had cleared 3 to 4 weeks before delivery. On the other hand, the experience of 283 women with genital herpes suggests that those women who suffer from genital herpes during pregnancy are three times more likely to abort than other women during the first 20 weeks of pregnancy. In this same study, the risk of neonatal infection was 10 percent if infection occurred after 32 weeks of pregnancy, and increased to 40 percent if infection was present at confinement. Neonatal infection from infected mothers is almost certainly of the HSV-2 type, acquired by passage through an infected birth canal. In addition HSV-2 may be transmitted from infant to infant in the hospital nursery by its personnel.

The epidemiology of recurrent herpes is complicated by unknown factors that cause reactivation of the virus. Because the epidemiology of recurrence depends on recollection, the most acceptable studies of reccurent herpes labialis come from students in health care professions. These show inexplicable differences in recurrence: 45 percent in Wales and the United Kingdom, 40 percent in North America, 30 percent in Europe and Africa, 17 percent in Asia, and 16 percent in South America.

The possible relationship of HSV-2 to carcinoma of the cervix has been explored in recent years in light of its ability to transform cells in vitro, the incidence of antibodies to HSV-2 in cancer patients, and the demonstration of viral RNA in cancer cells from the cervix. No conclusive studies have been published to date.

Distribution and Incidence

Infection by herpes virus is reported worldwide, as determined by antibody studies, and is related to the socioeconomic state. The prevalence of positive antibody tests to HSV-1 approaches universality (100 percent) in the lower strata, falling to 30 to 50 percent among those of higher socioeconomic levels. Obviously, transmission is more likely among those living in a crowded and unhygienic environment. The prevalence of positive antibody response begins in early childhood and rises to its peak in adult life. Transplacental antibodies are present in infants up to 6 months of age. Then a sharp rise in antibodies occurs for those aged 1 to 4 years, mainly to HSV-1. This is followed by a slight rise from 5 to 14 years, and after 14 there is a marked rise in antibodies through late adulthood, which is in part due to HSV-2 infection (see Figure VIII.64.1).

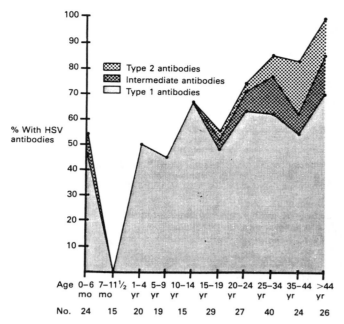

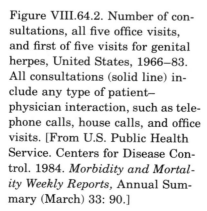

Figure VIII.64.1. Percentage distribution of antibodies to HSV-1, HSV-2, and intermediate form (types 1 and 2) in 239 patients of various age groups. (From A. J. Nahmius and D. E. Campbell. 1983. Infections caused by herpes simplex viruses. In *Infectious Diseases*, 3d edition, ed. Paul D. Hoeprich, 859, by permission of Harper & Row, publishers.)

Because HSV-2 infection is a sexually transmitted disease, it has been studied more intensively in recent years than the more common HSV-1 infection.

On the other hand, most observers agree that herpes genitalis has been on the increase in recent years, and in 1983 the National Institutes of Health estimated that there were 20 million cases in the United States, with 300,000 to 500,000 new cases developing annually. Undoubtedly, contributing factors include increased sexual activity as well as a preference for the use of oral contraceptives over the condom, although a wider use of diagnostic tests may account for some of the apparent increased prevalence. Certainly, publicity concerning herpes genitalis has alerted the medical profession to the disease and has made the public aware that "chafing of a menstrual pad" and lesions on the male genitals may entail more than temporary annoyance.

In any event, beginning with its *1983 Annual Summary, Morbidity and Mortality Reports,* the U.S. Public Health Service has included herpes genitalis. The report for 1984, based on physician consultations, office visits, and the first office visits for the disease, "reflects a 16 fold increase from 28,000 to 423,000 in the number of consultations for genital herpes in the period 1966–1983" (see Figure VIII.64.2).

Immunology

Antibodies to the herpes viruses last throughout the patient's lifetime. An antigen common to both HSV-1 and HSV-2 produces crossreacting antibodies to both strains that can be differentiated immunologically by immunofluorescence and microneutralization tests. Antibody to one type, however, precludes neither an infection with the other nor the development of specific antibodies to the second infection. Yet previous infection with HSV-1 does mitigate the clinical manifestations of the first episode of genital herpes caused by HSV-2. The antibodies that respond to an initial herpes simplex virus infection are complement-fixing, neutralizing, cytotoxic, pre-

Figure VIII.64.2. Number of consultations, all five office visits, and first of five visits for genital herpes, United States, 1966–83. All consultations (solid line) include any type of patient–physician interaction, such as telephone calls, house calls, and office visits. [From U.S. Public Health Service. Centers for Disease Control. 1984. *Morbidity and Mortality Weekly Reports,* Annual Summary (March) 33: 90.]

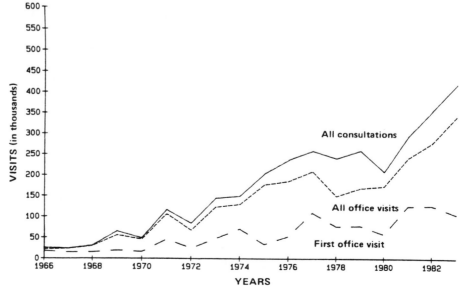

cipitating, and nonprecipitating antibodies, and appear early in the infection. Lawrence Corey (1984) has stated that although complement-fixing and neutralizing "antibodies usually are maintained and in high titer, and inactivate extracellular virus, continued replication of virus by cell to cell transfer ensues. These data help explain frequent reactivation of the disease in the presence of high levels of antibody titer." The relation of humoral antibodies to reactivation of disease is unclear. Whereas the humoral immune response remains at high levels, the in vitro cellular immune response to HSV antigens appears to fluctuate.

Pathology and Clinical Manifestations

The virus multiplies in the epithelium at the portal of entry. The epithelial cells increase in size and contain an enlarged nucleus with intranuclear inclusions. The developing blisterlike vesicle is intradermal and is surrounded by inflammatory cells, edema, and congestion. Viremia may develop in malnourished infants as an accompaniment to measles, and in patients with extensive burns or in those on immunodepressant drugs. Systematic disease accompanies viremia.

The initial lesion at the site of inoculation or at the site of recurrence, whether in the skin or mucous membrane, is a small reddened area that develops into a small, thin-walled, blisterlike vesicle filled with clear fluid. Equally as common is the appearance of a group of small vesicles on the erythematous base.

Gingivostomatitis is the usual type of primary or initial HSV-1 lesion in infants and young children and is seen occasionally in adults. There may be several days of prodromal symptoms such as malaise, fever, and usually cervical lymphadenopathy. Commonly, by the time a physician is consulted, the gums are inflamed and ulcerated. Pain is distressing and may interfere with eating; the course is normally a week to 10 days.

Labial herpes only occasionally represents the initial HSV-1 lesion, but the "cold sore" or "fever blister" of the lip is the most common lesion of recurrent disease. Here a cluster of vesicles appears after a couple of days of hyperesthesia and erythema, to last from several to 10 days. Most commonly these appear at the vermilion line of the skin of the lower lip or on the skin of the upper lip, at times extending to or into the nostril. The term "fever blister" stems from the frequency with which herpetic recurrence accompanies febrile illnesses. Before the age of antibiotics, it was more likely to accompany pneumococ-

cal pneumonia than other types of pneumonia or febrile disease.

Conjunctivitis with or without *keratitis* may be the primary lesion of herpes virus infection. Then the preauricular lymph node commonly is enlarged. Keratitis is characterized by dendritic ulceration.

Cutaneous herpes (HSV-1) may involve the skin of the body, anywhere above the waist and including the feet. (HSV-2 has been isolated from fingers from autoinoculation or genital-to-finger contact in sexual play.) It may be accompanied by edema, fever, lymphangitis, and lymphadenopathy.

Herpes genitalis also has the incubation period of several days following exposure to infection. It may be subclinical, especially in women having lesions only in the vagina or the cervix rather than on the vulva. Herpetic infection is more obvious in men with localized pain, erythema, and the development of one or a group of vesicles on the glans, prepuce, or elsewhere on the penis. The inguinal lymph nodes may be swollen and tender. Urethral involvement in both sexes is manifested by dysuria (painful or difficult urination), and a discharge may be noted in male patients. Pelvic pain accompanying the dysuria is common in women. (The virus can be isolated from the urethra of both sexes. Primary infection with HSV-2 virus often is accompanied by systemic symptoms during the first several days (see Figure VIII.64.3). Complications of primary infection reveal a generalized infection, especially as aseptic meningitis and other indications of viral invasion of the central nervous system.

In a study of 148 newborns with herpes, A. J. Nahmias and colleagues (1970) reported an incubation period of up to 21 days; almost all were infected with HSV-2 and had evidence of dissemination. The overall fatality rate was 71 percent, and 95 percent among those with disseminated infection. Of those recovering, 15 percent had sequelae, especially defects in the central nervous system.

Some studies show recurrences within the first year in 80 percent of infections with HSV-2. Recurrent lesions commonly present with milder symptoms initially, are generally of shorter duration, and are rarely accompanied by overt systemic symptoms. These lesions commonly appear on the genitalia, but may appear on the buttocks and elsewhere adjacent to the genital area. Latent infection presumably is established in the sacral-nerve-root ganglia. From a study of 375 patients, Stanley Bierman (1983) found that recurrences ceased in half of them after some 7 years following the onset of disease. In others, however, the recurrences may span many years.

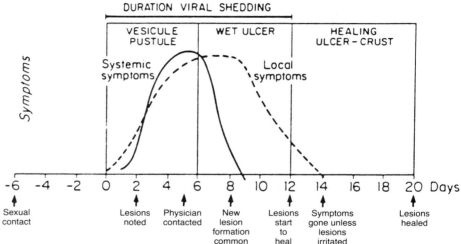

Figure VIII.64.3. Schematic graph of the clinical course of primary genital herpes. (From L. Corey. 1984. Genital herpes. In *Sexually Transmitted Diseases,* ed. King K. Holmes et al., 453, by permission of the McGraw Hill Book Company.)

It is unclear what triggers recurrent genital herpes. Emotional stress, fever, heat, trauma, coitus, and the menses have all been suggested. But they lack the certainty that a febrile illness seems to play as a provoking factor in HSV-1 recurrences.

History and Geography

The word *herpes* is derived from the Greek verb "to creep," and the identification of disease in ancient writings depends upon one's interpretation of the description of physical signs. Thus, one may decide either that a described lesion was of the herpetic type or accept the translation of the term "herpes" itself. No doubt aphthae and herpetic lesions were not differentiated.

The oldest record of disease of the genitalia appears in the *Ebers Papyrus* (c. 1550 B.C.). The translator commented on the inflammation of the vulva and thighs of a woman in nonspecific terms, but in the same papyrus describes treatment for "herpes of the face." Hippocrates spoke of "herpetic sores" and, again in his *Epidemics,* that "many have aphthae and ulcerations of the mouth, frequent fluxations of the genital organs and ulcers." Herodotus described herpetic eruptions "which appear about the mouth at the crisis of simple fevers." H. Haeser (1875), in reviewing the medical writings of the Byzantine Empire, quotes from three physicians (the fourth to seventh centuries) concerning "superficial aphthae" and "vesicular eruptions" of the vulva. J. Preuss (1911), a Biblical scholar, in referring to the Talmud's permission to delay the rite of circumcision, said, *"Mila betzaraath* is probably harmless herpes of the foreskin."

The first definitive description of herpes appears in Jean Astruc's 1736 publication of *De Morbis Venereis,* translated into English and published in

London in 1754. His description of vesicles in both male and female patients unmistakably indicates those of herpes genitalis. Toward the end of the eighteenth century, the English physician Robert Willan developed a classification, published in 1808, of the bewildering varieties of skin diseases, among which was a category of vesiculae.

In his *Synopsis of Cutaneous Diseases* (1818), Thomas Bateman described herpes labialis, which "occasionally appears as an idiopathic affection . . . frequently in the course of disease of the viscera of which it is symptomatic." His accurate description of herpes praeputialis emphasized the hazard of interpreting a cluster of vesicles as a syphilitic chancre. He described the prodromes, development of the erythema and vesicles, and their course to healing, ending with, "I have not been able to ascertain the causes of this eruption on the prepuce. . . . Whencesoever it may originate, it is liable to recur in the same individual at intervals of six or eight weeks."

Jean Louis Alibert (1832) not only described herpes praeputialis but stated that the lesion may occur at the introitus of the vagina. F. L. Legendre (1853) described three instances of herpes of the vulva, with the observation that herpes may recur 2 or 3 days before menstruation.

The most descriptive paper on herpes progenitalis was presented by Boston physician F. B. Greenough (1881), at the meeting of the American Dermatological Association. He documented its frequency among private patients and its rarity among patients in the Venereal Disease Clinic of the Boston Dispensary. His explanation for this discrepancy was that patients in a charitable institution were less apt to complain of a trivial abnormality unless they believed it to be a manifestation of a more serious disease. He made the important observation that one of the "three" venereal diseases had existed before the appearance of herpes genitalis. His summary included the statement:

[S]ome of its most interesting and important characteristics are, its tendency to relapse, the very great frequency with which it will be found to have been preceded by the act of coitus, the fact that it rarely, if ever, is found in patients who have been perfectly free from all venereal trouble, and that it is confined to the period of youth and early manhood.

In addition, Greenough made the surprising observation that he had never seen an instance of genital herpes in a woman. Among the numerous discussants of Greenough's paper was Louis A. Duhring (1881), president of the association, who commented in his discussion that though others had seen the disease in women, he, too, had never seen such an instance. This phase of the discussion prompted a paper 2 years later by Paul Unna of Hamburg (1883), published in an American journal. He, too, had never seen herpes genitalis in his private female patients, but cited observations made in Germany and France where medical examination of prostitutes was under police surveillance. In addition, he pointed out that among women admitted to the syphilis department of the Hamburg General Hospital, from 1878 to 1881, with admission of 1,357 to 1,459 patients annually, the incidence of herpes genitalis was 64, 126, 121, and 112 cases during the 4 years. For the same years, males admitted to the syphilis department, with admissions of 634 to 795 annually, had an incidence of herpes genitalis of 4, 9, 4, and 0, respectively.

Unna (1883) summarized:

It is now evident that the conclusions arrived at by members of the American Dermatological Society are correct, in so far as the *general rarity* of herpes vulvae is concerned; but, on the contrary, the conclusion that *women as such are therefore less* susceptible of being thus affected *is erroneous.* Indeed, herpes progenitalis is found more frequently in women *who are only distinguished by their vocation* than in men. We may therefore say only this much: *that women are just as susceptible to herpes as men* are; there is no immunity from herpes for the female *sex.* On the contrary, the exciting cause that induces virile herpes is usually absent in women; but when this is present (as in puellae publicae) herpes is frequently found; for women *herpes is so to say a vocational disease.* (Italics added)

Unna dismissed the usual theories to account for the disease and suggested that it was a variant of herpes zoster, triggered by genital irritations: Just as there are "men who are habitually attacked by herpes after each act of coition, so, too, there are prostitutes who have an eruption of herpes every time they menstruate."

R. Bergh of Copenhagen (1890) confirmed a high incidence of herpes genitalis among prostitutes, reporting that the episodes were related to the menses in 73.4 percent of 877 women admitted to the hospital for the disease. Aware of the relationship of herpes labialis to bacterial infection, he was puzzled by the lack of such a relationship in herpes genitalis in spite of the not infrequent coincidence of herpes labialis and genitalis. He did not accept any relationship between herpes genitalis and venereal disease because he had seen it in a recently married woman and in youths who masturbated frequently. Therefore, he concluded the lesions were of a nervous origin, being due to congestion of the parts, as after masturbation or coitus in men and with menses in prostitutes. E. Levin (1906) reported observations on 1,584 women admitted to the venereal disease shelter in Berlin in 1898–9. There were 112 with herpes of whom 83 had genital herpes. Twenty-nine women had recurrent episodes, and thus 154 episodes were analyzed: 118 genital and 26 at other sites. Coincidence with menstruation occurred in 70 percent of the episodes.

A few years later, Prague physician O. Baum (1920) reported herpetic keratitis, following inoculation of rabbit corneas with vesicular fluid from two cases of herpes labialis, two of herpes genitalis (one in a recurrence), one of herpes faciei, and one each of herpes after the injection of bismuth and salvarsan. Results of such experiments with material from three cases of herpes zoster and several other vesicular skin diseases were negative. Four years later, investigators at the University of Turin, while carrying out successful experiments of inoculating blood and cerebrospinal fluid from patients having herpetic disease (or during a period between recurrences) into corneas, found instances of positive reaction among control subjects. This led to experiments with blood and cerebrospinal fluid from subjects who had not had herpetic eruptions for a long time; of 21 patients, only 3 gave negative results with both blood and spinal fluid. In 4, the spinal fluids were abnormal, and in 4 the Wassermann reaction was positive.

In 1921, B. Lipschütz successfully inoculated material from vesicles on the genitalia into the skin of human subjects. Four years later, S. Flexner and H. L. Amos (1925) demonstrated the herpes virus, and in 1934 Albert Sabin and colleagues isolated it. K. E. Schneweiss (1962) identified two strains of herpes virus by neutralization tests, a finding confirmed by W. R. Dowdle and Nahmias in 1967. The literature in subsequent years has contributed to knowledge concerning epidemiology and immunology.

R. H. Kampmeier

Bibliography

Alibert, J. L. 1832. *Monographie des dermatoses.* Paris.

Bateman, Thomas. 1818. *A practical synopsis of cutaneous diseases.* Longman.

Baum, O. 1920. Ueber die Uebertragbarkeit des Herpes Simplex auf die Kaninchenhornhaut. *Dermatologische Wochenschrift* 70: 105–6.

Bergh, R. 1890. Ueber Herpes Menstralis. *Monatshefte für Praktische Dermatologie* 10: 1–16.

Beswick, T.S.L. 1962. The origin and the use of the word herpes. *Medical History* 6: 214–32.

Bierman, Stanley M. 1983. A retrospective study of 375 patients with genital herpes simplex infections seen between 1973 and 1980. *Cutis* 31: 548–65.

Bolognese, R. J. 1976. Herpesvirus hominis type II infections in asymptomatic pregnant women. *Obstetrics and Gynecology* 48: 507–10.

Corey, Lawrence. 1984. Genital herpes. In *Sexually transmitted diseases,* ed. King K. Holmes et al. New York.

Dowdle, W. R., and A. J. Nahmias. 1967. Association of antigenic type of herpes virus hominis with site of viral recovery. *Journal of Immunology* 99: 974–80.

Duhring, Louis A. 1881. Discussion of Greenough paper. *Archives of Dermatology* 7: 29.

Flexner, S., and H. L. Amos. 1925. Contributions to the pathology of experimental encephalitis: II. Herpetic strains of encephalitogenic virus. *Journal of Experimental Medicine* 41: 223–43.

Greenough, F. B. 1881. Herpes progenitalis. *Archives of Dermatology* 7: 1–29.

Haeser, H. 1875. *Lehrbuchgeschichte der Medizin und der epidemischen Krankheiten,* 3 vols. Jena.

Hoeprich, P. D., ed. 1983. *Infectious diseases,* 3d edition. New York.

Holmes, King K., et al., eds. 1984. *Sexually transmitted diseases.* New York.

Kampmeier, R. H. 1984. Herpes genitalis: A clinical puzzle for two centuries. *Sexually Transmitted Diseases* 11: 41–5.

Legendre, F. L. 1853. Mémoire sur l'herpes de la vulve. *Archives Générales de Médecine* 2: 171–204.

Levin, E. 1906. Ueber Herpes bein Frauen und seine Beziehungen zur Menstruation. *Deutsche Medizinische Wochenschrift* 26: 277–9; 293–6.

Lipschütz, B. 1921. Untersuchungen über die Aetiologie der Krankheiten den Herpesgruppe (Herpes zoster, Herpes genitalis, Herpes febrilis). *Archiv für Dermatologie und Syphilis* 136: 428–82.

Morton, R. S. 1975. Herpes genitalis. In *Recent advances in sexually transmitted diseases,* ed. R. S. Morton and J. R. W. Harris. London.

Nahmias, A. J., C. A. Alford, and B. K. Sheldon. 1970. Infection of the newborn with *Herpes virus hominis. Advances in Pediatrics* 17: 185–226.

Nahmias, A. J., and Donald E. Campbell. 1983. Infections caused by herpes simplex viruses. In *Infectious diseases,* ed. Paul D. Hoeprich, 3d ed. Philadelphia.

Nahmias, A. J., H. L. Keyserling, and G. M. Kerrick. 1983. Herpes simplex virus. In *Infectious diseases of the fetus and newborn infants,* ed. J. Remington and J. O. Klein, 2d ed. Philadelphia.

Nahmias, A. J., et al. 1969. Genital infection with type 2 herpes virus hominis: A commonly occurring venereal disease. *British Journal of Venereal Diseases* 45: 294–8.

1981. Clinical aspects of infection with herpes simplex viruses 1 and 2. In *The human herpesviruses,* ed. Andre J. Nahmias, Walter R. Dowdle, and Raymond F. Schinazi. New York.

Preuss, J. 1978. *Biblical and Talmudic medicine (1911).* New York.

Rapp, Fred, ed. 1984. *Herpesviruses: Proceedings of a Burroughs Wellcome–UCLA Symposium,* April 8–13, 1984.

Rawls, W. E., et al. 1971. Genital herpes in two social groups. *American Journal of Obstetrics and Gynecology* 110: 682–9.

Sabin, Albert B., A. Bond, and A. M. Wright. 1934. Acute ascending myelitis following a monkey bite, with isolation of a virus capable of reproducing the disease. *Journal of Experimental Medicine* 59: 115–36.

Schneweiss, K. E. 1962. Serologische Untersuchungen zur Typendifferenzierung des *Herpesvirus Hominis. Zeitschrift für Immunitätsforschung und Experimentelle Therapie* 124: 24–48.

Unna, P. G. 1883. On herpes progenitalis, especially in women. *Journal of Cutaneous and Venereal Diseases* 1: 321–34.

U.S. Public Health Service. 1984. *Morbidity and Mortality Weekly Report. Annual Summary,* March 33: 90.

Willan, Robert. 1808. *On Cutaneous Diseases, Vol. 1.* London.

VIII.65
Herpesviruses

The family of herpesviruses (Herpetoviridae) includes herpes simplex 1 and 2 viruses, varicella zoster virus, Epstein–Barr virus, and the cytomegalovirus. All are double-stranded DNA viruses of icosahedral form, enclosed in a lipid-containing envelope, and ranging in size from 120 to 180 nanometers.

R. H. Kampmeier

VIII.66
Histoplasmosis

Histoplasmosis is an infection caused by *Histoplasma capsulatum*, a soil fungus. Exposure occurs by inhalation, and the primary infection is in the lung. The disease is usually benign and self-limited, despite a strong tendency for invasion of the bloodstream during the primary infection. This fungemia seeds reticuloendothelial organs throughout the body. Under favorable conditions, the organism can cause progressive disease in one or in multiple sites, resulting in a wide variety of clinical manifestations.

Distribution and Incidence

H. capsulatum has been isolated from soil of more than 50 countries. It is most common in temperate climates along river valleys and has been found in North, Central, and South America; India; Southeast Asia; and rarely Europe.

By far the most heavily endemic area in the world is the east central United States, particularly the Mississippi and Ohio River valleys. It is most prevalent in the states of Ohio, Kentucky, Indiana, Illinois, Kentucky, Tennessee, and Arkansas. Surrounding states also have many infections.

Infection is almost universal in the most heavily endemic areas. Skin test surveys reveal that over 90 percent of persons living in some counties in the central United States have had histoplasmosis before age 20 (Edwards et al. 1969). Based on skin test surveys, there are probably 40 to 50 million people in the central United States who have had histoplasmosis, and there are several hundred thousand new cases each year. The number of serious infections requiring diagnosis and treatment is very small, perhaps 1 or 2 percent of the total.

In contrast to the highly endemic central United States, only a handful of individual cases have been documented in Europe. Skin test surveys show about 0.5 percent of the population positive to histoplasmin. In Italy, positive skin tests are slightly more common (about 2 percent) (Mantovani 1972).

Etiology and Epidemiology

H. capsulatum is a thermal dimorphic fungus. At 25°C, it grows on Sabouraud agar as a fluffy-white mycelium, which bears microconidia and also characteristic tuberculate macroconidia. The organism is free-living in nature in this form. At 37°C, it grows as a small (2- to 4-μm diameter) yeast. The organism is found in this form in infected tissue.

A minor disturbance of fungus-laden soil may scatter spores into the air. The microconidia are inhaled, causing infection. Within the lung the organism converts to the yeast phase, which is not infectious. Person-to-person transmission does not occur. So-called epidemics of histoplasmosis are more accurately point-source outbreaks.

Within a highly endemic area, the organism is widely but not uniformly distributed. Microfoci with high concentrations of organisms are found by chicken coops and starling roosts, and in caves inhabited by bats. The nitrogen-rich excrement of birds and bats provides a favorable growth environment for the fungus. Exposure of small groups of people to high concentrations of organisms at such sites may result in outbreaks of symptomatic infection. These are fairly easy to identify because a severe respiratory illness occurs simultaneously in a group of people who were together for a particular activity 14 days earlier. Extremely large outbreaks of longer duration have occurred during excavation for road or building construction. A good example is the community-wide outbreak of histoplasmosis that occurred during the building of a swimming pool and tennis court complex in Indianapolis, Indiana, infecting perhaps over 100,000 people (Wheat et al. 1981).

Most cases of histoplasmosis, however, are sporadic and result from casual exposure to environmental spores. Patients with sporadic illness probably inhale fewer spores and are more likely to be asymptomatic or minimally symptomatic. The vast majority of these infections are never recognized and are known to exist only as a result of skin test surveys.

Immunology

Cell-mediated immunity is crucial in host defense. Inhalation of spores causes patchy areas of pneumonitis. The spores are transformed into the yeast form, which is engulfed by macrophages. The yeasts multiply intracellularly with a generation time of 11 hours (Howard 1965). The regional lymph nodes are quickly involved, and hematogenous spread occurs. The fungus is cleared from the blood by reticuloendothelial cells throughout the body. Specific cell-mediated immunity develops and rapidly checks the infection in the lung and at distant sites. Granuloma formation and necrosis occur at sites of infection.

Humoral antibody also develops. Although circulating antibodies are the basis of many diagnostic tests, they have little importance in limiting the infection. Hyperimmune serum is of no benefit in experimental infections, and hypogammaglobulinemic patients are not prone to progressive infections.

Clinical Manifestations and Pathology

Primary Pulmonary Histoplasmosis

This disease is asymptomatic at least half of the time. Symptomatic patients become ill about 2 weeks after exposure. They have an influenza-like illness with fever, chills, myalgias, headache, and a nonproductive cough. Rare manifestations include arthralgias, arthritis, and erythema nodosum. With or without symptoms, the chest roentgenogram may show patchy areas of pneumonitis and prominent hilar adenopathy.

A primary fungemia probably occurs in most cases. The calcified granulomas commonly found in spleens and livers of patients from endemic areas result from this primary, self-limited fungemia, not from progressive dissemination.

Following exposure to an unusually heavy inoculum, a more diffuse pulmonary involvement may occur, with an extensive nodular infiltrate on the chest roentgenogram. Dyspnea may be added to the other symptoms, and symptoms are more severe and last longer. Most patients recover without treatment, but extreme cases may progress to respiratory failure.

The chest roentgenogram often returns to normal after a primary pulmonary infection, but a variety of residual abnormalities may be seen. Initial soft infiltrates may harden and contract, leaving one or several nodules. Central necrosis may result in a dense core of calcium (a "target" lesion), but this is not universal. Infrequently, alternate periods of activity followed by healing may result in concentric rings of calcium as the lesion slowly enlarges. Lymph node calcification, either in association with a parenchymal nodule or as a solitary finding, is common. Finally, small "buckshot" calcifications may be scattered over both lung fields, a pattern characteristic of uneventful recovery after exposure to a heavy inoculum of organisms.

Primary histoplasmosis has several uncommon local complications within the chest. Involvement of the pericardium can cause a nonspecific acute pericarditis (Wheat et al. 1983). The inflammation probably represents a response to adjacent infection in the lung, as the cultures of pericardial fluid are usually sterile. Many cases are probably misdiagnosed as benign viral pericarditis. Rarely, the process progresses to chronic constrictive pericarditis. More delayed and more serious, an extensive fibrosing process in the mediastinum can cause vascular compression and result in the superior vena caval syndrome with edema of the head and upper extremities and development of superficial venous collaterals across the chest wall. Inflammation adjacent to the esophagus may cause a traction diverticulum. A lymph node impinging on a bronchus may cause a chronic cough. If a calcified lymph node erodes through a bronchus, it becomes a broncholith. Hemoptysis is a common clinical manifestation.

Chronic Cavitary Histoplasmosis

Although it may occur anywhere in the lung, chronic cavitary histoplasmosis usually involves both upper lobes and closely resembles reinfection tuberculosis in its roentgenographic appearance. The mechanism of infection, however, is not endogenous reactivation. Rather the infection is the result of a primary infection in abnormal lungs, typically the lungs of middle-aged or older male smokers who have centrilobular emphysema (Goodwin et al. 1976). Acute pulmonary histoplasmosis in this setting usually resolves uneventfully although very slowly. In about a third of cases, infected air spaces persist. A progressive fibrosing and cavitary process gradually destroys adjacent areas of the lung. Chronic cough is the most common symptom. Constitutional symptoms, including low-grade fever, night sweats, and weight loss, increase as the illness progresses.

Disseminated Histoplasmosis

This condition refers to any progressive extrapulmonary infection. There is a range of infection with different tissue responses. At one extreme there are massive numbers of organisms in all reticuloendothelial organs with little tendency to granuloma formation. Clinical features include high fever, hepatosplenomegaly, lymphadenopathy, and pancytopenia due to bone marrow involvement. This type of disseminated histoplasmosis has been called the "infantile" form and may lead to death within days or weeks. Other patients, often older adults, have a more indolent illness, many months in duration, characterized by low or moderate fever, weight loss, and skin and mucous membrane lesions. Biopsies of involved tissues show well-formed granulomas similar to sarcoidosis. Organisms are scanty and often are demonstrated only with special stains.

Disseminated histoplasmosis also occurs as an opportunistic infection. The degree of granulomatous tissue response may vary from none to a considerable amount and has prognostic value. If the bone marrow biopsy shows epitheloid granulomas or even recognizable aggregates of macrophages, the response to treatment is quite good. If the biopsy shows no granulomas, tissue necrosis, and a large number of organisms, the prognosis is very poor (Davies, McKenna, and Sarosi 1979).

Disseminated histoplasmosis often presents as a nonspecific systemic febrile illness rather than as a pulmonary infection. There is usually no cough. The chest roentgenogram may be normal. If abnormal, it often shows a diffuse infiltrate, suggesting hematogenous spread to the lung, rather than a focal infiltrate.

Immunosuppressed patients probably get disseminated histoplasmosis in two ways. If they inhale the organisms while immunosuppressed, the primary infection will progress, as documented in the Indianapolis outbreak (Wheat et al. 1982). On the other hand, if they become profoundly immunosuppressed long after their primary infection, the disease may reactivate (Davies, Kahn, and Sarosi 1978). This is suggested by the systemic, nonpulmonary nature of the illness and is supported by the recent experience with the acquired immune deficiency syndrome (AIDS). Patients with past exposure to endemic areas are developing disseminated histoplasmosis while living in nonendemic areas such as New York City (Huang et al. 1988), San Francisco, and Los Angeles.

Disseminated histoplasmosis may also present as a more localized infection. Examples include central nervous system histoplasmosis, meningeal histoplasmosis, and isolated gastrointestinal histoplasmosis, which often involves the terminal ileum. All are extremely rare.

Diagnosis

The *histoplasmin skin test* is a valuable epidemiological tool that has permitted mapping of the endemic area. However, it is worthless in individual case diagnosis. A positive skin test means only that the person is one of many millions who have had histoplasmosis, probably remotely and without sequelae. It does not mean that a current illness under investigation is being caused by the fungus.

Primary histoplasmosis is usually not diagnosed at all. Sputum cultures are positive in less than 10 percent of cases. Most recognized cases are diagnosed by serology. Serologic tests include *immunodiffusion* (M and H bands) and *complement fixation* (yeast and mycelial antigens) tests. An M band by immunodiffusion is fairly specific. The H band is never found alone. When present with the M band (10 to 20 percent of the time), it adds further to specificity. Unfortunately, the immunodiffusion test is insensitive and appears slowly after primary infection. Less than 25 percent of symptomatic patients have a positive test 2 weeks after the onset of clinical illness (Davies 1986). The complement fixation test is more sensitive but less specific. The titer against the mycelial antigen is not important because it is almost always lower than the titer against the yeast antigen. A titer of 1 to 32 or higher against the yeast antigen is diagnostic if the clinical picture suggests histoplasmosis. Unfortunately, only 60 percent of patients have a positive test 2 weeks after the onset of clinical illness, and many have 1:8 or 1:16 titers (Davies 1986). What this means is the serologic tests are most useful for diagnosing patients who have already recovered. Patients with rapidly progressive pneumonias not responding to antibacterial antibiotics need urgent diagnosis, especially if respiratory failure is impending or actually develops. Some patients are diagnosed by serology. Others require lung biopsy for histopathological diagnosis, because a negative serology cannot exclude the diagnosis, and empirical treatment for all possible causes of progressive pulmonary infection is not possible.

Chronic cavitary histoplasmosis is easier to diagnose. The pace is slower. Tuberculosis is suspected first, but the tuberculin skin test is negative and the sputum is negative for tuberculosis by smear and culture. Sputum cultures for *H. capsulatum* are usually positive, as are serologic tests (immunodiffusion: 75 percent; complement fixation: 90 percent).

Disseminated histoplasmosis is difficult to diagnose because the illness is so nonspecific. Serologic tests are positive in over half of cases and may provide an important clue. Serodiagnostic tests are least helpful in the immunosuppressed because they are less sensitive and because the pace of the illness may be so fast that there is no time to wait for the results. Histopathological examination of tissue biopsies is the method of diagnosis in most cases. Bone marrow biopsy is particularly valuable in febrile illnesses without localizing features. Special stains, such as one of the many modifications of the silver stain, are necessary to ensure visualization of the organisms. Cultures of blood, bone marrow, and other tissues and of body fluids may also give the diagnosis in some cases.

History and Geography

Infection with *H. capsulatum* was first described in April 1906 by Samuel Darling (1906). From an autopsy of a laborer who died while working on the Panama Canal, he described a disseminated infection of the reticuloendothelial system caused by an organism that he believed was protozoan. Macrophages were filled with small organisms. Within a few years he reported two other similar cases. In 1913, H. da Rocha-Lima discussed the published photomicrographs of Darling's cases and speculated that the organism might be a fungus rather than a protozoan (Rocha-Lima 1913).

Another autopsy case was reported in Minnesota in 1926 by W. A. Riley and C. J. Watson (1926), who credited Darling with being the first to describe the infection in 1906. Later, however, there was some confusion as to whether a case report of R. P. Strong (1906) from the Philippines in January 1906 had described histoplasmosis first. But in a personal letter many years later, Strong stated his belief that the case he had described was not histoplasmosis, but rather a rare human infection with *Cryptococcus farciminosus,* the cause of farcy in horses (Parsons and Zarafonetis 1945). Thus credit for the first case description remains with Darling, who recognized that the disease was previously undescribed and who named the organism and the illness.

After Riley and Watson's paper, scattered autopsy reports of similar cases followed, mostly from the central United States. Then in 1934, the first premortem diagnosis of such a patient was made by finding the characteristic intracellular organisms on a peripheral blood smear (Dodd and Tompkins 1934). W. A. DeMonbreun (1934) isolated the infectious agent, proved that it was a fungus, and demonstrated its thermal dimorphism.

In January 1945, R. J. Parsons and C. J. Zarafonetis (1945) reported 7 cases, reviewed 71 previous

cases, and concluded that histoplasmosis was a rare systemic infection that was nearly always fatal. However, in the same year, A. Christie and J. C. Peterson (1945) and also C. E. Palmer (1945), using antigen derived from the first isolate, demonstrated that great numbers of asymptomatic persons in the central United States had been infected with the fungus. Furthermore, they showed that almost all tuberculin-negative persons with calcifications on chest roentgenogram had positive histoplasmin skin tests. Quickly the endemic area was mapped and fungus was isolated from soil in areas with high skin-test positivity. The new conclusion was that histoplasmosis is very common and almost invariably benign and self-limited. The fatal cases were rare and exceptional.

Most of the skin-test reactors in the early surveys had had asymptomatic or minimally symptomatic nonspecific infections. The retrospective discovery of a highly symptomatic but also self-limited form of primary histoplasmosis soon followed. Small groups of patients exposed to high concentrations of organisms, often in closed spaces, had been verified as victims of epidemics of an unknown but relatively severe acute pulmonary illness. An epidemiological investigation of one such outbreak, which occurred in 1944 and was reported 3 years later (Cain et al. 1947), demonstrated convincingly that *H. capsulatum* had been the offending agent.

Upper-lobe cavitary histoplasmosis resembling tuberculosis was first described in Missouri in 1956 by M. L. Furculow and C. A. Brasher among sanitorium patients being treated for tuberculosis. The mechanism of infection was most likely progressive primary infection in an abnormal lung, and not reactivation (Goodwin et al. 1976).

In 1955, the isolation of amphotericin B was described by W. Gold and colleagues, and within a few years the drug was available for treatment of a wide variety of fungal infections. This drug, despite some toxicity, proved highly effective for histoplasmosis and remains the agent to which newer alternatives must be compared. Ketoconazole, a nontoxic oral imidazole, arrived in the 1980s. It is not as effective as amphotericin B but is reasonable therapy for mild to moderately ill patients with chronic cavitary disease and indolent forms of disseminated disease.

With the increase in the use of glucocorticoids and cytotoxic drugs for malignant and nonmalignant diseases, disseminated histoplasmosis assumed increasing importance (Davies, Khan, and Sarosi 1978; Kaufman et al. 1978). Endogenous reactivation was suspected as a mechanism in some cases because the illness presented as a nonspecific febrile illness. Treatment with amphotericin B was very effective if the diagnosis was made quickly and if the patient had some degree of cell-mediated immune response.

Finally, as previously noted, AIDS brought a new level of suppression of the cell-mediated immune system. The concept of endogenous reactivation received further support, for, unlike other immunosuppressed patients, even those AIDS patients who respond to treatment are not cured but require long-term suppressive therapy to prevent relapse of infection (Johnson et al. 1986).

Scott F. Davies

Bibliography

Cain, J. C., et al. 1947. An unusual pulmonary disease. *Archives of Internal Medicine* 79: 626–41.

Christie A., and J. C. Peterson. 1945. Pulmonary calcification in negative reactors to histoplasmin. *American Journal of Public Health* 35: 1131–47.

Darling, S. T. 1906. A protozoan general infection producing pseudo tuberculosis in the lungs and focal necrosis of the liver, spleen and lymph nodes. *Journal of the American Medical Association* 46: 1283–6.

Davies, S. F. 1986. Serodiagnosis of histoplasmosis. *Seminars in Respiratory Infections* 1: 9–15.

Davies, S. F., M. Khan, and G. A. Sarosi. 1978. Disseminated histoplasmosis in immunologically suppressed patients: Occurrence in non-endemic area. *American Journal of Medicine* 64: 94–100.

Davies, S. F., R. W. McKenna, and G. A. Sarosi. 1979. Trephine biopsy of the bone marrow in disseminated histoplasmosis. *American Journal of Medicine* 67: 617–77.

DeMonbreun, W. A. 1934. The cultivation and cultural characteristics of Darling's histoplasma capsulatum. *American Journal of Tropical Medicine* 14: 93–125.

Dodd, K., and E. H. Tompkins. 1934. Case of histoplasmosis of Darling in an infant. *American Journal of Tropical Medicine* 14: 127–37.

Edwards, L. D., et al. 1969. An atlas of sensitivity to tuberculin, PPDB, and histoplasmin in the United States. *American Review of Respiratory Disease* 90 (Supplement) 1: 132.

Furcolow, M. L., and C. A. Brasher. 1956. Chronic progressive (cavitary) histoplasmosis as a problem in tuberculosis sanitoriums. *American Review of Tuberculosis and Pulmonary Disease* 73: 609–19.

Gold, W., et al. 1955. Amphotericins A and B, antifungal antibiotics produced by a streptomycete. *Antibiotics Annual* 579–86.

Goodwin, R. A., et al. 1976. Chronic pulmonary histoplasmosis. *Medicine* 55: 413–52.

Grayston, J. T., and M. L. Furcolow. 1953. Occurrence of histoplasmosis in epidemics: Epidemiological studies. *American Journal of Public Health* 43: 665–76.

Howard, D. H. 1965. Intracellular growth in histoplasma capsulatum. *Journal of Bacteriology* 89: 518–23.

Huang, C. T., et al. 1988. Disseminated histoplasmosis in the acquired immunodeficiency syndrome: Report of 5 cases from a non-endemic area. *Archives of Internal Medicine* 2147: 1181–4.

Johnson, P. C., et al. 1986. Progressive disseminated histoplasmosis in patients with the acquired immunodeficiency syndrome. *Seminars in Respiratory Infections* 1: 1–8.

Kaufman, C. A., et al. 1978. Histoplasmosis in immunosuppressed patients. *American Journal of Medicine* 64: 923–32.

Mantovani, A. 1972. Histoplasmosis in Europe. *Annales de la Société Belge de Médecine Tropicale* 52: 421–34.

Palmer, C. E. 1945. Non-tuberculosis pulmonary calcification and sensitivity to histoplasmin. *Public Health Reports* 60: 513–20.

Parsons, R. J., and C. Zarafonetis. 1945. Histoplasmosis in man: A report of 7 cases and a review of 71 cases. *Archives of Internal Medicine* 75: 1–23.

Riley, W. A., and C. J. Watson. 1926. Histoplasmosis of Darling with report of a case originating in Minnesota. *American Journal of Tropical Medicine* 6: 271–82.

Rocha-Lima, H. da. 1913. Beitrag zur Kenntnis der Blastomykosen: lymphangitis epizootica und histoplasmosis. *Zentralblatt für Bakteriologie, Parasitenkunde, Infektionskrankheiten; and Hygiene Seminars in Respiratory Infections* 1: 9–15.

Strong, R. P. 1906. A study of some tropical ulcerations of the skin with particular reference to their etiology. *Philippine Journal of Science* 1: 91–115.

Wheat, L. J., et al. 1981. A large urban outbreak of histoplasmosis: Clinical features. *Annals of Internal Medicine* 94: 331–7.

  1982. Risk factors for disseminated or fatal histoplasmosis. *Annals of Internal Medicine* 95: 159–63.

  1983. Pericarditis as a manifestation of histoplasmosis during two large urban outbreaks. *Medicine* 62: 110–18.

VIII.67
Hookworm Disease

Ancylostomiasis, or hookworm disease, is caused by hookworm infection and is characterized by progressive anemia. In 1989, it was estimated that perhaps as many as one billion people, most of them living in tropical and subtropical regions, are afflicted to some extent with hookworm infection, although it is not known how many thus infected can be said to be victims of hookworm disease. It is difficult to define the difference between hookworm infection and hookworm disease because a host whose diet contains adequate amounts of iron may sustain a worm burden without debilitating consequences that would render a malnourished person anemic. A person exhibiting signs of the anemia associated with hookworm infestation, therefore, may be said to have hookworm disease regardless of the number of parasites present. Hookworm disease does not appear on the short list of major causes of death in developing countries, but it should be regarded as an important contributing factor in millions of deaths annually and as a source in its own right of widespread human suffering.

Two species of intestinal nematode, *Ancylostoma duodenale* and *Necator americanus,* are the parasites that cause ancylostomiasis. Although they apparently cause the same disease, there are important differences between the two species. *A. duodenale* is slightly larger, sickle-shaped, with hooks or teeth; *N. americanus* is smaller, "S" shaped, with shell-like semilunar cutting plates instead of teeth. Despite being named the "American killer," *N. americanus* is less pathogenic than *A. duodenale,* as measured by comparative blood loss. *A. duodenale* has a higher reproductive rate and a shorter life-span. It is also able to infect the host in more ways than can *N. americanus.* Hookworm disease has been called by nearly 150 different names, taxonomic as well as colloquial. Many, such as *geophagia* and *langue blanche,* describe physical symptoms, clinical features, or unusual behavior associated with the affliction. The name *Ancylostoma duodenale* itself was a subject of disagreement among parasitologists, until resolved in 1915 by the International Commission on Zoological Nomenclature. Commonly used variations at one time or another have included *Agchylostoma, Anchylostomum, Ankylostoma,* and *Uncinaria.* Ancylostomiasis was also known as uncinariasis.

Etiology and Epidemiology

Although *A. duodenale* can be ingested in contaminated food, water, or possibly breast milk, the more common route of infection, and the only one for *N. americanus,* is through penetration of the skin. Larvae in the soil typically enter through the skin of the feet, frequently causing dermatitis, once called "ground itch" or "dew poison" in the southern United States, and "water itch" or "coolie itch" in India. Then the parasites travel through the bloodstream to the alveoli of the lungs, climb the respiratory tree, and make their way into the esophagus. During their migration through the airways into the esophagus, the host sometimes develops a cough, wheeziness, or temporary hoarseness. The hookworms are then swallowed and pass into the gut, where some will successfully attach themselves to the small intestinal mucosa and begin nourishing themselves on their host's blood. In the small intestine, hookworms will grow to a length of about 1 centimeter and mature in 6 to 8 weeks after initial infection. Depending on the species, hookworms generally live from 1 to 5 years, although a few apparently live longer. The adult female may produce thousands of ova per day, which pass out of the body with the host's feces. Egg production varies with the species, the age of the worm, the number of worms in the gut, and the degree of the host's resistance. If deposited on warm, moist soil, the eggs will produce larvae that will molt twice over 2 weeks before becoming infective and can survive in a free-living state for over a month before finding a host.

Hookworms thrive on human ignorance and poverty. If the billions of people living in areas of hookworm infestation were able to eat moderately well, wear good shoes, and defecate in latrines, hookworm disease would soon no longer pose a serious threat to human health. Understood as an index of socioeconomic status, hookworm infection will likely remain a daunting public health problem as long as there are poor people, inadequately educated, living in warm climates. The historical record is not reassuring: Documentary and physical evidence suggest that hookworms have infected humans in different parts of the world for millennia. In the early decades of the twentieth century, massive campaigns launched to eradicate hookworm disease ended in disillusionment and failure. Modern public health officials now pursue the more modest goal of containment, with reductions in the incidence of acute infection. If anything resembling the optimism of the early days of antihookworm work still survives, it is in the possibility that a vaccine may yet be produced, thus permitting overmatched agencies to finesse the intractable political problems of malnutrition and poverty.

Distribution and Incidence

The earliest global survey of hookworm distribution was conducted in 1910, in preparation for a campaign against hookworm disease carried out by the Rockefeller Foundation. Responses from 54 countries led to a preliminary description of a "hookworm belt" girdling the Earth between 30° south latitude and 36° north. Another survey conducted at the same time estimated that 40 percent of the inhabitants of the southern United States suffered in varying degrees from hookworm infection. The larvae prefer shade, and light sand or loam soils. They thrive in the southeastern coastal plains of the United States, but not in the Piedmont clays. Although infection has not been eliminated in the United States, the public health menace of hookworm disease has disappeared, only in part because of the earlier treatment and control programs, but largely as an incidental consequence of the concentration of the population in cities and towns with sewer systems, and the general improvement in sanitary conditions and the standard of living for those remaining on the farms. Likewise in Europe and the United Kingdom, where the disease was sometimes found in mines, hookworm infection is no longer a problem. In Japan as well, rising living standards and antihookworm campaigns have eradicated the disease.

It is still, however, a chronic fact of life in most of the rest of the regions within the old "hookworm belt." In the Caribbean, Central and South America, Africa, China, India, Southeast Asia, and Oceania, endemic hookworm infection remains widespread and largely untreated. After a flurry of activity in the first three decades of the twentieth century, hookworm prevention and treatment programs have been sporadic and uncoordinated. This recent history of neglect has made it difficult even to estimate the incidence of hookworm disease in areas of the world where hookworm infection is known to be prevalent. A combination of factors helps to explain why hookworm lost the attention it once received from philanthropic organizations and public health agencies. The failure of earlier intensive efforts to make quick, dramatic reductions in the incidence of hookworm infection and hookworm disease led public health officials with limited budgets to conclude that a concentration of resources elsewhere would produce better results. Hookworm infection came to be regarded as a stubborn condition of rural poverty in developing nations. The campaigns of the 1910s and 1920s seemed to demonstrate the futility of treating the condition in a systematic way without major improvements in the general standard of living. Other diseases such as smallpox and malaria were both deadlier and less obviously the consequences of social and economic circumstances beyond the control of public health workers.

Other parasitic diseases for which there are no effective anthelmintics were given research priority and funding, thus distracting workers in developed countries and signaling public health officials in developing countries that hookworms and other soil-transmitted parasites were no longer as important as they once had seemed. Geopolitical factors – the economic depression of the 1930s, the Second World War, the dismantling of the European and American colonial empires, the Cold War, and political instability in many of the countries where hookworm infection is endemic – have also contributed to the reduction of support for elaborate countermeasures.

Clinical Manifestations and Pathology

Theoretically, the presence of a single parasite is detrimental in some way to the host. In reality, however, adequately nourished persons with light infections are not likely to suffer discernible ill effects or to exhibit the clinical features associated with hookworm anemia. Children and pregnant women will begin to manifest symptoms of hookworm disease at lower levels of infection, as greater demands on their normal iron stores already exist. Efforts to establish a threshold of infection above which the host might be expected to begin to show signs of hookworm anemia have been frustrated by the inability to control other significant variables such as nutrition and general health in a population large enough to be statistically valid. An otherwise healthy person with a normal daily intake of iron can apparently tolerate several hundred hookworms without patently adverse effects. The likelihood of hookworm disease in an individual varies in direct proportion to the worm burden and in inverse proportion to iron intake.

Hookworm disease shares many of the same clinical symptoms accompanying other kinds of anemia. Persons suffering from severe hookworm infection often have a pale and wan appearance, a tell-tale yellow-green pallor to the skin that helps to explain why the disease was sometimes called "Egyptian chlorosis" or "tropical chlorosis" in the years before the parasite was discovered and described in the medical literature. In children, growth may be significantly retarded. A distended abdomen and pronounced, sharply pointed shoulder blades ("pot belly" and "angel wings" in the American South) were once thought to identify children with hookworm disease, although the same features often accompany malnutrition as well. In pregnant women, hookworm infection increases the likelihood of fetal morbidity. Victims of hookworm anemia, regardless of age or sex, may be chronically sluggish, listless, and easily tired, symptoms that prompted a facetious American newspaper reporter early in the twentieth century to dub hookworm the "germ of laziness." Dropsy, dizziness or giddiness, indigestion, shortness of breath, tachycardia, and in very extreme cases congestive heart failure have also all been associated with advanced hookworm disease. Hookworm sufferers will sometimes eat dirt, chalk, or clay as well.

A diagnosis of hookworm infection can be made easily if ova are detected during a microscopic examination of a fecal smear. Quantitative methods have made it possible to estimate both the total number of eggs based on a quick count in the area under the cover slip and the quantity of hookworms lodged in the intestine. Since the nineteenth century, dozens of anthelmintic drugs have been tried, including thymol, oil of chenopodium, carbon tetrachloride, and tetrachloroethylene. More recently developed hookworm vermifuges include bephenium, mebendazole, pyrantel, and thiabendazole. A regimen combining chemotherapy with the simultaneous administration of iron tablets now seems to be the most effective way to eliminate the parasites and at the same time to restore the hemoglobin to a normal level quickly.

The probability of reinfection is high, however, if a person thus treated continues to walk barefooted on ground contaminated with hookworm larvae. This discouraging realization has bedeviled public health workers since the days of the massive early control programs. Numerous designs for sanitary latrines have come and gone over the years; their construction costs placed them beyond the means of impoverished agricultural workers. Cheaper and less sanitary latrines were often worse than no latrines at all, as they tended to concentrate the locus of infection in a small area where people habitually went to defecate. Reinfection would occur rapidly in such instances, although it would take somewhat longer to reach pretreatment worm burdens.

The problems posed by unsanitary latrines were universal. Other difficulties were specific to certain regions or cultures, though no less imposing for that.

For example, an extensive treatment and control campaign in China in the early 1920s foundered on the age-old practice of fertilizing mulberry trees with human feces, often infested with hookworm ova, acquired in massive quantities from brokers who collected it for that purpose in nearby villages. For centuries, then, the Chinese silk industry had sustained a disease afflicting its workers whose contaminated feces nourished the crop on which their livelihoods depended.

History and Geography

From Ancient Times Through the Nineteenth Century

Hieroglyphic entries on the *Ebers Papyrus* (c. 1550 B.C.) describe a mysterious affliction, *a-a-a disease*, thought by some to be hookworm anemia, but by others, schistosomiasis. In the fifth century B.C., Hippocrates described a pathological condition marked by dirt eating, intestinal distress, and a yellowish complexion. A handful of other sketchy descriptions from the Mediterranean basin in the ancient and early medieval periods now appear to be reports of hookworm disease. From the Western Hemisphere in the centuries after European colonization came scattered accounts from English, French, Spanish, and Portuguese settlers of epidemics among their slaves, called by a rich variety of colloquial names and now thought to be descriptions of widespread hookworm infestation.

The Italian physician Angelo Dubini was the first to report the discovery of hookworms in a human. He detected them first during an autopsy in 1838 and again in 1842. His interest aroused, Dubini examined 100 cadavers for hookworms and found them in more than 20. His 1843 article provided a detailed description of the parasite, which he named "*Agchylostoma*" (a faulty transliteration of the Greek words for "hook" and "mouth") *duodenale*. Dubini did not believe that hookworms had caused the deaths of any of the people he had examined, although he did detect a slight inflammation of the intestinal mucosa at the point of attachment. By 1846, Dubini's parasites had been found in Egypt and, by 1865, in Brazil. In 1878, a trio of Italian scientists – Giovanni Battista Grassi, Corrado Parona, and Ernesto Parona – announced that they had detected hookworm ova in the feces of anemic patients, thus making it possible for anyone with access to a microscope to diagnose hookworm infection.

In 1880, an outbreak of anemia among the miners digging the St. Gotthard tunnel in the Alps generated a wave of public concern in Italy. Within weeks, hundreds of miners were examined and found to be infected with hookworms. Edoardo Perroncito, a pathologist at the University of Turin who had found over 1,500 hookworms in a postmortem examination of a miner, argued that the presence of hookworms in large numbers and the epidemic of anemia were causally related. In 1881, Camillo Bozzolo reported that he had had success using thymol to treat the infection. For the next 35 years, thymol remained the most widely used drug in the treatment of hookworm disease.

Twentieth-Century Writings

In 1898, Arthur Looss in Cairo first suggested that hookworm larvae could penetrate the skin. He had accidentally infected himself by spilling water contaminated with hookworm larvae on his hand. Shortly afterward, the spot on his hand where the water had spilled began to burn and turned red. He surmised that the hookworm larvae were responsible. Two to three months later, he found hookworm ova in his feces. Although Looss's announcement was initially greeted with considerable skepticism, further experimentation by himself and others had by 1901 confirmed beyond doubt the percutaneous route of infection. Looss was later to describe the migratory path of the hookworm within the host.

While Looss was developing his theory of skin penetration in Egypt, a U.S. Army physician stationed in Puerto Rico, Bailey K. Ashford, discovered in 1899 that hookworm infection was rampant among the agricultural workers in the sugar cane fields (Ashford 1900). In 1903, Ashford persuaded the governor to budget funds for the creation of the Anemia Commission of Puerto Rico, the first large antihookworm program of its kind in the world.

Ashford had believed that the hookworms he found in Puerto Rico were *A. duodenale*. At the time of his discovery, no other species was known to infect humans. Charles W. Stiles, a zoologist trained in Germany working for the U.S. Department of Agriculture, examined a sample of Ashford's hookworms and others sent to him from different parts of the United States. He compared them with samples of *A. duodenale* and concluded in 1902 that these hookworms were indigenous to the Western Hemisphere and were a different species, which he named *Necator americanus*. In 1905, Looss found *N. americanus* in six Central African pygmies brought to Cairo for a music hall exhibition. He speculated that *N. americanus* originated in the Eastern Hemisphere and was brought to the Americas by African

slaves. Within 2 years, *N. americanus* had been found extensively not only in Africa but also in India and Australia. Whether *A. duodenale* might also have been introduced into the Americas at about the same time by the first Spanish explorers and the conquistadors has been the subject of some disagreement. The theory that *A. duodenale* existed in pre-Columbian America seems to have been bolstered by the discovery in 1974 of what appears to be an *A. duodenale* in the intestine of a Peruvian mummy dating from about A.D. 900. Both species are widespread in both hemispheres, although their origins remain murky.

In 1909, John D. Rockefeller created an organization to eradicate hookworm disease in the southern United States. Stiles, who maintained that eradication was an unrealistic goal, had nevertheless persuaded Rockefeller's principal philanthropic advisor, Frederick T. Gates, that hookworm infection was a serious problem. With $1 million at its disposal, the Rockefeller Sanitary Commission established operations in 11 American states. Over its 5-year existence, the Rockefeller Sanitary Commission awakened the public to the nature and extent of the threat, stimulated widespread concern for improved sanitation, treated almost 700,000 people suffering from hookworm infection, and invigorated long-moribund state boards of health. It failed, however, to eradicate hookworm infection anywhere.

At the invitation of the British Colonial Office, the Rockefeller Foundation in 1914 undertook a worldwide campaign modeled on the experience of the Rockefeller Sanitary Commission. They opened operations in the British possessions in the West Indies before extending the work into British Guiana, Egypt, Ceylon, and Malaya. By the end of the First World War, Rockefeller programs were underway or ready to begin in Central America, Brazil, and China. Shortly thereafter, Rockefeller-sponsored campaigns were in place in most of the countries in the tropics. Their earlier experience in the southern United States had led administrators of the Rockefeller Foundation programs to employ a combination of two approaches to the problem of hookworm infection. The dispensary method attracted people from the surrounding area to a day-long demonstration conducted by a Rockefeller physician assisted by microscopists during which examinations were carried out and treatments dispensed, while the crowd heard lectures on prevention and improved sanitation. The intensive method was based on a different approach to the problem of hookworm infection. A clearly delimited area was selected for a saturation campaign of aggressive hookworm treatment and latrine construction.

Beginning in the early 1920s, the Rockefeller Foundation had begun to rethink its basic approach to hookworm work. The early days of extensive, protracted campaigns had produced negligible results. The incidence of hookworm infection in Puerto Rico, for example, was as high in 1920 as it had been in 1903, just before Ashford's Anemia Commission began to go to work. Not yet prepared to abandon hookworm work altogether, the Rockefeller Foundation gradually withdrew from massive treatment campaigns and began to redirect its efforts toward laboratory research, with field work restricted to the gathering of data and the testing of hypotheses and drugs. By the mid-1920s, disillusionment had set in and the days of the antihookworm crusades were over. Since then, although laboratory work has revealed much more about the relationship between humans and hookworms, little has been done in a practical way to rid the former of the latter, except where there have been improvements in living conditions.

John Ettling

Bibliography

Ashford, Bailey K. 1900. Ankylostomiasis in Puerto Rico. *New York Medical Journal* 71: 552–6.

1934. *A soldier of science*. New York.

Boccaccio, Mary. 1972. Ground itch and dew poison: The Rockefeller Sanitary Commission, 1909–14. *Journal of the History of Medicine and Allied Sciences* 27: 30–53.

Brown, E. Richard. 1979. *Rockefeller medicine men: Medicine and capitalism in America*. Berkeley.

Cassedy, James H. 1971. The "germ of laziness" in the South, 1909–1915: Charles Wardell Stiles and the paradox. *Bulletin of the History of Medicine* 45: 159–69.

Chandler, A. C. 1929. *Hookworm disease: Its distribution, biology, epidemiology, pathology, diagnosis, treatment, and control*. London.

Dock, G., and C. Bass. 1910. *Hookworm disease*. St. Louis.

Ettling, John. 1981. *The germ of laziness: Rockefeller philanthropy and public health in the New South*. Cambridge, Mass.

Fosdick, Raymond B. 1952. *The story of the Rockefeller Foundation*. New York.

Gates, Frederick T. 1977. *Chapters in my life*. New York.

Hoeppli, R. 1959. *Parasites and parasitic infections in early medicine and science*. Singapore.

Kean, B. H., K. E. Mott, and A. J. Russell. 1978. *Tropical medicine and parasitology: Classical investigations*. Ithaca, N.Y.

Keymer, Anne, and Don Bundy. 1989. Seventy-five years of solicitude. *Nature* 337: 114.

Lane, Clayton. 1932. *Hookworm infection*. London.

Link, William. 1988. Privies, progressivism, and public schools: Health reform and education in the rural south, 1909–1920. *Journal of Southern History* 54: 623–42.

Rockefeller Foundation. 1913/14–1929. *Annual Report*. New York.

1922. *Bibliography of hookworm disease*. New York.

Rockefeller Sanitary Commission. 1910–1915. Publication Nos. 1–9. Washington D.C.

Savitt, Todd L., and James Harvey Young. 1988. *Disease and distinctiveness in the American South*. Knoxville, Tenn.

Schad, G. A., and J. G. Banwell, 1989. Hookworms. In *Tropical and geographical medicine,* ed. K. S. Warren and A. A. F. Mahmoud, 379–92. New York.

Schad, G. A., T. A. Nawalinski, and V. Kochar. 1983. Human ecology and the distribution and abundance of hookworm populations. In *Human ecology and infectious diseases,* ed. N. Croll and J. Cross, 187–223. New York.

Schad, G. A., and K. S. Warren. 1990. *Hookworm disease: Current status and new directions*. London.

Stiles, C. W. 1939. Early history, in part esoteric, of the hookworm (uncinariasis) campaign in our southern states. *Journal of Parasitology* 25: 283–308.

Warren, K. S. 1989. Hookworm control. *Lancet* 1 (8616): 897–900.

Williams, Greer. 1969. *The plague killers*. New York.

VIII.68
Huntington's Disease (Chorea)

Huntington's disease (HD) is a rare progressive neurological disorder, in which normal central nervous system development is succeeded in early adulthood by premature and selective neuronal death. First-rank symptoms consist of rapid, involuntary jerking movements, or *chorea,* due to lesions in the putamen and the caudate nucleus, and a progressive *dementia* due to loss of cells in the cerebral cortex (Hayden 1981). Onset of symptoms is typically in the third or fourth decade, and the clinical course is progressive and relentless over a period of 10 to 30 years. At autopsy, gross examination of HD brains reveals severe, symmetrical atrophy of the frontal and temporal lobes as well as, to a lesser degree, the parietal and occipital lobes. The caudate nucleus is profoundly involved, and diffuse neuronal loss extends into the cerebral cortex, basal ganglia, thalamus, and spinal motor neurons. Various neurotransmitter systems have also been shown to be progressively affected (Rosenberg 1986).

References to the disorder have been found as early as 1841, but the first full description of the disease was made by George S. Huntington in 1872 (Gates 1946). Referring to a large family on Long Island, Huntington distinguished this condition from other known choreiform movement disorders such as Sydenham chorea, or St. Vitus dance. The remarkable history of HD in the New World was recounted in a paper by P. R. Vessie (1932). The carriers of the mutant gene responsible for nearly all known cases of the disease sailed for Massachusetts from Suffolk in 1630. Upon arrival, these individuals founded family lines that included not only the Long Island cases but also the celebrated "Groton witch," whose violent and uncontrollable movements were recorded in 1671 as evidence of possession (Vessie 1932). Compilations of the pedigrees encompassing the various branches of the families founded in seventeenth-century Massachusetts demonstrated a clear pattern of autosomal dominant transmission, meaning that the disease will appear in one-half the offspring of an affected parent.

During the century that has passed since the first description of HD, numerous biochemical and histological studies have been carried out. However, the primary defect in HD remains unknown. A major breakthrough occurred in 1983 when J. F. Gusella and colleagues announced the discovery of an anonymous DNA sequence closely linked to the putative HD gene (Gusella et al. 1983, 1985). This molecular probe, which has been refined by subcloning, is now a tool for presymptomatic diagnosis of HD (Folstein et al. 1985). An effort is underway to clone and sequence the HD gene itself in order to determine the precise nature of the pathological changes leading to clinical HD (Gilliam et al. 1987).

Eric J. Devor

Bibliography

Folstein, S. E., et al. 1985. Huntington's disease: Two families with differing clinical features show linkage to the G8 probe. *Science* 229: 776–9.

Gates, R. R. 1946. *Human genetics*. New York.

Gilliam, T. C., et al. 1987. Localization of the Huntington's disease gene to a small segment of chromosome 4 flanked by D4S10 and the telomere. *Cell* 50: 565–5711.

Gusella, J. F., et al. 1983. A polymorphic DNA marker genetically linked to Huntington's disease. *Nature* 306: 75–8.

Gusella, J. F., et al. 1985. Deletion of Huntington's

disease-linked G8 (D4S10) locus in Wolf – Hirschhorn syndrome. *Nature* 318: 75–78.

Hayden, M. R. 1981. *Huntington's chorea*. New York.

Rosenberg, R. N. 1986. *Neurogenetics: Principles and practices*. New York.

Vessie, P. R. 1932. On the transmission of Huntington's chorea for 300 years: The Bures family group. *Journal of Nervous and Mental Diseases* 76: 553–73.

VIII.69
Hypertension

Arterial hypertension is a condition characterized by abnormally high systolic and/or diastolic blood pressure levels. Systolic and diastolic blood pressure levels are usually estimated indirectly by use of an inflatable rubber bladder to compress the artery in the upper arm. The pressure exerted on the artery by the bladder is registered by a device called a *manometer*. The level of the blood pressure is a measure of the force exerted against the walls of the artery during each heart beat or pulse. The peak of the pressure wave occurs when the heart beats or contracts (systole) and is called the *systolic pressure*. The valley of the pressure wave occurs when the heart relaxes (diastole) and is termed the *diastolic pressure*. Blood pressure is recorded as systolic over diastolic.

Although longitudinal research studies such as the one in Framingham, Massachusetts, and the life insurance industry have noted that even slight elevations of blood pressure are associated with increased risk of premature death, the World Health Organization has recommended that the following blood pressure levels be used to classify adults (blood pressure levels defining juvenile hypertension are under review):

Hypertensive: Greater than or equal to 160 millimeters of mercury (mmHg) systolic and/or greater than or equal to 95 mmHg diastolic.
Normotensive: Less than or equal to 140 mmHg systolic and less than or equal to 90 mmHg diastolic.
Borderline Hypertensive: Between hypertensive and normotensive.

The condition is also divided etiologically into two types: *secondary* and *primary* or *essential* hypertension. Secondary hypertension, resulting from some known cause (including diseases of the kidney or the adrenal glands), represents less than 10 percent of all the cases of the disease. Essential hypertension, occurring in over 90 percent of the cases, is defined as high blood pressure without evident cause. Most of the discussion that follows deals with this latter, more prevalent type of the disease.

Distribution and Incidence

In most societies the average blood pressure levels and the diseases associated with higher blood pressure increase as people get older. However, blood pressure does not increase with age in all populations. Indeed, the disease appears to be totally absent from societies described as "stone age." In such societies, blood pressure does not rise with age, and hypertension is extremely rare. However, a 1988 World Health Organization literature survey on high blood pressure in less developed countries revealed that the prevalence of hypertension there is increasing.

A recent international survey, the INTERSALT study, highlights the wide geographic variability of hypertension throughout the world. INTERSALT, a 52-center, 32-country study, found that the prevalence of hypertension (hypertensives were defined as anyone having greater than 140 mmHg systolic or greater than 90 mmHg diastolic or of persons on antihypertensive medication) between the ages of 20 and 59 ranged from zero percent in the Yanomamo Indians of northern Brazil to over 33 percent in an African-American population in Jackson, Mississippi. There was a significant within-continent variability as well (see Table VIII.69.1). It is likely that this wide variability in the prevalence of hypertension is due to differences in both environmental and genetic factors.

Etiology and Epidemiology

Many have hypothesized that environmental factors are primarily responsible for the development of high blood pressure. Principal evidence for this view consists of reports that unacculturated or "primitive" populations are virtually free of hypertension, but when members of these populations migrate to urban areas their blood pressures rise. There are conflicting interpretations of this phenomenon: Some postulate that the change in diet (especially salt intake) and/or the weight gain that often accompany the move to a modern area are the primary reasons for the development of high blood pressure in populations that were previously free from it. Others suggest that an increase in the level of psy-

Table VIII.69.1. *Prevalence of hypertension in 20- to 59-year-olds, by region, in ascending order by prevalence: 52 populations, INTERSALT Study, 1988*

Rank of 52	Prevalence hypertension (%)	Site, country (race)	n
Africa			
4	05.0	Kenya	176
42	24.0	Zimbabwe	195
Asia			
2	00.8	Papua New Guinea	162
6	08.1	South Korea	198
7	08.5	Beijing, P.R. China	200
8	10.0	Ladakh, India	200
9	10.0	Toyama, Japan	200
10	10.9	Tochigi, Japan	194
11	11.7	Osaka, Japan	197
17	13.5	Nanning, P.R. China	200
18	13.6	New Delhi, India	199
20	15.0	Tianjin, P.R. China	200
28	17.6	Taiwan	181
Europe			
12	12.5	Iceland	200
14	13.0	Naples, Italy	200
15	13.1	Heidelberg, F.R. Germany	196
19	15.0	Birmingham, U.K.	200
21	15.5	Soviet Union	194
22	15.5	Torrejon, Spain	200
23	16.0	Manresa, Spain	200
24	16.2	Gubbio, Italy	199
25	16.6	Bernried, F.R. Germany	197
26	17.0	Ghent, Belgium	200
30	18.6	Belfast, U.K.	199
31	19.0	Krakow, Poland	200
33	19.7	Charleroi, Belgium	157
34	20.5	Mirano, Italy	200
36	20.7	German Democratic Republic	198
37	21.0	South Wales, U.K.	199
39	23.0	Joensuu, Finland	200
40	23.0	Malta	200
43	24.2	The Netherlands	199
45	24.6	Bassiano, Italy	199
46	25.0	Warsaw, Poland	200
47	26.0	Turku, Finland	200
49	26.6	Denmark	199
50	31.0	Hungary	200
51	32.0	Portugal	198

Table VIII.69.1 *(cont.)*

Rank of 52	Prevalence hypertension (%)	Site, country (race)	n
North America			
13	12.6	Chicago, U.S.	196
32	19.2	Goodman, U.S. (white)	198
35	20.6	Jackson, U.S. (white)	199
38	22.6	Labrador, Canada	161
41	23.2	Hawaii, U.S.	187
44	24.5	St. Johns, Canada	200
48	26.1	Goodman, U.S. (black)	186
52	33.5	Jackson, U.S. (black)	184
South America			
1	00.0	Yanomamo, Brazil	195
3	01.0	Xingu, Brazil	198
5	05.9	Mexico	172
16	13.5	Argentina	200
27	17.1	Colombia	191
29	18.0	Trinidad and Tobago	176

Note: At each site the investigators randomly chose about 200 individuals from population-based registries from 4 equally sized age groups between the ages of 20 and 59 years. Subjects were defined as hypertensive if systolic blood pressure was ≥ 140 mmHg, or if diastolic BP was ≥ 90 mmHG, or if the subject was on antihypertensive medication. Total $N = 10,079$.

Source: INTERSALT (1988).

chosocial stress is the culprit. Still others surmise that those who experienced the greatest rise in blood pressure may have inherited a genetic predisposition to the disease that is sparked by some environmental phenomena such as dietary salt or psychosocial stress. Interestingly, salt and stress have been assumed to be related to the disease for eons. A Chinese physician stated over 4,000 years ago that "if too much salt is used in food, the pulse hardens [and] when rebellious emotions rise to Heaven, the pulse expires and leaves the body."

A gain in body weight as a result of a generalized increase in food intake is most definitely associated with high blood pressure, and a sustained reduction in body weight is one of the most effective methods of lowering blood pressure.

Specific dietary factors that may affect blood pressure include salt (sodium chloride), potassium, mag-

nesium, calcium, fat, and even licorice. Most interest has centered around salt – more specifically, the sodium portion of the molecule. The most compelling evidence for the influence of salt on blood pressure is the fact that every low-salt-intake population ever studied has manifested very low blood pressure that does not rise with age. Significantly, INTERSALT reported a positive and statistically significant relationship between salt intake and blood pressure in their 52-center study.

Psychosocial stress is also believed to be associated with hypertension. In some population surveys, investigators have reported that societies under high stress also have higher mean blood pressure levels than those under low stress. Unfortunately, stress has been a difficult phenomenon to measure, and the association between stress and blood pressure has been difficult to demonstrate in human populations. One of the most compelling animal models for stress-induced hypertension has been that developed by J. P. Henry and associates (1975). This model makes it necessary for mice to compete for food and territory; most animals in the system develop very high blood pressure and die from kidney failure. Notable exceptions are dominant males whose blood pressure is less elevated. Some believe that this is a valid model applicable to human societies as well.

Heredity is known to be an important contributor to blood pressure regulation, and hence to abnormally elevated blood pressure or hypertension. Like many quantitative genetic traits such as height, levels of blood pressure tend to run in families; some have higher blood pressure, some have lower blood pressure. Other evidence of genetic influence is revealed by the concordance of hypertension in siblings, especially identical, or monozygotic (MZ), twins: If one member of a set of MZ twins has hypertension, there is a strong likelihood that the other will have the disease as well. Genetic influences on arterial pressure have also been demonstrated in inbred strains of rats, mice, and other animals. The hereditary mediators of these genetic influences on blood pressure are not known but probably reside in genetic influences on the major blood pressure control systems.

Many investigators believe that neither genetic nor environmental factors act alone, that in fact there is an interactive relationship between genes and environment. A compelling example of this is the simple breeding experiments in rats carried out by L. K. Dahl and colleagues in the early 1960s. By selective breeding they were able, in a very few generations, to develop two strains of rats: One, extremely sensitive to the blood pressure-raising effects of salt in the diet, was called "salt sensitive"; the other, resistant to the blood pressure-raising effects of salt, was termed "salt resistant." Humans manifest similar differences, in that some are "salt sensitive" and others are not, and the Dahl model may be applicable to understanding the evolution of "salt sensitivity" in human populations as well.

In former times, as isolated populations diverged and migrated into different ecological systems, they may also have experienced different "selection pressures" related to salt metabolism. These included different temperatures, salt intake, and mortality from salt-depletive diseases such as diarrhea and fever. These "selection pressures" may have resulted in a new genotype that enhanced survival in the new ecology environment by protecting against premature mortality from salt-depletive conditions. If this protective genotype included an enhanced ability to conserve sodium, then it is likely that these adaptations predispose to salt-sensitive hypertension today. It is argued that this may have occurred when many sub-Saharan Africans were forced to migrate to the Western Hemisphere. Mortality rates were very high from salt-depletive diseases, and it is surmised that those with the superior salt-retaining abilities survived and passed their genes on to present-day African Americans. This enhanced genetically based ability to conserve salt may, therefore, be found in greater frequency in Western Hemisphere blacks than in West African blacks, and may be part of the reason the former group today has a higher prevalence of hypertension than does the latter.

Clinical Manifestations

Although in the past a "hard pulse" or "dropsical swellings" (edema) may have signaled hypertension, today the only acceptable way to detect the condition is through the use of the blood pressure cuff (sphygmomanometer). Because the disease is usually asymptomatic, essential hypertension has been appropriately termed the "silent killer." Undetected and uncontrolled, it can damage the arteries, the kidneys, and the heart, and, as several important long-term studies revealed, hypertension is a precursor to premature death from coronary heart disease, stroke, congestive heart failure, kidney (renal) failure, and atherosclerosis.

History

For centuries, the only way to assess "blood pressure" was to feel the pulse, and interpreting its force and rhythm proved to be a useful predictor of disease and death. In about 2500 B.C., for example, a Chinese physician remarked: "[W]hen the pulse is abundant but tense and hard like a cord, there are dropsical swellings."

More than 4,000 years later, in 1827, the British physician Richard Bright suggested that the dropsical swellings he encountered in a patient were due to obstruction in the kidney's circulatory system. Bright's argument was so persuasive that throughout the remainder of the nineteenth century most physicians considered a strong or tense pulse a symptom of kidney disease.

By the late nineteenth century, the earlier discoveries on the measurement of systolic blood pressure by Stephen Hales, Samuel von Basch, and others led to the invention of the sphygmomanometer (blood pressure cuff). Coupled with the 1905 description of diastolic blood pressure by N. Korotkoff, this device effectively replaced diagnosis by "pulse," and its widespread use led observers to the realization that most patients with elevated arterial pressure did not have a kidney disorder. This newly discovered condition was given various names including angiosclerosis, presclerosis, hyperpiesis, primary hypertensive cardiovascular disease, and essential hypertension. The condition was soon recognized as one of the most common types of cardiovascular disorders. Insurance companies led the way in quantifying the association between this new disease and premature death.

In the 1910s, the medical director of the Northwestern Mutual Life Insurance Company, J. W. Fisher, reported the results of several years of study of the relationship between blood pressure levels and premature death. Table VIII.69.2 provides a brief summary of the findings.

It was obvious to Fisher that the higher the systolic blood pressure, the greater the risk of death. Those with systolic blood pressure levels above 160 mmHg had a probability of premature death about 2.5 times greater than those with a systolic blood pressure of about 140 mmHg. In recommending that any insurance application with a persistent blood pressure of "15 mm Hg above the average for his or her age" should be investigated further, Fisher was probably the first to offer a quantifiable definition of "high blood pressure" (see Table VIII.69.3).

The scientific world was interested in what caused this newly discovered, deadly, and extremely prevalent disease. During the 1930s and 1940s, researchers conducted detailed examinations on the influence of the sympathetic nervous system, the endocrine system, and the renal system on arterial pressure, and were successful in cataloging several types of

Table VIII.69.2. *Relationship between blood pressure and mortality: Northwestern Mutual Life Insurance Company, 1907–14*

Age	Insurance status	Systolic BP	Observed deaths	Expected deaths	Proportion obs/expected
40–60	insured	142.43	85	91.17	0.93
"All ages"	insured	152.58	33	23.62	1.40
"All ages"	not insured	161.44	83	34.95	2.37

Note: Expected deaths = expected deaths in company (80% of M.A. table in source); systolic BP = systolic blood pressure; observed deaths = observed deaths of those with noted systolic blood pressure.

Source: Adapted from Fisher (1914).

secondary hypertension. Pheochromocytoma was first reported in 1929, Cushing's syndrome in 1932, pyelonephritis in 1937, renal artery stenosis in 1938, and Conn's syndrome (primary aldosteronism) in 1955. In very few cases these "secondary" causes of high blood pressure were cured through surgery, but in the great majority of cases – those with essential hypertension – the ultimate determinant of elevated arterial pressure remained a mystery. One very important breakthrough in understanding the pathophysiology of essential hypertension occurred among investigators working in animal physiology.

In the 1920s, Harry Goldblatt progressively constricted blood flow to the kidney in a dog, which produced a rapidly developing high blood pressure that resulted in death due to heart failure. The experiment, said by T. A. Stamey to have "stimulated more medical research than any single experiment in medical history," sparked a worldwide search for a kidney (renal)-based pressor substance that produced hypertension. By the end of the 1930s, two

Table VIII.69.3. *"Normal" and "unacceptable" systolic blood pressures by age: Northwestern Mutual Life Insurance Company, 1914*

Age group	"Normal" systolic blood pressure	"Unacceptable" systolic blood pressure
15–20	119.85	>134.85
21–25	122.76	>137.76
26–30	123.65	>138.65
31–35	123.74	>138.74
36–40	126.96	>141.96
41–45	128.56	>143.56
46–50	130.57	>145.57
51–55	132.13	>147.13
56–60	134.78	>149.78

Source: Adapted from Fisher (1914).

teams, one in the United States and one in Argentina, simultaneously discovered that the blood from a "Goldblatt kidney" contained a substance that caused vasoconstriction (squeezing of the arteries). The American group called their substance "angiotonin," while the Argentine group christened the compound "hypertensin." These two teams met and, deciding they were working on the same substance, combined their two names for the compound; the substance became *angiotensin*. These discoveries led to extensive biochemical research into the neural, cellular, and hemodynamic systems that control blood pressure, and eventually to the development of the most widely prescribed antihypertensive medications today. The discovery and elucidation of the biochemical mechanisms controlling blood pressure were extremely important in understanding and controlling high blood pressure, but researchers were still a long way from finding the ultimate cause of the disease.

In the 1950s and 1960s, an important debate occurred between two British physicians over the influence of heredity on high blood pressure in humans. Robert Platt argued that essential hypertension was a "qualitative" disease, controlled by a single gene, with a bimodal population distribution. George Pickering, on the other hand, reasoned that what was termed "hypertension" was only the upper end of a continuous unimodal distribution of blood pressure levels. He thought that hypertension was a "quantitative" disease and was controlled by multiple genes in combination with environmental influences. The debate was never resolved by the two participants. Epidemiological research since then has tended to favor Pickering's quantitative definition; however, in 1983 the analysis of a biostatistician showed the bimodal distribution of blood pressure values in a very large sample from Norway.

Today, both environmental and genetic factors are under intense study as possible etiologic factors at the individual level and the population level. However, it is still the case that the cause of abnormally elevated blood pressure in over 90 percent of the cases remains unknown. Fortunately, however, successful efforts are being made to lower blood pressure through diet, stress reduction, exercise, weight control, medication, and other means, in the hope that the frequency of premature deaths from hypertension will be reduced throughout the world.

Thomas W. Wilson and Clarence E. Grim

Bibliography

Allanby, K. D. 1958. The evolution of the treatment of essential hypertension. *Guy's Hospital Review* 107: 515–30.

Dahl, L. K., M. Heine, and L. Tassinari. 1962. Role of genetic factors in susceptibility to experimental hypertension due to chronic excess salt ingestion. *Nature* 194: 480–2.

Fasciolo, J. C. 1977. Historical background on the renin–angiotensin system. In *Hypertension: Physiopathology and treatment,* ed. E. Koiw Genest and O. Kuchel, 134–9. New York.

Fisher, J. W. 1914. The diagnostic value of the sphygmomanometer in examinations for life insurance. *Journal of the American Medical Association* 63: 1752–4.

Flexner, M. 1959. The historical background of medical therapy in essential hypertension. *Journal of the Kentucky Medical Association* 57: 1210–13.

Henry, J. P., P. M. Stephens, and G. A. Santisteban. 1975. A model of psychosocial hypertension showing reversibility and progression of cardiovascular complications. *Circulation Research* 36: 156–64.

INTERSALT Cooperative Research Group. 1988. INTERSALT: An international study of electrolyte excretion and blood pressure. Results from 24 hour urinary sodium and potassium excretion. *British Medical Journal* 297: 319–28.

Janeway, T. C. 1915. Important contributions to clinical medicine during the past thirty years from the study of human blood pressure. *Bulletin of the Johns Hopkins Hospital* 26: 341–50.

Kannel, W. B., M. J. Schwartz, and P. M. McNamara. 1969. Blood pressure and risk of coronary heart disease: The Framingham study. *Diseases of the Chest* 56: 43–52.

Kaplan, N. M. 1986. *Clinical hypertension.* Baltimore.

Laragh, J. H., and B. M. Brenner, eds. 1990. *Hypertension: Pathophysiology, diagnosis, and management,* 2 vols. New York.

Lew, E. A. 1973. High blood pressure, other risk factors and longevity: The insurance viewpoint. *American Journal of Medicine* 55: 284.

Major, R. 1930. The history of taking blood pressure. *Annals of Medical History* 2: 47–55.

Nissinen, A., et al. 1988. Hypertension in developing countries. *World Health Statistics Quarterly* 41: 141–54.

Page, I. H. 1988. *Hypertension research: A memoir, 1920–1960.* New York.

Ruskin, A. 1956. *Classics in arterial hypertension.* Springfield, Ill.

Stamey, T. A. 1963. *Renovascular hypertension.* Baltimore.

Swales, J. D., ed. 1985. *Platt versus Pickering: An episode in recent medical history.* London.

Wakerlin, G. E. 1962. From Bright to light: The story of hypertension research. *Circulation Research* 11: 131–6.

Waldron, I., et al. 1982. Cross-cultural variation in blood pressure: A quantitative analysis of the relationships of blood pressure to cultural characteristics, salt consumption, and body weight. *Social Science Medicine* 16: 419–30.

White, P. D. 1946. The heart in hypertension since the days of Richard Bright. *Canadian Medical Journal* 54: 129–36.

Wilson, T. W., and C. E. Grim. 1992. Unnatural selection: The history of the trans-Atlantic slave trade and blood pressures today. In *The Atlantic slave trade: Effects on economics, societies, and peoples in Africa, the Americas, and Europe,* ed. J. E. Inikori and S. Engerman, 339–59. Durham, N.C.

World Health Organization. 1988. *Arterial hypertension.* Technical Report Series N. 628.

VIII.70
Infectious Hepatitis

Hepatitis literally refers to any inflammation of the liver. Even when restricted by the term "infectious," it has many causes, including malaria and many viruses including that of yellow fever. By convention, however, infectious hepatitis usually refers to a small group of diseases caused by several unrelated viruses, whose most obvious and most consistent symptoms are due to liver damage. Because these diseases are unrelated, except in liver involvement, they will be treated individually. Only their early undifferentiated history can be reviewed in general terms.

Even the distinction between infectious and noninfectious hepatitis is a problem. Autoimmune chronic active hepatitis will not be considered here, although there is evidence of viral involvement in triggering the autoimmune reaction. Liver cancer will be included as a late consequence of infection with hepatitis B virus, because that seems to be the main cause. Other clinically similar diseases that are not covered here are cirrhosis due to toxins such as alcohol, and jaundice due to physical obstruction of the bile duct.

History

Until the mid-1900s, hepatitis was frequently equated with jaundice, although jaundice is only a sign of a failure to clear normal breakdown products from the blood. Under this terminology, hepatitis and other liver diseases played a very important role in early medical writings, but it is difficult to determine which references relate to hepatitis as we now know it, and which refer to the various other causes of jaundice. It is even more difficult to distinguish one type of hepatitis from another in the early references. Hippocrates identified at least four kinds of jaundice, one of which he considered epidemic and thus, by implication, infectious. Another was "autumnal hepatitis"; this condition, which appeared after an interval appropriate to the incubation period following the dry Mediterranean summer when water supplies would have shrunk, could have been hepatitis A. An emphasis on the liver has persisted into modern times in French popular medicine, where the liver is commonly blamed for ill-defined ailments.

Postclassical writers continued to have difficulty in distinguishing infectious forms from noninfectious forms of jaundice because of the long and variable incubation periods of the infectious diseases. Clear recognition of the infectivity of hepatitis is usually ascribed to Pope Zacarias (St. Zachary), who in the eighth century advocated a quarantine of cases. This had little effect on general thinking, however, because of the variety of circumstances that were associated with different outbreaks. Many cases seemed to be sporadic, but epidemics of what must have been hepatitis A, or enterically transmitted non-A, non-B, were known from the early seventeenth century to be common in troops under campaign conditions. An epidemic of hepatitis B, associated with one lot of smallpox vaccine of human origin, was well described by A. Lürman in 1885. In spite of this, as late as 1908, the dominant medical opinion held that all hepatitis was due to obstruction of the bile duct. The picture did not really begin to clear until the middle of the twentieth century.

Hepatitis A

Etiology

Hepatitis A is caused by an RNA virus 27 nanometers in diameter. It is very similar to poliovirus in general structure and also in its ability to spread through fecal contamination of food and water. The virus is very fastidious in its host range. It is known to infect only humans, apes, and marmosets, and it replicates in vitro only in a few primate cell lines.

Geography and Epidemiology

The virus of hepatitis A is essentially worldwide in its distribution, but it is very much commoner where drinking water is unsafe and sanitation inadequate. Like poliomyelitis, however, the prevalence of disease is often inversely related to the prevalence of virus. In the less developed countries most people become immune through infection in childhood, often with no apparent illness. In semideveloped countries, porcelain water filters may be used to remove the causes of acute bacterial and protozoal diseases, but not the cause of hepatitis virus. Persons from developed countries, especially when traveling in lesser developed areas, are likely to become infected as adults with serious consequences.

Clinical Manifestations

Hepatitis A is manifested by general malaise, loss of appetite, and often, jaundice. Definitive diagnosis of hepatitis requires the demonstration of elevated blood levels of bilirubin and of certain enzymes. Specific diagnosis can be confirmed only by electron microscopic examination of the feces or, more practically, by demonstration of specific antibodies. The disease is seldom fatal when uncomplicated by other conditions, and rarely leaves sequelae. Recovery normally occurs in 4 to 8 weeks.

History

As noted above, although the existence of a hepatitis transmitted by conventional infectious routes could be inferred from the early literature, specific identification of hepatitis A was not accomplished until the late 1960s and 1970s. Then, the development of methods for recognizing hepatitis B, and Saul Krugman's (1967) demonstration of two distinct agents in his studies of children in a home for the retarded, made its existence apparent. The agent of this disease remained enigmatic because it could not be propagated, except in humans. S. M. Feinstone, A. Z. Kapikian, and R. A. Purcell identified the virus in feces in 1973. F. W. Deinhardt and others showed in 1972 that the marmoset was susceptible. Finally, in 1979, P. J. Provost and M. R. Hilleman found a tissue culture line that could be used to grow the virus. An attenuated vaccine has been produced and successfully tested, but not marketed because of continuing production problems.

Hepatitis B

Etiology

The cause of hepatitis B is a very unusual virus. Most important, it is unusually stable and can withstand boiling temperatures and drying without inactivation. Although the virus is of moderate size, 45 nm in diameter, it has the smallest DNA genome known. It accomplishes all its necessary functions by using overlapping stretches of the same genetic information to produce different proteins. The protein that is used for the external surface of the virus is produced in such great excess that the host immune system cannot cope, and becomes paralyzed. To reproduce itself, the virus first makes a copy of its genome in RNA, then recopies that back into DNA. The virus DNA can be integrated into the human genetic material, to provide a secure resting place for the virus and, perhaps, to interfere with the host's growth control mechanism and cause cancer.

Geography and Epidemiology

The stability of hepatitis B virus means that it can persist on any article that is contaminated with blood, most significantly, used needles and surgical instruments. In developed countries it has usually been transmitted in this way. Disposable needles, and tests to make certain that blood for transfusion is free of the virus, have reduced the incidence of this disease in most of the population, but it continues to be a serious problem among intravenous drug abusers.

Hepatitis B can also be sexually transmitted. It is excreted in the semen and transmitted from male to female and from male to male in this way. Because the heterosexual transmission does not form a complete cycle, this has been less of a problem among heterosexuals than in the male homosexual communities of Europe and North America.

The ability of the virus to remain infectious when dried means that it can persist on sharp stones and thorns along paths and, perhaps, also on the proboscises of mosquitos. This provides a particularly important mode of spread in primitive societies, where shoes are not worn and scant clothing is used. There, hepatitis B attains very high prevalence levels through gradual exposure over a lifetime.

The most serious pattern of hepatitis B infection is seen in South Asia and sub-Saharan Africa, where transmission from mother to child is common. Infection may occur during birth or via the mother's milk. The significance of this pattern of transmission is that persistent infection is particularly likely to follow infection in early life, and liver cancer is a common sequela to persistent infection. In these parts of the world, cancer of the liver is the most common of all cancers and a major cause of death in middle age. The situation is self-perpetuating, in that persons infected in infancy are most likely to become carriers and, hence, most likely to transmit to the next generation.

Clinical Manifestations and Prevention

Infection with hepatitis B can have a variety of outcomes. It may be inapparent, or it may cause a disease indistinguishable from that caused by hepatitis A. It may also, however, cause chronic active hepatitis with or without cirrhosis. Any of these forms may lead to a chronic carrier state in which large quantities of surface antigen, and sometimes infectious whole virus, circulate in the blood. This may damage the kidneys or, as described above, lead to cancer. Thus, although uncomplicated hepatitis B is not often fatal in the acute phase, the total mortality that it causes can be great.

A good vaccine is available. It was proven effective in an extraordinary trial, published by Wolf Szmuness and others in 1980, which was carried out with the help of the New York male homosexual community. Thousands participated, either as vaccine recipients or as part of a placebo group. Because of the high homosexual transmission rate, the incidence of disease in the unvaccinated group was high enough to provide a good level of significance in the results. The first vaccine was produced by purifying hepatitis B antigen from the blood of carriers. This method was efficient, and never proved unsafe, but it left open the possibility that some other disease might be transmitted with the vaccine. Bacterial clones have now been developed that carry the gene for the virus antigen, and the product of these clones has now replaced blood as a source of antigen in the United States. This technology has been expensive, however, and blood-derived vaccine is still used elsewhere. The Chinese of Taiwan have used this type of vaccine to immunize children of infected mothers, and, it is hoped, to break the cycle leading to liver cancer.

It must be remembered that the vaccine only prevents infection. There is as yet no way to cure the disease or abort the carrier state. A person who becomes a carrier is likely to remain so for many years. This means that many people already infected are still doomed to liver cancer, and it emphasizes the need for vaccination of health workers who may be exposed frequently.

History

Although it had been clear for many years that blood products could transmit hepatitis, the full import of this fact did not register on the medical profession. Normal human serum continued to be used to prevent measles in children and to stabilize vaccines. In 1942, a new yellow fever vaccine, mixed with human serum, was administered to U.S. troops headed overseas: Of those vaccinated, 28,000 developed hepatitis, and many died.

The discovery of hepatitis B virus followed an unusual course. In the early 1960s, Baruch Blumberg was studying blood groups in diverse populations and found a new antigen in the blood of Australian aborigines. Later, he found that one of his staff, who worked with the blood samples, had acquired the "Australia antigen," and he recognized that it was infectious. Ultimately, it turned out that this antigen was the surface protein of the hepatitis B virus.

Hepatitis C

Etiology

The virus of hepatitis C has neither been seen nor cultured to the time of writing. However, in 1989, a 3,000-kiloDalton strand of RNA from the blood of an experimentally infected chimpanzee was transcribed into DNA by Qui-Lim Choo and his associates. Propagated into a bacterial clone, this DNA codes for an antigen that crossreacts with the agent of an important transfusion-transmitted hepatitis virus. The discoverers suggested that this "hepatitis C Virus" might be structurally similar to the virus of yellow fever or equine encephalitis. This implies that the virus genetic material was the original RNA strand, not DNA. Hepatitis C is inactivated by chloroform, showing that, unlike the viruses of hepatitis A or B, it has a lipid-containing envelope. The agent of some other transfusion-transmitted non-A, non-B hepatitis is resistant to chloroform, indicating the existence of at least one more unidentified agent of this disease.

Geography and Epidemiology

Wherever hepatitis A and B have been distinguished, a residuum of non-A, non-B cases have remained. Some of these cases are associated with blood transfusions, whereas others, as described below, are not. Hepatitis C is the most common transfusion-transmitted non-A, non-B in the United States, but its role in the rest of the world is unknown. Although it is important as a cause of posttransfusion hepatitis, this is not its main mode of transmission, and it is encountered sporadically in untransfused persons. Transmission by intravenous drug use is more frequent, and sexual transmission seems also to occur.

Clinical Manifestations

Hepatitis C is a serious disease in that a high proportion of cases develop permanent liver damage. In spite of the paucity of our knowledge about this disease, it is almost unique among viral infections in being treatable. Alpha interferon results in dramatic improvement of hepatitis C liver disease. Unfortunately, the disease often recurs when treatment stops, and the treatment is both expensive and accompanied by unpleasant side effects.

Hepatitis Associated with Delta Agent

Etiology

A fourth hepatitis virus, the delta agent, is unable to grow independently; it grows only in cells that are also infected with hepatitis B. Its defect is an inability to make coat protein, and it must, therefore, wrap itself in the surface protein of another virus to become infectious. As has been noted, hepatitis B produces large quantities of coat protein; in this way, delta can attain very high titers in the blood. Envelopment in the other's coat also gives delta the advantage of hepatitis B virus's freedom from immune attack, and the fact that hepatitis B is commonly persistent in infected persons gives delta a reasonably large field in which to forage. Like hepatitis A, but not B, delta virus has an RNA genome. It does produce one distinctive protein that permits serologic identification of the infection. Wrapped in the hepatitis B coat, it is intermediate in size between A and B, at 36 nanometers.

Geography and Epidemiology

Delta virus has been found in most countries of Europe and North America as well as in much of the rest of the world. Its distribution, however, seems to be more spotty than that of the A or B virus. Although there is no evidence that delta shares the unusual stability of hepatitis B virus, they are often transmitted together by parenteral injection.

Clinical Manifestations

Infection with delta virus, which is always superimposed on an underlying hepatitis B infection, has the highest acute fatality rate of all the hepatitides. Outbreaks of unusually severe hepatitis have often proven to have been caused by it. Otherwise, the symptoms caused by delta are not distinctive.

History

The antigen of delta virus was first recognized in Italy in 1977. Since that time, there has been a number of studies of its distribution and its molecular characteristics. No vaccine is available as yet.

Enterically Transmitted Non-A, Non-B Hepatitis (ET-NANBH)

Etiology

ET-NANBH is a virus structurally similar to but immunologically distinct from hepatitis A. It has recently been associated with a number of previously inexplicable hepatitis epidemics. As yet the virus has not been grown in culture, but it can be serially passed through monkeys and has been identified by electron microscopy. Biochemical characterization remains to be done.

Geography and Epidemiology

Most epidemics attributed to ET-NANBH have occurred in less developed countries at times when even the normally limited sanitation procedures have broken down. Most of these have been in South Asia, but there have also been epidemics in the southern former Soviet Union, ir. refugee camps in Somaliland, and in Mexican villages, where water supplies became grossly contaminated. All ages are commonly affected, but there may actually be a preponderance of adult cases. These circumstances suggest that ET-NANBH virus is less infectious than hepatitis A and that, even in conditions of generally poor sanitation, most people remain only minimally susceptible.

Clinical Manifestations

ET-NANBH usually causes a hepatitis that is indistinguishable from that caused by hepatitis A or B. However, infected pregnant women have an unusually high mortality rate, which may reach 20 percent.

History

A major epidemic of ET-NANBH occurred in New Delhi in 1955. The New Delhi sewage emptied into the Ganges River a little below the point of a water supply intake. In that year there was a drought, the river became low, and the sewage began to flow upstream. Alert water technicians recognized the problem and raised chlorination levels, so that there was no unusual outbreak of bacterial disease. However, a month or so later, 68 percent of the exposed population developed jaundice, and more than 10 percent of the affected pregnant women died. Careful investigations were made at the time, but the cause of the epidemic remained undetermined until recently, when Daniel Bradley and his associates developed a test based on reactions (observed in the electron microscope) of immune sera and virus from feces of patients in a more recent Burmese epidemic.

Francis L. Black

Bibliography

Alter, Marion J., and R. F. Sampliner. 1989. Hepatitis C: And miles to go before we sleep. *New England Journal of Medicine* 321: 1538–9.

Beasley, R. Palmer, et al. 1981. Hepatocellular carcinoma and hepatitis B virus, a prospective study of 27,707 men in Taiwan. *Lancet* 2: 1129–33.

Blumberg, Baruch S., et al. 1967. A serum antigen (Australia antigen) in Down's syndrome, leukemia and hepatitis. *Annals of Internal Medicine* 66: 924–31.

Bonino, Ferrucio, et al. 1984. Delta hepatitis agent: Structural and antigenic properties of the delta-associated particle. *Infection and Immunity* 43: 1000–5.

Bradley, Daniel W., and James E. Maynard. 1986. Etiology and natural history of post-transfusion and enterically transmitted non-A, non-B hepatitis. *Seminars in Liver Disease* 6: 56–66.

Deinhardt, F. W., et al. 1972. Viral hepatitis in nonhuman primates. *Canadian Medical Association Journal* 106 (Supplement): 468–72.

Feinstone, S. M., A. Z. Kapikian, and R. A. Purcell. 1973. Hepatitis A: Detection by immune electron microscopy of a viruslike antigen associated with acute illness. *Science* 182: 1026–8.

Hadler, S. C., and H. S. Margolis. 1989. Viral hepatitis. In *Viral infections of humans*, ed. Alfred S. Evans. New York.

Hilleman, Maurice, R. 1984. Immunologic prevention of human hepatitis. *Perspectives in Biology and Medicine* 27: 54357.

Krugman, Saul. 1967. Infectious hepatitis: Evidence for two distinctive clinical, epidemiological and immunological types of infection. *Journal of the American Medical Association* 200: 365–73.

Krugman, Saul, and Joan P. Giles. 1970. Viral hepatitis. *Journal of the American Medical Association* 212: 1019–29.

Lürman, A. 1885. Eine Icterusepidemie. *Berliner klinische Wochenschrift* 22: 20–3.

Murray, K. 1987. A molecular biologist's view of viral hepatitis. *Proceedings of the Royal Society of Medicine, Biology* 230: 107–46.

Provost, P. J., and M. R. Hilleman. 1979. Propagation of human hepatitis A virus in cell culture in vitro. *Proceedings of the Society for Experimental Biology and Medicine.* 160: 213–21.

Szmuness, Wolf, et al. 1980. Hepatitis B vaccine demonstration of efficacy in a controlled clinical trial in a high risk population. *New England Journal of Medicine* 303: 833–41.

Vyas, Girish H., and Jay H. Hoofnagle, eds. 1984. *Viral hepatitis and liver disease*. Orlando.

Zuckerman, Arie J. 1975. *Human viral hepatitis*. Amsterdam.

VIII.71
Infectious Mononucleosis

Infectious mononucleosis is an acute infectious disease of children, adolescents, and young adults. It is caused by the Epstein–Barr virus (EB virus) and is followed by lifelong immunity.

Distribution and Incidence

On the basis of the populations investigated, it would seem that infectious mononucleosis occurs worldwide but attacks only those persons who have had no EBV antibodies. The virus replicates in the salivary glands, is present in the oropharyngeal secretions of patients ill with the disease, and continues to be shed for months following convalescence. As a lifelong inhabitant of the lymphoid tissues, it is excreted intermittently into the oropharynx.

In the underdeveloped countries it is a disease of childhood, and, since it spreads by contact with oral secretions, crowding and unhygienic surroundings favor its ready transmission. In more developed countries, it strikes especially those of the 15- to 25-year age group and is recognized clinically as infectious mononucleosis. In the United States, on college campuses, the disease is commonly known as the "kissing disease."

Children of low socioeconomic state almost universally show antibodies to the virus. (In Ghana, 84 percent of infants have acquired antibodies by age 21 months.) In a worldwide prospective study of 5,000 children and young adults without EB virus antibodies, 29 percent developed antibodies within a period of 4 to 8 years. Among susceptible college students the annual incidence of the disease is about 15 percent.

Immunology

Specific antibodies to EB virus are demonstrable early after the onset of the disease. Although the higher titers may decrease in subsequent months, they remain at detectable levels throughout life, along with immunity to the disease.

Pathology and Clinical Manifestations

Although the pathological findings may be multivisceral, the predominant finding is follicular hyperplasia of the lymph nodes. The lymphoid tissues show diffuse proliferation of the atypical lymphocyte that is present in the spleen and the walls of blood vessels, is periportal in the liver, and appears in the peripheral bloodstream. These monocytoid lymphocytes (Downey cells) may make up 10 percent or more of the white cells and are of diagnostic significance.

In childhood the disease is subclinical or masquerades as one of many episodes of upper respiratory infection. In the typical youthful adult, after an incubation period of about 5 or 6 weeks, clinical disease shows itself with prodromes of malaise, fatigue, headache, and chilliness followed by high fever, sore throat, and tender swollen cervical lymph nodes. Examination shows, in addition to the lymphadenopathy, paryngitis often with scattered petechiae and swelling of the pharyngeal lymphoid structures, hepatosplenomegaly, and, not infrequently, a transient maculopapular rash. Palpebral and periorbital edema may develop. Mild jaundice appears in some 10 percent of patients. Rarely are symptoms related to the central nervous system. Following an initial leukopenia, a leucocytosis of 15,000 to 20,000 or higher appears with an absolute lymphocytosis and with atypical lymphocytes prominent as noted above.

In most patients the disease is mild, and recovery occurs within several weeks. College students are generally up and about within a week or so. Complications in the nervous system may occasionally occur in adults, but death from the disease is extremely rare, splenic rupture being the most serious complication.

History and Geography

This disease was described first by a Russian pediatrician, Nil F. Filatov, in 1885, as idiopathic adenitis. Four years later, a German physician, Emil Pfeiffer, also described a disease that was epidemic in children and characterized by glandular enlargement. He gave it the name *Drüsenfieber* (glandular fever). In 1896, J. P. West wrote of a similar epidemic in the United States, but it was only in 1920 that Thomas Sprunt, of Baltimore, gave it the name infectious mononucleosis. H. Downey and C. A. McKinly described the characteristic mononuclear leucocytes in 1923. The Epstein – Barr virus was identified by W. Henle and associates in 1968.

R. H. Kampmeier

Bibliography

Epstein, M.A., and B. G. Achong. 1977. Pathogenesis of infectious mononucleosis. *Lancet* 2: 1270–2.

Davidsohn, I., and P. H. Walker. 1935. Nature of heterophile antibodies in infectious mononucleosis. *American Journal of Clinical Pathology* 5: 455–65.

Downey, H., and C. A. McKinly. 1923. Acute lymphadenosis compared with acute lymphatic leukemia. *Archives of Internal Medicine* 2: 82–112.

Henle, W., and G. Henle. 1979. The virus as the etiologic agent of infectious mononucleosis. In *Epstein–Barr virus,* ed. B. G. Epstein and B. G. Achong, New York.

1981. Clinical spectrum of Epstein – Barr virus infection. In *The human herpesviruses: An interdisciplinary perspective,* ed. Andre J. Nahmias, Walter R. Dowdle, and Raymond F. Schinazi. New York.

Niederman, James C. 1982. Infectious mononucleosis. In *Cecil's textbook of medicine,* ed. James B. Wyngaarden and Lloys H. Smith, Jr. Philadelphia.

Paul, John R., and Walls W. Bunnell. 1932. Presence of heterophile antibodies in infectious mononucleosis. *American Journal of Medical Science* 183: 90–104.

Pfeifer, Emil. 1889. Drüsenfieber. *Jahrbuch Kinderheilkunde* 29: 257–64.

Sprunt, Thomas, and Frank A. Evans. 1920. Mononucleosis leucocytosis in reaction to acute infections ("infectious mononucleosis"). *Bulletin of Johns Hopkins Hospital* 31: 410–17.

Strauss, Stephen E. 1987. Editorial – EB or not EB – that is the question. *Journal of American Medical Association* 257: 2335–6.

VIII.72 Inflammatory Bowel Disease

The inflammatory bowel diseases (IBD) – ulcerative colitis and Crohn's disease – constitute a group of disorders of the small and large intestine whose causes and interrelationships remain obscure (Kirsner and Shorter 1988). Their course is acute and chronic, with unpredictable remissions and exacerbations, and numerous local and systemic complications. Treatment is symptomatic and supportive. The economic drain imposed by these diseases in terms of direct medical, surgical, and hospitalization expenses, loss of work, and interrupted career development is enormous. The emotional impact upon the patient and upon the family is equally substantial. In these contexts, the inflammatory bowel diseases today are one of the major worldwide challenges in medicine.

Ulcerative Colitis

Clinical Manifestations, Pathology, and Diagnosis

The principal symptoms of ulcerative colitis are rectal bleeding, constipation early (in ulcerative proctitis), diarrhea usually, abdominal cramping pain, rectal urgency, fever, anorexia, fatigue, and weight loss. The physical findings depend upon the severity of the colitis, ranging from normal in mild disease, to fever, pallor from loss of blood, dehydration and malnutrition, and the signs of associated complications. X-ray and endoscopic examinations demonstrate diffuse inflammation and ulceration of the rectum and colon in 50 percent of patients, and the adjoining terminal ileum. Ulcerative colitis begins in the mucosa and submucosa of the colon (the inner bowel surface); in severe colitis the entire bowel wall may be involved. The principal histological features are the following: vascular congestion, diffuse cellular infiltration with polymorphonuclear cells, lymphocytes, plasma cells, mast cells, eosinophils, and macrophages; multiple crypt abscesses; and shallow ulcerations. Chronic ulcerative proctitis is the same disease as ulcerative colitis, except for its restriction to the rectum and its milder course.

The laboratory findings reflect the severity of the colitis. The white blood cell count usually is normal except in the presence of complications. The hemoglobin, red cell, and hematocrit are decreased in proportion to the loss of blood. The sedimentation rate may be elevated but frequently is normal. Blood proteins including serum albumin often are diminished. The stools contain blood. Cultures are negative for known pathogenic bacteria.

Complications are numerous. In the colon, they include pericolitis, toxic dilatation, perforation, peritonitis, hemorrhage, obstruction, polyps, carcinoma, and lymphoma. The many systemic complications include iron-deficiency anemia, hemolytic anemia, protein loss, malnutrition, retardation of growth in children, arthritis, iritis, sacroileitis, metabolic bone disease, skin problems (erythema nodosum, pyoderma gangrenosum), pyelonephritis, nephrolithiasis, liver disease (fat infiltration, hepatitis, pericholangitis, sclerosing cholangitis), and vascular thromboses.

The differential diagnosis includes specific bacterial infections, ischemic colitis, diverticulitis, and Crohn's disease of the colon.

Treatment

The therapeutic emphasis in ulcerative colitis involves a general program of nutritional restoration, emotional support, sulfasalazine, 5-aminosalicylic acid, antispasmodics, antibacterial drugs, adrenocorticotropin (ACTH), and adrenal corticosteroids. Proctocolectomy and ileostomy is a highly successful operation for ulcerative colitis. The Kock continent pouch, and total colectomy together with ileoanal anastomoses, with and without ileal pouch, offer useful surgical alternatives in selected patients. The prognosis of ulcerative colitis has improved considerably, and the mortality has diminished to less than 1 percent as a result of the many medical and surgical therapeutic advances.

Etiology

Ulcerative colitis is common among young people, especially below the age of 40 years, but no age range is exempt and the number of older patients is increasing. There is no sex predominance. The circumstances of onset of ulcerative colitis in most instances are not known. Patients usually appear to be in good health; occasionally, symptoms appear after visits to countries such as Mexico and Saudi Arabia, implicating an enteric infection. Initial thoughts as to etiology emphasized a microbial infection, and this possibility continues today. Many organisms have been implicated and discarded, including diplostreptococcus, *Streptococcus, Escherichia coli, Pseudomonas aeruginosa, Clostridium difficile, Sphaerophorus necrophorus,* Morgan's bacillus, *Shigella* organisms,

Salmonella paratyphi, Proteus organisms, viruses (e.g., lymphopathia venereum), parasites, and fungi (*Histoplasma,* Monilia). Immunologic mechanisms have been implicated on the basis of clinical, morphological, and experimental observations. The immunologic disorder may be one of defective immunoregulation, as in an altered response to a microbial infection or to usual bowel organisms. Nutritional deficiencies are common but are secondary developments.

Various circumstances such as acute respiratory illness, enteric infections, and antibiotics may act as a "trigger mechanism," precipitating the disease in genetically "vulnerable" persons. Genetic influences may be expressed through the immune response genes and the mucosal immune system of the bowel. Emotional disturbances are common in patients with ulcerative colitis, but they probably do not initiate the disease. The important interactions among the central nervous system, the gut, and the endocrine and immune systems now under investigation may clarify these issues.

Crohn's Disease

Crohn's disease, also called regional enteritis, jejunoileitis, ileocolitis, and Crohn's colitis, is an acute and chronic inflammatory disease of the small intestine, especially the terminal ileum, but actually involving the entire gastrointestinal tract, from the mouth to the anus. The disease occurs frequently among children, adolescents, and young adults, but is increasing in people over the age of 60. There is a slight female:male predominance.

Clinical Manifestations

The clinical manifestations include fever, diarrhea, cramping abdominal pain, anemia, and weight loss. Initial symptoms may include arthralgias suggesting an arthritis, gynecological difficulties, urinary symptoms (frequency, dysuria), or a combination of severe loss of appetite, weight loss, and depression, suggesting anorexia nervosa. Slowing or retardation of growth may be the first clinical indication of illness in children. Occasionally, the initial presentation is indistinguishable from an acute appendicitis.

The physical findings include fever, "toxemia," tenderness in the mid abdomen and right lower abdominal quadrant, and often a tender loop of bowel or an inflammatory mass composed of adherent inflamed bowel, thickened mesentery, and enlarged abdominal lymph nodes, palpated in the right lower abdominal quadrant. The laboratory findings include a normal or elevated white blood cell count, increased sedimentation rate, anemia, decreased total proteins and serum albumin, and evidence of undernutrition. By X-ray, the intestinal lumen is found to be ulcerated and narrowed. Fistulas to adjacent structures are not uncommon. The histological features include transmural disease, knifelike ulcerations overlying the epithelium of lymphoid aggregates in Peyer's patches, profuse cellular accumulations, lymphatic dilatation, prominent lymphoid follicles, and granuloma formation.

The complications of regional enteritis include most of the problems enumerated for ulcerative colitis and, in addition, perianal abscess, perineal fistulas, abdominal abscess and fistual formation, intestinal narrowing and obstruction, carcinoma of the small and large intestine, and obstructive hydronephrosis. In patients with multiple bowel resections and significant loss of intestinal digestive capacity, the complications include altered bile salt metabolism, steatorrhea, increased absorption of dietary oxalate and hyperoxaluria, increased frequency of kidney stones, zinc and magnesium deficiencies, other nutritional deficits including vitamins B_{12} and D, bone demineralization, and osteopenia.

Treatment

As in ulcerative colitis, medical treatment is symptomatic, supportive, and individualized, with emphasis upon restoration of nutrition, antispasmodic medication, and antibacterial and antiinflammatory medication. Corticotropin and adrenal steroids reduce the inflammatory reaction, but do not necessarily cure the disease. Immunosuppressive drugs (6-mercaptopurine, azathioprine) may be helpful adjuncts but require continuing administration. Surgical treatment is necessary for complications, especially abscess and fistula formation, unrelenting intestinal obstruction, and uncontrollable hemorrhage. The recurrence rate is high.

Etiology

As in ulcerative colitis, etiologic hypotheses vary widely, from the excessive eating of cornflakes, refined sugars, or margarine, to bottle-feeding rather than breastfeeding, environmental pollutants, the indiscriminate administration of antibiotics, and the use of oral contraceptives among young women. A wide variety of bacteria and viruses have been implicated, and although none has achieved etiologic status, the "new" microbial pathogens now being identified have renewed interest in microbial possibilities including mycobacteria. Other suggested but unproven etiologies have included blunt trauma to the abdominal wall (e.g., seat belt injury); the ingestion

of foreign material (e.g., talc), producing an obstructive lymphangitis; sarcoidosis; altered intestinal neurohumoral mechanisms; and nutritional deficiencies.

Ulcerative Colitis and Crohn's Disease: General Aspects

Epidemiology, Distribution, and Incidence

Ulcerative colitis and Crohn's disease share similar epidemiological and demographic features. The incidence of ulcerative colitis, still considerable, apparently has stabilized or possibly diminished in many areas of the world, with several exceptions (Norway, Japan, Faroe Islands, northeast Scotland). Ulcerative colitis appears to be more prevalent in the United Kingdom, New Zealand, Australia, the United States, and northern Europe. It is less frequent in central and southern Europe, infrequent in the Middle East, uncommon in South America and Africa, but increasing in Japan.

Similarly Crohn's disease is most common in the United Kingdom, the United States, and Scandinavia, on the rise in Japan, but less frequent in central and northern Europe and uncommon in Africa and South America. The incidence of Crohn's disease has been increasing throughout much of the world (Great Britain, the United States, Norway, Finland, Switzerland, Israel, and South Africa) but appears to have stabilized in such diverse cities as Aberdeen (Scotland), Baltimore (United States), Cardiff (Wales), and Stockholm (Sweden). B. M. Mendeloff and A. I. Calkins (1988) estimate that in the United States the annual incidence "for the sum of both disorders" is 5 to 15 new cases per 100,000 population. The worldwide prevalence of Crohn's disease, especially in industrialized areas, and the worldwide similarity of its clinical, radiological, and pathological features, regardless of geographic, ethnic, dietary, and sociocultural differences, are noteworthy.

The inflammatory bowel diseases are more frequent among white than black populations; but Crohn's disease in particular is increasing among the black populations of the United States and Great Britain. Ulcerative colitis and especially Crohn's disease are much more common among the Jewish population of the United States, the United Kingdom, and Sweden than among other members of the population. In Israel, Crohn's disease is more common among Ashkenazi than among Sephardic Jews. Overall, ulcerative colitis and Crohn's disease occur among all ethnic groups, including the Maoris of New Zealand, Arabs (e.g., Kuwait, Saudi Arabia), and probably the Chinese, albeit infrequently. An intriguing and unexplained epidemiological observation has to do with the scarcity of cigarette smokers in patients with ulcerative colitis and the apparently increased vulnerability of former smokers to ulcerative colitis, whereas by contrast there is an excess of smokers in Crohn's disease populations. It should be noted that the "smoking connection" does not obtain among children with IBD.

Genetic (Familial) Aspects

Ulcerative colitis and Crohn's disease are not "classic" genetic disorders. There are no inheritable protein or metabolic abnormalities, no antecedent chromosomal defects, no genetic markers, no consanguinity, and no Mendelian ratios. However, genetic influences are important in the development of ulcerative colitis and even more so in Crohn's disease, as reflected in their familial clustering (20 percent for ulcerative colitis and up to 40 percent for Crohn's disease). In addition to the initial patient, one more member of the family is usually affected, but up to 8 patients in a single family have been observed. IBD occurs with a high degree of concordance among monozygotic twins. The nature of the genetic influence in IBD is not known. Thus far, no universally distinctive histocompatibility haplotype linkage has been demonstrated. The occasional occurrence of Crohn's disease or ulcerative colitis in adopted children or later in the initially healthy mate of a patient with IBD supports an environmental (possibly viral) rather than a genetic mechanism. Current etiologic studies focus upon a genetically mediated abnormality in the immune response genes (defective immunoregulation in the bowel's mucosal immune system), possible linkage with a known genetic locus, or with specific T-cell antigen receptor genes.

Comparisons and Contrasts

Is there a pathogenetic relationship between ulcerative colitis and regional ileitis/colitis? In the absence of differentiating biological markers, a definitive answer to this important question is not possible at present. The simultaneous presence or sequential evolution of both active ulcerative colitis and active regional ileitis/colitis, and the sequential development of ulcerative colitis followed by Crohn's disease in a single patient, though they may occur, probably have never been documented to everyone's satisfaction.

The Similarities. Both disorders have significant familial associations. Approximately 25 percent of families with multiple instances of IBD show an intermingling of ulcerative colitis and Crohn's disease. Both diseases share the same epidemiological and demographic features. They also share many symptoms (abdominal pain, diarrhea, weight loss, rectal bleeding), local complications (hemorrhage, perforation, toxic dilatation of the colon), and systemic complications (erythema nodosum, pyoderma gangrenosum, arthritis, liver disease, kidney stones).

The Differences. Ulcerative colitis is a continuous mucosal disease, at least initially, with diffuse involvement of the colon. Crohn's disease is a transmural process, focal in distribution, penetrating through the bowel wall, and producing microabscesses and fistulas. Histologically, granulomas and prominent lymphoid aggregates are much more common in Crohn's disease than in ulcerative colitis.

Ulcerative colitis is limited to the colon and occasionally a short segment of terminal ileum; Crohn's disease focally may involve any segment of the alimentary tract, mouth to anus. Ulcerative colitis is a continuous inflammatory reaction; Crohn's disease, wherever located, is a discontinuous, focal process. Perianal suppuration and fistula formation (enterocutaneous, enteroenteric, enterocolonic, enterovesical, enterouterine) characterize Crohn's disease, but not ulcerative colitis. Immune-modulating drugs are more helpful in Crohn's disease than in ulcerative colitis. Proctocolectomy and ileostomy are curative in ulcerative colitis, but the same operation in Crohn's disease carries a recurrence rate of approximately 15 to 20 percent.

The answer to the question whether the two ailments are related would seem to be that ulcerative colitis and Crohn's disease are probably separate disorders, with limited morphological and clinical expressions accounting for overlapping manifestations.

History of IBD

Ulcerative Colitis

Early Literature to 1920

In all probability, we shall never know for certain who first described ulcerative colitis (UC) . . . for although the disease was initially referred [to] by name in the latter half of the century, it seems likely that its existence was recognized for over two millennia before that time. (Goligher et al. 1968)

Hippocrates was aware that diarrhea was not a single disease entity, whereas Aretaeus of Cappadocia in the second century described many types of diarrhea, including one characterized by "foul evacuations," occurring chiefly in older children and adults. Instances of an "ulcerative colitis" apparently were described by Roman physicians, including Ephesus in the eleventh century. "Noncontagious diarrhea" flourished for centuries under a variety of labels, such as the "bloody flux" of Thomas Sydenham in 1666. In 1865, medical officers of the Union Army during the American Civil War described the clinical and pathological features of an "ulcerative colitis-like" process in patients with chronic diarrhea. Several of these cases actually suggested Crohn's disease more than ulcerative colitis but in the absence of modern microbiological studies, the question is moot (Kirsner and Shorter 1988).

S. Wilks and W. Moxon (1875) wrote: "We have seen a case affected by discharge of mucus and blood, where, after death, the whole internal surface of the colon presented a highly vascular soft, red surface covered with a tenacious mucus and adherent lymph. . . . In other examples there has been extensive ulceration." Because the concept of microbial illnesses had not yet emerged, the possibility of a specific infection, in at least some instances, cannot be excluded. W. H. Allchin (1885), W. Hale-White (1888), and H. Folet, writing in 1885, are among those cited by G. Placitelli and colleagues (1958), who provided accurate clinical accounts. G. N. Pitt and A. E. Durham in 1885 described a woman of 29 years with a 5-year history of diarrhea:

[M]ore than half of the area of the whole colon was covered with small friable villous polypi . . . the intervening depressed white areas in the muscular coat, the mucous coat having entirely ulcerated away. . . . the circumference of the bowel is only 1⅓ – 2 inches, being narrower than the small intestine. (Kirsner 1988)

During the 1880s and 1890s, instances of an ulcerative colitis were reported by numerous physicians from England, France, Germany, Italy, and other European countries (Kirsner 1988). In 1888 Hale-White, a contemporary of Wilks at Guy's Hospital, described 29 cases of ulcerative colitis and remarked that "[t]he origin of this ulceration is extremely obscure . . . it is not dysentery." He cited similar observations by W. Leube (*Ziemssen's Cyclopedia*), K. Rokitansky ("Pathological Anatomy"), H. Nothnagel (*Beitrage zur Physiologie und Pathologie des Darmes*, 1884), and A. Bertrand and V. Fontana ("De l'enterocolite chronique endémique des Pays Chauds"), but again complete confirmation is not possible.

In 1895 Hale-White reported the association of liver disease and ulcerative colitis, and in 1920 R. F. Weir performed the operation of appendicostomy to facilitate "colonic drainage" in ulcerative colitis. J. P. Lockhart-Mummery (1907) described seven instances of colon carcinoma among 36 patients with ulcerative colitis, and emphasized the diagnostic value of sigmoidoscopy at the Royal Society of Medicine. By 1909, approximately 317 cases of patients with "ulcerative colitis" had been collected (between 1888 and 1907) from London hospitals, and in 1909 Allchin recorded perhaps the first instance of "familial" ulcerative colitis. Additional instances of ulcerative colitis were noted at the Paris Congress of Medicine in 1913. J. Y. Brown (1913) of the United States may have been the first to suggest the procedure of ileostomy in the surgical management of ulcerative colitis.

American and European Literature, 1920–45. During the 1920s, the number of reports increased steadily and included those by H. Rolleston, C. E. Smith, J. M. Lynch and J. Felsen of New York, A. F. Hurst, and E. Spriggs. During the same decade, Hermann Strauss of Berlin may have been the first to recommend blood transfusions in the treatment of ulcerative colitis. In 1924 J. A. Bargen of the Mayo Clinic published his experimental studies implicating the diplostreptococcus in the etiology of ulcerative colitis – a notion later discarded. More important was his (1946) comprehensive clinical study of the course, complications, and management of "thrombo-ulcerative colitis." C. D. Murray first drew public attention to the psychogenic aspects of ulcerative colitis in 1930, which were confirmed by A. J. Sullivan and C. A. Chandler (1932). This initiated the period (1930–60s) of intense psychiatric interest in ulcerative colitis.

Worldwide attention was directed to "*colites ulcereuses graves non-ambienne*" at the 1935 International Congress of Gastroenterology in Brussels; the amount of literature on the disease increased rapidly after this, with clinical contributions initiated by many physicians from many countries.

By the 1940s, ulcerative colitis, if not increasing in prevalence, at least was recognized more often than regional ileitis and was the dominant IBD disease. However, by the end of World War II, Crohn's disease (regional enteritis, Crohn's colitis) had become more frequent. Concurrently with an apparent stabilization of the frequency of ulcerative colitis in the United States, Crohn's disease has been the more prominent of the two prototypes of nonspecific IBD.

Crohn's Disease

Literature before 1900. The initial description of Crohn's disease may date back to Giovanni Battista Morgagni who, in 1761, described ileal ulceration and enlarged mesenteric lymph nodes in a young man who died of an ileal perforation; or, perhaps even earlier, to the "iliac passion" – claims that can never be substantiated. More suggestive early instances of Crohn's disease include an 1806 report by H. Saunders and that by C. Combe and Saunders (1813). Nineteenth-century descriptions of ileocecal disease consistent with today's concept of Crohn's disease, regional ileitis, or ileocolitis were authored by J. deGroote, J. Abercrombie, J. S. Bristowe, N. Moore, and Wilks. Wilks's (1859) description of the postmortem examination on the celebrated Isabella Bankes is of interest:

The intestines lay in a coil adherent by a thin layer of lymph indicative of recent inflammation; the ileum was inflamed for three feet from the ileo-caecal valve though otherwise the small intestine looked normal. The large intestine was ulcerated from end to end with ulcers of various sizes mostly isolated [t]hough some had run together.... Inflammation was most marked at the proximal colon and the caecum appeared to be sloughing causing the peritonitis.

Thirty years later, Samuel Fenwick (1889) described the necropsy findings suggestive of Crohn's disease, in a 27-year-old female:

Many of the coils of intestine were adherent and a communication existed between the caecum and a portion of the small intestine adherent to it, whilst the sigmoid flexure was adherent to the rectum, and a communication also existed between them. The lower end of the ileum was much dilated and hypertrophied, and the ileocecal valve was contracted to the size of a swan's quill.

Literature after 1900. Early in this century, T. Kennedy Dalziel (1913) of Glasgow described a group of 13 patients dating back to 1901 with findings closely resembling those recorded by B. B. Crohn, L. Ginzburg, and G. D. Oppenheimer (1932): "The affected bowel gives the consistence and smoothness of an eel in a state of rigor mortis, and the glands, though enlarged, are evidently not caseous." Many reports of single instances of a chronic stenosing inflammation of the last portion of the small bowel ("terminal ileitis") appeared subsequently. In addition, F. J. Nuboer (1932) of Holland described two patients with "chronic phlegmonous ileitis," manifesting the same gross and histological findings that Crohn and associates described. Similarly, M. Golob (1932) reported a "chronic infectious granuloma" involving the ileocecal region in a 44-year-old male presenting with rectal bleeding.

Soon after Crohn's (1932) paper, A. D. Bissell (1934) of the University of Chicago reported on two patients. The first patient was a 39-year-old male with symptoms of 4 years' duration, including abdominal cramps, diarrhea, and weight loss who required resection of an ileocecal mass. The second patient, a 28-year-old male, also required resection of the terminal ileum and cecum. These early case reports depicted Crohn's disease ("regional ileitis") as a mass-producing, bowel-narrowing process, virtually always requiring surgical intervention.

The principal clinical differentiation in the early part of the twentieth century included intestinal tuberculosis and granuloma formation simulating tumor in the bowel. E. Moschowitz and A. D. Wilensky (1923), from New York's Mount Sinai Hospital, reflecting that center's interest in granulomatous inflammations of the bowel, described four patients with nonspecific granulomatous disease of the intestine. Ginzburg and Oppenheimer, in the Pathology Department of the same hospital, identified a dozen instances of a localized hypertrophic, ulcerative stenosis of the distal 2 or 3 feet of the terminal ileum. Specific causes such as amebiasis, actinomycosis, intestinal tuberculosis, and syphilis were ruled out. In 1930, Crohn had two patients with a similar process. Crohn's first case was a 16-year-old boy with diarrhea, fever, a mass in the right lower abdominal quadrant, and pain, requiring ileocecal resection. Interestingly, the patient's sister also required an operation for regional ileitis several years later – the first recorded instance of "familial regional ileitis." Bargen, anticipating the more extensive involvement of the small intestine, suggested the term *regional enteritis* instead of "terminal ileitis."

In 1925 T. H. Coffen of Portland, Oregon, referring to earlier reports of intestinal granulomas, described a 20-year-old man with abdominal symptoms since 1915, diagnosed as phlegmonous enteritis. In 1916, 8 inches of thickened bowel were removed because of obstruction. A second obstruction 5 months later necessitated the removal of 24 inches of ileum. Eight months later a third resection was performed for the same condition. The pathological description of the resected bowel today would be consistent with a diagnosis of Crohn's disease.

In other notable articles, H. Mock in 1931 and R. Colp in 1933 chronicled involvement of the colon. C. Gotlieb and S. Alpert (1937) described regional jejunitis, and J. R. Ross (1949) identified "regional gastritis." W. A. Jackman and J. L. Kantor in 1934 and R. Marshak in 1951 described the roentgenographic appearance of Crohn's disease of the small bowel and the colon, and in 1936 Harold Edwards described a resected terminal ileum, with "the consistency of a hosepipe" from a 23-year-old woman with a history of persistent diarrhea, abdominal pain, and weight loss. R. Shapiro (1939) comprehensively reviewed the literature through the 1930s and identified numerous case reports mainly in the earlier German surgical literature of "inflammatory tumors" of the gastrointestinal tract, especially the colon; some of these probably were instances of Crohn's disease.

Authoritative descriptions of the pathological features of Crohn's disease have been provided by S. Warren and S. C. Sommers (1948), G. Hadfield (1939), and H. Rappaport and colleagues (1951). In 1952, Charles Wells of Liverpool distinguished between ulcerative colitis and what he termed "segmental colitis," and suggested that this latter form of colonic lesion was a variant of Crohn's disease. In 1955 Bryan Brooke and W. Trevor Cooke of England were among the first to recognize "right-sided colitis" as Crohn's disease of the colon rather than as ulcerative colitis, but it was not until reports in 1959 and 1960 by Lockhart-Mummery and B. C. Morson (1960) that Crohn's disease of the colon was generally accepted as a valid entity.

Eponym of Crohn's Disease. New instances of granulomatous inflammation of the small bowel were reported in Great Britain, occasionally designated as Crohn's disease, in 1936. In America the term "Crohn's disease" was first employed as a synonym by F. Harris and colleagues (1933) and later by Hurst of Great Britain. But others have also claimed priority. In Poland this entity was called "Lesniowski–Crohn's disease," whereas in Scotland the eponym of "Dalziel's disease" was recorded. H. I. Goldstein designated the condition "Saunders–Abercrombie–Crohn's ileitis."

To some American observers, this entity might well have been called "CGO disease," to include the important contributions of not only Crohn, but also Ginzburg and Oppenheimer, who provided 12 of the 14 cases constituting the (1932) *JAMA* paper. Whatever the "labeling" circumstances, the entity today carries the eponym "Crohn's disease" as the most convenient designation, which is now sanctioned by worldwide usage to designate a unique inflammatory process involving any part of the gastrointesti-

nal tract. It is to the credit of Crohn, Ginzburg, and Oppenheimer that their clinical description stimulated worldwide interest in this disease. Certainly much credit belongs to Crohn for his long clinical interest in the illness, his many publications and lectures on the subject, and his encouragement of others in the further investigation of the problem.

On the matter of eponyms, the comment of Thomas Lewis (1944) seems appropriate: "Diagnosis is a system of more or less accurate guessing, in which the end point achieved is a name. These names applied to disease come to assume the importance of specific entities . . . whereas they are, for the most part, no more than insecure and therefore temporary conceptions."

Joseph B. Kirsner

Bibliography

Allchin, W. H. 1885. A case of extensive ulceration of the colon. *Transactions of the Pathological Society of London* 36: 199.

Bargen, J. A. 1946. Chronic ulcerative colitis. In *The cyclopedia of medicine, surgery, and specialties,* ed. G. M. Piersol, Vol. 4: 382, 398. Philadelphia.

Bissell, A. D. 1934. Localized chronic ulcerative ileitis. *Annals of Surgery* 99: 957–66.

Brown, J. Y. 1913. The value of complete physiological rest of the large bowel in the treatment of certain ulcerative and obstructive lesions of this organ. *Surgery, Gynecology and Obstetrics* 16: 610.

Combe, C., and H. Saunders. 1813. A singular case of stricture and thickening of ileum. *Medical Transactions of the Royal College of Physicians, London* 4: 16.

Crohn B. B., L. Ginzburg, and G. D. Oppenheimer. 1932. Regional ileitis – a pathological and clinical entity. *Journal of the American Medical Association* 99: 1323–9.

Dalziel, T. K. 1913. Chronic intestinal enteritis. *British Medical Journal* 2: 1068–70.

Fenwick, S. 1889. *Clinical lectures on some obscure diseases of the abdomen.* London.

Goligher, J. C., et al. 1968. *Ulcerative colitis.* Baltimore.

Golob, M. 1932. Infectious granuloma of the intestines. *Medical Journal and Record* 135: 390–3.

Gotlieb, C., and S. Alpert. 1937. Regional jejunitis. *American Journal of Roentgenology and Radium Therapy* 38: 861–83.

Hadfield, G. 1939. The primary histological lesions of regional ileitis. *Lancet* 2: 773–5.

Hale-White, W. 1888. On simple ulcerative colitis and other rare intestinal ulcers. *Guy's Hospital Reports* 45: 131.

Harris, F., G. Bell, and H. Brunn. 1933. Chronic cicatrizing enteritis: Regional ileitis (Crohn). *Surgery, Gynecology, and Obstetrics* 57: 637–45.

Hawkins, C. 1983. Historical review. In *Inflammatory bowel disease*, ed. R. N. Allan et al., Vol. 1: 1–7. London.

Kirsner, J. B. 1988. Historical aspects of inflammatory bowel disease. *Journal of Clinical Gastroenterology* 10: 286–97.

Kirsner, J. B., and R. G. Shorter. 1988. *Inflammatory bowel disease*. Philadelphia.

Lewis, T. 1944. Reflections upon reform in medical education. I. Present state and needs. *Lancet* 1: 619–21.

Lockhart-Mummery, H. E., and B. C. Morson. 1960. Crohn's disease (regional enteritis) of the large intestine and its distinction from ulcerative colitis. *Gut* 1: 87–105.

Lockhart-Mummery, J. P. 1907. The causes of colitis: With special reference to its surgical treatment, with an account of 36 cases. *Lancet* 1: 1638.

Mendeloff, A. I., and B. M. Calkins. 1988. *The epidemiology of idiopathic inflammatory bowel disease*. London.

Morris-Gallart, E., and P. D. Sanjmane, eds. 1935. *Colitis ulcerosa graves non ambianac – etiologia, diagnostica y tratemiento*. Salvat. La Barcelone.

Moschowitz, E., and A. O. Wilensky. 1923. Nonspecific granulomata of the intestine. *American Journal of Medical Science* 166: 48–66.

Nuboer, F. J. 1932. Chronische Phlegmone vas let ileum. *Mededelingen uit het Geneeskundig laboratorium te Weltevreden* 76: 2989.

Placitelli, G., A. Franchini, M. Mini, and L. Possati. 1958. *La Colite ulcerosa*. Rome.

Rappaport, H., F. H. Bergoyne, and F. Smetana. 1951. The pathology of regional enteritis. *Military Surgeon* 109: 463–502.

Ross, J. R. 1949. Cicatrizing enterocolitis and gastritis. *Gastroenterology* 13: 344.

Shapiro, R. 1939. Regional ileitis. *American Journal of Medical Science* 198: 269–92.

Sullivan, A. J., and C. A. Chandler. 1932. Ulcerative colitis of psychogenic origin: Report of six cases. *Yale Journal of Biology and Medicine* 4: 779.

Warren, S., and S. C. Sommers. 1948. Cicatrizing enteritis (regional ileitis) as a pathologic entity. *American Journal of Pathology* 24: 475–521.

Wells, C. 1952. Ulcerative colitis in Crohn's disease. *Annals of the Royal College of Surgeons* 11: 105–20.

Wilks, S. 1859. Morbid appearances in the intestine of Miss Bankes. *London Medical Gazette* 2: 264–65.

Wilks S., and W. Moxon. 1875. *Lectures on pathological anatomy*, 2d edition, ed. J. and A. Churchill, 408, 762. London.

VIII.73
Influenza

Influenza, also known as flu, grip, and grippe, is a disease of humans, pigs, horses, and several other mammals, as well as of a number of species of domesticated and wild birds. Among humans it is a very contagious respiratory disease characterized by sudden onset and symptoms of sore throat, cough, often a runny nose, and (belying the apparent restriction of the infection to the respiratory tract) fever, chills, headache, weakness, generalized pain in muscles and joints, and prostration. It is difficult to differentiate between single cases of influenza and of feverish colds, but when there is a sudden outbreak of symptoms among a number of people, the correct diagnosis is almost always influenza.

There is at present no specific cure that is effective against this viral disease. In mild cases the acute symptoms disappear in 7 to 10 days, although general physical and mental depression may occasionally persist. Influenzal pneumonia is rare, but often fatal. Bronchitis, sinusitis, and bacterial pneumonia are among the more common complications, and the last can be fatal, but seldom is if properly treated. Influenza is generally benign, and even in pandemic years, the mortality rate is usually low – 1 percent or less – the disease being a real threat to life for only the very young, the immunosuppressed, and the elderly. However, this infection is so contagious that in most years multitudes contract it, and thus the number of deaths in absolute terms is usually quite high. Influenza, combined with pneumonia, is one of the 10 leading causes of death in the United States in the 1980s. The sequelae of influenza are often hard to discern and define – prolonged mental depression, for instance – but there is evidence that the global pandemic of encephalitis lethargica (parkinsonism) of the 1920s had its origin in the great pandemic of 1918–19.

Distribution and Incidence

In seemingly every year, there are at least some cases of influenza in every populated continent and in most of the large islands of the world. During epidemics, which occur somewhere almost annually, the malady sweeps large regions, even entire continents. During pandemics, a number of which have occurred every century for several hundred years, the disease infects a large percentage of the world's population and, ever since the 1889–90 pandemic, in all probability a majority of that population. Not everyone so infected becomes clinically sick, but nonetheless influenza pandemics are among the most vast and awesome of all earthly phenomena. The disease strikes so many so quickly and over such vast areas that the eighteenth-century Italians blamed it on the influence of heavenly bodies and called it *influenza*.

Etiology and Epidemiology

The causative agents of influenza are three myxoviruses, the influenza viruses A, B, and C. The B and C viruses are associated with sporadic epidemics among children and young adults, and do not cause pandemics. The A virus is the cause of most cases during and between pandemics. It exists and has existed in a number of subtypes, which usually do not induce cross-immunity to one another. In most instances, influenza viruses pass from person to person by breath-borne droplets, and from animal to animal by this and other routes. Although the disease can spread in warm weather, its epidemics among humans in the temperate zones usually appear in the winters, when people gather together in schools, houses, buses, and so forth under conditions of poor ventilation. Geographically, the malady spreads as fast as its victims travel, which in our time can mean circumnavigation of the globe in a few months, with the pandemic veering to the north and south of the tropics with the changing seasons.

Immunology

Influenza A virus is distinctive in its genetic instability, which probably makes permanent immunity to the disease impossible, no matter how many times it is contracted. This, plus its short incubation period of 1 to 2 days and the ease with which it passes from person to person, enables the disease to swing around the globe in pandemics and, between them, to maintain itself not only in epidemics among the previously unexposed and newborn, but also among the previously exposed and adult majority. Between pandemics the proteins on the shell of the virus undergo slow but constant genetic change, rendering acquired immunity ever more obsolete. This genetic instability is the likeliest explanation for the fact that even during pandemics the virus seems to change sufficiently to produce repeating waves of the infection, often two and three in a given locale. Several times a century, the virus has changed radically, rendering obsolete the immunologic defenses of the great majority of humans vis-à-vis influenza,

including immunologically experienced adults. In the mildest of these pandemics, millions fall ill and thousands die.

The cause of the major changes in the virus that set off the pandemics is still a matter of mystery. Many theories have been devised, including those pertaining to the influence of sun spots and such. Currently the three most plausible theories are the following:

1. The influenza A virus currently circulating through the human population undergoes a series of mutations, which rapidly and radically transform the virus into an infection-producing organism for which human immune systems are unprepared.
2. An animal influenza virus abruptly gains the ability to cause disease in humans, with the same results.
3. A human influenza virus and an animal influenza virus recombine ("cross-breed") to produce a new virus that retains its capacity to infect humans but has a surface with which human immune systems are unfamiliar.

In the present state of research, the first of these three seems the least likely and the last the most likely explanation. Nothing, however, is certain yet, and the cause of influenza pandemics remains unknown.

History and Geography

Through the Eighteenth Century

The origins of influenza are unknown. It is not an infection of our primate relations, and so it is probably not a very old human disease. It has, as far as we know, no latent state, and it does create a usually effective (though short-lived) immunity, and so it was unlikely to have been common among our Paleolithic ancestors or those of our herd animals before the advent of agriculture, cities, and concentrated populations of humans and domesticated animals. In small populations, it would have burnt itself out by killing or immunizing all available victims quickly. But because the immunity engendered is ephemeral, it does not require the large populations that measles and smallpox do to maintain itself.

Although influenza could be among the older diseases of civilization, acquired from pigs or ducks or other animals thousands of years ago, there is no clear evidence of its spread among humans until Europe's Middle Ages, and no undeniable evidence until the fifteenth and sixteenth centuries. Yet, since that time, the malady has been our unfailing companion, never absent for more than a few decades, if that. The association of the disease with Old World domesticated animals, and the extreme vulnerability to it of isolated peoples such as Amerindians, suggest that it was restricted to the Old World until the end of the fifteenth century. In that and the following centuries it spread overseas with Europeans and their livestock, and may account for much of the clinically undefined morbidity and mortality among the indigenes of Europe's transatlantic and transpacific empires. Large-scale epidemics of influenza did roll over Europe in 1510, 1557, and 1580. The last, the first unambiguously pandemic explosion of the disease, extended into Africa and Asia as well. There were further epidemics in Europe in the seventeenth century, but seemingly of only a regional nature.

At least three pandemics of influenza occurred in Europe in the eighteenth century – 1729–30, 1732–3, and 1781–2 – and several epidemics, two of which – 1761–2 and 1788–9 – may have been extensive enough to be termed pandemics. The pandemic of 1781–2 was, in its geographic spread and the number of people infected, among the greatest manifestations of disease of all history. Physicians guessed, for instance, that two-thirds of the people of Rome and three-quarters of the population of Britain fell ill, and influenza spread widely in North America, the West Indies, and Spanish America.

Nineteenth Century

By the end of the eighteenth century, accelerating population growth, urbanization, and improvements in transportation were changing the world in ways that enhanced the transmission of microbes across long distances. There were at least three influenza pandemics in the nineteenth century: 1830–1, 1833, and 1889–90, and a number of major epidemics as well. Even so, one of the most intriguing aspects of the history of influenza in this century was the long hiatus between the second and third pandemics. In fact, in Europe, from the epidemic of 1847–8 (defined a pandemic by some) to 1889, there were only a few minor upsurges of this disease.

When influenza rose up again in 1889, most physicians had only a textbook acquaintance with the disease, but by this time the medical sciences were making rapid advances, and public health had become a matter of governmental concern. The 1889–90 pandemic was the first for which we have detailed records. It reached Europe from the east (hence its nickname, the Russian flu), and such was

the efficiency of transatlantic shipping that it swept over western Europe and appeared in North America in the same month, December of 1889. It struck Nebraska, Saskatchewan, Rio de Janeiro, Buenos Aires, Montevideo, and Singapore in February, Australia and New Zealand in March. By spring the pandemic was firmly established and widespread in Asia and Africa. Some Africans, who had never seen the disease in their lifetimes, called it a "white man's disease." Waves of this infection continued to roll across large regions of the world for the rest of the century, and although the mortality rates in this pandemic were quite low, the total of deaths was high. By conservative estimate, 250,000 died in Europe, and the world total must have been at the very least two or three times greater. Influenza killed many more than cholera did in the nineteenth century, but much of the mortality was restricted to the elderly, and thus its reputation as an unpleasant but not dangerous infection was preserved.

Early Twentieth Century

Its history for the first 17 years of the next century reinforced this view. Although rarely absent for long, influenza attracted little attention until 1918–19, when a pandemic of unprecedented virulence appeared. What was probably its first wave rose in the spring of 1918, perhaps first in the United States, attracting little attention because its death rate was low. Its most ominous characteristic was that many of the dead were young adults, in contradistinction to the malady's previous record. That spring and summer, this new influenza circumnavigated the globe, infecting millions and killing hundreds of thousands, and making ever more difficult the waging of wars in Europe and the Middle East. The name given this new disease was the Spanish flu, not because morbidity and mortality were higher there than elsewhere, but because Spain was not a belligerent and thus the ravages of the malady in that country were not screened from world attention by censorship. As in previous pandemics and epidemics, morbidity rates were vastly greater than mortality rates, and the latter, as a percentage of the former, were not impressive.

In August, that changed, as death rates doubled, tripled, and more. A second wave arose, sending hundreds of millions to sickbeds, as if they were as immunologically inexperienced as children, and killing millions. This wave tended to subside toward the end of the year, but returned again in a third wave in the winter and spring. In both the fall and winter waves, about half the deaths were in the 20- to 40-

year-old group. Fully 550,000 died in the United States, about 10 times the number of battle deaths of Americans in World War I.

In remote parts of the world, where influenza had never or rarely reached before, the death rate was often extremely high. In Western Samoa, 7,542 died out of a population of 38,302 in the last 2 months of 1918. The total of deaths in the world was in excess of 21 million, that number being an estimate made in the 1920s before historians and demographers sifted through the records of Latin America, Africa, and Asia, adding many more – millions, certainly – to the world total. It is possible that the 1918–19 pandemic was, in terms of absolute numbers, the greatest single demographic shock that the human species has ever received. The Black Death and World Wars I and II killed higher percentages of the populations at risk, but took years to do so and were not universal in their destruction. The so-called Spanish flu did most of its killing in a 6-month period and reached almost every human population on Earth. Moreover, its impact was even greater than these numbers indicate because so many young adults died. To this day, we do not know what made the 1918–19 influenza such a killer. Theories about wartime deprivation are clearly invalid because the death rates in well-fed America and Australasia were approximately the same as in the nations immediately engaged in the fighting. Perhaps as has been suggested, a chance synergy of viral and bacterial infection produced an exceptionally deadly pneumonia, or perhaps the 1918 virus was so distinctive antigenically that it provoked a massive immune response, choking the victims with inflammation and edema. We have no way of proving or disproving these theories.

In 1920, another wave of the disease rolled over the world, and in the United States this was, with the exceptions of the two preceding years, the worst for influenza mortality of all time. But morbidity and mortality rates soon shrank back to normal levels, and the disease lost most of its power to kill young adults. The medical profession, however, has subsequently worried about a resurgence of the killer virus, and has devoted great energy to identifying it, learning its secrets, and how to disarm it.

Prevention and Control

The medical profession, grappling with the great pandemic, labored under three major disadvantages: First, in the 1890s one of the premier bacteriologists of the world, Richard F. J. Pfeiffer, thought he had discovered the causative organism, common

in his time and again in the fall of 1918. Unfortunately, Pfeiffer's bacillus was not the cause, although it doubtlessly played a role in many secondary infections. Its chief significance is probably that it inveigled many scientists into wasting a lot of time discovering its insignificance. Second, influenza was believed to be an exclusively human disease, making it very awkward to work with in the laboratory. Third, bacteriologists of the early decades of the twentieth century had no means by which to see anything as small as the true cause of the disease, the influenza virus.

About 1930, Richard E. Shope discovered that he could transfer a mild influenza-like disease from one pig to another via a clear liquid from which all visible organisms had been filtered. (If Pfeiffer's bacillus was also present in the pigs, they became much sicker, a phenomenon that is one of the sources of the theory that the 1918 influenza may have been the product of synergistic infections.) In 1933, W. Smith, C. H. Andrewes, and P. P. Laidlaw succeeded in infecting ferrets with a filtrate obtained from a human with influenza, and after these events, researchers knew what to look for. In the following years, the A, B, and C viruses were isolated and identified and, thanks to the new electron microscope, seen and photographed.

It is possible that more is now known about the influenza virus than about any other virus, but its changing nature has defeated all efforts thus far to make a vaccine against the disease that will be effective for more than a few years at most. Vaccines were produced in the 1940s to protect the soldiers of World War II from a repetition of the pandemic that had killed so many of them in World War I, and influenza vaccines developed since have enabled millions, particularly the elderly, to live through epidemics without illness or with only minor illness. But the ability of the A virus to change and sometimes to change radically – as at the beginning of the 1957–8 and 1968 pandemics – and to race around the globe faster than suitable vaccines can be produced and delivered to large numbers of people, has so far frustrated all efforts to abort pandemics. Vaccines were effective in damping neither the pandemic of the so-called Asian flu of 1957–8 nor the Hong Kong flu of 1968.

At present, a worldwide network of 100 or so centers, most of them national laboratories, cooperate under the direction of the World Health Organization to identify new strains of influenza virus as quickly as they appear in order to minimize the time between the beginning of epidemics and the production and distribution of relevant vaccines. The efficiency of this organization has been impressive, and certainly has saved many lives, but influenza is not yet under control. The frustration of flu fighters of the United States reached a peak in 1976, when a virus closely resembling Shope's swine virus and that of the 1918 pandemic began to spread among soldiers at Fort Dix, New Jersey. The medical profession and the U.S. government mobilized in order to prevent a recurrence of the disaster that had occurred 60 years before. Scores of millions of dollars were spent to devise a vaccine, to produce it in quantity, and to deliver it into the arms of millions of Americans. No pandemic appeared, not even an epidemic, and the single long-lasting medical result of this enormous effort seems to have been a number of cases of Guillain–Barré syndrome, a paralytic and occasionally fatal disorder, which were associated with the vaccinations. The number of these cases was tiny, relative to the tens of millions of doses of the vaccine administered, but the result in litigation has been massive.

Alfred W. Crosby

Bibliography

Beveridge, W. I. B. 1977. *Influenza: The last great plague: An unfinished story of discovery*. New York.

Crosby, Alfred W. 1989. *America's forgotten pandemic: The influenza of 1918*. New York.

Guerra, Francisco, 1985. La epidemía Americana de influenza en 1493. *Revista de Indias* 45: 325–47.

Hoyle, L. 1968. *The influenza viruses*. New York.

Jordan, Edwin O. 1927. *Epidemic influenza: A survey*. Chicago.

Kaplan, Martin M., and Robert G. Webster. 1977. The epidemiology of influenza. *Scientific American* 237: 88–106.

Kilbourne, Edwin D. 1975. *The influenza viruses and influenza*. New York.

1987. *Influenza*. New York.

Kingsley, M. Stevens. 1918. The pathophysiology of influenzal pneumonia in 1918. *Perspectives in Biology and Medicine* 25: 115–25.

MacDonald, Kristine L., et al. 1987. Toxic shock syndrome, a newly recognized complication of influenza and influenza-like illness. *Journal of the American Medical Association* 257: 1053–8.

Neustadt, Richard E., and Harvey V. Fineberg. 1978. *The swine flu affair: Decision-making on a slippery slope*. Washington, D.C.

Osborn, June E. 1977. *Influenza in America, 1918–1976*. New York.

Patterson, K. David. 1981. The demographic impact of the 1918–19 influenza pandemic in sub-Saharan Africa: A preliminary assessment. In *African historical de-* mography, 2d edition, ed. C. Fyfe and D. McMaster, 401–31. Edinburgh.

1986. *Pandemic influenza, 1700–1900*. Totowa, N.J.

Ravenholt, R. T., and William H. Foege. 1982. 1918 influenza, encephalitis lethargica, parkinsonism. *Lancet* 2: 860–64.

Silverstein, Arthur M. 1981. *Pure politics and impure science: The swine flu affair*. Baltimore.

Stuart-Harris, Charles. 1981. The epidemiology and prevention of influenza. *American Scientist* 69: 166–71.

VIII.74
Japanese B Encephalitis

Japanese B encephalitis is a relatively uncommon disease, even in areas where the infection is endemic. The disease is one of several caused by arthropod-borne viruses (arboviruses); carried by mosquitoes of the genus *Culex,* this one is a member of the family Togaviridae and genus *Flavivirus* and thus is an RNA virus. The species of *Culex* that is the most common insect vector for Japanese B encephalitis is *Culex tritaeniorhyncus.*

The disease was first recognized and described in 1871, and the virus was first isolated in 1935. The infection may appear in epidemic or in sporadic outbreaks, and is carried particularly in swine, but also has been isolated from a variety of birds and from equine animals. The virus is distributed principally in East and Southeast Asia.

Epidemiology

Epidemic outbreaks of Japanese B encephalitis, like those of arboviruses in general, tend to occur in regions that are usually dry and arid and, therefore, relatively free of viral activity; such areas may accumulate a large number of individuals who, because of lack of previous exposure, are relatively susceptible. Then with rain and the appearance of conditions favorable to the proliferation of the insect vector, epidemic outbreaks may occur, particularly where there are relatively high population densities of the human host and of the amplifying hosts such as equine or porcine animal species. In addition, there is evidence that for some arboviruses a change occurs in the relative virulence of the infecting strain, which may also account for an epidemic outbreak. Why, given the presence of Japanese B encephalitis virus in birds with wide-ranging migratory patterns, the disease remains localized to certain geographic areas is not entirely clear, but presumably has to do with the specificity of the insect vector in carrying the infectious agent. The mosquito vector, *C. tritaeniorhyncus,* is found in rice fields and feeds on pigs and birds, as well as human and other hosts. However, the Japanese custom of raising pigs in the fall, after the flooding of rice paddies is over, and of taking the pigs to market early the following year, may also help to account for the general lack of large outbreaks as well as for the usual pattern of sporadic cases. As might be expected with such a pattern, the few large outbreaks tend to occur in more rural areas, street antibody to the virus is relatively common, and clinical cases account for about 2 percent of all of the infections, as judged by antibody surveys.

Pathology

Most of the information on the early stages of the disease has been gained from studies in the mouse. Pathological features of fatal human cases have generally been consistent with the experimental findings. Early in the disease, focal hemorrhages, congestion, and edema are found in the brain. Microscopically widespread damage to Purkinje cells of the cerebellum is noted, with pervascular inflammation and multiple foci of degeneration and necrosis. Extraneural evidence of spread of the virus is found in the form of hyperplasia of the germinal centers of the lymph nodes and of the spleen; multiple foci of round-cell infiltration in many organs, including the heart, kidneys, and lungs; and, in pregnancy, infiltration of the placenta with corresponding abortion and stillbirth. Multiple lesions in the offspring indicate cross-placental passage of the virus.

Clinical Manifestations

The clinical disease consists of the usual signs and symptoms of encephalitis, and no syndrome has been elicited that is specific for Japanese B encephalitis. Within a few days to several weeks (mean of 10 days) after a bite by a mosquito carrying the virus, susceptible patients manifest fever and evidence of damage to the central nervous system, which may include meningism, delirium, drowsiness, confusion, stupor, paralyses especially of the facial muscles, and, in the most severe cases, coma and death within a few days after onset.

The cerebrospinal fluid shows the presence of a nonpyogenic infection, with increased numbers of mononuclear cells, rarely over 1,000 per cubic millimeter, and elevated protein; sugar is therefore not generally decreased and may be elevated in the spinal fluid.

Diagnosis

The definitive diagnosis is made only from studies of the antibody status of the affected individual, with evidence of the absence of specific antibody at the time of onset of the disease followed by a 4-fold or greater rise in titer of the antibody during the following days or weeks. Complement-fixing antibody is the first to appear in most patients, but hemagglutinating and neutralizing antibodies are usually demonstrable shortly thereafter. More recently, antibody tests using fluorescein- or enzyme-labeled antibody, or the various modifications of these, showing specific rise in titer, are sufficient to establish the diagnosis. Antigenic variation is common among viral isolates, and at least two immunotypes have been delineated; thus the serodiagnosis must be performed in laboratories that have on hand the several subtypes that may be needed for a full serologic analysis of a given case or outbreak.

The disease is one of the most fatal among arboviruses, with case fatality rates of 50 to 70 percent having been recorded in outbreaks. Recovery may be complete, or there may be residual damage to the central nervous system; Japanese B encephalitis, in contrast to other arboviral encephalitides, is accompanied by relatively high rates of complete recovery despite the high case fatality rates.

There is no specific treatment, and supportive care is the major intervention that can be offered. The protective effect of antibody suggests that convalescent serum or other sources of antibody might have some therapeutic value, but this has not been systematically investigated on a suitable scale.

Prevention and Control

Vaccines have been available for many years for immunization of humans and of livestock. Live attenuated vaccines have been available in Japan since 1972, and in China more recently, and their effectiveness is shown by seroconversion rates of up to 96 percent. Vaccines are prepared by purification of viral suspensions from mouse brains, or from hamster kidney cultures, but several newer technologies are presently under active investigation. Widespread immunization campaigns have been successful in Japan, Taiwan, and China. At present, the vaccines are composed principally of the prototype Nakayama strain, and reasonable control of the disease has taken place. It is therefore unclear how necessary or desirable the addition of the newer isolates, with slightly different antigenic specificities, would be.

Currently used vaccines require primary immunization with two injections at 7- to 14-day intervals, a booster within 1 year, and further boosters at 3- to 4-year intervals. Fortunately, the vaccine produces relatively few side reactions, and postvaccinal encephalitis must be exceedingly rare because few if any reliable reports of this complication following administration of the vaccine are in evidence.

Vector control has been investigated in some detail. Larvicides and adulticides aimed at the chief mosquito vector have reduced attack rates in areas where these have been tested, and programs of control of insect vectors, coupled with elimination of aquatic vegetation in irrigation channels and with spraying of insecticides in livestock pens, have had some success in China. Under epidemic conditions, spraying with appropriate insecticides has sometimes been necessary.

Edward H. Kass

Bibliography

Buescher, E. L., and W. F. Scherer. 1959. Ecologic studies of Japanese encephalitis virus in Japan. IX. Epidemiologic correlations and conclusions. *American Journal of Tropical Medicine and Hygiene* 8: 719–22.

Buescher, E. L., et al. 1959a. Ecologic studies of Japanese encephalitis virus in Japan. IV. Avian infection. *American Journal of Tropical Medicine and Hygiene* 8: 678–88.

1959b. Ecologic studies of Japanese encephalitis virus in Japan. II. Mosquito infection. *American Journal of Tropical Medicine and Hygiene* 8: 651–64.

Fukumi, H., et al. 1975. Ecology of Japanese encephalitis virus in Japan. I. Mosquito and pig infection with the virus in relation to human incidences. *Tropical Medicine* 17: 97–110.

Hayashi, K., et al. 1978. Ecology of Japanese encephalitis virus in Japan, particularly the results of surveys in every interepidemic season from 1964 to 1976. *Tropical Medicine* 20: 81–96.

Hayashi, M. 1934. Uebertragung des Virus von encephalitis epidemica auf Affen. *Proceedings of the Imperial Academy of Tokyo* 10: 41–4.

Konno, J., et al. 1966. Cyclic outbreaks of Japanese encephalitis among pigs and humans. *American Journal of Epidemiology* 84: 292–300.

Mifune, K. 1965. Transmission of Japanese encephalitis virus to susceptible pigs by mosquitoes of *Culex tritaeniorhynchus* after experimental hibernation. *Endemic Diseases Bulletin of Nagasaki University* 7: 178–91.

Sabin, A. B. 1950. Search for virus of Japanese B encepha-litis in various arthropods collected in Japan in 1946–1947. *American Journal of Hygiene* 51: 36–62.

Umenai, T., et al. 1985. Japanese encephalitis: Current worldwide status. *Bulletin of the World Health Organization* 63: 625–31.

VIII.75
Lactose Intolerance and Malabsorption

Lactose malabsorption describes a physiological situation. It is the basis for lactose intolerance. The inability to digest lactose is a quantitative phenomenon related to the enzyme lactase and its amount and activity in the intestine. Lactose intolerance, then, is a clinical definition. It involves the concept that the individual is unable to tolerate physiologically the lactose present in milk and other dietary products because of an inability to digest the carbohydrate, due to insufficient activity of the lactase enzyme. Intolerance to lactose as a clinical entity has been recognized for some time. Early in this century, Abraham Jacoby hinted at the existence of lactose intolerance in speeches to the American Pediatric Society; later, in 1926, John Howland, in his presidential address to that same organization, was somewhat more explicit when he indicated that many of the infantile diarrheas were the result of a lack of "ferments" necessary for the digestion of carbohydrate (Flatz 1989).

More recently, interest of physicians and nutritionists in the digestion of lactose stimulated reports during the late 1950s. One by A. Holzel and colleagues (1959) reported on a severe diarrhea associated with the ingestion of lactose in two young siblings who, as a consequence, were "failing to thrive." Another report, by P. Durand (1958), diagnosed two patients with lactose malabsorption and lactosuria. Since then, innumerable articles and reviews have appeared in the world's literature (Scrimshaw and Murray 1988). Evaluations of that literature may be obtained by consulting G. Semenza and S. Auricchio (1989), G. Flatz (1989), and N. Kretchmer (1971).

Lactose: Chemistry, Digestion, and Metabolism

Lactose is a galactoside composed of glucose and galactose. This compound is found in the milk of most mammals, although in marsupials and mono-tremes it appears in conjugated form. It is entirely lacking in the milk of the California sea lion and related pinnipedia of the Pacific Basin. The reason for the latter is that lactose is synthesized in the mammary gland from two monosaccharides, glucose and galactose, by the enzyme galactosyltransferase, which requires the presence of alpha-lactalbumin – not produced by the mammary glands of the sea lion. Thus the concentration of lactose in the milk of placental animals ranges from a low of zero to a high of 7 percent (Sunshine and Kretchmer 1964).

Lactose is digested in the small intestine by the lactase (a galactosidase), which is located in the brush border of the epithelial cells of intestinal villi. This enzyme is anchored to the membrane by a hydrophobic tail of amino acids. Detailed descriptions have recently been published of the intimate intracellular metabolism of lactase (Castillo et al. 1989; Quan et al. 1990).

In most mammals the activity of lactose-digesting lactase is high during the perinatal period; after weaning the activity declines to about 10 percent of its original value. But in certain human groups the enzyme activity remains elevated throughout the lifetime of most of their members (Kretchmer 1977). Examples of these groups include northern Europeans, people of Magyar-Finnish extraction, and two African tribes, the Fulani and the Tussi.

Clinical Manifestations

The clinical manifestations of lactose intolerance include increasing abdominal discomfort, borborygmus, flatulence, and finally fermentative diarrhea. Although an inordinate amount of any carbohydrate in the diet will produce a similar symptomatology, intolerance to lactose is the most prominent of these clinical syndromes. The basis of this phenomenon is primarily the activity of the lactase relative to dietary lactose. The lower the activity, the less the capacity for the hydrolysis of the lactose, although other factors – such as intestinal motility and the presence of other nutrients – also play a role in this phenomenon.

When the capacity of the lactase is exceeded, the nonhydrolyzed dietary lactose passes into the large bowel where it is fermented by the myriad of colonic bacteria. This action in turn yields propionic acid, hydrogen, methane, and alcohols, and results in a watery diarrhea, the pH of which is acidic.

In general, the activity of lactase in the intestine in almost all mammals by the time of weaning has decreased to about 10 percent of that encountered during the perinatal period. This does not mean, however, that weaning is directly related to the decrease in activity of lactase. There has been no documentation indicating that there is any inductive relationship between the activity of the enzyme and the ingestion of milk. In fact, all the careful studies indicate that there is no relationship between the two events (i.e., the ingestion of milk and the activity of lactase).

Classification

Lactose malabsorption can be classified into three categories:

1. Congenital malabsorption of lactase, a rare phenomenon, which has been documented in only a few cases.
2. Primary malabsorption of lactose, a worldwide situation that is encountered in humans after the age of 5 to 7 years, and in other animals after weaning. (This is considered to be a normal physiological process, transmitted genetically; indeed it resembles a classical Mendelian recessive trait.)
3. An acquired malabsorption of lactose that can be encountered at any age in infants and children under 7 years, as well as in adults who had previously been lactose absorbers. This form can also be associated with nonspecific and specific diarrhea of infancy, drugs that affect the intestinal mucosa, and diseases such as cystic fibrosis and gluten-sensitive enteropathy.

An interesting phenomenon is that the colonic flora of the lactose-intolerant individual seems able to adapt to a nonfermentive type of bacteria. A study was launched in Nigeria in which six medical students, all proven lactose nondigesters, were fed graded doses of 5 grams of lactose to a final amount of 50 grams over a 6-month period. At the end of this time, all six of the individuals could tolerate the 50 grams of lactose, but were shown to be unable to digest it. Adults who should be intolerant to lactose can drink a glass, or even a pint, of milk with relative impunity, but nonetheless manifest no increase in lactase activity and consequently cannot digest the lactose.

History and Geography

The ability to digest lactose is a nutritional event that can be clearly associated with evolutionary pressures. During the Neolithic period, human adults began to drink milk, probably in association with the domestication of animals. These ancient pastoralists who originated in the Euphrates River Valley were nomadic, constantly in search of new pastures for their animals. It is assumed that they migrated in two main directions: to the northwest, toward Europe; and to the southwest, across the then-fertile Sahara toward east and west Central Africa. The exact time of these migrations is unknown, but presumably the nomadic pastoralists of Africa (e.g., the Fulani, the Tussi, the Masai, and others) have their origins in these migrations as do those of northern Europe.

In the Americas, by contrast, there were no indigenous pastoral groups, and thus, in the Western Hemisphere, there was no ingestion of milk after weaning until the Europeans arrived. An absence of dietary milk after weaning was also the case in Australia, the islands of the Pacific, Japan, and the rest of Asia. In these regions the individual after weaning obtained calcium from small bones, limestone, dark-green vegetables, and fermented or pressed (and thus much reduced in lactose) dairy products.

Thus the present-day geographic distribution of peoples who can or cannot digest lactose fits with our historical knowledge of the distribution of ancient pastoral groups and the milking of their animals. Nonetheless, confusion arises over questions of levels of lactose intolerance among peoples with no history of pastoral activity. In the case of a native American population – the Pima-Papagos, for example – the inability to digest lactose has been reported at only 60 percent (see Tables VIII.75.1 and VIII.75.2). The 40

Table VIII.75.1. *Lactose absorption and malabsorption correlated with degree of Indian blood (children ≥4 years, and adults)*

	No. of absorbers	No. of malabsorbers[a]	Percentage of malabsorbers
Full-blood Indians (100% Pima or all Pima-Papago)			
	3[b]	59	95
Mixed Anglo (Northern European)-Indian			
⅟₁₆ Anglo	0	2	100
⅛ Anglo	5	16	76
¼ or ½ Anglo	11	7	39
Total	16	25	61

[a]Malabsorbers represent 21 adults (> 18 years), 38 children (4–18 years).
[b]Ages 4, 4½, and 6 years.

Source: Johnson et al. 1977. Lactose malabsorption among the Pima Indians of Arizona. *Gastroenterology* 73(6): 1229–1304, p. 1391, by permission of *Gastroenterology*.

Table VIII.75.2. *Distribution of the adult lactase phenotypes in human populations*

Population or country	Subgroup	Number of subjects	High LDC	Low LDC	Percent low LDC
Finland	Finns	449	371	78	17
	Lapps	521	305	216	41
	Swedes	91	84	7	8
Sweden	Swedes	400	396	4	1
Denmark	Danes	761	743	18	3
Britain	British	96	90	6	6
Ireland	Irish	50	48	2	4
Netherlands	Dutch	14	14	0	0
Germany	Germans	1872	1596	276	15
France	North	73	56	17	23
	South	82	47	35	43
Spain	Spaniards	265	225	40	15
Switzerland	Swiss	64	54	10	16
Austria	Austrians	528	422	106	20
Italy	North	565	301	264	47
	South	128	41	78	68
	Sicily	100	29	71	71
Yugoslavia	Slovenians	153	99	54	35
	South	51	25	26	51
Hungary	Hungarians	707	446	61	37
Czechoslovakia	Czechs	217	189	28	13
Poland	Poles	296	187	109	37
Former U.S.S.R.	Leningrad	248	210	38	15
	Estonians	650	467	183	28
Greece	Greeks	972	452	520	53
Cyprus	Greeks	67	19	48	72
Gypsies	European	253	83	170	67
Turkey	Turks	470	135	335	71
Morocco	Maghrebi	55	12	43	78
Egypt		584	157	427	73
Sudan	Arabs	387	179	208	54
	Beja	303	252	51	17
	Other nomads	61	42	19	31
	South	366	92	274	75
Ethiopia		58	6	52	90
Somalia		244	58	186	76
Kenya	Bantu	71	19	52	73
Uganda, Rwanda	Bantu	114	14	100	88
	Hima, Tussi	70	65	5	7
	Mixed	75	38	37	49
Central Africa	Bantu	112	6	106	95
South Africa	Bantu	57	3	54	95
	Bushmen	65	3	62	95
	Mixed	152	26	126	83
Nigeria	Ibo, Yoruba	113	12	101	89
	Hausa	48	9	39	81
	Fulani (Fulbe)	9	7	2	22
Niger	Tuareg	118	103	15	13
Senegal	Agricultural	131	85	46	35
	Peuhl (Fulbe)	29	29	0	0
Israel	Israeli	272	92	180	66
	Arabs	67	13	54	80
Jordan	Agricultural	204	43	161	79
	Bedouins	162	123	39	24
Saudi Arabia	Bedouins	22	17	5	23
	Other Arabs	18	8	10	56
Lebanon		225	48	177	79
Syria		75	7	68	91
Arabs	Mixed groups	30	5	25	83
Iran	Iranians	40	7	33	83
Afghanistan	Afghans	270	47	223	83
Pakistan		467	195	272	58

Table VIII.75.2. *(cont.)*

Population or country	Subgroup	Number of subjects	High LDC	Low LDC	Percent low LDC
India	North	264	194	70	27
	Central	125	46	79	63
	South	60	20	40	67
Indians	Overseas	87	22	65	75
Sri Lanka	Sinhalese	200	55	145	73
Thailand	Thai	428	8	420	98
Vietnamese	In U.S.A.	31	0	31	100
China	Han North	641	49	592	93
	Han South	405	17	388	96
	Mongols	198	24	174	88
	Kazakhs	195	46	149	76
	Uighurs	202	37	165	82
	Hui	177	24	153	86
	Koreans	198	12	186	94
	Hakka	202	22	180	89
	Bai/Zhuang	359	27	332	93
	Taiwan	71	0	71	100
Chinese	Overseas	94	23	71	76
Japan	Japanese	66	10	56	85
Indonesia	Javanese	53	5	48	91
Papua New Guinea	Tribals	123	12	111	90
Fiji	Fijians	12	0	12	100
Australia	Whites	133	127	6	5
	Aborigines	145	48	97	67
Greenland	Eskimo	119	18	101	85
	Mixed	108	67	41	38
Canada	Whites	16	15	1	6
	Indians	30	11	19	63
U.S.A.	Alaska	36	6	30	83
	Indians	221	11	210	95
	Whites	1101	887	214	19
	Blacks	390	138	252	65
	Mexicans	305	147	158	52
Mexico	Mexicans	401	69	332	83
Colombia	Mestizos	45	30	15	33
	Chami Indians	24	0	24	100
Peru	Mestizos	94	26	68	72
Bolivia	Aymara	31	7	24	77
Brazil	Whites	53	27	26	49
	Nonwhites	31	8	23	74
	Japanese	20	0	20	100

Note: LDC = lactose digestion capacity.

Source: G. Flatz. 1989. The genetic polymorphism of intestinal lactase activity in adult humans. In *The metabolic basis of inherited disease,* 6th edition, ed. G. R. Scriver, A. Z. Beaudet, W. S. Sly, and D. Valle, p. 3003. New York. By permission of McGraw-Hill Book Company.

percent who can drink milk, however, represent the genetic penetrance of the pure genetic pool of native Americans with a gene that affords them the ability to digest lactose. Without that genetic penetrance, the percentage that could not digest lactose would have reached 100.

Flatz (1989) has compiled a list of figures that report the distribution of lactose phenotypes for many populations of the world (see Table VII.75.2). These data support the cultural hypothesis first promulgated by Frederick Simoons (1970), which states that the ability to digest lactose is associated only with a population that has a history of pastoralism. The hereditary pattern for the ability to digest lactose appears to be simple and to follow straightforward Mendelian genetics. The individual who can digest lactose carries the mutated gene, which in this case, is dominant. The lactose nonabsorber carries a recessive gene. Consequently, the cross between lactose malabsorbers always yields progeny who are lactose malabsorbers, thus perpetuating the absolute inability to digest lactose among a lactose-intolerant population.

Summary

Lactase has been shown in a number of careful investigations to be the same enzyme in the infant as in the adult who can digest lactose, and in the residual activity found in the nondigester. In general, the lactose digester has 10 times more enzymatic activity than the lactose nondigester. Thus, the biochemical genetics of lactose digestion is related to the amount and activity of lactase.

Today, lactose malabsorbers who would like to be able to drink milk can purchase various "lactase" preparations now on the market that "digest" the lactose in milk before it is ingested. Others who do not drink milk can overcome the potential dietary calcium deficiency by consuming fermented milks, pressed cheeses, dark-green vegetables, and small bones as in sardines.

The worldwide distribution of an inability to digest lactose after weaning in most human adults and all other mammals argues for this condition to be the normal physiological state. The ability to digest lactose would seem then to be evidence of a genetic polymorphism. It is only the bias of the milk-oriented societies of northern Europe and North America that casts lactose malabsorption as an abnormality.

Norman Kretchmer

Bibliography

Castillo, R., et al. 1990. Intestinal lactase in the neonatal rat. *Journal of Biological Chemistry* 265: 15889–93.

Debongnie, J. C., et al. 1975. Absorption of nitrogen and fat. *Archives of the Diseases of Childhood* 50: 363–6.

Durand, P. 1958. Idiopathic lactosuria in a patient with chronic diarrhea and acidosis. *Minerva Pediatrica* 10: 1083–1147.

Flatz, G. 1989. The genetic polymorphism of intestinal lactase activity in adult humans. In *The metabolic basis of inherited disease,* 6th edition, ed. C. R. Scriver et al. New York.

Holzel, A., V. Schwartz, and K. W. Sutcliff. 1959. Defective lactose absorption causing malnutrition in infancy. *Lancet* 1: 1126–8.

Johnson, J., et al. Lactose malabsorption among the Pima Indians of Arizona. *Gastroenterology* 73(6): 1299–1304.

Kretchmer, N. 1971. [Memorial lecture] Lactose and lactase: A historical perspective. *Gastroenterology* 61: 805–13.

1977. The geography and biology of lactose digestion and malabsorption. *Postgraduate Medical Journal* 53: 65–72.

Lebenthal, E., et al. 1981. Recurrent abdominal pain and lactose absorption in children. *Pediatrics* 67: 828–32.

Quan, R., et al. 1990. Intestinal lactase: Shift in intracellular processing to altered, inactive species in the adult rat. *Journal of Biological Chemistry* 265: 15882–8.

Ransome-Kuti, O., et al. 1975. A genetic study of lactose digestion in Nigerian families. *Gastroenterology* 68: 431–6.

Sahi, T. 1974. The inheritance of selective adult-type lactose malabsorption. *Scandinavian Journal of Gastroenterology* (Supplement 30): 1–73.

Scrimshaw, N. S., and E. B. Murray. 1988. The acceptability of milk and milk products in populations with high prevalence of lactose intolerance. *American Journal of Clinical Nutrition* (Supplement 48(4)): 1083–1147.

Semenza, G., and S. Auricchio. 1989. Small-intestinal disaccharidases. In *The metabolic basis of inherited disease,* 6th edition, ed. C. R. Scriver et al. New York.

Simoons, F. J. 1970. Primary adult lactose intolerance and the milking habit: A problem in biologic and cultural interrelations. II. A culture-historical hypothesis. *American Journal of Digestive Diseases* 15: 695–710.

Sunshine, P., and N. Kretchmer. 1964. Intestinal disaccharidases: Absence in two species of sea lions. *Science* 144: 850–1.

Wald, A., et al. 1982. Lactose malabsorption in recurrent abdominal pain of childhood. *Journal of Pediatrics* 100: 65–8.

VIII.76
Lassa Fever

Recognition of Africa's major endemic diseases of human beings was apparently well advanced by 1900. Malaria, trypanosomiasis, yellow fever, schistosomiasis, typhoid fever, brucellosis, and a long list of other afflictions had been characterized. But then, in 1969, a new member of the coterie of major endemic diseases of Africa entered the scene: Lassa fever.

The events leading to the discovery were dramatic. A nurse, Laura Wine, in a mission hospital in Lassa, Nigeria, became ill, progressed unfavorably, and died, despite the marshaling of antimalarials, antibiotics, antimicrobial agents, and supportive therapy. This death, as a statistic, would probably have been labeled "malaria" and thus been registered as such in national and World Health Organization disease records. But another nurse, Charlotte Shaw, who attended the first, also became ill. She was taken by small plane from Lassa to the Evangel Hospital in Jos, Nigeria, operated by the Sudan Interior Mission, where she died while being attended by physicians Harold White and Janet Troup, and nurse Lily Pinneo. Again, there was no firm diagnosis. Pinneo then got sick. Doctors at the hospital were thoroughly alarmed. She was evacuated, via Jos and Lagos, to America by plane, and was admitted to the College of Physicians and Surgeons at Columbia University, where she was attended by John Frame, E. Leifer, and D. J. Gocke.

The Yale Arbovirus Research Unit in New Haven, Connecticut, was alerted by Frame, who helped to get specimens for the unit. By a combination of serendipity and skill, an agent was isolated – a virus, unknown hitherto to humans. It was called "Lassa virus" (Buckley, Casals, and Downs 1970). Two laboratory-acquired cases occurred in Yale personnel working on the virus. One of them, Juan Roman, died. The other, Jordi Casals, was given immune plasma from the recently recovered nurse, Pinneo, and made a full recovery. In due course and with unfailing collaboration from many services, the agent was established as belonging to a grouping including lymphocytic choriomeningitis virus of nearly worldwide distribution. (Examples are Tacaribe virus from bats in Trinidad; Junin virus, the causative agent of Argentine hemorrhagic fever; and Machupo virus, causative agent of Bolivian hemorrhagic fever.) The grouping of these agents has

Table VIII.76.1. *Lassa fever outbreaks: West Africa, 1969–88*

Location	Dates	Statistics
Lassa and Jos, Nigeria	Jan.–Feb. 1969	3 cases, 2 deaths
Jos, Nigeria	Jan.–Feb. 1970	23 cases, 13 deaths
Zorzor, Liberia	Mar.–Apr. 1972	10 cases, 4 deaths
Panguma and Tongo, Sierra Leone	Oct. 1970–Oct. 1972	64 cases, 23 deaths
Onitsha, Nigeria	Jan. 1974	2 cases, 1 death
Sierra Leone, inland	Feb. 1977–Jan. 1979	441 cases, 76 deaths
Vom (near Jos), Nigeria	1976–7	5 cases, 2 deaths
Bombereke, Benin	Feb. 1977	1 case, 1 death

Note: Seropositive individuals have been detected in Senegal, Guinea, Central African Republic, and the Cameroons.

been officially designated *Arenavirus* in the family Arenaviridae (Fenner 1976). As portrayed in Table VIII.76.1, seven other outbreaks of Lassa fever are known to have occurred in Africa since 1969. Unfortunately, Nurse Troup, who attended cases in the 1969 outbreak at Jos, became infected through a finger prick in an outbreak at Jos the following year and died.

Clinical Manifestations, Morbidity, and Mortality

High fever associated with malaise, muscle and joint pains, sore throat, retrosternal pain, nausea, manifestation of liver involvement, bleeding tendency of variable severity, proteinuria, and erythematous maculopapular rash with petechiae are features of the illness, but not of themselves particularly diagnostic. The presence of an enanthem in the oropharynx has been considered by some to have specific diagnostic importance.

In early stages, the disease can simulate many illnesses occurring in Central Africa, prominent among them malaria (Downs 1975), although typhoid fever, rickettsial diseases, brucellosis, hepatitis (before appearance of jaundice), and even yellow fever can also be mimicked. Sporadically occurring Lassa cases are certainly not often diagnosed. When epidemics arise, the clumping of cases of mysterious illness can and has attracted attention, leading to diagnosis. It has become recognized from studies, such as one in Sierra Leone, that there are many

mild Lassa cases (McCormick et al. 1987a). This study of several years' duration was conducted by personnel from the Centers for Disease Control, U.S. Public Health Service, in two hospitals in central Sierra Leone. It determined that Lassa was the causative agent (determined by virus isolation) in 10 to 16 percent of all adult medical hospital admissions and in about 30 percent of adult hospital deaths. The fatality rate for 441 hospitalized patients was 16.5 percent.

Karl M. Johnson and colleagues (1987) have shown that mortality is directly associated with level of viremia, although it must be noted that by the time figures for viremia have been received from the overseas laboratory, the patient is either recovered or dead. Joseph B. McCormick and colleagues (1987b) estimate the ratio of fatalities in infections in general to be 1 to 2 percent, a rate lower than estimates based on hospitalized patients. How widely the findings on rates and outcome can be extrapolated to other hospitals and other settings in West Africa is not yet known. Studies simply have not been done to determine this. However, it is clear that when seriously ill patients are seen, the prognosis is highly unfavorable, even when the best of currently recognized therapeutic regimes are applied.

Virus Morphology, Size, and Structure

F. A. Murphy and S. G. Whitfield (1975) have given a detailed account of the morphology and morphogenesis of the virion and have related it to the other members of the *Arenavirus* group. The virus particles, on budding from the cell membrane, may be round, oval, or pleomorphic, with mean diameters of 110 to 130 nanometers and with spike-covered envelopes. The center of the particle contains variable numbers of fine granulations, measuring 20 to 25 nanometers, a characteristic that prompted the name *Arenavirus*. The nucleosome consists of single-stranded RNA. In 1984, F. Lehmann-Grube furnished a detailed account of the development and pathogenetic characteristics of the Arenaviridae.

Diagnosis

Laboratory findings include leukopenia and increasing thrombocytopenia, proteinuria, and hematuria, and evidence of coagulation. Diagnostic tests have been developed. Viremia is a constant feature in Lassa cases, and the virus can be isolated and identified in cell culture, using procedures that take a week or more to run. By this time, the patient, if indeed a Lassa patient, may be in dire straits. A rapid diagnostic test is sorely needed. Progress has been made in survey methodology. Serum specimens from suspected patients, taken a few weeks after illness, and those taken in samplings of populations, can be examined for the presence of antibody to Lassa, using a special test plate developed in U.S. Army laboratories. "Spots" of inactivated antigens are made on a test plate, called colloquially a *CRELM plate*. A drop of serum from an individual is placed on each of the "spots" of, respectively, Congo-Crimean fever, Rift Valley fever, and Ebola, Lassa, and Marburg inactivated viruses, and incubated. A fluorescein-tagged anti-human globulin is then added to each drop. Development of fluorescence in one of the "spots" after incubation indicates presence of human antibody, coupled to the signaled antigen. This method has led to greater knowledge of several deadly diseases in Africa, and is a major step toward understanding the geographic location of these diseases.

Treatment

Treatment modalities are being explored. Ribavirin shows promise of benefits if administered early enough in the course of disease (McCormick et al. 1987a,b). An early hope in treatment, administration of plasma from recovered cases, has not been very successful. If given early enough, before a positive laboratory diagnosis is possible, it may have some value. Given later, there have been occasional dramatic recoveries, as in the case of Yale's Jordi Casals. But there have also been many failures. Renal shutdown has been a fatal feature of such treatment in some instances. All work with Lassa virus must be conducted under conditions of highest security (MMWR 1983), which slows down laboratory work. Several human deaths have occurred among laboratory workers, nonetheless.

Epidemiology

The association with the *Arenavirus* group helped to orient the studies in Africa, relating to determination of the transmission cycle of the Lassa virus. Predictably, like its congeners, it was determined to be an infection of small rodents, usually house-frequenting rodents. *Praomys (Mastomys) natalensis* in sub-Saharan, equatorial, and southern Africa is the most common house-frequenting rodent and has been found infected to varying degrees in several regions in Africa afflicted with Lassa (McCormick et al. 1987a,b). The infection in the rodent is persistent, with virus in the urine a common feature. As epidemics occurred in other localities in Nigeria, Liberia, and Sierra Leone over the course of several years, it became apparent that Lassa virus is widespread in West Africa and also may be found in East Africa (McCormick et al. 1987). Studies of distribution are far from complete.

Control

Control must proceed at several levels. At the village level, community-wide rodent control may be implemented, which should include rodent proofing of grain storage facilities, general trash cleanup, and rodent poisoning campaigns. At the householder's level, measures should include rodent proofing of dwellings, rodent trapping, and rodent poisoning. At the clinic level, the possibility of Lassa should be considered whenever fever cases are seen, and appropriate measures taken to protect the examiner and other patients at the clinic. At the hospital level, attention must be given to rodent control, and in addition, diagnosed or suspected Lassa patients should be isolated, with staff taking full precautions to avoid close contact with them. Special precautionary measures are indicated for obstetrical, gynecological, and surgical services. At the governmental level, Lassa should be made a reportable disease, and at the international level, Lassa *must* be made a reportable disease.

Wilbur G. Downs

Bibliography

Auperin, David D., and Joseph B. McCormick. 1989. Nucleotide sequence of the Lassa virus (Josiah strain) S genome RNA and amino acid sequence of the N and GPC proteins to other arenaviruses. *Virology* 168: 421–5.

Buckley, Sonya M., Jordi Casals, and Wilbur G. Downs. 1970. Isolation and antigenic characterization: Lassa virus. *Nature* 227: 174.

Downs, Wilbur G. 1975. Malaria: The great umbrella. *Bulletin of the New York Academy of Medicine* 51: 984–90.

Fenner, Frank. 1976. Classification and nomenclature of viruses. *Second Report of the International Committee on Taxonomy of Viruses: Intervirology* 7: 1–116.

Fuller, John G. 1974. *Fever: The hunt for a new killer virus*. New York.

Johnson, Karl M., et al. 1987. Clinical virology of Lassa fever in hospitalized patients. *Journal of Infectious Diseases* 155: 456–64.

McCormick, Joseph B., et al. 1987a. A case-control study of the clinical diagnosis and course of Lassa fever. *Journal of Infectious Diseases* 155: 445–55.

1987b. A prospective study of the epidemiology and ecology of Lassa fever. *Journal of Infectious Diseases* 155: 437–44.

MMWR. 1983. Viral hemorrhagic fever: Initial management of suspected and confirmed cases. *Morbidity and*

Mortality Weekly Report Supplement 32, No. 2S: 27S–39S.

Murphy, Fred A., and S. G. Whitfield. 1975. Morphology and morphogenesis of arenaviruses. *Bulletin of the World Health Organization* 52: 409–19.

Saltzmann, Samuel. 1978. *La Fièvre de Lassa*. Editions des Groupes Missionnaires. Annemasse, France.

Vella, Ethelwald L. 1985. *Exotic new disease: A review of the emergent viral hemorrhagic fevers*. United Kingdom Ministry of Defence. Section One: Lassa fever – the multimammate rat disease.

VIII.77
Lead Poisoning

Lead poisoning (*plumbism*) is defined simply as the undesirable health effects induced by that metal. Many of these, however, are "nonspecific"; that is, they are similar to or identical with symptoms and signs produced by causes other than lead, and some of the toxic effects are so subtle they require laboratory identification. This historical and geographic discussion concerns itself primarily with those overt effects obviously apparent upon even casual observation by nonmedical observers, which therefore are most likely to appear in the historical record. Principal among these are abdominal colic, muscle paralysis due to lead-damaged nerves, and convulsions.

Physiology
Lead gains access to the human body principally through the air we breathe and the substances we ingest. Residents of industrialized nations acquire about half of their "body burden" of lead from polluted respired air. Healthy adults only absorb about 10 percent of ingested lead, but children may absorb as much as half of the lead they eat or drink. Lead absorption is enhanced by a low level of calcium in the diet. Lead may also be absorbed through the skin. Prolonged applications of lead-containing substances such as poultices or cosmetics may result in health-threatening absorption of lead.

Absorbed lead is distributed throughout the body by the blood. The human body's ability to excrete absorbed lead is so limited, however, that normal life activities in Western countries will produce lead absorption in excess of the body's excretory capacity. About 5 percent of unexcretable lead is deposited in the liver, brain, and other viscera, where its resi-

dence time is only a matter of a few weeks. The other 95 percent is stored in bone for an extraordinarily long time, measurable in decades in the adult. If absorption ceases, such lead will be leached slowly from the skeleton over a period of many years, and is then excreted through the kidneys. Lead may be transferred to the fetus via the placenta.

Methods of exposure to lead as well as the nature of toxic episodes are discussed under History and Geography.

Clinical Manifestations
For many decades the appellation "lead poisoning" has referred to the clinically apparent symptoms manifested by this metal's toxic effects on the intestine, brain, and nerves. Before dealing with them in detail, however, the less obvious effects of lead poisoning are noted briefly.

Lead can interfere with the physiology of almost every body function. At "low" blood concentration (less than 40 micrograms [μg] lead/100 ml blood [dl]), there is some evidence that it can impair intellectual capacity development in children, an effect of potentially greater significance for a population than the more overt symptoms usually associated with the concept of lead poisoning. In the mouth, lead may combine with sulfur produced by local bacteria, producing a linear, black precipitate on the gums sufficiently apparent and unique to be of diagnostic value. Episodes of intense lead exposure may cause temporary arrest of long bone growth visible as a horizontal band of radiodensity ("bone lead line").

Lead produces moderate anemia with resulting facial pallor by poisoning enzymes necessary for the formation of hemoglobin, the blood's principal oxygen carrier. Lead excreted through the kidneys can poison the renal cells, eventually terminating in fatal renal failure. Effects well documented in animals, though less convincingly in humans, include suppression of gonadal function (with consequent decreased fertility or sterility) as well as carcinogenic and teratogenic activity associated with increased rates of abortion, stillbirth, and neonatal mortality.

The symptom of lead poisoning most commonly encountered in the historical literature is abdominal pain. Its cause is usually attributed to intestinal spasm, though the abdominal muscles may participate in the painful, uncontrolled contractions usually termed "colic." When they are severe and prolonged, such affected individuals may be driven to desperate measures for relief. Similar pain may be seen in the common forms of diarrhea, but that associated with lead poisoning is accompanied by constipation, and hence the common reference to the abdominal pain of lead intoxication as "dry bellyache." In individual cases such a state could be simulated by inflammation of the gallbladder, pancreas, or stomach, and by stones in the kidney or bile passages, but these conditions neither would be accompanied by other symptoms or signs of lead toxicity, nor would they affect large segments of a population or occupation.

Lead also has a destructive effect on nerves (*peripheral neuropathy*), whose ability to transmit the electrical impulses to the muscle is then reduced or completely blocked, producing muscle paralysis. Peculiarly (and diagnostically) the nerves supplying those muscles (extensors), which normally raise the wrist or foot, are especially commonly affected, causing the unique affliction of "wrist drop" (often termed "the dangles" in the past) and "foot drop."

Serious disturbances of behavior leading to convulsions, coma, and death are the most severe and feared of lead's effects. Children are notoriously more susceptible to such brain toxicity, and even a single episode of convulsions, when not fatal, often causes permanent, residual cerebral damage. Meningitis, tumors, trauma, and other diseases may result in identical convulsive seizures, and their lead etiology may be recognizable in the literature only through their association with other features of lead toxicity.

Finally it should be noted that lead poisoning may cause gout. This condition is due to the reduced ability of the lead-poisoned kidney to excrete uric acid, a product of normal protein metabolism. The retained uric acid is frequently deposited in the soft tissue, often near joints, resulting in exquisitely tender inflammation. The etiology of the renal toxicity underlying most cases of gout is unknown, but when the kidney injury is caused by lead, it is known as "saturnine gout," in reference to the association of lead with that planetary god by the ancients.

A rough correlation exists between the amount of lead in the blood and the presence of these various signs and symptoms. At lead levels below 40 μg/dl, clinically evident effects are uncommon, but with progressively increasing concentrations above 80 μg/dl, symptoms become more probable. Many modifying and influencing factors, however, give rise to diagnostic difficulties.

Distribution and Incidence

The geographic distribution of lead poisoning is global, but it is not of equal frequency everywhere.

Because circumstances leading to lead exposure are of anthropogenic origin, the prevalence of plumbism correlates with practices and traditions of lead use. Predictably, the geographic pattern of such episodes has varied with time.

Although there are few recorded instances of major health problems due to lead in antiquity, some perspective on the extent of lead poisoning can be gained by reviewing lead production records. Figure VIII.77.1 represents an approximation calculated by C. C. Patterson and others. Because *galena* is the most abundant form of natural lead ore in Europe and Asia, and because its very low solubility produces little toxicity for its miners, one could reasonably surmise that lead poisoning probably was not common prior to the popularization of the smelting process about 3500 B.C.

The *cupellation* process, discovered about 3000 B.C., permitted the separation of the small amounts of the commonly "contaminating" silver from the much larger quantities of smelted lead, and was followed by a substantial increase in lead production as a by-product of the pursuit of silver in the Mediterranean area. We only speculate about the degree to which lead toxicity affected those involved in lead production in the Middle East and Mediterranean area during these periods, though the crude nature of the furnace facilities must have exposed many to a toxigenic degree.

Introduction of coinage during Greece's Classical Period resulted in a phenomenal increase in silver (and therefore, lead) production, which was exaggerated by Roman exploitation to the point of ore exhaustion, leading to a marked reduction of that form of mining after the decline of the Roman Empire. Reference to lead intoxication can be found in the various Greek and Roman writers of antiquity (details under History and Geography: *Historical Antiquity*). It was then not until the late Middle Ages that lead production rose again, this time in Europe, with recognition of lead's utility now justifying its acquisition for its own sake. Although the Spanish pursuit of silver in the New World was second only to that of gold, the miners' mortality was largely due to factors other than poisoning from lead in the ore, and heavy metal toxicity during the silver extraction process was related primarily to the mercury used after 1570. It was the Industrial Revolution, with its enormous surge in lead production, that was responsible for the recurrent endemics in France, Italy, Spain, Germany, and especially Great Britain, and later, their New World colonies. Even so, the 80,000 tons of lead generated annually worldwide at the apex of

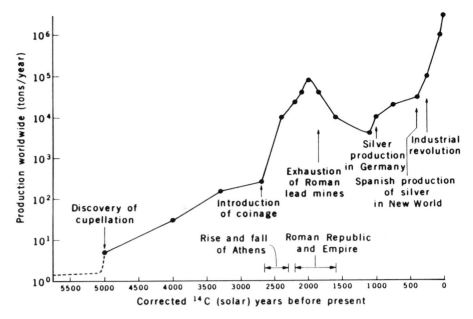

Figure VIII.77.1. World lead production during past 5,500 years. [Adapted from Roger L. Boeckx. 1986. Report. *Analytical Chemistry* 58 (February): 275A, reprinted by permission from *Analytical Chemistry,* 1986, American Chemical Society.]

Roman productivity has expanded exponentially to reach more than 3 million tons worldwide today. With this exponential rise has come a staggering degree of lead exposure in the populations of Western nations.

History and Geography

Because various cultures indulged in activities producing serious lead exposure in different periods, this discussion focuses on those periods specifically relevant to lead poisoning.

Prehistory

By definition, this period contains no written record of lead intoxication, but some concept of the extent of lead use and the degree of presumed lead exposure by its consumers is made available by the archaeological record. A few lead pieces from Iraq about 5000 to 4500 B.C.; multiple lead items at the Troy I site; lead tumblers from Mesopotamian tombs; and galena beads in predynastic Egyptian graves from about 3500 to 3000 B.C.; lead pipes at Ur; leaded glazes from Babylon; and leaded bronzes from Thailand between 2000 and 1500 B.C. – all imply an active, working knowledge of lead smelting. Artifacts also reveal early experimentation with leaded bronzes in China's ancient metallurgical centers in the southwestern provinces by about 1700 B.C. Skeletal lead analyses by several workers, such as the study by Philippe Grandjean and others (1979) of the Nubian population from as early as 3300 B.C., demonstrate negligible quantities of lead stored in bone, suggesting that lead toxicity in this period was probably limited to the few people directly involved in the smelting process.

Historical Antiquity

In Asia Minor, Cappadocian tablets record lead use as an exchange item as early as the third millennium B.C. By 2000 B.C., not only had the smelting of lead ore (conversion to and extraction of metallic lead from the ore compounds) become common knowledge, but also the process of cupellation – the separation of silver from the smelted lead – was widely practiced, as shown by the use of silver as the principal unit of exchange in Susa, Persia, at that time. Old Testament Biblical references testify that lead had broad utilitarian applications and was widely traded even prior to the Israelite departure from Egypt, though there are no comments on its negative health effects. Early dynastic Egyptians used lead for votive statuettes, net sinkers, and cosmetics. Mycenaeans exploited the later well-known mines at Lavrion near Athens and fashioned the product into lead straps. Amulets and loom weights from this period have been found in India. Surely such widespread use of lead must have been accompanied by lead intoxication on occasion, at least among the industrial workers and users of certain lead products including foodwares, but the record remains silent on such matters, implying a probable failure of recognition of its toxic manifestations.

Much of our knowledge about the use of lead in the Greco-Roman period is related to the mines such as the one at Lavrion (called *Laurium* after the Roman conquest) near Athens. The hilly terrain of the area is laced with intersecting veins of "argentiferous galena," a lead sulfide ore including as much as 0.5 percent silver as a minor element. This silver was sought by the Athenians, who referred to Lavrion as a "silver mine," even though they needed to separate 100 to 200 ounces of lead for each ounce of silver retrieved from the ore. This same silver was also one of the sources of Athens's wealth and power, for with it Themistocles built the navy that defeated the invading Persians and established Athens as the premier Mediterranean sea power. Similar mines were also operated on a number of Mediterranean islands, Asia Minor, and the European continent. Mines have been identified in Spain, France, Italy, and Great Britain. Interestingly, the silver component of ores in England and Wales was so low that these were mined primarily for their lead content.

With the generation of huge quantities of metallic lead as a by-product of the silver refinement process, the obvious utilitarian value of lead was also exploited. Applications included household tableware, storage containers for oil and other fluids, encasement of iron bars to bind construction stones together, sheathing for ships' hulls, coins, toys, statues, bronze and pewter alloys, coffins, tablets, solder, and a thousand other purposes. During the three centuries of its peak production period, the Lavrion mine is estimated to have yielded over 2 million tons of ore. The most intensive Roman use of lead related to their water system. In addition to lining with sheet lead parts of their extensive aqueductal system and cisterns, Romans also rolled such sheets into tubular form and soldered them to produce pipes through which the water was distributed.

An even more dangerous application of lead lay in its use as a food or beverage container lining and, even worse, as a food additive. In the absence of sugar, Romans used concentrated fruit juice, commonly grape, as a sweetening and flavoring agent (sapa or defrutum). Such juice was concentrated by boiling in lead-lined containers to avoid the undesirable flavor imparted by copper. During the concentration process lead was leached from the container by the acid fruit juice. Replications of this product using original Roman recipes are reported to have resulted in lead concentrations of up to nearly 800 milligrams per liter, about 16,000 times greater than the upper limit for potable water defined by the U.S. Environmental Protection Agency! Eventually Romans acquired such an addiction to the sweet flavor of lead acetate that it was often made available as an optional seasoning additive to wine.

This massive production and utilization of lead in all its forms clearly exposed the majority of urban Romans to lead. Roman customs, however, probably resulted in unequal exposure. Poor and middle-class citizens of Rome and other major communities closely shared ingestion of the lead-contaminated water delivered through the lead-lined aqueducts and pipes of the public water systems. The wealthier class, however, additionally contaminated their wine and food through the more extensive use of lead-lined containers, expensive pewter tableware, and the food additives described above.

It is difficult to imagine that the health problems associated with excessive lead ingestion had not been recognized during this period, and references by contemporary authors indicate many were indeed aware of them. The Greek physician-poet Nicander is normally credited with the first, clear, unequivocal description of plumbism in the second century B.C., when he noted colic, constipation, paralysis, and pallor resulting from the ingestion of the lead compounds litharge and cerusse. Lucretius in the following century described "deadly exhalations of gold and silver mines" and the pallor of miners' complexions, calling attention to their "short life." The Roman architect Vitruvius, also in the first century B.C., cautioned that drinking water from surface pools in the vicinity of lead mines was apt to produce muscle cramps and gout. Pliny (first century A.D.) warned against the deadly fumes of silver mines, calling attention to their lethality by their effect on dogs and advising all exposed to such fumes to emulate the miners' and smelters' custom of tying an animal bladder over their faces as a mask. Pliny also identified red lead as a deadly poison, whereas his contemporary Celsus described an antidote to white lead. Vitruvius additionally condemned the use of lead for water conduits, noting that lead fumes poison the blood, with consequent pallor as seen in lead workers. Emperor Augustus prohibited the use of lead for water pipes, though there is little evidence of enforcement of his edict. One of the clearest descriptions of lead poisoning affecting large numbers of the population during late Roman times is that by Paul of Aegina, who described an epidemic of colic, lower limb paralysis, and epilepsy in Rome and elsewhere during the seventh century. S. C. Gilfillan (1965) speculated that the well-documented precipitous decline in numbers of the Roman aristocracy during the century following A.D. 60 may have resulted from lead's toxic effects on fertility (noting that prohibition of wine drinking by women of child-bearing age was lifted about that time) and believes this may have been a major factor in the decline of the Roman Empire. J. Nriagu (1983) suggests further that lead-contaminated wine could explain the bizarre behavior of many Roman emperors and may be the cause of Celsus's comment that most of them suffered from gout. Although some scholars of Roman history regard the suggestions of Gilfillan and Nriagu as extrapolations beyond available evidence, wine consumption by the wealthy does appear to have increased during the imperial age, and conformity to contemporary suggestions for its preparation would have increased its lead content.

The Industrial Revolution and Modern Europe

With the rapid increase in lead production during the Industrial Revolution and the explosive growth that followed, including the modern era of lead fuel additives, the scene of lead poisoning shifted to the European stage. During the sixteenth to the eighteenth and even into the nineteenth century, recurrent waves of tardily recognized lead poisoning epidemics swept the various continental countries and the British Isles, frequently in temporally overlapping inundations. Most of these were eventually traced either to industrial exposure to lead or to ingestion of lead-contaminated beverages or food.

The concept of industrial exposure as a cause of disease was crystallized for eighteenth-century physicians by the masterful studies so meticulously recorded by Bernardino Ramazzini in 1700 (De Morbis Artificum Diatriba), although he was not the first to suggest it. His publications established the clear relationship between certain diseases and occupations. Among them were lead poisoning in miners, potters, and painters.

The French epidemic of crampy abdominal pain termed the "colic of Poitou" began in 1572, but more than a century passed before the consumption of lead-contaminated wine was identified as its etiology. A half-century-long endemic of abdominal colic was initiated in Madrid about 1730. The suggestion that lead was its cause was not taken seriously until 1797, when the fact was made clear that its distribution among the poor was due to their use of badly glazed lead food containers. In the middle of the eighteenth century, Théodore Tronchin realized the "colica pictonum" in Holland constituted poisoning from the use of water draining from lead roofs and from lead water pipes. The eighteenth and nineteenth centuries also were characterized by British importation of Portuguese port wine in prodigious

quantities when the 1703 Treaty of Methuen reduced its price to less than that of the French products. The brandy used to fortify the natural wines was often prepared in stills containing lead parts. Such fortified wines are believed to have been responsible for a concurrent frequency of gout so high that this period is often called "the golden age of gout" in England.

Two eighteenth-century workers – Sir George Baker in England and L. Tanquerel des Planches in France – most clearly epitomize publicized recognition of lead ingestion and industrial exposure to lead as the etiology of specific symptom complexes. In the region of Devonshire, England, an epidemic of abdominal colic ("the colic of Devonshire") raged for decades in the middle of the eighteenth century. Occasional writers had noted its relationship to cider drinking, but its absence in the cider-producing neighboring regions remained puzzling. In 1767, Baker, a Devonshire native, published his report now acknowledged as a milestone in the history of lead poisoning. Baker established the feature that characterized the Devonshire colic: lead contamination of the cider. He had traced the origin of the lead to a type of millstone used in the cider's manufacturing process. The Devonshire millstones were unique in that they were made in multiple segments bonded together by lead keys exposed on the stone's surface. He also noted the custom of cider storage in lead-lined containers and the addition of lead to the cider as a flavoring and preservative agent. His publication, clearly indicting lead as the epidemic's cause, was followed by preventive practices and a gradual subsidence of the epidemic.

Similarly, for many decades in the eighteenth and early nineteenth centuries, Paris's Charity Hospital had become famous for its treatment of patients with the various "dry colic" syndromes. In 1839 Tanquerel des Planches reported how he had studied these patients' complaints, scoured their hospital charts, and eventually demonstrated that most were engaged in an occupation involving unequivocal lead exposure. His detailed clinical observations included paralysis, encephalomalacia, and such a thorough description of the other items comprising the lead poisoning syndrome that it can be used as a medical teaching exercise today.

The New World Colonial Period

There was hardly a pause in the spread of the European colics before they also appeared in the American colonies. These settlers had arrived in the New

World with a restricted hoard of tools and machinery; malleable lead could be and was employed to create substitutes for a myriad of items manufactured out of steel in Europe with consequent opportunities for lead exposure.

One such source exposure was the consumption of lead-contaminated liquor. The coiled condensation tube (usually called the "worm") of an alcohol still was most easily fashioned out of lead. The distillation of fermented sugar products in such a still for rum production caused sufficient lead leaching from the "worm" to render the rum toxic. By 1685, epidemics of abdominal colic ("dry bellyache" or "dry gripes") were common in North Carolina and Virginia. Upon suggestions from those consumers that their illness might be the result of lead-contaminated New England rum, Massachusetts protected its trade market with remarkable alacrity by enacting the Massachusetts Bay Law of 1723, prohibiting the use of lead parts in a liquor distillation apparatus. Although the law is often hailed as the first public health law in the colonies, it should be noted there is no evidence of any serious, objective investigation regarding the role of lead in the origin of the rum-drinkers' symptoms, nor does the medical profession seem to have been the principal instigator for the law's passage. It appears the legislators were responding primarily to customer complaints, motivated more by trade than by health concerns.

Both the continent and the West Indies had a similar problem. Whereas slaves on North American continental plantations developed lead poisoning infrequently, the afflicted individuals on Caribbean island plantations included both Caucasians and black slaves. Barbados was especially affected, with the literature from the latter seventeenth and much of the eighteenth centuries replete with references to "dry bellyache," clearly a clinical entity well known to both physicians and the laity but of undetermined cause. Jerome Handler and others (1986) provided the chemical support for the diagnosis of lead poisoning in the slaves of a Barbadian population from the eighteenth century by finding sufficient lead in their archaeologically excavated bones to predict that at least one-third of them probably had had lead poisoning symptoms of moderate or greater severity.

The reason for high bone lead values in island plantation slaves in contrast to those on continental plantations lay in the nature of the product: sugar in the islands; cotton, fruit, or tobacco on the continent. The sugar was collected in lead-lined tubs, ducted

through lead pipes into a lead-lined copper cauldron in the boiling-house (whose fumes would expose the boiling-house workers), and stored in lead containers, to be distilled later into rum through a lead still. In addition, the lead-laden rum was used as a work incentive with subsequent consumption in large quantities of this lead-contaminated liquor by the afflicted slaves.

In 1745 Benjamin Franklin published Thomas Cadawaler's treatise on dry gripes in which the role of lead was defined. This knowledge may have been carried to Europe by Franklin because Baker of Devonshire quoted Franklin in his well-known 1767 article. By the mid-eighteenth century, knowledge about the lead etiology of the dry bellyache was reaching Barbados. In 1788 John Hunter (*Observations on the Diseases of the Army in Jamaica*) detailed dry gripes symptoms and specifically attributed them to lead. The condition gradually subsided in the West Indies during the last quarter of the century.

Another common source of lead poisoning in colonial America was houseware, especially those items used in the preparation, serving, or storage of food and beverages. In England, expensive pewterware, some with more than 20 percent lead composition, was the symbol of social and economic success, and this was emulated in the colonies. Plates and goblets were commonly of pewter in the wealthier colonial homes; perishables such as milk, cream, or fruit juices were stored in lead-lined containers as were wine, drinking water, and other beverages. Indeed, in such a wealthy home almost everything the family ate or drank contained some lead. In a continental plantation where access to such lead-contaminated food was tightly controlled, Arthur Aufderheide and colleagues (1981) could demonstrate that the extent of differential lead exposure had a socioeconomic basis. The slave labor force of a 1670–1730 Virginia plantation had no more lead in their bones than the average, modern North American does, but the skeletons of their wealthy Caucasian masters contained a sixfold greater quantity. Colonists were also exposed through their use of lead bottles, funnels, nipple shields, dram cups, candlesticks, lamps, pipes, roof gutters, and many other items.

Mining also claimed its colonial victims. The eastern American mines were largely of the poorly soluble galena ore and generated little morbidity. It was in the western Utah mines, whose ore was predominantly lead carbonate, that lead poisoning reached epidemic proportions, with many thousands of miners suffering from plumbism between 1870 and 1900.

The Present Era

Even though we have a more sophisticated understanding of lead poisoning today, our ongoing use of lead seems to provide new opportunities for exposure. Lead encephalopathy acquired by infants nursing at the breasts of mothers using lead-containing cosmetics constituted the fourth most common, fatal, pediatric malady in Manchuria in 1925. A poisoning episode from lead fumes occurred in a Baltimore neighborhood in 1933 when poor families there burned discarded battery casings as cheap fuel. Until C. C. Patterson (1982) called attention to it recently, lead solder was used to seal many food cans. The common practice of *pica* (dirt eating), partly biological and partly cultural in origin, has become especially dangerous for children playing in yards whose soils are badly contaminated from inner-city factory and vehicle-exhausted lead. Chips of lead-laden, old paint peeling from their aging houses constitute a toxic time bomb for the very young. Many surviving victims of childhood lead poisoning in Australia were found to suffer failure of lead-poisoned kidneys several decades later. A 1910 American pharmacopoeia still listed both a variety of therapeutic lead compounds and antidotes to lead poisoning! There is probably no purer example of the price exacted by historical ignorance than the plumbism rampant among the modern illicit liquor producers ("moonshiners") using lead-containing distillation units (automobile radiators soldered with lead) in the United States today.

American lead production peaked about 1975, with at least half of it converted into automobile fuel additive. Recent partial control of automobile exhaust fumes has been accompanied by a 37 percent reduction in average blood lead levels in Americans.

Statistical data for lead poisoning are difficult to acquire, but in the United States, 831 adult deaths could be identified between 1931 and 1940; whereas in England, Tony Waldron (1982) describes a reduction from about 115 deaths annually in 1900 to only an occasional few by 1960. In view of the known diagnostic inefficiency of lead poisoning, these are surely minimal figures.

Prevention and Control

For many centuries, humanity's flirtation with lead frequently has been its undoing. Its romance with this pedestrian metal has been inspired not by any gemlike allure it possesses but, rather, by its irresist-ible utility. No other metal is so easily extracted from the soil and so readily fashioned into unlimited numbers of needed items. In every age, however, writers sounding the warning of its toxic hazards were ignored or decried. Reasons for such resistance remain enigmatic.

It may be that the nonspecificity of the lead intoxication syndrome confused earlier diagnosticians because other conditions can simulate some of lead's toxic effects. The mine fumes that several Greco-Roman period authors held responsible for lead miners' health problems were perhaps the obvious and unpleasant sulfur dioxide odors emitted by galena ore rather than by lead compounds. Yet Pliny even complained specifically that the practice of "adulterating" wine (adding lead to improve the flavor) produces nerve injury manifested by paralyzed, dangling hands. His contemporary, the physician Dioscorides, clearly described colic and renal failure resulting from drinking the lead oxide compound called *litharge*. Most ancient miners were slaves whose ailments may not have been treated by physicians. It is, of course, possible that Romans were not exposed to as much lead as we presume today and that a lack of concern by Roman physicians simply reflects a low frequency of lead poisoning in ancient times. This can be evaluated objectively only by lead analysis of appropriately selected ancient bones. To date, some of Waldron's (1982) Romano-British cemetery excavation studies have revealed elevated bone lead values, but further investigations on Italian samples with sharply defined socioeconomic status of the studied individuals will be needed to resolve this question.

Perhaps even more relevant is the fact that during most of history the cause-and-effect relationship between a specific agent like lead and a specific symptom was only vaguely appreciated by physicians whose theoretical concepts did not readily embrace such an association. More concerned with the balance of postulated body humors, they were apt to attribute a broad range of symptoms to general environmental (often climatic) disturbances. Even nineteenth-century French naval surgeons accepted lead as the etiology of the lead poisoning syndrome but rejected it as the cause of an identical symptom complex in their tropical sailors. They attributed it instead to the effect of high tropical temperatures, thus delaying recognition of its true origin in their custom of shipboard food storage in lead containers.

Surely, lack of a system for regular publication and wide dissemination of medical knowledge also contributed to delay in grasping the etiology of lead poisoning. As early as 1656, Samuel Stockhausen, a physician to the lead miners of northern Germany, published his realization that their affliction was the toxic effect of the lead ore they mined. Forty years later, that observation led his south German colleague, Eberhard Gockel, to recognize lead contamination of wine as the cause of an identical problem in his clerical patients, and it was to be more than another century (and many more "colicdemics") before the translation of Stockhausen's report into French enabled Tanquerel to identify the same problem at Paris's Charity Hospital.

Josef Eisinger (1982) has noted the recurring need throughout most of Western history for governments to enact legislation restricting the population's exposure to lead. Serious and major efforts to reduce lead exposure, such as the 1971 Lead-Based Poisoning Prevention Act in the United States and more recent legislation involving lead air pollution by automobiles, are phenomena primarily since the 1970s. The history of the past two millennia, however, suggests that our knowledge of lead's potential hazards will not prevent at least some continuing problems with its health effects.

Arthur C. Aufderheide

Bibliography

Aufderheide, A. C., et al. 1981. Lead in bone II. Skeletal-lead content as an indicator of lifetime lead ingestion and the social correlates in an archaeological population. *American Journal of Physical Anthropology* 55: 285–91.

Boeckx, Roger L. 1986. Report. *Analytical Chemistry* 58(2): 275A.

Eisinger, J. 1982. Eberhard Gockel and the colica Pictonum. *Medical History* 26: 279–302.

Gifillan, S. C. 1965. Lead poisoning and the fall of Rome. *Journal of Occupational Medicine* 7: 53–60.

Gockel, Eberhard. 1697. *Eine curiose Beschreibung dess An 1694.95 und 96 durch Silberglett versussten sauren Weins. . . .* Ulm.

Grandjean, Philippe, O. Vag Nielson, and Irving M. Shapiro. 1979. Lead retention in ancient Nubian and contemporary populations. *Journal of Environmental Pathology and Toxicology* 2: 781–7.

Handler, J. S., et al. 1986. Lead contact and poisoning in Barbados slaves: Historical, chemical, and biological evidence. *Social Science History* 10: 399–425.

Hirsch, August. 1883–6. *Handbook of geographic and historical pathology*, 3 vols. London.

McCord, C. P. 1953. 1954. Lead and lead poisoning in early America. *Industrial Medicine and Surgery* 22: 393–9, 534–9, 573–7; 23: 27–31, 75–80, 120–4, 169–72.

Nriagu, J. 1983. *Lead and lead poisoning in antiquity.* New York.

Patterson, Clair C. 1982. Natural levels of lead in humans. *California Environment Essay,* Ser. 3, Institute for Environmental Studies, University of North Carolina. Chapel Hill.

Stockhausen, Samuel. 1656. *Libellus de lithargyrii fumo noxio morbifico, metallico frequentiori morbo vulgo dilto Die Huettenkatze.* Goslar.

Waldron, H. A., and D. Stofen. 1974. *Subclinical lead poisoning.* London.

Waldron, Tony. 1982. Human bone lead concentrations. In *Romano-British cemeteries at Circencester,* ed. Alan McWhirr, Linda Viner, and Calvin Wells, 203–4. Circencester, England.

VIII.78
Legionnaires' Disease

Legionnaires' disease is an acute infection of humans, principally manifested by pneumonia, that occurs in a distinctive pattern in epidemics and is caused by bacteria of the genus *Legionella*. Typically the incubation period – the interval between exposure to the bacterium and the onset of illness – is 2 to 10 days, with an average of 5 to 6 days, and the attack rate – the proportion of people exposed to the bacterium who become ill – is less than 5 percent. Without specific antibiotic treatment, 15 percent or more of the cases are fatal, although the percentage of fatal cases rises sharply in immunosuppressed patients.

Legionnaires' disease is one form of presentation of *Legionella* infections, which are generally referred to by the umbrella term *legionellosis*. Another distinctive clinicoepidemiological pattern of legionellosis is *Pontiac fever*. Pontiac fever affects 45 to 100 percent of those exposed and has an incubation period of 1 to 2 days. Pneumonia does not occur, and all patients recover. More than 20 species of *Legionella* have been identified, 10 of which are proven causes of legionellosis in humans. The most common agents of human infection are *Legionella pneumophila, Legionella micdadei, Legionella bozemanii, Legionella dumoffii,* and *Legionella longbeachae.*

Legionellae are distinguished from other bacteria in being weakly staining, gram-negative, aerobic rods that do not grow on blood agar or metabolize carbohydrates, and have large proportions of branched-chain fatty acids in their cell walls and ma-

jor amounts of ubiquinones with more than 10 iso-
prene units on the side chain.

Distribution and Incidence

Legionellosis is easily overlooked, but has been
found essentially wherever it has been sought. The
weak staining of *Legionella* and its failure to grow
on the usual bacterial diagnostic media allowed it to
be missed for many years in the evaluation of persons with pneumonia. Once the right combination of
staining and other diagnostic culture procedures
was identified, *Legionella* was found to cause 1 to 2
percent of the pneumonia cases in the United States,
or perhaps 25,000 to 50,000 cases annually.

Formal surveys of the incidence of legionellosis
have not been done in most countries, but large
numbers of cases have been identified in Great Britain and several European countries, and cases have
been reported on all continents.

Epidemiology and Etiology

Legionellae live in unsalty water and are widely distributed in nature. They thrive particularly well at or
slightly above human body temperature, and thus
are commonly found on the hot water side of potable
water systems and in the recirculating water in cooling towers and other heat exchange devices.

The various ways in which *Legionellae* can go
from their watery environment to infect humans are
not all worked out, but one method is clear. Aerosols
created by some mechanical disturbance of contaminated water, such as in the operation of a cooling
tower, can on occasion infect people downwind. It is
likely that, after the aerosol is generated, the droplets of water evaporate, leaving the bacteria airborne. Once airborne, they can travel a considerable
distance, be inhaled, and then be deposited in the
lungs. Potable water systems also can act as the
source of legionellosis outbreaks, but it is not known
whether this occurs through aerosols (as might be
generated by sinks, showers, or toilets), by colonization of the throat and then aspiration into the lungs,
by direct inoculation (as into the eye or a wound), or
by ingestion.

Many outbreaks have been recognized, but most
cases occur individually (or sporadically). The risk of
Legionella pneumonia (including Legionnaires' disease) increases with age and is two to four times
higher in men than in women. No racial predisposition has been seen. Cigarette smokers are more susceptible, as are people whose cellular immune system is compromised – for example, by medication

(such as corticosteroids) or underlying illness. Nosocomial (hospital-acquired) legionellosis is an important problem, probably because particularly susceptible people are gathered in a building with water
systems that *Legionella* can contaminate.

Few children have been shown to have legionellosis, but one prospective study showed that one-
half developed serum antibodies to *L. pneumophila*
before 4 years of age, indicating that inapparent
infection may be common, at least at that age. In
contrast, studies of adults during Legionnaires' disease outbreaks have generally shown that fewer
than one-half of the *Legionella* infections are
inapparent.

Legionellosis can occur throughout the year but is
most common from June through October in the
Northern Hemisphere. The summer season predominates even in outbreaks unrelated to air-conditioning
systems, but whether warmer weather causes the
bacteria to flourish or, rather, humans to increase
contact with their environment is not known. The
fact that most bacterial and viral pneumonias are
most common in the winter makes the seasonality of
legionellosis one clue in diagnosis. Legionellosis does
not seem to spread from one person to another.

Travel and certain occupations put people at increased risk of legionellosis. Several outbreaks have
occurred in tourist hotels, and a disproportionate
number of sporadic cases are in people who recently
have traveled overnight. Disease caused by *Legionella* and serologic evidence of previous *Legionella* infection are more common in power plant
workers who have close exposure to cooling towers.
Other outbreaks have occurred in people who used
compressed air to clean river debris out of a steam
turbine condenser, and in workers exposed to aerosols of contaminated grinding fluid in an engine
assembly plant.

Legionellosis outbreaks can be stopped by turning
off the machinery that is making infectious aerosols,
disinfecting that machinery, and heating or rechlor-
inating contaminated drinking water. Several chemical additives that are used in the routine maintenance of cooling towers and evaporative condensers
can limit the growth of *Legionella* if used in combination with regular cleaning. Certain rubber materials
used in plumbing washers seem to provide nutrients
for *Legionella;* using different components may help
prevent legionellosis associated with drinking water. Maintaining a temperature of 60°C on the hot
water side of institutional plumbing systems has
stopped some legionellosis outbreaks by lowering
the concentration of *Legionella* sharply.

Immunology

Legionella organisms live *inside* cells of all types, from various protozoa and freshwater amoebae in the external environment to various phagocytic cells in the human body. Given the location of *Legionella* inside cells, it might be expected that cell-mediated immunity is more important than humoral (antibody-mediated) immunity, and such seems to be the case in legionellosis.

This may explain why people with defective cellular immunity are particularly susceptible to legionellosis and why so few people exposed in an epidemic of Legionnaires' disease become sick even though usually fewer than 20 percent (and often fewer than 5 percent) have preexisting elevations of titers of specific antibody to *Legionella*.

Clinical Manifestations and Pathology

Two distinct clinical and epidemiological syndromes of legionellosis have been identified: Legionnaires' disease and Pontiac fever. Legionnaires' disease is a multisystem disease, characterized by pneumonia, high fever, chills, muscle aches, chest pain, headache, diarrhea, and confusion. Chemical evidence of involvement of the liver and kidneys may also be found. Pneumonia usually worsens over the first week of illness and resolves gradually thereafter. Without specific antibiotic therapy, the disease is fatal in about 15 to 20 percent of otherwise healthy people, and in up to 50 percent of those with compromised cellular immunity. It is not readily distinguished on clinical observation alone from several other forms of bacterial pneumonia.

Pathological changes are usually confined to the lungs, which often show a pattern of lobar pneumonia. Air sacs (alveoli) are filled with macrophages, other inflammatory cells, and fibrin. With the proper stain, large numbers of *Legionella* can be seen, mostly in the macrophages. The trachea and larger airways are generally spared, which may explain the relative lack of sputum in most cases and the lack of contagiousness.

Pontiac fever is characterized by fever, chills, muscle aches, and headache. Cough and chest pain are much less common than in Legionnaires' disease, and no cases have pneumonia. Victims are very ill for 2 to 7 days, but all recover.

History and Geography

From July 21 through 24, 1976, the Pennsylvania Department of the American Legion, a fraternal organization of military veterans, held its annual meeting in Philadelphia, with headquarters in the Bellevue Stratford Hotel. Within days of the end of the convention, reports began to reach Legion headquarters of conventioneers who had developed pneumonia and died. A massive investigation, begun on August 3, uncovered 221 cases in Legionnaires who had attended the convention and others who had been in or near the headquarters' hotel. The earliest case had its onset on July 20, the peak occurrence extended from July 24 through August 1, and decreasing numbers of cases continued through August 16. Ninety percent of those who became ill developed pneumonia, and 16 percent died.

Diagnostic tests for all known agents of pneumonia, infectious and otherwise, were negative. The epidemiological investigation suggested airborne spread of the agent, because risk of "Legionnaires' disease," as the press had dubbed it, increased with the amount of time spent in the lobby of the hotel and on the nearby sidewalk, but was unrelated to contact with other sick people or animals, eating, or participation in specific events at the convention. Those who drank water at the Bellevue Stratford had a higher risk than others, suggesting the possibility of a waterborne agent, but 49 of the cases had only been on the sidewalk outside and had drunk no water there.

The outbreak received considerable notoriety and prompted a congressional investigation. The failure to find immediately the agent led to much public speculation about toxic chemicals and sabotage, but the answer came through the more usual route of persistent scientific work.

In August, Joseph McDade, who worked on rickettsia at the U.S. Public Health Service Centers for Disease Control, had tested specimens from Legionnaires for evidence of rickettsia by inoculating lung specimens into guinea pigs and, if the animals died, putting tissue from them into embryonated eggs. The experiments were complicated by what seemed to have been some bacterial contamination, but overall the results appeared clearly negative. In late November, McDade received a draft report of the status of the investigation to that point. He noted that the liver was involved in many of the cases, a fact that was reminiscent of Q fever, the rickettsial infection most commonly associated with pneumonia. After mulling upon that coincidence, he returned to his laboratory over the Christmas holidays to reexamine the specimens from his August experiments. After some hours, he came across a cluster of what looked to be large rickettsiae or small bacteria in a section of liver from a guinea pig that had been inoculated with lung tissue from a fatal case of Legionnaires' disease. Repeating the inoculation of eggs, he was able to grow these organisms in the yolk sacs. Using the infected yolk sac suspension as the antigen in an indirect fluorescent antibody (IFA) test, he was then able to show that the serum collected during the field investigation from patients who had recovered from Legionnaires' disease (but not that from unaffected people) had sharply rising titers of specific antibody to the yolk sac organism – indicating convincingly that this (which has since become known as *Legionella pneumophila*) was the causative agent.

In the 11 years before the Legionnaires' disease outbreak, the Centers for Disease Control had investigated two other large epidemics of respiratory disease for which an agent had not been found. One, in 1965, had involved 81 patients at St. Elizabeth's Hospital, a psychiatric institution in Washington, D.C. John V. Bennett, the epidemiologist who had led the original St. Elizabeth's investigation, communicated to the author in the early fall of 1976 that he was certain that the two outbreaks were caused by the same agent. Fortunately, serum specimens from the St. Elizabeth's outbreak had been stored at the Centers since 1965. When tested in early January of 1977, they unequivocally proved Bennett right.

In 1968, a remarkable outbreak of a severe, self-limited illness involved 95 of 100 employees in a health department building in Pontiac, Michigan. Some of the investigators from the Centers for Disease Control succumbed also, but only those who entered the building when the air conditioning system was turned on. Guinea pigs were placed in the building without any protection, with antibiotic prophylaxis, or in an isolator that filtered the air, and then were killed to look for evidence of pneumonia or other ill effects. Inspection of the air conditioning system showed two major defects. The exhaust from the evaporative condenser discharged on the roof just a few feet from the fresh air intake. In addition, the exhaust duct and a horizontal chilled air duct that was adjacent to the exhaust duct had defects that allowed water droplets from the exhaust to puddle in the chilled air duct. Water recirculating in the evaporative condenser was aerosolized (with or without prior attempts to sterilize it) in laboratory tests to expose guinea pigs in an attempt to induce disease.

When materials from the 1968 investigation of Pontiac fever were used in the tests that succeeded for Legionnaires' disease, scientists were intrigued to find positive results. Not only did people recovering from Pontiac fever show rising titers of specific antibody to *L. pneumophila*, but also *L. pneumophila*

could be recovered from the stored lung tissue of guinea pigs that had been exposed, unprotected, to the air in the health department building or to the evaporative condenser water. Thus a very different disease – both epidemiologically and clinically – was shown to be caused by a bacterium which, to this day, cannot be distinguished from the one that caused Legionnaires' disease.

Within a few weeks of the isolation of *L. pneumophila* in embryonated eggs, Robert Weaver found a way to grow it on agar plates. Subsequent improvements led to the development of charcoal yeast extract agar, which greatly facilitates the isolation of *Legionella*.

Investigations of legionellosis proceeded both forward and backward in time. In the summer of 1977, outbreaks of Legionnaires' disease were quickly recognized in Vermont, Ohio, and Tennessee. In 1978 an outbreak of 44 cases at a hospital in Memphis, Tennessee, started shortly after a flood knocked out the usual cooling tower, and required turning on an auxiliary that had been out of use for 2 years. Cases clustered downwind from the auxiliary cooling tower but stopped occurring 10 days after it was shut off. *L. pneumophila* was isolated from both patients and the cooling tower water, confirming the epidemiological evidence that Legionnaires' disease, like Pontiac fever, could be caused by *L. pneumophila* contamination of heat-rejection devices in air-conditioning systems.

But air conditioning systems were not the whole answer. Public health authorities in Scotland and Spain were investigating a series of pneumonia cases acquired by Scottish visitors to a hotel in Benidorm, Spain, over several seasons. The hotel was not air-conditioned, but the cases proved to be Legionnaires' disease. It would be some time before the source was found.

Other previously "unsolved" outbreaks were found to have been legionellosis. In 1973, all 10 men involved in cleaning a steam turbine condenser at a power plant on the James River in Virginia had developed what in retrospect seemed to have been Pontiac fever. Testing of stored serum specimens confirmed this. An outbreak of 78 hospitalized cases of pneumonia in Austin, Minnesota, in the summer of 1957 had been investigated at the time. Although the records had been preserved, the serum specimens had been lost in a refrigeration mishap. Survivors were recontacted in 1979, and they and the appropriate controls were bled to confirm the diagnosis of Legionnaires' disease in what is to date the earliest documented epidemic of legionellosis.

In 1979 reports began to appear of agents, some of which caused pneumonia, that resembled the *L. pneumophila* type strain in some ways but were clearly distinct. McDade and colleagues isolated an organism on artificial media that Hugh Tatlock had recovered in 1943 by inoculating into guinea pigs blood from a soldier at Fort Bragg, North Carolina, who seemed to have a case of "pre-tibial fever," an illness subsequently shown to be caused by *Leptospira*. Later that year, A. William Pasculle and colleagues isolated the "Pittsburgh pneumonia agent" in embryonated eggs but could not grow it in artificial media. Subsequently, the Tatlock organism and the Pittsburgh pneumonia agent were shown to be the same, and were named *L. micdadei*.

McDade and colleagues also grew the OLDA strain on artificial media. OLDA was another organism that resembled a rickettsia and had originally been isolated in 1947 by E. B. Jackson, by inoculating a guinea pig with blood from a patient with fever of unknown origin. When characterized in 1979, it turned out to be *L. pneumophila*. It remains the earliest documented isolate of that species.

In 1959 F. Marilyn Bozeman and colleagues isolated a rickettsia-like organism in guinea pigs from a navy man who developed pneumonia after practicing with scuba gear in freshwater swimming pools. Lester G. Cordes and colleagues isolated it on artificial media in 1979 and showed that it was distinct from *L. pneumophila*. It was subsequently named *L. bozemanii*.

Another line of discovery first reported in 1979 had important consequences in defining the biology of *Legionella*. George K. Morris and his colleagues reported the recovery of *L. pneumophila* from environmental water specimens, collected in the course of investigation of outbreaks of Legionnaires' disease. This quickly led to the discovery that *Legionella* organisms were widespread in nature, and could be found in about one-half of cooling towers. It also, for example, led to the discovery of additional *Legionella* species, not previously recognized to cause human disease.

In 1980, John O. H. Tobin reported the first isolation of *Legionella* from potable water systems, as part of an investigation of two kidney transplant patients who acquired Legionnaires' disease while in the same hospital room in England. Subsequent studies in hospitals in England and in the United State showed the importance of such systems as the sources for dissemination of *Legionella*.

As these studies were reported, the picture emerged of *Legionella* as a group of freshwater-associated bacteria widely distributed in nature, causing pneumonia in humans when particularly susceptible people are exposed by aerosols, or perhaps otherwise, to contaminated water. The presence of running hot water and other thermal pollution, often from industrial processes, favors its growth, suggesting that legionellosis may be expected to be particularly common in the developed world. However, the disease appears to be worldwide in its distribution.

David W. Fraser

Bibliography

Balows, Albert, and David W. Fraser, eds. 1979. International symposium on Legionnaires' disease. *Annals of Internal Medicine* 90: 489–703.

Brenner, Don J. 1986. Classification of Legionellaceae: Current status and remaining questions. *Israel Journal of Medical Sciences* 22: 620–32.

Broome, Claire V., and David W. Fraser. 1979. Epidemiologic aspects of legionellosis. *Epidemiologic Reviews* 1: 1–16.

Dondero, Timothy J., Jr., et al. 1980. An outbreak of Legionnaires' disease associated with a contaminated air-conditioning cooling tower. *New England Journal of Medicine* 302: 365–70.

Edelstein, P. H. 1987. Laboratory diagnosis of infections caused by legionellae. *European Journal of Clinical Microbiology* 6: 4–10.

England, A. C., and D. W. Fraser. 1981. Sporadic and epidemic nosocomial legionellosis in the United States. *American Journal of Medicine* 70: 707–11.

Fisher-Hoch, S. P., M. G. Smith, and J. S. Colbourne. 1982. *Legionella* pneumophila in hospital hot water cylinders. *Lancet* 2: 1073.

Fraser, David W., et al. 1977. Legionnaires' disease: Description of an epidemic of pneumonia. *New England Journal of Medicine* 297: 1189–97.

Glick, Thomas H., et al. 1978. Pontiac fever. An epidemic of unknown etiology in a health department: I. Clinical and epidemiologic aspects. *American Journal of Epidemiology* 107: 149–60.

Kaufmann, Arnold F., et al. 1981. Pontiac fever: Isolation of the etiologic agent (*Legionella pneumophila*) and demonstration of its mode of transmission. *American Journal of Epidemiology* 114: 337–47.

Kirby, B. D., et al. 1980. Legionnaires' disease: Report of sixty-five nosocomially acquired cases and review of the literature. *Medicine* 59: 188–205.

McDade Joseph E., et al. 1977. Legionnaires' disease: Isolation of a bacterium and demonstration of its role in other respiratory diseases. *New England Journal of Medicine* 297: 1197–1203.

Shands, Kathryn N., et al. 1985. Potable water as a source of Legionnaires' disease. *Journal of the American Medical Association* 253: 1412–16.

Thornsberry, Clyde, et al., eds. 1984. *Legionella: Proceedings of the 2nd international symposium of the American Society for Microbiology.* Washington, D.C.

VIII.79
Leishmaniasis

Leishmaniasis is primarily a skin disease produced by a number of different species of protozoa (genus *Leishmania*). The disease occurs in three basic clinical forms, each of which has several variants caused by different species, subspecies, or strains of the pathogen. The intermediate host is the sandfly.

Distribution and Incidence

Cutaneous leishmaniasis (often called "oriental sore") is found in Armenia, Azerbaijan, Turkmenistan, Uzbekistan (republics of the former Soviet Union), Afghanistan, India, Iran, much of the Middle East and North Africa, the Sahara, the savanna states from Sudan to Senegal, and in Kenya and Ethiopia. In the New World, species of *Leishmania* cause various clinical forms of the disease in Central America, the Amazon Basin, the Guyanas, and the Andes, especially Venezuela and Peru. In eastern South America a form of the disease mainly afflicting children extends from Argentina to Venezuela and north through Central America to Mexico.

Mucocutaneous leishmaniasis is restricted to the New World and occurs in Brazil, eastern Peru, Paraguay, Ecuador, Colombia, and Venezuela.

Visceral leishmaniasis is found in India, Burma, Bangladesh, China, Thailand, Somalia, Chad, Kenya, Gabon, Sudan, and Niger. A variant occurring primarily among children is spread over southern Europe, North Africa, and the Middle East as well as Romania and the southern part of the former Soviet Union.

As a result of high levels of disease in rodent and dog populations, leishmaniasis is so common in endemic areas that it leaves its mark on every inhabitant. Recent estimates indicate that some 12 million individuals have one form or another of this infection. Thus leishmaniasis can be regarded as second in importance only to malaria among the protozoal diseases of humans. Although the mortality is low for the skin disease, it is almost always fatal for *kala-azar,* an organ variant.

Epidemiology and Etiology

All forms of leishmaniasis are zoonoses transmitted to human beings from wild or domestic animals via the sandfly (usually *Phlebotomus*). The leishmanial form of the parasite lives in reticuloendothelial cells of the mammalian host where it divides by binary fission to destroy the host cell. The parasites are taken up by the sandfly while feeding on the skin of the host, and in the insect's intestine they develop into leptomonad forms. These divide, producing enormous numbers, and work their way to the pharynx and buccal cavity. There is a natural restriction of individual leishmaniae to specific sandflies, even though a wide variety of these insect species may be available.

Cutaneous leishmaniasis is caused by several members of the *Leishmania tropica* species complex. All produce chronic skin lesions, which tend to ulcerate. Some forms tend to be "urban" and closely linked to dogs as alternating hosts. Others are "rural," with nonhuman reservoirs including various rodents, marsupials, and foxes. In the Americas, sandflies of the genus *Lutzomyia* are often vectors. The initial lesion usually heals spontaneously, but often leaves a disfiguring scar.

Mucocutaneous leishmaniasis is caused by *Leishmania braziliensis*. In the form known as *espundia* in Brazil, the initial lesion develops into an infection of the mucosal tissues of the nose and mouth, resulting in gross deformities and sometimes death from secondary infections. *Lutzomyia* flies are the major vectors. (A clinically similar form, believed to be caused by *L. tropica*, has been described in Ethiopia.)

Visceral leishmaniasis, or kala-azar, is caused by at least three members of the *Leishmania donovani* complex. In visceral leishmaniasis, unlike other forms of the disease, the organisms parasitize reticuloendothelial cells beyond the subcutaneous and mucosal tissue, and a number of internal organs may be involved. Symptoms include swelling of the liver and spleen, fever, diarrhea, emaciation, anemia, darkening of the skin, and gross abdominal enlargement. Mortality in untreated cases has reached 75 to 95 percent over a 2-year period.

Clinical Manifestations and Pathololgy

Old World cutaneous leishmaniasis has an incubation period of 6 weeks to a year, depending on the species of *Leishmania*. The lesions may be multiple, and it is thought that they are the result of multiple bites. There is much local induration and possible lymphatic spread to the regional lymph nodes. Healing is slow, with the formation of scar tissue in a year or so.

The New World disease takes several different forms:

1. A self-limiting ulcer of 6 months' duration without metastases, caused by *Leishmania tropica mexicana,* is found in the Yucatan. It has a rodent reservoir in flat, low, rain forests.
2. *Espundia,* due to *L. braziliensis,* exists in the jungles of Panama through Amazonia to Paraguay. It starts as a painless ulcer and metastasizes to the oronasal or anorectal area in 5 to 23 years. The host is thought to be the paca (*Cuniculus paca*), a nocturnal American rodent.
3. A solitary ulcerative lesion known as *uta,* usually found at the base of the nose with no metastasis, exists in the Andean valleys of Peru and Argentina. The agent is *Leishmania peruviana,* and the host is the dog.
4. Leproid leishmaniasis is seen in Venezuela. It begins as a fleshy cutaneous nodule that slowly spreads over the body without ulcerating and is difficult to distinguish from leprosy. It is thought to be due to an immune response and is very chronic.

In the absence of demonstrable leishmania, reliance rests on the *leishmanin skin test,* which is positive in cutaneous disease when there is a tuberculoid histology. Generally it becomes positive early and remains so after healing is complete. Although most lesions are self-limiting, antimony, pyrimethamine, and amphotericin B are used to treat metastases. A persistent positive serology is an important sign of continued survival of the parasite, which may live for decades in asymptomatic individuals.

History and Geography

Leishmaniasis is an ancient disease of both the Old and the New Worlds. Old World cutaneous leishmaniasis was first described in English by Alexander Russell in the mid-eighteenth century. Designs on Indian pottery of the New World clearly show the disfiguring disease. The pre-Columbian Incas knew of the dangers of the disease in the lowlands east of the Andes where coca grew and thus used captives to cultivate it. The Spaniards who later took over the coca trade were less aware of the problem, and consequently, their labor policies resulted in much disfigurement and death.

Visceral leishmaniasis was known to nineteenth-century British doctors in India as kala-azar or *Dumdum fever* with its symptoms attributed vari-

Figure VIII.79.1. The *uta* form of leishmaniasis.

ously to malaria, Malta fever, and other diseases. It was in 1900 that W. B. Leishman, working at Nettley, noticed the similarity of the parasite to that of trypanosomiasis, and shortly thereafter Leishman's bodies were discovered to be the cause of kala-azar. Leishman published his findings in 1903, yet his work was duplicated independently by Charles Donovan. Leishman's name was given to the entire genus, but the agent of kala-azar got its specific name from Donovan.

Old World leishmaniasis or *oriental sore* had long been in northern Africa and India, where it was known geographically as the *Delhi boil, Aleppo boil,* and so forth. Its agent, *L. tropica,* was probably seen as early as 1885, but the first clear description was not published until 1898, by Peter Fokitsch Borovsky in a Russian military journal. However, the paper did not become known to the West, and thus credit for the discovery of the organism is often given to James Homer Wright of Baltimore, who in 1903 found it in an ulcer of a child from Armenia.

The first cases of cutaneous disease in the Americas were described by A. Carini and V. Paranhos in southern Brazil in 1909 – the same year that mucocutaneous leishmaniasis was described as a distinct disease, this also in Brazil. Gasper Oliveira de Vianna named the etiologic agent *Leishmania braziliensis* in 1911. The visceral form in the Americas was first seen in Paraguay in 1913. *Phlebotomus* was suspected of being the vector as early as 1911, but this was not proven until 1941.

The cutaneous and mucocutaneous form of the disease are relatively common problems among people working in heavily forested areas, such as the original area of Amazonia in Brazil. In Peru the *uta* form is seen on the lower eastern slopes of the Andes. In the Arica area of northern Chile there is an interesting case of what is probably the *uta* form (Figure VIII.79.1) of this disease dating back about 1,000 years. It is known that contacts were common with the jungle area for trade purposes, and this case is probably an example of an imported exotic disease to the Pacific coast.

Marvin J. Allison

Bibliography

Gade, Daniel W. 1979. Inca and colonial settlement, coca cultivation and endemic disease in the tropical forest. *Journal of Historical Geography* 5: 263–79.

Herrer, Aristides, and Howard A. Christensen. 1975. Implication of *Phlebotomus* sand flies as vectors of bartonellosis and leishmaniasis as early as 1764. *Science* 190: 154–5.

Jones, T. C., et al. 1987. Epidemiology of America: Cutaneous leishmaniasis due to *Leishmania braziliensis. Journal of Infectious Diseases* 156: 73–83.

Kean, B. H., Kenneth E. Mott, and Adair J. Russell, eds. 1978. *Tropical medicine and parasitology: Classic investigations,* Vol. I, 228–70. Ithaca.

Lainson, R., and J. J. Shaw. 1978. Epidemiology and ecology of Leishmaniasis in Latin America. *Nature (Parasitology* Supplement) 273: 595–600.

Markell, Edward K., Marietta Voge, and David T. John. 1986. *Medical parasitology,* 6th edition. Philadelphia.

Strong, R. P. 1944. *Stitts diagnosis, prevention and treatment of tropical disease.* 7th edition. Philadelphia.

Vianna, Gaspar Oliveira de. 1911. Sobre o tratemento de leishmaniose tegumentar. *Anais Paulistas de Medicina e Cirurgia* 2: 167–9.

VIII.80
Leprosy

Leprosy occurs naturally only in humans and is caused by infection with *Mycobacterium leprae.* Known also in the twentieth century as "Hansen's disease," after the Norwegian microbiologist A. G. H. Hansen who first isolated the microorganism in 1873, true leprosy is a chronic, debilitating, and disfiguring infection. However, the long history of disease attributed to leprosy undoubtedly includes a broad range of skin and systemic afflictions that only resembled leprosy symptoms.

The leprosy bacillus multiplies quite slowly, usually in the sheaths of peripheral nerves. Losing sensation in discrete, patchy areas of the skin is often the earliest, but ignored, symptom of infection. Lacking adequate innervation, the affected dermis can be damaged without evoking a pain response as, for example, by a burn or a cut. Repair of the tissue is then hindered by poor regulation of local blood supply. Hence, secondary infection and inflammation of an involved area are common, leading to scarring and callusing of surviving tissues. This long process can result in the loss of fingers, toes, nasal tissue, or other parts of the body frequently exposed to the

elements. A "bear claw" foot or hand becomes one of the characteristically maiming and stigmatizing features of the leper. Involvement of the nasal cartilage and vocal cords, common sites for the organism's growth, leads to profound disfiguration of the center of the face and also to the raspy, honking voice described in some historical accounts of true leprosy.

The early and more subtle physiological changes caused by leprosy have been noted consistently only since the nineteenth century. Owing to the involvement of nerves supplying the dermis, the heavily innervated face loses "free play" of expression and affect. Eyelashes and the lateral part of the eyebrows disappear long before other, grosser signs betray infection.

Distribution and Incidence

In the late twentieth century, leprosy occurs commonly only in tropical and subtropical regions, as indicated in Map VIII.80.1. There are at least 15 million lepers worldwide, most of them residing in Africa, South and Southeast Asia, and South America. However, this geographic distribution of the disease more likely reflects the poverty of these regions than it does the possibility that elevated temperatures and humidity facilitate infection. Despite cheap and effective medication (dapsone) to arrest the relentless progression of leprosy in infected individuals, the disease continues to spread in the rural regions of Africa, Southeast Asia, and the Indian subcontinent. Often because leprosy stigmatizes its victims socially, leading to loss of employment, alienation from family and community, and, ultimately, to confinement in a leprosarium, lepers deny infection or evade treatment as long as they can. In the process they ensure transmission of the disease to others. Leprosy is normally passed from one individual to another only with sustained exposure, but the disease continues to spread even in areas served by Western medical practitioners, because of the high social costs of early identification and treatment.

In the past, leprosy probably extended as far north as the Arctic Circle. Extensive paleopathological investigations of medieval gravesites thought to have belonged to leper colonies have produced evidence of leprosy among Danes and Norwegians of the thirteenth century. Interestingly, the distribution of leprosy in medieval Europe, like that of today, appears to have been rural, and the written or physical evidence of leprosy disappears with urbanization. The disappearance of leprosy in Europe historically progressed gradually northward from the urban Mediterranean areas of Italy and Spain. Cases of leprosy were still reported in England and Scotland during

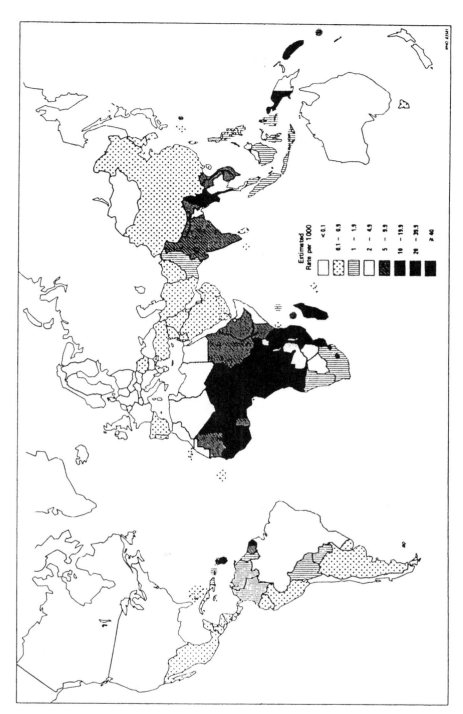

Map VIII.80.1. Estimated endemicity of leprosy in the world, 1983. (From World Health Organization. 1985. *Epidemiology of leprosy in relation to control: Report of a WHO Study Group.* World Health Organization Technical Report Series 716. Geneva.)

Estimated
Rate per 1000

< 0.1
0.1 – 0.9
1 – 1.9
2 – 4.9
5 – 9.9
10 – 19.9
20 – 39.9
≥ 40

the fourteenth and fifteenth centuries, and the disease persisted in Scandinavia until the late nineteenth century, where Hansen discovered the bacillus that causes the disease.

One of the odd features of the geographic distribution of leprosy is the increased prevalence on islands or near seacoasts. Late medieval and early modern theorists even attributed the cause of the disease to an exclusively fish diet, an explanation now discredited. Undoubtedly the low infectivity of the disease and its association with poverty and poor sanitation contribute to the slow spread inland once leprosy is introduced into a region.

Epidemiology

It is possible that the history of *Mycobacterium tuberculosis,* an organism related to leprosy and one that creates a limited cross-immunity to *M. leprae* infection, has affected the long-term distribution and incidence of leprosy, as may also have other atypical mycobacterial infections such as scrofula and avian tuberculosis. Increased population density in urban areas facilitates the spread of tuberculosis infection, which may have contributed to a declining incidence of leprosy as cities and large towns appeared. In large regions of West Africa today, leprosy's hold over rural, remote villages increases with distance from a city (Hunter and Thomas 1984), whereas tuberculosis infection, evidenced by positive reactions to a tine or tuberculin purified protein derivative (PPD) test, increases dramatically with population density. There is almost no evidence that leprosy existed in the Western Hemisphere, Australia, or Oceanic Islands before it was introduced from the Old World.

This epidemiological relationship between tuberculosis and leprosy, however, is obscured in individual patients. For despite cross-immunity, the most common associated cause of death in leprosaria is tuberculosis, illustrating how long-sufferers of leprosy lose the ability to combat other chronic infections. Moreover, geographic determinants of leprosy infection alone cannot explain the high prevalence of leprosy in densely settled eastern India. It could be, however, that more successful control of tuberculosis in the region permitted the persistence of leprosy and that stigmatization of lepers effectively delayed treatment of the illness by medical and public health authorities.

Etiology

M. leprae belongs to a large group of intracellular bacterial pathogens widely distributed in nature. Members of the family Mycobacteriaceae can infect mammalian and avian hosts, and, as exemplified by bovine tuberculosis and avian tuberculosis, a pathogen dominant in one host species can successfully infect an altogether different host. Thus humans have suffered from bovine tuberculosis transmitted through contaminated cow's milk and from atypical mycobacterial infections in the form of "scrofula" or infected lymphatic glands. But among these, only leprosy and tuberculosis can be successfully transmitted from one human to another, although *M. leprae* is the only one of these genera that cannot be transmitted naturally to species other than humans.

This feature of leprosy made difficult the search for a suitable experimental animal for research, and only during the mid-1960s did medical scientists succeed in transmitting the infection to armadillos of the American Southwest. In what period of human history *M. leprae* appeared, and from what other mycobacterial species it evolved are a mystery. Paleopathological evidence confirms the existence of true leprosy in the ancient eastern Mediterranean basin. It was probably African in origin and steadily disseminated among human communities from Pleistocene times onward (Grmek 1983).

The organism usually enters a new human host through respiratory passages or the skin. Because the period of incubation (i.e., the interval between infection and the manifestation of symptoms) is so long, the actual process of the microorganism's growth and dissemination through the body is not well understood. Commonly, early symptoms of disease appear 3 to 5 years after infection, but clinical evidence of infection may appear in as little as 6 months, or as long as 20 years post infection.

Clinical Manifestations and Pathology

Typically leprosy first appears on the skin as a patch or area thickened and differing in color from the surrounding skin. It may be darker or lighter in color, but is usually distinguishable because the area is unresponsive to touch or pain. As is true of other chronic infectious diseases, such as tuberculosis, syphilis, or acquired immune deficiency syndrome, the clinical features of leprosy can vary from one sufferer to another. Leprosy is in fact described as a "bipolar" disease because of two very different clinical forms of the illness, with "mixed" or "indeterminate" reactions to infection possible but less frequent. The intermediate type is sometimes called "borderline" as well. Individuals whose clinical course vacillates between the two polar types are also viewed as intermediate.

In tuberculoid leprosy, one of the polar types, the

areas of "patchy anesthesia" on the skin heal relatively quickly after injury, but new areas appear, more extensive and severe, and the untreated disease involves peripheral nerves to such an extent that desensitized skin cannot be protected from burns, exposure, or other insults to the body surface. Even though tuberculoid leprosy is thought to be milder than lepromatous leprosy, possibly because of a stronger immune response to infection, the secondary infections after skin injury make it a serious disease.

In the "leonine facies" of lepromatous leprosy, the other polar type, the reaction on the skin surface is dramatic and severely disfiguring, because the intermediate healing of involved skin produces thick, corrugated scar tissue. The lesions are often teeming with infective bacilli. The two clinical forms are not caused by morphologically distinguishable forms of *M. leprae*. Thus either a strong or a weak immunologic response (if this difference is the "cause" of the two forms of disease) produces crippling and disfigurement.

The leonine form is more distinctive by sight and thus is more frequent in historical accounts closely describing leprosy. Chinese surgeon Hua T'o's description (around A.D. 150) is a good one:

The skin is first numb without sensation, gradually red spots appear on it, when it is swollen and ulcerated without any pus. And later the disease develops to such an extent that the eyebrows fall, the eyes may become blind, the lips deformed and the voice hoarse. The patient may also experience ringing in his ears and the soles of his feet develop rotted holes; his finger joints may become dislocated and the bridge of his nose flattened. (Skisnes 1973)

On the other hand, exaggerated, grossly disfiguring ulceration of face and limbs is not necessarily caused by leprosy. Syphilis, repeated frostbite injury, and diabetes could also account for the features given in this eighteenth-century Japanese description:

[I]t is useless to attempt to cure a patient whose eyes have a yellow hue [a reflection of either liver damage or the destruction of red blood cells], whose fingernails have no white crescents at the bottom, whose hands are wholly anesthetic, whose palm or sole bleeds, whose eyeballs are ulcerated, whose penis is putrified, whose hands or feet are clawed, whose skin is spotted with black, whose fingers have melted off leaving frog-foot shaped ends, whose body hairs fall off, whose nose is gone, whose bones are poisoned and putrified. (Skisnes 1973)

In addition, secondary infection by many noninfectious diseases such as psoriasis, pellagra, eczema, and lupus erythematosis could easily have led to this historical diagnosis of leprosy. Thus the more subtle changes of early leprosy, such as the loss of the lateral third of the eyebrows, the hoarse voice, the areas of patchy anesthesia, and the loss of free play in facial musculature – all features of the diagnostic procedure described by tenth-century Persian physician Avicenna – provide more assurance of a correct diagnosis of leprosy than does simply loathesome appearance.

Untreated, the established leprosy infection today usually progresses slowly, although there are periods of rapid worsening in a person's overall ability to contain the disease. During these periods of exacerbation, severe pain can be caused by involvement of the nerves, and nodules on the skin may appear rapidly and in crops of lesions. It is rare to die, however, from unchecked Hansen's disease; secondary infection usually leads to the patient's demise.

Immunology

Because leprosy is caused by an intracellular pathogen, production of circulating humoral antibodies (the immunoglobulins) is of little use in combatting the infection of cells and the multiplication of the organism in human tissues. Cell-mediated, or T-cell, immunity is thus the principal bodily means of combating leprosy. Individuals in whom the expression of cell-mediated immunity is compromised or poorly developed, such as pregnant women and children younger than 2 years of age, are at greater risk for both infection (when initially exposed) and progression of the disease unimpeded by the immune system. Others with intact cellular immunity can live almost 20 years before the first serious, debilitating consequences of infection occur. It is not known to what extent recurrent viral infection, which also challenges cellular immunity, may hasten the onset of clinical leprosy.

Genetic factors may further mediate the clinical expression of leprosy among those already infected, predisposing some individuals to a more or less rapid course of the disease, or perhaps influencing the appearance of severe, lepromatous leprosy rather than the milder tuberculoid form. Nevertheless, there are only a limited number of cases in which some clear genetic determinant of susceptibility can be differentiated from the socioeconomic factors mediating exposure to the agent.

History and Geography

The history of leprosy has been dominated by three questions or problems. One question concerns stigmatization. Most ancient societies identified some individuals as "lepers," and the leper was stigmatized, although surely lepers as a group included many suffering from something besides Hansen's disease. Stigmatization of the leper has persisted into the late twentieth century despite advances and refinements in the medical diagnosis and treatment of leprosy. The second problem focuses on medical evidence for leprosy's changing incidence and prevalence over time, particularly in western European history during the period between 500 and 1500 of the present era. Finally, the world distribution of leprosy and failures to impede its spread have emerged as a historical problem of the past 250 years.

In the Old Testament Book of Leviticus, the disease *zara'ath* or *tsara'ath* was identified by priests and its victims were cast "outside the camp" as unclean and uncleansable. They were viewed as both chosen and rejected by God and, consequently, not exiled altogether from the community, as were criminals, but rather made to live apart as if the living dead. Thus, central problems posed by the disease *zara'ath* involved, on the one hand, the spiritual identity of diseased individuals who, although probably morally "tainted," were not, apparently, personally responsible for their disease; and on the other hand, the delegation of the process of making the diagnosis to religious, not medical, authorities.

Because the opprobrium attached to leprosy was handled dramatically by writers of the Biblical Old Testament and because this Judaeo-Christian tradition was of central importance to western European history for the next 2,000 years, stigmatization of the leper was derived from religious, medical, and social responses to individuals carrying the diagnosis. Thus, during the High Middle Ages (A.D. 1100–1300), lepers were identified by priests or other spiritual authorities, and then separated from the general community, often ritualistically. Considered "dead to society," last rites and services might be said in the leper's presence, sometimes as the victim stood symbolically in a grave. Thereafter the person's access to his or her city or village was severely limited. Italian cities, for example, posted guards at the city gates to identify lepers and deny them entrance except under carefully controlled circumstances. Leprosaria, or isolation hospitals to house lepers, were constructed at church or communal expense, although medical services to these facilities were limited. Where public services were less well organized, lepers had to depend upon begging or alms.

Laws in western Europe illustrated the exaggerated fear of contagion lepers generated. Lepers had to be identifiable at a distance, leading to the creation of legendary symbols of the leper: a yellow cross sewn to their cape or vestment; a clapper or bell to warn those who might pass by too closely; a long pole in order to point to items they wished to purchase, or to retrieve an alms cup placed closer to a road than lepers were allowed to go.

The stigmatization of lepers, however, was not limited to Western tradition, and in most societies of the past those labeled as lepers were denied legal rights in addition to being socially ostracized. In traditions of both East Asia and the Indian subcontinent, marriage to a leper or the offspring of a leper was prohibited, and, as in Western tradition, the disease was often attributed to moral causes (sin) as well as to contagion. Interesting in this regard is the iconographic representation of the leper in Tibetan art, a man covered with vesicles and ulcers, which parallels Western depictions of Job as a man covered by sores in punishment by God for his sins. The stereotype of the leper as filthy, rotten, nauseating, and repulsive is so strong that most "hansenologists" today advocate rejection of the name "leprosy" in favor of Hansen's disease. The only exception to this pattern of stigmatization seems to be in Islamic society, where the leper is neither exiled nor considered perverse, promiscuous, or otherwise morally repulsive (Dols 1983).

In contrast to ancient Chinese texts of approximately the same period, in which leprosy destroying the center of the face is well described, the clinical evidence for leprosy in the ancient Mediterranean is meager. Nowhere in the Biblical tradition is there more than a general description of the disease that created such a severe response. Hippocratic texts provide no evidence that true leprosy existed in ancient Greece, but the Hippocratic, Greek word *lepra*, probably describing psoriasis, gave origin to the disease's name. Thus a coherent and powerful tradition in the West stigmatizing the leper was begun in what appears to have been the absence of any organized and reasonably accurate medical description of how these sufferers could be identified. Indeed, the earliest clinical description of leprosy in the West appears neither in the Hippocratic corpus (written in Greek between 400 and 100 B.C.) nor in the 20 surviving volumes of the works of the great second-century Greek physician, Galen, but rather in the writings of the tenth-century Persian physician Avicenna, and it is his *Canon of Medicine* that provides the description upon which medieval European physicians relied.

The decline of leprosy in Europe coincided with increasing medical sophistication in diagnosing what we might recognize as leprosy. This decline may be due in part to an increase in another mycobacterial disease such as tuberculosis; to improvements in living standards; to high catastrophic mortality from plague and other epidemics, effectively reducing the number of lepers in the general population; or to the simple fact that medical authorities began to share the burden of diagnosis with religious and communal leaders. Surely other skin infections and afflictions that might earlier have been taken for leprosy were better recognized in the late Middle Ages. Nonetheless true leprosy certainly existed in Europe, as the exhumations of medieval skeletal materials from northern Europe have well illustrated (Møller-Christensen 1961; Andersen 1969; Steinbock 1976).

Knowledge of leprosy in modern medical terms evolved during the nineteenth century, coincident with development of the germ theory of disease. During this period, the precise description of the clinical characteristics of lepromatous leprosy by Danish physician Daniel C. Danielssen in the 1840s; the discovery of the microorganism by Hansen in 1873; and widespread attention to the contemporary geographic distribution of leprosy in European colonial territories served to identify the disease as a contagious tropical infection. As such it was believed to be eradicable by Western medical efforts in public health intervention. Methods of quarantine and isolation were enthusiastically employed, despite skepticism about these methods in general public health control.

In the same year that Hansen found the causal organism of leprosy, a devoted Catholic priest, Father Damien de Veuster, drew worldwide attention in an attempt to humanize the treatment of leprosy by going to live among lepers in Hawaii. But he may have underscored fear of the contagion of leprosy because he eventually contracted the disease. Thus in modern times, increasing medical knowledge of the incidence and prevalence of *M. leprae* may have served to increase alarm and fear as leprosy was "discovered" to be the resilient global problem it remains to this day.

Ann G. Carmichael

Bibliography

Andersen, J. G. 1969. Studies in the mediaeval diagnosis of leprosy in Denmark. *Danish Medical Bulletin* (Supplement) 16: 1–142.

Brody, Saul Nathanial. 1974. *The disease of the soul: A study in the moral association of leprosy in medieval literature.* Ithaca.

Clay, Rotha Mary. 1909. *The medieval hospitals of England.* London.

Clark, George A., et al. 1987. The evolution of mycobacterial disease in human populations: A reevaluation. *Current Anthropology* 28: 45–62.

Demaitre, Luke. 1985. The description and diagnosis of leprosy by fourteenth-century physicians. *Bulletin of the History of Medicine* 59: 327–44.

Dols, Michael W. 1983. The leper in medieval Islamic society. *Speculum* 4: 891–916.

Ell, Stephen R. 1984. Blood and sexuality in medieval leprosy. *Janus* 71: 153–64.

Grmek, Mirko D. 1983. *Les Maladies à l'aube de la civilisation occidentale: Recherches sur la réalité pathologique dans le monde grec préhistorique, archaïque et classique.* Paris.

Grön, K. 1973. Leprosy in literature and art. *International Journal of Leprosy* 41: 249–83.

Gussow, Z., and G. S. Tracy. 1970. Stigma and the leprosy phenomenon: The social history of a disease in the nineteenth and twentieth centuries. *Bulletin of the History of Medicine* 44: 425–49.

Hunter, John M., and Morris O. Thomas. 1984. Hypothesis of leprosy, tuberculosis, and urbanization in Africa. *Social Science and Medicine* 19: 26–57.

Møller-Christensen, V. 1961. *Bone changes in leprosy.* Copenhagen.

Palmer, Richard J. 1982. The church, leprosy and plague in Medieval and Early Modern Europe. In *The church and healing: Studies in church history*, No. 19. ed. W. J. Shields. Oxford.

Richards, Peter. 1977. *The medieval leper and his northern heirs.* Cambridge.

1971. Leprosy in Tibetan art and religion. *International Journal of Leprosy* 39: 60–65.

Skisnes, Olaf K. 1973. Notes from the history of leprosy. *International Journal of Leprosy* 41: 220–37.

Steinbock, R. T. 1976. *Paleopathological diagnosis and interpretation.* Springfield, Ill.

World Health Organization. 1985. *Epidemiology of leprosy in relation to control: Report of a WHO Study Group.* Technical report series 716. Geneva.

VIII.81
Leptospirosis

The kind of leptospirosis manifested by severe jaundice was first described as a human disease in 1886 by A. Weil. Named *Weil's disease* the following year, the term was meant to designate a distinctive infectious jaundice, and it would not be known until much later that leptospirosis was caused by numerous leptospires that triggered various clinical syndromes. The first of the causative pathogens were independently discovered in 1915 by R. Inada among Japanese mine workers and by P. Uhlenhut and W. Fromme among German soldiers. *Leptospira,* a genus of the family Treponemataceae, order Spirochaetales, is a fine threadlike organism with hooked ends (see Figure VIII.81.1) that is pathogenic for humans and other mammals, producing meningitis, hepatitis, and nephritis both separately and together. In the past, the disease killed between 15 and 40 percent of those infected. Modern treatment has reduced mortality to about 5 percent. As a zoonosis, the disease is generally maintained in rodent reservoirs.

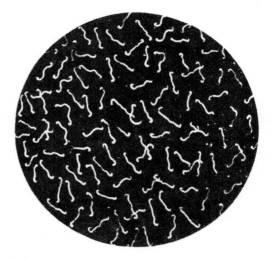

Figure VIII.81.1. Leptospires on dark field. (From O. Gsell. 1978. Leptospires and relapsing fever. In *Handbook of Clinical Neurology,* Part III, Chapter 18, 395–418, by permission of Elsevier Science Publishing.)

Etiology and Epidemiology

Leptospires are obligate aerobes and classified serologically as a bacterium, subdivided into two species. One is *Leptospira biflexa,* which includes the various water spirochetes, whereas the other, *Leptospira interrogans,* embraces the parasitic strains. The species *interrogans* (so named because of an appearance like a question mark) is now subdivided by the main antigen into 187 serotypes or serovars. Human leptospirosis generally results from direct or indirect exposure to the urine of infected animals, although it can also be transmitted by handling infected animal tissue, by animal bites, and by the ingestion of contaminated food and water. The leptospires can enter the body through breaks in the skin, as well as through the lining of the mouth, nose, and eyes.

Persons of all ages are susceptible to the infection, and although the disease may occur at any time, it is most often seen during warmer weather and periods of heavy rainfall. Its presence in mud and swamps has often placed soldiers at special risk. As a rule, it appears as isolated cases, but it can also manifest itself in small clusters and even in large outbreaks, depending on the type and the circumstances of its transmission.

In most of the world, leptospirosis is an occupational disease. Field workers and those who work around farm animals are at risk, as are employees of slaughter houses and poultry and fish production plants, and persons employed in sewers, mines, and in other wet places infested with rodents. Infected wild animals such as rats and mice are the source of infection for domesticated animals, especially dogs (*Leptospira canicola*), pigs (*Leptospira pomona*), and cattle (*Leptospira hardjo*), who may in turn infect humans.

As Table VIII.81.1 indicates, localized leptospirosis infections produced by one or another strain of the pathogen occur across the globe. The pig-raising areas of the European alpine region, northern Australia, and parts of Argentina see one form of the disease caused by *L. pomona* and *Leptospira hyos* or *tarassovi* and called *swineherd's disease.* Similarly, the sugarcane plantation regions of East Asia and rice-growing regions of Spain and Italy harbor other forms, which are the result of infection by field mice. Local names for the various forms of leptospirosis often reflect the circumstances under which it is contracted. Thus there is "harvest" or "swamp" fever, caused by *Leptospira grippotyphosa.* In Germany, agricultural workers contracted "field fever"; in Silesia, there was "mud fever"; in Russia, "water fever"; and in Germany and Switzerland, "pea pickers disease." On the other hand, leptospirosis can also be an urban disease carried by the ubiquitous *Rattus norwegicus,* as well as by dogs.

Table VIII.81.1. *Serologic classification of leptospires*

Important serogroups	Principal human diseases	Rare serogroups
1. *L. icterohaemorrhagiae*	Morbus Weil	10. *L. pyrogenes*
2. *L. bataviae*	Indonesian Weil, rice field fever	11. *L. javanica*
3. *L. canicola*	canicola fever	12. *L. ballum*
4. *L. grippotyphosa*	field or swamp fever	13. *L. celledoni*
5. *L. pomona*	swineherd's disease	14. *L. cynopteri*
6. *L. hyos = tarassovi*	swineherd's disease	15. *L. panama*
7. *L. australis*	cane fever	16. *L. shermani*
8. *L. autumnalis*	Japanese autumnal fever	17. *L. semeranga*
9. *L. hebdomadis*	7-day fever	18. *L. andamana*
		19. *L. sejroe*, including serovar *L. hardjo*

Source: O. Gsell. 1978. Leptospiroses and relapsing fever. In *Handbook of Clinical Neurology,* Part III, Chapter 18, 397. New York: Elsevier Science Publishing, by permission of publisher.

Clinical Manifestations

Figure VIII.81.2 shows the phases of leptospirosis and the relevant diagnostic procedures. The first phase of the disease is characterized by an acute onset of high fever, headache, malaise, conjunctival reddening, muscle pain, often meningism, renal irritation, hypotonia, and relative bradycardia (see Table VIII.81.2). In the second stage, there is danger of organ involvement, which is accompanied by the appearance of specific antibodies in the serum. The disease frequently causes the liver to become enlarged and painful, and can be life-threatening when renal damage is severe. Icterus, when it occurs, can be very intense and last for several weeks. Leptospirosis also causes kidney damage, although the most common second-stage symptom is serosal meningitis, and less frequently encephalomyelitis or neuritis. Swineherds' meningitis is particularly well known (Gsell 1952). Meningitis symptoms usually subside completely in the third week.

As Figure VIII.81.2 indicates, there can be other damage from the disease, but only rarely. When it causes death, postmortem findings reveal renal and hepatic failure represented by renal tubular necroses, hemoglobinemia, and liver cell necrosis with general jaundice and anemia. Hemorrhages can be found in almost any organ, and in muscles and subcutaneous tissue.

Treatment

Antibiotics are quite effective against leptospires but only if employed within the first 3 or, at the most, 4 days. After this, efforts should be directed at avoiding complications. Severe kidney insufficiency requires hemodialysis or peritoneal dialysis, and infusions or transfusions may be necessary as well.

History and Geography

Much of the history of leptospirosis appears as an effort to separate leptospiral jaundice and meningitis from other infections. The clinical portion of this history began with Weil's description of the disease in 1886; the bacteriologic phase began with isolation

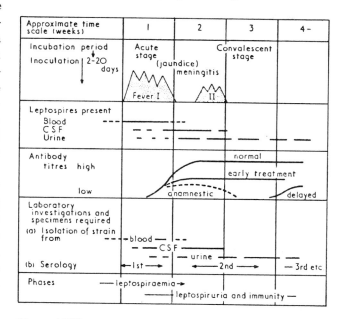

Figure VIII.81.2. Phases and relevant diagnostic procedures of leptospiroses. (Reproduced with slight modification from L. H. Turner 1973, in O. Gsell. 1978. Leptospiroses and relapsing fever. In *Handbook of Clinical Neurology,* Part III, Chapter 18, 395–419; 399, by permission of Elsevier Science Publishing.)

Table VIII.81.2. *Symptoms occurring in leptospiroses*

Symptom	% cases
Fever	100
Headaches	96
Biphasic fever	96
Meningitis serosa	90–96
Pathological urinary sediment	84
Conjunct. hyperaemia	60
Pharyngitis	60
Hypotonia	38
Myalgias, arthralgias	28
Exanthema	14
Icterus	1–2
Duration of fever	
Up to 8 days	77
9–14 days	16
15–19 days	7
Leukopenia under 6000	
First phase	30
Second phase	43
Leukocytosis upwards of 9000	
First phase	25
Second phase	25
Shift to the left in blood formula	
First phase	81
Second phase	72

Source: O. Gsell. 1978. Leptospiroses and relapsing fever. In *Handbook of Clinical Neurology*, Part III, Chapter 18, 399. New York: Elsevier Science Publishing, by permission of the publisher.

of the pathogenic germs in 1915 by Inada and Uhlenhut and Fromme. In 1918, H. Noguchi gave the name *Leptospira* to the newly discovered bacteria. During the years 1917–18 Y. Indo, H. Ito, and H. Wani found cases of the disease that were not characterized by jaundice – described as the 7-day fever *"Nanukayami"* which has the field mouse as a carrier. In the following decades, numerous different serotypes were found throughout the world. Among these are *Leptospira pyrogenes* (Indonesia, 1923), *Leptospira autumnalis* (Japan, 1925), *Leptospira bataviae* (Indonesia, 1926), *L. grippotyphosa* (Russia, 1928), *Leptospira andaman* (Andaman Islands, 1931), *L. canicola* (Netherlands, 1933), *Leptospira australis* as well as *L. pomona* (Australia, 1937), and *Leptospira hebdomadis hardjo* (Great Britain, 1968).

In Switzerland during the year 1944, *L. pomona* was found to be the cause of swineherds disease with the pig as its carrier, and 4 years later *L. tarassovi*

and *L. hyos* were discovered to be of the same serotype and also carried by the pig. Numerous other serovars have been discovered subsequently, and after 1950 a new classification of the serotypes was accepted which classified the clinical groups into malignant and benign human leptospires, while in serology it permitted the allocation of animal and human leptospires to different serovars. In looking back on a century of research on leptospirosis, it seems remarkable that serious and widespread epidemics have been so infrequent. Today the incidence of the disease has been reduced in developed countries, probably because of a decrease in the rodent populations and because of improved human hygiene in the presence of domestic animals.

Otto R. Gsell

Bibliography

Alston, J. M., and J. C. Broom. 1958. *Leptospiroses in man and animal*. London.

Faine, S. 1982. Guidelines for the control of leptospirosis. *World Health Organization* Offset Publication No. 67.

Gsell, O. 1952. Leptospirosen. In *Handbuch der Inneren Medizen,* 4th edition, 21–45. Berlin.

  1974. Leptospirosen. *Klinik der Gegenwart,* Vol. 2, ed. H. E. Bock, W. Gerock, and F. Hartmann. München.

 1978. Leptospiroses and relapsing fever. In *Handbook of Clinical Neurology,* Part III: 395–419. New York.

  1984. History of leptospiroses: 100 years. *Zentralblatt für Bakteriologie und Hygiene* A257: 473–8.

  1990. Leptospiroses. *Zentralblatt für Bakteriologie und Hygiene* 281: 109–26.

Symposium of the leptospiroses, December 1952. 1953. Washington, D.C.

Turner, L. H. 1973. Leptospiroses III. *British Medical Journal* 1: 537–40.

VIII.82
Leukemia

Leukemia, commonly known as cancer of the blood, describes a group of malignant disorders that arise in the blood-forming cells. The bone marrow, where the cells of the blood are made, malfunctions to produce abnormal white cells (*leukemic cells*) in an uncontrolled manner to the detriment of all the other essential blood cells. Blood consists of a clear fluid (*plasma*), containing chemical substances essential to the body's needs, and three types of blood cells. The red blood cells (*erythrocytes*) are by far the most numerous; their main function is to transport oxygen to all the tissues of the body. They contain *hemoglobin,* an iron-rich protein that gives the blood its red color. A reduction in hemoglobin concentration is known as *anemia.* The white blood cells, *leukocytes,* of which there are three major groups, namely *monocytes, granulocytes,* and *lymphocytes,* play different roles in defending the body against infection. Platelets help to control bleeding.

Hematopoiesis

Blood cell formation, known as *hematopoiesis,* starts in the bone marrow, the spongy interior of the large bones, with a pool of immature or undifferentiated cells known as pluripotent stem cells, which contain the characteristics of all the major blood cell lines. These cells divide, either producing themselves exactly or producing more specialized cells that contain the characteristics of only one of the two major cell lines: One of these two specialized cells, known as the *mixed myeloid progenitor cell,* consists of the progenitor cells to the red blood cells, the monocytes and granulocytes (white cells), and the platelets. The other, the *lymphoid stem cell,* produces the lymphocytes that make up about 30 percent of the circulating white blood cells. The two types of lymphocytes – *T cells* and *B cells* – have different functions: The T cells attack and destroy virus-infected cells, foreign tissue, and cancer cells; B cells produce antibodies, which are proteins that help destroy infectious agents. The two types of white cells interact in complex ways to regulate the immune response.

The production process is continual through division and differentiation, with cell characteristics becoming increasingly defined with each division. The result is that cells are "committed" to evolution into one specific cell type, and thus, as mature cells, they are released into the bloodstream at a rate consistent with the body's needs and the death of old cells. The exception is the lymphocytes: These are allowed to leave the bone marrow as immature cells, but they mature in the lymph system (thymus, spleen, lymph nodes, and so forth) before entering the bloodstream. In normal health, immature stem cells or *blasts* are present in the circulating blood only in very small numbers, and healthy bone marrow does not contain more than 5 percent of the total cell population.

From 6 weeks until about 6 to 7 months in utero, liver and the spleen are the main organs involved in blood formation. Thereafter, the bone marrow takes over. In infants, practically all the bones are involved, but in adults the production is limited to the vertebrae, ribs, sternum, skull, sacrum, pelvis, and the proximal ends of the femur. Because the entire blood cell formation, growth, maintenance, destruction, and replacement cycle is most efficiently organized, it follows that any abnormal reproduction of any type of cell will disrupt the blood cell balance and, in the absence of a self-regulating mechanism, will affect the body's general health.

Every day at least 200 billion red cells, 10 billion white cells, and over 400 billion platelets are produced in the marrow. The averagel life-span of the cells varies according to the cell type, and ranges from 1 to 2 days for white cells, to about 7 days for platelets, to 120 days for red cells. In normal circulating blood there are approximately 1,000 red cells to each white cell. But in leukemia, the normal production of blood cells fails. In all but its rarest form, one or more of the types of white blood cells reproduces abnormally and creates useless, immature blast cells or poorly developed cells of inferior quality. These leukemic cells begin to overpopulate the bone marrow, spill into the bloodstream and the lymph system, and infiltrate vital organs and glands, causing them to enlarge and malfunction. Because the bone marrow is severely impaired, it is unable to maintain production of sufficient levels of red cells and platelets. As a consequence, the whole balance of the blood cell population is seriously disturbed, and the body's defense mechanisms provided by the white blood cells and the platelets are rendered ineffective.

Classification of the Leukemias

Leukemia types are classified according to the type of white cell that is affected. The two main types of the disease are *myeloid* (also called *granulocytic* or *myelogenous*) and *lymphatic* (or *lymphocytic*). These two main types are derived from the two major cell lines: the mixed myeloid progenitor cell line, which

produces the white blood cell monocytes or granulocytes; and the lymphoid cell line, which gives rise to
the lymphocytes. These are further subdivided into
acute (progressing rapidly) and *chronic* (progressing
slowly). In the acute form, there is abnormal growth
of immature or blast cells whereas in chronic leukemia, more mature cells proliferate, although abnormal immature cells may also be present. The following are the diseases that mainly arise:

1. *Acute myeloid leukemia* (AML), also called
acute myelogenous leukemia, acute myelocytic leukemia, acute myeloblastic leukemia, and acute
granulocytic leukemia, is synonymous with the
group known as *acute nonlymphocytic leukemia*
(ANLL), which includes some of the rarer subtypes
of the disease (e.g., monocytic leukemia). AML involves the neutrophils (one of the granulocytes) that
stem from the myeloid progenitor cell line.

2. *Chronic myeloid leukemia* (CML), also called
chronic myelogenous leukemia, chronic myelocytic
leukemia, and chronic granulocytic leukemia (CGL),
produces excessive numbers of granulocytes that accumulate in the bone marrow and blood stream.

3. *Acute lymphoblastic leukemia* (ALL), also
known as acute lymphocytic leukemia and acute
lymphatic leukemia, arises as a result of abnormal
immature lymphocytes, which proliferate in the
bone marrow and the bloodstream and affect the
lymphocytes (the B cells and T cells) stemming from
the lymphoid cell line.

4. *Chronic lymphocytic leukemia* (CLL), also
known as chronic lymphatic leukemia and chronic
lymphogenous leukemia, produces an abnormal increase in lymphocytes that lack their infection-
fighting ability. It is the major type of a group of
diseases known as lymphoproliferative disorders,
which includes such rarer forms of leukemia as
hairy cell leukemia and adult T cell leukemia.

Distribution and Incidence

Leukemia occurs worldwide and represents just over
5 percent of all cancers. The disease does not present
in a regular pattern, and its comparative rarity
helps to explain its irregularity. Leukemia can
strike anyone, at any time, and at any age. The
difficulties in collecting statistics relating to leukemia in populations throughout the world are due not
only to the different methods of reporting cases and
identifying the true leukemia cell-type specificity,
but also to the variable standards and access to medical care. Comparing the incidence of leukemia and
other cancers on a worldwide basis can therefore
present problems.

The specific types of leukemia are very different in
their age patterns and presentation:

1. *Acute myeloid leukemia* (AML) is the major
form of leukemia. Its rate of incidence increases with
age, yet it also occurs in early infancy and in those in
their early 20s. With a mean estimated presentation
at around the age of 40 years, the disease affects
both sexes equally.

2. *Chronic myeloid leukemia* (CML) is considered
an "adult" leukemia, attacking those in the 30- to
50-year age bracket, although it also presents in the
older age groups. It, too, has an equal rate of incidence in males and females.

3. *Acute lymphoblastic leukemia* (ALL) is often
referred to as "childhood leukemia" for the reason
that it accounts for 85 percent of leukemia in children and only 15 percent of cases in adults. ALL has
been reported in all races and all geographic areas;
yet, for every child with leukemia there are about 10
adults with it.

4. *Chronic lymphocytic leukemia* (CLL) is primarily a disease of the elderly; it rarely presents in
anyone below the age of 40. It is more common in
males than females, with a male/female ratio of 2:1.

The estimated incidence of all cases of leukemia in
the developed countries of the world is 10 per
100,000 of population, the most common now being
CLL including the lymphoproliferative disorders,
followed by AML and its subgroups, then CML,
and lastly ALL. Incidence rates vary in some
countries of the world and among some ethnic
groups, but no variation is of great significance.
The male/female incidence ratio is about 1.7:1.

Etiology

The etiology of leukemia is at present unknown. The
basic question is what causes a healthy cell to
change to become malignant and to proliferate in
that state. The consensus of opinion is that the disease results from the interaction of a number of
factors, including environmental agents, and investigations are being pursued on the following:

1. Genetic factors, involving chromosomal abnormalities and changes.
2. Disorders of the immune system (the body's defense system against infection).
3. Exposure to ionizing radiation from a single large
   dose or from repeated small doses.
4. Chemicals that suppress bone marrow function.
5. Infection – viruses: Retroviruses are known to
   cause leukemia and lymphomas in certain animal
   species but not in humans, although recently a

type of RNA virus has been isolated from patients with adult T cell leukemia known as human T cell leukemia virus HTLV1.

Epidemiology

As the cause of leukemia remains obscure, epidemiology has assumed an importance in two directions: first, the incidence, age, and sex differences in the various forms of the disease related to their geographic presentation, and second, the hunt for etiologic clues.

One of the first epidemiology studies on leukemia was by W. R. Gowers, based upon 154 cases and published in London in 1879. The study comprised age and sex data collected at a time when leukemia was recognized only as a chronic disease. It offered few etiologic clues other than exposure to malaria, which was then not confined to tropical countries.

Toward the close of the nineteenth century, a small number of cases of leukemia in its acute form were reported in Europe, and attention was focused on this new form of the disease, particularly in America. George Dock of the University of Michigan was a leading investigator of the complicated aspects of acute leukemia and its rapid onset. The literature, which Dock reviewed extensively in 1903, regarded infection and "some microscopic germ" as suspects.

The infective theory of acute leukemia was further discussed in a 1917 publication in the *British Journal of Children's Diseases* by G. Ward, who had collected a series of 1,457 cases of leukemia. This work added to the knowledge of the age–sex distribution of the disease and suggested that although acute leukemia resembled an infectious disease in many respects (e.g., the feverlike symptoms it caused), there was little evidence to suggest that it was by nature infectious or that it was hereditary.

Leukemia tends to present in an irregular pattern, evidenced by the number of "clusters" of cases that are regularly reported, clusters being defined as more cases of the disease than would be expected to occur in a specific area. The first report of a cluster of leukemia cases came from Paris in 1922, where four patients living within a short distance of one another were diagnosed with acute leukemia in a period of 7 weeks. It was the commonly held view that the cause was the water from a canal in the area. In this event, as with most clusters, the pattern was of normal or less than normal incidence of the disease both before and after the appearance of the cluster of cases.

Because of the sudden presentation of clusters of the disease, investigations are often launched to find a cause. The identification of possible contributory factors within the environment is one approach, although the prime concentration is on what influences the basic cells and genes to change and begin the malignant process. The most established etiologic factor in human leukemias is ionizing radiation. The atom bombs dropped on Hiroshima and Nagasaki in 1945, for example, brought a rise in the incidence of leukemia, which began about 3 years after the atomic attack and reached a peak at 6 years, but then slowly declined to a normal incidence of the disease at 20 years. On investigation it was found that the greatest incidence was among those closest to the explosion, whereas at 2,000 meters or more the risk of leukemia was no greater than among unirradiated people.

Altogether some 250 cases of leukemia occurred between 1946 and 1965 in the 183,000 people exposed to radiation in Hiroshima and Nagasaki. From this information it followed that only a small proportion of those irradiated developed leukemia, and this led to the suggestion of individual susceptibility. Later, public concern about nuclear power causing leukemia was heightened by the number of clusters of cases of the disease reported in areas surrounding nuclear power stations. Indeed many questions have been raised on this issue, particularly because childhood cases appear to be more prominent in these reported clusters. The pattern – which became apparent in the aftermath of the attacks on Hiroshima and Nagasaki – seems to emerge in these clusters as well; for if nuclear power stations are emitting radiation, relatively few people are actually affected – again raising the etiologic question of possible susceptibility.

The issue of genetic susceptibility was studied by Frederick Gunz, a distinguished research physician at Sydney Hospital in Australia, whose biological approach to epidemiology resulted in his publications in 1974 and 1975 on the genetics of human leukemia. Gunz concluded that evidence from family studies reinforced the theory of a genetic basis in some people for chronic lymphatic leukemia in particular. Gunz also reported that certain chemicals, notably benzene along with viruses, were identified as triggering factors in some animal leukemias, but evidence for such a conclusion in human leukemia remained elusive.

A major epidemiology study embracing a population base of some 20 million people was started in 1984 in England and Wales, at the University of Leeds, by the Leukaemia Research Fund. This computerized program with diagnostic check controls will be of major importance in assessing current trends in the presentation of the disease.

Clinical Manifestations and Pathology

Some of the first symptoms of acute leukemia are similar to those of common infectious illness. All the leukemias share common signs and symptoms arising from the infiltration of the bone marrow, with leukemic cells replacing the normal tissues. The lack of red cells causes fatigue and anemia, the lack of normal white cells results in infections and fever, and the lack of platelets produces bleeding and bruising. The lymph nodes, spleen, and liver may become enlarged as they are infiltrated with leukemic cells. Bone or joint pains are associated symptoms, and purpura is often present. Although the basic features of the leukemias are common, marked differences exist between the acute and chronic leukemias in their mode of presentation. In the acute leukemias, influenza-type symptoms and fever (present for only days or weeks) signal the sudden and rapid progress of the acute form of the disease. Weakness, exhaustion, enlargement of the lymph nodes, abnormal bleeding (from the gums for example), and a tendency to bruise easily are some of the chief symptoms.

By contrast, the symptoms of chronic leukemias are generally far more subtle. It is not uncommon for the disease to be discovered accidentally when a blood test is carried out for an unrelated reason. The most common symptoms are loss of energy, tiredness, fever, night sweats, and loss of appetite. There may also be enlargement of the liver and spleen and the lymph nodes.

Leukemia can be diagnosed only by microscopic examination of the blood and the bone marrow. A blood test may show low hemoglobin, low levels of normal white cells, and a low platelet count; and leukemic blast cells may be present. A bone marrow biopsy will confirm the diagnosis of leukemia and the predominant cell type involved, which will enable the leukemia to be correctly classified.

Treatment

The remedies for leukemia in the nineteenth century were few, and none was useful in controlling the disease for any length of time. In the first 50 years following its recognition (Bennett 1845), leukemia was generally accepted as a chronic disease, and the limited therapeutics in the armory of the general physician were applied. Quinine was used for combating fever; morphine and opium, for diarrhea; iron, for anemia; iodine, for external use as an antibacterial; and arsenic. In 1786, Thomas Fowler

of York, England, introduced a solution of arsenic trioxide for the cure of agues, remittent fevers, and headaches. In addition, it became a general tonic for animals and humans alike, and in 1865 a German physician prescribed this solution in the treatment of a woman with chronic myeloid leukemia. The patient became temporarily restored to health, and as a result, arsenic became the first agent of some beneficial use in the treatment of certain forms of leukemia, causing a shrinkage of the enlarged spleen and lymph nodes and a reduction in the leukemic cells.

The discovery in 1895 of X-rays by Wilhelm Röntgen soon led to X-ray therapy of leukemias with results similar to those produced by arsenic. However, X-ray therapy had a greater advantage because it was discovered to have the ability to prevent cell division and to inhibit cell growth. On the other hand, patients could eventually become resistant to treatment with X-rays. Thus William Osler commented in 1914 that he had not seen any striking permanent improvement in patients who had undergone X-ray therapy, and C. E. Forkner of Cornell University, New York, writing on the etiology of leukemia in 1938, stated that although much could be done to add to the comfort of patients with chronic forms of leukemia, acute leukemia did not respond to any form of therapy.

In 1946, two American research groups reported on nitrogen mustard therapy, which arose from the poisonous mustard gas research study initiated during World War II. It was found that the chemical analogues of the gas could cause depression of the blood cells, and that some patients in cases of leukemia and lymphoma who had become resistant to X-ray therapy responded to treatment with this agent. This new treatment triggered intensive efforts to find less toxic and more specific therapeutic agents. The result was the introduction of chemotherapy. The aim of all treatment of leukemia is to achieve a prolonged remission of the disease, a state in which all clinical signs of abnormal blood cells disappear and the normal balance of less than 5 percent of blasts in the bone marrow is restored.

Chemotherapy is the form of induction therapy used to effect a remission. A variety of drugs are used to attack the leukemic cells in diverse ways, and they are often given in combination to enhance the efficacy of treatment. However, as these drugs can affect both the leukemic and normal cells, their doses and the sequence of their use must be controlled with great care. Usually combinations of drugs belonging to different groups of chemical compounds are used to attack leukemic cells at different stages of their growth to prevent leukemic cells from becoming resistant to the therapy.

Radiotherapy by deep X-irradiation may also be given; and in certain instances it is used to attack leukemic cells that may accumulate in certain areas of the body – for example, in the central nervous system, the testis, and the eye – and for which chemotherapy is less effective. The treatment and choice of drugs differ for each of the main types of the disease. The slowly progressing chronic leukemias are less responsive to the currently available therapies than are the acute leukemias, although in nearly all cases modern therapy can effect remission. The next stage is to keep the patient in remission through a second level of treatment known as *consolidation therapy,* to be followed by *maintenance therapy,* which aims to destroy any remaining or undetected leukemic cells. Antibiotics are available to treat infections, to which the immunosuppressed patient has an increased susceptibility. Complete remission does not always mean cure because some residual leukemic cells may still be present and remain undetected even by means of microscopic examination and will multiply over a period of time. If leukemic cell growth recurs, treatment is restarted to achieve a second remission. Survival rates differ for each type of leukemia. The most encouraging results are achieved in children with acute lymphoblastic leukemia; over half of those diagnosed are now long-term survivors.

A further form of treatment in suitable cases is bone marrow transplantation. This new therapy involves high-dose chemotherapy and total body irradiation followed by an infusion of bone marrow from either a suitable donor (an *allogeneic* transplant) or from the patient's own marrow taken and stored during remission (an autograft transplant). Apart from suitable donor availability, a major complication at present is graft-versus-host disease resulting from the reaction of the infused marrow with the recipient and, in autologous transplant, the risk of residual disease still being present in the marrow. This form of therapy has been responsible for the control of the disease in cases where other means would not have been successful.

History and Geography

Leukemia was identified as a new disease in 1845 by two independent observers. John Hughes Bennett, lecturer in clinical medicine and pathologist to the Royal Infirmary at Edinburgh, published his observations in the *Edinburgh Medical Journal* of October 1845, a month before Rudolph Virchow published his findings under the title *Weisses Blut.* Two years later, Virchow named the disease *leukemia,* Greek for "white blood," and Bennett in 1851 called it *leucocythemia,* Greek for "white cell blood." Both men, who were keen observers and in the early stages of what were to become distinguished careers in medicine, made their observations at the autopsy table. However, it is unlikely that the disease was new in 1845, for there had been earlier reports of what was described as peculiar conditions of the blood, pus in the blood, and "milky" blood, with some symptoms compatible with those of leukemia. David Craigie in Edinburgh and Alexandre Donné in Paris, among others, were physicians who in the decade previously were alert to something odd in the condition of the blood of certain patients.

The microscope at that time was a crude instrument, and there was no satisfactory means of illuminating the specimens being observed. In fact, what is remarkable is that the disease was recognized at all, when one considers its rarity, on the one hand, and the continual epidemics of infectious diseases as well as chronic ailments of the last century which occupied the medical profession, on the other. But after recognition, reports of suspected or actual cases of leukemia began to appear in the literature, slowly revealing its worldwide distribution. Case reports from Europe and America also indicated the ineffectual nature of any known therapy.

Two breakthroughs occurred in the last half of the nineteenth century. The first was the discovery by Ernst Neumann in 1868 of the importance of the bone marrow in the formation of blood; a year later, he published his report on the changes in the bone marrow in leukemia, which introduced the term *myelogenous leukemia.* The second came in 1877, when Paul Ehrlich, a medical student at the time, developed a stain that permitted the cells to be clearly defined. By then, the microscope had been improved, and the new technique of staining enabled features of the blood to be studied that had hitherto been unseen or unsuspected.

Thus began a new era in hematology, but it was to be nearly 70 years before any progress was to be made in the treatment of leukemia. This began with the realization that folic acid was important to blood cell formation, and that its lack caused anemia and, significantly, a decrease in the white cells. Ensuing experiments showed that some preparations containing folic acid inhibited growth of experimental tumors, whereas other observations indicated that it might stimulate the growth of leukemic cells. This led a group of researchers in the United States to develop a series of new drugs that were designed as antagonists of folic acid for trial in the treatment of human cancers. Aminopterin was one of these new drugs and was used with much success in the treatment of acute leukemia by Sidney Farber and his group at Boston Children's Hospital in the late 1940s. Much research followed in a quest for new and more successful drugs to combat leukemia, with the result that by the late 1980s there was an established armamentarium of drugs used mostly in combination to achieve a remission and to maintain it.

Leukemia is a disease of major interest in both hematology and cancer research where much progress has been and is still being made, measured in terms of patient survival. Moreover, the outstanding "problem areas" of research are now more clearly defined and recognized, and current research efforts (in both pure and applied settings) within the fields of cell and molecular biology, immunology, cytogenetics, and virology are directed toward investigating such problems as the following:

1. Application of molecular mechanisms in therapy to destroy leukemic cells
2. Role of viruses in influencing the development of the disease
3. Nature of environmental triggers of leukemia
4. How to achieve earlier recognition of leukemia
5. How to understand the scientific basis for remission and thus how it can be maintained
6. How to eliminate residual disease

It is hoped that improved therapy for both adult and childhood cases will result from these complex and concentrated research efforts and that survival rates will be increased even more. Virchow wrote the following in 1858: "I do not wish by any means to infer that the disease in question [leukemia] is absolutely incurable; I hope on the contrary that for it too remedies will at length be discovered." Today there is optimism that Virchow's hope will be realized.

Gordon J. Piller

Bibliography

Ackerknecht, E. H. 1953. *Rudolf Virchow: Doctor, statesman, anthropologist.* Madison, Wis.
Bennett, J. H. 1845. Case of hypertrophy of the spleen and liver in which death took place from suppuration of the blood. *Edinburgh Medical Journal* 64: 413–23.
International Agency for Research on Cancer. 1982. *Cancer incidence in five continents,* Vol. IV. Lyons.
Doll, R. 1966. The incidence of leukaemia and the significance of environmental factors. In *Lectures on Haematology,* ed. F. G. J. Hayhoe, 138–51. Cambridge.
Garrison, F. H., and L. T. Morton. 1970. *A medical bibliography.* 3d edition. London.
Gunz, F. W. 1974. Genetics of human leukaemia. *Series Haematologica* 7: 164–91.
Hoffbrand, A. V., and J. E. Pettit. 1985. *Essential haematology.* Oxford.
Leukaemia Research Fund of Britain. Various publications.
Leukemia Society of America. Various publications.
Linet, M. 1985. *The leukaemias: Epidemiological aspects.* New York.
Metcalf, D. 1989. Haemopoietic growth factors (1) & (11). *Lancet* i: 825–7, 885–6.
Osler, W. 1914. *The principles and practice of medicine,* 8th edition. Oxford.
U.S. Department of Health and Human Services. National Cancer Institute. 1985. *Research report – Leukemia.* Washington, D.C.
Virchow, R. 1858. *Cellular pathology.* New York.
Wintrobe, M. M. 1980. *Blood pure and eloquent.* New York.

VIII.83
Lupus Erythematosus

Lupus erythematosus (LE) is a clinical syndrome that has multiple, but largely unknown causes. It exhibits an extremely broad spectrum of symptoms, and it can range in severity from being potentially fatal within a few weeks to eliciting minor indolent symptoms which, prior to immunologic testing, are virtually undiagnosable. When limited to the skin, it is called *discoid lupus erythematosus* (DLE); when the viscera are symptomatically affected, it is termed *systemic lupus erythematosus* (SLE). The inciting causes activate immunologic mechanisms that mediate the pathological, predominantly inflammatory, tissue responses.

History
Medical use of the term *lupus* has been traced to the fifteenth century, when it designated a variety of cancer. The term was reintroduced by London physician Robert Willan in 1808 to designate cutaneous tuberculosis, particularly when it affected the face. Cutaneous tuberculosis eventually received the synonym *lupus vulgaris.* In 1851 P. L. Alphée Cazenave of Paris used the term *lupus erythemateaux* to describe the condition that came to be called discoid lupus erythematosus (DLE) by Vienna's Moriz Kaposi in 1872 (Jarcho 1957). During 1866–70,

Kaposi diagnosed this disease in 22 patients and concluded that it was more common and more severe in women. All 3 deaths occurred among his 15 female patients. Although one of these had pulmonary tuberculosis, and cutaneous tuberculosis was common, Kaposi believed that DLE is not related to tuberculosis. Such a causal relationship, however, came to be advocated, particularly by French dermatologists, and remained under discussion until the 1930s. During the 5 years in which Kaposi saw 22 cases of DLE, 279 cases of lupus vulgaris were seen in the same department (Kaposi 1872). One generation later, among 30,000 dermatologic patients seen in Manchester, England, between 1893 and 1913, a diagnosis of DLE was made in 142 instances (0.47 percent), and lupus vulgaris in 1.5 percent. Of the DLE cases, 66 percent were female, ranging in age from 15 to 63 years, whereas males ranged in age from 8 to 66 years.

Kaposi (1872) used the term *disseminated lupus erythematosus,* but referred thereby to cases with widespread skin lesions rather than visceral involvement. Nevertheless, he described some cases having fever, pleuropneumonia, arthralgia, and arthritis. Recognition developed slowly that various visceral manifestations are attributes of the systemic disease rather than coincidences. From 1894 to 1903, William Osler saw 29 patients (17 aged 3–15 years; 12 aged 18–57 years), who had an "erythema with visceral lesions." He is credited with having provided the first clear descriptions of *systemic lupus erythematosus* (SLE) although, by modern criteria, the diagnosis that resulted from those descriptions does not fit all of the cases.

Osler (1904) added involvement of the kidneys and central nervous system to the description of Kaposi, whereas Alfred Kraus and Carl Bohac (1908–9) recognized that pneumonia belongs to the syndrome. Before the 1940s, most publications on lupus erythematosus were written by dermatologists, and consequently, skin lesions were considered essential to satisfy the diagnosis. Emanual Libman and Benjamin Sacks (1923) described four cases of noninfectious endocarditis (heart inflammation) of which three had the skin lesions of LE. A review of 11 cases of Libman–Sacks endocarditis in 1932 found that 5 lacked the skin eruption. George Belote and H. S. Ratner (1936) concluded that this form of heart disease nevertheless is a manifestation of SLE. Leukopenia and sensitivity to sunlight were convincingly related to SLE in 1939, but it was only in the 1940s that it became accepted that a skin eruption is not a necessary component of

SLE. Recent data indicate that even with the current longer life expectancy of SLE patients, only about 40 percent ever have the "butterfly" facial rash, and that an eruption occurs somewhere on the body in about 75 percent of the cases. The concept that DLE and SLE are manifestations of the same disease was first proposed by Harry Keil in 1937, but two decades passed before the concept became generally accepted.

SLE was perceived to be rare and uniformly fatal because only the most severe cases identified by their rash were being diagnosed. For example, at the University Hospital in Prague there were just eight cases from 1897 to 1908. At the Johns Hopkins Hospital, only three cases were diagnosed between 1919 and 1923. In fact among 7,500 autopsies of cases above 13 years of age reviewed at the same hospital in 1936, there were just five instances of SLE. Five cases were diagnosed at the Mayo Clinic between 1918 and 1921 (Goeckerman 1923), but, as the disease became more familiar, 132 cases were recognized during the decade 1938 to 1947 (Montgomery and McCreight 1949).

In 1948, Malcolm Hargraves, a hematologist at the Mayo Clinic, reported a discovery, which he said "has been called an L.E. cell in our laboratory because of its frequent appearance in the bone marrow in cases of acute disseminated L.E." (Hargraves 1969). In the next 4 years, numerous modifications of Hargrave's procedure were devised in various laboratories to make demonstration of the LE cell easier and more reliable.

In 1954 it was discovered that the formation of LE cells results from a reaction between a factor in the serum and leukocyte nuclei. This led in 1957 to the development of a quantifiable test of this antigen–antibody reaction. The determination of antinuclear antibodies (ANA) has gradually replaced the LE cell as the principal diagnostic test for SLE. These tests have greatly increased case finding and thereby have led to the recognition that SLE exhibits a broad range of severity. Nevertheless, the ANA test may cause confusion because many circumstances induce ANA reactions, at least in low titer. In North America and Europe, "false positive" reactions are most often due either to a drug or to another connective tissue disease, whereas in tropical Africa they have been related to endemic malaria.

The next advance was the standardization of criteria for the diagnosis of SLE. For this purpose, a committee of American rheumatologists in 1971 published a battery of clinical and laboratory findings of which a specified number had to be present for the diagnosis to be probable. This schema was well received, and a modification prepared in 1982 has been adopted in many countries (Tan et al. 1982).

Drug-Induced SLE

A syndrome that was indistinguishable from SLE was recognized at the Cleveland Clinic in 1954 in patients who were taking the antihypertensive drug hydralazine. Since then, many drugs have been suspected or have been proven potentially to have such an effect. By far the most consistent SLE-inducing agent is procainamide; this drug, used to treat cardiac arrhythmias, was first reported to induce SLE in 1962. After 6 months of therapy, ANA develop in at least half of these cases; and after 1 year, a quarter of the cases may exhibit symptoms of SLE. In patient populations in which potentially lupus-inducing drugs, such as procainamide, hydralazine, phenytoin, and isoniazid are widely used, about 10 percent of the cases of SLE are drug-induced (Lee, Rivero, and Siegel 1966). Drug-induced SLE is relatively benign. The female preponderance is diminished and its most frequent symptoms are pleurisy and arthralgia. Fever, leukopenia, and skin lesions occur about half as frequently as in idiopathic SLE; renal involvement and pericarditis are rare, and central nervous system involvement does not occur. Only the development of ANA warrants close observation. If it is possible to discontinue the inciting drug after symptoms have developed, those symptoms will disappear within several weeks.

Treatment and Mortality

In the 1940s it was generally acknowledged that there was no effective treatment for either DLE or SLE. The initial breakthrough occurred in 1949, with the discovery that the *corticosteroids* cortisone and corticotropin can exert a dramatic suppression of most symptoms of SLE. Prednisone, a synthetic derivative of cortisone, was introduced in 1955 and has become the most commonly used orally administered corticosteroid (Urman and Rothfield 1977). Only the cutaneous and renal manifestations are frequently refractory. In 1951, quinacrine, an antimalarial drug, was found to be effective against DLE. Soon thereafter, the *antimalarials* chloroquine and hydroxychloroquine were found similarly useful, and the latter is now principally employed. In SLE the antimalarials are also most effective against the rash, but they may also ameliorate some visceral symptoms. The third major therapeutic category is the *immunosuppressive drugs*. The first to be tried was nitrogen mustard, in 1950. Now the most commonly used drugs in this category are azathioprine and cyclophosphamide (Wagner 1976). This type of treatment is reserved for severe renal involvement and refractoriness to corticosteroid therapy.

Modern therapy has not only improved the quality of life of the SLE patient but has also greatly prolonged his or her survival. Before the advent of corticosteroids, one-half of these patients died within 2 to 3 years of being diagnosed. Now the mean survival of 15 years after diagnosis has reached 75 percent. Two factors in addition to the therapeutic agents cited above help to account for this improvement: (1) better antibiotic therapy for potentially fatal bacterial infections; and (2) recognition of much milder cases for which a more benign course is likely even with minimal therapy.

Mortality is influenced by race and sex. According to U.S. data for 1968 to 1976, the annual mortality rate, relative to 1.0 for white males, was 1.6 for black males; 3.7 for white females; and 10.5 for black females (Gordon, Stolley, and Schinar 1981).

Epidemiology, Distribution, and Incidence

Reviews of the proportion of cases of DLE in the clientele of dermatology clinics began to be reported at the beginning of this century. An incidence of between 0.25 percent and 0.75 percent has been consistently found in various parts of the world (Gahan 1942). The early belief that the disease is rare in the tropics and among black populations has been disproved in Africa and in the United States (Rothfield et al. 1963; Findlay and Lups 1967).

The only epidemiological conclusion about SLE reached until the 1950s was that the disease occurs predominantly in young women. In 1952 an ethnic predisposition was postulated, based on the observation of the often deleterious effect of sun exposure: Redheaded, freckled persons with an inability to tan were deemed most susceptible (Brunsting 1952). This conclusion was contradicted, however, by M. Siegel and his colleagues (1964), whose epidemiological data indicated that SLE is actually more common among blacks. Studies in San Francisco (Fessel 1974) and Baltimore (Hochberg 1987) substantiated this increased susceptibility of blacks, particularly among black women. National data from Veterans Administration hospitals have confirmed the racial difference among men as well (Siegel and Lee 1973). Unlike infectious diseases such as rheumatic fever or tuberculosis, the occurrence of SLE appears not to be related to socioeconomic factors. In terms of total population, the annual incidence of SLE in the United States has been estimated at about 5 per 100,000, with black females about three times more susceptible and black males two times more susceptible than their white counterparts. The mean age of onset is 28 to 30 years, but the preponderance of female patients varies with age. *About twice as many females as males suffer from the disease during the first decade of life and from the seventh decade on.* But between ages 20 and 40, there are 8 female patients for every male.

The prevalence, sex ratio, and mortality rates for SLE in northern Europe resemble those of U.S. white populations (Helve 1985; Hochberg 1987). In other parts of the world, as recognition of the disease has increased, more cases are being diagnosed. For example, SLE was rarely diagnosed in India before 1970, but from 1974 to 1985, 181 cases were seen in one hospital in New Delhi (Malaviya et al. 1987). Studies in Hawaii (Serdula and Rhoads 1979) and Malaysia (Frank 1980) indicate greater susceptibility of Chinese than other ethnic groups, and the death rate due to SLE for Oriental women in the United States (nearly three times that of white women) is similar to that of black women (Kaslow 1982). The prevalence of SLE among Polynesians also exceeds that of Caucasians (Serdula and Rhoads 1979; Hart, Grigor, and Caughey 1983).

In the predominantly black population of Jamaica, SLE constitutes a remarkably large proportion of treated rheumatic diseases. Indeed, 22 percent of all outpatients and 37 percent of inpatients with rheumatic disease suffer from SLE (Wilson and Hughes 1979). In view of the prevalence of SLE among nonwhite populations elsewhere, the apparent rarity of the disease among African blacks has been perplexing. The first case was reported from Senegal in 1960. Between 1967 and 1978, only 21 cases were recorded in Kampala, Uganda. A 5-year prospective analysis of cases of polyarthritis in Zimbabwe reported in 1969 found no case of SLE, whereas another study during 1979–84 discovered 31 cases (30 female, ages 13 to 46 years) (Taylor and Stein 1986). The possibility of differences in susceptibility of various African ethnic groups must be considered. During 1960–72, for example, 130 cases of SLE were admitted to two hospitals in Cape Town, South Africa. These included 86 "coloureds" (mainly Indian), 36 whites, and only 8 "Bantu." In terms of each 1,000 female admissions, this meant a rate of 4.9 "coloured," 3.8 "Bantu," and 2.3 white (Jessop and Meyers 1973). The data from much of the world remain inadequate to draw firm conclusions about ethnic and other possible variables related to SLE.

Thomas G. Benedek

Bibliography

Beck, J. S. 1969. Antinuclear antibodies: Methods of detection and significance. *Mayo Clinic Proceedings* 44: 600–19.

Belote, G. H., and H. S. Ratner. 1936. The so-called Libman–Sacks syndrome: Its relation to dermatology. *Archives of Dermatology and Syphilology* 33: 642–64.

Brunsting, L. A. 1952. Disseminated (systemic) lupus erythematosus. *Proceedings of the Staff of the Mayo Clinic* 27: 410–12.

Fessel, W. J. 1974. Systemic lupus erythematosus in the community. Incidence, prevalence, outcome and first symptoms; the high prevalence in black women. *Archives of Internal Medicine* 134: 1027–35.

Findlay, G. H., and J. G. Lups. 1967. The incidence and pathogenesis of chronic discoid lupus erythematosus: An analysis of 191 consecutive cases from the Transvaal. *South African Medical Journal* 41: 694–8.

Frank, A. O. 1980. Apparent predisposition to systemic lupus erythematosus in Chinese patients in West Malaysia. *Annals of the Rheumatic Diseases* 39: 266–9.

Gahan, E. 1942. Geographic distribution of lupus erythematosus. *Archives of Dermatology and Syphilology* 45: 1133–7.

Goeckerman, W. H. 1923. Lupus erythematosus as a systemic disease. *Journal of the American Medical Association* 80: 542–7.

Gordon, M. F., P. D. Stolley, and R. Schinar. 1981. Trends in recent systemic lupus erythematosus mortality rates. *Arthritis and Rheumatism* 24: 762–76.

Greenwood, B. M., E. M. Herrick, and E. J. Holbrow. 1970. Speckled antinuclear factor in African sera. *Clinical and Experimental Immunology* 7: 75–83.

Hargraves, M. M. 1969. Discovery of the LE cell and its morphology. *Mayo Clinic Proceedings* 44: 579–99.

Hart, H. H., R. R. Grigor, and D. E. Caughey. 1983. Ethnic difference in the prevalence of systemic lupus erythematosus. *Annals of the Rheumatic Diseases* 42: 529–32.

Helve, T. 1985. Prevalence and mortality rates of systemic lupus erythematosus and causes of death in SLE patients in Finland. *Scandinavian Journal of Rheumatology* 14: 43–6.

Hench, P. S., et al. 1950. Effects of cortisone acetate and pituitary ACTH on rheumatoid arthritis, rheumatic fever and certain other conditions. *Archives of Internal Medicine* 85: 545–666.

Hochberg, M. C. 1985. The incidence of systemic lupus erythematosus in Baltimore, Maryland, 1970–1977. *Arthritis and Rheumatism* 28: 80–6.

1987. Mortality from systemic lupus erythematosus in England and Wales, 1974–1983. *British Journal of Rheumatism* 26: 437–41.

Jarcho, S. 1957. Notes on the early modern history of lupus erythematosus. *Journal of the Mount Sinai Hospital* 24: 939–44.

Jessop S., and O. L. Meyers. 1973. Systemic lupus erythematosus. *South African Medical Journal* 47: 222–5.

Kaposi, M. 1872. Neue Beiträge zur Kenntniss des Lupus erythematosus. *Archiv für Dermatologie und Syphilis* 4: 18–41.

Kaslow, R. A. 1982. High rate of death caused by systemic lupus erythematosus among U.S. residents of Asian descent. *Arthritis and Rheumatism* 2: 414–18.

Keil, H. 1937. Conception of lupus erythematosus and variants. *Archives of Dermatology and Syphilology* 36: 729–57.

Kraus, A., and C. Bohac. 1908. Bericht über acht Fälle von Lupus erythematodes acutus. *Archiv für Dermatologie und Syphilis* 43: 117–56.

Lee, S. L., I. Rivero, and M. Siegel. 1966. Activation of systemic lupus erythematosus by drugs. *Archives of Internal Medicine* 117: 620–6.

Libman, E., and B. Sacks. 1924. A hitherto undescribed form of valvular and mural endocarditis. *Transactions of the Association of American Physicians* 38: 46–61.

MacLeod, J. M. 1913. Discussion on the nature, varieties, causes and treatment of lupus erythematosus. *British Medical Journal* 2: 313–19.

Malaviya, A. N., et al. 1987. Systemic connective tissue diseases in India – IX. Survival in systemic lupus erythematosus. *Journal of the Association of Physicians of India* 36: 509–11.

Montgomery, H., and W. G. McCreight. 1949. Disseminated lupus erythematosus. *Archives of Dermatology and Syphilology* 60: 356–72.

Osler, W. 1904. On the visceral manifestations of the erythema group of skin diseases. *American Journal of the Medical Sciences* 127: 1–23, 751–4.

Page, F. 1951. Treatment of lupus erythematosus with mepacrine. *Lancet* 2: 755–8.

Rose, E., and D. M. Pillsbury. 1939. Acute disseminated lupus erythematosus – a systemic disease. *Annals of Internal Medicine* 12: 951–63.

Rothfield, N. F., et al. 1963. Chronic discoid lupus erythematosus: A study of 65 patients and 65 controls. *New England Journal of Medicine* 269: 1155–61.

Serdula, M. K., and G. G. Rhoads. 1979. Frequency of systemic lupus erythematosus in different ethnic groups in Hawaii. *Arthritis and Rheumatism* 22: 328–33.

Siegel, M., and S. L. Lee. 1973. The epidemiology of systemic erythematosus. *Seminars in Arthritis and Rheumatism* 3: 1–54.

Tan, E. M., et al. 1982. The 1982 revised criteria for the classification of systemic lupus erythematosus. *Arthritis and Rheumatism* 25: 1271–7.

Taylor, H. G., and C. M. Stein. 1986. Systemic lupus erythematosus. *Annals of the Rheumatic Diseases* 45: 645–8.

Urman, J. D., and N. F. Rothfield. 1977. Corticosteroid treatment in systemic lupus erythematosus: Survival studies. *Journal of the American Medical Association* 238: 2272–6.

Wagner, L. 1976. Immunosuppressive agents in lupus nephritis: A critical analysis. *Medicine* 55: 239–50.

Wilson, W. A., and G. R. Hughes. 1979. Rheumatic disease in Jamaica. *Annals of the Rheumatic Diseases* 38: 320–5.

VIII.84
Lyme Borreliosis (Lyme Disease)

Lyme borreliosis is a tick-borne spirochetal bacterial disease caused by *Borrelia burgdorferi*. Lyme borreliosis is a systemic illness with potential involvement of the skin, neurological, cardiac, and articular systems. It can mimic a variety of other diseases such as juvenile rheumatoid arthritis, multiple sclerosis, and syphilis.

Epidemiology

The disease is the most frequently diagnosed tick-transmitted illness in the United States. The three major geographic loci of Lyme disease in the United States are the Northeast and middle Atlantic coastal regions, the upper Midwest, and the Pacific Northwest. The disease is found in Europe, Australia, the former U.S.S.R., China, Japan, and several African countries. The vector of Lyme disease is the tick, *Ixodes dammini*, or related *Ixodes* ticks such as *pacificus, scapularis,* or *ricinus. B. burgdorferi* has been found in other ticks such as the *Dermacentor variabilis, Amblyomma americanum,* and *Haemaphysalis leporispalustris;* however, transmission has not been proved.

B. burgdorferi has been found in horseflies, deerflies, and mosquitoes, but proof that these insects are possible secondary vectors has not been established. The reservoirs of *B. burgdorferi* occur in animals parasitized by infected ticks. The *Ixodes* tick is a three-host tick with a life cycle of 2 years. Adult ticks mate and feed primarily on deer in late fall; the female deposits eggs on the ground, which produce larvae that are active late the following summer. The tiny larvae obtain a blood meal from infected rodents such as white-footed mice, shrews, chipmunks, and squirrels, which are primary reservoirs for *B. burgdorferi*. Ground foraging birds are also important hosts for the larvae and nymphs. After a blood meal, the larvae molt to a nymphal form, which is active the following spring and early to midsummer. It seeks an animal host, obtains a blood meal, and molts to an adult stage to complete the 2-year life cycle. The animal hosts can include humans, dogs, deer, cows, horses, raccoons, cats, skunks, black bears, and Virginia opossums.

Each developmental stage of the tick requires feeding once and may take several days. *B. burgdorferi* is transmitted to the host during the blood meal. The longer the time of attachment of the infected tick to the host, the greater probability of transmission.

Etiology

The detection of *B. burgdorferi* in human tissue or body fluids is the most reliable technique to prove the cause of an infectious disease. In Lyme borreliosis, cultivation of the organism has been difficult, probably because of slow growth of *B. burgdorferi* and its low density in body tissues.

An alternative method to establish proof of infection by *B. burgdorferi* relies on the detection of its antibody. In early Lyme borreliosis, the immunoglobulin (Ig) M form of the antibody response appears first, peaks 3 to 6 weeks after exposure, and then declines. The IgG then becomes detectable and is present in late-stage disease states. However, antibodies are frequently not detectable in the early stages of the disease by current techniques. In the late stages of the disease, they are almost always positive. Other spirochetal diseases, such as yaws, pinta, or syphilis, may give false-positive results, but can be excluded by clinical evaluation.

Clinical Manifestations

Lyme borreliosis is a multisystem disease. Its primary target organs include the skin initially and later, potentially, the neurological, cardiac, and articular systems. Lyme borreliosis is categorized in three phases. Arbitrarily:

Stage I involves the dermatologic system and is diagnosed by the classic rash, erythema chronicum migrans (ECM).

Stage II involves the neurological or cardiac system months to years after exposure to the organism.

Stage III, involving the joints, also can occur months to years after the initial exposure.

These three stages may overlap and occasionally can present simultaneously. Moreover, any of these stages may occur in the absence of the others.

Erythema chronicum migrans (ECM) is pathognomonic for Stage I Lyme borreliosis. The average incubation period is 1 to 3 weeks (range: 3 days to 16 weeks). This rash is a diagnostic marker of the disease and begins as a small flat (macule) or swollen (papule) spot at the site of the tick bite and then expands to a very large (10 to 20 centimeters) oval or round lesion with a red to pink outer border and a very clear central area. Viable *B. burgdorferi* occasionally can be cultured in the advancing margins. Blood-borne spread of the spirochete may produce multiple, secondary lesions days to weeks later. The rash persists for a few days to weeks, and is usually unaccompanied by systemic symptoms, although occasionally fever, chills, and fatigue may occur. Because the rash can be asymptomatic or on areas of the body that may not be observed, many people may go undiagnosed. More than 20 percent of adults who have Lyme borreliosis will not remember having the rash, and the percentage is much higher in children.

Stage II of Lyme borreliosis may involve the neurological system. Of patients, 10 to 15 percent may have this involvement and present with a meningitis-type picture or have cranial nerve palsies. The most commonly involved cranial nerve is the seventh (facial) nerve, which results in an inability to control properly the facial musculature. In individuals with meningeal irritation, episodic headaches, neck pain, and stiffness may occur. Cerebrospinal fluid analysis frequently shows a predominance of mononuclear white blood cells. Occasional patients with stroke syndromes including hemiparesis as well as cases mimicking multiple sclerosis or encephalitis have been reported. Individuals may have associated confusion, agitation and disorientation, and memory loss. The symptoms and signs may wax and wane over weeks and months.

Heart involvement is rare as part of Stage II manifestations of Lyme borreliosis. Cardiac manifestations are commonly detected only as first-degree heart block on electrocardiographic tracings, although some patients can have a more serious second- or third-degree heart block and present with episodic fainting spells. Both the neurological and cardiac manifestations may occur within weeks to months or even longer after infection with the *B. burgdorferi* organism, and they can occur without any antecedent rash.

The most common late manifestation of Lyme borreliosis is arthritis. It usually occurs several months after the tick bite, but the range is 1 week to over 10 years after exposure. It is usually an oligoarticular form of arthritis (fewer than four joints) involving the large joints such as the knee or ankle. The attacks may last from a few days to several months. Some individuals will have recurrence with variable periods of remission between attacks. The intensity of articular involvement is variable, because some patients complain only of aches (*arthralgias*), whereas others demonstrate joint swelling (*arthritis*). In children the symptoms and signs of Stage III Lyme borreliosis can mimic juvenile rheumatoid arthritis. Antibody testing to *B. burgdorferi* can provide valuable clues to diagnosis of Lyme borreliosis in those individuals who present with Stage II or III without antecedent history of ECM or tick bite exposure.

B. burgdorferi infection can be spread transplacentally in humans. Infections during pregnancy can result in spontaneous abortion, premature delivery, low birth weight, and congenital malformation. These complications are similar to those caused by the spirochete *Treponema pallidum,* the causative agent of syphilis.

Lyme borreliosis is treated with antibiotics. The best results are achieved with prompt administration of oral antibiotics at the time of initial infection (Stage I). The duration of the rash and associated symptoms is abbreviated by a 3-week course of oral tetracycline, penicillin, or erythromycin therapy. In Stage III Lyme borreliosis, 3 weeks of parenteral penicillin or ceftriaxone are the drugs of choice. The earlier antibiotics are instituted, the more likely a cure may be achieved. A delay in starting antibiotics may result in lifelong, intermittent or even chronic, residual symptoms from the disease.

History

In 1909, in Stockholm, Swedish dermatologist Arvid Afzelius (1910) described a rash (which he labeled *erythema migrans*) on a female patient following a bite from an *Ixodes* tick. In 1913 an Austrian physician described a similar lesion on a patient and labeled it *erythema chronicum migrans* (ECM). Recognition that ECM was associated with systemic symptoms occurred in France in 1922. Investigators described patients with tick bites who developed subsequent erythema migrans and lymphocytic meningoradiculitis (nervous system involvement). In 1934 a German dentist described six patients with erythema migrans and associated joint symptoms. And in 1951 beneficial effects of penicillin in the treatment of a patient with ECM and meningitis suggested a bacterial etiology.

In the United States the first documented case of ECM occurred in a grouse hunter in Wisconsin in 1969. In 1975, two homemakers reported to the Connecticut State Health Department that several children living close together in Lyme, Connecticut, had developed arthritis. A following investigation by Al-

len C. Steere revealed an associated rash (ECM) in 25 percent of patients. He named the syndrome Lyme disease in honor of the town in which it was first observed.

In 1977 it was observed that an *I. dammini* tick bite preceded the ECM rash on a human subject. Willy Burgdorfer and his colleagues (1982) isolated a spirochete from the midgut of the *I. dammini* tick; this spirochete was subsequently named *Borrelia burgdorferi.* The following year, Steere isolated the spirochete from blood, skin, and spinal fluid from patients with the Lyme disease syndrome and concluded that it was the causative agent. Also, in 1983 in West Germany, H. W. Pfister and his colleagues (1984) concluded that *B. burgdorferi* isolated in spinal fluid from a patient with lymphocytic meningoradiculitis (Bannwarth's syndrome) was causative, and they implied that the original description of 13 patients provided by A. Bannwarth (1941) may have been due to the same organism. Dermatologist Klaus Weber and his colleagues (1984), working in West Germany, noted an elevation of IgG antibodies in the blood of patients with the skin lesion *acrodermatitis chronica atrophicans* (ACA). ACA is an uncommon late dermatologic manifestation of Lyme borreliosis. The first description of ACA was given by the German physician Alfred Buchwald (1883), and may have been the first reported case of Lyme borreliosis.

Robert D. Leff

Bibliography

Afzelius, A. 1910. Verhandlungen der dermatologischen Gesellschaft zu Stockholm on October 28, 1909. *Archives of Dermatology and Syphilis* 101: 404.

Anderson, John. 1988. Mammalian and avian reservoirs of *Borrelia burgdorferi*. In *Lyme disease and related disorders,* ed. Jorge Benach and Edward Bosler, 180–91. New York.

Bannwarth, A. 1941. Chronische lymphozytare Meningitis, entzündliche Polyneuritis und "Rheumatismus." *Archive von Psychiatry und Nervenkrankheit* 113: 284–376.

Buchwald, A. 1883. Ein Fall von diffuser idiopathischer Hautatrophie. *Archives of Dermatology and Syphilis* 10: 553–6.

Burgdorfer, Willy, et al. 1982. Lyme disease – a tick-borne spirochetosis. *Science* 216: 1B, 1317–19.

Craft, Joseph E., and Allen C. Steere. 1986. Lyme disease. In *New frontiers in pediatric rheumatology,* Proceedings of a symposium held on June 2, 1985 at the College of Physicians and Surgeons of Columbia University, New York, 38–42. New York.

Garin, Bujadoux C. 1922. Paralysie par les tiques. *Journal of Medicine Lyon* 71: 765–7.

Hellerstrom, S. 1930. Erythema chronicum migrans Af-
    zelii. *Acta Dermatology Venereology (Stockholm)* 11:
    315–21.

Johnson, Russell. 1988. Lyme borreliosis: A disease that
    has come into its own. *Laboratory Medicine:* 34–40.

Lipschütz, B. 1913. Ueber eine seltene erythemform
    (erythema chronicum migrans). *Archives Dermatol-
    ogy and Syphilis* 118: 349–56.

Magnarelli, Louis. 1986. The etiologic agent of Lyme dis-
    ease in deer flies, horse flies, and mosquitoes. *Journal
    of Infectious Diseases* 154(2): 355–8.

Markowitz, Lauri E., et al. 1986. Lyme disease during
    pregnancy. *Journal of the American Medical Associa-
    tion* 255(24): 3394–6.

Pfister, H. W., et al. 1984. The spirochetal etiology of
    lymphocytic meningoradiculitis of Bannwarth (Bann-
    warth's syndrome). *Journal of Neurology* 231: 141–4.

Stadelmann R. 1934. Ein Beitrag zum Krankheitsbild des
    Erythema chronicum migrans Lipschütz. Ph.D. disser-
    tation, Marburg.

Steere, Allen C., and Stephen E. Malawista. 1985. Lyme
    disease. In *Textbook of rheumatology,* Vol. 2, 2d edition,
    ed. William N. Kelley et al., 1557–63. Philadelphia.

Weber, Klaus, et al. 1984. European erythema migrans
    disease and related disorders. *Yale Journal of Biology
    and Medicine* 57: 463–71.

VIII.85
Malaria

Malaria is the disease resulting from infection by one
or more of four species of protozoan parasites of the
genus *Plasmodium*. These parasites are normally
transmitted from one human host to the next by the
bite of an infected female mosquito of the genus
Anopheles. Although malaria has receded from many
temperate regions in this century, the disease continues to be a major cause of morbidity and mortality in
many tropical and subtropical countries. Three of the
species – *Plasmodium vivax, Plasmodium falciparum,* and *Plasmodium malariae* – are widely distributed; the fourth, *Plasmodium ovale,* is principally a
parasite of tropical Africa. *P. vivax* (the agent of benign tertian malaria) and *P. falciparum* (causing malignant tertian malaria) are responsible for the great
majority of cases and deaths attributed to malaria
throughout the world.

Malaria is characteristically paroxysmal, and often periodic. The classical clinical episode begins
with chills, extends through a bout of fever, and ends
with sweating, subsiding fever, a sense of relief, and,
often, sleep. Between the early paroxysms the infected person may feel quite well; as the disease
progresses, however, the patient may be increasingly burdened by symptoms, even in the periods
between febrile paroxysms. Although infection by
any species may have serious, even fatal, consequences, *P. falciparum* infection is particularly dangerous because of complications associated with this
parasite.

The term *malaria,* from the Italian *mala* and *aria*
("bad air"), was certainly in use in Italy by the seventeenth century to refer to the cause of intermittent
fevers thought to result from exposure to marsh air
or miasma. Horace Walpole wrote home from Italy in
1740 about "[a] horrid thing called mal'aria, that
comes to Rome every summer and kills one." This is
said to be the first use of the term in English, and it
may well have been the first appearance of the word
in print (Russell et al. 1963). However, Walpole and
other writers of the eighteenth century, and later,
used the term to refer to the presumed cause rather
than the disease. It was only after the pathogenic
agents were identified at the end of the nineteenth
century that usage shifted so that the term "malaria" came to refer to the disease rather than the
agent.

Etiology

Protozoa assigned to the genus *Plasmodium* are
parasitic in many species of vertebrate animals including birds, reptiles, amphibians, and mammals.
Most Old and New World primate species serve as
hosts for plasmodia, and some of these parasites are
closely related to the species established in human
populations. It is generally accepted that the human
malaria parasites evolved in association with early
human beings, perhaps differentiating into the four
species recognized today in the mid-Pleistocene
(Garnham 1966; Bruce-Chwatt and Zulueta 1980).

All of the mammalian plasmodia have similar
two-phase life cycles: an asexual (*schizogonic*) phase
in the vertebrate host and a sexual (*sporogonic*)
phase in female *Anopheles* mosquitoes. These cycles
reflect ancient anopheline and vertebrate host–
parasite relationships that seem to date from at
least the Oligocene.

The sexual phase in the mosquito is initiated as
the female anopheline takes a blood meal from a
human or other vertebrate host. Parasites in ingested red blood cells are released as male and female gametes in the stomach of the mosquito. Fusion of the gametes produces a *zygote,* which, after

rapid development, migrates and encysts in the stomach wall. At maturity, after some 10 to 20 days, this oocyst releases thousands of *sporozoites,* motile forms that migrate to the salivary glands. When the now infective mosquito bites and probes for vertebrate blood, many of these sporozoites are likely to be injected into the new host in released saliva. The duration of the sexual or sporogonic phase of the cycle is controlled principally by environmental temperature and humidity. *P. vivax* requires a minimum temperature of 16°C; *P. falciparum,* at least 18°C. The duration of *P. vivax* sporogony is 9 to 16 days and that of *P. falciparum,* 12 to 24 days, when environmental temperatures range between 20° and 25°C (Bruce-Chwatt 1987).

Most of the sporozoites injected by the biting mosquito are phagocytosed, but some, traveling in the bloodstream, reach the liver, enter parenchymal cells, and (as tissue *schizonts*) proceed by nuclear division to form large numbers (10,000 to 20,000) of merozoites. Eventually, about 6 to 16 days after initial infection, the preerythrocytic schizont ruptures, releasing its *merozoites* into the bloodstream. Those merozoites that escape phagocytosis invade red blood cells and, as *trophozoites,* initiate the erythrocytic portion of the asexual phase. The trophozoite form breaks down the hemoglobin of the host erythrocyte, leaving hematin pigment as a digestive product. As it grows, the parasite (now called an erythrocytic schizont) divides, producing 8 to 24 merozoites, depending on the species. For the human malaria parasites, schizogony in the red cell lasts about 48 hours or, for *P. malariae,* about 72 hours. When the schizont reaches maturity, the erythrocyte bursts and the merozoites are released. Again some will be phagocytosed whereas others will invade uninfected red cells. Erythrocytic schizogony may then continue through repeated cycles with increasing synchronism, manifest as clinical periodicity. As a consequence, more and more red cells are parasitized and destroyed. Immune responses or therapeutic intervention can check the process short of profound anemia, complications, and death.

Following clinical recovery, *P. vivax* and its close relative *P. ovale* are capable of causing relapse, even after several years. Recrudescence of quartan malaria (*P. malariae* infection) may occur after many years, even 30 or more years after initial infection. *P. vivax* and *P. ovale* infections can persist because of the survival in the host liver of dormant stages capable of reinitiating erythrocytic schizogony. Recrudescent *P. malariae* infection appears to be due to longterm survival of erythrocytic-stage parasites.

P. falciparum parasites, on the other hand, are much more limited in time of survival; if the disease is left untreated and is not fatal, *P. falciparum* infection will terminate spontaneously without relapse, usually in less than a year. Instead of developing as trophozoites, small numbers of red cell merozoites differentiate as male and female forms (*gametocytes*). These circulate in erythrocytes and may eventually be ingested by a female *Anopheles* mosquito – to begin a new sexual phase of the life cycle.

Although malaria transmission normally follows the bite of the infected mosquito, several other routes have been recorded, including congenital transmission and direct transfer of parasites by blood transfusion or by contaminated needles shared by drug abusers. Before the advent of antibiotic therapy, malaria infections were also sometimes induced by injection for therapeutic purposes – for example, to produce high fevers in the treatment of late-stage syphilis.

Distribution and Incidence

Although the eradication campaigns of the 1950s and 1960s contributed to substantial declines in the incidence of malaria in many countries, and to the elimination of transmission in some, malaria persists as a major contributor to ill health in vast areas of the tropical and subtropical world. Reported cases of malaria are increasing from year to year, especially in areas of Asia and the Americas undergoing agricultural colonization with forest clearing and pioneering of unexploited lands. Eradication campaigns have given way to long-term control programs in most areas where the disease remains endemic, and in some countries control is now being linked to or integrated with systems of primary health care (Bruce-Chwatt 1987; Hilton 1987).

The present global situation has been categorized by David Clyde (1987) as follows:

1. Areas where malaria never existed or disappeared spontaneously (with a current population totaling some 1.3 billion)
2. Areas where control and eradication campaigns, in combination with other factors, have eliminated endemic malaria in recent years (population about 800 million)
3. Areas under continuing control, including most endemic countries of Asia and the Americas (population about 2.2 billion)
4. Areas with little or no organized control, mainly in Africa south of the Sahara (population about 400 million)

Table VIII.85.1. *Malaria in 1984*

Geographic areas	No. of cases reported to the World Health Organization	Population at risk (millions)	Estimated incidence per 1,000 population at risk
The Americas	914,000	179	11.8
Europe, including Turkey and former Soviet Union	60,000	47	2.1
Africa south of the Sahara	5,000,000[a]	385	202.6
North Africa and western Asia	305,000	166	5.4
Central and South Asia	2,711,000	844	10.5
Eastern Asia and Oceania	1,300,000	1,069	7.5
Total	10,290,000		

[a]Estimated; mainly clinical diagnoses.

Source: Adapted from World Health Organization data and Clyde (1987, tables 1 and 2).

Reported cases, and estimates for Africa south of the Sahara, are summarized in Table VIII.85.1 for 1984, together with incidence estimates. The total of some 10 million cases probably represents less than 10 percent of actual cases for that year because of reporting and surveillance deficiencies. Clyde (1987) believes that the infected population in 1984 may actually have exceeded 100 million in a population at risk of 2.6 billion. Malaria-related deaths are also poorly reported; David Hilton (1987) notes that worldwide estimates of deaths are still in the range of hundreds of thousands every year.

The Americas. The United States, Canada, and most countries of the Caribbean are essentially free of malaria transmission and report only small numbers of imported cases. Costa Rica, Panama, and several southern South American countries are also nearly free of local transmission. Haiti and the Dominican Republic report only *P. falciparum* cases, although in substantial numbers. *P. vivax* is the prevailing species in Mexico, Central America, and northern South America, although many *P. falciparum* cases are also reported, especially from Brazil, Colombia, and Ecuador.

Europe, Turkey, and the former Soviet Union. Malaria is no longer endemic in Europe and the Soviet Union, but Turkey still reports some autochthonous cases.

Africa south of the Sahara. About 90 percent of the population in this region is still at risk, and transmission is high in many areas, especially in rural West Africa (Spencer 1986). *P. falciparum* is the predominant species.

North Africa and western Asia. Only a few small foci of autochthonous transmission persist in this region.

Central and South Asia. Malaria remains endemic in most countries of the region. *P. vivax* is predominant, but *P. falciparum* is also important, and this species appears to be increasing in relative prevalence (Spencer 1986).

Eastern Asia and Oceania. The northeastern area of Asia, including Japan, is free of transmission, as are many of the smaller islands and island groups in Oceania. Endemic foci persist in some of the larger island areas (e.g., the Philippines, the Solomon Islands, Papua New Guinea, and Indonesia) and in most of mainland Southeast Asia and China. *P. vivax* prevails in China, where the incidence is steadily declining. In Thailand, which is also experiencing a decline in incidence, *P. falciparum* is somewhat more prevalent than *P. vivax*.

Epidemiology and Control

Malaria transmission in any locale depends upon the complex interactions of parasites; vector mosquitoes; physical, socioeconomic, and environmental factors; and human biology, demography, and behavior.

The four species of plasmodia differ in many biological characteristics. Each species, for example, has somewhat different environmental temperature requirements for sporogony; each is different in many features of its schizogonia cycle, and as a consequence, each has distinctive clinical manifestations. *P. falciparum* differs so much from the other three species (of the subgenus *Plasmodium*) that it has been assigned to its own subgenus, *Laverania* (Garnham 1966). Within each species, variation in strains is also important. Differences in strains influence sporogonic development in mosquitoes, virulence and thus the clinical course, and the development of resistance to antimalarial drugs.

The presence of anopheline mosquitoes capable of supporting sporogony is fundamental for natural malaria transmission. Although more than 400 species of *Anopheles* have been described, natural sporozoite infections have been found in only about 67 species, and only some 30 species are recognized as important vectors (Spencer 1986). Usually, in any endemic area, only one, two, or three vector species are responsible for most of the malaria transmission. Parasite species and strain differences affect anopheline receptivity to infection. Vector competence for transmission is also influenced by mosquito population densities, flight ranges, feeding and resting habits, blood meal preferences (anthropophilic for human blood; zoophilic for animal blood), blood meal frequencies, and the lifespan of the female anopheline. In recent decades, resistance to insecticides has also become a major vector-related determinant of transmission.

Vector, parasite, and host interactions are profoundly affected by factors in the environment. Physical factors, such as temperature, rainfall, and humidity, control mosquito survival and the duration of sporogony. Other factors such as latitude, altitude, and landscape characteristics (natural or human-modified) influence mosquito breeding, vector densities, and vector survival, as well as many kinds of human behavior. In addition, features of the social and economic environment contribute in many ways to patterns of transmission.

Age, gender, and a variety of human demographic variables, together with genetic factors, immune mechanisms, and health conditions (e.g., nutritional status, pregnancy, and concurrent infections), constitute the final host-related set of determinants in the malaria epidemiological complex that must be well understood before fully effective control can be instituted in any setting.

The incidence and prevalence of clinical cases may be useful measures for describing the status of malaria in an area, but parasite and spleen rates are even more helpful for determining the level of endemicity – spleen rates particularly, because enlarged spleens are indicative of past or recent active erythrocytic schizogony. The *spleen rate* is the proportion of persons, usually children 2 to 9 years old, with enlarged spleens at a particular time, whereas the *parasite rate* is the proportion of persons in a population with microscopically confirmed parasitemia at a particular time.

Malaria endemicity is classified on the basis of spleen or parasite rates:

1. *Hypoendemic malaria:* spleen or parasite rates up to 10 percent in 2- to 9-year-old children
2. *Mesoendemic malaria:* spleen or parasite rates of 11 to 50 percent in 2- to 9-year-olds
3. *Hyperendemic malaria:* spleen or parasite rates over 50 percent in 2- to 9-year-olds together with a high adult spleen rate
4. *Holoendemic malaria:* spleen or parasite rates over 75 percent in 2- to 9-year-olds with low adult spleen rates and high infant parasite rates

In a pioneering work, George Macdonald (1957) attempted to fit many of the variables noted above into an epidemiological model. His ideas continue to be influential in contemporary malariology despite many advances in epidemiological and mathematical modeling sophistication. Macdonald's principles in defining stable and unstable malaria, for example, continue to be helpful in studies of epidemiological patterns. Stable malaria is characteristically endemic, often hyper- or holoendemic. There is little seasonal change; transmission continues through most or all of the year; epidemics of malaria are very unlikely to occur; and most of the population, except infants, has some immunity as a result of experience with the disease. Control under these circumstances is likely to be very difficult. Malaria in much of tropical Africa south of the Sahara corresponds to Macdonald's stable extreme.

Unstable malaria may be endemic, but transmission varies from year to year and may be strictly seasonal, reflecting the strong seasonal change typical in unstable areas. Seasonal epidemics may occur, collective immunity varies and may be low, and children as well as infants may be nonimmune. Control is relatively easy, and indeed, many of the countries only recently freed from endemic malaria were in the unstable category.

Immunity

Acquired and innate immunity are important factors in the epidemiology of malaria. Innate resistance has been recognized in some human populations. In parts of Central and West Africa, many individuals lack the Duffy blood group antigens Fy[a] and Fy[b] and are thus resistant to *P. vivax* infection. Generally, in these areas, *P. ovale* replaces *P. vivax* as the prevailing cause of benign tertian malaria. In endemic *P. falciparum* areas of Africa, those individuals heterozygous for hemoglobin AS or sickle trait are more likely to survive malignant tertian malaria than are hemoglobin A homozygotes. The persistence of sickle-cell disease (in hemoglobin SS homozygotes), with its unfortunate consequences, is balanced by the substantial advantage conferred by the AS condition, but only as long as *P. falciparum* remains endemic in the area. Several other hemoglobin variants have been thought to provide some protection against *P. falciparum* infection; it is known that persistent hemoglobin F (fetal Hb) delays development of falciparum parasites (Bruce-Chwatt 1987). Another genetic condition, deficiency of the red blood cell enzyme glucose 6-phosphate dehydrogenase (G6PD), also provides a degree of protection against falciparum infection.

Acquired immunity in malaria is species-specific and also specific to stage, that is, to the sporozoite, to the asexual forms in the blood, or to the sexual stages (Clyde 1987). In endemic areas, newborns may be protected for a few months by maternal antibodies that have crossed the placenta. After this phase of protection, however, infants and toddlers are especially vulnerable; most of the severe illnesses and deaths due to malaria in endemic regions occur in these early years. Older children and adults gradually acquire immunity with repeated exposure to infection. This partial immunity (*premunition*) is sustained in the presence of low densities of parasites in the blood. In premune individuals the spleen may remain enlarged; hence the spleen rate may be relatively high in an adult population despite a low parasite rate. With prolonged exposure and infection, however, as in a holoendemic area, eventual spleen scarring and shrinkage leads to a low adult spleen rate. Attenuated malaria certainly contributes to impaired resistance to other diseases; thus improved malaria control in endemic areas generally results in declines in morbidity and mortality from all causes (Bruce-Chwatt 1987).

Clinical Manifestations and Pathology

The classical malaria paroxysm is initiated by a chill, lasting up to an hour and often accompanied by headache, nausea, and vomiting. The chill is followed by a period of spiking fever lasting several hours. The subsiding fever is accompanied by sweating, often profuse. The relieved patient may drift off to sleep, to awaken feeling relatively well. The early paroxysms may be asynchronous. As the clinical episode progresses, *P. malariae* paroxysms occur about every 72 hours (*quartan* periodicity), whereas those of the other three species occur with *tertian* (48-hour) periodicity. *P. falciparum* infection is less likely to become clearly synchronous, and the classic

clinical picture may never develop. Mixed infections of two or even three species may produce atypical and confusing clinical manifestations.

These clinical events are related to the behavior of the parasites in the bloodstream. The onset of chill reflects the escape of parasites and metabolic products from great numbers of ruptured red cells. By the end of the paroxysm, the parasites will have invaded new red cells to initiate another generation of erythrocytic schizogony. With each cycle of invasion, multiplication, and rupture, more red cells are destroyed. In the absence of treatment and immune defenses, severe anemia may develop, particularly in falciparum malaria. The spleen enlarges during the acute episode, in part because of its function in filtering out of the bloodstream the detritus resulting from red cell destruction. The liver may also increase in size.

Although malaria caused by the other three species may be fatal, most of the serious complications and deaths are caused by *P. falciparum*. This species can invade a high proportion of the total red cell mass, and the parasitized cells tend to agglutinate, occluding capillaries in almost any organ. These occlusions are considered to underlie cerebral, gastrointestinal, adrenal, and other complications in falciparum malaria. Cerebral malaria begins with headache and may progress to convulsions, delirium, and coma. Gastrointestinal complications resemble bacillary dysentery or cholera.

The initial uncomplicated and untreated episode of malaria usually lasts 2 to 4 weeks (about twice as long for *P. malariae*). Relapses commonly occur in untreated malaria. Drug-resistant strains of *P. falciparum* may also cause relapses after inadequate treatment.

Blackwater fever is a distinctive intravascular hemolytic disorder associated with longstanding and repeated falciparum malaria infection, especially in hyper- and holoendemic areas. The incidence of blackwater fever has fallen considerably in the second half of this century as malaria control has improved and as drug prophylaxis and treatment has expanded from an earlier dependence on quinine. Quinine is not an essential etiologic factor, but the onset of blackwater fever has often been noted to follow the administration of therapeutic doses of the drug. It is also known that the disorder rarely occurs in persons who have taken quinine regularly as a prophylactic. Blackwater fever is characterized by abrupt onset, chill, fever, jaundice, nausea, vomiting, and red or dark-brown urine containing hemoglobin. The case mortality rate, resulting principally from anuria and uremia, usually falls between 10 and 30 percent.

History and Geography

Since at least the mid-Pleistocene, many thousands of generations of humans have been parasitized by the plasmodia (Garnham 1966). Species very similar to the human plasmodia have also been described from gorillas and chimpanzees; indeed the relationships of the malaria parasites of humankind and the African apes are extremely close (Dunn 1966; Garnham 1966). It is therefore certain that human malaria is an Old World disease in its origins. There has, however, been some debate about the timing of malaria's appearance in the Western Hemisphere (McNeill 1976). Some have suggested that malaria was present in the New World long before the time of European contact, but a strong case can be made that the hemisphere was malaria-free until the end of the fifteenth century (Dunn 1965; McNeill 1976).

Malaria could have reached the New World before 1492 only as an infection of migrants from northeast Asia or by pre-Columbian sea-borne introductions. The possibility that humans brought malaria overland into North America from Siberia can almost certainly be discounted; conditions for malaria transmission were unsuitable in the far north during and after the Pleistocene, as they are today. It is equally unlikely that the Vikings could have introduced malaria in the centuries before Columbus. These voyagers came from regions of Europe and the North Atlantic (Greenland, Iceland) presumably free of malaria at that time, and they seem to have visited northeastern North American coasts that were north of any possible receptive anopheline mosquito populations. Similarly, any voyagers landing on American shores from the central or eastern Pacific could not have carried the parasites with them because islands in that region are free of anopheline vectors and thus of locally transmitted malaria. Voyagers reaching American coasts from eastern Asia (e.g., fishermen adrift from Japan) could conceivably have introduced malaria, but this possibility too is remote.

Moreover, and more to the point, colonial records indicate that malaria was almost certainly unknown to the indigenous peoples of the Americas. It is also evident that some areas that supported large pre-Columbian populations soon became dangerously malarious after European contact (McNeill 1976). The absence in aboriginal American populations of any of the blood genetic polymorphisms associated with malaria elsewhere in the world is another kind of evidence consistent with the conclusion that the Western Hemisphere remained free of the disease until contact (Dunn 1965).

In the first two centuries after 1492, malaria parasites must have been introduced many times from Europe and Africa. Anopheline vectors were at hand, species native to the Americas. Together with smallpox, measles, and other infectious diseases brought across the Atlantic from the Old World, malaria soon began to contribute to the depopulation of the indigenous peoples, especially those of the lowland American tropics (Borah and Cook 1963; Crosby 1973; McNeill 1976).

From its early, usually coastal, sites of introduction, malaria spread widely in North, Central, and South America, limited principally by altitude and latitude – that is, by factors controlling the distribution of vector mosquitoes. By the nineteenth century in North America, the disease was prevalent in much of the Mississippi Valley; seasonal transmission occurred even in the northernmost areas of the Mississippi basin (Ackerknecht 1945). Malaria transmission, unstable and seasonal, also extended into the northeastern United States, well north in California, and far to the south in South America. By the eighteenth and nineteenth centuries, malaria had also become established as a stable endemic disease in the American subtropics and tropics, including most of the islands of the Caribbean.

The Old World gave malaria to the New; the New World, however, provided the first effective remedy for the disease. It is recorded that a sample of cinchona bark, taken from a Peruvian tree as a medicinal, was carried to Europe in 1632 by a Spanish priest (Russell et al. 1963). The bark was soon discovered to provide relief from certain intermittent fevers. This therapeutic action allowed Richard Morton and Thomas Sydenham in England in 1666, and Francesco Torti in Italy in 1712, to begin the process of defining malaria as a clinical entity separable from other fevers, which failed to respond to cinchona (Russell et al. 1963). By the end of the seventeenth century, cinchona bark was an important export product from Peru, well established in the treatment of intermittent fevers.

The human malaria parasites have evolved in association with their evolving hosts and have followed the human species through most, but not all, of its dispersal in Africa, Asia, and Europe. Transmission, dependent on suitable anopheline mosquitoes, has always been limited by all those environmental conditions, influenced by latitude and altitude, that control vector breeding and survival.

The antiquity of the human–*Plasmodium* association in the Old World is symbolized, biologically, by the existence in modern populations of some of the blood genetic polymorphisms. Early texts – Chinese, Hindu, Chaldean, Greek – give us other evidence of this ancient association (Russell et al. 1963; McNeill 1976; Bruce-Chwatt and Zulueta 1980). Malaria was probably endemic in Greece by the fourth century, B.C.; Hippocrates described the types of periodicity of intermittent fevers – quotidian, tertian, quartan – and took note of the enlargement of spleens in those who lived in low, marshy districts. In Italy, too, the intermittent fevers were well known, for example, to Cicero, and well described by Celsus, Pliny the Elder, and Galen (Russell et al. 1963).

Malaria was certainly a disease of some importance in the centuries of Roman domination of Europe and the Mediterranean basin. However, in their review of malaria in early classical times, especially in relation to military operations, L. J. Bruce-Chwatt and J. de Zulueta (1980) reached the conclusion that malaria was much less destructive than it has been in recent centuries, primarily because *P. falciparum* was absent or rare and the other species were less intensely transmitted. The conclude that *P. falciparum* failed to spread in those centuries because *Anopheles atroparvus* was refractory as a vector for the falciparum strains then introduced from time to time by travelers. *A. atroparvus*, basically a zoophilic species, was also a poor vector for *P. malariae* and *P. vivax*. By late classical times, however, it appears that two other anopheline species, *Anopheles labranchiae* and *Anopheles sacharovi*, had been introduced and dispersed along the coasts of southern Europe from their North African and Asian origins. These anthropophilic species were much more effective as vectors for all three of the species of plasmodia. By the final centuries of the Roman Empire, malaria was a more lethal force and may have contributed to the social, political, and cultural decline that had set in.

After the fall of the Roman Empire, the history of malaria in Europe and the Mediterranean region is obscure for many centuries (Bruce-Chwatt and Zulueta 1980). With few exceptions medieval medical writers provide only sketchy and confusing accounts of cases and outbreaks that may have been due to malaria. During the Renaissance, the historical record is clearer and richer, but malaria appears not to have represented a major problem to society in those centuries. It is not until the seventeenth and eighteenth centuries that malaria became resurgent in Europe, not only in the south but, in periodic outbreaks, as far north as the Netherlands, Ger-

many, southern Scandinavia, Poland, and Russia (Bruce-Chwatt and Zulueta 1980).

Through all of these centuries the record of malaria's human impact in Asia and Africa is fragmentary. With the onset of European colonization, however, it soon became obvious that endemic malaria was a threat almost everywhere in the Old World tropics, especially to the colonizers (who were, of course, generally nonimmune upon arrival in the tropics). The beginnings of tropical medicine and modern malariology are entangled in this recognition (Dunn 1984).

The modern era in malariology began in the last two decades of the nineteenth century with the identification of the causal parasites and the recognition of the role of anopheline mosquitoes as vectors. These discoveries provided the rationale for new strategies in malaria control, developed during the first third of the twentieth century. Malaria control itself was not a new concept; nor was the control of mosquitoes a new idea at this time. Humankind had sought from ancient times to control biting mosquitoes as pests (Russell et al. 1963). The new rationale, however, provided for much more specific vector control, directed principally at those anophelines that proved to be important in transmission. Malaria control was further strengthened in the 1930s with the introduction of synthetic antimalarials, useful not only in treatment but also in prophylaxis. The 1940s brought further advances in chemotherapy together with the first of the residual insecticides, DDT.

By the late 1940s and early 1950s, the resources for treatment and control of malaria appeared to be sufficiently formidable to justify attempts at national eradication in a few countries (e.g., Venezuela, Italy, the United States). Early success in local or aerial eradication, based on residual spraying, together with concerns about the emergence of anopheline resistance to DDT and other insecticides, led to a decision in 1955 to commit the World Health Organization to malaria eradication. This commitment pushed many countries into supposedly time-limited eradication campaigns, often with considerable WHO financial and adivsory support. Some of these campaigns were successful, especially in countries with unstable malaria, but others faltered after dramatic initial reductions in incidence. By the end of the eradication era, in the early 1970s, some hundreds of millions of people were living in areas where campaigns had eliminated endemic malaria (Clyde 1987), but in many other areas malaria continued to prevail, forcing a return to long-term control strategies.

In 1980 the World Health Organization began to recommend that malaria control be coordinated with primary health care. The experiences, especially the difficulties, of the eradication years also made it imperative that modern malaria control be strongly supported by epidemiological field work with recognition of local variability in transmission patterns and of sociocultural, economic, and human behavioral influences on transmission and control (Bruce-Chwatt 1987). Malaria control and therapy continues to be complicated by mosquito resistance to insecticides and by parasite resistance to drugs. Vaccine development proceeds, although slowly. The problems posed by malaria persist, but they are not insoluble. Malaria will remain endemic in many countries in the twenty-first century, but the prospects are good for steady improvement in control.

Frederick L. Dunn

Bibliography

Ackerknecht, E. H. 1945. Malaria in the Upper Mississippi Valley, 1860–1900. *Bulletin of the History of Medicine,* Supplement No. 4.

Borah, Woodrow W., and Sherburne F. Cook. 1963. The aboriginal population of Central Mexico on the eve of the Spanish Conquest. *Ibero-Americana* No. 45.

Bruce-Chwatt, L. J. 1987. Malaria and its control: Present situation and future prospects. *Annual Review of Public Health* 8: 75–110.

Bruce-Chwatt, L. J., and J. de Zulueta. 1980. *The rise and fall of malaria in Europe: A historico-epidemiological study.* London.

Clyde, David F. 1987. Recent trends in the epidemiology and control of malaria. *Epidemiologic Reviews* 9: 219–43.

Crosby, Alfred W., Jr. 1973. *The Columbian exchange: Biological and cultural consequences of 1492.* Westport, Conn.

Dunn, Frederick L. 1965. On the antiquity of malaria in the Western Hemisphere. *Human Biology* 37: 385–93.

  1966. Patterns of parasitism in primates: Phylogenetic and ecological interpretations, with particular reference to the Hominoidea. *Folia Primatologica* 4: 329–45.

  1984. Social determinants in tropical disease. In *Tropical and geographical medicine,* ed. K. S. Warren and A. A. F. Mahmoud, 1086–96. New York.

Garnham, P. C. C. 1966. *Malaria parasites and other haemosporidia.* Oxford.

Hilton, David. 1987. Malaria: A new battle plan. *Contact* 95: 1–5.

Macdonald, George. 1957. *The epidemiology and control of malaria.* London.

McNeill, William H. 1976. *Plagues and peoples.* Garden City, N.Y.

Russell, P. F., et al. 1963. *Practical malariology,* 2d edition. London.

Spencer, Harrison C. 1986. Epidemiology of malaria. In *Clinics in tropical medicine and communicable diseases,* Vol. 1: *Malaria,* 1–28.

VIII.86
Marburg Virus Disease

History

In 1967, a disease outbreak occurred in a laboratory in Marburg, Germany, where the kidneys of cercopithecoid (Green African; vervet) monkeys were being taken out for preparation of cell cultures. Twenty-seven laboratory workers (including a worker in Yugoslavia) fell ill with a grave illness, and seven died. There were four secondary cases in total (including the wife of an infected laboratory worker in Yugoslavia secondarily infected by sexual intercourse), but none fatal. Early suspicions focused on yellow fever, but this was soon ruled out (Casals 1971). In due course, a virus was isolated and found to be quite distinct from any other known viruses. Electron micrographs revealed a virus with bizarre morphology of a type never seen before (Peters, Muller, and Slenckza 1971). Pictures taken resembled photographs of a bowl of spaghetti. The agent was named Marburg virus and the disease Marburg disease. Strict monkey quarantines were initiated. No further cases were seen in laboratory workers.

An intensive and extensive series of field studies were initiated in East Africa, which had been the monkeys' homeland (Henderson et al. 1971; Hennessen 1971; Kalter 1971). No virus recoveries were made from any of the monkeys examined. In later years, serologic studies involving humans and primates, and also rodents, have been carried out in many regions, as can be seen in Table VIII.86.1.

The first Marburg cases seen in Africa occurred in February of 1975. A young Australian couple touring in Rhodesia (Zimbabwe) became ill by the time they got to South Africa. They were admitted to a major hospital in Johannesburg where the young man died and the young lady recovered. A nurse tending them also sickened and recovered. After the disease was determined to be Marburg, a thorough epidemiological inquest was carried out all along the

Table VIII.86.1. *Serologic studies of Marburg virus in humans and other primates*

Study area	Date	No. examined	No. positive	Percent positive	Remarks
Humans					
Senegal: northern provinces	1977	159	0	0	
Central African Republic	1980	499	7	1.4	several regions
Liberia	1982	400+	4	1	several regions
Gabon	1982	253	0	0	
Kenya	1982	58	0	0	
Cameroons	1982	1517	15	1	several regions
Sudan: northern provinces	1979–82	231	0	0	very desert region
Sudan: central provinces	1979–82	240	0	0	savannah regions
Sudan: southern provinces	1979–82	176	1	0.6	agri and forest
Kenya	1983	741	0	0	several regions
Kenya	1983	1899	8	4.2	several regions
Liberia	1986	215	2	2	
Nigeria	1988	1677	29	1.1	several regions
Primates					
Kenya	1981	136	4	3	vervet monkeys
Kenya	1981	184	1	0.6	baboons
Gabon	1982	48	0	0	chimpanzees

route of passage of the victims, concentrating particular attention on every locale where they spent a night. Animal, insect, and human populations were sampled. No evidence of endemic disease was found (Gear et al. 1975).

On January 14, 1980, a 58-year-old man from western Kenya was seen in a Nairobi hospital. He died 6 hours after admission, and a physician who attended him also became ill but recovered. A Marburg virus was isolated from his blood (Centers for Disease Control 1980). Subsequent epidemiological investigations carried on in western Kenya produced a positive finding: Antibodies against the Marburg virus were found in two vervet monkeys from among many primates examined.

The latest episode involved a boy in Kenya in 1987 who became infected in a visit to a park in the western part of Kenya. The boy died. There were no secondary cases reported.

Etiology

Electron microscopic examination of blood, liver, and spleen of guinea pigs infected with materials from patients show a long, viruslike agent, quite unlike any virus particle ever before visualized. The particles vary in length, up to several microns. The width of the particles is also variable, with limits of 720 to 1100 Å (7,200 to 11,000 nanometers). There is an outer shell, an intermediate clear zone, and a nucleo-

capsid core of approximately 280 Å width (Peters et al. 1971). Marburg virus was shown (Casals 1971) to be unrelated to the many arboviruses against which it was tested, and most closely resembles the Ebola virus agent discovered in 1976. In fact, both Marburg and Ebola viruses have since been placed in a new family, Filoviridae (Kiley et al. 1982), which includes but the two members thus far.

It was discovered that the Marburg virus could be inactivated by gamma irradiation (Elliot, McCormick, and Johnson 1982); this finding made the preparation of inactivated diagnostic reagents possible. Cultivation of Marburg in cell culture has allowed observation of growth and multiplication taking place in a number of mammalian and avian cell types. A cytopathic effect on cells was observed in *Cercopithecus* kidney cell lines, and human amnion cell lines (Hoffmann and Kunz 1971).

Immunoglobulin responses have been studied (Wulff and Johnson 1979), measured by immunofluorescence. Immunoglobulin M antibodies appear in sera of patients infected with Marburg virus 4 to 7 days after onset of illness. Titers peak 1 to 2 weeks later, and by 1 to 2 months have decreased considerably. Antiviral IgG antibodies appear at the same time as or a little later than IgM antibodies and persist much longer (Wulff and Johnson 1979). In autopsy material, antigenic material is present in large amounts, and can be demonstrated as late as 3 hours after death by use of immunofluorescent techniques (Wulff, Slenczka, and Gear 1978).

Clinical Manifestations and Diagnosis

The incubation period following exposure varied from 5 to 7 days. In six cases for which data are available, death occurred between days 7 and 16. The onset was indicated by malaise, myalgia, and often prostration (Martini 1971). Vomiting frequently occurred by the third day, and conjunctivitis by the fourth, by which time the temperature had reached 40°C. A rash occurred on the fifth day, was macular in type, and progressed usually to a maculopapular rash that later coalesced into a more diffuse rash. In severe cases, a diffuse dark livid erythema developed on face, trunk, and extremities. An enanthem of the soft palate developed at the same time as the rash. Spleen and liver were not palpable. Lymph node enlargement was noted in the nuchal region and the axillae. A diarrhea appeared, often with blood in the stools. The South African cases differed only in that there were no enanthem and no lymph node enlargement.

The above description was declared by several clinicians to make diagnosis easy. This may be true when there is a clustering of cases, and epidemiologists are on the alert; however, in much of Africa, the occurrence of single cases, however severe, would not be likely to arouse suspicion. Moreover, during the first 5 to 6 days, the symptoms could be mistaken for those of many other diseases. Laboratory diagnosis is accomplished by means of immunofluorescence techniques, by electron microscopic examination of a serum sample from a patient, which has been centrifuged and placed on a grid (Wulff et al. 1978), and by inoculation of laboratory animals. None of these methods is readily accessible in the usual field situation; yet early diagnosis is imperative in order to abort a possible developing epidemic.

Mortality

Because descriptions of Marburg virus pathology are equally applicable to Ebola virus, some pathologists feel that the findings are not distinctive enough to permit a positive diagnosis of either on the basis of pathology alone, especially in regions where there are many causes of fever and death.

Guinea pigs and rhesus and vervet monkeys are susceptible to the virus. The infection is fatal for the monkeys and, often but not always, fatal for the guinea pigs. Guinea pigs that recover may have persistent virus in serum and urine for several weeks. The same has been observed for human beings.

Ebola virus infection is considerably more fatal in humans than is the Marburg virus. In the four secondary Marburg cases studied, it was clear that their clinical course was less severe than that seen in primary cases, and there was no mortality.

Treatment and Prophylaxis

No effective therapy has been found. In one case in a London treatment center, therapy was instituted using interferon in conjunction with immune plasma. The patient, a secondary exposure case, recovered. Further clinical trials on human beings await further cases.

Basic methods for the management of patients with suspected viral hemorrhagic fever include strict isolation and precaution in examination and in taking specimens from patients, as well as in handling material from suspect cases in the laboratory. Such procedures are not readily applicable in bush clinics in many parts of Africa. Further precautions are necessary in the movement of suspected cases internationally and in the shipment of specimens internationally (Simpson 1977; Centers for Disease Control 1988).

Prophylaxis and control await further epidemiological information on animal reservoirs of disease, modes of transmission from animal reservoirs (if indeed there are animal reservoirs) to humans, and modes of persistence of the virus in nature.

Wilbur G. Downs

Bibliography

Casals, J. 1971. Absence of a serological relationship between the Marburg virus and some arboviruses. In *Marburg virus disease,* ed. G. A. Martini and R. Siegert, 98–104. New York.

Elliot, L. H., J. B. McCormick, and K. M. Johnson. 1982. Inactivation of Lassa, Marburg and Ebola viruses by gamma irradiation. *Journal of Clinical Microbiology* 16: 704–8.

Evans, A. S., ed. 1978. *Viral infections of humans: Epidemiology and control,* 2d edition. New York.

Fields, B. N., ed. 1985. *Virology.* New York.

Gear, J. H. S. 1988. *CRC handbook of viral and rickettsial fevers.* Boca Raton, Fla.

Gear, J. H. S., et al. 1975. Outbreak of Marburg virus disease in Johannesburg. *British Medical Journal,* November 29: 489–93.

Haas, R., and G. Maass. 1971. Experimental infection of monkeys with the Marburg virus. In *Marburg virus disease,* ed. G. A. Martini and R. Siegert, 136–43. New York.

Henderson, B. E., et al. 1971. Epidemiological studies in Uganda relating to the "Marburg" agent. In *Marburg virus disease,* ed. G. A. Martini and R. Siegert, 166–76. New York.

Hennessen, W. 1971. Epidemiology of Marburg virus disease. In *Marburg virus disease,* ed. G. A. Martini and R. Siegert, 161–5. New York.

Hoffmann, H., and C. Kunz. 1971. Cultivation of the Marburg virus (*Rhabdovirus simiae*) in cell cultures. In *Marburg virus disease,* ed. G. A. Martini and R. Siegert, 112–16. New York.

Isaäcson, M. 1988. Marburg and Ebola virus infections. In *CRC handbook of viral and rickettsial fevers,* ed. J. H. S. Gear, 185–97. Boca Raton, Fla.

Johnson, K. M. 1978. African hemorrhagic fevers due to Marburg and Ebola viruses. In *Viral infections of humans: Epidemiology and control,* ed. A. S. Evans, 95–103. New York.

Kalter, S. S. 1971. A serological survey of primate sera for antibody to the Marburg virus. In *Marburg virus disease,* ed. G. A. Martini and R. Siegert, 177–87. New York.

Kiley, M. P., et al. 1982. Filoviridae: A taxonomic home for Marburg and Ebola viruses? *Intervirology* 18: 24–32.

Martini, G. A. 1971. Marburg virus disease, clinical syndrome. In *Marburg virus disease,* ed. G. A. Martini and R. Siegert, 1–9. New York.

Murphy, F. M. 1985. Marburg and Ebola viruses. In *Virology,* ed. B. N. Fields, Chapter 47. New York.

Peters D., G. Muller, and W. Slenckza. 1971. Morphology, development and classification of the Marburg virus. In *Marburg virus disease,* ed. G. A. Martini and R. Siegert, 68–83. New York.

Siegert, R., and W. Slenckza. 1971. Laboratory diagnosis and pathogenesis. In *Marburg virus disease,* ed. G. A. Martini and R. Siegert, 157–60. New York.

Siegert, R., H.-L. Shu, and W. Slenczka. 1968. Zur Diagnostic und Pathogenese der Infektion mit Marburg-virus. *Hygiene Institut of Philipps University (Marburg University) Marburg/Lahn:* 1827–30.

Simpson, D. I. H. 1977. *Marburg and Ebola virus infections: A guide for their diagnosis, management and control.* WHO Offset Publication No. 36, Geneva. 1–28.

U.S. Public Health Service. Centers for Disease Control. 1988. Management of patients with suspected viral hemorrhagic fever. *Morbidity and Mortality Weekly Report* 37 (Feb. 26): 1–15.

Wulff, H., and K. M. Johnson. 1979. Immunoglobulin M and G responses measured by immunofluorescence in patients with Lassa or Marburg infections. *Bulletin of the World Health Organization* 57: 631–5.

Wulff, H., W. Slenczka, and J. S. S. Gear. 1978. Early detection of antigen and estimation of virus yield in specimens from patients with Marburg virus disease. *Bulletin of the World Health Organization* 56: 633–9.

VIII.87
Mastoiditis

Infections of the middle ear and mastoid encompass a spectrum of potentially serious medical conditions and sequelae. Decreased hearing from ear infections may have a lifelong impact on speech, learning, and social and vocational development, causing these conditions to remain a major health concern. Because of the anatomic relationship of the middle ear and mastoid to the middle and posterior cranial compartments, life-threatening complications may occur.

Classification

Inflammatory diseases of the middle ear and mastoid are categorized according to the underlying disease process and location:

1. *Acute suppurative otitis media* (AOM) is characterized by obstruction of the eustachian tube, allowing the retention and suppuration of retained secretions. AOM is the medical term associated with, most commonly, the acute ear infection of childhood. Generally the course of this infection is self-limited, with or without medical treatment, and the retained infected secretions are discharged through either the eustachian tube or a ruptured tympanic membrane.

Acute coalescent mastoiditis can result from failure of these processes to evacuate the abscess. Coalescence of disease within the mastoid leads to pus under pressure and ultimately dissolution of surrounding bone. This condition may require urgent surgical evacuation because the infection is capable of spreading to local and regional structures.

3. *Otitis media with effusion* (OME) is an inflammatory condition of the middle ear in which serous or mucoid fluid accumulates. Both AOM and OME are precursor conditions to tympanic membrane retractions and perforations. Ongoing eustachian tube dysfunction predisposes to persistent retained secretions in the ear and recurrent acute attacks of otitis media. A small percentage of these patients develop a chronic tympanic membrane perforation which, in most cases, allows eventual aeration of the middle ear and mastoid air-cell spaces and resolution of the underlying disease process.

4. *Chronic suppurative otitis media* (CSOM) is defined as an ear with a tympanic membrane perforation. Benign CSOM is characterized by a dry tympanic membrane perforation, unassociated with

active infection. Active CSOM is the result of intermittent bacterial infection often in the presence of ingrown skin in the middle ear and mastoid cavities. This skin ingrowth is known as *cholesteatoma formation. Primary acquired cholesteatoma* occurs through a tympanic membrane retraction into the attic of the middle-ear space, with a subsequent potential for extension into the middle ear and mastoid air-cell systems. *Secondary acquired cholesteatoma* is defined as skin growth through a tympanic membrane perforation into the ear.

Distribution and Incidence

Surveys of large pediatric populations demonstrate that 80 percent of all children will experience one or more episodes of AOM by the age of 6. Together AOM, OME, and CSOM comprise one of the most common disease entities affecting human populations. Indeed, AOM is thought to be the most common disease treated with antibiotics.

Prevalence studies have demonstrated an extraordinarily high incidence of complicated infections of the middle ear in African, American Indian, Alaskan and Canadian Eskimo, Australian aboriginal, and New Zealand Maori pediatric populations, suggesting that disease-manifesting tissue destruction of the middle-ear and mastoid structures is much more prevalent in these areas. By contrast, studies of children in different geographic areas indicate that the incidence of uncomplicated disease in the middle ear is similar in all areas.

The incidence of complicated infections producing mastoiditis has dramatically declined since the advent of antibiotics in the 1930s and 1940s. Prior to that time, acute coalescent mastoiditis complicated AOM in approximately 20 percent of the cases. Initially, antibiotics cut into mortality rates from mastoiditis, but overall moribidity remained unchanged. By the 1950s, however, the incidence of acute mastoiditis resulting from AOM had declined to 3 percent. Current reports indicate that mastoiditis and other infectious complications will develop in less than 0.5 percent of cases of AOM.

Epidemiology

A variety of host and environmental factors, as well as infectious etiologic agents, have been linked to infection of the middle ear and mastoid. AOM occurs most commonly between 6 and 24 months of age. Subsequently, the incidence of AOM declines with age except for a limited reversal of the downward trend between 5 and 6 years of age, the time of entrance into school. The incidence of uncomplicated AOM is not significantly different in boys from that in girls. Mastoiditis, however, would appear to be more common among males.

Studies of eastern coast American children have demonstrated a higher incidence of middle ear infections in Hispanic and Caucasian children than in black children. The higher incidence of middle ear and mastoid infections in certain peoples is not readily explained. Variability in eustachian tube size, orientation, and function among racial groups has been suggested as being responsible for differences in disease incidence. Genetic predisposition to middle ear infection and associated complications has also been demonstrated. Down syndrome, cleft palate, and other craniofacial anomalies are also associated with a high risk of developing AOM, OME, and CSOM.

The severity of otitic infections is related to factors such as extremes of climate (temperature, humidity, and altitude) and poverty with attendant crowded living conditions, inadequate hygiene, and poor sanitation. There is a well-recognized seasonal variance in the incidence of AOM. During the winter months, outpatient visits for AOM are approximately 4-fold higher than in the summer months. Although intake of mother's milk and avoidance of cigarette smoke appear to confer some protection against OME, no effect on the incidence of suppurative complications has been shown.

Etiology

Eustachian tube dysfunction is the most important factor in the pathogenesis of middle ear infections. The most commonly cited problem is an abnormal palatal-muscle, eustachian-tube vector, which commonly occurs in young children. With adolescent growth, descent of the soft-palate-muscle sling relative to the eustachian tube orifice improves the eustachian tube opening. However, poor tubal function may persist with mucosal disease (allergic, inflammatory, immunologic impairment, or immotile cilia), extrinsic compression (enlarged adenoid or nasopharyngeal tumor), or palatal muscle dysfunction (cleft palate and other craniofacial anomalies). Persistent eustachian-tube dysfunction induces a relative negative pressure in the middle-ear space. The lack of aeration and the accumulation of effusions provide an environment conducive to the development of OME or AOM.

Bacteriologic studies identify *Streptococcus pneumoniae* and *Hemophilus influenzae* most frequently as the pathogenic organisms in AOM. Group A beta-hemolytic streptococcus, *Staphylococcus aureus,* and *Branhamella catarrhalis* are less frequent causes of AOM. Gram-negative enteric bacilli are isolated on occasion in infants up to 6 weeks of age with AOM.

When AOM continues beyond 2 weeks as a result of inadequate antimicrobial therapy, progressive thickening of the mucosa lining the middle ear obstructs free drainage of purulent secretions, thereby permitting bone destruction and extension of infection. This process may eventuate in mastoiditis and possibly other local or intracranial extensions of suppuration.

Immunology

The respiratory mucosal membrane that lines the middle-ear space and mastoid air cells is an immunologic defense consisting of constantly renewed mucus that contains lysozyme, a potent, bacteria-dissolving enzyme. In response to an invading organism, production of mucus is increased. Inflammatory dilation of vessels, white blood cell migration, and proteolytic enzyme and antibody deposition contribute to the formation of mucopurulent (containing both mucus and pus) secretions. All of the major classes of immunoglobulins have been identified in middle-ear effusions of patients with AOM. A significant type-specific antibody response in the serum to the bacteria responsible for AOM has been demonstrated. The presence of this type-specific antibody in middle-ear effusions is associated with clearance of mucopurulent secretions and an early return to normal middle-ear function.

The incidence of otitis media and attendant complications is higher in individuals with congenital or acquired immunologic deficiencies. The presence of a concomitant malignancy, the use of immunosuppressive drugs, uncontrolled diabetes, and previous irradiation are also associated with a higher risk of developing AOM and related complications.

Clinical Manifestations

The onset of AOM in childhood is often associated with fever, lethargy, and irritability. Older children may experience earaches and decreased hearing. Examination with a hand-held otoscope demonstrates tympanic membrane redness, opacity, bulging, and poor mobility when pneumatic pressure is applied. However, there is considerable variability in the symptoms and signs of acute otitis media.

OME is often characterized by hearing loss and a history of recurrent episodes of AOM. Otoscopic findings usually consist of fluid visible behind a retracted tympanic membrane.

CSOM in its active form often presents with foul-smelling drainage and longstanding hearing loss. Otoscopy reveals tympanic membrane retraction, perforation or hyalinization, and often, evidence of bony erosion, with the development of a cystlike mass called *cholesteatoma.* Development of pain in such an ear is a foreboding sign, as it often represents the obstruction of drainage of the infection, and pus under pressure. Local complications of CSOM include bone erosion producing hearing loss, facial nerve dysfunction, sensorineural hearing loss, ringing sounds in the ear, and vestibular disturbances. On occasion, infection will extend into the bony skull or into the soft tissues of the neck and scalp, either through normal preformed pathways such as vascular channels, or through progressive bone destruction. Catastrophic intracranial complications include abscesses, abnormal fluid accumulation, lateral sinus thrombosis, meningitis, and brain herniation.

Pathology

Pathological findings associated with AOM demonstrate inflammatory changes in the lining of the middle ear as well as suppurative exudates in the middle-ear cleft. The quantity of the exudate increases with time and exerts pressure on the tympanic membrane. The bulging tympanic membrane may rupture spontaneously in the central or marginal portions. Marginal perforations are more likely to lead to ingrowth of skin and the formation of a secondary acquired cholesteatoma. Primary acquired cholesteatomas arise in retraction pockets of the tympanic membrane that are induced by eustachian tube dysfunction. Cholesteatoma can also arise from congenital or traumatic implantation of skin into the middle ear as well as from abnormal changes in the middle-ear mucosal lining in response to inflammation.

Suppurative AOM persisting beyond 2 weeks can initiate the development of acute coalescent mastoiditis. The progressive thickening of the mucosa of the middle ear begins to obstruct the drainage of mucopus through the eustachian tube. Stoppage of blood in the veins and the high acidity of that blood promote demineralization and the loss of bony partitions. As a consequence, separate air cells of the mastoid coalesce into large cavities filled with mucopurulent secretions and thickened mucosal granulations. The erosion of bone, however, may not be confined to the air cell partitions within the mastoid bone. Other portions of the temporal bone including the posterior wall of the external canal, the mastoid cortex, and the thin, bony plates separating air cells from the sigmoid sinus and dura may likewise be eroded. Extension of the infection beyond the mucosal lining of the middle ear and mastoid air cells may produce an intracranial complication, generally by passage of the infection along preformed bony pathways or through inflamed veins in intact bone.

History and Geography

Antiquity Through the Sixteenth Century

It is likely that humanity has always suffered from acute infections of the middle ear and attendant suppurative complications such as mastoiditis. Studies of 2,600-year-old Egyptian mummies reveal perforations of the tympanic membrane and destruction of the mastoid air-cell system. Evidence of suppurative destruction of the mastoid is also apparent in skeletal specimens from early Persian populations (1900 B.C. to 800 B.C.).

Hippocrates appreciated the potential seriousness of otitic complications and noted that "acute pain of the ear with continued high fever is to be dreaded for the patient may become delirious and die." Early in the Roman era, the Roman physician Aulus Cornelius Celsus observed that "inflammation and pain to the ear lead sometimes to insanity and death." The Arabian physician Avicenna related suppuration of the ear and mastoid with the brain, reasoning incorrectly that the ear discharge was caused by the brain disease. For centuries, middle-ear and mastoid infections producing discharges from the ear were considered virtually normal conditions because they occurred so frequently.

Although the seriousness of ear suppuration was appreciated much earlier, the concept of opening the mastoid to relieve infection did not occur until the sixteenth century. The great medieval surgeon Ambroise Paré was called to the bed of Francis II of France. Paré found the young king febrile and delirious with a discharging ear. He proposed to drain the pus through an opening in the lateral skull. The boy-king's bride, Mary, Queen of Scots, consented. However, the king's mother, Catherine de Médici, refused to let the surgery take place, causing Mary to lose her first husband and throne while she was only 18 years old.

Seventeenth Through Eighteenth Century

Notable advances in understanding the pathophysiology of aural suppuration were made in the late seventeenth century. Joseph DuVerney wrote *Traité de l'Organe de l'Ouie* (1683), which is generally regarded to be the first monograph published on the subject of otology. It was the first book to contain an account of the structure, function, and diseases of the ear, whereas earlier works were devoted to purely normal otologic anatomy. In this work, DuVerney described infectious aural pathology and the mechanisms producing earache, otorrhea, and hearing loss. He was the first to describe extension of tympanic cavity infection posteriorly to the mastoid air cells to produce the characteristic symptoms and findings of mastoiditis.

Noteworthy contributions were made by Antonio Valsalva (1704), who still believed that aural suppuration was secondary to cerebral abscess formation and was not the primary lesion. He did, however, suggest a method for removing purulence from the ear. This procedure consisted of blowing out strongly while holding the mouth and nose firmly closed, thus forcing air to pass into the middle ear by way of the eustachian tube. He suggested this maneuver as a means of expelling pus in cases of otitis. Valsalva's student Giovanni Morgagni, in his great work *On the Sites and Causes of Disease* (1761), revealed postmortem evidence that demonstrated that aural suppuration was the primary source of lethal, intracranial abscesses.

In the early eighteenth century, Jean Petit of Paris performed what is generally believed to have been the first successful operation on the mastoid for the evacuation of pus. He demonstrated recovery "after the compact layer had been taken away with gouge and mallet." He stressed the need for early drainage of mastoid abscesses because of the potential for "accidents which may supervene and render the disease infinitely complicated and fatal."

S. Stevenson and D. Guthrie, in their *History of Otolaryngology* (1949), describe how, in 1776, a Prussian military surgeon apparently treated a painful, swollen, draining mastoid by removing a portion of the overlying mastoid cortex. The surgeon was probably unaware of Petit's work, and the authors quote him saying, "Perhaps this is no new discovery, but for me it is quite new."

Performance of the mastoidectomy operation suffered a setback when the procedure was performed on Baron von Berger, personal physician to the King of Denmark. The baron, hearing of the success of Petit and others, persuaded a surgeon to operate upon his mastoid to relieve tinnitus and hearing loss. The operation was performed before the importance of surgical asepsis was realized, and resulted in a wound infection. The baron died of meningitis 12 days later, and the mastoidectomy operation fell into disrepute until the middle of the nineteenth century.

France was one of the first countries to remove otology from the sphere of the general surgeon and to give it a place of its own. One of the first to specialize in this discipline was Jean Marie Gaspard Itard. Itard was a military surgeon in Paris who carried out extensive study of otologic physiology and pathology, and published a textbook on these subjects, *Traité des Maladies de l'Orielle et de l'Audition,* in 1821. He exposed many errors of his predecessors, particularly their opening of the mastoid cavity as a cure for deafness. Like Itard, Jean Antoine Saissy, a Parisian surgeon, was strongly opposed to puncturing the tympanic membrane for aural suppuration as recommended by his predecessors. Instead, he treated middle ear and mastoid suppuration by rinsing through a eustachian catheter. He described the technique in his *Essai sur les maladies de l'oreille interne* (1829).

In 1853, Sir William Wilde of Dublin – father of the poet Oscar Wilde – published the medical classic *Practical Observations on Aural Surgery and the Nature and Treatment of Diseases of the Ear.* In this publication he recommended incision of the mastoid through the skin and periosteum for fluctuant mastoiditis when symptoms and findings were life-threatening.

The nineteenth century saw the successful employment of ether in a surgical operation by William Thomas Green Morton in 1846 and the introduction of chloroform by James Young Simpson in 1847. These, coupled with bacteriologic discoveries made by Louis Pasteur and the work of Joseph Lister on antisepsis, the invention of the electric light by Thomas Edison, and the work of Rudolph Virchow in cellular pathology, had profound effects upon the development of otologic surgery for suppuration.

James Hinton, a London surgeon, and Hermann Hugo Rudolf Schwartze of Halle are credited with establishing the specific indications and method of simple mastoidectomy. This operation involved removal of the bony cortex overlying the mastoid air cells. The insight and work of Schwartze led to the first systematic account of the operation as a scientific procedure to be performed when specific indications were present and according to a definite plan. His rationale was so convincing that by the end of the nineteenth century, the operation had attained widespread acceptance and had overcome more than a century of prejudice against it.

In 1861 the German surgeon Anton von Troltsch had reported successful treatment of a case of apparent mastoiditis with a postauricular incision and wound exploration. He subsequently recognized that failure to address disease deeper within the middle ear recesses and mastoid invariably resulted in recurrence of otorrhea. In 1873 he proposed extensions of Schwartze's simple mastoidectomy to treat surgically these problematic areas.

Following a similar line of reasoning, Ernst von Küster and Ernst von Bergmann, in papers read before the German Surgical Society in 1889, recommended extending Schwartze's mastoidectomy procedures to include removal of the posterior wall of the external canal and middle ear structures "to clear away all disease and so fully to expose the source of the suppuration that the pus is nowhere checked at its outflow." This extended procedure became known as the *radical mastoidectomy.*

Prior to these remarkable advances in the surgical treatment of mastoiditis, the "mastoid operations" frequently failed because of delayed surgical intervention in cases in which infections had already extended beyond the mastoid process to involve intracranial structures. George Shambaugh, Jr., has noted that these patients died most likely despite, not because of, their mastoid operation (Shambaugh and Glasscock 1980). Many surgeons trained before 1870 were unable to absorb and practice Listerian doctrines, and this fact may have contributed to an overly conservative approach to surgical procedures. Properly indicated and performed, mastoidectomy for a well-localized coalescent infection proved to be extremely effective in removing the risk of serious complication from an abscess within the mastoid and in preventing continued aural suppuration. The addition of techniques for exteriorizing infectious processes in the less accessible apex of the temporal bone, as well as progress in making earlier diagnosis of mastoiditis, capped this important phase of otologic surgery for aural suppuration.

In many cases of chronic otorrhea treated with radical mastoidectomy, previous infection had destroyed the middle-ear sound-conducting system. Removal of the tympanic membrane and ossicular remnants was necessary in order to extirpate the infection completely. However, it soon became apparent that in a subset of cases of chronic otorrhea, the infectious process did not involve the inferior portions of the tympanic membrane or ossicular chain. In 1899, Otto Körner demonstrated that, in selected cases, the majority of the tympanic membrane and ossicular chain could be left intact during radical mastoidectomy, thus maintaining the preoperative hearing level.

In 1910 Gustav Bondy formally devised the modified radical mastoidectomy for cases in which the inferior portion of the tympanic membrane (pars tensa) and the ossicular chain remained intact. He demonstrated that the removal of the superior bone overlying infected cholesteatoma adequately exteriorized and exposed disease while preserving hearing. Despite the successful demonstration of this less radical approach in selected patients, otologic surgeons were slow to accept Bondy's procedure. Most likely, the preoccupation with preventing intracranial suppurative complications forestalled acceptance of this less aggressive approach. Shambaugh and others in America and abroad recognized the utility of the Bondy procedure, and it finally gained widespread acceptance by the 1930s.

A marked decline in the need for mastoid operations developed with the use of sulfanilamide and penicillin. The favorable results that were achieved with the use of these antibiotics in many cases encouraged their application at earlier stages of severe infections including mastoiditis. At first, otologic surgeons were hesitant to abandon the established surgical drainage procedures for mastoiditis, fearing that antibiotics would mask the clinical picture and lead to late complications. It soon became evident, however, that if antibiotics could be given before localized collections of pus were established, fewer complications requiring surgical intervention would result. Nonetheless, modern-day physicians have recognized that too low a dose of an antibiotic given for too brief a time, or the use of a less effective antibiotic in the early stages of otitis media, may indeed mask a developing mastoiditis.

Interest in hearing-preservation in conjunction with surgical treatment of chronic ear infections continued to grow. The German surgeons F. Zöllner and H. Wullstein share credit for performing the first successful repairs of the tympanic membrane using free skin grafting techniques in 1951. The ability to repair perforations of the tympanic membrane and seal the middle ear reduced the likelihood of persistent aural suppuration and associated mastoid and intracranial complications.

The emphasis on preservation and restoration of hearing in conjunction with the management of chronic ear infections has fostered the development of methods of ossicular reconstruction since the 1950s. Techniques in ossicular reconstruction are designed to simulate the middle-ear sound-conducting mechanism. Alloplastic prostheses made of polyethylene and Teflon and bioceramic materials have produced mixed results with respect to long-term hearing and prosthesis stability and acceptance.

The incus interposition technique of ossicular re-

construction was introduced by William J. House in 1966. C. L. Pennington and R. E. Wehrs are credited with refinement of this technique for reestablishing ossicular continuity between the tympanic membrane and the cochlea.

In 1954 B. W. Armstrong reintroduced a procedure, first suggested by Adam Politzer in 1869, to reverse the effects of eustachian tube dysfunction. The procedure entails a limited incision of the tympanic membrane and insertion of a tympanostomy tube. Theoretically, a functioning tympanostomy tube exerts a prophylactic effect by maintaining ambient pressure within the middle ear and mastoid and providing aeration and drainage of retained middle-ear secretions. Tympanostomy tubes appear to be beneficial in restoring hearing and preventing middle-ear infections and structural deterioration while in place.

This review of the historical development of otology reports an evolution in the understanding and management of aural infections. Interestingly, current principles of the surgical treatment of chronic ear infections recapitulate this evolution. The essential principles and objectives upon which modern surgical procedures are based are (1) removal of irreversibly infected tissue and restoration of middle-ear and mastoid aeration; (2) preservation of normal anatomic contours, and avoidance of an open cavity, when possible, by maintaining the external ear canal wall; and (3) restoration of the middle-ear sound-transformer mechanism in order to produce usable postoperative hearing.

The historical lessons learned by otologists underscore the importance of adequate surgical exposure and removal of irreversibly infected tissue followed by regular, indefinite postoperative follow-up in order to maintain a safe, dry ear.

John L. Kemink, John K. Niparko, and
Steven A. Telian

Bibliography

Armstrong, B. W. 1954. New treatment for chronic secretory otitis media. *American Medical Association Archives of Otolaryngology* 59: 653–4.

Bluestone, C., and S. Stool. 1983. *Pediatric otolaryngology.* Philadelphia.

Bergmann, Ernst von. 1888. Krankenvorstellung: Geheilter Hirnabszess. *Berliner Klinische Wochenschrift* 25: 1054–6.

Bondy, Gustav. 1910. Totalaufmeisselung mit Erhaltung von Trommelfell und Gehörknöchetchen. *Münchener Ohrenheilkunde* 44: 15–23.

Clements, D. 1978. Otitis media and hearing loss in a

small aboriginal community. *Medical Journal of Australia* 1: 665–7.

DuVerney, Guichard Joseph. 1683. *Traité l'organe de l'ouie; contenant la structure, les usages et les maladies de toutes les parties de l'oreille.* Paris.

Hinton, James. 1847a. *Atlas of the membrana tympani.* London.

    1847b. *The questions of aural surgery.* London.

House, W. J., M. E. Patterson, and F. H. Linthicum, Jr. 1966. Incus homografts in chronic ear surgery. *Archives of Otolaryngology* 84: 148–53.

Hughes, G. 1985. *Textbook of clinical otology.* New York.

Itard, Jean Marie Gaspard. 1821. *Traité des maladies de l'oreille et de l'audition,* 2 vols. Paris.

Küster, Ernst Georg Ferdinand von. 1889. Ueber die Grundsätze der Behandlung von Eiterungen in starrwandigen Hölen, mit besonderer Berücksichtigung des Empyems der Pleura. *Deutsche Medizinische Wochenschrift* 15: 254–7.

Morgagni, Giovanni Batista. 1966. *On the sites and causes of disease,* trans. B. Alexander. New York.

Palva, T., and K. Palkinen. 1959. Mastoiditis. *Journal of Laryngology and Otology* 73: 573.

Pennington, C. L. 1973. Incus interposition techniques. *Annals of Otology, Rhinology and Laryngology* 82: 518–31.

Politzer, Adam. 1878–82. *Lehrbuch der Ohrenheilkunde,* 2 vols. Stuttgart.

Saissy, Jean Antoine. 1829. *Essai sur les maladies de l'oreille interne.* Paris.

Schuknecht, H. 1974. *Pathology of the ear.* Cambridge.

Schwartze, Hermann Hugo Rudolf, and Adolph Eysell. 1873. Ueber die künstliche Eröffnung des Warzenforsatzes. *Archiv für Ohren- Nasen- und Kehlkopfheilkunde vereinigt mit Zeitschrift für Hals- Nasen- und Ohrenheilkunde* 1: 157–87.

Shambaugh, G., and M. Glasscock. 1980. *Surgery of the ear.* Philadelphia.

Sonnenschein, R. 1936. The development of mastoidectomy. *Annals of Medical History* 8: 500.

Stevenson, S., and D. Guthrie. 1949. *History of otolaryngology.* Edinburgh.

Teele, D., S. Pelton, and J. Klein. 1981. Bacteriology of acute otitis media unresponsive to initial antimicrobial therapy. *Journal of Pediatrics* 98: 537.

Timmermans, F., and S. Gerson. 1980. Chronic granulomatous otitis media in Inuit children. *Canadian Medical Association Journal* 122: 545.

Valsalva, Antonio Maria. 1704. *De aure humana tractatus.* Bologna.

Wehrs, R. E. 1972. Three years' experience with the homograft tympanic membrane. *Transactions of the American Academy of Ophthalmology and Otolaryngology* 76: 142–6.

Wilde, Sir William Robert Wills. 1853. *Practical observations on aural surgery and the nature and treatment of diseases of the ear.* London.

Wullstein, H. 1952. Funktionelle Operationen im Mittelohr mit Hilfe des freien spaltlappen Transplantates. *Archiv für Ohren- Nasen- und Kehlkopfheilkunde vereinigt mit Zeitschrift für Hals- Nasen- und Ohrenheilkunde* 161: 422–35.

Zöllner, F. 1952. Plastische Eingriffe an den Labyrinthfenstern. *Archiv für Ohren- Nasen- und Kehlkopfheilkunde vereinigt mit Zeitschrift für Hals- Nasen- und Ohrenheilkunde* 161: 414–22.

VIII.88
Measles

Measles (rubeola; hard measles; red measles; 9-day measles; morbilli) is a common, acute, viral infectious disease, principally of children, with worldwide distribution, that is clinically characterized by fever and a typical red, blotchy rash combined with cough, coryza, or conjunctivitis. It is a vaccine-preventable disease, and its vaccine is one of the vaccines included in the Expanded Programme on Immunization (EPI) of the World Health Organization (WHO). The disease is known by many local names throughout the world.

Etiology and Epidemiology

Measles is caused by a virus, which is in the genus *Morbillivirus* of the family Paramyxoviridae. Although the virus does not survive drying on a surface, it can survive drying in microdroplets in the air.

Measles is one of the most highly communicable diseases, transmitted by contact of susceptible individuals with the nose and throat secretions of infected persons, primarily by droplet spread. Infection also occurs by direct contact, and by indirect contact through freshly soiled articles and airborne transmission. There is no reservoir for measles other than human beings, which means that a continuous chain of susceptible contacts is necessary to sustain transmission. The period of communicability is from slightly before the beginning of the prodromal phase of the disease to 4 days after the start of the rash. There is no carrier state. Measles has an incubation period from time of exposure to onset of fever of about 10 days with a range from 8 to 13 days. The incubation period from time of exposure to rash onset is about 14 days.

In populated areas with no or low vaccination coverage, measles is primarily an endemic disease of children, with epidemics occurring every 2 to 5 years. In such areas, the greatest incidence is in children under 2 years of age. Epidemic measles has a winter–spring seasonality in temperate climates and a less marked hot–dry seasonality in equatorial regions. This seasonality may be primarily the result of the indirect effect of climate on socioeconomic conditions and population movements. In more remote isolated populations, measles is not endemic and disease is dependent upon introduction of the virus from the outside, at which time an epidemic may occur, affecting all age groups born since the last epidemic. There is no evidence for a gender difference with respect to incidence or severity of measles, or a racial difference with respect to incidence. Differences in severity among certain populations are most likely the result of nutritional and environmental factors.

Measles mortality is highest in the very young and the very old. In malnourished children in the developing world, the case fatality rate may be as high as 5 to 10 percent or more. Some studies have indicated that multiple cases within a family group may lead to higher mortality rates.

Distribution and Incidence

Measles has a worldwide distribution, and the Expanded Programme on Immunization of the World Health Organization maintains an information system on reported cases and vaccination coverage in member countries. Because of underreporting, worldwide reported measles incidence represents only a small fraction of an estimated 50 million cases and 1.5 million deaths caused annually by measles in developing countries. It should be emphasized that reported incidence is subject to completeness of reporting and also to a general trend of improving disease surveillance. Measles vaccination as part of the Expanded Programme on Immunization, with global coverage estimated at 55 percent for children under 1 year of age (52 percent in developing countries), is currently averting over 40 million cases and over 1 million deaths resulting from the disease each year in Third World countries.

In populated areas where measles is both endemic and epidemic, over 90 percent of the adult population will show serologic evidence of prior infection. In remote or island populations where measles is not endemic, a significant proportion of the population can be susceptible, which may produce large outbreaks when the measles virus is introduced from the outside. In some countries, such as the United States, a national goal of measles elimination has been adopted, and impressive progress toward its control has been achieved.

Immunology

Infants usually have a passive immunity to measles as a result of maternal antibodies acquired transplacentally from immune mothers. This passive immunity protects the infant from measles infection for 6 to 9 months, depending on the amount of maternal antibody acquired.

Measles infection induces a lifelong immunity. Several methods for confirming infection and immunity have been developed, including the following: serologic tests, fluorescent antibody techniques, and isolation of the virus from patients during the acute phase of the disease.

A single dose of live attenuated measles virus vaccine confers long-term, probably lifelong, immunity in over 95 percent of susceptible individuals. The optimal age for vaccination is related to the persistence of passive immunity from maternal antibodies and patterns of disease transmission. For developed countries with low incidence, such as the United States, vaccination at 15 months of age is recommended, whereas in developing countries the Expanded Programme on Immunization recommends vaccination at 9 months of age.

Measles vaccine may confer immunity if given within 72 hours of exposure; and immune globulin (IG), if given within 6 days of exposure, may provide a limited-duration protection from measles, owing to passively acquired antibodies from the immune globulin.

Clinical Manifestations and Pathology

The prodromal phase of measles disease typically includes symptoms and signs of fever, cough, coryza, and conjunctivitis. During this stage, small whitish specks on reddened areas of the mucosal lining of the mouth called *Koplik's spots* are diagnostic of measles. The prodromal period continues for 3 to 7 days until the characteristic blotchy reddish rash appears. This rash usually appears first on the head and then spreads down the body and outward to the limbs, lasting about 4 to 7 days. After its peak, in uncomplicated cases, all the symptoms and signs begin to recede and the rash fades in the same order it appeared.

Complications due to viral replication or secondary bacterial infection may occur, however, and result in middle-ear infections and pneumonia. Diarrhea may also complicate measles and, in the developing world, is one of the most important causes of measles-associated mortality. Neurological involvement may also occur, resulting in encephalitis during or soon after the acute illness or in the rare subacute sclerosing panencephalitis (SSPE) after a lengthy incubation period. Measles is uncommon during pregnancy, and the limited data available do not appear to demonstrate clearly any increased risk of fetal mortality or congenital malformations.

History and Geography

Ancient Times Through the Eighteenth Century

The origin of measles is unknown. Francis Black (1976) has noted that populations of a sufficient size to allow for a continuous chain of susceptibles required to sustain measles transmission would not have developed until sometime after 2500 B.C. He has suggested that measles may have arisen as an adaptation of one of the other viruses of the same genus (which includes rinderpest and canine distemper). It is interesting to note that Hippocrates, writing in the fourth century B.C., did not describe a rash illness that would be consistent with measles, even though his recorded case histories document the existence of many other infections in ancient Greece.

The history of measles is confused with that of smallpox in much of the early literature. Although records are scanty, major unidentified epidemics with high mortality rates spread through the Roman Empire in A.D. 165–80 and again in 251–66. William McNeill (1976) has noted that there are some suggestive circumstances that make it tempting to believe that these two "demographic disasters" signaled the arrival of measles and smallpox. In China, two major epidemics with high mortality were recorded in A.D. 161–2 and 310–12, but again there is uncertainty of the diseases, and McNeill states that, given the fragmentary and imperfect data, it is possible to conclude only that "some time between A.D. 37 and A.D. 653 diseases like smallpox and measles arrived in China." The Persian physician known as Rhazes is generally credited with the first authentic written record of measles by differentiating the two diseases in approximately A.D. 910 in his *Treatise on the Small-Pox and Measles*. Rhazes, however, quoted previous writers, including the famous Hebrew physician El Yahudi, who lived 300 years ear-

lier. Rhazes used the word *hasbah* for measles and believed that "the measles arise from very bad blood." He considered the disease "more to be dreaded than smallpox." Around the year 1000, Avicenna of Baghdad also wrote about measles, and translators of his writings are said to have introduced the term *rubeola* for the disease.

During medieval times, measles was referred to by the Latin term *morbilli*, the diminutive of *morbus*, meaning the "little disease." August Hirsch (1883–6) notes that measles was also called *rubeola, rossalia, rosagia,* as well as the colloquial names *fersa* or *sofersa* (Milanese), *mesles* and later *measles* (English), *maal* and *masern* (German), and the *masura* or *spots* (Sanskrit). The derivation of the English name "measles" is in some doubt. One suggestion is that it may have come from the Latin term *miscellus* or *misella,* a diminutive of the Latin *miser,* meaning "miserable" – a term given to those suffering from leprosy. The sores on the legs of leprosy patients were known as *mesles,* and John of Gaddesden in the early fourteenth century unjustifiably coupled these *mesles* with the disease *morbilli* of medical authors. Eventually the term "measles" lost its connection with leprosy.

Measles, smallpox, and other rash illnesses continued to be confused in Europe during the Middle Ages. The seventeenth-century physician and epidemiologist Thomas Sydenham studied measles epidemics in 1670 and 1674 and made observations on the clinical features of the illness and its complications. He is generally credited with differentiating and describing measles in northern Europe, and his famous descriptions of the disease in "Of Measles in the Year 1670" and "On the Measles" were published in *Process Integri* in 1692. The first clear demonstration that measles was an infectious disease is attributed to Francis Home who, in 1758, attempted to prevent the illness and provide immunity by placing blood from measles patients beneath the skin or into the nose of susceptible persons. Numerous measles epidemics were reported in the seventeenth and eighteenth centuries in the English medical literature.

Nineteenth Century

The most famous epidemiological study of measles was conducted by Peter Panum and reported in his classic *Observations Made During the Epidemic of Measles on the Faroe Islands in the Year 1846* (1940). Measles attacked about 6,100 islanders during 1846 and was associated with the deaths of 102 of the 7,864 inhabitants, who had been completely free of the disease for 65 years. Panum confirmed the respiratory route of transmission, the incubation period, and the lifelong immunity acquired from previous infection. Hirsch (1883–6) built on Panum's work and recorded the universal geographic distribution of measles by noting accounts of epidemics that had occurred in most parts of the world. He noted that measles reached the Western Hemisphere soon after the arrival of the first European colonists and followed the westward movement of the settlers. He suggested that introduction of the disease into the Australian continent occurred in 1854 after first appearing in the Hawaiian Islands in 1848.

A particularly vivid account of the dramatic 1876 measles epidemic in Fiji quoted by Hirsch illustrates the conditions that accounted for the relatively high mortality:

Later in the epidemic, when it is said to be like plague, . . . the people, seized with fear, had abandoned their sick. . . . The people chose swampy sites for their dwellings, and whether they kept close shut up in huts without ventilation, or rushed into the streams and remained in the water during the height of the illness, the consequences were equally fatal. The excessive mortality resulted from terror at the mysterious seizure, and [from] the want of the commonest aids during illness. . . . Thousands were carried off by want of nourishment and care, as well as by dysentery and congestion of the lungs. . . .

It was especially dramatic when measles struck a "virgin soil" population that had no prior or recent exposure to measles disease or measles vaccine, and thus the outbreak affected most persons. With regard to the introduction of measles by the Spaniards from the Old World into the Amerindian populations of the New World, McNeill (1976) noted that "measles followed hard upon the heels of smallpox, spreading through Mexico and Peru in 1530–1. Deaths were frequent, as is to be expected when such a disease encounters a virgin population dense enough to keep the chain of infection going." High mortality was also reported in measles epidemics that occurred in virgin soil island populations in the Pacific Ocean in the nineteenth century: 40,000 deaths out of a population of 150,000 in Hawaii in 1848, 20,000 deaths comprising 20 to 25 percent of the population of Fiji in 1874, and 645 deaths out of 8,845 cases in Samoa in 1911. High mortality in these settings was likely due to some of the same factors that result in high mortality rates among unvaccinated individuals in many areas of the developing world today, including lack of supportive care, lack of treatment for complications, and malnutrition. In virgin soil

settings where populations were well nourished and where better medical care was available, the mortality rate was much lower, as noted in the outbreak of measles in southern Greenland in 1951 where, in one district, 4,257 persons out of a population of about 4,400 contracted measles and 77 deaths occurred (Christensen et al. 1953).

Not until 1896 did Henry Koplik publish a description of Koplik's spots, although apparently their significance was independently recognized about a century earlier by John Quier in Jamaica and Richard Hazeltine in Maine.

Prevention and Control

Research leading to the development of current measles vaccines began around the beginning of this century. John Anderson and Joseph Goldberger (1911) demonstrated that the illness was caused by a virus, by injecting filtered material from patients with acute diseases into monkeys. Harry Plotz (1938) and Geoffrey Rake and Morris Shaffer (1940) reported the cultivation of measles virus in tissue culture. In 1954, with the advent of reliable tissue culture techniques, J. F. Enders and T. C. Peebles were able to isolate the measles virus. Subsequent research by S. L. Katz, M. J. Milanovic, and J. F. Enders (1958) resulted in the development of an attenuated strain of measles vaccine which was produced in 1958. In 1963, after field trials, the attenuated ("live") measles vaccine was licensed for general use in the United States. An inactivated ("killed") measles vaccine was also developed, but was shown to be inferior and is no longer available.

With the establishment of the World Health Organization Expanded Programme on Immunization in 1974, measles vaccine has been introduced into the national immunization programs of most countries. The current levels of immunization coverage for measles vaccine show wide geographic variation. Except for more remote isolated populations where the occurrence of measles disease is not endemic and is subject to infrequent introduction of virus, the geographic occurrence in the world today is related to the immunization coverage with measles vaccine. In countries with sustained, large-scale immunization programs and reliable disease surveillance, the impact of control efforts has been documented through decreasing numbers of reported cases. Global measles eradication is considered to be technically possible, but it is increasingly recognized that extremely high immunization coverage levels will be necessary to achieve such a goal.

Robert J. Kim-Farley

This chapter was written in the author's private capacity. No official support or endorsement by the Centers for Disease Control is intended or should be inferred.

Bibliography

Anderson, J. F., and J. Goldberger. 1911. Experimental measles in the monkey. *Public Health Reports* 26: 847–8, 887–95.

Benenson, Abram S., ed. 1985. *Control of communicable disease in man.* Washington, D.C.

Bett, Walter R., ed. 1954. *The history and conquest of common diseases.* Norman, Okla.

Black, Francis. 1976. Measles. In *Viral infections of humans: Epidemiology and control,* ed. Alfred S. Evans, 451–69. New York.

Caufield, E. 1943. Early measles epidemics in America. *Yale Journal of Biology and Medicine* 15: 521–6.

Centers for Disease Control. 1987. Measles – United States, 1986. *Morbidity and Mortality Weekly Report* 36: 301–5.

Christensen, Pov Elo, et al. 1953. An epidemic of measles in southern Greenland, 1951. *Acta Medica Scandinavica* 6: 448.

Enders, J. F., and T. C. Peebles. 1954. Propagation in tissue cultures of cytopathogenic agents from patients with measles. *Proceedings of the Society for Experimental Biology and Medicine* 86: 277–86.

Expanded Programme on Immunization. 1986. *Update: Measles – spots that kill.* Geneva.

Feigin, Ralph D., and James D. Cherry, eds. 1981. *Textbook of pediatric infectious diseases.* Philadelphia.

Gastel, Barbara. 1973. Measles: A potentially finite history. *Journal of the History of Medicine* 28: 34–44.

Goerka, H. 1956. The life and scientific works of Mr. John Quier. *West Indian Medical Journal* 5: 23.

Hirsch, August. 1883–6. *Handbook of geographical and historical pathology,* 3 vols. London.

Home, Francis. 1759. *Medical facts and experiments.* London.

Howe, G. Melvyn, ed. 1977. *A world geography of human diseases.* London.

Katz, S. L., M. V. Milanovic, and J. F. Enders. 1958. Propagation of measles virus in cultures of chick embryo cells. *Proceedings of the Society for Experimental Biology and Medicine* 97: 23–9.

Koplik, Henry. 1896. The diagnosis of the invasion of measles from a study of the exanthema as it appears on the buccal mucous membrane. *Archives of Pediatrics* 13: 918–22.

Major, Ralph H. 1945. *Classic descriptions of disease.* Springfield, Ill.

McNeill, William H. 1976. *Plagues and peoples.* Garden City, N.Y.

Panum, P. L. 1940. *Observations made during the epidemic of measles on the Faroe Islands in the year 1846.* New York.

Plotz, Harry. 1938. Culture 'in vitro' du virus de la rougeole. *Bulletin de l'Académie de Médecine de Paris* 119: 598–601.

Rake, Geoffrey, and M. F. Schaefer. 1940. Studies on measles. I. The use of the chorio-allantois of the developing chicken embryo. *Journal of Immunology* 38: 177–200.

Wilson, G. S. 1962. Measles as a universal disease. *American Journal of Diseases of Children* 103: 49–53.

VIII.89
Meningitis

Meningitis is an acute inflammation of the meninges, the membranes covering the brain and spinal cord. The disease is usually the result of bacterial infection, but a number of viruses, fungi, and other microbial agents can also cause it. Meningitis can develop as well from noninfectious conditions such as tumors, lead poisoning, and reactions to vaccines. Meningococcal meningitis, caused by a bacterium, *Neisseria meningitidis,* is the only form that occurs in major epidemics. Also called *cerebrospinal meningitis* (CSM), it has been known in the past as "spotted fever," cerebrospinal fever, typhus cerebralis, and meningitis epidemica. Aseptic meningitis refers to inflammations of the meninges without detectable bacterial involvement. The most common causes are any of a number of viruses.

Etiology and Epidemiology

Many species of bacteria can cause meningitis, but over 80 percent of all cases in developed countries in recent years have been due to only three: *N. meningitidis, Hemophilus influenzae,* and *Streptococcus (Diplococcus) pneumoniae.* Other common members of the human bacterial flora such as *Escherichia coli* and various streptococci and staphylococci can also produce meningitis under special circumstances, as can members of the genera *Listeria, Pseudomonas,* and *Proteus.* Meningitis sometimes develops as a complication of tuberculosis.

Aseptic meningitis is usually the result of viral infection. Among the many types of viruses that can be involved are mumps, echovirus, poliovirus, coxsackievirus, herpes simplex, herpes zoster, hepatitis, measles, rubella, and several mosquito-borne agents of encephalitis. Fungi, most commonly *Cryptococcus,* are other possible agents.

Laboratory study is necessary to determine the cause of any particular case of meningitis, so it is generally difficult to be certain of the exact etiology of past meningitis cases or epidemics. However, despite the current relative significance of *Hemophilus* and *Streptococcus, Neisseria* is the most important pathogen for meningococcal meningitis; it is the only type that commonly occurs in major epidemics, and is the most likely to attack adults.

N. meningitidis is a nonmotile, gram-negative coccus closely related to the organism that causes gonorrhea. Its protective capsule is composed of one of several possible large sugar polymers (polysaccharides), which provide the basis for assigning a given specimen into 1 of about 13 currently recognized serogroups. Serogroups B, C, W-135, and Y have been especially active in the Americas in recent years; group A organisms are the most likely to cause large-scale epidemics and have historically been very prevalent in Africa. Serogroups can be divided into serotypes; these finer distinctions are often crucial in tracing connected cases or determining if a given outbreak has a common origin. Humans are the only natural host.

N. meningitidis is a common inhabitant of the mucosal membranes of the nose and throat, where it normally causes no harm. As many as 5 to 50 percent of a population may be asymptomatic carriers without any cases of meningitis developing, but such carriers are crucial to the spread of the disease. The organism is transmitted by droplets sneezed or coughed from the noses and throats of carriers or, less commonly, meningitis patients. It is very susceptible to desiccation and to sunlight, so close and prolonged contact is favorable to propagation.

The majority of victims, especially in sporadic cases and small outbreaks, are children under age 5. Among adults, new military recruits crowded into barracks have traditionally been prime targets. Throughout the nineteenth and twentieth centuries, wartime mobilization in Europe and America was always accompanied by sharp increases in meningitis case rates.

Meningitis is a highly seasonal disease. In temperate regions, a large preponderance of cases develop in the winter and early spring. The reasons for this are not clear, but indoor living, crowding, and the effects of cold temperature and low humidity on potential hosts' mucous membranes may all play a role. Epidemics in sub-Saharan Africa develop during the cool, dry season, when people travel more and sleep indoors to keep warm. African outbreaks tend to end abruptly when the rains come.

Immunology

N. meningitidis stimulates the production of serotype-specific antibodies in persons who have experienced infection. The antibodies in most serogroups develop against the polysaccharides of the bacterial capsule, but the basis for antigenicity in serogroup B is unclear. Infants can acquire passive immunity from their mothers and be protected for a few months. Vaccines are available for protection against several serogroups, including A, C, Y, and W-135.

Clinical Manifestations and Pathology

Infection with *N. meningitidis* can result in one of three conditions. In the large majority of cases, bacteria are carried in the nose and pharynx without any symptoms or with just a sore throat. Serious disease develops only if the bacteria reach the bloodstream. This can produce fulminating blood infection or meningococcemia, which is characterized by sudden prostration, high fever, skin blotches (*ecchymoses*), and collapse. Most of these cases are fatal unless promptly treated, and death may ensue in a matter of hours, before the meninges become involved.

Meningitis, however, is the more common result, occurring when bacteria travel through the blood to infect the membranes of the brain and spinal cord. Fever, violent headache, stiff neck, and vomiting are typical symptoms, and, as in meningococcemia, many victims show a petechial rash due to blockage of small blood vessels. A thick, purulent exudate covers the brain, and arthritis, cardiac damage, and shock may develop. Coma, convulsions, and delirium are frequent, and death rates for untreated cases range from 50 to 90 percent. Even in epidemic conditions, however, only a small minority of persons harboring the organism develop clinical disease. It is not known why most people remain healthy carriers whereas others become desperately ill. Individual susceptibility, damage to mucous membranes, and concomitant infections with other bacteria may all play a role.

Diagnosis is based on clinical signs and the recovery of pathogens from the cerebrospinal fluid or, in meningococcemia, from the blood. Culture of organisms from throat swabs is used to monitor carrier rates and circulating strains.

Therapy was revolutionized with the introduction of sulfa drugs in the late 1930s, and sulfonamides were widely used as a prophylaxis for exposed populations. The appearance and spread of sulfonamide-resistant bacteria after 1963 has forced a shift in preventive tactics, but the pathogen is still very sensitive to treatment with penicillin. Military recruits are routinely vaccinated in most countries, and extensive inoculation campaigns have helped control epidemics in Africa. Better ventilation and reductions in crowding in living and sleeping areas are useful in barracks and other institutional settings. Prophylaxis with rifampin is helpful in reducing carrier rates and preventing outbreaks after cases have occurred in specific populations, as, for example, children in day-care centers.

History and Geography

Meningococcal and other forms of meningitis occur throughout the world. Meningitis is endemic in tropical and temperate regions and in both urban and rural settings, and sporadic cases and small epidemics can develop anywhere. In this century, epidemic cerebrospinal meningitis (CSM) has repeatedly cut a wide swath throughout African savanna country in a belt south of the Sahara; these unusual epidemics are caused by serotype A of *N. meningitidis*.

Antiquity Through the Nineteenth Century

Meningitis was not described in a form recognized as definitive until after 1800, so the antiquity of the disease is unknown. Mention of "epidemic convulsion" in tenth-century China and a possible description by T. Willis in England in 1684 could indicate earlier recognition of meningococcal meningitis. There are many other possible references to meningitis outbreaks in European medical literature of the sixteenth, seventeenth, and eighteenth centuries. An episode described in Munster in 1788 could well have been meningococcal meningitis. Indeed, although the first clear clinical description was of cases in Geneva in 1805, it seems highly unlikely that meningitis of meningococcal or other etiology is really such a new infection in humans.

In the early months of 1805, a small epidemic of CSM was described in Geneva by Gaspard Vieusseux. Most victims were infants and children. Clinical accounts, complemented by autopsy studies by A. Matthey, establish the identity of the disease. In March 1806, a cluster of 13 or 14 cases were described in Medfield, Massachusetts. As in Switzerland, the victims were infants and children. Nine patients died, despite frantic application of an array of depletive and stimulating therapies. The case descriptions and five autopsies confirmed a diagnosis of CSM. An epidemic of apparent meningitis afflicted British troops in Sicily in 1808, and French garrisons in Grenoble and Paris were struck in early 1814. In North America, meningitis epidemics were reported in Canada in 1807, in Virginia, Kentucky,

and Ohio in 1808, in New York State and Pennsylvania in 1809, among American troops during the War of 1812, and were described as "sinking typhus" or "spotted fever" in New England from 1814 to 1816.

Relatively little more was heard about this deadly and apparently quite new disease until the years 1837 through 1842, when a series of outbreaks occurred in French garrisons, and civilians also came under attack in some nearby towns. Thus epidemics in Algeria from 1840 to 1847 began among French troops, but caused many deaths among the indigenous Moslem population as well, especially in the Algiers and Constantine areas during 1846 and 1847. Meningitis was also widespread in southern Italy from 1839 to 1845, and there were scattered reports from Corfu, Ireland, and especially Denmark in the period 1845 to 1848. There was also a series of small epidemics in the United States in the 1840s, primarily in the South.

The first recorded major epidemic of CSM began in Sweden in 1854, starting in Göteborg in the late winter and slowly spreading to the north and east during the next five winters. It died out in the summers and resumed a slow, irregular progress during winters, reaching 61° north in 1857 and 63° north in 1858. The epidemic declined in 1859, with scattered cases reported in the next several years and a small flare-up in the years 1865 to 1867. Government returns showed a total of 4,158 meningitis deaths from 1854 to 1860 and 419 in 1865–7.

During the 1860s, numerous small but deadly epidemics occurred in Germany, the Netherlands, England, France, Italy, Portugal, Austria, Hungary, Greece, Turkey, Poland, and Russia. There were numerous outbreaks in the United States during the same decade, with both Union and Confederate troops suffering during the Civil War. In the United States and elsewhere, recruits and small children continued to be the most common victims. Scattered cases and sporadic outbreaks continued for the rest of the century, with flurries of activity in the mid-1880s and at the end of the century.

Twentieth Century

There was a new burst of meningitis activity in the first decade of the twentieth century. The first cases from Australia were recorded in 1900–1. Portugal had more than 5,000 cases from 1901 to 1905; a series of North American epidemics from 1904 to 1907 involved much of the United States and Canada, with 2,755 patients in New York alone in 1905. A severe epidemic in Silesia caused almost 10,000 cases from 1905 to 1908.

For most of the twentieth century, meningitis in the developed countries has followed a pattern of small, local epidemics and scattered cases, mostly among children. The two world wars caused major spurts as military authorities crammed large numbers of recruits into crowded barracks. In England and Wales, for example, cases rose from a few hundred a year prior to World War I to a peak of more than 3,500 by 1915. Similarly, annual cases and deaths rose more than fivefold in the early 1940s, with over 23,000 cases in 1940 and 1941. But except for a peak of almost 1,300 cases in 1974, there have been fewer than 1,000 cases a year reported since the early 1950s.

For the United States, there were 5,839 cases and 2,279 deaths among soldiers during World War I. In 1942 and 1943, however, although there were 13,922 military cases, thanks to new therapy there were only 559 deaths. Moreover, except for a spurt to about 14 cases per 100,000 people in 1942, civilian case rates in the United States have remained under 4 per 100,000 since the late 1930s. Total meningococcal infections have rarely exceeded 3,000 a year, but reported cases of aseptic meningitis have risen steadily and have totaled two to four times the meningococcal figure during the 1980s.

The situation in non-Western countries is quite different. Incidence rates tend to be much higher, and there are still major epidemics like those that afflicted Sweden and Silesia in the past. For example, China has experienced three major epidemics of serogroup A meningococcal meningitis since 1949, with peak incidence rates of 50 to 400 per 100,000 in 1959, 1967, and 1977. During the 1963–9 epidemic, which coincided with the upheavals of the Cultural Revolution, there were more than 3 million cases and 166,000 deaths.

Africa has had two kinds of experience with the disease. In most of the continent, meningitis is a sporadic disease that behaves much as it does in the West, although often with higher incidence and fatality rates. Much of north, central, east and southern Africa falls into this pattern. In South Africa, scattered cases were reported in the 1880s. Mining compounds have had favorable conditions for meningitis, with newly hired African workers forced to live in conditions similar to those of military recruits. CSM is endemic in east Africa, producing a few hundred cases in most countries in recent years.

On the other hand, there has been at least one terrible epidemic. In 1913 CSM swept Kenya and Tanganyika, killing over 20,000 people in Kenya alone and, partly as a result of military activity,

lingering in Tanganyika until 1919. Both territories, as well as neighboring Uganda, had dramatic surges during World War II. In North Africa, Algeria and Egypt experienced meningitis epidemics in the nineteenth century, and the disease has been reported throughout the region in recent decades. Morocco had over 6,000 cases in 1967.

The classic area for epidemic CSM, however, has been the savanna zone south of the Sahara Desert from Sudan to Senegal. This "CSM belt" has been swept by a series of great epidemics during the twentieth century. Indeed, there the disease has behaved in a very different fashion, advancing on a regular front and killing tens of thousands of people in a season. Only the Swedish epidemic of the 1850s seems to have displayed a similar broad geographic pattern. In both places, macroscopic examination indicated that the disease advanced in a regular manner from season to season, but also that actual cases were scattered widely within the afflicted zone in a totally unpredictable manner. The epidemic hopped about, skipping many large communities and sometimes striking hard at small, relatively isolated places. Areas struck in one CSM season were usually spared in the next.

The reasons for the unusual behavior of CSM in the African "CSM belt" are unclear. Open grassland country facilitates mobility, and much of the region has a fairly dense population. A long, cool dry season creates dusty conditions and may dry out mucous membranes of the nose and throat while it also allows people to travel easily and encourages them to sleep indoors. Housing is often crowded and poorly ventilated. Perhaps the savanna dry season is analogous to the Swedish winter; people are forced to congregate indoors, and the seasonal low humidity in Africa was replicated in Sweden by home heating. The Swedish outbreaks ceased every year with the arrival of spring, whereas the sub-Saharan zone experiences relief with the first rains.

Although there has been a tendency, exemplified in the studies of the British colonial physician B. B. Waddy, to view the entire savanna belt as a single epidemiological unit, there have been distinct geographic zones of CSM. Thus the disease did not spread in great waves from southern Sudan across the grasslands to West Africa. Epidemics in southern Sudan and northern Uganda, especially destructive in the late 1920s, have been independent of developments in central and northern Sudan. And, with an exception in 1934 and 1935, central Sudanese epidemics have not been linked to those in Chad and westward.

The antiquity of meningitis in the savanna zone is not known, but some evidence exists that the disease had occurred in central Sudan and the densely populated Hausa country of northern Nigeria by the 1880s. Small outbreaks in troops in Senegal in the 1890s and in the Gold Coast (Ghana) in 1900 did not afflict wide regions. The first of the great West African epidemics began in northern Nigeria in early 1905. It spread westward as far as French Sudan (Mali) and northwest Ghana in 1906, lingering in these places until the rains of 1908. British authorities guessed the 3-year death toll in Ghana at some 34,000; case mortality was estimated at 80 percent. Total deaths in the 1905–8 epidemic are not known, but there clearly was a major disaster.

The second CSM cycle in the western savanna began in northwest Ghana in 1919, spread to Upper Volta (Burkina Faso) in 1920, and swept northern Nigeria and Niger from 1921 to 1924. Weak political and medical infrastructures precluded accurate estimates of cases or deaths, but the death toll in one northern Nigerian province, Sokoto, was put at over 45,000 in 1921 alone, and French officials assumed that at least 15,000 persons died in Niger over the 4-year period.

The third great cycle of CSM activity in West Africa began in 1935, when Chad was attacked by an epidemic that had raged during the previous year in the Kordofan and Darfur provinces of central Sudan. This was the first and only time that a clear pattern of east–west spread from Sudan has been demonstrated. Carriers brought infection westward during the rainy seasons to Chad, to northern Nigeria, and thence to Niger, with disastrous epidemics developing in early 1937. CSM hit Upper Volta in 1938 and Mali and northern Ghana in 1939, and local outbreaks continued through 1941. Mortality statistics are very unreliable, but even with the advent of sulfa drugs, several tens of thousands died. CSM was again epidemic in the years 1943–7, with major outbreaks reported from Chad to Senegal. Upper Volta, western Niger, and northwest Ghana were especially seriously afflicted.

Another cycle of epidemics developed in 1949 from foci in northern Ghana, northern Nigeria, and Upper Volta, spreading eastward as far as Sudan by 1952. By this time, meningococcal meningitis had become well established throughout the region, and geographic patterns of spread were much less distinct. At least 250,000 and perhaps a million or more people died of CSM in West Africa between 1905 and the end of the colonial period in 1960. The disease remains a very serious public health problem in the entire CSM belt, despite the advent of sulfa and penicillin therapy and vaccines against serogroup A pathogens.

The puzzlingly late discovery of meningitis as a clinical entity did not retard development of knowledge of its etiology. The sporadic nature of outbreaks and the apparent lack of transmissibility of infection by victims led many nineteenth-century writers to believe that the disease was not contagious and was somehow linked to climate or environmental conditions such as crowding. By about 1860, however, it was widely assumed that there was some sort of specific poison or agent involved. In 1887 an Austrian pathologist, Anton Weichselbaum, described the meningococcus under the name *Diplococcus intracellularis meningitidis*. This organism was suspected of being the primary pathogen for many years, but its role was not proven until studies done in 1904 and 1905 in connection with the great Silesian epidemic. By 1910 it was recognized that the meningococcus was responsible for epidemics and that other bacteria could cause sporadic cases. Lumbar puncture, introduced in 1891 by Heinrich Quincke, provided an easy method to get cerebrospinal fluid for study, and was sometimes used to provide relief from the terrible headaches caused by the disease. The crucial epidemiological role of asymptomatic carriers was appreciated by the turn of the century.

After 1905, inspired by success against diphtheria, there were many attempts to develop a therapeutic serum. Some early successes were reported, especially in France, but by 1909 it was clear that there were important serologic differences among strains. Workers in Britain, the United States, and France had established four major serogroups by the end of World War I. Vaccine therapy remained of limited value, but in the absence of anything else, it was frequently tried. In the 1930s, French efforts to protect Africans against serogroup A by vaccination had inconclusive results, and similar British trials in Sudan were unsuccessful.

The development of sulfa drugs in the 1930s revolutionized meningitis therapy. Gerhardt Domagk published on one such drug in 1935; French workers at the Institut Pasteur introduced a more effective active form, sulfanilamide, later in the same year. Clinical trials showed the almost miraculous impact of sulfanilamide on meningococcal infections in 1937. This drug, one of a group of chemicals called *sulfonamides*, reduced case-fatality rates from between 50 and 80 percent to 20 percent and less, and saved many thousands of lives during the meningitis epidemics of World War II. Sulfa drugs were successfully used for prophylaxis and to reduce carrier rates by the U.S. Army beginning in 1943; the technique was widely adopted for troops and during outbreaks.

The advent of this class of "wonder drugs" had an especially dramatic impact in the CSM belt of Africa, where they were introduced in early 1938 in the midst of major epidemics in Sudan and West Africa. Prior to this date, Africans had been well aware that European therapy was useless. Preventive measures seemed equally futile and were often arbitrary and very harsh. Victims were usually quarantined, and cordons were sometimes thrown around whole villages and districts. Such efforts disrupted trade and care of the sick, but, given the key role of asymptomatic carriers and the use of bush paths to avoid police checkpoints, they did nothing to impede the spread of the disease. Annoying procedures like "nasopharyngeal disinfection" of travelers in Chad or destroying houses or removing their roofs in Sudan did not encourage African cooperation with colonial medical authorities. Indeed, Africans very sensibly tried to hide cases, preferring not to add government public health measures to the burdens of an epidemic. Sulfa drugs were, however, extremely effective. Africans responded pragmatically to this new treatment and, seeing death rates plummet, eagerly began to report cases and seek treatment for themselves and their children. In many areas, a shortage of medical workers forced authorities to give supplies of drugs to chiefs to pass along to the sick. This and the introduction of drug prophylaxis meant that CSM, in sharp contrast to earlier decades, was overreported during the 1940s and 1950s.

In 1963 sulfa-resistant strains of *N. meningitis* were detected by U.S. military doctors and the spread of such strains has forced an end to sulfa prophylaxis. Penicillin therapy is still very effective, but this antibiotic has no preventive value. Vaccines against serogroup C and A organisms were introduced in 1971 and 1973, respectively. Improved vaccines for these and other serogroups have been developed in recent years, although there is still no protection against serogroup B bacteria. Meningitis will probably remain a public health problem, especially in underdeveloped countries. Death occurs in about 5 percent of all cases, even with prompt treatment. Poverty, logistical problems, and financial difficulties make meningitis a continuing threat in the traditional CSM belt of Africa.

K. David Patterson

Bibliography

Centers for Disease Control. 1986. *Summary of notifiable diseases, United States, 1986.* Atlanta.

Danielson, L., and E. Mann. 1983. The first American account of cerebrospinal meningitis. *Reviews of Infectious Diseases* 5: 967–72. [Reprint of 1806 article.]

Dowling, Harry F. 1977. *Fighting infection: Conquests of the twentieth century.* Cambridge, Mass.

Hirsch, August. 1886. *Handbook of geographical and historical pathology,* Vol. III. London.

Lapeyssonie, L. 1963. La Méningite cérébro-spinale en Afrique. *Bulletin of The World Health Organization* 28 (Supplement).

Netter, Arnold, and Robert Debré. 1911. *La Méningite cérébrospinale.* Paris.

Patterson, K. David, and Gerald W. Hartwig. 1984. *Cerebrospinal meningitis in West Africa and Sudan in the twentieth century.* Los Angeles.

Solente, Lucy. 1938. Histoire de l'évolution des méningites cérébro-spinales aiguës. *Révue de Médicine* 55: 18–29.

Vedros, Neylan A., ed. 1987. *Evolution of meningococcal disease,* 2 vols. Boca Raton, Fla.

Waddy, B. B. 1957. African epidemic cerebro-spinal meningitis. *Journal of Tropical Medicine and Hygiene* 60: 179–89, 218–23.

VIII.90
Milk Sickness (Tremetol Poisoning)

Milk sickness, usually called *milksick* by early nineteenth-century American pioneers, denotes what we now know to be poisoning by milk from cows that have eaten either the white snakeroot or the rayless goldenrod plants. The white snakeroot, common in the Midwest and upper South, is a member of the Compositae called *Eupatorium urticaefolium.* It is also known as white sanicle, squaw weed, snake weed, pool wort, and deer wort. A shade-loving plant, it is frequently seen growing on roadsides, in damp open areas of the woods, or on the shaded north side of ridges. The rayless goldenrod, *Haplopappus heterophyllus,* is the cause of the disease in southwestern states, such as Arizona and New Mexico.

Milk sickness has been called variously alkali poisoning, puking disease, sick stomach, the slows or sloes, stiff joints, swamp sickness, tires, and trembles (when it occurs in animals). It is now known as *tremetol poisoning* after an identified toxic ingredient of the white snakeroot and rayless goldenrod. Tremetol, obtained from the leaves and stems of these plants by extraction with ether, is an unsaturated alcohol with the empirical formula $C_{16}H_{22}O_3$. In consistency and odor, it resembles turpentine.

Distribution and Incidence

Milk sickness was unknown in Europe or in any other region of the world except North America. It appeared in North Carolina as early as the American Revolution near a mountain ridge named Milk Sick. Its highest incidence was in dry years when cows wandered from their brown pastures into the woods in search of forage. As more forests were cleared so that cattle had more adequate pasture, and as fences were built, the incidence of milk sickness decreased rapidly.

The disease wrought havoc in the Midwest, especially in Illinois, Indiana, and Ohio, and in the upper southern states of Kentucky, North Carolina, Tennessee, and Virginia. Milk sickness was, in some years and some localities, the most important obstacle to settlement by the pioneers. Beginning about 1815, a flood of pioneers moved west. As they penetrated the forest wilderness of the Midwest they all too frequently came upon evidence of epidemics of the disease as several villages were abandoned. Physicians in Kentucky and Tennessee described milk sickness as being so widespread that the Kentucky legislature appointed a committee in 1827 to investigate its cause. A few years later, the state medical society of Indiana also attempted a similar investigation. Interestingly, in that state it has been noted that "Evansville, Indiana, owes its prominent position . . . today, in part at least, [to] the fact that its early competitor, Darlington, was abandoned" because of milk sickness (Snively 1967).

Epidemiology and Etiology

In 1811, an anonymous author wrote that milk sickness was a true poisoning because it involved no fever. He also believed that it was caused by poisonous milk that had a peculiar taste and smell. The source of the poison, he wrote, was vegetation eaten by the cows. He further advised that finding the offending plant would remove a major stumbling block to emigration westward.

In the years that followed, the theories as to the cause of milk sickness were numerous. One suggested that the cause was arsenic; another claimed it was a mysterious soil organism, whereas another attributed the disease to a mysterious exhalation from the soil. Still others incriminated various poisonous minerals and springs. Nonetheless there was no definite identification of one specific toxic plant during the nineteenth century. In the 1880s, the medical revolution following the discoveries of Louis Pasteur in France and Robert Koch in Germany led to the expectation that many obscure diseases such as milk sickness would prove to be of bacterial etiology. This expectation appeared to have been realized when Edwin Jordan and Norman Harris (1909) reported that *Bacillus lactimorbi* was the cause of milk sickness in humans and trembles in cattle. Needless to say, they were wrong.

Beginning in 1905, however, Edwin Moseley of what is now Bowling Green State University in Ohio began a scientific study of the white snakeroot that lasted for over three decades. In careful animal-feeding trials, he established the toxic dose of snakeroot for animals at 6 to 10 percent body weight. He also found that the stems were less poisonous than the leaves and that neither freezing nor drying destroyed the poison. His book, published in 1941, is the definitive work on milk sickness.

Finally James Couch (1928) reported that he had isolated three poisonous substances from the white snakeroot: a volatile oil and a resin acid that did not produce trembles, and an oily liquid with the characteristics of a secondary alcohol that did. The last he identified as $C_{16}H_{22}O_3$ and, drawing on the Latin *tremēre* meaning "tremble," named it *tremetol*.

Heating reduces somewhat the toxicity of poisoned milk, and oxidation readily destroys the toxic properties of tremetol. Because only a small number of cows are likely to be secreting toxic milk at one time, human illness is seen chiefly when milk from a single animal or herd is consumed. It is now thought that the dilution that occurs in the usual dairy collection and distribution of milk from a large milk source, rather than pasteurization, is the reason for the failure of milk sickness to develop in urban areas. For that reason, milk sickness has become extremely rare. Moreover, in rural areas, farmers are now well aware that to avoid trembles or milk sickness, one need only abandon woodland grazing, for the white snakeroot is a woodland plant and almost never found in bright and open pastures.

Clinical Manifestations

When milk sickness occurs in animals, chiefly cattle, it is called trembles. The animals suffer from anorexia, weakness, falling, stiffness, and trembling.

In humans the symptoms of milk sickness include anorexia, listlessness, severe constipation, and –

most important of all, and underlying most of the symptoms – profound acidosis; the latter, if untreated, leads to coma and death. Because of the acidosis, the breath smells of acetone, described in the past as an overpowering "fetor." The weakness is thought to be due chiefly to hypoglycemia, and death, to ketoacidosis and marked fatty degeneration of the liver, kidney, and muscles. The disease can be chronic or latent, and is likely to recur if the patient is subjected to fatigue, starvation, intercurrent infection, or vigorous exercise.

The lethargy that characterizes the patient who has not completely recovered from an attack of milk sickness helped give it the name of slows (or sloes). Abraham Lincoln knew it by that name, and, annoyed by the desultory progress of the Army of the Potomac in the early months of the Civil War, he once tartly remarked that General McClellan "seemed to have the slows."

History and Geography

Milk sickness has vanished from the list of major concerns of modern Americans. Although endemic in the Midwest and upper South, it had never been seen elsewhere in the United States, in Europe, or in any other continent. The settlers along the Atlantic seaboard knew nothing of it, and if the Indians or their cattle suffered from the disease, they did not inform the early settlers. Not until the pioneers began to push westward beyond the Alleghenies did the disease attract attention.

The first sporadic cases to be recognized occurred in North Carolina in the years preceding the Revolution. It was generally known that on the western side of the Allegheny Mountains from Georgia to the Great Lakes a disorder called trembles prevailed among cattle, and that wherever it appeared, the settlers were likely to get a disease, which from its most prominent symptom received at first the name "sick stomach" and from a theory concerning its cause that of "milk sickness."

In 1811, the *Medical Repository* of New York contained an anonymous report entitled "Disease in Ohio, Ascribed to Some Deleterious Quality in the Milk of Cows." This appears to be the earliest surviving reference to a disease that was to become a frequent cause of death and a major source of misery and mystification in the rural South and Midwest through a large part of the nineteenth century.

William Snively and Louanna Furbee (1956) described a discovery made in 1834 by Anna Pierce Hobbs, a pioneer doctor, in southeastern Illinois. Having learned from a Shawnee medicine woman

that white snakeroot caused trembles and milk sickness, she had a calf fed several bunches of the root. The calf developed typical trembles, enforcing her conviction that she had found the cause of milk sickness. John Rowe, a farmer of Fayette County, Ohio, wrote in 1838 that he had discovered through similar experimentation that trembles was caused by ingestion of white snakeroot.

During the second half of the nineteenth century, milk sickness occurred sporadically, which made sequential observations difficult to make, and the reason for its cause was lost in the widely held medical belief in miasmas and exhalations from the ground. Moreover, because milk sickness was limited to the Midwest, upper South, and Southwest, influential eastern physicians tended to ignore it or even discount the possibility that it really existed as a disease *sui generis*.

Nonetheless, the solution was eventually found when attention was turned back to the poisonous plant theory advanced during the first half of the century. Although many plants were suspected, such as poison ivy, water hemlock, Virginia creeper, coralberry, spurge, mushrooms, and march marigold, scrutiny finally centered once again on white snakeroot. Yet it was not until 1928 that the white snakeroot was established with certainty as the cause of milk sickness – over a century after the anonymous 1811 article appeared.

The question that Snively has asked remains: "How could a disease, perhaps the leading cause of death and disability in the Midwest and Upper South for over two centuries, go unrecognized by the medical profession at large until 1928?"

Thomas E. Cone, Jr.

Bibliography

Anon. 1811. Disease in Ohio ascribed to some deleterious quality in milk of cows. *Medical Repository [N.Y.]* 3: 92–4.

Couch, James F. 1928. Milk sickness, result of richweed poisoning. *Journal of the American Medical Association* 91: 234–6.

Furbee, Louanna, and William D. Snively, Jr. 1968. Milk sickness, 1811–1966: A bibliography. *Journal of the History of Medicine* 23: 276–85.

Hartmann, Alexis F., Sr., et al. 1963. Tremetol poisoning – not yet extinct. *Journal of the American Medical Association* 185: 706–9.

Jordan, Edwin O., and Norman MacL. Harris. 1909. Milk sickness. *Journal of Infectious Diseases* 6: 401–91.

Jordan, Philip D. 1944. Milk sickness in the western country together with an account of the death of Lincoln's mother. *Ohio State Medical Journal* 40: 848–51.

McKeever, George E. 1976. Milk sickness: A disease of the Middle West. *Michigan Medicine* 72: 775–80.

Moseley, Edwin L. 1941. *Milk sickness caused by white snakeroot*. Ann Arbor, Mich.

Snively, William D., Jr. 1967. Mystery of the milksick. *Minnesota Medicine* 50: 469–76.

Snively, William D., Jr., and Louanna Furbee. 1956. Discovery of the cause of milk sickness. *Journal of the American Medical Association* 196: 1055–60.

VIII.91
Multiple Sclerosis

Multiple sclerosis is a disease of the central nervous system characterized clinically by recurring episodes of neurological disturbance which, especially early in the course of the disease, tend to remit spontaneously, although as time goes by there is often a gradual accumulation of disability. The course of the disease is quite variable, at one extreme lasting for 50 years without the development of significant disability, and at the other terminating fatally in a matter of months. Overall, about one quarter of patients remain able to work for up to 15 years after the first recognized clinical manifestation, and the mean duration of life is approximately 25 years from that time. Nevertheless, because the disease commonly affects young adults and produces disability in the prime of life, the economic burden is heavy, in the United States averaging $15,000 per annum per family with a member afflicted (Inman 1983 data, cited in McDonald and Silberberg, eds. 1986, 180).

Overview

Multiple sclerosis is a remarkable disease. It was first clearly described more than 120 years ago in a way which we would recognize as a modern, pathologically based account that discusses the clinical features of the illness and their possible pathophysiology (Charcot 1868). It is only since the early 1970s, however, that real progress has been made in understanding its nature, course, and pathogenesis. It was discussed in treatises on pathology by R. Carswell (1838) and J. Cruveilhier (1835–42), and more knowledge was added by E. Rindfleisch (1873), but the French school did most to delineate the disease. Good descriptions were appearing in standard textbooks of neurology before the end of the nineteenth

century, and in 1916 J. W. Dawson gave an exhaustive account of the pathology of the disease which has remained a standard reference.

Three personal accounts of multiple sclerosis by sufferers are worth reading for the insights that they give into its course and its consequences. The first two take the form of diaries, one written in the nineteenth century by Augustus d'Esté, one of King George III's illegitimate grandsons, and the other early in the twentieth century by a young naturalist who used the pseudonym W. N. P. Barbellion (Barbellion 1919; Firth 1948). The third, a well-illustrated account of the visual experience of optic neuritis (one of the common manifestations of multiple sclerosis the main symptoms of which are well described by d'Esté), was recently provided by Peter MacKarell (1986), a professional painter who was afflicted by it.

The geography of multiple sclerosis is interesting because it is strange and because understanding it may provide a crucial clue to the nature of the disease (see Matthews et al. 1985; McDonald 1986). Geographic peculiarities were first noted 85 years ago when Byron Bramwell argued that the higher incidence of multiple sclerosis in his practice in Edinburgh than that of neurologists in New York reflected a real difference in frequency between the two cities.

Forty years ago, the notion of the relevance of genetic background as well as latitude was pointed out by Geoffrey Dean on the basis of the lower prevalence of multiple sclerosis among Boers than among British descendants in South Africa; in both groups the prevalence of the disease in Africa was the same as in their countries of origin. The idea that genetic background was important also received support from the discovery of the rarity of multiple sclerosis among the Japanese. In the past 20 years, strenuous efforts have been made to determine the consequences of migration at different ages from areas of high to low prevalence, and vice versa. These studies support the general idea of an interaction between latitude and genetic factors determining the geographic distribution of the disease.

Pathology

The characteristic lesion of multiple sclerosis is the *plaque of demyelination* – a patch varying from a few cubic millimeters to many cubic centimeters in which the myelin sheath of nerve fibers is destroyed, leaving the axons relatively intact. Small plaques are oriented around small veins (the venules), though this orientation is often obscured in large lesions. The venules in areas of active demyelination, as judged by the presence of inflammatory cells and myelin breakdown products, are surrounded by cells derived from the immune system. Such cells are also present in the substance of the brain itself — in the lesions, especially at the edges, where it has been suggested that they may play a role in limiting the spread of damage.

The outstanding feature of the chronic lesion is the formation of a fibrous scar as a result of proliferation of the astrocytes, one of the supporting cells of the central nervous system. Remyelination, at least in most cases coming to post mortem, is scanty, although it is an open question whether it may be more extensive early in the course of the disease.

The plaques are distributed asymmetrically throughout the brain and spinal cord, but there are certain sites of predilection which determine the characteristic clinical pattern of the disease. The important functional consequence of demyelination is block of electrical conduction in the nerve fibers which leads to many of the clinical features of the disease.

Clinical Manifestations

In at least 80 percent of patients, the disease follows a relapsing and remitting course, often in the later stages entering a steadily progressive phase. Fully 5 to 10 percent of patients experience a steadily progressive course from onset. The typical episode of neurological disturbance develops over a matter of days or a week or two, persists for a few weeks, then resolves over a month or two. Common manifestations include reversible episodes of visual loss (optic neuritis), sensory disturbance or weakness in the trunk or limbs, vertigo, and bladder disturbance. Obvious disturbance of intellectual function is uncommon, except in severe cases. Recently, however, subtle defects have been demonstrated early in the course of the disease.

Certain special clinical patterns are of interest. Steadily progressive spastic weakness is more common in late-onset cases (older than 40 years). In Orientals generally, severe and persistent visual loss and limb weakness are particularly common. In the same group, a curious form of spasmodic disorder of the limbs is also frequent. The reasons for these well-documented ethnic differences in the pattern of clinical involvement are unknown.

Distribution and Incidence

Multiple sclerosis affects principally individuals of northern European Caucasoid origin living in temperate zones, though it does occur infrequently in the tropics and in other racial groups. Because the course of the disease is so prolonged and the manifestations are so variable, it is difficult to determine its true incidence, and prevalence rates are generally used to compare the frequency of the disease in different populations. Females are affected about twice as commonly as men. The average age of onset is 30 years old, and it rarely starts over the age of 60 or before puberty. In Caucasoid populations, approximately 10 percent of patients have an affected relative. The concordance rate in twins (i.e., the frequency with which both members of a twin pair have the disease) is about 30 percent for identical twins and 2 percent for nonidentical twins, the latter being similar to the frequency in siblings. The difference in concordance rate between identical and nonidentical twins provides strong evidence for the implication of a genetic factor in the etiology of the disease, but the rather low concordance rate in identical twins suggests that an environmental factor is also involved. Further evidence implicating both environmental and genetic factors comes from a consideration of the geography and epidemiology of the disease.

Geography and Epidemiology

There are two relevant geographic aspects: the distribution of the disease and the distribution of its genetic associations. Among Caucasoids the prevalence of multiple sclerosis is generally higher in higher latitudes. In the United Kingdom, for example, the prevalence in the Orkney and Shetland Islands is 309 per 100,000, in northern Scotland 178 per 100,000, and in the south of England 100 per 100,000. It must be pointed out, however, that these prevalence studies have been conducted at different times, and the reliability of ascertainment varies. Nevertheless, data from other regions suggest that the trends are real: Multiple sclerosis is more common in the northern United States and Canada than in the southern United States, and in the more temperate south of New Zealand and Australia than in their northern portions.

The influence of migration on risk has been studied in several populations. Migration from high prevalence (e.g., northern Europe and the northern United States) to low prevalence areas (e.g., Israel, South Africa, or the southern United States) before puberty appears to decrease the risk of developing the disease, while migration after puberty does not. The total number of patients involved in these studies is small, but the consistency of the results suggests that the observation is significant. Studies of migration from low-risk to high-risk zones (Vietnam to Paris, New British Commonwealth to the Old) are based on even smaller numbers, though they have yielded concordant results. These observations provide further, albeit rather weak, evidence for the operation of an environmental factor in the etiology of multiple sclerosis, although this would seem to be the case if the risk of developing the disease is influenced by where individuals spend their first 15 years.

On the face of it, stronger evidence comes from the study of apparent clusters of cases in the Faroe Islands in the North Sea. No cases had been identified in the Faroe Islands prior to World War II. But between 1943 and 1973, there were 32 cases; there have been no new cases since. Although it cannot be certain that cases prior to 1943 were not missed, the balance of evidence is in favor of there being an unusual run of them in the 30 years after that date. J. F. Kurtzke and K. Hyllested (1986) have analyzed the data minutely and have suggested that there were two mini-epidemics within the main one. In addition, they have pointed out that the pattern of presentation of the cases suggests a point source epidemic and, noting that the places of residence of the patients were close to the location of army camps during World War II, have proposed that an infection was introduced by the British troops occupying the islands during that period. C. M. Poser and P. L. Hibberd (1988) have challenged these conclusions. Nonetheless, the overall clustering of cases is striking and probably a phenomenon of biological significance, indicating exposure to a newly introduced environmental agent in the early 1940s. Other examples of clustering have been reported but are less convincing.

Multiple sclerosis is much less frequent in non-Caucasoid populations. No postmortem-proved case has yet been described in African blacks, and prevalence of the disease is lower in American blacks than in whites living in the same areas. The disease is similarly rare among American Indians, the Maoris in New Zealand, the gypsies in Hungary, and Orientals living in California and Washington State but not in the larger populations they live among. Multiple sclerosis is also rare among the Japanese in Japan; among the Chinese in Taiwan, China, and Hong Kong; and among Indians living in India. It is so far unreported in the Eskimo. In many of these groups (but not Orientals in the United States and Japan), problems of ascertainment may have led to a significant underestimate of the true frequency of the disease. Nevertheless, it is clear that there are real differences in the frequency of the disease in different ethnic groups, again suggesting the operation of a genetic factor in determining susceptibility.

Genetics

The most intensively studied genetic associations of multiple sclerosis are those within the human leukocyte antigen (HLA) region of the sixth chromosome. The most frequent association in Caucasoid populations is with HLA-DR2, though others, including DQwl, have been reported. The strength of the associations varies in different population groups. R. J. Swingler and D. A. S. Compston (1986), though cautious in interpreting their data, have reported that in the United Kingdom the north–south gradient of prevalence of multiple sclerosis is mirrored by a similar gradient in the frequency of DR2 in the control population. In the New World, G. C. Ebers and D. Bulman (1986) have shown that in the United States the areas of highest prevalence correspond with the areas of immigration from Finland and Scandinavia (where there is a high frequency of DR2), and D. C. G. Skegg and colleagues (1987) have shown that multiple sclerosis is three times less common in the north than in the south of New Zealand – the latter a site of preferential migration for the Scots, who have a particularly high frequency of DR2.

There are fewer data for non-Caucasoid populations. In a small study, multiple sclerosis was found to be associated with the Dw2 (related to DR2) in blacks in Philadelphia. Among the Arabs, multiple sclerosis is associated with DR2 in some groups, and DR4 in others. No HLA association has been found in the Japanese and Israelis.

It should be noted that multiple sclerosis is rare in two populations in which DR2 is common: the Hungarian Gypsies (of whom 56 percent of controls are DR2 positive) as well as the Maoris – raising the possibility of the existence of an overriding genetic protective effect. Protective genes have also been postulated in Mongoloid and Caucasoid populations. Moreover, current research suggests that multiple sclerosis may be associated with peculiarities in the structure of certain genes in the HLA region.

What is one to make of this mass of confusing and sometimes conflicting data? The frequency with which some association with the HLA system is found suggests that the observations are significant. Yet it is clear that none of the factors so far identified alone confer susceptibility to the disease. The simplest explanation would be that DR2 is acting as a marker for another gene (or genes) conferring susceptibility, and that other genetic factors are involved as well.

Other possible genetic associations have been little studied, although there is evidence for an association with genes concerned with the control of antibody structure located on the fourteenth chromosome. A consistent pattern has not yet emerged. What is common to all the genetic associations so far identified is that they are concerned in one way or another with the genetic control of the immune response.

Pathogenesis and Etiology

In considering how the geographic, epidemiological, genetic, and pathological data might fit together, it must be stressed that there is no wholly satisfactory framework within which to incorporate all the data.

Pathogenesis

Much evidence has accumulated suggesting an immunologic basis for the disorder in patients with multiple sclerosis. There is abnormal synthesis of antibodies, both inside and outside the brain; there are changes in the number and functional activity of peripheral blood lymphocyte subsets in active disease; and there are immune-competent cells around the venules in the lesions and in the brain itself. The occurrence of such changes in the retina (where there is no myelin) is evidence that the vascular events are not secondary to myelin breakdown produced in some other way. This, combined with the results of recent functional vascular studies and other evidence, suggests that a vascular change is a critical early event in development of the new lesion.

Etiology

These processes provide a plausible though incomplete explanation for the development of the lesions in established multiple sclerosis. What of its initiation? There is good evidence from family studies and epidemiology that an environmental trigger, probably infective, is required in the genetically susceptible individual. The most likely infective agent would be a virus, though interest in spirochetes has been revived recently on rather slender grounds.

Two possible mechanisms for demyelination following viral infection are now known that occur only in genetically susceptible hosts. With visna, a retrovirus infection of certain strains of sheep, there are recurring episodes of demyelination of the central nervous system dependent on a direct attack of the virus; the remissions are due to the formation of neutralizing antibodies, whereas the exacerbations are due to mutations that lead to the loss of antibody control and renewed multiplication of the virus

(Johnson 1982). There are, however, a number of important clinical and pathological differences between visna and multiple sclerosis, including the consistent failure to isolate, reproducibly from the latter, a virus or fragments of one.

The second plausible mechanism involves the development of an autoimmune form of demyelination (after complete elimination of the virus) in mice inoculated intracerebrally with corona virus (Watanabe, Wege, and Ter Meulen 1983). The limitations of this model are that it is not known whether the process occurs after a natural route of infection, and whether in appropriate strains of animals a spontaneously relapsing and remitting disease can develop.

In conclusion, a solution to the problem of the nature and cause of multiple sclerosis would seem to be within sight. When we understand the reasons for the peculiar distribution of the disease, we are also likely to understand its etiology and pathogenesis.

W. I. McDonald

Bibliography

Barbellion, W. N. P. 1919. *The journal of a disappointed man.* London.

Carswell, R. 1838. *Pathological anatomy: Illustrations of the elementary forms of disease.* London.

Charcot, J. M. 1968. Histologie de la sclérose en plaques. *Gazette Hôpital (Paris)* 41: 554–5, 557–8, 566.

Cruveilhier, J. 1835–42. *Anatomie pathologique du corps humain: Descriptions avec figures lithographiées et coloriées: Des diverses alterations morbides dont le corps humain est susceptible.* Paris.

Dawson, J. W. 1916. The histology of disseminated sclerosis. *Transactions of the Royal Society of Edinburgh* 50: 517–740.

Ebers, G. C., and D. Bulman. 1986. The geography of MS reflects genetic susceptibility. *Neurology* 36 (Supplement 1): 108.

Firth, D. 1948. *The case of Augustus d'Esté.* Cambridge.

Johnson, R. T. 1982. *Viral infections of the nervous system.* New York.

Kurtzke, J. F., and K. Hyllested. 1986. Multiple sclerosis in the Faroe Islands. II. Clinical update, transmission and the nature of MS. *Neurology* 36: 307–28.

MacKarell, P. 1986. Interior journey and beyond: An artist's view of optic neuritis. In *Optic neuritis,* ed. R. F. Plant and G. T. Hess. Cambridge.

Matthews, W. B., et al. 1985. *McAlpine's multiple sclerosis.* London.

McDonald, W. I. 1986. The mystery of the origin of multiple sclerosis. Gowers Lecture. *Journal of Neurology, Neurosurgery, and Psychiatry* 49: 113–23.

McDonald, W. I., and D. H. Silberberg, eds. 1986. *Multiple sclerosis.* London.

Poser, C. M., and P. L. Hibberd. 1988. Analysis of the

epidemic of multiple sclerosis in the Faroe Islands. II. Biostatistical aspects. *Neuroepidemiology* 7: 181–9.

Rindfleisch, E. 1873. *A manual of pathological histology*, Vol. III. London.

Skegg, D. C. G., et al. 1987. Occurrence of multiple sclerosis in the north and south of New Zealand. *Journal of Neurology, Neurosurgery and Psychiatry* 50: 134–9.

Swingler, R. J., and D. A. S. Compston. 1986. The distribution of multiple sclerosis in the United Kingdom. *Journal of Neurology, Neurosurgery and Psychiatry* 49: 115–24.

Watanabe, R., H. Wege, and V. Ter Meulen. 1983. Active transfer of EAE-like lesions from rats with corona virus-induced demyelinating encephalomyelitis. *Nature* 305: 150–3.

VIII.92
Mumps

Mumps (infectious parotitis; epidemic parotitis) is a common, acute, viral infectious disease, principally of children, with worldwide distribution. It is frequently clinically characterized by fever and painful enlargement of one or more salivary glands. Inapparent infection is common and occurs in about one-third of infections. Sometimes postpubertal males with mumps may develop painful swelling of the testicles, usually only on one side, with sterility an extremely rare complication. Mumps is a vaccine-preventable disease, but the vaccine is not yet widely used on a global basis.

Etiology and Epidemiology

Mumps is caused by the mumps virus, a member of the genus *Paramyxovirus* of the family Paramyxoviridae. Mumps virus has an irregular spherical shape averaging about 200 nanometers in diameter and contains a single-stranded RNA genome.

Mumps is a contagious disease, only slightly less contagious than rubella and measles, transmitted from infected persons to susceptible individuals by droplet spread and by direct contact with saliva. Mumps virus has also been shown to be transmitted across the placenta to the fetus. There is no natural reservoir for mumps other than human beings, which means that a continuous chain of susceptible contacts is necessary to sustain transmission. Although the period of communicability may be from 6 days before salivary gland symptoms to 9 days after-

wards, the period of greatest infectivity is about 48 hours before salivary gland involvement. There is no carrier state. Mumps has an incubation period from time of exposure to onset of salivary gland swelling of about 18 days with a range of 2 to 3 weeks.

In populated areas with no or low vaccination coverage, mumps is primarily an endemic disease of children, with epidemics occurring in closely associated groups such as schools. Its peak incidence is found in the age group 6 to 10 years, and mumps is rare before 2 years of age. Outbreaks may occur at intervals ranging from 2 to 7 years. There is a concentration of cases in the cooler seasons in temperate climates, and there is no apparent seasonality in tropical areas. In more remote isolated populations, mumps is not endemic, and disease depends upon introduction of the virus from the outside, at which time an epidemic may occur, affecting all age groups born since the previous epidemic. There is no evidence for a sex or racial difference in incidence of mumps, although clinically apparent mumps may be more common in males than in females.

Distribution and Incidence

Serologic surveys as well as recorded outbreaks have demonstrated the existence of mumps throughout the world. Mumps is not a reportable disease in most countries, is underreported even in countries where it is a notifiable disease, and may be clinically inapparent in 30 to 40 percent of infections. In populated areas where mumps is both endemic and epidemic, over 80 percent of the adult population will show serologic evidence of prior infection. In remote or island populations where mumps is not endemic, a significant proportion of the population can be susceptible which may lead to large outbreaks when the mumps virus is introduced from the outside.

In some countries, such as the United States, where mumps is a reportable disease and mumps vaccine has been extensively used (often in combination with measles and rubella vaccine), there have been impressive declines in reported cases of mumps.

Immunology

Infants usually have a passive immunity to mumps because of maternal antibodies acquired transplacentally from their immune mothers. This passive immunity protects the infant from mumps infection for about 6 months, depending on the amount of maternal antibody acquired.

Mumps infection in both clinically apparent and inapparent cases induces a lifelong immunity. Because a significant percentage of mumps infections are clinically inapparent, persons may develop immunity without recognizing they have been infected. Several serologic tests for confirming infection or immunity have been developed, and it is also possible to isolate the virus from patients during the acute phase of the disease. Skin tests for immunity are not considered reliable.

A single dose of live attenuated mumps virus vaccine confers long-term, probably lifelong, immunity in over 90 percent of susceptible individuals.

Clinical Manifestations and Pathology

The prodromal phase of mumps disease may be absent or include symptoms of low-grade fever, loss of appetite, malaise, and headache. Salivary gland swelling will often follow the prodromal period within a day, although it sometimes will not begin for a week or more. The salivary gland swelling progresses to maximum size in 1 to 3 days. The gland is painful and tender to the touch. Typically both the parotid salivary glands are affected, usually with one gland enlarging a few days after the other; hence the name "infectious or epidemic parotitis." One-sided parotid gland involvement occurs in approximately one-fourth of patients who have salivary gland involvement. The fever may last for a variable period (from 1 to 6 days), and the parotid gland enlargement may be present for 6 to 10 days. It should be emphasized that approximately one-third of mumps cases may go unrecognized or be completely asymptomatic.

A common manifestation of mumps in approximately 20 to 30 percent of postpubertal males is painful testicular swelling (orchitis), usually one-sided. Sterility is an extremely rare outcome of testicular involvement on both sides, which occurs in only approximately 2 percent of cases. The next most common manifestation of mumps is central nervous system involvement in the form of a usually benign meningitis, which may occur in about 10 percent of all infections. Uncommon manifestations of mumps include involvement and sometimes painful swelling of other glands such as the ovaries, breasts, thyroid, and pancreas. Mumps-associated complications are rare and may include encephalitis, neuritis, arthritis, nephritis, hepatitis, pericarditis, and hematologic complications. Deafness, usually one-sided and often permanent, is reported to occur once per 20,000 cases of mumps. Although increased fetal mortality has been reported in women who contracted mumps during the first trimester, there is no evidence that mumps in pregnancy increases the risk of fetal malformations.

History and Geography

In the fifth century B.C., Hippocrates is believed to have first recognized mumps as a distinct clinical entity in his work *Epidemics I*. He described an outbreak of an illness on the island of Thasus, noting that "swelling appeared about the ears, in many on either side, and in the greatest number on both sides . . . in some instances earlier, and in others later, inflammations with pain seized sometimes one of the testicles, and sometimes both." Greek and Roman medical writers of antiquity as well as medieval practitioners at various times recorded cases of mumps-like illnesses, but there was relatively little study of the disease. Outbreaks of mumps in Paris in the sixteenth century were recorded by Guillaume de Baillou. In 1755 Richard Russell described mumps and expressed his opinion that the disease was communicable.

Mumps is called *Ziegenpeter* or *Bauerwetzel* in German and *oreillons* in French. The origin of the term "mumps" is unclear although it may come from the English noun *mump,* meaning a "lump," or the English verb *mump,* meaning "to be sulky," or even perhaps from the pattern of mumbling speech in individuals with significant salivary gland swelling.

In 1790, Robert Hamilton presented a very full description of mumps to the Royal Society of Edinburgh. He emphasized that orchitis was a manifestation of mumps and suggested that some mumps patients had symptoms of central nervous system involvement. In the beginning of the eighteenth century, interest in the study of epidemics helped to establish the communicability and wide geographic distribution of the disease.

August Hirsch collected references to some 150 epidemics occurring between 1714 and 1859 in temperate latitudes in both hemispheres as well as in cold, subtropical, and equatorial regions. He specifically mentioned accounts of outbreaks that had occurred in diverse countries and places: "Iceland, the Faroe Islands, Lapland, Alaska, Egypt, Arabia, India, Malay Archipelago, Polynesia, the West Coast of Africa, Mexico, the West Indies, Peru, Italy, Sweden, Prussian Saxony, Schleswig and Holstein, the departments of Dusseldorf and Treves, the Cologne department, Martinique, Canton Zurich, Denmark, Lower Bavaria, Central Franconia, the quondam Duchy of Nassau, New York, Halle, Moscow, Bombay, and Berlin." He also stated that during the American Civil War, 11,216 cases among Confederate troops were reported during the first year of the war and 13,429 cases during the second year. He concluded that mumps "occurs in widest diffusion over the globe, no part of the world being exempt from this strange malady."

Data have also demonstrated the occurrence of epidemic mumps in the closely associated populations of prisons, orphanages, boarding schools, garrisons, and ships. Indeed, Haven Emerson noted that mumps was the most important disease in terms of days lost from active duty in the American Expeditionary Force in France during World War I; and Surgeon General T. Parran of the U.S. Public Health Service stated in 1940 that mumps was one of the most disabling of the acute infections among armed forces recruits, exceeded only by the venereal diseases.

Despite earlier animal experiments suggesting that the fluid of the salivary glands was infective, C. D. Johnson and E. W. Goodpasture were not able to prove conclusively the viral etiology of mumps until 1934. They demonstrated that mumps was caused by a filtrable virus in saliva by transmitting mumps from patients to rhesus monkeys. In 1945 K. Habel successfully cultivated mumps virus in chick embryos. In 1948 G. Henle and associates experimentally confirmed the significant percentage of clinically inapparent infections by deliberately exposing 15 susceptible subjects to mumps, then following their clinical condition, isolating the virus, and performing serologic studies. In 1951, an experimental killed-virus vaccine was used in humans. A live mumps virus vaccine has been used in the former U.S.S.R. since the early 1960s. In 1966 E. B. Buynak and M. R. Hilleman reported on the development of a live attenuated mumps virus vaccine, and they, R. E. Weibel, and others conducted a successful trial of the vaccine, which led to its licensure in 1967 in the United States.

The worldwide geographic distribution of mumps is well documented, even in Hirsch's collection of some 150 epidemics noted earlier. In populous countries without any sustained, large-scale immunization programs, mumps is widespread. In island or remote communities, large numbers of susceptible persons may exist. In countries with sustained, large-scale immunization programs, the impact of control efforts has been documented through decreasing numbers of cases of reported mumps.

Robert J. Kim-Farley

This chapter was written in the author's private capacity. No official support or endorsement by the Centers for Disease Control is intended or should be inferred.

Bibliography

Amstey, Marvin S., ed. 1984. *Virus infection in pregnancy.* New York.

Benenson, Abram S., ed. 1985. *Control of communicable diseases in man.* Washington, D.C.

Bett, Walter R., ed. 1954. *The history and conquest of common diseases.* Norman, Okla.

Bunyak, E. B., and Hilleman, M. R. 1966. Live attenuated mumps virus vaccine. I. Vaccine development. *Proceedings of the Society of Experimental Biology and Medicine* 123: 768–75.

Evans, Alfred S., ed. 1976. *Viral infections of humans: Epidemiology and control.* New York.

Gordon, John E., and Ralph H. Heeren. 1940. The epidemiology of mumps. *American Journal of the Medical Sciences* 200: 412–28.

Habel, K. 1945. Cultivation of mumps virus in the developing chick embryo and its application to studies of immunity to mumps in man. *Public Health Reports* 60: 201–12.

Hamilton, Robert. 1790. An account of a distemper, by the common people in England vulgarly called the mumps. *Transactions of the Royal Society of Edinburgh* 2: 59–72.

Henle, G., and F. Deinhardt. 1955. Propagation and primary isolation of mumps virus in tissue culture. *Proceedings of the Society of Experimental Biology and Medicine* 89: 556–60.

Henle, G., et al. 1948. Isolation of mumps virus from human beings with induced apparent or inapparent infections. *Journal of Experimental Medicine* 88: 223.

Hirsch, August. 1886. *Handbook of historical and geographical pathology,* trans. Charles Creighton. London.

Johnson, C. D., and E. W. Goodpasture. 1934. An investigation of the etiology of mumps. *Journal of Experimental Medicine* 59: 1–19.

Krugman, S., and S. L. Katz. 1981. *Infectious diseases of children.* St. Louis.

Major, Ralph H. 1945. *Classic descriptions of disease.* Springfield, Ill.

U.S. Public Health Service. Centers for Disease Control. 1987. Mumps – United States, 1985–1986. *Morbidity and Mortality Weekly Report* 36: 151–5.

Weibel, R. E., et al. 1967. Live attenuated mumps-virus vaccine. III. Clinical and serologic aspects in a field evaluation. *New England Journal of Medicine* 245–51.

VIII.93
Muscular Dystrophy

The muscular dystrophies are a group of genetically determined, almost exclusively pediatric diseases. Generally, the earlier the age at which symptoms begin, the poorer is the prognosis. Because of a considerable overlap of manifestations and rates of progression and, until recently, the lack of any biochemical test, their classification is still unsettled. As a group, the principal differential diagnosis of the muscular *dystrophies* is from the muscular *atrophies*. In the former, the primary defect is in the voluntary muscle fibers; in the latter, it is in the innervation of muscles.

Classification

The most common of the dystrophies and the first to be described was that delineated by Guillaume B. A. Duchenne, a French neurologist, in 1868. *Duchenne muscular dystrophy* (DMD) is a sex-linked recessive disorder. Consequently, it clinically affects only males and is inherited through female carriers of the gene. Although affected boys have abnormally elevated concentrations of muscle cell enzymes such as creatine phosphokinase in their blood, this abnormality is also found in about three-fourths of the asymptomatic female carriers. DMD appears to have a rather uniform incidence worldwide, with a mean incidence estimated to be about 1 case per 4,000 live male births, or 15 to 33 cases per 100,000. Most surveys have been of predominantly Caucasian populations, but the results of a study in Japan were consistent with the others. A family history of DMD can be obtained in only about one-third of cases. The others are attributed to either a previously unexpressed carrier state or to a new mutation.

Cases can be identified during the first week of life by an excessive concentration of creatine phosphokinase in the blood, although the infant appears to be normal. The boy learns to walk somewhat late, falls easily, and has difficulty in getting up again. The gait gradually becomes broad based and waddling. Nevertheless, the diagnosis usually is not made before the age of 5 years. Unless the boy has been identified by biochemical screening during infancy and the parents receive genetic counseling, their risk of producing additional dystrophic children remains high.

The appearance of the child may be perplexing because, although he is weak, his muscles may appear to be unusually well developed. This *pseudohypertrophy* is due to the infiltration of muscle and replacement of muscle fibers by fat and connective tissue. As the disease progresses, muscle fibers increasingly appear abnormal microscopically, and others disappear. The upper extremities are affected later but in the same fashion as the pelvic girdle and lower limbs. Smooth muscle (e.g., intestinal tract, bladder) is not affected. As a result of subnormal stress on the developing skeleton from the weak musculature, ossification of long bones is delayed, and the mineral content of bones is deficient. Once weakness has resulted in confinement to wheelchair or bed, contractures of extremity joints and *kyphoscoliosis* (deformity of the vertebral column) supervene. A moderate degree of mental retardation frequently is an associated problem. Death is generally due to respiratory failure before the age of 20.

The defective gene of DMD was identified in 1986. Soon thereafter it was discovered that this genetic abnormality causes a deficiency of a protein, now called *dystrophin,* in the membrane of muscle fibers. Although this substance normally constitutes only 0.002 percent of the total muscle protein, its deficiency can now be detected and can serve as a specific diagnostic test.

At the other extreme from DMD in the spectrum of severity, there is *facio-scapulo-humeral dystrophy* (FSHD), which was described by the French neurologists Louis T. Landouzy and Joseph J. Déjerine in 1884. Onset usually occurs during adolescence, but can be much later. Its incidence has been estimated to be from 5 percent to 50 percent of the incidence of DMD. Inheritance is autosomal dominant, and FSHD occurs equally in both sexes. As the name indicates, the muscles of the face and shoulder girdle are affected first. Sometimes only facial muscles are involved. An affected person may be unable to close the eyelids completely or to purse the lips. Muscular involvement progresses downward to the pelvic girdle and legs, but it may become arrested at any time. Reproduction is not impaired. Death from sudden heart failure occurs in some cases. So far there is no effective treatment for the underlying abnormality of any of the muscular dystrophies.

Thomas G. Benedek

Bibliography

Drummond, L. M. 1979. Creatine phosphokinase levels in the newborn and their use in screening for Duchenne muscular dystrophy. *Archives of Disease in Childhood* 54: 362–66.

Emery, A. E. 1980. Duchenne muscular dystrophy: Genetic aspects, carrier detection and antenatal diagnosis. *British Medical Bulletin* 36: 117–22.

Gardner-Medwin, D. 1980. Clinical features and classification of the muscular dystrophies. *British Medical Bulletin* 36: 109–15.

Hoffman, E. P., et al. 1988. Characterization of dystrophin in muscle biopsy specimens from patients with Duchenne's or Becker's muscular dystrophy. *New England Journal of Medicine* 318: 1363–8.

Hyser, C. L., and J. R. Mendell. 1988. Recent advances in Duchenne and Becker muscular dystrophy. *Neurologic Clinics* 6: 429–53.

Kakulas, B. A., and R. D. Adams. 1985. *Diseases of muscle*, 4th edition. Philadelphia.

Kazadov, V. M., et al. 1974. The facio-scapulo-limb (or the facioscapulohumeral) type of muscular dystrophy: Clinical and genetic study of 200 cases. *European Neurology* 11: 236–60.

Leth, A., et al. 1985. Progressive muscular dystrophy in Denmark. *Acta Paediatrica Scandinavica* 74: 881–5.

Tangsrud, S. E. 1989. Child neuromuscular disease in southern Norway: The prevalence and incidence of Duchenne muscular dystrophy. *Acta Paediatrica Scandinavica* 78: 881–5.

VIII.94
Myasthenia Gravis

Myasthenia gravis is a disorder of skeletal muscle characterized by weakness and easy fatigability due to autoimmune destruction of the acetylcholine receptor in the postsynaptic membrane of the neuromuscular junction.

Distribution and Incidence

The disease has a worldwide distribution and has been identified as the primary cause of death at the average annual rate of 1.5 per million in the United States. If cases coded as contributory or as a complication are included, then the total would be 2 to 2.5. This seems to be the safest method of reckoning the actual incidence of myasthenia gravis, and previous estimates of 1 in 1,600 of the population probably vastly overestimate the incidence of myasthenia. There is no difference between whites and nonwhites, and there is no difference in nationality. The death rate is slightly higher for women than men. In age-adjusted death rates for all ages, there is no appreciable difference in nine geographic regions of the United States. Thus myasthenia gravis seems to

be uniformly distributed throughout the United States, and probably is uniformly distributed throughout the world. There is no difference between city and country in the incidence of myasthenia gravis, and the age-specific death rates for the United States, based on a survey of 675 death certificates listing myasthenia gravis as the primary cause of death, showed that 90 percent of the decedents were older than 15 years of age. For this population the age-specific death rate is less than 1 per million until age 35, when there is a steady increase in the incidence of death for myasthenia gravis up to age 75. There appears to be a twin-peaked incidence, with females peaking between the ages of 15 and 24, and men peaking between ages 40 and 60. But if all ages are considered together, the sex ratio is probably close to 1. Morbidity data in surveys of the United States, Canada, England, Norway, and Iceland over a 10-year period using retrospective analysis show that the incidence of myasthenia is probably 0.2 to 0.5 per 100,000, with the prevalence being 3 to 6 per 100,000. In other words, the prevalence is approximately 10 times the incidence.

Etiology and Immunology

The overwhelming evidence is that myasthenia gravis is due to an immune system dysfunction that produces an autodirected antibody against the acetylcholine receptor in the postsynaptic membrane of the neuromuscular junction. The evidence is clinical, laboratory, serologic, and therapeutic. The clinical evidence that myasthenia is an autoimmune disease is based on the association of myasthenia with vaccination, insect sting, infection, or trauma; and its association with autoimmune diseases such as hypothyroidism, systemic lupus, and polymyositis. Many laboratory abnormalities point to the immune system dysfunction in myasthenia gravis. These include serologic abnormalities, increased incidence of a specific human leukocyte antigen (HLA-B8) in certain types of disease, histologic abnormalities of thymus and skeletal muscle, and abnormal responsiveness of lymphocytes to mitogens. Antinuclear antibodies are positive in uncomplicated myasthenia in about 18 percent of cases and in 54 percent of myasthenic patients who have thymoma, a tumor derived from elements of the thymus. Antistriated muscle antibodies are present in about 11 percent of patients with uncomplicated myasthenia and in all patients who have myasthenia associated with thymoma. Perhaps the most important serologic test in myasthenia is the IgG antibody directed against the acetylcholine receptor.

This antibody is probably positive in 70 to 95 percent of clinically diagnosed myasthenic patients and is the cause of the weakness and easy fatigability in the disease. Myasthenia gravis can be readily produced in animals by immunizing them against their acetylcholine receptor. Experimental autoimmune myasthenia gravis usually develops 2 to 3 weeks after immunization with the receptor and has all the features of human myasthenia gravis. Myasthenia gravis responds to all of the manipulations against the immune system that one would expect to see if the disease were of autoimmune origin. Thymectomy is effective, as are prednisone, Cytoxan, plasma exchange, and any other treatment that neutralizes the effect of excessive autoimmunity.

Clinical Manifestations

The single most important clinical feature of myasthenia gravis is weakness of skeletal muscle worsened by exercise and relieved by rest. Without this feature there can be no diagnosis. Weakness with easy fatigability is the only constant in this disease; all other features are variable. For instance, the weakness is usually worse in the afternoon and evening, although some patients are weaker in the morning when they first awaken. Usually the muscles supplied by the cranial nerves are the first and most severely affected, with resultant diplopia, ophthalmoplegia, dysphagia, dysphonia, dyspnea, and dysmimia. The disease may involve proximal lower- and upper-extremity muscles. In rare instances, however, proximal muscles weaken first. Involvement of individual muscles may be symmetrical, but is often asymmetrical with a dominant leg and arm usually weaker than a nondominant counterpart. Myasthenia gravis can also present as weakness of a single muscle – for example, the external rectus or superior oblique in one eye – or as a single complaint – for instance, jaw ptosis from inability to close the mouth. It can also present as a symptom seemingly unrelated to the neuromuscular system – for instance, burning eyes from exposure to keratitis, from incomplete eye closure during sleep, or a sore throat on awakening from mouth breathing during sleep. The disease may affect people at any age or of either sex and varies in severity from mild nonprogressive disease involving the eyes only (ocular form) to severe cases that may be rapidly fatal such as acute myasthenia gravis afflicting older men.

Diagnosis and Pathology

No two myasthenic patients look alike or have the same signs and symptoms. The classical appearance is unmistakable and is usually associated with bilateral ptosis, weakness of the face, and difficulty in smiling, chewing, and talking. The clinical diagnosis is confirmed by demonstrating electrical defects in transmission at the neuromuscular junction, responsiveness to anticholinesterase drugs, or the presence of the anti-acetylcholine receptor antibody circulating in the patient's blood. The consistent pathology found in every patient is autoimmune destruction of the postsynaptic receptor, simplification of the postsynaptic membrane, widening of the synaptic gap, and reduction in the acetylcholine receptor numbers and efficiency. Thymic pathology is also present in myasthenia gravis. Approximately 80 percent of patients have germinal centers and enlarged thymus, and about 10 percent of patients have a thymic tumor, a thymoma.

History

Seventeenth Century

Although myasthenia gravis was not described with any pretense of completeness as a clinical entity until the last quarter of the nineteenth century, a reference by Thomas Willis, an astute seventeenth-century English clinician, indicates that Willis probably knew of the disease and recognized the chief symptom of asthenia of the voluntary muscles with recovery after rest. The description of weakness in his patients occurs in his book on the physiology and pathology of disease with illustrated cases, *De anima brutorum* (1672), published in two separate editions the same year in Oxford and in London. The book was translated into English by S. Pordage in 1683 and published as "Two Discourses Concerning the Souls of Brutes" in Willis's *Practice of Physick* (London 1684). The significant part is as follows:

There follows another kind of this disease i.e., the palsy, depending on the want and fewness of spirits in which although motion be not deficient in any part or member wholly, yet it is not performed in any but the weakly and depravedly only. For though the distempered are free from want of motion they are not able however to move their member strongly or to bear any weight. Moreover, in every motor endeavor, they labor with a trembling of their limbs which is only a defect of debility and of a broken strength in the mode of power.

He then goes on to say that the patients with this affliction, although languishing in their limbs, are well in their stomachs and have a good and laudable pulse and urine. "Yet, they are as if they were innervated and cannot stand upright and dare scarce enter upon local motions, or if they do cannot perform them long. Yea, some without any notable sickness are for a long time fixed in their bed as if they were everyday about to die" Willis then goes on to state what has been often quoted:

At this time I have under my charge a prudent and honest woman who for many years have been obnoxious to this sort of spurious palsy, not only in her members, but also in her tongue. She for sometimes can speak freely and readily enough, but after she has spoke long or hastily or eagerly, she is not able to speak a word but becomes mute as a fish, nor can she recover the use of her voice under an hour or two.

Thus did Willis note that his patients developed general, "although partial paralysis," and that they were not able to move their members strongly or bear any weight. This seems to be a description of myasthenia gravis, although, of course, we will never really know.

Nineteenth Century

Nearly 200 years were to pass from the time of Willis before myasthenia gravis was again mentioned in the medical literature. The next recorded observation appears to have been made by an English physician, Samuel Wilks in 1877, one of the physicians to Guy's Hospital, London, who, when describing some cases of bulbar paralysis, described a patient with symptoms slightly similar to myasthenia gravis. He talked about a woman who could scarcely walk and had defective extraocular movement. Her speech was slow and deliberate, and she fatigued easily. Subsequently, she developed trouble swallowing and was unable to cough and died of respiratory paralysis. This is an incomplete discussion, but is the first fatal case of myasthenia gravis ever described in the medical literature. This report by Wilks was of some importance because the patient was autopsied and no abnormality could be found in the nervous system, indicating that the patient's trouble was due to some kind of functional defect.

The first really complete report of myasthenia gravis was given by Wilhelm W. Erb in 1879; he described a patient, age 55, who was seen in 1868, 11 years prior to the publication of the case record. The patient's illness had developed over a period of four months, and the first principal symptoms, which were clearly described, included ptosis, neck weakness, and dysphagia. Some atrophy was noticed in the neck muscles, and the patient seemed to respond to faradism (induced current). The patient was probably one of the first to be treated by Erb with electricity. The patient, George Fuss, a day laborer, went

into remission, and it was natural for Erb to attribute the improvement to his electrical treatment. Erb's second case was Magdalene Meisel, a peasant 30 years of age, first seen in 1870. Her symptoms were double vision, ptosis, dysphagia, and weakness. She died suddenly at night, and no autopsy was done. She had clear-cut exacerbations and remissions. The third patient reported by Erb, August Thal, a merchant, age 47 years, had difficulty holding his head up, and showed bilateral ptosis and facial weakness.

Subsequently, a score more cases were reported by 1893, when Samuel V. Goldflam reported a detailed study of myasthenia gravis. Goldflam mentions all of the currently accepted clinical signs and symptoms of the disease, which he summarized as follows:

1. The disease occurs in early life.
2. Both sexes are equally affected.
3. It is a disease of the motor system.
4. Chewing, swallowing, and eye movements are most affected at first, followed by involvement of trunk extremity.
5. Trunk involvement is usually but not necessarily always symmetrical.
6. Most patients are worse in the afternoon and evening and are improved by rest.

Goldflam also mentioned that daily exacerbations and remissions may occur, and that death may be due to respiratory impairment, and may occur suddenly. His article in many ways is the most important ever written in the history of myasthenia gravis.

The next major advance occurred a year later, in an 1894 paper by F. Galle. He was the first to analyze the reaction of muscles in myasthenia gravis to electrical stimulation and to name the disease. He also suggested physostigmine as a form of drug treatment, but he does not seem to have followed up on this important point; it was left to Mary Walker, 40 years later, to demonstrate the therapeutic value of physostigmine.

Twentieth Century

Modern studies of the pathological physiology of myasthenia gravis started with the work of A. M. Harvey (1948), and a series of illustrious colleagues, including Richard Masland, D. Grob, and T. R. Johns. These men recognized the characteristic response of the evoked muscle action potential to repetitive stimulation of nerve, thereby localizing the defect of myasthenia gravis to the neuromuscular junction.

In 1964, E. Elmquist and colleagues, using microelectrode techniques on human intercostal muscle, seemed to show that there was too little acetylcholine in each quantum released from the nerve terminal, an abnormality that could be explained by the presence of a false transmitter or by an abnormal binding or packaging of acetylcholine quanta. This particular finding, as it subsequently turned out, was in error, and we now know that the postsynaptic membrane is poorly sensitive to infused acetylcholine and that the defect in myasthenia gravis has nothing to do with any presynaptic defect. In fact, presynaptic release of acetylcholine in myasthenia gravis is normal.

In the meanwhile, evidence was accumulating that there was an immunologic disorder in myasthenia. This was first suggested by D. W. Smithers in 1959, who recognized the histological parallel between the thymus in myasthenia and the thyroid gland in thyroiditis. The following year, J. A. Simpson drew attention to the increased frequency, in myasthenia gravis, of other diseases regarded as autoimmune, especially rheumatoid arthritis. But the major advance occurred in 1973, when J. Patrick and J. M. Lindstrom injected rabbits with acetylcholine receptors purified from electric eel, intending to make antibodies to the acetylcholine receptor. In the process, they induced and recognized experimental autoimmune myasthenia gravis. This led to experiments indicating the nature of the human disease. We now know that the disease is caused by a circulating antibody directed against the acetylcholine receptor and that treatments directed against the abnormal antibody are effective in modifying the clinical signs and symptoms of myasthenia gravis.

Bernard M. Patten

Bibliography

Blalock, A., et al. 1941. The treatment of myasthenia gravis by removal of the thymus gland. *Journal of the American Medical Association* 117: 1529.

Brunner, N. E., T. Namba, and D. Grob. 1972. Corticosteroids in management of severe, generalized myasthenia gravis: Effectiveness and comparison with corticotropin therapy. *Neurology* 22: 603–10.

Elmquist, D., and J. O. Josefsson. 1962. The nature of the neuromuscular block produced by neomycin. *Acta Physiologica Scandinavica* 54: 105–10.

Grob, D., and A. M. Harvey. 1951. Effect of adrenocorticotropic hormone (ACTH) and cortisone administration in patients with myasthenia gravis and report of onset of myasthenia gravis during prolonged cortisone administration. *Johns Hopkins Medical Journal* 91: 125–36.

Harvey, A. M. 1948. Some preliminary observations on the clinical course of myasthenia gravis before and after thymectomy. *Bulletin of the New York Academy of Medicine* 24: 505–22.

Lindstrom, J. M., et al. 1976. Antibody to acetylcholine receptor in myasthenia gravis: Prevalence, clinical correlates and diagnostic value. *Neurology* 26: 1054–9.

Lisak, R. P., and R. L. Barchi. 1982. *Myasthenia gravis*. London.

Mann, J. D., T. R. Johns, and J. F. Campa. 1976. Long-term administration of corticosteroids in myasthenia gravis. *Neurology* 26: 729.

Newsom-Davis, J. 1979. Plasma exchange in myasthenia gravis. *Plasma Therapy* 1: 17.

Osserman, K. E. 1958. *Myasthenia gravis*. New York.

Patrick, J., and J. M. Lindstrom. 1973. Autoimmune response to acetylcholine receptor. *Science* 180: 871–2.

Patten, B. M. 1978. Myasthenia gravis. *Muscle and Nerve* 1: 190.

Schwab, R. S., and C. C. Leland. 1953. Sex and age in myasthenia gravis as critical factors in incidence and remission. *Journal of the American Medical Association* 153: 1270.

Simpson, J. A. 1966. Myasthenia gravis as an autoimmune disease: Clinical aspects. *Annals of the New York Academy of Sciences* 135: 506–16.

Vincent, A. 1980. Immunology of acetylcholine receptor in relation to myasthenia gravis. *Physiological Reviews* 60: 756.

Walker, M. B. 1934. Treatment of myasthenia gravis with physostigmine. *Lancet* 1: 1200.

Whitaker, J. N. 1980. Myasthenia gravis and autoimmunity. *Advances in Internal Medicine* 26: 489.

VIII.95
Nematode Infections

The roughly 500,00 species in the phylum Nemathelminthes, the nematodes or roundworms, include both free-living forms and important parasites of plants and animals. Many species of nematodes parasitize humans, and several of them are major public health problems in poor countries, especially in the tropics. Some species reside as adults in the intestine; others are found in the blood and tissues. See *Ascariasis, Dracunculiasis, Enterobiasis, Filariasis, Onchocerciasis, Strongyloidiasis, Trichinosis,* and *Trichuriasis.*

K. David Patterson

VIII.96
Onchocerciasis

Onchocerciasis is caused by a filarial nematode, the roundworm *Onchocerca volvulus*. Humans are infected by larval microfilariae transmitted by blood-feeding female flies of the genus *Simulium*. Symptoms include skin damage, extreme itching, and ocular lesions, which can lead to permanent blindness. Synonyms include river blindness in West Africa, *sowda* in Yemen, and *enfermedad de Robles* in Latin America.

Distribution and Incidence

Onchocerciasis is widely distributed in Africa south of the Sahara, especially in the savanna grasslands from Senegal to Sudan. Its range extends southward into Kenya, Zaire, and Malawi. The region encompassing the headwaters of the Volta River system in northern Ghana, northeastern Ivory Coast, southern Burkina Faso (Upper Volta), and adjacent territories has been a major center for the disease. Onchocerciasis was almost certainly indigenous to Africa, but it has been transmitted by the slave trade to the Arabian Peninsula (Saudi Arabia and Yemen) and to the Caribbean basin, where scattered foci exist in Mexico, Guatemala, Colombia, Venezuela, Ecuador, and Brazil. The disease has a patchy distribution within its range; infection rates in particular villages may range from zero to virtually 100 percent.

In the 700,000 square-kilometers of the Volta Basin region alone, the World Health Organization estimated that in the early 1970s, about 1 million of the 10 million inhabitants were infected, with about 70,000 classified as "economically blind." In northern Ghana alone, surveys in the early 1950s determined that about 30,000 people, roughly 3 percent of the population, were totally blind because of onchocerciasis. In some West African villages, adult blindness rates of from 10 to 30 percent have been observed. Conversely, dermatologic symptoms predominate in Arabia, and ocular involvement is rare.

Clinical Manifestations, Diagnosis, and Treatment

O. volvulus, one of several filarial worms that are important human parasites, lives in the cutaneous and subcutaneous tissues. Humans are the only definitive host; there is no animal reservoir. Numbers of adult worms, the females of which may reach a length of 50 centimeters, live in large coiled masses, which usually become surrounded by fibrotic tissue generated by the host. In these nodules, which may reach the size of a walnut and are often easily visible on the head, trunk, hips, or legs, the adults can live and breed for as long as 16 years. Thousands of larvae, the microfilariae, emerge from the nodules and migrate in the tissues of the skin. Host immune reactions to dead or dying microfilariae cause various forms of dermatologic destruction, including loss of elasticity, depigmentation, and thickening of the skin. These changes are complicated by the host's reaction to the extreme pruritis caused by the allergic reactions to the worm proteins; the victim may scratch him- or herself incessantly in a vain attempt to relieve the tormenting itch. This condition is sometimes called "craw-craw" in West Africa. Wandering microfilariae can also cause damage to the lymphatic system and inguinal swellings known as "hanging groin." Microfilariae that reach the eye cause the most damage. Larvae dying in various ocular tissues cause cumulative lesions that, over a period of one to several years, can lead to progressive loss of sight and total blindness. There appear to be distinct geographic strains, which help to explain different pathological pictures in parts of the parasite's range; for example, in forest regions of Cameroon a smaller percentage of infected persons experience ocular complications than do inhabitants of the savanna.

Diagnosis is by detection of nodules, by microscopic demonstration of microfilariae in skin snips, and, in recent years, by a number of immunologic tests. Therapy includes surgical removal of nodules, which has been widely practiced in Latin America to combat eye damage, and various drugs to kill the wandering microfilariae. The first drug to be widely used was diethylcarbamiazine (DEC), but in heavily infected people it may cause serious side effects when the immune system reacts to the allergens released by large numbers of dying worms. Dermatologic complications of DEC can be severe, but these are treatable with antihistamines and corticosteroids; ophthalmologic complications are less common but more dangerous. Suramin, a drug used to combat trypanosomiasis, is effective against both microfilariae and adult worms, but it has serious side effects and, like DEC, is too dangerous to use in mass campaigns. Some success has been reported with antihelminthics like mebendazole, but only ivermectin, a microfilaricide introduced in the early 1980s, seems safe and effective enough for widespread use in rural areas of developing countries.

Etiology and Epidemiology

The vectors and intermediate hosts of the pathogen are blood-feeding flies of the genus *Simulium,* especially members of the species complex *Simulium damnosum.* These annoying and appropriately named insects, sometimes called buffalo gnats, are close relatives of the familiar "black flies" of the northern United States and southern Canada. The females bite people, cattle, goats, wild animals, or birds to obtain blood meals. Flies feeding on infected humans may ingest microfilariae. These migrate from the insect's stomach to the muscles of the thorax, where they undergo about a 1-week developmental process before migrating to the salivary glands. Here, as infective larvae, they await the opportunity to enter a new host when the fly feeds again. Once this happens, the larvae wander briefly in the skin before settling down in clumps to mature, breed, and produce microfilariae.

Simulium females lay eggs on rocks and vegetation in swiftly flowing, richly oxygenated water. Ripples around rocks, bridge abutments, and dam spillways provide favorable conditions for the larval development of the vector. There is no transovarial transmission, so newly emerged adults must acquire onchocerca in a blood meal. Adult flies have extensive flight ranges: Infected females aided by winds and weather fronts can move hundreds of kilometers to establish new foci of disease. However, because of the vector's breeding preferences, most flies and hence most onchocerciasis cases are found within a few kilo-

meters of a stream with suitable breeding sites. The term "river blindness" accurately reflects the geographic distribution of the disease.

Onchocerciasis often has dramatic effects on human activities and settlement patterns. In many heavily infested areas, notably in the headwaters of the Volta River, swarming flies, tormenting skin infestation, and progressive blindness among a significant proportion of the population have resulted in progressive abandonment of rich, well-watered farmlands near the rivers. Depopulation of river valleys due to onchocerciasis has been going on for decades in much of northern Ghana, with people being forced to cultivate crowded and eroding lands away from the streams. In many areas, land-hungry people were settling the river valleys in the early twentieth century, but, as John Hunter has shown in his classic study of Nangodi on the Red Volta, in recent decades the line of settlement has been retreating from the rivers. It is possible that a cycle of colonization and retreat, with farmers caught between malnutrition and land shortages on the one hand and the perils of onchocerciasis on the other, has been going on for centuries in parts of the Volta basin.

History

As stated above, onchocerciasis is almost certainly a disease that originated in Africa and has spread to Arabia and the New World as an unintended by-product of the slave trade. Skin lesions caused by onchocerciasis were first described by J. O'Neill, who detected microfilariae from Africans in the Gold Coast (modern Ghana) suffering from the tormenting itch of "craw-craw." The organism was first described in 1893 by the eminent German parasitologist K. G. Friedrich Rudolf Leuckart, who studied adults in nodules extracted from Gold Coast Africans by a missionary. In 1916 the disease was first recognized in the Americas when the Guatemalan investigator Rodolfo Robles discovered onchocerciasis in the highlands of his country. Robles linked nodules to eye disease and suggested that the distribution of infection implicated two species of *Simulium* as vectors. D. B. Blacklock, working in Sierra Leone, showed in 1926 that *S. damnosum* was the vector. In 1931 J. Hissette, working in the Belgian Congo, linked onchocerciasis with blindness for the first time in Africa, but despite confirmation in the Sudan a year later, colonial doctors generally considered onchocerciasis only a skin disease. Just before World War II, French doctors in what is now Burkina Faso began to link the disease with mass blindness and river valley abandonment. Their colleagues across the frontier in the British

Gold Coast did not make a similar discovery until 1949. Although British physicians and administrators were aware of river valley depopulation, onchocerciasis, and substantial blindness in the northern part of the colony, they did not link these phenomena, partly because doctors who became interested in the problem in the 1930s were repeatedly distracted by other duties or transferred. After the war, the association was finally made, especially in a crucial 1949 report by B. B. Waddy. A series of investigations in the 1950s confirmed the widespread incidence and serious consequences of the disease in a number of African countries, and Latin American foci were delimited.

Control

In 1975 the World Health Organization, supported by a number of donor and afflicted countries, began the Onchocerciasis Control Programme, an ambitious and expensive 20-year effort to eliminate onchocerciasis in the entire Volta Basin. The basic strategy was to kill fly larvae by aerial spraying of an organophosphate called Abate (generic name: temephos) over breeding sites scattered over a huge and repeatedly extended portion of West Africa. The absence of an effective agent to kill adult flies has not prevented tremendous success in reducing and sometimes eliminating *Simulium* populations. Although treatment of victims was less successful until very recently because existing drugs were too dangerous for mass use, the vector control program, though costly and constantly faced with the problem of reintroduction of adult flies from places beyond the limits of the control program, has resulted in dramatic declines in biting rates, infection, and blindness in most of the region. Recently, treatment of thousands of victims with ivermectin, a safe and effective microfilaricide, has helped to reduce blindness among infected persons and has reduced the chances that a feeding fly would ingest infective microfilariae. The absence of an agent to kill adult worms and the logistical and financial difficulties of the massive larviciding campaign make total eradication unlikely, but vector control and microfilaricidal treatment can reduce the number of infected persons and lessen or eliminate severe clinical symptoms. Success at this level could help make thousands of square kilometers of valuable farmland safe for use in many regions of Africa. It is, however, clear that there must be a long-term commitment to the campaign for many years into the future, or river blindness will reconquer its old haunts.

K. David Patterson

Bibliography

Hunter, John M. 1966. River blindness in Nangodi, Northern Ghana: A hypothesis of cyclical advance and retreat. *Geographical Review* 66: 398–416.

　1981. Progress and concerns in the World Health Organization Onchocerciasis Control Program in West Africa. *Social Science and Medicine* 15D: 261–75.

Kean, B. H., Kenneth E. Mott, and Adair J. Russell. 1978. *Tropical medicine and parasitology: Classic investigations,* Vol. 2, 444–57. Ithaca, N.Y.

Patterson, K. David. 1978. River blindness in Northern Ghana, 1900–1950. In *Disease in African history: An introductory survey and case studies,* ed. Gerald W. Hartwig and K. David Patterson, 88–117. Durham, N.C.

Puyelo, R., and M. M. Holstein. 1950. L'Onchocercose humaine en Afrique noire française: Maladie sociale. *Médicine Tropicale* 10: 397–510.

Waddy, B. B. 1969. Prospects for the control of onchocerciasis in Africa. *Bulletin of the World Health Organization* 40: 843–58.

VIII.97
Ophthalmia (Conjunctivitis and Trachoma)

In its broadest sense, ophthalmia is an inflammation of the eye, especially of the conjunctiva of the eye. The term derives from the Greek word *ophthalmos* (the eye). Hence, almost any disease that attacked the eye was called *ophthalmia* in many Greco-Roman and later European sources until the beginning of the twentieth century. As medical knowledge was refined, defining terms were attached, such as "purulent ophthalmia," "neonatorum ophthalmia," or "Egyptian ophthalmia." The problem for historians attempting to define eye diseases in the past is that the term "ophthalmia" meant many diseases that attack the eyes or that manifest symptoms in the eye, and that blindness due to "ophthalmia" had many causes. Two important causes of ophthalmia were trachoma and conjunctivitis; this essay is limited to these.

Trachoma (also called *granular conjunctivitis* and *Egyptian ophthalmia*) has been defined as a contagious keratonconjunctivitis caused by *Chlamydia trachomatis* (serotypes A, B, Ba, and C). It is characterized by the formation of inflammatory granulations on the inner eyelid, severe scarring of the eye in the fourth stage, and blindness (but not in all cases). It was one of the leading causes of blindness in the past, and still blinds millions in Asia, the Middle East, and Africa (Bietti and Werner 1967; Rodger 1981; Insler 1987).

Conjunctivitis (purulent ophthalmia) may appear with trachoma and may complicate the progression of the disease so that blindness rather than healing occurs. Although conjunctivitis may denote any inflammation of the conjunctiva ("the mucous membrane lining the inner surface of the eyelids and covering the front part of the eyeball"), bacteria often infect the conjunctiva at the same time as does trachoma, thus causing an acute bacterial conjunctivitis. In the Middle East, for example, "spring and fall epidemics of gonococcal and Koch–Weeks conjunctivitis account for much of the corneal scarring seen in these populations" (Thygeson 1964). If trachoma attacks as well, the two in combination may blind many individuals. Viruses can also cause conjunctivitis, and historical descriptions that stress mild cases of ophthalmia often point to a viral or bacterial conjunctivitis. By contrast, the more severe ophthalmia that scarred the eye or permanently blinded individuals was often trachoma. It was almost impossible to identify the various forms of conjunctivitis before twentieth-century scientific methods of testing, but even at present, in desert and tropical areas, forms of bacterial and viral conjunctivitis are still confused with trachoma, with which they often occur.

Ophthalmia neonatorum is a term used for eye disease in newborns since the Greeks, but vague historical references make it difficult to identify the actual disease. Blindness in newborns may be due to various infections acquired in the birth canal. Before the twentieth century, ocular gonorrhea may have been the major cause of blindness in newborns, but in the twentieth century (at least in the industrialized nations) chlamydial infection is the most common type of ophthalmia neonatorum (Thygeson 1971; Rodger 1981; Insler 1987).

Distribution and Incidence

Trachoma remains widespread in the twentieth century. Two estimates place the number of victims worldwide at 400 million to 500 million, with millions suffering from sight defects and perhaps 2 million totally blinded (Bietti and Werner 1967; Rodger 1981).

In 1935 Adalbert Fuchs found that the greatest frequency of the disease was in Egypt, "where 98 percent of schoolchildren in the fourth grade are afflicted by trachoma" (Fuchs 1962). In the 1960s,

Egypt still led the list of areas where a majority of the population was affected. Because a dry climate seems to affect incidence, among the highest rates of infection are the countries of North Africa and the Muslim Middle East – that is, from Morocco to Egypt and the Sudan in North Africa, and from the Red Sea to Turkey and Iran in the Middle East. It is also widespread in Asia, with 20 to 50 percent of the population infected in Burma, Pakistan, India, China, Southwest Asia, Indonesia, and Borneo. These rates also occur in Africa south of the Sahara, except for West Africa, where the incidence falls below 20 percent. Similar trachoma rates continue along the Mediterranean coast of Europe, in Eastern Europe, parts of Russia, Korea, Japan, Australia, New Zealand (among the Maoris), and the Pacific Islands. In the Western Hemisphere, Brazil and Mexico have the highest incidences, but trachoma also infects Indians and Mexican-Americans in the southwestern United States. Sporadic cases appear in parts of Europe, the Philippines, and some Central and South American countries. The disease is practically extinct in Canada, Switzerland, Austria, and northern Europe – that is, in the countries with the highest standards of living and sanitary conditions and without pockets of extreme poverty. Where living conditions have improved, trachoma has declined or disappeared (Bietti and Werner, 1967). It is, however, a disease that still afflicts the impoverished who live in crowded conditions in the desert and tropical regions of Africa, the Middle East, Asia, and Latin America (Bietti and Werner 1967; Rodger 1981).

Etiology and Epidemiology

Trachoma generally requires prolonged contact among individuals in filthy and overcrowded living conditions for transmission. In endemic areas, infection first occurs in childhood as a result of close family contact. Transmission may be from mother to baby, from eye to eye, by fingers, and by eye-seeking flies. In urban slums or poor villages where people live crowded together under unsanitary conditions, garbage and raw sewage attract flies that breed copiously. As the insects swarm on the faces of infants and children, they feed on the infected eye discharges of those with trachoma and carry it to the eyes of other victims. Most children in endemic areas have trachoma at an early age, but hosting the disease in childhood does not provide a lifelong immunity.

Trachoma transmission may also occur by direct touch, by the contamination of clothing or bedding, possibly by bathing in pools in which people swim and wash, and by sexual means. According to B. R. Jones:

[I]n the vast majority of cases infection (with the TRIC agent) is transmitted from person to person by intimate sexual contact involving at various times genital, rectal, oral or other mucosal surfaces. No doubt it can be directly transferred to the eye during such activities. However, in the vast majority of cases it appears to be transferred to a genital mucosal area, and then by means of transferring a genital discharge by hand, or other vectors, it reaches the eye. (Cited by Rodger 1981)

Factors that contribute to the severity of trachoma are ocular irritants and bacterial conjunctivitis. It is most prevalent where the climate is hot and dry, and low humidity leads to excessive drying of the conjunctiva. Winds and dust, along with smoke in unventilated huts, further irritate the eyes. Bacterial infections, particularly the seasonal outbreak of bacterial purulent conjunctivitis, often cause the worst cases. Frederick Rodger (1981) suspects that such infections are "related to the peak period of reproduction of the fly population."

Clinical Manifestations and Pathology

Trachoma

The clinical features of trachoma are usually divided into four stages, following the classification system of A. F. MacCallan published in 1931:

Stage 1 (incipient trachoma) is characterized by increasing redness of the conjunctiva lining the upper lids and covering the tarsal plate. Magnification reveals many small red dots in the congested conjunctiva. As the organism proliferates, larger pale follicles appear. Both features then spread across the upper conjunctival surface. A minimal exudate occurs, which may be more profuse if there is a secondary bacterial infection. This stage is difficult to distinguish from the similar follicles of folliculosis and follicular conjunctivitis. Another characteristic of this acute stage is that the upper part of the cornea becomes edematous and infiltrated with inflammatory cells that invade the upper part of the cornea from its edge. In the last phase of incipient trachoma, *pannus* ("an abnormal membranelike vascularization of the cornea, due to granulation of the eyelids") appears in the upper cornea. Rarely does pannus appear in the lower cornea, and then only with pannus in the upper cornea. The duration of Stage 1 is several weeks to several months.

Stage 2 (established trachoma) marks the increase of all the symptoms established in Stage 1 and is often termed the "florid stage" because of the "florid inflammation mainly of the upper tarsal conjunctiva with the formation of follicles" and then of papillae with the "follicles appearing like sago grains." The pannus increases toward the apex of the cornea. Because the red vessels in the cornea are dilated, they are visible to the naked eye. In severe cases, because a secondary bacterial infection may worsen the appearance of the eye, there will be purulent and copious secretions. In dark-skinned populations the conjunctiva may take on pigment, which remains after the healing stage. The duration is 6 months to several years.

Stage 3 (cicatrizing trachoma) is the scarring and healing stage. The follicles rupture, and scar tissue forms on the undersurface of the upper lids. Scar tissue also appears elsewhere on the conjunctiva. At first, the scars are pink but later turn white. It is not uncommon for a new infection of *C. trachomatis* to occur at this stage and to start the process all over again. Thus Stages 2 and 3 may coexist for many years and may be further complicated by repeated bacterial infections. With each new attack, more scar tissue appears, and an ever-increasing pannus covers the cornea. This phase may be several years in duration.

Stage 4 (healed trachoma) is the final stage of the disease in which healing has been completed without any signs of inflammation, and the disease is no longer infectious. Trachomatous scarring remains, however, and may deform the upper lid and cause opaqueness in the cornea. The thickening of the upper lids gives a "hooded appearance to the eyes." Because scarring of the upper lids involves the tarsal plate, which buckles, twists, and inturns, these features indicate a past trachoma. When the inturning occurs, the lashes often rub on the cornea (*trichiasis*), causing constant irritation and tearing until the corneal surface is scarred. Ulcers may develop, and bacterial infection of the ulcers can lead to blindness. Another complication may be drying of the conjunctiva and cornea. The combination of corneal scarring, opacification, and vascularization plus secondary bacterial infections all account for impaired vision and blindness (Thygeson 1964; Yanoff and Fine 1975; Grayson 1979; and Rodger 1981).

Conjunctivitis

Simple acute conjunctivitis is a common eye infection, caused by a variety of microorganisms. Its most characteristic sign is the red or bloodshot eye. In mild cases, there may be a "feeling of roughness or sand in the eyes," but in serious cases there is "great pain" and photophobia (dread of light). In its early stages discharges from the eyes are thin and serous, but after a few days they may become so purulent that the secretions gum the lids together, and it becomes difficult to open the eyes, especially upon waking. The infection often begins in one eye before spreading to the other one. An acute conjunctivitis may last for 1 to 2 weeks (Thomson 1984).

Severe forms of conjunctivitis include *ophthalmia neonatorum,* due to infectious discharges in the birth canal; *follicular conjunctivitis,* which is often confused with the early stages of trachoma; *phlyctenular conjunctivitis,* which may lead to ulceration in the cornea; and a highly infectious *hemorrhagic conjunctivitis,* which affected 15 to 20 million in India in 1981 (Thomson 1984).

Gonococcal conjunctivitis, due to *Neisseria gonorrhea,* infects newborns as well as children and adults. Whereas newborns acquire the eye disease in the birth canal from their mother's vaginal secretions, others may contract the disease by direct or indirect contact. Although there may be nonvenereal transmission – especially in the tropics – the disease is now transmitted mainly by sexual intercourse. In infants the eyelids may be very swollen, and ulceration of the cornea often follows. Ocular gonorrhea infection used to be one of the principal causes of blindness in Europe until the 1880s, when a silver nitrate solution came into use in newborns. Since then, "the dramatic decrease in blindness that has resulted" is "one of great victories of scientific medicine" (Thygeson 1971; Insler 1987).

In contrast to gonococcal conjunctivitis, which has declined in the developed world, *chronic follicular conjunctivitis* and *acute conjunctivitis* in newborns have been on the increase along with other sexually transmitted diseases. "*Chlamydia trachomatis* [serotypes D through K] is now the most common sexually transmitted infection in the developed world" (Insler 1987). It causes not only conjunctivitis in newborns and adults but also genital tract infections. In adults symptoms of chronic follicular conjunctivitis include "foreign body sensation, tearing, redness, photophobia, and lid swelling." In newborns *inclusion conjunctivitis* or *blennorrhea* of the newborn usually appears 5 to 14 days after birth, since the baby acquires the chlamydial infection during its passage through the birth canal. Descriptions of infants with purulent ophthalmia – abnormal discharges of mucus some days after birth – may suggest this disease. Because purulent ophthalmia usually does not lead to severe visual loss, blindness in newborns is more likely due to gonococci and other bacteria that often complicate chlamydial infection.

The herpes simplex virus, other viral infections, or other bacterial infections (due to *Staphylococcus* or *Pseudomonas*) may also cause an ophthalmia neonatorum (Insler 1987).

History and Geography

Antiquity

Trachoma is an ancient disease. It was known in China in the twenty-seventh century B.C. (Bietti and Werner 1967) and ancient Egypt from the sixteenth century B.C. In 1872 George Ebers discovered a medical papyrus at Thebes that clearly described a chronic conjunctivitis (ophthalmia, lippitudo, chronic granular disease). The ancient Egyptians called the disease *Hetae,* and their symbol for it was the rain from heaven, which means a flowing downward of fluid. The papyrus also describes the white spot (*sehet*) or leukoma of the cornea, but still more clearly "the hairs in the eye" (*shene m mert*) or trichiasis (inward-growing eyelashes). All of this is very suggestive of trachoma (Worms and Marmoiton 1929; Hirschberg 1982; Meyerhof 1984).

Greek and Latin.   By the time of the ancient Greeks, eye inflammations (ophthalmia) were frequently described and sometimes defined, and in about A.D. 60 the term *trachoma* ("roughness") first was used by Dioscorides (Worms and Marmoiton 1929; Chance 1939). Although the Hippocratic books do not define ophthalmia precisely for us, Galen defines it as "an inflammation of the conjunctiva." The Greeks also used the term *lippitudo* (exudation from an eye) for the secreting eye, which is a possible reference to trachoma. Later Greek authors distinguished among a severe irritation of the conjunctiva, the true conjunctivitis or secreting eye, and a simple conjunctivitis. The most important reference to trachoma comes from the book *On Vision,* in which the Hippocratic corpus describes not the disease but rather its treatment. It stresses the scraping of the lids of the eye along with the cutting away from their inner side of the fleshy granulations followed by cauterization of the lid with a hot iron. Another book in the Hippocratic corpus describes an early operation for trichiasis (Meyerhof 1984). Possibly one reason for the amount of attention given to trachoma in the Hippocratic corpus is that there appears to have been a major outbreak of the disease among the Athenians during the Peloponnesian War (431 to 404 B.C.) (Chance 1939; Cornand 1979).

For the treatment of trachoma, Greek physicians stressed scraping thickened lids with fig leaves or the rough skins of sea animals, such as sharks. Writing in Latin in the first century A.D., Celsus describes trachoma, which was then called *aspiritudo*. "This [roughness] often follows inflammations of the eyes, sometimes more sometimes less violently. Sometimes this roughness is followed by a running eye." He also recommended treatment for trichiasis. About A.D. 45, a younger contemporary of Celsus wrote a book of remedies for many diseases, including several for trachoma. The Greek physician Dioscorides recommended fig leaves and the shell of octopus for scouring the "rough and fig-like granulations of the lids." Galen also refers to the octopus-shell as well as to the skin of sharks for scraping the lid in severe cases of trachoma (Meyerhof 1984).

The Romans were also well acquainted with trachoma. The movement of Roman troops throughout the empire must have dispersed trachoma from the Mediterranean region to wherever the Roman soldiers sought to extend the empire. Some evidence for trachoma on the frontiers of the Roman Empire (France, England, and Germany) comes from the stone-seals of Roman oculists, which record the names of remedies used for trachoma (James 1933; Chance 1939). Roman medical books also include typical remedies for the ailment. In the fourth century A.D., Theodorus Priscianus reported his personal experiences with patients who suffered from "the malady of roughness (*asperitatis vitium*)"; he used garlic juice to anoint the conjunctiva. In the sixth century A.D., Christian physicians from Asia Minor – Alexander of Tralles and Aetius of Amida – referred to trachoma and trichiasis. Aetius distinguished four stages of trachoma (*dasytes* = "density" = slight thickening of the conjunctiva; *trachytes* = "roughness"; *sykosis* = "figlike granulation"; and *tylosis* = "callousness" = cicatricial trachoma) (Chance 1939; Meyerhof 1984). To some extent this understanding of the disease is reflected in the trachoma descriptions in the seventh century A.D. of Paul of Aegina, an Alexandrian physician:

Trachoma is a roughness of the inner surface of the lids. When the disease is of greater intensity it is also called "fig disease." If the disease is chronic and cicatricial then it is called "scar." Topical medications are indicated. They consist of wine and two kinds of red iron ore. These are washed and then the inner surface of the lid is gently cauterized. (Hirschberg 1982)

Paul also provides descriptions of trachoma treatments. He refers to everting the lid and scraping it with pumice, octopus shell, fig leaves, or an instrument. Patients with trichiasis were operated on with a needle and thread, a procedure that was reinvented in 1844. To prevent inflammation of the eyes, he recommended the method of "cutting and of burning the forehead and temples" – a treatment that was used on St. Francis of Assisi in medieval Italy and that was still common among Egyptian peasants in the twentieth century (Meyerhof 1984; Green 1987). Paul and Aetius were also familiar with eye diseases in newborns. Paul, for example, referred to a "purulent exudation" in the eyes of newborns, while Aetius recommended the irrigation of the eyes of a newborn – "oil should be dropped into them" (Hirschberg 1982).

Arabic. After the important medical writings in Greek or Latin, the next significant surviving treatises on eye diseases are in Arabic, dating from the eighth and ninth centuries A.D. Unfortunately, earlier texts by Syriac-speaking Christians of Syria, Mesopotamia, and Persia have been lost except for one that follows Galen. The later Arabic authors, however, enable us to continue to track trachoma through accurate medical descriptions. In the ninth century, the first attempt, by Ibn Masawaih, does not provide a good description of trachoma but does refer to pannus and trichiasis. His successor and pupil, Hunain ibn Is-haq, distinguished the four forms of trachoma, using the Greek names but with Arabic explanations. He also called pannus "varicose ophthalmia" (Meyerhof 1984).

According to Max Meyerhof, the best Arabic sources on eye diseases including trachoma were composed after A.D. 1000. The first and best of these is *The Memorandum-Book of a Tenth-Century Oculist (Tadhkirat al-Kahhalin)*, composed in the early eleventh century A.D. by a Christian oculist living in Baghdad, Ali ibn Isa. As well as distinguishing 13 diseases of the conjunctiva and 13 of the cornea (Hirschberg 1985), he clearly describes trachoma:

Trachoma is of four kinds: the *first* exhibits redness at the surface of the inner side of the lid. Its symptom is that you see, when you evert the lid, something like grains resembling those of dry mange (*hasaf*). It is less severe and painful than the three other kinds. It is accompanied by lachrymation: it mostly follows an acute ophthalmia (*ramad* = acute conjunctivitis). In general, the causes of all the kinds of trachoma are saline humours, long exposure to the sun, dust and smoke and improper treatment of ophthalmia. . . .

The *second kind* of trachoma exhibits more roughness that [*sic*] the first; it is associated with pain and heaviness, and both kinds produce in the eye moisture and lachrymation. . . .

The *third kind* of trachoma: It is stronger and more severe than the second kind and has more roughness. Its symptom is that you see the surface of the inner side of the lid like a split-up fig; therefore this kind [is] called the "figlike" (sycosis). . . .

The *fourth kind* of trachoma is more grave than the three other kinds and exhibits still more roughness; it is more dangerous and chronic. It is associated with severe pain and callosity, and it is impossible to root it out in a short space of time, on account of the thickening of the lid, especially when it is old. Sometimes it causes the growth of superfluous lashes. Its symptom is that you see on the everted lid a dark-red blackish colour and on it a kind of prominent crust (cicatricial tissue). (Meyerhof 1984; Hirschberg 1985)

This is the first time that the connection between trichiasis and trachoma was made in the literature (Meyerhof 1984). It is also the best description of trachoma and its treatment written in antiquity and probably the best until the work of J. N. Fischer of Prague in 1832. Certainly subsequent works in Arabic do not improve on Ali ibn Isa's, because most copied his chapters on trachoma. One exception is *The Luminous Support on Eye-Diseases* by the Cairo oculist Sadaqa ibn Ibrahim al-Sadhili, who used his personal experience in ophthalmic operations to write his textbook in the second half of the fourteenth century. For the first time, as Meyerhof (1984) notes, we have a reference to the "frequency of certain eye-diseases in Egypt. . . . The inhabitants of Egypt suffer mostly from ophthalmia, on account of the abundance of dust and sand in their land." He goes on to describe the four kinds of trachoma, but what is new, he notes, is that "one of the forms develops [*sic*] from the preceding form by inappropriate treatment. He insists on the frequency of trichiasis with the fourth and most severe form of trachoma" and states that "pannus is often a sequela of ingrown lashes." Furthermore, he reported that "pannus is often observed after a neglected acute ophthalmia or a very chronic trachoma."

The Greeks and the Arabs thus knew far more about trachoma than did their counterparts in Europe until the nineteenth century. They recognized different forms of trachoma (MacCallan's four stages in contemporary language); the follicles and papillae, which they compared to the appearance of a halved fig; the scars; the contagiousness (sometimes referred to as "heredity," meaning "in the family"); and the danger of old trachoma, or reinfection. The Arabs were also able to recognize the connection of trichiasis and pannus with trachoma, and their operative and topical treatments of tra-

choma were superior to those in the West (Meyerhof 1984). From the accuracy of their descriptions, it is clear that they had had a long acquaintance with the disease.

Europe from Medieval Times Through the Eighteenth Century

In contrast, Medieval Europe was poorly prepared to confront trachoma when it appeared in epidemic forms, often accompanying returning Crusader armies from North Africa or the Middle East (Cornand 1979). Because Arab authors used the term *jarab* (scabies), medieval Latin translators from the Arabic called trachoma "scabies." As late as 1561, Pierre Franco would term the disease *scabie et prurit en oeil* (Hirschberg 1985). That trachoma existed in Jerusalem is attested by the writings of Benvenutus of Jerusalem (thirteenth century), whose description of his surgical treatment of trachoma survives (Chance 1939; Hirschberg 1985). Because of the frequent movement of Italian merchants and crusading armies between Italy and the Middle East, it is not surprising that Italy and especially Salerno became a center of knowledge about eye diseases (Chance 1939). Arabic and Greek writers were translated into Latin and influenced Italian concepts of trachoma and its treatment. At the end of the thirteenth century, Lanfranchi of Milan referred to a trachoma treatment (Worms and Marmoiton 1929). One possible description of trachoma from medieval Italy appears in a biography of St. Francis of Assisi, which traces the progression of his ophthalmia, acquired on a trip to Egypt and the Middle East. "Wiping the tears from his sore eyes," he returned to Italy, in the early stages of the disease. As his sight deteriorated, he sought treatment at an ophthalmia center in Rieti and later underwent cauterization on both temples with a hot iron, an ancient treatment for trachoma. He was finally blinded shortly before his death (Green 1987).

In the fourteenth century, French surgeon Guy de Chauliac provided a "recognisable description" of trachoma (Boldt 1904; Chance 1939), whereas in England one medical tract on eye diseases survives from the same century. Written by John of Arderne in 1377, it concentrates on treatments that seem characteristic of folk medicine, but some references suggest trachoma, although a form of conjunctivitis is more likely. Crocus, for example, "relieves the redness of the eyes and stays the flux of humours to the eye, it deletes pannus, which is macula of the eye, for it becomes dissolved and wasted away." His cure for *lippitudo* (the Greek term for "secreting eye") and watery eye included fresh butter and a man's urine (James 1933).

Although trachoma was poorly identified, one suspects that it remained established in medieval and early modern Europe and did not die out between the period of the Crusades and the sixteenth century, when notable epidemics of "ophthalmia" occurred in connection with the movement of armies. A well-known epidemic occurred in 1556, and was described by Forestus. English doctors characterized the disease by the term *paupières mûrales,* because the conjunctiva seemed to them to be like a wall (Worms and Marmoiton 1929). A little later, Jean Costoeus referred to the treatment of trachoma by cautery. Other epidemics similar to the 1556 epidemic occurred at Breslau in 1699 and 1700, and again among the English troops at Westphalia in 1762. In the second half of the eighteenth century, trachoma epidemics swept through Sweden and Finland (Worms and Marmoiton 1929).

Napoleonic Period

Although trachoma was a problem in Europe long before 1800, it could also be imported, as it was after Napoleon Bonaparte's campaign in Egypt (1798–1801), when an ophthalmia epidemic swept Europe. Many of the returning French troops had lost their sight as a result of "ophthalmia." Trachoma and forms of conjunctivitis were still endemic in Egypt. Indeed European travelers to Egypt, especially those of the eighteenth century, referred to Egypt as "the land of the blind." A Bohemian visitor even described the "masses of flies on the eyes of the natives, especially children," and he attributed the prevalence of eye disease to the "general filthiness" of the poor. Meyerhof (1932) suggests that the incidence of trachoma and blindness had increased in Egypt under the rule of the Mamelukes and Turks, when 2 million peasants were living in misery. Perhaps it was that combination of poverty and the arrival of a foreign army that set the stage for the terrible epidemic or epidemics of "ophthalmia" that would torment Europe for half a century.

In any event, when Napoleon's 40,000 troops invaded Egypt in the summer of 1798, they first suffered from a contagious ophthalmia, which was probably the conjunctivitis caused by the Koch–Weeks bacillus, prevalent in Egypt during the summer months. By September, "few soldiers had escaped ophthalmia," and cases had become acute. Some were suffering from gonorrheal conjunctivitis and trachoma, and soldiers had "eyes completely blinded by the swelling of the lids." Of one group of 3,000 soldiers, 1,400 were unable to fight because of "ophthalmia." Thousands of others suffered from eye diseases, and the blinded were either hospitalized, sent home, or, in their helpless condition, massacred by local people or armies. Many veterans of the Egyptian campaigns continued to suffer from eye problems for years after their return to Europe (Meyerhof 1932).

The Turkish and British armies in Egypt also contracted ophthalmia. It was the British who first characterized it as contagious, a theory not always accepted in the nineteenth century. A British surgeon, George Power, described the disease as a "purulent conjunctivitis," which had been prevalent among the Irish peasantry about 1790. Actually, epidemics of ophthalmia had been common among the peasants of Ireland in the eighteenth century, and Power regarded it as infectious and of "a species of the same disease" as Egyptian ophthalmia (Collins 1904; Meyerhof 1932). The French military surgeon Dominique Jean Larrey referred to the contagious disease of "granular conjunctivitis" in 1802 (Chance 1939).

"Egyptian ophthalmia" accompanied the British troops on their return to England and Ireland, where it became known to "almost every medical practitioner" by 1806 (Meyerhof 1932). As early as 1802, Patrick MacGregor described granulations that he observed on the conjunctivae of 56 veterans who had returned from Egypt. "In all of them the eye-lids were more or less affected; and when the inner surface of the eye-lids was examined with a magnifying glass, the small sebaceous glands situated there were found increased in size, and of a redder colour than natural" (Meyerhof 1932). Most writers on that epidemic, according to E. Treacher Collins (1904), stress "the purulent character of the discharge, the acuteness of the symptoms, and the rapid and destructive ulceration of the cornea which was liable to ensue – characteristics which we associate today with gonorrhoeal ophthalmia rather than Trachoma."

When the British tried to capture Egypt in 1807, the troops again came down with acute ophthalmia; and when they moved on to Sicily, they spread the disease there. Ophthalmia continued to ravage the British army for about 10 more years. By 1818, over 5,000 men had been invalided from the British army for blindness. The epidemics, of course, had spread to the other armies who fought during the Napoleonic period. The Italian troops were infected in 1801 at Elba and Leghorn by the French. This epidemic lasted until 1826. The Italians carried the disease to the Hungarian (1809) and Austrian (1814) armies. One of the most severe epidemics was in the Prussian army from 1813 to 1817, when 20,000 to 25,000 men were affected. From there it passed to the Swedish troops in 1814, and to the Dutch in 1815. More than 17,000 troops were attacked in the Russian army during the years 1816 to 1839, and by 1834, 4,000 Belgian soldiers had become completely blind. In fact, in 1840 one in five in the Belgian army still suffered from ophthalmia. When the epidemic hit Portugal in 1849, it affected 10,000 soldiers over an 8-year period. It even reached Cuba in the New World in 1813, where it devastated 7,000 soldiers, "most" of whom "became blind." Because of its association with soldiers in the nineteenth century, the disease had become known as "military ophthalmia," with some even believing that it was an "eye affection exclusively found among soldiers" (Boldt 1904; Worms and Marmoiton 1929; Meyerhof 1932; Hirschberg 1986).

The interesting question, of course, concerns the identity of the ophthalmia contracted in Egypt and disseminated in Europe. According to Meyerhof (1932), the diseases that afflicted the French, Turkish, and British forces were the same eye diseases that prevail in Egypt: two forms of conjunctivitis – (1) acute catarrhal conjunctivitis caused by the Koch–Weeks bacillus and (2) acute purulent conjunctivitis caused by the gonococcus, sometimes blended with streptococcus or pneumococcus, which is often followed by postgonorrheal conjunctivitis – and genuine trachoma in its various stages. When trachoma occurs along with an acute form of conjunctivitis, such as the Koch–Weeks, and when it attacks adults, it tends to be more severe and contagious. Lack of sanitation in the armies and among the local population facilitated the rapid spread of the ophthalmias. Meyerhof also contrasts the high incidence of ophthalmia among the British troops in the early nineteenth century with only scattered cases among them in the twentieth century. This he attributes to the vastly improved hygienic conditions among the troops.

Not all the eye ailments that afflicted nineteenth-century European armies, however, came from Egypt. As we saw, trachoma had existed in Europe before Napoleon's time and, in fact, according to J. Boldt (1904), had long been endemic in Central Europe – from the Gulf of Finland to the Carpathian Mountains. Thus, when the Prussian army of the Napoleonic period became infected with trachoma, it was not due to the Egyptian epidemic, he believes, but rather to massive troop mobilizations that en-

listed trachomatous recruits from endemic areas in Central Europe. It may have been the case, then, that the war of the Napoleonic period facilitated the dissemination of trachoma and other eye diseases throughout Europe, only some of which owed their origin to the Egyptian campaigns.

Nineteenth Century

With the disbanding of armies and the return of peace in the first half of the nineteenth century, trachoma virulence declined in Europe; but as European nations turned their attention to imperial wars in Asia and Africa, the disease was on hand to attack the armies stationed abroad. Indeed, Collins (1904) notes that wherever British troops were quartered in the nineteenth century, ophthalmia "flourished." Soldiers came down with the disease in Africa, India, Ceylon, the West Indies, the Mediterranean, and Canada. In the German protectorate of the South Sea Islands, the Germans encountered a high incidence of ocular disease, including trachoma (1910–12). Military records thus permit historians to trace trachoma incidence throughout the world in the nineteenth century (Boldt 1904; Collins 1904; Cornand 1979; Kluxen and Bernsmeier 1980).

But the civilians carried the disease as well. Both voluntary and forced immigrants brought ophthalmia with them to the Americas. The British recorded cases of trachoma among immigrants from Poland, Finland, Russia, and Armenia, who were in transit to the United States or Canada. The problem of contagious eye diseases was so serious that the United States and Canada declared trachoma to be a "dangerous" disease and prohibited the entry of those infected with it. Nonetheless, many immigrants escaped detection. Among the immigrants with a high incidence of the disease were the Irish, for ophthalmia epidemics had been severe in the famine-plagued Ireland of the 1840s (Boldt 1904; Collins 1904).

Ophthalmia also attacked the "involuntary immigrants" of the nineteenth century. What was called "Egyptian ophthalmia" or just "ophthalmia" was one of the most feared diseases of the slave trade, as it could sweep through slave ships, blinding the entire cargo and crew of a slaver. If fortunate, a few of the crew would regain their sight and bring the ship into port. Ships where this was not the case were on occasion discovered drifting helplessly on the open seas. In 1819, the French slave ship Le Rôdeur experienced one of the best-documented cases of ophthalmia. The ship had traded at Bonny in West Africa. About 2 weeks into the voyage, the first symptoms of the disease appeared among the slaves in the intermediate deck, and soon after this, the crew was infected:

In the morning when the patient wakes up he notices a slight irritation and itching at the lid margins which appear red and swollen. On the next day the lids are more swollen and the patient experiences severe pain. . . . On the third day there is a secretion which appears yellow and thick, but later turns green and stringy; the secretion is so ample that every 15 minutes when the patients open their lids a few drops escape. There is from the beginning considerable photophobia and epiphora . . . the pain increases from day to day, similarly, the number of blinded patients; . . . Some of the sailors were three times affected by the disease. When the lid swelling decreased one could see a few vesicles on the bulbar conjunctiva. (Hirschberg 1986)

When the ship arrived in Guadeloupe, those afflicted found their condition quickly improved by eating fresh fruit and by washing their eyes with fresh water and a lemon extract, which a black woman had recommended; but the epidemic had blinded 39 blacks and 12 crew members. The others lost vision only in one eye or had severe corneal scars (Hirschberg 1986).

Descriptions of ophthalmia also came from British reports on the conditions aboard slave ships that the Royal Navy detained in the nineteenth century. Thomas Nelson, a British surgeon, recorded two shipboard epidemics of blinding ophthalmia on slave ships off the coast of Brazil (1846). He reported on "swollen eyelids," a "discharge which keeps constantly trickling down their cheeks," and "ulcers on the cornea." Of particular interest is his description of the treatment of infected slaves with silver nitrate, which is now used in newborns to prevent blindness due to ocular gonorrhea.

When slave dealers unloaded the infected slaves in the markets of Brazil, epidemics of ophthalmia broke out in the port cities. In the 1830s and 1840s, slave ships from Angola and Benguela repeatedly introduced the disease into the slave market of Rio de Janeiro, and from there it spread into the city and to surrounding plantations. The exact cause of the ophthalmias in slaves is, however, difficult to determine.

On the other hand, ophthalmia was not the only cause of eye disease among slaves. Although descriptions of the blind (Luccock 1820) and the medical study of J. F. X. Sigaud (1844) suggest that trachoma was responsible for some blindness in Rio, Julius Hirschberg (1982-6) blames the epidemic aboard the *Le Rôdeur* on an acute or contagious form of blennorrhea. Blinding ophthalmias also seemed to

have appeared frequently in the same slaves suffering from measles or smallpox; one of the slave ships Nelson examined, for example, that had been struck with ophthalmia had also experienced an epidemic of smallpox. Interestingly, during the North American Civil War, many soldiers had ophthalmia after virulent smallpox and measles epidemics (Cunningham 1958). Furthermore, blacks in the eastern United States seemed to escape trachoma. Swan Burnett of Washington observed only six "suspicious cases" of trachoma among 10,000 blacks (Boldt 1904). In Cuba, blacks had a lower incidence of the disease than whites – 1.1 per 100, with a slightly higher rate of 2.3 for mulattoes. In sharp contrast, the incidence for whites was 42 per 100 (Santos Fernández 1901). Although Africans and their descendants clearly contracted trachoma in Brazil, Cuba, and Africa (Rodger 1959, 1981; Fuchs 1962), such descriptions suggest that historians cannot attribute *all* ophthalmias in black slaves to trachoma. Along with acute conjunctivitis, other diseases that affect the eye, such as smallpox, measles, leprosy, tuberculosis, syphilis, and onchocerciasis (river blindness), doubtless also blinded slaves.

By the nineteenth century, the term ophthalmia had come to cover an extraordinary variety of identifiable and imaginary eye diseases in medical textbooks. Hence, such terms as cachectic, senile, menopausal, abdominal, and scrofulous were attached to the word ophthalmia (Furnari 1845; Hirschberg 1986). Only in the twentieth century were the actual causes of eye diseases isolated, and more accurate scientific descriptions of trachoma and conjunctivitis made possible.

Mary C. Karasch

I am grateful for the assistance of Professors Leo Gerulaitis and Barry Winkler of Oakland University.

Bibliography

Bietti, Giambattista, and Georges H. Werner. 1967. *Trachoma: Prevention and treatment*. Springfield, Ill.

Boldt, J. 1904. *Trachoma*, trans. J. Herbert Parsons and Thos. Snowball. London.

Chance, Burton. 1939. *Clio medica: Ophthalmology*. New York.

Choyce, D. P. 1967. Tropical eye diseases. In *The eye in systemic disease*, Vol. 1, ed. Dan M. Gordon. Boston.

Collins, E. Treacher. 1904. Introduction. In *Trachoma* by J. Boldt. London.

Cornand, Pr. G. 1979. Trachome et armées. *Revue Internationale du Trachome et de Pathologie Oculaire Tropicale et Subtropicale* 56 (3–4): 99–110.

Cunningham, H. H. 1958. *Doctors in gray: The Confederate medical service*. Baton Rouge, La.

Fuchs, Adalbert. 1962. *Geography of eye diseases.* Vienna.

Furnari, S. 1845. *Voyage médical dans l'Afrique Septentrionale ou de l'ophthalmologie . . .* Paris.

Grayson, Merrill. 1979. *Diseases of the cornea.* St. Louis.

Green, Julien. 1987. *God's fool: The life and times of Francis of Assisi,* trans. Peter Heinegg. San Francisco.

Hirschberg, Julius. 1982–6. *The history of ophthalmology,* Vols. 1–7, trans. F. C. Blodi. Bonn.

Insler, Michael S., ed. 1987. *Aids and other sexually transmitted diseases and the eye.* Orlando.

James, R. Rutson. 1933. *Studies in the history of ophthalmology in England prior to the year 1800.* Cambridge.

Kluxen, G., and H. Bernsmeier. 1980. Endemic ocular infections of the South Seas in the German colonial era. *Papua and New Guinea Medical Journal* 23 (4): 197–9.

Luccock, John. 1820. *Notes on Rio de Janeiro and the southern parts of Brazil.* London.

Meyerhof, Max. 1932. A short history of ophthalmia during the Egyptian campaigns of 1798–1807. *British Journal of Ophthalmology* (March): 129–52.

   1984. *Studies in medieval Arabic medicine: Theory and practice,* ed. Penelope Johnstone. London.

Nelson, Thomas. 1846. *Remarks on the slavery and slave trade of the Brazils.* London.

Rodger, Frederick C. 1959. *Blindness in West Africa.* London.

   1981. *Eye disease in the tropics.* Edinburgh.

Santos Fernández, Juan. 1901. *Las Enfermedades de los ojos en los negros y mulatos.* Trabajo leido en el XIII Congreso Médico Internacional celebrado en Paris del 2 al 9 de Agosto de 1900. Havana.

Sigaud, J. F. S. 1844. *Du Climat et des maladies du Brésil ou statistique médicale de cet empire.* Paris.

Thomson, William A. R. 1984. *Black's medical dictionary,* 34th edition. Totowa, N.J.

Thygeson, Phillips. 1964. Diagnosis and treatment of trachoma. In *Viral diseases,* Vol. 4, ed. Herbert E. Kaufman. Boston.

   1971. Historical review of oculogenital disease. *American Journal of Ophthalmology* 71: 975–85.

Worms, G., and J. E. Marmoiton. 1929. *Le Trachome.* Paris.

Yanoff, Myron, and Ben S. Fine. 1975. *Ocular pathology: A text and atlas.* Hagerstown, Md.

VIII.98
Osteoarthritis

Osteoarthritis (OA) is the most common rheumatic disorder afflicting humankind and vertebrates in general. The most common alternative terms, *osteoarthrosis* and *degenerative joint disease,* are used because of divergent concepts of the nature and cause of the disorder. One school maintains that OA is a family of systemic inflammatory disorders with similar clinical and pathological end results. Another supports the use of the term "osteoarthrosis" because inflammation is not present. Still another uses the term "degenerative joint disease" because it is held that aging and "wear and tear" are responsible for its occurrence.

William Heberden, an eighteenth-century English physician, gained immortality by describing what we now term *Heberden's nodes,* a common heritable form of osteoarthritis, especially common in women. In his *Commentaries,* he writes:

What are those little hard knots, about the size of a small pea, which are frequently seen upon the fingers, particularly a little below the top, near the joint? They have no connection with the gout, being found in persons who never had it: They continue for life; and being hardly ever attended with pain, or disposed to become sores, are rather unsightly, than inconvenient, though they must be some little hindrance to the free use of the fingers (Heberden 1802)

Modern research provides new data for a comprehensive definition encompassing clinical, biochemical, and anatomic features (Denko 1989). OA is a multifactorial systemic inflammatory disorder with clinical symptoms of pain and stiffness in movable joints, showing radiographic evidence of cartilage loss and bony overgrowth. The anatomic changes — cartilage loss and a kind of bony overgrowth and spurs — may occur physiologically without clinical symptoms. Osteoarthritis is classified as *primary (idiopathic)* when there is no known predisposing factor; or *secondary,* when there is a clearly defined, underlying condition contributing to its etiology, such as trauma, metabolic diseases, or gout. Several symptom complexes are grouped as variant subsets such as generalized osteoarthritis or erosive inflammatory osteoarthritis.

Distribution and Incidence

Osteoarthritis spares no race or geographic area. In the majority of patients, especially the younger group, the disease is mild and does not cause significant disability. However, in patients in the older age group it is more severe and often produces disability with loss of time from work and thus economic loss. The disease occurs with increased severity and frequency in older populations as a result of prolonged exposure to pathophysiological processes responsible for its development.

OA occurs with more frequency and more severity in women than in men. There is a sex difference in distribution of the joints involved. Lower spine and hip disease are more common in men, whereas cervical spine and finger arthritis are more common in women. The most commonly affected joints are the distal interphalangeal joints (*Heberden's nodes*); the proximal interphalangeal joints of the fingers (*Bouchard's nodes*); the first metatarsophalangeal (*bunion*) joints of the feet; and the spine, the hips, and the knees (Peyron 1984).

Studies of the incidence of osteoarthritis produce divergent data because of differences in definition and diagnostic techniques. For example, when the definition includes only pathological anatomic changes (cartilage loss and bony growth), investigators find evidence for the disorder in 90 percent of persons over age 40. Only about 30 percent of persons with radiographic changes of degenerative joint disease complain of pain in relevant joints (Moskowitz 1984). The frequency and severity of symptoms of the illness increase with age so that osteoarthritis is a major cause of symptomatic arthritis in the middle-aged and elderly population.

Epidemiology

The first epidemiological studies on osteoarthritis were reported about 60 years ago in England, using only questionnaires and clinical examination to evaluate incapacity and invalidism due to the disease. These methods, however, lacked diagnostic reliability, and classification of the disease was difficult. Later, use of roentgenograms to detect changes allowed for the classification of OA ranging from mild to severe, depending on the loss of cartilage and the presence of bony overgrowth. The cartilage loss is seen as joint space narrowing, whereas bony overgrowth can be one or more of the following: osteophytes, bony eburnation, or increased bone density. Early physical findings such as Heberden's nodes may precede radiographic changes.

Various surveys have explored demographic factors associated with osteoarthritis. A study of skeletal remains of contemporary white and black Americans, twelfth-century Native Americans, and

protohistoric Alaskan Eskimos showed that those who underwent the heaviest mechanical stresses suffered the most severe joint involvement (Denko 1989). Climate does not influence the prevalence of OA. In two groups of Native Americans of the same ethnic descent but with one living in a cold mountain region and the other in a hot desert, no differences were found in radiographs of the hands and feet. Hereditary predisposition to Heberden's nodes have been found in half of the observed cases. The remaining cases are thought to be traumatic.

Differences in patterns of affected joints occur in different ethnic groups. Heberden's nodes are rare in blacks, as is nonnodal generalized osteoarthritis. Occupational factors may play a role in the incidence, especially in males. Studies from Great Britain, United States, and France show osteoarthritis to be a major cause of incapacity, economic loss, and social disadvantage in persons over the age of 50. Hip disease is more common in white populations than in blacks and Native Americans. Asian populations have a low incidence of hip disease, but incidence of OA of the fingers in Asia is high, as is the incidence in Europeans. Knee disease shows less difference among ethnic groups, being similarly prevalent in whites and blacks in South Africa and Jamaica (Peyron 1984).

Protective factors are few, including mainly the absence of mechanical stress such as that resulting from motor impairment, hemiplegia, or poliomyelitis. Predisposition to osteoarthritis occurs in individuals who have pseudogout (calcium pyrophosphate deposition disease). Deposits of urate crystals such as that occurring in gout also predispose the individual to osteoarthritis.

Etiology

The popular concept that osteoarthritis is a single disease resulting from attrition of cartilage due to age and wear-and-tear is not tenable in light of modern experimental studies. Osteoarthritis can be regarded as the result of aberrations in a complex pattern of biological reactions whose failure leads to anatomic changes in joint structure and function. One or more biological feedback loops may lead to malfunction of the complex system. Biological modifiers induce variable effects, depending on the target mechanism. A recent hypothesis proposes that OA is a multifactorial metabolic inflammatory disorder in which too little cartilage and too much bone are synthesized because of impaired liver function in processing growth hormone and insulin. Hepatic dysfunction results in altered neuropeptide levels: too little insulin-like growth factor-1, which is required for cartilage growth, and too much insulin, which accelerates bony growth and osteophyte formation (Denko, Boja, and Moskowitz 1987).

Clinical Manifestations

Osteoarthritis usually has an insidious onset depending on the specific joints afflicted and the patient's tolerance to pain. The characteristic symptoms are pain and stiffness localized to the involved joints. In early disease the pain occurs with use of the joint; later pain occurs during rest. Morning stiffness is usually of short duration, less than 30 minutes. Frequently it is related to changes in the weather. The affected joint creaks on movement, and its motion is reduced.

The affected joint is enlarged, owing to bony overgrowth and to synovitis with accumulation of fluid. It is tender and painful. Late in the disease, subluxation and muscle atrophy occur. Rarely is there ankylosis or fusion with complete loss of motion.

Radiographic examination shows cartilage loss, causing joint-space narrowing with bony overgrowth. The bony changes include eburnation in the subchondral region as well as spur development around the margin of the joint. Subchondral erosions are common, as are subchondral cysts. Osteophytes usually form as these changes occur.

In a related disorder, excessive osteophytes occur along the anterior and anterolateral surfaces of the vertebrae and bridge the disk spaces. These patients are diagnosed as having diffuse idiopathic skeletal hyperostosis (DISH), a disorder different from osteoarthritis in its biochemical changes.

History and Geography

Since prehistory, vertebrates have presumably suffered from osteoarthritis. Bones of dinosaurs show bony spurs and ankylosed spinal segments that are markers of the disease. The same changes occurred in prehistoric humankind as well as in animals, modern and ancient, such as horses and dogs (Rothschild 1989). Clinical descriptions of arthritis date back to the fifth century B.C., to Hippocrates, who described the Scythians as having markedly lax or hypermobile joints:

I will give you strong proof of the hypermobility (laxity) of their constitutions. You will find the greater part of the Scythians, and all the Nomades, with marks of the cautery on their shoulders, arms, wrists, breasts, hip-joints, and loins, and that for no other reason but the hypermobility and flabbiness of their constitution, for they can neither strain with their bows, nor launch the javelin from their

shoulder owing to their laxity and atony: but when they are burnt, much of the laxity in their joints is dried up, and they become braced, better fed, and their joints get into a more suitable condition.... They afterwards became lame and stiff at the hip joint, such of them, at least, as are severely attacked with it. (Adams 1891)

The disorder was attributed to divine retribution for the destruction of the Temple of Ashkelon which the Scythians wrought during an invasion of Palestine. D. G. Rokhlin (1965) has illustrated severe shoulder OA, deforming arthrosis, in a Scythian skeleton derived from this Hippocratic period (fifth to third century B.C.). Evidently, shoulder OA was common among the Scythians despite their treatment.

Over the centuries, the names of disorders encompassing OA have changed and have included terms such as "rheumatism" and "lumbago," which are no longer scientifically used. Today we can recognize dozens of forms and subsets of OA.

The prevalence of OA and the pattern of joint involvement show wide geographic differences. Factors influencing the prevalence of osteoarthritis are very complex. Climate is often blamed for rheumatic troubles. Sixteen worldwide population samples – 13,200 Caucasians, blacks, and Native Americans aged 35 and over – were examined with X-rays, all of which were read by one observer. The following observations resulted, in part. OA was most prevalent in the north of England, where 67 percent of men and 73 percent of women had OA. The lowest incidence was in Nigeria and Liberia. Prevalence of OA was also low in Soweto, South Africa, and in Piestany, Czechoslovakia.

The incidence of OA also varied with the specific joint being studied. For exmple, OA of the hips was common in males over 55 in the north of England; 22 to 25 percent were affected. These men were mainly coal miners and shepherds. In contrast, only 1 to 3 percent of black men, and only 2 to 4 percent of the black women, were affected in Jamaica, Liberia, Nigeria, and South Africa. Data on Heberden's nodes in 10 of the population samples revealed the highest frequency – 32 percent – in the population of Watford, England; 30 percent in the Blackfeet Indians of Montana; and 26 percent in the people of Azmoos, Switzerland. All the black populations had low prevalence, as did inhabitants of Oberholen, Germany. The Pima Indians of Arizona had an 11 percent incidence in the women, whereas in the men 20 percent were affected, a reversal of the normal sex distribution. (For more examples see Lawrence and Sebo 1980.)

Factors influencing the prevalence of osteoarthritis in populations include heredity, occupation, and possibly diet and resultant body build. Comparison of figures for populations living in very different parts of the world indicates no correlation with latitude, longitude, or any type of climate. Comparison was made of radiographs of hands and feet for 17 different European, African, and American groups of individuals living from 54° north to 26° south. Nine were white, four black, and four Native American. Eleven of the population groups lived in rural areas, six in urban areas. No significant differences were found among the different groups in the prevalence of osteoarthritis. A survey in Sweden showed that the highest incidence of OA was in the southeast and central northern regions of the country and seemed to correlate more closely with the occupations of the patients than with climatic conditions. More workers in farming and forestry had the disease than did workers in other occupations (Peyron 1984).

Charles W. Denko

Bibliography

Adams, F. 1891. *The genuine works of Hippocrates.* New York.

Denko, Charles W. 1989. Osteoarthritis: A metabolic disorder. In *New developments in antirheumatic therapy,* Inflammation and drug therapy series, Vol. 3, ed. Kim D. Rainsford and G. D. Velo, 29–35. Lancashire, U.K.

Denko, Charles W., B. Boja, and R. W. Moskowitz. 1987. Serum levels of insulin and insulin-like growth factor-1 (IGF-1). In osteoarthritis (OA). *Arthritis and Rheumatism* 30 (Supplement, ab): 29.

Heberden, William. 1802. *Commentaries on the history and cure of disease.* Reprinted under the auspices of the Library of the New York Academy of Medicine. New York, 1962.

Howell, D. S. 1984. Etiopathogenesis of osteoarthritis. In *Osteoarthritis: Diagnosis and management,* ed. R. W. Moskowitz et al., 129–46. Philadelphia.

Lawrence, J. S., and M. Sebo. 1980. The geography of osteoarthrosis. In *The aetiopathogenesis of osteoarthrosis,* ed. G. Nuki, 155–83. Kent, U.K.

Moskowitz, Roland W. 1984. Osteoarthritis: Symptoms and signs. In *Osteoarthritis: Diagnosis and management,* ed. R. W. Moskowitz, D. S. Howell, and V. M. Goldberg, 149–54. Philadelphia.

Peyron, Jacques G. 1984. The epidemiology of osteoarthritis. In *Osteoarthritis: Diagnosis and management,* ed. Roland W. Moskowitz et al., 9–27. Philadelphia.

Rokhlin, D. G. 1965. Paleolithic and Mesolithic osseous finds [in Russian]. In *Diseases of ancient man,* Chapter 5, 216–43. Moscow-Leningrad.

Rothschild, Bruce M. 1989. Skeletal paleopathology of rheumatic diseases: The subprimate connection. In *Arthritis and allied conditions: A textbook of rheumatology,* 11th edition, ed. Daniel J. McCarty, 3–7. Philadelphia.

VIII.99
Osteoporosis

Osteoporosis is defined as a proportional decrease of both bone mineral and bone matrix, leading to fracture after minimal trauma. It differs from osteomalacia in which there is a normal amount of bone matrix (osteoid) but decreased mineralization. There are two clinical syndromes of osteoporosis. Type I, or postmenopausal osteoporosis, occurs in women aged 51 to 75; it involves primarily trabecular bone loss, and presents as vertebral crush fractures or fracture of the distal radius. Type II, or senile osteoporosis, occurs in both men and women, particularly after the age of 60; it involves trabecular and cortical bone loss, and more commonly presents with hip and vertebral wedge fractures. Postmenopausal osteoporosis is associated with decreased serum levels of parathyroid hormone and a secondary decrease in activation of vitamin D, whereas senile osteoporosis is associated with a primary decrease in activation of vitamin D and increased parathyroid hormone.

Osteoporosis is an enormous public health problem, responsible for at least 1.2 million fractures in the United States each year. Fractures of the vertebral bodies and hip comprise the majority, and the complications of hip fracture are fatal in 12 to 20 percent of cases. Nearly 30 percent require long-term nursing home care. The direct and indirect costs of osteoporosis in the United States are estimated at over 8 billion in 1989 dollars annually.

Age-related bone loss or involutional osteoporosis begins about age 40 in both sexes at an initial rate of about 0.5 percent per year. The bone loss increases with age until slowing very late in life. In women, an accelerated postmenopausal loss of bone occurs at a rate of 2 to 3 percent per year for about 10 years. Over their lifetime, women lose about 35 percent of their cortical bone and 50 percent of their trabecular bone, whereas men lose about two-thirds of these amounts (Riggs and Melton 1986). The skeletal bone mass is comprised of 80 percent cortical and 20 percent trabecular bone. Trabecular or spongy bone has a much higher turnover rate, nearly eight times that of cortical or compact bone.

Etiology

The process of age-related osteoporosis is universal, although certain populations are affected to a greater degree or at an earlier age. Osteoporosis in the elderly is exceedingly common and involves multiple factors of age, sex, endocrine system, genetics, environment, nutrition, and physical activity. Age-related factors include decreased osteoblast function, decreased intestinal calcium absorption, decreased renal activation of vitamin D, and increased parathyroid hormone secretion combined with decreased clearance of the hormone by the kidney.

In women, decreased estrogen production in menopause accounts for 10 to 20 percent loss of total bone mass. Although men do not undergo the equivalent of menopause, gonadal function declines in many elderly men and contributes to osteoporosis. Multiple pregnancies and extended breastfeeding in premonopausal females may also produce negative calcium balance and subsequent bone loss. Underlying medical conditions or medications can contribute to osteoporosis, particularly hyperthryoidism, hemiplegia or paralysis, alcoholism, use of glucocorticoid steroids, and smoking.

Population and familial studies implicate both genetic and environmental factors in causing or inhibiting osteoporosis. Blacks, for example, tend to have greater initial bone mass or bone density than do Caucasian populations. Even with similar rates of bone loss, their osteoporosis begins at a later age than that of their white counterparts. Black females living in Michigan had similar relative vertebral density by age to blacks living in Puerto Rico. Both black groups had significantly less osteoporosis by age group than did Caucasian females living in Michigan. Within the Caucasian group, women of British Isles' ancestry had a higher incidence of osteoporosis than did whites of other national origins (Smith and Rizek 1966).

Nutrition, particularly calcium intake, plays a role in the inhibition of osteoporosis. Long-term trials of calcium supplementation, however, have had mixed results in postmenopausal women. Such supplementation may be more effective if initiated in women years before onset of menopause. A high-protein diet increases urinary excretion of calcium and may therefore induce a negative calcium balance. The decreased renal activation of vitamin D with age may also be a contributing factor in populations without vitamin D supplementation or with the elderly confined indoors.

Physical activity decreases the rate of bone loss in the elderly. The skeletal stresses from weight bearing and muscle contraction stimulate osteoblast function, and muscle mass and bone mass are directly related.

Epidemiology, Distribution, and Incidence

Osteoporosis was defined as a clinical entity by Fuller Albright and colleagues in 1941. Since that time a large number of epidemiological studies have been performed to evaluate the varying rates of osteoporosis and osteoporosis-related fractures in different populations. The process of age-related and postmenopausal bone loss occurs in all populations. It appears to start earlier for women in Japan and India as compared to women in Britain and the United States. It occurs later in Finnish women, and age-related rates of bone loss of women between 35 and 64 years of age are lower in Jamaica and the four African countries studied than in the other countries examined (Nordin 1966).

Relating the differing rates to calcium intake correlates well with the populations in Japan, India, and Finland but not Jamaica or the African countries. Other factors such as genetically determined initial bone density or increased physical activity may also be involved. The rate of hip fracture varies according to the age distribution of osteoporosis in all countries. This distribution involves a much broader age group in India secondary to the prevalence of rickets and osteomalacia.

Black females in both Puerto Rico and Michigan have less osteoporosis than do white females in Michigan. However, both groups demonstrate a very high prevalence with advanced age: 60 percent of those over 65 years in Puerto Rico and 80 percent over 65 years in Michigan (Smith and Rizek 1966). The incidence rates of hip fracture are higher in white populations in all geographic areas including Israel and Singapore, compared to the indigenous populations. A very low incidence rate is also noted among the Maoris of New Zealand and Bantu of South Africa compared to white populations in both areas. The age-adjusted incidence rate of hip fracture for females and males per 100,000 is 5.3 and 5.6 among the Bantu compared to 101.6 and 50.5 among blacks in the United States (Cummings et al. 1985).

In the United States, over 90 percent of all hip fractures occur in individuals over age 70 years. By age 90, a third of all women will have sustained a hip fracture. Vertebral fractures are present in 25 percent of women over age 70.

History

Age-related bone loss has also been examined in prehistoric skeletal populations. Archaic Indians dating back to 2500 B.C. and subsisting as hunter-gatherers showed differential rates between females and males as well as overall rates of osteoporosis quite similar to those of a modern hospital population. A more recent Hopewell Indian population showed greater age-related bone loss, probably resulting from genetic or nutritional factors (Perzigian 1973). A study of three ancient Nubian skeletal populations found that osteoporosis occurred earlier in life among these women as compared to modern Western samples, perhaps secondary to inadequate calcium intake or extended lactation (Dewey et al. 1969).

R. Ted Steinbock

Bibliography

Albright, F., et al. 1941. Post-menopausal osteoporosis. *Journal of the American Medical Association* 116: 2465–8.

Chalmers, J., and K. C. Ho. 1970. Geographical variations in senile osteoporosis. *Journal of Bone and Joint Surgery* 52B: 667–75.

Cummings, S. R., et al. 1985. Epidemiology of osteoporosis and osteoporotic fractures. *Epidemiology Review* 7: 178–208.

Dewey, J. R., et al. 1969. Femoral cortical involution in three Nubian archaeological populations. *Human Biology* 41: 13–28.

Ericksen, M. F. 1976. Cortical bone loss with age in three native American populations. *American Journal of Physical Anthropology* 45: 443–52.

Garn, S. M. 1970. *The earlier gain and the later loss of cortical bone.* Springfield, Ill.

Nordin, B. E. C. 1966. International patterns of osteoporosis. *Clinical Orthopedics* 45: 17–30.

Perzigian, A. J. 1973. Osteoporotic bone loss in two prehistoric Indian populations. *American Journal of Physical Anthropology* 39: 87–96.

Resnick, N. M., and S. L. Greenspan. 1989. Senile osteoporosis reconsidered. *Journal of the American Medical Association* 261: 1025–9.

Riggs, B. L., and L. J. Melton. 1986. Involutional osteoporosis. *New England Journal of Medicine* 314: 1676–86.

Smith, R. W., and J. Rizek. 1966. Epidemiologic studies of osteoporosis in women of Puerto Rico and southeastern Michigan with special reference to age, race, national origin and to other related or associated findings. *Clinicial Orthopedics* 45: 31–48.

VIII.100
Paget's Disease of Bone

Paget's disease of bone was described as "osteitis deformans," a "chronic inflammation of bone" by Sir James Paget in an address to the Royal Medical Chirurgical Society of London in 1876.

His original description was masterful and thus has withstood the test of time. Paget's disease of bone describes an abnormal osseous (bony) structure whereby isolated and sometimes contiguous areas of the skeleton undergo changes leading to clinical deformity for some of those affected. Clinically affected people may have the appearance of enlarged bone, bowed extremities, shortened stature, and simian posturing because the body's usual system for maintaining strong and healthy bone malfunctions. Normal bone turnover is altered in the affected areas. The resorption process accelerates, and the repair process responds by building a heavy, thickened, and enlarged bone. Although the new bone contains normal or increased amounts of calcium, the material of the bone is disorganized, and the bone is structurally weak. The result may be pain, deformity, fracture, and arthritis.

Distribution and Incidence

The disease appears to have its greatest prevalence in Europe and in regions inhabited by European emigrants such as Australia, New Zealand, and areas of South America. For no apparent reason, the disease is distinctly uncommon in African blacks, Orientals, and inhabitants of India and Scandinavia. Where studied, the incidence ranges between 3.5 and 4.5 percent of the population in high prevalence regions of the world, with a high of 8.3 percent in a part of Lancashire, England, to a low of 0.4 percent in Sweden. In a U.S. survey of Paget's disease based on pelvic X-rays, the incidence was 3.9 percent in Caucasians residing in Brooklyn and 0.9 percent in Caucasians residing in Atlanta. Similarly, 1,000 pelvic X-rays revealed no Paget's disease in Lexington, Kentucky, and 1.1 percent pelvic Paget's disease in Providence, Rhode Island.

Epidemiology and Etiology

Males are more at risk from Paget's disease than are females by a 3:2 ratio. There is evidence of heritability: A survey, for example, revealed that 13.8 percent of patients with Paget's disease had relatives with Paget's disease. Approximately half were from successive generations and half from siblings. Familial cases had an earlier onset than did isolated cases. An autosomal dominant pattern was suggested.

The etiology remains unknown. Paget named this disease "osteitis deformans" in the belief that the basic process was inflammatory and had an infectious origin. Recent ultrastructural studies of involved bone have revealed nuclear and cytoplasmic inclusions. They have not been found in bone cells of patients with other skeletal disorders, with the exception of giant cell tumors of bone. Morphologically the nuclei resemble those of cells infected with paramyxoviruses such as parainfluenza, mumps, and measles, and the cells resemble cultured cells infected with respiratory syncytial virus (RSV).

This tubular morphological finding has raised the question as to whether Paget's disease is a slow virus infection of bone. Other slow virus infections of human beings have similarly demonstrated a long clinical latent period, absence of an acute inflammatory response, a slowly progressive course, restriction of disease to a single organ system, patchy distribution in the body, and genetic predisposition.

Immunohistological studies of bone biopsy specimens have demonstrated antigen from RSV and measles. An indirect immunofluorescence antibody assay has demonstrated evidence for both measles and RSV antigens in Pagetic bone grown in culture from 30 patients. The suggestion of different RNA viruses (measles is a member of the genus *Morbillivirus*, whereas RSV is a member of the genus *Pneumovirus*) seems incompatible. It has been proposed that Paget's disease stems from a previously uncharacterized virus, perhaps of the *Pneumovirus* group. According to this hypothesis, Paget's disease patients are infected with a slow virus at an early age, probably under the age of 30. The slow virus isolates to particular areas of the skeleton by growth pattern and/or blood supply. As the metabolic activity of the skeleton decreases with age, the infested osteoclasts increase their metabolic activity, eventually producing diseased bone some 20 to 40 years following the initial infestation.

Clinical Manifestations

It is estimated that 80 percent of people with Paget's disease are asymptomatic and have no clinical findings suggestive of the disease. When symptomatic, the clinical manifestations are often defined by the complications of the disease. Clinical findings may include some or all of the following: frontal bossing, scalp vein dilatation, angioid streaks, simian pos-

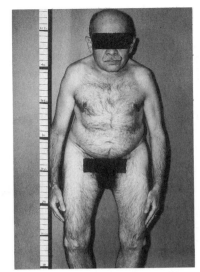

Figure VIII.100.1. Severe Paget's disease of the bone in a 66-year-old male. Note the anthropoid appearance and simian posturing, with the anterior and lateral bow to the arms, thighs, and legs. There are functional flexion contractures of the hips and knees.

ture, short stature, flexion contractures at hips and knees, anterior and lateral bowing of long bones, warmth of involved extremity, periosteal tenderness, and compressive neuropathy. Figure VIII.100.1 shows a man with severe Paget's disease of bone.

Pagetic bone pain is uncommon, but when present it is aching, deep, poorly described, and occasionally continuous at night. It is often aggravated by pressure or weight bearing.

The following deformities may develop: (1) The involved skull may become soft, thickened, and enlarged; (2) the femora tend to migrate medially and superiorly deforming the softened pelvis; (3) enlargement of vertebrae alters the spine, resulting in an anthropoid appearance; (4) the affected long bones soften and bow from weight-bearing or from the force of the surrounding muscles.

Pathological fractures can also occur in the form of compression fractures of vertebrae, incomplete or stress fractures of the long bones, or completed fractures of long bones.

The relation of secondary osteoarthritis to Paget's disease has recently been emphasized. Low back pain is the most common clinical presentation of Paget's disease and is often related to secondary osteoarthritis.

Sarcomatous degeneration, although uncommon, does occur in approximately 1 percent of patients with Paget's disease, representing a 40-fold increase over that of the general adult population. It is most often heralded by increasing pain.

Skull symptoms may include headaches, vertigo, rushing sensations, and noise in the head. Maxillary exceeds mandibular involvement by a 2:1 ratio, and both may disrupt the lamina dura or cause unsightly deformity. Hearing loss may be severe but is most often moderate.

Neural compression may occur from spinal stenosis or a spinal lateral recess syndrome. Paraparesis – paraplegia in Paget's disease – is most often related to Paget's disease of dorsal or cervical vertebrae.

History and Geography

Paget's disease is not a new disease, having been suspected in a Neanderthal skull. Although isolated case reports in the mid-nineteenth century describe what is now called Paget's disease, the classical clinical description by Paget and a pathological description by Henry Butlin clarified this entity in 1876. Paget was a major figure in the medical community, having been knighted at the age of 43, at which time he began his observations of the first patient with the bone disease that would bear his name. He is also credited with having defined such diseases as Paget's disease of the breast, rectum, and skin; carpal tunnel syndrome; and trichinosis. Paget's disease of bone is unique in that it affects only adult humans; reports of Paget's disease in animals are not convincing. A childhood osseous condition called *juvenile Paget's disease* appears to be a separate entity.

At present, it is difficult to reconcile the geographic isolation of this disease to Europeans (exclusive of Scandinavians) and their descendants. Theories of a slow virus infection in susceptible individuals seem dubious, for if this were the case, then theoretically the disease would have a more worldwide distribution. Isolated case reports of Paget's disease in South African blacks, Japanese, and Indians (from India) only serve to confuse the issue of transmission.

Temperature cannot be implicated, as high prevalence areas include disparate climatic regions of Italy, Spain, Germany, and eastern Russia. Similarly, occupation and degree of physical activity do not appear related to the cause of Paget's disease as the blend of geographic areas involves all types of lifestyles. Interestingly, the black population of the United States appears to sustain a higher frequency of Paget's disease than might be expected, given the rarity of the disease in Africa. An explanation in part involves intermarriage with those of European ancestry.

Roy D. Altman

Bibliography

Altman, R. D., and B. Collins. 1980. Musculoskeletal manifestations of Paget's disease of bone. *Arthritis and Rheumatism* 23: 1121–7.

Altman, R. D., and R. Winchester. *HLF-A, B, C, D, Dr* loci in Paget's disease. School of Medicine, University of Miami. Miami, Fla. (Unpublished data.)

Barry, H. C. 1969. *Paget's disease of bone*. Edinburgh and London.

Cullen, P., et al. 1976. Frequencies of HLA-A and HLA-B: Histocompatibility antigens in Paget's disease of bone. *Tissue Antigens* 7: 55–6.

Dickson, D. D., et al. 1945. Osteitis deformans: Paget's disease of bone. *Radiology* 44: 449–70.

Fotino, M., et al. 1977. Evidence for linkage between HLA and Paget's disease. *Transplant Proceedings* 9: 1867–8.

Howatson, A. F., and V. L. Fornasier. 1982. Microfilaments associated with Paget's disease of bone: Comparison with nucleocapsids of measles virus and respiratory syncytial virus. *Intervirology* 18: 150–9.

Mills, B. J., et al. 1980. Cell cultures form bone affected by Paget's disease. *Arthritis and Rheumatism* 23: 1115–20.

1984. Evidence for both respiratory syncytial virus and measles virus antigens in the osteoclasts of patients with Paget's disease of bone. *Clinical Orthopaedics and Related Research* 183: 303–11.

Morales, A., et al. 1980. Manifestaciones articulares de la enfermedad de Paget. Revisión de 84 casos. *Revista Clínica Española* 159: 195–8.

Paget, J. 1877. On a form of chronic inflammation of bones (osteitis deformans). *Medico-Chirurgical Transactions* 60: 37–64.

Rebel, A., et al. 1974. Particularités ultrastructuales des osteoclastes de la maladie de Paget. *Revue du Rhumatisme et des Maladies Osteo-articulaires* 41: 767–71.

1980. Viral antigens in osteoclasts from Paget's disease of bone. *Lancet* 2: 344–6.

Rosenbaum, H. D., and D. J. Hanson. 1969. Geographic variation in the prevalence of Paget's disease of bone. *Radiology* 92: 959–63.

Sofaer, J. A., et al. 1983. A family study of Paget's disease of bone. *Journal of Epidemiology and Community Health* 37: 226–31.

Tilyard, M. W., et al. 1982. A probable linkage between familial Paget's disease and the HLA loci. *Australian and New Zealand Journal of Medicine* 12: 498–500.

VIII.101
Paragonimiasis

Several species of the genus *Paragonimus,* the lung flukes, can parasitize human beings. The most important, *Paragonimus westermani,* is found in China, Japan, Korea, Southeast Asia, Papua New Guinea, and parts of India and Central Africa. It was first discovered in the lungs of tigers in European zoos in 1878. Other species occur in Asia, in Africa, and in Central America and parts of South America. Wild and domestic members of the cat and dog families and other carnivorous animals are also hosts, and in many places humans are accidental hosts for worms that normally reside in other mammals. Adult worms produce eggs in the lungs, which reach fresh water either in the sputum or by being coughed up, swallowed, and passed in the feces.

Motile larvae hatch, penetrate an appropriate type of snail, undergo two reproductive cycles, and emerge to seek the second intermediate host, a crab or crayfish. Here they penetrate between the joints of the crustacean's exoskeleton, and encyst there to await ingestion by humans or other definitive host. They then burrow through the intestinal wall and the diaphragm and enter the lungs, where they may survive for many years. Slow, chronic lung damage may become very serious in heavy infestations. Migrating flukes sometimes wander widely lost and reach atypical (ectopic) sites like the brain, where they cause a variety of neurological symptoms and may prove fatal.

Diagnosis of paragonimiasis depends on detection of the eggs in sputum or feces. Treatment of the lung form of the disease is usually effective, but may be prolonged. Prevention is achieved by avoidance of raw, poorly cooked, pickled, or marinated freshwater crabs and crayfish.

K. David Patterson

Bibliography

Burton, K. 1982. Pulmonary paragonimiasis in Laotian refugee children. *Pediatrics* 70: 246–8.

Kean, B. H., et al. eds. 1978. *Tropical medicine and parasitology: Classic investigations,* Vol. II, 601–14. Ithaca and London. [Five early papers.]

Nwokolo, C. 1974. Endemic paragonimiasis in Africa. *Bulletin of the World Health Organization* 50: 569–71.

Yokagama, M. 1965. *Paragonimus* and paragonimiasis. In *Advances in Parasitology,* ed. B. Dawes, Vol. II, 99–158. New York.

VIII.102
Parkinson's Disease

Parkinson's disease, or parkinsonism, is a syndrome (i.e., a constellation of clinical signs and symptoms) consisting of four cardinal features: resting tremor, bradykinesia (physical and mental sluggishness), rigidity, and impaired postural reflexes. The diagnosis is made on the basis of finding any three of the four cardinal features.

Distribution and Incidence

This disease occurs throughout the world, with no population protected against the condition. Most surveys have investigated Caucasian populations of northern European or of Anglo-Saxon descent, and few studies have been done on the occurrence of Parkinson's disease in other populations. In Caucasians the prevalence is 84 to 187 per 100,000 of population, with no geographic patterns and no clusters of increased incidence. Two studies seem to indicate a lower prevalence in blacks; this has been the clinical experience as well, probably indicating a decreased risk of Parkinson's disease for blacks. The annual incidence varies from 5 to 24 per 100,000 of the white population. These figures, of course, depend on the methods of ascertainment, the population studied, the length of time that data have been collected, and many other factors. If the prevalence is divided by the annual incidence, the average duration of the illness is approximately 10 years.

Epidemiology

Parkinson's disease usually occurs in late middle life or beyond. The mean age of onset is 58 to 62. Onset before age 30 is rare but is not unknown, and there is a juvenile form of Parkinson's disease. The greatest incidence is in the decade age 70 to 79 years, with an incidence of 1 to 2 per 1,000 population per year. Later the incidence of parkinsonism seems to decline, a finding which, if true, would have important implications about pathogenesis, indicating that the disease is not simply a result of the operation of the aging process on the nervous system. There appears to be no difference between the sexes in regard to the risk of being affected by Parkinson's disease; early studies in this respect were in error because of decreased ascertainment in females. It is now generally accepted that the ratio is almost or exactly the same for both sexes. Parkinson's disease was known before 1817, the year of publication of the famous manuscript by James Parkinson, but prevalence studies have been possible only since the 1960s, and they indicate no substantial change in incidence.

In 1917 an epidemic of encephalitis lethargica started in Vienna and spread throughout the world. Following this illness, about half of the victims developed Parkinson's disease with tremor, bradykinesia, and rigidity often associated with oculogyric crises, parkinsonian crises (sudden episodic worsening of signs and symptoms), behavioral abnormalities, cranial nerve palsies, and a host of other central nervous system abnormalities. The age of onset of the postencephalitic Parkinson's disease is early compared to other types of Parkinson's disease. A popular and now discarded theory, the *Cohort theory,* hypothesized that all Parkinson's disease was caused by the encephalitis lethargica agent and that Parkinson's disease would therefore disappear in the 1980s. Since 1961 when the Cohort theory was promulgated, evidence against it has been overwhelming, and we now know that there is no decrease in the prevalence of Parkinson's disease, but of course, the postencephalitic Parkinson's disease has almost disappeared.

Mortality

The mortality rate from parkinsonism varies from 0.5 to 3.8 per 100,000 of population, and the duration averages about 10 years, with a large range of 1 to 33 years, depending on the age of onset, the rate of progression, the patient's general health, and the treatments received. M. M. Hoehn and M. D. Yahr found that victims of Parkinson's disease have a range of mortality 2.9 times greater than the norm, but treatment with levodopa increases the quality of life, decreases the symptoms of the disease, and also reduces this excess mortality. Genetic studies failed to show significant risks of parkinsonism in families, and careful analysis of monozygotic twins indicates a lack of concordance for this disease. The twin studies clearly show that the major factor in the cause of parkinsonism is not hereditary.

Etiology

The signs and symptoms of parkinsonism are caused by a decrease in striatal dopamine due to the loss of dopaminergic neurons in the substantia nigra of the midbrain. At the present time, environmental agents are the primary known cause of parkinsonism; exposure to manganese, carbon disulfide, and carbon monoxide are recognized environmental toxins that can produce the disorder. It is also known that drugs that interfere with dopaminergic pathways or receptors – such as phenothiazines, reserpine, and alpha-methyldopa – can produce the Parkinson's syndrome, and multiple head traumas, probably causing atrophy of the substantia nigra, also may do the same. The recent discovery that 1-methyl-4-phenyl-1,2,3,6-tetrahydropyridine (MPTP), a commercially available chemical intermediate used in the synthesis of organic compounds, induces parkinsonism, has again supported the concept that environmental chemicals play a major role in the pathogenesis of this disorder. Varying amounts of MPTP may be formed as a byproduct in the synthesis of potent analgesic drugs, one of which is MPPP (1-methyl-4-phenyl-4-proprionoxypiperidine), the reverse ester of meperidine, a strong analgesic drug similar to heroin and morphine. The self-administration of small amounts of MPTP by young drug abusers who were using MPPP as an alternative to heroin has resulted in a severe and permanent Parkinson's syndrome that resembles Parkinson's disease in its clinical, pathological, and biochemical features as well as its responsiveness to the drugs usually used in the treatment of Parkinson's patients. Primate models of parkinsonism using MPTP demonstrate that a Parkinson-like syndrome can be produced in the monkey, and it is now known that metabolic conversion by monoamine oxidase B of MPTP to MPP+ (1-methyl-4-phenylpyridinium) is the reaction that results in the ultimate toxin MPP+. It therefore follows that blocking monoamine oxidase B with a selective inhibitor such as L-deprenyl completely prevents the toxicity of MPTP, but administration of a selective monoamine oxidase A inhibitor such as clorgylin does not. Thus, MPTP turns out to be the first toxin positively known to cause Parkinson's disease whose neuropharmacology is known and whose toxicity can be prevented by preventing its metabolic conversion to the ultimate toxin, which is MPP+ (see Figure VIII.102.1).

Pathology

Nigrostriatal dopaminergic system failure is the important pathological feature of parkinsonism. Loss of pigment cells in the substantia nigra and the dopaminergic neurons associated with them results in a deficiency of dopa in the striatum and produces the clinical signs and symptoms of the disease.

Clinical Manifestations

The cardinal features of Parkinson's disease are resting tremor, bradykinesia, rigidity, and postural instability. The resting tremor usually is 4 to 6 cycles per second and is present at rest and decreases with

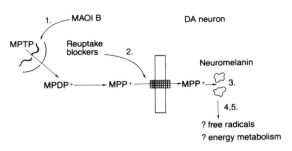

Figure VIII.102.1. Scheme illustrating the mechanism of MPTP toxicity at nigral dopamine neurons in primates. MPTP, which is lipophilic, enters the brain where it is transformed into MPP$^+$ by monoamine oxidase B located in glial cells or in serotonergic neurons. MPP$^+$ is taken up into the dopaminergic (DA) neurons, where it accumulates, by dopamine reuptake mechanisms. The binding of MPP$^+$ to neuromelanin might assist in the accumulation of MPP$^+$, or might contribute to its toxicity. MPP$^+$ within the neurons is assumed not to undergo redox cycling to reproduce free radical species but, rather, to be actively accumulated by mitochondria, where it inerferes with mitochondrial energy metabolism, leading to cell death. The precise mechanism of MPP$^+$ toxicity remains unknown. The sequence of events leading to MPTP toxicity can, in theory, be inhibited at a number of points: (1) Selective monoamine oxidase B inhibitors (MAOI B) such as deprenyl inhibit the conversion of MPTP to MPP$^+$; (2) dopamine reuptake blockers such as nomifensine inhibit the entry and accumulation of MPP$^+$ into dopaminergic neurons; (3) chloroquine might inhibit the binding of MPP$^+$ to neuromelanin and thus limit its toxicity for protective substances such as antioxidants (e.g., alpha-tocopherol); or substances such as acetyl-L-carnitine that protect mitochondria from toxic insults might inhibit the toxic mechanism of MPP$^+$; (4,5) other substances as yet unknown might inhibit the production of free radicals or boost energy metabolism. (From Joseph Jankovic and Eduardo Tolosa, eds. 1988. *Parkinson's disease and movement disorders.* Baltimore, Maryland: Urban and Schwarzenberg, by permission of the publisher.)

action. The tremor usually starts in the upper extremity on one side and then spreads to the lower extremity on the same side. Upper and lower extremities are usually time-locked, with the lower extremity a half cycle behind the upper extremity. Once the tremor has spread to one side of the body, the opposite upper extremity is usually involved, and then the opposite lower extremity. Postural tremor is also present in the majority of Parkinson's patients, and postural tremor is usually slightly faster than the resting tremor. *Bradykinesia,* which literally means "slow movement," is not the same as *hypokinesia,* meaning "decreased movement," or

akinesia, "no movement." All of these movement disorders can be part of Parkinson's disease. The bradykinesia shows up as a delay in the execution and initiation of voluntary movement, and also there is difficulty arresting the movement once it has been started. Akinesia is simply an extreme state of immobility, and some Parkinson's patients, particularly before treatment with levodopa became available, eventually ended their days totally rigid and immobilized. *Rigidity* is resistance to passive stretch of muscle, and the patients with parkinsonism have a characteristic stiffness of the muscles of the body. This stiffness can be brought out by passive rotation of the wrist or flexion–extension at the forearm. It is also present in the truncal muscles and can be examined by placing one's hands on the dorsal aspect of the patient's back muscles and having the patient flex and extend the body at the waist. The rigidity that is characteristic of parkinsonism is the rigidity that usually gives way in little catches and, hence, has been called *cogwheel rigidity.* The most disabling of the cardinal features of parkinsonism is the postural instability. This one symptom alone accounts for most of the falls that occur in this disease. The instability results in loss of balance with propulsion and retropulsion, and such patients are unable to anticipate a change in their posture and thereby correct for the change, and thus they often follow their center of gravity as they fall to the ground. Little postural corrections that are normally made automatically cannot be done, and this is the major motor defect in the disease. Other clinical features of parkinsonism include masked facies and decreased blinking, increased saliva production called *sialorrhea, hyperhidrosis* (profuse sweating) or oily skin, a low-pitched monotonous voice, stooped posture, scoliosis, decreased upward gaze, a tendency toward low blood pressure, micrographia, and a shuffling and small-stepped gait.

History

Tremor was mentioned in the writings of Hippocrates, Celsus, and Galen, but the real history of Parkinson's disease does not start until 1817, the year Parkinson's essay on the shaking palsy was published – when he was 62 years old. Parkinson called the disease the "shaking palsy," but he also provided a Latin term: *paralysis agitans.* He reported on six patients. The first was personally observed, two others were noticed casually in the street; case 4 had an abscess on the chest wall but was lost to follow-up; case 5 was evidently seen at a distance, and there are no details of that patient available; and case 6 was a 72-year-old man who was visually inspected but evidently not examined.

In other words, by modern standards Parkinson's great essay on Parkinson's disease would not have passed muster. It is clear that the information he conveys in his essay is basically from visual inspection: He did not examine the patients personally. Despite that his paper was well received by the medical community, and subsequently, clinicians added to his description.

Armand Trousseau, in 1859, included a lecture in clinical medicine on parkinsonism and discussed the rigidity and the bradykinesia. The great French neurologist Jean Martin Charcot considered Parkinson's disease a neurosis because there was no proper central nervous system lesion to explain it, and the condition was characteristically worsened by stress or emotion. Charcot frequently commented that everything possible had been used to treat parkinsonism but with very little effect. He recommended belladonna alkaloids, especially hyoscyamine, an etropine isomer, now known to us as scopolamine. According to our modern biochemical understanding of parkinsonism, this agent should have a partial effect in improving the signs and symptoms of Parkinson's disease. In an interesting paper in 1893, Paul Oscar Blocq reported the case of a patient with hemiparkinsonism, who at autopsy was found to have a lesion in the inferior peduncle with complete destruction of the substantia nigra. This, of course, suggested that the neuroanatomic substrate of Parkinson's disease was the substantia nigra and probably is the first description in the medical literature of a lesion that produces parkinsonism. Many other descriptions were made by William R. Gowers and other famous physicians, but these merely added to the fundamental and original observations of Parkinson.

The road to effective therapy was paved in the 1960s by A. Carlsson, who showed in animals that reserpine produces a bradykinesia that could be reversed by the administration of L-dopa, a dopamine precursor. Because it was known that reserpine administration to humans produces a condition that resembles parkinsonism, L-dopa was administered to reserpinized humans to ameliorate the signs and symptoms of the reserpine-induced parkinsonism. O. Hornykiewicz and colleagues then studied the concentration of dopamine in patients dying of parkinsonism, comparing the results to those in normal controls, and reported that there was a marked decrease in dopamine in the caudate nucleus. In 1962 André Barbeau tried the oral administration of L-dopa (100 to 200 mg), and in 1961 W. Birkmayer and

Hornykiewicz experimented with intravenous levodopa (50 to 150 mg), both reporting temporary benefits in parkinsonism. Others, however, were unable to confirm any major effect until George C. Cotzias and colleagues initiated the modern era of therapy in parkinsonism by showing that much larger oral doses of the L-dopa, 1.6 to 12.6 grams per day, resulted in dramatic improvement in many patients. The improvements were so dramatic that the efficacy of levodopa treatment was established beyond any doubt, and a new era in the management of Parkinson's disease began.

Geography

As was previously mentioned, an increased incidence of Parkinson's disease has not been shown anywhere in the world. However, there is an increased incidence of a complex of parkinsonism, dementia, and amyotrophic lateral sclerosis (ALS) in Guam, the Kii Peninsula of Japan, Rota, and the western highlands of New Guinea. This peculiar disease, in which patients manifest abnormalities referable to almost every level of the neuraxis, resembles a combination of parkinsonism, Alzheimer's disease, and ALS. Two major theories have emerged to explain the increased incidence of this condition in areas of the world bordered by the Mariana volcanic fault. The first theory implicates a secondary hyperparathyroidism, which increases the deposition of toxic environmental metals in the nervous system. This theory is supported by the finding of increased manganese and calcium levels in nervous tissue taken from patients dying of this condition. The secondary theory implicates the ingestion of two toxic amino acids – beta-oxaloamine-1-alanine (BOAA) and beta-methylamino-1-alanine (BMAA) – by people in this area of the world. This theory is supported by the finding that infusions of toxic amino acids can produce nervous system disease in primates that does seem to resemble some of the degenerative diseases including parkinsonism, ALS, and Alzheimer's disease. Further work needs to be done to clarify the role of these toxic amino acids, if any, in the pathogenesis of the Parkinson's disease–ALS–dementia complex on Guam. Both theories, implicating environmental factors as the cause, are supported by the fact that the incidence of this peculiar combination of disorders is steadily decreasing.

Bernard M. Patten

Bibliography

Barbeau, André. 1962. The pathogenesis of Parkinson's disease. *Canadian Medical Association Journal* 87: 802–7.

Birkmeyer, W., and O. Hornykiewicz. 1961. The L-3,4-dioxyphenylalanine (DOPA) effect in Parkinson-akinesia. *Wiener Klinische Wochenschrift* 37: 787–8.

Cotzias, G. C. et al. 1967. Aromatic amino acids and the modification of parkinsonism. *New England Journal of Medicine* 276: 347.

Duvoisin, R. C. 1984. *Parkinson's disease: A guide for patient and family.* New York.

Duvoisin, R. C. et al. 1963. Parkinsonism before and since the epidemic of encephalitis lethargica. *Archives of Neurology* 8: 232.

Hoehn, M. M., and M. D. Yahr. 1967. Parkinsonism: Onset, progression, and mortality. *Neurology* 17: 427.

Hornykiewicz, O. 1966. Dopamine (3-hydroxytyramine) and brain function. *Pharmacological Reviews* 18: 925.

Koller, W. C., ed. 1987. *Handbook of Parkinson's disease.* New York.

Parkinson, J. 1817. *An essay on the shaking palsy.* London.

VIII.103
Pellagra

Pellagra is a recurring nutritional disease associated with a severe deficiency of niacin, a vitamin of the B-complex group that includes both nicotinic acid and nicotinamide. Because the body can convert the essential amino acid *tryptophan* into niacin, inclusion of enough tryptophan in the diet is as effective as niacin in preventing the disease. Pellagra is usually associated with signs of deficiencies of other B complex vitamins and nearly always is linked with poverty and a diet composed substantially of maize. In recent years, pellagra in India and Egypt has been tied to consumption of another grain, *jowar,* a type of millet or sorghum.

Pellagra is characterized by dermatitis, diarrhea, and dementia, and thus is known as the *disease of the "3 D's."* If untreated, a fourth "D," death, may ensue. Before the cause of the disease was known, mortality was as high as 70 percent. As knowledge about the disease increased, however, and many mild cases, previously undiagnosed, were recognized, the mortality rate was reduced substantially.

Dermatitis is the characteristic symptom of pellagra and the one on which diagnosis is based. Symmetrical lesions appear on the hands and arms, on the tops of the feet and around the ankles, on the back of the neck, and across the face in a butterfly-shaped design. Weakness, a sense of malaise, and a reddened skin, sometimes confused with sunburn, are the first indications of the disease. Later the skin crusts and peels, revealing a smooth glossy skin underneath. In Spain, where the disease was first described in the eighteenth century, it was called *mal de la rosa;* in France, peasants named it *mal de la misère.* In Italy, it was called *mal del sole* because its peak came with the spring equinox. Late in the eighteenth century, the Italian physician Francesco Frapolli named the disease pellagra, which means "rough or dry skin."

Distribution and Incidence

In the two centuries between 1730 and 1930, pellagra caused much death and chronic misery, first in Europe, then in the Middle East, parts of Africa and Asia, and in North America. It was associated always with a maize diet. Since the 1930s the disease has virtually disappeared from the United States and southern Europe, and its incidence is decreasing in the Middle East. It continues to be a problem in Egypt, among the Bantu in parts of Africa, and in India, particularly in the Hyderabad region, where consumption of jowar, not maize, apparently is the precipitating factor. The disease may appear whenever famine exists.

The greatly reduced incidence of the disease in the United States may be attributed to a changed economic status in the South, where it was once prevalent; to the widespread distribution of brewer's yeast, which is a pellagra preventive; and to the enrichment of bread, flour, and cornmeal with vitamins. An occasional diagnosis of pellagra is still made in the United States, usually in association with alcoholism or a malabsorption malady.

Even in those countries where pellagra continues to be a public health problem, it no longer appears in epidemic form, but rather in endemic foci. It is most likely to occur among agricultural workers whose diets are unsatisfactory, in adults rather than children, and in men rather than women.

Epidemiology and Etiology

Observations about pellagra made in Spain in the early eighteenth century have stood the test of time: The disease is associated with a maize diet and occurs mainly among the poor. These observations were repeated over the years, and their scientific validity was confirmed more than 200 years later by work done in the United States during the second and third decades of the twentieth century.

The U.S. Public Health Service, working in the southern states, linked pellagra conclusively to the peculiar *"3 M" diet* of the region – meat, meal, and molasses – and to the poverty of which this diet was a symbol. Bread made from cornmeal was the largest component of the pellagrin's daily fare. Meat was pork fat back, and molasses was syrup made from cane. Widespread pellagra was found among tenant farmers and mill workers, in orphanages and mental institutions. The diet of pellagrins was always both monotonous and cheap. In what would become one of the classic studies in epidemiology, pellagra was linked irrevocably to economics. A systematic analysis of diet in relation to the income of workers in South Carolina mill villages showed that pellagra appeared wherever income was marginal and variety in diet was limited.

The missing element in the pellagrin's diet at first was called the pellagra-preventing or *"P-P" factor*. Although its exact nature was unknown, it was proved to exist in a number of foods including meat, milk, eggs, and certain vegetables, particularly turnip greens. One of the richest and least expensive sources was found in yeast. In 1937, the P-P factor was identified specifically as nicotinic acid, or niacin, a B-complex vitamin. Adding niacin to the diet almost magically eliminates even the worst symptoms of pellagra.

The discovery of niacin as the pellagra-preventive factor, however, did not answer all the questions about the disease. It did not explain why milk, a poor source of niacin, would prevent pellagra, nor why a diet based mostly on corn, which possesses more niacin than milk, causes it. The answer to part of the riddle lay in the discovery that the liver can convert the amino acid tryptophan, of which milk is a rich source, into niacin. The mystery of corn's association with pellagra lies in the type of niacin it contains.

Niacin is distributed in a wide variety of foods including cereals, legumes, oilseeds, meat, tea, and coffee. Its presence in food, however, does not mean that it is always available to the body. Niacin may appear in a free form ready to be absorbed; or it may appear in a bound form called *niacytin* and be biologically unavailable, as is the case with maize. Niacytin is released only after the grain is treated with an alkali such as lime. In Mexico and Central America, where pellagra has seldom been a problem even though corn is the dietary staple, the grain is soaked in lime and heated before being baked as tortillas. Treatment with lime also lowers the content of the amino acid leucine in corn.

It is the high leucine content of millet jowar (*Sorghum vulgare*) that is thought to be responsible for the appearance of pellagra in Egypt and India where this grain constitutes a large part of the diet. Niacin is found in jowar in a free form and is therefore nutritionally available, but the grain's protein has an imbalance between leucine and the amino acid isoleucine. Like maize, jowar contains a relative excess of leucine, about 12 percent, as compared with a level of below 8 percent in most other cereals. This excess brings about a conditioned niacin deficiency, one in which pyridoxine, vitamin B_6, appears to play a role.

The amount of niacin required in the diet is affected by the quality of protein consumed because tryptophan is a precursor of niacin. The term *niacin equivalent* is used because 60 milligrams of tryptophan supply 1 milligram of niacin. An adequate diet contains 6 to 9 milligrams of niacin-equivalents per day for infants, 11 to 18 for children, and 13 to 19 for adults.

Thus the etiology of pellagra is incredibly complex. The disease may result from either a niacin deficiency or an amino acid imbalance. Three essential amino acids – tryptophan, leucine, and isoleucine – and two vitamins – niacin and vitamin B_6 – are involved. The interaction of these nutrients is not fully understood, and other nutrients as well as hormones may have a role. There is also an apparent association of pellagra with sunshine.

Regular consumption of alcohol is related to the development of pellagra, as are parasitic infections, particularly schistosomiasis. Pellagra also may be precipitated by treatment with certain drugs. Isoniazid, used to treat tuberculosis, and 3-mercaptopurine, used to treat leukemia, can lead to a niacin deficiency. In patients with malignant carcinoid, tryptophan is diverted mainly to serotonin rather than to niacin, and pellagra may follow. *Hartnup's disease,* a genetic disorder that causes errors in tryptophan metabolism, looks much like pellagra and is responsive to niacin therapy.

Clinical Manifestations and Pathology

Pellagra usually appears in the winter or spring and seems to disappear a few months later, only to recur the following year. Symptoms become progressively worse. In the early stages of the disease, patients feel weak, tire easily, lose their appetites, and cannot sleep. The first definite sign of the disease, however, is a reddening of the skin, frequently mistaken for sunburn. In severe cases, the skin manifestation progresses rapidly and makes the disease easy to distinguish. It may appear on the feet and ankles, hands and forearms ("pellagra gloves"), or around the neck, and across the face. Lesions on the neck are called *Casal's necklace,* after the Spanish physician Gaspar Casal, who first identified *mal de la rosa* in 1735. In all cases, the skin manifestations are symmetrical and bilateral.

The first published description of pellagra, written by the French physician François Thièry in 1755, was graphic. The skin, he wrote, is "a horrible crust, dry, scabby, blackish, crossed with cracks, which causes much pain to the sufferer and throws off a very foetid odor." Although lesions usually occur on those parts of the body exposed to the sun, the genitals and pressure points may be affected. There is a clear demarcation between the affected and normal skin. Pellagra lesions sometimes peel, beginning from the center and spreading to the edges. In acute cases blisters occur. These may rupture, leaving weeping areas that resemble third-degree burns.

Although dermatitis is the diagnostic feature, the disease also affects the gastrointestinal tract. Patients may be nauseated or suffer from excessive salivation, have a reddened tongue, or experience a burning sensation in the abdomen. These symptoms, although associated with pellagra, are usually due to deficiencies of B-complex vitamins other than niacin. Diarrhea, sometimes intense, is characteristic of the disease.

Particularly distressing are the neurological symptoms. Insomnia is an early complaint, and patients are often apprehensive. Peripheral neuritis makes the movements of pellagrins uncertain. Mental aberrations are varied. Some patients suffer only mild depression, confusion, or loss of memory. Others manifest psychotic changes severe enough for admission to a mental hospital. Some are suicidal. All these symptoms are caused by biochemical changes still imperfectly understood. The amino acid composition of the skin is altered, and the collagen markedly reduced. The low level of urocanic acid in the skin may be related to pellagra's characteristic photosensitive rash since urocanic acid acts as an ultraviolet ray trap. There are also changes in the electrical rhythms of the brain, even if mental symptoms are not present. The majority of pellagra victims show an absence of normal alpha rhythms, but theta wave activity and high-voltage delta wave activity are found. These changes are believed to be related to an altered metabolism, in the brain, of serotonin, which is synthesized from tryptophan. Serotonin is one of the biogenic amines that modulate behavior.

History and Geography

Europe

Pellagra has always been associated with maize or corn, a grain native to America and the staple food of the American Indians. Carried to Europe as early as the third voyage of Christopher Columbus, maize was at first of interest chiefly to herbalists investigating the medicinal properties of plants. By the middle of the seventeenth century, however, at least one herbalist observed that the grain might have a deleterious rather than a sanguine effect if consumed in large quantities. An herbal of Caspar Bauhinus, published posthumously in 1658 at Basel, described how boys of the Guineas roasted and burned the grains and ate them in place of bread: "[I]f they take it a little too often [they] cannot rid themselves of the itch, since the plant produces blood that is too hot and virtually burned."

Despite this caveat, the obvious advantages of maize ensured its spread beyond the botanical gardens of Europe and into the fields. Its ease of cultivation and prolific yields made it an attractive substitute for wheat, barley, or millet. By the end of the eighteenth century, maize was widely grown in Italy, and from there spread into what is now Yugoslavia and into France, Austria, and Hungary. The ruling Hapsburgs of Austria-Hungary actively fostered its production not only because maize provided a staple food for the peasants, but because its greater yields meant larger tithes for the royal coffers.

Pellagra was first identified by Casal, a physician at the royal court of Spain. In 1735 in the town of Oviedo in the Austrias, he first noticed a kind of leprosy the peasants called *mal de la rosa*. "Since I never saw a more disgusting indigenous disease," he wrote, "I thought I should explain its characteristics." There followed the description of the disease with its extreme weakness, sensations of burning, crusts on the skin, and melancholia. Casal noted that victims of the disease lived primarily on maize, and he emphasized that the "rose" could be treated by adding to the diet milk, cheese, and other foods seldom seen by the poor. Thièry, then a physician at the court of Spain, read Casal's manuscript and wrote a brief description of the disease for a French journal, published in 1755. Casal's own work, *História natural y médica de la principado de Austrias*, was not published until 1762, 3 years after his death. In it, the section on *mal de la rosa* is set apart from other diseases discussed. It contains the volume's only illustration and is written in Latin rather than Spanish. Within 10 years, the disease was noted in Italy and given the name pellagra by Frapolli.

Accounts of pellagra in Spain are scarce after Casal's report, but by the nineteenth century the disease was rampant in northern Italy and southwestern France. Estimates were that 5 percent of the population of Lombardy was affected and that in the worst areas, the ratio was 1:5. In Milan in 1817, a visiting English physician found that about 66 percent of the inmates of a mental institution were pellagrins. The lack of reports of the disease from Spain during this period puzzled the French physician Théophile Roussel; visiting Spain in the 1840s, he determined that some diseases called by various other names were indeed pellagra, and thus published a report to this effect. Although Spanish physicians resented his interference in their medical affairs, Roussel's insistence that there was unity in endemic pellagra-like diseases was a step forward.

In retrospect, it is possible to see why pellagra spread as it did with the cultivation of maize. It was not the grain itself that was to blame for the malady, but the social and economic conditions that forced the poorest segment of the populace to eat an increasingly monotonous diet. In Spain, for example, the disease occurred in the region where the once powerful guild that controlled the raising of Merino sheep had lost its influence. There were 321 different sheep taxes in 1758, and the formerly prosperous sheep industry was badly crippled. Peasants were left to fend for themselves. In Italy, a system of land tenure called *mezzadria* kept peasants impoverished, half their crops going to the landowner to pay rent. In southern France, maize was not an important crop until the late eighteenth century, and its production in the environs of Paris was not encouraged until 1829, the year the first pellagra case was reported in the country. The peasants who fell victim to the disease were primarily sheep herders. Their land was poor, and money and food were so scarce that they ate an exclusively vegetable diet. The French, however, were luckier than their neighbors. They benefited from the work of Roussel, who believed so strongly that pellagra was caused by eating maize that he encouraged reforms to improve the food supply and the working and living conditions of the peasants. He wrote two books on pellagra, the second appearing in 1866. In this volume, he wrote that the problem of pellagra would be solved not by scientific discovery but through social progress. His arguments were persuasive enough for the French government to decrease maize cultivation for human food and encourage animal husbandry. By the turn of the century, pellagra had virtually disappeared from France.

Few people were willing to accept the idea that a disease as horrible as pellagra was caused by economic conditions. Many, however, were ready to associate it with maize. The proponents of this view were called *Zeists*, from *zea mays*, the botanical name of maize. They were led by an Italian physician, Giovanni Battista Marzari, who suggested that there were two problems with the corn diet of pellagrins. The grain was picked before it was ripe and molded in storage. More important, he believed that corn was lacking in certain nutritive elements. His followers tended to accept the spoiled corn theory and for years searched diligently for a toxin. Lodovico Balardini thought he had found it in copper-green molds growing on corn. Cesare Lombroso of Turin, who was as much interested in criminology as medicine, spent a quarter of a century studying these molds. The spoiled corn theory was used to explain why pellagra broke out in Yucatan in 1882, when locusts destroyed the Indian corn crop and the grain had to be imported from New York. Brought in the holds of ships as ballast, the grain spoiled en route. The poorer classes ate it anyway, and pellagra followed. When corn crops failed again in the early years of the twentieth century, corn was again imported to Yucatan. Again it arrived spoiled, and there were outbreaks of pellagra.

Not everyone was convinced that corn was responsible for pellagra. The Anti-Zeists thought that heredity played a part, that bad air was responsible, or that the disease was caused by some unseen organism, which they termed a virus. In the nineteenth century, however, the Zeists were for the most part triumphant, and when they were able to persuade governments to act in curtailing the consumption of corn, as they were in France, they met with a measure of success.

America and the Third World

For a century and a half after pellagra was first described, the magnitude of the problem outside Europe was not appreciated. Not until the 1890s, when the British epidemiologist Fleming Sandwith went to Egypt to serve on the staff of a hospital in Cairo, was anything about pellagra written in English. Sandwith found that many of his hookworm patients had pellagra, and he later discovered that they suffered from malaria and syphilis as well as other ailments. Sandwith noted that the disease was principally "country-bred," and he associated it with a diet of corn. He believed, however, that diseased corn, not good corn, was responsible. During the Boer War, when he was surrounded by poor Bantu people living on maize, he expected to find pellagra among them and he did, although the medical men of South Africa assured him that no such disease existed there.

When pellagra was identified in the southern United States, Sandwith was not surprised. Because this was an area where much corn was eaten, he had long suspected that the disease must be present. He expressed the "confident hope" that long unsolved pellagra problems would be mastered in the United States. The chief threat he saw to eventual success was that "enterprising" people in the South would diagnose everything as "doubtful pellagra." If that happened, he thought, the whole question of pellagra's etiology would fall into disrepute. Both his hopes and his fears were realized.

Pellagra came to the attention of the American medical profession in the spring of 1907 with the diagnosis of an epidemic at a mental hospital in Alabama. The mortality rate was a shocking 64 percent. In the months that followed, hundreds and then thousands of cases were identified, and there was a frantic search for a cause and a cure. The Zeists had their advocates in America, as in Europe, but there was also much interest in looking for an insect vector. The *Simulium* fly appeared to be the most likely suspect. This theory, advanced by Louis Sambon of the London School of Tropical Medicine, was greeted with relief by agriculturists in the United States. Because of the discovery that malaria, yellow fever, and Rocky Mountain spotted fever had insect vectors, pellagra might well have one, too. Some American physicians blamed foodstuffs other than corn, notably cane sugar and cottonseed oil.

While the search for a cause was underway, so was one for a cure. More than 200 remedies are recorded in the literature. Those most frequently tried were various arsenic compounds, both inorganic and organic, the most popular being Salvarsan, used in the treatment of syphilis.

The U.S. Public Health Service began its work on pellagra soon after the first cases were diagnosed in Alabama, but it was not until 1914, when Joseph Goldberger was assigned to the problem, that real progress was made. In a matter of weeks, Goldberger identified the essential cause of the disease: Something was missing in the diet. In a logical systematic way, he did what no one before him had done. He proved his case and found the missing element, although he did not specifically identify it.

Only 3 weeks after Goldberger began his work, he completely revamped the pellagra investigations of the U.S. Public Health Service and set them on a course that yielded fruitful results. His most important innovation was to introduce a new diet into selected institutions where pellagra was prevalent to see if the disease would disappear. Succeeding in that experiment, he then induced pellagra with a poor diet in a population of volunteer prisoners. To boost acceptance of the then novel idea that a disease could be caused by a dietetic deficiency and to squelch his critics, Goldberger next attempted to transmit the disease to himself and several colleagues. In several experiments over a course of 2 months in 1916, he used all the time-honored ways of experimentally transmitting a disease: blood, nasal secretions, epidermal scales from skin lesions, urine, and feces. Neither he nor anyone else got pellagra.

While these "filth parties" were underway, Goldberger began a study of the relationship of pellagra to economics. He noted that rural victims of the disease were sharecroppers and tenant farmers caught in a cycle of poverty tied to a one-crop agriculture. They grew little but cotton and used their meager share of profits to buy the "3 M" dietary articles which were all they could afford. Few grew much in the way of foodstuffs or kept a cow. Most were chronically in debt. In the mill villages, wages were kept notoriously low so as to attract industry into the so-called New South arising out of the debacle of Civil War. It was in the company-owned South Carolina mill villages that Goldberger demonstrated that poverty begets disease. Conducted over a period of 2 or 3 years, this epidemiological study conclusively proved that pellagrins were sick because they were poor. The study itself became a model in epidemiology. Victims of pellagra in the mill villages were poorer than those who escaped the disease.

In the 1920s, Goldberger turned from epidemiological studies to a search for the specific cause of pellagra. Working at the Hygienic Laboratory in Washington, D.C., a forerunner of the National Institutes of Health, he began a systematic search for the specific element missing in the pellagrin's diet. He was aided in this work by two fortuitous events. He got an animal model for his studies when research workers at Yale University determined that black tongue in dogs is an analogue of human pellagra, and, almost accidentally, he and his associates found one of the richest sources of the missing pellagra-preventive factor. In an effort to improve the dogs' appetite for the monotonous pellagra-producing diet, they added a cake of commercial yeast to the daily ration. The results were magical. Within 4 days after a dog with pellagra was given yeast, its condition had markedly improved.

The efficacy of yeast in preventing and treating pellagra was dramatically proved during the flood of the Mississippi River in the spring of 1927, when thousands of people were driven from their homes and forced to subsist on a diet even more restricted than usual. With Goldberger's help and encouragement, the American Red Cross distributed tons of yeast to flood victims. Distribution of yeast became a standard feature of aid to people during the depression of the 1930s. It was from yeast and liver extracts, also found to be an effective pellagra preventive, that the missing dietary element was finally isolated.

Goldberger was studying liver extracts at the time of his death in 1929. That year there were probably more than 200,000 cases of pellagra in the United States, and the mortality rate was 33 percent. Ironically, it was in the years of economic depression which followed that the incidence of pellagra began to decrease in the United States as both the economy and government programs forced Southerners to grow something other than cotton. With diversification of agriculture and government programs that provided jobs, distributed surplus commodities, and encouraged people to grow more foodstuffs and preserve them for winter use, the disease began to disappear.

After Goldberger's work, the next scientific breakthrough in conquering the disease came from laboratories at the University of Wisconsin, where in 1937 nicotinic acid, later named niacin, was found to be the pellagra-preventive factor. Conrad A. Elvehjem and his associates found that a deficiency of nicotinic acid caused black tongue in dogs. Subsequently, they learned that nicotinamide is as effective in treating black tongue as is nicotinic acid.

Numerous studies were made to transfer the results of this research on dogs afflicted with black tongue to humans with pellagra. Tom Spies used nicotinic acid to treat pellagra patients with considerable success at a hospital in Cincinnati and later extended and expanded his work to Alabama. Commenting on the work of Elvehjem and Spies and fellow workers, the New York Times noted that "an ailment which has baffled medicine for centuries has at last been relegated to the curable diseases and . . . American Medicine has to its credit a triumph comparable with the conquest of yellow fever."

The incredible complexity of pellagra has provided years of work for researchers. Grace A. Goldsmith and her co-workers at Tulane University proved that the amino acid tryptophan is a precursor of niacin, and she helped establish the recommended dietary allowances for that vitamin. Physicians in India have been responsible for the observation that pellagra is associated with the consumption of millet.

Coluthur Gopalan linked the high incidence of pellagra on the Deccan Plateau to consumption of millet and to the grain's high leucine content. Another Indian physician, P. S. Shankar, also noted the association of millet with the disease and found that the drug isoniazid, given for treatment of tuberculosis, may precipitate pellagra.

The disappearance of pellagra from so much of the world where it was once endemic is due as much to economic and social factors as to advances in medicine. In the southern United States, enrichment of bread and flour with vitamins, begun in World War II, has certainly played a part in eliminating the disease, but so has burgeoning prosperity. The example of France in the late nineteenth century showed that government policy that encouraged a varied agriculture could result in important health benefits. Pellagra was finally brought under control in Italy by the 1930s, probably because of a rising standard of living.

From the time when pellagra was first described in the eighteenth century, members of the upper classes have tended either to deny the existence of the disease or to blame its appearance on the inherent moral weaknesses of its victims. In the American South, pellagra became a political and social issue. Its presence bespoke a distinctiveness for the region that many Southerners did not welcome. In the late twentieth century, the disease appears in only isolated pockets in Egypt, Lesotho, and India. Its victims are poor, just as were the Spanish peasants who consulted Don Gaspar Casal in Asturias in 1735.

Elizabeth W. Etheridge

Bibliography

Barakat, M. R. 1976. Pellagra. In *Nutrition in preventive medicine: The major deficiency syndromes, epidemiology and approaches to control*, 126–35. Geneva.

Barrett-Connor, Elizabeth. 1967. The etiology of pellagra and its significance for modern medicine [Editorial]. *American Journal of Medicine* 42: 859–67.

Carpenter, Kenneth, ed. 1981. *Pellagra,* Benchmark Papers in Biochemistry No. 2. Stroudsburg, Penna.

Conquest of Pellagra. 1980. Symposium presented by the American Institute of Nutrition, Anaheim, Cal., April 14. *Federation Proceedings* 40: 1519–35.

Elvehjem, C. A., et al. 1937. Relation of nicotinic acid and nicotinic acid amide to canine black tongue. *Journal of American Chemical Society* 59: 1767–8.

  1938. The isolation and identification of the anti-black tongue factor. *Journal of Biological Chemistry* 123: 137–49.

Etheridge, Elizabeth W. 1972. *The butterfly caste: A social history of pellagra in the South*. Westport, Conn.

Gopalan, C[oluthur], and Kamala S. Jaya Rao. 1975. Pellagra and amino acid imbalance. *Vitamins and hormones* 33: 505–28.

Narasinga Rao, B. S., and C. Gopalan. 1984. Niacin. *Nutrition Reviews' present knowledge in nutrition,* 5th edition, 318–31. Washington, D.C.

Roe, Daphne A. 1973. *A plague of corn: The social history of pellagra.* Ithaca, N.Y.

Schultz, Myron G. 1977. Joseph Goldberger and pellagra. *American Journal of Tropical Medicine and Hygiene* 26: 1088–92.

Srikantia, S. G. 1982. Endemic pellagra. In *Human nutrition: Current issues and controversies,* ed. A. Neuberger and T. H. Jukes, 209–16. Lancaster, U.K.

    1984. Pellagra. *Hunter's tropical medicine,* 6th edition, ed. G. Thomas Strickland, 855–7. Philadelphia.

Terris, Milton, ed. 1964. *Goldberger on pellagra.* Baton Rouge, La.

VIII.104
Periodontal Disease (Pyorrhea)

The word "pyorrhea" comes from the Greek *pyon* ("pus") and *rhoia* ("to flow"). Thus the definition is a graphic description of the disease in which there is an outflowing of pus from the gingival (gum) tissues of the oral cavity. The term "pyorrhea" has been used in Europe since the mid-1500s and in America since the late 1800s. However, it was not until 1937 that the American Academy of Periodontology abandoned the term in favor of "periodontal disease."

The term "periodontal disease" is used in reference to any disease of the supporting structures of the teeth. These structures include the gingiva, periodontal ligament, and alveolar bone. In simplest terms, periodontal disease can be divided into two distinct, but not mutually exclusive, disease processes. The first involves inflammation of the gingival tissues, called "gingivitis," and the second, a destructive loss of bone and connective tissue attachment termed "periodontitis."

Distribution, Incidence, and Epidemiology
Epidemiological research during the past 25 years indicates that periodontal disease is one of the most common diseases affecting humankind. There is a direct cause-and-effect relationship between the bac-terial colonization on the surface of the tooth and the inflammation (and often consequential destruction) of the tooth's supporting structures. The rate of destruction varies, and is dependent on the individual's response to the bacterial irritation.

Periodontal disease is a widespread chronic disease and remains as the primary reason for the loss of teeth in the adult population throughout the world. In fact, virtually all individuals in any population exhibit manifestations of the disease. The prevalence and severity of periodontal disease increase with advancing age, tend to be greater in nonwhites than whites, and are greater for males in both races. There appears to be a trend toward an increase in the prevalence and severity of periodontal disease in the over-35 age group. This increase is most pronounced in the lower socioeconomic groups and is highly correlated with differing levels of personal and professional oral hygiene care.

Many individuals in the older population have had fewer teeth extracted as a consequence of a lower caries (cavities) incidence, which is a result of fluoride use, improvements in dental care, and better public health education. Paradoxically, this increase in the retention rate of teeth in the aging population provides an increase in the number of teeth at risk to the development of periodontitis. The only improvement that has been noted since the 1970s has been a slight reduction in the incidence and severity of gingivitis among the under-35 age group.

Etiology
Numerous studies have firmly established the primary etiologic agent in periodontal disease as "plaque." Plaque is a colorless, soft, sticky film of bacteria that constantly forms on the teeth. Plaque is composed primarily of different and numerous types of microorganisms as well as adherent mucin (a protein and polysaccharide combination), foodstuffs, and cellular debris. One gram of dental plaque contains more than 10^{11} bacteria. Plaque can calcify to form a local tissue irritant – *calculus* (tartar) – to which new colonies of plaque can readily adhere. The microbial population of plaque is variable, and is determined by its location on the tooth surface, the intraoral environment at the time of the plaque formation, and the length of time that the colony has been present in the mouth. When plaque is removed, a new plaque may form, having different characteristics in its quantity, quality, and spatial arrangement. The microorganisms in plaque

produce metabolic products and cellular constituents that affect the underlying periodontal tissues. These include exotoxins, endotoxins, antigens, and enzymes.

Any microbial plaque within the gingival crevice causes at least gingivitis. In some areas of the mouth, plaque and gingivitis lead to a destructive periodontitis. Periodontal disease is not caused by the intraoral invasion of foreign pathogens, but rather by colonization of microorganisms of the normal oral flora that exists even in the absence of disease. Certain species of this bacterial plaque play a more significant part in the development and progress of the disease because they increase in relative proportions as well as in absolute numbers. These species are also relevant in that their virulent mechanisms act to disrupt the host's defenses.

Inadequate or improper oral hygiene techniques must be considered one of the etiologic factors in the development of periodontal disease. Other causative influences include food impaction between teeth, defective dental restorations, malposed teeth, physiological gingival stress due to high frenum attachment, effects of dry mouth, and, to a minor extent, heredity. Of course, there is a strong relationship between all of the etiologic factors and the host's resistance. The capacity to resist or repair depends on many factors such as adequate nutrition and assimilation, antibody production, hormonal influences, white cell defenses, and formative cell capabilities.

Clinical Manifestations and Pathology

The pathogenesis of periodontal disease must be considered in four stages: colonization, invasion, destruction, and healing.

During colonization, plaque accumulates on the teeth and microbial growth ensues. If the plaque is not removed through adequate oral hygiene, the formation of calculus may begin, and the early stages of microbial invasion into the adjacent gingival tissues commence. Clinical signs may consist of gingival tissues that are tender, swollen, and red. This tissue may bleed upon probing or during brushing. However, periodontal disease usually progresses over the course of many years, and discomfort is a rarity. It is because of this asymptomatic evolution that persistent bacterial invasion and local irritation can progress into the destructive phase of the disease in which loss of connective tissue and loss of alveolar bone take place. Signs and symptoms of the destructive stage can include pocketing around the tooth within the gingival crevice, gingival recession, sup-

purative exudate (pus) from the gingiva, and looseness or separation of the permanent teeth.

An examination of the teeth may entail numerous tests and measurements for the evaluation of the presence and severity of periodontal disease. These may include visual signs of inflammation, probing pockets' depths around teeth, evaluation of bleeding on probing, assessment of plaque or calculus accumulation above and below the gingival margin, phase-contrast microscopic analysis of the bacteria recovered from the crevice, assaying the crevicular fluid flow, and interpretation of dental radiographs.

The healing phase is the least understood of the four stages of the disease. However, studies reveal that periodontal disease is episodic, and undergoes periods of remission and exacerbation. Although colonization, invasion, and destruction are interrelated and overlapping, this fourth stage, healing, is clearly distinct in that it is characterized by reduction of inflammation, the repair of gingival tissues, and the sclerosis and remodeling of the alveolar bone.

History and Geography

Antiquity Through the Seventeenth Century

Although periodontology has been practiced as a specialty only during this century, the recognition of periodontal disease in various forms has persisted for millennia. The condition of the dental structures of teeth and bone of our ancestors has been revealed through examination and radiographs of skulls discovered in archaeological excavations. There is evidence that periodontal disease existed in some of the earliest members of humankind.

Egyptian mummies show signs of dental caries and periodontal disease as well as primitive, yet valiant, attempts at repairing these dental pathoses. Indeed, it is believed that the Papyrus of Ebers, which was written around 1550 B.C. by Egyptians, and describes various conditions of the oral cavity, is the earliest written record of dentistry as a distinctive branch of the healing arts. The Greek historian Herodotus described Egypt as being the home of medical specialties, including dentistry.

About 1300 B.C., Aesculapius, the mythical physician, supposedly recognized the importance of dental hygiene by recommending cleaning of the mouth and teeth. The physician to the King of Babylon, Arad-Nana, in the sixth century B.C., suggested removing the "film" and "deposits" from the teeth with a cloth-covered index finger. More aggressive periodontal therapy appears about 25 B.C., when Celsus, a Roman physician, treated gums and loose teeth with gold wire and seared the gingiva with red-hot iron. Oral hygiene techniques can also be traced to the Mayan culture and to those living around Central America between 200 B.C. and A.D. 800.

Pliny, a Roman, published his book *Natural History* in the first century A.D.; in it he describes the prevalence of periodontal disease among the Romans as well as various remedies for its prevention and care. The most notable prescriptions were the use of dentifrices, mouthwashes, and toothpicks; the first mention of "toothbrushing" seems to have been made by the Roman poet Ovid in his *Art of Love-making,* in the first century A.D. The siwak, a fibrous wood product which preceded the toothbrush, was used by the Arabians since the ninth century, and can still be found in use in some areas today. The modern-day toothbrush, however, was invented in China only in 1498.

In 1530, Zene Artzney wrote a book dealing with dental therapeutics in which he discusses the formation and modes of prevention of calculus. He also noted in his writing that loose teeth and their premature loss were a result of "carelessness, weakness, or . . . disease." In 1575 Ambroise Paré coined the term "pyorrhea alveolaris," and describes the teeth attaching to the jaw via "a ligament which goes from the root of the tooth."

Eighteenth Century to the Present

Pierre Fauchard, the founder of modern dentistry, in his now famous 1728 publication *Le Chirurgien Dentiste,* or *Traité des Dents,* stated that the "relation between the gums and teeth is such that the diseases of one may easily extend to the other." In 1820, Eleazar Parmly recommended that for the "constant security of the teeth," all deposits on the teeth must be removed. He later became known as the "Apostle of Dental Hygiene." In the latter half of the nineteenth century, John Riggs, who was to become "the father of periodontology," described periodontal disease as a "progressive process from marginal gingivitis to the final exfoliation of the teeth." He developed preventive as well as surgical treatments for what he called "scurvy of the gums." For decades, any such condition was called "Rigg's disease."

Our understanding of periodontal disease, including its etiology and pathogenesis, grew enormously during the 1900s. Periodontal disease is currently under attack on several fronts, through preventive care, improvements in oral hygiene techniques, mechanical and chemical plaque inhibitors, nutrition,

surgical intervention, drugs, and immunology. Much work, however, remains ahead, especially in the relationship of the disease to the host's immune system.

Jeffrey Levin

Bibliography

Douglass, Chester, et al. 1983. National trends in the prevalence and severity of the periodontal diseases. *Journal of the American Dental Association* 3: 403–12.

Dummett, Clifton O. 1983. Epidemiology of periodontal disease: A review. *Military Medicine* 7: 606–11.

Genco, Robert 1984. Pathogenesis of periodontal disease: New concepts. *Journal of the Canadian Dental Association* 5: 391–5.

Goldman, Henry. 1986. Periodontal disease (Parts I through V). *Compendium of Continuing Education* 7: 12–325.

Imberman, Michael, and Susan Wilson. 1985. Current trends in periodontal diagnosis. *CDA Journal* 13: 75–82.

Lindhe, Jan. 1983. *Textbook of clinical periodontology.* Munksgaard.

Ramirez, Juan, and Richard Stallard. 1970. A historical review of periodontology. *Periodontal Abstracts* 18: 139–42.

Schonfeld, Steven, and Luigi Checchi. 1985. Review of immunology for the periodontist. *Journal of the Western Society of Periodontology* 2: 53–64.

Theilade, Else. 1986. The non-specific theory in microbial etiology of inflammatory periodontal diseases. *Journal of Clinical Periodontology* 13: 905–11.

Pica is usually described as a pathological craving for nonfoods, although it can mean a craving for substances generally accepted to be food as well. Medical science has long been interested in this disorder, for although it does not constitute a disease, it is often a symptom of disease and frequently is associated with nutritional deficiencies, especially those connected with minerals. In addition, psychiatry and psychology find that pica is often connected with mental problems, including those of retardation. Anthropologists study it as a cultural phenomenon, since it has been associated with some religions and also perhaps because the use of nonfoods is indicative of food shortages in the distant past.

The word "pica" comes from the Latin for "magpie," a bird that eats practically anything. The term was first used by Ambroise Paré in the 1500s, although references to pica consumption can be found in many ancient and medieval writings. M. H. Boezo, in his 1638 work *De Pica*, was the first to draw a distinction between "pica," which he believed was an appetite for "absurd things," and which was common in both men and women, and "malacia," which referred to a voracious desire for normal food substances. He observed that the latter occurred most often in pregnant women, and believed the cause was a mental alteration caused by the pregnancy.

Classification

Probably the type of pica that has received the most scientific and lay scrutiny is the consumption of earth, called *geophagy*. This word was first applied by Aristotle, and it means, literally, "dirt eating." Since that time, it has gone under many names, including *allotriophagia* (Sophocles), *erdessen* (medieval Germany), *mal d'estomac* (French), *citta*, and *cachexia Africana*. The last, from the Latin, meaning "the wasting away of Africans," was a condition first noted by slave owners in the West Indies. Unlike some of the other types of pica, geophagy is and has been a nearly universal phenomenon. There are records of earth consumption on all continents, and at nearly all times. Throughout history, it seems humankind has been consuming dirt, clay, mud, chalk, and various other types of earth for nutritional, cultural, and psychological reasons.

Still another type of pica is called *papophagia*, although some believe that it is not a disorder at all. The word is from the Greek and means "the eating of frost or ice," and was coined by a U.S. Air Force doctor, Charles Coltman. Some modern weight loss plans recommend the chewing or sucking of ice as a method of appetite control, and those who work with people trying to quit smoking often suggest that smokers chew ice as a substitute.

Amylophagia refers to the consumption of laundry starch, which is almost exclusively associated with women. It was first noticed in the rural American South, and is believed to have begun with women who originally consumed clay, but switched to laundry starch. Hilda Hertz, in a 1947 article, observed that although the tastes of clay and starch are quite different, the texture is similar. Later research indicated that pregnant women ate starch because it relieved nausea, vomiting, and morning sickness. Local black culture held that if a woman consumed laundry starch while pregnant, her baby would "slide out" more easily during delivery.

Trichophagia is the ingestion of hair. Those suffering from trichophagia and its associated problems are almost always young, English-speaking females with long hair who exhibit the nervous habit of chewing strands of it. It is usually related closely to "mouthing" behaviors (chewing on pencils, fingernails, and so on but not swallowing them); if hair is accidentally ingested over a long period of time, "hairballs" can form in the stomach, causing serious gastrointestinal problems.

There are many other types of picas, including *lithophagia*, the eating of rocks or pebbles. Sometimes the danger arises not from the items consumed but from their effect on the digestive system or the body in general. One of the most dangerous, the consumption of paint chips by small children, can result in lead poisoning.

Incidence

The reasons for the practice of pica are almost as numerous as its types. The interpretation of data on the disorder is complicated because definitions of pica are unreliable and because there is a natural reluctance on the part of practitioners to admit to the ingestion of nonfoods. This is especially true of geophagy, since "dirt-eating" is generally considered to be degenerate behavior.

Pica has been closely associated with women and pregnancy since classical times, and until recently it was believed that pregnancy caused mental instability in a woman, and thus provoked her cravings for both food and nonfood substances. Recent studies, however, have indicated that changes in sense of taste are not a constant in pregnancy, despite the desire for sharp-tasting foods. There have been many studies of the incidence of pica among pregnant women in the United States since World War II, most carried out in rural areas. One of the most prominent of the few urban studies was done by Harry Roselle (1970), a New York medical doctor. He discovered that some of his nonpregnant patients consumed laundry starch or clay, and thought that this practice might be associated with iron-deficiency anemia. He prescribed iron for these patients, but their lack of cooperation did not allow him to form a firm generalization about the link between iron deficiency and pica. He did observe that hemoglobin values were unchanged while they were consuming clay and starch, which led him to believe that pica was a symptom, rather than a cause, of the anemia.

Most medical investigations of pica tend to be most concerned with children. The practice is usually associated with those in poverty, especially black children in rural areas or urban slums. Reports conflict as to whether pica in this group is nutritionally motivated. There seems to be no difference in prevalence between male and female children. However, during adolescence, girls are more likely than boys to take up or continue the practice.

As babies explore their environment, they put a variety of things in their mouths. The actual ingestion of nonfood substances seems to start as early as 6 months of age, but tends to decline with a developmental increase in hand–mouth activity and to drop sharply after the child reaches 3 years of age. Often, when pica is encountered after that age, the possibility of mental disturbance is explored.

Pica is usually described as rare among adult males, although some claim that it is merely underreported and the most common picalike practice among men – chewing tobacco – is not generally viewed to be pica. A study, carried out in Columbus, Ohio, in 1968 by J. A. Halsted found that 25 percent of 302 general patients admitted to eating clay, starch, or dirt at one time or another. Of these, only 24 percent (18 patients) were male.

Etiology

The causes of pica are not clear, and the search for them has been the subject of medical speculation since antiquity. Pica has been seen by most modern doctors and nutritionists chiefly as a means of alleviating nutritional deficiency. Similarly, most ancient and medieval scholars concerned with the subject stressed the importance of good nutrition and recommended fresh fruit and vegetables as a remedy. Despite innumerable recent studies, however, no definite connection has been established between pica and dietary imbalance. Nutrients in which pica practitioners are thought to be deficient include vitamins C and D, phosphorus, calcium, zinc, and especially iron. As early as A.D. 1000, Avicenna was treating pica with iron, and the search for the relationship between iron deficiency and pica continues today.

Psychiatrists and psychologists often feel that both nutritional deficiencies and psychological disorders are linked in pica patients. Some believe it is merely a continuation of infantile hand–mouth behavior patterns. Paulette Robischon (1971) conducted a study of 90 children between the ages of 19 to 24 months, and demonstrated that children who practice pica after infancy generally are slower to develop than those who do not. Other studies have found that black children are more likely than white children to exhibit pica, which has been linked to the overall lower income levels of their parents rather than to any racial cause. Reginald S. Lourie and his associates (1957, 1963), in their numerous studies, discovered that the pattern of pica in youngsters is very close to that of addiction. They termed it "a distorted form of the instinctual seeking of satisfaction." Often pica seems a defense against loss of security, such as that occasioned by separation from one or both parents, or emotional difficulties of the parents. Most young children who practice pica exhibit other oral activities, including thumbsucking, nailbiting, and so on.

There is also a "cultural" etiology for pica. Anthropologists have long been searching the past for practical reasons to explain why certain cultures and religions require the consumption of nonfood items. Symbolic geophagy was practiced in ancient times in Europe (so-called *terra sigilata,* or "sealed earth"), in the Middle East (consumption of a bit of dust from Mohammed's tomb), and even among early Christians. In parts of Africa it is thought that clay eating promotes fertility in women and lactation during pregnancy. John M. Hunter (1973) has postulated a culture–nutrition hypothesis, which attempts to demonstrate how geophagy, a type of pica, evolved from a nutritional activity and physiological imperative into a cultural institution in some societies. Pregnant women in Nigeria consumed clay in a culturally acceptable way, purchased loaves in the marketplace, and gained needed calcium and magnesium as a result.

A last reason for pica is for pharmacological purposes. It has been suggested that individuals engaged in pica practice may be attempting to medicate themselves for real or imagined illnesses. Physiological problems that have been thought to cause pica include gastrointestinal malaise, stress, hunger, parasitic infestations (such as worms), and toxicosis.

History and Geography

Antiquity

Pica was well known to the ancients: Aristotle and Socrates both wrote of the practice of earth eating, and it is known that in Greece, as early as 40 B.C., the sacred "sealed earth" was used as a sort of magical "cure-all." The clays of the islands of Samos, Chios, and Selinos in the Aegean Sea were said to be especially effective. Galen took 20,000 lozenges of the clay from Lemnos back to Rome, and used them to treat poison victims.

Pliny the Elder noted that some residents of the province of Campania mixed white chalk with their porridge, to give it some color and texture. The chalk came from a hill called *Leucogauem,* which in Greek means "white earth." Supposedly, Caesar Augustus ordered 20,000 sesterces to be paid yearly to the Neapolitans on behalf of the Campanians for the lease of the hill, without which, the Campanians claimed, they could not make their porridge. Pliny also noted a region in northern Africa where a similar porridge was made with gypsum mixed in.

Many of the earliest medical writers tended to concentrate on the pica habits of pregnant women. In the sixth century, Aetius of Amida claimed that the urge to consume nonfoods was caused by a suppression of the menstrual flow, which in turn was caused by pressure from the fetus. He recommended exercise and fresh fruits and vegetables.

The Middle Ages

Avicenna described pica (although not by that name) and employed various iron preparations, among them iron dross steeped in fine wine and strained through a plant known as "Hippocrates' sleeve." Avicenna felt that an excessive appetite for sour and sharp-tasting foods was more easily remedied than one for dry things such as clay and charcoal. He further believed that pica in pregnant women was treatable by this method, but if the children of that pregnancy began practicing pica, they could not be cured of it. This disorder must have been fairly widespread, because Avicenna wrote of the need to control it in young boys, and recommended imprisonment if necessary, although pregnant women were to be treated more gently, for fear of damaging the infant.

Medical writers of the Middle Ages tended to view mental instability and food as important causes of pica. J. Ledelius, for example, stated that bits of leftover food in the stomach rotted and gave off four humors that ruined an individual's sense of taste and caused the craving of all sorts of odd substances. H. Betten, by contrast, argued that the cause of pica was not foul humors in the stomach but weakness of the mind. An individual whose mind was controlled by emotion was far more likely to consume nonfoods than one whose mind was controlled by discipline. He concluded that this was the reason women exhibited pica symptoms more often than men. However, he did not advocate denying women the substances they craved, for to do so, he thought, would damage the fetus. He recommended that nonpregnant women be given stern lectures to strengthen their wills, and various prescriptions to strengthen their stomachs.

Famine was often the cause of pica use. During periods of famine in China, individuals would consume clays of various colors and types in place of rice. Usually grass, foliage, weeds, and tree bark were used as famine food, but in truly desperate times, such as the famine of 1640 in what is now Hunan Province, the people ate not only clay but also boiled shoes, leather, and wood.

Similarly, in Europe, during the Thirty Years' War, while armies were ravaging the countryside and taking food from every village they encountered, the peasants of Pomerania turned to baking bread with dough mixed with powdered earth. The practice of baking earth into bread was also observed in Germany during the War of the Austrian Succession, not only in peasant villages but even in the castle of Wittenberg.

Nineteenth Century: Pica, Exploration, and Empire

As Europeans began to explore Africa, Asia, and the Western Hemisphere, they discovered that pica seemed to exist, or to have existed, on almost every continent of the globe. Alexander von Humboldt and A. Bonpland (1804) found that some of the natives of South America engaged in pica. The Otomac Indian tribe, who lived along the Orinoco River, were particularly fond of consuming an iron-rich clay during the lean months when the river overflowed its banks. Pica was also discovered among the natives of some mountainous regions of Peru, where powdered lime mixed with coca leaves was sold in the marketplaces.

The Indians of the Rio de la Hacha, however, preferred to consume the lime without additives, and usually carried it about with them in small boxes.

In central Africa, David Livingstone (1870) reported that some of the tribes were clay eaters. The Africans referred to the practice as *safura;* it was most notable among pregnant women of the area, but it was also practiced by males of all classes. The availability of food seemed to have no bearing on whether an individual chose to consume clay or not.

The literature of India indicates that geophagy was practiced on the subcontinent in ancient times; yet none of the early Portuguese or English accounts of India in the seventeenth and eighteenth centuries makes any mention of pica. By the end of the nineteenth century, however, British colonial physicians began to write about the earth eaters of India, believing that it was universal there. Native-born physicians also wrote about the subject, and one, Sarat Chandra Mitra (1904–7), thought it was a racial characteristic. Although he acknowledged that clay eating was practiced in many areas of the world, he thought that the Aryan and Dravidian races were unique in that they tended to use it for food on a regular basis, whereas other races ate it for sustenance only occasionally, or for pharmaceutical reasons.

David Hooper and Harold Mann (1906) published a more extensive study of pica in India a year later, in which they took issue with Mitra's assertion that clay eating was a racial characteristic. They believed that the reason people in all cultures of India consumed clay was to alleviate the symptoms of disease: gastric or intestinal irritation, anemia, even as a remedy for cholera.

Pica and Slavery

Plantation owners and managers in all areas of the slaveholding New World were concerned with the practice of pica by their slaves, because those who consumed earth appeared to become addicted to it, and the addiction was thought to be fatal. Planters referred to pica as a disease, calling it *mal d'estomac, cachexia Africana,* stomach evil, or dirt eating. Contemporary authors described the practice as widespread in the British West Indies. The dirt eaters usually became sick, suffering from stomach pains and difficult breathing. This was often followed by nausea and diarrhea, depression, and listlessness. Death followed within 2 or 3 months. Plantation owners and managers tried every means at their disposal to break the habit in those slaves who acquired it, but were generally unsuccessful.

John Imray, an Edinburgh-trained physician who resided in Dominica, wrote in 1843 that pica in the West Indies had become much rarer after the slaves were emancipated. He was convinced that a change in life-style was sufficient to cure earth eating. Slaves, in many cases, had been expected to feed themselves with their provision grounds, but because they had been overworked by the sugar planters, they had little energy left for their own crops. In desperation, they turned to earth eating. Freedom gave the blacks more time to grow and prepare their food. On the other hand, the diet and system of feeding slaves on the North American continent were much different from and nutritionally better than the diet and feeding system in the West Indies. Yet pica was also reportedly a serious problem among slaves in the southern United States.

Twentieth Century

The association of iron deficiency with earth eating, which we have seen since earliest times, has continued into the twentieth century, as physicians came increasingly to believe that anemia was the cause of geophagy, and that iron preparations were the cure. At the same time, however, the dangers of the consumption of some kinds of pica materials were discovered.

In 1924 J. C. Ruddock suggested, in an article in the *Journal of the American Medical Association,* that lead poisoning was the result of some types of pica. As awareness of the dangers of the consumption by children of paint chips increased, the U.S. government moved to limit the lead content of commercially available paints and plasters in the early 1940s. Unfortunately, pica continued to be a major cause of lead poisoning in children. In New York City alone, there were about 52 reported cases of lead poisoning every year, with case-mortality rates ranging between 13 and 27 percent. The cause of the poisoning was almost always the ingestion of plaster and chips of lead-based paint in old, run-down tenements.

Geographic studies of pica, especially geophagy, began to appear in the late nineteenth and twentieth centuries. In Germany, R. Lasch (1898) wrote a preliminary study, which was the basis for Berthold Laufer's larger study of geophagy, published by the Field Museum of Natural History in 1930. Laufer's approach was different from previous works in that he surveyed every continent on the globe in which geophagy had been reported, and for the first time, information of the practice in ancient China was published in English.

Articles by physicians and nutritionists appeared

in the late 1940s and early 1950s, as the practice of clay eating in the southern and urban areas of the United States was given a clinical examination. In their 1942 survey of black children in rural Mississippi, Dorothy Dickens and R. N. Ford found that of the 209 children in the sample, 25 percent of the girls and 26 percent of the boys had eaten either dirt or clay in the previous 2 weeks. Hertz (1947) observed the practice among pregnant black women in North Carolina, and because there were no reports of clay eating among the male population, she concluded that the practice was related to gender. Albert Whiting (1947), following up Hertz's study in that same year, examined the types of clays used in pica, and reported on the consumption of soot from stove pipes. Pica users did not eat the soot directly, but placed it in bags and soaked them in water, making a sort of tea. In the 1950s, Cecile Hoover Edwards and her colleagues (1954, 1959) undertook a study of rural women in Alabama, examining why pregnant women craved certain nonfood items. They issued questionnaires to 47 health agencies and 91 individual health workers in the southeastern region of the United States, and found that superstition and oral tradition played a large role in the selection of pica materials. In a subsequent study, intending to determine the nutritive value of the clays consumed, they discovered that women who ate clay and cornstarch had diets that were otherwise low in calories, calcium, iron, thiamine, and niacin.

Two major studies of pica appeared in the late 1950s. In 1957 Marcia Cooper published a book-length study of pica, which included its history and association with mental and physical illness, physical defects, and nutrition. According to Cooper, pica becomes established in children because they lack an understanding of dietary taboos. Poor nutrition leads them to practice pica with any number of substances that might be mouthed or eaten. Cooper acknowledged that the exact causes of pica were not completely demonstrated by her work, but was certain that more clinical studies in the future would elucidate them.

The other major work on pica, published by Bengt Anell and Sture Lagercrantz in Sweden in 1958, was focused on the geography of the disorder, and scrutinized geophagy in Indonesia and Oceania, as well as among blacks in Africa and America.

Throughout the century, most studies have assumed that a nutritional deficiency leads to pica, and, although iron deficiency is assumed to be the major cause, other trace elements, especially zinc, have also been investigated. Yet, despite the fact that the connection between iron-deficiency anemia and pica has been recognized for centuries, the question of whether pica is a cause or an effect of the anemia is still sometimes debated. Moreover, although both children and pregnant women engage in pica, there is no clear understanding of the physiological mechanisms that drive them to it. Thus, although pica has been recognized by practitioners of medicine since the beginning of recorded history, medicine seems little closer today to understanding its causes.

Brian T. Higgins

Bibliography

Aëtius of Amida. 1950. *The gynecology and obstetrics of the VIth century, A.D.*, trans. J. V. Ricci from the Latin edition of Coronarius, 1542. Philadelphia.

Albin, Jack B. 1977. The treatment of pica (scavenging) behavior in the retarded: A critical analysis and implications for research. *Mental Retardation* 15: 14–17.

Anell, Bengt, and Sture Lagercrantz. 1958. *Geophagical customs*. Uppsala.

Burde, Brigitte de la, and Betty Reames. 1973. Prevention of pica, the major cause of lead poisoning with children. *American Journal of Public Health* 63: 737–43.

Bradley, Francis. 1964. Sandlappers and clay eaters. *North Carolina Folklore* 12: 27–8.

Carpenter, W. M. 1845. Observations on the cachexia Africana, or the habit and effects of dirt-eating in the Negro race. *New Orleans Medical and Surgical Journal* 1: 146–68.

Coltman, Charles A. 1969. Papophagia and iron lack. *Journal of the American Medical Association* 207: 513–14.

1971. Papophagia. *Archives of Internal Medicine* 128: 472–3.

Cooper, Marcia C. 1957. *Pica*. Springfield, Ill.

Craigin, F. W. 1811. *Practical rules for the management and medical treatment of slaves in the sugar plantations by a practical planter*. London.

1835. Observations on the cachexia Africana or dirt-eating. *American Journal of Medical Science* 17: 365–74.

Crosby, William H. 1971. Food pica and iron deficiency. *Archives of Internal Medicine* 127: 960–1.

1976. Pica: A compulsion caused by iron deficiency. *British Journal of Haematology* 34: 341–2.

Danford, D. E. 1982. Pica and nutrition. *Annual Review of Nutrition* 2: 303–22.

Dickens, D., and R. N. Ford. 1942. Geophagy (dirt eating) among Mississippi school children. *American Sociological Review* 7: 59–65.

Edwards, C. H., H. McSwain, and S. Haire. 1954. Odd dietary practices of women. *Journal of the American Dietary Association* 30: 976–81.

Edwards, C. H., et al. 1959. Clay- and cornstarch-eating women. *Journal of the American Dietary Association* 35: 810–15.

Greenberg, M., et al. 1958. A study of pica in relation to lead poisoning. *Pediatrics* 22: 756–60.

Halsted, James A. 1968. Geophagia in man: Its nature and nutritional effects. *American Journal of Clinical Nutrition* 21: 1384–93.

Hertz, Hilda. 1947. Notes on clay and starch eating among Negroes in a southern urban community. *Social Forces* 25: 343–4.

Hooper, David, and H. H. Mann. 1906. Earth-eating and the earth-eating habit in India. *Memoirs of the Asiatic Society of Bengal* 1: 249–70.

Humboldt, Alexander von, and A. Bonpland. 1804. *Personal narrative of travels to the equinoctial regions of the new continent during the years 1799–1804.* London.

Hunter, John M. 1973. Geophagy in Africa and in the United States: A culture–nutrition hypothesis. *Geographical Review* 63: 170–95.

Hunter, John M., Oscar H. Horst, and Robert N. Thomas. 1989. Religious geophagy as a cottage industry: The holy clay tablet of Esquipulas, Guatemala. *National Geographic Research* 5: 281–95.

Imray, J. 1843. Observations on the *mal d'estomac* or cachexia Africana, as it takes place among the Negroes of Dominica. *Edinburgh Medical and Surgical Journal* 59: 304–21.

Keith, Louis, E. R. Brown, and C. Rosenberg. 1970. Pica: The unfinished story. Background: Correlations with anemia and pregnancy. *Perspectives in Biology and Medicine* 13: 626–32.

Kiple, Kenneth F. 1984. *The Caribbean slave: A biological history.* Cambridge.

Lanzowsky, P. 1959. Investigation into the aetiology and treatment of pica. *Archives of the Diseases of Childhood* 34: 140–8.

Lasch, R. 1898. Ueber Geophagie. *Mitteilungen der Anthropologischen Gesellschaft* 28: 214–22.

Laufer, Berthold. 1930. Geophagy. *Field Museum of Natural History Anthropological Series* 18: 101–98.

Layman, E. M., et al. 1963. Cultural influences and symptom choice: Clay-eating customs in relation to the etiology of pica. *Psychological Record* 13: 249–57.

LeConte, J. 1846. Observations on geophagy. *Southern Medical and Surgical Journal* 1: 417–44.

Livingstone, David. 1870. *Last journals.* London.

Lourie, R. S., et al. 1957. A study of the etiology of pica in young children, an early pattern of addiction. In *Problems of addiction and habituation,* ed. Paul H. Hoch and J. Zogin. New York.

  1963. Why children eat things that are not food. *Children* 10: 143–6.

Maxwell, James. 1835. Pathological inquiry into the nature of cachexia Africana. *Jamaica Physical Journal* 2: 409–35.

Mitra, S. C. 1904–7. Note on clay-eating as a racial charac-

teristic. *Journal of the Anthropological Society of Bombay* 7: 284–90.

Morgan, R. F. 1984. Pica. *Journal of the Royal Society of Medicine* 77: 1052–4.

Mustacchi, Piero. 1971. Cesare Bressa (1785–1836) on dirt eating in Louisiana: A critical analysis of his unpublished manuscript "De la dissolution scorbutique." *Journal of the American Medical Association* 218: 229–32.

Robischon, Paulette. 1971. Pica practice and other hand–mouth behavior and children's developmental level. *Nursing Research* 20: 4–18.

Roselle, H. A. 1970. Association of laundry starch and clay ingestion with anemia in New York City. *Archives of Internal Medicine* 125: 57–61.

Thompson, C. J. S. 1913. Terra sigilata, a famous medicament of ancient times. *Seventeenth International Congress of Medical Sciences* 433–4.

Vermeer, Donald E. 1979. Geophagia in rural Mississippi: Environmental and cultural contexts and nutritional implications. *American Journal of Clinical Nutrition* 32: 2129–35.

Whiting, A. N. 1947. Clay, starch and soot-eating among southern rural Negroes in North Carolina. *Journal of Negro Education* 16: 601–12.

VIII.106
Pinta

Pinta (meaning "spotted") is also called *mal de pinto* and *carate.* It is the least destructive of the treponematoses that are pathogenic for humans. Although the taxonomy of these treponemes is by no means resolved, pinta is sufficiently distinctive to argue for a separate causal species, *Treponema carateum.* As a specific treponemal variety, it was not described until 1938. The disease is chronic, predominantly affects the skin, and is now found only among isolated rural groups in Central and South America and Mexico, where it is endemic. Local names for the illness are *tiña, empeines,* and *vitiligo.*

Distribution and Incidence

According to one historian of treponemal diseases, pinta may have had a considerable world distribution at the end of the Paleolithic period, some 10,000 years ago. However, its past geographic distribution is in some doubt, and an alternative view suggests that it may have evolved purely in Amerindian communities of the New World, as a final level of microevolutionary change in the treponematoses there. Because it is not a very destructive condition, and may remain untreated in many individuals of the Third World countries of Latin America, it has been estimated that as many as a million individuals may have the disease.

Epidemiology and Etiology

Pinta is caused by *T. carateum,* which cannot be distinguished from *Treponema pallidum* (the causative agent of endemic and venereal syphilis). These treponemes are found mainly in the lower Malpighian layers of the epidermis, and may be present for years before the skin lesions eventually become inactive and depigmented. Large areas may be infected, and the disease may remain infectious for a long period. It is unusual for other areas of the body, such as the genitals, to be involved. In contrast to the other human treponematoses, the skeleton is never affected.

This chronic clinical condition usually begins in childhood and lasts into adulthood, if not for most of the lifetime of an infected individual. Social and hygienic factors result in the differential incidence of the disease in varying components of Latin American societies, with native Indians, mestizos, and blacks being most affected. Infection seems most likely to be by skin contact. Insect vectors have also been suggested as a means of transmission, but this has not been substantiated.

Immunology

Serologic reactions are positive early, then increase in degree. Experiments show that there is cross-immunity to a varying extent in individuals infected with *T. carateum, T. pallidum,* and *Treponema pertenue.*

Clinical Manifestations and Pathology

There is no chancre, and the condition begins as an extragenital papule, usually situated in the lower extremity (and perhaps associated with damage to the skin surface). Within 3 weeks, the papule has expanded into a reactive patch of circinate form, termed a *pintid.* In the next few months, a more general rash occurs on the face and limbs, which can be similar in appearance to such diseases as psoriasis, ringworm, and eczema.

Histologically, hyperkeratosis and intercellular edema are evident, with an increase of lymphocytes and plasma cells. In adults, there are usually pigmentary changes in the later stages. Bluish patches

are perhaps most characteristic, but lesions may be white. Pigmentary function is clearly disturbed, and in the white patches pigment is absent. It should be emphasized that other treponematoses can start out to some extent like pinta, but that the others progress beyond purely skin changes. The disease is not transmitted to the fetus.

History and Geography

Pinta is believed to be most prevalent in Mexico, Venezuela, Colombia, Peru, and Ecuador. It is an "old" disease in the Americas, clearly present before the arrival of the Europeans. Although a relatively mild disease, it has tended historically to evoke a variety of social responses. In some instances the *pintados* or "spotted ones" have been shunned, much like lepers in the Old World. Yet in other circumstances their distinctive appearance has brought them high status. For example, Montezuma, the Aztec emperor, selected such individuals to bear his litter, and they were apparently frequently formed into special and elite battalions in Mexican history.

It appears, however, that the earliest recognizable description of pinta as a separate disease was not recorded until 1757 in Mexico. Because of the possible similarities to leprosy in regard to the skin changes, it is not so surprising that a medical commission in 1811 reported on it as leprosy. In 1889 pinta was viewed as perhaps linked to syphilis and was thought to be transmitted by venereal contact. Indeed, this hypothesis seemed to "square" with accounts that reported the efficacy of mercury in the treatment of pinta, and the fact that infected individuals who worked in mercury mines felt better. The positive Wassermann reaction was demonstrated in 1925, but the true nature of this distinctive treponemal condition was not recognized until 1938.

Don R. Brothwell

Bibliography
Brothwell, Don. 1981. Microevolutionary change in the human pathogenic treponemes: An alternative hypothesis. *International Journal of Systematic Bacteriology* 31: 82–7.

Holcomb, R. C. 1942. Pinta, a treponematosis: A review of the literature. *United States Navy Medical Bulletin* 40: 517–52.

Hudson, Ellis Herndon. 1949–51. Treponematosis. In *Oxford medicine* 5: 656(9)–656(122). New York.

Saunders, George M. 1949–51. Yaws: Framboesia tropica. In *Oxford medicine* 5: 707–720 (130). New York.

Sosa-Martinez, J., and S. Peralta. 1961. An epidemiologic

study of pinta in Mexico. *American Journal of Tropical Medicine and Hygiene* 10: 556–65.

Wood, Corinne Shear. 1978. Syphilis in anthropological perspective. *Social Science and Medicine* 12: 47–55.

VIII.107
Plague of Athens

The Greek historian Thucydides interrupts his history of the Peloponnesian War between Athens and Sparta to describe the following epidemic in 430 B.C.:

It was generally agreed that in respect of other ailments no season had ever been so healthy. Previous diseases all turned off into the plague; and the rest of the people were attacked without exciting cause, and without warning, in perfect health. It began with violent sensations of heat in the head, and redness and burning in the eyes; internally, the throat and tongue were blood-red from the start, emitting an abnormal and malodorous breath. These symptoms developed into sneezing and hoarseness, and before long the trouble descended into the chest, attended by violent coughing. Whenever it settled in the heart, it upset that organ, and evacuations of bile ensued, of every kind for which the doctors have a name; these also together with great distress. Most patients suffered an attack of empty retching, inducing violent convulsions, in some cases soon after the abatement of the previous symptoms, in others much later. The body was neither unduly hot externally to the touch, nor yellowish in color, but flushed and livid, with an efflorescence of small blisters and sores. Internally, the heat was so intense that the victims could not endure the laying-on of even the lightest wraps and linens; indeed nothing would suffice but they must go naked, and a plunge into cold water would give the greatest relief. Many who were left unattended actually did this, jumping into wells, so unquenchable was the thirst which possessed them; but it was all the same, whether they drank much or little. The victims were attacked throughout by inability to rest and by sleeplessness. Throughout the height of the disease the body would not waste away but would hold out against the distress beyond all expectation. The majority succumbed to the internal heat before their strength was entirely exhausted, on the seventh or ninth day. Or else, if they survived, the plague would descend to the bowels, where severe lesions would form, together with an attack of uniformly fluid diarrhea which in most cases ended in death through exhaustion. Thus the malady that first settled in the head passed through the whole body, starting at the top. And if the patient recovered from the worst effects, symptoms ap-

peared in the form of a seizure of the extremities: the private parts and the tips of the fingers and toes were attacked, and many survived with the loss of these, others with the loss of their eyes. Some rose from their beds with a total and immediate loss of memory, unable to recall their own names or to recognize their next of kin. (Text of Thucydides [book 2, chap. 49], trans. W. L. Page, 1953)

Expanding rapidly in the early summer, the epidemic was far more lethal than others Thucydides had known, and he claimed that the novelty of this disease left Greek physicians powerless to deal with it. The epidemic was said to have begun in Africa, south of Ethiopia, spreading first to Egypt and Libya, then to Persia, then to Greece.

The stricken initially complained of "violent heat in the head," coryza, swollen and inflamed eyes, throat, and tongue, proceeding to violent coughing. Then the victims usually began to vomit, the disease bringing on "all the vomits of bile to which physicians have ever given names." Death claimed many of the sufferers in 7 to 9 days, a merciful end to wrenching convulsions, intense internal heat, and extreme thirst. Thucydides described an exanthem characterizing many cases: The skin, not hot to the touch, took on a livid color, inclining to red, and breaking out in pustules and ulcers. However, he did not offer clear comment about the distribution of the rash, thus permitting much disagreement in the literature.

Causing almost equal difficulty for medical observers today is Thucydides' description of the behavior of sufferers, hurling themselves into wells and cisterns in order to assuage the "inner heat" and satisfy their thirst. Thucydides does not identify any age group, sex, or socioeconomic category among those most at risk, rather emphasizing that the previously healthy were as likely to suffer and die as those previously debilitated by illness. He claims that 1,050 out of 4,000 adult male soldiers perished of the Plague – a high mortality rate even if all were afflicted. Pericles, the great orator and leader of Athens, apparently perished from the sickness, but Thucydides and Socrates did not. Thucydides assumes that the disease was contagious, and no one has questioned that assumption.

The epidemic lingered for 4 years in southern Greece, killing up to 25 percent of the population (if one accepts the highest mortality estimates). No subsequent epidemics in the Hellenic and Hellenistic Greek hegemony are comparable to this epidemic in magnitude. Because the epidemic, according to Thucydides and to many later historians of ancient Greece, was responsible for Athenian military losses to Sparta, many have judged the Plague of Athens to be a "turning point" in the history of Western civilization.

Epidemiology and Etiology

Although many have speculated on causal questions surrounding the Plague of Athens and are convinced of their retrospective diagnoses, no consensus is likely to emerge. Fairly well supported arguments have advanced epidemic typhus, measles, and smallpox as candidates because all produce some of the dominant clinical and epidemiological features of Thucydides' description. Less frequently, bubonic plague, ergotism, streptococcal diseases, and, most recently, tularemia have found scholarly proponents.

Epidemic Typhus (Rickettsial Infection)

The facts that (1) the Plague of Athens occurred during wartime, (2) the severe clinical course lasted 7 to 10 days, (3) the fever was accompanied by first respiratory, then gastrointestinal, complaints and finally delirium associated with a rash – all have led several physician–historians to a diagnosis of epidemic typhus. Typhus is a louse-borne disease and severe cases could lead to circulatory collapse, accounting for the loss of distal extremities (fingers and toes) as well as damage to the optic nerve.

Insofar as Thucydides mentions vision loss as well as loss of the use of the extremities among some survivors, William MacArthur (1954) and Harry Keil (1951) find more support for this diagnosis of the clinical symptoms than for that of smallpox. By contrast, Hans Zinsser, in his 1935 classic *Rats, Lice, and History,* was not persuaded that the description Thucydides offered bore any resemblance to the typhus that cost so many lives in the two world wars. Yet other clinicians, citing their clinical experiences in wartime, have been equally persuaded that the description of Thucydides does suggest typhus. J. C. F. Poole and A. J. Holladay (1982) have most recently summarized this older literature.

J. F. D. Shrewsbury (1950) argues against a diagnosis of typhus, pointing out that Thucydides made no mention of either cloudy mental state or depression, both among the symptoms most frequently reported to accompany typhus infection over the last 500 years. Shrewsbury emphasizes the generally good personal and domestic cleanliness of the ancient Greeks, in order to argue that they were not lousy and thus could not have transmitted typhus with such ease. Yet Keil has provided an extensive survey of the words for lice found in Greek texts of the fifth century B.C., which indicates that they were hardly uncommon. Even so, Shrewsbury argues that typhus is too mild a disease to have killed a quarter of those who fell ill, and consequently, he holds that some "virgin soil" epidemic of a viral nature was the more probable cause of the Plague of Athens.

Measles Virus

Indeed, Shrewsbury favored a diagnosis of measles, as did classicist D. L. Page (1953). Shrewsbury points to similar levels of mortality in the severe, virgin soil epidemics of measles in the Fiji Islands in 1876, where more than 25 percent of the native population died. He considered the most significant passage in Thucydides to be the description of sufferers plunging themselves into cool water for relief. The Fiji Islanders displayed an identical behavior. Because even in the twentieth century, measles in adults could be malignant, causing severe diarrhea and pneumonia, he argued that the Plague of Athens may have been measles in its "pristine, virulent, early form," not the "emasculated" modern virus. Page agrees that the Plague of Athens was measles, feeling that the clarity of Thucydides' account was such that little support can be found in the text for other diagnoses; that is to say, Thucydides, although a layman, was not guilty of omitting crucial diagnostic details that medical contemporaries would have noted.

Smallpox Virus

Robert J. Littman and M. L. Littman (1969), however, argue for smallpox as the disease called the Plague of Athens, on the basis of the specific terms used by Thucydides to describe the exanthem or rash of the infection in question. Using Page's careful retranslation, the Littmans place emphasis on both the term φλύκταιναί ("small blister" or "pustule") and word ἕλκος ("ulcer" or "sore"), and contend that the description could refer only to a vesicle-forming eruption. In other words, Thucydides' description suggests a diagnosis of smallpox, because neither measles nor typhus typically forms vesicles in the exanthem. Moreover, the description hints strongly at the centrifugal spread of the rash, from face and trunk to extremities, again confirming a diagnosis of smallpox. The fact that Thucydides does not mention pockmarks among the survivors is found by the Littmans to be without import because they believed he was more concerned with the military impact of the disease than long-term effects on the survivors. In addition, the Littmans point to the absence of reference to pockmarking, even in some twentieth-century medical accounts of smallpox.

Other Explanations

Edna Hooker (1958) has been the last scholar to incline toward a diagnosis of bubonic plague, although many scholars found this a popular diagnosis during the first third of the twentieth century. Littman and Littman, however, argue against the bubonic plague, dismissing any possibility that the terms Thucydides chose could refer to buboes (lymphadenopathy associated with plague).

Another hypothesis, put forth by P. L. Salway and W. Dell (1955), suggests that ergotism, caused by fungal toxins in grain, explains the Plague of Athens even though Athenians rarely ate rye bread, the grain on which ergot usually grows. The occurrence of gangrene in extremities of victims who survived is, they maintain, an important symptom, which does not support the other diagnoses, but does support one of ergotism. John Wylie and Hugh Stubbs (1983) have provided a review of those infections with a wide host range that might have caused this level of human mortality 2,400 years ago, and thus they consider zoonoses other than plague and typhus. More recently, Alexander Langmuir and his colleagues (1985) have revived a pre-twentieth-century diagnosis of influenza virus, but emphasize that concurrent or subsequent staphylococcal infection could easily have created a "toxic shock" syndrome, with severe respiratory symptoms, bullous (or vesicular) skin infections, and violent gastrointestinal symptoms. As staphylococcal infection heightened the mortality from influenza in 1918, so a similar combination of viral and bacterial infection could explain the great Plague. On the other hand, Holladay (1986) takes issue with this latter explanation.

Methods of Historical Epidemiology

Study of the epidemic briefly described by Thucydides has inspired discussions of how diseases in the distant past can be identified, and thus discussions of the methods of historical epidemiology. There are three difficulties that emerge in the literature of the Plague of Athens that can and have presented themselves in other retrospective diagnostic efforts. First has to do with "virgin soil" epidemics. Although Thucydides only implies that all members of society were at risk of contracting the sickness, that no one was immune, and that immunity was conferred on the survivors of infection, he does specifically state that the disease was previously unknown to lay and medical Athenians. Some scholars hold that a new disease among a population immunologically virgin to the microorganism in question need display neither the expected seasonal onset characterizing the disease

nor the case-fatality rates usually seen. Those who oppose this methodological stance hold that this principle of retrospective analysis calls into question all diagnostic precepts. Many assume that supramortality would cause a breakdown in normal nursing care and hygienic services, leading to excess mortality; therefore, they stress the need for distinguishing the socioeconomic effects of a virgin soil epidemic from discussions of the virulence of the disease or the immunologic vulnerability of the population.

The second difficulty pertains to the changing epidemiology (or even clinical presentation) of diseases over time and thus is a variation of what is called "virgin soil epidemics argument": that infections of the past may have been caused by an organism known today but that the organism behaved quite differently in past individuals and populations. As Littman and Littman (1969) observed, "[A]s diseases adapt to new hosts under changing environments over the passage of years the symptomatology may change." From a historical standpoint, this can be a particularly pessimistic argument, and, in fact, James Longrigg (1980) has disallowed the possibility of ever discovering the cause of the Plague on much these grounds: "Epidemic diseases inevitably become modified in the course of centuries of alternating widespread prevalence and quiescence and . . . symptoms can, in any case, vary considerably in accordance with diet." Poole and Holladay (1979) go even further in denying any possible resemblance of the Plague of Athens to an infectious disease known in more recent times, whereas Langmuir and colleagues (1985) suggest that the discussion abandon altogether the hope for a one-to-one correspondence with a modern infectious disease and look instead to a physiological understanding of the processes involved.

The third difficulty focuses on the intent and fidelity of Thucydides' account to actual events. Of the authors discussed in this essay, only Watson Williams (1957) argues that Thucydides himself might not have been terribly well informed about the epidemic, because he did not write his history until after 404 B.C., approximately 25 years after the epidemic had taken place. Williams further suggests that even if Thucydides wrote from notes or consulted one of the few physicians who survived (the account claims that most died early in the epidemic), individuals tended to believe that their own experience with an infection was characteristic of all those who suffered from it.

Most assume, however, that Thucydides' account of the events lacks some crucial details from a modern point of view, but is otherwise accurate. Since

Page's review, which offers abundant detail that Thucydides was particularly well versed in medical terms and ideas, most have come to believe that the account was informed by contemporary medical knowledge. Longrigg (1980) argees, but skeptically considers the possibility that Thucydides "dramatically exploited [the Plague] for historiographical purposes." On the other hand, Jody Rubin Pinault (1986), tracing an ancient legend that Hippocrates himself devised the successful remedy of building fires to combat the epidemic at Athens, argues that Thucydides' "silence about this remarkable achievement of Hippocrates" is compelling evidence that he was not at all well versed about the Plague.

Clearly, discussions of the causes of the Plague of Athens form an important and instructive example of the study of the history of human infectious diseases. In addition, such a study reveals the many pitfalls connected with this type of integration and points to the need for still more sophisticated methods and techniques.

Ann G. Carmichael

Bibliography

Eby, Clifford H., and Harold D. Evjen. 1958. The plague at Athens: A new oar in muddied waters. *Journal of the History of Medicine and the Allied Sciences* 17: 258–63.

Holladay, A. J. 1986. The Thucydides syndrome: Another view. *New England Journal of Medicine* 315: 1170–3.

Hooker, Edna M. 1958. Buboes in Thucydides? *Journal of Hellenic Studies* 78: 84–8.

Keil, Harry. 1951. The louse in Greek antiquity, with comments on the diagnosis of the Athenian plague as recorded by Thucydides. *Bulletin of the History of Medicine* 25: 305–23.

Langmuir, Alexander D., et al. 1985. The Thucydides syndrome: A new hypothesis for the cause of the Plague of Athens. *New England Journal of Medicine* 313: 1027–30.

Littman, Robert J., and M. L. Littman. 1969. The Athenian plague: Smallpox. *American Philosological Association, Proceedings* 100: 261–73.

Longrigg, James. 1980. The great Plague of Athens. *History of Science* 18: 209–25.

MacArthur, William P. 1954. The Athenian plague: A medical note. *Classical Quarterly* 48: 171–4.

Page, D. L. 1953. Thucydides: Description of the great plague at Athens. *Classical Quarterly* 47: 97–119.

Pinault, Jody Ruin. 1986. How Hippocrates cured the plague. *Journal of the History of Medicine and Allied Sciences* 41: 52–74.

Poole, J. C. F., and A. J. Holladay. 1979. Thucydides and the Plague of Athens. *Classical Quarterly* 29: 282–300.

1982. Thucydides and the plague: A footnote. *Classical Quarterly* 32 (new series): 235–6.

Salway, P. L., and W. Dell. 1955. Plague at Athens. *Greece and Rome* 2 (2nd ser.): 62–70.

Shrewsbury, J. F. D. 1950. The Plague of Athens. *Bulletin of the History of Medicine* 24: 1–25.

Williams, E. Watson. 1957. The sickness at Athens. *Greece and Rome,* 2d ser., 4: 98–103.

Wylie, John A. H., and Hugh W. Stubbs. 1983. The Plague of Athens: 430–28 B.C.: Epidemic and epizootic. *Classical Quarterly* 33: 6–11.

VIII.108

Pneumocystis Pneumonia (Interstitial Plasma Cell Pneumonia, Pneumocystosis)

This form of pneumonia is caused by *Pneumocystis carinii*, a protozoan of uncertain taxonomic status in the class Sporozoa. An extracellular parasite of the lungs of humans, dogs, rodents, and other mammals, the organism occurs worldwide. It appears to be of low virulence and almost never causes disease except in weak or immunosuppressed individuals. *P. carinii* was discovered in guinea pigs in 1909, but human disease was first recognized in the 1940s in malnourished and premature infants. Patients suffering from leukemia, Hodgkin's disease, and other immunosuppressive diseases, or organ transplant recipients and other patients whose treatment requires suppression of the immune system, are also vulnerable to infection. In the early 1980s, pneumocystis pneumonia achieved prominence as the most common opportunistic infection afflicting patients with acquired immune deficiency syndrome (AIDS). Over half of all AIDS victims suffer from this form of pneumonia, and it frequently is the proximate cause of death.

Transmission is usually by airborne droplets, although transplacental passage resulting in fetal death has been reported. Latent infection may be common, with clinical disease and droplet transmission developing only in weakened hosts. The parasite damages the alveolar walls and induces an abundant foamy exudate and fibrosis. Death results from asphyxiation due to the exudate. Although initial response to chemical therapy is common, treatment is difficult because of side effects of the drugs and the debilitated state of the patients.

K. David Patterson

Bibliography

Frenkel, J. K. 1974. Toxoplasmosis and pneumocystosis: Clinical and laboratory aspects in immunocompetent and compromised hosts. In *Opportunistic pathogens,* ed. J. E. Prier and H. Friedman. Baltimore.

Gajdusek, D. C. 1957. *Pneumocystis carinii* – etiologic agent of interstitial plasma cell pneumonia of premature and young infants. *Pediatrics* 19: 543–65.

Marx, J. L. 1982. New disease baffles medical community. *Science* 217: 618–21.

Meer, G. van der, and S. L. Brug. 1942. Infection à pneumocystis chez l'homme et chez les animaux. *Annales de la Société Belge de Médecine Tropical* 22: 301–7.

VIII.109
Pneumonia

Pneumonia is an acute inflammatory condition of lung parenchyma (lung tissue excluding the airways) caused by a variety of infectious agents and toxins and favored by aspects of the environment and/or the general physical status of the patient. The term "pneumonia" is derived from the Greek word περιπλευμονιη meaning "condition about the lung"; the word refers to a clinicopathological state that arises in several different yet specific disease patterns. All of these are characterized by some degree of fever, cough, chest pain, and difficulty in breathing. Technically speaking, *pneumonitis,* which means "inflammation of the lung," is a synonym for pneumonia, but the former is usually reserved for benign, localized, and sometimes chronic inflammation without major toxemia (generalized effects). Many modifiers and eponyms are applied to the term pneumonia to reflect the cause (e.g., *embolic* pneumonia) or the localization (e.g., *pleuro-* or *broncho*pneumonia). The classic form is *lobar* pneumonia, an infectious but not particularly contagious condition usually localized to part or all of one of the five lobes of the lungs, and caused by a pneumococcus, the gram-positive organism *Streptococcus pneumoniae* (formerly called *Diplococcus pneumoniae*). Untreated lobar pneumonia has a mortality of about 30 percent, but the advent of antibiotic treatment has improved survival rates.

Several other pathogens (bacterial, viral, fungal, and parasitic) are recognized causative agents. The extent of the pulmonary involvement; the onset, pattern, and duration of symptoms; as well as the mortality rate depend on both the causative organism and precipitating factors. Chemical irritation, environmental exposure to noxious substances, or hypersensitivity can occasionally cause pneumonia. *Aspiration pneumonia* is a chemical-related condition, arising when vomited gastric acid is taken into the lung (along with oropharyngeal bacteria) by a patient in a weakened or semicomatose state induced by drugs, alcohol, anesthesia, or other disease. This type of pneumonia is readily complicated by superinfection by one or more organisms.

In many cases, pneumonia is only one manifestation of another specific disease such as the acquired immune deficiency syndrome (AIDS), ascariasis, cytomegalovirus, influenza, Legionnaire's disease, plague, pneumocystis, Q fever, rickettsial diseases, tuberculosis, tularemia, and varicella.

Etiology and Epidemiology

Many pathogens have been associated with infectious pneumonia. Bacterial varieties include *Escherichia coli, Hemophilus influenzae, Klebsiella pneumoniae, Legionella pneumophila, Mycobacterium tuberculosis,* staphylococci, and streptococci. Common viral agents are arbovirus, cytomegalovirus, influenza, measles, respiratory syncytial virus, and varicella. Other pathogens include *Mycoplasma pneumoniae, Blastomyces, Nocardia, Pneumocystis carinii,* and the rickettsial pathogen *Coxiella burnetii.* This list is far from exhaustive.

Despite the large number of pneumonia pathogens, the disease develops only if other host or environmental conditions are met. Normally the airways and lung tissue distal to the throat (glottis) are sterile. Occasionally, organisms that are always present in the upper airway, in the digestive tract, or on the skin enter the lung. Ordinarily they are rapidly eliminated either by mechanical means, such as by coughing and the microscopic action of cilia, or by immune mechanisms. Infection and the resultant inflammation of pneumonia can occur in healthy individuals, but are often associated with a breakdown in one or more of the usual defense mechanisms or, more rarely, with exposure to a particularly virulent strain of pathogen or an unusually high aerosol dose of organism (as in Legionnaire's disease). Occasionally, *bacterial pneumonia* will occur as a result of septicemic spread from an infectious focus elsewhere in the body.

Immune defenses are altered by underlying debility, be it nutritional (starvation and alcoholism), infectious (tuberculosis and AIDS), neoplastic (cancer or lymphoma), or iatrogenic. Iatrogenic causes of immune depression are becoming more important with the increasingly frequent use of immunosuppressive or cytotoxic drugs in the treatment of cancer, autoimmunity, and organ transplantation. One special form of immune deficiency resulting from absent splenic function leads to an exaggerated susceptibility to *S. pneumoniae* infection and lobar pneumonia. This condition, called *functional asplenia,* can arise following splenectomy or as a complication of sickle-cell anemia. Thus a relative predisposition to pneumococcal infection can be found in the geographic regions containing a high frequency of hemoglobin S.

Mechanical defenses are hampered by immobility due to altered consciousness, paralysis or pain, endotracheal intubation, and prior viral infection of the upper airway, such as bronchitis or a cold. Controversy surrounds the ancient etiologic theory about cold temperatures. August Hirsch (1886) found a high incidence of pneumonia in months having wide variability in temperature. Two factors do tend to support an indirect correlation between cold and pneumonia: Predisposing viral infections are more common in winter, and some evidence suggests that the mechanical action of cilia is slowed on prolonged exposure to cold.

Lobar pneumonia appears in all populations. Its incidence and mortality rate are higher in individuals or groups predisposed to one or more of the factors described above. Elderly patients frequently develop pneumonia as the terminal complication of other debilitating illness, hence the famous metaphor "friend of the aged" (Osler 1901).

Mortality rates for pneumonia are difficult to estimate because of its multifactorial nature and the fact that it can complicate other diseases. As mentioned previously, untreated lobar pneumonia can result in death in 30 percent of cases. With antibiotics, fatalities are reduced to a varying extent depending on the underlying condition of the patient, but in persons over the age of 12 years the mortality is at least 18 percent and in immunocompromised persons it is much higher. In the late nineteenth century, Hirsch suggested that the annual death rate averaged 1.5 per 1,000 in a survey of European and American municipal statistics (Hirsch 1886). Pollution of the atmosphere may have contributed to the apparent rise in pneumonia mortality in Britain during the last half of the nineteenth century (Howe 1972). William Osler saw pneumonia mortality as one of the most important problems of his era and applied to it John Bunyan's metaphor (originally intended for tuberculosis), "Captain of all these men of death." Contemporary pneumonia mortality combined with influenza is still the sixth most common cause of death in the United States, where mortality is estimated to be approximately 0.3 per 1,000 (U.S. Public Health Service Centers for Disease Control 1989). Pneumococcal vaccination of high-risk groups with functional asplenia and other forms of debility has contributed to a decrease in incidence.

Other forms of pneumonia follow epidemiological patterns that reflect the frequency of the organism or causative toxins in the host's environment, as for example *Legionella,* which favors water in air-conditioning systems.

Clinical Manifestations

The incubation period for pneumonia is variable, depending on the causative organism, but pneumococcal pneumonia has a fairly uniform pattern. There may be a brief prodrome of coldlike symptoms, but usually the onset is sudden, with shaking chills and a rapid rise in temperature, followed by a rise in heart and respiratory rates. Cough productive of "rusty" blood-tinged sputum and dyspnea are usual. Most patients experience pleuritic chest pain. In severe cases, there can be inadequate oxygenation of blood, leading to cyanosis. If untreated, the fever and other symptoms persist for at least 7 to 10 days, when a "crisis" may occur consisting of sweating with defervescence and spontaneous resolution. With antibiotic treatment, the fever usually falls within 48 hours. Untreated, or inadequately treated, the disease may progress to dyspnea, shock, abscess formation, empyema, and disseminated infection. When empyema occurs, surgical drainage is essential.

Diagnosis is based on the classic history and physical findings. Dullness to percussion is detected over the involved lobe(s) of lung, and auscultation may reveal decreased air entry, crepitant rales, bronchophony, whispering pectoriloquy, and variable alteration in fremitus, which reflects the pathological state of the lung tissue as it progresses through edema to consolidation and resolution or suppuration. Confirmation of the diagnosis is made by chest X-ray, and the specific pathogen is identified in sputum stains and culture. Treatment consists of rest, hydration, oxygen if necessary, and antibiotics. The selection of the last is based on, or endorsed by, the culture results.

In the nonlobar forms of pneumonia with diffuse inflammation, the history may be atypical and physical examination unreliable. In these cases, chest X-ray and special cultures may be necessary. In some cases, the precise identity of the pathogen is confirmed by serologic tests for specific and/or nonspecific antibodies (viral and mycoplasma pneumonia) or by immunofluorescence techniques (*Legionella*). When the patient is unable to cough or the inflammation is nonpyogenic, lung biopsy for microscopic inspection and culture is required (pneumocystis).

History

Antiquity Through the Eighteenth Century

Lobar pneumonia has probably always afflicted humans. Pneumococcal organisms have been found in prehistoric remains, and evidence of the disease itself has been observed in Egyptian mummies from 1200 B.C. (Ruffier 1921; Janssens 1970; Grmek 1983). Epidemics of this disease are probably less common than has previously been thought, however. In his pre-germ-theory observations, Hirsch cited sixteenth- to late-nineteenth-century reports of epidemic outbreaks of "pneumonia" in numerous places on six continents. He emphasized that nearly all these records drew attention to "the malignant type of disease" and the "typhoid symptoms" (Hirsch 1886). These qualifiers raise doubts about whether or not these outbreaks were truly pneumonia. It is probable that most, if not all, were caused by organisms other than pneumococcus. Conditions now called by another name and known to have pneumonic manifestations, like plague and influenza, are far more likely candidates for retrospective diagnosis (Stout 1980).

Pneumonia is not only an old disease, it is also one of the oldest *diagnosed* diseases. Hippocratic accounts of a highly lethal illness called *peripleumonin* give a readily identifiable description of the symptoms, progression, and suppurative complications of classic pneumonia and localize the disease to the lung. This disease was a paradigmatic example of the Greek theory that held that all illness progressed through *coction* (approximately, incubation and early illness) to crisis and lysis (breaking up), while certain days in this sequence were "critical" to the outcome (Sigerist 1951). These writers based the diagnosis on the symptoms, but the physical sign of "clubbing" or "Hippocratic nails" was associated with prolonged pneumonia. Auscultation was also recommended to confirm the presence of pus in the chest. Variant pneumonic conditions of the lung were also described, including lethargy, moist and dry pneumonia, also called *erysipelas* of the lung. Therapy included bleeding, fluids, expectorants, and, only if absolutely necessary, surgical

evacuation of empyemic pus (Hippocrates 1988; Potter 1988).

In the first century A.D., Aretaeus of Cappadocia distinguished this disease from pleurisy, and four centuries later Caelius Aurelianus recognized that it could be confined to only certain parts of the lung. Except for a few subtle modifications, little change occurred in the clinical diagnosis and treatment of pneumonia until the early nineteenth century.

Nineteenth Through Twentieth Century

It is true that eighteenth-century pathological anatomists drew attention to the microscopic appearance of the lung in fatal cases of lobar pneumonia. This work, however, had little impact on diagnosis until 1808, when Jean-Nicolas Corvisart translated and revised the 1761 treatise on percussion by Leopold Auenbrugger. This technique made it possible to detect and localize the presence of fluid or consolidation in the lung and to follow its evolution. Eight years later, Corvisart's student, René Laennec, carried this one step further when he invented the stethoscope. In calling his technique "*médiate auscultation*," Laennec readily gave priority to Hippocrates for having practiced the "immediate" variety by direct application of the ear to the chest. Laennec recommended both percussion and auscultation of the breath sounds and voice to confirm the physical diagnosis of pneumonia. With this combination he was able to distinguish consolidated lung from pleural fluid or pus in the living patient. He introduced most of the technical terms for pathological lung sounds – including "rale," "rhoncus," "crepitation," "bronchophony," "egophony" – some of which became pathognomonic for disease states. In addition, he adopted Giovanni Morgagni's notion of "hepatisation of the lung," as a descriptive term for consolidation. Percussion and auscultation changed the concept of pneumonia from a definition based on classic symptoms to one based on classic physical findings. This conceptual shift was endorsed but not altered by the advent of the chest X-ray at the turn of this century.

The Italians Giovanni Rasori and Giacomo Thommasini had recommended high-dose antimony potassium tartrate (tartar emetic) as a treatment for pneumonia, and Laennec used the new method of statistical analysis with historical controls to suggest that this was an effective remedy. Yet in spite of its potential utility, the extreme toxicity of the drug guaranteed its unpopularity (Duffin 1985). Benjamin Rush, an American, and Laennec's contemporary, Jean Baptiste Bouillaud, were proponents of copious *"coup sur coup"* phlebotomy. Until the late nineteenth century, when salicylates became available for fever, pneumonia therapy consisted of various combinations and quantities of the ancient remedies, emetics, mercury, and especially bleeding (Risse 1986; Warner 1986).

Germ theory had a major impact on the concept of pneumonia, but it was rapidly apparent that despite its fairly homogeneous clinical manifestations this disease was associated not with a single germ (like tuberculosis and cholera) but with a variety of pathogens. This situation cast some doubt on the imputed role of each new pathogen. In December 1880, Louis Pasteur isolated the organism that would later become the pneumococcus. Carl Friedlander discovered the first lung-derived pneumonia organism, *K. pneumoniae* (Friedlander's bacillus) in 1883. Albert Frankel identified the pneumococcus (*D. pneumoniae*) in 1884, and Anton Weichselbaum confirmed his findings in 1886. *Klebsiella* was found to be quite rare and seemed to favor the upper lobes, whereas the pneumococcus favored the lower lobes; however, there was some overlap between the pneumonic states induced by these organisms. Specific diagnoses could be made only by isolation of the pathogen in culture.

Gradually many other organisms and viruses came to be associated with pneumonia, usually in clinical settings that deviated more or less from classic lobar pneumonia. For example (and to name only a few), *H. influenzae* was isolated in 1918; *Mycoplasma pneumoniae* (the "Eaton agent" of "atypical pneumonia") in 1944; *L. pneumophila* in 1977 (Hudson 1979; Denny 1981; Stevens 1981; Levin 1984). It is likely that new pathogens will be recognized as antibiotics and vaccination alter the ecology of the lung.

Knowledge of the pneumococcus led to improvement in treatment and reduction in mortality from pneumonia, but it also had a major impact on the broad fields of immunology, bacteriology, and molecular genetics. Study of the capsule – its antigenic properties and capacity to transform – provided key information about drug resistance in bacteria: Acquired assistance of pneumococci was first recognized in 1912, long before the antibiotic era (Austrian 1981). Rufus Cole, Raymond Dochez, and Oswald Avery developed typologies for the pneumococci before and during World War I, and in 1929 René Dubos discovered a bacterial enzyme that decomposed the capsular polysaccharide of type III pneumococcus, a discovery that contributed to the later work of Jacques Monod (Benison 1976).

Treatment and prevention of pneumonia have been dramatically improved in the twentieth century. Oxygen therapy was introduced by William C. Stadie during the 1918 New York influenza epidemic (Harvey 1979). Typing of pneumococci led to the 1912 introduction of antisera by Rufus Cole, who claimed that, by 1929, this therapy reduced mortality in some populations to 10.5 percent (Dowling 1973). Antisera were effective only when the exact type of pneumococcus was known. Gerhard Domagk's Pronotosil (sulfanilamide) was not particularly effective against pneumococcus, but it did control other predisposing conditions. Its successor, sulfapyridine, was more effective. The advent of penicillin in the mid-1940s led to further reduction in mortality; however, it also led to the evolution of penicillin-resistant strains of pneumococci and the now seemingly endless chase after effective derivatives against so-called new organisms (Weinstein 1980).

Pneumonia control programs relied at first on antipneumococcal serum therapy, but as early as 1911, Almroth E. Wright conducted vaccination trials on thousands of black South African gold miners (Dowling 1973; Austrian 1981). These trials, conducted before the diversity of capsular types was fully appreciated, were inconclusive. It was not until 1945 that unequivocal demonstration of protection against type-specific pneumococcal infection in humans was demonstrated by Colin M. MacLeod and Michael Heidelberger using a tetravalent vaccine. Contemporary vaccines contain at least 23 capsular antigens and are 80 to 90 percent effective in immunocompetent persons, but may be useless in some forms of immunodeficiency.

Jacalyn Duffin

Bibliography

Aretaeus. 1856. *The extant works of Aretaeus the Cappadocian,* trans. Francis Adams. London.

Auenbrugger, Leopold. 1808. *Nouvelle méthode pour reconnaître les maladies de la poitrine.* Paris.

Aurelianus, Caelius. 1950. *On acute diseases and on chronic diseases,* trans. I. E. Drabkin. Chicago.

Austrian, Robert. 1981. Pneumococcus: The first one hundred years. *Review of Infectious Diseases* 3: 183–9.

1987. Pneumococcal pneumonia. In *Harrison's principles of internal medicine,* ed. E. Braunwald et al., 534–7. New York.

Benison, Saul. 1976. René Dubos and the capsular polysaccharide of pneumococcus: An oral history memoir. *Bulletin of the History of Medicine* 50: 459–77.

Denny, Floyd W. 1981. Atypical pneumonia and the Armed Forces Epidemiological Board. *Journal of Infectious Diseases* 143: 305–16.

Dowling, Harry F. 1973. The rise and fall of pneumonia-control programs. *Journal of Infectious Diseases* 127: 201–6.

    1977. *Fighting infection: Conquests of the twentieth century.* Cambridge, Mass., and London.

Duffin, Jacalyn. 1985. Laennec: Entre la pathologie et la clinique. Doctoral thesis, Sorbonne University. Paris.

Grmek, Mirko D. 1983. *Les Maladies à l'aube de la civilisation occidentale.* Paris.

Harvey, A. McGehee. 1979. Anoxemia in pneumonia and its successful treatment by oxygen. *American Journal of Medicine* 66: 193–5.

Hippocrates. 1988. *Loeb Classical Library,* Vols. 5 and 6, trans. Paul Potter. Cambridge, Mass.

Hirsch, August. 1883–6. *Handbook of geographical and historical pathology,* trans. Chas. Creighton. London.

Hirschmann, Jan V., and John F. Murray. 1987. Pneumonia and lung abscess. In *Harrison's principles of internal medicine,* ed. E. Braunwald et al., 1075–82. New York.

Howe, G. Melvyn. 1972. *Man, environment and disease in Britain: A medical geography of Britain through the ages.* New York.

Hudson, Robert P. 1979. Lessons from Legionnaire's disease. *Annals of Internal Medicine* 90: 704–7.

Janssens, Paul A. 1970. *Paleopathology: Diseases and injuries of prehistoric man.* London.

Laennec, René T. 1826. *De l'auscultation médiate ou traité du diagnostic des maladies des poumons et du coeur,* 2d edition. Paris.

Levin, Stuart. 1984. The atypical pneumonia syndrome. *Journal of the American Medical Association* 251: 945–8.

McGrew, Roderick E. 1985. *Encyclopedia of medical history.* New York.

Osler Club Symposium. 1952. Recent history of pneumonia. *British Medical Journal* 1: 156–7.

Osler, William. 1901. *Principles and practice of medicine,* 4th edition. New York.

Potter, Paul. 1988. *Short handbook of Hippocratic medicine.* Quebec.

Risse, Guenter. 1986. *Hospital life in Enlightenment Scotland: Care and teaching at the Royal Infirmary of Edinburgh.* Cambridge.

Ruffier, Marc Armand. 1921. *Studies in the paleopathology of Egypt,* trans. Roy L. Moodie. Chicago.

Sigerist, Henry. 1951. *A history of medicine. II: Early Greek, Hindu and Persian medicine.* New York and Oxford.

Stevens, Kingsley M. 1981. The pathophysiology of influenzal pneumonia in 1918. *Perspectives in Biology and Medicine* 25: 115–25.

Stout, G. 1980. The 1888 pneumonia in Middlesbrough. *Journal of the Royal Society of Medicine* 73: 664–8.

U.S. Public Health Service. Centers for Disease Control. 1989. Mortality trends – United States, 1986–88. *Morbidity and Mortality Weekly Reports* 38: 117.

Warner, John Harley. 1986. *The therapeutic perspective: Medical practice, knowledge and identity in America, 1820–1885.* Cambridge, Mass., and London.

Weinstein, Louis. 1980. The "new" pneumonias: The doctor's dilemma. *Annals of Internal Medicine* 92: 559–61.

VIII.110
Poliomyelitis

Poliomyelitis is an acute disease caused by inflammation and destruction of motor neurons after infection by a poliovirus. Sensory functions are not affected. Although frequently asymptomatic, the infection may cause fever and a number of other general symptoms, described as abortive polio or minor illness. Occasionally, however, these prodromal symptoms are followed a few days later by infection of the central nervous system (CNS) and fever, with meningitis, or paresis (weakness) or paralysis of one or more muscles. Many patients recover use of the muscle or some muscles affected in the following months, although some have permanent paralysis or paresis. When the muscles of respiration are affected, death may follow.

Other enteroviruses of the ECHO (Enteric Cytopathic Human Orphan virus) and Coxsackie groups may also cause meningitis and paresis, or temporary paralysis. In the past, cases of abortive polio and those with paralysis who later recovered were often included in statistics as polio cases. Today, only cases with paralysis or paresis after 3 months are recorded as paralytic polio.

Poliomyelitis was known by several names until the 1870s, when it became known as acute anterior poliomyelitis. Among them was Heine–Medin disease (after two early researchers, Jacob von Heine and Karl Oscar Medin) and infantile paralysis because it affected mainly young children. As more adults and older children were affected, poliomyelitis – inflammation of the gray marrow – became the name of choice and is often shortened to polio.

Etiology and Immunology

There are three immunologic types of poliovirus, with strain differences in each, and there may be minor cross-reactions between types 1 and 2. Within each type there is a wide range of ability to cause paralysis, from the highly virulent type 1 Mahoney strain to avirulent wild and vaccine strains. Wild

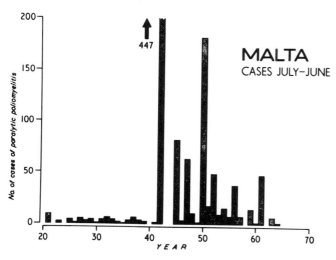

Figure VIII.110.1. Cases of paralytic poliomyelitis in Malta, 1920–64. Epidemics always occurred in the winter, with no cases in June to July even in other years; the cases are counted from July of one year to June of the next to emphasize the epidemics. Cases are those notified except for 1942, when late-diagnosed cases are included. In the late 1950s and early 1960s, inactivated poliovirus vaccine (IPV) was given to groups already mostly immune. In 1964 oral poliovirus vaccine (OPV) was given to all age groups and, from then on, to young babies and children.

strains may cause only a few cases of paralysis while immunizing other children. The introduction of a new virulent strain, however, may cause an epidemic, as in Malta in 1942 (Figure VIII.110.1). Strains differ widely in their transmissibility: In Malta, the pattern of cases among children in villages, among British servicemen, and in the next epidemic suggests that everyone in the island was rapidly infected. There are many other examples, however, of small epidemics without further cases in the region. The new technique of genomic sequencing has shown that small epidemics, many hundreds of miles apart, may be caused by viruses that are very similar.

The virus spreads from person to person via the fecal–oral route, although a few epidemics may have been caused by contaminated milk. Ingested virus replicates in the gut and associated lymphoid tissue. After 2 to 3 days, there is viremia lasting until about day nine, when the virus is neutralized by serum antibody. The level of viremia correlates with virulence; there is little or no viremia with avirulent strains. Animal experiments suggest that the level of antibody that protects is below the threshold of detection.

Exposure to virus leads to lifelong immunity to viruses of the same type. Although people who are immune have some gut immunity, they may still be infected but they have no viremia and shed less virus for a shorter time. Humans are the only natural host and reservoir, although other primates may be infected experimentally or accidentally.

Since 1910 it seemed that immunization might be feasible. The first attempts in 1935 ended with cases and deaths attributed to the vaccines. Many vaccines were made for experimental use only, but a vaccine for humans was not possible until the virus could be grown in quantity outside the central nervous system of monkeys, the number of antigenic types could be established, and cheap methods of titrating virus and antibody could be developed. J. F. Enders, T. H. Weller, and F. C. Robbins grew poliovirus in human tissue culture in late 1948 and solved all three problems. In 1951 Hilary Koprowski fed an attenuated virus to 20 adults.

In 1953 Jonas Salk injected an inactivated vaccine (IPV) into over 100 children, and in the following year the vaccine was given to 400,000 children in an elaborate field trial involving 1.8 million children. The effort was successful, but a slightly different vaccine was finally licensed. Vaccine from at least one manufacturer – Cutter Laboratories – contained live virions, and there were about 250 resulting cases in what was called the "Cutter incident" of 1955. Manufacture and safety testing of the Salk vaccine were tightened but at the cost of reduced antigenicity. In the 1980s, a purified and more antigenic IPV was produced that required two doses instead of three to produce lasting immunity.

Two early attenuated oral poliovaccines (OPV), the Koprowski and Cox–Lederle vaccines, had been given trials in several countries but were abandoned. Use of the Cox–Lederle vaccine in West Berlin in the spring of 1960 was followed by a few cases that might have been vaccine-associated. On the other hand, inflammation in a muscle, caused by an injection, can greatly increase the chance of paralysis, and it may be that a drug such as thalidomide, which causes peripheral neuritis, might act in the same way, although without the localization that is the hallmark of provocation polio. Thalidomide, which was in use in 1960, caused peripheral neuritis, and analysis of the cases is consistent with the theory that thalidomide made those taking it more susceptible to CNS invasion by the vaccine virus.

In the 1950s A. B. Sabin produced an oral polio vaccine (OPV), which has been used extensively throughout the world. The advantages of the Sabin vaccine are many: (1) It can be given by nonmedical staff under supervision; (2) it induces gut immunity;

(3) it is inexpensive; and (4) immunity spreads to others not given the vaccine. Yet there are disadvantages: (1) Three separate doses are required; (2) it is quickly inactivated by heat; and (3) the virus reverts toward virulence and causes some vaccine-associated cases (VAC). Although there is no evidence that it can harm pregnant women, the Sabin vaccine is not given to them. About one child in a million given OPV develops paralysis. Early figures of risk were based on doses, not children, and included large numbers who were already immune and so not at risk. Hypogammaglobulinemic children are at risk from OPV, and a small number (about 2 percent) develop a chronic CNS infection with paralysis. A very small number of contact VAC occur, mainly among mothers of children given OPV. The number of such cases depends on the number of people who have not been immunized by vaccine or wild viruses.

Oral polio vaccine has been used very successfully in countries with temperate climates but less so in many warmer developing countries. The problems have been largely due to lack of cold-chain facilities (to prevent heat inactivation) and organization. The most effective method of immunization is the once or twice a year "polio day" pulse program. Distribution of the vaccine is made a few days before immunization to local immunization posts throughout the whole country, reducing the problems presented by the cold chain. On the day of immunization, which is heavily advertised in the media, all children 2 years and younger who are present are given OPV. The flood of virus shed by vaccinees then vaccinates any who did not receive OPV and displaces circulating wild virus.

Inactivated polio vaccine is more stable and may be combined with other vaccines such as that of diphtheria–pertussis–tetanus (DPT), thus simplifying immunization schedules and reducing cost. The latest IPV is very safe, highly purified, and antigenic. Although one dose may suffice, at least two doses are recommended.

Epidemiology

In most years it is very difficult to assess epidemics because there may be several polioviruses of different virulence and types circulating. Thus the extent of the circulation of the virulent viruses will not be known and the cases will not necessarily correspond to the geographic boundaries used for reporting. Moreover, because viruses change their virulence, the number of nonimmunes will be unknown. Surveys of immune status and examination of feces for virus are expensive and time-consuming, and sam-

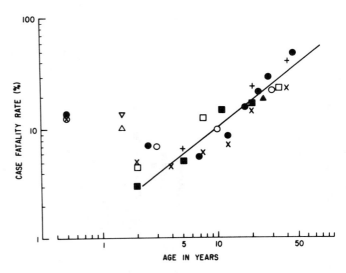

Figure VIII.110.2. Case-fatality rates for poliomyelitis based on records from (X) England and Wales, 1947–50 (average of male and female rates; 28 notified cases); (○) Denmark, 1947–50 (28 paralytic cases); (●) France, 1952 (average of male and female rates; 28 notified cases); (■) Sweden, 1935–44 (28 confirmed paralytic cases); (+) Eskimos, Chesterfield Inlet (14 cases); (□) Cutter vaccinees (27 cases); (△) West Virginia (18 cases); (▲) Malta, 1942–3 (service cases, 20–30 years of age, no. of cases not specified); (▽) Sweden, 1911–13 (5 cases). [From Harold V. Wyatt. 1975. *Medical Hypotheses* 1 (1): 35–42, by permission of Churchill-Livingstone, publishers.]

ple only a tiny fraction of a given population. Thus our epidemiological knowledge of the disease is very dependent on virgin soil epidemics in islands and isolated communities with definite boundaries that contain many nonimmunes.

After an epidemic in 1919, polio was made a notifiable disease in Malta. About three cases were reported each year (Figure VIII.110.1) until 1942, when almost 3 percent of children under 3 years of age were stricken. Other epidemics followed at intervals of 2 or 3 years. Some of these epidemics were probably caused by the importation of virulent viruses from Egypt by returning Maltese in 1919, 1945, and 1947 and by the arrival by overnight flight of about 250 RAF men in 1942. Nearly all the Maltese cases were children under 5 years of age.

Prior to the 1930s, most polio cases occurred in young children, except in small isolated communities where older children, adolescents, and even adults were sometimes affected. Beginning in the 1930s, however, there was a shift to older children and adolescents, first in Scandinavia and the United States, and then in Europe. The older children suffered less paralysis, and, as Figure VIII.110.2 shows, the case-fatality rate was low. By contrast, young adults had paralysis and case-fatality rates like those of small children. In many severe epidemics, the case-rate for 2-year-olds has been about 2 percent with increasing rates up to about 10 years of age, when the rate stabilizes at 25 percent. In a virgin soil epidemic among an Eskimo population in 1948, 2 out of 53 children and 25 percent of adolescents and adults were paralyzed.

Incidence in monozygotic and dizygotic twins suggests genetic susceptibility, and there are families who have had many cases over several generations. Yet, the overall level of familial incidence is low, and genetic susceptibility has been largely discounted. On the other hand, the changes in paralysis and case-fatality rates at about 3 years of age can be explained if two groups are genetically susceptible – the 2 percent of the population who are homozygotes and the 24 percent who are heterozygotes. This model suggests that genetic susceptibility is a maturation process, with about half the homozygotes becoming phenotypically susceptible at 1 year of age and all at 2 years. Heterozygotes would mature more slowly, reaching 24 percent at about 10 years.

Early epidemiological surveys often included all cases whether there was residual paralysis or not, and cases of abortive polio were also frequently included, although diagnosis in these cases is difficult and uncertain. From the late 1930s, it became increasingly common to restrict inclusion in the statistics to those with paralysis, and later only to those with residual paralysis. In countries where there is universal immunization and very few cases, each suspected case is investigated. A positive virus isolation or a rise in antibody titer between acute and convalescent sera is evidence of poliovirus involvement. Polioviruses are tested for affinity to vaccine and wild strains.

Distribution and Incidence

At all ages, there are more male than female cases. However, pregnant females have a higher incidence of poliomyelitis than nonpregnant females of the same age. Attempts to explain these differences have been unsuccessful. The case-fatality rates of males and females are similar. Studies of many hundred pregnant women with polio showed no increase in miscarriages, and there were no affected births. Moreover, 48 stillborn or aborted fetuses showed no signs of polio. A few fetuses have been examined for virus, which was isolated from many organs. The one stillborn fetus tested was positive for virus in the CNS (Wyatt 1979).

Yet when the mother had suffered paralysis between 7 days before and 10 days after birth, 40 percent of the babies suffered concurrent paralysis, with a 56 percent case-fatality rate. By contrast, babies born of mothers who had experienced paralysis earlier in the pregnancy (nonconcurrent) had a less than 0.01 percent chance of polio in the month after birth and only a 10 percent case-fatality rate. The few babies born by Caesarian section of mothers who contracted polio just before birth were not affected. Babies with paralysis 0 to 10 days after birth had a very short incubation time – 6 days – as compared with 12 days for concurrent cases in babies with paralysis 11 to 28 days after birth.

When a nonimmune person who is infected with a virulent poliovirus receives an injection of an inflammatory substance into a muscle, the chance of paralysis occurring 7 to 18 days later is much increased. In many cases, the muscle receiving the injection is the first paralyzed and the extent and severity of paralysis may also be increased. The phenomenon, called *provocation,* was recognized in 1950, when mass immunization with diphtheria–pertussis–tetanus vaccine (DPT) began. Risk of provocation was much reduced by giving DPT in winter when circulation of poliovirus was minimal. Sterile saline and human gammaglobulin did not provoke. Provocation had first been described, but not named, in 1914 when nearly a quarter of 22 babies with congenital syphilis were paralyzed with polio after treatment with multiple injections of Salvarsan. Further epidemics with 25 percent case-rates were noted in Rome between 1936 and 1947 among similar children given multiple injections of Salvarsan (arsphenamine) and, later, penicillin. Similarly, nonepidemic polio among children with congenital syphilis in Rome and London showed case-rates up to 25 times the rate in ordinary children, and simliar rates were seen in epidemics in the South Pacific in 1932 and 1951.

The degree of provocation increases with the ability to produce inflammation: Thus vaccines with adjuvants are more provocative than those without. Single injections may increase the risk up to 8 times, whereas multiple injections may increase the risk 25 times.

Injection of live poliovirus, as in the Cutter incident, may cause paralysis with features similar to provocation polio but with a shorter incubation. *Toxocara* infection increases the risk of polio: The dead larvae in the muscles may act as centers of provocation.

Tonsillectomy – but probably not tonsillotomy – increases the risk of paralysis and especially the risk

Table VIII.110.1. *Comparison of paralysis of lower limbs in temperate and developing countries*

Regions	N	Percent of cases with involvement of:		Coincident injections
		Lower limbs only (mean %)	Lower limbs plus other paralysis (mean %)	
Tropical and sub-tropical, 1938–78[a]	6,278	85	89	very common
Temperate, 1905–50[b]	10,694	49	79	probably none
Singapore, 1946	116	48	72	few or none
Malta, 1942	420	51	–	very few

[a]Based on 12 papers: from Sri Lanka (1 paper), Madagascar (1), India (5), Nigeria (2), Congo (1), Cameroun (1), and Bahrain and Kuwait (1).
[b]Based on 9 papers: from the United States (4), the United Kingdom (2), Sweden (1), Denmark (1), and Germany (1).

of bulbar polio. The increased risk not only is immediate but also persists for 5 or more years. The incubation time immediately after the operation is from 7 to 17 days – the same as for ordinary polio – which implies that entry of the virus does not occur directly in the oropharynx but only after viremia.

As immunity to polio is mediated by antibody, all hypogammaglobulinemics should be particularly susceptible. Before antibiotics, most of these children probably died of bacterial infections, but from 1950 to 1960, of 154 children and adults with inherited or acquired hypogammaglobulinemia, only 8 developed polio – about the number expected on the genetic model. Only about 2 percent of hypogammaglobulinemic children – about 10 percent of VAC children – develop polio after OPV has been given. The incubation is longer than 28 days; there is a high mortality after a long chronic illness, with abnormal lesions in the CNS and no reversion to virulence of the virus. Hypogammaglobulinemics are about 10,000 times more likely than other children to develop polio after the oral administration of polio vaccine.

Clinical Manifestations and Pathology
During the prodromal stage, there is viremia, and replication of virus occurs in the muscles. There may be muscle pains as well as fever. About 25 percent of those infected may show signs of abortive polio. There are two theories as to how virus reaches the CNS. The first suggests that virus crosses the blood–brain barrier (BBB) and travels along neuronal pathways in the CNS. However, David Bodian showed that virus traveled up the sciatic nerve at 2.4 mm per hour. Postmortems reveal that lesions in the CNS can be discrete and separate, suggesting that virus enters at numerous endplate junctions of motor neurons in the muscles and reaches the CNS at many different places. The time taken to reach the CNS from any muscle depends on the length of the nerve to be traveled, during which time the virus would be shielded from antibody. Virus could enter a nerve at any time from about the second to the ninth day. Virus entering from a foot muscle on the ninth day in a tall adult would reach the CNS about 18 days later. This model would account for the incubation of about 3 to 28 days. As viremia ends about the ninth day, the BBB model requires the virus to be 18 days in the CNS before producing symptoms.

Leg muscles are more often affected than arms, as indicated in Table VIII.110.1. In general, the larger the muscle the greater the chance of paralysis, and the smaller the muscle the greater the chance of paresis. Muscles are not affected at random. The neurons serving them lie in adjacent and overlapping bundles in the CNS: Damage in one bundle will often spill over into an adjacent bundle, so there is a high probability that both muscles will be affected.

Up to 60 percent of the neurons serving a muscle may be destroyed before there is a loss of function, and thus patients who have had nonparalytic CNS infection may still have suffered considerable damage. In one such patient who was examined after death from an unrelated accident, there were a number of separate regions of damage. Many survivors

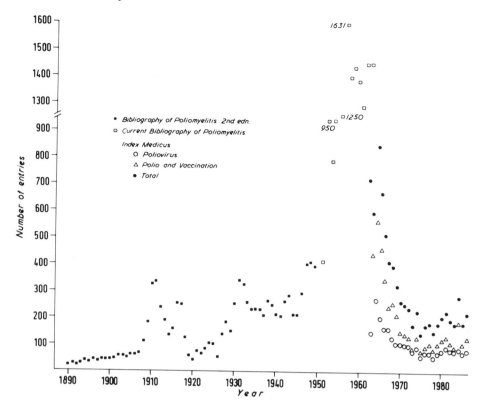

Figure VIII.110.3. Numbers of publications about polio by year, 1890 to 1986. The figures are not entirely comparable: The *Current Bibliography of Poliomyelitis* includes some papers about other viruses; *Index Medicus* puts the entry for a single paper in more than one section, so that the number of papers is overestimated by perhaps 5 percent. Entries in the *Bibliography of Infantile Paralysis* are listed by year of publication, whereas other bibliographies list entries by year of appearance in the secondary serial (e.g., 6 months later). The effects of world wars, slumps, large epidemics, and notable research findings are apparent (see J. R. Paul 1971). The peak of papers in 1984 is due to an international conference held in 1983.

are suffering late effects of polio (LEP) more than 30 years later. Previously unaffected muscles become weak; already affected muscles become weaker; and in addition, generalized weakness and fatigue occur. The muscles most commonly affected are those that recovered well from the initial attack and have been used strenuously ever since. There is continual loss of motor neurons with age, and LEP may be the effect of normal aging superimposed on previous loss through polio.

In the acute stage, there is massive proliferation of lymphocytes in lymph nodes, and the picture in the CNS resembles a host-versus-graft reaction. Infected neurons are destroyed, although the inflammation does not correspond with the location of virus. Delayed hypersensitivity to poliovirus does not occur, even after many injections of vaccine. Moreover, the short response time suggests that the lymphocyte proliferation is a secondary response. Sabin showed that some adults gave a skin response to primate gray matter. One explanation could be that infected neurons are damaged with loss of function, but that more damage is caused by lymphocytes sensitized to motor neuron antigen. The proportion of damage caused by virus and lymphocytes may depend on the presence of antibody. In animal experiments, Bodian observed that 75 percent of infected neurons recover.

Second attacks by a virus of a different type presumably should occur; yet only 44 have been reported – far less than one might expect. This and animal experiments, however, suggest that second attacks are not blocked by antibody against poliovirus. Some hypogammaglobulinemics suffer a chronic infection, and animal experiments show that coincident infections with other enteroviruses can be synergistic.

History and Geography

Polio may be as old as humankind, but there are very few early indicators of the disease. An Egyptian stele from about 1400 B.C., now in the Carlsberg Glyptothek, Copenhagen, shows a young priest with a shortened, deformed foot in the typical equinus position of polio. In the 1830s, three small epidemics of the disease were reported from England, the United States, and the island of Saint Helena. In the 1890s and early 1900s, there were more serious epidemics reported in Scandinavia, Massachusetts, and Vermont, and then the great New York epidemic of 1916 occurred with over 9,000 cases in the city itself. Almost all the patients in the New York epidemic were under 5 years of age, and 2 percent of the children aged 2 years were affected. After this, polio cases in the United States fell to a low level, then showed peaks and troughs, and rose again to an annual average of some 40,000 cases from 1951 to 1955. As Figure VIII.110.3 shows, polio research accompanied these peaks and troughs.

After 1955, with the widespread use of the IPV in the United States, Canada, South Africa, Australia, and some countries in Europe, the number of cases fell dramatically. As not all children were immunized, small epidemics still occurred among the poor living in substandard conditions. But soon almost all the countries in temperate climates were using polio vaccine, and the potency of the vaccine was improved. Nonetheless, by 1960 in the United States in particular, there were doubts that IPV would eliminate polio.

By the end of 1960, however, Sabin OPV, given to more than 115 million people in Russia and Eastern Europe, had almost completely eliminated polio there. Gradually, opinion swung toward the routine use of the OPV instead of IPV, although Scandinavia and Holland continued to use IPV.

With these exceptions, beginning in 1961, OPV was increasingly used in countries with the most temperate climate, and the number of polio cases fell to even lower levels, although there were still small epidemics where wild virus struck communities that refused immunization or were not receiving primary health care. In the United States there are now about 10 cases a year, roughly half of which are vaccine-associated in vaccines or their contacts, or in hypogammaglobulinemic children.

In Holland, by contrast, there is a large community that rejects immunizations on religious grounds, and thus these people have suffered eight epidemics since 1960. The disease has not, however, spread to the immunized population. The last epidemic, which occurred in 1978, produced 110 cases of which 79 were paralytic (one baby died) and as a result of which the virus was carried to Canada. There were cases in Alberta, British Columbia, and Ontario, from which it was carried to Pennsylvania, and then to Iowa, Wisconsin, and Missouri, and then back to Canada, causing 21 cases and three nonparalytic attacks in North America. Genomic sequencing of virus isolates from this epidemic confirms that the same virus was involved for over 15 months and on two continents and that it may well have come from Turkey originally.

Polio was previously thought to have been of very low incidence in developing countries, although the disease occurred in such diverse and remote places as Saint Helena, isolated Greenland villages, and Nauru in the southern Pacific, which suffered very severe epidemics. Individual cases in undeveloped countries were noted especially among older Europeans, but it was assumed that almost all infants were infected while still protected by maternal antibodies, and that very few developed paralysis. Despite an outbreak among New Zealand troops in Egypt in 1941 and, during the next few years, among British and U.S. servicemen in the Middle and Far East and India, little attention was paid to the disease, the epidemics in Singapore, the Andaman Islands, and Bombay not withstanding.

Early data from developing countries were based on acute admissions to hospitals and, consequently, seriously underestimate the true number of cases. Indeed, even in the mid-1980s, statistics sent to the World Health Organization (WHO) from individual countries may represent only 10 percent of the true number of the cases. In 1977, by way of illustration, in Nigeria more children attended one physiotherapy clinic than the officially notified number of polio cases for that year for the entire country. A truer estimate of cases can be made by lameness surveys of children in schools supplemented by searches of villages for children so disabled that they do not attend school. Unfortunately, such investigations are always out of date, and do not include those who died of polio. It seems likely that the deaths among girls with polio may be quite high in communities where girls are not as highly regarded as boys.

Moreover, case-fatality rates for polio in developing countries are usually based on admission to hospitals and may therefore grossly distort those rates, as only the more serious cases reach those hospitals. Reporting polio cases as an incidence per 100,000 population can also be misleading, as the proportion of children in the population can differ considerably from country to country. The prevalence, based on the total number of cases by the age of 5 years (Figure VIII.110.4), is a better statistic for developing countries.

Even when data on all hospital cases are collected in developing countries, only about half of the cases are found. Up to 10 percent of these cases occur in babies under 6 months, although few studies are this specific (Figure VIII.110.4). Because they will have already had many infections, adults can be expected to have a high level of protective antibodies which mothers should pass on to their babies. Nonetheless, despite repeated infections, pregnant women may still have very low levels of antibodies, and consequently, about 20 to 40 percent of all polio cases occur before the first birthday. For immunization to be effective, all children must be immune by 6 months of age. As Figure VIII.110.4 indicates, giving vaccine to individual children over 1 year is wasteful, and resources should be targeted for the youngest age possible.

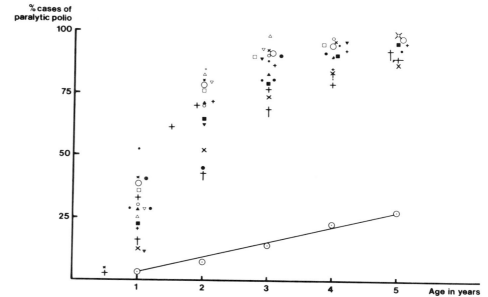

Figure VIII.110.4. Age of onset of cases of poliomyelitis in developing countries, compared with Miami, Florida, United States, 1948–9 (lower points and line). Remaining symbols represent data from samples: Africa (11), India (4), Malta (1), and Singapore (1). (Author's compilation.)

OPV can be given at birth but is more usually given at intervals some time after. The WHO has set up the Expanded Programme on Immunization (EPI), and Rotary International, Save the Children, and UNICEF are also involved in immunization projects. Thus, by June 1987, WHO estimated that 45 percent of children under 1 year in developing countries (excluding China) had received three doses of vaccine.

Very promising programs are underway in South America; and Argentina, Brazil, Chile, Costa Rica, Cuba, Nicaragua, and Paraguay have programs that reach more than 80 percent of their children below 1 year of age.

In Central Africa, by contrast, few countries achieve a 50 percent immunization rate of children under 1 year of age. Similarly, India, with 22 million children born each year, immunizes less than half, and many lameness surveys show a rising prevalence among older children in the 5- to 10-year age group, despite increased use of vaccine during the period. Indeed, in India, surveys of all kinds since 1945 have revealed a steady increase in prevalence. This increase may reflect better reporting and investigation or could be due to the widespread use of unsterile syringes and injections causing provocation polio.

The pattern of muscle paralysis in children in Nigeria is consistent with provocation after injections in the two large muscles. Many children with polio have a history of injections in the paralyzed muscles.

H. V. Wyatt

Bibliography

Bodian, David. 1976. Poliomyelitis and the sources of useful knowledge. *Johns Hopkins Medical Journal* 138: 130–6.

Enders, John Franklin. 1949. Cultivation of the Lansing strain of poliomyelitis virus in cultures of various human embryonic tissues. *Science* 109: 85–7.

Flexner, Simon, and Paul A. Lewis. 1910. Experimental poliomyelitis in monkeys: Active immunization and passive serum protection. *Journal of the American Medical Association* 54: 1780–2.

Hedley, O. F. 1940. *Public Health Reports* 55: 1647–91.

Koprowski, Hilary, et al. 1952. Immune responses in human volunteers upon oral administration of a rodent-adapted strain of poliomyelitis virus. *American Journal of Hygiene* 55: 108–26.

Lambert, A. 1920. Acute rheumatic fever. *Journal of the American Medical Association* 74: 993–5.

Paul, John R. 1971. *A history of poliomyelitis.* New Haven.

Sabin, Albert B. 1955. Characteristics and genetic potentialities of experimentally produced and naturally occurring variants of poliomyelitis virus. *Annals of the New York Academy of Sciences* 61: 924–38.

Sabin, Albert B., and Peter K. Olitsky. 1936. Cultivation of poliomyelitis virus in vitro in human embryonic nervous tissue. *Proceedings of the Society for Experimental Biology and Medicine* 34: 357–9.

Salk, Jonas E., et al. 1953. Studies in human subjects on active immunization against poliomyelitis. I. A preliminary report of experiments in progress. *Journal of the American Medical Association* 151: 1081–98.

Underwood, Michael. 1789. *Treatise on the diseases of children.* London.

Wickman, Ivan. 1913. *Acute poliomyelitis.* Nervous and mental diseases monograph series No. 16. New York.

World Health Organization. 1955. *Poliomyelitis*. Monograph series No. 26. Geneva.

Wyatt, Harold V. 1973a. Hypogammaglobulinemia and poliomyelitis. *Journal of Infectious Diseases* 128: 802–6.

  1973b. Is polio a model for consumer research? *Nature* 241: 247–9.

  1975a. Is poliomyelitis a genetically-determined disease? I. A genetic model. *Medical Hypotheses* 1: 23–32.

  1975b. Is poliomyelitis a genetically-determined disease? II. A critical examination of the epidemiological data. *Medical Hypotheses* 1: 35–42.

  1975c. Risk of live poliovirus in immunodeficient children. *Journal of Pediatrics* 87: 52–3.

  1976a. Is poliomyelitis an auto-allergic disease triggered by virus? *Medical Hypotheses* 2: 262–8.

  1976b. Provocation poliomyelitis and entry of poliovirus to the CNS. *Medical Hypotheses* 2: 269–74.

  1978a. Abortive poliomyelitis or minor illness as a clue to genetic susceptibility. *Medical Microbiology and Immunology* 166: 37–42.

  1978b. Polio immunization: Benefits and risks. *Journal of Family Practice* 7: 469–74.

  1979. Poliomyelitis in the fetus and the newborn. A comment on the new understanding of the pathogenesis. *Clinical Pediatrics* 18: 33–8.

  1981. Provocation poliomyelitis: Neglected clinical observations from 1914 to 1950. *Bulletin of the History of Medicine* 55: 543–57.

  1984. The popularity of injections in the Third World: Origins and consequences. *Social Science and Medicine* 19: 911–15.

  1985. Provocation of poliomyelitis by multiple injections. *Transactions of the Royal Society for Tropical Medicine and Hygiene* 79: 355–8.

  1989. Poliomyelitis in developing countries: Lower limb paralysis and injections. *Transactions of the Royal Society for Tropical Medicine and Hygiene* 83: 545–9.

  1990. Incubation of poliomyelitis as calculated from the time of entry into the central nervous system via the peripheral nerve pathways. *Reviews of Infectious Diseases* 12: 547–56.

VIII.111
Protein–Energy Malnutrition

Protein–energy malnutrition (PEM) or, as it is still sometimes called, *protein–calorie malnutrition* (PCM), is a term of convenience that refers to a range of syndromes among infants and children of preschool age in whom manifestations of growth failure occur because of protein and energy deficiencies. In most instances this condition besets those in the less developed world of Asia, Africa, and Latin America, where dietary factors are thought to be a crucial part of the etiology. PEM thereby tends to exclude what is conventionally known as "failure to thrive" in Europe and North America, in which the vast majority of cases result from organic disorders such as cystic fibrosis or congenital heart disease problems and are not so directly associated with diet as such.

PEM is best described in its two clinical versions of *kwashiorkor* and *marasmus*. In the former, edema is always present, whereas extreme wasting (commonly defined as below 60 percent that of normal weight for height) identifies the latter. Much of the research in the 1950s and 1960s focused on differentiating between the symptoms and etiologies of kwashiorkor and marasmus, but since then it has become evident that cases purely of one or the other are the exception rather than the rule. The majority display both edema and extreme wasting, plus a variable mix of other symptoms, that have earned them the rather inelegant designation of *marasmic kwashiorkor*. In addition, far more common than all of the three put together are numerous subclinical syndromes, usually referred to as mild-to-moderate PEM. A frequent analogy for PEM, therefore, is an iceberg; only a very small proportion of the total is clearly visible. Most cases remain below the surface and go undetected except under close analysis.

Numerous attempts have been made to develop a logically ordered, comprehensive classification of PEM, but several problems have prevented the achievement of one that satisfies the demands of both clinicians and field workers. A particular dilemma is that the various syndromes are not static. Mild-to-moderate cases fluctuate considerably and can move in the direction of kwashiorkor, marasmus, or marasmic kwashiorkor in ways that remain unclear. Also, once established, the clinical conditions do not always stay constant until they are resolved. Kwashiorkor can become marasmus, and vice versa.

Another problem is what to measure, especially in the subclinical stages. Biochemical tests are expensive to perform, and in any event, they have not proved to be very reliable discriminators. As a result, anthropometric characteristics are relied upon. The simplest such indicator, and longest in use, is that of *weight-for-age,* a measurement that gives a reasonably good picture of current nutritional status, assuming, of course, that age is known accurately, which all too often is not the case. More critically, weight-for-age fails to differentiate between chronic and acute malnutrition. Because of these liabilities, the tendency today is to try to combine *weight-for-height,* which measures the degree of wasting, and thus the presence of acute malnutrition, with *height-for-age,* an indicator of stunting or chronic malnutrition. Other measures that have frequently been used in the field such as head and upper arm circumference and skin fold thicknesses add nothing to clarify the picture. They simply indicate if malnutrition is present but do not help in specifying the type.

Overriding the issue of anthropometric classification are the growth standards employed. Those in longest use were derived from studies of middle-class white Americans and are known as either the Harvard or Boston standards. More recently these have been superseded in international comparisons by those developed at the U.S. National Center for Health Statistics (USNCHS) based on a larger sample that cuts across ethnic and socioeconomic groupings. Most authorities tend to accept the position that with proper nourishment and general good health there are no significant human differences in infant and child growth patterns. However, some, especially in India, argue that there are differences, and that by using growth standards based on children of predominantly European ethnic backgrounds, a serious overestimation of malnutrition in many other parts of the world results. In point of fact, the issue of differential growth is still unresolved. Until it is, the safest procedure is probably to accept the USNCHS standards, while remembering that these are designed for comparative purposes only and do not necessarily represent growth objectives that should be sought for each and every population.

Etiology

Traditional interpretations have stressed the predominant role of diet in the etiology of PEM, with protein singled out as the most important missing ingredient. Critical shortages of protein alone, it was believed, would lead to kwashiorkor, and when these were combined with severe energy deficits, created by famine or other food crises, either marasmus or marasmic kwashiorkor would result. Mild-to-moderate syndromes simply reflected lesser shortages of the two essential dietary requirements, protein and calories.

Beyond food supplies, the behavioral variables deemed most critical in the past appeared to be the duration of breastfeeding and subsequent food habits. Too early weaning onto poor-quality substitutes for mother's milk such as rice water, sugar water, diluted milk or formula, and corn starch mixtures, was associated with marasmus. These substances are often contaminated with bacteria because of polluted water supplies and unsanitary preparation and cooking utensils, and consequently, repeated bouts of diarrhea were seen to accentuate the nutritional shortages. In addition, many cultures use starvation to treat diarrhea, a therapy that has further negative repercussions for the victim. Later-aged weaning onto predominantly bulky carbohydrate–low amino acid foodstuffs, notably cassava and plantains, was seen as the pathway to kwashiorkor. Abrupt weaning was believed to be especially hazardous, particularly if the child had to compete for food from a "common pot" with older siblings and adult males who often monopolize the high-quality protein foods such as meat, fish, eggs, and milk. With kwashiorkor the problem was the balance of protein and energy, not the quantity of food consumed, which generally appeared ample.

This portrayal has proved to be not so much erroneous as somewhat oversimplified. Clinical research has verified that kwashiorkor is always associated with low serum proteins, but considerable variation has been found in energy intake. Some cases show deficits, whereas in others energy levels are adequate and occasionally even excessive. Protein deficiency is clearly quite secondary to energy deficiency in marasmus and, in all probability, marasmic kwashiorkor. Indeed, if energy was not so severely restricted, it is unlikely that signs of protein shortages would be observable.

An extremely important finding is that diet does not seem to play quite the overarching role in PEM that was initially believed. What is critical is the availability of nutrients to the cells, and thus infections can act as an equal if not more important limiting factor. Included in these infections are not only the various diarrhea-producing gastrointestinal disorders, but also such widespread childhood diseases as pneumonia, measles, tuberculosis, and malaria. All can initiate symptoms of PEM by inducing anorexia and by lowering amino acid levels, and it is clear that malnourished children are more susceptible to serious episodes of infection. The various syndromes of PEM, therefore, are best construed as resulting from complex nutrition–infection interactions. Based on current knowledge, it would appear that how they develop depends on how the life history of a child unfolds within a particular environmental context.

Many cases undoubtedly begin in the uterus. Because of widespread maternal malnutrition, low birthweights are common throughout Asia, Africa, and Latin America. Breastfeeding on demand during the first 4 to 6 months of life tends to compensate for any fetal growth deficit, while at the same time providing important disease immunities, but those infants who are not so fortunate as to be breastfed are well along a pathway to some PEM syndrome. If a serious infection should ensue at this time, then symptoms of marasmus might very likely develop. If not, then at the least, growth failure will continue, and the child will remain at risk.

After about the first half year of life, breastfeeding alone no longer provides adequate nutrition, and it is now that many children often begin to show signs of mild-to-moderate PEM. Food supplies might be limited generally, or perhaps there is little knowledge of proper supplements. In any event, the course PEM takes will depend on the severity of the food shortage – a "hungry season" seems to be especially dangerous – and once again on the infections to which the child is exposed. When nutrition–infection stress is extreme, then overt clinical symptoms of PEM can be expected.

Weaning is frequently a time of stress, and, when it occurs after 18 to 24 months of age, symptoms of kwashiorkor tend to predominate over those of marasmus, assuming that there is not a gross deficiency of energy in the new diet. However, weaning by itself does not appear to produce kwashiorkor; this is true even if the staple foods are overwhelmingly of the starchy variety. The child must enter this stage of life already nutritionally disadvantaged or otherwise in poor health before discernible symptoms of kwashiorkor emerge. Some analysts refer to a "prekwashiorkor state," but how such a state differs from other mild-to-moderate syndromes has not been demonstrated.

The overriding etiologic issue, of course, is poverty, and PEM is a problem only where poverty is pervasive. Poverty means that local food shortages cannot be overcome by purchases, that living conditions will foster recurring infections, that education

for effective intervention will be inadequate, that proper parental supervision of the feeding of infants and young children is likely to be missing, and that preventive and curative health services will not be readily available. In a very real sense, then, PEM is the outcome of "total deprivation." An acceptance of this fact has led to recent shifts in policies designed to combat it. For many years emphasis was placed on providing protein-fortified and energy-rich food substitutes or developing meat and dairy industries, but these approaches have proven to be too costly for most people in need, and they address only a small part of the problem. PEM must be attacked on a broad front, including economic and political as well as nutritional intervention.

Clinical Manifestations and Pathology

In the earliest stages of PEM, the child simply appears smaller than he or she should be for that age. If the condition deteriorates further, however, clinical symptoms will begin to emerge. Although the mix is likely to be complex, for ease of description the symptoms are still best portrayed as those characterstics of either kwashiorkor or marasmus.

The edema that defines all cases of kwashiorkor varies. It can be mild and localized on the extremities and sacrum or more severe and general. Although muscle wasting is discernible, subcutaneous fat is usually retained, and consequently the child takes on a bloated appearance, known as the "sugar baby" look in the West Indies. There also tends to be some growth retardation in head length and circumference.

More often than not there are skin changes, including ulcerating areas, open and healed sores, scabies, and a condition known as "flaky-paint dermatosis," in which removal of the flakes reveals lighter patches of skin. When kwashiorkor persists, the hair begins to be affected; it loses its luster, and dark hair becomes lighter. Curly hair straightens, and eventually the hair becomes brittle and falls out, leaving bare areas of scalp clearly visible.

Upon examination, the liver and spleen frequently are found to be enlarged, and a range of other symptoms have been documented. Among the more common are anemia and vitamin A deficiency, with some vision impairment, a range of micronutrient deficiencies, plus tendencies to hypothermia, higher bilirubin, hyponatremia, hypoglycemia, and very low plasma albumin.

Behavioral changes are quite marked. Vomiting and diarrhea become persistent; without resolution, anorexia usually sets in. As the child's strength wanes, motor skills regress, and eventually he or she becomes almost totally apathetic to external stimuli. It is as if the burden of life has become too great to bear. Because of this withdrawal, treatment is difficult outside of a clinical setting where the child can be fed intravenously.

The overt symptoms of classical marasmus are far fewer and less medically unusual. There is extreme wasting of both muscles and subcutaneous tissues, and stunting is quite marked. Because the victim is so emaciated, the head appears abnormally large, especially the eyes. The skin tends to be dry and patchy, but dermatosis is not seen, nor are there any significant hair changes. Anorexia is uncommon, and, in fact, the appetite is usually good, which helps to simplify therapy. As in kwashiorkor, there is likely to be hypothermia and a tendency to hypoglycemia. Dehydration is a problem as marasmus worsens, and behavior changes from being fretful and highly irritable to a semicomatose state that immediately precedes death.

With severe PEM, mortality is high – over 20 percent. It is seldom, however, that starvation is the final cause of death; rather it is one or more of the infections that brought on the condition, and these usually run their fatal course in just a few days. Although there is some debate among authorities, the onset of hypothermia and hypoglycemia probably signals the need for immediate treatment.

For those children who have suffered mild-to-moderate PEM or who have recovered from one of the clinical syndromes, the question of long-term effects remains. The available evidence does support a relationship between chronic PEM and some permanent stunting, but this by itself cannot be considered a serious impairment to performance later in life. Indeed, stunting can be viewed as an adaptation to food shortages that conserves energy supplies. Nevertheless, there is one possible impact on skeletal development that does have serious repercussions. In areas where chronic PEM is prevalent, there also appears to be a high incidence of cephalopelvic disproportion among women, a condition that leads to birth difficulties, notably miscarriages, stillbirths, and heightened maternal mortality. The theory is that PEM somehow interferes with calcium metabolism, thereby producing incomplete pelvic development, but this has yet to be proven conclusively. Although the data are even less adequate, there is also some suggestion that later-aged cardiovascular, liver, and pancreas diseases might somehow be connected with childhood PEM.

The issue that has stimulated the most interest and controversy, however, is the effect of PEM on the brain. A considerable amount of research has shown that subnormal mental and psychomotor functioning tends to follow PEM, and during the 1960s and 1970s it was common for direct causal connections to be made. Some investigators even hypothesized that severe attacks of PEM resulted in permanent mental disabilities. But once again important reassessments have been forthcoming. The earlier tests generally failed to control for the learning environment of their subjects, and thus to sort out all the other factors that might be contributing to poor performance, such as reduced mother–child interaction and a lack of stimulating surroundings upon which the child could act in order to learn. This illustrates yet another dimension of the "total deprivation" that surrounds PEM. Currently, the prevailing view is that neither mild-to-moderate nor acute clinical PEM seems to be associated with long-term intellectual and psychological disabilities, assuming, of course, that the necessary social interventions are made. The matter of permanent injury caused by chronic PEM, notably of the marasmic variety during the first year of life, however, remains unresolved. There may very well be irreversible brain damage in the more serious of these cases, as is strongly suggested by research on laboratory animals.

History and Geography

In one form or another, PEM is undoubtedly as old as humankind, and indeed, the term marasmus has been used to refer to starvation for centuries. However, other than implying its incidence on the basis of reported past famines and general living conditions, the medical literature fails to mention PEM specifically until about the middle of the nineteenth century. It was around this time that concepts of malnutrition were beginning to develop, most notably among the new pediatric specialists in France and Germany, who were treating the numerous serious health problems of childhood, especially illnesses seen among foundlings and infants sent out to wet-nurse. One disorder, in particular, began to receive considerable attention. Known as *mehlnährschaden,* it was attributed to diets that were based excessively on flour, usually breads or thin gruels, with little milk or meat included.

At the same time, in the wake of colonial expansion, doctors in the field began to send back reports of a similar disorder from many tropical areas. Although the disease was initially thought to be caused by parasites (as virtually all diseases of the tropics were thought to be in the early days of diagnosis), by the 1920s a dietary etiology began to gain some acceptance. A proliferation of terms ensued, the more common being infantile pellagra, nutritional edema, infantile edema, starchy dystrophy, and fatty-liver disease. These were all describing, of course, what is now known as kwashiorkor, a term that was first used by Cecily Williams in the 1931–2 *Annual Medical Report of the Gold Coast* (now Ghana). She took the term from the local Ga language, in which it designates an ill child who has been "deposed" from the breast because of a new pregnancy.

Although terminological and etiologic arguments continued, by the 1950s the concept of kwashiorkor had become firmly entrenched in the nutrition literature and accepted by the medical community as a certifiable human disease resulting from a deficiency of protein. Continuing research into its causes and consequences led to the discovery of other syndromes and to the formulation of the more general concept of protein–calorie malnutrition. The word "calorie," however, was subsequently replaced by "energy" in the early 1970s when the international system of unit measures was adopted by the United Nations.

Some analysts argue that too much attention has been paid to kwashiorkor. They feel that researchers' obsession with this condition has diverted attention away from more important PEM problems and, in the process, has led to many inappropriate policy decisions because of a mistaken emphasis placed on the limiting role of protein. But a more plausible argument can be made that far less would be known about PEM today had it not been for the efforts expended on kwashiorkor. It provided the important first entry into the maze that PEM is now understood to be. In time, we hope, the full maze will eventually be mapped.

Distribution

At one time the general geography of PEM seemed straightforward. Kwashiorkor existed in the year-round wet tropical forest zones of Asia, Africa, and Latin America, where root and tree crops make up the predominant food staples. By contrast, marasmus was found in wet/dry areas because of seasonal or longer shortages of the staple cereal grains. Marasmus also predominated in the cities as a result of the substitution of bottlefeeding for breastfeeding. Changing etiologic knowledge has put this neat generalization to rest, and, in point of fact, little can be said about the precise distribution of PEM. Field surveys are limited in number, and many of them are of small sample size. Additionally, studies are difficult

to compare because of temporal differences and differences in measurements. About the best that can be done with the data at hand is to portray a rough regional patterning, knowing that there will be many shortcomings and, in the process, hope to identify the main trouble spots. Two recent studies have attempted just such an exercise; one has used the more widely available weight-for-age information, whereas the other has relied upon weight-for-height (wasting) calculations, converting other measures where possible. Both have employed USNCHS growth standards and a variable sample of countries within the parameters of the World Health Organization's regionalization scheme.

What emerges from these two efforts is a focus of PEM in the Southeast Asia region. Some 52 percent of preschool children are estimated to fall below 80 percent of the weight-for-age standard, led by Bangladesh with 91 percent and India with 75 percent. No country in the region shows a prevalence of wasting (defined as greater than 2 standard deviations below the norm) among 12- to 23-month-olds under 10 percent. Once again, Bangladesh and India are at the upper extreme, with 53 percent and 43 percent, respectively.

Both the Africa and Eastern Mediterranean regions show 35 percent deficient by the weight-for-age criteria, and of the countries included in the surveys, only Yemen and Mali stand above 50 percent. Wasting totals are generally in the vicinity of 10 percent, but there are two countries that register exceptionally high totals: Malawi (36 percent) and Somalia (66 percent).

On both measurement scales, the less developed countries in the Americas fare much better. The regional below-weight-for-age average is 21 percent, and all countries except one show a less than 10 percent incidence of wasting. That lone exception is Haiti, where the figure is calculated at 18 percent, still far lower than figures for many places in Asia and Africa.

Limited trend data suggest some lessening of the incidence of PEM since the 1960s, an observation supported by declining infant and child mortality rates. This is true even in Africa, where scenes of famine have created the image of spreading malnutrition. Still, there is little room for complacency, given the magnitude of the problem that remains and the fact that poverty has proved to be intractable in many areas. Certain populations, notably landless rural laborers and the rapidly growing numbers of urban unemployed, seem to be sinking ever deeper into poverty and therefore could well be experiencing an increase in PEM. Also, wars and civil strife provide ideal breeding grounds for PEM. The examples of Ethiopia and Kampuchea are vivid reminders of what can happen in the wake of political turmoil.

James L. Newman

Bibliography

Alleyne, G. A. O., et al. 1977. *Protein–energy malnutrition.* London.

Baxter, K., and J. C. Waterlow. 1985. *Nutritional adaptation in man.* London.

Bhandari, B., and S. L. Mandowara. 1982. Does grading of PEM with reference to the Harvard standard need a change? *Indian Journal of Pediatrics* 49: 161–6.

Bhattacharyya, A. K. 1986. Protein–energy malnutrition (kwashiorkor–marasmus syndrome): Terminology, classification and evolution. *World Review of Nutrition and Dietetics* 47: 80–133.

Diener, P. 1980. Meat, markets, and mechanical materialism: The great protein fiasco in anthropology. *Dialectical Anthropology* 5: 171–92.

Greene, L. S., ed. 1977. *Malnutrition, behavior, and social organization.* New York.

Haaga, J., et al. 1985. An estimate of the prevalence of child malnutrition in developing countries. *World Health Statistics Quarterly* 38: 331–47.

Keller, W., and C. M. Fillmore. 1983. Prevalence of protein–energy malnutrition. *World Health Statistics Quarterly* 36: 129–67.

Kerpel-Fronius, E. 1983. *The pathophysiology of infantile malnutrition, protein–energy malnutrition, and failure to thrive.* Budapest.

Pan American Health Organization. 1984. Global trends in protein–energy malnutrition. *Pan American Health Organization Bulletin* 18: 404–6.

Tomkins, A. M. 1986. Protein–energy malnutrition and risk of infection. *Proceedings of the Nutrition Society* 45: 289–304.

Trowell, H. C., J. N. P. Davies, and R. F. A. Dean. 1954. *Kwashiorkor.* London.

White, P. L., and N. Selvey. 1984. *Malnutrition: Determinants and consequences.* New York.

VIII.112
Protozoan Infections

Protozoa are one-celled animals or animal-like eukaryotic (having an organized nucleus) organisms. Older classifications treated the Protozoa as a phylum in the animal kingdom, but modern taxonomists generally consider them members of a distinct kingdom, the Protista, along with other simple eucaryotes. Three phyla (or classes) of Protozoa have species pathogenic for humankind: (1) The Sarcomastigophora – the flagellates and amebas – include trypanosomes, leishmanias, and parasitic amebas; (2) the Ciliophora – the ciliates – have only one human pathogen – *Balantidium coli*, an intestinal parasite with wide distribution but, usually, little clinical significance; (3) the Apicomplexa – the sporozoans – include many important pathogens, including the four species of *Plasmodium* that cause malaria.

K. David Patterson

VIII.113
Puerperal Fever

Historically the terms *puerperal fever* and *childbed fever* referred to any acute fever occurring in puerperae during the first few days after delivery. Less frequently, the terms were also applied to symptomatically similar diseases that occurred during pregnancy or even among the newborn. From a modern point of view, what was formerly called puerperal fever includes a range of disorders most of which would now be referred to as puerperal sepsis. Typically, puerperal sepsis involves postpartum infection in the pelvic region, but it can refer to disorders focused in other areas, such as mastitis. In modern usage, the term puerperal fever occurs mainly in discussions of the great fever epidemics that afflicted maternity clinics in earlier centuries.

Etiology and Epidemiology

A wide range of aerobic and anaerobic microorganisms have been associated with acute pelvic inflammation and with other postpartum inflammations that could be identified as puerperal fever. Group A streptococci (pyogenes) were probably the leading causal agent in most puerperal fever epidemics in earlier centuries. However, since the 1970s, group B streptococci (agalactiae) have become the most prevalent causal agent.

Clinical Manifestations and Pathology

Among puerperae the clinical manifestations of puerperal sepsis include acute fever, profuse lochial flow, and an enlarged and tender uterus. Onset is generally between 2 and 5 days after delivery. Normally there is inflammation of the endometrium and surrounding structures as well as of the lymphatic and vascular systems. One also finds pelvic cellulitis, septic pelvic thrombophlebitis, peritonitis, and pelvic abscesses. Among neonates, infection usually becomes apparent in the first 5 days after birth, but onset is sometimes delayed by several weeks. Symptoms include lethargy, poor feeding, and abnormal temperature. Infection by group B streptococci is often clinically indistinguishable from other bacterial infections.

History and Geograpy

The Hippocratic corpus contains case histories of puerperal fever. Various epidemics were recorded in the sixteenth and seventeenth centuries. The disease was first characterized and named in the eighteenth century when serious epidemics began to appear with regularity in the large public maternity clinics of Europe. In the late eighteenth and early nineteenth centuries, various English and American obstetricians concluded that puerperal fever was sometimes contagious. Alexander Gordon and Oliver Wendell Holmes argued that physicians could transmit the disease from one patient to another, and they recommended various measures to reduce the frequency of such accidents. By the early nineteenth century, the disease was responsible for a mortality rate of between 5 and 20 percent of maternity patients in most major European hospitals. Smaller hospitals had outbreaks in which, through a period of several months, 70 to 100 percent of maternity patients died from puerperal fever. The etiology of the disease was unclear, although seasonal patterns and its high incidence in the maternity clinics seemed to suggest that it was usually due to a local poison conveyed through the atmosphere. By the middle of the nineteenth century, the disease was receiving a great deal of attention in the medical literature, and cases were being reported from around the world.

In 1847, Ignaz Semmelweis became assistant in the Vienna maternity clinic. The incidence of puerperal fever in the Vienna hospital was about 7 percent, which compared favorably with other hospitals around Europe. However, the Vienna clinic consisted of two divisions, one for obstetricians and the other for midwives; the first division consistently had a mortality rate three to five times greater than the second division. After several months of intensive investigation, Semmelweis concluded that the difference was due to decaying organic matter, usually from autopsied corpses, which was conveyed to patients on the hands of the medical personnel in the first clinic. He introduced washing in a chlorine solution for decontamination, with the result that the mortality rate in the first clinic dropped below that of the second. However, incidence of the disease had always been seasonal, and most obstetricians were unpersuaded.

By 1850 Semmelweis had become convinced that decaying organic matter was responsible for all cases of puerperal fever – even for the relatively few cases that occurred in the second clinic. Indeed, he provided an etiologic characterization of puerperal fever in which it became true by definition that all cases of the disease were due to contamination. Given Semmelweis's definition it also followed trivially that puerperal fever was not a unique disease but only a form of sepsis. Semmelweis had virtually no evidence for this strong position. His critics immediately cited cases in which women died from puerperal fever without ever having been exposed to decaying organic matter. Semmelweis responded that in such cases the decaying matter must have been produced internally, perhaps by the decomposition of blood or of placental fragments. Even the physicians who accepted his initial results rejected this bold and apparently unwarranted claim.

By the 1860s, Louis Pasteur's work on fermentation and putrefaction drew attention to the possible significance of microorganisms in some disease processes. Building on Pasteur's work, and certainly aware of Semmelweis's theories, Carl Mayrhofer examined the vaginal discharges of more than 100 healthy and diseased patients in the Vienna maternity clinic. In 1865 he identified and described various microorganisms that seemed to be present only in discharges from women suffering from puerperal fever.

Using the best techniques that he had available, Mayrhofer isolated these organisms, cultured them in solutions of sugar, ammonia, and water, and then reproduced the disease by introducing the organisms into healthy test animals.

Mayrhofer's work was unimpressive to his colleagues in Vienna, but it received considerable attention in Berlin. Within a few years a number of writers, many of whom explicitly based their work on the discoveries of Semmelweis and of Mayrhofer, were studying the microorganisms that were identified in puerperal fever and in other forms of sepsis. Through the middle decades of the nineteenth century, most of those who wrote on wound infections gave prominent attention to puerperal fever. These included Edwin Klebs, Robert Koch, and Pasteur. In 1879 Pasteur identified the streptococci that were the principal cause of the disease. By this time, it was apparent to most observers that puerperal fever was actually a form of sepsis. In this sense, therefore, puerperal fever ceased to exist as a unique diagnostic or theoretical entity.

Classical studies in the early decades of the twentieth century led to the serologic classification of streptococci and to the recognition that group A strains were the most prevalent agent in puerperal fever. Group B streptococci were first reported in puerperal sepsis in 1935 and recently have displaced the group A strains as the most prominent agents in puerperal sepsis in the United States and Great Britain. Infections of group A streptococci are generally exogenous and affect puerperae, whereas infections of group B pathogens are usually endogenous and, although the mother may be affected, generally strike the fetus or neonate. The change in relative frequency of causal agents, therefore, has had important ramifications in clinical manifestations, prophylaxis, and therapy. The development and use of various antibacterial agents have obviously revolutionized the management of puerperal sepsis. Improved care for delivering mothers has also had an important impact, and in recent years liberalization of abortion laws has reduced the incidence of puerperal sepsis associated with illegal abortions. However, control of sepsis is now recognized to be more difficult and complex than might once have been believed, and it remains a particularly difficult problem in Third World countries where medical care is not readily available. Therefore, although the incidence of puerperal sepsis has been drastically reduced, taken collectively the various forms of this disorder continue to be a leading cause of maternal and neonatal death throughout the world.

K. Codell Carter

Bibliography

Carter, K. Codell. 1985. Ignaz Semmelweis, Carl Mayrhofer, and the rise of germ theory. *Medical History* 29: 33–53.

Charles, David, and Bryan Larsen. 1986. Streptococcal puerperal sepsis and obstetric infections: A historical perspective. *Reviews of Infectious Diseases* 8: 411–22.

Eickhoff, Theodore C., et al. 1964. Neonatal sepsis and other infections due to group B beta-hemolytic streptococci. *New England Journal of Medicine* 271: 1245–7.

Lancefield, Rebecca Craighill. 1933. A serological differentiation of human and other groups of hemolytic streptococci. *Journal of Experimental Medicine* 57: 571–95.

Mayrhofer, Carl. 1865. Zur Frage nach der Aetiologie der Puerperalprozesse. *Monatsschrift für Geburtskunde und Frauenkrankheiten* 25: 112–34.

Pasteur, Louis. 1880. De l'extension de la théorie des germes à l'étiologie de quelques maladies communes. *Comptes rendus hebdomadaires des séances de l'Académie des Sciences* 90: 1033–44.

Peckham, C. H. 1935. A brief history of puerperal infection. *Bulletin for the History of Medicine* 3: 187–212.

Russell, J. K. 1983. *Maternal mortality in obstetrical epidemiology*, ed. S. L. Barron and A. M. Thomson. London.

Semmelweis, Ignaz. 1983. *The etiology, concept and prophylaxis of childbed fever*, trans. K. Codell Carter. Madison, Wis. (Originally published in German in 1861.)

VIII.114

Q Fever

The "Q" in Q fever stands for "query," the designation applied by E. H. Derrick to an acute illness with fever and severe headache of unknown cause occurring in abattoir workers and dairy farmers in Queensland, Australia, in 1935. Despite the discovery of the causative agent, a rickettsia-like organism, this unenlightening name has remained current, although an alternative is abattoir fever. Q fever, occurring in epidemics in military personnel stationed in the Balkans and Italy during World War II, was known as *Balkan influenza* or *Balkan grippe*.

Q fever is caused by infection with *Coxiella burnetii*, previously known as *Rickettsia burnetii*, and is the sole member of the genus *Coxiella*, family Rickettsiaceae. It was initially confused with viruses, but though *C. burnetii* is an obligate intracellular parasite, it has a true bacterial cell wall.

Q fever is a zoonosis of worldwide distribution, and many species of animals, birds, ticks, and other biting insects are natural hosts. In animals, naturally acquired infection appears to be asymptomatic so that Q fever is not of any economic significance to farmers. Transmission to humans occurs via inhalation of contaminated dust while infected animals, carcasses, or animal products are being handled; via laboratory accidents; and sometimes via tick bite and the consumption of unpasteurized milk. Asymptomatic infection is common. Illness may take two forms. *Acute* Q fever is usually a self-limiting febrile flulike illness or atypical pneumonia lasting up to 4 weeks. Untreated, the fatality rate is less than 1 percent. *Chronic* Q fever may develop months to years later, presenting as endocarditis and/or hepatitis. Endocarditis usually occurs in those with preexisting heart valve disease; untreated, it is usually fatal.

Distribution and Incidence

The distribution of acute Q fever is worldwide, but chronic Q fever appears to be more limited, most cases being reported from the United Kingdom, Australia, and Ireland. In the United Kingdom, *Coxiella* infection accounted for 3 percent of all cases of endocarditis reported by laboratories during 1975–81. In other countries, it is still rare enough for individual cases to be reported in the medical literature. This anomaly may be due to underdiagnosis in most countries or perhaps to differences in the virulence of prevalent strains. Acute Q fever affects predominantly adult men, and there is a well-recognized association with certain occupational groups such as farmers, abattoir workers, and veterinarians. Q fever often occurs in seasonal spring and autumn peaks associated with lambing and calving.

It is certain that Q fever is very considerably underdiagnosed so that accurate national incidence figures are not available. In the United States by 1960, Q fever was recognized to be endemic in dairy herds throughout the country. Reports of human cases were uncommon but increased steadily from 1948 to 1977. Over this period, 1,164 cases were reported to the Centers for Disease Control. Although most states reported cases, fully 67 percent of them were from California, where there is a very high prevalence of infection in cattle and consequently a high proportion of cattle excreting organisms in milk. Reported infection in humans, however, is relatively rare, with only 148 being reported from 1970 to 1978. Seroprevalence surveys of cattle in the United Kingdom suggest that about 3 to 5 percent of dairy cattle and 2 to 6 percent of sheep have been infected. About 100 to 200 cases are reported by laboratories each year, and 10 percent of these are chronic infections.

Epidemiology and Etiology

Coxiellae differ from other rickettsiae in not needing an arthropod vector for transmission. Two cycles of natural infection have been recognized. In the wildlife cycle, transmission between wild animals and birds occurs from tick bites, from inhalation of dust, and, possibly in carnivores, from ingestion of infected placentas and meat. Ticks are infected from the blood of an infected host, but transovarial spread has also been documented. Coxiellae multiply in the tick gut and salivary gland, and transmission occurs by biting or when tick feces contaminate broken skin. In the domestic animal cycle and in human infection, tickborne infection is considered less important, and transmission occurs usually from inhalation of contaminated dust and possibly from direct contact with infected animals. Cows, sheep, and goats are the main reservoirs for human infection. In these animals, coxiellae localize in the genital tract and udder and are excreted in vast numbers in milk, birth fluids, and placentas without usually causing disease or a drop in milk yield in cows, although abortion may occur in sheep and goats. Recent investigations have implicated rabbits and parturient cats as possible sources of human infection.

Coxiellae are very resistant to environmental conditions, surviving for months or years in dust or animal litter. Experiments have shown that these organisms can survive in 1 percent formalin for 24 hours, on wool for 7 to 9 months at 20°C, in dried blood for at least 6 months at room temperature, and in tick feces for at least 18 months at room temperature; they can also survive temperatures of 63°C for up to 30 minutes. The latter observation is important since it places coxiellae at the border of resistance to high-temperature, brief-interval milk pasteurization. However, there is still dispute about whether symptomatic Q fever can be acquired from drinking contaminated milk, although the prevalence of antibodies is raised in raw milk drinkers. Person-to-person spread has been documented but is very unusual. Laboratory accidents are a serious hazard when working with live organisms, and for this reason routine diagnostic laboratories seldom attempt isolation.

The vast number of organisms excreted by infected animals, the dissemination of the organisms in dust by wind, the hardy nature of the organism, and the low infective dose for humans (said to be one organism) explain a characteristic feature of Q fever – the occurrence of localized, explosive outbreaks often without an obvious source of infection. Moreover, even when the source of infection is identified, such as sheep used in medical research institutions, human cases occur in people only indirectly exposed by being in the vicinity of the animals.

Immunology

The serologic diagnosis of acute, as opposed to chronic, Q fever was considerably helped by the discovery of phase variation in the organism. Coxiellae isolated directly from animals or ticks are in phase 1; in this phase, specific antibodies are induced that are detectable by complement fixation and other serologic tests. When coxiellae are passed serially through chick embryo yolk sacs, phase 2 organisms become predominant. Passage of phase 2 organisms through animals causes the predominant phase to revert to phase 1. It has been found that phase 1 antigen reacts with late convalescent serums from inoculated guinea pigs; and phase 2, with early convalescent serums in guinea pigs.

Within 2 weeks of acute infection in humans, all or most patients will develop IgM, IgG, and IgA antibodies against phase 2 and IgM antibodies against phase 1, detectable by indirect immunofluorescence tests, as well as complement-fixing antibodies to phase 2. The IgM antibody titer declines rapidly after 2 to 3 months. Phase 1 IgG, IgA, and complement-fixing antibodies may be detectable after about 4 weeks, but do not reach high titers unless chronic infection ensues. In chronic Q fever, there are usually high titers of IgG antibodies detectable by immunofluorescence and complement fixation to both phase 1 and 2. However, IgM antibody is either absent or present in very low titers, and there are high titers of IgG to phase 1.

The presence of IgG antibodies is associated with immunity, but cell-mediated immunity is known to be important as well. The phase 1 antigen used in vaccines gives far better protection than phase 2 vaccines. The intradermal skin test using diluted vaccine may be employed to identify patients who are already immune and who are more likely to have hypersensitivity reactions to the vaccine. Vaccination is followed by a rise in phase 1 IgM antibodies and phase 2 IgM, IgG, and complement-fixing antibodies at low levels.

Clinical Manifestations and Pathology

Subclinical infection is common. Only 191 of 415 newly infected persons were symptomatic in an outbreak in Switzerland in 1983, caused when infected sheep were driven from mountain pastures through several villages on the way to market. The clinical features of acute Q fever are shared by several other infectious agents, and diagnosis depends upon serologic confirmation. Illness begins 2 to 4 weeks after exposure, with the incubation period possibly varying with the infecting dose. There is sudden onset of fever, sweating, shivering, rigors, malaise, joint and limb pains, very severe frontal headache, retro-orbital pain and photophobia, and a mild nonproductive cough. Rash is uncommon. Untreated fever usually lasts 1 to 2 weeks, but pneumonia may persist for several weeks. Abnormal liver function tests are usual, but jaundice is less common. More than half of patients show "ground glass" infiltration due to pneumonitis on chest X-ray, even though severe respiratory symptoms are unusual. Rarer complications of acute Q fever are meningoencephalitis, cerebellar ataxia, coma, myocarditis, pericarditis, infiltration of the bone marrow by granulomas leading to bone marrow failure, orchitis, and placentitis. There may be splenomegaly and lymphocytosis.

Liver biopsy reveals small granulomas containing fibrinoid material. In animal models, coxiellae persist for long periods in liver, spleen, and lymph nodes and may multiply in the placenta during pregnancy and so be excreted in vast numbers during parturition. There is some evidence that this may occur also in humans.

Chronic Q fever is usually considered a rare occurrence, particularly, but not exclusively, affecting patients with preexisting aortic or mitral valve malformations or disease and occurring from several months up to many years after acute infection. However, the absence of a history of acute Q fever, preexisting heart valve disease, or exposure to animals and animal products does not exclude the possibility of chronic Q fever. Illness begins as a low-grade fever with night sweats, anemia, joint pains, finger clubbing, heart murmur, and developing heart failure. There is usually hepatosplenomegaly. Coxiellae can be isolated from vegetations on damaged or prosthetic heart valves. Vegetations may embolize. Abnormal liver function tests are usual, and chronic Q fever may sometimes present as chronic liver disease.

Acute Q fever can be treated successfully with tetracyclines, chloramphenicol, and erythromycin, but chronic Q fever is difficult to treat. Prolonged administration of combinations of tetracyclines, rifampicin, lincamycin, clindamycin, and cotrimoxazole have been recommended, but eventually heart valve replacement may be unavoidable. Reinfection of prosthetic valves has been described, possibly occurring as a result of persistent extracardiac infection.

History and Geography

In 1935, an outbreak of a febrile illness among meat workers in Brisbane, Australia, was investigated by E. H. Derrick, director of the Laboratory of Microbiology and Pathology, Queensland Health Department, at the request of the director-general of Health and Medical Services for Queensland. In 1937, Derrick published the first report of a new disease which he called Q fever "until further knowledge should allow a better name." He went on to show that guinea pigs could be infected by inoculating blood or urine from febrile patients, and that extracts of guinea pig liver and spleen could transmit infection to other guinea pigs. In collaboration with Derrick, F. M. Burnet and Mavis Freeman (1937) searched for a virus in extracts of guinea pig liver using animal inoculation experiments and identified a rickettsia-like agent that was called *Rickettsia burnetii*. In the United States, G. E. Davis and H. R. Cox (1938) reported the isolation of an organism from *Dermacentor andersoni* ticks collected at Nine Mile Creek in Montana in 1935, which they called *Rickettsia diaporica* because of the ability of the agent to pass through bacterial filters. It was later proved to be identical with *R. burnetii*. Its infectivity for humans was unhappily demonstrated by laboratory-acquired infections. Cox showed that the Q fever agent differed significantly from other rickettsias, and it has been placed in a separate genus, *Coxiella*.

The most significant aspects of the history of Q fever, following its discovery, were the discovery of the importance of the domestic animal cycle, the recognition of the military significance of Q fever, the high risk for laboratory workers, and the development of vaccines.

In his original paper, Derrick speculated that transmission was due to blood-sucking insects and that the organism had an animal reservoir. He identified the bandicoot as a reservoir of infection. However, the wildlife cycle initially suspected by Derrick has not proved to be a significant source of human infection. The domestic animal cycle is far more important and explained the epidemic of Q fever during and after World War II when thousands of troops in the Balkans and Italy were infected.

The epidemic in question began in southern Yugoslavia in March 1941, and involved more than 600 troops. Further outbreaks occurred in northern Yugoslavia, the Crimea, Greece, the Ukraine, and Corsica. A German physician, H. Dennig (1947), described more than 1,000 cases, half of whom had pneumonia. Risk of illness was associated with sleeping on hay or straw. Further outbreaks in 1942, 1943, and 1944 were noted in German troops exposed to sheep and goat flocks. Following the Allied invasion of Italy, Allied troops shared the Q fever epidemic. From February to March 1945, 511 cases

of atypical pneumonia were admitted to two military hospitals in Naples. Other outbreaks occurred in Italy, Greece, and Corsica.

The military significance of Q fever was now clear. The attack rate among exposed troops was very high and illness was prolonged. For example, of 160 men billeting in a hay barn, 53 (or 33 percent) developed Q fever. Of 900 men on a training exercise, which included sitting in a barn loft to watch training films, 267 (or 30 percent) became ill. From December 1944 to June 1945, more than 1,700 cases were diagnosed in Allied forces. After the war, outbreaks occurred from 1946 to 1956 among Greek and Swiss troops, in 1951 among U.S. servicemen in Libya, and in 1955 among French soldiers in Algeria. The factors contributing to the epidemic among troops were the sudden exposure of susceptible people to infection, particularly by sleeping on straw and hay (the local indigenous population was apparently unaffected by the epidemic), the rapid movement of infected flocks during wartime, and the mixing of infected and uninfected flocks. This was well illustrated in 1974 and 1975 in Cyprus. An outbreak of abortion affected sheep and goats from flocks herded together to escape the Turkish invasion. In a camp near the place where the flocks grazed, 78 British soldiers developed Q fever.

The importance of domestic animals as the reservoir for human infection was further emphasized by outbreaks in the United States, where the first naturally acquired U.S. cases were reported in 1941 in two patients from western Montana who had not received tick bites. In March 1946, 55 of 132 livestock and meat handlers in a plant in Amarillo, Texas, developed Q fever, and two died. In August of the same year, a similar outbreak occurred in Chicago. Further studies revealed sporadic cases, particularly in California. During outbreaks that occurred in 1947, city residents living near dairy farms were infected, probably by dust carried in the wind. In northern California, cases were associated with sheep. *Coxiella* was isolated from cow and sheep milk as well as from air and dust.

Laboratory-acquired infection was one of the earliest problems caused by Q fever. During 1938–55, 22 incidents involving over 250 cases were recorded. In one military institution, 50 cases were recorded during 1950–65. In 1940 an outbreak occurred in the U.S. National Institutes of Health in which 15 workers were infected. In this and other laboratory-associated incidents, infections occurred not only in those directly handling the organism but also in those who worked near or walked through the laboratory buildings, an observation that emphasized the importance of the respiratory route of infection. In the 1970s, attention was drawn to the serious risk of working on infected animals in research institutions, and interest in developing a safer and more effective vaccine was restimulated in the United States. In the 1980s, in both the United States and the United Kingdom, large outbreaks occurred that were associated with operative procedures on pregnant sheep.

The first vaccines for Q fever were developed principally to protect laboratory workers from infection. Used in the late 1940s and early 1950s, they had the drawback of provoking severe local skin reactions. In the 1950s, M. G. P. Stoker and P. Fiset (1956) reported the unique phenomenon of phase variation of *C. burnetii* (see Immunology section), which has proved of great value not only in diagnosing chronic Q fever but also in developing an effective vaccine. The first killed vaccines used were predominantly phase 2 antigens. In the 1970s in Australia, an upsurge of infection in abattoir workers as a result of a high number of feral goats slaughtered for export led to renewed efforts in vaccine development. Vaccines currently undergoing trials in Australia are derived from phase 1 organisms.

Following the original work in Australia, the United States, and the Mediterranean area, many other countries quickly identified cases. The first recorded human case of Q fever in the United Kingdom occurred in 1949, but seroprevalence surveys of domestic animals in 1952 showed infection to be widespread, with about 6 percent of dairy farms and 2 percent of cattle and sheep infected. These were statistics that did not significantly differ from surveys done in the 1970s. By 1953, 23 countries were known to be infected, and further surveys sponsored by the World Health Organization revealed that by 1956, 51 countries in all continents were infected. Only Scandinavia, Ireland, New Zealand, and the Netherlands were said to be free of infection. Since then, in Ireland there is good evidence that infection was introduced through importation of infected sheep from England in the 1960s, with the first indigenous cases being identified, retrospectively, in 1962. Today Q fever is known to be global in distribution, and it is likely that any patchiness in distribution reflects as much the differing levels of awareness of the disease as differences in disease incidence.

S. R. Palmer

Bibliography

American Journal of Hygiene. 1946. Reports. Paper on Q fever. 44: 1–182.

Baca, O. G., and D. Paretsky. 1983. Q fever and *Coxiella burnetii*: A model for host–parasite interactions. *Microbiological Reviews* 47: 127–49.

Burnet, F. M., and M. Freeman. 1937. Experimental studies on the virus of "Q" fever. *Medical Journal of Australia* 2: 299–305.

Burnet, M. 1967. Derrick and the story of Q fever. *Medical Journal of Australia* 54: 1067–8.

Davis, G. E., and H. R. Cox. 1938. A filter-passing infectious agent isolated from ticks. 1. Isolation from *Dermacentor andersoni*, reactions in animals, and filtration experiments. *Public Health Reports* 53: 2259–67.

Dennig, H. 1947. Q fever (Balkan influenza). *Deutsche medizinische Wochenschrift* 72: 369–71.

Derrick, E. H. 1937. Q fever, a new fever entity: Clinical features, diagnosis and laboratory investigation. *Medical Journal of Australia* 2: 281–99.

Kaplan, M. M., and P. Bertagna. 1955. The geographical distribution of Q fever. *Bulletin of the World Health Organization* 13: 829–60.

Leedom, J. M. 1980. Q fever: An update. In *Current clinical topics in infectious disease*. Vol. I, ed. J. S. Remington and M. N. Swartz, 304–13. New York.

Marmion, B. P. 1967. Development of Q fever vaccines 1937 to 1967. *Medical Journal of Australia* 54: 1074–8.

Palmer, S. R., and Susan Young. 1982. Q fever endocarditis in England and Wales, 1975–81. *Lancet* 2: 1448–9.

Saah, A. J., and R. B. Hornick. 1985. *Coxiella burnetii* (Q fever). In *Principles and practice of infectious diseases,* 2d edition, ed. G. L. Mandell et al., 1088–90. New York.

Spicer, A. J. 1978. Military significance of Q fever: A review. *Journal of the Royal Society of Medicine* 71: 762–7.

Stoker, M. G. P., and P. Fiset. 1956. Phase variation of the Nine Mile and other strains of *Rickettsia burnetii*. *Canadian Journal of Microbiology* 2: 310–21.

Turck, W. P. G., et al. 1976. Chronic Q fever. *Quarterly Journal of Medicine* 45: 193–217.

Worswick, D., and B. P. Marmion. 1985. Antibody responses in acute and chronic Q fever and in subjects vaccinated against Q fever. *Journal of Medical Microbiology* 19: 281–96.

Rabies is an acute viral encephalomyelitis or inflammation of the brain and spinal cord of humans and other mammals, especially carnivores. The disease, known since antiquity, is almost always transmitted to human beings in the saliva of biting animals and is almost invariably fatal. The name *hydrophobia*, "fear of water," and the French term *la rage* illustrate two common symptoms.

Distribution and Incidence

Rabies occurs in most of the world, including Africa, Asia, the Americas, and most of Europe. It has never occurred in, or has been eliminated from, Britain, Ireland, Sweden, Norway, Japan, Australia, New Zealand, Hawaii, and many other islands in the Pacific and the Caribbean. Rabies is primarily a disease of wild carnivores, particularly canids such as the fox, wolf, jackal, and coyote. Skunks and raccoons are also common hosts, as are many species of bats. Virtually any species of mammal can contract the disease when bitten by an infected animal. Domestic dogs are the major threat to humans; cats are a growing danger in North America. Cattle, horses, sheep, and other livestock may also be affected. Outbreaks among farm animals may cause considerable economic loss, but bovine or equine rabies usually poses little danger for humans.

Rabies is a relatively uncommon disease in humans, occurring sporadically as isolated cases or in small clusters. Epizootics develop at irregular intervals in wild carnivores, and may infect humans mainly through dogs or rarely directly. Persons working alone in remote areas, such as hunters, trappers, or shepherds, are vulnerable to attack by infected animals. Wolves are especially dangerous because their size and strength allow them to inflict multiple bites. Most human cases, particularly in developing countries, are acquired by the bites of "mad dogs," which were themselves victims of attacks by feral animals. Vampire bats in Trinidad and parts of northern South America are a source of rabies for cattle and, on rare occasions, human beings. Elsewhere, other species of bats can infect people and terrestrial animals, but this seems to be uncommon.

Human rabies has become a rare disease in developed countries. There were 236 cases in the United States between 1946 and 1965; only 11 occurred after 1960, and no cases at all have been reported in many of the subsequent years. Canada reported only 21 cases from 1924 to 1986, but Mexico recorded 76 fatalities in 1985 and 81 in 1986. In Africa, Ghana confirmed 102 cases from 1977 to 1981, whereas Ethiopia recorded 412 in 1982. India reported the highest annual number of cases in the early 1980s – that is, 20,000 – as well as the highest rate of infection – 28.8 per million individuals.

Etiology

Rabies is caused by a virus of the rhabdovirus group. The virus is a rod-shaped particle with a single strand of RNA for its genetic material. Large concentrations of virus are present in the saliva of sick animals and enter a new host through bite wounds. The virus is neurotrophic; it migrates along nerves to the brain, where it multiplies, causing grave damage manifested in part by behavioral changes in the victim. New viruses descend through efferent nerves to the salivary glands and hence into the saliva.

Epidemiology

Rabies circulates primarily in wild carnivores and only incidentally attacks domestic ones. Canids – notably foxes, wolves, and jackals – are the major reservoir in much of the world, although skunks, raccoons, mongooses, and other carnivores can also be significant hosts. Human beings are accidental and terminal hosts. The spread of rabies in skunks and raccoons, two species that have adapted with great success to suburban habitats, has caused concern in the United States during the 1970s and 1980s, but so far no human cases have been attributed. Opossums, rabbits and hares, rodents, and hoofed mammals can suffer and die from rabies, but they rarely transmit it.

Bats in Europe and the Americas are commonly infected, but, except for the blood-feeding "vampire" bats that plague cattle and even people in the Caribbean and parts of northern South America, their epidemiological significance is unclear. Transmission to humans and other animals is possible, but serologic studies of viral strains in the United States and Canada suggest that bat rabies is largely self-contained. Slightly different area-specific strains are found in terrestrial species in given areas, suggesting, for example, that foxes and skunks exchange a specific viral type. Species of bats in the same region tend to have a greater variety of strains, with none identical to that prevailing in local ground-dwelling animals. High-resolution serologic studies have been possible only since the early

1980s, and much more research will be needed to clarify fully the epizootiology of wildlife rabies.

Wildlife rabies tends to occur in irregular waves, and may spread over thousands of miles in a matter of a few decades. Control of rabies in wild animals by population reduction has generally been unsuccessful, and vaccines for use in wild mammals are still in the experimental stage. Monitoring local reservoir hosts can, however, alert public health authorities to the danger of possible cases among dogs and cats, and provide time to warn people to avoid wild animals and to control and vaccinate their pets. In the United States, where canine rabies has steadily declined for decades, the number of cases in cats began to exceed cases in dogs in 1980. This has resulted in widespread campaigns to vaccinate felines.

Animals may exhibit either "furious rabies," with agitated, aggressive behavoir preceding paralysis and death, or "dumb rabies," where the victim is lethargic and progressively immobile. The classic "mad dog," foaming at the mouth and wandering menacingly in the streets, does exist, but not all sick dogs display such dramatic symptoms. In northern Canada rabid foxes and wolves may become "crazy," wandering about settlements, mingling with sled dogs, and sometimes attacking the dogs or their owners. Normally nocturnal animals like skunks or raccoons may wander through inhabited areas in daytime and exhibit little or no fear of people or other animals. Unfortunately, such abnormal behavior can make small furry creatures seem "tame" and "cute"; many people have had to undergo an expensive series of rabies vaccine shots after handling "friendly" raccoons.

Although infection by virus-laden saliva is the only common way to contact rabies, two other mechanisms have been reported. Inhalation of virus in dust and contamination in surgery are possible, but both are very rare. High concentrations of virus may occur in dust in caves heavily populated by bats, and spelunkers have died of rabies after inhaling the virus. Laboratory inhalation of virus-laden aerosols has also caused infections. Cornea transplants from the cadavers of undiagnosed rabies victims have caused at least two deaths in recipients, but immunologic testing of donors should prevent future incidents.

Pathology and Clinical Manifestations

If infective saliva enters a break in the skin, viruses are carried from the site of the wound through the nerves to the brain. The incubation period of the disease varies from 2 to 16 weeks, depending on the site, severity, and location of the wound, and the size of the viral inoculation. Severe bites on the face and head are the most dangerous and have the shortest incubation periods, because the virus does not have far to travel. Infection results in destruction of cells in several regions of the brain and spinal cord and damage to the myelin sheaths of nerves. Clumps of viruses called Negri bodies are often seen on microscopic examination of affected cells and are useful in diagnosis.

Rabies patients commonly show restless, agitated behavior and hypersensitivity to minor stimuli. They frequently become extremely apprehensive or aggressive shortly after the onset of the disease. Convulsions and excessive salivation are common. Patients often suffer intense thirst, but have severe muscle spasms in the throat when they attempt to drink. This frequently develops into extreme hydrophobia, with the sight or even mention of liquids inducing terror and spasms. Within a few days this "furious" phase is followed by depression, paralysis, and death. The gruesome symptoms and the inevitability of death have made rabies one of the most frightening diseases in any culture where it is known.

There have been a handful of reports of survivors, but even the most intensive supportive care is generally futile, and there are no specific drugs or other therapies. Prevention is the only solution. Vaccinating dogs and cats, controlling strays, monitoring wildlife populations, and education are all essential. A preexposure human vaccine is available for persons at special risk, such as game wardens, veterinarians, and laboratory workers.

Fortunately, persons bitten by a rabid or possibly rabid animal can still be effectively vaccinated before the disease completes its long incubation period. If the biting animal is captured and shown to be rabid, or if it escapes but there are grounds to suspect that it might be rabid, prompt treatment is essential. Careful cleansing of the wound to remove as much virus as possible is followed by a series of injections of a serum (gamma globulin) that contains preformed antibodies to the virus. Human rabies immune globulin (RIG) has replaced an equine preparation in recent years. The key measure, a series of shots with a specific vaccine, is then begun.

The earliest vaccines were developed by Louis Pasteur in the 1880s, using rabbit spinal cord tissue. Preparations from brain tissues of sheep, goats, or mice are still used in some developing countries, but these vaccines are being replaced because they can cause severe allergic reactions. Duck embryo cultures were used to produce vaccine until human diploid cell vaccine (HDCV) was developed in France and the United States in the late 1970s. This vaccine is cheaper and safer, and requires a shorter series of injections. A new, improved vaccine was released in the United States in 1988.

Proper postexposure prophylaxis is very effective, and must be given if there is any reasonable possibility of infection. It is, however, time-consuming and expensive. In the United States, where cases have averaged only one or two per year since 1965, some 20,000 to 30,000 people are treated annually, at a cost of about $400 each. India provided treatment to about 3 million victims of animal bites annually in the early 1980s, whereas El Salvador treated the world's highest rate of 4,570 persons per million population. A World Health Organization survey of 30 developing countries in 1980 showed an average of 3.7 rabies cases and 867 treatments per million population. The costs of rabies in lives, terror, and medical resources are considerable, especially in the Third World.

History

Literature

Rabies is one of the oldest documented diseases of humankind. Rare, but with spectacular symptoms and fatal outcome, it was and is an easily observed disease. Although some cases (particularly when an animal bite was not documented) could be confused with tetanus or with a neurological disorder like epilepsy, rabies cases are generally easy to recognize, even in old accounts.

Antiquity. Rabies may have been described in Mesopotamian texts as early as 2300 B.C., and was well known to ancient writers from China to Rome. The first certain reference in Chinese texts dates from the sixth century B.C., and the disease is described in a first-century Indian text. Rabies is also mentioned in a number of literary works from ancient Greece, including plays by Euripides, Xenophon's *Anabasis,* and perhaps Homer's *Iliad.* Aristotle's fourth-century *History of Animals* describes rabies in dogs and other domestic animals.

Roman medical writers of the first and second centuries, such as Dioscorides, Pliny, Galen, and especially Celsus, wrote extensively on rabies and established a number of ideas about the disease, which were influential in European and Islamic medicine well into the eighteenth century. In accordance with prevailing humoral doctrines, it was believed that dogs (or other animals) developed the disease from a "corruption" of their humors, due to factors such as stress, cold, heat, or poisoning. Their saliva became poisonous, and bites carried the rabies poison or "virus" to humans or other animals. Celsus advocated bloodletting and cauterizing the wound with hot irons, a practice that, although harsh, might at times have cleansed the bite and one that was followed well into the nineteenth century. Celsus also suggested sudden immersion of the victim in hot or cold water, a practice that was also employed, at least sporadically, into the nineteenth century. Like his contemporaries, Celsus described a wide array of internal and external remedies of animal, mineral, and vegetable origins, none of which, based on modern knowledge, could have done any good. Pliny's unfounded belief that a "tongueworm" of dogs was responsible for rabies lasted as long as the ideas of Celsus.

Medieval Period Through the Sixteenth Century. Rabies continued to interest many medical and other writers after the fall of Rome and into the Middle Ages. Jewish authorities wrote about rabies in several passages of the Talmud. Numerous Christian writers in the West and the Byzantine Empire discussed the disease, following the humoral theories of Classical times. Medieval Islamic authorities such as Rhazes in the tenth century and Avicenna (Ibn Sina) in the eleventh century also worked in the Galenic humoral tradition and were strongly influenced by the views of Celsus. Avicenna gave good accounts of rabies in dogs, wolves, foxes, and jackals. He thought that their humors, notably the black bile, were disrupted by heat, cold, or ingesting putrified food or polluted water, resulting in rabies and "mad" behavior.

As in most medical matters, commentators on rabies in medieval western Europe had little to add to the comments of ancient and Islamic writers. In the thirteenth century, Arnold of Villanova wrote wrongly that dogs became rabid after eating corpses, but he did rightly stress the importance of thoroughly washing the bite wounds. Once symptoms of rabies appeared, many persons resorted to religious methods of healing. In much of western Europe, pilgrimages and prayers were directed to the shrine of Saint Hubert (who died in 727), a patron of hunters whose relics were kept in the Ardennes. Other saints were invoked elsewhere in Europe and among the Coptic Christians of Egypt.

Early modern medical authorities had little to add to the works of their predecessors. Girolamo Fracastoro, sometimes hailed as a sixteenth-century forerunner of the formulators of the germ theory, considered rabies one of many diseases caused by "seminaria," something more like a seed or a self-replicating poison than a microorganism. He thought that it affected the heart and advocated cauterization of the wound. The sixteenth-century French surgeon Ambrose Paré gave a good clinical description and recognized central nervous system involvement.

Eighteenth Through Mid-Nineteenth Century. Perhaps because the disease was more common, or perhaps because of the growing volume of medical research and writing in general, the literature on rabies became much more abundant in the eighteenth and early nineteenth centuries. Autopsy studies were done (although without results, as the lesions are microscopic) and many more case reports and epidemiological observations were published. The growth of the literature was especially notable in France, where the Société Royale de Médecine, founded in 1776, took considerable interest in the problem. As of about 1750, many French and other physicians believed in the spontaneous appearance of rabies, possibly because some apparent cases were really tetanus, resulting from puncture wounds rather than animal bites. But within a few decades it was generally recognized that rabies resulted only from bites of rabid animals and that not all such bites, especially bites through clothes, transmitted the disease. Joseph-Ignace Guillotin, the inventor of the execution device popularized during the French Revolution, proposed an experimental approach to therapy. He wanted condemned criminals to be bitten by mad dogs so that clinical trials of various remedies could be conducted on them.

This scheme was not adopted, but some important experiments were undertaken in the 1790s and the first two decades of the 1800s. The prominent English physician John Hunter proposed saliva inoculation experiments in 1793 and in 1799. An Italian investigator, Eusebio Valli, claimed that the "virus" in saliva was made less virulent by gastric juice from frogs. He did not, however, publish his results, and his work seems to have had little impact. The first saliva inoculation experiments are credited to the German investigator Georg Gottfried Zinke, who published in 1804. Zinke, who was aware of Hunter's work and may have been inspired by it, was able to infect dogs, cats, rabbits, and birds; saliva treated with acids was not infective. In 1813 the French researchers François Magendie and Gilbert Breschet infected dogs and several other animals with saliva from a human rabies victim. Such results, repeated and extended by others, discredited the views of some students of mental disease, who believed that rabies was not a physical disease but only the product of terror and imagination.

Nineteenth-century therapy, however, remained a hopeless melange of useless remedies, many inherited from medieval and ancient times. Doctors tried every possible treatment from drugs and purges to electric shock and immersion in the sea. Sedatives were often employed to ease the patient's suffering, and euthanasia may have been practiced.

Late Nineteenth Century. Modern knowledge of rabies etiology and prevention dates from the last half of the nineteenth century and is closely linked to the rise of experimental methodology and germ theory. Rabies was not common enough to be a major public health hazard, but it was spectacular enough to attract a fair amount of research. The work of Pierre-Victor Galtier, a French veterinarian, was especially important. In 1879 he published the results of experiments in which he maintained rabies in a series of rabbits. Galtier continued to publish on rabies, but the development of a vaccine was the climax of the career of another person, Louis Pasteur.

Pasteur published his first paper on rabies in 1881. Working with rabbits as advocated by Galtier, Pasteur was able to use dried spinal cord material as a dependable source of infectious material. By 1884 he had developed a method of attenuating the still unknown agent in dried rabbit spinal cords. The weakened infective agent, suspected by Pasteur of being a "microbe of infinite smallness," was injected into dogs. Unlike fresh preparations, it did not cause sickness, but instead provided protection against injections of virulent virus.

The first human trials were conducted in 1885. Pasteur and his associates could not inject a person with the virus in order to test the vaccine but, rather, had to treat a victim of a recent attack in hopes that the weakened virus in the vaccine would convey immunity before the virulent virus from the bite could cause disease. In July 1885, a 9-year-old boy, who had been badly bitten by a rabid dog, was brought to Paris within 2 days of exposure. Doctors were convinced that he had been infected, and Pasteur knew that the prognosis was hopeless unless the new vaccine was effective. The boy was given a series of injections with progressively fresher rabbit spinal cord vaccine. He lived, and eventually became concierge at the Institut Pasteur. A second victim was treated successfully in October, and 350 others were inoculated over the next several months. Only one died – a girl who did not receive vaccine until over a month after exposure.

The Pasteur treatment was a major theoretical and practical breakthrough. It caused a public sensation, and people bitten by rabid or suspicious animals flocked to Pasteur's laboratory from all over Europe. Success rates were consistently high, especially if vaccine was promptly administered and if wounds were not on the head. Even with a long train ride to delay treatment, 35 of 38 Russians who had been bitten by rabid wolves were saved by injections. The French government promptly began to fund the work of the Institut Pasteur, branches of which were soon established elsewhere in France and its empire as centers of vaccine production and medical research.

Pasteur's associates, notably Emile Roux, and other workers developed methods of vaccine production and treatment. Research suggested a route from the bite through the nerves to the brain, but this was not proven until well into the twentieth century. The etiology of rabies remained a mystery.

Twentieth Century.   In 1903 Adelchi Negri working in Italy discovered microscopic dark bodies in nerve cells of rabid dogs. He thought they were protozoans that caused the disease, but, although this proved erroneous, the Negri bodies were a useful diagnostic sign. Tests with mouse inoculation of suspect tissue, introduced in 1935, and various serologic methods have largely replaced histological examination for Negri bodies as tests for rabies in dogs and other animals.

Although Negri's protozoan theory attracted some attention, the search for the etiologic agent centered around the concept of "filterable viruses" – entities too minute to be retained by filters with pores small enough to hold bacteria. The virus was first seen in 1962; electron microscope studies in 1965 showed that the Negri bodies were clumps of viruses and antibodies.

Epidemics and Epizootics

Rabies epidemics and epizootics are difficult to trace before the twentieth century. In Europe, although there are many case reports, most descriptions are of isolated cases or small outbreaks. In 1271 rabid wolves invaded towns in Franconia (Germany), attacking herds and flocks and killing 30 persons. There was a fox epizootic in Frankfurt in 1563. Rabies seems to have been widespread in western Europe during the eighteenth and nineteenth centuries, possibly because population growth was disturbing the wildlife habitat and causing greater contact between feral mammals and domestic dogs. In 1701 Nancy, France, was beset by canine rabies and enacted laws against stray dogs. Paris responded to rabies cases in 1725 with a leash law, and other European cities followed with similar ordinances. Such restraints, as well as campaigns to rid the streets of strays, were seldom strictly enforced until there was a rabies scare.

A widespread epizootic in 1719–28 involved France, Germany, Silesia, and Hungary, and there also were many animal and human cases in Britain in 1734–5. Rabies was common in the greater London area in 1759–62 and in France, Italy, and Spain in 1763. A major epizootic developed in foxes in the Jura region of France in 1803; this outbreak apparently lasted until the late 1830s and spread over Switzerland and much of Germany and Austria. Outbreaks among wolves, foxes, and dogs continued throughout the century and caused hundreds of human deaths.

Rabies declined in the twentieth century, in wild and domestic animals as well as in humans. The disease was exterminated in Britain in 1922 and became rare throughout western Europe. In the early 1940s, however, a fox epizootic developed in Poland and since then has spread westward at a rate of 30 to 60 kilometers a year, reaching France in 1968. Denmark has defended itself by intensive fox control in a belt of territory near the German border; Britain is still protected by the Channel.

The history of rabies on other continents is little known. Sporadic cases and scattered epidemics occurred in Ethiopia prior to the twentieth century, a pattern that must have been common in other African and Asian countries. Rabies did not exist in Australia or New Zealand prior to English colonization in 1788, and seems to have been absent from the Pacific islands as well.

The antiquity of rabies in the New World is unclear. It is certainly possible that bat rabies existed in pre-Columbian times, and Arctic foxes and wolves could just as possibly have carried the virus from Siberia to Alaska and northern Canada centuries or millennia ago. Eskimo oral traditions suggest that the Eskimos were aware of rabies long before European contact. However, early European sources do not mention rabies among the American fauna, and a Spanish work published in 1579 specifically denied the existence of rabies anywhere in the "Indies." The first accounts of the disease are from Mexico in 1709, Cuba in 1719, Barbados in 1741, Virginia in 1753, North Carolina in 1762, New England in 1768, Jamaica and Hispaniola in 1783, and Peru in 1803. Because rabies is such an obvious disease, at least when it afflicts domestic animals and people, and because it was so well known to both lay and medical observers, the absence of early reports could well indicate that rabies, at least in temperate and tropical America, was a late biological importation from Europe.

Fox rabies was known in the eighteenth century, and the disease was widespread in North American wildlife populations in the nineteenth century. Rabid skunks (hydrophobic or "phobey cats") were described in the Great Plains in the 1830s and in California in the 1850s. Most U.S. cases in the twentieth century have been reported in dogs, but since canine rabies is in decline as a result of vaccination and animal control measures, greater attention has been given to wild animals. Raccoon rabies was first described in 1936, and bat rabies, now recognized in 47 states, was first detected in 1953. An epizootic developed among raccoons in Florida in 1955, and spread slowly northward into Georgia and South Carolina in the 1960s and 1970s. Sportsmen transported infected raccoons from this focus to the Virginia–West Virginia border for hunting in the mid-1970s; and rabies has spread in both states and into Pennsylvania, Maryland, and Washington, D.C. Skunk rabies has been spreading slowly from two foci in the Midwest for several decades, and now extends from Texas and Tennessee to Montana and Manitoba. Fox rabies is widespread in the Appalachians. In Canada, an epizootic was recognized in the far north in 1947, but probably began in the 1930s or earlier. Foxes and wolves are the primary victims, and the epizootic has spread south into Ontario, Quebec, and the northeastern United States.

Wildlife rabies still represents a potential threat to Europeans and North Americans, but vaccination of pets should prevent more than an occasional human case. In developing countries such as Mexico or India, canine rabies is still a real danger, and relatively little attention has been given to wildlife reservoirs of the virus.

K. David Patterson

Bibliography

Baer, George M., ed. 1975. *The natural history of rabies*, 2 vols. New York.

Bögel, K., and E. Motschwiller. 1986. Incidence of rabies and post-exposure treatment in developing countries. *Bulletin of the World Health Organization* 64: 883–7.

Carter, K. Codell. 1982. Nineteenth-century treatments for rabies as reported in the *Lancet. Medical History* 26: 67–78.

Held, Joe R., Erbest Tierkel, and James Steele, 1967. Rabies in man and animals in the United States, 1946–65. *Public Health Reports* 82: 1009–18.

McLean, Robert G. 1970. Wildlife rabies in the United States: Recent history and current concepts. *Journal of Wildlife Diseases* 6: 229–35.

Pankhurst, Rchard. 1970. History and traditional treatment of rabies in Ethiopia. *Medical History* 14: 378–89.

Plummer, P. J. G. 1954. Rabies in Canada, with special reference to wildlife reservoirs. *Bulletin of the World Health Organization* 10: 767–74.

Steele, James H. 1975. History of rabies. In *The natural history of rabies,* ed. George M. Baer, 1–29. New York.

Théodoridés, Jean. 1986. *Histoire de la rage: Cave canem.* Paris.

U.S. Public Health Service. Centers for Disease Control. 1987. *Rabies Surveillance* 1986. *Morbidity and Mortality Weekly Report* 36 (Supplement 3S): 1S–27S.

Wilkinson, Lise. 1977. The development of the virus concept as reflected in corpora of studies on individual pathogens. 4. Rabies – two millennia of ideas and conjecture on the aetiology of a virus disease. *Medical History* 21: 15–31.

VIII.116
Relapsing Fever

Relapsing fever is a disease characterized by the occurrence of one or more relapses after the primary febrile paroxysm has subsided. Various types of relapsing fever are caused by blood parasites of the *Borrelia* group. There are two chief forms of the disease: the *endemic,* transmitted to humans by various ticks of the genus *Ornithodoros,* and maintained among a variety of rodents; and the *epidemic,* caused by a parasitic spirochete, *Borrelia recurrentis,* which is transmitted by human head and body lice. *B. recurrentis* is less virulent than the tick-borne forms. Under favorable conditions, mortality is about 5 percent, but in times of distress, as in war or famine, it can reach 60 to 70 percent.

It is also known as famine fever and tick fever, and in the past as yellow fever, because of associated jaundice. The term "relapsing fever" was first used by David Craigie of Edinburgh in 1843. The disease was often, and frequently is still, confused with malaria and typhus, whose symptoms are similar.

Etiology and Epidemiology

Tick-borne relapsing fever is normally contained within the relationship between tick and rodent host; human beings become affected only when they accidentally become involved in that relationship. For example, if human shelters such as log cabins attract rodents, they may in turn become tick habitats. Transmission of relapsing fever is through the infected saliva or coxal fluid of the tick, making it essentially a disease of locality. In the case of louse-borne relapsing fever, the only reservoir of *B. recurrentis* is human beings, despite the fact that the disease is spread by lice, either in the bite, or by contact with the body fluids of the louse through scratching. The louse is infected by ingesting infected human blood; once infected, it remains so for the rest of its life which is generally about 3 weeks. The infection is not congenital in the offspring. As in typhus fever, the febrile condition of the patient encourages the departure of lice because they are sensitive to temperature and, consequently, prefer the temperature in the clothing of healthy persons.

Tick-borne relapsing fever tends to be more severe than the louse-borne variety, but both types vary greatly in severity and fatality. In 1912, for example, louse-borne relapsing fever was very severe in Indochina and India but very mild in Turkey and Egypt. There are also indications that levels of individual and residual immunity are important. Illustrative are *Borrelia* infections, which are severe in European populations in North and East Africa, but mild in the local populations. On the other hand, in West Africa the disease is equally severe among Europeans and the local inhabitants. Case fatality depends not only on the type of infection and the availability of treatment, but also on the individual's nutritional status and resilience. Thus after World War II, adult fatalities from the disease averaged 8.5 percent among the poorer classes but only 3.6 percent among the well-to-do. Children suffered the most, with death the outcome for 65 percent of cases.

Because mortality varies inversely with living conditions, louse-borne relapsing fever is a true famine fever, generally manifesting itself in times of distress, when overcrowding, diminished personal hygiene, and undernutrition encourage its spread and increase its deadliness. It is said to be "the most epidemic of the epidemic diseases" (Topley and Wilson 1984); and Alexander Collie (in 1887) noted that it rarely occurs except as an epidemic. The factors involved in the survival of the disease between epidemics are still not fully understood.

Distribution and Incidence

Endemic foci of tick-borne relapsing fever exist in most parts of the world, but not in Australia, New Zealand, and the Pacific islands. Louse-borne relapsing fever has been reported worldwide, but since 1964, Ethiopia is the only country that has continuously reported large numbers of cases. Foci of the disease appear, however, to be present in other African countries, and no information on its prevalence is available for the Soviet Union or China.

As with tyhpus fever, there is a marked seasonal incidence coinciding with the winter months. Warm winter clothes (and in the past, deficient winter hygiene) favor the growth of louse populations, whereas rising heat and humidity in spring and summer cause lice to die.

Clinical Manifestations

After an incubation period of some 5 to 8 days, the disease manifests itself suddenly, with shivering, headache, body pains, and high temperature. Nausea and vomiting are occasionally present. The spleen and liver are enlarged and tender; bronchitis is present in 40 to 60 percent of cases and jaundice in 20 to 60 percent. In cases with a favorable outcome, there is a crisis of 1 to 2 hours or longer within 3 to 9 days, followed by a fall in temperature. Relapse, shorter and less severe than the primary attack, follows in 11 to 15 days. A diminishing proportion of patients suffer up to four relapses. Not all cases relapse, however, and in some epidemics no more than 50 percent of the patients suffer relapse. Death is due to liver damage, lobar pneumonia, subarachnoid hemorrhage, or rupture of the spleen.

The causal organisms are present in the blood during the febrile attacks, but absent in the intermissions. After one or more relapses, the active immunity produced by the patient is sufficient to prevent further invasion of the blood by the spirochetes. It is doubtful, however, that this represents a true end of the disease for the patient. Rather it would seem that an equilibrium is established between host and parasite, and like all equilibria is liable to disturbance.

History and Geography

The history of relapsing fever is difficult to trace with any certainty before the louse-borne form was clinically distinguished from typhus and typhoid by William Jenner in 1849. Louse-borne relapsing fever was the first of the communicable diseases to have its causal organism identified, when Otto Obermeier made his observations of spirelli in the blood of patients during the Berlin epidemic of 1867–8. His findings were publicized in 1873. The louse was identified as the vector by F. P. Mackie (1907), then working in India, and the epidemiology of the disease was finally worked out by Charles Nicolle and his colleagues at the Institut Pasteur in Tunis between 1912 and 1932.

Moving back in time, Hippocrates describes an apparent outbreak of relapsing fever on the island of Thassus, off Thrace, and it is possible that the "yellow fever" of seventh-century Europe may have been relapsing fever. The disease may also have been among those constituting the epidemics of "sweating sickness" that affected England in 1485–1551. There were probably a series of relapsing fever epidemics in late-eighteenth-century Gloucestershire, and the first reliable observation of the illness was recorded in Dublin by John Rutty in 1739. The disease was observed principally in Britain and Ireland before the mid-nineteenth century, when it became more active. An outbreak in Scotland in 1841 spread south into England, and from there to the United States. The disease was present, with typhus, in Ireland during the Great Famine of 1846–50. Epidemics also occurred in Prussia (1846–8) and Russia (1864–5), which presaged repeated outbreaks in Germany and Russia during the remainder of the century.

Relapsing fever was reintroduced into the United States by Irish immigrants, resulting in outbreaks in Philadelphia in 1844 and 1869, and in New York in 1847 and 1871. There was an extensive epidemic in Finland in 1876–7. Egypt, Russia, central Europe, and Poland all suffered great epidemics during World War I, and widespread outbreaks occurred in Russia and central Europe in 1919–23. There were further outbreaks in the Middle East, notably in Egypt, after World War II. The disease was shown to be endemic in China along the Yangtse River in the 1930s, and its appearance in Korea after the Korean War suggests that a Chinese focus persists.

Since the 1950s, however, the major continuing focus of louse-borne relapsing fever has been in Africa. In 1910 it was present in Tunisia and Algeria; in 1921 a virulent outbreak appeared in North Equatorial Africa, and spread across the continent as far as Sudan. In 1943 a serious epidemic in North Africa spread into the eastern Mediterranean and Europe. From the 1950s, at least, the disease has had an endemic focus in Ethiopia, making excursions into neighboring Sudan. A. D. M. Bryceson and his colleagues (1970) believed there to be not less than 1,000 cases in Addis Abbaba every year, with a mortality of 5 percent, and they suggested a figure of some 10,000 cases annually for Ethiopia as a whole. The most recently available World Health Organization statistics suggest a modest 2,000 cases in Ethio-

pia in 1980, but an enormous rise to over 22,000 cases (from fewer than 50 in 1978–9) in Sudan in 1981.

Conditions in Ethiopia and the Sudan during the last 10 years have not been conducive to the collection of satisfactory statistical information. Reports from the field, however, suggest a continuing low endemic prevalence of relapsing fever, while at the same time indicating confusion of the disease with malaria and typhus by fieldworkers. It seems likely, however, that any major epidemic escalation would have received attention, and thus the fear of an epidemic escalation in Sudan, expressed by Bryceson (1970) and W. Burgdorfer (1976), have so far proved unfounded.

The history of tick-borne relapsing fever is less well documented, probably because of the local, non-epidemic character of the disease. It was first recognized in Africa in 1847, and in the United States soon after the West had been settled. Among recent recorded outbreaks are two from the western United States among people occupying tick-infested log cabins. The first took place among a group of 42 Boy Scouts and scoutmasters camping at Browne Mountain in March 1968, of whom 11 became ill. The second and the largest outbreak known in the Western Hemisphere resulted in 62 cases among visitors and Park Service employees who spent the night in log cabins on the north rim of the Grand Canyon in Arizona, during the summer of 1973.

Anne Hardy

Bibliography

Bryceson, A. D. M., et al. 1970. Louse-borne relapsing fever. *Quarterly Journal of Medicine* 153: 129–70.

Burgdorfer, Willy. 1976. The epidemiology of relapsing fevers. In *The biology of parasitic spirochaetes,* ed. Russell C. Johnson, 191–200. London.

Collie, Alex. 1887. *On fevers.* London.

Edell, Timm [*sic*] A., et al. 1979. Tick-borne relapsing fever in Colorado. *Journal of the American Medical Association* 249, No. 21: 2279–82.

Felsenfeld, Oscar. 1971. *Borrelia.* St Louis, Mo.

MacArthur, William P. 1957. Medical history of the famine. In *The Great Famine,* ed. R. Dudley Edwards and T. Desmond Williams, 263–315. New York.

Mackie, F. P. 1907. The part played by *Pediculus corporis* in the transmission of relapsing fever. *British Medical Journal* ii: 1706.

1920. The transmission of relapsing fever. *British Medical Journal* i: 380–1.

Murchison, Charles. 1884. *Continued fevers of Great Britain and Ireland,* 3d edition. London.

Topley, William, and Graham S. Wilson, eds. 1984. *Princi-*

ples of bacteriology, virology and immunity, 7th edition, Vol. 3, 524. London.

VIII.117
Rheumatic Fever and Rheumatic Heart Disease

Acute rheumatic fever is a noncontagious disease characterized by febrile, nonsuppurative inflammation, primarily of articular and cardiac tissues, less frequently affecting the skin and brain. The cerebral manifestation – Sydenham's chorea – and the superficial manifestations – subcutaneous nodules and erythema marginatum – are limited to children and young adults.

Etiology and Treatment

The disease is caused by infection, most often of the throat, with type A beta-hemolytic strains of streptococcus. Fever, migratory joint pains and tachycardia, the most frequent symptoms, typically begin 1 to 3 weeks after the onset of untreated streptococcal pharyngitis. However, only 0.1 to 3.0 percent of untreated bouts of this infection result in a first attack of rheumatic fever. Consequently, various largely unidentified permissive factors must participate in initiating the immunologic pathogenesis of the disease.

First attacks of acute rheumatic fever can be prevented by timely treatment of the streptococcal infection with penicillin or another appropriate antibiotic, but such treatment does not influence the course of the disease once it has begun. Rheumatic fever recurs only as a result of a new infection with a pathogenic strain of streptococcus. Prophylactic antibiotic treatment diminishes, but does not eradicate recurrences (Taranta et al. 1964). The shorter the interval since the previous bout of rheumatic fever, the greater is the likelihood that a new attack will be elicited. An infection that occurs within 2 years of an attack has a 20 to 25 percent chance of inducing a recurrence. If the first attack does not affect the heart, a recurrence usually spares it as well, but if the heart has been involved, a second bout it likely to result in greater damage (Spagnuolo, Pasternack, and Taranta 1971). An attack of rheumatic fever usually lasts several weeks, but is rarely fatal. Death most often is a consequence of chronic heart failure, which is the end result of damage to heart valves (predominantly the mitral and aortic valve). Rheumatic heart disease in about one-half the cases develops in the absence of any history of acute rheumatic fever, the infection having slightly initiated the pathogenic immunologic mechanism in the heart (Vendsborg, Hansen, and Olesen 1968).

History

Clinical Manifestations and Diagnosis

The major clinical manifestations of rheumatic fever were first described separately, their relationships not being recognized until the ninteenth century. Thomas Sydenham in 1685 distinguished an acute, febrile polyarthritis "chiefly attacking the young and vigorous" from gout. One year later, he described as "St. Vitus' dance" the neurological disorder that is now called Sydenham's chorea (Murphy 1943). It was Richard Bright who in 1839 first connected the condition with rheumatic fever (Schechter 1935).

In 1797, Matthew Baillie of London noted a thickening of some heart valves in autopsies of patients who had had acute rheumatism, and a few years later David Dundas, surgeon to King George III, described nine cases of "a peculiar disease of the heart" that "is always the consequence of, or is connected with, rheumatic affection" (Dundas 1809). Four years later, William C. Wells, also of London, published a series of 16 cases of "rheumatism of the heart" (median age, 15 years), and added the description of subcutaneous nodules. However, the occurrence of nodules was largely ignored until a comprehensive study by Thomas Barlow and Francis Warner was published in 1881 (Benedek 1984).

Before the introduction of auscultation by René T. Laennec in 1818, rheumatic heart disease was recognized from abnormalities of the pulse, respiration, and palpation of the chest in the presence or recent history of fever and joint pains. Laennec had described murmurs caused by deformities of the mitral valves. In 1835 James Hope also described murmurs that originated from the other valves and concluded that rheumatic fever is the most frequent cause (Hope 1846). This opinion was soon confirmed by Jean B. Bouillaud. The "Aschoff nodule," the myocardial granuloma that came to be considered pathognomonic of rheumatic carditis, had been recognized as early as 1883, but was described definitively by Ludwig Aschoff of Marburg only in 1904 (Benedek 1984).

Bacteriologic studies, beginning in the 1870s, were made on blood and joint fluid aspirates. This approach was justified in 1883 by the demonstration of the cause of gonococcal arthritis. The normal bacterial flora of the throat was not understood. Yet contrary to most investigators of the time, a Berlin physician writing at the turn of the twentieth century concluded that because one finds the same bacteria in the throats of persons with or without rheumatic fever, the disease must be caused not by a specific microbe but by a peculiar reactivity of susceptible individuals.

When Homer F. Swift of New York began his investigations of the cause of rheumatic fever in 1916, he was still culturing blood and joint fluid. In retrospect, the successful cultures that prolonged efforts to find a directly infectious agent (rather than an immunologic incitor) were due either to contamination or to the presence of bacterial endocarditis, an infection that usually is superimposed on rheumatic or congential heart disease. By 1928 Swift had concluded that an allergic response to repeated streptococcal infections is the most likely cause of rheumatic fever, but erroneously believed that nonhemolytic strains were the principal pathogens. The investigations begun by Alvin F. Coburn in New York in the mid-1920s resulted in the correction and extension of Swift's conclusions. On the basis of detailed epidemiological correlations of the bacterial flora of the throat with the onset of initial and recurrent bouts of rheumatic fever, Coburn inferred that the true pathogen is the hemolytic streptococcus, serologic type A (Benedek 1987). The hypothesis that the disease is mediated immunologically was supported by the discovery by E. W. Todd in London of antibodies to streptococci in the blood of rheumatic fever patients (Todd 1932).

Early Epidemiological Studies

The first statistical report, by John Haygarth in 1805, found that 4.5 percent of the admissions to the Chester Infirmary between 1767 and 1801 had "rheumatism" and that 36 percent of those, or 1.6 percent of the total, had acute febrile rheumatism or "rheumatick fever." How many of these actually were cases of this disease is uncertain (a problem that continued to vex many surveys). Eleven of the 70 cases of whom age was recorded involved patients 50 to 70 years old, and unequivocal symptoms of heart failure were not described even in fatalities.

Most reports since then have also described the experience in an individual hospital. Regional surveys and mandatory reporting of rheumatic fever have been rare, occurring mainly in Great Britain, Scandinavia, and the United States. Nearly a century after Haygarth's monograph, a report on the occurrence of "rheumatism" at St. Bartholomew's Hospital, London, demonstrated the vagaries of diagnosis in more detail, as well as the great prevalence of rheumatic fever. During the 15-year span 1863 to 1877, an average of 323 patients with "rheumatism" were admitted annually. This constituted about 14 percent of all medical admissions. Beginning in 1867, gonorrheal rheumatism and rhematoid arthritis were diagnosed separately. However, this change only slightly reduced the cases of presumed acute rheumatic fever with or without heart disease – to 311 per year. The associated mortality was 1.3 percent (Southey 1878). This result is consistent with more recent U.S. data according to which the acute mortality has ranged from 3.5 percent during 1935–42 to 0.9 percent during 1951–8 (Mayer et al. 1963). At St. Bartholomew's during 1867–77, a total of only 716 cases of scarlet fever (also caused by infection with the hemolytic streptococcus) were admitted, and the mortality among these was 14.0 percent (Southey 1878).

Acute rheumatic fever occurred more frequently in older persons in the nineteenth century than in the more recent preantibiotic period. A questionnaire sent to physicians by the British Medical Association during 1882–6 regarding their cases of rheumatic fever indicated the mean age of an attack among 647 cases to have been 25.4 years, with 4 percent of the patients over 60 years of age (Whipham 1888). Of 400 cases admitted to Roosevelt Hospital in New York during 1872–82, 7 percent of the attacks occurred in patients older than 55. By contrast, 25 percent of first attacks occurred between ages 20 and 25, whereas 49 percent of first attacks and 34 percent of all attacks occurred in the third decade of life (May 1884). The latter is similar to the experience at Bellevue Hospital in New York 40 years later, where, as Table VIII.117.1 shows, 34.5 percent of the cases of acute rheumatic fever were in the third decade. By the 1930s, however, only 13.8 percent of patients admitted to Philadelphia hospitals for acute rheumatic fever were in their third decade. Similarly, a review of 3,129 cases in New York, the majority of whom had their first attack between 1920 and 1940, showed a mean age of onset of 15 years (Lambert 1920).

In the 1880s, it was estimated in London that about 20 percent of patients without symptoms or history of rheumatic fever who were admitted to a hospital for any reason had a sibling or parent who had had rheumatic fever; such familial cases were present in about 35 percent of the patients who were hospitalized because of rheumatic fever (Garrod and

Table VIII.117.1. *Age distribution of admissions for acute rheumatic fever*

	Bellevue Hospital, 1911–18[a]		Philadelphia hospitals, 1930–4[b]		
	Cases	Percent	Cases	Percent	% Cardiac
<5	11	0.3	66	5.0	65.2
5–9	69	1.9	272	20.6	69.9
10–14	118	3.3	273	20.6	70.7
15–19	279	7.8	177	13.4	71.2
20–4	667	18.6	151	11.4	58.3
25–9	571	15.9	117	8.8	57.3
30–4	521	14.5	101	7.6	51.5
35–9	419	11.7	63	4.8	31.7
40–4	324	9.0	42	3.2	61.9
45–9	263	7.3	26	2.0	53.8
50–4	168	4.7	19	1.4	63.2
55–9	93	2.6	6	0.5	33.3
60+	87	2.4	9	0.7	33.3
Total	3,590		1,322		63.3

Sources: Data from [a]Lambert (1920); and [b]Hedley (1940).

Cooke 1888). It had been noted in a British Medical Association survey that rheumatic fever "greatly preponderates in the lower over the middle and upper classes" (Whipham 1888). The occurrence of multiple cases in a family was at first attributed to inheritance. As bacteriologic findings came to be accepted in the 1880s and 1890s, however, the concept that both familial occurrence and the association with poverty could best be explained by the easier spread of an infectious agent in crowded living conditions also became accepted. The possibility of racial predisposition was considered because of the greater prevalence of rheumatic fever in populations as disparate as American blacks, South African Bantus, and New Zealand Maoris as compared to white nationals. Most investigators, however, concluded that susceptibility was due to the greater poverty and poorer housing of certain racial groups in various societies, although several investigations have suggested that there is a heritable factor that influences susceptibility to rheumatic fever (Wilson and Schweitzer 1954).

The importance of crowded living conditions gained further attention because of the prevalence of the diagnosis of rheumatic fever in military encampments during the First World War. Between April 1917 and December 1919, for example, 24,770 U.S. soldiers, representing 27 percent of all rheumatologic cases, received this diagnosis. Crowded train-

ing camps were believed to have contributed to the disproportionately large percentage of cases (Hench and Boland 1946). The development of epidemiological data about rheumatic fever has been difficult because the acute phase of the disease may be brief or actually imperceptible, so that its occurrence may become recognized only from findings of valvular heart disease, perhaps years later in an uncertain proportion of the cases. Many estimates of the prevalence of rheumatic fever have been extrapolated from the prevalence of heart disease in those between the ages of 5 and 19 years, because their disease is most likely to be rheumatic. Widely differing diagnostic criteria, examining techniques, and reporting practices have made epidemiological comparisons unreliable. This problem began to be addressed in 1943 by the Cardiovascular Diseases Subcommittee of the [U.S.] National Research Council, which sought more precise diagnostic criteria so as to assess the problem of rheumatic fever in military training camps. In response, T. Duckett Jones, a Boston cardiologist, devised a set of five "major" and seven "minor" criteria and proposed that "any single major manifestation with at least two of the minor manifestations would seem to place the diagnosis on reasonably safe grounds." The Jones criteria received international acceptance quite rapidly and have been modified twice. The main revision in 1955 altered the importance that was assigned to some clinical signs, whereas the revision in 1965 placed increased importance on laboratory evidence of recent streptococcal infection (Stollerman et al. 1965).

Treatment

Salicylate preparations introduced between 1876 and 1879 were found to be particularly effective in counteracting the fever and joint pain of acute rheumatic fever. In 1899 aspirin came on the market, and for the next 50 years the basic treatment consisted of the maximum tolerated dose of either sodium salicylate or aspirin (Rodnan and Benedek 1970). Greater understanding of the cause of rheumatic fever did not have an immediate effect on its treatment because there was no way to eradicate a streptococcal infection. Sulfanilamide was found to prevent recurrences when taken prophylactically (Swift, Moen, and Hirst 1938; Thomas and France 1939). Penicillin became available in 1945 and quickly proved to be safer and more reliable as a preventive agent (Spink et al. 1946). The most reliable prophylactic method, a monthly injection of slowly excreted benzathine penicillin, was introduced in 1951.

The introduction in 1949 of cortisone and corticotropin was perceived as the first possible improvement over salicylate therapy for acute rheumatic fever. During the first few years in which these hormones were available, most investigators found that control of fever and joint pain was achieved more rapidly with these drugs than with salicylates; moreover, if given early enough, they seemed to minimize heart damage. Uncertainty about the latter impression, however, led to the establishment in 1955 of an elaborate Anglo-American prospective therapeutic comparison of salicylate with cortisone or corticotropin therapy. After 10 years, it was concluded that the long-term results from both modalities were similar (U.K. and U.S. Joint Report 1965).

Decline of Rheumatic Fever

London physician G. B. Longstaff (1905) may have been the first to suggest that the prevalence of rheumatic fever was decreasing. He deduced this from death certificates in England and Wales during 1881–1900. During these 20 years, 51,666 deaths were attributed to "rheumatic fever" or "rheumatism of the heart," and 3.3 times as many (171,298) to "valvular disease of the heart." In comparing the 5-year periods 1881–5 and 1896–1900, death rates per million due to rheumatic fever declined 15.6 percent, from 97.6 to 82.4, and those for "residual rheumatism" declined 19.1 percent from 35.0 to 28.3. Data collected by J. A. Glover (1930) for the same region showed a lower incidence of deaths for 1901 than Longstaff had calculated (67 per million), but indicated continuity of the decline: to 46 per million in 1910 and 38 per million in 1928.

The two most common sources of epidemiological data other than death reports have been hospital admissions and recurrence rates among patients who were being followed in rheumatic fever clinics. In order for hospitalization data to be intrinsically comparable, one must assume a socioeconomically stable service area and consistent admissions policies, both of which assumptions are risky. Clinic data tend to yield the most detailed information, but if the clinic is effective, its prevalence information cannot be extrapolated to communities that lack similar services.

Annual admissions data for rheumatic fever were recorded between 1906 and 1925 for hospitals in Montreal, Boston, New York, New Orleans, and the Panama Canal Zone. A comparison of the proportion of total admissions for rheumatic fever between 1906–8 and 1923–5, as reflected in Table VIII.117.2, shows a decline from 59 percent (New York Bellevue) to 79 percent (New Orleans Charity) (Seegal and Seegal 1927).

Table VIII.117.2. *Cases of rheumatic fever per 1,000 admissions, various hospitals*

Hospital/City	1906–10	1921–25	1906–25
Royal Victoria Hospital, Montreal	33.5	14.6	22.6
Mass. General Hospital, Boston	25.3	12.4	16.1
Charity Hospital, New Orleans	12.9	2.7	6.9
Bellevue Hospital, New York	16.8	7.5	8.6
General Hospital, Ancon, Panama Canal Zone	7.00	2.00	3.35

Source: Data from Seegal and Seegal (1927).

A comparison of the prevalence of rheumatic fever among U.S. military personnel during the two world wars shows that, as serious as the problem was during World War II, this diagnosis was made in only 10 percent as many army and 38 percent as many navy personnel. The contribution of more precise diagnosis and prophylactic programs to this improvement is uncertain.

The lengthiest clinical evaluation of rheumatic fever patients was carried out by M. G. Wilson and collaborators (1958) in New York. Beginning in 1916 and continuing in the same area for 40 years, it reported a steady decline in recurrences of rheumatic fever, unrelated to treatment. During 1921–43, 25 percent of children 6 to 13 years of age and 6.1 percent of those aged 14 to 20 suffered recurrences, whereas during 1944–56 only 15.1 percent of the younger and 2.8 percent of the older age group were so affected.

Antimicrobial prophylaxis began to be used in 1952. Yet the age-adjusted recurrence rate for the 5 years 1942–6 was 7.9 percent, and for 1952–6 it was 6.1 percent; this difference was not significant. The socioeconomic circumstances of the area served by the clinic had improved during these decades, but no improvement in the recurrence rate was observed in the poorest segment of the population (Wilson, Lim, and Birch 1958).

A study of the economic correlates of the occurrence of primary and recurrent rheumatic fever in Baltimore during 1960–4 also demonstrated a strong correlation between low economic status and the occurrence of the disease, but only among the white subjects. The annual incidence was consistently greater among blacks, with only slight improvement related to higher socioeconomic category, whereas the incidence among whites diminished markedly with higher socioeconomic category. Thus, the annual incidence of rheumatic fever among blacks in the lowest fifth on the socioeconomic scale was 56 percent greater than among comparable whites, whereas the difference reached 478 percent when the most affluent fifths were compared (Gordis, Lilienfeld, and Rodriguez 1969).

In weighing the relative importance of rheumatic fever and rheumatic heart disease against other potentially lethal problems of childhood, we find that in the United States during 1939–41, the pair still ranked second, behind accidents, as the leading causes of death in the 10- to 14-year age group. There was a significant sex- and race-related gradient, from 11.2 deaths per 100,000 white boys to 17.4 deaths per 100,000 nonwhite girls (Wolff 1951). This amounted to an average of 4,000 deaths per year for that period. But by 1972–4, an average of only 179 deaths were reported annually, and by 1982–4, deaths had declined to 78 cases per year. Similarly, as Table VIII.117.3 indicates, the reported national incidence of rheumatic fever declined from 10,470 cases in 1961 to 2,793 cases in 1971 and 264 cases in 1981.

Geography

Rheumatic fever was thought to be rare in the tropics, as judged by observations on English troops and native populations in India in the mid-nineteenth century. Seeming to confirm that view were clinical and autopsy reports, primarily from India and the Malay Peninsula, which started to appear in the 1890s and were still cited in the 1930s (Clarke 1930). But these publications are somewhat perplexing, for beginning in 1925, substantial numbers of cases of rheumatic heart disease were being reported from tropical India.

Nevertheless, rheumatic fever has been found to occur less frequently in tropical than in temperate regions despite the fact that poverty, aspects of which appear to facilitate the occurrence of the disease, is in general more prevalent in the tropics. Thus, observations on military personnel that minimize the economic factor have shown a lower incidence in tropical encampments. For example, the mean incidence of rheumatic fever among white U.S. Army enlisted men stationed in the United States during 1913–25 was 5.00 plus or minus 2.46 per 1,000, whereas the incidence among similar personnel stationed in the Philippines was 1.74 plus or minus 1.23 per 1,000 (Faulkner and White 1924). Paradoxically, however, during the decade 1914–23

there were slightly more admissions for rheumatic fever to the General Hospital of Manila than to the Johns Hopkins Hospital in Baltimore – 7.90 versus 7.19 per 1,000 medical admissions (Seegal and Seegal 1927).

A north-to-south declining gradient of rheumatic fever within the United States was suggested during the 1920s (Harrison and Levine 1924). This was confirmed by numerous studies, including one in which the prevalence of rheumatic heart disease was compared among Indian children on reservations in Montana, Wyoming, and Arizona (Paul and Dixon 1937). A similar gradient has been reported from China. An altitude gradient has been demonstrated in Kenya for hospitalizations for acute rheumatic fever, and in Mexico for the proportion of rheumatic heart disease among cardiac patients. In both countries there was significantly more disease in the more temperate highlands.

The "classical" manifestations of rheumatic fever were described in northern Europe, and whether its acute manifestations differ in the tropics has long been debated. If one considers, however, the wide variation in the frequency with which various acute manifestations of the disease have occurred in temperate regions, as presented in Table VIII.117.3, it seems doubtful that there are consistent biological differences in the presentation of rheumatic fever in the tropics. Some of the reported inconsistencies reflect selection biases related to cultural attitudes and medical and other resources, whereas others reflect over- or underdiagnosis. For example, the fact that virtually all of the patients in a small series of cases from Nigeria and Uganda had carditis probably indicates that childhood cases of lesser severity were simply not seen rather than nonexistent.

The wide range of the occurrence of "arthritis" in rheumatic fever cases may be attributed in part to the differentiation by some authors between objective signs of joint inflammation and mere arthralgia. Nevertheless, there can be striking differences in the occurrence of arthritis, even when rigorous diagnostic criteria may be assumed; for example, 42 percent and 71 percent of the patients had arthritis in two series of cases at two different times from Toronto. But the extreme variations in the occurrence of chorea – ranging from 2 percent to 52 percent – are the most inexplicable. Erythema marginatum is rarely described in dark-skinned children, but this eruption is sufficiently uncommon in fair-skinned individuals that, assuming some underdiagnosis in the former, a significant difference seems unlikely.

Table VIII.117.3. Signs of acute rheumatic fever worldwide

Area	Years	Cases	% M/F	Cardiac	Arthritis	Chorea	Nodules	E. Marg.	Reference
Rochester, N.Y.	?–1934	1,240	46/54	64.2%	39.0%	29.0%	1.3%	1.9%	JAMA 103: 886, 1934
Boston, Mass.	1921–31	1,000	29/71	65.3	41.0	51.8	8.8	7.1	Circulation 4: 836, 1951
Boston, Mass.	1941–51	457		52.5	90.1	13.3	11.8	10.5	Am J Cardiol 1: 436, 1958
U.S. Multicenter	1951–2	257	56/44	67.7	47.7	7.0	7.4	3.9	Circulation 11: 343, 1955
New York, N.Y.	1958–60	275		42	76	7.6	1	4	Medicine 41: 279, 1962
Toronto, Canada	1937–40	178	49/51	46.0	42.1	41.0	6.2	2.2	Can Med Assoc J 94: 1027, 1966
Toronto, Canada	1957–60	218	41/59	44.0	70.6	15.1	1.3	5.0	Can Med Assoc J 94: 1027, 1966
U.K. Multicenter	1951–2	240	47/53	82.9	40.0	15.0	21.7	7.9	Circulation 11: 343, 1955
England	?–1968	1,006	40/60	72	62.4	25.5	8	2	Ann Rheum Dis 28: 471, 1969
Dublin, Ireland	1957–66	160	42/58	68	78	31	4	5	Irish J Med Sci 3: 307, 1970
Puerto Rico	1953–61	101	42/58	77	89	12	6	5	Am Heart J 63: 18, 1962
Puerto Rico	1962–4	101	48/52	68	78	19	5	9	Am J Dis Child 110: 239, 1965
Trinidad	1970–1	93	47/53	73	82	3			J Pediatr 92: 325, 1978
Cairo, Egypt	1961–4	1,000	37/63	79.5	13.2	12.3			Ann Rheum Dis 24: 389, 1965
Kenya	1962–3	56	59/41	57	68	20			E Afr Med J 40: 593, 1963
Nigeria	1975–9	66	64/36	98	61	1.5	3	1.5	Am J Dis Child 135: 236, 1981
S. Afr. (Bantu)	1962–4	127	32/68	87	36	5	1	0	S Afr Med J 40: 899, 1966
Uganda	1968–73	150	40/60	95.3	68.0	8.7	1.3	3.3	E Afr Med J 51: 710, 1974
Ceylon	1953–7	560		36.1		2.3	0.5		Arch Dis Child 34: 247, 1959
South India	1955–9	166	63/37	97	25.3	5.4	1.2		Ind J Child Health 9: 240, 1960
North India	1967–71	102	55/45	33.3	66.7	20.6	2	2	Circulation 49: 8, 1974
North India	1980–3	100	58/42	51	68	16	5	0	Bull WHO 64: 573, 1986
New Delhi, India	1968–77	450		42	30	2.6	6	0.2	Ind Heart J 33: 264, 1981
Bombay, India	1981–4	168	58/42	57.1	32	14.3	3.0	0	J Trop Pediatr 31: 273, 1985
Indonesia	1969–72	170		57	40	3.5	0.1	1.7	Jpn Heart J 20: 237, 1974
Iran	1957–67	55	64/36	82	38	4	2	2	Am J Dis Child 118: 694, 1969
Shiraz, Iran	1958–69	100		83	56	4	1	3	Clin Pediatr 10: 530, 1971
Japan	1958–75	220		66	55	9.5	3.6	16.4	Jpn Heart J 20: 237, 1974
Pakistan	1964–5	57	51/49	73	59	7	3	3	Clin Therapeutics 4: 240, 1981
Philippines	1974	208		94	66	1	5	0.5	Clin Therapeutics 4: 240, 1981
Taiwan	1946–75	400		84	33	5.7	2.2	6	Jpn Heart J 20: 237, 1979
Thailand	1961–75	325		60	36	2.5	1.5	0.3	Jpn Heart J 20: 237, 1979
Rotorua, N. Z.	1972–83	188	57/43	72.6	49	10	0	2.7	NZ Med J 97: 675, 1984

The relationship of subcutaneous nodules to carditis may indicate real geographic differences in disease expression. Nodules have occurred in 8 to 12 percent of several large series of cases from temperate regions (Benedek 1984), whereas they have been less common in others and have consistently been rare in the tropics. In temperate climates nodules are almost always associated with acute carditis and may be predictive of more severe valve damage. Thus, according to the long-term experience of Wilson and W. Lim (1957) in New York, 3 percent of cases of mitral insufficiency, 9 percent of cases of combined mitral insufficiency and stenosis, and 30 percent of cases of combined mitral and aortic valve damage had exhibited nodules during the acute phase of illness. In tropical areas there is a weaker association between the occurrence of nodules and carditis and a difference in the valvular involvement, or at least this seems to be the case of India. There, carditis not only results in permanent valve injury more rapidly and is more likely to be acutely fatal, but also has a peculiar tendency to cause pure mitral stenosis. This has been described repeatedly since 1935. According to the largest reported experience involving 2,050 cases of rheumatic heart disease in New Delhi, 81 percent of whom were below 30 years of age, 43.5 percent had pure mitral stenosis (Wilson et al. 1958). Reports from other countries do not resolve the question of whether this finding represents an ethnic difference or is a result of delayed initial medical care.

Rheumatic Heart Disease and Its Surgical Repair

Wilson and associates evaluated 385 patients up to 49 years of age who had heart murmurs and had had rheumatic fever before the age of 20. Fully 89 percent were asymptomatic; 45 percent of the cohort had pure mitral insufficiency; 41.8 percent had combined mitral insufficiency and stenosis; 10.3 percent had both mitral lesions and aortic insufficiency; and 2.9 percent had double mitral and double aortic valve defects (Gordis et al. 1969). Of 78 fatal cases from the population of which those just mentioned were among the survivors, 15.4 percent had only mitral insufficiency, 37.2 percent had mitral insufficiency and stenosis, and 47.3 percent also had aortic insufficiency (Magida and Streitfeld 1957).

The surgical treatment of rheumatically damaged heart valves began in the late 1940s when Dwight E. Harken in Boston performed the first successful mitral commissurotomy (Harken et al. 1948). The procedure was improved by Charles P. Bailey of Philadelphia a year later (Bailey et al. 1960). This was "closed" heart surgery. No attempt to repair a damaged aortic valve was possible until an oxygenating system to bypass blood temporarily around the heart was developed; this technique made "open" heart surgery possible. The first practical apparatus was employed by John W. Kirklin. The first valve operations to ameliorate aortic insufficiency were performed by Bailey in 1959 and to correct aortic stenosis in the same year by Donald G. Mulder in Los Angeles. The next technical phase was the replacement of an active valve. This began with the ball valve devised by Albert Starr and Lowell Edwards (1961). Such plastic valves, however, tend to destroy red blood cells, and thus valves were developed with leaflets of pig, cattle, or sheep tissue. This type of prosthesis was first inserted to replace an aortic valve in 1965, and a mitral valve in 1967, both by A. Carpentier in Paris.

In 1983 about 16,000 mitral and 33,000 aortic valve replacements were performed in the United States. However, the cause of the injury, particularly of the aortic valve, has gradually shifted from rheumatic to other varieties of heart disease (Gillum 1986).

Thomas G. Benedek

Bibliography

Arora, R., et al. 1981. Clinical profile of rheumatic fever and rheumatic heart disease: A study of 2,500 cases. *Indian Heart Journal* 33: 264–9.

Bailey, C. P., J. Zimmerman, and W. Likoff. 1960. The complete relief of mitral stenosis: Ten years of progress toward this goal. *Diseases of the Chest* 37: 543–60.

Benedek, T. G. 1984. Subcutaneous nodules and the differentiation of rheumatoid arthritis from rheumatic fever. *Seminars in Arthritis and Rheumatism* 13: 306–21.

1987. A century of American rheumatology. *Annals of Internal Medicine* 106: 307–12.

Clarke, J. T. 1930. The geographical distribution of rheumatic fever. *Journal of Tropical Medicine and Hygiene* 33: 249–57.

Dundas, D. 1809. An account of a peculiar disease of the heart. *Medico-Chirurgical Transactions* 1: 36–46.

Faulkner, J. M., annd P. D. White. 1924. The incidence of rheumatic fever, chorea and rheumatic heart disease. *Journal of the American Medical Association* 83: 425–6.

Garrod, A. E., and E. H. Cooke. 1888. Frequency of rheumatic family histories amongst non-rheumatic patients. *Lancet* 2: 110.

Gillum, R. F. 1986. Trends in acute rheumatic fever and chronic rheumatic heart disease: A national perspective. *American Heart Journal* 111: 430–2.

Glover, J. A. 1930. I. The incidence of acute rheumatism. *Milroy lectures on the incidence of rheumatic fever,* 1: 499–505.

Gordis, L., A. Lilienfeld, and R. Rodriguez. 1969. Studies in the epidemiology and preventability of rheumatic fever. *Journal of Chronic Diseases* 21: 645–66.

Harken, D. E., et al. 1948. The surgical treatment of mitral stenosis. I. Valvuloplasty. *New England Journal of Medicine* 239: 801–9.

Harris, T. R., and S. A. Levine. 1924. Notes on the regional distribution of rheumatic fever and rheumatic heart disease in the United States. *Southern Medical Journal* 12: 914–15.

Hedley, O. F. 1940. Rheumatic heart disease in Philadelphia hospitals, part II. *Public Health Reports* 55: 1647–91.

Hench, P. S., and E. W. Boland. 1946. The management of chronic arthritis and other rheumatic disorders among soldiers of the United States Army. *Annals of Internal Medicine* 24: 808–25.

Hope, J. 1846. *A treatise on the diseases of the heart and great vessels, and on the affections which may be mistaken for them,* 2d American edition, from 3d London edition, 95–113. Philadelphia.

Lambert, A. 1920. The incidence of acute rheumatic fever at Bellevue Hospital. *Journal of the American Medical Association* 74: 993–5.

Longstaff, G. B. 1905. A contribution to the etiology of rheumatic fever. *Transactions of the Epidemiological Society of London,* new ser., 24: 33–83.

Magida, M. G., and F. H. Streitfeld. 1957. The natural history of rheumatic heart disease in the third, fourth and fifth decades of life. II. Prognosis with special reference to morbidity. *Circulation* 16: 713–22.

May, C. H. 1884. Statistics of four hundred cases of rheumatism, with special reference to treatment: treated at the Roosevelt Hospital. *Medical Record* 25: 57–62, 87–93, 116–21, 173–8.

Mayer, F. E., et al. 1963. Declining severity of first attack of rheumatic fever. *American Journal of the Diseases of Childhood* 105: 146–52.

Murphy, G. E. 1943. The evolution of our knowledge of rheumatic fever. *Bulletin of the History of Medicine* 14: 123–47.

Paul, J. R., and G. L. Dixon. 1937. Climate and rheumatic heart disease: A survey among American Indian school children in northern and southern localities. *Journal of the American Medical Association* 108: 2096–100.

Rodnan, G. P., and T. G. Benedek. 1970. The early history of antirheumatic drugs. *Arthritis and Rheumatism* 13: 145–65.

Schechter, D. C. 1975. St. Vitus' dance and rheumatic disease. *New York State Journal of Medicine* 75: 1091–102.

Seegal, D., and B. C. Seegal. 1927. Studies in the epidemiology of rheumatic fever. *Journal of the American Medical Association* 89: 11–17.

Southey, R. 1878. Observations on acute rheumatism. *St. Bartholomew's Hospital Reports* 14: 1–22.

Spagnuolo, M., B. Pasternack, and A. Taranta. 1971. Risk of rheumatic fever recurrences after streptococcal infections. *New England Journal of Medicine* 285: 641–7.

Spink, W. W., et al. 1946. Sulfadiazine and penicillin for hemolytic streptococcus infections of the upper respiratory tract. *Archives of Internal Medicine* 77: 260–94.

Starr, A., and M. L. Edwards. 1961. Mitral replacement: Clinical experience with a ball-valve prosthesis. *Annals of Surgery* 154: 726–40.

Stollerman, G. H., et al. 1965. Jones criteria (revised) for guidance in the diagnosis of rheumatic fever. *Circulation* 32: 664–8.

Swift, H. F., J. K. Moen, and G. K. Hirst. 1938. The action of sulfanilamide in rheumatic fever. *Journal of the American Medical Association* 110: 426–34.

Taranta, A., et al. 1964. Rheumatic fever in children and adolescents. IV. Relationship of the rheumatic fever recurrence rate per streptococcal infection to the titers of streptococcal antibodies. *Annals of Internal Medicine* 60 (Supplement 5): 47–57.

Thomas, C. B., and R. France. 1939. A preliminary report of the prophylactic use of sulfanilamide in patients susceptible to rheumatic fever. *Bulletin of the Johns Hopkins Hospital* 64: 67–77.

Todd, E. W., 1932. Antigenic streptococcal haemolysin. *Journal of Experimental Medicine* 55: 267–80.

U.K. and U.S. Joint Report. 1965. The natural history of rheumatic fever and rheumatic heart disease: Cooperative clinical trial of ACTH, cortisone, and aspirin. *Circulation* 32: 457–76.

Vendsborg, P., L. F. Hansen, and K. H. Olesen. 1968. Decreasing incidence of a history of acute rheumatic fever in chronic heart disease. *Cardiologia* 53: 332–40.

Whipham, T. 1888. Reports of the Collective Investigation Committee of the British Medical Association. III. Acute rheumatism. *British Medical Journal* i: 387–404.

Wilson, M. G., and M. Schweitzer. 1954. Pattern of hereditary susceptibility in rheumatic fever. *Circulation* 10: 699–704.

Wilson, M. G., and W. N. Lim. 1957. The natural history of rheumatic heart disease in the third, fourth and fifth decades of life. I. Prognosis with special reference to survivorship. *Circulation* 16: 700–12.

Wilson, M. G., W. N. Lim, and A. M. Birch. 1958. The decline of rheumatic fever: Recurrence rates of rheumatic fever among 782 children for twenty-one consecutive calendar years (1936–1956). *Journal of Chronic Diseases* 7: 183–97.

Wolff, G. 1951. Death toll from rheumatic fever in childhood. *Journal of the American Medical Association* 145: 719–24.

Rickets and osteomalacia are diseases with multiple etiologies primarily related to abnormal metabolism of vitamin D and secondarily to calcium and phosphate metabolism. Of the many causes, by far the most important relate to dietary vitamin D deficiency and the activation of vitamin D precursors by the kidney and sunlight. Rickets and osteomalacia are characterized pathophysiologically by a failure of normal mineralization of bone and epiphyseal cartilage and clinically by skeletal deformity. Rickets occurs in growing infants and children, and both bone and epiphyseal cartilage are affected. Osteomalacia occurs in adults after closure of the epiphyses, and its manifestations are often much less prominent.

History

Historically, rickets was among the earliest diseases to be described. As early as 300 B.C., Lu-pu-wei described crooked legs and hunchback; however, these can occur with other disorders. More specifc references are found in the separate writings of three Chinese physicians of the seventh and eighth centuries A.D., including enlarged head, body wasting, pigeon breast, and delayed walking. By the tenth century, Chien-i, the Father of Chinese pediatrics, described many cases of rickets (Lee 1940).

In the second century A.D., Soranus of Ephesus mentioned characteristic deformities of the legs and spine in young children and remarked on the higher frequency in urban Rome compared to Greece. Slightly later, Galen's work included a description of skeletal deformities in infants and young children, particularly the knock-knee, bow leg, and funnel-shaped chest, and pigeon breast seen in rickets. Sporadic and somewhat ambiguous references to the disease were made until the mid-seventeenth century, when the classic descriptions of Daniel Whistler and Francis Glisson appeared.

In 1645 Whistler published his medical thesis in Latin, *On the Disease of English Children which is Popularly Termed the Rickets*. Five years later, Glisson wrote the classic text on the subject, still unsurpassed as a clinical description of rickets. Both physicians considered the disorder of recent origin, and indeed the northern climate, crowded living conditions, and socioeconomic changes may have influenced its prevalence at that time. Glisson himself noted a number of cases affecting the "cradles of the rich," perhaps related to the use of swaddling clothes and the vitamin D-deficient diet of pap and starch.

The word "rickets" was first used in the London Bill of Mortality report for 1634. The derivation of the word has been a source of contention since that time. Possibilities include *rucket* in Dorset dialect, meaning "short of breath"; the verb *rucken,* meaning "to rock or reel"; the Middle English word *wricken,* denoting "to twist"; the Saxon word *rick,* meaning "heap" or "hump"; or the Norman word *riquets,* for hunchback. Glisson suggested the term "rachitis" derived from the Greek word for spine, and this term remains in use in many countries today.

Nearly 250 years passed before the specific role of vitamin D and its active metabolites was elucidated via biochemical studies. L. Findlay (1908) reproduced the disease in puppies raised in a confined, darkened space. A year later, Georg Schmorl (1909) demonstrated the striking seasonal variation of the disease by autopsy findings. In 1917 Alfred F. Hess and L. J. Unger described the prevention of rickets by use of cod liver oil or by ultraviolet irradiation. Shortly thereafter, a number of researchers, particularly the group of Elmer V. McCollum (1922), isolated vitamin D and related compounds. A better understanding of the exact mechanisms and conversion of vitamin D metabolism into more active forms was gained only since the mid-1960s and 1970s (Lund and DeLuca 1966; Fraser and Kodicek 1970).

Vitamin D is classified more accurately as a prohormone rather than a vitamin. It is formed by the interaction of ultraviolet light with a cholesterol derivative in the deeper layers of the skin, but small amounts of vitamin D may also be derived from dietary sources such as dairy product and fish liver oils. Vitamin D is then hydroxylated once in the liver, and a second hydroxylation into the highly active hormone occurs in the kidney. It acts upon the target organs, intestine, and bone to regulate serum calcium and phosphate levels and the mineralization of bone.

Paleopathology

As a disease producing characteristic skeletal deformities, rickets can be traced back to antiquity by direct examination of the skeletal evidence. As expected, the disease was extremely rare in ancient Egypt. Only one or two possible cases have been described in skeletal remains from North and South America. Most reported examples of ancient rickets come from Europe. A few date back to Neolithic times in Norway, Sweden, and Denmark. Examples become more plentiful during the Middle Ages in cities across northern and central Europe, again confirming the central role of inadequate sunlight in causing the disease (Steinbock 1976).

Epidemiology, Distribution, and Geography

As early as 1890, Theobald A. Palm gathered data via correspondence with medical missionaries worldwide and concluded that the main etiologic factor in rickets is the lack of sunlight. It was much later before scientists linked the variable pigmentation in the races of men with the regulation of vitamin D synthesis (Loomis 1967). The processes of pigmentation and keratinization of the outer layer of the skin (stratum corneum) directly affect the amount of solar ultraviolet radiation reaching the deeper stratum granulosum, where vitamin D is synthesized. White or depigmented skin of the northern latitudes allows maximum ultraviolet penetration. Black or heavily pigmented skin and Oriental or keratinized skin minimize UV penetration in southern latitudes to maintain vitamin D synthesis within physiological limits. The skin pigmentation or keratinization also plays a role in preventing sun-induced skin cancer, a greater problem among light-skinned groups who move to sunnier climates.

A cautionary note should be included when discussing the incidence or prevalence of rickets. The diagnosis of rickets will vary, depending on the nature of the criteria utilized – clinical, radiographic, or biochemical. Moreover, the sensitivity of each of these methods varies considerably according to the stage of the disease or age of the individual.

Historically, the incidence of rickets increased with the rise of sunless, crowded urban centers as part of the Industrial Revolution. Indeed, rickets may, among other things, be considered as an air pollution disease since factory-produced smog filters and decreases the available ultraviolet light (Loomis 1970). As Palm (1890) deduced from this worldwide correspondence: "It is in the narrow alleys, the haunts and playgrounds of the children of the poor, that this exclusion of sunlight is at its worst, and it is there that the victims of rickets are to be found in abundance."

In 1899 Theodor Escherich reported that in Vienna 97 percent of infants between 9 and 15 months had clinical evidence of rickets. An autopsy analysis in Dresden, Germany, by Schmorl (1909) showed that 89 percent of all children between 2 months and 4 years of age exhibited evidence of active or healed rickets. Schmorl also noted a striking seasonal variation in the presence of rickets. Similar high numbers were reported near the turn of the century for Oslo, Bergen, Berlin, Glasgow, Dublin, Belfast, Edinburgh, Paris, Florence, and Moscow (cf. Owen 1889; Hess 1929). Some authorities noted a general decrease in rickets at higher altitudes in the Scottish Highlands and Swiss Alps, related to the increased ultraviolet component of solar radiation. However, cases became more numerous and severe at the highest altitudes, presumably related to the practice of keeping the infants heavily bundled or indoors nearly year round (see Feer 1916).

Large American cities also had a high prevalence of rickets. In 1900 John L. Morse estimated that 80 percent of all infants under 2 years of age in Boston had rickets. Hess reported in 1921 that 75 percent of New York City children had clinical evidence of rickets (see also Hess 1929). Martha M. Eliot (1925) found that 83 percent of infants under 8 months of age in New Haven had radiographic findings of mild rickets. L. R. Du Buys (1924) noted that rickets was widespread in New Orleans, and the clinical manifestations were more marked in blacks than whites.

As a deficiency disease involving sunlight and diet, cultural and socioeconomic factors interacting with climate are important in the epidemiology and geographic distribution of rickets and osteomalacia. In general, rickets is uncommon in sunny climates; however, even sun-rich areas may have rickets. For example, nearly 30 percent of children seen at an Ethiopian clinic had clinical evidence of rickets, primarily related to a shortened period of breast feeding and swaddling of infants to avoid the "evil eye" (Mariam and Sterky 1973). In many Moslem countries, the custom of *purdah* – the complete shielding of women and young children indoors or with veils – is a major factor in rickets and osteomalacia. A study of 1,482 Moslem girls in India, aged 5 to 17 years, showed that 40 percent had skeletal evidence of rickets (Wilson 1931).

Among many Asian groups the use of Chupatti flour as a dietary staple also contributes to the prevalence of rickets. The high phytate content in the wheat fiber binds calcium and zinc, resulting in decreased intestinal absorption of these minerals. In addition, the lignin component of wheat fiber binds to bile salts and ingested vitamin D, decreasing their absorption (Reinhold 1976). The use of *raghif,* an unleavened bread rich in phytates, is also a factor in osteomalacia among Bedouin women of childbearing age (Shany et al. 1976).

An unfortunate synergistic effect of decreased sunlight and high cereal, rice, or maize diet has been reported in both epidemiological and experimental studies (Robertson et al. 1984; Sly et al. 1984). Indeed, the effects of phytates, lignin, and other components in these grains may be rachitogenic even in the presence of adequate sunlight (Wilson 1931; Pettifor et al. 1978).

With the addition of synthetic vitamin D to dairy products and bread in the United States, there has been a dramatic decline in the incidence of rickets. Between 1956 and 1960, fewer than 0.4 cases per 100,000 pediatric admissions were for rickets. Vitamin D supplementation is not practiced in Britain, and 9 percent of young children in Glasgow had radiographic evidence of rickets (Richards et al. 1968). Osteomalacia among the elderly remains a significant public health problem related to decreased exposure to sunlight, intestinal malabsorption, poor diet, and decreased hydroxylation of vitamin D by the liver and kidneys. Osteomalacia in combination with osteoporosis is therefore an important factor in the occurrence of hip fracture among the elderly.

R. Ted Steinbock

Bibliography

Du Buys, L. R. 1924. A clinical study of rickets in the breast-fed infant. *American Journal of Diseases of Children* 27: 149–60.

Eliot, M. M. 1925. The control of rickets. *Journal of the American Medical Association* 85: 656–8.

Escherich, T. 1899. Rickets. *Comptes Rendu du XII Congrès Internationale de Médecine* 3, Section 6.

Feer, E. 1916. Zur geographischen Verbreitung und Aetiologie der Rachitis. *Medizin Klink* 8: 1–225.

Findlay, L. 1908. The etiology of rickets. *British Medical Journal* ii: 859–62.

Fraser, D. R., and E. Kodicek. 1970. Unique biosynthesis by kidney of a biologically active vitamin D metabolite. *Nature* 228: 764.

Glisson, F. 1650. *Rachitide sive Morbo Puerili, qui vulgo The Rickets dicitur.* London.

Hess, A. F. 1929. *Rickets, including osteomalacia and tetany.* Philadelphia.

Hess, A. F., and L. J. Unger. 1917. Prophylactic therapy for rickets in a Negro community. *Journal of the American Medical Association* 69: 1583–6.

Lee, T. 1940. Historical notes on some vitamin deficiency diseases in China. *Chinese Medical Journal* 58: 314–23.

Loomis, W. F. 1967. Skin-pigment regulation of vitamin D-biosynthesis in man. *Science* 157: 501–6.

  1970. Rickets. *Scientific American* 223: 77–91.

Lund, J., and H. F. DeLuca. 1966. Biologically active metabolite of vitamin D3 from bone, liver, and blood serum. *Journal of Lipid Research* 7: 739.

Mariam, T. W., and G. Sterky. 1973. Severe rickets in infancy and childhood in Ethiopia. *Journal of Pediatrics* 82: 876–8.

McCollum, E. V., et al. 1922. Studies in experimental rickets XXI. An experimental demonstration of the existence of a vitamin which promotes calcium deposition. *Journal of Biological Chemistry* 53: 293–313.

Morse, J. L. 1900. The frequency of rickets in infancy in Boston and vicinity. *Journal of the American Medical Association* 34: 724–6.

Owen, J. 1889. Geographical distribution of rickets, acute and chronic rheumatism, cancer and urinary calculus in the British Islands. *British Medical Journal* i: 113–17.

Palm, T. A. 1890. The geographical distribution and etiology of rickets. *Practitioner* 45: 270–4.

Pettifor, J. M., et al. 1978. Rickets in children of rural origin in South Africa: Is low dietary calcium a factor? *Journal of Pediatrics* 92: 320–4.

Reinhold, J. G. 1976. Rickets in Asian immigrants. *Lancet* ii: 1132.

Richards, I. D. G., et al. 1968. Infantile rickets persists in Glasgow. *Lancet* 1: 803–5.

Robertson, I., et al. 1984. The role of cereals in the aetiology of nutritional rickets: The lesson of the Irish National Nutrition Survey 1943–48. *British Journal of Nutrition* 45: 17–22.

Schmorl, G. 1909. Die pathologisische Anatomie der rachitischen Knochenerkrankung mit besonderer Berucksichtigung ihrer Histologie und Pathogenese. *Ergebnisse der Inneren Medezin und Kinderheilkunde* 4: 403–54.

Shany, S., J. Hirsh, and G. M. Berlyne. 1976. 25-Hydroxycholecalciferol levels in Bedouins in the Negev. *American Journal of Clinical Nutrition* 29: 1104–9.

Sly, M. R., et al. 1984. Exacerbation of rickets and osteomalacia by maize: A study of bone histomorphometry and composition in young baboons. *Calcified Tissue International* 36: 370–9.

Steinbock, R. T. 1976. *Paleopathological diagnosis and interpretation: Bone diseases in ancient human populations.* Springfield, Ill.

Whistler, D. 1645. *De morbo puerili Anglorum, quem patrio idiomate indigenae vocant The Rickets.* London.

Wilson, D. C. 1931. Osteomalacia (late rickets) studies. *Indian Journal of Medical Research* 18: 951–78.

VIII.119
Rickettsial Diseases

The rickettsial diseases are a group of related maladies with common characteristics such as arthropod vectors, obligate intracellular etiologic agents, and similar symptoms, including skin rashes, high fever, and headache. The prototype is classic, epidemic, louse-borne typhus fever. Most other rickettsial diseases were originally described as "typhus-like" and were differentiated from the classic disease during the twentieth century.

Those whose etiologic agents share the *Rickettsia* genus with the historic disease are murine, or flea-borne typhus, Rocky Mountain spotted fever and other members of the spotted fever group of diseases, and scrub typhus or tsutsugamushi. Two other diseases, Q fever and trench fever, are also known as rickettsial diseases. In recent decades, however, key differences in the clinical manifestations, in mode of transmission, and in the physiology of the etiologic agents of these two diseases have caused them to be placed in separate genera.

Pathological rickettsiae were discovered early in the twentieth century and named after Howard Taylor Ricketts, a University of Chicago investigator, who lost his life in research on typhus in Mexico after several years of fruitful research on Rocky Mountain spotted fever. Although smaller than most bacteria, rickettsiae are visible under the light microscope. Unlike common bacteria, they are obligate intracellular parasites – that is, they metabolize and multiply only inside living cells, a characteristic shared with the viruses. This peculiar combination of traits caused the rickettsiae to be classified for several decades as organisms midway between bacteria and viruses. By the late 1960s, however, research revealed that they were true, if highly fastidious, bacteria.

Most of the rickettsial maladies are "diseases of nature," normally existing as infections of arthropods (insects, ticks, and mites) and their mammalian hosts. Humans are accidental intruders into the natural cycle. Like bubonic plague and yellow fever, the manifestations of infection are often more severe in humans than in the arthropods and mammals to which the organisms have adapted over eons. The geographic distribution of the rickettsial diseases is linked to environments favorable to host arthropods. In addition, these diseases tend to be found in "islands of infection" within favorable environments. This phenomenon has been attributed to ecological conditions in the case of scrub typhus or tsutsugamushi and to antigenic incompatibility between pathogenic and nonpathogenic rickettsiae seeking to establish themselves in the ovaries of female ticks in Rocky Mountain spotted fever.

The common clinical manifestations of these diseases reflect their pathological physiology as infections of the human circulatory system. Their etiologic agents multiply inside endothelial cells lining small blood vessels. Affected cells become swollen and may impede blood flow. Electrolyte imbalance and capillary permeability establish a vicious circle that progresses to circulatory collapse in fatal cases. Blood seeping from the capillaries into the skin causes the typical rash, and capillary blockage in the brain contributes to the neurological symptoms. Since the introduction of broad-spectrum antibiotics in 1948, the rickettsial diseases have been curable, if diagnosed before the diseases have progressed too far.

Victoria A. Harden

Bibliography

Burgdorfer, Willy, and Robert L. Anacker, eds. 1987. *Rickettsiae and rickettsial diseases.* New York.

Harden, Victoria A. 1987. Koch's postulates and the etiology of rickettsial diseases. *Journal of the History of Medicine and Allied Sciences* 42: 277–95.

Horsfall, Frank L., Jr., and Igor Tamm, eds. 1965. *Viral and rickettsial infections of man,* 4th edition. Philadelphia.

Moe, James B., and Carl E. Pedersen, Jr. 1980. The impact of rickettsial diseases on military operations. *Military Medicine* 145: 780–5.

Moulton, F. R., ed. 1948. *Rickettsial diseases of man.* Proceedings of a symposium of the American Association for the Advancement of Science, Boston, December 26–28, 1946 [Washington, D.C.: American Association for the Advancement of Science].

Rivers, Thomas M., ed. 1952. *Viral and rickettsial infections of man,* 2d edition. Philadelphia.

Rivers, Thomas M., and Frank L. Horsfall, Jr., eds. 1959. *Viral and rickettsial infections of man,* 3d edition. Philadelphia.

U.S. Army Chemical Corps Technical Library. 1952. *Bibliography on epidemic, endemic, and scrub typhus fevers.* Frederick, Md.

Virus and rickettsial diseases, with especial consideration of their public health significance. 1939. A symposium held at the Harvard School of Public Health, June 12–17, 1939. Cambridge, Mass.

Walker, David H., ed. 1988. *Biology of rickettsial diseases,* 2 vols. Boca Raton, Fla.

Woodward, Theodore E. 1973. A historical account of the rickettsial diseases with a discussion of unsolved problems. *Journal of Infectious Diseases* 127: 583–94.

Zdrodovskii, P. F., and H. M. Golinevich. 1960. *The rickettsial diseases*. English trans. of Russian text. Oxford.

VIII.120
Rocky Mountain Spotted Fever and the Spotted Fever Group Diseases

Rocky Mountain spotted fever is a severe, acute, rickettsial disease transmitted by ticks and limited to the Western Hemisphere. Its major symptoms are similar to those of epidemic typhus, but its rash covers the entire body, including the face, the palms of the hands, and the soles of the feet. Between 20 and 25 percent of untreated victims die, making Rocky Mountain spotted fever the most severe rickettsial infection in the Americas. First identified in the Rocky Mountain region of the United States, this place name has never been dislodged, even though it is inaccurate and even misleading.

Etiology and Epidemiology

The severity with which Rocky Mountain spotted fever treats its victims underscores its natural existence as an infection of ticks and their mammalian hosts. The microbial cause of the disease, *Rickettsia rickettsii,* normally inhabits *ixodid,* or hard shell, ticks, apparently causing little harm to the host. Although small mammals are susceptible to a mild infection with *R. rickettsii* and may transmit it to uninfected ticks, the principal means by which the organism is maintained in nature is from one generation to the next in the eggs of the female tick.

The epidemiology of Rocky Mountain spotted fever is linked to areas favorable for the habitation of the vector ticks. The Rocky Mountain wood tick, *Dermacentor andersoni,* and the American dog tick, *Dermacentor variabilis,* are the most common vectors in the United States, although the Lone Star tick, *Amblyomma americanum,* also transmits the disease in the south central and southeastern parts of the United States. Two other ticks, *Rhipicephalus sanguineus* and *Amblyomma cajennense,* also carry the disease in Mexico, Central America, and South America. Only a small percentage of ticks – generally less than 5 percent – are usually infective.

Humans typically contract Rocky Mountain spotted fever when they accidentally become a part of the disease's biosystem. In the western United States, hikers, backpackers, and the like may become subjected to infection when traveling in areas where ticks are plentiful, especially during the spring months. In the eastern United States, where most cases now occur, changing land-use patterns have brought humans into the habitat of the tick. The development of suburban housing developments and the transformation of agricultural land into wooded recreation areas are two examples.

Rocky Mountain spotted fever characteristically appears in "islands" of infection. During early research on a particularly virulent form in Montana's Bitterroot Valley, for example, investigators were baffled by the fact that Rocky Mountain spotted fever appeared on the west side of the Bitterroot River but not on the east side (see Map VIII.120.1). Recently, Rocky Mountain Laboratory investigator Willy Burgdorfer has shown that this peculiar epidemiological occurrence is related to an antigenic "interference phenomenon." Nonpathogenic rickettsiae in the ovaries of ticks on the east side of the river "interfere" with the establishment of pathogenic rickettsiae in these tissues, thus preventing the pathogenic *R. rickettsii* from being passed on to the next generation of ticks.

Distribution and Incidence

Known only in the Western Hemisphere, Rocky Mountain spotted fever has been identified in Canada, the United States, Mexico, Costa Rica, Panama, Brazil, and Colombia. Before 1940, most cases were reported in the Rocky Mountain region, but since that time, the number of cases in the southeastern and southwestern United States (sometimes called the "tick belt" region) has far outstripped those reported from the west. In the 1970s, case incidence in the United States began to rise, reaching a peak of 1,192 cases in 1981. In recent years, the number of cases has declined slightly and leveled off. At present, Oklahoma has the highest infection rate in relation to its population, whereas North Carolina reports the largest number of cases. A small number of cases continues to occur in Canada. In Mexico and Central and South America, the disease is poorly reported, and consequently it is difficult to estimate its actual incidence in these areas.

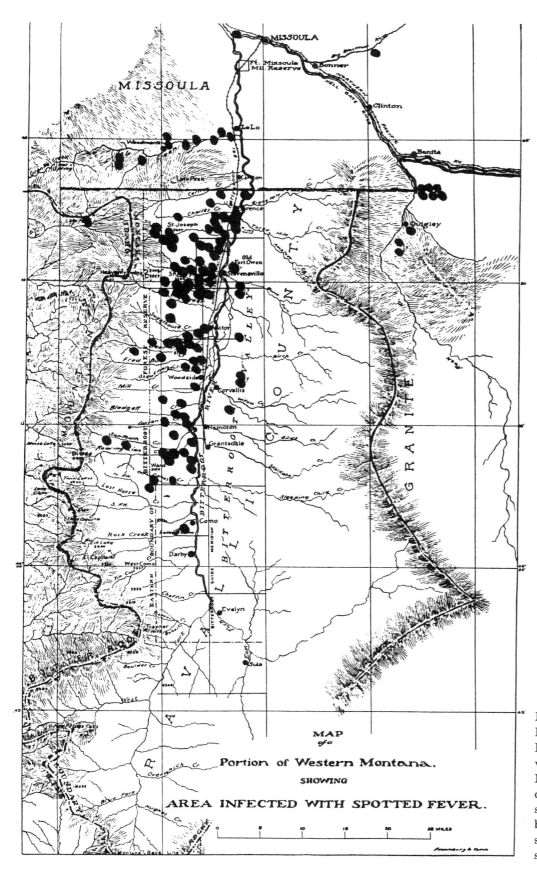

Map VIII.120.1. Epidemiological map of Rocky Mountain spotted fever in Bitterroot Valley, Montana, 1902. Recorded cases are highlighted to show the predominant distribution of cases on the west side of the valley. (From Wilson and Chowning 1904.)

Clinical Manifestations

After an incubation period of from 3 to 12 days, typical typhuslike symptoms appear abruptly: severe headache, joint and back pains, prostration, and a high fever. About the fourth day of fever, the characteristic skin rash appears. Usually beginning on the wrist and ankles, it spreads to cover the entire body. Because few diseases cause rashes on the palms of the hands and the soles of the feet, this sign, when accompanied by high fever and history of tick exposure, is considered diagnostic. The fever continues for 2 to 3 weeks, usually subsiding gradually in cases that recover. In fatal cases, neurological symptoms of deafness, confusion, delirium, and coma are accompanied by circulatory collapse, and, often, kidney failure. In addition, the rash may darken, becoming almost black, and may spread, becoming confluent in some cases. These characteristics contributed to two early names for the disease, "black measles" and "blue disease."

If diagnosed early in the course of illness, Rocky Mountain spotted fever may be treated effectively with broad-spectrum antibiotics. Patients at risk of dying are usually those in whom the disease is not diagnosed in time to begin effective treatment. On their first visit to a physician, such patients do not report a history of tick exposure, do not yet have a visible rash, and often complain of abdominal symptoms that may be confused with other illnesses. At special risk are people who suffer from glucose-6-phosphate dehydrogenase (G6PD) deficiency, a genetic-linked disorder, which has a high frequency in black males relative to most other peoples and to black females. Thus mortality rates from Rocky Mountain spotted fever are significantly higher for black males than for the general population.

History and Geography

Rocky Mountain spotted fever as a specific disease entity is essentially twentieth century in origin. Retrospective diagnoses have identified the disease in the eighteenth and nineteenth centuries, but the first reports differentiating it from other fevers were published only in the late 1890s. Pioneers traveling the western trails of North America encountered a disease in the spring variously known as "trail typhus," "spotted fever," "spotted typhus," or other such descriptive names. Mortality varied from under 5 percent in Idaho to approximately 70 percent in the Bitterroot Valley of western Montana.

In 1901, public outcry for action against the deadly disease in the Bitterroot Valley stimulated the newly created Montana State Board of Health to launch a scientific investigation of the disease. In 1902, two pathologists from the University of Minnesota suggested that the wood tick might be the vector of the disease, which they believed was caused by a protozoan organism. Their etiologic theory was discredited, but in 1906 the tick was independently confirmed as the disease vector by Howard Taylor Ricketts of the University of Chicago and by Walter King of the U.S. Public Health Service. Ricketts continued the investigations, seeking to produce a vaccine or therapeutic serum against the disease. In 1909, when funding for Ricketts's research was delayed in the Montana state legislature, he accepted an invitation to study tabardillo, the Mexican typhus fever, in Mexico City. Tragically, he contracted typhus and died in May 1910.

Between 1910 and 1920, efforts to combat Rocky Mountain spotted fever focused on tick eradication programs. Modeled on the successful tick control program that had eliminated Texas cattle fever throughout the South, the campaign failed against Rocky Mountain spotted fever for two reasons. The Texas cattle fever tick was a one-host tick, whereas the Rocky Mountain wood tick chose different hosts for each stage in its life cycle. This characteristic made control much more difficult. Second, cold spring weather in Montana interfered with livestock dipping when the ticks first emerged.

In 1916 S. Burt Wolbach of Harvard University Medical School described the etiologic agent of Rocky Mountain spotted fever, which he labeled "a wholly new kind of micro-organism." Wolbach originally named it *Dermacentroxenus rickettsi*, the genus name after its vector tick and the species name after Ricketts. Taxonomists later classified this organism in the same genus with the typhus germs, changing its name to *Rickettsia rickettsii*.

In 1921 the U.S. Public Health Service renewed the effort to prepare a vaccine against Rocky Mountain spotted fever. Working jointly, physician Roscoe R. Spencer and entomologist Ralph R. Parker succeeded in 1924 in preparing a vaccine from infected ticks, the first successful vaccine made from the bodies of arthropod vectors. From 1925, when clinical trials began, through 1948, when effective antibiotics were introduced, the Spencer–Parker vaccine was the chief means of fighting Rocky Mountain spotted fever.

In 1931 the disease was discovered to exist on the eastern seaboard of the United States, and shortly thereafter, pockets of infection were identified in São Paulo, Brazil; in Tobia, Colombia; in Choix, Mexico; as well as in Canada and other areas of the Western

Hemisphere. The original names by which the disease was known sometimes underscored its character as a "place" disease. For example, it was called *febre maculosa brasileira* but also "São Paulo typhus" in Brazil, "Tobia petechial fever" in Colombia, and *fiebre de Choix* as well as *fiebre manchada* in Mexico. As additional information became known about other rickettsial diseases, numerous investigators suggested more appropriate names for the disease, such as tick-borne typhus, tick spotted typhus, American spotted fever, or, simply, spotted fever. None successfully supplanted Rocky Mountain spotted fever.

After the introduction of the broad-spectrum antibiotics in 1948, Rocky Mountain spotted fever incidence in the United States dropped to about 250 cases per year, with only about 24 deaths. To some extent, the early and widespread use of antibiotics may have obscured the true incidence of the disease. Beginning in 1969 and continuing through the 1970s, the incidence of Rocky Mountain spotted fever rose inexorably in the United States, probably as a result of the development of suburban housing and the transformation of agricultural land into wooded recreational areas. Although this phenomenon was not reported from other countries of the hemisphere, it was reported in the Mediterranean basin, where *boutonneuse fever,* a related but milder spotted fever group disease, was known. The increase in Rocky Mountain spotted fever cases and deaths during the 1970s stimulated new research into diagnosis and prevention of the disease.

Unlike epidemic typhus, Rocky Mountain spotted fever poses no threat of erupting into epidemics. As a disease of nature, however, it is unlikely to be eradicated as a human hazard. If the public and physicians are alert to the possibility of infection during "tick seasons," effective antibiotic therapy can be administered and Rocky Mountain spotted fever need not cause unnecessary loss of life.

Other Diseases of the Spotted Fever Group

Three other major tick-borne rickettsioses are known throughout the world. Usually mild diseases, these three spotted fever group maladies are generally fatal only to the aged or debilitated patients. All exhibit a distinctive diagnostic characteristic, an *eschar,* or dark scab, that forms over the wound caused by the initial tick bite. Lymph nodes draining the eschar also swell and become tender.

Boutonneuse fever, named for the buttonlike eschar, was the earliest of these spotted fever group diseases identified. Described by Alfred Conor in North Africa in 1910, the disease has also been known by many other local names, including Mediterranean spotted fever, *fièvre boutonneuse,* Marseilles exanthematic fever, Indian tick-typhus, South African tick-bite fever, and Italian eruptive fever. Its most common etiologic agent is *Rickettsia conorii,* the species name given in honor of Conor. In recent decades, other variant spotted fever group strains have also been identified as causing this disease. A number of different ticks are responsible for its transmission, the most common being *R. sanguineus.* In Africa, many people apparently gain immunity during childhood through a mild infection, for the disease is primarily seen in tourists or in new residents. From its local names, it is apparent that boutonneuse fever is known from Africa throughout the Mediterranean basin and into India. During the 1970s an increase paralleling that of Rocky Mountain spotted fever in the United States was reported in the Mediterranean basin.

Siberian tick-typhus was first documented during the 1930s, when exploitation of Siberian forest and steppes brought many people into the habitat of its vector ticks. Transmitted by several species of ixodid ticks, it is believed to be far more widespread than reported statistics indicate. Its etiologic agent is *Rickettsia siberica.* Known as well as North Asian tick-typhus, this disease is also found in China and in other north Asian republics.

Queensland tick-typhus, caused by *Rickettsia australis,* was first reported in North Queensland, Australia, in 1946. Its vector tick, *Ixodes holocyclus,* parasitizes marsupials in addition to wild rodents. In general, people working in forest and scrub areas in northern and southern Queensland are at risk of contracting this disease, although in 1979 an urban focus was reported in Sydney.

The final member of the spotted fever group of diseases is unique in being the only member not transmitted by a tick. Its name, *rickettsialpox,* clearly reflects its history as a disease defined by the investigators who first studied it. In 1946 a strange disease resembling mild chickenpox and exhibiting an eschar, or initial lesion, was reported in a New York apartment building. Charles Pomerantz, a local exterminator and amateur entomologist, had alerted New York health authorities to the possibility of some sort of arthropod-borne disease after he found mite-infected mice in the apartment-complex basement. New York investigators collaborated with the U.S. Public Health Service, and within 8 months the entire picture of the disease had been elucidated. The etiologic agent of the disease was shown to be a hitherto unknown rickettsia of the spotted fever group. Because the organism was found to inhabit the mite *Allodermanyssus sanguineus,* a parasite of the house mouse, it was named *Rickettsia akari,* the species designation meaning "mite." Epidemiological research determined that the disease was contracted wherever mites had access to human living areas. In the case of the original apartment complex, the mites climbed up a central incinerator and infested the carpeting in apartments, thus rendering young children especially susceptible. In 1949–50 the illness was also identified in the Soviet Union, and was known there as *vesicular rickettsiosis.* A mild, nonfatal disease, rickettsialpox has not been reported in recent years in the United States and only sporadically in the former Soviet Union.

Victoria A. Harden

Bibliography

Aikawa, Jerry K. 1966. *Rocky Mountain spotted fever.* Springfield, Ill.

Harden, Victoria A. 1985. Rocky Mountain spotted fever research and the development of the insect vector theory. *Bulletin of the History of Medicine* 59: 449–66.
    1990. *Rocky mountain spotted fever: A twentieth-century disease.* Baltimore.

Hoogstraal, Harry. 1981. Changing patterns of tickborne diseases in modern society. *Annual Reviews of Entomology* 26: 75–99.

Lackman, David B. 1963. A review of information of rickettsialpox in the United States. *Clinical Pediatrics* 2: 296–301.

McDade, Joseph E., and Verne F. Newhouse. 1948. Natural history of *rickettsia rickettsii. Annual Review of Microbiology* 40: 287–309.

Price, Esther Gaskins. 1948. *Fighting spotted fever in the Rockies.* Helena, Montana.

Roueche, Berton. 1947. The alerting of Mr. Pomerantz. *New Yorker* August 30: 28.

U.S. Public Health Service. Centers for Disease Control. 1985. Rocky Mountain spotted fever – United States, 1985. *Morbidity and Mortality Weekly Reports* 35 (April 18): 247–9.

Wilson, Louis B., and William M. Chowning. 1904. Studies in pyroplasmosis hominis: 'Spotted fever' or 'tick fever' of the Rocky Mountains. *Journal of Infectious Diseases* 1: 31–57.

Woodward, Theodore E., and Elizabeth B. Jackson. 1965. Spotted fever rickettsiae. In *Viral and rickettsial infections of man,* ed. Frank L. Horsfall, Jr., and Igor Tamm, 1095–129. Philadelphia.

VIII.121
Rubella

Rubella (German measles; 3-day measles) is a common, acute, viral infectious disease, principally of children and young adults, with worldwide distribution frequently characterized clinically as a mild rash illness. Inapparent infection is common and may occur in as many as half of infections. Rubella has special significance when a pregnant woman contracts the disease in early pregnancy because fetal infection can ensue and result in developmental abnormalities known as the congenital rubella syndrome (CRS). Rubella is a vaccine-preventable disease, but the vaccine is not yet widely used on a global basis.

Etiology and Epidemiology

Rubella is caused by the rubella virus, which is in the genus *Rubivirus* of the family Togaviridae. Rubella virus is 50 to 60 nanometers in diameter and contains a single-stranded RNA genome.

Rubella is a highly contagious disease transmitted by contact of susceptible individuals with the nose and throat secretions of infected persons, primarily by droplet spread. Infection also occurs by direct contact, by indirect contact through freshly soiled articles, and by airborne transmission. There is no reservoir for rubella other than human beings, which means that a continuous chain of susceptible contacts is necessary to sustain transmission. The period of communicability is from about 1 week before rash onset to at least 4 days after. There is no carrier state except for infants with congenital rubella, who may shed virus for many months after birth. Rubella's incubation period from time of exposure to onset of rash is 16 to 18 days, with a range of 14 to 23 days.

In populated areas with no or low vaccination coverage, rubella is primarily an endemic disease of children with periodic epidemics. However, a significant proportion of adults remain susceptible, and thus congenital rubella may result if a pregnant woman contracts rubella. In more remote isolated populations, rubella is not endemic and disease is dependent upon introduction of the virus from the outside, at which time an epidemic may occur, affecting all age groups born since the last epidemic. There is no evidence for a sex difference in incidence or severity of rubella, although more cases may be reported in women because of concern for congenital rubella. There is no evidence for a racial difference in incidence or severity.

The risk of congenital rubella is related to gestational age at the time of maternal infection. Fetal or placental infection has been shown to accompany 85 percent of maternal infections that occur during the first 8 weeks of pregnancy. Data from the last major epidemic in the United States, which occurred from 1964 to 1965 and resulted in 20,000 infants born with congenital rubella syndrome, showed that the risk of developmental defects was about 50 percent in infants whose mothers were infected during the first month of pregnancy, 22 percent during the second, 6 percent during the third, and about 1 percent during the fourth month of pregnancy. Other investigators have shown that infection in the first 8 weeks of pregnancy also leads to high rates of abortion or stillbirth.

Distribution and Incidence

Rubella has a global distribution. Although it is not a reportable disease in most countries, is underreported in countries where it is a notifiable disease, and may be clinically inapparent in as many as 50 percent of infections, serologic surveillance demonstrates its existence throughout the world. In populated areas where rubella is both endemic and epidemic, between 80 and 90 percent of the adult population will show serologic evidence of prior infection. In remote or island populations where rubella is not endemic, a significant proportion of the population can be susceptible, which may lead to large outbreaks when the virus is introduced from the outside.

In some countries with extensive use of rubella vaccine and where rubella is a reportable disease, such as the United States and the United Kingdom, there have been impressive declines in reported cases of rubella and congenital rubella syndrome.

Immunology

Infants usually have a passive immunity to rubella because of maternal antibodies acquired transplacentally from immune mothers. This passive immunity protects the infant from infection for 6 to 9 months, depending on the amount of maternal antibody acquired.

Rubella infection in both clinically apparent and inapparent cases induces a lifelong immunity. Because a significant percentage of rubella infections are clinically inapparent, persons may develop im-

munity without recognizing that they have been infected. Several serologic tests for confirming infection or immunity have been developed, and it is also possible to isolate the virus from patients during the acute phase of the disease.

A single dose of live attenuated rubella virus vaccine confers long-term, probably lifelong, immunity in approximately 95 percent of susceptible individuals.

Clinical Manifestations and Pathology

The prodromal phase of postnatally acquired rubella usually occurs from 1 to 5 days prior to rash onset, but may be completely lacking, especially in children. Prodromal symptoms may include headache, low-grade fever, malaise, conjunctivitis, mild rhinitis, and lymphadenopathy (most commonly tender swelling of the lymph nodes behind the ears and at the base of the skull). The rash phase of illness begins with a reddish, discrete rash, sometimes itchy, usually appearing first on the face and then spreading to the hands and feet. Although the progression, duration, and extent of the rash vary greatly, it typically covers the whole body within 24 hours and has disappeared completely by the end of the third day – hence the name 3-day measles. It is important to note that the variability and sometimes the absence of prodromal symptoms as well as rash make a clinical diagnosis uncertain, and laboratory serologic tests are necessary for confirmation of the diagnosis.

Complications in postnatally acquired illness may include arthritis and arthralgia, which are more common in adults and women than in prepubertal children and men. Neurological involvement, including encephalitis, is a rare complication of rubella.

In congenitally acquired rubella, the fetal infection may result in abortion, stillbirth, congenital malformations, or growth retardation. The congenital rubella syndrome is the result of inhibition of cell multiplication in the developing fetus and a chronic infective state that may persist for many months after birth. Some consequences of fetal infection may not become apparent until years after birth. Common congenital abnormalities and active infective processes at birth include cataracts, deafness, central nervous system defects leading to mental retardation, structural defects of the heart and myocarditis, bone lesions, pneumonitis, and hepatitis.

History and Geography

The early history of rubella is confused with that of other illnesses that produce a rash such as measles and smallpox. Although it has been suggested that the early Arabian physicians differentiated rubella as a form of measles known as *Hhamikah,* the disease appears to have been first described in 1619 by Daniel Sennert, who used the term *Rotheln* (*röteln*) and attributed the name, which seems to have been a popular term, to the red color of the rash. Two German physicians are generally credited with clinically describing rubella as a separate entity during the 1750s, and it continued to be called *Rotheln* by German investigators from the mid-eighteenth to the mid-nineteenth century. The early interest in the disease by German physicians apparently led to the use of the term "German measles" in other countries. It has, however, also been suggested that the word may have actually been "germane" rather than "German," with derivations meaning "closely akin to." In other words, "germane measles" was intended to indicate a disease similiar to measles.

In 1866 Henry Veale, a Scottish physician serving in India, published a description of 30 cases of rubella and proposed the name "rubella" as being "short for the sake of convenience in writing, and euphonious for ease in pronunciation." At the International Congress of Medicine in London in 1881, a general consensus was reached that rubella was an independent entity. William Squire summarized this consensus, noting, "A century was required to complete the separation of measles from smallpox. Another century passed from Thomas Sydenham to William Withering before scarlet fever was finally distinguished from measles. . . . The century is fulfilled that should give autonomy to rubella." During the next 60 years attention was focused on differentiating the characteristics and further describing the symptomatology and course of rubella, which was considered an inconsequential infection of childhood. The fact that rubella was due to a virus and transmissible by the injection of throat washings was established by Y. Hiro and S. Tasaka in 1938.

Then, in 1941, Norman McAlister Gregg, an Australian ophthalmologic surgeon, published a landmark work on his observations of an epidemic of congenital cataracts and other ocular and cardiac abnormalities in infants of mothers who had contracted rubella in the first trimester of their pregnancy. Although skepticism at first prevailed in the medical community, his observations were confirmed by other investigators in Australia, the United States, and the United Kingdom who also described other congenital abnormalities associated with rubella in pregnancy. The comprehensive paper on rubella published by Conrad Wesselhoeft in 1947 helped to draw world attention to the importance of Gregg's findings, and in 1953, Saul Krugman, Robert Ward, and their colleagues were able to document, through volunteer studies, that rubella infection can occur without rash.

The rubella virus was isolated and propagated in tissue culture in 1962 simultaneously by T. H. Weller and F. A. Neva at the Harvard School of Public Health in Boston and by P. D. Parkman, E. L. Buescher, and M. S. Artenstein at the Walter Reed Army Institute of Research in Washington, D.C. In addition to providing the tools needed to further understanding of the epidemiology of the disease, including the hemagglutination-inhibition test introduced in 1967, this isolation also led to subsequent research and development of vaccines. In 1969 a live attenuated rubella virus vaccine was licensed for use in the United States, and shortly thereafter other vaccine virus strains were adopted for use in the United States and in several European countries.

The World Health Organization (WHO) has coordinated collaborative seroepidemiological studies of rubella documenting geographic patterns. In countries without any sustained, large-scale immunization programs, it has been shown that rubella infection is widespread. It was also possible to show through serial seroepidemiological studies that rubella epidemics may occur even when clinical records do not document an outbreak of overt rubella. Urban areas demonstrate sustained circulation of virus, whereas rural areas may show patterns of lower immunity rates. In island or remote communities, many persons may be susceptible. In countries with sustained, large-scale immunization programs, the impact of control efforts has been demonstrated by a decrease in the numbers of cases of reported rubella and congenital rubella syndrome and of susceptibles in the population.

Robert J. Kim-Farley

This chapter was written in the author's private capacity. No official support or endorsement by the Centers for Disease Control is intended or should be inferred.

Bibliography

Amstey, Marvin S., ed. 1984. *Virus infection in pregnancy.* New York.

Assaad, F., and K. Ljungars-Esteves. 1985. Rubella – world impact. *Reviews of Infectious Diseases* 7 (Supplement 1): S29–36.

Benenson, Abram S., ed. 1985. *Control of communicable diseases in man.* Washington, D.C.

Bett, Walter R., ed. 1954. *The history and conquest of common diseases.* Norman, Okla.

Cockburn, Charles W. 1969. World aspects of the epidemiology of rubella. *American Journal of Diseases of Children* 118: 112–22.

Cooper, Louis Z. 1985. The history and medical consequences of rubella. *Reviews of Infectious Diseases* 7 (Suppl. 1): S2–9.

Emminghaus, H. 1870. Ueber Rubeolen. *Jahrbuch für Kinderheilkunde und physische Erziehung* 4: 47–59.

Feigin, Ralph D., and James D. Cherry, eds. 1981. *Textbook of pediatric infectious diseases*. Philadelphia.

Forbes, John A. 1969. Rubella: Historical aspects. *American Journal of Diseases of Children* 118: 5–11.

Goodall, E. W. 1934. *A short history of the epidemic infectious diseases*. London.

Gregg, Norman McA. 1941. Congenital cataract following German measles in the mother. *Transactions of Ophthalmological Society of Australia* 3: 35–46.

Hiro, Y., and S. Tasaka. 1938. Die Röteln sind eine Viruskrankheit. *Monatschrift für Kinderheilkunde* 76: 328–32.

Krugman, S., et al. 1953. Studies on rubella immunization. I. Demonstration of rubella without rash. *Journal of the American Medical Association* 151: 285–8.

Parkman, P. D., et al. 1962. Recovery of rubella virus from Army recruits. *Proceedings of the Society for Experimental Biology and Medicine* 111: 225–30.

Squire, William. 1881. On rubella: Rubeola sine catarrho: Rotheln, or German measles. *Transactions of the International Congress of Medicine* 4: 27–31.

U.S. Public Health Service. Centers for Disease Control. 1987. Rubella and congenital rubella – United States, 1984–1986. *Morbidity and Mortality Weekly Reports* 36: 664–6, 671–5.

Veale, Henry. 1866. History of an epidemic of Rotheln, with observations on its pathology. *Edinburgh Medical Journal* 12: 404–14.

Weller, T. H., and F. A. Neva. 1962. Propagation in tissue culture of cytopathic agents from patients with rubella-like illnesses. *Proceedings of the Society for Experimental Biology and Medicine* 111: 215–25.

Wesselhoeft, Conrad. 1947. Rubella (German measles). *New England Journal of Medicine* 236: 943–50.

Withering, William. 1779. *An account of the scarlet fever and sore throat, or scarlatina anginosa; particularly as it appeared at Birmingham in the year 1778*. London.

VIII.122
St. Anthony's Fire

This disease is generally associated with *ergotism*, a disease resulting from the ingestion of the ergot fungus that grows on rye. Most authorities assume that the name St. Anthony's fire refers to St. Anthony the Great, a third-century A.D. hermit and founder of Christian ascetic monasticism. This saint renounced the world for the deserts of Egypt and, according to hagiographers, there combatted the devil numerous times. His visions of the devil took the form of worldly pleasures, seductive women, dragons, banquet tables, and the like. However, St. Anthony of Padua, born in the late twelfth century, may also be connected to the name of the disease. This saint was a noted preacher, popular for his ability to exorcise demons. He was also known for restoring the insane to health, and was credited with miraculously healing an individual whose limb had been amputated.

Supposedly the "fire" part of the name refers to the painful skin infections, gangrene, and neurological disturbances that occur with ergot poisoning. Thus, in France north of the Loire where rye was a traditional staple grain, attributing most cases of *mal des ardents* to ergotism has seemed reasonable to historians. Sufferers there reportedly lost limbs, attributable to the gangrenous form of ergotism, if they survived both the initial inflammatory process and the generalized famine that accompanied epidemics of the disease. On the other hand, it is also quite possible that erysipelas and other bacterial skin infections were at the root of the symptoms mentioned, for these diseases also flourish under conditions of famine.

The disease we think of as St. Anthony's fire was commonly described in western Europe from 900 to 1700. During the eleventh century, recurrences of the "sacred fire" (usually associated with erysipelas in classical medicine) led to the creation of hospitals and also to an appeal to many different interceding saints, of whom Anthony was only one. In the Dauphiné region of France, however, Count Gerlin II acquired the relics of St. Anthony the Great and returned them in 1070 to Vienne (on the Rhône River). By 1090 healing miracles were being attributed to the bones, and local nobles helped a small group of lay hospitalers to form a pilgrimage site for sufferers of "fire." By the twelfth century, this hos-

Figure VIII.122.1. Woodcut of St. Anthony by Johannes Wechtlin. (From Hanns von Gersdorff. 1517. *Feldtbuch de Wundartznev.* Strassburg, by courtesy of the Lilly Library, Bloomington, Indiana.)

pice was run by regular clergy, calling themselves "friars of the blue Tau," for the large Greek letter that came to symbolize Anthony iconographically. Wine or water steeped in the bones of the saint was offered sufferers as the miraculous cure; however, additional food supplements at the hospices of St. Anthony may have arrested ergot intoxication.

During the later Middle Ages, the cult of St. Anthony spread well beyond the regions of southern France and Savoy, where it had gained rapid popularity, into central Europe as far east as Russia. There the people often commemorated cures with votive art that has come to symbolize the disease to posterity. For example, in Figure VIII.122.1, a victim stretches his fiery hand toward the saint for help.

The earliest unambiguous references to the ergot fungus occur in the late sixteenth century; by the late seventeenth century, ergotism was described independently of the popular attribution to St. Anthony. The older name – perhaps the older "disease"

as well – rapidly disappeared from learned descriptions, in part because of the association of ergot fungus on rye and other grains with epidemics of convulsive and other neurological disorders, rather than with the skin infections and subsequent gangrene that characterized "St. Anthony's fire."

Ann G. Carmichael

Bibliography

Barger, George. 1931. *Ergot and ergotism.* London.

Bové, Frank, J. 1970. *The story of ergot.* Basel, N.Y.

Carbonelli, G. 1920. Del fuoco di S. Antonio e due documenti iconografici del XV secolo. *Bolletino di Istituto Storico, Italiano dell'Arte Sanitaria* 19: 144–53.

Chaumartin, Henry. 1946. *Le Mal des ardents et le feu Saint Antoine: Etudes historique, médicales, hagiographiques et légendaire.* Vienne.

Dotz, Warren. 1980. St. Anthony's fire. *American Journal of Dermatopathology* 2: 249–53.

Frey, Emil F. 1979. Saints in medical history. *Clio Medica* 14: 35–70.

VIII.123
Scarlet Fever

Scarlet fever is an acute infectious disease, caused by certain types of group A hemolytic streptococci. The disease is characterized by sudden onset of soreness on swallowing, with fever and headache. A rash appears within 2 days of onset, and desquamation follows.

The term "scarlet fever" was supposedly first used by Thomas Sydenham in 1683, but it appeared in a diary of Samuel Pepys in an entry for November 10, 1664. From the seventeenth to the early twentieth century, the word *scarlatina* was popularly used to denote a mild form of the disease.

Distribution and Incidence

Like the streptococcal sore throat to which it is closely related, scarlet fever is a disease of temperate climates, prevailing generally in the winter months. It occurs principally in young children, although adults may suffer sore throats as a result of the same infection.

Etiology and Epidemiology

The group A hemolytic streptococci are responsible for a range of afflictions other than scarlet fever, including erysipelas, rheumatic fever, and the sore throats known as tonsillitis in Great Britain and as pharyngitis in the United States. Scarlet fever is caused only by certain strains that produce (or release) a soluble toxin, whose absorption causes the rash characteristic of the disease. Different strains of streptococci produce different amounts of toxin. Epidemics thus vary greatly in severity, with mortality rates ranging from 0 to 30 percent. Transmission of the infection is by intimate contact, such as occurs in overcrowded homes and classrooms, and evidence of airborne or droplet nuclei infection is slight. In the past, scarlet fever occasionally occurred as a hospital infection, and the disease was also transmitted in contaminated milk.

Susceptibility to the skin rash differs according to the immune and hypersensitivity status of the individual. Those who have experienced scarlet fever once are unlikely to do so again, but remain vulnerable to streptococcal sore throats when exposed to infection with a new serologic type. Research on the susceptibility of different population groups, as defined by a positive skin test (Dick test), suggests that more than half of young infants are immune to the disease, but that by the age of 2 years, only some 20 percent remain so. Thereafter the proportion of immunes rises steadily through childhood, reaching 77 percent at 10 to 15 years and 86 percent in adults.

The rare occurrence of second attacks of scarlet fever with rash is probably due to infection with a new antigenic erythrogenic toxin. The available evidence suggests that the geographic dominance of particular strains of scarlet fever streptococci is long-term, varying from country to country and from time to time. In Britain, during the years 1936 to 1956, type 4 streptococci were isolated more often from scarlet fever than from tonsillitis cases. In 1964–5, the commonest type associated with scarlet fever was type 4 in Britain, type 22 in East Germany, and type 1 in the former Soviet Union and Holland. With all types, the disease appears to follow a general pattern of alternate severity and mildness. At present, it is very common, though very mild, in both Europe and North America. Fatalities have ceased to occur, and the prevailing mildness of type means that cases tend to escape notification.

Clinical Manifestations

The initial symptoms of scarlet fever are the same as those of streptococcal sore throat: sudden onset of soreness on swallowing, accompanied by fever and headache. Vomiting and nausea are often early symptoms in young children. The characteristically erythemateous and punctuate rash appears within 2 days, at first on the upper chest and back, then spreading to the rest of the body. In white patients the rash does not commonly appear on the face, but in about half of all black patients it does. The rash is accompanied by the characteristic raspberry tongue. In general, the rash is variable in its manifestations. Desquamation usually occurs, beginning sometimes as early as the fifth day, sometimes as late as 4 to 5 weeks after the onset of the disease. A range of complications, principally affecting young children, add to the dangers of the disease. These include anemia, otitis media, rheumatic fever, and meningitis. In rare cases, scarlet fever appears in severe septic or toxic forms.

History and Geography

The early history of scarlet fever prevalence is obscure. It is possible that outbreaks were observed by Near Eastern practitioners of the Arabian school, but the first undoubted account of a disease with a fiery rash as a characteristic was provided by Giovanni Filippo Ingrassia of Palermo in 1553. The disease was apparently present in Germany and Italy in the early seventeenth century, and we know of a severe outbreak in Poland in 1625. At that time, the disease was variously known as *rossalia, purpurea epidemica maligna,* and *febris miliaria rubra.* It is clear from observations by Daniel Sennert in 1619, Michael Düring in 1625, and Johann Schultes in 1665 that the scarlatinal manifestations of desquamation, nephritis, and dropsy were well known before the disease received its modern name. Although in 1683 Sydenham wrote of the disease as having a mild character, he nevertheless established its autonomy, and distinguished it from other acute exanthema, notably measles, by naming it. By the end of the seventeenth century, the identity of scarlet fever was well recognized, although much epidemiological confusion remained, and still remains, over the respective roles of scarlet fever, streptococcal sore throat, and diphtheria (cynanche maligna) in seventeenth-century and eighteenth-century epidemics.

During the eighteenth century, scarlet fever was present in epidemic form throughout Europe and the United States. It appeared in Copenhagen in 1677, in Scotland in 1684, in the United States in 1735, and in Sweden in 1744. In general, however, the evidence suggests that the disease made irregular epidemic appearances, and that its mortality varied considerably. During the early eighteenth century, it seems to have been of fairly mild character, but

Dutch and Swedish evidence suggests that by mid-century a very virulent strain was also present.

The character of scarlet fever as a relatively new disease may be reflected in the age incidences reported during this period. Sydenham noted that it attacked whole families, though more especially the infants, whereas Nils Rósen von Rosenstein observed in 1744 the simultaneous occurrence of sore throat without rash in children in infected households. This pattern was observed in adults by Maxmilian Stoll in 1786. In the last years of the century, scarlet fever was extensive and virulent in Europe, with severe outbreaks in Denmark and Finland in 1776–8, and in central Germany in 1795–1805. By 1814 it was again very mild, but continued its global spread, appearing in South America in 1892, in Greenland in 1847, and in Australia and New Zealand in 1848.

During the 1820s and 1830s, however, a more virulent form reappeared, and consequently, the disease was the leading cause of death among infectious childhood maladies until 1875. During the 1880s, the disease continued to be widely prevalent but began to decline as a cause of death, and by the 1890s its character was again relatively mild, although not as mild as it has become today. This decline in severity was first apparent in Britain and western Europe, although a malignant form was still present in Poland, Russia, and Romania during the 1930s. Observations by Edward Wilberforce Goodall made in the Metropolitan Asylums' Board's Eastern Hospital, London, showed that as fatality dwindled, so did the more serious clinical forms.

Streptococci were first isolated from the blood of scarlet fever patients by Edward Klein in 1887, but he failed to reproduce the disease in animals. In 1911 Kari Landsteiner produced a similar disease in monkeys by inoculating them with faucial exudate from scarlet fever patients, but until about 1922 the streptococci were generally considered to be secondary invaders.

It was ultimately observation of human beings that proved scarlet fever to be a result of streptococcal infection. Seminal work by George Dick and Gladys Dick in the early 1920s proved scarlet fever to be primarily a local infection of the throat caused by type A hemolytic streptococci. In 1923 the Dicks successfully inoculated volunteers, and in 1924 developed the *Dick test:* the intradermal injection of a diluted filtrate of a broth culture of a scarlatinal strain of streptococcus which, by the resultant appearance or not of a local erythemateous reaction, determines the susceptibility of the subject to scarlet fever. In other words, a negative Dick test is an indication of antitoxic immunity.

Anne Hardy

Bibliography

Rolleston, J. D. 1937. *The history of acute exanthema.* London.

Smith, Francis B. 1979. *The people's health, 1830–1910.* London.

Wilson, L. G. 1986. The historical riddle of milk-borne scarlet fever. *Bulletin of the History of Medicine* 60: 321–42.

VIII.124
Schistosomiasis

Schistosomiasis (bilharzia), known also by many local names such as "red-water fever," "snail fever," "big-belly," and "Katayama disease," is an "immunologic disease" induced by eggs of blood-vessel-inhabiting worms of the class Trematoda, genus *Schistosoma.* These eggs induce an immunologic response after they become trapped in the body organs, especially the liver, gut wall, and urogenital tract.

There are three major human schistosome species: *Schistosoma haematobium,* which inhabit the veins of the bladder area and whose eggs are discharged in the urine; and *Schistosoma mansoni* and *Schistosoma japonicum,* which inhabit the mesenteric veins supplying the intestines and whose eggs are discharged in the feces. In every case, however, the worms may also be found in the liver and portal system. There are also a few other species that can parasitize humans. These include the japonicum-like *Schistosoma mekongi* from the lower Mekong River basin, and some African schistosomes, such as *Schistosoma intercalatum,* that normally parasitize cattle and wild animals.

Terminology

The terminology of this disease is very confusing. Theodor Bilharz, the discoverer of the trematode worm responsible for the disease, placed it in the genus *Distoma,* a broad genus that was soon abandoned as more trematode species were discovered. Numerous generic names were thereafter invented to label the worm, including *Schistosoma* in 1858 (the name that must stand according to the rules of zoological nomenclature), *Gynaecophorus* in 1858, *Bilhar-*

zia in 1859, and *Thecosoma* in 1860. Before World War II, however, in an understandable desire to honor the name of Bilharz, the disease was commonly called *bilharziasis*. But in 1949, members of the World Health Organization's Study Group on Bilharziasis in Africa, ignorant of the tight rules of zoological nomenclature, recommended that the name *Bilharzia* be used for the worm and "bilharziasis" for the disease. A recommendation to this effect was made to the International Commission of Zoological Nomenclature which ruled, in 1954, that the disease should be called bilharziasis, while retaining the name *Schistosoma* for the worms.

This ruling makes little sense. The name bilharziasis would be used only for the disease if the generic name of the worm were *Bilharzia*, just as trypanosomiasis is used to denote the disease caused by protozoans of the genus *Trypanosoma*. But because the generic name *Schistosoma* must be retained, the term "bilharziasis" becomes invalid, although the word "bilharzia" could be used to denote the disease.

Logic, however, has frequently ruled over historical awareness, and since World War II, the Americans, in particular, have used the word "schistosomiasis," or even its ugly derivative, "schisto," to denote a disease whose causal agent belongs to the genus *Schistosoma*.

Distribution and Prevalence

The disease has an almost worldwide tropical distribution, but is mercifully absent from the Indian subcontinent. *S. haematobium* is highly endemic in the Nile Valley, and has an irregular distribution in the Middle East and North Africa (Map VIII.124.1). It occurs in most West and Central African countries, along the coastal countries of East Africa from Somalia to Natal, and in the islands off the east coast. *S. mansoni* is highly endemic in the Nile Delta and now seems to be spreading into the Nile Valley (Map VIII.124.2). In Africa it has a distribution similar to (although more irregular than) that of *S. haematobium*. But, unlike *S. haematobium*, *S. mansoni* also occurs in South America (Brazil, Surinam, and Venezuela) and in some islands in the Caribbean (Dominican Republic, Puerto Rico, St. Lucia, and others) (Map VIII.124.3); the parasite was transported from Africa to the New World as an unintended by-product of the slave trade. Oriental schistosomiasis, caused by *S. japonicum,* is endemic to the Yangtze Valley and many coastal provinces of mainland China (Map VIII.124.4). It also occurs in Central Sulawesi and the Philippines, and there are

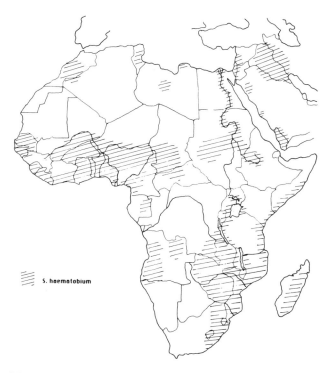

Map VIII.124.1. Distribution of *Schistosoma haematobium* in Africa and the Middle East. (From Farley 1991.)

Map VIII.124.2. Distribution of *Schistosoma mansoni* in Africa and the Middle East. (From Farley 1991.)

Map VIII.124.3. Distribution of *Schistosoma mansoni* in the Western Hemisphere. (From Farley 1991.)

Map VIII.124.4. Distribution of *Schistosoma japonicum* and *Schistosoma mekongi*. (From Farley 1991.)

a series of smaller foci in Malaysia, Thailand, and Japan.

Over 200 million people are said to be infected with the disease, although the data on which such figures are based are extremely variable and unreliable. There is little doubt, however, that in villages of the Nile Delta and other areas where there is constant contact of the human host with water, the prevalence can be as high as almost 100 percent. On a worldwide scale, a recent World Health Organization survey revealed that in 42 countries surveyed, 21 percent of the population was infected.

Etiology

The worms are acquired in fresh water by contact with their larval stages. The worm eggs, which are highly diagnostic for each species, are shed in the urine or feces of the human host and hatch to produce a minute short-lived larval stage called a *miracidium*. The miracidium of each species invades the tissues of a specific snail host where it undergoes asexual reproduction, eventually to produce the final larval stage. The final stage, the *cercaria,* is released daily in very large numbers from the snail, swims freely in the water, and then bores into the skin of the human host. In the human the parasite migrates to the liver via the heart and lungs, eventually to mature in the veins of the liver, gut, or bladder. Eggs appear in the urine or feces approximately 30 to 40 days after infection.

Epidemiology

The disease has a very complex epidemiology, resulting in part from a quite intricate relationship between the parasite and the snail intermediate host. Not only are there strains of each schistosome species, but also there are a multiplicity of snails that vary in their susceptibility to these strains and have a taxonomy that is in a constant state of revision. Historically this has long been a source of total confusion.

In very general terms, the snail hosts of *S. haematobium* belong to the genus *Bulinus,* which has been divided into two subgenera: one with three species complexes, including the *Bulinus truncatus–tropicus* group; and the other with one species complex, the *Bulinus africanus* group. The *B. truncatus–tropicus* species complex act as intermediate hosts to *S. haematobium* in Egypt and other countries north of the Sahara, whereas the *B. africanus* species complex generally serve as the most important intermediate hosts south of the Sahara. The genus *Biomphalaria* acts as the intermediate host for *S. mansoni.* As in

Bulinus, the genus has been divided into species complexes, with the *Biomphalaria pfeifferi* group acting as the most important complex in Africa south of the Sahara and in the Middle East, and *Biomphalaria alexandrina* the host in the Nile Delta. In the Americas, *Biomphalaria glabrata* acts as the most effective host. Whereas *S. haematobium* and *S. mansoni* are transmitted by species of pulmonate freshwater snails, *S. japonicum* is transmitted by amphibious prosobranch snails belonging to the species *Oncomelania hupensis,* of which there are six geographic subspecies. The aquatic prosobranch snail, *Tricula aperta,* endemic to the Mekong River, acts as the intermediate host of *S. mekongi.*

Schistosomiasis can be a serious chronic disease in poor rural areas, where children and adults, because of recreational, domestic, religious, and occupational reasons, come regularly into contact with fresh water contaminated with the schistosome cercariae. In most endemic areas, the prevalence of the disease and the intensity of infection (i.e., the number of eggs released, which is an indication of the number of worms carried) peak among those in their teenage years. Indeed in areas of high endemicity virtually all children become infected at some time. Thereafter, a decrease in prevalence and a decline in intensity occur. Even in highly endemic areas the rate of transmission of the disease is low. This follows, in part, from the patchy distribution of the surprisingly low numbers of infected snails.

Reservoir hosts play an important role in Oriental schistosomiasis, where the parasite is naturally transmitted between humans and other vertebrates, including many domesticated animals such as cattle, pigs, and dogs. Although animals are believed to play little if any role in the transmission of the two schistosome species in Africa, rodents are thought to act as important reservoirs of *S. mansoni* in South America.

The human schistosomes belong to a large family of trematodes, the Schistosomatidae, which also parasitize birds and mammals. In many parts of the world, particularly in the lake country of the central and western United States and Canada, the cercariae of these nonhuman schistosomes can penetrate the skin of humans by accident. Although these cercariae are destroyed in the skin, they nevertheless cause a harmless but very irritating rash – "swimmer's itch" or "schistosome dermatitis."

Pathology

Disease pathology is due to embolized eggs that induce inflammatory reactions in various body organs, from which arise the classic symptoms of chronic schistosomiasis. This pathology is, however, very variable and is generally related to the intensity of infection. There are also pathological differences among the various species and among strains of the same species.

In *S. haematobium* lesions occur in the bladder and ureter around the entrapped and calcifying eggs, with the eventual laying down of fibrous connective tissue. The symptoms include blood in the urine (hematuria), painful and excessive urination (dysuria), and various symptoms associated with obstructions of passages, such as distension of the ureters (hydroureter) and distension and atrophy of the kidneys through blockage of the urethras (hydronephrosis). In the intestinal schistosomes, the lesions occur in the gut wall and liver, leading to the deposition of fibrous connective tissue. The venous obstruction produced by these lesions results in a compensatory increased arterial flow that leads to portal hypertension and the classic enlargement of the liver and spleen (hepatosplenomegaly). Eggs of all three species may also become trapped in the lungs, and with *S. japonicum,* nervous disorders or "cerebral schistosomiasis" can also occur if egg aggregates come to rest in the brain.

Immunology

The post-teenage decline in the disease has often been taken as evidence for a gradually acquired immunity, but this probably plays a less significant role in the decline than do changing patterns of water contact. However, "concomitant immunity" is known to occur in experimental animals. The adult worms induce an immune response that has no effect on the adult worms but that protects the host from reinfection by destroying many of the invading cercariae. The adult worms, themselves, are able to circumvent this immune response 2 to 3 days after boring into the skin by acquiring host antigens that become bound to the surface of the parasite; the host is no longer able to recognize the worms as foreign organisms. Whether concomitant immunity plays any significant role in humans has yet to be determined.

History

Pre–World War I

Human schistosome worms were first described from Egypt by Theodor Bilharz in 1851, and their presence was related to disease symptoms by Wilhelm Griesinger shortly thereafter. Both men naturally assumed the worm to be a single species,

Distoma haematobium (later named *S. haematobium*), occurring in the blood vessels of the gut or bladder. That there were two Egyptian species with different egg types was first suggested by Louis Sambon in 1907, who named the second species *S. mansoni*. A year later, Piraja da Silva in Brazil gave the first description of *S. mansoni,* but unfortunately assumed it to be another species distinct from both *S. mansoni* and *haematobium.* A long and testy controversy over the existence of two species in Egypt, with different morphologies and egg types, was finally resolved by Robert Leiper in 1915. Meanwhile, in 1905 Fujiro Katsurada had described eggs and worms from patients and cats in the Yamanashi district of Japan, and named them *Schistosoma haematobium japonicum.*

The life cycles of the worms long remained a mystery, although it was usually assumed that an intermediate host was involved. But Arthur Looss, the foremost authority on the disease at the turn of the century, argued in 1894 that there was no intermediate host, and that the miracidia bored directly back into human beings. This bizarre theory likewise generated a controversy that was finally resolved by experimental work in Japan. There, in 1913 Keinosuke Miyairi and Masatsuga Suzuki discovered the snail host into which the miracidia penetrated, and for the first time described the fork-tailed schistosome cercariae emerging from the snails a few weeks later.

Leiper had been sent to China at this time to uncover the mysterious life cycle of the worm, and, hearing of the Japanese success, had hurried to Japan to confirm the life cycle. In 1914 he was posted to Egypt, where he quickly resolved the life-cycle problem in that country, distinguishing the two species of schistosome worm in Egypt not only by their morphologies and egg types but also by their different snail hosts.

With these problems resolved, interest in schistosomiasis subsided a bit, particularly because the disease was thought curable by the drug antimony tartrate and preventable by the snail-killing chemical copper sulfate.

The Interwar Years

Between the two world wars, campaigns against the disease using these chemicals were carried out in Egypt, the Gezira irrigated area of the Sudan, Southern Rhodesia, and South Africa, particularly after schistosomiasis was found among the children of "poor whites" in rural Transvaal. In addition, the high prevalence of the disease among African mine laborers recruited for the South African mines generated research on the disease by members of the South African Institute for Medical Research. The interwar years also witnessed the first involvement with the disease by the International Health Division of the Rockefeller Foundation, which financed an attempted eradication campaign against hookworm and schistosomiasis in Egypt between 1929 and 1940. Moreover, in 1924 Ernest Faust and E. Meleney, two faculty members at the Rockefeller-funded Peking Union Medical College, first discovered the life cycle of *S. japonicum* in China.

Post–World War II

After World War II, interest in the disease dramatically increased, especially in the British, French, and Belgian colonies in Africa. By 1950, schistosomiasis, previously considered to be unimportant outside Egypt, Sudan, South Africa, and to some extent China, was recognized as the most important tropical disease in the world, after malaria. In America this interest followed from an outbreak of the infection among American troops in Leyte, in the Philippines, where in 1944 over 1,000 troops of combat engineering companies involved in bridge building and road construction came down with the disease. The scientists and physicians, who were posted to Leyte to deal with the problem, brought the disease to the attention of American academics immediately after the war and initiated the growth in schistosomiasis research.

In British Africa, where medical work had long been hampered by the policies of a penny-pinching empire, a series of Colonial Development and Welfare Acts passed every 5 years between 1940 and 1955 transformed the Colonial Office into an agent of colonial development. Money was made available for medical research, most of which was allocated for work on trypanosomiasis and the tsetse fly. But a helminth subcommittee of the Medical Research Advisory Committee was also formed, which began to stress the danger of schistosomiasis, particularly as new irrigation schemes, built as part of the new emphasis on colonial agricultural development, threatened to spread the disease. The subcommittee initiated, for example, testing of a new drug, Miracil D, discovered by the British after occupation of the Bayer laboratories in Elberfeld toward the end of World War II.

The first major British work on the epidemiology of the disease in colonial Africa took place between 1955 and 1965, a period that saw the East Africa Medical Survey conducted while the Nationalist Government of South Africa initiated surveys of the disease and supported laboratory research on experimental schistosomiasis in animals.

The 1950s also witnessed the first mass campaign against the disease that involved more than the usual introduction of latrines, drugs, and mollusc-killing chemicals by foreign experts. In 1958, as part of the Great Leap Forward, the Schistosomiasis Subcommittee of the Chinese Communist Party initiated another such campaign against schistosomiasis. Utilizing a host of methods including the mass reclamation of swamp land, the Chinese eradicated the disease from many areas of the country. In 1949 perhaps 10 million Chinese were heavily infected with *S. japonicum,* whereas today the number is reported to have dropped to 2.4 million lightly infected cases.

The threat posed by irrigation schemes led to the postwar development of better molluscicides to replace the ineffective copper sulfate. Niclosamide, selling under the trade name of Bayluscide, became the chemical of choice, but results were disappointing. Chemotherapy has now become the favored weapon, particularly after the important 15-year experimental control campaign in St. Lucia (1966–81), sponsored by the Rockefeller Foundation, and after the development of single-dose drugs to replace the highly toxic antimony compounds and Miracil-D, used earlier. Oral oxamniquine proved effective against *S. mansoni,* and metrifonate against *S. haematobium,* whereas the newly developed praziquantel is emerging as a "wonder drug" effective against all schistosome species.

Today, with major support from the McConnnell Clark Foundation, a great deal of emphasis is being placed on problems of schistosome immunity and the development of vaccines.

John Farley

Bibliography

Abdel-Wahab, M. F. 1982. *Schistosomiasis in Egypt.* Boca Raton, Fla.

Basch, P. 1986. Schistosomiasis in China: An update. *American Journal of Chinese Medicine* 14: 17–25.

Cerqueira Falcão, E. de. 1953. *Novas achegas ao estudo da determinação da especificidade do S. mansoni.* Rio de Janeiro.

Farley, John. 1988. Bilharzia: A problem of native health. In *Imperial medicine and indigenous societies,* ed. D. Arnold, 189–207. Manchester.

1991. *Bilharzia: A history of imperial tropical medicine.* Cambridge.

Hartwig, G., and K. Patterson. 1984. *Schistosomiasis in twentieth century Africa: Historical studies on West Africa and Sudan.* Los Angeles.

Hoffmann, D. B., and K. S. Warren. 1978. *Schistosomiasis IV. Condensation of the selected literature, 1963–75.* Washington, D.C.

Jordan, Peter. 1985. *Schistosomiasis: The St. Lucia project.* Cambridge.

Jordan, Peter, and Gerald Webbe. 1982. *Schistosomiasis: Epidemiology, treatment and control.* London.

Kean, B., et al., eds. 1978. *Tropical medicine and parasitology. Classic investigations.* Ithaca, N.Y.

Maldonado, J. F. 1967. *Schistosomiasis in America.* Barcelona.

Nelson, G. 1977. A milestone on the road to the discovery of the life cycles of the human schistosomes. *American Journal of Tropical Medicine Hygiene* 26: 1093–100.

Report of the American schistosomiasis delegation to the People's Republic of China. 1977. *American Journal of Tropical Medicine Hygiene* 26: 427–57.

Sandbach, F. R. 1976. A history of schistosomiasis research and policy for its control. *Medical History* 20: 259–75.

1977. Farewell to the god of plague – the control of schistosomiasis in China. *Social Science and Medicine* 14: 27–33.

Sasa, M. 1972. A historical review of the early Japanese contributions to the knowledge of schistosomiasis japonica. In *Research in filariasis and schistosomiasis,* ed. M. Yokogawa, Vol. 2, 235–61. Baltimore.

Warren, K. S. 1973. *Schistosomiasis. The evolution of a medical literature, selected abstracts and citations, 1852–1972.* Cambridge.

Warren, K. S., and D. B. Hoffman. 1978. *Schistosomiasis III: Abstracts of the complete literature, 1963–1974.* Washington, D.C.

Warren, K. S., and A. Mahmoud. 1967. *Tropical and geographical medicine.* New York.

Warren, K. S., and V. A. Newill. 1967. *Schistosomiasis: A bibliography of the world's literature from 1852 to 1962.* Cleveland, Ohio.

Scrofula can be defined only historically. That is, scrofula is a term about which there was some measure of consensus in the past, but one that has now been largely superseded by terms that indicate some form of tuberculosis. It must be emphasized, however, that scrofula is *not* simply an old name for what we call tuberculosis. Our ontology of disease centers on the tubercle bacillus, and we would commit a grave historical error if we assume that with its aid we can know what was actually there in old discussions of scrofula. To understand these old discussions, we need to know how and why the old picture of scrofula was put together.

The distribution of scrofula, as we shall see below, has much more to do with the religious and political convictions of those who saw it than with physical geography or economic conditions or other circumstances normally considered conducive to diseases. Likewise in regard to its clinical manifestations, we may note, first, that this term itself implies an underlying entity that becomes manifest. But, second, scrofula, historically, *was* its collection of symptoms and signs. What we need to understand is what went into that collection, and why.

History and Geography

"Scrophula," like "scurvy" and "syphilis," is not a term that was used by the ancients. Whereas there may be special reasons why the latter two were unknown (a distribution to the north of the ancient Mediterranean and a possible Columbian origin, respectively), there seems to be no reason to suspect that scrofula was a new disease. Or, at least, so it seemed to many of the humanist doctors of the Renaissance, trying to reconstitute Greek medicine. In fact, the best they could do in the case of scrofula was to claim that one of its chief symptoms, tumors in the neck, was to be identified with the *struma* of the classical physicians. But simple strumae in the ancient descriptions were not associated with the other features that Renaissance physicians knew were part of scrofula. But how did they "know" this? Where did their picture of scrofula come from?

The answer is that there were medieval descriptions of scrofula. Partly these came from a surgical tradition, which was less Hellenizing than the physicians' medicine of the Renaissance. And in part they came from a popular tradition in which scrofula was

identified as the "King's Evil," and it was believed curable by the touch of a king. The essence of the medieval ceremony of touching in order to dispel the evil was that it demonstrated the quasi-sacerdotal nature of the office of kingship. The political advantages were clear, for a king, in performing the cure, showed that he was king in accordance with God's will. This was the important point in the seventeenth and eighteenth centuries, when the nature of scrofula was most energetically explored: The power of curing by the Royal Touch was a power vouchsafed by God only to the *true line* of kings. It could therefore be used to legitimate claim and accession to the throne. The kings of France continued to touch until the Revolution, and were emulated by other monarchs. In France and pre-Reformation England, the religious nature of the ceremony cemented the relationships and mutual stability of church and throne. It was a ceremony too miraculous for the taste of some Protestants, although the English Puritans at first tolerated it, and James I, although of a Calvinist background, found it increasingly expedient to use the Touch. But by the time of Charles I, his opponents saw it as a justification of absolute royal rule by a king who claimed to act as a representative of God. The Stuarts, whether on the throne or in temporary or permanent exile, continued to touch for the King's Evil, and their supporters continued to claim that their success in curing scrofula was a sure sign of their descent in the true line and thus the only legitimate monarchs. The Puritans and Parliamentarians saw the Touch as politically dangerous and tried to suppress it. Queen Anne was the last British monarch to use the Touch. The Hanoverians, as kings of political convenience, made no attempt to practice it, and their Whig supporters professed horror at a medieval and superstitious ritual.

The strongest passions were aroused in the conflicts that surrounded the issue. Crowds pressing around the Stuart kings to receive the Touch contained thousands of individuals; and there is no need to emphasize that in the Civil War the questions that split families were ones of religion and personal salvation, and of liberties and duties on Earth. Because the King's Evil was intimately bound up with the person of the king, if we look for a "distribution" of scrofula — for example, by examining seventeenth-century medical works — we find abundant references to the disease in Britain and France. But elsewhere the texts may be completely silent about the disease. Thus in Holland, recently freed from the rule of an absolutist and Catholic monarch, and a republic of sorts, scrofula had no place in the medical consciousness. Nor did Italian or German medical men, with no national attachment to a true line of kings, have much reason to emphasize scrofula as a disease entity, but rather viewed its separated symptoms as different entities. By the eighteenth century, some medical reference works betray an Enlightenment embarrassment in identifying scrofula as a disease that had a nonmedical cure, the Touch. In discussing the disease, British writers of the eighteenth century drew on a tradition of literature that rested on the works of Richard Wiseman, surgeon to Charles II. In the earlier nineteenth century, with the disappearance of the French line of kings, scrofula continued to be identified, although perhaps more regularly in its adjectival form and applied to a symptom. The notion that lay behind the name did not long survive germ theory, when attention turned away from collections of symptoms to causative microorganisms.

Clinical Manifestations: Contemporaneous Observations

To this point we have seen something of the nature, geography, and history of scrofula. We should next examine what it was that contemporaneous observers saw when describing the disease. The classic description was that of Wiseman (1705), a passionate royalist, to whom the Restoration seemed an expression of God's will, which had placed the rightful line of kings back on the throne. The power of the king to cure by the Touch was triumphantly demonstrated again, and if it was good to show that the king cured, it was better to show that he cured a disease that medicine or surgery could not. Thus Wiseman selected only the most extensive and difficult cases to go forward to the king. He rejected the simple identification of scrofula and struma and said that "none of these definitions seem to describe sufficiently the Disease which we in England call the Kings-Evil." Scrofula, he insisted, included more than the tumors-in-their-own-membranes that was struma: There were the bifurcated swelling of the upper lip; the tumors of the muscles, ligaments, tendons, and bones; the fistulae of the tonsils and of the lachrymal region of the eyes; together with ophthalmia. The cases sent to the king had a characteristic tumor near the mastoid muscle, and protrusion of the eyes – *lipitudo*.

Wiseman, of course, was in a position to insist on his definition of scrofula in that he both chose who would receive the Royal Touch and published the most authoritative account of the condition. But he drew together his description of the disease partly from descriptions made by other practitioners, and there must have been something like a national consensus of what the disease consisted of. There would not otherwise have been any perception of the disease or the king's role in its cure among the thousands of ordinary people, or among their parsons or squires who, we may suppose, encouraged them to go to London for the Touch.

The term "scrofula" remained in use in mainly British and French medical texts through the eighteenth century, and we can gather more information from medical practice in hospitals about what physicians saw the disease to be. The voluntary hospitals of the eighteenth century were charitable institutions of one form or another. Demand for effective use of charitable funds (and the utility of recovered patients for advertising purposes) often led to pressure for a quick turnover of patients. This meant that chronic cases were generally not admitted, nor were infectious cases, on the grounds that they would endanger the other patients. So when we see scrofulous patients being admitted to an eighteenth-century hospital, we can assume that the physician or surgeon who made the admissions did not think that the disease was chronic or infectious. In practice, admissions to hospitals show the same ambivalence about the nature of scrofula as the eighteenth-century medical world at large. Sometimes the term simply did not exist in the language of the physician in charge or in his hospital, and at other times scrofulous men and women were refused admission as incurable or even infectious. Often a physician could not tell whether the patient's symptoms were scrofulous, and took in the patient for tests. Sometimes admittedly scrofulous patients were taken into hospitals in the belief that they were not infectious and that a course of mercury-sweats would cure them.

From the records we can see that the physician or surgeon was looking for a number of things to establish that his patient was scrofulous: an itch and tumors in the glands, joints, and other tissues. As the disease progressed, the physician saw these tumors change into ulcers, which became deep and ultimately produced caries in the bones. Exploratory surgery was used to discover whether the last stage of the disease had been reached and what, accordingly, the prognosis was. Sometimes patients were sent home as incurable, sometimes they were treated in a hot room with mercury-sweats to unblock their glands and vessels of the impediment that was held to cause scrofula. Which of these many alternatives was used probably depended on where the doctor had been trained.

The politics of early-nineteenth-century Europe no longer supported the idea of the "true line of kings." Without true kings, there was no King's Evil, and scrofula was seen as a disease entity less often than in the preceding century. It is true that a system so influential as that of William Cullen retained the disease entity, but in fact his subdivision of it helped to destroy the unit of scrofula as a term. He distinguished, first, "scrofula vulgaris" as the disease in its external form, without complications. This is probably the scrofulous itch of the hospitals. Cullen's second type was "scrofula mesenterica," the internal form of the disease, with swelling abdomen, pale countenance, and loss of appetite. The third type was "scrofula fugax," consisting of swelling about the neck and corresponding to the old struma. Cullen's fourth category was "scrofula americana," which by the 1830s was thought of as European scrofula combined with the yaws.

The term "scrofula" survived largely in the adjectival form, so that scrofulous tumors or ulcers could be seen and described on their own without a necessary connection to the other defining characteristics of the seventeenth-century disease. With the new emphasis on postmortem pathological anatomy of the first half of the nineteenth century, cases of internal scrofula were often found to be characterized by tubercles in the lungs. The discovery (by Robert Koch in 1882) of the bacillus responsible for these created an ontology of disease around tuberculosis, thus rendering scrofula peripheral to medicine and accessible only to the historian.

Roger K. French

Bibliography
Barlow, Frank. 1980. The King's Evil. *English Historical Review* 95: 3–27.
Blancard, S. 1715. *The physical dictionary*, 6th edition. London.
    1735. *Lexicon medicum renovatum.* Leyden.
Bloch, M. 1973. *The royal touch.* London.
Boerhaave, H. 1727. *Institutiones medicae in usus annuae exercitationis domesticos.* Leyden.
    1738. *Aphorismsi de cognoscendis et curandis morbis.* Paris.
Dunglison, Robley. 1833. *Medical lexicon: A dictionary of medical science,* ed. Richard Dunglison. Philadelphia, 1874.
Hooper, R. 1801. *A compendious medical dictionary,* 2d edition. London.
    1831. *Lexicon medicum; or medical dictionary,* 6th edition. London.
James, R. 1743–5. *A medical dictionary,* 3 vols. London.

Longmore, T. 1891. *Richard Wiseman, sergeant surgeon to Charles II.* London.
Nicholaus, E. 1747. *Methodus concinnandi formulas medicamentorum.* Magdeburg.
Quincy, J. 1713. *Lexicon physico medicum graeco-latinum.* Leipzig.
Swieten, G. van. 1787–92. *Commentaria in Hermanni Boerhaave aphorismos de cognoscendis et curandis morbis.* Wurzburg.
Wiseman, R. 1705. *Severall chirurgical treatises,* 4th edition. London.

VIII.126
Scurvy

Scurvy is a deficiency disease, arising from a lack of vitamin C (ascorbic acid) in the diet. It occurs most characteristically in the absence of fresh fruit and vegetables, but can still be avoided when these are not consumed if the diet is rich in uncooked meat as in the case of Eskimos (heat destroys the vitamin). Scurvy does not appear in a regularly recognizable way in the ancient medical literature, and its name is not classical but, rather, derived from the north European vernaculars of the Renaissance. It was, for example, *schverbaujck* in Dutch and *scorbuck* in Danish, and Latinized in 1541 by Johannes Echthius, a Dutch physician living in Cologne, as *scorbutus*. In the slave trade it was often called the *mal de Luanda*.

Etiology, Epidemiology, and Distribution
Human beings, like guinea pigs and monkeys but unlike many other animals, do not synthesize vitamin C. No doubt this reflects a period of evolution in a vitamin C–rich environment; and, with the expansion of the species to all parts of the Earth, less generous climates have inevitably taken a toll due to scurvy. The disease occurs where economic, social, or climatic factors prevent access to an appropriate diet, and frequently has appeared under circumstances where diets are circumscribed, including long sea voyages, during military operations, in prisons, with the failure of crops, and during the Gold Rush. In the modern period, infantile scurvy has been a problem, for example, in Canada during the decades 1945–65, where it occurred mostly among the lower socioeconomic groups. As with other occur-

rences of infantile scurvy, this period was associated with a trend away from breast feeding, combined with maternal ignorance about substitute foods. The same causes were at work in cases in Australia.

Scurvy occurs occasionally in slavish followers of fad diets, and more commonly in middle-aged men living on their own and neglecting their diets. The disease is not widely reported from the Third World, perhaps because of a comparatively greater availability of fresh fruit and vegetables in some countries, but more generally no doubt because of a lack of the medical services that would be the normal route of reporting the disease.

It can be said in general that scurvy is a disease of northern countries although, as observed, the traditional diet of the Eskimo is sufficient to prevent it. Until recent times adult scurvy was endemic in Russia. This was not the case with infantile scurvy, however, for properly suckled infants do better than adults when the general diet tends toward the scorbutic.

Clinical Manifestations

Various individuals in the modern period have subjected themselves experimentally to a diet free of vitamin C, and the characteristic features of the disease have been carefully monitored. At about 12 weeks the first sign, a feeling of lethargy, appears. The first physical sign appears at 19 weeks, when the skin becomes dry and rough and the hair follicles form lumps. Small hemorrhages in the legs begin at about 23 weeks, and a bit later fresh wounds will no longer heal. One of the classical signs of scurvy, the swollen, purple, and soft gums, does not appear until about 30 weeks of a diet free of vitamin C. In a wartime study on a group of conscientious objectors, one of the volunteers developed a tubercular lesion at 26 weeks, and two more suffered what seems to have been cardiac hemorrhage, at 36 and 38 weeks. They were clearly close to that stage of the disease that had killed another self-experimenter in the eighteenth century, not to mention many thousands of sailors. At this point, the volunteers were given large doses of ascorbic acid, and all made complete recoveries.

In the young, scurvy produces reabsorption at the end of the long bones and a disappearance of cartilage. Postmortem examination, particularly in animals, reveals a characteristic subperiosteal hemorrhage. Historical evidence, which includes cases far more severe than modern cases, reveals loss of elasticity of the flesh, loosening of the teeth, and the reopening of old wounds and fractures.

History

Outbreaks

Antiquity. No doubt scurvy appeared often in ancient times – perhaps during sieges – and no doubt was treated by medical personnel. But we cannot claim that the disease was really known to the ancients unless we can give evidence of some sort of consensus about it. To discuss an illness and write about it means, at least, that the disease has a name; but the ancients did not seem to have had a name for scurvy. In any event scurvy could not be found in the writings of Hippocrates or Galen by individuals of the late fifteenth and sixteenth century, to whom the disease was so obvious, and for whom medicine was founded on Hippocrates and Galen. As with the other apparently new disease of the Renaissance, syphilis, it was important for humanist physicians to believe that, notwithstanding a change of name, the old writers had known the disease. Only then could it be fitted into the newly classical body of theory and practice of medicine and an effective treatment sought. Attempts were made by scholars to show that Hippocrates was not ignorant of scurvy, but the disease was treated as new by practical persons like the ships' surgeons who saw so much of it.

Renaissance Through the Eighteenth Century: Maritime Scurvy. Of course, the circumstances surrounding scurvy's appearance during the Renaissance and Early Modern Europe were very different from those that surrounded the diseases discussed by Galen and Hippocrates. The economic power of northern European countries was growing rapidly, and their desire to trade was matched by the technical developments of shipbuilding and navigation. The Europeans' theater of action was the Atlantic, not merely the enclosed Mediterranean, and all of these factors meant that the ships stayed at sea for periods long enough for scurvy to develop. In 1498 Vasco da Gama, reaching the east coast of Africa, found that many of his men suffered from what appears to have been scurvy. Twelve weeks at sea on the return journey renewed the disease.

The earliest battles for trade routes were between Spain and Portugal, and Fernando Magellan, for example, saw much scurvy among his crew when at sea for 15 weeks in 1519. These two nations established control over the southern routes to the Far East, but were quickly followed by the French and English, who tried to find a northern route.

A French expedition of 1523 explored the east

coast of North America, and a second expedition sent in 1534 that had to overwinter on the Saint Lawrence River suffered a great deal of scurvy.

The English, too, were interested in North America since making an expedition to Newfoundland under the command of John Cabot in 1497. Francis Drake's circumnavigation of 1577–80 indicates the extent of the technical developments in shipbuilding and navigation since the previous century, and the defeat of the Spanish Armada in 1588 was a stimulus to trading voyages. The next century saw the expeditions of the big trading companies like the East India Company, and the establishment of colonies by countries other than Spain and Portugal. It also, as a consequence, witnessed more and more sea voyages of long duration. The East India Company, for example, sent out an expedition to trade with Sumatra in 1601; it was 29 weeks at sea before reaching the Cape, and scurvy was widespread, almost to the point of paralyzing the expedition. The only ship exempted from the disease was that of the expedition's general, Sir James Lancaster, who had provided lemon juice for his sailors.

Observers of the early voyages noted the surprisingly rapid recovery of scorbutic sailors on reaching a port where fresh food was available. Empirical experience showed in particular the value of citrus fruits (the variant forms of "lime" and "lemon" in the different vernaculars are easily confused). In the subsequent history of maritime scurvy, the question looms as to why this knowledge was not used to prevent the disease.

The answer lies partly in the logistical and technical problems of provisioning the ever larger ships and squadrons: Citrus fruits are not native to the northern countries where big merchant fleets were based; these fruits did not keep well over long voyages; and attempts to concentrate or preserve the juice must have often reduced its effectiveness. The Dutch East India Company tried to ensure regular supplies by planting orchards at Mauritius and St. Helena, and even attempted laying out gardens on board ship. The Dutch Company's statistics show that the mortality in its ships over a 5-year period during the last decade of the seventeenth century, from all causes, was a little more than 13 percent, although where distilled water was used, the rate dropped to 9.5 percent. It is not known what proportion of these deaths were due to scurvy, but it appears that in regular trading voyages at least, with known landfalls and provisions for the crews including fruit juice, scurvy was not very deadly.

This was not the case, however, in the European navies, particularly during the following century. Their business was military, not commercial, and their operations were far from regular. In any military operation there is the expectation that the lives of men will have to be expended, and experience showed that disease would take many. Control of the seas rather than mere coastal defense was now the prize of naval warfare, and fully 855 men out of 1,000 succumbed, largely to scurvy, when Commodore George Anson fulfilled his commission of 1740 to capture the Spanish treasure-galleon.

Subsequent wars involved navies not only in long-distance operations but also in blockades of long duration. The supply of citrus fruits was simply not adequate for operations on this scale, when a complement of 500 men for a single ship of the line was not unusual. Although some physicians even advised against lemons or limes, generally a substitute was sought. One was found in cider, to which a land-based tradition attributed antiscorbutic properties. Edward Ives, a ship's surgeon in the early 1740s, was losing the usual large number of men to scurvy, when he persuaded his admiral to provision with the best Devon cider. While it lasted, he lost none of the 500 men aboard: The scurvy came only afterwards, all other conditions remaining the same.

This was essentially a forced clinical experiment, a technique taken up (after correspondence with Ives) and used in a more elaborate way by the better known James Lind. Lind divided his scorbutic patients into those taking fresh oranges and lemons, those taking cider, and those to whom he gave other current remedies. The first group improved rapidly, followed by those drinking cider; the remainder did not improve. Lind has been much celebrated for this early clinical trial, but doubt has recently been cast on his results on the grounds that modern research shows no vitamin C in cider. Yet modern cider is generally preserved in some way to give it a longer shelf life, whereas cider made in the eighteenth-century manner is high in vitamin C.

By 1753 Lind had incorporated his results into a large and very scholarly historical, bibliographical, and clinical work entitled *A Treatise of the Scurvy*. It was the most authoritative argument that had been made for the use of citrus fruits to prevent scurvy, but it was not until the end of the eighteenth century that, because of the work of an administrator, Sir Gilbert Blane, lime juice was issued to British sailors as a matter of course.

Nineteenth Century.   The lessons learned at sea enabled the occasional small-scale outbreak of scurvy in the prisons of the earlier nineteenth century to be handled adequately. But there was no remedy for the scurvy produced by the great failure of the potato crop in 1845–6. Potatoes are rich in vitamin C, and the population of Ireland, more than other European countries, depended upon them as food. Scotland also suffered. Scurvy later in the century appeared regularly where conditions prevented access to fresh fruit and vegetables. Examples are the California Gold Rush of 1848 and later, during which the long trek over mountains much resembled a long voyage at sea and the war in the Crimea (1854–6) and the siege of Sebastopol, when the French and British armies' supply routes were interrupted. American experiences with scurvy also occurred during a circumnavigation in 1838, during a blockade of the Mexican coast in 1846, and during the Civil War, particularly in prisoner-of-war camps, where the mortality rose to 9 percent per month.

The circumstances that made scurvy a disease of the northern countries made it a special danger in the Arctic regions. When there was regular commerce – for example, by the Hudson Bay Company – scurvy was only a minor threat, and, since its origin in the seventeenth century the Company had shipped out lime juice. Fresh meat killed locally was also recognized as valuable, a truth that had been learned the hard way in some early overwintering disasters. Government-backed explorations, however, generally encountered scurvy, particularly when small parties left the iced-in ship for exploration on foot.

Perhaps the least expected occurrence of scurvy was that of the infantile variety from the 1870s to the First World War, in Europe and America. The odd feature was that infantile scurvy occurred in the higher social classes, where there was no economic reason for vitamin C deficiency. The reason was that mothers of the upper classes tended to avoid breast feeding their own children, and the various forms of preserved milk newly available did not contain vitamin C. Thus scurvy often occurred before the child began consuming adult food. In previous periods, upper-class mothers also avoided breast feeding, but then the infants would have been given to a wet nurse as a substitute mother.

Etiological Theories

Changing Concepts and Implications for Treatment. Theories on the causation of scurvy were, on the whole, more destructive than helpful to its successful treatment in the period before the discovery of vitamin C. By and large, government officials, offi-

cers, and surgeons of big trading companies, and eventually naval and military administrators, were convinced of the empirical fact that certain fruits prevented and cured the disease. But when they took advice about scurvy from educated physicians, it was sometimes bad. Because medical theory had its impact upon practice, we must look briefly at theories about scurvy.

There is one central feature of the story of scurvy theories which had an enormous effect. This was the rise of the germ theory of disease in the second half of the nineteenth century, which changed medicine more than anything else had done in the preceding 2,000 years. Disease was now seen to be caused by a living organism, in some cases visible under a microscope. The organism was s species of living thing, perceptible (perhaps) and classifiable. Here was the essence, the cause of the disease: Clinical symptoms were now viewed as secondary reactions, varying with the nature of the patient. And the new medicine, by the end of the century, proved spectacularly successful in combatting infectious diseases. The effect was a whole new ontology of disease, centered on the infective organism; thus for scurvy, the effect of this revolution was to encourage a search for a causal organism, or at least a poison. In other words, the research ran counter to the previous consensus that incomplete diets could cause scurvy, and led to numerous disputes about the nature of the disease.

To understand why, we must look at the nature of medical theory in the earlier period. Up to and even including the eighteenth century in some places, the medical person had seen the human body as a microcosm located in a similar but larger macrocosm. Traditional European medicine, based on Galen's rationalization of Hippocratic principles, recognized the body as consisting of seven "Naturals" – its humors, spirits, faculties, and parts. The "Non-Naturals" were the points at which the body intereacted with the macrocosm and the results of its activity – the regimen of diet, exercise, sleep, and so on. "Contra-Naturals" were things that caused disturbance in the body. The microcosm corresponded to the macrocosm because they both consisted of the same principles, the four elements and four qualities, appearing in the body as the four humors. Food was elementary and qualitative and needed only refining to become the substance of the body. The effect of the environment – its airs, waters, and places – was similarly qualitative. The notion that scurvy was a disease that arose from an improper diet fitted naturally into this scheme. An impropriety of the diet was generally believed to affect bodily organs, and early writers such as Echthius in 1541 made scurvy a melancholic disease of the spleen.

He attributed it to the spleen because in discussing splenetic diseases Hippocrates listed some symptoms that look scorbutic; and Echthius's argument was the Hippocratic–Galenic one – that a disordered spleen could not fulfill its normal function of excreting black bile (melancholia, one of the four humors), and that the excess of black bile in the body in turn caused scurvy. Similar humoral theories of scurvy were widely held, and many writers attributed the presumed damage to the spleen to a dietary cause – the salt meat, stale water, and preserved food of long sea voyages.

The theory of the disease changed with the theory of medicine. In the later seventeenth century, when chemical notions of the body were proving attractive, some writers distinguished an "acid" from an "alkaline" scurvy. When mechanism was employed in the medicine of the eighteenth century, doctors talked about sharp, corrosive particles in the blood. These were still humoral theories, and although the humors were no longer viewed as qualitative in action, their vice still derived from diet. Hermann Boerhaave, the most authoritative voice of the eighteenth century, blamed salt; dried and smoked meats, including fish and sea birds; ships' biscuits (*panis biscoctum*); dried peas and beans; old, sharp, and salty cheese; and so on. Such a diet, he argued, led to the proximate cause of the disease: The blood became thin and sharp, whether acid or alkaline. From this all the symptoms could be deduced, and all treatment was to be directed to restoring the proper nature of the blood. Boerhaave had the whole armory of eighteenth-century medical techniques with which to attempt this, because some kind of disturbance of the blood was believed to be at the root of many diseases in the medical theory of the time.

Citrus fruits were mentioned by Boerhaave, but only in a long list of other remedies and without special attention, and without an explanation of how such remedies work. The use of citrus juice, after all, was a mere empirical discovery, which had little part in a medicine so rational as that of Boerhaave. Perhaps Boerhaave, like Beaudouin Ronsse (Ronsseus) more than a century before, was embarrassed at something so empirical. His rationalist view attributed the cause of scurvy not to anything necessary lacking in the diet, but to the excess of things undesirable. His student Gerard L. B. van Swieten, however, took the more usual line that the cause of the disease was the lack of something.

Scurvy, he argued, appeared more often in besieged cities than in the army besieging, which had access to fresh provisions.

The practice of treating scurvy was again affected by medical theory later in the eighteenth century. Contemporary interest in medical chemistry centered on the nature of various "airs" (in our terms, "gases") of which "fixed air" was sometimes held to prevent putrefaction. It was also commonly held that scurvy was a putrefactive disease, and attention naturally was given to the possibility that it could be treated with fixed air. There were attempts to use water impregnated with fixed air on board ship, and a wider movement to treat scurvy with malt. It was argued that just as malt digested in water became a wort that ferments into beer, giving off fixed air, so wort drunk by scorbutics would ferment in their bodies, correcting the tendency to putrefy.

Captain James Cook's report to the Admiralty in 1776 spoke highly of malt, and also of sauerkraut, both of them in his view being preferable to the contemporary citrus fruit concentrate – "rob" – of oranges and lemons. The expense of the latter was clearly the reason for the search for substitutes. Cook's apparently empirical observations agreed with theories of fermentation shared by his influential colleagues in the Royal Society and elsewhere, and helped to lengthen the period of the use of malt-wort in the navy. In 1795, however, Gilbert Blane was appointed commissioner of the Board of Sick and Wounded Sailors, and, supported by some recent experiments with lemon juice, he persuaded the Lords of the Admiralty to authorize a daily dose of three quarters of an ounce of the juice to each sailor. Over the next 20 years, this amount totaled more than 1.5 million gallons; Admiral Horatio Nelson alone accounted for 50,000 gallons for the Mediterranean fleet.

Although, after this, scurvy virtually disappeared from the British fleet (but not from other fleets as, for example, the French, during the Napoleonic Wars), on land the theories of medical professionals continued to threaten practice. The Seige of Paris (1870–1) produced an outbreak of scurvy and once again focused attention on its cause at a time when ideas about contagion and germs were becoming more widespread. At a debate in the French Academy of Medicine in 1874, the view was aired that scurvy was a contagious miasm, and was no more caused by a lack of fresh fruit than malaria was caused by a lack of the medicine quinine. The revolution in medical thought about disease causation now made *positive* causes of scurvy (the presence of a noxious agent) more attractive than a *negative* (the absence of a factor).

A British expedition of 1894 spent three winters in Franz-Joseph Land, remaining healthy on a diet that included fresh meat but very little lime juice. The medical explanation for the absence of scurvy was that the disease was caused by chemical products resulting from bacterial action in poorly kept meat, and it was realized that no one had studied scurvy in the light of Louis Pasteur's germ theory. This new line of inquiry was made possible by a grant from the Royal Society, whose president was Lord Joseph Lister, the man who revolutionized surgery by killing Pasteurian germs with carbolic acid. It was Lister who presented the results of the inquiry to the Royal Society, and those results were taken to support a germ theory of scurvy. So thoroughly was germ theory implicated in the etiology of scurvy that one naval surgeon, at least, explained that the benefit obtained from lime juice was simply that it acted as an antibacterial mouthwash.

Evolution of the Deficiency Disease Concept. The final recognition of scurvy as a deficiency disease is a twentieth-century story. From the last years of the nineteenth century, there had been concern in Norway at the incidence of "ship beriberi." It was studied by Axel Holst, who had had experience at the Pasteur Institute and had also worked with Robert Koch. He knew of the experimental use of chickens in a study of beriberi in the Dutch East Indies, but chose guinea pigs as his experimental animals, feeling them to be more convenient and closer to humans in physiology. Under a restricted diet, the animals developed the symptoms of scurvy as it appeared in humans. Guinea pigs had also been used in Germany as models for "Barlow's disease" (infantile scurvy, long thought a separate condition).

The work (up to 1913) of Holst and his collaborator Theodor Frölich (a specialist in infantile scurvy) was to show that scurvy was indeed a disease of a deficient diet. Meanwhile, in 1912, Casimir Funk, working at the Lister Institute in London, proposed that scurvy was one of a group of four diseases (the others were beriberi, rickets, and pellagra) that were caused by dietery deficiency. Each missing factor, he believed, was a nitrogenous base, for which he coined the name "vitamine." At the same time, in the United States E. V. McCollum and others showed that some fats contained a factor necessary for the growth of rats. The "deficiency" thesis met some opposition from bacteriologists, and in 1916 and 1917 workers in the United States cultured bacteria from the tissues of scorbutic animals. Inoculated into healthy animals, this culture produced some signs of scurvy. Related to the bacterial theory was the "positive" notion of McCollum that scurvy was due to poisons developing by bacterial action in the accumulating feces in the intestines of the experimental animals. (The animals were rats, which synthesize their own vitamin C.)

Despite all these opposing doctrines, however, the results obtained by Holst and Frölich prompted later efforts to identify and isolate the active component. McCollum had already identified a fat-soluble factor – "A" – and a water-soluble factor – "B" – necessary for the growth of experimental rats, and it was natural for those who believed in the deficiency thesis to look for a "vitamine C."

The presence of scurvy during the First World War and its aftermath in central Europe prompted systematic assays on various antiscorbutics, particularly in guinea pigs at the Lister Institute. There too, from 1918, S. S. Zilva and others attempted to isolate the active component of vitamin C. This was achieved by the Hungarian Albert Szent-Györgyi, who was working in Hopkin's laboratory in Cambridge on a different problem. He was interested in the powers of chemical reduction of organic substances, including the sugars of lemon juice. Between 1928 and 1932, Glen King at the University of Pittsburgh also had been trying to isolate vitamin C, and in the latter year published results that combined the findings of Szent-Györgyi with his own and with trials with guinea pigs. Vitamin C had been discovered, and scurvy was vanquished.

Roger K. French

Bibliography

Carpenter, K. J. 1986. *The history of scurvy and vitamin C.* Cambridge.

Eddy, W., and G. Dalldorf. 1941. *The avitaminoses.* London.

French, R. K. 1982. *The history and virtues of cyder.* London–New York.

Hughes, R. E. 1975. James Lind and the cure of scurvy: An experimental approach. *Medical History* 19: 342–51.

Lind, J. 1753. *A treatise of the scurvy.* Edinburgh.

Roddis, L. H. 1951. *James Lind.* London.

Stewart, C. P., and D. Guthrie. 1953. *Lind's treatise on scurvy.* Edinburgh.

Woodall, J. 1978. *The surgions mate, 1671.* Facsimile edition, ed. J. Kirkup. Bath.

VIII.127
Sickle-Cell Anemia

Sickle-cell disease is an inherited disorder resulting from an abnormality in the structure of a protein in the red blood cell called hemoglobin. It represents a spectrum of disorders ranging from the full-blown form, sickle-cell anemia, to the carrier state called sickle-cell trait. Also included in this spectrum are several other variant hemoglobin disorders, which all have the sickle hemoglobin. Sickle-cell anemia is the prototype for most molecular diseases and was the first disease to have its cause isolated to a single molecular change in the human genetic structure. This single change is responsible for all of the dramatic physiological changes and clinical events that occur in this disease.

Sickle-cell trait occurs when the individual is heterozygous for the sickle-cell gene and results in red blood cell concentrations of the abnormal hemoglobin (hemoglobin S) of less than 50 percent. It generally does not result in serious illness although this generalization has recently been disputed. In addition to sickle-cell trait, several sickle-cell syndromes occur when hemoglobin S is present in a heterozygous state with other hemoglobin variants – some with similar properties. Common examples of these include hemoglobin C and hemoglobin E.

Distribution and Incidence
Sickle-cell anemia is found in as many as 4 percent of Africans and in 1 percent of black Americans (1 per 500). Upward of 40 percent of Africans carry the sickle-cell trait as compared to 9 percent of black Americans. In some Mediterranean cultures the trait is also present. It is now generally believed that the sickle-cell gene mutation occurred independently in several areas of Africa. Therefore, its presence across several different peoples is easily explained.

Hemoglobin S is transmitted as an autosomal recessive gene. So if both parents have sickle-cell trait, the chances are 1 in 4 that any child born to them will have hemoglobin SS and thus sickle-cell anemia; 1 in 4 that it will have hemoglobin AA and be normal; and 2 in 4 that it will have hemoglobin AS and have the sickle-cell trait.

The pattern of death in persons who have sickle-cell anemia is bimodal, with the first peak occurring in childhood and the second occurring among people in their late 30s. Deaths during childhood are related to infectious causes, whereas those during adulthood are due to organ failure from repeated tissue destruction.

Etiology
Hemoglobin is responsible for carrying oxygen in the bloodstream and is found inside the red blood cell. It is a protein made up of four chains called globins and four iron groups called heme. Each globin chain is composed of a series of building blocks called amino acids that in turn are built from the genetic material known as deoxyribonucleic acid (DNA). The structure of a particular piece of DNA determines the structure of a particular protein. In the case of sickle-cell anemia the structure of the DNA molecule is changed through a single genetic mutation and results in a change in the amino acid composition of the protein chain. This change is a substitution of valine for glutamic acid in the sixth position of the amino end of the molecule. This simple substitution causes marked changes in the solubility and interactive properties of hemoglobin. Under appropriate conditions, this results in a dramatic conformational change in the red cell from a flexible biconcaved disk to an inflexible sickled cell.

Sickling results from a low oxygen state and tends to occur in the acidotic and hypertonic milieu of small blood vessels. It is a two-step process. Initially, small submicroscopic aggregates of hemoglobin form, followed by rapid polymer formation into long tubular helical fibers that twist the red cell into the sickle shape. This fiber formation is reversible and results from noncovalent chemical bonds between hemoglobin molecules.

Sickling is also accompanied by a dynamic process at the cell membrane. Ion fluxes that occur normally at the membrane become disrupted during sickling, and a rapid influx of calcium occurs. This calcium is later pumped out of the cell by an energy-dependent mechanism utilizing an intercellular energy source known as adenosine triphosphate (ATP). Recurrent sickling results in early depletion of ATP and is one contributor to premature cellular death. Recurrent sickling can cause the cellular membrane to become permanently calcified, resulting in rigid, irreversibly sickled cells. These cells are found in all persons afflicted with sickle-cell disease and may represent from 5 to 50 percent of the red cell mass.

Functionally, hemoglobin S has a lower affinity for oxygen especially at low hydrogen-ion concentrations and increased tonicity. This results in early release of oxygen and the inability to oxygenate tissues adequately. In the sickled form, these cells have significant difficulty traversing the small vasculature of the capillary bed. Vascular occlusion and destruction of tissues result. The life-span of a single cell is also decreased from 120 to 60 days and is manifested as a hemolytic anemia. This condition results from a combination of acquired membrane abnormalities from recurrent sickling and destruction of irreversibly sickled cells. There is also increased incidence of infection owing to gradual destruction of the spleen and alterations in the immune system.

The presence of other forms of hemoglobin can modify the ability of hemoglobin S to form fibrils. One such hemoglobin is fetal hemoglobin. Hemoglobin F is normally present at birth in large concentrations. After birth its production is decreased and is replaced with adult hemoglobin (hemoglobin A), such that by 6 months of life the individual has hemoglobin in adult percentages. In some individuals, however, hemoglobin F persists in abnormally high levels. This persistence of hemoglobin F alters the final hemoglobin concentration in the red blood cell and reduces the percentage of hemoglobin S in patients with sickle-cell disease. Hemoglobin F is a poor participant in hemoglobin S fibril formation and thus inhibits sickling. Clinically this results in a milder form of the disease and in some patients produces an asymptomatic state.

Clinical Manifestations

Sickle-cell disease can be diagnosed prenatally by a procedure known as amniocentesis. After birth the diagnosis is generally made by hemoglobin electrophoresis using cord or peripheral blood. Early diagnosis is now encouraged because of the benefits of new preventive therapies for infection.

Sickle-cell anemia is characterized clinically by a chronic hemolytic anemia and recurrent states called *crises*. These crisis states are further divided into three types: *pain, sequestration,* and *aplastic.*

Pain crisis is the most common and occurs on the average of three times a year. It first presents after 6 months of life when the level of fetal hemoglobin has decreased to a low level. At this age the first signs are often a painful inflammation of the bones of the hands or feet, known as the hand–foot syndrome. Older patients generally develop a recurrent syndrome of joint, back, abdominal, or long-bone pain, which may last for approximately 7 days. Other serious manifestations of vascular occlusion include strokes, heart attacks, leg ulcers, priapism, and pulmonary infarcts.

Splenic sequestration occurs when a large portion of the red cell mass becomes trapped in the spleen,

resulting in acute shock. With age, recurrent vascular occlusion of small blood vessels in the spleen results in functional destruction of this organ. Because the spleen is required for destruction of certain types of bacteria, patients with sickle-cell anemia are at increased risk of bacterial infections.

In rare instances, the blood-forming bone marrow becomes exhausted or suppressed for short periods of time, resulting in an acute reduction in red blood cells. This is known as red cell aplasia. This is a temporary condition but one that may require blood transfusions until the bone marrow recovers.

By contrast, sickle-cell trait occurs when individuals' genes carry only one hemoglobin S gene. These persons are phenotypically normal in most respects, although sickling has occasionally been reported to occur in these individuals at high altitudes or low oxygen tension, resulting in splenic infarction. Bleeding from the kidney and a gradual decrease in the concentrating ability of the kidneys have also been shown to occur with increased frequency in people with sickle-cell trait. This condition is almost always benign in nature, however. Nevertheless, concerns have been raised recently that individuals with sickle-cell trait are at increased risk for acute muscle destruction and sudden death. These reports require further confirmation and are highly controversial.

Various other hemoglobins have been shown to sickle in a manner similar to hemoglobin S. Careful chemical analysis is required to differentiate these from sickle hemoglobin.

History and Geography

Sickle-cell anemia has been traced back to at least 1670, where it was noted to be present in the Krobo tribe in Ghana. This disorder was first described clinically by James B. Herrick, a Chicago physician, in 1910. During the 10 years following Herrick's report, three cases of sickle-cell anemia were reported. Thirteen years later, J. G. Huck reported a series of 14 patients and first noted the reversibility of sickling. In 1939 J. Bibb and L. W. Diggs described irreversibly sickled cells, and in 1946 M. Sherman demonstrated that hemoglobin S has an ordered structure. This finding encouraged Linus Pauling to investigate the physical chemistry of hemoglobin S by electrophoresis. On the basis of his findings he reasoned that the genetic basis of sickling was due to a single gene. V. M. Ingram, using peptide mapping techniques, then demonstrated that the condition resulted from a single amino acid substitution of valine for glutamic acid. M. Murayama noted that this change resulted in the loss of two negative charges and postulated that noncovalent interactions took place, resulting in hemoglobin stacking. In 1949 A. B. Raper noted the high incidence of sickle-cell trait in areas endemic for malaria and suggested that the trait protected against infestation. But it was not until 1954 that geneticist A. C. Allison correlated sickle trait with regions in which falciparum malaria was or had been endemic.

Further analysis of this observation showed that this gene change was the result of a genetic principle known as balanced polymorphism. Generally a gene such as the sickle-cell gene, which results in severe morbidity and mortality, dies out in a population unless certain conditions result in a more favorable survival. Such is the case with the sickle-cell gene. Africa and the Mediterranean are areas endemic for the parasite *Plasmodium falciparum,* which causes a malignant form of malaria. But when persons with sickle-cell hemoglobin are infected with malaria, the infected cells tend to sickle and are selectively destroyed by the body's immune system. Therefore, the sickle-cell gene promotes survival in persons infected with a disease that is potentially fatal and, paradoxically, prolongs survival. In parts of the world such as the United States where *P. falciparum* is no longer endemic, the sickle-cell gene becomes the sole determinant of morbidity and does not prolong life. This explains why the frequency of the sickle-cell gene has decreased in much of the Americas.

Georges C. Benjamin

Bibliography

Allison, A. C. 1954. Protection afforded by sickle-cell trait against subtertian malaria infection. *British Medical Journal* i: 290–4.

Benjamin, G. C. 1983. Sickle cell trait and sickle cell anemia: A review. *Military Medicine* 148: 701–6.

Dean J., and A. N. Schechter. 1978. Sickle cell anemia: Molecular and cellular basis of therapeutic approaches. Part I. *New England Journal of Medicine* 299: 752–62.

   1978b. Sickle cell anemia: Molecular and cellular basis of therapeutic approaches. Part II. *New England Journal of Medicine* 299: 804–11.

   1978c. Sickle cell anemia: Molecular and cellular basis of therapeutic approaches. Part III. *New England Journal of Medicine* 299: 863–70.

Foget, B. G. 1979. Molecular genetics of hemoglobin synthesis. *Annals of Internal Medicine* 91: 605–16.

Glader, B. E. 1986. Screening for anemia and erythrocyte disorders in children. *Pediatrics* 78: 368–9.

Herrick, J. B. 1910. Peculiar elongated and sickle-shaped red blood corpuscles in a case of severe anemia. *Archives of Internal Medicine* 25: 553–61.

Kark, J. A., et al. 1987. Sickle cell trait as a risk factor for sudden death in physical training. *New England Journal of Medicine* 317: 781–7.

Motulsky, A. G. 1973. Frequency of sickling disorders in U.S. blacks. *New England Journal of Medicine* 288: 31–3.

Savitt, Todd L., and Morton F. Goldberg. 1989. Herrick's 1910 case report of sickle cell anemia: The rest of the story. *Journal of the American Medical Association* 261: 266–71.

Scott, R. B. 1985. Advances in the treatment of sickle cell disease in children. *American Journal of the Diseases of Childhood* 139: 1219–22.

Sears, D. A. 1978. The morbidity of sickle cell trait: A review of the literature. *American Journal of Medicine* 64: 1021–36.

VIII.128
Smallpox

Smallpox (*variola*) no longer is an active infection. Its virus exists only in laboratories. It was an acute viral disease usually transmitted by airborne droplets and entering the body through the upper respiratory tract. It infected as many as 90 percent or more of people at risk. It affected all races, and neither age nor gender seems to have influenced susceptibility directly. There never was a cure, but during its last decades of existence antibiotics were often prescribed to prevent or limit secondary infections. Closely related diseases exist, like cowpox and monkeypox, but smallpox appears to have been an exclusively human infection. Virologists recognized two kinds of smallpox: *Variola major,* with a mortality rate commonly of 25 to 30 percent; and *Variola minor,* with mild symptoms and a death rate of 1 percent or less. The characteristics of smallpox viruses varied over the centuries, and strains intermediate in virulence between *V. major* and *V. minor* in all probability existed. The worst strains, of course, attracted the most attention, and the recorded history of smallpox is for the most part a history of *V. major.*

Etiology and Epidemiology

Within the range of recorded history, as far as we know, the source of smallpox was always a human being with the infection. There was no animal reservoir. The virus could survive in scabs for considerable periods, and laundry workers on occasion contracted the disease from clothing and bedding of smallpox patients, but most transmissions were airborne and occurred over distances of no more than a few meters. In the second to the very last recorded transmission – in Birmingham, England in 1978 – the virus must have drifted from a laboratory on one floor of a building through an air duct to an unimmunized person on the floor above. Quarantine was effective against this malady, as long as it was applied early (even before the appearance of symptoms) and strictly enforced.

Clinical Manifestations and Pathology

The incubation period was about 12 days. Onset was abrupt and prostrating: high fever, headache, and pain in the back and muscles; and, in children, sometimes vomiting and convulsions. In the severest infections, extreme toxemia and massive hemorraging into the skin, lungs, and other organs could cause death swiftly before the appearance of more than a slight rash. In the great majority of cases, the sufferer survived to experience the characteristic rash 2 to 5 days after onset. In most cases the rash appeared more densely on the face, palms, and soles than on the trunk. In another few days, the small pimples of the rash turned to pustules, which in extreme cases were confluent, almost always indicating a lethal infection. William Bradford observed cases like this among Amerindians near Plymouth in North America in 1633–4. He describes their pustules as "breaking and mattering and running one into another." Complications may have been common in Amerindians. Those cited just above seem to have had a pneumonic secondary infection: "And then, being very sore, what with cold and other distempers, they die like rotten sheep."

Drying and crusting of the pustules began on the eighth or ninth day after the first eruptions. The scabs fell off 3 or 4 weeks after onset, and the victim was well again, barring complications. Among the possible sequelae were blindness and, at least occasionally, male infertility. The probable sequel was a pocked and scarred face, appalling to others as well as to the survivor. Literature is full of references to women thus robbed of their smooth skins, from Ben Jonson's cry – "Envious and foule Disease, could there not be One beautie in an Age, and free from thee?" – to Charles Dickens's heroine of *Bleak House,* who after recovery remarks bravely, "It matters very little . . . I hope I can do without my old face very well."

Immunology

Except in the rarest instances, smallpox infection ended in one of only two ways: death or long-lasting immunity. Lacking an animal reservoir and the ability to remain latent within the human body, smallpox existed only as an active infection. It was one of the classic epidemic diseases, surviving in many eras and parts of the world only as rolling waves of infection. It could achieve endemicity only in large and, often, cosmopolitan populations, where it could pass in unbroken sequence through the bodies of travelers newly arrived from areas free from the malady, and through the bodies of the immunologically innocent newborn. Where it was endemic, it was usually a childhood disease, and trial by smallpox was a prerequisite for adulthood for all but a small minority.

History

Antiquity

Because it only persisted by passing from one human to another, smallpox could not have existed with its historical characteristics among the sparse populations of the Paleolithic Age. It may have first appeared sporadically among the village dwellers of the Neolithic Age, derived from pox diseases of livestock, or from similar infections circulating among wild animals with whom humans were often in contact. In our own time, Africans occasionally contract monkeypox, which has symptoms similar to smallpox, but which is, fortunately, very unlikely to spread from human to human.

Smallpox may well have circulated among the ancient Egyptians. The face, neck, and shoulders of the mummy of Pharoah Ramses V, who died in 1157 B.C., are disfigured by a rash of elevated pustules like those of smallpox, but researchers cannot be absolutely sure of the infection that caused them. Dreadful epidemics rolled back and forth through the Old World in ancient times, but rarely were the symptoms described clearly enough for researchers to make diagnoses confidently. In the second and third centuries A.D., two pandemics devastated the Roman Empire, one or both of which may have been smallpox, but we know very little about the diseases clinically. There is some indication of smallpox in China by the fourth century, and stronger evidence for its arrival in Japan in the 730s.

Ninth Through Fifteenth Century

With *The Treatise on Smallpox and Measles* at about the turn of the ninth century by Rhazes, a Baghdad physician, we are finally on solid ground. He clearly differentiated between the two diseases, and revealed smallpox to be a common childhood disease in southwest Asia in his time. The density of population centers extending west to the Mediterranean and Atlantic and east to China and the Pacific in that era suggests strongly that smallpox was prevalent, at least in epidemic form, throughout the area of advanced Old World civilizations before the end of the first Christian millennium. In the same general period, the malady may have invaded peripheral areas: sub-Saharan Africa, northern Europe, and the Indonesian archipelago.

Smallpox, though widespread in the first millennium and a half of the Christian era, seems not to have been among humanity's chief curses in those centuries. It ranked behind plague, tuberculosis, and probably other maladies prevalent in the Old World in the period Europeans call the Middle Ages, and did not become a major demographic check in Europe until the sixteenth and seventeenth centuries.

Sixteenth Through Seventeenth Century
The most important effect of smallpox historically was as a solvent exuded by dense populations of the Old World. For example, it was an important ally of the Russian invaders of Siberia, as it was of the Hollanders in Cape Colony, South Africa. On the other hand, smallpox was a merciless enemy of barbarians trying to penetrate concentrations of dense population. The Manchus, who rode south into China and founded the Ch'ing Dynasty in the seventeenth century, were obliged to excuse princes and dignitaries from the thinly populated steppes (who had not yet contracted smallpox) from coming to Beijing to make obeisance to the Emperor. For their safety and survival, special audiences were provided in Jehol, north of the Great Wall.

No later than 1519, smallpox crossed the Atlantic to a New World still free from the disease; decimated the Arawaks of the West Indies, a people already in steep decline; accompanied the Spaniards to Mexico; and rolled on ahead of them into the Incan Empire. Amerindians had, at very best, no more resistance to the disease than did Europeans, and they must have suffered similarly high or even higher morbidity rates. The Spanish estimates of death rates among Amerindians in this, the first of their many pandemics of smallpox, ran from about one-fourth to one-half – that is, rates comparable to those of European children afflicted with the disease. The psychological effect of such experiences on peoples who believed in a direct connection between pestilence and the supernatural was considerable. The Amerindians quaked in confusion and terror; and the Europeans preened themselves as the chosen people. John Winthrop, first governor of Massachusetts Bay Colony in North America, noted on May 22, 1634: "For the natives, they are neere all dead of the small Poxe, so as the Lord hathe cleared our title to what we possess" (Winslow 1974).

Eighteenth Century
The final major chapter in the history of the expansion of smallpox opened in 1789, when the infection appeared among the Australian aborigines in contact with the newly arrived English settlers at Sydney Harbor. It destroyed half the indigenes, by English estimate, and spread over the Blue Mountains into the interior, although no one knows how far. This epidemic was probably the single greatest demographic shock ever dealt the Aborigines.

By the eighteenth century, smallpox accounted for 10 to 15 percent of all deaths in some European countries annually, 80 percent of the victims being under 10 years of age. It is likely that similar rates were common in major cities in North Africa and civilized Eurasia. Outside these areas of dense population the disease was epidemic, killing high percentages of adults essential to the functioning of the economy and society. The peoples of the Old World, living in the presence of this threat for generation after generation, were bound to devise means of defending themselves, if such could be found.

Variolation.   Our modern techniques of inoculation and vaccination began – no one knows when or where – with *variolation* (the artificial infection with smallpox of healthy people) in the hope that this would produce mild cases of the disease but solid immunity. In China, smallpox scabs were blown up the nostril, seemingly a very dangerous method because it might produce infection through the upper respiratory tract, as in naturally incurred smallpox, but the scabs were apparently aged first, attenuating the virus. Elsewhere in the Old World, variolation was generally accomplished by obtaining material, usually fluid, from pustules of an active case of smallpox and then scratching this into the skin. If variolation was done expertly, the infection was mild, and the death rate no more than 3 or 4 percent and, when done by the most skilled practitioners, as low as 1 percent.

Variolation was practiced for a long time, not by formally trained physicians, but by folk healers. For example, Cotton Mather, a minister in the Massachusetts Bay Colony in North America, first heard of it about 1706 from his African slave, who told him that smallpox and variolation were both common in Africa. Peasants in remote parts of Scotland, Wales, Greece, the Middle East, and elsewhere in Eurasia were "buying the smallpox," as those who spoke English put it, long before the rich and well-born learned of variolation. The most famous figure of that latter event was Lady Mary Wortley Montagu, a woman whose brother died of the disease and who, attacked by smallpox as an adult, lost her beauty and even her eyebrows. While in Constantinople as wife of the British ambassador, she learned of a method practiced there of "ingrafting" the disease, which usually led to a mild infection and yet stout immunity. Lady Montagu had her son variolated in Constantinople in 1717, and her daughter, in London in 1721.

In that same year, smallpox broke out in Boston, Massachusetts, where the people, too few to maintain the disease endemically, periodically suffered terrifying epidemic waves of it. Mather knew nothing of Lady Montagu's experiments, but he had heard of variolation from his slave and had read reports about it. He persuaded Zabdiel Boylston to experiment with the new practice in Boston. Despite fierce opposition from those who viewed the practice as dangerous (which it certainly was), Boylston scratched pus from a smallpox pustule into the skins of his son and two slaves. In all, he variolated 244 people, while in nearby Cambridge and Roxbury other physicians variolated 36 more. This was the first large-scale test of the practice, at least in the West. Also – amazingly – it may have been the first example of careful quantitative analysis of the effects of a medical procedure. Boston had a population of about 11,000, thousands of whom fled during the epidemic. Of the remainder, 5,980 caught the disease naturally, and 844 – or 14 percent – died. But only 6 – or just 2.4 percent – of the 244 variolated by Boylston died.

The practice of variolation was not adopted as rapidly as the statistics above suggest that it should have. After an initial flurry of variolating among some members of the upper classes and their domestics in the 1720s, the spread of the new procedure slowed and may even have retreated. British North Americans resorted to it only during epidemics, when contracting the disease naturally seemed just as likely as, and a good deal more dangerous than, embracing it via variolation.

Acceptance of the practice was contingent on several developments. One was a rise in the fear of smallpox, which a surge of the disease around 1750 stimulated. Others were the reduction of what were at first high fees for variolation, and the improvement in technique so as to reduce the chances of dying from this procedure to a tolerable minimum. These changes were accomplished by a handful of physicians, among them the American James Kirkpatrick, and more importantly, the Britons Robert Sutton and his sons, especially Daniel. The Suttons reduced variolation to a slight pricking of the skin, rather than, as had previously often been the case, deep incisions that thrust the virus directly and dangerously into the bloodstream and that increased chances of secondary infection. The establishment of smallpox hospitals, where variolated patients could be isolated, helped to quell fears of artificially triggered epidemics.

In the 1760s and for the rest of the century, variolation became increasingly common in the British Empire, and on the continent of Europe, as well, though more slowly. The death of Louis XV of smallpox in May and the variolation of Louis XVI in June of 1774 spurred the practice everywhere. By the end of the century, many thousands had been variolated in Europe and America. How many we will never know because physicians kept poor records, and there were many itinerent inoculators, who kept no records at all. Some experts claim that the spread of this new way of promoting immunization was one of the chief causes of the beginnings of our present population explosion in the last half of the eighteenth century, but it is impossible to tease out this factor from others, such as improved nutrition. In addition, there is the question of how many deaths were caused by epidemics unintentionally started by variolation. Yet we can be sure that in the long run variolation stimulated population growth, at least indirectly, by accustoming people in general to the benefits of producing immunity by deliberately incurring mild infections.

Vaccination. The greatest windfall of variolation (and the greatest in the history of medicine) occurred in the last decades of the eighteenth century when an experienced English variolator and scientist, Edward Jenner, noticed that the variolation failed to produce symptoms of illness in people who had previously contracted a mild pox disease from livestock, usually cattle. He *vaccinated* (a new word derived from the Latin for "cow") several people, including his own son, with cowpox matter, and then attempted variolation. Inoculation with smallpox matter uniformly failed to produce pustules or much else in the way of illness. He published his results in June of 1798 as *An Inquiry into the Causes and Effects of Variolae Vaccinae, a Disease, Discovered in some of the Western Counties of England, particularly Gloucestershire, and known by the Name of Cow Pox.* Vaccination may have been practiced before by common folk, like variolation, but now a member of the elite had introduced an account of the technique into print for the whole world to read, and that made all the difference.

Nineteenth Century

It was as if, to quote a nineteenth-century historian, "an Angel's trumpet had sounded over the earth" (Winslow 1974). England led the way in the new practice – more than 100,000 were vaccinated there by 1801 – and the rest of the world came treading on her heels. Within 3 years of the publication of Jenner's *Inquiry*, it was translated into German, French, Spanish, Dutch, Italian, and Latin. In France 1.7 million were vaccinated between 1808 and 1811, and in Russia about 2 million in the decade ending 1814, and so on across the world.

Getting potent vaccine across the great oceans as scabs or bits of thread soaked in matter from pustules was problematical, and often the virus proved dead and useless when scratched into transatlantic arms. Sometimes the virus survived and did the job, to the benefit, for instance, of the clients of Benjamin Waterhouse of Boston, Massachusetts, in 1800. The surest way of preserving the infectiousness of cowpox virus while traveling great distances was by the *serial method:* Recruit a number of unimmunized people, vaccinate one, and then, when his pustules are ripe, transfer the disease to another, and so on in sequence until the destination is reached with an active case on board.

This was the technique used by Don Francisco Xavier Balmis who, empowered and financed by the Spanish monarchy, led an expedition around the world from 1804 to 1806, from Spain to the New World and thence to the Philippines, China, and St. Helena, vaccinating thousands as he went. He used young boys, usually orphans, as reservoirs of the cowpox, the first set obtained in Spain and the others as required in America and elsewhere.

During the 1800s, humanity began to win its battle with smallpox. Vaccination continued to spread, and in some countries was even made compulsory, at least for infants. Its benign effect on death rates, unlike that of variolation, was obvious, and literally millions of children, who would have died without Jenner's discovery, lived to enrich their societies

with their skills and labor, and to fuel the population explosion. In a few advanced and disciplined societies, such as England and Prussia, where doctors, officials, and the public cooperated to smother smallpox, deaths due to the disease were near zero by the end of the century. Elsewhere success was equivocal, even though the benign influence of vaccination was supplemented by the appearance of *V. minor* toward the end of the century, displacing the more virulent form of the disease in some regions of the world.

Twentieth Century

Jenner realized that his discovery could mean "the annihilation of smallpox – the most dreadful scourge of the human race" – but not until the middle of the twentieth century did this seem not just a theoretical but also a practical possibility. By 1950 a number of wealthy societies in the temperate zones with strong governments, large numbers of skilled medical personnel, and scientifically sophisticated populations were free or nearly free of the disease. But most of the smallpox in the world raged in the tropics, where few or none of the factors just cited existed, and where smallpox vaccine lost its potency quickly in the heat. Freeze-drying, invented in the 1940s and adapted for mass production of vaccine in the 1950s, solved that problem.

In 1966, the Nineteenth World Health Assembly issued a call for the eradication of smallpox from the Earth. Donald A. Henderson, an officer of the World Health Organization, took charge of the Smallpox Eradication Programme. During its first year, 1967, smallpox existed in every continent except North America and Europe, and the estimate was that 10 to 15 million people contracted the disease each year. By 1972 it was gone from South America, as well. By the end of 1973 it was restricted to the Indian subcontinent and the horn of Africa, Ethiopia, and Somalia. In October of 1975, Rahima Banu of Bangladesh came down with *V. major,* the last case of smallpox in Asia. On October 26, 1977, the rash of *V. minor* appeared on the skin of Ali Maow Maalin of Somalia. This was the last case of this kind of smallpox and the last case of naturally occurring smallpox in the world. In August of 1978, smallpox virus somehow escaped from a laboratory in Birmingham, England, infecting Janet Parker and, subsequently, her mother. The daughter died; the mother survived. The director of the laboratory committed suicide while in quarantine. These were the last deaths associated with the ancient and now defunct scourge of smallpox. In 1979 the Global Commission for the Certification of Smallpox Eradication officially announced the demise of the disease. As of 1980, stocks of vaccine sufficient for 200 million vaccinations were being maintained in the unlikely case that smallpox should somehow arise again.

Humanity won the victory against the smallpox virus by displacing it with the vaccine virus. Almost everyone for nearly a century and a half believed that virus to be the organism of cowpox, but in 1939 careful comparison of vaccinia virus (which does not exist naturally) of cowpox virus and of smallpox virus showed them to be related but clearly distinct entities. One expert claims that the Jenner strain of vaccinia virus was contaminated with a mild strain of smallpox very early, and that vaccination was a continuation of variolation not only in technique but also in the identity of the virus, as well. Decades of variolation, according to this theory, produced a very attenuated strain (or strains) of smallpox virus, and vaccinia virus is no more than one of these tamed varieties. Other experts suggest that Jenner was not dealing with cowpox, but horsepox, which cattle occasionally contracted. Unfortunately, horsepox died out early in the twentieth century, and so we have no way of testing this hypothesis. Still others suggest that vaccinia virus was the product of hybridization of two or more pox viruses in the nineteenth century. Careful analysis of the DNA of the viruses of vaccinia and possible "parents" has uncovered little indication of a close and recent relationship. The stuff of smallpox vaccination is a mystery, perhaps the greatest happy accident in the history of the relationship of humans and pathogens.

Alfred W. Crosby

Bibliography

Baxby, Derrick. 1981. *Jenner's smallpox vaccine: The battle of vaccinia virus and its origin.* London.

Bowers, John Z. 1981. The odyssey of smallpox vaccination. *Bulletin of the History of Medicine* 55: 17–33.

Butlin, N. G. 1983. *Our original aggression: Aboriginal populations of southeastern Australia, 1788–1850.* Sydney.

Carmichael, Ann, and Arthur M. Silverstein. n.d. *Smallpox before the seventeenth century.* (Unpublished ms.)

Clendenning, Philip H. 1973. Dr. Thomas Dimsdale and smallpox inoculation in Russia. *Journal of the History of Medicine and Allied Sciences* 28: 109–25.

Crosby, Alfred W. 1972. *The Columbian exchange: Biological and cultural consequences of 1492.* Westport, Conn.

1976. Virgin soil epidemics as a factor in the aboriginal depopulation in America. *The William and Mary Quarterly,* 3d Series, 33: 289–99.

1986. *Ecological imperialism: The biological expansion of Europe, 900–1900.* Cambridge.

Cumpston, J. H. L. 1914. *The history of smallpox in Australia, 1788–1908.* Melbourne.

Derbes, Vincent J. 1958. Smallpox in English poetry of the seventeenth century. *A.M.A. Archives of Dermatology* 77: 430–2.

Dixon, D. W. 1962. *Smallpox.* London.

Farris, William. 1985. *Population, disease and land in early Japan, 645–900.* Cambridge.

Fenner, F., et al. 1988. *Smallpox and its eradication.* Geneva.

Flinn, Michael W. 1981. *The European demographic system, 1500–1820.* Baltimore.

Greenough, Paul R. 1980. Variolation and vaccination in South Asia, c. 1700–1865: A preliminary note. *Social Science and Medicine* 14: 345–7.

Henderson, Donald A. 1988. *Smallpox eradication.* Geneva.

Hopkins, Donald R. 1983. *Princes and peasants: Smallpox in history.* Chicago.

Miller, Genevieve. 1957. *The adoption of inoculation for smallpox in England and France.* Philadelphia.

Perrenoud, Alfred. 1979. *La Population de Genève du seizième au début du dix-neuvième siècle.* Geneva.

Razzell, Peter. 1977a. *Edward Jenner's cowpox vaccine: The history of a medical myth.* Sussex, England.

1977b. *The conquest of smallpox: The impact of inoculation on smallpox mortality in eighteenth century Britain.* Sussex, England.

Saunders, Paul. 1982. *Edward Jenner: The Cheltenham years, 1795–1823.* Hanover, N.H.

Serruys, Henry. 1980. Smallpox in Mongolia during the Ming and Ch'ing dynasties. *Zentralasiastische Studien* 14: 41–63.

Smith, Michael M. 1974. *The "real expedición maritima de la vacuna" in New Spain and Guatemala.* Philadelphia.

Stern, E. Wagnere, and Allen E. Stearn. 1945. *The effect of smallpox on the destiny of the American Indian.* Boston.

Twitchett, Denis. 1979. Population and pestilence in T'ang China. In *Studia Sino-Mongolica: Festschrift um Herbert Franke,* 35–68. Wiesbaden.

Winslow, Ola Elizabeth. 1974. *A destroying angel: The conquest of smallpox in colonial Boston.* Boston.

VIII.129
Streptococcal Diseases

Streptococci are responsible for many common and not so common human and animal diseases. Streptococcal pharyngitis, scarlet fever, impetigo, erysipelas, neonatal meningitis and sepsis, puerperal sepsis, and bacterial endocarditis all follow infection with streptococci. In addition, some streptococci provoke two peculiar postinfectious conditions: acute rheumatic fever and acute glomerulonephritis. Rebecca Lancefield (1933) divided streptococci into distinct serologic groups, labeled *A, B, C, D . . .*, each with a number of separate subgroups. In addition to these groups, microbiologists further classify streptococci on whether and how they hemolyze red blood cells (*alpha:* incomplete or green hemolysis; *beta:* complete or clear hemolysis). According to this tradition, the streptococcus responsible for pharyngitis is known as a "group A beta-hemolytic streptococcus." Another member of the genus *Streptococcus* is the *Streptococcus pneumoniae*, the bacteria responsible for pneumonia.

The streptococcus has a number of biological peculiarities that alter its ability to infect humans. The genetic insertion of a bacteriophage produces a toxin responsible for the rash of scarlet fever. A group of proteins, known as the M protein, renders the streptococcus impervious to the normal bodily defense of phagocytosis. Hemolysins and enzymes, when present, help the streptococcus to invade the host. One can speculate that this potential biological variability is responsible for the abrupt changes that streptococcal illnesses have made in the past (Gallis 1984).

Streptococcal illness can be extremely common. Few have escaped streptococcal pharyngitis or superficial impetigo of the skin. Alternately, some forms of streptococcal illness are rare. An example is streptococcal endocarditis. Most streptococcal diseases are spread through respiratory droplets. Others can be spread by bacterial contamination of food or milk, by soiled hands or instruments touching open wounds, or when normal resident bacteria invade the bloodstream (for example, when endocarditis follows dental work).

Group A streptococci produce several common illnesses. *Streptococcal pharyngitis* presents a clinical picture of fever, headache, sore throat, and abdominal discomfort. Before therapy with penicillin, the disease was often self-limited, but in certain cases the streptococci could disseminate to other ana-

tomic sites, producing otitis media, mastoiditis, tonsillar abscesses, or osteomyelitis. *Puerperal sepsis,* or childbed fever, occurs when streptococci, introduced at delivery, invade the internal lining of the uterus. Group A streptococci can cause *impetigo* (a superficial skin infection), *cellulitis,* and *erysipelas* (a life-threatening, rapidly progressing soft tissue infection).

Group A streptococci are responsible for two striking postinfectious conditions: The first is *acute rheumatic fever,* which follows streptococcal pharyngitis after 2 to 3 weeks. Rheumatic fever can include one or more of the following: carditis (pericarditis, myocarditis, and/or endocarditis); migratory, nondeforming arthritis; chorea; subcutaneous, fibrous nodules; and erythema marginatum. The second postinfectious condition is *acute glomerulonephritis,* a usually temporary form of renal failure.

Group B streptococci form part of the normal flora of the vagina and usually do not produce illness in adult women. These bacteria, however, can infect babies during delivery, producing meningitis and sepsis.

Group C streptococci are usually pathogenic only for animals.

Group D streptococci, normal residents of the human body, can produce endocarditis in people with deformed heart valves. Some streptococci cannot be so readily grouped, such as *Streptococcus viridans*. These can also cause endocarditis, and they play a role in the formation of dental caries.

History and Geography

Women have suffered from puerperal fever, presumably due to streptococci, since ancient times. Many case studies in the books of *Epidemics* within the Hippocratic corpus indicate that women suffered from postpartum fever, debility, and death. Nevertheless, childbed fever was probably never common. Oliver Wendell Holmes, in his masterfully argued "Contagiousness of Puerperal Fever" (1842–3), claimed that childbed fever was rare. When it occurred, it clustered around the practice of an individual physician. Holmes pointed to the need for cleanliness to prevent further victims.

Similarly, in the other classical study of puerperal sepsis first published in 1861, Ignaz Semmelweis (1983) demonstrated that physicians who followed their dead patients to the autopsy room and then returned to the lying-in room to deliver more babies had more of their patients die of puerperal fever than did midwives who did not perform autopsies. These observations of Holmes and Semmelweis (each unaware of the work of the other) point to the tremendous gulf in personal cleanliness that existed between the pre- and post-germ-theory practitioners.

Holmes, for example, tells of distinguished obstetricians who carried pelvic organs removed at autopsy in their street coat pockets. Both accounts also underscore the irony in the fact that the most scientifically oriented physicians, the ones who performed autopsies, were responsible for spreading the illness! Those accounts, however, treat with silence the plight of infants born of infected mothers. We know from twentieth-century experience that many infants emerged unscathed. But in the past, some may have developed a fatal infection, and even the lucky surviving infants would have faced an uncertain future if their mothers were unable to nurse them.

Erysipelas's role in history was an inevitable accompaniment of wounds, whether accidental or surgical (Simpson 1872). Any deep cut through uncleansed skin risked injecting streptococci into susceptible tissue. Erysipelas also accompanied other streptococcal-related illnesses, such as childbed fever. Scarlet fever (streptococcal pharyngitis produced by peculiar strains of streptococci that release a toxin yielding a rash) crosses medical history in a number of places. In the early years of bacteriology, Friedrich Löffler (1884) had to sort out scarlet fever cocci from diphtheria bacilli (both produced sore throats). Scarlet fever often occurred in epidemics passed both in the usual droplet fashion and in contaminated food – especially milk – supplies.

Streptococcal pharyngitis, with or without rash, provoked a prominent postinfectious state: acute rheumatic fever. For a period of about a century, rheumatic fever injured more hearts than any other disease. It struck children and young adults, usually less than 25 years of age, in temperate climates. Although mentioned by prominent seventeenth-century writers, such as Thomas Sydenham, rheumatic fever appears not to have become a major problem until the late eighteenth and early nineteenth centuries, when carditis emerged as the major component of rheumatic fever. This seems to have been the result of a biological change in the way the streptococcus provoked the body to respond (rheumatic fever is not an infection in the usual sense, but rather an immunologic response to the streptococcus), coupled with the introduction of the stethoscope that made diagnosis easier (Cheadle 1889).

All streptococcal diseases, except newborn sepsis and meningitis, have become less virulent since the end of the nineteenth century, a phenomenon that has yet to be explained. Their incidence was clearly on the decline before the arrival of specific measures to treat these illnesses. The puzzle to be sorted out is the possibility that the streptococcus, with its biological variability, could have become less inherently invasive in natural fashion. But it did so at the precise time in history (at least in Europe and the United States) when nutrition, housing, and standards of living substantially improved.

Today, however, the streptococcus is usually sensitive to sulfonamides and to penicillins; thus most infections are curable with appropriate antibiotics.

Peter C. English

Bibliography

Cheadle, Walter Butler. 1889. *Various manifestations of the rheumatic state*. London.

Gallis, Harry A. 1984. Streptococcus. In *Zinser microbiology*, 18th edition, ed. Wolfgang K. Joklik, Hilda P. Willett, and D. Bernard Amos. Norwalk. Conn.

Hippocrates. 1978. *Hippocratic writings*, ed. G. E. R. Lloyd, trans. J. Chadwick and W. N. Mann. New York.

Holmes, Oliver Wendell. 1842–3. On the contagiousness of puerperal fever. *New England Quarterly Journal of Medicine* 1: 503–30.

Lancefield, Rebecca C. 1933. A serological differentiation of human and other groups of hemolytic streptococci. *Journal of Experimental Medicine* 57: 571.

Löffler, Friedrich. 1884. Untersuchungen über die Bedeutung der Micro-Organismen für die Entstehung der Diphtherie beim Menschen, bei der Taube und beim Kalbe. *Mittheilungen aus dem Kaiserlichen Gesundheitsamte* 2: 421.

Semmelweis, Ignaz. 1983. *The etiology, concept, and prophylaxis of childbed fever*, trans. K. Codell Carter. Madison, Wis.

Simpson, James Y. 1872. *Anesthesia, hospitalism, hermaphroditism, and a proposal to stamp out smallpox and other contagious diseases*. New York.

VIII.130
Strongyloidiasis

Strongyloidiasis, or *Cochin-China diarrhea,* is caused by a minute nematode, the threadworm *Strongyloides stercoralis.* The organism was first discovered in 1876 in French troops who had suffered severe diarrhea in the Cochin-China region of Vietnam. *Strongyloides* occurs around the world, with a range similar to that of the hookworms. Millions of people harbor the organism. Because poor sanitation and going without shoes favor transmission, it is especially prevalent in poor tropical countries. Like hookworm disease, strongyloidiasis prevalence has declined greatly in the southern United States since the early twentieth century, but it still exists in foci in Kentucky and other states.

The worm has a complex life cycle. Parasitic males may not exist, but if they do, they are eliminated from the body shortly after infection. The females burrow in the mucosa of the intestine, where they feed and lay their eggs, apparently by parthenogenesis. The eggs pass into the lumen of the intestine, where they hatch into a rhabditiform larval stage. In most cases these larvae are voided in the feces to the soil and either transform themselves directly into an infective filariform larval stage, or, if conditions are favorable, undergo one or more generations of sexual reproduction before filariform larvae appear. Like the hookworms, the filariform *Strongyloides* larvae penetrate human skin, often on an unshod foot, enter the venous circulation, and are carried through the heart to the lungs. Here they burrow through the walls of the air sacs, ascend to the throat, and are swallowed. The adult females bore into the walls of the small intestine and sometimes into the wall of the large intestine as well. Autoinfection is also possible and can maintain the parasite for years after the host has left endemic areas. In this variation of the life cycle, rhabditiform larvae develop into infective filariforms while still in the intestine. These larvae penetrate the mucosa, enter the bloodstream, and are eventually swallowed to continue the cycle.

Migrating larvae may produce itching when they penetrate the skin, and cough and chest pain when they are active in the lungs. Light intestinal infections are often asymptomatic, but heavier worm loads may cause abdominal pain, nausea, alternating diarrhea and constipation, anemia, weight loss, and low fever. Autoinfection can produce an enormous number of worms and can be fatal. Persons with immune deficiencies from diseases such as cancer or acquired immune deficiency syndrome, or whose therapy requires immune suppression, may develop devastating hyperinfections from mild or inapparent strongyloidiasis.

Diagnosis is made by detection of larvae in stool specimens. Therapy is usually effective, although side effects from drugs are common. Prevention is largely a matter of education and better living conditions. Improved rural sanitation and wearing shoes break the worm's life cycle in most cases, and treatment prevents autoinfection.

Strongyloides fülleborni, a parasite of monkeys, has been found in many people in Zaire, Zambia, and other central African countries; larvae may possibly be transmitted in mother's milk. The same or a very similar species has been found in 80 to 100 percent of infants in a region of Papua New Guinea.

K. David Patterson

Bibliography

Ashford, R. W., et al. 1979. Strongyloides infection in a mid-mountain Papua New Guinea community: Results of an epidemiological survey. *Papua New Guinea Medical Journal* 22: 128–35.

Hira, P. R., and B. G. Patel. 1980. Human strongyloidiasis due to the primate species *Strongyloides fülleborni. Tropical and Geographical Medicine* 32: 23–9.

Kean, B. H., et al., eds. 1978. *Tropical medicine and parasitology: Classic investigations,* Vol. II, 325–45. Ithaca and London. [Five early papers.]

Scowden, E. B., et al. 1978. Overwhelming strongyloidiasis: An unappreciated opportunistic infection. *Medicine* 57: 527–44.

Walzer, Peter D., et al. 1982. Epidemiological features of *Strongyloides stercoralis.* Infection in an endemic area of the United States. *American Journal of Tropical Medicine and Hygiene* 31: 313–19.

VIII.131
Sudden Infant Death Syndrome

The sudden infant death syndrome (SIDS) is a difficult condition to define because medical scientists do not yet fully understand its nature. In the typical SIDS case, an apparently healthy infant, who may recently have suffered some minor respiratory ailment, is put to bed in the evening and is found dead in the crib next morning. The baby shows no signs of having been distressed; autopsy reveals no significant findings to explain the cause of death (Bergman et al. 1974; Golding, Limerick, and Macfarlane 1985).

The Second International Conference on Causes of Sudden Death in Infants, held in Seattle in 1969, described SIDS as "the sudden death of any infant or young child which is unexpected by history, and in which a thorough postmortem examination fails to demonstrate an adequate cause for death" (Bergman, Beckwith, and Ray, eds. 1970). That definition still applies. Physicians make the diagnosis of SIDS by excluding other causes of death in infants between one month and one year.

In attempting to understand SIDS, medical professionals have identified epidemiological patterns that characterize its victims, their parents, and the settings in which SIDS death occur. These characteristics will be discussed in subsequent sections.

Distribution and Incidence

The vast majority of reported and published SIDS cases come from countries and continents in the Earth's temperate zones (e.g., the United States, Canada, Europe, Australia, New Zealand, Japan, Hong Kong, and Israel) (Golding et al. 1985; Culbertson, Krous, and Bendell, eds. 1988; Guntheroth 1989; Irgens, Skjaerven, and Lie 1989; Lee et al. 1989). But SIDS occurs worldwide, in countries in tropical and frigid zones, in the mountains and at sea level (Golding et al. 1985; Culbertson et al. 1988; Guntheroth 1989). SIDS tends to receive less attention in countries with high infant death rates from problems such as infectious diseases and malnutrition. Autopsies are rarely performed on adults, much less on children, in these countries, making it almost impossible scientifically to label a sudden infant death as SIDS (Bergman 1986). SIDS becomes a significant factor in a country when the infant death rate approaches

approximately 15 per 1,000 live births. The lower the death rate from other causes of infant mortality, the higher the proportion of deaths from SIDS (Culbertson et al. 1988).

The occurrence of SIDS has probably not changed much over the centuries around the world (Bergman 1986; Culbertson et al. 1988). Rates range generally from 1.5 to 3.5 cases per 1,000 live births per year, though the incidence varies from country to country. It is difficult to compare these rates because of differences in the way each study team obtains and analyzes its data (Culbertson et al. 1988). In the United States, SIDS rates have ranged from 1.2 to 3.4 deaths per 1,000 live births. The range is higher in Britain (2.1 to 4.0) and the Antipodes (New Zealand and Australia) (1.6 to 4.1), and lower on the European continent (0.5 to 2.7), in Israel (0.3 to 0.7), Japan (0.5 to 1.2), and Hong Kong (0.036 to 0.3) (Golding et al. 1985; Culbertson et al. 1988; Guntheroth 1989; Irgens et al. 1989; Lee et al. 1989).

SIDS accounts for approximately 6,000 to 7,000 infant deaths per year in the United States (Bergman 1986). It is the greatest killer of infants between 1 month and 1 year of life (Culbertson et al. 1988).

Epidemiology

SIDS' outstanding epidemiological characteristic is the age at which it strikes children. Most deaths occur at between 1 month and 6 months of age, with a peak between ages 2 and 3 months. Very vew cases occur before 1 month; the incidence drops significantly after 6 months old. SIDS deaths thus occur at an age when babies are undergoing their most rapid systemic development, and when their needs for efficient bodily processes and outside sources of energy to fuel them are greatest. Infants at this time are adjusting, for example, their sleep patterns to changing internal needs and to the outside environment, their gastrointestinal systems to changing foods, their immune systems to new antigens and pathogens, and their nervous systems to a variety of new motor and sensory stimuli. Life outside the womb is very different from life inside the womb.

SIDS strikes children of both sexes, of all social, economic, ethnic, and racial groups, and at all times of the year. The distribution of SIDS within these groups and seasons is not equal, however. About 60 percent of SIDS deaths occur among boys. SIDS occurs more commonly, but by no means exclusively, during the colder months of the year (autumn and winter), in both the northern and southern hemispheres. Members of lower socioeconomic groups generally suffer a higher incidence of SIDS than do others. The distribution of SIDS also seems to follow racial lines in the United States: Afro-Americans (blacks) show the highest incidence, followed by Euro-Americans (whites), followed by Asian-Americans. That racial distribution may be deceptive, as it probably reflects more the generally lower socioeconomic status (SES) of blacks in the United States compared to other groups. Low SES does not always translate into high risk for SIDS, however. Studies in both Chicago (Guntheroth 1989) and California (Grether and Schulman 1989) show, interestingly and, at present, inexplicably, that Hispanics of low SES have a SIDS rate comparable to or lower than that for whites.

Certain other characteristics of babies, mothers, and families appear to be risk factors associated with a higher incidence of SIDS in infants. None of these factors is predictive of SIDS and none will be found in all SIDS cases, but all increase the risk in a child vulnerable to SIDS. All, it should be noted, can be related to low SES. Prematurity and low birth weight are both important risk factors in SIDS. SIDS occurs more frequently in children of the following: multiple births (increased risk due to small birth size or prematurity), younger mothers, mothers who smoke, mothers of greater parity, higher birth rank in the family, single mothers, mothers who are drug abusers, mothers with poor prenatal care, and families in which a SIDS death has previously occurred (slightly increased risk).

Etiology and Pathology

At present, the etiology of SIDS remains a mystery. It is not even clear whether SIDS has a single cause, has several causes, or is the result of a combination of factors working together.

Before the medical profession took an interest in the sudden, unexplained deaths of infants in the eighteenth century, people attributed the demise of these children to accidental suffocation in bedclothes, or to accidental smothering and overlaying by sleeping parents. Less charitable people accused parents or nursemaids of infanticide. These theories persisted throughout the nineteenth and early and mid-twentieth centuries concomitantly with medical theories that ascribed sudden infant deaths to an enlarged thymus or a thymic condition (see the History section for more on this). Since the 1940s, when researchers took a renewed interest in the etiology of sudden unexplained infant deaths, medicine has proposed numerous theories to explain why these children die.

When medical examiners in the 1940s and 1950s tested the blood of infants who had died suddenly and inexplicably, they often found fulminant infections that could easily have caused death. For the next several years, bacterial and viral infections were considered a major cause of sudden infant deaths. But when those deaths from infection were weeded out, there still remained a large number for which pathologists could find no infectious agents. Researchers then found other possible causes of death, including the following: powerful allergic reactions to cow's milk, to house dust mites, or to some unidentified allergen; botulism, beginning in 1976 when a number of infants infected with *Clostridium botulinum* were discovered in California; a severe, undetected respiratory viral infection; a response to vaccination against childhood diseases; overheating; hypothermia; high sodium in the blood; deficiency of a trace element like magnesium, zinc, copper, calcium, selenium, or manganese; a vitamin deficiency; and high or low levels of thyroid hormones. Some physicians reiterated the old view that a proportion of parents committed infanticide. Further research into these and other proposed etiologies continues.

Most current research relates the "final pathway" of SIDS to a malfunctioning or immaturity of the respiratory or cardiovascular system. Etiologic theories under consideration include preexisting hypoxia, heart conduction problems (arrhythmias), and apnea (Culbertson et al. 1988; Schwartz, Southall, and Valdes-Dapena 1988; Guntheroth 1989). Evidence indicates that children who die of SIDS possess physical risk factors such as small size, slower growth rate, fatty changes in the liver, and thymic changes campatible with previous infection. These risk factors are not specific to SIDS but, like the social factors listed in the Epidemiology section, reflect increased risk to all infant deaths. When a young patient possesses what Abraham Bergman (1986) calls a "critical mass" of these physical and social factors, all that is needed is a trigger to cause SIDS to occur. "Something must happen during sleep to tip the balance," he speculates, because virtually all SIDS deaths occur during sleep. The nature of that trigger is the mystery of SIDS.

SIDS leaves few pathological footprints in its young victims' bodies. Postmortem examination reveals little for the physician to use in understanding the pathology of the condition. The very definition of SIDS incorporates this fact, stating that negative postmortem findings help to classify an infant's cause of death as SIDS. Pathologists studying large numbers of SIDS cases have, over the years, noted only a few consistent postmortem findings that might at some time help explain the nature of SIDS. These include, according to one SIDS researcher (Guntheroth 1989), "intrathoracic petechiae, patchy pulmonary edema and emphysema," indicative of respiratory problems; "histopathology suggesting pre-existing hypoxia, such as changes in pulmonary arteries and right ventricle, smaller thymus, extra-medullary erythropoiesis, increased peri-adrenal brown fat cells, [and] enlarged adrenal chromaffin cells"; and neuropathological changes such as "astroglial proliferation in brain stem, leukomalacia, and delayed loss of dendritic spines in reticular substance," consistent with underdevelopment or a subtle chronic disorder. The pathological changes so far discovered fail to provide enough information for medical scientists to understand the etiology or mechanism behind SIDS deaths.

History

The medical profession and society did not recognize SIDS until the late twentieth century. And yet people from Biblical times onward described sudden unexplained infant deaths that matched the typical history of a SIDS death of today. Because the deaths almost always occurred at home or in private situations, and to seemingly healthy children, most people, including parents and caregivers, generally ascribed the cause of death to accidental or intentional smothering or suffocation. When discovering their infants, with whom they regularly slept, dead next to them after a night's sleep, with no signs of any disease or disturbance, and no cries during the night, parents believed that they had unknowingly overlaid and smothered their children. Or, if they had not slept with their infant, but found it lifeless where they had put it down for the night or for a nap, parents assumed the child had suffocated in its bed clothes. In either circumstance, parents blamed themselves for the tragedy. Worse, community members suspected not just parental negligence, but overt infanticide. Because SIDS leaves no telltale marks on its little victims, no one could determine if the infant's demise was truly accidental or if it was intentional. As a result, society assumed parental negligence and punished the parents or whoever was responsible for the child's care. Medical people were not consulted in these situations except perhaps to confirm the death. It was purely a societal matter dealt with by religious, and later by secular, authorities.

Perhaps the first recorded Western case of SIDS is found in the famous Bible story in 1 Kings 3:19 of the two women who went before King Solomon with claims to motherhood of an infant boy. One of the women had awakened, found her son dead, thought she had overlaid him, and secretly switched the child with another. Solomon's proposed solution was to cut the living boy in half so each mother could have part of the child. Medieval church rules enunciated specific punishments for those who overlaid their children, and forbade parents from taking infants to bed with them. As early as the sixteenth century, Florentine craftsmen designed a wooden arch that fit over, and kept blankets away from, the child, thus preventing potential suffocation with bed clothes.

The power of ecclesiastical courts began to wane in the Renaissance. As secular authorities gained power during the subsequent centuries, civil courts investigated cases of overlaying and smothering to determine causes of death. At this same time, medicine was learning more about human anatomy and physiology. In 1761 an Italian physician, Giovanni Morgagni, published his book *On the Seats and Causes of Disease,* which correlated specific autopsy findings with disease signs and symptoms during a patient's illness. The resultant development of pathological anatomy in the early nineteenth century helped medicalize the previously nonmedical conditions of sudden unexplained infant death. As autopsies of these children revealed large thymuses (actually a normal finding), physicians explained death on the basis that the thymus gland cut off the tracheal airway or overly reduced the size of the thoracic cavity in which the heart and lungs had to function. Such explanations relieved parents of blame for their children's deaths. Despite evidence presented by other physicians during the nineteenth and early twentieth centuries that neither an enlarged thymus nor a similar but more complex condition called status thymico-lymphaticus could cause sudden infant death (Cone 1979), many people, including judges in courts, used thymic death to absolve parents of guilt. By the end of the nineteenth century, medical people were divided over sudden unexplained infant deaths. For example, a police surgeon in Dundee, Scotland, in 1892 openly accused parents of neglect, ignorance, carelessness, and drunkenness in overlaying their children (Templeman 1892), whereas William Osler (1904) still wrote of thymic enlargement as a cause of sudden infant death in the 1904 edition of his influential and widely used textbook of medicine.

Recognition of the condition now known as SIDS began to occur in the 1940s and 1950s with the publication of studies (e.g., Werne and Garrow 1953) demonstrating the extreme difficulty of overlaying a child or smothering a child in bed clothes, and the importance of performing full autopsies on these children. As medical scientists and epidemiologists gathered information during the 1960s and 1970s, they better characterized SIDS (Bergman 1986; Guntheroth 1989). Public awareness and political campaigns since the 1970s have succeeded in removing much of the parental stigma associated with sudden infant deaths (Bergman 1986).

Todd L. Savitt

Bibliography

Beckwith, J. Bruce. 1973. The sudden infant death syndrome. *Current Problems in Pediatrics* 3: 1–36.

Bergman, Abraham B. 1986. *The "discovery" of sudden infant death syndrome: Lessons in the practice of political medicine.* New York.

Bergman, Abraham B., J. B. Beckwith, and C. G. Ray, eds. 1970. *Sudden infant death syndrome: Proceedings of the second international conference on causes of sudden deaths in infants.* Seattle.

Bergman, Abraham B., et al., eds. 1974. *Sudden unexpected death in infants.* New York.

Cone, Thomas E., Jr. 1979. *History of American pediatrics.* Boston.

Culbertson, Jan L., Henry F. Krous, and R. Debra Bendell, eds. 1988. *Sudden infant death syndrome: Medical aspects and psychological management.* Baltimore.

Golding, Jean, Sylvia Limerick, and Aidan Macfarlane. 1985. *Sudden infant death: Patterns, puzzles and problems.* Seattle.

Grether, Judith K., and Jane Schulman. 1989. Sudden infant death syndrome and birth weight. *Journal of Pediatrics* 114: 561–7.

Guntheroth, Warren G. 1989. *Crib death: The sudden infant death syndrome,* 2d revised edition. New York.

Irgens, L. M., R. Skjaerven, and R. T. Lie. 1989. Secular trends of sudden infant death syndrome and other causes of post-perinatal mortality in Norwegian birth cohorts 1967–1984. *Acta Paediatrica Scandinavica* 78: 228–32.

Johnson, Michael P. 1981. Smothered slave infants: Were slave mothers at fault? *Journal of Southern History* 47: 493–520.

Kiple, Kenneth F., and Virginia H. King. 1981. *Another dimension to the black diaspora: Diet, disease, and racism.* Cambridge, U.K.

Lee, Natalie N. Y., et al. 1989. Sudden infant death syndrome in Hong Kong: Confirmation of low incidence. *British Medical Journal* 298: 721–2.

Osler, William. 1904. *The principles and practice of medicine.* New York.

Russell-Jones, D. L. 1985. Sudden infant death in history and literature. *Archives of Disease in Childhood* 60: 278–81.

Savitt, Todd L. 1975. Smothering and overlaying of Virginia slave children: A suggested explanation. *Bulletin of the History of Medicine* 41: 400–4.

1979. The social and medical history of crib death. *Journal of the Florida Medical Association* 66: 853–9.

Schwartz, Peter J., David P. Southall, and Marie Valdes-Dapena, eds. 1988. The sudden infant death syndrome: Cardiac and respiratory mechanisms and interventions. *Annals of the New York Academy of Sciences* 533: 1–474.

Templeman, C. 1892. Two hundred and fifty-eight cases of suffocation of infants. *Edinburgh Medical Journal* 38: 322–9.

Werne, J., and I. Garrow. 1953. Sudden apparently unexplained death during infancy. I. Pathologic findings in infants found dead. *American Journal of Pathology* 29: 633–76.

VIII.132
Sudden Unexplained Death Syndrome (Asian)

Sudden unexplained death syndrome (SUDS) occurs when a relatively young healthy person, usually male and Asian, dies unexpectedly while sleeping. The victim has no known antecedent illnesses, and there are no factors that might precipitate cardiac arrest. At autopsy, no cause of death can be identified in the heart, lung, or brain. Postmortem toxicologic screening tests reveal no poisons. A sudden fatality during sleep in a previously healthy member of an ethnic group subject to SUDS, but whose death is not investigated with an autopsy, is defined as a presumptive case of SUDS.

Distribution and Incidence

SUDS has occurred in the 1980s among Southeast Asian refugees and immigrants in the United States, mainly among Laotians, Hmong, Kampucheans, and Filipinos. In Asia, SUDS has been described in the Japanese and Filipino medical literature and is also observed in refugee camps in Thailand. In 1983 the death rate ascribed to SUDS in the 25- to 44-year age group of Laotian and Hmong males in the United States, 87 per 100,000, was comparable to the sum of the four leading causes of natural death among other U.S. males in that age group. The incidence of SUDS has decreased since 1983, and there is evidence that the longer a refugee has been in the United States, the lower the risk.

Epidemiology

The first comprehensive report of SUDS in the United States was published by the Centers for Disease Control (CDC) on December 4, 1981; it described 38 victims, all Southeast Asian refugees. All but one of the cases were males: 25 Hmong, 8 Laotian, 4 Vietnamese, and 1 Kampuchean. Median period of time in the United States was 5 months (range, 5 days to 52 months) before death. Geographic distribution of the deaths reflected the distribution of the Southeast Asian refugees in the United States. The deaths occurred between 9:30 P.M. and 7:00 A.M.

Clinical Manifestations and Pathology

The victims whose deaths were witnessed by relatives appeared to be asleep prior to death or were just falling asleep. None of them had complained of illness or symptoms before going to bed, and all were considered by family members to have been in good health.

Witnesses of SUDS deaths become aware of abnormal breathing sounds, in some cases preceded by a brief groan. Victims cannot be aroused. Terminal respirations are said to be labored and deep, irregular and without wheezing or stridor. The victims remain flaccid during these events, although a few are described as having tonic rigidity. Some of the victims are incontinent of urine or feces. Witnesses recall no signs of pain or terrifying dreams. A few of the victims who are still alive when paramedics reach them are found to be in ventricular fibrillation.

Interviews with family members yield no clues as to why the victims have died. Spouses have not noted symptoms consistent with sleep apnea syndrome.

Etiology

In discussing the significance of SUDS cases, CDC investigators note that they "may constitute a new syndrome" because of the differences in the epidemiological pattern between these cases and other victims of sudden death. The quickness of the deaths is unusual, and there is a lack of any ascribed cause after extensive postmortem investigation.

The etiology of SUDS remains unknown. In 1982 researchers at the CDC performed a case control study using the first 26 cases of SUDS among Hmong and Laotians in the United States. Results were meager. No single variable was found that differentiated cases from controls. The victims tended to have been in the country less than 6 months, to have left Laos less than 3 years earlier, to have spent a greater proportion of their income on housing, and to have acquired fewer possessions in the United States than had other immigrants. Although cases had similar amounts of English training, they had less job training. Cases had gained weight less frequently than controls and lost weight more frequently. The authors of the study concluded that factors that enhance emotional stress or result from such stress are a "possible precipitating element in these deaths."

History and Geography

Sudden death in healthy individuals is a phenomenon that has occurred throughout history and in many cultures. Because of their sudden and unexpected nature, many of these deaths have been attributed to supernatural or psychological causes. There has been speculation that SUDS among Southeast Asian refugees in the United States may be triggered by such factors as stress, night terror, evil spirits, or culture shock.

Yet a number of older reports in the medical literature of the Philippines have identified a sudden nocturnal death syndrome known as *Bangungut*. Previously healthy males die during the night, making moaning, snoring, or choking noises. *Bangungut* means "to rise and moan in sleep" in Tagalog, reflecting the folk belief that the deaths are caused by terror from nightmares. The victims are men 20 to 50 years old. No consistent cause has been found for these sudden deaths, even though they have been extensively evaluated with autopsies. The main postmortem finding is hemorrhagic pancreatitis, a condition most observers believe is not a cause of the syndrome but, rather, an effect after death.

Physicians in the Emergency Department at Philippine General Hospital in Manila state that they see numerous cases of SUDS every year. The typical profile of a victim is a young male adult with a stocky build, usually a poorly educated construction worker who migrated from the Visayan Islands to work in Manila and who had either been on a drinking spree shortly before sleeping or had just eaten a fatty meal prior to retiring for the night. The victim is brought to the Emergency Room by fellow workers who are unable to wake him, but who remember his moaning and groaning in sleep. Nearly universally Filipinos have heard about *Bangungut* and believe in its authenticity. Many of them describe experiences as children being assigned to watch over their fathers' afternoon naps.

Similar episodes of sudden death among Filipinos living in the Hawaiian Islands were described in the medical and popular literature during 1930–60.

In Japan, there is a disease referred to as *pokkuri,* which is a sudden death similar to those described in Southeast Asians in the United States and in the Philippines. A study of 18,515 consecutive autopsies in Japan found cardiac death of unknown etiology in 76 cases. Almost all of these deaths occurred in young men who had been considered to be in good health and who died suddenly during sleep. Some Japanese pathologists believe that the cause of death is a fulminant deletion of myoglobin from myocardial fibers during a state of acute cardiac failure.

An American anthropologist and epidemiologist has studied SUDS in the refugee camps in Thailand. Although autopsies are not common in such settings, the deaths were very similar to SUDS deaths occurring among similar refugees in the United States.

Emotional trauma, voodoo, spirits, and magic have all been suggested as important factors for sudden unexplained death in folk cultures. Modern biomedical beliefs prescribe that psychological factors cannot cause deaths per se, but may trigger a fatal event. A different emphasis occurs in reports of sudden death among persons living in cultures where the concept of psychological sudden death has greater currency than in scientific Westernized cultures. For example, in Australia there was a belief among the northern Aborigines that a person who has been pointed at with a bone will die as a result. A government surgeon among the people of that region in 1897 wrote that he had witnessed three or four such cases. A phenomenon of wishful dying has been described among rural Bantu people in South Africa.

Several studies of the Hmong, the group hardest hit by SUDS in the United States, have proposed psychological triggers as explanations for their deaths. An extensive cultural study of SUDS focused on Hmong religion and its relationship to health concepts, but no correlation could be found between the deaths and religious preference, degree of belief in traditional religion, or anxiety over religious questions. The author concluded that one possible triggering mechanism for SUDS might be overwhelming and inescapable stress. Another study conducted in the United States by two anthropologists also considered stress as a potential trigger in SUDS. The authors interviewed relatives of 28 victims of the syndrome and concluded that night terror might have contributed to their deaths. The researchers speculated that such terror was brought on by exhaustion, culture shock, family quarrels, or even the violent images found on television.

Neal R. Holtan

Bibliography

Aponte, G. E. 1960. The enigma of Bangungut. *Annals of Internal Medicine* 52: 1258–63.

Baron, R. C., et al. 1983. Sudden death among Southeast Asian refugees: An unexplained nocturnal phenomenon. *Journal of the American Medical Association* 250: 2947–51.

Bliatout, B. 1982. *Hmong sudden unexpected nocturnal death syndrome: A cultural study.* Portland, Ore.

Cannon, W. B. 1942. Voodoo death. *American Anthropologist* 44: 169–81.

Ishiyama, I., et al. 1982. Fulminant deletion of myoglobin from myocardial fibers in state of acute cardiac failure inducing sudden cardiac death. *Lancet* 2: 1468–9.

Lemoine, J., and C. Mougne. 1983. Why has death stalked the refugees? *Natural History,* November, 6–19.

Munger, R. G. 1982. Sudden adult death in Asian populations: The case of the Hmong. In *The Hmong in the West,* ed. B. Downing and D. Olney, 307–19. Minneapolis.

Otto, C. M, R.V. Tauxe, and L.A. Cobb. 1984. Ventricular fibrillation causes sudden death in southeast Asian immigrants. *Annals of Internal Medicine* 100: 45–7.

Parrish, R. G., et al. 1987. Sudden unexplained death syndrome in southeast Asian refugees: A review of CDC surveillance. *Morbidity and Mortality Weekly Reports* 36 (Supplement): 43ss–53ss.

Sugai, Masayoshi. 1959. A pathological study on sudden and unexpected death, especially on the cardiac death autopsy by medical examiners in Tokyo. *Acta Pathologica Japonica* 9 (Supplement): 723–52.

VIII.133
Sweating Sickness

History and Geography

The sweating sickness, or *sudor anglicus,* is one of the great puzzles of historical epidemiology because no modern disease corresponds very well to its principal epidemiological and clinical features. Thus it is a topic that has generated much speculation and debate in the understanding of what caused the five English epidemics attributed to the "Sweat."

The first description was written in 1486, which indicated that the earliest epidemic occurred (northern England) during June of 1485, where strictly contemporary accounts use the words "plague" and "pestilence" to describe the local mortality crisis (Wylie and Collier 1981). However, Charles Creighton (1891), whom most authors follow, claims that the initial outbreak began later, in London, on September 19, 1485, brought back with Henry VII's mercenaries from France and Flanders.

Once in London the epidemic displayed some of its most characteristic and consistent features: higher mortality among men than women, peaking during middle adulthood among the economically advantaged, and a sudden, acute fever accompanied by profuse sweating. Its victims generally lapsed into coma and died within 24 to 48 hours. Similar outbreaks have been identified: in 1508, 1517, 1528, and 1551. Oddly, the disease favored Englishmen at home and abroad. In the British Isles, Scots, Welsh, and Irish were spared.

The "Sweat" had no important demographic repercussions, as the numbers affected were always small in comparison to the poxes and plagues of this period. Nonetheless, each recurrence of the disease produced widespread fear (Gottfried 1977; Slack 1979). In 1528–9, the Sweat uncharacteristically extended to Calais and to many German regions, but was clearly associated with severe famine, as well as an epidemic of typhus (petechial fever) and plague. As might be expected, a body of literature on the disease had accumulated at the time as well as later, and it has fueled continued interest in the Sweat's identity.

In 1508 Sir Thomas More informed Cardinal Wolsey of the Sweat's progress among young scholars at Oxford and Cambridge, but little discussion was generated. In fact, the 1517 and 1551 epidemics are the only two epidemics for which we have substantial contemporary accounts. Edward Hall's chronicle reports that in 1517, "this malady was so cruel that it killed some within three houres, some within two houres, some merry at dinner and dedde [dead] at supper. Many died in the Kynges court, the lord Clinton, the lorde Gray of Wilton, and many Knightes, gentlemen and officers" (Wylie and Collier 1981).

Court historian Polydore Vergil's graphic description of the disease was based on his experience during the Sweat's 1508 and 1517 appearances and written from memory. First published in 1534, it directly follows this text. In addition, there is some speculation that Vergil may have had access to chronicled reports contemporary with the 1485 outbreak. The earliest description provided by a physician was not written until 1552, when noted humanist John Caius published his *Boke, or Counseill against the Disease Commonly called the Sweate or Sweatyng Sicknesse* (text in Hecker 1844). His advice, however timely or expert, was to no avail, for the disease never recurred.

Etiology

The early nineteenth-century historical epidemiologist J. F. K. Hecker, who was fascinated by the Sweat's abrupt appearances and disappearances, felt that English methods of therapy were partly responsible for the high case-fatality rates. Writing over a century later, Maurice Strauss (1973) concurred, arguing that efforts to encourage perspiration and to stimulate vigorous purging of the bowels would have exacerbated fluid and salt losses associated with a high fever and led to circulatory collapse. Hecker (1844), however, also blamed the English climate and the habits of the English nobility.

[T]he English sweating sickness was a spirit of the mist, which hovered amid the dark clouds. Even in ordinary years the atmosphere of England is loaded with these clouds during considerable periods, and in damp seasons they would prove the more injurious, as the English of these times were not accustomed to cleanliness, moderation in their diet, or even comfortable refinements. Gluttony was common among the nobility as well as among the lower classes; all were immoderately addicted to drinking.

Building on the suggestion that peculiarities of the sixteenth-century English diet might account for the disease, Adam Patrick (1965) argued that the Sweat resembled a shock reaction, with its hyperacute *pyrexia* (fever) and sweating, occasionally associated with evidence of circulatory collapse. Among the most likely toxins, he passed over bacterial endotoxins and exotoxins in favor of fungal toxins associated with food poisoning. Ultimately, he felt that the sweating sickness was a form of ergotism.

Writing in 1891, Creighton, by contrast, denied the possibility that local conditions could alone explain the appearances of the Sweat, and he was loath to identify it with any one known infection. He was, however, convinced that it was introduced by the Flemish mercenaries hired by Henry Tudor, "a swarm of disreputable free-booters from Normandy, natives of a soil which developed the sweat as an indigenous malady in the long course of generations." An opponent of the germ theory of disease, Creighton believed that the soil of the lower basin of the Seine perennially harbored the disease, its epidemic appearances dictated by variations in weather conditions. He concluded firmly that "it must have come from the persons of the foreign soldiers": He contrasted the ability of the French to host the disease and survive, and the partial immunity many Africans displayed when exposed to yellow fever, with the susceptibility of the English and drew a parallel with the effect, on unprotected flocks of cattle, of bringing an animal infected with Texas cattle-fever into the fold.

Most recent authorities concur with Creighton that whatever caused the Sweat, it was a disease that found "virgin soil" in England or among the English. In so doing, they follow Hans Zinsser's assessment that the Sweat was caused by a viral illness to which the uniquely susceptible English population gradually acquired immunity (Zinsser 1935). Zinsser departed from earlier twentieth-century physicians in ascribing the cause of the Sweat to influenza (Hamer 1906; Crookshank 1919), and today there seems to be agreement that the Sweat was not an influenza virus, although it spread in a similar manner (Shaw 1933; Roberts 1965).

Finally, John Wylie and Leslie Collier (1981) speculate that a novel arbovirus infection, transmitted by an insect vector, accords with most of the clinical and epidemiological information. By the mid-sixteenth century, the disease was becoming endemic in England, affecting children more than adults and in the process losing some of its terror.

Ann G. Carmichael

Polydore Vergil's (1534) description of the Sweating Sickness (from Shaw, 1933, 270–1)

The same year (1485), a new disease pervaded the whole kingdom, during Henry's first descent into the island, a pestilence horrible indeed, and before which no age could endure, a well-known fact; suddenly a fatal sweat attacked the body wracking it with pains in the head and stomach, moreover there was a terrific sensation of heat. Therefore the patients cast off the bed coverings from the beginning, as some of them suffered less heat if they lay in bed; if they were dressed they stripped off their clothes, the thirsty ones drank cold water, others suffering from this fetid heat, provoked a sweat which had a foul odor, by adding bed clothes, all of them dying immediately or not long after the sweat had begun; so that not one in a hundred evaded it. Nor did any art of medicine or science avail to help it, meanwhile, for this strange disease escaped all their knowledge. In fact, after twenty four hours (the severity of the disease continued for that length of time) the sweat departed bringing this conclusion, i.e., that they were not cleansed by the sweat, as many of them perished. But that fact pointed out a final measure in the treatment for this great torture; those who had sweat once, since they sickened again put into use those things which they had discovered to have been beneficial in the first attack. Even so, when the calamity befell the sickly race again (1508), from earlier observations they had forgotten how to care for themselves, in order that they might bear more easily the strenuous sweating. Thus from experience, after such a huge slaughter of human beings, it follows that the most prompt relief should have been found, which was this: if anyone was seized during the daytime he should go to bed forthwith, with his clothes on; if, while he was in bed at night, he should lie quietly and not move from that place, remaining so for twenty four hours exactly, covered with not enough bed clothes to provoke the sweat but just enough to allow him to sweat spontaneously, taking no food, if possible to bear the hunger, and drinking no more water than usual or of less warmth, which should satisfy in a way and quench the thirst; in the first stages of this treatment care should be taken that there should be no occasion either for warming up or cooling off the hands or feet as to do so means death. Such was the treatment found for this plague which covered so much of England at this time and in times past has so often afflicted it, for the first year that Henry began to reign was remarkable for the plague, which was taken by many as a bad omen.

Bibliography

Brossollet, J. 1974. Expansion européenne de la suette anglaise. *Proceedings of the XXIII International Congress of the History of Medicine, 1972,* Vol. 1: 595–600. London.

Creighton, Charles. 1891. *A history of epidemics in Britain,* Vol. 1. Cambridge.

Crookshank, F. G. 1919. The history of epidemic encephalomyelitis in relation to influenza. *Proceedings of the Royal Society of Medicine, Section of the History of Medicine* 12: 1–21.

Gottfried, Robert S. 1977. Population, plague and the sweating sickness: Demographic movements in late fifteenth-century England, *Journal of British Studies* 17: 12–37.

Hamer, (Sir) William H. 1906. *Epidemic disease in England*. Milroy Lecture. London.

Hecker, J. F. K. 1844. *Epidemics of the Middle Ages*, trans. B. G. Babbington. London.

Patrick, Adam. 1965. A consideration of the nature of the English sweating sickness. *Medical History* 9: 272–84.

Roberts, R. S. 1965. A consideration of the nature of the English sweating sickness. *Medical History* 9: 385–9.

Shaw, M. B. 1933. A short history of the sweating sickness. *Annals of Medical History*, new ser., 5: 246–74.

Slack, Paul. 1979. Mortality crises and epidemic disease in England, 1485–1610. In *Health, medicine and mortality in the sixteenth century*, ed. Charles Webster. New York.

Strauss, Maurice B. 1973. A hypothesis as to the mechanism of fulminant course and death in the sweating sickness. *Journal of the History of Medicine and Allied Sciences* 28: 48–51.

Wylie, John A. H., and Leslie H. Collier. 1981. The English sweating sickness (sudor anglicus): A reappraisal. *Journal of the History of Medicine and Allied Sciences* 36: 425–45.

Zinsser, Hans. 1935. *Rats, lice and history*. Boston.

VIII.134
Syphilis

Syphilis or, more properly, venereal syphilis is a chronic communicable disease, which, until the acquired immunodeficiency syndrome emerged in the early 1980s, was the most serious and dreaded of the so-called sexually transmitted diseases (STD) – formerly, venereal diseases (VD). Caused by *Treponema pallidum* subspecies pallidum, a spirochetal bacterium, the only known natural host of which is the human being, venereal syphilis is thus one of the human treponematoses – along with pinta, yaws, and endemic syphilis. Although predominantly transferred by sexual contact, *T. pallidum* is also capable of being transmitted from an infected mother to her fetus across the placenta at any stage of pregnancy (congenital syphilis).

Syphilis develops naturally through three clinical stages (primary, secondary, and tertiary or late), each separated by a subclinical period. Of the subclinical periods, the one between the secondary and tertiary stages (latent syphilis) is the most pronounced. Clinical manifestations of syphilis are extremely protean, and capable, at the tertiary stage, of affecting any system of the human body.

Syphilis took its name from Girolamo Fracastoro's well-known poem, *Syphilis, sive morbus gallicus* (1530), in which the Italian humanist-physician invented this phrase to name the disease then known all over Europe as *morbus gallicus*. However, the term syphilis did not become widely used until the late eighteenth century, and that usage was vague and applied to many other symptoms besides those of venereal syphilis until the development of the germ theory in the late nineteenth and early twentieth centuries.

Distribution and Incidence

Unlike human nonvenereal treponematoses (pinta, yaws, and endemic syphilis), venereal syphilis has managed to establish a worldwide distribution, although its incidence patterns are somewhat different in developed and developing countries.

The incidence of syphilis, for example, has continuously declined in the Western world since the 1860s, although major wars have momentarily interrupted this trend. After the Second World War, late and congenital syphilis almost disappeared, mainly as a result of public health measures and penicillin. Since the 1950s, however, both primary and secondary syphilis have steadily increased (nearly 29,000 cases in the United States in 1984) with its peak incidence in the 15- to 34-year age group. A strikingly high male/female ratio (2.6:1 in the United States in 1983) is due to a considerable incidence of syphilis in male homosexuals. In 1980, 58 percent of all syphilitic men in England were homosexuals as were 50 percent in the United States (Csonka 1987; Holmes and Lukehart 1987).

In developing countries, syphilis continues to be a widespread disease, although interpretative problems of serologic tests for syphilis make it difficult to estimate the numbers of infected people in those regions. Syphilis is increasing in areas where yaws was previously endemic, such as tropical and equatorial America and Africa, and Southeast Asia. Infected prostitutes seem to play an important role in the spread of syphilis in these areas, most noticeably in the Far East. The risk of congenital syphilis continues to be considerable in many developing countries, resulting in fetal wastage, neonatal mortality, and infant morbidity (WHO 1986; Csonka 1987).

Etiology and Epidemiology

Although syphilis is transferred predominantly by sexual contact, it may also be transmitted in nonsexual ways, such as by close contact with either an open lesion of early syphilis or infected fomites, by

Table VIII.134.1. *Etiology, epidemiology, and clinical manifestations of the human treponematoses*

	Venereal syphilis	Endemic syphilis	Yaws	Pinta
Organism	*T. pallidum*	*T. pallidum endemicum*	*T. pertenue*	*T. carateum*
Occurrence	Sporadic, urban	Endemic, rural	Endemic, rural	Endemic, rural
Geographic distribution	Worldwide	Southwest Asia, sub-Saharan regions of Africa, Bosnia	Africa, Southeast Asia, Western Pacific, South America, Caribbean	Central and South America, Mexico
Climate in which the disease mostly occurs	All types	Arid, warm	Humid, warm	Semiarid, warm
Age group with peak incidence (years)	18–30	2–10	2–10	15–30
Transmissibility	High	High	High	Low
Reservoir of infection	Adults	Children 2–15 years old; contacts in home, school and village; latent cases capable of becoming active	Children 2–15 years old; contacts in home, school and village; latent cases capable of becoming active	Cases with long-standing skin lesions
Mode of transmission	Sexual, transplacental[a]	Household contacts: mouth-to-mouth or via drinking, eating utensils	Skin-to-skin; ? insect vector	Skin-to-skin; ? insect vector
Usual age	Adult	Early childhood	Early childhood	Adolescent
Primary lesion	Cutaneous ulcer (chancre)	Rarely seen	Framboise (raspberry), or "mother yaw"	Nonulcerating papule with satellites
Secondary lesion	Mucocutaneous; occasional periostitis	Florid mucocutaneous lesions (mucous patch, split papule, condyloma latum); osteoperiostitis	Cutaneous papulo-squamous lesions; osteoperiostitis	Pintides
Tertiary lesion	Gumma, cardiovascular, and CNS lues	Destructive cutaneous osteoarticular gummas	Destructive cutaneous osteoarticular gummas	Dyschromic, achromic macules

[a]Because the nonvenereal treponematoses are usually acquired in childhood, and because treponemal bacteremia ceases with time, only in adult-onset venereal syphilis is there any likelihood of a mother giving birth to an infected child.

Sources: Adapted from Perine et al. (1984, 2); Perine (1987, 650).

infection of an unborn infant in utero, and by transfusions of infected blood.

As noted above, *T. pallidum,* the causal agent of syphilis, is a member of the order Spirochetales. This order of bacteria includes three genera pathogenic for humans and several other animals: (1) *Borrelia,* responsible for Vincent's angina (*Borrelia recurrentis*), relapsing fever (*Borrelia vincentii*), and Lyme disease (*Borrelia burgdorferi*); (2) *Leptospira,* which causes human leptospirosis; and (3) *Treponema,* responsible for a group of diseases known as treponematoses (Holmes and Lukehart 1987).

The *Treponema* genus includes several pathogenic species and subspecies responsible for four different human diseases: (1) *pinta,* a Central and South American disease, which affects the skin, caused by *Treponema carateum;* (2) *yaws,* a disease of skin and

bones occurring in rural populations of the humid tropics, caused by *Treponema pallidum* subspecies *pertenue;* (3) *endemic syphilis,* similar to yaws, but found only in warm, arid climates, and caused by *T. pallidum* subspecies *endemicum;* and (4) *venereal syphilis,* which has no climatic restrictions and may affect any tissue of the body including internal organs, and is caused by *T. pallidum* subspecies *pallidum.* These and other major features concerning the human treponematoses are indicated in Table VIII.134.1. Surprisingly, in spite of the differentiated (both clinically and epidemiologically) disease entities they produce, these four treponemes cannot be morphologically distinguished from one another. Moreover, they elicit the same immunologic reactions, and are all susceptible to penicillin (Hackett 1963; Perine et al. 1984; Csonka 1987).

Almost from the time of Columbus's arrival in America, but particularly from the European Enlightenment, the uncertain geographic and historical origins of syphilis have been the object of scholarly controversy (Guerra 1987). Since the 1950s, however, the rise of molecular biology has pushed anthropologists and historical epidemiologists to frame this problem progressively in terms of the evolutionary origins of all the human treponematoses. At present, two major theories – the unitarian and the nonunitarian – contend with each other in providing an explanation for the surprising similarities of the human treponematoses.

For E. H. Hudson, the most outstanding defender of unitarian theory, there is only one treponematosis, although it assumes different clinical patterns under different epidemiological conditions. Thus, the changing physical and sociocultural environment of human beings has caused treponematosis to change into one or another of those four different clinical syndromes already mentioned: pinta, yaws, endemic syphilis, and syphilis. From the unitarian viewpoint, then, it does not make sense to talk about transmission of syphilis from the New World to the Old, or vice versa (Hudson 1965).

By contrast, C. J. Hackett, the main upholder of nonunitarian theory, maintains that the clinical variety of human treponematoses is probably due to *mutational changes* in the treponemal strains themselves. His thesis is that successive mutations have been responsible for the different human treponematoses starting from a lost ancestral animal treponematosis. The earliest of the treponematoses seems to have been pinta, which might have extended from Africa and Asia into America about 15,000 B.C.; that is, during the last part of the last glaciation and before the subsequent melting of the polar icecaps that formed the Bering Strait.

By about 10,000 B.C., a warm humid environment caused either the pinta treponemes themselves (hypothesis A) or the lost ancestral animal treponemes (hypothesis B) to mutate in Afro-Asia, bringing forth yaws, a disease that extended through Africa, Southeast Asia, and eventually Australia and the Pacific islands, but that did not reach the Americas.

Around 7000 B.C., in the warm arid climates that developed after the last glaciation, another mutation occurred, this time from yaws to endemic syphilis. The latter appeared in northern and Saharan Africa, southwestern and central Asia, and central Australia, whereas yaws itself remained unchanged in the warm and more humid climates.

Finally, about 3000 B.C., the development of large

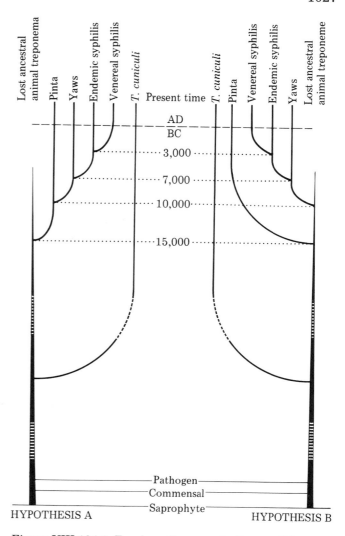

Figure VIII.134.1. Two hypotheses as to the possible evolution of the organisms responsible for human treponematoses (according to C. J. Hackett 1963, 25). [From C. J. Hackett. 1963. On the origin of the human treponematoses (pinta, yaws, endemic syphilis, and venereal syphilis). *Bulletin of the World Health Organization* 29: 7–41.]

urban areas and the increasing use of clothing in the eastern Mediterranean and southwestern Asia became selective agents for still another mutation as syphilis changed from a nonvenereal disease of rural children (endemic syphilis) to a venereal disease of urban adults (venereal syphilis). According to Hackett, at any rate, by the first century B.C., as Figure VIII.134.1 indicates, syphilis had spread throughout the Mediterranean. He suggests, however, that this early venereal syphilis was a "mild" form of the disease, which may explain why there is no evidence of the illness in Europe before the end of the fifteenth century, when a new successful treponeme mutation – probably favored by environmental and social conditions in congested European cities at that time – gave rise to a far more serious disease. Initially extremely virulent, this form of syphilis is supposed to have become progressively less destructive from around the 1530s onward (Hackett 1963). As will be discussed below, however, still other scholars trace the sudden epidemic of venereal syphilis to the post-Columbian importation of an American parasite to Europe, and thence to Asia and Africa.

Immunology

There is no natural immunity to infection by pathogenic treponemes. However, "only about 50 percent of the named contacts of primary and secondary syphilis become infected," and 25 percent after a single exposure. The chance of infection is influenced – in undefined proportions – by sexual and hygienic practices, inoculum size, environmental and body temperature, and other factors.

Acquired immunity is related to inoculum size and duration of infection prior to treatment. Intradermal inoculation of *T. pallidum* usually causes primary lesions and serologic response in those who have previously been treated for early syphilis. By contrast, it produces no symptoms or responses in those with untreated latent syphilis, or in those previously treated for late latent (more than 1 year's duration) syphilis (Holmes and Lukehart 1987).

Clinical Manifestations and Pathology

When William Osler asserted that "who knows syphilis, knows medicine," he was doing no more than stressing the extreme clinical variety of this disease, which is capable of affecting any system of the human body. As noted previously, the natural course of venereal syphilis includes three consecutive clinical stages, each stage separated by a latent period with no visible signs of infection (Perine et al. 1984; Csonka 1987; Holmes and Lukehart 1987).

Primary Syphilis

T. pallidum penetrates intact mucous membranes and abraded skin. After an incubation period ranging from 2 to 6 weeks (average 3 weeks), the primary lesion – the *chancre* – appears at the site of entry. it is a single, small, and painless ulcer with undurated edges, usually appearing in the genitalia (penis, vulva, labia, cervix) and, less frequently, in other regions such as the anus, mouth, buttocks, and fingers. Chancres of the penis and vulva are usually accompanied by moderate bilateral enlargement of inguinal lymph nodes. The chancre heals spontaneously over a period of 2 to 6 weeks.

Secondary Syphilis

In most patients, after a brief latent period (6 to 8 weeks), there is a secondary clinical stage characterized by the appearance of disseminated lesions on the skin and in the internal organs. In women, these lesions are often the first overt clinical sign of syphilis. Secondary lesions consist of a symmetrical, evolutive, and painless rash, very variable in appearance and localization, and usually accompanied by fever, malaise, aches in the bones (often worse at night), and generalized enlargement of lymph nodes. After a few weeks – generally 2 to 6 – secondary lesions and symptoms spontaneously disappear. In 25 percent of untreated patients, however, there is a recurrence of secondary lesions during the first 2 years of infection.

Tertiary or Late Syphilis

The tertiary stage develops only in about one-third of untreated cases, and only after another latent period lasting from 1 to 20 years, or even longer. This stage is characterized by progressively destructive lesions of the skin and mucous membranes, bones, and internal organs. The most typical lesion is the *gumma,* a small rubbery tumor that is a benign manifestation of tertiary syphilis, which can develop in any part of the body.

Particularly serious forms of late syphilis involve the cardiovascular and central nervous systems. Cardiovascular syphilis may cause aneurism of the thoracic aorta, and dilatation of the aortic valve. Neurosyphilis includes a loss of positional sense and sensation (tabes dorsalis, locomotor ataxia) or a form of insanity (general paresis [GPI], dementia paralytica).

As a result of the introduction of antibiotic therapy, tertiary syphilis has almost disappeared. Thus the most reliable information available on it today has been provided by two major studies on the course of untreated syphilis, the Oslo Study (1891–1951) and the Tuskegee Study (1932–72). The former surveyed retrospectively a group of nearly 2,000 patients with primary and secondary syphilis diagnosed clinically before immunologic tests came into use. The latter studied prospectively 431 black men with seropositive latent syphilis of 3 or more years' duration, who were deliberately kept untreated. Because of the ethical issues raised by this racist experiment, the Tuskegee Study has been crucial in formulating the present guidelines concerning medical experimentation on humans (Jones 1981; Holmes and Lukehart 1987).

Congenital Syphilis

The risk of congenital syphilis to the fetus is high during the first 2 years after the mother has acquired the infection. An infected fetus may die during pregnancy, be stillborn, or be born prematurely. Secondary-type lesions are present at birth or appear within the first 6 months of life (Perine et al. 1984; Csonka 1987; Holmes and Lukehart 1987).

History and Geography

Medical historiography has in the past usually identified the disease known today as venereal syphilis with the morbus gallicus that was mentioned for the first time in European medical and lay writings of the late fifteenth century. Indeed, nineteenth- and twentieth-century medical historians, in looking at past medical and lay descriptions of morbus gallicus, have systematically practiced a retrospective diagnosis of syphilis.

According to them, the history of syphilis began with the eruption of morbus gallicus in Europe in the 1490s, and can be traced throughout the centuries until today, although neither its geographic origins nor the precise date of its appearance has been established. Since the European Enlightenment, both of these questions have been the object of a continuous – and often tart – controversy between the defenders of an American origin of syphilis and those who have claimed that syphilis *did* exist in the Old World long before Columbus arrived in the New World. The most varied documental proofs (medical and lay writings, iconography) and – increasingly since the late nineteenth century – material proofs (paleopathological remains) have been wielded in this debate. It is an unfinished debate, however, for in claiming that present-day venereal syphilis was already known and had been described under several names before or after the Europeans' arrival in America, historians have produced the kind of contradictory conclusions that serve only to keep it alive (Guerra 1978; Wood 1978).

A second way of approaching the history of syphilis has already been referred to in the section on the etiology and epidemiology of syphilis. This approach lies in studying the disease and the germ responsible for it in the broad biological and epidemiological context of the development of human treponematoses, and integrates results provided by both paleopathological and historicoepidemiological studies. A result of this approach has been some attractive and promising hypotheses on the history of syphilis, but at the moment, no definitive conclusions have

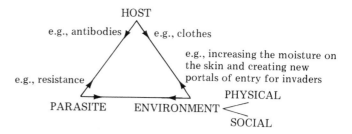

Figure VIII.134.2. Infectious diseases considered as a dynamic triangular interaction among host, parasite, and environment (according to E. H. Hudson, 1958, 8–9.) (Adapted from E. H. Hudson. 1958. *Non-venereal syphilis*. Edinburgh-London.)

been reached (Hackett 1963; Hudson 1965; Wood 1978).

Given these circumstances, a third approach seems appropriate, which actually deals with the history of the concept of syphilis, rather than with the history of the disease itself. This third way renounces retrospective diagnosis of syphilis and insists on the need to contemplate the disease entity called syphilis within the strict historicocultural context in which it occurs, and from which it receives its true significance. Put plainly, every disease entity is an intellectual construction that is peculiar to some form of medicine; and every form of medicine is nothing but a historical variable in any human community. Thus the disease entity known today as venereal syphilis can be conceived of, at this point, as a paradigmatic example as was demonstrated by a Polish microbiologist, Ludwik Fleck, in the mid-1930s in a monograph in which there has been renewed interest since the late 1970s (Fleck 1979).

Furthermore, in looking at what we call infectious diseases, we must distinguish between what may be termed disease entities and the diseases themselves. As disease entities, infectious illnesses assumed their present shape only in late nineteenth- and early twentieth-century Western medicine as a result of the development of germ theory. But as diseases in themselves they have existed for a long time.

Infectious diseases, moreover, cannot be regarded ontologically as natural beings in the same way as the microbiological agents that cause them can be regarded (Reznek 1987). Rather, as Hudson (1958) has demonstrated, in the case of human treponematoses, they should be considered the result of a dynamic interaction among host, parasite, and environment, as portrayed in Figure VIII.134.2. Moreover, any such interaction that has occurred in the past can neither be reproduced under experimental conditions, nor be easily reconstructed historically.

To be precise, venereal syphilis took shape in Western scientific medicine only as a result of deep changes, both intellectual and social, during the second half of the nineteenth and the first decade of the twentieth century; foremost among these changes was the formulation of germ theory. Yet an exhaustive bibliographical survey on venereal diseases done by J. K. Proksch in 1889–1900 makes clear that the term syphilis, though invented by Fracastoro in the sixteenth century, did not become widely used until the late eighteenth or early nineteenth century. So, it may be anachronistic to refer to as syphilis either *the* disease entity that we call "venereal syphilis" before the late nineteenth or early twentieth century, or *a* disease entity named "syphilis" before the late eighteenth or early nineteenth century.

Let us now consider the origins, emergence, and development of the concept of syphilis. Our departure point will be the disease entity that began to be called *morbus gallicus* in late fifteenth-century Europe. Although for the above-mentioned reasons we cannot agree with those who have identified morbus gallicus with syphilis, it is obvious that the former may well be considered the earliest identifiable conceptual ancestor of the disease entity that we now call venereal syphilis (Fleck 1979).

1400–1600

Morbus gallicus is the name that soon became dominant in designating a disease generally considered as new in Europe of the 1490s. It was perceived as an incurable and loathsome disease consisting of severe aches in the bones, and of sores usually beginning in the genitals, but eventually covering most or all of the body. Contemporary medical and lay evidence concurred in including it among the numerous calamities (floods, earthquakes, epidemics, famines, wars) that Europeans – especially Italians – suffered at the end of the fifteenth century.

Italian sources show us that the "French Pox" spread in Italy during the period 1494–5, after the clash between the armies of France and Spain over the question of the kingdom of Naples. The notoriety the phrase *morbus gallicus* soon achieved all over Italy was closely associated with the tragic consequences of the impact of the French invasion on the fragile Italian political equilibrium. Similarly, the prompt acceptance in early sixteenth-century Italy of the theory of an American origin for morbus gallicus may be explained by the fact that Spaniards

were regarded as the newest *barbari stranieri* to devastate Italy. The great prestige of Renaissance Italy and its cultural hegemony throughout Europe were important factors, among others, in ensuring the rapid popularization of both the term morbus gallicus and the theory of its American origin.

Through the sixteenth century, the phrase "French Pox" achieved in Europe and overseas an overwhelming dominance over any other names for the disease, not only in the medical academic world, but also at popular levels. Only French physicians – those native to or settled in France – seem, understandably, to have rejected this name, and put forth others. For example, in 1552 Thierry de Héry of Paris suggested *maladie vénérienne* or *grosse vairolle;* in 1553 Auger Ferrier of Toulouse proposed *pudendagra* or *lues hispanica;* in 1560 Antoine Chaumette of Paris put forth the denomination *morbus venereus;* and in 1563 Leonardo Botallo, also of Paris, used the term *lues venerea,* as did Jean Fernel in posthumous publication in 1579.

1600–1750

During the seventeenth century this new term, *lues venerea* (venereal disease), was adopted all over Europe, sharing an *ex aequo* leadership with that of morbus gallicus. In eighteenth-century Europe the term "lues venerea" eventually superseded that of morbus gallicus, and the use of the latter declined dramatically.

Two points may be raised about the expression lues venerea. First, the adjective "venerea" stresses the direct relationship existing between the French Pox and the pleasures of Venus and, thus, the individual responsibility of those who contract the disease. Applied to the morbus gallicus, this adjective seems to have appeared for the first time in 1527 in a work by French physician Jacques de Bethencourt, entitled *Nova poenitentialis Quadragesima, nec non Purgatorium in Morbum Gallicum sive Venereum.* Both the title and contents of this book evoke the climate of religious exaltation and of moral rearmament present in Reformation Europe (Temkin 1977). The second point has to do with the name "lues," which underscores the perception of the disease, at that time, as a contagious and calamitous one from a physical, and even from a moral, viewpoint.

A good example of the dominance exerted by the expression "lues venerea" on eighteenth-century European university medicine is offered to us by an influential work of the French royal physician Jean Astruc, *De Morbis Veneris,* published in 1736, which was reissued many times and translated into a great number of European languages before the end of the nineteenth century. The work argues that the lues venerea was caused by a unique and specific virus venereum. It treats the particular morbi venerei as species making up the genus *Lues venerea,* and it differentiates between *lues venerea incipiens* and *confirmata.* The first was composed of different morbi venerei (gonorrhea, hernia venerea, bubones venerei, caries pudendorum, and porri, among others); whereas the second, the lues venerea confirmata, also called morbus venereus universalis, comprised numerous complaints affecting the whole human body. Among these were morbi genitalium, vitia cutis, morbi oris et narium, dolores venerei, morbi ossium, tumores, glandulosi et lymphatici, oculorum morbi, morbi aurium, and lesiones functionum.

1750–1850

Whether venereal disease was caused by an animated contagion or by a chemical poison, until the mid-eighteenth century almost every intellectual stream in European academic medicine seems to have defended the unity of lues venerea on the basis of a unique and specific virus venereum. However, after 1750 the concept of lues venerea began to be challenged as a result of nosographic and nosological efforts made by Enlightenment pathologists, who (with the support of clinical observations, anatomopathological analyses, and inoculation experiments) began to question whether lues venerea was a single disease entity after all. The result of this challenge was the progressive disappearance of the expression lues venerea from the literature. And although it did not entirely disappear until the nineteenth century, it was increasingly replaced by the plural expression *morbi venerei* (venereal diseases), which began to be used at the beginning of the eighteenth century. At about the same time, specific denominations given to each one of the "morbi venerei" (chancre, gonorrhea, bubo, and syphilis, among others) started to appear with increasing frequency. From the early nineteenth century, the number of medical works specifically devoted to certain among these diseases – mainly to gonorrhea and syphilis – began to proliferate.

Let us look in more detail at how the concept of lues venerea was destroyed during the period 1750–1850, while keeping in mind that it was during this period that specialized hospitals emerged, including those for the treatment of venereal disease and that dermatovenerology was born as a medical specialty. Enlightenment controversies over lues venerea came to concentrate mostly on whether the blennorrhagic

discharge – usually called gonorrhea – happening in many venereal patients, constituted a disease entity different from lues venerea, or (as thought before), was just a peculiar clinical form or stage of lues venerea (Flegel 1974). The beginning of this process of disease differentiation, which, roughly speaking, took place in Europe and North America throughout the century 1750–1850, may be found in the influential work by Giovanni Battista Morgagni, *De Sedibus et Causis Morborum per Anatomen Indagatis,* published in Venice in 1761. He found at autopsy that venereal patients with blennorrhagic discharge and no evidence of chancre rarely had hidden in the genital passages the expected chancre, which was supposed to provoke the discharge in the first place.

During the following decades, numerous physicians argued the single or dual nature of lues venerea, resorting to anatomoclinical observations and to autoinoculative and heteroinoculative experiments with pus from venereal lesions. This controversy did not end until the 1830s in part, at least, because there was tremendous ambiguity in the use of terms referring to venereal complaints. Although terms like syphilis, *maladie(s) syphilitique(s),* and so forth spread rapidly in the European medical literature during the first two decades of the nineteenth century, the term syphilis became almost dominant after the 1820s. The word nonetheless continued to appear in some works as an alternative term or one complementary to that of "venereal diseases."

The controversy, however, over whether venereal disease was a single disease entity or more than one illness was brought to an end in the late 1830s. During this period the French venereologist Philippe Ricord had developed a vast clinical and experimental program at the Paris Hôpital du Midi, including both the systematic use of the uterine speculum and numerous (more than 2,500) autoinoculative experiments with pus from venereal patients. In 1838 he presented his results and conclusions in *Traité pratique sur les maladies vénériennes, ou recherches critiques et experimentales sur l'inoculation appliquée à l'étude de ces maladies.* These experiments, asserted Ricord, had permitted him to demonstrate the existence of the so-called *virus syphilitique,* so that chancre and blennorrhagia could be definitely separated. Moreover the expectations had also allowed him to distinguish the primary lesions of *vérole* from those that are not primary, and primary symptoms from secondary symptoms. As a result, Ricord proposed the division of syphilis symptoms into primary, successive, secondary, transitional, and tertiary.

1850–1950

During the second half of the nineteenth and the beginning of the twentieth century, Ricord's concept of syphilis was gradually reshaped, as other disease entities recognized today as sexually transmitted diseases (gonorrhea, chancroid, lymphogranuloma venereum, genital herpes, venereal warts, and others) were emerging. If most of these new disease entities were first shaped according to anatomoclinical criteria, each one of them (syphilis included) eventually got its definitive "identity card" when the relevant germ causing it was isolated.

Gonorrhea and chancroid are two illustrative examples in this respect. Ricord, who definitely separated chancre and blennorrhagia, asserted that the latter might be the result of local irritation, excessive sexual intercourse, or excessive sexual excitement. The present clinical picture of gonorrhea was completed only in 1879, when Albert Neisser discovered the germ responsible for it, which he called gonococcus. On the other hand, chancroid or soft sore (ulcus molle) emerged as a disease entity in 1852, when a pupil of Ricord, Léon Bassereau, demonstrated that the two kinds of luetic chancre – one hard, painless, and unique; the other soft, painful, and frequently multiple – resulted from exposure to a like lesion. In addition, the latter was autoinoculable. Almost 40 years later, in 1889, August Ducrey identified the bacillum responsible for it (Kampmeier 1984).

As for the concept of syphilis, it developed and changed profoundly during the second half of the nineteenth century as the disease became a major research area in Western scientific medicine. Perhaps the person who contributed most to the development of the concept of syphilis during this period was the French venereologist Jean-Alfred Fournier. It was Fournier who propounded the concept of latency in both acquired and congenital syphilis, definitely established the relationship between syphilis and so-called parasyphilitic affections (mainly tabes dorsalis and general paresis of the insane), and began a social campaign against the disease.

But the discovery of the germ responsible for syphilis did not occur until 1905, when Fritz Schaudinn and Erich Hoffmann isolated it in serum from a lesion of secondary syphilis. In 1906 the collective work of August von Wassermann, Albert Neisser, Carl Bruck, and others made possible the invention, in Germany, of the first serologic procedure for the diagnosis of syphilis. This was the complement-fixation test, which soon became well known as the *Wassermann Reaction* (WR). In the following years,

T. pallidum was also found in lesions of tertiary syphilis, verifying Fournier's theory. Karl Reuter, for example, in 1906 found the germ in the wall of a syphilitic aorta, whereas Hideyo Noguchi in 1913 proved its presence in brain tissue from paretics (Quétel 1986).

By way of conclusion it should be emphasized that, as has been the case with many other disease entities, a crisis of a disease entity concept based upon its specific biological cause (Laín-Entralgo 1982) has also ensnared venereal syphilis. In 1935, whereas most bacteriologists and pathologists still claimed specificity of a causal microorganism to be the definitive nosographic criterion for an infectious disease, Fleck lucidly insisted upon the essential incompleteness of the concept of syphilis (Fleck 1979).

Time has confirmed Fleck's insight. Put plainly, it should be obvious from the foregoing that Western medicine has had enormous difficulties in establishing scientific criteria that delimit precisely the so-called venereal syphilis from the remaining human treponematoses (Hackett 1963; Hudson 1965; Perine et al. 1984).

Jon Arrizabalaga

Bibliography

Baker, Brenda J., and George J. Armelagos. 1988. The origin and antiquity of syphilis: Paleopathological diagnosis and interpretation. *Current Anthropology* 29: 703–37.

Bardet, Jean-Pierre, et al. 1988. *Peurs et terreurs face à la contagion: Choléra, tuberculose, syphilis: XIX–XXᵉ siècles.* Paris.

Crosby, Alfred W. 1972. *The Columbian exchange: Biological and cultural consequences of 1492.* Westport, Conn.

Csonka, G. W. 1987. Syphilis. In *Oxford textbook of medicine,* 2d edition, ed. D. J. Weatherall et al., Vol. 1: 5.386–5.403. Oxford.

Fleck, Ludwik. 1979. *Genesis and development of a scientific fact,* trans. Fred Bradley and Thaddeus J. Trenn, ed. Thaddeus J. Trenn and Robert Merton. Chicago–London.

Flegel, Kenneth M. 1974. Changing concepts of the nosology of gonorrhea and syphilis. *Bulletin of the History of Medicine* 48: 571–88.

Grmek, Mirko. 1988. *Diseases in the Ancient Greek world.* Baltimore.

Guerra, Francisco. 1978. The dispute over syphilis: Europe versus America. *Clio Medica* 13: 39–61.

Hackett, C. J. 1963. On the origin of the human treponematoses (pinta, yaws, endemic syphilis and venereal syphilis). *Bulletin of the World Health Organization* 29: 7–41.

Holmes, King K., and Sheila A. Lukehart. 1987. Syphilis.

In *Harrison's principles of internal medicine,* 11th edition, ed. E. Braunwald et al., 639–49. New York.

Hudson, E. H. 1958. *Non-venereal syphilis.* Edinburgh–London.

1965. Treponematosis and man's social evolution. *American Anthropologist* 67: 885–901.

Jones, J. H. 1981. *Bad blood: The Tuskegee syphilis experiment.* New York and London.

Kampmeier, Rudolph H. 1984. Early development of knowledge of sexually transmitted diseases. In *Sexually transmitted diseases,* ed. K. K. Holmes et al., 19–29. New York.

Laín-Entralgo, Pedro. 1982. *El diagnóstico médico: Historia y teoría.* Barcelona.

Perine, Peter L. 1987. Nonvenereal treponematoses: Yaws, pinta, and endemic syphilis. In *Harrison's principles of internal medicine,* 11th edition, ed. E. Braunwald et al., 650–2. New York.

Perine, Peter L., et al. 1984. *Handbook of endemic treponematoses.* Geneva.

Proksch, J. K. 1889–1900. *Die Literatur über die venerischen Krankheiten von den ersten Schriften über Syphilis aus dem Ende des fünfzehnten Jahrhunderts . . . ,* 5 vols. Bonn.

Quétel, C. 1986. *Le mal de Naples: Histoire de la syphilis.* Paris.

Reznek, Lawrie. 1987. *The nature of disease.* London and New York.

Temkin, Owsei. 1977. On the history of "morality and syphilis." In *The double face of Janus and other essays in the history of medicine,* ed. O. Temkin, 472–84. Baltimore.

Wood, Corinne Shear. 1978. Syphilis in anthropological perspective. *Social sciences and medicine* 12: 47–55.

World Health Organization. Expert Committee on Venereal Diseases and Treponematoses. 1986. *Sixth report.* Geneva.

VIII.135
Syphilis, Nonvenereal

Nonvenereal syphilis has apparently occurred in many forms and places, and one interpretation of this phenomenon is that venereal syphilis can revert to nonvenereal transmission. Others see it as a discrete disease with its own etiologic epidemiology. The most common and enduring form of the disease is called *bejel;* it occurs in the arid regions of North Africa, the Middle East, and the eastern Mediterranean, and seems to have antedated venereal syphilis as a disease entity by a considerable period of time. It is one of the endemic treponematoses caused by spirochetes, bacteria belonging to the genus *Treponema.* Other diseases in this group are *yaws* and *pinta.* Like yaws, bejel is essentially a disease of children, although those who escape the illness as children are likely to acquire it as adults, often from their own children. Its specific cause seems to be *Treponema pallidum,* the same agent as that of syphilis, although it may be a treponema intermediary between *T. pallidum* and *Treponema pertenue,* the agent of yaws. Although treponemal disease has been transferred experimentally to animals, humans appear to be the only natural reservoir.

Etiology, Epidemiology, and Clinical Manifestations

Because the treponemas that cause yaws, nonvenereal syphilis, pinta (an American disease), and syphilis are morphologically and serologically indistinguishable, it is believed that at least the Old World diseases may represent an evolutionary continuum running from south to north. Yaws, thought to be the oldest, spreads by skin-to-skin contact and flourishes in the hot and moist regions of Africa south of the Sahara where individuals have historically worn little clothing. Syphilis, by contrast, seems to be the newest of the treponematoses. Venereal transmission allows it to spread among peoples of colder climates whose clothing would frustrate skin-to-skin transmission.

Bejel or nonvenereal syphilis seems to be intermediate between the two both bacteriologically and geographically. It has been conceived of as yaws modified by a desert environment, and as juvenile, nonvenereal syphilis. It is not transmitted congenitally. The disease spreads from child to child in dry, mostly rural areas where a lack of cleanliness facilitates transmission. The spirochetes of nonvenereal syphilis, like those of yaws and syphilis, perish in the presence of atmospheric oxygen, soaps, detergents, and antiseptics, and are very sensitive to drying. *T. pallidum* is able to penetrate mucous membranes, but intact skin presents it with a formidable barrier. The primary lesion is often in the region of the mouth, probably the result of sharing drinking vessels or eating utensils or by direct mouth-to-mouth contact. It can also spread from direct nonsexual contact, and flies, lice, and fleas may also have a role in transmission.

The stages of the disease – primary, secondary, and late or tertiary – are not so pronounced as are those of syphilis. In the case of bejel, the primary lesion is soon followed by the appearance of moist papules in skin folds and by drier lesions on the trunk and extremities. Late lesions, when they occur, can be ugly. Huge ulcers may form, and ulceration of the palatal and nasal bones can cause them to erode. Other possible physical symptoms are changes in pigment distribution and in the deformity of other bones, especially long bones such as the tibia.

Immunology and Pathology

Although pinta has been given experimentally to syphilitics, a high degree of cross-immunity between *T. pallidum* and *T. pertenue* seems to exist. Thus, one who has suffered nonvenereal syphilis is not only safe from another attack but is also at least partially protected against syphilis and yaws.

The pathogenic mechanisms in this and other treponemal infections are not yet fully understood. The pathogens do not kill cells, and they produce no known toxic substances. Thus it would seem that much of the pathology stems from the immune response of the host. Nonvenereal syphilis or bejel is similar to yaws in some respects, among them, juvenile acquisition, an absence of chancres, and congenital transmission. Moreover, both diseases rarely involve the cardiovascular and the central nervous systems. Yet nonvenereal syphilis resembles syphilis in its affinity for the mucous membranes, and in many of its pathological aspects. And, like syphilis, it occurs outside of the tropics. Finally, the usual serologic tests for syphilis are positive in nonvenereal syphilis.

History and Geography

The story of bejel is intimately bound up with the work of Ellis Herndon Hudson, a physician and medical historian. He first described the disease in 1928, after observing it among the Bedouin Arabs. In 1937 he summarized all available information on this form of nonvenereal syphilis and stated that the Arab word *bejel* had been introduced into the literature to distinguish this nonvenereal and endemic form of syphilis from the venereal variety.

In 1946 he emphasized the intermediary nature of bejel between yaws and syphilis and presented a unitarian concept of treponematosis, which stressed the evolutionary relationship among yaws, endemic syphilis, pinta, and venereal syphilis, and held that they were all varieties of a single disease caused by one parasite, *T. pallidum*.

Not all agree. Some, for example, argue that the various treponemal infections are due to changes in the treponemal strains themselves – to mutations. Others feel that the treponemal infections are essentially different diseases, caused by different parasites, whereas E. I. Grin has advanced the argument that venereal syphilis has reached villages (in the Sudan at least) from towns, only to become endemic (i.e., nonvenereal) in a rural environment.

There is, however, general agreement that nonvenereal syphilis is a very old disease. Hudson argues that it flourished in the villages that first appeared during the early Neolithic period and that it was the "venereal leprosy" of the Middle Ages, the "sibbens" of Scotland, the "button-scurvy" of Ireland, the *radesyge* of the Scandinavian countries, and the *skerljevo* of the Balkans. Apparently, it never took root in the Americas.

Because endemic syphilis fades in the face of the cleanliness associated with civilization, and because of the high efficacy of penicillin as a cure, the disease has withdrawn from most of Europe. But the bejel of the Middle East has its counterparts in the *njovera* of Rhodesia, the *dichuchwa* that plagues the Bushmen, and the *irkintia* of the Australian aborigines.

Kenneth F. Kiple

Bibliography

Cockburn, Thomas A. 1961. The origin of the treponematoses. *Bulletin of the World Health Organization* 24: 221–28.

Grin, E. I. 1961. Endemic treponematoses in the Sudan. *Bulletin of the World Health Organization* 24: 229–38.

Hackett, C. J. 1963. On the origin of the human treponematoses. *Bulletin of the World Health Organization* 29: 7–41.

Hudson, Ellis Herndon. 1949. Treponematosis. In *Oxford medicine*, Vol. 5, ed. Henry A. Christian, 9–121. New York.

   1958. *Non-venereal syphilis: A sociological and medical study of Bejel.* Edinburgh and London.

Perrine, Peter L. 1984. Syphilis and the endemic treponematoses. In *Hunter's tropical medicine*, 6th edition, ed. G. Thomas Strickland, 247–56.

Wood, Corinne Shear. 1978. Syphilis in anthropological perspective. *Social Science and Medicine* 12: 47–55.

VIII.136
Tapeworm

Tapeworms are flatworms in the class Cestoda of the phylum Platyhelminthes. The body of an adult worm consists of a small head or *scolex*, which is usually armed with hooks or suckers to attach the animal to the wall of its host's small intestine, and a chain of segments or *proglottids*. New proglottids arise by budding from the scolex region. As they mature, they are pushed away from the head by the formation of new proglottids and develop both male and female sex organs. After fertilization, eggs or gravid proglottids are excreted with the host's feces. Tapeworm life cycles are complex. In general, the eggs must be ingested by an intermediate host, where they typically become saclike larvae in the tissues. When the host of the adult form (the definitive host) eats an infected intermediate host, adult worms develop in its intestine. Some species have two or more intermediate hosts and can use several species as the definitive host. Serious clinical disease often occurs when a parasite becomes established in an atypical host or when larval forms are able to develop in what is normally a definitive host.

History

Because tapeworms can exceed 30 feet in length and strings of segments are often passed in the feces, it is not surprising that they were described by ancient writers in China, India, and the Mediterranean world. Encysted larvae – bladderworms or cysticerci – have been known in beef and pork for millennia, but their relationship to adult worms was not suspected until the eighteenth century and not proved until 1855, when F. Küchenmeister fed larval pork tapeworms concealed in food to condemned criminals and recovered adult worms on autopsy. The three large species that infect humans were not clearly differentiated until 1782. The notion of spontaneous generation of adult tapeworms in the human intestine was widely accepted until about 1820, and the theory was not inconsistent with the then known facts.

Diagnosis, Treatment, and Prevention

Intestinal infections are discovered when proglottids are passed or when eggs are found by microscopic examination of the feces. Diagnosis of larval infections is much more difficult and depends on serologic tests or surgery. Drugs are effective against adult tapeworms, but larval infections are much more difficult to treat and may require surgery. Prevention is basically a matter of personal hygiene, especially in rural areas, and thorough cooking of meat or fish.

Important Species

Five species are important parasites of humans: *Echinococcus granulosis* and *Taenia solium* are dangerous as larvae; *Taenia saginata, T. solium, Hymenolepsis nana,* and *Diphyllobothrium latum* live as adults in the intestine. Several other species can also infect humankind, but usually have other hosts. For example, *Dipylidium canium,* the dog tapeworm, can spread to children who accidentally eat fleas. Larval stages of several species of the genus *Spirometra,* normally parasitic in other vertebrates, can cause a dangerous condition called *sparaganosis* if a person swallows them in their copepod hosts. The Oriental custom of treating wounds or inflamed eyes with a poultice of fresh frog flesh can permit larvae to become established in the patient.

T. saginata, the beef tapeworm, inhabits human intestines around the world, although it is no longer common in developed countries. Cattle and other bovids are the intermediate hosts. If a cow or water buffalo eats grass contaminated with feces and eggs, the eggs hatch in the animal's intestine into a larva that migrates through the intestinal wall and forms a bladderlike sac, a *cysticercus,* in the muscles. Humans acquire the worm by eating raw or poorly cooked beef, as in steak tartare. Infections are sometimes asymptomatic, but many people experience mild to severe abdominal discomfort and a few have convulsions and develop problems of malnutrition. Prevention is by meat inspection, improved rural sanitation, and proper cooking. In the last instance, as is the case with many other parasites, higher prices for fuels in poor countries are often accompanied by increasing incidence.

T. solium, the pork tapeworm, is much less common than the beef tapeworm, but potentially is a considerably more dangerous parasite. It occurs around the world, except where Islamic or Jewish customs restrict pork consumption. The life cycle resembles *T. saginata,* except that wild and domestic swine are the intermediate hosts. Human infection usually results from eating poorly cooked pork; sausages can be especially dangerous. People can also serve as intermediate hosts if they ingest eggs in food or water or from soiled hands. The resulting larval infection, *cysticercosis,* can be very serious and even fatal, especially if cysticeroids develop in the brain. Adults cause symptoms like those of the beef tapeworm. Inspection and thorough cooking or freezing of pork are important for prevention, and adult infections should be treated to avoid the danger of cysticerosis.

H. nana, the dwarf tapeworm, is only 1 to $1\frac{1}{2}$ inches long. It occurs around the world, including the southern United States, and is a common parasite of domestic mice was well as humans. Infection results from eating larvae in fleas or in the grain beetle *Tenebrio.* Autoinfection is also common. In this direct life cycle, eggs hatch in a person's intestine, and the larvae attach to the intestinal wall to mature. Heavy infection can cause severe diarrhea, abdominal pain, and convulsions, especially in young children.

D. latum, the broad fish tapeworm, was described in 1602 and recognized as a distinct species in 1758, but its complex life cycle was not fully worked out until 1917. *D. latum* is an old parasite of humankind; eggs have been discovered in pre-Christian archaeological sites in northern Germany. This large tapeworm is found in the Baltic region, the Alps, the lower Danube, in much of European Russia, in scattered places in Central Asia, the Far East, Africa, and Alaska, and in the Great Lakes area of North America. The worm was probably introduced into the United States and Canada by Scandinavian immigrants. *D. latum* has a complex life cycle, with the first larval stage in small freshwater crustaceans and the second stage, the *pleurocercoid,* in the muscles of fish of the trout, pike, and perch families. People become infected by eating raw or undercooked or undersalted fish. Cooks preparing gefilte fish or pickled or salt fish dishes become infected as they sample the product to see if it is properly seasoned. Adult worms produce as many as a million eggs a day. If the host defecates in or near water, motile larvae emerge that seek a crustacean to complete the cycle. A related species with a life cycle involving marine fish and sea lions has afflicted inhabitants of coastal Peru and Chile since pre-Columbian times.

D. latum may exceed 35 feet in length and, like the beef and pork tapeworms, can thrive for many years in its host's gut. Symptoms are similar to those of other tapeworms, but in rare cases this worm can produce a form of anemia by robbing the host of vitamin B_{12}. There seems to be a genetic component to this complication, with Finnish populations most vulnerable. Treatment is effective, and prevention consists of better sanitation and cooking fish to kill the pleurocercoid larvae.

K. David Patterson

Bibliography

Bornsdorff, Bertil von. 1977. *Diphyllobothriasis in man.* London.

Desowitz, Robert S. 1978. On New Guinea tapeworms and Jewish grandmothers. *Natural History* 85: 22–7.

Ferreira, L. F., A. J. G. de Araújo, U. E. C. Confalonieri, and L. Nuñez. 1984. The finding of eggs of *Diphyllobothrium* in human coprolites (4,100–1,950 B.C.) from northern Chile. *Memorias do Instituto Oswaldo Cruz* 79: 175–80.

Foster, W. D. 1965. *A short history of parasitology.* Edinburgh and London.

Kean, B. H., Kenneth E. Mott, and Adair J. Russell, eds. 1978. *Tropical medicine and parasitology: Classic investigations,* Vol. II, 615–35; 653–71. Ithaca and London.

Ward, W. B. 1930. *The introduction and spread of the fish tapeworm (Diphyllobothrium latum) in the United States.* Baltimore.

VIII.137
Tay–Sachs Disease

Tay–Sachs disease (TSD) is the best known of the sphingolipidoses, a group of genetic disorders that includes Niemann–Pick disease, Gaucher's disease, and others. Specifically, TSD is G_{M2} (beta) gangliosidosis, an autosomal recessive disease with complete penetrance. Affected individuals (recessive homozygotes) produce virtually no functional hexosaminidase A (hex A), an enzyme necessary for normal neurological development and function. TSD is very rare in most populations, but is, overall, about 100 times more prevalent among Ashkenazi Jews. This indicates that the TSD gene frequency is about 10 times higher in the Ashkenazi Jewish population. Persons with the disease usually show clinical symptoms of neurological degeneration by 6 months of age. Their condition steadily deteriorates, and they seldom live beyond the age of 4 years. There is no cure, but heterozygous "carriers" of the defective gene can be identified by clinical test, and amniocentesis can detect an affected fetus.

History

The British ophthalmologist Warren Tay (1881) first reported some of the early clinical signs of TSD. In the United States, Bernard Sachs (1887) further documented the clinical course and pathology of the disease he later called "amaurotic family idiocy" (Sachs 1896). It was Sachs who first noted the familial nature of the disease, and its seemingly exclusive occurrence in Jewish families. However, reports were soon made of non-Jewish cases. D. Slome (1933) was the first to survey the literature on the population characteristics of TSD and confirmed the disease's autosomal recessive mode of transmission as well as the TSD gene's higher frequency among Jews. E. Klenk (1942) discovered that the nerve cells of individuals who died from TSD contained an excess of a lipid he called *ganglioside*. L. Svennerholm (1962) later described the specific G_{M2} ganglioside. The hexosaminidase enzyme was discovered by D. Robinson and J. L. Stirling (1968) to have two components, A and B, and S. Okada and J. S. O'Brien (1969) found that hex A deficiency was associated with high levels of G_{M2} ganglioside in the neurological tissues of TSD patients. L. Schneck and colleagues (1970), R. Navon and B. Padeh (1971), and O'Brien and colleagues (1971) demonstrated that prenatal diagnosis of hex A deficiency was possible. More recently, the hex A gene has been mapped to chromosome 15 (see Kidd, Klinger, and Ruddle 1989), and different variants (alleles) of the hex A gene, each one of which leads to TSD, have been discovered.

Clinical Manifestations and Mortality

E. H. Kolodny (1979) gives a concise outline of the symptoms and course of TSD. Between birth and age 6 months, the affected child may begin displaying apathy, hypotonia, and an exaggerated startle reaction to noise. Between 6 and 12 months of age, the characteristic cherry-red spot in the eye becomes evident, and the child also displays psychomotor retardation, spasticity, and rigidity. From 12 to 18 months of age, the child may have excessive drooling, bouts of unmotivated laughter, and convulsions. Between 18 and 24 months, megacephaly, cortical blindness, and quadriplegia commonly occur. After age 2 years, the child is in a vegetative state, and most affected children die sometime during the next 2 years. Until then their condition steadily worsens, with flexor contractures, episodes of autonomic dysfunction, neurogenic bladder, and skin yellowing being common signs.

Pathology

B. W. Volk, Schneck, and M. Adachi (1970) and Adachi and Volk (1975) detail the pathology of TSD. The key pathological features of TSD are most apparent in the brain and related structures, and become more obvious as the disease progresses. The most striking gross change in the brain is its marked increase in weight, especially in individuals who live beyond 2 years of age. Another gross change, most apparent in later stages of the disease, is cerebellar atrophy. At the cellular level, the most noticeable changes involve the neurons, especially those in the cortex. After about 1 year of age, the cerebral neurons have lost their characteristic angular shape and are swollen with material. Later in the disease process there is loss of these neurons. These characteristic neuronal changes are also seen in the spinal cord. The cherry-red spot in the eye observed by Tay (1881) is caused by the loss of ganglion cells and thinning of the nerve cell layer in the macula, which exposes more of the underlying choroidal coat to ophthalmologic examination (Adachi and Volk 1975).

Biochemistry

Gangliosides are a family of acidic complex lipids called *glycosphingolipids*. Gangliosides are present to some degree in most of the body's tissues, but are found primarily in the brain (Svennerholm 1980). More than 40 different molecular forms have been discovered, four of which comprise 65 percent to 85 percent of the total ganglioside content of mammalian brains (Rapport 1981). Though the role of gangliosides in neural physiology is not completely understood, the basic biochemical cause of TSD remains straightforward. In persons with TSD, unusually large amounts of G_{M2} ganglioside accumulate in the brain and associated tissues, thus disrupting their normal development and function. This accumulation is due to the lack of a functional specific enzyme, hex A, that breaks down the G_{M2} ganglioside. Hex A activity can be assessed by a serum enzyme assay (O'Brien et al. 1970). This has led to the discovery by many investigators that heterozygous carriers of the TSD gene have roughly only half the hex A activity of individuals homozygous for the normal allele. This is apparently enough, however, for normal catabolism of the G_{M2} ganglioside. In fact, G. Bach and colleagues (1976) reported a healthy adult TSD heterozygote woman with only 22 percent hex A activity.

Molecular Genetics

P. A. Lalley, M. C. Rattazzi, and T. B. Shows (1974) and F. Gilbert and colleagues (1975) used somatic cell hybrids to determine that the hex A gene is linked to genes on chromosome 15. Using the same technology, but with cells from a person with a translocation of the distal half of the long arm (q) of chromosome 15 to chromosome 17, C. J. Chern and colleagues (1977) were able to assign the hex A gene to the q22–qter region of chromosome 15. R. Myerowitz and colleagues (1985) isolated a cDNA clone (a copy of a particular length of DNA) that contains the entire hex A gene. This cDNA clone can be used as a "probe" to look for variants of the normal Hex A gene. Myerowitz and N. D. Hogikyan (1986) used the probe to find that different mutations of the Hex A gene result in TSD in Ashkenazi Jews and non-Jewish French Canadians. H. Nakai, M. G. Byers, and Shows (1987) also used this probe to narrow down the location of the hex A gene to 15q23–q24. B. L. Triggs-Raine and colleagues (1989) used molecular genetic techniques to screen for TSD gene variants in the Ashkenazi Jewish population, and in the Ashkenazi Jews tested they found two different mutations of the hex A gene that result in the usual infantile onset TSD. They also found a different mutation of the hex A gene that gives rise to a rare adult-onset TSD. The use of molecular genetic methods is leading to a more complete understanding of the genetic basis of TSD (see Tanaka et al. 1990).

Genetic Epidemiology

Certainly contributing to the amount of attention paid to TSD over the last century is the enigma it (and other deleterious genetic disorders such as sickle-cell anemia) presents: How can a lethal gene get to a high frequency in a population? How can that high frequency be maintained? Why is that gene found at a relatively high level in a particular population? In addressing this problem, one first examines in turn the basic evolutionary forces that change gene frequencies: mutation, gene flow, genetic drift, and natural selection.

Forces of Evolution Affecting Gene Frequencies

Mutations. Mutations are the original source of all genetic variability, occurring at generally very low, but constant, rates. Thus (at least once, but probably more than once) mutation gave rise to each TSD gene variant found among the Ashkenazim and non-Ashkenazim. Mutation alone, however, cannot explain the unusually high frequency of the TSD genes in the Ashkenazim. The reason is simply that there would need to be an unprecedentedly high mutation rate of this gene in Ashkenazi Jews to account for its presently observed frequency in that population. There is no evidence of this being the case.

Gene Flow. Gene flow, the movement of genes from one population to another as individuals move, plays a greater or lesser role in the various explanations of the high TSD gene frequency in the Ashkenazim. Gene flow could have its biggest role if the intriguing scenario proposed by A. Koestler (1976) is correct. He suggests that the Ashkenazim are in large part descended from members of the Khazar Empire. The Khazar Empire existed from the seventh to the tenth century A.D. in an area north of the Caucasus Mountains, and during that time some Khazars converted to Judaism. It is speculated that after the fall of the Khazar Empire, those converts moved northwestward into areas of central Europe where Jews from western Europe were also emigrating. Thus, if those Khazars carried the TSD genes, they delivered them as part and parcel of their contribution to the Ashkenazi gene pool. As was the case with mutation, though, it is unlikely that gene flow in and of itself can account for the high frequency of the TSD genes among Ashkenazi Jews. The reason is that such an explanation would suggest that there was a group (perhaps the Khazars, perhaps some other group) with a high frequency of the TSD gene that provided the Ashkenazi Jewish population with a large number of carriers. There is no evidence of such an occurrence (see Neel 1979), which leaves natural selection and genetic drift as more likely reasons for the high frequency of the TSD genes among Ashkenazi Jews.

Natural Selection. N. C. Myrianthopoulos (1962) and A. G. Knudson and W. D. Kaplan (1962) first suggested that heterozygote carriers of the TSD gene may have a selective advantage over the normal homozygote. Myrianthopoulos and S. M. Aronson (1966, 1967) calculated that a selective advantage of about 1.25 percent on the part of the heterozygous carrier of the TSD allele would be sufficient to maintain the allele at its present frequency of approximately 1.3 percent among the Ashkenazim, despite the loss of TSD genes through the deaths of recessive homozygotes afflicted with TSD.

They then showed that over the course of 50 generations (roughly from the time of the Diaspora to the present), a heterozygote-selective advantage of about 4.5 percent would increase the TSD allele frequency from 0.13 percent to 1.3 percent, again despite losses of TSD alleles through the deaths of recessive homozygotes. In order to provide support for their hypothesis, they compared sibship sizes of the parents of TSD offspring to the sibship sizes of a control group. They found the former to be slightly larger than the latter. Although the differences were not statistically significant, they indicated a heterozygote advantage sufficient to result in the observed present-day TSD gene frequency in the Ashkenazi population (assuming that the heterozygote advantage had remained more or less constant over time).

Two conditions are essential for a natural selection explanation to hold: (1) a selective agent of sufficient magnitude to affect negatively the reproductive success of individuals, and (2) a physiological basis for the advantage one genotype has over the others. Following up on their earlier work, Myrianthopoulos and Arsonson (1972) suggested that heterozygous carriers of the TSD allele were less susceptible to tuberculosis, a disease especially common in many urban centers of Europe during the nineteenth century. Although they found a negative association between indirect estimates of TSD and tuberculosis prevalence, the association was too small to be statistically significant. Furthermore, no physiological basis was offered to explain why heterozygote carriers of the TSD allele might have a selective advantage with regard to tuberculosis. More recently, J. Zlotogora, M. Zeigler, and Bach (1988) have posited that selection is the reason for the high prevalence of not only TSD in the Ashkenazi population, but also sphingolipid storage disorders in general among all Jews. However, they conclude that the nature of the hypothesized selective forces has yet to be fully elucidated.

Founder Effect and Genetic Drift. G. A. Chase and V. A. McKusick (1972) suggested that founder effect and genetic drift, rather than heterozygote advantage and natural selection, explain better the high TSD gene frequencies in the Ashkenazi Jewish population. D. C. Rao and N. E. Morton (1973) calculated that it was possible that drift could account for the high frequency of the TSD genes in the Ashkenazim, and D. Wagener and colleagues (1978) came to a similar conclusion. T. E. Kelly and colleagues (1975) studied a semi-isolated non-Jewish population with

a high frequency of TSD, concluding that founder effect is the most likely cause and suggesting that this case illustrated, in microcosm, how the high frequency of the TSD genes might have occurred. A. L. Fraikor (1977) also favors a genetic drift explanation in a detailed study in which genetic drift (broadened to include founder effect as well as some other population processes) is argued to be the most parsimonious explanation for the high TSD gene frequency among the Ashkenazim.

Genetic drift refers specifically to random changes in gene frequencies from one generation to the next (i.e., "sampling errors"). Sampling error is most pronounced in small populations in which, simply because of the chance combination of a relatively small number of gametes out of millions of genetically different contenders, the offspring generation's gene pool may not contain the same genes in the same frequencies as the parental generation's gene pool. Thus, gene frequencies "drift" up or down through time. Unfortunately, there is no way to tell whether or not genetic drift has occurred in a population. Nonetheless, the probability of genetic drift of a certain magnitude occurring under certain circumstances can be estimated. Population size and changes in population size through time are the most important parameters in these calculations (see Wilson and Bossert 1971). A process related to genetic drift, *founder effect,* refers to the genetic impact that one or a few individuals may, by chance, have on the genetic structure of a new population after either migration or population decline. It is because of the chance factor that founder effect is usually considered in the context of genetic drift.

Fraikor (1977) chronicles the population history of Ashkenazi Jewry and finds that the conditions most conducive for genetic drift (especially small and semi-isolated local populations and large fluctuations in overall population size) were present throughout much of Europe for hundreds of years. However, A. Chakravarti and R. Chakraborty (1978) calculate that even in some situations highly conducive to genetic drift, the probability of observing the present discrepancies in TSD gene frequencies between the Ashkenazim and non-Ashkenazim is low. They conclude that heterozygote advantage and genetic drift should be considered together as the most probable explanation for the high TSD frequency in the Ashkenazi Jewish population. This conclusion serves as a worthwhile reminder that the forces of evolution are not necessarily mutually exclusive explanations of genetic variation, a point made explicit by S. Wright (1977) in his "shifting balance" theory of evolution.

Up to now the difference between Ashkenazi Jews and non-Ashkenazi Jews (and non-Jews) in TSD prevalence and gene frequencies has been emphasized. Indeed, in the extensive literature on TSD, this difference is often the only one considered. There is, however, evidence of considerable disparity among Ashkenazi Jewish groups in the prevalence of TSD. These differences are also important in assessing the reasons for the overall high frequency of TSD genes among the Ashkenazim. Aronson (1964) found that the ancestors of the majority of Jewish TSD cases in the United States came from the northeastern provinces of Poland and the Baltic States. Myrianthopoulos and Aronson (1967) confirmed this finding, stating that with regard to TSD prevalence in central Europe "some variation, as high as fivefold, existed between Ashkenazi communities of these areas and that this variation is not random but shows a definite geographic trend."

As it happens, these findings can be incorporated into both the natural selection hypothesis and the genetic drift hypothesis. The search for natural selection is made somewhat easier because a selective agent in the environment that might give the heterozygote a reproductive advantage no longer needs to exist across Europe, but needs only to be shown to exist in a delimited geographic area. TSD genes spread out from there through gene flow, and it would have been some time before they would have been removed in appreciable numbers through the deaths of the recessive homozygotes; by then the carrier frequency may have become rather high. The case for genetic drift is made somewhat stronger because the Ashkenazim no longer need to be considered a large interbreeding population, but instead can be viewed as a subdivided population made up of a number of smaller semi-isolates in each of which genetic drift is more likely to take place. The TSD genes spread from areas of high frequency to neighboring areas of low frequency through gene flow, thus explaining the geographic distribution observed by Myrianthopoulos and Aronson (1967) of the ancestors of TSD-affected individuals.

A Combination of Factors. In the absence of much substantive data, and the fact that evolutionary forces most often work in concert, the conclusion reached by Chakravarti and Chakraborty (1978), that a combination of heterozygote advantage and genetic drift is the most probable reason for the high TSD gene frequencies in the Ashkenazim, is appeal-

ing. In a similar vein, although not incorporating heterozygote advantage, Fraikor (1977) does not rely solely on genetic drift, but favors a combination of factors. She writes of Ashkenazi Jewish communities over the last few hundred years:

The combination of polygamy, inbreeding, small effective population size, and large numbers of progeny could have elevated the frequency of the TSD allele in the descendants of these populations. The subsequent period of seminomadism resulted in numerous individual carriers being scattered in many parts of Eastern Europe. Some carriers probably also remained in Germany or Western Europe. During the Golden Age of the sixteenth century, the rapid population expansion and freedom of migration within the territory of Poland greatly enhanced the chances for carriers to marry noncarriers. Such marriages would further increase the number of carriers in the total population, and selection against the gene would be reduced because affected homozygotes were not being produced in significant numbers. (Fraikor 1977)

Alternative Theories

Before leaving this issue, we must consider other explanations for the high frequency of TSD in the Ashkenazi Jewish population. One of these, inbreeding, was mentioned previously. *Inbreeding* does not change gene frequencies, but because it increases homozygosity generally (dependent on the level of inbreeding), it increases the probability of deleterious alleles coming together in individuals. Inbreeding is, in fact, the likely cause of the high prevalence of other sphingolipid disorders in other Jewish populations (see Zlotogora et al. 1980; Towne 1987; Zlotogora, Zeigler, and Bach 1988), and as Fraikor (1977) hypothesizes, may have played a role in some of the smaller and more isolated Ashkenazi Jewish communities.

Finally, Wagener and Cavalli-Sforza (1975) suggest that either "hitchhiking" or *epistasis* may have increased TSD gene frequencies in the Ashkenazim. When two genes are in close proximity to each other on a chromosome, they are likely to be inherited together over the generations. Thus, a deleterious allele may "hitch" an evolutionary ride with a selectively favorable allele. With the human genome map becoming more and more detailed, some hitchhiking hypotheses can increasingly be tested. What remains to be seen in this case is whether a highly favorable allele can be found in the Ashkenazim that happens to be on chromosome 15 in the area of q23–q24. Epistasis refers to the interactions between unlinked genes. J. V. Neel (1979) notes the following:

[An] epistasis hypothesis is theoretically possible but difficult to visualize as a general explanation for recessive deleterious genes in high frequencies in defined groups, given what we know about the usual heterozygous effects of these genes. Specifically, in the case of TSD, it is difficult to visualize a genetic interaction that converts half-levels of hex-A into a selective advantage.

The Disease in the Future

There has been some debate on whether or not the incidence of TSD is increasing. R. F. Shaw and A. P. Smith (1969) argue that it is, basing their conclusion on a calculation that assumes a heterozygote advantage of approximately 5.3 percent, a value slightly higher than that calculated by Myrianthopoulos and Aronson (1966). On the other hand, Myrianthopoulos, A. F. Taylor, and Aronson (1970) doubt that the TSD gene is increasing because the conditions (high prevalences of tuberculosis) that may have offered the heterozygote an advantage in the past are no longer present. Chase and McKusick (1972) suggest that the present high incidence of TSD is "a transient phenomenon due to the chance encounter of recessive genes whose frequency has reached a high level partly as a consequence of diminished inbreeding." It must also be kept in mind, though, that present-day high levels of TSD may be an artifact of better diagnosis and case reporting.

Aside from the continuing study and debate about the different aspects of TSD touched on here, there are some more immediate concerns. At the present time, there is no cure for TSD. However, because heterozygote carriers of a TSD gene can be identified by a clinical test, as can an affected fetus through amniocentesis, individuals have available to them some important options. M. M. Kaback and R. S. Zeiger (1972) conducted the first major effort to identify TSD heterozygote carriers. Kolodny (1979) gives three reasons for the success of this screening program:

1. The testing program was targeted toward a defined subgroup of the population, namely, Ashkenazi Jews in their childbearing years.
2. A relatively simple, accurate, and inexpensive method was available for determining heterozygote status in an individual.
3. An in utero test for Tay–Sachs disease existed.

Kolodny (1979) went on to note that as a result of this and other screening programs more than 100 TSD births had been averted. Kaback and colleagues (see his 1979, 1981) present detailed information and updates on various aspects of TSD screening programs. D. A. Greenberg and Kaback (1982) report that at the time of their writing, over 200,000 adults in the United States had been screened for TSD carrier status. Estimates of TSD carrier frequencies vary somewhat from one study to another. O'Brien (1983) predicts a U.S. Ashkenazi Jewish population carrier frequency of 2.6 percent, whereas Kolodny (1979) estimates the frequency to be 3.7 percent.

Bradford Towne

I would like to thank Dr. Jean W. MacCluer for her comments and suggestions on this article.

Bibliography

Adachi, M., and B. W. Volk. 1975. Pathology. In *The gangliosidoses*, ed. B. W. Volk and L. Schneck, 125–58. New York.

Aronson, S. M. 1964. Epidemiology. In *Tay–Sachs disease*, ed. B. W. Volk, 118–53. New York.

Bach, G., et al. 1976. Tay–Sachs disease in a Moroccan Jewish family: A possible new mutation. *Israeli Journal of Medical Science* 12: 1432.

Chakravarti, A., and R. Chakraborty. 1978. Elevated frequency of Tay–Sachs disease among Ashkenazic Jews unlikely by genetic drift alone. *American Journal of Human Genetics* 30: 256–61.

Chase, G. A., and V. A. McKusick. 1972. Controversy in human genetics: Founder effect in Tay–Sachs disease. *American Journal of Human Genetics* 24: 339–40.

Chern, C. J., et al. 1977. Assignment of the structural genes for the α subunit of hexosaminidase A, mannose phosphate isomerase, and pyruvate kinase to the region q22–qter of human chromosome 15. *Somatology of Cell Genetics* 3: 553.

Fraikor, A. L. 1977. Tay–Sachs disease: Genetic drift among the Ashkenazic Jews. *Social Biology* 24: 117–34.

Gilbert, F., et al. 1975. Tay–Sachs' and Sandhoff's diseases: The assignment of genes for hexosaminidase A and B to individual human chromosomes. *Proceedings of the National Academy of Sciences of the United States of America* 72: 263–7.

Greenberg, D. A., and M. M. Kaback. 1982. Estimation of the frequency of hexosaminidase A variant alleles in the American Jewish population. *American Journal of Human Genetics* 34: 444–51.

Kaback, M. M. 1979. *Tay–Sachs disease: Screening and prevention*. New York.

  1981. Heterozygote screening and prenatal diagnosis in Tay–Sachs disease: A worldwide update. In *Lysozymes and lysosomal storage diseases*, ed. J. W. Callahan and J. A. Lowden, 331–42. New York.

Kaback, M. M., and R. S. Zeiger. 1972. Heterozygote detection in Tay–Sachs disease: A prototype community screening program for the prevention of recessive genetic disorders. In *Sphingolipids, sphingolipidoses, and allied disorders,* ed. B. W. Volk and S. M. Aronson, 613–32. New York.

Kelly, T. E., et al. 1975. Tay–Sachs disease: High gene frequency in a non-Jewish population. *American Journal of Human Genetics* 27: 287–91.

Kidd, K. K., H. P. Klinger, and F. H. Ruddle, eds. 1989. *Human gene mapping,* Vol. 10. Basel.

Klenk, E. 1942. Ueber die Ganglioside des Gehirns bei der infantilen amaurotischen idiotie vom Typus Tay–Sachs. *Berichte der Deutschen Chemischen Gesellschaft* 75: 1632.

Knudson, A. G., and W. D. Kaplan. 1962. Genetics of the sphingolipidoses. In *Cerebral sphingolipidoses: A symposium on Tay–Sachs disease and allied disorders,* eds. S. M. Aronson and B. W. Volk, 395–411. New York.

Koestler, A. 1976. *The thirteenth tribe.* New York.

Kolodny, E. H. 1979. Tay–Sachs disease. In *Genetic diseases among Ashkenazi Jews,* ed. R. M. Goodman and A. G. Motulsky, 217–29. New York.

Lalley, P. A., et al. 1974. Human β-D-ε-Acetylhexosaminidases A and B: Expression and linkage relationship in somatic cell hybrids. *Proceedings of the National Academy of Sciences of the United States of America* 71: 1569–73.

Myerowitz, R., and N. D. Hogikyan. 1986. Different mutations in Ashkenazi Jewish and non-Jewish French Canadians with Tay–Sachs disease. *Science* 232: 1646–8.

Myerowitz, R., et al. 1985. Human β-hexosaminidase α chain: Coding sequence and homology with the chain. *Proceedings of the National Academy of the United States of America* 82: 7830–4.

Myrianthopoulos, N. C. 1962. Some epidemiologic and genetic aspects of Tay–Sachs disease. In *Cerebral sphingolipidoses: A symposium on Tay–Sachs disease and allied disorders,* ed. S. M. Aronson and B. W. Volk, 359–74. New York.

Myrianthopoulos, N. C., and S. M. Aronson. 1966. Population dynamics of Tay–Sachs disease. I. Reproductive fitness and selection. *American Journal of Human Genetics* 18: 313–27.

1967. Reproductive fitness and selection in Tay–Sachs disease. In *Inborn disorders of sphingolipid metabolism,* ed. S. M. Aronson and B. W. Volk, 431–41. New York.

1972. Population dynamics of Tay–Sachs disease. II. What confers the selective advantage upon the Jewish heterozygote? In *Sphingolipids, sphingolipidoses, and allied disorders,* ed. B. W. Volk and S. M. Aronson, 561–70. New York.

Myrianthopoulos, N. C., A. F. Naylor, and S. M. Aronson. 1970. Tay–Sachs disease is probably not increasing. *Nature* 227: 609.

Nakai, H., M. G. Ryers, and T. B. Shows. 1987. Mapping HEX A to 15q23–q24. *Cytogenetics and Cell Genetics* 46: 667 [A1188].

Navon, R., and B. Padeh. 1971. Prenatal diagnosis of Tay–Sachs genotypes. *British Medical Journal* 4: 17–20.

Neel, J. V. 1979. History and the Tay–Sachs allele. In *Genetic diseases among Ashkenazi Jews,* ed. R. M. Goodman and A. G. Motulsky, 285–99. New York.

O'Brien, J. S. 1983. The gangliosides. In *The metabolic basis of inherited disease,* ed. J. B. Stanbury et al., 945–69. New York.

O'Brien, J. S., et al. 1970. Tay–Sachs disease: Detection of heterozygotes and homozygotes by serum hexosaminidase assay. *New England Journal of Medicine* 283: 15–20.

1971. Tay–Sachs disease: Prenatal diagnosis. *Science* 172: 61–4.

Okada, S., and J. S. O'Brien. 1969. Tay–Sachs disease: Generalized absence of β-D-ε-acetylhexosaminidase component. *Science* 165: 698–700.

Rao, D. C., and N. E. Morton. 1973. Large deviations in the distribution of rare genes. *American Journal of Human Genetics* 25: 594–7.

Rapport, M. M. 1981. Introduction to the biochemistry of gangliosides. In *Gangliosides in neurological and neuromuscular function, development, and repair,* ed. M. M. Rapport and A. Gorio, xv–xix. New York.

Robinson, D., and J. L. Stirling. 1968. ε-Acetyl-β-glucosaminidases in human spleen. *Biochemical Journal* 107: 321–7.

Sachs, B. 1887. On arrested cerebral development with special reference to its cortical pathology. *Journal of Nervous and Mental Disease* 14: 541–53.

1896. A family form of idiocy, generally fatal, associated with early blindness. *Journal of Nervous and Mental Disease* 23: 475–9.

Schneck, L., et al. 1970. Prenatal diagnosis of Tay–Sachs disease. *Lancet* 1: 582–4.

Shaw, R. F., and A. P. Smith. 1969. Is Tay–Sachs disease increasing? *Nature* 224: 1214–15.

Slome, D. 1933. The genetic basis of amaurotic family idiocy. *Journal of Genetics* 27: 363–72.

Svennerholm, L. 1962. The chemical structure of normal human brain and Tay–Sachs gangliosides. *Biochemical and Biophysical Research Communications* 9: 436–41.

1980. Gangliosides and synaptic transmission. In *Structure and function of gangliosides,* ed. L. Svennerholm et al., 533–44. New York.

Tanaka, A., et al. 1990. G_{M2}-gangliosidosis B_1 variant: Analsyis of β-hexosaminidase α gene abnormalities in seven patients. *American Journal of Human Genetics* 46: 329.

Tay, W. 1881. Symmetrical changes in the region of the yellow spot in each eye of an infant. *Ophthalmological Society of the United Kingdom* 1: 155.

Towne, B. 1987. Population structure and anthropometric variation among the Habbani Yemeni Jews. Ph.D. dissertation, University of Utah.

Triggs-Raine, B. L., et al. 1989. Ashkenazi Tay–Sachs

disease: A comparison of DNA- and enzyme-based methods for carrier testing. *American Journal of Human Genetics* (supplement) 45: A226.

Volk, B. W., L. Schneck, and M. Adachi. 1970. Clinic, pathology and biochemistry of Tay–Sachs disease. In *Handbook of clinical neurology*, Vol. 10: *Leucodystrophies and poliodystrophies*, ed. P. J. Vinken and G. W. Bruyn, 385–426. Amsterdam.

Wagener, D., and L. L. Cavalli-Sforza. 1975. Ethnic variation in genetic disease: Possible roles of hitchhiking and epistasis. *American Journal of Human Genetics* 27: 348–64.

Wagener, D., L. L. Cavalli-Sforza, and R. Barakat. 1978. Ethnic variation of genetic disease: Roles of drift for recessive lethal genes. *American Journal of Human Genetics* 30: 262–70.

Wilson, E. O., and W. H. Bossert. 1971. *A primer of population biology*. Sunderland, Mass.

Wright, S. 1977. *Evolution and the genetics of populations*, Vol. 3: *Experimental results and evolutionary deductions*. Chicago.

Zlotogora, J., et al. 1980. Metachromatic leukodystrophy in the Habbanite Jews: High frequency in a genetic isolate and screening for heterozygotes. *American Journal of Human Genetics* 32: 663–9.

Zlotogora, J., M. Zeigler, and G. Bach. 1988. Selection in favor of lysosomal storage disorders? *American Journal of Human Genetics* 42: 271–3.

VIII.138
Tetanus

Tetanus is an acute disease caused by the production of a neurotoxin, *tetanospasmin*, by a bacterium, *Clostridium tetani*, when the spores of the organism enter a wound, and develop into the toxin-producing vegetative form. The case-fatality rate averages 50 percent in adults and is higher in neonates (especially those in developing nations) and in patients over 60 years of age.

Etiology and Epidemiology

C. tetani is an obligate anerobe, a spore-forming, gram-positive motile rod. The terminal spore caused the organism to be called the "drumstick" rod. The protein toxin, tetanospasmin, blocks acetylcholine release at the motor end-plates. The toxin travels up the nerve trunks, as well as fixing directly on nerve cells. The spinal cord is the primary target organ, with chromatolysis of the motor neurons and inhibition of antagonists accounting for the spasm and rigidity that characterize the disease. Toxin fixation to central nervous system neurons may lead to seizures; involvement of the sympathetic nervous system may evoke vascular irregularities.

Humans may be considered accidental interveners in the life cycle of the organism, which is a soil saprophyte and a harmless inhabitant of the intestines of many herbivores. The organism requires a wound to invade mammals. Traumatic, surgical, dental, umbilical, burn, and cosmetic wounds are the most common causes of infection in humans. "Skin popping" of addictive drugs, insect bites, and nonmedical abortions are less common causes of infection. As an obligate anaerobe, the organism can reproduce and produce toxin only when local oxidation–reduction processes reduce tissue oxygen to near zero; deep, infected wounds are thus ideal culture media.

There may be 300,000 to 500,000 cases of tetanus a year worldwide, with perhaps 120,000 of those being neonates whose umbilical wounds become infected. The United States reported 101 cases in 1987 and 1988.

Clinical Manifestations, Diagnosis, and Pathology

There is no special characteristic or diagnostic pathology. Lysis of myofibrils and muscle bleeding are secondary to the muscle spasm. The usual incubation period ranges from 2 to 14 days after wounding. Cases of "dormant" tetanus have been reported after several months, probably because spores have remained in a closed wound as a silent abscess. The diagnosis is based entirely on the history and the clinical findings; there are no specific laboratory findings. The differential diagnosis includes strychnine poisoning and dystonic reactions to phenothiazines and metoclopramide.

The clinical manifestations are usually classified into three forms:

1. *Localized tetanus* presents with spasm near the site of the injury, usually in an extremity. The fatality rate is 1 percent or less.
2. *Generalized tetanus*, the more common form, is marked by the classic trismus (lock jaw), fixed grin (risus sardonicus), and backward arching of the trunk (opisthotonos). Tonic seizures of the muscle groups occur in spasms, lead to rigidity, and are very painful. They may be precipitated by any stimulus. Pneumonia may follow respiratory muscle involvement or laryngeal spasm with as-

piration. Cardiovascular disturbances are common, especially vasoconstriction and a labile blood pressure. Severe spasms may cause vertebral fractures. The course of this form, in survivors, is from 1 to 2 weeks.

3. *Cephalic tetanus,* an uncommon form of the disease, follows facial wounds, involves the facial nerves, and may be followed by generalized tetanus.

4. *Neonatal tetanus* following infection of the umbilical cord (discussed in the next chapter) usually begins by the third to tenth day after birth, and then progresses to generalized tetanus.

Death from tetanus is usually due to respiratory failure with hypoxia or pneumonia, and occasionally to circulatory collapse, especially in patients over 60 years old.

Treatment

Treatment may be summarized as measures to decrease the presence of the organism: debridement of the wound and antibiotics; neutralization of the toxin by antitoxin; and control of the effects of the toxin by drugs with specific neuropharmacological effects. Curarization and artificial respiration for 2 weeks have been used in severe cases. Careful continuous nursing care is essential.

History

A man who was struck from behind by a sharp dart a little below the neck had a wound which did not look serious because it did not go deep. But sometime later when the point had been extracted the patient was seized with backward-bending convulsions like those of opisthotonus. His jaws were locked, and any liquid that he attempted to swallow was returned through his nostrils. He died on the second day.

So Hippocrates recorded an obvious case of tetanus. At least one other case is recorded in the same volume. In *Diseases III,* the general case is given: "[W]hen tètanus occurs, the jaws become as hard as wood, patients cannot open their mouths . . . their backs become rigid . . . he suffers great pain . . . generally dies on the third, fifth, seventh or fourteenth day – if he survives that many, he recovers." Further it is noted that "the patient is drawn backwards . . . his pains are violent . . . his elbows become flexed . . . he holds his fingers in a fist . . . vomits through his nostrils. If one survives for fourteen days, he recovers." The treatment regimens varied: "pepper, black, hellbore, fat bird soup, vapour baths, cold water baths," and "phlobotomy relieves lumbar tetanus."

But the terseness of the aphorism "A convulsion supervening upon a wound is deadly" may mark the more general outcome of a case of generalized tetanus. Certainly Aretaeus (Adams 1956), writing some 700 years later, found tetanus to be "An inhuman calamity! An incredible sight! A spectacle painful even to the beholder! An incurable malady!" He believed the prayers of spectators for the death of the patient to be useful, "being a deliverance from the pains." He also pitied the attending physician's inability to afford relief, "for if he should wish to straighten the limbs, he can only do so by cutting and breaking those of a living man." It is a "great misfortune of the physician." Aretaeus, after an excellent clinical description of the disease, urged a wide variety of therapeutic maneuvers, including special diets, forcing liquids, a quiet house, phlebotomy, massage with oils, fomentations, cupping, specific treatment of any wound, and more.

The clinical descriptions have not been bettered. Therapy has changed, but it is possible that the number of survivors "after the fourteenth day" may not have markedly improved. William Osler (1892), in his seminal text, noted the clinical and epidemiological data given above, cited Hippocrates, and summarized the unchanged clinical findings. He found an 80 percent rate mortality within 4 days. Therapy had improved: The nasogastric tube was in use for feeding and hydration, morphine for sedation, and chloroform for muscle relaxation. He emphasized antiseptic care of the wound. It is fair to say that from Hippocrates to Osler – and to today – there have been no changes in diagnostic techniques, and there has been only a small reduction in mortality rates in established cases. Tetanus is a disease that must be prevented, and prevention had to begin with isolation of the organism and advances in immunology.

Isolation of the Tetanus Organism

The discovery of the tetanus organism was part of the microbiological revolution that proved the theory that a specific organism caused a specific disease. In 1884 Arthur Nicolaier produced tetanus-like symptoms and death by injecting soil samples into animals. He isolated a rod-shaped bacillus and suggested that it secreted a toxin resembling strychnine in its action. He did not isolate the organism in pure culture. Neither did D. Rosenbach in 1886, although he was able to produce classic tetanus in guinea pigs by injecting tissue from a fatal human case. He did describe the "drumstick" appearance and correctly deduced that these were terminal spores. It remained for Shibasaburo Kitasato to isolate the organism in pure culture, in 1889, from a fatal case of a soldier in Berlin. He described the anaerobic culture requirements, said he had confirmed Nicholaier's observations, and also concluded that the clinical effects were due to a toxin. The study of tetanus toxin and antitoxin followed directly and in parallel with the research of Emil Behring and Kitasato on diphtheria toxin, a much more important disease.

Tetanus Toxin and Antitoxin

Tetanus and diphtheria investigations provided the framework upon which Behring built his understanding of the principles of serum therapy. In an 1892 (1892b) paper, he argued that the serum of a patient should contain material protective and curative for another individual with the disease. In a series of studies, he and his co-workers proved this point in animal studies, but did not recommend serum use in humans until the mechanism of action was better understood. They noted that even if treatment of the animal began very early, at least 1,000 times as much antitoxin was needed to cure as to protect before infection, and that, as the symptoms became general, the antitoxin was useless in any amount.

The availability of horse antitoxin soon led to clinical trials, with widely varying results. Analysis eventually showed that antitoxin had to be given very early in the disease; that dosage – empirical at first – was critical; and that it was essentially useless once the toxin was fixed to neurons and the patient was symptomatic. As Henry Parish (1965) and E. Haberman (1978) both suggest, better understanding of wound care and more aseptic surgery accompanied the rising rate of successful use of antitoxin and a decreased death rate, especially in selected populations like soldiers.

Given that soldiers often have fought in well-manured farmland and do not have clean skins, and that until very recently armies lived in close proximity to horses used for transport and cavalry, it is not surprising that tetanus was a common problem in wounded soldiers. In 1808, for example, the rate of tetanus before immunization was 12.5 per 1,000; by contrast, the rate was only 0.04 per 1,000 in World War II (Boyd 1958).

It was World War I that saw the general introduction of early, near-universal use of antitoxin, accompanied by meticulous debridement of wounds. The effect of these measures may be seen in the British army. There was an incidence of 8 per 1,000 wounded from August to October 1914. As improved wound management and routine antitoxin use developed, the rate fell to 1.5 per 1,000 wounded. World War I patients, perhaps because the antitoxin produced a *forme fruste,* had a syndrome of "local tetanus" – not fatal, and usually confined to one extremity. U.S. forces, entering the war in 1917, had the advantage of the experience of their allies and thus had an incidence of only 0.16 per 1,000 wounded. Allergic reactions to horse serum occurred, more commonly after repeated doses of antitoxin.

Tetanus Toxoid

Although Arthur Silverstein (1989) credits Paul Ehrlich with the first discussion of toxoids, the practical use of formaldehyde to produce a toxoid (a *formalin-inactivated antitoxin*) was introduced for tetanus by Gaston Ramon in 1927 following the preliminary work by P. Descomby in 1924. As opposed to the passive immunity conferred by antitoxin, the toxoid produced an active immunity that would protect against tetanus. Also in 1927, Ramon along with Charles Zoeller tested the immunogenicity of the toxoid in humans, and later worked out the duration of immunity and the timing and effect of booster doses.

A fluid toxoid was in use because of its harmlessness and its efficacy (although it caused more local reactions than does the modern aluminum phosphate absorbed vaccine). This toxoid, a combined diphtheria–tetanus toxoids vaccine, was given to infants in parts of France in the late 1920s and, by regulation, to French soldiers in 1931.

Immunization with the much more epidemiologically important diphtheria toxoid began in the 1920s in parts of the United States and just before World War II in Britain. The absorbed tetanus toxoid was used by the armies of Britain, France, and Canada by 1939; the United States began its use in 1941. During World War II, the American army had 5 fatal tetanus cases (2 in nonimmunized patients) and 7 nonfatal cases (all in immunized patients) in over 500,000 wounded soldiers. The reaction rate to the immunization series of three doses was 21 per 100,000, none fatal.

After World War II, the routine use of a combined vaccine of diphtheria and tetanus toxoids (DT) was urged for childhood immunization. Soon the triple vaccine, with pertussis added (DPT), became legally required for school admission in the United States. Childhood immunization programs in Europe vary, but tend to be on similar schedules and under similar laws. Nonfatal anaphylactic reactions occur at a rate of 1 per 1.5 to 2 million doses. The benefit/risk ratio for tetanus immunization is thus extraordinarily good. A worldwide infant and child immunization campaign, coupled with a booster upon injury, would essentially eliminate the disease as a clinical entity.

Robert J. T. Joy

Bibliography

Adams, Francis. 1956. *The extant works of Aretaeus, the Cappadocian.* London.

Beaty, Harry N. 1987. Tetanus. In *Harrison's principles of internal medicine,* ed. Eugene Braunwald et al., 558–61. New York.

Behring, Emil. 1892a. *Das Tetanusheilserum und seine Anwendung auf tetanuskranke Menschen.* Leipzig.

1892b. Die Blutserumtherapie bei Diphtherie und Tetanus. *Zeitschrift für Hygiene und Infektionskrankheiten* 12: 1–9.

Behring, Emil, and Shibasaburo Kitasato. 1890. Ueber das Zustandekommen der Diphtherie-Immunität und der Tetanus-Immunität bei Thiereu. *Deutsche Medizinische Wochenschrift* 16: 1113–45.

Behrman, Richard E., and Victor C. Vaughn, III. 1983. *Nelson textbook of pediatrics.* 686–9. Philadelphia.

Boyd, John. 1958. Tetanus in two world wars. *Proceedings of the Royal Society of Medicine* 52:109–110.

Chamberlain, Weston P., and Frank W. Weed. 1926. *Medical department of the United States Army in the World War,* Vol. VI: *Sanitation.* Washington, D.C.

Courtois-Suffit, M., and R. Giroux. 1918. *The abnormal forms of tetanus.* London.

Davis, Bernard D., et al., eds. 1990. *Microbiology.* Philadelphia.

Dowling, Harry P. 1977. *Fighting infection.* Cambridge, Mass.

Haberman, E. 1978. Tetanus. In *Handbook of clinical neurology,* Vol. 33, Part 1, ed. P. J. Ninken and G. W. Bruyn, 491–547. New York.

Hill, Gale B., Suydam Osterhaut, and Hilda P. Willet. 1988. Clostridium. In *Zinsser microbiology,* ed. Wolfgang K. Jolik et al., 545–48. Norwalk, Conn.

Hippocrates. 1931. *Aphorisms V,* trans. and ed. W. H. S. Jones. Cambridge.

1973. *Epidemics V.* In *Greek medicine,* trans. E. D. Phillips, 70–1. London.

Kitasato, Shibasaboro. 1889. Ueber den tetanus bacillus. *Zeitschrift für Hygiene und Infektionskrankheiten* 7: 225–34.

Long, Arthur P. 1955. The Army immunization program. In *Personal health measures and immunization: Medical department of the U.S. Army in World War II,* ed. Ebbe C. Hoff, 271–341. Washington, D.C.

National Institute of Medicine. 1985. *Vaccine supply and innovation,* ed. Jay P. Sanford. Washington, D.C.

Nicolaier, Arthur. 1884. Ueber infectiösen Tetanus. *Deutsche Medizinische Wochenschrift* 10:842–44.

Osler, Sir William. 1892. *The principles and practice of medicine.* New York.

Parish, Henry J. 1965. *A history of immunization.* London.

Ramon, Gaston, and P. Descomby. 1927. L'Anatoxine tétanique et la prophylaxe du tétanos chez le cheval et les animaux domestiques. *Annales de l'Institut Pasteur* 41: 835–47.

Ramon, Gaston, and Charles Zoeller. 1927. L'Anatoxine tétanique et l'immunisation active de l'homme vis-à-vis du tétanos. *Annales de l'Institut Pasteur* 41: 803–33.

1933. Sur la valeur et la durée de l'immunité conférée par l'anatoxine tétanique dans la vaccination de l'homme contre le tétanos. *Compte Rendus des Séances de la Société de Biologie* 112: 347–50.

Rosenbach, D. 1886. Zur Aetiologie des Wundstarrkrampfes beim Menschen. *Archiv für Klinische Chirurgie* 306–17.

Silverstein, Arthur. 1989. *A history of immunology.* New York.

U.S. Department of Health and Human Services. Centers for Disease Control. 1990. Tetanus. *Morbidity and Mortality Weekly Report* 39(3):37–40.

Willems, J. S., and C. R. Saunders. 1981. Cost-effectiveness and cost-benefit analysis of vaccines. *Journal of Infectious Diseases* 144 (5): 486–93.

VIII.139
Tetanus, Neonatal

Neonatal tetanus is a form of tetanus, an acute toxic illness confined to the newborn. It is characterized as a neurological disease resulting in severe muscle spasms, which can persist for at least a week and commonly results in death. The agent is *Clostridium tetani,* which usually enters the bloodstream or motor nerves through an infected umbilicus. *C. tetani* produces two toxins, including tetanospasmin, the extremely potent neurotoxic component causing spasms. This toxin reaches the nervous system and eventually becomes fixed in the ganglion cells of the spinal cord or cranial nerves. Neonatal tetanus differs from numerous other bacterial diseases in that it is not transferred from person to person; instead, *C. tetani* is found in soil and is introduced into the body through an exposed area. The disease has been known by various names, including *tetani neonatoria, trismus nascentium, lockjaw,* and the "9-day illness" or "fits" because it normally occurs during the first 9 days of life. Its association with filth and rural conditions means that neonatal tetanus is still common in Third World nations and is one of their greatest public health problems. Mortality rates are high, even with modern treatment, and preventive measures are essential to avoid the disease.

Distribution and Incidence

Neonatal tetanus today is a problem confined primarily to Africa, Asia, and the West Indies, although before the twentieth century, it was global in occurrence. The bacillus, found in soil, water, intestines, and the feces of animals and humans (where it can survive for years if not exposed to sunlight) is ubiquitous. Although it was once common in rural areas like much of Ireland and the southern United States, this disease is virtually unknown anywhere in North America and western Europe today. Its incidence depends on soil conditions, type of agriculture and animal husbandry, level of economic development, available health services, and quality and type of obstetrical procedures.

The most important reasons for the decline of neonatal tetanus in the past century have been improved standards of living, urbanization, and an understanding of sepsis. Efforts are being made by the World Health Organization to educate women and birth attendants on preventive measures and to bring obstetrical procedures and concepts of cleanliness to areas where the disease still exists. Statistics have shown that higher standards of obstetrical hygiene significantly decrease the chance of infection.

Neonatal tetanus occurs when *C. tetani* enters the body as a result of a dirty dressing or poor care of the umbilicus. Where the disease is common, the umbilicus is often cut with an unclean instrument such as a knife, razor, sickle, or piece of sharpened rock or bamboo. Often the umbilicus stump is covered with ashes, charcoal powder, cow dung poultices, ghee, powdered pepper, snail saliva, turmeric, or other contaminated substances, and is dressed with leaves or dirty rags, or is left exposed. Rural tribes might blame evil spirits for the disease, but efforts to keep spirits away from a new baby often increase unhygienic postnatal procedures. Observers have found the disease to be more common among male newborns than among females, although this reported difference may reflect greater parental concern for the health of sons than daughters in some cultures. There is a question of whether race affects the frequency of neonatal tetanus, but unclean habits and living conditions of certain populations are probably much more important reasons why some people seem to suffer from it more than others. It seems to occur more often in warm months, perhaps because during these times babies are more exposed to soil and possible infection. All infants are susceptible unless they receive passive immunity from mothers who have been previously immunized.

Next to prematurity, neonatal tetanus is the most frequent cause of infant death in poor communities where traditional birth attendants serve mothers. Current estimates are that it kills some 10 percent of those being born alive in these areas. It has taken an enormous toll in developing nations and, during the first half of the nineteenth century, accounted for many infant slave deaths in the southern United States.

Mortality rates of infants developing the disease vary from 40 to 80 percent in Third World nations, although accurate statistics are difficult to obtain, since many infants are delivered outside a hospital or clinic, and numerous deaths are never registered. Current estimates are that 750,000 newborns die annually from neonatal tetanus. The mortality rate is inversely proportional to the age of the infant. It is often as high as 90 percent if it is contracted by the newborn during the first week after birth, and 50 percent if contracted during the second.

One of the paradoxes concerning neonatal tetanus, and a major problem in eradicating the disease, is that immunization is more difficult in areas where the illness is most common. Such populations are often suspicious of modern obstetrical procedures or are located far from clinical care. Yet the actual cost of preventing the disease is minimal and uncomplicated.

Epidemiology and Etiology

Because neonatal tetanus is usually caused by an infection of the umbilicus (though circumcision leads to a few cases), it does not occur as an epidemic. It strikes individuals rather than communities and, therefore, is difficult to study and does not generate the kind of public interest that epidemics do. Consequently, the disease has not yet received the attention it deserves.

C. tetani is an obligate anaerobe (a microorganism that can grow only in the complete absence of molecular oxygen), a gram-positive, nonencapsulated, slender, motile rod. It is introduced into an injured area as spores. The disease develops if the spores are converted to vegetative organisms, producing the potent toxin, tetanospasmin. The toxin reaches the nervous system via the bloodstream or by traveling along the axon cylinders of motor nerves, eventually becoming fixed in the spinal cord and cranial nerves. Reflex convulsive activity follows.

Clinical Manifestations

A baby with neonatal tetanus is beset with symptoms that are easy to recognize and usually appear 3 to 10 days after birth. Signs include difficulty with feeding and swallowing, generalized stiffness, spasms, and convulsions. The newborn can develop special problems relating to ventilation, hydration, and sedation. The first and most distinctive sign of neonatal tetanus is *trismus,* or a stiffening of the jaw, resembling a smile. The mouth will not open fully, resulting in a condition that has become known as *risus sardonicus.* Patients often have their legs and arms partially flexed, arms crossed over their abdomen, hands clenched, excessive flexion of the toes, stifled cry, and wrinkled face. Their body temperatures can reach 100° or higher. Sucking is impaired, thus making regular nursing impossible. That and general fussiness are the first symptoms most mothers notice. Respiratory complications commonly arise. Infants who die within 48 hours generally succumb to uncontrolled spasms or intense congestion of the liver, lungs, or brain. Newborns who die from the disease after 2 days generally die from bronchopneumonia. Other complications include aspiration pneumonia, acute gastroenteritis, and umbilical hernia.

Treatment

The best means of controlling the disease are those that prevent the organism from entering – namely ensuring sterile conditions for the birth. The umbilicus should be treated conservatively and cleaned with hydrogen peroxide; foreign objects should be removed, and thimerosal (Merthiolate) applied.

Most medical observers conclude that in order to lessen the incidence of neonatal tetanus in Third World nations, obstetrical procedures must be improved by teaching traditional birth attendants about sepsis. The transfer of maternal tetanus antibodies across the placenta has been found to be effective in conferring passive immunity to the neonate for several months, though it is better if the mother is immunized before, rather than during, pregnancy. Nevertheless, researchers have recently discovered that injections of absorbed tetanus toxoid given to pregnant women who have not been inoculated previously for tetanus (at least 2 injections spaced about 6 weeks apart) can successfully prevent infant infection.

Babies who do develop neonatal tetanus are often sedated with phenobarbital and chlorpromazine given intramuscularly, although diazepam is frequently used now because it works quickly. Antibiotics are also administered. The infant should be kept quiet, fed through a tube, and, if having difficulty breathing, given mouth-to-mouth resuscitation. The aim is first to control muscle spasms with sedatives and then to keep the baby breathing with a tracheotomy and a respirator if available. Medical attendants in hospitals or clinics commonly place the infant in intensive care, give an antitoxin, apply antibacterial therapy, and ensure airway clearance.

History and Geography

The term tetanus is from the Greek verb *tano,* meaning "to stretch." Hippocrates described three varieties of the infant disease. Aristotle noted infant convulsions that occurred before the seventh day. Galen first named the disease *trismus.* Moschion (Muscio), writing about three centuries later, claimed that it was caused by stagnant blood in the umbilical cord, as did André Levret and others some 1,500 years after Galen. Indeed, by the early nineteenth century, doctors were still attributing neonatal tetanus to this cause as well as a variety of others, including irritation within the intestinal canal, poverty, filth, poor diet, falls, impure atmosphere, rough handling, a vaginal disease, cold or sea air, costiveness, smoke from chimneys, and mismanagement by female midwives. In 1793 M. Bartram of South Carolina ascribed the disease to the umbilicus, and his theory generated much debate. Some physicians urged cleanliness and washing the umbilicus with a weak solution of silver nitrate and dressing the area with an ointment formed of lard and lead acetate.

But attention strayed again from the umbilicus. A study at the Dublin Lying-In Hospital in 1782 noted that of 17,650 infants born, 2,944 died within a fortnight from neonatal tetanus. The institution's impure atmosphere and poorly ventilated chambers were blamed for the high rate. In 1846 J. Marion Sims concluded that a depression of the occipital bone during birth caused the disease, and he urged his colleagues to observe bone formation closely in newborns.

In 1818 Abraham Colles, however, first noted the similarity between neonatal tetanus and tetanus and attributed its incidence to inflammation and ulceration of the umbilicus. He suggested that air be purified, that the umbilicus be dressed with spirits of turpentine, and that the baby be plunged into cold water. Efforts were made to bleed patients to remove the noxious influences and produce relaxation. During the nineteenth century, accounts demonstrate a

99 percent fatality for those who were affected. No disease of infancy was more fatal, and few parents saw any reason to call a doctor.

The bacterial theories of Louis Pasteur and Robert Koch have been important in eradicating the disease in the twentieth century. In 1884 Arthur Nicolaier found the bacillus in soil, and was able to produce the disease in animals. He found the same bacillus in human wounds. Shibasaburo Kitasato (1889) obtained the germ in pure culture. The tetanus toxoid was first used effectively during World War II. Immunization, along with the benefits of urbanization and industrialization, and a rise in the standard of living, have helped to eradicate the disease from developed nations.

Another preventive measure evolved when in 1923 C. T. Broeck and J. H. Bauer showed that tetanus antitoxin could cross the placenta. L. Nathan-Larrier, G. Ramon, and E. Grassett (1927) suggested that this could protect the newborn from tetanus by providing passive immunity. Later F. D. Schofield, G. R. Westbrook, and V. M. Tucker (1961), studying the disease in New Guinea, and K. W. Newell and others in Colombia (1964), proved that immunizing a pregnant woman with two or three injections of tetanus toxoid would decrease incidence of the disease. Unfortunately, it is difficult to provide such medical services to the people who need it most.

The World Health Organization continues to monitor the incidence of neonatal tetanus, to survey mortality rates of home and clinic deliveries, and to hold worldwide conferences to discuss means for improving the care of newborns. Its goal is to eradicate neonatal tetanus by the year 2000.

Sally McMillen

Bibliography

Bytchenko, B. 1964. Geographical distribution of tetanus in the world: A review of the problem. *Bulletin of the World Health Organization* 34: 71–104.

Hartigan, J. F. 1884. *The lock-jaw of infants (trismus nascentium) or nine day fits, crying spasms, etc.* New York.

Hirsch, August. 1883–6. *Handbook of geographical and historical pathology,* Vol. 3: 616–25. London.

International Conference on Tetanus. 1967. *Principles on tetanus: Proceedings of the International Conference on Tetanus,* ed. Leo Eckmann, sponsored by the Swiss Academy of Medical Sciences with support of the World Health Organization. Bern.

Islam, M. Shafiquel, et al. 1980. *Birth care practice and neonatal tetanus in a rural area of Bangladesh.* Dacca.

Nathan-Larrier, L., G. Ramon, and E. Giasset. 1927. Contribution à l'étude du passage des antégenes et des anticorps à travers le placenta. *Annales de l'Institut Pasteur* 41: 862–7.

Schofield, F. D., G. R. Westbrook, and V. M. Tucker. 1961. Neonatal tetanus in New Guinea. Effect of active immunization in pregnancy. *British Medical Journal* No. 5255: 785–9.

Senecal, J., 1978. Tetanus. In *Diseases of children in the subtropics and tropics,* 3d edition, ed. Errick R. Jelliffe and J. P. Stanfield, 696–704. London.

Varela, Luis R., et al. 1985. Tetanus antitoxin titers in women of childbearing age from nine diverse populations. *Journal of Infectious Diseases* 151: 850–3.

Watson, John McClaran. 1859. *A treatise on the history, etiology and prophylaxis of trismus nascentium,* 3d edition. Nashville, Tenn.

World Health Organization. Regional Office for the Eastern Mediterranean. 1982. *Prevention of neonatal tetanus: Report of a meeting: February 22–25, 1982.*

VIII.140
Tetany

Tetany is a symptom complex characterized by painful and prolonged contractions of the (generally smooth) muscles. These often appear as convulsions and are usually triggered by hypocalcemia. Adult varieties of the condition that result from calcium or magnesium deficiencies include maternal tetany, parathyroid tetany, osteomalacic tetany, and magnesium tetany. Alkalosis can also produce tetany. Examples include gastric tetany and hyperventilation tetany, following a lengthy period of forced inspiration and expiration. Another form of the disease — grass tetany caused by magnesium deficiency — is found in cattle. Despite these many forms, however, the disease occurs chiefly in infants (*neonatal* tetany) and young children (*infantile* tetany) in whom it is normally associated with rickets. It affects males far more than females and, in the absence of proper treatment, frequently proves deadly.

Distribution and Incidence

Because tetany has so often been confused with tetanus, very few data are available on the geographic distribution of the disease. It probably occurs worldwide in the temperate zones, with the highest frequency of neonatal tetany among bottle-fed, black, and prematurely born infants. An abundance of year-round sunshine and, hence, vitamin D may have the effect of reducing the incidence of infantile tetany in the tropics. The incidence of neonatal tetany recorded at New York Hospital between 1940 and 1958 was between 1 per 500 and 1 per 700 births.

Etiology

Tetany is a disease whose etiology is incompletely understood. It was originally associated with calcium deficiency and more recently with magnesium deficiency, although it can also be produced by alkalosis. The disease can follow the removal or incapacity of the parathyroid glands and can be a complication of alcoholism and a consequence of prolonged diarrhea and vomiting. Protein–energy malnutrition (PEM) may also precipitate the disease.

As a rule, neonatal tetany strikes during the first 14 days of life, and the spasms, twitches, rigid body, and turned-down corners of the mouth (carp mouth) that it produces are nearly identical to the symptoms of neonatal tetanus. Full-term newborn infants generally have significantly higher levels of serum calcium than do their mothers. However, these levels fall rapidly during the first 2 or 3 days of life, and perhaps the high phosphorus content of cow's milk places the bottle-fed baby at special risk from tetany because it impairs the alimentary absorption of calcium. Another contributing factor is, doubtless, parathyroid immaturity, whereas still another can be the poor nutritional status of the mother. Maternal tetany can develop in malnourished and multiparous mothers whose serum calcium falls with each succeeding pregnancy. Thus there is a positive correlation among frequent pregnancies, maternal dietary deficiency, and hypocalcemic (or hypomagnesemic) convulsions in infants.

At greatest risk are infants born prematurely, born with low birth weights, and born of multiparous or diabetic mothers as well as those who are products of a difficult labor. Males are much more susceptible than females, suggesting that an androgen may be involved. The peak incidence of neonatal tetany for full-term infants occurs about the sixth day of life, and the disease seldom appears before the third day. In those who are born prematurely or whose mothers suffered a difficult birth, the condition frequently develops within the first 24 hours.

Infantile tetany, the most common form of the disease, occurs chiefly between 6 months and 2 years of age and is the most prevalent between 4 and 8 months of age. As with neonatal tetany, males again predominate among the victims, and bottle-fed babies are at substantially greater risk than their breast-fed counterparts. In neonatal tetany, vitamin D has the para-

doxical effect of raising the incidence of hypocalcemia, perhaps because of its suppressive effect on the parathyroid glands. But a deficiency of vitamin D to promote the absorption of calcium is strongly implicated in the etiology of infantile tetany, and indeed, evidence of rickets is nearly always present. The disease is much more frequent during the winter months when sunlight and, thus, vitamin D are in shortest supply. Because of pigment, black children in temperate zones have in the past proved the most susceptible to rickets during these months. Doubtless they are also more susceptible to infantile tetany than are their white counterparts.

Clinical Manifestations and Pathology

Tetany, characterized by neuromuscular irritability, is often signaled by a tingling sensation in the fingers, and it may become impossible to open and close the hands. Carpopedal spasms (of the wrist and ankle joints) are common, as are stiffness, pain, and spasms in other muscles. Vomiting is also common. Infants in particular may develop a rigid face, "carpmouth," and body – all symptoms that mimic neonatal tetanus. Mental symptoms include hallucinations, dullness, and distortion. Cardiac spasms may develop, and coma, along with respiratory failure (following asthma-like attacks), leads to death. Mortality from neonatal tetany is low today in developed countries because of treatment with calcium. However, in the 1950s and previously, it has been suggested that over half of the victims died. Necropsy findings of hyperplasia of parathyroid glands are confined to children fed cow's milk.

History

It is probable that tetany due to mineral (and perhaps vitamin D) deficiencies has always plagued humankind to some limited extent. In children the convulsions of tetany in the past were often attributed to "teething." But it was not until the beginning of the nineteenth century, with increased bottle feeding, that a syndrome resembling tetany was first described in England (Clarke 1815). François Rémy Lucien Corvisart gave the syndrome its name in 1852, and in 1854 Armand Trousseau described tetany in lactating women. In 1881 H. Weiss observed that tetany appeared on occasion in patients whose goiter had been removed, and in the 1880s the disease appeared in near-epidemic proportions in Vienna. Yet August Hirsch (1883–6) had nothing to say about tetany in his massive *Handbook*.

In 1913 E. Kehrer penned a description of neonatal tetany and suggested the administration of calcium salts in its treatment, but according to Paul D. Saville and Norman Kretschmer (1960), the first satisfactory chemical study was the work of J. Howland and W. M. Marriott (1918). It was this work that distinguished rickets from tetany and reported a substantial reduction of serum calcium in infantile tetany patients. It also reported that the administration of calcium salts would relieve the symptoms.

Alfred Hess (1929) pointed out that in the United States the peak incidence of tetany was in the early spring, that cases seldom developed in the summer, and that the black young were "markedly susceptible." This suggests a role for vitamin D, given its shortage during the winter months in temperate climates and the difficulties blacks have had historically with vitamin D while wintering in those climates.

During the late 1950s and early 1960s, much attention was focused on the disease, and Arthur Bloomfield (1959) and Saville and Kretschmer (1960) surveyed the literature on what had been an important killer of the young. Subsequently, however, as more has been learned about mineral metabolism and as the disease has gone into decline, so has the name "tetany." Although it is still in the literature, the tendency since the 1960s has been to write of *hypocalcemic* and *hypomagnesemic*, rather than tetanic, convulsions.

Kenneth F. Kiple

Bibliography

Beaton, G. H. 1976. Some other nutritional deficiencies. In *Nutrition in preventive medicine*, ed. G. H. Beaton and J. M. Bengoa. Geneva.

Bloomfield, Arthur. 1959. A bibliography of internal medicine: Tetany. *Stanford Medical Bulletin* 17: 1–12.

Clarke, John. 1815. *Commentaries on some of the most important diseases of children*. London.

Clarke, Patrick, and I. J. Carré. 1967. Hypocalcemic, hypermagnesemic convulsions. *Journal of Pediatrics* 5: 806–9.

Cockburn, F., et al. 1973. Neonatal convulsions associated with primary disturbance. *Archives of Diseases in Childhood* 48: 99–108.

Hess, Alfred. 1929. *Rickets including osteomalacia and tetany*. Philadelphia.

Hirsch, August. 1883–6. *Handbook of geographical and historical pathology*, 3 vols., trans. Charles Creighton. London.

Howland, J., and W. McKim Marriott. 1918. Observations upon the calcium content of the blood in infantile tetany and upon the effect of treatment by calcium. *Quarterly Journal of Medicine* 2: 289–93.

Keen, J. H. 1969. Significance of hypocalcemia in neonatal convulsions. *Archives of Diseases in Childhood* 44: 356–61.

Purvis, R. J., et al. 1973. Enamel hypoplasia of the teeth associated with neonatal tetany: A manifestation of maternal vitamin D deficiency. *Lancet* ii: 811–14.

Saville, Paul D., and Norman Kretschmer. 1960. Neonatal tetany: A report of 125 cases and review of the literature. *Biology of the Neonate* 2: 1–18.

Tsang, Reginald, and William Oh. 1970. Neonatal hypocalcemia in low birth weight infants. *Pediatrics* 45: 773–81.

VIII.141
Toxoplasmosis

The agent of this disease, the sporozoan protozoan *Toxoplasma gondii*, is a common parasite of many species of birds and mammals. The organism was first seen in 1908 in the tissues of a Tunisian rodent, the gundi, and fully described in 1909. Human disease was first described in 1923 and congenital neonatal disease was reported in 1939, but the complex life cycle of the parasite was not elucidated until 1970. Serologic tests show that humans around the world harbor *T. gondii*, but because almost all infections are asymptomatic, very few have the disease. The protozoan is an intracellular parasite of a variety of tissues in warm-blooded vertebrates. It multiplies by binary fission in a host cell, eventually rupturing the cell and releasing parasites to attack other cells. Sexual reproduction can take place only in cats and other felines. These definitive hosts release oöcysts, the stage infective for herbivores, in their feces. Asexual intracellular replication takes place in the herbivore, and, if the tissues containing *T. gondii* are eaten by a carnivore, asexual reproduction may also occur in their tissues. Humans can become infected by eating poorly cooked or raw meat or poultry, by ingesting oöcytes from the feces of cats, or congenitally.

Clinical Manifestations

Human infections are usually inapparent, although they sometimes can lie dormant for years and flare up in weakened or immunodeficient hosts. Most cases in otherwise healthy people are mild and cause vague symptoms like fever and weakness. The disease often mimics infectious mononucleosis. Chronic cases can cause diarrhea, headache, and eye damage. Rare fulminating infections cause severe symptoms and may affect the brain. Uterine transmission of toxoplasmosis often has grave consequences. Five to 15 percent of cases result in fetal death, and 18 to 23 percent result in moderate to severe brain and eye abnormalities. Some apparently normal infants later develop severe retinal disease or mental retardation. In persons whose immune systems have been suppressed by therapy or disease, as, for example, organ transplant recipients or acquired immune deficiency syndrome victims, old or latent infections can become activated. Cerebral toxoplasmosis is a fairly common and very serious complication of AIDS.

Distribution and Incidence

The highest known prevalence rate, 93 percent, was found in Parisian women who enjoy eating raw beef. By age 25, roughly 70 percent of El Salvadorians and 30 percent of white residents of New York City harbor antibodies against *Toxoplasma*. It is estimated that about 3,000 babies are born each year in the United States with congenitally acquired toxoplasmosis.

Diagnosis, Treatment, and Prevention

The diagnosis of toxoplasmosis is complicated by its wide range of symptoms and depends on serologic tests. Therapy is often difficult, especially in weak patients, and is ineffective for fetuses. Prevention is by thorough cooking of meat and poultry and by careful handling of cat feces. Pregnant women should not empty cat litter boxes, and children's sandboxes should be covered when not in use.

K. David Patterson

Bibliography

Frenkel, J. K. 1984. Toxoplasmosis. In *Microbiology,* ed. L. Leive and D. Schlessinger, 212–17. Washington, D.C.

Kean, B. H. 1972. Clinical toxoplasmosis – 50 years. *Transactions of the Royal Society of Tropical Medicine and Hygiene* 66: 549–67.

Kean, B. H., Kenneth E. Mott, and Adair J. Russell, eds. 1978. *Tropical medicine and parasitology: Classic investigations,* Vol. I, 271–84. Ithaca and London.

Kennou, M. F. 1986. Propos sur *Toxoplasma gondii* (Nicolle et Manceaux, 1909). *Archives de l'Institut Pasteur de Tunis* 63: 123–31.

Wong, B., et al. 1984. Central-nervous-system toxoplasmosis in homosexual men and parental drug abusers. *Annals of Internal Medicine* 100: 36–42.

VIII.142
Trematode Infections

Trematodes or flukes are flatworms of the class Trematoda of the phylum Platyhelminthes. They have complex life cycles that usually involve a snail as an intermediate host. The definitive host that harbors the adult worms, generally a mammal, acquires the parasite by ingesting an encysted form in a second intermediate host or on vegetation. Many species can infect human beings, but most of these are normally resident in other mammals, and humans are just accidental hosts.

K. David Patterson

Bibliography

Goldsmid, J. M. 1975. Ecological and cultural aspects of human trematodiasis (excluding schistosomiasis) in Africa. *Central African Journal of Medicine* 21: 49–53.

Healy, G. R. 1970. Trematodes transmitted to man by fish, frogs, and crustacea. *Journal of Wildlife Diseases* 6: 255–61.

VIII.143
Trench Fever

Trench fever is a nonfatal, acute disease first described in 1915 during World War I, when it afflicted at least 1 million soldiers on both sides of the conflict. Although initially known by several names, including Polish fever, Meuse fever, and Russian intermittent fever, the descriptive appellation *trench fever* given to the disease by the British armies in northern France has endured.

Clinical Manifestations

After an incubation period lasting between 14 and 30 days, trench fever elicits typical typhuslike symptoms: sudden onset, chills, headache, dizziness, and body aches and pains. Two of its descriptive names, shin fever and shank fever, recall its characteristic leg pains. Although also known as 5-day fever or quintan fever, the disease usually disables its victims for 5 or 6 weeks. About half of those afflicted suffer only one bout of fever, but the other half may have a number of relapses. Although trench fever is never fatal, it caused a greater loss of manpower during World War I than did any other malady except influenza.

History and Geography

Also known as Wolhynian fever and His–Werner disease, trench fever occurred in Russia, England, France, the Middle East, Italy, Germany, and Austria. It is carried by body lice; hence it follows the pattern of its more deadly relative, epidemic typhus fever, in plaguing armies where hygiene is substandard. The disease became quiescent after World War I ended, but it appeared again on the eastern European front during the second global conflict.

Etiology

The etiological agent of this disease, *Rochalima quintana,* was first studied during World War I by a commission of the American Red Cross Medical Research Committee. Their report found that the organism, unlike other rickettsiae, would pass through porcelain filters. Later, in another departure from typical rickettsial characteristics, the trench fever organism was cultivated on lifeless, cell-free, blood agar media. Because of these and other differences, in 1961 it was removed from the genus *Rickettsia* and placed in a separate genus, *Rochalima.*

Victoria A. Harden

Bibliography

American Red Cross. Medical Research Committee. 1918. *Trench fever: Report of Commission, Medical Research Committee, American Red Cross,* ed. Richard P. Strong. Oxford.

Bruce, David. 1921. Trench fever: Final report of the War Office Trench Fever Investigation Committee. *Journal of Hygiene* 20: 258–88.

Liu, Wei-tung. 1984. Trench fever: A resumé of literature and a note on some obscure phases of the disease. *Chinese Medical Journal* 97: 179–90.

Swift, H. F. 1920. Trench fever. *Archives of Internal Medicine* 26: 76–98.

Warren, Joel. 1965. Trench fever Rickettsia. In *Viral and rickettsial infections of man,* 4th edition, ed. Frank L. Horsfall, Jr., and Igor Tamm. Philadelphia.

VIII.144
The Treponematoses

The members of genus *Treponeme,* family Treponemataceae, and order Spirochaetales consist of *Treponeme pallidum* (first described in 1905), which causes syphilis and nonvenereal syphilis; *Treponeme pertenue* (first described in 1905), which is responsible for yaws; and *Treponeme carateum* (first described in 1938), which produces pinta. Or at least this is the way that most medical texts would have it. It may be, however, that the three pathogens in question are actually only one, for although they produce different pathological processes, the pathogens themselves are virtually indistinguishable under the microscope, and the diseases they cause respond to the same treatment. The origin of this infamous family and the relationship of its members to one another have been topics of considerable and very interesting debate since the 1970s, largely because such questions bear directly on the centuries-old debate of whether the Americans bestowed syphilis on the rest of the world.

Many agree that the treponemes probably evolved from microorganisms that originally parasitized decaying organic matter, and which later – perhaps hundreds of thousands of years ago – came to specialize in human hosts, but probably only after first parasitizing another animal host (Wood 1978). There is little disagreement that the first treponemes to parasitize humans did so by entering their bodies through traumatized skin and were subsequently passed on to other humans by skin-to-skin transmission. Real disagreement begins, however, over questions of where the first humans were infected, and the identity of the disease they were infected with.

E. H. Hudson (1958) has argued that the first of the treponemal infections was *yaws* and that it probably emerged in Central Africa where it quickly became endemic. Then, about 100,000 years ago, it accompanied migrating humans from Africa to spread around the globe. C. J. Hackett (1963), on the other hand, portrays *pinta* as the first treponemal disease, arising only about 20,000 years ago in Eurasia to spread throughout the rest of the world.

At issue here are two very different concepts of treponematosis. Hudson feels that the distinctions among the treponematoses – *T. pallidum, T. pertenue,* and *T. carateum* – are artificial. In this so-called *unitarian view,* all of the human treponematoses actually constitute a single disease, but one that has different manifestations depending on climate and culture. Hackett, however, argues that the distinctions are very real – the consequence of *mutations* of the treponemal strains themselves. T. A. Cockburn (1961) has shown along Darwinian lines how human geographic isolation, especially after the Ice Age, could have led to treponemal speciation. Similarly, Don Brothwell (1981) has also speculated on the evolution of the treponemes and suggests that there may have been six lines of *Treponema,* which have undergone separate microevolutionary development to reach the four in existence today.

Historically, yaws has been prevalent in the hot and moist regions of Asia and Africa where little in the way of clothing is worn, facilitating transmission from skin to skin. By contrast, nonvenereal syphilis has flourished in hot but dry regions, where it spreads mostly from mouth to mouth. Both of these illnesses are normally rural, fostered by unsanitary living conditions, and are usually endemic and thus diseases of children. Venereal syphilis, on the other hand, is a disease of adults, seems to have first become manifest in the urban areas of temperate climates, and has been portrayed by Hudson, Cockburn, and others as a consequence of improving hygienic conditions. Put succinctly, in colder climates where people were better clothed and washed, the treponemas were denied their established patterns of skin-to-skin or mouth-to-mouth transmission among youngsters. As a consequence, persons reached sexual maturity without exposure to them, and sexual intercourse became one more means of transmission for the treponemas, particularly in urban areas where sexual promiscuity and prostitution were common (Hudson 1958).

The historical gradation of treponemal infections from the yaws of warm, moist Africa south of the Sahara, through the nonvenereal syphilis in hot and dry North Africa, to venereal syphilis in a cooler and urbanizing Europe, has constituted a compelling geographic model for both Hudson and Hackett and their followers. They point out, nonetheless, that yaws, and both nonvenereal and venereal syphilis, may all be present in a relatively small geographic area, with yaws and perhaps nonvenereal syphilis dominating the rural area surrounding a city, which harbors syphilis. Moreover, both views hold that venereal syphilis was present in Eurasia long before the voyages of Columbus, but its symptoms were lumped with those other disfiguring illnesses including yaws and nonvenereal syphilis, usually under the rubric of leprosy.

Needless to say, this challenge to the long-held notion that syphilis was introduced from the Ameri-

cas has encountered some heavy opposition (Dennie 1962; Crosby 1969, 1972). Yet we know that pinta was present in the Americas when Columbus arrived, and both the unitarian and the mutation hypotheses accommodate the notion that other treponemal diseases could have developed there as well. In fact, Brothwell (1981) has argued that Asia was probably the cradle for the evolution of the treponemes pathogenic to humans, and that they diffused from there to the Americas via migrants across the Bering Straits landbridge to the New World, as well as throughout the Old World. In other words, it is conceivable that all the pathogenic human treponemes were present in each of the major land masses of the globe by 1492. Yet Hudson (1964) believes that endemic syphilis and yaws reached the Americas via the slave trade and there evolved into syphilis; Francisco Guerra (1978) holds that all four treponemal infections were present in the New World, but only endemic and venereal syphilis resided in the Old World until yaws, not syphilis, was imported from the Americas; whereas Corinne Wood (1978), after reviewing the arguments and evidence, finds the Columbian hypothesis for the origin of syphilis the most plausible.

Much of the evidence upon which this last conclusion is based is skeletal in nature, embracing both negative and positive findings. Most of the negative findings have to do with the Old World, where it turns out that those buried in leper cemeteries would seem to have been mostly lepers and not syphilitics, as those who placed syphilis in Europe prior to the Columbian voyages felt would be the case. Moreover, there is (at least thus far) a dearth of evidence in Old World skeletal remains that would testify to the presence of syphilis in Eurasia prior to 1493, although the presence of yaws and endemic syphilis has been occasionally reported.

In the New World, by contrast, there is a great deal of positive skeletal evidence of pre-Columbian treponematosis. This evidence is not, however, of pinta (spotted), which causes changes in pigmentation but does not affect the bones as the other treponemal illnesses are capable of doing. Thus yaws, endemic nonvenereal syphilis, and syphilis are all possibilities for the American infection in question, as is perhaps some other treponemal infection now extinct. Of these candidates, however, venereal syphilis seems the least promising, because of an apparent absence of congenital syphilis in the skeletal material.

Brenda Baker and George Armelagos (1988), in providing us with the latest extensive review of the literature on the treponematoses, have also provided us with the latest hypothesis as to their origin and antiquity. Given the scarcity of skeletal evidence of treponematosis in the Old World, and its abundance in the Americas, they suggest that treponematosis is a relatively new disease that arose in the Americas as a nonvenereal infection that spread by "casual contact." However, after the men of the Columbian voyages contracted the illness and carried it back to Europe, the circumstances of urban environments transformed the nonvenereal American disease into the venereal syphilis that raged across Europe and much of the globe for the next century or so before subsiding into the considerably more tame disease we know today.

Clearly, then, despite decades of debate about the nature of the treponematoses, there is still no agreement on their place or places of origin, nor on their antiquity. It does seem to be generally accepted that a transition in the method of transmission of the treponemal syndromes can be, and was, rather swiftly brought on by changing environmental and social circumstances, and thus, that syphilis is the youngest of these syndromes. But like so many other surveys of the treponematoses this one, too, must end with the hope that more evidence will be uncovered in the future to shed light on the many continuing paradoxes posed by this fascinating family, which may or may not consist of a single member.

Kenneth F. Kiple

Bibliography

Baker, Brenda J., and George J. Armelagos. 1988. The origin and antiquity of syphilis: Paleopathological diagnosis and interpretation. *Current Anthropology* 29: 703–37.

Brothwell, Don. 1981. Microevolutionary change in human pathogenic treponemes: An alternative hypothesis. *International Journal of Systematic Bacteriology* 31: 82–7.

Cockburn, Thomas A. 1961. The origin of the treponematoses. *Bulletin of the World Health Organization* 24: 221–8.

Crosby, Alfred W., Jr. 1969. The early history of syphilis: A reappraisal. *American Anthropologist* 71: 218–27.

1972. *The Columbian exchange: Biological and cultural consequences of 1492*. Westport, Conn.

Dennie, Charles C. 1962. *A history of syphilis*. Springfield, Ill.

Guerra, Francisco. 1978. The dispute over syphilis: Europe versus America. *Clio Medica* 13: 39–61.

Hackett, C. J. 1963. On the origin of the human treponematoses. *Bulletin of the World Health Organization* 29: 7–41.

Hudson, Ellis Herndon. 1958. *Non-venereal syphilis*. Edinburgh.

1964. Treponematosis and African slavery. *British Journal of Venereal Diseases* 40: 43–52.

Wood, Corinne Shear. 1978. Syphilis in anthropological perspective. *Social Science and Medicine* 12: 47–55.

VIII.145
Trichinosis

Trichinosis, also known as trichinellosis, trichiniasis, or trichinelliasis, is a disease of humans and of other mammals infected with the nematode worm *Trichinella spiralis*. The pathological changes and the symptomatology of *Trichinella* infection are manifestations of three successive stages in the life history of the worm: (1) penetration of adult female worms into the intestinal mucosa, (2) migration of juvenile worms, and (3) penetration of juvenile worms and subsequent encystment in muscle cells.

Distribution and Incidence

Although trichinosis occurs worldwide, in humans it is found principally in the United States, Canada, and eastern Europe. It is also well known in Mexico, parts of South America, Africa, southern Asia, and the Middle East. People acquire trichinae by ingesting uncooked or poorly cooked meat, especially pork. Home-made sausages have caused many recent outbreaks in the United States. Hence, the prevalence of trichinosis is less in the tropics and subtropics, where less meat is consumed. Trichinosis does not occur among Hindus, Jews, and Moslems, for whom there are religious bans on eating pork.

Although the prevalence of trichinosis in human populations is low (probably 2.2 percent or less in the United States, based on autopsy surveys), epidemic outbreaks are not infrequent. Incidence of infection is likely to be higher than suspected because of the vagueness of symptoms, which usually suggest other conditions.

Epidemiology and Etiology

T. spiralis is unusual in that a single individual animal serves as both intermediate and definitive (final) host, with the juvenile and adult worms located in different organs.

Humans acquire infections by ingesting infective juveniles, which are encysted in striated muscle of swine or other animals. The worms are freed from their cysts by gastric juices and invade the intestinal mucosa where they copulate. Males die shortly after copulation, and the females migrate through the intestinal epithelium, each giving birth to as many as 1,500 live young over a period of 4 to 16 weeks. Spent females eventually die and are absorbed by the host.

Young juveniles are carried throughout the body via the arterial system. They finally reach skeletal muscle, where they penetrate individual fibers and grow in a spiral fashion, eventually becoming encysted by a blunt, ellipsoidal capsule of host origin. The time required for complete encapsulation is about 3 months. Calcification of the capsule begins as early as 6 months and may take up to 2 years to complete. Eventually the worms also become calcified, although they may remain viable for several years prior to calcification.

Not all striated muscles are parasitized to the same degree. Among muscles most heavily affected are the diaphragm, tongue, and masticatory muscles, intercostals, and muscles of the arms and legs.

Most mammals are susceptible to *Trichinella* infections. Infections are maintained in nature by flesh-eating animals. Humans are regarded as accidental hosts because, barring cannibalism or the consumption of cadavers by other mammals, the infection reaches a dead end. Most human infections result from eating pork or pork products, but numerous fatal cases of trichinosis have been recorded from among those who eat undercooked or underfrozen bear or walrus meat.

Cooking meat is of importance in preventing trichinosis. Pork should be cooked until the pink color turns to gray. Alternatively, freezing of meat at −15°C for 20 days will destroy all parasites.

Immunology

Trichinella infection results in the development of serum antibodies, including IgE, and cell-mediated immune responses. Resistance to reinfection has been demonstrated in experimental animals by an allergic IgE-mediated inflammatory response that expels adult worms from the intestine. Eosinophils may also play a role in immunity to *Trichinella* because experimental depletion of eosinophils has been shown to result in increased numbers of larvae recovered from infected animals.

Clinical Manifestations and Pathology

The first symptoms of *Trichinella* infection occur 1 to 2 days after ingestion of infected meat. Initial symptoms are vague and often lead to misdiagnosis, if apparent at all. As a host reacts to the waste products produced by the worms, lesions develop and enteric bacteria are introduced into them. Nausea, toxic diarrhea, sweating, and vomiting may occur, mimicking an acute food-poisoning syndrome. Respiratory symptoms may follow between the second and sixth day, and last for 6 days. In addition, there may be red blotches erupting on the skin.

During the period of migration of juveniles, there are muscular pains as inflammatory processes develop in the muscles. Difficulty in breathing, chewing, and swallowing develops. Edema around the face and hands is due to endovascular and perivascular inflammation. Edema around the eyes is a common early sign. Lymph nodes become enlarged and tender. Enlarged parotid or sublingual glands often lead to misdiagnosis of mumps. Eosinophilia may be present but often does not occur, even in the most extreme cases. Myocarditis, peritonitis, pneumonia, encephalitis, pleurisy, meningitis, and eye damage may result from migrating juveniles. Death from myocarditis may occur at this stage.

Penetration by juveniles into muscle cells, and subsequent encystment, may result in toxic edema, cachexia, or dehydration. Blood pressure drops rapidly, and the patient may display nervous disorders such as defects of vision, altered or lost reflexes, hallucinations, delirium, and encephalitis. Severe cases can result in death 4 to 6 weeks after infection. Death may occur as a result of toxemia, myocarditis, nephritis, peritonitis, or other complications.

It is important to recognize that most cases of trichinosis go undetected and that in milder cases no special series of symptoms may be present. Accurate diagnosis is made by employing muscle biopsy, pressing the tissue between glass slides, and examining it under a microscope. Alternatively, tissue may be digested in artificial gastric juice and the sediment examined for freed juveniles. *Xenodiagnosis* (feeding biopsy material to laboratory rats) is a useful diagnostic technique. *Immunodiagnostic* techniques may be useful when carried out by competent workers.

There is no thoroughly effective treatment for trichinosis. Thiabendazole has been somewhat effective, but serious side effects are known to occur. Steroids are given if myocarditis develops or if there are central nervous system complications. However, because corticosteroid therapy will inhibit the inflammatory reaction, an increase in larvae in the muscles will accompany this treatment.

History and Geography

Antiquity

Although knowledge of the parasite causing trichinosis was first obtained in 1835, knowledge of the disease dates back to antiquity. Dietary laws prohibiting the eating of swine are thought to have been engendered by the observation that human illness sometimes followed the eating of such flesh. In 1940 Asa Chandler stated: "There can be little doubt that this worm, with the pork tapeworm as an accomplice, was responsible for the old Jewish law against the eating of pork." Historians have surmised that Muhammad recognized that certain epidemics could have been caused by ingestion of pork, and thus followed the example of Moses in prohibiting pork consumption.

Nineteenth Century

The first person to actually see trichinae was James Paget, a 21-year-old freshman medical student at St. Bartholomew's Hospital in London. In 1835 Paget noted a curious pathological condition in the cadaver of a middle-aged man that was brought in for study. The cadaver had "spicules of bone" in the muscles. They were so hard that they blunted the scalpel. Others had seen these gritty particles previously, but it was Paget who had natural history training and the intense desire to observe new things, and thus he was the first to note that the particle was a worm in its capsule. Paget did not have a microscope, but eventually secured the use of one from the botanist Robert Brown of the British Museum. Specimens of the worm were taken to Richard Owen, who was to become England's greatest comparative anatomist. Owen subsequently presented a paper on the worm at the Zoological Society, and gave the parasite its name. Owen's presentation at the Zoological Society occurred just 18 days after Paget's announcement.

Although Paget's discovery was overshadowed by the detailed and complete memoir by Owen, Paget retained his intense spirit of scientific inquiry and published many papers on medical subjects. Later, he became Sir James Paget, one of the most distinguished surgeons of his time.

Trichinae in animals other than humans were first noted in 1846. Joseph Leidy, a professor of anatomy working in Philadelphia, found the worms in the extensor muscles of the thigh of a hog. Leidy had previously seen trichinae in human bodies in a dissection room, and he could perceive no distinction in the worms from the two hosts. In 1850 Ernst Herbst, working in Göttingen, established that trichinae from meat eaten by an animal may invade its muscles. Herbst infected a badger with trichinous dog meat and then fed the infected badger meat to three dogs. All three dogs were infected at autopsy.

The significance of Herbst's experiments, as well as Leidy's observations, was not appreciated at the time because leading authorities believed that the trichinae from nonhumans were of a different species from those of humans. Herbst himself believed that trichinae were actually the larvae of filarial worms.

The problem of determining the life cycle of trichinae soon caught the attention of two of the leading researchers of their time, Rudolf Virchow of Berlin and Rudolph Leuckart of Giessen. Leuckart, in 1850, observed that the female intestinal trichinae are viviparous, but he believed that the trichinae were derived from the intestinal nematode *Trichuris trichiura*. Virchow, in 1859, fed encapsulated trichinae from a human to a dog, where the worms reached sexual maturity. Virchow refuted Leuckart's claim that the trichinae were identical with *Trichuris*.

Verification of the life cycle of trichinae and the discovery of the pathogenesis of trichinous infections represent monumental contributions by Friedrich Albert Zenker in 1860. Zenker performed an autopsy on a 20-year-old servant girl in Dresden whose illness had been diagnosed as typhoid fever. He examined muscle fibers from the arm and was startled to see "dozens of trichinae, lying free in the muscle, either coiled or extended, and exhibiting the plainest signs of life." Other skeletal muscles examined were likewise inhabited by the worms. Upon examining intestinal contents, Zenker saw sexually mature worms. It was apparent to him that the parasite underwent its entire life cycle in one and the same host.

Zenker subsequently investigated the household in which the servant girl worked, and found the parasite in sausage that had been prepared just prior to the onset of the girl's illness. Furthermore, other members of the household who had eaten the meat had become seriously ill with the same symptoms as shown by the unfortunate servant girl.

Following the establishment of the details of the life cycle and pathogenesis of trichinae, several outbreaks of infection were recorded. Some 140 epidemics of trichinosis were noted in Europe between 1860 and 1877, in which 3,044 persons were known to have fallen ill and 231 to have died.

Beginning in 1863, examination of pork for

trichinae was practiced in parts of Germany, and in 1879 a law was enacted in Prussia whereby all pork was required to be examined for trichinae. In this same year, ordinances were passed in Italy, Austria, and Hungary forbidding the importation of swine or pork products from the United States, and other countries followed with similar bans. Subsequently, the U.S. Department of Agriculture, although not providing for specific examination for trichinae, did specify methods for the processing of pork products that are customarily eaten raw. Such procedures will destroy the infectivity of any trichinae present. Public education, and heat treatment of the garbage used to feed hogs, have also helped to reduce the incidence of the disease in North America and Europe.

Donald E. Gilbertson

Bibliography

Blumer, G. 1939. Some remarks on the early history of trichinosis (1822–1866). *Yale Journal of Biology and Medicine* 11: 581–8.

Brown, Harold W., and Franklin A. Neva. 1983. *Basic clinical parasitology.* Norwalk, Conn.

Campbell, W. C., ed. 1982. *Trichinellosis.* New York.

Chandler, Asa C. 1940. *Introduction to parasitology.* New York.

Gould, S. E., ed. 1970. *Trichinosis in man and animals.* Springfield, Ill.

Reinhard, Edward G. 1958. Landmarks of parasitology. II. Demonstration of the life cycle and pathogenicity of the spiral threadworm. *Experimental Parasitology* 7: 108–23.

VIII.146
Trichuriasis

The nematode *Trichuris trichiura,* the whipworm or threadworm, is a very common parasite that occurs worldwide but is most abundant in warm, moist climates. It still exists in the southern United States, but it has declined there and in other developed countries in recent decades with improved sanitation; it is now found mostly in poor tropical countries. Adult worms range up to 2 inches in length, so whipworms were probably seen by ancient observers, but they were first clearly recognized by an early Portuguese writer on tropical medicine, Aleixo de Abreu, in 1623. Several scientists described the species in the mid-eighteenth century. Archaeological evidence shows that the worm infected people in the Americas prior to the voyage of Columbus.

Trichuris attaches itself to the wall of the large intestine and passes its eggs in the host's feces. Eggs require 10 to 14 days in the soil to mature or "embryonate." Embryonation is most successful in warm, moist soils in shady places. Like *Ascaris,* which has a similar range, *Trichuris* infects people who have swallowed embryonated eggs in soil or in contaminated food or water. Unlke *Ascaris,* however, the whipworm does not require an elaborate period of larval migration in the host. The eggs hatch in the small intestine, where the larvae spend some time before moving to their home in the cecum.

Trichuriasis rarely causes much harm unless there is a heavy worm load. Severe infections can cause abdominal discomfort, bloody or mucoid diarrhea, weight loss, weakness, and anemia. Masses of worms can cause appendicitis, and prolapse of the rectum can occur in children harboring large numbers of worms. Symptoms, including anemia, tend to be more severe in children. Diagnosis of trichuriasis is by discovery of eggs in the feces. Drug treatment is effective. Prevention of whipworm infection, like prevention of ascariasis, which often coexists with trichuriasis, is by improved sanitation, personal hygiene, and composting of night soil before it is used for fertilizer.

K. David Patterson

Bibliography

Gilman, R. H., et al. 1983. The adverse effects of heavy *Trichuris* infection. *Transactions of the Royal Society of Tropical Medicine and Hygiene* 77: 432–38.

Kean, B. H., Kenneth E. Mott, and Adair J. Russell, eds.

1978. *Tropical medicine and parasitology: Classic investigations,* Vol. II, 360–2. Ithaca and London.

Stoll, N. R. 1947. This wormy world. *Journal of Parasitology* 33: 1–18.

VIII.147
Tuberculosis

Tuberculosis is an infectious disease most commonly associated with the lungs, but which can affect almost any tissue or organ in the body. Its primary cause is an acid-fast bacillus, *Mycobacterium tuberculosis.* It is usually a chronic disease that lingers for months and sometimes years, but acute forms, which most commonly strike infants and young children, can prove fatal in a matter of weeks or days. One acute form is called *miliary* tuberculosis because of the small, grainlike tubercles it creates simultaneously in almost every organ of the body. From ancient times, tuberculosis was endemic in most populations of Eurasia, North Africa, and possibly the Americas, affecting relatively small numbers of people and maintaining low prevalence rates. But with the rise of urban and industrial development between the eighteenth and twentieth centuries, it became epidemic in much of Europe, North and South America, and Africa and Asia. In some places during this time most people were exposed to this disease, and its prevalence rates approached 100 percent of the population. Tuberculosis killed millions of people, placing it, despite its chronicity, on a historical par with the great global epidemic diseases of bubonic plague, cholera, measles, smallpox, typhoid, typhus, and the like. Until 1944, there was no specific drug therapy for it. In that year, researchers discovered streptomycin, which proved effective in inhibiting the disease. Two more drugs, *para*-aminosalicylic acid (PAS) and isoniazid (isonicotinic acid hydrazide, or INH), discovered in 1946 and 1952, respectively, provided an extremely effective treatment when used in combination with streptomycin. Together, they made all but the most advanced cases curable. Tuberculosis is no longer epidemic, but it still afflicts people worldwide, from the most highly industrialized to developing countries; the latter, however, suffer most severely from it because their populations are more likely to be exposed to the bacillus, placing them at higher risk of developing the disease when they are malnourished and/or in old age.

Etiology and Epidemiology

Perhaps no other disease better illustrates the principle of multifactorial causation: The tubercle bacillus is a necessary but not the only condition. In addition, the host and the host's environment contribute numerous other causes central to its pathogenesis.

Species Classification

Over 30 species of the genus *Mycobacterium* have been identified, more than 15 of which can cause disorders similar, but not identical, to tuberculosis. Human disease typically is caused by members of the species *Mycobacterium tuberculosis.* In addition, mycobacteria can cause disease in a wide variety of animals, including birds, fish, rodents, elephants, and cattle. Of its animal forms, only the bovine can infect people. Some bacteriologists consider the bovine form a separate species of the tubercle bacillus, whereas others group it with several variants that they classify together as the *M. tuberculosis* complex.

The human bacillus has also been divided into three types according to immunologic responses (phage types), which show marked variations in virulence. These are *type I,* found in India; *type A,* found in Africa, China, and Japan as well as in Europe and North America; and *type B,* found exclusively in Europe and North America. Type I is the least virulent of the three, making Indians more susceptible to disease when infected with type A or B. These differences probably result from the evolution of widely separated organisms over long periods of time. However, all forms of *M. tuberculosis* show a strong resistance to mutation, and thus it is unlikely that an increase in virulence caused the disease to become epidemic, or that a decrease in virulence prompted the decline in tuberculosis mortality rates that occurred in England, the United States, and other Western nations before the introduction of streptomycin and other specifics.

Transmission

Except for the bovine types, tubercle bacilli reach human hosts almost exclusively through aerial transmissions. By talking, coughing, sneezing, spitting, singing, and other respiratory functions, people produce airborne particles called *droplet nuclei,* which, if emitted by a tubercular individual, can contain between one and three bacilli. Just one is enough to establish a tuberculosis infection when inhaled. Once airborne in a closed space, these particles disperse and some remain suspended like tobacco smoke. Larger ones fall to the floor or ground where they present little threat of infection, although dry tubercle bacilli can remain viable for months. Their transmission in dust particles is possible but rare; yet, from the late nineteenth century, this was believed to be the main form of transmission, and many countries passed laws that forbade spitting in public places. Bovine bacilli are ordinarily ingested through the digestive tract via milk and milk products and usually cause intestinal disease, but infrequently lead to pulmonary or miliary tuberculosis. The pasteurization of milk eliminates this source of infection.

Incubation Period

After entering the body, tubercle bacilli are remarkably durable and persistent. They can remain viable throughout their host's lifetime, dormant until resistance fails, whereupon they can cause active disease even if they failed to do so when they first entered the body. In contrast to most other infectious diseases, tuberculosis has an indefinite and variable incubation period.

Host-Dependent Factors

Whether or not tubercle bacilli cause active disease upon entering the body depends primarily on several host-dependent factors. Age, gender, and immunogenetic factors along with a number of environmental factors such as crowding, quality of nutrition, and working conditions are all of importance.

Age.   Once a person becomes infected with the bacillus, age has a powerful influence on what follows. Infancy, puberty, and old age are periods of low resistance and high susceptibility to tuberculosis. The younger the individual, the more likely that primary infection will become active disease and result in death. Infants are particularly susceptible to acute miliary tuberculosis. Unlike the organisms in many infectious diseases, however, the tubercle bacillus does not produce immunity in those exposed to it: Exposure early in life usually leads to relatively high mortality rates from tuberculosis in later middle or old age.

Gender.   Gender is also an important determinant. Although the reasons remain as yet undiscovered, more females die from tuberculosis than do males in populations where tuberculosis epidemics are just beginning, and the converse is usually true where the disease is declining. In youth and early adulthood, females generally experience greater mortality from tuberculosis than males, but after age 30 years the mortality of males surpasses that of fe-

males. Biological evidence suggests that the onset of the menses brings on metabolic changes that increase the body's need for protein, and that when it is unavailable, resistance drops. Childbirth can induce or aggravate the disease by lowering resistance to infection and this contributes to increased mortality in females up to age 30.

Genetic Factors.   Extensive research on heredity in tuberculosis has produced only ambiguous results. Some families experience more tuberculosis than others in similar circumstances, and specialists do agree that heredity influences an individual's risk of developing the disease, but the mechanisms of heredity have not been demonstrated. The role of race in tuberculosis also presents a difficult problem to researchers. For decades, American scientists attempted to ascertain whether blacks, who long had higher rates of mortality from the disease than whites, were biologically more susceptible to it because of an inherited characteristic. Results have been indeterminate, because in this case constitution and environment remain inseparably intertwined. Nevertheless, a population's genetic pool is an important influence on resistance to the tubercle bacillus. A long history of inhabiting urban environments seems to have made Jews more resistant to the disease than are most other ethnic groups. By contrast, a population's previous lack of exposure to tuberculosis can lead to acute epidemics of the disease, as exemplified by those that occurred among the Maori of New Zealand and the Eskimos of Alaska.

Some epidemiologists assert that natural selection determines the course of tuberculosis epidemics, based on the idea that genetic background and resistance to the disease are of paramount importance. Mortality rates drop, they say, as the more susceptible are weeded out. Others oppose this theory, in part because tuberculosis epidemics in Europe and the United States subsided more quickly than the theory would have predicted. Moreover, although natural selection has doubtless reinforced resistance to the disease, it has not played a leading role in the decline of its epidemics. Rather it would seem that economic and social changes made the most important contributions to the decline in tuberculosis mortality rates until the late 1940s, when medicinal cures became available.

Primary Environmental Factors

Where tuberculosis is present, the specific factors most important in the etiology of the disease are crowding, quality of nutrition, and working conditions.

Crowding. Crowding, as a function of persons per room, increases a person's chances of infection when diseased individuals are constantly releasing the bacilli into the air of small and cramped quarters. Population density, on the other hand, which is a ratio of persons per measure of land area, has little impact on tuberculosis mortality rates. Indeed, in most industrial nations, those rates are higher in rural than in urban areas because in sparsely populated rural areas, substandard living conditions, including crowded housing, often make the disease a major health problem.

Nutrition. Nutrition also plays a key role in the etiology of tuberculosis. Both epidemiological and laboratory evidence demonstrate the importance of protein in resistance to tuberculosis.

Working Conditions. Occupation and working conditions also can affect its pathogenesis and outcome. Textile mill laborers, masons, pottery factory operatives, metal grinders, and other workers in the "dusty trades" inhale particulate matter that inflames the lungs and increases their risk of developing the disease. The physical exertion and stress of exhausting work also magnify an individual's risk of developing tuberculosis, as does smoking. Socioeconomic status, which obviously has a powerful influence on all of these factors, may indirectly affect a population's tuberculosis mortality rates as well. Numerous studies have shown that groups with the lowest income levels suffer the most from the disease, and also that a rising income greatly reduces tuberculosis mortality.

This combination of factors means that industrialization alternatively exacerbates and improves rates of mortality from tuberculosis. The early stages of an industrial economy are generally those in which crowded and impoverished living conditions prevail for numerous people and lead to increased tuberculosis mortality. Eventually, however, industrialization's material benefits improve housing and nutrition, and reduce risks for infection and reinfection, thereby lowering both morbidity and mortality rates.

Other Environmental Factors. Other environmental factors seem to have little influence on tuberculosis mortality. Researchers long considered climate an important factor in the pathogenesis and treatment of tuberculosis, but recent studies have not found that temperature, humidity, or other climatic factors influence either one's risk of developing tuberculosis or its course once the disease is developed.

Epidemiologists have faced numerous difficulties in the study of tuberculosis, and found it particularly difficult to determine the mortality from the disease until the advent of mass screening programs using tuberculin and X-ray photography. Nonetheless they have played a primary role in unraveling some of the mysteries of tuberculosis and determining the factors, such as age and nutritional deficiencies, which put populations at greater or lesser risk of developing the disease.

Clinical Manifestations and Pathology

Tuberculosis most commonly infects the lungs, but it can infect almost any other part of the body, and frequently causes disease in the meninges, intestines, bones, lymph glands surrounding the neck, skin, spine, kidneys, and genitals. Most of these forms, with the exception of tubercular meningitis, are chronic, taking months and sometimes years before resulting in either recovery or death. Miliary tuberculosis concurrently affects almost every vital organ.

Because pulmonary tuberculosis is by far the most common form of this disease, it usually brings to mind its most familiar symptom: an increasingly frequent and violent cough that produces a purulent sputum sometimes streaked with blood. Coughing up larger amounts of blood hemorrhaged in the lungs is not uncommon in advanced cases, but this is by no means a universal symptom. Indeed, until the disease reaches its advanced stages, many victims are completely free of symptoms or experience only the mild respiratory symptoms similar to those of influenza or a common cold. The systemic symptoms of tuberculosis generally include fatigue, lethargy, anorexia, weight loss, irregular menses, ill-defined anxiety, chills, muscular aches, sweating, and low-grade fevers that continue indefinitely. In the past, however, many people developed mild or even asymptomatic cases of the disease and recovered before realizing it, as autopsies, and later X-rays, revealed.

Because in its early stages tuberculosis has only unalarming symptoms and myriad possible manifestations, diagnosis is difficult even today. Preliminary diagnosis can be made with a *tuberculin test,* which usually indicates whether a person has become infected with the tubercle bacillus. On the other hand, although tuberculin testing is highly reliable today, false-positive responses are not unknown.

The tubercle bacillus by itself does not damage the normal human body; it neither contains nor exudes any toxic materials. Rather cellular and tissue damage arises from an allergic reaction in the body, or *hypersensitivity,* which occurs in response to contact with the bacillus. In other words, after the body has become allergic to invading tubercle bacilli, the immune system destroys them. This process, however, releases proteins and fatty substances that in turn can cause inflammation and can damage surrounding tissue and cells. This same process also creates the *tubercles* that distinguish the disease. Experts sometimes refer to tubercles as caseous areas because they often have a cheesy consistency, although they can become as hard as rocks. Alternatively, caseous areas can liquefy, leaving a cavity. If this occurs close to a major blood vessel, it may result in a hemorrhage.

Immunology

The immune system's role in the development of tuberculosis is complicated, and part of that role still remains obscure. The complexity of the role has made it difficult to determine the extent to which antibodies protect the body against active disease and to what extent they cause it. Individual resistance to tuberculosis undergoes marked fluctuations: Quiescent infections often flare up under conditions that depress resistance, only to be suppressed when resistance is recovered. Acquired resistance to the tubercle bacillus confers no stable and durable protection as it does in diseases such as measles and smallpox, and can, to the contrary, make the development of active disease even more likely.

The efficacy of immunization against tuberculosis is still debated. Antituberculosis vaccination usually consists of administering the famous strain BCG (bacillus Calmette–Guérin), an attenuated form of the bovine bacillus first isolated in 1921 by the French bacteriologists A. Calmette and C. Guérin after years of laboratory cultivation. Clinical tests and epidemiological evidence indicate that it offers some degree of immunity when the recipient has not been infected before.

History

Antiquity

Archaeological evidence indicates that tuberculosis afflicted prehistoric men and women in Eurasia and Africa at least from the Neolithic period. Stone Age skeletons with lesions apparently caused by tuberculosis of the spine have been unearthed in Britain and Germany, and spinal tuberculosis has been found in numerous Egyptian mummies dating from the third millennium before Christ. In China, a woman's mummified body dating from the early Han dynasty (206 B.C. – A.D. 7) clearly displays tuberculosis scars on her lungs. Trade and migration patterns ensured the dissemination of China's chronic diseases throughout East Asia during the first three centuries of the present era. Skeletal evidence strongly suggests that native Americans suffered from the disease as early as 800 B.C., and pulmonary lesions that contain acid-fast bacilli dating from A.D. 290 have been discovered in Chilean mummies.

This physical evidence suggests two important points concerning the prehistory of tuberculosis. First, the disease quite possibly evolved together with humans from the earliest of times. Some specialists have presented the view that tuberculosis was originally limited to animals and first affected humans only after people started to domesticate cattle and other beasts. Others have contested this view, asserting that in the case of such a chronic disease, no animal intermediary is necessary to maintain viable bacilli even in relatively small populations. The second point is that tuberculosis afflicted most people worldwide from prehistoric times, save for small numbers of peoples, such as the Maori, who lived in isolation for centuries. Because of this, most epidemics of the disease resulted not from the introduction of foreign pathogens into virgin populations but from changes in the host population and its environment.

Textual sources support these conclusions, although not always with complete clarity because of marked differences in the ways people in different times and cultures have perceived the symptoms and course of tubercular disease. Until the present concept of tuberculosis – as a single disease caused by the tubercle bacillus – emerged during the last decades of the nineteenth century, its various forms were often known by separate names and thought of as different diseases. For example, the pulmonary forms were commonly called phthisis or pulmonary consumption; infections of the lymph glands surrounding the neck were termed scrofula; and those of the skin referred to as lupus vulgaris. This nosological confusion makes identification of the disease from historical texts difficult, and consequently conclusions concerning tuberculosis based on most written sources up to the mid-nineteenth century necessarily engender some skepticism.

Nevertheless, classical Hindu, Babylonian, Assyrian, Chinese, Greek, and Roman sources all describe the signs and symptoms of tuberculosis. Hindu texts dating from 1200 B.C. and perhaps earlier, along with Mesopotamian texts from the seventh century B.C., had established procedures for treating pulmonary tuberculosis and scrofula. The first description of the disease in Chinese may date back to 2700 B.C., and texts from around 400 B.C. clearly describe the symptoms of tuberculosis. The first Greek mention of what probably was tuberculosis is that of Homer, about 800 B.C. Hippocratic writings from approximately 400 B.C. discuss *phthisis,* the Greek term for consumption, which they attributed to the effects of evil airs. Phthisis then became the standard European term that signified a cluster of symptoms akin to and including those of pulmonary tuberculosis. Other Greek and Roman writers of both medical and nonmedical texts use the term extensively, including Galen, who during the second century of the Christian era recommended a change of climate as therapy for consumption. René and Jean Dubos, in their classic study of tuberculosis, *The White Plague* (1952), note that the ancient cultures that described the signs and symptoms of the disease were primarily urban, whereas pastoral cultures make scarce mention of the disease. Biblical literature, for example, makes scant reference to it.

Medieval Period

Medieval Europeans suffered considerably from tuberculosis, although contemporary documents mention it more often in its glandular form rather than its pulmonary form – that is, as scrofula or tuberculosis. This was because of the custom of the "king's touch," in which kings of France and England were believed to have the power to cure scrofula simply by touching its victims. The custom originated in the twelfth century and continued through the eighteenth to its demise along with the divine right of kings at the end of that century.

Chinese medical texts that provide the most detailed treatments of the disease were written during the Sui (581–617) and Tang (618–907) dynasties. Japanese physicians appropriated the Chinese texts, and with their aid clearly described the symptoms of tubercular diseases in their own country. By the twelfth century, Chinese Taoist priests had attributed phthisis both to infection by evil airs (*qi*) and to animalculae, which attacked a physically or mentally exhausted individual. The disease was said to pass through six stages in which these animalculae underwent a series of metamorphoses and in the last stage became highly infectious. In positing this systematic germ theory of tuberculosis, the Chinese

anticipated Western medical theorizing by two centuries. In the first half of the sixteenth century, Girolamo Fracastoro, better know as Fracastorius, became the first Western physician to propose such a theory. Unlike the Chinese theory, however, Fracastorius's was not limited to phthisis, which he believed was only one of many diseases caused by the spread of animalculae.

Sixteenth Through Eighteenth Century

During the sixteenth century, mortality from tuberculosis increased noticeably in countries with growing urban populations. In England, for example, it caused about 20 percent of all deaths at midcentury, with the greatest concentrations of the disease found in London. A similar phenomenon occurred in Japan at nearly the same time: Contemporary observers remarked that phthisis had become widespread in the rapidly growing administrative capital of Edo at the beginning of the seventeenth century. It was during the eighteenth century, however, that the world's great epidemics of tuberculosis began, and they were well underway by the beginning of the following century. The nations that suffered most severely from tuberculosis at this time also were experiencing intense urbanization and industrialization. Thus physicians and other writers reported that phthisis was common in the cities of England, the United States, Italy, and France.

Autopsies showed that close to 100 percent of some urban populations, such as those of London, Paris, and other major industrial cities, had at some point in their lives developed the disease, although they had died of some other cause. Rates of mortality from tuberculosis in most major American cities during the early nineteenth century ranged from 400 to 500 per 100,000 of population, and in Philadelphia (1811–20) they reached 618. Women workers in textile industries generally led other groups in tuberculosis mortality in every country where modern textile factories were appearing. When statistics for tuberculosis mortality became available for most industrial countries of western Europe and the United States after 1860, they showed that its epidemics were declining. In the developing countries of the time, however, including most eastern European nations and Japan, tuberculosis epidemics were just starting at the end of the nineteenth century.

Increasing attention was given to tuberculosis by European physicians beginning with the seventeenth century, in part because of major changes in medical theory and in part because of growing mortality from phthisis and scrofula. In 1685 Richard

Morton became the first Western physician to publish a single text on phthisis, a term which he used to embrace a number of wasting diseases, including pulmonary consumption and scrofula. Morton depended on traditional humoral theory to describe the etiology of phthisis. By the eighteenth century, however, physicians were redefining their concepts of diseases, and searching for new explanations for their causes. As a result, the nineteenth century became a period of intense research into and speculation about tubercular diseases. In Europe and especially in the United States, physicians and laypersons alike looked for elements in both life-style and environment that made a person "susceptible" to it. Among those "elements" were dissolute and immoral living, alcohol and tobacco consumption, along with various developmental crises in the host's physical well-being such as puberty or childbirth. In addition, damp soil and filth in general could make an individual susceptible to consumption. Others, however, believed that pulmonary consumption was a hereditary affliction – a belief that became a powerful social stigma in much of the world. Indeed, throughout much of the nineteenth century, popular (and some medical) concepts of tuberculosis resonated with the notion that the disease expressed a person's inherent nature as opposed to just being something that one had. In fact, those considered susceptible to tuberculosis were said to have a phthisical diathesis.

Nineteenth Through Twentieth Century

Theories of Etiology. A major break with previous theories of tubercular diseases occurred at the beginning of the nineteenth century, which initiated a process that had transformed their classification by the 1880s, especially among European medical scientists. From the early 1800s, the French clinical school analyzed pathological phenomena by comparing the course of disease observed at the bedside with autopsy observations. René Théophile Hyacinthe Laennec, a leading physician of this school, postulated the theory that all tubercular phenomena, including phthisis, scrofula, and miliary tubercles, in fact constituted a single disease.

German physicians of the "physiological" school, who opposed the "ontological" view of diseases, which posits clearly definable entities for which distinct species can be established, vigorously attacked Laennec's theory of tuberculosis. A leading theoretician of German "physiological medicine," Karl Wunderlich, asserted that it was impossible to draw a distinct line between, for example, dysentery and enteric diarrhea. Wunderlich thought of disease names only as conveniences, not as linguistic symbols for specific entities. In his views of tuberculosis, Wunderlich echoed the ideas of his contemporary, Rudolph Virchow. Virchow, in many respects one of the greatest medical theoreticians of the nineteenth century, also repudiated the ontological theory of diseases, including Laennec's idea that all tubercular phenomena manifested a single, specific disease. Rather, he divided tubercular manifestations into the two separate categories of inflammatory and neoplastic phenomena, and thought that some forms fundamentally resembled cancer. Virchow considered the important difference between diseases not to be one of cause but of pathological processes within individual cells.

Despite Virchow's views, however, the tradition of combining clinical and pathological investigations continued in France, most notably in the work of Jean-Antoine Villemin, who followed Laennec in saying that tuberculosis was a specific disease caused by a specific agent, but went one step beyond him by demonstrating in practice what Laennec had postulated in theory. In 1865 Villemin caused tuberculosis in rabbits by injecting them with matter from human tubercles. Although this work had a negligible impact on German ideas concerning tuberculosis, the notion that it was a specific disease was provided an unshakable scientific foundation in the work of the Prussian bacteriologist Robert Koch.

Using the clearly defined bacteriologic methods he had developed, Koch proved in 1882 that it was possible to give animals tuberculosis by inoculating them with bacteria – and not simply tubercular matter – that he had isolated from human tubercles. Although a number of problems in the identification of tuberculosis remained (such as the identity of scrofula, which some still maintained was a separate disease), the discovery of the tubercle bacillus finally established tuberculosis as a single disease clearly distinguishable by a single cause. It is true that for several more years, some circles, particularly the group led by Virchow, disputed Koch's methods and conclusions. Nonetheless his discovery of the tubercle bacillus changed the way not only members of the medical profession thought about tuberculosis but also how most people viewed the disease: No longer was it the result of an inherent susceptibility but, rather, something that one "had."

Early Attempts at Prevention. Koch's discovery had little effect on attempts to treat tuberculosis, but it had important implications for prophylaxis. Observers attempting to establish the most important routes of infection concluded that dry tubercle bacilli in dried sputum presented the greatest threat. To prevent the disease, they recommended the general removal of dust from all public and private places, restrictions on spitting and the use of spittoons in all places, and the disinfection or destruction of the belongings and surroundings of tuberculosis victims. In some places, such procedures were already "on the books," because many national and local governments had passed laws specifying some or all of them. It was not until the 1930s that researchers demonstrated that, in most cases, infection was the result of airborne infection and that dried sputum or other forms of contact with the bacillus played little role in the transmission of the disease.

Early Treatment. The primary interest of most practicing physicians at this time, however, was not in ascertaining the etiology of tuberculosis but, rather, in treating the disease. The many hundreds of thousands of tuberculosis victims worldwide were desperate to be cured, and created an unbounded demand for remedies, making equally large opportunities for both physicians and quacks – although by today's standards it is often difficult to separate the two. Some of the most popular cures for tuberculosis that physicians advocated during the nineteenth century included creosote, carbolic acid solutions, gold, iodoform, arsenic, and menthol oil; at various times all were administered orally, inhaled, or injected directly into the lungs. More unusual treatments ranged from drinking papaya juice to enemas of sulfur gases. Starting during the late nineteenth century and continuing well into the twentieth, physicians practiced surgical therapies, including pneumothorax, or collapsed-lung treatments, and the surgical removal of ribs with the objective of reducing the size of the thoracic cavity.

Advances in Diagnosis. It was the search for a remedy, rather than his discovery of the tubercle bacillus, that brought Koch international fame. In 1890, at the strong urging of Kaiser Wilhelm II's government, he announced that he had discovered a cure for tuberculosis, which attracted hundreds of scientists and thousands of the afflicted to his laboratory in Berlin. Within a year, however, many were questioning the efficacy of "Koch's lymph" (a glycerol-based extract from the tubercle bacillus). As a cure it was not effective; in fact, it proved harmful in advanced cases. On the other hand, it soon became the extremely important diagnostic tool better known as *tuberculin* and the primary means of determining infection by the tubercle bacillus.

Along with the discoveries of the tubercle bacillus and tuberculin, the X-ray, discovered in 1895, helped change the way in which both physicians and laypersons thought about tuberculosis. It made visible to the eye lesions in the lungs and other parts of the body caused by the disease long before its symptoms became noticeable, allowing physicians to start treatment at a much earlier stage in the disease. Although they did not become a dependable diagnostic tool until the end of the second decade of the twentieth century, X-ray photographs together with tuberculin became the basic tools of the mass screening programs that governments and antituberculosis associations implemented from the 1920s to the 1950s.

Later Therapies and Prevention. As diagnostic techniques improved but medicinal cures remained ineffective, therapies based on climate and regimen became increasingly popular. Hippocrates had first recommended a change of climate as a treatment for phthisis, and from the seventeenth century onward physicians in both the West and the East continued to recommend healthful climates and life-styles as consumption cures. From the mid-nineteenth century, open-air and rest therapies became increasingly popular throughout Europe and the United States, and as an extension of rest therapy, pneumothorax, or the collapsing of a heavily diseased lung so that it could "rest," became popular in the late 1800s and remained common in many countries until the 1940s. The systematic integration of these therapies with other forms of treatment culminated in the sanitorium. From the 1880s, luxury sanitoria for the wealthy, like the one in Davos, Switzerland (immortalized in Thomas Mann's *The Magic Mountain*), drew patients from around the world. And about 1900, state-sponsored sanitoria began to appear throughout western Europe, North America, and Japan.

Where sanitoria were not feasible, such as in inner cities, public health bureaucrats and physicians developed alternatives that offered open-air treatment for the diseased as well as preventive regimens for those who seemed susceptible.

Many sanitoria and prevention programs were sponsored or managed by private or semiprivate antituberculosis organizations. These had been established in most of western Europe and North America from the 1890s, and in much of the rest of the world during the first two decades of the twentieth century. Such organizations also supported educational programs, which became a mainstay of tuberculosis control movements. Their purpose was to inform the public of the ways in which the disease was transmitted and developed, and to encourage people to secure frequent checkups and early treatment if they were infected. The most commonly afflicted groups, however – factory laborers, other industrial workers, and the urban poor – rarely had the necessary resources to secure treatment for the disease even if they received an early diagnosis.

Mortality and Incidence. Understandably, medical scientists, public health bureaucrats, and workers in such prevention movements where rates of mortality from tuberculosis declined dramatically from the late nineteenth century onward concluded that the decline was the direct result of their efforts. This was especially the case in Great Britain, Germany, and the United States. Yet the experience of others contradicted such claims. During the first four decades of the twentieth century, the Japanese, for example, implemented almost all the tuberculosis control measures that Western countries had developed, including extensive legislation aimed at the control of tuberculosis, state-sponsored sanitoria in the major urban centers, intensive education programs, and government-administered mass screenings and BCG immunizations. Throughout the first three decades of this period, however, Japan's rates of mortality from tuberculosis hovered at around 200 per 100,000, and then actually increased from the early 1930s. It was not until the late 1940s that the rates of tuberculosis mortality began a sustained fall. In the case of Japan, the prevention movement was much less important than later improvements in living standards and working conditions and even later government intervention with nationwide treatment programs using streptomycin, PAS, and, after 1952, isoniazid.

Since the 1950s, the countries with the highest tuberculosis mortality rates have been those with low standards of living, poor working conditions, and inadequate treatment programs. Medicine has learned that the mere availability of specifics against tuberculosis is not enough to stem the disease; their administration must be coordinated with reforms that raise living standards and improve working conditions, or the incidence of the disease will remain inordinately high. During the early 1970s, over 20 nations worldwide – all of them developing countries – had new case rates for tuberculosis of over 150 per 100,000 per year; Macau (in 1973),

Swaziland (in 1970), and Bolivia (in 1972) all had incidence rates of over 400.

Thus although the leaders of antituberculosis movements long spoke of eradicating the disease, it remains a major health problem in many countries, and serves as an index of social conditions worldwide. Even in developed, industrial countries, when social conditions deteriorate, the incidence of tuberculosis rises quickly. Clearly, the disease remains far from eradicated in the developing world. But even in the developed world, tuberculosis retains the potential of becoming a significant health problem during times of economic depression, war, and social unrest.

William D. Johnston

Bibliography

Ackerknecht, Erwin H. 1982. *A short history of medicine.* Baltimore.

Bloch, Marc. 1973. *The royal touch: Sacred monarchy and scrofula in England and France,* trans. J. E. Anderson. London.

Bowditch, Henry I. 1862. *Consumption in New England: Or locality one of its chief causes.* Boston.

Bryder, Linda. 1988. *Below the magic mountain.* Oxford.

Buikstra, Jane E., ed. 1981. *Prehistoric tuberculosis in the Americas.* Evanston, Ill.

Caldwell, Mark. 1988. *The last crusade: The war on consumption, 1862–1954.* New York.

Chapin, Charles V. 1888. *What changes has the acceptance of the germ theory made in measures for the prevention and treatment of consumption?* Providence, R.I.

    1924. Deaths among taxpayers and non-taxpayers, income tax, Providence, 1865. *American Journal of Public Health* 14: 647–51.

Collins, C. H., M. D. Yates, and J. M. Grange. 1982. Subdivision of *Mycobacterium tuberculosis* into five variants for epidemiological purposes: Methods and nomenclature. *Journal of Hygiene (Cambridge)* 89: 235–42.

Comstock, George W. 1975. Frost revisited: The modern epidemiology of tuberculosis. *American Journal of Epidemiology* 101: 363–82.

Crosby, Alfred W. 1986. *Ecological imperialism: The biological expansion of Europe, 900–1900.* Cambridge.

Dannenberg, Arthur M., Jr. 1980. Pathogenesis of tuberculosis. In *Pulmonary diseases and disorders,* ed. Alfred P. Fishman, 1264–81. New York.

Dubos, René, and Jean Dubos. 1952. *The white plague: Tuberculosis, man and society.* Reprint. New Brunswick, N.J.

Dubos, René J., and Cynthia Pierce. 1948. The effect of diet on experimental tuberculosis of mice. *American Review of Tuberculosis* 57: 287–93.

Esmond, R. Long. 1941. Constitution and related factors in resistance to tuberculosis. *Archives of Pathology* 32: 122–62, 286–310.

Faber, Knud. 1930. *Nosography: The evolution of clinical medicine in modern times*. New York.

1938. Tuberculosis and nutrition. *Acta Tuberculosea Scandanavica* 12: 287–335.

Framingham Community Health and Tuberculosis Demonstration. 1919. *Tuberculosis findings*. Framingham, Mass.

Frost, Wade Hampton. 1937. How much control of tuberculosis? *American Journal of Public Health* 27: 759–66.

1939. The age selection of mortality from tuberculosis in successive decades. *American Journal of Hygiene* 30: 91–6.

Fujikawa, Yû. 1904. *Nihon igaku shi* [A history of Japanese medicine]. Tokyo.

Grange, John M. 1979. The changing tubercle. *British Journal of Hospital Medicine* 22: 540–8.

Grange, John M., et al. 1978. The correlation of bacteriophage types of *Mycobacterium tuberculosis* with guinea-pig virulence and in-vitro indicators of virulence. *Journal of General Microbiology* 108: 1–7.

Grange, John M., C. H. Collins, and M. D. Yates. 1980. Epidemiological studies on tuberculosis: The role of microbiological investigations. *British Journal of Diseases of the Chest* 75: 315.

Grigg, E. R. N. 1958. The arcana of tuberculosis. *American Review of Tuberculosis and Pulmonary Diseases* 78: 151–72, 426–53, 583–603.

Grzybowski, Stephan. 1983. *Tuberculosis and its prevention*. St. Louis.

Grzybowski, Stephan, and W. B. Marr. 1963. The unchanging pattern of pulmonary tuberculosis. *Canadian Medical Association Journal* 89: 737–40.

Guillaume, Pierre. 1986. *Du Désespoir au salut: Les Tuberculeux aux XIX$_e$ et XX$_e$ siècles*. Paris.

Kaplan, Gary J., et al. 1972. Tuberculosis in Alaska, 1970. *American Review of Respiratory Diseases* 105: 920–6.

Kass, Edward H. 1971. Infectious diseases and social change. *Journal of Infectious Diseases* 123: 110–14.

Katz, Julius, and Solomon Kunofsky. 1961. Trends of tuberculosis morbidity and mortality. *American Review of Respiratory Diseases* 84: 217–25.

King, Lester S. 1982. *Medical thinking: A historical preface*. Princeton, N.J.

Klebs, Arnold C. 1909. *Tuberculosis: A treatise by American authors*. New York.

Koch, Robert. 1987. *The essays of Robert Koch*. New York.

Lester, William. 1980. Treatment of tuberculosis. In *Pulmonary diseases and disorders*, ed. Alfred P. Fishman, 1305–23. New York.

Liu Ts'un-yan. 1971. The Taoists' knowledge of tuberculosis in the twelfth century. *T'oung Pao* 57: 285–301.

Lowell, Anthony M. 1956. *Socio-economic conditions and tuberculosis prevalence*. New York.

Lowell, Anthony M., Lydia B. Edwards, and Carroll E. Palmer. 1969. *Tuberculosis*. Cambridge, Mass.

Lurie, Max B. 1964. *Resistance to tuberculosis*. Cambridge, Mass.

McKeown, Thomas. 1976. *The modern rise of population*. London.

McKeown, Thomas, R. G. Brown, and R. G. Record. 1972. An interpretation of the modern rise of population in Europe. *Population Studies* 26: 345–82.

Meachen, G. Norman. 1936. *A short history of tuberculosis*. Reprint. New York.

Morse, Dan. 1967. Tuberculosis. In *Disease in antiquity*, ed. D. R. Brothwell and A. T. Sandison, 249–71. Springfield, Ill.

Nakano Yasuaki, and Kurokawa Keikan. 1940. Tôyô igaku ni okeru kekkaku gainen narabini sono chihô no hensen ni tsuite. [On changes in the concept of tuberculosis and its therapeutic methods in Eastern medicine]. *Nihon rinshô kekkaku* [The Japanese Journal of Clinical Tuberculosis] 1: 142–8, 263–70, 388–97, 495–505, 635–48, 747–54, 879–86.

Ochs, Charles W. 1962. The epidemiology of tuberculosis. *Journal of the American Medical Association* 179: 247–52.

Pope, Alton S., and John E. Gordon. 1955. The impact of tuberculosis on human populations. *American Journal of the Medical Sciences* 230: 317–53.

Rather, Leland J. 1978. *The genesis of cancer: A study in the history of ideas*. Baltimore.

Reichman, Lee B., and Robert O'Day. 1978. Tuberculosis infection in a large urban population. *American Review of Respiratory Diseases* 117: 705–12.

Rich, Arnold R. 1951. *The pathogenesis of tuberculosis*. Springfield, Ill.

Riley, Richard L. 1980. The changing scene in tuberculosis. In *Pulmonary diseases and disorders*, ed. Alfred P. Fishman, 1229–33. New York.

Riley, Richard L., et al. 1955. Aerial dissemination of pulmonary tuberculosis: A two-year study of contagion in a tuberculosis ward. *American Journal of Hygiene* 70: 185–96.

Rosenkrantz, Barbara G. 1985. The trouble with bovine tuberculosis. *Bulletin of the History of Medicine* 59: 155–75.

1987. Introductory essay: Tuberculosis, Dubos and master teachers. In René Dubos and Jean Dubos. *The white plague: Tuberculosis, man, and society*, xiii–xxxiv. New Brunswick, N.J.

Selye, Hans. 1955. Stress and disease. *Science* 122: 625–31.

Shimamura Kikuji. 1972. Kekkaku [Tuberculosis]. In *Kôshû eisei* [Public Health], ed. Kagoyama Takashi, 159–99. Tokyo.

Shryock, Richard Harrison. 1977. *National Tuberculosis Association, 1904–1907: A study of the voluntary health movement in the United States*. New York.

Sigerist, Henry E. 1943. *Civilization and disease*. Ithaca, N.Y.

Smith, Francis B. 1988. *The retreat of tuberculosis*. London.

Stead, William W., and Joseph H. Bates. 1980. Epidemiology and prevention of tuberculosis. In *Pulmonary dis-

eases and disorders, ed. Alfred P. Fishman, 1234–54. New York.

Taylor, Robert. 1986. *Saranac: America's magic mountain.* Boston.

Teller, Michael E. 1988. *The tuberculosis movement.* Westport, Conn.

Terris, Milton. 1984. Relation of economic status to tuberculosis mortality by age and sex. *American Journal of Public Health* 38: 1061–70.

Thorpe, Ethel L. M. 1989. *The social histories of smallpox and tuberculosis in Canada: Culture, evolution and disease.* Winnipeg.

Virchow, Rudolf. 1850. Tuberculosis and its relation to inflammation, scrofulosis and typhus. In *Collected essays on public health and epidemiology,* ed. and trans. Leland J. Rather, Vol. 1, 346–50. Canton, Mass.

  1860. *Cellular pathology as based upon physiological and pathological histology,* trans. Frank Chance. New York.

Wayne, Lawrence G. 1980. Microbiology of tuberculosis. In *Pulmonary diseases and disorders,* ed. Alfred P. Fishman, 1255–63. New York.

Weg, John G. 1982. Chronic respiratory tract infections. In *Pulmonary medicine,* ed. Clarance A. Geunter, 390–429. Philadelphia.

Wells, W. F. 1934. On air-borne infection. Study II. Droplets and droplet nuclei. *American Journal of Hygiene* 20: 611–18.

Wolff, Georg. 1938a. Tuberculosis and civilization: Part I. Basic facts and figures in the epidemiology of tuberculosis. *Human Biology* 10: 106–23.

  1938b. Tuberculosis and civilization: Part II. Interpretation of the etiological factors in the epidemiology of tuberculosis. *Human Biology* 10: 251–84.

  1940. Tuberculosis mortality and industrialization. *American Review of Tuberculosis* 42: 1–27, 214–42.

Youmans, Guy P. 1979. *Tuberculosis.* Philadelphia.

VIII.148
Tularemia

Tularemia is primarily a specific, infectious disease of rodents and lagomorphs. The causative organism, however, has been isolated from over 100 species of mammals, 9 species of domestic animals, 25 species of birds, 70 species of insects, and several species of fish and amphibians. Humans can become infected by being bitten by infected blood-sucking insects, by handling infected animal carcasses, and by ingesting contaminated water or poorly cooked meat. In humankind, tularemia is an acute, infectious, moderately severe, febrile disease, which has a mortality rate of approximately 7 percent in untreated cases. The causative agent, *Francisella (Pasteurella) tularensis,* is a tiny gram-negative, pleomorphic coccobacillus requiring special media for isolation and growth. Tularemia is also know as deer-fly fever, Pahvant Valley plague, rabbit fever, Ohara's disease, yatobyo, and lemming fever.

Etiology and Epidemiology

Two variants (biovars) of the causative organism are recognized. *F. tularensis* biovar *tularensis* (type A) has been isolated in nature only in North America and is the most virulent in human beings. The second is designated *F. tularensis* biovar *palaearctica* (type B) and is found in all areas where tularemia is endemic in the Northern Hemisphere.

Tularemia is unique in the number of ways in which humans can become infected, and the clinical picture of the disease depends upon the infection route. The most common route is via the skin, either by insect bite or by direct passage through intact skin by contact with infected carcasses or a scratch from an infected animal. Of the numerous insects that transmit the disease, the tick is the most important. The wood tick (*Dermacentor andersoni*) and three species of rabbit tick are especially important in the United States. Biting insects such as the deer fly (*Chrysops discalis*) and the stable fly (*Stomoxys calcitrans*) also carry the disease to humans. Of the several species of mosquitoes shown to harbor the disease organism, only two species act as vectors to humans: *Aedes cinereus* and *Aedes excrucians* in Sweden and the former Soviet Union. Infection of the intestinal canal follows ingestion of contaminated water and undercooked meat. Humans can also contract infection via the respiratory route by inhaling the organism from such sources as contaminated hay and wool.

Susceptibility to tularemia is independent of age, sex, race, and health status. That men are more often infected is related to their intrusion into the transmission cycle through hunting and handling of infected, fur-bearing animals. Human-to-human transmission is extremely rare, and the disease is largely confined to rural areas. The disease may occur in any season but is least prevalent in winter when insect vectors are least abundant and small animals are not much hunted.

The fatality rate in North America, prior to the widespread use of streptomycin in the late 1940s, ranged from 5 to 9 percent. Today that figure has been reduced to less than 1 percent. In Europe, the mortality rate has always been much lower, in the realm of 1 percent owing, probably, to the lower virulence of *F. tularensis* strain. An attack confers relatively solid lifelong immunity. A live attenuated vaccine is now available that reduces the severity of the ulceroglandular infection and reduces the incidence of typhoid-type tularemia. However, the vaccine is still being investigated and used primarily for laboratory workers who are always at high risk in working with the tularemia organism.

Distribution and Incidence

Tularemia, in humans, is confined to the Northern Hemisphere with three main areas of epidemicity: North America, Europe, especially eastern Europe and Russia, and to a lesser extent Japan. It is not found in nature in the British Isles. Tularemia has been reported everywhere in the United States except Hawaii. In Canada, the disease is endemic in the central and western provinces, as well as the Northwest Territories, but seldom is reported from the eastern provinces. Other countries that have reported the disease include Mexico, Norway, Sweden, Belgium, France, Germany, Poland, Czechoslovakia, Austria, Yugoslavia, Turkey, and Tunisia. Sporadic cases have been reported from northern South America including Venezuela, Ecuador, and Colombia, but these have not been confirmed.

In the United States, tularemia became a reportable disease in 1927 and rose to a peak incidence in 1939 with 2,291 cases reported (17.5 per million population). Since the 1950s, the disease has undergone a dramatic decline. In 1984 in the United States only 291 cases were reported (1.2 per million). Since 1931 in Canada nearly 400 cases have been reported but with a steady decline over the years. In Russia a similar decrease has been observed. In the mid-1940s, 100,000 cases per year were reported; yet these were reduced to a few hundred cases per year by the mid-1960s. The reasons for this worldwide decline are controversial. The reasons advanced range from ecologically induced selection against the more virulent strains of *F. tularensis* and reduction of the organism circulating in wild reservoirs, to an increased awareness of the disease through mass education, to a failure to detect and report cases.

Clinical Manifestations and Pathology

Tularemia may manifest an extremely variable clinical picture depending upon the site of inoculation and the extent of its spread. In general, the incubation period averages about 3 days, varying from 1 to 9. The disease begins with headache, chills, vomiting, fever, with generalized aches and pains. An ulcer develops at the site of initial entry, while associated lymph nodes become enlarged and tender. The disease lasts 3 to 4 weeks, with sweating, weight loss, and general debility. Convalescence requires 2 to 3 months.

Several clinical types of the disease have been described:

1. The cutaneous (ulceroglandular) type in which an inflamed papule develops at the site of inoculation, which soon breaks down, leaving a punched-out ulcer. There is painful enlargement of associated lymph nodes, which may last 2 to 3 months. The usual signs of infection, fever, and prostration are common.

2. The ophthalmic (oculoglandular) type, which occurs when the bacterium enters via the conjunctival sac. Local inflammation occurs with enlargement of the lymph nodes of the neck. Permanent impairment of vision may occur.

3. The pleuropulmonary type, which develops secondary to the other forms. Milder forms resemble atypical pneumonia and may include shortness of breath, malaise, chills, and pleuritic pain.

4. The gastrointestinal (oropharyngeal) form that is contracted from the ingestion of contaminated food and water and may be accompanied by acute abdominal symptoms such as pain, vomiting, and diarrhea with ulcerative lesions in the intestinal mucosa.

5. The glandular form, which develops without a primary lesion but with enlargement of regional lymph nodes.

6. The typhoidal (septicemic) form that also develops without a primary lesion and without enlarge-

ment of the regional nodes. Infection arises via the respiratory route or is the late result of local infection.

7. The meningitic type, which is rare in North America but not infrequent in Asia, under certain conditions of insect transmission.

In all these types, subclinical infections may be more common than previously supposed. A recent study in Sweden showed that about 23 percent of the population had been infected, but 32 percent of these were subclinical cases.

History and Geography

Tularemia enjoys a unique place in medical history as it is the first disease to be identified and entirely described by American investigators. In 1910 G. W. McCoy of the U.S. Public Health Service, while studying plague in California ground squirrels, reported a "plague-like disease of rodents" in these animals. The following year, he and C. W. Chapin, using a special nutrient medium, succeeded in culturing the causative organism and named it *Bacterium tularense* after Tulare County, California, where infected squirrels were first discovered. W. B. Wherry and B. H. Lamb were the first to diagnose bacteriologically a human case of the disease in 1914. The infected patient, an Ohio meat cutter, showed ulcerative conjunctivitis and lymphadenitis.

Earlier, in 1911, R. A. Pearse had described several cases of deer-fly fever in humans from Utah and suggested that the disease was caused by the bite of *Chrysops discalis,* the common deer fly. It was left to Edward Francis, a surgeon with the U.S. Public Health Service, to piece together the complicated etiologic connection among deer-fly fever in humans, the plaguelike disease of rodents in California, and similar illnesses in small mammals of Utah and Indiana. Francis isolated the organism in 1921 and proved that it was indeed spread by the bite of the deer fly as well as by direct contact with infected meat. The role of the tick in the spread of tularemia was determined in 1924 by R. R. Parker, R. R. Spencer, and Francis. It was also Francis who coined the term "tularemia" after finding the organism in the blood of infected individuals. In the late 1950s the genus name of the organism was changed to *Pasteurella* because of a supposed relationship to the causative organism of plague. In 1974, upon recommendation of microbiologists in the Soviet Union and the United States, the genus name was changed to *Francisella* to honor Francis who, through more than 30 years of investigation into tularemia, was

the man most responsible for sorting out its complexities and many manifestations.

In 1925, Hachiro Ohara, a Japanese scientist, published a paper entitled "Concerning an Acute Febrile Disease Transmitted by Wild Rabbits," followed shortly by a second paper describing how an illness that would become known as *Ohara's disease* was successfully transmitted to humans. Other papers by Japanese scientists soon followed, but none made reference to American investigations of tularemia.

Francis and a colleague, recognizing that Ohara's disease seemed similar to tularemia in every way, requested serums from convalescent Japanese patients. Examination of the sera quickly confirmed that Ohara's disease and tularemia were actually the same illness.

The first isolation of *F. tularensis* outside North America and Japan occurred in the Soviet Union in 1926, and by 1928 almost 800 cases were reported, rising to a peak incidence in 1941–2 of approximately 100,000 cases, but, as in North America, there has subsequently been a dramatic delcine in cases.

Although tularemia is often described as a "new disease," it is perhaps best to consider it new only in terms of its discovery. Medical historians believe there is good evidence that tularemia was endemic in the United States, Scandinavia, and the Soviet Union in the eighteenth and nineteenth centuries. Many travelers in Russia as early as 1741 noted a disease with all the characteristics of tularemia and termed "Siberian ulcer."

In the United States at least three written records survive describing the disease, including one from California in 1904 and another from Arizona in 1907. In fact, the wide distribution of the disease and its adaptation to a wide variety of animals suggest that the disease is ancient in nature, perhaps dating to the latter end of the Miocene or early Pliocene periods.

Despite the dramatic decline in the incidence of tularemia since the 1950s, it would appear that tularemia will remain a hazard to humans for many years to come. In spite of the great amount of research over the past 70 years, numerous questions remain unanswered because of the very complex interactions among hosts, vectors, and varied environments. Because of these complex ecological interactions, eradication of tularemia seems unlikely.

Patrick D. Horne

Bibliography

Foshay, L. 1950. Tularemia. *Annual Review of Microbiology* 4: 313–30.

Francis, E. 1925. Tularemia. *Journal of the American Medical Association* 84: 1243–50.

Gelman, A. C. 1961. Tularemia. In *Studies in disease ecology,* ed. J. M. May, 89–108. New York.

Jellison, W. L. 1972. Tularemia: Dr. Edward Francis and his first 23 isolates of *Francisella tularensis. Bulletin of the History of Medicine* 46: 477–85.

Olsen, P. F. 1975. Tularemia. In *Diseases transmitted from animals to man,* 6th edition, ed. W. T. H. Hubbert et al., 191–233. Springfield, Ill.

Pollitzer, R. 1967. *History and incidence of tularemia in the Soviet Union.* New York.

Simpson, W. M. 1929. *Tularemia: History, pathology, diagnosis and treatment.* New York.

VIII.149
Typhoid Fever

Typhoid fever is a systemic infection caused by the bacterium *Salmonella typhi,* usually manifested by the slow onset of a sustained fever and a variety of other symptoms including headache, cough, digestive disturbances, abdominal pain, and profound weakness. In a minority of sufferers, findings more specific for typhoid fever may be present, such as enlargement of the spleen or liver, or a characteristic "rose spot" rash. Untreated, the illness lasts 3 to 4 weeks; it claims the lives of about 10 percent of those affected and leaves about 2 percent as permanent carriers of the organism. Three-quarters of the world's population live in areas where typhoid is endemic, and 1 out of every 300 of the world's population contracts the disease each year. One million persons die of it annually, mostly children.

A variant illness, called paratyphoid fever, has many of the same features as typhoid fever, but is caused by members of the *Salmonella* bacterial family other than *S. typhi.* Typhoid and paratyphoid fevers are sometimes lumped together under the term *enteric fever.*

Etiology

The microorganism responsible for typhoid fever is a member of one of the largest and most widespread families of bacteria on Earth with over 1,700 serotypes recognized. The salmonellae are rod-shaped bacteria that have a cell wall and flagella, which give the bacterium motility.

Salmonellae can colonize the gastrointestinal tract of a broad range of animal hosts including mammals, birds, reptiles, amphibians, fish, and insects. Some types of salmonellae are highly adapted to specific animals; others have a wide range of hosts. Because of this versatility and the enormous consequent animal reservoir, the eradication of all salmonellosis would be essentially impossible.

Salmonellosis is generally a mild disease in humans, characterized by a few hours or days of vomiting and diarrhea (gastroenteritis), followed by weeks to months during which the organism is shed asymptomatically in the feces. The disease is usually acquired by ingestion of foods that are contaminated with the organism, but other routes – person-to-person, animal-to-person – may sometimes play a role. In the 1970s in the United States, more than 10 percent of the nation's salmonellosis was acquired from baby turtles, a favored pet of children in those days.

Almost unique among the salmonellae, the typhoid bacillus is adapted to human beings alone. *S. typhi* also possesses a protective envelope, called the "virulence antigen" or *Vi antigen,* which appears to help the organism resist the immunologic defenses of the host. The exclusive adaptation of *S. typhi* to human beings makes control possible through public health measures.

Epidemiology

Typhoid fever is spread by the fecal–oral route: Bacteria shed in the stool by infected persons can be ingested by someone else, usually through contaminated food or water.

Control of typhoid fever depends on maintaining a separation between sewage and drinking water. In certain areas of the world, as many as 3 percent of adults may be shedding *S. typhi.* Thus with poor sanitation, the population is continuously exposed, and the disease is constantly present. Such areas are termed *endemic.* Many of the least developed regions of the world are highly endemic for typhoid fever.

In contrast, where effective sanitation barriers are suddenly breached, transmission follows an epidemic pattern with a sudden rise in the incidence of a disease within a limited geographic area. For example, typhoid fever is almost unknown in Switzerland; yet contamination of Zermatt's water supply in 1963 resulted in 280 cases in a brief period of time. Ten years later, a similar compromise of the water supply of a migrant laborers' camp in Florida permitted an outbreak of 222 cases, with a single carrier as the apparent origin.

The other main vehicle for typhoid transmission is

food. Though denied another animal host, *S. typhi* can grow well on many types of food, and contaminated foods have been responsible for large-scale outbreaks. Five hundred cases of typhoid fever in Aberdeen, Scotland, in 1964 were traced to imported canned beef which, after processing under sterile conditions in Argentina, had been cooled in a sewage-laden river where microscopic cracks in the seams of the cans permitted contamination.

Foodborne transmission may be important in maintaining high levels of endemicity in areas where drinking water is pure. In Santiago, Chile, 10 percent of water samples from the irrigation canals are positive for *S. typhi*, and contamination of produce, rather than drinking water, appears to be an important factor in the city's typhoid problem.

In fact, even when food is initially free of *S. typhi*, handling by persons who shed the bacillus can be enough to produce disease in those who eat it, particularly where refrigeration is absent and basic standards of hygiene are not maintained.

Minor roles in *S. typhi* transmission are also played by shellfish harvested from contaminated waters and flies lighting first on excrement and then on food. Transmission may also occur accidentally in the microbiology laboratory while workers are handling infected human specimens.

The percentage of persons who develop typhoid fever after exposure to the bacillus depends upon a number of factors, among them the virulence and number of organisms ingested, and the host's health and immune status.

Experiments conducted with adult volunteers demonstrate that the attack rate of typhoid fever depends directly on the number of organisms ingested. Illness was produced in about 25 percent of volunteers each ingesting 100,000 bacilli; ingestion of 10 million bacilli resulted in illness in 50 percent; and ingestion of 1 billion organisms virtually guaranteed the development of typhoid fever. The incubation period varied inversely: The larger the dose, the shorter the incubation period. Some strains, however, are able to produce disease at very low numbers: Only 10 organisms of the type involved in the 1963 Zermatt epidemic were needed to make half of volunteers ill. Attack rates of epidemics in the developed world suggest that most such outbreaks are initiated by exposure to only a few hundred or thousand organisms.

With typhoid, whatever the degree of community exposure, maintaining personal hygiene, boiling drinking water, and cooking food just before eating it play an important role in preventing typhoid fe-

ver. Predisposing factors for the development of all *Salmonella* infections include red cell breakdown diseases (e.g., sickle-cell disease, malaria), immunodeficiency (e.g., AIDS), malignancy, or dysfunction of various organs such as stomach, liver, or kidney. Other conditions such as gastric hypoacidity and the use of antibiotics that inhibit normal gut bacterial flora are risk factors that favor *Salmonella* infections. Adults in endemic areas are more resistant to typhoid than are children in the same area or previously unexposed persons from other areas.

A distinctive feature of the epidemiology of typhoid is the existence of a large number of asymptomatic carriers: persons who excrete *S. typhi* yet manifest no signs of illness.

In the normal course of typhoid fever, fecal excretion of the organism persists for a few weeks, but about 2 percent of infected persons will never clear the bacillus from their stools. In such persons, the organism appears to colonize the biliary tract – that is, the tubules that conduct bile from the liver and the gallbladder. Persons with preexisting disease of the biliary tract – for example, inflammation or gallstones – are at risk for becoming carriers. *S. typhi* appears to have a particular affinity for bile and gallstones. It grows best on media enriched with bile by-products. Once a stone is infected, it forms a focus of infection sheltered from antibiotics and the host's immune system.

The likelihood of becoming a carrier increases with age and peaks at 55 years of age, with women carriers outnumbering their male counterparts 3 to 1 – a pattern similar to that seen in biliary disease, but contrasting sharply with acute typhoid fever, which is a disease of the young and which affects both sexes equally. In Chile, where the incidence of both biliary disease and typhoid fever is high, there is an estimated 1 carrier per 150 persons. The lack of symptoms often makes the carrier difficult to identify, and sequestration of the bacillus on gallstones makes its eradication difficult or impossible.

Distribution and Incidence

Since the beginning of the twentieth century, typhoid fever has been largely a disease of the developing world, and the same factors that interfere with the provision of health care in these regions also interfere with the gathering of health statistics.

For northern Europe, North America, Japan, and Australia, the annual incidence of typhoid fever is less than 1 case per 100,000 persons, and half of these cases are acquired by foreign travel rather than by indigenous exposure. The annual incidence in southern and eastern Europe averages about 10 per 100,000, whereas in the developing world it is 40 in Egypt, 100 in Chile, 850 in rural South Africa, and ranges from 500 to 1,000 for some areas of South and Southeast Asia.

These crude estimates in turn suggest that the global incidence averages 300 cases of typhoid fever per 100,000 persons per year or 15 million cases of typhoid fever each year.

Regarding age, sex, and race, the following generalizations can be made: In endemic areas, 75 percent of cases of typhoid fever occur in persons 3 to 18 years old. Typhoid is only rarely described in children younger than 2 years, although studies in Chile indicate that typhoid fever may be unsuspected clinically because the characteristic features of the disease are blurred in this age group. For acute typhoid fever, the ratio of the sexes is equal, but three-quarters of carriers are women; no susceptibility to typhoid fever has been identified by race.

Poverty is usually associated with poor sanitation and poor health care, and thus constitutes a risk factor for acquisition of typhoid. Blacks in South Africa have four times the incidence of typhoid, with eight times the mortality rate of whites. In Israel, the rate for the Jewish population is similar to that for Europe; for the non-Jewish population, it is similar to that for the Middle East.

In endemic areas, typhoid tends to peak in the summer months. Whether this pattern is due to greater consumption of water or enhanced proliferation of the bacteria in food is unknown. In the developed world, to judge by the United States, seasonality reflects foreign travel patterns, with peaks in January and February and again in the summer months.

Pathology

Most ingested typhoid bacilli are killed by stomach acid. Factors that reduce stomach acid (antacids) and speed transit time through the stomach (infancy, surgery, water rather than food as a bacterial vehicle) enhance the chances of infection.

Once in the small intestine, the bacilli penetrate the mucosal lining and are ingested by white cells located in gut lymph nodes. Perhaps because of its protective envelope (Vi antigen), *S. typhi* resists intracellular digestion and proceeds to multiply within the cells that normally destroy bacteria. Bacteria multiply and pass into the bloodstream. Initially, they are cleared from the blood by white cells located in the liver and spleen, but there, too, the bacilli multiply intracellularly, and reenter the

bloodstream. It is during this second period of bacteremia that the clinical symptoms of typhoid begin.

Lymph nodes in the small intestine become particularly laden with bacilli, occasionally to such an extent that they and the surrounding tissues die, leading to intestinal hemorrhage or perforation – the major causes of mortality in typhoid. The biliary tract is infected, and the patient may begin shedding *S. typhi* in the stool. Delirium, inflammation of the heart, and shock may occur and are caused not by direct infection but, rather, by toxins released either by the bacilli or by the white cells. Over a period of weeks, the body's intracellular immune system recognizes the typhoid bacillus, permitting the host to destroy the invader.

Clinical Manifestations

Typhoid fever is an illness characterized by fever and headache. Other early symptoms that may occur are abdominal distension or tenderness, constipation and a few loose bowel movements, cough or bronchitis, and "rose spots" – a transient rash that usually begins on the abdomen. As the illness progresses, the headache may be more severe and be associated with mental confusion or stupor, the liver and spleen usually become enlarged, and complications such as intestinal hemorrhage, intestinal perforation, and pneumonia may occur.

If the disease is untreated, mortality ranges between 10 and 20 percent; 1 in 5 persons experiences gastrointestinal hemorrhage, and 1 in 50 suffers from perforation of the gut. Relapse occurs in about 10 percent of patients, usually after a week free of illness, but the symptoms are frequently milder and the duration shorter than during the original attack.

With early effective antibiotic treatment and supportive care, the course of the disease is markedly changed: Fever is usually gone within 3 days, and mortality is cut to less than 1 percent.

Diagnosis

Signs and symptoms so distinctive of typhoid as to render a clinical diagnosis secure are present only in a minority of patients. Particularly at the onset where fever may be the only complaint, typhoid is easily confused with a host of other diseases that share its geographic patterns: malaria, hepatitis, tuberculosis, brucellosis, and typhus, to name a few.

The usual method of diagnosis is the culture of *S. typhi* from some part of the body. In persons with typhoid fever, culture of bone marrow is positive in 80 to 90 percent, and blood cultures are positive in

70 percent. Cultures of duodenal fluid are positive in 50 percent. Stool and urine cultures have positivity rates of only 30 and 10 percent, respectively.

In 1896, Fernand Widal determined that most persons infected with *S. typhi* develop antibodies to its cell wall (O antigen) and flagellae (H antigen). Since that time, the Widal test for O and H antibodies in the blood has been used extensively to diagnose typhoid fever. But although the test uses inexpensive materials and is rapid, it is not always reliable. Persons with typhoid fever may never show a rise in antibody levels, and past exposure to *S. typhi* (such as is common among adults in endemic areas) can mean a positive Widal test, whatever the patient's current ailment. In unimmunized children in endemic areas, however, the Widal test may be of value.

Treatment

Until 1948, little other than supportive measures could be offered the typhoid patient, but with the discovery of the antibiotic chloramphenicol, mortality was markedly reduced. For 20 years chloramphenicol was an entirely effective treatment, but resistance to it emerged in the early 1970s almost simultaneously in Mexico and Vietnam. Within a few years, 75 percent of all isolates of *S. typhi* in Vietnam were resistant. In developed areas, where infections were less frequent and antibiotic use was more tightly controlled, the percentage of resistant strains remained below 5 percent. Antibiotics such as trimethoprim, sulfamethoxazole, ampicillin, and others are now the drugs of choice for typhoid fever.

Control

Strategies for control of typhoid are divided into three categories:

Elimination of the Reservoir

Identification of carriers in an endemic population is difficult, and eradication of the carrier state costly. This option appears impractical.

Interruption of Transmission

Where pure water and food can be assured, typhoid transmission is minimal. Solely by improvement of sanitary conditions in the past century in developed countries, the incidence of typhoid fever has declined from 1 in 200 to 1 in 250,000. Mathematical models suggest that the building of privies in endemic areas would be among the least costly methods of reducing typhoid prevalence. Unfortunately, the pace of progress in making such sanitary improvements is slow.

Immunization

Exposure to the typhoid bacillus appears to confer some degree of protection against subsequent infection. Volunteer trials in the twentieth century verified this, and the extent of protection was quantified at 75 percent. However, the immunity was relative; it seemed to decay after a number of years, and could be overcome, at any stage, by the administration of a sufficient number of bacilli. Nevertheless, a relative immunity was better than none, and attempts to induce it artificially began almost as soon as the bacillus was isolated in the last decades of the nineteenth century. Since that time, most clinical vaccine trials indicate a protective effect of about 75 percent. At present, three major formulations exist:

Injection of Killed S. typhi *Bacilli.* This version contributed to the elimination of typhoid from the British and American armies during World War I, and, when administered to Thai schoolchildren in the 1970s, it was apparently instrumental in decreasing endemic typhoid fever. It is cheap and easy to produce, but there is a high rate of adverse reactions (fever, pain at the site of injection), as well as the need for refrigeration, sterile administration, and one to two boosters.

Injection of Vi Antigen. Vi Antigen (the protective polysaccharide envelope of *S. typhi*) provides, for persons in endemic areas, a degree of protection that is similar to that of the killed vaccine. The efficacy of this vaccine in Western travelers is not known. Only one dose is required, no refrigeration is needed, and no adverse effects have been noted. It requires sterile administration and is relatively expensive.

Oral Vaccine. This vaccine consists of a mutant strain of *S. typhi* incapable of causing typhoid fever. Studies in Egypt and Chile have documented its efficacy, with no adverse reactions observed. Refrigeration, but not sterile administration, is required. Disadvantages include the problems of storage and administration of a live vaccine, the need for at least three doses, and the higher cost.

Although control of typhoid fever is best accomplished with improvement of sanitary conditions, immunization with the more acceptable oral and polysaccharide vaccines may play an important public health role in developing countries.

History

Antiquity Through The Seventeenth Century

Typhoid fever has surely been a disease of human beings since prehistory, but for ancient physicians its nonspecific symptoms did not make it distinct from other illnesses. Hippocrates described a case of what appears to have been typhoid, and Caesar Augustus was cured of a fever with the characteristics of typhoid by the use of cold baths, a remedy that persisted well into the twentieth century.

Although meaningful reports from ancient and medieval times are lacking, the early mercantile and colonial enterprises of European expansion were clearly affected by typhoid epidemics. In the early seventeenth century, 6,500 out of 7,500 colonists at Jamestown, Virginia, died most likely from typhoid fever.

At about the same time this epidemic was occurring, the Belgian anatomist Adriaan van den Spieghel (Spigelius) described lesions in the lymphoid tissue of the small intestine of a patient who had died of a protracted fever, the first report of the characteristic pathological findings of typhoid. Later in the century, a British physician, Thomas Willis, cataloged the symptoms, signs, and course of a disease he called "putrid malignant fever," which was clearly typhoid.

Eighteenth Through Nineteenth Century

In the mid-eighteenth century, the Frenchman François Boissier de Sauvages consolidated a variety of ailments, including what Willis had called putrid malignant fever, into the term "typhus." In the 1830s, Pierre Louis, dissatisfied with the heterogeneity of the concept of typhus, proposed isolating a particular constellation of symptoms under the name "typhoid fever," or typhus-like fever. Later the American William W. Gerhard, studying an epidemic in Philadelphia, established typhoid fever as an entity independent of typhus, a term that now refers only to diseases caused by the rickettsial family of bacteria.

Though the illness now had a clinical definition, its mode of transmission was still in dispute. Somewhat earlier in the century, Pierre Bretonneau had argued that typhoid was contagious and that an attack conferred immunity. In the 1840s, the Englishman William Budd virtually inaugurated the science of epidemiology by his demonstration that typhoid was spread from infected individuals to new hosts by means of water and food. Budd's position was actively opposed by those who believed in spontaneous generation, and little was done to implement his recommendations of public health measures. As a result, the annual incidence in Europe at that time remained as high as 1 per 200 people.

Finally, in 1875 Budd's warnings were heeded, and the British Public Health Act was passed, radically improving sanitary practices. Within a decade, typhoid mortality was cut in half. This lesson was not lost on other developed nations who enacted sanitary laws of their own. Since that time, the incidence of typhoid in the developed world has steadily declined to its current annual rate of 1 case per 250,000 individuals.

This profound revolution in public health had begun before the microbial etiology of typhoid, or any other infection, had been established. Yet just 2 years after the Public Health Act was passed in England, the German Robert Koch demonstrated that a microorganism was the cause of anthrax; 3 years later his countrymen Carl Eberth and Edwin Klebs identified the typhoid bacillus in intestinal lymph nodes, making typhoid one of the earliest diseases for which a bacterial agent was known.

The next 2 decades saw an explosion of knowledge about the organism which was then called *Eberthella typhosa* in honor of its discoverer. In 1884 Georg Gaffky succeeded in culturing the bacillus from lymph nodes, and shortly thereafter it was isolated from blood and stool.

Despite these rapid advances, therapeutic interventions against typhoid were lacking. During the Spanish-American War of 1898, one-fifth of the American army fell ill from typhoid fever, with a mortality six times the number of those who died of wounds. At about this time in England, Almroth Wright developed a vaccine of heat-killed bacilli, which reduced the attack rate among soldiers in India by 75 percent. Despite these impressive results, the vaccine was little used 2 years later in the South African (Boer) War, and the disastrous experience of the American army in the war against Spain was virtually repeated among British troops in South Africa.

Twentieth Century

Early in this century, both the British and American commands ordered mandatory typhoid immunization and better military sanitation. The effect a decade later was dramatic: During World War I, the typhoid attack rate was reduced from 1 in 5, to 1 in 2,000, and since then, perhaps for the first time in human history, typhoid has not played a major role in armed conflicts.

In 1906 George Soper, then a sanitary engineer for the New York Department of Health, was called upon to investigate an outbreak of typhoid. It had occurred in a summer home in Oyster Bay, a well-to-do town where the disease was unknown. Yet 6 of 11 people in the house had become ill. Soper determined that 3 weeks before the outbreak a new cook had been hired but had left after the first persons began falling ill. The cook's name was Mary Mallon, and she was destined to become inextricably linked with typhoid fever.

Four years earlier, Koch had proposed that a person might chronically shed the typhoid bacillus and thus infect others, yet remain healthy and unaffected by the disease. His carrier hypothesis lacked adequate supporting evidence and was doubted by many. It occurred to Soper, however, that the perplexing cluster of typhoid cases in Oyster Bay might be explained if the cook were a carrier.

Soper's investigations showed that over the previous 10 years inexplicable typhoid outbreaks had occurred in seven of the eight families for which Mary Mallon had worked. A year later, Soper located her working once again in a home where typhoid fever had just broken out. She was removed against her will to a hospital where culture of her stool proved that she was indeed shedding S. typhi in great numbers. After a 3-year detention on North Brother Island in Long Island Sound (a detention that raised many civil liberty questions), she was released on the promise that she would never again handle food. Five years later, however, she was found to be the source of an epidemic of 25 cases of typhoid that occurred at Women's Hospital in Manhattan. She was arrested and spent the rest of her life on North Brother Island. "Typhoid Mary" had established beyond scientific doubt that a carrier state existed in typhoid.

In 1933 Eberthella typhosa became Salmonella typhi, thereby joining a family of bacilli named after D. E. Salmon, who in the 1880s had discovered an organism (Salmonella cholerasuis) responsible for bacteremia in humans and diarrhea in swine. The discovery in 1948 of antibiotics active against S. typhi converted typhoid in the developed world from a rare but dread disease to just a rare one, acquired mainly by travel abroad.

On a global scale, however, there has been little evidence that typhoid is fading into obscurity. Although inexpensive vaccines place typhoid control within reach of those nations with limited health resources, the huge worldwide reservoir of carriers and the continuation of poor sanitation in endemic areas suggest that it will be some time before the developing nations can significantly reduce the incidence of typhoid fever.

Charles W. LeBaron and David W. Taylor

This chapter was written in the authors' private capacities. No official support or endorsement by the Centers for Disease Control is intended or should be inferred.

Bibliography

Acharya, I. L., et al. 1987. Prevention of typhoid fever in Nepal with the Vi capsular polysaccharide of *Salmonella typhi*. *New England Journal of Medicine* 317: 1101–4.

Blaser, M. J., and L. S. Newman. 1982. A review of human salmonellosis: 1. Infective dose. *Reviews of Infectious Diseases* 4: 1096–106.

Bodhidatta, L., et al. 1987. Control of typhoid fever in Bangkok, Thailand, by annual immunization of schoolchildren with parenteral typhoid vaccine. *Reviews of Infectious Diseases* 9: 841–5.

Claman, G. 1979. A typhoid epidemic and the power of the press in Denver in 1879. *Colorado Magazine* 56: 143–60.

Feldman, R. E., et al. 1982. Epidemiology of *Salmonella typhi* infection in a migrant labor camp in Dade County, Florida. *Journal of Infectious Diseases* 146: 724–6.

Gadeholt, H., and S. T. Madsen. 1963. Clinical course, complications and mortality in typhoid fever as compared with paratyphoid B. *Acta Medica Scandinavica* 174: 753–60.

Hornick, R. B. 1979. Immunization against typhoid fever. *Annual Reviews of Medicine* 30: 457–72.

Huckstep, R. L. 1962. *Typhoid fever and other salmonella infections*. Edinburgh.

Koppes, Clayton R., and William P. Norris. 1985. Ethnicity, class, and mortality in the industrial city: A case study of typhoid fever in Pittsburgh, 1890–1910. *Journal of Urban History* 11: 259–79.

Levine, M. M., R. E. Black, C. Lanata, and the Chilean Typhoid Committee. 1982. Precise estimation of the numbers of chronic carriers of *Salmonella typhi* in Santiago, Chile, an endemic area. *Journal of Infectious Diseases* 146: 724–6.

Osler, W. 1906. *The principles and practice of medicine, designed for the use of practitioners and students of medicine*. New York.

Popkiss, M. E. E. 1980. Typhoid fever, a report on a point-source outbreak of 69 cases in Cape Town. *South African Medical Journal* 57: 325–9.

Rubin, R. H., and L. Weinstein. 1977. *Salmonellosis*. Stratton, N.Y.

Smith, Dale, ed. 1985. *William Budd: On the causes of fever. On the causes and mode of propagation of the common continued fevers of Great Britain and Ireland.* The Henry E. Sigerist Supplements to the *Bulletin of History of Medicine,* No. 9. Baltimore.

Stevenson, Lloyd G. 1982. Exemplary disease: The typhoid pattern. *Journal of the History of Medicine and Allied Sciences* 32: 159–81.

Stuart, B. M., and R. L. Pullen. 1946. Typhoid, clinical analysis of three hundred and sixty cases. *Archives of Internal Medicine* 78: 629–61.

Sufin, Mark. 1970. The case of the disappearing cook. *American Heritage* 21: 37–43.

Thomison, J. B. 1974–5. Typhoid fever in medical history. Parts I, II, and III. *Journal of the Tennessee Medical Association* 67: 991–7; 68: 106–11; 68: 373–7.

VIII.150
Typhomalarial Fever

Typhomalarial fever as a specific disease is not recognized by medical authorities today, but for the last half of the nineteenth century it was a frequently useful diagnostic category of diverse and often imprecise meaning. Joseph J. Woodward, a U.S. Army surgeon, defined the term during the American Civil War for those camp diseases "in which the malarial and typhoid elements are variously combined with each other and with the scorbutic taint." Woodward considered the disease "a new hybrid of old and well known pathological conditions," but one that was distinct, both clinically and at postmortem, from malarial and typhoid fevers.

Distribution and Incidence

William Osler once wrote that typhomalarial fever existed "in the minds of doctors but not in the bodies of patients." If so, it existed in the minds of many American doctors in the South, Midwest, and western regions of the country as well as in the minds of military and other European physicians practicing in the unsanitary, malarious regions of the globe, particularly the Mediterranean, British India, and some areas of China. It was primarily an Anglo-American phenomenon, although there are a few reports from southern Europe, which indicate that the possibility of the diagnosis was at least considered.

Etiology and Epidemiology

Typhomalarial fever was generally regarded as a noncontagious, infectious disease that resulted from exposure to the atmospheric or environmental infections or toxins that caused malarial fevers and typhoid fevers. Most commonly, patients were previously debilitated, or their vital powers were depressed in some way. In Woodward's classic formulation, this was the result of the depression produced by army camp life and malnutrition – particularly incipient scurvy. The disease required an area of endemic malarial fever, frequently a marsh, into which the animal causes of typhoid fever – crowding and improper sanitation – intruded. The debilitated individual in such an environment was almost sure to contract typhomalarial fever.

Clinical Manifestations and Pathology

The clinical course of the disease was extremely varied, depending on whether the malarial or typhoid elements predominated. When the malarial element was dominant, the symptoms were those of periodic fever – usually of the remittent rather than the intermittent variety. It was frequently quotidian but could be tertian, quartan, or irregularly remittent. However, the patient was more than usually depressed; there were frequent central nervous system symptoms, commonly stupor or coma, as well as gastrointestinal complaints, most commonly diarrhea. The disease was of more rapid onset than classic typhoid fever, but if the typhoid elements dominated, the disease would clinically resemble typhoid fever except for a definite periodicity, frequent hepatic tenderness, and a greater degree of splenomegaly, often with pain on palpitation. The convalescence would be more rapid than typical typhoid fever.

At postmortem there was a "greater tendency to the deposit of black pigment in the enlarged follicles" of the small bowel in typhomalarial than in typhoid fever. Furthermore, there were, in Woodward's (1863) formulation, some differences in the enlargement of the intestinal glands, the glands rising more gradually from the surrounding tissue in typhomalarial fever cases than in typhoid. By 1876, however, Woodward denied the significance of this supposed difference.

History and Geography

Woodward's concept was born of the frustrations of mid-nineteenth-century medicine, particularly in America.

1800–50

At the beginning of the nineteenth century, diagnosis was based almost entirely upon patient descriptions of their complaints – that is, the perceived functional derangements that resulted in a consultation with the physician. The physicians placed these complaints in the context of their own experience and knowledge, made a diagnosis, and offered the patient their professional advice. Diseases were collections of symptoms appearing in known orders in particular locations; adjectives were frequently part of a diagnosis, providing further refinement to a relatively limited array of disease nouns. The most common disease was "fever," of which fever was the chief symptom. The symptom fever was essentially the subjective sensation of chill and heat and was related by the medical profession to a quickened pulse. Elevated body temperature was related to fever but was not objectively measured by most physicians until the last third of the nineteenth century. If there was an observed cause of the fever, particularly an inflammation, then the fever was symptomatic. Both pneumonia and erysipelas had symptomatic fevers associated with them. If there was not an observed cause of the fever, then the fever was *essential* – that is, a disease itself. The essential fevers were categorized by symptom variation, severity, location, pathological associations, and so forth.

The two main categories were *periodic* and *continued* fever, but they were also categorized by such terms as malignant, pernicious, epidemic, putrid, spotted, and bilious, based upon the understandings of the physician observing a particular case. Periodic fevers – intermittent and remittent fevers, which had a classic periodicity – were believed to be caused by the atmospheric contamination of vegetable decomposition associated with marshes and other well-recognized areas of periodic-fever endemicity. During the nineteenth century, this poison came to be called "malaria," and the fevers it caused were "malarial" fevers. The continued fevers were more variable: Some were of short duration and only an inconvenience to the patient, whereas others were long and grave of prognosis. Those continued fevers with coma or stupor and of severe aspect were frequently called typhus by the Anglo-American medical world of the late eighteenth century. The adjective "typhoid" was applied to fevers that were typhus-like but not true typhus.

During the first half of the nineteenth century, a group of research-oriented, urban hospital-based physicians began to define disease on the basis of the postmortem findings as correlated with the clinical course. This hospital-based medicine was most strongly associated with the hospitals and pathologists of Paris, particularly René Laennec, Jean Corvisart, and Pierre Louis. In Great Britain, the Irish clinicians William Stokes and Robert Graves and the London hospital physicians Richard Bright, Thomas Addison, and Thomas Hodgkins were part of the same movement. This approach to medicine spread through the world but did not fully replace the purely clinical approach, particularly among those whose chief interests were in medical practice. In 1829 Louis described a specific fever with lesions of Peyer's patches of the small bowel and named it "typhoid" because he thought it was the disease British authorities of the previous generation had called "typhus." This is, of course, the disease known today as typhoid fever.

All of this nosographic confusion was reflected in the American medical literature. Daniel Drake, the great medical geographer of the interior valley of North America, wrote about the typhoid stage of autumnal fever, by which he probably meant what we might call pernicious malaria. Louis's American students brought his view of typhoid to America, and one of them, James Jackson, Jr., demonstrated that what was commonly called autumnal fever in New England was the same disease Louis called typhoid. Another student of Louis, William Gerhard of Philadelphia, proved that the disease his mentor had termed typhoid was distinct from the disease usually called autumnal fever in Philadelphia.

Based largely on his New England practice and experience, Elisha Bartlett described typhoid fever as the most common disease in the United States. By 1847, however, he realized that malarial fevers were the dominant concern of physicians in the South and Midwest, but not enough people learned of the revised opinion. Support for almost any interpretation could be found in the medical literature of the period.

1850s–1870s

In the 1850s, as the American South became increasingly isolated culturally, there arose a campaign for a distinctively southern medicine. In part, this desire reflected real geographic differences in disease, but in part it was a result of the increasingly strident southern nationalism that led to the Civil War. As a result of this campaign and the preexisting nosological confusion, there was, by 1860, a belief in a southern typhoid fever that was occasionally periodic and frequently cured by quinine therapy.

Etiologic theories of the mid-nineteenth century also contributed to the confusion. Urban diseases, like typhus and typhoid, were believed to be the result of the unsanitary conditions of life in the early industrial city. Crowding, a general lack of cleanliness, and a combination of animal and human waste, gave rise to a distinct and unpleasant odor in the cities. Where the smell was worst was also frequently the area of greatest morbidity, and it was believed that there were animal miasmas that caused urban fevers, much like the marsh miasmas (malaria) that caused rural fevers. If the two causes were simultaneously present, a combined or composite disease state should be expected. In the camps of the Civil War, that is exactly what was experienced, and typhomalarial fever was the name officially sanctioned for the camp disease that was not obviously a malarial or typhoid fever.

During and immediately after the war, an era when disease theory was changing and the diagnostic precision of the profession was limited, physicians found the concept of typhomalarial fever to be very useful and flexible in diagnosis. There were, however, serious doubts on the part of leading medical theorists concerning the specific nature of typhomalarial fever. In the 1870s, these doubts increased, but so did the utilization of the diagnosis. By the late 1870s, the specificity, in pathological terms, of typhomalarial fever was an idea of the past, but the clinical reality remained, and the name seemed to explain the etiology of the symptom complexities so described.

For the same reasons physicians in other parts of the world began seriously to consider the American diagnosis in the 1870s. In the 1860s, British army surgeons stationed on Malta had identified a new disease originally called gastric remittent fever and later Malta fever. We know it today as brucellosis. In 1875 W. C. Maclean, professor of military medicine at the Army Medical School at Netley, suggested that Malta fever might be typhomalarial fever. James Donaldson, on the other hand, suggested the name "faeco-malarial fever" to reflect more accurately the current understanding of dual causes. By the 1870s, the special role of human fecal matter in the propagation of typhoid fever was becoming accepted in Great Britain, largely as a result of the work of Charles Murchison and William Budd. Similar new diseases reported by the British doctors in the Indian Medical Service and the Chinese Imperial Customs Medical Service were also considered as typhomalarial fever by some authorities.

The primary interest of these physicians was in disease prevention, and the name "typhomalarial" lent force to their campaign for cleanliness. J. Lane Notter explained:

The cause then of this disease is, I maintain, a preventable one. It essentially consists in defective drainage, in having to sleep in houses and breathe air impregnated with faecal organic vapours given off from saturated subsoil or filthy watercloses, aided by climatic conditions which make enteric fever in Malta assume a malarial type, and which would, under similar conditions in England, simply produce typhoid fever.

1880s

In the 1880s the miasmatic etiologic speculations began to give way to the new germ theory of disease based in medical microbiology. Alphonse Laveran observed the malaria plasmodium; Georg Gaffky isolated *Salmonella typhi.* David Bruce discovered an organism that caused Malta fever; he called it *Micrococcus melitensis,* but the genus was subsequently named *Brucella.* However, the germ theory and medical microbiology were not immediately accepted by all or even most practitioners. Debate on typhomalaria remained lively, particularly in the American medical literature. Leading physicians saw etiologic research and eventual etiologic definition of disease as the way to resolve the clinical difficulties, but microbiological techniques remained largely in the realm of experimental pathology, not yet overly useful to practitioners. The possibility of specific diseases similar to typhoid and malaria yet etiologically unique remained viable, but the profession was divided on how prevalent such diseases might be. Periodic typhoid and severe malaria were clinically real and needed names. Debate continued, but the terms were changing.

1890s–1900s

In the 1890s, progress in medical microbiology and the development of serum diagnostic tests for typhoid and Malta fevers made etiologic definitions of disease more useful to practitioners, and doubts increased about the utility of typhomalarial fever as a diagnosis.

When America mobilized volunteers for the war with Spain in 1898, the sanitation in the camps was very bad. Disease was widespread and Army Surgeon General George Miller Sternberg appointed a commission of experts composed of Walter Reed, Victor Vaughan, and E. O. Shakespeare to investigate. Using modern techniques – blood smear examinations and Fernand Widal's serodiagnostic test – the commission proved that most of the cases diagnosed as typhomalarial fever were typhoid. Because the conditions, particularly in camps in the Deep South, approximated those under which Woodward had originally postulated the existence of typhomalarial fever, these results were particularly significant. By the early twentieth century, the diagnosis of typho-malarial fever was widely regarded as an admission of diagnostic failure, and slowly it vanished from the medical literature.

Dale Smith

Bibliography

Donaldson, J. 1876. On the diagnosis and causation of faecomalarial fever. *Report of the Army Medical Department for 1876*, 238–42.

Drake, Daniel. 1850. *A systematic treatise, historical, etiological, and practical, on the principal diseases of the interior valley of North America.* Cincinnati, Oh.

Maclean, W. C. 1875. On Malta fever: With a suggestion. *British Medical Journal* ii: 224–5.

Notter, J. L. 1876. On Malta fever. *Edinburgh Medical Journal* 22: 289–98.

Smith, Dale C. 1982. The rise and fall of typhomalarial fever. *Journal of the History of Medicine* 37: 182–220, 287–321.

Reed, Walter, Victor C. Vaughan, and Edward C. Shakespeare. 1904. *Report on the origin and spread of typhoid fever in U.S. military camps during the Spanish War of 1898*, 2 vols. Washington, D.C.

Woodward, Joseph J. 1863. *Outlines of the chief camp diseases of the United States armies.* Philadelphia.

VIII.151
Typhus, Epidemic

Epidemic typhus fever is an acute rickettsial disease transmitted among victims by the human body louse, *Pediculus humanus corporis.* Its characteristic symptoms include high fever, prostration, headache and body aches, and a widespread rash that covers the trunk and limbs of the body. Mortality rates in untreated cases vary widely. Broad-spectrum antibiotics provide an effective therapy for the disease.

Because of its association with conditions of human misery, typhus has been known by many names. *Jail distemper* and its variations – *morbus carcerum,* gaol fever, and jayl fever – indicate the prevalence of typhus in detention facilities. Ship fever, camp fever, and famine fever reflect the poor hygiene characteristic of travel, of military expeditions, and of refugee populations. The characteristic rash of typhus has elicited other descriptive names, including spotted fever in English, *Fleckfieber* and *typhus exanthematicus* in German, *typhus exanthé-*

matique in French, *tifo exantemático* and *tabardillo* in Spanish (the latter meaning "red cloak"), and *typhus-esantematico* in Italian. Although Hippocrates applied the word *typhus,* from the Greek word meaning smoky or hazy, to confused or stuporous states of mind frequently associated with high fevers, the word was not associated with the disease as it is currently known until the eighteenth century. After murine typhus was identified, the appellation *typhus historique* was sometimes applied to the classic, epidemic disease.

Etiology and Epidemiology

Occurring as a natural infection only in humans, epidemic typhus is caused by *Rickettsia prowazekii.* It is spread from host to host by the human body louse, *P. humanus corporis,* and less often by the human head louse, *Pediculus humanus capitis.* The body louse spends its entire existence in the clothes of humans. Eggs laid in the seams of the undergarments hatch after about 8 days, and the nymphs become adults in about 2 weeks, going through three molts. Each louse takes four to six blood meals a day from its host under natural conditions. Human blood constitutes its only food.

Once typhus organisms in infected human blood are ingested by a louse, they multiply rapidly in the cells lining the louse's intestines and are secreted in the feces of infected lice. Since rickettsiae are not found in other tissues (such as the salivary glands) of the louse, they are transmitted to new human hosts mechanically. This is usually accomplished by contact of infected louse feces with a small abrasion of the skin incurred when the human scratches the unpleasant itch caused by feeding lice. The disease spreads when lice leave feverish or dead victims for new hosts with normal temperatures. Unlike other rickettsial organisms, *R. prowazekii* is not passed from generation to generation in the eggs of its host arthropod. In fact, as Hans Zinsser of Harvard Medical School pointed out in his 1935 history of typhus fever, humans constitute a great threat to the health and happiness of these small creatures, for humans usually recover from typhus fever, whereas the disease is inevitably deadly for infected lice.

Typhus is widely known as a disease of cold climates, appearing in epidemics that usually reach their peaks in late winter and taper off in the spring. This pattern is clearly related to the ideal conditions for multiplication of lice and their rapid transmission to new hosts. Typhus flourishes when people are crowded together in unsanitary surroundings and lack fuel, circumstances that predispose them to wear the same garments day and night for months at a time.

Persons of all ages are susceptible to typhus. Mortality rates in untreated typhus fever vary between 5 and 25 percent, occasionally reaching 40 percent. In children under 15 years of age, however, the disease is generally mild. As age increases, so does mortality.

Clinical Manifestations and Pathology

After an incubation period that may vary from 5 to 15 days, the onset of typhus is abrupt. Many patients are able to state the exact hour at which they noted the beginning of their illness. Headache, loss of appetite, and general malaise are followed by a rapidly rising fever. Bouts of chills, nausea, and prostration characterize the first week of illness. The most characteristic symptom of typhus is a widespread rash that appears about the fourth to sixth day after onset. Dark, reddish, discrete spots 2 to 5 millimeters in diameter appear scattered over the body and limbs. These lesions at first are bright red, but they rapidly become darker in color and more petechial in character. After recovery, the rash usually fades, but in rare cases it may leave a brownish stain that persists for several months.

During the first 2 or 3 days, the fever reaches its maximum, between 102° to 105°F, and is sustained for another 5 days, after which it falls rapidly if the outcome is favorable. In fatal cases, however, prostration becomes more progressive, with neurological symptoms increasing. These may include deafness, stupor, delirium, and eventually coma preceding death. Since 1948, however, when chloramphenicol and the tetracyclines (known collectively as broadspectrum antibiotics) were introduced, no one need die of typhus if diagnosis is made in a timely manner.

Immunology

An attack of typhus confers long immunity. Many children in regions where typhus is frequent may contract subclinical or mild cases that protect them somewhat from a later, more severe infection. Because *R. prowazekii* persists in the tissues of its victims even after recovery from the disease, however, symptoms of the disease may reappear years later, especially under conditions of stress when a victim's immune system is depressed. This phenomenon was noted but not recognized in 1898, when New York physician Nathan Brill described a disease frequently diagnosed as typhoid but having symptoms

more closely related to typhus. In 1910 Brill published an exhaustive study of 221 cases, and his thoroughness led to the designation of "Brill's disease" as a catchall for unknown, typhus-like symptoms. Two years later, U.S. Public Health Service investigators John F. Anderson and Joseph Goldberger demonstrated reciprocal cross-immunity in monkeys between Brill's disease and epidemic typhus.

For the next two decades, moreover, because of ignorance surrounding many other rickettsial diseases, illnesses exhibiting typhuslike symptoms anywhere in the world were often classified as Brill's disease. In 1934 Zinsser correctly hypothesized from epidemiological data that Brill's disease was a recrudescence of epidemic typhus in persons who had earlier suffered an attack of the classic disease. During the 1950s, laboratory investigations confirmed his hypothesis, and the disease was renamed *Brill–Zinsser disease*.

The first laboratory diagnostic test for typhus grew out of a chance observation in 1916 by Viennese physician Edmund Weil and his English colleague Arthur Felix that a strain of *Bacillus proteus* was agglutinated by the sera of typhus patients. Later studies revealed that the phenomenon was a chance antigenic "fit," but the *Weil–Felix reaction,* as it came to be called, provided a laboratory tool that became useful in several rickettsial diseases. In 1941 a more specific complement-fixation test was developed, and during the 1970s a variety of new techniques have improved the sensitivity and accuracy of laboratory diagnosis.

Distribution and Incidence

In all areas of the world where public health and sanitation measures have been rigorously enforced, the incidence of typhus has declined dramatically. Cases may erupt in urban slums, and the disease remains a threat to many isolated rural regions. Reporting of cases is poor in many regions of the world where typhus is most prevalent. Map VIII.151.1 shows the worldwide distribution of epidemic typhus during World War II. A recent study indicates that the major areas where typhus-infected lice are widespread have been reduced to three: the Himalayan region of Asia, the Andean regions of South America, and the horn of Africa, especially famine-ridden Ethiopia. In November 1984, for example, 68 cases were serologically confirmed in one Ethiopian refugee camp. Following treatment with tetracycline antibiotics, however, only three people died. Thus typhus, although causing considerable morbidity, is not at present as great a killer as in past centuries.

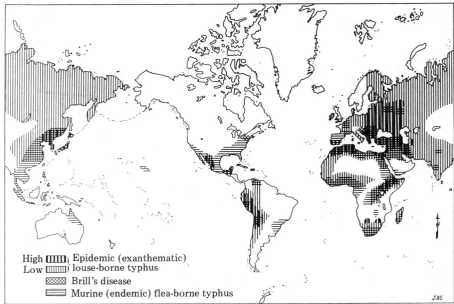

Map VIII.151.1. Outline map of the world (c. World War II), showing the approximate geographic distribution of epidemic (exanthematic) louse-borne typhus, murine (endemic) flea-borne typhus, and Brill's disease. (From Stanhope Bayne-Jones, in U.S. Army Medical Department 1964, 177.)

High ▨▨▨ ⎫ Epidemic (exanthematic)
Low ▥▥▥ ⎭ louse-borne typhus
        ▨▨▨ Brill's disease
        ▤▤▤ Murine (endemic) flea-borne typhus

History and Geography

Antiquity Through The Sixteenth Century

As a disease having a human reservoir, epidemic typhus has undoubtedly existed for centuries. Although it has been speculated that certain ancient plagues were probably typhus, the first contemporary accounts of a disease that may well have been typhus appeared near the end of the fifteenth century. In 1489–90 during the civil wars of Granada, Spanish physicians described a typhus-like disease that killed 17,000 Spanish soldiers – six times the number killed in combat with the Moors.

In the early sixteenth century, a similar malady appeared in Italy. During the French siege of Naples in 1528, an apparent typhus epidemic may have altered the subsequent course of European history. The French were at the point of decisive victory over the forces of Charles V when the disease appeared and struck down 30,000 French soldiers, forcing the remnants of the army to withdraw. In 1546 Girolamo Fracastoro (Fracastorius), who had observed the epidemics in Italy, published the first clear description of what he termed a "lenticular or punctate or petechial" fever also characterized by headache and general malaise.

In the Balkan regions, where German, Italian, and French troops assembled to combat the Turks, many soldiers were struck by typhus even before they reached the battlefield. As it was disseminated across Europe by forces returning from Hungary, typhus became known as *morbus hungaricus*. Toward the end of the sixteenth century, typhus was also recorded in the Mexican highlands, where it killed more than 2 million Amerindians. It remains unclear, however, whether the disease was brought to the New World by Spanish explorers or, as some evidence indicates, was known to the Aztecs and some pre-Columbian Indians in Mexico.

Early to Mid-Nineteenth Century

Typhus increased dramatically in the early nineteenth century. In 1812 Napoleon's catastrophic expedition to Russia was plagued by typhus. Between 1816 and 1819, moreover, a great epidemic of the disease struck 700,000 people in Ireland, whose population was only 6 million. For several decades, however, confusion characterized medical understanding of the disease. By the late eighteenth century, the medical nosologist Boissier de Sauvages had begun using the word *typhus* to describe the neurological symptoms of typhus, but few attempts were made to distinguish pathologically between typhus and typhoid fever, which also produced a red rash. Even into the twentieth century, confusion between typhoid and typhus was perpetuated in the nomenclature. In many European countries, the former was known as *typhus abdominalis* and the latter as *typhus exanthematicus*.

In 1837 Philadelphia physician William Wood Gerhard, who had studied the distinctive intestinal lesions of typhoid as a student of Pierre Louis in Paris, noted their absence in victims of typhus fever, which had been epidemic in Philadelphia the previous year. Gerhard's work, however, was not immediately embraced by physicians who clung to older theories of the unity of fevers. It was not until mid-century that additional pathological and epidemiological research, especially by William Jenner and Austin Flint, convinced most American physicians that typhus and typhoid were distinct disease entities.

The European revolutions of 1848 spawned typhus epidemics in eastern Europe, as did warfare in Ethiopia. During a particularly severe typhus epidemic in Upper Silesia, the German physician and politician Rudolph Virchow published a radical assessment of the epidemic that subsequently cost him his government post. Observing that the disease afflicted the poor, the uneducated, and the unclean, Virchow called for democracy, education, and public health measures as the proper "treatment" of the epidemic.

Late Nineteenth Century Through World War I

Although typhus itself subsided during the latter half of the nineteenth century, the advent of the germ theory of disease during the 1870s spurred bacteriologists to search for a microbial cause for the classic scourge. In 1909, exploiting recent discoveries about the role of insect and other arthropod vectors of microorganisms, Charles Nicolle, director of the Institut Pasteur in Tunis, North Africa, demonstrated that the body louse was the vector of typhus. The following year, Howard Taylor Ricketts, who was investigating typhus in Mexico City, described small bacteria he found in the blood of typhus victims, in infected lice, and in lice feces. Before Ricketts could confirm his observations, he contracted typhus and died. In 1916 the Brazilian Henrique da Rocha Lima described similar organisms, which he named *Rickettsia prowazekii,* the genus name after Ricketts and the species name after Polish researcher Stanislaus von Prowazek, who had also died from a laboratory-acquired typhus infection.

During World War I, military forces on both sides of the conflict acted on Nicolle's discovery, instituting delousing procedures to combat typhus. These included bathing and steam-treating clothing to kill lice. Among poor civilian populations in war-torn eastern Europe, where such preventive measures were not enforced, the disease continued to exact a high rate of mortality. In 1915 Serbia was particularly hard hit, and typhus settled with a vengeance on Russia and Poland after 1918. Typhus research in Poland after World War I, sponsored by the League of Red Cross Societies, confirmed Rocha Lima's assertion that *R. prowazekii* was the cause of typhus. Even so, because rickettsiae could not be cultured on lifeless media like ordinary bacteria, their etiologic relationship to typhus and other rickettsial diseases was not firmly established until the late 1930s.

Postwar Period Through World War II

During the 1920s and 1930s, empirical research on a vaccine against typhus was hampered because the organisms could not be grown in necessary quantities outside of living cells. Displaying ingenuity in the face of this limitation, researchers prepared vaccines from infected lice intestines, from lice feces, and from the typhus-infected lungs of rats. Then in 1937 U.S. Public Health Service investigator Herald R. Cox discovered that rickettsiae grew luxuriously in the yolksacs of fertile hens' eggs. This method simplified vaccine production and made it commercially feasible just as the onset of World War II again raised concern about large-scale typhus epidemics.

The threat of typhus was a key factor in Allied military plans during World War II, and in 1942 President Franklin D. Roosevelt created an extraordinary body, the U.S.A. Typhus Commission, to combat typhus wherever it might threaten the U.S. military efforts. The so-called Cox vaccine was administered to all Allied military personnel, and although experience during the hostilities indicated that it did not actually prevent the disease, it clearly ameliorated its course. Intensive research on antilouse agents by government and private groups, moreover, demonstrated that lice could be effectively controlled by dichlorodiphenyl-trichloroethane, more commonly called DDT. This powder could be applied with a "blowing machine" to puff it under clothes without their owners having to remove them. The method was not only faster, it was also accepted by even the most modest civilians. DDT also proved to be highly effective in the typhus epidemic that occurred during the winter of 1943–4 in Naples, Italy. With astonishing rapidity, the nascent epidemic collapsed. Within two decades, however, the ability of lice to become resistant to DDT had been documented. In addition, the chemical's ecological hazards were found unacceptable, and it is no longer widely used to prevent typhus.

Prophylaxis and control of typhus with the Cox vaccine and with DDT during World War II reduced typhus from a major threat to a mere nuisance among Allied troops. Only 104 cases occurred among U.S. military personnel, with no deaths. In contrast, severe epidemics occurred among civilians in North Africa, Yugoslavia, the German concentration camps, Japan, and Korea.

Mid-Twentieth Century to Present

In 1948 the tetracyclines and chloramphenicol, known together as broad-spectrum antibiotics, were discovered to be effective treatments for rickettsial diseases. Since the late 1940s, efforts to combat typhus have depended almost exclusively on these antibiotics. In 1980 concern about the limited efficacy and side effects of the Cox vaccine halted its production, and at the present writing, no typhus vaccine is commercially available. Recent research, moreover, has indicated that the humoral immunity stimulated by all existing rickettsial vaccines is less important than is cell-mediated immunity. At present, genetic engineering techniques are being employed in research on a more effective vaccine.

Since 1950, typhus has been reported most frequently from the horn of Africa, from the high plains of the Andes in South America, and from the Himalayan regions of Asia – all areas characterized by rural poverty and cold weather. In one survey of Bolivian army recruits, for example, 80 percent had antibodies against the disease. Another study in a Bolivian village near the Peruvian border found mild typhus in children often confused with measles. Typically, the disease was more severe in afflicted adults than in children.

In Ethiopia, with its frequent famines, thousands of cases of typhus have been documented in recent years, especially in refugee camps. Similar ecological and sociological conditions in neighboring countries suggest that the disease may also be widespread in them but masked by poor reporting. Reliable statistics are also virtually impossible to obtain from the Himalayan regions of Asia.

Since Nicolle's identification of the body louse as the vector of typhus, the slogan "no lice, no typhus" has been the watchword of public health efforts against this disease. But as Hans Zinsser noted in 1935, typhus will always remain a smoldering threat, ready to break out at any time that war, famine, or other catastrophes remove the public health barriers against it.

Victoria A. Harden

Bibliography

Anderson, John F., and Joseph Goldberger. 1912. The relation of so-called Brill's disease to typhus fever. *Public Health Reports* 27: 149–60.

Brill, Nathan E. 1910. An acute infectious disease of unknown origin: A clinical study based on 221 cases. *American Journal of Medical Science* 139: 484–502.

Edlinger, E. 1986. Actualité des Rickettsioses. *Archives de l'Institut Pasteur de Tunis* 63: 75–90.

Fracastoro, Girolamo. 1589. De morbis contagious. In *Opera omnia.* Venice.

Gear, J. H. S. 1984. Studies of the rickettsial diseases at the South African Institute for Medical Research: Epidemic louse-borne typhus fever. *Adler Museum Bulletin* 10: 8–15.

Gerhard, William Wood. 1837. On the typhus fever, which occurred at Philadelphia in the spring and summer of 1836. *American Journal of Medical Science* 19: 289–92, 298–9, 302–3.

Loeffler, W., and H. Mooser. 1952. Ein weiterer Fall von Brill-Zinsserscher Krankheit in Zürich (Später Rückfall bei klassischem Fleckfieber). *Schweizer Medizinische Wochenschrift* 82: 493.

Pankhurst, Richard. 1976. Some notes for the history of typhus in Ethiopia. *Medical History* 20: 384–93.

Smith, Dale C. 1980. Gerhard's distinction between typhoid and typhus and its reception in America, 1833–1860. *Bulletin of the History of Medicine* 54: 368–85.

Snyder, John C. 1965. Typhus fever rickettsiae. In *Viral and rickettsial infections of man,* 4th edition, ed. Frank L. Horsfall, Jr., and Igor Tamm, 1059–94. Philadelphia.

U.S. Army. Medical Department. 1964. *Preventive medicine in World War II,* Vol. 7: *Communicable diseases: Arthropodborne diseases other than malaria.* Washington, D.C.

Virchow, Rudolf. 1985. Report on the typhus epidemic in Upper Silesia. English trans. In *Rudolf Virchow: Collected essays on public health and epidemiology,* 2 vols., ed. L. J. Rather, Vol. 2, 205–319. Canton, Mass.

Zinsser, Hans. 1934. Varieties of typhus virus and the epidemiology of the American form of European typhus fever (Brill's disease). *American Journal of Hygiene* 20: 513–32.

1935. *Rats, lice and history.* Boston.

Murine typhus is an acute illness characterized by symptoms similar to those of epidemic typhus but milder in character. Unlike its epidemic relative, it is a natural infection of the rat and transmitted sporadically to humans by the rat flea, *Xenopsylla cheopis*. Its relation to the rat is reflected in the name *murine* typhus. The etiologic agent is *Rickettsia typhi*.

Clinical Manifestations

Symptoms and the course of illness in murine typhus are similar to those in epidemic, louse-borne typhus. For this reason, distinguishing between the two diseases has been difficult. The flea-borne illness, however, is almost never fatal, with about a 2 percent mortality in persons over age 50.

Etiology and Epidemiology

Murine typhus is found worldwide and is infectious for persons of all ages (see previous chapter, Map VIII.151.1). Those living or working in areas where rats are abundant are most susceptible. Like epidemic typhus, murine typhus is transmitted mechanically, through rubbing infected feces of the flea *Xenopsylla cheopis* into a skin abrasion, through the eye, or through mucous membranes of the respiratory tract. In the years following World War II, active campaigns against rats and their fleas with DDT and rodenticides sharply reduced the incidence of murine typhus in the United States.

The causative agent of epidemic typhus is known as *R. typhi*, although some investigators prefer to call it *Rickettsia mooseri* in honor of Herman Mooser, a Swiss pathologist who, working in Mexico, differentiated between this organism and *Rickettsia prowazekii*. In guinea pigs, *R. typhi* causes a characteristic reaction in scrotal cells useful for distinguishing between murine and epidemic typhus. First noticed in 1917 by U.S. Public Health Service investigator Mather H. Neill and confirmed nearly two decades later by Mooser, the reaction became known as the Neill–Mooser phenomenon.

History and Geography

Although murine typhus was identified only during the twentieth century, it may be an even older disease than classic, epidemic typhus. Neither of the two hosts of *R. typhi*, the rat and the rat flea, suffer ill effects from their infection with the organism, whereas *R. prowazekii* inevitably kills its vector louse and causes a serious illness in its human host.

Sporadic cases of typhuslike fevers in areas free from lice were reported early in the twentieth century in the United States, Malaya, and Australia. Often these infections were designated by local names, such as "urban" or "shop" typhus. It was not until 1926, however, that the distinctiveness of this disease was recognized. During an epidemiological investigation of such cases in the southeastern United States, U.S. Public Health Service investigator Kenneth F. Maxcy described an *endemic* form of typhus fever and postulated that some ectoparasite of the rat might be its vector. By 1931, infected fleas had been found in nature, confirming Maxcy's hypothesis. Although the name "endemic typhus" was used for some time, it was shortly observed that the disease could occur in epidemics as well as sporadically. In 1932 Mooser proposed that the disease be called "murine typhus" instead to indicate its relationship to rats.

Although broad-spectrum antibiotics provide effective treatment against this disease, its mild course and low fatality rate make these measures almost unnecessary. By the time the disease is diagnosed, the patient is usually in convalescence.

Victoria A. Harden

Bibliography

Biraud, Y., and S. Deutschman. 1936. Typhus and typhuslike rickettsia infections. *Epidemiological Reports* 15: 90–160.

Dyer, R. E., et al. 1932. Endemic typhus fever of the United States: History, epidemiology and mode of transmissions. *Journal of the American Medical Association* 99: 795–801.

Mooser, Herman. 1932. Essai sur l'histoire naturelle du typhus exanthématique. *Archive de l'Institut Pasteur de Tunis* 21: 1–19.

Williams, C. L. 1949. The control of murine typhus with DDT. *Military Surgeon* 104: 163–7.

Zinsser, Hans, and M. R. Castaneda. 1932. Studies on typhus fever IX. On the serum reactions of Mexican and European typhus rickettsia. *Journal of Experimental Medicine* 56: 455–67.

VIII.153
Typhus, Scrub (Tsutsugamushi)

Tsutsugamushi, like epidemic typhus, has been known in the Orient for centuries. In 1810 the Japanese Hakuju Hashimoto described a *tsutsuga* (disease) along the tributaries of the Shinano River. A similar disease, thought to be carried by mites, or *mushi* in Japanese, had also been known at least since the sixteenth century in southern China. Sometimes called Japanese flood fever, tsutsugamushi is more commonly known in the United States as scrub typhus – a name used widely by English-speaking troops during World War II. The disease exhibits characteristic typhuslike symptoms of high fever, headache, duration of 2 weeks, and a widespread rash.

Distribution and Incidence

The geographic boundaries of this malady are defined by the range of its vectors, primarily the trombiculid mites, *Lentotrombidium akamushi* and *Leototrombidium deliensis,* and their vertebrate hosts. They extend from India and Pakistan in the West, to Japan and the northern portions of Australia, including all the countries of Southeast Asia, southern China, Korea, the Philippines, and Indonesia, as well as additional islands in the Pacific Ocean (see Map VIII.153.1). During World War II, the incidence of scrub typhus rose dramatically among military troops, reaching 900 per 1,000 personnel in some areas. It continues to remain a problem in isolated, rural areas.

Etiology and Epidemiology

The etiologic agent of scrub typhus, *Rickettsia tsutsugamushi,* is a natural infection of several trombiculid mites, most commonly *L. deliensis.* Maintained in

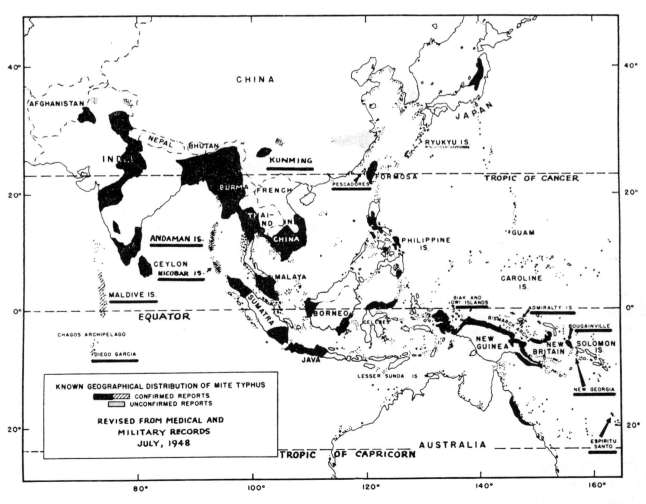

Map VIII.153.1. Known geographic distribution of mite (scrub) typhus in Asia, July 1948.

nature by generational transmission through the eggs of the female, the disease is communicated to humans only during the larval stage of the mite's life cycle. At this time, the six-legged larval mite, often called a "chigger," seeks an animal on which to find a meal of tissue juices, or lymph. Usually they feed on field mice, rats, tree-shrews, and other small mammals, but humans are satisfactory if they happen into the mite's environment. Ground-frequenting birds may also become infected and transport infected mites to a new location. In later stages of their lives, the mites live in the soil and not in animals.

Because of the wide geographic area across which tsutsugamushi is spread, its epidemiological pattern varies. In the Niigata region of Japan, for example, the disease is most common during the summer months, associated with increased incidence of the mite *L. akamushi*, whereas in the Chiba and the Kanagawa prefectures and the Izu Schichito Islands, it occurs in mild form throughout autumn and winter. In Malaya, a hot, tropical climate supports the disease throughout the year, and near the India–Burma border it is usually associated with the monsoon season.

Similarly, a variety of terrains may support the development of the vector mites, including grassy fields, river banks, neglected or abandoned rice fields, overgrown clearings, forests, jungles, and border areas between field and forest. The key requirements in any area include a suitable rodent population and sufficient ground moisture to support the mites. The "islands of infection" in which scrub typhus typically occurs apparently represent favorable ecological conditions for the mites.

Clinical Manifestations

Scrub typhus incubates in human hosts for about 10 to 12 days, after which it manifests itself suddenly, with chills and fever, headache, and other typical typhuslike symptoms. In most Caucasians and, less frequently, in Asians, an *eschar* or initial lesion from the mite bite occurs and causes lymph-gland swelling. During the first week of the disease, the fever increases to 104° or 105°F. Between the fifth and the eighth day, a red macular rash appears on the trunk of the body, and it may extend to the arms and the legs. During the second week, the pulse rate may increase to 120 or 140, blood pressure falls, and neurological symptoms such as deafness, stupor, delirium, and muscle twitching may appear in untreated patients. Pneumonia and signs of circulatory failure may also occur, but by the beginning of the third week, those untreated individuals who recover

begin to experience a reduction in fever and other symptoms. Those who die usually do so by the end of the second week from circulatory failure or from secondary pneumonia or encephalitis. Even in recovered patients, however, neurological effects may continue, and convalescence is usually long. Fortunately, the broad-spectrum antibiotics have reduced the mortality in treated patients to nearly zero.

Unfortunately, the immunity conferred by this infection is specific to the scrub typhus strain only. Current infections may occur when the individual is infected by other strains.

History and Geography

Reports of tsutsugamushi reach back to at least the sixteenth century in the Orient. Bacteriologic investigations of the disease began in Japan in the early 1890s when it captured the attention of Shibasaburo Kitasato, who had returned from his work with Robert Koch in Germany to found the Institute for Infectious Diseases in Tokyo. Various other researchers, principally Japanese, continued to study the disease through the first three decades of the twentieth century, identifying its causative microbe as a rickettsiae.

Renewed investigation by Western scientists was stimulated by severe outbreaks of scrub typhus in the Pacific and the China–Burma–India theaters during World War II. With the Allied countermove to stem the rapid Japanese advance in the Pacific, the occupation of islands often took place in haste, and groups of soldiers would shortly become very ill. Between January 1943 and August 1945, scrub typhus disabled some 18,000 Allied troops, including 6,685 American servicemen. Fatality rates varied from a low of 0.6 percent in some regions to as high as 35 percent in others; there were 234 deaths among U.S. troops.

Throughout the 1920s and 1930s, British researchers and their colleagues at the Institute of Medical Research in Kuala Lumpur, Federated Malay States, had observed that tsutsugamushi was distinguished from other typhuslike diseases by its reaction to a particular strain of bacteria used in the Weil–Felix test. When the U.S. Typhus Commission began to study scrub typhus ("because of its last name" as Commission Director Stanhope Bayne-Jones noted) the Weil–Felix diagnostic test was virtually the only laboratory tool available. Numerous experts in medicine, epidemiology, and entomology were called upon to examine the problem, and, by the end of the war, two major lines of defense against the disease had been developed.

The first was prevention. The army launched education efforts, including posters describing the mite, where it was likely to be found, and how soldiers should prepare their campsites to avoid it. In addition, chemicals were developed to impregnate clothing that would repel the tsutsugamushi mite. Benzyl benzoate proved to be effective and lasted 2 weeks before reapplication was necessary. The second line of defense focused on intensive research to develop an antiserum or a vaccine against tsutsugamushi. World War II ended, however, before either could be made practical. In 1948, the broad-spectrum antibiotic chloramphenicol was tested at the Institute of Medical Research in Kuala Lumpur and found to be highly effective as treatment for the disease.

Victoria A. Harden

Bibliography

Blake, Francis G., et al. 1945. Studies on tsutsugamushi disease (scrub typhus, mite-born typhus) in New Guinea and adjacent islands: Epidemiology, clinical observations, and etiology in the Dobadura area. *American Journal of Hygiene* 41: 243–372.

Kawamura, Rinya. 1926. Studies on tsutsugamushi disease (Japanese flood fever). *Bulletin of the College of Medicine of the University of Cincinnati* 4 (special Nos. 1 and 2): 1–229.

Philip, Cornelius B. 1964. Scrub typhus and scrub itch. In *Preventive medicine in World War II, Vol. 7: Communicable diseases: Arthropodborne diseases other than malaria,* 275–347. Medical Department, U.S. Army.

Santana, Frederick J., et al. 1976. *Annotated bibliography of scrub typhus in Taiwan and the Pescadores Islands (1911–1975).* A special publication of U.S. Naval Medical Research Unit No. 2. Taipei, Taiwan.

Smadel, Joseph E., and Bennett L. Elisberg. 1965. Scrub typhus rickettsia. In *Viral and rickettsial infections of man,* 4th edition, ed. Frank L. Horsfall, Jr., and Igor Tamm, 1130–43. Philadelphia.

VIII.154
Urolithiasis (Renal and Urinary Bladder Stone Disease)

The major forms of urolithiasis consist of either upper tract stones within the kidneys or ureters (renal stones) or lower tract stones formed within the bladder. These two forms of urolithiasis have distinct differences in etiology, chemical composition, and epidemiological features, and should therefore be considered two separate diseases.

Historical evidence has shown a striking increase in incidence of renal stone disease in more developed countries over the past 100 years. There has been a simultaneous decrease in bladder stone incidence, demonstrating an inverse relationship between the two disorders. Changes in the environment have a profound effect on the epidemiology of human diseases. An unusual example of this interplay is the role of dietary change in the shifting epidemiological pattern from bladder stone to renal stone disease.

Etiology

The large majority of bladder stones occur in young boys from rural or impoverished areas. In these regions, the disorder is known as endemic bladder stone disease. Information from both historical and experimental sources points to a nutritional deficiency during infancy or possibly in utero as the major factor in endemic bladder stone formation. Other less common causes of bladder stone are schistosomiasis (producing bladder wall thickening, stricture, and outlet obstruction) as well as obstruction in elderly males from benign prostatic hypertrophy.

Although deficiencies of vitamin A, vitamin B_6, or magnesium have been suggested in endemic bladder stone disease, low intake of animal protein in combination with high intake of grain carbohydrate is more important. Indeed, it seems that whereas low animal protein intake in infancy may cause bladder stone, a high animal protein diet provokes renal stones (Robertson 1978). This probably explains the epidemiological enigma of the disappearance of endemic bladder stone as areas improved economically, with a concomitant increasing incidence of renal stone (Table VIII.154.1).

Low intake of animal protein and high intake of grain carbohydrate produce more acidic urine and decreased urinary phosphate excretion. These in turn

Table VIII.154.1. *Major features differentiating bladder and renal stone disease*

Features	Bladder stone	Renal stone
Age	Young children	Adults
M/F ratio	12:1	1.2:1
Socioeconomic class	Poor, usually rural areas	All classes affected in more developed countries
Diet	Almost strictly vegetarian; animal protein intake <10 g; high grain intake	Increased meat consumption; animal protein >40 g; high intake of refined sugar
Chemical composition	Ammonium acid urate, uric acid, calcium oxalate	Calcium phosphate, calcium oxalate, other
Recurrence	Rare	Frequent

decrease the solubility of calcium oxalate and uric acid leading to bladder stone formation. Conversely, greater animal protein intake produces more urinary phosphate. An increased intake of refined sugar plus a decreased intake of fiber increase the intestinal absorption of calcium. Increased protein and sucrose intake cause increased urinary calcium excretion, possibly secondary to a distal renal tubular acidosis. This sets the stage for calcium phosphate or calcium oxalate stone formation in the kidneys.

Other less common types of renal stones have specific etiologies. For example, cysteine stones are created by a genetic defect in renal tubule reabsorption of certain amino acids. Repeated urinary infections can result in magnesium ammonium phosphate stones. A number of systemic diseases can cause hypercalcemia with subsequent calcium stone formation. These include hyperparathyroidism and Cushing's syndrome.

Finally, a multitude of other factors also operate in renal stone formation or prevention. Substances known as stone inhibitors are normally present in the urine. Dehydration, by producing relative stasis and more concentrated urine, is an added factor in stone formation and partially explains the increased incidence in hot and arid climates and seasonal increases during summer months.

Epidemiology and Geographic Distribution

Bladder Stone Disease

Among early authors, Galen during the second century in Rome and Albucasis during the eleventh century in Spain observed the frequent occurrence of bladder stone in young boys. Bladder stone still primarily affects boys under 10 years of age. Among approximately 7,000 cases from Thailand, the median age at operation was 4.5 years. Almost 95 percent of all patients were male (Halstead 1961). Numerous clinical studies of the disease in other regions confirm the occurrence at an early age and a marked predominance of male patients (Thomson 1921; Racic 1935; Brown and Brown 1941; Eckstein 1961).

Anatomic differences in the urethra of males and females probably account for the infrequency of bladder stone in females. The female urethra is short, wide, and straight, allowing stronger flow of urine and passage of gravel before large stones are formed.

Bladder stone disease occurs in agricultural regions, particularly in the lower economic classes. Fifty years ago, bladder stone commonly occurred in the inland districts of the Balkans, where living conditions were very primitive. At the same time, the disease was rare along the Adriatic coast, where better living conditions prevailed (Anderson 1972). Bladder stone was quite common in the economically depressed rural areas of Norfolk, England, during the eighteenth and nineteenth centuries, whereas the disease was rare among the more affluent people living in the adjacent urban centers (Thomas 1949; Batty Shaw 1970). A similar disparity is seen today between the rural farmers and city dwellers of Thailand and northern India (Halstead 1961; Anderson 1969, 1972).

Accurate figures on the prevalence of bladder stone disease come from northeast Thailand, where over 20,000 people were interviewed. A history of past or present bladder stone was obtained in 3.8 percent. A small group (0.33 percent) had required surgical removal of the bladder stone (Halstead and Valyasevi 1967). Contrary to this low number, nearly 2 percent of all admissions to the Norfolk and Norwich Hospital during the period 1772–1816 were for removal of bladder stone (Batty Shaw 1970).

Historical accounts from the 1500s to the mid-1800s document the prevalence of the disease throughout Europe, Asia, and America (Anderson 1962; Lonsdale and Mason 1966; Batty Shaw 1970; Prien 1971). Bladder stone remains quite common in Egypt, northwest India, southern China, Thailand, Afghanistan, Iraq, Turkey, and Madagascar. Prior to 1940, bladder stone was also common in portions of Iceland, Russia, Hungary, Indonesia, Tunisia, and Sicily.

Renal Stone Disease

Renal stone disease has mainly been an affliction of the more industrialized and affluent countries of Europe, North America, and Japan and has been uncommon or unknown in impoverished regions and primitive societies. However, people in these areas have developed a similar prevalence with improvement in living conditions and subsequent dietary changes (Modlin 1967).

Population studies in both America and Europe reveal prevalence rates for renal stone ranging from 3 to 13 percent. Nearly 75 percent of these people with so-called idiopathic calcium stone disease have one or more recurrences, implying a continuous exposure to risk factors such as diet. The incidence of the disease has risen continuously since the turn of the century except for brief declines during both world wars – again pointing to dietary changes as an important factor.

Unlike bladder stone disease, renal stones occur predominantly in adults. Men are affected slightly more often than women.

History and Paleopathology

Epidemiological studies have shown that bladder stone is a disease of communities where the diet is high in grain or rice and low in animal protein. With dietary changes resulting from improved technology, migration, or cultural shift, bladder stone disease is replaced by renal stone disease. This is well demonstrated over the past two centuries in parts of Britain, France and other European countries, Russia, China, and Turkey. It is therefore not surprising that ancient references to stone disease deal almost entirely with bladder stone, with rare mention of the renal colic characteristic of upper tract stones.

Bladder stone was common in ancient Persia (600–300 B.C.), particularly in infants, and was considered a result of ingesting sour milk, fruits, or acidic drinks. The Babylonian *Talmud* contains references to bladder stone disease and includes the ingenious suggestion that patients should urinate on the doorstep in order to see the stone.

In India, the *Rig Veda* and *Atharva Veda*, inscribed around 1500 B.C., consist of incantations against disease, including bladder stone. The *Ayur Veda,* published much later, around the first century A.D., described suprapubic incision for removing bladder stones. In the second century A.D., Charaka described four types of stones, almost certainly originating in the bladder. The first was white and as large as a hen's egg; the second was rough and covered with spines; the third was of a dark color; and the fourth was composed of sperm. The first three stones were probably urate and calcium oxalate bladder stones typical of endemic disease.

Early Chinese literature contains few references to any recognizable disease. However, detailed case histories of 25 patients treated by Shunyü I in the second century B.C. have been preserved. They include a palace superintendent afflicted with hematuria, urinary retention, and bladder stones. This may represent a case of either schistosomiasis or endemic stone disease (Lu and Needham 1967).

In Greece, Hippocrates had earlier recognized both renal and bladder stone and recommended diuretics and ingestion of large quantities of water for their removal. He considered wounds of the bladder wall as invariably fatal and therefore specifically forbade his followers to cut for the stone.

The Assyrian *Book of Medicine,* probably written around 300 B.C., includes much of the work of Hippocrates. Among the numerous prescriptions for various maladies are two elaborate potions for flushing out or dissolving renal stones. The latter recipe contains 50 substances with particular emphasis on camphor and vinegar. Other Assyrian works contain directions for infusing various preparations into the bladder through a bronze tube to dissolve bladder stones (Thompson 1934).

In Alexandria around 100 B.C., Ammonios developed an instrument for crushing stones within the bladder. In the first century A.D. in Alexandria, Rufus of Ephesus gave detailed instructions for removing bladder stones through a transverse perineal incision.

In Rome during the same century, Celsus performed numerous operations for bladder stone in boys 9 to 14 years of age. His eight-volume *De Medicina* contains a precise description of transverse perineal lithotomy followed almost without modification until the sixteenth century. Galen described the lateral perineal lithotomy, but, more importantly, noted the frequent occurrence of bladder stone in young boys. He also tried giving stone solvents (lithotryptics) in an effort to dissolve the stones.

In Arabic medicine, Rhazes at about the turn of the tenth century described both renal and bladder stones, and he implicated increased salt intake and hot weather as factors in renal stone formation. Around a century later, Avicenna thought that bladder stones formed when the urine contained an excess of matter (Bitschai 1952).

By the eighteenth century, more and more sur-

Table VIII.154.2. *Paleopathological specimens of renal and bladder stones*

Approx. date	Location	Age/Sex	Size (cm)	Type	Composition
3500 B.C.	El Amrah, Egypt	16/M	6.5	bladder	urate
3500 B.C.	Egypt	–	4.5 × 3.0	bladder	urate, and magnesium ammonium phosphate
			4.5 × 3.0		
			4.0 × 2.5		
3100 B.C.	Helouan, Egypt	–	3.5 × 3.0	?renal	–
			(5 stones)		
		–	3.0 × 2.0	?renal	–
		–	3.5 × 2.0	?renal	–
2800 B.C.	Naga-el-Dier, Egypt	–	1.6	renal	oxalate/phosphate
			(4 stones)		
1000 B.C.	Egypt	adult/M	large	bladder	–
1000 B.C.	Sudan	(32 cases)	3.0–3.9 ave.	bladder	calcite/apatite
	Egypt			ureter	–
A.D. 0–200	Sinai Desert, Egypt	adult/M	3.0 × 3.5 × 1.5	renal	phosphate
			(2 stones)		
8500 B.C.	Trapani, Sicily	20–25/M	2.0 × 1.0	bladder	–
2100 B.C.	Lot, France	adult	4.1 × 3.5 × 3.0	bladder	–
2000–700 B.C.	Yorkshire, England	adult	4.0 × 3.0 × 3.0	bladder	–
2000–700 B.C.	Yorkshire, England	adult	0.5 × 1.0	bladder	–
A.D. 450–1000	Somerset, England	adult	–	?bladder	–
A.D. 1300–1500	Aebelholt, Denmark	40/F	0.4 × 0.3	renal	oxalate
3300 B.C.	Indian Knoll, Ky.	24/M	4.0 × 2.7 × 2.3	bladder	oxalate
		24/F	3.3 × 2.3 × 1.2	renal	oxalate/phosphate
		40/M	3.3 × 1.6 × 1.0	renal	oxalate/phosphate
1500 B.C.	Fulton Co., Ill.	20/F	1.7 × 1.0 × 0.7	renal	phosphate
100 B.C.–A.D. 500	Northeastern, Ariz.	18/M	4.2 × 3.7 × 2.7	bladder	oxalate/urate
A.D. 500–750	Vandal Cave, Ariz.	30–40/M	3.0 × 2.7 × 2.5	bladder	oxalate/urate
A.D. 1000	Arica, Chile	45–50/F	1.5 × 1.5 × 0.6	ureter	phosphate
A.D. 1500	Marion Co., Ind.	50/F	0.7–2.0	renal	phosphate
			(31 stones)		
A.D. 1600–1700	Putnam Co., W.Va.	–	3.1 × 2.0 × 0.5	renal	phosphate

geons were attempting the dangerous lateral perineal lithotomy. Special hospitals for bladder stone patients were opened in England, France, Holland, and elsewhere. In 1753, Frère Come opened such a hospital in Paris and operated on over 1,000 patients. The Norfolk and Norwich Hospital was founded in 1771, and one of every 55 admissions in this endemic region was for removal of bladder stone.

Through paleopathology and careful archaeological technique, actual specimens of ancient renal and bladder stones have been recovered from skeletal and mummified remains. This material has been extensively reviewed elsewhere and is summarized in Table VIII.154.2 (Steinbock 1985).

R. Ted Steinbock

Bibliography

Anderson, D. A. 1962. The nutritional significance of primary bladder stones. *British Journal of Urology* 34: 160–77.

1969. Historical and geographical differences in the pattern of incidence of urinary stones considered in relation to possible etiological factors. In *Renal stone research symposium,* ed. A. Hodgkinson and B. C. Nordin. London.

1972. Environmental factors in the etiology of urolithiasis. In *Urinary calculi: International symposium on renal stone research,* 130–44. Madrid.

Assendelft, E. 1900. Bericht über 630 stationär behandelte Steinkranke. *Archiv für Klinische Chirurgie* 60: 669–80.

Batty Shaw, A. 1970. The Norwich School of lithotomy. *Medical History* 14: 221–59.

1979. East Anglian bladder stone. *Journal of the Royal Society of Medicine* 72: 222–8.

Bitschai, J. 1951. Calculosis of the urinary tract in Egypt. *Journal of the Mount Sinai Hospital* 17: 630–43.

1952. The history of urology in Egypt. *American Journal of Surgery* 83: 215–24.

Brown, R. K., and E. C. Brown. 1941. Urinary stones: A study of their etiology in small children in Syria. *Surgery* 9: 415–24.

Eckstein, H. B. 1961. Endemic urinary lithiasis in Turkish children. *Archives of Disease in Children* 36: 137–45.

Ellis, H. 1970. *A history of bladder stone.* Oxford.

Halstead, S. B. 1961. Bladder stone in Thailand: A review of the problem. *American Journal of Tropical Medicine and Hygiene* 10: 918–25.

Halstead, S. B., and A. Valyasevi. 1967. Studies of bladder stone disease in Thailand: Epidemiologic studies in Ubol province. *American Journal of Clinical Nutrition* 20: 1329–39.

Halstead, S. B., A. Valyasevi, and P. Umpoaivit. 1967. Studies of bladder stone disease in Thailand: Dietary habits and disease prevalence. *American Journal of Clinical Nutrition* 20: 1352–61.

Heyadat, S., and P. Amirshahy. 1970. Urinary lithiasis in Iran. *Tropical and Geographical Medicine* 22: 416–22.

Lonsdale, K. 1968. Human stones. *Science* 159: 1199–207.

Lonsdale, K., and P. Mason. 1966. Uric acid, uric acid dihydrate, and urates in urinary calculi, ancient and modern. *Science* 152: 1511–12.

Loutfi, A., R. van Reen, and G. Abdel-Hamid. 1974. Studies on bladder stone disease in Egyptian children. *Journal of the Egyptian Medical Association* 57: 96–114.

Lu, G. D., and J. Needham. 1967. Records of diseases in ancient China. In *Diseases in antiquity*, ed. D. R. Brothwell and A. T. Sandison, 222–37. Springfield, Ill.

Madden, F. C. 1913. The incidence of stone in Egypt. *Lancet* 2: 132–5.

McCarrison, R. 1931. The causation of stone in India. *British Medical Journal* i: 1009–14.

Modlin, M. 1967. The etiology of renal stone. *Annals of the Royal College of Surgeons* 40: 155–78.

Prien, E. L. 1971. The riddle of urinary stone disease. *Journal of the American Medical Association* 216: 503–7.

Racic, J. 1935. Calculus of the bladder in Dalmatia. *Urologic and Cutaneous Review* 39: 158–63.

Robertson, W. G. 1978. Risk factors in calcium stone disease of the upper urinary tract. *British Journal of Urology* 50: 449–54.

Robertson, W. G., et al. 1979. The effect of high animal protein intake on the risk of calcium stone formation in the urinary tract. *Clinical Science* 52: 285–8.

Stark, H. 1970. Childhood urolithiasis in northern Israel. *Israel Journal of Medical Science* 6: 341–5.

Steinbock, R. T. 1985. The history, epidemiology, and paleopathology of kidney and bladder stone disease. In *Health and disease in the prehistoric southwest*, ed. C. F. Merbs and R. J. Miller, 177–209. Tempe, Ariz.

Thomas, J. M. R. 1949. Vesical calculus in Norfolk. *British Journal of Urology* 21: 20–3.

Thompson, R. C. 1934. Assyrian prescriptions for diseases of urine. *Babyloniaca* 14: 96–120.

Thomson, J. O. 1921. Urinary calculi at Canton Hospital, China. *Surgery* 32: 44–56.

Valyasevi, A., and A. Dhanamitta. 1968. Current research on pediatric bladder stone disease in Thailand. *Journal of Vitaminology* 14: 40–7.

VIII.155
Varicella Zoster

Varicella (chickenpox) is an acute infection of short duration caused by *Varicella–Zoster virus* (VZV), which is spread in the early stages of disease by droplets of secretions from the nasopharynx. It is followed by lifetime latency that may be broken in occasional patients by reactivation of virus in sensory ganglia manifested as *herpes zoster* (shingles).

Epidemiology and Incidence

Chickenpox is endemic worldwide, is highly communicable, and commonly appears as epidemics among children who are usually attacked between 2 and 8 years of age. (Infants are protected by transplacental maternal antibodies.) Few escape infection until adult life, and these usually live in isolated rural communities. Probably most of those who have seemed to escape the disease had subclinical infections. (The annual *Report of Morbidity and Mortality in the United States* shows, for 1984, 221,983 cases of varicella reported from 33 states, an incidence of 138 cases per 100,000 population. The age was known in 28 percent; 56 percent of these cases appeared in the 5- to 9-year age group, less than 6 percent were 15 years of age or older.)

The sporadic reactivation of the virus as shingles is unrelated to exposure to exogenous infection and, in general, is uncommon even in populations in which practically all have had chickenpox. Its peak incidence is after age 50. Of those who develop shingles, only 1 percent have two attacks. Patients with impaired cellular immunity are at risk, and herpes zoster is not uncommon in those suffering from malignant disease.

Immunology

A viremia develops promptly after infection with VZV of which there is only one serotype. Circulating antibody is demonstrable within 1 to 4 days after the appearance of the rash. Although immunity is lifelong, it has been suggested that a waning of immunity in older age explains shingles, and viremia would seem to account for a varicella-like rash in some instances. Reactivation of humoral and cellular antibodies might then account for the termination of a bout with herpes zoster. Patients receiving cancericidal drugs or adrenocortical steroids are at high risk for serious complications from VZV infection.

Clinical Manifestations and Pathology

Presumably the virus enters and replicates briefly in the cells of the respiratory mucosa followed by an intermittent viremia. The histopathology is identical with that described for herpes simplex infection. The virus is present in the vesicles. During viremia the virus travels from cutaneous sensory nerve endings to the posterior ganglia where it remains latent to be reactivated in some patients as herpes zoster. Then the dorsal ganglia show intense inflammation even with hemorrhagic necrosis, leptomeningitis, and myelitis of the posterior spinal columns. Although VZV has been isolated from ganglia during active disease, it has not been found during quiescent periods.

After an incubation period of 10 to 20 days and some 24 hours before the rash of varicella appears, the prodromes of mild headache, malaise, and moderate fever appear. Because these are commonly unrecognized in young children, the rash seemingly is the initial evidence of disease. It appears as a cutaneous blush, with the development of successive crops of macules, papules, and superficial vesicles surrounded by a red areola, which go on to crusting within 24 hours. The acute phase lasts about a week.

Although the rash may be generalized, it usually involves the trunk and face, with fewer lesions on the extremities. Vesicles may appear in the mouth, and laryngeal involvement may cause dyspnea. Chickenpox is a benign disease in children unless they suffer from leukemia or are taking corticosteroids. Other than acute encephalitis, an occasional circumstance late in the disease, complications have been reported very rarely in almost all the body systems. In adults varicella tends to be less benign, and commonly the X-ray reveals pulmonary infiltrates.

An attack of herpes zoster may be ushered in with 1 or 2 days of fever, chills, malaise, and gastrointestinal symptoms before symptoms of local disease appear. Either with or without prodromal symptoms the patient becomes aware of some pain, at times with itching, in the area of the affected segmental nerves. After several days, crops of vesicles on an erythematous base appear in the distribution of the nerves of one or several posterior root ganglia, usually accompanied by hyperesthesia and pain. The vesicles dry and become crusted in about a week, although the course may be slower in aged persons. Hyperesthesia or pain may last for weeks and months especially in those patients with malignant disease. In an occasional aged patient, these residua never disappear. Herpes of the ophthalmic branch of the trigeminal nerve is not uncommon and may be accompanied by keratoconjunctivitis, which may be followed by serious corneal scarring and glaucoma. Zoster of the geniculate ganglion produces Ramsey Hunt's syndrome. The characteristic pain syndrome of zoster may run its course without skin eruption, contrary to the clinician's initial prediction.

History and Geography

Both J. E. Schmidt (1959) and F. H. Garrison (1960) credit Giovanni Filippo Ingrassia, an Italian physician, with differentiating chickenpox from scarlet fever in 1553, and state that the English physician William Heberden (1785) gave the earliest clear description of varicella and distinguished it from smallpox in 1768. Jean Alibert (1832) included varicella in his group II category of exanthematous dermatoses – acute febrile contagious diseases. E. E. Tyzzer (1905), an American pathologist, described cellular inclusion bodies, and T. M. Rivers and W. S. Tillett (1924) reported isolation of the virus.

P. A. Rayer, in his 1845 treatise on diseases of the skin, described the microscopic contents of zoster vesicles and of the underlying skin. F. von Bärensprung (1861–3) concluded that zoster was due to disease of the posterior roots. In the following years, several case reports of herpes zoster in which there were postmortem findings of inflammation of the posterior root ganglia appeared. Bärensprung's suspicion that the Gasserian ganglion was affected in herpes zoster of the face was confirmed by O. Wyss (1872). A. W. Campbell and Henry Head (1900) established that herpes zoster results from a hemorrhagic inflammation of the posterior nerve roots and the homologous cranial ganglia. In 1925, Karl Kundratitz described the inoculation of susceptible children with zoster vesicle fluid resulting in varicella.

R. H. Kampmeier

Bibliography

Alibert, J. L. 1832. *Monographie des dermatoses.* Paris.

Bärensprung, F. von. 1861–3. Ueber die Gurtel Krankheit. *Annalen Charite Krankenhaus* 9: 40–128, 10: 27–53, 11: 96–116.

Bokay, Janos. 1892. Das Auftreten von Varizellen unter eigentümlichen Verhältnissen. *Magyar orvosi Archivum.* Nov 3.

Campbell, A. W., and Henry Head. 1900. Hemorrhagic inflammation of posterior nerve roots and homologous spinal ganglia. *Brain* 23: 353–523.

Crissey, John T., and Lawrence C. Parish. 1981. *The dermatology and syphilology of the nineteenth century.* New York.

Garrison, Fielding Hudson. 1960. *History of medicine,* 4th edition. Reprint. Philadelphia.

Heberden, William. 1785. On the chickenpox. *Medical Transactions of the Royal College of Physicians of London* i: 427–36.

Kibrick, Sidney. 1982. Varicella and herpes zoster. In *Cecil's textbook of medicine,* 16th edition, ed. James B. Wyngaarden and Lloyd H. Smith, Chapter 300. Philadelphia.

Kundratitz, Karl. 1925. Experimentelle Uebertragung von Herpes Zoster auf den Menschen and Beziehungen von Herpes Zoster zu Varizellen. *Monatschrift für Kinderheilkunde* 29: 516–23.

Marcy, S. Michael, and Sidney Kibrick. 1983. Varicella and herpes zoster. In *Infectious diseases,* 3d edition, ed. Paul D. Hoeprich, Chapter 93. Philadelphia.

NIH Conference. 1978. Herpes zoster varicella infections in immunosuppressed patients. Moderator R. Dolan. *Annals of Internal Medicine* 89: 375–88.

Rivers, T. M., and W. S. Tillett. 1924. The lesions in rabbits experimentally infected by a virus encountered in the attempted transmission of varicella. *Journal of Experimental Medicine* 40: 281–7.

Schmidt, J. E. 1959. *Medical discoveries: Who and when.* Springfield, Ill.

Tyzzer, E. E. 1905. The histology of the skin lesions of varicella. *Journal of Medical Research* 14: 361–89.

Weller, T. H., and A. H. Coons. 1954. Fluorescent antibody studies with agents of varicella and herpes zoster propagated in vitro. *Proceedings of the Society for Experimental Biology and Medicine* 86: 789–94.

Weller, T. H., H. M. Witton, and E. J. Bell. 1958. The etiology agents of varicella and herpes zoster: Isolation, propagation, and cultural characteristics in vitro. *Journal of Experimental Medicine* 108: 843–86.

Wyss, O. 1872. Beitrag zur Kenntnis des Zoster. *Archiv für Dermatologie und Syphilis* 4: 449–50.

Zulia, J. A. 1981. Clinical spectrum of varicella zoster virus infection. In *The human herpesviruses – An interdisciplinary perspective,* ed. Andre J. Nahmias, Walter Dowdle, and Raymond F. Schinzi. New York.

VIII.156
Whooping Cough

Whooping cough, otherwise known as pertussis, after the causative bacillus *Bordetella pertussis,* is an acute infectious disease of childhood. Affecting the respiratory tract, it is characterized by paroxysms of coughing, culminating in the prolonged inspiration which gives the disease its name. Before the present century, the popular name was generally spelled without the initial "w," and did not come into general use until the end of the eighteenth century. Until the early nineteenth century, the commonest appellation was *chincough.* The term *pertussis* was first used by Thomas Sydenham in the latter part of the seventeenth century.

Distribution and Incidence

The distribution of whooping cough is now worldwide. It is generally an endemic disease that erupts in sporadic epidemics, but in most developed countries it has been controlled by immunization programs. Of clinical cases, 80 percent occur in the under-10 age group, and unlike most other communicable diseases, whooping cough develops more often in females than in males.

Etiology and Epidemiology

Although included among the more important diseases of childhood, whooping cough has been relatively neglected, and various aspects of its epidemiology are not yet fully understood. Transmission seems to be mainly airborne, apparently by droplet infection. Human beings are the only reservoir of the disease; *B. pertussis* cannot survive long outside the host, and quickly succumbs to drying, ultraviolet light, and temperatures above 120° to 130°F. It spreads primarily through household and schoolroom contact, although mild subclinical cases, perhaps in adolescents and adults, may play a further (undemonstrated) role in transmission. One attack confers immunity, and rare second attacks are probably explained by infection with the much milder, and less common, *Bordetella parapertussis.*

Clinical Manifestations

An incubation period of 7 to 10 days is followed by an initial catarrhal stage, lasting 1 to 2 weeks. During this phase the disease is highly communicable, but the symptoms are nonspecific and resemble those of many other infectious diseases, and of minor respiratory ailments. An increasingly persistent cough develops, which in the third stage becomes more severe and spasmodic, terminating in the characteristic whoop. In acute cases, paroxysms may occur 40 or 50 times in 24 hours. The whoop is frequently followed by vomiting. In young infants, who are unable to produce the whoop and resume effective breathing quickly, episodes of cyanosis follow the paroxysm. The acute stage lasts up to 4 weeks, but paroxysms may continue for 3 months or longer. The patient is considered convalescent when vomiting ceases, and the severity of the paroxysms diminishes. Complications include collapsed lungs, anoxic convulsions, and exhaustion; secondary bacterial infections may cause otitis media or pneumonia. Bronchiectasis has become rare since the introduction of antimicrobial agents.

History and Geography

The history of whooping cough before the twentieth century is obscure. It cannot with certainty be traced back further than the mid-sixteenth century and it was almost certainly unknown to the ancient world. Although the term "chincough" was current in the early sixteenth century, the first medical description of the disease dates from 1578, when Guillaume Baillou observed a severe epidemic in Paris. He wrote of it as a familiar affliction, for which there seemed to be several names already. Moreover, it was apparently the subject of medical discussions.

Nonetheless, the prevalence of the disease remains largely obscure until the mid-eighteenth century. August Hirsch in 1886 suggested that the native habitat of the disease was originally northern Europe. But the existence of a widespread folklore with regard to its treatment may indicate a more ancient existence in such places as southern India and Malabar.

Thomas Willis in 1675 described the chincough as an epidemic disease of infants and children, usually occurring during the summer and autumn. In his view, the cough, although difficult to cure, was rarely fatal or very dangerous.

By contrast, his contemporary, Sydenham, thought it so formidable as to require the most rigorous treatment. The earliest statistics regarded as in any way reliable come from mid-eighteenth-century Sweden, where Nils Rósen von Rosenstein described it as a familiar epidemic disease of variable fatality. The terms "whooping cough" and "chincough" first appear as causes of death in the London Bills of Mortality in 1701, and an increasing number of deaths were attributed to them. Indeed, the toll rose from 119, in the 15-year period 1702–17, to 4,252 in the period 1762–77. With the introduction of the civil registration of deaths in 1838, English mortality figures became more reliable. Deaths from whooping cough reached a peak of some 1,500 per million population under age 15 per annum in England and Wales in about 1870, after which the death rate from the disease began to decline. This fall was first manifest in agricultural areas, whereas in urban and industrial countries the death rates were slower to fall. During the 1880s, case fatality, so far as can be ascertained, stood at 10 percent, compared to 1.1 percent during World War II, and 0.1 percent in recent years. In underdeveloped countries today, hospital case-fatality rates are about 15 percent.

Although the infectious character of whooping cough was appreciated from at least the early eighteenth century, the nature of the clinical disease was simultaneously a matter of debate. Both Willis and Sydenham, for example, thought the disease seated chiefly in the chest, whereas William Harvey and his followers held it to be in the stomach and the alimentary canal. Not until Robert Watt of Glasgow, stimulated by the deaths of two of his children from the disease, undertook a series of dissections in 1812–13 did the involvement of the respiratory tract become clear. Medical interest in the disease during the nineteenth century was minimal, until discussion began about the possibilities of prevention in the 1880s.

In London, during the nineteenth century, the highest whooping cough mortality was experienced by the children of the working classes, and death was generally due to complications involving the respiratory organs. Whooping cough cases were not received into the Metropolitan Asylums' Board's hospitals (London) before 1910. The disease was made notifiable in the United States in 1922, but not until somewhat later in Great Britain.

Mortality and morbidity from whooping cough have declined greatly in developed countries during the twentieth century. The causative organism was first isolated by Jules Bordet and Octave Gengou in 1900, but was not grown in vitro until 1906, when its morphology and cultural characteristics were established. Vaccines against the disease were first introduced in the 1930s, and were in widespread use by the later 1940s.

But recently, there has been increasing public awareness of possible complications from whooping cough vaccine, which has been stimulated by the publicity surrounding the relatively small number of cases in which the vaccine is supposed to have caused brain damage to children. The result was that during the 1970s rates of vaccination fell off in both Britain and Japan, where immunization is voluntary. In both countries the disease subsequently began to increase in prevalence, and epidemic outbreaks in 1978 and 1982 were similar in scale to those of the 1950s, when the immunization program was new. Another large outbreak was anticipated in 1986, but was aborted by intensive publicity concerning the benefits of vaccination, which caused immunization rates to rise.

Anne Hardy

Bibliography

Brooks, G. F., and T. M. Buchanan. 1970. Pertussis in the United States. *Journal of Infectious Disease* 122: 123–5.

Radbill, Samuel X. 1943. Whooping cough in fact and fantasy. *Bulletin of the History of Medicine* 13: 33–55.

Smith, Francis B. 1979. *The people's health, 1830–1910.* London.

Watt, Robert. 1813. *A treatise on the history, nature, and treatment of chincough.* Glasgow.

VIII.157
Yaws

This disease has suffered from variable and confusing descriptions. It is now generally called yaws, although the term *framboesia* is also still in common use. Although primary, secondary, and tertiary stages of the condition are recognized, further subdivisions have been made that are associated with various alternative terminology.

Yaws is generally considered to be a highly contagious disease in tropical areas of the world, and in populations with limited hygiene. It is characterized in the early stages by variable cutaneous changes, and eventually affects joints and bones. The causal organism is considered to be *Treponema pertenue,* although the taxonomy of the pathogenic treponemes is in some doubt, and some reclassification may well take place in the near future. An incubation period of up to 28 days is followed by the appearance of the primary lesion, 2 to 5 centimeters in diameter, which develops into granular excrescences at times with lymph node enlargement. Further eruptions take place, which can be characterized by a "waxing and waning" of successive lesions. Single

or multiple lesions can eventually develop on the feet ("crab yaws," "ulcerative plantar papules") and are some of the most painful and disabling lesions of all. Eventually, in what some would see as a tertiary stage, there can be patchy depigmentation, deep destruction and remodeling of bones, and gangosa (changes to nasopharyngeal structures). The internal organs are not normally involved, and in this respect it contrasts markedly with the sister treponematosis venereal syphilis.

Distribution and Incidence

As a result of the intensive campaign against yaws that was carried out in the 1950s by the World Health Organization, the disease is no longer present in many populations where previously it was a serious health threat. Nevertheless, some comment on its previous geography and ecology is worthwhile, particularly as this may tell us something about its adaptive evolution. Indeed, it would seem true to say that of the treponematoses, yaws is the one that appears to be adapted to infecting human populations in tropical or subtropical climates (so there are the combined factors of heat, humidity, poor living conditions and hygiene, and limited clothing worn). Thus although it has been estimated that 80 percent of the yaws-afflicted populations lived within the mean annual isotherm of 80°F, it has to be recognized that various environmental and social factors must be taken into account in order to understand the variable incidences of this disease.

Exceptions to the geographic rules that might be seen to govern this condition are not difficult to find. For instance, in the case of mean annual rainfall, yaws was usually found in areas where there is 50 to 75 inches of rain a year, but it has occurred in drier climates as represented by parts of Madagascar, India, and Bolivia. In all, there were probably some 50 million yaws cases in the world half a century ago.

In the 1940s and early 1950s, estimates of yaws prevalence were made in various areas of the world, partly in relation to yaws eradication programs. Although regional figures have now dropped radically, it is pertinent to the history of the subject to note the extent of the previous evidence, and the variation found. In the case of most of the New World, although yaws was probably introduced by slaves centuries ago, no significant incidence has remained into this century. However, in the Caribbean area, which had been varyingly affected by the slave trade, yaws displayed some contrasts. Thus, Cuba was reported as having a low frequency of yaws, whereas in Haiti 60 to 80 percent of the rural population were estimated to have had yaws. Similarly, Jamaica registered 70 to 80 percent frequency figures in some districts. In South America, Brazil was known to have many cases, especially in the northern regions where 350,000 cases were at one time noted. In Colombia, there was also regional variation, with the Pacific coast regions reporting 80,000 cases (with a general rate of 43.5 per 100,000). In contrast to these two countries, yaws appears to have been only a very modest health problem in Peru and Venezuela.

In the Old World, the disease was endemic in parts of Africa, Asia, and the Pacific. In Africa, quite high frequencies were found in some areas, although possibly the highest incidences occurred in Asia and the Pacific. In 1945, in the area then designated the Belgian Congo, there were 325,994 cases; and, in the same year, Tanganyika recorded 69,000 cases. Also about this time, frequencies in French West Africa varied from 0.02 percent (Niger) to 6.3 percent (Ivory Coast). French Equatorial Africa similarly had frequencies ranging from 0.1 percent (Chad) to 4.3 percent (Gabon), and the regional incidences in Uganda varied from 2 percent to 17.5 percent.

Yaws was also an important disease in the more tropical areas of Asia. In the Indian territory of Madhya Pradesh, 5.6 percent of the population was recorded as having yaws. Indonesia may have had as many as 10 million yaws cases before its anti-yaws campaign had any effect, and in some areas possibly 60 percent of the population had some experience of the disease. Thailand may also have had some 1.4 million cases prior to its current reduction, and in Laos, too, 1 to 15 percent of the population was thought to be affected.

Territories of the Pacific area showed some surprising frequencies, and clearly the relatively small populations of most of the islands did not prevent the spread of this disease. It was frequent on Guam, and, in 1953, on Simbo Island 20 percent of the general population had experienced yaws (and 78 percent of the children had been affected at some time). Also in the early 1950s, it was recorded that 17 percent of the population of Wallis Island and 18 percent of 80,000 Western Samoans had yaws.

This evidence of yaws in various parts of the world just prior to the antibiotic campaigns for its eradication helps to emphasize points of historical interest. One is that yaws probably had a relatively limited distribution in the New World. In some areas where notable frequencies have been attained, the phenomenon was probably linked to the history of the arrival of yaws-affected African slaves on the one

hand, and environmental and social variable conducive to the survival and expansion of yaws on the other. A second point of historical interest is that in the Old World it is clear that yaws affects widely divergent ethnic groups distributed from Africa to the Pacific and that the history of the disease in these areas is likely to be hundreds if not thousands of years old.

Etiology and Epidemiology

Yaws is one of the four chronic infectious treponemal diseases that affect humans, and, in contrast to pinta, endemic syphilis, and venereal syphilis, it appears to be especially adapted to hot and humid tropical and subtropical environments. Rural populations were probably more affected than urban groups. The causal organism has been given separate species status, *Treponeme pertenue,* but the taxonomy of the treponematoses deserves reevaluation. The microorganism was discovered by Aldo Castellani in 1905, and since then its morphology has been to some extent revealed, especially by electron microscopy. Differences between the pathogenic treponemes have not, however, been resolved at this level, and it now seems unlikely that significant morphological differences will appear between *T. pertenue* and *Treponeme pallidum* (which causes syphilis).

Only humans appear to be the natural hosts of all the pathogenic human treponemes. None have so far been cultivated in artificial media, and there is still much to learn about their biological characteristics. In terms of the nature of the lesions produced, the most divergent forms are yaws and venereal syphilis. There is variable cross-protection once an individual has one variety of treponeme and comes into contact with another form.

The site of entry for yaws treponemes is not usually the genitalia, but often the legs. Large numbers of treponemes are probably unnecessary to instigate the disease. Infectious yaws lesions are mainly the early-stage papillomas, the infection being spread perhaps to small abrasions by direct or hand contact (via lesions). Transmission by flies is still considered to be unimportant. The yaws organisms are known to remain infectious in serum for up to 2 hours, provided the temperature remains at about 28°C.

Like endemic syphilis, yaws characteristically develops during childhood by nonvenereal contact. Eventually, after chronic progress of the disease, over 8 months or more, individuals commonly undergo spontaneous cure, although some cases continue to a tertiary stage.

Immunology

There appears to be no significant natural resistance to infection by yaws or other pathogenic treponemes. However, there is clear evidence that some individuals can develop specific resistance or immunity following infection with these treponemes. Thus, early clinical lesions can disappear, so there can be an asymptomatic or latent period, and this may or may not be followed by later-stage symptoms. The plasma cells and lymphocytes present in treponemal lesions indicate local antibody formation and some degree of immunologic response. Sera from yaws and the other pathogenic treponemes react to the same antigens.

Clinical Manifestations and Pathology

The progress of yaws seems best described in two major stages: an early phase with initial and secondary lesions; then a late stage, which usually develops after some years.

The clinical features of early yaws can be summarized as follows. In the region of entry of the treponemes, the primary lesions develop within the first 8 weeks. It is usual to find that the legs are involved first, the lesion being in the form of a large rounded itching papule, which is usually less than 5 or 6 centimeters in size. There is the possibility that it will ulcerate or become secondarily infected. Crusting of the ulceration occurs, and eventually a raspberry-like granuloma develops beneath. Bleeding may occur, and there can be a yellowish discharge.

Within 3 to 6 weeks after the initial lesion, secondary eruptions occur, and extend all over the body. These can continue for up to 2 years. Variants of these yearly yaws lesions have been given a confusing range of names. According to the 1951 WHO nomenclature, they may be summarized as follows.

Circinate (annular or ringworm) yaws lesions tend to encircle an area of skin, which may be several centimeters in diameter. Macular eruptions may occur and can be depigmented or partly hyperpigmented (peripherally). These disappear within a few weeks or months. The papular or "lichenous" rash can be regional or cover the whole body with small papules, usually for not more than a few weeks. Plantar and palmar lesions can be ulcerative or nonulcerative. In the case of painful ulcerating soles, the individual tends to walk on the outer border of the foot in a crablike fashion ("crab yaws"). Alternatively, in the nonulcerating lesions, there may later be a worm-eaten appearance associated with thickened dry hyperkeratotic skin. In the moist parts of the body (anus, vagina, mouth, nose, axillae), raised condylomatous areas resembling the condylomata of venereal and endemic syphilis can occur.

In the later stages of yaws, usually after 5 years, further lesions may occur in individuals whose condition has not become fully latent. In particular, there can be a nodular "lupoid" involvement of the skin, with the formation of granulation tissue, ulceration, and scar formation. In this late stage, there may also be one or a few large ulcers ("gummatous ulceration") lasting for years. Disturbances in pigmentation may further occur, being usually patchy. Possibly the most significant of the late stages of yaws are those that cause significant changes in the bones, for these can clearly be searched for archaeologically and thus may provide an ancient perspective to the history of this disease. Parts of the skeleton, especially the long bones, may show a range of changes from periostitis to deep cavitation and shaft swelling. In children there can also be dactylitis, which can produce remodeling and expansion of one or more phalanges, especially of the fingers. Also, the vault of the skull may be affected, causing localized cratering or more widespread osteitis and eventual stellate scarring. Most destructive of all is gangosa (rhinopharyngitis mutilans), which is characterized by massive destruction of the nose, palate, turbinates, and vomer.

History and Geography

It is important to emphasize at the outset that the history of yaws has been, to some extent, mixed up and confused by studies of syphilis. This, of course, is understandable, in that they are closely related treponemal diseases, and even now can be confused at a clinical level. It is thus small wonder that earlier writers could mistake one condition for the other, or are vague about the actual nature of the disease. Possibly the best example of this confusion is provided by writings on the Australian aborigines, in whose tribes yaws may have been a long-term pre-European problem. Indeed, the Aranda tribe has an old established name, *irkintja,* for the condition that many observers believed was syphilis (Hackett 1936b). This does not mean that all of the earlier medical writers were wrong, and Robert Koch, in a 1900 report to the German government, perceptively wrote that in the Bismarck Archipelago he had seen places where practically all children were infected with yaws, and that framboesia was frequently mistaken for syphilis by both laypersons and medical practitioners. Koch went on to say that the alleged great epidemics of syphilis in the South Seas were in large part the result of this same misdiagnosis.

Antiquity Through the Fifteenth Century

Although it has been suggested that the biblical condition "blains" (Exodus IX) could have been yaws, and similarly that the reference by Pliny the Elder (first century A.D.) to a yawslike eruption of the face could have indicated early treponemal disease, there is really no ancient written records that can be taken seriously as good evidence. On the other hand, the archaeological record does appear to provide clear proof of the antiquity of the treponemal diseases.

Regarding the medieval period, European history provides some facts that seem relevant to a full understanding of the history and spread of yaws. In 1367 Marco Pizziani explored along the African coast, and by 1470 others had sailed south as far as the Equator. Portuguese settlements were established, linked to the slave trade, and these intimate contacts between widely different peoples and environments provided opportunities for the movement of disease as well as people. Although the estimated figure of between 300,000 and 400,000 Negro slaves arriving in Portugal by the end of the fifteenth century may well be too high, there is no doubt that we must recognize this as a significant corridor for the potential shunting of disease, including yaws, to other areas, including northern Europe. Moreover, the slaves did not simply move toward Europe and western Asia.

Sixteenth Through Eighteenth Century

At the very beginning of the sixteenth century, the first consignment of slaves from Africa arrived in Hispaniola and, following this, millions more reached the New World. It was thus that yaws became established to varying degrees, depending on social and environmental factors, in various parts of the Americas. In 1648 Willem Piso, a Leiden doctor associated with the Dutch West India Company, which occupied a part of Brazil for a few decades, wrote in his *Historia Naturalis Brasiliae* of treponematosis in that country, mentioning a condition called "bubas" which he distinguished from the "Spanish pocks."

Earlier, in 1642, Jacobus Bontius, another Leiden doctor, had written of witnessing yaws as a result of his travels in the East Indies. In the Moluccas, the frequency of yaws led Bontius to call it a "common plague."

From the middle of the seventeenth to the end of the eighteenth century, there were a series of writings that consolidated the view that yaws was a distinct disease. Some of this evidence is so skimpy as to provoke only the suspicion of yaws as, for example,

the 1720 "epidemic" in Scotland of "sibbens," with symptoms suggestive of intruded yaws.

On the other hand, John Brickell of North Carolina, writing in the 1730s, distinguished yaws and syphilis, and noted that the former condition was "brought hither by the Negroes from Guinea" and was "seldom cured by mercurials." In the West Indies physicians who attended slaves came to know the disease well. They, too, believed its origin was in Africa. As in Africa, yaws was a disease mostly of children in the Caribbean, and many plantations erected yaws houses. Edward Bancroft, an eighteenth-century physician who gained experience with yaws in Guiana, South America, concluded that it could be transmitted by flies. This view was accepted by various medical writers in the following decades.

In this closing period of the eighteenth century and the first decades of the next, the stages of yaws development were slowly being understood. Vaccination was also tried in an attempt to prevent the disease, and positive results were claimed. Somewhat more alarming in humanitarian terms, the experimental injecting of slaves was carried out, at times with "success." Of special value were experiments on humans known to have already suffered from yaws, the negative results showing that immunity to secondary infection was possible.

Nineteenth Through Twentieth Century

Gangosa, meaning nasal voice, was first mentioned in the literature by a Spanish medical committee in 1828, and by 1891 J. Numa Rat had discussed these lesions in rhinopharyngitis mutilans and viewed them as an indication of the tertiary stage of yaws. Similarly, E. C. Stirling in 1894 was the first to note "boomerang leg" (also called *sabre tibia*), which was a later-stage yaws feature he saw in Australian aborigines.

The question of the taxonomy of the pathogenic treponemes was opened up for debate in 1900, when Joseph Hutchinson agreed that, contrary to growing opinion, yaws and syphilis were simply different patterns of the same disease – an argument that was to be strongly defended later by Ellis H. Hudson (1946, 1958). But during this century, the treponemal diseases have tended to be worked on more and more in isolation. Thus, R. L. Spittel (1923) concentrated not only on yaws but specifically on *parangi*, the form with which he had had considerable experience in Ceylon. Perhaps the most versatile treponematologist has been C. J. Hackett, whose field work in the 1930s took him to tribal communities in Australia and Africa. His contributions dealing with the bone changes in yaws and syphilis have been especially significant. These findings in turn are helping physical anthropologists to trace the history of these diseases in human skeletal materials. It is hoped that such efforts will soon produce major breakthroughs in our knowledge of the history of the treponematoses.

Don R. Brothwell

Bibliography

Brickell, John. 1737. *Natural history of North Carolina.* New York.

Castellani, Aldo. 1905. On the presence of spirochaetes in two cases of ulcerated parangi (yaws). *British Medical Journal* ii: 1280, 1330–1, 1430.

Dijke, M. J. V., C. Bakker, and H. W. Hoesen. 1921. On the etiology of rhinopharyngitis mutilans. In *Transactions of the Fourth Congress of the Far Eastern Association of Tropical Medicine,* 2: 129–37. Weltevreden.

Fox, H. 1944. Yaws (framboesia tropica). In *Clinical tropical medicine,* ed. A. T. Bercovitz, Chapter 23, New York.

Guthe, T., and R. R. Willcox. 1954. Les tréponématoses: Problème mondial. *Chronique de l'Organisation Mondiale de la Santé* 8: 41–122.

Hackett, Cecil J. 1936a. *Boomerang leg and yaws in Australian aborigines,* Monograph No. 1. Royal Society of Tropical Medicine and Hygiene. London.

1936b. A critical survey of some references to syphilis and yaws among the Australian aborigines. *Medical Journal of Australia* i: 733–45.

1951. *Bone lesions of yaws in Uganda.* Oxford.

Hackett, Cecil J., and L. J. A. Loewenthal. 1960. *Different diagnosis of yaws lesions.* World Health Organization Monograph Series No. 45. Geneva.

Hermans, E. H. 1931. Framboesia tropica. *Acta Leidensia Scholae Medicinae Tropicae,* Vol. 6. Lugduni-Batavorum.

Hill, K. R., R. Kodijat, and M. Sardadi. 1951. *Atlas of framboesia.* World Health Organization Monograph Series No. 5. Geneva.

Hudson, Ellis H. 1946. *Treponematosis.* New York.

1958. *Non-venereal syphilis.* Edinburgh.

Hutchinson, J. H. 1900. A discussion on yaws. *British Medical Journal* ii: 561.

May, Jacques M. 1958. The ecology of yaws. In *The ecology of human disease,* Chapter 16. New York.

Rat, J. N. 1891. *Framboesia (yaws).* London.

Schell, R. F., and D. M. Musher, eds. 1983. *Pathogenesis and immunology of treponemal infection.* New York.

Spittel, R. L. 1923. *Framboesia tropica (parangi of Ceylon).* London.

VIII.158
Yellow Fever

Yellow fever is an acute group B virus disease of short duration transmitted to humans by different genera of mosquitoes, but especially by the *Aedes aegypti* (known previously as the *Stegomyia fasciata*). It remains endemic in the tropical regions of Africa and the Americas in a sylvan or jungle form, but historically its greatest impact on humans has been in an epidemic or urban form. The disease can appear with symptoms ranging from extremely mild to malignant; in classic cases it is characterized by fever, headache, jaundice, albuminuria (high-protein content in the urine), and hemorrhage into the stomach and intestinal tract. High mortality rates were frequently recorded during epidemics (20 to 70 percent), although today we know that yellow fever mortality is actually relatively low, suggesting of course that the majority of the cases were mild and went undiagnosed. The jaundice has prompted the appellation yellow fever, and other designations such as the *mal de Siam, fièvre jaune, gelbfieber,* and *virus amaril,* whereas the hemorrhaging of black blood led to the name "black vomit" or *vomito negro.*

Known early in the New World as the "Barbados distemper," "bleeding fever," the *"maladie de Siam," "el peste," vomito negro,* and later yellow jack (because of the yellow quarantine flag flown by ships), the disease has been called by some 150 names. It was first termed "yellow fever" apparently by Griffin Hughes in his *Natural History of Barbados* (1750).

Etiology and Epidemiology

Generally speaking, humans suffer most from those illnesses for which they are not the intended host. Bubonic plague, for example, is normally a disease of rodents that has, from time to time, incidentally infected humans with devastating consequences. Similarly, yellow fever is normally a disease of nonhuman primates, particularly monkeys. The disease is transmitted among them by mosquito vectors, but not mosquitoes that are ordinarily attracted to human beings. In this form the disease is called sylvan or jungle yellow fever, and is enzootic, meaning that the pattern of transmission is from nonhuman primate to mosquito to nonhuman primate.

When the disease leaves the treetops (as, for example, when a tree is felled), and when mosquitoes such as *Aedes africanus* and *Aedes simpsoni* in Africa and

Haemogogus genera in the Americas link jungle yellow fever with humans and begin a cycle of transmission from nonhuman primate to mosquito to human, the disease is often called *endemic;* when the yellow fever virus is taken in the blood of an infected human to heavily populated areas where the cycle is one of human to the female *A. aegypti* mosquito to human, the disease is termed *epidemic* or *urban* yellow fever.

The habits of the female *A. aegypti* have much to do with shaping the characteristics of an epidemic. She is a domestic mosquito that lives close to humans, depending on them for blood meals and breeding in puddles or containers of water in and around their places of dwelling. Her range is very short, generally a few hundred yards at most, which means that *A. aegypti* requires a fairly closely packed human population. Because *A. aegypti* can survive only a few days without water (although her eggs can survive for years in dehydrated form) and requires water in which to breed, adequate rainfall is a prerequisite for urban yellow fever, and indeed, many of the classic epidemics have taken place shortly after a period of extended rainfall. Warm weather is another prerequisite, for *A. aegypti* will not bite when the temperature falls below 62°F (or 17°C), and extended chilly weather will send her into hibernation.

The virus also has some distinctive requirements, especially for transmission – a process in which humans are best thought of as the site where the virus changes mosquitoes. This exchange can take place only during the first 3 to 6 days of infection of the yellow fever victim while the virus still remains in the blood (viremia); after the virus has entered the mosquito, it must incubate for another 9 to 18 days before the mosquito can infect another human being. After this period of extrinsic incubation, however, the mosquito will remain infective for the remainder of its life, which could be upward of 180 days, although generally the life-span of the female *A. aegypti* is closer to a month or two.

Although it has generally been thought that monkeys serve as the reservoir for the virus, other mammals (marsupials and armadillos) are also suspected of carrying the virus in endemic areas, and for short periods of time the mosquito populations can act as a reservoir.

Distribution and Incidence

In the Americas epidemic yellow fever has been in rapid decline during the twentieth century, essentially due to efforts aimed at eradicating *A. aegypti*

from major population centers. The last outbreak of urban yellow fever took place in Trinidad in 1954.

Nonetheless the yellow fever virus remains very much alive in the monkeys that inhabit the forests of Central and South America, and consequently a small number of human cases (between 50 and 300) continue to be reported annually among individuals who work in or live in close proximity to those forests. The vast majority of the cases occur in regions of Brazil, Ecuador, Venezuela, Colombia, and Peru that are drained by river networks contributing to the Orinoco, Magdalena, and Amazon systems. A bit earlier in the century, human cases of the disease were also reported with some regularity in Central America, Bolivia, Argentina, and Paraguay.

In Africa, severe epidemics of urban yellow fever still occur from time to time; a notable recent example is the Ethiopian epidemic of 1961, which cost thousands of lives. Still more recently a major outbreak in western and southwestern Nigeria claimed thousands of lives. Isolated human cases, however, are not reported with systematic regularity despite the vast belt of endemic yellow fever that stretches across much of that continent, and despite the presence of antibodies in a great number of the inhabitants of that belt, indicating past yellow fever infection.

One mystery surrounding yellow fever is that it has never occurred in Asia, despite the presence there of the *Aedes* mosquito vector. Some think that the mosquitoes themselves in that part of the world are resistant to infection. Others suspect that a population may be able to support only so many group B arboviruses and that entrenched illnesses in this category such as dengue and Japanese encephalitis may have forestalled the advance of the yellow virus.

Immunology

An attack of yellow fever confers on the host a lifetime of immunity against reinfection. Because the disease generally reserves its most severe symptoms for young adults and (as some illnesses) treats children more gently, whole populations in endemic areas or in areas frequently visited by yellow fever can become more or less quietly immune as children experience the illness as just one more in a train of childhood ailments. Under such circumstances an epidemic is never seen, unless or until large groups of newcomers suddenly arrive, such as was so often the case with immigrants, soldiers, and sailors reaching the Americas. It was this phenomenon that gave rise to yellow fever nicknames such as "strangers' fever," the "disease of acclimation," and "patriotic fever."

On the basis of the experience of both slave and free black populations in the hemisphere, however, many came to believe that blacks possessed a special (today some would say innate) ability to resist the disease. The question remains unresolved. Some have denied this ability, by pointing to urban epidemics in Ethiopia or Sudan and western Nigeria in which thousands of blacks lost their lives. These regions are on the edge of the endemic belt where many presumably would not have been exposed regularly to yellow fever, and thus would have included many with no acquired immunity. By contrast, most of the slaves reaching the Americas originated from deep within the endemic zone, and consequently would have acquired immunity to yellow fever before they ever stepped aboard a slaving ship. Thus it is possible to explain much of blacks' refractoriness to yellow fever on the basis of acquired immunity.

On the other hand, genetic selection for yellow fever resistance as a result of prolonged exposure cannot be discounted, for many of the West African descendants of those first arrivals to the Americas lived for generations in areas untouched by yellow fever, yet, without any opportunity to acquire immunity in advance, suffered much less than whites when the disease finally did make an appearance. It has been suggested that related arboviruses or flaviviruses (dengue or Japanese encephalitis, for example) may confer some cross-protection against yellow fever, whereas others believe that certain strains of the illness may vary in mildness or severity, depending on the groups of individuals under attack. In this latter connection it may be significant that Chinese in the New World were reputed to be almost as resistant to the illness as blacks because although yellow fever has never invaded Asia, dengue and Japanese encephalitis are endemic to much of the region.

Fortunately today one need not suffer through the illness in order to ensure resistance to it. Rather immunization can be gained with a strain of living virus called 17D, and immunization projects have been in effect since the 1930s in many regions of endemic yellow fever.

Clinical Manifestations and Pathology

The onset of symptoms generally occurs 3 to 6 days after the virus is injected into the blood. In the range of moderately severe to malignant cases, the symptoms arrive suddenly with flushed features, severe chills, high fever, intense headache, and perhaps a backache and other muscular aches and pains. Quite often there is nausea. These symptoms continue throughout a restless, agitated 2 or 3 days, after which the patient characteristically experiences a remission.

From this point forward, most patients fortunately will recover, but for others, the remission will be short-lived, jaundice may set in, hallucinations frequently will take place, and internal hemorrhaging will occur, with the victim vomiting huge quantities of black vomitus. This frequently terminal signal is confirmed by convulsions, coma, and, generally from the seventh to the tenth day of the illness, death.

Early in the course of the illness the virus sets up an infection – primarily in the liver – and multiplies to the extent that just one drop of blood contains millions of virus particles. This volume of foreign matter in the blood quickly summons an antibody response, which, if the patient recovers, remains in the blood for a lifetime to ensure that he or she never will be called upon to repeat the experience. If the patient dies, pathological findings usually reveal extensive internal damage such as cardiac enlargement and kidney congestion; hemorrhages of the stomach, duodenum, bladder, and mucous membranes; and liver necrosis.

Diagnosis

Because of its wide range of symptoms, diagnosis of yellow fever has always been difficult, and in the past the disease has doubtless been confused with many other ailments that present similar symptoms. Examples of such illnesses are infectious Weil's disease, dengue, tick-borne relapsing fever, lassa fever, malaria (especially blackwater fever), scurvy, and typhoid and typhus; even illnesses such as influenza easily could have camouflaged mild yellow fever.

History and Geography

American Versus African Hypothesis of Origin

Much historical interest in yellow fever has focused on its place of origin: Africa or the Americas? Those who believe it to have been the latter have emphasized that the disease was described and epidemics were recorded in the Western Hemisphere well over a century before it was recognized in Africa, with the first recognizable epidemic striking Barbados in 1647 and then spreading during the next 2 years to Guadeloupe, St. Kitts, Cuba, and the Yucatan Peninsula. Moreover, Amerindian accounts and records of the early Spanish conquistadores make mention of diseases that could have been yellow fever, such as an epidemic of 1454 on the Mexican plateau, a 1477–

97 epidemic that raged in the Yucatan, and an outbreak of disease in Santo Domingo that assaulted the men of Columbus in 1493.

By contrast, the protagonists of the African hypothesis dismiss these outbreaks as typhus, malaria, or some other disease but not yellow fever, in large part because of immunologic evidence. Whatever the illnesses might have been they argue, the Indians were very susceptible to them; however, any endemic presence of yellow fever should have created a high degree of immunity to it. In addition, American monkeys are demonstratively susceptible to the illness, whereas West African populations of both humans and monkeys have shown themselves to be quite resistant to it, suggesting a history of long exposure.

Indeed, the West Africans' ability to resist yellow fever would explain why recognition of the disease was so slow in coming to that region. In the case of Europeans in Africa, it was difficult to distinguish among the "fevers" that fell upon them (and, in the case of portions of the British army during the early nineteenth century, were eliminating more than half of the troops annually). But judging from the extraordinarily low (by comparison) death rates of black troops serving alongside the Europeans, yellow fever must have been prominent among them, and in this connection it is worth noting that even in this century, physicians in Africa have almost routinely misdiagnosed yellow fever as malaria. Interestingly, too, J. P. Schotte, who is credited with first describing yellow fever in West Africa in 1778, did not claim that it was the first epidemic of the disease in the region. Rather, he discussed previous epidemics, in which he reported (significantly) that only the Europeans had suffered greatly.

A final piece of evidence that may point to an African cradle of yellow fever has to do with the prevalence of its *A. aegypti* vector. In Africa, many species of mosquitoes are more or less closely allied to the Aedes, whereas very few are thusly related in the Americas, suggesting that the vector, at least, is an import. On the other hand, it is possible (although unlikely) that the yellow fever virus was present in the monkey populations of the New World prior to the arrival of the Europeans but had to await the arrival of the vector in order to be transmitted to humans.

Certainly the timing of yellow fever's recorded appearance in the New World does nothing to detract from the case for an African origin of the vector, and probably of the virus as well, for the decade of the 1640s was one of accelerated slave trade activity to Barbados as that island was converting its economy to one of a sugar plantation system based on slave labor. The same slave ships that could have delivered the virus in black bodies doubtless did carry the mosquito in their water casks. However, whether the disease achieved endemicity by establishing itself in the monkey populations of those few Caribbean islands that contained monkeys can only be speculated upon, for so many of the serious outbreaks to follow also seem to be traceable directly back to Africa via the slave trade. It does seem, however, that the Yucatan Peninsula and the region around Vera Cruz became endemic foci.

Disease Outbreaks: Seventeenth Through Nineteenth Century

Having reached the Caribbean, the disease began making summer visits northward, striking New York in 1668, Philadelphia and Charleston in 1690, and Boston in 1691, while to the south, yellow fever became a regular visitor to the port cities of Colombia, Ecuador, and Peru. Interestingly, it disappeared from Cuba in 1655 after raging there since 1649 and, save for a visit to Santiago de Cuba in 1695, did not return until 1761, apparently because of the islands' sparse population during this century-long period.

A similar phenomenon appears in the medical literature on Brazil. There seems no doubt that the *bicha* or *molestia da terra* that struck Pernambuco in November of 1685 was yellow fever. It killed thousands in Recife and Olinda and spread into Ceará before burning out about 5 years later. As was the case in the Caribbean, the outbreak in Brazil has been attributed to a ship that arrived from the African coast. However, despite a thriving slave trade that presumably could have brought the vector and virus to Brazil in countless ships, and a monkey population that some believe already harbored the virus, the region reputedly was free of the disease for the next century and a half. It is true that many slaves reaching Brazil came from Angolan and, to a lesser extent, East African regions that were outside the endemic zone of yellow fever. But many also came from regions within that zone, which makes it so perplexing that when yellow fever was allegedly reintroduced, some say that it arrived not from Africa but from North America, in 1849, on the brig *Brazil*, whose crew had been infected either in New Orleans or Havana when the ship had put in to those ports.

Equally perplexing is the selectivity yellow fever demonstrated in seeking out victims as the disease spread from Bahia to other coastal cities, for, although it fell upon European newcomers with considerable fury, it treated local blacks and whites far more gently, suggesting, of course, that the disease may have been present in the region all along – in its jungle or sylvan form – quietly immunizing the population by periodically producing mild cases in the young. Significantly, in the years immediately prior to the outbreak of the 1849 epidemic, Brazil had been the recipient of a sizable influx of European immigrants, in addition, the population of Rio de Janeiro still included a number of individuals on their way to California. Thus in this epidemic, as in the countless ones to follow, it would be the newcomers who were the chief sufferers of the illness.

Yet yellow fever did not limit its assaults on Europeans to Africa and the Americas, but rather on notable occasions sought them out in their homelands as well, apparently reaching the continent from the Caribbean. The Iberian Peninsula was the most common target, with periodic epidemics reported there throughout the eighteenth and nineteenth centuries. The coastal cities of Oporto, Lisbon, and Barcelona bore the brunt of these attacks, although the disease did penetrate to the heart of the peninsula from time to time, even reaching Madrid in 1878. Small outbreaks also occurred on occasion in France, England, and Italy.

Without doubt, however, yellow fever gained its most fearsome reputation in the Caribbean because of Europeans on hand to host it, often in the form of military personnel who provided the disease with a seemingly endless stream of nonimmunes. In 1655, of the 1,500 French soldiers sent to occupy Saint Lucia, only 89 were reported to have survived an onslaught of disease led by yellow fever. The decade of the 1690s saw yellow fever sweep much of the Caribbean, and whole populations of many islands thinned considerably. In 1693 the English attack on the French at Martinique collapsed in face of yellow fever, whereas in 1741, Admiral Edward Vernon's abortive attack on Cartagena saw the loss of close to half of an original landing force of 19,000 (including many North Americans) to yellow fever.

Prisoners sent as workmen from Vera Cruz to Havana in 1761 are credited with reintroducing yellow fever to Cuba where it proved a formidable ally of the Spaniards the following year in a nearly successful effort to deny Havana to the English. However, it was during European attempts to invade St. Domingue around the turn of the century that yellow fever deaths really peaked in the Caribbean. Over the years 1793–6 the British army in the West Indies lost some 80,000 men, with over half of the

deaths attributed to yellow fever. The disease also decimated the French soon after they began their invasion of Hispaniola in 1802 and accounted for a sizable portion of the 40,000 men lost in the first 10 months of the war. After the French retreat to the islands of Martinique and Guadeloupe, yellow fever destroyed any French notions of attempting a second assault by raging among the survivors for another 3 years. It was this tremendous loss of European life to yellow fever (and to malaria) that prompted the English to begin to fill West Indies regiments with black troops who were thought to be immune to the disease and demonstrated over and over again that, indeed, many were.

Because of Philadelphia's brisk trade with the West Indies, yellow fever found its way frequently to that port city during the eighteenth century, with epidemics recorded for the years 1741, 1747, 1762, 1793, 1794, and 1797. The epidemic of 1793 was carried to the city by French refugees from revolution-torn San Domingue. With the turn of the nineteenth century, however, as the West Indian trade was shared to a greater extent by southern ports, it was the South that began to receive most of yellow fever's attention, with New Orleans, Savannah, Mobile, and Charleston the most frequent ports of call for the disease.

During the first 6 decades of the nineteenth century, Savannah suffered from 15 epidemics, Charleston had 22, and New Orleans at least 33. The most notable of the New Orleans epidemics occurred in 1853 during which the city lost almost 8,000 individuals to the disease. Chief among the victims of this and all other epidemics were Northerners and foreigners (especially the Irish), along with white Southerners from the interior. Permanent white residents, however, seldom suffered from fatal yellow fever. Among blacks, it was reported by physicians that mulattoes were the most susceptible (to about the same degree as local whites), and until late in the antebellum period, "pure" blacks were believed to be totally immune. Yet in the decade or so before the Civil War, physicians began to notice that blacks did take the disease in a very mild form during epidemics – so mild that it had heretofore escaped notice.

In Brazil, too, blacks were reputed to be extraordinarily resistant to yellow fever, whereas the European immigrants flocking to South America in large numbers became the primary target. With the end of the slave trade in 1850, the chances of the disease entering the country from Africa were reduced. There was always the possibility that the disease would be imported from the Caribbean or North America as supposedly occurred in 1849, but in view of the almost continual epidemic onslaught of yellow fever on Brazilian coastal cities for the remainder of the century, it seems a reasonable supposition that the disease was endemically established in the country.

Cuba, too, was the nineteenth-century destination of European laborers (from Catholic Europe and the Canary Islands), and these, as well as numerous refugees from Spanish America and numerous Spanish soldiers, assured yellow fever a plenitude of hosts on that island. Moreover, a contraband slave trade continued contact with the reservoir of yellow fever in Africa, and regular trade with Vera Cruz kept Cuba in touch with another endemic focus of the disease. Thus it is not surprising that Cuba became the yellow fever capital of the Caribbean. By contrast, the disease began to wane in most of the rest of the islands as the end of the British and French slave trades and the decline of the sugar industry turned them into economic backwaters seldom visited by outsiders.

The northern blockade of southern ports during the American Civil War, rather ironically, kept the South free of yellow fever for the duration by curtailing West Indian shipping traffic. However, the disease returned to New Orleans in 1867, assaulted inland Montgomery in 1873 and Savannah in 1876, before beginning an ascent of the Mississippi River in 1878 that left countless yellow fever dead in a wake that stretched from New Orleans to Memphis, Tennessee, where 5,000 alone went to a yellow fever grave.

This 1878 epidemic almost certainly reached the United States from Cuba, where the influx of Spanish soldiers sent since 1876 to end the Ten Years' War had provided the tinder for an epidemic that raged on that island from 1876 until 1879. Whether the Cuban epidemic also reached out to slaughter French workers arriving in Panama from 1878 onward to work on Ferdinand de Lesseps' abortive attempt to build a canal across the isthmus, or whether that outbreak came from an endemic jungle source is a matter of speculation. But like their predecessors, who between 1851 and 1855 lost thousands of their numbers to yellow fever in building the Panamanian railroad for American financiers, the French canal workers died in droves, many even bringing their own caskets with them to the isthmus.

Transmission and Control: Twentieth Century

The beginning of the end of yellow fever's seemingly endless onslaughts on the Atlantic coastal regions of the hemisphere came just 3 years after the disastrous yellow fever year of 1878, when Carlos Finlay y Barres of Cuba put forth his theory that the *A. aegypti* mosquito transmitted the disease. The theory was confirmed in 1900 through the use of human volunteers (three of whom died) by the U.S. Army Commission on Yellow Fever in Havana headed by Walter Reed. Armed with this knowledge, William Gorgas was able, by eradicating the *A. aegypti,* to rid Havana and consequently much of Cuba (which just 3 years previously had registered 6,000 yellow fever deaths) of the disease. Following this, Gorgas applied the same mosquito eradication methods in Panama, making it possible for workers on the American canal to avoid the fate of so many of their French predecessors. The measures were also quickly applied elsewhere so that the 1905 outbreak of yellow fever in New Orleans and the 1908–9 appearance of the disease in Barbados represented, respectively, the last of the disease on North American soil, and the last reported appearance in the Caribbean for decades.

Plans for eradicating the disease from the entire globe were put forth by Gorgas, and in 1915 the Rockefeller Foundation launched this effort with the creation of its Yellow Fever Commission. The commission began by concentrating on sites in Latin America, but in 1920 shifted much of its attention to Africa. In 1925 the Second Commission to West Africa established itself at Lagos, Nigeria, where, among other things, it was discovered that the rhesus monkey from India, unlike African monkeys, was susceptible to yellow fever. With that discovery, it became possible to use monkeys rather than human volunteers for yellow fever experiments. Nonetheless, yellow fever research remained a dangerous affair, and Adrian Stokes, Hideyo Noguchi, William A. Young, and Theodore B. Hayne all perished from the disease in Africa during these "heroic days" of yellow fever research, which by 1929 had demonstrated beyond doubt that yellow fever was the result of infection by a virus.

In Brazil, the knowledge gained by the Reed Commission in Havana was quickly applied by Oswaldo Cruz to a mosquito eradication campaign that freed major coastal cities from the terror of almost unremitting yellow fever assaults for the first time in over a half-century. Despite the campaign, however, the disease stubbornly refused to disappear from Brazil. Sporadic outbreaks continued with puzzling frequency in that country, and in Peru, Ecuador, and Venezuela and Colombia as well, all of which shared portions of South America's great rain forest.

In 1923 the International Health Division of the Rockefeller Foundation accepted Brazil's invitation to administer the Brazilian Yellow Fever Service and, under the direction of Fred Soper, conducted immunologic surveys which showed that many Brazilians residing close to the forest regions had hosted yellow fever in the past. In 1928 a yellow fever epidemic in Rio, which had been free from the disease for over two decades, triggered investigations revealing that yellow fever could spread in the absence of the *A. aegypti* mosquito, and that the disease was very much alive in the monkey inhabitants of the great South American rain forest. Jungle yellow fever had been discovered, and with that discovery most of the final riddles connected with yellow fever transmission were resolved.

Meanwhile, as mentioned previously, by the late 1920s workers in Africa had demonstrated that the rhesus monkey was susceptible to yellow fever; thus with an animal that could be used in laboratory experiments, efforts to isolate the yellow fever virus were begun. Shortly afterward Max Theiler discovered that the disease could also be transmitted to white mice, which were less expensive and certainly easier to handle experimental animals. Next Theiler showed that if the virus was transmitted from mouse to mouse, it became sufficiently weakened that it could be used to inoculate and immunize monkeys against yellow fever. More effort on the part of Theiler and co-workers led, by the late 1930s, to a further attenuation of the virus, called the *17D Valline strain,* which is a mutation of the virus achieved by successive passage of virus in cultures and chick embryo tissues. It is harmless to humans, but immunizes them against the disease.

The development of a vaccine against yellow fever was crucial, for with the discovery of jungle yellow fever came the realization that yellow fever could not be wiped out after all. This vaccination became the only method of yellow fever prevention in regions where mosquito eradication was not practical. The virus is always present in monkeys and perhaps other wild creatures of the forests, and consequently cannot be pinpointed.

For this reason epidemiologists are particularly alarmed at the relaxation of mosquito control measures in the Western Hemisphere, where very few have been vaccinated. In the southern portions of the United States and much of the Caribbean and Central America, *A. aegypti* has reestablished itself, and Brazil, once apparently free from the mosquito, has reimported it from North America. With modern air travel, an infected individual – or even

mosquito – could easily be whisked from the South American or African forests to any number of large cities where *A. aegypti* again resides in large numbers, and stands ready to spread the disease throughout nonimmune populations. In addition, *Aedes albopictus,* a close relative of *A. aegypti,* has recently (within the last decade) been introduced to the United States from its native habitat in the Orient. Laboratory studies have revealed *A. albopictus* to be fully susceptible to the yellow fever virus and capable of transmitting it to vertebrates, and it is known to be a prominent vector of dengue as well. Its habits, feeding preferences, and general biology closely resemble those of its more famous congener, and both can inhabit the same areas. Moreover, the newcomer is more tolerant of cold weather, and it has spread widely in the United States. Its spread to the West Indies, and Central and South America is feared. As Wilbur Downs stated in a personal communication, "It could prove to be a most unwelcome contributor to yellow fever epidemiology in coming decades."

Donald B. Cooper and Kenneth F. Kiple

Bibliography

Blake, John B. 1968. Yellow fever in eighteenth century America. *Bulletin of the New York Academy of Medicine,* 2d Ser., 44: 673–86.

Carter, Henry Rose. 1931. *Yellow fever: An epidemiological and historical study of its place of origin,* ed. Laura A. Carter and W. H. Frost. Baltimore.

Coleman, William. 1984. Epidemiological method in the 1860s: Yellow fever at Saint-Nazaire. *Bulletin of the History of Medicine* 58: 145–63.

Cooper, Donald B. 1975. Brazil's long fight against epidemic disease, 1849–1917, with special emphasis on yellow fever. *Bulletin of the New York Academy of Medicine* 51: 672–96.

Downs, Wilbur G. 1982a. History of epidemiological aspects of yellow fever. *Yale Journal of Biology and Medicine* 55: 179–85.

    1982b. The Rockefeller Foundation virus program: 1951–1971 with update to 1981. *Annual Reviews in Medicine* 33: 1–29.

Duffy, John. 1966. *Sword of pestilence: The New Orleans yellow fever epidemic of 1853.* Baton Rouge, La.

Franco, Odair. 1969. *Historia da febre-amarella no Brasil.* Rio de Janeiro.

Guerra, Francisco. 1966. The influence of disease on race, logistics and colonization in the Antilles. *Journal of Tropical Medicine and Hygiene* 69: 23–35.

Kiple, Kenneth F. 1985. *The Caribbean slave: A biological history.* New York.

Kiple, Kenneth F., and Virginia H. Kiple. 1977. Black yellow fever immunities both innate and acquired as revealed in the American South. *Social Science History* 1: 419–36.

Powell, J. H. 1965. *Bring out your dead: The great plague of yellow fever in Philadelphia in 1793.* New York.

Strode, George K., ed. 1951. *Yellow fever.* New York.

Theiler, Max. 1964, 1951. Nobel lecture: The development of vaccines against yellow fever. *Nobel lectures: Physiology and Medicine 1942–1962,* 351–9. Amsterdam.

Ward, James S. 1972. *Yellow fever in Latin America: A geographical study.* Liverpool.

Indexes

Our approach to indexing this work was guided, in part, by the desire to make available substantive information that seemed best omitted in the text. As a consequence, the Name Index gives a brief biographical sketch, including dates of birth and death, for each (normally pre–twentieth-century) figure of prominence in the history of medicine who is mentioned by more than one of our authors.

Yet this work is less a history of medicine than it is the history (and geography) of human disease promised by the title, and it is this promise that dictates the primary focus of the Subject Index. This index first divides the globe into its major regions and then subdivides these regions geographically and chronologically so that, for example, the diseases of Japan in the premodern period are found listed alphabetically under Asia, East, Japan, premodern.

If, however, the reader is interested only in smallpox in premodern Japan, then the smallpox entry in the Subject Index may also be consulted, where a chronology of epidemics during the period in question is provided along with a listing of the outbreaks of this disease noted by our authors in every portion of the globe, from its earliest recorded appearance to the most recently reported cases.

Other areas of interest, such as the history of medicine or infant mortality or public health, can be accessed through topical entries such as medicine and medical history; mortality, infant; and public health and sanitation. In addition, in the Subject Index we have provided cross-referencing among topics covered in the text, and we have also attempted to include, whenever possible, synonyms that have been used historically for modern diseases.

Name Index

Leishman, Sir William Boog (1865–1926): Leishman received his medical degree from the University of Glasgow (1886), after which he served in the British Royal Army Medical Corps. He discovered the protozoal parasite of kala-azar and his name was subsequently given to the genus of parasitic protozoa, the family of Trypanosomatidae, which causes a variety of tropical ailments around the globe. 417, 833

Lejeune, Jerome, 122

Leme, Caramuru Paes, 538

Leonardo da Vinci, *see* Vinci, Leonardo da

Leonides of Alexandria, 102

Leopold, king of Belgium, 557

Lepine, R., 668

Lereboullet, Dominique, 652

LeRoy Ladurie, Emmanuel, 285

Leslie, Charles, 34

Leube, W., 804

Leuckart, Karl Georg Friedrich Rudolf (1823–98): A German zoologist, Leuckart was a pioneer in parasitology and animal ecology who described the morphology and life history of *Taenia echinococcus,* as well as the relationship between hydatid cysts and tapeworms in dogs. 896, 1057

Levan, A., 122

Lever, John, 706

Levin, E., 777

Levine, P., 572

Levret, André, 1048

Lewis, Meriwether, 320

Lewis, Sir Thomas (1881–1945): A pioneer in the use of the electrocardiogram, Lewis also did important work on blood vessels. 92, 695, 806

Lewis, Timothy Richards (1841–86): Lewis was a pioneer in the field of tropical medicine. He was the first to describe a trypanosome (*T. lewisi*) in a mammal (1877) and, independent of Demarquay and Wucherer, discovered microfilariae, being the first to use the term (1872). 648, 727–8

Lhermitte, J., 585

Liao, Y.-C. J., 124

Libman, Emanuel, 849

Lieber, Charles S., 653

Lieberman, Leslie Sue, 6

Liebermeister, Karl von, 653

Liebig, Justus von (1803–73): A German chemist, Liebig introduced the concept of metabolism into physiology and divided foods into fats, carbohydrates, and proteins. 18, 152

Li Gao (Li Kao), 25, 57

Lilienfeld, A. M., 686

Lillard, Harvey, 164

Lillie, R. D., 595

Lim, W. N., 976

Lincoln, Abraham, 882

Lind, James (1716–94): A British naval surgeon, Lind is considered the founder of the study of naval hygiene in England. He is best remembered, however, for his classic work on scurvy (1753), which urged the issue of citrus juice to seamen. Thanks in part to the work of Lind, scurvy was eventually eliminated from British naval vessels. 142, 645, 1002

Lindstrom, J. M., 894

Linnaeus, *see* Linné

Linné (Linnaeus), Carl von (1707–78): A Swedish botanist and taxonomist, Linné first studied botany and natural history, as well as medicine. He is known as the father of modern systematic botany. He established a system of plant classification based on sexual characteristics, which utilized a binomial system of nomenclature (genus and species) still followed today. His attempt to classify diseases in the same manner, however, was almost useless. 16, 47, 148, 688

Linscoten, Jan Huygen van, 645

Lipschütz, Benjamin, 777

Li Shih-chen, 25

Lister, Lord Joseph (1827–1912): A British surgeon and biologist, Lister used carbolic acid as an antiseptic to reduce the high degree of sepsis following operations and thus became the founder of antiseptic surgery. He was elected a Fellow of the Royal Society (1860) and raised to the peerage (1897) in honor of his accomplishments. 103, 127, 204, 302, 744, 869, 1005

Littman, M. L., 735, 935, 936

Littman, Robert J., 935, 936

Liu Tsung-hüan, 56

Liu Wan-su, 25

Livingstone, David (1813–73): A Scottish explorer and physician, Livingstone became a medical missionary in Africa where he described relapsing fever that often results from a tick bite. He also studied the tsetse fly and sleeping sickness in cattle transmitted by its bite. 296, 297, 930

Livy (Titus Livius), 268

Locke, John, 61, 201

Lockhart-Mummery, H. E., 804, 806

Loeb, Leo, 103

Löffler, Friedrich August Johann (Loeffler) (1852–1915): A German bacteriologist, Löffler's many discoveries in bacteriology include devising a new medium to culture the bacillus of diphtheria. In 1882 he discovered the causative agent of glanders and he also made an important contribution to virology with his demonstration that foot-and-mouth disease in cattle is caused by a filtrate virus. 266, 656, 681, 682, 1015

Lombroso, Cesare (1836–1909): An Italian criminologist and anthropologist, Lombroso is remembered for his notion of the "criminal type," which he believed was the result of degeneration, and atavism. 70, 921

Longrigg, James, 936, 937

Longstaff, G. B., 973

Looss, Arthur (1861–1923): Looss discovered that hookworms can penetrate human skin as he became infected himself. He was the foremost authority on hookworm disease at the turn of the century and also on schistosomiasis. 787, 996

Lopez, Robert, 509

Lösch, Fedor, 570

Loubère, S. de la, 429

Loudon, Irvine, 640, 721

Louis XV, king of France, 1011

Louis, Pierre Charles Alexandre (1787–1872): A French physician, Louis was the founder of clinical statistics whose methods were calculated to show the importance or worthlessness of various medical treatments. Among the latter was the bloodletting panacea of F. J. B. Broussais. He also introduced the term typhoid fever and described the rose spots characteristic of the disease. Louis was the teacher of many American physicians including W. W. Gerhard, Oliver Wendell Holmes, and H. I. Bowditch. 17, 708, 1075, 1078, 1082

Louis XVI, king of France, 1011

Lourie, Reginald S., 928

Lovejoy, C., 308

Low, George C., 729

Lowe, Peter, 748

sickle-cell anemia is inherited in a simple Mendelian manner. 113, 120, 575, 667, 1040

Neergaard, K. von, 706

Negri, Adelchi, 966

Neill, Mather H., 1085

Neisser, Albert Ludwig (1855–1916): A German dermatologist, Neisser discovered the causal organism of gonorrhea in 1879 and named it gonococcus. He also did important work on syphilis and leprosy. 760, 1032

Nelson, Horatio, 1004

Neumann, Ernst, 847

Neva, Franklin Allen, 988

Newell, K. W., 1049

Newman, George, 155

Newman, M. T., 523

Newsholme, Arthur, 225

Newton, Isaac, 16, 61

Nicander, 823

Nicholson, Marjorie, 286

Nicolaier (Nikolaier), Arthur (1862–1942): A German physician, Nicolaier has been credited with the discovery of the tetanus bacillus in 1884 although he did not isolate the organism in a pure culture. 1044, 1049

Nicolle, Charles Jules Henri (1866–1936): A French physician and epidemiologist, Nicolle is best known for his demonstration in 1909 that typhus was transmitted by lice that also carry relapsing fever and trench fever. He was awarded the Nobel Prize in 1928. 969, 1083

Nicot, Jean, 177

Niemann, Albert, 173

Ninsho, 382

Nitze, Max, 18

Noe, G., 729

Noguchi Hideyo (1876–1928): A Japanese-born bacteriologist and pathologist, Noguchi studied medicine in Japan, served in China as a quarantine doctor during an epidemic of bubonic plague, and later settled permanently in the United States. He developed the first pure cultures of *Treponema pallidum* as well as a number of other cultures, and studied Oroya fever and the *verruga peruana* of Peru and Ecuador, demonstrating that they were caused by the same organism. Noguchi became a part of the Rockefeller-led effort to discover the causes of yellow fever and eradicate it. He died of the disease in Africa. 79, 635, 842, 1032, 1105

Norris, John, 612

Norwood, H., 526

Nossal, Gustav, 134

Nothnagel, H., 804

Notter, J. Lane, 1079

Nriagu, J., 824

Nuboer, F. J., 805

Nugent, John, 168

Nutton, Vivian, 196

Nyswander, Marie, 172

Oakley, K., 308

Obermeier, Otto, 968

O'Brien, J. S., 1037

Oedipus, 507

Ohara, Hachiro, 1070

Okada, S., 1037

Oliver, Thomas, 189, 190

Onan, 86

O'Neill, J., 896

Onjo, king of Paekche, 390

Oppenheimer, G. D., 805

Opuls, W., 732

Orellana, Francisco de, 536

Oribasius (325–403): One of the last of the great Greek compilers, Oribasius preserved the writings of countless Greek physicians. His *Synagoge* is a 70-volume compilation of medical knowledge from Hippocrates to his own times. 12, 264–5, 267

Orta (Horta), Garcia da (c. 1490–1570): A Portuguese physician, Orta studied medicine at the universities of Salamanca and Acala de Henares and practiced briefly in Portugal before leaving for Portuguese territories in the Far East. He was the first European to describe cholera in modern times and, according to H. Harold Scott, the first European to leave behind works in tropical medicine. The Portuguese regard Orta as the father of tropical medicine. 415, 643, 645

Ortner, Donald J., 251, 252, 309, 602

O'Shaughnessy, W. B., 649

Osler, Sir William (1849–1919): A Canadian-born physician and medical historian, Osler was an authority on the heart but was also responsible for advances in numerous other areas of medicine. His textbook on *The Principles and Practice of Medicine* (1892) was considered the best work in English on medicine at the time. Osler was successively professor of medicine at McGill University, the University of Pennsylvania, Johns Hopkins University, and Oxford University. He became a Fellow of the Royal Society in 1898. 179, 639, 712, 939, 1019, 1028, 1044, 1077

Otis, G. A., 178

Otto, John Conrad, 622

Ovid, 926

Owen, Norman, 427, 433

Owen, Ray, 133

Owen, Richard, 1057

Owen, Robert, 202

Pacini, Filippo, 643, 648

Padeh, B., 1037

Page, D. L., 935

Paget, Sir James (1814–99): An English surgeon and pathologist, Paget was associated with St. Bartholomew's Hospital during most of his career and was surgeon extraordinary to Queen Victoria. He wrote a classical description of osteitis deformans, an illness now called "Paget's disease" and discovered a cancerous disease of the nipple, now "Paget's disease of the nipple." 116, 178, 911, 1057

Painter, T. S., 122

Palm, Theobald A., 979

Palmer, Bartlett Joshua, 166–7

Palmer, C. E., 782

Palmer, Daniel David, 164, 165, 166

Palmer, Richard, 196

Panum, Peter, 873–4

Paracelsus (Philippus Aureolus Theophrastus Bombastus von Hohenheim) (1493–1541): A Swiss physician and chemist, Paracelsus studied in Italy and may have received his medical degree there. He travelled incessantly but authored many works on medicine, chemistry, and natural philosophy. He attacked the overreliance of physicians on the works of the ancients and especially humoral theory while advocating chemically prepared medicines instead of herbal remedies. 14, 47, 340, 692, 693, 694, 750

Paranhos, V., 833

Paré, Ambroise (c. 1510–90): A French military surgeon, Paré introduced improved methods in treating gunshot wounds and amputation. Although a lowly barber-

Subject Index